DOCUMENTS ON THE LITURGY

1963–1979

DOCUMENTS ON THE LITURGY

1963 – 1979

Conciliar, Papal, and Curial Texts

International Commission on English in the Liturgy
A Joint Commission of Catholic Bishops' Conferences

THE LITURGICAL PRESS
Collegeville   Minnesota

The collection is based on the plan and list of documents prepared by Gaston Fontaine, CRIC, of Service de Documentation Pastorale, Inc., Montreal, Que., Canada and was edited and translated by Thomas C. O'Brien of the ICEL Secretariat.

Library of Congress Catalog Card Number: 82-83580
ISBN 0-8146-1281-4

CONTENTS

FOREWORD   xi

INTRODUCTION   xiii

CHAPTER ONE. GENERAL PRINCIPLES (DOL 1–173)

Section	1.	Conciliar Documents (DOL 1–19)	3
Section	2.	Launching the Reform (DOL 20–76)	83
Section	3.	Work of the Agencies of the Holy See (DOL 77–102)	213
Section	4.	The Holy See and the Hierarchy (DOL 103–107)	257
Section	5.	Languages of the Liturgy (DOL 108–133)	267
Section	6.	Publication of Liturgical Books (DOL 134–140)	303
Section	7.	The Holy See and Religious Superiors (DOL 141–143)	311
Section	8.	Ecumenism (DOL 144–167)	315
Section	9.	Other Documents (DOL 168–173)	357

CHAPTER TWO. THE EUCHARIST (DOL 174–287)

Section	1.	General Documents (DOL 174–194)	375
Section	2.	The *Ordo Missae* prior to 1969 (DOL 195–201)	447
Section	3.	New Roman Missal in General (DOL 202–221)	457
Section	4.	Concelebration (DOL 222–226)	553
Section	5.	The Lectionary (DOL 227–238)	565
Section	6.	General Intercessions (DOL 239–240)	593
Section	7.	The Eucharistic Prayer (DOL 241–251)	607
Section	8.	Communion (DOL 252–273)	
		A. Minister and Rites (DOL 252–267)	637
		B. Communion under Both Kinds (DOL 268–270)	661
		C. Eucharistic Fast (DOL 271–273)	667
Section	9.	Special Directories (DOL 274–276)	671
Section	10.	Worship of the Eucharist outside Mass (DOL 277–279)	689
Section	11.	Mass Intentions and Stipends (DOL 280–287)	701

CHAPTER THREE. THE OTHER SACRAMENTS
  AND THE SACRAMENTALS (DOL 288–417)

Section	1.	The Sacraments and Sacramentals in General (DOL 288–291)	709
Section	2.	Baptism (DOL 292–302)	717
Section	3.	Confirmation (DOL 303–308)	765
Section	4.	Holy Orders (DOL 309–335)	
		A. The Sacrament (DOL 309–323)	779
		B. Ordinations (DOL 324–325)	815
		C. The Pastoral Office (DOL 326–331)	821
		D. Priestly Formation (DOL 332–335)	843
Section	5.	Ministries (DOL 336–346)	903

Section   6.   Marriage (DOL 347–357)
              A. The Rite of Marriage (DOL 347–350)   919
              B. Mixed Marriages (DOL 351–357)   927
Section   7.   Penance (DOL 358–390)
              A. Christian Penance (DOL 358–359)   935
              B. Sacrament of Penance in General (DOL 360–378)   945
              C. First Confession of Children (DOL 379–382)   985
              D. Indulgences (DOL 383–390)   993
Section   8.   Religious Life (DOL 391–406)
              A. Rites (DOL 391–399)   1017
              B. Liturgy and Religious Life (DOL 400–406)   1035
Section   9.   Sacraments of the Sick (DOL 407–412)   1049
Section 10.   Funerals (DOL 413–418)   1065

CHAPTER FOUR. THE DIVINE OFFICE (DOL 419–439)

Section   1.   The Office prior to 1970 (DOL 419–423)   1077
Section   2.   *The Liturgy of the Hours* (DOL 424–436)   1085
Section   3.   Monastic Orders (DOL 437–439)   1147

CHAPTER FIVE. THE LITURGICAL YEAR (DOL 440–499)

Section   1.   General Principles (DOL 440–443)   1151
Section   2.   The Lord's Day (DOL 444–452)   1169
Section   3.   Temporal Cycle (DOL 453–461)   1183
Section   4.   Sanctoral Cycle (DOL 462–479)
              A. The Blessed Virgin Mary (DOL 462–468)   1195
              B. The Saints and the Blessed (DOL 469–479)   1229
Section   5.   Particular Calendars and Propers (DOL 480–483)   1243
Section   6.   Holy Years (DOL 484–494)
              A. Jubilee of 1966 (484–489)   1259
              B. The Holy Year 1975 (490–494)   1267
Section   7.   Other Documents (DOL 495–499)   1281

CHAPTER SIX. MUSIC (DOL 500–538)

Section   1.   General Documents (DOL 500–528)   1285
Section   2.   Chants for Mass (DOL 529–538)   1337

CHAPTER SEVEN. ART AND FURNISHINGS (DOL 539–554)

Section   1.   General Documents (DOL 539–541)   1353
Section   2.   Places of Worship (DOL 542–548)   1361
Section   3.   Vestments and Vesture (DOL 549–554)   1389

APPENDIX:

Document Titles by Date of Issue   1405
Document Numbers by Classification   1423
Incipits   1429
Replies from *Notitiae*   1433

ABBREVIATIONS   1437

GENERAL INDEX   1443

FOREWORD

With joy and confidence I present this volume to all in the English-speaking world and beyond its confines who will find in it a valuable addition to their liturgical collections and libraries. Among those who I am sure will welcome its appearance are the conferences of bishops and individual bishops, chanceries and secretariats, academic personnel and students, priests, religious, and laity active in the pastoral ministry. The book contains the English version of all the official pronouncements on liturgy issued to the universal Church over the period of sixteen years, 1963–1979.

For all interested in liturgy the volume is indispensable, conducive as it is to rapid and rewarding consultation. This is guaranteed by the method of classification, which is based on the chapters of the conciliar Constitution on the Liturgy, and the system of abundant cross-references. For the painstaking work involved in this there cannot but be an enthusiastic expression of gratitude to the staff members of the ICEL Secretariat who undertook the work.

A good reference book is always a boon, but this is more than a reference book. It is an attractive invitation to the intellectual, spiritual, and pastoral assimilation of the liturgical reform launched by the Second Vatican Council. As the first General Instruction of 26 September 1964 puts it, the conciliar Constitution on the Liturgy "will have ever richer effects as pastors and faithful alike deepen their understanding of its genuine spirit and with goodwill put it into practice" (*Inter Oecumenici* no. 1).

Eighteen years have gone by since the liturgical Constitution was promulgated and a great richness of liturgical progress has been achieved. But perhaps we are losing breath, running out of steam, and allowing routine to do its deadening work. Or perhaps in the case of many there has been little true experience of what liturgical reform means and of the spirit it endeavors to promote.

In both cases this book has much to offer—the vision, the insights, the norms and practical directives that under Christ and his Spirit provide the driving force for the growth of liturgical life.

No limit can be set in advance to healthy growth. Since we have come to realize that the Church is a growing ferment of spirit related to an evolving world, we must expect its liturgy to manifest continual signs of growth, of healthy growth, that is, growth emerging from the essentials of the Church's tradition of worship and sacraments, maintaining the sound acquisitions of the past and paying due deference to the regulative role of authority.

This book contains the liturgical record of sixteen dramatic years in the history of the Church. As a record it is precious, but as a spur to reflection, assimilation, and action it is a thousand times more precious. Under the impulse of the Spirit and in full accord with the priestly ministry of Christ in his Church may it fulfill these noble functions.

Denis E. Hurley, OMI
Archbishop of Durban
Chairman, International Commission
on English in the Liturgy

INTRODUCTION

The Constitution on the Liturgy *Sacrosanctum Concilium* of 4 December 1963 set in motion a total reform of the liturgy of the Roman Catholic Church. The progress of that reform is marked in part by the texts connected with carrying out the conciliar intent and decrees. To provide an English edition of these texts the Advisory Committee of the International Commission on English in the Liturgy (ICEL) proposed in 1972 the project that has led to *Documents on the Liturgy*. Work of more pressing pastoral urgency delayed the realization of that proposal. But the intervening period has made possible a thoroughly comprehensive compilation of texts and their organization into a cohesive and functional arrangement.

PLAN OF THE EDITION

The overall arrangement of *Documents on the Liturgy* is not chronological but topical; the texts are grouped according to subject matter, since subject matter most often occasions recourse to a reference work. The arrangement into seven chapters corresponds to the sequence of the seven chapters of the Constitution on the Liturgy. Within each chapter the subject matter is further divided into sections and subsections according to the distinct facets of the general topic. Within that thematic framework the texts appear in chronological sequence, according to their official date of issue.

A further element in the arrangement of *Documents on the Liturgy* is the cross-referencing within the text to documents placed elsewhere in the collection that have bearing on the subject matter at hand. The cross-references are inserted according to their date of issue; where pertinent, the specifically related paragraphs are cited.

CONTENT OF THE EDITION

TEXTS INCLUDED

The 554 texts in *Documents on the Liturgy* cover the years 1963–1979.[1] The collection begins with the entire text of the Constitution on the Liturgy and with excerpts of liturgical import from other conciliar documents. The remainder of the texts come from three popes and the agencies of the Roman Curia. The compilation includes, of course, the documents that have determined the general lines of the liturgical reform and those involving the revision of the liturgical books and rites. The introductions (*praenotanda*) of all the rites, "revised by decree of Vatican Council II and promulgated by authority of Pope Paul VI," are given in their entirety because of the special significance of their content. Also part of the collection are excerpts on the liturgy from documents of a different or broader scope. A notable feature of *Documents on the Liturgy* is the number of less formal texts—papal addresses or homilies, letters marking particular occasions. They are included because of their importance to the history of the reform, as indications of its emphases, elaborations on its themes, or evidence of its problems.

---

[1] Three documents (DOL 413, 500, 103) antedate the Constitution on the Liturgy, but were included because of their immediate relevance to later documents. In addition to R. Kaszinski, ed., *Enchiridion Documentorum Instaurationis Liturgicae* (1976), the general index for the years 1965–76 of *Notitiae*, and the indexes of canonical and pastoral liturgical reviews, the following have been used as a check list: Carlo Braga, "Recensio documentorum annis 1963–1974 editorum," *Ephemerides liturgicae* 88 (1974) 479-523; Armando Cuva, "Documentazione liturgica di un decennio, 4 dicembre 1963–2 dicembre 1973," *Salesianum* 36 (1974) 117–130; "I documenti della riforma liturgica del Vaticano II (1963–1973)," *Rivista liturgica* 61 (1974) 102–163.

Particular decrees, replies, or rescripts are also presented, since they often have broad implications or were preliminary steps toward later general discipline.

In addition to the official documents that make up the text, this edition includes in notes most of the administrative decisions—replies on rubrics or comments on official texts—that have appeared in *Notitiae* 1965–1979.[2]

TRANSLATION OF TEXTS

Documents originally issued in English or, as in the case of the *General Catechetical Directory* (DOL 169), where the English translation is officially approved, are given in the official English version. In a few cases public-domain translations have been used; for some particular replies, rescripts, or letters the original was unavailable. All other documents have been translated from the Latin or other language of the original.[3] The collaboration of a single translator and a group of experts reviewing the translations has, it is hoped, served to ensure the fidelity and consistency so important to the understanding of the texts. Particular attention has been given to earlier ICEL translations of the introductions (*praenotanda*) of the liturgical books in the interest of exactness and consistent usage. The translation has been governed throughout by criteria different from those appropriate to the various genres of liturgical texts meant for singing or recitation in the liturgical assembly. The aim has been to render the exact meaning of texts that are often technical into sound, comprehensible, and accurate English.

APPENDIX, ABBREVIATIONS, GENERAL INDEX

The Appendix consists of: a list of documents, by title, according to their date of issue; a list of documents, by number, according to their specific, technical classification within the general grouping, "conciliar," "papal," or "curial"; an alphabetical list of incipits; a list of the replies or comments from *Notitiae* that annotate the text.

The Abbreviations include those for the biblical books, the conciliar documents, and a composite list of common abbreviations and sigla adopted for the sake of economy of reference.

The General Index is intended especially to provide access to the specific terms in the text that have direct liturgical relevance.

FORMAT OF THE EDITION

TEXT

Each chapter and each section or subsection begins with a summary. Each document begins with a heading, consisting of the following, typographically distinguished elements: the number of the document in the collection, the originator, the technical classification[4] and the incipit (where pertinent), the addressee, the subject matter, date of issue, bibliographical reference to the official publication and language (other than Latin) in which the document appeared originally. In the case of texts not published in *Acta Apostolicae Sedis*, *Notitiae*, or by the Vatican Polyglot Press, the source and

---

[2] The distinction of these replies or comments from official texts is made clear in *Notitiae* 1 (1965) 137 in a note prefixed to the section *Documentorum explanatio.* "The solution offered has no official character, but has only the value of serving as a guideline: Any official solutions will be published where necessary by the competent authority in the *Acta Apostolicae Sedis.*"

[3] This includes the 1979 Instruction on Liturgical Formation in Seminaries (DOL 325); because of its defectiveness the English version published by the originator was not used.

[4] The weight of documents corresponds to this technical classification; see Francis G. Morrisey, *The Canonical Significance of Papal and Curial Pronouncements* (Canon Law Society of America, Washington, D.C., n.d.).

language of the text is given in a footnote. Particular decrees, replies, or rescripts are recognizable by the parenthetical inclusion of the recipient after the classification.

All texts are printed with the headings in the typographical subordination corresponding to the original and with its internal enumeration of paragraphs. The edition carries a marginal number, running sequentially throughout, to the principal paragraphs of the text.

The cross-references inserted between documents in each section bear the edition's document number and the heading in the abbreviated form. Each is set off typographically by the symbol ▶ prefixed and by type size. When cross-references are given to specific paragraphs, the DOL marginal paragraph number is added in brackets after the subject matter of the paragraph.

FOOTNOTES

Footnotes are of four kinds: asterisked notes (*), numbered notes, lettered notes, "R" notes.

Asterisked notes are bibliographical, giving the source of the original text not published in an official organ, or the edition on which the translation is based (together with the system for indicating variants in earlier editions), or the source of a translation.

Numbered notes are those of the original text. When the original documentation involves references to documents in the collection a cross-reference to the document number and paragraph number is appended in square brackets, for example, [DOL 4 no. 141] appended to a reference to *Lumen gentium* no. 11. (In the few cases where the original texts employed a symbol rather than a number, DOL uses a dagger [†] for the reference.) Retention of the original's numbering of notes explains the irregularity of sequence in the case of documents that are excerpts.

Lettered notes (a, b, c, etc.) are editorial and consist chiefly in cross-references for documents alluded to in the original or variants in earlier editions of a text.

"R" notes are supplementary material, mainly the administrative decisions that have appeared in *Notitiae*. These "R" notes are numbered sequentially throughout a section (R1, R2, R3, etc.), which allows for precise cross-references to these notes in later sections.

ACKNOWLEDGMENTS

For the gracious permission to use the translations given for DOL 255, 256, 262, 280, 282, 312, and 457 ICEL wishes to thank James I. O'Connor, SJ, publisher of the *Canon Law Digest*.

The initial collection of documents was planned and principally compiled by Kevin Seasoltz, OSB. The present, expanded collection resulted from the planning and organization of Gaston Fontaine, CRIC.

DOCUMENTS ON THE LITURGY

1963–1979

CHAPTER ONE

GENERAL PRINCIPLES

SUMMARY (DOL 1–173). In the Constitution on the Liturgy *Sacrosanctum Concilium* a short preamble (art. 1–4) precedes its first and longest chapter of 42 articles, "General Principles for the Reform and Promotion of the Sacred Liturgy." This momentous chapter covers: the nature and importance of the liturgy (art. 5–13); the objectives of liturgical formation and active participation (art. 14–20); the essential norms for reform of the liturgy (art. 21–40); the ideal of the liturgical life in the diocese and the parish (art. 41–42); recommendations on organizing pastoral-liturgical activity on a diocesan and national scale (art. 43–46).

In *Documents on the Liturgy* the first chapter has 173 documents that deal with all these topics, either in a general way or in their details. The chapter does not adopt the detailed division of the Constitution, but organizes the same themes into nine sections that cover the "General Principles for the Reform and Promotion of the Sacred Liturgy."

Section 1. Conciliar Documents

SUMMARY (DOL 1–19). This collection must unquestionably begin with the conciliar documents, since the liturgical reform is a major accomplishment of Vatican Council II, the new Pentecost for the Church. In this section there are 19 documents:

—The complete text of the Constitution on the Liturgy of 4 December 1963 is preeminent (DOL 1) and the cross-references throughout *Documents on the Liturgy* keep this foundational text constantly in the foreground. Adjoined to it is Pope Paul VI's address on the day of promulgation (DOL 2).

—There are excerpts from thirteen other conciliar texts. These documents address, in greater or less detail, the nature of liturgical celebrations, their importance, or their pastoral demands (DOL 3–7, 10, 12–14, 16–19). Annexed to the conciliar documents concerned are four replies on their interpretation made by the competent curial agencies (DOL 8, 9, 11, 15).

3

1. VATICAN COUNCIL II, **Constitution on the Liturgy** *Sacrosanctum Concilium,* 4 December 1963: AAS 56 (1964) 97–138; ConstDecrDecl 3–69.

1   1.   This Sacred Council has several aims in view: it desires to impart an ever increasing vigor to the Christian life of the faithful; to adapt more suitably to the needs of our own times those institutions that are subject to change; to foster whatever can promote union among all who believe in Christ; to strengthen whatever can help to call the whole of humanity into the household of the Church. The Council therefore sees particularly cogent reasons for undertaking the reform and promotion of the liturgy.

2   2.   For the liturgy, "making the work of our redemption a present actuality,"[1] most of all in the divine sacrifice of the eucharist, is the outstanding means whereby the faithful may express in their lives and manifest to others the mystery of Christ and the real nature of the true Church. It is of the essence of the Church to be both human and divine, visible yet endowed with invisible resources, eager to act yet intent on contemplation, present in this world yet not at home in it; and the Church is all these things in such wise that in it the human is directed and subordinated to the divine, the visible likewise to the invisible, action to contemplation, and this present world to that city yet to come which we seek.[2] While the liturgy daily builds up those who are within into a holy temple of the Lord, into a dwelling place for God in the Spirit,[3] to the mature measure of the fullness of Christ,[4] at the same time it marvelously strengthens their power to preach Christ and thus shows forth the Church to those who are outside as a sign lifted up among the nations,[5] under which the scattered children of God may be gathered together,[6] until there is one sheepfold and one shepherd.[7]

3   3.   Wherefore the Council judges that the following principles concerning the promotion and reform of the liturgy should be called to mind and practical norms established.

Among these principles and norms there are some that can and should be applied both to the Roman Rite and also to all the other rites. The practical norms that follow, however, should be taken as applying only to the Roman Rite, except for those that, in the very nature of things, affect other rites as well.

4   4.   Lastly, in faithful obedience to tradition, the Council declares that the Church holds all lawfully acknowledged rites to be of equal right and dignity and wishes to preserve them in the future and to foster them in every way. The Council also desires that, where necessary, the rites be revised carefully in the light of sound tradition and that they be given new vigor to meet the circumstances and needs of modern times.

---

[1]   MR, prayer over the gifts, 9th Sunday after Pentecost [RM, prayer over the gifts, Holy Thursday and 2nd Sunday in Ordinary Time].

[2]   See Heb 13:14.

[3]   See Eph 2:21–22.

[4]   See Eph 4:13.

[5]   See Is 11:12.

[6]   See Jn 11:52.

[7]   See Jn 10:16.

CHAPTER I
GENERAL PRINCIPLES FOR THE REFORM AND PROMOTION OF THE SACRED LITURGY

I. NATURE OF THE LITURGY AND ITS IMPORTANCE IN THE CHURCH'S LIFE

5.   God who "wills that all be saved and come to the knowledge of the truth" (1   5
Tm 2:4), "who in many and various ways spoke in times past to the fathers by the
prophets" (Heb 1:1), when the fullness of time had come sent his Son, the Word
made flesh, anointed by the Holy Spirit, to preach the Gospel to the poor, to heal
the contrite of heart;[1] he is "the physician, being both flesh and of the Spirit,"[2] the
mediator between God and us.[3] For his humanity, united with the person of the
Word, was the instrument of our salvation. Therefore in Christ "the perfect
achievement of our reconciliation came forth and the fullness of divine worship
was given to us."[4]

The wonderful works of God among the people of the Old Testament were a
prelude to the work of Christ the Lord. He achieved his task of redeeming humanity and giving perfect glory to God, principally by the paschal mystery of his blessed
passion, resurrection from the dead, and glorious ascension, whereby "dying, he
destroyed our death and, rising, he restored our life."[5] For it was from the side of
Christ as he slept the sleep of death upon the cross that there came forth the
sublime sacrament of the whole Church.[6]

6.   As Christ was sent by the Father, he himself also sent the apostles, filled with   6
the Holy Spirit. Their mission was, first, by preaching the Gospel to every creature,[7] to proclaim that by his death and resurrection Christ has freed us from
Satan's grip[8] and brought us into the Father's kingdom. But the work they preached
they were also to bring into effect through the sacrifice and the sacraments, the
center of the whole liturgical life. Thus by baptism all are plunged into the paschal
mystery of Christ: they die with him, are buried with him, and rise with him;[9] they
receive the spirit of adoption as children "in which we cry: Abba, Father" (Rom
8:15), and thus become true adorers whom the Father seeks.[10] In like manner, as
often as they eat the supper of the Lord they proclaim the death of the Lord until he
comes.[11] For that reason, on the very day of Pentecost when the Church appeared
before the world, "those who received the word" of Peter "were baptized." And
"they continued steadfastly in the teaching of the apostles and in the communion
of the breaking of bread and in prayers . . . praising God and being in favor with all
the people" (Acts 2:41–47). From that time onward the Church has never failed to

---

[1]   See Is 61:1; Lk 4:18.

[2]   Ignatius of Antioch, *Ad Eph.* 7, 2: Funk PA 1, 218.

[3]   See 1 Tm 2:5.

[4]   Mohlberg SacrVeron 162, no. 1265.

[5]   MR, preface of Easter [RM, preface I of Easter].

[6]   See Augustine, *Enarr. in Ps. 138*, 2: CCL 40, 1991. MR, prayer after the second reading on Holy
Saturday before the restoration of Holy Week [RM, prayer after the seventh reading, Easter Vigil].

[7]   See Mk 16:15.

[8]   See Acts 26:18.

[9]   See Rom 6:4; Eph 2:6; Col 3:1.

[10]   See Jn 4:23.

[11]   See 1 Cor 11:26.

come together to celebrate the paschal mystery: reading those things "which were in all the Scriptures concerning him" (Lk 24:27); celebrating the eucharist, in which "the victory and triumph of his death are again made present";[12] and at the same time giving thanks "to God for his inexpressible gift" (2 Cor 9:15) in Christ Jesus, "in praise of his glory" (Eph 1:12), through the power of the Holy Spirit.

7. To accomplish so great a work, Christ is always present in his Church, especially in its liturgical celebrations. He is present in the sacrifice of the Mass, not only in the person of his minister, "the same now offering, through the ministry of priests, who formerly offered himself on the cross,"[13] but especially under the eucharistic elements. By his power he is present in the sacraments, so that when a man baptizes it is really Christ himself who baptizes.[14] He is present in his word, since it is he himself who speaks when the holy Scriptures are read in the Church. He is present, lastly, when the Church prays and sings, for he promised: "Where two or three are gathered together in my name, there am I in the midst of them" (Mt 18:20).

Christ always truly associates the Church with himself in this great work wherein God is perfectly glorified and the recipients made holy. The Church is the Lord's beloved Bride who calls to him and through him offers worship to the eternal Father.

Rightly, then, the liturgy is considered as an exercise of the priestly office of Jesus Christ. In the liturgy, by means of signs perceptible to the senses, human sanctification is signified and brought about in ways proper to each of these signs; in the liturgy the whole public worship is performed by the Mystical Body of Jesus Christ, that is, by the Head and his members.

From this it follows that every liturgical celebration, because it is an action of Christ the Priest and of his Body which is the Church, is a sacred action surpassing all others; no other action of the Church can equal its effectiveness by the same title and to the same degree.

8. In the earthly liturgy we take part in a foretaste of that heavenly liturgy celebrated in the holy city of Jerusalem toward which we journey as pilgrims, where Christ is sitting at the right hand of God, a minister of the holies and of the true tabernacle;[15] we sing a hymn to the Lord's glory with the whole company of heaven; venerating the memory of the saints, we hope for some part and fellowship with them; we eagerly await the Savior, our Lord Jesus Christ, until he, our life, shall appear and we too will appear with him in glory.[16]

9. The liturgy does not exhaust the entire activity of the Church. Before people can come to the liturgy they must be called to faith and to conversion: "How then are they to call upon him in whom they have not yet believed? But how are they to believe him whom they have not heard? And how are they to hear if no one preaches? And how are men to preach unless they be sent?" (Rom 10:14–15).

---

12 Council of Trent, sess. 13, 11 Oct. 1551, Decr. *De ss. Eucharist.* cap. 5: CT 7, *Actorum* pt. 4, 202.

13 Council of Trent, sess. 22, 17 Sept. 1562, Doctr. *De ss. Missae sacrif.* cap. 2: CT 8, *Actorum* pt. 5, 960.

14 See Augustine, *In Ioannis Evangelium Tractatus 6,* cap. 1, n. 7: PL 35, 1428.

15 See Rv 21:2; Col 3:1; Heb 8:2.

16 See Phil 3:20; Col 3:4.

Therefore the Church announces the good tidings of salvation to those who do not believe, so that all may know the true God and Jesus Christ whom he has sent and may be converted from their ways, doing penance.[17] To believers, also, the Church must ever preach faith and penance, prepare them for the sacraments, teach them to observe all that Christ has commanded,[18] and invite them to all the works of charity, worship, and the apostolate. For all these works make it clear that Christ's faithful, though not of this world, are to be the light of the world and to glorify the Father in the eyes of all.

10. Still, the liturgy is the summit toward which the activity of the Church is directed; at the same time it is the fount from which all the Church's power flows. For the aim and object of apostolic works is that all who are made children of God by faith and baptism should come together to praise God in the midst of his Church, to take part in the sacrifice, and to eat the Lord's Supper.   10

The liturgy in its turn moves the faithful, filled with "the paschal sacraments," to be "one in holiness";[19] it prays that "they may hold fast in their lives to what they have grasped by their faith";[20] the renewal in the eucharist of the covenant between the Lord and his people draws the faithful into the compelling love of Christ and sets them on fire. From the liturgy, therefore, particularly the eucharist, grace is poured forth upon us as from a fountain; the liturgy is the source for achieving in the most effective way possible human sanctification and God's glorification, the end to which all the Church's other activities are directed.

11. But in order that the liturgy may possess its full effectiveness, it is necessary that the faithful come to it with proper dispositions, that their minds be attuned to their voices, and that they cooperate with divine grace, lest they receive it in vain.[21] Pastors must therefore realize that when the liturgy is celebrated something more is required than the mere observance of the laws governing valid and lawful celebration; it is also their duty to ensure that the faithful take part fully aware of what they are doing, actively engaged in the rite, and enriched by its effects.   11

12. The spiritual life, however, is not limited solely to participation in the liturgy. Christians are indeed called to pray in union with each other, but they must also enter into their chamber to pray to the Father in secret;[22] further, according to the teaching of the Apostle, they should pray without ceasing.[23] We learn from the same Apostle that we must always bear about in our body the dying of Jesus, so that the life also of Jesus may be made manifest in our bodily frame.[24] This is why we ask the Lord in the sacrifice of the Mass that "receiving the offering of the spiritual victim," he may fashion us for himself "as an eternal gift."[25]   12

---

[17] See Jn 17:3; Lk 24:47; Acts 2:38.

[18] See Mt 28:20.

[19] MR, prayer after communion, Easter Vigil, and Easter Sunday [RM, prayer after communion, Easter Vigil].

[20] MR, opening prayer, Mass for Tuesday within the octave of Easter [RM, opening prayer, Mass for Monday of Easter Week].

[21] See 2 Cor 6:1.

[22] See Mt 6:6.

[23] See 1 Thes 5:17.

[24] See 2 Cor 4:10–11.

[25] MR, prayer over the gifts, Monday within the octave of Pentecost [RM, prayer over the gifts, Saturday after the 2nd, 4th, and 6th Sundays of Easter].

13   13. Popular devotions of the Christian people are to be highly endorsed, provided they accord with the laws and norms of the Church, above all when they are ordered by the Apostolic See.

Devotions proper to particular Churches also have a special dignity if they are undertaken by mandate of the bishops according to customs or books lawfully approved.

But these devotions should be so fashioned that they harmonize with the liturgical seasons, accord with the sacred liturgy, are in some way derived from it, and lead the people to it, since, in fact, the liturgy by its very nature far surpasses any of them.

II. PROMOTION OF LITURGICAL INSTRUCTION
AND ACTIVE PARTICIPATION

14   14. The Church earnestly desires that all the faithful be led to that full, conscious, and active participation in liturgical celebrations called for by the very nature of the liturgy. Such participation by the Christian people as "a chosen race, a royal priesthood, a holy nation, God's own people" (1 Pt 2:9; see 2:4–5) is their right and duty by reason of their baptism.

In the reform and promotion of the liturgy, this full and active participation by all the people is the aim to be considered before all else. For it is the primary and indispensable source from which the faithful are to derive the true Christian spirit and therefore pastors must zealously strive in all their pastoral work to achieve such participation by means of the necessary instruction.

Yet it would be futile to entertain any hopes of realizing this unless, in the first place, the pastors themselves become thoroughly imbued with the spirit and power of the liturgy and make themselves its teachers. A prime need, therefore, is that attention be directed, first of all, to the liturgical formation of the clergy. Wherefore the Council has decided to enact what follows.

15   15. Professors appointed to teach liturgy in seminaries, religious houses of study, and theological faculties must be thoroughly trained for their work in institutes specializing in this subject.

16   16. The study of liturgy is to be ranked among the compulsory and major courses in seminaries and religious houses of studies; in theological faculties it is to rank among the principal courses. It is to be taught under its theological, historical, spiritual, pastoral, and canonical aspects. Moreover, other professors, while striving to expound the mystery of Christ and the history of salvation from the angle proper to each of their own subjects, must nevertheless do so in a way that will clearly bring out the connection between their subjects and the liturgy, as also the underlying unity of all priestly training. This consideration is especially important for professors of dogmatic, spiritual, and pastoral theology and for professors of holy Scripture.

17   17. In seminaries and houses of religious, clerics shall be given a liturgical formation in their spiritual life. The means for this are: proper guidance so that they may be able to understand the sacred rites and take part in them wholeheartedly; the actual celebration of the sacred mysteries and of other, popular devotions imbued with the spirit of the liturgy. In addition they must learn how to observe the liturgical laws, so that life in seminaries and houses of religious may be thoroughly permeated by the spirit of the liturgy.

18. Priests, both secular and religious, who are already working in the Lord's   18
vineyard are to be helped by every suitable means to understand ever more fully
what it is they are doing in their liturgical functions; they are to be aided to live the
liturgical life and to share it with the faithful entrusted to their care.

19. With zeal and patience pastors must promote the liturgical instruction of the   19
faithful and also their active participation in the liturgy both internally and exter-
nally, taking into account their age and condition, their way of life, and their stage
of religious development. By doing so, pastors will be fulfilling one of their chief
duties as faithful stewards of the mysteries of God; and in this matter they must
lead their flock not only by word but also by example.

20. Radio and television broadcasts of sacred rites must be marked by discretion   20
and dignity, under the leadership and direction of a competent person appointed for
this office by the bishops. This is especially important when the service to be
broadcast is the Mass.

21. In order that the Christian people may more surely derive an abundance of   21
graces from the liturgy, the Church desires to undertake with great care a general
reform of the liturgy itself. For the liturgy is made up of immutable elements,
divinely instituted, and of elements subject to change. These not only may but
ought to be changed with the passage of time if they have suffered from the
intrusion of anything out of harmony with the inner nature of the liturgy or have
become pointless.

   In this reform both texts and rites should be so drawn up that they express
more clearly the holy things they signify and that the Christian people, as far as
possible, are able to understand them with ease and to take part in the rites fully,
actively, and as befits a community.

   Wherefore the Council establishes the general norms that follow.

A. General Norms

22. § 1. Regulation of the liturgy depends solely on the authority of the Church,   22
that is, on the Apostolic See and, accordingly as the law determines, on the bishop.

   § 2. In virtue of power conceded by the law, the regulation of the liturgy
within certain defined limits belongs also to various kinds of competent territorial
bodies of bishops lawfully established.

   § 3. Therefore, no other person, not even if he is a priest, may on his own add,
remove, or change anything in the liturgy.

23. That sound tradition may be retained and yet the way remain open to legiti-   23
mate progress, a careful investigation is always to be made into each part of the
liturgy to be revised. This investigation should be theological, historical, and pastoral. Also the general laws governing the structure and meaning of the liturgy must
be studied in conjunction with the experience derived from recent liturgical reforms
and from the indults conceded to various places. Finally, there must be no innovations unless the good of the Church genuinely and certainly requires them; care
must be taken that any new forms adopted should in some way grow organically
from forms already existing.

   As far as possible, marked differences between the rites used in neighboring
regions must be carefully avoided.

24. Sacred Scripture is of the greatest importance in the celebration of the liturgy. 24
For it is from Scripture that the readings are given and explained in the homily and

that psalms are sung; the prayers, collects, and liturgical songs are scriptural in their inspiration; it is from the Scriptures that actions and signs derive their meaning. Thus to achieve the reform, progress, and adaptation of the liturgy, it is essential to promote that warm and living love for Scripture to which the venerable tradition of both Eastern and Western rites gives testimony.

25   25. The liturgical books are to be revised as soon as possible; experts are to be employed in this task and bishops from various parts of the world are to be consulted.

B. Norms Drawn from the Hierarchic and Communal Nature of the Liturgy

26   26. Liturgical services are not private functions, but are celebrations belonging to the Church, which is the "sacrament of unity," namely, the holy people united and ordered under their bishops.[26]

Therefore liturgical services involve the whole Body of the Church; they manifest it and have effects upon it; but they also concern the individual members of the Church in different ways, according to their different orders, offices, and actual participation.

27   27. Whenever rites, according to their specific nature, make provision for communal celebration involving the presence and active participation of the faithful, it is to be stressed that this way of celebrating them is to be preferred, as far as possible, to a celebration that is individual and, so to speak, private.

This applies with special force to the celebration of Mass and the administration of the sacraments, even though every Mass has of itself a public and social character.

28   28. In liturgical celebrations each one, minister or layperson, who has an office to perform, should do all of, but only, those parts which pertain to that office by the nature of the rite and the principles of liturgy.

29   29. Servers, readers, commentators, and members of the choir also exercise a genuine liturgical function. They ought to discharge their office therefore with the sincere devotion and decorum demanded by so exalted a ministry and rightly expected of them by God's people.

Consequently, they must all be deeply imbued with the spirit of the liturgy, in the measure proper to each one, and they must be trained to perform their functions in a correct and orderly manner.

30   30. To promote active participation, the people should be encouraged to take part by means of acclamations, responses, psalmody, antiphons, and songs, as well as by actions, gestures, and bearing. And at the proper times all should observe a reverent silence.

31   31. The revision of the liturgical books must ensure that the rubrics make provision for the parts belonging to the people.

32   32. The liturgy makes distinctions between persons according to their liturgical function and sacred orders and there are liturgical laws providing for due honors to be given to civil authorities. Apart from these instances no special honors are to be

---

[26]   Cyprian, *De cath. eccl. unitate* 7: CSEL 3, 1; see also *Ep.* 66, n. 8, 3: CSEL 3, pt. 2, 732–733.

paid in the liturgy to any private persons or classes of persons, whether in the ceremonies or by external display.

C. Norms Based on the Teaching and Pastoral Character of the Liturgy

33. Although the liturgy is above all things the worship of the divine majesty, it likewise contains rich instruction for the faithful.[27] For in the liturgy God is speaking to his people and Christ is still proclaiming his Gospel. And the people are responding to God by both song and prayer.

Moreover, the prayers addressed to God by the priest, who presides over the assembly in the person of Christ, are said in the name of the entire holy people and of all present. And the visible signs used by the liturgy to signify invisible divine realities have been chosen by Christ or the Church. Thus not only when things are read "that were written for our instruction" (Rom 15:4), but also when the Church prays or sings or acts, the faith of those taking part is nourished and their minds are raised to God, so that they may offer him their worship as intelligent beings and receive his grace more abundantly.

In the reform of the liturgy, therefore, the following general norms are to be observed.

34. The rites should be marked by a noble simplicity; they should be short, clear, and unencumbered by useless repetitions; they should be within the people's powers of comprehension and as a rule not require much explanation.

35. That the intimate connection between words and rites may stand out clearly in the liturgy:

1. In sacred celebrations there is to be more reading from holy Scripture and it is to be more varied and apposite.

2. Because the spoken word is part of the liturgical service, the best place for it, consistent with the nature of the rite, is to be indicated even in the rubrics; the ministry of preaching is to be fulfilled with exactitude and fidelity. Preaching should draw its content mainly from scriptural and liturgical sources, being a proclamation of God's wonderful works in the history of salvation, the mystery of Christ, ever present and active within us, especially in the celebration of the liturgy.

3. A more explicitly liturgical catechesis should also be given in a variety of ways. Within the rites themselves provision is to be made for brief comments, when needed, by the priest or a qualified minister; they should occur only at the more suitable moments and use a set formula or something similar.

4. Bible services should be encouraged, especially on the vigils of the more solemn feasts, on some weekdays in Advent and Lent, and on Sundays and holydays. They are particularly to be recommended in places where no priest is available; when this is the case, a deacon or some other person authorized by the bishop is to preside over the celebration.

36. § 1. Particular law remaining in force, the use of the Latin language is to be preserved in the Latin rites.

§ 2. But since the use of the mother tongue, whether in the Mass, the administration of the sacraments, or other parts of the liturgy, frequently may be of great advantage to the people, the limits of its use may be extended. This will apply in the first place to the readings and instructions and to some prayers and chants,

33

34

35

36

---

27   See Council of Trent, sess. 22, 17 Sept. 1562, Doctr. *De ss. Missae sacrif.* cap. 8: CT 8, 961.

according to the regulations on this matter to be laid down for each case in subsequent chapters.

§ 3. Respecting such norms and also, where applicable, consulting the bishops of nearby territories of the same language, the competent, territorial ecclesiastical authority mentioned in art. 22, § 2 is empowered to decide whether and to what extent the vernacular is to be used. The enactments of the competent authority are to be approved, that is, confirmed by the Holy See.

§ 4. Translations from the Latin text into the mother tongue intended for use in the liturgy must be approved by the competent, territorial ecclesiastical authority already mentioned.

D. Norms for Adapting the Liturgy to the Culture and Traditions of Peoples

37 37. Even in the liturgy the Church has no wish to impose a rigid uniformity in matters that do not affect the faith or the good of the whole community; rather the Church respects and fosters the genius and talents of the various races and peoples. The Church considers with sympathy and, if possible, preserves intact the elements in these peoples' way of life that are not indissolubly bound up with superstition and error. Sometimes in fact the Church admits such elements into the liturgy itself, provided they are in keeping with the true and authentic spirit of the liturgy.

38 38. Provisions shall also be made, even in the revision of liturgical books, for legitimate variations and adaptations to different groups, regions, and peoples, especially in mission lands, provided the substantial unity of the Roman Rite is preserved; this should be borne in mind when rites are drawn up and rubrics devised.

39 39. Within the limits set by the *editio typica* of the liturgical books, it shall be for the competent, territorial ecclesiastical authority mentioned in art. 22, § 2 to specify adaptations, especially in the case of the administration of the sacraments, the sacramentals, processions, liturgical language, sacred music, and the arts. This, however, is to be done in accord with the fundamental norms laid down in this Constitution.

40 40. In some places and circumstances, however, an even more radical adaptation of the liturgy is needed and this entails greater difficulties. Wherefore:

1. The competent, territorial ecclesiastical authority mentioned in art. 22, § 2, must, in this matter, carefully and prudently weigh what elements from the traditions and culture of individual peoples may be appropriately admitted into divine worship. They are to propose to the Apostolic See adaptations considered useful or necessary that will be introduced with its consent.

2. To ensure that adaptations are made with all the circumspection they demand, the Apostolic See will grant power to this same territorial ecclesiastical authority to permit and to direct, as the case requires, the necessary preliminary experiments within certain groups suited for the purpose and for a fixed time.

3. Because liturgical laws often involve special difficulties with respect to adaptation, particularly in mission lands, experts in these matters must be employed to formulate them.

IV. PROMOTION OF LITURGICAL LIFE IN DIOCESE AND PARISH

41 41. The bishop is to be looked on as the high priest of his flock, the faithful's life in Christ in some way deriving from and depending on him.

Therefore all should hold in great esteem the liturgical life of the diocese centered around the bishop, especially in his cathedral church; they must be convinced that the preeminent manifestation of the Church is present in the full, active participation of all God's holy people in these liturgical celebrations, especially in the same eucharist, in a single prayer, at one altar at which the bishop presides, surrounded by his college of priests and by his ministers.[28]

42. But because it is impossible for the bishop always and everywhere to preside over the whole flock in his Church, he cannot do otherwise than establish lesser groupings of the faithful. Among these the parishes, set up locally under a pastor taking the place of the bishop, are the most important: in some manner they represent the visible Church established throughout the world.

And therefore both in attitude and in practice the liturgical life of the parish and its relationship to the bishop must be fostered among the faithful and clergy; efforts must also be made toward a lively sense of community within the parish, above all in the shared celebration of the Sunday Mass.

V. PROMOTION OF PASTORAL–LITURGICAL ACTION

43. Zeal for the promotion and restoration of the liturgy is rightly held to be a sign of the providential dispositions of God in our time, a movement of the Holy Spirit in his Church. Today it is a distinguishing mark of the Church's life, indeed of the whole tenor of contemporary religious thought and action.

So that this pastoral-liturgical action may become even more vigorous in the Church, the Council decrees what follows.

44. It is advisable that the competent, territorial ecclesiastical authority mentioned in art. 22, § 2 set up a liturgical commission, to be assisted by experts in liturgical science, music, art, and pastoral practice. As far as possible the commission should be aided by some kind of institute for pastoral liturgy, consisting of persons eminent in these matters and including the laity as circumstances suggest. Under the direction of the aforementioned territorial ecclesiastical authority the commission is to regulate pastoral-liturgical action throughout the territory and to promote studies and necessary experiments whenever there is question of adaptations to be proposed to the Apostolic See.

45. For the same reason every diocese is to have a commission on the liturgy, under the direction of the bishop, for promoting the liturgical apostolate.

Sometimes it may be advisable for several dioceses to form among themselves one single commission, in order to promote the liturgy by means of shared consultation.

46. Besides the commission on the liturgy, every diocese, as far as possible, should have commissions for music and art.

These three commissions must work in closest collaboration; indeed it will often be best to fuse the three of them into one single commission.

---

[28]   See Ignatius of Antioch, *Ad Magn.* 7; *Ad Philad.* 4; *Ad Smyrn.* 8: Funk PA 1, 236, 266, 281.

CHAPTER II
THE MOST SACRED MYSTERY OF THE EUCHARIST

47   47. At the Last Supper, on the night when he was betrayed, our Savior instituted the eucharistic sacrifice of his body and blood. He did this in order to perpetuate the sacrifice of the cross throughout the centuries until he should come again and in this way to entrust to his beloved Bride, the Church, a memorial of his death and resurrection: a sacrament of love, a sign of unity, a bond of charity,[1] a paschal banquet "in which Christ is eaten, the heart is filled with grace, and a pledge of future glory given to us."[2]

48   48. The Church, therefore, earnestly desires that Christ's faithful, when present at this mystery of faith, should not be there as strangers or silent spectators; on the contrary, through a good understanding of the rites and prayers they should take part in the sacred service conscious of what they are doing, with devotion and full involvement. They should be instructed by God's word and be nourished at the table of the Lord's body; they should give thanks to God; by offering the immaculate Victim, not only through the hands of the priest, but also with him, they should learn to offer themselves as well; through Christ the Mediator,[3] they should be formed day by day into an ever more perfect unity with God and with each other, so that finally God may be all in all.

49   49. Thus, mindful of those Masses celebrated with the assistance of the faithful, especially on Sundays and holydays of obligation, the Council makes the following decrees in order that the sacrifice of the Mass, even in its ritual forms, may become pastorally effective to the utmost degree.

50   50. The Order of Mass is to be revised in a way that will bring out more clearly the intrinsic nature and purpose of its several parts, as also the connection between them, and will more readily achieve the devout, active participation of the faithful.

      For this purpose the rites are to be simplified, due care being taken to preserve their substance; elements that, with the passage of time, came to be duplicated or were added with but little advantage are now to be discarded; other elements that have suffered injury through accident of history are now, as may seem useful or necessary, to be restored to the vigor they had in the tradition of the Fathers.

51   51. The treasures of the Bible are to be opened up more lavishly, so that a richer share in God's word may be provided for the faithful. In this way a more representative portion of holy Scripture will be read to the people in the course of a prescribed number of years.

52   52. By means of the homily the mysteries of the faith and the guiding principles of the Christian life are expounded from the sacred text during the course of the liturgical year; as part of the liturgy itself therefore, the homily is strongly recommended; in fact, at Masses celebrated with the assistance of the people on Sundays and holydays of obligation it is not to be omitted except for a serious reason.

53   53. Especially on Sundays and holydays of obligation there is to be restored, after the gospel and the homily, "the universal prayer" or "the prayer of the faithful." By

---

[1]   See Augustine, *In Ioannis Evangelium Tractatus 36*, cap. 6, n. 13: PL 35: 1613.

[2]   BrevRom, antiphon for the Magnificat, second vespers, feast of Corpus Christi [LH, antiphon for Canticle of Mary, evening prayer II, feast of Corpus Christi].

[3]   See Cyril of Alexandria, *Commentarium in Ioannis Evangelium* lib. 11, cap. 11–12: PG 74, 557–565, esp. 564–565.

this prayer, in which the people are to take part, intercession shall be made for holy Church, for the civil authorities, for those oppressed by various needs, for all people, and for the salvation of the entire world.[4]

54. With art. 36 of this Constitution as the norm, in Masses celebrated with the people a suitable place may be allotted to their mother tongue. This is to apply in the first place to the readings and "the universal prayer," but also, as local conditions may warrant, to those parts belonging to the people.

Nevertheless steps should be taken enabling the faithful to say or to sing together in Latin those parts of the Ordinary of the Mass belonging to them.

Wherever a more extended use of the mother tongue within the Mass appears desirable, the regulation laid down in art. 40 of this Constitution is to be observed.

55. That more complete form of participation in the Mass by which the faithful, after the priest's communion, receive the Lord's body from the same sacrifice, is strongly endorsed.

The dogmatic principles laid down by the Council of Trent remain intact.[5] In instances to be specified by the Apostolic See, however, communion under both kinds may be granted both to clerics and religious and to the laity at the discretion of the bishops, for example, to the ordained at the Mass of their ordination, to the professed at the Mass of their religious profession, to the newly baptized at the Mass following their baptism.

56. The two parts that, in a certain sense, go to make up the Mass, namely, the liturgy of the word and the liturgy of the eucharist, are so closely connected with each other that they form but one single act of worship. Accordingly this Council strongly urges pastors that in their catechesis they insistently teach the faithful to take part in the entire Mass, especially on Sundays and holydays of obligation.

57. § 1. Concelebration, which aptly expresses the unity of the priesthood, has continued to this day as a practice in the Church of both East and West. For this reason it has seemed good to the Council to extend permission for concelebration to the following cases:

    1. a.   on Holy Thursday, both the chrism Mass and the evening Mass;

       b.   Masses during councils, bishops' conferences, and synods;

       c.   the Mass at the blessing of an abbot.

    2. Also, with permission of the Ordinary, who is the one to decide whether concelebration is opportune, to:

       a.   the conventual Mass and the principal Mass in churches, when the needs of the faithful do not require that all the priests on hand celebrate individually;

       b.   Masses celebrated at any kind of meeting of priests, whether secular or religious.

   § 2. 1. The regulation, however, of the discipline of concelebration in the diocese pertains to the bishop.

     2. This, however, does not take away the option of every priest to celebrate Mass individually, not, however, at the same time and in the same church as a concelebrated Mass or on Holy Thursday.

54

55

56

57

---

[4] See 1 Tm 2:1–2.

[5] Council of Trent, sess. 21, Doctr. *De Communione sub utraque specie et parvulorum* cap. 1–3, can. 1–3: CT 8, 698–699.

58   58. A new rite for concelebration is to be drawn up and inserted into the Roman Pontifical and Roman Missal.

CHAPTER III
THE OTHER SACRAMENTS AND THE SACRAMENTALS

59   59. The purpose of the sacraments is to make people holy, to build up the Body of Christ, and, finally, to give worship to God; but being signs they also have a teaching function. They not only presuppose faith, but by words and objects they also nourish, strengthen, and express it; that is why they are called "sacraments of faith." They do indeed impart grace, but, in addition, the very act of celebrating them disposes the faithful most effectively to receive this grace in a fruitful manner, to worship God rightly, and to practice charity.

It is therefore of the highest importance that the faithful should readily understand the sacramental signs and should with great eagerness frequent those sacraments that were instituted to nourish the Christian life.

60   60. The Church has, in addition, instituted sacramentals. These are sacred signs bearing a kind of resemblance to the sacraments: they signify effects, particularly of a spiritual kind, that are obtained through the Church's intercession. They dispose people to receive the chief effect of the sacraments and they make holy various occasions in human life.

61   61. Thus, for well-disposed members of the faithful, the effect of the liturgy of the sacraments and sacramentals is that almost every event in their lives is made holy by divine grace that flows from the paschal mystery of Christ's passion, death, and resurrection, the fount from which all sacraments and sacramentals draw their power. The liturgy means also that there is hardly any proper use of material things that cannot thus be directed toward human sanctification and the praise of God.

62   62. With the passage of time, however, certain features have crept into the rites of the sacraments and sacramentals that have made their nature and purpose less clear to the people of today; hence some changes have become necessary as adaptations to the needs of our own times. For this reason the Council decrees what follows concerning the revision of these rites.

63   63. Because the use of the mother tongue in the administration of the sacraments and sacramentals can often be of considerable help for the people, this use is to be extended according to the following norms:

a.   With art. 36 as the norm, the vernacular may be used in administering the sacraments and sacramentals.

b.   Particular rituals in harmony with the new edition of the Roman Ritual shall be prepared without delay by the competent, territorial ecclesiastical authority mentioned in art. 22, § 2 of this Constitution. These rituals are to be adapted, even in regard to the language employed, to the needs of the different regions. Once they have been reviewed by the Apostolic See, they are to be used in the regions for which they have been prepared. But those who draw up these rituals or particular collections of rites must not leave out the prefatory instructions for the individual rites in the Roman Ritual, whether the instructions are pastoral and rubrical or have some special social bearing.

64   64. The catechumenate for adults, divided into several stages, is to be restored and put into use at the discretion of the local Ordinary. By this means the time of the

catechumenate, which is intended as a period of well-suited instruction, may be sanctified by sacred rites to be celebrated at successive intervals of time.

65. With art. 37–40 of this Constitution as the norm, it is lawful in mission lands to allow, besides what is part of Christian tradition, those initiation elements in use among individual peoples, to the extent that such elements are compatible with the Christian rite of initiation.

65

66. Both of the rites for the baptism of adults are to be revised: not only the simpler rite, but also the more solemn one, with proper attention to the restored catechumenate. A special Mass "On the Occasion of a Baptism" is to be incorporated into the Roman Missal.

66

67. The rite for the baptism of infants is to be revised and it should be suited to the fact that those to be baptized are infants. The roles as well as the obligations of parents and godparents should be brought out more clearly in the rite itself.

67

68. The baptismal rite should contain alternatives, to be used at the discretion of the local Ordinary, for occasions when a very large number are to be baptized together. Moreover, a shorter rite is to be drawn up, especially in mission lands, for use by catechists but also by the faithful in general when there is danger of death and neither a priest nor a deacon is available.

68

69. In place of the rite called the "Order of Supplying What Was Omitted in the Baptism of an Infant," a new rite is to be drawn up. This should manifest more clearly and fittingly that an infant who was baptized by the short rite has already been received into the Church.

69

Similarly, a new rite is to be drawn up for converts who have already been validly baptized; it should express that they are being received into the communion of the Church.

70. Except during the Easter season, baptismal water may be blessed within the rite of baptism itself by use of an approved, shorter formulary.

70

71. The rite of confirmation is also to be revised in order that the intimate connection of this sacrament with the whole of Christian initiation may stand out more clearly; for this reason it is fitting for candidates to renew their baptismal promises just before they are confirmed.

71

Confirmation may be conferred within Mass when convenient; as for the rite outside Mass, a formulary is to be composed for use as an introduction.

72. The rite and formularies for the sacrament of penance are to be revised so that they more clearly express both the nature and effect of the sacrament.

72

73. "Extreme unction," which may also and more properly be called "anointing of the sick," is not a sacrament for those only who are at the point of death. Hence, as soon as any one of the faithful begins to be in danger of death from sickness or old age, the fitting time for that person to receive this sacrament has certainly already arrived.

73

74. In addition to the separate rites for anointing of the sick and for viaticum, a continuous rite shall be drawn up, structured so that the sick person is anointed after confessing and before receiving viaticum.

74

75   75. The number of the anointings is to be adapted to the circumstances; the prayers that belong to the rite of anointing are to be so revised that they correspond to the varying conditions of the sick who receive the sacrament.

76   76. Both the ceremonies and texts of the ordination rites are to be revised. The address given by the bishop at the beginning of each ordination or consecration may be in the vernacular.

When a bishop is consecrated, all the bishops present may take part in the laying on of hands.

77   77. The marriage rite now found in the Roman Ritual is to be revised and enriched in such a way that it more clearly signifies the grace of the sacrament and imparts a knowledge of the obligations of spouses.

"If any regions follow other praiseworthy customs and ceremonies when celebrating the sacrament of marriage, the Council earnestly desires that by all means these be retained."[1]

Moreover, the competent, territorial ecclesiastical authority mentioned in art. 22, § 2 of this Constitution is free to draw up, in accord with art. 63, its own rite, suited to the usages of place and people. But the rite must always conform to the law that the priest assisting at the marriage must ask for and obtain the consent of the contracting parties.

78   78. Marriage is normally to be celebrated within Mass, after the reading of the gospel and the homily and before "the prayer of the faithful." The prayer for the bride, duly emended to remind both spouses of their equal obligation to remain faithful to each other, may be said in the vernacular.

But if the sacrament of marriage is celebrated apart from Mass, the epistle and gospel from the nuptial Mass are to be read at the beginning of the rite and the blessing is always to be given to the spouses.

79   79. The sacramentals are to be reviewed in the light of the primary criterion that the faithful participate intelligently, actively, and easily; the conditions of our own days must also be considered. When rituals are revised, in accord with art. 63, new sacramentals may also be added as the need for them becomes apparent.

Reserved blessings shall be very few; reservations shall be in favor only on bishops and Ordinaries.

Let provision be made that some sacramentals, at least in special circumstances and at the discretion of the Ordinary, may be administered by qualified laypersons.

80   80. The rite for the consecration to a life of virginity as it exists in the Roman Pontifical is to be revised.

A rite of religious profession and renewal of vows shall be drawn up with a view to achieving greater unity, simplicity, and dignity. Apart from exceptions in particular law, this rite should be adopted by those who make their profession or renewal of vows within Mass.

Religious profession should preferably be made within Mass.

81   81. The rite of funerals should express more clearly the paschal character of Christian death and should correspond more closely to the circumstances and traditions of various regions. This applies also to the liturgical color to be used.

---

[1] Council of Trent, sess. 24, Decr. *De reformatione* cap. 1: CT 9, *Actorum* pt. 6, 969. See also RR, tit. 8, cap. 2, n. 6.

82. The rite for the burial of infants is to be revised and a special Mass for the   82
occasion provided.

CHAPTER IV
DIVINE OFFICE

83. Christ Jesus, High Priest of the new and eternal covenant, taking human   83
nature, introduced into this earthly exile the hymn that is sung throughout all ages
in the halls of heaven. He joins the entire human community to himself, associating
it with his own singing of this canticle of divine praise.

For he continues his priestly work through the agency of his Church, which is
unceasingly engaged in praising the Lord and interceding for the salvation of the
whole world. The Church does this not only by celebrating the eucharist, but also
in other ways, especially by praying the divine office.

84. By tradition going back to early Christian times, the divine office is so arranged   84
that the whole course of the day and night is made holy by the praises of God.
Therefore, when this wonderful song of praise is rightly performed by priests and
others who are deputed for this purpose by the Church's ordinance or by the
faithful praying together with the priest in the approved form, then it is truly the
voice of a bride addressing her bridegroom; it is the very prayer that Christ himself,
together with his Body, addresses to the Father.

85. Hence all who render this service are not only fulfilling a duty of the Church,   85
but also are sharing in the greatest honor of Christ's Bride, for by offering these
praises to God they are standing before God's throne in the name of the Church,
their Mother.

86. Priests engaged in the sacred pastoral ministry will offer the praises of the   86
hours with greater fervor the more vividly they realize that they must heed St.
Paul's exhortation: "Pray without ceasing" (1 Thes 5:17). For the work in which
they labor will effect nothing and bring forth no fruit except by the power of the
Lord who said: "Without me you can do nothing" (Jn 15:5). That is why the
apostles, instituting deacons, said: "We will devote ourselves to prayer and to the
ministry of the word" (Acts 6:4).

87. In order that the divine office may be better and more completely carried out in   87
existing circumstances, whether by priests or by other members of the Church, the
Council, carrying further the restoration already so happily begun by the Apostolic
See, has seen fit to decree what follows concerning the office of the Roman Rite.

88. Because the purpose of the office is to sanctify the day, the traditional sequence   88
of the hours is to be restored so that once again they may be genuinely related to
the hour of the day when they are prayed, as far as it is possible. Moreover, it will
be necessary to take into account the modern conditions in which daily life has to
be lived, especially by those who are called to labor in apostolic works.

89. Therefore, when the office is revised, these norms are to be observed: 89

a. By the venerable tradition of the universal Church, lauds as morning
prayer and vespers as evening prayers are the two hinges on which the daily office
turns; hence they are to be considered as the chief hours and celebrated as such.

b. Compline is to be so composed that it will be a suitable prayer for the end
of the day.

c. The hour known as matins, although it should retain the character of nocturnal praise when celebrated in choir, shall be adapted so that it may be recited at any hour of the day; it shall be made up of fewer psalms and longer readings.

d. The hour of prime is to be suppressed.

e. In choir the minor hours of terce, sext, and none are to be observed. But outside choir it will be be lawful to choose whichever of the three best suits the hour of the day.

90   90. The divine office, because it is the public prayer of the Church, is a source of devotion and nourishment also for personal prayer. Therefore priests and all others who take part in the divine office are earnestly exhorted in the Lord to attune their minds to their voices when praying it. The better to achieve this, let them take steps to improve their understanding of the liturgy and of the Bible, especially the psalms.

In revising the Roman office, its ancient and venerable treasures are to be so adapted that all those to whom they are handed on may more fully and readily draw profit from them.

91   91. So that it may really be possible in practice to observe the course of the hours proposed in art. 89, the psalms are no longer to be distributed over just one week, but over some longer period of time.

The work of revising the psalter, already happily begun, is to be finished as soon as possible and is to take into account the style of Christian Latin, the liturgical use of psalms, including their being sung, and the entire tradition of the Latin Church.

92   92. As regards the readings, the following shall be observed:

a. Readings from sacred Scripture shall be arranged so that the riches of God's word may be easily accessible in more abundant measure.

b. Readings excerpted from the works of the Fathers, doctors, and ecclesiastical writers shall be better selected.

c. The accounts of the martyrdom or lives of the saints are to be made to accord with the historical facts.

93   93. To whatever extent may seem advisable, the hymns are to be restored to their original form and any allusion to mythology or anything that conflicts with Christian piety is to be dropped or changed. Also, as occasion arises, let other selections from the treasury of hymns be incorporated.

94   94. That the day may be truly sanctified and the hours themselves recited with spiritual advantage, it is best that each of them be prayed at a time most closely corresponding to the true time of each canonical hour.

95   95. In addition to the conventual Mass, communities obliged to choral office are bound to celebrate the office in choir every day. In particular:

a. Orders of canons, of monks and of nuns, and of other regulars bound by law or constitutions to choral office must celebrate the entire office.

b. Cathedral or collegiate chapters are bound to recite those parts of the office imposed on them by general or particular law.

c. All members of the above communities who are in major orders or are solemnly professed, except for lay brothers, are bound individually to recite those canonical hours which they do not pray in choir.

96. Clerics not bound to office in choir, if they are in major orders, are bound to   96
pray the entire office every day, either in common or individually, following the
norms in art. 89 .

97. Appropriate instances are to be defined by the rubrics in which a liturgical   97
service may be substituted for the divine office.

    In particular cases and for a just reason Ordinaries may dispense their subjects
wholly or in part from the obligation of reciting the divine office or may commute
it.

98. Members of any institute dedicated to acquiring perfection who, according to   98
their constitutions, are to recite any parts of the divine office are thereby performing the public prayer of the Church.

    They too perform the public prayer of the Church who, in virtue of their
constitutions, recite any little office, provided this has been drawn up after the
pattern of the divine office and duly approved.

99. Since the divine office is the voice of the Church, that is, of the whole Mystical   99
Body publicly praising God, those clerics who are not obliged to office in choir,
especially priests who live together or who meet together for any purpose, are
urged to pray at least some part of the divine office in common.

    All who pray the divine office, whether in choir or in common, should fulfill
the task entrusted to them as perfectly as possible: this refers not only to the
internal devotion of their minds but also to their external manner of celebration.

    It is advantageous, moreover, that the office in choir and in common be sung
when there is an opportunity to do so.

100. Pastors should see to it that the chief hours, especially vespers, are celebrated   100
in common in church on Sundays and the more solemn feasts. The laity, too, are
encouraged to recite the divine office either with the priests, or among themselves,
or even individually.

101. § 1. In accordance with the centuries-old tradition of the Latin rite, clerics are   101
to retain the Latin language in the divine office. But in individual cases the Ordinary has the power of granting the use of a vernacular translation, prepared in
accord with art. 36, to those clerics for whom the use of Latin constitutes a grave
obstacle to their praying the office properly.

    § 2. The competent superior has the power to grant the use of the vernacular
in the celebration of the divine office, even in choir, to nuns and to members of
institutes dedicated to acquiring perfection, both men who are not clerics and
women. The version, however, must be one that has been approved.

    § 3. Any cleric bound to the divine office fulfills his obligation if he prays the
office in the vernacular together with a group of the faithful or with those mentioned in § 2, provided the text of the translation has been approved.

CHAPTER V
THE LITURGICAL YEAR

102. The Church is conscious that it must celebrate the saving work of the divine   102
Bridegroom by devoutly recalling it on certain days throughout the course of the
year. Every week, on the day which the Church has called the Lord's Day, it keeps
the memory of the Lord's resurrection, which it also celebrates once in the year,
together with his blessed passion, in the most solemn festival of Easter.

Within the cycle of a year, moreover, the Church unfolds the whole mystery of Christ, from his incarnation and birth until his ascension, the day of Pentecost, and the expectation of blessed hope and of the Lord's return.

Recalling thus the mysteries of redemption, the Church opens to the faithful the riches of the Lord's powers and merits, so that these are in some way made present in every age in order that the faithful may lay hold on them and be filled with saving grace.

103   103. In celebrating this annual cycle of Christ's mysteries, the Church honors with special love Mary, the Mother of God, who is joined by an inseparable bond to the saving work of her Son. In her the Church holds up and admires the most excellent effect of the redemption and joyfully contemplates, as in a flawless image, that which the Church itself desires and hopes wholly to be.

104   104. The Church has also included in the annual cycle days devoted to the memory of the martyrs and the other saints. Raised up to perfection by the manifold grace of God and already in possession of eternal salvation, they sing God's perfect praise in heaven and offer prayers for us. By celebrating their passage from earth to heaven the Church proclaims the paschal mystery achieved in the saints, who have suffered and been glorified with Christ; it proposes them to the faithful as examples drawing all to the Father through Christ and pleads through their merits for God's favors.

105   105. Finally, in the various seasons of the year and according to its traditional discipline, the Church completes the formation of the faithful by means of devout practices for soul and body, by instruction, prayer, and works of penance and of mercy.

Accordingly the sacred Council has seen fit to decree what follows.

106   106. By a tradition handed down from the apostles and having its origin from the very day of Christ's resurrection, the Church celebrates the paschal mystery every eighth day, which, with good reason, bears the name of the Lord's Day or Sunday. For on this day Christ's faithful must gather together so that, by hearing the word of God and taking part in the eucharist, they may call to mind the passion, the resurrection, and the glorification of the Lord Jesus and may thank God, who "has begotten them again unto a living hope through the resurrection of Jesus Christ from the dead" (1 Pt 1:3). Hence the Lord's Day is the first holyday of all and should be proposed to the devotion of the faithful and taught to them in such a way that it may become in fact a day of joy and of freedom from work. Other celebrations, unless they be truly of greatest importance, shall not have precedence over the Sunday, the foundation and core of the whole liturgical year.

107   107. The liturgical year is to be so revised that the traditional customs and usages of the sacred seasons are preserved or restored to suit the conditions of modern times; their specific character is to be retained, so that they duly nourish the devotion of the faithful who celebrate the mysteries of Christian redemption and above all the paschal mystery. If certain adaptations are considered necessary on account of local conditions, they are to be made in accordance with the provisions of art. 39 and 40.

108   108. The minds of the faithful must be directed primarily toward those feasts of the Lord on which the mysteries of salvation are celebrated in the course of the year. Therefore, the Proper of Seasons shall be given the precedence due to it over the feasts of the saints, in order that the entire cycle of the mysteries of salvation may be celebrated in the measure due to them.

109. Lent is marked by two themes, the baptismal and the penitential. By recalling   109
or preparing for baptism and by repentance, this season disposes the faithful, as
they more diligently listen to the word of God and devote themselves to prayer, to
celebrate the paschal mystery . The baptismal and penitential aspects of Lent are to
be given greater prominence in both the liturgy and liturgical catechesis. Hence:

a. More use is to be made of the baptismal features proper to the Lenten
liturgy; some of those from an earlier era are to be restored as may seem advisable.

b. The same is to apply to the penitential elements. As regards catechesis, it is
important to impress on the minds of the faithful not only the social consequences
of sin but also the essence of the virtue of penance, namely, detestation of sin as an
offense against God; the role of the Church in penitential practices is not to be
neglected and the people are to be exhorted to pray for sinners.

110. During Lent penance should be not only inward and individual, but also   110
outward and social. The practice of penance should be fostered, however, in ways
that are possible in our own times and in different regions and according to the
circumstances of the faithful; it should be encouraged by the authorities mentioned
in art. 22.

Nevertheless, let the paschal fast be kept sacred. Let it be observed everywhere
on Good Friday and, where possible, prolonged throughout Holy Saturday, as a
way of coming to the joys of the Sunday of the resurrection with uplifted and
welcoming heart.

111. The saints have been traditionally honored in the Church and their authentic   111
relics and images held in veneration. For the feasts of the saints proclaim the
wonderful works of Christ in his servants and display to the faithful fitting examples for their imitation.

Lest the feasts of the saints take precedence over the feasts commemorating
the very mysteries of salvation, many of them should be left to be celebrated by a
particular Church or nation or religious family; those only should be extended to
the universal Church that commemorate saints of truly universal significance.

CHAPTER VI
SACRED MUSIC

112. The musical tradition of the universal Church is a treasure of inestimable   112
value, greater even than that of any other art. The main reason for this preeminence
is that, as sacred song closely bound to the text, it forms a necessary or integral part
of the solemn liturgy.

Holy Scripture itself has bestowed praise upon sacred song[1] and the same may
be said of the Fathers of the Church and of the Roman pontiffs, who in recent
times, led by St. Pius X, have explained more precisely the ministerial function
supplied by sacred music in the service of the Lord.

Therefore sacred music will be the more holy the more closely it is joined to
the liturgical rite, whether by adding delight to prayer, fostering oneness of spirit,
or investing the rites with greater solemnity. But the Church approves of all forms
of genuine art possessing the qualities required and admits them into divine worship.

---
[1] See Eph 5:19; Col 3:16.

Accordingly, the Council, keeping the norms and precepts of ecclesiastical tradition and discipline and having regard to the purpose of sacred music, which is the glory of God and the sanctification of the faithful, decrees what follows.

113   113. A liturgical service takes on a nobler aspect when the rites are celebrated with singing, the sacred ministers take their parts in them, and the faithful actively participate.

As regards the language to be used, the provisions of art. 36 are to be observed; for the Mass, those of art. 54; for the sacraments, those of art. 63; for the divine office, those of art. 101.

114   114. The treasure of sacred music is to be preserved and fostered with great care. Choirs must be diligently developed, especially in cathedral churches; but bishops and other pastors of souls must be at pains to ensure that whenever a liturgical service is to be celebrated with song, the whole assembly of the faithful is enabled, in keeping with art. 28 and 30, to contribute the active participation that rightly belongs to it.

115   115. Great importance is to be attached to the teaching and practice of music in seminaries, in the novitiates and houses of study of religious of both sexes, and also in other Catholic institutions and schools. To impart this instruction, those in charge of teaching sacred music are to receive thorough training.

It is recommended also that higher institutes of sacred music be established whenever possible.

Musicians and singers, especially young boys, must also be given a genuine liturgical training.

116   116. The Church acknowledges Gregorian chant as distinctive of the Roman liturgy; therefore, other things being equal, it should be given pride of place in liturgical services.

But other kinds of sacred music, especially polyphony, are by no means excluded from liturgical celebrations, provided they accord with the spirit of the liturgical service, in the way laid down in art. 30.

117   117. The *editio typica* of the books of Gregorian chant is to be completed and a more critical edition is to be prepared of those books already published since the reform of St. Pius X.

It is desirable also that an edition be prepared containing the simpler melodies for use in small churches.

118   118. The people's own religious songs are to be encouraged with care so that in sacred devotions as well as during services of the liturgy itself, in keeping with rubrical norms and requirements, the faithful may raise their voices in song.

119   119. In certain parts of the world, especially mission lands, people have their own musical traditions and these play a great part in their religious and social life. Thus, in keeping with art. 39 and 40, due importance is to be attached to their music and a suitable place given to it, not only in forming their attitude toward religion, but also in adapting worship to their native genius.

Therefore, when missionaries are being given training in music, every effort should be made to see that they become competent in promoting the traditional music of the people, both in schools and in sacred services, as far as may be practicable.

120. In the Latin Church the pipe organ is to be held in high esteem, for it is the   120
traditional musical instrument that adds a wonderful splendor to the Church's
ceremonies and powerfully lifts up the spirit to God and to higher things.

But other instruments also may be admitted for use in divine worship, with
the knowledge and consent of the competent territorial authority and in conformity
with art. 22, § 2, art. 37, and art. 40. This applies, however, only on condition that
the instruments are suitable, or can be made suitable, for sacred use, are in accord
with the dignity of the place of worship, and truly contribute to the uplifting of the
faithful.

121. Composers, filled with the Christian spirit, should feel that their vocation is to   121
develop sacred music and to increase its store of treasures.

Let them produce compositions having the qualities proper to genuine sacred
music, not confining themselves to works that can be sung only by large choirs, but
providing also for the needs of small choirs and for the active participation of the
entire assembly of the faithful.

The texts intended to be sung must always be consistent with Catholic teaching; indeed they should be drawn chiefly from holy Scripture and from liturgical
sources.

CHAPTER VII
SACRED ART AND SACRED FURNISHINGS

122. The fine arts are deservedly ranked among the noblest activities of human   122
genius and this applies especially to religious art and to its highest achievement,
sacred art. These arts, by their very nature, are oriented toward the infinite beauty
of God, which they attempt in some way to portray by the work of human hands.
They are dedicated to advancing God's praise and glory to the degree that they
center on the single aim of turning the human spirit devoutly toward God.

The Church has therefore always been the friend of the fine arts, has ever
sought their noble help, and has trained artists with the special aim that all things
set apart for use in divine worship are truly worthy, becoming, and beautiful, signs
and symbols of the supernatural world. The Church has always regarded itself as
the rightful arbiter of the arts, deciding which of the works of artists are in accordance with faith, with reverence, and with honored traditional laws and are thereby
suited for sacred use.

The Church has been particularly careful to see that sacred furnishings worthily and beautifully serve the dignity of worship and has admitted changes in materials, design, or ornamentation prompted by the progress of the technical arts with
the passage of time.

Wherefore it has pleased the Fathers to issue the following decrees on these
matters.

123. The Church has not adopted any particular style of art as its very own but has   123
admitted styles from every period, according to the proper genius and circumstances of peoples and the requirements of the many different rites in the Church.
Thus, in the course of the centuries, the Church has brought into being a treasury
of art that must be very carefully preserved. The art of our own days, coming from
every race and region, shall also be given free scope in the Church, on condition
that it serves the places of worship and sacred rites with the reverence and honor
due to them. In this way contemporary art can add its own voice to that wonderful
chorus of praise sung by the great masters of past ages of Catholic faith.

124   124. In encouraging and favoring art that is truly sacred, Ordinaries should strive after noble beauty rather than mere sumptuous display. This principle is to apply also in the matter of sacred vestments and appointments.

Let bishops carefully remove from the house of God and from other places of worship those works of artists that are repugnant to faith and morals and to Christian devotion and that offend true religious sense either by their grotesqueness or by the deficiency, mediocrity, or sham in their artistic quality.

When churches are to be built, let great care be taken that they are well suited to celebrating liturgical services and to bringing about the active participation of the faithful.

125   125. The practice of placing sacred images in churches so that they may be venerated by the faithful is to be maintained. Nevertheless there is to be restraint regarding their number and prominence so that they do not create confusion among the Christian people or foster religious practices of doubtful orthodoxy.

126   126. When deciding on works of art, local Ordinaries shall give hearing to the diocesan commission on sacred art and, if need be, to others who are especially expert, as well as to the commissions referred to in art. 44, 45, and 46. Ordinaries must be very careful to see that sacred furnishings and valuable works of art are not disposed of or damaged, for they are the adornment of the house of God.

127   127. Bishops should have a special concern for artists, so as to imbue them with the spirit of sacred art and liturgy. This they may do in person or through competent priests who are gifted with a knowledge and love of art.

It is also recommended that schools or academies of sacred art to train artists be founded in those parts of the world where they seem useful.

All artists who, prompted by their talents, desire to serve God's glory in holy Church, should ever bear in mind that they are engaged in a kind of sacred imitation of God the Creator and are concerned with works intended to be used in Catholic worship, to uplift the faithful, and to foster their devotion and religious formation.

128   128. Along with the revision of the liturgical books, as laid down in art. 25, there is to be an early revision of the canons and ecclesiastical statutes regulating the supplying of material things involved in sacred worship. This applies in particular to the worthy and well-planned construction of places of worship, the design and construction of altars, the nobility, placement, and security of the eucharistic tabernacle, the practicality and dignity of the baptistery, the appropriate arrangement of sacred images and church decorations and appointments. Laws that seem less suited to the reformed liturgy are to be brought into harmony with it or else abolished; laws that are helpful are to be retained if already in use or introduced where they are lacking.

With art. 22 of this Constitution as the norm, the territorial bodies of bishops are empowered to make adaptations to the needs and customs of their different regions; this applies especially to the material and design of sacred furnishings and vestments.

129   129. During their philosophical and theological studies clerics are to be taught about the history and development of sacred art and about the sound principles on which the production of its works must be grounded. In consequence they will be able to appreciate and preserve the Church's treasured monuments and be in a position to offer good advice to artists who are engaged in producing works of art.

130. It is fitting that the use of pontifical insignia be reserved to those ecclesiastical
persons who have either episcopal rank or some definite jurisdiction.

APPENDIX
DECLARATION OF THE SECOND VATICAN ECUMENICAL
COUNCIL ON REVISION OF THE CALENDAR

131. The Second Vatican Ecumenical Council recognizes the importance of the
wishes expressed by many on assigning the feast of Easter to a fixed Sunday and on
an unchanging calendar and has considered the effects that could result from the
introduction of a new calendar. Accordingly the Council issues the following declaration:

1. The Council is not opposed to the assignment of the feast of Easter to a
particular Sunday of the Gregorian Calendar, provided those whom it may concern,
especially other Christians who are not in communion with the Apostolic See, give
their assent.

2. The Council likewise declares that it does not oppose measures designed to
introduce a perpetual calendar into civil society .

Among the various systems being suggested to establish a perpetual calendar
and to introduce it into civil life, only those systems are acceptable to the Church
that retain and safeguard a seven-day week with Sunday and introduce no days
outside the week, so that the present sequence of weeks is left intact, unless the
most serious reasons arise. Concerning these the Apostolic See will make its own
judgment.

The Fathers of the Council have given assent to all and to each part of the
matters set forth in this Constitution. And together with the venerable Fathers, we,
by the apostolic power given to us by Christ, approve, enact, and establish in the
Holy Spirit each and all the decrees in this Constitution and command that what
has been thus established in the Council be promulgated for the glory of God.

▶   See also Chapter One, Section 2. Launching the Reform.

2. PAUL VI, **Address** to the Fathers at the end of the second period of
Vatican Council II, excerpt on the liturgy, 4 December 1963: AAS 56 (1964)
31–40.

[. . .] The difficult, complex debates have had rich results. They have brought
one topic to a conclusion, the sacred liturgy. Treated before all others, in a sense it
has priority over all others for its intrinsic dignity and importance to the life of the
Church and today we will solemnly promulgate the document on the liturgy. Our
spirit, therefore, exults with true joy, for in the way things have gone we note
respect for a right scale of values and duties. God must hold first place; prayer to
him is our first duty. The liturgy is the first source of the divine communion in
which God shares his own life with us. It is also the first school of the spiritual life.
The liturgy is the first gift we must make to the Christian people united to us by
faith and the fervor of their prayers. It is also a primary invitation to the human
race, so that all may lift their now mute voices in blessed and genuine prayer and

thus may experience that indescribable, regenerative power to be found when they join us in proclaiming the praises of God and the hopes of the human heart through Christ and the Holy Spirit.

133   We do not want to pass over in silence the faithful of the Eastern Churches, the high honor they hold for divine worship, and their precise care in celebrating the sacred rites. For them the liturgy has always been the school of truth and the spark of charity.

134   The first achievement of the Council must be treasured as something that will quicken and put its imprint on the life of the Church. The Church is above all a worshiping society, a praying community; it is a people alive with the purity of conscience and devotion to religion that faith and the gifts of grace vitalize. We are now in the process of simplifying the forms of worship so that they will be better understood by the faithful and better adapted to the language of our times. Still, the Council in no way intends thereby to lessen the importance of prayer, nor to subordinate it to other concerns of ministry or activity. Neither is there any intent to deprive liturgical prayer of its expressive power or ancient beauty. The purpose rather is to make the liturgy purer, truer to the marks of its own nature, closer to the sources of its truth and grace, readier to serve as a spiritual treasury for the faithful.

135   For the successful achievement of these goals it is our wish that no one violate the order of the Church's public prayer by introducing personal innovations or ritual novelties. We want no one by usurpation to lay claim to the power of the Constitution being promulgated today; all must await the publication of the relevant and clear norms on the liturgy and the lawful approval of those changes that will be provided by the postconciliar commissions established for the purpose. Let this preeminent prayer of the Church, then, resound in harmony throughout the world; let no one distort or pervert it.

3. VATICAN COUNCIL II, Decree on the Media of Social Communication *Inter mirifica*, 4 December 1963: AAS 56 (1964) 145–153; ConstDecrDecl 73–79 (excerpt).

136   18. Moreover, that the varied apostolates of the Church with respect to the media of social communication may be strengthened effectively, each year in every diocese of the world, by determination of the bishops, a day should be celebrated on which the faithful are instructed in their responsibilities in this regard. They should be invited to pray and contribute funds for this cause. Such funds are to be expended exclusively on the promotion, maintenance, and development of organizations and undertakings sponsored by the Church in this area, according to the needs of the whole Catholic world.

▶   170. PONTIFICAL COMMISSION FOR THE MEDIA OF SOCIAL COMMUNICA-
        TION, Instruction *Communio et progressio*, on application of the Decree on the
        Media, 23 May 1971.

4. VATICAN COUNCIL II, **Dogmatic Constitution on the Church** *Lumen gentium,* 21 November 1964: AAS 57 (1965) 5–67; ConstDecrDecl 93–206 (excerpts).

CHAPTER I
MYSTERY OF THE CHURCH

3.   The Son, therefore, came, sent by the Father. It was in him, before the founda-   137
tion of the world, that the Father chose us and predestined us to become adopted
children, for in him it pleased the Father to reestablish all things (see Eph 1:4–5,
10). To carry out the Father's will, Christ inaugurated the kingdom of heaven on
earth and revealed to us the mystery of that kingdom; by his obedience he brought
about redemption. The Church or, in other words, the kingdom of Christ already
present now in mystery, grows visibly through the power of God in the world. The
Church's inauguration and growth are symbolized by the blood and water that
flowed from the open side of Jesus crucified (see Jn 19:34) and are foretold in the
words of the Lord referring to his death on the cross: "And I, if I be lifted up from
the earth, will draw all things to myself" (Jn 12:32, Gr.). As often as the sacrifice of
the cross in which "Christ our Passover was sacrificed" (1 Cor 5:7) is celebrated on
the altar, the work of our redemption is carried on and, in the sacrament of the
eucharistic bread, the unity of all believers who form one Body in Christ (see 1 Cor
10:17) is both expressed and brought about. We are all called to this union with
Christ, who is the light of the world, from whom we go forth, through whom we
live, and toward whom our whole life presses forward.

6.   [. . .] Often the Church has also been called the "building" of God (see 1 Cor   138
3:9). The Lord himself compared himself to the stone that the builders rejected, but
which was made into the cornerstone (see Mt 21:42 and par.; Acts 4:11; 1 Pt 2:7; Ps
117 [118]:22). On this foundation the Church is built by the apostles (see 1 Cor
3:11) and from it the Church receives its stability and cohesiveness. This edifice has
many names to describe it: the house (see 1 Tm 3:15) of God in which his "family"
dwells as the household of God in the Spirit (see Eph 2:19–22); the "dwelling place
of God with us" (Rv 21:3); and, especially, the holy "temple." This temple the
Fathers of the Church point to as symbolized by places of worship built of stone
and the liturgy rightly likens to the holy city, the new Jerusalem.[5] Within it we, like
living stones, are being built up here on earth (see 1 Pt 2:5). John saw this holy city
coming down from heaven at the renewal of the world as "a bride made ready and
adorned for her husband" (Rv 21:1–2). [. . .]

7.   In the human nature united to himself, the Son of God, by overcoming death   139
through his own death and resurrection, redeemed us and refashioned us into a new
creation (see Gal 6:15; 2 Cor 5:17). By communicating his Spirit, Christ made us his
brothers and sisters, called together from all nations, to be mystically his own Body.

In that Body the life of Christ is bestowed on believers; through the sacraments they are united in a hidden and real way with Christ who suffered and was
glorified.[6] For through baptism we are formed in the likeness of Christ: "For in one

---

[5]   See Origen, *In Matth.* 16:21: PG 13, 1443. Tertullian, *Adv. Marcionem* 3, 7: PL 2, 357; CSEL 47, 3, 386.
Liturgical texts, see *Sacramentarium Gelasianum*: PL 78, 160; Mohlberg LibSacr 111, XC: "Deus qui ex omni
coaptacione sanctorum aeternum tibi condis habitaculum. . ."; hymns *Urbs Ierusalem beata: Breviarium mona-
sticum*; BrevRom [LH, Common of Dedication of a Church, evening prayer II]; *Coelestis urbs Ierusalem*:
BrevRom.

[6]   See ST 3a, 62.5 ad 1.

Spirit we were all baptized into one Body" (1 Cor 12:13). In this sacred rite our being joined to Christ's death and resurrection is both symbolized and brought about: "For we were buried with him by baptism into death"; and if "we have been united with him in a death like his, we shall certainly be united with him in a resurrection like his" (Rom 6:4–5). Really partaking of the body of the Lord in the breaking of the eucharistic bread, we are taken up into communion with him and with one another: "Because there is one bread, we who are many, are one Body, for we all partake of the one bread" (1 Cor 10:17). In this way all of us are made members of his Body (see 1 Cor 12:27), "but individually members one of another" (Rom 12:5). [. . .]

CHAPTER II
PEOPLE OF GOD

140

10. Christ the Lord, the High Priest taken from among us (see Heb 5:15), made the new people "a kingdom and priests to God the Father" (Rv 1:6; see 5:9–10). By rebirth and the anointing of the Holy Spirit, the baptized are consecrated as a spiritual house and a holy priesthood, so that through all the works proper to Christians, they may offer spiritual sacrifices and proclaim the power of him who has called them out of darkness into his wondrous light (see 1 Pt 2:4–10). Therefore all the disciples of Christ, persevering in prayer and praising God (see Acts 2:42–47), should present themselves as a living sacrifice, holy and pleasing to God (see Rom 12:1). Everywhere on earth they should bear witness to Christ and give answer to those who seek an account of that hope of eternal life that is in them (see 1 Pt 3:15).

Though they differ from one another in essence and not only in degree, the universal priesthood of believers and the ministerial or hierarchic priesthood are nonetheless interrelated: each of them in its own special way is a sharing in the one priesthood of Christ.[1] The ministerial priest, by the sacred power he possesses, builds up and guides the priestly people; acting in the person of Christ, he makes present the eucharistic sacrifice and offers it to God in the name of all the people. The faithful on their part, in virtue of their royal priesthood, join in the offering of the eucharist.[2] They likewise exercise that priesthood in receiving the sacraments, in prayer and thanksgiving, in the witness of a holy life, and in self-denial and active charity.

141

11. The sacraments and the exercise of the virtues give actual expression to the sacred, organically structured nature of the priestly community. Incorporated into the Church through baptism, the faithful are deputed by the baptismal character for the worship of the Christian religion. Reborn as children of God, they must confess before men the faith they have received from God through the Church.[3] By the sacrament of confirmation they are more fully bound to the Church and the Holy Spirit endows them with special strength, so that they are more strictly obliged to spread and defend the faith, both by word and by deed, as true witnesses of Christ.[4] Taking part in the eucharistic sacrifice, the fount and apex of the whole

---

[1] See Pius XII, Addr. *Magnificate Dominum,* 2 Nov. 1954: AAS 46 (1954) 669; Encycl. *Mediator Dei,* 20 Nov. 1947: AAS 39 (1947) 555.

[2] See Pius XI, Encycl. *Miserentissimus Redemptor,* 8 May 1928: AAS 20 (1928) 171. Pius XII, Addr. *Vous nous avez,* 22 Sept. 1956: AAS 48 (1956) 714.

[3] See ST 3a, 63.2.

[4] See Cyril of Jerusalem, *Catech.* 17, de Spiritu Sancto 2, 35–37: PG 33, 1009–12. Nicolas Cabasilas, *De vita in Christo* lib. 3, de utilitate chrismatis: PG 150, 569–580. ST 3a, 65.3 and 72.1 and 5.

Christian life, they offer the divine victim to God and offer themselves along with him.[5] Thus by reason of both the offering and holy communion all take part in this liturgical service, not indeed all in the same way, but all in their proper way. Strengthened in holy communion by the body of Christ, they then manifest in a concrete way the unity of the people of God that this sacrament aptly signifies and wondrously causes.

Those who approach the sacrament of penance obtain from God's mercy pardon for having offended him and at the same time reconciliation with the Church, which they have wounded by their sins and which by charity, example, and prayer seeks their conversion. By the sacred anointing of the sick and the prayer of priests the entire Church commends the sick to the suffering and glorified Lord, asking that he lighten their suffering and save them (see Jas 5:14-16); the Church exhorts them, moreover, to contribute to the welfare of the whole people of God by associating themselves freely with Christ's passion and death (see Rom 8:17; Col 1:24; 2 Tm 2:11-12; 1 Pt 4:13). Those of the faithful who are consecrated by holy orders are appointed to feed the Church in Christ's name with the word and the grace of God. Finally, Christian spouses, in virtue of the sacrament of marriage, whereby they signify and partake of the mystery of that unity and fruitful love existing between Christ and his Church (see Eph 5:32), help each other to attain to holiness in their married life and in the rearing and education of their children. By reason of their state and rank in life they have their own special gift among the people of God.[6] From the marriage of Christians comes the family, in which new citizens of human society are born; in baptism by the grace of the Holy Spirit they are made the children of God in order to perpetuate the people of God through the ages. The family is, so to speak, the Church of the household. In it, by their word and example, parents should be the first preachers of the faith to their children; they should encourage them in the vocation proper to each and with special care in a vocation to a sacred state.

Endowed with so many and such powerful means of salvation, all the faithful, whatever their condition or state, have from the Lord, in a way proper to each, the vocation to that perfect holiness by which the Father himself is perfect.

12. The holy people of God share also in Christ's prophetic office and spread abroad a living witness to him, especially by means of a life of faith and charity and by offering to God a sacrifice of praise, that is, the fruit of lips giving thanks to his name (see Heb 13:15). The entire body of the faithful, anointed as they are by the Holy One (see Jn 2:20, 27), cannot err in matters of belief. They manifest this special endowment by means of the whole people's supernatural discernment in matters of faith (*sensus fidei*) when "from the bishops down to the last of the lay faithful"[7] they show universal agreement in matters of faith and morals. That discernment in matters of faith is enlivened and sustained by the Spirit of truth. It is exercised under the guidance of the sacred teaching authority (*magisterium*); in faithful and respectful obedience to this authority the people of God receive not just the word of men but truly the word of God (see 1 Thes 2:13). Through it the people of God adhere unwaveringly to the "faith given once and for all to the saints" (Jude 3), penetrate it more deeply with right thinking, and apply it more fully in their lives.

142

---

⁵ See Pius XII, Encycl. *Mediator Dei*, 20 Nov 1947: AAS 39 (1947) esp. 552.

⁶ 1 Cor 7:7: "But each has his own gift (*idion charisma*) of God, one of this kind and one of another." See Augustine, *De dono persever.* 14, 37: PL 45, 1015: "It is not only continence that is a gift of God, but the chastity of the married as well."

⁷ Augustine, *De praed. Sanctorum* 14, 27: PL 44, 980.

143   13. All are called to belong to the new people of God. Wherefore this people,
while remaining one and only one, is to be spread throughout the whole world and
must exist in all ages. This is the way the purposes of God's will are to be fulfilled;
in the beginning he made human nature one and decreed that all his children,
scattered as they were, would finally be gathered together as one (see Jn 11:52). For
this purpose God sent his Son, whom he appointed heir of all things (see Heb 1:2),
that he might be teacher, king, and priest for all, the head of the new and universal
people of the children of God. For this too God at the last sent the Spirit of his Son
as Lord and giver of life. He is the source of the coming together of the whole
Church and of each and everyone of those who believe, as well as of their unity in
the teaching of the apostles and in fellowship, in the breaking of bread and in
prayers (see Acts 2:42, Gr.). [. . .]

144   17. As the Son was sent by the Father, so he too sent the apostles (see Jn 20:21),
saying: "Go, therefore, make disciples of all nations, baptizing them in the name of
the Father and of the Son and of the Holy Spirit, teaching them to observe all things
whatsoever I have commanded you. And behold I am with you always even to the
close of the age" (Mt 28:19–20). The Church has received from the apostles this
solemn mandate of Christ to proclaim the saving truth and must carry it out to the
very ends of the earth (see Acts 1:8). Wherefore it makes the words of the Apostle
its own, "Woe to me, if I do not preach the Gospel" (1 Cor 9:16), and continues
unceasingly to send heralds of the Gospel until such time as the infant Churches are
fully established and can themselves carry on the work of evangelizing. For the
Holy Spirit impels the Church to do its part for the full accomplishment of the plan
by which God has constituted Christ as the source of salvation for the whole world.
By the proclamation of the Gospel the Church draws those who hear to receive and
profess the faith, disposes them for baptism, rescues them from the bondage of
error, and incorporates them into Christ so that through charity they may grow up
into full maturity in him. Through the work of the Church whatever good is in the
human mind and heart, whatever good lies latent in the religious practices and
cultures of diverse peoples, is not only saved from destruction but is also cleansed,
raised up, and made perfect unto the glory of God, the confounding of the devil,
and the happiness of man. On all Christ's disciples, according to the capability of
each, rests the obligation to spread the faith.[8] Even though anyone can baptize
those who believe, the priest alone can complete the building up of the Body in the
eucharistic sacrifice. Thus are fulfilled the words of God, spoken through his prophet: "From the rising of the sun to its setting my name is great among the nations and
in every place a pure offering is sacrificed and offered up in my name (Mal 1:11)."[9]
In this way the Church both prays and labors for the entire world to become the
people of God, the Body of the Lord, and the temple of the Holy Spirit and for all
honor and glory to be rendered to the Creator of all, in Christ the Head of all.

CHAPTER III
HIERARCHIC STRUCTURE OF THE CHURCH
AND IN PARTICULAR THE EPISCOPATE

145   21. In the bishops, therefore, who have priests as their helpers, our Lord Jesus
Christ, the supreme High Priest, is present in the midst of those who believe. Seated

---

[8]   See Benedict XV, Apostolic Epistle, *Maximum illud*: AAS 11 (1919) 440, esp. 451ff. Pius XI, Encycl.
Rerum Ecclesiae: AAS 18 (1926) 68–69. Pius XII, Encycl. *Fidei Donum*, 21 April 1957: AAS 49 (1957) 236–237.

[9]   See *Didache* 14: Funk DidConst 1, 32. Justin Martyr, *Dial.* 41: PG 6, 564. Irenaeus, *Adv. Haer.* 4, 17, 5:
PG 1, 1023; Harvey 2, 199. Council of Trent, sess. 22, cap. 1: Denz-Schön 1742.

at the right hand of the Father, Christ is not absent from the gathering of his high priests.[1] First of all, through their excellent service he preaches the word of God to all nations and constantly administers the sacraments of faith to those who believe. Through their fatherly care (see 1 Cor 4:15) he incorporates new members into his Body by a heavenly rebirth. Finally, through the bishop's wisdom and prudence he directs and guides the people of the New Covenant in their pilgrimage toward eternal happiness. These pastors, chosen to shepherd the Lord's flock of the elect, are servants of Christ and stewards of the mysteries of God (see 1 Cor 4:1); they are entrusted with bearing witness to the Gospel of God's grace (see Rom 15:16; Acts 20:24) and with the splendor of the new dispensation of the Spirit and of righteousness (see 2 Cor 3:8–9).

For the carrying out of these great offices, Christ empowered the apostles through a special outpouring of the Holy Spirit, who descended upon them (see Acts 1:8, 2:4; Jn 20:22–23); they passed on their spiritual gift to their helpers by the laying on of hands (see 1Tm 4:14; 2 Tm 1:6–7) and it has been handed down to us in episcopal consecration.[2] This Council teaches that episcopal consecration bestows the fullness of the sacrament of orders, that fullness of power, namely, which in both the Church's liturgical practice and the language of the Fathers is called the high priesthood, the summit of the sacred ministry.[3] But episcopal consecration, together with the office of sanctifying, also confers the offices of teaching and governing, offices which, of their very nature, can be exercised only in hierarchic communion with the head of the college and its members. For from tradition, expressed especially in liturgical rites and in the usage of the Church of both East and West, it is clear that the laying on of hands and the words of consecration bestow the grace of the Holy Spirit[4] and impress a sacred character[5] in such a way that bishops in an eminent and visible way carry on the roles of Christ himself as teacher, shepherd, and high priest and act in his person.[6] Admission of newly elected members into the episcopal body by means of the sacrament of orders belongs to the bishops.

26. Marked with the fullness of the sacrament of orders, a bishop is "the steward   146 of the grace of the supreme priesthood,"[7] especially in the eucharist, which he offers or causes to be offered[8] and by which the Church continually lives and grows. This Church of Christ is truly present in all lawful, local congregations of

---

[1]   See Leo the Great, *Serm.* 5, 3: PL 54, 154.

[2]   The Council of Trent in sess. 23, cap. 3 quotes the text of 2 Tm 1:6–7 to prove that holy orders is a true sacrament: Denz-Schön 1766.

[3]   The *Traditio Apostolica* of Hippolytus 3 attributes to the bishop the "primacy of priesthood": Botte, ed., SC 11 bis, 27–30. See *Sacramentarium Leonianum* in Mohlberg SacrVeron 119: "ad summi sacerdotii ministerium . . . Comple in sacerdotibus tuis mysterii tui summam". . . Mohlberg LibSacr 121–122: "Tribuas eis, Domine, cathedram episcopalem ad regendam Ecclesiam tuam et plebem universam." See PL 78, 224.

[4]   See *Traditio Apostolica* of Hippolytus 2: ed. cit., 27.

[5]   See Council of Trent, sess. 23, cap. 4, the teaching that the sacrament of orders imprints a sacramental character: Denz-Schön 1767. See also John XXIII, Addr. *Iubilate Deo*, 8 May 1960: AAS 52 (1960) 446. Paul VI, Homily at St. Peter's, 20 Oct. 1963: AAS 55 (1963) 1014.

[6]   See Cyprian, *Epist.* 63, 14: PL 4, 386; CSEL 3.2, 713: "The priest truly acts in the place of Christ." John Chrysostom, *In 2 Tim.*, Homil. 2, 4: PG 62, 612: The priest is the "symbol" of Christ. Ambrose, *In Ps.* 38, 25–26: PL 14, 1051–52; CSEL 64, 203–204. Ambrosiaster, *In 1 Tim.* 5, 19 and *In Eph.* 4, 11–12: PL 17, 479 and 387. Theodore of Mopsuestia, *Hom. catech.* 15, 21 and 24: Tonneau, ed., 497 and 503. Hesychius of Jerusalem, *In Lev.* 50, 2, 9, 23: PG 93, 849.

[7]   Prayer of consecration of a bishop in the Byzantine rite: *Euchologion to mega* (Rome, 1873) 139.

[8]   Ignatius of Antioch, *Smyrn.* 8,1: Funk PA 1, 282.

the faithful, which, united with their pastors, are themselves called Churches in the New Testament.[9] For in their own locality these Churches are the new people called by God in the Holy Spirit and in great fullness (see 1 Thes 1:5). In them the faithful are gathered together by the preaching of Christ's Gospel and the mystery of the Lord's Supper is celebrated, so that "by the food and blood of the Lord's body the whole brotherhood is joined together."[10] Any community of the altar, under the sacred ministry of the bishop,[11] stands out clearly as a symbol of that charity and "unity of the Mystical Body, without which there can be no salvation."[12] In these communities, though frequently small and poor or living in isolation, Christ is present and the power of his presence gathers together one, holy, catholic, and apostolic Church.[13] For "the sharing of the body and blood of Christ does nothing less than transform us into what we receive."[14]

Every lawful celebration of the eucharist is regulated by the bishop, to whom is committed the office of offering to the divine majesty the worship of Christian religion and of administering it in accordance with the Lord's commandments and the Church's laws, as further specified by his particular judgment for his diocese.

By praying and laboring for the people bishops thus in many ways and in great abundance cause the fullness of Christ's holiness to flow upon their people. Through the ministry of the word they communicate God's power to those who believe unto salvation (see Rom 1:16) and through the sacraments, the regular and fruitful administration of which they direct by their authority,[15] they sanctify the faithful. They oversee the conferral of baptism, which bestows a share in Christ's royal priesthood. They are the primary ministers of confirmation, dispensers of sacred orders, and the moderators of penitential discipline; they also earnestly exhort and instruct their people to carry out, with faith and reverence, their part in the liturgy, especially in the holy sacrifice of the Mass. Lastly, by the example of their way of life they must be an influence for good on those in their charge, keeping their own way of life free of evil and with God's help turned in every way possible toward the good, so that together with the flock committed to their care they may reach eternal life.[16]

147   27.   As vicars and ambassadors of Christ,[17] bishops govern the particular Churches entrusted to them through their counsel, exhortation, example, but also through their authority and sacred power, which indeed they use only for the building up of their flock in truth and holiness, mindful that the greater should become as the less and the chief as one who serves (see Lk 22:26–27). The power that they personally exercise in Christ's name is theirs by right and is ordinary and immediate, even though ultimately its exercise is governed by the supreme authority in the Church and can be circumscribed by definite limits for the advantage of the Church or of

---

[9] See Acts 8:1, 14:22–23, 20:17 and passim.

[10] Prayer from the Mozarabic Rite: PL 96, 759 B.

[11] See Ignatius of Antioch, *Smyrn.* 8,1: Funk PA 1, 282.

[12] ST 3a, 73.3.

[13] See Augustine, *Contra Faustum* 12, 20: PL 42, 265; *Serm.* 57, 7: PL 38, 389, etc.

[14] Leo the Great, *Serm.* 63, 7: PL 54, 357 C.

[15] See *Traditio Apostolica* of Hippolytus 2–3: ed. cit., 26–30.

[16] See the texts for the examination of the candidate at the beginning of an episcopal consecration and the prayer after the *Te Deum* at the end.

[17] Benedict XIV, Brief *Romana Ecclesia,* 5 Oct. 1752, § 1: *Bullarium Benedicti XIV,* v. 4 (Rome, 1758) 21: "Episcopus Christi typum gerit, Eiusque munere fungitur." Pius XII, Encycl. *Mystici Corporis:* AAS 35 (1943) 211: "Assignatos sibi greges singuli singulos Christi nomine pascunt et regunt."

the faithful. In virtue of this power bishops have the sacred right and the duty before the Lord of making laws for their subjects, of passing judgment, and of controlling whatever belongs to the right order of worship and the apostolate. [. . .]

28. Christ, whom the Father has sanctified and sent into the world (see Jn 10:36), through his apostles has made their successors, the bishops, sharers in his consecration and mission.[18] They in turn have lawfully handed on to different individuals in the Church in varying degrees a participation in this ministry. Thus the divinely established ecclesiastical ministry is exercised at different levels by those who from antiquity have been called bishops, priests, and deacons.[19] Even though they do not possess the fullness of the priesthood and in the exercise of their power are subordinate to the bishops, priests are nevertheless linked to the bishops in priestly dignity.[20] By virtue of the sacrament of orders,[21] in the image of Christ the eternal High Priest (see Heb 5:1–10, 7:24, 9:11–28), they are consecrated to preach the Gospel, to shepherd the faithful, and to celebrate divine worship as true priests of the New Testament.[22] Partakers of the function of Christ, the sole Mediator (see 1 Tm 2:5), at their own level of ministry they announce the divine word to all. They exercise their sacred function above all in the eucharistic worship or celebration of Mass, by which, acting in the person of Christ[23] and proclaiming his mystery, they unite the prayers of the faithful with the sacrifice of their Head and until the Lord's coming (see 2 Cor 11:26) make present again and apply in the sacrifice of the Mass the single sacrifice of the New Testament, namely, that of Christ offering himself once to the Father as spotless victim (see Heb 9:11–28).[24] For the repentant and the sick among the faithful they exercise the ministry of reconciliation and alleviation and they present the needs and the prayers of the faithful to God the Father (see Heb 5:1–3). Exercising within the limits of their authority the function of Christ as shepherd and Head,[25] they gather together God's family as a community all of one mind,[26] and lead them in the Spirit, through Christ, to God the Father. In the midst of the flock they adore him in spirit and in truth (see Jn 4:24). Finally, they labor in word and teaching (see 1 Tm 5:17), believing what they have read meditatively in the Law of God, teaching what they have believed, and putting into practice in their own lives what they have taught.[27]

148

---

[18] See Ignatius Martyr, *Ad Ephes.* 6, 1: Funk PA 1, 218.

[19] See Council of Trent, *De sacramento Ordinis* cap. 2 and can. 6: Denz-Schön 1765 and 1776.

[20] See Innocent I, *Epist. ad Decentium*: PL 20, 554 A; Mansi 3, 1029; Denz-Schön 215: "Presbyteri, licet secundi sint *sacerdotes*, pontificatus tamen *apicem* non habent." See also Cyprian, *Epist.* 61, 3: CSEL 3.1, 696.

[21] See Council of Trent, loc. cit. and esp. can. 7: Denz-Schön 1763–78, esp. 1777. Pius XII, Ap. Const. *Sacramentum Ordinis* : Denz-Schön 3857–61.

[22] See Innocent I, loc. cit. Gregory of Nazianzus, *Apol.* 2, 22: PG 35, 432. Dionysius the Pseudo-Areopagite, *Eccl. hier.* 1, 2: PG 3, 372 D.

[23] See Council of Trent, sess. 22: Denz-Schön 1743. Pius XII, Encycl. *Mediator Dei*: AAS 39 (1947) 553; Denz-Schön 3850.

[24] See Council of Trent, sess. 22: Denz-Schön 1739–40. Vatican Council II, SC art. 7 and 47 [DOL 1 nos. 7 and 47].

[25] See Pius XII, Encycl. *Mediator Dei* loc. cit.

[26] See Cyprian, *Epist.* 11, 3: PL 4, 242 B; CSEL 2.2, 497.

[27] See PR, *Ordo consecrationis sacerdotalis* bestowal of vestments [RP, Ordination of Priests, no. 14].

Priests, prudent cooperators with the episcopal order,[28] its aid and instrument, called to serve the people of God, constitute one priestly college with their bishop,[29] charged with different duties. Associated with their bishop in a spirit of trust and generosity, they make him present in a certain sense in the individual local congregations and in their day-to-day tasks do their part to carry out his functions and concerns. As they sanctify and govern, under the bishop's authority, that part of the Lord's flock entrusted to them, they make the universal Church visible in their own locality and contribute effectively to the building up of the whole Body of Christ (see Eph 4:12). Intent always upon the welfare of God's children, they must strive to lend their effort to the pastoral work of the whole diocese and even of the entire Church. On account of this sharing in their priesthood and mission, let priests sincerely look upon the bishop as their father and reverently obey him. Let the bishop regard his priests as his co-workers, as sons and friends, just as Christ called his disciples now not servants but friends (see Jn 15:15). All priests, both diocesan and religious, by reason of orders and ministry, are joined to the body of bishops and priests and serve the good of the whole Church in accord with their calling and the grace given to them. [. . .]

149   29. At a lower level of the hierarchy are deacons, who receive the laying on of hands "not unto priesthood but only for a ministry of service."[30] Strengthened by sacramental grace they have as their service for the people of God, in communion with the bishop and his college of presbyters, the *diakonia* of liturgy, word, and charity. Insofar as competent authority assigns them, the duties of the deacon are to: administer baptism solemnly; care for the eucharist and give holy communion; assist at and bless marriages in the name of the Church; carry viaticum to the dying; read the Scriptures to the people and exhort and instruct them; preside over worship and prayer; administer sacramentals; officiate at funeral and burial rites. Dedicated to duties of charity and service, deacons should be mindful of the admonition of St. Polycarp: "Be compassionate and conscientious, following the model set by the Lord, who made himself the servant of all."[31]

As the discipline of the Latin Church currently stands, these diaconal functions, supremely necessary to the Church's life, can be carried out in many places only with great difficulty. Henceforth, therefore, it will be permissible to restore the diaconate as a distinct and permanent rank of the hierarchy. To the various sorts of authorized territorial bodies of bishops it belongs to decide, with papal approval, whether and where it is advantageous to create permanent deacons for the care of souls. With the pope's consent, the permanent diaconate may be conferred on men of mature years, even married men, and upon qualified young men. For the last, however, the law of celibacy must remain in force.

CHAPTER IV
LAITY

150   33. Gathered together in the people of God and made members of the Body of Christ under one Head, all the laity are called upon as living members to expend

---

[28] See ibid., preface [RP no. 22].

[29] See Ignatius Martyr, *Philad.* 4: Funk PA 1, 266. Cornelius I, quoted in Cyprian, *Epist.* 48, 2: CSEL 3.2, 610.

[30] *Constitutiones Ecclesiae aegyptiacae* 3, 2: Funk DidConst 2, 103. *Statuta Eccl. Ant.* 37–41: Mansi 3, 954.

[31] Polycarp, *Ad. Phil.* 5, 2: Funk PA 1, 300: Christ is said to "become the *diaconus* of all." See Didache 15, 1: Funk PA 1, 32. Ignatius Martyr, *Trall.* 2, 3: Funk 1, 242. *Constitutiones Apostolorum* 8, 28, 4: Funk DidConst 1, 530.

every resource they have received through the kindness of the Creator and the grace of the Redeemer for the growth of the Church and its continuous sanctification.

The apostolate of the laity is a participation in the salvific mission of the Church itself; through their baptism and confirmation all are commissioned to that apostolate by the Lord himself. Moreover, by the sacraments, especially the eucharist, that charity toward God and neighbor which is the soul of the apostolate is communicated and nourished. The laity are called in a special way to make the Church to be present and at work in those places and circumstances where only through them can it become the salt of the earth.[1] Thus all the laity, in virtue of the very gifts bestowed upon them, are at the same time witnesses and living instruments of the mission of the Church itself "according to the measure of Christ's gift" (Eph 4:7). [. . .]

34. The supreme and eternal Priest, Christ Jesus, since he wills to continue his witness and service also through the laity, quickens them in his Spirit and increasingly urges them on to every good and perfect work.   151

For besides intimately linking them to his life and his mission, he also gives them a share in his priestly office of offering spiritual worship for the divine glory and human salvation. Thus the laity, dedicated to Christ and anointed by the Holy Spirit, are sublimely called and prepared so that ever more abundant fruits of the Spirit may be brought forth in them. For, if carried out in the Spirit, all their works, their prayers and apostolic endeavors, their ordinary married and family life, their daily occupations, their physical and mental relaxation, and even the hardships of life, when patiently borne, become spiritual sacrifices acceptable to God through Jesus Christ (see 1 Pt 2:5). All these are most fittingly offered to the Father in union with the offering of the body of the Lord in the celebration of the eucharist. Thus as adorers acting with holiness in all things, the laity consecrate the world itself to God.

35. Christ, the great prophet who proclaimed the kingdom of his Father by both the testimony of his life and the power of his words, continually fulfills his prophetic office until the complete manifestation of glory. He does so not only through the hierarchy, who teach in his name and with his authority, but also through the laity, whom he has made his witnesses and endowed with understanding of the faith (*sensu fidei*) and the grace of speech (see Acts 2:17–18; Rv 19:10) so that the power of the Gospel may shine forth in their daily social and family life. [. . .]   152

Just as the sacraments of the New Law, which nourish the life and the apostolate of the faithful, prefigure a new heaven and a new earth (see Rv 21:1), so too the laity go forth as powerful heralds of a faith in things to be hoped for (see Heb 11:1), when they unwaveringly join to their profession of faith a life prompted by faith. This evangelization, that is, this announcing of Christ by living witness as well as by spoken word, takes on a specific quality and a singular power in that it is carried out in the ordinary surroundings of the world.

In this service of the laity, that state of life which is sanctified by a special sacrament is obviously of great value, namely, married and family life. [. . .]

Even when preoccupied with temporal cares, the laity can and must perform a work of great value for the evangelization of the world. Some of them, in fact, have to supply the sacred services, to the extent that they can, when there are no sacred ministers or in times of persecution; many devote all their energies to apostolic

---

[1] See Pius XI, Encycl. *Quadragesimo anno*, 15 May 1931: AAS 23 (1931) 221ff. Pius XII, Addr. *De quelle consolation*, 14 Oct. 1951: AAS 43 (1951) 790ff.

work; all, however, must cooperate for the spread and the growth of Christ's kingdom in the world. Therefore, let the laity devotedly strive to acquire a more profound grasp of revealed truth and plead constantly with God for the gift of wisdom.

153   37. The laity have the right, as do all Christians, to receive from their bishops in abundance the spiritual goods of the Church, especially the assistance of the word of God and of the sacraments;[2] they should, in turn, openly reveal to these pastors their needs and desires with the freedom and confidence that befits children of God whose brother is Christ. [. . .]

[. . .] Nor should the laity fail to pray for their bishops, so that with joy and not grief (see Heb 13:17) these pastors may keep watch as men charged with giving an account of the souls of their people.

CHAPTER V
UNIVERSAL CALL TO HOLINESS IN THE CHURCH

154   42. "God is love, and he who abides in love, abides in God, and God abides in him" (1 Jn 4:16). But, since God has poured out his love into our hearts through the Holy Spirit, who has been given to us (see Rom 5:5), the first and most necessary gift is love, by which we love God above all things and our neighbor because of God. Indeed, in order that like the good seed love may grow and bring forth fruit in the soul, all the faithful must willingly hear the word of God and in their works carry out his will through the help of his grace. Such works consist in the use of the sacraments and especially the eucharist, frequent participation in the sacred rites of the liturgy, application to prayer, self-abnegation, lively mutual service, and the constant exercise of all the virtues. For charity, as the bond of perfection, the fulfillment of the Law (see Col 3:14; Rom 13:10), rules over all the means of attaining holiness, gives life to them, and bears them toward their goal.[1] Thus love for God and the love for neighbor are the mark of the true disciple of Christ. [. . .]

CHAPTER VI
RELIGIOUS

155   44. Through the vows, or other sacred bonds analogous to the vows in their own way, members of the faithful oblige themselves to the evangelical counsels and bind themselves totally to God as loved above all. These faithful of Christ thereby have a new and distinctive kind of relationship to the service and honor of God. For baptism has made them die to sin and consecrated them to God; but in order that they may attain the effects of baptismal grace more abundantly they propose by their profession in the Church of the evangelical counsels both to rid themselves of the obstacles that could stand in the way of the intensity of charity and the completeness of their worship of God, and to consecrate themselves more radically to the divine service.[1] [. . .]

156   45. [. . .] The Church not only raises religious profession to the dignity of being a canonical state by its law, but by its liturgy shows that it is a state consecrated to

---

2   See CIC, can. 682.

1   See Augustine, *Enchiridion* 121, 32: PL 40, 288. ST 2a2ae, 184.1. Pius XII, Ap. Exhort. *Menti nostrae*, 23 Sept. 1950: AAS 42 (1950) 660.

1   See ST 2a2ae, 184.3 and 188.2. Bonaventure, Opusc. 11, *Apologia Pauperum* cap. 3, 3: *Opera*, v. 8 (ed. Quaracchi, 1898) 245a.

God. For the Church itself, by the authority committed to it by God, receives the vows of those making profession; by its public prayer it entreats God that help and grace be given to them; it puts them in his hands and bestows on them a spiritual blessing, as it conjoins their offering to the eucharistic sacrifice.

CHAPTER VII
ESCHATOLOGICAL NATURE OF THE PILGRIM CHURCH
AND ITS UNION WITH THE CHURCH IN HEAVEN

49. [. . .] All those who belong to Christ, possessing his Spirit, come together into   157
the one Church and are joined together in Christ (see Eph 4:16). The union between those who are still pilgrims and their brothers and sisters who have died in the peace of Christ is therefore not broken, but rather strengthened by a communion in spiritual blessings; this has always been the faith of the Church. Because those in heaven are more closely united with Christ, they ground the whole Church more firmly in holiness, lend nobility to the worship the Church offers to God here on earth, and in many ways contribute to its upbuilding (see 1 Cor 12:12–27).[1] For after they have been received into their heavenly home and are present to the Lord (see 2 Cor 5:8), through him and with him and in him they do not cease to intercede with the Father for us.[2] They show forth the merits they have won on earth through the one Mediator between God and us (see 1 Tm 2:5) by serving God in all things and filling up in their flesh those things that are lacking of the sufferings of Christ for his Body which is the Church (see Col 1:24).[3] Thus their familial concern brings us great aid in our weakness.

50. Fully conscious of this communion of the entire Mystical Body of Jesus Christ,   158
the pilgrim Church from the very first ages of the Christian religion has devotedly revered the memory of the dead[4] and, "because it is a holy and wholesome thought to pray for the dead that they may be loosed from their sins" (see 2 Mc 12:46), also offers prayers for them. The Church has always believed that the apostles and Christ's martyrs, who have given the supreme witness of faith and charity by the shedding of their blood, are closely joined with us in Christ and has always venerated them with special devotion, together with the Blessed Virgin Mary and the holy angels,[5] and has devoutly implored the aid of their intercession. To these were soon added those also who had more closely imitated Christ's virginity and poverty,[6] then those whom heroic practice of the Christian virtues[7] and their divine charisms recommended to the devotion and imitation of the faithful.[8]

When we look at the lives of those who have faithfully followed Christ, we are inspired with a new reason for seeking the city that is to come (see Heb 13:14,

---

[1]   See the synthetic exposition of this teaching of St. Paul in Pius XII, Encycl. *Mystici Corporis*: AAS 35 (1943) 200 and passim.

[2]   See, e.g., Augustine, *Enarrat in Ps.* 85, 24: PL 37, 1099. Jerome, *Liber contra Vigilantium* 6: PL 23, 344. Thomas Aquinas, *In 4ᵐ Sent* ., d.45, q.3, a.2. Bonaventure, *In 4ᵐ Sent.*, d.45, a.3, q.2; etc.

[3]   See Pius XII, loc. cit.: 245.

[4]   Thus the many inscriptions in the Catacombs of Rome.

[5]   See Gelasius I, *De libris recipiendis* 3: PL 59, 160; Denz-Schön 353.

[6]   See Methodius, *Symposion* 7, 3: GCS 74.

[7]   See Benedict XV, *Decretum approbationis virtutum in causa beatificationis et canonizationis Servi Dei Ioannis Nepomuceni Neumann*: AAS 14 (1922) 23. See also addresses on the saints by Pius XI, *Discorsi e Radiomessaggi*, vv. 1–3 (1941–42). Pius XII, *Discorsi e Radiomessaggi*, v. 10 (1949) 37–43.

[8]   See Pius XII, Encycl. *Mediator Dei*: AAS 39 (1947) 581.

11:10) and at the same time we are shown a secure path along which, amid the vicissitudes of this world, in keeping with the state in life and condition proper to each of us, we will be able to arrive at perfect holiness.[9] In the lives of those who, although sharing in our humanity, yet are more fully transformed into the image of Christ, God strikingly manifests his presence and his countenance to us. He speaks to us in them and gives us a sign of his kingdom,[10] to which we are powerfully drawn by so great a host of witnesses before us (see Heb 12:1) and their proof of the truth of the Gospel.

Nor is it in virtue of example alone that we hold dear the memory of those in heaven, but even more so in the interest of strengthening the union of the whole Church in the Spirit through the practice of mutual charity (see Eph 4:1–6). For just as Christian communion among wayfarers brings us closer to Christ, so our companionship with the saints joins us to Christ, from whom as from its source and Head issue every grace and the very life of the people of God.[11] It is supremely fitting, therefore, that we love those friends, coheirs of Jesus Christ, who are also our brothers and sisters, our special benefactors; that we render the thanks due to God for them;[12] that "we call on them in supplication and have recourse to their prayers and help to obtain favors from God through his Son, Jesus Christ, our Redeemer and Savior."[13] For every genuine expression of our love toward them by its very nature has as its term Christ, "crown of all the saints,"[14] and through him God, wonderful in his saints and in them glorified.[15]

Our union with the Church in heaven has as its supreme form of expression our celebrating together in joint exultation the praise of God's majesty, especially in the liturgy — wherein the Holy Spirit's power acts upon us through the signs of the sacraments[16] — when we all, from every tribe and tongue and people and nation redeemed in Christ's blood (see Rv 5:9) and gathered together into the one Church, glorify the triune God with one hymn of praise. Celebration of the eucharistic sacrifice, therefore, joins us most closely to the Church in heaven, as we enter into communion with and honor the memory, first of all, of the glorious Mary, ever virgin, then of the blessed Joseph, the blessed apostles and martyrs, and all the saints.[17]

159   51. This Council accepts with great devotion the revered faith of our ancestors regarding this vital communion with our own who are in heavenly glory or who after death are still being purified and it reaffirms the decrees of the Council of Nicaea II,[18] of Florence,[19] and of Trent.[20] At the same time, in conformity with our

---

⁹   See Heb 13:7; Sir ch. 44–50; Heb 11:3–40. See also Pius XII, loc. cit.: 582–583.

¹⁰   See Vatican Council I, Const. Dogm. *De fide catholica*, cap. 3: Denz-Schön 3013.

¹¹   See Pius XII, Encycl. *Mystici Corporis*: AAS 35 (1943) 216.

¹²   On gratitude toward the saints themselves, see E. Diehl, *Inscriptiones latinae christianae veteres*, v. 1 (Berlin, 1925) nos. 2008, 2382, and passim.

¹³   Council of Trent, sess. 25, *De invocatione . . . Sanctorum*: Denz-Schön 1821.

¹⁴   BrevRom, Invitatorium, feast of All Saints.

¹⁵   See, e.g., 2 Thes 1:10.

¹⁶   See Vatican II, SC art. 104 [DOL 1, no. 104].

¹⁷   See MR, Canon of the Mass [RM, Eucharistic Prayer I].

¹⁸   See Council of Nicaea II, Act. 7: Denz-Schön 600.

¹⁹   See Council of Florence, *Decretum pro Graecis*: Denz-Schön 1304.

²⁰   See Council of Trent, sess. 25, loc. cit.: Denz-Schön 1821–24; Decr. *De purgatorio*: Denz-Schön 1820; sess. 6, Decr. *De iustificatione* can. 30: Denz-Schön 1580.

own pastoral interests, we urge all concerned, if any abuses, excesses, or shortcomings have crept in here or there, to do what is in their power to remove or correct them and to reform all things for a fuller praise of Christ and of God. Let them therefore teach the faithful that the authentic veneration of the saints consists not so much in the multiplying of external acts as in the greater intensity of our love, whereby, for our own greater good and that of the whole Church, we seek from the saints "example in their way of life, company in their communion, and aid in their intercession."[21] On the other hand, let them teach the faithful that our communion with those in heaven, provided it be understood in the full light of faith, in no way weakens but instead more thoroughly enriches the worship of adoration we give to God the Father, through Christ, in the Spirit.[22]

All of us who are children of God and constitute one family in Christ (see Heb 3:6), as long as we remain in communion with one another in mutual charity and in one praise of the most holy Trinity, are living up to the Church's inmost vocation and in foretaste are sharing the liturgy of the final glory.[23] For when Christ appears and the glorious resurrection of the dead takes place, the glory of God will light up the heavenly city, whose lamp will be the Lamb (see Rv 5:12). Then the whole Church of the saints in the supreme blessedness of charity will adore God and "the Lamb who was slain" (Rv 5:12), proclaiming with one voice: "To him who sits upon the throne and to the Lamb, blessing, and honor, and glory, and might for ever and ever" (Rv 5:13).

CHAPTER VIII
BLESSED VIRGIN MARY, MOTHER OF GOD,
IN THE MYSTERY OF CHRIST AND THE CHURCH

IV. VENERATION OF THE BLESSED VIRGIN IN THE CHURCH

66. Mary, as the Mother of God, placed by grace next to her Son above all angels and saints, has shared in the mysteries of Christ and is justly honored by a special veneration in the Church. From earliest times she has been honored under the title of Mother of God, under whose protection the faithful take refuge in all their perils and needs. Hence from the Council of Ephesus onward the devotion of the people of God toward Mary wonderfully increased in veneration and love, in invocation and imitation, according to her own prophetic words: "All generations shall call me blessed, because he that is mighty hath done great things for me" (Lk 1:48–49). Devotion to Mary as it has always existed in the Church, even though it is altogether special, is essentially distinct from the worship of adoration paid equally to the Word incarnate, the Father, and the Holy Spirit. Honoring Mary contributes to that adoration. For the various forms of Marian devotion sanctioned by the Church, within the limits of sound orthodoxy and suited to circumstances of time and place as well as to the character and culture of peoples, have the effect that as we honor the Mother we also truly know the Son and give love, glory, and obedience to him, through whom all things have their being (see Col 1:15–16) and "in whom it has pleased the eternal Father that all fullness should dwell" (Col 1:19).

160

---

21   MR, Preface for Saints, for use by the dioceses of France [RM, Preface for Holy Men and Women I, P 69] .

22   See Peter Canisius, *Catechismus Maior seu Summa doctrinae Christianae* cap. 3., P. Streicher, ed., pt. 1, 15–16, no. 44 and 100–101, no. 49.

23   See Vatican II, SC art. 8 [DOL 1 no. 8].

161   67. It is the express intent of this Council to profess this Catholic teaching and at
the same time to counsel all the Church's children to foster wholeheartedly the
cultus — especially the liturgical cultus — of the Blessed Virgin, to treasure those
Marian devotions and practices commended over the centuries by the Church's
magisterium, and to adhere religiously to those decrees laid down of old regarding
veneration of images of Christ, the Blessed Virgin, and the saints.[1] The Council also
strongly urges theologians and preachers of God's word as they treat of the unique
dignity of the Mother of God to refrain alike from exaggerating and from minimizing.[2] Devoted under the guidance of the magisterium to the study of sacred Scripture, of the Fathers and doctors, and of the liturgies of the Church, they should
explain soundly the offices and privileges of the Blessed Virgin in their inseparable
relationship to Christ, the source of all truth, holiness, and devotion. They are to
guard conscientiously against anything in word or act that might lead Christians
separated from us or anyone else to a mistaken idea of what precisely the Church
teaches on Mary. For their part, the faithful must be mindful that true devotion
does not consist in sheer, passing feeling, or in mindless credulity, but that it issues
from an authentic faith that leads us to acknowledge the exaltedness of the Mother
of God and inspires us to a filial love for her as our Mother and to an imitation of
her virtues.

5. VATICAN COUNCIL II, Decree on the Eastern Catholic Churches *Orientalium Ecclesiarum*, 21 November 1964: AAS 57 (1965) 76–85; ConstDecr-Decl 223–240 (excerpts).

PARTICULAR CHURCHES OR RITES

162   2. The Holy Catholic Church, the Mystical Body of Christ, is made up of the
faithful who are organically united in the Holy Spirit by the same faith, the same
sacraments, and the same government and who, coming together into various
groups conjoined by their hierarchy, form the particular Churches or Rites. A
marvelous communion exists among them with the result that diversity within the
Church in no way harms its unity, but instead manifests it. For it is the intent of the
Catholic Church that each individual Church or Rite should retain its traditions
whole and entire; the Church wishes as well to adjust the character of its life to
needs differing with time and place.[2]

163   3. Although differing somewhat among themselves as what are called "rites,"
that is, by their liturgy, ecclesiastical discipline, and spiritual heritage, nevertheless
these individual Churches, whether of the East or the West, each as much as the

---

[1] See Council of Nicaea II, A.D. 787: Mansi 13, 378–379; Denz-Schön 600–601. Council of Trent,
sess. 25: Mansi 33, 171–172.

[2] See Pius XII, Radio Message, 24 Oct. 1954: AAS 46 (1954) 679; Encycl. *Ad caeli reginam*, 11 Oct.
1954: AAS 46 (1954) 637.

[2] See Leo IX, Litt. *In terra pax*, A.D. 1053, "Ut enim." Innocent III, Lateran Council IV, A.D. 1215, cap.
4, "Licet Graecos"; Litt. *Inter quatuor*, 2 Aug. 1206, "Postulasti postmodum." Innocent IV, Ep. *Cum de cetero*, 27
Aug. 1247; Ep. *Sub Catholicae*, 6 March 1254, prooem. Nicholas III, Instr. *Istud est memoriale*, 9 Oct. 1278. Leo X,
Litt. Ap. *Accepimus nuper*, 18 May 1521. Paul III, Litt. Ap. *Dudum*, 23 Dec. 1534. Pius IV, Const. *Romanus
Pontifex*, 16 Feb. 1564, § 5. Clement VIII, Const. *Magnus Dominus*, 23 Dec. 1595, § 10. Paul V, Const. *Solet
circumspecta*, 10 Dec. 1615, § 3. Benedict XIV, Encycl. *Demandatam*, 24 Dec. 1743, § 3; Encycl. *Allatae sunt*, 26
June 1755, §§ 3, 6–19, 32. Pius VI, Encycl. *Catholicae communionis*, 24 May 1787. Pius IX, Litt. *In suprema*, 6 Jan.
1948, § 3; Litt. Ap. *Ecclesiam Christi*, 26 Nov. 1853; Const. *Romani Pontificis*, 6 Jan. 1862. Leo XIII, Litt. Ap.
Praeclara, 20 June 1894, n. 7; Litt. Ap. *Orientalium dignitas*, 30 Nov. 1894, prooem.; etc.

others, are entrusted to the pastoral government of the Roman pontiff, the divinely appointed successor of St. Peter in primacy over the universal Church. Consequently, they are of equal dignity, so that none of them is superior to the others on the basis of rite and they enjoy the same rights and are under the same obligations, even with respect to preaching the Gospel to the whole world (see Mk 16:15) under the guidance of the Roman pontiff.

4.   [. . .] All clerics and those aspiring to sacred orders should be instructed in the   164
rites and especially in the practical norms that must be applied in interritual questions. The laity, too, as part of their catechetical education should be taught about rites and their rules. Finally, Catholics as a group and individually, as also the baptized of every non-Catholic Church or Community who enter into the fullness of Catholic communion, must everywhere retain their own rite, cherish it, and observe it to the best of their ability.[4] This is stated without prejudice, in special cases of persons, communities, or areas, to the right of recourse to the Apostolic See, which, as the supreme judge of interchurch relations, will, acting itself or through other authorities, meet the needs of the occasion in an ecumenical spirit, by the issuance of opportune directives, decrees, or rescripts.

SAFEGUARDING THE SPIRITUAL HERITAGE OF THE EASTERN CHURCHES

6.   All the faithful of the Eastern Churches should know and be convinced that   165
they can and must always preserve their lawful liturgical rites and their church discipline and that these may not be altered except for the sake of their own organic development. [. . .] Those who, by reason of office or apostolic ministries, are in close contact with the Eastern Churches or their faithful should, in proportion to their responsibilities, be trained in knowledge and respect regarding the ritual, discipline, teaching, history, and genius of Eastern Catholics.[6] [. . .]

DISCIPLINE OF THE SACRAMENTS

12.   This Council expresses its endorsement, praise, and its hope for any needed   166
reform of the ancient discipline of the sacraments observed in the Eastern Churches and also of the practice connected with sacramental celebration and administration.

13.   Regarding the minister of confirmation the practice existing in the Eastern   167
Churches from the most ancient times is to be fully restored. Priests, therefore, using chrism blessed by a patriarch or a bishop, are empowered to confer this sacrament.[14]

---

[4]   Pius XII, Motu Proprio *Cleri sanctitati*, 2 June 1957, notes in can. 8, "without the permission of the Holy See," according to centuries-old practice; can. 11 notes in regard to baptized non-Catholics, "they may choose the rite they prefer"; the same document proposes an arrangement for the observance of their own rite by all and everywhere: AAS 49 (1957) 438–439.

[6]   See Benedict XV, Litt. Ap. *Orientis Catholicae*, 15 Oct. 1917. Pius XI, Encycl. *Rerum orientalium*, 8 Sept. 1928; etc.

[14]   See Innocent IV, Ep. *Sub catholicae*, 6 March 1254, § 3, n. 4. Council of Lyons II, A.D. 1274, (profession of faith of Michael Palaeologus made to Gregory X). Eugene IV, Const. *Exsultate Deo*, at Council of Florence, 22 Nov. 1439, § 2: COeD 520. Clement VIII, Instr. *Sanctissimus*, 31 Aug. 1595. Benedict XIV, Const. *Etsi pastoralis*, 26 May 1742, § 2, n. 1; § 3, n. 1; etc. Synod of Laodicea, A.D. 347/381, can. 48: Mansi 2, 571–572. Synod of Sis (Armenians), A.D. 1342: Mansi 25, 1240–41. Synod of Lebanon (Maronites), A.D. 1736, P. 2, cap. 3, n. 2: Mansi 38, 48. Also other local synods.

168   14. All Eastern-rite priests, either in conjunction with baptism or separately from it, can confer this sacrament validly on all the faithful of any rite, including the Latin; however, for lawfulness they are to follow the regulations of both the general and particular law.[15] Latin-rite priests, in accordance with the faculties they have for the administration of this sacrament, may administer it also to faithful of the Eastern Churches, without prejudice to the rite and, in what concerns lawfulness, observing the regulations of both the general and particular law.[16]

169   15. The faithful of the Eastern Churches on Sundays and holydays are bound by precept to assist at the Divine Liturgy or, depending on the law or custom of their own rite, at the celebration of the Divine Praises.[17] To facilitate their satisfying this obligation, the available time (tempus utile) for fulfillment of the precept is from vespers of the vigil to the end of the Sunday or holyday.[18] The faithful are strongly encouraged to receive the eucharist on these days, or more often, and even daily.[19]

170   16. Since the faithful of the various particular Churches within the same region or territory are in daily contact with each other, the faculty to hear confessions granted lawfully and unconditionally by their own hierarchs to priests, whatever their rite, is hereby extended to the entire territory of the granting authority and for all places and people, whatever their rite, within that territory. There is an exception if the local hierarch has expressly withheld such a faculty in the places belonging to his own rite.[20]

171   17. With a view to reviving in the Eastern Churches the full ancient discipline regarding the sacrament of orders, this Council strongly desires restoration of the permanent diaconate wherever it has fallen into disuse.[21] The legislative authority of each particular Church should see to the subdiaconate, the orders below it, and to their rights and obligations.[22]

172   18. To prevent invalidity in the case of marriages between Eastern Catholics and other baptized Eastern Christians and to provide for the stability and sanctity of marriage and for family peace, this Council decrees that for such marriages the canonical form is obligatory only as to their lawfulness; for their validity the

---

[15] See Holy Office, Instr. (to the bp. of Szepes) [Spisske] , A.D. 1783. SC Propagation of the Faith, (for Copts), 15 March 1790, n. 13; Decr., 6 Oct. 1863, C, a. SCEC, 1 May 1948. Holy Office, Resp., 22 April 1896, with letter of 19 May 1896.

[16] CIC can. 782, § 4. SCEC, Decr. De sacramento confirmationis administrando [. . .], 1 May 1948.

[17] See Synod of Laodicea, A.D. 347/381, can. 29. Nicephorus of Constantinople cap. 14: PG 111, 749–760. Synod of Dvin (Armenians), A.D. 719, can. 31. Theodore the Studite, sermo 21: PG 99, 536–538. Nicholas I, Litt. Ad consulta vestra, 3 Nov. 866: PL 119, 984–985 and 993–994. Also other local synods.

[18] An innovation, at least where the obligation to assist at the Divine Liturgy is in force; otherwise the point is consistent with the liturgical day of the Eastern Churches.

[19] See Canones Apostolorum 8 and 9: Mansi 1, 29–32. Council of Antioch, A.D. 341, can. 2: Mansi 2, 1309–10. Timothy of Alexandria, interrogat. 3. Innocent III, Const. Quia divinae , 4 Jan. 1215. Also several later synods of the Eastern Churches.

[20] While respecting the territorial character of jurisdiction, this canon intends, for the good of souls, to make available a plurality of jurisdictions within the one territory.

[21] See Council of Nicaea I, can. 18: COeD 13–14. Synod of Neocaesarea, A.D. 314–325, can. 12: Mansi 2, 543–546. Synod of Sardica, A.D. 343, can. 8: Mansi 8:11–12. Leo the Great, Litt. Omnium quidem, 13 Jan. 444: PL 54, 616–620. Council of Chalcedon can. 6: COeD 66. Council of Constantinople IV, can. 23 and 26: COeD 159 and 161; etc.

[22] Many Eastern Churches look on subdiaconate as a minor order, but Pius XII in the Motu Proprio Cleri sanctitati prescribed for it the obligations of the major orders. This canon proposes a return to ancient practice regarding the obligations of subdeacons, thus repealing the general law of Cleri sanctitati.

presence of a sacred minister suffices, as long as the other requirements of law are met.[23]

DIVINE WORSHIP

19. Henceforth only an ecumenical council or the Holy See has competence to establish, transfer, or suppress holydays common to all the Eastern Churches. With regard to the holydays proper to any particular Church, the same competence is shared with the Holy See by its patriarchal or archiepiscopal synod, with due consideration, however, always being given to the whole region and the other particular Churches.[24]

20. Until attainment of the desired agreement among all Christians on a common date for the celebration of Easter, it is left to patriarchs or the highest territorial ecclesiastical authorities, in order to promote unity among Christians of the same region or nation, to concur, with unanimous consent and after consultation of all interested parties, on celebrating Easter on the same Sunday.[25]

21. In regard to the law on the sacred seasons, any of the faithful who are outside the region or territory of their own rite may follow the practice prevailing in the place they are living. Families of mixed rites may follow such laws in conformity with one of the rites.[26]

22. Clerics and religious of the Eastern Churches are to celebrate, in keeping with their own laws and traditions, the Divine Praises, which all the Eastern Churches from earliest antiquity have held in high esteem.[27]

23. The right to rule on the languages to be used in liturgical services and, after reporting to the Holy See, of approving the vernacular translations of texts belongs to the patriarch with his synod or to the highest ecclesiastical authority with his council of hierarchs.[28]

173

174

175

176

177

---

[23] See Pius XII, Motu Proprio *Crebrae allatae* , 22 Feb. 1949, can. 32, § 2, no. 5 (the faculty of patriarchs to dispense from canonical form): AAS 41 (1949) 96; *idem*, Motu Proprio *Cleri sanctitati*, 2 June 1957, can. 267 (faculty of patriarchs for *sanatio in radice*): AAS 49 (1957) 514. The Holy Office and SCEC in 1957 granted (for five years) the faculty for dispensation from canonical form and for *sanatio* because of a defect in the form "outside of a patriarchate, to metropolitans and other local Ordinaries who have no higher authority except the Holy See."

[24] See Leo the Great, Litt. *Quod saepissime*, 15 April 454, "Petitionem autem": PL 54, 1094–96. Nicephorus of Constantinople, cap. 13. Synod of the Patriarch Sergius, 18 Sept. 1596, can. 17. Pius VI, Litt. Ap. *Assueto paterne*, 8 April 1775; etc.

[25] See SC Appendix [DOL 1 no. 131].

[26] See Clement VII, Instr. *Sanctissimus*, 31 Aug. 1595, § 6, "Si ipsi graeci." Holy Office, 7 June 1673, Reply to 1 and 2; 13 March 1727, Reply to 1. SC Propagation of the Faith, Decr. 18 Aug. 1913, art. 33: AAS 5 (1913) 398; Decr. 14 Aug. 1914, art. 27: AAS 6 (1914) 462–463; Decr. 27 March 1916, art. 14: AAS 8 (1916) 107. SCEC, Decr. 1 March 1929, art. 36: AAS 21 (1929) 158; Decr. 4 May 1930, art. 41: AAS 22 (1930) 352–353.

[27] See Synod of Laodicea, A.D. 347/381, can. 15: Mansi 2:567–568. Synod of Mar Isaac of the Chaldeans, A.D. 410, can. 15. Nerses of Lambron (Glaiensis), A.D. 1166. Innocent IV, *Sub catholicae*, 6 March 1254, § 8. Benedict XIV, Const. *Etsi pastoralis*, 26 May 1742, § 7, n. 5; Instr. *Eo quamvis tempore*, 4 May 1745, §§ 42ff. Also later synods: Armenian (1911), Coptic (1898), Maronite (1736), Rumanian (1872), Ruthenian (1891), Syrian (1888).

[28] Based on Eastern practice.

RELATIONS WITH CHRISTIANS OF CHURCHES SEPARATED FROM US

178   26. Divine law itself forbids any *communicatio in sacris* (shared worship) that harms the Church's unity or includes danger of error in faith, scandal, or indifferentism.[31] With regard to Eastern Christians separated from us, however, pastoral experience attests that account can and must be taken of varied conditions affecting individuals that do no injury to the Church's unity and involve none of the dangers to be avoided, but in which the need for salvation and the good of souls are the urgent issues. Accordingly, the Catholic Church, in keeping with the circumstances of the times, places, and people, has followed and continues to follow a more lenient policy in ensuring for all the means of salvation and a witness to the charity prevailing between Christians through shared sacraments and other sacred functions and things. With such points in mind, "in order not to be, through harshness in judgment, a stumbling block to those who are saved,"[32] and in order to promote union with the Eastern Churches separated from us, this Council decrees the policy that follows.

179   27. On the basis of the principles already stated, when Eastern Christians separated in good faith from the Catholic Church request it of their own accord and are rightly disposed, they may be admitted to the sacraments of penance, eucharist, and anointing. Moreover, Catholics may request these same sacraments of ministers of other Eastern Churches having valid sacraments on any occasion of need or genuine spiritual benefit when access to a Catholic priest is physically or morally impossible.[33]

180   28. Given the same principles, *communicatio in sacris,* as to functions, articles and places of worship, between Catholics and Eastern Christians separated from us is allowed for a just reason.[34]

181   29. The more lenient policy regarding *communicatio in sacris* with members of the Eastern Churches separated from us is entrusted to the watchfulness and direction of the local hierarchs with a view to their guiding the relations between Christians — after consultation with one another and, where feasible, with hierarchs of the Churches separated from us — by means of appropriate and effective precepts and directives.

---

[31]   This teaching is in force also in the Churches separated from us.

[32]   Basil the Great, *Ep. canonica ad Amphilocium:* PG 32, 669 B.

[33]   This leniency is based on: 1. the validity of sacraments; 2. good faith and dispositions; 3. need of eternal salvation; 4. absence of the person's own priest; 5. exclusion of danger and of any formal assent to error.

[34]   The meaning is extrasacramental *communicatio in sacris;* the Council grants the mitigation *servatis servandis.*

6. VATICAN COUNCIL II, **Decree on Ecumenism** *Unitatis redintegratio*, 21 November 1964: AAS 57 (1965) 90–107; ConstDecrDecl 243–274 (excerpts).

CHAPTER I
CATHOLIC PRINCIPLES OF ECUMENISM

2.   God's love was revealed in our midst in this: the Father sent his only begotten   182
Son into the world in order that having become man he would by his redemptive
act give a new birth to the whole human race and gather it together as one.[2] Before
he offered himself as a spotless victim on the altar of the cross, Christ prayed to his
Father for those who believe, in these words: ". . . That they may all be one, even
as you, Father, are in me and I in you, that they also may be one in us, so that the
world may believe that you have sent me" (Jn 17:21).

In his Church Christ has established the sublime sacrament of the eucharist as
the sign and cause of the Church's unity. [. . .]

Jesus Christ wills the increase of his people and brings about their unity in
communion (profession of one faith, celebration together of divine worship, concord as God's family) through the work of the apostles and their successors, the
bishops united to their head, the successor of Peter: through their faithful preaching
of the Gospel, administration of the sacraments, and governance in love under the
action of the Holy Spirit.

3.   [. . .] Among our separated brothers and sisters are celebrated many sacred   183
services of the Christian religion that, in ways differing with the different conditions of each Church or Communion, have unquestionably the power of causing
grace and that must be acknowledged as effective in opening the way into the
community of salvation. [. . .]

4.   [. . .] Safeguarding unity in essentials, let all members of the Church, accord-   184
ing to the offices committed to each, respect genuine freedom in regard to diversity
in the spiritual life and in discipline as well as in the liturgical rites and even the
theological formulation of revealed truth; in all things they are to foster charity. By
such a course they will more and more allow the genuine catholicity and apostolicity of the Church increasingly to shine forth. [. . .]

CHAPTER II
ECUMENISM IN PRACTICE

6.   [. . .] Christ summons the Church in its pilgrim journey to the continuous   185
reformation it always needs as a human and earthly institution. [. . .]

Such renewal is of singular ecumenical significance. The biblical and liturgical
movements, the preaching of God's word and catechesis, the lay apostolate, new
forms of religious life, the spirituality of marriage, the Church's social teaching and
action — all such phases of the Church's life that are bringing about renewal are to
be viewed as pledges and promises holding out high hope of future progress in
ecumenism.

8.   [. . .] The custom has grown of Catholics coming together in large numbers to   186
offer the prayer for church unity that on the eve of his death our Savior himself
fervently offered to the Father: "That they all may be one" (Jn 17:21).

---

[2]   See 1 Jn 4:9; Col 1:18–20; Jn 11:52.

On certain special occasions, such as prayer services for Christian unity, and at ecumenical meetings, it is both lawful and even greatly desirable that Catholics join in prayer with Christians separated from us. Such shared prayer is an extremely effective means of asking for grace and is a natural expression of the abiding bond that links Catholics with those separated from us: "Where two or three are gathered together in my name, there am I in the midst of them" (Mt 18:20).

Communicatio in sacris, however, may not be regarded as a means to be used indiscriminately toward restoring Christian unity. Such sharing is dependent mainly on two principles: the unity of the Church, of which it is a sign, and the sharing in the means of grace. Its function as sign often rules out *communicatio in sacris*. Its being a source of grace sometimes favors it. Unless the conference of bishops, following the norms of its own statutes, or the Holy See has ruled otherwise, the local bishop is the authority competent to decide with prudence what the right course of action should be in view of all the circumstances of time, place, and people.

CHAPTER III
CHURCHES AND ECCLESIAL COMMUNITIES
NOT IN UNION WITH THE HOLY SEE

I. THE SPECIAL CASE OF THE EASTERN CHURCHES

187   15. Eastern Christians, as everyone knows, carry out the sacred liturgy with the utmost love, especially the eucharistic liturgy, that source of the Churches' life and pledge of the glory to come in which the faithful united with their bishop and having access to the Father through the Word incarnate, crucified, and glorified, by the outpouring of the Holy Spirit, attain communion with the Trinity as those who have become "partakers in the divine nature" (2 Pt 1:4). Therefore, the celebration of the eucharist in each of these Churches builds up and gives increase[1] to the Church of God and their celebrating it together shows these Churches to be in communion with one another.

With the most beautiful hymns the Eastern Christians in their liturgies exalt the Virgin Mary, whom the Ecumenical Council of Ephesus solemnly proclaimed as the Mother of God, in order that Christ would be confessed, in keeping with Scripture, as truly and literally the Son of God and the Son of Man. Eastern Christians also sing the praises of many saints, among them the Fathers of the Church universal.

Because these Churches, even though separated from us, have true sacraments and especially, by virtue of apostolic succession, the eucharist and the priesthood — all bonds still linking them closely to us — some form of *communicatio in sacris* is not only admissible but even advisable in the right circumstances and with the approval of church authority. [. . .]

All should be convinced that the knowledge, respect, preservation, and furtherance of the rich liturgical and spiritual patrimony of Eastern Christians is of utmost importance to the faithful safeguarding of Christian tradition and to the achievement of reconciliation between Eastern and Western Christians.

188   17. [. . .] With thankfulness to God that many Eastern members of the Catholic Church, guarding their heritage and desiring to live it more purely and fully already are in full communion with those of the Western tradition, this Council declares

---

[1]   See St. John Chrysostom, *In Ioannem Homilia 46*: PG 59, 260–262.

that this entire heritage, spiritual and liturgical, disciplinary and theological in the various traditions, forms part of the full catholicity and apostolicity of the Church.

II. WESTERN CHURCHES AND ECCLESIAL COMMUNITIES NOT IN UNION WITH US

22. Whenever the sacrament of baptism is conferred rightly in accord with the Lord's institution and received with the required disposition of spirit, it truly incorporates the recipient into the crucified and glorified Christ and brings the new birth of a share in the divine life: "You were buried with him in baptism, in which you were also raised with him through faith in the working of God, who raised him from the dead" (Col 2:12).[3]

189

Baptism, accordingly, forms the sacramental bond of unity existing between all who have a new birth through it. But of its nature baptism is but a beginning, a prelude pointed toward attainment of the fullness of life in Christ. As such its direction is toward a complete profession of faith, complete incorporation into the plan of salvation as willed by Christ, and, finally, complete entrance into eucharistic communion.

The Ecclesial Communities separated from us do not have the full unity with us that derives from baptism and, we believe, especially because of their lack of the sacrament of orders, have not kept the authentic and integral substance of the eucharistic mystery. Nevertheless when in the Lord's Supper they commemorate his death and resurrection, they attest to the sign of their life in communion with Christ and they await his glorious Second Coming. Their teaching, therefore, on the Lord's Supper, the rest of the sacraments, the worship and ministry of the Church provides apt topics for dialogue.

23. Faith in Christ inspires the Christian way of life of these Christians, the grace of baptism and the preached word of God sustain it. That Christian life shows itself in private prayer, meditation on the Bible, Christian family life, the worship of the community gathered to praise God. In addition, their forms of worship often are marked by elements from the ancient liturgy we share.

190

Their faith in Christ yields its fruit in praise and thanksgiving for blessings received from God; and joined to it is a keen sense of justice and a sincere love of neighbor. [. . .]

▶   See also Chapter One, Section 8. Ecumenism.

---

[3]   See also Rom 6:4.

7. VATICAN COUNCIL II, **Decree on the Pastoral Office of Bishops** *Christus Dominus*, 28 October 1965: AAS 58 (1966) 673–696; ConstDecrDecl 277–321 (excerpts).

CHAPTER II
BISHOPS AND THE PARTICULAR CHURCHES, I.E., DIOCESES

I. DIOCESAN BISHOPS

191   11. The diocese forms that part of the people of God entrusted to the pastoral care of the bishop with the assistance of the presbyterate. In allegiance to its pastor and by him gathered together in the Holy Spirit through the Gospel and the eucharist, the diocese stands as a particular Church, in which Christ's one, holy, catholic, and apostolic Church is truly present and at work. By carrying out the office of teaching, sanctifying, and governing, each bishop entrusted with the care of a particular Church feeds his sheep in the Lord's name as their proper, ordinary, and immediate pastor. Bishops, however, must also respect the rights belonging to patriarchs or other hierarchic authorities.[1] [. . .]

192   12. In carrying out their office as teachers, bishops are to preach Christ's Gospel to people; of all their principal duties this one is preeminent.[2] They should fulfill it by courageously in the Spirit inviting people to faith or by strengthening them in a faith already alive. Let them proclaim the mystery of Christ in its entirety, namely, those truths which being unknown leave Christ unknown and which are the divinely revealed way to glorify God and to obtain blessedness from God.[3] [. . .]

193   14. Bishops should see to it that children and adolescents, young people and adults, receive careful catechetical instruction, the aim of which is that faith, elucidated through teaching, become living, explicit, and expressed in action. Bishops should see to it that such teaching follows an order and method suited not simply to the subject matter but also to the character, capacities, age, and circumstances of those being instructed. Also that this instruction has as its foundation Scripture, tradition, liturgy, and the Church's magisterium and life. [. . .]

They should also take steps toward restoring the instruction of adult catechumens or toward adapting it more effectively.

194   15. In carrying out their office of sanctifying, bishops are to be mindful that they have been taken from among the people and appointed for the people in those things that are of God, to offer gifts and sacrifice for sins. Bishops possess the fullness of holy orders and on them both priests and deacons depend in the exercise of their own power of orders. Priests, appointed to be prudent cooperators of the order of bishops, are themselves consecrated as true priests of the New Testament; deacons serve as those ordained to service for the people of God in communion with the bishop and his priests. The bishops themselves are the chief stewards of the mysteries of God and the overseers, promoters, and guardians of all liturgical life in the particular Churches entrusted to their care.[8]

---

[1]   See OE nos. 7–11: AAS 57 (1965) 79–80; ConstDecrDecl 228–230.

[2]   See Council of Trent, sess. 5, Decr. *De reformatione* cap. 2: Mansi 33, 30; sess. 24, Decr. *De reformatione* cap. 4: Mansi 33, 159. LG cap. 3, no. 25: AAS 57 (1965) 29ff; ConstDecrDecl 138–141.

[3]   See LG, loc. cit.

[8]   See SC [DOL 1 no. 22]. Paul VI, Motu Proprio *Sacram Liturgiam* [DOL 20 nos. 288–289].

Bishops are thus to work constantly toward the faithful's deeper knowledge and living of the paschal mystery through the eucharist in order to fashion the one Body, closely bound together in the unity of Christ's charity.[9] "Devoted to prayer and to the ministry of the word" (Acts 6:4), they should expend every effort that those entrusted to their care become of one mind in prayer,[10] grow in grace by receiving the sacraments, and bear witness to the Lord in faith.

Mindful of their own obligation to give an example of holiness in charity, humility, and simpleness of life, the bishops as leaders in the way of perfection should be intent on furthering the holiness of their own clergy, religious, and laity in keeping with each one's particular vocation.[11] They should sanctify the Churches entrusted to them in such a way that their Churches will fully manifest the sense of Christ's universal Church. To this end, bishops should intensely promote vocations to the priesthood and religious life, with special attention to mission vocations.

III. COOPERATORS OF THE DIOCESAN BISHOP IN THE PASTORAL OFFICE

3. DIOCESAN CLERGY

28. All priests, diocesan and religious, share with the bishop and exercise the one priesthood of Christ. They are thus made the prudent cooperators of the order of episcopacy. [. . .]   195

30. [. . .] 2. In carrying out their teaching office pastors have these responsibilities: to preach the word of God to all the people so that, grounded in faith, hope, and charity, they may grow in Christ and the Christian community may bear that witness of charity which the Lord has counseled;[17] to lead the faithful by catechetical instruction to the full knowledge of the mystery of salvation befitting their age. [. . .]   196

In their work of sanctifying, pastors should see to it that the celebration of the eucharistic sacrifice is the center and high point in the whole life of the Christian community. They should also strive for the strengthening of the faithful by the devout and frequent reception of the sacraments and an intelligent, intense participation in the liturgy. Pastors are also to keep in mind that the sacrament of penance is of the greatest assistance toward furthering the Christian life. In consequence they should make themselves readily available for confessions of the faithful and, if necessary, bring in other confessors conversant with foreign languages. [. . .]

4. RELIGIOUS

35. [. . .] 4. All religious, exempt or not, are subject to the power of the local Ordinary, in whatever relates to: public worship services, but without prejudice to differences of rite; the care of souls; preaching to the faithful; the religious and moral education, catechetical instruction, and liturgical formation of the faithful, especially the young. Religious are also subject to the local Ordinary in regard to conduct proper to the clerical state and activities involving the apostolate. [. . .]   197

---

[9]   See Pius XII, Encycl. *Mediator Dei*, 20 Nov. 1947, AAS 39 (1947) 521ff. Paul VI, Encycl. *Mysterium fidei* [DOL 176 nos. 1184–87].

[10]   See Acts 1:14; 2:46.

[11]   See LG nos. 44–45 [DOL 4 nos. 155–156].

[17]   See Jn 13:35.

CHAPTER III
COOPERATION BETWEEN BISHOPS FOR THE COMMON
GOOD OF SEVERAL CHURCHES

I. SYNODS, COUNCILS, AND ESPECIALLY CONFERENCES OF BISHOPS

198   37. [. . .] The Council decrees the following concerning conferences of bishops.

199   38. 1.   A conference of bishops is a type of organization in which the bishops of a particular country or territory carry out their pastoral office collaboratively with a view to promoting the greater good the Church offers to people, and especially through forms of the apostolate and programs designed for present-day conditions.

4.   Decisions of a conference of bishops, on condition that they have been reached lawfully and by vote of two-thirds of the voting members and have been reviewed by the Apostolic See, possess juridical binding force only in those matters that the general law has stipulated or that a mandate of the Holy See, whether given *motu proprio* or in answer to the petition of the conference itself, has decreed.

5.   Where special circumstances so require, the bishops of several nations may, upon approval by the Holy See, form one conference of bishops.

Communication between conferences of bishops of different countries should be encouraged as a way to promote and to safeguard the greater good.

6.   The Council strongly urges prelates of the Eastern Churches, in the synods of their own Churches held to improve discipline and further works for the good of religion, to take into consideration the general good of the whole territory where there are several Churches of different rites and to make use of interritual consultation in keeping with norms to be established by competent authority.

▶   See also Chapter One, Section 4. The Holy See and the Hierarchy; Chapter Three, Section 4. Holy Orders: C. Pastoral Office.

▶   169.   SC Clergy, *General Catechetical Directory*, 11 April 1971.

8. PONTIFICAL CENTRAL COMMISSION FOR COORDINATING POSTCONCILIAR WORK AND FOR INTERPRETING THE DECREES OF VATICAN II, **Reply** to a query, on the Decree *Christus Dominus* no. 38, § 4, 10 June 1966: AAS 60 (1968) 361; Not 4 (1968) 364.

200   May the legislative power that, according to *Christus Dominus* no. 38, § 4,[a] is granted within definite limits to conferences of bishops be delegated to the episcopal committees established by the same conferences?

The Central Commission for Coordination of Postconciliar Work and for Interpreting the Decrees of Vatican Council II, after considering the matter fully in its meeting of 24 May 1966, has decided that the proper response is: No.

Pope Paul VI, at an audience granted to the undersigned [Cardinal A. Cicognani] on 10 June 1966, confirmed and approved this decision.[R1]

---

[a]   See DOL 7 no. 199.

[R1]   Not 4 (1968) 364–365 carried the following commentary. The following are included among the decisions belonging to the conference of bishops in the area of liturgy: 1. "whether and to what extent the vernacular is to be used. [. . .] The *acta* of the competent authority are to be approved, that is, confirmed by the Holy See" (SC art. 36, § 3 [DOL 1 no. 36]); 2. to approve vernacular translations (see SC art. 36, § 4

9. PONTIFICAL COMMISSION FOR THE INTERPRETATION OF THE DECREES OF VATICAN COUNCIL II, **Reply** to a query, on the Decree *Christus Dominus* and the Motu Proprio *Ecclesiae Sanctae*, 5 February 1968: AAS 60 (1968) 362.

Query: After the conciliar Decree *Christus Dominus*, 28 October 1965, and the   201
Motu Proprio *Ecclesiae Sanctae*, 6 August 1966,[a] which made determinations concerning conferences of bishops, do those norms still remain in force that the Constitution *Sacrosanctum Concilium*, 4 December 1963, the Motu Proprio *Sacram Liturgiam*, 25 January 1964, and the Instruction *Inter Oecumenici*, 26 September 1964,[b] established provisorily?

Reply: No.   [Pope Paul VI approved this decision 5 February 1968.]

10. VATICAN COUNCIL II, **Decree on the Appropriate Renewal of Religious Life** *Perfectae caritatis*, 28 October 1965: AAS 58 (1966) 702–712; Const-DecrDecl 333–353 (excerpts).

2.   An appropriate renewal of religious life includes at the same time, first, a   202
continuous return to the sources of all Christian life and to the originating inspiration of the institutes; second, the adaptation of these elements to the changed conditions of the age. Under the influence of the Holy Spirit and the guidance of the Church such a renewal must go forward on the basis of the principles that follow. [. . .]

c.   All religious institutes are to share in the life of the Church. They are to take to heart, in keeping with their own distinctive character, and to further with all their energies the Church's endeavors and aims regarding Scripture, liturgy, dogmatic and pastoral matters, ecumenism, the missions, and social questions.

3.   The plan of life, prayer, and work of religious institutes should effectively   203
match the present-day physical and psychological conditions of their members and, in accord with the requirements of the spirit of each institute, should everywhere, but especially in mission lands, also answer the needs of the apostolate, cultural demands, social and economic conditions.

The form of governance should be examined against the same criteria.

Accordingly, religious institutes should appropriately revise their constitutions, directives, books of customs, prayers and ceremonies, or any similar collections and,

---

[DOL 1 no. 36]); 3. "Within the limits set by the *editio typica* of the liturgical books . . . to specify adaptations, especially in the case of the administration of the sacraments, the sacramentals, processions, liturgical languages, sacred music, and the arts. This, however, is to be done in accord with the fundamental norms laid down in this Constitution." (SC art. 39 [DOL 1 no. 39]); 4. to suggest to the Apostolic See more radical adaptations to the traditions and mentality of the individual peoples (see SC art. 40, 1 [DOL 1 no. 40]). Decisions on these matters may not be entrusted to liturgical commissions, the council of the conference president, or other such instrumentalities of the conference of bishops.

Similarly, in the matter of definitively approving the texts of vernacular translations, which requires confirmation by the Apostolic See, the vote of the members of the conference must be taken. The *acta* to be forwarded to the Consilium must be signed by the president and the secretary of the conference of bishops; the *acta* must also report the result of the voting (see InterOec nos. 29, 30, 31 [DOL 23 nos. 321, 322, 323]). National liturgical commissions or other agencies of the conference are empowered *by mandate of the conference itself*, to approve only *ad interim* vernacular texts.

a   See DOL 7 no. 199 and DOL 106 no. 755.

b   See DOL 1 no. 22; DOL 20 no. 288; DOL 23 nos. 315–323.

discarding obsolete regulations, bring them into line with the documents of this Council.

204   6.   Those professing the evangelical counsels should above all else seek and love God who has first loved us (see 1 Jn 4:10). In all circumstances they should be intent on developing a life hidden with Christ in God (see Col 3:3), the source and impetus of love of neighbor directed toward the salvation of the world and the building up of the Church. That love also enlivens and guides the practice of the evangelical counsels themselves.

Drawing from the authentic sources of Christian spirituality, the members of religious institutes are to cultivate sedulously the spirit and practice of prayer.

They should turn daily to sacred Scripture, there to learn by reading and meditation the "surpassing knowledge of Jesus Christ" (Phil 3:8). With heart and voice they should enter into the liturgy, especially the mystery of the eucharist and from this abundant source nurture their spiritual life.

Thus strengthened at the table of the divine Law and the sacred altar, they are to love Christ's members as brothers and sisters and to respect and love their pastors with a filial spirit. In life and spirit they should more and more be united with the Church, totally dedicated to its mission.

205   7.   In the Mystical Body of Christ, in which "all the members do not have the same function" (Rom 12:4), a place apart, whatever the pressures of the apostolate, will always belong to those institutes totally dedicated to contemplation, those, namely, whose members in solitude and silence, in constant prayer and willing penance devote themselves entirely to God. They offer up to God a sublime sacrifice of praise; by their abundant signs of holiness they are a shining light among the people of God, whom they inspire by their example and increase by their hidden apostolic power.

206   8.   In the Church there are a great many institutes, both clerical and nonclerical, that are dedicated to the various works of the apostolate. All of them have their own, different charisms, according to the grace which has been given to them: the charism of ministry for serving; of doctrine for teaching; of speech for exhorting; of giving with simplicity; of showing mercy with cheerfulness (see Rom 12:5–8). "For there are varieties of gifts, but the same Spirit" (1 Cor 12:4). In such institutes activities of the apostolate and of mercy form part of the very essence of the religious life, because they are a holy service and a true work of charity, entrusted to religious by the Church and carried out in its name. Accordingly the entire religious life of the members should be imbued with an apostolic spirit and their entire apostolic activity enlivened by the spirit of the religious life. It is altogether necessary therefore that the members' apostolic activity have its source in close union with Christ in order that they may answer their call to follow him before all else and to serve him in his members. This is the way that their love for God and neighbor will be nurtured. [. . .]

207   9.   The Council's wish is that the venerable institution of monastic life in both East and West should be faithfully maintained and radiate its authentic spirit ever more resplendently. For in the long course of the centuries it has earned the well-deserved respect of both the Church and human society. The principal duty of monks is to pay service, at once humble and exalted, to God's majesty within the monastic walls, whether in the hidden life of complete dedication to divine worship or in lawfully taking on certain works of the apostolate or of Christian charity. Respecting the spirit of their own community, monks should renew their ancient traditions, the source of so much good, and so adapt them to the contemporary

needs of souls that their monasteries will become like seed beds for the growth of the Christian people.

Religious orders that by rule or statute combine the apostolic life with choral office and monastic observances should strike a balance between their manner of life and the demands of their particular apostolate in such a way that they still faithfully preserve their proper form of life as a source of inestimable benefits to the Church.

10. The nonclerical religious life for both men and women constitutes a distinct state of professing the evangelical counsels. This Council therefore has high regard for this form of life, so useful to the pastoral mission of the Church in the education of youth, care for the sick, and other ministries. The Council encourages the members of these institutes in their vocation and urges them toward the adaptation of their life to today's requirements.

The Council declares that in religious institutes of brothers, as long as their proper, nonclerical character is preserved, there is no objection to the general chapter's deciding on the reception of holy orders by some members in order to provide for the need for priestly ministry in the houses of the institute.

15. The common life, lived after the example of the early Church, in which the many believers were of one heart and one mind (see Acts 4:32), should continue in prayer and in like-minded communion, strengthened by gospel teaching, the liturgy, and above all the eucharist. [. . .]

11. PONTIFICAL CENTRAL COMMISSION FOR COORDINATING POSTCONCILIAR WORK AND FOR INTERPRETING THE DECREES OF VATICAN II, **Reply** to a query, on the Decree *Perfectae caritatis*, 10 June 1966: AAS 60 (1968) 360.

I. Does the Latin expression *Sacra Synodus declarat nihil obstare* in the Decree of the Second Ecumenical Vatican Council *Perfectae caritatis* no. 10, § 2,[a] imply a positive recommendation of the matters that follow? Or rather does it indicate merely the opportunity for all lay institutes to have some members receive sacred orders, under the conditions stated?

II. Does or does not the conciliar text cited contain the explicit recognition of a right proper to the general chapter of each institute to judge the expediency of using the faculty in question?

The Central Commission for Coordinating Postconciliar Work and for Interpreting the Decrees of Vatican II, having thoroughly considered the issue, decided at a meeting held 24 May 1966 that the reply should be:

To I: No to the first part; Yes to the second: in other words, the expression involves merely the opportunity for all lay institutes to have some members receive sacred orders.

To II: Yes to the first part; No to the second: in other words, the right does belong to the general chapter of each institute to judge on the expediency of using the faculty in question in the second part of the first query, the requirements of the law being observed.

---

[a]   See DOL 10 no. 208.

[Pope Paul VI approved this decision on 10 February 1966.]

▶   See also Chapter Three, Section 8. Religious Life: B. Liturgy and Religious Life.

12. VATICAN COUNCIL II, **Decree on Priestly Formation** *Optatam totius*, 28 October 1965: AAS 58 (1966) 713–727; ConstDecrDecl 357–384 (excerpts).

II. MORE URGENT PROMOTION OF VOCATIONS TO THE PRIESTHOOD

211   2.   [. . .] The active cooperation of all the people of God in promoting vocations is a response to the workings of the providence of God, who has endowed the men divinely chosen to share in the ministerial priesthood of Christ with the qualities needed and who helps them by his grace. At the same time, God also leaves it in the hands of the lawful ministers of the Church to issue the call to the candidates seeking this great office with a right intention and in full freedom and to consecrate them with the seal of the Holy Spirit for divine worship and service to the Church, once the suitableness of such candidates has been certified.[4]

This Council endorses the well-tested means of general cooperation in the work of vocations, namely, fervent prayer, Christian penance, an ever-deepening instruction of the faithful, whether by preaching and catechesis or imparted through the various communications media, in order to bring out the need and the sublimity of the vocation to the priesthood. [. . .]

III. RIGHT ORGANIZATION OF MAJOR SEMINARIES

212   4.   Major seminaries are needed for the formation of priests. The whole training of the seminarians must have as its objective to fashion genuine pastors of souls having as their model our Lord Jesus Christ, teacher, priest, and shepherd. Their preparation should accordingly be aimed at: the ministry of the word, that they grow in understanding of God's word, in possessing it by meditation, in expressing it in word and life; the ministry of worship and sanctification, that by prayer and sharing in the celebration of the liturgy they may carry out the work of salvation through the eucharistic sacrifice and the sacraments; the pastoral ministry, that they may come to learn how to be Christ's representative who "came not to be served, but to serve and to give his life for the ransom of many" (Mk 10:45; see Jn 13:12–17) and that, having become servants of all, they may gain more souls (see 1 Cor 9:19).

Accordingly, all programs of formation — spiritual, intellectual, and disciplinary — together with their corresponding practice are to be directed to this pastoral aim. To the achievement of such an aim all seminary officials and teachers are to devote their earnest, collaborative efforts, with loyal respect toward the bishop's authority.

---

4   Pius XII, Ap. Const. *Sedes Sapientiae*, 31 May 1956: AAS 48 (1956) 357.

IV. NEED FOR GREATER CARE OF SPIRITUAL FORMATION

8.   The spiritual formation of the seminarians is closely connected with their   213
intellectual and pastoral formation. With the help especially of the spiritual director,[13] the instruction imparted should be such that they learn to live in close and
continuous relationship to the Father, through his Son Jesus Christ, in the Holy
Spirit. Destined to be configured to Christ the Priest through ordination, they
should become accustomed as his friends to stay near him in close companionship
for all of their lives.[14] They should live Christ's paschal mystery in such a way that
they will be able to lead the people to be entrusted to them to enter into this
mystery. Seminarians are to be taught to look for Christ in faithful meditation on
God's word, their active sharing in the holy mysteries of the Church, especially in
the eucharist and the divine office;[15] to look for Christ as well in the bishop who
sends them and the people to whom they are sent, above all in the poor, the little
ones, the sick, sinners, unbelievers. They should have the love and devotion of filial
trust in the Blessed Virgin Mary, whom Christ dying on the cross gave as mother to
his disciples.

Devotional practices endorsed by long usage of the Church should be earnestly
observed. There must, however, be caution against making spiritual formation
consist entirely in these or against fostering mere religious feeling. Seminarians
should instead learn to live after the pattern of the Gospel and to be grounded in
faith, hope, and charity, so that in practicing these they may acquire a spirit of
prayer,[16] possess strength and protection in their vocation, be endowed with the
other virtues, and grow in zeal to win all for Christ.

V. REVISION OF ECCLESIASTICAL STUDIES

16.   [. . .] Dogmatic theology is to be so planned as to set forth biblical themes first.   214
The students should be shown what the Fathers of the Church in both East and
West have contributed toward the faithful transmittal and explanation of each of
the truths of faith. They should learn the later history of dogma and see it in
relationship to the general history of the Church. Then through systematic reasoning, under the tutelage of St. Thomas Aquinas, the students should learn to go
deeply into and grasp the interconnection of the mysteries of salvation in order that
these may as far as possible be seen as a whole.[36] The students should learn also to

---

   [13]   See Pius XII, Ap. Exhort. *Menti Nostrae*, 23 Sept. 1950: AAS 42 (1950) 674. SC Seminaries and
Universities, *La formazione spirituale del candidato al sacerdozio* (Vatican City, 1965).

   [14]   See St. Pius X, Exhort. ad Clerum *Haerent animo*, 4 Aug. 1908: *S. Pii X Acta* 4, 242–244. Pius XII, loc.
cit. 659–661. John XXIII, Encycl. *Sacerdotii Nostri primordia*, 1 Aug. 1959: AAS 51 (1959) 550ff.

   [15]   See Pius XII, Encycl. *Mediator Dei*, 20 Nov. 1947: AAS 39 (1947) 547ff.; 572ff. John XXIII, Ap.
Exhort. *Sacrae Laudis*, 6 Jan. 1962: AAS 54 (1962) 69. SC art. 16 and 17 [DOL 1 nos. 16–17]. SCR, Instr.
InterOec, 26 Sept. 1964, nos. 14–17 [DOL 23 nos. 306–309].

   [16]   See John XXIII, Encycl. *Sacerdotii Nostri primordia*: AAS 51 (1959) 559ff.

   [36]   See Pius XII, Sermon to Seminarians, 24 June 1939: AAS 31 (1939) 247: "The endorsement of St.
Thomas's teaching does not stifle but rather stimulates and soundly directs rivalry in the search and
spread of the truth." Paul VI, Address at the Gregorian University, 12 May 1964: AAS 56 (1964) 365:
"[Professors] should with reverence heed the voice of the doctors of the Church, among whom Aquinas
holds the first place. So great is his genius, so sincere his love of truth, such is his wisdom in investigating,
explaining, and bringing together in a coherent bond of unity the loftiest truths, that his teaching is not
only a supremely effective instrument for safeguarding the foundations of faith, but also for achieving in a
useful and safe way the fruits of sound progress." See also *idem*, Address to the Sixth International
Thomistic Congress, 10 Sept. 1965: AAS 57 (1965) 788–792.

perceive the presence and the working of these mysteries in the services of the liturgy[37] and in the entire life of the Church; to learn as well to seek the answers to human problems in the light of revelation; to apply its eternal truths to the actual condition of human affairs; and to share these truths in a way suited to their contemporaries.[38]

The other theological disciplines ought also to be revised out of a more intense contact with the mystery of Christ and the history of salvation. [. . .] The liturgy, which is to be regarded as the primary and necessary source of a truly Christian spirit, is to be taught according to the intent of the Constitution on the Liturgy, articles 15 and 16.[39] [. . .]

VI. FURTHERING STRICTLY PASTORAL FORMATION

215   19. The pastoral concern that should animate the entire formation of seminarians demands also that they be carefully instructed in matters having a special bearing on the sacred ministry, thus in catechesis and preaching, liturgical worship and sacramental administration, works of charity, the responsibility to seek out the erring and the unbelieving, and similar pastoral functions.

▶   See also Chapter Three, Section 4. Holy Orders: D. Priestly Formation.

13. VATICAN COUNCIL II, Declaration on Christian Education *Gravissimum educationis*, 28 October 1965: AAS 58 (1966) 728–739; ConstDecrDecl 387–408 (excerpt).

216   2. A Christian education is the right of all Christians, because having become a new creature by being born again of water and the Holy Spirit,[8] they are called and truly are the children of God. Such an education does not have as its aim simply the growth of the human personality as already described. The primary objective is rather that the baptized, as they are led step by step to knowledge of the mystery of salvation, may likewise grow in awareness of the gift of faith they have received; that they learn to worship the Father in spirit and in truth (see Jn 4:23) — especially in the liturgy; that they be trained to live their own lives on the model of the new being created in righteousness and the holiness of truth (see Eph 4:22–24). In this way they are to develop into mature humanity, to the measure of the fullness of Christ (see Eph 4:13) and to contribute their part to the increase of the Mystical Body. [. . .]

217   4. The Church, while at pains in the fulfillment of its office as teacher to use every effective aid, has as the primary concern its own distinctive resources. The first of these is catechesis,[16] which sheds light on the faith and strengthens it,

---

37   See SC art. 7 and 16 [DOL 1 nos. 7 and 16].

38   See Paul VI, Encycl. *Ecclesiam Suam*, 6 Aug. 1964: AAS 56 (1964) 640ff.

39   See SC art. 10, 14, 15, 16 [DOL 1 nos. 10, 14, 15, 16]. SCR, Instr. InterOec, 26 Sept. 1964, nos. 11 and 12. [DOL 23 nos. 303–304].

8   See Pius XI, Encycl. *Divini Illius Magistri*: AAS 22 (1930) 83.

16   See Pius XI, Motu Proprio *Orbem Catholicum*, 29 June 1923: AAS 15 (1923) 327–329; *idem*, Decr. *Provida sane*, 12 Jan. 1935: AAS 27 (1935) 145–152; CD nos. 13, 14.

nurtures a life in keeping with the spirit of Christ, opens the way to an aware and active share in the mystery of the liturgy,[17] and is an impetus toward the apostolate. [. . .]

14. VATICAN COUNCIL II, Dogmatic Constitution on Divine Revelation
Dei Verbum, 18 November 1965: AAS 58 (1966) 817–830; ConstDecrDecl 423–447 (excerpts).

PREFACE

1.   This Council hears the word of God in reverence and proclaims it in trust, thereby making its own the words of St. John: "We proclaim to you the eternal life that was with the Father and was made manifest to us. That which we have seen and heard we proclaim also to you so that you may have fellowship with us and our fellowship is with the Father and with his Son Jesus Christ" (1 Jn 1:2–3). [. . .]

218

CHAPTER I
REVELATION ITSELF

2.   In his goodness and wisdom God has seen fit to reveal himself and to make known the mystery of his will (see Eph 1:9), namely, that through Christ, the Word made flesh, all may have access to the Father in the one Holy Spirit and may become sharers in the divine nature (see Eph 2:18; 2 Pt 1:4). [. . .] The plan of divine revelation is carried out both through deeds and through the words connected with them: the deeds God works in the history of salvation light up and confirm the teaching and realities signified by words; the words in turn proclaim God's works and illumine the mystery they contain. The inner truth of the revelation about God and human salvation becomes a light for us in Christ, who is at once the mediator and the fullest expression of divine revelation.[2]

219

CHAPTER II
TRANSMITTAL OF REVELATION

7.   [. . .] In order that the Church would continue to keep the Gospel intact and alive, the apostles left the bishops as their successors, "handing on to them their own office of teaching."[3] This sacred tradition and sacred Scripture of the Old and New Testament serve as the mirror in which the Church as a pilgrim here on earth contemplates God, the source of all that it receives, until it is brought to see him face to face as he is (see 1 Jn 3:2).

220

8.   The apostolic preaching, expressed in a special way in the inspired books, must be safeguarded by an uninterrupted succession. [. . .]

      [. . .] What the apostles handed down contains everything needed for the people of God to live a life of holiness and to grow in faith. Thus the Church in

221

---

   17   See SC art. 14 [DOL 1 no. 14].

    2   See Mt 11:27; Jn 1:14 and 17, 14:6, 17:1–3; 2 Cor 3:16 and 4:6; Eph 1:3–14.

    3   Irenaeus, *Adv. Haer.* 3, 3, 1: Harvey 2, 9.

teaching, life, and worship keeps alive and passes on to every generation all that it is, all that it believes.

This tradition deriving from the apostles develops in the Church under the influence of the Holy Spirit.[5] The sources of this development are the contemplation and study of believers who ponder over these things in their heart (see Lk 2:19,51), their deep understanding of their own experience of spiritual realities, and the preaching of those who together with their succession to the episcopate have received the sure charism of truth. Thus with the passage of the centuries the Church advances toward the fullness of divine truth until God's words are wholly accomplished in the Church.

The words of the church Fathers bear witness to the life-giving presence of this tradition, the riches of which are showered upon the practice and life of the believing, praying Church. This same tradition makes known to the Church the entire canon of sacred Scripture, gives to the Church a deepening perception of the pages of Scripture, and makes them always living. In this way God, who has spoken once of old, speaks anew and without interruption to the Bride of his beloved Son; the Holy Spirit, through whom the living voice of the Gospel resounds in the Church and thereby in the world, leads those who believe to all truth, making the word of Christ richly dwell in them (see Col 3:26).

222   10. Sacred tradition and sacred Scripture make up the one sacred deposit of the word of God entrusted to the Church. Holding fast to this, the entire holy people, united to their bishops in doctrine and communion, persevere together in the breaking of the bread and in prayer (see Acts 2:42, Gr.). This is the source of the incomparable concord of bishops and faithful in holding to, practicing, and confessing the faith handed down.[7]

The office of authentically interpreting the word of God in Scripture or tradition[8] has been entrusted exclusively to the living teaching authority (*magisterium*) of the Church,[9] which it exercises in the name of Jesus Christ. The magisterium does not stand above the word of God but is rather its servant, teaching only what has been handed on. With the help of the Holy Spirit, the magisterium hears that word devoutly, guards it zealously, expounds it faithfully. From that one deposit of faith alone the Church derives all the truths it proposes to be believed in as divinely revealed.

Clearly, then, tradition, Scripture, and the Church's magisterium are, in accord with God's wise plan, so joined together and coordinated that none stands without the others, but all three together, each in its own way under the influence of the Holy Spirit, contribute effectively to the salvation of souls.

CHAPTER IV
OLD TESTAMENT

223   15. The divine plan for the Old Testament was above all arranged so as to prepare, to proclaim in prophecy (see Lk 24:44; Jn 5:39; 1 Pt 1:10), and to prefigure through types (see 1 Cor 10:11) the coming of Christ, the Redeemer of all, and of his

---

5   See Vatican Council I, Const. dogm. de fide catholica *Dei Filius* cap. 4: Denz-Schön 3020.

7   See Pius XII, Ap. Const. *Munificentissimus Deus*, 1 Nov. 1950: AAS 42 (1950) 756, with the words of St. Cyprian: "The Church is a people joined to the priest and a flock staying close to its shepherd" (*Ep.* 66, 8: CSEL 3, 2, 733).

8   See Vatican Council I, loc. cit. cap. 3: Denz-Schön 3011.

9   See Pius XII, Encycl. *Humani generis*, 12 Aug 1950: AAS 42 (1950) 568–569; Denz-Schön 3886.

messianic kingdom. Therefore, the books of the Old Testament provide, in a way suited to humanity's condition before Christ restored the way of salvation, a knowledge of God and of human beings and of God's ways of dealing with them in justice and mercy. Even though what they contain is incomplete and transient, these books point out a genuinely divine plan of instruction.[1] The books of the Old Testament give expression to a vivid sense of the divine; they contain sublime teaching about God, a sound wisdom about human life, and a wondrous treasury of prayers; finally, within them lies hidden the mystery of salvation. Christian people must therefore accept them with reverence.

CHAPTER VI
SACRED SCRIPTURE IN THE CHURCH'S LIFE

21. The Church has always revered sacred Scripture even as it has revered the body of the Lord, because, above all in the liturgy, it never ceases to receive the bread of life from the table both of God's word and of Christ's body and to offer it to the faithful. The Church has always held and continues to hold that the Scriptures along with sacred tradition are the supreme rule of its own faith, because being inspired by God and consigned once and for all to writing, the Scriptures impart without change the word of God himself and cause the voice of the Holy Spirit to be heard in the words of the apostles and prophets. All preaching in the Church, even as the Christian religion itself, must have the Scriptures as its source and norm. In the sacred books the Father who is in heaven lovingly comes to meet his children and converses with them. Such are the force and power present in God's word that it stands as the support and vitality of the Church and the Church's children, the stronghold for their faith, food for their soul, a pure and never-failing source for their spiritual life. Thus these words apply par excellence to Scripture: "The word of God is living and active" (Heb 4:12); "It is able to build you up and give you the inheritance among all those who are sanctified" (Acts 20:32; see also 1 Thes 2:13).   224

22. The Scriptures must be made readily accessible to the faithful. For this reason the Church from the very beginning received as its own the Septuagint version of the Old Testament; the Church also has held in honor other translations of the East as well as Latin translations, above all the one called the Vulgate. The word of God must be available in all ages; with maternal care, therefore, the Church has taken pains for proper and accurate translations into the various languages and especially for translations based on the original texts of the sacred books. Given the opportunity and with the approval of Church authority, when such translations are done as a collaborative effort with Christians separated from us, all Christians will be able to make use of them.   225

23. The Church, Bride of the Word incarnate, endeavors under the guidance of the Holy Spirit to reach an ever more penetrating understanding of the Scriptures, so that it may unfailingly nourish its children on God's own words. This is the reason also why the Church duly encourages the study of the Fathers as well as the liturgies of both East and West. [. . .]   226

25. All the clergy, above all priests and others lawfully engaged in the ministry of the word as deacons or catechists, must by constant reading and painstaking study   227

---

[1] See Pius XI, Encycl. *Mit brennender Sorge*, 14 March 1937: AAS 29 (1937) 151.

hold fast to the Scriptures. This is to guard against anyone's becoming "a preacher of the word of God empty on the outside because inwardly he is not a listener,"[4] whereas his duty is to share with the faithful in his care the abundant treasures of God's word. This Council likewise strongly and explicitly urges all the faithful, and religious especially, toward the learning of the "surpassing knowledge of Jesus Christ" (Phil 3:8) by their frequent reading of the holy Scriptures. "Not to know the Scriptures is not to know Christ."[5] All, then, should eagerly turn to the sacred text, whether through the liturgy so packed with God's word, through their own devout reading, or through the biblical institutes and other resources that, in virtue of the approval and efforts of the bishops, are in our day available everywhere. All should be mindful of the need that prayer accompany the reading of Scripture so that this may become a conversation between God and ourselves; "when we pray we speak to him; when we read the Scriptures he speaks to us."[6] [. . .]

228   26. Through the reading and study of the Bible, then, "may the word of the Lord speed on and triumph" (2 Thes 3:1); may the treasure of revelation entrusted to the Church more and more fill up the hearts of all. Even as the life of the Church receives increase from constantly turning to the mystery of the eucharist, so too there is reason to hope for a new awakening of the spiritual life deriving from an increased dedication to God's word, which "abides forever" (Is 40:8; 1 Pt 1:23–25).

15. PONTIFICAL COMMISSION FOR THE INTERPRETATION OF THE DECREES OF VATICAN COUNCIL II, **Reply** to a query, on the Constitution *Dei Verbum* no. 21, 5 February 1968: AAS 60 (1968) 362.

229   Query: In the words, "The Church has always revered sacred Scripture *even as* it has the body of the Lord, because, above all in the liturgy, it never ceases to receive from the altar and to offer to the faithful as the bread of life both the word of God and the body of Christ" does the term "even as" (*sicut*) in the Dogmatic Constitution *Dei Verbum*[a] have the force of meaning that the same or equal reverence is due to Scripture as to the eucharist?

Reply: Veneration is due to both sacred Scripture and the eucharist, but in a different way and from a different consideration, as can be gathered from the Constitution on the Liturgy *Sacrosanctum Concilium* art. 7,[b] the Encyclical *Mysterium fidei*, 3 September 1965: AAS 57 (1965) 764,[c] the SCR Instruction *Eucharisticum mysterium*, 25 May 1967, no. 9: AAS 59 (1967) 547.[d]

---

   [4] Augustine, *Serm.* 179, 1: PL 38, 966.

   [5] Jerome, *Comment. in Is.*, Prol.: PL 24, 17. See also Benedict XV, Encycl. *Spiritus Paraclitus: Enchiridion Biblicum* (EB) 475–480. Pius XII, Encycl. *Divino afflanto Spiritu*: EB 544.

   [6] Ambrose, *De officiis ministrorum* 1, 20, 88: PL 16, 50.

   [a] See DOL 14 no. 224.

   [b] DOL 1 no. 7.

   [c] DOL 176 no. 1183.

   [d] DOL 179 no. 1238.

16. VATICAN COUNCIL II, **Decree on the Apostolate of the Laity** *Apostoli-cam actuositatem*, 18 November 1965: AAS 58 (1966) 837–864; ConstDecrDecl 459–508 (excerpts).

PREFACE

1.   Since the apostolic activity of the people of God is something this Council wishes to intensify,[1] it turns attentively to the Christian laity. The Council has already elsewhere reviewed the roles proper to the laity in the Church's mission.[2] Deriving as it does from the vocation to be Christians, their apostolate can never be missing from the Church's life.   230

CHAPTER I
LAITY'S CALL TO THE APOSTOLATE

2.   [. . .] In the Church there are different ministries but one mission. Upon the apostles and their successors Christ bestowed the office of teaching, sanctifying, and governing in the power of his name. But the laity also, made sharers in the priestly, prophetic, and kingly office of Christ, carry out in the Church and in the world their own proper part in the mission of the people of God as a whole.[3] They exercise their apostolate by their involvement in evangelizing and sanctifying others and in making the spirit of the Gospel penetrate and better the temporal order. As a result the laity's involvement in the secular order provides a clear witnessing of Christ and contributes to the salvation of humankind. [. . .]   231

3.   The laity derive their responsibility and rights for the apostolate from their own union with Christ, the Head of the Church. For as they become members of Christ's Mystical Body through baptism and are strengthened in the power of the Holy Spirit through confirmation, they are commissioned to be apostles by the Lord himself. They are consecrated to be a kingly priesthood and a holy people (see 1 Pt 2:4–10) to the end that in all that they do they may offer up spiritual sacrifices and bear witness to Christ in all the earth. The sacraments, the eucharist above all, bring to them and sustain that charity which is the soul of all apostolic activity.[4] [. . .]   232

      For the carrying out of the apostolate, the Holy Spirit, sanctifying the people of God by means of ministry and sacraments, bestows special gifts on believers (see 1 Cor 12:7), "apportioning them to each one individually as he wills" (1 Cor 12:11). The purpose is this: "As each has received a gift, employ it for another, as good stewards of God's varied grace" (1 Pt 4:10), for the building up of the whole Body in charity (see Eph 4:16). [. . .]

4.   Since Christ as emissary of the Father is the source and the beginning of the Church's entire apostolate, clearly the effectiveness of the apostolate of the laity depends on their personal, vital union with Christ. [. . .] That life of close union receives its nurture in the Church from the spiritual resources that all the faithful share, above all from an intense participation in the liturgy.[5] The laity must use   233

---

    [1]   See John XXIII, Ap. Const. *Humanae salutis*, 25 Dec. 1961: AAS 54 (1962) 7–10.

    [2]   See LG nos. 33–38 [DOL 4 nos. 150–153]; SC art. 26–40 [DOL 1 nos. 26–40]; IM: AAS 56 (1964) 145–153; ConstDecrDecl 73–89; UR [DOL 6]. See also CD nos. 16, 17, 18; GE nos. 3, 5, 7.

    [3]   See LG no. 31.

    [4]   See LG no. 33, also no. 10 [DOL 4 no. 150, also no. 140].

    [5]   See SC art. 11 [DOL 1 no. 11].

these resources in such a way that as they rightly attend to their secular responsibilities in the day-to-day circumstances of life they do not isolate union with Christ from their life, but rather increase it as they fulfill their duties in conformity to God's will. [. . .]

Only by the light of faith and by meditating on the word of God has anyone the power to perceive always and everywhere the God in whom "we live and move and have our being" (Acts 17:28); the power to look for his will in every happening; the power to see Christ in all people, whether friends or strangers; the power to evaluate properly the true meaning and worth of the things of this world, both in themselves and in their relationship to humanity's final destiny. [. . .]

CHAPTER II
OBJECTIVES TO BE ACHIEVED

234   6.   The Church's mission bears upon human salvation as achieved through faith in Christ and through his grace. Consequently, the objective of the apostolate of the Church and of all its members is to make Christ's message known to the world by word and deed and to be the channel of his grace. The principal means is the ministry of word and sacrament, entrusted in a special way to the clergy, but in which the laity have an important part to play "as fellow workers in the truth" (3 Jn 8). In this area especially the pastoral ministry and the lay apostolate complement each other. [. . .]

The lay apostolate does not consist simply in the witness of personal life; the true apostle looks for opportunities to proclaim Christ in words both to nonbelievers in order to bring them to faith and to believers in order to instruct and strengthen them and to encourage them to a more devout life. "The love of Christ impels us" (2 Cor 5:14) and in all our hearts the words of St. Paul must resound: "Woe to me if I do not preach the Gospel" (1 Cor 9:16).[6] [. . .]

235   8.   [. . .] In its earliest days the Church showed itself to be completely united around Christ in the bond of charity by combining the agape with the eucharistic meal. Similarly in every era the Church bears this sign of charity as its distinguishing mark; while it rejoices in similar efforts of others, it claims the works of charity as its own inalienable responsibility and right. [. . .]

CHAPTER III
THE MANY FIELDS OF THE APOSTOLATE

236   10.   Sharing in Christ's office as priest, prophet, and king, the laity have their own active roles in the life and works of the Church. [. . .] Drawing their strength from an intense participation in the liturgical life of their own community, they also do their part conscientiously in the community's apostolic endeavors: in leading back to the Church people who may have strayed afar; in being devoted co-workers in the spread of God's word, especially through catechetical instruction; in making more effective through their own talents the Church's care of souls and even its financial management.

237   11.   The Creator of all things has established marriage as the beginning and foundation of all human society and by his grace turned it into a great sacrament in

---

6   See Pius XI, Encycl. *Ubi arcano*, 23 Dec. 1922: AAS 14 (1922) 659. Pius XII, Encycl. *Summi Pontificatus*, 20 Oct. 1939: AAS 31 (1939) 442–443.

Christ and the Church (see Eph 5:32). Therefore, the apostolate of married couples and of families has a unique importance for both the Church and civil society. [. . .]

The family has received from God the mission to be the first living cell of society. The family will accomplish its mission if, by the loyalty of its members to each other and their prayer to God together, it shows itself to be a sanctuary of the Church in the home; if the whole family enters into the Church's liturgical worship; if the family offers warm hospitality and fosters justice and other good works to serve as brothers and sisters all those burdened with need. [. . .]

CHAPTER IV
THE MANY WAYS OF THE APOSTOLATE

16. [. . .] We should all remember that we can reach other people and contribute   238
to the salvation of the whole world by public prayer and worship, by penance, and in the trials and tribulations of life by a willing acceptance that conforms us to the suffering Christ (see 2 Cor 4:10; Col 1:24).

17. The apostolate of the individual is a compelling need in regions where the   239
freedom of the Church is seriously hampered. In such trying circumstances lay people, substituting as far as they can for priests and jeopardizing their personal freedom, sometimes even their life, are teaching their neighbors Christian doctrine, instructing them in Christian living and a Catholic mentality, and influencing them to receive the sacraments often and above all to develop devotion to the eucharist.[7]
[. . .]

CHAPTER V
GOOD ORDER

24. The hierarchy has the responsibility of encouraging the apostolate of the laity,   240
of providing them with the spiritual principles and resources for it, of directing the carrying out of this apostolate toward the general well-being of the Church, and of overseeing it in order to safeguard doctrine and good order. [. . .]

[. . .] The hierarchy, finally, entrusts to lay people some responsibilities more closely linked to the pastoral office — in the teaching of Christian doctrine, in certain rites in the liturgy, in the care of souls. In the exercise of any such role the laity by reason of the mission they have received are completely subject to higher ecclesiastical supervision. [. . .]

17. VATICAN COUNCIL II, **Decree on the Church's Missionary Activity** *Ad gentes*, 7 December 1965: AAS 58 (1966) 947–990; ConstDecrDecl 543–615 (excerpts).

1.   Sent by God to all nations as "the universal sacrament of salvation,"[1] the   241
Church, obedient to the mandate of its Founder[2] out of the inner demands of its own catholicity, strives to proclaim the Gospel to all people. The apostles them-

---

[7]   See Pius XII, Addr. to the First International Congress for the Lay Apostolate, 14 Oct. 1951: AAS 43 (1951) 788.

[1]   See LG no. 48: AAS 57 (1965) 53; ConstDecrDecl 181.

[2]   See Mk 16:15.

selves, on whom the Church was built, following in Christ's footsteps "preached the word of truth and became the fathers of Churches."[3] The responsibility of their successors is to perpetuate that work, so that "the word of God may speed on and triumph" (2 Thes 3:1) and God's kingdom may be proclaimed and established in all the earth. [. . .]

CHAPTER I
DOCTRINAL PRINCIPLES

242   5. [. . .] The Church accomplishes its mission through activity whereby, in obedience to Christ's command and prompted by the grace and charity of the Holy Spirit, it becomes fully present to all peoples. The purpose is to lead them by example, preaching, the sacraments, and other channels of grace to Christ's faith, freedom, and peace and so to open up to them the free and sure way to share fully in the mystery of Christ. [. . .]

243   6. [. . .] "Missions" is the name generally given to those special endeavors by which heralds of the Gospel sent by the Church and going out into the whole world fulfill the office of preaching the Gospel and of implanting the Church among peoples or groups not yet believing in Christ. Missionary activity carries out these endeavors and as a rule in specific territories determined by the Holy See. [. . .] The chief means for establishing the Church is the preaching of the Gospel of Jesus Christ. The Lord sent his disciples to proclaim his Gospel to the whole world so that those reborn by God's word[35] would by baptism become part of the Church, which as the Body of the Word incarnate feeds and lives on God's word and the eucharistic bread.[36]

244   9. [. . .] Missionary activity is nothing other and nothing less than the appearance, that is, the epiphany, and the fulfillment of God's will in the world and its history; there through missions God is clearly unfolding the history of salvation. Missionary activity makes Christ the author of salvation to be present through preaching the word and celebrating the sacraments, of which the eucharist is the center and the crowning point. All that the Church discovers of truth and grace among peoples as, so to speak, the hidden presence of God, it rids of any evil elements and restores to Christ their source, who defeats the devil's empire and holds in check the manifold evil powers of sin. Thus whatever of good lies rooted in the human mind and heart or in the rituals and cultures of peoples is not destroyed but healed, raised up, and brought to fulfillment for God's glory, the confounding of the devil, and the blessedness of people.[52] [. . .]

---

[3]   Augustine, *Enarr. in Ps.* 44, 23: PL 36, 508; CCL 38, 150.

[35]   See 1 Pt 1:23.

[36]   See Acts 2:42.

[52]   See LG no. 17 [DOL 4 no. 144]. Augustine, *De civitate Dei* 19, 17: PL 41, 646. SC Propagation of the Faith, Instr.: *Collectanea* 1, no. 135, p. 42.

CHAPTER II
MISSION WORK

ARTICLE 1. CHRISTIAN WITNESS

11. The Church has to become present among the different peoples through its children who are already with them or who are sent to them. For all Christian believers, wherever they are, have the obligation to show forth by living example and the spoken word that new person they have put on through baptism and that power of the Holy Spirit that has strengthened them through confirmation. Then others, beholding their good works, may give glory to the Father and come to realize fully the true meaning of human life and of the universal bond of human communion. [. . .]

245

ARTICLE 2. PREACHING THE GOSPEL AND
GATHERING GOD'S PEOPLE TOGETHER

14. Those who through the Church have accepted from the Father faith in Christ[17] should be admitted to the catechumenate by means of liturgical ceremonies. The catechumenate means not simply a presentation of teachings and precepts, but a formation in the whole of Christian life and a sufficiently prolonged period of training; by these means the disciples will become bound to Christ as their master. Catechumens should therefore be properly initiated into the mystery of salvation and the practices of gospel living; by means of sacred rites celebrated at successive times,[18] they should be led gradually into the life of faith, liturgy, and charity belonging to the people of God.

246

Next, freed from the power of darkness,[19] dying, buried, and risen again together with Christ through the sacraments of Christian initiation, they receive the Spirit[20] of adoption of children,[21] and with the whole people of God celebrate the memorial of the Lord's death and resurrection.

There is a great need for a reform of the Lenten and Easter liturgy so that it will be a spiritual preparation of the catechumens for the celebration of the paschal mystery, the rites of which will include their being reborn to Christ through baptism.

Christian initiation during the catechumenate is not the concern of catechists or priests alone, but of the whole community of believers and especially of godparents, so that from the outset the catechumens will have a sense of being part of the people of God. Moreover, because the Church's life is apostolic, catechumens should learn to take an active share in the evangelization and the building up of the Church through the witness of their life and the profession of their faith.

Finally, the new code of canon law should set out clearly the juridic status of catechumens; they are already joined to the Church,[22] already part of Christ's household,[23] and are in many cases already living a life of faith, hope, and charity.

---

17 See LG no. 17 [DOL 4 no. 144].

18 See SC art. 64–65 [DOL 1 nos. 64–65].

19 See Col 1:13. On being freed from slavery to the devil and darkness, see Mt 12:28; Jn 8:44 and 12:31 (cf. 1 Jn 3:8; Eph 2:1–2). See also RR, liturgy of baptism.

20 See Rom 6:4–11; Col 2:12–13; 1 Pt 3:21–22; Mk 16:16.

21 See 1 Thes 3:5–7; Acts 8:14–17. [Ed.: for note 21, see 1 Thes 4:8.]

22 See LG no. 14: AAS 57 (1965) 19; ConstDecrDecl 119.

23 See Augustine, *Tract. in Ioann.* 11, 4: PL 35, 1476.

ARTICLE 3. BUILDING A CHRISTIAN COMMUNITY

247   15. The Holy Spirit calls all to Christ through the seed of the word and the preaching of the Gospel and inspires in hearts the obedience of faith. When in the womb of the baptismal font the Spirit gives birth into a new life to those who believe in Christ, he gathers them all together into the one people of God, "a chosen race, a royal priesthood, a holy nation, God's own people" (1 Pt 2:9).[24]

As God's co-workers,[25] therefore, missionaries are to create congregations of believers of a kind that, living in a way worthy of their calling,[26] will carry out the divinely appointed offices of priest, prophet, and king. This is how the Christian community becomes a sign of God's presence in the world: by the eucharistic sacrifice it goes constantly with Christ to the Father;[27] stengthened by God's word,[28] it bears witness to Christ;[29] it walks in charity and burns with the apostolic spirit.[30] Right from the beginning the Christian community should be trained to be as far as possible self-sufficient in regard to its own needs. [. . .]

248   16. [. . .] This Council's decrees on the vocation and formation of priests are to be followed exactly from the time the Church is implanted and by the new Churches. Great importance is to be attached to the directives on correlating spiritual, theological, and pastoral formation, on living according to the model of the Gospel in disregard of personal or family interests, on cultivating a sense of the mystery of the Church. Priests will thus learn in a special way how to dedicate themselves completely to serving the Body of Christ and the work of the Gospel, to be loyal to their bishop as his trusted co-workers, and to offer their fraternal assistance to their brother priests.[35]

Toward this broad objective the whole formation of seminarians is to be planned in light of the mystery of salvation as set forth in the Scriptures. The seminarians should discover and live out this mystery of Christ and human salvation in the liturgy.[36] [. . .]

Where the conferences of bishops deem it advisable, the order of diaconate as a permanent state of life is to be restored in accord with the norm of the Constitution on the Church.[41] To make their ministry more effective through sacramental grace, it is advantageous to strengthen and bind closer to the altar through the apostolic tradition of the laying on of hands those men who are actually exercising diaconal functions: preaching God's word as catechists; presiding in the name of a pastor or bishop over scattered Christian communities; engaging in social or charitable works.

249   17. Also worthy of praise and well-deserving for their work in the missions to all peoples are the many catechists, both men and women, who, filled with the apos-

---

[24]   See LG no. 9: AAS 57 (1965) 13; ConstDecrDecl 108.

[25]   See 1 Cor 3:9.

[26]   See Eph 4:1.

[27]   See LG nos. 10, 11, 34 [DOL 4 nos. 140, 141, 151].

[28]   See DV no. 21 [DOL 14 no. 224].

[29]   See LG nos. 12, 35 [DOL 4 nos. 142, 152].

[30]   See LG nos. 23, 36: AAS 57 (1965) 28, 41–42; ConstDecrDecl 134, 167–173.

[35]   See OT nos. 4, 8, 9: AAS 58 (1966) 716, 718, 719; ConstDecrDecl 363, 367, 368.

[36]   See SC art. 17 [DOL 1 no. 17].

[41]   See LG no. 29 [DOL 4 no. 149].

tolic spirit, contribute by their immense labors a singular and indispensable assistance to spreading the faith and the Church. [. . .]

It is therefore imperative to have more diocesan and regional schools where future catechists will learn Catholic teaching, especially on the Bible and the liturgy, catechetical methods, and pastoral practice; where also they will become formed in the ways of Christian life[42] by devoting themselves to growth in devoutness and holiness. [. . .] The Churches should also give grateful recognition to the assistant catechists, whose help is so essential. These people preside over prayer in their communities and are the teachers of religion. There is need, then, to ensure their careful doctrinal and spiritual formation. It is also highly desirable that, where it seems appropriate, catechists, once they have gone through the required formation, receive a canonical mission at a public liturgy so that among their people they may act in the service of faith with greater authority.

CHAPTER III
LOCAL CHURCHES

19. [. . .] In the new Churches the life of the people of God ought to grow at all   250
levels of the Christian life as it is to be renewed in accord with the norms of this
Council. This means that the congregations of the faithful consciously become
more and more communities of faith, of charity, and of the liturgy. [. . .] The faith
is taught by means of an effective catechesis; it is celebrated in a liturgy congenial
to the culture of the people; it is integrated by suitable canonical legislation into the
laudable practices and customs established in the region.

20. [. . .] The native priests in the new Churches should enter wholeheartedly into   251
evangelization, establishing cooperation with foreign missionaries. The two form
but one presbyterate, under the authority of the bishop, not only to be pastors to
the faithful and celebrants of divine worship, but also to be preachers of the Gospel
to those still outside the Church. [. . .]

CHAPTER V
RIGHT ORGANIZATION OF MISSIONARY ACTIVITY

31. By consulting with each other the conferences of bishops should deal with the   252
more serious issues and problems, but without any disregard of circumstances that
differ from place to place.[12] To forestall wasting the short supply of personnel and
resources or needlessly duplicating projects, the conferences of bishops are advised
to establish, by pooling their assets, facilities that will be of service to all: for
example, seminaries, upper-level and technical schools, pastoral, catechetical, liturgical, and communication centers. [. . .]

Where it is advantageous, a similar form of cooperation should be set up
between several conferences. [. . .]

CHAPTER VI
COOPERATION

36. As members of the living Christ who through baptism and through   253
confirmation and the eucharist have been incorporated into him and configured to

---

    42   See John XXIII, *Princeps Pastorum*, 28 Nov. 1959: AAS 51 (1959) 855.

    12   See CD nos. 36–38: AAS 58 (1966) 692–694; ConstDecrDecl 314–317.

him, all the faithful are under an obligation to cooperate in the growth and spread of his Body, the Church, so that they may bring it quickly to its fullness.[1]

Accordingly, all the members of the Church should be keenly aware of their responsibility toward the world, develop in themselves a genuinely Catholic spirit, and devote their energies to evangelization. But all should recognize that their first and most urgent duty in the cause of spreading the faith is a life profoundly Christian. For their ardor to serve God and their charity toward others will send a fresh breath of life throughout the entire Church, which will then appear as a sign raised up before the nations,[2] as the "light of the world" (Mt 5:14), and the "salt of the earth" (Mt 5:13). This life-witness will achieve its effect all the more readily if it is presented in union with that of other Christians, as the norms of the Decree on Ecumenism provide.[3]

This renewed spirit will be the source of prayers and penitential acts offered to God so that by his grace missionary work will bear fruit, vocations to the missions will take root, and the needed resources will be forthcoming. [. . .]

254   37. Communities, particularly the diocese and the parish, are where the people of God live and are in a sense visible: therefore these communities also have a part in bearing witness to Christ before all peoples. [. . .]

Through its members, whom God chooses for this sublime task, the whole community prays, works together, and carries on its activities among peoples. [. . .]

255   38. Because they are members of the body of bishops, the successor to the apostolic college, all bishops have been consecrated not just for a particular diocese but for the salvation of the whole world as well. Christ's commandment to preach the Gospel to every creature[5] rests primarily and immediately on them, with Peter and under Peter. [. . .]

The bishop has the responsibility to raise up among his people, especially the sick and the suffering, souls who will wholeheartedly offer to God prayer and penance for the evangelization of the world. [. . .]

256   39. Priests are Christ's representatives and the co-workers with the order of bishops in the threefold sacred office that has an inherent relationship to the Church's mission.[11] They ought, therefore, to have a profound understanding that their life has been consecrated to the service of mission. Since through their ministry — consisting above all in the eucharist as this builds up the Church — they enter into communion with Christ the Head of the Church and bring others into that communion, they cannot help but experience how much remains unachieved for the full measure of Christ's Body and how much is yet to be added for its continued growth. They shall therefore have as one objective for their pastoral ministry that it serve the spread of the Gospel among non-Christians.

Priests in their pastoral ministry are to arouse and maintain among the faithful a zeal for the evangelization of the world. This they will do by instruction through catechesis and by preaching on the duty of the Church to proclaim Christ to all

---

[1]   See Eph 4:13.

[2]   See Is 11:12.

[3]   See UR no. 12: AAS 57 (1965) 99; ConstDecrDecl 260.

[5]   See Mk 16:15.

[11]   See LG no. 28 [DOL 4 no. 148].

peoples; [. . .] they should teach the faithful to pray for the missions and, becoming beggars for the sake of Christ and the salvation of souls,[12] unabashedly appeal for money for the missions.

18. VATICAN COUNCIL II, Decree on the Ministry and Life of Priests
Presbyterorum Ordinis, 7 December 1965: AAS 58 (1966) 991–1024; Const-DecrDecl 619–678 (excerpts).

CHAPTER I
PRIESTHOOD IN THE MISSION OF THE CHURCH

2.   The Lord Jesus, "whom the Father has consecrated and sent into the world" (Jn 10:36), has made his whole Mystical Body the sharer in the Spirit's anointing by which he himself has been anointed.[2] For in him all the faithful are made a holy and royal priesthood. They offer spiritual sacrifices to God through Jesus Christ and they proclaim the perfections of him who has called them out of darkness into his marvelous light.[3] Hence, there is no member who does not have a part in the mission of the whole Body. Rather, all ought to revere Christ in their hearts[4] and bear witness to him in the spirit of prophecy.[5]

That all might grow together into the one Body in which "not all the members have the same function" (Rom 12:4), the Lord has established certain of the faithful as ministers, possessing the sacred power of orders to offer sacrifice in the community, to forgive sins,[6] and in Christ's name to exercise publicly the office of priest on behalf of the people. [. . .]

As connected with the order of bishops, the priestly office shares in the authority by which Christ himself builds up, sanctifies, and rules his Body. Their sacerdotal office presupposes the sacraments of Christian initiation, but it is conferred by that special sacrament through which priests, by the anointing of the Holy Spirit, are marked with a distinct sacramental character and are so configured to Christ the Priest that they have the power to act in the person of Christ the Head.[11]

Since in their own degree priests participate in the office of the apostles, God gives them the grace to be ministers of Christ Jesus among the people so that their carrying out of the sacred service of the Gospel may make the offering of the people acceptable, sanctified in the Holy Spirit.[12] For through the apostolic proclamation of the Gospel the people of God are called together and gathered in such a way that all who belong to this people because they have been sanctified by the Holy Spirit, offer themselves as a "sacrifice, living, holy, acceptable to God" (Rom 12:1). Through the ministry of priests the spiritual sacrifice of the faithful is brought to

257

---

[12]   See Pius XI, *Rerum Ecclesiae*, 28 Feb. 1926: AAS 28 (1926) 72.

[2]   See Mt 3:16; Lk 4:18; Acts 4:27, 10:38.

[3]   See 1 Pt 2:5 and 9.

[4]   See 1 Pt 3:15.

[5]   See Rv 19:10; LG no. 35 [DOL 4 no. 152].

[6]   See Council of Trent, sess. 23, cap. 1 and can. 2: Denz-Schön 1764 and 1771.

[11]   See LG no. 10 [DOL 4 no. 140].

[12]   See Rom 15:16, Gr.

completion in union with the sacrifice of Christ, the sole Mediator; through the hands of priests and in the name of the whole Church, that sacrifice is offered in the eucharist in a sacramental and unbloody manner until he himself returns.[13] This is the purpose and supreme exercise of the priest's ministry. For that ministry, which has its origin from the gospel message, derives its power and force from the sacrifice of Christ. Its aim is that "the entire city of the redeemed, that is, the community and society of the saints, may be offered as a universal sacrifice to God through the High Priest who in his passion offered his very self for us that we might be the Body of so exalted a Head."[14] The purpose, therefore, that priests pursue by their ministry and life is the glory of God the Father to be accomplished in Christ. That glory consists in this: that men and women knowingly, freely, and gladly accept the work God has accomplished in Christ and manifest it in their lives. Hence, whether engaged in prayer and adoration, preaching the word, offering the eucharistic sacrifice, administering the other sacraments, or performing any of the works of the ministry for others, priests are contributing to the spread of God's glory as well as to the development of divine life in people. Even as all of these activities result from Christ's Passover, they will be crowned in the glorious return of the same Lord when he himself hands over the kingdom to God the Father.[15]

258   3.   Priests, taken from among the people and appointed for the people in the things that pertain to God in order to offer gifts and sacrifices for sins,[16] live among others as their brothers. [. . .]

CHAPTER II
MINISTRY OF PRIESTS

I. FUNCTIONS OF THE PRIEST

259   4.   The people of God are first gathered together by the word of the living God,[1] which they have a right to seek from the mouth of priests.[2] No one can be saved except by first having believed.[3] Priests, therefore, as the co-workers of the bishops, have for their first responsibility the proclaiming of God's Gospel to all,[4] so that in fulfilling the Lord's command, "Go into the whole world, preach the Gospel to the whole creation" (Mk 16:15),[5] they may establish and build up the people of God.

---

[13]   See 1 Cor 11:26.

[14]   Augustine, *De civitate Dei* 10, 6: PL 41, 284.

[15]   See 1 Cor 15:24.

[16]   See Heb 2:17, 4:15.

[1]   See 1 Pt 1:23; Acts 6:7, 12:24. Augustine: "[The apostles] preached the word of truth and so have fathered Churches" (*Enarr. in Ps.* 44, 23: PL 36, 508).

[2]   See Mal 2:7; 1 Tm 4:11–13; 2 Tm 4:5; Ti 1:9.

[3]   See Mk 16:16.

[4]   See 2 Cor 11:7. What is said of bishops applies also to priests as their co-workers. See also *Statuta Ecclesiae antiqua* cap. 3: C. Munier, ed. (Paris, 1960) 79. Gratian, *Decretum*: E. Friedberg, ed. (repr. 1955) 1:307. Council of Trent, sess. 5, Decr. 2, no. 9: COeD 88; sess. 24, Decr. *De reformatione*, cap. 4: COeD 739. LG no. 25:AAS 57(1965) 29–31; ConstDecrDecl 107.

[5]   See *Constitutiones Apostolorum* 2, 26, 7: "[Priests] are the teachers of the knowledge about God, because the Lord himself has commanded us, 'Going, therefore, teach'. . .": Funk DidConst, 105. See also the Leonine Sacramentary and others up to the time of the *Pontificale Romanum*; the preface [prayer of consecration] for the ordination of priests: "With the same loving care you gave companions to your Son's apostles to help in teaching the faith: they preached the Gospel in the whole world" [RP 213]; *Liber Ordinum Liturgiae Mozarabicae*, preface for ordination of priests: "As teacher of the people and ruler of his subjects may he hold rightly to the Catholic faith and announce to all the true salvation": M. Férotin, ed.,

For "faith comes from what is heard and what is heard comes by the preaching of Christ" (Rom 10:17). Thus the saving word gives birth to faith in the hearts of nonbelievers and nurtures it in the hearts of believers. Faith, then, is what begins and increases the community of believers. [. . .]

The exercise of the ministry of the word, therefore, is manifold, in keeping with the needs of the hearers and the charisms of the preacher. In non-Christian regions or groups the proclamation of the Gospel brings people to the faith and the sacraments;[9] in the community of Christians, especially in the case of those who seem to understand or believe little of what they observe, the preaching of the word is necessary for the administration of the sacraments. For the sacraments are sacraments of faith and faith has its origin and sustenance in the word.[10] All this applies above all to the liturgy of the word in the celebration of Mass: there is an inseparable union between the proclamation of the death of the Lord, the response of the people listening, and the offering whereby Christ has confirmed the New Covenant in his blood. The people share in that offering by their inner intentions and their reception of the sacraments.[11]

5.   God, who alone is holy and the author of holiness, willed to take to himself as   260
companions and helpers men who would humbly dedicate themselves to the work of making others holy. Through the ministry of the bishop God consecrates priests to be sharers by a special title in the priesthood of Christ. In exercising sacred functions they act therefore as the ministers of him who in the liturgy continually fulfills his priestly office on our behalf by the action of his Spirit.[12] By baptism men and women are brought into the people of God and the Church; by the oil of the sick those who are ill find relief; by the celebration of Mass people sacramentally offer the sacrifice of Christ. But in administering all the sacraments, as St. Ignatius the Martyr already attested in the early days of the Church,[13] priests, on various grounds, are linked hierarchically with their bishop and so, in a certain way, bring his presence to every gathering of the faithful.[14]

The other sacraments, like every ministry of the Church and every work of the apostolate, are linked with the holy eucharist and have it as their end.[15] For the eucharist contains the Church's entire spiritual wealth,[16] that is, Christ himself. He is our Passover and living bread; through his flesh, made living and life-giving by the Holy Spirit, he is bringing life to people and thereby inviting them to offer themselves together with him, as well as their labors and all created things. The

---

Le Liber Ordinum et usage dans l'Eglise Wisigothique et Mozarabe d'Espagne: Monumenta Ecclesiae Liturgica, v. 5 (Paris, 1905) col. 55, lines 4–6.

[9]   See Mt 28:19; Mk 16:16. Tertullian, De baptismo 14, 2: CCL 1, 289, 11–13. Athanasius, Adv. Arianos 2, 24: PG 26, 237 A-B. Jerome: "First they teach all nations, then baptize those taught; the body cannot receive the sacrament unless first the soul has received the truth of faith" (In Matth. 28:19: PL 26, 226 D). Thomas Aquinas: "As he sent forth his disciples to preach, our Lord enjoined three duties upon them: the first to teach the faith; the second to grace those who believe with the sacraments. . ." (Expos. primae Decretalis § 1: Opuscula theologica [Turin and Rome, 1954] 1138).

[10]   See SC art. 35, 2 [DOL 1 no. 35].

[11]   See SC art. 33, 35, 48, 52 [DOL 1 nos. 33, 35, 48, 52].

[12]   See SC art. 7 [DOL 1 no. 7]. Pius XII, Encycl. Mystici Corporis, 29 June 1943: AAS 35 (1943) 230.

[13]   Ignatius of Antioch, Smyrn. 8, 1–2: Funk PA 1, 240. Constitutiones Apostolorum 8, 12, 3 and 8, 29, 2: Funk DidConst 496 and 532.

[14]   See LG no. 28 [DOL 4 no. 148].

[15]   See Thomas Aquinas: "The eucharist stands at the summit of the whole spiritual life and is the reason for all the other sacraments" (ST 3a, 73.3). See also ibid., 65. 3.

[16]   See ST 3a, 65.3 ad 1; 79.1 and ad 1.

eucharist therefore stands as the source and apex of all evangelization: catechumens are led gradually toward a share in the eucharist and the faithful who already bear the seal of baptism and confirmation enter through the eucharist more fully into the Body of Christ.

The eucharistic assembly is thus central for the community of the faithful over which the priest has charge. That explains why priests instruct the faithful to offer the divine victim to the Father in the sacrifice of the Mass and with Christ to make an offering of their own life. In the spirit of Christ the Good Shepherd, priests guide the faithful to bring their sins with contrite heart to the Church in the sacrament of penance for the sake of an ever more complete conversion to the Lord, heeding the words: "Repent, for the kingdom of heaven is at hand" (Mt 4:17). They also teach the people to take part in the liturgy in a way that will bring them to true prayer. Priests lead their people along, in keeping with the graces and needs of each, toward the practice of an increasingly intense spirit of prayer all through life. They call on all their people to discharge the duties of their state in life and invite the more devout to practice, in a way suited to each person, the evangelical counsels. They show their people how they can sing to the Lord in their hearts with spiritual hymns and songs, always and for everything giving thanks in the name of our Lord Jesus Christ to God the Father.[17] That praise and thanksgiving which they offer in the eucharist priests themselves spread out over the hours of the day by fulfilling the divine office. Through it they pray to God in the name of the Church for all the people in their care and indeed for the entire world.

The church, the house of prayer, must be well cared for and suited to prayer and liturgy.[18] There the eucharist is celebrated and reserved and the faithful gather for worship. There the presence of the Son of God, our Savior offered on the altar of sacrifice for us, is treasured as the aid and solace of the faithful. There priests and people are called together to respond gratefully to the gift of Christ, who through his humanity never ceases to pour forth the divine life upon the members of his Body.[19] Priests should carefully devote themselves to the science and art of liturgy, so that through their liturgical ministry the Christian communities in their care will offer an always more perfect praise to God, Father, Son, and Holy Spirit.

261   6.   Carrying out to the degree of their authority the office of Christ the Head and Shepherd, priests gather together the family of God in the bishop's name as a community one in spirit and lead it through Christ in the Spirit to the Father.[20] To carry out this as well as other functions proper to them, priests receive a spiritual power, given for the building up of the Church.[21] [. . .]

[. . .] Ceremonies, whatever their beauty, or organizations, whatever their success, will be of little use if they do not have as their purpose, leading people to Christian maturity.[26] [. . .]

---

[17]   See Eph 5:19–20.

[18]   See Jerome: ". . .the chalices, veils, and other articles having a part in the worship of the Lord's passion should, because of their closeness to the Lord's body and blood, be respected with the reverence due to that body and blood" (Ep. 114, 2: PL 22, 934). See also SC art. 122–127 [DOL 1 nos. 122–127].

[19]   See Paul VI: "In the course of the day they should not omit to visit the blessed sacrament, which, in keeping with liturgical law, is to be reserved in the worthiest place and with utmost reverence. Such visits are a proof of gratitude, a pledge of love, a service of adoration owed to the Lord Christ there present" (Encycl. Mysterium fidei no. 66 [DOL 176 no. 1210]).

[20]   See LG no. 28 [DOL 4 no. 148].

[21]   See 2 Cor 10:8, 13:10.

[26]   Jerome: "Of what use is it to have walls splendid with jewels and Christ in the poor man exposed to starvation?" (Ep. 58, 7: PL 22, 584).

No Christian community is ever built up unless it has its roots and center in the eucharistic liturgy, which, therefore, is the indispensable starting point for leading people to a sense of community.[31] The eucharistic celebration itself to be genuine and complete, must lead both to the various works of charity and mutual help and to mission activity.

Further, an ecclesial community by charity, prayer, example, and penitential practices fulfills a true form of motherhood in bringing souls to Christ. [. . .]

In raising up a community of Christians, priests are never to be the advocates of an ideology or of any human party but are to spend themselves as heralds of the Gospel and pastors in the Church having as their goal the spiritual growth of Christ's Body.

II. PRIESTS AS RELATED TO OTHERS

7.   All priests, together with the bishops, share in one and the same priesthood in such a way that the very unity of their consecration and mission requires their hierarchical communion with the order of bishops.[32] At times they express this communion in a most striking way by concelebration, as a clear sign that they celebrate the eucharistic communion joined to their bishop.[33] Accordingly, by reason of the gift of the Holy Spirit given to priests in sacred ordination, bishops should regard them as needed helpers and counselors in ministry and in the office of teaching, sanctifying, and shepherding the people of God.[34] This is a point that liturgical texts, even from the early days of the Church, declare emphatically, for example, when they solemnly entreat God to pour forth on the ordinand to priesthood the spirit "of grace and counsel so that he may help and rule the people with a pure heart,"[35] even as in the desert the spirit of Moses was spread to the minds of the seventy prudent men,[36] "whom he then used as helpers to rule with care over countless multitudes of people."[37] [. . .]

262

---

[31]   See *Didascalia* 2, 59, 1–3: "Teacher, command and exhort the people to go often to church and never to miss, but to gather together every time and not to leave it empty by absenting themselves and so making Christ's Body diminish in its members. . . . Because you are members of Christ, do not yourselves be far away from the church, not gathering together there; having Christ as your Head and, according to his promise, present in your midst and sharing with you, do not neglect him yourselves or separate the Savior from his members; do not tear or scatter Christ's Body": Funk DidConst 1, 170. See Paul VI, Addr. to Italian clergy at the 13th Week on Pastoral Renewal, Orvieto, 6 Sept. 1963: AAS 55 (1963) 750–755.

[32]   See LG no. 28 [DOL 4 no. 148].

[33]   See the so-called *Constitutio Ecclesiastica Apostolorum* 18, designating priests as the *symmystai* [helpers] and *synepimachoi* [co-workers] of bishops: T. Schermann, ed., *Die allgemeine Kirchenordnung*, v.1 (Paderborn, 1914). A. Harnack, *Die Quellen der sogleich apostolischen Kirchenordnung*, in *Texte und Untersuchungen zur Geschichte der altchristlichen Literatur*, II, 5, p. 13, nos. 18 and 19. Pseudo-Jerome: ". . .as they bless with bishops they are their associates in the mysteries (*De septem ordinibus Ecclesiae*: A. W. Kalff, ed. [Würzburg, 1937] 45). Isidore of Seville: "[Priests] preside in Christ's Church and in consecrating his body and blood are the associates of the bishops; the same is true of their teaching of the people and their office of preaching" (*De ecclesiasticis officiis* 2, cap. 7: PL 83, 787).

[34]   See *Didascalia* 2, 28, 4: Funk DidConst 1, 108. *Constitutiones Apostolorum* 2, 28, 4 and 2, 34, 3: Funk DidConst 1, 109 and 117.

[35]   *Constitutiones Apostolorum* 8, 16, 4: Funk DidConst 1, 523. See also *Epitome Constitutionum Apostolorum* 6: Funk DidConst 2, 80, lines 3–4. *Testamentum Domini*: ". . .give him the spirit of grace, counsel, and magnanimity, the spirit of priesthood. . .to assist and guide your people by his work, with fear and a pure heart." I.E. Rahmani, tr. (Mainz, 1899) 69; also in *Traditio Apostolorum*, B. Botte, ed., *La Tradition Apostolique de S. Hippolyte* (Münster, W., 1963) 20.

[36]   See Nm 11:16–25.

[37]   *Pontificale Romanum*, De Ordinatione Presbyterorum, preface; words also found in the Leonine, Gelasian, and Gregorian Sacramentaries. Similar expressions are found in the liturgies of the East: see *Traditio Apostolorum*: ". . .look upon this your servant and bestow upon him the spirit of priestly grace and counsel that he may assist and guide your people with a pure heart, even as you have had regard for your

263   8.   Ranked in the priestly order by ordination, all priests are linked together in a close bond of brotherhood. They make up the one presbyterate, particularly in the diocese they are assigned to serve under their bishop, because no matter how diverse their responsibilities the priestly ministry they exercise for the people is one. [. . .] Each therefore has a special bond of apostolic charity, ministry, and brotherhood with his fellow members in this presbyterate. From antiquity the liturgy has given expression to this as the presbyters present are invited to lay hands together with the ordaining bishop upon the ordinand and to concelebrate the eucharist in a spirit of concord. Each priest, then, is joined to his confrères by the bond of charity, prayer, and cooperation in all things; this bond manifests the unity that Christ willed to become complete among those belonging to him so that the world might know that the Father has sent his Son.[46] [. . .]

III. DISTRIBUTION OF PRIESTS AND VOCATIONS TO THE PRIESTHOOD

264   11. [. . .] "Since the captain of the ship and passengers have the same concern,"[64] the entire people of God should be taught that they have a duty to share, by constant prayer and other means at their disposal, in the work of providing the Church with the priests needed to carry on its divine mission. [. . .]

CHAPTER III
LIFE OF THE PRIEST

I. CALL TO CHRISTIAN PERFECTION

265   13.   Priests will come to holiness in the way proper to them by carrying out their offices sincerely and untiringly in the Spirit of Christ.

Being the ministers of God's word, they read and listen each day to the word they are to teach to others. As they strive to receive it within themselves, they will become ever more completely disciples of the Lord: "Meditate on these things; devote yourself to them, so that all may see your progress. Take heed to yourself and to your teaching; hold to that, for by so doing you will save both yourself and your hearers" (1 Tm 4:15–16). Intent on ways of bringing to others more effectively the fruits of their own contemplation,[8] they will treasure more deeply the "unsearchable riches of Christ" (Eph 3:8) and the manifold wisdom of God.[9] Mindful that it is the Lord who opens hearts[10] and God's power not their own that raises the spirit,[11] they will closely associate themselves in the act of preaching God's word

---

Chosen People and commanded Moses to choose elders whom you filled with the spirit you had given to your servant" (ancient Veronese Latin version: B. Botte, ed. cit. 20). *Constitutiones Apostolorum* 8, 16, 4: Funk DidConst 1, 522, 16–17. *Epit. Const.Apost.* 6: Funk DidConst 2, 80, 5–7. *Testamentum Domini*, I.E. Rahmani, tr. (Mainz, 1899) 69. *Euchologion Serapionis* 27: Funk DidConst 2, 190, lines 1–7. *Ritus Ordinationis in ritu Maronitarum*: H. Denzinger, tr., in *Ritus Orientalium* 2 (Würzburg, 1863) 161. Among the Fathers the following are examples: Theodore of Mopsuestia, *In 1 Tim* 3:8: Swete, ed., 2, 119–121. Theodoret, *Quaestiones in Numeros* 18: PG 80, 369 C–372 B.

46   See Jn 17:23.

64   PR, De Ordinatione Presbyterorum.

8   See ST 2a2ae, 188.7.

9   See Eph 3:9–10.

10   See Acts 16:14.

11   See 2 Cor 4:7.

with Christ the Teacher and surrender themselves to the Spirit of Christ. Thus united to Christ, they share in God's love, the mystery of which, hidden for ages,[12] has been revealed in Christ.

As ministers of the sacred, above all in the sacrifice of the Mass, priests in a particular way represent the person of Christ, who made himself a victim in order to make humankind holy. They therefore are called upon to imitate the holy realities they deal with, namely, that as celebrants of the mystery of the death of the Lord, they themselves seek to die to sin and evil desires.[13] In the mystery of the eucharistic sacrifice, the fulfillment of the priest's chief office, the work of redemption is continuously actual.[14] Hence daily celebration is urged upon priests; it remains the act of Christ and the Church even when the faithful cannot attend.[15] Priests, therefore, as they unite themselves with the act of Christ the Priest, are offering themselves completely each day; as they are nourished on the body of Christ, they are sharing deeply in the love of him who gives himself to be the food of those who believe. As they administer the sacraments, they also are united with Christ's intention and love. This is true in a particular way when they make themselves completely and at all times available to administer the sacrament of penance whenever the people reasonably request it. In reciting the divine office they give their own voice to the Church, which continues praying in the name of all together with Christ, who "always lives to make intercession for us" (Heb 7:25). [. . .]

14. [. . .] To continue unfailingly to do his Father's will through the Church,   266
Christ acts through his ministers; he therefore stands always as the origin and source of the unity of their lives. Accordingly, priests will achieve that same unity as they join themselves to Christ in obeying the Father's will and in making a gift of themselves for the flock committed to their care.[22] Thereby serving like the Good Shepherd, they will find in the actuality of pastoral charity the bond of priestly perfection creating unity between their lives and ministry. Such pastoral charity[23] has its source above all in the eucharistic sacrifice. This, therefore, stands as the center and basis of the priest's life in such a way that what happens on the altar of sacrifice the priest seeks to reflect within his own spirit. That, however, can only come about if priests by prayer enter ever more deeply into the mystery of Christ. [. . .]

III. HELPS FOR THE PRIEST'S LIFE

18. To preserve their union with Christ in all of life's turnings, priests have, in   267
addition to the attentive exercise of their ministry, the means, both the general and those proper to themselves, both the old and the new, that the Holy Spirit never

---

12   See Eph 3:9.

13   PR, De Ordinatione Presbyterorum.

14   MR, prayer over the gifts, Ninth Sunday after Pentecost [RM, Holy Thursday and 2nd Sunday in Ordinary Time].

15   "Every Mass, even though a priest may offer it in private, is not something private; it is an act of Christ and of the Church. In offering this sacrifice, the Church learns to offer itself as a sacrifice for all and applies the single, boundless, redemptive power of the sacrifice of the cross for the salvation of the entire world. . . . Therefore, from a paternal and solicitous heart, we earnestly recommend to priests, our special crown and happiness in the Lord, that . . . they worthily and devoutly offer Mass each day" (Paul VI, Encycl. *Mysterium fidei* nos. 32, 33 [DOL 176 nos. 1176, 1177]). See SC art. 26 and 27 [DOL 1 nos. 26 and 27].

22   See 1 Jn 3:16.

23   "Let it be the work of love to feed the Lord's sheep" (St. Augustine, *Tract. in Ioann.* 123, 5: PL 35, 1967).

ceases to create among the people of God and that the Church commends, sometimes even enjoins, for the sanctification of its members.[54] Preeminent among such
resources are the acts whereby the faithful receive sustenance from God's word at
the twofold table of Scripture and the eucharist.[55] The urgency for priests to have
recourse to both for their sanctification is obvious.

The ministers of sacramental grace are united closely to Christ the Savior and
Shepherd by their own fruitful reception of the sacraments and especially by the
frequent use of the sacrament of penance. Prepared for by a daily examination of
conscience, this sacrament greatly furthers the needed conversion of heart toward
the love of the Father of mercies. Strengthened by the Scriptures read in the light of
faith, priests have the power to search attentively for the signs of God's will and the
promptings of his grace in the varying occurrences of life and so to become day by
day more docile to the mission they have taken up in the Holy Spirit. The striking
model of such docility they find always in the Blessed Virgin Mary, who, led by the
Holy Spirit, gave herself completely to the mystery of human redemption.[56] Priests
should always revere and with a filial devotion and homage love the Mother of the
High Priest and the Queen of Apostles.

As a means of fulfilling their ministry with fidelity, they should set aside a
place for daily communion with Christ the Lord in visits of personal devotion to the
eucharist. They should welcome retreats and esteem spiritual direction. In many
ways, especially regular mental prayer and their own chosen prayer forms, priests
search and ask God for a spirit of genuine adoration. Through it they and their
people with them unite themselves closely to Christ, the Mediator of the New
Covenant, and so are enabled as adopted children to cry out: "Abba, Father" (Rom
8:15).

▶   See also Chapter Three, Section 4. Holy Orders: A. The Sacrament of Orders; B.
            Ordinations.

19. VATICAN COUNCIL II, Pastoral Constitution on the Church in the Modern World Gaudium et spes, 7 December 1965: AAS 58 (1966) 1025–1115; ConstDecrDecl 681–835.

PREFACE

268   1.   (*The intimate ties of the Church with the whole family of peoples*). The joy and hope, the
struggle and anguish of the people of this age and especially of the poor and those
suffering in any way are the joy and hope, the struggle and anguish of Christ's
disciples and there is nothing genuinely human that does not find a response in
their hearts. For the community of Christians is made up of people; brought together in Christ, they are guided by the Holy Spirit in their pilgrimage toward the
kingdom of the Father and have received the message of salvation to be proclaimed
to all. The Christian community experiences itself, therefore, as linked to all humankind and its history.

---

[54]   See CIC can. 125ff.

[55]   See PC no. 7 [DOL 10 no. 204]; DV no. 21 [DOL 14 no. 224].

[56]   See LG no. 65: AAS 57 (1965) 64–65; ConstDecrDecl 202.

PART I. THE CHURCH AND HUMANITY'S CALLING

CHAPTER I
DIGNITY OF THE HUMAN PERSON

18. (*The mystery of death*). The enigma of the human condition has as its most baffling   269
point the confrontation with death. The human person is tortured not merely by
pain and gradual physical decline, but most of all by fear of total extinction. In
being horrified by and recoiling from total destruction and the final eclipse of self,
the person is judging correctly out of an instinct of the heart. The seed of eternity
existing in each one of us reacts against death because that seed is itself not reduc-
ible to mere matter. [. . .]

At the prospect of death, all imagining fails, but the Church, taught by divine
revelation, affirms that God has created the human being for happiness as an end
beyond the limits of earthly wretchedness. Christian faith teaches further that
bodily death, from which we would have escaped had we not sinned, [14] is meant to
be conquered when we are restored by the almighty and merciful Savior to the
salvation lost by sin. For God has called us and continues to call us to cling with all
our being to an everlasting share in the imperishable divine life. Christ, freeing us
from death by his own death, in rising to life has already won that victory. [15]
Therefore, to every reflective person anxious about the destiny to come, faith,
presented with solid supporting reasons, offers the answer. At the same time faith
makes possible communion in Christ with loved ones already taken away in death
as it gives hope that they have reached true life with God.

CHAPTER III
HUMAN ENDEAVOR IN THE UNIVERSE

38. (*Human endeavor brought to fulfillment in the paschal mystery*). [. . .] Undergoing death   270
for us sinners, [12] [the Word made flesh] by his own example teaches us that we too
must carry the cross that the flesh and the world place on the shoulders of those
who seek peace and justice. Made Lord by his resurrection, Christ, to whom all
power on earth and in heaven has been given, [13] continues to work through the
power of his Holy Spirit in the hearts of people. In them he not only arouses the
longing for the life of the world to come, but at the same time stirs up, purifies, and
strengthens all those generous aspirations by which the human family endeavors to
make its own life more human and to bring all the earth into the serving of this end.
But there are diverse gifts of the Spirit: some he calls to bear bold witness to the
longing for a home in heaven and to keep that desire burning within the human
family; others, to devote themselves to serve their neighbor on earth and by this
ministry to prepare the ground for the kingdom of God. All, however, he makes
free so that, setting aside self-love and raising all earthly resources toward a truly
human life, they may strain forward to the future when all humanity will become
an offering pleasing to God. [14]

---

[14]   See Wis 1:13, 2:22–24; Rom 5:21, 6:23; Jas 1:15.

[15]   See 1 Cor 15:56–57.

[12]   See Jn 3:14–16; Rom 5:8–10.

[13]   See Acts 2:36; Mt 28:18.

[14]   See Rom 15:16.

PART II: PARTICULARLY PRESSING PROBLEMS

CHAPTER I
PROMOTING THE DIGNITY OF MARRIAGE AND THE FAMILY

271   48. (*The holiness of marriage and the family*). [. . .] True marital love is taken up into
divine love, ruled and enriched by Christ's redeeming power and the Church's
salvific work. The goal is to lead spouses to God, to help and strengthen them in the
sublime office of being mother or father.[6] This is also the reason why there is a
distinct sacrament for them that gives them the power and a kind of consecration
for their duties and dignity of state.[7] As they fulfill their office through this sacramental power and Christ's spirit fills their life with faith, hope, and charity, husband and wife draw ever closer to the full development of their own personality
and mutual sanctification, thus to giving glory to God together.

With parental example and family prayer to guide them, children, and indeed
all who come into the family circle, will more readily discover the path to true
humanity, salvation, and holiness. [. . .]

272   49. (*Conjugal love*). [. . .] A respect for the equal personal dignity of man and woman
through a mutual and complete love will give rich evidence of the unity of marriage
as ratified by the Lord. A steadfast living out of this Christian vocation calls for
high virtue. Strengthened by grace for their life, spouses therefore need to develop
and in prayer to plead for magnanimity, a solidity for their love, and the spirit of
sacrifice. [. . .]

273   52. (*Promoting marriage and the family, a common concern*). [. . .] Equipped with the
knowledge required of them on the subject of the family, priests have the duty of
encouraging the vocation of husbands and wives by a variety of pastoral measures,
among them the preaching of God's word, worship in liturgy, and other spiritual
helps for conjugal and familial life. With kindness and patience priests must also
support parents in their times of difficulty and comfort them in charity, so as to
develop truly happy families.

CHAPTER II
PROMOTION OF CULTURAL PROGRESS

SECTION 2. PRINCIPLES

274   58. (*The many relationships of Christ's Gospel with human culture*). Many links exist between the message of salvation and human culture. For God, revealing himself to
his people until the full self-disclosure in his incarnate Son, has spoken in a way
corresponding to the culture proper to each different age. Living in diverse circumstances over the centuries, the Church has also made use of the discoveries of
different human cultures to spread and explain Christ's message to all peoples, to
study it and deepen understanding, to give it a more effective expression in the
liturgy and in the life of the community of believers that is marked by great
diversity. [. . .] Christ's Gospel constantly renews the life and culture of fallen
humanity, counteracts and dispels the errors and evils deriving from the ever
threatening seduction of sin. The Gospel unceasingly purifies and elevates the

---

6   See LG nos. 40, 41, 47: AAS 57 (1965) 15–16, 40–41; ConstDecrDecl 166, 169, 180.

7   See Pius XI, Encycl. *Casti connubii*: AAS 22 (1930) 583.

morality of peoples. With heaven-sent riches it enlarges from within, confirms, completes, and renews in Christ[6] the particular endowments and good qualities of every people and every period. Thus also the Church by the very fact of carrying out its proper office [7] gives impetus to human and civil culture, contributes to it, and by its own activity, the liturgy included, leads humanity toward freedom of spirit.

SECTION 3. CERTAIN MORE PRESSING OBLIGATIONS OF CHRISTIANS IN REGARD TO CULTURE

62. (*The right way to combine human and civil culture with Christian education*). [. . .] The Church respects new art forms suited to the people of today according to the mentality of the many different nations and regions. They are to be admitted into the sanctuary whenever, by being expressed in a way adapted and conformed to the demands of the liturgy, they raise the mind to God.[13] [. . .]

275

---

[6]   See Eph 1:10.

[7]   See Pius XI, words addressed to M. Roland-Gosselin: "We must never lose sight of the fact that the objective of the Church is to evangelize, not to civilize. If the Church does bring civilization, it is through evangelization" (Semaine Sociale de Versailles, 1936, 461–462).

[13]   See SC art. 123 [DOL 1 no. 123]. Paul VI, Address to artists of Rome, 7 May 1964: AAS 56 (1964) 439–442.

Section 2. Launching the Reform

SUMMARY (DOL 20–76). Since the beginning of 1964 the Holy See has exercised a continuing leadership aimed at guiding the implementation of the conciliar reform of the liturgy, supporting and protecting it, and when necessary correcting its course. The present, longest section in Chapter One is evidence of the constant involvement of the popes and their closest co-workers in the reform. There are 57 documents.

—Of chief importance are the four that precisely set out major steps for fulfilling the conciliar decrees: the papal Motu Proprio *Sacram Liturgiam* (DOL 20) and the three curial general instructions for the correct carrying out of the Constitution on the Liturgy (DOL 23, 39, 52).

—The personal engagement of three popes is reflected in thirty documents. Paul VI's unflagging commitment stands out clearly in his own letters, one to the bishops of the United States (DOL 60) and two on the Lefebvre case (DOL 58, 61), as well as in letters written on his behalf to liturgical meetings by the Secretariat of State (DOL 51 and 66). There are also twenty-three of Pope Paul's addresses: four to the cardinals (DOL 22, 30, 59, 65), four to groups of bishops (DOL 21, 44, 63, 68), three to particular groups (DOL 25, 33, 64), and twelve to general audiences (DOL 24, 27, 34, 45, 46, 47, 49, 50, 53, 55, 56, 57); there are also two texts with his remarks at the Angelus (DOL 26, 48). John Paul I touched on the issue of liturgical aberrations in the homily on the occasion of taking possession of his cathedral church, St. John Lateran (DOL 69). From John Paul II there are extracts from seven documents: his televised inaugural address (DOL 70), four other addresses (DOL 71, 72, 73, 75), one homily (DOL 74), and an apostolic exhortation (DOL 76).

—The Consilium gave expression to its proper responsibilities for the reform in five letters to presidents of the conferences of bishops (DOL 28, 31, 32, 40, 41). The Consilium and three other curial agencies issued documents occasioned by the specific problem of arbitrary liturgical innovations (DOL 29, 35, 36, 37).

—In addition there are two editorials and a rescript on cultural adaptation from the Consilium (DOL 38, 42, 43); particular letters from the Congregation for Divine Worship and the Congregation for the Sacraments and Divine Worship (DOL 54, 62); and, because of the renewed emphasis on the word of God in the liturgy, a document of the 1977 Synod of Bishops (DOL 67).

20. PAUL VI, **Motu Proprio** *Sacram Liturgiam,* on putting into effect some prescriptions of the Constitution on the Liturgy, 25 January 1964: AAS 56 (1964) 139–144.

276   That the sacred liturgy be carefully safeguarded, developed, and, where necessary, reformed has been the concern of earlier popes, of ourself, and of the bishops of the Church. The many published documents on liturgical topics, known to all, confirm this. So does the Constitution on the Liturgy, approved with near unanimity by Vatican Council II in solemn session and promulgated 4 December 1963.

    The concern for the liturgy rests on the fact that "in the earthly liturgy we take part in a foretaste of that heavenly liturgy celebrated in the holy city of Jerusalem toward which we journey as pilgrims, where Christ is sitting at the right hand of God, a minister of the holies and of the true tabernacle (see Rv 21:2; Col 3:1; Heb 8:2); we sing a hymn to the Lord's glory with the whole company of heaven; venerating the memory of the saints, we hope for some part and communion with them; we eagerly await the Savior, our Lord Jesus Christ, until he, our life, shall appear and we too will appear with him in glory (see Phil 3:20; Col 3:2)."[1]

    The hearts of the faithful who so worship God, the source and exemplar of all holiness, are therefore drawn, even compelled, to seek this holiness and in this way to become in this earthly pilgrimage "seekers of holy Zion."[2]

277   Accordingly, our foremost concern is clearly that the faithful, and especially priests, dedicate themselves first of all to the study of the Constitution on the Liturgy and from this moment on prepare themselves to carry out its prescriptions wholeheartedly as soon as these take effect. Because by the very nature of the case the understanding and dissemination of liturgical laws must go into effect without delay, we earnestly exhort bishops of dioceses to an immediate, intense effort, aided by their sacred ministers, "the stewards of God's mysteries,"[3] so that their own faithful, in keeping with their age, particular state in life, and level of culture will grasp the innate power and value of the liturgy and at the same time participate[a] devoutly, body and soul, in the rites of the Church.[4]

278   Many of the prescriptions of the Constitution clearly cannot be put into effect in a short period of time, since some of the rites must first be revised and new liturgical books prepared. In order that this work may be carried out in the wisdom and prudence required, we are setting up a special commission with the principal task of seeing that the prescriptions of the Constitution are put into effect.

    Other norms of the Constitution, however, are applicable now; we desire their immediate observance, so that the faithful may no longer be without the anticipated fruits of grace.

    By apostolic authority and *motu proprio,* therefore, we prescribe and decree that the following norms shall go into effect beginning with the First Sunday of Lent, 16 February 1964, the expiration date of the established *vacatio legis.*

---

  [1]   SC art. 8 [DOL 1 no. 8].

  [2]   Hymn of lauds, feast of the Dedication of a Church.

  [3]   1 Cor 4:1.

  [a]   The definitive text in AAS emended the text as published in OR, 29 Jan. 1964, p. 1. The two texts will be noted throughout where the changes occur. Here:
      AAS: *participent.*   OR: *intersint.*

  [4]   See SC art. 19 [DOL 1 no. 19].

I.   The norms in art. 15, 16, and 17 on the teaching of liturgy in seminaries,   279
houses of study of religious, and theological faculties are to be incorporated into
their programs of study in such a way that with the beginning of the next academic
year students may devote themselves to liturgical studies in an orderly and intense
way.

II.   In keeping with the norms of art. 45 and 46, in all dioceses there is to be[b] a   280
commission that is entrusted, under the bishop's direction, with the duty of increasing the knowledge and furthering the progress of the liturgy.

In this matter it may be advantageous for several dioceses to have a joint
commission.

Each diocese should also, as far as possible, have two other commissions,[c] one
for music, the other for art.

In some dioceses it will often be advisable to merge the three commissions
into one.[d]

III.   On the date already established, the norms of art. 52 shall take effect, namely,   281
that there be a homily during Mass[e] on Sundays and holydays of obligation.

IV.   We direct the implementation of the part of art. 71 that permits the sacrament   282
of confirmation to be celebrated, when convenient, within Mass after the reading of
the gospel and the homily.[f]

V.   Regarding art. 78, the sacrament of marriage is normally to be celebrated   283
within Mass, after the gospel has been read and the homily given.[g]

Should marriage be celebrated without a Mass, the following regulations,
pending revision of the entire rite, are to be observed: at the beginning of the rite,
following a brief instruction,[5] the epistle and gospel of the nuptial Mass are to be
read in the vernacular; then the blessing found in the *Rituale Romanum*, tit. VIII, cap.
III is always to be given to the spouses.[h]

------

[b]   AAS: . . . art. 45 et 46, in singulis dioecesi-
bus Consilium habeatur, . . .

    OR: art. 45 et 46, quam primum in singulis dioe-
cesibus Consilium condatur, . . .

[c]   AAS: Praeterea in quavis dioecesi, quantum
fieri potest, duo alia habeantur Consilia: . . .

    OR: Praeterea in quavis dioecesi duo alia consti-
tuantur Consilia: . . .

[d]   AAS: Quae tria Consilia in singula dioecesi
non raro congruet, ut in unum coalescant.

    OR: Quae tria Consilia in singula dioecesi, si
opus erit, in unum concedere poterunt.

[e]   AAS: . . . in Missis habendae . . .

    OR: . . . inter Eucharisticum sacrificium haben-
dae . . .

[f]   AAS: . . . statuimus, ex qua Sacramentum
Confirmationis, pro opportunitate, intra Missam, post lectionem Evangelii et homiliam, con-
ferri potest . . .

    OR: . . . statuimus, qua venia datur Sacramen-
tum Confirmationis inter Eucharisticum sacrificium
pro opportunitate conferendi . . .

[g]   AAS: . . . attinet, Matrimonii Sacramentum
de more intra Missam celebretur, post lectum
Evangelium et habitam homiliam.

    OR: . . . attinet, omnes quorum interest, mone-
mus, Matrimonii Sacramentum de more inter Eucharisticum sacrificium celebrandum esse, post lectum Evangelium et habitam homiliam.

[5]   See SC art. 35, § 3 [DOL 1 no. 35].

[h]   AAS: Quodsi Matrimonium sine Missa
celebretur . . . haec serventur: . . . post brevem
habitam admonitionem legantur lingua vernacu-

    OR: Quodsi Matrimonium extra Eucharisticum
sacrificum celebretur . . . haec servari iubemus: ini-
tio sacrae huius caeremoniae, post brevem habitam

284 VI. Although the order for divine office has not yet been revised and reformed, in keeping with art. 89, those not bound by choral obligation[i] now have our permission, from the expiration date of the *vacatio legis*, to omit the hour of prime and to choose from among the other little hours the one best suited to the time of day.

We make this concession with the full confidence that sacred ministers will not grow slack in devotion, but rather that, if they diligently carry out the duties of their priestly office for the love of God, they will see themselves as going through the day closely united in spirit with him.

285 VII. Also in regard to the divine office, Ordinaries may, in particular cases and for just cause, dispense their subjects from the obligation, in whole or in part, or may replace it with something else.[6, j]

286 VIII. In regard also to recitation of the office, we declare that[k] members of any institute of religious perfection who by reason of their own rule recite either some part of the divine office or a little office, structured like the divine office and duly approved, shall be counted as celebrating public prayer with the Church.[7]

287 IX. To those bound to recite the divine office art. 101 of the Constitution grants the faculty — in various ways and for various classes of people — to use the vernacular instead of Latin. Therefore it seems advisable to make it clear that the various vernacular versions must be drawn up and approved by the competent, territorial ecclesiastical authority, as provided in art. 36, §§ 3 and 4; and that, as provided in art. 36, § 3, the acts of this authority require due approval, that is, confirmation, of the Holy See.[l] This is the course to be taken whenever any Latin liturgical text is translated into the vernacular by the authority already mentioned.

288 X. Whenever the Constitution (art. 22, § 2), entrusts regulation of the liturgy, within certain specified limits, to various types of competent, lawfully constituted, territorial assemblies of bishops, we decree that for the present these must be national bodies.

---

la Epistula et Evangelium e *Missa pro Sponsis* deprompta; ac deinde ea benedictio Sponsis semper impertiatur quae. . .

[i] AAS: . . . tamen iam nunc iis qui chori obligatione non astringuntur. . .

[6] See SC art. 97 [DOL 1 no. 97].

[j] AAS: . . . pertinet, in casibus singularibus et de iusta causa, Ordinarii possunt. . .

[k] AAS: De eadem divini Officii recitatione declaramus, cuiusvis. . .

[7] See SC art. 98 [DOL 1 no. 98].

[l] AAS: . . . opportunum ducimus significare, varias huiusmodi populares interpretationes, a competente auctoritate ecclesiastica territoriali conficiendas et approbandas esse, ad normam art. 36, §§ 3 et 4; acta vero huius auctoritatis, ad normam eiusdem art. 36, § 3, ab Apostolica Sede esse rite probanda seu confirmanda. Quod ut semper. . .

exhortationem . . . legantur Epistula et Evangelium e *Missa pro Sponsis* deprompta; ac deinde ea benedictio, uti vocant, Sponsis impertiatur quae. . .

OR: . . . tamen iam nunc iis qui illius recitandi obligatione non astringuntur. . .

OR: . . . pertinet, est ea venia iam nunc obtineant praecipimus cuius vi in casibus singularibus et de iusta et bene considerata causa, Ordinarii possunt. . .

OR: De eadem divini Officii recitatione constare volumus, cuiusvis. . .

OR: . . . opportunum ducimus significare varias huiusmodi populares interpretationes a competente auctoritate ecclesiastica territoriali propositas, ab Apostolica Sede de esse rite recognoscendas atque probandas. Quod ut semper. . .

In such national assemblies, besides the residential bishops, all those mentioned in CIC can. 292 may participate and vote; coadjutor and auxiliary bishops may also be summoned to meetings.

Passage of lawful decrees in these bodies requires two-thirds of the votes, cast by secret ballot.

XI.   Finally, we want it understood that over and above the liturgical matters   289
changed by this Apostolic Letter or made effective before the date established, regulation of the liturgy depends exclusively on the authority of the Church, i.e., of the Holy See and of the bishop in accordance with the law; therefore no other person, not even a priest,[m] may add, take away, or change anything in matters of liturgy.[8]

We order that all matters decreed by this Letter, issued *motu proprio*, are confirmed and established, anything to the contrary notwithstanding.

21. PAUL VI, **Address** to bishops at a plenary meeting of the assembly of Italian bishops, excerpt on liturgical reform, 14 April 1964: AAS 56 (1964) 378–387 (Italian).

[. . .] The first point clearly is religion in life. This must be our dominant   290
interest, taking precedence over every merely civil issue, however relevant, of our nation's life. "Seek first the kingdom of God."[3] The liturgical reform provides us with an excellent opportunity in this regard: it calls us back to the theological view of human destiny that the action of grace, and thus of the life of the sacraments and prayer, has primacy. The liturgical reform opens up to us a way to reeducate our people in their religion, to purify and revitalize their forms of worship and devotion, to restore dignity, beauty, simplicity, and good taste to our religious ceremonies. Without such inward and outward renewal there can be little hope for any widespread survival of religious living in today's changed conditions. We take it on ourself to make but two pertinent recommendations. The first is that you take the greatest pains over the sanctifying of days of precept, devoting all your energies to the end that the celebration of the Sunday and holyday Mass with the word of God and the participation of the people will be an occasion of the most intense involvement for all. The second is that you promote sacred song, the religious, congregational singing of the people. Remember, if the faithful sing they do not leave the Church; if they do not leave the Church, they keep the faith and live as Christians.

A present-day phenomenon calling for a particular pastoral concern is ever-   291
increasing travel on holydays of obligation. As a consequence there is a need to provide adequate religious services for the faithful in the more frequented centers. It therefore seems necessary to make appropriate plans and arrangements on both the diocesan and national levels. It would be extremely useful to have any suggestion that, after an accurate investigation and evaluation of the general facts, could

---

[m] AAS: . . . penes Episcopum; atque idcirco   OR: . . . penes Episcopum, atque idcirco nemini
nemini omnino alii, ne sacerdoti quidem, li-   omnino alii, etiamsi sacerdoti, licere. . .
cere. . .

[8]   See SC art. 22, §§ 1 and 3 [DOL 1 no. 22].

[3]   Mt 6:33.

point to helpful measures that would more effectively ensure for all the fulfillment of their religious obligations on holydays.

The fact of these periodic movements of people is also a reminder to us of another needy category of the faithful, those who emigrate in order to find work. Far from their former surroundings, their families and friends, they are often exposed to the danger of letting their religious obligations slip away or even of embracing ideas and organizations that would alienate them even further from the faith. For these also the hierarchy must take the steps necessary so that the different groups of these people may have the possibility and the means to join and take an active part in the life and the organizations of their host dioceses.

22. PAUL VI, **Address** to a consistory, on carrying out the reform of the liturgy, 23 June 1964: AAS 56 (1964) 581–589 (Italian).

292   [. . .] The results of the intense work [of the Council] are the first two great conciliar documents, the comprehensive and carefully structured Constitution on the Liturgy and the Decree on the Media of Social Communications. Both have been promulgated and are beginning to work in the Church with great promise for their increasingly effective application on behalf of the spiritual life of the faithful and the spread throughout the world of the Christian message and Christian thought.

With the motu proprio of 25 January 1964,[a] we have indicated our will that certain of the norms of the Constitution go into effect immediately and have put into the hands of a special Consilium the responsibility both for preparing the overall liturgical reform on the basis of the norms of the Constitution and for studying how the decisions of the Council may be applied in letter and spirit through ways that are effective and proper to the Holy See.

We are extremely pleased to learn that in the various countries of the world the bishops are already intently engaged in studying and settling on the particular adaptations required by local conditions for the liturgical reform to correspond more closely to concrete needs and requirements. [. . .]

23. SC RITES (Consilium), **Instruction** (first) *Inter Oecumenici*, on the orderly carrying out of the Constitution on the Liturgy, 26 September 1964: AAS 56 (1964) 877–900.

INTRODUCTION

I. NATURE OF THIS INSTRUCTION

293   1.   Among the Second Vatican Ecumenical Council's primary achievements must be counted the Constitution on the Liturgy, since it regulates the most exalted sphere of the Church's activity. The document will have ever richer effects as pastors and faithful alike deepen their understanding of its genuine spirit and with good will put it into practice.

---

    [a] i.e., *Sacram Liturgiam* [DOL 20].

2.   The Consilium, which Pope Paul VI established by the Motu Proprio *Sacram*   294
Liturgiam,[a] has promptly taken up its two appointed tasks: to carry out the directives
of the Constitution and of *Sacram Liturgiam* and to provide the means for interpreting
these documents and putting them into practice.

3.   That these documents should immediately be properly carried out everywhere   295
and any possible doubts on interpretation removed are matters of the utmost importance. Therefore, by papal mandate, the Consilium has prepared the present
Instruction. It sets out more sharply the functions of conferences of bishops in
liturgical matters, explains more fully those principles stated in general terms in the
aforementioned documents, and authorizes or mandates that those measures that
are practicable before revision of the liturgical books go into effect immediately.

II. PRINCIPLES TO BE KEPT IN MIND

4.   The reason for deciding to put these things into practice now is that the liturgy   296
may ever more fully satisfy the conciliar intent on promoting active participation of
the faithful.[R1]

   The faithful will more readily respond to the overall reform of the liturgy if
this proceeds step by step in stages and if pastors present and explain it to them by
means of the needed catechesis.

5.   Necessary before all else, however, is the shared conviction that the Constitu-   297
tion on the Liturgy has as its objective not simply to change liturgical forms and
texts but rather to bring to life the kind of formation of the faithful and ministry of
pastors that will have their summit and source in the liturgy (see SC art. 10).[b] That
is the purpose of the changes made up to now and of those yet to come.

6.   Pastoral activity guided toward the liturgy has its power in being a living   298
experience of the paschal mystery, in which the Son of God, incarnate and made
obedient even to the death of the cross, has in his resurrection and ascension been
raised up in such a way that he communicates his divine life to the world. Through
this life those who are dead to sin and conformed to Christ "may live no longer for
themselves but for him who for their sake died and was raised" (2 Cor 5:15).

---

   [a]   See DOL 20 no. 278.

   [R1]   1. Query: "In this diocese there are several monasteries of nuns. In some cases the major superiors
have directed that during Mass the screen be opened in order that the nuns may better take part in the
liturgy. Is it lawful to extend this rule to all monasteries, whether of diocesan or pontifical right?" Reply:
The issue belongs to the Congregation of Religious, to which any petition requesting an indult is to be
addressed. Clearly, however the practice of the Congregation of Religious in such cases is to suggest that
to facilitate liturgical participation the nuns be so situated that they are able to see all the rites carried out
at the altar. If there are small windows, they are opened or the curtains are drawn back from the screens. If
they are not in view of the people, the nuns also raise their veils from over their faces: Not 1 (1965) 190,
no. 57.
   2. Query: May sign language be used in the celebration of the liturgy for the deaf? Reply: Yes. For
it is the only way for the deaf actually to take an active part in the liturgy. In fact, at the request of several
bodies of bishops, Pope Paul has recently (14 Dec. 1965) kindly granted that sign language may be used in
the celebration of the liturgy for the deaf whenever pastoral reasons make it advisable. This concession
extends to all the parts that are said in the vernacular [see DOL 274]. The celebration may have the
following arrangement:
   1. The readings to the congregation are done in sign language.
   2. As to participation for the other parts belonging to the congregation: a. the priest at the
same time pronounces and makes the signs for words belonging to him alone; the people make their
responses in signs; b. in the parts that are to be said by the celebrant and people together, e.g., *Gloria, Credo,
Sanctus-Benedictus, Agnus Dei*, etc., the people follow the celebrant's signs with their own: Not 2 (1966) 30–
31, no. 95.

   [b]   See DOL 1 no. 10.

Faith and the sacraments of faith accomplish this, especially baptism (see SC art. 6)[c] and the mystery of the eucharist (see SC art. 47),[d] the center of the other sacraments and sacramentals (see SC art. 61)[e] and of the cycle of celebrations that in the course of the year unfold Christ's paschal mystery (see SC art. 102–107).[f]

299   7.   The liturgy, it is true, does not exhaust the entire activity of the Church (see SC art. 9);[g] nevertheless the greatest care must be taken about rightly linking pastoral activity with the liturgy and carrying out a pastoral liturgy not as if it were set apart and existing in isolation but as it is closely joined to other pastoral works.

Especially necessary is a close, living union between liturgy, catechesis, religious formation, and preaching.

III. RESULTS TO BE HOPED FOR

300   8.   Bishops and their assistants in the priesthood should, therefore, attach ever greater importance to their whole pastoral ministry as it is focused toward the liturgy. Then the faithful themselves will richly partake of the divine life through sharing in the sacred celebrations and, changed into the leaven of Christ and the salt of the earth, will proclaim that divine life and pass it on to others.

CHAPTER I
GENERAL NORMS

I. HOW THE NORMS APPLY

301   9.   The practical norms, in the Constitution and in this Instruction, as well as practices this Instruction allows or mandates even before revision of the liturgical books, even if they are part of the Roman Rite, may be applied in other Latin rites, due regard being given to the provisions of law.

302   10.   Matters that this Instruction commits to the power of the competent, territorial ecclesiastical authority can and should be put into effect only by such authority through lawful decrees.

In every case the time and circumstances in which such decrees begin to take effect are to be stipulated, with a reasonable preceding interval (*vacatio*) provided for instruction and preparation of the faithful regarding their observance.

II. THE LITURGICAL FORMATION OF CLERICS (SC art. 15–16 and 18)

303   11.   Regarding the liturgical formation of the clergy:

a.   In theological faculties there shall be a chair of liturgy so that all students may receive the requisite liturgical instruction; in seminaries and religious houses of studies local Ordinaries and major superiors shall see to it that as soon as possible there is a properly trained specialist in liturgy.

b.   Professors appointed to teach liturgy shall be trained as soon as possible, in keeping with the norms of the Constitution art. 15.[h]

---

c   See DOL 1 no. 6.

d   See DOL 1 no. 47.

e   See DOL 1 no. 61.

f   See DOL 1 nos. 102–107.

g   See DOL 1 no. 9.

h   See DOL 1 no. 15.

   c. For the continuing liturgical education of clerics, especially those already working in the Lord's vineyard, institutes in pastoral liturgy shall be set up wherever possible.

12. The course in liturgy shall be of appropriate duration, to be fixed in the curriculum of studies by competent authority, and shall follow a method patterned on the norm of the Constitution art. 16.

                  304

13. Liturgical celebrations shall be carried out as perfectly as possible. Therefore:

                  305

   a. Rubrics shall be observed exactly and ceremonies carried out with dignity, under the careful supervision of superiors and with the required preparation beforehand.

   b. Clerics shall frequently exercise the liturgical functions proper to their order, i.e., of deacon, subdeacon, acolyte, reader, as well as those of commentator and cantor.

   c. Churches and chapels, all sacred furnishings and vestments shall bear the mark of genuine Christian art, including the contemporary.

III. LITURGICAL FORMATION OF THE CLERIC'S SPIRITUAL LIFE (SC art. 17)

14. In order that clerics may be trained for a full participation in liturgical celebrations and for a spiritual life deriving from them and to be shared later with others, the Constitution on the Liturgy shall be put into full effect in seminaries and religious houses of studies in keeping with the norms of the documents of the Holy See, the superiors and faculty all working together in harmony to achieve this goal. In order to guide clerics properly toward the liturgy: books are to be recommended on liturgy, especially in its theological and spiritual dimensions, and made available in the library in sufficient numbers; there are to be meditations and conferences, drawn above all from the fonts of sacred Scripture and liturgy (see Const. art. 35, 2);[i] and those communal devotions are to be observed that are in keeping with Christian customs and practice and are suited to the various seasons of the liturgical year.

                  306

15. The eucharist, center of the whole spiritual life, is to be celebrated daily and with the use of different forms of celebration best suited to the condition of the participants.

                  307

     On Sundays and on the other greater holydays a sung Mass shall be celebrated, with all who live in the house participating;[R2] there is to be a homily and, as far as possible, all who are not priests shall receive communion. Once the new rite has been published, concelebration is permitted for priests, especially on more solemn feasts, if pastoral needs do not require individual celebration.[R3]

---

   [i] See DOL 1 no. 35.

   [R2] Query: Is the expression "with all who live in the house participating" to be taken to mean also superiors and teachers who are residing in the seminary or house of religious formation at the time of this Mass? Reply: Yes. If the superiors are priests and, in keeping with the same article of this Instruction, there is concelebration, it is fitting that they concelebrate: Not 1 (1965) 136, no. 1.

   [R3] Query: This seminary community must take part in two Masses on Sunday: an early recited Mass with communion; a solemn Mass later without communion. Would it not be preferable to have one, solemn Mass, with the whole seminary taking part and with communion? Reply: The intent and spirit of the Instruction no. 15 requires in seminaries on Sundays and holydays a Mass of greater solemnity than on other days and with all the elements of the Mass, particularly the homily, general intercessions, and communion. If this more complete celebration makes participation in another Mass difficult or impossible, the other, it seems, should be eliminated or made optional, without prejudice to genuine devotion. There is all the more reason for this since the singing of lauds (see Instr. no. 16), a celebration of the word of God (ibid. no. 38) or other spiritual practices, e.g., mental prayer, can be substituted: Not 1 (1965) 305, no. 79.

At least on the great festivals it would be well for seminarians to participate in the eucharist gathered round the bishop in the cathedral church.

308   16. Even if not yet bound by obligation to divine office, clerics should each day recite or sing in common lauds in the morning as morning prayer and vespers in the evening as evening prayer or compline at the end of the day. Superiors should, as far as possible, themselves take part in this common recitation. Sufficient time shall be provided in the daily schedule for clerics in sacred orders to pray the divine office.

At least on major festivals it would be well, when possible, for seminarians to sing evening prayer in the cathedral church.

309   17. Religious devotions, arranged according to the laws or customs of each place or institute, shall be held in due esteem. Nevertheless, care should be taken that, especially if they are held in common, they harmonize with the liturgy, in keeping with the Constitution art. 13,[j] and that they take into account the seasons of the liturgical year.

IV. LITURGICAL FORMATION OF MEMBERS OF RELIGIOUS INSTITUTES

310   18. The foregoing articles on the liturgical formation of clerics' spiritual life are to be applied, with the required modifications, to both men and women members of religious institutes.

V. LITURGICAL FORMATION OF THE FAITHFUL (SC art. 19)

311   19. Pastors shall strive diligently and patiently to carry out the mandate of the Constitution on the liturgical formation of the faithful and on their active participation, both inward and outward, "in keeping with their age and condition, their way of life, and stage of religious development" (SC art. 19).[k] They should be especially concerned about the liturgical formation and active participation of those involved in lay religious associations; such people have the responsibility of sharing more fully in the Church's life and of assisting their pastors in the effective promotion of parish liturgical life (see SC art. 42).[l]

VI. COMPETENT AUTHORITY IN LITURGICAL MATTERS (SC art. 22)

312   20. Regulation of the liturgy belongs to the authority of the Church; no one, therefore, is to act on individual initiative in this matter, thereby, as might well happen, doing harm to the liturgy and to its reform under competent authority.[R4]

---

[j]   See DOL 1 no. 13.

[k]   See DOL 1 no. 19.

[l]   See DOL 1 no. 42.

[R4]   Query: Is it lawful to make changes at will in vernacular liturgical texts approved by competent authority? Reply:

1. According to the Constitution on the Liturgy regulation of the liturgy belongs solely to the Apostolic See and, as the law determines, to the bishops and territorial bodies of the bishops. "Therefore no other person, not even if he is a priest, may on his own add, remove, or change anything in the liturgy" (SC art. 22, §§ 1–3 [DOL 1 no. 22]).

2. The competent territorial authority has the responsibility of deciding on the fact and mode of allowing the vernacular in the liturgy and of approving texts translated into the vernacular (SC art. 36, §§ 3–4 [DOL 1 no. 36]; InterOec nos. 23–31).

3. In addition, recall the words of Pope Paul VI to those taking part in a meeting on vernacular translations of liturgical texts, 10 Nov. 1965: "The last remark to be made is that liturgical texts, approved by competent authority and confirmed by the Holy See, are as such to be respected religiously. No one has the right to change, shorten, amplify, or omit them to suit himself. What has been lawfully established has the force of ecclesiastical law, which all must obey in conscience and all the more so when the laws at issue regulate the most sacred of all actions" [DOL 113 no. 790]: Not 2 (1966) 289, no. 99.

21. The Holy See has the authority to reform and approve the general liturgical books; to regulate the liturgy in matters affecting the universal Church; to approve or confirm the *acta* and decisions of territorial authorities; and to accede to their proposals and requests.   313

22. The bishop has the authority to regulate the liturgy within his own diocese, in keeping with the norms and spirit of the Constitution on the Liturgy, the decrees of the Holy See, and competent territorial authority.[R5]   314

23. The various territorial assemblies of bishops that have responsibility for the liturgy by virtue of the Constitution art. 22[m] should for the time being be taken to mean one of the following: 315

  a. an assembly of all the bishops of a nation, in accordance with the norm of the Motu Proprio *Sacram Liturgiam* X;[n]

  b. an assembly already lawfully constituted and consisting of the bishops — or of the bishops and other local Ordinaries — of several nations;

  c. an assembly yet to be constituted, with the permission of the Holy See, and consisting of the bishops — or of the bishops and local Ordinaries — of several nations, especially if the bishops in the individual nations are so few that it would be more advantageous for a group to be formed of those from various nations sharing the same language and culture.

  If particular local conditions suggest another course, the matter should be referred to the Holy See.

24. The following must be included in the call to any of the above-mentioned assemblies: 316

  a. residential bishops;

  b. abbots and prelates *nullius*;

  c. vicars and prefects apostolic;

  d. permanently appointed apostolic administrators of dioceses;

  e. all other local Ordinaries, except vicars general.

  Coadjutor and auxiliary bishops may be called by the president, with the consent of the majority of the voting members of the assembly.

25. Unless there is some other lawful provision for certain places and in view of special circumstances, the assembly must be convened: 317

  a. by the one who is the president, in the case of assemblies already lawfully constituted;

  b. in other cases, by the archbishop or bishop having right of precedence under the norm of law.

[R5] Query: When the rubrics provide several options, may the competent territorial authority for the whole region or the bishop for his diocese direct all to observe a single way of doing things, for the sake of uniformity? Reply: Strictly speaking this is lawful. But always to be kept in mind is the preservation of that freedom, envisioned by the new rubrics, to adapt the celebration *in an intelligent way* to the particular church and assembly of the faithful in such a way that the whole rite is a living reality for living people: Not 1 (1965) 254, no. 76.

[m] See DOL 1 no. 22.

[n] See DOL 20 no. 288.

318   26. The president, with the consent of the fathers, establishes the rules of order for dealing with issues and opens, transfers, extends, and adjourns the sessions of the assembly.

319   27. A deliberative vote belongs to all those named in no. 24, including coadjutor and auxiliary bishops, unless the convening instrument expressly provides other- wise.

320   28. Lawful enactment of decrees requires a two-thirds vote by secret ballot.

321   29. The *acta* of the competent territorial authority, to be transmitted to the Holy See for approval, that is, confirmation, should include the following:

   a. the names of participants in the assembly;

   b. a report on matters dealt with;

   c. the outcome of the vote on each decree.

   These *acta*, signed by the president and secretary of the assembly and stamped with a seal, shall be sent in duplicate to the Consilium.

322   30. With regard to *acta* containing decrees on use of the vernacular and the manner of its introduction into the liturgy, the *acta*, following the Constitution on the Liturgy art. 36, § 3° and the Motu Proprio *Sacram Liturgiam* no. IX,ᵖ should also contain:

   a. a list of the individual parts of the liturgy for which use of the vernacular has been decided;

   b. two copies of the liturgical texts prepared in the vernacular, one of which will be returned to the assembly of bishops;

   c. a brief report on the criteria used for the work of translation.

323   31. The decrees of the territorial authority needing the approval, that is, confirmation, of the Holy See shall be promulgated and implemented only when they have received such approval, that is, confirmation.

VII. PARTS TAKEN BY INDIVIDUALS IN THE LITURGY (SC art. 28)

324   32. Parts belonging to the choir or to the people and sung or recited by them are not said privately by the celebrant.

325   33. Nor are readings that are read or sung by the appropriate minister said private- ly by the celebrant.

VIII. DISCRIMINATION TO BE AVOIDED (SC art. 32)

326   34. Individual bishops, or, if it seems advisable, regional or national conferences of bishops shall see to it that the Council's prohibition against preferential treatment of individuals or a social class either in the ceremonies or by outward display is respected in their territories.

327   35. In addition, pastors shall not neglect to ensure prudently and charitably that in the liturgical services and more especially in the celebration of Mass and the admin- istration of the sacraments and sacramentals the equality of the faithful is clearly apparent and that any suggestion of moneymaking is avoided.

   ° See DOL 1 no. 36.

   ᵖ See DOL 20 no. 287.

IX. SIMPLIFICATION OF CERTAIN RITES (SC art. 34)

36. In order that liturgical services may manifest a noble simplicity more attuned   328
to the spirit of the times:

    a. the celebrant and ministers shall bow to the choir only at the beginning
and end of a service;

    b. incensation of the clergy, apart from those who are bishops, shall take place
toward each side of the choir, with three swings of the censer;[R6]

    c. incensation shall be limited to the one altar where the liturgical rite is being
celebrated;

    d. kissing of the hand and of objects presented or received shall be omitted.[R7]

X. CELEBRATIONS OF THE WORD OF GOD (SC art. 35, § 4)

37. In places without a priest and where none is available for celebration of Mass   329
on Sundays and holydays of obligation, a sacred celebration of the word of God
with a deacon or even a properly appointed layperson presiding, shall be arranged,
at the discretion of the local Ordinary.

    The plan of such a celebration shall be almost the same as that of the liturgy of
the word at Mass. Normally the epistle and gospel from the Mass of the day shall
be read in the vernacular, with chants, especially from the psalms, before and
between the readings. If the one presiding is a deacon, he shall give a homily; a
nondeacon shall read a homily chosen by the bishop or the pastor. The whole
celebration is to end with the universal prayer or prayer of the faithful and the
Lord's Prayer.[R8]

38. Celebrations of the word of God, to be promoted on the vigils of more solemn   330
feast days, should also follow the structure of the liturgy of the word at Mass,
although it is quite permissible to have but one reading.

    Where there are several readings, their arrangement, for a clear perception of
the progression of salvation history, should place the Old Testament reading before
the one from the New Testament and should show the reading of the gospel to be
the culmination of all.

39. The diocesan liturgical commissions shall be responsible for suggesting and   331
making available such resources as will ensure dignity and devotion in these celebrations of the word.

    [R6] Query: Is it lawful to sprinkle with holy water all those present in the sanctuary as is done with
incensation? Reply: Yes: Not 1 (1965) 136, no. 2.

    [R7] 1. Query: Does the rule on omitting kissing of the hand and of objects that are presented or
received apply when a bishop celebrates in both a solemn and nonsolemn form? Reply: Yes: Not 1 (1965)
185, no. 38.
    2. Query: Is the kissing of the ring of a bishop distributing communion to the faithful to be
omitted? Reply: Yes: ibid., no. 39.
    3. Query: Should the celebrant and the ministers as they receive such objects and the vestments
kiss them? Reply: No: ibid., no. 40.

    [R8] Query: In explaining the meaning of a celebration of the word of God on Sundays and holydays in
places lacking a priest the Instruction seems to exclude a prayer associating the congregation in spirit with
the sacrifice being offered in the parish church and a second prayer inviting the faithful to spiritual
communion. Is this really the intent of the Instruction? Reply: Not at all. In fact it is helpful in this
situation to conclude the prayer of the faithful with the opening prayer of the Mass: Not 1 (1965) 305, no.
80.

XI. VERNACULAR TRANSLATIONS OF LITURGICAL TEXTS (SC art. 36, § 3)

332   40. Vernacular translations of liturgical texts to be prepared in conformity with the norms of art. 36, § 3,[q] will benefit from observing the following criteria.

    a. The basis of the translations is the Latin liturgical text. The version of the biblical passages should conform to the same Latin liturgical text. This does not, however, take away the right to revise that version, should it seem advisable, on the basis of the original text or of some clearer version.

    b. The liturgical commission mentioned in the Constitution art. 44[r] and in the present Instruction art. 44 is to have special responsibility for the preparation of translations of liturgical texts, with the institute of pastoral liturgy providing as much assistance as possible. But where there is no such commission, two or three bishops are to share responsibility for the translating; they are to choose experts, including the laity, in Scripture, liturgy, the biblical languages, Latin, the vernacular, and music. Sound translation of a liturgical text into the language of a people has to answer many requirements simultaneously.

    c. Where applicable, there should be consultation on translations with bishops of neighboring regions using the same language.

    d. In nations of several languages there should be a translation for each language, to be submitted to the bishops involved for careful examination.

    e. Special attention should be given to the high quality of books used for reading the liturgical text to the people in the vernacular, so that even the book's appearance may prompt greater reverence for the word of God and for sacred objects.

333   41. Liturgical services held anywhere for people of a foreign language, especially for immigrants, members of a personal parish, or other like groups, may, with the consent of the local Ordinary, lawfully be celebrated in the native tongue of these faithful. Such celebrations are to conform to the limits for use of the vernacular and to the translation approved by the competent, territorial ecclesiastical authority for the language in question.

334   42. Melodies for parts to be sung in the vernacular by celebrant and ministers must have the approval of the competent, territorial ecclesiastical authority.[R9]

335   43. Particular liturgical books lawfully approved before the promulgation of the Constitution on the Liturgy and indults granted up to then, unless they conflict

---

    q   See DOL 1 no. 36.

    r   See DOL 1 no. 44.

    R9   Query: Must melodies for singing the Ordinary of the Mass in the vernacular be approved by the assembly of bishops? Reply: In Not 2 (1966) 243 there is the statement: "Melodies for chants of the Ordinary of the Mass do not require approval by the assembly of bishops" [DOL 23 no. 349, note R20]. In some instances, however, a conference of bishops or a national liturgical commission has reserved to itself the power to approve new melodies even for the parts of the Ordinary of the Mass. Thus the question arises of who has competence in this matter. The Instruction InterOec no. 42 clearly states that this approval on the part of the conference of bishops is required only for *new* melodies *to be sung by the celebrant and the ministers.* Nothing is required, therefore, regarding melodies for the Ordinary, i.e., the *Kyrie, Gloria, Credo, Sanctus-Benedictus, and Agnus Dei.* On this point nothing of the existing legislation is changed regarding melodies for these same texts in Latin, that is, it is enough to have the *imprimatur* of the Ordinary of the place where the musical text is published.

    It would be difficult for the conference of bishops to review every musical composition and more difficult still, because of the consequences, to make a judgment about each.

    For the present, however, when compositions with the vernacular texts are coming out for the first time, conferences of bishops or liturgical commissions can exercise a closer vigilance so that nothing unworthy or unsuited to divine worship intrudes: Not 2 (1966) 339, no. 103.

with the Constitution, remain in force until other dispositions are made as the reform of the liturgy is completed, in whole or in part.

XII. LITURGICAL COMMISSION OF THE ASSEMBLY OF BISHOPS (SC art. 44)

44. The liturgical commission, which should be expeditiously established by the territorial authority, shall as far as possible be chosen from among the bishops themselves or at least include one of them, along with priests expert in liturgical and pastoral matters and designated by name for this office.

336

The members and consultants of the commission should ideally meet several times a year to deal with issues as a group.

45. The territorial authority may properly entrust the following to the commission:

337

    a. to carry out studies and experiments in keeping with the norms of the Constitution art. 40, §§ 1 and 2;[5]

    b. to further practical initiatives for the whole region that will foster liturgical life and the application of the Constitution on the Liturgy;

    c. to prepare studies and the resources required as a result of decrees of the plenary assembly of bishops;

    d. to control pastoral liturgy in the whole nation, to see to the application of decrees of the plenary assembly, and to report on these matters to the assembly;

    e. to further frequent consultation and promote collaboration with regional associations involved with Scripture, catechetics, pastoral care, music, and art, as well as with every kind of lay religious association.

46. Members of the institute of pastoral liturgy, as well as experts called to assist the liturgical commission, shall be generous in aiding individual bishops to promote pastoral-liturgical activity more effectively in their territory.

338

XIII. DIOCESAN LITURGICAL COMMISSION (SC art. 45)

47. The diocesan liturgical commission, under the direction of the bishop, has these responsibilities:

339

    a. to be fully informed on the state of pastoral-liturgical activity in the diocese;

    b. to carry out faithfully those proposals in liturgical matters made by the competent authority and to keep informed on the studies and programs taking place elsewhere in this field;

    c. to suggest and promote practical programs of every kind that may contribute to the advancement of liturgical life, especially in the interest of aiding priests laboring in the Lord's vineyard;

    d. to suggest, in individual cases or even for the whole diocese, timely, step-by-step measures for the work of pastoral liturgy, to appoint and to call upon people capable of helping priests in this matter as occasion arises, to propose suitable means and resources;

    e. to see to it that programs in the diocese designed to promote liturgy go forward with the cooperation and mutual help of other groups along the lines mentioned above (no. 45 e) regarding the liturgical commission of the assembly of bishops.

---

    5 See DOL 1 no. 40.

CHAPTER II
MYSTERY OF THE EUCHARIST

I. ORDO MISSAE (SC art. 50)

340   48. Until reform of the entire *Ordo Missae*, the points that follow are to be observed:

a. The celebrant is not to say privately those parts of the Proper sung or recited by the choir or the congregation.

b. The celebrant may sing or recite the parts of the Ordinary together with the congregation or choir.R10

c. In the prayers at the foot of the altar at the beginning of Mass Psalm 42 is omitted. All the prayers at the foot of the altar are omitted whenever there is another liturgical rite immediately preceding.R11

d. In solemn Mass the subdeacon does not hold the paten but leaves it on the altar.

e. In sung Masses the secret prayer or prayer over the gifts is sung and in other Masses recited aloud.

f. The doxology at the end of the canon, from *Per ipsum* through *Per omnia saecula saeculorum. R. Amen,* is to be sung or recited aloud. Throughout the whole doxology the celebrant slightly elevates the chalice with the host, omitting the signs of the cross, and genuflects at the end after the *Amen* response by the people.

g. In recited Masses the congregation may recite the Lord's Prayer in the vernacular along with the celebrant; in sung Masses the people may sing it in Latin along with the celebrant and, should the territorial ecclesiastical authority have so decreed, also in the vernacular, using melodies approved by the same authority.

h. The embolism after the Lord's Prayer shall be sung or recited aloud.

i. The formulary for distributing holy communion is to be, *Corpus Christi.* As he says these words, the celebrant holds the host slightly above the ciborium and shows it to the communicant, who responds: *Amen,* then receives communion from the celebrant, the sign of the cross with the host being omitted.R12

j. The last gospel is omitted; the Leonine Prayers are suppressed.

k. It is lawful to celebrate a sung Mass with only a deacon assisting.

l. It is lawful, when necessary, for bishops to celebrate a sung Mass following the form used by priests.

II. READINGS AND CHANTS BETWEEN READINGS (SC art. 51)

341   49. In Masses celebrated with a congregation, the lessons, epistle, and gospel are to be read or sung facing the people:

R10   Query: At a recited Mass may one or other part of the Ordinary (*Kyrie, Gloria,* etc.) or of the Proper (e.g., the gradual, the communion antiphon) be sung? Reply: Yes: Not 1 (1965) 136, no. 3.

R11   See SCR, Reply, on prayers at the foot of the altar, 5 Feb. 1966 [DOL 200].

R12   1. Query: Is distributing communion before Mass a practice to be approved? Reply: Communion is the high point of participation in the Mass and should stand out as such. Therefore it is right that communion take place within Mass as can be gathered from the *Ordo Missae* no. 53 and the *Ritus servandus* no. 81. Should occasion arise when there is need to distribute communion before Mass, this should more properly be done in alb and stole rather than in the vestments required for the priest at Mass: Not 1 (1965) 308, no. 88.

2. Query: Is it lawful to distribute communion across the table? Reply: The meaning of the query is whether it is fitting to make the altar serve as a table, in such a way that the priest standing at it may give communion to the faithful approaching on the other side in order better to express participation in the same sacrifice. According to the Roman Ritual (tit. V, no. II, no. IV) communion is to be distributed to the faithful outside the sanctuary. Nor does it seem right to abandon the traditional practice whereby the faithful both present the gifts and receive communion at the entrance to the sanctuary: Not 2 (1966) 339–340, no. 104.

a. at the lectern or at the edge of the sanctuary in solemn Masses;

b. at the altar, lectern, or the edge of the sanctuary — whichever is more convenient — in sung or recited Masses if sung or read by the celebrant; at the lectern or at the edge of the sanctuary if sung or read by someone else.[R13]

50. In nonsolemn Masses celebrated with the faithful participating a qualified reader or the server reads the lessons and epistles with the intervening chants; the celebrant sits and listens.[R14] A deacon or a second priest may read the gospel and he says the *Munda cor meum*, asks for the blessing, and, at the end, presents the Book of the Gospels for the celebrant to kiss.[R15]

342

51. In sung Masses, the lessons, epistle, and gospel, if in the vernacular, may simply be read.

343

52. For the reading or singing of the lessons, epistle, intervening chants, and gospel, the following is the procedure.

344

a. In solemn Masses the celebrant sits and listens to the lessons, the epistle, and chants. After singing or reading the epistle, the subdeacon goes to the celebrant for the blessing. At this point the celebrant, remaining seated, puts incense into the thurible and blesses it. During the singing of the *Alleluia* and verse or toward the end of other chants after the epistle, the celebrant rises to bless the deacon. From his place he listens to the gospel, kisses the Book of the Gospels, and, after the homily, intones the *Credo*, when prescribed. At the end of the *Credo* he returns to the altar with the ministers, unless he is to lead the prayer of the faithful.

[R13] Query: If the first part of the Mass is carried out at the altar, may the celebrant remain at the middle of the altar, just as the arrangement is for the end of Mass? Reply: The right course is that churches be gradually furnished with a presidential chair, "making it plain that the celebrant presides over the whole community" (InterOec no. 92 [DOL 23, no. 384]), and with a place for a fitting proclamation of the word of God. The point is that "the intrinsic nature and purpose of the several parts of the Mass, as also the connection between them, may be more clearly manifested" (SC art. 50 [DOL 1 no. 50]). To these requirements for the current and future reform even the buildings for worship must be made to conform. Nevertheless where some particular reason *meantime* argues for the priest's remaining at the altar, he must conduct himself in the manner set forth in the *Ritus servandus* nos. 25 and 34. The rubrics now in force do not allow the entire first part of the Mass to be carried out at the middle of the altar. If, however, the readings are done from the altar (no. 47), they may be read facing the people from one and the same side of the altar. Thereby at least some sort of distinction between the two parts of the Mass is maintained: Not 2 (1966) 29, no. 91.

[R14] Query: Is it permissible for only the one reader to read all the parts of the Proper? Reply: The arrangement of the rite of the liturgy of the word as planned by the *Ritus servandus* and the *Ordo Missae* has as its purpose that "in liturgical celebrations each person, minister or lay person, who has an office to perform, should do all of, but only, those parts which pertain to that office by the nature of the rite and the principles of liturgy" (SC art. 28 [DOL 1 no. 28]). Care must therefore be taken lest now the reader do almost all that the celebrant used to do and become the principal center of attention. This is the case where the reader does all the parts of the Proper, the readings, and intervening chants and even sometimes serves as commentator and cantor. Measures are gradually to be taken for an arrangement of celebrations attuned to the spirit of the Constitution: each part of a celebration should have its own qualified minister — reader, psalmist or cantor, commentator. The parts of the Proper, indeed, are processional chants serving as the whole community's accompaniment of one of the rites and these of their nature belong to either the congregation or the *schola*. The right way, therefore, is to have at least a part of the community, a sort of choir of several persons, read or sing such chants. Where this course is not yet possible, there is at least to be provision that the one who reads these chants be a person distinct from the reader or server who does the readings and from the commentator: Not 2 (1966) 29–30, no. 92.

[R15] Query: May the deacon or a second priest who reads the gospel wear only surplice and stole or, if a religious, choral vesture? Reply: The prescription of the *Ritus servandus* no. 44 in no way envisions there being a second priest or a deacon who comes out to read or sing the gospel, then leaves. The intent of the *Ritus* is that a deacon, or in his absence a second priest, assist the celebrant throughout the entire rite. The deacon or second priest, therefore, is obliged to wear the liturgical vestments proper to his order, namely, the deacon an alb and diaconal stole; the priest, an alb and stole worn in the manner of a priest: Not 2 (1966) 30, no. 93.

b. The celebrant follows the same procedures in sung or recited Masses in which the lessons, epistle, intervening chants, and the gospel are sung or recited by the minister mentioned in no. 50.

c. In sung or recited Masses in which the celebrant sings or recites the gospel, during the singing or saying of the *Alleluia* and verse or toward the end of other chants after the epistle, he goes to the foot of the altar and there, bowing profoundly, says the *Munda cor meum*. He then goes to the lectern or to the edge of the sanctuary to sing or recite the gospel.

d. But in a sung or recited Mass if the celebrant sings or reads all the lessons at the lectern or at the edge of the sanctuary, he also, if necessary, recites the chants after the lessons and the epistle standing in the same place; then he says the *Munda cor meum*, facing the altar.

III. HOMILY (SC art. 52)[R16]

345   53. There shall be a homily on Sundays and holydays of obligation at all Masses celebrated with a congregation, including conventual, sung, or pontifical Masses.

On days other than Sundays and holydays a homily is recommended, especially on some of the weekdays of Advent and Lent or on other occasions when the faithful come to church in large numbers.[R17]

346   54. A homily on the sacred text means an explanation, pertinent to the mystery celebrated and the special needs of the listeners, of some point in either the readings from sacred Scripture or in another text from the Ordinary or Proper of the day's Mass.

347   55. Because the homily is part of the liturgy for the day, any syllabus proposed for preaching within the Mass during certain periods must keep intact the intimate connection with at least the principal seasons and feasts of the liturgical year (see SC art. 102–104),[a] that is, with the mystery of redemption.

IV. UNIVERSAL PRAYER OR PRAYER OF THE FAITHFUL (SC art. 53)

348   56. In places where the universal prayer or prayer of the faithful is already the custom, it shall take place before the offertory, after the *Oremus*, and, for the time being, with formularies in use in individual regions. The celebrant is to lead the prayer at either his chair, the altar, the lectern, or the edge of the sanctuary.

A deacon, cantor, or other suitable minister may sing the intentions or intercessions. The celebrant takes the introductions and concluding prayer, this being ordinarily the *Deus, refugium nostrum et virtus* (MR, Orationes diversae no. 20)[b] or another prayer more suited to particular needs.

[R16] Query: Does it go counter to the spirit of the Constitution art. 52 [DOL 1 no. 52] to provide in place of the homily a catechetical instruction of the faithful? Reply: The Instruction clarifies the Constitution art. 52 in the sense that if the competent authorities arrange a syllabus for the preaching during Mass, this preaching must be so planned as to safeguard a close connection with at least the chief seasons and feasts of the liturgical year, that is, with the mystery of redemption: Not 1 (1965) 137, no. 4.

[R17] Query: When Mass is celebrated for any deceased person, may there be a sermon after the gospel? Reply: Yes, provided any semblance of a eulogy is avoided, and the homily derives "from the sacred text" (SC art. 52 [DOL 1 no. 52]), presents the "paschal character of Christian death" (SC art. 81 [DOL 1 no. 81]), and directs the faith and hope of those present to the paschal mystery of Christ: Not 2 (1966) 30, no. 94.

[a]   See DOL 1 nos. 102–104.

[b]   RM, "General Intercessions: General Formula 1, Concluding Prayer."

In places where the universal prayer or prayer of the faithful is not the custom, the competent territorial authority may decree its use in the manner indicated above and with formularies approved by that authority for the time being.[R18]

V. PART ALLOWED THE VERNACULAR IN MASS (SC art. 54)

57. For Masses, whether sung or recited, celebrated with a congregation,[R19] the competent, territorial ecclesiastical authority on approval, that is, confirmation, of its decisions by the Holy See, may introduce the vernacular into: [R20]

349

[R18]   1. Query: In Masses celebrated with a congregation are the general intercessions obligatory on weekdays? Reply: There is no such obligation on weekdays: Not 1 (1965) 250, no. 58.

2. Query: Is it lawful for the local Ordinary to compose for his diocese the texts for the general intercessions or does this faculty belong exclusively to the national assembly of bishops? Reply: In the preparation of the texts it is most appropriate that the individual bishops be left with the right to add one or another intercession that fits in with the needs of each diocese or place: ibid., no. 59.

3. Query: Is it lawful for rectors of churches to add to a given text for the general intercessions one or another intention corresponding to local conditions? Reply: It is lawful and indeed very appropriate on the same grounds as those indicated in no. 59 in the case of the diocese: ibid., no. 60.

4. Query: May texts for the general intercessions be composed for a special group, e.g., for pastors, pilgrims, etc., that are relevant to the group? If so, who is the authority competent to approve them? Reply: The norms given by the Consilium (De Oratione communi seu fidelium, Vatican City, 1965, p. 6 no. 10 [DOL 239 no. 1900]) envision there being texts for votive celebrations, in which, while not totally by-passing the more general intercessions, "more scope is allowed for the appropriate votive intention." In the case of a particular group the texts must be approved by the local Ordinary involved. And until the reform becomes definitive, they do not require the confirmation of the Consilium (see Instruction no. 56): Not 1 (1965) 306, no. 81.

[R19]   Query: The Instruction says "[Text quoted, no. 57] " with a congregation. A decree for one of the countries says "with a concourse of the faithful." With a congregation seems to allude to active assistance of those taking part, whereas a concourse of the faithful is possible without active participation. Is the second case a sufficient reason to use the vernacular? Reply: Most assuredly and in fact a fortiori because passive assistance also stems from the fact that the faithful understand nothing, not even the words spoken to God at the altar. Furthermore the two expressions are completely equivalent: Not 1 (1965) 185–186, no. 41.

[R20]   1. Query: Is it lawful to sing the Mass in the vernacular? The question has been raised because some allege that the lawfulness can not be inferred from the Constitution on the Liturgy. Reply: The principles of a solution are contained in the Constitution itself.

The explicit and authentic interpretation of these principles is the Instruction on the orderly carrying out of the Constitution, 26 Sept. 1964 issued by the SCR.

Let us review the documents, keeping in view the mutual connection of the complete articles of each document with each other.

I. The general principle on allowing the vernacular in the liturgy is in the Constitution, art. 36, which states: "[Text quoted, see DOL 1 no. 36]." We conclude from this article:

a. Latin must be retained in Latin rites, i.e., Latin remains the language proper to the Latin rite, even though the conciliar decisions admit the vernacular into the liturgy.

b. The vernacular is allowed as a liturgical language into celebrations, under certain conditions.

c. These conditions are:

1. The conference of bishops for each country decree its use (i.e., the right to use it) and the mode thereof (i.e., the limits within which that use is lawful).

2. The norms respected that are indicated for the different parts of the liturgy in the individual chapters of the Constitution.

d. The examples adduced are only illustrative, since art. 36 says ". . . in the first place . . . to some prayers . . ." and refers the reader explicitly to the specifics given in subsequent chapters.

e. There is no distinction between sung and nonsung celebrations.

II. As for the Mass, the principles set out in art. 36 are made more explicit and applied in art. 54, which thus fulfills the statement in art. 36 that norms would be established in detail. This is the text of art. 54: "[Text quoted, DOL 1 no. 54]." We conclude from this article:

a. The vernacular is allowed in Masses with a congregation, without distinction between a sung Mass and a recited Mass.

b. There are degrees in this acceptance of the vernacular: especially, that is, because of their very nature, in the case of the readings and the general intercessions; as local conditions may warrant, that is, a broader or narrower extension accordingly as the capacity of the people for an aware and active participation requires, even in the parts that belong to the congregation.

c. The norms of art. 36 must be respected, particularly those of paragraphs three and four;

a. the proclaiming of the lessons, epistle, and gospel; the universal prayer or prayer of the faithful;

b. as befits the circumstances of the place, the chants of the Ordinary of the Mass, namely, the *Kyrie, Gloria, Credo, Sanctus-Benedictus, Agnus Dei,* as well as the introit, offertory, and communion antiphons and the chants between the readings;

c. acclamations, greeting, and dialogue formularies, the *Ecce Agnus Dei, Domine, non sum dignus, Corpus Christi* at the communion of the faithful, and the Lord's Prayer with its introduction and embolism.[R21]

---

paragraph one states the general principle on keeping Latin in the Latin rites and paragraph two is now made specific by the words of art. 54.

    III. To apply art. 54 concretely, therefore, all that is left is to decide which are the parts "that belong to the congregation."

    This phrase, which in art. 54 replaces and determines the more general terms of art. 36 "in some prayers and chants," derives from the SCR's Instruction of 3 Sept. 1958. The Instruction, sets forth degrees of the congregation's participation in both high (no. 25) and low Mass (no. 31); it also suggests the parts in which the faithful can properly take part.

    The Instruction *Inter Oecumenici* of 26 Sept. 1964, no. 57 obviously assumes these points and gives graduated organization to the material, in keeping with the principles of the Constitution.

    This is the text "[Text of InterOec no. 57 quoted]."

    This text eliminates all doubt. Not only by its silence on the point, like the Constitution, but by explicit rejection, it removes any distinction between a sung Mass and a recited Mass. "For Masses, whether sung or recited, celebrated with a congregation. . . ."

    IV. Therefore there is absolutely no way of agreeing to the interpretation by some that the words in art. 36 "in some prayers and chants" are to be understood only of the vernacular prayers and chants that the people at Mass may add over and above the liturgical texts.

    Such a practice was already allowed as a matter of course in a low Mass and in a high Mass on the basis of custom or indult (see Instr. 3 Sept. 1958, nos. 14 and 13c).

    Further, the nature of active participation requires that the faithful not say different prayers or different chants, as though carrying out a service other than that of the celebrant, but that they take their proper part in sharing in the same prayers and chants, so that there may be a clear expression of the unity of the liturgical rite.

    V. Therefore in practice it is lawful to sing the Mass in the vernacular provided:

    a. The national body of bishops has permitted this and has both approved the translations and received the confirmation of the Apostolic See.

    b. The chants to be used in the vernacular remain within the limits laid down by the body of bishops.

    c. Melodies to be sung by the priest and his ministers have been approved by the body of bishops. N.B. Melodies for chants of the Ordinary of the Mass do not require approval by the assembly of bishops [see DOL 23 no. 334, note R9].

    VI. What then of the treasury of sacred music developed in past centuries for the Latin texts?

    a. Even though the vernacular is admitted, Latin is not excluded. Therefore in celebrations partially or wholly in Latin, the traditional treasury of music is to be used, with forms being chosen that match the capacities of the individual assembly of the faithful and the individual *schola cantorum.*

    b. To this treasury handed down from the past is now being added, however, a new element of the same treasury for texts written in the vernacular. Of course time is needed in order to succeed in having works of excellence. Those who apply their talent and art to writing new melodies therefore are to be commended.

    c. Taking into account the idiom and distinctive features of each language, experts may point out clearly whether in the different celebrations some parts can be sung in Latin, others in the vernacular: Not 2 (1966) 240–243, no. 98.

    2. Query: What are the cases envisioned by the law when Latin may be used at a Mass attended by a congregation? Reply: Such cases are those planned for and stipulated by local Ordinaries for their own dioceses and in particular circumstances. For example, the Cardinal Vicar of Rome has ruled that for the spiritual benefit of pilgrims some Masses are to be in Latin in certain churches: Not 6 (1970) 104, no. 31.

    [R21] In the end of its "Summary of Decrees Which Confirm the Decisions of Conferences of Bishops" in Not 1 (1965) 7–9, the Consilium published the following *Decretum typicum:* Use of the vernacular is allowed:

    1. At Masses, whether sung or recited, that are celebrated with a congregation attending:

        a. in proclaiming the lessons, epistle, and gospel;

        b. in the general intercessions;

        c. in the chants of the Ordinary of the Mass, namely: the *Kyrie, Gloria, Credo, Sanctus-Benedictus,*

Missals to be used in the liturgy, however, shall contain besides the vernacular version the Latin text as well.

58. The Holy See alone can grant permission for use of the vernacular in those parts of the Mass that the celebrant sings or recites alone.   350

59. Pastors shall carefully see to it that the Christian faithful, especially members of lay religious institutes, also know how to recite or sing together in Latin, mainly with simple melodies, the parts of the Ordinary of the Mass proper to them.   351

VI. FACULTY OF REPEATING COMMUNION ON THE SAME DAY (SC art. 55)

60. The faithful who receive communion at the Mass of the Easter Vigil or the Midnight Mass of Christmas may receive again at the second Mass of Easter and at one of the Day Masses of Christmas.[R22]   352

CHAPTER III
THE OTHER SACRAMENTS AND THE SACRAMENTALS

I. PART ALLOWED THE VERNACULAR (SC ART. 63)

61. The competent territorial authority, on approval, that is, confirmation, of its decisions by the Holy See, may introduce the vernacular for: 353

    a. the rites, including the essential sacramental forms, of baptism, confirmation, penance, anointing of the sick, marriage, and the distribution of holy communion;

    b. the conferral of orders: the address preliminary to ordination or consecration, the examination of the bishop-elect at an episcopal consecration, and the admonitions;[R23]

    c. sacramentals;

    d. rite of funerals.

Whenever a more extensive use of the vernacular seems desirable, the prescription of the Constitution art. 40 is to be observed.

---

and Agnus Dei;
    d. in the chants of the Proper of the Mass, that is: the entrance, presentation, and communion antiphons with their psalms; the chants between the readings;
    e. in acclamations, greetings, and dialogic texts;
    f. in the Lord's Prayer, its introduction and embolism;
    g. in the formularies for the communion of the faithful;
    h. in the collect, prayer over the gifts, prayer after communion, and prayer over the people: Not 1 (1965) 9.

[R22] Query: Why is it lawful on only two days for the faithful to receive communion twice? Reply: The general law on communion only once each day remains intact. But the Church, basing itself on the principle of fuller participation in the liturgy through reception of the eucharist, on those days on which it celebrates two completely distinct liturgical offices for an entire community, grants permission to the faithful taking part in both to receive communion twice. The Church does not extend the permission to days when several celebrations amount only to a repetition of the same celebration to accommodate the faithful who could not be present if there were only one. In short: when one office is celebrated, even if repeatedly, communion is allowed only once; when two offices are celebrated, communion is allowed twice: Not (1965) 137, no. 5.

[R23] See SCR, Enumeration of the parts of the ordination rites that may be in the vernacular, 17 July 1965 [DOL 112].

II. ELEMENTS TO BE DROPPED IN THE RITE OF SUPPLYING CEREMONIES
FOR A PERSON ALREADY BAPTIZED (SC ART. 69)

354   62. In the rite of supplying ceremonies in the case of a baptized infant, *Rituale Romanum* tit. II, cap. 6, the exorcisms in no. 6 (*Exi ab eo*), no. 10 (*Exorcizo te, immunde spiritus — Ergo, maledicte diabole*), and no. 15 (*Exorcizo te, omnis spiritus*) are to be dropped.

355   63. In the rite for supplying ceremonies in the case of a baptized adult, *Rituale Romanum* tit. II, cap. 6, the exorcisms in no. 5 (*Exi ab eo*), no. 15 (*Ergo, maledicte diabole*), no. 17 (*Audi, maledicte satana*), no. 19 (*Exorcizo te — Ergo, maledicte diabole*), no. 21 (*Ergo, maledicte diabole*), no. 23 (*Ergo, maledicte diabole*), no. 25 (*Exorcizo te — Ergo, maledicte diabole*), no. 31 (*Nec te latet*), and no. 35 (*Exi, immunde spiritus*) are to be dropped.

III. CONFIRMATION (SC ART. 71)

356   64. If confirmation is conferred within Mass, the Mass should be celebrated by the bishop himself; in this case he confers the sacrament clad in Mass vestments.

The Mass within which confirmation is conferred may be celebrated as a second-class votive Mass of the Holy Spirit.

357   65. After the gospel and homily, before the reception of confirmation, it is well for those being confirmed to renew their baptismal promises, according to the rite in lawful use in individual regions, unless they have already done so before Mass.

358   66. If the Mass is celebrated by someone else, the bishop should assist at the Mass in the vestments prescribed for the conferral of confirmation; they may be either of the color of the Mass or white. The bishop himself should give the homily and the celebrant should resume the Mass only after the conferral of confirmation.

359   67. The conferral of confirmation follows the rite outlined in the *Pontificale Romanum*, but with a single sign of the cross at the words *In nomine Patris, et Filii, et Spiritus Sancti* that follow the formulary, *Signo te*.

IV. CONTINUOUS RITE FOR ANOINTING THE SICK AND VIATICUM (SC ART. 74)

360   68. When the anointing of the sick and viaticum are administered at the same time, unless a continuous rite already exists in a local ritual, the sequence of the rite is to be as follows: after the sprinkling with holy water and the prayer upon entering the room as given in the rite of anointing, the priest should, if need be, hear the confession of the sick person, then administer the anointing and finally give viaticum, omitting the sprinkling with its formularies, the *Confiteor*, and the absolution. If, however, the apostolic blessing with plenary indulgence at the hour of death is also to be imparted, it shall be given immediately before the anointing; the sprinkling with its formularies, the *Confiteor*, and absolution are omitted.

V. LAYING ON OF HANDS IN THE CONSECRATION OF A BISHOP (SC ART. 76)

361   69. At the consecration of a bishop all bishops present, clad in choral vesture, may participate in the laying on of hands. Only the consecrator and the two coconsecrators, however, pronounce the words, *Accipe Spiritum Sanctum*.

VI. RITE OF MARRIAGE (SC ART. 78)

362   70. Unless there is some good, excusing reason, marriage shall be celebrated within Mass, after the gospel and homily. The homily is never to be omitted.

363   71. Whenever marriage is celebrated within Mass, the *Missa votiva pro sponsis* shall always be celebrated, even in closed times, or a commemoration made from it, in keeping with the rubrics.

72. As far as possible, the pastor himself or the one he delegates to assist at the   364
marriage shall celebrate the Mass; if another priest assists at the marriage, the
celebrant shall not continue the Mass until the rite of marriage has been completed.

The priest who only assists at the marriage but does not celebrate the Mass
shall be vested in surplice and white stole and, if it is the local custom, also in cope;
he shall also give the homily. But the celebrant is always to give the blessing after
the *Pater noster* and before the *Placeat*.

73. The nuptial blessing shall always be given within the Mass, even in closed   365
times and even if one or both of the spouses is entering into a second marriage.

74. In the celebration of marriage outside Mass: 366

a. At the beginning of the rite, in keeping with the Motu Proprio *Sacram
Liturgiam* no. V,[a] a brief instruction shall be given, not a homily but simply an
introduction to the celebration of marriage (see SC art. 35, § 3).[b] After the reading
of the epistle and gospel from the *Missa pro sponsis*, there shall be a sermon or homily
based on the sacred text (see SC art. 52).[c] The order of the whole rite, then, is to be
as follows: the brief instruction,[R24] reading of the epistle and gospel in the vernacular, homily, celebration of marriage, nuptial blessing.

b. For the reading of the epistle and gospel from the *Missa pro sponsis*, if there is
no vernacular text approved by the competent territorial ecclesiastical authority, it
is lawful for the time being to use a text approved by the local Ordinary.

c. Singing is allowed between the epistle and gospel. After the rite of marriage and before the nuptial blessing it is most desirable to have the prayer of the
faithful in a form approved by the local Ordinary and incorporating intercessions
for the spouses.

d. Even in closed times and even if one or both of the spouses is entering a
second marriage, they are to receive the nuptial blessing, according to the formulary
in the *Rituale Romanum* tit. VIII, cap. 3, unless local rituals provide a different one.

75. If marriage is celebrated during closed times, the pastor shall advise the   367
spouses to be mindful of the proper spirit of the particular liturgical season.

VII. SACRAMENTALS (SC ART. 79)

76. For the blessing of candles on 2 February and of ashes on Ash Wednesday just   368
one of the prayers for these in the *Missale Romanum* suffices.

77. The blessings in the *Rituale Romanum* tit. IX, cap. 9, 10, 11, hitherto reserved,   369
may be given by any priest, except for: the blessing of a bell for the use of a blessed
church or oratory (cap. 9, no. 11); the blessing of the cornerstone of a church (cap. 9,
no. 16); the blessing of a new church or public oratory (cap. 9, no. 17); the blessing
of an antemensium (cap. 9, no. 21); the blessing of a new cemetery (cap. 9, no. 22);

---

[a]   See DOL 20 no. 283.

[b]   See DOL 1 no. 35.

[c]   See DOL 1 no. 52.

[R24]   Query: What should be the content of the brief instruction at the beginning of the rite of marriage?
Reply: In the celebration of marriage without a Mass, the brief instruction, kept to a very few words, calls
the attention of those present to what is to follow. This instruction can certainly be given by the
commentator: Not 1 (1965) 137, no. 6.

papal blessings (cap. 10, nos. 1–3); the blessing and erection of the stations of the cross (cap. 11, no. 1), reserved to the bishop.[d]

CHAPTER IV
DIVINE OFFICE

I. CELEBRATION OF DIVINE OFFICE BY THOSE BOUND TO CHOIR

370   78. Until reform of the divine office is completed:

a. Communities of canons, monks, nuns, other regulars or religious bound to choir by law or constitutions must, in addition to the conventual Mass, celebrate the entire divine office daily in choir.[R25]

Individual members of these communities who are in major orders or solemnly professed, except for lay brothers, are obliged, even if lawfully dispensed from choir, to private recitation each day of the hours they do not celebrate in choir.

b. Cathedral and collegiate chapters must, besides the conventual Mass, celebrate in choir those parts of the office imposed on them by common or particular law.

Individual chapter members, besides the canonical hours obligatory for all clerics in major orders (see SC art. 96 and 89),[a] must recite in private the hours that are celebrated by their chapter.

c. In mission regions, while preserving the religious or capitular choral discipline established by law,[R26] religious or capitulars who are lawfully absent from choir by reason of pastoral ministry may, with permission of the local Ordinary (not of his vicar general or delegate), use the concession granted by the Motu Proprio *Sacram Liturgiam* no. VI.[b]

II. FACULTY OF DISPENSING FROM OR COMMUTING DIVINE OFFICE (SC ART. 97)

371   79. The faculty given all Ordinaries to dispense their subjects, in individual cases and for a just reason, from the obligation of the divine office in whole or in part or

---

[d] See Apostolic Penitentiary, Declaration on indulgences attached to blessed articles, 6 March 1965 [DOL 384].

[R25] 1. Query: Are religious bound to choral recitation of the divine office obliged while traveling (even when guests in a house not obliged to choral recitation of the divine office) to recite all the canonical hours privately? Reply: Yes. By reason of CIC can. 14, §§ 1 and 3, these religious are not exempt from observing personal laws. But the law on the divine office is personal, in virtue of the constitutions of religious, that is, of solemn profession, or in virtue of holy orders: Not 1 (1965) 186, no. 42.

2. Query: Are religious "bound to choir" still obliged to the recitation of prime? Reply: In virtue of a recent concession (2 June 1965 [DOL 419]) the Apostolic See has left it up to religious major superiors to direct according to their prudent judgment that the hour of prime be retained or to declare it optional for their subjects: Not 1 (1965) 250, no. 61).

3. Query: In Not 1 (1965) 251, no. 61 there is the statement regarding prime for religious "bound to choir": "[Text of preceding reply quoted.]" What does "religious major superiors" mean? Reply: In this instance it means *religious superiors general*: ibid. 306, no. 82.

[a] DOL 1 nos. 96 and 89.

[R26] Query: May religious Ordinaries in virtue of the Constitution on the Liturgy art. 97 [DOL 1 no. 97] and the Motu Proprio *Sacram Liturgiam* no. VIII [DOL 20 no. 285] in individual instances and for a just reason dispense individual communities in whole or in part from recitation of the divine office or commute the obligation? Reply: No. The Constitution art. 97 is clear: "in individual instances." In no way is there question of dispensing communities bound to choir. This is why the Motu Proprio *Pastorale munus* no. 24 [DOL 103, no. 731] granted bishops the faculty of reducing the choral obligation of chapters. The interpretation in question, finally, is clearly excluded in the Instruction of 26 Sept. 1964, no. 78 c, which grants special faculties for mission regions, but "preserving the religious . . . choral discipline established by law": Not 1 (1965) 186, no. 43.

[b] DOL 20 no. 284.

to commute it is also extended to major superiors of nonexempt clerical, religious institutes and of societies of common life.

III. LITTLE OFFICES (SC ART. 98)[R27]

80. No little office can be classified as conformed to the divine office if it does not consist of psalms, readings, hymns, and prayers or if it has no relationship to the hours of the day and the particular liturgical season.

372

81. But little offices already lawfully approved suffice for the time being as a sharing in the public prayer of the Church, provided their make-up meets the criteria just stated.

373

For use as part of the public prayer of the Church, any new little office must have the approval of the Holy See.

82. The translation of the text of a little office into the vernacular for use as the public prayer of the Church must have the approval of the competent, territorial ecclesiastical authority, following approval, that is, confirmation, by the Holy See.

374

83. The Ordinary or major superior of the subject is the authority competent to grant use of the vernacular in the recitation of a little office to anyone bound to it by constitution or to dispense from or commute the obligation.

375

IV. DIVINE OFFICE OR LITTLE OFFICE CELEBRATED IN COMMON
BY RELIGIOUS INSTITUTES (SC ART. 99)

84. The obligation of celebrating in common all or part of the divine office or a little office imposed by their constitution on members of institutes of perfection does not take away the faculty of omitting prime and of choosing from among the little hours the one best suited to the time of day (see Motu Proprio *Sacram Liturgiam* no. VI).[c]

376

V. LANGUAGE FOR RECITATION OF DIVINE OFFICE (SC ART. 101)

85. In reciting the divine office in choir clerics are bound to retain the Latin language.

377

86. The faculty granted the Ordinary to allow use of the vernacular in individual cases by those clerics for whom the use of Latin constitutes a serious hindrance to fulfilling the obligation of the office is extended also to the major superiors of nonexempt, clerical religious institutes and of societies of common life.

378

87. The serious hindrance required for the concession of the faculty mentioned ought to be evaluated on the basis of the physical, moral, intellectual, and spiritual condition of the petitioner. Nevertheless, this faculty, conceded solely to make the recitation of the divine office easier and more devout, is not intended to lessen in any way the obligation of priests in the Latin rite to learn Latin.

379

88. The respective Ordinaries of the same language are to prepare and approve the translations of the divine office for the non-Roman rites. (For parts of the office shared with the Roman Rite, however, they are to use the version approved by competent territorial authority.) The Ordinaries are then to submit the translation for the Holy See's confirmation.

380

[R27] Query: Must little offices be abolished after the reform of the liturgy? Reply: The Constitution art. 89 [DOL 1 no. 89] and the Instruction nos. 80–84 assume the continuance of little offices even after the reform of the liturgy: Not 1 (1965) 186, no. 44.

[c] See DOL 20 no. 284.

381   89. Breviaries for clerics who, according to the provisions of art. 101, § 2,[d] have the right to use the vernacular for the divine office should contain the Latin text along with the vernacular.

CHAPTER V
DESIGNING CHURCHES AND ALTARS TO FACILITATE
ACTIVE PARTICIPATION OF THE FAITHFUL

I. DESIGN OF CHURCHES

382   90. In building new churches or restoring and adapting old ones every care is to be taken that they are suited to celebrating liturgical services authentically and that they ensure active participation by the faithful (see SC art. 124).[a]

II. MAIN ALTAR

383   91. The main altar should preferably be freestanding, to permit walking around it and celebration facing the people. Its location in the place of worship should be truly central so that the attention of the whole congregation naturally focuses there.[R28]

        Choice of materials for the construction and adornment of the altar is to respect the prescriptions of law.

        The sanctuary area is to be spacious enough to accommodate the sacred rites.

III. CHAIR FOR CELEBRANT AND MINISTERS

384   92. In relation to the plan of the church, the chair for the celebrant and ministers should occupy a place that is clearly visible to all the faithful and that makes it plain that the celebrant presides over the whole community.

        Should the chair stand behind the altar, any semblance of a throne, the prerogative of a bishop, is to be avoided.[R29]

---

        [d]   See DOL 1 no. 101.

        [a]   See DOL 1 no. 124.

        [R28] 1. Query: Is it lawful to construct an altar in the middle of the church in order that Mass may always be celebrated facing the people? Reply: The Instruction does not refer to the mathematical center of a church but to a conceptual center, saying "so that the attention of the whole congregation naturally focuses there": Not 1 (1965) 137–138, no. 7.
        2. Query: Until a church is suitably remodeled, is it lawful for celebration of Mass facing the people to place a portable altar (a simple table in form) in front of a main altar that is fixed and made of precious marble? Reply: Yes, provided: a. there is truly an observable space between both altars; b. ideally, the portable altar is placed outside the sanctuary; in this case it must have sufficient space around it in the manner of a sanctuary and be adequately separated from the body of the church: ibid., 138, no. 8.
        3. Query: For celebration of Mass facing the people is it lawful to construct a portable altar in a permanent manner in front of the main altar? Reply: Per se it is lawful, but it is not recommended. For the faithful take part very well in a Mass celebrated according to the norm of the new Ordo Missae even if the altar is made in such a way that the celebrant turns his back to them. The entire liturgy of the word is celebrated facing the people, at the chair, or at the lectern. If, in spite of this, the pastor of the church has decided to place another, portable altar in front of the main altar, this altar is to be set up as temporary. There is to be a truly observable space between both altars and the portable altar is to have enough space around it to serve as a kind of sanctuary: Not 1 (1965) 251, no. 62.

        [R29] Query: Some priests think that, lest the celebrant and ministers be hidden by the altar, the best place for them is behind it in the apse, but that the chair should be raised on at least three steps, in order that the people may see all the ministers and it is clear that the celebrant truly presides. Is this opinion admissible, especially if in the apse there is a throne for exposition of the blessed sacrament? Reply: To the first part, Yes. To the second part: if the tabernacle is in the apse or there is a throne for exposition of the blessed sacrament, the presidential chair is to be placed, somewhat raised, at the side of the altar: Not 1 (1965) 138, no. 9.

IV. MINOR ALTARS

93. There are to be fewer minor altars and, where the design of the building   385
permits, the best place for them is in chapels somewhat set apart from the body of
the church.

V. ALTAR APPOINTMENTS

94. At the discretion of the Ordinary, the cross and candlesticks required on the   386
altar for the various liturgical rites may also be placed next to it.R30

VI. RESERVATION OF THE EUCHARIST

95. The eucharist is to be reserved in a solid and secure tabernacle, placed in the   387
middle of the main altar or on a minor, but truly worthy altar, or, in accord with
lawful custom and in particular cases approved by the local Ordinary, also in
another, special, and properly adorned part of the church.R31

It is lawful to celebrate Mass facing the people even on an altar where there is
a small but becoming tabernacle.

VII. LECTERN (AMBO)

96. There should be a lectern or lecterns for the proclamation of the readings, so   388
arranged that the faithful may readily see and hear the minister.

R30   Query: Is a cross turned toward the people still to be placed on the altar? Reply: The problem arises
because of the photographs in Not 2 (1966) 176, used as illustrations of certain churches adapted to the
new requirements of pastoral liturgy; in these photographs no cross is visible. In fact a note (p. 162) states:
"A single large cross in the middle of the apse hangs over the whole liturgical assembly." Per se the
prescription of the *Codex rubricarum* no. 527 is still in force: "On the altar there is to be at the center a
sufficiently large cross bearing the image of the crucified." This cross, according to the *Caeremoniale Episcoporum* (lib. I, c. 12, n. 11) must be one "with the image of the crucified turned to the inner face of the altar."
     However the 1965 *Ritus Servandus* no longer prescribes that the priest raise his eyes toward the cross
during the celebration of Mass. Further, the Instruction no. 94 says: "[Text quoted]."
     If the altar faces the people, it seems more practical to use this option. Otherwise, either only the
letter of the law is kept and a cross is used that is so small as to be at times virtually invisible or the cross
prevents the people from seeing the rites well, especially at the elevations and the *Through him.*
     Away from the altar there are three alternatives: to place the processional cross before the altar,
with the face turned toward the celebrant, which does not always fit in well with other appointments of
the sanctuary; to have a large, pendant cross; to have a large cross affixed to the apse wall. In the last two
instances another cross for the altar is not required, the single large cross is enough; in celebrations facing
the people it is not incensed first but when the priest, going around the altar, stands in front of the cross
on the side of the altar near the people: Not 2 (1966) 290–291, no. 101.

R31   1. Query: When Mass is celebrated on an altar placed between the main altar and the people, may
the eucharist be reserved at the main altar, even though the celebrant turns his back to the eucharist?
Reply: Yes, provided: a. there is truly an observable space between both altars; b. the tabernacle on the
main altar is placed high enough that it is above the head of the celebrant as he stands at the foot of the
intermediate altar: Not 1 (1965) 138, no. 10.
     2. Query: On an altar facing the people may a tabernacle be placed at the left side and a cross or
book containing the Scriptures at the other side? Reply: No. Rather attention must be paid to the
Instruction no. 95, according to which "the tabernacle may be placed in particular cases . . . [text quoted] "
(e.g., in the right side of the sanctuary or in the apse): ibid. 138–139, no. 11.
     3. Query: If the main altar is built facing the people, is it in accord with the intent of the
Constitution and the Instruction no. 95 to reserve the eucharist at a minor altar distinct from the main
altar? Reply: Yes: Not 1 (1965) 251, no. 63.
     4. Query: Is it lawful to celebrate Mass in the presence of the exposed blessed sacrament at a
portable altar, distinct from the altar of exposition but in the same area? Reply: No. Nor can the *Codex
rubricarum* no. 349 be urged as an objection to this reply. This number concerns the Mass on the middle day
during forty hours, which must be celebrated "on an altar where the blessed sacrament is not exposed."
But the point in question is an altar distinct from the altar of exposition in such a way that there is no
interference with adoration of the blessed sacrament: ibid., no. 64. See also SCR, Reply on tabernacle veil,
3 July 1965 [DOL 542].

VIII. PLACE FOR CHOIR AND ORGAN

389   97. The choir and organ shall occupy a place clearly showing that the singers and the organist form part of the united community of the faithful and allowing them best to fulfill their part in the liturgy.

IX. PLACE FOR THE FAITHFUL

390   98. Special care should be taken that the place for the faithful will assure their proper participation in the sacred rites with both eyes and mind. Normally there should be benches or chairs for their use but, in keeping with the Constitution art. 32,[b] the custom of reserving places for special persons is to be suppressed.

Care is also to be taken to enable the faithful not only to see the celebrant and other ministers but also to hear them easily, even by use of modern sound equipment.

X. BAPTISTERY

391   99. In the construction and decoration of the baptistery great pains are to be taken to ensure that it clearly expresses the dignity of the sacrament of baptism and that it is a place well suited to communal celebrations (see SC art. 27).[c]

This Instruction was prepared by the Consilium by mandate of Pope Paul VI, and presented to the Pope by Cardinal Giacomo Lercaro, President of the Consilium. After having carefully considered the Instruction, in consultation with the Consilium and the Congregation of Rites, Pope Paul in an audience granted to Cardinal Arcadio Maria Larraona, Prefect of the Congregation of Rites, gave it specific approval as a whole and in its parts, confirmed it by his authority, and ordered it to be published and faithfully observed by all concerned, beginning on the first Sunday of Lent, 7 March 1965.

24. PAUL VI, **Address** to a general audience, including representatives of Catholic Action in Italy, on the recent Constitution on the Liturgy, 13 January 1965.*

392   [. . .] We must repeat that what brings joy to us redounds to your honor. To you, the beloved laity especially, we say: through your own endeavor to put the Constitution on the Liturgy into exact and vital effect you show yourselves to have that understanding of the times which Christ recommended to his first disciples (see Mt 16:4) and which the Church today is in the process of awakening and recognizing in adult Catholics. These times call for a spiritual revival, having its source in those genuine and inexhaustible fonts of truth and of grace that are the gifts of the Gospel to humanity. We refer to the liturgy of the word and the liturgy of the eucharistic sacrifice: turn your steps toward these fonts and there quench your thirst. You show that you understand the new way of religion which the current liturgical reform intends to restore and which is intimately connected with a broader movement as its central source of vitality. This movement is intrinsic to the constitutive principles of God's Church and is made easier and given greater thrust by the progress of human culture. This movement has as its end to make every Christian a member of the Mystical Body, living and active, not dead and passive, raised to a personal sharing in that activity which is the most exalted, beautiful,

---

    b   See DOL 1 no. 32.

    c   See DOL 1 no. 27.

    *   Text, OR 14 Jan. 1965, 1 (Italian).

effective, and mysterious that the pilgrim on earth can attain. In it every person enters into the unfolding course of human destiny, intercedes between God and the world. That activity is the liturgy. Entering in this way into the development of the plan of salvation, which today the Church is promoting with renewed fervor and directive norms, you accomplish a work not only of personal spirituality but of the apostolate. The apostolate is your own distinctive program. But the activity that you devote to understanding and sharing in the liturgy fully becomes translated into an activity revitalizing society. Only the genuine practice of religion can provide such an activity, imparting to souls spiritual, moral, and affective energies. Again we extend to you our good wishes and encouragement and with all our hearts give you our blessing. [. . .]

You will hear often during these times discourses on the liturgy from many   393
voices and on different themes, but always deriving from the Council's Constitution on the Liturgy and the various instructions instituting its gradual application. That is all to the good; the new legislation on the public, official worship of the Church has enough importance and merit to be widely publicized and explained. One special reason for that is one of its characteristics and purposes, the participation of the faithful in the rites that the priest directs and personalizes. It is also well to notice how it is proper to the Church's own authority to call, to promote, and to intensify this new manner of prayer. In this way the Church increases its own spiritual mission. It has been and remains the Church's first concern to safeguard orthodoxy in prayer; it has been the Church's continuing concern to preserve stability and uniformity in expressions of worship, a great work from which its spiritual life has received immense benefits. The Church's solicitude now broadens; today it is changing certain aspects of ritual discipline that are now inadequate and is seeking boldly but thoughtfully to plumb their essential meaning, the demands of community, and the supernatural value of ecclesial worship. The Church is doing so by making clearer above all the functions performed by the word of God, both in Scripture and in the instruction of catechesis and the homily, and by giving the celebration of the sacraments its illuminating yet mysterious central place.

To understand this religious program and to enjoy its hoped-for results we   394
must all change our settled way of thinking regarding sacred ceremonies and religious practices, especially if we think of the ceremonies merely as a carrying out of external rites and of religious practices as calling for no more than a passive, distracted assistance. We must be fully cognizant of the fact that with the Council a new spiritual pedagogy has been born. That is what is new about the Council and we must not hang back from making ourselves first the pupils and then the masters in this school of prayer now at its inception. It may well happen that the reforms will affect practices both dear to us and still worthy of respect; that the reforms will demand efforts that, at the outset, are a strain. But we must be devout and trusting: the religious and spiritual vista that the Constitution opens up before us is stupendous in its doctrinal profundity and authenticity, in the cogency of its Christian logic, in the purity and richness of its cultural and aesthetic elements, in its response to the character and needs of the modern man. Again, the authority of the Church teaches us and guarantees the soundness of the reforms carried out in its pastoral effort to strengthen faith in Christ and love for him in souls and to heighten religious awareness in our world.

Welcome this exhortation coming from the Pope; once again taste the experience of fruitfulness that obedience brings with it; obedience to the Church and to the one in the Church having the ministry of leading believers to adore the Father "in spirit and in truth" (Jn 4:23). That is our recommendation and our wish; we wish to seal both with the apostolic blessing.

25. PAUL VI, **Address** to pastors and Lenten preachers of Rome, excerpt on the liturgy, 1 March 1965: AAS 57 (1965) 325–330 (Italian).

CONSTITUTION ON THE LITURGY

395   [. . .] We desire to take advantage of this meeting to make a recommendation related to this singular phase of the Church's life, namely, the application, now at its starting point, of the conciliar Constitution on the Liturgy. At the end of the audience you will receive a booklet on this theme and, of course, you are already familiar with it. Thus our recommendation is this: devote the most intense care, especially in the first year, to learning, explaining, applying the new norms chosen by the Church to celebrate divine worship from now on. The matter is not easy, but delicate, requiring direct and systematic involvement, requiring your help given personally, patiently, lovingly, and in a genuinely pastoral way. Here are some of the issues: to change so many attitudes that in a number of respects are themselves worthy of honor and dearly held; to upset devout and good people by presenting new ways of prayer that they are not going to understand right away; to win over to a personal involvement in communal prayer the many people used to praying — or not praying — in church as they please; to intensify training in prayer and worship in every congregation, that is, to introduce the faithful to new viewpoints, gestures, practices, formularies, and attitudes, amounting to an active part in religion that many are unused to. In a word, the issue is engaging the people of God in the priestly liturgical life. Again, we say that it is a difficult and delicate matter, but adding that it is necessary, obligatory, providential, and renewing. We hope that it will also be satisfying. Perhaps your ministry will never be so full of outward results and inner consolation as when you begin to see the outcome of the teaching and pastoral power demanded of you, and when you come to experience the reality expressed in the words: "Behold how good it is and pleasant when brothers dwell in unity."[5] This profound, heartfelt, active unity of your people, making their prayers and offerings with you, will emerge before your eyes in its ever new and mystical beauty and will be a touching reward for all the care expended to achieve such a result. But take care: you must be convinced of the grandeur of the issues; you are faced with the sublimest of ideas, with divine truths and realities. You must be convinced that the objective is to reach the heart of today's people through the liturgy as the truest, most authoritative, sacred, and effective way and so to rekindle in them the flame of love for God and neighbor, the awesome, intoxicating power to commune with God — authentically, consolingly, redemptively. You need to have, together with such a lofty conception of the new state of the liturgy, the art of attending to the demands of the concrete: schedule, order, materials, gestures, movements, silence, speech, and perhaps the most difficult of all, music. The last is going to take years, but we must begin, and begin over and over, perseveringly, in order to succeed in giving to the congregation a voice that is reverent, harmonious, sweet, and sublime.

EXALTED MINISTRY OF THE WORD

396   Among the many matters requiring preparation, dedication, dignity, and relevance is the word, as well you know. Nothing less than a special part of the liturgy of the Mass is set aside for the word: we refer to the word of Scripture, the word of God, proclaimed and listened to with renewed worthiness and devotion; but we also refer to the word of the priest, acting as apostle, prophet, teacher, and guide for

---

⁵ Ps 132 (133): 1.

the people of God. To this word we refer here, you pastors and Lenten preachers who are listening to us, in order to strengthen your ministry, which the liturgy elevates to its pristine place as the herald of the mystery of salvation and which the liturgy fills and enriches with biblical content, links closely to the eucharistic sacrifice, strips of sham rhetoric, and animates with divine authority. You are well aware of all that has been spoken and written about preaching: the relationship it must bear with the preacher's own spiritual and moral life; the prayer that must precede — the preacher, says St. Augustine, is one who prays before being one who speaks;[6] the sincerity that must be its mark — "let the soul of Christ's priest match his speech," says St. Jerome;[7] the content that must be genuinely religious, addressed not to draw admiration from the people, but to instruct and build them up; the sublimity and the need of the ministry of the word in the manifold, age-old forms of its expression as instructive or admonitory, theological or exhortatory.

REASON FOR THE EFFECTIVENESS OF PREACHING

We will not repeat any of their instructions, but do wish to call to mind how many doctors and saints have dealt with this ministry. It would be an immense literature to collect and study. We limit ourself to the expression of one desire: that preaching be effective. The ability to accomplish this in today's world must be one of the most important practical disciplines in contemporary preparation for ministry. The example of speakers we hear daily through television is a stimulus. The increased sophistication of the public summons us. Modern people's intolerance of any kind of ineptitude, pompousness, rhetoric, affectation, substitution of the profane for the sacred, obligates us. Today's demand for words that are plain, simple and to the point, brief, and comprehensible is in our favor. There remains the difficulty of expressing the divine in human words, of endowing the sacred word with the hidden power that makes it persuasive and salvific; to make our poor speech sharp and lively like a sword: "For the word of God is living and active, sharper than any two-edged sword, piercing to the division of soul and spirit."[8] Dear pastors and Lenten preachers, remember, the religious vitality of our times may in great measure depend on this at once human and mysterious effectiveness of preaching. That is why our exhortation is intended to honor your ministry, to strengthen you in the dedication not only of your voice but of your mind, your devotion, your prayer, your suffering, and your fervor. That is why these words end in the wish that lying in store for you are all the joy and the merit of preaching that is truly sacred, truly effective.   397

You have come here to listen to such things. For you who have experienced and borne the fatigue of the preaching ministry, they amount to no more than you already know and want, except as an added and mysterious factor that we wish intently to join to your pastoral eloquence, to be for you a power and a consolation, namely, our mandate and our blessing. Both of these we impart to you with Christ's own words: *Euntes ergo docete . . . . Ecce vobiscum sum . . . .*[9]   398

---

6   Augustine, *De doctr. chr.*: PL 34, 103.

7   Jerome, *Ep.* 52, 7: PL 22, 533.

8   Heb 4:12.

9   Mt. 28:19,20.

26. PAUL VI, **Remarks at the Angelus** to the people in St. Peter's Square, on the beginning of the vernacular in the liturgy, 7 March 1965 (Italian).*,a

399   Today is a memorable Sunday in the spiritual history of the Church: the vernacular, as you have perceived this morning, has officially taken its place within liturgical worship. The Church has judged this measure — raised and debated at the Council — to be necessary to make its prayer understandable and grasped by all. The good of the faithful calls for this kind action, making possible their active share in the Church's public worship. The Church has sacrificed its native tongue, Latin, a language that is sacred, measured, beautiful, richly expressive, and graceful. The Church has made the sacrifice of an age-old tradition and above all of unity in language among diverse peoples to bow to a higher universality, an outreach to all peoples.

        That means you, the faithful, so that you may be able to unite yourselves more closely to the Church's prayer, pass over from being simply spectators to becoming active participants. If you can truly respond to this kindness of the Church, you will find the great joy, reward, and blessing of a genuine spiritual renewal. We are about to pray together to the Blessed Virgin — this time still in Latin — that she may fill us with desire for an intense and authentic spiritual life, with a reawakened sense of community, of being a family, an assembly praying together, of being the people of God. That will be the assurance of our deriving true profit from this great reform of the liturgy.

        Then the benefits of this great liturgical reform will be guaranteed to us.

27. PAUL VI, **Address** to a general audience, on reactions to the reform of the liturgy, 17 March 1965 (Italian).*

400   In an audience like this one our family conversation cannot help but turn to the theme of the day: the application of the reform of the liturgy to the Mass. If the public character of our meeting did not prevent it, we should like to have asked you — as we have asked others in private meetings — what your impressions are regarding this new departure that deserves to hold the attention of each one of us. In any case we believe that your answer to our question would not differ from those of others that have reached us recently.

401   What do people think about the reform of the liturgy? The replies can be grouped into two categories. First, there are those that give evidence of a degree of confusion and therefore of uneasiness. Until now people were comfortable; they could pray the way they wished; all were quite familiar with the way the Mass proceeded. Now on all sides there are new things, changes, surprises: it has even gone so far as to do away with ringing the Sanctus bell. Then there are all those prayers that no one can any longer find; standing to receive communion; the end of the Mass cut off abruptly after the blessing. Everyone makes the responses; there is much moving about; the prayers and the readings are spoken out loud. In short, there is no more peace, things are understood less than before, and so on.

---

    * Text, OR 8–9 March 1965, 1 (Italian).

    a This document is placed here because it calls attention to the beginning of such an important feature of the reform; see Section 5 of this Chapter.

    * Text, OR 18 March 1965, 1 (Italian).

We shall not criticize these remarks because that would require showing how great a lack of understanding about religious rites they manifest. They do not indicate a true devotion or a genuine perception of the import of the Mass. Rather they betray a certain spiritual laziness, the refusal to make the personal effort toward understanding and participation. That effort would open the way to a better grasp and carrying out of the most sacred of religious acts, one with which we are invited, indeed obliged to associate ourselves. We repeat what all pastors and all professors of religion are saying over and over again these days. 1. It is unavoidable that at the beginning there should be some confusion and uneasiness. It is simply normal that a spiritual and practical reform that affects ingrained and devoutly observed religious practices should cause confusion and that it should not always please everyone. 2. But a bit of explanation, preparation, assistance kindly given have quickly quieted uneasiness and made people understand and like the new order of things. 3. We should not think that after a while there can be a return to the former, undisturbed devotion or apathy. No, the new way of doing things will have to be different; it will have to prevent and to shake up the passivity of the people present at Mass. Before, it was enough to assist; now, it is necessary to take part. Before, being there was enough; now, attention and activity are required. Before, everyone could doze or perhaps even chatter; now all must listen and pray. We are hopeful that soon celebrants and people can have the new liturgical books and that their literary and typographical quality will be no less worthy than that of the former books. The assembly becomes alive and active; taking part means allowing the soul to become attentive, to enter into the dialogue, to sing, to act. The unity of a community action, consisting not only of outward gestures but also of an inner movement of faith and devotion, invests the rite with a special power and beauty. The rite thereby becomes a chorus, a concert; it takes on the rhythm of giant wings soaring toward the heights of joy and of the divine mysteries.

The second category of comments that have come to our attention on the   402
subject of the new liturgy is, in contrast, inspired by enthusiam and praise. At last, some are saying, we can grasp and follow the ceremonial of the Mass, which is so complex and mysterious. At last we can begin to enjoy the Mass. At last the priest speaks to the people and it is clear that he is acting with them and through them. We have the striking testimony of all kinds of people, the young, critics and observers, the devout in search of fervor and prayer, people of long and impressive experience and of a high level of culture. One distinguished old gentleman, of noble heart and a very sensitive, still unsatisfied spirituality, at the end of the first celebration of the new liturgy felt impelled to go up to the celebrant to express, in all simplicity, his own happiness at having at last — and perhaps for the first time in his life — taken part in the Mass with his whole soul.

Perhaps this wonder and holy enthusiasm will subside; perhaps they will change quickly into a new complacency. Is there anything that does not become routine? However, there is every reason to believe that there will be no lessening of the consciousness of religious intensity required by the new form of the rite. This is an awareness that there is need to achieve simultaneously two spiritual acts: a genuine, personal participation in the rite, with all its implications of the essential in religion; communion with the assembly of the faithful, with the *Ecclesia*. The first of these acts is bent upon love for God; the second, upon love for neighbor. Thus the Gospel of love becomes a reality in the souls of our time. Therein truly lies something beautiful, new, great, full of light and hope.

28. CONSILIUM, **Letter** *Ordo agendorum* of A. Bugnini to presidents of the conferences of bishops, requesting a report on the first steps of liturgical reform, 29 March 1965.*

403   The "agenda" set forth for the meetings of the Consilium, 26–30 April, includes reports on the first steps of the liturgical reform in the various countries.

I should therefore like to ask Your Excellency to prepare a short report on your own country. It should state the principal measures taken to prepare for the reform, the results of their execution, the problems arising, proposals for the next steps. It will be helpful if the *written* report not exceed two pages and most kind if it can be sent to the secretariat of the Consilium before the meetings.

29. CONSILIUM, **Declaration** *Passim quandoque*, on liturgical experimentation, 15 June 1965: Not 1 (1965) 145.

404   There are occasional reports of liturgical innovations here and there at variance with either the rubrics now in force or with the Constitution or Instruction on the Liturgy.[a] The innovators commonly claim that they have obtained a faculty or indult from the Consilium, authorizing liturgical experimentation.

The Consilium declares that, except for the indults granted from 3 July 1964 to 14 April 1965 for concelebration and communion under both kinds, it has issued no general indult of any kind authorizing experiments.

405   A reminder is hardly necessary that according to the Constitution art. 40, no. 2,[b] such a faculty is to be granted by the Holy See solely to territorial ecclesiastical authority; concession for experimentation is made only: a. within specified groups; b. to those qualified; c. for a fixed period.

If in the future the Consilium permits experiments, then, it will forward the faculty always to the territorial ecclesiastical authority, always in writing, and with a statement of the conditions and limits within which the experiments are allowed.

When, therefore, rites, ceremonies, or initiatives of any kind are seen to conflict with prevailing liturgical laws, they are to be regarded as "personal" and individualistic, and as such repudiated by the Constitution and by the Consilium.

30. PAUL VI, **Address** to a consistory, excerpt on the beginnings of liturgical reform, 24 June 1965: AAS 57 (1965) 638–645.

406   [. . .] During this year also the reform of the liturgy has begun to come into effect. This was planned by the relevant conciliar document with the purpose of making easier for the faithful — as is now happening — access to the sources of a more authentic spirituality and a deeper, more fruitful understanding of the content and meaning of the liturgical rites. We can, therefore, only rejoice in the many steps

----

*   Prot. N. 1466.

a   See InterOec [DOL 23].

b   See DOL 1 no. 40.

taken in the liturgical apostolate, always with the desire that they be in accord with the spirit and letter of the conciliar Constitution and the Instruction regarding it[a] as well as with the norms promulgated by the competent ecclesiastical authority. That will make the effects of such steps for the faithful safe, well ordered, and manifold. [. . .]

31. CONSILIUM, **Letter** *Le renouveau liturgique* of Cardinal G. Lercaro to presidents of the conferences of bishops, on furthering liturgical reform, 30 June 1965: Not 1 (1965) 257–264 (French; drawn up in six major languages).

The current liturgical renewal is a reassuring fact, an encouragement to go on   407
with the work. Entering into the stream of spiritual renewal initiated by Vatican Council II is not the business of an elite, but of the entire holy people of God, whose limits embrace the Church and all humanity.

With deep feeling and admiration we are witnessing this "new passage of the Holy Spirit over his Church," prophetically announced by Pope Pius XII nine years ago at the time of the audience concluding the first congress on pastoral liturgy at Assisi. We see the growth and consolidation of this "new school of the spirit," to which Pope Paul VI has so often referred, as one of the most precious results of the Council. It is not too much to say that Vatican Council II will pass into history having as its hallmark one of its boldest advances, the reform of the liturgy, as this becomes ever more luminous and dynamic.

If we had to describe, in all sincerity and objectivity, what has been occurring   408
in churches throughout the world since 7 March, we should each have to make a list of "the wonderful works of God." Evidence of this appears in reports on the different nations published in *Notitiae*, the Consilium's bulletin. Those reliable reports, made usually by the president or other qualified member of a national liturgical commission, brief as they are, demonstrate that in every part of the world the Church is witnessing an unexpected springtime. There is every right to predict that this spiritual flowering will be even more striking as the faithful, becoming more aware that they make up the people of God, enter more deeply into the mystery of the liturgy and as Christian life and heroic holiness, especially among the laity, flow from closer and closer contact with the genuine sources of grace, not only in a few privileged nations, but all over the world.

All of that is consoling to us who, in the service of souls, are the instruments of   409
"God's varied grace" (1 Pt 4:10). Still, we must see to it that this fullness of life does not weaken, that this river which "makes glad the city of God" (Ps 45:5 [46:4]) does not run off into dead streamlets at the risk of drying up. That is what could happen the moment the single, centralized direction of the practice of worship begins to pass little by little from the center to the periphery because of a failure to keep to the higher course of unity in intention and action.

We must face the fact that clouds here and there darken the horizon of the new day of the liturgy's vitality. For this reason the Consilium, with a view to the application of recent norms and documents, has thought it timely at the present moment, when liturgical weeks and study conferences are everywhere about to take place, to direct to Your Excellency, and through you to all the bishops and to

---

[a]   See InterOec [DOL 23].

the diocesan and regular clergy of your country, certain guidelines to be followed for a more fruitful liturgical life.

410   1.   The new liturgical norms have been devised with a certain flexibility that allows for adaptation and consequently for an increased pastoral effectiveness. That does not mean that every priest can do what he likes and redesign the sacred rites of the Church to suit his fancy. We must, first, bear in mind who has received from the Church the right to make such adaptations; secondly, we must take into consideration what the norms determine and judge to what extent they provide for adaptation.

411   2.   Further, there is the sense of community, of a gathered family. It is a sentiment that has already grown and must grow still more, since the liturgy fosters and extends it; it is in truth one of the most perceptible results of the ceremonies celebrated according to the reformed rites. But the sense of community cannot and must not smother the sense of hierarchy in the Church. This hierarchic sense must be expressed in a disciplined and harmonious cooperation of the college of priests with the bishop, with the college of bishops, in particular with the bishops of a nation united in conference, and in the cooperation of all with the vicar of Christ. Such cooperation will not deprive pastoral experiments in touch with life's reality of anything of their freshness and effectiveness. It will, however, put a brake on uncontrolled arbitrariness and on pointless variety, it will forestall the danger that the laity, in spite of their fuller participation in the life of the Church, will feel less genuinely the "people" and "family" of God and will end up lamenting and murmuring like the children of Israel against Moses and Aaron.

Unity does not mean stifling or eliminating variety, but it will express itself amidst variety in a vigilance against the descent of variety into chaos.

The filial virtue of Christian obedience — which is the expression of charity — will also be the bond and guarantee of union and unity.

412   3.   For fifteen months the Consilium has worked without letup in its forty study groups of experts and through a carefully composed body of forty-two bishops, the core of the Consilium. But a general reform of the liturgy that goes right to the roots cannot be achieved in a day. It takes time, research, painstaking development, critiques, and controls. It demands patience of all. I ask Your Excellency to emphasize that point to your clergy, in order to put a stop to any personal, precipitate, and harmful innovations; God does not bless them and they are therefore without power to achieve lasting results; on the contrary, they do damage to the devotion of the faithful and to a reform begun in so holy a manner. They also prejudice our own efforts, for such initiatives are usually arbitrary and end up by putting into a bad light a work being carried out with circumspection, a sense of responsibility, prudence, and true knowledge of pastoral needs. This work of the Consilium will not be interminable; we are pledged not to prolong it any more than necessary. But let no one presume to disturb our steady and well-considered pace by individualistic meddling.

Those who believe they have constructive suggestions will be doing a work of charity by submitting their proposals to the Consilium, which will examine them carefully so that reform may be the work of the whole Church.

4.   During the transition period the earlier liturgical legislation remains in force in   413
all points that have not been formally declared obsolete. In addition, the Constitution on the Liturgy, the Motu Proprio [*Sacram Liturgiam*],ᵃ the Instruction [*Inter Oecumenici*],ᵇ and its authorized interpretation, both by the Congregation of Rites and
the Consilium, and finally the norms drawn up by conferences of bishops, are the
texts constituting the law.

To go beyond these limits is not permissible. Thus nobody is allowed experimentation without explicit authorization. The Consilium has never given such
authorization in blanket form, since the Constitution itself envisions experimenta-
tions as something reserved to those best prepared and selected, as limited to a
definite period, and as supervised by ecclesiastical authority.ᶜ Every concession to
experiment will be given in writing and communicated to the competent authority,
with the restrictive limits clearly stated. All initiatives in conflict with the actual
determinations of law must therefore be considered as personal and arbitrary acts
and as such repudiated by the Constitution and the Consilium.

On the other hand, if this request to stay within the limits set by the authentic
legislation of the Church is necessary, so also is a fresh summons, addressed to all,
to an integral fulfillment of the new norms, both those contained in the conciliar
documents themselves and those added by way of application. There are two
attitudes equally injurious to the work of renewal undertaken by the Church: the
rash activity of some and the inactivity of others, caused either by lack of understanding or by sheer inertia. The words of Pope Paul are explicit in this regard: "We
must be fully cognizant of the fact that with the Council a new spiritual pedagogy
has been born. That is what is new about the Council and we must not hang back
from making ourselves first the pupils and then the masters in this school of prayer
now at its inception. It may well happen that the reforms will affect practices both
dear to us and still worthy of respect; that the reforms will demand efforts that, at
the outset, are a strain. But we must be devout and trusting: the religious and
spiritual vista that the Constitution opens up before us is stupendous in its doctrinal profundity and authenticity, in the cogency of its Christian logic, in the purity
and richness of its cultural and aesthetic elements, in its response to the character
and needs of the modern man. Again, the authority of the Church teaches us and
guarantees the soundness of the reforms carried out in its pastoral effort to
strengthen faith in Christ and love for him in souls, and to heighten religious
awareness in our world" (Address to a general audience, 13 January 1965).ᵈ

5.   The Constitution on the Liturgy has brought out the full meaning of eucharis-   414
tic devotion in its nature as "genuine worship fed by the Gospel and the teaching of
theology" (Address of Paul VI at the eucharistic congress in Pisa).ᵉ

This devotion finds its highest expression in the celebration of the holy sacrifice, which gathers up the whole people of God in active participation around the
one altar, in the one faith and the one prayer, under the presidency of the bishop or
his representative (see SC art. 41–42).ᶠ

Among the different forms of eucharistic celebration, one is of particular value,
namely, concelebration, which the Council has restored to common usage in the

---

ᵃ   See DOL 20.

ᵇ   See DOL 23.

ᶜ   See DOL 1 no. 40.

ᵈ   DOL 24 no. 394.

ᵉ   DOL 174 no. 1143.

ᶠ   See DOL 1 nos. 41 and 42.

Church. Concelebration must not be regarded solely as a means of surmounting such practical difficulties as may arise because of the multiplication of individual celebrations. It is to be perceived in the light of its true doctrinal meaning: as the manifestation of the unity between sacrifice and priesthood, of the unity of the entire people of God in the sacred service, and, finally, of the increase in true charity, fruit of the eucharist, among those who celebrate this unique sacrifice.

Promotion of concelebration, consequently, is worthwhile where it can be advantageous to the devotion of priests and faithful. But there must be care that concelebration is never at the cost of service to the faithful by an excessive reduction in the number of individual celebrations for them and that it does not keep priests who wish to celebrate individually from doing so. Individual celebration, even without a congregation, retains all its doctrinal and ascetical importance and the full approval of the Church. There must also be care that the practice of concelebration always is accompanied by due catechetical and liturgical preparation and is marked by the required dignity and solemnity as prescribed by the recently published rite.

415   6.   Since 7 March there has been a widespread movement toward celebrations facing the people; it has become clear that this practice is the most advantageous pastorally. The intention of an end that is good in itself, however, has in some cases given rise to measures that are in poor taste, illogical, and artificial. The Consilium has already in private form drawn up some norms on this subject. They will be completed as soon as possible and published officially. We wish to emphasize, however, that the celebration of the whole Mass facing the people is not absolutely indispensable for pastoral effectiveness. The entire liturgy of the word, in which the active participation of the faithful is amply achieved through dialogue and song, already proceeds facing the people and is all the more intelligible now that it uses the people's own language. Certainly it is right to wish that the liturgy of the eucharist itself might also be celebrated facing the people and that the faithful be enabled to follow the whole rite directly, thereby participating with a greater awareness. But that must not lead to the rash, often mindless rearrangement of existing churches and altars at the cost of a more or less irreparable damage to other values, also calling for respect.

The construction of altars facing the people is therefore desirable in new churches; elsewhere it will be achieved gradually through seriously studied adaptations that take all values into account.

If in the interim it seems useful to allow erection of portable altars that make celebration facing the people possible, careful attention is to be given to the dignity and beauty suited to the altar, the table of sacrifice and of the banquet of God's family.

416   7.   An issue closely linked to that of the altar is *the tabernacle*. We can hardly give here prescriptions of a general and uniform character. An attentive study needs to be made in each case, with due attention to the material and spiritual circumstances proper to each place.

Artists will little by little suggest the best solution. But it is the business of priests to advise them and call attention to the principles that must safeguard the respect and honor due to the eucharist. It is important to contribute to the development of eucharistic worship, which should continue under all those genuine forms recognized by the Church as embodying true Christian piety.

Particularly in larger churches, a chapel specially set aside for the reservation and adoration of the eucharist is advisable and might well be used for the eucharistic celebration during the week, when there are fewer of the faithful participating.

Whatever the solution chosen from among those recommended by the Instruction [InterOec] (no. 95),[g] the greatest care should be devoted to the dignity of the tabernacle. If the local Ordinary agrees to its location away from the altar, the place should be truly worthy and prominent, so that the tabernacle is readily visible and is not hidden by the priest during the celebration of the Mass. In a word, the location should make it possible for the tabernacle to serve unmistakably as a sign and to give a sense of the Savior's presence in the midst of his people.

It is therefore pertinent to take note of solutions sometimes proposed or already in effect that *do not seem really to achieve a satisfactory result*. They would include the following: tabernacles permanently inserted into the altar table or retracted automatically at the time of celebration; tabernacles placed in front of the altar, sometimes on a slightly lower pedestal, sometimes on another altar at a lower level and used in conjunction with the altar of celebration; finally, tabernacles built into the wall of the apse or those placed upon an already existing altar having the celebrant's chair in front of or below it.

More detailed information on this matter will be given, as has been said earlier, at the same time as that on the altar itself.

8.   In the adaptation of churches to the demands of liturgical renewal there has   417
sometimes been exaggeration regarding sacred images. At times, it is true, some churches have been cluttered with images and statues, but to strip bare and do away with absolutely everything is to risk the opposite extreme. The transformation of churches has sometimes been carried out without the accompaniment of a sufficient catechesis and has given rise to harmful reactions or at least has not been edifying to the faithful.

Without a doubt the mysteries of redemption and the eucharistic celebration must be at the center of worship; but according to the Constitution (art. 103, 104, 108, 111),[h] there is a consonant and perfectly subordinate place for the veneration of the Virgin Mary, Mother of God, and of the saints. That is a consoling and enlightening Catholic teaching.

A sensible zeal in the spirit of the Church respects the truth that in God's house everything has meaning, everything speaks, everything must safeguard the mark of the sacred and of mystery.

9.   Until 1947 the liturgical movement had been born, sustained, and guided by   418
the initiative of volunteers or of religious institutes, which generously bore the expense and the sacrifice in order to promote the knowledge and study of the liturgy through publications, liturgical weeks, and in other ways.

In 1947 Pius XII brought the movement directly under the auspices of the ecclesiastical hierarchy (see Encyclical *Mediator Dei* no. 108).

The arrangement has been reenforced and, so to speak, canonized by Vatican Council II, which gave to the conferences of bishops or to bishops and Ordinaries various faculties hitherto reserved to the Holy See. That fact has consequences of utmost importance. The liturgical movement has obtained from the Church the official recognition that was its aim. The groups, religious institutes, and individuals who have made themselves its promoters have done well and have rendered valuable service to the Church. But for that spiritual resource to which they have consecrated themselves to continue its sanctifying action, it needs to be more firmly

---

[g]   See DOL 23 no. 387.

[h]   See DOL 1 nos. 103, 104, 108, 111.

settled within the lines traced by the Church and to follow the forms and limits that the judgment of the hierarchy deems most advisable.

Let our search, in harmonious agreement, be for solutions best suited and conducive to close collaboration. Today no liturgical center should remain isolated on the fringes of the path traced by the Church.

Liturgical periodicals and those dedicated to pastoral activity are invited to continue with zeal their study, research, and intelligent and serious spread of the liturgy. But let them abstain from publishing new ideas or reform projects in outright opposition to existing legislation or evincing a questionable liturgical sense.

I wanted to write these things to Your Excellency to open my heart, with you as intermediary, to all those who at this time of special responsibility are working with zeal and enthusiasm to the end that all the faithful may through the liturgy intensely live the mystery of Christ; I am thinking particularly of the clergy as well as of the ranks of organized laity, above all young people, and of men and women religious.

I would like to express to you, by these assurances, my brotherly and sincere thanks for all that you may be pleased to do and for the dissemination and carrying out of these directives.

32. CONSILIUM, **Letter** *L'heureux développement* of Cardinal G. Lercaro to presidents of the conferences of bishops, on problems in the reform of the liturgy, 25 January 1966: Not 2 (1966) 157–161 (French; issued in six major languages).*

419   The favorable development of the liturgical reform and of the pastoral movement connected with it continues to have an ever deeper and more beneficial effect on the life of our parish communities. Generous perseverance in this effort, above all if carried out in harmony with the bishops and under their active and watchful guidance, will, one hopes, bear even richer fruits of spiritual renewal.

In view of this progress in the liturgical apostolate, I should like to speak with Your Excellency about some problems that have recently made themselves apparent.

1. RELATIONS BETWEEN HIERARCHIES AND LITURGICAL CENTERS

420   In his Allocution of 10 November 1965, to those taking part in the "Conventus de popularibus interpretationibus textuum liturgicorum," the Holy Father emphasized that liturgical centers and periodicals of a liturgical nature which are not the direct expression of the episcopal conference or of the national liturgical commission should have a much closer relationship with the episcopal conferences, in such a way that in the same nation directions on liturgical action should be one and the same, and coming directly from the hierarchy. "Cum sacra Liturgia universa moderationi Hierarchiae sit obnoxia (see Const. de sacra Lit., art. 22, par. 1–2; AAS 56, 1964, 106)," said the Holy Father, "omnes, sive singuli, sive coetus, sive praecipue in nationibus instituta rei liturgicae accurandae et provehendae, sive commentarii, quibus idem est propositum, in unaquaque regione plane pendeant ex Hierarchia. Competentis auctoritatis est huiusmodi arctioris necessitudinis vincula definire de iisque statuere. Summo igitur studio est annitendum, ut hac etiam in re omnium sit

---

 * English text from the Consilium.

una voluntas, una actio, quemadmodum unus est finis, ad quem contenditur, una perfectionis imago, quae mentibus obversatur et ad quam assequendam tot fiunt conatus."[a]

To put the Holy Father's desire into action, in a meeting of the presidents of the national liturgical commissions, held in the Palace of the Cancelleria Apostolica on 17 November 1965, the following guidelines were put forward to the Fathers assembled there:

a. By "centers" are meant those dealing with the liturgical and pastoral apostolate, and which promote public events in connection with this. Such centers are, for example, those organizing liturgical weeks or directing schools or institutes of liturgy.   421

b. "Periodicals" here mean those of a pastoral and not purely scientific nature; however, it is for the competent authority to be judge of the character of the various periodicals.   422

c. The same competent authority will decide how this closer link will best be established. It may well vary according to the place and circumstances: by means of a delegate on the staff or editorial board, or a reviser, or a director designated by the bishops, etc.   423

What matters is that throughout the region there should be uniform norms and directives, and a single control over the development of the liturgy, namely, control by the bishops. This does not mean that they will stifle those capable of furthering liturgical renewal; rather, it is for the bishops to sustain and protect them, to set them out on new initiatives, so that both clergy and faithful may better understand and take part in the liturgy.

These norms come into effect as from now, and the Consilium would be extremely grateful to know as soon as possible how, in the ambit of Your Excellency's own conference, these have been applied in practice.

2. MASSES IN LATIN

It is only right that where the use of the vernacular in the liturgy is concerned, one should be guided not only by the spirit of the Liturgy Constitution, but also by an awareness of the given situation in different places. Here and there, in fact, the adoption of the vernacular in the Mass has given rise to some signs of disquiet. It would be good if local Ordinaries were to consider the eventual suitability of preserving in some churches, especially in big cities and in places where there are large influxes of tourists, one, or more if necessary, Mass in Latin. This would be said according to an established and publicized timetable, insofar as and to the extent that it seemed necessary or desirable.   424

3. THE LANGUAGE IN BILINGUAL REGIONS

In the same pastoral spirit, the Ordinary in bilingual regions will lay down those dispositions which best provide for the needs of the various language groups. The use of Latin for example is one way, or, as is the praiseworthy practice in many places, by arranging that the sacred celebrations should be at different times for people speaking different languages. Every care must be taken that the use of the language adopted in worship should not be a cause of damage to the religious   425

---

[a] "Moreover, since the whole liturgy is subject to the regulation of the hierarchy (see SC art. 22, §§ 1 and 2 [DOL 1 no. 22]), in every nation the individuals, groups, and especially the principal national institutes for the care and promotion of liturgy, as well as all periodicals having the same purpose, should be wholly dependent on the hierarchy. The competent authority has the right to determine the means and establish rules for this close relationship. Every effort must be made for unity of will and of action in this matter, for we have a single goal to reach and a single ideal of perfection to keep before our minds and to make the aim of all our efforts" [DOL 113 no. 789].

practice of the people, nor should it lessen the harmony and charity of the parish community.

4. CHOIRS

426   There are some who think that the liturgical revival implies that choirs have had their day, that they have outlasted their usefulness and can quietly be scrapped. As a matter of fact this has already happened in certain cathedrals, colleges, and shrines, where the choir has been suppressed.

The principle upon which such action seeks to rest has no foundation in truth. If it is to be desired that the liturgical assembly be initiated, educated, and guided in its singing, a choir is indispensable. The choir, while adding dignity and solemnity by its own mastery of what it sings, must also undertake the moderating function of leading and sustaining the participation of the faithful in those parts which are proper to them.

5. THE SACRED QUALITY OF CHURCH MUSIC

427   It is necessary moreover that the principles of sacredness and dignity which distinguish church music, be it for its chant as for its sound,[b] should remain intact. All that which is merely secular should be proscribed from the house of God. Jazz, for example, cannot today be part of a musical repertoire designed for worship.

Where musical instruments are concerned, differing mentalities, cultures, and traditions are to be borne in mind, and those instruments which have an entirely secular connotation should not be allowed in church. The Church has immense possibilities for deep, effective and uplifting action, without having recourse to means which are very dubious and even, by common consent, harmful.

6. ALTARS VERSUS POPULUM AND TABERNACLES

428   I have already spoken about this in my letter of 30 June 1965,[c] but by your leave I intend to return briefly to the same subject.

The altar *versus populum*, certainly makes for a celebration of the eucharist which is truer and more communal; it also makes participation easier. Here too, however, prudence should be our guide. Above all because for a living and participated liturgy, it is not indispensable that the altar should be *versus populum*: in the Mass, the entire liturgy of the word is celebrated at the chair, ambo or lectern, and, therefore, facing the assembly; as to the eucharistic liturgy, loudspeaker systems make participation feasible enough. Secondly, hard thought should be given to the artistic and architectural question, this element in many places being protected by rigorous civil laws. It should not be forgotten that many other factors, on the part of the celebrant and on the part of the ministers and surroundings, are required to make the celebration genuinely worthy and meaningful.

Provisional altars, constructed in front of the main altars for celebration *versus populum*, should gradually disappear, giving way to a more permanent arrangement of the place of sacrifice.

In making these necessary arrangements regarding the altar where Mass is normally celebrated on Sundays and feast days, especial care should be taken concerning the positioning of the tabernacle, giving it a place completely worthy of it according to the indications and norms already given by this Consilium. In each and every case where it is intended to put the tabernacle in a place other than on the altar, the Ordinary must judge whether or not all requirements are met in the

---

[b]   *Sic*. The French has "in regard both to singing and to musical instruments."

[c]   See DOL 31 nos. 415–416.

alternative proposal. It is therefore excluded that a decision of this nature be left to the liturgical commissions, national or diocesan, and even less to individual priests.

7. WOMEN SERVING AT THE ALTAR

Finally, there have not been entirely wanting those who, acting on arbitrary   429
interpretations of one or other of the articles in the Constitution, have believed it lawful to allow women and girls to serve at the altar in the sacred ceremonies. A woman has a right and duty to a *munus liturgicum*, and quite how far this goes has yet to be accurately studied, but that under present-day legislation women have no *ministerium* at the altar is certain. The *ministerium* depends upon the will of the Church, and the Church has never extended this liturgical *ministerium* to women. Accordingly, any arbitrary innovation in this field is a grave infraction of church discipline and should be firmly eliminated.

Your Excellency is asked *to kindly pass on these points to the bishops, but "only" to the bishops*, of your conference. These points have as their aim, the giving of some norms in order that the conference and their excellencies themselves might formulate and communicate concrete directives to the liturgical commissions and clergy of their respective dioceses.

I wish to express my fraternal and earnest thanks for whatever you may be able to do in this regard.

33. PAUL VI, **Homily** at the Parish of Mary Immaculate in Rome, excerpt on themes and objectives of the Council regarding reform of the liturgy, 27 March 1966: Not 2 (1966) 121–122 (Italian).

A second undertaking of the Council is the reform of the liturgy, and in a most   430
beautiful and fruitful direction. The Council has taken the fundamental position that the faithful have to understand what the priest is saying and to share in the liturgy; to be not just passive spectators at Mass but souls alive; to be the people of God responsive to him and forming a community gathered as one around the celebrant.

Look at the altar, placed now for dialogue with the assembly; consider the remarkable sacrifice of Latin, the priceless repository of the Church's treasure. The repository has been opened up, as the people's own spoken language now becomes part of their prayer. Lips that have often been still, sealed as it were, now at last begin to move, as the whole assembly can speak its part in the colloquy with the priest, at least during the preparatory and dismissal rites of the Mass. No longer do we have the sad phenomenon of people being conversant and vocal about every human subject yet silent and apathetic in the house of God. How sublime it is to hear during Mass the communal recitation of the Our Father!

In this way the Sunday Mass is not just an obligation but a pleasure, not just fulfilled as a duty, but claimed as a right. To be entitled to go to Mass, to rest from work on Sunday, to devote at least one hour a week to the aspirations of the spirit is an inalienable possession: the capacity to speak to God of one's sorrows, hopes, toil, of every anxiety; it is to bring to God the experiences of the week with its daily trials and to offer all to him. At Mass the Lord transforms them all into himself, becoming in the eucharist our food and drink, as the bread and wine are symbols of all human strivings. In the eucharist, then, the Lord transforms our human existence into one that is divine.

Be, then, fervent at the Sunday Mass; hold on to it jealously; endeavor to fill every corner of your parish church, to be part of a host of people surrounding the altar. Say to your priests: make us understand; open the book to us. And learn to sing. A Mass celebrated with the song of the people makes for the full raising up of the spirit. St. Ambrose — one of the first bishops to introduce sacred singing into the Christian community — expressed this striking thought: "When I hear an entire assembly sing with one voice 'Holy, Holy, Holy, Lord God' my spirit is flooded with happiness; nothing in the world can possess such grandeur and majesty."

This is the sublime reality: humanity reaches the heights; it speaks to God and makes itself heard in heaven with the voices of all: of children, of men and women, of the suffering. Humanity sings a hymn to the glory of God "in the highest," asks for and receives "peace to his people on earth."

34. PAUL VI, **Address** to a general audience, on liturgical participation in Holy Week, 6 April 1966: Not 2 (1966) 122–123 (Italian).

431   You will find it natural, beloved sons and daughters, . . . for us to take this meeting as an opportunity for urging you to give this week the importance belonging to it and to look on it as the central and decisive point in the spiritual cycle of the entire year. To give this week its due value brings with it an obligation and a right to participate in Holy Week in some way and to some degree.

"Participation": here is one of the ecumenical Council's most often repeated and most forceful affirmations bearing on divine worship, on the liturgy. So much so that this affirmation can be termed one of the distinguishing principles of the conciliar teaching and reform. The word recurs most explicitly many times: ". . . Pastors [to them before all others the Council addresses its words] must therefore realize that when the liturgy is celebrated something more is required than the mere observance of the laws governing valid and lawful celebration; it is their duty also to ensure that the faithful take part fully aware of what they are doing, actively engaged in the rite, and enriched by its effects" (SC art. 11).[a] Then the Council turns to the faithful: "The Church earnestly desires that all the faithful be led to that full, conscious, and active participation in liturgical celebrations called for by the very nature of the liturgy. Such participation by the Christian people as 'a chosen race, a royal priesthood, a holy nation, God's own people' (1 Pt 2:9; see also 2:4–5) is their right and duty by reason of their baptism." The liturgy is "the primary and indispensable source from which the people are to derive the true Christian spirit" (SC art. 14).[b]

We could go on adding similar passages. The mind of the Church is unmistakable: the Christian people must not be merely passively present at the rites of divine worship; they must grasp its meaning and join themselves to it in such a way that the celebration is full, alive, and communal (see SC art. 21).[c] On this point we can say rightly that the *aggiornamento* of the Council has meant a return to both the historical and interior fonts of Christian spirituality (see J. Jungmann, *Tradition liturgique et problèmes actuels de pastorale*, 82).

---

[a]   DOL 1 no. 11.

[b]   DOL 1 no. 14.

[c]   See DOL 1 no. 21.

And so, dearest children, we offer these two remarks for your reflection. The   432
first concerns the qualities of liturgical participation as the Council proposes it.
First, that it be fully aware, a quality that of itself would suffice to inspire a
humanistic *apologia* for religion as the Church instills it into the faithful. The
Church's prayer is not esoteric, nor remote from people's comprehension; rather it
goes out to meet their capabilities and desire to know and to grasp. The Church's
prayer takes for its own the words of Christ: "They shall all be taught by God, *Erunt
omnes docibiles Dei*" (Jn 6:45). "Active and personal," this is a second quality of
liturgical participation, and the third is that it be "communal." If only we may fully
understand these realities! We will then say with Jesus: "If you know these things,
blessed are you if you do them, *Si haec scitis, beati eritis si feceritis ea*" (Jn 13:17).

The second remark brings us back to Holy Week. If there is any liturgy that
should find us all drawn together, attentive, earnest, and united through a participation that is ever more full, worthy, devout, and loving, it is the liturgy of Holy
Week. The reason is clear and it is profound: the paschal mystery that in Holy
Week has its most exalted and moving expression is not just one point in the
liturgical year; it is the source of all other celebrations of the year. All others point
to the mystery of our redemption — and that is the paschal mystery (see Jungmann,
op. cit. 341ff.).

35. SC RITES (Consilium), **Declaration** *Da qualche tempo*, repudiating arbi-
trary liturgical innovations, 29 December 1966: AAS 59 (1967) 85–86; Not
3 (1967) 37–38 (Italian).

For some time now certain newspapers and magazines have been providing for   433
their readers reports and pictures of liturgical ceremonies, especially celebrations of
the eucharist, that are foreign to Catholic worship and quite unbelievable. "Family
eucharistic meals" followed by dinner are celebrated in private homes; there are
Masses with novel and improvised rites, vestments, and texts, sometimes with
music of an altogether profane and worldy character, unworthy of a sacred service.
These travesties of worship, springing from mere private initiative, tend inevitably
to desacralize the liturgy, the purest expression of the worship the Church offers to
God.

Appeal to pastoral renewal as a motive is completely ruled out; renewal develops in an orderly way, not haphazardly. All the practices in question are at odds
with the letter and spirit of Vatican II's Constitution on the Liturgy and harmful to
the unity and dignity of the people of God.

Pope Paul VI said on 13 October of this year: "Diversity in language and
newness in ritual are, it is true, factors that the desire for reform has introduced into
liturgy. Nothing is to be adopted however that has not been duly approved by
authority of the bishops, fully mindful of their office and obligations, and by this
Apostolic See. Nothing should be allowed that is unworthy of divine worship,
nothing that is obviously profane or unfit to express the inner, sacred power of
prayer. Nothing odd or unusual is allowable, since such things, far from fostering
devotion in the praying community, rather shock and upset it and impede the
proper and rightful cultivation of a devotion faithful to tradition."[a]

While deploring the practices described and the attendant publicity, we ur-   434
gently invite Ordinaries, both local and religious, to watch over the right applica-

---
[a] DOL 84 no. 634.

tion of the Constitution on the Liturgy. With kindness but firmness they should dissuade those who, whatever their good intentions, sponsor such exhibitions. Where these occur, Ordinaries should reprove the abuses, banning any experiment not authorized and guided by the hierarchy and not conducive to a reform in keeping with the mind of the Council, so that the noble work of renewal may develop without deviation and produce those results in the life of Christians that the Church expects.

We add the reminder that apart from those cases envisioned by liturgical law and therein precisely defined, celebration of Mass in private homes is unlawful.

36. CONSILIUM, **Editorial** *Expériences liturgiques*, on liturgical experimentation, December 1966: Not 2 (1966) 345–346 (French).

435   In its responsibility for the reform of the liturgical books, the Consilium has, for three years and with the dedicated and able collaboration of its two hundred *periti*, been at work without letup. Approved provisorily by the Consilium and with the concurrence of Pope Paul VI, some of the reformed rites are actually being tested in certain countries, under immediate supervision by the local bishop: two cases in point are the rites for the baptism of adults and for the funerals of adults. Everyone is aware also that for a year now certain weekday lectionaries have been authorized *ad experimentum* during the interim until the complete revision of the Roman Lectionary. The rites for concelebration and communion under both kinds, during the intervening months since their promulgation on 7 March 1965, have undergone a productive period of testing. Such is the way for an intelligent reform of the liturgy to proceed, by testing the work of experts in the concrete conditions of actual use. It is hardly necessary to recall that this kind of experimentation is marked by *orderliness*, on the basis, that is, of planned projects that undergo long preparation and careful review, followed by authorized approval for their limited, controlled use and by regular reports on their status to higher authority.

"Experiments" that spring up here and there under individual initiative or as the vagaries of some special group are another matter altogether. You hear about them by chance as you travel or talk to priests or laypersons or even as you read periodicals. They leave you dumbfounded, speechless . . .

Cardinal G. Lercaro, President of the Consilium, on 30 June 1965 requested presidents of the conferences of bishops "to put a stop to any personal, precipitate, and harmful innovations; God does not bless them and they are, therefore, without power to achieve any lasting results" (see Not 1 [1965] 259).[a] Now more than a year and a half has passed and nothing has changed. In one place new formularies, created out of the blue, for the Mass, even for the canon, are being circulated secretly or openly and used in the liturgy. Elsewhere there is a total disregard for the actual legislation governing use of the vernacular. In other places there are liturgical gestures having no other justification than the personal opinion of the celebrant or the gathered community.

436   Now there even is a move toward legitimating this situation. The line taken is that a living liturgy is of its nature a creative liturgy. This creativity cannot be the narrow monopoly of the agencies of church authority; it is at work as well among all the Christian people as they celebrate the liturgy, which thereby receives a new birth, the manifestation of its vitality. There is, of course, the expected disclaimer

---

[a] DOL 31 no. 412.

about the need to avoid license that would lead to anarchy. But that simply means the need to have recourse to the discernment of spirits in order to distinguish genuine charism from misguided novelty . . .

The partial truth in this outlook cannot be allowed to destroy the basic character of Christian worship: that it is just as much hierarchic as it is communitarian. Official church documents repeat this over and over; on this issue it would be an affront to seek to go against the Constitution on the Liturgy and other supporting conciliar documents (Constitution on the Church; the Decree *Christus Dominus*, the Constitution *Gaudium et spes*).

In two passages the Constitution on the Liturgy speaks of "adaptation" (art. 40) and of the "research and experimentation required" (art. 44).[b] Both repeat that all of this must be carried out in right order, under immediate supervision by the hierarchy, and with explicit authorization from the Holy See *de consensu Apostolicae Sedis; ab Apostolica Sede facultas tribuatur*. As Cardinal Lercaro points out in the letter mentioned, these experiments "were envisioned as something reserved to those best prepared and selected, as limited to a fixed period of time, and as supervised by ecclesiastical authority . . . No one is allowed experimentation without explicit authorization" (loc. cit., 260).[c] The Consilium welcomes constructive suggestions, whatever the source, "to assure that the reform will be the work of the whole Church" (ibid., 259).[d] But the Consilium equally rejects and deplores individual or group innovations carried out arbitrarily; these badly hamper the advance of the liturgical reform. Patience and obedience: this is the price for the work in which we are engaged.

37. SC RITES (Consilium), **Press Conference** of A. Bugnini, regarding the Declaration of 29 December 1966,[a] 4 January 1967: Not 1 (1967) 39–45.

1.   Before anything else, there are three basic remarks to be made.   437

a.   First, we are in a peculiar period of transition regarding the liturgy. The Council has approved a constitution on it that to be put fully into effect requires time, reflection, and study. A reform of Catholic worship cannot be accomplished in a day or a month, nor even in a year. The issue is not simply one of touching up, so to speak, a priceless work of art; in some areas entire rites have to be restructured *ex novo*. Certainly this involves restoring, but ultimately I would almost call it a remaking and at certain points a creating anew.

Why a work that is so radical?

Because the vision of the liturgy the Council has given us is completely diverse from what we had before. From being regarded primarily as rubrical, formalistic, centralized, the liturgy has now been given an expression in its dogmatic, biblical, and pastoral character. The liturgy looks for ways to make itself intelligible in word, symbol, gesture, sign. The liturgy is striving to adapt itself to the mentality, genius, aspirations, and needs of every people and so to touch them deeply and bring Christ to them. As for its juridical aspects, the disposition of the liturgy is now to a great extent in the hands of the conferences of bishops, in some respects in

---

b   DOL 1 nos. 40 and 44.

c   DOL 31 no. 413.

d   DOL 31 no. 412.

a   See DOL 35.

those of the local Ordinary, even of the priest celebrating. If the restored liturgy — ineptly labeled by some the "new" liturgy — were to fail to reach its new horizons, then the work of renewal would be a failure. We are not working on a museum piece, but aiming at a living liturgy for the living people of our own times.

b. There is a second preliminary point I would make. I have spoken of a restoring and a creating anew. Clearly, these two must be brought into perfect harmony if the resulting work is still to be called the liturgy in the pure Roman tradition, created by the Church over the centuries, and at the same time is to be the liturgy suited to our age.

The first condition is basic and indispensable for the second. We build upon rock and not upon sand precisely because in its acts of worship the Church has expressed its faith and, in a sense, its own being.

What, however, are those truly ancient elements that form the core, the solid and indestructible center of the majestic tree that at once expresses the perennial faith of the Church and is capable of putting out new growth so as to sustain faith today?

To that question are directed the art, the secret, the delicate, and serious work of the 250 *periti* who labor in the Consilium.

c. One further remark. The work of reforming the liturgy is not an easy one and, what is more, in a certain sense time is running against us. The Constitution on the Liturgy is in everyone's hands, the liturgical movement, tirelessly in progress now for more than half a century, has created in the clergy and in a large segment of the laity an interest and a certain sophistication in matters of the liturgy. It has also, without doubt, created in them a right. Now three years have gone by since the Constitution; its applications have been, while important, too few.

The result has been the temptation in some places and settings to jump the gun and improvise.

Other factors, positive as well as negative, that prevail in all parts of today's world, including the ecclesiastical, encourage the overturning of apparent barriers and too great a readiness to bewail conservatism.

438   2.   These remarks indicate the background of the Declaration of 12 December 1966. What indeed is its import, in letter and spirit?

First of all, why did the two agencies of the Roman Curia charged with responsibility for the liturgy make so weighty a statement as a Declaration? Because everywhere[1] to some degree, like germs, those phenomena and events have appeared which have been so widely publicized in certain sectors of the press; and like germs they could grow and spread further.

The Declaration, therefore, serves as a red light signaling one direction that is blocked against those whose intentions are good but whose steps are impetuous.

That being said, I must add that since the Declaration was published there has been some confusion about it that should be cleared up. It refers to "family eucharistic meals," celebrated in a home and followed by dinner. Clearly a limited issue is involved.

First, the reason for this is that for the celebration of the eucharist, or for that matter of any liturgical rite, God has willed and the Church has set aside for God a separate site, a place, an altar, dedicated in solemn rites, where the Christian com-

---

[1]   It has been alleged that the Declaration was intended for one particular nation or another. Not at all: the phenomena at issue are quite universal, even if the reports and photographs in the press have focused on a specific region. That is why as spokesman I have avoided getting into the particulars highlighted by some, even the less suspect, organs of the press. To describe the Declaration as "ridiculous" or charge Rome with "insincerity" evinces either an irresponsible shallowness or contentiousness.

munity is gathered as God's living temple to offer him a sacrifice of praise. Private homes, or some other building, as well as the open air, are allowed for Mass absolutely as exceptions required by altogether peculiar circumstances; such cases cannot be brought up as precedents.[2]

Second, the eucharist, in which Christ is present under the appearances of bread and wine, is a reality quite distinct from a family meal, a convivial gathering, or, as the ancients called it, an agape. Never is the eucharist an ordinary meal. Christ instituted it during the Passover supper. In the first centuries of the Church the combining of the eucharistic celebration with the agape occurred. But it quickly became apparent that this combination had disadvantages and that it was necessary to set the agape off from the eucharistic celebration. By the third century nowhere in the Christian world did they any longer go together. This practice the Church has observed right up to the present. To try to go back to a worship form abandoned now for sixteen centuries would be an anachronism without doctrinal or pastoral justification.

A *third* point is perhaps not out of place. Celebration of the eucharist in private homes would minimalize and dilute the full meaning of the Church as the gathering of the holy people of God in their diverse, many-sided, and close-knit composition. To break down the act of worship, communal by its essence, into tiny groups of people would be to impoverish the universality of faith and of charity "toward all."

3.   The Declaration refers also to "Masses with novel and improvised rites, vest-   439
ments, and texts."[b]

Everyone knows that liturgical ceremonies are minutely determined in laws called rubrics, which only the Church has the right to specify and, as required, to change. This really is a matter of the Church's encasing with beauty the jewel received from Christ in order to guard it and to exhibit its precious value and mystery to every age. To set only at a human level all that involves the sacred, that is, all that touches on mystery, is not to draw nearer to God but rather to grow farther away. That is why the Church has no intention of confusing the sacred with the profane, the earthly with the supernatural.

4.   *Song*. There is also an allusion to music that is "profane and worldly."[c] The first   440
adjective, it seems to me, refers to the type of music; the second, to its style of performance.

A great deal could be said about this issue, which so much engages public opinion; but I will be brief.

St. Pius X, the first to deal with the issue of singing as a part of pastoral liturgy, in his well-known Motu Proprio *Tra le sollecitudini* (1903) forbade "lascivious" songs, and instruments that are "raucous and frivolous." It is, we must admit, not always

---

[2]   Altogether outside the point of the Declaration is the case where there is no church, or the group of Catholics is small, or the distance too great, or Christianity is just newly introduced, and where, with permission of the local Ordinary, Mass is celebrated in a decent place provided by a family where the faithful gather to take part in the Mass, especially on weekdays. Always with the Ordinary's permission and supervision, the same could occur in the crowded sections of the great cities or in the special circumstances of dechristianized areas, where the needs of a specialized, organized, and planned pastoral ministry requires such an arrangement at the beginning.

In such cases the conferences of bishops or at least the individual bishop would make the judgment on the advisability of this course and lay down the right conditions to be carried out for proper order. These, however, are all passing situations, which in no way ought to compromise the normal weekday church services and far less weaken or jeopardize the principle that the people of God assemble on Sunday.

[b]   DOL 35 no. 433.

[c]   DOL 35 no. 433.

easy to identify these two qualities. As to the words of songs, the question is easier because, reflecting as they do the fads and fashions of the moment, sentimental verses are readily recognized.

But what of melody? Every age has its tastes, preferences, and mode of expression. Like all art music is a sign revealing the times.

As for musical instruments, St. Pius X was quite explicit in banning those that are "raucous and frivolous" from places of worship. Clearly he had in mind the Western culture of the Latin Church. Is such a criterion valid today? Only partly so. This is the reason that, after recommending use of the traditional instruments, the Constitution on the Liturgy adds: "Other instruments also may be admitted for use in divine worship, with the knowledge and consent of the competent territorial authority [i.e., the conference of bishops]. This applies, however, only on condition that [1] the instruments are suitable, or can be made suitable, for sacred use, [2] are in accord with the dignity of the place of worship, and [3] truly contribute to the uplifting of the faithful" (art. 120).[d]

This is the necessary basis for judging new musical forms. The Declaration asserts that, at least in some instances, these three conditions have not been respected. The music it mentions is "profane," thus not worthy of the place of worship; "worldly," that is, of a style whose performance requires or seems to require movements, gestures, and attitudes unworthy of a sacred service.

Does that foreclose every further development of today's percussion music for liturgy?[3] The Declaration does not permit such an inference, but it is not difficult to perceive that there would have to be a great deal of sacralization before that kind of music can legitimately cross the church threshold.

441   5.   The Declaration also makes reference to a pastoral *aggiornamento* as motive.

It is the motive that reveals and, in a degree, proves the upright intention of those who have thrown themselves into personal and arbitrary innovations in the field of liturgy. Their intent in this has been to encourage the practice of the faith or to offer a remedy for a growing indifference and disaffection — often quite emphatic — toward religious practices. This is another case where the end does not justify the means.[4] Indeed in this instance the means chosen are quite unenlightened. We hardly need repeat that the liturgy is hierarchic, that is, the disposition of the liturgy cannot be the business of any individual, but belongs to the Church. All individualistic attempts "are contrary to the ecclesial meaning of the liturgy and harmful to the Church's unity," in addition to being shocking, disturbing, and confusing to the faithful.

At times some speak of experiments from a viewpoint altogether in conflict with and foreign to that of the Council.

---

[d]   DOL 1 no. 120.

[3]   This is the music the Declaration refers to and not, in any way, as those with preconceived notions would have it, the modern music composed, especially after 7 March 1965, for a vernacular liturgical text in various countries (entire Masses, or responsorial-psalm melodies or hymn tunes).

This kind of music, just as that by any composer for the Latin text, is subject to criticism, and so may vary in degree of merit. But it is not part either of the letter or spirit of the Declaration to repudiate such music. On the contrary the document serves as an impetus to the creation of a repertoire suited to liturgy in the vernacular. Time will be the judge of whether any failure here will have been due to lack of inspiration or lack of technique: that is the way time has judged so many compositions for Latin texts that have passed into oblivion.

[4]   Not even an ecumenical end can suffice, as a certain reporter seems to claim, overenthusiastically. The delicate issue of ecumenism is also guided and regulated by the Church with norms that are wise, safe, and prudent; the end is to reach a *union* that is enlightened, convinced, and lasting, not a union at any price. Thus in this area, as well, the measures of the "illuminati" do not help.

The argument goes like this: private individuals or groups conduct liturgical experiments, then from these the hierarchy will choose those that better answer to people's needs.

Anyone can see the latent danger of disorder, anarchy, and recalcitrance contained in such a position. The Constitution speaks of experimentation twice, in art. 40 and art. 44. The first text concerns experiments in preparation for the adoption of a rite. The competent, territorial ecclesiastical authority (that is, the conference of bishops) will permit and direct such experiments "within certain groups suited for the purpose and for a fixed time" *after having obtained the permission from the Holy See.*[e] Article 44 concerns experiments promoted by the territorial ecclesiastical authority (that is, the conference of bishops) with a view to *adaptations to be proposed to the Holy See,*[f] that is, the adaptations spoken of in art. 40. Whatever the liturgical experiment, in the mind of the Constitution it comes within the competence of the hierarchy: the conference of bishops and the Holy See. Any other experiment that does not follow this course is *contra legem.*

Every arbitrary measure is an injury to the Constitution, the liturgy, and the *sensus Ecclesiae.*

6.   Allow me, finally, to draw attention to the Declaration's appeal to Ordinaries   442
to watch over and promote the liturgical movement.

Their charge, then, is twofold.

The Constitution has in fact created a new situation in law between the center and the circumference, between the Holy See and its governing agencies and the bishops. The bishops are no longer, as they were before the Council, simply the faithful executors of the decisions of the Holy See; rather they have the responsibility of promoting liturgical life in the direction willed by the Council and of taking the initiative, within the sphere of their own competence, in organizing diocesan, regional, and national liturgical commissions, in preparing the translation of liturgical texts, in investigating and proposing adaptations and experiments, etc. The bishops have an immense area of work and great responsibility.

They must meet the challenge. Sometimes it is the inertia or slowness of the agencies charged with leading that opens the way to personal and arbitrary innovations that threaten the liturgical movement and do harm to everyone.

Out of respect for the truth, I must add that as far as I can judge the conferences of bishops and the national liturgical commissions, which ultimately bear the burden of the Declaration's appeal, are proceeding step by step, fully aware of their own responsibilities and the immense possibilities open to them. Almost all the liturgical commissions are hard at work on the preparation of texts and an effective catechesis of the people.

The course in process is one of great labor but also of great hope, above all of great love; for the liturgy is being revitalized, in the way St. Pius X wished, as the first and indispensable source of the genuine Christian spirit.

---

e   DOL 1 no. 40.

f   See DOL 1 no. 44.

38. CONSILIUM, **Editorial** *Mecanique et Liturgie*, on mechanical devices in the liturgy, January 1967: Not 3 (1967) 3–4 (French).

443   Three articles in the 1958 Instruction of the Congregation of Rites drew attention to the danger involved in the intrusion of mechanical musical instruments into the liturgical movement. A general principle is laid down in article 60 c: "The only musical instruments allowed in liturgy are those that a person must play; those operated mechanically or automatically are excluded." This is made more detailed further on: "Use in liturgy of instruments and 'automatic' devices, for example, the electric organ, phonograph, radio, dictaphone or tape recorder, and the like is absolutely forbidden. This applies to liturgies celebrated either inside a church or outdoors and includes broadcasts of sermons or sacred music, as well as records of singers or a congregation to replace or support the singing at a liturgy" (art. 71). Lastly, it is forbidden "to use in place of blessed bells any kind of mechanical means to imitate or amplify their sound" (art. 91).

Why in this era of remarkable inventions does divine worship insistently disdain progress?

Admittedly no one has any problem about using the countless, modern mechanical means for the construction, adornment, heating, and acoustics of places of worship. Microphones permit even those at the back of the largest churches to hear the voice of the celebrant, preacher, reader, or commentator (provided of course these have learned how to use a microphone).

When, however, the issue is the basic principles of celebration, the Church wishes at all cost fidelity to that "worship in spirit and truth" that the Lord Jesus has initiated. For that brings in human beings, in their complete person, body and soul; their participation in the mystery of salvation, present sacramentally and at work, engages their whole being. Neither the celebrant, the people in the body of the church, nor the organist can be reduced to the status of a machine, a robot, a tape recorder. Theirs must be the presence of the holy people of God, praying, singing, playing the music in a single-minded faith, a vital hope, and a burning charity. They do these things, to be sure, with the means they possess, their own physical and spiritual capacities (and it is to be hoped that these will always be improving). But the often quite modest quality of their praying, singing, or playing is of a level in the realm of sacred signs far surpassing the perfection of the recording of a prayer, a song, or instrumental music. To introduce such recordings would be artificial and, in fact, a lie. What is quite legitimate in the context of preparing a liturgy or in the many other expressions of religious culture is totally out of place within the liturgical assembly. For this necessarily means living, acting people entering into communion with mystery.[R32]

[R32] Query: Recently (20 Jan. 1977) a daily newspaper carried an advertisement for a "Mass for Parish Communities," a record and a tape of instrumental music to accompany voices for use in the eucharistic celebration by communities that have no musical instruments. In view of the high standard of the newspaper carrying this advertisement, we ask whether such a means is to be allowed in the celebration of the liturgy. Reply: The entire liturgy rests upon the use of signs and to be effective these signs must be authentic and truthful. The reform and sensitive adaptation of the liturgy has this as one of its main purposes. Sacred music and singing are signs and signs that are to be expressed as authentic and truthful by a living, praying congregation of the faithful, not by a simulated congregation. Already in 1958 Pope Pius XII's Instruction *De musica sacra et sacra Liturgia* stated the principle that sound equipment is most useful for the learning of chants and for supporting voices during open-air processions, but that they are barred from celebrations "in a place of worship." Since that time the norms in official documents have not been changed. The one exception is the Directory for Masses with Children no. 32 [DOL 276 no. 2165], which mentions use of recorded music, with, however, due caution and prudence. It is not by chance that the recent instruction of the bishops of Italy on Masses with children clearly states that the use of music which consists exclusively in recorded singing is unlawful: Not 13 (1977) 94, no. 1.

The demand for truth and authenticity, so compelling for the people of today, makes its presence felt throughout the entire sphere of worship. No electrical lighting will ever have the value of the living flame of wax or oil being visibly consumed as an offering to the Lord, the Light eternal, or as homage to the saints. The illumination of the Church with the candles of the congregation at the Easter Vigil is a rite simple yet full of meaning, bringing to mind both the resurrection and the faith. How ridiculous it would become if candles were exchanged for flashlights.

444

Recently someone has invented a wondrous gadget that by the press of a button drops the altar breads one by one into a ciborium and counts them, to the delight of the statisticians. How much more natural, beautiful, and symbolic of sharing in the sacred meal is the simple human action of each person placing a host into a ciborium or onto a paten.

The liturgical reform has its own distinctive way of safeguarding the nobility of objects and of actions. Any reaction it has against the danger of mechanization in worship is not based on antiquarianism. The motive rather is that the worship of God ought to lead people to a sense of the sacred and of mystery and to make the whole of creation be permeated with the renewal of the New Covenant.

39. SC RITES (Consilium), **Instruction** (second) *Tres abhinc annos*, on the orderly carrying out of the Constitution on the Liturgy, 4 May 1967: AAS 59 (1967) 442–448; Not 3 (1967) 169–194.

Three years ago the Instruction *Inter Oecumenici*, issued by the Congregation of Rites, 26 September 1964,[a] established a number of adaptations for introduction into the sacred rites. These adaptations, the firstfruits of the general liturgical reform called for by the conciliar Constitution on the Liturgy, took effect on 7 March 1965.

445

Their rich yield is becoming quite clear from the many reports of bishops, which attest to an increased, more aware, and intense participation of the faithful everywhere in the liturgy, especially in the holy sacrifice of the Mass.

To increase this participation even more and to make the liturgical rites, especially the Mass, clearer and better understood, the same bishops have proposed certain other adaptations. Submitted first to the Consilium, the proposals have undergone careful examination and discussion by the Consilium and the Congregation of Rites.

At least for the moment, not every proposal can be sanctioned. Others, however, do seem worth putting into effect immediately, because pastoral considerations commend them and they seem to offer no hindrance to the definitive reform of the liturgy yet to come. Further, they seem advantageous for the gradual introduction of that reform and are feasible simply by altering rubrics, not the existing liturgical books.

446

On this occasion it seems necessary to recall to everyone's mind that capital principle of church discipline which the Constitution on the Liturgy solemnly confirmed. "Regulation of the liturgy depends solely on the authority of the Church. Therefore no other person, not even if he is a priest, may on his own add, take away, or change anything in the liturgy" (SC art. 22, §§ 2–3).

---

[a] See DOL 23.

Ordinaries, both local and religious, should therefore be mindful of their grave duty before the Lord to watch carefully over observance of this norm, so important for church life and order. All ministers of sacred rites as well as all the faithful should also willingly conform to it.

Individual spiritual growth and well-being demand this, as do harmonious cooperation in the Lord and mutual good example among the faithful in any local community. It is required also by the serious responsibility of each community to cooperate for the good of the Church throughout the world, especially today when the good or evil that develops in local communities quickly has an impact on the fabric of the whole family of God.

All should heed the warning of the Apostle: "For God is not a God of discord but of peace" (1 Cor 14:33).

The following adaptations and changes are instituted to achieve the more specific actualization and measured progress of the liturgical reform.

I. OPTIONS IN THE TEXTS FOR MASS

447   1.   Outside Lent, on days of class III, the Mass either of the office of the day or of the commemoration made at morning prayer may be celebrated. If the second is chosen, the color of the office of the day may be used, in keeping with the *Codex rubricarum* no. 323.

448   2.   Once the conference of bishops in its own region has sanctioned an order of readings for weekdays in Masses with a congregation[b] this may also be used for Masses celebrated without a congregation and the readings may be in the vernacular.

This order of readings for weekdays may be used on certain days of class II, to be indicated in the lectionary itself, and in all Masses of class III and IV, whether Masses of the season or of saints, or votive Masses not having their own, strictly proper readings, that is, those that mention the mystery or person being celebrated.

449   3.   On weekdays in Ordinary Time, in the celebration of the Mass of the Sunday preceding, one of the Prayers for Various Needs or an opening prayer from the votive Masses for Various Needs may be taken from the Missal to replace the prayer of the Sunday Mass.

II. PRAYERS IN THE MASS

450   4.   In the Mass only one prayer is to be said; depending on the rubrics, however, there is added before the single conclusion:

      a.   the prayer proper to a rite (*Codex rubricarum* no. 447);

            the prayer from the Mass for the profession of men or women religious, displacing the Mass of the day (*Rubr. spec. Missalis*);

            the prayer from the votive Mass *Pro sponsis* displaced by the Mass of the day (*Codex rubricarum* no. 380).

      b.   the prayer from the votive Mass of thanksgiving (*Codex rubricarum* no. 382 and *Rubr. spec. Missalis*);

            the prayer for the anniversaries of the pope and the bishop (*Codex rubricarum* nos. 449–450);

            the prayer for the anniversary of the priest's own ordination (*Codex rubricarum* nos. 451–452).

---

   b   See DOL 229.

5. If in the same Mass several prayers were to be required before the single   451
conclusion, the only one added in fact is the one most in keeping with the celebration.

6. Instead of an imperated prayer, the bishop may insert one or more intentions   452
for particular needs into the general intercessions.

In them by decree of the conference of bishops intentions also may be included
for civil rulers (now used in various forms in the different countries) and special
intentions for the particular needs of a nation or region.

III. CHANGES IN THE ORDER OF MASS

7. The celebrant genuflects only: 453

    a. on going to or leaving the altar if there is a tabernacle containing the
blessed sacrament;

    b. after elevating the host and the chalice;

    c. after the doxology at the end of the canon;

    d. at communion, before the words *Panem caelestem accipiam*;

    e. after the communion of the faithful, when he has placed the remaining
hosts in the tabernacle.

All other genuflections are omitted.

8. The celebrant kisses the altar only: at the beginning of Mass, while saying the   454
Oramus te Domine, or on going to the altar, if the prayers at the foot of the altar are
omitted; at the end of Mass before the blessing and dismissal of the people.

The kissing of the altar is otherwise omitted.

9. At the offertory, after offering the bread and wine, the celebrant places on the 455
corporal the paten with host and the chalice, omitting the signs of the cross with
paten and with chalice.

He leaves the paten, with the host on it, on the corporal both before and after
the consecration.

10. In Masses celebrated with a congregation, even when not concelebrated, the   456
celebrant may say the canon aloud. In sung Masses he may sing those parts of the
canon that the rite for concelebration allows.

11. In the canon, the celebrant: 457

    a. begins the *Te igitur* standing erect and with hands outstretched;

    b. makes one sign of the cross over the offerings at the words *benedicas + haec
dona, haec munera, haec sancta sacrificia illibata*, in the prayer *Te igitur*. He makes
no other sign of the cross over the offerings.

12. After the consecration, the celebrant need not join thumb and forefinger;   458
should any particle of the host have remained on his fingers, he rubs his fingers
together over the paten.[R33]

[R33] Query: In view of the permission provided in the Second Instruction not to join the thumbs and
index fingers after the consecration, may the ablution of the fingers over the chalice be omitted? Reply:
The permission not to join the thumbs and index fingers after the consecration presupposes that no
particle of the host has remained on the fingers or, if it has, that it is shaken off the fingers onto the paten.
If, therefore, these points are carefully observed, it does not seem to exceed or contravene the spirit of the
law to omit the ablution of the fingers over the chalice (the ablution to be consumed afterward by the
priest). For in these cases there is no reason for the ablution of the fingers, even as there is no reason for

459   13. The communion rite for priest and people is to have the following arrangement: after he says *Panem caelestem accipiam*, the celebrant takes the host and, facing
the people, raises it, saying the *Ecce Agnus Dei*, then adding three times with the
people the *Domine, non sum dignus*. He then communicates himself with host and
chalice and immediately distributes communion in the usual way to the people.

460   14. The faithful receiving communion at the chrism Mass on Holy Thursday may
receive again at the evening Mass on the same day.

461   15. A Mass celebrated with a congregation should include, according to circumstances, either a period of silence or the singing or recitation of a psalm or canticle
of praise, e.g., Ps 33 [34], *I will bless the Lord*, Ps 150, *Praise the Lord in his sanctuary* or the
canticles *Bless the Lord* [Dn 3:35] or *Blessed are you, O Lord* [1 Chr 29:10].

462   16. At the end of Mass the blessing of the people comes immediately before the
dismissal. It is recommended that the priest recite the *Placeat* silently as he is leaving
the altar.

       Even Masses for the dead include the blessing and usual dismissal formulary,
Ite, Missa est, unless the absolution follows immediately; in this case, omitting the
blessing, the celebrant says: *Benedicamus Domino* and proceeds to the absolution.[R34]

IV. SOME SPECIAL CASES

463   17. In nuptial Masses the celebrant says the prayers *Propitiare* and *Deus, qui potestate*
not between the *Pater noster* and its embolism, but after the breaking of bread and the
commingling, just before the *Agnus Dei*.

       In a Mass celebrated facing the people the celebrant, after the commingling
and a genuflection, may go to the bride and groom and say the prayers just mentioned. He then returns to the altar, genuflects, and continues the Mass in the usual
way.

464   18. A Mass celebrated by a priest with failing sight or otherwise infirm and having
an indult to say a votive Mass, may have the following arrangement.

       a.   The priest says the prayers and the preface of the votive Mass.

       b.   Another priest, a deacon, reader, or server is to do the readings from the
Mass of the day or from a weekday lectionary. If only a reader or server is present,
he has permission also to read the gospel, but without the *Munda cor meum, Iube,
domne, benedicere*, and *Dominus sit in corde meo*. The celebrant however says the *Dominus
vobiscum* before the reading of the gospel and at the end kisses the book.

       c.   The choir, the congregation, or even the reader may take the entrance,
offertory, and communion antiphons, and the chants between the readings.

---

joining the fingers, that is no danger that any particle of the host will be lost or profaned. Hygienic reasons
also recommend this solution, especially after the distribution of communion: Not 3 (1967) 304, no. 108.

   [R34]   Query: In Masses for the dead and weekday Masses are those rubrics peculiar to them still to be
observed? Reply: These special rubrics remain in force in Masses for the dead: the book is not kissed after
the gospel; the water is not blessed; we kneel for the opening prayer. It does not seem absolutely contrary
to the spirit of the law for there to be uniformity even on these points and for the same norms to be
followed in Masses both for the living and for the dead. The same consideration applies to the rule on
kneeling at the prayers on penitential days and in Masses for the dead. In fact it seems advantageous for
the faithful's participation to avoid multiple changes in these same rites. Therefore, it seems also to be
more advisable not to kneel at the prayers, except only on those days and occasions when the faithful are
invited to kneel by the directive *Let us kneel*: Not 4 (1968) 136, no. 115.

V. VARIATIONS IN THE DIVINE OFFICE

19. Pending complete reform of the divine office, on days of class I and class II   465
with a matins of three nocturns, recitation of any one nocturn with three psalms
and three readings is permitted. The hymn *Te Deum*, when called for by the rubrics,
comes after the third reading. In the last three days of Holy Week the pertinent
rubrics of the Roman Breviary are to be followed.[R35]

20. Private recitation leaves out the absolution and blessing before the readings as   466
well as the concluding *Tu autem*.

21. In lauds and vespers celebrated with a congregation, in place of the *capitulum*   467
there can be a longer reading from Scripture, taken, for example, from matins or
from the Mass of the day, or from a weekday lectionary, and, as circumstances
suggest, a brief homily. Unless Mass immediately follows, general intercessions
may be inserted before the prayer.

   When there are such insertions, there need only be three psalms, chosen in this
way: at lauds one of the first three, then the canticle, then the final psalm; at vespers
any three of the five psalms.

22. At compline celebrated with a congregation participating the psalms can al-   468
ways be those of Sunday.

VI. SOME VARIATIONS IN RITES FOR THE DEAD

23. The color for the office and Mass for the dead may in all cases be violet. But   469
the conferences of bishops have the right to stipulate another color suited to the
sensibilities of the people, not out of keeping with human grief, and expressive of
Christian hope as enlightened by the paschal mystery.

24. At the absolution over the coffin and over the grave, other responsories taken   470
from matins for the dead, namely, *Credo quod Redemptor meus vivit, Qui Lazarum resusci-
tasti, Memento mei, Deus, Libera me, Domine, de viis inferni,* may replace the *Libera me,
Domine*.

VII. VESTMENTS

25. The maniple is no longer required.   471

26. The celebrant may wear the chasuble for the *Asperges* before Mass on Sundays,   472
for the blessing and imposition of ashes on Ash Wednesday, and for the absolution
over a coffin or grave.

27. A concelebrant must wear the vestments obligatory for individual celebration   473
of Mass (*Rite of Concelebration* no. 12).[c]

   When there is a serious reason, for example, a large number of concelebrants
and a lack of vestments, the concelebrants, with the principal celebrant always
excepted, may leave off a chasuble but never the alb and stole.

[R35] Query: On Sundays may the nocturn be said with only three psalms and three readings? Reply:
Sundays are either of class I or II. Matins, however, has only one nocturn with nine psalms and nine
readings. Thus the question arises: whether a person may on Sundays make use of the simplification of
matins in the Second Instruction, 14 May 1967, no. 19. The spirit of the law is to meet the needs of priests
who on Sundays are burdened with pastoral work and more pressed than on some other days of class I or
II that fall during the week. Therefore on Sunday also priests may arrange matins so that it consists of the
invitatory, hymn, three of the nine psalms given in the breviary, and three readings: Not 3 (1967) 303, no.
107.

[c] See DOL 223 no. 1805.

VIII. USE OF THE VERNACULAR

474   28. The competent territorial authority observing those matters contained in the
Constitution on the Liturgy art. 36, § 3 and § 4[d] may authorize use of the vernacular in liturgies celebrated with a congregation for:

  a. the canon of the Mass;[R36]

  b. all the rites of holy orders;[e]

  c. the readings of the divine office, even in choral recitation.

In the audience granted 13 April 1967 to the undersigned Cardinal Arcadio
Maria Larraona, Prefect of the Congregation of Rites, Pope Paul VI approved and
confirmed by his authority the present Instruction as a whole and in all its parts,
ordering its publication and its faithful observance by all concerned, beginning 29
June 1967.

40. CONSILIUM, **Letter** to presidents of the conferences of bishops and,
for their information, to presidents of the national liturgical commissions,
requesting a survey of the pastoral results of the reform of the liturgy, 15
June 1967.*

475   On a number of occasions in recent years, certain "movements" or "associations" have, in several areas, organized inquiries on the liturgical reform which
have been tendentious or based on unreal data. By falsifying the perspectives and
by captious devices, they have presented to the public false results regarding the
reaction of Catholics to the liturgical renewal promoted by the Council and desired
by our Holy Father, Pope Paul VI.

Higher authority therefore judges it opportune "to conduct an investigation,
with the cooperation of the episcopal conferences, regarding the results of the
liturgical reform, *on the pastoral level.*"

When the reform began, the Secretariat of the Consilium asked, through the
national liturgical commissions, for reports on how the first steps of the reform had
been received in different parts of the world.[a] The replies were later published in
Notitiae.

Now that we are in the third year of work on the reform, the request mentioned above offers an excellent opportunity to gather further and more precise
documentation. As far as possible, statistical data should be provided as to what has
been done in the various countries, on the results that have followed from this, and
on the reactions of people in different environments and of different social levels.

  [d] See DOL 1 no. 36.

  [R36] Query: If the priest recites the canon aloud, may the congregation respond? Reply: The priest
celebrant alone is to recite the canon, since it is a sacerdotal prayer. Therefore to the priest alone also
belong the concluding *Through Christ Our Lord* and its *Amen.* However, it is difficult to stop the faithful from
making the response *Amen* spontaneously and if they were asked not to make this response within the
canon, they might not take part at all in the concluding doxology. It therefore seems better not to disturb
the faithful if they do make the response *Amen* spontaneously within the canon: Not 4 (1968) 136, no. 114.

  [e] See Paul VI, Concession of the vernacular for the canon and for the rites of ordination, 31 Jan. 1967
[DOL 117], which is reconfirmed here.

  * English text from the Consilium.

  [a] See DOL 28.

Therefore, on behalf of His Eminence Cardinal Giacomo Lercaro, President of the Consilium, I approach Your Excellency in your capacity as president of the episcopal conference, in order that through the suitable organisms, and in particular through the national liturgical commission and diocesan liturgical commissions or other bodies normally used by the episcopal conference in inquiries of this nature, a survey may be conducted on the pastoral results of the liturgical reform in your nation.

Enclosed are indications of the points with which we are more particularly concerned. However, these are merely guidelines and more detailed questions may be drawn up in whatever way seems most fitting.

I would also ask that the reply be sent to the Consilium by 30 November of this year.

I should be very grateful to Your Excellency if you could let me know how the survey is drawn up and carried out in the area of your episcopal conference. If our Secretariat can help in any way, it is at your service.

SOME USEFUL POINTS FOR THE SURVEY

1.   On the pastoral level, has the liturgical reform brought advantages or disad-   476
vantages? Which especially?

2.   Has the number of faithful taking part in the Mass on Sundays, feasts, and weekdays, increased or decreased with the reform?

3.   Has the participation in other celebrations, in particular those of Holy Week, and above all with regard to the sacraments, increased or decreased?

4.   Has the use of the vernacular contributed to a participation which is more active and intelligent?

5.   Have the singing and the responses made in common, as an element in the participation, had a positive or a negative effect?

6.   What are the reactions of the faithful regarding the use of the vernacular, the simplification of the rites, the changes in the church and sanctuary, and church furnishings in general?[b]

41. CONSILIUM, **Letter** *Dans sa récente allocution* of Cardinal G. Lercaro to presidents of the conferences of bishops and, for their information, to presidents of the national liturgical commissions, on issues regarding reform of the liturgy, 21 June 1967: Not 3 (1967) 289–296 (French; issued in six major languages).[*]

In his recent Allocution to the Consilium, His Holiness Pope Paul VI said: "The   477
first results of the liturgical reform are, in certain respects, truly encouraging and full of promise." He invited us to optimism as we see "all that is finest and most hopeful in what our times have to offer to all who love Christ — these times which are so restless, enigmatic, yet full of earthly vitality." The Holy Father also reminded us of our serious responsibility: "It is you who, more than anybody else, are called to give that shape to the liturgy which will show its truth, beauty, and spirituality. You will ensure that the paschal mystery which lives in it may be seen

---

[b]   For replies, see Not 4 (1968) 15–33.

[*]   English text from the Consilium.

ever more clearly, for the glory of God and the spiritual renewal of the distracted but searching multitudes in the world of today" (Allocution, 19 April 1967).[a]

As I have had the pleasure of doing twice already, I should like, thanks to the assistance of Your Excellency, to address all the bishops of your conference. I should like them to join me in thanking the Lord for the marvelous fruits which are now maturing under the sun of the Holy Spirit. I wish also to ask their fraternal support for the solution of several grave problems which the realization of the first steps in liturgical reform has brought in its train.

1. OVERALL VIEW OF THE WORK COMPLETED AND COOPERATION WITH THE NATIONAL COMMISSIONS

478

The three recent Instructions of the Sacred Congregation of Rites, prepared by the Consilium and published in recent months (*Musicam sacram*, 5 March; *Tres abhinc annos*, 4 May; *Eucharisticum mysterium*, 25 May)[b] mark important steps in the putting into effect of the conciliar Constitution on the Liturgy. The work of the study groups for the reform of the liturgical books is proceeding quickly. In the foreseeable future it is possible to see the issue of this immense work of reform, impatiently awaited by the whole of the Catholic world.

Sharing with Your Excellency my satisfaction for all this labor and effort, I should like to recall to your attention the desire of the Consilium to work in close liaison with the national liturgical commissions. We continually need to have a more precise knowledge of the legitimate aspirations of the clergy and of the Christian people. For this we rely on the collaboration of the national commissions. These in fact, assisted by their specialized institutes, are in the best position to inform and document us. They can make us continually more aware of the pastoral needs for a liturgy which is genuinely expressive of contemporary man, and beneficial to him. Allow me then to ask for this necessary cooperation, the results of which will make themselves felt even in the details of the renewed rites.

2. EXPERIMENTS WITH THE NEW RITES

479

About a year ago, thanks to the work of the study groups, we began to experiment with some of the renewed rites. These were approved by the Consilium and permitted *ad experimentum* by the Holy Father. Up to now there have been the rites of adult baptism, *when it is linked with the catechumenate*, and the funeral rites for adults. Others will follow shortly. For example, there will be the rites for infant baptism, and for marriage; texts of some new prefaces will be ready, and three new forms of the eucharistic prayer.

These experiments are carried out "on projects prepared over a long period, carefully examined and emended, and duly approved for limited and controlled use, with regular reports to higher authority" (*Notitiae*, 2 [1966] 345).[c]

In order that a greater degree of uniform direction may be obtained for these experiments, and that there may be the necessary advice and help available, we have decided to entrust their execution not to private individuals, but to the national liturgical commissions. These will have the task and responsibility of preparing and organizing them. The commissions shall select the dioceses and parishes in which a serious liturgical and pastoral program will offer the best hopes for success.

[a]   DOL 86 no. 640.

[b]   See DOL 508; 39; 179.

[c]   See DOL 36 no. 435.

We have already used this procedure for some rites and intend to gradually extend it to the others when they are ready.

I should like to underline one of the more difficult and important tasks which, in the preparation of the experiments, are entrusted to the national liturgical commissions. It is for them to determine, adapting to local situations, some points for which the rites proposed *ad experimentum* leave the choice to the episcopal conferences or offer several possibilities. It is easy to see that the way of presenting these problems plays a great part in the success of the experiment and in the very future of the rite itself.

The observations and suggestions sent to the Consilium by the liturgical commissions as a result of the experiments that they have organized will be very important.

3. ARBITRARY LITURGICAL EXPERIMENTS

Besides these official experiments, it is necessary to speak, to deplore them once more, of another kind of liturgical experiment: namely, those that are introduced arbitrarily and on private initiative. I mentioned this in my letter to the presidents of the episcopal conferences on 30 June 1965 (*Notitiae*, 1 [1965] 259).[d] The situation today is considerably more alarming than two years ago, due to the widespread nature of these experiments. Many priests alter the gestures and texts of the liturgy in order to follow their own inclinations, personal tastes, or the desires of some group of the faithful. They change the translations duly approved by the episcopal conferences and confirmed by the Apostolic See. They justify this manner of acting by stating that it is necessary to have experiments in a living environment and that it is necessary to put into effect as quickly as possible the orientation given by the Council towards simplicity, truth, and intelligibility. It is asserted that not all can be done by the central organisms and that room must be made for the legitimate aspirations of the Christian people. Sometimes they even try to find in other conciliar documents arguments for insisting on the right to creative expression in liturgical matters by the living community.

480

Recently, renewing his confidence in the Consilium, the Holy Father did however express his sadness and concern regarding certain manifestations of community worship "which often deliberately take on arbitrary forms, sometimes in total disaccord with the norms in force in the Church." The Holy Father expressed "his hope that the bishops will keep a close watch on such episodes and that they will maintain the balance proper to Catholic worship in the liturgical and religious domain." He also addressed himself to religious, the clergy and all the faithful "in order that they may not let themselves be carried away by the attraction of capricious experiments but may try rather to give to the rites prescribed by the Church their perfection and plenitude" (Allocution of 19 April 1967).[e]

481

I know I may trust in Your Excellency's zeal that in the area of the conference in which you preside, clergy and people will respond with faithful, total, and filial obedience to the appeal of the Holy Father; that, in your country, these arbitrary experiments which are "dangerous for the peace and order of the Church" (ibid.)[f] may take no hold, or, if need be, may disappear. All can understand that the liturgical reform cannot be carried out arbitrarily, in disorder, and with ill-considered speed. On the contrary, it requires order, obedience, and patience.

---

[d]   See DOL 31 no. 412.

[e]   DOL 86 no. 639.

[f]   DOL 86 no. 639.

4. ADAPTATIONS IN THE LITURGY

482   In the same Allocution of 19 April 1967, the Holy Father also recalled that one of the tasks of the Consilium is that of "wisely directing each liturgical experiment, of which the use, if carried out responsibly and with careful study, is judged permissible."[8] There are in fact certain adjustments in the liturgy which are desirable in that they better respond to the character of a particular people, culture, or ethnic group.

Far from rejecting them, the Constitution on the Sacred Liturgy accepts this principle in articles 40–44.[h] The Instruction *Inter Oecumenici* of 26 September 1964, also refers to them (no. 45).[i]

The procedure to be followed in such cases is indicated clearly in these texts:

— the work of preparation by liturgical, pastoral, and theological experts;

— approval by the episcopal conference;

— the episcopal conference's request to the Holy See;

— the Holy See establishes the form of the experiments;

— the experiments are carried out "in suitable groups prepared for this, and for a limited time" (SC art. 40, par. 2)[j] under the control of the local hierarchy.

In this way, and only in this way, can there legitimately come into being the adaptations judged necessary both as regards rites and texts in the liturgy.

I think however that it is useful to ask the national commissions and the institutes to which they entrust the task of undertaking the studies preliminary to these adaptations kindly to keep before them, for certain rites, the new projects now in process at the Consilium. Experience has already shown in fact that many difficulties caused by the present rites are resolved by the new texts proposed by the Consilium. These in their turn need, at least in certain aspects, to be completed by the adaptations entrusted to the episcopal conferences.

5. LOCAL CHURCH AND UNIVERSAL CHURCH

483   It is certainly a cause for rejoicing that in our times the sense of the local Church is better developed and expressed, especially in the diocese and around the bishop, successor of the apostles and the head of the people of God. It is more easily understood that the whole of the liturgical assembly, presided over by the priest representing the bishop, is the visible and efficacious sign of the Church, and, like her, is "one, holy, catholic, and apostolic."

But this rediscovery must not weaken the no-less necessary awareness of the universal Church and of the solidarity by which all Christians are united in the one Body of Christ and all the assemblies in the one Church "spread over all the earth." Even with the legitimate adaptations duly approved by the competent authority, it is the same worship in "spirit and truth" that must be celebrated by all the assemblies, be they in cathedrals or modest mission chapels, in parish churches or oratories. In this age of ours, which knows no barriers of space, this sense of Christian solidarity in worship should play a greater role than in the past. Movement from one region to another, from one country to another, or from one continent to another, is becoming increasingly more frequent. Press, radio, and television spread

---

[8] DOL 86 no. 639.

[h] See DOL 1 nos. 40–44.

[i] See DOL 23 no. 337.

[j] DOL 1 no. 40.

news of events even in the farthest countries to all parts of the world with amazing speed, making them present through the attraction of image and sound. All this makes us understand that the liturgical celebration itself, wherever it may be, is open to the dimensions of the world and can no longer regard itself as isolated and obscure.

Every priest and each of the faithful, in accepting to celebrate worship as laid down by the competent authority, maintain their communion with the other priests and faithful. Each bishop, guardian of prayer and of the faith, is collegially united to all his brethren in the apostolic college. Here too, it is a question in the last analysis of that charity, fruit of the Holy Spirit, which unites us all in worship with the same Lord, the Christ who died and has risen, and through him, with him, and in him, in the worship of the same heavenly Father.

6. MIXED COMMISSIONS

On 16 October 1964, in my first letter (see *Notitiae* 1 [1965] 194–196) I ex-   **484**
pressed the thought of the Consilium on liturgical translations in countries which speak the same language, that is, that "there should be one official translation, and, possibly, even single liturgical editions for the same language."[k]

This was confirmed by the Holy Father Pope Paul VI in his Allocution of 10 November 1965, to the participants in the translators' Congress (*Notitiae*, 1 [1965] 380).[l]

From that time onwards enormous efforts have been made to attain unified liturgical translations in French, English, Spanish, Portuguese, and Dutch. Several liturgical books have been published by common accord between countries of the same language.

In this respect allow me to determine the following points: **485**

a. The principle of one translation for countries that speak the same vernacular language in the liturgy applies even to countries in different continents.

b. For each language spoken in several countries, it is desirable to set up a mixed commission, composed of bishops and experts from each of the countries involved.

c. The commission must organize the work of study and preparation of the translations.

d. When this work is completed, the vernacular text must be submitted to all the episcopal conferences, to whom the approval of liturgical translation pertains (see Instruction *Inter Oecumenici* nos. 23–28).[m] The subsequent observations of the bishops will be communicated to the mixed commission, which if need be, will make new proposals.

e. Each episcopal conference will ask from the Consilium the confirmation of vernacular translations approved by it, adhering faithfully to nos. 29–30 of the Instruction *Inter Oecumenici*,[n] which establishes that there should be sent to the Consilium an accurate report on the decisions of the conference, with the result of the prescribed *vote* by secret ballot.

---

[k] See DOL 108 no. 764.

[l] See DOL 113.

[m] See DOL 23 nos. 315–320.

[n] See DOL 23 nos. 321–322.

f. It is for each episcopal conference to decide how liturgical books are to be published (see Decree of the Sacred Congregation of Rites *Cum nostra aetate* of 27 January 1966, no. 3; *Notitiae* 3 [1966] 173).[o] Often it is more advantageous that there should be one edition for all the countries that use the same translations. The episcopal conferences may facilitate this solution, whenever there are reasonable grounds for judging it to be preferable.

7. TRANSLATION OF THE CANON AND RITE OF ORDINATION

486 Since last March the Holy Father has acceded to the request of numerous episcopates to admit the spoken tongue in the canon of the Mass and in the rites of holy orders.[p] This concession is in order to permit the Christian people to better understand the spiritual riches of these celebrations and to draw from them yet greater profit. This is in conformity with the principles of the Constitution on the Sacred Liturgy, which placed no restriction in principle on the use of the vernacular in the liturgy.

After the initial point of departure (see Instruction *Inter Oecumenici* nos. 57 and 61)[q] and the extension of the spoken language to the preface (27 April 1965),[r] this is the last step in the *gradual extension of the vernacular*. In liturgical celebrations it will no longer be necessary to pass frequently from one language to another: this will certainly be welcome. In particular the great eucharistic prayer will derive added dignity from this.

It should be borne in mind that for the canon the Holy See is not approving translations which are already found in the missals of the faithful and which have been allowed *ad interim* in past years. It will be necessary to prepare a new translation, and one that is made with care. Moreover, this translation should be *accurate and integral*. The texts should be taken as they are, without mutilations or simplifications of any kind. Adaptations to the character of the spoken tongue should be sober and prudent. The *periti* should accept this norm in good spirit, since its application is necessary at the present time. It is not opportune to "jump the gun." When the time has come to create, then it will no longer be necessary to be tied down to the restrictions of literal translation. But, for the present time, we are still at the point in which we must more fully uncover and live by all the riches of our liturgical heritage.

I should be most grateful to Your Excellency if you could communicate this letter to the bishops of your conference and to the major religious superiors of your nation, as soon as possible and in whatever way you judge to be most fitting.

42. CONSILIUM, **Editorial** *Des gestes qui révèlent*, on gestures in the liturgy, January 1968: Not 4 (1968) 8–9 (French).

487 The conciliar Constitution laid down the following principle covering the reform of gestures in the liturgy: "The rites should be distinguished by a noble simplicity; they should be short, clear, and unencumbered by useless repetition;

[o] See DOL 134 no. 921.

[p] See DOL 117.

[q] See DOL 23 nos. 349 and 353.

[r] See DOL 110.

they should be within the people's power of comprehension and as a rule not require much explanation" (art. 34).[a]

The Instruction *Inter Oecumenici* (26 Sept. 1964)[b] and especially the more recent one *Tres abhinc annos* (4 May 1967)[c] have brought about a sweeping simplification of many liturgical gestures. The same is the case with the two rites approved *ad experimentum* two years ago, those for adult baptism and for funerals of adults. The complete revision of the liturgical books will, of course, go still further in this direction as intended by Vatican II.

But if it is relatively simple to restore to the rites a noble simplicity and marked brevity, it is not at all simple to change old habits and mannerisms. The disciples at Emmaus knew the Lord in the breaking of the bread; but can today's Christians see through to this same presence in the way in which their priests carry out the breaking of the bread in the liturgy? The celebrant's gestures function as signs; they are meant to reveal Christ's presence. But they will be effective as such only to the degree that they are motivated directly by an inner vision, the contemplation of mystery. Careful observance of rubrics, necessary though it is, is not enough here. How can gestures that have become mechanical from habit, sloppy from routine, half-hearted from apathy still function as signs of the work of salvation? The Roman Ritual in one text from four and a half centuries ago demanded gestures of celebrants that by their dignity and gravity would serve as an effective message for the faithful, "making them attentive and lifting them up to the contemplation of heavenly things" (tit. 1, no. 11).

Television is constantly showing us gestures that are beautiful, decorous, and expressive. These pictures on the screen reflect hours of the most precise training and exacting rehearsal. Should the celebrants who handle, so to speak, the realities of the new and everlasting covenant be exempt from the same basic preparation? These are things that must be *learned*: how to stand erect, bow, genuflect; how to bend over to kiss the altar; how to make the sign of the cross over the offerings or trace it over the offerings or the congregation; how to raise the arms, extend the hands, join the fingers, etc. To be graceful yet remain simple and unstudied, liturgical gestures demand at least a minimum of preparation and care.   488

They also require at least a little *time*. Haste leaves no room at all for beauty. Liturgical gestures have to be performed unhurriedly and be of a measure suited to the gathered assembly, to which they are a revelation of the realities of the kingdom. An affected slowness that would provoke boredom or ridicule has to be avoided; but equal care is needed against the intrusion of haste, the fear of "wasting" time, the telescoping of gestures.

The celebrant himself is a sign of Christ; he bears witness to Christ and the Church only to the degree that his bearing, his gestures, and his words allow his inner contemplation to show through. Riveted body and soul on the Lord's Supper, the sacraments, and the other expressions of worship "in spirit and in truth," the celebrant will thus make his gestures "salvation events" by which the love of the Father revealed in Jesus Christ will be manifested and diffused through the Holy Spirit.

---

[a]   DOL 1 no. 34.

[b]   See DOL 23 no. 328.

[c]   See DOL 39 nos. 453–459.

43. CONSILIUM, **Rescript** (India), on liturgical adaptations to Indian culture, 25 April 1969.*

489   The Cardinal President of the Consilium, His Eminence Benno Cardinal Gut, has accepted the proposals of the Catholic Bishops' Conference of India for certain adaptations in the liturgy, according to articles 37–40 of the Liturgical Constitution. In his name I would like to establish what follows:

1. The posture during Mass, both for the priests and the faithful, may be adapted to the local usage, that is, sitting on the floor, standing, and the like; footwear may be removed also.

2. Genuflections may be replaced by the profound bow with the *anjali hasta*.

3. A *panchanga pranam* by both priests and faithful can take place before the liturgy of the word, as part of the penitential rite, and at the conclusion of the anaphora.

4. Kissing of objects may be adapted to local custom, that is, touching the object with one's fingers or palm of one's hand and bringing the hands to one's eyes or forehead.

5. The kiss of peace could be given by the exchange of the *anjali hasta* and/or the placing of the hands of the giver between the hands of the recipient.

6. Incense could be made more use of in liturgical services. The receptacle could be the simple incense bowl with handle.

7. The vestments could be simplified. A single tunic-type chasuble with a stole (*angavastra*) could replace the traditional vestments of the Roman Rite. Samples of this change are to be forwarded to the Consilium.

8. The corporal could be replaced by a tray (*thali* or *thamboola thattu*) of fitting material.

9. Oil lamps could be used instead of candles.

10. The preparatory rite of the Mass may include:

    a. the presentation of gifts;

    b. the welcome of the celebrant in an Indian way, e.g., with a single *arati*, washing of hands, etc.;

    c. the lighting of the lamp;

    d. the greetings of peace among the faithful in sign of mutual reconciliation.

11. In the *Oratio fidelium* some spontaneity may be permitted both with regard to its structure and the formulation of the intentions. The universal aspect of the Church, however, should not be left in oblivion.

12. In the offertory rite, and at the conclusion of the anaphora, the Indian form of worship may be integrated, that is, double or triple *arati* of flowers, and/or incense, and/or light.

The above-mentioned adaptations can be put into effect by the episcopal conference and local hierarchies in places where they see fit and in the degree and measure that they think fitting for the faithful. A catechesis, however, should precede such changes, and if necessary, a gradual implementation could be done.

The proposal to compose a new Indian anaphora in collaboration with experts in different fields is most welcomed. When completed, copies should be sent to the Consilium for study. It might help if this were not publicized too much.

---

* English text from the Consilium, Prot. N. 802/69.

44. PAUL VI, **Address** to a symposium of bishops from all of Africa at Kampala, excerpt on the liturgy and different cultures, 31 July 1969: AAS 61 (1969) 573–578; Not 5 (1969) 346 (English).

2. [. . .] The expression, that is, the language and mode of manifesting this one faith, may be manifold; hence, it may be original, suited to the tongue, the style, the character, the genius, and the culture of the one who professes this one faith. From this point of view, a certain pluralism is not only legitimate, but desirable. An adaptation of the Christian life in the fields of pastoral, ritual, didactic, and spiritual activities is not only possible, it is even favored by the Church. The liturgical renewal is a living example of this. And in this sense you may, and you must, have an African Christianity. Indeed, you possess human values and characteristic forms of culture which can rise up to perfection such as to find in Christianity and for Christianity a true superior fullness and prove to be capable of a richness of expression all its own and genuinely African. This may take time. It will require that your African soul become imbued to its depths with the secret charisms of Christianity, so that these charisms may then overflow freely, in beauty and wisdom, in the true African manner. It will require from your culture that it should not refuse, but rather eagerly desire to draw from the patrimony of the patristic, exegetical, and theological tradition of the Catholic Church those treasures of wisdom which can rightly be considered universal, above all, those which can be most easily assimilated by the African mind. [. . .]

490

45. PAUL VI, **Address** to a general audience at Castelgandolfo, on the liturgy and personal prayer, 13 August 1969: Not 5 (1969) 337–339 (Italian; excerpt).

[. . .] The liturgy is the community and ecclesial celebration of the word of God and the mysteries of redemption (see SC art. 2).[a] No one could rightly attribute to it any lessening of personal prayer, above all of spirituality, interior religion, of that *pietas*, understood as devotion and the expression of the gift of the Holy Spirit, by which we turn toward God in the depths of our heart with the intimacy of the name, "Father" (see Rom 8:15–16; ST 2a2ae, 121.1). Through an intense and prolonged religious movement, the liturgy, crowned and, as it were, canonized by Vatican II, has gained a new importance, dignity, accessibility, and participation in the consciousness and the spiritual life of the people of God and, we predict, this will continue even more in the future. The liturgy has a primacy and fullness, an effectiveness of itself, that we should recognize and promote. But the liturgy, by its nature public and official in the Church, should not come to replace or impoverish personal spirituality. The liturgy is not ritual alone; it is mystery and by that fact calls for all who share in it to be consciously, fervently wrapped up in it. The liturgy demands faith, hope, charity, and so many other virtues and sentiments, acts and conditions — like humility, repentance, pardoning offenses, intention, attention, inward and vocal expression — disposing the believer for immersion into the divine reality that liturgical celebration makes present and active. Personal religion, because it is within the reach of everyone, is the indispensable condition for a genuine and aware liturgical participation. But that is not all: personal religion is also the result, the consequence of such participation, which is meant precisely to sanctify

491

---

[a]   See DOL 1 no. 2.

souls and to strengthen in them the sense of union with God, with Christ, with the Church, with all humanity. [. . .]

46. PAUL VI, **Address** to a general audience at Castelgandolfo, excerpt on prayer prompted by joy and hope, 20 August 1969: Not 5 (1969) 339–342 (Italian).

492
    At an earlier gathering like this one[a] we spoke of the need today and always, but today especially [. . .], to foster a spirit and practice of personal prayer. Without a genuine, intimate, continuous inner prayer-life in faith and charity we cannot keep ourselves Christians; we cannot profitably and wisely share in the flourishing liturgical renaissance. [. . .]

It is our belief that many of the sad, spiritual and moral crises of people brought up in the Church and given a place at various levels of the ecclesial structure have been due to an apathy toward and perhaps a lack of a regular and intense prayer life, assisted all along by wise exterior practices; these being abandoned, prayer itself dries up and with it fidelity and joy.

[. . .] We wish each of you to put yourself into one of the categories that anyone can perceive at a glance.

THREE CATEGORIES

493
    The first category perhaps covers the most people; it is that of lethargy. The fire of the spirit is not out, but covered with ashes. The seed is not dead but, as the gospel parable says (Mt 13:7–22), it is choked with weeds, the "cares of the present world," and the "spell of riches." [. . .]

A second category, whose ranks have swelled with troubled people after the conciliar reform of the liturgy, includes the suspicious, the criticizers, the malcontents. Disturbed in their devotional practices, these spirits grudgingly resign themselves to the new ways, but make no attempt to understand the reasons for them. They find the new expressions of divine worship unpleasing. They take refuge in their moaning, which takes away their ancient flavor from texts of the past and blocks any taste for what the Church, in this *second spring of the liturgy*, offers to spirits that are open to the meaning and language of the new rites sanctioned by the wisdom and authority of the postconciliar reform. A not very difficult effort at acceptance and understanding would bring the experience of dignity, simplicity, and new-found antiquity in the new liturgies and would also bring to the sanctuary of each person's self the consolation and the life-giving force of community celebrations. The interior life would yield a greater fullness.

To a third category belong those who say that they are content with preaching charity toward their neighbors and with leaving charity toward God in the background or declaring it unnecessary. It is evident to all what a negative effect such an attitude has had, with its claim that it is action, not prayer, that keeps the Christian life alive and honest. [. . .]

---

    [a] See DOL 45.

47. PAUL VI, **Address** to a general audience at Castelgandolfo, on reform
of the liturgy and a new spirit of prayer in the Church, 3 September 1969:
Not 5 (1969) 342–345 (Italian).

For several weeks now we have been saying that those who wish to keep   494
themselves Christians and so to grow up in Christ (see Eph 4:15) need to enliven
their own faith and thereby to rekindle the spirit and practice of a personal prayer
life.[a]

We are convinced that divine worship as instituted and celebrated in the
hierarchic Church, that is, the liturgy, as well as popular and private devotions have
the power, as Christ foretold, to nurture "in spirit and in truth" (Jn 4:23) the
adoration of the Father, that is, the one true and effective relationship to God. Both
forms of prayer have the power to interpret what is in the heart of the people of
today no less than of yesterday and to offer them the most noble and beautiful
ways to express themselves. Both have the power to open the pathway to spiritual
knowledge, contained "in contemplative thought" (Dante, *Paradiso* 21:117), and to
the art of translating into prayer the pleas and praises of all humanity. Both have
the power to give voice to the simple and heartfelt words belonging to the critical
moments of life.

We must reread, dearest children, that noble document, the Constitution on
the Liturgy, and try to grasp what it contains that is continuous with the Church's
tradition of prayer and what it proposes to us that is new. Specifically, it reminds
us how the liturgical celebration reflects and embodies the mystery of the Church, a
pilgrim in time (see SC art. 2); it expresses the desire that we be not passively
present at the liturgy but as sharers "especially in the divine sacrifice of the eucharist."[b]

Praise be to God that the liturgical movement, taken up and advanced by the
Council, has spread throughout the Church and entered into the awareness of
clergy and people. The choral prayer of the Mystical Body, which the Church is, is
reaching and stirring the people of God, who are consciously becoming a community and experiencing an increase in faith and grace. Therefore, supernatural faith is
reawakening, eschatological hope is guiding ecclesial spirituality, charity is reas-
suming its life-giving, active primacy. And all of this in a pagan, worldly century,
deaf to the cries of the soul.

With all the capacity, work, and will that we possess, we wish to encourage
this immense effort to inspire the whole Catholic community with a new and vital
appreciation of affective prayer. The revision of rites and texts now under way calls
for great study and labor in those preparing the revision as well as for great patience
in those who must put it into effect, and great loyalty and filial cooperation in those
who must conform to it by adjusting their own devotional practices and by putting
aside their own preferences.

The current reform contains its dangers; one in particular is that of arbitra-   495
riness, which implies a threat to the spiritual unity of the ecclesial society, the
sublimity of prayer, and the dignity of ritual. This individualism may allege as
justification the many changes introduced into the traditional prayer of the whole
Church. It would be a great blow if the Church's maternal care to allow the use of
the vernacular, special adaptations to local preferences, a new variety of texts, and
innovation in ritual, were to create the opinion that there are no longer any general

---

[a]   See DOL 45, 46.

[b]   DOL 1 no. 2.

norms, fixed and obligatory, for the Church's prayer and that everyone can presume at will to rearrange and tamper with it. That would no longer mean a pluralism within the lawful limits, but a distortion of a kind that is such as to be not merely ritual but substantial (as, for example, sharing in communion with those not possessing a valid priesthood). Such disorder, which sadly exists here and there, poses a grave threat for the Church: it is an obstacle to the disciplined reform the Church validates and sanctions; it introduces a discordant note into the outward and inner harmony of the Church's concert of prayer; it spawns subjectivism as a religious criterion that infects clergy and people; it generates confusion and weakness in the community's religious education. Arbitrariness is an example — but neither a fraternal nor a good example.

Another possible pretext for this attitude is the desire for a worship modeled on personal taste, better understood and more compatible with the actual condition of the participants. The pretext may even go so far as to allege a more "spiritual" form of worship. We are willing to see in such justifications some degree of good will, which the wisdom of the bishops will know how to take into consideration. Thus our Congregation for Divine Worship has issued an Instruction on the celebration of Masses in special circumstances outside of places of worship.[c]

But we prefer to exhort people of good will, priests and laity, not to indulge in this undocile individualism. Besides violating canon law, it does injury to the heart of Catholic worship, namely, communion: communion with God and communion with each other, the mediator of which is the ministerial priesthood as authorized by the bishop. Individualism tends to create *ecclesiolae*, even sects. It tends to cut itself away from the celebration of a universal charity, to withdraw from the so-called institutional structure of the genuine, real, human Church. It deludes itself with the thought that it possesses a free, utterly charismatic Christianity; what it achieves in fact is something shapeless, ephemeral, "blown about by every breeze of doctrine" (Eph 4:14), exposed to passion and fashion, to temporal and political goals.

This tendency to shake off church authority and communion gradually and obdurately can, sad to say, lead people far: not, as some have claimed, to the catacombs, but right out of the Church. In the end it can mean flight, a breaking away, and therefore a scandal and a ruin. It does not build up, but tears down. Who does not remember the repeated, still resounding appeals of St. Ignatius of Antioch, martyred at the beginning of the second century: "Let there be but one altar as there is but one bishop" (*Ad Philad.* 4); "Do nothing apart from the bishop" (*Ad Trall.* 2, 2), etc. The reason is that the bishop is the head of the local Church, even as the pope is head of the universal Church (see Denz-Schön 3050–59).

In this matter the relationship between the Church and prayer is clear. We will not discuss it now, but we are sure that it is easy to perceive for anyone having on the one hand the *sensus Ecclesiae* and on the other a concern for a strong, living prayer-life. We must, dearest children, pray with the Church and for the Church. And that is what we urge you to do.

48. PAUL VI, **Remarks at the Angelus,** on the parish and liturgical life, 7 September 1969: Not 5 (1969) 345–346 (Italian; excerpt).

496   [. . .] There are some who attach no importance to their own parish and others who regard the parish as a now outmoded institution of the past. It is true that

---

today's society has changed much and that for this reason the parish must adapt its life to the new needs of the people. Nonetheless we must acknowledge the parish to be an ecclesial entity that is always living and indispensable.

The parish is the primary, structured community recognized by the diocesan Church and by virtue of that is, as the Council teaches, in communion with the universal Church. The parish is our first and normal spiritual family, developed not so much out of the homogeneity of the members (who in many cases are quite different from each other) but in virtue of a specific pastoral ministry and of the cohesive influence of the one faith and the one charity.

The parish stands as an institution of the highest moral and social value in view of its being the primary and responsible agency working to serve a necessary purpose that affects all. That end is the care of souls, which presupposes a qualified priest, the pastor, who dedicates himself completely to the community entrusted to him, and is ready at all times, like the Good Shepherd, to put the salvation of others ahead of his own life if necessary. The parish is the school of God's word, the table of the eucharistic bread. It is the home of the community's love. It is the temple of shared prayer; in a certain sense, as the Council says, it is the visible Church established concretely in all parts of the earth.

For this reason, again echoing the Council, the liturgical life of the parish and its bond with the bishop must be emphasized in the spirit and in the practice of the laity and clergy so that they will serve rightly to give vigorous growth to the sense of community in the parish. [. . .]

49. PAUL VI, **Address** to a general audience, on the Church as a praying community, 22 April 1970: Not 6 (1970) 157–160 (Italian; excerpt).

[. . .] What is the Church about? What is its purpose? What is its mark of   497
identity? What is the moment in which it expresses its essence, that full activity that justifies and characterizes its existence? The reply to these questions echoes back from the very walls of the Basilica of St. Peter. The Church is an association of prayer, a *societas Spiritus* (see Phil 2:1. St. Augustine, *Serm.* 71, 19: PL 38, 462). The Church is humanity finding, through the mediation of Christ the sole High Priest, the genuine way to pray, that is, to speak to God and about God. The Church is the family of those who adore the Father "in spirit and truth" (Jn 4:23).

It would be interesting to reconsider the correlation between the word "church" as applied to the edifice erected for prayer and as applied to the assembly of believers. They are "church" whether they are inside or outside the building where they gather to pray. Notice that among other things the material edifice intended to gather the faithful in prayer can, and to a certain degree (in this basilica to the point of majesty) must, be not simply a place of prayer, *domus orationis*, but in addition a sign of prayer, a spiritual edifice, a prayer itself, the expression of worship, a work of art meant for the spirit. These are the grounds for the practical need to build places of worship that will give the Christian people the opportunity to gather together and pray. They are also the grounds for the credit due to those who work to build the "new churches" that are to welcome and train for prayer the new communities that do not yet have their indispensable *domus orationis*, homes where they are to gather to celebrate the prayer of their community.

We wish, therefore, in this place and at this moment to bring to your mind the designation that so well defines Catholicism: *Ecclesia orans*, the Church that prays. This most precisely religious character of the Church is essential and providential and it is the truth the Council teaches in its first document, the Constitution on the Liturgy. We must keep this characteristic of the Church in mind, as well as its being necessary and primary. What would the Church be without prayer? Would a Christianity that did not teach people how they can and must converse with God be anything more than a philanthropic humanism or a purely temporal social theory?

498   The contemporary tendency toward universal secularization is well known, as is the fact that this tendency has penetrated the outlook even of Christians, including clergy and religious. We have spoken of it before, but it is helpful to do so again, because prayer today is in a state of decline. To go right to the point: community and liturgical prayer is in the process of becoming widespread again, of being shared in and understood; this is indeed a blessing for our people and our era. We also must take notice of the prescriptions of the liturgical reform as they are at work; they represent the will of the Council, have been studied with wise and patient care by foremost liturgists in the Church, and have been counseled by experts in pastoral ministry. It will be the liturgical life, carefully nurtured and fully assimilated into the minds and practice of the Christian people, that will keep awake and active the religious sense in these secular, desacralized times, and that will give to the Church a new spring in its spiritual, Christian life.

But at the same time we must lament the decline of personal prayer, which threatens the liturgy itself with an impoverishment of its interiority, with external ritualism, and an outward formalism. The religious sense can itself be lessened through lack of two indispensable qualities of prayer: that it be interior and that it be personal. There is a need for everyone to learn to pray within self and from self. All Christians must have their own personal prayer. [. . .]

The *Ecclesia orans* is a chorus of individual voices, alive, aware, full of life. In its process of renewal and its desire for us to be witnesses and apostles, what the Church asks is an inner spirituality, a personal devotion, a meditation developed from the heart, a degree of contemplation — thoughtful and adoring, pleading and rejoicing. [. . .]

50. PAUL VI, **Address** to a general audience, on the new pedagogy contained in the sense of community, 2 June 1970: Not 6 (1970) 233–235 (Italian; excerpt).

499   One of the salient ideas emerging from the Council for Christian spiritual formation is the sense of community.

Those intent on welcoming the conciliar spirit and criteria for renewal realize that they have a new pedagogy as model. This requires such persons to conceive and express their religious, moral, and social life in terms of the ecclesial community to which they belong. Throughout its documents the Council speaks of the Church: the Church now is the people of God; the Church is the Mystical Body of Christ; the Church is *communio*. If you wish to be Christians, to be Catholics, to be the faithful, you can no longer forget this existential reality. The life of religion cannot be lived as an individual's expression of the relationship between self and God, between the Christian and Christ, between the Catholic and the Church. Nor can it be conceived as an elitist expression, something that within an autonomous group, cut off from the larger ecclesial communion, finds its own satisfaction and avoids outside interference, whether of superiors, peers, or followers; these are kept out by the initiates' exclusivism, the typical attitude of a group closed in on itself and self-satisfied. For the believer, however, the spirit of community is the indispensable ambience.

Let us, however, express two reservations, or better two obvious observations. The religious fact in essence, in its profound and inescapable demands, remains a personal fact. This is the reason why it is free and proper to any person accepting it. The relationship between the person and God goes on within the individual conscience and precisely at the moment of self-experience as a person, fully responsible and dynamically set upon deciding on personal destiny.[1] Thus entrance into the community life of the Church, so far from leaving aside the personal engagement of the faithful, intensifies and demands it, whether in the practice of prayer — liturgical prayer — or in social relationships, that is, those of justice and charity. Is not the faith given to us through the Church as intermediary? Is not the Church's ministry the channel for receiving grace? What would we know of Christ without the Church as teacher?[2] "The liturgy itself requires the soul to press on toward contemplation; and sharing in the life of the liturgy . . . is an eminent way to prepare for union with God through loving contemplation."[3] We could go deeper into this theme by noting how the spirit of community that the Church is now instilling into us is not something new but a return to the origins of Christian spirituality. As such it is no suppression of the personal involvement of the believer but rather its revitalization, based on the remembrance and the attitude in practice of the "royal priesthood," which belongs to the baptized and is so much spoken of today, since the Council has proclaimed anew its existence, dignity, and exercise.[4]

500

LOCAL CHURCHES

Similar remarks could be made about the legitimate and providential existence of groups established as particular "religions"; they set before themselves as their ideal the imitation of Christ and the practice of the evangelical counsels, according to their own laws as authenticated by the Church's authority for the pursuit of Christian perfection.[5] Such groups, however, in their own distinctive style, also live in the Church, from the Church, for the Church. They are in no way cut off from inner and outer communion with it; they too, and often better than others, have the sense and the taste of the spirit of community and zeal for it.

501

We can speak in the same way of the not merely accepted, but honored existence of particular Churches with their own traditions, rites, and canonical rules. But for these, too, *communio* is the indispensable requirement for belonging to the single true Church of Christ. The sacred term *communio* is pivotal for the whole issue of ecumenism, to which the Council also summons us and whose meaning it wants us to learn.

We should also make mention of the local Churches, which are not splinter groups or autonomous within the unity of the universal Church, but are integrated parts, living members, flowering branches, endowed with their own vitality from the one source of faith and grace. But in their very effort to fulfill their own inner and original communion they also are expressions of the *communio* of the Church as a whole; they bear witness to the sweet, original harmony of variety within unity.[6]

---

[1]   ST 2a2ae, 81.

[2]   See J. A. Möhler, *Die Einheit in der Kirche* I, 1, 7; *L'unité dans l'Eglise* 21.

[3]   J. Maritain, *Liturgie et contemplation* 14.1.

[4]   See LG nos. 10–11, etc.

[5]   See LG no. 43.

[6]   See LG nos. 23, 26, etc.

All this being said, it remains true that the Church, revitalized and explained by the Council, stands out today more than in the past as a community. The more the Church is spread in the world, the more it defines itself, in virtue of an inherent and constitutive need, *as communio*.[7] Note the social aspect of this definition. Humanity can be seen as a mass, a numerical quantity, or as a mere category of human beings, an amorphous crowd, lacking any deep or tested or chosen bonds within. Or it can be seen as a pluralistic and corporate society or community, brought together for particular ends or interests: as a people, a nation, a society of nations . . . And in the last analysis as a *communio*; this is the humanity Christ wills.

THE CHURCH, ORGANIC BODY

502   You know what the requisites and elements are for this supreme expression of humanity: faith, the Spirit, the hierarchy; in short the Church, our Church.

If a *communio*, what are the implications? The Church as a communion implies a basic equality, namely, personal dignity and a shared common bond; it implies a progressive solidarity;[8] a disciplined obedience and loyal collaboration; a proportionate co-responsibility in the furtherance of the general well-being. But the Church does not imply an equality of function; for functions are also clearly marked out within ecclesial communion, because this is organic, hierarchic, a body with diverse and specified responsibilities, etc.

The conclusion is that we must increase in ourselves the sense of community and the practice of the relevant virtues. We must, that is, increase in charity, a term that must grow in meaning, value, practice. This is the spirit of community which the Council wished to be the model of our formation and the object of our fidelity. Right at the beginning of the Church St. Paul taught us: "Following the truth in charity, we are to grow in all things toward him who is the Head, Christ, from whom the whole Body . . . in the measure of each of its parts, achieves growth to build itself up in love."[9] This is the true spirit of community.

51. SECRETARIAT OF STATE, Letter of Cardinal J. Villot to Bishop A. Mistrorigo, President of the Italian Bishops' Committee on Liturgy, on the occasion of the 21st National Liturgical Week of Italy (Verona, 31 August – 4 September 1970), August 1970: Not 6 (1970) 305–308 (Italian; excerpt).

503   With great pleasure Pope Paul VI has received the announcement of the coming celebration at Verona. [. . .]

The Pope [. . .] wishes through me to communicate to the organizers his fatherly encouragement and at the same time to put before the participants certain thoughts that seem to him to be particularly useful for the gradual and orderly development of the reform of the liturgy in Italy.

1. The theme chosen for the liturgical week, "The Prayer of the Christian Community," that is, the divine office or, as we now say, the liturgy of the hours, is especially timely. With the publication of the new breviary imminent, this week can serve as a spiritual preparation for the Italian clergy to welcome it with love and enthusiasm.

---

[7]   See J. Hamer, *L'Eglise est une communion* (1962); *idem*, OR 12 May 1970.

[8]   Gal 6:2.

[9]   Eph 4:15–16.

Even just a partial restructuring and rearrangement of the divine office has produced in some countries reassuring results and a revived interest in the office. The same will surely be the case in Italy, where the traditional fidelity of the clergy and religious to the recitation of the canonical hours is worthy of every praise. The office always will remain for the priest the prayer to which the Church obliges him and to which he pledged himself on the day of his subdiaconate. Everyone should try to see in this rule not an onus but a privileged invitation; not an obligation but a maternal call to the *unum necessarium*.[1] Prayer, and this prayer in particular, is for the priest, the font of grace and the soul of his apostolate.

The "sacrifice of praise" spreads through the day the spiritual radiance of the eucharistic sacrifice and is in turn a preparation for it. This is especially true if each hour is celebrated at the corresponding time of day and with attention to the particular character of the office as being the practice of prayer spread throughout the other duties of pastoral ministry.

Nor should we forget that the *Officium divinum* is the *official prayer* of the praying Church. Priests and all who are deputed for the office by the Church have a mandate through the voice of one who calls them in the name of the divine Master. Accordingly, the Church both entrusts the priest with this treasure of graces, and gives him its form, structure, and words, so that in his voice may resound the echo of the love and the voice of the Bride of Christ. Consequently, the revised Roman Breviary, even though offering a greater flexibility for adaptation, will retain a form and a structure that are clearly defined so that public prayer may remain substantially one and homogeneous throughout the entire Church.

A richer and more varied choice of biblical and patristic readings will draw both clergy and people closer to the genuine sources of the Church's spirituality: sacred Scripture and the Fathers of the Church. The enlarged collection of prayers will not cause us to forget that the inspired song of the psalms is the fabric of the divine office. All will share through the psalms the comfort of continuing to pray in the same phrases as generations of the *sancti*, who have built up the Church throughout the centuries.

It is well also to recall that the priest would be fulfilling his responsibility only partially if he were to limit himself to nurturing only his personal devotion on the prayer of the hours and did not *try to bring the Christian people to share in it*. No step should be left untried toward restoring at least the more important hours, like morning prayer and evening prayer, to a place in the practice of the parish community, of youth groups, and of souls better trained in liturgical devotion; this is in fact being done with good results in many churches and communities.

A further hope is that gradually we will come to solemnize the celebration of the hours in song, both when the people are present and when groups of priests or other clergy gather.

2. There is cause for comfort in the increased measures to bring about a deeper knowledge of the liturgy and an ever more intelligent, active, and personal participation by the faithful in the rites of the Church. The postconciliar liturgical renewal without doubt has opened the way, by facilitating contact of the faithful with the sacred rites. There is, however, a need now to continue and intensify this methodical and prolonged catechesis; it will clarify and deepen the understanding of the rites and help the people of God to enter with awareness and vitality into the meaning of mystery and the sacred. 504

Were the liturgical movement and reform to open up in our age access to the genuine sources of piety, yet not protect and safeguard the sense of the sacred, then

---

[1] Lk 10:42.

all the efforts and measures of the Church would be in vain, because the very sources of devotion are the sources of the divine life in the soul.

505   3. Next, there is need to derive from the extraordinary spiritual wealth that all the new rites, above all the Roman Missal, provide a fuller advantage for the inner life of the Christian community, that is, for those souls consecrated to the Lord, and for the laity.

This now is the responsibility of pastors of souls and of liturgists. Sterile criticism or frenetic searching for ways other than those set forth by the Church would be foolish. Arbitary, individualistic innovations outside the established norms would be harmful. Obedience and fidelity are in this as in other matters the sure guarantee for a constructive and serious effort toward the building up and sanctification of souls.

506   4. We cannot omit commending the rise of schools, centers, and institutes for liturgy, including those at a regional or interdiocesan level. They are designed to make available to the greatest number of priests and laity the information developed by scholarly research so that it can be rightly applied to pastoral activity.

Biblical preparation needs particular attention. For this reason special courses in the Bible are strongly recommended for the laity and also the practice of preparing for the Sunday Mass at weekly meetings bringing together priests and the more interested laity. In such gatherings the priests can situate the liturgical texts, especially the readings, within their historical, literary, and theological context; the laity, in turn, can make the important and valued contribution of suggesting practical conclusions that can have specific bearing and relevance for the Sunday assembly.

The new Lectionary brings to the faithful, in much fuller proportions, the teaching of the Bible, but for this very reason it requires a greater effort on the part of pastors to help the people grasp and assimilate this teaching. The most welcome results will derive from a joint, diligent, and harmonious effort worked out between the clergy and the more involved laity.

507   5. Pope Paul wishes to extend a word of appreciation and praise for their service to the periodicals intended for the clergy, especially to those having as their particular field of work the study, explanation, and spread of the liturgy. None should hold back from this common responsibility. An immense area lies at hand: the history of the reformed rites; the theology behind them; their biblical setting; their ascetical and spiritual content; their pastoral values. To comment on and explain the new liturgical texts can mean a priceless and helpful service to the activity that Church, hierarchy, and pastors direct toward making the liturgical renewal comprehensible and living.

508   6. Finally, the liturgical formation of the young deserves special care. Many times Pope Paul has brought up the point that in the restlessness and impatience met with among the youth of today there is cause for worry but also for hope. One reason for hope is undoubtedly the reawakened sense of God expressed in the intelligent, attentive, and direct sharing in the liturgy by prayer and song. Altogether praiseworthy, therefore, are the attempts to have "youth Masses," provided these are conducted in keeping with the norms recently issued by the Congregation for Divine Worship (Instruction for Masses with Special Groups, 15 May 1969).[a] But it still is desirable that these youth groups be gradually integrated into the parish community so as to enliven the parish Masses with singing, readings, and instructions suited to them. [. . .]

---

[a]   See DOL 275.

52. SC DIVINE WORSHIP, **Instruction** (third) *Liturgicae instaurationes*, on the orderly carrying out of the Constitution on the Liturgy, 5 September 1970: AAS 62 (1970) 692–704; Not 7 (1971) 10–26.

The liturgical reforms put into effect thus far as applications of Vatican Council II's Constitution on the Liturgy have to do primarily with the celebration of the mystery of the eucharist. "For the eucharist contains the Church's entire spiritual wealth, that is, Christ himself. He is our Passion and living bread; through his flesh, made living and life-giving by the Holy Spirit, he is bringing life to people and thereby inviting them to offer themselves together with him, as well as their labors and all created things."[1] The repeated celebration of the sacrifice of the Mass in our worshiping communities stands as evidence that the Mass is the center of the Church's entire life, the focal point of all other activities, and that the purpose of the ritual renewal is to inspire a pastoral ministry that has the liturgy as its crown and source and that is a living-out of the paschal mystery of Christ.[2]

509

The work of reform, accomplished step by step over the past six years, has served as a passage from the earlier to a new liturgy, presented, since publication of the Roman Missal with its Order of Mass and General Instruction, in such a clearer and fuller form that it truly opens a new path for pastoral-liturgical life, permitting great achievements. In addition, the recently published Mass Lectionary together with the wealth of prayer forms contained in the Roman Missal provide a wide range of options for celebrations of the eucharist.

The many options regarding texts and the flexibility of the rubrics are a great advantage to a living, pointed, and spiritually beneficial celebration, that is, one adapted to local conditions and to the character and culture of the faithful. There is, then, no need for purely personal improvisations, which can only trivialize the liturgy.

Measured transition to new and fresh forms of worship, conducted with both the overall work of renewal and the wide range of local conditions as its criteria, has been welcomed by the majority of clergy and faithful.[3] Still, there have been here and there both resistance and impatience. In the cause of holding on to the old tradition, some have received the changes grudgingly. Alleging pastoral needs, others became convinced that they could not wait for promulgation of the definitive reforms. In consequence, they have resorted to personal innovations, to hasty, often ill-advised measures, to new creations and additions or to the simplification of rites. All of this has frequently conflicted with the most basic liturgical norms and upset the consciences of the faithful. The innovators have thus obstructed the cause of genuine liturgical renewal or made it more difficult.

510

The result is that many bishops, priests, and laity have asked the Apostolic See to bring its authority to bear on the preservation and growth in the liturgy of the effective union of spirit that is to be expected as the right and the characteristic of the family of Christians gathered in God's presence.

What seemed untimely during the process of the Consilium's assiduous work on the reform has now become possible in view of all that has now been solidly and clearly established.

---

[1] PO no. 5 [DOL 18 no. 260].

[2] See SCR, Instr. InterOec, 26 Sept. 1964, nos. 5–6 [DOL 23 nos. 297–298].

[3] See Paul VI, Addr. to a general audience, 21 Aug. 1969 [DOL 46].

511   The first appeal must be made to the authority of the individual bishops; the Holy Spirit has chosen them to rule the Church of God[4] and they are "the chief stewards of the mysteries of God, and the overseers, promoters, and guardians of all liturgical life in the particular Churches entrusted to their care."[5] They have the duty of governing, guiding, encouraging, or sometimes reproving, of lighting the way for the carrying out of true reform, and also of taking counsel, so that the whole Body of the Church may be able to move ahead single-mindedly and with the unity of charity in the diocese, the nation, and the entire world. Such efforts of the bishops are the more necessary and urgent because the link between liturgy and faith is so close that service to the one redounds to the other.

With the cooperation of their liturgical commissions, bishops should have complete information on the religious and social condition of the faithful in their care, of their spiritual needs, and of the ways most likely to help them; bishops should also use all the options the new rites provide. They will then be able to evaluate what favors or hampers true reform and with care and discernment to suggest and control courses of action in such a way that, all genuine needs being given their due, the entire undertaking will nevertheless evolve in accord with the norms set by the new liturgical laws.

The bishops' mastery of the knowledge needed greatly assists priests in the ministry they exercise in due hierarchic communion[6] and facilitates that obedience required as a fuller sign of worship and for the sanctification of souls.

With a view to making the bishop's function more effective for an exact application of liturgical norms, especially those of the General Instruction of the Roman Missal, as well as for the sake of restoring discipline and order in the celebration of the eucharist, center of the Church's life, "a sign of unity and a bond of charity,"[7] it seems worthwhile to review the following principles and suggestions.

512   1.   The new norms have made liturgical formularies, gestures, and actions much simpler, in keeping with that principle established in the Constitution on the Liturgy: "The rites should be marked by a noble simplicity; they should be short, clear, and unencumbered by useless repetitions; they should be within the people's powers of comprehension and as a rule not require much explanation."[8] No one should go beyond these defined limits; to do so would be to strip the liturgy of its sacred symbolism and proper beauty, so needed for the fulfillment of the mystery of salvation in the Christian community and, with the help of an effective catechesis, for its comprehension under the veil of things that are seen.

The liturgical reform bears absolutely no relation to what is called "desacralization" and in no way intends to lend support to the phenomenon of "secularizing the world." Accordingly the rites must retain their dignity, spirit of reverence, and sacred character.

The effectiveness of liturgy does not lie in experimenting with rites and altering them over and over, nor in a continuous reductionism, but solely in entering more deeply into the word of God and the mystery being celebrated. It is the presence of these two that authenticates the Church's rites, not what some priest decides, indulging his own preferences.

---

4   See Acts 20:28.

5   CD no. 15 [DOL 7 no. 194]; see SC art. 22 [DOL 1 no. 22].

6   See PO no. 15: AAS 58 (1966) 1014–15; ConstDecrDecl 660.

7   SC art. 47 [DOL no. 47].

8   SC art. 34 [DOL 1 no. 34].

Keep in mind, then, that the private recasting of ritual introduced by an individual priest insults the dignity of the believer and lays the way open to individual and idiosyncratic forms in celebrations that are in fact the property of the whole Church.

The ministry of the priest is the ministry of the universal Church: its exercise is impossible without obedience, hierarchic communion, and the will to serve God and neighbor. The hierarchic character and sacramental power of the liturgy as well as the respectful service owed to the believing community demand that the priest fulfill his role in worship as the "faithful servant and steward of the mysteries of God,"[9] without imposing any rite not decreed and sanctioned by the liturgical books.

2.   Of all the texts read in the liturgical assembly the books of sacred Scripture   513
possess the primacy of a unique dignity: in them God is speaking to his people;
Christ, in his own word, continues to proclaim his Gospel.[10] Therefore:

   a.   The liturgy of the word demands cultivation with the utmost attention. In no case is it allowed to substitute readings from other sacred or profane authors, ancient or modern. The homily has as its purpose to explain to the faithful the word of God just proclaimed and to adapt it to the mentality of the times. The priest, therefore, is the homilist; the congregation is to refrain from comments, attempts at dialogue, or anything similar. To have only a single reading is never allowed.

   b.   The liturgy of the word prepares and leads up to the liturgy of the eucha-rist, forming with it the one act of worship.[11] To separate the two, therefore, or to celebrate them at different times or places is not permitted. As for integrating some liturgical service or part of the divine office before Mass with the liturgy of the word, the guidelines are the norms laid down in the liturgical books for the case in question.

3.   The liturgical texts themselves, composed by the Church, are to be treated   514
with the highest respect. No one, then, may take it on himself to make changes,
substitutions, deletions, or additions.[12]

   a.   There is special reason to keep the Order of Mass intact. Under no consid-   515
eration, not even the pretext of singing the Mass, may the official translations of its formularies be altered. There are, of course, optional forms, noted in the context of the various rites, for certain parts of the Mass: the penitential rite, the eucharistic prayers, acclamations, final blessing.

   b.   Sources for the entrance and communion antiphons are: the *Graduale roma-*   516
num, The Simple Gradual, the Roman Missal, and the compilations approved by the conferences of bishops. In choosing chants for Mass, the conferences should take into account not only suitability to the times and differing circumstances of the liturgical services, but also the needs of the faithful using them.

   c.   Congregational singing is to be fostered by every means possible, even by   517
use of new types of music suited to the culture of the people and to the contempo-rary spirit. The conferences of bishops should authorize a list of songs that are to be used in Masses with special groups, for example, with youth or children, and that in text, melody, rhythm, and instrumentation are suited to the dignity and holiness of the place and of divine worship.

---

   9   See 1 Cor 4:1.
   10   See SC art. 7 and 33 [DOL 1 nos. 7 and 33].
   11   See SC art. 56 [DOL 1 no. 56].
   12   See SC art. 22, § 3 [DOL 1 no. 22].

The Church does not bar any style of sacred music from the liturgy.[13] Still, not every style or the sound of every song or instrument deserves equal status as an aid to prayer and an expression of the mystery of Christ. All musical elements have as their one purpose the celebration of divine worship. They must, then, possess sacredness and soundness of form,[14] fit in with the spirit of the liturgical service and the nature of its particular parts; they must not be a hindrance to an intense participation of the assembly[15] but must direct the mind's attention and the heart's sentiments toward the rites.

More specific determinations belong to the conferences of bishops or, where there are no general norms as yet, to the bishop within his diocese.[16] Every attention is to be given to the choice of musical instruments; limited in number and suited to the region and to community culture, they should prompt devotion and not be too loud.

518   d. Broad options are given for the choice of prayers. Especially on weekdays in Ordinary Time the sources are any one of the Mass prayers from the thirty-four weeks of Ordinary Time or the prayers from the Masses for Various Occasions[17] or from the votive Masses.

For translations of the prayers the conferences of bishops are empowered to use the special norms in no. 34 of the Instruction on translations of liturgical texts for celebrations with a congregation, issued by the Consilium, 25 January 1969.[18]

519   e. As for readings, besides those assigned for every Sunday, feast, and weekday, there are many others for use in celebrating the sacraments or for other special occasions. In Masses for special groups the option is granted to choose texts best suited to the particular celebration, as long as they come from an authorized lectionary.[19]

520   f. The priest may say a very few words to the congregation at the beginning of the Mass and before the readings, the preface, and the dismissal,[20] but should give no instruction during the eucharistic prayer. Whatever he says should be brief and to the point, thought out ahead of time. Any other instructions that might be needed should be the responsibility of the "moderator" of the assembly, who is to avoid going on and on and say only what is strictly necessary.

521   g. The general intercessions in addition to the intentions for the Church, the world, and those in need may properly include one pertinent to the local community. That will forestall adding intentions to Eucharistic Prayer I (Roman Canon) in the commemorations of the living and the dead. Intentions for the general intercessions are to be prepared and written out beforehand and in a form consistent with the genre of the prayer.[21] The reading of the intentions may be assigned to one or more of those present at the liturgy.

[13] See SCR, Instr. MusSacr, 5 March 1967, no. 9 [DOL 508 no. 4130].

[14] See MusSacr no. 4]DOL 508 no. 4125].

[15] See SC art. 119–120 [DOL 1 nos. 119–120].

[16] See MusSacr no. 9 [DOL 508 no. 4130].

[17] See GIRM no. 323 [DOL 208 no. 1713].

[18] See Consilium Instr. *Comme le prévoit*, 25 Jan. 1969, no. 34, also nos. 21–24 [DOL 123 no. 871, also nos. 858–861].

[19] See SCDW, Instr. *Actio pastoralis*, 15 May 1969, no. 6 e [DOL 275 no. 2127].

[20] See GIRM no. 11 [DOL 208 no. 1401].

[21] See GIRM nos. 45–46 [DOL 208 nos. 1435–36].

Used intelligently, these faculties afford such broad options that there is no reason for resorting to individualistic creations. Accordingly priests are instructed to prepare their celebrations with their mind on the actual circumstances and the spiritual needs of the people and with faithful adherence to the limits set by the General Instruction of the Roman Missal.

4.   The eucharistic prayer more than any other part of the Mass is, by reason of his office, the prayer of the priest alone.[22] Recitation of any part by a lesser minister, the assembly, or any individual is forbidden. Such a course conflicts with the hierarchic character of the liturgy in which all are to do all but only those parts belonging to them.[23] The priest alone, therefore, is to recite the entire eucharistic prayer.

522

5.   The bread for eucharistic celebration is bread of wheat and, in keeping with the age-old custom of the Latin Church, unleavened.[24]

523

Its authenticity as sign requires that the bread have the appearance of genuine food to be broken and shared in together. At the same time the bread, whether the small host for communion of the faithful or the larger hosts to be broken into parts, is *always* to be made in the traditional shape, in keeping with the norm of the General Instruction of the Roman Missal.[25]

The need for greater authenticity relates to color, taste, and thickness rather than to shape. Out of reverence for the sacrament the eucharistic bread should be baked with great care, so that the breaking can be dignified and the eating not offensive to the sensibilities of the people. Bread that tastes of uncooked flour or that becomes quickly so hard as to be inedible is not to be used. As befits the sacrament, the breaking of the consecrated bread, the taking of the consecrated bread and wine in communion, and the consuming of leftover hosts after communion should be done with reverence.[26]

6.   In its sacramental sign value communion under both kinds expresses a more complete sharing by the faithful.[27] Its concession has as limits the determinations of the General Instruction of the Roman Missal (no. 242)[a] and the norm of the Instruction of the Congregation for Divine Worship, *Sacramentali Communione*, on the extension of the faculty for administering communion under both kinds, 29 June 1970.[b]

524

a.   Ordinaries are not to grant blanket permission but, within the limits set by the conference of bishops, are to specify the instances and celebrations for this form of communion. To be excluded are occasions when the number of communicants is great. The permission should be for specific, structured, and homogeneous assemblies.

b.   A thorough catechesis is to precede admittance to communion under both kinds so that the people will fully perceive its significance.

---

[22]   See GIRM no. 10 [DOL 208 no. 1400].

[23]   See SC art. 28 [DOL 1 no. 28].

[24]   See GIRM no. 282 [DOL 208 no. 1672].

[25]   See GIRM no. 283 [DOL 208 no. 1673].

[26]   See SCR, Instr. EuchMyst, 25 May 1967, no. 48 [DOL 179 no. 1277].

[27]   See GIRM no. 240 [DOL 208 no. 1630].

[a]   See DOL 208 no. 1632.

[b]   See DOL 270.

c. Priests, deacons, or acolytes who have received institution should be present to offer communion from the chalice. If there are none of these present, the rite is to be carried out by the celebrant as it is set out in the General Instruction of the Roman Missal no. 245.[c]

c. The method of having the communicants pass the chalice from one to another or having them go directly to the chalice to receive the precious blood does not seem advisable. Instead of this, communion should be by intinction.

d. The first minister of communion is the priest celebrant, next deacons, then acolytes, in particular cases to be determined by the competent authority. The Holy See has the power to permit the appointment of other known and worthy persons as ministers, if they have received a mandate. Those lacking this mandate cannot distribute communion or carry the vessels containing the blessed sacrament.

The manner of distributing communion is to conform to the directives of the General Instruction of the Roman Missal (nos. 244–252)[d] and of the 29 June 1970 Instruction of this Congregation.[e] Should there be any concession of a manner of distribution differing from the usual, the conditions the Apostolic See lays down are to be observed.

e. Wherever, for want of priests, other persons — for example, catechists in mission areas — receive from the bishop, with the concurrence of the Apostolic See, the right to celebrate the liturgy of the word and distribute communion, they are to refrain absolutely from reciting the eucharistic prayer. Should it seem desirable to read the institution narrative, they should make it a reading in the liturgy of the word. In the kind of assemblies in question, then, the recitation of the Lord's Prayer and the distribution of holy communion with the prescribed rite immediately follow the liturgy of the word.

f. Whatever the manner of distributing, great care is to be taken for its dignified, devout, and decorous administration and for forestalling any danger of irreverence. There is to be due regard for the character of the liturgical assembly and for the age, circumstances, and degree of preparation of the recipients.[28]

525

7. In conformity with norms traditional in the Church, women (single, married, religious), whether in churches, homes, convents, schools, or institutions for women, are barred from serving the priest at the altar.

According to the norms established for these matters, however, women are allowed to:

a. proclaim the readings, except the gospel. They are to make sure that, with the help of modern sound equipment, they can be comfortably heard by all. The conferences of bishops are to give specific directions on the place best suited for women to read the word of God in the liturgical assembly.

b. announce the intentions in the general intercessions;

c. lead the liturgical assembly in singing and play the organ or other instruments;

d. read the commentary assisting the people toward a better understanding of the rite;

---

[c] See DOL 208 no. 1635.

[d] See DOL 208 nos. 1634–42.

[e] See DOL 270 [no. 2115].

[28] See SCDW, Instr. *Sacra Communione*, 29 June 1970, no. 6 [DOL 270 no. 2115].

e.   attend to other functions, customarily filled by women in other settings, as a service to the congregation, for example, ushering, organizing processions, taking up the collection.[29]

8.   Sacred vessels, vestments, and furnishings are to be treated with proper respect   526
and care. The greater latitude granted with regard to their material and design is intended to give the various peoples and artisans opportunity to devote the full power of their talents to sacred worship.

But the following points must be kept in mind.

a.   Objects having a place in worship must always be "of high quality, durable, and well suited to sacred uses."[30] Anything that is trivial or commonplace must not be used.

b.   Before use, chalices and patens are to be consecrated by the bishop, who will decide whether they are fit for their intended function.

c.   "The vestment common to ministers of every rank is the alb."[31] The abuse is here repudiated of celebrating or even concelebrating Mass with stole only over the monastic cowl or over ordinary clerical garb, to say nothing of street clothes. Equally forbidden is the wearing of the stole alone over street clothes when carrying out other ritual acts, for example, the laying on of hands at ordinations, administering other sacraments, giving blessings.

d.   It is up to the conferences of bishops to decide whether it is advisable to choose materials other than the traditional for the sacred furnishings. They are to inform the Apostolic See about their decisions.[32]

As to the design of vestments, the conferences of bishops have the power to decide on and to propose to the Holy See adaptations consistent with the needs and customs of the respective regions.[33]

9.   The eucharist is celebrated as a rule in a place of worship.[34] Apart from cases of   527
real need, as adjudged by the Ordinary for his jurisdiction, celebration outside a church is not permitted. When the Ordinary does allow this, there must be care that a worthy place is chosen and that the Mass is celebrated on a suitable table. If at all possible, the celebration should not take place in a dining room or on a dining-room table.

10. In applying the reform of the liturgy, bishops should have special concern   528
about the fixed and worthy arrangement of the place of worship, especially the sanctuary, in conformity with the norms set forth in the General Instruction of the Roman Missal[35] and the Instruction *Eucharisticum mysterium*.[36]

Arrangements begun in recent years as temporary have tended in the meantime to take on a permanent form. Even some repudiated by the Consilium con-

---

[29]   See GIRM no. 68 [DOL 208 no. 1458].

[30]   See GIRM no. 288 [DOL 208 no. 1678].

[31]   See GIRM no. 298 [DOL 208 no. 1688].

[32]   See SC art. 128 [DOL 1 no. 128].

[33]   See GIRM no. 304 [DOL 208 no. 1694].

[34]   See GIRM no. 260 [DOL 208 no. 1650].

[35]   See GIRM nos. 153–280 [DOL 208 nos. 1543–1670].

[36]   See SCR, Instr. EuchMyst nos. 52–57 [DOL 179 nos. 1281–86].

tinue, though in fact they are in conflict with the sense of the liturgy, aesthetic grace, and the smoothness and dignity of liturgical celebration.[37]

Through the collaboration of diocesan commissions on liturgy and on sacred art and, if necessary, through consultation with experts or even with civil authorities, there should be a complete review of the blueprints for new constructions and of the existing adaptations. The aim is to ensure a fixed arrangement in all churches that will preserve ancient monuments where necessary and to the fullest extent possible meet new needs.

529   11.   An understanding of the reformed liturgy still demands an intense effort for accurate translations and editions of the revised liturgical books. These must be translated in their entirety and other, particular liturgical books in use must be suppressed.

Should any conference of bishops judge it necessary and timely to add further formularies or to make particular adaptations, these are to be incorporated after the approval of the Holy See and by means of a distinctive typeface are to be clearly set off as separate from the original Latin text.

In this matter it is advisable to proceed without haste, enlisting the help not only of theologians and liturgists, but of people of learning and letters. Then the translations will be documents of tested beauty; their grace, balance, elegance, and richness of style and language will endow them with the promise of lasting use; they will match the requirements of the inner richness of their content.[38]

The preparation of vernacular liturgical books is to follow the traditional norms for publishing texts: translators or authors are to remain anonymous; liturgical books are for the service of the Christian community and editing and publication is by mandate and authority of the hierarchy, which under no consideration is answerable to outsiders. That would be offensive to the freedom of church authority and the dignity of liturgy.

530   12.   Any liturgical experimentation that may seem necessary or advantageous receives authorization from this Congregation alone, in writing, with norms clearly set out, and subject to the responsibility of the competent local authority.

All earlier permissions for experimentation with the Mass, granted in view of the liturgical reform as it was in progress, are to be considered as no longer in effect. Since publication of the *Missale Romanum* the norms and forms of eucharistic celebration are those given in the General Instruction and the Order of Mass.

The conferences of bishops are to draw up in detail any adaptations envisioned in the liturgical books and submit them for confirmation to the Holy See.

Should further adaptations become necessary, in keeping with the norm of the Constitution *Sacrosanctum Concilium* art. 40,[f] the conference of bishops is to examine the issue thoroughly, attentive to the character and traditions of each people and to specific pastoral needs. When some form of experimentation seems advisable, there is to be a precise delineation of its limits and a testing within qualified groups by prudent and specially appointed persons. Experimentation should not take place in large-scale celebrations nor be widely publicized. Experiments should be few and not last beyond a year. A report then is to be sent to the Holy See. While a reply is pending, use of the petitioned adaptation is forbidden. When changes in the structure of rites or in the order of parts as set forth in the liturgical books are involved,

---

[37]   See Consilium, Letter of Card. G. Lercaro to presidents of the conferences of bishops, 30 June 1965 [DOL 31 no. 415].

[38]   See Paul VI, Addr. to liturgical commissions of Italy, 7 Feb. 1969 [DOL 246 no. 1968].

[f]   See DOL 1 no. 40.

or any departure from the usual, or the introduction of new texts, a point-by-point outline is to be submitted to the Holy See prior to the beginning of any kind of experiment.

Such a procedure is called for and demanded by both the Constitution *Sacrosanctum Concilium*[39] and the importance of the issue.

13. In conclusion: it must be remembered that the liturgical reform decided on by   531
the Council affects the universal Church. It thus requires in pastoral meetings a study of its meaning and practice for the Christian education of the people to the end that the liturgy may become vital, touch the soul, and meet its needs.

The contemporary reform aims at making available liturgical prayer that has its origin in a living and honored tradition. Once available this prayer must appear clearly as the work of the entire people of God in all their orders and ministries.[40] The effectiveness and authenticity of this reform has as its sole guarantee the unity of the whole ecclesial organism.

Prompted by a ready obedience to church laws and precepts and by a spirit of faith, and putting aside purely personal preferences or idiosyncracies, pastors especially should be ministers of the community liturgy through personal example, study, and an intelligent, persistent catechesis. They will thus prepare for that flowering spring expected from this liturgical reform, which looks to the needs of the age and which repudiates the secular and arbitrary as lethal to itself.

Pope Paul VI has approved this Instruction, prepared at his mandate by the Congregation for Divine Worship, and confirmed it with his authority on 3 September 1970, ordering its publication and its observance by all concerned.

53. PAUL VI, **Address** to a general audience, excerpt on the Church as a community of prayer, 3 November 1971: Not 7 (1971) 377–378.

[. . .] What is the Church? The Church is a community that prays; a people   532
singing praise and voicing their petitions, a people of God. That is the mark of the Church's philosophy and theology. It is we human beings who need God (see 2 Cor 3:5), we who to him owe everything (see Mt 22:38). Thus our fundamental, characteristically human attitude is one of worship. The Church is before all else a society of worship; its most pressing concern is prayer. The Church sets before itself one primary aim: to put people in touch with God, indeed in communion with him; the Church, as the Council teaches, is "the sign and instrument of intimate union with God" (LG no. 1). The Church binds us to itself as its faithful in order to join us to God as his faithful. The Church through the word, through charity, through the sacraments makes present in history the Christ of the Gospel, the one effective and indispensable mediator between God and ourselves. That is the Church's basic mission, the mission of worship. And this collective mission requires the most solid and strong structures. The Church therefore claims, and with every right, to offer to humanity the definitive answer to the issue of religion, which, as everyone knows, has so much fascinated and weighed upon humanity. Even in the face of the all but universal indifference and the fierce denials of our age, the Church firmly maintains that religion always possesses, and today more than ever, a reason for being and,

---

[39]   See SC art. 40 [DOL 1 no. 40].
[40]   See GIRM no. 58 [DOL 208 no. 1448].

further, that the religious answer that the Church itself offers is the "foundation and the crown" of human life, of its knowledge, and of its striving. That answer is the light, the support, the terminus, the blessedness of our earthly existence; it is the first and the last word, the alpha and the omega for the world. Through its universal and supreme, human and cosmic view, that is, the Catholic religion, the Church is organized, exists, loves, works, and suffers. And always by carrying out its twofold conversation with God and with people, always by praying.

Like it or not, this is the figure of the Church: it is humanity arrayed as a choir of praise and prayer, adoring the Father "in spirit and in truth" (Jn 4:23). This Church presents to us a splendid countenance, radiant with spirituality and community, with moral strength and charity's goodness, with mystery and clarity. No other earthly institution can offer or claim to present such a countenance to the people of this age. This radiance shines out from the Church's face as the reflection of the countenance of God (see Ps 4:7). This is what the praying Church is.

PRAYER AS INTERIOR AND PERSONAL, PUBLIC AND COMMUNAL

533   The Church praying has received at the Council its most splendid idealization. We must not forget that regarding the stirring reality of liturgical reform. Great weight, even regarding the spiritual conditions of today's world, is due to that reform because of its originating, pastoral intent to reawaken prayer among the people of God. This is to be a pure and shared prayer, that is, interior and personal, yet at the same time public and communal. Its meaning is not simply a matter of ritual, pertaining to the sacristy or to an arcane and merely liturgical erudition. Prayer is to be a religious affirmation, full of faith and life: an apostolic school for all seekers of the life-giving truth; a spiritual challenge thrown down before an atheistic, pagan, and secularized world.

On the recent occasion of the publication of the new breviary, one of the personal and particularly expressive letters we received remarked among other things on the advantage of urging the faithful "at a time of widespread world tensions to remember the excellence of the reading, explanation of, and meditation on the word of God, with the assurance that such an exhortation would be received as salutary by everyone. It would be, as it were, a seal on the new liturgical book and at the same time a rightful recognition of the opportunity to share in a prayer composed by the labors of centuries and echoing the lasting voice of the Fathers, doctors, and theologians of the Church. . . ." This is quite true and it is such an exhortation that we now make in these informal remarks. We address them especially to the clergy and religious whose honor and duty it is in a particular way to keep the flame of prayer alight in the Church. We address them, as well to all those devout children of the Church who know that every renewal in the Church, its vitality, its surmounting of difficulties and crises, its capacity to serve the liberation and salvation of those who are near or far, are all sustained by prayer. That prayer is intimate and personal (see Mt 6:4) but nonetheless communal, priestly, and public: it is the prayer we call liturgy.

54. SC DIVINE WORSHIP, **Letter** *Durante los meses* of Cardinal A. Tabero to Bishop A. Brandão Vilela, President of CELAM, on certain aspects of the reform of the liturgy, 8 November 1972: Not 8(1972) 365–369 (Spanish; excerpt).

534   During the past August and September, I have had the opportunity to visit a great many of the countries of Latin America. This visit, undertaken at the kind

invitation of the secretary of CELAM and of several conferences of bishops, has allowed me: first, to take part in the meeting for study and reflection held at Medellín by the leaders in the liturgical movement and to engage in frequent dialogue with them; second, to meet in several countries with the body of bishops or at least with the national liturgical commissions. [. . .]

At this time the Congregation for Divine Worship feels the need to continue the dialogue thus begun, with the same spirit of fraternal cooperation. [. . .]

1.   In the first place we must acknowledge appreciatively the evident efforts ex-   535
pended to bring about in Latin America the welcome results in liturgical reform that the Council sought and intended. Evident at the same time, however, is the pressing need that bishops, priests, religious, and all the people of God enter ever more fully and deeply into the spirit of the measures introduced into the reformed liturgy. Then the result will be, as it should, that these measures will not remain something merely outward and passing, condemned to disappear when this novelty has worn off, but will stand as a continuous, strong, and enduring spiritual and pastoral advance for the dioceses and communities.

A genuine need that must be faced is that the prerequisites of any such success are concern and activity on the part of the bishops and of the national and diocesan liturgical commissions, which according to the Council must be established every-where (SC art. 44–45).[a]

Acting both within their conferences and as the responsible leaders in their own dioceses, the bishops must provide the liturgy with its true inspiration and animation. They must study and evaluate the circumstances of their people and the condition of the interchange between clergy and laity in the liturgy and the liturgical ministry. They must further and support the steps undertaken for the liturgical formation of all. They must propose the forms of celebration most suited to the individual circumstances of their people and see to the maximum use of all the pastoral resources that the revised liturgical books offer. They must engage in frequent dialogue with those taking individual liberties in the liturgy so that they may correct abuses and innovations based on imprecise ideas originating in unacceptable positions and so that they may inspire, direct, and give guidance toward a sound course of action, one based on a genuine liturgical spirit and pastoral concern.

All of us are convinced that in discharging their offices the bishops cannot restrict themselves to watchfulness and banning. Rather they have to devote themselves to proposing measures conducive to the solution of emerging problems and to ensuring that priests do not succumb to the temptation of the line of least resistance or adopt forms of celebration that are static and lifeless, but do what they can to bring quickly to realization what the Council's words describe: "The liturgy is the summit toward which the activity of the Church is directed; at the same time it is the fount from which all the Church's power flows" (SC art. 10).[b]

2.   An indispensable element for success in this matter is the *liturgical commission*,   536
the establishment of which, according to the Council, is obligatory in every diocese and country. Undoubtedly, a basic means for the liturgical reform to succeed and to become a unique pastoral resource is the furtherance of the creation and the work of commissions that are well organized and efficient, made up of experts fully prepared and dedicated, on whom the bishops can rely. Given the situation in some dioceses of Latin America, it will not always be possible to establish one at the

---

    [a]   See DOL 1 nos. 44–45.

    [b]   DOL 1 no. 10.

diocesan or even at the interdiocesan level. But an intelligent pooling of all available resources, under the direction of each national hierarchy as well as cooperation between countries with similar problems, will always be most important and effective for the end we have in mind.

Permit us to lay special emphasis on the need to vitalize and make effective the commission charged with the preparation of the translation of liturgical books for Latin America, which has recently replaced the joint CELAM-Spain commission and about which much is said in the report to the Department of Liturgy of the General Assembly of CELAM.

As we know, it is a commission that, like other agencies of CELAM, must be ready to serve the conferences of bishops and that will have to devote itself not only to the translation of the liturgical books into Spanish, but also to studying possible adaptations of the liturgy to concrete situations in Latin America and within each country, in keeping with the directives of the Council (SC art. 37–40).[c]

The workings and activities of this commission take on a greater necessity and urgency at the present time when liturgical commissions are reviewing the experiments of the past few years and reevaluating the first translations. Some conferences of bishops have already completed a first revision of, for example, the *Ordo Missae* and it has been or is about to be submitted to this Congregation for approval and confirmation. We note that the work of revision that may sometimes be required must not in any way jeopardize the necessary unity that has to be retained as the norm, at least in the parts of the liturgy intended for participation of the laity.

537   3.   We wish to insist on one further point: the pressing need to prepare *personnel specializing* in liturgy. In some parts of Latin America there could be a failure to attach sufficient importance to the liturgy because of more pressing human and material needs. But this want of esteem or appreciation for the liturgy arises usually and most frequently from the lack of preparation in pastors and people, who therefore do not put the liturgy in the place belonging to it in the life and activity of the Church. They are in need of guides to help in the discovery of the principles for reform outlined by the Council.

CELAM, through its Instituto Liturgico de Medellín, has the power to remedy this deficiency and possesses the means to raise the level of the liturgical-pastoral preparation of those people of Latin America who must carry out their activity in the parishes and dioceses. There are difficulties, sometimes serious difficulties, but no one can fail to perceive the benefits that in matters liturgical such preparation can bring to the renewal of the Church in Latin America. A similar institute, under the direction of CELAM, with expert administrative and teaching personnel, programs and teaching methods marked by fidelity to the doctrine and norms of the Church, and students carefully chosen will increasingly yield the happiest results: people who are knowledgeable and well prepared to serve the Latin American Church and to assist the bishops in the field of liturgical reform.

This Congregation cannot but recall a few beautiful and significant words of the Council that are a stimulus to all of us having responsibility in the reform of the liturgy: "Zeal for the promotion and restoration of the liturgy is rightly held to be a sign of the providential dispositions of God in our time, a movement of the Holy Spirit in his Church. Today it is a distinguishing mark of the Church's life, indeed of the whole tenor of contemporary religious thought and action" (SC art. 43).[d]
[. . .]

---

c   See DOL 1 nos. 37–40.

d   DOL 1 no. 43.

55. PAUL VI, **Address** to a general audience, proposing a decalogue for prayer, 22 August 1973: Not 9 (1973) 297–300 (Italian).

When we propose to further a religious reform, its very nature impels us to think anew about prayer, both private and communal. It is not without significance that the first of the documents of the recent Council is the Constitution on the Liturgy, i.e., on the Church's official prayer. Prayer (*oratio*) is the distinctive act of the virtue of religion (see ST 2a2ae, 83.3). Accordingly the desire to stamp the life of religion with a consciousness and an expression fitted to the needs and attitudes of the people of today calls on us to invite them and to teach them to pray. We know that the topic is limitless; allow us to keep this talk to the most basic observations.

First, a question: do people pray today?

Where the Church is alive, yes. Prayer is the breath of the Mystical Body, its conversation with God, the expression of its charity, its endeavor to reach the Father. Prayer is the acknowledgment of the Father's providence in the events of the world, the plea for his mercy and the intervention of his help where our powers fail, the confession of our need for him and of his glory. It is the joy of the people of God in praising him and all that comes to us from him; it is the school of the Christian life. That means that prayer is a flower that springs up from a double root, deep and living: the religious sense (its root in nature); the grace of the Holy Spirit (its root surpassing nature), who inspires us to pray (see Rom 8:26; H. Bremond, *Introduction à la philosophie de la Prière*, p. 224, etc.). We can say rightly that prayer is the Church expressing itself vertically; yet also that it is the Church's nourishment, its source. Prayer is the privileged moment when the divine life begins to course through the Church. We must, then, attend to prayer intensely and esteem it highly, remembering the words of the Council that "the liturgy does not exhaust the entire activity of the Church. Before people can come to the liturgy they must be called to faith and to conversion" (SC art. 9).[a]

That brings up another giant obstacle to the religious renewal intended by the Council and planned by the coming Holy Year: how do we bring today's people to pray?

We must acknowledge that the irreligion of so many people of today makes it very difficult to inspire in the spirits of our contemporaries a prayer that is prompt, spontaneous, and joyous. We would say, oversimplifying, that there are two classes of objection. The first assails at its roots the very reason for prayer's existence, alleging that prayer is without any divine respondent and so is vain, pointless, even damaging to the autonomy of the human person. The second objection is a refusal to trust itself in practice to the experience of prayer; it keeps lips and heart tightly shut, like a person afraid to speak in an unknown, foreign tongue, and it inures itself to regard life without any reference to God ("like Françoise Sagan, who one day told a reporter, 'God — I never give him a thought!'"; Ch. Moeller, *L'Homme moderne devant le salut*, p. 18).

We spoke of a giant obstacle; but it is not insuperable. And for one reason: like it or not the need of God is inborn in the human heart. The heart suffers so often, debases itself in an unreasoned skepticism because it has suppressed the voice within that through countless stirrings seeks to address itself to heaven; not as to an empty and terrifyingly inscrutable cosmos, but as to the First Being, the Absolute, the Creator, the living God (see R. Guardini, *Dieu vivant*; P. C. Landucci, *Il Dio in cui crediamo*; Simone Weil, who died at Ashford exactly thirty years ago, 24 August 1943, *Attente de Dieu*). Notice, even for their significance simply as psycho-social phenomena, the unusual expressions among the younger generations of a collective

538

---

[a] DOL 1 no. 9.

mysticism that is not always an affected mystification; rather it seems to be a thirst for God, perhaps still without awareness of the true fountain for quenching it, but unfeigned as the silent declaration of what it is: a thirst, a profound thirst.

In any case, our wish is to give to prayer, both personal (thus measured by the requirements of age and circumstances) and communal (thus corresponding to the life of the community) particular attention keyed to the spiritual renewal we are hoping and preparing for.

DECALOGUE FOR PRAYER

From many valiant workers in today's fields of the kingdom of God we are able to put together empirically a decalogue of suggestions they have proposed to us. This is it, in the form of simple but perhaps not useless information.

539   I.   There must be a faithful, intelligent, and careful application of the liturgical reform promoted by the Council and particularized by the competent church authorities. Whoever blocks it or slows it down without reason loses the providential opportunity for a true revitalization and spread of the Catholic religion in our times. Whoever exploits the reform as a way of indulging in arbitrary experiments dissipates energy and outrages the *sensus Ecclesiae*.

Now is the hour for honoring in God's Church with good will and with unanimity that solemn *lex orandi*: reform of the liturgy.

540   II.   Always to be recommended is catechesis — philosophical, scriptural, theological, pastoral — on divine worship as the Church proclaims it today. For prayer is not a blind feeling; it is the utterance of a soul enlightened by truth and impelled by charity (ST 2a2ae, 83.1 ad 2).

541   III.   The voices of authority advise us in carrying out reform to exercise great caution with regard to the traditional religious practices of people; to guard against extinguishing religious sentiment in the course of giving it a new and more authentically spiritual expression. A sense for what is true, beautiful, simple, a sense of the community, and of tradition — always deserving respect — must rule over the outward manifestations of worship, with a view to preserving the attachment of the people to them.

542   IV.   The family must be the great school of devotion, of spirituality, of fidelity to religion. The Church has deep trust in the sensitive, authoritative, irreplaceable activity of parents as religious teachers.

543   V.   *The obligation to observe Sundays and holydays of obligation* retains more than ever its fundamental importance. The Church has made concessions to make this observance possible. Anyone aware of the meaning and purpose of this precept of the Church must see it not simply as a basic duty, but as a right, a need, an honor, an opportunity; no real and intelligent believer can, without grave reasons, refuse to fulfill it.

544   VI.   The established community claims for itself the right to the presence of all its faithful. Should some be permitted a certain autonomy in the practice of religion as distinct, homogeneous groups, they must retain the understanding of the Church's nature: it is a people, with one heart and one soul; it is, even socially, a unity; it is a Church.

545   VII.   As it unfolds, a liturgical celebration, especially of the Mass, is always a very serious action. It must, then, be prepared and carried out with great care in its every

detail, even the externals (as to gravity, dignity, schedule, duration, etc., the unfailing simplicity and sacredness of the spoken word). Here the ministers of worship have a grave responsibility in regard to their own performance and example.

VIII.   Similarly, the assistance of the faithful must contribute to the worthy performance of worship: by their punctuality, orderliness, silence, above all their participation, the principal point of the liturgical reform. All of this has been said before, but how much remains be done.   546

IX.   Prayer in its full meaning is to have two levels, the personal and the communal, as the liturgical norms have indicated.   547

X.   Singing: what a great problem! But take heart: it is not insoluble. A new epoch is beginning for sacred music. Many have called for the preservation in all nations of the Latin, Gregorian chant of the *Gloria, Credo, Sanctus, and Agnus Dei.* May that be God's will. Then we can study what steps can be taken to achieve it.[R37]   548

So many things: yet how beautiful they are and ultimately how simple. If they are carried out, what power their new outpouring upon the community of the faithful would have to bring about in the Church and in the world the longed-for religious renewal.

56. PAUL VI, **Address** to a general audience, on the effects of liturgical participation, 26 March 1975.[*]

The liturgical celebration of Holy Week requires of us, the faithful (although we could just as well say this of every thinking person) a preparatory reflection on the objective meaning of the events that this celebration intends not only to recall and portray, but in a certain sense to reactualize.   549

The first feature of the liturgical act that impresses itself on our attention is one of supreme interest and one that a religious outlook, raised up to the transcendent, supratemporal sense of our relationship with God, finds to be obvious and compelling. It is this: a religious attitude is able to invest religious facts, which bear the mark of God's presence and even of his being in a place, with a power of permanence. Pascal has said: "Jesus will be in agony until the end of the world and we must not fall asleep during his agony" (*Le mystère de Jésus*). The paschal mystery mystically continues in time and goes on today.

That is why we are privileged not only to be present at the celebration of the liturgy, but permitted and urged to take part. Participation in the liturgy, always a point of church teaching, has become a program especially emphasized by the recent Vatican Council. We cannot, then, simply be present at a liturgical rite as spectators. If we are truly drawn into its meaning and intent, we must become, to an extent, the actors in it. Or we must at least become attuned to the celebration by transferring to the time and setting of its origins our religious thoughts and sentiments. We must therefore see ourselves sitting at table at the Last Supper, standing along the *Via Crucis*, lightning-struck at the mystery of the risen Jesus' appearances. The language of the liturgy is meant to be a transparent screen allowing our physical and actual humanity to unite itself to the events and statements that the language relates.

[R37]   See commentary on no. X in *Not* 9 (1973) 302–303.

[*]   Text, OR 27 March 1975, 1 (Italian; excerpt).

Today we are, as it were, under a kind of spell. The constant invasion of modern theater and films with their overwhelming power has inured us to this spell. But there is an essential difference in the liturgical drama. The theater or a film entertains and may even absorb us, but they do not lead us to mistake their shadow for substance, their fantasy for reality. They affect our senses, penetrate our imagination, perhaps move us. But we are aware that they have nothing to do with our own real existence: the spectator is purely passive, always free to draw back from the spell of the "diversion" in its etymological sense — as a turning away from the concrete reality of our lives (see Pascal, ibid. II; also Bossuet, *Sur la Comédie; Oeuvres* XII, 237). In contrast, the liturgical drama not only brings to mind again Christ's deeds but reactualizes his salvific action (see ST 3a, 56.1 and 3; Vagaggini, *Il senso teologico della liturgia*, 98ff.). Likewise very different are the memorial, however noble, of a great personality (Socrates, for example) and the human-divine memorial of Christ, as he is the always active source of our salvation. To memorialize him reactualizes the effects belonging to him, both as exemplars and as active causes (see Pius XII, *Mediator Dei* no. 163), which invest the liturgical celebration with its distinguishing mark and incomparable dignity. The celebration is a representation *sui generis* that makes it become part of our existence, of life as it is lived.

In any believer who participates in the liturgy there is no sense of remoteness or of being on the outside. Consequently in celebrating the paschal mystery the believer is taken into and overcome by the dramatic power of the "hour" of Christ, *"my hour"* as he called it (see Jn 2:4, 12:23, 17:1, etc.). [. . .]

57. PAUL VI, **Address** to a general audience, excerpt on the liturgy as the first source for renewal of the Christian life, 6 August 1975: Not 11 (1975) 217–219 (Italian).

550   [. . .] Renewal calls for many things that the Church can and must make use of. What is the first? First, as you know, is the liturgy: in dignity, in the understanding that the living Church has of the divine plan for salvation, in being what the Council has singled out first and recommended for the renewal of the Christian life in the world. It was to the liturgy that the first conciliar document addressed itself and it is this legislation that characterizes the Council itself as one of renewal: unlike others it was not directly dogmatic, but rather a pedagogic and pastoral council.

In the overall plan of human and Christian life the priority of prayer has thus been acknowledged, on the supposition and the demand that spiritual contact with God must be conscious and personal, as we have had other occasions to affirm.[a] We must, however, integrate this primary act of our religion (see L. De Grandmaison, *La religion personelle*) into the complete and rightful setting of its most authentic expression, which, by divine institution, is social, communal, and ecclesial, that is, sacerdotal and liturgical. The official form our religion takes is the liturgy. In the course of our eagerness to rekindle the vitality and authenticity of religion in the life of individuals, but especially in the life of the people of God, we must revere and promote the liturgy in our times, in ecclesial and collective life. As the Constitution states, "The liturgy does not exhaust the entire activity of the Church. . . . Nevertheless, the liturgy is the summit toward which the activity of the Church is

---

[a]   See DOL 45, 46, 49, 53, 55.

directed; at the same time it is the fount from which all the Church's power flows" (SC art. 9, 10).[b]

As much as the liturgy has been discussed before and since the Council, our hope, strengthened by the Council's own advocacy, is that such discussion will continue, so that liturgy becomes the law and the practice of our religious life. For us it suffices here to confirm the liturgical program that the Church has set before itself, to make stable and fruitful the idea and therefore the practice of the liturgy. In that program lies the secret of a new vitality for the Church's tradition, the face of the Church's beauty, the expression of the Church's interior and universal unity, and at the same time the manifold and pentecostal expression of every tongue and every people. Above all the liturgical program is the affirmation of two basic principles. Let us call them to mind. The liturgy is the celebration of the priesthood of Christ (see SC art. 7).[c] He is present among us especially in the eucharistic sacrifice of the Mass, in order to make present and accomplish, wherever we are, the divine and human drama of our redemption, the drama above all of a love that offers itself and saves, the drama we have now become used to calling the "paschal mystery." The liturgy wells up from the depths of religious truth, from the revelation of the active, divine plan of goodness, mercy, sharing, from the Father's charity toward humanity through the Word made flesh like us and for us, in the Spirit of love that descends upon us to make us ascend in return in the consummation of a new fullness of glorious and eternal life (see Eph 1:3ff.).

Let us say no more. But we must all hold fast and joyously to the conviction that the *lex orandi* (rule of prayer) possesses in the *lex credendi* (rule of faith) its guiding light and measure; the rule of faith is the word received; the liturgy, the word expressed (see M. Zundel, *Le poème de la sainte liturgie*, a preconciliar but pertinent work). But let us speak of the other fundamental principle of the liturgical reform: the people of God must be made up of believers who know, who participate, and up to a point concelebrate with the priest, the *alter Christus* who speaks for God to the people and for the people to God. The liturgy is a communion of minds, prayers, voices, agape or charity. Passive presence is not enough; participation is required. The people must see in the liturgy a school for listening and learning, a sacred celebration presented and guided by the priest, but in which, as a gathering of hearts and voices, they join by their response, their offerings, their prayers, and their song. If the Council and the Holy Year will have strengthened the people in their obligation to participate and sing in the liturgy, they will have succeeded in an achievement of immense value for religion and community. Whoever sings participates and whoever participates is not bored but full of joy. Whoever finds joy in prayer remains and develops as a Christian. Whoever is a Christian is saved.

551

Let no one think of this elation as an illusion or as an empty escape from the actual and social realities of our concrete, human existence. On the contrary the elation means the outpouring of wisdom and energy that makes Christians as citizens eager, generous, and active in the sphere of earthly realities even as they march and lead toward citizenship in heaven.

Remember that liturgy is believing, praising in song, alive to earthly experience, on pilgrimage toward the celebration of the eternal revelation.

---

[b]   DOL 1 nos. 9, 10.

[c]   See DOL 1 no. 7.

58. PAUL VI, **Epistle** (autograph) *Nous avons pris* to Cardinal J. Villot, Secretary of State, on the case of Archbishop M. Lefebvre, 21 February 1976.*

552   We have taken note of an interview given by Archbishop Marcel Lefebvre in the weekly, *France Catholique-Ecclesia* (no. 1322, 13 February 1976). Among the errors contained in this interview there is one which we wish to correct personally: it alleges that you stand between the Pope and Archbishop Lefebvre, as a barrier to his meeting with us in person. That is not the case.

Our judgment is that before being received in audience Archbishop Lefebvre must retract his unacceptable position on Vatican Council II and on the measures we have promulgated or approved in the areas of liturgy and church discipline (and, by implication, of doctrine). Unfortunately he continues to advocate his position in word and act. A genuine change of attitude is therefore required in order that the desired meeting may take place in the spirit of fraternity and ecclesial unity that we have so desired ever since the beginning of this painful affair and especially since we have on two separate occasions written personally to Archbishop Lefebvre.

We continue to hope that he will soon by his deeds give us a concrete proof of his loyalty to the Church and the Holy See, from which he has received so many signs of esteem and confidence. We know that you share this hope and for that reason we authorize you to make this letter public; this reflects our favor and affection toward you, our co-worker in the apostolic office.

59. PAUL VI, **Address** to a consistory, excerpt on loyalty to the Church and the Council, 24 May 1976: AAS 68 (1976) 369–378; Not 12 (1976) 217–223.

553   II.   As we have already remarked, a consistory stands as a very solemn and serious occasion in the Church's life, lived in its earthly conditions. On the occasion of your presence and participation we cannot under any consideration omit a discussion of several issues and affairs of the Church which are matters of concern to us, which we regard to be of great importance, and about which we desire to share with you our sentiments. These are on the one hand feelings of gratitude and joy, but on the other, of anguish and sorrow.

554   1.   The positive sentiments arise from the innate optimism — grounded on the secure promises of Christ[2] and on ever new and consoling happenings in the Church — that we keep alive in our heart. That optimism represents the vital flowering and youthfulness of the Church, for which there are such witnesses and examples at hand. These we have observed and come in contact with all during the recently ended Holy Year, which continues to be a light for our spirit. The essence of the Christian life lies in the life of the spirit, in that supernatural life which is God's gift. To us has been granted that singular solace of seeing that the spiritual life is growing and flourishing among so many nations and peoples through their bearing witness to the faith, through the liturgy, through a desire for prayer again felt and savored, through the joy springing from a clear spiritual vision and purity.

In addition, we see a constant increase of love for neighbor, which is inseparable from love for God and which sparks the ardor of desire in many of our children and their works of mercy for the poor, the outcast, the defenseless.

---

* Original French text, DocCath 73 (1976) 305.

[2] See Mt 28:20; Jn 16:33.

We know that the directive norms of the late Council are effectively guiding and sustaining the continuous effort of self-conformity to the Gospel of Christ through the cultivation of a truly Christian life and the practice of the theological virtues.

With intense admiration we look upon burgeoning mission initiatives and we perceive sure signs of progress in another matter of immense importance, the area, namely, of priestly and religious vocations. Without any doubt in several countries, after an interval of decline, vocations are reviving.

We observe on every continent young people magnanimously and in practice obeying the gospel precepts and in their lives giving witness to their will to preserve the necessary conjunction between the high ideals of a Christian life and the duty to put them into practice.

So, our Esteemed Brothers, the Spirit is indeed active in all areas of the Church, even those which for a time seemed most barren.

2.   There are, however, underlying causes for bitterness and grief that we have   555
no intention of concealing or understating. More often than not these causes proceed from a patent, sometimes incurable extremism regarding certain excesses that point to, in their opposing factions, an immature frivolousness or a defiant obstinacy. Such attitudes beget a regrettable refusal to listen to all those urgings and admonitions, that the priceless teaching of the Council issued more than ten years ago, to provide a sound balance, calming turbulent spirits.

a.   One extreme is made up of those who — claiming the strongest allegiance to the Church and the magisterium — reject and repudiate in practice the very principles of the Council and their subsequent application and reformation as well as the measured carrying out of these principles by the work of the Holy See and the conferences of bishops under our Christ-given authority. Such people diminish the Church's authority under pretext of tradition; their obedience to that authority is merely lip-service. They draw the faithful away from the ties of obedience to the See of Peter as well as from their lawful bishops. They repudiate the authority of today in favor of that of another age. It is all the more grievous and evil that the recalcitrance we refer to not only has certain priests as its defenders but has a bishop, Marcel Lefebvre, whom we still continue to reach out to with respect, as its leader and guide.

We make these observations with profound sorrow; but anyone can see that this course of action — whatever the goals or intentions of these people — involves the intent to pass beyond obedience to and communion with the successor of Peter and therefore with the Church.

Sadly, this is the natural consequence when anyone insists that on the pretext of keeping the faith intact and of working in his own way to defend the Church he would rather flout obedience than obey. That, of course, is utterly at variance with genuine obedience. And this is the openly declared position. These people do not even hesitate to claim that Vatican Council II has no obligatory force; that the Catholic faith is in jeopardy by reason of the conciliar norms; that the Council is to be disobeyed in order to safeguard certain traditions. What traditions? To their own circle — not to the pope, the college of bishops, an ecumenical council — should belong the right to choose among countless traditions those that are to be held as norms of faith. You must see, our Esteemed Brothers, that such a position calls into question the divine will that made Peter and his lawful successors the head of the Church, who being confirmed in faith would feed the whole flock,[3] and

---

[3]   See Lk 22:32; Jn 21:15ff.

the divine will that constitutes the head of the Church as the guarantor and guardian of the deposit of faith.

We must attach to this refusal to respect the liturgical norms laid down a special grievousness in that it introduces division where Christ's love has gathered us together in unity, namely, into the liturgy and the eucharistic sacrifice. For our part, in the name of tradition, we beseech all our children and all Catholic communities to celebrate the rites of the restored liturgy with dignity and fervent devotion. Use of the new *Ordo Missae* is in no way left up to the choice of priests or people. The Instruction of 14 June 1971 provided that celebration of Mass according to the former rite would be permitted, by faculty from the Ordinary, only for aged or sick priests offering the sacrifice *without a congregation*.[a] The new *Ordo Missae* was promulgated in place of the old after careful deliberation and to carry out the directives of Vatican Council II. For a like reason our predecessor St. Pius V, after the Council of Trent, commanded the use of the Roman Missal revised by his authority.

In virtue of the supreme authority granted to us by Jesus Christ we command the same ready obedience to the other new laws, relating to liturgy, discipline, pastoral activity, made in these last years to put into effect the decrees of the Council. Any course of action seeking to stand in the way of the conciliar decrees can under no consideration be regarded as a work done for the advantage of the Church, since it in fact does the Church serious harm.

Both personally and through our assistants and other friends we have warned Archbishop Lefebvre about the gravity of the measures he is taking; the unlawfulness of his principal, continuing undertakings; the emptiness and frequent falsity of the doctrinal tenets by which he tries to support both his position and his undertakings; and about the losses to the whole Church originating with him.[b]

556   With profound anguish, yet with the hope of a father, we turn our thoughts now to our brother in the episcopate, his collaborators, and all those who have been drawn in as followers. We are convinced that many of these Christians were honorably motivated, at least at the outset. We have a clear awareness of their devout affection for the traditional forms of worship and discipline from which for so long they drew spiritual strength and nurture. But we are equally sure that if they would begin, calmly and without bias, to think about it, they will admit that they can find today the strength and sustenance they seek in the renewed forms of religion that both to the Council and to us it has seemed necessary to introduce in order to advance the good of the Church, its progress in today's world, and its unity. Again, therefore, we exhort them, our brothers and sons, and implore them to take cognizance of the grave wounds they will otherwise inflict on the Church. We repeat the invitation to them to ponder again Christ's solemn pronouncements about the unity of the Church[4] and about obedience to the lawful shepherd he placed over his whole flock, since such obedience is a sign of that due to the Father and the Son.[5] We await them with open heart and with arms eager to embrace them; may all of them, giving us an example of humility, return to the path of unity and love to gladden the people of God.

557   b. At the other extreme are those who — proposing just the opposite teaching, but giving us equal cause for grief — falsely regard themselves as taking the road opened by the Council. Moved by their own one-sided opinions, which in

---

a   See DOL 216 no. 1772.

b   See DOL 58.

4   See Jn 17:21ff.

5   See Lk 10:16.

some cases seem beyond hope of correction, they are fiercely engaged in passing judgment on the Church and its institutions.

With equal firmness, therefore, we must repudiate the course of action taken by:

— Those who decide that they have the right to create a liturgy of their own, at times reducing the sacrifice of the Mass and the sacraments to a celebration of life or their own struggles and to the status of a symbol of their own spirit of community; or practice outlawed forms of intercommunion.

— Those who in teaching religion water down the teaching of Catholic doctrine, accommodating it to human desires or demands on the basis of opinions that entirely debase the Christian message. This we have already declared in the Apostolic Exhortation *Quinque iam annos*, issued 8 December 1971 five years after the close of the Council.[6]

— Those who by their attitude show outright scorn for the living tradition of the Church, from the Fathers on down to the teaching of the magisterium. They have a new method of interpreting the teaching of the Church, the Gospel itself, spiritual realities, the divinity of Christ, his resurrection, or the eucharist in such a way as to destroy utterly the genuine meaning of these truths. They thus are creating a new *gnōsis* in the Church and in a sense introducing "free thought." The effect is all the more dangerous since the persons involved are those to whom the sublime and supremely serious office of teaching sacred theology has been entrusted.

— Those who make light of the proper office of the priestly ministry.

— Those who deplorably violate the laws of the Church or the precepts of the moral life the Church instills.

— Those who understand the Christian life as though its purpose was to put order into earthly society. They in fact reduce Christianity to political action, employing to this end a spirit, means, and measures that contradict the Gospel. They go so far as to confuse the transcendent message of Christ, his preaching of the kingdom of God, his commandment of love toward others based on God's ineffable fatherhood, with points of view that effectively deny Christ's message. They substitute in its place a doctrine totally opposed to it and propose an uneasy marriage between two views of human life that are utterly incompatible — as various protagonists of this teaching acknowledge.

Christians of this stripe are surely not very numerous, but they are very noisy, since they foolishly believe that they are the interpreters of the needs of the whole Christian people or of the irreversible course of history. As they do so they can in no way appeal to the authority of Vatican Council II, since its correct interpretation and application give absolutely no grounds for license. Nor can they plead the demands of the apostolate for ways to approach people who do not practice their religion or who lack the Christian faith. Genuine apostles receive their mission from the Church as witnesses to the teaching and life of the Church. The leaven must permeate the whole dough, but it must remain the leaven of the Gospel, otherwise it too spoils along with the world.

Esteemed Brothers! Our desire has been to pass on to you these our innermost thoughts because we know well what kind of times threaten the Church. The Church is and will always remain a sign and a standard raised among the peoples,[7] because it has the task of announcing the truth to the world and sometimes, with

558

---

6   See AAS 63 (1971) 99.

7   See Is 5:26, 11:12.

good cause, of making that truth a reproach to the world as it beholds the Church. This is the truth of the faith that throws light on our final human destiny, of the hope that alone does not disappoint,[8] of the charity that delivers us from the excessive self-love that in various guises tries to take hold and cast us down. This is by no means a time for flight, for desertion, for yielding; much less is it a time for fright. Christian people are being summoned simply to be Christians true to their name; they will be that to the degree that they remain loyal to the Church and the Council.

We believe that no one will call into question the sum total of the instructions and exhortations that throughout the years of our pontificate we have addressed to the bishops and the people of God, indeed to all the world. We are grateful to those who from them have derived a course of action. We have taught all these things inspired by an intense hope and motivated by a serene optimism that did not interfere with our realistic evaluation of the way things are concretely. If today we have dwelt at length on certain reprehensible theories, we have done so because this special occasion and your benign trust led us to believe this advisable. The essence of the charism of prophecy, for the exercise of which the Lord has promised the help of his abiding Spirit, in fact bears upon our vigilance, our sounding the alram in danger, our peering for signs of a dawning light in the dark encircling night. "Watchman how goes the night? Watchman how goes the night?";[9] the prophet Isaiah puts these words into our own mouth. Until the gentle dawn restores joy and beauty to the human race, we wish to go on raising our voice as befits the office entrusted to us. You our friends and closest co-workers have the power before all the rest and better than all to repeat and to spread our words among so many of our brothers and children. As we get ready now to honor the Lord Jesus about to ascend to the right hand of the Father with the signs of his passion and glorious resurrection, we must stand gazing up to the opened heavens[10] full of hope, of joy, of courage. In the Name of the Lord! in that holy Name we bless all of you.

60. PAUL VI, **Epistle** "To Our Venerable" to the bishops of the U.S.A., on the occasion of the bicentennial, excerpt on the liturgy as the soul of the Christian people, 6 June 1976: AAS 68 (1976) 406–415 (English).

559   [. . .] We ask that everyone should assume the part that is his or hers. To priests, your conscientious collaborators of the presbyteral order and sharers in your responsibility, we lovingly recall the expression of the Acts of the Apostles: their priorities must be today and forever "in prayer and in the service of the word."[4] Deacons are to accomplish their ministry of service in the fullness of faith and of the Holy Spirit.[5] May the laity be "light in the Lord,"[6] giving a witness of good words before the world and may the home be a stronghold of true conjugal love, of unity, and of peace. In this regard we repeat what our predecessor Pius XII

---

[8] See Rom 5:5.

[9] Is 21:11.

[10] Acts 7:56.

[4] Acts 6:4.

[5] See Acts 6:5.

[6] Eph 5:8.

wrote to the American bishops: "What can there be on earth more serene and joyful than the Christian family?"[7] We renew our solicitude for the full participation of women, in accordance with their role, in the life of the Church.

We pray for the young, that having been given the undiluted message of the Gospel they may lend their total energy, in the authenticity of love and discipline, to the building up of the Christian community. For the elderly we ask respect and reverence. For all the various component groups of your society we ask the determination to work in unity — so "that the world may believe."[8] [. . .]

We have supreme pastoral solicitude for the future of your seminaries and we repeat to you what we said last year to a group of rectors of major seminaries: ". . .we rely on your devoted collaboration, so that our beloved seminaries may be always houses of deep faith and authentic Christian asceticism, as well as joyful communities sustained by eucharistic piety."[9]

The inheritance of the Holy Year to the entire Church is one of evangelization.   560
With immense joy we have been assured that you are committed with increased energy to this goal. Within this context we pray that the Church in the United States will generously keep alive the missionary spirit and indeed "intensify it in the moment of history in which we are living."[10] May the priestly and religious vocations which we beseech the Lord to multiply in your midst also include an increase of selfless missionaries who will help this generation to carry out Christ's command "to make disciples of all nations."[11] In this regard we cannot emphasize too forcefully the teaching of the Second Vatican Council wherein the eucharist is presented as "the source and summit of all evangelization,"[12] as well as "the source and summit of all Christian life."[13]

The true Christian spirit that must animate your people has today and always   561
its primary and indispensable source in their active participation in the eucharistic sacrifice and in the entire liturgical life of the Church.[14] We ask that your people be constantly invited to a deeper realization of the centrality of the eucharist in their lives and of their need to participate therein. This is indeed an important emphasis, especially in a year in which the Eucharistic Congress marks the special passage of the Lord among your people.

We exhort all our sons and daughters to a profound sense of reverence for the eucharistic mystery and above all we lovingly remind all the priests, who are called to act in the person of Christ, of their special duty: *sancta sancte tractanda*. The very holiness of God, of Jesus Christ — *Tu solus sanctus . . . Iesu Christe* — demands deep reverence and profound respect.

We are pleased to recall that the Holy See has authorized, under certain cir-   562
cumstances, the distribution of holy communion by extraordinary ministers duly deputed to this high task. But we wish to emphasize that this ministry remains an extraordinary ministry to be exercised in accordance with the precise norms of the

---

7   *Sertum laetitiae*, 1 Nov. 1939.

8   Jn 17:21.

9   Paul VI, Discourse, 16 April 1975.

10   Paul VI, *Evangelii nuntiandi* no. 53.

11   Mt 28:19.

12   PO no. 5 [DOL 18 no. 260].

13   LG no. 11 [DOL 4 no. 141].

14   See SC art. 10, 14 [DOL 1 nos. 10, 14].

Holy See. By its nature therefore the role of the extraordinary minister is different from those other roles of eucharistic participation that are the ordinary expression of lay participation.

As we have already told the president of your episcopal conference, we have deeply at heart the renewed discipline of the sacrament of penance or of reconciliation. We pray that the element of spiritual conversion, so necessary for this sacrament, will play a great role in the life of your people and that they will never lose a sense of sin and therefore of the need for confession and forgiveness. We ask for supreme vigilance in the question of auricular confession: that it may be held in honor by all and that its fervent and frequent use may be promoted with pastoral conviction and zeal. [. . .]

61. PAUL VI, **Epistle** *Cum te* to Archbishop Marcel Lefebvre, 11 October 1976: Not 12 (1976) 417–427.

563   When we received you at Castelgandolfo on 12 September last, we gave you the opportunity to state freely your thoughts and wishes, even though we already were well acquainted with the many aspects of your case. The remembrance we keep of those things that in times past have distinguished you as a man devoted to the service of the Church — your burning devotion to the faith and the apostolate as well as your accomplishments — have inspired the hope in us, and continue to do so, that you will again become one who, standing in complete communion with the Church, will contribute to its upbuilding. We have again implored you to think over, in God's presence and in recognition of your obligations of office, all your public statements after your singularly grievous deeds.

We have waited now for a month. Your attitude, evinced by your continuing public words and actions, apparently has not changed. As a matter of fact we have before us the letter you sent us on 16 September, in which you state: "One thing binds us together: the pressing desire to end the wrong practices that disfigure the Church. How I long to work with Your Holiness and under your authority in this saving work, to the end that the Church may recover its true countenance." How are we to interpret these words, so commendable in themselves, that are the sum and substance of your response? For you speak as though you have forgotten your own objectives and your scandalous actions, never repudiated, against the ecclesial community. Clearly you are not repentant over what you have done or over a course that has brought down upon you the penalty of suspension. You have given absolutely no plain statement of allegiance to the authority of Vatican Council II and the Holy See, the crux of the matter, and you continue with the movement you instigated, even though explicitly commanded by lawful authority to desist. Thus the ambiguity persists, the result of your double-talk. For our part, as promised, we now send you our conclusions, the product of long deliberation.

564   I.   You set yourself up as defender and advocate of the faithful and priests who "are torn in pieces by what is going on in the Church," sadly convinced that the Catholic faith and the essential values of tradition are neither respected in the minds nor observed in the lives of a portion of the people of God, at least in some countries. But the fact is that your explanation of matters, the role you have assumed and the way you are carrying it out, involve a seduction of the people of God with error and the deception of people of good will. They rightly look for loyalty and desire to know better and to live up to the reality of the spiritual and apostolic life.

Any present deviation from the right path in faith and the use of the sacraments must be without any doubt regarded as most grievous whenever it becomes evident. For a long time now, mindful of both doctrine and pastoral practice, we have been concerned about this. But that is no reason for any failure to consider the very positive signs of spiritual revitalization and of a heightened awareness of their responsibility on the part of many Catholics. Neither may we forget the implicit cause that has given rise to the turning point or crisis: the enormous change going on in the present-day world affects the deepest sentiments of the faithful and makes all the more urgent apostolic concern for those *who are far off*. It is equally true that there are both priests and faithful who give the name of "conciliar" prescriptions to their own interpretations — distorted, mischievous, frequently scandalous, sacrilegious. But to attribute such wicked practices to the Council or the ensuing work of renewal is unwarranted. Such practices are rather the contradiction of the Council because they lack fidelity to it. Yet you are trying to convince the faithful that the immediate cause of the crisis rather than being a false interpretation of the Council, originates from it.

Further, you present yourself as having a unique charge entrusted to you in   565
this whole matter. But the responsibility for detecting and correcting erroneous practices belongs first to ourself and all the bishops acting in consort with us. We have been unfailing in raising our voice to reject such unrestrained and ill-advised lines of thought and courses of action. We have again pronounced ourself on this matter clearly and forthrightly in our consistorial address of 24 May 1976.[a] We more than anyone else perceive the pain of troubled Christians and we are answering the plea of those athirst for faith and the life of the spirit. We have never in any way been remiss in giving evidence of our concern to preserve in the Church loyalty to genuine tradition or to carry out our own will that the Church may, with the help of God, have the capability of reaching out to the present age and the times to come.

You seem to have no clear idea of your own course of action. You claim to want to correct the erroneous practices defacing the Church; you complain that authority in the Church is not held in high enough esteem; you wish to defend the true faith, a right appreciation of priestly ministry, and the devotion of souls toward the eucharist in its fullness as sacrifice and sacrament. Such zeal would in itself deserve our approval and confirmation, since the issues are those which, together with evangelization and Christian unity, are our unceasing concern and the very theme of our apostolic ministry. But how can you carry out your role by claiming at the same time that you have the responsibility of repudiating the Council — thus rebuffing your confrères in the episcopate — of spurning the Holy See, with the accusation that "Rome is slanted toward neo-Modernism and neo-Protestantism," and openly refusing the obedience owed to us? If you really wish to work "under our authority," as you alleged in your last letter, you must first put an end to this double-talk, this disruptive and contradictory way of acting.

II. Let us move on to the specific demands you set forth in our conversation of 11   566
September. You asked for recognition of the right to celebrate Mass in some places of worship according to the rite originated by the Council of Trent. You also propose to conduct the training of candidates for the priesthood according to your own theories or criteria, namely, "the preconciliar," and in your own seminaries, as you are doing in the seminary in Ecône. Beneath these and similar issues that we will discuss in detail we must detect the key to the whole problem, which really and in

---

[a]   See DOL 59.

the strict sense is theological. These issues have become the sure and concrete ways of stating an ecclesiology that is patently false in its main theses.

The issue, and it must be termed basic, is that, as you have publicly stated, you reject altogether the authority of the Council and of the pope. Your actions have so well conformed to that refusal that your rebellion — for such it must regrettably be called — spreads and becomes in a way an institution. This is the capital and main issue; it cannot possibly meet with approval.

Do we really have to remind you of these things, you who are our brother in the episcopate, honored with the title of Assistant at the Pontifical Throne, so that you are even more closely bound to the Chair of Peter? Christ gave supreme authority in the Church to Peter and the apostolic college and thereby to the pope and episcopal college "together with its head." Every Catholic is convinced that the Lord's words to Peter refer to the office of his lawful successors, the popes: "Whatever you shall bind upon earth will be bound also in heaven" (Mt 16:19); "Feed my sheep" (Jn 21:16–17); "Confirm your brothers" (Lk 22:32). Vatican Council I expresses the assent owed to the pope in these words: "Pastors and faithful, whatever their rite or rank, are bound singly and collectively by the duty of hierarchic subordination and obedience, not only in matters of faith and morals, but also in matters related to the discipline and governance of the Church throughout the world. The purpose is that through the unity kept with the Roman Pontiff of both communion and the professing of one faith the Church of Christ will be one flock under one shepherd. This is the teaching of Catholic truth from which no one may deviate and still keep the faith and salvation" (Const. Dogm. *Pastor aeternus* c. 3: Denz-Schön 3060). As to the bishops in conjunction with the pope, they solemnly exercise power, to the extent that it affects the universal Church, in general councils, on the basis of the words Jesus spoke to all the apostles together: "Whatsoever you bind on earth shall be bound also in heaven" (Mt 18:18). The conclusion is that by the rationale you hold you are refusing to accept these two forms in which supreme authority functions in the Church.

Certainly every bishop is an authoritative teacher, having the office of teaching the faith to the people in his charge, so as to direct their minds and their conduct, and to forestall errors that can expose his people to danger. But we must note the following: "Episcopal consecration, together with the office of sanctifying, also confers the office of teaching and of governing, offices which, of their very nature, can be exercised only in hierarchical communion with the head and of the college and its members" (LG no. 21; see also no. 35).[b] Far less does an isolated bishop and one lacking canonical mission possess the effective faculty for decreeing universally what the rule of faith is and settling what tradition is. You want alone and on your own to decide what matters tradition embraces.

567   You claim to be subject to the Church and loyal to tradition, only because you are obedient to certain norms of the past — norms, namely, that were issued by the predecessors of him on whom God has in this day conferred the power committed to Peter. Consequently, even here the notion of tradition to which you appeal is flawed. For tradition is not inert and dead, or some static "given" that at a fixed and definite date in history has put constraints on the life of an entity that is organic and dynamic, namely, the Church or Mystical Body of Christ. It is for the pope and the councils to make the judgment distinguishing between those things in the traditions of the Church from which no one can depart without becoming unfaithful to Jesus Christ and the Holy Spirit, i.e., the deposit of faith, and the things that can and should be adapted to the needs of the times. Such adaptation is designed to

---

b   DOL 4 no. 145; see also no. 152.

make the character of prayer and the mission of the Church better meet the diversity of times and places and to express and communicate the divine message in a way more suited to the contemporary idiom, without, however, resorting to unacceptable compromise.

Tradition, therefore, cannot be detached from the living magisterium of the Church, any more than it can be separated from Scripture: "clearly tradition, Scripture, and the Church's magisterium are so joined together and coordinated that none can stand without the others, but all three together, each in its own way under the influence of the one Holy Spirit contribute effectively to the salvation of souls" (DV no. 10).[c]

The popes and ecumenical councils before Vatican II had always acted accordingly, assisted by a special help of the Holy Spirit, and this Council acted in the same way. In the matters it decreed and in the work of renewal through which we have determined that they should be put into practice, there is nothing touching fundamentals and essentials that is opposed to the two-thousand-year-old tradition of the Church. We ourself are the surety, the guarantor of this matter, not in virtue of personal qualities but in virtue of the office the Lord has entrusted to us as holder of the place of Peter by lawful succession and in virtue of that special assistance the Lord has promised to us as once he did to Peter: "I have prayed for you that your faith may not fail" (Lk 22:32). With us the guarantors are also the bishops throughout the world.

You have no right any more to bring up the distinction between the doctrinal and the pastoral that you use to support your acceptance of certain texts of Vatican Council II and your rejection of others. It is true that the matters decided in any Council do not all call for an assent of the same quality; only what the Council affirms in its "definitions" as a truth of faith or as bound up with faith requires the assent of faith. Nevertheless, the rest also form part of the solemn magisterium of the Church, to be trustingly accepted and sincerely put into practice by every Catholic.

You say, in addition, that in conscience you do not always understand how it is possible to reconcile certain conciliar texts or some of our own measures and decrees putting them into practice with the sound tradition of the Church and particularly with the Council of Trent or with pronouncements of our predecessors. You cite, for example, the collegiality of the bishops, the new *Ordo Missae*, ecumenism, religious freedom, the rationale for initiating dialogue, evangelization of the present-day world. This letter is not the place to go into these issues one by one. The tenor of the documents together with the necessarily nuanced positions they represent, the coherence of the discourse containing them, the authoritative explanations given, commentaries that have explored them deeply and, as they say, objectively, are such that they can help you to overcome the doubts and hesitations troubling you. There are excellent counselors, men versed in theology and spirituality, able with the aid of divine light, to assist you; and we too are ready to offer you our fraternal help at any time. But how can it be possible that your own spiritual problem — the grave disturbance of your spirit under which you labor and which we look upon with respect — gives you the right to make yourself the public judge of these matters that have been lawfully and almost unanimously established, then also the right deliberately to drive a part of the faithful into following you in your repudiation?

The reasons presented have their value in making a person more readily obey what has been commanded — and it is our desire that the faithful who are dis-

568

------

[c]   DOL 14 no. 222.

turbed or silent have the wisdom, honesty, and humility to enable them to accept such cogent arguments that by now have been fully brought forward. Nevertheless, proofs are not necessary per se for that assent, joined to obedience, that is due to an ecumenical council and the decisions of the pope. This is really a matter of an ecclesial sense.

If we look for the deeper truth of the matter, you and your followers are striving to stand fast at a certain fixed point of time in the Church's life. In so doing, you refuse allegiance to the living Church as it has always been. You separate yourselves from its lawful pastors, finding fault with their exercise of the offices they possess by law. Although you deplore the upheaval — or as you say the "subversion" — taking place in the Church, you admit that you are unmoved by the precepts of the pope or by your own suspension. Swayed by this attitude, have you not, without dimissorial letters and against an express ban, ordained priests, thus setting up a band of priests who are irregular in the Church and under grave ecclesiastical penalty? To this is added your assertion that the suspension you have incurred applies only to the celebration of sacraments according to the revised rites, as though these have been introduced into the Church against the law. You have gone so far as to call the Church schismatic, deciding that you can evade the penalty of suspension by administering the sacraments using the older rites in opposition to the norms decreed (see 1 Cor 14:40).

569   The unlawful practice of celebrating the "Mass of St. Pius V" results from the same mistaken attitude. You know very well that this Mass had already undergone changes in the course of time and that the Roman Canon is Eucharistic Prayer I. The contemporary reform of the liturgy has drawn its purposes and its guiding principles from the Council and the historical sources on liturgy. The work of reform has had the effect of feeding the faithful more fully on the word of God. As the faithful share more intensely in the liturgy, the office of the priest, acting in *persona Christi*, remains intact. We have sanctioned the reform with our own authority and directed its obligatory use by all who call themselves Catholics. The reason we have made the judgment, as a matter of general principle, to brook no delays in this regard or to allow no exceptions is the spiritual growth and unity of the whole ecclesial community; for Catholics the *Ordo Missae* of the Roman Rite is a singular sign of their unity. As for you, the former rite of Mass is a sign of your false ecclesiology and a matter on which to assail the Council and its work of reform. You take as pretext or as your alleged justification that only in the former rite are the authentic sacrifice of the Mass and the authentic ministerial priesthood preserved, their meaning unobscured. We reject out-of-hand this erroneous judgment and unjust accusation; we cannot permit the divine eucharist, sacrament of unity, to be made the source of division (see 1 Cor 11:18); we cannot permit you to make use of it as an instrument and symbol of your rebellion.

In the Church there is room for what is called pluralism, but only in things lawful and only within the limits of obedience. They have no understanding of this who flatly reject the reform of the liturgy or who make the real presence and the eucharistic sacrifice a subject of controversy. In the same line, priestly training not in accord with the plan of the Council cannot be approved.

We thus cannot bow to your demands, because they involve activities that are the consequences of your rebellion against the one, true Church. You can be sure that this inflexibility does not stem from a refusal to allow concession on points of liturgy or discipline, but from the fact that the import and the gravity of your activities are such that to accede would mean our opening the way to an utterly false conception of the Church and of tradition.

In full awareness of our office, therefore, we must tell you, Esteemed Brother, that you are in error. With the fraternal love in which we hold you and the authority whose weight we bear, we urge you to retract your words and your acts, to amend your ways, and to stop wounding Christ's Church.

III. WHAT IN PARTICULAR DO WE ASK OF YOU?

A.   First and foremost that you issue some statement, of a kind that will rectify   570
and settle all these matters both for our own sake and for all the people of God. They have a right to have things made clear and cannot without harm go on bearing with these equivocations of yours. Accordingly, this statement must clearly affirm that you have sincerely given your assent to Vatican Council II and to each of its documents, understood in their plain sense, as composed by the conciliar Fathers, approved and promulgated by our authority. Such assent to an ecumenical Council has from the beginning been a rule of action in the Church.

The statement also must make it plain that you accept the instructions and decrees we have issued since the Council, with the assistance of the different agencies of the Holy See, to put it into practice; you are to mention by name the *Ordo Missae*, as well as our right to command its acceptance and use by the whole Christian people.

You must further acknowledge the binding force of the norms of the canon law now in effect, which for the most part coincides with the *Codex Iuris Canonici* promulgated by our predecessor Benedict XV, and including those norms dealing with canonical penalties.

As to our own person, you will disown and retract all the grave accusations and insulting insinuations that you have publicly leveled against us, against the integrity of our faith and the loyalty we hold toward the authentic office of St. Peter's successor.

As to the bishops, you must equally acknowledge their authority to forbid you, within their own dioceses, to preach or administer the sacraments of the eucharist, confirmation, orders and the others when they have expressly forbidden this.

You must, finally, pledge that you will refrain from all activities (lectures, writings, publications) inconsistent with your statement and that you will publicly repudiate any undertakings in your name that are also contrary to your statement.

This of course involves only the bare minimum that any Catholic bishop must accept: this kind of assent and allegiance can admit of no half measures. Since, therefore, you have indicated your acceptance of the principle in the matter, we in turn explain the concrete conditions your statement is to contain. This is the first condition for the lifting of your suspension.

B.   There remains the question of your future occupation, your works, and espe-   571
cially your seminaries. You know very well, Esteemed Brother, that because of the ambiguities and the irregular acts, both past and present, involved in its programs, we cannot revoke the juridical suppression of the "Priestly Fraternity of St. Pius X." For it has fostered an attitude contrary to the Council and to its execution, which the Vicar of Christ has striven so intently to advance. Your public statement of 21 November 1974 attests to that same spirit; but as our commission of cardinals on 6 May 1975 rightly judged, no priestly training or formation consistent with the needs of Christ's Church can be built on such a foundation. This does not take away from the positive things present in your seminaries; but the gaps in regard to ecclesiology already referred to must be considered, as well as the ability to exercise the pastoral ministry in these times. In the face of this unfortunate mixture, our

concern is not to destroy but to correct and, as far as possible, to follow the safe course.

This also is the reason why, as guardian of the faith and of priestly training, we command you to leave up to us the responsibility for and governance of your works, especially the seminaries. Doubtless that is for you a very great sacrifice, but it is also a proof of your trust and obedience as well as being the one condition necessary for those seminaries, now lacking any canonical status, to achieve perhaps a place in the Church.

Only when you have agreed to these principles will we be able to turn our attention to and provide for the men who are involved, taking care to promote their genuine priestly vocations and for their duly meeting the requirements of the doctrine, discipline, and pastoral activity of the Church. At such a time as well, we will be able with good will to turn to your petitions and wishes and, together with the offices of our Curia, take whatever measures are required.

As for those ministers you have ordained to the priesthood in contravention of the law, it will be possible to lift the sanctions they have incurred by virtue of canons 985, 7 and 2374, if they first show that they are well disposed and if each signs his name to the statement we have demanded of you. We trust that out of a sense and love of the Church you will help make this step easier for them.

In regard to the other foundations, houses of formation, "priorates," and other kinds of institutes established with you as founder or sponsor, we command you equally to turn all of them over to the Holy See, which will weigh, under various aspects, the case of each of them with the local bishop. In particular, their life, governance, and apostolic activity will, as is generally the case in the whole Catholic Church, be subject to an agreement entered into with the local bishop — *nihil sine episcopo* — and in keeping with the mind and spirit that your statement will contain.

572   All the topics and themes found in this letter, and thoughtfully developed with the assistance of the prefects of the curial congregations involved, have been raised only for the greater good and advantage of the Church. You yourself in our conversation of 11 September have affirmed: "I am prepared for all things that are for the good of the Church." The response is now up to you.

If, God forbid, you should refuse to draft the statement of submission we ask, you will remain suspended. On the other hand, our pardon and the lifting of the suspension will be granted once you sincerely and unequivocally fulfill the conditions of this letter and repair the scandal given. The obedience and trust you show us will permit us to confer calmly with you about your difficulties.

May the Holy Spirit enlighten and guide you toward the one solution of this issue that will permit you to recover your peace of conscience, lost for a time; toward the one solution also that will safeguard the good of souls, strengthen the unity of the Church, the care of which God has entrusted to us, and avert the danger of schism. We understand, because of your present state of mind, how difficult it is for you to see things clearly and how bitter and hard it is for you to change your ways. Is it not then very necessary for you, as is usual in such cases, to settle upon a time and a place of silent retreat where you may prepare for the required turnabout? We admonish you in a spirit of brotherhood to beware of the urgings of those who prefer you to continue on in an unacceptable course and viewpoint. All of us, your brothers in the episcopate, as well as the great majority of Christians await at last from you that ecclesial way of acting that will do you honor.

To uproot the abuses we lament and to provide for a true renewal of the spirit and that needed, avid evangelization toward which the Holy Spirit inspires us more than ever before, there is now need for the help and wholehearted zeal of the whole ecclesial community around the pope and the bishops. Instead we have in some quarters extreme rebellion or direct disobedience, or, as you call it "subversion"; were it not for your own obduracy, Esteemed Brother, you could have been helping us all along, as your letter declares to be your wish, by your loyalty and under our authority to bring about the progress of the Church.

Esteemed Brother, without delay, in an intense and genuinely religious spirit, reflect as you receive this solemn adjuration of the lowly but lawful successor of Peter. Carefully weighing the seriousness of the times and of the matter at hand, may you take the only step worthy of a loyal son of the Church. This is our hope and our prayer.

62. SC SACRAMENTS AND DIVINE WORSHIP, **Letter** of Cardinal J. R. Knox, Prefect, to Cardinal N. Jubany Arnau, Archbishop of Barcelona, on the occasion of the symposium organized by the review *Phase* on the theme: The Liturgical Pastoral Ministry Today (Barcelona, 12–15 April 1977), 31 March 1977.*

It was with the greatest satisfaction that I just received the announcement of and the kind invitation to participate in the symposium on the liturgy to take place in Barcelona, 12–15 April 1977, organized in observance of the one-hundredth number of the review *Phase*.   573

Since 1960 *Phase* has provided a most noble service, not only as the organ of the Centro de Pastoral Liturgica, Barcelona, but also as a reliable vehicle for creating awareness throughout Spain and Spanish-speaking countries in the area of reflection and study on the liturgy. In covering the celebration of Vatican II and closely following the different steps in the reform of the liturgy, *Phase* has shown fidelity in communicating the directives emanating from the Apostolic See. It has directed careful consideration to the problems arising within the liturgical reform and those tangential to it. It has made investigations into the opportuneness of certain measures. When necessary, it has proposed solutions to concrete problems. For these reasons we can justly say that *Phase* reflects in a way all the vicissitudes of the reform of the liturgy; the appearance, therefore, of its one-hundredth number justifies the celebration that has been organized.

The demands of my position as Prefect of the Congregation for the Sacraments and Divine Worship prevent my accepting the invitation, which I would so much like to accept, to take part in the work of this symposium. But through this letter I wish to extend to the organizers and participants my sincere esteem, my cordial greetings, and my blessing. At the same time I wish to share some ideas that the theme of the symposium has suggested to me.

The concrete situation of the liturgy at this period of Church and world — both of which are in the midst of an evolving process whose consequences are hard to foresee — raises issues that are of interest to the whole Church but particularly to those involved in liturgical matters. Such issues are by no means, therefore, foreign to the interests of the Congregation for the Sacraments and Divine Worship, to which Pope Paul VI has entrusted the difficult mission of being the means of continuing, animating, and guiding the reform of the liturgy along the lines intended by Vatican Council II.   574

---

* Text, *Phase* 17 (1977) 352–355 (Spanish).

This symposium can be an excellent occasion for reflecting together on how much has been achieved up to now; on those problems actually before us for which there are not always easy solutions; and on the possibilities of discovering new paths and new forms for the future.

At this time, in particular, it is opportune to insist that the liturgy urgently demands the conjoined forces of pastors and faithful in order to penetrate with seriousness, awareness, and responsibility into the reality of the mystery of Christian worship. The immense treasure of duly reformed rites and texts that has been placed at the disposal of the Church must be the object of reflection, of study, and above all of an adequate presentation to the people who celebrate the liturgy. It is right to know, to present, and to celebrate in the light of the Church's genuine tradition the rites that enable us to share fully in the saving mystery of Christ, who is always active in the Church through the power of the Spirit.

575   It is by working in this direction that two lamentable situations can be overcome: of those who, adamant in retaining superseded forms, consider the reform to be reckless; at the opposite extreme, of those who, regarding the renewal as excessively cautious, set themselves on fashioning their own "liturgies," which may contain certain human values but are without any doubt not the liturgy of the Church. The entire Church, pastors and people alike, must share the conviction that the liturgical reform demanded by Vatican II does not come to an end with the publication of the last books for rites and celebrations. Rather it requires a continuous deepening in order that the Christian rites, in light of the proper liturgical texts, may become a living, fruitful, intelligible reality, and in consequence will have a genuine impact on the entire life and conduct of Christians.

Your Eminence, our own heartfelt wish is that the holding of this symposium will serve above all to guarantee in the participants the desire and the resolve to work together wholeheartedly in this effort at reflection and study regarding the treasures of the liturgy. That will serve to enable them to live the liturgy more intensely and to make possible among the entire people of God future effects of the reform that today we can only begin to imagine. It is our wish as well that the symposium will contribute to a close collaboration with the Apostolic See with a view to promoting the future of the liturgy, the abiding source of the Church's life.

63. PAUL VI, **Address** to the bishops of the southwestern region of France, excerpt on gravity and dignity in the liturgy, 18 April 1977: AAS 69 (1977) 472–476; Not 13 (1977) 198 (French).

576   A further point of importance; we are anxious to give explicit encouragement to your own and your priests' efforts to stir up in the Christian people a perceptive and vital participation in *the liturgy*, as was the mind of your recent meeting at Lourdes. We know about and esteem those celebrations in your urban and rural churches that demonstrate a genuine liturgical spirit and a model of fidelity to the norms of Vatican II. Your own joy in them is ours as well. We must also encourage your vigilance and firmness. Catholic liturgy must remain theocentric; that is its very nature and it inspires the reform the Council has brought about. Permit us to dwell for a moment on the celebration of the eucharist. It goes beyond being a gathering of friends and a sharing of life together. St. Paul did not hesitate to point this out to the Christians of Corinth (1 Cor 11:22). In its essence the eucharist is the reiteration of Christ's redemptive sacrifice. Over this reality no minister, no lay person has ownership. The eucharist is a sacred mystery, calling for an atmosphere

of gravity and dignity and it allows for no mediocrity or indifference regarding place, the appearance of the vestments, the articles used in worship. All must be simple, yes, but never careless. We congratulate and urge on the dioceses which in different ways are offering the faithful a liturgical formation worthy of the name. This kind of work, so different from a facile improvising, will permit Catholic worship to retain its identity, as well as to give expression to and cultivate the faith of the people born of baptism.

64. PAUL VI, **Address** to participants in the 40th anniversary of the Pontifical Greek College in Rome, excerpt on liturgical traditions as a pastoral resource, 30 April 1977: AAS 69 (1977) 343–348; Not 13 (1977) 199–200 (Italian).

Dear young men of this audience, especially those of you who are students of   577
theology. We turn to you not simply to include you in our remarks or just out of convention, but out of the great trust we place in the generosity you show. Your vocation is great and very important to today's Church. You are called to preach Christ to our contemporaries more and more, no matter what the contrary appearances may suggest, they are aware of the call and the claims of the Absolute. You have in your hands a doctrinal, spiritual, and ascetical heritage that is among the richest in the world, even at the level of human culture. We have in mind particularly Greek theological thought and liturgical practice. Are not some of you in training to celebrate the Divine Liturgy of St. John Chrysostom, remembered as the "Golden Mouthed" because of the power of his preaching the Good News? Will not some of you one day celebrate the Liturgy of St. Basil the Great? Do you not already sing daily the sacred songs of such great hymn writers as St. John of Damascus and Andrew of Crete? They have graced the celebration of the Christian mystery with inspired poetic form, effective to move the heart and open it to the contemplation of the divine. If you devote yourselves to your heritage with loving mind, you have already as your own the choicest instrument for catechetical and pastoral activity, one that will yield, as it already has done, the fruits of charity in abundance.

65. PAUL VI, **Address** to a consistory, excerpt on the beneficial results of the liturgical reform, 27 June 1977: AAS 69 (1977) 369–377; Not 13 (1977) 359–360.

III

Again today a special matter in the Church's life draws our attention to itself: 578
namely, the undoubtedly beneficial results of the liturgical reform. From the day that Vatican Council II issued its Constitution *Sacrosanctum Concilium*, great advances have been made that are in line with the state of things prepared by the liturgical movement of the late 19th century and that fulfill those dearly held objectives for which so many churchmen and scholars had worked and prayed. The new Order of Mass we have promulgated after the long and able preparatory work of the responsible groups, with its new eucharistic prayers added to the essentially unchanged Roman Canon, has yielded special fruit: namely, a wider participation in the liturgy,

a deeper, more reflective understanding of the sacred rites, a greater and fuller knowledge of the inexhaustible treasures of Scripture, an increased sense of the Church as community.

The passage of these last years has shown that we are on the right path. Sad to say there have been abuses and an excessive liberty in carrying out norms, although most of the priests and people have used sound and upright judgment in this matter. Now is the time once and for all to cast out the decaying leaven of harmful extremes and to put liturgical reform we have approved, following the will of the Council, into effect integrally, i.e., by respecting the balanced judgments or criteria that inspired it.

We sternly urge adherence to the established norms by those who raise an uproar or a challenge in the name of a misunderstood creative freedom, and thus inflict so much harm on the Church with their rash innovations, so vulgar, so frivolous — and sometimes even lamentably profane. Otherwise the essence of dogma and obviously of ecclesiastical discipline will be weakened, in line with the famous axiom, *lex orandi, lex credendi*. We therefore call for absolute loyalty so that the rule of faith may remain safe. We are sure that in this matter we have the help of the assiduous, prudent, and paternal action of the bishops, who bear an obligation in conscience regarding faith and prayer in their individual dioceses.

Equally we admonish those who are defiant and who persist in their obstinacy on the pretext of tradition that they heed the voice of the successor of Peter and of the bishops, as duty requires, and accept the value of the changes in accidentals introduced into the sacred rites. Such changes evidence a true continuity with and are in fact often a return to ancient rites adapted to present needs. We admonish these people not to remain obdurate and of closed mind out of a biased opinion that is utterly unsustainable. We entreat them earnestly in the name of the Lord: "We beg you in Christ's name to be reconciled to God."[8]

66. SECRETARIAT OF STATE, **Letter** of Cardinal J. Villot to Bishop R. Alberti, President of the Department of Liturgy of CELAM, on the occasion of the 2nd Latin American meeting on liturgy (Caracas, 12–24 July 1977), July 1977: Not 13 (1977) 459–467 (Spanish).

579   The meeting of the liturgical commissions of the Latin American continent in Caracas, called by the CELAM Department of Liturgy, of which you are president, is an event of great importance for the development of the liturgical and ecclesial life of that continent. For this reason Pope Paul VI has requested Cardinal James R. Knox, Prefect of the Congregation for the Sacraments and Divine Worship, to be the bearer of his words of encouragement and good wishes for the outcome of the meeting to the participants.

The liturgical movement is truly a strong part of renewal and is influencing the life of the Church. Described by Pius XII as a sign of the Spirit's passage through the Church, the liturgical movement since Vatican Council II has become a sign of hope and of budding youth, springing from the mystery of Christ celebrated in the liturgy and from which the Church constantly is reborn and renewed.

The liturgical movement is equally an important element of hope for the Latin American Church, today bent so intently upon its tireless work of evangelization and human development, in order to bring people to discover and to live out more

---

8   2 Cor 5:20.

genuinely their human dignity and their faith. In this undertaking the liturgy as the full sharing in the Christian mystery of salvation stands as the apex towards which pastoral work must aim and as the source that sustains energies along a difficult road.

1. FROM REFORM TO RENEWAL

In the light of a dearth of resources and personnel, the liturgical reform and its introduction into the ecclesial communities of Latin America has been a work of intense dedication. But, at least on the part of some, it has been sidetracked or has not been sufficiently grasped in its spiritual and vital content, which reform of the liturgy seeks to bring to the faith and to the lives of the individual ecclesial communities. In some cases there has been a lack of serious preparation of pastoral ministers or other urgent needs have arisen in the life of the community, limiting, at least in part, the efforts expended.

580

This is the reason for the need to undertake the journey anew or, if begun, to quicken its pace. All must hasten to pass from reform to renewal, from a change of ritual to a perception and assimilation of the contents of the reform, in order to bring about a renewal of conscience and of commitment to a Christian life that has its source in living the mystery of Christ in the liturgy and in an ever deeper sharing in the life of the Church.

The first and most important work that has to be accomplished is to lead the community to discover in the celebration of the liturgy the mystery of salvation in its full measure. That includes not simply the commemoration of an event of the past, nor just the reality present in the sacrament and offered for liturgical celebration, but the reality as it has direct and actual bearing on the life of today's people. Conversely, history as it is going on, with all its turnings lived and suffered by the Church and by humanity, is assimilated by the liturgy. There it is united to the divine salvation already accomplished and is effectively transformed into a history of salvation through the proclamation and presentation anew of God's action. Without such a perception of history and its relation to the liturgy, the liturgy is exposed to the risk of being cut away from life, being transformed into something purely ritualistic and aesthetic, and even of becoming a way of escaping from reality.

But to reach that kind of profound perception of the mystery so as to convert it into a source of internal renewal for the liturgical reform, a leadership effort is needed to bring the participating community to a grasp of the various signs characteristic of the liturgy.

First of these is the need to understand the value of the assembly, the gathering of the people of God in celebration, as a sign, as an actual expression of the Church's faith. Through this assembly, the Church appears before the world, bears witness of its presence as a royal, prophetic, and priestly people, intent upon the worship of God and the renewal of the world.

There must be an understanding of the value of God's word, which, by means of its proclamation in the assembly, continues to make God's saving acts present in the history of all ages through the continuous renewal of God's wonderful works. Belonging to the past, they continue to be alive in the present and to make the history of today's people to be a history of salvation.

There must be an understanding of the value of sacrament as an ecclesial act that continues the contact of people today with the saving humanity of Christ, with his mystery made present through the faith, prayer, and action of the Church, guided and sustained by the Holy Spirit. The eucharist must be appreciated as at once sacrament and true sacrifice.

There must be an understanding of the value of the gestures, postures, and actions that enter into the celebration of a sacrament and are not merely external, ritual elements, but the expression of the faith of the Christian community.

Finally, there must be an understanding of the commitment that the liturgy presupposes in the life of individuals and community. The liturgy is neither authentic nor really effective if it does not bring about a continous conversion that causes to be translated into reality, into a new way of living, the faith and charity toward all proclaimed, heard, prayed for, and lived in the liturgy.

If pastoral effort does not succeed in making these values a vital experience in the Christian community, to the point that they are assimilated into its own life, the liturgical reform will remain at the level of outward changes, curiosities turned quickly into disillusionment; the reform will not be the source of a genuine renewal of the Church's life.

The carrying on of this undertaking rests in the hands of the diocesan and national liturgical commissions, which must advance their efforts in the directions here described. The work also is in the hands of priests, ministers, and others engaged in pastoral activity, who must bring the meaning of liturgical celebration into contact with the community celebrating.

Therefore there is a need to assist priests and the faithful to perceive more exactly the true meaning of the liturgy, to pass from less precise ideas and evaluations to an authentic view of the living reality of Christ's mystery as this is at work in the sacraments of the Church through human activity. Following this path will also quicken the realization that the liturgy, because of its nature and proper purpose, is not a vogue in the Church's life that can fade away with the passage of time. The course to be followed, no matter what the particular context, can bring a sense also of the urgency of other aspects of the Church's life and work, for example, in the field of catechesis and human development. Moreover, it is easy to see how even in these matters the liturgy is the culmination toward which these other activities converge as their full actualization.

In order that liturgical communities may come more readily to perceive this profound, life-giving reality of mystery in the concrete conditions of their life, the liturgical commissions should help and instruct priests and ministers how to make the celebration alive and relevant. This means concretely the intelligent promotion of the resources that the liturgical books provide to prepare, organize, and carry out a celebration and to adapt it to the life and capacity of the participants. The means for this is the judicious choice of methods to advance participation in a way that will make it truly aware, active, and devout, that is, spiritually fruitful.

Guided and enlightened by these principles, the liturgy will be changed into a genuine element of the proclamation and incarnation of God's salvation in the concrete conditions of the celebrating community. The liturgy will take up not only the language and other cultural elements of the community, but also and most especially its cares and aspirations. The liturgy will be the expression of the community's faith, not abstractly but as the source of renewal for each individual, the entire community, and the world around it. All of this means, in a word, giving a new impetus to the life of the Church and the Church's obligation of service through a renewed liturgy.

2. LITURGY AND EVANGELIZATION

581   The pastoral programs of the whole Church are focused at this time on the problem of evangelization, as is evident from the work of the conferences of bishops, the Synod of Bishops [1974], and the plenary meeting of CELAM planned for 1978. These programs, important as they are for countries that are receiving the

message of salvation for the first time, are perhaps even more important for traditionally Christian countries like those of Latin America. These are called upon to live in their own time with a greater awareness of the faith that is their patrimony so that it becomes a matter of their self-commitment and of commitment for others.

In the work of evangelization the liturgy clearly holds a place of primary importance: it stands as a high point at which the preached mystery of salvation becomes actual; pastorally it offers to evangelization privileged occasions and a sound and effective formation. Further, evangelization and liturgy — or in the current phrase evangelization and "sacramentalization" — are not mutually exclusive but complementary. A sacramental celebration remains incomplete and ineffective without a prior, preparatory evangelization; evangelization in turn remains incomplete unless it leads naturally into sacramental celebration.

A sacrament, because it is a sacrament of faith, calls for prior evangelization that prepares the faith of the recipients so that they can grasp, live, and translate into action the sacrament to be received. Like all liturgical celebrations, a sacrament becomes a means and an element of evangelization when pastoral effort leads the community to comprehend the value of sign, gesture, word as components of the liturgy, and when evangelization takes as its point of departure the rites and texts, the content of the mystery celebrated, the cycle of celebrations, thus joining together the work of forming the community and the celebration of the liturgy. In this way the recurring rites and liturgical, sacramental celebrations help to bring evangelization and the formation of a Christian community gradually to completeness, to penetrate more and more the meaning of their formularies and rites, and to live them as the expression of faith, rather than as simply the Church's official prayer. The recurrence also helps evangelization to cause the message received through the sacramental words and actions to be applied to living.

The intimate union between evangelization and liturgy also gives rise to the duty of renewing the liturgical celebration; this will unfailingly have a strong impact on the life of the Church. Every celebration, because it involves evangelization, must be continually renewed not only in its outward elements, but above all in its spirit and in the way it is carried out. Then the Church, as the local community in celebration, will not be merely a passive recipient of evangelization; rather, by experiencing the inner dynamism that comes from the proclamation and actualization of the mystery in building itself up and growing, will feel impelled to share with the world the salvation God offers. From this impetus to mission the character and the structures of ecclestical communities will be the beneficiaries; they will feel themselves bound to be the catalysts of mission, renewal, and development, not just centers of ritual.

All of this requires a constant, effective cooperation between the departments and commissions on liturgy. At their different levels of obligation and responsibility, they are to work in the area of catechesis, liturgy, education, and human development, in order to achieve a joint effort and an integration that better shows the correlation and the work of each sector, as it strives toward a common pastoral objective. It is not superfluous to emphasize that this joint work must be illumined and guided by the central theme of all liturgy, the mystery of salvation, as the idea and the force that will create the convergence and unity of all pastoral activity.

3. LITURGY AND SOME PROBLEMS PECULIAR TO THE LATIN AMERICAN CHURCH

The renewal of the Church, which ought to be the result of the right application of liturgical reform, must also take into account the conditions proper to the Church on the Latin American continent. These conditions are the expression of a   582 history and a life reflecting a rich past and they can contribute to a new enrichment that is at once the basis for great hope. To act upon all of this will not cause a useless and odd separatism but a sign manifesting the richness springing from plurality in unity.

We wish, therefore, to underline some aspects of religion in Latin America that need to be kept in mind as the renewal of the liturgy goes on.

a. One of the characteristics of the Latin American people is what is called "popular religion." Sometimes that describes a faith not fully formed or enlightened; sometimes a faith expressed in forms marginal to liturgy or reflecting cultural and religious traditions of the past. Its imperfections aside, this complex of faith-expressions stands as a true value and it would be misguided to try to erase it from the lives of the people, especially without supplying an adequate substitute. On the contrary it needs study, comprehension, evaluation, purification from all that is aberrant. The popular religion must be the starting point for successful evangelization. There is need to enrich it with properly liturgical elements and to assist its development and emergence into a genuine liturgy, intelligently and wisely adapted to particular circumstances. The forms of popular faith and devotion, often an outgrowth compensating for a liturgy that was too far removed from the faithful's understanding and modes of expression, can and must be included, once properly purified, as a starting point for a liturgy wisely adapted to particular circumstances and groups that are still far from maturity and depth in faith.

b. The faith and Christian life of many communities has survived and developed, as is still the case, thanks to the gifts of ministry that the Spirit of the Lord continuously produces in the Church. There is need to promote and nurture vocations to the ministry of priesthood and diaconate. But one of the most pressing obligations also weighing on the Latin American Church is the discernment and actualization of new ministries. These ministries involve liturgical acts not reserved to the ordained and other aspects of the community's religious and human life, especially where there is no priest. Lay ministers in the past were engaged almost exclusively in the community's prayer life, contributing to the keeping of the faith through religious, largely devotional, practices. Today they have a much more extended sphere of action, including the liturgy. There is need to create and to develop these ministries and to give a proper formation to those engaged in them; they are the Spirit's gift to the Church and the hope for the future of the ecclesial communities.

c. The conditions peculiar to Latin America often give rise to the creation, within the traditional units, of smaller groups or communities. Clearly, they are of great importance as a source of Christian commitment, which for the most part is communicated through celebration of the liturgy. At the pastoral level these communities obviously cannot be a divisive element within the ecclesial community. Rather they must become living, conscious, effective nuclei that enable the Church to have more influence within the actual human situation in which it exists. At the level of liturgy as well, these smaller communities can have a genuine influence for renewal, if they assimilate the true values of the reform to the point of transforming them with a source of life and if they succeed in communicating these values to their fellow Christians by aiding and enlivening the liturgies of the wider, local community. This is all the more a reason for the liturgies of these smaller groups not to be arbitrary or uselessly recondite creations. Rather they should represent a more perceptive grasp of the meaning of the mystery celebrated, which ought to nourish their spiritual life more fully and thereby that of the whole local community.

d. The problem of how to manage adaptation of the Roman Rite liturgy is made pressing by the presence of the diverse cultures that enrich Latin America: indigenous cultures preserved with a degree of purity of tradition; cultures arising from the fusion of native elements with those imported from the Old World and from countries having distinct traditions of their own. The issue is not one of creating a new liturgy, much less of change for the sake of change, nor of resurrecting obsolete elements out of an antiquarian interest. A perceptive pastoral sensitivity, based on a faith that is sure and deep lived by the Christian community, combined with a close cooperation between pastors and persons expert in the various fields of science will be able to point to the way of evaluating certain sound elements of an authentic, local tradition. The objective is that liturgy, conformed to the wise objectives of Vatican II, will have the power to express itself more clearly in the language, mentality, and life of the various local Churches, while at the same time preserving the unity of faith and a profound communion in charity.

e. Finally, Pope Paul exhorts the bishops of the Latin American Church to continue devotedly the work of leading, organizing, directing, and advancing the liturgy in Latin America. May the agencies of CELAM be the providential means for a fruitful coordination of pastoral resources, including making up for the lack of local resources. The different national and regional agencies can and ought to intensify this effort, which has already yielded satisfying results, to vitalize the faith and prayer life of the people of God. May the bishops inspire their co-workers and be an example to them, showing how the liturgy, once its resources are used wisely and in conjunction with pastoral action, is a vital force for actualizing the Church's mission.

Through these wishes the Pope unites himself to the work of this meeting of national liturgical commissions, invokes upon it the grace and light of the Holy Spirit, and imparts to Your Excellency, your co-workers in organizing this meeting, and all participants the apostolic blessing.

67. SYNOD OF BISHOPS 1977, "Message to the People of God," 28 October 1977 (excerpts).*

INTRODUCTION

1. Since the Fourth General Assembly of the Synod of Bishops, called together at Rome by Pope Paul VI, to discuss giving catechesis in our time especially to children and young people, is now approaching an end, we bishops wish to give a message to you who, entrusted to us by virtue of the pastoral office in various parts of the world, belong to the people of God, and to all who have interest in the Church's activity and responsibility in human society, and by this share with you the principal conclusions of our work.

583

Examining our world, troubled indeed and filled with crises but at the same time open to the saving powers of grace, after the other synodal assembly had, in 1974, given attention to carrying out evangelization in our time, nothing seemed to be more useful to the Church, under the leadership of the Supreme Pontiff, than to continue on the same theme by study of that ecclesial activity which, constantly alive and active, is required for a diffusion of the word of God and for a deeper understanding of the person and of the message of salvation of our Lord Jesus Christ, and which consists of an ordered and progressive education in the faith, joined with a continuous process of maturation of the same faith, which we call *catechesis*.

---

* English text of the Publication Office, USCC (Washington, D.C., 1978).

It was necessary that we examine, always in the light of God's word, the signs of the times for renewing catechesis and for increasing its importance in pastoral work, and this especially since a certain vital vigor of the Church's whole catechetical effort almost everywhere was strongly felt, with fine fruit for renewal of the total ecclesial community. Known to us moreover were the desire and hunger for spiritual nourishment and formation in the faith especially among the rising generations which, desiring to fulfill their obligations and duty toward building up a just society, seek to enter a deeper knowledge of the mystery of God. We were also challenged in our faith by the various forms of human culture which strongly tend toward a greater perfection of man, though not always in consonance with the Gospel. It is also true that defects were known to us, in that the responsibility of all the faithful in the maturation of their own faith was sometimes given over to oblivion, or in that revelation was not always, as was right and just, everywhere rightly disseminated. We were not ignorant of the difficulties to which catechesis is subject in certain regions of the world, to the extent that opposing powers place new obstacles in the way of fulfilling the mission of Jesus Christ concerning the faith to be announced to all nations.

Concerned about these situations of children and young people who will in the future bear on their shoulders the task of building a new world, and listening to their aspirations, we gave them special attention.

Moreover, the bond of our theme with the question of education in the world of the present time escaped no one's attention. We were convinced that the pedagogy of God, which is noted in the history of salvation, contributes even today to solution of this problem for the good of the whole human race.

After the long and laborious preparation for the Synod, which involved consultation with all the particular Churches, our studies having been brought to an end and our wish having been expressed to the Supreme Pontiff by special recommendations conveyed to him that he, in his own time, might wish to offer the universal Church a document on Christian instruction through catechesis as he did after the 1974 Synod with his Apostolic Exhortation *Evangelii nuntiandi,*[a] we have agreed, with due approbation, to open our minds to you and to bare our thinking on certain more urgent things.

PART I

THE WORLD, YOUNG PEOPLE, AND CATECHESIS
(A REALISTIC VIEW OF THE SITUATION)

THE RADICAL CHANGES IN THE CONTEMPORARY WORLD

584   2.   The Synod, as an event of our times, could in no way ignore the real situation in which the world lives. The bishops are witnesses and sharers of the hope, tensions, and frustrations (see GS no. 1)[b] with which people of today are moved. In all nations, whatever their social system or cultural tradition, men and women are searching, struggling, and working for the common good and to build a new world. Old systems of values often are no longer accepted, and have even crumbled; human security is brought to crisis by force, oppression, and contempt of the person. Experience shows that the hope founded by some on ideologies and technical skill is insufficient.

Amid the many tumults of the conflict of ideas and systems, a new search for God is again emerging, new signs of divine unrest in man's unquiet heart are being

---

a   See DOL 236.

b   See DOL 19 no. 268.

uncovered, and at the same time a new sense of values, which pertain to the dignity of the human person, is being perceived.

THE PROBLEMS OF YOUNG PEOPLE

3.   The rising generations are more aware of themselves. Both by the proportion   585
of their number and by their qualities and the hope which they necessarily show
for the future, they signify a role of great importance for the human race. The
currents which pervade our society echo with a special vigor among these generations. They strongly show cultural division, the fruit of social change. Children
often pay the penalties for the errors and failures of adults. More often they are
victims of the machination of false leaders who profit from their generosity and
magnanimity.

Education work should take its beginning from the aspirations of the young
for creativity, justice, liberty, and truth. It also should respond to their aspirations
for co-responsibility in church and civil life, as well as to their tendency toward
love of God and of neighbor. For catechesis is an ecclesial action for this world and
especially for the rising generations, so that the life of Christ transforms the life of
young people and leads them to fulfillment.

THE COMPLEXITY OF CATECHETICAL ACTIVITY

5.   The same realistic sense invites us to consider the complexity of catechetical   586
activity. The diversity of *cultures* makes for catechesis a great plurality of situations.
As was indicated by the Second General Vatican Council, and as was recalled by
Paul VI in his Apostolic Exhortation *Evangelii nuntiandi*, it is necessary that the
Christian message plant roots in human cultures by taking them over and by
transforming them. In this sense one can say that catechesis is a certain instrument
of "inculturation." And this signifies that it evolves and at the same time illumines
from within the forms of life of those to whom it is directed. The Christian faith
must be implanted by catechesis into those cultures. A true "incarnation" of the
faith by catechesis supposes a process not only of "giving" but also of "receiving."

PART II
CATECHESIS AS A MANIFESTATION OF SALVATION IN CHRIST

CATECHESIS IS RELATED TO THE MYSTERY OF CHRIST AS TO ITS CENTER

7.   The Church does not cease repeating that it brings the message of salvation,   587
destined for all people. Its task is to proclaim and to bring to effect in the world
salvation in Christ. It is, then, a task of evangelization. Catechesis is an aspect of
this very task. It is related to the mystery of Christ as to its center. Christ, true God
and man, and his saving work carried out in his incarnation, life, death, and resurrection, should be the center of the message. Jesus Christ is the basis of our faith
and the source of our life. The whole history of salvation, then, tends toward
Christ. In catechesis we try to understand and experience how important he is for
our daily lives. Catechesis must proclaim how the Father reconciles us with himself
through his Son Jesus Christ and how the Holy Spirit guides us. To the extent that
it is a transmission of this mystery, catechesis is the living word, faithful to God and
at the same time to man.

In harmony with those things which were published in the Apostolic Exhortation *Evangelii nuntiandi*, the Synod calls to mind these aspects which follow. And they
are: catechesis is word; catechesis is memory; catechesis is witness.

CATECHESIS AS WORD

588   8.   This is one of the first aspects of the mission of the Church: for the Church speaks, proclaims, teaches, communicates with others. And these words signify one action, an action, that is, that pertains to making known, in the Spirit, the mystery of God the Savior: "For this is eternal life, that they know you, the only true God, and Jesus Christ whom you have sent" (Jn 17:3). This knowledge, however, is not just any system of knowing, for it is the knowledge of a mystery, a knowledge full of hope, it is knowing according to the Spirit, an organic comprehension of the mystery of Christ, to which it is related as to its center. It is not a system, an abstraction, or an ideology.

Catechesis arises from a profession of faith, and leads to this profession of faith. It makes it possible for a community of believers to proclaim that Jesus, the Son of God, the Christ, is alive and is the Savior.

For this reason, the example of any catechesis is the baptismal catechumenate, which is the peculiar form by which an adult converted to the faith is brought to the profession of baptismal faith on the Paschal Vigil. While this preparation is being made, the catechumens receive the Gospel (sacred Scripture) and the ecclesial expression of it, which is the Creed of faith.

Catechesis, however, can use many other forms as well (sacred preaching, religious instruction in schools, radio or television broadcasts), which at a certain time or at various times have come into use by means of social communication or by ways of teaching.

Whatever it is, it is necessary to distinguish criteria by which a certain and definite form of the word may be truly catechetical. Not every instruction, even though it treat of religious matter, is of itself ecclesial catechesis. On the other hand, certain words which touch man in his concrete situation and impel him to lead himself to Christ, can become catechumenal words. And these words indeed by their very foundation transmit the essential parts of vital substance of the gospel message, which can be neither changed nor passed over in silence (see *Evangelii nuntiandi* no. 25).

Certainly the complete vital substance which is transmitted by the Creed of faith hands on the fundamental nucleus of the mystery of the one and triune God as it was revealed to us through the mystery of God's Son, the Incarnate Savior, always living in his Church.

But to discern both faithfulness in handing on the whole message of the Gospel and the authentic catechetical form of the words by which faith is transmitted, it is necessary that one reverently attend to the magisterial and pastoral ministry of the Church.

CATECHESIS AS "MEMORY"

589   9.   This is another primary aspect of the Church's activity, to the extent that it recalls, commemorates, celebrates the sacred in memory of the Lord Jesus, and accomplishes "anamnesis."

Indeed, the word and action of the ecclesial community have an impact only to the extent that they are today the word and action which manifest Jesus and bind to Christ. Catechesis thus is connected with the whole sacramental and liturgical action.

Catechesis is the manifestation in our time of the mystery hidden from the ages in God (see Col 1:26). This is why the first language that catechesis uses is sacred Scripture and the Creed. In this way catechesis is an authentic introduction to *lectio divina*, that is, to the reading of sacred Scripture, but "according to the Spirit" who dwells in the Church, both present in the apostolic ministries and active in the faithful. Sacred Scripture, however, brings it about that Christians use a common language. Customarily, at the time of formation, it happens that certain biblical sentences, taken especially from the New Testament, or certain liturgical formulas with which the sense of these sentences is expressed most clearly, and other common prayers, are committed to memory.

The believing man also takes to himself those expressions of the faith, worked out by the living thought of Christians through the course of centuries, which have been collected in the creeds and in the principal documents of the Church.

Thus it happens that to be a Christian is the same thing as to enter into a living tradition, which through the history of men shows how, in Jesus Christ, the Word of God assumed human nature. In sum, catechesis is "a transmission of the teachings of faith." The themes which it selects and the way it explains them are in agreement with genuine fidelity toward God and toward man in Jesus Christ.

CATECHESIS AS WITNESS

10. The word, resting on a living tradition, is in this way a living word for our time. Expressions, to the extent they are witness, commitment, "inculturation," ecclesial action, spiritual life, personal and liturgical prayer, and holiness, manifest this same thing, that is, witness.   590

A community of believers is a community of men living today which brings into effect the history of salvation. Salvation, which the community carries within itself, offers to men of this time freedom from sin, violence, injustice, and egoism. Thus the words of Jesus are fulfilled: "The truth will set you free" (Jn 8:32).

Catechesis, therefore, cannot be separated from a studious and active giving in life: "Not those who say, 'Lord, Lord . . .'" (Mt 7:21). This giving, however, can take on multiple forms, both individual and collegial. It is indeed according to tradition the "following of Christ." Hence it is that teaching of moral doctrine, the "Law of Christ," has its place in catechesis. It should be affirmed without any ambiguity that there are laws and moral principles which catechesis must expound, and that the moral doctrine of the Gospel is equipped in a peculiar way which greatly exceeds the mere demands of natural ethics. Indeed, the law of Christ, or law of love, is inscribed in our hearts by the Holy Spirit who has been given to us (see Rom 5:5; Jn 13:34).

On the other hand, catechesis, to the extent it is witness, at the same time educates a Christian by making it possible that he is fully inserted into the community of the disciples of Jesus Christ, which is the Church, taking to himself the total truth of the state of grace and of sin of this believing people, which is the pilgrim on earth, and receiving all those senses of fraternal solidarity which the Christian ought to preserve by living with all who, believers and nonbelievers, share the same fate of the human family. Thus the ecclesial community in truth constitutes itself as the universal sacrament of salvation.

Yet this moral doctrine is not only "individual," since it at the same time shows the social dimension of the gospel message.

One of the principal tasks of catechesis today is that it introduce and stimulate new forms of that studious and active giving, especially in the field of justice.

Thus, from the experience of Christians, new ways of evangelical life will spring up. With the helping grace of Christ, they will bring forth new fruits of holiness.

THE SPECIAL CHARACTERISTIC OF THE PEDAGOGY OF FAITH

11. In all complete catechesis there should be united in an indissoluble way: knowledge of the word of God; celebration of the faith in sacraments; profession of the faith in daily life.   591

The pedagogy of faith, therefore, has a special characteristic: an encounter with the person of Christ, a conversion of the heart, and experience of the Spirit in ecclesial communion.

PART III
CATECHESIS IS THE WORK OF ALL IN THE CHURCH

FOR A COMMON CO-RESPONSIBILITY

592   12. Catechesis is a task of vital importance for the whole Church. It in truth affects all the faithful, each according to his circumstances of life and his particular gifts or charisms. Certainly all Christians, by virtue of sacred baptism, ratified by sacramental confirmation, are called to transmit the Gospel and to see the faith of their brethren — especially children and young people — in Christ. Yet it sometimes can, for causes quite diverse, bring with it certain tensions and dissensions. The Synod, therefore, urges all the faithful to overcome the difficulties that perhaps arise and thus always to favor a common co-responsibility. In this way aspects are indicated which will afterward be described more accurately.

THE CHRISTIAN COMMUNITY

593   13. a. The place or setting in which catechesis is normally given is the Christian community. Catechesis is not a merely "individual" task, but it is always carried out in the dimension of the Christian community.

The forms of communities, however, are evolving in our time. Aside from the communities which include the family, the first community where a person is educated, or the parish, where the Christian assembly is normally at issue, or the school, the community destined for education, there are today springing up many other communities, among which are small ecclesial communities, associations, youth groups, and others of this sort.

These new communities indeed offer an opportunity to the Church, for they can be as a leaven in the mass and a leaven in the world which is being transformed. They contribute to showing more clearly both the variety and the unity of the Church. They ought to show among themselves charity and communion. Catechesis can find in them new places where it can be brought to effect, for there the members of the community are to each other the proclaimers of the mystery of Christ. Certainly catechesis will at the same time present the mystery of the Church, the people of God, that is, and the Mystical Body of Christ, in which many groups of men and communities are united intimately with God and among each other.

THE BISHOP AND THE OTHERS DEDICATED TO CATECHESIS

594   14. b. The bishop in his own local Church should play the primary role in catechetical activity. Aside from those things which belong to him in coordinating the action of people who in his particular Church dedicate themselves to catechesis, the bishop should also give himself to the giving of catechesis. Together with him the rest, each in his own way, cooperate in fulfilling the catechetical ministry. The duty of catechizing does not belong to anyone alone, because many energies are needed to carry it out. Each according to his function and charism contributes to carrying out the same mission: bishops together with their priests, the deacons, parents, catechists, leaders, and animators of the Christian communities. To fulfill this task, persons consecrated to God can and should, under indeed many titles, offer their own inestimable assistance to the Church.

In many nations catechists, together with their priests, share in the duty of directing the Christian communities. In union with their bishop, they take on responsibility for transmitting the faith.

The Synod confirms to all the importance of this task and hopes that all will find the good will and assistance they need. The Synod asks that catechetical ministries or duties not be assumed unless there is a suitable prior formation, according to the twofold reckoning or dimension of catechesis, that is, fidelity toward God and man. This indeed brings with it a formation pertaining to the sacred disciplines and at the same time notions about man which, necessary according to nations or circumstance, contain acquaintance with what the sciences offer about man.

CONCLUSION

18. After we have spoken with you about the work we have gone through these days near the Chair of Peter, in union and communion with Peter's successor, Pope Paul VI, we wish to give thanks to God first of all: to God the Supreme Giver from whom all good things come (see Jas 1:17); to God to whom we have dedicated our lives; to God who through the Spirit of his Son was always present to us and enabled us to see, look upon, and touch with our hands (see 1 Jn 1:1) his wonders; to God who, it is our heartfelt desire, may be loved by you above all things. — 595

Then we give thanks to all who with us expend energies in the catechetical ministry. We think of priests, co-workers in our apostolic ministry, joined with us so intimately by virtue of the same sacrament of orders; we think of those who lead lives consecrated to God, whether in religious communities or in the world, affirming again our hope in the great spiritual fruitfulness in the world which life in the spirit of the beatitudes brings (see LG no. 42); we think of those whom we call by the particular name of catechists. How many are the men, women, young people, indeed even children who give up their time, often without any reward of this world, in so great a work, to build up the kingdom of God, filled with true charity since they form Christ Jesus in human hearts and strive to lead them to fullness. We think also of those parents who educate their children from earliest infancy in knowledge of Jesus Christ and in fear and love of God, and keep alive in the hearts of their children the faith received through baptism and ratified by confirmation, by building it up in such a way that they constantly bring forth fruits of eternal life. We think also of so many of our fraternal communities, dedicated to prayer, to the poor, which offer precious witness of life to a world oppressed by individualistic egoism.

68. PAUL VI, **Address** to the bishops of Holland, excerpt on celebrating the liturgy in faith and joy, 17 November 1977: AAS 70 (1978) 28–35; Not 13 (1977) 553–554[a] (French).

We turn our attention next to the Catholic communities of Holland, which celebrate the liturgy in faith and joy as it is a share in and a mirror of the liturgy of heaven, a sacred act and prayer of Christ, of the Church, and of all who seek to drink at the fountains of divine life, the sacraments. — 596

On this subject there is a twofold motive for special confidence.

---

[a] Erroneously dated 18 November in Not.

597   The first arises from the fact of publication at this time of the new Roman Missal in its Dutch translation. The Church in Holland will thus have in its hands a new instrument of adaptation, allowing the eucharistic celebration to regain the life-giving power and inner influence too often missing because of rash and unjustified innovations (see SC art. no. 22, § 3).[b]

The new Missal — one of the most treasured results of Vatican Council II (see SC art. 50)[c] — even though authorizing a sound diversity of forms, assures the necessary unity and, in its wealth of texts, elicits the conscious and active participation of the faithful. We are sure that you will zealously see to it that every parish and church of your dioceses is supplied with enough copies. May the Lord grant that the introduction of the new Roman Missal — which alone now is authorized — in its Dutch translation may bring with it a new flowering of devotion to the eucharist, the *sacramentum pietatis, signum unitatis, vinculum caritatis* (St. Augustine).

598   A second reason for confidence we find in the letter you have addressed to your priests in November 1976 on the occasion of the Dutch translation of the new *Rite of Penance*. You in effect have underlined the importance of the sacrament of penance in the process of conversion, reconciliation, and liberation from sin accomplished by Christ — in a word in the process of the renewal of Christian life. You have also rightly remarked how "without the sacrament of penance we would be without a source of reconciliation and salvation." In the light of these considerations and in keeping with the norms established by the Holy See, you have reaffirmed the need for confession and individual absolution. You have also confirmed that general confession and general absolution are limited to special cases, with the understanding, as well, that even in such cases at least those conscious of grave sins must go to confession individually in due time.

We urge you to tend to the growth of the seed you have planted. With your priests, search for the best pastoral means for the faithful even from childhood to benefit most surely from the joy, the comfort, and the enrichment of this sacrament. Overcome by your gentleness and patience the difficulties that can sometimes come from the very persons who are the ministers of the sacrament of salvation.

69. JOHN PAUL I, **Homily** on the occasion of taking possession of his cathedral, St. John Lateran, excerpt on liturgical irregularities, 23 September 1978: AAS 70 (1978) 747–751;[a] Not 14 (1978) 451–455 (Italian).

599   The master of ceremonies has chosen the three biblical readings for this solemn liturgy that he thought suited the occasion and I will try to explain them. [. . .]

600   The third reading (Mt 28:16–20) reminds the bishop of Rome of his duties. [. . .] The second duty, expressed in the word "baptize," refers to the sacraments and to the entire liturgy. The Diocese of Rome has followed the program of the Italian Conference of Bishops, "Evangelization and Sacraments," and knows already that evangelization, sacraments, and a holy life are but three steps along the one road. Evangelization is the preparation for the sacraments; the sacraments lead the recipients to live as Christians. My wish is that this great idea may be applied ever more extensively. My wish as well is that Rome may give a good example in its

---

    b   See DOL 1 no. 22.

    c   See DOL 1 no. 50.

    a   Erroneously dated 13 Nov 1978 (745 and 1014).

way of celebrating the liturgy fully and without misplaced "creativity." Abuses in liturgy have prompted as a reaction attitudes leading to positions that are unjustifiable in themselves and in conflict with the Gospel. In appealing with affection and trust to the sense of responsibility of all before God and the Church, my intention is to be able to ensure that every irregularity in liturgy will be scrupulously avoided.

70. JOHN PAUL II, **Address** (televised) to the world, from the Sistine Chapel, the day after his election, excerpt on fidelity to liturgical norms, 17 October 1978: AAS 70 (1978) 919–927.

[. . .] We wish first of all to state the lasting importance of the Second Vatican Ecumenical Council and we take it as our clear duty to devote our energies to putting it into effect. [. . .]   601

This general purpose of fidelity to Vatican Council II and our own express intention of putting it into effect can consist of many parts [. . .]; but there is one part on which more effort will be bent, the ecclesiological.

[. . .] Loyalty also includes respect for the liturgical norms issued by ecclesiastical authority and therefore opposes the practice either of introducing innovations arbitrarily and without approval or of obstinately refusing what has lawfully been laid down concerning liturgical rites and made part of them. Loyalty also has bearing on the church discipline spoken of by our predecessor. Such discipline is not of a kind that represses or, as they say, deadens, but has as its purpose the protection of right order in the Mystical Body of Christ, making it possible for the conjunction of all the members to fulfill its purpose in its established and natural way. [. . .]

71. JOHN PAUL II, **Address** to the bishops of the Byzantine-Ruthenian Province of the U.S.A., excerpt on the importance of the particular rites in the Church, 23 November 1978: Not 14 (1978) 569–570 (English).

The Church is indeed enriched by such venerable traditions and would be much poorer without them. Their variety contributes in no small measure to her splendor. They enshrine many great artistic and cultural values, the loss of which would be sorely felt. Each of them is in itself worthy of great admiration and wonder.   602

Yet these traditions are no mere adornment of the Church. United in brotherhood, they are important means at the disposal of the Church for displaying to the world the universality of Christ's salvation and fulfilling its mission of making disciples of all nations.

The variety within brotherhood that is seen in the Catholic Church, far from being detrimental to the Church's unity, rather manifests it, showing how all peoples and cultures are called to be organically united in the Holy Spirit through the same faith, the same sacraments, the same government.

Each tradition must value and cherish the others. The eye cannot say to the hand: "I have no need of you"; for, if all were a single organ, where would the body be (see Rom 12:19,21)? The Church is Christ's and the various parts of the Body are intended to serve the good of the whole and to collaborate with each other for that end.

Each individual tradition has its own contribution to make to the good of the whole. Each one's understanding of the faith is deepened by the doctrine contained in the works of the Fathers and spiritual writers of the others, by the theological riches stored in the others' liturgies as they have developed over the centuries under the guidance of the Holy Spirit and of legitimate ecclesiastical authority, and by the others' ways of living the faith that they have received from the apostles. Each one can find support in the examples of zeal, fidelity, and holiness that are provided by the others' history.

The Second Vatican Council declared that "all should realize that it is of supreme importance to understand, venerate, preserve, and foster the exceedingly rich liturgical and spiritual heritage of the Eastern Churches, in order faithfully to preserve the fullness of Christian tradition" (UR no. 15).[a] The Council also declared that the Eastern Churches' "entire heritage of spirituality and liturgy, of discipline and theology, in their various traditions, belongs to the full catholic and apostolic character of the Church" (UR no. 17).[b]

My brother bishops, I do most heartily respect and appreciate the venerable traditions to which you belong and I desire to see them flourish.

I would wish every member of the Catholic Church to cherish his or her own tradition. "It is the mind of the Catholic Church that each individual Church or rite retain its traditions whole and entire, while adjusting its way of life to the various needs of time and place" (OE no. 2).[c] You and the Churches over which you preside should accordingly treasure your heritage and take care to hand it on in its integrity to future generations.

I would also wish each member of the Catholic Church to recognize the equal dignity of the other rites within its unity. Each rite is called to assist the others, working together in harmony and good order for the good of the whole and not for its own particular welfare.

72. JOHN PAUL II, **Address** to priests, men religious, and seminarians at St. Charles Seminary, Philadelphia, excerpt on liturgical prayer, the guarantee of fidelity to the Church, 3 October 1979: Not 15 (1979) 608–609 (English).

603

To understand what it means to be faithful we must look to Christ, the "faithful witness" (Rv 1:5), the Son who "learned to obey through what he suffered" (Heb 5:8); to Jesus who said: "My aim is to do not my own will, but the will of him who sent me" (Jn 5:30). We look to Jesus, not only to see and contemplate his fidelity to the Father despite all opposition (see Heb 12:3), but also to learn from him the means he employed in order to be faithful: especially prayer and abandonment to God's will (see Lk 22:39ff.).

Remember that in the final analysis perseverance in fidelity is a proof, not of human strength and courage, but of the efficacy of Christ's grace. And so if we are going to persevere we shall have to be men of prayer who, through the eucharist, the liturgy of the hours, and our personal encounters with Christ, find the courage

---

[a]   DOL 6 no. 187.

[b]   DOL 6 no. 188.

[c]   DOL 5 no. 162.

and grace to be faithful. Let us be confident then, remembering the words of St. Paul: "There is nothing that I cannot master with the help of the one who gives me strength" (Phil 4:13).

73. JOHN PAUL II, **Address** to the Ukrainian community of Philadelphia, excerpt on diversity of rites as the presence of the Spirit in the Church, 4 October 1979: Not 15 (1979) 610–611 (English).

As history testifies, the Church developed a number of rites and traditions as   604
in the course of time she spread from Jerusalem to the nations and took flesh in the language, culture, and human traditions of the individual peoples who accepted the Gospel with open hearts. These various rites and traditions, far from being a sign of deviation, infidelity, or disunity, were in fact unfailing proof of the presence of the Holy Spirit, who continually renews and enriches the Church, the kingdom of Christ already present in mystery (See LG no. 3).[a]

The various traditions within the Church give expression to the multitude of ways the Gospel can take root and flower in the lives of God's people. They are living evidence of the richness of the Church. Each one, while united to all the others in the "same faith, the same sacraments, and the same government" (OE no. 2),[b] is nevertheless manifested in its own liturgy, ecclesiastical discipline, and spiritual patrimony. Each tradition combined particular artistic expressions and unique spiritual insights with an unparalleled lived experience of being faithful to Christ. It was in view of these considerations that the Second Vatican Council declared: "History, tradition, and numerous ecclesiastical institutions clearly manifest how much the universal Church is indebted to the Eastern Churches. Thus this sacred Synod not only honors this ecclesiastical and spiritual heritage with merited esteem and rightful praise, but also unhesitatingly looks upon it as the heritage of Christ's universal Church" (OE no. 5).

74. JOHN PAUL II, **Homily** to priests of the U.S.A. at the Civic Center, Philadelphia, excerpt on active participation in the liturgy as the goal of pastoral activity, 4 October 1979: AAS 71 (1979) 1198–1204; Not 15 (1979) 609–610 (English).

3.   [. . .] Just as Jesus was most perfectly a "man-for-others" in giving himself up   605
totally on the cross, so the priest is most of all servant and "man-for-others" when he acts *in persona Christi* in the eucharist, leading the Church in that celebration in which this sacrifice of the cross is renewed. For in the Church's daily eucharistic worship the "Good News" that the apostles were sent out to proclaim is preached in its fullness; the work of our redemption is reenacted.

How perfectly the Fathers at the Second Vatican Council captured this fundamental truth in their Decree on Priestly Life and Ministry: "The other sacraments, as every ministry of the Church and every work of the apostolate, are linked with

---

a   DOL 4 no. 137.

b   DOL 5 no. 162.

the holy eucharist and are directed toward it. . . . Hence the eucharist shows itself to be the source and the summit of all evangelization" (PO no. 5).ª In the celebration of the eucharist, we priests are at the very heart of our ministry of service, of "giving God's flock a shepherd's care." All our pastoral endeavors are incomplete until our people are led to the full and active participation in the eucharistic sacrifice. . . .

My brother priests: have we not here touched upon the heart of the matter — our zeal for the priesthood itself? It is inseparable from our zeal for the service of the people. This concelebrated Mass, which so beautifully symbolizes the unity of our priesthood, gives to the whole world the witness of the unity for which Jesus prayed to his Father on our behalf. But it must not become a merely transient manifestation, which would render fruitless the prayer of Jesus. Every eucharist renews this prayer for our unity: "Lord, remember your Church throughout the world; make us grow in love, together with John Paul our Pope, . . . our bishop, and all the clergy."

75. JOHN PAUL II, **Address** to the bishops of the U.S.A. at Quigley Seminary, Chicago, excerpt on bishops as the guardians and promoters of the Church's authentic liturgy, 5 October 1979: AAS 71 (1979) 1218–29; Not 15 (1979) 612–614 (English).

606   [. . .] Guided by the Holy Spirit, we must all be deeply convinced that holiness is the first priority in our lives and in our ministry. In this context, as bishops we see the immense value of prayer: the liturgical prayer of the Church, our prayer together, our prayer alone. In recent times many of you have found that the practice of making spiritual retreats together with your brother bishops is indeed a help to that holiness born of truth. May God sustain you in this initiative so that each of you, and all of you together, may fulfill your role as a sign of holiness offered to God's people on their pilgrimage to the Father. May you yourselves, like St. John Neumann, also be a prophetic anticipation of holiness. The people need to have bishops whom they can look upon as leaders in the quest for holiness — bishops who are trying to anticipate prophetically in their own lives the attainment of the goal to which they are leading the faithful. [. . .]

607   As bishops who are servants of truth, we are also called to be *servants of unity, in the communion of the Church*.

In *the communion of holiness* we ourselves are called, as I mentioned above, to conversion, so that we may preach with convincing power the message of Jesus: "Reform your lives and believe in the Gospel." We have a special role to play in safeguarding the sacrament of reconciliation, so that, in fidelity to a divine precept, we and our people may experience in our innermost being that "grace has far surpassed sin" (Rom 5:20). I, too, ratify the prophetic call of Paul VI, who urged the bishops to help their priests to "deeply understand how closely they collaborate through the sacrament of penance with the Savior in the work of conversion" (Address of 20 April 1978).ª In this regard I confirm again the Norms of *Sacramentum*

ª   DOL 18 no. 260.

ª   DOL 378 no. 3139.

Paenitentiae which so wisely emphasize the ecclesial dimension of the sacrament of penance and indicate the precise limits of general absolution,[b] just as Paul VI did in his *ad limina* address to the American bishops.

Conversion by its very nature is the condition for that union with God which reaches its greatest expression in the eucharist. Our union with Christ in the eucharist presupposes, in turn, that our hearts are set on conversion, that they are pure. This is indeed an important part of our preaching to the people. In my encyclical I endeavored to express it in these words: "The Christ who calls to the eucharistic banquet is always the same Christ who exhorts us to penance and repeats his 'Repent.' Without this constant and ever-renewed endeavor for conversion, partaking of the eucharist would lack its full redeeming effectiveness. . ." (*Redemptor hominis* no. 20).[c] In the face of a widespread phenomenon of our time, namely, that many of our people who are among the great numbers who receive communion make little use of confession, we must emphasize Christ's basic call to conversion. We must also stress that the personal encounter with the forgiving Jesus in the sacrament of reconciliation is a divine means which keeps alive in our hearts and in our communities, a consciousness of sin in its perennial and tragic reality, and which actually brings forth, by the action of Jesus and the power of his Spirit, fruits of conversion in justice and holiness of life. By this sacrament we are renewed in fervor, strengthened in our resolves, and buoyed up by divine encouragement.

As chosen leaders in *a community of praise and prayer*, it is our special joy to offer the eucharist and to give our people a sense of their vocation as an Easter people, with the *Alleluia* as their song. And let us always recall that the validity of all liturgical development and the effectiveness of every liturgical sign presupposes the great principle that the Catholic liturgy is theocentric, and that it is above all "the worship of divine majesty" (see SC art. 33)[d] in union with Jesus Christ. Our people have a supernatural sense whereby they look for reverence in all liturgy, especially in what touches the mystery of the eucharist. With deep faith our people understand that the eucharist — in the Mass and outside the Mass — is the body and blood of Jesus Christ, and therefore deserves the worship that is given to the living God and to him alone.

As ministers of *a community of service*, it is our privilege to proclaim the truth of Christ's union with his members in his Body, the Church. Hence we commend all service rendered in his name and to his brethren (see Mt 25:45). [. . .]

76. JOHN PAUL II, **Apostolic Exhortation** *Catechesi tradendae*, on catechesis in our time, 16 October 1979: AAS 71 (1979) 1277–1340; Not 15 (1979) 601–602 (excerpt).*

INTRODUCTION

1. The Church has always considered catechesis one of her primary tasks, for, before Christ ascended to his Father after his resurrection, he gave the apostles a   608

---

b   See DOL 361.

c   DOL 191 no. 1330.

d   See DOL 1 no. 33.

*   Official English text, Vatican Polyglot Press, 1979.

final command — to make disciples of all nations and to teach them to observe all that he had commanded.[1] He thus entrusted them with the mission and power to proclaim to humanity what they had heard, what they had seen with their eyes, what they had looked upon and touched with their hands, concerning the Word of life.[2] He also entrusted them with the mission and power to explain with authority what he had taught them, his words and actions, his signs and commandments. And he gave them the Spirit to fulfill this mission.

Very soon the name of catechesis was given to the whole of the efforts within the Church to make disciples, to help people to believe that Jesus is the Son of God, so that believing they might have life in his name,[3] and to educate and instruct them in this life and thus build up the Body of Christ. The Church has not ceased to devote her energy to this task.

III
CATECHESIS IN THE CHURCH'S PASTORAL AND MISSIONARY ACTIVITY

CATECHESIS AND SACRAMENTS

609   23. Catechesis is intrinsically linked with the whole of liturgical and sacramental activity, for it is in the sacraments, especially in the eucharist, that Christ Jesus works in fullness for the transformation of human beings.

In the early Church the catechumenate and preparation for the sacraments of baptism and the eucharist were the same thing. Although in the countries that have long been Christian the Church has changed her practice in this field, the catechumenate has never been abolished; on the contrary, it is experiencing a renewal in those countries[54] and is abundantly practiced in the young missionary Churches. In any case, catechesis always has reference to the sacraments. On the one hand, the catechesis that prepares for the sacraments is an eminent kind and every form of catechesis necessarily leads to the sacraments of faith. On the other hand, authentic practice of the sacraments is bound to have a catechetical aspect. In other words, sacramental life is impoverished and very soon turns into hollow ritualism if it is not based on serious knowledge of the meaning of the sacraments, and catechesis becomes intellectualized if it fails to come alive in sacramental practice.

IV
THE WHOLE OF THE GOOD NEWS DRAWN FROM ITS SOURCE

THE SOURCE

610   27. Catechesis will always draw its content from the living source of the word of God transmitted in tradition and the Scriptures, for "sacred tradition and sacred Scripture make up a single sacred deposit of the word of God, which is entrusted to the Church," as was recalled by the Second Vatican Council, which desired that "the ministry of the word — pastoral preaching, catechetics and all forms of Christian instruction — (should be) healthily nourished and (should) thrive in holiness through the word of Scripture."[57]

---

[1]   See Mt 28:19–20.

[2]   See 1 Jn 1:1.

[3]   See Jn 20:31.

[54]   See *Rite of Christian Initiation of Adults* [DOL 301].

[57]   DV nos. 10 and 24; see also *General Catechetical Directory* no. 45, where the principal and complementary sources of catechesis are well set out.

To speak of tradition and Scripture as the source of catechesis is to draw attention to the fact that catechesis must be impregnated and penetrated by the thought, the spirit, and the outlook of the Bible and the Gospels through assiduous contact with the texts themselves; but it is also a reminder that catechesis will be all the richer and more effective for reading the texts with the intelligence and the heart of the Church and for drawing inspiration from the two thousand years of the Church's reflection and life.

The Church's teaching, liturgy, and life spring from this source and lead back to it, under the guidance of the pastors and, in particular, of the doctrinal magisterium entrusted to them by the Lord.

VI
SOME WAYS AND MEANS OF CATECHESIS

THE HOMILY

48. This remark is even more valid for the catechesis given in the setting of the liturgy, especially at the eucharistic assembly. Respecting the specific nature and proper cadence of this setting, the homily takes up again the journey of faith put forward by catechesis and brings it to its natural fulfillment. At the same time it encourages the Lord's disciples to begin anew each day their spiritual journey in truth, adoration, and thanksgiving. Accordingly, one can say that catechetical teaching too finds its source and its fulfillment in the eucharist, within the whole circle of the liturgical year. Preaching, centered upon the bible texts, must then in its own way make it possible to familiarize the faithful with the whole of the mysteries of the faith and with the norms of Christian living. Much attention must be given to the homily: it should be neither too long nor too short; it should always be carefully prepared, rich in substance, and adapted to the hearers, and reserved to ordained ministers. The homily should have its place not only in every Sunday and feast-day eucharist, but also in the celebration of baptisms, penitential liturgies, marriages, and funerals. This is one of the benefits of the liturgical renewal.

611

VII
HOW TO IMPART CATECHESIS

THE CONTRIBUTION OF POPULAR DEVOTION

54. Another question of method concerns the utilization in catechetical instruction of valid elements in popular piety. I have in mind devotions practiced by the faithful in certain regions with moving fervor and purity of intention, even if the faith underlying them needs to be purified or rectified in many aspects. I have in mind certain easily understood prayers that many simple people are fond of repeating. I have in mind certain acts of piety practiced with a sincere desire to do penance or to please the Lord. Underlying most of these prayers and practices, besides elements that should be discarded, there are other elements which, if they were properly used, could serve very well to help people advance toward knowledge of the mystery of Christ and of his message: the love and mercy of God, the incarnation of Christ, his redeeming cross and resurrection, the activity of the Spirit in each Christian and in the Church, the mystery of the hereafter, the evangelical virtues to be practiced, the presence of the Christian in the world, etc. And why should we appeal to non-Christian or even anti-Christian elements, refusing to build on elements which, even if they need to be revised and improved, have something Christian at their root?

612

SECTION 3. WORK OF THE AGENCIES OF THE HOLY SEE

SUMMARY (DOL 77–102). This section centers on the succession of curial agencies immediately responsible for carrying out the reform decrees of the Constitution on the Liturgy.

—One group of texts presents the creation or reorganization of such entities: the Consilium (DOL 77), the Congregation of Rites (DOL 82, 87–89), the Congregation for Divine Worship (DOL 93–94), the Congregation for the Sacraments and Divine Worship (DOL 101). For their historical interest the respective lists of members are added (DOL 78, 95, 102), as well as a letter of Pope Paul VI to Cardinal Lercaro, first President of the Consilium (DOL 90),and an exchange of letters between Pope Paul and Cardinal Gut, first Prefect of the Congregation for Divine Worship (DOL 96, 97).

—The progress as well as problems involved in the work of these agencies are reflected in: Paul VI's addresses at the series of audiences for members of the Consilium (DOL 81, 84, 86, 92, 99), in the remarks addressed to the Pope by the presidents or prefects at these audiences (DOL 80, 83, 85, 91, 98); a letter of the Consilium to papal nuncios (DOL 79); the report to the Synod of Bishops 1974 by the prefect of the Congregation for Divine Worship (DOL 100).

77. SECRETARIAT OF STATE, **Letter** *Mi onore di communicare* of Cardinal A. Cicognani to Cardinal G. Lercaro, President of the Consilium, on the organization and work of the Consilium, 29 February 1964 (Italian).*

613   I have the honor of communicating to Your Eminence, in keeping with the directives of Pope Paul VI, the responsibilities of the Consilium for the Carrying out of the Constitution on the Liturgy, of which Your Eminence is President. They are as follows:

      a. to suggest the names of the persons charged with forming study groups for the revision of rites and liturgical books;

      b. to oversee and coordinate the work of the study groups;

      c. to prepare carefully an instruction explaining the practical application of the Motu Proprio *Sacram Liturgiam*ª and clearly outlining the competence of territorial ecclesiastical authorities, pending the reform of the rites and liturgical books;

      d. to apply, according to the letter and spirit of the Council, the Constitution it approved, by responding to the proposals of the conferences of bishops and to questions that arise involving the correct application of the Constitution.

Appeals of decisions of the Consilium as well as the solution of particularly sensitive and grave or completely new problems will be referred by the Consilium to the pope.

78. CONSILIUM, **List of members** (1964–1969).**

[The members are listed alphabetically, with title at time of appointment, date of appointment; other pertinent dates.]

614   AGAGIANIAN, Cardinal Peter Gregory, Prefect of SC Propagation of the Faith, 5 March 1964.

ANTONELLI, Ferdinando, OFM, 5 March 1964; Secretary of SC Rites, 17 January 1965; Titular Archbishop of Idiera, 19 February 1966; Secretary of SC Causes of Saints, 7 May 1969; cardinal, 5 March 1973.

BEA, Cardinal Augustin, SJ, President of the Secretariat for Christian Unity, 5 March 1964; President of the Pontifical Commission for the Neo-Vulgate, 1 December 1965; died 16 November 1968.ª

BEKKERS, William, Bishop of s'Herzogenbosh (Bois-le-Duc), Holland, 5 March 1964; died 9 May 1966.

BEVILACQUA, Giulio, Oratorian, 5 March 1964; cardinal, 25 February 1965; died 6 May 1965.ᵇ

---

  * Text, EDL 191.

  ª See DOL 20.

 ** Announcements: 5 March 1964: AAS 56 (1964) 479–480. 1 June 1965: AAS 57 (1965) 614. 30 December 1965: ibid. 1024. 2 February 1967: Not 3 (1967) 113. 18 July 1967: AAS 59 (1967) 825. 9 January 1968: AAS 60 (1968) 59. 29 January 1968: ibid. 237. 17 December 1968: ibid. 823.

  ª See Not 4 (1968) 360–362 (A. Bugnini).

  ᵇ See Not 1 (1965) 97–98.

BLUYSSEN, Jan, bishop at s'Herzogenbosh (Bois-le-Duc), Holland, 30 December 1965; Auxiliary Bishop s'Herzogenbosh, 11 October 1966; member of the Council of the Presidency, 11 October 1970.

BOTERO SALAZAR, Tulio, Archbishop of Medellín, Colombia, 5 March 1964.

BOUDON, René, Bishop of Mende, France, 5 March 1964; member of the Council of the Presidency, 11 October 1967.

BUGNINI, Annibale, CM, Secretary, 5 March 1964; Subsecretary of SC Rites, 26 January 1965; special secretary for liturgy of the first Synod of Bishops, September 1967; Delegate for Pontifical Ceremonies, 25 May 1968.

BYRNE, Leo Christopher, Coadjutor Archbishop of St. Paul and Minneapolis, Minn., U.S.A., 17 December 1968.

CARTER, Gerald Emmet, Bishop of London, Ont., Canada, 30 December 1965.

CLAVEL MENDEZ, Thomas Albert, Archbishop of Panama, Panama, 1 June 1965.

CODY, Cardinal John Patrick, Archbishop of Chicago, Ill., U.S.A., 18 July 1967.

CONFALONIERI, Cardinal Carlo, Proprefect of the Consistorial Congregation, Vice President, 5 March 1964.

CONWAY, Cardinal William, Archbishop of Armagh, Ireland, 1 June 1965; member of the Council of the Presidency, 11 October 1967.

DE KESEL, Leo, Auxiliary Bishop of Ghent, Belgium, 2 February 1967.

DWYER, George Patrick, Bishop of Leeds, England, 1 June 1965; Archbishop of Birmingham, England, 5 October 1965.

ENCISO VIANA, Jesús, Bishop of Mallorca, Spain, 5 March 1964; died 21 September 1964.

ENRIQUE Y TARANCÓN, Vicente, Archbishop of Oviedo, Spain, 1 June 1965; member of the Council of the Presidency, 11 October 1967; Archbishop of Toledo, 30 January 1969; cardinal, 28 April 1969.

FELICI, Pericle, 5 March 1964; President of the Pontifical Commission for the Revision of the Code of Canon Law, 21 February 1967; cardinal, 26 June 1967.

FEY SCHNEIDER, Bernardo, CSsR, Coadjutor Bishop of Potosí, Bolivia, 5 March 1964.

GIOBBE, Cardinal Paolo, Prefect of the Apostolic Datary, 5 March 1964.

GRACIAS, Cardinal Valerian, Archbishop of Bombay, India, 5 March 1964.

GRAY, Gordon J., Archbishop of St. Andrews and Edinburgh, Scotland, 2 February 1967; cardinal, 28 April 1969.

GRIMSHAW, Francis, Archbishop of Birmingham, England, 5 March 1964; died 22 March 1965.

GUANO, Emilio, Bishop of Livorno (Leghorn), Italy, 5 March 1964.

GUT, Benno, OSB, Abbot Primate of the Benedictine Confederation, 5 March 1964; cardinal, 26 June 1967; Prefect of SC Rites and President of the Consilium, 9 January 1968.

HALLINAN, Paul, Archbishop of Atlanta, Ga., U.S.A., 5 March 1964; died 27 March 1968.

HÄNGGI, Anton, Bishop of Basel-Lugano, Switzerland, 29 January 1968.

HERVAS Y BENET, Juan, Titutar Bishop of Dora, Ordinary of Ciudad Real (prelature), Spain, 5 March 1964.

HURLEY, Denis Eugene, OMI, Archbishop of Durban, South Africa, 1 June 1965.

ISNARD, Clemente José Carlos, OSB, Bishop of Nueva Friburgo, Brazil, 5 March 1964; member of the Council of the Presidency, 11 October 1967.

JENNY, Henri, Archbishop of Cambrai, France, 5 March 1964.

JOP, Franciszek, Titular Bishop of Daulia, Apostolic Administrator of Opole, Poland, 5 March 1964.

KABANGU, François, Bishop of Luebo, Zaire, 17 December 1968.

KERVÉADOU, François, Bishop of Saint-Brieuc, France, 5 March 1964.

KOVÁCS, Sándor (Alexander), Bishop of Szombathely, Hungary, 30 December 1965.

LARRAONA, Cardinal Arcadio, CMF, Prefect of SC Rites, 5 March 1964; resigned 9 January 1968; died 7 May 1973.

LAZÍK, Ambrosius, Titular Bishop of Appia, Apostolic Administrator of Trnava, Czechoslovakia, 30 December 1965; died 20 April 1968.

LERCARO, Cardinal Giacomo, Archbishop of Bologna, Italy, President, 19 February 1964; relator on the liturgy at the first Synod of Bishops, 27 October 1967; resigned 9 January 1968.[c]

LOPES DE MOURA, Agostinho Joaquim, CSSp, Bishop of Portalegre-Castelo, Branco, Portugal, 5 March 1964.

MALULA, Joseph, Archbishop of Kinshasa, Zaire, 5 March 1964; cardinal, 28 April 1969.

MANSOURATI, Clément Ignace, Titular Archbishop of Apamea in Syria, Lebanon, 5 March 1964.

MARTIN, Joseph Albert, Bishop of Nicolet, P.Q., Canada, 5 March 1964.

NAGAE, Laurentius Satoshi, Bishop of Urawa, Japan, 5 March 1964.

OŤCENAŠEK, Karel, Titular Bishop of Chersonesus in Crete, Apostolic Administrator of Hradec Králové, Czechoslovakia, 2 April 1969.

---

[c] See Not 4 (1968) 3–5 and DOL 90.

PELLEGRINO, Michele, Archbishop of Turin, Italy, 30 December 1965; member of the Council of the Presidency, 11 October 1967; cardinal, 26 June 1967.

PICHLER, Alfred, Bishop of Banjaluka, Yugoslavia, 5 March 1964.

RAU, Enrique, Bishop of Mar Del Plata, Argentina, 5 March 1964; died 11 August 1971.

RITTER, Cardinal Joseph Elmer, Archbishop of St. Louis, Mo., U.S.A., 5 March 1964; died 10 June 1967.

ROSSI, Carlo, Bishop of Biella, Italy, 5 March 1964.[d]

RUGAMBWA, Cardinal Laurean, Bishop of Bukoba, Tanzania, 5 March 1964; Archbishop of Dar-es-Salaam, Tanzania, 19 December 1968.

SILVA HENRÍQUEZ, Cardinal Raúl, Archbishop of Santiago de Chile, 5 March 1964.

SPÜLBECK, Otto, Bishop of Meissen, East Germany, 5 March 1964; member of the Council of the Presidency, 11 October 1967.

VAN BEKKUM, Guillaume, SVD, Bishop of Ruteng, Indonesia, 5 March 1964.

VAN ZUYLEN, Guillaume-Marie, Bishop of Liège, Belgium, 5 March 1964.

VOLK, Hermann, Bishop of Mainz, Germany, 5 March 1964; cardinal, 5 March 1973.

WEAKLAND, Rembert, OSB, Abbot Primate of the Benedictine Confederation, 29 January 1968.

YOUNG, Guilford Clyde, Archbishop of Hobart, Australia, 5 March 1964.

ZAUNER, Franz, Bishop of Linz, Austria, 5 March 1964.

79. CONSILIUM, **Letter** *Le sarei grato* to papal nuncios and apostolic delegates, on the course to follow in reform of the liturgy, 25 March 1964 (Italian).[*]

I will be grateful to you for conveying the following information to the presidents of the conferences of bishops or the bishop presiding at episcopal meetings convened for the discussions designed to carry out the Constitution on the Liturgy. In setting up the Consilium, Pope Paul VI has entrusted it, among other things, with these tasks: 1. to prepare an instruction explaining the practical application of the Motu Proprio *Sacram Liturgiam*[a] and outlining clearly the competence of territorial ecclesiastical authorities, pending revision of the rites and liturgical books; 2. to put into application, in the letter and spirit of the Council, the Constitution on the Liturgy, by examining and confirming the decisions of conferences of bishops and

615

---

d   See Not 16 (1980) 122.

*   Text, EDL 192–196.

a   See DOL 20.

by responding to questions that arise involving the correct application of the Constitution.[b]

Accordingly, the competent authority shall send to the Consilium the enactments of conferences of bishops on applying the Constitution.

The instruction already mentioned[c] is under the care of a capable group of experts, but its development and approval on the part of the Consilium will obviously take some time. For this reason it seems appropriate at this time to indicate certain points to be developed further in the instruction, which, in the meantime, can serve as directive norms for the episcopate.

616   1.   Every decision on liturgical matters requires passage by two-thirds of the votes cast by secret ballot (*Sacram Liturgiam* no. X).[d] The result of the vote on every decision is to appear clearly in the *acta* transmitted to the Holy See.

617   2.   On the issue of introducing the vernacular into the liturgy, it is not sufficient to report in a general way that a conference of bishops has approved its use, for example, in rites pertaining to the Roman Missal, Ritual, or Pontifical; instead there must be an indication of the particular rites, parts, formularies, and texts the conference decides on.

618   3.   On the same subject of the vernacular, "in the parts belonging to the people" (SC art. 54),[e] *doing one part at a time* seems appropriate, as does the principle of *proceeding gradually*. The point is to avoid an excessively abrupt transition from the present arrangement of almost complete fidelity to Latin to the new arrangement that provides for bringing in the vernacular more extensively.

For example, before the introduction of popular religious music into the vernacular as a substitute for the music traditional in the liturgy, there should be an effort in every nation to compile a collection of melodies with vernacular texts, fully suited to the liturgical rites and having artistic worth.

619   4.   The time does not yet seem right to petition, even for a whole nation, modifications, omissions, or variations in the present arrangement of the liturgical celebrations.

80. CONSILIUM, **Remarks** of Cardinal G. Lercaro, President of the Consilium, at a papal audience for the members of the Consilium, 29 October 1964.*

620   The Fathers and other members who here represent the large Consilium family wish to express to Your Holiness their sincere and devoted sentiments for your fatherly kindness and graciousness in granting the request to receive us in audience.

We wish above all to thank you for considering us worthy to be chosen as your associates in work of such importance. We see its increasing growth and splendor;

  b   See DOL 77 no. 613.
  c   See DOL 23.
  d   See DOL 20 no. 288.
  e   DOL 1 no. 54.
  *   Text, OR 31 Oct. 1964, 1.

we see how truly necessary and valuable it is for the salvation and sanctification of souls.

We regard our "call" as an extraordinary grace and special privilege. If you will allow me to say so candidly, voicing the feelings of all of us, it is a privilege, even though as the work goes on we feel the pressures increasing daily.

For we must thoroughly examine the rites and forms of divine worship and these are elements that through the centuries of the Church's history all Catholics, and especially we priests, have held dear. But a pastoral concern presses us to carry out this work as a sacred trust; the danger of harming souls forbids us to resist the holy principles of this work.

Ours therefore becomes an "ecclesial" task and a sacred pastoral charge. We bear with the work because we think of it as God's will, expressed clearly in the decisions of the teaching Church by the documents of the Council.

The Council's Constitution on the Liturgy has formulated the solid principles of liturgical reform. We also are greatly strengthened in our work by your fatherly kindness, understanding, reassurance, and encouragement. We thus are strongly motivated to complete our task, in the knowledge that this work answers the needs of souls and of the Church.

Holy Father, we are gladdened by the recently published *Instruction*,[a] which stands as the first fruits of the effective cooperation of all those who are working so that the liturgy will appear in a new splendor and authenticity. We are filled with a great joy because of the strong resource offered for pastoral ministry in the name of all of the Consilium — a large family that is daily increasing, numbering already two hundred and fifty, including cardinals, bishops, consultors, and advisors. In this joy we offer to you our sentiments of loyalty, dedication, and absolute obedience in all that either your commands or wishes express to us.

Holy Father, we ask your apostolic blessing on the Consilium, on both its absent and present members as well as on its works and undertakings.

81. PAUL VI, **Address** to the members and *periti* of the Consilium, 29 October 1964: AAS 56 (1964) 993–996.

To see all of you today is a great comfort and joy. As you gather for your   621
regular meeting in Rome, your laudable intent is to offer to the chief shepherd of the Church a gracious testimony of love and respect. We receive this token of reverence all the more gladly in that it gives us the long-awaited chance to congratulate you warmly and to offer well-earned thanks for your unflagging application and intense effort in carrying out your responsibilities.

You are well aware of our great esteem and constant concern to follow your work, which — and rightly so — we regard as so important. For yours is the task, along with the Congregation of Rites, of carrying out the norms of the Constitution on the Liturgy, so happily promulgated by Vatican Council II. Clearly, then, the most welcome results, which we are sure will benefit the Church, largely depend on your work. Through your activity especially, the wise prescriptions of the Council will be received gladly and daily be more appreciated; little by little the Christian people will shape their lives according to that model.

We think it timely, then, to bring to your attention certain ideas about liturgy. They are, we know, familiar to you, yet calling them to mind is useful, especially on

---

ᵃ See DOL 23.

the occasion offered by this meeting, from which you all desire to derive new energies and constructive incentives.

622   The portion of the work particularly entrusted to you involves taking up the revision of the liturgical books. That, it need hardly be said, is a work of immense importance and entails the most serious difficulties. Formulation of the prayers of the liturgy is the issue. To evaluate them, to revise them or compose new ones, you need not only the highest wisdom and perspicacity, but also an accurate sense of contemporary needs combined with a full understanding of the traditional liturgical heritage handed on to us.

You must have the conviction that the formularies of public prayer cannot be worthy of God unless they faithfully express Catholic teaching. They are to be so composed as to measure up to the norms of the highest art, as befits the majesty of divine worship. The prayers should breathe with the religious spirit of devotion; they should evince a splendor in their brevity and clear simplicity that will assure right understanding and the ready perception of their truth and beauty. Only then will the public prayer of the Church correspond to the nature and inner spirit of the liturgy and serve the Christian people's offering of the glory due to God.

623   Your outlook on the liturgical reform, to be adequate and rightly focused, requires attentiveness to another, equally important standard. You have to take into account the effectiveness of the sacred rites to teach. As you know, the conciliar Fathers, when they established the norms for promoting the liturgy, had before them the pastoral objective of a more intense liturgical participation on the part of the faithful, who would thereby learn more fully at the heavenly sources of truth and grace how better and more abundantly to derive sustenance for Christian living. As the Constitution on the Liturgy wisely counsels, although the liturgy consists chiefly in the worship of God's majesty, it also contains much instruction for the faithful. God in the liturgy is speaking to his own people; Christ continues there to proclaim his Gospel.[a] Yours, therefore, should be a special care that liturgical worship really turns out to be a school for the Christian people. Liturgy should be a schooling in devotion that teaches the faithful to cultivate an intimate exchange with God; a schooling in truth in which visible symbols lead the spirit to the understanding and love of things invisible; a schooling in Christian charity whereby everyone more and more experiences the unity of the Church through the bonds of familial communion.

624   Finally, a faithful carrying out of the Constitution requires you to blend in harmony and beauty the new with the old. Great caution is needed against an excessive eagerness for the new that pays little or no attention to the genius of the liturgical heritage handed down to us. Such a misguided course would have to be called the destruction, not the reform of the liturgy. For the liturgy is like a mighty tree, the continual renewal of whose leaves shows its beauty; the great age of whose trunk, with roots deep and firm in the earth, attests to the richness of its life. In matters of liturgy, therefore, no real conflict should arise between present and past. Rather everything should proceed in such a way that each new development is in continuity and accord with sound tradition and new forms grow spontaneously, as it were, out of those already existing.[b]

As you see, you have a long, rough trek ahead. Your application, however, has already produced the most welcome results — an outstanding example of which is

---

[a]   See SC art. 33 [DOL 1 no. 33].

[b]   See SC art. 23 [DOL 1 no. 23].

the Instruction on the Liturgy [*Inter Oecumenici*] promulgated recently by the Congregation of Rites.[c] Our high hopes, then, for your future work are well-founded. Meanwhile, be mindful that not only we ourself but the whole Church look to you with anxious anticipation. Remember always that it is a magnificent task to offer to the praying Church a voice and, so to speak, an instrument with which to celebrate the praises of God and to offer him the petitions of his children. A task of this kind, for whose success heaven and earth conspire, is a work at once human and divine: human, because it depends on your skill, learning, and piety; divine, because the inspiration and action of the Holy Spirit cannot be absent from it. Without the Holy Spirit nothing holy, nothing strong, nothing saving can be accomplished.

Gladly we beseech almighty God for his continuing, outpoured aid. Let the sign and witness of this be the apostolic blessing we lovingly in the Lord impart to each of you.

82. SECRETARIAT OF STATE, Letter *Compio il venerato incarico* of Cardinal A. Cicognani to Cardinal A. M. Larraona, Prefect of the Congregation of Rites, on the respective competencies of the Congregation and of the Consilium, 7 January 1965 (Italian).*

I write to discharge [. . .] the task entrusted to me of replying to Your Eminence's question on the respective competencies of the Consilium and the Congregation of Rites. I am able to confirm what has already been established: to the Consilium will fall attention either to issues or to liturgical texts that application of the Constitution on the Liturgy now requires.[a] To the Congregation of Rites will fall, with consultation of the Consilium, promulgation of the documents that will put into effect norms and liturgical texts as they become available. It seems advisable to reserve to the critical evaluation of the Consilium those conditions required for the applications of the Constitution now in the process of testing. The Consilium will thus have a basis for deciding what forms may be best for definitive and authoritative approval by the Congregation of Rites.   625

Promulgation of liturgical books of an official, permanent, and universal character, will naturally be reserved to the same Congregation. At the same time, it is clearly appropriate that the decree of promulgation also bear the signature of the Cardinal President of the Consilium, as was the case with publication of the recent Instruction [*Inter Oecumenici*].[b]

83. CONSILIUM, Remarks of Cardinal G. Lercaro, President of the Consilium, at a papal audience for the members of the Consilium, 13 October 1966: Not 2 (1966) 308–311.

We are filled with great joy to be able to stand in your presence today, the joy of sons who draw near to their father in close and loving conversation. Our joy is   626

---

[c]   See DOL 23.

*   Text, EDL 379.

[a]   See DOL 77.

[b]   See DOL 23.

all the greater because with wise and noble purpose you are, as it were, the supreme president of the Consilium, the results of whose work are, by your decision in establishing it, submitted directly to you.

We must also mention the light that your policies and decisions bring to us. You give us the heart to carry on the work when we perceive the importance you give to the liturgy in your many sermons, addresses, and documents. We are also grateful for the guidance that you so kindly bring to our work.

There are, however, three reasons why today's colloquium is of an exceptional seriousness.

627   1.   First of all, we are witnesses to the flourishing liturgical reform that began to take effect on 7 March 1965 and now is growing stronger throughout the world. We desired to meet with you in order to assure you that the Church is everywhere discovering purer and more vital sources of grace from an intense, devout, fruitful, and full sharing in the liturgy. The faithful are following and living the rites with a more intense love. The use of the vernacular in the liturgy almost everywhere has made its celebrations more effective and brought out more fully their sacred contents. The faithful's interest in religion has increased. Almost everywhere, as well, the clergy and faithful already are in possession of beautiful editions of the liturgical books, published in conformity with the norms set by the Holy See.

A sensible moderation and serenity have replaced that initial heated upheaval that gave rise to some uncertainty and confusion. For the national liturgical commissions have little by little become organized and stable and for the most part it is on their initiative that the decisions and directions depend that are needed in each country for the renewal of the liturgy to advance in a genuinely liturgical direction and with a pastoral inspiration. We should also recognize that not only the commissions already well organized in the larger countries, but also those established by the smaller conferences of bishops and with the bishops' direction have already set out timely and wise norms and promoted measures advantageous to both clergy and faithful.

Yet we are aware that not in all matters nor everywhere has there been success; here and there deviations from the right course, if I may so call them, have been a source of worry and pain for you. We trust that soon, in patience, gentleness, and courage, all will find their way to willing and filial acceptance of the norms laid down by the Holy See.

628   2.   A second reason for joy in the pleasure of this meeting is the opportunity it affords us to inform you that the work entrusted to us is progressing apace. Some drafts of the revised rites have already been completed and you have chosen to have them tried out within certain specified groups. These are the drafts for the rites of adult baptism and funerals. Other drafts — and in fact the greater part — have already reached partial completion. The compositon of the Consilium's study groups brings together many *periti* and consultors who are enthusiastically fashioning the main features of the liturgical reform. For the primary parts of the reform involve the Mass, the divine office, and the Ritual; these are so intimately interrelated that they must develop in balance with each other.

When we examine our work, we are moved to offer you our profound thanks for having allowed experiments here and there. These are the indispensable ways for judging what part of the work done is good and what needs modification, so that everything may grow and improve and have final success when handed to the Church in finished form.

In addition to the work for general reform of the liturgy there have been other achievements during the past year: two instructions, one on song and music in the liturgy;[a] the other, on the mystery of the eucharist,[b] soon to be presented to you; the *Graduale simplex*[c] and other work entrusted to the Consilium. The journal *Notitiae* has also begun publication and has clearly been welcomed everywhere with attention and pleasure, since it is a link between the Consilium and the liturgical commissions and their work.

3.   Finally, the third reason making this an occasion of celebration is that through   629
the Consilium the Church is reaching a goal you desire and treasure. The Consilium is fashioning bonds of cooperation with non-Catholic Ecclesial Communities that were already begun during the Council. Now for the first time the Consilium has welcomed into its study groups five observers, delegates of their own Ecclesial Communities. For us this is a precious and important event: it enters into the life and activity of the Church to give stability to the concord and charity that prompt the joint study of issues relating to ourselves and our separated brothers and sisters.

Holy Father. After the three years of experience with the method for the work of the Consilium, we are meeting to revise this method. It will be a pleasure for us to present to you the decisions that seem indicated in order that the Consilium, on which so many throughout the world fix their attention, may maintain its strength and keep up its pace. [. . .]

84. PAUL VI, **Address** to the members and *periti* of the Consilium, 13 October 1966: AAS 58 (1966) 1145–50; Not 2 (1966) 297–303, with Italian translation 303–308.

Present here today is the Consilium ad exsequendam Constitutionem de sacra   630
Liturgia; we owe loving and respectful greetings on the occasion of this plenary meeting to a body of men highly qualified by their authority and learning, brought wisely together from many parts of the world. They bring the fruits of their research and their prayer to achieve one complex objective of utmost importance. That objective includes revision of the Church's liturgical texts and the rearrangement of the norms and modes for the Church's celebration of the sacred mysteries in genuine divine worship and for its instruction of the faithful on participation in the liturgy and on a spiritual life that is deeper and more richly nourished from the sources of holiness.

We welcome you therefore with respect and with pleasure and thank you for this visit that allows our person and our thoughts to share in your most worthwhile work. For that work you have our thanks. What could be more profitable for the Church in these days after the Council? What could do more to spark the fire of devotion in the Church's heart, to win for it the help of the Holy Spirit, to provide it with the power that attracts, that teaches, that sanctifies?

Our own thoughts turn often to your exacting and discerning work for the revision of the liturgy according to the mind of the Council. Three points come to mind about the performance of a task so complex and demanding such prudence.

---

  a   See DOL 508.

  b   See DOL 179.

  c   See DOL 533.

631   Your first charge is an investigation into the sacred rites of long usage in the Church, which you are then to revise and to put into an improved form. The investigation presents no special problems, since the ceremonies are well known; it does, nevertheless, require certain qualities of spirit. One is a reverence for the sacred that prompts us to honor the ceremonies used by the Church in worshiping God. Another is respect for tradition, which has passed on a priceless heritage worthy of veneration. Necessary as well is a sense of history, which has bearing on the way the rites under revision were formed, on their genuine meaning, either as prayer or as symbol, and on other similar points.

No predisposition to change everything without reason must govern this investigation, nor a hastiness, typical of the iconoclast, to emend and revise everything. The guides must be a devout prudence and a reverence combined with wisdom. The search must be for what is best rather than for what is new. With the new, whatever bears the treasures of the most inspired ages of faith should receive preference over present-day inventions. Nevertheless, the voice of the Church today must not be so constricted that it could not sing a new song, should the inspiration of the Holy Spirit move it to do so.[1]

632   Your second, extremely delicate duty is this: an examination of the modes of liturgical expression — whether words, including music and song, or gestures and ritual actions. The biblical sources of the particular rites must receive the most careful consideration. Intense effort must be brought to bear on the agreement of the *lex orandi* with the *lex credendi*, so that in its meaning prayer preserves the riches of dogma and religious language is suited both to the dogmatic realities it bears and to the balanced expression of the scale of values among the realities celebrated. All of this requires you to expend your learning as men dedicated to doctrine, your special skills as men of letters and the arts; but it also requires you to give your hearts, burning with love for God, for Christ and his kingdom — hearts, we believe, that in prayer have experienced the mystical. Your abilities will be put to the test by this endeavor, which derives its energies and inner force from prayer addressed to God then lived and which enlists the help of the arts. The effect on your work of revision will be, besides the mysterious stamp of beauty, the heavenly gift or charism of being universal and lasting, the charism of being ever young. The liturgy deserves the adornment of such special gifts.

633   There is a third and thoroughly human task that the pressure on you to achieve a literary style worthy of the liturgy must not cause you to forget. That task, uppermost in the minds of those intent on reform, is to make the liturgical rites plain and clear to the majority of the faithful in their intelligibility, in their forms of expression, in the way they are carried out.[2] To match liturgical structure and language to pastoral needs, to the catechetical aims of liturgy, to the spiritual and moral formation of the faithful, to the desire for union with God, to the nature of the sign of the sacred that allows for comprehension and, by experience, perception of its religious power — that is your work. What practical knowledge and charity it demands of you who are the artisans of the new liturgy, the bearers of treasures hidden from us till now! For in the liturgy the aim is beauty and simplicity, depth and clarity of meaning, substance with brevity, the resonances of ages past joined to the voices of today in a new harmony. To you the Church of God confides this sublime undertaking.

---

[1]   See SC art. 23 [DOL 1 no. 23].

[2]   See SC art. 11, 14, etc. [DOL 1 nos. 11, 14].

We have said these things to you, Esteemed Brothers and dear sons, to show   634
the importance we attach to the work you are so earnestly bent upon. But we point
out, as well, its wider bearing, its other services and advantages for the guidance of
the broad and multiform reform efforts inspired by the Constitution on the Liturgy.
The ancient Congregation of Rites, so worthy of esteem, has the task of deciding
what new forms are to be established in law as well as of safeguarding those now in
force. Your own Consilium has a responsibility of vigilance during this period when
new forms of divine worship are being tested and introduced in the different
regions of the Church.[a] You must check misguided attempts that may here and
there appear and constrain those who follow their own preferences at the risk of
disturbing the right order of public prayer and of occasioning doctrinal errors.
Accordingly, it is for you to prevent abuses, to prod those who lag or resist, to
stimulate energies, to encourage promising initiatives, to praise those deserving
praise. Your supervisory function is of great importance at this time and we confirm
you in it in a special way. Mindful of how vigilantly and prudently you are
fulfilling it, we are grateful. Diversity in language and newness in ritual are, it is
true, factors that the desire for reform has introduced into the liturgy. Nothing is to
be adopted however that has not been duly approved by the authority of the
bishops, fully mindful of their office and obligations, and by this Apostolic See.
Nothing should be allowed that is unworthy of divine worship, nothing that is
obviously profane or unfit to express the inner, sacred power of prayer. Nothing
odd or unusual is allowable, since such things, far from fostering devotion in the
praying community, shock and upset it and impede the proper and rightful cultivation of a devotion faithful to tradition. In this whole matter the course that seems
best is to proceed step by step, in keeping with the principles of sound pedagogy.

We note with pleasure that your brief but valuable commentaries, published in
Notitiae, are already fulfilling a needed function. This small collection of commentaries has value for another reason, for which we gladly honor the Consilium: the
spread throughout the Church of information and new points related to liturgical
practice, thus serving to influence others by good example and to encourage at once
a legitimate variety in ways of liturgical expression and a unity in essentials that we
must always treasure in the Church's liturgical life.

We are also happy about the careful and well-organized work engaged in by
the Consilium, evincing a sense of dedication that is a shining example for others
and that bears results so welcome and so numerous as to hold great promise of what
is to come. The postconciliar Church, waiting for the Council's initiative to be
brought to completion and its decrees to be put into practice, rejoices in your
devout and noble work as it involves fidelity to the conciliar decrees that shape and
guide it, the magnitude of the matters your work advances, and a pace that is as
swift as is permitted by the difficult, complex character of that work and by the
need for it to be done well.

There are certain weighty issues, singled out by the Cardinal President, that   635
require careful attention, our own included. One is sacred music, which engages the
interest of both liturgical and musical experts. The topic needs thorough explora-
tion, which will undoubtedly come about as, on the one side, pastoral experience
and, on the other, the musical arts continue an exchange that, we hope, will progress amicably and profitably. An instruction guiding the interrelationship of music
and liturgy will make their cooperation easier.[b] We are confident that it will restore

---

[a]   See DOL 82.

[b]   See DOL 508.

a new collaboration between those two sublime voices of the human spirit, prayer and art. The congress on sacred music recently held in Chicago confirms our hope.[c] Here we should like to remind you of what the conciliar Constitution decreed on music and liturgy, doing honor to both.[3] It is enough to point out that the pastoral and community character marking liturgical renewal and intended by the Council requires the revision and refashioning of music and sacred song in regard to those qualities by which they are, as they should be already, conjoined to the actions of the rites. To each the way must be opened to gain new worth, as it were, and to be encouraged to claim in the field of art and religion a new glory: "Sacred music will be the more holy the more closely it is joined to the liturgical rite."[4]

636   A second issue, worthy of your most intent consideration, is the *Ordo Missae*. We are aware of the work done and of how much learned and thoughtful discussion has taken place with regard to composing both a new missal and a liturgical calendar. The issue is of such a serious and universal import that we cannot do otherwise than consult with the bishops on any proposals before approving them by our own authority.

In the meantime, Esteemed Brothers and experts in the study of liturgy, continue your research and work. Take heart from realizing what service your work renders to the cause of Christian belief, which has its public and solemn expression in divine worship and from the same source receives a strength that assists both individuals and society. The service we refer to as coming from your work is a service to Christ's epiphany, his manifestation, which the liturgy in word, sacrament, and priesthood makes so intense that it can be experienced, even felt, by the hearts of the faithful and there become alive. We refer as well to the service the Church receives from the liturgy, that is, the sacred word, which, made pure, raises the Church higher and offers it the vision of its true self as the Mystical Body joined to Christ its Head, as humanity redeemed, and as the dearly beloved Bride of Christ, offering all to him and receiving all from him. We speak, too, of a service whereby you aid the people of these times through the attractiveness of the humble yet sublime beauty of the liturgy; you invite them to rediscover that lost world proper to the spirit where the divine mystery is present in an inexpressible and incomparable way.

Continue on with hard work and with trust; may you be helped by the conviction that you have our trust and our respect. Finally, may the light of Christ the Lord, the sign of his love, help you. For him you have taken on these labors; in the name of him in whose person we unworthily act, we bless you.

85. CONSILIUM, **Remarks** of Cardinal G. Lercaro at a papal audience for the Consilium, 19 April 1967: Not 3 (1967) 129–130 (excerpt).

637   With great pleasure we again, after a short six months, stand before Your Holiness to present our filial respects and the results of our meeting. [. . .]

Our present session, Holy Father, is noteworthy especially for two of its projects: the review and the approval within our competence of new texts for the eucharistic prayer; the preparation of the drafts containing the principles and rules

---

    [c]   See DOL 506.

    [3]   See SC art. 39, 44, 112, 115, 116, 120, 121 [DOL 1 nos. 39, 44, 112, 115, 116, 120, 121].

    [4]   SC art. 112 [DOL 1 no. 112].

for the main phases of our work, which will be presented soon to the Synod of Bishops.

As we went about these tasks the words you chose in your last paternal address to bolster our energies echoed in our mind: "The voice of the Church today must not be so constricted that it could not sing a new song, should the inspiration of the Holy Spirit move it to do so."[a]

Our hope, therefore, is that these new formularies may put into the mouth of the Church "a new song" that will abundantly bring to the holy people of God the joy of soul and the gladness of the Holy Spirit.

In addition to these projects, which have taken up the greater part of our efforts, we have given some attention to other matters of no less importance but that cannot be said to have reached completion in all their details. These mainly involve the sacrament of baptism for infants and the sacrament of marriage and we hope this work will soon reach its conclusion. [. . .]

86. PAUL VI, **Address** to the members and *periti* of the Consilium, 19 April 1967: AAS 59 (1967) 418–421; Not 3 (1967) 121–125, with Italian translation, 125–129.

We thank Cardinal Giacomo Lercaro with a grateful heart for the distinguished and respectful words he has addressed to us on behalf of the group assembled here. In spite of many current pressing tasks, we wanted to accede to the request for this audience and so to greet the Consilium, which we set up to revise the liturgical books of the Latin rite in the light of the aims and norms of the Council and to provide ourself and the Congregation of Rites, responsible in this area, with wise and helpful assistance in an endeavor of such complexity and importance.

638

The Consilium fully deserves to receive renewed expression of our high esteem and confidence and its members our encouragement. For we know the men who make up this body and their qualifications, men outstanding for their knowledge and love of the liturgy. We know how massive is the material the Consilium must face, how serious and diverse are the questions it must bring to resolution, how rapid the pace it must set if it is to accomplish its assigned task in a reasonably short space of time.

We know, as well, the primary considerations that are the groundwork for a task so difficult and so demanding of prudence. They are stated in the Constitution on the Liturgy art. 23 and the Consilium has followed them with loyal and attentive spirit. The words bear repeating: "That sound tradition may be retained and yet the way remain open to legitimate progress, a careful investigation is always to be made into each part of the liturgy that is to be revised. This investigation should be theological, historical, and pastoral. Also the general laws governing the structure and meaning of the liturgy must be studied in conjunction with the experience derived from recent liturgical reforms and from the indults conceded to various places. Finally, there must be no innovations unless the good of the Church genuinely and certainly requires them; care must be taken that any new forms adopted should in some way grow organically from forms already existing."[1]

---

[a] DOL 84 no. 631.

[1] SC art. 23 [DOL 1 no. 23].

We understand that the undertakings engaging your efforts and providing the Holy See with data and support for its sublime responsibility to stir up and guide the prayer of the people of God sometimes and for varying reasons provoke the hostile reactions of certain people. New measures give rise to many different incidents and new issues; there are also interpretations contrary to both the law and to what is right; there are comments of doubtful worth. But even if there have in fact been misjudgments and defective application regarding some new measures, nevertheless we feel obliged to express our gratitude and general approval to the Consilium. We have, then, a shining occasion not only to praise and encourage its strenuous work, but also to urge the clergy and the laity to appreciate its merits and to promote its effectiveness.

639   We cannot, however, veil our disturbance over some facts, incidents, and preferences that without any doubt are not favorable to the success the Church expects from the hard work of the Consilium.

The first fact is the unjust and irreverent attack published recently against Cardinal Lercaro, the illustrious and eminent President of the Consilium. Obviously we do not agree with this publication, which surely in no one inspires piety nor helps the cause it pretends to advance, namely, that of preserving the Latin language in the liturgy. Latin is an issue certainly deserving serious attention, but the issue cannot be solved in a way that is opposed to the great principle confirmed by the Council, namely, that liturgical prayer, accommodated to the understanding of the people, is to be intelligible.[a] Nor can it be solved in opposition to another principle called for by the collectivity of human culture, namely, that peoples' deepest and sincerest sentiments can best be expressed through the vernacular as it is in actual usage. Setting aside the whole question of the use of Latin in the liturgy, harmed rather than helped by the above-mentioned publication, we wish to express to Cardinal Lercaro our regret and our support.

Another reason for sorrow and concern is the import of disciplinary irregularity that is spreading in the modes of communal worship in various regions. Frequently these celebrations take a form deliberately patterned on the personal preference of certain individuals and often are wholly at odds with the precepts now in force in the Church. This creates serious distress in faithful Christians and alleges pretexts that are completely reprehensible, imperil the peace and good order of the Church, and are baneful because they spread bad and upsetting examples. In this regard, we wish to recall what the Council had to say about the regulation of the liturgy, namely, that "regulation of the liturgy depends solely on the authority of the Church."[2] But it is of greater concern to us to express the hope that bishops will keep a close watch on such episodes and that they will safeguard the balance proper to Catholic worship in the liturgical and religious domain. In this postconciliar period this area is the object of very special concern. We wish to make the same plea to religious orders, from which the Church today more than ever expects the support of their loyalty and example. We turn also to the clergy and all the faithful so that they do not allow themselves to burn with the inane desire for experiments inspired by private preference, but rather strive to bring the rites prescribed by the Church to effective fulfillment. This exhortation is in line with one of the duties of the Consilium, namely, to control wisely the specific liturgical experiments that seem worth bringing to fruition in a responsible and considered way.[b]

---

[a] See SC art. 33 [DOL 1 no. 33].

[2] SC art. 22 [DOL 1 no. 22].

[b] See DOL 77 and 82.

An even greater source of anguish is a widening movement toward a liturgy, if   640
it can be called that, which is rashly described as "desacralized" and, as a necessary
consequence, toward a desacralized Christian religion. This new outlook, easily
traceable to its turbulent origins, and supporting the upheaval, as is its intent, of
genuine Catholic worship, opens the way to such distortions in teaching, discipline,
and ministry that we have no hesitancy in condemning it as erroneous. The error is
a source of sadness, not only because of its conflict with canon law and its mindless
passion for novelty, but also because its inevitable consequence is the disintegration
of religion.

Any emerging movement or idea can, of course, contain more than a particle of
truth and the originators of novelties are perhaps well-intentioned and learned
people. Furthermore, we are always prepared to give consideration to anything
relating to the Church that has value and deserves approval. But we cannot hide,
especially from you, our feeling that the above-mentioned tendency poses the
danger of spiritual ruin.

The objective must be to repel such a danger, to reclaim people, journals, and
institutions from its snares to a fruitful and wise cooperation for the Church and for
the defense of the teaching and norms of the ecumenical Council. To this end you
more than anyone else are called on to bring out that countenance of the liturgy
which shows its truth, beauty, and spiritual character and which reflects ever more
brightly the paschal mystery living within it. That will serve the glory of God and
the inner renewal of those of our age drifting aimlessly, yet beset by a deep yearning they do not recognize.

We are confident of success, with God's help, as we ponder the seriousness of
your own dedication and the early results of liturgical renewal, so favorable as to
promise even better things. The genuine prayer-life of the Church has renewed
vigor in the communities of the faithful, a thing of beauty and a sign of high hope
to anyone burning with love for Christ, in an age so confused yet full of earthly
vitality.

Carry on your work peacefully and cheerfully. "God wills it," we can truly say,
for his own glory, for the life of the Church, and for the salvation of the world. Our
apostolic blessing will always be with you.

87. PAUL VI, **Motu Proprio** *Pro comperto sane*, bringing in diocesan bishops as
members of the congregations of the Roman Curia, 6 August 1967: AAS 59
(1967) 881–884 (excerpt).

Well known to all is the teaching of the Second Vatican Ecumenical Council on   641
the nature of the Church as visible. Equally clear is the mind of the Council on the
need of adapting to the contemporary mentality all the resources and instruments
the Church uses to enable it to carry out more effectively its appointed work of
salvation. [. . .]

With good reason the Council expressed among the norms laid down by the
Decree *Christus Dominus* the desire that membership of the congregations of the
Roman Curia should include "a certain number of bishops, especially diocesan
bishops, so that they might have the power to report fully to the pope the thinking,
desires, and needs of all the Churches. . . ."[1]

---

[1] CD no. 10: AAS 58 (1966) 677; ConstDecrDecl 284.

In order that our Roman Curia may successfully face the grave responsibilities that have their origin in the decisions and desires of the Council and in order that the Curia, as needs increase, may have at its disposal the knowledge and prudence of our brothers in the episcopate, we have given considerable thought to the ways and means whereby the congregations charged with the governance of the entire Church might be able more and more to make use of the bishops' wise counsel and help. We are quite convinced that if the more important issues are faced through a sharing of views, orderliness, and care, all of Catholic life would be benefited and that such a procedure could be advantageous not only for dealing with the more serious affairs of the Church itself but also for confronting issues that perplex all our contemporaries.

Accordingly, having weighed all sides carefully, consulted with men of knowledge and competence, and prayed for God's heavenly light, we ordain and decree the following *motu proprio*.

642   I.   In addition to cardinals, a certain number of diocesan bishops are assigned to the congregations as full-fledged members.

643   II.   Such bishops take part as members in plenary sessions at which are treated matters that are of great importance and of universal applicability. The ordinary sessions of the congregations will continue as usual, with the participation of the cardinals and bishop-members who may be in Rome.

644   III.   To forestall any upset to the dioceses arising out of a too frequent or prolonged absence of their bishops, (and here we call attention to the stipulations of canon law on episcopal residency) we decree that, at a time to be duly set by the congregations, their plenary sessions may be held only once a year, unless some unusual occurrence indicates otherwise.

645   IV.   Nomination of bishops as members, which we reserve to ourself, will proceed thus: the cardinal prefects of the individual congregations are to arrange for inquiry and investigation within the conferences of bishops and, where applicable, even request a list of bishops for candidacy who possess peculiar competence in the areas involved. Once these steps have been taken, the cardinal prefects will present the names to us and we will make our own free choice.

646   V.   Each of the congregations will have as members seven diocesan bishops, chosen by preference over others because of their competence in the issues involved; due attention should also be given to the continents where the elected live, so as to bring out the Church's universality.

For plenary sessions of the Congregation of Religious, out of consideration for its distinctive area of concern, ten members will be nominated; three are to be chosen from a list of superiors general of orders or clerical congregations that the Roman Union of Superiors General of Men will prepare and submit to the cardinal prefect.

647   VI.   The term of membership will be five years, in order that the congregations may continually have the advantage of new members in good health. [. . .]

88. PAUL VI, **Apostolic Constitution** *Regimini Ecclesiae universae*, on reform of the Roman Curia, 15 August 1967: AAS 59 (1967) 885–928 (excerpt).

III.   THE CONGREGATIONS

CHAPTER I
CONGREGATION FOR THE DOCTRINE OF THE FAITH

29. The Congregation for the Doctrine of the Faith has charge of safeguarding teaching on faith and morals throughout the Catholic world.[13] 648

31. Its competence extends to all issues having a direct bearing on teaching regarding faith and morals or having a connection with faith. 649

36. In defense of the dignity of the sacrament of penance, the Congregation acts in accord with its own revised and approved procedures, which it will make known to local Ordinaries. Anyone accused is to be given the right to defend himself, either personally or by choosing an advocate from those approved by the Congregation. 650

CHAPTER II
CONGREGATION FOR THE EASTERN CHURCHES

45. § 1. The Congregation possesses all faculties the other congregations have for the Latin Church. But it is to refer to the other congregations matters belonging to them and it is to respect the rights of the Apostolic Penitentiary. 651

CHAPTER IV
CONGREGATION FOR THE DISCIPLINE OF THE SACRAMENTS

54. The Congregation for the Discipline of the Sacraments, in charge of a cardinal prefect assisted by a secretary and subsecretary, looks to all issues relating to the seven sacraments. With regard to teaching, however, the Congregation for the Doctrine of the Faith retains competency, as does the Congregation of Rites in regard to the rites and ceremonies for the celebration, administration, and reception of the sacraments; [. . .] 652

55. The same Congregation takes care of the usual decrees and concessions regarding the discipline of the sacraments and the celebration of Mass. It also has the power to grant dispensations outside the power of bishops,[a] including power to dispense from the eucharistic fast the faithful and, after any necessary consultation with the Congregation for the Doctrine of the Faith, priest celebrants. 653

CHAPTER V
CONGREGATION OF RITES

58. The Congregation of Rites has competency over all matters related directly and immediately to divine worship in the Roman Rite and other Latin rites, without prejudice to the competency of other congregations in matters involving doctrine or discipline or requiring a judicial process. 654

---

[13]   See Motu Proprio *Integrae servandae*, 7 Dec. 1965: AAS 57 (1965) 952.

[a]   See DOL 103 and 105.

655   59. It deals also with all matters concerning beatifications, canonizations, or relics.

656   60. The Congregation, in charge of its cardinal prefect assisted by a secretary, has two sections: liturgical, that is, for worship; judicial, that is, for the causes of servants of God.

Section I

657   61. § 1. The Worship Section, made up of its own members and consultants, covers all matters relating to liturgical or nonliturgical worship; a subsecretary is the one immediately in charge.

§ 2. The Worship Section comprises three Offices:

§ 2. 1. The First Office is responsible for the right ordering of divine worship in the liturgy under its pastoral and ritual aspects.

§ 2. 2. The Second Office promotes relations with the conferences of bishops and liturgical institutes, gathers and evaluates both information on the Church's liturgical life and publications devoted to liturgy, but without prejudice to the responsibilities of the Consilium until completion of the reform of the liturgy.

§ 2. 3. The Third Office, namely, of nonliturgical worship, exists to take care of the sacred devotional practices of the Christian people, without prejudice to the competence of the Congregation for the Doctrine of the Faith.

§ 3. The Worship Section receives the assistance both of its group of consultants — to be chosen by the pope from experts in liturgy from all over the world — and of special commissions appointed to study more complex issues of the liturgy.

§ 4. Revision of the liturgical books and execution of the reform of the liturgy are the responsibility of the Consilium; its final decisions, however, are to be submitted to a plenary session of the Worship Section.[21]

Consultants of the Consilium are ipso facto *periti* of the Congregation of Rites.

Section II

658   62. § 1. The Judicial Section, or Section for the Causes of Servants of God, under the immediate supervision of a secretary and auditor general, is in charge of matters both concerning beatification and canonization processes, including those related to the Eastern Churches, and concerning relics.

659   63. Both the Worship Section and the Judicial Section have the assistance of the historico-hagiographical Office, which has its proper statutes given in Pius XI's Motu Proprio, *Già da qualche tempo*, 6 February 1930.

660   64. The two Sections, each retaining its specific competence, work together on issues involving relics or the regulation of the veneration of saints in keeping with the norms of Catholic teaching.

The two Sections likewise have common archives, records, treasury, and other similar resources.

CHAPTER VI
CONGREGATION FOR THE CLERGY

661   65. So that its name better fits its functions, the Congregation of the Council will henceforth be called the Congregation for the Clergy.

---

[21]   See CIC can. 244.

66. The Congregation for the Clergy, in charge of its cardinal prefect assisted by a secretary and subsecretary, has competence in all matters involving the persons, offices, and pastoral ministries of clergy carrying out the apostolate in dioceses. The Congregation comprises three Offices.

662

67. § 1. Through the First Office the Congregation investigates, proposes, and promotes ways and means for priests to strive for holiness[26] and to continue their education[27] so that from their learning in divine revelation, theology, liturgy, and the humanities they may fulfill their ministry more effectively. This Office also promotes institutes of pastoral liturgy, sees to the setting up of libraries for the clergy[28] and to the establishment everywhere of regularly scheduled courses, as they are called, whereby priests, especially the younger, will develop and broaden pastoral knowledge and methods, share with each other their practical experiences, and coordinate their pastoral activities.[29]

663

§ 2. It will see to the same matters, with the adaptations to their proper ministries, on behalf of deacons.

68. Through this First Office the Congregation also has the following responsibilities:

664

§ 1. to attend to all matters belonging to: the duties and discipline of diocesan clergy, cathedral and collegial chapters, pastors, curates, and other priests engaged in parish ministry, and of religious — except for matters purely of religious life;[30] the celebration of Mass and stipends; the bestowal of offices and nonconsistorial benefices and, where they still exist, popular elections to these preferments;[31] the obligation to recite the divine office; devotional practices.

69. Through the Second Office, the Congregation:

665

1. endeavors especially to promote whatever concerns the preaching of the word of God; [. . .]

2. revises and approves the catechetical directories and preaching programs or syllabuses that the conferences of bishops prepare in view of the different ages and circumstances of the faithful; promotes national catechetical congresses or sanctions or convenes international catechetical congresses. [. . .]

89. SECRETARIAT OF STATE, **Rescript** *Cum notae causae,* delaying the effective date of the Apostolic Constitution *Regimini Ecclesiae universae,* 30 December 1967: AAS 60 (1968) 50.

Well-known causes have prevented the general norms for the Roman Curia, i.e., its regulation, from being completed and therefore from being put into effect on the day determined by the Apostolic Constitution *Regimini Ecclesiae universae* no. 12.

666

---

26 See PO no. 15: AAS 58 (1966) 1014; ConstDecrDecl 660.

27 See PO no. 19: AAS 58 (1966) 1019; ConstDecrDecl 670.

28 See ibid.

29 See ibid.

30 See CD no. 35, 4 [DOL 7 no. 197].

31 See Motu Proprio *Ecclesiae Sanctae,* 6 Aug. 1966, I, no. 18: AAS 58 (1966) 767.

Pope Paul VI has therefore decreed that this Constitution shall begin to have its full and absolute force on 1 March 1968 rather than on 1 January 1968.

The same effective date applies for those points involving the Papal Household in no. 134 of the same Constitution.

90. PAUL VI, **Epistle** *Nell' atto in cui* to Cardinal G. Lercaro, President of the Consilium, at the end of his term of office, 9 January 1968: Not 4 (1968) 4 (Italian).

667   At this time, when with an admirable spirit of service and dedication you relinquish the responsibilities of the presidency of the Consilium, mainly for reasons of health, we wish to express to you again our lively and sincere thanks.

We are conscious of the work you have devoted to directing this institution, which originated from the concern and work of the conciliar Fathers. We know how much effort you have put into establishing a method of work and strengthening the activity of the Consilium.

The Lord Jesus, the eternal High Priest, will not leave unrewarded the rich crown of merits you have acquired by a faithful service that has taken so much of your energies. This is what we ask of him for the sake of your continued well-being and happiness.

As a testimony of our constant good will, we gladly bestow our special apostolic blessing on you and with affection extend it to the entire beloved Archdiocese of Bologna.

91. CONSILIUM, **Remarks** of Cardinal B. Gut at a papal audience for the Consilium, 14 October 1968: Not 4 (1968) 346–347 (excerpt).

668   [. . .] This year also the holy people of God have had the occasion to rejoice in the fruits of the labor of the *periti*, whose work is hidden but carried on with great enthusiasm. The new eucharistic prayers have given a new song to the Church, a beginning, but one of great hope, of the new creation that the Holy Spirit always teaches the chosen Bride of Christ to pour forth as a new song.

In the same period other documents have simplified some of the rites and made them more in keeping with the contemporary mentality, while preserving the nobility of the rites and their power to instruct the minds of the faithful. We expect that the new rites for the ordination of bishops, priests, and deacons, already approved by you, will be published and will bring fruits of holy joy and edification.

We also have been able to judge, after a fairly prolonged trial period, how the rites approved *ad experimentum* have been received and we have reason to hope that in the light of comments about them they can be put into final form and presented.

You yourself, Holy Father, have used some of these rites on the occasion of the International Eucharistic Congress [Bogotá] . Undoubtedly in your own mind you still hear the chorus of voices, countless in number but one in spirit, that graced the celebrations and joined together into the one prayer the aspirations of so many people. [. . .]

92. PAUL VI, **Address** to the members and *periti* of the Consilium, 14 October 1968: AAS 60 (1968) 732–737; Not 4 (1968) 335–340, with Italian translation, 341–346.

You can well understand how attentively we have listened to the brief but eloquent words of your most worthy and beloved President reviewing for us the varied activities of the Consilium during the past year.[a] We have noted the great volume of work accomplished, clear evidence that the task of liturgical renewal entrusted to you is moving ahead quickly and with ever increasing intensity.   669

Actually, your present meeting here in Rome occurs at a point when we can, and indeed must, look back over the road traversed in order to ponder and evaluate the results of your labors so far. We gladly acknowledge that they are rich and that they raise our spirits high in hope. The new rites and the new prayer forms introduced into the liturgy have added to the splendor of the age-old and beautiful sacred patrimony of the Church and we observe with joy a new flowering in divine worship everywhere because of a more lively participation of the faithful.

For this we give thanks first of all to almighty God, for "every good gift and every perfect gift is from above, coming down from the Father of lights."[1]

But to you also, to whom these results are in large part due, we wish to express our gratitude, even as we also take this opportunity to thank the conferences of bishops for the support promptly and generously given to you; clearly this has made your work easier. We also are well aware that all the bishops of the Church are sparing neither pains nor energies to see to it that the liturgical reform leads the people of God to a more flourishing Christian life and to "that full, conscious, and active participation in liturgical celebrations" which is to be counted among the chief aims of the ecumenical Council.[2] We are confirmed in the conviction that the present age, when interest in prayer, when faith, piety toward God, and the hope for eternal blessings grow ever weaker, presents us with the opportunity to call not only the Church but also the entire human community back to a love for a genuine religious life.

But we did not want to talk to you just to congratulate you for work well done. Even more intense is the desire to exhort you and encourage you for the long road yet to be traveled. First, there is the revision of the Roman Missal, now on the verge of completion; then the revision of the Roman Breviary, Ritual, Pontifical, and Martyrology. You will still need a long time to revise all these liturgical books properly.   670

Clearly the Church today attaches supreme importance to the liturgy, which must be regarded, in the words of the Council, "as the summit toward which the activity of the Church is directed and at the same time as the fount from which all its power flows."[3] It is also clear how necessary it is that as you go about your work you keep always in mind the close relationship between the Church's *lex orandi* and the other sectors of religious life, especially faith, tradition, and canon law.

Since the *lex orandi* must be in harmony with the *lex credendi* and serve to manifest and corroborate the faith of the Christian people, the new prayer formularies you are preparing cannot be worthy of God unless they are the faithful reflections of Catholic teaching. It is easy to see that for these formularies to match

---

[a] See DOL 91.

[1] Jas 1:17.

[2] SC art. 23 [DOL 1 no. 23].

[3] SC art. 10 [DOL 1 no. 10].

the nature and character of liturgical worship, they must clearly bear the marks of majesty, simplicity, beauty, and have the power to stir the spirit and to spark devotion.[4]

671   A further point is that reform of the liturgy must not be taken to be a repudiation of the sacred patrimony of past ages and a reckless welcoming of every conceivable novelty. You are well aware of the objective the conciliar Fathers set for themselves in this regard when they promulgated the Constitution on the Liturgy, namely, that the new should be in harmony with sound tradition so that "any new forms adopted should in some way grow organically from forms already existing."[5] Hence a sound reform is to be seen as one having the power to combine the new and the old harmoniously.

These remarks clearly imply that to guarantee a true reform it is important that all accept the ecclesial and hierarchic character of the liturgy. That is to say, the rites and prayer formularies must not be regarded as a private matter, left up to individuals, a parish, a diocese, or a nation, but as the property of the whole Church, because they express the living voice of its prayer. No one, then, is permitted to change these formularies, to introduce new ones, or to substitute others in their place. The very dignity of the liturgy forbids this, for through the liturgy we are in contact with God. The good of souls and the effectiveness of pastoral activity, which would be imperiled, also forbid it. Remember that norm of the Constitution on the Liturgy: "Regulation of the liturgy depends solely on the authority of the Church."[6]

672   As we speak to you about the norms that must rule your endeavor, we cannot pass over in silence certain courses of action appearing here and there in the Church that are causing us anxiety and pain.

We refer, first of all, to the attitude of those who receive with bad grace whatever comes from ecclesiastical authority or is lawfully commanded. This results at times even in conferences of bishops going too far on their own initiative in liturgical matters. Another result is arbitrary experimentation and the introduction of rites that are flagrantly in conflict with the norms established by the Church. Anyone can see that this way of acting not only scandalizes the conscience of the faithful, but does harm to the orderly accomplishment of liturgical reform, which demands of all concerned prudence, vigilance, and above all discipline.

673   A cause of even greater worry is the behavior of those who contend that liturgical worship should be stripped of its sacred character and who therefore erroneously believe that no sacred objects or ornaments should be used, but that objects of common, everyday use should be substituted. Their own rashness leads some so far that they do not spare the sacred place of celebration. Such notions, we must insist, not only distort the genuine nature of the liturgy, but the true meaning of the Catholic religion.[7]

In simplifying liturgical rites, formularies, and actions, there must be care not to go further than necessary and not to neglect the importance to be given to liturgical "signs." That would open the way to weakening the power and

---

[4]   See R. Guardini, *Lo spirito della liturgia* (Morcelliana) 43, 44.

[5]   SC art. 23 [DOL 1 no. 23].

[6]   SC art. 22, 1; see also art. 33. [DOL 1 no. 22; also no. 33].

[7]   See L. Bouyer, *La vie de la liturgie* (Ed. du Cerf, "Lex orandi") 324.

effectiveness of the liturgy. To remove from the sacred rites whatever today seems repetitive, obsolete, or pointless is one thing;[b] it is something else to strip the liturgy of the signs and splendor that, if kept within their proper bounds, are needed for the Christian people to perceive rightly the hidden realities and truths concealed under the veil of external rites.

Therefore your great and noble task, beloved sons, is to see to it that the liturgy manifests the true splendor of its countenance before all humanity and brings its power to bear to further the spiritual life of society. Nor is that all. You must also see to it that the present eagerness of the people of God for liturgical reform does not wane as time passes.

In this matter we must obviously proceed step by step, because the work you have in hand calls for continuously assessing the degree of preparation of the faithful. Accordingly, the method and timing for introducing new rites should be such as to ensure their readier acceptance and comprehension.

Permit us to propose for your careful attention a final recommendation and one   674
close to our heart. It is this: be careful that what you produce does not wander away from the usages of the Roman tradition. Rome is where the Latin liturgy has had its origins, development, and culmination.

The motivation for this recommendation is not history or place or a desire to tighten our own control. Our view and judgment look rather to theological reasons and the very nature of the Church, which at Rome has the center of its unity and the bulwark of its catholicity.

Rather than to our words, listen to those of two illustrious liturgical scholars.

The first of these, Father Gabriel M. Brasó, OSB says: "He who does not feel Roman will find it difficult to experience fully the spirit and inspiration of the liturgy. *Romanità* is the safeguard of the undiminished purity of the liturgy's spirit. Deviations in the field of liturgy and its aims, as in many other ways of thinking and in the practice of the Christian life, usually have as their root a lack of *Romanità*. An excessive and narrow-minded patriotism treats Rome as a rival, its norms as incomprehensible, and its laws as a manifestation of an unchecked despotism. But *Romanità* is the basis of our catholicity."[8]

The other testimony we wish to cite is that of E. Bishop, famous as an outstanding scholar in the field of liturgical studies, who, in his study on the essential character of the Roman Rite warns: "The Roman way has its own virtues, which appear all the more necessary and worthy of esteem because the religious history of Europe at various times enables us to perceive the harm resulting from neglecting them."[9]

Therefore beloved sons, put aside mistrust or fear of Rome. Rome knows how to welcome your efforts warmly, to evaluate them correctly, and to make them lasting and truly Catholic, not for its own honor but for that of the Church and for the glory of Christ our Redeemer.

These are the guidelines we have chosen to set before you, urged on by the sense of our apostolic office. That you may promptly and rightly carry them out, may God grant you an abundance of heavenly grace, in pledge of which we bestow on each of you our apostolic blessing.

---

b   See DOL 1 nos. 21 and 34.

8   G. M. Brasó, *Liturgia e spiritualità*, (Ed. Liturgische) 307–308.

9   E. Bishop, *Le Génie du Rite Romain* (Libr. de l'art catholique) 66–67.

93. PAUL VI, **Address** to a consistory, excerpt on the liturgy and on the division of the SC Rites into two congregations, 28 April 1969: AAS 61 (1969) 425–432; Not 5 (1969) 128.

675   [. . .] The Church has an innate need to pray that finds its preeminent expression in the eucharistic sacrifice. That need is the abiding, pure source for all liturgical norms [. . .]. That is the context of the new Order of Mass. After the long and laborious work to simplify the rites for the beginning of Mass, the offertory, the sign of peace, and the breaking of the bread, the Order of Mass should be seen as the culmination of the new structure of the Mass desired by the conciliar Fathers and designed to assist the faithful to take an ever more conscious and active part in the eucharistic sacrifice. To the same end the Roman Canon, after some slight revision, has received a more complete unity and become easier to recite. As you well know, several formularies for the canon, that is, anaphoras, have been added to the new Roman Missal. Soon therefore you will have in your hands this new Roman Missal, as well as the other liturgical books that after painstaking care the Consilium has revised.

676   In the new General Roman Calendar you will notice that the liturgical year has not been altered radically. Rather the criterion for its revision was that the elements making up the individual parts of each liturgical season would give clearer expression to the truth that Christ's paschal mystery is the center of all liturgical worship. Further, to the extent possible, the General Roman Calendar has retained the celebration of the saints' "birthdays," but in such a way that for the whole Church those saints have been chosen who seemed to be the most important both historically and as examples. Other saints of less general significance were left to be honored by the local Churches. There has also been care to ensure the historical truth of the elements pertaining to the saint's lives and feasts. The purpose of all these measures has been to bring out clearly that holiness in the Church belongs to all parts of the world and to all periods of history and that all peoples and all the faithful of every social rank are called to attain holiness, as the Dogmatic Constitution *Lumen gentium* has solemnly taught.[8] [. . .]

677   To carry out the great work of facilitating the Church's office of guiding and furthering the prayer-life of the faithful we have accepted the argument and the desire for dividing the Sacred Congregation of Rites into two separate congregations. The one will be concerned with divine worship; the other, with handling the causes of saints. We have judged this to be very necessary. In the case of the first congregation, the one principal agency will thereby have as its sole responsibility the strengthening and preservation everywhere of the Church's life of prayer, especially since Vatican Council II has done so much to advance the cause of liturgy in all its aspects. In the case of the second, there will thus be an agency, distinct by a name having a historical connotation, that will specifically deal with the causes of saints, since this work is both so extensive and difficult. We have thoroughly weighed the arguments for the advisability of this change and therefore will promulgate the norms for the newly established congregations in an apostolic constitution soon to be published.[a] In this we will describe the nature of these congregations, outline their organization, and specify their duties and competence.

---

[8]   See LG nos. 39–42.

[a]   See DOL 94.

94. PAUL VI, **Apostolic Constitution** *Sacra Rituum Congregatio*, establishing the new SC Divine Worship and SC Causes of Saints, 8 May 1969: AAS 61 (1969) 297–305; Not 5 (1969) 129–133 (excerpt).

The Sacred Congregation of Rites, which our predecessor Pope Sixtus V estab-   678
lished in 1588,[1] has had from the beginning a double function, namely, to have charge of and to regulate the sacred rites of the Latin Church; to carry out in the whole Church everything pertaining in any way to the canonization of saints. This second function was entrusted to the congregation in charge of rites because causes of canonization have always had bearing on honoring by public cultus throughout the Church those servants of God enrolled in the heavenly register of saints.

For almost four centuries the Congregation of Rites has fulfilled this double function with such wisdom that it has won high praise. As for liturgy, it is enough to mention that after St. Pius V had published the carefully revised Roman Breviary and Roman Missal,[2] the Congregation of Rites, following the prescriptions of the Council of Trent,[3] revised and published the other liturgical books. The Congregation, having rid them of distortions from the Middle Ages, restored the liturgical formularies and rites of the Latin Church to their original purity and rightful conciseness. Having eliminated an excessive variety in the liturgical books, the Congregation reduced them to a certain liturgical unity, thereafter firmly maintained.[4]

In this century the Congregation, fulfilling the mandate of our predecessor St. Pius X, opened the way for a general liturgical renewal by a revision of the Roman Breviary,[5] named for the same Pope. Following on that start, at the order of Pope Pius XII, the Congregation restored the Easter Vigil in 1951[6] and in 1955 published the new rites for Holy Week.[7] From these and many other measures the Constitution on the Liturgy approved by Vatican Council II[8] in a sense takes its origins.

Not to be less esteemed is the work of the Congregation devoted to the preparation and examination of the causes of saints. The list of those who, after examination of their heroic virtues or martyrdom, have been inscribed in the catalogue of saints from 1588 to the present time clearly attests to this work.

But at the present time the general reform of the liturgy decreed by Vatican Council II and a revision of laws relative to causes of saints in tune with the times seem to suggest and require new research, new attention and carefulness in dealing with and settling such matters.

Further, reflection clearly shows that the liturgy is one matter, the causes of saints another, and that each calls for its distinct specialization, training of mind, and method of procedure.

We ourself, therefore, in that section of the Apostolic Constitution *Regimini Ecclesiae* dealing with the Congregation of Rites,[9] ordered that it be divided into two

---

[1] See Bull, *Immensa aeterni Dei: Bullarium Romanum* 8 (Turin ed., 1863) 989.

[2] See Ap. Const. *Quo primum*, 13 July 1570.

[3] See Council of Trent, sess. 22, 24, 25, canons and decrees.

[4] The five volumes published by the Council, containing its authoritative decrees, are evidence enough of its merits in the area of liturgy.

[5] See Ap. Const. *Divino afflatu*, 1 Nov. 1911: AAS 3 (1911) 633–635.

[6] See SCR, Decr. *Dominicae Resurrectionis*: AAS 43 (1951) 128ff.

[7] See SCR, Decr. *Maxima Redemptionis nostrae mysteria*: AAS 47 (1955) 838ff.

[8] See SC [DOL 1].

[9] See Ap. Const. *Regimini Ecclesiae* nos. 58–64 [DOL 88 nos. 656–660].

parts or sections, one concerned with divine worship, the other with the causes of saints.

Now, however, having reflected on the matter and sought the advice of experts, we have decided to separate the sections from each other completely so that each is autonomous.

679   By virtue of the present Apostolic Constitution, then, in place of the Congregation of Rites as it has existed up till the present, we substitute two new Congregations, the one to have the official title *Sacra Congregatio pro Cultu Divino*, the other *Sacra Congregatio pro Causis Sanctorum*.

The Congregation for Divine Worship, in addition to its proper competence, to be specified below, will also take on the duties of the Consilium, which, consequently, we wish to be terminated as an entity in its own right and declare to be constituted as a special intra-Congregational Commission for the duration of the work begun on the liturgical books.

Wherefore, we repeal the provisions of the Apostolic Constitution *Regimini Ecclesiae*[10] and decree the following to be observed.

SACRED CONGREGATION FOR DIVINE WORSHIP

680   1.   The Congregation for Divine Worship, in charge of a cardinal prefect assisted by a secretary and subsecretary, has competence over all matters related directly and immediately to divine worship in the Roman Rite and other Latin rites, without prejudice to the rights of other congregations in matters involving the teachings of the faith or church discipline requiring judicial process.

681   2.   The Congregation is divided into three Offices.

§ 1. The First Office attends to: the liturgical worship of God both from a ritual and pastoral point of view; the revision and composition of liturgical texts; the review of particular calendars and the propers of Masses and offices, for either dioceses or religious orders; the granting of appropriate dispensations in these areas; the authentic and lawful interpretation of the norms and rubrics found in liturgical books; control over the veneration of relics; confirmation of patron saints; and the conferral of the title of minor basilica.

§ 2. The Second Office maintains relations with the conferences of bishops, whose liturgical enactments, in conformity with the provisions of the Constitution on the Liturgy art. 36, § 3,[11] it approves, that is, confirms. In the light of both general liturgical laws and the needs, traditions, and culture of individual peoples, it makes a careful evaluation of those adaptations proposed by the conferences of bishops to which the Constitution art. 40 refers.[12] Finally this Office concerns itself with paraliturgical worship, that is, with the devotional practices of the Christian people, without prejudice to the competence of the Congregation for the Doctrine of the Faith.

§ 3. The Third Office maintains relations with liturgical commissions, with the joint commissions of several countries, with institutes dedicated to the liturgical apostolate, music, chant, or art. It gathers not only reports about liturgical life in the Church, but also publications on the same topic, then prepares statistical tables. It studies how the media of social communication may contribute to the promotion of

---

10   See ibid.

11   See SC art. 36, § 3 [DOL 1 no. 36].

12   See SC art. 40 [DOL 1 no. 40].

divine worship. Finally, it encourages pastoral initiatives, international associations, and congresses directed to the liturgical apostolate.

3.   The Congregation receives the assistance both of its own group of consultants, experts in liturgical matters to be chosen by the pope from all over the world, and of special commissions appointed to study the more complex issues.[13]   682

4.   In order to complete the liturgical reform, the Congregation may for the present make use of the members and *periti* of the Consilium. The way this is to be carried out is as follows: 683

   § 1. Cardinal-members of the Consilium become ipso facto members of the Congregation for Divine Worship. If it seems advisable, other cardinals can be added.

   § 2. Diocesan bishops, who are to be appointed members of this Congregation in virtue of the Motu Proprio *Pro comperto sane*,[14] will, for this one time, be elected by those who are already members of the Consilium from among their own members.

   § 3. In meetings in which final decisions on the publication of liturgical books are to be approved the members of the special commission formed out of the replaced Consilium and the members of the Congregation shall be official participants.

14.   What we have prescribed in this Constitution comes into effect on this very day.   684

   Furthermore, it is our will that these statutes and prescriptions be now and remain for the future firm and effective, notwithstanding, should the case arise, the apostolic constitutions and ordinances issued by our predecessors or other prescriptions, even those that might be cited for special mention or as exceptions.

95. SC DIVINE WORSHIP, List of members (1969–1975).*

[The members are listed alphabetically, with title at time of appointment, date of appointment; other pertinent dates.]

AGAGIANIAN, Cardinal Peter Gregory, Prefect of SC Evangelization of Peoples, 8 May 1969; died 16 May 1971.   685

BAGGIO, Cardinal Sebastiano, Archbishop of Cagliari, Italy, 8 May 1969.

BENGSCH, Cardinal Archbishop Alfred, Bishop of Berlin, Germany, 21 August 1970; died 13 December 1979.

BERTOLI, Cardinal Paolo, Prefect of SC Causes of Saints, 19 February 1972.

BOUDON, René, Bishop of Mende, France, 13 January 1970.

---

[13]   See Ap. Const. *Regimini Ecclesiae* no. 61, 3[DOL 88 no. 659].

[14]   See Motu Proprio *Pro comperto sane* [DOL 87].

*   Announcements: 7 and 8 May 1969: AAS 61 (1969) 352–353; Not 5(1969) 133. 13 January and 21 August 1970: AAS 62 (1970) 75 and 572; Not 6 (1970) 336–228. 27 February 1972: AAS 64 (1972) 255–256. 25 January 1974: AAS 66 (1974) 47.

BUGNINI, Annibale, CM, Secretary, 7 May 1969, elected Titular Bishop of Diocletiana, 6 January 1972, ordained bishop, 13 February 1972.[a]

CARTER, Gerald Emmet, Bishop of London, Ont., Canada, 13 January 1970.

CODY, Cardinal John Patrick, Archbishop of Chicago, Ill., U.S.A., 8 May 1969.

CONFALONIERI, Cardinal Carlo, Prefect of SC Bishops, 8 May 1969.

CONWAY, Cardinal William, Archbishop of Armagh, Ireland, 8 May 1969.

DEARDEN, Cardinal John Francis, Archbishop of Detroit, Mich., U.S.A., 21 August 1970.

ENRIQUE Y TARANCÓN, Cardinal Vicente, Archbishop of Toledo, Spain, 8 May 1969.

FELICI, Cardinal Pericle, President of the Pontifical Commission for the Revision of the Code of Canon Law, 8 May 1969.

GIOBBE, Cardinal Paolo, 8 May 1969; died 14 August 1972.

GRACIAS, Cardinal Valerian, Archbishop of Bombay, India, 8 May 1969.

GRAY, Cardinal Gordon J., Archbishop of St. Andrews and Edinburgh, Scotland, 8 May 1969.

GUT, Cardinal Benno, OSB, Prefect, 7 May 1969; died 8 December 1970.[b]

HÄNGGI, Anton, Bishop of Basel-Lugano, Switzerland, 13 January 1970.

HURLEY, Denis Eugene, OMI, Archbishop of Durban, South Africa, 13 January 1970.

ISNARD, Clemente José Carlos, OSB, Bishop of Nueva Friburgo, Brazil, 13 January 1970.

JUBANY ARNAU, Cardinal Narciso, Archbishop of Barcelona, Spain, 12 April 1973.

KISBERK, Imre, Titular Bishop of Christianopolis, Apostolic Administrator of Székesfehérvár, Hungary, 21 August 1970.

KNOX, Cardinal James R., Prefect, 25 January 1974.[c]

LERCARO, Cardinal Giacomo, 8 May 1969; died 18 October 1976.[d]

LUCIANI, Cardinal Albino, Patriarch of Venice, Italy, 12 April 1973.

MARTY, Cardinal François, Archbishop of Paris, France, 21 August 1970.

---

[a] See Not 8 (1972) 33–35; 11 (1975) 216.

[b] See Not 5 (1969) 134; 7 (1971) 3–5.

[c] See Not 10 (1974) 41 and 115.

[d] See Not 7 (1971) 329–331; 8 (1972) 181; 10 (1974) 238; 13 (1977) 40–44.

NAGAE, Laurentius Satoshi, Bishop of Urawa, Japan, 13 January 1970.

NOÈ, Virgilio, Subsecretary, 7 May 1969; Master of Pontifical Ceremonies, 9 January 1970.

PELLEGRINO, Cardinal Michele, Archbishop of Turin, Italy, 8 May 1969.

RUGAMBWA, Cardinal Laurean, Archbishop of Dar-es-Salaam, Tanzania, 8 May 1969.

SALAZAR LOPÉZ, Cardinal José, Archbishop of Guadalajara, Mexico, 12 April 1973.

SAMORÈ, Cardinal Antonio, Prefect of SC Discipline of the Sacraments, 19 February 1972.

SILVA HENRÍQUEZ, Cardinal Raúl, Archbishop of Santiago de Chile, 8 May 1969.

SPÜLBECK, Otto, Bishop of Meissen, East Germany, 13 January 1970; died 27 June 1970.[e]

TABERA ARAOZ, Arturo, CMF, Archbishop of Pamplona, Spain, 21 August 1970; Prefect, 20 February 1971; member PCIDV, 31 March 1973; Prefect of SC Religious and Secular Institutes, 13 September 1973; died 13 June 1975.[f]

WILLEBRANDS, Cardinal Jan, President of the Secretariat for Christian Unity, 8 May 1969.

WOJTYLA, Cardinal Karol, Archbishop of Krakow, Poland, 21 August 1970.

96. SC DIVINE WORSHIP, **Epistle** *La Sacra Congregazione* of Cardinal B. Gut, Prefect, to Pope Paul VI, from the first meeting of the SC Congregation for Divine Worship, 12 May 1969: Not 5 (1969) 134 (Italian).

The Sacred Congregation for Divine Worship, meeting for the first time, in reverence and filial devotion turns its first thought to Your Holiness for having given to the Church the gift of this new Congregation. Our hope is that it will be a source of blessing and grace for souls and of consolation to yourself. We thank you also for having called on us to continue the work that we have been able to develop so far with such enthusiasm, total dedication, and joy.

686

May you be sure, Holy Father, that we revere the Consilium ad exsequendam Constitutionem de Sacra Liturgia, born out of your own heart. It was like a banner heralding the ideal of renewal and youth in the field of liturgy.

We will hold just as dear this new Congregation, in which today we begin our ecclesial service, humbly yet moved by an equal and, if possible, a greater dedication. Holy Father, we implore a special apostolic blessing on all of us, your workers, on this Congregation, on all the members and *periti* of the Commission that is the special heir of the Consilium.

---

e   See Not 6 (1970) 338–339.

f   See Not 7 (1971) 291; 8 (1972) 31–32 and 345–346; 9 (1973) 304–305; 11 (1975) 175.

97. PAUL VI, **Epistle** (autograph) *Rispondiamo subito* in reply to Cardinal B. Gut, Prefect of the new SC for Divine Worship, 12 May 1969: Not 5 (1969) 134 (Italian).

687   We hasten to reply to the letter which you, together with Father Bugnini and his co-workers in the Consilium, have sent us today at the beginning of the activity of your Congregation. The Congregation's purpose is to make ever more effective the incomparably important work that the Holy See, following its own centuries-old traditions and in keeping with the norms and mind of Vatican Council II, directs to the practice and advancement of the Church's prayer. We thank you profoundly for the sentiments and resolve expressed, from which we derive the surest promise for the successful continuation and fruitful increase of the work already in progress and already of such distinguished merit. Surely the Lord will come to the aid of such activity, since it centers completely on his glory and the spread of his Spirit among the people of God. We confirm these good wishes with our apostolic blessing in Christ.

98. SC DIVINE WORSHIP, **Remarks** of Cardinal B. Gut, Prefect, at a papal audience for the Consilium, 10 April 1970: Not 6 (1970) 224–225.

688   Holy Father. For the fifth time we come together before you during our plenary sessions devoted to reform of the liturgy and this is the last session at which we will all gather as members of the Consilium.

In these last six years we have lived through a remarkable period in the Church's history. It has been a period of hard and difficult work, not without problems; it has at times been marked by controversy; its passage has been measured by wise and often courageous experimentation. It is a period of history that has been at once serious and happy, bringing joy to the spirit.

Looking back over the course we have traveled, we gladly offer thanks to you, Holy Father, for having been so kind as to choose us to devote our energies to the work of renewing the inmost life of the Church. This work brings to realization those things by which Vatican Council II has marked the Church and its structure with the spirit of genuine reform. That is a starting point from which the Church, entering on a new course pointed out by God, will advance toward more sublime and shining goals.

Like a ship that after a long voyage nears the harbor, the reform of the liturgy is fast approaching its successful outcome. The soon-to-be-published Roman Missal as well as the divine office that we hope to be able to put in the hands of the people of God in a short time stand as the more notable achievements of the latest phase of the process.

Thirteen plenary and innumerable particular sessions, three hundred sixty-five schemata prepared for the plenary sessions, many other kinds of documents, including constitutions, decrees, instructions — this sums up the work done. By their silent but assiduous and dauntless work the fifty Fathers, cardinals and bishops, and the one hundred fifty *periti*, chosen from all parts of the world, have given a new form to the Church's *lex orandi*, in which the whole of God's family is raising a beautiful chorus of celebration.

Future historians will have the advantage of archives full of priceless records should they wish to reconstruct the development of the individual reformed rites or examine their texts, deriving from tradition or newly composed, or evaluate the particular reformed rubrical and pastoral norms. Then it will be utterly clear how conscious of their responsibility before God and the Church the members of that institution were in doing their work. It is the institution that you, Holy Father, with such foresight created on 3 January 1964 and that will be remembered in history as "the Consilium."

Further, we are happy to acknowledge that you have made our fervent wish come true when you initiated the Congregation for Divine Worship.[a] This new agency will continue to guide along the same course the work of liturgical reform so happily begun.

Finally, we wish to thank you because you have continually supported, favored, and guided our work. There have been days not only of calm, but days also when the seas surged around the prow and imperiled the fragile ship. Your strong hope, your encouragement, your enlightening words, above all your faith in the good work begun have constantly supported us. For this reason the reform of the liturgy that has taken its name from you stands clearly and in fact as your work and will be counted as one of the brightest jewels in the history of your pontificate.   689

Now the Consilium or special commission for the completion of the liturgical reform is dissolved and gives way to a new congregation. Nevertheless we deeply desire that this family which has worked together in shared joys and sorrows may not be dissolved. May it remain united so that all the members in their own Churches will stand always at the forefront, leading the liturgical reform, which promises such great benefits in the Church.

We promise you our service to the Church all the days of our lives. At the same time we ask your fatherly blessing on us so that through sacrifice and the praise of God, our humble work also will serve to bring about the sanctification of the faithful and the unity of believers and in all things will do honor to God.

99. PAUL VI, **Address** to the members and *periti* of the Consilium on the occasion of its final plenary meeting, 10 April 1970: AAS 62 (1970) 272–274; Not 6 (1970) 222–224.

We are happy to welcome you warmly and address you, who, under the presidency of Cardinal Benno Gut, have made up the Consilium, now being dissolved, with the establishment of the Congregation for Divine Worship.   690

A review of the work you have accomplished over the years, moves us to offer you the most profound thanks for such great and numerous efforts. With ready willingness and expert competence you have given yourselves to a complex and extremely difficult task, seeking no reward but intent only on service to the Church. Yours has been an arduous undertaking: the preparation of instructions that would gradually apply the conciliar Constitution on the Liturgy to practice;[a] the recasting of long-standing liturgical texts into a new format; even the creation of entirely new formularies.

In the light of such difficulties, it is amazing that so much is already finished; to mention only the highlights: the several instructions and other documents issued; the supporting writings of some of your members; the new Order of Mass; the

----

[a] See DOL 94.

[a] See DOL 23 and 39.

changes for the liturgy of Holy Week; the rites for the baptism of infants, for diaconate, priesthood, episcopacy, and marriage; the rite of funerals and of religious profession; the Roman Calendar. Soon to be published, after much hard work, is the Roman Missal, then (among other things) the Roman Breviary, the rites for confirmation and for the baptism of adults, the revised Roman Martyrology, the second book of the Roman Pontifical, and the Roman Ceremonial.

The principles approved by the Council's Constitution on the Liturgy has been the guiding light for all of your work. That "Magna Charta" of liturgical reform has initiated in the Church a new impetus in divine worship toward empowering people for a genuine, effective expression of their deepest sentiments in the liturgy and toward the preservation, as far as possible, of the heritage of the Latin Church.

Working along these two lines, not always easily coordinated, you have pursued the reform of the liturgy. Whether ancient or newly adapted and revised to suit the contemporary mind, texts have now been provided that are more numerous than those of former usage and richer in spiritual meaning; so too are new rites, simplified in accord with the intention of the Council and more clearly expressive of the realities they celebrate.

You have striven particularly to see to it that the word of God in Scripture receives greater prominence; that theology more strongly influences liturgical texts for a closer correspondence between the *lex orandi* and the *lex credendi*; that as divine worship is ennobled by a genuine simplicity the people of God, especially with the sanctioning of a wider use of the vernacular, can understand the liturgical formularies more clearly and participate in the celebrations more actively.

The welcome outcome is that Vatican Council II, in no small measure because of your own efforts and care, is accomplishing a healthy renewal in the Church's life as to what concerns the encounter between God and his people that takes place in the liturgy.

691   As the Consilium comes to an end after its outstanding service and the Congregation for Divine Worship is already carrying out its mandate as a permanent part of the Roman Curia, we want to express some wishes for the present and for the future. Our desire is that every care must be taken to carry out the reform of the liturgy with devotion, with wisdom, and with fidelity, not at the whim of any individual. Let there be an end at last to experimentation not approved by competent ecclesiastical authority. No sacrifice is pleasing to God that is offered without regard for the Church's directives. The liturgical reform will achieve fulfillment through loyalty to the will of the Council; in a cause so holy because it involves divine worship and the spiritual life, we must preserve, safeguard, and promote without reserve unity and harmony of spirit.

May the prayer of the Church keep its integrity and devotion and grow in strength from day to day. May it ever increase the honor of God and the religious fervor of the faithful.

In the hope for these things, we impart to each and all of you with special sentiments of charity the apostolic blessing.

100. SC DIVINE WORSHIP, **Report** *Sacra Congregatio* of Cardinal J. R. Knox, Prefect, to the Synod of Bishops (27 September–26 October 1974), September 1974: Not 10 (1974) 355–362.

The Congregation for Divine Worship, established by Pope Paul VI, 9 May 1969,[a] continues the work of the Consilium begun in 1964, in keeping with the norms laid down by Vatican Council II for the reform of the liturgy.

It is the smallest of the Roman congregations, comprising, in addition to the cardinal prefect, a staff of not more than ten, twenty-seven members from among the cardinals and bishops, and twenty consultors. But it gladly makes use of the cooperation of experts from all parts of the world, especially from the national liturgical commissions and from liturgical and pastoral institutes. The help of these experts enables the Congregation to be aware of and to study reactions, problems, wishes, and new needs in the different parts of the world.

At present the Congregation is faced with two main tasks: bringing to a conclusion the reform of the liturgical books and discussing as well as solving problems arising out of new needs.

I. REFORM OF THE LITURGICAL BOOKS

We can say that the reform of the liturgical books has all but reached its conclusion; only the following books are yet to be published:

1. The *Pontificale Romanum*. The rites relative to persons, formerly found in volume one of the Roman Pontifical (holy orders, blessing of an abbot or abbess, consecration to a life or virginity, etc.) have all been promulgated.

The rites relative to objects, such as the dedication of a church and an altar, formerly found in volume two of the Roman Pontifical, will be published before the end of this year.

2. The *Rituale Romanum*. The rites for the celebration of the sacraments have all been promulgated. Blessings, or sacramentals, found in the second part of the former Ritual, will, with God's help, be published within the first six months of 1975. After the completed revision of the Roman Ritual and of the rites now contained in the Roman Pontifical, we will examine the possibilities for arrangement of the material and make suggestions with a view to the collection of the various rites into volumes in a way that is convenient for use of pastors, traveling missionaries, and bishops.

3. The *Martyrologium*. After four years of work, this book also is nearing completion. There is reason to hope that it will be offered to the Church within the next year. It should not be regarded as though it were simply a catalogue of the saints and the blessed, but as truly a *liturgical* book, offering for pastoral advantage the saints and the blessed historically authenticated and venerated by the universal Church. A *Sanctorale romanum*, therefore, more selective and richer than a martyrology, it has been composed in order that its public reading may provide spiritual sustenance.

4. The *Caeremoniale Episcoporum*. The new edition of this book must in no way be looked on as a mere handbook of ceremonies. For each rite a brief explanation will be provided on the meaning of the rite and its guiding pastoral principles. The result will be a *Caeremoniale romanum* that like a crown will regulate the reformed liturgy.

692

693

---

[a] See DOL 94.

5. The *Liber precum*. This will appear as a small, careful guide for devotional practices that complement or prepare for liturgical services. In order that devotional practices may retain their worth, they must fit in with liturgical norms, supplementing and not disregarding or contradicting them.

As to devotion to the Virgin Mary, there is a shining model in the recent Apostolic Exhortation *Marialis cultus*,[b] on the right formation and growth of veneration of the Blessed Virgin Mary. The same path must be followed regarding devotion to the adorable person of Christ: the Stations of the Cross as a contemplation of the Lord's passion; devotion to the Sacred Heart of Jesus, the Precious Blood, the Holy Name.

The *Liber precum* will chiefly suggest norms for the benefit of conferences of bishops and local Ordinaries.

II. CARRYING OUT REFORM OF THE LITURGY

694   We must not say that reform of the liturgy has reached its objective once the new books are published. New problems arise, the needs of peoples emerge in clearer light, as does the comparison between the style of language of the liturgical texts and that of our own contemporaries. Clearly it is altogether necessary to weigh all these matters carefully.

During the past year the Congregation for Divine Worship published as an adjunct of the General Instruction of the Roman Missal, the Directory for Masses with Children.[c] It has been received everywhere with praise, especially by those who are in charge of catechesis for children and of their initiation into taking part in the Mass. Resources for liturgical texts suited to children and especially eucharistic prayers must be added to the Directory.

The phenomenon of private persons creating new texts for liturgical celebration has in recent years frequently been the cause of anxiety and confusion. Here and there this still goes on with its attendant dangers to the purity and integrity of faith as expressed by liturgical prayer and to the unity of the Church, local, diocesan, and universal. We have pondered this problem from every angle, especially as it relates to the eucharistic prayers. Finally, after consultation with the other departments of the Roman Curia, the decision was published through the circular letter to presidents of the conferences of bishops, 27 May [April] 1973.[d] On the basis of what was set forth in that letter, some conferences of bishops have requested a distinct eucharistic prayer for situations or circumstances that are altogether special. In some places new prayers over and above those of the Roman Missal have been composed. Our Congregation is weighing all these matters with due responsibility.

In addition there are two questions now at issue among the national liturgical conferences as they busily carry on their work; I wish to put them before you.

A. CELEBRATIONS WITH LAYPERSONS PRESIDING

695   A great many Christian communities exist in a "diaspora" situation; many in Latin America, Asia, Africa, but also in some parts of Europe are without the permanent presence of a priest; in many cases a priest can visit such communities only very rarely — once or twice a year.

Among the heavier and more pressing tasks and concerns of bishops beset by the shortage of priests this one must be included: to strive by every means that

---

b   See DOL 467.

c   See DOL 276.

d   See DOL 248.

communities habitually without a priest will not be deprived of spiritual care. They must be given the chance to gather in order to offer prayer together, to hear the word of God, to sing his praises, to celebrate the sacraments of baptism and marriage, to receive the eucharist, especially on Sunday, under the presidency of one of the faithful, a religious, or a catechist who has received from the bishop a mandate to care for that community. In different parts of the world, measures have begun and experiments are under way. Regrettably, however, very often nothing is being done and the faith is dying out little by little. In some places certain things are being done that are not right, with the danger of a confusion in the people's minds between a sacramental and nonsacramental celebration, between the eucharist and a simple thanksgiving service. We have accordingly submitted the issue to study under all of its aspects; we have made an inquiry into measures already being taken. We are very confident of providing the bishops with some broad pastoral and liturgical principles, suggestions, and models for the carrying out of community celebrations with a layperson presiding.

B. Instruments of Social Communication (Audiovisuals) in the Liturgy

The instruments of social communication are everywhere in today's society 696 and their even wider use is foreseen in the coming years. The Church cannot forget this, but instead must consider the fact that people are so affected by them that audiovisual education is more effective than education through oral or written communication. Therefore these means must be dealt with not only because they can be of assistance in catechetics, especially in communities not having priests, but also because it is no longer possible to disregard them.

There are, as well, requests and experiments regarding use of audiovisual resources in liturgical celebrations themselves and in almost every country there are radio or television broadcasts of liturgical services, especially the Mass.

With regard to this issue there must be careful reflection; it is already undergoing the review of our Congregation.

ADAPTATION

The books of the reformed liturgy supply the basic structure of the liturgical 697 services of the Roman Rite. Within this "substantial unity," however, the Constitution on the Liturgy itself allows for "legitimate variations and adaptations to different *groups, regions, and peoples*, especially in mission lands" (SC art. 38),[e] depending on the characteristics, culture, and spiritual endowments of various nations and persons. This is an absolutely essential course in order that the liturgy may really take hold of the minds of the faithful and help them to take part in Christ's paschal mystery and so to be fashioned in his likeness. Liturgical adaptation is the chief program for pastoral liturgy once the reform of the liturgical books is completed. Of course, the qualities, traditions, usages of various nations and peoples must be considered with sympathy and indeed fostered. But at the same time the dangers of particularism or subjectivism must be avoided, as also whatever in the progress of culture quickly passes or whatever is inextricably tied up with superstition and error, or whatever does not square with the rationale of the true and authentic liturgical spirit. The Congregation for Divine Worship plans to treat this issue more fully with the conferences of bishops, in the interest of promoting a true and authentic adaptation that pays heed to the traditions and needs of peoples and at

---

e   DOL 1 no. 38.

the same time respects the structure of the liturgical books and the tradition of the Church.

DEEPENING LITURGICAL FORMATION

698   In every nation there is intense activity in providing translations of liturgical books and the aids needed for the faithful's participation in the liturgy. Liturgical commissions and experts have expended great effort on this task. Often great sacrifices and heavy burdens have been faced, a clear sign of the Church's vitality. Pastoral activity is more and more planned around the liturgy, which in some parts of the world remains almost the sole occasion for meeting the Christian community and giving catechetical instruction. But as has been forcefully asserted from the beginning, changes in the liturgy itself are not enough. There is need to acquire a deeper sense of celebration, of community, of participation and to increase the knowledge of rites and prayers. Only when celebrations of the liturgy, and particularly of the sacraments, are prepared with thorough care and the people are led to them through a catechumenate as it were, does the liturgical reform preserve its vitality and yield the results of genuine Christian life and holiness. Therefore, there must be futherance of the liturgical formation of priests and people and of groups of servers, cantors, acolytes, and readers. No less important is the work of experts to provide every part of the world with its own repertoire of hymns and songs as means to imbue the community with Christian truths and to lead it to take part in the liturgy.

699   There are some liturgical measures undertaken that are ill-conceived, not to be approved, and based on private judgment; sometimes they are publicized and spread more than they should be, and they still continue. They often originate because the liturgical books in their full import are not known or not yet put into practice. Another reason for their origin is stubbornness or dawdling in carrying out the liturgical reform fully and correctly. Either course of action must be repudiated. Not only are those to be reproved who on their own initiative go too far either against or outside liturgical laws, but also those who oppose liturgical renewal on frivolous, even false grounds. This applies above all to those who violently assert that nonuse of the new Roman Missal is lawful and that Mass with a congregation can be celebrated according to the Tridentine form established by St. Pius V, in spite of the contrary determinations made by the Apostolic Constitution of Pope Paul VI[f] and by the conferences of bishops. All of this is the worse by reason of the fact that those opposing the new Roman Missal dare in defense of their position to level accusations at Pope Paul himself and invent false interpretations of documents and texts that confuse the Christian community.[g]

The Missal of Paul VI presents the Church's integral faith regarding the Mass. The traditional teaching is clearly set forth in the Apostolic Constitution and in the General Instruction with its Introduction that preface the Missal.[h] These documents clearly state that the Mass is at once and inseparably a sacrifice perpetuating the sacrifice of the cross, a memorial of the Lord's death and resurrection, a sacred meal. All of these points must be kept in mind in catechesis so that there is a clear awareness of what the Church is doing, even if it expresses this in various ways.

---

[f] See DOL 202.

[g] See DOL 61.

[h] See DOL 208.

There is, for example, a complaint that the new eucharistic prayers do not   700
bring out the sacrificial aspect of the eucharist. What really should be said is that
they do so more clearly than the Roman Canon. For the high point of the eucharistic prayer is the narrative of institution, when above all the priest acts in the person
of Christ. In these "words and actions of Christ that sacrifice is celebrated which he
himself instituted at the Last Supper when under the appearances of bread and
wine he offered his body and blood" (GIRM no. 55 d).[i] Through Christ's own
words also the sacrificial character of the celebration is stated: for it is the body
"which will be given up for you" — words added by the new Missal — and "the
blood which will be shed for you and for all men."

The sacrificial character of the eucharist is expressed as well through the
offering that is part of all the eucharistic prayers: "the Church and in particular the
Church here and now assembled — offers the spotless victim to the Father in the
Holy Spirit" (GIRM no. 55 f).[j]

If more evidence is required, listen to the explicit words of the new eucharistic
prayers:

Eucharistic Prayer II: *Father, . . . we offer to you . . . this holy and perfect sacrifice,*
                              the bread of life and the cup of eternal salvation.

Eucharistic Prayer III: *We offer you . . . this holy and living sacrifice.*
                              See the victim whose death has reconciled us to yourself.
                              Lord, may this sacrifice which has made our peace with you.

Eucharistic Prayer IV: *We offer you his body and blood, the acceptable sacrifice which*
                              brings salvation to the whole world.

On this point these words are certainly clearer than those of the Roman
Canon.

CONCLUSION

The *via media* that the Congregation for Divine Worship is following with the   701
purpose of achieving a gradual transition to a reformed liturgy in keeping with the
letter and spirit of the liturgical books and of the Constitution on the Liturgy is also
set before the bishops. The basis of their responsibility is that they are "the chief
stewards of the mysteries of God and the overseers, promoters, and guardians of all
liturgical life in the particular Churches entrusted to their care" (CD no. 15).[k] Their
task is to regulate, to direct, sometimes to correct, and at all times to explain by a
constant and clear catechesis the meaning of the liturgy; they are to encourage
celebrations that are carried out worthily and in full conformity with genuine
renewal; they are to give an example in celebrations at which they themselves
preside. Also resting on them is the duty to promote studies and surveys on the way
liturgical life is developing in the diocese, on the needs and real requirements of the
faithful, and on the best way to help them.

Thus through the liturgy rightly celebrated, which above all expresses the
Church's true faith and which is the gathering place for the feelings, desires, joys
and sorrows, struggles and frustrations of the people, the renewal of the Christian
life takes place and the faithful, steeped in the mystery of Christ, are enabled to live
it more fully and express it outwardly.

For the Church's intent is to proclaim the living God and Jesus Christ whom he
has sent so that people might hold fast to him in unfeigned faith. But Christ sent

   [i]   DOL 208 no. 1445.

   [j]   DOL 208 no. 1445.

   [k]   DOL 7 no. 194.

the apostles not only to preach the Gospel but also to put into effect through the sacrifice and the sacraments the work of salvation they were proclaiming (see SC art. 5).[1] The purpose of evangelization is that those believing in Christ may be reborn through baptism into a new life and may be gathered together into the one people of God (see AG no. 15),[m] and in this way be brought to offer their own labors and all created things with Christ to God the Father in the eucharistic sacrifice, "the source and apex of all evangelization" (PO no. 5).[n] Evangelization is linked necessarily to the liturgy. Otherwise, it will not achieve its purpose. For by the gospel message people must be led to *faith* and to the *sacraments*; the *preaching* of the word in turn requires the ministry of the *sacraments*. All of this stands out prominently in all the rites of the reformed liturgy: the celebration of the word and the celebration of the sacrament are intimately joined together and make up the one act of worship.[o]

101. PAUL VI, Apostolic Constitution *Constans Nobis*, establishing the SC for the Sacraments and Divine Worship, 11 July 1975: AAS 67 (1975) 417– 420; Not 9 (1975) 209–211.

702   Our constant effort and intense concern, especially in these years following Vatican Council II, have gone into organizing the Roman Curia in such a way that its departments, through which we provide for the well-being and the progress of the universal Church, may effectively carry out the wide range of their assignments and respond in the best way possible to the increasing demands of pastoral activity. The first step, taken with publication of the Apostolic Constitution *Regimini Ecclesiae universae*, was a new and more detailed organization, in keeping with the wishes of the Council,[1] regarding the congregations, tribunals, secretariats, offices, and councils of the Curia.[2] While this reorganization made soundly based changes in older forms, that is, *structures*, it did not foreclose either the capability or the avenue for introducing different structures or abolishing yet others as circumstances might require.

We think it pointless to review these structures now, since they were duly published as they were established.[3] It is more useful to see the fact of the many present changes in the Church's governing in relation to two other facts. The first is the extremely rapid tempo of contemporary society. The second is the conspicuous care and concern of the Church to respond, through the best means possible, to the tempo of modern life as one of the "signs of the times," in order to pursue the supernatural mission entrusted to it by its divine Founder.

----

[1]   See DOL 1 no. 5.

[m]   See DOL 17 no. 247.

[n]   DOL 18 no. 260.

[o]   See DOL 1 no. 56.

[1]   See CD no. 9.

[2]   See Ap. Const. *Regimini Ecclesiae universae* [DOL 88].

[3]   See Ap. Const. *Sacra Rituum Congregatio*, dividing the SCR into two congregations [DOL 94]; Motu Proprio *Apostolicae caritatis*, establishing the Pontifical Commission for Migration and Tourism: AAS 62 (1970) 193–197; Epistle *Amoris officio* to Cardinal Jean Villot, establishing the Pontifical Council "Cor Unum": AAS 63 (1961) 669–673; Motu Proprio *Quo aptius*, transferring the duties of the Apostolic Chancery to the Secretariat of State: AAS 65 (1973) 113–116.

From 1969, when we established the Congregation for Divine Worship,[4] to the present, our experience makes clear the closeness and convergence of the mutual interests of this Congregation and the Congregation for the Discipline of the Sacraments. This is the origin, first of the suggestion, then of the firm decision that it would be truly useful and in fact necessary to entrust the business of these two congregations to one new entity. At least in a certain sense, there is theologically only a single kind of interest at issue, one in which the liturgico-cultural or pastoral aspects are so linked to the canonical and juridical as to be virtually inseparable. Consequently, we are fully convinced that a more efficient arrangement of the matters that these two departments have handled up to the present time can be of even greater help and improvement for the renewal of the liturgy, wisely decreed by Vatican Council II and already so far advanced, and for the right execution of that great undertaking. For it we feel we must labor unceasingly and from it so many welcome benefits for the religious life have poured forth upon the whole people of God.

703

Having carefully weighed the whole matter, then, and having heard the views of serious and competent men, we have decided, in view of the opportuneness of unifying matters relevant to the discipline of the sacraments and to divine worship, to replace the two former congregations with one new one.

To this end, we decree the following.

1.   The Congregation for the Discipline of the Sacraments and the Congregation for Divine Worship cease to exist in the form they have had up to now.

704

2.   A new congregation is instituted with the official name *Sacra Congregatio pro Sacramentis divinoque Cultu.*

705

3.   This new congregation, under the care of a cardinal prefect assisted by a secretary, is divided into two parts or sections: one for the discipline of the sacraments; the other for divine worship. A subsecretary is assigned to each section.

706

4.   The first section has for its assigned responsibility the matters previously pertaining to the Congregation for the Discipline of the Sacraments as set forth in the Apostolic Constitution *Regimini Ecclesiae universae* nos. 54–57;[a] the second section, the matters previously pertaining to the Congregation for Divine Worship as set forth in the Apostolic Constitution *Sacra Rituum Congregatio* nos. 1–4.[b]

707

5.   The effective date for all the prescriptions of the present Constitution will be the first day of this coming month of August.

708

Furthermore, it is our will that these statutes and prescriptions be now and remain for the future firm and effective, notwithstanding, should the case arise, the apostolic constitutions and ordinances issued by our predecessors or other prescriptions, even those that might be cited for special mention or as exceptions.

---

[4] See Ap. Const. *Sacra Rituum Congregatio* [DOL 94 nos. 680–683].

[a] See DOL 88 nos. 652–653.

[b] See DOL 94 nos. 680–683.

102. SC SACRAMENTS AND DIVINE WORSHIP, List of members (1975–1979).*

[The members are listed alphabetically, with title at time of appointment, date of appointment; other pertinent dates.]

709   ALESSIO, Luis, Subsecretary, Section for Divine Worship, 21 October 1977.

ARNS, Cardinal Paulo Evaristo, OFM, Archbishop of São Paulo, Brazil, 30 September 1975.

AROKIASWAMY, Packiam, Archbishop of Bangalore, India, 30 September 1975.

BENGSCH, Cardinal Archbishop Alfred, Bishop of Berlin, Germany, 30 September 1975; member of SC Catholic Education, 21 February 1977; died 13 December 1979.

COLOMBO, Cardinal Giovanni, Archbishop of Milan, Italy, 30 September 1975.

CORRIPIO AHUMADA, Cardinal Ernesto, Archbishop of Mexico City, Mexico, 24 July 1979.

D'ALMEIDA TRINIDADE, Manuel, Bishop of Aveiro, Brazil, 30 September 1975.

DARMOJUWONO, Cardinal Justinus, Archbishop of Semarang, Indonesia, 30 September 1975.

DEARDEN, Cardinal John Francis, Archbishop of Detroit, Mich., U.S.A., 30 September 1975.

DUVAL, Cardinal Léon-Etienne, Archbishop of Algiers, Algeria, 30 September 1975.

FELICI, Cardinal Pericle, President of the Pontifical Commission for the Revision of the Code of Canon Law, 30 September 1975; Prefect of the Apostolic Signatura, 15 August 1977; member of the General Secretariat of the Synod of Bishops, 26 October 1977.

FORTIER, Joseph Louis Jean Marie, Archbishop of Sherbrooke, P.Q., Canada, 30 September 1975.

FRANIC, Frane, Archbishop of Split, Yugoslavia, 30 September 1975.

GRAY, Cardinal Gordon J., Archbishop of St. Andrews and Edinburgh, Scotland, 30 September 1975.

INNOCENTI, Antonio, Titular Archbishop of Aeclanum, Secretary, 17 July 1975; consultor of SC Eastern Churches, 25 April 1978; consultor of SC Doctrine of the Faith, 26 June 1978.

JUBANY ARNAU, Cardinal Narciso, Archbishop of Barcelona, Spain, 30 September 1975; member of SC Religious and Secular Institutes, 22 May 1978.

---

*   Announcements: 17 July 1975; 18 Aug. 1975; 30 Sept. 1975; 30 Oct. 1975: AAS 67 (1975) 463–464; 507; 601; 684. 24 May 1976; 27 Sept. 1976; 15 Dec. 1976: AAS 68 (1976) 427; 684; 749. 21 Feb. 1977; (2) 21 Feb. 1977; 15 Aug. 1977; 21 and 26 Oct. 1977: AAS 69 (1977) 235; 619; 684. 25 April 1978; 19 and 22 May 1978; 26 June 1978: AAS 70 (1978) 536–539. 17 Jan. 1979; 24 July 1979: AAS 71 (1979) 385; 1056.

KNOX, Cardinal James R., Prefect, 17 July 1975; member of the Administration of the Patrimony of the Holy See, 18 August 1975; papal legate to the International Eucharistic Congress at Philadelphia, 7 July 1976 [See DOL 183]; member of the PCIDV, 25 April 1978; papal legate for celebration of the centenary of the Church in Uganda, 17 January 1979.

LUCIANI, Cardinal Albino, Patriarch of Venice, Italy, 30 September 1975; Pope John Paul I, 26 August 1978; died 28 September 1978.

MAGNONI, Antonio, Subsecretary of the Section for the Sacraments, 17 July 1975.

MARTY, Cardinal François, Archbishop of Paris, France, 30 September 1975.

MUÑOZ DUQUE, Cardinal Anibal, Archbishop of Bogotá, Colombia, 30 September 1975.

NASALLI ROCCA DI CORNELIANO, Cardinal Mario, 30 September 1975.

NOÈ, Virgilio, Subsecretary of the Section for Divine Worship, 17 July 1975; Adjunct Secretary of the Section for Divine Worship, 21 Oct. 1977; consultor, Special Commission for the Liturgy of the Congregation for Eastern Churches, 25 April 1978.

OTUNGA, Cardinal Maurice, Archbishop of Nairobi, Kenya, 30 September 1975.

PIGNEDOLI, Cardinal Sergio, President of the Secretariat for Non-Christians, 30 September 1975; died 15 June 1980.

PIRONIO, Cardinal Eduardo, Proprefect of SC Religious and Secular Institutes, 24 May 1976; Prefect of the same, 29 May 1976; councilor of the Pontifical Commission for Latin America, 27 September 1976; member of the PCIDV, 25 April 1978; member of SC Eastern Churches, 19 May 1978.

POLETTI, Cardinal Ugo, Vicar of Rome, 30 September 1975; member of SC Eastern Churches, 19 May 1978; member of SC Religious and Secular Institutes, 22 May 1978.

PRIMATESTA, Cardinal Raúl Francisco, Archbishop of Córdoba, Argentina, 30 September 1975; member of the General Secretariat of the Synod of Bishops, 26 October 1977.

ROSSI, Cardinal Opilio, 24 May 1976; President of the Pontifical Council for the Laity, 15 December 1976; member of SC Eastern Churches, 10 April 1978; member of SC Religious and Secular Institutes, 22 May 1978.

RYAN, Dermot J., Archbishop of Dublin, Republic of Ireland, 30 September 1975.

SALAZAR LÓPEZ, Cardinal José, Archbishop of Guadalajara, Mexico, 30 September 1975.

SEPER, Cardinal Franjo, Prefect of SC Doctrine of the Faith, 30 September 1975.

STAFFA, Cardinal Dino, Prefect of the Apostolic Signatura, 30 September 1975; died 7 August 1977.

TENHUMBERG, Heinrich, Bishop of Münster, Germany, 30 October 1975; member of the Pontifical Commission for Justice and Peace, 30 April 1977; died 16 September 1979.

TOMIZAWA, Benedict, Bishop of Sapporo, Japan, 30 September 1975.

TRIN-NHU-KHUÉ, Cardinal Joseph Marie, Archbishop of Hanoi, Vietnam, 24 May 1976; died 27 November 1978.

WILLEBRANDS, Cardinal Jan, President of the Secretariat for Christian Unity, 30 September 1975; Archbishop of Utrecht, Holland, 21 December 1976.

WOJTYLA, Cardinal Karol, Archbishop of Krakow, Poland, 30 September 1975; Pope John Paul II, 16 October 1978.

Section 4. The Holy See and the Hierarchy

SUMMARY (DOL 103–107). At the outset of the reform the most important documents on the general role of the bishops and the conferences of bishops were the Constitution on the Liturgy itself and the first Instruction *Inter Oecumenici*. On specific subjects, the correspondence of Rome with the bishops and the conferences of bishops is given in context throughout *Documents on the Liturgy*. The present section contains only 5 documents, having to do mainly with faculties granted to bishops in regard to liturgy.

—From three of these issued *motu proprio* by Paul VI extracts are given from *Pastorale munus* (DOL 103) and *De Episcoporum muneribus* (DOL 105), on the powers of bishops, and from *Ecclesiae Sanctae*, on the role of bishops and the conferences of bishops in carrying out certain decrees of the Council and on multinational conferences of bishops (DOL 106). In connection with *Pastorale munus*, there is an authentic interpretation of one of its provisions (DOL 104).

—From the SC Bishops' Index of Faculties, those related to the liturgy granted by SC Clergy and SC Rites are listed (DOL 107).

103. PAUL VI, **Motu Proprio** *Pastorale munus*, on the powers and privileges granted to bishops, 30 November 1963: AAS 56 (1964) 5–12 (excerpt).

710   The pastoral office was linked by Christ to the grave responsibilities of teaching and sanctifying, of binding and loosing. Bishops in all ages have fulfilled this charge with shining examples of the highest charity, in spite of facing many obstacles.

    As the concerns and works of the Church have increased with the passing of centuries, the Holy See has been always intently and readily responsive to the requests of bishops bearing on their pastoral concern. The Holy See has not only used its peculiar authority and jurisdiction to increase the number of diocesan bishops, but has also bestowed on them the special faculties and privileges required to meet current needs effectively.

    As the second session of Vatican Council II draws to a close, out of a strong desire to assure the conciliar Fathers of our high esteem for all our brothers in the episcopate, we have decided to accede gladly to the bishops' petitions and to make those concessions to them that will highlight their episcopal dignity and at the same time make their pastoral charge more effective and unencumbered. This we believe to be eminently consistent with our own office as universal pastor. As we extend these concessions to bishops, we ask at the same time that, joining themselves to Christ and to ourself, his vicar on earth, and animated by a burning charity, they strive by the help of their own work to lighten the "care of all the Churches" (see 2 Cor 11:28) that rests on our shoulders.

711   The faculties in question are extraordinary and consequently we grant them in such a way that bishops may not delegate them to anyone else except a coadjutor or auxiliary bishop and a vicar general, unless the formula conceding specific faculties determines otherwise.

    In keeping with the rule of law currently in force, the faculties that we declare to belong by law to residential bishops belong also by law to vicars and prefects apostolic, to appointed apostolic administrators, to abbots and prelates *nullius*. All of these possess personally within their own territory those rights and faculties belonging to residential bishops within their own dioceses. Vicars and prefects apostolic, although not authorized to appoint a vicar general, have, nevertheless, the power lawfully to delegate the faculties in question to their pro-vicar or pro-prefect.

    With all due deliberation and by reason of our respect and love toward all the bishops of the Catholic Church, we therefore decree and establish *motu proprio* and in virtue of our apostolic authority, that from 8 December 1963 bishops may at once make use of the following faculties and privileges.

I. FACULTIES THAT BELONG BY RIGHT TO A RESIDENTIAL BISHOP FROM THE MOMENT HE TAKES CANONICAL POSSESSION OF HIS DIOCESE, BUT THAT, WITH THE EXCEPTION OF HIS COADJUTOR AND AUXILIARY BISHOPS AND THE VICAR GENERAL, HE CANNOT DELEGATE TO OTHERS UNLESS THE CONTRARY IS EXPRESSLY STATED IN THE FACULTIES:

712   1.   To extend for just cause but not beyond one month the lawful use of expired rescripts or indults granted by the Holy See, without petition for their extension having to be sent first to the Holy See, but with the obligation of immediate recourse *pro gratia* or, if petition has already been made, to obtain a response.

713   2.   To permit priests, because of the scarcity of clergy and for just cause, to celebrate Mass twice on weekdays and even three times on Sundays and holydays of obligation, provided there is genuine pastoral need.

3. To permit priests who celebrate two or three Masses to take something to drink even though an interval of one hour does not intervene before the celebration of the next Mass.

714

4. To permit priests, for a just cause, to celebrate Mass at any hour of the day and to distribute communion in the evening, but with due observance of other requirements of the law.

715

5. To permit priests suffering from poor eyesight or some other infirmity to celebrate daily the votive Mass of the Blessed Virgin Mary or a Mass for the dead, assisted, if necessary, by another priest or a deacon and observing the Instruction issued by the Congregation of Rites on 15 April 1961.

716

6. To grant the same faculty to priests who are totally blind, provided they are always assisted by another priest or deacon.

717

7. To permit priests to celebrate Mass outside a place of worship on an altar stone, provided the place is decent and becoming; never, however, in a bedroom. This faculty can be granted in individual cases for a just cause, but it can be granted as a permanent faculty only for a more serious reason.

718

8. Likewise, to grant permission to celebrate Mass for just cause at sea and on rivers, but with due precautions.

719

9. To permit priests having the indult for a portable altar to use in place of an altar stone, for a just and serious cause, a Greek *antimensium* or a linen cloth blessed by a bishop, in the right-hand corner of which must be placed relics of martyrs also approved by a bishop. The other prescriptions of the rubrics, especially concerning altar cloths and the corporal, must be observed.

720

10. To permit infirm or elderly priests to celebrate Mass daily at home (but not in a bedroom) even on the more solemn feasts. They must observe the liturgical requirements, but have permission to sit if they are unable to stand.

721

11. On the basis of diminished revenue and for as long as this continues, to reduce, on the ratio of the lawfully prevailing stipend in the diocese, the number of Masses required by an autonomous bequest. The condition is that there is no one bound by the obligation to increase the bequest who can in any practical way be constrained to do so.

722

12. Likewise, to reduce Mass obligations or endowments binding on benefices or other ecclesiastical institutions, if the income from the benefices or institutions proves insufficient for the adequate support of the beneficiary and for the fulfillment of the sacred ministries attached to the benefice or for the attainment of the goal proper to the ecclesiastical institution.

723

13. To grant chaplains of any kind of hospital, orphanage, or prison the faculty to administer the sacrament of confirmation, in the absence of the pastor, to those faithful who are in danger of death. The norms set forth by the Congregation of the Sacraments in its Decree *Spiritus Sancti munera*, 14 September 1946, for a priest administering the sacrament of confirmation are to be observed.

724

14. To grant to confessors eminent for their knowledge and prudence the faculty of absolving, in conjunction with sacramental confession, any of the faithful from all censures, even though reserved, except: a. censures *ab homine*; b. censures re-

725

served *specialissimo modo* to the Holy See; c. censures attached to the violation of the secret of the Holy Office; d. excommunication for priests and their partners who presume to contract marriage, even civilly, and are actually living together.

726   15. To dispense ordinands for a just cause from the defect of being underage, provided no more than six complete months is involved.

727   16. To dispense from the impediment that bars sons of non-Catholics from receiving orders as long as their parents continue to be in error.

728   17. To dispense those already ordained from every kind of irregularity, arising from either delict or defect, in order that they may celebrate Mass and receive and retain ecclesiastical benefices. This faculty requires that no scandal come from its use and that the ministry of the altar be rightly performed. Excluded from the faculty are those irregularities mentioned in CIC can. 985, nos. 3 and 4. If the crime of heresy or schism is involved, an abjuration in the hands of the one absolving must precede the dispensation.

729   18. To confer holy orders outside the cathedral church and outside the canonical times, and even on weekdays, if pastoral considerations so require.

730   23. To permit, for serious cause, the interpellations of the nonbelieving spouse that are to take place before the baptism of the spouse converting; also for serious cause, to dispense from the interpellations before or after the baptism of the one converting, providing that it is clear, from at least a summary and extrajudicial process, that the interpellations would be impossible or pointless.

731   24. To reduce, for a good cause, the obligation of cathedral or collegiate chapters of canons to the daily recitation of the divine office in choir by granting satisfaction of this obligation through the choral recitation on certain days only or through recitation of a certain part of the office only.

732   25. To assign, in case of need, some canons to works of ministry, teaching, or the apostolate, excusing them from choir, but without prejudice to their rights to receive prebendary income. But any right to the daily distributions or those referred to as *inter praesentes* is excluded.

733   26. To commute the divine office to a daily recitation of at least a third part of the rosary of the Blessed Virgin Mary, or of other prayers, because of poor eyesight or another reason as long as such conditions last.

734   27. To depute in particular cases or for a time the vicar general, or another priest holding an office, to consecrate portable altars, chalices, and patens according to the form prescribed in the Roman Pontifical and with the use of the sacred oils blessed by the bishop.

735   28. To permit minor clerics, lay religious as well as devout women to perform even the first washing of palls, corporals, and purificators.

736   29. To use the faculties and privileges, in accord with their scope and tenor, that religious institutes having houses in the diocese possess for the welfare of the faithful.

737   30. To grant priests the faculty to erect, observing the rites prescribed by the Church, the Stations of the Cross, even outdoors, and to attach all the indulgences imparted to those who practice this devotion. This faculty, however, may not be

used in a parish territory in which there is a house of religious who by apostolic indult possess the privilege of erecting the Stations of the Cross.

33.   To confirm up to even a fifth three-year term an ordinary confessor for reli-   738
gious women. This may be done if a shortage of priests suitable for this office leaves no other course or if a majority of the religious, including those who have no voting rights in other matters, agree to the confirmation. In this case, however, other provisions are to be made for the minority.

II.   PRIVILEGES THAT IN ADDITION TO THOSE ENUMERATED IN THE CIC BELONG TO ALL BISHOPS, BOTH RESIDENTIAL AND TITULAR, FROM THE RECEIPT OF AUTHENTIC NOTICE OF THEIR CANONICAL APPOINTMENT:

1.   To preach the word of God everywhere in the world, unless a local Ordinary   739
expressly disapproves.

2.   To hear confessions of the faithful, even of women religious, everywhere in   740
the world, unless a local Ordinary expressly disapproves.

3.   To absolve anyone of the faithful anywhere from all reserved sins, with the   741
exception of the sin of false denunciation, by which an innocent priest is accused before ecclesiastical judges of the crime of solicitation.

4.   To absolve anyone of the faithful anywhere in the act of sacramental confes-   742
sion from all, even reserved, censures with the exception of: a. censures *ab homine*; b. censures reserved *specialissimo modo* to the Holy See; c. censures for the violation of the secret of the Holy Office; d. the excommunication for priests and their partners who presume to contract marriage, even civilly, and are actually living together.

     Residential bishops may use this faculty in their subjects' favor even in regard to the external forum.

5.   To reserve the blessed sacrament in an oratory in their home, provided the   743
prescriptions of liturgical law are properly observed.

6.   To celebrate Mass for just cause at any hour of the day and to distribute   744
communion even in the evening, with due observance of the other prescriptions of law.

7.   To bless anywhere with one sign of the cross, and with all the indulgences   745
customarily granted by the Holy See, rosaries and other chaplets, crosses, medals, and scapulars approved by the Holy See and to impose the scapulars without the obligation of enrolling the names.

8.   To erect in churches and oratories, even private ones, with only one blessing,   746
the Stations of the Cross, attaching all the indulgences that have been granted to those who practice this devotion.

     These faculties and privileges we gladly grant to our brothers in the episcopate with the intention and desire mentioned already, namely, that all these favors may form part of the beauty and well- being of the Church of Christ, to which we owe all that we are and all that we have.

     All things to the contrary notwithstanding, even those worthy of special mention.

▶   1.   VATICAN COUNCIL II, Constitution on the Liturgy *Sacrosanctum Concilium*, 4
           December 1963:

> art. 22:   Authority of bishops to regulate the liturgy [no. 22].
>   23:   Authority of conferences of bishops [no. 23].

▶   23.   SC RITES (Consilium) Instruction *Inter Oecumenici*, 26 September 1964:

> nos. 22:   Authority of the bishop [no. 314].
>   23–29:   Conferences of bishops [no. 315–321].

104. PONTIFICAL COMMISSION FOR THE INTERPRETATION OF THE DECREES OF VATICAN COUNCIL II, **Reply to a query,** on the Motu Proprio *Pastorale munus*, nos. 11–12, 1 July 1971: AAS 63 (1971) 860.

747   Query: By virtue of the faculties granted through the Motu Proprio *Pastorale munus* of 30 November 1963, nos. 11–12,[a] may bishops reduce or even, if the situation warrants, suppress an obligation of funded Masses that has been culpably not fulfilled in the past.

Reply: Yes, as to the reduction of funded Masses, but as far as possible respecting the founder's or donor's will; no, as to suppression of the obligation.

105. PAUL VI, **Motu Proprio** *De Episcoporum muneribus*, on norms relating to bishops' power of dispensation, 15 June 1966: AAS 58 (1966) 467–472 (excerpt).

IX.   Excepting those faculties specially granted to papal legates and Ordinaries, we expressly reserve to ourself the following dispensations:

748   17. From the canonical form required for contracting marriage validly.

749   18. From the law of renewing matrimonial consent in cases of a *sanatio in radice* whenever:

> c.   the case involves a mixed marriage where the conditions prescribed by the Instruction already mentioned [SCDF, *Matrimonii Sacramentum* no. I, 18 March 1966] had not been observed; [. . .]

750   20. From the time prescribed for the eucharistic fast.

106. PAUL VI, **Motu Proprio** *Ecclesiae Sanctae*, norms for carrying out certain of the decrees of Vatican Council II, 6 August 1966: AAS 58 (1966) 757–787 (excerpts).

751   The holy Church's governance requires that after Vatican Council II new norms be established and that a new regulation of church matters be fixed. These should more and more fit the needs brought to light by the Council and be shaped to the goals and areas of the apostolate the Council has opened up for the Church in

---

[a]   See DOL 103 nos. 722–723.

the profoundly changed world of today, a world in need of a light to guide it and in search of the supernatural warmth of charity.

Urged on by these considerations, as soon as the Ecumenical Council came to an end we appointed study commissions that would apply their learning and experience to the task of proposing definite norms for executing those decrees of the Council for which a *vacatio legis* had already been provided. These commissions, as we were happy to report in the Motu Proprio *Munus apostolicum* of 10 June 1966, have worked faithfully at their task and at the time assigned have informed us of their conclusions.

Having carefully reflected on these conclusions, we believe that it is now time to issue the norms already mentioned. The matter, however, is one of discipline, about which experience may suggest still further changes. Moreover a special commission is at work revising and correcting the body of canon law and the laws of the universal Church will have an organization that is more apposite and exact. Therefore we think that our acts will be more wise and judicious if we issue the present norms *ad experimentum*.

During this trial period, then, the conferences of bishops may share with us the observations and comments that the carrying out of these norms suggests and may submit to us new recommendations.

Therefore, after due deliberation, *motu proprio* and by our apostolic authority, we decree and promulgate the following norms for carrying out those decrees of the Council bearing the *incipits*: *Christus Dominus* (The Pastoral Office of Bishops in the Church); *Presbyterorum Ordinis* (The Ministry and Life of Priests); *Perfectae caritatis* (The Appropriate Renewal of Religious Life); *Ad Gentes* (The Missionary Activity of the Church). We order that the norms be observed *ad experimentum*, that is, until a new code of canon law is promulgated, unless in the meanwhile the Holy See makes other provisions. 752

The effective date for these norms will be 11 October 1966, the feast of the Maternity of the Blessed Virgin Mary, the day on which, four years ago, our predecessor Pope John XXIII solemnly opened the Council.

Whatever we have established by this Motu Proprio we order to be settled and valid, all things to the contrary notwithstanding, even those worthy of special mention. [. . .]

I
NORMS FOR CARRYING OUT THE DECREES OF VATICAN COUNCIL II, *CHRISTUS DOMINUS* AND *PRESBYTERORUM ORDINIS*

RELIGIOUS
(CD NOS. 33–35)

26. In their churches and public or semipublic oratories attended regularly by the faithful, religious are also bound by the laws and decrees that the local Ordinary enacts canonically regarding the public exercise of worship.[a] This is without prejudice to any particular rite that religious may lawfully use for their own community only and with allowance made for the order of choral office and the sacred services related to the special end of the religious institute. 753

38. In regard to observance of the general laws and episcopal decrees on divine worship, the local Ordinary has the right to conduct a visitation of the churches and oratories, even semipublic, of religious, including the exempt, if such places are 754

---

[a] See DOL 7 no. 197.

regularly open to the faithful. If he discovers any abuse in this matter and has notified the superior to no avail, he can take appropriate action on his own authority.

CONFERENCES OF BISHOPS
(CD NO. 38)[b]

755   41. § 4. Multinational or international conferences of bishops can be formed only with the approval of the Holy See, which alone has the power to establish the proper norms for such conferences. Each time conferences of bishops engage in a course of action or relations among themselves that take on an international aspect, the Holy See must be advised in advance.

§ 5. Interconference relations, especially of neighboring nations, can be carried on in timely and practical ways through their secretariats. These relations can, among other things, look to the following:

a. sharing plans of action, especially in the area of pastoral ministry;

b. exchanging written or printed reports on decisions of a conference of bishops or on the *acta* and documents that the bishops publish jointly;

c. informing each other of various apostolic enterprises proposed or recommended by a conference of bishops and of anything else that might be helpful in similar matters;

d. posing the more serious problems that seem to be of the greatest importance currently and in specific circumstances;

e. pointing out the dangers or errors prevalent in their respective nations and liable also to affect other peoples, with a view to the use of effective resources for their prevention, elimination, or control; and other such matters.

II
NORMS FOR CARRYING OUT THE DECREE OF VATICAN COUNCIL II,
PERFECTAE CARITATIS

PART II
ELEMENTS IN RELIGIOUS LIFE TO BE ADAPTED AND RENEWED

I. THE DIVINE OFFICE OF BROTHERS AND SISTERS (PC NO. 3)[c]

756   20. Although religious who recite a duly approved little office perform the public prayer of the Church (see SC art. 98),[d] still it is recommended to the religious institutes that in place of the little office they recite the divine office, either in whole or in part, so as to share more intimately in the liturgical life of the Church. Religious of the Eastern rites, however, should recite the doxologies and the Divine Praises according to their own liturgical books and customs.

II. MENTAL PRAYER (PC NO. 6)[e]

757   21. With a view to religious' sharing more deeply and effectively in the mystery of the eucharist and the public prayer of the Church and to a fuller nurturing of their spiritual life, more time should be set aside for mental prayer instead of multiplying vocal prayers. Devotional practices customary in the Church are, however, to be

---

b   See DOL 7 no. 199.

c   See DOL 10 no. 203.

d   See DOL 1 no. 98.

e   See DOL 10 no. 204.

maintained and due care is to be given to the formation of religious in the spiritual life.

III
NORMS FOR CARRYING OUT THE DECREE OF VATICAN COUNCIL II
AD GENTES DIVINITUS

3. To increase the mission spirit in the Christian people their prayers and daily   758
sacrifices should be encouraged, to the end that the annual day dedicated to missions will take on the character of a spontaneous expression of that spirit (AG no.
36).ᶠ

Bishops or conferences of bishops should compose intentions for the missions
for inclusion in the general intercessions of the Mass.

18. It is to be hoped that conferences of bishops will join together in organizations   759
based on the various socio-cultural regions. [. . .] Accordingly, the Congregation for
the Propagation of the Faith (AG no. 29) is to promote such collaboration between
the conferences of bishops.

The conferences, in conjunction with the Congregation, will: [. . .]

20. Establish groups of experts to study the views of the various peoples concerning the world and humankind and their attitude of mind toward God and to make
whatever is good or true part of their theological reflection.

Such a theological study provides the basis needed for missionary adaptation,
research into which is also a responsibility of the groups of experts mentioned.
Missionary adaptation encompasses, among other elements, methods of evangelization, styles of liturgy, the religious life, and ecclesiastical legislation (AG no. 19).ᵍ

In what concerns styles of liturgy, the study groups are to send their findings
and proposals to the Consilium. [. . .]

▶   9.   PCIDV, Reply to a query, on the Decree *Christus Dominus* no. 38 and the Motu
        Proprio *Ecclesiae Sanctae* I, no. 41, 5 February 1968.

107. SC BISHOPS, **Index** of quinquennial faculties granted to local Ordinaries, 1 January 1968.*

I. FROM SC CLERGY

To transfer Mass obligations to days, churches, or altars different from those   760
stipulated by the terms of a foundation, provided there is a genuine need for doing
so and nothing prejudicial to the convenience of the people is entailed. Excluded
from this are legacies that in some places can be readily augmented by increasing
the offering. Individual celebrants are also cautioned to inform the diocesan curia
each year regarding the satisfaction of transferred Masses.

ᶠ   See DOL 17 no. 253.

ᵍ   See DOL 17 no. 250.

*   Text, CommRel 49 (1970) 179–180 (excerpt).

III. FROM SC RITES

761 1.   To depute priests, if possible those holding some ecclesiastical office, to consecrate fixed, immovable altars, observing the rites and formularies in the revised Roman Pontifical.

762 2.   To bless the holy oils on Holy Thursday in the presence of as many priests and ministers as it is possible to gather according to local circumstances and conditions.

763 3.   To celebrate himself a requiem Mass of class IV, that is, a daily requiem Mass, once a week in his own chapel, provided the liturgical day is not a class I or class II day and except during the whole of Advent and Lent.

Section 5. Languages of the Liturgy

SUMMARY (DOL 108–133). In addition to the important cross-references on the acceptance of the vernacular as a liturgical language, there are 26 texts here. They are chiefly directives or reflections on the general issue of liturgical translations. (Directives on the translation of the particular liturgical books are given in the decrees of promulgation and the introductions to the rites.)

—Paul VI's major statement on languages is his address to liturgical translators (DOL 113). In two other addresses he established a sound working balance between Latin and the vernacular (DOL 116, 121) and he personally authorized the use of the vernacular for the preface at Mass (DOL 110), the Roman Canon, and the rites of ordination (DOL 117). His own respect for tradition shapes the letter of the Secretariat of State addressed to the abbot of Hauterive (DOL 122).

—The Consilium's major contribution is the 1969 instruction on translation, issued in six major languages (DOL 123). The Consilium also addressed a letter to the conferences of bishops on uniform translations (DOL 108) and published particular directives on specific texts (DOL 111, 115, 118, 120, 124).

—The Congregation of Rites gave specific directives on the language for the rites of ordination (DOL 112). On the language for celebrations of religious the same Congregation and the Congregation of Religious issued one document jointly (DOL 109) and one each separately (DOL 114, 119).

—The new Congregation for Divine Worship continued the main policies of the Consilium in a general declaration (DOL 125) and in its norms on uniform translations (DOL 126), which received particular application to Spanish-speaking countries (DOL 128, 129). This Congregation also issued a document on the translation of the rite of religious profession (DOL 127) and of the essential form of the sacraments (DOL 130, 132), a point on which the Congregation for the Doctrine of the Faith published a doctrinal declaration (DOL 131).

—The Congregation for the Sacraments and Divine Worship reviewed the whole topic of liturgical translation in a letter to the conferences of bishops (DOL 133).

▶   1.   VATICAN COUNCIL II, Constitution on the Liturgy *Sacrosanctum Concilium*, 3
          December 1963:

          art. 36:   Latin and the vernacular [no. 36].
                39:          Role of the conferences of bishops [no. 39].
                54:          Language for the Mass [no. 54].
                63:          Language for the sacraments [no. 63].
                76:          Language for ordinations [no. 76].
                78:          Language for marriage [no. 78].
                101:         Language for divine office [no. 101].
                113:         Language and singing [no. 113].

▶   20.   PAUL VI, Motu Proprio *Sacram Liturgiam*, on putting into effect some prescriptions
          of the Constitution on the Liturgy, 25 January 1964:

          IX: Language for divine office [no. 287].

▶   79.   CONSILIUM, Letter *Le sarei grato* to papal nuncios and apostolic delegates, 25
          March 1964:

          nos. 2–3   Introduction of the vernacular [nos. 617–618].

▶   23.   SC RITES (Consilium), Instruction (first) *Inter Oecumenici*, 26 September 1964:

          nos. 30–31   Decisions of the conferences of bishops
                               [nos. 322–323].
                40–42   Norms for translators [nos. 332–334].
                57–59:   Language for the Mass [nos. 349–351].ᵃ
                61:           Language for the sacraments [no. 353].
                82–83:   Language for little offices [nos. 374–375].
                85–89:   Language for divine office [nos. 377–381].

108. CONSILIUM, **Letter** *Consilium ad exsequendum* of Cardinal G. Lercaro to
presidents of the conferences of bishops, on uniform translation in a language common to several countries, 16 October 1964: Not 1 (1965) 195–
196.

764   The Consilium, in the course of "confirming" the *acta* of conferences of bishops
regarding liturgy, has frequently called attention to a special, often quite difficult
point arising from the wider place in the liturgy that the Constitution on the
Liturgy gives to the vernacular.ᵃ

          As the centuries-old unity of liturgical language gives way and the various
vernaculars are coming into use alongside Latin, we must see to it that the spiritual
and pastoral effectiveness of the liturgy is not imperiled. Transition to a new state
of things should come about with the deliberateness and prudence required.

          The Consilium accordingly wishes to make known its mind on the special
issue of vernacular versions in regions using the same language: in these regions
uniformity is to be maintained in the texts for vernacular celebration of the liturgy.
Approval of multiple versions, texts, and editions in one and the same language,

---

     ᵃ   See also DOL 23 no. 349, note R20.

     ᵃ   See DOL 1 no. 36.

especially in such major languages as English, French, German, and Spanish, seems ill-advised; it would be detrimental both to the importance of the texts themselves and to the dignity of the liturgical books.

Your Excellency, I transmit the wishes of the Consilium to you, relying on you to inform the president of the liturgical commission of your national conference so that through an authorized person consultations may take place in whatever way is feasible between the conferences of bishops — a course already being followed in some instances.

We will be grateful if Your Excellency will kindly inform the Consilium Secretariat regarding the results of this suggestion, indicating any problems encountered, so that, if possible, we may offer help to solve them.

109. SC RITES, **Reply** (Capuchins) to a query, on recitation of the divine office by lay brothers, 9 January 1965.*

The procurator general of the Order of Friars Minor Capuchin, prostrate at the   765
feet of Your Holiness, earnestly requests:

I.   That lay brothers and priests present together in choir may recite lauds, vespers, and compline in the vernacular, using a lawfully approved translation. [. . .]

The Congregation of Rites, using the powers granted to it by Pope Paul VI and taking into consideration the special circumstances cited in the request, replies: To I: No.

▶   26.   PAUL VI, Remarks at the Angelus, on the beginning of the vernacular in the liturgy, 7 March 1965.

110. SECRETARIAT OF STATE, **Letter** *Ho l'onore* of Cardinal A. Cicognani, informing Cardinal G. Lercaro, President of the Consilium, of Pope Paul VI's concession allowing the preface at Mass to be in the vernacular, 27 April 1965.**

I have the honor of referring to the request addressed to Pope Paul VI by you   766
on 22 March 1965. In your capacity as President of the Consilium you asked that the Pope kindly grant permission for the vernacular in the preface of the Mass.

It is now my honored task to inform Your Eminence that Pope Paul has graciously directed that the resolution of this matter be left to the decision of each conference of bishops.

---

*   Text, CommRel 44 (1965) 206–207.

**   Text, EDL 395 (Italian). See also Not 1 (1965) 149.

111. CONSILIUM, **Instruction** *Popularibus interpretationibus* to superiors general and to presidents of the conferences of bishops, on the translation of the propers belonging to dioceses and religious families, 1–2 June 1965: Not 1 (1965) 197–198.

767   The translations of the Roman Missal and Breviary for the various countries have been confirmed as they are given in the texts approved by the conferences of bishops. What remains to be done is to submit the translations of propers belonging to each diocese or religious family for confirmation by the Apostolic See.

The Consilium is frequently asked for a method of procedure in this matter. It seems advisable, therefore, to provide the rules that follow.

768   1.   Use of the vernacular in diocesan or religious propers is subject to the limitations lawfully established by the national conferences of bishops and approved, that is, confirmed, by the Apostolic See (SC art. 36, § 3).[a]

769   2.   The translation of such propers is to be prepared and receive approval, in keeping with the intent of the Instruction of 26 September 1964, no. 88, "by the respective Ordinaries of the same language";[b] therefore:

a.   in the case of diocesan propers, by the bishop or bishops concerned;

b.   in the case of propers for religious by the major superiors in regions having the same language.

770   3.   Preparation of translations is to observe the same Instruction no. 40,[c] with the appropriate modifications.

771   4.   For the sake of the maximum uniformity possible in liturgical texts:

a.   Parts of the proper that exist in texts already translated and approved by the conference of bishops and confirmed by the Apostolic See, are to be taken from such texts. For example, parts from the common or proper of the Roman Breviary or Missal are to be used in the translation approved already for a whole country; readings are to be taken from the translation of the Scriptures approved by the conference of bishops; any formularies of a ritual that already exist in a text approved by the conference of bishops are to be taken from that text, etc.

b.   Parts that happen to be common to several dioceses or religious families are to be prepared conjointly; the points already stated are to be observed.

772   5.   Texts that are proper to only one church must be approved by the competent Ordinary.

773   6.   In the meantime, that is, until a better translation is prepared, it is permissible to adopt texts already familiar to the faithful. Such texts, however, require the Apostolic See's approval, that is, confirmation, for use in the liturgy.

774   7.   Confirmation is to be obtained in this way: the bishop in the case of diocesan propers and the general superior in the case of propers for religious sends the text to

---

[a]   See DOL 1 no. 36.

[b]   DOL 23 no. 380.

[c]   See DOL 23 no. 332.

the Consilium in duplicate, appending a brief report on the criteria on which the translation was based (see Instruction nos. 29 and 30).[d]

8.   Texts may be published and put into use only after the Apostolic See has given approval, that is, confirmation.   775

112. SC RITES, **Enumeration** *Constitutio de sacra Liturgia* of the parts of the rites of ordination that may be in the vernacular, 17 July 1965: Not 1 (1965) 277–279.

The Constitution on the Liturgy art. 76 states: "The address given by the   776
bishop at the beginning of each ordination or consecration may be in the vernacular."[a]

The Instruction [InterOec] no. 61 determines the matter in greater detail: "The competent territorial authority, on approval, that is, confirmation of its decisions by the Holy See, may introduce the vernacular for: . . . b. the conferral of orders: the preliminaries for ordination or consecration, the examination of the bishop-elect at an episcopal consecration, and the admonitions."[b]

Bishops have requested an exact statement of which parts in particular may be in the vernacular in each ordination rite. Therefore the Congregation of Rites on 17 July 1965 has enumerated these parts as follows.

CREATION OF CLERICS
The call.   777
V. Adiutorium nostrum etc.
"Oremus, fratres carissimi."
"Filii carissimi, animadvertere debetis."

ORDINATION OF PORTERS
The call.   778
"Suscepturi, filii carissimi."
"Deum Patrem omnipotentem."
Oremus. Flectamus genua. Levate.

ORDINATION OF READERS
The call.   779
"Electi, filii carissimi."
"Oremus, fratres carissimi."
Oremus. Flectamus genua. Levate.

ORDINATION OF EXORCISTS
The call.   780
"Ordinandi, filii carissimi."
"Deum Patrem omnipotentem."
Oremus. Flectamus genua. Levate.

---

[d]   See DOL 23 nos. 321 and 322.

[a]   DOL 1 no. 76.

[b]   DOL 23 no. 353.

ORDINATION OF ACOLYTES

781   The call.
"Suscepturi, filii carissimi."
"Deum Patrem omnipotentem."
Oremus. Flectamus genua. Levate.

ORDINATION OF SUBDEACONS

782   The call.
"Accedant qui ordinandi sunt diaconi et presbyteri."
"Filii dilectissimi, ad sacrum."
"Recedant in partem, qui ordinandi sunt diaconi et presbyteri."
"Adepturi, filii carissimi."
In the admonition "Adepturi" the last words are to be emended as follows:
"in vera et catholica fide fundati. Quod ipse vobis praestare dignetur, qui
vivit et regnat, Deus, in saecula saeculorum.
R. Amen. "Oremus Deum."
Oremus. Flectamus genua. Levate.

ORDINATION OF DEACONS

783   The call.
"Reverendissime Pater. . . Deo gratias."
"Auxiliante Domino."
"Provehendi, filii dilectissimi."
"Commune votum."
"Oremus, fratres carissimi. . . vivit et regnat Deus."
Oremus. Flectamus genua. Levate.

ORDINATION OF PRIESTS

784   The call.
"Reverendissime Pater . . . Deo gratias."
"Quoniam, fratres carissimi."
"Consecrandi, filii dilectissimi."
Oremus. Flectamus genua. Levate.
"Quia res."
"Benedictio Dei omnipotentis."
"Filii dilectissimi."

CONSECRATION OF A BISHOP-ELECT

785

Examination of the bishop-elect.
"Episcopum oportet."
"Oremus, fratres carissimi."

113. PAUL VI, **Address** to translators of liturgical texts, 10 November 1965:
AAS 57 (1965) 967–970; Not 1 (1965) 378–381.

786   We greet all of you who, in the interest of your assigned task of translating
liturgical texts, have gathered in Rome at this time in order to consider and discuss
the matters that are your special concern. You have come back to Rome, to the See
of Peter, where the whole undertaking engaging your energies had its beginnings,
namely, the reform of the liturgy, and especially in what relates to the participation

of the faithful. You have come back to drink limpid and health-giving waters from their source.

We fully approve the purpose for holding this meeting. The translation of those texts into the vernacular languages is a matter of such great discernment, importance, and difficulty that it seems achievable only through an exchange of views by all involved. Nor can it be left up to the judgment of just anyone, lest the work fall short of the expectations of the Church and the faithful.

St. Jerome, easily the ablest in this art, experienced the magnitude of this task: "If I translate word by word, it sounds absurd; if I am forced to change something in the word order or style, I seem to have stopped being a translator."[1]

You must be convinced that there are not as many liturgies as there are languages used by the Church in the sacred rites; the voice of the Church remains one and the same in celebrating the divine mysteries and administering the sacraments, although that voice speaks in a variety of tongues.

Like a caring mother, the Church, through the teaching of Vatican Council II, has called on its children, in full awareness of their responsibility in the Body of Christ, to share actively in the liturgical prayers and rites. For this reason, the Church has permitted the translation of texts venerable for their antiquity, devotion, beauty, and long-standing use. That is proof of the exalted duty and weighty responsibilities of those who translate such texts. The translations published here and there prior to promulgation of the Constitution on the Liturgy had as their purpose to assist the faithful's understanding of the rite celebrated in Latin; they were aids to people untrained in this ancient language. The translations now, however, have become part of the rites themselves; they have become the voice of the Church.

787

The vernacular now taking its place in the liturgy ought to be within the grasp of all, even children and the uneducated. But, as you well know, the language should always be worthy of the noble realities it signifies, set apart from the everyday speech of the street and the marketplace, so that it will affect the spirit and enkindle the heart with love of God. Obviously, the translator must not use the same kind of language for passages from Scripture, containing the divine word, as for prayers and hymns. Hence those dedicated to this work must know both Christian Latin and their own modern language. Translators also have to take the rules of music into account and so must choose words to be sung that fit the kind of melody suited to the culture and nature of each people, whose spirits may through song rise more readily and fervently to God.

With acumen and tireless devotion let the intent of all your efforts be that the liturgical community can be clothed in a spotless and graceful vesture of speech and "find a beautiful mantle for the realities within."[2] For pastoral reasons, the beauty and richness of Latin, which the Latin Church used for centuries for prayers, petitions, and thanksgiving to God, have been partially lost. Nevertheless your wise and diligent efforts should make a similar clarity of language and dignity of expression shine forth in the vernacular translations of liturgical texts.

This occasion moves us to add a fatherly warning to all concerned about certain matters related not to the office and art of translators but rather to the use of what they translate.

---

[1]   Jerome, *Interpret. Chron. Euseb. Pamph.*, Praef.: PL 27, 35.

[2]   Jerome, op. cit.: PL 27, 36.

788   First, it seems right to recall the norm that was published in a letter from our dear son, Cardinal Giacomo Lercaro, President of the Consilium, 16 October 1964. It advised that in bringing the vernacular into the liturgy the transition to new forms should be made gradually and with discretion; that, especially in countries of a common language, uniformity should be preserved in the liturgical texts and multiplicity of versions, harmful to gravity and dignity, avoided.[a]

789   Moreover, since the whole liturgy is subject to the regulation of the hierarchy,[3] in every nation the individuals, groups, and especially the principal national institutes for the care and promotion of liturgy, as well as all periodicals having the same purpose, should be wholly dependent on the hierarchy. The competent authority has the right to determine the means and establish rules for this close relationship. Every effort must be made for unity of intent and of action in this matter, for we have a single goal to reach and a single ideal of perfection to keep before our minds and to make the aim of all our efforts.

790   The last remark to be made is that liturgical texts, approved by competent authority and confirmed by the Holy See, are as such to be held in all reverence. No one has the right to change, shorten, amplify, or omit them to suit himself. The Church in liturgical matters shows itself to be a kind and generous mother so that its children may take part in the liturgy "actively, consciously, and with devotion"; nevertheless those matters that have been lawfully established have the force of ecclesiastical laws that all must obey in conscience. This is all the more the case when the laws at issue regulate the most sacred of all actions.

          Nor is it permitted for anyone to introduce new elements into the liturgy for the sake of experiment; this threatens grave harm to divine worship or to the Christian faithful. Indeed, according to the norm of the Constitution on the Liturgy[4] the Holy See alone has the right to permit such experiments. [. . .]

114. SC RITES and SC RELIGIOUS, Instruction *In edicendis normis*, on the language to be used in the recitation of divine office and the celebration of the "conventual" or "community" Mass among religious, 23 November 1965: AAS 57 (1965) 1010–13; Not 2 (1966) 84–87.*

791   In publishing the norms for the language to be used in the recitation of the divine office in choir, in common, or in private, the Second Vatican Council had in mind both the preservation of the long-standing tradition of church Latin and the promotion of the spiritual good of all those who are officially deputed for this prayer or who take part in it. For this reason, it deemed it fitting to grant permission for the use of the vernacular in certain circumstances and to certain well-determined categories of persons.

          Thereupon, a number of petitions were addressed to the Holy See requesting that the norms of the Sacred Council in this regard be more precisely determined and that the use of the vernacular be permitted also to clerics, even in the choral

---

    [a]   See DOL 108 no. 764.

    [3]   See SC art. 22, §§ 1 and 2 [DOL 1 no. 22].

    [4]   See SC 40, 2 [DOL 1 no. 40].

    *   English text from the Congregations, Vatican Polyglot Press, 1966.

recitation of the divine office, in special circumstances either of place or of pastoral activities confided to some communities.

Having carefully considered these petitions, the Sacred Congregation of Rites, the Sacred Congregation of Religious, and "The Council for the Proper Implementation of the Constitution on Sacred Liturgy" have, by common consent, made the following decisions in order to establish a suitable uniformity and to provide well-defined norms.

I. CLERICAL RELIGIOUS INSTITUTES BOUND BY THE OBLIGATION OF THE CHOIR

1.   Clerical religious institutes "bound by the obligation of the choir" must recite   792
the divine office in choir in Latin, according to the prescriptions of art. 101, § 1 of the Constitution on the Sacred Liturgy and of no. 85 of the Instruction of 26 September 1964 for the proper implementation of the same Constitution.[a]

2.   Nevertheless, by special disposition, provision is to be made for monasteries   793
which are located in missionary countries and which are made up for the greater part of native members to be permitted to use the vernacular according to the sense of art. 40 of the Constitution.[b]

3.   The competent authority for the permission mentioned in the foregoing para-   794
graph is the Sacred Congregation of Religious.

II. CLERICAL RELIGIOUS INSTITUTES NOT BOUND BY THE OBLIGATION OF THE CHOIR

4.   Clerical religious institutes not bound by the obligation of the choir may recite   795
in common those parts of the divine office in the vernacular in which the lay religious, by virtue of the constitutions, are also bound to take part.

5.   The right to decide on the use of the vernacular in the parts of the divine office   796
mentioned in the preceding paragraph, belongs to the general chapter or, after the mind of members has been ascertained, to the general council of the institute.

6.   When, however, a decision of this kind involves a change in the constitutions,   797
it must be approved by the Sacred Congregation of Religious in the case of institutes of pontifical right, or by the local Ordinaries in the case of congregations of diocesan right (see CIC can. 495, 2).

III. CLERICAL RELIGIOUS COMMUNITIES ENGAGED IN THE PASTORAL MINISTRY IN PARISHES, SHRINES, OR CHURCHES ATTENDED BY LARGE NUMBERS OF THE FAITHFUL

7.   Clerical religious communities, even those bound by the obligation of the   798
choir, which are engaged in the service of a parish, a shrine, or a church attended by large numbers of the faithful, may use the vernacular for those parts of the divine office which, for pastoral reasons, they recite together with the people.

8.   The following are to decide on the granting of this permission: 799

   a.   the local Ordinary, with the assent of the major religious superior and the approval of the Sacred Congregation of Religious in the case of a community bound by the obligation of the choir;

   b.   the local Ordinary with the assent of the major religious superior, in the case of a community which is not bound by the obligation of the choir.

---

   [a]   See DOL 1 no. 101 and DOL 23 no. 377.

   [b]   See DOL 1 no. 40.

IV. NUNS

800   9.   Nuns may request permission to recite the divine office in the vernacular even in choir.

In those monasteries, however, in which, according to their own traditional usage, the divine office is recited solemnly and Gregorian chant is especially cultivated, the Latin language is to be preserved as far as possible.

801   10.   In particular, permission is to be granted to monasteries which are located in missionary countries and which are composed for the greater part of native members, to use the vernacular.

802   11.   Where Latin is retained in the choral recitation of the divine office, it is permitted nevertheless to read the lessons in the vernacular.

803   12.   The competent authority for permitting the use of the vernacular in the choral recitation of the divine office for nuns is the Sacred Congregation of Religious. The petition is to be made by the chapter of the monastery with the consent of the local Ordinary or, if the monastery is under the jurisdiction of the order, of the religious superior.

804   13.   Nuns who are not present at the choral recitation may use the vernacular when reciting the divine office alone.

V. LAY RELIGIOUS INSTITUTES

805   14.   For lay communities or institutes of the state of perfection, whether of men or of women, the competent superior may grant, in accordance with the prescriptions of art. 101, 2 of the Constitution on the Sacred Liturgy,ᶜ that the vernacular be used in the recitation of the divine office, even in choir.

806   15.   The competent superior is the general chapter of the institute or, after the members of the institute have been duly consulted, the general council.

807   16.   When, however, a decision of this kind involves a change in the constitutions, it must be approved by the Sacred Congregation of Religious in the case of institutes of pontifical right or by the local Ordinaries in the case of congregations of diocesan right (see CIC can. 495, 2).

VI. THE LANGUAGE TO BE USED IN THE "CONVENTUAL" MASS

808   17.   Clerical religious institutes bound by the obligation of the choir, in the "conventual" Mass:

a.   are bound to retain the Latin language, following the same reasoning as given above for the divine office (nos. 1–2); the lessons however may be recited in the vernacular;

b.   may use the vernacular, within the limits laid down by the competent territorial authority, when the religious community is engaged in the pastoral ministry in some parish, shrine, or church attended by large numbers of the faithful and the "conventual" Mass is celebrated for the convenience of the faithful.

809   18.   Nuns, according to what has been laid down for the recitation of the divine office in choir (nos. 9–11), may either retain the Latin language or may use the vernacular, within the limits determined by the competent territorial authority.

ᶜ   See DOL 1 no. 101.

VII. THE LANGUAGE TO BE USED IN THE CELEBRATION OF THE "COMMUNIY" MASS, IN CLERICAL RELIGIOUS INSTITUTES NOT BOUND BY THE OBLIGATION OF THE CHOIR AND IN LAY RELIGIOUS INSTITUTES EITHER OF MEN OR OF WOMEN

19. Clerical religious institutes not bound by the obligation of the choir may, in the celebration of the "community" Mass, use the vernacular in addition to Latin, within the limits set down by the competent territorial authority, several times a week (for example, two or three times).   810

20. The "community" Mass, as it is called, for lay religious institutes of men or women may be habitually celebrated in the vernacular, within the limits laid down by the competent territorial authority.   811

Provision should be made, however, for the members of these institutes to be able to recite or sing together in Latin also the parts of the Ordinary or the Proper which pertain to them (see SC art. 54).[d]

The Supreme Pontiff in an audience granted to His Eminence Cardinal Arcadio M. Larraona, Prefect of the Sacred Congregation of Rites, benignly approved and, by his authority, confirmed and ordered to be published this present Instruction prepared by common consent by the Sacred Congregation of Rites, by the Sacred Congregation of Religious, and by the "Council for the Implementation of the Constitution on the Sacred Liturgy," determining likewise that it should become effective on 6 February 1966, Septuagesima Sunday.

115. CONSILIUM, **Communication** *Per Litteras Apostolicas* to presidents of the conferences of bishops, on norms for the translation of the Mass of the Jubilee, 21 January 1966: Not 2 (1966) 43.

By the Apostolic Letter *Mirificus eventus* Pope Paul VI proclaimed an extraordinary Jubilee that is to be celebrated from 1 January to 29 May 1966.[a]   812

By order of the Pope, the Congregation of Rites has prepared and promulgated a proper Mass that brings out more clearly the purpose established for the Jubilee.

The *editio typica* of this Mass, published by the Vatican Polyglot Press, provides texts for both Ordinary Time and the Easter season, with proper general intercessions and preface, and with chants taken from the *Graduale simplex* or set to simple melodies.

In order that this Mass may be put to use even in the vernacular, Pope Paul VI makes these concessions:

1. In regions sharing a common language the individual conferences of bishops are empowered to adopt the vernacular translation properly prepared by a joint commission without obligation in this instance of obtaining confirmation of the text from the Consilium.   813

2. Other conferences of bishops are to see to the preparation of an accurate and suitable translation. They are to give the approval for the translation and the permission for its use, in this instance without confirmation of the text by the Consilium.   814

---

d   See DOL 1 no. 54.

a   See DOL 484.

▶   32.   CONSILIUM, Letter *L'heureux développement* to presidents of the conferences of
            bishops, on the reform of the liturgy, 25 January 1966.

116. PAUL VI, Address to participants in an international congress on the
study of Latin, excerpt on the pastoral advantage of the vernacular in the
liturgy, 16 April 1966: AAS 58 (1966) 359–362; Not 2 (1966) 156.

815   [. . .] In this cause [of Latin] the Church exercises its diligence and efforts and
will continue to do so. The Second Ecumenical Vatican Council in its wise decrees
granted the use of the vernacular in liturgical rites whenever considerations of
pastoral advantage required.[a] Since by their nature words express thoughts, it is not
right to make language more important than the mind's understanding, especially
when it comes to divine worship and conversation with God. Rather, no matter
what the language, it must be made to serve the thoughts of the mind and the
affections of the heart, whether spoken by sacred ministers or by the people calling
on God's name and praising him. The words of St. Augustine are as clear in their
meaning as they are telling in their support on this point: "I would rather be
reproved by the grammarians than not be understood by the people" (*Enarr. in Ps.
138*: PL 37, 1796). "In Latin 'Jesus' is *Christus salvator*. It is not the grammarian's
question about the Latin style that matters, but the Christian's question about the
truth" (*Serm.* 299: PL 38, 1371).

▶   8.   PONTIFICAL CENTRAL COMMISSION FOR COORDINATING POSTCON-
           CILIAR WORK AND INTERPRETING THE DECREES OF VATICAN
           COUNCIL II, Reply to a query on the Decree *Christus Dominus* no. 38, § 4, 10 June
           1966.

117. PAUL VI, Concession, allowing, *ad experimentum*, use of the vernacular
in the canon of the Mass and in ordinations, 31 January 1967: Not 3 (1967)
154.

816   At the request of many conferences of bishops, Pope Paul VI on 31 January
1967 has graciously granted use of the vernacular, *ad experimentum*, in the canon of
the Mass and in the conferral of holy orders (the essential sacramental form being
excepted, should this seem advisable to the conference of bishops).

             This concession received confirmation through the second Instruction on the
liturgy of the Congregation of Rites, 4 May 1967, no. 28.[a] Its use is subject to the
following conditions.

817   a.   The conference of bishops is to prepare the text of the translation for these
two items, approve it, and submit it to the Consilium for confirmation (SC art. 36, §
3).[b]

---

[a]   See DOL 1 no. 36.

[a]   See DOL 39 no. 474.

[b]   See DOL 1 no. 36.

b. Besides the vernacular text, editions of the Missal and Pontifical are re-   818
quired to contain the Latin text (see the Instruction of 26 September 1964, no. 57;ᶜ
the Decree of the Congregation of Rites on publishing liturgical books, 27 January
1966, no. 5ᵈ).

c. A decree of publication is to be promulgated and made effective only after   819
the Holy See's approval, that is, confirmation, of the translated text (Instruction
Inter Oecumenici no. 31).ᵉ

▶   1.   VATICAN COUNCIL II, Constitution on the Liturgy *Sacrosanctum Concilium*, 4
         December 1963:

         art. 22:   Authority of bishops to regulate the liturgy [no.
                                22].
                23:             Authority of conferences of bishops [no. 23].

▶   39. SC RITES (Consilium), Instruction (second) *Tres abhinc annos*, 4 May 1967:

         no. 28:   Use of the vernacular.

▶   41. CONSILIUM, Letter *Dans sa récente allocution* to presidents of the conferences of
         bishops, on issues of the reform, 21 June 1967:

         no. 7:   Translation of the canon and rites of ordination
                               [486].

118. CONSILIUM, **Communication** *Aussitôt après* of A. Bugnini to presidents of the conferences of bishops and, for their information, presidents of
national liturgical commissions, on the translation of the Roman Canon, 10
August 1967: Not 3 (1967) 326–327 (French; issued in six major languages).*

As soon as the Holy See allowed the use of the vernacular to include the canon   820
of the Mass, the "Consilium" asked study groups from the various commissions
and the national liturgical commissions to prepare the necessary translations. The
work of translation and revision necessarily requires time, dealing as it does with so
serious and important a liturgical document, touching the very heart of the Mass.

Moreover, it is the desire of the Holy See that the work proceed in such a way
that the different translations of the Roman Canon correspond among themselves.
Thus, as far as possible, a certain uniformity would be preserved, at least in this
very sacred text of the celebration of the eucharist.

At the present time, in order that the work develop with all necessary calm and
in keeping with the directives already given and that the clergy should not have to
wait too long for the practical application of this generally awaited decree and
pursuant to instructions received from higher authority, it is my pleasure, in the
name of His Eminence, the Most Reverend Giacomo Cardinal Lercaro, President of

---

ᶜ   See DOL 23 no. 349.

ᵈ   See DOL 134 no. 923.

ᵉ   See DOL 23 no. 323.

*   English text from the Consilium.

the Consilium, together with the other competent departments of the Holy See, to communicate to Your Grace, the following.[R1]

821   1.   The version which is in the process of preparation, the sole version for the languages spoken in several countries, is to render faithfully the text of the Roman Canon, without variations, omissions, or insertions which would make it different from the Latin text.

822   2.   The language is to be that normally used in liturgical texts, avoiding exaggerated classical and modern forms.

823   3.   The style is to display a certain rhythm, making the text easy to speak and sing.

824   4.   Since it is expected that a considerable period will be needed for the revision and confirmation of the versions prepared by the episcopal conferences, and since, while there is no official translation, provision should be made to supply the necessary uniformity between the various texts, the episcopal conferences may, *in the meantime*, approve and permit one of the translations already in use with the permission of ecclesiastical authority.

There is to be no more than a single translation adopted by any nation during the interim period.

825   5.   It is the desire of the Holy Father that missals, whether they are for feast days or daily use, in complete or partial editions, should always carry the Latin text next to the vernacular version, in double columns, or facing pages, and not [be] in pamphlet form or separate books. This is in accordance with the Instruction *Inter Oecumenici* of 26 September 1964, nos. 57 and 98[b] and with the Decree of the Sacred Congregation of Rites *De editionibus librorum liturgicorum* of 27 January 1966, no. 5.[c]

I hope that the complex and delicate work, preparing and revising the translation of the Roman Canon, so worthy of respect, will lead to a more perfect presentation of the text, a better aid to understanding, and be of greater advantage to the devotion of the faithful.

119. SC RELIGIOUS, **Rescript** (Capuchins), to the minister general, on the vernacular in the divine office, 20 September 1967.*

826   This Congregation, on the basis of a recent, favorable decision of Pope Paul VI, graciously grants the power you have earnestly requested: you may permit your communities to recite the divine office in the vernacular whenever lay religious take part in the recitation.

[R1]   The norms in this letter in part amend the precepts in the letter of the president of the Consilium, 21 June 1967 [DOL 41] and allow adoption of a provisory translation of the Roman Canon; see Not 3 (1967) 326.

[b]   See DOL 23 nos. 349 and 390.

[c]   See DOL 134 no. 923.

*   Text, CommRel 47 (1968) 64.

You are charged, however, with ensuring that all interpret this power and the use of this concession in conformity with the mind and the precept in the Pope's letter of 6 June 1967. By this letter he authorized the Congregation of Religious to grant use of the vernacular in altogether special circumstances, namely:

1.   "This indult may in no way be viewed as rescinding the Instruction *In edicendis*   827
normis, 23 November 1965.[a] The norms of this Instruction are in complete harmony with the prescriptions of Vatican Council II, a point the Pope has strongly repeated in the Letter *Sacrificium laudis*, 15 August 1966."[b]

2.   "Monasteries and religious institutes that respect these norms and cultivate the   828
chant proper to the Roman Church (see SC art. 116),[c] are to be highly commended and strongly encouraged in their commitment."

3.   "With a view to preserving intact in the Church its priceless heritage of liturgi-   829
cal prayer, it is supremely desirable that communities receiving permission to recite the divine office in the vernacular make use of Latin for the celebration of the office in Gregorian chant."

4.   You are empowered to grant the present indult "provided the communities   830
themselves request the permission by the free and secret vote of all the members."[d]

120. CONSILIUM, **Communication** *Instantibus pluribus* to presidents of the national liturgical commissions, on norms for translation of the *Graduale simplex*, 23 January 1968: Not 4 (1968) 10.

At the request of many conferences of bishops, the Consilium has decided to   831
declare the following on translation of the *Graduale simplex* into the vernacular.

1.   The conferences of bishops have the power to allow use of the vernacular for   832
all or some of the chants contained in the *Graduale simplex* and to give approval to a text for such chants, in keeping with the Constitution on the Liturgy art. 38[a] and the Instruction *Inter Oecumenici*, 26 September 1964, nos. 28–31 and 40.[b]

2.   Every formulary for a Mass or part of a Mass is to retain the psalm, antiphon,   833
and type of chant that correspond to the tenor of the liturgical rite, as given in the *Graduale simplex* (see Instruction *Musicam sacram*, 15 March 1967, nos. 6 and 9).[c]
     In particular:
     a.   For the psalm verses it is permissible to use a vernacular translation of the psalms approved by competent authority; it should, however, be a translation

---

     [a]   See DOL 114.

     [b]   See DOL 421.

     [c]   See DOL 1 no. 116.

     [d]   CommRel 66 notes a similar concession to the Dominicans, 5 July 1967 (*Analecta S. Ordinis Fratrum Praedicatorum* 38 [1967] 302), without the requirement of lay religious taking part in the office.

     [a]   See DOL 1 no. 38.

     [b]   See DOL 23 nos. 320–323 and 332.

     [c]   DOL 508 nos. 4127 and 4130.

suited to singing. If such a translation has its own division of verses, this may be kept.

b. The texts of antiphons, even those taken from the psalter, sometimes need modification: to achieve fully the meaning appropriate to a liturgical season or particular feast; to ensure the people's understanding of the text; to match the rhythmical and vocal requirements of chant in the vernacular (see Instruction *Musicam sacram* no. 54).[d]

c. The types of chant in the *Graduale simplex* (namely, either with the antiphon repeated after the psalm verse or a short response terminating the melody of a versicle) may be adapted to the style of music and song typical of individual peoples. But any sort of secular or profane melody is excluded.

834   3. Sometimes the texts of antiphons, of the psalm verse, or of the psalm itself as given in the *Graduale simplex* may create problems, with the result that a different choice of texts seems preferable:

— either because the text in the translation being used presents pastoral problems;

— or because it seems advisable to use collections of psalms and antiphons that may already be in use, familiar to many, and well accepted.

In such cases the conference of bishops may choose other texts, but in a way consistent with the principles set forth in the Introduction[e] of the *Graduale simplex*.[f]

121. PAUL VI, **Address** to Latinists, excerpt on Latin and the vernacular in the Church, 26 April 1968: Not 4 (1968) 144–145.

835   Today in the presence of this assembly of men of great wisdom, we desire to repeat: the study of Latin must still be cultivated in our times and above all in seminaries and houses for the religious formation of the young. In no way is it permissible to ignore this language if there is to be any genuine attempt to create keen minds in the young, to train them in humane letters, to probe and reflect on the words of the Fathers, and above all to prepare them to share fully in the ancient treasures of the liturgy. Without the knowledge of Latin something is altogether missing from a higher, fully rounded education — and in particular with regard to theology and liturgy. The people of our times expect such an education of their priests and the Fathers of Vatican Council II repeatedly endorsed it, in the Decree *Optatam totius* on priestly formation, in the Constitution on the Liturgy (art. 16),[a] and in other conciliar norms.

Because of the power and effectiveness of Latin to develop the mind and to open the way to the more advanced fields of study, we have the strong desire that it continue to receive the attention it deserves. At the same time the whole world knows that, in willing and eager obedience to the wise norms of Vatican Council II, we ourself have taken every step to have all the modern languages introduced into the liturgy. No lack of regard for Latin has moved us in this direction, but rather the keen awareness of our own pastoral responsibility and a deep sense of the need for

---

d   See DOL 508 no. 4175.

e   See DOL 533.

f   These norms were confirmed by Pope Paul VI, 23 January 1968.

a   See DOL 1 no. 16.

pastors to provide plentifully the food of God's word contained in the liturgy. But it must also be presented in such a way as to be understood and in a way that will lead Christ's faithful to experience the loveliness of the liturgical rites and to take part in them eagerly and intently.

We want to say something very plainly to those whose shallow minds or unthinking passion for the new lead them to the idea that the Latin language must be totally spurned by the Latin Church. To them we say that it is absolutely clear that Latin must be held in high honor and especially for the excellent and serious reasons that we have mentioned. On the other hand, we also address those who, out of an empty aestheticism that goes too far in seeking to preserve what is old or out of a prejudice against anything new, have bitterly denounced the changes recently introduced. To them we say that we must clearly never forget that Latin must be subordinate to the pastoral ministry and is not an end in itself. Any defense, therefore, of the rights this language has acquired in the Church must avoid at all costs impeding or constricting the renewal of pastoral service mandated by the Council. In this matter, too, the highest law must be the well-being of souls.

836

122. SECRETARIAT OF STATE, **Letter** of Cardinal A. Cicognani to Bernard Kaul, OCSO, Abbot of the Cistercian monastery of Hauterive (Posieux, Canton of Fribourg, Switzerland), on Latin in the liturgy, 14 June 1968.*

Through your letter of 21 May 1968 you requested of Pope Paul VI that "with his blessing he entrust to the monks of Hauterive as their particular apostolic task celebration of the liturgy in Latin and with the Gregorian chant, while preserving for the divine office the structure provided for it in the Rule of St. Benedict and maintained up to the present by the monastic orders."

837

I am happy to inform you that your wish has been so welcome to the Pope that not only does he wholeheartedly accede to it and commend it, but also regards it as especially worthy of sons of St. Benedict.

Nothing could be more appreciated by the Pope than to see you take on as your proper apostolate a trust that he regards so highly: the fervent and vital preservation in the Church of the monastic liturgy, that priceless heritage bequeathed by our forefathers, which in the course of so many centuries has yielded such rich results for devotion, the beauty of worship, and holy joy.

Grateful for the comfort that your wish brings him, the Pope willingly grants the apostolic blessing you have requested. May it be for you and your monks the pledge of abundant heavenly graces and may it make your apostolate of celebrating the liturgy in Latin and with the Gregorian chant advantageous for the Church and a source of the fruits of holiness.

---

* Text, DocCath 65 (1968) 1837–38 (French translation from Latin original).

123. CONSILIUM, **Instruction** *Comme le prévoit*, on the translation of liturgical texts for celebrations with a congregation, 25 January 1969: Not 5 (1969) 3–12 (French; issued in six major languages).*

838   1.   The Constitution on the Sacred Liturgy foresees that many Latin texts of the Roman liturgy must be translated into different languages (art. 36). Although many of them have already been translated, the work of translation is not drawing to a close. New texts have been edited or prepared for the renewal of the liturgy. Above all, after sufficient experiment and passage of time, all translations will need review.

839   2.   In accordance with art. 36 of the Constitution *Sacrosanctum Concilium*[a] and no. 40 of the Instruction of the Congregation of Rites *Inter Oecumenici*,[b] the work of translation of liturgical texts is thus laid down: It is the duty of the episcopal conferences to decide which texts are to be translated, to prepare or review the translations, to approve them, and "after approval, that is, confirmation, by the Holy See" to promulgate them.

When a common language is spoken in several different countries, international commissions should be appointed by the conferences of bishops who speak the same language to make one text for all (letter of Cardinal Lercaro to the presidents of episcopal conferences, dated 16 October 1964).[c]

840   3.   Although these translations are the responsibility of the competent territorial authority of each country, it seems desirable to observe common principles of procedure, especially for texts of major importance, in order to make confirmation by the Apostolic See easier and to achieve greater unity of practice.

841   4.   The Consilium has therefore thought fit in this declaration to lay down, in common and nontechnical terms, some of the more important theoretical and practical principles for the guidance of all who are called upon to prepare, to approve, or to confirm liturgical translations.

I. GENERAL PRINCIPLES

842   5.   A liturgical text, inasmuch as it is a ritual sign, is a medium of spoken communication. It is, first of all, a sign perceived by the senses and used by men to communicate with each other. But to believers who celebrate the sacred rites a word is itself a "mystery." By spoken words Christ himself speaks to his people and the people, through the Spirit in the Church, answer their Lord.[d]

843   6.   The purpose of liturgical translations is to proclaim the message of salvation to believers and to express the prayer of the Church to the Lord: "Liturgical translations have become . . . the voice of the Church" (address of Paul VI to participants in the congress on translations of liturgical texts, 10 November 1965).[e] To achieve this end, it is not sufficient that a liturgical translation merely reproduce the expressions and ideas of the original text. Rather it must faithfully communicate to a

---

*   English text from the Consilium.

[a]   See DOL 1 no. 36.

[b]   See DOL 23 no. 332.

[c]   See DOL 108.

[d]   See DOL 1 no. 33.

[e]   DOL 113 no. 787.

given people, and in their own language, that which the Church by means of this given text originally intended to communicate to another people in another time. A faithful translation, therefore, cannot be judged on the basis of individual words: the total context of this specific act of communication must be kept in mind, as well as the literary form proper to the respective language.

7. Thus, in the case of liturgical communication, it is necessary to take into account not only the message to be conveyed, but also the speaker, the audience, and the style. Translations, therefore, must be faithful to the art of communication in all its various aspects, but especially in regard to the message itself, in regard to the audience for which it is intended, and in regard to the manner of expression.   844

8. Even if in spoken communication the message cannot be separated from the manner of speaking, the translator should give first consideration to the meaning of the communication.   845

9. To discover the true meaning of a text, the translator must follow the scientific methods of textual study as used by experts. This part of the translator's task is obvious. A few points may be added with reference to liturgical texts: 846

10. a. If need be, a critical text of the passage must first be established so that the translation can be done from the original or at least from the best available text.   847

11. b. Latin terms must be considered in the light of their uses — historical or cultural, Christian or liturgical. For example, the early Christian use of *devotio* differs from its use in classical or more modern times. The Latin *oratio* means in English not an oration (one of its senses in classical Latin) but a *prayer* — and this English word bears different meanings, such as prayer of praise or prayer in general or prayer of petition. *Pius* and *pietas* are very inadequately rendered in English as *pious* and *piety*. In one case the Latin *salus* may mean *salvation* in the theological sense; elsewhere it may mean *safety, health* (physical health or total health), or *well-being*. *Sarx-caro* is inadequately rendered in English as *flesh*. *Doulos-servus* and *famula* are inadequately rendered in English by *slave, servant, handmaid*. The force of an image or metaphor must also be considered, whether it is rare or common, living or worn out.   848

12. c. The translator must always keep in mind that the "unit of meaning" is not the individual word but the whole passage. The translator must therefore be careful that the translation is not so analytical that it exaggerates the importance of particular phrases while it obscures or weakens the meaning of the whole. Thus, in Latin, the piling up of *ratam, rationabilem, acceptabilem* may increase the sense of invocation. In other tongues, a succession of adjectives may actually weaken the force of the prayer. The same is true of *beatissima Virgo* or *beata et gloriosa* or the routine addition of *sanctus* or *beatus* to a saint's name, or the too casual use of superlatives. Understatement in English is sometimes the more effective means of emphasis.   849

13. d. To keep the correct signification, words and expressions must be used in their proper historical, social, and ritual meanings. Thus, in prayers for Lent, *ieiunium* now has the sense of *lenten* observance, both liturgical and ascetic; the meaning is not confined to abstinence from food. *Tapeinos-humilis* originally had "class" overtones not present in the English *humble* or even *lowly*. Many of the phrases of approach to the Almighty were originally adapted from forms of address to the sovereign in the courts of Byzantium and Rome. It is necessary to study how far an attempt should be made to offer equivalents in modern English for such words as *quaesumus, dignare, clementissime, maiestas*, and the like.   850

851   14. The accuracy and value of a translation can only be assessed in terms of the purpose of the communication. To serve the particular congregations who will use it, the following points should be observed in translating.

852   15. a. The language chosen should be that in "common" usage, that is, suited to the greater number of the faithful who speak it in everyday use, even "children and persons of small education" (Paul VI in the allocution cited).[f] However, the language should not be "common" in the bad sense, but "worthy of expressing the highest realities" (ibid.).[g] Moreover, the correct biblical or Christian meaning of certain words and ideas will always need explanation and instruction. Nevertheless no special literary training should be required of the people; liturgical texts should normally be intelligible to all, even to the less educated.[h] For example, *temptation* as a translation of *tentatio* in the Lord's Prayer is inaccurate and can only be misleading to people who are not biblical scholars. Similarly, *scandal* in the ordinary English sense of gossip is a misleading translation of the scriptural *scandalum*. Besides, liturgical texts must sometimes possess a truly poetic quality, but this does not imply the use of specifically "poetic diction."

853   16. b. Certain other principles should be observed so that a translation will be understood by the hearers in the same sense as the revealed truths expressed in the liturgy.

854   17. 1. When words are taken from the so-called sacral vocabulary now in use, the translator should consider whether the everyday common meaning of these words and phrases bears or can bear a Christian meaning. These phrases may carry a pre-Christian, quasi-Christian, Christian, or even anti-Christian meaning. The translator should also consider whether such words can convey the exact Christian liturgical action and manifestation of faith. Thus in the Greek Bible, the word *hieros* (*sacer*) was often avoided because of its connection with the pagan cults and instead the rarer word *hagios* (*sanctus*) was substituted. Another example. The proper meaning of the biblical *hesed-eleos-misericordia*, is not accurately expressed in English by *mercy* or *pity*. Again, the word *mereri* in classical Latin often signifies *to be worthy of something*, but in the language of the liturgy it carries a meaning very different from the ancient meaning: "I do something because of which I am worthy of a prize or a reward." In English the word *to deserve* when used by itself retains the stricter sense. A translation would lead to error if it did not consider this fact, for example, in translating *Quia quem meruisti portare* in the hymn *Regina caeli* as *Because you deserved to bear*. . . .

855   18. 2. It often happens that there is no word in common use that exactly corresponds to the biblical or liturgical sense of the term to be translated, as in the use of the biblical *iustitia*. The nearest suitable word must then be chosen which, through habitual use in various catechetical texts and in prayer, lends itself to take on the biblical and Christian sense intended by the liturgy. Such has been the evolution of the Greek word *doxa* and the Latin *gloria* when used to translate the Hebrew *kabod*. The expression *hominibus bonae voluntatis* literally translated as *to men of good will* (or *good will to men* in order to stress divine favor) will be misleading; no single English word or phrase will completely reflect the original Latin or the Greek which the Latin translates. Similarly in English there is no exact equivalent for *mysterium*. In English, *mystery* means something

f   DOL 113 no. 787.

g   DOL 113 no. 787.

h   See DOL 1 no. 34.

which cannot be readily explained or else a type of drama or fiction. Nor can the word *venerabilis* (as in *sanctas et venerabiles manus*) be translated as *venerable*, which nowadays means *elderly*.

19. 3. In many modern languages a biblical or liturgical language must be created   856
by use. This will be achieved rather by infusing a Christian meaning into common words than by importing uncommon or technical terms.

20. c. The prayer of the Church is always the prayer of some actual community,   857
assembled here and now. It is not sufficient that a formula handed down from some other time or region be translated verbatim, even if accurately, for liturgical use. The formula translated must become the genuine prayer of the congregation and in it each of its members should be able to find and express himself or herself.

21. A translation of the liturgy therefore often requires cautious adaptation. But   858
cases differ:

22. a. Sometimes a text can be translated word for word and keep the same   859
meaning as the original, for example, *pleni sunt caeli et terra gloria tua*.

23. b. Sometimes the metaphors must be changed to keep the true sense, as in   860
locum refrigerii in northern regions.

24. c. Sometimes the meaning of a text can no longer be understood, either   861
because it is contrary to modern Christian ideas (as in *terrena despicere* or *ut inimicos sanctae Ecclesiae humiliare digneris*) or because it has less relevance today (as in some phrases intended to combat Arianism) or because it no longer expresses the true original meaning "as in certain obsolete forms of lenten penance." In these cases, so long as the teaching of the Gospel remains intact, not only must inappropriate expressions be avoided, but others found which express a corresponding meaning in modern words. The greatest care must be taken that all translations are not only beautiful and suited to the contemporary mind, but express true doctrine and authentic Christian spirituality.

25. A particular form of expression and speech is required for spoken communica-   862
tion. In rendering any liturgical text, the translator must keep in mind the major importance of the spoken or rhetorical style or what might, by extension of the term, be called the literary genre. On this matter several things should be noted:

26. 1. The literary genre of every liturgical text depends first of all on the nature   863
of the ritual act signified in the words — acclamation or supplication, proclamation or praying, reading or singing. Each action requires its proper form of expression. Moreover a prayer differs as it is to be spoken by one person alone or by many in unison; whether it is in prose or in verse; spoken or sung. All these considerations affect not only the manner of delivery, but also the choice of words.

27. 2. A liturgical text is a "linguistic fact" designed for celebration. When it is in   864
written form (as is usually the case), it offers a stylistic problem for translators. Each text must therefore be examined to discover the significant elements proper to the genre, for example, in Roman prayers the formal structure, cursus, dignity, brevity, etc.

28. Among the separate elements are those which are essential and others which   865
are secondary and subsidiary. The essential elements, so far as is possible, should be

preserved in translation, sometimes intact, sometimes in equivalent terms. The general structure of the Roman prayers can be retained unchanged: the divine title, the motive of the petition, the petition itself, the conclusion. Others cannot be retained: the oratorical cursus, rhetorical-prose cadence.

866   29. It is to be noted that if any particular kind of quality is regarded as essential to a literary genre (for example, intelligibility of prayers when said aloud), this may take precedence over another quality less significant for communication (for example, verbal fidelity).

II. SOME PARTICULAR CONSIDERATIONS

867   30. Among liturgical texts, sacred Scripture has always held a special place because the Church recognizes in the sacred books the written voice of God (DV no. 9). The divine word has been transmitted to us under different historical forms or literary genres and the revelation communicated by the documents cannot be entirely divorced from these forms or genres. In the case of biblical translations intended for liturgical readings, the characteristics of speech or writing are proper to different modes of communication in the sacred books and should be preserved with special accuracy. This is particularly important in the translations of psalms and canticles.

868   31. Biblical translations in the Roman liturgy ought to conform "with the Latin liturgical text" (Instruction *Inter Oecumenici*, 26 September 1964, no. 40 a).[i] In no way should there be a paraphrasing of the biblical text, even if it is difficult to understand. Nor should words or explanatory phrases be inserted. All this is the task of catechesis and the homily.

869   32. In some cases it will be necessary that "suitable and accurate translations be made into the different languages from the original texts of the sacred books. And if, given the opportunity and the approval of church authority, these translations are produced in cooperation with the separated brethren as well, all Christians will be able to use them" (DV no. 22).[j] Translations approved for liturgical use should closely approximate the best versions in a particular language.

870   33. Some euchological and sacramental formularies like the consecratory prayers, the anaphoras, prefaces, exorcisms, and those prayers which accompany an action, such as the imposition of hands, the anointing, the signs of the cross, etc., should be translated integrally and faithfully, without variations, omissions, or insertions. These texts, whether ancient or modern, have a precise and studied theological elaboration. If the text is ancient, certain Latin terms present difficulties of interpretation because of their use and meaning, which are much different from their corresponding terms in modern language. The translation will therefore demand an astute handling and sometimes a paraphrasing, in order to render accurately the original pregnant meaning. If the text is a more recent one, the difficulty will be reduced considerably, given the use of terms and a style of language which are closer to modern concepts.

871   34. The prayers (opening prayer, prayer over the gifts, prayer after communion, and prayer over the people) from the ancient Roman tradition are succinct and abstract. In translation they may need to be rendered somewhat more freely while

---

i   DOL 23 no. 332.
j   DOL 14 no. 225.

conserving the original ideas. This can be done by moderately amplifying them or, if necessary, paraphrasing expressions in order to concretize them for the celebration and the needs of today. In every case pompous and superfluous language should be avoided.

35. All texts which are intended to be said aloud follow the laws proper to their delivery and, in the case of written texts, their literary genre. This applies especially to the acclamations where the act of acclaiming by voice is an essential element. It will be insufficient to translate only the exact meaning of an idea unless the text can also be expressed by sound and rhythm.

36. Particular care is necessary for texts which are to be sung.

    a. The form of singing which is proper to every liturgical action and to each of its parts should be retained (antiphon alternated with the psalm, responsory, etc. See Instruction *Musicam sacram*, 5 March 1967, nos. 6 and 9).[k]

    b. Regarding the psalms, in addition to the division into versicles as given in Latin, a division into stanzas may be particularly desirable if a text is used which is well known by the people or common to other Churches.

    c. The responses (versicles, responsories) and antiphons, even though they come from Scripture, become part of the liturgy and enter into a new literary form. In translating them it is possible to give them a verbal form which, while preserving their full meaning, is more suitable for singing and harmonizes them with the liturgical season or a special feast. Examples of such adaptations which include minor adaptations of the original text are numerous in ancient antiphonaries.

    d. When the content of an antiphon or psalm creates a special difficulty, the episcopal conferences may authorize the choice of another text which meets the same needs of the liturgical celebration and the particular season or feast.

    e. If these same texts are likewise intended for recitation without singing, the translation should be suitable for that purpose.

37. Liturgical hymns lose their proper function unless they are rendered in an appropriate verse rhythm, suitable for singing by the people. A literal translation of such texts is therefore generally out of the question. It follows that hymns very often need a new rendering made according to the musical and choral laws of the popular poetry in each language.

III. COMMITTEES FOR TRANSLATING

38. To make the translations, committees should be formed of experts in the various disciplines, namely, liturgy, Scripture, theology, pastoral study, and especially languages and literature, and, according to circumstances, music. If several committees are concerned with the different parts of liturgical texts, their work should be coordinated.

39. Before a text is promulgated, sufficient opportunity should be allowed for experiment by selected congregations in different places. An *ad interim* translation should be properly approved by the liturgical commission of the conference of bishops.

872

873

874

875

876

---

   k See DOL 508 nos. 4127 and 4130.

877 40. Close collaboration should be established between the committee of experts and the authorities who must approve the translations (such as a conference of bishops), so that:

a. the same people, for the most part, share in the work from beginning to end;

b. when the authority asks for emendations, these should be made by the experts themselves and a new text then submitted for the judgment of the authority. Otherwise, it should give the task to a new committee which is more suitable, but also composed of qualified people.

878 41. Those countries which have a common language should employ a "mixed commission" to prepare a single text. There are many advantages to such a procedure: in the preparation of a text the most competent experts are able to cooperate; a unique possibility for communication is created among these people; participation of the people is made easier. In this joint venture between countries speaking the same language it is important to distinguish between the texts which are said by one person and heard by the congregation and those intended to be recited or sung by all. Uniformity is obviously more important for the latter category than for the former.

879 42. In those cases where a single text is prepared for a large number of countries, the text should satisfy the "different needs and mentalities of each region" (letter of Cardinal Lercaro to the presidents of episcopal conferences, 16 October 1964).[1] Therefore:

1. Each episcopal conference sharing the same language should examine the translation program or the first draft of a text.

2. Meanwhile, to avoid anxiety and unnecessary delay for priests and people, the coordinating secretariat should provide a provisional text which, with the consent of the proper authority (see no. 39), can be published and printed as an *ad interim* text in each country. It is preferable that the same provisional text be used everywhere since the result will contribute to a better final text for all the countries.

3. Each of the countries will receive the definitive text at the same time. If a particular episcopal conference requires a change or substitution for specific local needs, it should propose the change to the "mixed commission," which must first agree. This is necessary in order to have a single text which remains substantially unchanged and under the supervision of the "mixed commission."

4. Each country can publish texts which are provisional as well as texts which are officially approved by the Holy See, but ought to contribute, on a prorated basis according to the extent it publishes, to the expenses of the "mixed commission," which must pay the periti and bishops of the commission. National liturgical commissions should make prior arrangements with the secretariat regarding these publications.

5. In the publications of works from the "mixed commissions," the appropriate notice should appear on the first page: "A provisional text prepared by the 'mixed commission' . . . ." or "Text approved by the 'mixed commission' . . . and confirmed by the Consilium for the Implementation of the Constitution on the Sacred Liturgy." If a change or substitution is desirable in an individual country, as indicated in no. 42, 3, a further notice is necessary, namely: "with adaptations authorized by the episcopal conference of . . . and the 'mixed commission'."

---

[1] DOL 108 no. 764.

43. Texts translated from another language are clearly not sufficient for the cele- 880
bration of a fully renewed liturgy. The creation of new texts will be necessary. But
translation of texts transmitted through the tradition of the Church is the best
school and discipline for the creation of new texts so "that any new forms adopted
should in some way grow organically from forms already in existence" (SC art.
23).m

124. CONSILIUM, **Declaration** *Circa Instructionem*, on *ad interim* translations
of liturgical texts, March 1969: Not 5 (1969) 68.

The Instruction on the preparation of vernacular translations, published in the 881
preceding issue of *Notitiae* and transmitted to presidents of the conferences of bishops and to presidents of national liturgical commissions and of joint commissions,
has given rise to a query on interim texts: must these be transmitted to the Consilium before they are promulgated.

The Instruction speaks of this matter twice in no. 42, which *seemed* to state that
such texts should be promulgated under the *sole* responsibility of the liturgical
commission of the conference of bishops.a

The text of the Instruction is not clear: 1. in regard to the power seemingly
given to liturgical commissions; 2. in regard to confirmation of the provisional texts
by the Consilium.

As to point 1: the decision of the Central Commission for Interpretation of 882
Conciliar Decrees, reported in *Notitiae*, 1968, 364 (see AAS 60 [1968] 361) remains in
force: the conference cannot delegate to the liturgical commission the task of preparing vernacular translations and *approving them* for *ad interim* use.b Hence at least the
executive council of the conference president ought to approve them.

As to point 2: what was laid down and published in *Notitiae*, 1968, 365 remains 883
in force: even interim translations must be sent to the Consilium for confirmation
after the national liturgical commission *and* at least the executive committee of the
conference of bishops has approved them.R2

At issue are texts and formularies, often extremely important, for public and
official use in liturgical celebration; hence the concern that they exhibit all the
requisites for completeness and accuracy. Furthermore, in the absence of approval

---

m   DOL 1 no. 23.

a   See DOL 123 [no. 879].

b   See DOL 8.

R2   Query: It has been asked how long the trial period for a vernacular texts granted *ad interim* can be
extended. Reply: Concessions of this kind are given by the Consilium at the request of a conference of
bishops when some problem may arise in obtaining the necessary approval of a text that must be given in
a plenary meeting of the bishops. This is the case mainly when the bishops meet only yearly or reside at a
great distance from each other and are without any means of ready communication. The same concession
is sometimes made in the case of texts of special importance, in order that opinions useful for making a
final translation may be gathered on the basis of experience. In such instances the national liturgical
commission prepares a text and with the consent of the president of the conference of bishops petitions
the Consilium for *approval ad interim* of the text. But within *six months* or at most *within a year* this text must be
submitted for the approval of the conference of bishops, then presented to the Consilium for
confirmation. In the case of those conferences involved in completely special circumstances, provision will
be made by means of particular law: Not 4 (1968) 365.

by the whole conference of bishops, the confirmation by the Consilium stands as the seal and guarantee of unity and harmony.

125. SC DIVINE WORSHIP, Declaration *Plures liturgicae*, on the translation of new liturgical texts, 15 September 1969: Not 5 (1969) 333–334.

884   Several liturgical commissions, charged with the translation of liturgical texts, have asked this Congregation whether the texts of the reformed rites printed or to be printed must be carried in their entirety or whether they may be shortened when the translations are being done.

The Constitution on the Liturgy art. 63,b contains a clear reply to this query, at least regarding the rites for the sacraments: "Those who draw up these rituals or particular collections of rites must not leave out the introductory instructions for the individual rites in the Roman Ritual, whether the instructions are pastoral and rubrical or have some special social bearing."[a]

The same point applies to the other books: official editions, that is, those for use by the priest or qualified minister, must contain everything given in the Latin *editio typica*; this law does not apply to the booklets or pamphlets intended for use by the faithful.[R3]

---

[a]   DOL 1 no. 63.

[R3]   Everywhere the work of liturgical renewal is advancing apace. Diocesan commissions together with pastors are engaged in putting into practice the pastoral principles established for the renewal; national commissions are hard at work translating the liturgical books into the vernacular. This process of translation has given rise to several queries that have been submitted for decision to the Congregation for Divine Worship.

1.   Query: Must the General Instruction of the Roman Missal and of the Liturgy of the Hours as well as the Introductions (*Praenotanda*) for each of the rites be included in editions of liturgical texts? Reply: *Yes*. The Introductions and Instructions are prerequisites for understanding the spirit of the reformed rites; they are indispensable for grasping the specific theological and practical value of the changes, additions, and variants.

2.   Query: Must rubrics be printed? Reply: *Yes*. All rubrics must be printed. They may be elaborated, but may not be compressed. For they remain a support for the entire structure of the liturgical service.

3.   Query: May the Latin Appendix of the Roman Missal be printed separately or must it be printed as part of the vernacular edition of the missal? Reply: *The Latin Appendix must be printed as part of the vernacular edition*. A priest visiting or passing through a country whose language he does not know can then, when using the local missal, readily find the Latin text and celebrate Mass. A separate publication containing the Latin Appendix would easily be lost and with it the purpose the Appendix serves. The Latin Appendix is not to be confused with the *Missale parvum*, which contains a fuller collection of Masses.

4.   Query: May the Latin Appendix of the *Missale Romanum* or the *Missale parvum* be translated? Reply: *No*. The reason is clear from the purpose of the Appendix already mentioned. There is also a danger to be avoided, namely, of using only the Mass formularies found in the Appendix and the *Missale parvum*. That would conflict with the norms for the liturgy, particularly with the principles of reform designed as an effort toward offering the faithful a richer assortment of biblical and euchological texts that would contribute to the understanding of the mystery of Christ and attune the celebration of the liturgy to the needs and character of a diversity of communities.

5.   Query: Must the four-week cycle of the psalter, all hymns, responsories, and antiphons be printed in editions of the liturgy of the hours? Reply: *Yes*. Everything contained in the Latin *editio typica* of the liturgy of the hours is to be included. Hymns are not excepted because they are among the distinguishing marks for each of the hours. An Appendix, however, may include alternative hymns, which are taken from existing collections or newly composed and are approved by the conference of bishops (see GILH no. 178 [DOL 426 no. 3608]).

6.   Query: Must the "various texts," i.e., prayers or biblical readings, be included? Reply: *Yes*. These form part of the prized riches of liturgical reform. For the most part such texts are left up to the judgment of the celebrant, who is to shape the liturgy for the assembly he presides over by choosing the most apposite texts. If such texts are missing from the volume published, this option of the celebrant is made pointless and the celebration impoverished.

The reason for this norm lies above all in the fact that the increased resources of the present liturgical reform are present in:

1. the pastoral instructions given as introductions to the rites or interspersed throughout them;

2. the extensive collection of biblical texts, formularies, and prayers offered for optional use.

To drop these is to nullify the liturgical reform; in a short time there would be a return to the ritual formalism that the conciliar Constitution sought above all to remedy.

What powers, therefore, do the conferences of bishops have?

Many of these are already indicated in their proper contexts. In general the task of the conferences is:

1. to preserve and increase the biblical and euchological resources provided   885
by the reformed rites. They are empowered therefore to add certain formularies that may be more in keeping with the mentality and culture of their own
people. In such a case the added formulary must be printed with a distinguishing symbol attached so that it is clearly identifiable as proper to the ritual of
this or that country;

2. to formulate those rites which the rubrics leave up to the determination of   886
the conferences of bishops;

3. to weigh carefully and sympathetically whether a particular rite is less   887
suited to the practices and outlook of the people; or whether in the local
customs or tradition there is anything that may usefully "be admitted into
divine worship," provided it is not bound up with pagan superstition and error
and is in keeping with the truth and the authentic spirit of the liturgy (see SC
art. 37 and 40).[b]

▶   209. SC DIVINE WORSHIP, Instruction *Constitutione Apostolica*, 20 October 1969:

         no. 4:   Translation of the Order of Mass [no. 1736].

▶   212. PAUL VI, Address on the new Order of Mass, 26 November 1969:

                          Latin and the vernacular [no. 1762].

---

7. Query: Must the parts of the books left to the discretion of the conferences of bishops be
printed? Reply: *Yes*. Everyone, especially priests, must know the extent of their own competency and what
remains in the hands of the conference of bishops. This will expedite the making or proposing of decisions
by the agencies of the conferences of bishops.
    8. Query: Must the decrees of the Congregation for Divine Worship promulgating an *editio typica*
or confirming a vernacular version be printed? Reply: *Yes*. The decrees promulgating an *editio typica* must be
published in their entirety. The decrees of confirmation may either be published in their entirety or by a
summary statement that such and such a vernacular edition was confirmed on such a date, with the
protocol number of the Congregation.
    9. Query: Is there still such a person as the censor of liturgical books, appointed by competent
authority and charged with declaring that the *editio typica* of any vernacular version corresponds to the
Latin *editio typica*? Reply: *Yes*. The vernacular edition must carry a statement on its conformity to the Latin
editio typica and the name of the censor(s) and of the bishop granting the imprimatur: Not 9 (1973) 153–154.

    b   See DOL 1 nos. 37 and 40.

126. SC DIVINE WORSHIP, **Norms** *In confirmandis actis,* on uniform translation of liturgical texts in the same language: 6 February 1970: Not 6 (1970) 84–85.

888

In confirming the enactments of conferences of bishops on points related to the vernacular, the Holy See is particularly mindful of ensuring uniformity in liturgical texts in regions sharing the same language. Hence, it has promoted the establishment of mixed commissions common to several conferences of bishops so that a single vernacular version of liturgical texts would be prepared (see letter of Cardinal Lercaro, 16 October 1964: Not 1 [1965] 195;ᵃ address of Pope Paul VI to the participants of a meeting on the vernacular versions of liturgical texts, 10 November 1965: Not 1 [1965] 380ᵇ).

What the mixed commissions have prepared with enormous labor shows the benefits and advantages of this cooperation (see "Instruction on the Translation of Liturgical Texts for Celebration with a Congregation," 25 January 1969, no. 41: Not 5 [1969] 11ᶜ). But admittedly there have been certain difficulties in adapting the translations prepared by the mixed commissions to the needs of different peoples, especially because the documents cited required a *single* translation for *all* texts.

Consequently, having weighed the repeated petitions from conferences of bishops, Pope Paul VI has established that uniformity is required only in the text of the Order of Mass and in the parts that *require the direct participation of the people.*

This new norm, which was made known directly to the conferences of bishops of the Portuguese language (12 November 1968, Prot. N. 2578/68) and to those of the Spanish language (5 August 1969, Prot. N. 905/69), was provided for the other conferences in the Instruction on the gradual carrying out of the Apostolic Constitution *Missale Romanum,* 20 October 1969, no. 4 (Not 5 [1969] 420).ᵈ

To clarify and expedite relations between the mixed commissions and the conferences of bishops, over and above the prescriptions in no. 4 of the Instruction on translation already cited,ᵉ the following are decreed:

889

1. There is to be a single vernacular version for:

a. such parts of the liturgy as acclamations, responsories, and dialogues, which require direct participation by the congregation;

b. the parts of the Order of Mass;

c. the psalms and hymns in the divine office and the *preces* [intercessions] at lauds and vespers.

890

2. For other texts a single vernacular version is preferable; nevertheless, where there is a true need, the individual conferences of bishops are empowered to make adaptations in the common translation or to make a new one.

891

3. The texts mentioned in no. 1 must be approved by all the conferences of bishops obliged to its use before the Holy See confirms such texts. The report of the president of the joint commission to this Congregation will attest to such approval by the conferences of bishops.

ᵃ   See DOL 108.

ᵇ   See DOL 113.

ᶜ   See DOL 123 no. 878.

ᵈ   See DOL 209 no. 1736.

ᵉ   *Sic.* The correct reference is to nos. 41–42 [see DOL 123 nos. 878–879].

This new arrangement does not lessen the benefit and advantage of collabora- 892
tion by the joint commissions; the intent rather is to ease the process of agreement
between the conferences of bishops on a draft of a text in their common language.
This Congregation earnestly desires that the work of the joint commissions will
continue to go forward with increased success.

127. SC DIVINE WORSHIP, **Circular Letter** *Die 2 Februarii* to the presidents
of the national liturgical commissions, on the vernacular translation of the
rite of religious profession, 15 July 1970: Not 6 (1970) 317–318.

On 2 February 1970, this Congregation for Divine Worship, as all know, pro- 893
mulgated, by the express mandate of Pope Paul VI, the *editio typica* of the *Ordo
professionis religiosae.*

The *Rite of Religious Profession* has been inserted into the "Roman Ritual as Revised by Decree of the Second Vatican Ecumenical Council and Published by
Authority of Pope Paul VI"; it therefore is lawfully and rightly numbered among
the books of the Roman liturgy. Accordingly, it belongs to the conferences of
bishops to see to the vernacular translations of the *Ordo professionis religiosae*, as the
Decree itself instructs: "The conferences of bishops (where applicable, the joint
commissions of countries with a common language) are to arrange for accurate
vernacular translations of this rite, after consultation with the associations of religious superiors that plan and administer programs for religious in each country"
(Decree, 2 February 1970: Prot. N. 200/70).[a]

I am not unmindful of the number and importance of the labors now facing
the liturgical commissions, especially since the welcome publication of the Roman
Missal. However, many religious institutes are waiting for the translation in order
to make their own adaptations of the *Rite of Religious Profession*. Therefore, I presume
to appeal to you for a vernacular translation of the *Ordo professionis* as soon as
possible.

I wish to assure you that this Congregation, out of the respect due to the
conferences of bishops and their *periti*, has not approved and never will approve, not
even *ad interim*, any translation that in whole or in part has been prepared on private
initiative.

As I have said, the conferences of bishops are at this time overburdened with
work. But the task of translating the *Ordo professionis* is eased somewhat. All that is
asked of the conferences is a translation that is integral, faithful, and accurate; the
individual religious institutes will take care of making their own adaptations in due
time.

It will be a kindness to me if you write a word on the progress of the work; I
hope that a text may soon reach this Congregation for its confirmation.

▶   216.   SC DIVINE WORSHIP, Notification *Instructione de Constitutione*, on the Roman
          Missal, the book of the liturgy of the hours, the General Calendar, 14 June 1971:

ᵃ   DOL 391 no. 3229.

no.   4:   Language of Mass and liturgy of the hours [no.
                           1773].

128. SC DIVINE WORSHIP, **Letter** *Al comenzar* of Cardinal A. Tabera to presidents of the conference of bishops and liturgical commissions of the Spanish-speaking countries, on translations into Spanish, 29 October 1971: Not 8 (1972) 38–40 (Spanish).

894   To begin the work of liturgical reform, the Holy See has insisted in regard to achieving translations of the liturgical books from Latin into the different vernacular languages on the establishment of joint commissions for countries sharing a common language. In accord with this rule, such a commission was set up between Spain and the Spanish-speaking countries of Latin America that formed the membership of CELAM. The work of the joint commission "CELAM-España" has won praise both for its speed in the translation and publication of the liturgical books and for the fraternal cooperation that has united around the same ideal the bishops and *periti* of both Spain and Latin America in the endeavor to produce texts worthy of a noble liturgical and literary tradition.

        The progess of the liturgical reform has, however, reached a new development in this very work of preparing liturgical books. This work has now passed — and not just in Spanish-speaking countries — from the stage of simply translating to that of adapting the texts and rites in a way that respects and expresses the mentality, the traditions, and the positive values of the different peoples and cultures, especially from a pastoral viewpoint.

        Thus, in view of the desire expressed by both the Department of Liturgy and the majority of bishops in the plenary meeting of CELAM in May at San José, Costa Rica, the office of the president of CELAM has put before this Congregation the question of whether it is time for the Latin American countries and Spain to be more independent of each other in regard to the Spanish translation of the liturgical books.

        The Congregation has carefully studied this issue in consultation with both parties as well as at a joint meeting that took advantage of the presence in Rome of the Spanish and Latin American bishops on the occasion of the Synod of Bishops. As a result the Congregation is able now to communicate what follows.

895   1.   In the preparation of books a pastoral development with its consequences in the field of liturgy is to be considered, as also the resulting development in the norms affecting the work of the joint commission. Therefore the Congregation regards as useful and approves the autonomy of Spain and of the countries of Latin America in the work of translating and preparing their own liturgical books.

896   2.   In this new arrangement it seems advisable that Latin America should form, under the responsibility of CELAM and its Department of Liturgy, a commission charged with preparing the liturgical books for the Latin American countries. This Congregation has full confidence that the new texts, through the cooperation of experts in the various disciplines, will be of merit, from the standpoint of both liturgy and language.

897   3.   The new arrangement does not preclude the composition of a common text in a particular case at the discretion of the Holy See and, if helpful, by agreement

between CELAM and the liturgical commission of the conference of bishops of Spain. The procedures in effect hitherto would be followed in fraternal cooperation.

4.   So that this cooperation may run smoothly, there is to be respect both for the   898
autonomy and jurisdiction of the conferences of bishops, which have charge of
church law in matters of pastoral import, and for proprietary rights according to
civil law in the individual countries.

5.   The conferences of bishops are to adopt only those books that are prepared   899
expressly for their regions and that therefore better meet pastoral conditions in
those regions. It will be useful to emphasize this point at every opportunity by
instructing and appealing to the clergy. In addition, the national commissions
should lend their support to ensure that publishers and booksellers in the individual countries respect these same pastoral considerations.

6.   As to proprietary rights and use of already existing common texts, as well as of   900
any future common texts, the agencies involved are to make the financial arrangements they think appropriate.

This Congregation has complete confidence that the new arrangement will
further the work in a way more in keeping with concrete pastoral requirements of
each country so as to promote an ever deepening, active, and beneficial participation of the faithful in the Church's liturgy.

129. SC DIVINE WORSHIP, **Circular Letter** *El 6 febrero* of Cardinal A.
Tabera to the Spanish-speaking conferences of bishops in Latin America, on
uniform translation of the parts of the liturgy belonging to the people, 20
November 1972: Not 9 (1973) 70–71 (Spanish).

On 6 February 1970 this Congregation, standardizing as the norm the decisions   901
already made in particular instances, underscored the need that in countries sharing
a common language there be a single translation for those parts of the liturgy calling
for the direct participation of the congregation (see Not 6 [1970] 84–85).[a]

During my recent visit to some of the Latin-American nations I was able to
observe for myself the sensibleness of such a policy. This Congregation, therefore,
insists on it to the end that liturgical participation may become both possible and
simpler in these times of frequent travel and communication between the various
countries.

I am pleased to forward the list of those parts of the Mass and of the sacramental rites that must be uniform in translation.

All the parts engaging the direct participation of the faithful must have the
same translation in all the countries sharing a common language.

In particular:

1) For Mass: 902
    1. the greeting (*In the name of the Father*; the salutation and its response);
    2. the penitential rite;
    3. the *Kyrie*;

---

   a   See DOL 126.

4. the *Gloria*;

5. the dialogue before the gospel;

6. the *Credo*;

7. the invitation to pray (*Orate fratres*);

8. the dialogue introducing the preface and the *Sanctus*;

9. the institution narrative and the words of consecration;

10. the acclamation after the consecration;

11. the Lord's Prayer;

12. the acclamation after the *Deliver us*;

13. the greeting of peace;

14. the *Agnus Dei*;

15. the *Lord, I am not worthy*;

16. the dismissal formularies.

903   2) For other sacraments:

1. the people's responses;

2. the essential forms of the sacraments.

130. SC DIVINE WORSHIP, **Circular Letter** *Dum toto terrarum* to presidents of the conferences of bishops, on the translation of the forms of the sacraments, 25 October 1973: AAS 66 (1974) 98–99; Not 10 (1974) 37–38.

904   During the period that liturgical commissions everywhere have been engaged in translating liturgical books with commendable speed and in publishing the translations, the Congregation for Divine Worship has gradually developed norms for the confirmation of the texts submitted to it, in keeping with the Constitution on the Liturgy art. 36, § 3[a] and the Instruction *Inter Oecumenici* of 26 September 1964 no. 40.[b] The result has been the facilitation of the whole enterprise and the acceleration of the practical carrying out of the reform of the liturgy.

I have the pleasure of informing you at this time of norms to be followed that have been laid down recently.

905   1. Pope Paul VI reserves to himself the power to approve personally all translations of the sacramental forms into the vernacular. After consultation with the conferences of bishops concerned, this Congregation will supply such translations into the principal modern languages (namely, English, French, German, Spanish, Dutch, Italian, and Portuguese).

906   2. Sacramental forms translated into the vernacular should not only completely convey right theological teaching, but also correspond as closely as possible to the Latin text, which the congregations responsible have composed with the utmost thought and care.

---

[a] See DOL 1 no. 36.

[b] See DOL 23 no. 332.

3. For languages other than those mentioned in no. 1, the liturgical commissions concerned should prepare their own translations of the sacramental forms. Upon approving such translations, the conference of bishops will submit them to this Congregation, with a detailed explanation in one of the more widely known languages (for example, English or French) of the import and sense of every word.

907

Should the sacramental forms, part of the essence of the sacraments, not be translated word for word, convincing reasons are to be given for changing them vis-à-vis the Latin text.

These norms will greatly facilitate approval of texts, especially in the case of translations into languages common to many countries, hence to many conferences of bishops. Before the definitive approval of any text, this Congregation will take the most effective steps possible to consult with the conferences, to the end that both in the quality of their language and style and in their address to spiritual needs the forms translated will meet the requirements of the people for whom they are intended.

908

131. SC DOCTRINE OF THE FAITH, **Declaration** *Instauratio liturgica*, on the translation of the forms of the sacraments, 25 January 1974: AAS 66 (1974) 661; Not 10 (1974) 395.

Reform of the liturgy as carried out in keeping with the Constitution of Vatican Council II has brought about changes even in the forms of the sacraments that are part of the essence of the sacramental rites. Like every other text, the new words of these sacramental forms should be translated in a way that conveys their original sense according to the idiom of the vernacular. This gives rise to certain difficulties that are coming to light as the conferences of bishops submit translations of the sacramental forms for the Holy See's approval. In this situation, therefore, this Congregation for the Doctrine of the Faith issues the reminder that a translation of the sacramental forms belonging to the essence of the sacramental rites must faithfully render the original meaning of the Latin prototype. With that in mind the Congregation declares:

909

The Holy See examines the translation of a sacramental form into the vernacular and, when it judges that the translation rightly expresses the meaning intended by the Church, approves and confirms the translation. In so doing the Holy See is stipulating that the meaning of the translation is to be understood in accord with the mind of the Church as expressed by the original Latin text.

Pope Paul VI has given his approval to this Declaration at an audience granted on 25 January 1974 to the Cardinal Prefect of the Congregation.

▶ 523. SC DIVINE WORSHIP, Letter *Voluntati obsequens* to bishops, accompanying the booklet *Iubilate Deo*, 14 April 1974.

▶ 524. SC DIVINE WORSHIP, *Iubilate Deo*, Introduction, 14 April 1974.

132. SC DIVINE WORSHIP, **Letter** to presidents of the English-speaking conferences of bishops, on papal approval of the translation of the sacramental form of confirmation, 5 May 1975.*

910   In a letter dated the twenty-sixth June 1974, this Sacred Congregation had consulted episcopal conferences responsible for English in the liturgy concerning the essential formula to be used in the sacrament of confirmation.

The replies received were presented to the Holy Father, who directed that a further study be made. His Holiness has now approved the following definitive formula: BE SEALED WITH THE GIFT OF THE HOLY SPIRIT.

This should now be adopted as the only authorized English text. Since texts with interim approval have been in use for some time, it is left to the individual conferences to determine how the new translation will be introduced, fixing even a period of *vacatio legis* if this is deemed opportune.

I would be grateful if Your Eminence/Your Excellency could see that this Sacred Congregation is informed of the decision of the episcopal conference in this matter.

▶   538.   SC DIVINE WORSHIP, Note *Passim quaeritur*, on music in vernacular editions of the Roman Missal, May 1975.

133. SC SACRAMENTS AND DIVINE WORSHIP, **Letter** *Decem iam annos* to presidents of the conferences of bishops, on use of the vernacular in the liturgy, 5 June 1976: Not 12 (1976) 300–302.

911   For the past ten years the conferences of bishops and their liturgical commissions have been engaged in translating the liturgical books into the vernacular, a task not yet brought to completion. Following on the temporary and experimental versions prepared as a start, final texts and editions are now being prepared in all nations. This involves public and authorized texts through which the Church at prayer expresses its faith. Consequently, this work clearly calls for the utmost wisdom and imposes on conscience the grave responsibility to see to it that these books also when published in the vernacular are sure and precise in doctrine and worthy of the worship owed to God. Such books must, moreover, bear those marks that will show them to be the authorized texts of the local Churches, texts on which, in the bond of ecclesial communion, the Holy See has put its stamp of unity and authenticity.

The Holy See, therefore, by its timely norms and counsel, and moved by a spirit of the brotherly service binding it to the local Churches, has continually shown its interest in the work of translating liturgical texts into the vernacular and has given it encouragement. This spirit of service and the objective of the Holy See's speedier confirmation of the texts — a confirmation prescribed by the Constitution *Sacrosanctum Concilium* — suggest a number of norms that are to be followed when texts are submitted to this Congregation.

912   1.   The conferences of bishops have responsibility for decision on the introduction and on the extent or limits of the vernacular in the liturgy. For multilingual nations they also are responsible for deciding which languages are to be introduced

*   Text of the SCDW, Prot. N. 610/75.

into the liturgy. The Holy See, however, must approve, that is, confirm, conference decisions (see SC art. 36, § 3).[a]

Idioms coming from a dialect or proper and peculiar only to a certain locale are unacceptable and therefore cannot be approved, that is, confirmed. Such idioms are those that are replaceable by a language that is recognized and supported by the usual course of instruction in the schools, especially if this instruction is prescribed and compulsory by law and carried out in the schools throughout a nation. The point is to prevent an idiom or strictly local dialect from displacing the more widely used language and to preclude an excessive number of particular languages in the liturgy. A manageable uniformity of liturgical language within a country is an advantage for the participation of the faithful and for the editing and printing both of translations that are sound and precise in doctrine, worthy and complete, and of other resources serving the faithful.

If in the past a plan or criterion different from those just outlined has sometimes been observed, permissions already granted do not cease. But conferences of bishops are kindly advised to make every effort to see that this new arrangement is correctly understood with a view to correcting liturgical practices conflicting with this Instruction, even those lawfully adopted before publication of this Circular Letter.

2.   The responsibility for approving translations of liturgical texts into the vernac-   913
ular belongs to the conferences of bishops. The approval must be duly given by vote (see Instruction *Inter Oecumenici*, 26 September 1964, no. 28;[b] Central Commission for Coordinating Postconciliar Work and Interpreting the Decrees of Vatican Council II, Reply, AAS 60 [1968] 361[c]).

Any different procedure that the conferences of bishops should prefer in special circumstances must be specified in the statutes of the conference approved by the Apostolic See.

3.   The *acta* of a conference attesting to the approval secured for texts and indicat-   914
ing the result of the vote shall be forwarded to this Congregation along with any motions on the request for confirmation; the *president* and the *secretary* of the conference shall sign the *acta* (see Instruction *Inter Oecumenici* no. 29).[d]

Two copies of the liturgical text are also to be sent for purposes of confirmation. All are advised that the translation of the liturgical books must be complete, including optional texts, decrees for the front matter (preliminaries), and introductions to the rites.

4.   The report should show the rationale or criteria followed in the translation and   915
any differences introduced vis-à-vis the Latin *editio typica* (see ibid. no. 30).[e]

5.   Translation and approval of the forms of the sacraments must receive particu-   916
lar attention. On this point special norms were brought to the attention of the

---

    [a]   See DOL 1 no. 36.

    [b]   See DOL 23 no. 320.

    [c]   See DOL 8.

    [d]   See DOL 23 no. 321.

    [e]   See DOL 23 no. 322.

conferences of bishops by the Congregation for Divine Worship on 25 October 1973 (see AAS [1974] 98–99)[f] and by the Congregation for the Doctrine of the Faith on 25 January 1974 (see AAS 66 [1974] 661).[g]

In particular as to less well-known languages, the following should be observed:

a.   The meaning of every single word in the vernacular text should be given in one of the more widely known languages, namely, French, English, Italian, Portuguese, Spanish, German.

b.   If the translation departs from the original text, the reasons for *introducing such a translation* should be listed.

c.   The president and secretary of the conference of bishops are to certify the fact of approval by the conference and the authenticity of that version as a word-by-word translation of the text into one of the languages already mentioned.

917   6.   The confirmation given by the Holy See is to appear in the printed texts, two copies of which are to be transmitted to this Congregation.

----

[f]   See DOL 130.

[g]   See DOL 131.

Section 6. Publication of Liturgical Books

SUMMARY (DOL 134–140). The 7 documents here may be divided into two groups.

—On editions of liturgical books there is a decree of SC Rites (DOL 134), notable particularly for its precision of the term *editio typica*, and a letter of the Congregation for Divine Worship (DOL 138), as well as an excerpt from a decree on the more general issue of the bishops' vigilance in regard to books from the Congregation for the Doctrine of the Faith (DOL 140).

—On royalties due to the Holy See there are three letters (DOL 135, 136, 137) and a declaration (DOL 139) from the curial agencies concerned.

▶   23.   SC RITES (Consilium), Instruction (first) *Inter Oecumenici*, 26 September 1964:

no.   40 e: Dignity of editions of liturgical books [no. 332].

134. SC RITES (Consilium), **Decree** *Cum, nostra aetate,* on editions of the liturgical books, 27 January 1966: AAS 58 (1966) 169–171; Not 2 (1966) 172–174.

918   At the present time new editions of liturgical books, particularly vernacular editions, are being prepared almost everywhere and it therefore seems advisable to issue the following norms. Their purpose is to safeguard the dignity and appearance of liturgical books in such a way that, following a long-standing tradition in the Church, the best that human talent can produce will be given to the worship of God and the faithful will thereby be inspired toward the reverence due to the sacred.

919   1.   The name *editio typica* of liturgical books carrying only the Latin text belongs to the edition published by the *Vatican Polyglot Press* in virtue of a decree from the Congregation of Rites.

The name *editio typica* belongs also to the edition of liturgical books containing the vernacular translation, with or without the Latin text, that is published under the aegis of the conference of bishops in each country. The decree declaring this to be the *editio typica* is issued by the president of the conference or, by virtue of his mandate, by the president of the national liturgical commission. The same decree must make mention of the confirmation of the text given by the Holy See.

920   2.   Regarding the right to prepare editions *juxta typicam:*

a.   The right to publish books containing the Latin text alone is reserved to publishers having a pontifical patent.

b.   The right to publish books containing the Latin and the vernacular or the vernacular text alone is in the power of the national conference of bishops to assign to publishers of its choice.

921   3.   The conference of bishops in each country would do well, taking into account both the requirements of civil law and the publishing practices of the country, to decide on the publishers to be entrusted with publishing the vernacular texts for use in the liturgy.

922   4.   The size, design, and everything related to the typography of books for use in the liturgy are to be of a kind that enhance the beauty and worthiness such books should have.

923   5.   Editions of the Roman Missal and Breviary for use in the liturgy and containing the vernacular translation must also carry the Latin text, according to the norms of the Instruction of the Congregation of Rites, 26 September 1964, nos. 57 and 89.[a]

The same norms apply to editions of the Roman Pontifical.

924   6.   The vernacular is to be placed side by side with the Latin text only for the parts that, by decree of the conference of bishops, may be recited in the vernacular.

---

[a]   See DOL 23 nos. 349 and 381.

7.   The brief commentaries to be spoken by the priest or other qualified minister   925
(see Constitution on the Liturgy art. 35, § 3)[b] as a helpful prelude to certain parts of
the liturgy must be clearly set off from the liturgical text itself.

8.   The requirements before a publisher may go ahead with publication of books   926
for use in the liturgy are these:

     a.   For books containing the Latin text alone, permission obtained for each
instance from this Congregation of Rites and an agreement with the Administration
of the Patrimony of the Holy See on the conditions covering distribution of these
books.

     b.   For books containing the Latin text together with the vernacular or the
vernacular alone, permission obtained from the president of the conference of
bishops and an agreement with him on the conditions covering publication of these
books as to both the Latin text, controlled by the Administration of the Patrimony
of the Holy See, and the vernacular text, controlled by the conference of bishops.

9.   The statement of conformity with the *editio typica* of both the Latin and the   927
vernacular text, which according to CIC can. 1390 the local Ordinary authorizes, is
to be signed only after thorough and careful examination.

10.   Without prejudice to no. 5, the norms of this Decree apply to both complete   928
and partial editions of the following for use in the liturgy: Roman Breviary, Roman
Missal, Roman Ritual, Roman Pontifical, Roman Martyrology, and the Ceremonial
for Bishops, as well as books of Gregorian chant.

11.   In order that there may be one center where it will be possible to find a   929
complete collection of all liturgical books in use throughout the world, the presidents of the conferences of bishops are to:

     a.   send to the Consilium a list of the names of those publishers commissioned
to publish editions of such books;

     b.   see that two copies of liturgical books issued in their territory are sent to
the Secretariat of the Consilium.

     The present Decree was prepared by the Congregation of Rites and the Consi-
lium. At an audience granted 27 January 1966 to Cardinal Arcadio M. Larraona,
Prefect of the Congregation of Rites, Pope Paul VI by his authority approved and
confirmed the Decree and ordered it to be published for exact fulfillment by all
concerned.

135. SC RITES, **Letter** *Non latet sane* to presidents of the conferences of
bishops, on royalties for Latin editions of liturgical books, 5 August 1966.[*]

     Well known to Your Excellency is the great care that the Holy See has always   930
exercised regarding editions of the liturgical books.

     The Congregation of Rites twenty years ago, 10 August 1946, by the Decree *De
facultate edendi libros liturgicos* regulated these editions in such a way that, first, the *editio
typica* of the liturgical books would be assigned to the *Typographia Vaticana*, second, an
edition *juxta typicam* would be granted to distinguished "Pontifical Printers."

---

   b   See DOL 1 no. 35.

   *   SCR, Prot. N.R. 25/966.

At the present time, however, with the use of the vernacular brought into the liturgy and duly approved, the matter of publishing liturgical books has changed a great deal. For while the Holy See as ever takes care of the Latin text, the individual conferences of bishops worldwide have charge of the vernacular texts that are developed from the Latin text in their own translations.

The recent Decree *De editionibus librorum liturgicorum* published by this Congregation of Rites, 27 January 1966,[a] regulates the current state of affairs.

Therefore to obtain permission to print books carrying the Latin text only and intended for use in the liturgy a publisher is to send, along with the petition that must be submitted to the Congregation of Rites, a document in evidence that the payments due to the Administration of the Patrimony of the Holy See have already been made.

136. ADMINISTRATION OF THE PATRIMONY OF THE HOLY SEE, **Letter** to presidents of the conferences of bishops, on royalties for editions of liturgical books, 10 September 1966.*

931   In accordance with the regulations concerning the publishing of liturgical books laid down in the Decree of the Sacred Congregation of Rites, 10 August 1946, the Pontifical Publishers to whom the preparation and distribution of the *juxta typicam* editions was reserved, paid annually, in recognition of the rights of the Holy See, a certain royalty with each edition.

The recent Decree *De editione librorum liturgicorum*, issued by the same Sacred Congregation of Rites, 27 January 1966,[a] in order to adapt the preceding regulations to the new situation created by the introduction of the vernacular into the liturgy, lays down a new procedure regarding the rights of the Holy See.

In order to put this into effect: since every vernacular text in the liturgical books is based on the corresponding Latin original, the amount to be paid to the Administration of the Patrimony of the Holy See is determined as 1.50 percent of the total selling price of each book.

The amount will be paid by the publishers to the national liturgical commissions.

The national liturgical commissions will send the sum to this Administration in annual payments, to be made on 1 January each year, using the attached forms.

---

[a]   See DOL 134.

*   English text from the Administration of the Patrimony of the Holy See, Prot. N. 33242.

[a]   See DOL 134.

137. ADMINISTRATION OF THE PATRIMONY OF THE HOLY SEE, **Letter** to presidents of the conferences of bishops, on royalties for editions of liturgical books, 8 January 1968.*

On 10 September 1966, I had the pleasure of sending you a letter (N. 33242)[a]   932
which concerned the norms given in the Decree of 27 January 1966, issued by the
Sacred Congregation of Rites, entitled *De editione librorum liturgicorum.*[b] Today I take
the liberty of pointing out article 8, paragraph b, which states that every publisher
of liturgical Latin and vernacular books is obliged to pay the Holy See a royalty of
1.5 percent of the selling price of each book.[c] In this way the publishers contribute
to the costs of studying and editing the liturgical texts.

The above-mentioned letter instructed the publishers to pay these royalties to
the national liturgical commissions, which, in turn, would send the final amount to
the Administration of the Patrimony of the Holy See at the end of the year.

Appropriate forms were included in the letter of 10 September 1966 to help
facilitate payment.

I regret to communicate that up to the present time no reply has arrived. I
therefore would appreciate it very much if the respective offices were urged to make
their remittances for the years 1966 and 1967.

▶   125. SC DIVINE WORSHIP, Declaration *Plures liturgicae*, on the translation of new
           liturgical texts, 15 September 1969:

                    Completeness of editions [no. 884].

▶   210. SC DIVINE WORSHIP, Letter *Cum nonnullae Conferentiae*, on the Latin Appendix
           of the Roman Missal, 10 November 1969.

138. SC DIVINE WORSHIP, **Letter** *Tandis que cette Congrégation* to presidents
of the conferences of bishops and the national liturgical commissions, on
the publication of liturgical books, 25 February 1970.*

This Congregation is bringing to an end the publication of liturgical books,   933
updated according to the desires of Vatican II. In all countries a rather intense work
on translations of these texts into the various languages is being done. It is opportune, therefore, to call the attention of the episcopal conferences to some formalities
with regard to the printing of liturgical books.

Before the publication of editions in the vernacular, the printing of Latin texts
iuxta typicam was reserved to pontifical editors. These publications were regulated by
particular norms of the Sacred Congregation of Rites with the Decree *De facultate
edendi libros liturgicos*, 10 August 1946, and again on 23 November 1955.

These norms foresaw that the editors make the necessary agreements with the
Holy See's Administration for Material Goods.

---

* English text from the Administration of the Patrimony of the Holy See, Prot. N. 42141.

[a] See DOL 136.

[b] See DOL 134.

[c] The royalty is mentioned only in the letter of 10 September 1966.

* English text from SCDW, Prot. N. 1134/70.

The new situation, determined by the publication of liturgical books in bilingual editions, is regulated by the Decree of the Sacred Congregation of Rites *De editionibus librorum liturgicorum*, 27 January 1966 (AAS 58 [1966] 167–171).[a] This establishes that the editors, commissioned by the conferences of bishops to publish liturgical books, should regulate, for the publication of the Latin text, the administrative part with the Holy See's Administration for Material Goods; for vernacular texts, the conference of bishops. The quota established by the Holy See for the Latin text was 1.5% on the total price of each volume (see Letter of Administration for Material Goods, 10 September 1966 and 8 January 1968).[b]

The application of this administrative disposition indicated above has met with some difficulty.

Furthermore, this Congregation has dispensed with the obligation of publishing the Latin text in the new missals beside the vernacular text (10 November 1969: Not 5 [1969] 442–443).[c]

Nevertheless, I do feel obliged to recall to you the effort sustained by the Holy See in realizing the liturgical reform: consultation of bishops and experts; study groups and plenary sessions; schemata and preliminary studies; and, finally, the printing of the liturgical books in Latin.

It seems only just to meet the expenses of the Holy See for a work of interest and common utility for the *whole* Church.

Taking into consideration the new situation, the internal difficulties of some countries, and the burden confronted by the Holy See, permit me to ask your episcopal conference for suggestions as to how this situation can be solved in a dignified way both for the Holy See and the episcopal conference.

Your response would be appreciated *before 30 April 1970.*

139. SC DIVINE WORSHIP, **Declaration** *Nonnullae Commissiones*, on the publication of liturgical books, 15 May 1970: Not 6 (1970) 153.

934   Some national liturgical commissions have asked:

1. In publishing vernacular editions of liturgical books may the name of the author or authors who translated them be printed or should the translations remain anonymous?

2. May the copyright be assigned to one or other private person or publisher or should it remain in the hands of the conference of bishops or the national liturgical commission?

After weighing all factors and listening to the opinions of experts from several countries, the Congregation for Divine Worship declares the following:

As to 1: all vernacular versions of any liturgical documents or liturgical texts are to remain completely anonymous, as is the case with Latin texts published officially under the name and the authority of this Congregation. In books for use at the altar by the celebrant or ministers the authors' names must not appear either in the text or in the front matter.

---

[a]   See DOL 134.

[b]   See DOL 136 and 137.

[c]   See DOL 210.

As to 2: the copyright for all versions should remain in the hands of the conference of bishops or of the national liturgical commission.[R1]

▶   434.   SC DIVINE WORSHIP, Note *Liturgiae Horarum interpretationes*, on vernacular editions of *The Liturgy of the Hours*, 15 January 1973.

140. SC DOCTRINE OF THE FAITH, Decree *Ecclesiae Pastorum*, on the vigilance of the bishops of the Church with regard to books, 19 March 1975: AAS 67 (1975) 281–284; Not 11 (1975) 99 (excerpt).

ARTICLE 3

1.   Liturgical books, including vernacular translations or parts thereof, are to be published only by mandate of the conference of bishops and under its supervision, after confirmation by the Holy See.   935

2.   For republication of books approved by the Holy See and of vernacular translations made and approved in keeping with the prescription of par. 1, as well as of parts of either, the local Ordinary where the books are published must attest to their conformity to the approved edition.   936

3.   Prayer books for private use are also to be published only by permission of the local Ordinary.[R2]   937

▶   538.   SC DIVINE WORSHIP, Note *Passim quaeritur*, on music to be incorporated into vernacular editions of the Roman Missal, May 1975.

[R1]   See DOL 125 no. 884, note R3.

[R2]   Commentary in Not 11 (1975) 99–100: In keeping with this document and in view of the SCDW's directions on various occasions, the procedure for publishing liturgical books may be summarized.
   a.   Any liturgical books to be published *in Latin* are to be printed on the basis of the consent of the Apostolic See. The local Ordinary giving the *concordat cum originali* must be mentioned. The conferences of bishops may assign this task to the liturgical commissions.
   b.   Liturgical books in the vernacular must be promulgated by the president of the conference of bishops after the confirmation of the Apostolic See has been obtained.
   b.   This vernacular edition is an *editio typica* and must carry the decree of promulgation, which also gives the period of the *vacatio legis*. The edition must also carry a statement that confirmation has been granted by the Apostolic See and give the date and protocol number of the SCDW's decree of confirmation. A confirmation given *ad interim* must be explicitly designated as such.
   b.   The conference of bishops or, at its mandate, the national liturgical commission gives the *concordat cum originali*.
   c.   Texts proper to dioceses or institutes of Christian perfection, whether in Latin or in the vernacular, are published at the mandate of the Ordinary, once they have been confirmed by the Apostolic See. They must carry the decree of confirmation by the SCDW, as indicated above, and the *concordat cum originali* issued by the Ordinary.
   d.   Vernacular editions *iuxta typicam*, whether for the altar or for the people's participation, are permitted on the basis of the consent of the conference of bishops to which the texts belong. They must state the permission obtained as well as the *concordat cum originali* granted by the local Ordinary where the editions are published.

Section 7. The Holy See and Religious Superiors

SUMMARY (DOL 141–143). There are 3 general documents on powers and responsibilities of religious related to the liturgy.

—On religious superiors' faculties related to the liturgy the Secretariat of State issued a pontifical rescript (DOL 141) and the Congregation of Religious a decree (DOL 143).

—On religious' participation in the liturgical apostolate the same Congregation issued a notice to superiors in 1965 (DOL 142).

141. SECRETARIAT OF STATE, **Pontifical Rescript** *Cum admotae*, on faculties delegated to the superiors general of clerical religious institutes of pontifical rank and to the abbots-president of monastic congregations, 6 November 1964: AAS 59 (1967) 374–378 (excerpt).

938   Petitions have been made to the Holy See that superiors general of clerical religious institutes possess certain faculties in order to facilitate carrying out their responsibilities. At an audience granted 6 November of this year to me, the undersigned Cardinal for the Public Affairs of the Church, Pope Paul VI has acceded to these requests and has decreed the following. The intent is both to facilitate the internal government of religious institutes and at the same time to offer to these religious institutes a deserved testimony of his good will.

I. THE FACULTIES HERE LISTED ARE DELEGATED TO SUPERIORS GENERAL OF CLERICAL RELIGIOUS INSTITUTES OF PONTIFICAL RANK AND TO ABBOTS-PRESIDENT OF MONASTIC CONGREGATIONS:

939   1.   To permit, for the benefit of the religious, only their own priest-subjects to celebrate Mass and distribute holy communion at any hour of the day in their own houses when there is good reason, provided all other requirements are observed and without prejudice to the rights of the local Ordinary regarding celebration of Mass for the convenience of the faithful.

With the consent of their council, superiors general can subdelegate this faculty to other major superiors of the same religious institute.

940   2.   To allow their own priest-subjects afflicted with poor eyesight or suffering from some other infirmity to celebrate daily the votive Mass of the Virgin Mary, Mother of God, or a Mass for the dead, with the assistance, if needed, of another priest or deacon and observing the liturgical norms and prescriptions laid down in this matter by the Holy See.

941   3.   To grant the same faculty to their own priest-subjects who are totally blind, provided, however, another priest or a deacon assist such celebrants.

942   4.   To grant to their own priest-subjects the faculty to celebrate Mass within the religious house but outside of a place of worship (not however in a bedroom), upon an altar stone or, in the case of those of an Eastern rite, upon an *antimensium*. This faculty can be granted only for individual instances and for a good reason; in cases of regular celebration of this kind, a more serious reason is required.

With the consent of their council, superiors general are empowered to subdelegate this faculty to other major superiors of the same religious institute.

943   5.   To permit their own priest-subjects who are infirm or elderly to celebrate Mass seated if they are unable to stand; they are to follow the other liturgical laws.

944   8.   With the consent of their council, to dispense their own subjects who have already received sacred orders, but only that they may celebrate Mass, from every kind of irregularity arising from either delict or defect. The dispensation is conditional on the proper carrying out of the ministry of the altar and the absence of possible scandal. Excepted from the faculty, however, are the cases mentioned in CIC can. 985, nos. 3 and 4; in cases of the crime of heresy or schism, there must first be an abjuration before the one who absolves.

945   12. To grant not only to their own priest-subjects but also to those priests of any rite whatever, of the diocesan clergy, or of another religious institute, as long as these are approved by their own Ordinary or their own major superior, delegated

jurisdiction to hear the confessions of professed religious, novices, and others mentioned in CIC can. 514, § 1 and can. 46, § 1 of the Motu Proprio *Postquam apostolicis litteris* of 9 February 1952, namely, in the case of religious institutes not enjoying this kind of faculty by law (CIC can. 875, § 1).

With the consent of their council, superiors general can subdelegate this faculty not only to other major superiors but also to the superiors of individual houses of the same religious institute.

II. AS TO THE EXTENT, SUBJECT, AND USE OF THESE FACULTIES, THE FOLLOWING DECLARATIONS ARE MADE:

1.   The aforementioned faculties apply to clerical religious institutes of pontifical rank, regardless of their rite or the Congregation of the Holy See to which they are subject.

946

2.   The aforementioned faculties must be considered as granted also to superiors general of clerical societies of pontifical right living in common without public vows (see CIC, Bk. 2, ch. 17). The faculties listed under nos. 9 and 14 must be considered as granted also to superiors general of secular institutes of pontifical rank. Such superiors general can use the remaining faculties, however, only for those clerical subjects not incardinated in any diocese.

947

3.   The recipient of these same faculties is the person who is superior general or abbot-president or the person who, in the absence of these, pro tempore and by approved constitutions succeeds them in governing.

948

4.   If the superior general or the abbot-president is impeded in the discharge of his office, he is empowered to subdelegate those same faculties totally or partially to the religious who functions in his place and who, as a result, can himself use the faculties and again subdelegate them to others in individual cases and according to the limitations and provisos already stipulated.

949

5.   The matters decreed take effect from 21 November of this year and do not need what is called a formula of execution.

950

142. SC RELIGIOUS, **Notice** to the Roman Union of Superiors General, regarding the involvement of religious in the liturgical apostolate, 14 December 1965.*

Cardinal Ildebrando Antoniutti, Prefect of the Congregation of Religious, has notified the Roman Union of Superiors General of the following requirement. All religious orders and congregations with members engaged in the liturgical apostolate — through centers, publications, liturgical weeks, etc. — are to act, in agreement with the hierarchy, to preserve uniformity everywhere. Nothing, however, is taken away from the rites proper to individual orders.

951

---

* Text, CommRel 45 (1966) 332–333.

143. SC RELIGIOUS, **Decree** *Religionum laicalium*, delegating certain faculties to the superiors general of lay religious institutes of pontifical rank, both of men and of women, 31 May 1966.*

952   Lay religious institutes both of men and of women have presented petitions that they might enjoy certain faculties that have been delegated to the superiors general of clerical religious institutes by pontifical rescript, 6 November 1964,[a] to the extent that such faculties are not connected with the clerical state. Having considered these petitions and made its report to Pope Paul VI, the Congregation of Religious, in virtue of the task entrusted to it by the Pope in order to offer to the religious institutes in question a deserved sign of its good will, has decided to decree the following:

I. THESE FACULTIES ARE GRANTED TO THE SUPERIORS GENERAL OF RELIGIOUS INSTITUTES OF PONTIFICAL RANK, BOTH OF MEN AND OF WOMEN:

953   9.   To the superioresses general of orders of nuns, the faculty of dispensing, for a good reason, individual nuns from the obligation of reciting the divine office — if they are bound to this in virtue of the general law — when they have missed choir; or of commuting this obligation in favor of other prayers. With consent of the general council, this faculty may be subdelegated to the superioresses of individual houses.

    The same faculty is also granted to all superioresses of *sui iuris* monasteries of nuns.

II. AS TO THE EXTENSION, SUBJECT, AND USE OF THESE FACULTIES, WE DECLARE THE FOLLOWING:

954   3.   The subject of these faculties is the person of the superior general or superioress general or the person who, in their absence, replaces them *ad interim* as superior according to approved constitutions; for the faculty that is in question at the end of I, no. 9, it is the person of the superioress of a *sui iuris* monastery and, in her absence, the person who replaces her *ad interim* as superioress.

955   4.   If the superior general or superioress general is impeded from the exercise of office, the same faculties may be subdelegated in whole or in part to any member of the same institute who acts as substitute; such a person can, therefore, use the faculties personally and, in individual cases, subdelegate them according to the limits and qualifications already laid down.

▶   See also Chapter One, Section 5. Languages of the Liturgy; Chapter Four, The Divine Office.

** Text, CommRel 45 (1966) 252–254.

a See DOL 141.

Section 8. Ecumenism

SUMMARY (DOL 144–167). Liturgical implications of the new emphasis on ecumenism inspired by the Council are covered here in 24 documents.

—Papal involvement includes the joint statements of popes and heads of other Churches (DOL 145, 148, 152, 154, 156, 165, 166), the ecumenical correspondence of Paul VI on the date of Easter (DOL 146) and the question of the ordination of women (DOL 161, 162), and his apostolic exhortation on prayers for Christian unity (DOL 144). John Paul II in a homily expressed the hope for eucharistic sharing (DOL 167).

—The Secretariat for Christian Unity is the source of the general directives for Catholics in its two-part Ecumenical Directory (DOL 147, 151), with a note on its application (DOL 149), and guidelines for ecumenical collaboration with other Christians (DOL 159). On specific points, the Secretariat issued guidelines on Jewish-Christian relations (DOL 158), a declaration (DOL 150) and an instruction on eucharistic sharing (DOL 155, 157), two letters on a common date for the celebration of Easter (DOL 160, 164), and in a particular reply with universal import explained the admission of other Christians as godparents in the rite of Christian initiation (DOL 153).

—The Congregation for the Doctrine of the Faith issued a decree on another specific issue, the celebration of Mass for deceased non-Catholics (DOL 163).

—The extensive material on mixed marriages is assigned to Chapter Three. Section 6 (DOL 351–357).

144. PAUL VI, **Apostolic Exhortation** *E peregrinatione*, on prayer for the unity of Christians, 15 January 1964: AAS 56 (1964) 183–188 (excerpt).

956 Having come back from the pilgrimage during which, out of the desire for prayer and penance, we have venerated the places Christ consecrated by the mysteries of his redemption, we are constrained to turn with joyful spirit to all our brothers in the episcopate. [. . .]

Esteemed Brothers, we have seen how your devotedness, love for the Church, and singular pastoral concern have resulted in enthusiastic crowds of the faithful all along our journey of prayer and penance, showering us with love everywhere we went and uniting themselves to our apostolic purposes. [. . .]

957 We above all treasure the meetings with the heads of the Eastern Churches, from which we have been so long and so sadly estranged, and in particular the conversations we have had with the Ecumenical Patriarch of Constantinople, himself a pilgrim to Palestine. We have exchanged that holy kiss customary between the disciples of Christ and have together read that radiant prayer by which our Redeemer, before undergoing the torments of the Cross, asked the Father for the unity of his disciples so that the world might believe. We have together recited the Lord's Prayer by which we call upon God as our Father and are taught to give mutual forgiveness to each other. We rejoice in all these things as the firstfruits of the complete unity of Christ's Church, even though its attainment may still be far off. [. . .]

958 Above all, of course, we must with humble and sincere reverence offer to God a grateful heart and a mind conscious of his favors. He is guiding his Church through all its human vicissitudes and leading it to its eternal goals, so that from the shared experience of our pilgrimage we have a foretaste of new beginnings that give special promise of peace for the strengthening and progress of the kingdom of God. [. . .]

Of course we do not know when, in the counsels of God's providence, it will come about that the seeds so hopefully planted in our presence will grow to maturity. Nonetheless, we do hold it as certain that the unflagging prayers of generous Christians offered to God and their oftentimes hidden acts of penance have prepared the ways of the Lord in which we have been privileged to walk exultantly these past days. We also have no doubt that our humble, constant, trustful prayers and works of penance — offered to God out of Christian faith and love — will overcome the difficulties and adversities that lie ahead on the path yet to be trodden. In this way the longed-for goal can be reached safely and soon.

Accordingly, Esteemed Brothers, we have the greatest desire to join all the children of the Church to ourself in offering thanks to God for the happy outcome of our pilgrimage. Even as all the faithful desired through their prayers to prepare for our journey and to follow it intently, so also it is altogether right that they all join together in seeing to it that its salutary results are safeguarded. Those results are what we constantly and with full confidence, in the places consecrated by Christ the Lord's suffering and love, besought God to grant for the well-being of the Church and the good of the whole human family.

We therefore request, Esteemed Brothers, that in each parish of your dioceses you arrange for special services of thanksgiving and supplication to almighty God. We wish particularly to recommend the Week of Prayer for Christian Unity, which begins in a few days. Its purpose is that people of the different Christian confessions, united in the one zeal for religion, each year address their shared prayer to

God in order to plead for the unity that Christ the Lord enjoined upon all his followers.

On this point it is worthwhile to recall that our predecessor Pope John XXIII,   959
on 25 January 1959, the day ending the Week of Prayer, first announced the convocation of Vatican Council II for the purpose of a renewal of the Church and the restoration of the unity of all Christians. Let us remember as well that Pope John throughout his first encyclical, *Ad Petri Cathedram*, called all Christians his "dearest brothers" and invited them all without distinction to ask God for unity through their prayers. Taking the name of Paul the Apostle on being elevated to the papacy, we too have always honored the Week of Prayer in carrying out the ministry that the Lord has at various times assigned to us. With a spirit of joy we have each year celebrated the end of the Week of Prayer, in the Roman liturgy the feast of the Conversion of St. Paul.

We have come to know that countless people from the various Christian confessions have dedicated themselves to this noble cause of unity and are addressing their humble and fervent prayers to God for the accomplishment of his will. Do not let it happen, Esteemed Brothers, that the children of the Catholic Church, because they are, from God's freely given favor, the recipients of the fullness of truth, show themselves less concerned about furthering this most sacred cause of unity. On the contrary they must, from a deep religious concern, espouse this cause in union with other Christians who are separated from the Holy See. Because they are the recipients of this surpassing gift of God, full membership in his Church, let them be motivated to pursue this cause with greater generosity through their prayers and penitential acts. Led by their bishops, who during the Council clearly showed how close to their hearts Christian unity is, let all Catholics this year address more intense prayers to God that the grace of the Holy Spirit will bring about very soon the unity of all Christians.

To this end we grant to all pastors of the Catholic Church who conduct the special services we have recommended the power to impart in our name to all the faithful present, the papal blessing once on a day of their choice and also a plenary indulgence, which can be gained by all who receive the sacraments of penance and the eucharist and who pray for the pope's intentions. [. . .]

▶   6.   VATICAN COUNCIL II, Decree on Ecumenism *Unitatis redintegratio*, 21 November
            1964.

▶   446.   SC COUNCIL, Circular Letter *Omnibus in comperto* to local Ordinaries, on tourists'
            participation in Sunday and holyday Masses, 19 March 1966:

                          Ecumenical spirit [no. 3834].

145. PAUL VI and MICHAEL RAMSEY (Archbishop of Canterbury), Joint Statement, 24 March 1966: AAS 58 (1966) 286–287 (English; excerpt).

In this city of Rome, from which St. Augustine was sent by St. Gregory to   960
England and there founded the cathedral see of Canterbury, towards which the eyes of all Anglicans now turn as the center of their Christian Communion, His Holiness Pope Paul VI and His Grace Michael Ramsey, Archbishop of Canterbury, representing the Anglican Communion, have met to exchange fraternal greetings. [. . .]

They express their desire that all Christians belonging to these two Communions may be guided by these same sentiments of respect, esteem, and fraternal love. To help these develop to the full, they intend to inaugurate between the Roman Catholic Church and the Anglican Communion a serious dialogue which will have the Gospels and their common ancient traditions as their foundation and which may lead to that unity in truth for which Christ prayed.

These conversations should include not only theological matters such as Scripture, tradition, and liturgy, but also matters of practical difficulty felt on either side. His Holiness the Pope and His Grace the Archbishop of Canterbury are, indeed, aware that serious obstacles stand in the way of restoring a complete communion in faith and sacramental life; nevertheless, they are of one mind in their determination to promote responsible exchanges between their Communions in all those spheres of church life where collaboration is likely to lead to a greater understanding and a deeper charity, and to work together to find solutions for all the great problems that face those who believe in Christ in the world of today.

146. PAUL VI, **Epistle** *Nous nous apprêtons* to His Beatitude Christophoros, Pope and Patriarch of Alexandria, on a common date for Easter, 31 March 1966 (excerpt).*

961   We are about to celebrate with hearts full of love and gratitude the glorious resurrection of our Lord Jesus Christ, who has loved us to the point of becoming one of us and giving up his life "that he should gather together as one the children of God who were scattered" (Jn 11:52). The contemplation of the Father's love, "who in Christ, reconciling the world to himself, . . . has committed to us the word of reconciliation" (2 Cor 5:19), invites us quite naturally, beloved brother, to express to you our own union in charity. Our joy is greater still this year because we celebrate this great feast on the same date and so give common witness to the world of the identity of our faith in this central mystery of our religion. For St. Paul tells us: "If Christ be not risen, our own preaching is vain and your faith also is vain" (1 Cor 15:14).

962   We know that Your Beatitude shares this joy with us, for you also have the wish that Christians will agree on the date of Easter. Is not your Church examining the issue of the date of Easter, which is part of the program of the Orthodox pro-Synod? It has also been studied by the non-Chalcedonian Eastern Churches and has also been raised in the World Council of Churches.

Your Beatitude is aware that the Catholic bishops assembled in the recently concluded Second Vatican Council have declared that there is no objection to the fixing of a date for Easter on a set Sunday; but the will of the Council was that nothing should be done except in concert with the other Christian Churches.[a]

We realize that it is a complex issue, but we wish to let you know that we would happily consider any proposal aimed at achieving collaboration on this matter. Such collaboration, designed to bring us to a common solution, would be wholly in line with the decision of the Council of Nicaea, which asked that all Christians be in agreement on the same date for the celebration of the resurrection of our great God and Savior Jesus Christ.

---

*   Text, DocCath 64 (1967) 312–313 (French).
a   See DOL 1 no. 131.

We hasten also to assure Your Beatitude of the great interest with which we are following the preparatory work for the pan-Orthodox pro-Synod, which will have to address so many of the problems that the times impose on all the Christian Churches. Here again, we would give the most favorable consideration to any form of exchange of views that you might deem possible and desirable.

We should be pleased if the contacts established because of the sending of observers from your Church to the Vatican Council — for which we again wish to express our thanks to Your Beatitude — not only do not end with the Council, but continue and grow into an ever stronger mutual bond between our Churches. [. . .]

147. SECRETARIAT FOR CHRISTIAN UNITY, **Ecumenical Directory,** Part I, *Ad totam Ecclesiam*, excerpts on liturgy, 14 May 1967: AAS 59 (1967) 574–592.

II. VALIDITY OF BAPTISM BY MINISTERS OF CHURCHES AND ECCLESIAL COMMUNITIES SEPARATED FROM US

9.   The practice of the Church in this matter is guided by two principles: baptism is necessary for salvation; it can be conferred only once.

963

10.   The importance of the sacrament of baptism in ecumenical matters is highlighted by several documents of Vatican Council II: "As he was explicitly teaching the need of faith and baptism (see Mk 16:16; Jn 3:5), [Jesus] at the same time affirmed the need of the Church, which people enter through baptism as through a door" (LG no. 14).

964

"The Church recognizes that it is linked on many counts with those who, being baptized, have the honor of being called Christians, but do not profess the faith in its entirety nor preserve unity of communion under Peter's successor" (LG no. 15).

"Those who believe in Christ and have rightly received baptism are placed in a certain, even if not full, communion with the Catholic Church. . . . Those who have been justified by faith are in baptism incorporated into Christ; they therefore have a right to the honor of being called Christians and are rightly acknowledged as brothers and sisters in the Lord by the members of the Catholic Church" (UR no. 3).

"On the other hand, Catholics must gladly acknowledge and esteem the genuinely Christian treasures deriving from our common heritage that Christians separated from us possess" (UR no. 4).

11.   Baptism is thus the sacramental bond of unity and the very foundation of communion between all Christians. Hence, both its dignity and the manner of conferring it are matters of supreme importance for all disciples of Christ. A right esteem for this sacrament, however, and the mutual recognition of baptism conferred in Ecclesial Communities are sometimes made difficult because of a prudent doubt about baptism conferred in some particular instance. To avoid such difficulties when a separated Christian, led by the grace of the Holy Spirit and by conscience, seeks full communion with the Catholic Church, there are several guiding norms.

965

966   12. There can be no doubt about the validity of baptism among separated Eastern Christians.[5] It suffices, therefore, that a baptism be an established fact. Since in the Eastern Churches the priest always lawfully administers the sacrament of confirmation (chrism) along with baptism, it frequently happens that there is no mention of this sacrament in the canonical record of the baptism itself; this does not establish the existence of a doubt about the fact of its conferral.

967   13. As to other Christians, there can sometimes be a doubt.

        a. *Matter and form.* Baptism conferred by immersion, by infusion, or by sprinkling and in name of the Trinity is *per se* valid.[6] If therefore the rituals and liturgical books or customs of a Church or religious Community prescribe one of these ways of baptizing, cause for doubt can arise only on the chance occurrence of the minister's not observing the norms of the Community in question. Therefore testimony to the fidelity of the baptizing minister toward the norms of that Community or Church is required and suffices.

        To secure this, the normal requirement is a written baptismal certificate with the name of the baptizing minister. Often it can happen that a request for the cooperation of the separated Community is in order for the purpose of establishing in general or in a particular case whether a minister is to be regarded as one who conferred baptism in keeping with the authorized books.

        b. *Faith and intention.* Because some think that the minister's insufficiency in faith or intention can create a doubt about the baptism, the following are to be noted:

        —The minister's lack of faith never of itself invalidates a baptism.

        —Sufficient intention in the minister who confers baptism is to be presumed, unless there are serious grounds for doubting his intention to do what Christians do.[7]

        c. *Application of the matter.* In cases in which a doubt arises about the application of the matter, reverence toward the sacrament and respect for the ecclesial nature of the Communities separated from us demand initiation of a serious investigation about the practice of the Community and the circumstances of the baptism itself prior to any decision that the sacrament is invalid because of the manner of administration.[8]

968   14. The practice of the conditional baptism of all without distinction who desire to enter full communion with the Catholic Church cannot be approved. The sacrament of baptism cannot be repeated[9] and therefore it is not permitted to confer it again conditionally, unless there is a reasonable doubt about the fact or validity of the baptism already conferred.[10]

969   15. It may happen that after a thorough investigation of a baptism's right administration it is necessary to administer it again conditionally. In due recognition of the

---

        [5] With regard to all Christians a danger of invalidity must be taken into account in the case of baptism by sprinkling, especially administered collectively.

        [6] See CIC can. 758.

        [7] See Reply of the Holy Office, 30 Jan. 1833: "It is enough that they do what Christians do." Congregation of the Council, Decr. approved by Pius V, 19 June 1570, quoted by the Provincial Council of Evreux, 1576.

        [8] See CIC can. 737, § 1.

        [9] See CIC can. 732, § 1.

        [10] See Council of Trent, sess. 7, can. 4. CIC can. 732, § 2.

teaching that there is only one baptism, the minister is to: a. properly explain both the reasons why in this case he is baptizing conditionally and the significance of the rite of administration; b. use the nonsolemn rite of baptism.[11]

16. The whole issue of the theology and practice of baptism should be made the subject of dialogue between the Catholic Church and the Churches or Communities separated from us. It is suggested that the ecumenical commissions hold these discussions with the Churches or councils of Churches in various regions and, where useful, that both parties come to an agreement on the agenda for this project.   970

17. Out of reverence toward the sacrament of initiation that the Lord instituted for the New Covenant and in order to make clearer the requirements for its right administration, it is most desirable not to restrict the dialogue with Christians separated from us simply to the issue of the elements absolutely necessary for validity. The fullness of the sacramental sign and of the reality signified (*res sacramenti*) as deriving from their New Testament foundations should also receive attention, in order to facilitate agreement between the Churches on their recognition of each other's baptism.   971

18. A just esteem for the baptism conferred by ministers of Churches and Ecclesial Communities separated from us has great ecumenical import. For that effectively demonstrates that baptism forms "the sacramental bond of unity existing between all who have a new birth through it" (UR no. 22ᵃ).[12] The hope therefore must be that all Christians will more and more attend to its celebration with reverence and fidelity toward the Lord's teaching.   972

19. According to the intent of the Decree on Ecumenism, those Christians born and baptized outside the visible communion of the Catholic Church must be carefully distinguished from those who, being baptized in the Catholic Church, have knowingly and publicly rejected its faith. For according to the Decree, "Those who are now born into Communities of this kind [separated] and are imbued with the faith of Christ cannot be accused of the sin of separation" (UR no. 3). In the absence of such fault, therefore, those freely wishing to embrace the Catholic faith do not need to be absolved from the penalty of excommunication; after making a profession of faith according to norms set down by the local Ordinary, they are to be admitted into the full communion of the Catholic Church. The prescriptions of canon 2314 apply only in the case of those who have culpably fallen away from the faith or from Catholic communion and then with a contrite heart seek to be reconciled with the Church.   973

20. What has just been said about absolution from censures must, for the same reason, clearly be said about the abjuration of heresy.   974

III. PROMOTING SPIRITUAL ECUMENISM IN THE CATHOLIC CHURCH

21. "Conversion of heart and holiness of life, together with private and public prayer for the unity of Christians, should be regarded as the soul of the whole ecumenical movement and may rightly be called spiritual ecumenism" (UR no. 8).   975

---

[11] See CIC can. 737, § 2.

ᵃ DOL 6 no. 189.

[12] See LG no. 15. See also the Report of the Joint Commission of the Roman Catholic Church and the World Council of Churches: OR, 20 Feb. 1966, 7. Report of the Fourth International Meeting of "Faith and Order," Montreal, 1966, nos. 111, 113, 154.

In these few words the Decree on Ecumenism defines spiritual ecumenism and insists on its importance in order that Christians in their prayers, in the celebration of the eucharist, and indeed in their entire daily life will unfailingly keep before them the intention of unity.

All Christians, even if not living among those separated from us, always and everywhere have a personal part in the ecumenical movement by renewing their whole Christian life according to the spirit of the Gospel, stressed by Vatican Council II, and by shutting out nothing from the shared Christian heritage.[13]

976   22. It is fitting that prayers for unity be offered regularly at special times, such as:

a. the week of 18–25 January, called the Week of Prayer for Christian Unity, in which many Churches and Ecclesial Communities pray together to God for unity;

b. the days from the Ascension of the Lord to Pentecost, which commemorate how the Jerusalem community waited and prayed for the coming of the Holy Spirit to confirm them in unity and in a universal mission.

Further examples are:

a. the days around Epiphany, commemorating the manifestation of Christ to the world and the connection between the Church's mission and its unity;

b. Holy Thursday, commemorating the institution of the eucharist, the sacrament of unity, and the prayer of Jesus Christ the Savior in the upper room for the Church and its unity;

c. Good Friday or the feast of the Triumph of the Holy Cross, commemorating the mystery of the cross, which gathers together the scattered children of God;

d. the Easter solemnities, when the joy of the resurrection of the Lord is a power bringing all Christians together;

e. the occasion of meetings or other important events that ecumenism might prompt or that can have a special bearing on ecumenical interests.

977   23. "The custom has grown of Catholics coming together in large numbers to offer the prayer for Church unity that on the eve of his death our Savior himself fervently offered to the Father: 'That all may be one.'" (UR no. 8).[b]

Thus also all Christians should pray for unity in a way consonant with Christ's prayer at the Last Supper so that all of us may draw nearer to "that fullness of unity which Jesus Christ wants" (UR no. 4).

978   24. Pastors should take care to arrange gatherings of the faithful, suited to the various circumstances of place and people, to pray for unity. Since the eucharist is that marvelous sacrament "which both signifies and brings about the Church's unity" (UR no. 2),[c] there is much to be gained from reminding the faithful of the importance of the eucharist and from encouraging public prayers for Christian unity within the eucharistic celebration (e.g., in the general intercessions or in the litanies called *Ectenes*) and in the celebration of the votive Mass for the Unity of the Church. The parts of liturgical rites that have special prayers of petition, for example, the supplications called the *Litia* and the *Moleben* can very fittingly be celebrated for the intention of Christian unity.

---

13   See UR no. 6 [DOL 6 no. 185]; AG no. 36 [DOL 17 no. 253].

b   DOL 6 no. 186.

c   DOL 6 no. 182.

IV. COMMUNICATIO IN SPIRITUALIBUS WITH
CHRISTIANS SEPARATED FROM US

A. Introduction

25. To foster the restoration of unity among all Christians it is not enough that   979
they exercise mutual charity in their everyday contacts. It is also appropriate to
allow them in some degree to share together in those spiritual blessings that Christians possess in common. This sharing should be of a form and character consistent
with what is acceptable in the present situation of division. Of those elements or
endowments "that taken together go to build up and give life to the Church itself,
some and even many, can exist outside the visible confines of the Catholic Church"
(UR no. 3). The elements "that come from Christ and lead back to him belong by
right to the single Church of Christ" (UR no. 3); they can rightly serve the offering
of prayer for the grace of unity and express and strengthen the bonds that still link
Catholics with Christians separated from us.

26. Since, however, these spiritual endowments are present in different ways in   980
the various Christian Communities, sharing together in the spiritual is conditioned
by this diversity and must be handled in different ways according to the situation
of persons, Churches, and Communities. To regulate *communicatio in spiritualibus*, then,
the following are set forth as suited to the present state of affairs.

27. There should be an effort toward mutuality ("reciprocity") so that a sharing in   981
the sacred with mutual good will and charity, even though kept within narrow
limits, may contribute to a sound advance in agreement among Christians. Therefore dialogues and consultations on this matter between Catholic authorities, local
or territorial, and the authorities of other Communions are strongly recommended.

28. Where this reciprocity and mutual understanding are more difficult — by   982
reason of the fact that in some places and in regard to some Communities, sects, and
persons the ecumenical movement and the desire for peace with the Catholic
Church have not yet become strong[14] — the local Ordinary or, if need be, the
conference of bishops may indicate suitable ways of forestalling the danger of
indifferentism or proselytism[15] among the faithful in such circumstances. It is to be
hoped however that, through the grace of the Holy Spirit and the wise pastoral care
of the Ordinaries, an ecumenical sense and mutual respect will so increase both on
the part of the Catholic faithful and on the part of Christians separated from us that
the need for these special norms will gradually disappear.

29. Under the name *communicatio in spiritualibus* should be understood all prayers   983
offered in common, common use of sacred articles or places, and all *communicatio in
sacris* properly so called.

30. *Communicatio in sacris* occurs when anyone takes part in liturgical worship or in   984
the sacraments of another Church or Ecclesial Community.

31. The term "liturgical worship" refers to worship in a form that follows the   985
books, prescriptions, or usages of any Church or Community and that is celebrated
by a minister or delegate of such a Church or Community acting as such.

---

14   See UR no. 19.

15   The term *proselytism* is taken here as a manner of acting at odds with the spirit of the Gospel because
it employs dishonest motivation to draw people into a community, taking advantage, for example, of their
ignorance, poverty, etc. (see DH no. 4).

B. COMMON PRAYER SERVICES

986   32. "In certain special circumstances, such as gatherings to pray for unity and during ecumenical meetings, it is lawful and indeed greatly desirable that Catholics join in prayer with Christians separated from us. Such common prayers are an especially effective means for asking for the grace of unity and they are a genuine expression of the bonds that still link Catholics with Christians separated from us" (UR no. 8).[d]

The point of the Decree is prayer services in which members of different Communities, including ministers, take an "active" part. For Catholics the direction and furtherance of this kind of participation are in the hands of local Ordinaries. The following points are to be noted concerning it.

987   33. It is most desirable that Catholics join with Christians separated from us in prayer for any common concern in which they can and should cooperate, for example, to promote peace, social justice, mutual charity among all people, the dignity of the family, and similar matters. To be considered in the same way are those occasions when a nation or community wishes to offer a general thanksgiving to God or beg his help, as on national holidays, in time of disaster or national mourning, on a day of memorial for those who have died for their country. Such common prayer, insofar as it is possible, is also recommended when there is a meeting of Christians for study or action.

988   34. But common prayer services should be concerned above all with the restoration of unity among Christians. For a celebration of this kind examples of possible themes are: the mystery of the Church and its unity; baptism as the sacramental, though incomplete, bond of unity; the reforming of life, both personal and social, as a necessary way to achieve unity; other themes treated in no. 22.

FORM OF THE CELEBRATION

989   35. a. Preparation for a celebration of this kind should result from common agreement and cooperation of all the participants who represent the various Churches or Communities. (In this way, for example, the persons who are to take part should be chosen and the themes, hymns, scripture readings, prayers, and the like decided.)

b. Such a celebration may include any reading, prayer, or hymn that expresses something about the faith or spiritual life shared by all Christians. There is also a place for an exhortation, address, or biblical meditation that develops elements of the shared Christian heritage, favors mutual good will, and promotes unity between Christians.

c. Whether held by Catholics alone or together with Christians separated from us, these celebrations should be so structured that they conform to the "community" prayer modeled on the program of the liturgical movement.[16]

d. In preparing prayer services that are to be celebrated in the church building of an Eastern Church, it should be kept in mind that the established form of the liturgy of Eastern Christians is to be regarded as especially suited to prayer of petition. Therefore the character of the liturgical order of such a Church must be taken into account.

---

d   DOL 6 no. 186.

16   See SC, for example, art. 30, 34, 35 [DOL 1 nos. 30, 34, 35].

PLACE OF CELEBRATION

36. a. The place chosen is to be one acceptable to all the participants. Care should   990
be taken that everything about it is suitable and likely to foster a sense of devotion.

  b. A church or religious edifice is the place where a Community normally
celebrates its own liturgy. Nevertheless, where there is need and with approval of
the Ordinary, there is nothing against holding the common celebrations (mentioned
in nos. 32–35) in the church of one or another of the Communities concerned; in
fact in proper circumstances this might be the advisable thing to do.

  c. When prayer services are held with Eastern Christians separated from us, it
should be remembered that all of them regard the church itself as the most suitable
place for public prayer services.

VESTURE

37. The use of choir dress is not excluded when this is in keeping with the circum-   991
stances and mutually agreed on by the participants.

C. COMMUNICATIO IN SACRIS

38. "*Communicatio in sacris* may not be regarded as a means to be used indiscrimi-   992
nately toward restoring Christian unity. Such sharing is dependent mainly on two
principles: the unity of the Church, of which it is a sign, and the sharing in the
means of grace. Its function as sign often rules out *communicatio in sacris*; its being a
source of grace sometimes favors it" (UR no. 8).[e]

1. COMMUNICATIO IN SACRIS WITH EASTERN CHRISTIANS SEPARATED FROM US

39. "Because these Churches, even though separated from us, have true sacra-   993
ments and especially, by virtue of apostolic succession, the eucharist and the priesthood — all bonds still linking them closely to us — some form of *communicatio in
sacris* is not only admissible but even advisable in the right circumstances and with
the approval of church authority" (UR no. 15).[17,f]

40. Between the Catholic Church and the Eastern Churches separated from us   994
there is still a rather close communion in matters of faith;[18] "the celebration of the
eucharist in each of these Churches builds up and gives increase to the Church of
God," and "these Churches, even though separated, have true sacraments and
especially, by virtue of apostolic succession, the eucharist, and the priesthood . . ."
(UR no. 15).[g] Hence, an ecclesiological and sacramental basis exists for allowing and
even at times encouraging some sharing in liturgical worship, including the eucharist, with these Churches, "in the right circumstances and with the approval of
church authority" (UR no. 15).[h]

  Pastors should carefully instruct the faithful so that they will come to a clear
understanding of the rationale of common worship in this case.

41. The norms governing common worship established in the Decree *Orientalium*   995
Ecclesiarum[19] must be observed with that prudence advised by the Decree itself. The

---

  e   DOL 6 no. 186.

  17   See also OE nos. 24–29.

  f   DOL 6 no. 187.

  18   See UR no. 14.

  g   DOL 6 no. 187.

  h   DOL 6 no. 187.

  19   See OE nos. 26–29.

norms that, according to the Decree, apply to the faithful of the Eastern Catholic Churches apply as well to Catholics of any rite, including the Latin.

996   42. In regard to reception or administration of the sacraments of penance, the eucharist, and anointing of the sick, it is highly advisable that the Catholic authorities — the local Ordinary, the diocesan synod, or the conference of bishops — not grant the faculty for sacramental sharing until consultation with at least the local, authorized officials of the separated Eastern Church has reached a favorable outcome.

997   43. In the concession of faculties for sacramental sharing it is especially appropriate to take into account legitimate considerations of "reciprocity."

998   44. Over and above cases of necessity, the physical and moral impossibility of receiving the sacraments in a person's own Church for an extended period because of special circumstances can be counted as a just cause for recommending sacramental sharing, lest one of the faithful be deprived without good reason of the spiritual fruits of the sacraments.

999   45. The practices of Catholic and separated Eastern Christians differ regarding the frequency of communion, sacramental confession before communion, and the eucharistic fast. Therefore in the matter of intercommunion care must be taken against any failure of Catholics to respect the Eastern usages, in order not to give rise to shock or suspicion among separated Eastern Christians. A Catholic lawfully receiving communion with such Christians in the circumstances already indicated should therefore make every effort to follow their usages.

1000   46. In the absence of available confessors of their own Church, Eastern Christians who, of their own accord, wish to do so are free to go to a Catholic confessor. In similar circumstances it is permissible for a Catholic to confess to a confessor of an Eastern Church separated from Rome. "Reciprocity" should be observed in this matter also. But both parties should guard against arousing any suspicion of proselytism.[20]

1001   47. A Catholic who on occasion, for reasons dealt with in no. 50, assists at the Divine Liturgy (Mass) on a Sunday or holyday with separated Eastern Christians has no further obligation to the precept of hearing Mass in a Catholic church. Moreover, on such days Catholics who, for just reasons, cannot go to the sacred liturgy in a Catholic church should, if possible, assist at the liturgy with Eastern Christians separated from us.

1002   48. Because of the close communion, pointed out in no. 40, between the Catholic Church and the separated Eastern Churches, it is permissible for a just reason to accept one of the faithful of an Eastern Church as godparent along with a Catholic godparent at the baptism of a Catholic infant or adult, as long as the Catholic upbringing of the one being baptized is provided for and there is assurance that the person is fit to be a godparent. A Catholic invited to stand as a godparent at a baptism in an Eastern Church is not forbidden to do so. In such cases the duty of looking out for the Christian upbringing of the baptized falls first upon the godparent belonging to the Church in which the child is baptized.

---

[20]   See note 15 of this Directory.

49. At a marriage celebrated in a Catholic church, Christians separated from us are   1003
not excluded from acting as bridesmaid or best man. A Catholic may act as bridesmaid or best man at a marriage celebrated between Christians separated from us.

50. Catholics are permitted to be present at the liturgical worship of other Chris-   1004
tians for a just cause, for example, the performance of public duty or office, kinship,
friendship, the desire for better knowledge, etc. In these cases Catholics are not
barred from joining in the congregational responses, the hymns, and the actions of
the Church, whose guests they are, so to speak. As to receiving holy communion,
the rules set down in nos. 42 and 44 are to be observed. Because of the close
communion mentioned in no. 40, the local Ordinary can permit a Catholic invited
to do so to serve as reader at the worship service. All of this applies conversely to
Christians separated from us who are present at liturgies held in Catholic churches.

51. As to participation in ceremonies not requiring sacramental sharing, the fol-   1005
lowing must be observed:

    a. In Catholic ceremonies a minister of an Eastern Church representing his
own Church must receive the place and liturgical honor proper to Catholic ministers of the same order or rank in the Catholic Church.

    b. By mutual agreement a Catholic minister present in an official capacity at
religious services of Eastern Christians can wear the choir dress or the insignia
proper to his ecclesiastical rank.

    c. There should be the utmost respect for the point of view proper to the
clergy and faithful of Eastern Churches and for their customs, which may vary
according to times, places, or circumstances.

52. "*Communicatio in sacris* as to functions, articles, and places of worship between   1006
Catholics and Eastern Christians separated from us is allowed for a just reason" (OE
no. 28). Accordingly, should they so request, Eastern priests of communities with no
place to celebrate the liturgy properly and with dignity should, with permission of
the local Ordinary, be granted use of a Catholic building, cemetery, or church for
their rites and whatever else is needed.

53. The administrators of Catholic schools and institutions should be sure that   1007
Eastern ministers have the opportunity to offer their ministry and the sacraments to
their faithful who attend Catholic institutions. As far as circumstances will allow
and with permission of the local Ordinary, this assistance can be made available
inside the Catholic building, including a church.

54. In hospitals and other similar institutions conducted by Catholics, the admin-   1008
istrators should see that they advise the priest of the separated Eastern Church in
good time about the presence of his faithful and give him the opportunity to visit
the sick and administer the sacraments to them in a dignified and reverent way.

2. COMMUNICATIO IN SACRIS WITH OTHER CHRISTIANS SEPARATED FROM US

55. Celebration of the sacraments is an action of the celebrating Community,   1009
carried out within the Community itself as a sign of its own unity in faith, worship,
and life. Where such unity in faith regarding the sacraments is lacking, then,
participation by Christians separated from us, especially in the Catholic sacraments
of the eucharist, penance, and anointing of the sick, is forbidden. Nevertheless,
since the sacraments are both signs of unity and sources for gaining grace,[21] the
Church can for sufficient reasons permit separated Christians individually to receive

---

[21]   See UR no. 8 [DOL 6 no. 186].

these sacraments. This reception is permissible in danger of death or in a case of pressing need (in persecution, in prisons), if such persons do not have access to a minister of their own Communion and if they voluntarily ask for the sacraments from a Catholic priest. The only conditions are some sign of a belief in these sacraments consonant with the faith of the Church and the individual's own right dispositions. For other cases of necessity the local Ordinary or the conference of bishops should decide.

A Catholic in similar circumstances, however, may request these sacraments only of a minister who has validly received the sacrament of orders.

1010   56. Within the celebration of the eucharist the office of reader of sacred Scripture or of preacher must not be given to a Christian separated from us; the same holds for a Catholic in the celebration of the Lord's Supper or of a major liturgical service of the word held by separated Christians. At other services, even liturgical, both may be permitted to carry out certain parts with the previous permission of the local Ordinary and the consent of the authority of the other Community.

1011   57. The office of godparent at baptism or confirmation, in its liturgical and canonical sense, cannot be fulfilled by a Christian belonging to a separated Community, with the exception of what is laid down in no. 48. For it is not simply as a relative or friend of the one to be baptized or confirmed that the godparent has responsibility for the Christian upbringing of the recipient; in acting as the guarantor of the faith of the candidate, the godparent also is the representative of the community of faith. Likewise, a Catholic cannot fulfill this function for a member of a Community separated from us. However, for reasons of kinship or friendship, a Christian of another Communion, having a convinced faith in Christ, can be admitted along with the Catholic godparent as a Christian witness to a baptism. In similar circumstances, a Catholic can fulfill this role for a member of a Community separated from us. In these cases the responsibility for the Christian upbringing of the candidate falls *per se* on the godparent who is a member of the Church or Ecclesial Community in which the infant is baptized. Pastors should carefully instruct the faithful about the evangelical and ecumenical reason for this regulation so as to prevent any misunderstanding.

1012   58. In the celebration of Catholic marriages Christians separated from us may fulfill the role of official witness; the same is applicable to a Catholic at a marriage celebrated between Christians separated from us.

1013   59. The presence of Catholics is permissible on an occasional basis at the liturgy of other Christians for a good reason, for example, the performance of a public duty or service, kinship, friendship, the desire for a better knowledge, an ecumenical meeting, etc. In such cases, with due regard to what has already been said, Catholics are not forbidden to join in the congregational responses, hymns, and actions of that Community, whose guests they are, so to speak, provided they do nothing contrary to Catholic faith. All of this applies conversely to the presence of Christians separated from us at liturgies held in Catholic churches.

Their participation, from which reception of the eucharist is always excluded, should lead them to an appreciation of the spiritual riches existing among us and at the same time make them more aware of the gravity of separation.

1014   60. As to participation in ceremonies not calling for sacramental sharing, those ministers of other Communions present at the ceremonies may by mutual consent be given a place consistent with their rank. Likewise, Catholic ministers present at ceremonies celebrated by other Communions may wear choir dress, with due regard for local customs.

61. If Christians separated from us do not have a place in which to carry out their   1015
rites properly and with dignity, the local Ordinary can allow their use of Catholic
buildings, cemeteries, and churches.

62. The administrators of Catholic schools and institutions should see to it that the   1016
ministers of other Communions have the opportunity to give spiritual and sacramental help to their own faithful attending Catholic institutions. They may do so,
in accordance with circumstances, even inside Catholic buildings. The norm in no.
61 is followed.

63. In hospitals and other similar institutions conducted by Catholics, the admin-   1017
istrators should see to it that the ministers of separated Communions are advised in
good time of the presence of their faithful and that the ministers have the opportunity for visiting the sick and offering them spiritual and sacramental help.

    In an audience granted to the Secretariat for Promoting Christian Unity on 28
April 1967, Pope Paul VI approved and confirmed this Directory by his authority
and ordered it to be published. All things to the contrary notwithstanding.

148. PAUL VI and ATHENAGORAS I (Patriarch of Constantinople), **Joint
Statement**, 28 October 1967: AAS 59 (1967) 1054–55 (French; excerpt).

    [. . .] With a view to making possible the preparation of fruitful exchanges   1018
between the Roman Catholic Church and the Orthodox Church, the Pope and the
Patriarch give their blessing and pastoral support to every cooperative effort between Catholic and Orthodox professors in the areas of history, church traditions,
patristics, liturgy and in a presentation of the Gospel that corresponds at once to the
authentic message of the Lord and the needs of the world today. Animating these
efforts must be a spirit of loyalty to truth and of mutual understanding, as well as
the effective resolve to avoid past animosity and any sort of claim to superiority,
spiritual or intellectual. [. . .]

149. SECRETARIAT FOR CHRISTIAN UNITY, **Note** *In questi ultimi mesi* of
Cardinal A. Bea, on the application of the Ecumenical Directory, 6 October
1968.*

1.   During the last several months in different parts of the world, Protestant and   1019
Anglican Christians have been here and there admitted to sharing in communion at
the celebration of Mass, in spite of the absence of the conditions required by
current law and, therefore, in spite of disapproval by the competent ecclesiastical
authority.

---

*   Text, OR 6 Oct. 1968, 1 (Italian).

1020   2.   It seems to us necessary to recall here Vatican II's regulations on this issue and their application by the Ecumenical Directory (approved by Pope Paul VI on 27 April 1967 and published in AAS, 5 July 1967, 574–592).[a]

1021   3.   *"Communicatio in sacris,* however, may not be regarded as a means to be used indiscriminately toward restoring Christian unity. Such sharing is dependent mainly on two principles: the unity of the Church, of which it is a sign, and the sharing in the means of grace. Its function as sign often rules out *communicatio in sacris.* Its being a source of grace sometimes favors it. Unless the conference of bishops, following the norms of its own statutes, or the Holy See has ruled otherwise, the local bishop is the authority competent to decide with prudence what the right course of action is to be in view of all the circumstances of time, place, and people" (UR no. 8).[b]

1022   4.   "Celebration of the sacraments is an action of the celebrating Community, carried out within the Community itself as a sign of its own unity in faith, worship, and life. Where such unity in faith regarding the sacraments is lacking, then, participation by Christians separated from us, especially in the Catholic sacraments of the eucharist, penance, and anointing of the sick is forbidden. Nevertheless, since the sacraments are both signs of unity and sources for gaining grace (UR no. 8), the Church can, for sufficient reasons, permit separated Christians individually to receive these sacraments. This reception is permissible in danger of death or in a case of pressing need (in persecution, in prisons), if such persons do not have access to a minister of their own Communion and if they voluntarily ask for the sacraments from a Catholic priest. The only conditions are some sign of a belief in these sacraments consonant with the faith of the Church and the individual's own right dispositions. For other cases of necessity the local Ordinary or the conference of bishops should decide.

    "A Catholic in similar circumstances, however, may request sacraments only of a minister who has validly received the sacrament of orders" (Ecumenical Directory *Ad totam Ecclesiam* no. 55).[c]

1023   5.   These texts spell out quite precisely the conditions required for admitting an Anglican or Protestant to eucharistic communion in the Catholic Church. It is not enough that Christians belonging to one of the Confessions in question have the right spiritual dispositions and of their own accord ask for communion from a Catholic minister. Over and above these, two other conditions must obtain: they must have the same eucharistic faith as that professed by the Catholic Church; they must be unable to approach a minister of their own Confession.

    The Ecumenical Directory, by way of example, gives three situations beyond the individual's control, where these conditions prevail: danger of death, persecution, prison. In other instances the local Ordinary or the conference of bishops has the power to give permission, if it is requested, but under the condition that it is a question of urgent necessity similar to those cited in the example and in which the same conditions obtain.

    Where any one of these conditions is missing, admission to eucharistic communion in the Catholic Church is not possible.

---

[a]   See DOL 147.

[b]   DOL 6 no. 186.

[c]   DOL 147 no. 1009.

▶   326.   SC CLERGY, General Directory *Peregrinans in terra*, on the pastoral ministry in
          tourism, 30 April 1969:

          II, 3, B, g: Ecumenism [no. 2621].

150. SECRETARIAT FOR CHRISTIAN UNITY, **Declaration** *Dans ces derniers temps*, on the position of the Catholic Church regarding eucharistic sharing between Christians of different Confessions, 7 January 1970: AAS 62 (1970) 184–188 (French).

1.   Recently, in various parts of the world, something new has happened in regard   1024
to eucharistic sharing, involving, on the one side, faithful and clergy of the Catholic
Church and, on the other, Christians and pastors of other Churches and Ecclesial
Communities. This may involve admission of Catholic faithful to a Protestant or
Anglican eucharistic communion; participation by Protestants and Anglicans in the
eucharistic communion of the Catholic Church; a communal eucharist celebrated
together by ministers belonging to still-separated Churches and Ecclesial Communities and shared in by the faithful of these Communities.

Concerning this issue of great theological, pastoral, and above all ecumenical
importance, we wish to recall the norms of the Church as they have been recently
formulated.

2.   Vatican Council II declared itself on this subject in the Decree on Ecumenism,   1025
Unitatis redintegratio. Having noted that common prayers for unity are an effective
means of asking for the grace of unity and stand as a genuine expression of the
abiding bonds that continue to unite Catholics with other Christians, the Decree
continues:

"Communicatio in sacris, however, may not be regarded as a means to be used
indiscriminately toward restoring Christian unity. Such sharing is dependent mainly on two principles: the unity of the Church, of which it is a sign, and the sharing
in the means of grace. Its function as sign often rules out *communicatio in sacris.* Its
being a source of grace sometimes favors it. Unless the conference of bishops,
following the norms of its own statutes, or the Holy See, has ruled otherwise, the
local bishop is the authority competent to decide with prudence what the right
course of action is to be in view of the circumstances of time, place, and people"
(UR no. 8).[a]

3.   The Council bids us in the application of these general principles to take into   1026
account "the special status of the Eastern Churches" (UR no. 14) and to draw the
conclusions this calls for.

"Because these Churches, even though separated from us, have true sacraments and especially, by virtue of apostolic succession, the eucharist, and the priesthood — all bonds still linking them closely to us — some form of *communicatio in
sacris* is not only admissible but even advisable in the right circumstances and with
the approval of church authority" (UR no. 15).[b]

Going into greater detail, the Decree on the Eastern Catholic Churches *Orientalium Ecclesiarum* allows Eastern Christians who are not in full communion with the

---

[a]   DOL 6 no. 186.

[b]   DOL 6 no. 187.

Apostolic See of Rome to receive the sacraments of penance, the eucharist, and anointing of the sick when the required conditions are present. It likewise authorizes Catholics to ask for the same sacraments from Eastern priests whenever necessity or genuine spiritual benefit calls for it and when access to a Catholic priest is physically or morally impossible. The Decree also encourages contacts on this subject between the ecclesiastical authorities of the Churches concerned (see OE nos. 27, 29).[c]

1027   4.   In the section of the Decree on Ecumenism *Unitatis redintegratio* devoted to the "Western Churches and Ecclesial Communities not in Union with Us," which make up quite diverse Christian confessional families, the Council faced up to the theological problem underlying the sacramental, eucharistic relations with Christian Communities in which the same conditions as those of the Eastern Churches are not present:

"The Ecclesial Communities separated from us do not have the full unity with us that derives from baptism and, we believe, have not, especially because of their lack of the sacrament of orders, kept the authentic and integral substance of the eucharistic mystery. Nevertheless, when in the Lord's Supper they commemorate his death and resurrection, they attest to the sign of their life in communion with Christ and they await his glorious Second Coming. Their teaching, therefore, on the Lord's Supper, the rest of the sacraments, the worship and ministry of the Church provide apt subjects for dialogue" (UR no. 22).[d]

Notice that the regard for the eucharist in the doctrine of these Communities is joined to a call for dialogue on the eucharist and the entire sacramental life, with special mention of the ministries of the Church. The Catholic Church, of course, attaches critical importance to the traditional teaching on the need and essential conditions of a ministerial priesthood with its origins in apostolic succession.

1028   5.   The provisions of Vatican Council II were applied in the Ecumenical Directory approved by Pope Paul VI on 27 April 1967 (published in AAS, 5 July of the same year).[e]

As to eucharistic relations with Eastern Christians not in full communion with Rome, the Directory repeats the provisions of the Council, adding some especially practical details on the subject of "reciprocity" and prior agreement between the ecclesiastical authorities of the Churches concerned (Ecumenical Directory nos. 39–47).[f]

1029   6.   The Directory entered into greater detail regarding Christian Communities with which we do not share the ecclesiological and sacramental base that so markedly unites us with the Churches of the East. It formulates the following norms, after giving them theological support:

"Celebration of the sacraments is an action of the celebrating Community, carried out within the Community itself, as a sign of its own unity in faith, worship, and life. Where such unity in faith regarding the sacraments is lacking, then, participation by Christians separated from us, especially in the Catholic sacraments of the eucharist, penance, and anointing of the sick, is forbidden. Nevertheless,

c   DOL 5 nos. 179, 181.

d   DOL 6 no. 189.

e   See DOL 147.

f   See DOL 147 nos. 993–1001.

since the sacraments are both signs of unity and sources for gaining grace (see UR no. 8),[g] the Church can for sufficient reasons permit separated Christians individually to receive these sacraments. This reception is permissible in danger of death or in a case of pressing need (in persecution, in prisons), if such persons do not have access to a minister of their own Communion and if they voluntarily ask for the sacraments from a Catholic priest. The only conditions are some sign of a belief in these sacraments consonant with the faith of the Church and the individual's own right dispositions. For other cases of necessity the local Ordinary or the conference of bishops should decide.

"A Catholic in similar circumstances, however, may request these sacraments only of a minister who has validly received the sacrament of orders" (Directory no. 55).[h]

7.   Commenting on this passage a month before his death, Cardinal Bea, President   1030
of the Secretariat for Christian Unity, took pains to shed light on its exact sense:

"These texts spell out quite precisely the conditions required for admitting an Anglican or Protestant to eucharistic communion in the Catholic Church. It is not enough that Christians belonging to one of the Confessions in question have the right spiritual dispositions and of their own accord ask for communion from a Catholic minister. Over and above these, two other conditions must obtain: they must have the same eucharistic faith as that professed by the Catholic Church; they must be unable to approach a minister of their own Confession.

"The Ecumenical Directory, by way of example, gives three situations beyond the individual's control, where these conditions prevail: danger of death, persecution, prison. In other instances the local Ordinary or the conference of bishops has the power to give permission, if it is requested, but under the condition that it is a question of urgent necessity similar to those cited in the example and in which the same conditions obtain.

"Where one of these conditions is missing, admission to eucharistic communion in the Catholic Church is not possible" (Note on the application of the Ecumenical Directory, published in OR, 6 October 1968).[i]

8.   Concerning the role the Directory is called upon to play in the pastoral activity   1031
of the Church, it seems to us pertinent to recall here the words that Pope Paul addressed to the members of the Secretariat for Christian Unity on 13 November 1968:

"We need not tell you that to promote ecumenism effectively there is a need to guide it by putting its implementation under very exact rules. In our mind the Ecumenical Directory is not a collection of suggestions that anyone is free to accept or ignore. It is a genuine instruction, a detailed explanation of that discipline to which those who truly wish to serve the cause of ecumenism must submit" (OR, 14 November 1968).

9.   The Secretariat for Christian Unity is following this problem very closely. On   1032
its own it has taken various measures in this area and devoted great attention to it during its plenary session (*Congregatio plenaria*, i.e., one made up of forty bishops from throughout the world) held at Rome, 18–28 November 1969. The Secretariat also rejoices in the efforts being made throughout the world to achieve, within the historical context of the division between Christians, a more profound theology of

---

[g]   See DOL 6 no. 186.

[h]   DOL 147 no. 1009.

[i]   DOL 149 no. 1023.

the Church, the ministry, and the eucharist, both as sacrament and as sacrifice. With interest and profit the Secretariat notes the efforts made to clarify the problems involved and to sharpen terminology. Above all it is pleased with the interconfessional dialogue on this subject actually in progress on the local and worldwide levels. It expresses the hope that these conversations will serve to bring the positions closer together. At the same time the Secretariat is aware that up to the present time these dialogues have not yet achieved results that could be adopted on both sides by those who have the positions of responsibility in the Churches and the Ecclesial Communities concerned.

As regards the Catholic Church, then, there is no reason at this time to modify the norms cited earlier from the Ecumenical Directory. The line of conduct they trace results from the reflection of the Church on its own faith and from an assessment of the pastoral needs of the faithful. Before looking toward another approach in the matter of a shared eucharist, it will be necessary to have a clear assurance that any change that develops will remain in absolute conformity with the Church's profession of faith and will be advantageous to the spiritual life of its members.

1033   10.   At the time when the Week of Prayer for Christian Unity is about to begin, we give full weight to the desire for a shared eucharist as a powerful stimulus toward the search for the kind of complete ecclesial unity that Christ desired. This aspiration can be expressed very pointedly in the services about to take place during this Week of Prayer. Besides the biblical readings and meditation, these services could well include elements directed toward the hoped-for shared eucharist: our thanksgiving for the partial unity already achieved; our regret over the divisions remaining, with the firm resolve to take every measure to overcome them; finally, our prayer to the Lord to hasten the day when we will be able to celebrate together the mystery of the body and blood of Christ.

151. SECRETARIAT FOR CHRISTIAN UNITY, **Ecumenical Directory**, Part II, *Spiritus Domini*, on ecumenism in higher education, 16 April 1970: AAS 62 (1970) 705–724 (excerpts).

PART TWO
ECUMENISM IN HIGHER EDUCATION

INTRODUCTION

1034   (64)† The Spirit of the Lord is at work in the contemporary ecumenical movement so that, "the obstacles to complete ecclesiastical communion being overcome,"[1] the union of all Christians will be restored and become resplendent.[2] For all peoples are called to be the one new people in their confession of Jesus Christ as Savior and Lord, in their profession of the one faith, and in their celebration of the one eucharistic mystery[3] in order that, as the Lord says, "the world will believe that you have sent me" (Jn 17:21).

---

   † The paragraph numbers in parentheses continue the enumeration of the Ecumenical Directory, Part I, published 14 May 1967: AAS 59 (1967) 574–592 [DOI. 147].

  [1] UR no. 4.

  [2] See UR no. 1.

  [3] See UR no. 4.

All Christians must be animated by the spirit of ecumenism, above all those who have been entrusted with a special office and duty in the world and society. Accordingly, the principles of ecumenism that the decrees of Vatican Council II laid down must be appositely brought to bear in all institutions of higher education.[4] Many persons have in fact requested principles and guidelines for action in order that the energies of all concerned may work together effectively for the general good of the Catholic Church and of other Churches and Ecclesial Communions.

CHAPTER I
GENERAL PRINCIPLES AND AIDS ON EDUCATION
ABOUT ECUMENICAL AFFAIRS

3. AIDS TO ACHIEVE THE END

(69) d. Prayers offered not only during the Week of Prayer for Christian Unity but on other appropriate occasions throughout the year should rightly be numbered among those measures that must receive particular emphasis.[11] Depending on circumstances of place and persons and in conformity with the norms established for common worship (*communicatio in sacris*), the possibility is open for shared retreats lasting one or more days and under the direction of a reliable retreat master.[12]

1035

CHAPTER II
THE ECUMENICAL DIMENSION OF RELIGIOUS AND
THEOLOGICAL EDUCATION

4. THE ECUMENICAL ASPECT IN THE INDIVIDUAL THEOLOGICAL DISCIPLINES

(73) In every theological discipline the ecumenical aspect amounts to the consideration of the link between that discipline and the mystery of the Church's unity. Further, the course in each discipline should imbue the students with an appreciation for the wealth of the Christian tradition in its teaching, spirituality, and ecclesiastical discipline. That appreciation in the students can be achieved when their own tradition is related to the riches of the Christian traditions of the East and the West, both as to the ancient forms of these traditions and as to the contemporary modes of expressing them.

1036

This method of directing attention to the heritage of other Christian Churches and Ecclesial Communities has a truly great significance: [. . .] in liturgical studies, which carry out a scientific, comparative examination of the the various forms of divine worship and their doctrinal and spiritual implications; [. . .]

6. ECUMENISM AS A DISTINCT DISCIPLINE

(75) The fact that there is an ecumenical aspect throughout all theological education does not make a distinct course in ecumenism superfluous. In such a discipline the following are elements for possible inclusion, depending on varying circumstances and the time available:

1037

e. a survey of the "institutional" aspect and contemporary life of the different Christian Communions, covering doctrinal orientations, the true causes of disagreements, missionary activities, spirituality, forms of divine worship;

f. a host of ecumenical issues, i.e., issues specifically arising out of the ecumenical movement, regarding hermeneutics, ministry, worship, "intercom-

---

4 "Institutes of higher education" in this document means all university departments, academic institutions, diocesan seminaries, institutes, centers, or houses of formation for both men and women religious; high schools or secondary schools are not included.

11 See Ecumenical Directory I nos. 22, 32–34 [DOL 147 nos. 976, 986–988].

12 Following the norms established by competent authority. [. . .]

munion," tradition, a perverse proselytism vs. genuine evangelization, false irenicism, the laity, the ministry of women in the Church;

g. the spiritual approach to ecumenism and especially the meaning of prayer for unity and the various forms of spiritual ecumenism.

152. PAUL VI and VASKEN I (Patriarch of the Armenians), **Joint Statement**, 12 May 1970: AAS 62 (1970) 416–417 (French; excerpt).

1038   Paul VI, Bishop of Rome, and Vasken I, Supreme Catholicos-Patriarch of all the Armenians, give thanks to the Lord for allowing them, especially at this period of preparation for the great feast celebrating the descent of the Holy Spirit upon the apostles, to pray together, to meet, and to exchange the kiss of peace. [. . .]

Nevertheless, the quest for unity is at risk of remaining fruitless if it is not deeply rooted in the entire life of the entire Church. For this reason the Pope and the Patriarch share in the wish that a closer collaboration may develop in all possible spheres of the Christian life. Shared prayer, mutual spiritual assistance, cooperation aimed at finding genuinely Christian solutions to the problems of the world today are among the valuable measures at the disposal of that quest for complete unity so deeply desired.

This conjoint search and cooperation must have as their foundation the acknowledgment of each other's Christian faith and the sacramental life common to both, as well as mutual respect between persons and between the Churches.

153. SECRETARIAT FOR CHRISTIAN UNITY, **Reply** (Colombia) of J. Hamer, Secretary, to Msgr. José de Jesús Pimiento Rodriguez, Bishop of Garzon-Neiva, Huila, on non-Catholic Christians as godparents, 3 December 1970: Not 7 (1971) 92–93 (Italian).

1039   The Congregation for Divine Worship has passed on to this Secretariat, as the office responsible, your letter of 12 September, addressed to Cardinal Benno Gut. In it Your Excellency writes that the General Introduction no. 10 to the rite of baptism in the new ritual "exceeds the norms of the Ecumenical Directory, which provides that a member of an Eastern Church may be a godparent, but excludes this for a member of other Christian groups separated from us. The serious reason for this is that 'it is as a representative of the community of faith that anyone takes the responsibility for the faith of the recipient' (no. 57).[a] The most that can be allowed for another such Christian is to be a 'Christian witness' to the baptism."

1040   The objection Your Excellency raises has been carefully examined. However, what the General Introduction no. 10 of the new ritual states is this: "A baptized and believing Christian from a separated Church or Community may act as a godparent or Christian witness along with a Catholic godparent, at the request of the parents and in accordance with the norms laid down for various ecumenical cases."[b]

---

[a] See DOL 147 no. 1011. The translation here follows the Spanish of the letter quoted.

[b] DOL 294 no. 2259.

As Your Excellency will observe, there is explicit reference to the norms of the Ecumenical Directory *pro variis casibus*. These norms are in the Directory no. 48, as to the possibility "of accepting one of the faithful of an Eastern Church as godparent along with a Catholic godparent"[1] and in no. 57 as to the possibility of allowing a member of the faithful of another Church or Ecclesial Community as witness to the baptism "along with the Catholic godparent."[2] Accordingly the General Introduction no. 10 of the new baptismal ritual does not exceed the norms of the Directory. Even if the concise expression in the General Introduction no. 10 might seem unclear, still the Directory is explicitly cited. The Directory stated the norms in a way that is precise and clear. It differentiates between the case of a member of an Eastern Church and a member of another Church or Ecclesial Community: the first case involves admission as a godparent along with the Catholic godparent, the second, admission as a witness along with the Catholic godparent.

154. PAUL VI and MAR IGNATIOS JAKOB III (Patriarch cf the Church of Antioch of the Syrians), **Joint Statement,** 27 October 1971: AAS 63 (1971) 814–815 (English; excerpt).

As they conclude their solemn meeting, which marks a new step in the rela-   1041
tions between the Roman Catholic Church and the Syrian Orthodox Church, His Holiness Pope Paul VI and His Holiness Mar Ignatius Jacob III humbly render thanks to almighty God for having made possible this historic opportunity to pray together, to engage in a fraternal exchange of views concerning the needs of the Church of God, and to witness to their common desire that all Christians may intensify their service to the world with humility and complete dedication.

The Pope and the Patriarch have recognized the deep spiritual communion which already exists between their Churches. The celebration of the sacraments of the Lord, the common profession of faith in the Lord Jesus Christ, the Word of God made man for man's salvation, the apostolic traditions which form part of the common heritage of both Churches, the great Fathers and Doctors, including St. Cyril of Alexandria, who are their common masters in the faith — all these testify to the action of the Holy Spirit, who has continued to work in their Churches even when there have been human weakness and failings. The period of mutual recrimination and condemnation has given place to a willingness to meet together in sincere efforts to lighten and eventually remove the burden of history which still weighs heavily upon Christians.

Progress has already been made and Pope Paul VI and the Patriarch Mar Ignatius Jacob III are in agreement that there is no difference in the faith they profess concerning the mystery of the Word of God made flesh and become really man, even if over the centuries difficulties have arisen out of the different theological expressions by which this faith was expressed. They therefore encourage the clergy and faithful of their Churches to even greater endeavors at removing the obstacles which still prevent complete communion among them. This should be done with love, with openness to the promptings of the Holy Spirit, and with mutual respect for each other and each other's Church. They particularly exhort the scholars of their Churches, and of all Christian Communities, to penetrate more deeply into the mystery of Christ with humility and fidelity to the apostolic tradi-

---

[1]   Ecumenical Directory no. 48: "[Text quoted, DOL 147 no. 1002]."

[2]   Ibid. no. 57: "[Text quoted, DOL 147 no. 1011]."

tions, so that the fruits of their reflections may help the Church in her service to the world which the incarnate Son of God has redeemed. [. . .]

155. SECRETARIAT FOR CHRISTIAN UNITY, **Instruction**, on special instances of admitting other Christians to eucharistic communion in the Catholic Church, 1 June 1972: AAS 64 (1972) 518–525; Not 8 (1972) 270–277.

1. THE QUESTION

1042   We are often asked: In what given situations and under what conditions may the members of other Churches or Ecclesial Communities be admitted to eucharistic communion in the Catholic Church?

The question is not altogether new. The Second Ecumenical Vatican Council (Decree on Ecumenism *Unitatis redintegratio*) and the Ecumenical Directory have dealt with it already.[1]

The pastoral norms here set forth are in no way meant to alter but simply to explain the norms now in force by shedding light on their originating, doctrinal principles so as to make it easier to carry out the existing norms.

2. THE EUCHARIST AND THE MYSTERY OF THE CHURCH

1043   There is a very close connection between the mystery of the Church and the mystery of the eucharist.

1044   a. The eucharist contains really what is the foundation of the Church's existence and unity, the body of Christ, offered as sacrifice and given to the faithful as the bread of eternal life. The sacrament of the body and blood of Christ given as the Church's very constitution immediately implies:

> — the power of ministry, conferred by Christ on the apostles and their successors, bishops along with priests, to carry out sacramentally his own priestly act whereby he offered himself once and for all to the Father in the Holy Spirit and gave himself to believers that they might be one in him;

> — the unity of this ministry, which must be carried out in the name of Christ, the Head of the Church, and therefore in a hierarchic communion of the ministers;

> —the faith of the Church, which it proclaims in the very celebration of the eucharist and through which it responds in the Holy Spirit to Christ's gift in a way that conforms to the true reality of this gift.

---

[1] UR no. 8: *"Communicatio in sacris . . .* in view of all the circumstances of time, place, and people" [Text quoted; DOL 6 no. 186]. See also OE no. 27 [DOL 5 no. 179].

    Directorium ad ea quae a Concilio Vaticano Secundo de re oecumenica promulgata sunt exsequenda (Ecumenical Directory): AAS 59 (1967) 574–592:

    1. *Communicatio in sacris with Eastern Christians separated from us.* "Over and above cases of necessity, [Text quoted] " (no. 44; DOL 147 no. 998).

    2. *Communicatio in sacris with other Christians separated from us.* "Celebration of the sacraments [Text quoted] " (no. 55, DOL 147 no. 1009).

    See also Secretariat for Christian Unity, *Declaration on the position of the Catholic Church regarding eucharistic sharing between Christians of different Confessions:* OR 12–13 Jan. 1970; AAS 62 (1970) 184–188 [DOL 150].

The sacrament of the eucharist, taken with these three inseparable elements, is the sign of the real unity it causes, the visible unity of the Church of Christ, which cannot be lost.[2]

b. "The celebration of Mass, as the action of Christ and the people of God   1045
arrayed hierarchically, is for both the universal and local Church and for each
person the center of the whole Christian life."[3] In the sacrifice of the Mass the
Church in celebrating the mystery of Christ celebrates the mystery of its own being
and in this concrete way shows forth its own unity.

The faithful gathered at the altar offer the sacrifice through the hands of
the priest acting in Christ's name; they are an expression of the community of the
whole people of God joined together in the profession of one faith. The faithful
thus stand as a sign and as a kind of delegation representing a larger presence.

The celebration of Mass is itself a profession of faith; in that celebration
the entire Church recognizes and gives expression to itself. For a reflection on the
sublime meaning of the eucharistic prayers and on the other parts of the Mass —
both the fixed parts and those varying with the cycle of the liturgical year — and
the realization that the liturgy of the word and the liturgy of the eucharist form
one, single act of worship,[4] will bring out fully the truth of the maxim: *lex orandi lex
credendi.*[5] The Mass thus takes on that catechetical impact which the current liturgical reform has rightly recognized and emphasized. The Church, furthermore, has
through the centuries taken pains to bring into the liturgy the more significant
themes and the more important enrichments of our shared faith gained from experience. This has been accomplished both by the addition of new texts and by the
inauguration of new liturgical feasts.

c. The relationship between the local celebration of the eucharist and the   1046
entire ecclesial *communio* stands out even by the special mention in the eucharistic
prayers of the pope, the local bishop, and the other bishops belonging to the college
of bishops.

These statements about the eucharist as the center and apex of the whole
Christian life are applicable as well to the whole Church and to its every member,
but especially to those taking an active part in the celebration of Mass and most of
all to those who in it receive the body of Christ. Eucharistic communion within the
celebration of Mass is truly the fullest way of sharing in the eucharist, because it
means obeying the words of the Lord: "Take and eat."[6]

3. THE EUCHARIST: SPIRITUAL FOOD

Another effect of the eucharist is to give spiritual nourishment to those who   1047
receive it for what it truly is according to the Church's faith: the body and blood of
the Lord, given as food for everlasting life (see Jn 6:54–58). The eucharist is spiritual food for the baptized; through it they live Christ's life, are incorporated into him,

---

² See LG no. 3 [DOL 4 no. 137]; UR no. 4.

³ GIRM ch. 1, no. 1 [DOL 208 no. 1391].

⁴ See PO no. 4.

⁵ See Pius XI, Encycl. *Quas primas,* 28 Dec. 1925: AAS 17 (1925) 598. PO no. 5 [DOL 18 no. 260]; SC
art. 2 and 6 [DOL 1 nos. 2 and 6].

⁶ For "fuller participation in the Mass" see SC art. 55 [DOL 1 no. 55]. See also Instr. EuchMyst, 25
May 1967, no. 12 [DOL 179 no. 1241].
    The fact of having received one and the same baptism is not enough to allow reception of the
eucharist. For sharing in the eucharist expresses a complete profession of faith and complete incorporation
into the Church; for these baptism is the introduction. This sacrament "accordingly forms the sacramental
bond [Text quoted] into eucharistic communion" (UR no. 22 [DOL 6 no. 189]).

and more fully become sharers in the unfolding plan of the whole mystery of salvation. "Those who eat my flesh and drink my blood abide in me and I in them" (Jn 6: 56).

a. As the sacrament of closer union with Christ[7] and of the perfecting of the spiritual life, the eucharist is needed by every believer, just as the Lord says: "If you do not eat the flesh of the Son of Man and drink his blood, you will not have life in you" (Jn 6:53). Those who live the life of grace more intensely experience a compelling need for this spiritual food. The Church, moreover, recommends daily reception of the eucharist.

b. As spiritual food whose effect is to join the Christian more closely with Christ, the eucharist is in no way merely a means for satisfying purely individual aspirations, however exalted. The union of the faithful with Christ the Head of the Mystical Body gives rise to their bond with each other. This union of all the faithful is grounded on their sharing together the bread of the eucharist. "Because there is one bread, we who are many are the one Body, for we all partake of the one bread" (1 Cor 10:17). In virtue of this sacrament "a person is incorporated into Christ and united to Christ's members."[8] The continued reception of the eucharist incorporates the faithful more and more into the Body of Christ and makes them share more fully in the mystery of the Church.

c. Thus the spiritual need for the eucharist involves not merely the individual's growth in the spiritual life, but simultaneously and in the most intimately connected way also a deeper integration into Christ's Church, "which is his Body, the fullness of him who fills all in all" (Eph 1:23).

4. GENERAL NORMS FOR THE DIFFERENT INSTANCES OF ADMISSION TO THE EUCHARIST

1048   As to members of the Catholic Church, there is an inseparable connection between the following two aspects of the eucharist: its being the celebration of the ecclesial community, entire and integral, joined together in the one faith; its being the nourishment that meets the needs of the spiritual life, both personal and ecclesial, of each member of the community. The same will hold true when by God's will all the followers of Christ will be gathered together in the one, same Church. But what is the present situation, given the division of Christians? In every baptized person there exists a connatural spiritual need for the eucharist. Those not in full communion with the Catholic Church, at the dictate of their conscience go to the ministers of their own Community. But what are those among them to do who do not have access to their own minister or who for other motives come to ask for the eucharist from a priest of the Catholic Church?

The Ecumenical Directory has already pointed out the need of preserving intact two requirements: the integrity of ecclesial communion and the good of souls. Its directives derive from two general norms:

a. Never is it permitted to weaken the strict relationship between the mystery of the Church and the mystery of the eucharist, whatever the pastoral measures required in the clearly specified cases. For the celebration of the eucharist is intrinsically the sign of the completeness of the faith professed and of ecclesial communion. This principle may never be obscured but in this matter must show us the right course of action.

---

8   Council of Florence, *Decretum pro Armeniis*: Denz-Schön 1322. St. Thomas Aquinas often uses the phrase "sacrament of church unity" (e.g., ST 3a, 73.2, 5). The eucharist produces the unity of the Church or more formally speaking, produces the Mystical Body, because the eucharist contains Christ's real body.

b.   The principle will not in fact be obscured if admission to Catholic eucharistic communion in particular instances applies exclusively to those Christians: who give signs of a belief consistent with the Church's faith regarding the eucharist and experience a genuine spiritual need for the food of the eucharist, yet not having for a prolonged period access to a minister of their own Communion, ask for the sacrament of their own accord; who are rightly disposed to receive it and maintain a manner of life befitting a Christian. The spiritual need mentioned must be taken in the sense already described (see no. 3 b and c), i.e., as the need for growth in the spiritual life and for a deeper entrance into the mystery of the Church and its unity.

Even when these conditions are present, pastoral care must see to it that the admission of other Christians to eucharistic communion presents no danger nor upsets the faith of Catholics.[9]

5. ON THE BASIS OF THESE PRINCIPLES, DIFFERENCES BETWEEN MEMBERS OF THE EASTERN CHURCHES AND OTHER CHRISTIANS

Regarding admission to eucharistic communion in the Catholic Church, the   1049
Ecumenical Directory[10] contains norms for Eastern Christians separated from us that are distinct from the norms applying to other Christians. The reason for the distinction is that the Eastern Churches, even if separated from us, possess true sacraments and especially, because of apostolic succession, priesthood and eucharist. These sacraments link them to us in a very close bond, which results in some lessening of the danger of obscuring the relationship between eucharistic and ecclesial communion.[11] Pope Paul VI has remarked recently that between "our Church and the honored Orthodox Churches an almost but not quite complete communion already exists, deriving from our shared participation in the mystery of Christ and his Church."[12]

But it is another matter when it comes to Christians belonging to Communities in which faith in the eucharist differs from the Catholic Church's faith and the sacrament of orders is lacking. The admission of such Christians to the Catholic eucharist does bring with it the danger of obscuring the essential relationship between eucharistic and ecclesial communion. This is the reason why the Directory deals with this situation in a way differing from its treatment of Eastern Christians and why admission to the eucharist is lawful only in somewhat rare cases, that is, cases of "pressing necessity." These Christians are required in such cases to give signs that their belief in the eucharist is consistent with the faith of the Catholic Church, i.e., in the eucharist as Christ instituted it and as the Church teaches it. This question, however, is not put to Orthodox Christians, because they belong to a Church with a faith consistent with our own.

---

[9]   See OE no. 26 [DOL 5 no. 178].

[10]   See Ecumenical Directory nos. 44 and 55 [DOL 147 nos. 998 and 1009].

[11]   The two following texts of the *Directory*, taken in part from the conciliar documents, are extremely important, namely no. 39: "[Text quoted; DOL 147 no. 993]." See also OE nos. 24–29; no. 40: "[Text quoted up to (UR no. 15); DOL 147 no. 994]."

[12]   Paul VI, Letter to Patriarch Athenagoras I, 8 Feb. 1971, given to Metropolitan Melitos of Chalcedon at his visit on the same date. First published in OR, 7 March 1971.

6. AUTHORITY COMPETENT TO JUDGE IN INDIVIDUAL INSTANCES —
MEANING OF THE ECUMENICAL DIRECTORY NO. 55

1050   The Directory no. 55[a] grants to episcopal authority quite broad powers of decision on the presence of the conditions required to constitute the somewhat rare cases mentioned already. When such cases do occur in any region fairly often and regularly, the conference of bishops will doubtless be able to set forth some of the clearly applicable norms. Often, however, it is up to the local Ordinary to make the decision, because only he will be able to weigh all the circumstances in a given case and judge accordingly what is to be done.

Apart from danger of death, the Directory gives two instances, as examples, namely, imprisonment and persecution; but it also mentions "other similar cases of this kind of pressing necessity." That does not limit the cases in question to the situations of confinement and peril. The situation can also be that of Christians experiencing grave spiritual need and unable to reach their own Communities. Take for example the "diaspora," i.e., in the present age when there is such widespread migration of peoples, it happens more than formerly that non-Catholic Christians are scattered here and there within Catholic areas. Such Christians frequently are without any help from their own Community or can seek such help only at great expense and difficulty. If they meet the other conditions set forth in the Directory, these Christians may be admitted to eucharistic communion. But it is left up to the local bishop to weigh each case.

By letter of the Cardinal Secretary of State to the Cardinal President, 25 May 1972, Pope Paul VI approved this Instruction and ordered its publication.

156. PAUL VI and SHENOUDA III (Patriarch of the See of St. Mark of Alexandria), **Joint Statement,** 10 May 1973: AAS 65 (1973) 299–301 (English; excerpt).

1051   [. . .] The divine life is given to us and is nourished in us through the seven sacraments of Christ in his Church: baptism, chrism (confirmation), holy eucharist, penance, anointing of the sick, matrimony, and holy orders.

We venerate the Virgin Mary, Mother of the True Light, and we confess that she is ever Virgin, the God-bearer. She intercedes for us and, as the *Theotokos*, excels in her dignity all angelic hosts. [. . .]

Our spirituality is well and profoundly expressed in our rituals and in the liturgy of the Mass, which comprises the center of our public prayer and the culmination of our incorporation into Christ in his Church. We keep the fasts and feasts of our faith. We venerate the relics of the saints and ask the intercession of the angels and of the saints, the living and the departed. These compose a cloud of witnesses in the Church. They and we look in hope for the Second Coming of our Lord, when his glory will be revealed, to judge the living and the dead.

We humbly recognize that our Churches are not able to give more perfect witness to this new life in Christ because of existing divisions which have behind them centuries of difficult history. In fact, since the year 451 A.D., theological differences, nourished and widened by nontheological factors, have sprung up. These differences cannot be ignored. In spite of them, however, we are rediscovering ourselves as Churches with a common inheritance and are reaching out with

---

ᵃ   See DOL 147 no. 1009.

determination and confidence in the Lord to achieve the fullness and perfection of that unity which is his gift.

As an aid to accomplishing this task, we are setting up a joint commission representing our Churches, whose function will be to guide common study in the fields of church tradition, patristics, liturgy, theology, history, and practical problems, so that by cooperation in common we may seek to resolve, in a spirit of mutual respect, the differences existing between our Churches and be able to proclaim together the Gospel in ways which correspond to the authentic message of the Lord and to the needs and hopes of today's world. At the same time we express our gratitude and encouragement to other groups of Catholic and Orthodox scholars and pastors who devote their efforts to common activity in these and related fields. [. . .]

157. SECRETARIAT FOR CHRISTIAN UNITY, **Communication** *Dopo la pubblicazione,* on the interpretation of the Instruction of 1 June 1972 regarding special instances of admitting other Christians to eucharistic communion, 17 October 1973: AAS 65 (1973) 616–619.

A note on certain interpretations of the Instruction on special instances of admitting other Christians to eucharistic communion in the Catholic Church: 1052

1.   After publication of the Instruction of 1 June 1972 "on special instances admitting other Christians to eucharistic communion in the Catholic Church," different interpretations have been given and some of them deviate from the letter and spirit of that document. In order to forestall the spread of similar interpretations and their consequences we think it useful to call attention to several points.   1053

2.   By this Instruction, pastoral in nature, the Secretariat for Christian Unity in no way intended to alter the norms laid down by the conciliar Decree on Ecumenism and concretely applied in the Ecumenical Directory. The intent rather was to explain that the existing discipline has its source in the demands of faith and thus retains all its force.   1054

3.   The basic principles of the Instruction are these: 1055

a.   An indissoluble bond exists between the mystery of the Church and the mystery of the eucharist, between ecclesial communion and eucharistic communion. Of its nature the eucharist is a sign of the completeness of the faith professed and of ecclesial communion.[1]

b.   The eucharist is for the baptized a spiritual nourishment that brings about their living by the very life of Christ, their deeper incorporation into Christ, and their more intense sharing in the whole unfolding plan of Christ's mystery.[2]

4.   Within a complete communion in faith eucharistic sharing is the expression of such unity and therefore the expression of the unity of believers; at the same time it is the means sustaining and reenforcing their unity.   1056

Conversely, eucharistic communion by people not in complete ecclesial communion with each other cannot be the expression of the complete unity that the

---

[1]   See Instruction no. 2 a, b, c [DOL 155 nos. 1044, 1045, 1046].

[2]   See ibid. no. 3 [DOL 155 no. 1047].

eucharist of its nature signifies: in this case such unity does not exist. Eucharistic sharing in this case, therefore, cannot be viewed as a means to reach full ecclesial communion.

1057   5.   At the same time both the Ecumenical Directory and the Instruction, on the basis of what was said in the conciliar Decree on Ecumenism, acknowledge the possibility of exceptions in that the eucharist is a spiritual food, needed for the Christian life.

1058   6.   It is for the local Ordinary to weigh exceptional cases and make the concrete decisions. The Instruction[3] mentions that the Ecumenical Directory[4] grants to the local bishop the power to decide whether the conditions prevail that are required to constitute those exceptional cases.

This power of the bishops to investigate and to decide is governed by the criterion established by the Ecumenical Directory[5] and explained by the Instruction.[6] According to the Instruction, "Admission to Catholic eucharistic communion in particular instances applies exclusively to those Christians: who give signs of a belief consistent with the Church's faith regarding the eucharist and experience a genuine spiritual need for the food of the eucharist, yet for a prolonged period having no access to a minister of their own Communion, ask for the sacrament of their own accord; who are rightly disposed to receive it and maintain a manner of life befitting a Christian."[7]

That criterion has to be respected in its entirety, as embracing all the required conditions. It is not lawful, therefore, to neglect any one of them in the process of an investigation that is objective and pastorally responsible. Notice should also be taken of the fact that the Instruction speaks of particular cases and thus of cases that have to be weighed individually. Ruled out therefore is the issuance of a general norm that would turn an exceptional case into standard practice; nor is it permissible to make decisions on the basis of equity (*epikeia*) by making this the general norm.

Bishops, however, have the power to set the requirements in which the exceptions (i.e., the particular cases) apply and to establish the process for verifying that all the required conditions obtain in any given instance. When it is a matter of particular cases recurring frequently in a particular region, and in a certain constant pattern, the conferences of bishops can institute norms to ensure that in every given instance all the conditions are present. Even so it will normally be up to the local Ordinary to make the decision in such cases.

1059   7.   For admission of other Christians to the eucharist in the Catholic Church, the Instruction requires that they give signs of a faith consistent with the Catholic Church's faith regarding this sacrament. Such faith does not consist simply in the acceptance of the real presence, but implies as well the doctrine on the eucharist as taught by the Catholic Church.

---

3   See ibid. no. 6 [DOL 155 no. 1050].

4   See Ecumenical Directory I no. 55 [DOL 147 no. 1009].

5   See ibid.

6   See Instruction no. 4 b [DOL 155 no. 1048].

7   See ibid.

8.   The Instruction also calls to mind[8] the fact that the Ecumenical Directory[9] for   1060
Eastern Christians not in full communion with the Catholic Church supplies norms
distinct from those applying to other Christians.[10] For example:

   a.   Eastern Christians as members of a Church in which faith in the eucharist
conforms to the faith of the Catholic Church are not asked, on the occasion of their
admission to the eucharist, for a personal affirmation of faith in the sacrament; in an
Orthodox Christian such faith is presupposed.

   b.   Since the Orthodox Churches possess true sacraments, above all, in virtue
of apostolic succession, the priesthood and the eucharist, the Directory notes that
attention should be given to a legitimate reciprocity when sacramental sharing is
granted.[11]

   c.   Just reason for deciding in favor of sacramental sharing is much broader.[12]

9.   The issue of reciprocity has relevance exclusively to those Churches that have   1061
kept the substance of eucharistic teaching, the sacrament of orders, and apostolic
succession. The consequence of this is that a Catholic can request the eucharist
"only from a minister who has validly received the sacrament of orders."[13]

10.   The desire for eucharistic sharing is after all the expression of the desire for the   1062
full ecclesial unity of all Christians in the way Christ has willed it.

   Interconfessional dialogue on the theology of the eucharist (as sacrament and   1063
sacrifice), of ministry, and of the Church is pursuing its course within the ecumenical movement. The dialogue proceeds in reliance on the promises and prayers of the
Lord; it proceeds in the light of faith, urged on and enlivened by the charity that is
poured forth in our hearts by the Holy Spirit who has been given to us. We express
the hope that the ecumenical movement may lead us to a shared profession of faith
among Christians and thus allow us to be able to celebrate the eucharist within an
ecclesial unity by fulfilling the words: "Because there is but one bread we who are
many are the one Body."[14]

   This note has been approved and its publication authorized by Pope Paul VI.

158. SECRETARIAT FOR CHRISTIAN UNITY (Commission for Religious
Relations with Judaism), **Guidelines and Suggestions** *Datée du 28 octobre,* for
the application of the conciliar Declaration *Nostra aetate* no. 14, 1 December
1964, 28 October 1975: AAS 67 (1975) 73–79 (French; excerpt).

                              II. LITURGY

   All should be mindful of the common bonds existing between the Christian   1064
liturgy and the Jewish liturgy. Both liturgies share as a common characteristic

---

   [8]   See ibid. no. 5 [DOL 155 no. 1049].

   [9]   See Ecumenical Directory nos. 39–54 [DOL 147 nos. 993–1008].

   [10]   See ibid. nos. 55–63 [DOL 147 nos. 1009–17].

   [11]   See ibid. no. 43 [DOL 147 no. 997].

   [12]   See ibid. no. 44 [DOL 147 no. 998].

   [13]   Ibid. no. 55 [DOL 147 no. 1009].

   [14]   1 Cor 10:17.

community of life in the service of God and of humanity out of love for God as this service is made effective in the liturgy. Important to Jewish-Christian relations is a consciousness of the common elements in liturgical life (formularies, feasts, rituals, etc.); for all of them the Bible holds an essential place.

There should be an effort with regard to the Old Testament to understand better whatever in it retains its own, abiding value.[3] This is not cancelled by the later interpretation as the New Testament gives this value its full meaning, even while itself receiving clarification and explanation from the Old Testament.[4] The point is all the more urgent by reason of the fact that the reform of the liturgy more and more places the Old Testament texts before the Christian faithful.

Without lessening what is original in Christianity, commentaries on biblical texts should bring out the continuity of our faith with that of the Old Covenant as both have their origins in God's promises. Believing that these promises have been fulfilled with Christ's first coming, we are no less truly in a state of expectation as to their complete fulfillment at the moment of Christ's glorious second coming at the end of time.

With regard to liturgical readings, care should be taken in the homily to give them a correct interpretation, especially when it comes to passages that seem to cast the Jewish people in an unfavorable light. There should be every effort to instruct the Christian people in such a way that they will come to grasp all the texts in their authentic meaning and in their import for the modern believer.

Commissions responsible for liturgical translations should take special pains over how they translate terms and passages that poorly instructed Christians could take in a prejudicial sense. The biblical text is obviously unalterable, but at the same time in a translation intended for use in the liturgy care must be taken to make the meaning of a text clear in the light of exegetical studies.[5]

The preceding remarks apply also to the introductions to biblical readings as well as to the general intercessions and to commentaries incorporated into missals for the faithful.

159. SECRETARIAT FOR CHRISTIAN UNITY, *Ecumenical Collaboration at the Regional and Local Levels,* 22 February 1975 (excerpt).*

III
VARIOUS FORMS OF LOCAL ECUMENISM

A. Sharing in Prayer and Worship

1065   At the level of the local Churches there are many occasions for seeking the gifts of the Holy Spirit and that "change of heart and holiness of life which, along

---

3   See DV nos. 14–15.

4   See DV no. 16.

5   Thus in John's Gospel the designation "the Jews" often, according to the context, refers to "the leaders of the Jews" or "the enemies of Jesus"; such terms more accurately convey the thought of the evangelist and avoid any suggestion of indicting the Jewish people as such. A further example is the use of the terms "Pharisee" and "Pharisaism," both of which have taken on a mainly pejorative connotation.

*   English text from the Secretariat.

with public and private prayer for the unity of Christians, would be regarded as the soul of the whole ecumenical movement."[12] Many forms of this "spiritual ecumenism" are emerging today in prayer groups in which members of various confessions assemble.

The Ecumenical Directory expressed the hope that "Catholics and their other brethren will join in prayer for any common concern in which they can and should cooperate, e.g., peace, social justice, mutual charity among men, the dignity of the family, and so on. The same may be said of occasions when, according to circumstances, a nation or community wishes to make a common act of thanksgiving or petition to God, as on a national feast day, at a time of public disaster or mourning, on a day set aside for remembrance of those who have died for their country. This kind of prayer is also recommended as far as possible at times when Christians hold meetings for study or common action."[13]

The Prayer for Unity, as observed in January or in the week preceding Pentecost, is widespread and continues to be in most places the chief occasion on which Catholics and other Christians pray together. It is promoted by special committees set up for the purpose by ministers' fraternals or associations and very often by councils of Churches.

In certain places, some of the great festivals of the liturgical year are marked by joint celebrations in order to express the common joy of Christians in the central events of their faith.

On the Catholic side, participation in sacramental worship is regulated by the Decree on Ecumenism (no. 8),[a] the Ecumenical Directory I (nos. 42–44, 55),[b] the 1972 Instruction, and the Note issued in 1973.[14]

Both participation in common worship and an exact observance of the present canonical limits are a feature of normal Catholic ecumenical activity.

D. Shared Premises

The rule is that Catholic churches are reserved for Catholic worship. As consecrated buildings they have an important liturgical significance. Further, they have a pedagogical value for inculcating the meaning and spirit of worship. Therefore, sharing them with other Christians or constructing new churches jointly with other Christians can be only by way of exception. However, the Ecumenical Directory I has stated:

1066

"If the separated brethren have no place in which to carry out their religious rites properly and with dignity, the local Ordinary may allow them the use of a Catholic building, cemetery or church" (no. 61).[c]

"Because sharing in sacred functions, objects, and places with all the separated Eastern brethren is allowed for a reasonable cause (see Decree on Eastern Catholic Churches no. 28), it is recommended that, with the approval of the local Ordinary, separated Eastern priests and communities be allowed the use of Catholic churches, buildings, and cemeteries and other things necessary for their religious rites, if they

---

[12] UR no. 8.

[13] Ecumenical Directory no. 33 [DOL 147 no. 987].

[a] See DOL 6 no. 186.

[b] See DOL 147 nos. 996–998, 1009.

[14] *Instruction* regarding special cases of admitting other Christians to eucharistic communion in the Catholic Church: AAS 64 (1972) 518–525 [DOL 155]; *Communication* regarding special cases of admitting other Christians to eucharistic communion in the Catholic Church: AAS 65 (1973) 616–619 [DOL 157].

[c] DOL 147 no. 1015.

ask for this and have no place in which they can celebrate sacred functions properly and with dignity" (no. 52).[d]

Because of developments in society, because of rapid growth in population and building, and for financial motives, where there is a good ecumenical relationship and understanding between the Communities, the sharing of church premises can become a matter of practical interest. It does not seem possible to adduce any one mode for this kind of sharing, since it is a question of responding to a need or an emergency.[21]

1067   The building of an interconfessional place of worship must be an exception and should answer real needs which cannot otherwise be met. An airport chapel or a chapel at a military camp are examples that meet this condition. An exceptional pastoral situation could also be the reason for such a building, as when a government would forbid the multiplication of places of worship or in the case of the extreme poverty of a Christian community. There the simultaneous use of a church could be allowed.

1068   In a shared church, judicious consideration needs to be given to the question of the reservation of the blessed sacrament so that this is done in a way that is consonant with sound sacramental theology, as well as respectful of the sensitivities of those who use the building. In addition to strictly religious consideration, due attention ought to be paid to the practical, financial, and administrative problems, as well as to the questions of civil and canon law which are involved.

1069   Clearly, initiatives in the matter of shared premises can be undertaken only under the authority of the bishop of the diocese and on the basis of the norms for the application of those principles fixed by the competent episcopal conference. Before making plans for a shared building, the authorities of the respective Communities concerned ought first to reach agreement as to how their various disciplines will be observed, particularly in regard to the sacraments. Arrangements should be made so that the rules of the Catholic Church concerning *communicatio in sacris* are respected.

It is important that any project for a shared church be accompanied by suitable instruction of the Catholic people concerned, so that the meaning of this sharing may be grasped and any danger of indifferentism avoided.

160. SECRETARIAT FOR CHRISTIAN UNITY, **Letter** *Le deuxième Concile du Vatican* of Cardinal J. Willebrands to presidents of the conferences of bishops, on a common date for Easter, 18 May 1975.*

1070   The Second Vatican Council, in the Appendix to the Constitution on the Liturgy, "recognizes the great importance of the wishes expressed by many concerning the assignment of the feast of Easter to a fixed Sunday," and states that "it would not object if the feast of Easter were assigned to a particular Sunday of the

---

    [d]   DOL 147 no. 1006.

    [21] The experience of shared premises is not yet wide but in a number of places, as in some new towns in England and in "covenanted" parishes in [the] U.S.A., it has led to a situation where certain joint social and pastoral activities are undertaken in common, while the identities of the Catholic Church and the other Confessions involved are maintained and their discipline of worship respected.

    *   English text from the Secretariat, Prot. N. 1578/75; French version: Not 12 (1976) 59–60.

Gregorian calendar, provided that those whom it may concern give it their consent, especially the men and women who are not in communion with the Apostolic See."[a]

This desire had in fact been expressed by many bishops in reply to the questionnaire of the Pontifical Antepreparatory Commission, and it had already been manifested in 1918 in the course of an inquiry conducted on the occasion of the application of the liturgical reform of St. Pius X.

In 1964 the Holy Father instructed the Secretariat for Promoting Christian Unity to deal with this problem in liaison with the other Christian Churches and in particular with the Orthodox Churches. Numerous contacts were made. The Joint Working Group between the Catholic Church and the World Council of Churches dealt with this question at almost all its meetings; in 1970 a consultation was organized by the department "Faith and Order" of the World Council of Churches: Catholics, Orthodox, Anglicans, and Protestants took part in it.

The lines of a possible solution were thus being traced out at the same time as the faithful, especially those living in regions where Christian Communities celebrate Easter on different dates, were becoming aware of the need to give a visible witness of their community of faith in this central mystery of the gospel message.

The Holy Father, after recent consultation, has considered that the moment has come to attempt to set in motion a process of decision. He himself touched on the matter in his Easter letter to the Orthodox Patriarchs.[b] He has further directed me to present a concrete proposal to the Orthodox Churches, the Anglican Communion, and the World Confessional Families.

In 1977 all Christians, using their own different calculations, will celebrate Easter on the same day, 10 April, the Sunday following the second Saturday of April. In declarations made by various heads of Churches and in the conclusions reached by different authoritative Christian groups who have studied this question, this Sunday seems the date most frequently considered appropriate for the celebration of Easter.

1071

In the name of the Holy Father, I have proposed that from 1977 Easter should always be celebrated on the Sunday following the second Saturday of April.

The proposed solution is not the imposition of one tradition on another; on the contrary, it could well be the expression of an agreement to which we have been led by the Holy Spirit, in obedience to the intentions of the Fathers of the first ecumenical council, who desired above all else the unity of all in the celebration of the Lord's resurrection.[c]

At the same time, we have been in contact with the World Council of Churches, which is to submit a similar proposal to the consideration of its member Churches, with a request for their reactions.

We are also asking those Churches which have reasons preventing them from accepting the proposal to inform us whether they would object to the Catholic Church's fixing the celebration of Easter on this date in the event that the greater number of Churches are favorable to the proposal.

We have wished to inform your episcopal conference of this initiative in order that you may be able, if you judge it opportune, to exchange views on the matter with the other Christian Churches in your region, exchanges which would be conducive to favoring an agreement.

---

[a]   DOL 1 no. 131.

[b]   See, for example, DOL 146.

[c]   See DOL 146 no. 962.

No decision has yet been taken. In order to remain faithful to the orientation given by the Second Vatican Council, this decision will depend upon the acceptance or otherwise of the Holy Father's proposal by the other Christian Churches.

161. PAUL VI, **Epistle** "We write" to Dr. Frederick Donald Coggan, Archbishop of Canterbury, on the ordination of women to priesthood, 30 November 1975: AAS 68 (1976) 599–600 (English).

1072   We write in answer to your letter of 9 July last. We have many times had occasion to express to your revered predecessor, and more lately to yourself, our gratitude to God and our consolation at the growth of understanding between the Catholic Church and the Anglican Communion and to acknowledge the devoted work both in theological dialogue and reflection and in Christian collaboration which promotes and witnesses to this growth.

It is indeed within this setting of confidence and candor that we see your presentation of the problem raised by the developments within the Anglican Communion concerning the ordination of women to the priesthood.

Your Grace is of course well aware of the Catholic Church's position on this question. She holds that it is not admissible to ordain women to the priesthood, for very fundamental reasons. These reasons include: the example recorded in the sacred Scriptures of Christ choosing his Apostles only from among men; the constant practice of the Church, which has imitated Christ in choosing only men; and her living teaching authority, which has consistently held that the exclusion of women from the priesthood is in accordance with God's plan for his Church.

The Joint Commission between the Anglican Communion and the Catholic Church, which has been at work since 1966, is charged with presenting in due time a final report. We must regretfully recognize that a new course taken by the Anglican Communion in admitting women to the ordained priesthood cannot fail to introduce into this dialogue an element of grave difficulty which those involved will have to take seriously into account.

Obstacles do not destroy mutual commitment to a search for reconciliation. We learn with satisfaction of a first informal discussion of the question between Anglican representatives and those of our Secretariat for Promoting Christian Unity, at which the fundamental theological importance of the question was agreed on. It is our hope that this beginning may lead to further common counsel and growth of understanding.

Once again we extend every fraternal good wish in Christ our Lord.

162. PAUL VI, **Epistle** "As the tenth" to Dr. Frederick Donald Coggan, Archbishop of Canterbury, on the ordination of women to priesthood, 23 March 1976: AAS 68 (1976) 600–601 (English).

1073   As the tenth anniversary comes round of your revered predecessor's visit to Rome, we write to reciprocate with all sincerity the gratitude and the hope which, in recalling that historic occasion, you express in a letter recently handed to us by Bishop John Howe.

It is good to know that the resolves taken, the dialogue entered upon ten years ago, have continued and spread to many places and that a new spirit of mutual consideration and trust increasingly pervades our relations.

In such a spirit of candor and trust you allude in your letter of greeting to a problem which has recently loomed large: the likelihood, already very strong it seems in some places, that the Anglican Churches will proceed to admit women to the ordained priesthood. We had already exchanged letters with you on this subject and were able to express the Catholic conviction more fully to Bishop John Howe when he brought your greetings. Our affection for the Anglican Communion has for many years been strong and we have always nourished and often expressed ardent hopes that the Holy Spirit would lead us, in love and in obedience to God's will, along the path of reconciliation. This must be the measure of the sadness with which we encounter so grave a new obstacle and threat on that path.

But it is no part of corresponding to the promptings of the Holy Spirit to fail in the virtue of hope. With all the force of the love which moves us we pray that at this critical time the Spirit of God may shed his light abundantly on all of us and that his guiding hand may keep us in the way of reconciliation according to his will.

Moreover, we sincerely appreciate the fact that you have expressed a desire to meet us and we assure you that on our part we would look upon such a meeting as a great blessing and another means of furthering that complete unity willed by Christ for his Church.

163. SC DOCTRINE OF THE FAITH, **Decree** *Accidit in diversis regionibus,* on celebration of Mass in the Catholic Church for other deceased Christians, 11 June 1976: AAS 68 (1976) 621–622.

The case arises in different parts of the world that Catholic ministers are   1074
requested to celebrate Mass for the repose of the soul of deceased persons who were baptized in other Churches or Ecclesial Communities. This happens particularly when the deceased have shown special respect and honor to the Catholic religion or have devoted public service to the well-being of the entire civil community.

Private celebration of Mass for such persons obviously raises no problem; on the contrary, such Masses can be unreservedly encouraged on grounds of patriotism, friendship, gratitude, etc.

As to public Masses, however, the legislation now in force prohibits their celebration for those who die outside the full communion of the Catholic Church.[1]

The religious and social conditions that prompted such legislation have now changed. Consequently the question has come to this Congregation from various parts of the world whether in certain cases even a public Mass may be celebrated for such deceased persons.

The Fathers of the Congregation meeting in ordinary session, 9 July 1976, after weighing the matter, have passed the following decree.

I.   The current legislation regarding celebration of public Masses for the repose of   1075
the soul of other Christians is to be retained for the future as the general rule. This in part is out of the respect due to the conscience of the deceased who have not fully professed the Catholic faith.

---

[1] See CIC can. 1241, together with can. 1240 § 1, 1º.

1076   II. Exception to this general rule is permitted, until promulgation of a new code of canon law, whenever the following conditions are present simultaneously:

    1. The relatives, friends, or subjects of the deceased person request public celebration of Mass out of a genuinely religious motive.

    2. In the judgment of the Ordinary there is nothing shocking to the faithful.

    These two conditions are more likely to be present in the case of Christians of the Eastern Churches, with whom a closer, even though not complete, communion exists in matters of faith.

1077   III. In the cases in question public Mass may be celebrated, however, under the condition that the name of the deceased is not mentioned in the eucharistic prayer. This mention in fact presupposes full communion with the Catholic Church.

    In case other Christians join with Catholics to take part in the celebration of these Masses, the norms on *communicatio in sacris* laid down by Vatican Council II[2] and the Holy See[3] are to be observed with absolute compliance.

    Pope Paul VI at an audience granted on 11 June 1976 to the Cardinal Prefect of the Congregation for the Doctrine of the Faith confirmed the decision of the Fathers, approved it, and ordered its promulgation, amending as necessary can. 809 (together with can. 2262 § 2, no. 2) and can. 1241, all things to the contrary notwithstanding.

164. SECRETARIAT FOR CHRISTIAN UNITY, **Letter** *Dans ma lettre* of Cardinal J. Willebrands, President, to presidents of the conferences of bishops, on a common celebration of Easter, 16 March 1977.*

1078   In a letter of 18 May 1975 (Prot N. 1578/75)[a] I informed the episcopal conferences of consultations which had taken place, at the request of the Holy Father, concerning the possibility of arriving at a common Christian celebration of the feast of Easter, preferably on a fixed Sunday. I further informed them that I had been authorized by the Holy Father to present to the Orthodox Churches, the Anglican Communion and the World Confessional Families a proposal that from 1977 on Easter should always be celebrated on the Sunday following the second Saturday of April.

    At the same time the World Council of Churches made an inquiry among its member Churches concerning the possibility of implementing such a proposal.

    I would like to express my gratitude to the many episcopal conferences who sent us their observations and reflections on this proposal, whose purpose was to bring about a unity of all Christians in the public celebration of the Lord's resurrection.

    The reactions of the Churches and Communities stemming from the Western traditions of Christianity were almost unanimously favorable to the proposal as

---

    [2]   See OR nos.26–29; UR no. 8 [DOL 6 no. 186].

    [3]   See Ecumenical Directory nos. 40–42 and nos. 55–56 [DOL 147 nos. 994–996 and nos. 1009–10]; Instruction on special instances of admitting other Christians to eucharistic communion in the Catholic Church nos. 5–6 [DOL 155 nos. 1049–50].

    *   English text from the Secretariat, Prot. N. 956/77; French version, 15 March 1977: Not 13 (1977) 201–202.

    [a]   See DOL 160.

presented. All stressed, however, that such a change should be made only in consultation with the various Churches of the East and with their agreement.

The Orthodox Churches have given serious attention to this proposal. They have publicly stated their desire to see all Christians celebrate Easter together. Because of serious pastoral difficulties existing in certain local Churches, however, they feel that further study and reflection should be made by their Churches before a definite answer can be given. This study is already under way but it is clear that no decision will be possible in the immediate future. Furthermore it seems clear that, if the Churches and Communities of the Western tradition were to take their own immediate decision on the proposal, this would not assist us in arriving at the goal of a common celebration by all Christians of the central mystery of their faith.

Under these circumstances, the Holy Father has judged that the situation is not   1079
yet ripe enough for the Roman Catholic Church to change its present method of determining the date of Easter or to put into effect this year the proposal that this great feast be celebrated on a fixed Sunday of April.

Circumstances will make it possible for all Christians to celebrate together this year of 1977 the resurrection of our common Savior. Although it will not be possible to continue this practice in the immediate years to come, it is our conviction, arising out of the serious reactions to the original proposal made, that the entire Christian world is committed to arriving at a solution to this problem as soon as possible.

165. PAUL VI and FREDERICK DONALD COGGAN (Archbishop of Canterbury), **Joint Statement**, 29 April 1977: AAS 69 (1977) 286–289 (English).

1.   After four hundred years of estrangement, it is now the third time in seventeen   1080
years that an Archbishop of Canterbury and the Pope embrace in Christian friendship in the city of Rome. Since the visit of Archbishop Ramsey eleven years have passed and much has happened in that time to fulfill the hopes then expressed and to cause us to thank God.

2.   As the Roman Catholic Church and the constituent Churches of the Anglican   1081
Communion have sought to grow in mutual understanding and Christian love, they have come to recognize, to value, and to give thanks for: a common faith in God our Father, in our Lord Jesus Christ, and in the Holy Spirit; our common baptism into Christ; our sharing of the holy Scriptures, of the Apostles' and Nicene Creeds, the Chalcedonian definition, and the teaching of the Fathers; our common Christian inheritance for many centuries with its living traditions of liturgy, theology, spirituality, and mission.

3.   At the same time, in fulfillment of the pledge of eleven years ago to "a serious   1082
dialogue which, founded on the Gospels and on the ancient common traditions, may lead to that unity in truth, for which Christ prayed,"[1] Anglican and Roman Catholic theologians have faced calmly and objectively the historical and doctrinal differences which have divided us. Without compromising their respective allegiances, they have addressed these problems together and in the process they have discovered theological convergences often as unexpected as they were happy.

---

[1]   Paul VI and Michael Ramsey, *Common Declaration*, 1969 [DOL 145 no. 960].

1083   4.   The Anglican/Roman Catholic International Commission has produced three documents: on the eucharist, on ministry and ordination, and on Church and authority. We now recommend that the work it has begun be pursued, through procedures appropriate to our respective Communions, so that both of them may be led along the path toward unity.

The moment will shortly come when the respective authorities must evaluate the conclusions.

1084   5.   The response of both Communions to the work and fruits of theological dialogue will be measured by the practical response of the faithful to the task of restoring unity, which, as the Second Vatican Council says, "involves the whole Church, faithful and clergy alike" and "extends to everyone according to the talents of each."[2] We rejoice that this practical response has manifested itself in so many forms of pastoral cooperation in many parts of the world, in meetings of bishops, clergy, and faithful.

1085   6.   In mixed marriages between Anglicans and Roman Catholics, where the tragedy of our separation at the sacrament of union is seen most starkly, cooperation in pastoral care[3] in many places has borne fruit in increased understanding. Serious dialogue has cleared away many misconceptions and shown that we still share much that is deep-rooted in the Christian tradition and ideal of marriage, though important differences persist, particularly regarding remarriage after divorce. We are following attentively the work thus far accomplished in this dialogue by the Joint Commission on the Theology of Marriage and its Application to Mixed Marriages. It has stressed the need for fidelity and witness to the ideal of marriage set forth in the New Testament and constantly taught in Christian tradition. We have a common duty to defend this tradition and ideal and the moral values which derive from it.

1086   7.   All such cooperation, which must continue to grow and spread, is the true setting for continued dialogue and for the general extension and appreciation of its fruits and so for progress toward that goal which is Christ's will — the restoration of complete communion in faith and sacramental life.

1087   8.   Our call to this is one with the sublime Christian vocation itself, which is a call to communion; as St. John says: "That which we have seen and heard we proclaim also to you, so that you may have fellowship with us; and our fellowship is with the Father and his Son Jesus Christ."[4] If we are to maintain progress in doctrinal convergence and move forward resolutely to the communion of mind and heart for which Christ prayed, we must ponder still further his intentions in founding the Church and face courageously their requirements.

1088   9.   It is this communion with God in Christ through faith and through baptism and self-giving to him that stands at the center of our witness to the world, even while between us communion remains imperfect. Our divisions hinder this witness, hinder the work of Christ,[5] but they do not close all roads we may travel together. In a spirit of prayer and of submission to God's will, we must collaborate more

---

   [2] UR no. 5.

   [3] See *Matrimonia mixta* no. 14 [DOL 354 no. 3011].

   [4] 1 Jn 1:3.

   [5] Paul VI, Ap. Exhort. *Evangelii nuntiandi* no. 77.

earnestly in a "greater common witness to Christ before the world in the very work of evangelization."[6] It is our desire that the means of this collaboration be sought: the increasing spiritual hunger in all parts of God's world invites us to such a common pilgrimage.

This collaboration, pursued to the limit allowed by truth and loyalty, will create the climate in which dialogue and doctrinal convergence can bear fruit. While this fruit is ripening, serious obstacles remain, both of the past and of recent origin. Many in both Communions are asking themselves whether they have a common faith sufficient to be translated into communion of life, worship, and mission. Only the Communions themselves through their pastoral authorities can give that answer. When the moment comes to do so, may the answer shine through in spirit and truth, not obscured by the enmities, the prejudices, and the suspicions of the past.

10. To this we are bound to look forward and to spare no effort to bring it closer: to be baptized into Christ is to be baptized into hope — "and hope does not disappoint us because God's love has been poured into our hearts through the Holy Spirit which has been given us."[7]   1089

11. Christian hope manifests itself in prayer and action — in prudence but also in courage. We pledge ourselves and exhort the faithful of the Roman Catholic Church and of the Anglican Communion to live and work courageously in this hope of reconciliation and unity in our common Lord.   1090

166. JOHN PAUL II and DEMETRIOS I (Ecumenical Patriarch), **Joint Statement**, 29 November 1979: AAS 71 (1979) 1603–05 (French).

We, Pope John Paul II and the Ecumenical Patriarch Demetrios I, give thanks to God for his gift of our meeting to celebrate the feast of St. Andrew, first-called of the apostles and brother of St. Peter. "Blessed be the God and Father of our Lord Jesus Christ, who in Christ has blessed us with every spiritual blessing in the heavenly places" (Eph 1:3).   1091

A single purpose, God's glory through the fulfillment of his will, moves us to restate our determined intention to take every step possible in order to hasten that day when full communion will be reestablished between the Roman Catholic Church and the Greek Orthodox Church and when we can at last concelebrate the divine eucharist.

We are full of thanks to our predecessors Pope Paul VI and Patriarch Athenagoras I for all they did to reconcile our Churches and to bring about their progress in unity.

The advances achieved in the preparatory stages enable us to announce the beginning of theological dialogue and to publish the list of members of the joint, Catholic-Orthodox commission charged with carrying on such a dialogue.   1092

Its purposes will be not simply progress toward the reestablishment of full communion between the two sister Churches, the Catholic and the Orthodox, but

---

6   Ibid.

7   Rom 5:5.

also a contribution to the many dialogues being pursued throughout the Christian world in the search for unity.

The dialogue of charity (see Jn 13:34; Eph 4:1–7), rooted in an absolute adherence to the only Lord, Jesus Christ, and to his will regarding his Church, has opened the way toward a better understanding of the theological positions of the partners to the dialogue. That in turn has led to new approaches in the work of theology and to a new attitude regarding the past that our Churches share. This purifying of the collective memory of our Churches is an important result of the dialogue of charity and an indispensable condition for any advances in the future. This dialogue of charity must continue and become more intense in the complex situation that we have inherited from the past and that creates the actual setting in which our present efforts unfold.

Our wish is that advances in unity will open up new possibilities for dialogue and of cooperation with believers of other religions and with all people of good will. The aim is that love and brotherhood may put an end to hatred and enmity between people. We hope thereby to contribute to the coming of a genuine peace in the world. We beseech this gift from him who was, who is, and who is to come, Christ our only Lord and our true peace.

167. JOHN PAUL II, **Homily** at the Church of the Holy Spirit, Istanbul, excerpt on full communion in the eucharistic celebration, 29 November 1979: AAS 71 (1979) 1593–98; Not 15 (1979) 674–675 (French).

1093

[. . .] Thanks be to God, for several years now we have been celebrating with each other the feasts of the protectors of our Churches, as the pledge of a genuine desire for full concelebration: at Rome we have been celebrating the feast of St. Peter and St. Paul in the presence of an Orthodox delegation; at the Orthodox Patriarchate the feast of St. Andrew is celebrated with Catholics present.

Communion in prayer will lead us to full communion in the eucharist. I dare to hope that the day for it is near; personally I desire it to be very near. Do we not already share the same eucharistic faith and the true sacraments by reason of apostolic succession? Let us hope that complete communion in faith, especially in regard to ecclesiology, will soon allow our complete *communicatio in sacris*. My revered predecessor longed to see this day, as did Patriarch Athenagoras I. About him Pope Paul spoke these words shortly after the Patriarch's death: "He always summed up his sentiments in one single, supreme hope: to be able to 'drink the chalice' together with us, that is, to celebrate together the eucharistic sacrifice as the synthesis and crown of a ecclesial identification with Christ. We too have deeply desired that same thing. Now this unfulfilled desire must remain as our heritage and our commitment" (Remarks at the Angelus, 9 July 1972). For my part, in taking up this heritage, I share ardently in this desire, which time and progress in union only intensify.

▶ See also Chapter Two, Section 6. Marriage: B. Mixed Marriages.

Section 9. Other Documents

SUMMARY (DOL 168–173). This last section groups 6 documents that are of importance, but difficult to assign elsewhere in the collection:

—Three deal in general with faith and catechesis in their relationship to liturgy (DOL 168, 169, 171) and one with the particular issue of eschatology (DOL 173).

—A letter of Paul VI is of interest to the history of the liturgical movement (DOL 172).

—There is also an extract from an instruction on use of the media of social communication (DOL 170).

168. PAUL VI, **Solemn Profession of Faith** (Credo of the People of God), excerpt pertaining to the liturgy, 30 June 1968: AAS 60 (1968) 433–445.

1094   18. We confess and believe that there is one baptism, instituted by our Lord Jesus Christ for the forgiveness of sins and that baptism is to be administered even to infants "who themselves have not yet the power to commit any sin," so that those who lack supernatural grace from the beginning may be reborn "of water and the Holy Spirit" to divine life in Christ Jesus.[24]

1095   19. [. . .] The Lord Jesus in the course of time fashions his Church through the sacraments that derive from his own fullness.[26] By means of the sacraments the Church causes its members to share in the mystery of the death and resurrection of Jesus Christ through the grace of the Holy Spirit who gives the Church life and guidance.[27] The Church is therefore holy even though it has sinners in its midst, for the life on which it lives is none other than the life of grace. Nourished from this, the members of the Church are made holy; cutting themselves off from it, they incur sin and stain of soul, which prevent the spread of the Church's radiant holiness. The Church itself grieves and does penance for the sins from which it has the power to free its children by the blood of Christ and the gift of the Holy Spirit.

1096   24. We believe that the Mass, celebrated in the person of Christ by the priest in virtue of the power of orders and offered by him in the name of Christ and the members of Christ's Mystical Body, is truly the sacrifice of Calvary made present sacramentally on our altars. We believe that just as the bread and wine our Lord consecrated at the Last Supper were changed into the body and blood about to be offered for us on the cross, so too the bread and wine the priest consecrates are changed into the body and blood of Christ, seated in heavenly glory. We believe that the presence of the Lord hidden under the appearances of bread and wine, which to our senses remain the same as before, is true, real, and substantial.[37]

1097   25. In this sacrament, therefore, Christ cannot become present in any other way than by the change of the whole substance of the bread into his body and the whole substance of the wine into his blood, only the properties perceptible to our senses remaining intact. The Church aptly and correctly terms this mysterious change transubstantiation. To remain compatible with Catholic faith, any theological interpretation seeking some degree of understanding of this mystery must affirm unequivocally that in reality itself, that is, as distinct from merely in our minds, the bread and wine after the consecration no longer exist; consequently the body and blood of the Lord Jesus are present and to be adored under the appearances of bread and wine.[38] This is the way the Lord himself chose in order to give himself as our food and to bring us together in the unity of his Mystical Body.

1098   26. The one and undivided existence of Christ the Lord, glorious in heaven, is not multiplied, but becomes present through the sacrament in various places of the world where the eucharistic sacrifice is celebrated. That same existence after the sacrifice has been celebrated continues in the blessed sacrament present in the tabernacle as the living heart of our churches. Ours is the welcome duty therefore

---

[24] Council of Trent, sess. 5, *Decr. De peccato originali*: Denz-Schön 1514.

[26] See LG nos. 7, 11 [DOL 4 nos. 139, 141].

[27] See SC art. 5, 6 [DOL 1 nos. 5,6]; LG nos. 7, 12, 50 [DOL 4 nos. 139, 142, 158].

[37] Council of Trent, sess. 13, *Decr. De ss. Eucharistia*: Denz-Schön 1651.

[38] See ibid.: Denz-Schön 1642, 1651. Paul VI, Encycl. *Mysterium fidei* [DOL 176 no. 1190].

of offering homage and, in the host we gaze on, of adoring the incarnate Word, who is beyond our gaze yet has become present to us without leaving heaven.

169. SC CLERGY, *General Catechetical Directory*, 11 April 1971, AAS 64 (1972) 97–176 (excerpts).*

PART II. MINISTRY OF THE WORD

CHAPTER II
CATECHESIS IN THE PASTORAL MISSION OF THE CHURCH
(NATURE, PURPOSE, EFFICACY)

MINISTRY OF THE WORD IN THE CHURCH

17. The ministry of the word takes many forms, including catechesis, according to the different conditions under which it is practiced and the ends which it strives to achieve.   1099

There is the form called evangelization or missionary preaching. This has as its purpose the arousing of the beginnings of faith[22] so that men will adhere to the word of God.

Then there is the catechetical form, "which is intended to make men's faith become living, conscious, and active, through the light of instruction."[23]

And then there is the liturgical form, within the setting of a liturgical celebration, especially that of the eucharist (for example, the homily).[24]

Finally, there is the theological form, that is, the systematic treatment and the scientific investigation of the truths of faith.

For our purpose it is important to keep these forms distinct, since they are governed by their own laws. Nevertheless, in the concrete reality of the pastoral ministry, they are closely bound together. Accordingly, all that has so far been said about the ministry of the word in general is to be applied also to catechesis.

CATECHESIS AND THE LIFE OF LITURGICAL AND PRIVATE PRAYER

25. "Every liturgical celebration, because it is an action of Christ the Priest and of his Body the Church, is a sacred action surpassing all others. No other action of the Church can match its claim to efficacy, nor equal the degree of it."[31] And the more mature a Christian community becomes in faith, the more it lives its worship in spirit and in truth[32] in its liturgical celebrations, especially at the eucharist.   1100

Therefore, catechesis must promote an active, conscious, genuine participation in the liturgy of the Church, not merely by explaining the meaning of the ceremonies, but also by forming the minds of the faithful for prayer, for thanksgiving, for repentance, for praying with confidence, for a community spirit, and for under-

---

* English text of the *Directorium catechisticum generale*, approved by SCC, published by USCC Publications Office (Washington, DC, 1971).

22   See CD nos. 11, 13; AG nos. 6, 13, 14.

23   CD no. 14 [DOL 7 no. 193].

24   See SC art. 33, 52 [DOL 1 nos. 33, 52]. SCR, Instr. InterOec no. 54 [DOL 23 no. 346].

31   SC art. 7 [DOL 1 no. 7].

32   See Jn 4:23.

standing correctly the meaning of the creeds. All these things are necessary for a true liturgical life.

"The spiritual life, however, is not confined to participation in the liturgy. The Christian is assuredly called to pray with his brethren, but he must also enter into his chamber to pray to the Father in secret,[33] indeed, according to the teaching of the Apostle Paul,[34] he should pray without ceasing."[35]

Therefore, catechesis must also train the faithful to meditate on the word of God and to engage in private prayer.

PART III. THE CHRISTIAN MESSAGE

CHAPTER II
THE MORE OUTSTANDING ELEMENTS OF THE CHRISTIAN MESSAGE

GENUINE WORSHIP OF GOD IN A SECULARIZED WORLD

1101   48. "The God and Father of our Lord Jesus Christ"[14] is "the living God."[15] He is a holy, just, and merciful God; he is God the author of the covenant with men; God who sees, frees, and saves; God who loves as a father, as a spouse. Catechesis joyfully proclaims this God who is the source of our every hope.[16]

Catechesis, however, cannot ignore the fact that not a few men of our era strongly sense a remoteness and even absence of God. This fact, which is part of the process of secularization, surely constitutes a danger for the faith; but it also impels us to have a purer faith and to become more humble in the presence of the mystery of God, as we ought: "Truly you are a hidden God, the God of Israel, the Savior."[17] With this perspective, it is possible also to understand more easily the true nature of the worship which God demands and which glorifies him, a worship, that is, which includes a resolve to fulfill his will in every field of activity and faithfully to increase in charity the talents given by the Lord.[18] In the sacred liturgy the faithful bring the fruits of every kind of act of charity, of justice, of peace in order to make a humble offering of them to God and to receive in return the words of life and the graces they need to enable them in the world to profess the truth in love[19] in communion with Christ, who offers his body and blood for men.

THE SACRAMENTS, ACTIONS OF CHRIST IN THE CHURCH, THE PRIMORDIAL SACRAMENT

1102   55. The mystery of Christ is continued in the Church, which always enjoys his presence and ministers to him. This is done in a specific way through the signs that Christ instituted, which signify the gift of grace and produce it and are properly called sacraments.[48]

---

[33]   See Mt 6:6.

[34]   See 1 Thes 5:17.

[35]   SC art. 12 [DOL 1 no. 12].

[14]   Eph 1:3.

[15]   Mt 16:16.

[16]   See 1 Pt 1:3–4.

[17]   Is 45:15.

[18]   See Mt 25.14ff.

[19]   See Eph 4:15.

[48]   See Council of Trent, *Decr. de sacramentis*: Denz-Schön 1601 [–08].

The Church itself, however, is in some way to be considered the primordial sacrament, since it is not only the people of God but also in Christ a kind of "sign and instrument of the intimate union with God and of the unity of the entire human race."[49]

Sacraments are the principal and fundamental actions whereby Jesus Christ unceasingly bestows his Spirit on the faithful, thus making them the holy people which offers itself, in him and with him, as an oblation acceptable to the Father. The sacraments are surely to be considered inestimable blessings of the Church. To the Church, then, belongs the power of administering them; and yet they are always to be referred to Christ, from whom they receive their efficacy. In reality, it is Christ who baptizes. It is not so much a man who celebrates the eucharist as Christ himself, for he it is who offers himself in the sacrifice of the Mass by the ministry of the priests.[50] The sacramental action is, in the first place, the action of Christ and the ministers of the Church are as his instruments.

FULL MEANING OF THE SACRAMENTS

56. Catechesis will have the duty of presenting the seven sacraments according to their full meaning.   1103

First, they must be presented as sacraments of faith. Of themselves they certainly express the efficacious will of Christ the Savior; but men, on their part, must show a sincere will to respond to God's love and mercy. Hence, catechesis must concern itself with the acquisition of the proper dispositions, with the stimulation of sincerity and generosity for a worthy reception of the sacraments.

Second, the sacraments must be presented, each according to its own nature and end, not only as remedies for sin and its consequences, but especially as sources of grace in individuals and in communities, so that the entire dispensation of grace in the life of the faithful may be related in some way to the sacramental economy.

CATECHESIS ON THE SACRAMENTS

57. Baptism cleanses man from original sin and from all personal sins, gives him rebirth as a child of God, incorporates him into the Church, sanctifies him with the gifts of the Holy Spirit, and, impressing on his soul an indelible character, initiates him in Christ's priestly, prophetic, and kingly roles.[51] Confirmation binds the Christian more perfectly to the Church and enriches him with a special strength of the Holy Spirit, that he may live in the world as a witness of Christ.   1104

Since the life of Christians, which on earth is a warfare, is liable to temptations and sins, the way of the sacrament of penance is open for them, so that they may obtain pardon from the merciful God and reconcile themselves with the Church.

Holy orders in a special way conforms certain members of the people of God to Christ the Mediator by conferring on them a sacred power that they may shepherd the Church, nourish the faithful with the word of God and make them holy, and, in the first place, that they, representing Christ's person, may offer the sacrifice of the Mass and preside at the eucharistic banquet.

"By the sacred anointing of the sick and the prayer of its priests, the whole Church commends those who are ill to the suffering and glorified Lord, that he may lighten their sufferings and save them."[52]

---

[49]   LG no. 1.

[50]   See Council of Trent, *Doctrina de sacrificio Missae*: Denz-Schön 1743.

[51]   See 1 Pt 2:9. LG no. 31.

[52]   LG no. 11 [DOL 4 no. 141]. Jas 5:14–16.

In catechesis on the sacraments much importance should be placed on the explanation of the signs. Catechesis should lead the faithful through the visible signs to ponder God's invisible mysteries of salvation.

THE EUCHARIST, CENTER OF THE ENTIRE SACRAMENTAL LIFE

1105   58. The primacy of the eucharist over all the sacraments is unquestionable, as is also its supreme efficacy in building up the Church.[53]

For in the eucharist, when the words of consecration have been pronounced, the profound (not the phenomenal) reality of bread and wine is changed into the body and blood of Christ and this wonderful change has in the Church come to be called "transubstantiation." Accordingly, under the appearances (that is, the phenomenal reality) of the bread and wine, the humanity of Christ, not only by its power but by itself (that is, substantially), united with his divine Person, lies hidden in an altogether mysterious way.[54]

This sacrifice is not merely a rite commemorating a past sacrifice. For in it Christ by the ministry of the priests perpetuates the sacrifice of the cross in an unbloody manner through the course of the centuries.[55] In it too he nourishes the faithful with himself, the Bread of Life, in order that, filled with love of God and neighbor, they may become more and more a people acceptable to God.

Having been nourished with the victim of the sacrifice of the cross, the faithful should by a genuine and active love remove the prejudices because of which they are at times accused of a sterile worship that keeps them from being brotherly and from cooperating with other people. By its nature the eucharistic banquet is meant to help the faithful to unite their hearts with God more each day in frequent prayer and thence to acknowledge and love other men as brothers of Christ and sons of God the Father.

THE SACRAMENT OF MATRIMONY

1106   59. In our days, with the preeminence that the Christian message ascribes to consecrated virginity being preserved,[56] a special importance must be assigned to religious education on matrimony, which the Creator himself instituted and endowed with various blessings, purposes, and laws.[57]

Supported by the words of faith and by the natural law, under the guidance of the magisterium of the Church, which is responsible for authoritative interpretation of both the moral and the natural law,[58] and at the same time taking due account of contemporary advances in the anthropological sciences, catechesis must make matrimony the foundation of family life with regard to its values and its divine law of unity and indissolubility and with regard to its duties of love, which by its natural character has been ordered toward the procreation and education of offspring. In regulating procreation, conjugal chastity must be preserved in accord with the teaching of the Church.[59]

Since Christ elevated matrimony to the dignity of a sacrament for the baptized, the spouses, who are the ministers of the sacrament when they give personal and

---

[53] See LG nos. 11, 17 [DOL 4 nos. 141, 144]. SCR, Instr. EuchMyst nos. 5, 15 [DOL 179 nos. 1234, 1244].

[54] See Paul VI, Encycl. *Mysterium fidei* no. 46 [DOL 176 no. 1190].

[55] See SC art. 47 [DOL 1 no. 47].

[56] See 1 Cor 7:38. Council of Trent, *Canones de sacramento matrimonii*: Denz-Schön 1810.

[57] See GS no. 48.

[58] See Paul VI, Encycl. *Humanae vitae* no. 4: AAS 60 (1968) 483.

[59] See ibid. no. 14: AAS 60 (1968) 490.

irrevocable consent, living in Christ's grace imitate and in a certain way represent the love of Christ himself for his Church.[60] Christian spouses are strengthened and as it were consecrated by this special sacrament for fulfilling the duties of their state and for upholding its dignity.[61]

Finally, it is part of the family's vocation to become a community, one which is also open to the Church and to the world.

PART V. CATECHESIS ACCORDING TO AGE LEVELS

INFANCY AND ITS IMPORTANCE

78. The first roots of religious and moral life appear at the very beginning of human life. In the families of believers the first months and years of life, which are of the greatest importance for a man's balance in the years to come, can already provide the right conditions for developing a Christian personality. The baptism of infants takes on its full meaning when the Christian life of the parents, of the mother especially but not exclusively, makes it possible for the baptismal grace to produce its fruits. For the infant absorbs into himself, as though through an "osmosis" process, the manner of acting and the attitudes of the members of his family. And so it is that the immense number of his experiences will be, as it were, pressed together within him to form a foundation of that life of faith which will then gradually develop and manifest itself.

1107

The right orientation of a trusting spirit depends at first on a good relationship between the infant and his mother and then also on one between him and his father; it is nourished by sharing their joyfulness and by experiencing their loving authority. The theological virtues depend in part upon the growth of that healthy orientation for their own unimpeded development and at the same time they tend to strengthen that orientation. At this time, too, there arises the affirmation of personality or autonomy; this is needed for the acquisition of the moral virtues and for leading a life in community. It itself demands a balance between firmness and acceptance. Next, the capacity for spontaneous action can gradually develop; this will be most necessary for beginning social life as well as for promoting and strengthening the service of God and of the Church. An education in prayer must accompany all these acquisitions, so that the little child may learn to call upon the God who loves us and protects us, and upon Jesus, the Son of God and our brother, who leads us to the Father, and upon the Holy Spirit, who dwells within our hearts; and so that this child may also direct confident prayers to Mary, the Mother of Jesus and our mother. [. . .]

CHILDHOOD AND ITS IMPORTANCE

79. When the child goes to school he enters a society wider than that of his family and he is initiated into the society of adults in an intensive way that absorbs a great part of his resources and concerns. He gets his first experience of working in school.[1]

1108

Before this point, the family served a mediating role between the child and the people of God. But now the child is ready to begin sharing directly in the life of the Church and can be admitted to the sacraments. [. . .]

---

[60]   See Eph 5:25.

[61]   See GS no. 48 [DOL 19 no. 271].

[1]   See GE no. 5.

OLD AGE

1109   95. The importance of old age is still not sufficiently recognized in the pastoral ministry. [. . .]

Catechesis should teach the aged to have supernatural hope, by virtue of which death is considered a crossing over to true life and as a meeting with the divine Savior. In this way old age can become a sign of the presence of God, of immortal life, and of the future resurrection. This will, indeed, be an eschatological witness that the aged can bear by their patience toward themselves and toward others, by their benevolence, by their prayers poured out in praise of God, by their spirit of poverty and the trust that they put in God. [. . .]

SPECIAL FORMS OF CATECHESIS FOR ADULTS

1110   96. There are conditions and circumstances that demand special forms of catechesis.

a. There is the catechesis of Christian initiation or the catechumenate for adults. [. . .]

c. There is a catechesis which is to be given on the occasion of the principal events of life, such as marriage, the baptism of one's children, first communion and confirmation, the more difficult periods of the children's education, one's illness, and so forth. These are times when people are moved more strongly than ever to seek the true meaning of life. [. . .]

PART VI. PASTORAL ACTIVITY IN THE MINISTRY OF THE WORD

CHAPTER II
PROGRAM OF ACTION

NORMS

1111   106. The norms that can be given with regard to catechesis are many and they vary with the ends to be attained. In comparison with the others, the norms for preparing the faithful for the sacraments have a special importance. These include, for example, norms for the catechumenate of adults, for the sacramental initiation of children, and for the preparation of families for the baptism of their children.

To be effective, all such norms should be few in number, simple in character, and set external rather than internal criteria.

As is obvious, no particular norm can derogate from the Church's general laws and common practice without the approval of the Apostolic See.

CHAPTER III
CATECHETICAL FORMATION

SPIRITUAL LIFE OF CATECHISTS

1112   114. The function entrusted to the catechist demands of him a fervent sacramental and spiritual life, a practice of prayer, and a deep feeling for the excellence of the Christian message and for the power it has to transform one's life; it also demands of him the pursuit of the charity, humility, and prudence which allow the Holy Spirit to complete his fruitful work in those being taught.

FORMATION OF CATECHISTS

1113   115. It is necessary that ecclesiastical authorities regard the formation of catechists as a task of the greatest importance.

This formation is meant for all catechists,[3] both lay and religious, and also for Christian parents, who will be able to receive therefrom effective help for taking care of the initial and occasional catechesis for which they are responsible. This formation is meant for deacons, and especially for priests, for "by the power of the sacrament of orders, and in the image of the eternal High Priest,[4] they are consecrated to preach the Gospel, shepherd the faithful, and celebrate divine worship as true priests of the New Testament."[5] Indeed, in individual parishes the preaching of the word of God is committed chiefly to the priests, who are obliged to open the riches of sacred Scripture to the faithful and to explain the mysteries of the faith and the norms of Christian living in homilies throughout the course of the liturgical year.[6] Hence it is of great importance that a thorough catechetical preparation be given students in seminaries and scholasticates, which should be completed afterward by the continuing formation mentioned above.[7]

Finally, the formation is meant for teachers of religion in public schools, whether these belong to the Church or to the state. To carry out a task of such great importance only persons should be selected who are distinguished for talent, doctrine, and spiritual life.[8] [. . .]

CHAPTER VI
COORDINATION OF PASTORAL CATECHETICS WITH ALL PASTORAL WORK

CATECHUMENATE FOR ADULTS

130. The catechumenate for adults, which at one and the same time includes cate-   1114
chesis, liturgical participation, and community living, is an excellent example of an institution that springs from the cooperation of diverse pastoral functions. Its purpose is to direct the spiritual journey of persons who are preparing themselves for the reception of baptism and to give direction to their habits of thought and changes in moral living. It is a preparatory school in Christian living, an introduction to the religious, liturgical, charitable, and apostolic life of the people of God.[15] Not only the priests and catechists, but the entire Christian community, through sponsors who act in its name, is engaged in this work.

ADDENDUM
THE FIRST RECEPTION OF THE SACRAMENTS OF PENANCE
AND THE EUCHARIST

Among the tasks of catechesis, the preparation of children for the sacraments   1115
of penance and the eucharist is of great importance. With regard to this, it is held opportune to recall certain principles and to make some observations about certain experiments that have been taking place very recently in some regions or places of the Church.

---

³ See AG nos. 17 [DOL 17 no. 249] and 26.

⁴ See Heb 5:1–10, 7:24, 9:11–28.

⁵ LG no. 28 [DOL 4 no. 148].

⁶ See SC art. 51, 52 [DOL 1 nos. 51, 52].

⁷ See no. 110 of this document.

⁸ See GS no. 5.

¹⁵ See AG nos. 13, 14 [DOL 17 no. 246]; SC art. 65 [DOL 1 no. 65]; CD no. 14 [DOL 7 no. 193].

THE AGE OF DISCRETION

1116   1.   The suitable age for the first reception of these sacraments is deemed to be that which in documents of the Church is called the age of reason or of discretion. This age "both for confession and for communion is that at which the child begins to reason, that is, about the seventh year, more or less. From that time on the obligation of fulfilling the precepts of confession and communion begins."[1] It is praiseworthy to study by research in pastoral psychology and to describe this age, which develops gradually, is subject to various conditions, and which presents a peculiar nature in every child. One should, however, be on guard not to extend beyond the above-mentioned limits, which are not rigid, the time at which the precept of confession and communion begins to oblige *per se*.

FORMATION AND GROWTH OF THE MORAL CONSCIENCE OF CHILDREN

1117   2.   While the capacity to reason is evolving gradually in a child, his moral conscience too is being trained, that is, the faculty of judging his acts in relation to a norm of morality. A number of varying elements and circumstances come together in forming this moral conscience of a child: the character and discipline of his family, which is one of the most important educative factors during the first years of a child's life; his associations with others; and the activities and the witness of the ecclesial community. Catechesis, while carrying out its task of instructing and forming in the Christian faith, puts order into these various factors of education, promotes them, and works in conjunction with them. Only in this way will catechesis be able to give to the child timely direction toward the heavenly Father and correct any going astray or incorrect orientations of life that can occur. Without doubt children at this age should be told in the simplest possible way about God as our Lord and Father, about his love for us, about Jesus, the Son of God, who was made man for us and who died and rose again. By thinking about the love of God, the child will be able gradually to perceive the malice of sin, which always offends God the Father and Jesus and which is opposed to the charity with which we must love our neighbor and ourselves.

IMPORTANCE OF EXPLAINING THE SACRAMENT OF PENANCE TO CHILDREN

1118   3.   When a child begins to offend God by sin, he also begins to have the desire of receiving pardon, not only from parents or relatives, but also from God. Catechesis helps him by nourishing this desire wholesomely and it instills a holy aversion to sin, an awareness of the need for amendment, and especially love for God. The special task of catechesis here is to explain in a suitable way that sacramental confession is a means offered children of the Church to obtain pardon for sin and furthermore that it is even necessary per se if one has fallen into serious sin. To be sure, Christian parents and religious educators ought to teach the child in such a way that above all he will strive to advance to a more intimate love of the Lord Jesus and to genuine love of neighbor. The doctrine on the sacrament of penance is to be presented in a broad framework of attaining purification and spiritual growth with great confidence in the mercy and love of God. In this way, children not only can little by little acquire a delicate understanding of conscience, but do not lose heart when they fall into some lesser fault.

The eucharist is the summit and center of the entire Christian life. In addition to the required state of grace, great purity of soul is clearly fitting for the reception of communion. One must be very careful, however, that the children do not get the impression that confession is necessary before receiving the eucharist even when one sincerely loves God and has not departed from the path of God's commandments in a serious way.

---

[1]   Decr. *Quam singulari* 1: AAS 2 (1910) 582.

CERTAIN NEW EXPERIMENTS

4.   In very recent times in certain regions of the Church experiments relative to   1119
the first reception of the sacraments of penance and of the eucharist have been
made. These have given rise to doubt and confusion.

So that the communion of children may be appropriately received early and so
that psychological disturbances in the future Christian life which can result from a
too early use of confession may be avoided and so that better education for the
spirit of penance and a more valid catechetical preparation for confession itself may
be fostered, it has seemed to some that children should be admitted to first communion without first receiving the sacrament of penance.

In fact, however, going to the sacrament of penance from the beginning of the
use of reason does not in itself harm the minds of the children, provided it is
preceded, as it should be, by a kind and prudent catechetical preparation. The spirit
of penance can be developed more fully by continuing catechetical instruction after
first communion; likewise, there can be growth in knowledge and appreciation of
the great gift that Christ has given to sinful men in the sacrament of the pardon
they will receive and of reconciliation with the Church.[2]

These things have not prevented the introduction in certain places of a practice
in which some years regularly elapse between first communion and first confession.
In other places, however, the innovations made have been more cautious, either
because first confession was not so much delayed, or because consideration is given
the judgment of the parents who prefer to have their children go to the sacrament
of penance before first communion.

THE COMMON PRACTICE IN FORCE MUST BE HIGHLY ESTEEMED

5.   The Supreme Pontiff Pius X declared: "The custom of not admitting children to   1120
confession or of never giving them absolution, when they have arrived at the use of
reason, must be wholly condemned."[3] One can scarcely have regard for the right
that baptized children have of confessing their sins, if at the beginning of the age of
discretion they are not prepared and gently led to the sacrament of penance.

One should also keep in mind the usefulness of confession, which retains its
efficacy even when only venial sins are in question and which gives an increase of
grace and of charity, increases the child's good dispositions for receiving the eucharist, and also helps to perfect the Christian life. Hence, it appears the usefulness of
confession cannot be dismissed in favor of those forms of penance or those ministries of the word, by which the virtue of penance is aptly fostered in children, and
which can be fruitfully practiced together with the sacrament of penance, when a
suitable catechetical preparation has been made. The pastoral experience of the
Church, which is illustrated by many examples even in our day, teaches it how
much the so-called age of discretion is suited for effecting that the children's
baptismal grace, by means of a well-prepared reception of the sacraments of penance and of the eucharist, shows forth its first fruits, which are certainly to be
augmented afterward by means of a continued catechesis.

Having weighed all these points and keeping in mind the common and general
practice, which *per se* cannot be derogated without the approval of the Apostolic
See, and also having heard the conferences of bishops, the Holy See judges it fitting
that the practice now in force in the Church of putting confession ahead of first
communion should be retained. This in no way prevents this custom from being

---

[2]   See LG no. 11 [DOL 4 no. 141].

[3]   Decr. *Quam singulari* 7: AAS 2 (1910) 583.

carried out in various ways, as, for instance, by having a communal penitential celebration precede or follow the reception of the sacrament of penance.

The Holy See is not unmindful of the special conditions that exist in various countries, but it exhorts the bishops in this important matter not to depart from the practice in force without having first entered into communication with the Holy See in a spirit of hierarchical communion. Nor should they in any way allow the pastors or educators or religious institutes to begin or to continue to abandon the practice in force.

In regions, however, where new practices have already been introduced which depart notably from the pristine practice, the conferences of bishops will wish to submit these experiments to a new examination. If after that they wish to continue these experiments for a longer time, they should not do so unless they have first communicated with the Holy See, which will willingly hear them, and they are at one mind with the Holy See.

Pope Paul VI, by a letter of his Secretariat of State, no. 177335, dated 18 March 1971, approved this General Directory together with the Addendum, confirmed it by his authority, and ordered it to be published.

170. PONTIFICAL COMMISSION FOR THE MEDIA OF SOCIAL COMMUNICATION, Instruction *Communio et progressio*, on the right application of the conciliar Decree *Inter mirifica*, 23 May 1971: AAS 63 (1971) 593–656 (excerpts).

PART III. CATHOLIC INVOLVEMENT IN THE COMMUNICATIONS MEDIA

CHAPTER THREE
CATHOLICS' INTEREST AND USE OF EACH OF THE MEDIA

3. RADIO AND TELEVISION

1121   150. The various religious broadcasts made possible by radio and television give rise to new contacts between the faithful and wonderfully enrich their devotional and religious life. The media have great power for the religious education of the faithful and as an aid to their efforts on behalf of Church and world. The media also serve those who are so ill or so elderly that they are prevented from direct participation in the life of the Church. The media establish contact with those many people who, even if they take no part in the Church's life or have even left it, yearn unconsciously for the food of the spirit. The media also carry the Gospel to regions where Christ's Church has not yet carried out its work. The Church, therefore, must exert every effort to make such broadcasts possible and to improve them with new techniques.

1122   151. The most desirable and fitting religious broadcasts are those of the celebration of Mass and other sacred rites. Everything about the liturgy itself and the technical details must be prepared with absolute care. The diversity of the audience must be taken into consideration as also, in the case of international broadcasts, regional religious opinions and customs. In number and length these broadcasts should respect the desires of the audience.[R1]

[R1]   Query: May the Mass be broadcast via radio or television at an hour or on a day other than its time

152. Religious language and speaking style must be adapted to the nature of the   1123
medium used. Those who are to engage in this work should be picked judiciously
and carefully and not before they have developed the requisite knowledge and
experience.

157. In those nations where the Church is barred from the use of the media, listen-   1124
ing to religious radio broadcasts from abroad is the one way open to the faithful to
learn about the life of the universal Church and to hear the word of God. Their
unfortunate condition lays a grave burden on both the pastors and the laity of other
countries to join their own hearts and minds willingly with such Christians according to the demands of Christian solidarity, as it is called, and to assist their brothers
and sisters in Christ by providing radio or television broadcasts with a religious
message answering their needs.

171. SC DOCTRINE OF THE FAITH, Declaration *Mysterium Ecclesiae*, on Catholic teaching about the Church, against certain contemporary errors, 24 June 1973: AAS 65 (1973) 396–408 (excerpts).

6. THE CHURCH AS ASSOCIATED WITH THE PRIESTHOOD OF CHRIST

Christ the Lord, High Priest of the new and everlasting covenant, willed to   1125
conjoin and to configure to his perfect priesthood (see Heb 7:20–22 and 26–28,
10:14 and 21) the people he has purchased with his own blood. He therefore graced
his Church with a share in his own priesthood, namely, the universal priesthood of
believers and the ministerial or hierarchic priesthood. Even though these differ from
each other in essence and not just in degree, they nevertheless stand in mutual
relationship within the communion of the Church.

The sacrament of baptism bestows the universal priesthood of believers, which
is also called by right a royal priesthood (see 1 Pt 2:9; Rv 1:6, 5:9ff.), because it joins
the faithful to their heavenly king as members of a messianic people. By baptism
the faithful, "incorporated into the Church, are deputed for the worship of the
Christian religion" in virtue of an indelible sign, called a character; "reborn as
children of God, they must profess before all the faith they have received from God
through the Church."[44] Those born again through baptism therefore, "in virtue of
their royal priesthood, join in the offering of the eucharist. They likewise exercise
that priesthood in receiving the sacraments, in prayer and thanksgiving, in the
witness of a holy life, by self-denial, and by an active charity."[45]

In addition Christ, the Head of the Church, his Mystical Body, appointed as   1126
ministers of the priesthood, to act in his person in the Church,[46] the apostles and

---

of celebration? Reply: The purpose of broadcasts of the Mass is that those unable to participate may join
in mind and heart with the actual celebration. Should grave difficulties make it impossible for the
broadcasts of the celebration to be live, the listeners or viewers should be advised accordingly: Not 5
(1969) 406, no. 23.

44   LG no. 11 [DOL 4 no. 141].

45   Ibid. no. 10 [DOL 4 no. 140].

46   See Pius XI, Encycl. *Ad catholici sacerdotii*: AAS 28 (1936) 10; Denz-Schön 3755. See also LG no. 10
[DOL 4 no. 140]; PO no. 2 [DOL 18 no. 257].

through them their successors, the bishops; these in turn have lawfully handed down to priests, in a subordinate degree, the ministry they themselves received.[47] This is the origin in the Church of the apostolic succession of the ministerial priesthood, having as its purpose God's glory and service to his people and to the conversion of the entire human family to God.

In virtue of this priesthood bishops and priests "are in a way set apart in the midst of the people of God, not as though being separated from them or from any human being, but for their total consecration to the work for which the Lord has raised them up,"[48] namely, the work of sanctifying, teaching, and ruling. Hierarchic communion more precisely specifies that work.[49] In this many-sided task, the unceasing preaching of the Gospel is both primary and fundamental;[50] the eucharistic sacrifice is its high point and is the source of the whole Christian life.[51] Acting in the person of Christ the Head, in his name and in the name of the members of his Mystical Body,[52] priests offer that sacrifice to God the Father in the Holy Spirit; the sacrifice has as its complement the sacred meal by which the faithful, sharing in the one body of Christ, all become the one Body (see 1 Cor 10:16ff).

1127   The Church has more and more deeply examined the nature of the ministerial priesthood, the bestowal of which has been fixed by sacred rites from apostolic times (see 1 Tm 4:15; 2 Tm 1:6). With the assistance of the Holy Spirit the Church has perceived with the passage of time the understanding willed by God that this rite endows priests not only with an increase of grace for the holy fulfillment of their ecclesial offices but also with the sacramental character, the indelible seal of Christ. Those who receive it are set aside for sacred offices with the necessary power that derives from Christ. Theologians have explained the nature of the sacramental character in different ways; its permanent existence, however, is a teaching of the Council of Florence,[53] confirmed in two decrees by the Council of Trent.[54] The recent Vatican Council II cited this teaching several times[55] and the second General Assembly of the Synod of Bishops correctly mentioned that the existence of a sacerdotal character, lifelong in duration, is a matter belonging to the teaching of faith.[56] The faithful must acknowledge this permanent existence of the priestly character and it must be a basis for a correct evaluation of the nature of the priest's ministry and suited to its fulfillment.

1128   Holding fast to sacred tradition and to many documents of the Church's magisterium, Vatican Council II has taught the following about the power proper to the priest's ministry: "Even though anyone can baptize those who believe, the priest alone can complete the building up of the Body by the eucharistic sacrifice."[57]

---

[47] See LG no. 28 [DOL 4 no. 148].

[48] PO no. 3: ConstDecrDecl 625.

[49] See LG no. 24: ConstDecrDecl 137; nos. 27–28 [DOL 4 nos. 147–148].

[50] See PO no. 4 [DOL 18 no. 259].

[51] See LG no. 11 [DOL 4 no. 141]. See also Council of Trent, sess. 22, *Doctrina de Missae sacrificio* cap. 1 and 2: COeD 732–734; Denz-Schön 1739–43.

[52] See Paul VI, Solemn Profession of Faith no. 24 [DOL 168 no. 1096].

[53] Council of Florence, Bulla unionis Armenorum *Exsultate Deo*: COeD 546; Denz-Schön 1313.

[54] Council of Trent, *Decr. de Sacramentis* can. 9 and *Decr. de Sacramento ordinis* cap. 4 and can. 4: COeD 685, 742, 744; Denz-Schön 1609, 1767, 1774.

[55] See LG 21 [DOL 4 no. 145]; PO no. 2 [DOL 18 no. 257].

[56] See *Documenta Synodi Episcoporum*: I. *De sacerdotio ministeriali*, pars prima, n. 5: AAS 63 (1971) 907.

[57] LG no. 17 [DOL 4 no. 144].

"That all might grow together into one Body in which 'not all the members have the same function' (Rom 12:4), the Lord has established certain of the faithful as ministers, possessing the sacred power of orders to offer sacrifice in the community and to forgive sins."[58]

In similar fashion the second General Assembly of the Synod of Bishops correctly affirmed that only the priest has the power to act in the person of Christ by presiding over and bringing to completion the sacrificial meal which unites the people of God with Christ's sacrifice.[59] Leaving aside at this time the issue of the ministers of the individual sacraments, it is clear from the witness of sacred tradition and the magisterium that the faithful who, without ordination to the priesthood, arrogate to themselves the office of consecrating the eucharist, attempt something that is not only totally unlawful, but also invalid. The bishops must suppress such an abuse wherever it springs up.

172. PAUL VI, **Epistle** (autograph) *Cum proximae celebrationes* to Dom J. Prou, Abbot General of the Congregation of Solesmes, on the occasion of the centenary of the death of Dom Prosper Guéranger, 20 January 1975: Not 11 (1975) 170–172.

Celebrations are soon to be held commemorating the one-hundredth anniversary of the death of Dom Prosper Guéranger, founder of your abbey and restorer of the Benedictine Order in France. It is our pleasure through this letter to express our feelings of veneration toward the devoted man who is so well-deserving of the Church and at the same time to give evidence of our esteem toward the monks who continue his work and his spirit.   1129

Now, a century after his death, we are afforded a view that assures us of how sound was the course he took in establishing communities to carry out fully St. Benedict's monastic ideal. They were, that is, to direct their whole spiritual life toward a close-knit union with the prayer of the Church; at the same time they were to contemplate the mystery of God and to guide their own spiritual life along the path traced by the Church through the celebrations of the liturgical year (L. Duchesne, *Origines du culte chrétien*, Préface, p. VII).

There is every reason therefore to call Dom Guéranger the author of that movement of spirituality which, issuing from his writings and the monasteries associated with him, has had as its result that the intense participation of the Christian people in the liturgy is to be considered as "the first and indispensable source from which the faithful are to derive the true Christian spirit" (SC art. 14).[a] We can acknowledge that this new springtime of the spiritual life now being experienced by the Church from the liturgical renewal is the fruit of the seed that Dom Guéranger took care to sow patiently and arduously.

[58] PO no. 2 [DOL 18 no. 257]. See also: 1. Innocent III, Ep. *Eius exemplo* with the profession of faith required of the Waldensians: PL 215, 1510; Denz-Schön 794. 2. Lateran Council IV, Const. 1: De fide Catholica: COeD 230; Denz-Schön 802. The passage on the sacrament of the altar is to be read with the text following on the sacrament of baptism. 3. Council of Florence, Bulla unionis Armenorum *Exsultate Deo*: COeD 546; [Denz-Schön 1321]. The text on the minister of the eucharist is to be compared with adjoining texts on the ministers of the other sacraments. 4. Council of Trent, sess. 23, Decr. de Sacramento ordinis, cap. 4: COed 742ff. (Denz-Schön 1767–69). 5. Pius XII, Encycl. *Mediator Dei*: AAS 39 (1947) 552–556; Denz-Schön 3844–52.

[59] Documenta Synodi Episcoporum: I. *De sacerdotio ministeriali*, pars prima, n. 4: AAS 63 (1971) 906.

[a] DOL 1 no. 14.

It is also helpful to call to mind his intense devotion to the Virgin Mary, which is to be regarded "as a distinctive note of the Church's devotion" (Apostolic Exhortation *Marialis cultus*).[b] His own intent to bring back the liturgy into the center of Christian life and to restore its purity, dignity, and beauty, uniting this effort to his care to promote devotion to the Virgin Mother of God, is a clear model of what we ourself have recently taught and implored. There should be, namely, a correlation between the renewal and progress of Christian worship and the increase in Marian devotion, entering into the stream of the single worship which is offered to God and to which Marian devotion of its very nature should be related as to its center.[c]

1130   The charism Dom Guéranger seems to have received from the Holy Spirit is still at work in the Church through his confrères. To their well-deserved credit they have not only never ceased to keep burning the flame of monastic discipline he kindled, but have also given their unfailingly willing and generous assistance to the revision of the liturgical books. In particular, it is a pleasure to mention the critical texts of Gregorian chant published by the Abbey of Solesmes, as well as the more recent books required by the reform of the liturgy, especially the *Graduale simplex*, *Ordo cantus Missae*, and latest of all, the *Graduale sacrosanctae Romanae Ecclesiae*. By such efforts these monks will contribute soundly to safeguarding the heritage that the Church holds as "a treasure of inestimable value" (SC art. 112)[d] and to the solemn and dignified celebration of the liturgy in the Latin language. Along with our desire to offer you our own and the whole Church's sentiments of gratitude for this work, we wish also to single out in your patient and generous service the respect and love of your founder toward the Holy See and the pope that you still preserve. May the sons of Dom Guéranger feel themselves moved deeply by those sentiments of respect and love so that they put all their energies into a deep appreciation of the riches contained in the reformed Roman liturgy — the liturgy Dom Guéranger himself regarded as a preeminent form of prayer. You are under a debt to carry out a responsibility of vital necessity in the Church. You will do so by offering yourselves as an example in welcoming the reformed liturgy. Henceforward it will be the sign and the characteristic of your monastic life, through your full and solemn celebration of the liturgy of the hours and of the eucharistic sacrifice. We accordingly exhort you to bend your efforts toward integrating the reformed Roman liturgy into your daily life, as you devotedly preserve that commitment inherited from your forefathers toward the full ideal of the monastic life. Such a life is fostered by work, by the silence conducive to contemplation, by prayer, by the desire to seek God above all. That life is meant to empower you to present to the eyes of the world your witness to unseen realities. In this way, as well, Benedictine monasteries will truly flourish as enclaves of spiritual renewal, where, with God being put before everything else, "the human is directed and subordinated to the divine, the visible likewise to the invisible, action to contemplation, and this present world to that city yet to come" (SC art. 2).[e]

We offer you our most earnest desire that the spiritual riches you experience by your lives may pass beyond the monastic walls, with Dom Guéranger providing the light of his own example. By his writings he has for generations made a marvelous contribution to the right liturgical formation of countless priests and religious, to their grasp of its power and meaning, to their appreciation of its beauty, and above all to their translating it deeply and willingly into their own lives.

---

b   DOL 467 no. 3897.

c   See DOL 467 no. 3897.

d   DOL 1 no. 112.

e   DOL 1 no. 2.

173. SC DOCTRINE OF THE FAITH, **Letter** *Recentiores Episcoporum Synodi* to presidents of the conferences of bishops, on points regarding eschatology, 17 May 1979: AAS 71 (1979) 939–943; Not 15 (1979) 566–570 (excerpts).

The last two Synods of Bishops, addressing the subjects of evangelization [1974] and catechetics [1977], intensified the conviction of the need to preserve complete fidelity to the basic truths of faith, especially in these times. [. . .]   1131

Those concerned, therefore, must show an alertness against anything that might affect the general mentality of the faithful with a gradual distortion and progressive destruction of any element in the baptismal creed. Every element of the creed is necessary for the cohesiveness of faith and is linked by an unbreakable bond with certain received usages of great import in the life of the Church.

We have judged it necessary and urgent to draw attention to one such element. [. . .]

The issue is the article of the creed regarding life everlasting and thus covering   1132
all that is to happen after death. Dilution or any incomplete or uncertain approach cannot be allowed in expounding this teaching; that would imperil the faith and salvation of the people.

No one can fail to see the importance of the last article of the baptismal creed: it expresses the terminus and the goal of God's plan, which is the process that the creed outlines. If there is no resurrection, the whole structure of faith collapses, as St. Paul so strongly attests (see 1 Cor 15). Unless the faithful are clear about the content of the words "life everlasting," the promises of the Gospel and the meaning of creation and redemption become pointless and even life on earth must be described as lacking all hope (see Heb 11:1). [. . .]

The first thing necessary is that those carrying out the office of teaching should plainly spell out those matters the Church judges to belong to the essentials of faith. Theological research must have as its objective nothing else but to penetrate and explain those essentials.

This Congregation, charged with furthering and guarding the faith, proposes here to summarize what the Church teaches in Christ's name, especially in regard to what transpires between a person's death and the general resurrection.

1.   The Church believes[3] in the resurrection of the dead.   1133

2.   The Church's understanding of this resurrection is that it applies to the *complete*   1134
person; for the elect this means simply the extension of Christ's own resurrection to all.

3.   The Church affirms the continuing existence after death of the spiritual part of   1135
the person, possessed of consciousness and will, in such a way that the "human I," although for a time lacking the completeness given by the body, continues to have an independent existence. To designate this spiritual element the Church makes use of the term *anima* (soul), which it has received from the usage of Scripture and tradition. The Church is aware that in the Scriptures that term takes on many meanings, but nonetheless judges that there is no sound reason for rejecting the term and further that there must be a verbal means to convey the meaning of faith.

---

3   See the Apostles' Creed.

1136   4.   The Church rules out any kind of thought or expression that would make absurd or unintelligible its prayer, funeral rites, concern for the dead: all of these in what they express constitute *loci theologici* (sources for theology).

1137   5.   In fidelity to the Scriptures the Church awaits the "glorious manifestation of our Lord Jesus Christ."[4] The Church, however, believes this to be distinct from and later than the state of a person immediately after death.

1138   6.   In stating its teaching on the fate of the person after death, the Church rules out any kind of explanation that would cancel out the meaning of Mary's Assumption, in regard to what pertains to Mary uniquely, namely, that the bodily glorification of Mary is the anticipation of what is destined for all the other elect.

1139   7.   Holding fast to the New Testament and tradition, the Church believes in the blessedness of the just, who will some day be with Christ. The Church also believes that the doomed sinner will undergo everlasting punishment, the loss of the vision of God, and that this punishment will have its impact on the whole esse of the sinner. With regard to the elect, the Church believes in the possibility of a purification preceding the vision of God, but one entirely diverse from the punishment of the damned. This is what the Church has in mind in speaking of hell and purgatcry.

1140   A particular vigilance is needed against portrayals of the state of people after death that are based on imagination and fancy. This kind of excess is often a significant source of difficulties against Christian faith. On the other hand there must be respect for the imagery found in biblical use. Perception of its hidden meaning is needed and removal of the danger of carrying the imagery to extremes; this often blots out the realities it portrays.

Neither Scripture nor theologians supply enough light to define life after death clearly. Christians must steadfastly hold to two principal tenets. First, they must believe in a fundamental continuity that, by the power of the Holy Spirit, exists between life now in Christ and the life to come (for charity is the law of God's kingdom and our heavenly sharing in the divine glory is to be measured by our charity here on earth). Second, Christians must clearly recognize that the meanings of life now and of the life to come are completely different. For the economy of clear vision supplants the economy of faith; we will be with Christ and "will see God."[5] The essence of our hope lies in these promises and sublime mysteries; our power of imagination cannot approach such matters, but the reach of our heart does. [. . .]

---

4   DV no. 4.

5   1 Jn 3:2.

CHAPTER TWO

THE EUCHARIST

SUMMARY (DOL 174–287). The relatively brief second chapter of the Constitution on the Liturgy bears as its title "The Mystery of the Eucharist" and its 12 articles rapidly present a doctrinal and pastoral overview (art. 47–49), general principles for the reform of the Order of Mass (art. 50), specifics on the biblical readings at Mass (art. 51), the homily (art. 52), the general intercessions (art. 53), Latin and the vernacular (art. 54), communion, including communion under both kinds (art. 55), the unity of the parts of the Mass (art. 56), the restoration of concelebration (art. 57–58).

The eucharist is at the heart of the reform of the liturgy, since in its celebration "we have the high point of the work that in Christ God accomplishes to sanctify the world and the high point of the worship that in adoring God through Christ, his Son, we offer to the Father" (GIRM no. 2 [DOL 208 no. 1391]). Moreover, the reform of the Order of Mass was for a long time to be the most prominent feature of the great work of the Council in the awareness of many Catholics.

An immense amount of material had to be organized for the present chapter, since its detailed coverage extends from revision of the Roman Missal to the worship of the eucharist outside Mass. The 114 documents are therefore grouped under 11 sections, with one (Section 8) subdivided into three subsections.

Section 1. General Documents

SUMMARY (DOL 174–194). The 21 documents here treat the general doctrine on the eucharist and the various aspects of eucharistic worship.

—The major doctrinal texts are Paul VI's Encyclical *Mysterium fidei* (DOL 176) and the Instruction *Eucharisticum mysterium* (DOL 179) prepared by the Congregation of Rites with the Consilium and giving practical application to the encyclical on eucharistic catechesis and celebration. To these are added an excerpt relevant to the eucharist from a letter of the Congregation for the Doctrine of the Faith on contemporary doctrinal errors (DOL 178).

—The subsidiary texts are from Paul VI and John Paul II. Paul VI continually expressed the Church's eucharistic faith: in a letter to the Dutch bishops (DOL 175), on the occasion of national or international eucharistic congresses (DOL 174, 177, 180, 182, 183, 184, 185, 187), in celebrating the feast of Corpus Christi (DOL 181, 186, 188), and in the last liturgical address before his death, on the eucharist as center of the Church's unity (DOL 189). From John Paul II there are excerpts from the Encyclical *Redemptor hominis* (DOL 191), a letter written in anticipation of the 42nd International Eucharistic Congress at Lourdes (DOL 190), an address to bishops on the eucharist and penance (DOL 192), and two homilies given during his 1979 visits to Ireland and the United States (DOL 193, 194).

▶ 103. PAUL VI, Motu Proprio *Pastorale munus*, on the powers and privileges of bishops, 30 November 1963:

    I, nos. 2, 4–12:   Priests' celebration of Mass [nos. 713, 715–723].
    II, no. 6:   Bishops' celebration of Mass [no. 744].

▶ 1. VATICAN COUNCIL II, Constitution on the Liturgy *Sacrosanctum Concilium*, 4 December 1963:

    Ch. 2 (art. 47–58):   Mystery of the eucharist [nos. 47–58].

▶ 141. SECRETARIAT OF STATE, Pontifical Rescript *Cum admotae*, on faculties delegated to religious superiors, 6 November 1964:

    I, nos. 1–5:   Celebration of Mass [nos. 939–943].

▶ 4. VATICAN COUNCIL II, Dogmatic Constitution on the Church *Lumen gentium*, 21 November 1964:

    nos. 3, 6, 7:   The eucharist and the Church [nos. 137, 138, 139].

▶ 453. PAUL VI, Apostolic Epistle *Investigabiles divitias Christi*, on the Sacred Heart, 6 February 1965.

174. PAUL VI, **Address** to the 17th national Italian eucharistic congress at Pisa, 10 June 1965: AAS 57 (1965) 587–592 (Italian; excerpt).

1141   [. . .] We have come to this congress to share personally in its theme: "God is with us because Christ is with us." The sacred eucharistic signs are not just symbols and figures of Christ or ways of declaring his love, not just symbols of his action toward those sharing in his supper. They also contain him, the true and living Christ; they are the signs of his presence as he is, living in eternal glory. They represent him in the act of his sacrifice to show that the eucharistic sacrifice mirrors in an unbloody way the bloody sacrifice of Christ on the cross and makes those who worthily receive Christ's body and blood, under the signs of bread and wine, sharers in the blessings of redemption. This is the truth.

1142   We are aware that in expressing such a reality we are expressing mystery. We are also aware that in affirming the truth about the eucharist as the Church teaches it, we are implicitly affirming an extremely complex and wondrous cluster of other truths, essentially bound up with the eucharistic mystery; they are equally mysterious, but equally grounded in reality. Among such truths it is enough to cite: the priesthood with its tremendous powers to make actual by divine power the hidden presence of Christ in the eucharist; the essential relationship of this presence with the Mystical Body of Christ,[1] with the Church, that is, which possesses in the eucharist the sign and the most powerful source of its structure and sanctification — Christ himself in his actual exercise of supreme charity. There is more: this real and hidden presence is beneath signs no longer possessing their own real entity (the bread and wine, which are so full of the spiritual signification proper to the eucharist, as spiritual nourishment for us in our journey to eternal life). This presence has such profoundly theological, religious, spiritual, moral, and liturgical implications

---

[1] See ST 3a, 73.3.

as to constitute the heart of the Church, Jesus, who says: *"Ibi sum in medio."* "There am I in the midst of them."[2] Among such implications are: the analogy with the word resounding identically yet manifoldly in the listeners; the allusions to the Gospel — like the discourses at Capernaum and at the Last Supper; the origins of liturgy, the Mass first of all; application to worship — think of the silence and wondrous mystery of the countless tabernacles that irradiate light over the world, visible only to the angels, the saints, and believers; spiritual fruitfulness — think of the liturgical fullness of the gathering of the faithful around the altar and of the conversations of individual souls who are nourished by Christ or through faith and charity in adoration and prayer are gripped by God's presence.

This is all true. Again we are aware that we are expressing mystery. But that is the way it is. This is our witness, one with that of this Congress, and it brings to you what our apostolic teaching office authorizes and obliges us to profess. Christ is really present in the sacrament of the eucharist. We say this in order to rejoice with you, faithful children, who make the eucharist your spiritual nourishment, and to strengthen your devotion to that authentic worship, fed by the Gospel and the theological teaching to which the recent conciliar Constitution on the Liturgy exhorts us and shows the way. We speak this way also to put to flight the uncertainties stemming in the last few years from the attempt to give interpretations that side step the Church's tradition and its authentic teaching on this matter of such importance. We speak thus, also, to invite all of you, the people of this age, to center your attention on this ancient but always new message that the Church repeats: Christ, living and hidden under the sacramental signs that he offers us, is really present. These are not empty words, not a superstitious claim, or a mythical fantasy. They are the truth, no less real for being situated on a different plane than [. . .] scientific truths. [. . .]

1143

175. PAUL VI, **Epistle** Pastoralem Episcoporum Hollandiae to Cardinal B. Alfrink, Archbishop of Utrecht, on the pastoral letter of the bishops of Holland regarding the eucharist, 19 July 1965: AAS 57 (1965) 857.

Beloved Son, our greetings and apostolic blessing. We have received with joy and read with care the pastoral letter of the bishops of Holland that you have recently taken the trouble to send in French translation.

1144

Your choice of this topic for the consideration of your flock has pleased us beyond words and especially because it is further proof of the kind of vigilant concern that the demands of the times and the spiritual well-being of your flock call for and of your unstinting and tireless efforts to keep flourishing the sound devotion of your people and to preserve their faith from any stain of insidious error. Nothing, indeed, can be more advantageous or salutary than to direct the thoughts, minds, and desires of the faithful to the eucharistic sacrifice, the everlasting remembrance of Christ's passion, and to lead them often to the august sacrament of the altar. There Christ is present as the heavenly food of our souls, there he presents himself to all who adore him in the tabernacle, as the inexhaustible source of grace.

Accordingly, we are glad to have this opportunity to encourage you to be steadfast in your pastoral aims. We are happy to assure you of our continuing approval of whatever measures you may take either to explain, in accord with

---

2 Mt 18:20.

church documents, the doctrine of this great mystery or to increase love and devotion toward this august sacrament.

Please accept our congratulations and commendation for this proof of your pastoral concern. We add as well the ardent prayer that with the help of Christ's grace, whatever you propose or effect out of a sense of pastoral responsibility may achieve the hoped-for success and may be a source of comfort for you and your colleagues.

With such hopes, we affectionately in the Lord bestow our apostolic blessing on you, Beloved Son, the other bishops of Holland, and all the faithful under your care.

176. PAUL VI, **Encyclical** *Mysterium fidei*, on the doctrine and worship of the eucharist, 3 September 1965: AAS 57 (1965) 753–774.

1145   1.   The mystery of faith is the indescribable gift of the eucharist that the Catholic Church has received from Christ, its Bridegroom, as a pledge of his boundless love. The Church has always guarded it devoutly as a most precious treasure and in Vatican Council II has made a new and most solemn profession of the faith and the worship centered on this mystery.

1146   2.   When treating the reform of the liturgy, the Fathers of the Council, in keeping with their pastoral concern for the whole Church, considered nothing to be more important than urging the faithful to participate actively with sound faith and utmost devotion in the celebration of this most holy mystery; to offer it with the priest to God as a sacrifice for their own salvation and for that of the whole world; to nourish themselves with it as a spiritual food.

1147   3.   For if the liturgy is first in the life of the Church, the mystery of the eucharist is the heart and center of the liturgy itself. It is in fact the font of life; purified and strengthened by it, we live not for ourselves but for God and are joined to each other by the closest bonds of love.

1148   4.   The Fathers of the Council wished to make evident the indissoluble relationship that exists between faith and devotion. Confirming, therefore, the doctrine that the Church has always held and taught and that the Council of Trent solemnly defined, they decided to preface their treatise on the mystery of the eucharist with this summary of truths.

"At the Last Supper, on the night when he was betrayed, our Savior instituted the eucharistic sacrifice of his body and blood. He did this in order to perpetuate the sacrifice of the cross throughout the centuries until he should come again and so to entrust to his beloved Bride, the Church, a memorial of his death and resurrection: a sacrament of love, a sign of unity, a bond of charity, a paschal banquet in which Christ is eaten, the mind is filled with grace, and a pledge of future glory is given to us."[1]

1149   5.   In these words are emphasized both the sacrifice, which belongs to the essence of the Mass celebrated daily, and the sacrament. Those partaking in this sacrament eat the flesh of Christ and drink the blood of Christ in communion, receiving both grace, the beginning of eternal life, and the "medicine of immortality." This is in

---

[1]   SC art. 47 [DOL 1 no. 47].

accord with the words of the Lord: "Those who eat my flesh and drink my blood have everlasting life and I will raise them up on the last day."[2]

6.   We earnestly hope therefore that rich fruits of eucharistic devotion will grow out of the reformed liturgy, so that the holy Church, with this saving sign of its devotion raised on high, may go forward from day to day until it arrives at perfect unity[3] and may invite all who bear the name of Christian to the unity of faith and love and draw them gently together by the workings of divine grace.   1150

7.   It seems to us that we are seeing these results and gathering the firstfruits as it were in the great joy and enthusiasm with which the children of the Catholic Church have received the Constitution on the Liturgy and its liturgical reform. We perceive this as well in the many carefully prepared works being published in order to provide a deeper grasp and more effective appreciation of the teaching on the eucharist, especially as it relates to the mystery of the Church.   1151

8.   All of this is to us a cause of much consolation and joy. It is a very great pleasure for us to share this with you, our Esteemed Brothers, so that along with us you may give thanks to God, the giver of all gifts, who with his Spirit rules and continually enriches the Church.   1152

REASONS FOR PASTORAL CONCERN AND ANXIETY

9.   But in the very matter we are discussing, Esteemed Brothers, there are reasons for serious pastoral concern and anxiety. Conscious of our apostolic office, we cannot be silent in the face of these problems.   1153

10.   We are aware of the fact that, among those who treat of this mystery in written or spoken word, there are some who, with reference either to Masses celebrated in private or to the dogma of transubstantiation or to devotion to the eucharist, spread abroad opinions that upset the faithful and fill their minds with great confusion about matters of faith. They act as though it were permissible to consign to oblivion doctrine already defined by the Church or to interpret it in such a way as to weaken the genuine meaning of the words or the established import of the ideas behind them.   1154

11.   To corroborate the point with examples: it is not allowable to emphasize what is called the Mass "of the community" to the extent of disparaging Masses celebrated in private; or to stress the sign value of the sacrament as if the symbolism, which to be sure all acknowledge in the eucharist, expresses fully and exhaustively the meaning of Christ's presence; or to discuss the mystery of transubstantiation without mentioning the marvelous changing of the whole substance of the bread into the body and of the whole substance of the wine into the blood of Christ as stated by the Council of Trent, so that only what is called "transignification" or "transfinalization" is involved; or finally, to propose and to act on the opinion according to which Christ the Lord is no longer present in the consecrated hosts left after the celebration of the sacrifice of the Mass is ended.   1155

12.   Everyone sees that these and similar opinions now in circulation do great harm to eucharistic faith and worship.   1156

---

[2]   Jn 6:55.

[3]   See Jn 17:23.

1157 13. In order therefore that the hopes raised by the Council for a new light of eucharistic devotion throughout the Church are not frustrated by the seed of false opinions already sown, we have with apostolic authority decided to address you, Esteemed Brothers, and to express our mind on this subject.

1158 14. We certainly do not deny in those who are spreading these astonishing opinions an admirable desire to investigate this sublime mystery, to set forth its inexhaustible riches, and to explain its meaning to our contemporaries; rather we acknowledge and approve that desire. However, we cannot approve the opinions expressed and we have the duty to warn you of the grave danger these opinions involve for a right faith.

THE HOLY EUCHARIST IS A MYSTERY OF FAITH

1159 15. We wish, first of all, to recall a point well known to you but altogether necessary as a defense against the poison of any form of rationalism. It is something to which many illustrious martyrs have borne witness with their blood, which the leading Fathers and Doctors of the Church have constantly professed and taught: the eucharist is a very great mystery. It is literally *the* "mystery of faith," as the liturgy says. "Indeed, in it alone," as our predecessor Leo XIII very wisely remarked, "are contained, in a remarkable richness and variety of miracles, all supernatural realities."[4]

1160 16. We must therefore approach this mystery above all with humble obedience, not relying on human considerations, which ought to be given no voice, but adhering firmly to divine revelation.

1161 17. St. John Chrysostom, who, as you know, treated of the eucharistic mystery with such nobility of language and reverent insight, on one occasion while instructing his faithful about this mystery, expressed these most apposite words:

"Let us submit to God in all things and not contradict him, even if what he says seems contrary to our reason and intellect. Over reason and intellect let his words prevail. Let us also do this with regard to the [eucharistic] mysteries, not merely looking at what lies before our senses but fixing upon his words. His word cannot lead us astray."[5]

1162 18. The scholastic doctors often said the same thing. That the true body of Christ and his true blood are in this sacrament is something that "cannot be detected by sense," as St. Thomas says, "but only by faith, which rests on divine authority. Hence on Luke 22:19: 'This is my body which will be given up for you,' St. Cyril says: 'Do not entertain doubts on the truth of this; rather take the Savior's words with faith, for since he is truth, he does not lie.'"[6]

1163 19. Thus the Christian people, echoing the words of the same St. Thomas, frequently sing the words, "Sight, touch, and taste in thee are each deceived, the ear alone most safely is believed. I believe all the Son of God has spoken — than truth's own word there is no truer token."

---

4   Leo XIII, Encycl. *Mirae caritatis: Acta Leonis* 13, 22 (1902–03) 122.

5   *In Matth. homil.* 82, 4: PG 58, 743.

6   ST 3a, 75.1.

20. St. Bonaventure asserts: "There is no difficulty about Christ's presence in the   1164
eucharist as in a sign, but that he is truly present in the eucharist as he is in heaven,
this is most difficult. Therefore to believe this is especially meritorious."[7]

21. Moreover, the holy Gospel alludes to this when it tells of the many disciples of   1165
Christ who, after listening to the words about eating his flesh and drinking his
blood, turned away and left our Lord, saying: "This is a hard saying, and who can
accept it?" Peter, on the other hand, in reply to Jesus' question whether the twelve
also wished to leave, expressed his faith and that of the others promptly and
resolutely with the marvelous answer: "Lord, to whom shall we go? You have the
words of everlasting life."[8]

22. Therefore we should follow as a guiding star in our investigations of this   1166
mystery the magisterium of the Church, to whose care and interpretation the divine
Redeemer entrusted God's word, written or handed down. Ours should be the firm
conviction that "what since the days of antiquity was preached and believed
throughout the whole Church with true Catholic faith is true, even if it is proved
by no argument, explained by no words."[9]

23. But this is not enough. Not only the integrity of the faith, but also its proper   1167
mode of expression must be safeguarded, lest, God forbid, by the careless use of
words we introduce false notions about the most sublime realities. St. Augustine
gives a stern warning about this by reflecting on the way philosophers employ
words and the way Christians must do so. "The philosophers," he says, "use words
loosely and in matters very difficult to understand are not deterred from offending a
sense of religious reverence. We, however, have the obligation to speak according to
a definite norm lest the carelessness of our words give rise to impious ideas about
the very realities signified by these words."[10]

24. We must religiously respect the rule of terminology; after centuries of effort   1168
and under the protection of the Holy Spirit the Church has established it and
confirmed it by the authority of councils; that norm often became the watchword
and the banner of orthodox belief. Let no one arbitrarily or under the pretext of
new science presume to change it. Would we allow the dogmatic formulas of the
ecumenical councils concerning the mysteries of the most blessed Trinity and the
incarnation to be declared unsuited to our contemporaries and other formulas to be
rashly substituted? In like manner we must not put up with anyone's personal wish
to modify the formulas in which the Council of Trent set forth the mystery of the
eucharist for belief. Like others that the Church uses to express the dogmas of the
faith, the Tridentine formulas express concepts that are not tied to one specific form
of human culture, to a definite period of scientific progress, or to one school of
theological thought. They present the human mind's perception of the realities,
deriving from universal and necessary experience, and its expression of them in
suitable and accurate words, taken either from general or more specialized usage.
For this reason, these formulas are suited to people of all times and all places.

25. The dogmatic formulas are, it is true, open to clearer and plainer explanation   1169
and such explanation does come about and with the most advantageous results. But

---

7   *In IV Sent.* d. 10, P. 1, art. un., qu. 1: *Opera Omnia* 4 (Quaracchi, 1889) 217.

8   Jn 6:61–69.

9   Augustine, *Contra Iulianum* 6, 5, 11: PL 44, 829.

10   Augustine, *De civitate Dei* 10, 23: PL 41, 300.

that is in continuity with the sense the formulas had originally, so that as the understanding of the faith increases, its truth remains the same. This is the teaching of Vatican Council I on the dogmas of faith: "That meaning which holy Mother Church has once defined must forever be retained and we may never depart from that meaning under the pretext and name of a more profound learning."[11]

THE MYSTERY OF THE EUCHARIST IS MADE ACTUAL IN THE SACRIFICE OF THE MASS

1170   26. For the edification and joy of all, we wish to review with you, Esteemed Brothers, the doctrine that has been handed down concerning the mystery of the eucharist and that the Catholic Church holds and teaches with single-minded accord.

1171   27. We desire to recall at the outset what may be termed the very essence of this teaching, namely, that the mystery of the eucharist makes present again in a unique manner the sacrifice of the cross, which was once offered on Calvary, continuously calls it to mind, and applies its saving power for the forgiveness of those sins we commit daily.[12]

1172   28. Just as Moses with the blood of oxen once ratified the Old Covenant,[13] so also Christ our Lord, through the institution of the mystery of the eucharist, with his own blood ratified the New Covenant, whose Mediator he is. For, as the evangelists record, at the Last Supper: "And having taken bread, he gave thanks and broke, and gave it to them, saying, 'This is my body, which is being given for you; do this in remembrance of me.' In like manner he took also the cup after supper, saying, 'This cup is the New Covenant in my blood, which shall be shed for you.'"[14] And by bidding the apostles to do this in memory of him, he made clear his will that the same sacrifice should be ever made actual. The infant Church faithfully carried out this intention of Christ by holding fast to the teaching of the apostles and gathering to celebrate the eucharistic sacrifice. As St. Luke carefully testifies: "They continued steadfastly in the teaching of the apostles and in the communion of the breaking of bread and in prayers."[15] From this practice the faithful derived such spiritual strength that it was said of them: "The multitude of the believers were of one heart and soul."[16]

1173   29. Moreover, Paul the Apostle, who faithfully transmitted to us what he had received from the Lord,[17] is clearly speaking of the eucharistic sacrifice when he points out that Christians, because they have been made partakers at the table of the Lord, must not take part in pagan sacrifices. "The cup of blessing that we bless," he says, "is it not the partaking of the blood of Christ? And the bread that we break, is it not the partaking of the body of the Lord? . . . You cannot drink the cup

---

[11]   Vatican I, Const. Dogm. *De fide catholica* cap. 4: [Denz-Schön 3020].

[12]   See Council of Trent, *Doctrina de SS. Missae Sacrificio* cap. 1 [Denz-Schön 1740].

[13]   See Ex 24:8.

[14]   Lk 22:19–20; see Mt 26:26–28; Mk 14:22–24.

[15]   Acts 2:42.

[16]   Acts 4:32.

[17]   See 1 Cor 11:23ff.

of the Lord and the cup of devils; you cannot be partakers of the table of the Lord and of the table of devils."[18] Foreshadowed by Malachi,[19] this new sacrifice of the New Testament has always been offered by the Church, in accordance with the teaching of our Lord and the apostles, "not only for the sins, punishment, expiation, and needs of the living faithful, but also for those who have died in Christ but have not yet been completely purified."[20]

30. Passing over other citations, we recall simply the testimony of St. Cyril of Jerusalem, who wrote the following memorable instruction for his neophytes: "After the spiritual sacrifice, the unbloody act of worship, has been completed, relying on this propitiatory offering we beg God to grant peace to all the Churches, to give harmony to the whole world, to bless our rulers, our soldiers, and our companions, to aid the sick and afflicted, and in general all of us pray for those who stand in need. Then we offer the victim also for our deceased holy fathers and bishops and for all our dead. As we do this, we are filled with faith that this sacrifice will be of the greatest help to those souls for whom prayers are being offered, since as we pray that holy and awe-inspiring victim lies before us." St. Cyril closes his instruction by referring as an example to a crown fashioned for the emperor in order to move him to pardon exiles: "Similarly, when we offer our prayers to God for the dead, even though they be sinners, we fashion no crown, but instead we offer Christ slain for our sins, beseeching our merciful God to take pity both on them and on ourselves."[21] St. Augustine testifies that this manner of offering even for the dead "the sacrifice which ransomed us" was the practice observed in the Church at Rome,[22] and at the same time he remarks that the whole Church observed the practice as one handed down from the Fathers.[23]

1174

31. We may also add another point, because it sheds light on the mystery of the Church, namely, that the whole Church, exercising with Christ the role of priest and victim, offers the sacrifice of the Mass and the whole Church is offered in it. This sublime teaching was taught by the Fathers long ago,[24] our predecessor Pius XII brought it out in 1947,[25] and recently Vatican Council II expressed it in its Constitution on the Church when treating of the people of God.[26]

1175

This teaching, it is our own strong wish, should be brought out again and again and deeply impressed on the minds of the faithful (without diminishing the distinction not merely of degree but of essence between the universal and hierarchic priesthood[27]). For this teaching is a most effective means of developing eucharistic devotion, emphasizing the dignity of all the faithful, and inspiring their pursuit of holiness, which is identical with a generous, total self-offering to the service of God's majesty.

---

[18]   1 Cor 10:16.

[19]   See Mal 1:11.

[20]   Council of Trent, *Doctrina de SS. Missae Sacrificio* cap. 2 [Denz-Schön 1743].

[21]   Cyril of Jerusalem, *Catechesis* (myst. 5) 8–18: PG 33, 1115–18.

[22]   See Augustine, *Confessiones* 9, 12, 32: PL 32, 777; see also ibid. 9, 11, 27: PL 32, 775.

[23]   See Augustine, *Sermo* 172, 2: PL 38, 936; see also *De cura gerenda pro mortuis* 13: PL 40, 593.

[24]   See Augustine, *De civitate Dei* 10, 6: PL 41, 284.

[25]   See Pius XII, Encycl. *Mediator Dei*: AAS 39 (1947) 552.

[26]   See LG 11 [DOL 4 no. 141].

[27]   See LG 10 [DOL 4 no. 140].

1176   32. We should also mention "the public and social nature of every Mass,"[28] a conclusion that clearly emerges from the teaching we have been discussing. Every Mass, even though a priest may offer it in private, is not a private matter; it is an act of Christ and of the Church. In offering this sacrifice, the Church learns to offer itself as a sacrifice for all and applies the single, boundless, redemptive power of the sacrifice of the cross for the salvation of the entire world. For every Mass celebrated is offered not for the salvation of only a few, but for the salvation even of the whole world. Hence it follows that although it is eminently in accord with the very nature of the celebration of Mass that large groups of the faithful participate actively, nevertheless, there is to be no disparagement but full approval of a Mass that, in conformity with the prescriptions and lawful traditions of the Church, a priest for a sufficient reason offers in private, that is, with no one present except the server. From such a Mass an abundant outpouring of special, salutary graces enriches the celebrant, the faithful, the whole Church, and the entire world — graces that are not obtained in the same abundance simply by reception of holy communion.

1177   33. Therefore as a father we earnestly recommend to priests, our special crown and happiness in the Lord, that they be mindful of their power, received through the hands of the ordaining bishop, of offering sacrifice to God and of celebrating Masses both for the living and for the dead in the name of the Lord[29] and thus worthily and devoutly offer Mass each day in order that both they and the rest of the faithful may enjoy the benefits that flow so richly from the sacrifice of the cross. Thus also they will contribute much to the salvation of the human race.

IN THE SACRIFICE OF THE MASS CHRIST BECOMES SACRAMENTALLY PRESENT

1178   34. The few points we have touched on regarding the sacrifice of the Mass move us also to set forth others on the eucharist as sacrament: both sacrifice and sacrament form inseparable parts of the same mystery. The Lord is immolated in an unbloody manner in the sacrifice of the Mass, which presents anew the sacrifice of the cross and applies its saving power, at the moment when through the words of consecration he begins to be sacramentally present as the spiritual food of the faithful under the appearances of bread and wine.

1179   35. All of us know well that there is more than one way in which Christ is present in his Church, but it is useful to dwell on this beautiful teaching that the Constitution on the Liturgy brought out briefly.[30] Christ is present in his Church when it prays, since it is he "who prays for us and in us, and is prayed to by us; he prays for us as our Priest and in us as our Head; as our God he is prayed to by us."[31] He himself has promised: "Where two or three are gathered together in my name, I am there in their midst."[32] He is present in his Church as it performs works of mercy, not only because we do to Christ whatever good we do to one of the least of his brothers and sisters,[33] but also because it is Christ, performing these works through the Church, who continually assists by his divine charity. He is present in his

---

  [28]   See SC art. 27 [DOL 1 no. 27].

  [29]   See PR [Ordination of Priests].

  [30]   See SC art. 7 [DOL 1 no. 7].

  [31]   Augustine, *In Ps.* 5, 1: PL 37, 1081.

  [32]   Mt 18:20.

  [33]   See Mt 25:40.

pilgrim Church longing to reach the harbor of eternal life, since it is he who through faith dwells in our hearts[34] and through the Holy Spirit whom he gives us pours forth his love in the Church.[35]

36. In yet a different but most real way, he is present in the Church as it preaches. The Gospel that is proclaimed is the word of God and thus is preached only in the name of and by the authority of Christ, the incarnate Word of God and with his help, so that there may be "one flock which is safe with one shepherd."[36]

1180

37. He is present in his Church as it shepherds and guides the people of God, since the Church's sacred power comes from Christ and since Christ, "the shepherd of shepherds,"[37] is present in the shepherds who exercise that power, according to the promise made to the apostles.

1181

38. In a manner even more sublime, Christ also is present in his Church when it offers the sacrifice of the Mass in his name and administers the sacraments. In regard to Christ's presence in the offering of the sacrifice of the Mass, it is well to recall what St. John Chrysostom, overcome with wonder, said with no less truth than eloquence: "I wish to add something thoroughly amazing, but do not be astonished or disturbed. What is it? The sacrifice is the same, no matter who offers it, be it Paul or Peter; the sacrifice is the same that Christ gave to his disciples and that priests now offer, one Mass is not inferior to another, because it is not men who make this offering holy, but the one who sanctified it in the first place. For just as the words that God spoke are the same as those that the priest now uses, so also is the sacrifice the very same."[38] As for the sacraments, they are, as all know, the actions of Christ, who administers them through human ministers. The sacraments therefore are in themselves holy and by the power of Christ pour grace into the soul as they touch the body. These ways in which Christ is present fill the mind with wonder and present the mystery of the Church for contemplation. But there is another, indeed most remarkable way, in which Christ is present in his Church in the sacrament of the eucharist. This therefore among all the sacraments is "sweeter in devotion, lovelier in meaning, holier in content";[39] for it contains Christ himself and is "as it were the high point of the spiritual life and the purpose of all the other sacraments."[40]

1182

39. This presence is called the *real presence* not to exclude the other kinds as though they were not real, but because it is real par excellence, since it is substantial, in the sense that Christ whole and entire, God and man, becomes present.[41] Anyone is in error who explains the meaning of this presence by inventing a so-called pneumatic, omnipresent nature for Christ's glorified body or by confining the meaning within the limits of symbolism, as though this august sacrament amounted to nothing more in reality than an effective sign "of a spiritual presence of Christ and of his close union with the faithful, his members in the Mystical Body."[42]

1183

---

[34] See Eph 3:17.

[35] See Rom 5:5.

[36] Augustine, *Contra Litt. Petiliani* 3, 10, 11: PL 43, 353.

[37] *Idem, In Ps.* 86, 3: PL 37, 1102.

[38] John Chrysostom, *In Epist. 2 ad Tim. homil.* 2, 4: PG 62, 612.

[39] Giles of Rome, *Theoremata de Corpore Christi* theor. 50 (Venice, 1521) 127.

[40] ST 3a, 73.3.

[41] See Council of Trent, *Decr. de SS. Eucharistitia* cap. 3: [Denz-Schön 1635 and 1638].

[42] Pius XII, Encycl. *Humani generis*: AAS 42 (1950) 578.

1184   40. It is true that the Fathers and the scholastics developed many points on eucharistic symbolism, especially with reference to the unity of the Church. Summarizing their thoughts, the Council of Trent taught that our Savior bequeathed the blessed euc﹍ rist to his Church "as a symbol . . . of that unity and charity by which he wished all Christians to be united as closely as possible to each other," and hence "as a symbol of that one Body of which he is the Head."[43]

1185   41. At the very beginnings of Christian literature, the unknown author of a work entitled the *Didachē* or The Teaching of the Twelve Apostles wrote as follows on this subject: "In regard to the eucharist, give thanks in this manner: . . . As this broken bread was scattered upon the mountains, and then, when gathered, was made one, so may your Church be gathered into your kingdom from the ends of the earth."[44]

1186   42. Likewise St. Cyprian, insisting on the unity of the Church against schism, says: "Finally, the sacrifices of the Lord proclaim the unity of Christians fashioned by firm and inviolable charity. For when the Lord calls the bread, produced by the compacting of many grains of wheat, his body, he is describing our people whom he brought together in unity; when he refers to wine, pressed from many grapes, as his blood, he is speaking of our flock, joined together by the fusing of many into one."[45]

1187   43. What is more, before any of these, St. Paul had written to the Corinthians: "Because the bread is one, we though many, are one Body, all of us who share in the one bread."[46]

1188   44. But if the eucharistic symbolism brings us to understand rightly the effect proper to this sacrament, namely, the unity of the Mystical Body, it does not explain or bring out what it is that makes this sacrament different from all others. The Catholic Church's constant instruction imparted to catechumens, the Christian people's understanding of faith, the Council of Trent's defined teaching, the very words used by Christ when he instituted the most holy eucharist, compel us to acknowledge that "the eucharist is the flesh of our Savior Jesus Christ, which suffered for our sins and which the Father in his loving kindness raised again."[47] To these words of St. Ignatius of Antioch, we may add those which Theodore of Mopsuestia, on this point an authentic witness to the faith of the Church, addressed to the faithful: "The Lord did not say: 'This is a symbol of my body,' and 'This is a symbol of my blood,' but: '*This is my body and my blood*.' He teaches us not to look to the nature of the thing that lies before us and is perceived by the senses, for by the prayer of thanksgiving and the words spoken over it, it has been changed into flesh and blood."[48]

1189   45. Basing itself on this faith of the Church, the Council of Trent, "clearly and sincerely professes that in the holy sacrament of the eucharist, after the consecration of the bread and wine, our Lord Jesus Christ, true God and true man, is really, truly, and substantially contained under the appearances of these perceptible things." Therefore, the Savior in his humanity is present not only at the right hand

---

[43]   Council of Trent, *Decr. de SS. Eucharistia* prooem. and cap. 2: [Denz-Schön 1635 and 1638].

[44]   *Didachē* 9, 1: Funk PA 1, 20.

[45]   Cyprian, *Epist. ad Magnum* 6: PL 3, 1189.

[46]   1 Cor 10:17.

[47]   Ignatius of Antioch, *Epist. ad Smyrn.* 7, 1: PG 5, 714.

[48]   Theodore of Mopsuestia, *In Matth. Comm.* cap. 26: PG 66, 714.

of the Father according to the natural manner of existence, but at the same time also in the sacrament of the eucharist "by a mode of existence that we can hardly express in words, but that, with a mind enlightened by faith, we can grasp as possible to God and must most firmly believe."[49]

CHRIST OUR LORD PRESENT IN THE EUCHARIST BY TRANSUBSTANTIATION

46. To avoid misunderstanding this sacramental presence, which surpasses the laws of nature and in its meaning constitutes the greatest miracle of all,[50] we must listen with docility to the voice of the teaching and praying Church. This voice, which constantly echoes the voice of Christ, assures us that the way Christ becomes present in this sacrament is none other than by the change of the whole substance of the bread into his body and of the whole substance of the wine into his blood and that this unique and truly wonderful change the Catholic Church rightly calls transubstantiation.[51] After transubstantiation has taken place, the appearances of bread and wine undoubtedly take on a new meaning and a new purpose, for they no longer remain ordinary bread and ordinary drink, but become the sign of something sacred and the sign of a spiritual nourishment. But the reason they take on this new meaning and this new purpose is that they contain a new "reality," which with good reason we term *ontological*. There now underlies those appearances not what was there before, but something else entirely. This is true not merely because the faith of the Church accepts it as so, but objectively, because once the substance or nature of bread and wine has been changed into the body and blood of Christ, only the appearances of bread and wine remain. Under them Christ is present whole and entire, even "bodily" in his physical reality, although not in the same way that bodies are present in a given place.

1190

47. For this reason the Fathers regularly reminded the faithful that in thinking about this most august sacrament, they should not heed their senses, which bear on only the properties of bread and wine, but rather the words of Christ, which have power to change, transform, and "transmute" the bread and wine into his body and blood. For, as those same Fathers often said, the power that accomplishes this is the same power of God almighty that at the beginning of time created all things out of nothing.

1191

48. At the end of a sermon on the mysteries of faith, St. Cyril of Jerusalem says: "We have been instructed in these matters and filled with an unshakable faith that what seems to be bread is not bread, though it tastes like it, but the body of Christ, and that what seems to be wine is not wine, though it tastes like it, but the blood of Christ. Strengthen your heart by receiving this bread as spiritual food and gladden the countenance of your soul."[52]

1192

49. St. John Chrysostom emphasizes this point, saying: "It is not man who makes what is put before us the body and blood of Christ, but Christ himself who was crucified for us. The priest standing there in the place of Christ says these words but their power and grace are from God. 'This is my body,' the priest says, and these words transform what lies before him."[53]

1193

---

49   Council of Trent, *Decr. de SS. Eucharistia* cap. 1: [Denz-Schön 1636].

50   See Leo XIII, Encycl. *Mirae caritatis: Acta Leonis* 13, 22 (1902–03) 173.

51   See Council of Trent, *Decr. de SS. Eucharistia* cap. 4 and can. 2: [Denz-Schön 1642 and 1652].   ·

52   Cyril of Jerusalem, *Catecheses* (myst. 4): PG 33, 1103.

53   John Chrysostom, *De proditione Iudae, homil.* 1, 6: PG 49, 380; see also *In Matth. homil* 82, 5: PG 58, 744.

1194   50. Cyril, Bishop of Alexandria, agrees with John, Bishop of Constantinople, when he writes in his commentary on the Gospel of St. Matthew: "Christ used the demonstrative pronoun in saying: 'This is my body,' and 'This is my blood,' in order that you might not think what you see to be a mere figure. He wished rather that you know that, by the hidden power of God who has power over all things, the offerings are changed into Christ's body and blood; by partaking of these we receive the life-giving and sanctifying power of Christ."[54]

1195   51. Ambrose, Bishop of Milan, dealing with the eucharistic change, clearly says: "Let us be assured that this is not what nature formed, but what the blessing has consecrated and that greater power lies in the blessing than in nature, for by the blessing nature itself is changed." To confirm the truth of this mystery, he recounts many of the miracles described in the sacred Scriptures, among them Christ's birth of the Virgin Mary. Then, turning to the work of creation, he concludes: "The word of Christ, therefore, which could make out of nothing what did not exist, can it not change things already in existence into what they were not? For to give things their natures is not something less than to change them."[55]

1196   52. But there is no need to multiply supporting texts. Rather it is useful simply to recall that firmness of faith with which the Church with one accord opposed Berengarius. Yielding to the difficulties of human reasoning, he was the first who dared deny the eucharistic change and the Church repeatedly called for him to retract or be condemned. Therefore our predecessor St. Gregory VII ordered him to take an oath in the following words: "I believe inwardly and profess outwardly that the bread and wine placed on the altar are, by the mystery of the sacred prayer and the words of the Redeemer, substantially changed into the true and life-giving flesh and blood of Jesus Christ our Lord and that after the consecration the true Body of Christ is present that was born of the Virgin, that as an offering for the salvation of the world hung on the cross, and that is now seated at the right hand of the Father. I believe that the true blood of Christ is present that flowed from his side. They are present not only through the sign and power of the sacrament, but also in the very reality and truth of their nature and substance."[56]

1197   53. Continuous with these words, as an example of the stability of the Catholic faith, is the constant teaching on the eucharistic change by the ecumenical Councils of the Lateran, Constance, Florence, and lastly Trent, both in stating Catholic doctrine and in condemning error.

1198   54. After the Council of Trent, our predecessor Pius VI, on the occasion of the errors of the Synod of Pistoia, strongly reminded parish priests that in carrying out their office of teaching they not neglect to speak of transubstantiation, which is one of the articles of the faith.[57] Similarly, our predecessor Pius XII recalled the bounds that those who engage in learned discussions of the mystery of transubstantiation may not cross.[58] In fulfillment of our apostolic office, we also have openly borne solemn witness to the faith of the Church at the national Italian eucharistic congress held recently at Pisa.[59]

---

[54] Cyril of Alexandria, *In Matth.* 26, 27: PG 72, 451.

[55] Ambrose, *De mysteriis* 9, 50–52: PL 16, 422–424.

[56] Mansi 20, 524 D.

[57] Pius VI, Constitution *Auctorem fidei*, 28 Aug. 1794: [Denz-Schon 2629].

[58] Pius XII, Address, 22 Sept. 1956: AAS 48 (1956) 720.

[59] See AAS 57 (1965) 588–592 [DOL 174].

55. Moreover the Catholic Church has held to this faith in the presence of the   1199
body and blood of Christ in the eucharist, not only in its teaching but also in its life,
since it has at all times honored this great sacrament by the worship that is known
as *latria* and that is the worship due to God alone. As St. Augustine says: "It was in
his flesh that Christ walked among us and it is his flesh that he has given us to eat
for our salvation. No one, however, eats of this flesh without having first adored it
. . . and not only do we not sin by adoring, but we would sin by not adoring."[60]

LATREUTIC WORSHIP OF THE EUCHARIST

56. The Catholic Church has always offered and still offers the worship of *latria* to   1200
the sacrament of the eucharist, not only during Mass, but also outside it. It does so
by reserving consecrated hosts with the utmost care, exposing them to solemn
veneration by the faithful, and carrying them in processions to the joy of great
crowds of the faithful.

57. The most ancient of church practices provide evidence of this veneration. It   1201
was the custom of the Church's pastors to urge the faithful that they show the
greatest reverence toward the consecrated hosts they took to their homes. "The
body of Christ is meant to be eaten, not to be treated with irreverence," St. Hippolytus solemnly reminds the faithful.[61]

58. In fact the faithful thought themselves guilty, and rightly so, as Origen records,   1202
if after they had taken the body of the Lord and kept it with all care and reverence,
a small particle fell because of negligence.[62]

59. Novatian, on this point a reliable witness, states that these same pastors se-   1203
verely censured any failure in due reverence that may have crept in. He considers as
worthy of being condemned that person "who after dismissal from the Lord's
sacrifice and still, as is the custom, carrying with him the eucharist, the sacred body
of the Lord" does not go to his home but runs off to the theater.[63]

60. Indeed St. Cyril of Alexandria rejects as madness the opinion of those who   1204
maintained that the eucharist had no sanctifying power if any part were left over
for another day. "For," he says, "neither Christ is altered nor his holy body
changed, but its blessed force and power and life-giving grace always remain with
it."[64]

61. Nor may we forget that in ancient times the faithful, whether beset by the   1205
violence of persecution or living in solitude out of love for the monastic life,
nourished themselves even daily, receiving communion by their own hands in the
absence of a priest or deacon.[65]

62. We say this not in order to change that way of reserving the eucharist and of   1206
receiving holy communion which was later prescribed by the church laws now in

---

[60] Augustine, *In Ps.* 98, 9: PL 37, 126.

[61] Hippolytus, *Tradit. Apost.*: B. Botte, ed., *La Tradition Apostolique de St. Hippolyte* (Münster-W., 1963) 84.

[62] Origen, *In Exod. fragm.*: PG 12, 391.

[63] Novatian, *De spectaculis*: CSEL 3³, 8.

[64] Cyril of Alexandria, *Epist. ad Calosyrium*: PG 76, 1075.

[65] See Basil, *Epist.* 93: PG 32, 483–486.

force, but rather that we may rejoice together over the faith of the Church, which is always one and the same.

1207 63. This faith also gave rise to the feast of Corpus Christi, which was first celebrated in the Diocese of Liège, especially through the efforts of the servant of God Blessed Juliana of Mont-Cornillon, and which our predecessor Urban IV extended to the universal Church. From it have originated many practices of eucharistic devotion that, under the inspiration of divine grace, have increased from day to day and that the Catholic Church uses eagerly to show ever greater homage to Christ, to thank him for so great a gift, and to implore his mercy.

EXHORTATION TO PROMOTE THE WORSHIP OF THE EUCHARIST

1208 64. We entreat you, therefore, Esteemed Brothers, that among the people entrusted to your care and vigilance, you keep this faith pure and integral, freed of false and pernicious opinions; that faith allows for nothing but maintaining absolute fidelity to the words of Christ and the apostles. We entreat you to promote, without stinting word or work, worship of the eucharist, toward which all other forms of devotion must lead and there come to rest.

1209 65. May the faithful, thanks to your efforts, come to realize and experience ever more and more the truth of these words: "Those who desire life find here a place and a source of life. Let them approach, let them believe, let them be incorporated so that they may receive life. Let them not refuse union with the other members, let them not be putrid members, deserving to be cut off, or twisted members, a source of shame. Let them be beautiful, fitting, comely, and healthy members, let them cleave to the Body, live for God and through God. Let them now labor here on earth that they may afterward reign in heaven."[66]

1210 66. The faithful should, as we all hope, every day and in great numbers actively participate in the sacrifice of the Mass, receive communion with a pure heart, and make a fitting thanksgiving to Christ our Lord for so great a gift. Let them remember these words: "The desire of Jesus Christ and of the Church that all the faithful receive daily communion means above all that through the sacramental union with God they may obtain the strength necessary for mastering their passions, for purifying themselves of their daily venial faults, and for avoiding the grave sins to which human frailty is prone."[67] Moreover, in the course of the day the faithful should not omit to visit the blessed sacrament, which must, in keeping with liturgical laws, be reserved in the churches with great reverence in a most honorable location. Such visits are a proof of gratitude, a pledge of love, a service of adoration owed to Christ the Lord there present.

1211 67. No one can fail to understand that the divine eucharist bestows on the Christian people an incomparable dignity. Not only while the sacrifice is being offered and the sacrament celebrated but also after the sacrifice has been offered and the sacrament has been received, as long as the eucharist is kept in our churches and oratories, Christ is truly the Emmanuel, that is, "God with us." Day and night he is in our midst; full of grace and truth,[68] he dwells with us. He forms our moral life, nourishes virtues, consoles the afflicted, strengthens the weak, moves all those who draw near to imitate him, learning from his example to be meek and humble of

---

[66] Augustine, *In Ioann. tract.* 26, 13. PL 35, 1613.

[67] SC Council, *Decree* 20 Dec. 1905, approved by St. Pius X: *Acta Sanctae Sedis* 38 (1905) 401.

[68] See Jn 1:14.

heart and to seek not what is their own but the things of God. Anyone, therefore, who approaches this august sacrament with special devotion and endeavors to return generous love for Christ's own infinite love, experiences and fully understands, with great spiritual joy and profit, how precious is the life hidden with Christ in God[69] and how great is the value of communing with Christ, for there is nothing more consoling on earth, nothing more effective for advancing along the road of holiness.

68. Further, you realize, Esteemed Brothers, that the eucharist is reserved in churches and oratories as in the spiritual center of a religious community or parish, yes, of the universal Church and of all humanity, since beneath the veil of the eucharistic elements Christ is contained, the invisible Head of the Church, the Redeemer of the world, the center of all hearts, "through whom all things are and through whom we exist."[70]

1212

69. From this it follows that the worship paid to the divine eucharist strongly impels the soul to cultivate a "social" love,[71] by which we place the general good before the good of the individual, make our own the interests of the community, of the parish, of the entire Church, and extend our charity to the whole world, because we know that the members of Christ are everywhere.

1213

70. The sacrament of the eucharist is the sign and source of the unity of the Mystical Body of Christ and stirs up in those fervently devoted to it an intense ecclesial spirit. Therefore, Esteemed Brothers, may you never stop seeking to convince your people that in drawing near to the eucharistic mystery they learn to take the interests of the Church as their own, to entreat God unceasingly, and to offer themselves to the Lord as an acceptable sacrifice on behalf of the Church's unity and peace. May you teach all children of the Church to be one and to realize they are one, to have no factions among them but to be, as St. Paul enjoins, completely joined together in the same mind and in the same judgment.[72] May all who are not yet joined in complete communion with the Catholic Church, our separated brothers and sisters, but are graced with and glory in the name Christian, soon, with the help of God's grace, rejoice with us in the unity of faith and communion that Christ willed to be the mark of his disciples.

1214

71. Let religious, both men and women, realize that zeal in praying and in dedicating themselves to God for the unity of the Church is something that belongs particularly to them, since they are persons bound in a special manner to the adoration of the most blessed sacrament and in virtue of the vows they have made are, as it were, its honor guard here on earth.

1215

72. A foremost and fond desire of the Church has been and remains the desire for the unity of all Christians. We wish to express it again in the very words used by the Council of Trent at the close of its decree on the eucharist: "Finally, the holy Council, with fatherly affection, admonishes, exhorts, prays, and beseeches 'through the merciful kindness of our God'[73] that each and all who bear the name Christian will now at last agree and be of one mind in this *sign of unity, this bond of charity*, this symbol of concord, and that, mindful of such great majesty and such

1216

---

[69] See Col 3:3.

[70] 1 Cor 8:6.

[71] See Augustine, *De Genesi ad litt.* 11, 15, 20: PL 34, 437.

[72] See 1 Cor 1:10.

[73] Lk 1:78.

boundless love of Jesus Christ our Lord who gave his beloved life as the price of our salvation and 'his flesh to eat,'[74] they may believe and adore these sacred mysteries of his body and blood with such constancy and firmness of faith, with such devotion of mind, with such reverence and worship, that they can receive frequently that supersubstantial bread[75] and that it may truly be for them the life of the soul and unfailing health of mind. Then in the strength of that food[76] they will be able after the journey of this careworn pilgrimage to arrive in their heavenly home, there to eat without any veil the same 'bread of angels'[77] that now they eat under the sacred veils."[78]

1217   73. May the most loving Redeemer, who just before his death prayed to the Father that all who were to believe in him would be one even as he and the Father were one,[79] deign speedily to hear our most ardent prayer and that of the entire Church, that we may all with one voice and one faith celebrate the eucharistic mystery and, having been made partakers of the body of Christ, become the one Body,[80] be linked by those same bonds with which he himself desired it to be joined.

1218   74. And we turn with fatherly affection also to those who belong to the revered Churches of the East, from which so many of the most illustrious Fathers came whose testimony to the belief concerning the eucharist we have so gladly cited in this Letter. Our soul is filled with intense joy as we consider your faith in the eucharist, which is also ours, and as we listen to the liturgical prayers with which you celebrate so great a mystery; we rejoice to behold your eucharistic devotion and to read your theologians as they explain or defend the teaching concerning this most august sacrament.

1219   75. May the Most Blessed Virgin Mary, from whom Christ our Lord took the flesh that under the appearances of bread and wine "is contained, offered, and received in this sacrament,"[81] and all the saints of God, especially those who had a more ardent devotion to the divine eucharist, intercede with the Father of mercies so that from this same faith in the eucharist and devotion to it a perfect unity between all who bear the name Christian may come about and flourish. Firmly impressed on our mind are the words of the holy martyr Ignatius as he warned the faithful of Philadelphia against the evils of division and schism, the remedy for which lies in the eucharist: "Strive then," he says, "to make use of one form of thanksgiving, for the flesh of our Lord Jesus Christ is one and one is the chalice in the union of his blood, one the altar, one the bishop."[82]

1220   76. Encouraged by the most consoling hope of the blessings that will accrue to the whole Church and the entire world from an increase in devotion to the eucharist, with profound affection we impart to you, Esteemed Brothers, to the priests, religious, to all those associated in your work and to all the faithful entrusted to your care, the apostolic blessing as a pledge of heavenly graces.

---

[74] Jn 6:48ff.

[75] Mt 6:11.

[76] 1 Kings 19:8.

[77] Ps 77 [78]:25.

[78] Council of Trent, *Decr. de SS. Eucharistia* cap. 8 [Denz-Schön 1649].

[79] See Jn 17:20–21.

[80] See 1 Cor 10:17.

[81] CIC, can. 801.

[82] Ignatius of Antioch, *Epist. ad Philadelph.* 4: PG 5, 700.

177. PAUL VI, **Epistle** *Vox laetitiae* to Cardinal Paul M. Richaud, papal legate to the national eucharistic congress of France at Bordeaux, 25 March 1966: AAS 58 (1966) 356–358 (excerpt).

[. . .] This mystery of faith is the origin and end of the other sacraments and surpasses them all. It not only possesses the power to signify and effect divine grace, but, beyond the pattern of nature, it contains Christ the Lord, author of all charisms, truly, really, and substantially under the appearances of bread and wine. It brings him to those who receive it in order to nurture divine life and bring it to fulfillment in the faithful individually and in Christ's entire Mystical Body.   1221

"It is called and in reality is communion because in it we are in communion with Christ and share in his humanity and divinity, as well as bringing us into communion and joining us with one another. For we who partake of the one bread are all the one body and blood of Christ and because we are of the one Body, we become members of one another."[2]

The unbloody renewal of the offering that was made in blood on Calvary, the one sacrifice of the New Law, is a sacrifice of adoration, thanksgiving, impetration, and expiation for the living and the dead. It enables the Church, united in the person of Christ, to honor and worship the divine majesty with a supreme act of reverence, to possess the sign and cause of its own unity and peace, and to be quickened by the surge of that charity which is its bond. That occurs as often as and wherever the Church celebrates the eucharist, because every Mass is of its nature social and public. "Every Mass, even though a priest may offer it in private, is not a private matter; it is an act of Christ and the Church. . . . For every Mass celebrated is offered not for the salvation of only a few, but for the salvation even of the whole world. . . . From such a Mass an abundant outpouring of special, salutary graces enriches the celebrant, the faithful, the whole Church, and the entire world."[3]   1222

It will be well to call to mind a point that must be believed with unwavering faith: in the eucharist after the twofold consecration of the bread and the wine Christ is present immediately and not by a fleeting and passing presence; he remains in the hosts that are reserved after the consecration as the bread of life that came down from heaven and under the veils of the sacrament he is worthy of divine worship in reverence and in the homage of adoration. The divine goodness, to which the words "my delight has been to be with the children of men"[4] supremely apply, has so disposed things. That must rightly be a motive for us to offer endless thanks to God, as we possess in our conjoined love the sustenance for everlasting life and the pledge of eternal glory. [. . .]   1223

---

2   John Damascene, *De fide orthodoxa* 4, 13.

3   Paul VI, Encycl. *Mysterium fidei* no. 32 [DOL 176 no. 1176].

4   Prov 8:31.

178. SC DOCTRINE OF THE FAITH, **Letter** *Cum Oecumenicum Concilium* to presidents of the conferences of bishops, on errors of interpretation concerning the teachings of Vatican Council II, 24 July 1966: AAS 58 (1966) 659–661 (excerpts).[†]

1224   The Second Ecumenical Vatican Council, recently successfully concluded, has promulgated documents full of wisdom in matters of both doctrine and discipline in order to advance the Church's life effectively. Therefore, a serious duty rests on the whole people of God, namely, that of bending every effort toward the accomplishment of whatever, under the prompting of the Holy Spirit, has been solemnly taught or decreed in that great gathering of bishops with the pope presiding.

To the hierarchy belongs the right and the responsibility of watching over, guiding, and advancing the movement begun by the Council. The aim is that the conciliar teachings and decrees be given a correct interpretation and an application in keeping with their exactly respected force and intent. It is the bishops who are to defend the conciliar teaching; it is they who possess the office of teaching authoritatively under Peter as head. To their credit, many of them already have undertaken the work of properly explaining the teaching of the Council.

Regrettably, however, there has been unwelcome news from various parts of the world about growing abuses in interpreting conciliar teaching and of aberrant and rash opinions springing up here and there that deeply disturb the minds of many of the faithful. The study and effort to go more deeply into the truth, separating matters of faith from those of opinion, deserve praise. But from evidence reviewed by this Congregation it is clear that there are a number of positions which, stepping heedlessly beyond the bounds of mere opinion and hypothesis, seem in some degree to do injury to dogma and the foundation of faith.

It is useful to touch on some of these positions, by way of example, as they are known from the reports of scholars and from published writings.

1225   1.   First there is the matter of revelation itself. There are those who approach the Scriptures deliberately putting aside tradition, but they also restrict the power and scope of biblical inspiration and inerrancy and have a distorted opinion about the weight of historical texts.

1226   6.   In the theological treatment of the sacraments some elements are either ignored or given too little weight; this applies especially to the eucharist. Regarding Christ's real presence under the appearances of bread and wine, there are even some who theologize as partisans of an exaggerated symbolism, as though there were no conversion of the bread and wine into the body and blood of Christ through transubstantiation, but their mere transference through some sort of signification. There are some who in regard to the Mass emphasize the concept of the agape at the expense of the idea of sacrifice.

1227   7.   Some prefer to explain the sacrament of penance as a means of reconciliation with the Church and say too little about reconciliation with the God who has been offended. They also claim that the personal confession of sins is not required for this sacrament, but are intent on bringing out only the social function of reconciliation with the Church.

[†] Permission was given to us to publish this letter in order that its genuine tenor may become known. Certain daily newspapers, even though the nature of this letter calls for discretion, have not hesitated to publish some parts of the text, without, however, respecting the proper character of the document. The result has been that doubts have arisen regarding the true contents of the letter and the aim intended through it by the Apostolic See [Editorial Note of AAS].

10.   To all of these points a word must be added on ecumenism. The Apostolic See   1228
certainly commends those who, in the spirit of the conciliar Decree on Ecumenism,
promote measures to foster the bond of charity with other Christians and to draw
them toward the unity of the Church. But it is also painful to the Apostolic See that
there are some who, interpreting the conciliar Decree in their own way, press for the
kind of ecumenical activity that does injury to the truth concerning the unity of
faith and of the Church. They cultivate a perilous irenicism and indifferentism far
removed from the mind of the Council.

These errors and dangers, spread individually here and there, are reported   1229
summarily by this Letter to local Ordinaries in order that each one in keeping with
his office and responsibility will take every step to destroy or to prevent them.

This Congregation earnestly requests that the same local Ordinaries, meeting
together in their own conferences of bishops, deal with these matters, make a
suitable report to the Holy See about them, and express their own recommendations before Christmas 1966.

Obvious prudential reasons bar publication of this Letter. Ordinaries and all
others with whom they decide for good reason to share it are to keep it under strict
secrecy.

179. SC RITES, **Instruction** *Eucharisticum mysterium,* on worship of the eucharist, 25 May 1967: AAS 59 (1967) 539–573; Not 3 (1967) 225–260.

INTRODUCTION

MORE RECENT DOCUMENTS ON THE EUCHARISTIC MYSTERY

1.   The eucharistic mystery is truly the center of the liturgy and indeed of the   1230
whole Christian life. Consequently the Church, guided by the Holy Spirit, continually seeks to understand this mystery more fully and more and more to derive its
life from it.

In our day Vatican Council II has stressed several important aspects of this
mystery.[1]

Through the Constitution on the Liturgy, after first recalling certain realities
about the nature and importance of this sacrament, the Council established the
norms for the reform of the rites of the sacrifice of the Mass so that the celebration
of this mystery would further the active and full participation of the faithful.[2] In
addition, the Constitution broadened the practice of concelebration and communion under both kinds.[3]

In the Constitution on the Church the Council set forth the close connection
between the eucharist and the mystery of the Church.[4] In other documents the
Council frequently stressed the important place of the eucharistic mystery in the
life of the faithful[5] and its power to shed light on the meaning of human labor and

[1]   See SC art. 2, 41, 47 [DOL 1 nos. 2, 41,47].

[2]   See SC art. 48–54, 56 [DOL 1 nos. 48–54, 56].

[3]   See SC art. 55, 57 [DOL 1 nos. 55, 57].

[4]   See LG nos. 3, 7, 11, 26, 28, 50 [DOL 4 nos. 137, 139, 141, 146, 148, 158].

[5]   See UR nos. 2, 15 [DOL 6 nos. 182, 187]; CD nos. 15, 30 [DOL 7 nos. 194, 196]; PO nos. 2, 5–8,
13–14, 18 [DOL 18 nos. 257, 260–263, 265–266, 267].

indeed of all creation insofar as in it "natural elements, after being fashioned by human hands, are changed into the glorious body and blood of Christ."[6]

For many of these pronouncements of the Council Pius XII had prepared the way, especially by his encyclical *Mediator Dei*.[7] In his encyclical *Mysterium fidei*[8] Pope Paul VI has recalled the importance of certain aspects of eucharistic teaching, especially on the real presence of Christ and the worship due to this sacrament outside Mass.

NEED TO ATTEND SIMULTANEOUSLY TO THE COMPLETE TEACHING OF THESE DOCUMENTS

1231   2.   In recent times certain aspects of the traditional teaching on this mystery have been considered more thoroughly and have been presented with new zeal to the devotion of the faithful. Research and practical measures of various kinds, especially in the field of liturgy and Scripture, have provided assistance.

There is, consequently, a need to draw out practical norms from the total teaching of such documents, in order to indicate what the relationship of the Christian people toward this mystery should be so that they may achieve that understanding and holiness which the Council set before the Church as an ideal.

It is important that the eucharistic mystery, fully considered under the many facets of its own reality, appear with the clarity it should have before the minds of the faithful; and also that the relationships that are recognized in church teaching as existing objectively between the various facets of the mystery become reflected in the life and mind of the faithful.

THE MOST NOTEWORTHY DOCTRINAL THEMES IN THE RECENT DOCUMENTS

1232   3.   Among the doctrinal principles formulated in the Church's recent documents concerning the eucharist, it is useful to cite those that follow: they address the attitude of Christians toward this mystery and, therefore, have direct bearing on the purpose of this Instruction.

a.   "In the human nature united to himself the Son of God, by overcoming death through his own death and resurrection, redeemed us and refashioned us into a new creation (see Gal 6:15; 2 Cor 5:17). By communicating his Spirit, Christ made us his brothers and sisters, called together from all nations, to be mystically his own Body. In that Body the life of Christ is bestowed on believers, who through the sacraments are united in a hidden and real way with Christ who suffered and was glorified."[9]

Therefore, "at the Last Supper, on the night he was betrayed, our Savior instituted the eucharistic sacrifice of his body and blood. He did this in order to perpetuate the sacrifice of the cross throughout the centuries until he should come again and so to entrust to his beloved Bride, the Church, a memorial of his death and resurrection: a sacrament of love, a sign of unity, a bond of charity, a paschal banquet in which Christ is eaten, the heart filled with grace, and a pledge of future glory given to us."[10]

Hence the Mass, the Lord's Supper, is at once and inseparably:

— the sacrifice in which the sacrifice of the cross is perpetuated;

---

[6] See GS 38 [DOL 19 no. 270].

[7] See Pius XII, Encycl. *Mediator Dei*: AAS 39 (1947) 547–572; *idem*, Address to International Meeting on Pastoral Liturgy, Assisi, 22 Sept. 1956: AAS 48 (1956) 715–724.

[8] See Paul VI, Encycl. *Mysterium fidei* [DOL 176].

[9] LG no. 7 [DOL 4 no. 139].

[10] SC art. 47 [DOL 1 no. 47].

— the memorial of the death and resurrection of the Lord who said: "Do this in memory of me" (Lk 22:19);

— the sacred banquet in which, through the communion of the body and blood of the Lord, the people of God share the benefits of the paschal sacrifice, renew the New Covenant with us made once and for all by God in Christ's blood, and in faith and hope foreshadow and anticipate the eschatological banquet in the Father's kingdom as they proclaim the death of the Lord "until he comes."[11]

b. In the Mass, therefore, the sacrifice and sacred meal form part of the same mystery in such a way that the closest bond conjoins the one with the other.

In the sacrifice of the Mass the Lord is offered when "he begins to be sacramentally present as the spiritual food of the faithful under the appearance of bread and wine."[12] The reason that Christ entrusted this sacrifice to the Church was that the faithful might share in it both spiritually, by faith and charity, and sacramentally, through the sacred meal of communion. A sharing in the Lord's Supper is always a communion with Christ offering himself to the Father for us as a sacrifice.[13]

c. The celebration of the eucharist at Mass is the action not only of Christ but also of the Church. It is Christ's act because, perpetuating in an unbloody way the sacrifice consummated on the cross,[14] he offers himself to the Father for the salvation of the world through the ministry of priests.[15] It is the Church's act because, as the Bride and minister of Christ exercising together with him the role of priest and victim, the Church offers him to the Father and at the same time completely offers itself together with him.[16]

In this way, especially in the great eucharistic prayer, the Church gives thanks together with Christ to the Father in the Holy Spirit for all the benefits he gives us in creation and in a singular way in the paschal mystery and asks the Father for the coming of his kingdom.

d. Hence no Mass, in fact no liturgical service, is a merely private act, but the celebration of the Church as a society composed of different orders and ministries in which all the members have an active part in keeping with their proper order and office.[17]

e. The celebration of the eucharist in the sacrifice of the Mass is truly the origin and the purpose of the worship that is shown to the eucharist outside Mass. For the sacred elements that remain after Mass come from the Mass and they are reserved after Mass so that the faithful who cannot be present at Mass may be united to Christ and the celebration of his sacrifice through sacramental communion received with the right dispositions.[18]

---

[11] See SC art. 6, 10, 47, 106 [DOL 1 nos. 6, 10, 47, 106]; PO no. 4 [DOL 18 no. 259].

[12] Paul VI, Encycl. *Mysterium fidei* [DOL 176 no. 1178].

[13] See Pius XII, Encycl. *Mediator Dei*: AAS 39 (1947) 564–566.

[14] See SC art. 47 [DOL 1 no. 47].

[15] See Council of Trent, sess. 22, *Decr. de Missa* cap. 1: Denz-Schön 1741.

[16] See LG no. 11 [DOL 4 no.141]; SC art. 47–48 [DOL 1 nos. 47–48]; PO nos. 2, 5 [DOL 18 nos. 257, 260]. Pius XII, loc. cit.: 552. Paul VI, Encycl. *Mysterium fidei* [DOL 176 no. 1175].

[17] See SC art. 26–28 [DOL 1 nos. 26–28] and no. 44 of this Instruction.

[18] See no. 49 of this Instruction.

Hence the eucharistic sacrifice is the source and the summit of all the Church's worship and of the entire Christian life.[19] The faithful participate more fully in this sacrifice of thanksgiving, expiation, petition, and praise not only when they wholeheartedly offer the sacred victim and in him offer themselves to the Father with the priest, but also when they receive the same victim in the sacrament.

f.   It should be absolutely clear "that all the faithful show this holy sacrament the worship of adoration that is due to God himself, as has always been the practice recognized in the Catholic Church. Nor is the sacrament to be less the object of adoration on the grounds that it was instituted by Christ the Lord to be received as food."[20] For even in the reserved sacrament he is to be adored,[21] because he is substantially present there through the conversion of the bread and wine that, following the Council of Trent,[22] is most accurately termed transubstantiation.

g.   Therefore, the eucharistic mystery must be considered in its entirety, both in the celebration of Mass and in the worship of the sacred elements reserved after Mass in order to extend the grace of the sacrifice.[23]

The principles stated must be the source of the norms on the practical arrangement of the worship of this sacrament even after Mass and of its correlation with the proper arrangement of the Mass in conformity with the directives of Vatican Council II and of other pertinent documents of the Apostolic See.[24]

GENERAL INTENT OF THIS PRESENT INSTRUCTION

1233   4.   For this reason Pope Paul VI ordered the Consilium for the Implementation of the Constitution on the Liturgy to prepare a special instruction that would issue such practical norms, fitted to contemporary circumstances.

The purpose intended for these norms is both to provide the broad principles for catechesis of the faithful about the eucharistic mystery and to make more understandable the signs through which the eucharist is celebrated as the memorial of the Lord and worshiped in the Church as a lasting sacrament.

For although this mystery has a supreme and unique excellence, namely, the presence of the very author of holiness, nevertheless in common with the other sacraments, it too is the symbol of a sacred reality and the visible expression of an invisible grace.[25] Hence the more pertinent and clear the signs involved in its celebration and worship, the more surely and effectively will it penetrate the minds and lives of the faithful.[26]

---

[19]   See LG no. 11 [DOL 4 no. 141]; SC art. 41 [DOL 1 no. 41]; PO nos. 2, 5, 6 [DOL 18 nos. 257, 260, 261]; UR no. 15 [DOL 6 no. 187].

[20]   Council of Trent, sess. 13, *Decr. de Eucharistia* cap. 5: Denz-Schön 1643.

[21]   See Paul VI, Encycl. *Mysterium fidei* [DOL 176 nos. 1200–04]. Pius XII, loc. cit.: 569.

[22]   See Council of Trent, loc. cit. cap. 4: Denz-Schön 1652.

[23]   See the treatment of the Mass in the documents already cited; all of them deal with the twofold aspect of the eucharist: PO nos. 5, 18 [DOL 18 nos. 260, 267]. Paul VI, Encycl. *Mysterium fidei* [DOL 176 nos. 1146–49]. Pius XII, Encycl. *Mediator Dei*: AAS 39 (1947) 547–572; *idem*, Address at Assisi: AAS 48 (1956) 715–723.

[24]   See Paul VI, Encycl. *Mysterium fidei* [DOL 176 nos. 1200–10]. Pius XII, Encycl. *Mediator Dei*: AAS 39 (1947) 547–572. SCR, Instr. de musica sacra, 3 Sept. 1958: AAS 50 (1958) 630–663; *idem*, Instr. InterOec, 26 Sept 1964 [DOL 23 nos. 340–352].

[25]   See Council of Trent, sess. 13, *Decr. de SS. Eucharistia* cap. 3: Denz-Schön 1639. See also ST 3a, 60.1.

[26]   See SC art. 33, 59 [DOL 1 nos. 33, 59].

PART I
GENERAL PRINCIPLES TO BE GIVEN PROMINENCE IN
CATECHIZING THE PEOPLE ON THE EUCHARISTIC MYSTERY

REQUIREMENTS OF PASTORS WHO ARE TO GIVE INSTRUCTION ABOUT THIS MYSTERY

5.   Effective catechesis is necessary so that the eucharistic mystery might suffuse   1234
the minds and lives of the faithful.

To hand on this instruction properly, pastors should not only keep in mind the
integral teaching of faith, which is contained in the documents of the magisterium,
but also with heart and life enter deeply into the spirit of the Church on this
matter.[27]Then they will more readily judge which of the many aspects of this
mystery best suits the faithful in any given situation.

In view of what was said in no. 3, the following points, among others, deserve
special attention.

THE EUCHARISTIC MYSTERY AS CENTER OF THE WHOLE LIFE OF THE CHURCH

6.   Catechesis on the eucharistic mystery should aim at helping the faithful realize   1235
deeply that its celebration is the true center of the whole Christian life, both for the
universal Church and for the local congregations of that Church. For "the other
sacraments, like every ministry of the Church and every work of the apostolate, are
linked with the holy eucharist and have it as their end. For the most blessed
eucharist contains the Church's entire spiritual wealth, that is, Christ himself. He is
our Passover and living bread; through his flesh, made living and life-giving by the
Holy Spirit, he is giving people life and thereby inviting and leading them to offer
themselves together with him, as well as their labors and all created things."[28]

The eucharist is the effective sign and sublime cause of the sharing in divine
life and the unity of the people of God by which the Church exists.[29] It is the
culmination both of God's action sanctifying the world in Christ and of the worship
we offer to Christ and through him to the Father in the Holy Spirit.[30] Its celebration
"is the outstanding means whereby the faithful may express in their lives and
manifest to others the mystery of Christ and the real nature of the true Church."[31]

THE EUCHARISTIC MYSTERY AS THE CENTER OF THE LOCAL CHURCH

7.   Through the eucharist "the Church continually lives and grows. This Church   1236
of Christ is truly present in all lawful, local congregations of the faithful, which,
united with their bishops, are themselves called Churches in the New Testament.
For in their own locality these Churches are the new people called by God in the
Holy Spirit and in great fullness (see 1 Thes 1:5). In them the faithful are gathered
together through the preaching of Christ's Gospel and the mystery of the Lord's
Supper is celebrated, so that 'through the meal of the body and blood of the Lord
the whole brotherhood is joined together.'[32] Any community of the altar, under the
sacred ministry of the bishop,[33] or of a priest who takes his place,[34] "stands out

---

27   See SC art. 14, 17–18 [DOL 1 nos. 14, 17–18].

28   PO no. 5 [DOL 18 no. 260].

29   See LG no. 11 [DOL 4 no. 141]; UR nos. 2, 15 [DOL 6 nos. 182, 187].

30   See SC art. 10 [DOL 1 no. 10].

31   SC art. 2; see also art. 41 [DOL 1 no. 2; also no. 41].

32   Prayer from the Mozarabic Rite: PL 96, 759 B.

33   LG no. 26 [DOL 4 no. 146].

34   See SC art. 42 [DOL 1 no. 42].

clearly as a symbol of that charity and 'unity of the Mystical Body without which there can be no salvation.'[35] In these communities, though frequently small and poor or living in isolation, Christ is present and the power of his presence gathers together the one, holy, catholic, and apostolic Church. For 'the sharing of the body and blood of Christ does nothing less than transform us into what we receive.'"[36,37]

THE EUCHARISTIC MYSTERY AND THE UNITY OF CHRISTIANS

1237   8.   In addition to those things that concern the ecclesial community and the individual faithful, pastors should pay special attention to that part of the doctrine in which the Church teaches that the memorial of the Lord, celebrated in accord with his will, signifies and brings about the unity of all who believe in him.[38]

In compliance with the Decree on Ecumenism of Vatican Council II,[39] the faithful should be led to a proper appreciation of the values that are preserved in the eucharistic tradition through which their brothers and sisters in other Christian Confessions have continued to celebrate the Lord's Supper. For "when in the Lord's Supper they commemorate his death and resurrection, they attest to the sign of their life in communion with Christ and they await his glorious Second Coming."[40] Those, moreover, who have preserved the sacrament of orders in the celebration of the eucharist, "united with the bishop and having access to God the Father through the Word incarnate, crucified and glorified, attain communion with the Trinity by the outpouring of the Holy Spirit as people who have become 'partakers in the divine nature' (2 Pt 1:4). In each of these Churches, therefore, the celebration of the eucharist builds up and gives increase 'to the Church of God and its concelebration shows forth the communion of these Churches with each other.'"[41]

Above all in the celebration of the mystery of unity all Christians should be filled with sadness over the divisions separating them. Therefore, they should fervently pray to God that all Christ's disciples may daily come to a deeper understanding of the eucharistic mystery conformed to his own mind. They should celebrate it in such a way that, made partakers in the body of Christ, they may become the one Body (see 1 Cor 10:17), "linked by those same bonds with which he himself desired it to be joined."[42]

THE DIFFERENT MODES OF CHRIST'S PRESENCE

1238   9.   In order to achieve a deeper understanding of the eucharistic mystery, the faithful should be instructed in the principal modes by which the Lord is present to his Church in liturgical celebrations.[43]

He is always present in an assembly of the faithful gathered in his name (see Mt 18:20). He is also present in his word, for it is he who is speaking as the sacred Scriptures are read in the Church.

---

[35]   See ST 3a, 73.3.

[36]   Leo the Great, *Serm.* 63, 7: PL 54, 357 C.

[37]   LG no. 26 [DOL 4 no. 146].

[38]   See LG nos. 3, 7, 11, 26 [DOL 4 nos. 137, 139, 141, 146]; UR no. 2 [DOL 6 no. 182].

[39]   See UR nos. 15 and 22 [DOL 6 nos. 187 and 189].

[40]   UR no. 22 [DOL 6 no. 189].

[41]   UR no. 15: AAS 57 (1965) 102; ConstDecrDecl 265.

[42]   Paul VI, Encycl. *Mysterium fidei* [DOL 176 no.1217].

[43]   See SC art. 7 [DOL 1 no. 7].

In the eucharistic sacrifice he is present both in the person of the minister, "the same now offering through the ministry of the priest who formerly offered himself on the cross,"[44]and above all under the eucharistic elements.[45] For in that sacrament, in a unique way, Christ is present, whole and entire, God and man, substantially and continuously. This presence of Christ under the elements "is called the real presence not to exclude the other kinds, as though they were not real, but because it is real par excellence."[46]

CONNECTION BETWEEN THE LITURGY OF THE WORD AND THE LITURGY OF THE EUCHARIST

10. Pastors should, therefore, "insistently teach the faithful to take their part in the entire Mass," by showing the close connection that exists between the liturgy of the word and the celebration of the Lord's Supper, so that they may clearly perceive how the two constitute a single act of worship.[47] "The preaching of the word is necessary for the administration of the sacraments. For the sacraments are sacraments of faith and faith has its origin and sustenance in the word."[48] This is especially true of the celebration of Mass, in which the purpose of the liturgy of the word is to develop in a specific way the close link between the proclamation and hearing of the word of God and the eucharistic mystery.[49]

1239

The faithful, therefore, hearing the word of God, should realize that the wonders it proclaims achieve their summit in the paschal mystery, whose memorial is celebrated sacramentally in the Mass. In this way, the faithful, receiving the word of God and nourished by it, will be led in a spirit of thanksgiving to a fruitful participation in the mysteries of salvation. In this way the Church feeds upon the bread of life as it comes from the table of both the word of God and the body of Christ.[50]

THE UNIVERSAL PRIESTHOOD AND THE MINISTERIAL PRIESTHOOD IN THE CELEBRATION OF THE EUCHARIST

11. The more clearly the faithful recognize the place they have in the liturgical assembly and the parts they are to fulfill in the eucharistic celebration the more conscious and fruitful will be the active participation that belongs to a community.[51]

1240

Catechesis, then, should explain the teaching on the royal priesthood, which consecrates the faithful through their rebirth and the anointing of the Holy Spirit.[52]

There should also be further explanation both of the role of the ministerial priesthood in the celebration of the eucharist, which differs from the universal priesthood of the faithful in essence and not merely in degree,[53] and of the parts

---

44   Council of Trent, *Decr. de Missa* cap. 2: Denz-Schön 1743.

45   See SC art. 7 [DOL 1 no. 7].

46   Paul VI, Encycl. *Mysterium fidei* [DOL 176 no. 1183].

47   See SC art. 56 [DOL 1 no. 56].

48   PO no. 4 [DOL 18 no. 259].

49   See PO no. 4 [DOL 18 no. 259]; see also no. 3 of this Instruction.

50   See DV no. 21 [DOL 14 no. 224].

51   See SC art. 14, 26, 30, 38 [DOL 1 nos. 14, 26, 30, 38].

52   See LG no. 10 [DOL 4 no. 140]; PO no. 2 [DOL 18 no. 257]. Paul VI, Encycl. *Mysterium fidei* [DOL 176 no. 1175].

53   See LG no. 10 [DOL 4 no. 140]; PO nos. 2, 5 [DOL 18 nos. 257, 260].

fulfilled by others who exercise some ministry.[54]

THE NATURE OF ACTIVE PARTICIPATION IN THE MASS

1241   12. It should be explained that all who gather for the eucharist are that holy people who, together with the ministers, have a part in the sacred rites. The priest alone, insofar as he acts in the person of Christ, consecrates the bread and wine. Nevertheless the active part of the faithful in the eucharist consists in: giving thanks to God as they are mindful of the Lord's passion, death, and resurrection; offering the spotless victim not only through the hands of the priest but also together with him; and, through the reception of the body of the Lord, entering into the communion with God and with each other that participation is meant to lead to.[55] For there is a fuller share in the Mass when the people, properly disposed, receive the body of the Lord sacramentally in the Mass itself, out of obedience to his own words: "Take and eat."[56]

Like Christ's own passion, this sacrifice, though offered for all, "has no effect except in those who are united to Christ's passion by faith and charity. . . . Even for these, its benefits are greater or less in proportion to their devotion."[57]

All these things should be explained to the faithful in such a way that in consequence they share actively in the celebration of the Mass by both their inner affections and the outward rites, in keeping with the principles laid down by the Constitution on the Liturgy,[58] which have been further specified by the Instruction *Inter Oecumenici* of 26 September 1964,[a] the Instruction *Musicam sacram* of 5 March 1967,[59] and the Instruction *Tres abhinc annos* of 4 May 1967.[b]

INFLUENCE OF THE EUCHARISTIC CELEBRATION ON THE DAILY LIFE OF THE FAITHFUL

1242   13. What the faithful have received through faith and the sacrament in the celebration of the eucharist they should hold to by the way they live. They should strive to live their whole lives joyfully in the strength of this heavenly food, as sharers in the death and resurrection of the Lord. After taking part in the Mass therefore all should be "eager to do good works, to please God, and to live rightly, devoted to the Church, putting into practice what they have learned and growing in devotion."[60] They will seek to fill the world with the Christian spirit and "in all things, even in the midst of human affairs," to become witnesses of Christ.[61]

For "no Christian community is ever built up unless it has its roots and center in the eucharistic liturgy, which, therefore, is the indispensable starting point for leading people to a sense of community."[62]

---

[54] See SC art. 28–29 [DOL 1 nos. 28–29].

[55] See SC art. 48, 106 [DOL 1 nos. 48, 106].

[56] See SC art. 55 [DOL 1 no. 55].

[57] ST 3a, 79.7 ad 2.

[58] See SC art. 26–32 [DOL 1 nos. 26–32].

[a] See DOL 23.

[59] See SCR, Instr. *Musicam sacram*, 5 March 1967 [DOL 508].

[b] See DOL 39.

[60] Hippolytus, *Traditio Apostolica* 21: B. Botte, ed., 58–59. See SC art. 9, 10 [DOL 1 nos. 9, 10]; AA no. 3 [DOL 16 no. 232]; AG no. 39 [DOL 17 no. 256]; PO no. 5 [DOL 18 no. 260].

[61] See GS no. 43: AAS 58 (1966) 1063; ConstDecrDecl 746.

[62] PO no. 6 [DOL 18 no. 261].

CATECHESIS FOR CHILDREN ON THE MASS

14. Those who take care of the religious instruction of children, especially parents, pastors, and teachers, should be careful, when introducing them gradually to the mystery of salvation,[63] to give catechesis on the Mass the importance it deserves. This catechesis, suited to children's age and capacities, should, by means of the main rites and prayers of the Mass, aim at conveying its meaning, including what relates to taking part in the Church's life.

1243

All these things should be kept in mind in the special situation of preparing children for first communion, so that it will be very clear to them that this communion is their complete incorporation into the Body of Christ.[64]

THE RITES AND PRAYERS AS STARTING POINTS FOR CATECHESIS ON THE MASS

15. The Council of Trent prescribes that pastors should frequently "either themselves or through others, elaborate on some part of what is read at Mass and, among other things, explain something of the mystery of this sacrament."[65]

1244

Pastors should therefore guide the faithful to a full understanding of this mystery of faith by suitable catechesis, which should take as its starting point the mysteries of the liturgical year and the rites and prayers that are part of the celebration. Pastors should do this by explaining the meaning of these rites and prayers, especially those of the great eucharistic prayer, and lead the people to grasp the mystery that the rites and prayers signify and accomplish.

PART II
CELEBRATION OF THE MEMORIAL OF THE LORD

I. SOME GENERAL NORMS ON STRUCTURING CELEBRATION OF THE MEMORIAL OF THE LORD IN THE COMMUNITY OF THE FAITHFUL

UNITY OF THE COMMUNITY SHOWN IN THE CELEBRATION

16. In virtue of baptism "there is neither Jew nor Greek, slave nor freeman, male nor female," but all are one in Christ Jesus (see Gal 3:28). Therefore the assembly that most fully manifests the nature of the Church in the eucharist is one in which the faithful of every class, age, and condition are joined together.

1245

Nevertheless the unity of the community, which is derived from the one bread in which all share (see 1 Cor 10:17), has a hierarchic structure. For this reason it requires that "each one, minister or layperson, who has an office to perform, should do all of, but only, those parts which pertain to that office by the nature of the rite and the principles of liturgy."[66]

The best example of this unity is found "in the full, active participation of all God's holy people . . . in the same eucharist, in a single prayer, at one altar at which the bishop presides, surrounded by his college of priests and by his ministers."[67]

AVOIDING THE SCATTERING AND DISTRACTING OF THE COMMUNITY

17. In liturgical celebrations, any breakup or distraction of the community must be avoided. Care must be taken, accordingly, not to have two liturgical celebrations

1246

---

[63]   See GE no. 2: AAS 58 (1966) 730–731; ConstDecrDecl 391–392.

[64]   See PO no. 5 [DOL 18 no. 260].

[65]   Council of Trent, sess. 22, *Decr. de Missa* cap. 8: Denz-Schön 1749.

[66]   SC art. 28 [DOL 1 no. 28].

[67]   SC art. 41 [DOL 1 no. 41]; see also LG no. 26 [DOL 4 no. 146].

going on in the same church at the same time, since this would distract the attention of the people.

Above all this must be stressed in regard to the celebration of the eucharist. Hence the scattering of the people that generally occurs when Masses are celebrated at the same time in the same church should be carefully avoided on Sundays and holydays of obligation when Mass is celebrated for the people.

The same rule should be applied as far as possible on other days as well. The best way of achieving this is concelebration, in conformity with the law, by priests who want to celebrate Mass at the same time.[68]

Similar precautions must be taken against the communal or choral recitation of the office, sermons, the administration of baptisms, and the celebration of marriages at the same time and in the same church as a scheduled Mass for the people is being celebrated.

SENSE OF THE LOCAL AND UNIVERSAL COMMUNITY FOSTERED

1247   18. In the celebration of the eucharist, a sense of community should be fostered so that all will feel united with their brothers and sisters in the communion of the local and universal Church and even in a certain way with all humanity. For in the sacrifice of the Mass Christ offers himself for the salvation of the whole world and the congregation of the faithful is the type and sign of the unity of the human family in Christ its Head.[69]

WELCOMING VISITORS INTO THE LOCAL CELEBRATION OF THE EUCHARIST

1248   19. The faithful who take part in the celebration of the eucharist outside their own parish should join in the form of the sacred services that the local community uses.

Pastors have the responsibility of providing suitable ways to assist the faithful from other regions to join with the local community. This should be of particular concern in the churches of large cities and in places where many of the faithful gather for vacations.

Where there are many visitors or expatriates of another language, pastors should provide them with the opportunity, at least occasionally, to participate in the Mass celebrated in the way customary for them. "Nevertheless steps should be taken enabling the faithful to say or to sing together in Latin those parts of the Ordinary of the Mass belonging to them."[70]

CAREFULNESS ABOUT THE MANNER OF CELEBRATING

1249   20. To ensure that the celebration is conducted properly and that the faithful take an active part, the ministers should not only fulfill their role correctly according to the norms of liturgical laws, but their very bearing should communicate a sense of the sacred.

The people have the right to be nourished by the word of God proclaimed and explained. Accordingly priests are to give a homily whenever it is prescribed or seems advisable; but they are also to see to it that anything that their functions require them and the ministers to pronounce is said or sung so distinctly that the people hear it clearly, grasp its meaning, and are thus drawn to respond and partici-pate willingly.[71] To this end ministers should be prepared through the right kind of training, especially in seminaries and religious houses.

---

[68] See no. 47 of this Instruction.

[69] See LG no. 3 [DOL 4 no. 137].

[70] SC art. 54 [DOL 1 no. 54].

[71] See SC art. 11 [DOL 1 no. 11].

CANON OF THE MASS

21. a. According to the provisions of the Instruction *Tres abhinc annos*, 4 May 1967,   1250
no. 10, in Masses celebrated with a congregation, even when not concelebrated, the
priest celebrant may say the canon aloud. In sung Masses he may sing those parts of
the canon that may be sung according to the *Rite of Concelebration*.[c]

b. In printing the words of consecration the custom of setting them in type
different from the general text should be maintained in order that they may stand
out more clearly.

RADIO AND TELEVISION BROADCASTS OF MASS

22. Where, according to the intent of the Constitution on the Liturgy art. 20,[d] the   1251
Mass is televised or broadcast, local Ordinaries should see that the prayer and
participation of the faithful in attendance are not disturbed; furthermore, the celebration should be marked with such care and dignity that it is a model of celebrating the sacred mysteries according to the laws of the liturgical reform.[72]

PHOTOGRAPHS DURING THE CELEBRATION OF THE EUCHARIST

23. Strict care should be taken to ensure that liturgical celebrations, especially of   1252
the Mass, are not disturbed by the practice of taking photographs. Where a reasonable cause for them exists, everything should be done with great restraint and
according to the norms established by the local Ordinary.

IMPORTANCE OF THE ARRANGEMENT OF CHURCHES FOR WELL-ORDERED
CELEBRATIONS

24. "The church, the house of prayer, must be well cared for and suited to prayer   1253
and liturgy. There the eucharist is celebrated and reserved and the faithful gather
for worship. There the presence of the Son of God, our Savior, offered on the altar
of sacrifice for us, is treasured and revered as the aid and solace of the faithful."[73]

Pastors should understand, therefore, that the becoming arrangement of the
place of worship contributes much to a right celebration and to the active participation of the faithful.

For this reason the rules and directives given in the Instruction *Inter Oecumenici*
(nos. 90–99)[e] should be followed regarding: the building of churches and their
adaptation to the reformed liturgy; the construction and appointment of altars; the
suitable placement of chairs for the celebrant and ministers; the provision of a
proper place for the proclamation of the readings; the arrangement of places for the
faithful and the choir.

Above all, the main altar should be so placed and constructed that it always
appears as a sign of Christ himself, as the place in which the sacred mysteries are
carried out, and as the focal point for the gathered faithful, which demands the
highest respect.

Care should be taken against destroying treasures of sacred art in the course of
remodeling churches. On the judgment of the local Ordinary, after consulting experts and, when applicable, with the consent of other concerned parties, the decision may be made to relocate some of these treasures in the interest of the liturgical
reform. In such a case this should be done with good sense and in such a way that

---

c   See DOL 39 no. 456.

d   See DOL 1 no. 20.

72   See SCR, Instr. MusSacr, 5 March 1967, nos. 6, 8, and 11 [DOL 508 nos. 4127, 4129, 4132].

73   PO no. 5 [DOL 18 no. 260].

e   See DOL 23 nos. 382–391.

even in their new locations they will be set up in a manner befitting and worthy of the works themselves.

Pastors should remember that the material and the design of vestments greatly contribute to the dignity of liturgical celebrations. Vestments should be designed "for a noble beauty rather than mere sumptuous display."[74]

II. CELEBRATIONS ON SUNDAYS AND WEEKDAYS

CELEBRATION OF THE EUCHARIST ON SUNDAY

1254   25. Whenever the community gathers to celebrate the eucharist, it shows forth the death and resurrection of the Lord in the hope of his glorious coming. But the Sunday assembly shows this best of all, for this is the day of the week on which the Lord rose from the dead and on which, from apostolic tradition, the paschal mystery is celebrated in the eucharist in a special way.[75]

In order that the faithful may willingly fulfill the precept to keep this day holy and may understand why the Church calls them together to celebrate the eucharist every Sunday, right from the beginning of their Christian formation it should be set before them and instilled into them that Sunday is the original holyday.[76] On this day above all, gathered as one, they are to hear the word of God and share in the paschal mystery.

Futhermore, all measures should be encouraged that are designed to make Sunday "a day of joy and freedom from work."[77]

CELEBRATION OF SUNDAY WITH THE BISHOP AND IN THE PARISH

1255   26. It is fitting that the sense of ecclesial community, fostered and expressed especially by the shared celebration of Mass on Sunday, should be carefully developed. This applies to assemblies with the bishop, above all in the cathedral church, and to the parish assembly, whose pastor takes the place of the bishop.[78]

It is of great advantage to promote that active participation of the whole people in the Sunday celebration which is expressed in singing. In fact as far as possible the sung form of celebration should be the first choice.[79]

Especially on Sundays and holydays the celebrations that take place in other churches and oratories must be coordinated with the celebrations in the parish church so that they contribute to the overall pastoral program. It is indeed advantageous that small, nonclerical, religious communities and other such communities, especially those that work in the parish, take part in the parish Mass on those days.

As to the hours and the number of Masses to be celebrated in parishes, the convenience of the parish community must be kept in mind and the number of Masses not so multiplied as to harm pastoral effectiveness. Such would be the case, for example, if because there were too many Masses, only small groups of the faithful would attend each one in churches that can hold many people; or if, also because of the number of Masses, the priests were to be so overwhelmed with work that they could fulfill their ministry only with great difficulty.

---

[74] SC art. 124 [DOL 1 no. 124].

[75] See SC art. 6 and 106 [DOL 1 nos. 6 and 106].

[76] See SC art. 106 [DOL 1 no. 106].

[77] SC art. 106 [DOL 1 no. 106].

[78] See SC art. 41–42 [DOL 1 nos. 41–42]; LG no. 28 [DOL 4 no. 148]; PO no. 5 [DOL 18 no. 260].

[79] SCR, Instr. MusSacr, 5 March 1967, nos. 16 and 27 [DOL 508 nos. 4137 and 4148].

MASSES WITH PARTICULAR GROUPS

27. So that the unity of the parish community may stand out in the eucharist on   1256
Sundays and holydays, Masses for such particular groups as parish societies should,
if possible, preferably be held on weekdays. If they cannot be transferred to weekdays, care should be taken to maintain the unity of the parish community by
incorporating these particular groups into the parish celebrations.

SUNDAY AND HOLYDAY MASSES ANTICIPATED ON THE PREVIOUS EVENING[R1]

28. Where indult of the Apostolic See permits fulfillment on the preceding Satur-   1257
day evening of the obligation to participate in the Sunday Mass, pastors should
carefully teach the faithful the meaning of this favor and should take steps to
prevent its lessening in any way the sense of what Sunday is. This concession is
meant to enable the faithful in today's conditions to celebrate more easily the day
of the Lord's resurrection.

All concessions and contrary customs notwithstanding, this Mass may be
celebrated only on Saturday evening, at hours to be determined by the local Ordinary.

On the Saturday evening, the Mass is to be celebrated as assigned in the
calendar for the Sunday and the homily and general intercessions are not to be
omitted.

All these points apply also to the celebration of Mass that, for the same reason,
is anywhere allowed on the evening before a holyday of obligation.

The evening Mass before Pentecost Sunday is the Mass of the Saturday vigil
with the *Credo*. Likewise the evening Mass before Christmas is the Mass of the vigil
celebrated in a festal way with white vestments and with the *Alleluia* and the
preface from the Mass of the Nativity. The evening Mass before Easter may not be
started before dusk or certainly not before sunset. This Mass is always the Mass of
the Easter Vigil, which by reason of its special significance in the liturgical year and
in the whole Christian life must be celebrated with the liturgical rites for this holy
night according to the rite for the Easter Vigil.

The faithful who begin to celebrate the Sunday or holyday of obligation on the
evening of the preceding day may go to holy communion even if they have already
done so that morning. Those who "receive communion during the Mass of the
Easter Vigil or during the Mass of the Lord's Nativity may receive again at the
second Mass of Easter and at one of the Day Masses of Christmas."[80] Likewise "the
faithful receiving communion at the chrism Mass on Holy Thursday may receive
again at the evening Mass on the same day," in accordance with the norm of the
Instruction *Tres abhinc annos*, 4 May 1967, no. 14.[f]

MASSES CELEBRATED ON WEEKDAYS

29. The faithful should be invited to take part in Mass often on weekdays as well,   1258
even daily.

This is especially recommended for those weekdays that should be celebrated
with particular attention, above all in Lent and Advent; also on lesser feasts of the
Lord and on certain feasts of the Blessed Virgin Mary or of the saints that are held
in special honor in the universal or the local Church.

[R1] See DOL 448.

[80] InterOec no. 60 [DOL 23 no. 352].

[f] See DOL 39 no. 460.

MASS AT GATHERINGS TO FOSTER THE CHRISTIAN LIFE

1259   30. It is very fitting that meetings or congresses aimed at fostering the Christian life or the apostolate or at promoting religious studies, as well as spiritual retreats of various kinds, should be planned in such a way that the eucharistic celebration is their high point.

III. COMMUNION OF THE FAITHFUL

COMMUNION OF THE FAITHFUL AT MASS

1260   31. The faithful share more fully in the celebration of the eucharist through sacramental communion. It is strongly recommended that they should receive it as a rule in the Mass itself and at that point in the celebration which is prescribed by the rite, that is, right after the communion of the priest celebrant.[81]

In order that the communion may stand out more clearly even through signs as a participation in the sacrifice actually being celebrated, steps should be taken that enable the faithful to receive hosts consecrated at that Mass.[82]

It is proper for the priest celebrant especially to be the minister of communion; nor should he continue the Mass until the communion of the faithful has been completed. Other priests or deacons may, if need be, assist the priest celebrant.[83]

COMMUNION UNDER BOTH KINDS

1261   32. Holy communion has a more complete form as a sign when it is received under both kinds. For in this manner of reception (without prejudice to the principles laid down by the Council of Trent,[84] that under each element Christ whole and entire and the true sacrament are received), a fuller light shines on the sign of the eucharistic banquet. Moreover there is a clearer expression of that will by which the new and everlasting covenant is ratified in the blood of the Lord and of the relationship of the eucharistic banquet to the eschatological banquet in the Father's kingdom (see Mt 26:27–29).

From now on, therefore, at the discretion of the bishops and preceded by the required catechesis, communion from the chalice is permitted in the following cases, granted already by earlier law[85] or granted now by this Instruction:

   1. to newly baptized adults in the Mass following their baptism; to confirmed adults in the Mass of their confirmation; to baptized persons who are received into the communion of the Church;

   2. to the spouses in the Mass of their wedding;

   3. to those ordained in the Mass of their ordination;

   4. to an abbess in the Mass of her blessing; to the consecrated in the Mass of their consecration to a life of virginity; to religious in the Mass of their first profession or of renewal of religious profession, provided they take or renew their vows within the Mass;

   5. to lay missionaries in the Mass at which they are publicly sent out on their mission and to others in the Mass in which they receive an ecclesiastical mission;

---

[81]   See SC art. 55 [DOL 1 no. 55].

[82]   See SC art. 55 [DOL 1 no. 55]. [SCR] *Missale Romanum*, Ritus servandus in celebratione Missae, 27 Jan. 1965, no. 7.

[83]   SCR, Rubricae Breviarii et Missalis Romani, 26 July 1960, no. 502: AAS 52 (1960) 680.

[84]   See Council of Trent, sess. 21, *Decr. de communione eucharistica* cap. 1–3: Denz-Schön 1726–29.

[85]   See [SCR], *Rite of Communion under Both Kinds*, 7 March 1965, no. 1 [DOL 268 no. 2105].

6. in the administration of viaticum, to the sick person and to all who are present when Mass is celebrated, with conformity to the requirements of the law, in the house of the sick person;

7. to the deacon, subdeacon, and ministers exercising their proper office in a pontifical or solemn Mass;[R2]

8. when there is a concelebration:

a. to all exercising a genuine liturgical ministry in that concelebration, even lay people, and to all seminarians present;

b. in their own churches, to all members of institutes professing the evangelical counsels and members of other societies in which the members dedicate themselves to God either through religious vows or oblation or promise, and also to all who reside in the house of the members of these institutes and societies;

9. to priests present at large celebrations and unable to celebrate or concelebrate;

10. to all groups making retreats, in a Mass celebrated especially for those actually participating; to all taking part in the meeting of some pastoral commission, at the Mass they celebrate in common;

11. to those listed under nos. 2 and 4, in the Mass of their jubilee;

12. to the godfather, godmother, parents, and spouse of baptized adults, and to the laypersons who have catechized them, in the Mass of initiation;

13. to the relatives, friends, and special benefactors taking part in the Mass of a newly ordained priest.

COMMUNION OUTSIDE MASS

33. a. The faithful are to be led to the practice of receiving communion in the actual eucharistic celebration.[86] But priests are not to refuse to give communion to those who request it for a just reason even outside Mass. This is permissible even in the afternoon hours with the permission of the local bishop, in keeping with the norm of the Motu Proprio *Pastorale munus* no. 4, or by permission of the supreme moderator of a religious institute, in keeping with the norm of the Rescript *Cum admotae* art. 1, no. 1.[87]

b. When communion is distributed outside Mass at the prescribed hours, a short celebration of the word of God may, if opportune, precede it, in accordance with the provisions of the Instruction *Inter Oecumenici* (nos. 37, 39).[g]

c. When Mass cannot be celebrated because there is no priest available and communion is distributed by a minister with the faculty to do this in virtue of an indult of the Apostolic See, the rite laid down by the competent authority is to be followed.[R3]

1262

[R2] Query: When may communion under both kinds be given to a priest who has already celebrated Mass? Reply: The Instruction on the worship of the mystery of the eucharist, no. 32, 7 grants communion under both kinds to a deacon and subdeacon "exercising their proper offices in a pontifical or solemn Mass." The reference is to true deacons or subdeacons. Therefore, if any priest fulfills the function of deacon or subdeacon and has already celebrated Mass or is going to, he cannot receive communion under both kinds. On the other hand, in the case of concelebration the conditions are more generous: "all exercising a genuine liturgical function" (no. 37, 8). In this case all who exercise a liturgical office may be allowed communion under both kinds, even if they are priests who have already celebrated Mass or are going to later: Not 4 (1968) 133, no. 109.

[86] See Pius XII, Encycl. *Mediator Dei*: AAS 39 (1947) 565–566.

[87] See Paul VI, Motu Proprio *Pastorale munus* [I] no. 4 [DOL 103 no. 715]. Secretariat of State, Pontifical Rescript *Cum admotae* I, no. 1 [DOL 141 no. 939].

[g] See DOL 23 nos. 329, 331.

[R3] Query: Have the formularies for use in communion outside Mass (e.g., the *Confiteor*, *This is the Lamb*

THE WAY OF RECEIVING COMMUNION

1263   34. a. In accordance with the custom of the Church, the faithful may receive
communion either kneeling or standing. One or the other practice is to be chosen
according to the norms laid down by the conference of bishops and in view of the
various circumstances, above all the arrangement of the churches and the number
of the communicants. The faithful should willingly follow the manner of reception
indicated by the pastors so that communion may truly be a sign of familial union
among all those who share in the same table of the Lord.

b. When the faithful communicate kneeling, no other sign of reverence
toward the most holy sacrament is required, because the kneeling itself expresses
adoration.

When they receive communion standing, it is strongly recommended that,
approaching in line, they make a sign of reverence before receiving the sacrament.
This should be done at a designated moment and place, so as not to interfere with
the coming and going of the other communicants.

SACRAMENT OF PENANCE AND COMMUNION

1264   35. The eucharist should also be proposed to the faithful "as a remedy that frees
us from our daily faults and preserves us from mortal sins."[88] They should also
receive an explanation of how to make use of the penitential parts of the Mass.

"Those wishing to receive communion should be reminded of the precept 'let
them examine themselves' (1 Cor 1:28). Ecclesiastical custom shows that this examination is necessary so that none who are conscious of having committed mortal sin,
no matter how contrite they believe themselves to be, should approach the holy
eucharist without first making a sacramental confession."[89] "In a case of necessity,
however, and when no confessor is available, a person should first make an act of
perfect contrition."[90]

The faithful are to be constantly encouraged in the practice of receiving the
sacrament of penance outside Mass, especially at the scheduled hours, so that the
administration of the sacrament may be unhurried and genuinely useful and that
people will not be impeded from active participation in the Mass. Daily or frequent
communicants should be instructed to go to confession regularly, depending on
their individual needs.

COMMUNION ON SPECIAL OCCASIONS

1265   36. It is most fitting that whenever the faithful are beginning a new state or a new
way of working in the vineyard of the Lord, they take part in the sacrifice through
sacramental communion, thereby dedicating themselves again to God and renewing
their covenant with him.

This may well be done, for example, by the assembly of the faithful when they
renew their baptismal vows at the Easter Vigil; by young people when they do the
same thing in the presence of the Church, in a manner in keeping with their age; by
the bride and groom when they are united by the sacrament of marriage; by those
who dedicate themselves to God when they pronounce their vows or other forms of

---

of God) been changed? Reply: No. In distributing communion outside Mass those formularies are to be
used which are given in the Order of Mass (nos. 133–135), the *Confiteor* and absolution included (Order of
Mass no. 3), until other provisions are made: Not 6 (1970) 264, no. 40.

[88]   Council of Trent, sess. 13, *Decr. de Eucharistia* cap. 2: Denz-Schön 1638; see also sess. 22, *Decr. de Missa*
cap. 1 and 2: Denz-Schön 1740 and 1743.

[89]   Council of Trent, sess. 13, *Decr. de Eucharistia* cap. 7: Denz-Schön 1740 and 1743.

[90]   CIC can. 859.

commitment; by the faithful when they are to devote themselves to apostolic service.

FREQUENT AND DAILY COMMUNION

37. Since "it is clear that the frequent or daily reception of the most blessed eucharist increases union with Christ, nurtures the spiritual life more richly, forms the soul in virtue, and gives the communicant a stronger pledge of eternal happiness, pastors, confessors, and preachers . . . will frequently and zealously exhort the Christian people to this devout and salutary practice."[91]

1266

PRIVATE PRAYER AFTER COMMUNION

38. On those who partake of the body and blood of Christ the gift of the Spirit is poured out abundantly like living water (see Jn 7:37–39), provided communion is received both sacramentally and spiritually, that is, in living faith that works through love.[92]

1267

But the union with Christ that is the reason for the sacrament itself is to be sought not only at the time of the eucharistic celebration but is also to be prolonged all during the Christian's life. This means that the faithful of Christ, dwelling constantly on the gift they have received, should live their daily lives in continual thanksgiving under the Holy Spirit's guidance and should produce more abundant fruits of charity.

In order to continue more surely in the thanksgiving that in the Mass is offered to God in an eminent way, those who have been nourished by communion should be encouraged to remain for some time in prayer.[93]

VIATICUM

39. Communion received as viaticum should be considered as a special sign of sharing in the mystery celebrated in the Mass, the mystery of the death of the Lord and his return to the Father. Viaticum seals the faithful in their passage from life with the pledge of the resurrection as they are strengthened by Christ's body.

1268

Therefore, the faithful who are in danger of death from any cause whatever are bound by precept to receive communion;[94] pastors must guard against delay in the administration of this sacrament and see to it rather that the faithful receive it while still in full possession of their faculties.[95]

Even if the faithful have already communicated on the same day, and then the danger of death arises, it is strongly recommended that they receive communion again.

COMMUNION OF THOSE UNABLE TO COME TO CHURCH

40. It is right for those prevented from being present at the celebration of the community eucharist to receive the eucharist often; in this way they will also realize that they are part of the eucharistic community, borne up by its charity.

1269

Pastors should take care that the sick and the elderly be given the opportunity, even if they are not gravely ill or in danger of death, to receive the eucharist often, even daily if possible, especially during the Easter season. They may receive communion at any hour of the day.

---

[91] SC Council, *Decr. de quotidiana Ss. Eucharistiae sumptione*, 20 Dec. 1905, no. 6: *Acta Sanctae Sedis* 38 (1905–06) 401ff. Pius XII, Encycl. *Mediator Dei*: AAS 39 (1947) 565.

[92] See Council of Trent, sess. 13, *Decr. de Eucharistia* cap. 8: Denz-Schön 1648.

[93] See Pius XII, Encycl. *Mediator Dei*: AAS 39 (1947) 566.

[94] See CIC can. 864, 1.

[95] See ibid. can. 865.

COMMUNION UNDER THE FORM OF WINE ALONE

1270   41. In case of necessity and at the discretion of the bishop, it is permissible for the eucharist to be given under the form of wine alone to those who are unable to receive it under the form of bread.

In this case the celebration of Mass in the presence of the sick person is permissible, at the discretion of the local Ordinary.

If, however, Mass is not celebrated in the presence of the sick person, the blood of the Lord should be preserved in a properly covered chalice and placed in the tabernacle after Mass; it should not be carried to the sick person unless it is enclosed in a container that prevents any danger of spilling. In administering the sacrament, the method best suited to the individual case should be chosen from among those indicated in the rites for use in distributing communion under both kinds. If, after communion has been given, some of the precious blood remains, the minister is to consume it; he is also to see to the required ablutions.

IV. CELEBRATION OF THE EUCHARIST IN THE LIFE AND MINISTRY OF THE BISHOP AND PRIEST

CELEBRATION OF THE EUCHARIST IN THE LIFE AND MINISTRY OF THE BISHOP

1271   42. The celebration of the eucharist expresses in a special way the public and social nature of the liturgical celebrations of the Church, "which is the sacrament of unity, namely, the holy people united and ordered under their bishops."[96]

Hence "marked with the fullness of the sacrament of orders, a bishop is the steward of the grace of the supreme priesthood, especially in the eucharist, which he offers or causes to be offered. . . . Every lawful celebration of the eucharist is regulated by the bishop, to whom is committed the office of offering the worship of Christian religion to the divine majesty and of administering it in accordance with the Lord's commandments and the Church's laws, as further defined by his particular judgment for his diocese."[97] The celebration of the eucharist at which the bishop presides, surrounded by his college of priests and ministers, with the whole people of God actively taking part, is the preeminent manifestation of the hierarchically constituted Church.[98]

APPROPRIATENESS OF THE PARTICIPATION OF PRIESTS IN THE EUCHARIST, EXERCISING THEIR PROPER OFFICE

1272   43. In the celebration of the eucharist, priests also are deputed, by reason of a special sacrament, namely, orders, to fulfill the office proper to them. For they too "as ministers of the sacred, especially in the sacrifice of the Mass, . . . represent the person of Christ in a particular way."[99] Because of the sign value, it is therefore right that they take part in the eucharist by exercising the order proper to them,[100] that is, by celebrating or concelebrating the Mass and not simply by receiving communion like the laity.

DAILY CELEBRATION OF MASS

1273   44. "In the mystery of the eucharistic sacrifice, the fulfillment of the priest's chief office, the work of redemption is continually actual. Hence, daily celebration is

---

[96]   SC art. 26 [DOL 1 no. 26].

[97]   LG no. 26 [DOL 4 no. 146].

[98]   See SC art. 41 [DOL 1 no. 41].

[99]   PO no. 13 [DOL 18 no. 265]; see also LG no. 28 [DOL 4 no. 147].

[100]   See SC no. 28 [DOL 1 no. 28].

urged upon priests; it remains the act of Christ and the Church even when the faithful cannot attend";[101] in it the priest always acts for the salvation of the people.

FAITHFUL OBSERVANCE OF THE LAWS OF THE CHURCH IN CELEBRATING MASS

45. Especially in the celebration of the eucharist, only the supreme authority of the Church and, according to the norm of law, the bishops and the conferences of bishops, no one else, not even a priest, may, on his own initiative add, leave out, or change anything in the liturgy.[102] Therefore, priests should be intent on presiding over the celebration of the eucharist in such a way that the faithful know that they are participating not in a rite decided on by private authority,[103] but in the public worship of the Church, the direction of which has been entrusted by Christ to the apostles and their successors.

    1274

PRIORITY OF PASTORAL EFFECTIVENESS IN THE CHOICE OF THE DIFFERENT FORMS OF CELEBRATION

46. "When the liturgy is celebrated, something more is required than the mere observance of the laws governing valid and lawful celebration; it is also their duty to ensure that the faithful take part fully aware of what they are doing, actively engaged in the rite, and enriched by its effect."[104] Hence, from among the forms of celebration permitted by law priests should take care to choose those that in each situation seem best suited to the needs or well-being of the faithful and to their taking part actively.

    1275

CONCELEBRATION

47. Concelebration of the eucharist aptly expresses the unity of the sacrifice and the priesthood; whenever the faithful take an active part, the unity of the people of God stands out in a special way,[105] particularly if the bishop presides.[106]

    1276

Concelebration also symbolizes and strengthens the fraternal bond between priests, because "by virtue of the ordination to the priesthood that they share all are linked together in a close bond of brotherhood."[107]

Unless the needs of the faithful (which always must be regarded with a deep pastoral concern) rule it out, then, and without prejudice to the option of every priest to celebrate Mass individually, this excellent way for priests to celebrate Mass is preferable in the case of communities of priests, their periodic meetings, or in other similar circumstances. Those who live in community or serve the same church should gladly welcome visiting priests to concelebrate with them.

The authorized superiors should therefore facilitate and encourage concelebration whenever pastoral needs or another reasonable cause does not demand otherwise.

The faculty to concelebrate also applies to the principal Masses in churches and public and semipublic oratories of seminaries, colleges, and ecclesiastical institutions, as well as in those of religious orders and societies of common life without vows. Where there are a great many priests, the authorized superior can allow

---

101 PO no. 13 [DOL 18 no. 265]. See also Paul VI, Encycl. *Mysterium fidei* [DOL 176 no. 1176].

102 See SC art. 22 [DOL 1 no. 22].

103 See ST 2a2ae, 93, 1.

104 SC art. 11; also art. 48 [DOL 1 no. 11; also no. 48].

105 See SC art. 57 [DOL 1 no. 57]. SCR, Decr. generale *Ecclesiae semper*, 7 March 1965 [DOL 222].

106 See SC art. 41 [DOL 1 no. 41]; LG no. 28 [DOL 4 no. 147]; PO no. 7 [DOL 18 no. 262].

107 LG no. 28: AAS 57 (1965) 35; ConstDecrDecl 148; see also PO no. 8 [DOL 18 no. 263].

several concelebrations to take place on the same day, but at different times or in different places of worship.

BAKING OF THE BREAD FOR CONCELEBRATION

1277   48. If a large host is baked for concelebration, as permitted in the *Rite of Concelebration* no. 17,[h] care must be taken that, in keeping with traditional usage, it is of a form and appearance worthy of the eucharistic mystery.

PART III
WORSHIP OF THE EUCHARIST AS A PERMANENT SACRAMENT

I. REASONS FOR RESERVING THE EUCHARIST; PRAYER IN THE PRESENCE OF THE BLESSED SACRAMENT

REASONS FOR RESERVING THE EUCHARIST OUTSIDE MASS

1278   49. "It is pertinent to recall that the primary and original purpose of reserving the sacred elements in church outside Mass is the administration of viaticum; secondary ends are the distribution of communion outside Mass and the adoration of our Lord Jesus Christ hidden beneath these same elements."[108] For "the reservation of the sacred elements for the sick . . . led to the praiseworthy custom of adoring the heavenly food that is reserved in churches. This worship of adoration has a sound and firm foundation,"[109] especially since faith in the Lord's real presence has as its natural consequence the outward and public manifestation of that belief.

PRAYER IN THE PRESENCE OF THE BLESSED SACRAMENT

1279   50. When the faithful adore Christ present in the sacrament, they should remember that this presence derives from the sacrifice and has as its purpose both sacramental and spiritual communion.

Therefore, the devotion prompting the faithful to visit the blessed sacrament draws them into an ever deeper share in the paschal mystery and leads them to respond gratefully to the gift of him who through his humanity constantly pours divine life into the members of his Body.[110] Abiding with Christ the Lord, they enjoy his intimate friendship and pour out their hearts before him for themselves and for those dear to them and they pray for the peace and salvation of the world. Offering their entire lives with Christ to the Father in the Holy Spirit, they derive from this sublime colloquy an increase of faith, hope, and charity. Thus they foster those right dispositions that enable them with due devotion to celebrate the memorial of the Lord and receive frequently the bread given us by the Father.

The faithful should therefore strive to worship Christ the Lord in the blessed sacrament in a manner fitting in with their own way of life. Pastors should by example show the way and by word encourage their people.[111]

---

h   See DOL 223 no. 1810.

108   SC Sacraments, Instr. *Quam plurimum* 1 Oct. 1949: AAS 41 (1949) 509–510. See also Council of Trent, sess. 13, *Decr. de Eucharistia* cap. 6; Denz-Schön 1645. St. Pius X, Decr. *Sacra Tridentina Synodus*, 20 Dec. 1905: Denz-Schön 3375.

109   Pius XII, Encycl. *Mediator Dei*: AAS 39 (1947) 569.

110   See PO no. 5 [DOL 18 no. 260].

111   See PO no. 18 [DOL 18 no. 267].

CHURCHES READILY ACCESSIBLE TO THE FAITHFUL

51. Pastors should see to it that all churches and public oratories where the blessed   1280
sacrament is reserved are open at least several hours in the morning and evening so
that the faithful may easily pray before the blessed sacrament.

II. PLACE FOR EUCHARISTIC RESERVATION

THE TABERNACLE

52. Where the eucharist is allowed to be reserved in keeping with the provisions of   1281
law, only one altar or location in the same church may be the permanent, that is,
regular place of reservation.[112] As a general rule, therefore, there is to be but one
tabernacle in each church and it is to be solid and absolutely secure.[113,R4]

CHAPEL OF RESERVATION

53. The place in a church or oratory where the eucharist is reserved in a tabernacle   1282
should be truly a place of honor. It should also be suited to private prayer so that

---

[112] See CIC can. 1268, § 1.

[113] See SCR, Instr. InterOec, 26 Sept. 1964, no. 95 [DOL 23 no. 387]. SC Sacraments, Instr. *Nullo
umquam tempore*, 28 May 1938, no. 4: AAS 30 (1938) 199–200.

[R4] Query: In the rearrangement of churches according to the new requirements of the reform of the
liturgy tabernacles of glass have been suggested. Their function would be to permit the faithful to see,
through the glass, the vessels containing the eucharistic elements. Are such tabernacles acceptable?
    The idea of making tabernacles of glass can find some justification, both theoretical and historical.
Over the centuries the manner of reserving the eucharistic elements has taken various forms. Nevertheless
it seems that the proposal would amount to a return to medieval forms of eucharistic devotion that moved
ecclesiastical authority to forbid "sacrament houses" and tabernacles with a grating.
    Furthermore it would give the impression of having a kind of permanent exposition of the blessed
sacrament in the church and that is unacceptable. Accordingly:
    1. The documents of the reform instill a careful balance and a proportionate emphasis regarding
the different elements that bring out the character of the church as a house of prayer and of community:
place of the congregation, the altar, the lectern, the celebrant's chair, the place of eucharistic reservation.
        In the case proposed, the place of reservation would have an excessive prominence, especially if
it were located within the sanctuary, and would create some inconvenience in the celebration of the
liturgical rites.
        Eucharisticum mysterium in fact states: "[Text quoted no. 55]." Thus celebration of Mass in the
presence of the exposed blessed sacrament is forbidden. The difficulties indicated in the Instruction would
not be avoided if the celebration of Mass were to take place in proximity to a tabernacle of glass.
    2. Among the forms of eucharistic devotion recognized and endorsed by the Church, there are
certain ones that serve to summon the community to an awareness of "the sublime presence of Christ" in
the eucharist and invite it "to inner communion with him" (*Eucharisticum mysterium* no. 60). Adoration
during prolonged or short exposition of the blessed sacrament, in the traditional form of the forty hours or
in others more suited to the present day, is an excellent opportunity to lead the faithful to meditation and
prayer that are inspired by the abiding sacrament. If the sacrament were exposed continuously, there
would be a lessening of the value of these occasions as reminders of their proper place in the spiritual life
and of their character as high points for reflection on the eucharist.
        It seems more spiritually advantageous and more in keeping with the specific character of each
liturgical service to reserve exposition of the blessed sacrament for set occasions. Otherwise there could be
a danger, after the initial fervor aroused by the novelty of the situation, of minimizing the importance of
the real presence, of reducing it to the level of other signs in the church — the images, the ambry, the
baptismal font, etc.
        This is why the Church regulates the exposition of the blessed sacrament with appropriate
legislation; continuous exposition, such as would happen with a glass tabernacle, would in some way go
counter to this.
    3. All that has been said does not intend to assert that glass or crystal is altogether excluded as
material suitable for constructing the tabernacle. The tabernacle may be made out of these materials,
provided they are "solid and unbreakable," the tabernacle is then covered with a veil, and the showing of
the blessed sacrament is reserved to particular times, that is, to the times and manners envisioned in the
present legislation regarding short or prolonged exposition (see *Eucharisticum mysterium* nos. 60–66): Not 7
(1971) 414–415 (Italian).

the faithful may readily and to their advantage continue to honor the Lord in this sacrament by private worship.[114] Therefore, it is recommended that as far as possible the tabernacle be placed in a chapel set apart from the main body of the church, especially in churches where there frequently are marriages and funerals and in places that, because of their artistic or historical treasures, are visited by many people.

TABERNACLE IN THE MIDDLE OF ALTAR OR IN ANOTHER PART OF THE CHURCH

1283   54. "The eucharist is to be reserved in a solid and secure tabernacle, placed in the middle of the main altar or on a minor, but truly worthy altar, or else, depending on lawful custom and in particular cases approved by the local Ordinary, in another, special, and properly adorned part of the church.

"It is also lawful to celebrate Mass facing the people even on an altar where there is a small but becoming tabernacle."[115]

TABERNACLE ON AN ALTAR WHERE MASS IS CELEBRATED WITH A CONGREGATION

1284   55. In the celebration of Mass the principal modes of Christ's presence to his Church[116] emerge clearly one after the other: first he is seen to be present in the assembly of the faithful gathered in his name; then in his word, with the reading and explanation of Scripture; also in the person of the minister; finally, in a singular way under the eucharistic elements. Consequently, on the grounds of the sign value, it is more in keeping with the nature of the celebration that, through reservation of the sacrament in the tabernacle, Christ not be present eucharistically from the beginning on the altar where Mass is celebrated. That presence is the effect of the consecration and should appear as such.

THE TABERNACLE IN THE CONSTRUCTION OF NEW CHURCHES AND IN THE REMODELING OF EXISTING CHURCHES AND ALTARS

1285   56. It is fitting that the principles stated in nos. 52 and 54 be taken into account in the building of new churches.

Remodeling of already existing churches and altars must be carried out in exact compliance with no. 24 of this Instruction.

MEANS OF INDICATING THE PRESENCE OF BLESSED SACRAMENT IN THE TABERNACLE

1286   57. Care should be taken that the faithful be made aware of the presence of the blessed sacrament in the tabernacle by the use of a veil or some other effective means prescribed by the competent authority.

According to the traditional practice, a lamp should burn continuously near the tabernacle as a sign of the honor shown to the Lord.[117]

III. EUCHARISTIC DEVOTIONS

1287   58. Devotion, both private and public, toward the sacrament of the altar even outside Mass that conforms to the norms laid down by lawful authority and in the present Instruction is strongly advocated by the Church, since the eucharistic sacrifice is the source and summit of the whole Christian life.[118]

---

[114]   See PO no. 18 [DOL 18 no. 267]. Paul VI, Encycl. *Mysterium fidei* [DOL 176 no. 1210].

[115]   SCR, Instr. InterOec no. 95 [DOL 23 no. 387].

[116]   See no. 9 of this Instruction.

[117]   See CIC can. 1271.

[118]   See LG no. 11 [DOL 4 no. 141].

In structuring these devotional exercises, account should be taken of the norms determined by Vatican Council II concerning the relationship to be observed between the liturgy and other, nonliturgical sacred services. Particular attention should be paid to this one: "These devotions should be so fashioned that they harmonize with the liturgical seasons, accord with the liturgy, are in some way derived from it, and lead the people to it, since, in fact, the liturgy by its very nature far surpasses any of them."[119]

IV. EUCHARISTIC PROCESSIONS

59. In processions in which the eucharist is carried through the streets solemnly with singing, especially on the feast of Corpus Christi, the Christian people give public witness to their faith and to their devotion toward this sacrament.   1288

However, it is for the local Ordinary to decide on both the advisability of such processions in today's conditions and on a place and plan for them that will ensure their being carried out with decorum and without any loss of reverence toward this sacrament.

V. EXPOSITION OF THE BLESSED SACRAMENT

60. Exposition of the blessed sacrament, either in a ciborium or a monstrance, draws the faithful to an awareness of the sublime presence of Christ and invites them to inner communion with him. Therefore, it is a strong encouragement toward the worship owed to Christ in spirit and in truth.   1289

In such exposition care must be taken that the signs of it bring out the meaning of eucharistic worship in its correlation with the Mass. This end is served in the case of solemn and prolonged exposition by having it take place at the end of the Mass in which the host to be exposed for adoration has been consecrated. The Mass itself ends with the *Benedicamus Domino*, without the blessing. In the surroundings of exposition,[120] anything must be carefully avoided that could in any way obscure Christ's intention of instituting the holy eucharist above all in order to be near us to feed, to heal, and to comfort us.[121]

PROHIBITION OF MASS BEFORE THE EXPOSED BLESSED SACRAMENT

61. The celebration of Mass is prohibited within the body of the church during exposition of the blessed sacrament, all contrary concessions and traditions hitherto in force, even those worthy of special mention, notwithstanding.   1290

For, in addition to the reasons given in no. 55 of this Instruction, the celebration of the eucharistic mystery includes in a higher way that inner communion to which exposition is meant to lead the faithful and does not need the support of exposition.

If exposition of the blessed sacrament goes on for a day or for several successive days, it should be interrupted during the celebration of Mass, unless it is celebrated in a chapel separate from the area of exposition and at least some of the faithful remain in adoration.

In those places where a break with long-established, contrary custom would upset the faithful, the local Ordinary should fix a sufficient but not overly long period for instructing them before the present norm takes effect.

---

[119]   SC art. 13 [DOL 1 no. 13].

[120]   See no. 62 of this Instruction.

[121]   See St. Pius X, Decr. *Sacra Tridentina Synodus*, 20 Dec. 1905: Denz-Schön 3375.

ARRANGEMENT OF THE RITE OF EXPOSITION

1291   62. For brief exposition, the ciborium or monstrance should be placed on the altar table; for a longer exposition a throne can be used and set in a prominent, but not too elevated or distant position.[R5]

During the exposition everything should be so arranged that the faithful can devote themselves attentively in prayer to Christ the Lord.

To foster intimate prayer, readings from sacred Scripture, together with a homily or brief inspirational words that lead to a better understanding of the eucharistic mystery, are permitted. It is proper for the people to respond to the word of God with singing. There should also be suitable intervals of silence.[R6] At the end of the exposition, benediction is given.[R7]

When the vernacular is used, another eucharistic hymn, at the discretion of the conference of bishops, may be substituted for the *Tantum ergo* as the hymn to be sung before the benediction.

[R5]   Query: Does the bishop possess the faculty to grant sisters the right to expose the blessed sacrament in the monstrance for adoration? Reply: No. This faculty belongs to the SCDW: Not 6 (1970) 104, no. 32. [See, however, *Holy Communion and Worship of the Eucharist outside Mass* no. 91 (DOL 279 no. 2217).]

[R6]   1. Query: May prayers in honor of the Blessed Virgin Mary or the saints be allowed during exposition of the blessed sacrament? Reply: Until now in communities or particular groups there was a custom of having, with the blessed sacrament exposed, prayers in honor of the Blessed Virgin Mary, e.g., the rosary, or prayers to the saints, e.g., the Litany of the Saints, a novena in preparation for a saint's feast, etc.
    The question now is whether this is in keeping with the letter and spirit of the Instruction on the worship of the eucharistic mystery.
    On the one hand, notice that there is no explicit prohibition in the text of the Instruction.
    On the other, however, it is preferable to take in a restrictive sense the words, "During the exposition everything should be so arranged that the faithful can devote themselves attentively in prayer to Christ the Lord," so that the words amount to ". . .to Christ the Lord *alone*."
    The small word *alone*, often applied by commentators here, aptly conveys the intent of the law, even though it does not appear in the text of the Instruction. The people's adoration together before the exposed blessed sacrament achieves its purpose when it directs their minds and prayer to the eucharistic mystery, through silence, readings — especially from Scripture, singing, and petitions.
    Other devotions, although laudable and commendable, take the attention away to a different object and should therefore be assigned to another time, either before or after exposition and benediction of the blessed sacrament.
    Even the rosary must be classified as a Marian prayer, not as addressed to Christ. Nor is the prescribed meditation on the mysteries of Christ during the saying of the Hail Mary a counterargument. For the essential part of the rosary consists in the repeated prayer addressed to the Blessed Virgin. In fact this devotion would in some way require a reevaluation so that there may be closer concord between the voice and mind of the one praying: Not 4 (1968) 133–134, no. 110.
    2. Query: May evening prayer be sung in the presence of the exposed blessed sacrament? Reply: In some places, benediction immediately follows evening prayer, especially on Sundays. Since publication of the Instruction the arrangement sometimes is this: first there is exposition, then evening prayer is sung, and at the end there is benediction. This does not seem to be in accord with what has just been said. A better arrangement is possible.
    Benediction must not take on the appearance of being a conclusion to evening prayer. As a liturgical service in its own right, inviting the faithful to worship God, it can have a more advantageous place on Sunday. Once evening prayer has been sung, there can be exposition and, after a period of silence, benediction. If there has been a reading from Scripture and a homily during evening prayer, it certainly seems that there should not be a repetition.
    Depending on the differing circumstances of place and people, it would seem better to leave some interval of time between the two services: Not 4 (1968) 134, no 111.

[R7]   Query: To give benediction with the pyx [or ciborium] must the priest cover it with a humeral veil? Reply: By time-honored and accepted custom the priest, as a sign of reverence, takes the pyx or monstrance with hands covered by a humeral veil. This procedure does not mean *covering* the pyx; it rather should be shown to the faithful while the benediction is given, even as is the case when a monstrance is used. It therefore seems more in conformity with the true meaning of what is being done to use a humeral veil in picking up the pyx, but not to cover it: Not 5 (1969) 327, no. 10.

ANNUAL SOLEMN EXPOSITION

63. In churches where the eucharist is regularly reserved, there may be an annual,   1292
solemn exposition of the blessed sacrament for an extended period of time, even if
not strictly continuous, so that the local community may meditate on this mystery
more deeply and adore.

Exposition of this kind may take place only if the participation of a reasonable
number of the faithful is ensured, the local Ordinary consents, and the established
norms are followed.

PROLONGED EXPOSITION

64. For any serious and general need, the local Ordinary may order prayer before   1293
the blessed sacrament exposed over a longer period (which may be strictly continuous) in those churches to which the faithful come in large numbers.

INTERRUPTION OF EXPOSITION

65. Where there cannot be uninterrupted exposition, because there is not a   1294
sufficient number of worshipers, it is permissible to replace the blessed sacrament in
the tabernacle at fixed hours that are announced ahead of time. But this may not be
done more than twice a day, for example, at midday and at night.[R8]

This reposition can be simple and without singing: the priest vested in surplice
and stole, after a brief adoration of the blessed sacrament, places it in the tabernacle. At a set time, the exposition is resumed in a similar way, following which the
priest, after a brief period of adoration, leaves.

EXPOSITION FOR SHORT PERIODS

66. Even short expositions of the blessed sacrament, conducted in accord with the   1295
norms of the law, must be so arranged that before the benediction reasonable time
is provided for readings of the word of God, hymns, prayers, and silent prayer, as
circumstances permit.

Local Ordinaries will make certain that these expositions of the blessed sacrament are always and everywhere marked with proper reverance.

Exposition merely for the purpose of giving benediction after Mass is prohibited.

[R8] 1. Query: Must a veil [umbraculum] be placed in front of the monstrance during sermons? Reply:
Sermons in the presence of the exposed blessed sacrament are forbidden. "A homily or brief inspirational
words" mentioned in the Instruction [no. 62] is not a sermon, but a short explanation of the texts of the
readings "that leads to a better understanding of the eucharistic mystery" [ibid]. No veil is to be placed in
front of the monstrance during the homily or exhortation, any more than during the readings from
Scripture: Not 4 (1968) 135, no. 112.
        2. Query: In the case of prolonged exposition, is it lawful to put the blessed sacrament back in the
tabernacle more than twice in the day? Reply: The problem arises from the fact that in modern conditions
it is difficult to have a large number of people present continuously for several hours; it is only possible at
certain times, e.g., early in the morning, at noonday, and in the evening. The purpose of the law is to avoid
solemn exposition, with perhaps, some external display, but with only a few people present for adoration.
The better course seems to be to plan the times for community adoration as far as possible at fixed hours
at which to bring together a great number of adorers, rather than to spread out the numbers with small
groups over the different hours of the day. Then it is permissible to put the blessed sacrament back in the
tabernacle for the *night* and twice during the day, in such a way that it remains on the altar when there is a
large attendance of the faithful. A more frequent reposition, however, must be avoided. But, in religious
communities that by their constitutions have daily adoration, there seems to be nothing contrary to the
law to have a few members take turns in continuing the adoration before the blessed sacrament outside
the times of community adoration: Not 4 (1968) 135, no. 113.

VI. EUCHARISTIC CONGRESSES

1296   67. In eucharistic congresses, the faithful seek to understand this holy mystery more deeply through a consideration of its various aspects (see no. 3 of this Instruction). Their celebration of the eucharist should, moreover, be in keeping with the norms of Vatican Council II and they should offer their worship through private prayers and devotions, especially in solemn processions, in such a way that all these forms of devotion have their culmination in the solemn celebration of Mass.

All during a eucharistic congress of at least an entire region, it is proper to designate some churches for continuous adoration.

In the audience granted 13 April 1967 to Cardinal Arcadius M. Larraona, Prefect of this Congregation, Pope Paul VI by his authority approved and confirmed this Instruction and ordered it to be published, fixing the feast of the Assumption of the Blessed Virgin Mary, 15 August 1967, as its effective date.

▶   168.   PAUL VI, Solemn Profession of Faith, 30 June 1968:

nos. 24–26:   The eucharist [nos. 1096–98].

180. PAUL VI, **Epistle** *Inclitae Columbiae* to Cardinal G. Lercaro, papal legate to the 39th International Eucharistic Congress at Bogotá (18–25 August 1968), 16 July 1968: AAS 60 (1968) 523–525 (excerpts).

1297   [. . .] The sublimity of the eucharistic mystery is such that the mind falls completely short in studying and contemplating it and human eloquence is altogether unequal to the task of extolling its greatness. The days at Bogotá devoted to the sacrament of the altar will place it before our eyes as the bond of charity, and it will be the center of intense thought and ardent devotion. It is our thought that this is an event pertinent to the needs of the present and promising welcome results for the future.

Even though all the Church's sacraments bear in their very nature a social quality, this is present in the highest degree in the eucharist. The eucharist, in a singular way, is indeed the nourishment for personal spiritual life, but it is also preeminent in its social character and effectiveness.

The reason is that the eucharist is the sacrament of charity, the bond of perfection, the living fountain of an abundant life. What the heart is in the human body, what the sacred heart is in Christ's body, the eucharist by its analogous, life-giving function is in the Church, the Body of Christ. The blessed sacrament is the sun of the Church, the source of its life, suffusing all with its rays, casting its light on all, the seen and the unseen, joining time with eternity. "At the Last Supper, on the night when he was betrayed, our Savior instituted the eucharistic sacrifice of his body and blood. He did this in order to perpetuate the sacrifice of the cross throughout the centuries until he should come again and thereby to entrust to his beloved Bride, the Church, a memorial of his death and resurrection: a sacrament of love, a sign of unity, a bond of charity, a paschal banquet in which Christ is eaten, the heart filled with grace, and a pledge of future glory given to us."[4][. . .]

▶   169.   SC CLERGY, *General Catechetical Directory*, 11 April 1971:

---

⁴   SC art. 47 [DOL 1 no. 47].

no. 58:   The eucharist, center of the entire sacramental life
                           [no. 1105].

181. PAUL VI, **Address** to a general audience, on the feast of Corpus Christi, 7 June 1971: Not 7 (1971) 244–246 (Italian; excerpt).

Tomorrow is "Corpus Domini," the feast dedicated to the eucharist. [. . .]   1298

The lateness of the establishment of this feast in relation to those of the early centuries should not surprise us, nor should the spread of eucharistic worship. These facts serve to witness the progressive consciousness that the Church acquires of its own inner treasures of grace and truth and to the growing charity with which it responds to the great and sublime divine gift. The Church has always had faith in Christ's presence under the sacramental elements even apart from and outside the celebration of the eucharistic sacrifice. [. . .] This is one of the proofs that in the Church's liturgy content comes before rite, the *res* before the *sacramentum*. For this reason, also, we must honor the eucharist for the reality it presents to us even more than for the historical and ritual forms of its celebration. Eucharistic devotion extends beyond the brief moment of celebrating the sacrificial meal of the Lord. He remains under the sacramental appearances and his remaining not only justifies but demands such proper forms of worship as communion outside Mass when it is not possible during it and the solemn procession and rites belonging to tomorrow's feast.

Approaching the eucharist requires preparation. Think only of what holy communion means, of how urgently we are invited to it by the Church and by the very nature of the sacrament. The presence of God has always struck fear in people rather than attracting them (see Lk 5:8); but the eucharist, under its form as food and drink, elicits an immediate attraction rather than fear. Through its nature, so familiar, simple, and inviting, the eucharist presents itself to us and says, as it were: "Come to me all of you. . ." (see Mt 11:28; *Imitation of Christ* 4, 1). But this indescribable meeting of our soul with Christ, living and real, cannot take place without deep reverence, without even an attempt at appreciation, without bowing to the will of Jesus who awaits and invites us. What does the Lord want of us when we draw near to the eucharist?

On this the masters of the spiritual life have pointed out so many beautiful   1299
things. Let us at this time choose three elements that we must never forget.

The first is faith. It is to the mystery of faith that we dare to draw near. We must never forget faith, that is, the active power of the word of God, witnessed by the Church, as we enter within the sphere of reality that the word of God and of Christ reveal to us as present and active. Let us repeat with the humble person in the gospel: "Lord I believe, help my unbelief" (Mk 9:23). What psychological insight, what an outburst of the spirit these words provide for us! And that is what Christ asks of those who seek him out as the food for eternal life. He teaches: "This is the work of God [that you must do]: to believe in him whom God has sent" (Jn 6:29).

Second, there is the examination of conscience. In the midst of his eucharistic   1300
catechesis to the Corinthians, St. Paul says sternly: "Wherefore those who eat this bread and drink this cup of the Lord unworthily will be guilty of the body and blood of the Lord. But let all examine themselves and so let them eat of that bread and drink of that cup. For those who eat and drink unworthily eat and drink

damnation to themselves, not discerning the Lord's body" (1 Cor 11:27–29). Before approaching Christ's embrace it is necessary to have a pure soul, to have regained grace through penance, the sacrament of restoration. There are some today who try to release the faithful from this indispensable condition; but are those who exempt themselves from it really "the faithful"?

1301   Finally, there is a third preparation, also imposed by Christ. He warns us in the Sermon on the Mount: "Therefore, if you bring your gift to the altar and remember there that your brother has something against you, leave your gift at the altar and . . . first be reconciled to your brother and then come and offer your gift" (Mt 5: 23–24). That means that we cannot enter into communion with God, with Christ, if we are not in communion with one another. A preparation by familial charity is needed if we wish to enjoy the sacrament of charity and of unity, the eucharist. This too is a great lesson. What a change of heart our frequent communion calls for! What practical and social results our religious devotion can and must bring about: peace, pardon, concord, love for each other, goodness! How noble is the human setting that should surround the superhuman act of communion with Christ! Truths we know well, but what truths they are! We repeat the words of Jesus, in conclusion: "If you know these things, you are blessed if you do them" (Jn 13:17). [. . .]

182. PAUL VI, **Address** to a special audience for members of the Permanent Council on International Eucharistic Congresses, on the Melbourne Eucharistic Congress, "Eucharistic worship in the Church's life," 1 March 1972: AAS 64 (1972) 287–292; Not 8 (1972) 105–108 (Italian; excerpt).

1302   [. . .] The coming International Eucharistic Congress [. . .] will be a summons to honor the mandate of charity, as the motto of the Congress reminds us: "Love each other as I have loved you."[1] The eucharist, indeed, exists as the font, the source, and the "bond of charity."[2] This extends to practical applications in the sphere of human, social living. The Congress will be an invitation to unity and for unity, of which the eucharist is the simple but powerful sign.

At this stage of history, the ardor of our longing for the unity of the human family is equaled by the ominous and real threats and assaults against it. There is, therefore, a need to reassert solemnly the value of the eucharist as "sign of unity,"[3] as a means toward staying together, as a "symbol of concord."[4] In virtue of that inexpressible and mysterious mandate enjoined upon us in the person of Peter to confirm our brothers in the faith,[5] we wish to throw open to the entire Church and with it to all people of good will the invitation to await with particular expectation and hope the great event that is intended to be a demonstration of such an important aspect of the eucharistic mystery. Our predecessor Pius XII has given a marvelous definition of the sacrament of the eucharist: "the striking and awe-inspiring image of the unity of the Church."[6] With loving insistence contemporary theology

---

[1] Jn 13:34.

[2] See Augustine, *In Io. tractatus* 26, cap. 13: PL 35, 1613.

[3] Augustine, loc. cit.

[4] Council of Trent, sess. 13, cap. 8: [Denz-Schön 1649].

[5] See Lk 22:32.

[6] Pius XII, Encycl. *Mystici Corporis*: AAS 35 (1943) 233.

repeats the theme that the eucharist constitutes the Church. The same idea is the center of a constant, preferred reflection in recent studies, in the meditation of priests, of consecrated souls, and of the faithful, who are today more than ever open to the communitarian applications of their own faith. But the idea is as old as the Church itself. Participation in our Lord's sacrifice is the actualization of community with Christ Jesus and between the faithful. Revelation underlines this with great force: "For we who are many are one bread and one body; for we are all partakers of that one bread";[7] the Acts of the Apostles[8] put right before our eyes, so to speak, this unity, this sharing together in life and possessions, which was brought about in the young Christian community by constant participation in the "breaking of the bread."

Sitting down together at the same table to be nourished with the one body of Christ creates between Christians the closest, undivided unity, arising out of their dedication to God in worship and to each other in charity. By the sober force in its words and the expressive, allusive power in its gestures, the liturgy has put this truth completely within our grasp and has become the powerful instrument to put this truth into action. It is scarcely necessary to recall the solemn, mystical, and evocative eucharistic prayer in the *Didache*,[9] well known to all; or to mention the rite of the *fermentum*, in which the pope and in their dioceses the bishops sent to priests for the celebration of Mass, as a "symbol of the unity of the local Church and in particular of their close union in the celebration of the eucharistic mystery."[10] This is a very ancient rite, to which Irenaeus is an early witness,[11] which was fixed as a canonical rule by Popes Miltiades and Siricius and was the usage in Rome on Holy Thursday until the end of the eighth century.[12] *Lex orandi, lex credendi*: in the life of the early Church these ritual forms bore singular witness to the faith of the Christian community in the eucharist as sacrament of unity. It was the center of the community's coming together, the expression of its charity in the mutual communion, signified even visibly, between the hierarchy, the clergy, and the faithful, all joined together from near and far in their sharing in the single sacrifice and the single body of Christ. Bringing together that centuries-old heritage from revelation and Christian worship, Vatican Council II has synthesized for our own age this profound meaning of the eucharistic mystery: "Any community of the altar, under the sacred ministry of the bishop, stands out clearly as a symbol of that charity and 'unity of the Mystical Body, without which there can be no salvation.'[13] In these communities, though frequently small and poor or living in isolation, Christ is present and the power of his presence gathers together one, holy, catholic, and apostolic Church."[14]

1303

A eucharistic congress, summoning throngs of adorers before the blessed sacrament, is itself also a symbol, and an effective symbol, of that inward and outward ecclesial unity. Christ present beneath the eucharistic elements calls the entire Church to himself and causes it to reflect on its own vocation to unity and charity.

1304

---

[7] 1 Cor 10:17.

[8] Acts 2:42ff.

[9] *Didache* 9, 4.

[10] L. Duchesne, *Le Liber Pontificalis* 1 (Paris, 1955) no. 4, 169.

[11] See Eusebius, *Hist. eccl.* 5, 24. See also Mansi 2, 566.

[12] De Rossi, *Inscript. christ.* 2, 34.

[13] ST 3a, 73.3.

[14] LG no. 26 [DOL 4 no. 146].

Christ as he is solemnly and publicly adored today brings the Christian community back to the primordial fonts of its life and of its very reason for existing.

A eucharistic congress is therefore an act of faith in Christ's sovereign love that emanates from his eucharistic presence;[15] it is a reconfirmation of eucharistic worship in all its fullness and ramifications. We know well that the sacrifice of the Mass holds first place in the liturgy; all the documents of the magisterium, right up to the most recent, stand as the affirmation of that. But we wish also to recall, for all our brothers and all our sons and daughters, that, in spite of certain recent, ill-advised theological or practical positions, all the forms of eucharistic worship remain unchanged in their validity, their irreplaceable functions, their pedagogic and formative value as a school of education in faith, prayer, and holiness. From its very beginnings the Church has always surrounded with the highest reverence the eucharistic elements, the *caelestia membra*, as they are called in an inscription from the time of Pope Damasus on the tomb of St. Tarsisius. It memorializes the young martyr to eucharistic faith, who was ready to give his life rather than to leave the members of the Lord at the mercy of his cruel enemies.[16] From the second century on, the eucharist was brought to anyone unable to be present at the liturgical celebration or in danger of death and this was the purpose of reservation. Later witnesses clearly confirm this: Council of Lyons I;[17] Pope Gregory XI;[18] and finally the solemn declarations of the Council of Trent "on the worship and veneration to be offered toward this sacrament."[19] We will not bring up other well-known points, especially since Pius XII, in the Encyclical *Mediator Dei*, after recapitulating the testimony of Christian antiquity, the conciliar definitions, the statements of the Fathers,[20] stated this conclusion: "The worship of adoration rests on a sound and firm motive. The eucharist . . . differs from the other sacraments because it not only causes grace, but also in a permanent manner contains the very author of grace. When therefore the Church commands us to adore Christ hidden under the veil of the eucharist and to ask of him the supernatural and earthly gifts of which we stand always in need, it is showing that living faith in its divine Bridegroom, present under the veil of the eucharist; it is manifesting its thanks and rejoicing in its familial communion with him."[21]

1305   Preparation for the coming Eucharistic Congress, therefore, must have as its focus this reality: "Christ is with us all days, even until the end of the world";[22] that he is present in the little ones and in the poor; present in his revealed word; present in the eucharistic celebration; present above all, always and everywhere, and in a singular way, in the blessed sacrament. The reason is, as we sought to emphasize in our Encyclical *Mysterium fidei*, that this presence "is called real not to exclude the other kinds as though they were not real, but because it is real *par excellence*, since it is substantial, in the sense that Christ whole and entire, God and man, becomes present."[23]

---

15   See Pius XI, Encycl. *Quas primas*: AAS 17 (1925) 606.

16   A. Ferrua, *Epigrammata Damasiana* (Vatican City, 1942) 117–119.

17   A.D. 1245; see Denz-Schön 834.

18   A.D. 1370; see Denz-Schön 1101–03.

19   A.D. 1551; see Denz-Schön 1043ff.; 1656.

20   "No one eats this food without first having adored it" (Augustine, *Enarr. in Ps.* 98, 9: PL 37, 1264).

21   Pius XII, Encycl. *Mediator Dei*: AAS 39 (1947) 569.

22   Mt 28: 20.

23   Paul VI, Encycl. *Mysterium fidei*: [DOL 176 no. 1183].

Christ's real presence is the prolongation of the sacrifice in the liturgy; it makes the eternal liturgy of heaven to be present,[24] as we await the eschatological encounter with Christ, and more extensively applies the fruits of holy communion. Over and above these basic points of dogma, however, the real presence gives to the worship of the eucharist outside Mass irreplaceable importance. From a cultic standpoint it is a form of adoration, thanksgiving, expiation, and supplication — in other words it embraces the same ends as Christ's sacrifice. From an ascetical and mystical standpoint, without genuine devotion to the eucharist the apostolate lacks its vital sustenance; fidelity to ecclesiastical vocation and priestly ministry lacks any guarantee.[25] From the standpoint of ecclesial communion "the eucharist is reserved in churches and oratories as in the spiritual center of a religious community or parish, yes, of the universal Church and of all humanity."[26] From a social and human standpoint, it is the spark of charity and of social living. From an ecumenical standpoint, it is the source and sustainer of unity, as the principles of *Mysterium Fidei* indicate.[a][. . .]

183. PAUL VI, **Epistle** *Eventus religiosus* to Cardinal J.R. Knox, papal legate to the 41st International Eucharistic Congress at Philadelphia (1–8 August 1976), 7 July 1976: AAS 68 (1976) 454–456 (excerpt).

Since you are, as it were, our own voice, take pains that this sublime sacrament, which not only contains God's grace but truly, really, and substantially contains the author of grace, may receive worthy and reverent adoration and that a new flame of love may be kindled in people's hearts toward this indescribable gift from heaven. As Vatican Council II teaches, the eucharist is "the center and crowning point of all the sacraments."[2] In the eucharist "the sacrifice of Christ, the sole Mediator, is offered in an unbloody and sacramental manner until he himself returns."[3] The eucharist is spiritual sustenance causing us to live for the sake of the one whom we eat.[4] To it is due the worship of adoration even outside Mass "by reserving consecrated hosts with the utmost care and by exposing them to solemn veneration by the faithful."[5]

1306

Further, this sacrament is the sign of unity and the bond of charity. "It bears the name and in reality is communion because through it we come into communion with Christ, partake of his humanity and divinity, and enter into communion and conjunction with them. For we who share in the one bread are the one body and the one blood of Christ and become members of one another because we are of the one Body."[6] None who are nourished at this banquet allow themselves to be unaware of the suffering members of the one Body, but feel impelled to respond, as far as possible, to their needs. This is indeed the exalted meaning of the words, "The

1307

---

[24]   See Heb 7:25.

[25]   See PO nos. 4–5 [DOL 18 nos. 259–260].

[26]   Paul VI, Encycl. *Mysterium fidei* [DOL 176 no. 1212].

[a]   See DOL 176 nos. 1216–17.

[2]   AG no. 9 [DOL 17 no. 244].

[3]   PO no. 2 [DOL 18 no. 257].

[4]   See Jn 6:58.

[5]   Paul VI, Encycl. *Mysterium fidei* [DOL 176 no. 1200].

[6]   John of Damascus, *De fide orthodoxa* 4, 13.

Eucharist and the Hungers of the Human Family," which are proposed as the distinctive theme for this Eucharistic Congress. The hungers of the human family are, of course, many, embracing the spiritual and the physical. In particular, one hunger is the hunger for God, from whom so many are alienated. There is the hunger of the spirit, inasmuch as priests and religious must bear witness to those things that go beyond the natural. There is hunger for liberty, justice, truth, love, and peace — blessings so deeply longed for. There is the hunger for food, the lack of which torments so many people. The charity that has its source and sustenance in the eucharist and is the mark of the Christian calls for the resolve of self-dedication, imposes duties and burdens, and at this time especially presses us to come to the aid of our brothers and sisters suffering those hungers. [. . .]

184. PAUL VI, **Message** (televised) to the 41st International Eucharistic Congress at Philadelphia, 8 August 1976: AAS 68 (1976) 561–562 (English).

1308   To you, Americans; to you, men and women from all parts of the world, assembled for the International Eucharistic Congress.

It is the Bishop of Rome who speaks to you, the Successor of the Apostle Peter, the Pope of the Catholic Church, the Vicar of Christ on earth.

He speaks to greet you, to assure you of his prayers, to have you hear in his voice the echo of Christ's word, and thus, to some extent, to open up to you the deep meaning of the mystery that you are celebrating.

We ask you to be silent, to be silent now and to try to listen within yourselves to an inner proclamation!

The Lord is saying: "Be assured, I am with you."[1] I am here, he is saying: because this is my body! This is the cup of my blood!

1309   The *mystery of his presence* is thus enacted and celebrated: the mystery of his sacramental, but real and living presence. Jesus, the teacher of humanity, is here; he is calling for you.[2]

Yes, he is calling you, each one by name! The mystery of the eucharist is, above all, a personal mystery: personal, because of his divine presence — the presence of Christ, the Word of God made man; personal, because the eucharist is meant for each of us: for this reason Christ has become living bread and is multiplied in the sacrament, in order to be accessible to every human being who receives him worthily and who opens to him the door of faith and love.

1310   The eucharist is a *mystery of life*! Christ says: "He who eats this bread shall live!"[3]

The eucharist is a mystery of suffering, yes and a mystery of death! A mystery of redemptive passion, a *mystery of sacrifice*, consummated by Christ for our salvation. It is the mystery of the cross, reflected and commemorated in the sacrament which makes us share in the Lord's immolation, in order to associate us in his resurrection. Today, in time, the eucharist is the food for our earthly pilgrimage; tomorrow, in the life to come, it will be our everlasting happiness.

---

[1]   See Mt 28:20.

[2]   See Jn 11:28.

[3]   Jn 6:51.

The eucharist is therefore a *mystery of love*. It makes all of us who eat the same bread into a single body,[4] living by means of one Spirit. It makes us one family: brothers and sisters united in solidarity with one another[5] and all of us dedicated to giving witness, in mutual love, to the fact that we really are the followers of Christ.[6]

May it always be this way, beloved Brethren, and sons and daughters!

With our apostolic blessing: In the name of the Father and of the Son and of the Holy Spirit. Amen!

1311

185. PAUL VI, **Homily** at Bolsena, on the International Eucharistic Congress at Philadelphia, 8 August 1976: AAS 68 (1976) 558–561 (Italian; excerpt).

[. . .] However short the time at our disposal for reflection on so sublime and inexhaustible a mystery, we cannot pass over the central theme that the Philadelphia Eucharistic Congress has chosen as an occasion to bring together and elaborate on our thoughts about the eucharistic mystery.

1312

The eucharistic mystery is in essence the mystery of Jesus' real presence and of the true memorial of his passion under the appearance of bread and wine. In substance they are no longer anything but Christ himself present under those outward signs. Why does the Philadelphia Congress present us this mystery as Christ our Bread and Christ our Wine? [. . .]

It will suffice for us to underline two points about this teaching. The first is that of hunger and thirst, a continuous, manifold, inescapable need that forms part of the very nature of the human being — a being of hunger and thirst. That means that humans are not self-sufficient beings: they are beings in continuous, many-sided need of nourishment whose present existence depends on satisfying that need. They need air to breathe and mothers' milk at the threshold of life, food and drink many times a day; by a natural necessity a hundred other things are goals of life, knowledge, possession, and enjoyment; and they stand always in need of obtaining from outside whatever is lacking for their existence, development, well-being, and happiness. This is why human beings yearn, why they seek, why they work, why they love, suffer, pray, hope, wait; they are always in tension *toward something*, some fulfillment to support them and allow them to live life to the full and, if possible, for ever. This picture of existence, of the reality facing all, can be summed up under one caption: the human being is a being in need of bread, of one bread that nourishes, makes whole, expands, and extends an always questing and fragile human existence. It is an existence constrained to preserve and develop itself, yet condemned to experience its own inadequacy and transitoriness and in the end to undergo inescapable death. On this earth there is no bread that suffices; there is no earthly bread that can give immortality.

1313

But at this point, hear the word of Jesus: "I am the bread of life . . . those who eat this bread will live for ever."[2] In Christ human life has, for anyone with faith, its fulfillment, its pledge of immortal life.

---

[4] See 1 Cor 10:17.

[5] See Eph 4:16.

[6] See Jn 13:35.

[2] Jn 6:48–51.

1314   [. . .] Christ is the bread of life. And this means something further and of considerable importance. It is our second point. As ordinary bread satisfies ordinary hunger, Christ, the bread extraordinary, satisfies an extraordinary hunger, the boundless hunger of the human being, capable of boundless aspirations and longing to be open to them.[3] We often face the temptation of thinking that Christ does not really hold the answer to human needs, desires, and destiny. That is especially true of today's people who delude themselves into thinking that they are born for some other, higher food than the divine and that they have succeeded in fulfilling themselves through attainments other than those of faith; they often think religion to be a pseudo-food, empty and useless for the realities of life.

No. Christ does not conceal himself beneath a specious food to betray our nobler hungers, but clothes himself in the appearances of material food not only to make us desire that spiritual nourishment, but also to acknowledge and to justify the legitimate needs of natural life. It is Christ who, before proclaiming himself to be the bread from heaven, multiplied earthly loaves for all those to have their fill who had followed him to a desert place to listen to him and had nothing to eat.[4] It was Christ who addressed to humankind the incomparable invitation: "Come to me all you who labor and are heavily burdened and I will refresh you."[5] It is Christ, no longer under the appearances of bread and wine but of every suffering, needy human being, who will reveal on the last day, the day of judgment, that whenever we have come to the aid of anyone, we have come to the aid of Christ: "I was hungry and you gave me to eat; I was thirsty and you gave me to drink. . . ."[6]

May the eucharist become for us not only the food for each of our souls, for each of our Christian communities, but the stimulus of a charity toward our brothers and sisters of every condition (remember the parable of the good Samaritan) who are in need of help, understanding, solidarity. In this way we will instill social action with an energy, an idealism, a hope that will never grow less as long as Christ is with us with his eucharist. Christ is the bread of life. Christ is needed by every person, by every community, by every social reality that is genuine, based, that is, on love and self-sacrifice for the world. How we need Christ, the bread of life!

186. PAUL VI, **Homily** at St. Paul's-outside-the-Walls, on the feast of Corpus Christi, 12 June 1977: Not 13 (1977) 262–265 (Italian; excerpt).

1315   [. . .] The first purpose of this celebration is pedagogy, education: to make us attentive to the eucharistic mystery, keenly aware of it and rejoicing in it. Human beings get used to the extraordinary and often reduce the striking impression of a given moment to a conventional, superficial, and trite expression. Human beings get used to things and even when it comes to realities that surpass their normal capacity for understanding, they treat them as normal and as though contained in the purely verbal wrapping of a label, without any longer recognizing and acknowledging the abundant richness in the inner meaning of such realities. This often applies to ourselves and the inexpressible sacrament of the eucharist, which presents to our external perceptions only the outward images, the appearances of bread and wine. In reality the bread and wine cloak flesh and blood and on the altar contain the

---

[3]   See Augustine, *Confessions* 1,1.

[4]   See Jn 6:11ff.

[5]   Mt 11:28.

[6]   Mt 25:35.

elements of a sacrifice, of a victim immolated, of Christ crucified; they contain his body united to his own blood, to his soul, and to the divinity of the Word. This indeed is the "mystery of faith" present in the eucharist (see Council of Trent, *Decr. De Eucharistia* cap. 3). This is the first spiritual effort, to which this sacrament invites and obliges us, a straining for knowledge, not just one based on outward experience . . . but an effort of faith, that is, of holding fast to a word in control of all created things, a word, the Word of God, here present.

To draw near to the sacrament of love we must cross the threshold of faith (ST 3a, 73.3 ad 3). The mystery of faith! We enter into the sphere of faith, which invites us to perceive in the sacramental signs the sublime reality that they localize and represent, Christ sacrificed and made our spiritual food. Then a question at once timid and bold arises in our rapt thoughts: Why? why, Lord, have you chosen to take on these appearances? Why have you come to us hidden and veiled in this way? Let us hold our breath for a moment and listen. A word of Jesus is, so to speak, spoken by the eucharistic gift put before us; let us hear it again from the gospel. Jesus says again and always: "Come to me all you that labor and are heavily burdened and I will refresh you" (Mt 11:28). Jesus, then, is in an attitude of invitation, of knowing us, of compassion toward us; an attitude also of offering, of promising, of friendship, of goodness, of healing our ills, of comforting; in an attitude of being our nourishment, our bread, the source of our energies and life. "I am the bread of life" (Jn 6:68), our Lord replies in his eloquent silence, Jesus who is our bread. Is Jesus food? How far does the Lord wish to go? Is it not already too much that he has come into the world for us? Has he also made himself so accessible as to multiply his sacramental presence by means of every altar, every table, where another, representative and active form of his presence, that of the priest, makes possible the unlimited repetition of this miracle? (See M. de la Taille, *Mysterium Fidei*, Eluc. 36ff.).

The facets of this doctrine expand and increase progressively as we reflect on it, to the point of confounding our mind were it not that the supreme intent of our Lord has been made clear to us by a well-known word of the Apostle Paul, to whom this basilica is dedicated. His word has become a commonplace in our accustomed religious language. What is Christ's divine and supreme intention and what is the word that expresses it for us? The word is "communion," in Greek, *koinōnia*; it is a term that always comes to our lips whenever we intend to refer to the reception of this sacrament. "To go to communion" means to approach the eucharist, to receive Jesus in the sacrament that in its deepest reality consists in the unity of the Mystical Body of the Lord (see ST 3a, 73.3). In our human expression we give our own, subjective meaning to the word "communion," as though the act of our approaching the eucharist were an adequate expression of "communion." We pay too little attention to the initiative of Christ, who makes it possible for us to receive him, who offers himself to us by instituting and renewing this wonderful sacrament with his blessed words: "Take and eat; this is my body given in sacrifice for you. . . . This is the chalice of my blood, shed for you." Here is revealed Christ's ultimate intention toward those called to his religion; and in the end it means his love: "Greater love no one has than this, that one lay down one's life for one's friends. . . . You are my friends" (Jn 15:13ff.; see Prov 8:31).

We certainly are not worthy, but are we capable of entering into the heart of this religious exaltation? How many are they who cannot comprehend and how many are they who see the secret, yet cannot accept it. Here love for God, the first and greatest of God's commandments, becomes the first and greatest of God's gifts. We are the ones loved before we are made ready to love; he has first loved us (1 Jn 4:10–19). How many times we have withdrawn ourselves from that love; we who were created and made by him have refused the encounter with him (see the

1316

parable of the man invited to a great feast, Mt. 22:1–10; Lk 14:15–24), perhaps by the base and secret fear of being overcome by a love that would change our life. [. . .] The eucharist is the most direct, the most powerful invitation to friendship, to the following of Christ. The eucharist is, as well, the sustenance that gives the energy and the joy to respond to love. The eucharist thus puts the problem of our life as a supreme challenge of love, of choice, of fidelity; if we accept the challenge, the issue from being simply religious becomes social, according to the revealing words of the Apostle Paul, which we will repeat as a conclusion and as the memento of our celebration together. Love received from Christ in the eucharist is communion with him and is therefore transformed into and expressed by our communion with our brothers and sisters — that is with all human beings, who actually or potentially are our brothers and sisters. Nourished by the real and sacramental body of Christ, we become ever more fully the Mystical Body of Christ: "Is not the cup of blessing that we bless the communion of the body of Christ?. . . For we who are many are one bread and one body, for we are all partakers of that one bread" (1 Cor 10:16–17).

Let us repeat St. Augustine: "O sacrament of piety! O sign of unity! O bond of charity! Whoever wishes to live has this to live on" (*In Io. Tr.* 26, 19: PL 35, 1615). May it be that for us, dear brothers, dear sons and daughters.

187. PAUL VI, **Homily** to the 19th National Eucharistic Congress of Italy at Pescara, 17 September 1977: AAS 69 (1977) 568–570 (Italian; excerpt).

1317

[. . .] "Behold I am with you always, even unto the end of the world."[1] This is a divine word, an eternal word, and a word for here and now: Jesus Christ remains with us. Jesus is hidden, but he continues to be in our midst. But how? Through his word? Yes, he has guaranteed this kind of presence: "Heaven and earth will pass away, but my words will not pass away."[2] Is he with us by his mystical, unseen presence wherever his faithful followers gather in his name? Yes, he has entrusted this secret to us: "Wherever two or three are gathered in my name, I am there in the midst of them."[3] But this takes place in a manner beyond the senses, inwardly, indescribably. Other words of the Gospel, of the New Testament, open up to us this supreme and universal intention of God through what we may call the constitutive plan of religion, the plan, namely, of the covenant, of the incarnation, of setting up between God and humanity relationships of friendship, of shared life, of redemption. "They shall call his name Emmanuel, which means *God with us.*"[4]

But no one surmised that this plan went so far as to include our having in Christ the bread of life. Remember Jesus' own unquestionable words: "I am the bread of life."[5] Remember also the ensuing words, presenting the picture of Christ the victim as one who not only offers himself as life-giving food, but as the lamb destined to be slain; as one who gave his flesh and blood in sacrifice for the salvation of us all. Recall this twofold statement, bearing on a permanent reality, an inescapable duty, and one concerning the entire Church. Commentators on these mysterious words of the Lord, the meaning of which he shows in the gospel dis-

---

1   Mt 28:20.

2   Mt 24:35.

3   Mt 18:20.

4   Mt 1:23.

5   Jn 6:35 and 48.

course to be the nourishment that is his own flesh and blood, have rightly interpreted the announcement both of the institution of the eucharist and of the sacrifice of the cross, of which the eucharist was to be the perpetual memorial. O Jesus, the indispensable Bread, the irreplaceable Lamb, did your followers understand that without you they cannot have true life, the victory over death? Will the world understand? "This is a hard saying, *Durus est hic sermo* ! and who can accept it?, *et quis potest eum audire?*"[6] That was the reaction on the very day of the Lord's discourse, after the astonishing miracle of the multiplication of the loaves. The miracle was not enough to amaze and reassure the people who had benefited by it and to arouse in them that hunger for a heavenly bread that Christ the miracle-worker immediately made the subsumption in the logic of revelation. His listeners were disappointed and went away. They would have preferred the repetition of the material miracle and showed incomprehension and distrust toward a miracle of a different, higher level, a miracle having to do with a bread from heaven.

In the same way today sociological psychology, with a narrow view of the human reality, but a view that is gaining adherents even in the ranks of Christ's followers, would prefer to have from him the radical solution of socio-economic problems. It accuses Christ's school, concentrated on mystery and the attainment of the supernatural world, of failure in its mission by not having yet succeeded in satisfying the rightful hunger for material bread. It fails to attach due value to the twofold force of Christ's providence, which, elevating human aspirations to the higher sphere of the economy of faith and grace, satisfies the loftier and inescapable needs of the human spirit, while at the same time urging and making possible the fulfillment of the temporal needs of earthly life. The kingdom of God, the kingdom of charity, is aware of this twofold richness and makes the one the consequence of the other: "Seek you first," the Gospel teaches, "the kingdom of God and his justice," and all the things needed for the level of this present life will be given to you as a consequence.[7]

1318

This view of history and of the human condition does not touch on all the difficulties involved in understanding the eucharistic mystery. In the teaching on this mystery physical and metaphysical laws undergo alterations so far exceeding and surpassing, not to say opposing, the experience of the senses that the mind wavers in the face of Christ's words on the eucharistic bread and wine: "This is my body; this is my blood." But, in celebrating this eucharistic congress, we put these words at the forefront of our faith and, therefore, of our adoration. [. . .]

▶   330.   SC BISHOPS, Decree *Apostolatus maris*, on the pastoral care of seamen and ship passengers, 24 September 1977:

    nos. 1–6:   Celebration of Mass aboard ship (no. 2669).
         7:          Reservation of the eucharist aboard ship (no. 2669).

---

⁶   Jn 6:60.

⁷   See Mt 6:33.

188. PAUL VI, **Homily** at St. Paul-outside-the-Walls, on the feast of Corpus Christi, 28 May 1978: Not 14 (1978) 238–241 (Italian; excerpt).

1319   [. . .] We wish to propose to you, by suggestion rather than elaboration, a starting point for reflection.

And first on the value as memorial of the rite we are celebrating. You realize why there are two eucharistic elements. Jesus willed to be with us under the appearances of bread and wine, the figures of his body and blood, in order to make actual in the sacramental sign the reality of his sacrifice, that is, of his immolation on the cross that has brought salvation to the world. We cannot forget the words of the Apostle Paul: "For as often as you eat this bread and drink this cup, you proclaim the death of the Lord until he comes" (1 Cor 11:26). In the eucharist Jesus is therefore present as "the man of sorrows" (Is 53:3), as the "Lamb of God" who offers himself as victim for our sins (see Jn 1:29).

To grasp this meaning is to open our vision to limitless vistas: in this world there is no redemption without sacrifice (see Heb 9:22) and there is no redeemed existence that is not at the same time an existence as victim. The eucharist offers to Christians of all times the possibility of investing their daily Calvary of suffering, of bewilderment, sickness, death, with the value of a redemptive offering. This joins each person's pain to Christ's passion, directing each one's existence to the immolation in faith that in its completion opens onto the Easter morning of the resurrection.

How we long for the opportunity to repeat to each one in person this message of faith and hope, especially to every person who is burdened at this moment by sorrow or illness. The pain is not pointless. United to Christ, human pain takes on a degree of redemptive value from the passion of God's Son.

1320   The eucharist is a communion event; this is the second reflection we would put before you. The Lord's body and blood are offered as the nourishment that redeems us from every form of slavery and brings us into communion with the Trinity, making us share in Christ's own life and in his communion with the Father. It is no accident that the great priestly prayer of Jesus is closely linked with the eucharistic mystery and that his impassioned prayer *ut unum sint* (Jn 17) occurs in the very midst of the setting and the reality of this mystery.

The eucharist calls for communion. St. Paul, to whom this basilica is dedicated, understood this well; writing to the Christians of Corinth he asked: "The cup of blessing we bless, is it not the communion of Christ's blood? The bread we break, is it not the communion of Christ's body?" From this basic perception the Apostle in strictest logic drew out the well-known conclusions: "For we being many are the one bread and the one body: for we are all partakers of that one bread" (1 Cor 10: 16–17).

The eucharist is communion with Christ and by that very fact becomes and shows itself to be our communion with each other. The eucharist is the summons to make concord and union real between all of us to further whatever joins us as a family, to build up the Church, that Mystical Body of Christ of which the eucharist is the sign, the cause, and the sustenance. In the early Church the eucharistic assembly became the fountain of a communion in charity that made it an example to the pagan world. For us Christians of the twentieth century, as well, our sharing together at God's table must be the wellspring of a true love that is visible, that spreads, that creates history.

1321   There is yet a third aspect of the mystery: the eucharist is the anticipation and pledge of future glory. Celebrating this mystery daily, the pilgrim Church draws nearer each day to the Father's house; traveling along its way of sorrow and death, the Church comes closer to resurrection and life eternal. The eucharistic bread is the viaticum that sustains the Church along the somber road of this earthly existence and in a way brings it even now into the experience of the radiant existence of heaven. Repeating what Christ did at the Last Supper, we are building up in the fleeting moments of time the heavenly city that does not pass away. Therefore, it is our business as Christians to be, in the midst of other people, witnesses to this reality, heralds of this hope. Does not the Lord, present in the truth of the sacrament, say again and again in our hearts, perhaps at every Mass: "Fear not; I am the first and the last. I am he that lives" (Rv 1:17–18) ? What today's world probably needs most is for Christians, with humble courage, to raise the prophetic voice of their own hope. It will be from an intense and conscious eucharistic life that Christian witness will derive the warm openness and power to convince that are needed as the way to reach the human heart. [. . .]

189. PAUL VI, **Address** to bishops of Regions I and II of the United States, on the eucharistic sacrifice as center of the Church's unity, 15 June 1978: AAS 70 (1978) 419–423; Not 14 (1978) 324–327 (English; excerpt).

[. . .] Today we wish to consider the mystery of life in Jesus Christ. And since life in Jesus Christ is embodied in the eucharist, it is about the eucharist that we now wish to speak to you and to all the hierarchy in America. The eucharist is of supreme importance in our ministry as priests and bishops, making present Christ's salvific activity. The eucharist is of supreme relevance to our people in their Christian lives. It is of supreme effectiveness for the transformation of the world in justice, holiness, and peace. Precisely, therefore, because of the intimate relationship between the eucharist and the apostolate to which we dedicate ourselves, we wish to reflect with you on several aspects of this sacrament, which is the bread of life. — 1322

The Second Vatican Council has reminded all priests that the main source of their pastoral love is to be found in the eucharistic sacrifice.[2] It goes on to state that "the ministry of priests is directed toward this work and is perfected in it. For their ministry, which takes its start from the gospel proclamation, derives its power and force from the sacrifice of Christ."[3] And then it specifies that priests fulfill their chief duty in the mystery of the eucharistic sacrifice.[4] For us, Brethren, as for all our collaborators in the priesthood, who have dedicated their lives in order to lead the faithful to the fullness of the paschal mystery, this teaching is extremely important. It gives a decisive orientation to all our activities as shepherds of God's people and as heralds of the Gospel of salvation, whose highest proclamation is enacted in the eucharistic sacrifice.

Besides determining the priorities of our own ministry and that of our priests, the teaching of the Second Vatican Council gives immense joy to the Catholic people, reminding them that because the eucharist contains Christ himself it therefore contains "the Church's entire spiritual wealth."[5] — 1323

---

2 PO no. 14 [DOL 18 no. 266].

3 PO no. 2 [DOL 18 no. 257].

4 PO no. 13 [DOL 18 no. 265].

5 PO no. 5 [DOL 18 no. 260].

A few months before the promulgation of the Council's Decree on Priestly Ministry and Life, we ourself reiterated the Church's doctrine on the *real presence* of Christ in the eucharist, stating that "it is presence in the fullest sense: because it is a substantial presence by which the whole and complete Christ, God and man, is present."[6] We went on to state that the Catholic Church "has at all times given to this great sacrament the worship which is known as *latria* and which may be given to God alone."[7] And we are convinced today that an ever greater emphasis on this teaching will be a source of strength to all the pilgrim people of God. For this reason we encourage you and all your priests to preach frequently this rich doctrine of Christ's presence: the eucharist, in the Mass and outside of the Mass, contains the body and blood of Jesus Christ and is, therefore, deserving of the worship that is given to the living God and to him alone.

1324   Another clear enunciation of the importance of the eucharist is contained in the Dogmatic Constitution on the Church, in which participation in the eucharistic sacrifice is called "the source and summit of the whole Christian life."[8] The eucharistic sacrifice is itself the apex of the Church's liturgy, the entirety of which is the festive expression of salvation, and has as its primary role the glory of the Lord.[9] In the words of the Council: "the sacred liturgy is above all the worship of the divine majesty."[10] What a great service to the people of God: week after week, year after year to make them ever more conscious of the fact that they can draw unlimited strength from the eucharist to collaborate actively in the mission of the Church. It is the summit of their Christian lives, not in the sense that their other activities are not important, but in the sense that, for their full effectiveness, these activities must be united with Christ's salvific action and be associated with his redemptive sacrifice.

1325   The Vatican Council assures us that the eucharist is likewise "the source and summit of all evangelization."[11] The very identity of the Church, in her evangelizing mission, is effected by the eucharist, which becomes the goal of all our activities. All the pastoral endeavors of our ministry are incomplete until the people that we are called to serve are led to full and active participation in the eucharist. Every initiative we undertake in the name of God and as ministers of the Gospel must find fulfillment in the eucharist.

A year ago, at the canonization of John Neumann, we cited the importance that the eucharist held for him as a bishop of the Catholic Church, precisely in the context of evangelization. And the example we gave was the importance he attributed to the forty-hours devotion. Venerable Brothers, we do not hesitate today to propose to you and all your faithful the great practice of eucharistic adoration. At the same time we ask you and your priests to do all in your power so that the reverence due to the eucharist will be understood by all the faithful, that eucharistic celebrations everywhere will be characterized by dignity, and that all God's children will approach their Father through Jesus Christ, in a spirit of profound filial reverence. In this regard, we recall the words we spoke last year to a group of bishops on their *Ad limina* visit: "The Catholic liturgy must remain theocentric."[12]

---

[6]   Paul VI, Encycl. *Mysterium fidei* no. 39 [DOL 176 no. 1183].

[7]   Ibid. no. 55 [DOL 176 no. 1199].

[8]   LG no. 11 [DOL 4 no. 141].

[9]   See Paul VI, Address to the Swiss Bishops [DOL 290].

[10]   SC art. 33 [DOL 1 no. 33].

[11]   PO no. 5 [DOL 18 no. 260].

[12]   DOL 63 no. 576.

As we thank God for giving the people of his Church a greater awareness of their liturgical role, we believe that it is good to repeat — in order to help you to formulate the directives you give in your dioceses — what we mentioned in our Bicentennial Letter to the American Bishops: "We are pleased to recall that the Holy See has authorized, under certain circumstances, the distribution of holy communion by extraordinary ministers duly deputed to this high task. But we wish to emphasize that this ministry remains an extraordinary ministry to be exercised in accordance with the precise norms of the Holy See. By its nature therefore the role of the extraordinary minister is different from those other roles of eucharistic participation that are the ordinary expression of lay participation."[13] To give the eucharist to God's people remains in general therefore an honored pastoral function. Extraordinary ministers are envisioned by the Instruction *Immensae caritatis*[a] where there is a genuine lack of ministers, and under these conditions fulfill a providential role.

The Vatican Council assures us, moreover, that the eucharist is the root and   1326 center of the Church's unity.[14] No Christian community can be built up without the eucharist. In the eucharist the faithful must experience their oneness as God's people united in Christ: in his truth and in his love. This matter has been treated in the pastoral message "To Teach as Jesus Did," wherein the American Bishops emphasized that a spirit of fellowship "is fostered especially by the eucharist, which is at once sign of community and cause of its growth."[15]

From this viewpoint it is then easy to see how the eucharist is for the whole Church a bond of charity and a source of social love. The tradition of the Church speaks to us in every era of this marvelous truth. In our Encyclical *Mysterium fidei*, we stated that eucharistic worship leads to that social love "by which we place the common good before the good of the individual; we make the interests of the community, of the parish, of the entire Church our own; and extend our charity to the whole world because we know that everywhere there are members of Christ."[16]

Dear Brothers in Christ, with the full conviction of our being we believe that these truths will guide you and sustain you in your apostolic ministry, in the joyful hope of the coming of our Lord Jesus Christ. The eucharist is our source of hope because it is our pledge of life. Jesus himself has said: "I am the bread of life. . . . If anyone eats this bread he shall live for ever."[17] Amidst all the problems of the modern world let us remain constant in this hope. Our optimism is based, not on an unrealistic denial of the immense and manifest difficulties and opposition that beset the kingdom of God, but in a realization that, in the eucharist, the paschal mystery of the Lord Jesus is for ever operative and victorious over sin and death.

We thank you, Venerable Brethren, for your generous commitment to the Gospel, and for all your labors on its behalf; and we ask you to go forward in the power of Christ, the supreme Shepherd of the Church. We exhort you to be strong in proclaiming the mystery of life in Christ and in leading your people to the source of this life, the eucharist. We pray that you, in turn, will encourage the faithful in their eucharistic vocation. We ask especially that all our sons in the priesthood be

---

13   DOL 60 no. 562.

a   See DOL 264 nos. 2074–81.

14   See PO no. 6 [DOL 18 no. 261].

15   NCCB, *To Teach as Jesus Did* no. 24.

16   Paul VI, Encycl. *Mysterium fidei* no. 69 [DOL 176 no. 1213].

17   Jn 6: 48, 51.

sustained and supported in their inestimable role of building up God's people through the eucharist. In all sectors of the Church we pray that there will be a new era of eucharistic piety, generating confidence and fraternal love, and producing justice and holiness of life.

190. JOHN PAUL II, **Epistle** *Le Congrès eucharistique* to Cardinal J.R. Knox, announcing the theme of the International Eucharistic Congress at Lourdes in 1981, 1 January 1979: AAS 71 (1979) 335–337 (French; excerpt).

1327
[. . .] "Jesus Christ, the Bread Broken for the sake of a New World," is the theme chosen by the permanent Council for International Eucharistic Congresses and confirmed today by the Pope. [. . .] Like St. Paul (see 1 Cor 11:23) the pastors and theologians of the Congress must hand on what they themselves have received from living tradition that is guided by the Holy Spirit. From this will emerge, in the completeness of its mystery, the meaning of the "bread that is broken"; the "bread," in its full sense, refers not only to a generous distribution inspired by Jesus' example, but to the sacrifice of Christ who has given his body and shed his blood to take away the world's sin, to break down the wall between people who are enemies, and to open up to them the way to the Father's love. The Savior's basic statement recounted by St. John is this: "The bread that I will give to you is my flesh for the life of the world" (Jn 6:51). St. Paul, in turn, proclaims: "The cup of blessing we bless, is it not the communion of Christ's blood? The bread which we break, is it not the communion of the body of Christ?" (1 Cor 10:16). This lived tradition is the starting point from which the Congress can proceed toward seeing more deeply and expressing to today's world how and why the "new world" is bound up with the eucharist and the eucharist itself with Christ's passion and resurrection.

What a great grace it will be to achieve a heightened awareness that this sacrifice becomes present in each eucharist, that believers can take to themselves the fruit of the sacrifice as their daily bread and continue it in their own lives. The primary hours of the Eucharistic Congress, the source of all else, are the hours of contemplating the "mystery of faith" and of adoring it in union with the Virgin Mary who kept all these things in her heart (see Lk 2:51). What must reach the world is the force of this extraordinary message, of this "foolishness" and "wisdom" of God (see 1 Cor 1:21). The gathering at Lourdes will be indeed a success if it can further this genuine grasp of the eucharist, stir renewed gratitude for it, lead to a more reverent approach to it, to a more worthy celebration, to a more ardent desire to receive communion with greater effect because of better preparation.

1328
"Christ has laid down his life for us: and we ought to lay down our lives for one another" (1 Jn 3:16). The results expected from the bread of life that the Church breaks and distributes in Christ's name are a "new being" (Col 3:10), a new world bearing the sign of its filial relationships with God and its fraternal relationships between people, a new humanity. Needless to say, the deeper level at which this bond with the Body of Christ, this "osmosis" of his charity, is actual in communicants is beyond human power to perceive or measure. It belongs to the level of grace, of a mysterious sharing, through faith, in the life of Christ risen according to the spirit of holiness (see Rom 1:4). But from it must normally follow the great moral consequences that St. Paul lists in the second part of each of his letters. These consequences are at once invitations and demands: they presuppose in the participants at once an openness and a responsibility toward them. There are profound

implications here, first, regarding the relationship between communicants: "the eucharist creates the Church," it unites as members of one Body those who partake in the very body of Christ: "that all may be one" (Jn 17: 21). There are also profound consequences for society itself, for the way of drawing near to our fellow human beings, especially the poorest, to serve them, to share with them the bread of earth and the bread of love, to build with them a world more just and more worthy of God's children, and at the same time to prepare a "new world" yet to come. There God himself will bring about the ultimate renewal and a communion that will be complete and unfailing (see Rv 21:1–5. GS nos. 39, 45). The Lourdes Congress will have as its task to make clear in detail the entire spiritual and ethical dynamism that the eucharistic Christ brings to those who receive him with the right dispositions. The Congress will be at pains to set within the framework of the attitudes and beatitudes of the Gospel the possibilities for personal and social transformation through conversion, because conversion is at the heart of Christian renewal. On this point the message of the Eucharistic Congress will coincide with the abiding message of Lourdes. May the Immaculate Virgin assist in the purification of hearts on the occasion of this great gathering. [. . .]

191. JOHN PAUL II, **Encyclical** *Redemptor hominis*, excerpt on the eucharist, 4 March 1979: AAS 71 (1979) 257–324; Not 15 (1979) 193–198.

20. Within the mystery of redemption, the saving work accomplished by Jesus, the Church through fidelity to the Word and its ministry of truth becomes the sharer in its Master's Gospel. Further, through its full submission in hope and love, it becomes the sharer in the power of Christ's redemptive action, to which he has given sacramental expression and existence especially in the eucharist.[154] The eucharist, then, stands as the center and summit of that entire sacramental life through which the Christian passes from the mystery of baptism, the mystery of our burial with Christ into death and of our sharing in the resurrection, as St. Paul teaches.[155] On the basis of this teaching it becomes clearer why the sacramental life of the Church and of all Christians reaches its high point and completeness in the eucharist. In virtue of Christ's will this sacrament constantly makes actual again the mystery of the sacrifice by which he offered himself to the Father on the altar of the cross. This is the sacrifice that the Father accepted; because of that same complete self-donation of his Son, "become obedient unto death,"[156] the Father, from the beginning the first source and giver of life, responded in turn by his own fatherly gift, namely, of new, immortal life in the resurrection. This new life, which includes the bodily glorification of Christ crucified, has become the effective sign of a new gift given to humanity, the gift of the Holy Spirit. Through the Holy Spirit the divine life, possessed by the Father in himself and given to his Son,[157] is the gift to all those who are conjoined to Christ.

The eucharist is the fullest sacrament of this conjunction. As we celebrate and share together in the eucharist we are brought into contact with the Christ of earth and of heaven, who intercedes with the Father for us.[158] But this union is always

1329

---

154   See SC art. 10 [DOL 1 no. 10].

155   See Rom 6:3ff.

156   Phil 2:8.

157   See Jn 5:26; 1 Jn 5:11.

158   See Heb 9:24; 1 Jn 2:1.

through the saving, sacrificial act by which he has redeemed us so that we are "bought with a price."[159] Further, that "great price" of our redemption also is a proof of the value that God attaches to us humans and a confirmation of our dignity in Christ. For we are made children of God,[160] children by adoption;[161] we are at the same time fashioned in his image as "kings and priests," we receive a "royal priest-hood,"[162] that is, we are made sharers in the unique and irrevocable restoration of humanity and of the world to the Father that the Son, eternal[163] and at the same time true man, has accomplished once and for all. The eucharist is therefore the sacrament that is the fullest sign of our new life; in it Christ without interruption and ever in new ways "bears witness" in the Holy Spirit to our spirit[164] that, as sharers in the mystery of redemption, we are empowered to approach the eucharist in order to receive the fruits of the children of reconciliation[165] with God. Christ has achieved this reconciliation and is continually carrying it out among us through the ministry of the Church.

1330   The truth that is primary not only as true doctrine but as the truth of life is this: the eucharist builds up the Church[166] and fashions it into the true community of the people of God, into a congregation of believers, sealed with the same mark of unity that the apostles and first disciples of the Lord shared. The eucharist, more-over, is always building up this community and its unity, which it strengthens and renews through Christ's own sacrifice, because it commemorates his death on the cross,[167] the price of our redemption. Consequently, in the eucharist we touch, so to speak, the mystery of the Lord's body and blood, as the words used at its institution attest; because of the power of that institution these words have become the words in which those chosen for this ministry in the Church continue the celebration of the eucharist.

The Church lives on the eucharist, lives on the fullness of this sacrament, whose sublime essence and meaning have often been explained by the Church's magisterium from the earliest times down to our own.[168] Even so, we can say with certainty that this teaching — supported by the profound minds of theologians, by people of deep faith and prayer, by ascetics and mystics in their complete fidelity toward the eucharistic mystery — still is as it were only at its beginnings: their teaching cannot encompass in thought nor express in word what the eucharist is in its fullness, what it signifies, and what it brings to pass. The eucharist is literally the ineffable sacrament. The inescapable duty and the visible grace and origin of all the resources of the Church as the people of God are specifically these: to remain faithful and to go forward continuously in eucharistic life and devotion and to bring about spiritual progress centered around the eucharist. Consequently, it is completely impermissible for us, whether in thought, life, or deed, to take away

---

159   See 1 Cor 6:20.

160   See Jn 1:12.

161   See Rom 8:23.

162   Rv 5:10; 1 Pt 2:9.

163   See Jn 1:1–4, 18; Mt 3:17, 11:27, 17:5; Mk 1:11; Lk 1:32, 35, 3:22; Rom 1:4; 2 Cor 1:19; 1 Jn 5:5, 20; 2 Pt 1:17; Heb 1:2.

164   See 1 Jn 5:5–11.

165   See Rom 5:10, 11; 2 Cor 5:18ff.; Col 1:20, 22.

166   See LG no. 11 [DOL 4 no. 141]. Paul VI, Address 15 Sept. 1965: *Insegnamenti di Paolo VI* 3 (1965) 1036.

167   See SC art. 47 [DOL 1 no. 47].

168   See Paul VI, Encycl. *Mysterium fidei* [DOL 176].

from this blessed sacrament anything of its full nature and proper meaning. The eucharist is at once sacrament and sacrifice, sacrament and communion, sacrament and presence. No matter how clearly the eucharist has always been and must always remain the expression and celebration of the human community of Christ's disciples and followers, it still cannot be treated only as just another opportunity for professing this community. For in the celebration of the sacrament of the Lord's body and blood, the integral meaning of the divine mystery and the full force of this sacramental sign must be respected; in it Christ's presence is *real*, "the heart is filled with grace and a pledge of future glory given to us."[169] This is the basis for the obligation of the most reverential fulfillment of liturgical rules and of all those things that express the community's offering of worship to God. The obligation is all the more pressing because in this sacramental sign Christ has surrendered himself to us with an unbounded trust, as though taking no notice of our human weakness, of our unworthiness, of our becoming used to things and of our routine ways, even of the desecrations possible. All in the Church, but bishops and priests especially, must take care that this sacrament of love stands central in the life of the people of God, that all acts of due worship are a repayment of "love for love," to Christ, that he becomes in truth the life of our souls.[170] Nor can we ever forget these words of St. Paul: "Let all examine themselves and then let them eat of that bread and drink of that cup."[171] Obliquely at least, St. Paul's warning points to the close connection between the eucharist and penance. If the first statement in Christ's teaching and the first words of the Gospel — that is, the Good News — are "Repent (*metanoeïte*) and believe this Gospel,"[172] the sacrament of the passion, cross, and resurrection seems in a singular way to strengthen and confirm this appeal in our minds. The eucharist and penance in a sense stand as the two inwardly linked sides of a life in keeping with the spirit of the Gospel, a genuinely Christian life. For the Christ who invites us to his supper is the same Christ who urges us to penance, as he repeats: "Repent."[173] Without this constant and ever renewed intention toward conversion, sharing in the eucharist is deprived of its full redemptive effectiveness, it lacks altogether or possesses only in diminished degree the special readiness of spirit to offer spiritual sacrifice to God[174] that shows forth in its essential and full meaning our share in Christ's priesthood. For the priesthood in Christ is bound up with his self-sacrifice and self-giving to the Father. His gift, which is limitless, brings it about that there is a need for us as human beings, subject to so many limitations, to turn ourselves toward God in an ever more mature, constant, and radical conversion.

In recent years much effort has been directed — completely in accord with the   1331
Church's most ancient tradition — toward emphasizing the communitarian aspect of penance and especially of the sacrament in its use in the Church. These efforts are completely worthwhile and certainly will help towards the enrichment of the practice of penance in today's Church. But we have no right to forget that conversion is an inner act of great personal depth; one person cannot act in the place of the other; the community cannot supply for the individual person. Even though the fraternal community of the faithful united in communal celebration strikingly

---

169   SC art. 47 [DOL 1 no. 47].

170   See Jn 6:52, 58, 14:6; Gal 2:20.

171   1 Cor 11:28.

172   Mk 1:15.

173   Ibid.

174   See 1 Pt 2:5.

assists the act of conversion of the individual members, each one, from the inner recesses of personal conscience, must finally make the act of conversion a personal expression, with a complete sense of personal sin and of confidence in God. Like the psalmist, each individual must stand before God and say: "Against you alone have I sinned."[175] This is why the Church, while safeguarding the practice of this sacrament of penance as developed over many centuries, that is, the practice of individual confession with an act of contrition, purpose of amendment and expiation, is defending a particular right of the human soul. That right involves the encounter, proper to every person, with Christ crucified who forgives, with Christ who through the minister of the sacrament of reconciliation declares: "Your sins are forgiven";[176] "Go and sin no more."[177] Clearly, also, this right belongs to Christ and is a right that he possesses in regard to every person he has redeemed. It is the right of coming face to face with each person in the decisive moment of conversion and forgiveness. In protecting the sacrament of penance, the Church is openly confessing its faith in the mystery of redemption as in a reality that is living and life-giving and that also is consistent with the inner truth about human nature with the human sense of sin, and with the longing of the human conscience. "Blessed are they who hunger and thirst after justice, for they shall be filled."[178] The sacrament of penance is the means for us to thirst after the justice that comes from the same Redeemer.

In our times above all, the Church gathers around the eucharist and desires to appear unmistakably as a eucharistic community, the sign of the gradually growing union of all Christians. In the Church the need for penance must therefore be alive, in regard to penance both as sacrament[179] and as virtue. Paul VI has explained the meaning of the virtue of penance in his Apostolic Constitution *Paenitemini*.[180] One of the duties of the Church is to put into effect the teaching this document expounds. It is a theme that we ourself must investigate more deeply through consultation; in this regard we must gather much advice out of a collegial sense of the pastorate and with respect toward different traditions and toward the varying circumstances of the lives of people in our time. In any case, it is clear that the Church of the new Advent, the Church that is continually preparing itself for the Lord's Second Coming, must be the Church of the eucharist and of penance. Only on the basis of this spiritual vision is it the Church of divine mission, the Church *in the state of mission*, as Vatican Council II has shown the Church's true face to be.

192. JOHN PAUL II, **Address** to bishops of India from the Bengalese and northwest regions, on the eucharist and penance, 26 April 1979: AAS 71 (1979) 663–667; Not 15 (1979) 244–246 (English; excerpt).

1332   [. . .] The power of God was strikingly manifested in the paschal mystery of Jesus of Nazareth, it pervaded the teaching of the apostles, and it is active in our day. Above all, this power of God is active through the eucharistic sacrifice. It is

---

[175]   Ps 50(51): 6.

[176]   Mk 2:5.

[177]   Jn 8:11.

[178]   Mt 5:6.

[179]   See SCDF, Pastoral Norms on Giving General Sacramental Absolution [DOL 361]. Paul VI, Address to a group of bishops from the U.S.A. on their *Ad limina* visit, 20 April 1978 [DOL 378]. John Paul II, Address to a group of bishops from Canada on their *Ad limina* visit, 17 Nov. 1978 [DOL 291].

[180]   See DOL 358 nos. 3019–20.

here that we ourselves, together with our priests, must go to find the main source of
that pastoral love[6] which enables us to live a life of faith, a life of selfless love
modeled on that of the Good Shepherd.

In a full and active sharing in the eucharistic sacrifice and in the entire liturgical life of the Church all our people find the primary and indispensable source of
the true Christian spirit.[7] Here they draw the strength to be able to give to the
world the witness of faith, the witness of love. The joyful commitment of service to
humanity in need can only be sustained by power derived from the eucharistic
Christ. And it is he who inspires in the hearts of the faithful an ever greater
appreciation of the needs of his brethren.

The effectiveness of the laity, and in particular of Christian families, to give to
the world the witness of faith and love is conditioned by their spiritual dynamism,
which is nowhere more available than in the eucharist. The youth of your local
Churches can only come to full maturity in Christ through the power of the eucharist. God's gift of priestly and religious vocations is mysteriously related to the
reverent participation of God's people in the eucharist.

Brethren, in this hour of faith that we are celebrating together, it is fitting that
we should concentrate on the eucharist, which is the very mystery of faith. The
eucharist is our source of hope for the future. The success of our ministry is linked
to it; the well-being of God's people depends on it. With the Second Vatican
Council we must continually point out that the eucharist is "the source and summit
of all Christian life."[8] It is the heart of our ecclesial communities. To rededicate
ourselves to our ministry of faith as bishops requires a clear vision of our service in
the perspective of the eucharist. The full expression of human concern and love will
be effected only through the eucharist. All the great issues of your pastoral ministry
are related to the eucharistic Christ. He and he alone directs, through the power of
his presence and the dynamism of his salvific action, the inner life of the ecclesial
communities committed to your pastoral care. This profound truth motivated the
appeal which I made to the universal Church in my recent encyclical and which I
repeat today: "Every member of the Church, especially bishops and priests, must be
vigilant in seeing that this sacrament of love shall be at the center of the life of the
people of God. . . ."[9]

In the same encyclical, I spoke also about the close link between the eucharist   1333
and penance, emphasizing how personal conversion must constantly be pursued
with renewed endeavor so that partaking in the eucharist may not lack its full
redeeming effectiveness. In particular, I noted the need to guard the sacrament of
penance and I stressed that the faithful observance of the centuries-old "practice of
individual confession with a personal act of sorrow and the intention to amend and
make satisfaction" is an expression of the Church's defense of "man's right to a
more personal encounter with the crucified forgiving Christ," and of Christ's "right
to meet each one of us in that key moment . . . of conversion and forgiveness."[10]
Brethren, let us never grow tired of extolling the value of individual confession.
The documents that I cited in *Redemptor hominis* make reference to a point of capital

---

6   See PO no. 14 [DOL 18 no. 266].

7   See SC art. 14 [DOL 1 no. 14].

8   LG no. 11 [DOL 4 no. 141].

9   John Paul II, Encycl. *Redemptor hominis* no. 20 [DOL 191 no. 1330].

10 Ibid.

importance: "the solemn teaching of the Council of Trent concerning the divine precept of individual confession."[11]

Seen in this perspective, the diligent observance by all the priests of the Church of the Pastoral Norms of *Sacramentum Paenitentiae* in regard to general absolution[a] is both a question of loving fidelity to Jesus Christ and to his redemptive plan and the expression of ecclesial communion in what Paul VI called "a matter of special concern to the universal Church and of regulation by her supreme authority."[12] Of particular importance for all the bishops of the world is Paul VI's great pastoral appeal: "Moreover, we ask you, the bishops, to help your priests to have an ever greater appreciation of this splendid ministry of theirs as confessors.[13] The experience of centuries confirms the importance of this ministry. And if priests deeply understand how closely they collaborate, through the sacrament of penance, with the Savior in the work of conversion, they will give themselves with ever greater zeal to this ministry. . . . Other works, for lack of time, may have to be postponed or even abandoned, but not the confessional."[14]

Our ministry is indeed a ministry of faith and the supernatural means to effect our goal are commensurate with the wisdom and power of God. The eucharist and penance are great treasures of Christ's Church.

In all challenges and joys of our ministry, in all our hopes and disappointments, in all the difficulties inherent in proclaiming Christ and his uplifting message for the cause of man and human dignity, let us reflect, in faith, that Christ's power, and not our own, guides our steps and supports our efforts. Today in the fraternity of collegiality that is ours we can hear Christ speaking to us: *Ecce ego vobiscum sum.* And when you return to your people, endeavor to communicate the same message of faith, confidence, and strength to the whole community — to the priests, religious, and laity who make up with you the people of God: *Ecce ego vobiscum sum.* Particularly in the eucharist. [. . .]

▶ 335. SC CATHOLIC EDUCATION, Instruction *In ecclesiasticam futurorum sacerdotum*, on liturgical formation in seminaries, 3 June 1979:

nos. 22–27, 30–40: Mass and worship of the eucharist [nos. 2801–06, 2809–19].

193. JOHN PAUL II, **Homily** at Phoenix Park, Dublin: The eucharist contains the entire spiritual wealth of the Church, 29 September 1979: AAS 71 (1979) 1069–76; Not 15 (1979) 604–607 (English; excerpt).

1334   4. And so it becomes all the more urgent to steep ourselves in the truth that comes from Christ, who is "the way, the truth, and the life" (Jn 14:6), and in the strength that he himself offers us through his Spirit. It is especially in the eucharist that the power and the love of the Lord are given to us.

The sacrifice of the body and blood of Jesus Christ offered up for us is an act of supreme love on the part of the Savior. It is his great victory over sin and death — a

---

[11]   Ibid. note 179 [DOL 191 no. 1331]. Paul VI, Address to U.S. bishops, 20 April 1978 [DOL 378].

[a]   See DOL 361.

[12]   Paul VI, Address of 20 April 1978 [DOL 378 no. 3139].

[13]   See LG no. 30.

[14]   Paul VI, Address of 20 April 1978 [DOL 378 no. 3139].

victory that he communicates to us. The eucharist is a promise of eternal life, since Jesus himself tells us: "He who eats my flesh and drinks my blood has eternal life, and I will raise him up at the last day" (Jn 6:54).

The holy sacrifice of the Mass is meant to be the festive celebration of our salvation. In the Mass we give thanks and praise to God our Father for having given us redemption through the precious blood of Jesus Christ. The eucharist is also the center of the Church's unity, as well as her greatest treasure. In the words of the Second Vatican Council, the eucharist contains "the Church's entire spiritual wealth" (PO no. 5).[a] [. . .]

5.   Yes, it is from the eucharist that all of us receive the grace and strength for daily living — to live real Christian lives, in the joy of knowing that God loves us, that Christ died for us, and that the Holy Spirit lives in us.

Our full participation in the eucharist is the real source of the Christian spirit that we wish to see in our personal lives and in all aspects of society. Whether we serve in politics, in the economic, cultural, social, or scientific field — no matter what our occupation is — the eucharist is a challenge to our daily lives.

Dear brothers and sisters: there must always be consistency between what we believe and what we do. We cannot live on the glories of our past Christian history. Our union with Christ in the eucharist must be expressed in the truth of our lives today — in our actions, in our behavior, in our life-style, and in our relationships with others. For each one of us the eucharist is a call to ever greater effort, so that we may live as true followers of Jesus: truthful in our speech, generous in our deeds, concerned, respectful of the dignity and rights of all persons, whatever their rank or income, self-sacrificing, fair and just, kind, considerate, compassionate and self-controlled — looking to the well-being of our families, our young people, our country, Europe, and the world. The truth of our union with Jesus Christ in the eucharist is tested by whether or not we really love our fellow men and women; it is tested by how we treat others, especially our families: husbands and wives, children and parents, brothers and sisters. It is tested by whether or not we try to be reconciled with our enemies, on whether or not we forgive those who hurt us or offend us. It is tested by whether we practice in life what our faith teaches us. We must always remember what Jesus said: "You are my friends if you do what I command you" (Jn 15:14).

6.   The eucharist is also a great *call to conversion*. We know that it is an invitation to   1335
the banquet; that, by nourishing ourselves on the eucharist, we receive in it the body and blood of Christ, under the appearances of bread and wine. Precisely because of this invitation, the eucharist is and remains the call to conversion. If we receive it as such a call, such an invitation, it brings forth in us its proper fruits. It transforms our lives. It makes us a "new man," a "new creature" (see Gal 6:15; Eph 2:15; 2 Cor 5:17). It helps us not to be "overcome by evil, but *to overcome evil by good*" (see Rom 12:21). The eucharist helps love to triumph in us — love over hatred, zeal over indifference.

The call to conversion in the eucharist links the eucharist with that other great sacrament of God's love, which is penance. Every time that we receive the sacrament of penance or reconciliation, we receive the forgiveness of Christ, and we know that this forgiveness comes to us through the merits of his death — the very death that we celebrate in the eucharist. In the sacrament of reconciliation, we are all invited to meet Christ personally in this way, and to do so frequently. This encounter with Jesus is so very important that I wrote in my first encyclical letter these words: "In faithfully observing the centuries-old practice of the sacrament of

---

[a]   DOL 18 no. 260.

penance — the practice of individual confession with a personal act of sorrow and the intention to amend and make satisfaction — the Church is, therefore, defending the human soul's individual right: man's right to a more personal encounter with the crucified forgiving Christ, with Christ saying, through the minister of the sacrament of reconciliation: 'Your sins are forgiven'; 'Go, and do not sin again'."[b] Because of Christ's love and mercy, there is no sin that is too great to be forgiven; there is no sinner who will be rejected. Every person who repents will be received by Jesus Christ with forgiveness and immense love. [. . .]

I take this occasion to ask all of you to continue to hold this sacrament of penance in special honor, for ever. Let all of us remember the words of Pius XII in regard to frequent confession: "Not without the inspiration of the Holy Spirit was this practice introduced into the Church" (AAS 35 [1943] 235).

Dear brothers and sisters: the call to conversion and repentance comes from Christ, and always leads us back to Christ in the eucharist.

1336   7.   I wish also at this time to recall to you an important truth affirmed by the Second Vatican Council, namely: "The spiritual life, nevertheless, is not confined to participation in the liturgy" (SC art. 12).[c] And so I also encourage you in the other exercises of devotion that you have lovingly preserved for centuries, especially those in regard to the blessed sacrament. These acts of piety honor God and are useful for our Christian lives; they give joy to our hearts and help us to appreciate more the liturgical worship of the Church.

The visit to the blessed sacrament — so much a part of Ireland, so much a part of your piety, so much a part of your pilgrimage to Knock — is a great treasure of the Catholic faith. It nourishes social love and gives us opportunities for adoration and thanksgiving, for reparation and supplication. Benediction of the blessed sacrament, exposition and adoration of the blessed sacrament, holy hours and eucharistic processions are likewise precious elements of your heritage — in full accord with the teaching of the Second Vatican Council.

At this time, it is also my joy to reaffirm before Ireland and the whole world the wonderful teaching of the Catholic Church regarding Christ's consoling presence in the blessed sacrament, his real presence in the fullest sense: the substantial presence by which the whole and complete Christ, God and man, is present (see *Mysterium fidei* no. 39).[d] The eucharist, in the Mass and outside of the Mass, is the body and blood of Jesus Christ, and is therefore deserving of the worship that is given to the living God and to him alone (see *Mysterium fidei* no. 55; Paul VI, Address of 15 June 1978).[e]

And so, dear brothers and sisters, every act of reverence, every genuflection that you make before the blessed sacrament, is important because it is an act of faith in Christ, an act of love for Christ. And every sign of the cross and gesture of respect made each time you pass a church is also an act of faith. [. . .]

---

[b]   See DOL 191 no. 1331.

[c]   DOL 1 no. 12.

[d]   See DOL 176 no. 1183.

[e]   See DOL 176 no. 1199; DOL 189 no. 1323.

194. JOHN PAUL II, **Homily** at Grant Park, Chicago: The eucharist, unity of the people of God, 5 October 1979: AAS 71 (1979) 1230–34; Not 15 (1979) 611–612 (English; excerpt).

5.   [. . .] History does not exhaust itself in material progress, in technological   1337
conquest, or in cultural achievement only. Coming together around the altar of
sacrifice to break the bread of the holy eucharist with the successor of Peter, you
testify to this even deeper reality: to your unity as members of the people of God.

"We, though many, are one body in Christ" (Rom 12:5). The Church too is
composed of many members and enriched by the diversity of those who make up
the one community of faith and baptism, the one Body of Christ. What brings us
together and makes us one is our faith — the one apostolic faith. We are all one,
because we have accepted Jesus Christ as the Son of God, the Redeemer of the
human race, the sole Mediator between God and man. By the sacrament of baptism
we have been truly incorporated into the crucified and glorified Christ and through
the action of the Holy Spirit we have become living members of his one Body.
Christ gave us the wonderful sacrament of the eucharist, by which the unity of the
Church is both expressed and continually brought about and perfected.

6.   "One Lord, one faith, one baptism" (Eph 4:5), thus we are all bound together,
as the people of God, the Body of Christ, in a unity that transcends the diversity of
our origin, culture, education, and personality — in a unity that does not exclude a
rich diversity in ministries and services. With St. Paul we proclaim: "Just as each of
us has one body with many members, and not all the members have the same
function, so too we, though many, are one body in Christ, and individually members one of another" (Rom 12:4–5).

If then the Church, the one Body of Christ, is to be a forcefully discernible sign
of the gospel message, all her members must show forth, in the words of Paul VI,
that "harmony and consistency of doctrine, life, and worship which marked the
first day of her existence" (*Apostolic Exhortation on Reconciliation within the Church* no. 2),
when Christians "devoted themselves to the apostles' teachings and fellowship, to
the breaking of bread and the prayers" (Acts 2:42). [. . .]

7.   [. . .] In a few moments, we shall celebrate our unity by renewing the sacrifice
of Christ. Each one will bring a different gift to be presented in union with the
offering of Jesus: dedication to the betterment of society; efforts to console those
who suffer; the desire to give witness for justice; the resolve to work for peace and
brotherhood; the joy of a united family; or suffering in body or mind. Different
gifts, yes, but all united in the one great gift of Christ's love for his Father and for
us — everything united in the unity of Christ and his sacrifice. [. . .]

▶   75.   JOHN PAUL II, Address to the bishops of the United States at Chicago, 5 October 1979.

SECTION 2. THE ORDO MISSAE PRIOR TO 1969

SUMMARY (DOL 195–201). There are only 7 documents in this section, covering the interlude prior to promulgation of the revised Order of Mass in 1969.

—The main texts are two decrees. The first promulgated changes in accord with the Instruction *Inter Oecumenici* (DOL 196, 197); in connection with this decree there are extensive and interesting notes on the provisional *Ordo Missae* and the *Ritus servandus*. The second decree subsequent to the second Instruction *Tres abhinc annos* promulgated further changes (DOL 201).

—Other texts concern particular issues: preaching, from a section of Paul VI's Encyclical *Ecclesiam suam* (DOL 195); the deacon's function, in a decree for Rome but with universal import (DOL 199); a reply on the prayers at the foot of the altar (DOL 200).

—Finally, the booklet on Masses for the Fourth Period of Vatican II (DOL 198) exemplifies the provisional reform of the *Ordo Missae*.

▶   1.   VATICAN COUNCIL II, Constitution on the Liturgy *Sacrosanctum Concilium*, 4
          December 1963:

          art. 50–58:   Revision of the *Ordo Missae* [nos. 50–58].

▶   20.   PAUL VI, Motu Proprio *Sacram Liturgiam*, on putting into effect some prescriptions
          of the Constitution on the Liturgy, 25 January 1964:

          art. III: Homily at Sunday Mass [no. 281].

195. PAUL VI, Encyclical *Ecclesiam suam*, excerpt on the importance of
preaching, 6 August 1964: AAS 56 (1964) 609–659.

III

1338   90. [. . .] We wish again to lay stress on the supreme importance that the preach-
        ing of the word of God still has and on its even greater importance in these times
        for the area of the Catholic apostolate concerned with the dialogue we are discuss-
        ing. No other form of communication conceivable can take its place, even granted
        the technological power and effectiveness of press, radio, and television. The apos-
        tolate and preaching amount, in fact, to the same thing; preaching is the preeminent
        form of the apostolate. Our ministry before all else, Esteemed Brothers, is the
        ministry of the word. Even though we understand that, it seems necessary to call
        the fact to mind today in order to direct our pastoral activity to its true end. There is
        need for a return, not to human eloquence or empty rhetoric, but to the authentic
        art of proclaiming the word of God.

1339   91. We must rediscover the laws that make it simple and clear, powerful and
        possessed of authority so that we may cast aside the natural ineptness that holds us
        back in the use of so sublime and hidden a resource, the word of God; that by a
        noble competition we may make ourselves the equal of those who today by their
        words exert so much influence as molders of public opinion. We must plead again
        and again with the Lord for that powerful gift of touching hearts[60] so that we may
        be worthy to be men from whose efforts faith takes its true and effective begin-
        nings,[61] and our message reaches the ends of the earth.[62] With devotion and with
        full knowledge we should carry out what the Constitution on the Liturgy dictates
        concerning the ministry of the word.[a] Our catechesis of the Christian people, and as
        far as possible of others, should be marked by a mastery of words, effectiveness of
        method, and constancy in fulfilling this responsibility. It should be confirmed by
        the witness of genuine virtue, press onward toward progress, and be bent on bring-
        ing our hearers to a firm faith, to the knowledge of the relevance of God's word to
        human existence, and to some glimpse of the divine light. [. . .]

▶   23.   SC RITES (Consilium), Instruction (first) *Inter Oecumenici*, 26 September 1964:

          nos. 48:   The *Ordo Missae* [no. 340].

---

[60]   See Jer 1:6.

[61]   See Rom 10:17.

[62]   See Ps 18(19): 5; Rom 10:18.

[a]   See SC art. 51–56 [DOL 1 nos. 51–56].

49–52:	Readings and chants between them [nos. 341–344].
53–55:	Homily [nos. 345–347].
56:	Prayer of the faithful [no. 348].
57–58:	Use of the vernacular [nos. 349–350].
59:	Communion twice on the same day [no. 351].

▶   529.   SC RITES (Consilium), Decree *Quum Constitutio*, promulgating the *Kyriale simplex*, 14 December 1964.

▶   531.   SC RITES (Consilium), Decree *Edita Instructione*, promulgating the chants for the Roman Missal, 14 December 1964.

196. SC RITES (Consilium), **Decree** *Nuper edita Instructione*, promulgating the new *Ordo Missae* and the *Ritus servandus in celebratione Missae*, 27 January 1965: AAS 57 (1965) 408–409.*

The recently issued Instruction for the implementation of the Constitution on   1340
the Liturgy[a] has introduced a number of changes, varying in importance, especially into the celebration of Mass. Therefore, it has been judged necessary to prepare a revision, corresponding to the directives of the aforementioned Instruction, of both the *Ordo Missae* and the *Ritus in celebratione Missae servandus* and the *De defectibus in celebratione Missae occurrentibus* as they presently exist in the *Missale Romanum*.

The Consilium for the Implementation of the Constitution on the Liturgy accordingly has carefully completed such a revision, keeping in mind the overall rationale for the restructuring of the Mass. Applying the powers granted to it by Pope Paul VI, the Congregation of Rites has approved the revision and declared it to be the prototype. The Congregation directs that it be published and incorporated into any new editions of the *Missale Romanum*, so that the rules contained are exactly observed by all.[R1]

---

*   *Ordo Missae, Ritus servandus in celebratione Missae et De defectibus in celebratione Missae occurrentibus* (Vatican Polyglot Press, 1965).

a   DOL 23.

R1   The following replies appeared in *Notitiae* on the new *Ordo Missae* and the *Ritus servandus*, prior to publication of the new Roman Missal.

Replies on the *Ordo Missae*:
No. 18: Query: Is the invitation *Oremus* still to be given before the offertory antiphon? Reply: No. The prayer of the faithful prior to the offertory antiphon is introduced by the priest's invitation to pray. Thus the *Oremus* would make for duplication. This is the reason that the "Changes to be introduced into the *Ordo Missae*" [see DOL 201] have emended no. 1. This applies to all Masses, even when there is no prayer of the faithful, for the sake of uniformity: Not 3 (1967) 303, no. 106.
Nos. 44–45: 1. Query: May the deacon who reads or sings the gospel, according to the *Ritus servandus* nos. 44–45, also give the homily? Reply: Yes, once he has the permission of the local Ordinary required by CIC can. 1342, § 1: Not 1 (1965) 187, no. 46.
2. Query: May a deacon who in recited Masses reads the gospel, according to the *Ritus servandus* nos. 44–45, also assist as a deacon for the other parts of the Mass? Reply: Yes: ibid., no. 47.
Nos. 44–46. Query: I have seen a recited Mass celebrated facing the people in which the epistle was read at the right of the celebrant and the gospel at his left. Is this the correct way or should it be done just the opposite, as in the ancient basilicas? Reply: If there is but one lectern, all the readings are done from it. The one lectern may be placed to the right or the left of the altar, whichever is more in keeping with the design of the sanctuary and the church. If a church has two lecterns, a major one for the gospel and a minor one for the epistle, the readings are done from each according to its purpose. If the two lecterns are the same or two are to be set up, the epistle is read from the one on the left and the gospel from the one on the right, in relationship to the celebrant's chair in the apse of the church, behind the altar: ibid., no. 48.
No. 46. Query: Commentaries on Mass with a congregation say nothing about Mass celebrated in

the houses of women religious, girls' schools, etc. This is regrettable, especially in regard to the function of reader and commentator. It is generally not possible to have clerics in orders for these functions. Yet the rubrics say nothing about their being exercised by laypersons. What should be done? Reply: As to the function of reader: it can be taken by a server, even if he is not a cleric. When there is no server, the celebrant reads the lessons and epistle, according to the *Ritus servandus* no. 46 (see Not 1 [1965] 139–140, no. 16 [see notes on the *Ritus servandus* nos. 41 and 44]). As for the function of commentator: according to the SCR's Instruction of 3 September 1958 no. 96 a, it is generally enough if "a woman leads, as it were, . . . the singing and prayers": Not 1 (1965) 187–188, no. 49.

Nos. 46–57. Query: Is it permitted to read the gospel from the presidential chair from which the homily is also given? Reply: The *Ritus servandus* nos. 46 and 47 is to be followed: ". . .the celebrant reads or sings the lessons and epistle at the lectern or at the sanctuary steps. . . . Then standing in the same place . . . he sings or reads the gospel. But if there is no lectern or it seems more convenient, the celebrant may do all the readings from the altar, facing the people": Not 1 (1965) 188, no. 50.

No. 59. Query: The celebrant no longer signs himself during the prayers at the foot of the altar at the *Adiutorium nostrum in nomine Domini*. Should a bishop sign himself as he says the same words during the blessing at the end of Mass? Reply: No. It is a parallel situation, since in both cases the sign of the cross is omitted at the *Adiutorium nostrum* to avoid the celebrant's signing himself twice in succession: Not 1 (1965) 186–187, no. 45.

No. 60. Query: Is it true that the thurifer should no longer incense the acolytes at a solemn Mass? Reply: The acolytes are considered to be included when the thurifer incenses that part of the choir where they are standing: Not 1 (1965) 188, no. 51.

No. 83. Query: Should servers at a solemn Mass who are to receive communion kneel on the top step of the altar or may they stand at the foot of the altar? Reply: Local custom should be followed: ibid., no. 52.

Replies on the *Ritus servandus*:
No. 14. Query: In a Mass celebrated facing the people, is it permitted for the celebrant to recite the prayers at the foot of the altar with his back to the people? Reply: Yes: Not 1 (1965) 251, no. 65.

No. 22. 1. Query: May the prayers at the foot of the altar be omitted when lauds, recited by a community not obliged to choir, immediately precedes Mass? Reply: Yes, if the whole community takes part in the Mass in question. No, if after lauds the individual priests belonging to such a community celebrate Mass privately on side altars: Not 1 (1965) 139, no. 12.

2. Query: May the prayers at the foot of the altar be omitted according to the *Ritus servandus* no. 22 when communion is distributed immediately before Mass at the altar of celebration that has a tabernacle? It would mean repeating the *Confiteor*, *Misereatur*, and *Indulgentiam*, which are included in the communion rite. Reply: No. Two entirely distinct liturgical services are involved: ibid., no. 13.

No. 23. 1. Query: Should there still be a bow of the head at the *Gloria Patri* when it occurs in the Mass? Reply: Yes, in accord with general principles: ibid., no. 14.

2. Query: Since according to the Constitution art. 34 [see DOL 1 no. 34] repetitions must be avoided, should the reprise of the entrance antiphon after the *Gloria Patri* be omitted? Reply: This reprise is based on the very nature of an antiphon; it therefore should not be counted among the "useless repetitions" referred to by the Constitution art. 34: ibid., no. 15.

No. 35. Query: In Masses such as those of the Wednesday and Saturday ember days and the Wednesday after the Fourth Sunday of Lent, what procedure should a celebrant follow when in the absence of a qualified reader he must do all the readings himself? Must he go from the lectern to the chair (or altar) to read each prayer after the reading? Reply: In the case proposed he may also read the prayer from the lectern: Not 1 (1965) 251–252, no. 66.

Nos. 41 and 44. Query: At a Mass in which women alone take part (e.g., in houses of women religious) may a woman, properly trained, exercise the function of reader? Reply: No. The function of reader is liturgical and so is reserved to men. Therefore the celebrant reads the epistle: Not 1 (1965) 139–140, no. 16.

No. 47. Query: In the absence of a reader or server capable may the celebrant, facing the people from the altar, read also the gradual, *Alleluia*, tract, etc., if these are not sung or read by choir or congregation? Reply: Yes: Not 1 (1965) 252, no. 67.

No. 49. 1. Query: Should there be a genuflection at the *Et incarnatus est . . .* on Christmas only or also during the octave? Reply: On 25 December only: ibid., no. 68.

2. Query: Should there be a genuflection at the words *Veni, Sancte Spiritus* at the Mass on Pentecost Sunday or also during the octave? Reply: On Pentecost Sunday only: ibid., no. 69.

No. 50. 1. Query: In beginning the *Credo* should the celebrant still extend his hands? Reply: No. The words indicating this gesture slipped into the first edition of the *Ordo Missae* as a typographical error. They were later taken out; they are not found in the *Ritus servandus*: Not 1 (1965) 140, no. 17.

2. Query: Is it permitted to begin the *Credo* only at the chair or altar or also at the lectern or at the sanctuary steps? Reply: The *Ritus servandus* no. 50 is to be followed: ". . . if the *Credo* is to be said, the

celebrant begins it at the chair or altar": ibid., no. 18.

No. 51. 1. Query: How should the celebrant hold his hands during the prayer of the faithful? Reply: He should stand with hands joined: ibid., no. 19.

2. When there is a *Credo* in recited Masses should the celebrant go to the altar after the gospel or return to the chair, then again go to the lectern for the prayer of the faithful. Reply: In recited Masses when the celebrant himself reads the gospel, he is to intone the *Credo in unum Deum* "at the chair or at the altar" (*Ritus servandus* no. 50). He should lead the prayer of the faithful from the chair or altar as well, in order to avoid too many changes of place (see Ritus servandus no. 51): Not 1 (1965) 252, no. 70.

Nos. 55 and 56. Query: May the celebrant prepare the chalice for the offertory standing at the middle of the altar? Reply: No. He should do so in the usual way at the right side of the altar (except for the case indicated in the *Ritus servandus* no. 99, b): Not 1 (1965) 140, no. 20.

No. 58. Query: On days of fast and in Masses for the dead should there be a genuflection at the prayer over the gifts? Reply: Yes, in keeping with the intention of the *Codex rubricarum* no. 521, c: ibid., no. 21.

No. 62. Query: Since the dialogue preceding the preface and the *Sanctus* following may certainly be said in the vernacular, is the vernacular also lawful for the preface itself? Reply: On the basis of the recent concession of the Apostolic See (27 April 1965 [DOL 110]) and the Instruction no. 58 [DOL 23 no. 350], the competent, territorial ecclesiastical authority may allow use of this vernacular in prefaces, after the Consilium has confirmed the translation: ibid., no. 22.

No. 61. Query: What should the celebrant do when the *Sanctus* is sung polyphonically by the choir alone? Reply: For the time being it seems advisable to make no change and for the celebrant to begin the *Te igitur* immediately while the *Sanctus* is being sung: Not 1 (1965) 252, no. 71.

No. 69. 1. Query: In a solemn Mass is it permissible for the master of ceremonies to stand at the book, especially during the canon? Reply: The *Ritus servandus* no. 69 is to be followed: "In a solemn Mass, from the prayer over the gifts on, the deacon and subdeacon stand behind the celebrant, the deacon going to the celebrant's side whenever his ministry requires, then immediately returning to his place." When it is not possible for the deacon to assist at the book, the master of ceremonies does and once he has performed his service returns immediately to his place. The word *behind* in no. 69 indicates that the ministers must stand further away than the celebrant even if this is not actually in back of him: Not 1 (1965) 141, no. 23.

2. Query: At a prelate's recited Mass where should assistants or chaplains stand during the canon? Reply: They are to stand "after" the celebrant. That is, they are to station themselves in the same way as the *Ritus servandus* no. 69 indicates for the ministers: ibid., no. 24.

Nos. 76–77. Query: Must the celebrant wait for the completion of the singing of the *Agnus Dei* before going on with the prayer *Domine, Iesu Christe*? Reply: He may go on: ibid., no. 25.

No. 81. There is a certain church where Masses for the dead are celebrated at a special altar on the day of burial, on the seventh and thirtieth day after death, and on the anniversary. The faithful taking part who desire to receive communion must go to the altar of reservation. Is such a practice to be approved? Reply: It is better that in every Mass hosts be consecrated for the communion of the faithful (see *Ritus servandus* no. 7), even if these are few, in order to achieve that more complete participation discussed in the Constitution art. 55 [see DOL 1 no. 55]: Not 1 (1965) 306, no. 83.

No. 84. 1. Query: For the purification of his fingers after communion must the celebrant still go to the right side of the altar or may the servers go to him as he stands at the middle? Reply: After consuming the ablutions, the celebrant goes to the right side of the altar and there purifies his fingers (except in the case covered by the *Ritus servandus* no. 99, a): Not 1 (1965) 141, no. 26.

2. Query: The *Ritus servandus* no. 84 has: "Then the celebrant, standing at the middle of the altar with the book near him . . ." And no. 85: ". . . standing at the middle of the altar at the book says . . ." Should these words be interpreted to mean that the missal is to be placed at the middle of the altar? Reply: For the reading of the communion antiphon and the postcommunion, the missal may either be left at the left side where it was for the canon or, once the chalice has been removed, placed at the middle, whichever better suits the celebrant: ibid, no. 27.

3. Query: If, when there is no server able to remove the chalice, the celebrant places it a little to the right side, may the missal for the reading of the communion antiphon and the prayer following be placed at the middle of the altar? Reply: There is nothing against this: Not 1 (1965) 253, no. 73.

4. Query: Is it in keeping with the *Ordo Missae* no. 56, to omit the *Dominus vobiscum* before the postcommunion? Reply: The *Ordo Missae* is usually clarified and completed by the *Ritus servandus*, which in this instance has: "After consuming the ablutions, he kisses the altar, turns toward the congregation, and says: *Dominus vobiscum*, then turns around again toward the altar": Not 1 (1965) 142, no. 28.

5. Query: Is it permissible to complete the circle after the *Dominus vobiscum* before the postcommunion, when, as at the *Orate fratres*, the missal is at the celebrant's left? Reply: Yes: ibid., no. 29.

No. 87. 1. Query: When benediction of the blessed sacrament follows the Mass immediately, may the final blessing be omitted? Reply: No. Two distinct and unconnected services are involved. And in fact

197. SC RITES, **Letter** to publishers of liturgical books, listing the corrections for the rubrics of the *Missale Romanum*, 15 February 1965.

1341   "On 15 February 1965 by letter (SCR, Prot. R.11/965), the Congregation of Rites sent to the publishers of liturgical books a list of variations in the rubrics to be introduced throughout the *Missale Romanum*. These changes seemed necessary in order that the rubrics might be in conformity with both the norms of the Instruction of 26 September 1964[a] and the *Ordo Missae*, the *Ritus servandus*, and the chants for the *Missale Romanum* (see Not 1, 1965, 100–101).[b] Such rubrics, as is clear, are to be inserted also into bilingual editions of the missal": Not 1 (1965) 215.[c]

▶   222.   SC RITES (Consilium), Decree *Ecclesiae semper*, promulgating the new rites of concelebration and of communion under both kinds, 7 March 1965.

▶   31.   CONSILIUM, Letter *Le renouveau liturgique* to presidents of the conferences of bishops, on furthering liturgical reform, 30 June 1965:

it seems better that benediction not be given immediately after Mass: Not 1 (1965) 142, no. 30.
        2. Query: When (in virtue of an indult) there is solemn exposition of the blessed sacrament at the end of Mass, must the *Ite, Missa est* be said and the blessing be given? Or rather, as on Holy Thursday and Corpus Christi in the Mass before the procession, should the *Benedicamus Domino* be said and the *Placeat* without blessing (the second seems more in keeping with the situation)? Reply: Nothing is to be changed in the rite of such a Mass. Two distinct and unconnected services are involved: Not 1 (1965) 253, no. 74.

        General points:
        1. Query: Must servers at a recited Mass follow the old rubrics, prescribing that they kneel throughout the Mass (except at the gospel), or may they follow the pattern of the congregation's kneeling, standing, and sitting? Reply: In Masses with a congregation the servers certainly must follow the arrangement set for the congregation, acting as a model and mirror for the people. In recited Masses without a congregation ("private" Masses), the old rubrics may be followed : ibid., 254, no. 77.
        2. Query: How should a congregation of the faithful conduct itself in regard to the order of standing, kneeling, sitting, etc.? Reply: They should observe any directives given by competent authority; in the absence of these they should, as far as possible, observe the ceremonial, choral rules prescribed (*Codex rubricarum* 520–521): Not 1 (1965) 308, no. 89.
        3. Query: Do hand missals for the faithful retain their usefulness? Reply: Some are alleging that after the introduction of the vernacular into the liturgy hand missals no longer have any use and in fact interfere with active participation. The truth is that before promulgation of the Constitution on the Liturgy the purpose of these missals was "that the faithful might understand the rites celebrated in Latin; they were an aid to people who did not know the ancient language" (Paul VI, Address to meeting of translators [DOL 113 no. 787]). But an even more principal purpose was love and taste for the liturgy and the guidance of the faithful toward a gradually deeper understanding. This purpose still prevails. Hand missals edited in accord with the demands of the current reform of the liturgy and containing not only the Ordinary of the Mass, but the translation approved by proper authority of all the liturgical texts are needed on many counts: for a fuller perception of the mystery of salvation in its entirety as celebrated in the liturgical year; for the fostering of meditation and devotion out of the inexhaustible riches of the liturgical texts; for the facilitation of active participation. Such participation requires not only the proclamation and attentive hearing of the word of God in the assembled community, but also the holy people's response to the word received and their celebration of the parts of the Ordinary and Proper of the Mass by singing or reciting together the hymns and psalms. All of this can be done with the help of a hand missal or prayer book. Such a book will be all the more useful if it also contains parts pertaining to participation in the sacraments and other sacred rites, as for example *The Book of Catholic Worship* now being prepared by the Liturgical Conference in the U.S.A. (see Not 1 [1965] 318).
        Various groups seem to be in a special way in need of such a resource: communities that take part in daily Mass or wish to live and pray each day according to the spirit of the liturgy; those people who for reasons of sickness or some other obstacle cannot meet with their own liturgical community, in order that they may truly and closely join their prayer with the community; children who are to be gradually initiated into the mystery of the liturgy. This is a reason for applauding and spreading the custom of giving children at their first communion or confirmation a hand missal: it is the most appropriate gift of all: Not 2 (1966) 31–32, no. 96.

        [a]   See DOL 23.

        [b]   See DOL 531.

        [c]   The changes follow, 215–219.

nos. 5:   Concelebration [no. 414].

    6:                Altar facing the people [no. 415].

▶   543. SC RITES, Reply (Washington), on the altar facing the people and the celebration of Mass facing the people, 16 July 1965.

198. CONSILIUM, *Masses for the Fourth Period of Vatican Council II*, **Introduction** and **Order of Celebration**, 14 September 1965: Vatican Polyglot Press, 1965.

INTRODUCTION

1. This booklet provides for the conciliar Fathers the ordo and the texts for the   1342
Masses that are celebrated at the beginning of general congregations during the
Fourth Period of Vatican Council II.

2. The Council's Order of Celebration determines that each day the Mass of the   1343
Holy Spirit is said. In keeping with the intent of the Constitution on the Liturgy,
however, in place of this votive Mass the Mass of the day, whether of the season or
of a saint, will be celebrated on certain special days, namely:

    a. the ember days;

    b. feasts of the Dedication of the Archbasilica of the Holy Savior [St. John Lateran] and of the Basilica of St. Paul;

    c. feasts of the Blessed Virgin Mary;

    d. feasts of the apostles;

    e. feasts of popes;

    f. feasts of doctors of the Church;

    g. feasts of certain saints of "special significance" for the life of the Church or who are mentioned in the canon of the Mass.

3. To make better provision for due variety and for a fuller use of the treasures of   1344
liturgical texts, several sets of texts are given for the votive Mass of the Holy Spirit
and for the days when another Mass is celebrated. In addition, as outlined further
on, readings are taken in a semicontinuous sequence from Acts and the Gospel of
St. John.

4. The celebrations presented also have a didactic purpose, namely, to bring out,   1345
in keeping with recent documents on reform of the liturgy, the true rationale for a
eucharistic celebration in what relates either to the rites, the singing, or active
participation. Accordingly:

    a. Mass will be celebrated in keeping with the different forms of celebration
— that is, sung or not sung — established by the rubrics.

    b. The active participation of those assisting will be expressed in two ways:
by their singing or reciting together the parts belonging to the congregation; by the
distribution of holy communion to at least the Auditors during Mass.

    c. Different styles of singing will be used in order to bring out more clearly
the wide range of possibilities for using the repertoire of sacred music, according to
the capabilities of each individual worship assembly.

ORDER OF CELEBRATION

1346   1.   To emphasize the dignity and great importance of the Book of the Gospels, its enthronement will take place at the beginning of Mass, in preparation for its use for the reading of the gospel during the eucharistic celebration. The enthronement procession takes place as part of the entrance procession, during which the entrance antiphon with its psalm is sung.

1347   2.   Since another liturgical act, namely, this enthronement, comes first, the prayers at the foot of the altar are omitted.

1348   3.   The entire celebration follows the norms published in the *Ordo Missae*, 27 January 1965, by the Congregation of Rites.[a]

1349   4.   A bishop celebrant even in sung Masses follows the priest's manner of celebration, with only a deacon assisting, in accord with the faculty granted by the Instruction of the Congregation of Rites, 26 September 1964.[b]

1350   5.   The form of celebration, the parts of the Mass to be sung or recited, and the readings shall be posted for each day.

1351   6.   For the sake of a practical and complete example, the Mass shall contain all its elements, including the prayer of the faithful and the communion of the faithful. On certain special occasions there shall be a five-minute homily, prepared in writing.

1352   7.   Any special celebrations shall be announced well ahead of time.

199. SC RITES, **Decree** (Rome), on the functions of the deacon at Mass with a congregation and on concelebration, 12 January 1966: Not 2 (1966) 265–266.

1353   Cardinal Luigi Traglia, Vicar General of His Holiness in Rome, has submitted to the Congregation of Rites the following two queries for solution.

1.   According to the *Ritus servandus in celebratione Missae* no. 44, published 27 January 1965,[a] in Masses with a congregation participating the deacon or a second priest vested in alb and stole may sing or read the gospel. This, however, involves a certain difficulty in practice, because very often a priest appointed to hear confessions fulfills this function. Thus the question: In view of the situation described, may the deacon or priest vested only in surplice and stole read the gospel in Masses celebrated with a congregation participating?

2.   The *Ritus servandus in concelebratione Missae* article 3, when dealing with the regulation of the practice of concelebration, states: "The right to regulate, in accord with the law, the discipline for concelebration in his diocese, even in churches and semipublic oratories of exempt religious, belongs to the bishop. The right to decide on the advisability of concelebration and to permit it in his churches and oratories belongs to every Ordinary and even to every major superior of nonexempt, clerical religious institutes and of societies of clerics living in community without vows. He

---

    [a]   See DOL 196.
    [b]   See DOL 23 no. 340.
    [a]   See DOL 196.

also may limit the number of concelebrants, on the basis of the norms in no. 4, if, all circumstances being considered, he decides that the dignity of the rite requires this."[b] Thus the question: Does the major superior share equally with the local Ordinary the right to regulate concelebration in his own churches or instead is his right limited to allowing the use in his own churches of the permission already granted by the local Ordinary and to decide on the number of concelebrants?

The Congregation of Rites, after hearing the opinion of the liturgical commission and having fully considered the matter, has decided on these answers to the questions raised.   1354

1.   The intent of the *Ritus servandus* is that the deacon or, in his absence, a second priest, assist the celebrant with their ministry all during the entire rite. Thus each is obliged to wear the liturgical vestments of his own order: the deacon, an alb and deacon's stole; the priest, an alb and priest's stole. It therefore seems somewhat out of keeping with this intent that a priest appointed for confessions serve at the altar as a liturgical minister only for the reading of the gospel.[c]

2.   In churches of religious, permission of the local Ordinary is not required in regard to the faculty to concelebrate (see SC art. 57, § 1, 2 and the *Ritus servandus in concelebratione Missae* art. 3).[d] The faculty given to a major superior is threefold: a. to judge on the advisability of concelebration; b. to grant permission for it; c. to restrict, if necessary, the number of concelebrants.

It belongs to the bishop, that is, the local Ordinary, to regulate the practice of concelebration in his own diocese (see SC art. 57, § 2),[e] e.g., to forbid concelebration in other churches at the time of a concelebration in the cathedral; to prevent abuses; to ensure individual celebration of Masses for the benefit of the faithful; to give rules on the observance of the rite and its practice, on the prayer of the faithful, and on other like matters.

▶   32.   CONSILIUM, Letter *L'heureux développement*, to presidents of the conferences of bishops, on problems in the reform of the liturgy, 25 January 1966:

nos.	6:	Altar facing the people [no. 428].
	7:	The service of women at the altar [no. 429].

200. SC RITES, **Reply** to a query, on omitting the prayers at the foot of the altar, 5 February 1966: Not 2 (1966) 132.

The Instruction for the correct Implementation of the Constitution on the Liturgy art. 48, c states: "All the prayers at the foot of the altar are omitted whenever there is another liturgical rite immediately preceding."[a] Therefore, the following query has been submitted to the Congregation of Rites for the proper solution.   1355

May the prayers at the foot of the altar be omitted at the beginning of the conventual Mass in any community of women religious bound to choir immediate-

---

b   DOL 223 no. 1796.

c   See also DOL 23 no. 342, note R15.

d   See DOL 1 no. 57 and DOL 223 no. 1796.

e   See DOL 1 no. 57.

a   DOL 23 no. 340.

ly after the sisters' recitation of the divine office, even if the celebrant has not taken part in the office?

Having conferred with the Consilium and deliberated on this point the same Congregation has replied to this query: Yes.

▶ 239. CONSILIUM, *The Universal Prayer or Prayer of the Faithful*, 17 April 1966.

▶ 508. SC RITES (Consilium), Instruction *Musicam Sacram*, on music in the liturgy, 5 March 1967.

> nos. 27–36:   Singing during Mass [nos. 4148–57].

▶ 39. SC RITES (Consilium), Instruction (second) *Tres abhinc annos*, 4 May 1967:

> nos. 1–3:   Choice of texts [nos. 447–449].
> 4–6:   Prayers [nos. 450–452].
> 7–16:   Changes in the *Ordo Missae* [nos. 453–462].
> 18:   Mass of a blind or infirm priest [no. 464].
> 25–27:   Vestments [nos. 471–473].
> 28:   Use of the vernacular [no. 474].

201. SC RITES (Consilium), **Decree** *Per Instructionem alteram*, promulgating the text on changes in the Ordo Missae, 18 May 1967: Not 3 (1967) 195.*

1356   The Instruction *Tres abhinc annos*, issued 4 May of this year,[a] has introduced some further changes into the *Ordo Missae*. It has been judged advisable, therefore, to furnish the changes that, in conformity to *Tres abhinc annos*, are to be introduced into the *Ordo Missae*.

The Consilium for the Implementation of the Constitution on the Liturgy has carefully edited these variations and the Congregation of Rites has thoroughly reviewed them. Applying the powers granted it by Pope Paul VI, the Congregation of Rites has approved them and ordered their publication for their exact observance by all concerned.

▶ 532. SC RITES, Decree *Sacrosancti Oecumenici Concilii*, promulgating *The Simple Gradual*, 3 September 1967.

▶ 107. SC BISHOPS, Index of quinquennial faculties granted local Ordinaries, 1 January 1968:

> SC Rites, no. 3:   To celebrate once each week a Mass for the dead [no. 763].

* *Variationes in Ordinem Missae inducendae ad normam Instructionis S.R.C., die 4 Maii 1967* (Vatican Polyglot Press, 1967).

a See DOL 39.

Section 3. New Roman Missal in General

SUMMARY (DOL 202–221). There are 20 documents on this central element in the restructuring of the Mass of the Roman Rite.

—The major texts are the Apostolic Constitution *Missale Romanum* approving the new Roman Missal (DOL 202) and the decrees promulgating the new books for the Mass: the *editio typica* of the Order of Mass (DOL 203), the first *editio typica* of the Roman Missal (DOL 213), and the second *editio typica* (DOL 207). The order of presentation of these last documents is explained by the need to keep together the material on the four editions, from 1969 to 1975, of the General Instruction of the Roman Missal. This introduction, theological, pastoral, and rubrical in nature, was presented first through a Declaration of the Congregation for Divine Worship (DOL 204). The actual text of the General Instruction presented here is that of the 4th edition (DOL 208); the variants of the earlier editions are given in footnotes. The documents publishing these variants are also given (DOL 205, 206). Finally there is an authentic interpretation of one article of the General Instruction (DOL 215).

—Paul VI showed himself as the ardent defender and champion of the new Order of Mass in his addresses to general audiences (DOL 211, 212) and through two letters of the Secretariat of State (DOL 217, 220).

—The Congregation for Divine Worship's involvement consisted of an instruction and a notification on the gradual introduction of the new Order of Mass and Roman Missal (DOL 209 and 216), a particular reply and a notification on the obligatory use of the new Roman Missal (DOL 218 and 219), a letter to the conferences of bishops on the Latin Appendix, and remarks on the *Missale parvum* (DOL 210 and 214).

—Finally, the Vatican Press Office held a special press conference on alleged Protestant influences on the new Order of Mass (DOL 221).

▶ 441. SC RITES (Consilium), Decree *Anni liturgici ordinatione*, promulgating the new General Roman Calendar, 21 March 1969.

202. PAUL VI, Apostolic Constitution *Missale Romanum*, approving the new Roman Missal, 3 April 1969: AAS 61 (1969) 217–222; Not 5 (1969) 142–146.

1357   The *Missale Romanum* was promulgated in 1570 by our predecessor St. Pius V, in execution of the decree of the Council of Trent.[1] It has been recognized by all as one of the many admirable results that the Council achieved for the benefit of the entire Church of Christ. For four centuries it provided Latin-rite priests with norms for the celebration of the eucharistic sacrifice; moreover messengers of the Gospel brought this Missal to almost the entire world. Innumerable holy men and women nurtured their spiritual life on its readings from Scripture and on its prayer texts. In large part these prayer texts owed their arrangement to St. Gregory the Great.

A deep interest in fostering the liturgy has become widespread and strong among the Christian people and our predecessor Pius XII has viewed this both as a sign of God's caring will regarding today's people and as a saving movement of the Holy Spirit through his Church.[2] Since the beginning of this liturgical renewal, it has also become clear that the formularies of the Roman Missal had to be revised and enriched. A beginning was made by Pius XII in the restoration of the Easter Vigil and Holy Week services;[3] he thus took the first step toward adapting the Roman Missal to the contemporary mentality.

1358   The Second Vatican Ecumenical Council, in the Constitution *Sacrosanctum Concilium*, laid down the basis for the general revision of the Roman Missal: "Both texts and rites should be drawn up so that they express more clearly the holy things they signify";[4] therefore, "the Order of Mass is to be revised in such a way that the intrinsic nature and purpose of its several parts, as also the connection between them, may be more clearly brought out, and devout, active participation by the faithful more easily achieved."[5] The Council also decreed that "the treasures of the Bible are to be opened up more lavishly, so that a richer share in God's word may be provided for the faithful";[6] and finally that "a new rite for concelebration is to be drawn up and incorporated into the Roman Pontifical and Roman Missal."[7]

No one should think, however, that this revision of the Roman Missal has come out of nowhere. The progress in liturgical studies during the last four centuries has certainly prepared the way. Just after the Council of Trent, the study "of ancient manuscripts in the Vatican library and elsewhere," as St. Pius V attests in the Apostolic Constitution *Quo primum*, helped greatly in the correction of the Roman Missal. Since then, however, other ancient sources have been discovered and

---

¹   See Ap. Const. *Quo primum*, 14 July 1570.

²   See Pius XII, Addr. to the participants of the First International Congress on Pastoral Liturgy at Assisi, 22 May 1956: AAS 48 (1956) 712.

³   See SCR, Decr. *Dominicae Resurrectionis*, 9 Feb. 1951: AAS 43 (1951) 128ff.; Decr. *Maxima redemptionis nostrae mysteria*, 16 Nov. 1955: AAS 47 (1955) 838ff.

⁴   SC art. 21 [DOL 1 no. 21].

⁵   SC art. 50 [DOL 1 no. 50].

⁶   SC art. 51 [DOL 1 no. 51].

⁷   SC art. 58 [DOL 1 no. 58].

published and liturgical formularies of the Eastern Church have been studied. Accordingly many have had the desire for these doctrinal and spiritual riches not to be stored away in the dark, but to be put into use for the enlightenment of the mind of Christians and for the nurture of their spirit.

Now, however, our purpose is to set out at least in broad terms, the new plan of the Roman Missal. We therefore point out, first, that a General Instruction, for use as a preface to the book, gives the new regulations for the celebration of the eucharistic sacrifice. These regulations cover the rites to be carried out and the functions of each minister or participant as well as the furnishings and the places needed for divine worship.   1359

It must be acknowledged that the chief innovation in the reform concerns the eucharistic prayer. Although the Roman Rite over the centuries allowed for a multiplicity of different texts in the first part of the prayer (the preface), the second part, called the *Canon actionis*, took on a fixed form during the period of the fourth and fifth centuries. The Eastern liturgies, on the other hand, allowed a degree of variety into the anaphoras themselves. On this point, first of all, the eucharistic prayer has been enriched with a great number of prefaces — drawn from the early tradition of the Roman Church or recently composed — in order that the different facets of the mystery of salvation will stand out more clearly and that there will be more and richer themes of thanksgiving. But besides this, we have decided to add three new canons to the eucharistic prayer. Both for pastoral reasons, however, and for the facilitation of concelebration, we have ordered that the words of the Lord be identical in each form of the canon. Thus in each eucharistic prayer we wish those words to be as follows: over the bread: *Accipite et manducate ex hoc omnes: Hoc est enim Corpus meum, quod pro vobis tradetur;* over the chalice: *Accipite et bibite ex eo omnes: Hic est enim calix Sanguinis mei novi et aeterni testamenti, qui pro vobis et pro multis effundetur in remissionem peccatorum. Hoc facite in meam commemorationem.* The words *Mysterium fidei* have been removed from the context of Christ's own words and are spoken by the priest as an introduction to the faithful's acclamation.   1360

In the Order of Mass the rites have been "simplified, due care being taken to preserve their substance."[8] "Elements that, with the passage of time, came to be duplicated or were added with but little advantage"[9] have been eliminated, especially in the rites for the presentation of the bread and wine, the breaking of the bread, and communion.   1361

Also, "other elements that have suffered injury through accident of history" are restored "to the tradition of the Fathers,"[10] for example, the homily,[11] the general intercessions or prayer of the faithful,[12] and the penitential rite or act of reconciliation with God and the community at the beginning of the Mass, which thus, as is right, regains its proper importance.

According to the decree of the Second Vatican Council, that "a more representative portion of the holy Scriptures be read to the people over the course of a prescribed number of years,"[13] the Sunday readings are arranged in a cycle of three   1362

---

[8] SC art. 50 [DOL l no. 50].

[9] SC art. 50 [DOL 1 no. 50].

[10] SC art. 50 [DOL 1 no. 50].

[11] See SC art. 52 [DOL 1 no. 52].

[12] See SC art. 53 [DOL 1 no. 53].

[13] SC art. 51 [DOL 1 no. 51].

years. In addition, on Sundays and all the major feasts the epistle and gospel are preceded by an Old Testament reading or, at Easter, by readings from Acts. This is meant to provide a fuller exposition of the continuing process of the mystery of salvation, as shown in the words of divine revelation. These broadly selected biblical readings, which set before the faithful on Sundays and holydays the most important part of sacred Scripture, are complemented by other parts of the Bible read on other days.

All this has been planned to arouse among the faithful a greater hunger for the word of God.[14] Under the guidance of the Holy Spirit, this hunger will seem, so to speak, to impel the people of the New Covenant toward the perfect unity of the Church. We are fully confident that under this arrangement both priest and faithful will prepare their minds and hearts more devoutly for the Lord's Supper and that, meditating on the Scriptures, they will be nourished more each day by the words of the Lord. In accord with the teachings of the Second Vatican Council, all will thus regard sacred Scripture as the abiding source of spiritual life, the foundation for Christian instruction, and the core of all theological study.

1363   This reform of the Roman Missal, in addition to the three changes already mentioned (the eucharistic prayer, the Order of Mass, and the readings), has also corrected and considerably modified other of its components: the Proper of Seasons, the Proper of Saints, the Common of Saints, ritual Masses, and votive Masses. In all of these changes, particular care has been taken with the prayers. Their number has been increased, so that the new forms might better correspond to new needs, and the text of older prayers has been restored on the basis of the ancient sources. As a result, each weekday of the principal liturgical seasons, Advent, Christmas, Lent, and Easter, now has its own, distinct prayer.

1364   The text of the *Graduale Romanum* has not been changed as far as the music is concerned. In the interest of their being more readily understood, however, the responsorial psalm (which St. Augustine and St. Leo the Great often mention) as well as the entrance and communion antiphons have been revised for use in Masses that are not sung.

1365   After what we have presented concerning the new Roman Missal, we wish in conclusion to insist on one point in particular and to make it have its effect. When he promulgated the *editio princeps* of the Roman Missal, our predecessor St. Pius V offered it to the people of Christ as the instrument of liturgical unity and the expression of a pure and reverent worship in the Church. Even though, in virtue of the decree of the Second Vatican Council, we have accepted into the new Roman Missal lawful variations and adaptations,[15] our own expectation in no way differs from that of our predecessor. It is that the faithful will receive the new Missal as a help toward witnessing and strengthening their unity with one another; that through the new Missal one and the same prayer in a great diversity of languages will ascend, more fragrant than any incense, to our heavenly Father, through our High Priest, Jesus Christ, in the Holy Spirit.

1366   The effective date for what we have prescribed in this Constitution shall be the First Sunday of Advent of this year, 30 November.[a] We decree that these laws and prescriptions be firm and effective now and in the future, notwithstanding, to the

---

[14]   See Amos 8:11.

[15]   See SC art. 38–40 [DOL 1 nos. 38–40].

[a]   This sentence is left out of the first printing of the Apostolic Constitution *Missale Romanum* as it appeared in the *editio typica* of the *Ordo Missae* [see DOL 209].

extent necessary, the apostolic constitutions and ordinances issued by our predecessors and other prescriptions, even those deserving particular mention and amendment.

203. SC RITES (Consilium), **Decree** *Ordine Missae*, promulgating the *editio typica* of the *Ordo Missae* and issuing the General Instruction of the Roman Missal, 6 April 1969: Not 5 (1969) 147.

The *Ordo Missae* has been revised in keeping with the directives of the Consti-   1367
tution on the Liturgy[a] and has been approved by Pope Paul VI through the Apostolic Constitution *Missale Romanum*, 3 April 1969.[b] In virtue of an express mandate from the same Pope Paul, the Congregation of Rites promulgates this *Ordo Missae*, stipulating that its effective date is to be 30 November of this year, the first Sunday of Advent.

Along with the *Ordo Missae*, the General Instruction of the Roman Missal has been issued; it will replace the following preliminaries of the present Roman Missal: *Rubricae generales; Ritus servandus in celebratione et concelebratione Missae; De defectibus in celebratione Missae occurrentibus.* It is further stipulated that the General Instruction of the Roman Missal, which Paul VI likewise approved, also has 30 November 1969 as its effective date.[c]

SC RITES (Consilium), **General Instruction of the Roman Missal**, lst edition, 6 April 1969.[*]

204. SC DIVINE WORSHIP, **Declaration** *Institutio Generalis Missalis Romani*, on the occasion of a second printing of the *Ordo Missae*, clarifying the General Instruction of the Roman Missal, 18 November 1969: Not 5 (1969) 417–418.

The General Instruction of the Roman Missal will eventually serve as a prelim-   1368
inary to the Roman Missal as revised by decree of Vatican Council II; for the present it is prefixed to the *Ordo Missae*. The Instruction was drawn up by the Consilium for the Implementation of the Constitution on the Liturgy, with the collaboration of those highly expert in the theological and pastoral disciplines. It was approved, after careful review, by the cardinals and bishops of the Consilium who were appointed by the Pope to membership "from different parts of the world" (see SC art. 25).[a]

---

     [a]   See DOL 1 no. 50.

     [b]   See DOL 202 no. 1361.

     [c]   See DOL 202 nos. 1359, 1366; DOL 209.

     [*]   See DOL 208, note*.

     [a]   See DOL 1 no. 25.

The Instruction is an accurate resumé and application of those doctrinal principles and practical norms on the eucharist that are contained in the conciliar Constitution *Sacrosanctum Concilium* (4 December 1963),[b] Paul VI's Encyclical *Mysterium fidei*
(3 September 1965),[c] and the Congregation of Rites' Instruction *Eucharisticum mysterium* (25 May 1967).[d]

1369   Nevertheless the Instruction should not be looked on as a doctrinal, that is to
say, dogmatic document. Rather it is a pastoral and ritual instruction: it outlines the
celebration and its parts in the light of the doctrinal principles contained in the
documents noted. For the rites both have doctrine as their source and give to
doctrine its outward expression.

     The Instruction thus seeks to provide guidelines for catechesis of the faithful
and to offer the main criteria for eucharistic celebration to be used by those who
take part in the celebration according to their different orders and ranks.

1370   When the *editio typica* of the Roman Missal is published, the General Instruction
will therefore appear as a preliminary in place of the treatises on rubrics and rites in
the present Roman Missal. In view of what has been said, the Apostolic See will see
to any clarification of language that may be needed for a better pastoral and catechetical understanding and for improving rubrics.

SC DIVINE WORSHIP, **General Instruction of the Roman Missal**, 2nd edition, with Introduction issued with the 1st *editio typica* of the Roman Missal, 26 March 1970.[*]

205. SC DIVINE WORSHIP, **Presentation** *Edita Instructione* of the changes introduced into the General Instruction of the Roman Missal, May 1970: Not 6 (1970) 177.

1371   After its publication as a preliminary to the 1969 *Ordo Missae*, the General
Instruction of the Roman Missal became the object of many different doctrinal and
rubrical comments. Some points in it did not come across clearly, mainly because of
the difficulty of keeping all the contents in mind, since many points are covered in
different sections of the Instruction. Some complaints, however, were based on
prejudice against anything new; these were not deemed worth considering because
they are groundless: a review of the General Instruction both before and after its
publication by the Fathers and *periti* of the Consilium found no reason for changing
the arrangement of the material or any error in doctrine. The Instruction is a
pastoral and rubrical text[a] that structures the celebration of Mass in accord with the

---

  [b]   See DOL 1 nos. 47–58.

  [c]   See DOL 176.

  [d]   See DOL 179.

  [*]   See DOL 213. On the text of the 2nd edition, see DOL 208, note *.

  [a]   See DOL 204 no. 1369.

teaching of Vatican Council II, Paul VI's Encyclical *Mysterium fidei* (3 September 1965),[b] and the Instruction *Eucharisticum mysterium* (25 May 1967).[c]

But to overcome problems of any kind and to clarify some of the language of the General Instruction, the decision was made on the occasion of the *editio typica* of the new Roman Missal to supplement or rewrite the text of the General Instruction in some places (see SC Divine Worship, Declaration, 18 November 1969).[d] Nothing, however, has been completely revised and therefore the numbering of paragraphs remains the same as in the first edition.

The emendations are in fact few and sometimes quite minor or merely stylistic.[e] [. . .]

SC DIVINE WORSHIP, **General Instruction of the Roman Missal**, 3rd edition, after suppression of the subdiaconate, 23 December 1972.*

206. SC DIVINE WORSHIP, **Presentation** *Cum, die 1 Ianuarii* of the changes introduced into the General Instruction of the Roman Missal, 23 December 1972: Not 9 (1973) 34–38.

On 1 January 1973 a new discipline will become effective regarding first tonsure, minor orders, and subdiaconate, as established by the Motu Proprio *Ministeria quaedam* of 15 August 1972.[a] Accordingly, the order of subdiaconate will no longer exist in the Latin Church. A reader or acolyte, even one not formally instituted, will perform the subdeacon's functions. In the celebration of Mass all ministers should do all and only those parts that belong to them on the basis of the order they have received.[1] The ordained ministers at Mass are therefore to take part either by concelebrating if they are priests or by exercising their proper ministries if they are deacons. The function of subdeacon, then, is completely suppressed. If there are several deacons present, they may divide the parts of that ministry among themselves and perform them.[2] It is altogether out of place for a priest vested as a deacon to exercise the deacon's function. Finally, it should be kept in mind that "a liturgical service takes on a more sublime form when the rites are celebrated with singing, the ministers of each rank take their parts in them, and the congregation actively participates."[3]

1372

---

b   See DOL 176.

c   See DOL 179.

d   See DOL 204.

e   See Not 6 (1970) 177–193 for the complete text of these changes. They are indicated in the notes of DOL 208 on textual variants.

*   See DOL 208, note*.

a   See DOL 340.

1   See GIRM no. 58 [DOL 208 no. 1448].

2   See GIRM no. 71 [DOL 208 no. 1461].

3   SCR, Instr. MusSacr, 5 March 1967, no. 5 [DOL 508 no. 4126].

1373   In the General Instruction of the Roman Missal, therefore, everything about the subdeacon has to be deleted and the text in certain parts amplified or emended to correspond to the new discipline.

     For this reason this Congregation for Divine Worship has determined that the following changes are to be incorporated into the *editio typica* of the *Missale Romanum* published in 1970 [. . .].b

     These changes, composed by the Congregation, Pope Paul VI approved on 22 December 1972, ordering that they be published and incorporated into new editions of the Roman Missal.

SC DIVINE WORSHIP, General Instruction of the Roman Missal, 4th edition, issued with the 2nd *editio typica* of the Roman Missal, 27 March 1975.*

207. SC DIVINE WORSHIP, **Decree** *Cum Missale Romanum*, on the 2nd *editio typica* of the Roman Missal, 27 March 1975: Not 11 (1975) 297.

1374   Since the Roman Missal must be reprinted, variations and additions have been included in order that this new edition might be in accord with the documents published after the appearance of the first edition in 1970.

     In the General Instruction, the marginal numbers are unchanged, but a description of the liturgical functions of acolyte and reader is inserted in place of the paragraphs that formerly dealt with the subdeacon (nos. 142–152).

     There is another change of some importance in the section of the Roman Missal that contains the ritual Masses and the Masses for various needs and occasions. Certain formularies have been completed by supplying entrance and communion antiphons.

     Texts not found in the first edition have also been added, namely, among the ritual Masses, texts for the Mass of Dedication of a Church and an Altar and for the Mass of Reconciliation; among votive Masses, texts for Masses of Mary, Mother of the Church and of the Most Holy Name of Mary.

     Some other, less important changes have been introduced in headings and rubrics so that they may better correspond to the words or expressions occurring in the new liturgical books.

1375   Pope Paul VI has approved this second edition of the Roman Missal by his authority and the Congregation for Divine Worship now issues it and declares it to be the *editio typica*.

     It will be the responsibility of the conferences of bishops to introduce into the respective vernacular editions the changes contained in this second edition of the Roman Missal.

---

  b   The document here lists these changes and also includes changes introduced into the text of the Missal itself. On the 1972 text see DOL 208, note*.

  *   See DOL 208.

208. SC DIVINE WORSHIP, **General Instruction of the Roman Missal**, 4th ed. 27 March 1975: Vatican Polyglot Press, 1975.*

INTRODUCTION[a]

1. When Christ the Lord was about to celebrate the passover meal with his disciples and institute the sacrifice of his body and blood, he directed them to prepare a large room, arranged for the supper (Lk 22:12). The Church has always regarded this command of Christ as applying to itself when it gives directions about the preparation of the sentiments of the worshipers, the place, rites, and texts for the celebration of the eucharist. The current norms, laid down on the basis of the intent of Vatican Council II, and the new Missal that will be used henceforth in the celebration of Mass by the Church of the Roman Rite, are fresh evidence of the great care, faith, and unchanged love that the Church shows toward the eucharist. They attest as well to its coherent tradition, continuing amid the introduction of some new elements.

1376

A WITNESS TO UNCHANGED FAITH

2. The sacrificial nature of the Mass was solemnly proclaimed by the Council of Trent in agreement with the whole tradition of the Church.[1] Vatican Council II reaffirmed this teaching in these significant words: "At the Last Supper our Savior instituted the eucharistic sacrifice of his body and blood. He did this in order to perpetuate the sacrifice of the cross throughout the centuries until he should come again and in this way to entrust to his beloved Bride, the Church, a memorial of his death and resurrection."[2]

1377

The Council's teaching is expressed constantly in the formularies of the Mass. This teaching, in the concise words of the Leonine Sacramentary, is that "the work of our redemption is carried out whenever we celebrate the memory of this sacrifice";[3] it is aptly and accurately brought out in the eucharistic prayers. At the anamnesis or memorial, the priest, addressing God in the name of all the people, offers in thanksgiving the holy and living sacrifice: the Church's offering and the Victim whose death has reconciled us with God.[4] The priest also prays that the body and blood of Christ may be a sacrifice acceptable to the Father, bringing salvation to the whole world.[5]

---

* The translation of the GIRM that follows is not based on the Latin text accompanying the 1969 *Ordo Missae* but rather that in the 1975 *editio typica altera* of the *Missale Romanum*; variants in earlier Latin texts of the GIRM are carried in notes. The SCDW published, 27 March 1975, a declaration with the *editio typica altera* on the changes in the GIRM (see DOL 207).

The following versions of the GIRM preceded that accompanying the *editio typica altera*:

1. The GIRM issued with the new *Ordo Missae* promulgated 6 April 1969. Variants in this version are marked "OM."

2. The GIRM as emended in the *editio typica* of the *Missale Romanum*, promulgated 26 March 1970. Variants in this version are marked "MR'70."

3. The GIRM as emended by the variations published by the SCDW 23 Dec. 1972 (DOL 206), following the suppression of the subdiaconate and minor orders by the Motu Proprio *Ministeria quaedam*, 15 Aug. 1972 (DOL 340). Variants in this version are marked "MRVar." They appear in Not 9 (1973) 34–37.

[a] OM lacks this Introduction.

[1] See Council of Trent, sess. 22, 17 Sept. 1562: Denz-Schön 1738–59.

[2] SC art. 47 [DOL 1 no. 47]; see LG nos. 3, 28 [DOL 4 nos. 137, 148]; PO nos. 2, 4, 5 [DOL 18 nos. 257, 259, 260].

[4] See Eucharistic Prayer III.

[5] See Eucharistic Prayer IV.

In this new Missal, then, the Church's rule of prayer (*lex orandi*) corresponds to its constant rule of faith (*lex credendi*). This rule of faith instructs us that the sacrifice of the cross and its sacramental renewal in the Mass, which Christ instituted at the Last Supper and commanded his apostles to do in his memory, are one and the same, differing only in the manner of offering and that consequently the Mass is at once a sacrifice of praise and thanksgiving, of reconciliation and expiation.

1378   3.   The celebration of Mass also proclaims the sublime mystery of the Lord's real presence under the eucharistic elements, which Vatican Council II[6] and other documents of the Church's magisterium[7] have reaffirmed in the same sense and as the same teaching that the Council of Trent had proposed as a matter of faith.[8] The Mass does this not only by means of the very words of consecration, by which Christ becomes present through transubstantiation, but also by that spirit and expression of reverence and adoration in which the eucharistic liturgy is carried out. For the same reason the Christian people are invited in Holy Week[b] on Holy Thursday and on the solemnity of Corpus Christi to honor this wonderful sacrament in a special way by their adoration.

1379   4.   Further, because of the priest's more prominent place and office in the rite, its form sheds light on the ministerial priesthood proper to the presbyter, who offers the sacrifice in the person of Christ and presides over the assembly of a holy people. The meaning of his office is declared and detailed in the preface for the chrism Mass on Thursday of Holy Week,[c] the day celebrating the institution of the priesthood. The preface brings out the passing on of the sacerdotal power through the laying on of hands and, by listing its various offices, describes that power. It is the continuation of the power of Christ, High Priest of the New Testament.

1380   5.   In addition, the ministerial priesthood puts into its proper light another reality of which much should be made, namely, the royal priesthood of believers. Through the ministry of presbyters the people's spiritual sacrifice to God is brought to completeness in union with the sacrifice of Christ, our one and only Mediator.[9] For the celebration of the eucharist is the action of the whole Church; in it all should do only, but all of, those parts that belong to them in virtue of their place within the people of God. In this way greater attention will be given to some aspects of the eucharistic celebration that have sometimes been neglected in the course of time. For these people are the people of God, purchased by Christ's blood, gathered together by the Lord, nourished by his word. They are a people called to offer God the prayers of the entire human family, a people giving thanks in Christ for the mystery of salvation by offering his sacrifice. Finally, they are a people growing together into unity by sharing in Christ's body and blood. These people are holy by their origin, but becoming ever more holy by conscious, active, and fruitful participation in the mystery of the eucharist.[10]

---

[6]   See SC art. 7, 47 [DOL 1 nos. 7, 47]; PO nos. 5, 18 [DOL 18 nos. 260, 267].

[7]   See Pius XII, Encycl. *Humani generis*: AAS 42 (1950) 570–571. Paul VI, Encycl. *Mysterium fidei* nos. 33–55 [DOL 176 nos. 1177–99]; Solemn Profession of Faith, 30 June 1968, nos. 24–26 [DOL 168 nos. 1096–98]. SCR, Instr. EuchMyst, 25 May 1967, nos. 3, 9 [DOL 179 nos. 1232, 1238].

[8]   See Council of Trent, sess. 13, 11 Oct. 1551: Denz-Schön 1635–61.

[b]   MR'70 lacks.

[c]   MR'70: "Feria V in Cena Domini" for "Feria V Hebdomadae sanctae."

[9]   See PO no. 2 [DOL 18 no. 257].

[10]   See SC art. 11 [DOL 1 no. 11].

A WITNESS TO UNBROKEN TRADITION

6.   In setting forth its decrees for the revision of the Order of Mass, Vatican   1381
Council II directed, among other things, that some rites be restored "to the vigor
they had in the tradition of the Fathers";[11] this is a quotation from the Apostolic
Constitution[d] *Quo primum* of 1570, by which St. Pius V promulgated the Tridentine
Missal. The fact that the same words are used in reference to both Roman Missals
indicates how both of them, although separated by four centuries, embrace one and
the same tradition. And when the more profound elements of this tradition are
considered, it becomes clear how remarkably and harmoniously this new Roman
Missal improves on the older one.

7.   The older Missal belongs to the difficult period of attacks against Catholic   1382
teaching on the sacrificial nature of the Mass, the ministerial priesthood, and the
real and permanent presence of Christ under the eucharistic elements. St. Pius V
was therefore especially concerned with preserving the relatively recent developments in the Church's tradition, then unjustly being assailed, and introduced only
very slight changes into the sacred rites. In fact, the Roman Missal of 1570 differs
very little from the first printed edition of 1474, which in turn faithfully follows the
Missal used at the time of Pope Innocent III (1198–1216). Manuscripts in the
Vatican Library provided some verbal emendations, but they seldom allowed research into "ancient and approved authors" to extend beyond the examination of a
few liturgical commentaries of the Middle Ages.

8.   Today, on the other hand, countless studies of scholars have enriched the   1383
"tradition of the Fathers" that the revisers of the Missal under St. Pius V followed.
After the Gregorian Sacramentary was first published in 1571, many critical editions of other ancient Roman and Ambrosian sacramentaries appeared. Ancient
Spanish and Gallican liturgical books also became available, bringing to light many
prayers of profound spirituality that had hitherto been unknown.

   Traditions dating back to the first centuries before the formation of the Eastern
and Western rites are also better known today because so many liturgical documents have been discovered.

   The continuing progress in patristic studies has also illumined eucharistic theology through the teachings of such illustrious saints of Christian antiquity as
Irenaeus, Ambrose, Cyril of Jerusalem, and John Chrysostom.

9.   The "tradition of the Fathers" does not require merely the preservation of   1384
what our immediate predecessors have passed on to us. There must also be profound study and understanding of the Church's entire past and of all the ways in
which its single faith has been expressed in the quite diverse human and social
forms prevailing in Semitic, Greek, and Latin cultures. This broader view shows us
how the Holy Spirit endows the people of God with a marvelous fidelity in preserving the deposit of faith unchanged, even though prayers and rites differ so greatly.

ADAPTATION TO MODERN CONDITIONS

10.   As it bears witness to the Roman Church's rule of prayer (*lex orandi*) and guards   1385
the deposit of faith handed down by the later councils, the new Roman Missal in
turn marks a major step forward in liturgical tradition.

---

[11]   SC art. 50 [DOL 1 no. 50].

[d]   MR'70: "from the Apostolic Letter" for "from the Apostolic Constitution."

The Fathers of Vatican Council II in reaffirming the dogmatic statements of the Council of Trent were speaking at a far different time in the world's history. They were able therefore to bring forward proposals and measures of a pastoral nature that could not have even been foreseen four centuries ago.

1386   11. The Council of Trent recognized the great catechetical value of the celebration of Mass, but was unable to bring out all its consequences for the actual life of the Church. Many were pressing for permission to use the vernacular in celebrating the eucharistic sacrifice, but the Council, judging the conditions of that age, felt bound to answer such a request with a reaffirmation of the Church's traditional teaching. This teaching is that the eucharistic sacrifice is, first and foremost, the action of Christ himself and therefore the manner in which the faithful take part in the Mass does not affect the efficacy belonging to it. The Council thus stated in firm but measured words: "Although the Mass contains much instruction for the faithful, it did not seem expedient to the Fathers that as a general rule it be celebrated in the vernacular."[12] The Council accordingly anathematized anyone maintaining that "the rite of the Roman Church, in which part of the canon and the words of consecration are spoken in a low voice, should be condemned or that the Mass must be celebrated only[e] in the vernacular."[13] Although the Council of Trent on the one hand prohibited the use of the vernacular in the Mass, nevertheless, on the other, it did direct pastors to substitute appropriate catechesis: "Lest Christ's flock go hungry . . . the Council commands pastors and others having the care of souls that either personally or through others they frequently give instructions during Mass, especially on Sundays and holydays, on what[f] is read at Mass and that among their instructions they include some explanation of the mystery of this sacrifice."[14]

1387   12. Convened in order to adapt the Church to the contemporary requirements of its apostolic task, Vatican Council II examined thoroughly, as had Trent, the pedagogic and pastoral character of the liturgy.[15] Since no Catholic would now deny the lawfulness and efficacy of a sacred rite celebrated in Latin, the Council was able to acknowledge that "the use of the mother tongue frequently may be of great advantage to the people" and gave permission for its use.[16] The enthusiasm in response to this decision was so great that, under the leadership of the bishops and the Apostolic See, it has resulted in the permission for all liturgical celebrations in which the faithful participate to be in the vernacular for the sake of a better comprehension of the mystery being celebrated.

1388   13. The use of the vernacular in the liturgy may certainly be considered an important means for presenting more clearly the catechesis on the mystery that is part of the celebration itself. Nevertheless, Vatican Council II also ordered the observance of certain directives, prescribed by the Council of Trent but not obeyed everywhere. Among these are the obligatory homily on Sundays and holydays[17] and the permission to interpose some commentary during the sacred rites themselves.[18]

---

12   Council of Trent, sess. 22, *Doctr. de SS. Missae Sacrificio* cap. 8: Denz-Schön 1749.

e   MR'70 lacks "only."

13   Ibid. can. 9: Denz-Schön 1759.

f   MR'70: "on some matter that is read at Mass."

14   Ibid. cap. 8: Denz-Schön 1749.

15   See SC art. 33 [DOL 1 no. 33].

16   See SC art. 36 [DOL 1 no. 36].

17   See SC art. 52 [DOL 1 no. 52].

18   See SC art. 35, 3 [DOL 1 no. 35].

Above all, Vatican Council II strongly endorsed "that more complete form of participation in the Mass by which the faithful, after the priest's communion, receive the Lord's body from the same sacrifice."[19] Thus the Council gave impetus to the fulfillment of the further desire of the Fathers of Trent that for fuller participation in the holy eucharist "the faithful present at each Mass should communicate not only by spiritual desire but also by sacramental communion."[20]

14. Moved by the same spirit and pastoral concern, Vatican Council II was able to reevaluate the Tridentine norm on communion under both kinds. No one today challenges the doctrinal principles on the completeness of eucharistic communion under the form of bread alone. The Council thus gave permission for the reception of communion under both kinds on some occasions, because this more explicit form of the sacramental sign offers a special means of deepening the understanding of the mystery in which the faithful are taking part.[21]   1389

15. Thus the Church remains faithful in its responsibility as teacher of truth to guard "things old," that is, the deposit of tradition; at the same time it fulfills another duty, that of examining and prudently bringing forth "things new" (see Mt 13:52).   1390

Accordingly, a part of the new Roman Missal directs the prayer of the Church expressly to the needs of our times. This is above all true of the ritual Masses and the Masses for various needs and occasions,[g] which happily combine the traditional and the contemporary. Thus many expressions, drawn from the Church's most ancient tradition and become familiar through the many editions of the Roman Missal, have remained unchanged. Other expressions, however, have been adapted to today's needs and circumstances and still others — for example, the prayers for the Church, the laity, the sanctification of human work, the community of all peoples, certain needs proper to our era — are completely new compositions, drawing on the thoughts and even the very language of the recent conciliar documents.

The same awareness of the present state of the world also influenced the use of texts from very ancient tradition. It seemed that this cherished treasure would not be harmed if some phrases were changed so that the style of language would be more in accord with the language of modern theology and would faithfully reflect the actual state of the Church's discipline. Thus there have been changes of some expressions bearing on the evaluation and use of the good things of the earth and of allusions to a particular form of outward penance belonging to another age in the history of the Church.

In short, the liturgical norms of the Council of Trent have been completed and improved in many respects by those of Vatican Council II. This Council has brought to realization the efforts of the last four hundred years to move the faithful closer to the sacred liturgy, especially the efforts of recent times and above all the zeal for the liturgy promoted by St. Pius X and his successors.

---

[19]   SC art. 55 [DOL 1 no. 55].

[20]   Council of Trent, sess. 22, *Doctr. de SS. Missae Sacrificio* cap. 6: Denz-Schön 1747.

[21]   See SC art. 55 [DOL 1 no. 55].

[g]   MR'70: *"ad diversa"* for "for various needs and occasions."

CHAPTER I
IMPORTANCE AND DIGNITY OF THE EUCHARISTIC CELEBRATION

1391   1.   The celebration of Mass, the action of Christ and the people of God arrayed hierarchically, is for the universal and the local Church as well as for each person the center of the whole Christian life.[1] In the Mass we have the high point of the work that in Christ God accomplishes to sanctify us and the high point of the worship that in adoring God through Christ, his Son, we offer to the Father.[2] During the cycle of the year, moreover, the mysteries of redemption are recalled in the Mass in such a way that they are somehow made present.[3] All other liturgical rites and all the works of the Christian life are linked with the eucharistic celebration, flow from it, and have it as their end.[4]

1392   2.   Therefore, it is of the greatest importance that the celebration of the Mass, the Lord's Supper, be so arranged that the ministers and the faithful who take their own proper part in it may more fully receive its good effects.[5] This is the reason why Christ the Lord instituted the eucharistic sacrifice of his body and blood and entrusted it to the Church, his beloved Bride, as the memorial of his passion and resurrection.[6]

1393   3.   This purpose will best be accomplished if, after due regard for the nature and circumstances of each assembly, the celebration is planned in such a way that it brings about in the faithful a participation in body and spirit that is conscious, active, full, and motivated by faith, hope, and charity. The Church desires this kind of participation, the nature of the celebration demands it, and for the Christian people it is a right and duty they have by reason of their baptism.[7]

1394   4.   The presence and active participation of the people bring out more plainly the ecclesial nature of the celebration.[8] But even when their participation is not possible, the eucharistic celebration still retains its effectiveness and worth because it is the action of Christ and the Church,[9] in which the priest always acts on behalf of the people's salvation.

1395   5.   The celebration of the eucharist, like the entire liturgy, involves the use of outward signs that foster, strengthen, and express faith.[10] There must be the utmost care therefore to choose and to make wise use of those forms and elements provided by the Church that, in view of the circumstances of the people and the place, will best foster active and full participation and serve the spiritual well-being of the faithful.

---

[1]   See SC art. 41 [DOL 1 no. 41]; LG no. 11 [DOL 4 no. 141]; PO nos. 2, 5, 6 [DOL 18 nos. 257, 260, 261]; CD no. 30 [DOL 7 no. 196]; UR no. 15 [DOL 6 no. 187]. SCR, Instr. EuchMyst, 25 May 1967, nos. 3 e, 6 [DOL 179 nos. 1232, 1235].

[2]   See SC art. 10 [DOL 1 no. 10].

[3]   See SC art. 102 [DOL 1 no. 102].

[4]   See PO no. 5 [DOL 18 no. 260]; SC art. 10 [DOL 1 no. 10].

[5]   See SC art. 14, 19, 26, 28, 30 [DOL 1 nos. 14, 19, 26, 28, 30].

[6]   See SC art. 47 [DOL 1 no. 47].

[7]   See SC art. 14 [DOL 1 no. 14].

[8]   See SC art. 41 [DOL 1 no. 41].

[9]   See PO no. 13 [DOL 18 no. 265].

[10]   See SC art. 59 [DOL 1 no. 59].

6.   The purpose of this Instruction is to give the general guidelines for planning   1396
the eucharistic celebration properly and to set forth the rules for arranging the
individual forms of celebration.[11,a] In accord with the Constitution on the Liturgy,
each conference of bishops has the power to lay down norms for its own territory
that are suited to the traditions and character of peoples, regions, and various
communities.[12]

CHAPTER II
STRUCTURE, ELEMENTS, AND PARTS OF THE MASS

I. GENERAL STRUCTURE OF THE MASS

7.   At Mass or the Lord's Supper, the people of God are called together, with a   1397
priest presiding and acting in the person of Christ, to celebrate the memorial of the
Lord or eucharistic sacrifice.[13] For this reason Christ's promise applies supremely to
such a local gathering together of the Church: "Where two or three come together
in my name, there am I in their midst" (Mt 18:20). For at the celebration of Mass,
which perpetuates the sacrifice of the cross,[14] Christ is really present to the assembly gathered in his name; he is present in the person of the minister, in his own
word, and indeed substantially and permanently under the eucharistic elements.[15,a]

8.   The Mass is made up as it were of the liturgy of the word and the liturgy of the   1398
eucharist, two parts so closely connected that they form but one single act of
worship.[16] For in the Mass the table of God's word and of Christ's body is laid for
the people of God to receive from it instruction and food.[17] There are also certain
rites to open and conclude the celebration.

II. DIFFERENT ELEMENTS OF THE MASS

READING AND EXPLAINING THE WORD OF GOD

9.   When the Scriptures are read in the Church, God himself is speaking to his   1399
people, and Christ, present in his own word, is proclaiming the Gospel.

The readings must therefore be listened to by all with reverence; they make up
a principal element of the liturgy. In the biblical readings God's word addresses all
people of every era and is understandable to them, but a living commentary on the

---

[11]   For Masses with special groups see SCDW, Instr. *Actio pastoralis*, 15 May 1969 [DOL 275]; for
Masses with children, SCDW, *Directory for Masses with Children*, 1 Nov. 1973 [DOL 276]; for the manner of
joining the liturgy of the hours with the Mass, GILH nos. 93–98 [DOL 426 nos. 3523–28].

[a]   OM and MR '70 lack this note 11; their note 11 is note 12 here.

[12]   See SC art. 37–40 [DOL 1 nos. 37–40].

[13]   See PO no. 5 [DOL 18 no. 260]; SC art. 33 [DOL 1 no. 33].

[14]   See Council of Trent, sess. 22, cap. 1: Denz-Schön 1740. Paul VI, Solemn Profession of Faith, 30
June 1968, no. 24 [DOL 168 no. 1096].

[15]   See SC art. 7 [DOL 1 no. 7]. Paul VI, Encycl. *Mysterium fidei*, 3 Sept. 1965 [DOL 176 no. 1178]. SCR,
Instr. EuchMyst, 25 May 1967, no. 9 [DOL 179 no. 1238].

[a]   OM: "7. The Lord's Supper or Mass is the sacred assembly or congregation of the people of God
gathering together, with a priest presiding, in order to celebrate the memorial of the Lord. For this reason
Christ's promise applies supremely to such a local gathering together of the Church: 'Where two or three
come together in my name, there am I in their midst' (Mt 18:20)."

[16]   See SC art. 56 [DOL 1 no. 56]. SCR, Instr. EuchMyst no. 10 [DOL 179 no. 1239].

[17]   See SC art. 48, 51 [DOL 1 nos. 48, 51]; DV no. 21 [DOL 14 no. 224]; PO no. 4 [DOL 18 no. 259].

word, that is, the homily, as an integral part of the liturgy, increases the word's effectiveness.[18]

PRAYERS AND OTHER PARTS ASSIGNED TO THE PRIEST

1400   10. Among the parts assigned to the priest, the eucharistic prayer is preeminent; it is the high point of the entire celebration. Next are the prayers: the opening prayer or collect, the prayer over the gifts, and the prayer after communion. The priest, presiding over the assembly in the person of Christ, addresses these prayers to God in the name of the entire holy people and all present.[19] Thus there is good reason to call them "the presidential prayers."

1401   11. It is also up to the priest in the exercise of his office of presiding over the assembly to pronounce the instructions and words of introduction and conclusion that are provided in the rites themselves. By their very nature these introductions do not need to be expressed verbatim in the form in which they are given in the Missal; at least in certain cases it will be advisable to adapt them somewhat to the concrete situation of the community.[20] It also belongs to the priest presiding to proclaim the word of God and to give the final blessing.[b] He may give the faithful a very brief introduction to the Mass of the day (before the celebration begins), to the liturgy of the word (before the readings), and to the eucharistic prayer (before the preface); he may also make comments concluding the entire sacred service before the dismissal.

1402   12. The nature of the presidential prayers demands that they be spoken in a loud and clear voice and that everyone present listen with attention.[21] While the priest is reciting them there should be no other prayer and the organ or other instruments should not be played.[R1]

1403   13. But the priest does not only pray in the name of the whole community as its president; he also prays at times in his own name that he may exercise his ministry with attention and devotion. Such prayers are said inaudibly.

OTHER TEXTS IN THE CELEBRATION

1404   14. Since by nature the celebration of Mass has the character of being the act of a community,[22] both the dialogues between celebrant and congregation and the acclamations take on special value;[23] they are not simply outward signs of the community's celebration, but the means of greater communion between priest and people.

---

[18]   See SC art. 7, 33, 52 [DOL 1 nos. 7, 33, 52].

[19]   See SC art. 33 [DOL 1 no. 33].

[20]   See SCDW, Circular letter on the eucharistic prayers, 27 April 1973, no. 14 [DOL 248 no. 1988].

[b]   OM and MR'70: ". . .that are provided in the rites themselves, to proclaim the word of God, and to give the final blessing." Note 20 is lacking.

[21]   See SCR, Instr. MusSacr, 5 March 1967, no. 14 [DOL 508 no. 4135].

[R1]   Query: An organ accompaniment for the recitation of the eucharistic prayer is a practice that has developed in some places. Is this acceptable? Reply: The GIRM no. 12 clearly says: "[Text quoted]." This is a clear rule, leaving no room for doubt, since it is a reminder of wrong practices that have greatly impeded and diminished the people's participation in this central part of the Mass. Further, it is obvious that the organ's so-called background music often puts into the background what should be foremost and dominant. A "background" accompaniment of the priest's homily would be out of the question: but in the eucharistic prayer the word of the presider, *Toū proestoū* in Justin's expression, reaches the peak of its meaning: Not 13 (1977) 94–95, no. 2.

[22]   See SC art. 26, 27 [DOL 1 nos. 26, 27].

[23]   See SC art. 30 [DOL 1 no. 30].

15. The acclamations and the responses to the priest's greeting and prayers create a degree of the active participation that the gathered faithful must contribute in every form of the Mass, in order to express clearly and to further the entire community's involvement.[24]

1405

16. There are other parts, extremely useful for expressing and encouraging the people's active participation, that are assigned to the whole congregation: the penitential rite, the profession of faith, the general intercessions, and the Lord's Prayer.

1406

17. Finally, of the other texts:

1407

a. Some constitute an independent rite or act, such as the *Gloria*, the responsorial psalm, the *Alleluia* verse and the verse before the gospel,[c] the *Sanctus*, the memorial acclamation, and the song after communion.

b. Others accompany another rite, such as the songs at the entrance, at the preparation of the gifts, at the breaking of the bread (*Agnus Dei*), and at communion.

VOCAL EXPRESSION OF THE DIFFERENT TEXTS

18. In texts that are to be delivered in a clear, loud voice, whether by the priest or by the ministers or by all, the tone of voice should correspond to the genre of the text, that is, accordingly as it is a reading, a prayer, an instruction, an acclamation, or a song; the tone should also be suited to the form of celebration and to the solemnity of the gathering. Other criteria are the idiom of different languages and the genius of peoples.

1408

In the rubrics and in the norms that follow, the words *say* (*dicere*) or *proclaim* (*proferre*) are to be understood of both singing and speaking, and in accordance with the principles just stated.

IMPORTANCE OF SINGING

19. The faithful who gather together to await the Lord's coming are instructed by the Apostle Paul to sing psalms, hymns, and inspired songs (see Col 3:16). Song is the sign of the heart's joy (see Acts 2:46). Thus St. Augustine says rightly: "To sing belongs to lovers."[25] There is also the ancient proverb: "One who sings well prays twice."

1409

With due consideration for the culture and ability of each congregation, great importance should be attached to the use of singing at Mass; but it is not always necessary to sing all the texts that are of themselves meant to be sung.

In choosing the parts actually to be sung, however, preference should be given to those that are more significant and especially to those to be sung by the priest or ministers with the congregation responding or by the priest and people together.[26,d]

Since the faithful from different countries come together ever more frequently, it is desirable that they know how to sing at least some parts of the Ordinary of the

---

[24]   See SCR, Instr. MusSacr no. 16 a [DOL 508 no. 4137].

[c]   OM and MR'70 lack "the *Alleluia* verse and the verse before the gospel."

[25]   Augustine, *Sermo* 336, 1: PL 38, 1472.

[26]   See SCR, Instr. MusSacr nos. 7, 16 [DOL 508 nos. 4128, 4137]. MR, *Ordo cantus Missae*, ed. typica, 1972, Introduction [DOL 535].

[d]   OM and MR'70 lack second citation in note 26.

Mass in Latin, especially the profession of faith and the Lord's Prayer, set to simple melodies.[27]

MOVEMENTS AND POSTURES

1410 20. The uniformity in standing, kneeling, or sitting to be observed by all taking part is a sign of the community and the unity of the assembly; it both expresses and fosters the spiritual attitude of those taking part.[28]

1411 21. For the sake of uniformity in movement and posture, the people should follow the directions given during the celebration by the deacon, the priest, or another minister. Unless other provision is made, at every Mass the people should stand from the beginning of the entrance song or when the priest enters until the end of the opening prayer or collect; for the singing of the *Alleluia* before the gospel; while the gospel is proclaimed; during the profession of faith and the general intercessions; from the prayer over the gifts to the end of the Mass, except at the places indicated later in this paragraph. They should sit during the readings before the gospel and during the responsorial psalm, for the homily and the presentation of the gifts, and, if this seems helpful, during the period of silence after communion. They should kneel at the consecration unless prevented by the lack of space, the number of people present, or some other good reason.

But it is up to the conference of bishops to adapt the actions and postures described in the Order of the Roman Mass to the customs of the people.[29] But the conference must make sure that such adaptations correspond to the meaning and character of each part of the celebration.[R2]

1412 22. Included among the external actions of the Mass are those of the priest going to the altar, of the faithful presenting the gifts, and their coming forward to receive

---

[27] See SC art. 54 [DOL 1 no. 54]. SCR, Instr. InterOec, 26 Sept. 1964, no. 59 [DOL 23 no. 351]; Instr. MusSacr no. 47 [DOL 508 no. 4168].

[28] See SC art. 30 [DOL 1 no. 30].

[29] See SC art. 39 [DOL 1 no. 39].

[R2] 1. Query: After communion should the faithful be seated or not? Reply: After communion they may either kneel, stand, or sit. Accordingly the GIRM no. 21 gives this rule: "The people sit . . . if this seems useful during the period of silence after communion." Thus it is a matter of option, not obligation. The GIRM no. 121, should therefore be interpreted to match no. 21: Not 10 (1974) 407.

2. Query: In liturgical assemblies there is a great variety of gestures and postures during a celebration. For example should the people: a. stand during the prayer over the gifts; b. kneel after the *Sanctus* and during the entire eucharistic prayer; c. sit after communion? Reply: As usual the GIRM gives simple rules to solve these questions (GIRM no. 21): a. The people stand while the presidential prayers are being said, therefore, during the prayer over the gifts. b. They also stand throughout the eucharistic prayer, except the consecration. The practice is for the faithful to remain kneeling from the epiclesis before the consecration until the memorial acclamation after it. c. The people may sit during the silence after communion.

The points determined are in no way to be considered trivial, since their purpose is to ensure uniformity in posture in the assembly celebrating the eucharist as a manifestation of the community's unity in faith and worship. The people often give the impression immediately after the *Sanctus* and even more often after the consecration by their diverse postures that they are unmindful of being participants in the Church's liturgy, which is the supreme action of a community and not a time for individuals to isolate themselves in acts of private devotion: Not 14 (1978) 300–301, no. 1.

3. Query: In some places kneelers have been taken out of the churches. Thus the people can only stand or sit and this detracts from the reverence and adoration due to the eucharist. Reply: The appointments of a place of worship have some relationship to the customs of the particular locale. For example, in the East there are carpets; in the Roman basilicas, only since modern times, there are usually chairs without kneelers, so as to accommodate large crowds. There is nothing to prevent the faithful from kneeling on the floor to show their adoration, no matter how uncomfortable this may be. In cases where kneeling is not possible (see GIRM no. 21), a deep bow and a respectful bearing are signs of the reverence and adoration to be shown at the time of the consecration and communion: Not 14 (1978) 302–303, no. 4.

communion. While the songs proper to these movements are being sung, they should be carried out becomingly in keeping with the norms prescribed for each.

SILENCE

23. Silence should be observed at the designated times as part of the celebration.[30] Its function depends on the time it occurs in each part of the celebration. Thus at the penitential rite and again after the invitation to pray, all recollect themselves; at the conclusion of a reading or the homily, all meditate briefly on what has been heard;[R3] after communion, all praise God in silent prayer.

1413

III. INDIVIDUAL PARTS OF THE MASS

A. INTRODUCTORY RITES

24. The parts preceding the liturgy of the word, namely, the entrance song, greeting, penitential rite, *Kyrie, Gloria,* and opening prayer or collect, have the character of a beginning, introduction, and preparation.

1414

The purpose of these rites is that the faithful coming together take on the form of a community and prepare themselves to listen to God's word and celebrate the eucharist properly.

ENTRANCE

25. After the people have assembled, the entrance song begins as the priest and the ministers come in. The purpose of this song is to open the celebration, intensify the unity of the gathered people, lead their thoughts to the mystery of the season or feast, and accompany the procession of priest and ministers.

1415

26. The entrance song is sung alternately either by the choir and the congregation or by the cantor and the congregation; or it is sung entirely by the congregation or by the choir alone. The antiphon and psalm of the *Graduale Romanum* or the *The Simple Gradual* may be used, or another song that is suited to this part of the Mass,[R4] the day, or the season and that has a text approved by the conference of bishops.

1416

If there is no singing for the entrance, the antiphon in the Missal is recited either by the faithful, by some of them, or by a reader; otherwise it is recited by the priest after the greeting.

VENERATION OF THE ALTAR AND GREETING OF THE CONGREGATION

27. When the priest and the ministers enter the sanctuary, they reverence the altar. As a sign of veneration, the priest and deacon[a] kiss the altar; when the occasion warrants, the priest may also incense the altar.[R5]

1417

---

[30]   See SC art. 30 [DOL 1 no. 30]. SCR, Instr. MusSacr no. 17 [DOL 508 no. 4138].

[R3]   1.   Query: Is it appropriate to meditate for a short time in silence after the homily? Reply: Very much so.

2.   Query: May the organ be played softly during this interval of silence? Reply: Yes, as long as it really is played softly and is not a distraction to meditation: Not 9 (1973) 192.

[R4]   Query: In the GIRM no. 26 are the words *actioni sacrae* to be understood of the procession of the priest and ministers or of the entire eucharistic celebration? Reply: The words are to be understood of the procession, because the context is about the entrance song. Nevertheless the norm takes on a general applicability; whatever the singing during Mass, it should fit the character of the season and of the part of the rite actually taking place: Not 6 (1970) 404, no. 42.

[a]   OM and MR'70: "sacred ministers" for "deacon."

[R5]   Query: What is the accurate meaning of *ministri* and *ministri sacri* in the GIRM no. 27? Reply. The terms in GIRM no. 27 "[Text quoted]" refer to the deacon and subdeacon. This is made explicit in GIRM nos. 129 and 144: Not 6 (1970) 104, no. 29. [This material became irrelevant after MRVar in 1972.]

1418   28. After the entrance song, the priest and the whole assembly make the sign of the cross. Then through his greeting the priest declares to the assembled community that the Lord is present. This greeting and the congregation's response express the mystery of the gathered Church.

PENITENTIAL RITE

1419   29. After greeting the congregation, the priest or other qualified minister may very briefly introduce the faithful to the Mass of the day. Then the priest invites them to take part in the penitential rite, which the entire community carries out through a communal confession and which the priest's absolution brings to an end.[R6]

KYRIE ELEISON

1420   30. Then the *Kyrie* begins, unless it has already been included as part of the penitential rite. Since it is a song by which the faithful praise the Lord and implore his mercy, it is ordinarily prayed by all, that is, alternately by the congregation and the choir or cantor.

As a rule each of the acclamations is said twice, but, because of the idiom of different languages, the music, or other circumstances, it may be said more than twice or a short verse (trope) may be interpolated. If the *Kyrie* is not sung, it is to be recited.

GLORIA

1421   31. The *Gloria* is an ancient hymn in which the Church, assembled in the Holy Spirit, praises and entreats the Father and the Lamb. It is sung by the congregation, or by the congregation alternately with the choir, or by the choir alone. If not sung, it is to be recited either by all together or in alternation.

The *Gloria* is sung or said on Sundays outside Advent and Lent, on solemnities and feasts, and in special, more solemn celebrations.[R7]

OPENING PRAYER OR COLLECT

1422   32. Next the priest invites the people to pray and together with him they observe a brief silence so that they may realize they are in God's presence and may call their petitions to mind. The priest then says the opening prayer, which custom has

---

[R6]   1. Query: Does the *Asperges* rite still exist? Reply: Yes. For it is a rite that on Sunday helpfully calls to mind the baptismal washing. But this matter will be settled better in the new missal, in such a way that the *Asperges* will be coordinated with the penitential rite of the Mass: Not 5 (1969) 403, no. 11. See also DOL 208 no. 1477, note R22.

[R7]   1. Query: What is to be understood by the phrase "a special, more solemn celebration"? Reply: This occasion on which GIRM no. 31 calls for the singing of the *Gloria* is a celebration observed with solemnity or with a large number of people: Not 6 (1970) 263, no. 33.

2. Query: When the *Gloria* and *Credo* are not sung but just recited, sometimes the celebrant conducts the recitation in alternation with the congregation. But since a hymn and a profession of faith are at issue and these involve the assembly as a whole, does this practice seem to be in keeping with the rubrics? Reply: The rubrics of the Order of Mass, drawn up in a practical fashion, have only this on the *Gloria*: "the hymn is sung or recited" (no. 5) and on the *Credo*: "the profession of faith . . . is made" (no. 15). As is often the case, the GIRM shows progress of a spiritual order (nos. 31 and 43), by bringing out the community character proper to these texts and by stressing the dialogic style for their recitation.
a. As to the *Gloria*, the GIRM no. 31, to preserve its character as a hymn, says: "[Text quoted]." By preference, therefore, the *Gloria* should be sung. Otherwise it is recited by all either together or in alternation. The celebrant should join with the assembly's singing or reciting of the *Gloria* together or with one sector of the assembly's dialogic recitation or else he should recite the hymn in alternation with the assembly.
b. As to the *Credo*, the GIRM no. 44 says: "[Text quoted]." Therefore whether sung or recited the *Credo* belongs to the entire liturgical assembly, which says it together ("all") or sings it as two alternating choirs: Not 14 (1978) 538, no. 14.

named the "collect." This expresses the theme of the celebration and the priest's words address a petition to God the Father through Christ in the Holy Spirit.

The people make the prayer their own and give their assent by the acclamation, *Amen.*

In the Mass only one opening prayer[b] is said; this rule applies also to the prayer over the gifts and the prayer after communion.

The opening prayer ends with the longer conclusion, namely:

— if the prayer is directed to the Father: *We ask this (Grant this) through our Lord Jesus Christ, your Son, who lives and reigns with you and the Holy Spirit, one God, for ever and ever;*

— if it is directed to the Father, but the Son is mentioned at the end: *Who lives and reigns with you and the Holy Spirit, one God, for ever and ever;*

— if directed to the Son: *You live and reign with the Father and the Holy Spirit, one God, for ever and ever.*

The prayer over the gifts and the prayer after communion end with the shorter conclusion, namely:

— if the prayer is directed to the Father: *We ask this (Grant this) through Christ our Lord;*

— if it is directed to the Father, but the Son is mentioned at the end: *Who lives and reigns with you for ever and ever;*

— if it is directed to the Son: *You live and reign for ever and ever.*

B. Liturgy of the Word

33. Readings from Scripture and the chants between the readings form the main part of the liturgy of the word. The homily, profession of faith, and general intercessions or prayer of the faithful expand and complete this part of the Mass. In the readings, explained by the homily, God is speaking to his people,[31] opening up to them the mystery of redemption and salvation, and nourishing their spirit; Christ is present to the faithful through his own word.[32] Through the chants the people make God's word their own and through the profession of faith affirm their adherence to it. Finally, having been fed by this word, they make their petitions in the general intercessions for the needs of the Church and for the salvation of the whole world.

1423

SCRIPTURE READINGS

34. The readings lay the table of God's word for the faithful and open up the riches of the Bible to them.[33] Since by tradition the reading of the Scriptures is a ministerial, not a presidential function, it is proper that as a rule a deacon or, in his absence, a priest[c] other than the one presiding read the gospel. A reader[d] proclaims the other readings. In the absence of a deacon or another priest, the priest celebrant reads the gospel.[e,34]

1424

---

b   OM and MR'70: "oratio" for "collecta."

31   See SC art. 33 [DOL 1 no. 33].

32   See SC art. 7 [DOL 1 no. 7].

33   See SC art. 51 [DOL 1 no. 51].

c   OM and MR'70: "alter presbyter" for "alius sacerdos."

d   OM and MR'70: "a subdeacon or a reader." MRVar: as in present text.

e   OM and MR'70: "alio presbytero" for "alio sacerdote;" and "celebrant" for "priest celebrant."

34   See SCR, Instr. InterOec no. 50 [DOL 23 no. 342].

1425   35. The liturgy itself inculcates the great reverence to be shown toward the reading of the gospel, setting it off from the other readings by special marks of honor. A special minister is appointed to proclaim it and prepares himself by a blessing or prayer. The people, who by their acclamations acknowledge and confess Christ present and speaking to them, stand as they listen to it. Marks of reverence are given to the Book of the Gospels itself.

CHANTS BETWEEN THE READINGS

1426   36. After the first reading comes the responsorial psalm or gradual, an integral part of the liturgy of the word. The psalm as a rule is drawn from the Lectionary because the individual psalm texts are directly connected with the individual readings: the choice of psalm depends therefore on the readings. Nevertheless, in order that the people may be able to join in the responsorial psalm more readily, some texts of responses and psalms have been chosen, according to the different seasons of the year and classes of saints, for optional use, whenever the psalm is sung, in place of the text corresponding to the reading.

The psalmist or cantor of the psalm[f] sings the verses of the psalm at the lectern or other suitable place. The people remain seated and listen, but also as a rule take part by singing the response, except when the psalm is sung straight through without the response.

The psalm when sung may be either the psalm assigned in the Lectionary or the gradual from the *Graduale Romanum* or the responsorial psalm or the psalm with *Alleluia* as the response from *The Simple Gradual* in the form they have in those books.

1427   37. As the season requires, the *Alleluia* or another chant follows the second reading.

        a. The *Alleluia* is sung in every season outside Lent. It is begun either by all present or by the choir or cantor; it may then be repeated. The verses are taken from the Lectionary or the *Graduale*.

        b. The other chant consists of the verse before the gospel or another psalm or tract, as found in the Lectionary or the *Graduale*.

1428   38. When there is only one reading before the gospel:

        a. during a season calling for the *Alleluia*, there is an option to use either the psalm with *Alleluia* as the response, or the responsorial psalm and the *Alleluia* with its verse, or just the psalm, or just the *Alleluia*;

        b. during the season when the *Alleluia* is not allowed, either the responsorial psalm or the verse before the gospel may be used.

1429   39. If the psalm after the reading is not sung, it is to be recited. If not sung, the *Alleluia* or the verse before the gospel may be omitted.

1430   40. Sequences are optional, except on Easter Sunday and Pentecost.

HOMILY

1431   41. The homily is an integral part of the liturgy and is strongly recommended:[35] it is necessary for the nurturing of the Christian life. It should develop some point of the readings or of another text from the Ordinary or from the Proper of the Mass of the day, and take into account the mystery being celebrated and the needs proper to the listeners.[36]

---

    f   OM and MR'70. "Cantor psalmi, seu psalmista, ..."

    35   See SC art. 52 [DOL 1 no. 52].

    36   See SCR, Instr. InterOec no. 54 [DOL 23 no. 346].

42. There must be a homily on Sundays and holydays of obligation at all Masses   1432
that are celebrated with a congregation. It is recommended on other days, especially
on the weekdays of Advent, Lent, and the Easter season, as well as on other feasts
and occasions when the people come to church in large numbers.[37]

The homily should ordinarily be given by the priest[g] celebrant.[R8]

PROFESSION OF FAITH

43. The symbol or profession of faith in the celebration of Mass serves as a way   1433
for the people to respond and to give their assent to the word of God heard in the
readings and through the homily and for them to call to mind the truths of faith
before they begin to celebrate the eucharist.

44. Recitation of the profession of faith by the priest together with the people is   1434
obligatory on Sundays and solemnities. It may be said also at special, more solemn
celebrations.[R9]

If it is sung, as a rule all are to sing it together or in alternation.

GENERAL INTERCESSIONS

45. In the general intercessions or prayer of the faithful, the people, exercising   1435
their priestly function, intercede for all humanity. It is appropriate that this prayer
be included in all Masses celebrated with a congregation, so that petitions will be
offered for the Church, for civil authorities, for those oppressed by various needs,
for all people, and for the salvation of the world.[38]

46. As a rule the sequence of intentions is to be: 1436

    a. for the needs of the Church;

    b. for public authorities and the salvation of the world;

    c. for those oppressed by any need;

    d. for the local community.

In particular celebrations, such as confirmations, marriages, funerals, etc., the
series of intercessions may refer more specifically to the occasion.

47. It belongs to the priest celebrant to direct the general intercessions, by means   1437
of a brief introduction to invite the congregation to pray, and after the intercessions
to say the concluding prayer. It is desirable that a deacon, cantor, or other person
announce the intentions.[39] The whole assembly gives expression to its supplication
either by a response said together after each intention or by silent prayer.

---

[37] See ibid. no. 56 [DOL 23 no. 348].

[g] OM and MR'70 lack.

[R8] Query: Is it advisable to invite the faithful to bless themselves before or after the homily, to
address a salutation to them, for example, "Praised be Jesus Christ, etc."? Reply: It all depends on lawful
local custom. But generally speaking it is inadvisable to continue such customs because they have their
origin in preaching *outside Mass*. The homily is *part* of the liturgy; the people have already blessed themselves and received the greeting at the beginning of Mass. It is better, then, not to have a repetition before
or after the homily: Not 9 (1973) 178. See also PCIDV, on homilist, 11 Jan. 1971 (DOL 215). SC Clergy,
Letter on preaching by the laity, 20 Nov. 1973 (DOL 344).

[R9] Query: Is the *Credo* to be said during the Easter octave? Reply: Not per se; still, it may be said even
on these weekdays when there is a "more solemn" celebration: Not 7 (1971) 112, no. 2. See also DOL 208
no. 1421, note R7, Query 2.

[38] See SC art. 53 [DOL 1 no. 53].

[39] See SCR, Instr. InterOec no. 56 [DOL 23 no. 348].

C. LITURGY OF THE EUCHARIST

1438   48. At the last supper Christ instituted the sacrifice and paschal meal that make the sacrifice of the cross to be continuously present in the Church, when the priest, representing Christ the Lord, carries out what the Lord did and handed over to his disciples to do in his memory.[40,h]

Christ took the bread and the cup and gave thanks; he broke the bread and gave it to his disciples, saying: "Take and eat, this is my body." Giving the cup, he said: "Take and drink, this is the cup of my blood. Do this in memory of me." Accordingly, the Church has planned the celebration of the eucharistic liturgy around the parts corresponding to these words and actions of Christ:

1. In the preparation of the gifts, the bread and the wine with water are brought to the altar, that is, the same elements that Christ used.

2. In the eucharistic prayer thanks is given to God for the whole work of salvation and the gifts of bread and wine become the body and blood of Christ.

3. Through the breaking of the one bread the unity of the faithful is expressed and through communion they receive the Lord's body and blood in the same way the apostles received them from Christ's own hands.

PREPARATION OF THE GIFTS[R10]

1439   49. At the beginning of the liturgy of the eucharist the gifts, which will become Christ's body and blood, are brought to the altar.

First the altar, the Lord's table, which is the center of the whole eucharistic liturgy,[41] is prepared: the corporal, purificator, missal, and chalice are placed on it (unless the chalice is prepared at a side table).[i]

The gifts are then brought forward. It is desirable for the faithful to present the bread and wine, which are accepted by the priest or deacon at a convenient place. The gifts are placed on the altar to the accompaniment of the prescribed texts. Even though the faithful no longer, as in the past, bring the bread and wine for the

---

[40]   See SC art. 47 [DOL 1 no. 47]. SCR, Instr. EuchMyst no. 3 a,b [DOL 179 no. 1232].

[h]   OM: "48. The Last Supper, at which Christ instituted the memorial of his death and resurrection, becomes continually present in the Church as the priest, representing Christ the Lord, carries out what the Lord did and handed over to his disciples to do in his memory as he instituted the sacrifice and paschal meal."

[R10]   1. Query: What is the genuine meaning of the offertory rite? The description of the offertory of the Mass, it is pointed out, speaks only of the *preparation* of the gifts and of placing them on the altar, of the people's offerings for the church and for the poor, but nothing about the *offering* of the sacrifice. Reply: History teaches that the offertory rite is an action of preparation for the sacrifice in which the priest and ministers accept the gifts offered by the people. These are the elements for the celebration (the bread and wine) and other gifts intended for the church and the poor. This preparatory meaning has always been regarded as the identifying note of the offertory, even though the formularies did not adequately bring it out and were couched in sacrificial language. The new rite puts this specifying note in a clearer light by means both of the active part taken by the faithful in the presentation of the gifts and the formularies the celebrant says in placing the elements for the eucharistic celebration on the altar: Not 6 (1970) 37, no. 25.

2. Query: Does it not seem that the suppression of the prayers that accompanied the offering of the bread and wine has impoverished the offertory rite? Reply. In no way. The former prayers: *Suscipe, Sancte Pater . . .* and *Offerimus tibi, Domine . . .* were not accurate expressions of the genuine meaning of the "offertory" rites but merely anticipated the meaning of the true and literal sacrificial offering that is present in the eucharistic prayer after the consecration, when Christ becomes present on the altar as victim. The new formularies for the gifts bring out the giving of glory to God, who is the source of all things and of all the gifts given to humanity. They state explicitly the meaning of the rite being carried out; they associate the value of human work, which embraces all human concerns, with the mystery of Christ. The offertory rite, then, has been restored through that explicit teaching and shines forth with new light: ibid. 37–38, no. 26.

[41]   See SCR, Instr. InterOec no. 91 [DOL 23 no. 383].

[i]   OM and MR'70 lack "(unless . . . table)."

liturgy from their homes, the rite of carrying up the gifts retains the same spiritual value and meaning.

This is also the time to receive money or other gifts for the church or the poor brought by the faithful or collected at the Mass. These are to be put in a suitable place but not on the altar.

50. The procession bringing the gifts is accompanied by the presentation song, which continues at least until the gifts have been placed on the altar. The rules for this song are the same as those for the entrance song (no. 26). If it is not sung, the presentation antiphon is omitted.   1440

51. The gifts on the altar and the altar itself may be incensed. This is a symbol of the Church's offering and prayer going up to God. Afterward the deacon or other minister may incense the priest and the people.[R11]   1441

52. The priest then washes his hands as an expression of his desire to be cleansed within.[R12]   1442

53. Once the gifts have been placed on the altar and the accompanying rites completed, the preparation of the gifts comes to an end through the invitation to pray with the priest and the prayer over the gifts, which are a preparation for the eucharistic prayer.   1443

EUCHARISTIC PRAYER

54. Now the center and summit of the entire celebration begins: the eucharistic prayer, a prayer of thanksgiving and sanctification. The priest invites the people to   1444

[R11] Query: In Mass with a congregation celebrated more solemnly, different ways of incensation are being used: one plain and simple; the other, the same as the rite for incensation prescribed in the former Roman Missal. Which usage should be followed? Reply: It must never be forgotten that the Missal of Pope Paul VI has, since 1970, supplanted the one called improperly "the Missal of St. Pius V," and completely so, in both texts and rubrics. When the rubrics of the Missal of Paul VI say nothing or say little on particulars in some places, it is not to be inferred that the former rite should be observed. Therefore, the multiple and complex gestures for incensation as prescribed in the former Missal (see *Missale Romanum*, Vatican Polyglot Press, 1962: *Ritus servandus* VIII and *Ordo incensandi* pp. LXXX-LXXXIII) are not to be resumed.

In incensation the celebrant (GIRM nos. 51 and 105) proceeds as follows: a. toward the gifts: he incenses with three swings, as the deacon does toward the Book of the Gospels; b. toward the cross: he incenses with three swings when he comes in front of it; c. toward the altar: he incenses continuously from the side as he passes around the altar, making no distinction between the altar table and the base: Not 14 (1978) 301–302, no. 2.

[R12] Query: May the rite of washing the hands be omitted from the celebration of Mass? Reply: In no way. 1. Both the GIRM (nos. 52, 106, 222) and the Order of Mass (with a congregation, no. 24; without a congregation, no. 18) show the *Lavabo* to be one of the prescribed rites in the preparation of the gifts. A rite of major importance is clearly not at issue, but it is not to be dropped since its meaning is: "an expression of the (priest's) desire to be cleansed within" (GIRM no. 52). In the course of the Consilium's work on the Order of Mass, there were a number of debates on the value and the place to be assigned to the *Lavabo*, e.g., on whether it should be a rite in silence or with an accompanying text; there was, however, unanimity that it must be retained. Even though there has been no practical reason for the act of handwashing since the beginning of the Middle Ages, its symbolism is obvious and understood by all (see SC art. 34 [DOL 1 no. 34]). The rite is a usage in all liturgies of the West. 2. The Constitution on the Liturgy (SC art. 37–40 [DOL 1 nos. 37–40]) envisions ritual adaptations to be suggested by the conferences of bishops and submitted to the Holy See. Such adaptations must be based on serious reasons, for example, the specific culture and viewpoint of a people, contrary and unchangeable usages, the practical impossibility of adapting some new rite that is foreign to the genius of a people, and so on. 3. Apart from the envisioned exemptions from rubrics and differing translations of texts (see Consilium, Instr. 25 Jan. 1969 [DOL 123]), the Order of Mass is presented as a single unit whose general structure and individual components must be exactly respected. Arbitrary selectiveness on the part of an individual or a community would soon result in the ruin of a patiently and thoughtfully constructed work: Not 6 (1970) 38–39, no. 27.

lift up their hearts to the Lord in prayer and thanks; he unites them with himself in the prayer he addresses in their name to the Father through Jesus Christ. The meaning of the prayer is that the entire congregation joins itself to Christ in acknowledging the great things God has done and in offering the sacrifice.

1445   55. The chief elements making up the eucharistic prayer are these:

    a. Thanksgiving (expressed especially in the preface): in the name of the entire people of God, the priest praises the Father and gives thanks to him for the whole work of salvation or for some special aspect of it that corresponds to the day, feast, or season.

    b. Acclamation: joining with the angels, the congregation sings or recites the *Sanctus*. This acclamation is an intrinsic part of the eucharistic prayer and all the people join with the priest in singing or reciting it.

    c. Epiclesis: in special invocations the Church calls on God's power and asks that the gifts offered by human hands be consecrated, that is, become Christ's body and blood, and that the victim to be received in communion be the source of salvation for those who will partake.

    d. Institution narrative and consecration: in the words and actions of Christ, that sacrifice is celebrated which he himself instituted at the last supper, when, under the appearances of bread and wine, he offered his body and blood, gave them to his apostles to eat and drink, then commanded that they carry on this mystery.[i,R13]

    e. Anamnesis: in fulfillment of the command received from Christ through the apostles, the Church keeps his memorial by recalling especially his passion, resurrection, and ascension.

    f. Offering: in this memorial, the Church — and in particular the Church here and now assembled — offers the spotless victim to the Father in the Holy Spirit. The Church's intention is that the faithful not only offer this victim but also learn to offer themselves and so to surrender themselves, through Christ the Mediator, to an ever more complete union with the Father and with each other, so that at last God may be all in all.[42]

    g. Intercessions: the intercessions make it clear that the eucharist is celebrated in communion with the entire Church of heaven and earth and that the offering is

---

  i   OM: "d. Institution narrative: through the words and actions of Christ that last meal is again presented in which Christ the Lord himself instituted the sacrament of his passion and resurrection, when, under the appearance of bread and wine, he gave his body and blood to his apostles to eat and drink, then commanded that they carry on this mystery."

  R13 In certain vernacular versions of the text for consecrating the wine, the words *pro multis* are translated thus: English, *for all men*; Spanish, *por todos*; Italian, *per tutti*. Query: a. Is there a sufficient reason for introducing this variant and if so, what is it? b. Is the pertinent traditional teaching in the *Catechesism of the Council of Trent* to be considered superseded? c. Are all other versions of the biblical passage in question to be regarded as less accurate? d. Did something inaccurate and needing correction or emendation in fact slip in when the approval was given for such a version? Reply: The variant involved is fully justified: a. According to exegetes the Aramaic word translated in Latin by *pro multis* has as its meaning "for all": the "many" for whom Christ died is without limit; it is equivalent to saying "Christ has died for all." The words of St. Augustine are apposite: "See what he gave and you will discover what he bought. The price is Christ's blood. What is it worth but the whole world? What, but all peoples? Those who say either that the price is so small that it has purchased only Africans are ungrateful for the price they cost; those who say that they are so important that it has been given for them alone are proud" (*Enarr. in Ps.* 95, 5). b. The teaching of the *Catechism* is in no way superseded: the distinction that Christ's death is sufficient for all but efficacious for many remains valid. c. In the approval of this vernacular variant in the liturgical text nothing inaccurate has slipped in that requires correction or emendation: Not 6 (1970) 39–40, no. 28.

  42 See SC art. 48 [DOL 1 no. 48]; PO no. 5 [DOL 18 no. 260]. SCR, Instr. EuchMyst no. 12 [DOL 179 no. 1241].

made for the Church and all its members, living and dead, who are called to share in the salvation and redemption purchased by Christ's body and blood.[R14]

h. Final doxology: the praise of God is expressed in the doxology, to which the people's acclamation is an assent and a conclusion.

The eucharistic prayer calls for all to listen in silent reverence, but also to take part through the acclamations for which the rite makes provision.

COMMUNION RITE

56. Since the eucharistic celebration is the paschal meal, it is right that the faithful who are properly disposed[k] receive the Lord's body and blood as spiritual food as he commanded.[43] This is the purpose of the breaking of bread and the other preparatory rites that lead directly to the communion of the people:

1446

a. Lord's Prayer: this is a petition both for daily food, which for Christians means also the eucharistic bread,[l] and for the forgiveness of sin, so that what is holy may be given to those who are holy. The priest offers the invitation to pray, but all the faithful say the prayer with him; he alone adds the embolism, *Deliver us*, which the people conclude with a doxology. The embolism, developing the last petition of the Lord's Prayer, begs on behalf of the entire community of the faithful deliverance from the power of evil. The invitation, the prayer itself, the embolism, and the people's doxology are sung or are recited aloud.

b. Rite of peace: before they share in the same bread, the faithful implore peace and unity for the Church and for the whole human family and offer some sign of their love for one another.

The form the sign of peace should take is left to the conference of bishops to determine, in accord with the culture and customs of the people.

c. Breaking of the bread: in apostolic times this gesture of Christ at the last supper gave the entire eucharistic action its name. This rite is not simply functional, but is a sign that in sharing in the one bread of life which is Christ we who are many are made one body (see 1 Cor 10:17).

d. Commingling: the celebrant drops a part of the host into the chalice.

e. *Agnus Dei*: during the breaking of the bread and the commingling, the *Agnus Dei* is as a rule sung by the choir or cantor with the congregation responding; otherwise it is recited aloud. This invocation may be repeated as often as necessary to accompany the breaking of the bread. The final reprise concludes with the words, *grant us peace*.[R15]

R14　Query: In the intercessions of Eucharistic Prayer III, this parenthesis appears ("Saint N. — the saint of the day or the patron saint"). How should these words be interpreted? Must the saint of the day or the patron saint be mentioned? And even on a Sunday or on more solemn days? May the blessed also be mentioned? Reply: a. The words quoted, as is rightly noted, are in parentheses; therefore mention of the saint of the day or the patron saint is to be considered as optional. But it should not be omitted all the time, because mention of the saint adds something concretely relevant to the participants, the place, and the circumstances. b. There may therefore always be a mention of the saint of the day or of the patron saint, even if celebration of a Mass in honor of the saint is impeded, and even on Sunday and more solemn days. Special conditions of people and places may sometimes favor omission, for example, if mention of a little-known saint may cause puzzlement. The celebrant should always guard against imposing his own personal devotion on the faithful. c. What has been said about saints is applicable to the blessed, but only in keeping with places and ways established by law (see CIC can. 1277, § 2): Not 14 (1978) 594–595, no. 17.

k　OM lacks "the faithful who are rightly disposed."

43　See SCR, Instr. EuchMyst nos. 12, 33 a [DOL 179 nos. 1241, 1262].

l　OM: "This is a petition for daily food, which is given to Christians above all in the body of Christ."

R15　1. Query: May the singing of *Shalom* replace the singing of the *Agnus Dei*? Reply: No. The Ordinary of the Mass in all its parts must be followed as it appears in the Missal. Some slight adaptation is

f. Personal preparation of the priest: the priest prepares himself by the prayer, said softly, that he may receive Christ's body and blood to good effect. The faithful do the same by silent prayer.

g. The priest then shows the eucharistic bread for communion to the faithful and with them recites the prayer of humility in words from the Gospels.

h. It is most desirable that the faithful receive the Lord's body from hosts consecrated at the same Mass and that, in the instances when it is permitted, they share in the chalice. Then even through the signs communion will stand out more clearly as a sharing in the sacrifice actually being celebrated.[44,m]

i. During the priest's and the faithful's reception of the sacrament the communion song is sung. Its function is to express outwardly the communicants' union in spirit by means of the unity of their voices, to give evidence of joy of heart, and to make the procession to receive Christ's body more fully an act of community. The song begins when the priest takes communion and continues for as long as seems appropriate while the faithful receive Christ's body. But the communion song should be ended in good time whenever there is to be a hymn after communion.

An antiphon from the *Graduale Romanum* may also be used, with or without the psalm, or an antiphon with psalm from *The Simple Gradual* or another suitable song approved by the conference of bishops. It is sung by the choir alone or by the choir or cantor with the congregation.

If there is no singing, the communion antiphon in the Missal is recited either by the people, by some of them, or by a reader. Otherwise the priest himself says it after he has received communion and before he gives communion to the faithful.

j. After communion, the priest and people may spend some time in silent prayer. If desired, a hymn, psalm, or other song of praise may be sung by the entire congregation.

k. In the prayer after communion, the priest petitions for the effects of the mystery just celebrated and by their acclamation, *Amen*, the people make the prayer their own.

D. CONCLUDING RITE

1447   57. The concluding rite consists of:

a. the priest's greeting and blessing, which on certain days and occasions is expanded and expressed in the prayer over the people or another more solemn formulary;[R16]

---

countenanced in the *Directory for Masses with Children* no. 31 [DOL 276 no. 2164]. What is established for children, however, is not transferable to other assemblies: Not 11 (1975) 205.

2. Query: How many times must the *Agnus Dei* be said or sung, according to the indications in the Order of Mass? Reply: The point of the *Agnus Dei* is to accompany the breaking of the consecrated bread until a particle is dropped into the chalice (GIRM no. 56 e). In practice two situations are to be considered: a. If there is only one celebrant presiding or if there are only a few concelebrants, the breaking of the bread is done quite quickly. Usually the *Agnus Dei* said or sung three times, as indicated in the Order of Mass no. 131, is enough to accompany the rite. b. In the case when there are many concelebrants or the breaking of the bread takes a long time, then the *Agnus Dei* may be repeated until the completion of the breaking of the bread, following the rubric in the Order of Mass no. 131: "This may be repeated . . ." and the directive of the GIRM no. 56 e: "[Text quoted] ": Not 14 (1978) 306, no. 8.

[44] See SCR, Instr. EuchMyst nos. 31, 32, on communion twice in one day [DOL 179 nos. 1260, 1261]. See also SCDS, Instr. *Immensae caritatis*, 29 Jan. 1973, no. 2 [DOL 264 nos. 2082–84].

[m] OM and MR'70 lack second citation in note 44.

[R16] Query: What is the formulary a bishop is to use for the final blessing of Mass? Reply: Although nothing is said on this point in the new Order of Mass, at the end of Mass bishops bless the people either

b. the dismissal of the assembly, which sends each member back to doing good works, while praising and blessing the Lord.

CHAPTER III
OFFICES AND MINISTRIES IN THE MASS

58. All in the assembly gathered for Mass have an individual right and duty to contribute their participation in ways differing according to the diversity of their order and liturgical function.[45] Thus in carrying out this function, all, whether ministers or laypersons, should do all and only those parts that belong to them,[46] so that the very arrangement of the celebration itself makes the Church stand out as being formed in a structure of different orders and ministries.

I. OFFICES AND MINISTRIES OF HOLY ORDERS

59. Every authentic celebration of the eucharist is directed by the bishop, either in person or through the presbyters, who are his helpers.[47]

Whenever he is present at a Mass with a congregation, it is fitting that the bishop himself preside over the assembly and associate the presbyters with himself in the celebration, if possible by concelebrating with them.

This is done not to add external solemnity, but to express in a clearer light the mystery of the Church, which is the sacrament of unity.[48]

Even if the bishop is not the celebrant of the eucharist but assigns someone else,[a] he should preside over the liturgy of the word and give the blessing at the end of Mass.[b]

60. Within the community of believers, the presbyter is another who possesses the power of orders to offer sacrifice in the person of Christ.[49] He therefore presides over the assembly and leads its prayer, proclaims the message of salvation, joins the people to himself in offering the sacrifice to the Father through Christ in the Spirit, gives them the bread of eternal life, and shares in it with them.[c] At the eucharist he should, then, serve God and the people with dignity and humility; by his bearing and by the way he recites the words of the liturgy he should communicate to the faithful a sense of the living presence of Christ.

61. Among ministers, the deacon, whose order has been held in high honor since the early Church, has first place. At Mass he has his own functions: he proclaims

1448

1449

1450

1451

---

with the more solemn formulary that will appear in the new Roman Missal or with the formulary that has been customary until now, namely: *Blessed be the name of the Lord. . .; Our help is in the name of the Lord* (they do not cross themselves); *May almighty God bless you . . .*, as he makes the triple sign of the cross: Not 5 (1969) 403, no. 14. See also no. 1498, note R27.

45   See SC art. 14, 26 [DOL 1 nos. 14, 26].

46   See SC art. 28 [DOL 1 no. 28].

47   See LG nos. 26, 28 [DOL 4 nos. 146,148]; SC art. 42 [DOL 1 no. 42].

48   See SC art. 26 [DOL 1 no. 26].

a   OM: "Even if . . . but deputes someone else."

b   OM and MR'70: "and concludes the Mass with the dismissal rite."

49   See PO no. 2 [DOL 18 no. 257]; LG no. 28 [DOL 4 no. 148].

c   OM: "60. The priest celebrant also presides over the assembly, leads it in prayer, proclaims the message of salvation, joins the people to himself in offering the sacrifice through Christ in the Spirit to the Father, and shares with his brothers in the bread of eternal life." Note 49 is lacking.

the gospel, sometimes preaches God's word, leads the general intercessions, assists the priest, gives communion to the people (in particular, ministering the chalice), and sometimes gives directions regarding the assembly's moving, standing, kneeling, or sitting.[R17]

II. OFFICE AND FUNCTION OF THE PEOPLE OF GOD

1452   62. In the celebration of Mass the faithful are a holy people, a people God has made his own, a royal priesthood: they give thanks to the Father and offer the victim not only through the hands of the priest but also together with him and learn to offer themselves.[50] They should endeavor to make this clear by their deep sense of reverence for God and their charity toward all who share with them in the celebration.

They therefore are to shun any appearance of individualism or division, keeping before their mind that they have the one Father in heaven and therefore are all brothers and sisters to each other.

They should become one body, whether by hearing the word of God,[R18] or joining in prayers and song, or above all by offering the sacrifice together and sharing together in the Lord's table. There is a beautiful expression of this unity when the faithful maintain uniformity in their actions and in standing, sitting, or kneeling.

The faithful should serve the people of God willingly when asked to perform some particular ministry in the celebration.

1453   63. The *schola cantorum* or choir exercises its own liturgical function within the assembly. Its task is to ensure that the parts proper to it, in keeping with the different types of chants, are carried out becomingly and to encourage active participation of the people in the singing.[51] What is said about the choir applies in a similar way to other musicians, especially the organist.

1454   64. There should be a cantor or a choir director to lead and sustain the people in the singing. When in fact there is no choir, it is up to the cantor to lead the various songs, and the people take part in the way proper to them.[52]

[R17]   See DOL 309 no. 2536, note R1.

[50]   See SC art. 48 [DOL 1 no. 48]. SCR, Instr. EuchMyst no. 12 [DOL 179 no. 1241].

[R18]   Are hand missals still needed? Since reform of the liturgy the usefulness of hand missals for the faithful is often questioned. All now understand the words spoken at Mass; what is more, as far as the biblical readings are concerned, all ought to be listening attentively to the word of God. Nevertheless hand missals, it seems, remain necessary. People do not always hear well, especially in large churches, and what they do hear physically they do not always understand right away. They therefore often need to go back over the texts heard during a celebration. In addition, the liturgy, and the eucharistic celebration above all, is "the summit toward which the activity of the Church is directed; at the same time it is the fount from which all the Church's power flows" (SC art. 10 [DOL 1 no. 10]). All the concerns of the spiritual life must be brought to the liturgy and that happens if participation is truly actual and *aware*. This requires frequent meditation on the liturgical texts both before and after the celebration: Not 8 (1972) 195–196. See also the notes from Bp. R. Coffy, President of the Liturgical Commission of France, and the survey of vernacular missals available: ibid. 196–198. On the same point before 1969, see DOL 196 note R1: General Points, Query 3.

[51]   See SCR, Instr. MusSacr no. 19 [DOL 508 no. 4140].

[52]   See ibid. no. 21 [DOL 508 no. 4142].

III. SPECIAL MINISTRIES

65. The acolyte is instituted to serve at the altar and to assist the priest and deacon.   1455
In particular it is for him to prepare the altar and the vessels and, as a special
minister of the eucharist, to give communion to the faithful.[d]

66. The reader is instituted to proclaim the readings from Scripture, with the   1456
exception of the gospel. He may also announce the intentions for the general
intercessions and, in the absence of the psalmist, sing or read the psalm between the
readings.

The reader has his own proper function in the eucharistic celebration and
should exercise this even though ministers of a higher rank may be present.

Those who exercise the ministry of reader, even if they have not received
institution, must be truly qualified and carefully prepared in order that the faithful
will develop a warm and lively love for Scripture[53] from listening to the reading of
the sacred texts.[e]

67. The cantor of the psalm is to sing the psalm or other biblical song that comes   1457
between the readings. To fulfill their function correctly, these cantors should possess singing talent and an aptitude for correct pronunciation and diction.

68. As for other ministers, some perform different functions inside the sanctuary,   1458
others outside.

The first kind include those deputed as special ministers of communion[54] and[f]
those who carry the missal, the cross, candles, the bread, wine, water, and the
thurible.

The second kind include:

a. The commentator. This minister provides explanations and commentaries
with the purpose of introducing the faithful to the celebration and preparing them
to understand it better. The commentator's remarks must be meticulously prepared
and marked by a simple brevity.

In performing this function the commentator stands in a convenient place
visible to the faithful, but it is preferable that this not be at the lectern[g] where the
Scriptures are read.

---

[d] OM and MR 70: "65. The subdeacon has been ordained to serve at the altar and to assist the priest
and the deacon. In particular he is entrusted with the preparation of the altar and sacred vessels and with
the singing of the epistle." Changed by MRVar.

[53] See SC art. 24 [DOL 1 no. 24].

[e] OM and MR'70: "66. The reader, even if a layperson, has a proper function in the eucharistic
celebration and should exercise this even though ministers of a higher rank may be present. It belongs to
the reader to proclaim all the readings from Scripture, with the exception of the gospel and, if a subdeacon
is present, of the epistle. In the absence of a psalmist, the reader may also sing or read the psalm between
the readings. It is necessary that readers deputed for such a ministry be truly qualified and carefully
prepared so that the reading creates in the faithful a warm and living love for Scripture. The conference of
bishops may grant that when there is no man present capable of carrying out the reader's function, a
suitable woman, standing outside the sanctuary, may proclaim the readings preceding the gospel." (Note
51 is note 52 in the present text.)
    MRVar: As in present text; the lines "The conference of bishops . . ." remain in no. 66, but were
emended to the form they now have in no. 70 of the present text; note 54 here is note 51bis in MRVar.

[54] See SCDS, Instr. *Immensae caritatis*, 29 Jan. 1973, no. 1 [DOL 264 nos. 2074–81].

[f] OM and MR'70 lack "those . . . and" as well as note 54.

[g] OM and MR'70: ". . . but does not use the lectern."

    b. Those who, in some places, meet the people at the church entrance, seat them, and direct processions.

    c. Those who take up the collection.

1459   69. Especially in larger churches and communities, a person should be assigned responsibility for planning the services properly and for their being carried out by the ministers with decorum, order, and devotion.

1460   70. Laymen, even if they have not received institution as ministers, may perform all the functions below those reserved to deacons. At the discretion of the rector of the church, women may be appointed to ministries that are performed outside the sanctuary.

    The conference of bishops may permit qualified women to proclaim the readings before the gospel and to announce the intentions of the general intercessions. The conference may also more precisely designate a suitable place for a woman to proclaim the word of God in the liturgical assembly.[55,h]

1461   71. If there are several persons present who are empowered to exercise the same ministry, there is no objection to their being assigned different parts to perform. For example, one deacon may take the sung parts, another assist at the altar; if there are several readings, it is better to distribute them among a number of readers. The same applies for the other ministries.

1462   72. If only one minister is present at a Mass with a congregation, he may carry out several different functions.

1463   73. All concerned should work together in the effective preparation of each liturgical celebration as to its rites, pastoral aspects, and music. They should work under the direction of the rector of the church and should consult the faithful.

CHAPTER IV
THE DIFFERENT FORMS OF CELEBRATION

1464   74. In the local Church, first place should be given, because of its meaning, to the Mass at which the bishop presides surrounded by the college of presbyters and the ministers[56] and in which the people take full and active part. For this Mass is the preeminent expression of the Church.

1465   75. Great importance should be attached to a Mass celebrated by any community, but especially by the parish community, inasmuch as it represents the universal Church gathered at a given time and place. This is particularly true of the community's celebration of the Lord's Day.[57]

---

[55] See SCDW, Instr. *Liturgicae instaurationes*, 5 Sept. 1970, no. 7 [DOL 52 no. 525].

[h] OM and MR'70: "70. Laymen may perform all the ministries below those belonging to subdeacons. At the discretion of the rector of the Church, women may be appointed to ministries that are performed outside the sanctuary." [See note *e* of this chapter.]

    MRVar: "70. Laymen, even if they have not received institution, as ministers, may perform all the functions below those reserved to deacons. At the discretion . . . outside the sanctuary. With due regard for what has been said in no. 66 about the place from which scriptural readings are to be proclaimed, the conference of bishops may permit" etc., as in the present text, note 54 of which is note 51 in MRVar.

[56] See SC art. 41 [DOL 1 no. 41].

[57] See SC art. 42 [DOL 1 no. 42]. SCR, Instr. EuchMyst, 25 May 1967, no. 26 [DOL 179 no. 1255]. LG no. 28 [DOL 4 no. 148]; PO no. 5 [DOL 18 no. 260].

76. Of those Masses celebrated by some communities, the conventual Mass,   1466
which is a part of the daily office, or the "community" Mass have particular significance. Although such Masses do not have a special form of celebration, it is
most proper that they be celebrated with singing, with the full participation of all
community members, whether religious or canons. In these Masses, therefore, individuals should exercise the function proper to the order or ministry they have
received. All the priests who are not bound to celebrate individually for the pastoral
benefit of the faithful should thus concelebrate at the conventual or community
Mass, if possible. Further, all priests belonging to the community who are obliged
to celebrate individually for the pastoral benefit of the faithful may also on the
same day concelebrate at the conventual or community Mass.[58,a,R19]

I. MASS WITH A CONGREGATION

77. Mass with a congregation means a Mass celebrated with the people taking   1467
part. As far as possible, and especially on Sundays and holydays of obligation, this
Mass should be celebrated with song and with a suitable number of ministers.[59] But
it may be celebrated without music and with only one minister.

78. It is desirable that as a rule an acolyte, a reader, and a cantor[b] assist the priest   1468
celebrant; this form of celebration will hereafter be referred to as the "basic" or
"typical" form. But the rite to be described also allows for a greater number of
ministers.
    A deacon may exercise his office in any of the forms of celebration.

ARTICLES TO BE PREPARED
79. The altar is to be covered with at least one cloth. On or near the altar there are   1469
to be candlesticks with lighted candles, at least two but even four, six, or, if the
bishop of the diocese celebrates, seven.[R20] There is also to be a cross on or near the
altar. The candles and cross may be carried in the entrance procession. The Book of
the Gospels, if distinct from the book of other readings, may be placed on the altar,
unless it is carried in the entrance procession.

80. The following are also to be prepared: [c]   1470
    a. next to the priest's chair: the missal and, as may be useful, a book with the
        chants;

---

[a] OM: "76. Of those Masses celebrated by some communities the conventual Mass, which is part of
the daily office, has particular significance. Although . . . canons. In that Mass, therefore, . . . proper to
the order they have received. Moreover, all the priests who are not bound to celebrate individually for the
pastoral benefit of the faithful should concelebrate at it, if possible.[54] All who belong to the community,
both priests obliged to celebrate individually for the spiritual good of the faithful and those who are not
priests, may receive communion under both kinds."
    MR'70: "76. Of those Masses . . . the conventual Mass or the "community" Mass have special
significance. . . . In these Masses, therefore, individuals should exercise the ministry proper to the order
they have received. Moreover, all priests who are not bound to celebrate individually for the pastoral
benefit of the faithful should concelebrate at these Masses, if possible.[54] All who belong to the community, both priests obliged to celebrate individually for the spiritual good of the faithful and nonpriests, may
receive communion under both kinds [Note 54 in both these texts is note 58 in the present text]."

[R19] See DOL 223 no. 1796, note R3.

[59] See SCR, Instr. EuchMyst no. 26 [DOL 179 no. 1255]; Instr. MusSacr, 5 March 1967, nos. 16, 27
[DOL 508 nos. 4137, 4148].

[b] OM and MR'70: "It is desirable that a reader, cantor, and at least one server . . ."

[R20] See DOL 208 no. 1659, note R47.

[c] OM and MR'70: "80. To be prepared in the sanctuary are:"

b. at the lectern: the lectionary;

c. on a side table: the chalice, corporal, purificator, and, if useful, a pall; a paten and ciboria, if needed, with the bread for the communion of the ministers and the people, together with cruets containing wine and water, unless all of these are brought in by the faithful at the presentation of the gifts; a communion plate for the communion of the faithful;[d] the requisites for the washing of hands. The chalice should be covered with a veil, which may always be white.[R21]

1471   81. In the sacristy the vestments for the priest and ministers are to be prepared according to the various forms of celebration:

a. for the priest: alb, stole, and chasuble;

b. for the deacon: alb, stole, and dalmatic; the last may be omitted either out of necessity or for less solemnity;

c. for the other ministers: albs or other lawfully approved vestments.[e]

All who wear an alb should use a cincture and an amice, unless other provision is made.

A. Basic Form of Celebration

INTRODUCTORY RITES

1472   82. Once the congregation has gathered, the priest and the ministers, clad in their vestments, go to the altar in this order:

a. a server with a lighted censer, if incense is used;

b. the servers, who, according to the occasion, carry lighted candles, and between them the crossbearer, if the cross is to be carried;

c. acolytes and other ministers;[f]

d. a reader, who may carry the Book of the Gospels;

e. the priest who is to celebrate the Mass.

If incense is used, the priest puts some in the censer before the procession begins.

1473   83. During the procession to the altar the entrance song is sung (see nos. 25–26).

1474   84. On reaching the altar the priest and ministers make the proper reverence, that is, a low bow or, if there is a tabernacle containing the blessed sacrament, a genuflection.

If the cross has been carried in the procession, it is placed near the altar or at some other convenient place; the candles carried by the servers are placed near the altar or on a side table; the Book of the Gospels is placed on the altar.

1475   85. The priest goes up to the altar and kisses it. If incense is used, he incenses the altar while circling it.

---

[d] OM lacks "communion plate . . . faithful."

[R21] Query: In a great many places the veil is hardly ever used to cover the chalice prepared at a side table before Mass. Have any recent norms been given to suppress use of the veil? Reply: There is no norm, not even a recent one, to change the GIRM no. 80 c, which reads: "[Text quoted] ": Not 14 (1978) 594, no. 16.

[e] OM and MR'70: "c. for the subdeacon: alb and tunic; the tunic also may be omitted either out of necessity or for less solemnity"; "d. for the other ministers: albs or surplices."

[f] OM and MR'70: "b. the servers . . . the crossbearer; other ministers." Both lack present c, and have present d and e as c and d.

86. The priest then goes to the chair. After the entrance song, and with all stand-   1476
ing, the priest and the faithful make the sign of the cross. The priest says: *In the name
of the Father, and of the Son, and of the Holy Spirit*; the people answer: *Amen.*

Then, facing the people and with hands outstretched, the priest greets all
present, using one of the formularies indicated. He or some other qualified minister
may give the faithful a very brief introduction to the Mass of the day.

87. After the penitential rite,[R22] the *Kyrie* and *Gloria* are said, in keeping with the   1477
rubrics (nos. 30–31). Either the priest or the cantors or even everyone together may
begin the *Gloria.*

88. With his hands joined, the priest then invites the people to pray, saying: *Let us*   1478
pray. All pray silently with the priest for a while. Then the priest with hands
outstretched says the opening prayer,[g] at the end of which the people respond:
Amen.

LITURGY OF THE WORD

89. After the opening prayer,[h] the reader goes to the lectern for the first read-   1479
ing.[R23] All sit and listen and make the acclamation at the end.

90. After the reading, the psalmist or cantor of the psalm, or even the reader, sings   1480
or recites the psalm and the congregation sings or recites the response (see no. 36).

R22   Query: During the recitation of certain formularies, for example, the *Confiteor, Agnus Dei, Domine, non
sum dignus*, the accompanying gestures on the part of both priest and people are not always the same: some
strike their breast three times; others, once during such formularies. What is the lawful practice to be
followed? Reply: In this case it is helpful to recall: 1. gestures and words usually complement each other;
2. in this matter as in others the liturgical reform has sought authenticity and simplicity, in keeping with
SC art. 34: "The rites should be marked by a noble simplicity" [DOL 1 no. 34]. Whereas in the Roman
Missal promulgated by authority of the Council of Trent meticulous gestures usually accompanied the
words, the rubrics of the Roman Missal as reformed by authority of Vatican Council II are marked by their
restraint with regard to gestures. This being said:
    a. The words, *Through my own fault* in the *Confiteor* are annotated in the reformed Roman Missal with
the rubric: "They strike their breast" (*Ordo Missae* no. 3). In the former Missal at the same place the rubric
read this way: "He strikes his breast three times." Therefore it seems that the breast is not to be struck
three times by anyone in reciting the words, whether in Latin or another language, even if the tripled
formulary is said (*mea culpa, mea culpa, mea maxima culpa*). One striking of the breast is enough. Clearly, also,
one gesture is enough in those languages in which the words expressing fault are translated in a simpler
form, for example in English, *I have sinned through my own fault*; in French, *Oui, j'ai vraiment péché*. b. The special
restraint of the reformed Roman Missal is also clear regarding the other texts mentioned, the *Agnus Dei* and
Domine, non sum dignus, expressions of repentance and humility accompanying the breaking of the bread and
the call of the faithful to communion.
    As noted in the Reply no. 2 of the comments in Not 14 (1978) 301, when the rubrics of the Missal
of Paul VI say nothing, it is not to be thereby inferred that the former rubrics must be followed [see DOL
208 no. 1441, note R11]. The reformed Missal does not supplement but supplants the old Missal. The old
Missal at the *Agnus Dei* had the directive "striking his breast three times" and the same for the *Domine, non
sum dignus*. But because the new Missal says nothing on this point (*Ordo Missae*, nos. 131 and 133), there is
no reason for requiring any gesture to be added to these invocations: Not 14 (1978) 534–535, no. 10.

    g   OM and MR'70: "orationem" for "collectam."

    h   OM and MR'70: "oratione" for "collecta."

R23   Query: Before the biblical readings sometimes priests or lay readers announce subtitles for the
selection or even the rubric: "The first reading," "The second reading," etc. Is it permissible to follow this
practice? Reply: Clearly not. As with all rubrics, the titles, "The first reading," "The second reading," are
guides for the convenience of the reader. As to the captions, which consist either in a sentence drawn from
the text or in a summary statement of the reading, they too are guides useful for choosing among different
texts, especially in the Commons. The sole title to be announced is the one indicating the book of the
Bible or, where applicable, its author. For example: "A reading from the Letter of Paul to Timothy"; "A
reading from the holy Gospel according to Mark": Not 14 (1978) 303, no. 5.

1481 91. Then, if there is a second reading before the gospel, the reader reads it at the lectern as before. All sit and listen and make the acclamation at the end.

1482 92. The *Alleluia* or other chant, according to the season, follows (see nos. 37–39).

1483 93. During the singing of the *Alleluia* or other chant, if incense is being used, the priest puts some into the censer. Then with hands joined he bows before the altar and inaudibly says the prayer, *Almighty God, cleanse my heart.*

1484 94. If the Book of the Gospels is on the altar, he takes it and goes to the lectern, the servers, who may carry the censer and candles, walking ahead of him.

1485 95. At the lectern the priest opens the book and says: *The Lord be with you.* Then he says: *A reading from . . .,*[i] making the sign of the cross with his thumb on the book and on his forehead, mouth, and breast. If incense is used, he then incenses the book. After the acclamation of the people, he proclaims the gospel and at the end kisses the book, saying inaudibly: *May the words of the gospel wipe away our sins.* After the reading the people make the acclamation customary to the region.

1486 96. If no reader is present, the priest himself proclaims all the readings at the lectern and there also, if necessary, the chants between the readings. If incense is used, he puts some into the censer at the lectern and then, bowing, says the prayer, *Almighty God, cleanse my heart.*

1487 97. The homily is given at the chair or at the lectern.[R24]

1488 98. The profession of faith is said by the priest together with the people (see no. 44). At the words, *by the power of the Holy Spirit,* etc., all bow; on the solemnities of the Annunciation and Christmas all kneel.

1489 99. Next, with the people taking their proper part, follow the general intercessions (prayer of the faithful), which the priest directs from his chair or at the lectern (see nos. 45–47).

LITURGY OF THE EUCHARIST

1490 100. After the general intercessions, the presentation song begins (see no. 50). The servers place the corporal, purificator, chalice, and missal on the altar.

1491 101. It is fitting for the faithful's participation to be expressed by their presenting both the bread and wine for the celebration of the eucharist and other gifts to meet the needs of the church and of the poor.

The faithful's offerings are received by the priest, assisted by the ministers, and put in a suitable place; the bread and wine for the eucharist are taken to the altar.

1492 102. At the altar the priest receives the paten with the bread from a minister. With both hands he holds it slightly raised above the altar and says the accompanying prayer. Then he places the paten with the bread on the corporal.[R25]

---

i   OM: "Then he says: *The beginning of . . .* or *Continuation of . . . .*"

R24   Query: In the celebration of Mass may the bishop give the homily at the chair and seated ? Reply: By rule of the GIRM no. 97, in the celebration of Mass the homily is given at the chair or at the lectern. In keeping with custom, the bishop may certainly give the homily seated: Not 10 (1974) 80, no. 3. See also DOL 208 no. 1432, note R8.

R25   Query: How are the presentation of the bread and wine by the faithful and the presentation of the paten with the bread in GIRM no. 102 compatible? Reply: There is no problem. For the offerings that the priest receives from the people are put on a nearby table and the bread and wine are carried to the altar

103. Next, as a minister presents the cruets, the priest stands at the side of the altar   1493
and pours wine and a little water into the chalice, saying the accompanying prayer
inaudibly. He returns to the middle of the altar, takes the chalice, raises it a little with
both hands, and says the appointed prayer. Then he places the chalice on the corporal
and may cover it with a pall.

104. The priest bows and inaudibly says the prayer, *Lord God, we ask you to receive*.   1494

105. If incense is used, he incenses the gifts and the altar. A minister incenses the   1495
priest and the congregation.[R26]

106. After the prayer, *Lord God, we ask you to receive*, or after the incensation, the priest   1496
washes his hands at the side of the altar and inaudibly says the prescribed prayer as
a minister pours the water.

107. The priest returns to the center and, facing the people and extending then   1497
joining his hands, pronounces the invitation: *Pray, brothers and sisters*. After the people's response, he says the prayer over the gifts with hands outstretched. At the end
the people make the acclamation: *Amen*.

108. The priest then begins the eucharistic prayer. With hands outstretched, he says: 1498
The Lord be with you. As he says: *Lift up your hearts*, he raises his hands; with hands
outstretched, he adds: *Let us give thanks to the Lord our God*. When the people have
answered: *It is right to give him thanks and praise*, the priest continues the preface. At its
conclusion, he joins his hands and sings or says aloud with the ministers and people
the *Sanctus-Benedictus* (see no. 55 b).[R27]

109. The priest continues the eucharistic prayer according to the rubrics that are   1499
given for each of them. If the priest celebrant is a bishop, after the words *N. our Pope*
or the equivalent, he adds: *and for me your unworthy servant*. The local Ordinary must be
mentioned in this way: *N. our Bishop* (or *Vicar, Prelate, Prefect, Abbot*). Coadjutor and
auxiliary bishops may be mentioned in the eucharistic prayer. When several are
named, this is done with the collective formula, *N. our Bishop and his assistant bishops*.[60] All these phrases should be modified grammatically to fit with each one of the

---

(see GIRM no. 101), then the offertory rites take place. If the celebrant takes the paten or ciborium with
the bread from the faithful last, he may proceed directly to the altar and immediately recite the formulary
for offering the bread: Not 6 (1970) 404, no. 43.

[R26]   See DOL 208 no. 1441, note R11.

[R27]   Query: Some celebrants have the practice of raising then joining their hands during the dialogue
before the preface and at the beginning of the final blessing. Others omit such gestures. What is right?
Reply: As is often the case, at issue is a habit having its source in the rubrics of the former Roman Missal.
The current directives of the Order of Mass are to be followed, which are clear on the two points raised:
    a.   As to the dialogue before the preface, no. 27 (MR p. 392) says precisely: "With hands extended
he sings or says: *The Lord be with you*"; "He lifts up his hands and continues: *Lift up your hearts*"; "With hands
extended, he continues: *Let us give thanks to the Lord our God*"; "The priest continues the preface with hands
extended." Therefore the former rite is not to be continued; among other things it indicated at this point:
"He joins his hands before his breast and bows his head as he says: *Let us give thanks . . . ."*
    b.   As to the blessing at the end of Mass, the new Order of Mass says only: "The priest blesses the
people, with these words . . ." (no. 42). But the rubrics of the former Order of Mass, after the dismissal
Ite, Missa est, prescribed a gesture for the blessing having five steps: "Raising his eyes, extending, raising,
and joining his hands, and bowing his head to the cross, he says: *May almighty God bless you . . .* and turning
to the people . . . continues: *the Father. . . ."* Now, however, only that gesture is required which is
indicated by the relevant rubric, namely, the priest blesses the people, with the words: *May almighty God
bless you, the Father, and the Son, and the Holy Spirit*: Not 14 (1978) 536–537, no. 12.

[60]   See SCDW, Decr., 9 Oct. 1972 [DOL 247].

eucharistic prayers.[j]

    A little before the consecration, the server may ring a bell as a signal to the faithful. Depending on local custom, he also rings the bell at the showing of both the host and the chalice.[k,R28]

1500   110. After the doxology at the end of the eucharistic prayer,[l] the priest, with hands joined, says the introduction to the Lord's Prayer. With hands outstretched he then sings or says this prayer with the people.

1501   111. After the Lord's Prayer, the priest alone, with hands outstretched, says the embolism, *Deliver us*. At the end the congregation makes the acclamation, *For the kingdom*.

1502   112. Then the priest says aloud the prayer, *Lord Jesus Christ*. After this prayer, extending then joining his hands, he gives the greeting of peace: *The peace of the Lord be with you always*. The people answer: *And also with you*. Then the priest may add: *Let us offer each other the sign of peace*. All exchange some sign of peace and love, according to local custom. The priest may give the sign of peace to the ministers.[R29]

1503   113. The priest then takes the eucharistic bread and breaks it over the paten. He places a small piece in the chalice, saying inaudibly: *May this mingling*. Meanwhile the *Agnus Dei* is sung or recited by the choir and congregation (see no. 56 e).[R30]

1504   114. Then the priest inaudibly says the prayer, *Lord Jesus Christ, Son of the living God*, or *Lord Jesus Christ, with faith in your love and mercy*.[R31]

---

   [j] OM and MR'70 lack "If the priest celebrant . . . eucharistic prayers." and note 60.

   [k] OM lacks "A little before . . . chalice." MR'70: "elevation" for "showing of both the host and the chalice."

   [R28] Query: Is a bell to be rung at Mass? Reply: It all depends on the different circumstances of places and people, as is clear from GIRM no. 109: ["Text quoted"]. From a long and attentive catechesis and education in liturgy, a particular liturgical assembly may be able to take part in the Mass with such attention and awareness that it has no need of this signal at the central part of the Mass. This may easily be the case, for example, with religious communities or with particular or small groups. The opposite may be presumed in a parish or public church, where there is a different level of liturgical and religious education and where often people who are visitors or are not regular churchgoers take part. In these cases the bell as a signal is entirely appropriate and is sometimes necessary. To conclude: usually a signal with the bell should be given, at least at the two elevations, in order to elicit joy and attention: Not 8 (1972) 343.

   [l] OM and MR'70: "After the doxology following the eucharistic prayer."

   [R29] 1. Query: In churches without an altar facing the people should the priest in the celebration of Mass turn toward the congregation as he says: *The peace of the Lord be with you always* and *Let us offer each other a sign of peace*? Reply: Yes. The rubric in the Order of Mass with a congregation no. 128 directs that the priest speaks these words while facing the congregation: Not 6 (1970) 264, no. 39.

     2. Query: In some places there is a current practice whereby those taking part in the Mass replace the giving of the sign of peace at the deacon's invitation by holding hands during the singing of the Lord's Prayer. Is this acceptable? Reply: The prolonged holding of hands is of itself a sign of communion rather than of peace. Further, it is a liturgical gesture introduced spontaneously but on personal initiative; it is not in the rubrics. Nor is there any clear explanation of why the sign of peace at the invitation: *Let us offer each other the sign of peace* should be supplanted in order to bring a different gesture with less meaning into another part of the Mass: the sign of peace is filled with meaning, graciousness, and Christian inspiration. Any substitution for it must be repudiated: Not 11 (1975) 226.

   [R30] See DOL 208 no. 1446, note R15, Query 2.

   [R31] Query: After the commingling and during the prayer, *Lord, Jesus Christ, Son of the living God* or *Lord Jesus Christ, with faith*, some celebrants place their joined hands on the altar and, with bowed head, say the text of the prayer inaudibly. Is this procedure still to be followed? Reply: Traces of the former rites are here again discernible. To resolve this query the norms of the Order of Mass have to be heeded, with care not to add anything and with attention once again to the principle so kindly stated by Pope John XXIII: "Make complex and difficult matters simple; what is already simple leave alone." The former *Ritus servandus*

115. After the prayer the priest genuflects, takes the eucharistic bread, and, holding   1505
it slightly above the paten while facing the people, says: *This is the Lamb of God.* With
the people he adds, once only: *Lord, I am not worthy to receive you.*[R32]

116. Next, facing the altar, the priest says inaudibly: *May the body of Christ bring me to*   1506
everlasting life and reverently consumes the body of Christ. Then he takes the chalice,
saying: *May the blood of Christ bring me to everlasting life,* and reverently drinks the blood
of Christ.

117. He then takes the paten or a ciborium and goes to the communicants. If   1507
communion is given only under the form of bread,[m] he raises the eucharistic bread
slightly and shows it to each one, saying: *The body of Christ.* The communicants reply:
Amen and, holding the communion plate under their chin,[n] receive the sacrament.

118. For communion under both kinds, the rite described in nos. 240–252 is fol-   1508
lowed.

119. The communion song is begun while the priest is receiving the sacrament (see   1509
no. 56 i).

120. After communion the priest returns to the altar and collects any remaining   1510
particles. Then, standing at the side of the altar or at a side table,[o] he purifies the
paten or ciborium over the chalice, then purifies the chalice, saying inaudibly: *Lord,*
may I receive these gifts, etc.,[p] and dries it with a purificator. If this is done at the altar,
the vessels are taken to a side table by a minister.[q] It is also permitted, especially if
there are several vessels to be purified, to leave them, properly covered and on a
corporal, either at the altar or at a side table and to purify them after Mass when the
people have left.

121. Afterward the priest may return to the chair. A period of silence may now be   1511
observed,[r] or a hymn of praise or a psalm may be sung (see no. 56 j).[R33]

122. Then, standing at the altar or at the chair and facing the people, the priest says: *Let*   1512
us pray. There may be a brief period of silence, unless this has been already observed
immediately after communion. With hands outstretched, he recites the prayer after
communion, at the end of which the people make the response: *Amen.*

---

regarding this prayer directed (no. X, 3): "Then with joined hands placed on the altar, eyes fixed on the
sacrament, and bowing over he says inaudibly . . . ." The Order of Mass of Paul VI (no. 132) more
precisely determines what the GIRM says in no. 114: "Then the priest, with hands joined, says inaudibly
. . . ." Therefore, the celebrant stands upright with hands joined before his breast: Not 14 (1978) 537–
538, no. 13.

[R32]   See DOL 208 no. 1477, note R22.

[m]   OM and MR'70: "117. He then takes the paten or ciborium, goes to the communicants, raises the
host slightly and shows it to each one, saying . . ."

[n]   OM lacks "holding the communion plate under their chin."

[o]   OM lacks "or at a side table."

[p]   OM and MR '70 lack "saying quietly . . . *gifts.*"

[q]   OM: "The purified vessels are taken to a side table by a minister" for "If this is done . . . a
minister."

[r]   OM and MR'70 add "as all sit."

[R33]   See DOL 208 no. 1411, note R2, Query 1.

CONCLUDING RITES

1513   123. If there are any brief announcements, they may be made at this time.

1514   124. Then the priest, with hands outstretched, greets the people: *The Lord be with you.* They answer: *And also with you.* The priest immediately adds: *May almighty God bless you* and, as he blesses with the sign of the cross, continues: *the Father, and the Son, and the Holy Spirit.* All answer: *Amen.* On certain days and occasions another, more solemn form of blessing or the prayer over the people precedes this form of blessing as the rubrics direct.[R34]

Immediately after the blessing, with hands joined, the priest adds: *Go in the peace of Christ,* or: *Go in peace to love and serve the Lord,* or: *The Mass is ended, go in peace,* and the people answer: *Thanks be to God.*

1515   125. As a rule,[s] the priest then kisses the altar, makes the proper reverence with the ministers, and leaves.

1516   126. If another liturgical service follows the Mass, the concluding rites (greeting, blessing, and dismissal) are omitted.

B. Functions of the Deacon

1517   127. When there is a deacon present to exercise his ministry, the norms in the preceding section apply, with the following exceptions.

In general the deacon: a. assists the priest and walks at his side; b. at the altar, assists with the chalice or the book; c. if there is no other minister present, carries out other ministerial functions as required.

[R34]   1. Query: When at the end of Mass one of the solemn blessings or the prayer over the people is used, how is it to be integrated into the concluding rite? Reply: The GIRM no. 124 indicates [text paraphrased]. The rite in this case takes the following form. After the greeting, *The Lord be with you,* the deacon, or the priest himself if there is no deacon, says the invitation, *Bow your heads and pray for God's blessing* or something similar. Then the priest, with hands outstretched over the people, says the solemn blessing or the prayer over the people, then the words of the blessing; all reply: *Amen* (see MR 495 and 507): Not 6 (1970) 404, no. 41.

2. Query: The use of the solemn blessings and prayers over the people that are in the Roman Missal (MR, *ed. typica altera,* 1975, 495–511) expand and add solemnity to the conclusion of the Mass. This form of the concluding rite grows in use as the texts are translated and inserted into the missal proper to each region. But practice varies: a. The celebrant omits the greeting, *The Lord be with you,* before the blessing. b. The deacon or the celebrant omits the invitation, *Bow your heads and ask for God's blessing,* given in the Missal (MR 495 and 507). c. The priest omits extending his hands over the congregation (MR 495 and 507). d. At the blessing the priest sometimes uses the form, *May almighty God bless you . . .,* sometimes, *May the blessing of almighty God . . . .*

Reply: In this case also the queries arising from such diversity can be answered from a careful reading of the Roman Missal: a. The rubrics of the Missal (GIRM no. 124; Order of Mass no. 142) expressly lay down the steps in the conclusion of the celebration: first the greeting ("the priest . . . greets the people"), then the blessing ("he continues . . . blessing"), then the dismissal ("he adds immediately"). Furthermore, one of the solemn blessings or prayers over the people may be substituted for the usual formula for the blessing, *May almighty God bless you,* which follows the greeting of the celebrant. Clearly these formularies have the same status as the text of the usual blessing. Therefore, the celebrant's greeting, *The Lord be with you,* must precede them. b. The rubric at the beginning of this part of the Missal says: ". . . may give the invitation: *Bow your heads and pray for God's blessing*" (MR 495 and 507). Therefore the deacon or the priest celebrant is at liberty to use this invitation, to put it in different words, or to omit it altogether. c. But in contrast this same rubric also gives an explicit directive: "The priest extends his hands over the congregation while he says or sings the blessing." Therefore he holds his hands extended over the congregation during the entire blessing and during it the people respond: *Amen* to each part of this blessing. The priest performs the same gesture over the assembly during the prayer over the people. d. The celebrant as a rule uses the formulary: *May almighty God bless you . . ."* (MR, *ed. typica altera,* 1975, pp. 495–506): Not 14 (1978) 306–307, no. 9.

[s]   OM lacks "As a rule."

INTRODUCTORY RITES

128. Vested and carrying the Book of the Gospels,[t] the deacon precedes the priest on the way to the altar or else walks at the priest's side.

1518

129. With the priest he makes the proper reverence and goes up to the altar. After placing the Book of the Gospels[u] on it, along with the priest he kisses the altar. If incense is used, he assists the priest in putting some in the censer and in incensing the altar.

1519

130. After the incensing, he goes to the chair with the priest, sits next to him, and assists him as required.

1520

LITURGY OF THE WORD

131. If incense is used, the deacon assists the priest when he puts incense in the censer during the singing of the *Alleluia* or other chant. Then he bows before the priest and asks for the blessing, saying in a low voice: *Father, give me your blessing.* The priest blesses him: *The Lord be in your heart.* The deacon answers: *Amen.* If the Book of the Gospels is on the altar, he takes it and goes to the lectern; the servers, if there are any, precede, carrying candles and the censer when used. At the lectern the deacon greets the people, incenses the book, and proclaims the gospel. After the reading, he kisses the book, saying inaudibly: *May the words of the gospel wipe away our sins,* and returns to the priest.[v] If there is no homily or profession of faith, he may remain at the lectern for the general intercessions, but the servers leave.

1521

132. After the priest introduces the general intercessions, the deacon announces the intentions at the lectern or other suitable place.

1522

LITURGY OF THE EUCHARIST

133. At the presentation of the gifts, while the priest remains at the chair, the deacon prepares the altar, assisted by other ministers, but the care of the sacred vessels belongs to the deacon. He assists the priest in receiving the people's gifts. Next, he hands the priest the paten with the bread to be consecrated, pours wine and a little water into the chalice, saying inaudibly the prayer, *Through the mystery of this water and wine,* then passes the chalice to the priest.[w] (He may also prepare the chalice and pour the wine and water at a side table.) If incense is used, the deacon assists the priest with the incensing of the gifts and the altar; afterward he, or another minister, incenses the priest and the people.

1523

134. During the eucharistic prayer, the deacon stands near but slightly behind the priest, so that when necessary he may assist the priest with the chalice or the missal.

1524

135. At the final doxology of the eucharistic prayer, the deacon stands next to the priest, holding up the chalice as the priest raises the paten with the eucharistic bread, until the people have said the acclamation: *Amen.*

1525

---

[t]   OM and MR'70: "Vested, the deacon, if he carries the Book of the Gospels, precedes the priest . . ."

[u]   OM and MR'70: "After placing the Book of the Gospels on the altar, if he carries it . . ."

[v]   OM and MR'70: "celebrante" for "sacerdote."

[w]   OM and MR'70: ". . . pours wine and a little water into the chalice, then passes the chalice to the priest."

1526   136. After the priest has said the prayer for peace and the greeting: *The peace of the Lord be with you always*, and the people have made the response: *And also with you*, the deacon may invite all to exchange the sign of peace, saying: *Let us offer each other the sign of peace*. He himself receives the sign of peace from the priest and may offer it to other ministers near him.

1527   137. After the priest's communion, the deacon receives under both kinds and then assists the priest in giving communion to the people. But if communion is given under both kinds, the deacon ministers the chalice to the communicants and is the last to drink from it.

1528   138. After communion, the deacon returns to the altar with the priest and collects any remaining fragments. He then takes the chalice and other vessels to the side table, where he purifies them and arranges them in the usual way; the priest returns to the chair. But it is permissible to leave the vessels to be purified, properly covered and on a corporal, at a side table and to purify them after Mass, when the people have left.

CONCLUDING RITE

1529   139. Following the prayer after communion, if there are any brief announcements, the deacon may make them, unless the priest prefers to do so himself.

1530   140. After the priest's blessing, the deacon dismisses the people, saying: *Go in the peace of Christ*, or: *Go in peace to love and serve the Lord*, or: *The Mass is ended, go in peace.*

1531   141. Along with the priest, the deacon kisses the altar, makes the proper reverence, and leaves in the manner followed for the entrance procession.

C. FUNCTIONS OF THE ACOLYTE[x]

1532   142. The acolyte may have functions of various kinds and several may occur at the same time. It is therefore desirable that these functions be suitably distributed among several acolytes. But if there is only a single acolyte present, he should perform the more important functions and the rest are distributed among other ministers.

---

[x] OM and MR'70: Chapter IV, C. is "FUNCTIONS OF THE SUBDEACON," and comprises nos. 142–152. MRVar indicates that this section is to be deleted. The OM and MR'70 text follows:

INTRODUCTORY RITES

143. In the procession to the altar the acolyte may carry the cross, walking between two servers with lighted candles. When he reaches the altar, he places the cross near it and takes his own place in the sanctuary.

1533

144. Throughout the celebration it belongs to the acolyte to go to the priest or the deacon, whenever necessary, in order to present the book to them and to assist them

1534

C. FUNCTIONS OF THE SUBDEACON

142.   If the subdeacon exercises his function at Mass, he observes the following. In general he:

    a. serves the deacon or the priest;

    b. reads the epistle or the reading preceding the gospel;

    c. when no other minister is present, also reads the other readings preceding the gospel, and, as required, fulfills the functions of other ministers.

INTRODUCTORY RITES

143.   Wearing vestments, the subdeacon may carry the Book of the Gospels in the entrance procession, in which case he precedes the deacon; otherwise he walks at the priest's side or carries the cross, walking between two servers with lighted candles.

144.   After making the proper reverence, he goes up to the altar with the deacon and priest, places the Book of the Gospels on the altar and with the deacon and priest kisses the altar. If incense is used, he assists the priest in incensing the altar. He then goes to the chair with the priest and deacon and there assists the priest as required.

LITURGY OF THE WORD

145.   At the lectern he reads the epistle or other reading preceding the gospel, then returns to the priest.

146.   Before the gospel he assists the priest to put incense into the censer and accompanies the deacon to the lectern and assists him there for the proclamation of the gospel. After the gospel he returns to the priest with the deacon, in proper order.

LITURGY OF THE EUCHARIST

147.   After the general intercessions and while the chant for the presentation of the gifts is being sung, he prepares the altar with the assistance of the other ministers. During this time the priest and deacon remain at the chair. When the altar is ready, the subdeacon assists the deacon and priest to receive the gifts that may be presented by the people. He next accompanies the deacon and priest to the altar and there pours water into the chalice. If incense is used, he assists the priest in incensing the gifts and the altar.

148.   During the eucharistic prayer, the subdeacon stands near the priest, but slightly behind, so that he may, as required, assist with the missal.

149.   Once the deacon has given the invitation for the sign of peace, the subdeacon receives this from the priest after the deacon and may then offer the sign of peace to the ministers near him.

150.   The subdeacon receives communion after the deacon and, like the deacon, under both kinds.

151.   After communion, as the priest returns to the chair, the subdeacon assists the deacon in purifying and arranging the sacred vessels. Then with the deacon he rejoins the priest.

CONCLUDING RITE

152.   After the deacon's dismissal of the people, the subdeacon along with the priest and deacon kisses the altar, and, after the proper reverence to the altar; leaves in the same order as at the entrance.

in any other way required. Thus it is appropriate that, if possible, he have a place from which he can conveniently carry out his ministry both at the chair and at the altar.

LITURGY OF THE EUCHARIST

1535   145. After the general intercessions, when no deacon is present, the acolyte places the corporal, purificator, chalice, and missal on the altar, while the priest remains at the chair. Then, if necessary, the acolyte assists the priest in receiving the gifts of the people and he may bring the bread and wine to the altar and present them to the priest. If incense is used, the acolyte gives the censer to the priest and assists him in incensing the gifts and the altar.

1536   146. The acolyte may assist the priest as a special minister in giving communion to the people.[61] If communion is given under both kinds, the acolyte ministers the chalice to the communicants or he holds the chalice when communion is given by intinction.

1537   147. After communion, the acolyte helps the priest or deacon to purify and arrange the vessels. If no deacon is present, the acolyte takes the vessels to the side table, where he purifies and arranges them.

D. FUNCTIONS OF THE READER

INTRODUCTORY RITES

1538   148. In the procession to the altar, when no deacon is present, the reader may carry the Book of the Gospels. In that case he walks in front of the priest; otherwise he walks with the other ministers.

1539   149. Upon reaching the altar, the reader makes the proper reverence along with the priest, goes up to the altar, and places the Book of the Gospels on it. Then he takes his place in the sanctuary with the other ministers.

LITURGY OF THE WORD

1540   150. At the lectern the reader proclaims the readings that precede the gospel. If there is no cantor of the psalm, he may also sing or recite the responsorial psalm after the first reading.

1541   151. After the priest gives the introduction to the general intercessions, the reader may announce the intentions when no deacon is present.

1542   152. If there is no entrance song or communion song and the antiphons in the Missal are not said by the faithful, the reader recites them at the proper time.

II. CONCELEBRATED MASSES

INTRODUCTION

1543   153. Concelebration effectively brings out the unity of the priesthood, of the sacrifice, and of the whole people of God. In addition to the times when the rite itself prescribes it, concelebration is also permitted at:

    1. a. the chrism Mass and the evening Mass on Holy Thursday;[a]
        b. the Mass for councils, meetings of bishops, and synods;

---

[61]   See Paul VI, Motu Proprio *Ministeria quaedam*, 15 Aug. 1972, no. VI [DOL 340 no. 2931].

[a]   OM: "Feria V in Cena Domini" for "Feria V Hebdomadae sanctae."

c. the Mass for the blessing of an abbot;

2. in addition, with the permission of the Ordinary, who has the right to decide on the advisability of concelebration, at:

a. the conventual Mass and the principal Mass in churches and oratories when the needs of the people do not require that all the priests present celebrate individually;

b. the Mass for any kind of meeting of priests, either secular or religious.[62]

154. Where there is a large number of priests, the authorized superior may permit concelebration several times on the same day, but either at different times or in different places.[63]

155. The right to regulate, in accord with the law, the discipline for concelebration in his diocese, even in churches and semipublic oratories of exempt religious, belongs to the bishop. The right to decide on the advisability of concelebration and to permit it in his churches and oratories belongs to every Ordinary and even to every major superior of nonexempt clerical religious institutes and of societies of clerics living in community without vows.[64]

156. No one is ever to be admitted into a concelebration once Mass has already begun.[65]

157. A concelebration in which the priests of any diocese concelebrate with their own bishop, especially at the chrism Mass on Holy Thursday[b] and on the occasion of a synod or pastoral visitation, is to be held in high regard. Concelebration is likewise recommended whenever priests gather together with their bishop during a retreat or at any other meeting. That sign of the unity of the priesthood and of the Church itself which marks every concelebration stands out even more clearly in the instances mentioned.[66]

158. For a particular reason, having to do either with the meaning of the rite or of the liturgical feast, to celebrate or concelebrate more than once on the same day is permitted as follows:

a. One who has celebrated or concelebrated the chrism Mass on Holy Thursday[c] may also celebrate or concelebrate the evening Mass.

b. One who has celebrated or concelebrated the Mass of the Easter Vigil may celebrate or concelebrate the second Mass of Easter.

c. All priests may celebrate or concelebrate the three Masses of Christmas, provided the Masses are at their proper times of day.[d]

1544

1545

1546

1547

1548

---

[62] See SC art. 57 [DOL 1 no. 57].

[63] See SCR, Instr. EuchMyst no. 47 [DOL 179 no. 1276].

[64] See *Rite of Concelebration*, Introduction no. 3 [DOL 223 no. 1796].

[65] See ibid. no. 8 [DOL 223 no. 1801].

[b] OM: as in note a.

[66] See SCR, Decr. *Ecclesiae semper*, 7 March 1965 [DOL 222 no. 1792]; Instr. EuchMyst no. 47 [DOL 179 no. 1276].

[c] OM: as in note a.

[d] OM: "All priests may celebrate the three Masses of Christmas; they may also concelebrate them, provided the Masses are at their proper times of day.

d. One who concelebrates with the bishop or his delegate at a synod or pastoral visitation, or concelebrates on the occasion of a meeting of priests, may celebrate another Mass for the benefit of the people.[67] This holds also, in analogous circumstances, for gatherings of religious.[e,R35]

1549   159. The structure of a concelebrated Mass, whatever its form, follows the norms for an individual celebration, except for the points prescribed or changed in the next section.

1550   160. If neither a deacon nor other ministers assist in a concelebrated Mass, their functions are carried out by the concelebrants.

INTRODUCTORY RITES

1551   161. In the sacristy or other suitable place, the concelebrants put on the vestments usual for individual celebrants. For a good reason, however, as when there are more concelebrants than vestments, the concelebrants may omit the chasuble and simply wear the stole over the alb; but the principal celebrant always wears the chasuble.

1552   162. When everything is ready, there is the usual procession through the church to the altar. The concelebrating priests go ahead of the principal celebrant.

1553   163. On reaching the altar, the concelebrants and the celebrant make the prescribed reverence, kiss the altar, then go to their chairs. When incense is used, the principal celebrant incenses the altar, then goes to the chair.

LITURGY OF THE WORD

1554   164. During the liturgy of the word, the concelebrants remain at their places, sitting or standing as the principal celebrant does.

1555   165. As a rule the principal celebrant or one of the concelebrants gives the homily.

LITURGY OF THE EUCHARIST

1556   166. The rites for the preparation of the gifts are carried out by the principal celebrant; the other concelebrants remain at their places.

1557   167. At the end of the preparation of the gifts, the concelebrants come near the altar and stand around it in such a way that they do not interfere with the actions of the rite and that the people have a clear view. They should not be in the deacon's[f] way when he has to go to the altar in the performance of his ministry.

---

[67]   See *Rite of Concelebration*, Introduction no. 9 [DOL 223 no. 1802]. SCDW, Decl. on concelebration 7 Aug. 1972 [DOL 226].

[e]   OM: "d. One who concelebrates with the bishop or his delegate at a synod, pastoral visitation, or a gathering of priests, may, at the discretion of the bishop, celebrate again for the benefit of the faithful. This holds also, in analogous circumstances, for gatherings of religious with their own Ordinary."
    MR'70 adds to the last sentence: "or his delegate."

[f]   OM and MR'70 add: "or subdeacon's."

Manner of Reciting the Eucharistic Prayer[g,R36]

168. The preface is said by the principal celebrant alone; the *Sanctus* is sung or recited by all the concelebrants with the congregation and the choir.

1558

169. After the *Sanctus*, the concelebrants continue the eucharistic prayer in the way to be described. Unless otherwise indicated, only the principal celebrant makes the gestures.

1559

170. The parts said by all the concelebrants together are to be recited in such a way that the concelebrants say them in a softer voice and the principal celebrant's voice stands out clearly. In this way the congregation should be able to hear the text without difficulty.

1560

A. Eucharistic Prayer I, the Roman Canon

171. The prayer, *We come to you, Father*, is said by the principal celebrant alone, with hands outstretched.

1561

172. The intercessions, *Remember, Lord, your people* and *In union with the whole Church*, may be assigned to one of the concelebrants; he alone says these prayers, with hands outstretched and aloud.

1562

173. The prayer, *Father, accept this offering*, is said by the principal celebrant alone, with hands outstretched.

1563

174. From *Bless and approve our offering* to *Almighty God, we pray* inclusive, all the concelebrants recite everything together in this manner:

1564

    a. They say *Bless and approve our offering* with hands outstretched toward the offerings.

    b. They say *The day before he suffered* and *When supper was ended* with hands joined.

    c. While saying the words of the Lord, each extends his right hand toward the bread and toward the chalice, if this seems appropriate; they look at the eucharistic bread and chalice as these are shown[h] and afterward bow low.

---

  [g] OM and MR'70: this title is at no. 170.

  [R36] Query: In the manner of concelebrating we find the following differences: a. Sometimes the celebrant's voice stands out clearly, while the concelebrants recite the eucharistic prayer in a low or subdued voice. In other cases, conversely, a clash of loud voices is heard, as though each were striving to outdo the others. b. In carrying out the epiclesis before the consecration not all concelebrants stretch out their hands toward the gifts to invoke the action of the Holy Spirit, but they are extremely careful to do so during the consecration. c. During the epiclesis some bring their hands back as soon as the principal concelebrant has made the sign of the cross over the gifts; others keep their hands outstretched until the text of the epiclesis is concluded. Which ways are right?
    Reply: To decide which of these differences are right, it is enough to consider the nature of the functions that each concelebrant performs and the nature of the corresponding gesture: a. According to the GIRM no. 170 the assembly of the faithful must distinctly hear the voice of the one presiding. This can be achieved by use of a sensitive and well-placed microphone and especially by the modulation of the concelebrants' voices (*submissa voce*). Otherwise, as in the second case cited, the unity of tone and rhythm for the assembly's understanding of the text cannot be achieved. b. It is rather odd that the norms of the Missal envision a situation quite the opposite from the one alleged: during the epiclesis of the consecration all the concelebrants must hold their hands over the gifts (GIRM nos. 174 a, 180 a, 184 a, 188 a: "with hands outstretched toward the gifts") in invoking the action of the Holy Spirit. But during the consecration, the concelebrants hold the right hand toward the bread and the chalice, "if this seems appropriate" (GIRM nos. 174 c, 180 c, 184 c, 188 c) and they do so as they recite the *words of the Lord*, namely, up to "Do this in memory of me" inclusive. c. The act of holding the hands outstretched must accompany the words of the prayer. This is why the rubrics of the Order of Mass (nos. 90, 103, 110, 119) indicate the end of this action by saying: "He joins his hands": Not 14 (1978) 303–304, no. 6. See also DOL 242.

  [h] OM and MR'70: "elevated" for "shown."

d. They say *Father, we celebrate the memory of Christ* and *Look with favor* with hands outstretched.

e. From *Almighty God, we pray* to *the sacred body and blood of your Son* inclusive, they bow with hands joined; then they stand upright and cross themselves at the words, *let us be filled.*

1565 175. The intercessions, *Remember, Lord, those who have died* and *For ourselves, too,* may be assigned to one of the concelebrants; he alone says these prayers, with hands outstretched and aloud.

1566 176. At the words, *Though we are sinners,* all the concelebrants strike their breast.

1567 177. The prayer, *Through Christ our Lord you give us all these gifts,* is said by the principal celebrant alone.

1568 178. In this eucharistic prayer the parts from *Bless and approve our offering* to *Almighty God, we pray* inclusive and the concluding doxology may be sung.

B. Eucharistic Prayer II

1569 179. The prayer, *Lord, you are holy indeed,* is said by the principal celebrant alone, with hands outstretched.

1570 180. From *Let your Spirit come* to *May all of us who share* inclusive, all the concelebrants together say the prayer in this manner:

a. They say *Let your Spirit come* with hands outstretched toward the offerings.

b. They say *Before he was given up to death* and *When supper was ended* with hands joined.

c. While saying the words of the Lord, each extends his right hand toward the bread and toward the chalice, if this seems appropriate; they look at the eucharistic bread and the chalice as they are shown[i] and afterward bow low.

d. They say *In memory of his death* and *May all of us who share* with hands outstretched.

1571 181. The intercessions for the living, *Lord, remember your Church,* and for the dead, *Remember our brothers and sisters,* may be assigned to one of the concelebrants; he alone says the intercessions, with hands outstretched.

1572 182. In this eucharistic prayer the parts from *Before he was given up to death* to *In memory of his death* inclusive and the concluding doxology may be sung.

C. Eucharistic Prayer III

1573 183. The prayer, *Father, you are holy indeed,* is said by the principal celebrant alone, with hands outstretched.

1574 184. From And so, *Father, we bring you these gifts* to *Look with favor* inclusive, all the concelebrants together say the prayer in this manner:

a. They say *And so, Father, we bring you these gifts* with hands outstretched toward the offerings.

b. They say *On the night he was betrayed* and *When supper was ended* with hands joined.

---

[i] OM and MR'70: "elevated" for "shown."

c. While saying the words of the Lord, each extends his right hand toward the bread and toward the chalice, if this seems appropriate; they look at the eucharistic bread and chalice as these are shown[j] and afterward bow low.

d. They say *Father, calling to mind* and *Look with favor* with hands outstretched.

185. The intercessions, *May he make us an everlasting gift* and *Lord, may this sacrifice*, may be assigned to one of the concelebrants; he alone says these prayers, with hands outstretched. 1575

186. In this eucharistic prayer the parts from *On the night he was betrayed* to *Father calling to mind* inclusive and the concluding doxology may be sung. 1576

D. Eucharistic Prayer IV

187. The prayer, *Father, we acknowledge*, is said by the principal celebrant alone, with hands outstretched. 1577

188. From *Father, may this Holy Spirit* to *Lord, look upon this sacrifice* inclusive, all the concelebrants together say the prayer in this manner: 1578

a. They say *Father, may this Holy Spirit* with hands outstretched toward the offerings.

b. They say *He always loved those* and *In the same way* with hands joined.

c. While saying the words of the Lord, each extends his right hand toward the bread and toward the chalice, if this seems appropriate; they look at the eucharistic bread and chalice as these are shown[k] and afterward bow low.

d. They say *Father, we now celebrate* and *Lord, look upon this sacrifice* with hands outstretched.

189. The intercessions, *Lord, remember those*, may be assigned to one of the concelebrants; he alone says them, with hands outstretched. 1579

190. In this eucharistic prayer the parts from *He always loved those* to *Father, we now celebrate* inclusive and the concluding doxology may be sung. 1580

191. The concluding doxology of the eucharistic prayer may be sung or said either by the principal celebrant alone or together with all the concelebrants.[R37] 1581

---

[j]   OM and MR'70: "elevated" for "shown."

[k]   OM and MR'70: "elevated" for "shown."

[R37]   Query: It is apparent that practices differ greatly in the recitation or singing of the doxology concluding the eucharistic prayer: a. Sometimes the principal celebrant alone says or sings it. b. Or regularly all the concelebrants say or sing it. c. In some places the whole assembly says or sings it. What rule should be followed?
   Reply: In any meeting it customarily belongs to the one presiding to open and close the proceedings that are the purpose of the meeting. In the case of the eucharist the essential part of the entire celebration is clearly the eucharistic prayer, which extends from the preface to the final doxology inclusive. Therefore, it belongs to the one presiding to open this prayer with the preface; this is followed by the *Sanctus*, in which the assembly joins, then the one presiding alone recites the *Father, you are holy indeed* (or the parallel text). As to the concluding doxology, the three cases reported call for the following remarks: a. It is the right of the one who presides and who opened the eucharistic prayer also to close it by reciting the final doxology. This is exactly what the GIRM no. 191 indicates: "The concluding doxology of the eucharistic prayer is recited . . . by the principal celebrant alone." b. The second case reflects the prevailing usage, which almost everywhere concelebrants have quickly adopted in reciting or singing this conclusion together. This usage also conforms to the GIRM no. 191, the second part of which refers to it: ". . . or by all the concelebrants together with the principal celebrant." c. Unlike the two preceding cases, the recitation or singing of the conclusion by the whole assembly is an extension that is unlawful not merely from a disciplinary point of view — as being against the rules now in force — but at a deeper level, namely, as being in conflict with the very nature of ministries and texts.
   Even though someone could interpret this extension to the entire assembly as a sign of the desire

COMMUNION RITE

1582   192. Next, with hands joined, the celebrant introduces the Lord's Prayer; with hands outstretched, he then says this prayer itself with the other concelebrants and the congregation.

1583   193. The embolism, *Deliver us*, is said by the principal celebrant alone, with hands outstretched. All the concelebrants together with the congregation say the final acclamation, *For the kingdom*.

1584   194. After the deacon (or one of the concelebrants) says: *Let us offer each other the sign of peace*, all exchange the sign of peace. The concelebrants who are nearer the principal celebrant receive the sign of peace from him ahead of the deacon.

1585   195. During the *Agnus Dei*, some of the concelebrants may help the principal celebrant break the eucharistic bread for communion, both for the concelebrants and for the congregation.

1586   196. After the commingling, the principal celebrant alone says inaudibly the prayer, *Lord Jesus Christ, Son of the living God*, or *Lord Jesus Christ, with faith in your love and mercy*.

1587   197. After this prayer, the principal celebrant genuflects and steps back a little. One by one the concelebrants come to the middle of the altar, genuflect, and reverently take the body of Christ from the altar. Then holding the eucharistic bread in the right hand, with the left hand under it, they return to their places. The concelebrants may, however, remain in their places and take the body of Christ from the paten presented to them by the principal celebrant or by one or more of the concelebrants, or from the paten as it is passed from one to the other.

1588   198. Then the principal celebrant takes the eucharistic bread, holds it slightly raised above the paten, and, facing the congregation, says: *This is the Lamb of God*. With the concelebrants and the congregation he continues: *Lord, I am not worthy*.

1589   199. Then the principal celebrant, facing the altar, says inaudibly: *May the body of Christ bring me to everlasting life* and reverently consumes the body of Christ. The concelebrants do the same. After them the deacon receives the body of Christ from the principal celebrant.

1590   200. The blood of the Lord may be taken by drinking from the chalice directly, through a tube, with a spoon, or even by intinction.

1591   201. If communion is received directly from the chalice, either of two procedures may be followed.

        a. The principal celebrant takes the chalice and says inaudibly: *May the blood of Christ bring me to everlasting life*. He drinks a little and hands the chalice to the deacon or a concelebrant. Then he gives communion to the faithful or returns to the chair.

---

of the assembly for increased participation in the liturgy, it is necessary that this desire be realized in an orderly and authentic way. What seems like progress is in fact retrogression: it is a sign of forgetting the part that belongs to each individual in the liturgical celebration. See SC art. 28: ". . . each person, minister or layperson, who has an office to perform, should do all, but only those parts which pertain to that office by the nature of the rite and the principles of liturgy" [DOL 1 no. 28]. In the third case it happens often that the final *Amen* is said or sung by no one or almost no one. If, on the contrary, the directions given in the Order of Mass (nos. 100, 108, 115, 124, "The people respond: *Amen*") are followed, it is possible in order to give greater emphasis to this response to use more elaborate chants that give force and solemnity to the acclamation of all the people (for example, the triple *Amen* sung by all the people at a Mass celebrated by the pope or the more simple *Amen* in the French missal of 1974, p. [103]: Not 14 (1978) 304–305, no. 7.

The concelebrants approach the altar one by one or, if two chalices are used, two by two. They drink the blood of Christ and return to their seats. The deacon or a concelebrant wipes the chalice with a purificator after each concelebrant communicates.

b. The principal celebrant stands at the middle of the altar and drinks the blood of Christ in the usual manner.

But the concelebrants may receive the blood of the Lord while remaining in their places. They drink from the chalice presented by the deacon or by one of their number, or else passed from one to the other. Either the one who drinks from the chalice or the one who presents it always wipes it off. After communicating, each one returns to his seat.

202. If communion is received through a tube, this is the procedure. The principal celebrant takes the tube and says inaudibly: *May the blood of Christ bring me to everlasting life.* He drinks a little and immediately cleans the tube by sipping some water from a container at hand on the altar, then places the tube on the paten. The deacon or one of the concelebrants puts the chalice at a convenient place in the middle of the altar or at the right side on another corporal. A container of water for purifying the tubes is placed near the chalice, with a paten to hold them afterward.   1592

The concelebrants come forward one by one, take a tube, and drink a little from the chalice. They then purify the tube, by sipping a little water, and place it on the paten.

203. If communion is received by using a spoon, the same procedure is followed as for communion with a tube. But care is to be taken that after each communion the spoon is placed in a container of water. After communion has been completed, the acolyte[l] carries this container to a side table to wash and dry the spoons.   1593

204. The deacon receives communion last. He then drinks what remains in the chalice and takes it to the side table. There he or the acolyte washes and dries the chalice and arranges it in the usual way.[m]   1594

205. The concelebrants may also receive from the chalice at the altar immediately after receiving the body of the Lord.   1595

In this case the principal celebrant receives under both kinds as he would when celebrating Mass alone, but for the communion from the chalice he follows the rite that in each instance has been decided on for the concelebrants.

After the principal celebrant's communion, the chalice is placed on another corporal at the right side of the altar. The concelebrants come forward one by one, genuflect, and receive the body of the Lord; then they go to the side of the altar and drink the blood of the Lord, following the rite decided upon, as has just been said.

The communion of the deacon and the purification of the chalice take place as already described.[n]

206. If the concelebrants receive communion by intinction, the principal celebrant receives the body and blood of the Lord in the usual way, making sure that enough   1596

---

l   OM and MR'70: "subdeacon" for "acolyte."

m   OM and MR'70: "204. The deacon and subdeacon receive communion last. The subdeacon drinks the blood of Christ from the chalice offered to him by the deacon and answers: *Amen* when the deacon says: *The blood of Christ.* After the deacon has drunk the blood of Christ, draining all that remains, he brings the chalice to the side table and there purifies it; but the subdeacon dries and arranges the chalice in the usual way."

n   OM and MR'70: "ministers" for "deacon."

remains in the chalice for their communion. Then the deacon or one of the concelebrants arranges the paten with the eucharistic bread and the chalice conveniently in the center of the altar or at the right side on another corporal. The concelebrants approach the altar one by one, genuflect, and take a particle, dip part of it into the chalice, and, holding a paten under their chin, communicate. Afterward they return to their places as at the beginning of Mass.

The deacon receives communion also by intinction and to the concelebrant's words: *The body and blood of Christ*, makes the response: *Amen*. At the altar the deacon drinks all that remains in the chalice, takes it to the side table and there he or the acolyte purifies and dries it, then arranges it in the usual way.°

CONCLUDING RITE

1597   207. The principal celebrant does everything else until the end of Mass in the usual way; the other concelebrants remain at their seats.

1598   208. Before leaving, the concelebrants make the proper reverence to the altar; as a rule, the principal celebrant kisses the altar.

III. MASS WITHOUT A CONGREGATION

INTRODUCTION

1599   209. This section gives the norms for Mass celebrated by a priest with only one server to assist him and to make the responses.

1600   210. In general this form of Mass follows the rite of Mass with a congregation. The server takes the people's part to the extent possible.

1601   211. Mass should not be celebrated without a server, except out of serious necessity. In this case the greetings and the blessing at the end of Mass are omitted.

1602   212. The chalice is prepared before Mass, either on a side table near the altar or on the altar itself; the missal is placed on the left side of the altar.

INTRODUCTORY RITES

1603   213. After he reverences the altar, the priest crosses himself, saying: *In the name of the Father*, etc. He turns to the server and gives one of the forms of greeting. For the penitential rite the priest stands at the foot of the altar.

1604   214. The priest then goes up to the altar and kisses it, goes to the missal at the left side of the altar, and remains there until the end of the general intercessions.

1605   215. He reads the entrance antiphon and says the *Kyrie* and the *Gloria*, in keeping with the rubrics.

1606   216. Then, with hands joined, the priest says: *Let us pray*. After a suitable pause, he says the opening prayer, with hands outstretched. At the end the server responds: *Amen*.

°   OM and MR'70: "The deacon and subdeacon also receive communion by intinction and to the concelebrant's words: *The body and blood of Christ*, make the response: *Amen*. At the altar the deacon drinks all that remains in the chalice, takes it to the side table and there purifies it; the subdeacon dries it and arranges it in the usual way."

LITURGY OF THE WORD

217. After the opening prayer,[a] the server or the priest himself reads the first   1607
reading and psalm, the second reading, when it is to be said, and the *Alleluia* verse or
other chant.

218. The priest, remains in the same place, bows and says: *Almighty God, cleanse my*   1608
heart. He then reads the gospel and at the conclusion kisses the book, saying inaudibly: *May the words of the gospel wipe away our sins.* The server says the acclamation.

219. The priest then says the profession of faith with the server, if the rubrics call   1609
for it.

220. The general intercessions may be said even in this form of Mass; the priest   1610
gives the intentions and the server makes the response.

LITURGY OF THE EUCHARIST

221. The antiphon for the preparation of the gifts is omitted. The minister places   1611
the corporal, purificator, and chalice on the altar, unless they have already been put
there at the beginning of Mass.

222. Preparation of the bread and wine, including the pouring of the water, are   1612
carried out as at a Mass with a congregation, with the formularies given in the
Order of Mass. After placing the bread and wine on the altar, the priest washes his
hands at the side of the altar as the server pours the water.

223. The priest says the prayer over the gifts and the eucharistic prayer, following   1613
the rite described for Mass with a congregation.[R38]

224. The Lord's Prayer and the embolism, *Deliver us*, are said as at Mass with a   1614
congregation.

225. After the acclamation concluding the embolism, the priest says the prayer, *Lord*   1615
Jesus Christ, you said. He then adds: *The peace of the Lord be with you always*, and the server
answers: *And also with you.* The priest may give the sign of peace to the server.

226. Then, while he says the *Agnus Dei* with the server, the priest breaks the euchar-   1616
istic bread over the paten. After the *Agnus Dei*, he places a particle in the chalice,
saying inaudibly: *May this mingling.*

227. After the commingling, the priest inaudibly says the prayer, *Lord Jesus Christ, Son*   1617
of the living God, or *Lord Jesus Christ, with faith in your love and mercy.* Then he genuflects
and takes the eucharistic bread. If the server is to receive communion, the priest
turns to him and, holding the eucharistic bread a little above the paten, says: *This is*
the Lamb of God, adding once with the server: *Lord, I am not worthy.* Facing the altar, the
priest then receives the body of Christ. If the server is not receiving communion,

---

[a]   OM and MR'70: "orationem"/"oratione" for "collectam"/"collecta" in nos. 216, 217.

[R38]   Query: When there is no member of the faithful present able to make the acclamation after the
consecration, should the priest say: *Let us proclaim the mystery of faith?* Reply: No. The words *the mystery of faith,*
which have been removed from the context of Christ's own words and put after the consecration, "serve
as an introduction to the acclamation" (Ap. Const. *Missale Romanum* [DOL 202 no. 1360]). But when no
member of the faithful is present who is able to respond to the acclamation, the priest omits saying: *Let us*
proclaim the mystery of faith. The case is like that of a Mass which, because of serious need, is celebrated
without any server and therefore without the greetings and the blessing at the end of Mass (GIRM no.
211). The same reply applies to a concelebration by priests at which no member of the faithful is present:
Not 5 (1969) 324–325, no. 3.

the priest, after making a genuflection, takes the host and, facing the altar, says once inaudibly: *Lord, I am not worthy*, and eats the body of Christ. The blood of Christ is received in the way described in the Order of Mass with a congregation.

1618 228. Before giving communion to the server, the priest[b] says the communion antiphon.

1619 229. The chalice is washed at the side of the altar and then may be carried by the server to a side table or left on the altar, as at the beginning.[R39]

1620 230. After the purification of the chalice, the priest may observe a period of silence. Then he says the prayer after communion.

CONCLUDING RITES

1621 231. The concluding rites are carried out as at Mass with a congregation, but the dismissal formulary is omitted.

IV. SOME GENERAL RULES FOR ALL FORMS OF MASS

VENERATION OF THE ALTAR AND THE BOOK OF THE GOSPELS

1622 232. According to traditional liturgical practice, the altar and the Book of the Gospels are kissed as a sign of veneration. But if this sign of reverence is not in harmony with the traditions or the culture of the region, the conference of bishops may substitute some other sign, after informing the Apostolic See.

GENUFLECTIONS AND BOWS

1623 233. Three genuflections are made during Mass: after the showing of the eucharistic bread, after the showing[a] of the chalice, and before communion.

If there is a tabernacle with the blessed sacrament in the sanctuary, a genuflection is made before and after Mass and whenever anyone passes in front of the blessed sacrament.

1624 234. There are two kinds of bow, a bow of the head and a bow of the body:

a. A bow of the head is made when the three divine Persons are named together and[b] at the name of Jesus, Mary, and the saint in whose honor Mass is celebrated.

b. A bow of the body, or profound bow, is made: toward the altar if there is no tabernacle with the blessed sacrament; during the prayers, *Almighty God, cleanse* and *Lord God, we ask you to receive*; within the profession of faith at the words, *by the power of the Holy Spirit*; in Eucharistic Prayer I (Roman Canon) at the words, *Almighty God, we pray*. The same kind of bow is made by the deacon when he asks the blessing before the gospel. In addition, the priest bends over slightly as he says the words of the Lord at the consecration.[R40]

---

b   OM and MR'70: "celebrans" for "sacerdos."

R39   See DOL 208 no. 1628, note R42.

a   OM and MR'70: "elevation" for "showing."

b   OM lacks "when the three divine Persons are named together."

R40   Query: Some of the acts of reverence by both the celebrant and the people have fallen into disuse, for example, the profound bow to be made in place of the former genuflection at the words announcing the mystery of the incarnation in the *Credo*. Are such gestures still to be observed? Reply: Clearly people should express their faith, devotion, and reverence not only by words but also by gestures and posture. All the more care should be taken about this because the gestures now prescribed since the reform of the liturgy are fewer and simpler. Thus the Order of Mass and the GIRM assign a few instances when gestures are to accompany the words. It is enough to recall the GIRM no. 234 to recognize these various

INCENSATION

235. The use of incense is optional in any form of Mass: 1625

    a. during the entrance procession;

    b. at the beginning of Mass, to incense the altar;

    c. at the procession and proclamation of the gospel;

    d. at the preparation of the gifts, to incense them, as well as the altar, priest, and people;

    e. at the showing of the eucharistic bread and chalice after the consecration.[c]

236. The priest puts the incense in the censer and blesses it with the sign of the   1626
cross, saying nothing.

This is the way to incense the altar:

    a. If the altar is freestanding, the priest incenses it as he walks around it.

    b. If the altar is not freestanding, he incenses it while walking first to the right side, then to the left.

If there is a cross on or beside the altar, he incenses it before he incenses the altar. If the cross is behind the altar, the priest incenses it when he passes in front of it.

PURIFICATIONS

237. Whenever a particle of the eucharistic bread adheres to his fingers, especially   1627
after the breaking of the bread or the communion of the people, the priest cleanses
his fingers over the paten or, if necessary, washes them. He also gathers any particles that may fall outside the paten.[R41]

---

cases: "[Text quoted]." In the case of the words in the *Credo* the rubric of the Order of Mass also reads: "All bow." It is well to remember that at the Mass of the Christmas Vigil, the Mass at Midnight, the Mass at Dawn, and the Mass during the Day, there is a genuflection at the words *And he became man*, (see MR, pp. 153, 155, 156, 157); the same holds for Mass on the solemnity of the Annunciation of Our Lord (see MR p. 538).

    For the consecration of the bread and wine the GIRM no. 234 b prescribes: "[Text quoted]." Further the priest genuflects "after the showing of the host," and "after the showing of the chalice" (GIRM no. 233); "he genuflects in adoration" (Order of Mass, nos. 91–92, 104–105, 111–112, 120–121). As for concelebrants, they stand at the showing of the host and chalice, look at them, then bow profound- ly (GIRM nos. 174 c, 180 c, 184 c, 188 c).

    Likewise before communion there are gestures of reverence and faith made by both the celebrant and the people who receive communion. For the celebrant the GIRM no. 115 and the Order of Mass no. 133 have ". . . then the priest genuflects, takes the host," etc.; and for concelebrants the GIRM directs: "[Text quoted] " (GIRM no. 197). As for the people, when they receive the eucharist standing, they are to make some sign of reverence (GIRM nos. 244 c, 245 b, 246 b, 247 b): Not 14 (1978) 535–536, no. 11.

    [c] OM lacks "e."

  [R41] Query: The GIRM no. 237 says that particles of the eucharistic bread are to be collected after the consecration, but it is not clear what is to be done about them. Reply: The GIRM no. 237 must be taken in context with other articles that deal with the same point. The description of the basic form of celebration says clearly: "After communion the priest returns to the altar and collects any remaining particles. Then, standing at the side of the altar or at the side table, he purifies the paten or ciborium *over the chalice*, then purifies the chalice . . . and dries it with a purificator" (GIRM no. 120). The Order of Mass with a congregation no. 138 says: "After communion the priest or deacon purifies the paten *over the chalice* and the chalice itself." The Order of Mass without a congregation no. 31 says: "Then the priest purifies the chalice *over the paten* and the chalice itself." The point, therefore, is quite clear: Not 8 (1972) 195. See also DOL 278.

1628   238. The vessels are purified by the priest or else by the deacon or acolyte[d] after the communion or after Mass, if possible at a side table. Wine and water or water alone are used for the purification of the chalice, then drunk by the one who purifies it.[e] The paten is usually to be wiped with the purificator.[R42]

1629   239. If the eucharistic bread or any particle of it should fall, it is to be picked up reverently. If any of the precious blood spills, the area should be washed and the water poured into the sacrarium.

COMMUNION UNDER BOTH KINDS

1630   240. Holy communion has a more complete form as a sign when it is received under both kinds. For in this manner of reception a fuller light shines on the sign of the eucharistic banquet. Moreover there is a clearer expression of that will by which the new and everlasting covenant is ratified in the blood of the Lord and of the relationship of the eucharistic banquet to the eschatological banquet in the Father's kingdom.[68]

1631   241. For the faithful who take part in the rite or are present at it, pastors should take care to call to mind as clearly as possible Catholic teaching according to the Council of Trent on the manner of communion. Above all they should instruct the people that according to Catholic faith Christ, whole and entire, as well as the true sacrament are received even under one kind only; that, therefore, as far as the effects are concerned, those who receive in this manner are not deprived of any grace necessary for salvation.[69]

Pastors are also to teach that the Church has power in its stewardship of the sacraments, provided their substance remains intact. The Church may make those rules and changes that, in view of the different conditions, times, and places, it decides to be in the interest of reverence for the sacraments or the well-being of the recipients.[70] At the same time the faithful should be guided toward a desire to take part more intensely in a sacred rite in which the sign of the eucharistic meal stands out more explicitly.

---

    [d]   OM and MR'70 lack "or acolyte."

    [e]   OM, MR'70, and MRVar: "by the priest or deacon" for "by the one who purifies it."

    [R42]   Query: After the distribution of communion the priest often is observed purifying the vessels (chalice, paten, ciborium) at the middle of the altar. Cannot a better place and time be chosen to do this? May another minister purify the vessels?
    Reply: a. The directives in the GIRM are to be observed. There is a general principle in no. 238: "[Text quoted]." The directive as to time (whether after communion or after Mass) is completed in no. 229 with one regarding place (at the side of the altar). It is implicit in this regulation that the celebrant never stands at the middle of the altar as he purifies the vessels (see also no. 120). b. Other particulars are found elsewhere in the GIRM: As to the priest, no. 120: "[Text quoted]." As to the deacon, no. 138: "[Text quoted]." As to the acolyte, no. 147: "[Text quoted]."
    The remarks on the priest, deacon, and acolyte are applicable to a special minister who lawfully distributes communion (see SCDS, Instr. *Immensae caritatis* [DOL 264 nos. 2074–78]; RR, *Holy Communion and Worship of the Eucharist outside Mass* no. 17 [DOL 266 no. 2095]). See also GIRM no. 229 on a priest celebrating without a congregation; nos. 202–206 on a concelebrated Mass: Not 14 (1978) 593–594, no. 15.

    [68]   See SCR, Instr. EuchMyst no. 32 [DOL 179 no. 1261].

    [69]   See Council of Trent, sess. 21, *Decr. De Communione eucharistica* cap. 1–3: Denz-Schön 1725–29.

    [70]   See ibid. cap. 2: Denz-Schön 1728.

242. At the discretion of the Ordinary[f] and after the prerequisite catechesis, communion from the chalice is permitted in the case of:[71]

    1. newly baptized adults at the Mass following their baptism; adults at the Mass at which they receive confirmation; baptized persons who are being received into the full communion of the Church;

    2. the bride and bridegroom at their wedding Mass;

    3. deacons[g] at the Mass of their ordination;

    4. an abbess at the Mass in which she is blessed; those consecrated to a life of virginity at the Mass of their consecration; professed religious, their relatives, friends, and the other members of their community[h] at the Mass of first or perpetual vows or renewal of vows;[R43]

    5. those who receive institution for a certain ministry at the Mass of their institution;[i] lay missionary helpers at the Mass in which they publicly receive their mission; others at the Mass in which they receive an ecclesiastical mission;

    6. the sick person and all present at the time viaticum is to be administered when Mass is lawfully celebrated in the sick person's home;

    7. the deacon and ministers who exercise their office at Mass;[j]

    8. when there is a concelebration, in the case of:

        a. all who exercise a liturgical function at this concelebration and also all seminarians present;[k]

        b. in their churches or oratories, all members of institutes professing the evangelical counsels and other societies whose members dedicate themselves to God by religious vows or by an offering or promise; also all those who reside in the houses of members of such institutes and societies;

    9. priests who are present at major celebrations and are not able to celebrate or concelebrate;

    10. all who make a retreat at a Mass in which they actively participate and which is specially celebrated for the group; also all who take part in the meeting of any pastoral body at a Mass they celebrate as a group;

    11. those listed in nos. 2 and 4, at Masses celebrating their jubilees;

    12. godparents, relatives, wife or husband, and lay catechists of newly baptized adults at the Mass of their initiation;

    13. relatives, friends, and special benefactors who take part in the Mass of a newly ordained priest;

1632

---

    f   OM and MR'70: "of the bishop" for "of the Ordinary."

    71   See SCDW, *Instr. Sacramentali Communione*, 29 June 1970 [DOL 270; the list that follows in the text here is an Appendix to that Instruction, but is emended; see the notes following on the variants from OM and MR'70].

    g   OM and MR'70: "those ordained" for "deacons."

    h   OM lacks "their relatives, . . . community."

    R43   See DOL 269 on members of secular institutes.

    i   OM and MR'70 lack "those who . . . institution."

    j   OM: "7. the deacon, subdeacon, and ministers who exercise their office at a sung Mass." MR '70 has the same meaning but "implentibus in Missa cum cantu" for "in Missa in cantu implentibus."

    k   OM and MR'70: "a. all who exercise a genuine liturgical function at this celebration, even laypersons, and all seminarians present."

14. members of communities at the conventual or community Mass, in accord with the provisions of this Instruction no. 76.[1]

Further, the conferences of bishops have the power to decide to what extent and under what considerations and conditions Ordinaries may allow communion under both kinds in other instances that are of special significance in the spiritual life of any community or group of the faithful.

Within such limits, Ordinaries may designate the particular instances, but on condition that they grant permission not indiscriminately but for clearly defined celebrations and that they point out matters for caution. They are also to exclude occasions when there will be a large number of communicants. The groups receiving this permission must also be specific, well-ordered, and homogeneous.[m]

1633   243. Preparations for giving communion under both kinds:

a. If communion is received from the chalice with a tube, silver tubes are needed for the celebrant and each communicant. There should also be a container of water for purifying the tubes and a paten on which to put them afterward.

b. If communion is given with a spoon, only one spoon is necessary.

c. If communion is given by intinction, care is to be taken that the eucharistic bread is not too thin or too small, but a little thicker than usual so that after being partly dipped into the precious blood it can still easily be given to the communicant.

1. Rite of Communion under Both Kinds
Directly from the Chalice

1634   244. If there is a deacon or another assisting priest or an acolyte:[n]

a. The celebrant receives the Lord's body and blood as usual, making sure enough remains in the chalice for the other communicants. He wipes the outside of the chalice with a purificator.

b. The priest gives the chalice with purificator to the minister and himself takes the paten or ciborium with the hosts; then both station themselves conveniently for the communion of the people.

c. The communicants approach, make the proper reverence, and stand in front of the priest. Showing[o] the host he says: *The body of Christ.* The communicant answers: *Amen* and receives the body of Christ from the priest.

d. The communicant then moves to the minister of the chalice and stands before him. The minister says: *The blood of Christ,* the communicant answers: *Amen,* and the minister holds out the chalice with purificator. For the sake of convenience, communicants may raise the chalice to their mouth themselves. Holding the purificator under the mouth with one hand, they drink a little from the chalice, taking care not to spill it, and then return to their place. The minister wipes the outside of the chalice with the purificator.

e. The minister places the chalice on the altar after all who are receiving under both kinds have drunk from it. If there are others who are not receiving communion under both kinds, the priest gives these communion, then returns to

---

[1]   OM lacks 14.

[m]   See DOL 270 nos. 2111–12.

[n]   OM and MR'70 lack "or an acolyte" in nos. 244–247, 249–252; MRVar has the present text. OM and MR'70 in nos. 249–252: "deacon" for "minister" or "minister of the chalice" and "celebrans" for "sacerdos" or "sacerdos celebrans."

[o]   OM and MR'70: "Elevating" for "Showing."

the altar. The priest or minister drinks whatever remains in the chalice and carries out the usual purifications.

245. If there is no deacon, other priest, or acolyte: 1635

a. The priest receives the Lord's body and blood as usual, making sure enough remains in the chalice for the other communicants. He wipes the outside of the chalice with the purificator.

b. The priest then stations himself conveniently for communion and distributes the body of Christ in the usual way to all who are receiving under both kinds. The communicants approach, make the proper reverence, and stand in front of the priest. After receiving the body of Christ, they step back a little.

c. After all have received, the celebrant places the ciborium on the altar and takes the chalice with the purificator. All those receiving from the chalice come forward again and stand in front of the priest. He says: *The blood of Christ*, the communicant answers: *Amen*, and the priest presents the chalice with purificator. The communicants hold the purificator under their mouth with one hand, taking care that none of the precious blood is spilled, drink a little from the chalice, and then return to their place. The priest wipes the outside of the chalice with the purificator.

d. After the communion from the chalice, the priest places it on the altar and if there are others receiving under one kind only, he gives them communion in the usual way, then returns to the altar. He drinks whatever remains in the chalice and carries out the usual purifications.

2. Rite of Communion under Both Kinds by Intinction

246. If there is a deacon, another priest assisting, or an acolyte present: 1636

a. The priest hands this minister the chalice with purificator and he himself takes the paten or ciborium with the hosts. The priest and the minister of the chalice station themselves conveniently for distributing communion.

b. The communicants approach, make the proper reverence, stand in front of the priest, and hold the communion plate below their chin. The celebrant dips a particle into the chalice and, showing it,[p] says: *The body and blood of Christ*. The communicants respond: *Amen*, receive communion from the priest, and return to their place.

c. The communion of those who do not receive under both kinds and the rest of the rite take place as already described.

247. If there is no deacon, assisting priest, or acolyte present: 1637

a. After drinking the blood of the Lord, the priest takes the ciborium, or paten with the hosts, between the index and middle fingers of one hand and holds the chalice between the thumb and index finger of the same hand. Then he stations himself conveniently for communion.

b. The communicants approach, make the proper reverence, stand in front of the priest, and hold a plate beneath their chin. The priest takes a particle, dips it into the chalice, and, showing it, says: *The body and blood of Christ*. The communicants respond: *Amen*, receive communion from the priest, and return to their place.

c. It is also permitted to place a small table covered with a cloth and corporal at a suitable place.[q] The priest places the chalice or ciborium[r] on the table in order to make the distribution of communion easier.

---

q   OM and MR'70: "at the first step of the altar or at the edge of the sanctuary" for "at a suitable place."

d. The communion of those who do not receive under both kinds, the consumption of the blood remaining in the chalice, and the purifications take place as already described.

3. Rite of Communion under Both Kinds Using a Tube

1638   248. In this case the priest celebrant also uses a tube when receiving the blood of the Lord.

1639   249. If there is a deacon, another assisting priest, or an acolyte present:

a. For the communion of the body of the Lord, everything is done as described in nos. 224 b and c.

b. The communicant goes to the minister of the chalice and stands in front of him. The minister says: *The blood of Christ* and the communicant responds: *Amen.* The communicant receives the tube from the minister, places it in the chalice, and drinks a little. The communicant then removes the tube, careful not to spill any drops, and places it in a container of water held by the minister. The communicant sips a little water to purify the tube, then puts it into another container presented by the minister.

1640   250. If there is no deacon, other assisting priest, or acolyte present, the priest celebrant offers the chalice to each communicant in the way described already for communion from the chalice (no. 245). The minister standing next to him holds the container of water for purifying the tube.

4. Rite of Communion under Both Kinds Using a Spoon

1641   251. If a deacon, another assisting priest, or an acolyte is present, he holds the chalice and, saying: *The blood of Christ,* ministers the blood of the Lord with a spoon to the individual communicants, who hold the plate beneath their chin. He is to take care that the spoon does not touch the lips or tongue of the communicants.

1642   252. If there is no deacon, other assisting priest, or acolyte present, the priest celebrant himself gives them the Lord's blood, after all receiving communion under both kinds have received the Lord's body.

CHAPTER V
ARRANGEMENT AND FURNISHING OF CHURCHES FOR THE EUCHARISTIC CELEBRATION

I. GENERAL PRINCIPLES

1643   253. For the celebration of the eucharist, the people of God normally assemble in a church or, if there is none, in some other fitting place worthy of so great a mystery. Churches and other places of worship should therefore be suited to celebrating the liturgy and to ensuring the active participation of the faithful. Further, the places and requisites for worship should be truly worthy and beautiful, signs and symbols of heavenly realities.[72]

---

[72] See SC art. 122–124 [DOL 1 nos. 122–124]; PO no. 5 [DOL 18 no. 260]. SCR, Instr. InterOec, 26 Sept. 1964, no. 90 [DOL 23 no. 382]; Instr. EuchMyst, 25 May 1967, no. 24 [DOL 179 no. 1253].

254. At all times, therefore, the Church seeks out the service of the arts and wel-   1644
comes the artistic expressions of all peoples and regions.[73] The Church is intent on
keeping the works of art and the treasures handed down from the past[74] and, when
necessary, on adapting them to new needs. It strives as well to promote new works
of art that appeal to the contemporary mentality.[75]

In commissioning artists and choosing works of art that are to become part of a
church, the highest artistic standard is therefore to be set, in order that art may aid
faith and devotion and be true to the reality it is to symbolize and the purpose it is
to serve.[76]

255. It is preferable that churches be solemnly consecrated. The faithful should give   1645
due honor to the cathedral of their diocese and to their own church as symbols of
the spiritual Church that their Christian vocation commits them to build up and
extend.

256. All who are involved in the construction, restoration, and remodeling of   1646
churches are to consult the diocesan commission on liturgy and art. The local
Ordinary is to use the counsel and help of this commission whenever it comes to
laying down norms on this matter, approving plans for new buildings, and making
decisions on the more important issues.[77]

II. ARRANGEMENT OF A CHURCH FOR THE LITURGICAL ASSEMBLY

257. The people of God assembled at Mass possess an organic and hierarchical   1647
structure, expressed by the various ministries and actions for each part of the
celebration. The general plan of the sacred edifice should be such that in some way
it conveys the image of the gathered assembly. It should also allow the participants
to take the place most appropriate to them and assist all to carry out their individual
functions properly.[R44]

The congregation and the choir should have a place that facilitates their active
participation.[78]

The priest and his ministers have their place in the sanctuary, that is, in the
part of the church that brings out their distinctive role,[a] namely, to preside over the
prayers, to proclaim the word of God, or to minister at the altar.

Even though these elements must express a hierarchical arrangement and the
diversity of offices, they should at the same time form a complete and organic unity,
clearly expressive of the unity of the entire holy people. The character and beauty
of the place and all its appointments should foster devotion and show the holiness
of the mysteries celebrated there.

---

[73]   See SC art. 123 [DOL 1 no. 123].

[74]   See SCR, Instr. EuchMyst no. 24 [DOL 179 no. 1253].

[75]   See SC art. 123, 129 [DOL 1 nos. 123, 129]. SCR, Instr. InterOec no. 13 c [DOL 23 no. 305].

[76]   See SC art. 123 [DOL 1 no. 123].

[77]   See SC art. 126 [DOL 1 no. 126].

[R44] See DOL 208 no. 1662, note R48.

[78]   See SCR, InterOec nos. 97–98 [DOL 23 nos. 389–390].

[a]   OM and MR'70: ". . . their distinctive, hierarchic role."

III. SANCTUARY

1648   258. The sanctuary should be clearly marked off from the body of the church either by being somewhat elevated or by its distinctive design and appointments. It should be large enough to accommodate all the rites.[79]

IV. ALTAR

1649   259. At the altar the sacrifice of the cross is made present under sacramental signs. It is also the table of the Lord and the people of God are called together to share in it. The altar is, as well, the center of the thanksgiving that the eucharist accomplishes.[80]

1650   260. In a place of worship, the celebration of the eucharist must be on an altar, either fixed or movable. Outside a place of worship, especially if the celebration is only for a single occasion, a suitable table may be used, but always with a cloth and corporal.

1651   261. A fixed altar is one attached to the floor so that it cannot be moved; a movable altar is one that can be transferred from place to place.

1652   262. The main altar should be freestanding to allow the ministers to walk around it easily and Mass to be celebrated facing the people. It should be so placed as to be a focal point on which the attention of the whole congregation centers naturally.[81] The main altar should ordinarily be a fixed, consecrated altar.

1653   263. According to the Church's traditional practice and the altar's symbolism, the table of a fixed altar should be of stone and indeed of natural stone. But at the discretion of the conference of bishops some other solid, becoming, and well-crafted material may be used.[R45]

    The pedestal or base of the table may be of any sort of material, as long as it is becoming and solid.

1654   264. A movable altar may be constructed of any becoming, solid material suited to liturgical use, according to the traditions and customs of different regions.

1655   265. Altars both fixed and movable are consecrated according to the rite described in the liturgical books;[b,R46] but movable altars may simply be blessed. There is no obligation to have a consecrated stone in a movable altar or on the table where the eucharist is celebrated outside a place of worship (see no. 260).

---

[79] See ibid. no. 91 [DOL 23 no. 383].

[80] See SCR, Instr. EuchMyst no. 24 [DOL 179 no. 1253].

[81] See SCR, Instr. InterOec no. 91 [DOL 23 no. 383].

[R45] Query: Should an altar with a table of wood or metal be consecrated? Reply: Yes. The GIRM no. 263 says: "[Text quoted]." The consecration should be carried out according to the existing practice until a new rite is ready: Not 6 (1970) 263, no. 34. See DOL 547.

[b] OM and MR'70: "according to the rite of the Roman Pontifical" for "according to the rite described in the liturgical books."

[R46] Query: Has the formulary for the blessing of a movable altar been completed and where it is available? Reply: According to the GIRM no. 265, movable altars may only be blessed. The blessing formulary has not yet been completed: Not 6 (1970) 263, no. 35.

266. It is fitting to maintain the practice of enclosing in the altar to be dedicated or of plac-   1656
ing under this altar relics of saints, even of nonmartyrs. Care must be taken to have solid
evidence of the authenticity of such relics.

267. Minor altars should be fewer in number. In new churches they should be   1657
placed in chapels separated in some way from the body of the church.[82]

V. ALTAR FURNISHINGS

268. At least one cloth should be placed on the altar out of reverence for the   1658
celebration of the memorial of the Lord and the banquet that gives us his body and
blood. The shape, size, and decoration of the altar cloth should be in keeping with
the design of the altar.

269. Candles are to be used at every liturgical service as a sign of reverence and   1659
festiveness. The candlesticks are to be placed either on or around the altar in a way
suited to the design of the altar and the sanctuary. Everything is to be well balanced
and must not interfere with the faithful's clear view of what goes on at the altar or
is placed on it.[R47]

270. There is also to be a cross, clearly visible to the congregation, either on the altar   1660
or near it.

VI. CHAIR FOR THE PRIEST CELEBRANT AND THE MINISTERS, THAT IS, THE PLACE WHERE THE PRIEST PRESIDES

271. The priest celebrant's chair ought to stand as a symbol of his office of presiding   1661
over the assembly and of directing prayer. Thus the best place for the chair is at the
back of the sanctuary and turned toward the congregation, unless the structure or
other circumstances are an obstacle (for example, if too great a distance would
interfere with communication between the priest and people). Anything resembling
a throne is to be avoided. The seats for the ministers should be so placed in the
sanctuary that they can readily carry out their appointed functions.[83]

VII. LECTERN (AMBO) OR PLACE FROM WHICH THE WORD OF GOD IS PROCLAIMED

272. The dignity of the word of God requires the church to have a place that is   1662
suitable for proclamation of the word and is a natural focal point for the people
during the liturgy of the word.[84]

---

[82]   See SCR, Instr. InterOec no. 93 [DOL 23 no. 385].

[R47]   Query: Must the lighted candles that are to be placed in candlesticks for the celebration of Mass
consist in part of beeswax, olive oil, or other vegetable oil? Reply: The GIRM prescribes candles for Mass
"as a sign of reverence and festiveness" (nos. 79, 269). But it makes no further determination regarding the
material of their composition, except in the case of the sanctuary lamp, the fuel for which must be oil or
wax (see *Holy Communion and Worship of the Eucharist outside Mass*, Introduction no. 11 [DOL 279 no. 2203]).
The faculty that the conferences of bishops possess to choose suitable materials for sacred furnishings
applies therefore to the candles for Mass. That faculty is limited only by the condition that in the
estimation of the people the materials are valued and worthy and that they are appropriate for sacred use.
Candles intended for liturgical use should be made of material that can provide a living flame without
being smoky or noxious and that does not stain the altar cloths or coverings. Electric bulbs are banned in
the interest of safeguarding authenticity and the full symbolism of light: Not 10 (1974) 80, no. 4.

[83]   See SCR, Instr. InterOec no. 92 [DOL 23 no. 384].

[84]   See ibid. no. 96 [DOL 23 no. 388].

As a rule the lectern or ambo should be stationary, not simply a movable stand. In keeping with the structure of each church, it must be so placed that the ministers may be easily seen and heard by the faithful.[R48]

The readings, responsorial psalm, and the Easter Proclamation (*Exsultet*) are proclaimed from the lectern; it may be used also for the homily and general intercessions (prayer of the faithful).

It is better for the commentator, cantor, or choir director not to use the lectern.

VII. PLACES FOR THE FAITHFUL

1663   273. The places for the faithful should be arranged with care so that the people are able to take their rightful part in the celebration visually and mentally. As a rule, there should be benches or chairs for their use. But the custom of reserving seats for private persons must be abolished.[85] Chairs or benches should be set up in such a way that the people can easily take the positions required during various celebrations and have unimpeded access to receive communion.

The congregation must be enabled not only to see the priest and the other ministers but also, with the aid of modern sound equipment, to hear them without difficulty.[R49]

IX. CHOIR, ORGAN, AND OTHER MUSICAL INSTRUMENTS

1664   274. In relation to the design of each church, the *schola cantorum* should be so placed that its character as a part of the assembly of the faithful that has a special function stands out clearly. The location should also assist the choir's liturgical ministry and readily allow each member complete, that is, sacramental participation in the Mass.[86]

1665   275. The organ and other lawfully approved musical instruments are to be placed suitably in such a way that they can sustain the singing of the choir and congregation and be heard with ease when they are played alone.

[R48]   Query: When there is no celebrant's chair and no special place for carrying out the liturgy of the word, may a priest who celebrates with a small group present: a. remain at the altar during the liturgy of the word? b. set the missal on the right side of the altar or at the middle? c. and if so, which side of the altar is designated as the left or right? Reply: a. The liturgical norms in force make a clear distinction between the altar and the place for proclaiming the word of God (GIRM nos. 252–257). Where places have not yet been remodeled in keeping with the reformed liturgy (and such remodeling should be done without delay), it is necessary to provide at least a chair for the celebrant and a movable lectern for the reader. When the celebrant himself must act as reader, especially for the gospel, the reading should be at the movable lectern. In the very exceptional case when not even a bench can be set up, the priest may stay at the altar, where the missal and lectionary are set on a reading stand. b. This stand obviously should be placed conveniently for the celebrant's reading, for example, at the middle of the altar. The custom of setting the missal stand on the left side of the altar comes from the time when the chalice was placed at the center at the beginning of Mass. This is no longer the case, since reform of the liturgy, because the chalice is now placed on a side table, away from the altar. c. The left side of the altar is the side at the celebrant's left; the right side, at his right: Not 14 (1978) 302, no. 3.

[85]   See SC art. 32 [DOL 1 no. 32]. SCR, Instr. InterOec no. 98 [DOL 23 no. 390].

[R49]   See DOL 208 no. 1411, note R2, Query 3.

[86]   See SCR, Instr. MusSacr no. 23 [DOL 508 no. 4144].

X. RESERVATION OF THE EUCHARIST

276. Every encouragement should be given to the practice of eucharistic reservation in a chapel suited to the faithful's private adoration and prayer.[87,c] If this is impossible because of the structure of the church, the sacrament should be reserved at an altar or elsewhere, in keeping with local custom, and in a part of the church that is worthy and properly adorned.[88]   1666

277. The eucharist is to be reserved in a single, solid, unbreakable tabernacle. Thus as a rule there should be only one tablernacle in each church.[89]   1667

XI. IMAGES FOR VENERATION BY THE FAITHFUL

278. In keeping with the Church's very ancient tradition, it is lawful to set up in places of worship images of Christ, Mary, and the saints for veneration by the faithful. But there is need both to limit their number and to situate them in such a way that they do not distract the people's attention from the celebration.[90] There is to be only one image of any one saint. In general, the devotion of the entire community is to be the criterion regarding images[d] in the adornment and arrangement of a church.   1668

XII. GENERAL PLAN OF THE CHURCH

279. The style in which a church is decorated should be a means to achieve noble simplicity, not ostentation. The choice of materials for church appointments must be marked by concern for genuineness and by the intent to foster instruction of the faithful and the dignity of the place of worship.   1669

280. Proper planning of a church and its surroundings that meets contemporary needs requires attention not only to the elements belonging directly to liturgical services but also to those facilities for the comfort of the people that are usual in places of public gatherings.   1670

CHAPTER VI
REQUISITES FOR CELEBRATING MASS

I. BREAD AND WINE

281. Following the example of Christ, the Church has always used bread and wine with water to celebrate the Lord's Supper.   1671

282. According to the tradition of the entire Church, the bread must be made from wheat; according to the tradition of the Latin Church, it must be unleavened.   1672

---

87   See SCR, Instr. EuchMyst no. 53 [DOL 179 no. 1282]. RR, *Holy Communion and Worship of the Eucharist outside Mass, ed. typica*, 1973, Introduction no. 9 [DOL 279 no. 2201].

c   OM lacks "adoration and"; OM and MR'70 lack second reference in note 87.

88   See SCR, Instr. EuchMyst no. 54 [DOL 179 no. 1283]; Instr. InterOec no. 95 [DOL 23 no. 387].

89   See SCR, Instr. EuchMyst no. 52 [DOL 179 no. 1281]; Instr. InterOec no. 95 [DOL 23 no. 387]. SC Sacraments, Instr. *Nullo umquam tempore*, 28 May 1938, no. 4: AAS 30 (1938) 199–200. RR, *Holy Communion and Worship of the Eucharist outside Mass*, Introduction nos. 10–11 [DOL 279 nos. 2202–03].

90   See SC art. 125 [DOL 1 no. 125].

d   OM and MR'70 lack "regarding images."

1673   283. The nature of the sign demands that the material for the eucharistic celebration truly have the appearance of food. Accordingly, even though unleavened and baked in the traditional shape,[a] the eucharistic bread,[R50] should be made in such a way that in a Mass with a congregation the priest is able actually to break the host into parts and distribute them to at least some of the faithful. (When, however, the number of communicants is large or other pastoral needs require it, small hosts are in no way ruled out.) The action of the breaking of the bread, the simple term for the eucharist in apostolic times, will more clearly bring out the force and meaning of the sign of the unity of all in the one bread and of their charity, since the one bread is being distributed among the members of one family.

1674   284. The wine for the eucharist must be from the fruit of the vine (see Lk 22:18), natural, and pure, that is not mixed with any foreign substance.[R51]

1675   285. Care must be taken to ensure that the elements are kept in good condition: that the wine does not turn to vinegar or the bread spoil or become too hard to be broken easily.

1676   286. If the priest notices after the consecration or as he receives communion that water instead of wine was poured into the chalice, he pours the water into another container, then pours wine with water into the chalice and consecrates it. He says only the part of the institution narrative related to the consecration of the chalice, without being obliged to consecrate the bread again.

II. SACRED FURNISHINGS IN GENERAL

1677   287. As in the case of architecture, the Church welcomes the artistic style of every region for all sacred furnishings and accepts adaptations in keeping with the genius and traditions of each people, provided they fit the purpose for which the sacred furnishings are intended.[91]

---

[a]   OM lacks "and baked in the traditional shape."

[R50]   Query: In the GIRM no. 283 what does *eucharistic bread* mean? Reply: The term means the same thing as the *host* hitherto in use, except that the bread is larger in size. The term *eucharistic bread* in line 2 is explained by the words of line 4: "The priest is able actually *to break the host into parts.*" Thus line 2 is about this eucharistic element as to its *kind* and line 4 as to its *shape*. Therefore it was incorrect to interpret *eucharistic bread* in line 2 as a reference to its shape as though the term implies that bread in the shape designed for its everyday use may be substituted for the host in its traditional shape. The GIRM in no way intended to change the shape of the large and small hosts, but only to provide an option regarding size, thickness, and color in order that the host may really have the appearance of bread that is shared by many people: Not 6 (1970) 37, no. 24.

[R51]   Card. F. Seper, Prefect of the SCDF addressed the following letter, 2 May 1974, Prot. N. 88/74, to Card. J. Krol, President of the Conference of Bishops of the United States:

For some time different Ordinaries have asked this Sacred Congregation for the permission to allow priests who are undergoing a treatment for alcoholism or who have undergone this treatment, to celebrate Mass with unfermented grape juice.

With this situation in mind, the Congregation for the Doctrine of the Faith authorizes the Ordinaries of the United States of America to grant to those priests who have made this request the permission either to concelebrate with one or more priests a normal Mass but without receiving communion under the species of wine or, when this is not possible, to celebrate Mass using unfermented grape juice and to use water alone for the ritual ablutions after Communion. Also, one must avoid creating scandal for the faithful.

In the hope of meeting the concern shown by the bishops for those of their priests suffering from alcoholism and in asking you to inform the Ordinaries of the permission that is granted to them, I am sincerely yours.

[91]   See SC art. 128 [DOL 1 no. 128]. SCR, Instr. EuchMyst, 25 May 1967, no. 24 [DOL 179 no. 1253].

In this matter as well the concern is to be for the noble simplicity that is the perfect companion of genuine art.

288. In the choice of materials for sacred furnishings, others besides the traditional are acceptable that by contemporary standards are considered to be of high quality, are durable, and well suited to sacred uses. The conference of bishops is to make the decisions for each region.   1678

III. SACRED VESSELS

289. Among the requisites for the celebration of Mass, the sacred vessels hold a place of honor, especially the chalice and paten, which are used in presenting, consecrating, and receiving the bread and wine.   1679

290. Vessels should be made from materials that are solid and that in the particular region are regarded as noble. The conference of bishops will be the judge in this matter.[b] But preference is to be given to materials that do not break easily or become unusable.   1680

291. Chalices and other vessels that serve as receptacles for the blood of the Lord are to have a cup of nonabsorbent material. The base may be of any other solid and worthy material.   1681

292. Vessels that serve as receptacles for the eucharistic bread, such as a paten, ciborium, pyx, monstrance, etc., may be made of other materials that are prized in the region, for example, ebony or other hard woods, as long as they are suited to sacred use.   1682

293. For the consecration of hosts one rather large paten may properly be used; on it is placed the bread for the priest[c] as well as for the ministers and the faithful. 1683

294. Vessels made from metal should ordinarily be gilded on the inside if the metal is one that rusts; gilding is not necessary if the metal is more precious than gold and does not rust.   1684

295. The artist may fashion the sacred vessels in a shape that is in keeping with the culture of each region, provided each type of vessel is suited to the intended liturgical use.   1685

296. For the blessing or consecration of vessels the rites prescribed in the liturgical books are to be followed.[R52]   1686

IV. VESTMENTS

297. In the Church, the Body of Christ, not all members have the same function. This diversity of ministries is shown outwardly in worship by the diversity of 1687

---

b   OM lacks this sentence.

c   OM and MR'70: "celebrante" for "sacerdote."

R52   Query: In consecrating vessels not made of gold should the formularies of the Roman Pontifical be used? Reply: Yes. Whatever the material of their composition, provided this is solid and noble in the judgment of the conference of bishops, vessels are to be blessed or consecrated according to the rites appearing in the liturgical books (see GIRM no. 296). The formularies to be used remain those from the Roman Pontifical, with an anointing added in the case of consecration: Not 6 (1970) 263, no. 36. See DOL 547 nos. 4442–45.

vestments. These should therefore symbolize the function proper to each ministry. But at the same time the vestments should also contribute to the beauty of the rite.

1688   298. The vestment common to ministers of every rank is the alb, tied at the waist with a cincture, unless it is made to fit without a cincture. An amice should be put on first if the alb does not completely cover the street clothing at the neck. A surplice may not be substituted for the alb when the chasuble or dalmatic is to be worn or when a stole is used instead of the chasuble or dalmatic.[d]

1689   299. Unless otherwise indicated, the chasuble, worn over the alb and stole,[e] is the vestment proper to the priest celebrant at Mass and other rites immediately connected with Mass.[R53]

1690   300. The dalmatic, worn over the alb and stole,[f] is the vestment proper to the deacon.

1691   301. Ministers below the order of deacon may wear the alb or other vestment that is lawfully approved in each region.[g]

1692   302. The priest wears the stole around his neck and hanging down in front. The deacon wears it over his left shoulder and drawn across the chest to the right side, where it is fastened.

1693   303. The cope is worn by the priest in processions and other services, in keeping with the rubrics proper to each rite.

1694   304. Regarding the design of vestments, the conferences of bishops may determine and propose to the Apostolic See adaptations that correspond to the needs and usages of their regions.[92]

1695   305. In addition to the traditional materials, natural fabrics proper to the region may be used for making vestments; artificial fabrics that are in keeping with the dignity of the liturgy and the person wearing them may also be used. The conference of bishops will be the judge in this matter.[93]

1696   306. The beauty of a vestment should derive from its material and design rather than from lavish ornamentation. Representations on vestments should consist only of symbols, images, or pictures portraying the sacred. Anything out of keeping with the sacred is to be avoided.

[d]   OM: "298. The vestment common to ministers of every rank is the alb, tied at the waist with a cincture, if necessary. It may be well for an amice to be put on before the alb. A surplice may be substituted for the alb, but not when a chasuble or dalmatic is to be worn or when the stole is worn to replace the chasuble or dalmatic."
    MR'70: as in present text until "A surplice . . .," which is the same as OM.

[e]   OM lacks "worn over the alb and stole."

[R53]   Query: May the priest omit wearing the stole? Reply: No. The query arises from an interpretation of the GIRM no. 299. The contents of that number, "The chasuble is the vestment proper to the priest celebrant, at Masses and other rites . . .," must be understood as governed by nos. 81 and 302. From these it is altogether clear that the stole is a priestly vestment that never is to be left off at Mass and other rites directly connected with Mass: Not 6 (1970) 104, no. 30.

[f]   OM lacks "and stole."

[g]   OM and MR'70: "301. The subdeacon wears the tunic, which is put on over the alb." MRVar deletes no. 301.

[92]   See SC art. 128 [DOL 1 no. 128].

[93]   See ibid.

307. Variety in the color of the vestments is meant to give effective, outward   1697
expression to the specific character of the mysteries of the faith being celebrated
and, in the course of the year, to a sense of progress in the Christian life.

308. Traditional usage should be retained for the vestment colors.   1698

    a. White is used in the offices and Masses of the Easter and Christmas sea-
sons; on feasts and memorials[h] of the Lord, other than of his passion; on feasts and
memorials of Mary, the angels, saints who were not martyrs, All Saints (1 November), John the Baptist (24 June), John the Evangelist (27 December), the Chair of St.
Peter (22 February), and the Conversion of St. Paul (25 January).

    b. Red is used on Passion Sunday (Palm Sunday)[R54] and Good Friday,
Pentecost, celebrations of the Lord's passion, birthday feasts of the apostles and
evangelists, and celebrations of martyrs.

    c. Green is used in the offices and Masses of Ordinary Time.

    d. Violet is used in Lent and Advent. It may also be worn in offices and
Masses for the dead.

    e. Black may be used in Masses for the dead.

    f. Rose may be used on *Gaudete* Sunday (Third Sunday of Advent) and *Laetare*
Sunday (Fourth Sunday of Lent).

The conference of bishops may choose and propose to the Apostolic See adaptations suited to the needs and culture of peoples.

309. On solemn occasions more precious vestments may be used, even if not of the   1699
color of the day.

310. Ritual Masses are celebrated in their proper color, in white, or in a festive color; Masses   1700
for various needs and occasions are celebrated in the color proper to the day or the season
or in violet if they bear a penitential character, for example, Masses nos. 23, 28, and 40;
votive Masses are celebrated in the color suited to the Mass itself or in the color proper
to the day or season.[i]

V. OTHER REQUISITES FOR CHURCH USE

311. Besides vessels and vestments for which some special material is prescribed,   1701
any other furnishings that either have a liturgical use or are in any other way
introduced into a church should be worthy and suited to their particular purpose.

312. Even in minor matters, every effort should be made to respect the canons of art   1702
and to combine cleanliness and a noble simplicity.

---

   [h] OM: "commemorations" for "memorials."

   [R54] Query: On Passion Sunday is the color red worn only in the palms procession? Reply: No. Red is
the color for the Mass and office for the entire liturgical day on Passion, that is, Palm Sunday, namely, from
evening prayer I to evening prayer II. The same applies to Good Friday, on which red is the color for both
the office and the Celebration of the Lord's Passion: Not 5 (1969) 403, no. 12.

   [i] OM and MR'70: "310. Votive Masses are celebrated in the color appropriate to the Mass or in the
color proper to the day or season; Masses for various needs and occasions are celebrated in the color
proper to the day or season."

CHAPTER VII
CHOICE OF THE MASS AND ITS PARTS

1703   313. The pastoral effectiveness of a celebration will be heightened if the texts of readings, prayers, and songs correspond as closely as possible to the needs, religious dispositions, and aptitude of the participants. This will be achieved by an intelligent use of the broad options described in this chapter.

In planning the celebration, then, the priest should consider the general spiritual good of the assembly rather than his personal outlook. He should be mindful that the choice of texts is to be made in consultation with the ministers and others who have a function in the celebration, including the faithful in regard to the parts that more directly belong to them.

Since a variety of options is provided for the different parts of the Mass, it is necessary for the deacon, readers, psalmists, cantors, commentator, and choir to be completely sure beforehand of those texts for which they are responsible so that nothing is improvised. A harmonious planning and execution will help dispose the people spiritually to take part in the eucharist.

I. CHOICE OF MASS

1704   314. On solemnities the priest is bound to follow the calendar of the church where he is celebrating.

1705   315. On Sundays, on weekdays of Advent, the Christmas season, Lent, and the Easter season,[a] on feasts, and on obligatory memorials:

   a. if Mass is celebrated with a congregation, the priest should follow the calendar of the church where he is celebrating;

   b. if Mass is celebrated without a congregation, the priest may choose either the calendar of the church or his own calendar.

1706   316. On optional memorials:[b,R55]

[a] OM: "Advent and Lent" for "Advent . . . Easter season."

[b] OM: "316. When an optional memorial occurs, the priest may choose the weekday Mass, the Mass of the saint or one of the saints whose memorial it is, or the Mass of a saint inscribed in the martyrology for that day, or a Mass ad diversa, or a votive Mass. When a weekday in Ordinary Time occurs, he may choose the Mass of the weekday, or the Mass of a saint inscribed in the martyrology for that day, or a Mass ad diversa, or a votive Mass."

[R55] Query: May Masses for various needs and occasions and votive Masses be celebrated on weekdays of the Christmas and Easter seasons? Reply: The GIRM no. 316 [c] speaks only of the weekdays in Ordinary Time and not of the weekdays of the Christmas and Easter seasons. But a comparison of the GIRM with the General Norms for the Liturgical Year and the Calendar leads to the following interpretation.
   1. Masses for various needs and occasions or votive Masses are forbidden on solemnities, the Sundays of Advent, Lent, and the Easter season, as well as on Ash Wednesday and the weekdays of Holy Week, which "have precedence over all other celebrations" (see GNLYC no. 16 [DOL 442 no. 3782]).
   2. On the Sundays other than those just listed, on feasts, on the weekdays of Advent from 17 to 24 December and of Lent, such Masses may be said "in cases of serious need, at the direction of the local Ordinary or with his permission" (GIRM no. 332 [DOL 208 no. 1722]).
   3. On the weekdays of Advent, up to 16 December inclusive, during the Christmas season from 2 January to the Saturday after Epiphany, during the Easter season from the Tuesday after the octave of Easter until the Saturday before Pentecost, and on obligatory memorials, "if some real need or pastoral advantage requires, at the discretion of the rector of the church or the priest celebrant, the Masses corresponding to such need or advantage may be used in a celebration with a congregation" (GIRM no. 333 [DOL 208 no. 1723]). The need in question is to be understood in a pastoral sense, for example, if a large number of people gathers for a particular celebration, as is the case in some places on the first Friday of the month. Apart from such situations Masses for various needs and occasions are not allowed. During these seasons the weekday office has a certain priority in order that the mystery of salvation, rather than

a. On the weekdays of Advent from 17 December to 24 December, during the octave of Christmas, and on the weekdays of Lent, apart from Ash Wednesday and in Holy Week, the priest celebrates the Mass of the day; but he may take the opening prayer from a memorial listed in the General Roman Calendar for that day, except on Ash Wednesday and during Holy Week.

b. On the weekdays of Advent before 17 December, the weekdays of the Christmas season from 2 January on, and the weekdays of the Easter season,[c] the priest may choose the weekday Mass, the Mass of the saint or of one of the saints whose memorial is observed, or the Mass of a saint inscribed in the martyrology for that day.

c. On the weekdays in Ordinary Time, the priest may choose the weekday Mass, the Mass of an optional memorial, the Mass of a saint inscribed in the martyrology for that day, a Mass for various needs and occasions,[d] or a votive Mass.[R56]

If he celebrates with a congregation, the priest should first consider the spiritual good of the faithful and avoid imposing his own personal preferences. In particular, he should not omit the readings assigned for each day in the weekday lectionary too frequently or without sufficient reason, since the Church desires that a richer portion of God's word be provided for the people.[94]

For similar reasons he should use Masses for the dead sparingly. Every Mass is offered for both the living and the dead and there is a remembrance of the dead in each eucharistic prayer.

Where the faithful are attached to the optional memorials of Mary or the saints, at least one Mass of the memorial should be celebrated to satisfy their devotion.

When an option is given between a memorial in the General Roman Calendar and one in a diocesan or religious calendar, the preference should be given, all things being equal and depending on tradition, to the memorial in the particular calendar.

---

other feasts or commemorations, may be celebrated in the measure due to it (see SC art. 108 [DOL 1 no. 108]). This applies above all to the fifty days from Easter Sunday to Pentecost, days that are celebrated "as one feast day, or better as 'one great Sunday'" (GNLYC no. 22 [DOL 442 no. 3788]).

4. During Ordinary Time it is permissible to celebrate any of the Masses for various needs and occasions whenever the office is of the weekday or an optional memorial occurs.

5. Masses for the dead are regulated in the same way. a. The Mass of burial may be celebrated on any day, except the Easter triduum, the Sundays of Advent, Lent, and Easter, and solemnities. b. The Masses on the occasions of news of a death, final burial, and the first anniversary may be celebrated on the days indicated in nos. 3–4 (see GIRM no. 337 [DOL 208 no. 1727]). c. Daily Masses for the dead may be celebrated on the weekdays in Ordinary Time and when an optional memorial occurs, as in no. 4: Not 5 (1969) 323–324, no. 2.

[c] MR'70: "On the weekdays of the Christmas and Easter seasons" for "On the weekdays . . . of the Easter season."

[d] MR'70: "a Mass ad diversa" for "a Mass for various needs and occasions."

[R56] Query: On weekdays in Ordinary Time may the Mass of any saint one chooses be celebrated? Reply: Yes. The GIRM no. 316 c says: "[Text quoted]." The votive Masses listed are those "of the mysteries of the Lord or in honor of Mary or of a particular saint or of all the saints" (GIRM no. 329 c [DOL 208 no. 1719]).

Even though no. 316 c gives a certain precedence to those saints mentioned in the martyrology for the day, no. 329 c at the end allows, as an option in favor of the faithful's devotion, a votive Mass of any saint or all the saints. Texts for votive Masses to be celebrated in honor of the saints are to be chosen in keeping with no. 4, p. 514 of the *Missale Romanum* [RM: Proper of the Saints, Introduction no. 4]: Not 10 (1974) 145, no. 2.

94   See SC art. 51 [DOL 1 no. 51].

II. CHOICE OF INDIVIDUAL TEXTS

1707 317. In the choice of texts for the several parts of the Mass, the following rules are to be observed. They apply to Masses of the season and of the saints.

READINGS

1708 318. Sundays and holydays have three readings, that is, from the Old Testament, from the writings of an apostle, and from a Gospel. Thus God's own teaching brings the Christian people to a knowledge of the continuity of the work of salvation.

Accordingly, it is expected that there will be three readings, but for pastoral reasons and by decree of the conference of bishops the use of only two readings is allowed in some places. In such a case, the choice between the first two readings should be based on the norms in the Lectionary and on the intention to lead the people to a deeper knowledge of Scripture; there should never be any thought of choosing a text because it is shorter or easier.[R57]

1709 319. In the weekday lectionary, readings are provided for each day of every week throughout the year; therefore, unless a solemnity or feast occurs, these readings are for the most part to be used on the days to which they are assigned.

The continuous reading during the week, however, is sometimes interrupted by the occurrence of a feast or particular celebration. In this case the priest, taking into consideration the entire week's plan of readings, is allowed either to combine omitted parts with other readings or to give preference to certain readings.

In Masses with special groups, the priest may choose texts more suited to the particular celebration, provided they are taken from the texts of an approved lectionary.[a]

[R57] Query: The GIRM determines: "[Text no. 318 quoted]." What, therefore, is the mind of the legislator? How many readings should there be? Reply: The Introduction to the *Order of Readings for Mass* no. 3 a states concerning Sundays and holydays: "[Text quoted; DOL 232 no. 1845]." "Besides being of great advantage to the priest's preaching, this arrangement of the readings is in practice the only way to acquaint all the faithful with a certain number of Old Testament texts virtually unknown to most of them" (G. Fontaine, Not 5 [1969] 263). For pastoral reasons the conference of bishops, especially at the beginning, may allow use of only two readings (see GIRM no. 318). In some places it may seem necessary to prolong this arrangement in order to ensure the gradual biblical instruction of the Christian people.

In such cases, observing only what the conference of bishops has laid down, the priest presiding may choose either the first or the second reading, always, of course, retaining the gospel. The choice between the first or the second reading should meet the following criteria.

a. "There should never be any thought of choosing a text because it is shorter or easier" (GIRM no. 318).

b. "It is preferable to choose the reading that is more closely related to the day's gospel or is more helpful in presenting an organized and unified instruction [on the mystery of salvation] over a period of time" (*Order of Readings for Mass* no. 8 a [DOL 232 no. 1850]). In practice that reading is to be chosen which: is more closely related to the gospel; is more in keeping with the character of the liturgical season or feast; permits fuller catechesis of the faithful.

c. Preference is to be given to a continuous reading of some of the more important books of the Bible. For example, on the Sundays of Lent the two first readings constitute a continuous unit on the history of salvation; to omit the reading of texts of such high importance would be regrettable.

A second example: on Sundays in Ordinary Time it would be of greater advantage to give preference to a semicontinuous reading of one of the letters of the apostles.

d. "What must be avoided above all is reading from the Old Testament on one Sunday and on the next from the New Testament or vice versa; that would also make the texts more difficult to understand" (G. Fontaine, loc. cit. 275).

In certain circumstances it may be necessary, at the discretion of the local Ordinary, to provide for special cases not covered by the norms laid down by the conference of bishops. In Masses with special groups the Instruction *Actio pastoralis* (15 May 1969) no. 6 [DOL 275 no. 2127] grants the option of choosing texts better suited to the celebration: Not 8 (1972) 192–194.

[a] OM: "In Masses with special groups, the priest may choose from the readings occurring that week those that seem better suited to instruct the particular assembly."

320. The Lectionary has a special selection of texts from Scripture for Masses that   1710
incorporate certain sacraments or sacramentals or that are celebrated by reason of
special circumstances.

These selections of readings have been assigned so that by hearing a more
pertinent passage from God's word the faithful may be led to a better understanding of the mystery they are taking part in and may be led to a more ardent love for
God's word.

Therefore the texts for proclamation in the liturgical assembly are to be chosen
on the basis of their pastoral relevance and the options allowed in this matter.

PRAYERS

321. The many prefaces enriching the Roman Missal are intended to develop in   1711
different ways the theme of thanksgiving in the eucharistic prayer and bring out
more clearly the different facets of the mystery of salvation.

322. The choice of the eucharistic prayer may be guided by the following norms.   1712

a. Eucharistic Prayer I, the Roman Canon, which may be used on any day, is
particularly apt on days when there is a special text for the prayer, *In union with the
whole Church* or in Masses that have a special form of the prayer, *Father, accept this
offering*; also on the feasts of the apostles and saints mentioned in it and on Sundays,
unless for pastoral considerations another eucharistic prayer is preferred.[R58]

b. Eucharistic Prayer II has features that make it particularly suitable for
weekdays and special circumstances.

Although it has its own preface, it may also be used with other prefaces,
especially those that summarize the mystery of salvation, such as the Sunday
prefaces or the common prefaces.

When Mass is celebrated for a dead person, the special formulary may be
inserted in the place indicated, namely, before the intercession, *Remember our brothers
and sisters*.

c. Eucharistic Prayer III may be said with any preface. Its use is particularly
suited to Sundays and holydays.

The special formulary for a dead person may be used with this prayer in
the place indicated, namely, at the prayer, *In mercy and love unite all your children*.[R59]

d. Eucharistic Prayer IV has a fixed preface and provides a fuller summary of
the history of salvation. It may be used when a Mass has no preface of its
own.[b,R60]

[R58] Query: Are the formularies of the Roman Canon proper to the day still to be followed on Holy
Thursday? Reply: Yes. They are not in the new Order of Mass because they are given in their proper place,
that is, in the Roman Missal for the Mass of the Lord's Supper on Holy Thursday: Not 5 (1969) 403–404,
no. 15.

[R59] Query: When may the special formulary for the dead be used in Eucharistic Prayers II and III? The
source of this query is the phrasing of the rubric for Eucharistic Prayer III: "When this prayer is used *in
Masses for the dead . . . ."* (See *Preces eucharisticae et praefationes*, Vatican Polyglot Press, 1967, p. 35). This rubric
has been clarified in the new Order of Mass (GIRM no. 322 b): "When Mass is celebrated *for any dead person*
. . . ." Thus the special embolism for the deceased may be used in any Mass that is celebrated for a dead
person or in which a dead person receives special remembrance. The purpose of the law is to facilitate the
carrying out of the GIRM no. 316 on restraint in using the Masses for the dead: Not 5 (1969) 325, no. 4.

[b] OM and MR'70 add "and it is particularly appropriate in an assembly of the faithful who possess a
more thorough knowledge of sacred Scripture."

[R60] Query: When is a particular preface to be regarded as proper? Reply: The problem arises mainly
from the possibility of using Eucharistic Prayer IV, which has a fixed preface and consequently is governed by the rule that it may not be used when a Mass has its own proper preface (GIRM no. 322 d).
Further, the preface of the season is said on feasts and also during the particular seasons, some of which
are quite long, and this raises the question of the meaning of "proper preface." A preface is to be regarded

Because of the structure of this prayer no special formulary for the dead may be inserted.

e. A eucharistic prayer that has its own preface may be used with that preface, even when the Mass calls for the preface of the season.[c]

1713   323. In any Mass the prayers belonging to that Mass are used, unless otherwise noted.

In Masses on a memorial, however, the opening prayer or collect may be from the Mass itself or from the common; the prayer over the gifts and prayer after communion, unless they are proper, may be taken either from the common or from the weekdays of the current season.[R61]

On the weekdays in Ordinary Time, the prayers may be taken from the preceding Sunday, from another Sunday in Ordinary Time, or from the prayers for various needs and occasions[d] listed in the Missal. It is always permissible even to use the opening prayer from these Masses.

This provides a rich collection of texts that create an opportunity continually to rephrase the themes of prayer for the liturgical assembly and also to adapt the prayer to the needs of the people, the Church, and the world. During the more important seasons of the year, however, the proper seasonal prayers appointed for each day in the Missal already make this adaptation.

SONG

1714   324. The norms laid down in their proper places are to be observed for the choice of chants between the readings and the songs for the processions at the entrance, presentation of the gifts, and communion.

SPECIAL PERMISSIONS

1715   325. In addition to the permissions just given to choose more suitable texts, the conferences of bishops have the right in some circumstances to make further adaptations of readings, but on condition that the texts are taken from an approved lectionary.

---

as "proper" in a strict sense in Masses that are celebrated on the very day of a feast or during its *octave*. In the Proper of Seasons there is a corresponding preface, but this is not to be regarded as proper strictly speaking and during the season Eucharistic Prayer IV and Eucharistic Prayer II with their own prefaces may be used. In votive Masses there is the option to use either the preface corresponding to the Mass or the preface of any eucharistic prayer: Not 5 (1969) 323, no. 1.

    [c] OM lacks "e."

    [R61] Query: In Masses on a memorial may the prayer over the gifts and the prayer after communion, unless they are proper, also be taken from the votive Masses or from the votive prayers for various needs and occasions? Reply: The GIRM no. 323 says: "In Masses on a memorial, however, . . . the prayer over the gifts and the prayer after communion, unless they are proper, may be taken *either* from the common *or* from the weekday of the current season." For the celebration of a memorial is combined with the celebration of the current weekday; but Masses of saints cannot be combined with the Masses for various needs and occasions: Not 7 (1971) 112, no. 1.

    [d] OM and MR'70: "from the prayers *ad diversa*" for "from the prayers for various needs and occasions."

CHAPTER VIII
MASSES AND PRAYERS FOR VARIOUS NEEDS AND
OCCASIONS AND MASSES FOR THE DEAD

I. MASSES AND PRAYERS FOR VARIOUS NEEDS AND OCCASIONS[a]

326. For well-disposed Christians the liturgy of the sacraments and sacramentals causes almost every event in human life to be made holy by divine grace that flows from the paschal mystery.[95] The eucharist, in turn, is the sacrament of sacraments. Accordingly, the Missal provides formularies for Masses and prayers that may be used in the various circumstances of Christian life, for the needs of the whole world, and for the needs of the Church, both local and universal.

1716

327. In view of the broad options for choosing the readings and prayers, the Masses for various needs and occasions should be used sparingly, that is, when the occasion requires.

1717

328. In all the Masses for various needs and occasions, unless otherwise indicated, the weekday readings and the chants between them may be used, if they are suited to the celebration.

1718

329. The Masses for various needs and occasions are of three types:

1719

a. the ritual Masses, which are related to the celebration of certain sacraments or sacramentals;[b]

b. the Masses for various needs and occasions, which are used either as circumstances arise or at fixed times;

c. the votive Masses of the mysteries of the Lord or in honor of Mary or a particular saint or of all the saints,[c] which are options provided in favor of the faithful's devotion.

330. Ritual Masses are prohibited on the Sundays of Advent, Lent, and the Easter season, on solemnities, on days within the octave of Easter, on All Souls, on Ash Wednesday, and during Holy Week.[d] In addition, the norms in the ritual books or in the Masses themselves also apply.[e]

1720

331. From the selection of Masses for various needs and occasions, the competent authority may choose Masses for those special days of prayer that the conferences of bishops may decree during the course of the year.

1721

332. In cases of serious need or pastoral advantage, at the direction of the local Ordinary or with his permission, an appropriate Mass may be celebrated on any

1722

---

a   OM and MR '70: add "and votive Masses" in both headings.

95   See SC art. 61 [DOL 1 no. 61].

b   OM adds "or their anniversary."

c   OM and MR'70: "and of the saints" for "a particular . . . saints."

d   MR'70 lacks "on days within . . ., All Souls."

e   OM: "330. The use of ritual Masses is governed by norms proper to them that are given in the books of the rites or in the Masses themselves."

day except solemnities, the Sundays of Advent, Lent, and the Easter season, days within the octave of Easter, on All Souls,[f] Ash Wednesday, and during Holy Week.[g]

1723 333. On obligatory memorials, on the weekdays of Advent until 16 December, of the Christmas season after 2 January, and of the Easter season after the octave of Easter, Masses for various needs and occasions are per se forbidden. But if some real need or pastoral advantage requires, at the discretion of the rector of the church or the priest celebrant, the Masses corresponding to such need or advantage may be used in a celebration with a congregation.[h,R62]

1724 334. On weekdays in Ordinary Time when there is an optional memorial or the office is of that weekday,[i] any Mass or prayer for various needs and occasions is permitted, but ritual Masses are excluded.

II. MASSES FOR THE DEAD

1725 335. The Church offers Christ's paschal sacrifice for the dead so that on the basis of the communion existing between all Christ's members, the petition for spiritual help on behalf of some members may bring others comforting hope.

1726 336. The funeral Mass has first place among the Masses for the dead and may be celebrated on any day except solemnities that are days of obligation,[i] Holy Thursday, the Easter triduum,[k] and the Sundays of Advent, Lent, and the Easter season.[R63]

---

[f] MR'70 lacks "days within . . ., All Souls."

[g] OM: "332. In case of serious need, at the direction of the local Ordinary or with his permission, a Mass for this need may be celebrated on all days except solemnities and the Sundays of Advent, Lent, and the Easter season."

[h] OM: "333. On days when there is an obligatory memorial, if some real need requires, at the discretion of the rector of the church or the priest celebrant, Masses corresponding to this need may be used in a celebration with a congregation."
MR'70: "333. On days when there is an obligatory memorial or on a weekday of Advent, the Christmas and Easter seasons, when votive Masses are forbidden, if some real need or pastoral advantage requires, at the discretion of the rector of the church or the priest celebrating, Masses corresponding to this need or advantage may be used in a celebration with a congregation."

[R62] 1. Query: May the votive Masses of Jesus Christ the High Priest, the Sacred Heart, the Immaculate Heart of Mary be celebrated, respectively, on the first Thursday, Friday, and Saturday of the month even if an obligatory memorial occurs? Reply: They may be celebrated observing the rule of GIRM no. 333 "If some real need [text quoted] congregation." The decision about a real need is based on consideration of the sensibilities and devotion of the people: Not 5 (1969) 404, no. 17.
2. Query. What is meant by the weekdays of Advent, Christmas, and the Easter season on which "if some real need . . . [text quoted] congregation" (GIRM no. 333) ? Reply: These are the weekdays that are listed in the Table of Liturgical Days no. 13, i.e., "weekdays of Advent up to 16 December inclusive; weekdays of the Christmas season from 2 January until the Saturday after Epiphany; weekdays of the Easter season from the Monday after the octave of Easter until the Saturday before Pentecost inclusive" [DOL 442 no. 3825]. Since the GIRM no. 333 does not speak of the weekdays of Lent, neither does it intend to speak of the weekdays of Advent from 17 to 24 December inclusive nor of the days within the octave of Christmas, which in the Table of Liturgical Days no. 9 [DOL 442 no. 3825] are ranked with the weekdays of Lent: Not 10 (1974) 145, no. 1.

[i] OM: "334. On days when there is an obligatory memorial or the office is of the weekday in Ordinary Time . . ."

[j] OM lacks "that are days of obligation."

[k] OM and MR'70 lack "Holy Thursday, the Easter triduum."

[R63] 1. Query: May a funeral Mass be celebrated during the octaves of Christmas and Easter? Reply: Yes. The rule of the GIRM no. 336 is that of the Masses for the dead the one for a funeral may be celebrated on any day except holydays of obligation, the Sundays of Advent and Lent, and Easter Sunday.

337. On the occasions of news of a death, final burial, or the first anniversary, Mass   1727
for the dead may be celebrated even on days within the Christmas octave,[1] on
obligatory memorials, and on weekdays, except Ash Wednesday and during Holy
Week.[m,R64]

Other Masses for the dead, that is, daily Masses, may be celebrated on weekdays in Ordinary Time when there is an optional memorial or the office is of the
weekday, provided such Masses are actually offered for the dead.[n]

338. At the funeral Mass there should as a rule be a short homily, but never a   1728
eulogy of any kind. The homily is also recommended at other Masses for the dead
celebrated with a congregation.

339. All the faithful, and especially the family, should be urged to share in the   1729
eucharistic sacrifice offered for the deceased person by receiving communion.

340. If the funeral Mass is directly joined to the burial rite, once the prayer after   1730
communion has been said and omitting the rite of dismissal, the rite of final commendation or of farewell takes place, but only when the body is present.

341. In the planning and choosing of the variable parts of the Mass for the dead,   1731
especially the funeral Mass (for example, prayers, readings, general intercessions)
pastoral considerations bearing upon the deceased, the family, and those attending
should rightly be foremost.

Pastors should, moreover, take into special account those who are present at a
liturgical celebration or hear the Gospel only because of the funeral. These may be
non-Catholics or Catholics who never or rarely share in the eucharist or who have
apparently lost the faith. Priests are, after all, ministers of Christ's Gospel for all
people.

Therefore it may be celebrated during the octaves of Christmas or Easter: Not 6 (1970) 263, no. 37.
    2. Query: May a funeral Mass be celebrated on Holy Thursday and during the Easter triduum?
Reply: No. The directives in the Roman Missal apply. On Holy Thursday morning as a rule the chrism
Mass is celebrated (MR pp. 239–242). In addition to the evening Mass of the Lord's Supper "the local
Ordinary may permit another Mass to be celebrated in churches and public or semipublic oratories in the
evening or, in the case of genuine necessity, even in the morning, but exclusively for those who cannot in
any way take part in the evening Mass" (MR p. 243 [RM, Holy Thursday "Evening Mass of the Lord's
Supper"]). Other eucharistic celebrations on Holy Thursday are entirely forbidden. On Good Friday
"according to the Church's ancient tradition, the sacraments are not celebrated" (MR p. 250 [RM, Good
Friday, "Celebration of the Lord's Passion"]). "On Holy Saturday the Church waits at the Lord's tomb,
. . . and the sacrifice of the Mass is not celebrated" (MR p. 265 [RM, Holy Saturday]). In the case of
Easter Sunday, the GIRM no. 336 already forbids a funeral Mass, since this is a solemnity that is of
obligation: Not 10 (1974) 145–146. See also DOL 416 no. 3378, note R1.

  [1] MR'70 lacks "days within the Christmas octave."

  [m] OM: "337. A Mass for the dead may be celebrated even on days when there is an obligatory
memorial: on the occasions of the news of a death, the final burial, or the first anniversary.

  [R64] 1. Query: May the Masses for the dead referred to in the GIRM no. 337 be celebrated even on
weekdays of Lent? Reply: Yes. The Masses mentioned in no. 337 (on the occasions of news of a death,
final burial, or the first anniversary) may be celebrated on all weekdays, with the exception only of Ash
Wednesday and the weekdays of Holy Week: Not 6 (1970) 264, no. 38.
    2. Query: May a Mass for the dead after news of a death or on the day of final burial or the first
anniversary be celebrated even within the octave of Christmas? Reply: Yes. According to the GIRM no.
337 these Masses are allowed on weekdays from 17 to 24 December inclusive and on the weekdays of
Lent. Therefore they may be celebrated on days within the octave of Christmas, which the Table of
Liturgical Days no. 9 [DOL 442 no. 3825] ranks with those weekdays: Not 10 (1974) 146, no. 4.

  [n] OM and MR'70: "Other Masses for the dead, that is, daily Masses, may be celebrated on the same
days on which votive Masses are allowed, provided such Masses are actually offered for the dead."

▶   93.   PAUL VI, Address to a consistory, excerpt on the liturgy, 28 April 1969:

The new Order of Mass [no. 675].

209. SC DIVINE WORSHIP, **Instruction** *Constitutione Apostolica*, on the gradual carrying out of the Apostolic Constitution *Missale Romanum* (3 April
1969), 20 October 1969: AAS 61 (1969) 749–753; Not 5 (1969) 418–423.

1732   The Apostolic Constitution *Missale Romanum*, issued by Pope Paul VI on 3 April
of this year,ª approved the new *Missale Romanum* as revised by decree of Vatican
Council II. Up to the present, three parts of the Missal have appeared, the *Instructio
generalis Missalis Romani*, the *Ordo Missae* (promulgated by decree of the Congregation
of Rites, 6 April 1969),ᵇ and the *Ordo lectionum Missae* (issued by the Congregation for
Divine Worship, 25 May 1969).ᶜ The other parts of the Missal will appear very
soon.

The decrees mentioned stipulated that the effective date for use of the new
rites and texts is to be 30 November 1969, the First Sunday of Advent. But in fact
the carrying out of this phase of the revision of the Mass presents many major
difficulties: the immense work involved in preparing translations and new editions
of books; the need to impart precise and effective instruction; the need to change
smoothly the accustomed practices of priests and people.

Consequently, in response to the requests of many bishops and conferences of
bishops, the Congregation for Divine Worship, with the approval of Pope Paul VI,
has decided on the present norms for the gradual carrying out of the Apostolic
Constitution *Missale Romanum*. These norms supplement those issued by this
Congregation, 25 July 1969, on editions and use of the new *Lectionary for Mass*.[1]

I. ON THE ORDER OF MASS

1733   1.   The Latin text of the revised Order of Mass may be used beginning with 30
November 1969.

1734   2.   The conferences of bishops are to fix the date on which vernacular translations
of this Order of Mass may be used. But the best course is for translations of the text
for the new Order of Mass to be made as quickly as possible and, once approved, to
be put into use before the other texts of the Roman Missal have been translated.

1735   3.   Vernacular translations of the new Order of Mass are to be approved, at least
provisorily, by the conference of bishops (or by the national liturgical commission
together with at least an executive committee of the conference of bishops); they
are also to be submitted for the confirmation of this Congregation.[2]

ª   See DOL 202.

ᵇ   See DOL 203.

ᶜ   See DOL 232.

[1]   See AAS 61 (1969) 548–549 [DOL 233].

[2]   See Consilium, Declaration on the *ad interim* translation of liturgical texts: Not 5 (1969) 68 [DOL
124].

4.   There is to be a single translation of the text for the Order of Mass for all   1736
regions using the same language.[3] The same applies to other parts that call for direct
participation by the people.

5.   It is up to the conference of bishops to approve new melodies for parts of the   1737
Mass to be sung in the vernacular by celebrant and ministers.[4]

6.   The necessary catechesis is to precede actual use of the rites and texts for the   1738
new Order of Mass. Assistance for this is to come from national liturgical institutes
and diocesan liturgical commissions as well as from the use of all effective resources
(for example, study groups, conferences, articles published in newspapers or journals or circulated in some other way, or by explanations broadcast on radio and
television). The purpose is to help people and priests to have a thorough understanding and appreciation of the import of the new norms.

7.   The individual conferences of bishops are to appoint a date on which use of   1739
the new Order of Mass will become obligatory, except in those cases specified in
this Instruction nos. 19–20. That date is not to be later than 28 November 1971.

8.   Assisted by the respective bishops' committees and liturgical institutes, the   1740
conferences of bishops have the further responsibility of making the necessary
decisions on matters that the General Instruction of the Roman Missal leaves up to
them. They are to decide on:

    a.   the faithful's movements, standing, kneeling, and sitting during Mass;[5]

    b.   the reverences made to the altar and the Book of the Gospels;[6]

    c.   how the sign of peace is to be given;[7]

    d.   the permission to have only two readings at Mass on Sundays and holy-
days;[8]

    e.   the permission authorizing women to proclaim the scriptural readings be-
fore the gospel.[9]

II. OTHER TEXTS OF THE ROMAN MISSAL

9.   The Latin text of the Roman Missal may be used as soon as it is published.   1741

10.   The individual conferences of bishops are to set a date on which use of transla-   1742
tions of the texts of the new Roman Missal is authorized. It is permissible to
proceed step by step in this matter, introducing the translations one after the other
as soon as they have been approved; there is no need to wait until all the texts have
been translated. Accordingly, it will be possible to put into use, for example, texts
for the Proper of Seasons even though those for the Proper of Saints or of the
Commons, Masses for various needs and occasions, or for votive Masses are not yet

---

   [3]   See Letter to presidents of the conferences of bishops, "On uniform liturgical translations for a
language used in many places," 16 Oct. 1964 [DOL 108]. Instruction, "On the translation of liturgical
texts for celebrations with a congregation," 25 Jan. 1969, nos. 41–42 [DOL 123 nos. 878–879].

   [4]   See SCR, Instr. InterOec, 26 Sept. 1964, no. 42 [DOL 23 no. 334; Instr. MusSacr, 5 March 1967, no.
57 [DOL 508 no. 4178].

   [5]   See GIRM no. 21 [DOL 208 no. 1411].

   [6]   See GIRM no. 232 [DOL 208 no. 1622].

   [7]   See GIRM no. 56 b [DOL 208 no. 1446].

   [8]   See GIRM no. 318 [DOL 208 no. 1708].

   [9]   See GIRM no. 66 [DOL 208 no. 1456].

ready. It is best, however, to introduce parts of the new texts into the liturgy at the beginning of some season of the liturgical year (for example, Advent, Lent, the Easter season).

1743   11.   Translations of new texts of the Roman Missal also are to be approved, at least provisorily, by the conference of bishops (or by the national liturgical commission together with at least the executive council of the conference of bishops); they are also to be submitted for confirmation by this Congregation.[10]

1744   12.   It is up to the conferences of bishops to prepare a collection of vernacular texts for the songs at the entrance, presentation of the gifts, and communion.[11] Upon its approval of such a collection, the conference of bishops will at the same time strongly encourage experts in the field to add to and improve this collection, guided by the texts given in the new Roman Missal and by the genius and idiom of each language.

1745   13.   As the new Order of Mass is being used before publication of the new Roman Missal, the texts for antiphons and prayers are to be taken from the existing Missal, but with the following being observed.

    a.   If the entrance antiphon is not sung, it is said only once, without the psalm verse and *Gloria Patri*.[12]

    b.   If not sung, the antiphon for the presentation of the gifts is omitted;[13]

    c.   The prayer over the gifts and the prayer after communion are concluded with the short form.[14]

1746   14.   The individual conferences of bishops are to decide on the date when the texts of the new Roman Missal are to become obligatory, except for the cases that are specified in this Instruction nos. 20–21. It is better that such a date be no later than 28 November 1971.

III. LECTIONARY FOR MASS

1747   15.   The individual conferences of bishops are to fix a date on which the new *Lectionary for Mass* may be used or must be used.

1748   16.   While awaiting the translation as well as this Congregation's confirmation of the text of the new readings, the conferences of bishops are empowered to grant permission for interim use of one or more lawfully approved versions of the Bible. In this case the conferences will make sure that priests have available to them the requisite biblical listings as found in the *Lectionary for Mass* (that is, the chapter and verse numbers, the *incipits*, the divisions of the selected passages). This applies in a particular way to the readings for Year B of the Sunday cycle, use of which begins on 30 November 1969.

1749   17.   Until the texts of the new Lectionary are ready, the readings of the current Roman Missal are to be kept. It is also permissible *ad interim* to make use of orders of

---

    [10]   See no. 3 of this Instruction.

    [11]   See GIRM nos. 26, 50, 56 i [DOL 208 nos. 1416, 1440, 1446].

    [12]   See GIRM no. 26 [DOL 208 no. 1416].

    [13]   See GIRM no. 50 [DOL 208 no. 1440].

    [14]   See GIRM no. 32 [DOL 208 no. 1422].

readings approved for trial use and which are now being used for weekdays, ritual Masses for some of the sacraments, Masses for the dead, some votive Masses, etc.[15]

18. To safeguard the liturgical and pastoral importance of the responsorial psalm, the authorized national commissions are to draw up a temporary list, from the collection now being used, of psalms and verses that most closely correspond to the *Lectionary for Mass*.[16]   1750

These commissions should not fail to give strong encouragement to experts in the field to add to and improve the traditional collection of such texts and their melodies, guided by the texts available in the new *Lectionary for Mass* and the genius and idiom of each language.

The same sort of collection should be composed for the verses before the gospel.

IV. EXCEPTION

19. Elderly priests who celebrate Mass without a congregation and who might encounter serious difficulty in taking up the new Order of Mass and the new texts of the Roman Missal and *Lectionary for Mass*, may, with the consent of their Ordinary, keep to the rites and texts now in use.   1751

20. Special cases of priests who are infirm, ill, or otherwise disabled are to be submitted to this Congregation.   1752

Pope Paul VI approved this Instruction on 18 October 1969 and ordered its publication for the exact observance of all concerned.[R65]

210. SC DIVINE WORSHIP, **Letter** *Cum nonnullae Conferentiae* to presidents of the conferences of bishops, issuing norms on the Latin texts to be incorporated into vernacular editions of the Roman Missal, 10 November 1969: Not 5 (1969) 442–443.

Many conferences of bishops, engaged in the preparation of new vernacular editions of the Roman Missal, have inquired whether it is obligatory that such editions have an appendix containing the Latin text. Accordingly this Congregation, having weighed the matter, has decided on the following, with the approval of Pope Paul VI.   1753

---

   [15]   See the Instruction, "On preparing editions of the new *Lectionary for Mass* and on their use," 25 July 1969, nos. 4–5 [DOL 233 nos. 1874–75].

   [16]   See also the common texts for the singing of the responsorial psalm in the *Lectionary for Mass* nos. 174–175.

   R65   Not 5 (1969) 418–419 adds the following notation: When this Instruction was published certain second-rate writers made the unfounded claim that it had been prepared in response to the chidings and demands of a certain unfortunate pamphlet circulated in Rome in the second part of October. This is utterly naive. The Instruction has the following chronology and genesis. It was first proposed in September; the first draft was completed on 4 October. After several revisions of the text, as is the usual course in drawing up such documents, the final text was presented to Pope Paul VI and received approval on 20 October (which is its true, not fabricated date). Finally on 28 October a copy was sent to be published in *L'Osservatore Romano*. A comparing of the dates in question makes it altogether clear that this Instruction had an origin and development utterly unrelated to the pamphlet mentioned.

1754 1. The Latin text need not be printed in vernacular editions of the Roman Missal intended for liturgical use.

1755 2. But to facilitate celebration of Mass for priests not knowing the local language, all missals should, in addition to the vernacular text, carry in a convenient place (in an appendix, for example) the Latin text for:

a. the entire *Ordo Missae*, along with a selection of prefaces and the four eucharistic prayers;

b. several Mass formularies, usable in accord with the different liturgical days and seasons.

Texts to be added on such a basis are contained in an annex to this letter.[R66]

1756 3. Bishops should make sure that in all churches a copy of the Roman Missal in Latin is available. They should also make sure that in shrine churches the Latin text of the Mass proper to the place is available.

We take the occasion to inform Your Excellency also of the following:

a. The Vatican press has charge of printing the Latin *editio typica* of the Roman Missal; in addition to the Order of Mass this will include the texts for antiphons, prayers and prefaces for the entire cycle of the liturgical year.

b. The Vatican Press also is preparing an edition of the *Lectionary for Mass*, with not only the scriptural references but with the complete Latin text of the readings.

These volumes will be ready within the next few months.

211. PAUL VI, Address to a general audience, on the new Order of Mass about to be introduced, 19 November 1969: AAS 61 (1969) 777–780; Not 5 (1969) 409–412 (Italian).

1757 We wish to call your attention to an event that is on the verge of taking place in the Latin Catholic Church and to something that will become a matter of obligation in the dioceses of Italy on the First Sunday of Advent, which this year is on 30 November. We speak of the introduction into the liturgy of a new rite for the Mass. The Mass is to be celebrated in a form somewhat different from the one customary for the past four centuries, since the time of St. Pius V after the Council of Trent.

Because the Mass is the traditional and most inviolable expression of our religious worship and of the authenticity of our faith, the change is somewhat amazing and extraordinary. We may well ask these questions: How could such a change take place? In what does it consist? What effect will it have for those who attend Mass? The replies to these and other, similar questions prompted by something so singularly new will be amply provided and repeated in all churches, in religious publications, and in schools where Christian doctrine is taught. We urge you to pay heed to these replies and in this way to have as clear and appreciative an understanding as you can of the overwhelming and mysterious significance of the Mass.

For now, however, we shall use this brief and simple discourse to rid your minds of the first and quite natural perplexities that the change raises about the three questions already proposed.

[R66] See DOL 125, no. 884, note R3, Queries 3 and 4.

How could such a change take place? The answer is that it is due to the express will of the recent ecumenical Council. The Council has this to say: "The Order of Mass is to be revised in a way that will bring out more clearly the intrinsic nature and purpose of its several parts, as also the connection between them, and will more readily achieve the devout, active participation of the faithful. For this purpose the rites are to be simplified, due care being taken to preserve their substance; elements that, with the passage of time, came to be duplicated or were added with but little advantage are now to be discarded; other elements that have suffered injury through accident of history are now, as may seem useful or necessary, to be restored to that vigor they had in the tradition of the Fathers."[1]   1758

Thus the reform about to take place everywhere is the response to an authoritative mandate of the Church. It is an act of obedience, a matter of the Church's being consistent. It is a step forward in the Church's genuine tradition. It is a clear sign of faithfulness and vitality to which we must all give ready allegiance. It is not a fad, a fleeting or optional experiment, the invention of some dilettante. The reform is a law thought out by authorities in the field of liturgy, debated and studied at length. We would do well to welcome it with joyous enthusiasm and to put it into practice exactly and with one accord. This reform puts an end to uncertainty, arguments, and misguided experiments. It summons us back to that uniformity of rites and of attitudes that is proper to the Catholic Church, the heir and continuator of the first Christian community that was "of one heart and of one soul."[2] The harmonious chorus of its prayer is one of the signs and strengths of the Church's unity and catholicity. The change about to take place must not shatter or disturb that harmony, but rather intensify it and make it resound with a new, rejuvenated spirit.

The second question: In what does the change consist? You will find out. It involves a great many new ritual rules, which, especially at the outset, will call for a measure of attention and caution. Individual devotion and the sense of community will make it easy and agreeable to observe these new rules. But be very sure of one point: nothing of the substance of the traditional Mass has been altered. Some people might let themselves be persuaded that a particular ceremony or its accompanying rubric involves or implies an altering or lessening of the truth received once for ever and authoritatively guaranteed by Catholic faith. They might thus conclude that the equation between the *lex orandi* and the *lex credendi* has been jeopardized.   1759

That is absolutely not the case. Above all because no particular rite or rubric amounts in itself to a dogmatic definition. Such things are all subject to a theological evaluation, differing according to their context in the liturgy. They are all gestures and words related to a religious activity that is lived and living by reason of an inexpressible mystery, a divine presence, and that is carried out in diverse ways. Such religious activity is of a kind that only a theological critique can analyze and articulate in doctrinal formulas that satisfy logic. The second reason is that the Mass in its new order is and will remain the Mass it always has been and in some aspects bears increased evidence of being so. The unity between the Lord's Supper, the sacrifice of the cross, and the renewal representing both in the Mass is unfailingly affirmed and celebrated in the new rite, just as it was in the old. The Mass is and will remain the memorial of the Lord's Supper. There, changing bread and wine into his own body and blood, he instituted the sacrifice of the New Testament. By virtue of the priesthood conferred on his apostles, he willed that sacrifice to be

---

[1]   SC art. 50 [DOL 1 no. 50].

[2]   Acts 4:32.

renewed in its identical reality, but in a different mode, that is, unbloodily and sacramentally, as his perpetual memorial until his final coming.[3]

You will find set into the new rite with greater clarity the relationship between the liturgy of the word and the liturgy of the eucharist, so that the second corresponds to the first as its actualization.[4] You will also notice a fresh appeal for the assistance of the faithful at the eucharistic sacrifice; at Mass they are "the Church" and they have a sense that this is so. You may also see other wonderful marks of our Mass made more striking. Do not think that all this is meant to change the true, traditional essence of the Mass. Seek rather to learn to appreciate how the Church, through this new and more explicit language, wishes to give greater effectiveness to its liturgical message, and wishes, in a more direct and pastoral way, to draw near to each one of its children and to the people of God as a whole.

And so we come to reply to the third question: What effect will the change have on those who attend Mass? The result anticipated — or better, longed for — is the more intelligent, more effective, more joyous, and more sanctifying participation by the people in the liturgical mystery. That means their sharing in the hearing of the word of God, alive and resounding across the ages and in the history of our own souls; their sharing as well in the mystical reality of Christ's sacramental and propitiatory sacrifice.

Let us then not speak of a "new Mass," but of a "new age" in the life of the Church. We close with our apostolic blessing.

212. PAUL VI, **Address** to a general audience, on the new *Ordo Missae*, 26 November 1969: Not 5 (1969) 412–416 (Italian).

1760 Again we wish to invite you to direct your thoughts to the liturgical innovations in the new rite of Mass that will come into use in our celebration of the holy sacrifice next Sunday, 30 November, the First Sunday of Advent. A new rite of Mass means a change in a revered, centuries-old tradition. Hence it involves our religious heritage, a patrimony that had a right to an untouchable permanence, to put on our lips the prayer of our forefathers and saints, and to give us the assurance of fidelity to our spiritual past, which we make present so as to pass it on to the generations yet to come. Under the present circumstances we understand better the value of historical tradition and the communion of saints. The change affects the carrying out of the ceremonies of the Mass. We shall notice, perhaps with some uneasiness, that the rites at the altar are not proceeding with those words and gestures we had become so used to as to take them for granted. The change also affects the faithful. It should interest all those who are present, distracting them from their familiar personal devotions or usual lethargy.

We shall have to prepare for this many-sided upheaval, which, of course, is typical of any kind of newness introduced into our accustomed way of doing things. We might note that devout people are the ones who will be most disturbed; having their own laudable way of attending Mass, they will feel themselves torn away from their usual thoughts and obliged to replace them with others. Even priests themselves may find the experience troubling.

---

[3] See M. de la Taille, *Mysterium Fidei*, Elucid. 9.

[4] See Bouyer.

What should we do when we are faced with such an extraordinary and historic   1761
event? First of all, we must prepare ourselves. The innovation is no small matter.
We must not let ourselves be taken by surprise by the appearance, or perhaps even
the annoyance, of the external forms of the new rite. Intelligent people and an alert
faithful have a responsibility to become informed about the new measures we
speak of. Thanks to the many excellent measures taken in churches and in publications this is not difficult to do.

As noted on another occasion, we would do well to realize the reasons behind
the introduction of this serious change.[a] The first reason is obedience to the Council, which then becomes obedience to the bishops, who interpret and carry out its
prescriptions. This first reason is not a mere canonical matter, that is, one involving
only external precept; it is connected with the charism of the liturgical life, that is,
with the power and effectiveness of ecclesial prayer. This prayer finds its most
authoritative expression in the bishop and, therefore, in priests, who assist him in
his ministry and who, like him, act *in persona Christi*.[1] The will of Christ and the
inspiration of the Holy Spirit summon the Church to this change. We should
recognize the prophetic phase transpiring in the Mystical Body of Christ, the
Church. It is stirring the Church, awakening it, and obliging it to revitalize the
mysterious art of its prayer. The purpose of this movement in the Church is also, as
we have already said,[b] the second reason for the reform. That purpose is to unite
the assembly of the faithful as closely and effectively as possible to the official rite
of the liturgy of the word and of the eucharist, which make up the Mass. For the
faithful too are "a royal priesthood," that is, endowed with the power for supernatural communion with God.

Clearly the most noticeable new departure is that of language. From now on   1762
the vernacular, not Latin, will be the principal language of the Mass. For those who
appreciate the beauty of Latin, its power, and aptness to express the sacred, substitution of the vernacular certainly represents a great sacrifice. We are losing the
idiom of the Christian ages; we become like profane intruders into the literary
sanctuary of sacred language; we shall lose a large portion of that wonderful and
incomparable, artistic and spiritual reality, Gregorian chant. We indeed have reason
for sadness and perhaps even for bewilderment. What shall we put in the place of
this angelic language? We are sacrificing a priceless treasure. For what reason? What
is worth more than these sublime values of the Church? The answer may seem trite
and prosaic, but it is sound because it is both human and apostolic. Our understanding of prayer is worth more than the previous, ancient garments in which it
has been regally clad. Of more value, too, is the participation of the people, of
modern people who are surrounded by clear, intelligible language, translatable into
their ordinary conversation. If our sacred Latin should, like a thick curtain, close us
off from the world of children and young people, of work and the business of
everyday, then would we, fishers of men, be wise to allow it exclusive dominion
over the speech of religion and prayer?

What does St. Paul tell us? "In the church, I would rather speak five words of
my own understanding so that by my voice I may also instruct others, than ten
thousand words in an unknown tongue."[2] And St. Augustine seems to add his own

---

[a]   See DOL 211 no. 1758.

[1]   See Ignatius of Antioch, *Ad Eph*. IV.

[b]   See DOL 211 no. 1758.

[2]   1 Cor. 14:19.

comment when he says: "Provided all are instructed, there need be no fear of who the teachers are."[3] Moreover, the new Mass rite lays down the provision that the faithful "should know how to sing at least some parts of the Ordinary of the Mass in Latin, especially the profession of faith and the Lord's Prayer."[4] But let us remember well, as both an admonition and a consolation; that Latin will certainly not disappear in our Church. It will remain the noble language of the Apostolic See's official pronouncements, the academic vehicle for ecclesiastical studies, and the key that unlocks for us the heritage of our religious, historical, and literary culture, and, if possible, it will have a new and resplendent awakening.

1763   Finally, close examination will reveal that the fundamental plan of the Mass in its theological and spiritual import remains what it always has been. As a matter of fact, if the rite is carried out as it should be, that spiritual import will stand out in even greater richness. This will be so because of the greater simplicity of the ceremonies, the variety and number of biblical texts, the coordinated actions of the various ministers, the set moments of silence interspersed at the different stages of the rite, and above all because of the two indispensable requisites — the intimate participation of each individual present and the outpouring of hearts in a mutual charity. These two last requirements should make the Mass, more than ever before, a school of deep spirituality and a serene but exacting training for Christian social living. The soul's relationship with Christ and with other people acquires a new and vital intensity. Through the Church's minister, Christ the priest and victim renews and offers his redemptive sacrifice. He does so in the rite symbolizing his last supper, which left to us his body and blood under the appearances of bread and wine for our personal and spiritual nourishment and for our fusion into the unity of his redemptive love and immortal life.

1764   A practical difficulty remains, however, which is quite important because of the special nature of the sacred rite. How are we to celebrate this new rite when we do not yet have a complete missal and when so many uncertainties still surround the way it is to be carried out? To answer these questions, it will help to read you some of the following directives that come to us from the competent office, the Congregation for Divine Worship.

"As far as the obligatory aspects of the new rite are concerned:

1. *"Regarding the Latin text:* Priests who celebrate Mass in Latin, in private, or even in public for those cases provided for in the law, can use either the Roman Missal or the new rite until 28 November 1971.

"If they use the Roman Missal, they may use the three new anaphoras and the Roman Canon, with the options provided for in the latest text (omission of some saints, of the conclusions, etc.). The readings and the prayer of the faithful may be in the vernacular.

"If they use the new rite, they are to follow the official text, with the aforementioned permissions for use of the vernacular.

2. *"Regarding the vernacular text:* In Italy, effective 30 November this year, all those who celebrate Mass with a congregation are to use the Order of Mass published by the Italian conference of bishops or by another national conference.

"The readings for Sundays and holydays will be taken: either from the lectionary published by the Centro Azione Liturgica; or from the Roman Missal for Sundays and holydays that has been used up to now.

³   Augustine, *Serm.* 37: PL 38, 228; see also *Serm.* 299: PL 38, 1371.

⁴   GIRM no. 19 [DOL 208 no. 1409].

"On weekdays, they shall continue to use the weekday lectionary published three years ago.

"There is no problem for those who celebrate Mass in private because they *must celebrate Mass in Latin*. If, by virtue of a particular indult, they celebrate Mass in the vernacular: for the texts, they are to follow what has already been said concerning Mass with a congregation; for the rite, however, they are to follow the special *Ordo* published by the Italian conference of bishops."

Let us in every case and always remember that "the Mass is a mystery, in which we live through a death prompted by love. Its divine reality surpasses words. . . . It is the act without equal, the very act of our redemption in the memorial that makes it present."[5]

213. SC DIVINE WORSHIP, **Decree** *Celebrationes eucharisticae*, promulgating the first *editio typica* of the *Missale Romanum*, 26 March 1970: AAS 62 (1970) 554; Not 6 (1970) 169.

The Order of Mass has been established and the texts for the Roman Missal   1765
have been approved by Pope Paul VI in the Apostolic Constitution *Missale Romanum*, 3 April 1969.[a] This Congregation for Divine Worship, at the mandate of the Pope, now promulgates and declares to be the *editio typica* this new edition of the Roman Missal prepared in accord with the decrees of Vatican Council II.

As to use of the new Missal, the Latin edition may be put into use as soon as it is published, with the necessary adjustments of saints' days until the revised calendar is put into definitive effect. As to vernacular editions, the conferences of bishops are given the responsibility for their preparation and for setting the effective date for their use, after due confirmation by the Apostolic See.

214. SC DIVINE WORSHIP, **Comments** *Praesens Missale parvum*, accompanying the edition of the new *Missale parvum*, 18 October 1970: Vatican Polyglot Press, 1970.*

1.   The present *Missale parvum* provides the Masses that, by decree of the Congre-   1766
gation for Divine Worship (Prot. No. 1560/69), must be printed as an appendix in vernacular editions of the Roman Missal[a] to assist priests who do not have at hand in Latin or in another language in which they are able to celebrate Mass the text for the day's Mass.[R67]

It seemed helpful, however, to increase the collection of these Masses as a service for priest celebrants and as a way of avoiding a too frequent repetition of the same Mass texts.

---

[5]   Zundel.

[a]   See DOL 202.

*   Text also in *Missale parvum ad usum sacerdotis itinerantis* (Vatican Polyglot Press, 1974).

[a]   See DOL 210 no. 1755.

[R67]   See DOL 125 no. 884, note R3, Query 4.

1767   2.   As far as possible the priest should choose from these texts one that corresponds more closely to the liturgical day or season.

The Masses for various needs and occasions, votive Masses, or Masses for the dead are to be used when they are allowed according to the general norms.

215. PONTIFICAL COMMISSION FOR THE INTERPRETATION OF THE DECREES OF VATICAN COUNCIL II, **Reply** to a query, on the General Instruction of the Roman Missal no. 42, 11 January 1971: AAS 63 (1971) 329; Not 8 (1972) 370.

1768   Query: The words in the General Instruction of the Roman Missal no. 42, "The homily should ordinarily be given by the celebrant," put into practice the prescriptions of the Constitution *Sacrosanctum Concilium* art. 52[a] and the Dogmatic Constitution *Dei Verbum* no. 24 (see also the Motu Proprio *Sacram Liturgiam*, 29 January 1964, III,[b] and the Instruction of the Congregation for Divine Worship *Liturgicae instaurationes*, 5 September 1970, no. 2[c]). Should these words be interpreted in the sense that those also who are neither priests nor deacons, both men and women, but take part in the liturgy, may give the homily?

Reply: No.

At an audience granted to the undersigned Cardinal President, 11 January, 1971, Pope Paul VI confirmed and approved these decisions and ordered their publication.

216. SC DIVINE WORSHIP, **Notification** *Instructione de Constitutione*, on the Roman Missal, the book of the liturgy of the hours, and the Calendar, 14 June 1971: AAS 63 (1971) 712–715; Not 7 (1971) 215–217.

1769   The Instruction on the gradual carrying out of the Apostolic Constitution *Missale Romanum*, issued 20 October 1969 by this Congregation, set down certain rules that took into consideration particular instances and difficulties regarding use of the new Roman Missal and that granted to the conferences of bishops the faculty to extend the *vacatio legis* until 28 November 1971.[1]

This Congregation also decreed the continuance of the *ad interim* general and particular calendars during the present year 1971.[2]

In consideration of these facts, the Congregation for Divine Worship, with the approval of Pope Paul VI, lays down the following rules on the use of the *Missale Romanum*, the *Liturgia Horarum*, and the reformed Calendar and provides the solution to certain problems regarding the arrangement of the Calendar for the years 1972 and 1973.

---

    [a]   See DOL 1 no. 52.
    [b]   See DOL 20 no. 281.
    [c]   See DOL 52 no. 513.
    [1]   See AAS 61 (1969) 749–753 [DOL 209].
    [2]   See SCDW, Notification, 17 May 1970 [DOL 443].

1. THE MISSALE ROMANUM AND THE LITURGIA HORARUM

1.   In celebrations in Latin use of the *Missale Romanum* and the *Lectionarium Missae*   1770
published by this Congregation is already authorized.[3] The *Liturgia Horarum* may be
used as soon as the books have been published.

2.   The conferences of bishops are to see to completion as soon as possible of the   1771
translation and publication of these books in the vernacular.

With due regard for special problems attendant on these projects, the conferences should, however, settle on a definite date when translations, having their own
approval and the Apostolic See's confirmation, may or must be put into use in
whole or in part.

From the date on which the translated texts become obligatory for celebrations
in the vernacular only the revised form of the Mass and the liturgy of the hours will
be allowed, even for those who continue to use Latin.

3.   Continued use, in whole or in part, of the *Missale Romanum* in the 1962 *editio*   1772
typica, as emended by the 1965 and 1967 decrees[4] and of the *Breviarium Romanum*
formerly in use is allowed, with the consent of the Ordinary and only in celebrations without a congregation, for all those who because of their advanced years or
illness find serious difficulties in using the new Order of Mass in the Roman Missal,
the Lectionary for Mass, or the book of the liturgy of the hours.

4.   Regarding the language used: 1773

a.   *For Masses with a congregation* the conferences of bishops have the right to
decide on use of the vernacular for any part of the Mass.

In the case of conventual Mass in monasteries, particular law is to be
followed.

It is for local Ordinaries to judge, with the good of the faithful as the
decisive consideration, whether once use of the vernacular has begun it seems
advisable to have one or more Masses in Latin, especially sung Masses,[5] in certain
churches, especially those attended by people of a foreign language.

In Latin Masses it is better for the biblical readings and the general intercessions to be in the vernacular, but always with consideration for those taking part
who are of a foreign language.

b.   *In Masses without a congregation* every priest has the option of using either
Latin or the vernacular.

c.   With the consent of the Ordinary, celebration of the liturgy of the hours
whether individually, communally, or chorally, may be in the vernacular.

2. THE CALENDAR

5.   Taking into account the state of the work of translating the *Missale Romanum*   1774
and the *Liturgia Horarum*, the conferences of bishops are to fix a date on which the

---

[3]   See Decr. *Celebrationis eucharisticae*, 26 March 1970 [DOL 213]; Decr. *Ordine lectionum*, 30 Sept. 1970
[DOL 234].

[4]   See SCR, Decr. *Nuper edita*, 27 Jan. 1965 [DOL 196]; Decr. *Per Instructionem alteram*, 18 May 1967 [DOL
201].

[5]   See SCR, Instr. MusSacr, 5 March 1967, no. 48 [DOL 508 no. 4169].

General Calendar, promulgated 14 February 1969 by the Motu Proprio *Mysterii paschalis*,[a] will become obligatory in their territories.

Pending completion of the translation project, the conferences are to issue rules for the calendar that is to be followed in celebrations of the Mass and the liturgy of the hours both in Latin and in the vernacular.

1775   6.   While awaiting its revision, those using a proper calendar are, in the points proper to it, to follow that calendar as currently in force. The rank of celebrations is to be changed, however, to conform to the general norms on the calendar and alterations are to be made on points inconsistent with those general norms. In all else the norms issued by the conference of bishops are obligatory.

The work of revising particular calendars is to be completed within the period fixed by the instruction on this subject.[6]

1776   7.   In 1972 the solemnity of St. Joseph coincides with the Fifth Sunday of Lent. Accordingly it is to be anticipated, that is, celebrated on Saturday, 18 March.[7]

Where pastoral reasons suggest, local Ordinaries may allow use of the Mass for St. Joseph even at evening Masses on Saturday, 18 March, celebrated to fulfill the Sunday obligation.

1777   8.   In 1973, because several solemnities fall on the same day, the calendar is to have the following arrangement:

a.   Sunday, 24 June will be the solemnity of the Birth of St. John the Baptist.

In places where the solemnity of Corpus Christi is transferred to that Sunday, the solemnity of St. John the Baptist is observed the day before, Saturday, 23 June.

b.   Friday, 29 June will be the solemnity of SS. Peter and Paul, and the solemnity of the Sacred Heart is transferred to the following Sunday.

Wherever the solemnity of SS. Peter and Paul is not observed as a holyday of obligation and is ordinarily transferred to the following Sunday, the solemnity of the Sacred Heart will be celebrated on 29 June and the solemnity of St. Peter and St. Paul on 1 July.

217. SECRETARIAT OF STATE, Letter of Cardinal J. Villot to Bishop C. Rossi, President of the Centro di Azione Liturgica, on the occasion of the 22nd National Liturgical Week of Italy at Oropa (30 August – 3 September 1971), on the new Roman Missal, 30 August 1971.*

1778   Pope Paul IV has been informed that from 30 August to 3 September 1971 at the Marian shrine of Oropa the 22nd National Liturgical Week will be held on the theme: "The New Roman Missal."

---

[a]   See DOL 440.

[6]   See SCDW, Instr. on revising particular calendar and the propers for Mass and divine office, 24 June 1970, no. 4 [DOL 481 no. 3999].

[7]   See *General Roman Calendar*, General Norms for the Liturgical Year and the Calendar, no. 5 [DOL 442 no. 3771].

*   Text, OR 4 Sept. 1971, 1 (Italian).

This theme seems to the Pope to be particularly deserving of study and reflection.

1.   The Roman Missal is in fact the fundamental expression of the prayer of the   1779
Church: its purpose is to cast into formularies of doctrinal profoundity, spiritual
richness, and literary grace the praises and supplications that the Church in celebrating the eucharistic mystery addresses through Christ in the Spirit to the Father.

Further, the Missal takes up the whole mystery of Christ in the continuous
march of each liturgical year toward the Easter of the eternal Jerusalem and casts
the light of this mystery and its redemptive power on the Blessed Virgin, the saints,
the Church, human existence, and world events. Thus it expresses concretely how
in the Church the rule of prayer corresponds to the rule of faith.

What has always been true throughout the varied and progressive development of the Roman liturgy, from the ancient sacramentaries to the revered post-
Tridentine Missal of St. Pius V, is true also of the new Roman Missal. While
preserving the treasure of tradition, it has been rearranged and enhanced in consequence of the directives of Vatican Council II.

We might also say that in the new Missal there is further evidence and expression of the Church's perennial youth. That youth is the source of the Church's ever
rediscovering itself, through continuous renewal against the toll of time, in order to
present itself to humanity "without spot or wrinkle" (Eph 5:27), as its divine
Founder wished.

Accordingly this new Missal is marked by a greater cohesiveness in its texts.
But it also recommends itself because of the remarkable richness and variety of
these texts, embracing the new formularies added, especially for the more important seasons of the liturgical year, and the euchological collection, expanded to
some two thousand prayers and many new prefaces. The result is that in contrast to
the previous invariability of texts, explained in some providential way by special
historical conditions, the new Missal offers flexible and well-advised options.
While always respecting the norms for celebration, every celebrant has the opportunity and resources to meet the spiritual needs of the participating assembly more
effectively and to relate liturgical prayer in a vital way to the concrete situation of
today's people. This was the reason for recasting certain ancient formularies, for a
greater precision replacing the indefiniteness of certain prayers in the sanctoral
cycle, for adding, along lines that follow the directions set by the Council, Mass
texts and prayers "for special occasions."

Pope Paul therefore warmly urges priests to know the Missal, to study it, to
meditate on it. An experiential knowledge and wise use of these texts will bring
priests to see how it is possible and necessary to restore the style and spirit of
liturgical prayer without recourse to an out-of-place, arbitrary improvisation.

2.   There is yet another matter that the Pope would like to raise and to submit for   1780
careful consideration by those participating in the National Liturgical Week.

The preliminary and introduction to the new Missal is the *Institutio Generalis.*
This General Instruction is not a mere collection of rubrics, but rather a synthesis of
theological, ascetical, pastoral principles that are indispensable to a doctrinal
knowledge of the Mass, to its celebration, its catechesis, and its pastoral dimensions. A thorough catechesis on the Mass must take into account all aspects of the
eucharistic mystery and in particular its essential principles, which must be thoroughly explained. These are: the unity between the Lord's Supper and the sacrifice
of the cross; the continued renewal of both in the celebration of Mass; the close
relationship between the liturgy of the word and the liturgy of the eucharist as two
components of the one act of worship. Only a constant intensification of such a

catechesis will bring about the faithful's understanding of the meaning, the duty, and the joy of their own active and conscious participation. This means a participation that must receive expression in listening together, in praying and singing together, but also in a "sacred silence," the conversation of the individual with God, necessary because the prayer-dialogue of the assembly must truly be an ascent of faith and love in the Spirit through Christ to the Father.

All of this the General Instruction says and therefore it must be studied and gone into deeply with a loving attention.

1781   3.   The liturgy of the word, although not directly part of the Missal but of the Lectionary, is still an indispensable and requisite part of the celebration; it has now taken on an incomparable richness in the quantity and the variety of its readings. The new Lectionary of the Mass, in the three Sunday and two weekday cycles, offers a large collection of texts from which priests and faithful have at hand an abundance of material for reflection and prayer.

Regrettably it is true that the faithful generally are not sufficiently prepared to grasp the spiritual and sometimes even the literal sense of the splendid pages of the Bible, which, sad to say, they hardly know. For this reason the Pope urges an intense pastoral effort toward leading the people to a deeper knowledge of the Bible and toward making the clergy intent on imparting a catechesis that is more effective for an understanding and appreciation of the sacred texts. That undoubtedly involves on the part of priests a renewed application to both the study of sacred Scripture and the careful preparation of their preaching, especially of the homily. In the homily the genuine meaning of the word of God must, without ever being trivialized, take on forms that meet the needs of the present. [. . .]

218. SC DIVINE WORSHIP, **Reply** to the Abbé Charles Lardic (Diocese of Le Mans, France), on use of the Missal of St. Pius V, 16 June 1972: Not 9 (1973) 48.

1782   On 7 June 1972 the priest Charles Lardic, Diocese of Le Mans, wrote the following letter [in French] to the Congregation for Divine Worship:

"Reverend Father: On 19 May 1972 I had the honor of asking for information and ultimately for a permission regarding the Mass of St. Pius V. Allow me today to renew my request.

"Every year the Schola Saint-Grégoire of Le Mans (a school for Gregorian chant) organizes an international meeting for its students. The meeting ends with a Mass broadcast on the radio program France Culture. This year the Mass will be celebrated on 23 July, with, of course, the new *Ordo Missae* being used.

"But for the meeting itself, which takes place at the Grand Séminaire of Le Mans with only the students themselves present, the director, Mlle. Bellin, would like to use the Mass of St. Pius V.

"Since a specific and limited group is involved, may Mlle. Bellin consider having this Mass, in view of the current norms?

"If permission is required, in this given instance, may His Excellency Bishop Alix grant it?" [. . .]

The Congregation replied on 16 June that "the matter is to be referred to the diocesan Ordinary. It will be for him to decide according to pastoral prudence whether it is advisable to allow the celebration of *one* Mass according to the unreformed Roman Missal, on condition that there is no risk of dissension or disturbance within the community of the faithful."

Comment in *Notitiae*: "Some people, ignoring the petition of the writer, have concluded that a local Ordinary has the power to allow as a matter of course celebration of Mass according to the unreformed Roman Missal. The petition and the reply make it clear that this case involves a *single* Mass, 'for a specific and limited group,' and 'in a given instance.' Any other inference is unwarranted and false."   1783

219. SC DIVINE WORSHIP, **Notification** *Conferentiarum Episcopalium*, on the obligatory nature of the Roman Missal of Paul VI, 28 October 1974: Not 10 (1974) 353.

The responsibilities of the conferences of bishops to see to the preparation of translations of the liturgical books and the required petition for their confirmation by the Apostolic See have already been specified, with the approval of Pope Paul VI, by this Congregation through its notification of 14 June 1971.[a]   1784

Throughout the world the conferences have been in the process of carrying out these responsibilities, with the result that as sufficient time has passed the work is all but complete. When a conference of bishops decrees that the translation of the Roman Missal, or any part of it, for example, the Order of Mass, is obligatory in a region, Mass, whether in Latin or the vernacular, may be celebrated lawfully only according to the rite of the Roman Missal promulgated 3 April 1969 by authority of Pope Paul VI.[b]

As to the rules issued by this Congregation in favor of priests who because of their advanced years or infirmity find serious difficulties in using the new Order of Mass in the Roman Missal or the Lectionary for Mass, it is clear that an Ordinary has the power to grant them permission to use, in whole or in part, the *Missale Romanum* in the *editio typica* of 1962, as emended by the decrees of 1965 and 1967,[c] but *only* for celebration *without a congregation*.[d] Ordinaries cannot grant this permission for the celebration of Mass with a congregation. Both local and religious Ordinaries must rather see to it — without prejudice to non-Roman liturgical rites lawfully recognized by the Church but with no exception based on the claim of any, even immemorial custom — that all priests and people of the Roman Rite duly accept the Order of Mass in the Roman Missal; that through greater study and reverence they come to appreciate it for the treasures of both the word of God and of liturgical and pastoral teaching that it contains.

---

[a] See DOL 216 nos. 1771, 1773.

[b] See DOL 202.

[c] See DOL 196 and 201.

[d] See DOL 216 no. 1772.

220. SECRETARIAT OF STATE, **Letter** of Cardinal J. Villot to Bishop R. Coffy, President of the liturgical commission of France, on the obligatory use of the Roman Missal, 11 October 1975: Not 12 (1976) 81–83.

1785   Some time ago Pope Paul was presented with a copy of the one-volume French edition of the Roman Missal, produced by the Commission internationale franco-phone des traductions liturgiques with the collaboration of the publishing houses Mame and Desclée. The Pope has asked me to inform the president of the French bishops' liturgical commission, as well as all those whom it may concern, that he is grateful for this mark of respect and pleased at the immense labor so patiently accomplished. He rejoices in the thought that from now on the clergy and faithful will have for their use a resource meeting the requirements for a worthy celebration of the Mass.

    The preliminaries of this missal include the Apostolic Constitution *Missale Romanum* of Paul VI, promulgating the Roman Missal *ex decreto Concilii Oecumenici Vaticani II instauratum.* This document is a counterpart of the Constitution *Quo primum* of St. Pius V, promulgating four centuries ago the Roman Missal *ex decreto Sacrosancti Concilii Tridentini restitutum,* which was revised (*recognitum*) subsequently by several of the popes.

1786   Through the Constitution *Missale Romanum* Pope Paul, as you know, orders that the new Missal is to replace the former one, notwithstanding any constitutions or apostolic ordinances of his predecessors[a] — including, therefore, all the determina-tions of the Constitution *Quo primum.* No one, in France or anywhere else, can therefore claim an indult granted by *Quo primum* and allowing use of the former Missal. This can be used exclusively in the case envisioned by the notification of the Congregation for Divine Worship, 14 June 1971, approved by Pope Paul.[b] The notification of 28 October 1974 made it explicit once again that Ordinaries do not have the power to grant this permission (to use the former Order of Mass) for celebration with a congregation . . . notwithstanding any custom, even one from time immemorial.[c]

    Neglect or contempt regarding liturgical rules that are meant to safeguard the reverence owed to the blessed sacrament, the carrying out of unauthorized experi-mentation or capricious novelties, and in particular the substitution of unautho-rized eucharistic prayers must not be tolerated. The liturgy, above all the liturgy of the Mass, is the prayer of the Church. Even as the Church addresses the concrete life of the community in the parts of the liturgy designed for this purpose, it still is celebrating the mystery of Christ and this cannot be left up to the interpretation of the celebrant or those taking part.

    In a word, as the Constitution *Missale Romanum* puts it, in the Roman Missal, not anywhere else, must Catholics of the Roman Rite look for the sign and the means of their unity with each other; they must all look on it as the witness to the genuine worship of the Church.[d]

    On many occasions Pope Paul VI has brought to the attention of priests and faithful their grave duty of obedience and of safeguarding unity. Thus, for example, he said, on 22 August 1973: "There must be a faithful, intelligent, and careful application of the liturgical reform promoted by the Council and particularized by

---

    [a] See DOL 202 no. 1366.

    [b] See DOL 216.

    [c] See DOL 219.

    [d] See DOL 202 no. 1365.

the competent church authorities. Whoever blocks it or slows it down without reason loses the providential opportunity for a true revitalization and spread of the Catholic religion in our times. Whoever exploits the reform as a way of indulging in arbitrary experiments dissipates energy and outrages the *sensus Ecclesiae*. Now is the hour for honoring in God's Church with good will and unanimity that solemn *lex orandi*: reform of the liturgy."[e]

221. VATICAN PRESS OFFICE, **Reply,** on the alleged Protestant influences on the new Order of Mass, 25 February 1976.[*]

Questions (2 February 1976). Among the reasons advanced, at least in German-speaking Switzerland, against accepting the new Order of Mass, is the objection that six Protestant theologians are supposed to have had a part in composing new liturgical texts; that therefore the purity of traditional Catholic teaching has been compromised. With all due respect, this gives rise to the two following questions: 1787

Was there Protestant participation in the composition of the new Order of Mass?

If so, to what extent?

Reply (25 February 1976): The director of the Press Office of the Holy See may respond as follows to the question of the journalist, Georges Huber, on whether Protestant theologians had a part in composing the new Order of Mass:

1. In 1965 certain members of Protestant communities expressed the desire to follow the work of the Consilium.

2. In August 1968 six theologians of different Protestant denominations were allowed to become simple observers.

3. The Protestant observers did not take part in the composition of the texts of the new Missal.

▶   68.   PAUL VI, Address to bishops of Holland, 17 November 1977:

Translation of the new Roman Missal [no. 597].

---

[e]   DOL 55 no. 539.

[*]   Text, DocCath 73 (1976) 649.

Section 4. Concelebration

SUMMARY (DOL 222–226). Concelebration is unquestionably one of the most highly valued usages restored by Vatican Council II. This form of eucharistic celebration "effectively brings out the unity of the priesthood, of the sacrifice, and of the whole people of God" (General Instruction of the Roman Missal no. 153). There are 5 documents on this topic.

—The fundamental text is the 1965 *Rite of Concelebration* itself with its decree of promulgation (DOL 222, 223).

—The Congregation for Divine Worshp in 1972 issued a declaration (DOL 226) intended as a clarifying interpretation of the section of the General Instruction of the Roman Missal on concelebration (which largely incorporated the 1965 directives).

—Two subsidiary texts are on concelebration at the Mass of the ordination of priests (DOL 224) and on the stipend in the case of concelebration (DOL 225).

▶ 1. VATICAN COUNCIL II, Constitution on the Liturgy *Sacrosanctum Concilium*, 4 December 1963:

art. 57–58: Use and rite of concelebration [nos. 57–58].

▶ 23. SC RITES (Concilium), Instruction (first) *Inter Oecumenici*, 26 September 1964:

no. 15: Concelebration in major seminaries [no. 307].

▶ 531. SC RITES (Consilium), Decree *Edita Instructione*, promulgating the chants for the Roman Missal, 14 December 1964.

222. SC RITES (Consilium), Decree *Ecclesiae semper*, promulgating the *editio typica* of the rites of concelebration and of communion under both kinds, 7 March 1965: AAS 57 (1965) 410–412.

1788   The Church has always taken pains in guiding and reforming the celebrations of the sacred mysteries to ensure that the rites themselves express as effectively as possible the inexhaustible riches of Christ that the rites contain and impart to those rightly disposed. The Church's concern is that the rites will more deeply influence the attitudes and lives of the faithful taking part in them.

    This is the Church's intention in a special way in the case of the celebration of the eucharist. The Church coordinates and arranges the different forms of celebration so that they will express the diverse aspects of the eucharistic sacrifice and convey them to the faithful.

    In every form of its celebration, no matter how simple, all those marks and properties are present that belong to the Mass intrinsically and necessarily. But there is good reason for singling out the following elements.

1789   The first is the unity of the sacrifice of the cross. Many Masses are celebrated but they represent the one, single sacrifice of Christ[1] and they are sacrificial in nature by being the memorial of the bloody immolation on the Cross, the fruits of which are received through the unbloody offering of the Mass.

1790   The second is the unity of the priesthood. Many priests celebrate Mass but they are all individually simply the ministers of Christ; he exercises his priesthood through them and for this purpose makes them, through the sacrament of orders, sharers in his own priesthood in a distinctive way. Even when they offer the sacrifice individually, then, they all do so in virtue of the same priesthood and all act in the person of the one High Priest. He has the power to consecrate the sacrament of his body and blood through one priest or through many at one time.[2]

1791   The third is the more striking expression of an activity that belongs to the entire people of God. The Mass is the celebration of the sacrament of the Church's continued life and growth[3] and of the preeminent manifestation of the Church's

---

[1] See Council of Trent, sess. 22, cap. 1 [Denz-Schön 1739–40].

[2] See ST 3a, 82.3 ad 2 and ad 3.

[3] See LG no. 26 [DOL 4 no. 146].

true nature.[4] Every Mass, then, more than any other liturgical rite,[5] is the activity of the entire people of God, ordered and acting hierarchically.

Intrinsic to every Mass, these three characteristics are particularly conspicuous in the rite in which several priests concelebrate the same Mass.   1792

In this way of celebrating many priests act together with one will and one voice in virtue of the same priesthood and in the person of the one High Priest. Together they bring about and offer the single sacrifice by their single sacramental act and together they share in the sacrifice.

Especially when the bishop presides, such a celebration, with the conscious, active participation of the faithful as a community, is the preeminent manifestation of the Church[6] in the unity of sacrifice and priesthood and the single offering of thanks around the one altar with the ministers and holy people.

The rite of concelebration thus strikingly presents and deeply inculcates truths of utmost importance regarding the spiritual life and the pastoral formation of priests and faithful.

These are the reasons, much more than any at a purely practical level, that concelebration of the eucharistic mystery has been accepted in the Church, in different styles and forms, from the earliest days and, while developing in different ways, has remained in use in both East and West up to the present time.

These reasons also explain why those expert in liturgy did research on concelebration and advocated extension of the permission to concelebrate and appropriate reform of the rite.

After thorough deliberation Vatican Council II did extend the permission for concelebration to a number of occasions and decreed the preparation of a new rite   1793
that was to be incorporated into the Roman Missal.[7] Once the conciliar Constitution on the Liturgy had been solemnly approved and promulgated, therefore, Pope Paul VI commissioned the Consilium to prepare as quickly as possible a rite for concelebration. After this rite had been submitted to the repeated review of consultants and members and then put into final form, the Consilium on 19 June 1964 unanimously approved it and decided that, if agreeable to Pope Paul, the rite should be put to trial use in different parts of the world and in different settings before being approved definitively.

Also in obedience to the will of the Council, the Consilium drew up a rite for communion under both kinds, which sets out the occasions and the forms of celebration in which clergy, religious, and laity may receive the eucharist under both kinds.

Over a period of several months experiments in the use of both rites have therefore been conducted throughout the world with the most welcome results. The Secretariat of the Consilium has received reports on these experiments, together with pertinent observations and opinions. With all of these taken into consideration, both rites received a final revision and were then submitted to Pope VI by Cardinal Giacomo Lercaro, President of the Consilium.

With the assistance of the Consilium and the Congregation of Rites, the Pope gave due consideration to both these rites. At an audience granted on 4 March 1965 to Cardinal Arcadio M. Larraona, Prefect of the Congregation of Rites, the Pope

---

4   See SC art. 2 and 41 [DOL 1 nos. 2 and 41].

5   See SC art. 26 [DOL 1 no. 26].

6   See SC art. 41 [DOL 1 no. 41].

7   See SC art. 57 and 58 [DOL 1 nos. 57 and 58].

gave specific approval and by his authority confirmed the two rites in all and each of their parts and ordered their publication for universal observance beginning on 15 April 1965, Holy Thursday, and for their inclusion in the Roman Pontifical and Missal.

223. SC RITES (Consilium), *Rite of Concelebration*, **Introduction**, 7 March 1965: Vatican Polyglot Press, 1965, 13–18.

FACULTY TO CONCELEBRATE

1794   1.   Concelebration effectively expresses the unity of the priesthood and it has continued to this day as a practice in the Church of both East and West. For this reason Vatican Council II chose to extend permission for concelebration to the following instances:

    1. a.   both the chrism Mass and the evening Mass on Holy Thursday;[R1]

        b.   the Masses during councils, bishops' meetings, and synods;

        c.   the Mass at the blessing of an abbot.

    2. Also, with permission of the Ordinary competent to decide whether concelebration is opportune, to:

        a.   the conventual Mass and the principal Mass in churches when the needs of the faithful do not require that all priests available celebrate individually;

        b.   Masses celebrated at any kind of meeting of priests, whether secular or religious.[R2]

    The concession of concelebration does not, however, prejudice the option of every priest to celebrate Mass individually, not however at the same time and in the same church as a concelebrated Mass or on Holy Thursday (SC art. 57).[a]

1795   2.   In order to give proper expression to the unity of the priesthood, concelebration is allowed only once a day in any church or oratory. Where there is a large number of priests, however, the Ordinary or major superior referred to in no. 3 may give permission for several concelebrations on the same day, but not at the same time.

REGULATION OF THE PRACTICE OF CONCELEBRATION

1796   3.   The right to regulate, in accord with the law, the discipline for concelebration in his diocese, even in churches and semipublic oratories of exempt religious, belongs to the bishop.

    The right to decide on the advisability of concelebration and to permit it in his churches and oratories belongs to every Ordinary and even to every major superior

---

[R1]   Query: Is the Ordinary's permission needed for concelebration on Holy Thursday? Reply: No, unless there is a contrary indication based on special considerations (e.g., Mass being available for the people). The Constitution on the Liturgy art. 57, § 1, 1 a [DOL 1 no. 57] and the *Rite of Concelebration* no. 1, 1a grant *ipso iure* to all priests the permission to concelebrate at the evening Mass on Holy Thursday: Not 1 (1965) 307, no. 84.

[R2]   Query: Is concelebration on the occasion of a funeral preferable to having the several individual Masses during the funeral Mass, customary in some places? Reply: Yes: Not 1 (1965) 142, no. 31.

[a]   See DOL 1 no. 57.

of nonexempt, clerical religious institutes and of societies of clerics living in community without vows. He also may limit the number of concelebrants, on the basis of the norms in no. 4, if, all circumstances being considered, he decides that the dignity of the rite requires this.R3

R3   1. Query: In monastic communities may a priest-organist desiring to concelebrate stay at the organ during the liturgy of the word? Reply: Yes. It is very advantageous for the conventual Mass, so important in a community's spiritual life, to be celebrated with proportionate solemnity, all the members taking full part and each according to the order he has received (see GIRM no. 76 [DOL 208 no. 1466]). The organist carries out a genuine liturgical ministry (see GIRM no. 63 [DOL 208 no. 1453]) and in the case of the monk who is a priest this reaches its high point in concelebration. On these grounds, when the console of the organ is near the choir stalls, the organist concelebrating may stay at the organ until the prayer over the gifts or until the *Sanctus*, when he takes a place around the altar until the communion: Not 5 (1969) 405, no. 22.
2. Query: May those who have already celebrated Mass receive communion at the conventual or community Mass? Reply: Yes. The conventual or community Mass is treated explicitly in the GIRM no. 76 [DOL 208 no. 1466] and in the SCDW's later Declaration on Concelebration, 7 Aug. 1972 [DOL 226 no. 1814]. Because of the special importance of this Mass in the community's life, permission has been given to all the members who are obliged to celebrate Mass individually *for the pastoral benefit of the faithful* to receive communion under both kinds and to concelebrate.
Also to be taken into account, however, is the Instruction *Immensae caritatis*, 29 Jan. 1973, which also deals with the broadened permission to receive communion twice on the same day. Chapter 2, no. 6 of this document says that priests who have already celebrated Mass have permission to receive communion a second time on the same day at the principal Mass of any kind of meeting [DOL 264 no. 2084]. The conventual or community Mass must in fact be regarded as a special and indeed the principal meeting of a community.
These consequences of the law of the Church being stated, it will be of considerable advantage to propose several reasons that confirm the value and the intent of the concession given.
1. The Declaration on Concelebration emphasizes the great weight to be given to concelebration as "a sign and strengthening of the fraternal bond of priests and of the whole community, because this manner of celebrating the sacrifice in which all share consciously, actively, and in the way proper to each is a clearer portrayal of the whole community acting together and the preeminent manifestation of the Church in the unity of sacrifice and priesthood and in the single giving of thanks around the one altar" (SCDW, Declaration on Concelebration no. 1 [DOL 226 no. 1814]). The same document, however, also states: "Even though concelebration is to be regarded as the most excellent form of eucharistic celebration in communities, . . . the option of every priest to celebrate Mass alone must be respected" (ibid. no. 3 c [DOL 226 no. 1816]). Every priest must be accorded the freedom to choose the manner of celebrating he prefers; even one who as a rule concelebrates "may *on some occasions* wish to celebrate alone in the interest of his own spiritual progress or for some other reason" (Commentary on the Declaration: Not 8 [1972] 332). There can be many, legitimate considerations of personal devotion without taking away anything from the importance of concelebration: thus, for example, a special feast, an anniversary of the priest or his family, the death of relatives or friends. The conventual or community Mass does not afford the possibility of satisfying the individual priest's wish in certain circumstances to choose texts more in accord with his own requirements of the moment.
2. There would seem to be some infringement of freedom if a priest were forced either to concelebrate or, having celebrated alone, forced to take part in the conventual or community Mass without the opportunity for the full degree of participation that consists in sacramental communion. The following remarks of P. Gelineau are worth recalling: "Along with the restoration of frequent communion at the time of St. Pius X and of the meal as sign of the eucharist since Vatican II, the presence of noncommunicants at the second part of the Mass has introduced into the assembly an embarrassing separation of persons, especially in the case of a Mass with a group. There is a feeling that a shadow is cast on the sign of unity expressed in sharing the same bread and the same cup (as was formerly the case in so-called private Masses in which priests celebrated the same sacrament of unity side by side, but separately). This is sure proof that the eucharistic assembly involves more than hearing the word together and praying together. In a certain way it is a *new assembly*" (*Eglise qui chante*, nos. 135–136, July – August 1974, 15).
These points have their primary application to religious communities, where often there are no pastoral reasons for most of the priest-members to celebrate Mass with a congregation. These priests, therefore, either would be unable ever to celebrate Mass without a congregation — which is contrary to the liberty granted by the texts already cited — or would have to take part in the community Mass without being able to receive communion — in which case the full participation through which Mass is an *action of the entire community* would be lacking.
3. In order then that the conventual or community Mass truly possess its full meaning, sacramental communion must always be possible by means either of concelebration or of reception. Otherwise this Mass would lack an element of great importance for many priests taking part and the result might be that for them this Mass would lose something of its value. This same reason explains why of late in the Sistine Chapel communion has been distributed to cardinals, bishops, and priests even if they had already

1797   4.   In each case the number of concelebrants is to be settled by considering how many the church and the altar of concelebration can accommodate, even if all the concelebrants are not right next to the table of the altar.

      The faithful's clear view of the rite must be ensured; it is therefore better for the concelebrants not to be stationed between the altar and the people.

CONCELEBRATION AT THE CONSECRATION OF A BISHOP, THE BLESSING OF AN ABBOT, AND THE ORDINATION OF PRIESTS

1798   5.   It is highly appropriate that at an episcopal consecration the coconsecrators concelebrate with the consecrating bishop and the newly consecrated bishop.

      Similarly, at the blessing of an abbot it is desirable that all abbots present concelebrate with the bishop and newly blessed abbot.

      At the ordination of priests all the newly ordained are obliged to concelebrate with the bishop.

      On all these occasions the bishop who is the principal celebrant may welcome others to concelebrate.

RITE TO BE FOLLOWED IN CONCELEBRATION

1799   6.   The ritual norms that follow must be observed whenever a Mass according to the Roman Rite is concelebrated; they must also be applied, all *de iure* matters being respected, to all other Latin rites.

1800   7.   Any Latin-rite priest may concelebrate with other Latin-rite priests, even if the Mass is celebrated according to a liturgical rite other than his own.

EXCLUSION AFTER MASS HAS BEGUN

1801   8.   Under absolutely no consideration may anyone be admitted into a concelebration once Mass has begun.

MASS CELEBRATED OR CONCELEBRATED MORE THAN ONCE ON THE SAME DAY

1802   9.   a.   On Holy Thursday anyone who has celebrated or concelebrated the chrism Mass may also celebrate or concelebrate the evening Mass.

      b.   Anyone who has celebrated or concelebrated the first Mass of Easter at the Vigil may celebrate or concelebrate the second Mass of Easter.

      c.   On Christmas all priests may concelebrate the three Masses, provided each is at its proper time.

      d.   At a synod, a pastoral visitation, or priests' meeting anyone who has concelebrated with the bishop or his delegate may, at the discretion of the same bishop, celebrate a second Mass for the benefit of the faithful.

      In other cases anyone who concelebrates may not celebrate a second Mass on the same day.

---

celebrated Mass individually. The practice has contributed a great deal toward increasing the meaning of the papal Mass and participation in it: Not 11 (1975) 123–125.

STIPEND

10. Individual concelebrants may rightfully accept a stipend for Mass, in keeping with the norms of the law.[R4]

1803

PRIOR CATECHESIS

11. Pastors should make sure that through proper catechesis the faithful who are present at a concelebration are instructed beforehand about the rite and its significance.

1804

GENERAL NORMS

12. All the concelebrants must wear those vestments that they are obliged to wear when they celebrate Mass individually. Bishops concelebrating, however, wear only the amice, alb, cincture, pectoral cross, stole, chasuble, maniple, and miter.

1805

Vestments should be of the color proper for the Mass. When necessary, however, it is permissible for only the principal celebrant to wear the color proper to the Mass and for the other concelebrants to wear white, except at Masses for the dead.

In any exceptional cases, the issue is to be referred to the Apostolic See.

13. Except where the rubrics of the rite itself indicate otherwise, the principal celebrant carries out all the rites and says all the prayers that he usually does when celebrating alone, according to the different forms of Mass. Thus he bows, genuflects, kisses the altar, makes the sign of the cross over the offerings and other gestures, as the rubrics indicate. He is to take care to utter clearly and more audibly than the others the prayers that he is to sing or recite with the other concelebrants. This is to ensure that the others say the words at the same time as he does, especially the words of consecration; these must be pronounced by all and at the same time, but it suffices if the words are virtually simultaneous.

1806

14. The other concelebrants perform only those gestures and rites that are expressly assigned to them. They extend their hands only when saying the prayers that are to be said with hands outstretched or to be said aloud with the celebrant or alone; otherwise they keep their hands joined. Similarly, they say aloud only those prayers that they speak alone or along with the principal celebrant. They should, as far as possible, recite such parts from memory and not be so loud that their voices are heard above that of the principal celebrant. They should simply listen to the prayers not explicitly assigned to them or say them mentally.[R5]

1807

[R4] Query: May a priest with an indult for bination or trination on Sundays and holydays concelebrate the second or third Mass? What of the stipend in this case? Reply: To the first part: Permission to concelebrate granted to priests who have already celebrated Mass individually (whether once or twice) is not given to satisfy personal devotion but has in view determined circumstances serving the benefit of the concelebrants (see *Rite of Concelebration* no. 9). It is left to the discretion of the bishop to decide whether it is appropriate that a priest who concelebrates in such circumstances also be permitted to celebrate individually for the benefit of the faithful. The bishop must take the particular situation into account just as he does in allowing bination or trination.

To the second part: Taking a stipend for a concelebrated Mass follows the rule of the law. Thus if the concelebrated Mass is a second Mass for the priest, he is to follow the general rule of the Code of Canon Law or particular indult, if he has received one: Not 1 (1965) 253–254, no. 75; see also DOL 225, note R9.

[R5] See DOL 208 no. 1558, note R36.

1808   15. When a priest serves as deacon, assistant deacon, or subdeacon at a conceleb-rated Mass he is to refrain from concelebrating at that Mass.

The deacon, subdeacon, and assistant deacons may receive communion under both kinds. If they are priests, they may receive under both kinds even if they have already celebrated Mass or will do so later.[R6]

1809   16. The deacon, subdeacon, other ministers, and servers are to take care not to stand with the concelebrants, except when the rubrics call for their service; once this is performed, they are to withdraw immediately.

PREPARATION

1810   17. In addition to what is required for any form of Mass, the following are to be prepared:

a.   all the vestments that the principal celebrant must wear, in keeping with the various forms of Mass;

b.   amice, alb, cincture, maniple, stole, and chasuble for each of the concelebrants;

c.   depending on the number of concelebrants, one or more sufficiently large hosts, which will later be broken into parts; hosts for the communion of the people. When communion of the concelebrants is to be by intinction, the hosts provided are not to be too small or too thin, but a little thicker than usual, so that once partially dipped in the blood, they can be distributed without difficulty;

d.   a chalice of sufficient size or, if one is not available, two chalices, so that there is adequate provision for the communion of all the concelebrants;[R7]

e.   a burse with corporal, or several if necessary, a pall and purificator for the chalice, and other purificators for the concelebrants;

f.   patens for the communion of the concelebrants;

g.   for each of the concelebrants a silver tube or silver spoon and a vessel with water to purify them, if communion from the chalice is to be by tube or spoon;

h.   if needed, books for the concelebrants containing the Order of Mass;

i.   one or more vessels for washing the fingers;

j.   chairs or a bench for the concelebrants, placed next to the principal celebrant's chair or at a more convenient place in the sanctuary.[R8]

[R6] Query: May the sacred ministers who perform their office twice in one day at a concelebrated Mass also receive communion under both kinds twice? Reply: Yes: Not 1 (1965) 142, no. 32.

[R7] Query: May the concelebrants of a Mass continue to use small chalices? Reply: According to the *Rite of Concelebration* no. 17 d, for concelebration there is to be prepared "[Text quoted]." Were each concelebrant to have his own chalice, the Mass would be a synchronization of many individual Masses rather than a concelebration. For communion from the chalice one of the methods given in the *Rite of Concelebration* is to be chosen. Even were the use of small chalices only a means for communion, the pouring of the precious blood from the large to the small chalices and the very design of these chalices seem less consistent with concelebration. Therefore, it is better to maintain the rite of communion from the chalice in which the concelebrants receive communion from one and the same chalice, even with a tube or spoon: Not 1 (1965) 188–189, no. 53.

[R8] The following queries were raised concerning the ritual of concelebration itself:

No. 31. Query: Are even bishop concelebrants to be incensed as a group? Reply: Yes: Not 1 (1965) 142, no. 33.

No. 39 c. Query: In regard to the *Rite of Concelebration* no. 39 c: "The words of consecration,. . . with the right hand extended toward the bread and the chalice," is the right interpretation that the *palm of the hand* is sideward, not downward, so that the hand extended is seen as a pointing, in keeping with the demonstrative pronoun "This" in the consecration? Reply: Yes: Not 1 (1965) 143, no. 34.

No. 39. Query: Do the concelebrants who are standing at the altar table kiss the altar at the words

▶ 31.   CONSILIUM, Letter *Le renouveau liturgique*, on furthering liturgical reform, 30 June
         1965:

         no.   5:   Concelebration.

224. SC RITES, **Reply** (Zamora, Mexico), on concelebration at the ordination of priests, 26 November 1965: Not 2 (1966) 184.

His Excellency José Gabriel Anaya Diez de Bonilla, Bishop of Zamora, Mexico,   1811
submitted the following queries to the Congregation of Rites for appropriate solution:

1.   During the concelebration of the Mass in which they are ordained to priesthood, should the newly ordained say only those things that all the concelebrants
say?

2.   Besides the concelebrating priests, may there also be a deacon at such a concelebration? If so, what are his functions?

3.   When there are other priests concelebrating such a Mass, must the newly
ordained take the first places, by the side of the bishop?

After hearing the opinion of the liturgical committee and deliberating on the
matter, the Congregation of Rites has decided on the following replies:

To 1: Yes. See *Rite of Concelebration* nos. 109 and 115.

To 2: Yes to the first part; to the second: he is to fulfill the deacon's functions;
see *Rite of Concelebration* no. 109.

To 3: That is appropriate.

▶ 199.   SC RITES, Decree (Rome), on the functions of the deacon at Masses with a
          congregation and on concelebration, 12 January 1966.

225. SC COUNCIL, **Reply** to the SC Rites, on a query regarding the stipend for a concelebrated Mass, 18 April 1966: Not 2 (1966) 330.

We have received along with the esteemed letter of Your Excellency a copy of   1812
the opinions of three consultors concerning the stipend for a sung Mass in the case
of a concelebration, considered in the *Rite of Concelebration*, 7 March 1965.[a]

"as we receive from this altar"? Reply: Yes, following the *Rite of Concelebration* p. 68: ". . . the principal
celebrant and the concelebrants who are standing at the altar table kiss the altar, then all stand erect . . .":
Not 1 (1965) 143, no. 35.

   No. 46. Query: Does the bishop also, after the assisting deacons, give the kiss of peace to the
deacon and subdeacon? Reply: Yes, if they do not receive communion, since the bishop gives the kiss of
peace to deacon and subdeacon at communion (see also no. 50): Not 1 (1965) 307, no. 85.

   Nos. 76, 93, 108. Query: Must the principal celebrant say the *Quod ore sumpsimus* and wash his
fingers, saying the *Corpus tuum, Domine*? Reply: Standing at the middle of the altar he says the *Quod ore
sumpsimus*, then washes his fingers in the vessel prepared with water, saying the *Corpus tuum, Domine*, and
dries them: Not 1 (1965) 189, no. 54.

   Nos. 77, 78. Query: May a deacon assist at a concelebrated Mass as at a "Mass with deacon" (*Ritus
servandus* nos. 95–98), in order to exercise his proper diaconal functions? Reply: Yes, in keeping with the
Rite of Concelebration nos. 77 and 78: ibid., no. 55.

   a   See DOL 223 no. 1803.

In reply this Congregation holds that the stipend in question should belong only to the principal celebrant and not to the other concelebrants. Unless the contrary is explicitly stated, the donor who offers the stipend for the celebration of the sung Mass intends its celebration by an individual.[R9]

▶ 39. SC RITES (Consilium), Instruction (second) *Tres abhinc annos*, 4 May 1967:

    no. 27:   Vestments of concelebrants [no. 473].

▶ 179. SC RITES (Consilium), Instruction *Eucharisticum Mysterium*, on worship of the eucharist, 25 May 1967:

    nos. 47–48:   Concelebration [nos. 1276–77].

▶ 242. SC RITES (Consilium), Norms, on use of Eucharistic Prayers I-IV, 25 May 1968:

                      In concelebration [nos. 1932, 1934, 1937, 1940].

▶ 208. SC RITES (Consilium); SC DIVINE WORSHIP, General Instruction of the Roman Missal, 1st ed. 6 April 1969; 4th ed. 27 March 1975:

    nos. 59:   Concelebration with the bishop [no. 1449].
        76:           Concelebration at conventual and "community" Masses [no. 1466].
     153–208:   Rites at concelebrated Masses [nos. 1543–98].
     242, § 8:   Communion under both kinds at concelebrated Masses [no. 1632].

▶ 399. SC DIVINE WORSHIP, *Rite of Blessing of an Abbot*, Introduction, 9 November 1970:

    nos. 4–5:   Concelebrated Mass [nos. 3280–81].

[R9] Query: May a stipend be accepted in the concelebration of binated Mass? Reply: It was the custom in some places to have several Masses simultaneously, especially on the occasion of a funeral. This multiple celebration has decreased to some extent through the practice of concelebration. Accordingly, on the occasion of a funeral the priests in the area are invited to concelebrate; sometimes this involves bination, since some of them are obliged to celebrate Mass for the benefit of the faithful. Since the presence of a great number of people creates a pastoral reason, bishops themselves sometimes grant the faculty for bination in this case of concelebration. Thus a question arises on whether a stipend may be accepted as a contribution for some charitable work, the seminary, or the needs of the diocese. The following remarks seem to be in order:

1. Before all else the dignity and intrinsic meaning of concelebration must be safeguarded. Concelebration is not to be used merely for practical reasons or to add solemnity. Concelebration is a form of Mass in which there is present a fuller manifestation of the Church and a clearer expression of the unity of priesthood and sacrifice at the one altar and in a single giving of thanks. It therefore is a form of Mass proper to communities of priests and must not be introduced artificially. The liturgical formation of the faithful needs still to be completed on this point.

2. In every liturgical rite, but above all in the celebration of the Mass, the sacraments, and the sacramentals, preferential treatment of persons must be avoided "either in the ceremonies or in outward display" (InterOec no. 34 [DOL 23 no. 326]) in order that "the equality of the faithful is clearly apparent and that any suggestion of moneymaking is avoided" (InterOec no. 35 [DOL 23 no. 327]).

3. There must be complete adherence to the precept in the Declaration on Concelebration of 7 Aug. 1973: "[Text no. 3 c quoted; DOL 226 no. 1816]." Permission for concelebration even for priests who must celebrate individually for the benefit of the people in the case envisioned in this Declaration is granted exclusively on spiritual grounds. It is to enable priests to take part in the Mass "more fully and in their own distinctive way" [DOL 226 no. 1813]; to this may be added the consideration of fraternal cooperation of the priests, who thus assist each other in the pastoral ministry. The whole emphasis must be on these spiritual considerations so that they alone are the motives for concelebrating; under no consideration may a priest accept a stipend for a concelebration that is his second Mass: Not 11 (1975) 287–288.

▶   305.   SC DIVINE WORSHIP, *Rite of Confirmation*, Introduction, 22 August 1971:

no.   13:   Concelebrated Mass [no. 2522].

226. SC DIVINE WORSHIP, **Declaration** *In celebratione Missae*, on concelebration, 7 August 1972: AAS 64 (1972) 561–563; Not 8 (1972) 327–329.

In the celebration of Mass "all in the assembly gathered for Mass have an   1813
individual right and duty to contribute their participation in ways differing according to the diversity of their orders and functions . . . so that the very arrangement
of the celebration makes the Church stand out as being formed in a structure of
different orders and ministries."[1] Because of the distinct sacrament of orders,
priests exercise a function peculiar to them in the celebration of Mass when, either
individually or together with other priests, by a sacramental rite they bring about
the presence of Christ's sacrifice, offer it, and through communion share in it.[2]

Consistent with this, priests should celebrate or concelebrate in order to take
part in the Mass more fully and in their own distinctive way; nor should they
simply receive communion in the manner proper to the laity.[3]

Yet many petitions have been submitted on the correct interpretation of the
General Instruction of the Roman Missal (nos. 76, 158). This Congregation for
Divine Worship therefore declares the points that follow.

1.   Members of chapters and of any kind of community dedicated to perfection   1814
who are bound by their office to celebrate for the pastoral benefit of the faithful
may on the same day also concelebrate the conventual or "community" Mass.[4] The
reason is that in communities great weight is to be given to concelebration of the
eucharist. Concelebration is a sign and a strengthening of the fraternal bond of
priests and of the whole community,[5] because this manner of celebrating the sacrifice in which all share consciously, actively, and in the way proper to each is a
clearer portrayal of the whole community acting together and is the preeminent
manifestation of the Church in the unity of sacrifice and priesthood and in the
single giving of thanks around the one altar.[6]

2.   Anyone who, in keeping with the intent of the General Instruction of the   1815
Roman Missal no. 158,[a] concelebrates at the principal Mass on the occasion of a
pastoral visitation or other special meeting of priests, for example, at a pastoral
meeting, a congress, or a pilgrimage, has the right to celebrate Mass again for the
benefit of the faithful.

3.   The following, however, are to be observed.   1816

---

[1]   GIRM no. 58; see also SC art. 28 [DOL 208 no. 1448; also DOL 1 no. 28].

[2]   See SCR, General Decree *Ecclesiae semper*, 7 March 1965 [DOL 222 no. 1792].

[3]   See SCR, Instr. EuchMyst, 25 May 1967, no. 43 [DOL 179 no. 1272].

[4]   See GIRM no. 76 [DOL 208 no. 1466].

[5]   See LG no. 28 [DOL 4 no. 148]; PO no. 8 [DOL 18 no. 263].

[6]   See SCR, General Decree *Ecclesiae semper* [DOL 222 no. 1792]; Instr. EuchMyst no. 44 [DOL 179 no.
1273].

[a]   See DOL 208 no. 1548.

a.   Bishops and the authorized religious superiors[7] are carefully to ensure that concelebration in communities of priests and at priests' meetings is carried out with propriety and genuine reverence. To this end and to increase the spiritual benefits for those who take part, the freedom of the concelebrants must always be respected. Further, their inward and outward participation must be fostered by means of a celebration that is completely faithful to the General Instruction of the Roman Missal, that carries out all the parts of the Mass in accord with their individual meaning,[8] that respects the distinction of ministries and offices, and that has due regard for the importance of singing and silence.

b.   Those priests who celebrate one Mass for the pastoral benefit of the faithful and concelebrate a second Mass may not lawfully accept a stipend on any grounds for the concelebrated Mass.

c.   Although concelebration is to be regarded as the most excellent form of eucharistic celebration in communities, private celebration without a congregation also "remains as the center of the entire life of the Church and at the heart of the priest's existence."[9]

Therefore the option of every priest to celebrate Mass individually must be respected.[10] To preserve this freedom everything must be arranged regarding time, place, assistance of a server, and other requisites for celebration that will facilitate such celebration.

This Declaration was prepared in consultation with the Congregations concerned. Pope Paul VI on 7 August 1972 approved and confirmed it and ordered its publication.

[7]   See GIRM no. 155 [DOL 208 no. 1545].

[8]   See SCR, Instr. MusSacr, 5 March 1967, no. 6 [DOL 508 no. 4127].

[9]   See Synod of Bishops, *The Ministerial Priesthood*, part 2, no. 3 [DOL 318 no. 2572].

[10]   See SCR, Instr. EuchMyst no. 47 [DOL 179 no. 1276].

Section 5. The Lectionary

SUMMARY (DOL 227–238). The Constitution on the Liturgy repeatedly stressed the importance of the word of God in the liturgy and laid down practical rules for a better plan of biblical readings at Mass. This section includes cross-references to the major general documents on the lectionary and twelve specific texts that indicate the steps in the immense work of its revision.

—The Consilium provided the first information on the revision in connection with its publication of provisional lists of readings (DOL 229, 230).

—The fundamental documents regarding the new order of readings for Mass are the decree promulgating the first *editio typica* (DOL 231), the Introduction of the *Lectionary for Mass* (DOL 232), and an instruction on its editions and use (DOL 233).

—Publication of the *editio typica* of the Latin Lectionary for Mass involved its decree of promulgation (DOL 234) and when volume three of this Lectionary was issued it carried its own Introduction (DOL 235).

—There are also five subsidiary documents in this section: an excerpt on the homily from Paul VI's *Evangelii nuntiandi* (DOL 236); two texts from John Paul II on the occasion of publication of the complete Neo-Vulgate (DOL 237, 238); a Consilium note on one of the Lenten epistles (DOL 228); from the Pontifical Biblical Commission's instruction on the historical truth of the gospels, an extract pertinent to preaching (DOL 227).

▶   1.   VATICAN COUNCIL II, Constitution on the Liturgy *Sacrosanctum Concilium*, 4
         December 1963:

         art. 24:   Importance of Scripture [no. 24].
             33:               Dialogue, God and his people [no. 33].
             35:               Revision of the lectionary [no. 35].
             36, § 1:   Readings in the vernacular [no. 36].
             51:               Readings at Mass [no. 51].
             52:               The homily [no. 52].

▶   20. PAUL VI, Motu Proprio *Sacram Liturgiam*, on putting into effect some prescriptions
       of the Consitution on the Liturgy, 25 January 1964:

         art. III: The homily at Sunday and holyday Masses [no.
                               281].

227. PONTIFICAL BIBLICAL COMMISSION, Instruction *Sancta Mater Ec-clesia*, on the historical truth of the Gospels, 21 April 1964: AAS 56 (1964) 712–718 (excerpt).

1817   4.   Those *who instruct the Christian people through preaching* have need of the utmost
prudence. They should communicate their teaching mindful before all else of the
admonition of St. Paul: "Attend to yourself and to your teaching; hold fast to that,
for in doing so you will save both yourself and those who hear you."[32] They are to
refrain completely from expressing idle or ill-tested novelties. When it is necessary
to present new, already solidly established positions, they should do so with care,
taking into consideration who their hearers are. In recounting biblical events they
are not to embroider them with fictitious details at odds with truth.

▶   23.   SC RITES (Consilium), Instruction (first) *Inter Oecumenici*, 26 September 1964:

         nos. 37–39:   Celebrations of the word [nos. 329–331].
             40:               Translations of the biblical readings [no. 332].
             49–52:   Readings and chants between them [no. 341–344].
             53–55:   The homily [nos. 345–347].
             74:               Biblical readings at marriages [no. 366].

228. CONSILIUM, Note on the epistle for the Saturday after the third Sunday of Lent, 28 February 1965.*

1818   Some bishops have petitioned the Consilium for the option on the Saturday
after the Third Sunday of Lent to replace the text of the epistle, which tells the
story of Susanna, with another text.

        After careful consideration and consultation with the Congregation of Rites,
the Consilium has decided that for the time being, that is, until the new order of
readings for Mass has been settled, the epistle for the Saturday after the Third
Sunday of Lent may be replaced with the reading from Ephesians 6:10–17, which is

---

32   1 Tm 4:16.

*   Text, EphLit 79 (1965) 165.

the epistle for the Twenty-First Sunday after Pentecost and which fits in well with the season of Lent.

229. CONSILIUM, **Note** *Prima phasis renovationis,* on *ad interim* weekday lectionaries, 15 October 1965: Not 2 (1966) 6–7.

The first phase of reforming the liturgy through the documents published   1819
subsequent to the promulgation of the Constitution on the Liturgy had as its purpose to give the Scriptures their due honor and to give prominence to their importance as a first step toward "promoting that warm and living love for Scripture" on which "the reform, progress, and adaptation of the liturgy" depend (SC art. 24).[a]

The new structure of the liturgy of the word in the Mass and the use of the vernacular are already bringing about in the faithful a new love and fuller appreciation for Scripture.

In order to achieve the purpose intended by the Constitution more completely, the competent study group of the Consilium is working hard on "providing a richer share in God's word for the faithful, so that a representative portion of holy Scripture will be read to the people in the course of a prescribed number of years" (SC art. 51;[b] see also *De lectionibus in Missa*: Not 1 [1965] 333).

Meantime, the introduction of the vernacular into the liturgy has increased in pastors and faithful the desire to have immediately "in sacred celebrations a fuller, more varied, and more pertinent reading of Scripture." It is boring to repeat all through the week the Mass of the preceding Sunday or in Masses of the saints to repeat the same commons with the same scriptural selections.

Consequently, several groups of bishops have petitioned the trial use of an order of readings arranged over the course of a week and, in some cases, permission for a special cycle of readings suited to weekday Masses with children.

There is as yet not enough real experience to settle on a definitive order of   1820
readings and in some cases it is not possible to derive clear criteria from tradition that would make the work of the Consilium easier and surer and solve the problems already mentioned.

Pope Paul VI has therefore recently authorized the president of the Consilium to allow petitioning conferences of bishops the use of its own order of readings for weekdays. Each conference may submit its own arrangement of readings for examination and, if warranted, approval by the Consilium.

As an alternative, one conference may adopt an order prepared by another.

For the Consilium to grant permission for use of an order of weekday readings   1821
the conditions are:

1. The order of readings that must be used is the one annexed to the decree allowing the use.

2. The readings proposed are for use in Masses of the third and fourth class that do not have their own readings; their arrangement is to be such that in the first

---

[a]   DOL 1 no. 24.

[b]   DOL 1 no. 52.

year the series of gospel readings is combined with readings from other New Testament books and in the second year with readings from Old Testament books.

3. The readings can be used in Masses for the dead, even those of first and second class, except on All Souls Day.

4. Optional application of this concession is left up to the individual bishops, who will decide on the limits of the experiment and norms for carrying it out in their own jurisdictions.

5. All those with pastoral responsibilities will make a report on the experiment and its results to the bishops, who will forward the reports to the liturgical commission of their conference.

6. The liturgical commission will present a general report to the conference of bishops and it will be forwarded in turn to the Consilium.

7. The experiment will continue until other provisions are made.

▶ 7. VATICAN COUNCIL II, Decree on the Pastoral Office of Bishops *Christus Dominus*, 28 October 1965:

nos. 12: Preaching office [no. 192].
14: Catechesis [no. 193].

▶ 14. VATICAN COUNCIL II, Dogmatic Constitution on Divine Revelation *Dei Verbum*, 18 November 1965:

nos. 21–26: Scripture in the Church's life [nos. 224–228].

230. CONSILIUM, Note *Lectionarium feriale*, on the lectionary provided by the Consilium, January 1967: Not 3 (1967) 9–14.

1822   The Consilium offers a weekday lectionary, prepared by Study Group XI "On Readings for Mass," in response to the request of conferences of bishops that are not yet using existing orders of readings.

The new Order of Readings for weekdays (other than those with their own proper readings in the daily Roman Missal) serves as a daily calendar of the liturgical year, even for those parts of the year that very likely will be changed in the overall reform (for example, the season of Septuagesima and Passiontide, the ember days, the octave of Pentecost). In its general meeting of October 1966 the Consilium approved the broad principles of this Lectionary, along with the plan of readings for the weekdays of Advent, the Christmas-Epiphany season, and the Easter season. The usual reason why certain major texts are missing from this Order of Readings is that they have been reserved for the weekdays of Lent and for major feasts and will be so assigned in the definitive Lectionary.

These are the guiding principles for the new Order of Readings for weekdays.

The weekday Lectionary is independent, as it were, of the Lectionary for Sundays and the major feasts; there is, however, no reason why some passages should not appear in both Lectionaries.

I. ADVENT

1.   The first reading is a semicontinuous reading of Isaiah, leaving out the texts   1823
read on the Sundays of Advent or in the Christmas-Epiphany season. The gospel
readings are selected:

   a.   either because they fit harmoniously with the Old Testament reading and
   show the way Christ's life fulfilled prophecy;

   b.   or because they deal with those main events in John the Baptist's ministry
   that are not mentioned in the Sunday readings for Advent.

2.   On weekdays from 17 to 23 December a verse-by-verse reading of the first   1824
chapter of Luke sets forth the events immediately preparing for the birth of the
Lord. The Old Testament texts (prophecies from Micah, Malachi, Numbers, Isaiah,
Genesis, and 2 Kings) are chosen to fit harmoniously with the gospels.

II. CHRISTMAS-EPIPHANY SEASON

1.   From 29 December to 12 January there is a continous reading of the First Letter   1825
of John, because it concentrates attention on the incarnation.

2.   For 29, 30, 31 December the texts are passages from the end of the infancy   1826
gospel in Matthew and the account of the presentation in the temple in Luke.

3.   On the four weekdays preceding the Epiphany there is a repetition in its   1827
entirety of the prologue of John, because of the major importance of the last part of
this passage, and a continous reading of John Chapter 1, (except for verses 19–21,
read during Advent).

4.   The passages offered for the weekdays between Epiphany and the Baptism of   1828
the Lord recount the principal manifestations of Jesus and the great miracles that
liturgical tradition looks on as epiphanies "so that with due gladness we may honor
the beginning of those miracles that our Lord Jesus Christ kindly performed when
he was born as one of us" (*Missale Gothicum*, feast of the Epiphany).

5.   On the commemoration of the Baptism of the Lord the first reading is from the   1829
Letter to Titus 3:4–7, following the Roman usage of the 7th century (*Comes Wircebur-
gensis*[Wurzburg *Comes*]); thus Isaiah 60: 1–6 is reserved as proper to the *feast of the
Epiphany* and the epistle chosen (in the current Roman Missal it is the one for the
Mass at Dawn on Christmas) mentions "the washing of rebirth and of renewal by
the Holy Spirit."

III. EASTER SEASON

1.   After Low Sunday there is a semicontinuous reading of Acts that derives from   1830
both the Western (Ambrosian, Hispanic) and the Eastern tradition. This tradition
shows clearly that the whole life of the Church takes its beginning from Easter.

2.   On the earlier weekdays of the season the readings are about Christ's appear-   1831
ances recorded in Mark, Luke, and John that are not among the readings for Easter
week. Then, on the basis of a unanimous liturgical tradition, the readings until the
end of the Easter season are from John alone. John is the "spiritual" Gospel, going
more deeply into the mystery of Christ, the source of salvation. Until Thursday of
the Third Week after Easter the readings are from chapters 3, 4, 5, and 10, which
have a special relevance to the paschal season, and chapter 6 is read in its entirety.

From Friday of the Third Week after Easter until Friday before Pentecost, the Lord's discourse after the Last Supper is read in its entirety.

IV. WEEKS IN ORDINARY TIME

1832		1.	The heading *feriae per annum* (weekdays in Ordinary Time) covers the thirty-four weeks currently designated as the Weeks after Epiphany, of Septuagesima, and after Pentecost. The texts are read according to a single sequence of readings that goes from the time after Epiphany to Quinquagesima Sunday and then takes up again in the time after Pentecost.

1833		2.	The first reading is arranged in a two-year cycle that alternates between fairly long periods of selections from the Old Testament and of others from an apostle.

	The readings are divided over the two years in such a way that in some fashion there is a similar sequence of texts from the historical, prophetic, and sapiential books, on the one hand and, on the other, from the "great epistles," the pastoral and the catholic epistles.

	In each year the last week stands as an "eschatological week," because of the readings chosen from the Old Testament or the New (Revelation).

1834		3.	For the gospel there is a one-year cycle in a semicontinuous reading first of Mark (eight weeks), then of Luke (sixteen weeks), then of Matthew (ten weeks); to a certain extent this follows Byzantine usage.

OLD TESTAMENT READINGS

1835		4.	The historical texts have been selected so as to provide an overview of the history of salvation before the Lord's incarnation. But certain accounts of merely historical import have been omitted: it would be difficult to allow such readings in Mass (thus, for example, the Book of Judith is entirely passed over). In addition, the religious significance of historical events is brought out at times through selections from the sapiential books, interjected as an introduction or conclusion to a particular series of historical readings.

NEW TESTAMENT READINGS

1836		5.	Whereas it was necessary to select the Old Testament readings from such an abundant and varied material, the New Testament readings have a virtually continuous character. Still, passages that deal with issues having no pastoral usefulness for our age are omitted: for example, those about glossolalia, foods sacrificed to idols, or primitive church discipline.

1837		6.	The following were the principles for choosing gospel passages.

	a.	The literary structure, that is, principles of composition, distinguishing one Synoptic author from the others has been respected. Care was taken to ensure reading of nearly the entire Gospel. What is not given in readings from one evangelist is found in readings from another: in this way there are no words or deeds not proclaimed in the liturgical assembly.

	b.	The point of view proper to each evangelist has been respected. This includes not only the author's main direction or chief characteristic, but also the many personal touches or "colorations" each gives to the portrait of Christ.

	c.	This is the reason for the special care taken to find in each Gospel all the passages proper to the particular evangelist, even if these passages already were in the Lectionary for Sundays and major feasts. As a rule there is no repetition of passages already read on privileged weekdays. The parts proper to each of them are altogether necessary for a perception and presentation of the theology of the Synoptics.

d.　Parallel texts of the Synoptics are always given in the continuous reading when they fit into the context and are in different words. This occurs almost invariably because the point of view proper to each of the Gospels is present above all in such texts. The same holds for duplications within the same Gospel, where the two accounts (for example, of the multiplication of loaves) suggest different ideas.

e.　In each Gospel a complete portrait of Christ appears with the emphasis proper to the author; yet the three Synoptics frequently complement one another. The precedence of Mark seems to be more than a matter of chronology, because the Greek text of Luke and Matthew add significantly to the preaching schema that is preserved in its original form mainly in Mark. Even so, the two other Synoptics are not mere supplements to Mark: for example, the readings from Luke do not appear as a supplement to Mark because they present a complete picture of Christ, even though their structure leads to a perception of what is proper to Luke in relation to Mark.

f.　The readings from Matthew preserve almost in their entirety the sayings of Jesus, but in the context of a preparation. Great care has been taken to put together all the miracles along with their summary and to preserve the diverse phases of Christ's life, especially in certain geographical regions (for example, the ministry in Genesareth, Tyre and Sidon, Magdala, Perea, etc.).

QUESTIONS ON USE OF THE WEEKDAY LECTIONARY

Regarding concession of the weekday Lectionary, problems are frequently raised about the interpretation of certain words in the decree of concession. 　1838

1.　What does "weekdays" mean? 　1839

With the Order of Readings for weekdays, two cycles of readings, for feasts and for weekdays, are introduced in the Mass readings. They establish a continuous or semicontinuous reading of sacred Scripture in order that "the treasures of the Bible may be opened up more lavishly" (SC art. 51). The weekday cycle, therefore, is used in all Masses on the days of the week, whether the Mass itself is of the weekday, with the preceding Sunday's text, or of a saint.

2.　When may the weekday Lectionary be used? 　1840

"Proper readings" must be taken in the strict sense, that is, they are of the person or of the mystery the Mass celebrates. Examples are the feasts of the Conversion of St. Paul, the feasts of St. Barnabas, St. Martha, etc.

There are also *accommodated readings*, that is, readings not from a Common but selected because they bring out some feature of the spiritual life or the work of a saint. In such cases it does not seem necessary to insist on these accommodated readings, unless some pastoral reason for the celebration favors their precedence over the readings of the weekday cycle. For example, on the feast of St. Francis Xavier, even though the gospel reading is well suited to the feast, there does not seem to be a necessary reason for substituting it for the weekday reading except where there is a special celebration to stress a missionary theme.

With *votive Masses* a distinction seems in order. Some are celebrated at particular times for a special reason, for example, the Mass for Peace, for Christian Unity, for the Sick, etc; then it seems that the readings proper to the votive Mass ought to be used. There are also ordinary votive Masses assigned to certain days of the week and used regularly or frequently. In such cases use of the continuous reading seems preferable.

In votive Masses of *the Sacred Heart* celebrated on the first Friday of the month and in *Masses of the dead*, if the national conference of bishops has established a cycle of readings, the variable readings can be taken from this cycle; otherwise the readings should be those from the text of the Missal.

1841   3.   What should be done on certain days of the second class?

The days in question are the major weekdays of Advent (17–23 December) and the three days in the Christmas octave (29–31 December).

Whereas on these days the Mass should be that of the preceding Sunday or of the octave, with their readings being repeated, it is in keeping with the intent of the weekday Lectionary to vary texts and therefore the texts it assigns are used.[R1]

▶   123.   SC RITES (Consilium), Instruction *Comme le prévoit*, on translation of liturgical texts, 25 January 1969:

     nos. 30–32:   Translation of biblical readings [nos. 867–869].

▶   202.   PAUL VI, Apostolic Constitution *Missale Romanum*, 3 April 1969:

         On the new lectionary [no. 1362].

▶   208.   SC RITES (Consilium); SC DIVINE WORSHIP, General Instruction of the Roman Missal, 1st ed. 6 April 1969; 4th ed. 27 March 1975:

nos. 9:	Reading and explanation of the word of God [no. 1399].
33–42:	Liturgy of the word [nos. 1423–32].
66–67:	Functions of reader and psalmist [nos. 1456–57].
89–99:	Rites of the liturgy of the word [nos. 1479–89].
131–132:	Deacon's functions in the liturgy of the word [nos. 1521–22].
148–149:	Reader's functions [nos. 1538–39].
164–165:	Liturgy of the word in concelebrations [nos. 1554–55].
217–220:	Liturgy of the word at a Mass without a congregation [nos. 1607–10].
232:	Veneration of the Book of Gospels [no. 1622].
272:	Lectern, place for proclaiming the word of God [no. 1662].
318–320:	Choice of readings [nos. 1708–10].
325:	Choice of more pertinent readings [no. 1715].

[R1] In 1968 the Consilium published a list of "particular lectionaries" for use in pilgrimages to Marian shrines and in other special celebrations. The publication is prefaced by the following note: "The Council has directed that 'the treasures of the Bible are to be opened up more lavishly' [DOL 1 no. 51] and the Christian people have developed a greater taste for Scripture from hearing the new biblical passages in the weekday Lectionary. Both factors have fostered a desire also to have other biblical selections for certain special occasions. Consequently, study groups of experts and of pastors in different parts of the world have drawn up plans for readings. After obtaining authorization of the Consilium, some conferences of bishops have put these plans into use. For the use of such plans the conferences of bishops must submit their requests to the Consilium. No priest is allowed to use these plans for readings on his own initiative [. . .]": Not 4 (1968) 41.

For the complete list of these "particular lectionaries" approved provisionally, see Not 4 (1968) 43–88.

▶   275. SC DIVINE WORSHIP, Instruction *Actio pastoralis*, on Masses with special
          groups, 15 May 1969:

          no. 6 c, e,f,g: Biblical readings and homily [no. 2127].

231. SC DIVINE WORSHIP, **Decree** *Ordo lectionum*, promulgating the *editio typica* of the order of readings for Mass, 25 May 1969: AAS 61 (1969) 548–549; Not 5 (1969) 237.

The Constitution on the Sacred Liturgy directed that the treasures of the Bible   1842
be opened up more lavishly so that a richer share might be provided for the faithful
at the table of God's word and a more representative portion of sacred Scripture be
read to the people over a prescribed number of years (see SC art. 51).ᵃ In response to
these directives, the Consilium for the Implementation of the Constitution on the
Liturgy prepared this Lectionary for Mass and Pope Paul VI approved it in the
Apostolic Constitution *Missale Romanum*, 3 April 1969.ᵇ

This Congregation for Divine Worship, on the express directive of the Pope,
therefore publishes the *Order of Readings for Mass* to be used beginning 30 November
1969, the First Sunday of Advent. Since this date is the beginning of the liturgical
year 1970, the readings used will be from Year B of the Sunday readings and from
Week II of the first readings for the weekdays in Ordinary Time.

Since the *editio typica* of the new Order of Readings provides only text references, it is the responsibility of the conferences of bishops to prepare the complete
vernacular texts, following the norms in the Instruction on the translation of liturgical texts (Consilium for the Implementation of the Constitution on the Liturgy, 25
January 1969).ᶜ Vernacular texts may be taken from bible translations already lawfully approved for individual regions, with the confirmation of the Apostolic See. If
newly translated, they should be submitted for confirmation to this Congregation.

232. SC DIVINE WORSHIP, *Lectionary for Mass*, **Introduction**, 25 May 1969:
Vatican Polyglot Press, 1969.

INTRODUCTION
CHAPTER I
GENERAL ARRANGEMENT OF THE LECTIONARY FOR MASS

I. GENERAL PRINCIPLES

1.   The Church loves sacred Scripture and is anxious to deepen its understanding   1843
of the truth and to nourish its own life by studying these sacred writings. Vatican
Council II likened the Bible to a fountain of inner renewal within the community of

---

ᵃ   See DOL 1 no. 51.

ᵇ   See DOL 202 [no. 1362].

ᶜ   See DOL 123.

God's people and directed that in the revision of liturgical celebrations there should be "more reading from holy Scripture and it should be more varied and apposite."[1] The Council further directed that at Mass "the treasures of the Bible should be opened up more lavishly so that a richer share in God's word might be provided for the faithful. In this way a more representative portion of holy Scripture will be read to the people over a prescribed number of years."[2]

It is clear why the Council expressed such principles. By means of sacred Scripture, read during the liturgy of the word and explained during the homily, "God is speaking to his people, opening up to them the mystery of redemption and salvation, and nourishing their spirit; Christ is present to the faithful through his own word."[3] Thus the Church at Mass "never ceases to receive from the altar and to offer to the faithful as the bread of life both the word of God and the body of Christ."[4]

1844   2.   In response to the directives of the Council, the Consilium has prepared this Order of Readings, which lists texts for Sundays and the major feasts, for weekdays throughout the liturgical year, for Masses of the saints, and for other special occasions.

In arranging these texts the purpose was to assign those of greatest importance to Sundays and holydays of obligation, when the Christian people are bound to celebrate the eucharist together. In this way the faithful will be able to hear the principal portions of God's revealed word over a suitable period of time. Other biblical readings, which to some degree complement these texts, are arranged in a separate series for weekdays. Neither part of the Lectionary is dependent on the other: the readings for Sundays and major feasts proceed independently of the weekday readings and vice versa.

The set of readings for Masses of the saints, ritual Masses, votive Masses, and Masses for various needs and occasions is governed by its own rules.

II. LECTIONARY FOR SUNDAYS AND MAJOR FEASTS

1845   3.   The following are the characteristics of the Order of Readings for Sundays and holydays.

a.   Each Mass presents three readings: the first from the Old Testament, the second from the writings of the apostles (from an epistle or from Revelation, depending on the season of the year), and the third from the Gospels. This arrangement best illustrates the basic unity of both Testaments and of the history of salvation, in which Christ is the central figure, commemorated in his paschal mystery. This point should be one of the main subjects of catechesis. Furthermore, such an arrangement of the readings is traditional and has long been followed in the Western Church.

b.   This Lectionary provides a more extensive and varied reading of sacred Scripture on Sundays and holydays by arranging the texts in a three-year cycle. Thus the same text is read only once every fourth year.

Each year is designated A, B, or C. Year C is a year whose number is equally divisible by three, as if the cycle began with the first year of the Christian era. Thus 1968 is a Year C, 1969 is a Year A, 1970 is a Year B, 1971 is a Year C, etc.

---

[1]   SC art. 35 [DOL 1 no. 35].

[2]   SC art. 51 [DOL 1 no. 51].

[3]   GIRM no. 33 [DOL 208 no. 1423].

[4]   DV no. 21 [DOL 14 no. 224].

c. Readings for Sundays and holydays have been arranged according to two principles, called the principles of "thematic harmony" and of "semicontinuous reading." The different seasons of the year and the character of each liturgical season determine which principle applies in specific cases.

The best form of harmony between the Old and New Testament readings occurs when it is one that Scripture itself suggests. This is the case when the teachings and events recounted in texts of the New Testament bear a more or less explicit relationship to the teachings and events of the Old Testament. The Old Testament readings in this Lectionary have been chosen primarily because of their correspondence to the New Testament selections, especially the gospel reading.

Common themes provide another kind of harmonization between the readings for each Mass in the seasons of Advent, Lent, and Easter, each of which has its own spirit or character.

In contrast, the Sundays in Ordinary Time have no particular theme. The epistle and gospel readings for these days are arranged semicontinuously, while the Old Testament readings have been chosen because of their harmony with the gospel passages.

III. WEEKDAY LECTIONARY

4. The explanation of the arrangement of the weekday readings is as follows.   1846

a. The Lenten cycle has its own principles of arrangement, which reflect the baptismal and penitential themes of this season.

b. For other weekdays the gospel readings are arranged in a single cycle, resumed each year. The first reading is arranged over the thirty-four weeks of Ordinary Time in a two-year cycle. The cycle of Year I is for the odd-numbered years (e.g., 1969, 1971, etc.); the cycle of Year II, for the even-numbered years (e.g., 1970, 1972, etc.).

c. Either the principle of thematic harmony or the principle of semicontinuous reading is applied in the same way as in the Sunday Lectionary, that is, depending on whether a season has its own thematic notes.

IV. LECTIONARY FOR THE CELEBRATIONS OF THE SAINTS

5. Two groups of readings are provided for Masses of the saints.   1847

a. The Proper of the Saints provides the first group of readings for solemnities, feasts, and memorials, especially when there are proper texts for any of these. Sometimes in the Proper, however, the more appropriate text among those found in the Common is indicated as preferable.

b. The Common of the Saints provides a second group of readings, which is more complete. There are, first, readings appropriate for various classes of saints (martyrs, pastors, virgins), then a great number of texts dealing with holiness in general. These are for alternate use whenever the Common is indicated as the source for choosing readings.

Texts in this Common are arranged in the order in which they are to be read at Mass: Old Testament selections, texts from the writings of the apostles, psalms and verses between the readings, and finally gospel selections. Unless expressly stated otherwise, the plan of the arrangement is to enable the celebrant to choose the readings at will, considering the pastoral needs of the participating group.

V. LECTIONARY FOR RITUAL MASSES, MASSES FOR VARIOUS NEEDS AND OCCASIONS, AND VOTIVE MASSES

1848   6.   Texts for use at ritual Masses, votive Masses, and other special Masses are arranged in the same way. An extensive list of optional texts is provided, as in the Common of the Saints, to enable the celebrant to consider the particular occasion and the pastoral needs of the participating groups when he chooses from a variety of readings.

VI. MAIN CRITERIA APPLIED IN THE CHOICE AND ARRANGEMENT OF READINGS

1849   7.   In addition to the principles governing the arrangement of readings in specific parts of the Lectionary, there are others of a more general nature.

a.   Because of the importance of their subject matter and liturgical tradition, this new Lectionary *reserves certain scriptural books for specific liturgical seasons*. The tradition of reading the Acts of the Apostles during the Easter season is preserved, as common to East and West (in the Ambrosian and Spanish rites). These readings beautifully show that the entire life of the Church springs from the paschal mystery. The Eastern and Western traditions of reading the Gospel of John during the last weeks of Lent and throughout the Easter season is likewise honored, since it is the "spiritual" Gospel, which presents the mystery of Christ more deeply.

The reading of Isaiah, especially the first part of the book, is traditionally assigned to Advent. Parts of this prophet's writings are also read during the Christmas season, along with the First Letter of John.

b.   The new Lectionary endeavors to strike a balance in determining *the length of texts*. A distinction has been made between narratives, which demand a longer reading but are likely to hold the listener's attention, and other texts that should not be too lengthy because of their doctrinal depth.

Certain rather lengthy passages have been carefully abbreviated and appear in both long and short forms to meet different circumstances. The celebrant may decide which form to use. The verses that may be omitted must be indicated by appropriate typographical signs.

c.   On pastoral grounds, biblical texts that *are truly difficult* are not used in the readings for Sundays and solemnities. The difficulty may be objective, based on the serious literary, critical, or exegetical problems the texts raise or the difficulty may lie in the faithful's power to grasp the meaning of some texts. But there could be no justification for depriving the faithful of the spiritual riches in certain texts on the grounds of difficulty if its source is the inadequacy either of the religious education that every Christian should have or of the biblical formation that every pastor should have. Often a difficult reading is clarified by its correlation with another in the same Mass.

d.   Many liturgies, including the Roman liturgy, have traditionally omitted certain verses from biblical readings. This, it must be admitted, is not something to be done lightly, lest the meaning of the text or the intent and, so to speak, style of the Scriptures be distorted. But, for pastoral reasons, it seemed best to continue this tradition, taking care that the essential meaning of the text remain unchanged. Otherwise some texts would be too lengthy or readings of greater spiritual value to the people would have to be entirely omitted because of the one or two verses unsuitable pastorally or involving truly difficult questions.

VII. CELEBRANT'S CHOICE OF TEXTS

8.   This Lectionary sometimes provides the celebrant with a choice of two texts or   1850
a choice among several optional texts for one reading. This seldom occurs on
Sundays, solemnities, and feasts because such a choice might easily obscure the
spirit of the liturgical season or unduly interrupt the semicontinuous reading of a
book of the Bible. But such a choice is frequently possible in Masses of the saints,
ritual Masses, votive Masses, and Masses for various needs and occasions.

To keep a sound order in the choice of readings, these guidelines should be
followed.

a.   When three readings are assigned for a Mass, it is most desirable that all
three be read. If, however, for pastoral reasons, the conference of bishops permits
having only two readings, the choice between the first two should favor the reading
that is of greater value in presenting the mystery of salvation to the faithful. Unless
expressly stated otherwise in a particular part of the Lectionary, it is preferable to
choose the reading that is more closely related to the day's gospel or is more helpful
in presenting an organized and unified instruction over a period of time or that
permits a semicontinuous reading of a book of the Bible.

For instance, the Old Testament readings throughout Lent present the
development of salvation history. Semicontinuous selections from the writings of
an apostle are provided for Sundays in Ordinary Time. The priest should choose
the readings systematically for a number of Sundays in order to present his catechesis logically and coherently. It would hardly be right to choose a reading from the
Old Testament one week and from the writings of the apostles the next week,
without any order or any harmony with subsequent texts.

b.   When a text is given in a longer and shorter form, pastoral considerations
should determine the choice between the two forms. Such considerations include
the capacity of the hearers to listen to the longer or the shorter reading with profit,
their ability to understand difficult texts correctly, and their appreciation of a more
complete text that will be explained in the homily.

Whenever the choice between the long and short form is given, it should
be indicated typographically.

c.   When a choice between appointed texts is permitted, the needs of the
people should be considered. This involves choosing a text that is easier or more
suited to the congregation, or repeating or postponing a text appointed for a particular celebration then using it as an option on another occasion when it is helpful
pastorally.

These provisions are especially useful in circumstances when a text may
present difficulties for a certain group or when the same text might be repeated
within a few days, for instance, on Sunday and again during the week.

d.   When the weekday Lectionary is used, it is important to determine in
advance whether any feasts will occur in a given week to interrupt the course of
weekday readings. Then the priest, considering the entire week's readings, may
omit less important selections from the weekday Lectionary or combine them with
other readings when this will give a unified presentation of a specific theme.

e.   For Masses of the saints, *proper readings* are provided when they are available, that is, readings that are about the life of the saint or about the mystery
remembered in the Mass (as, for example, on the feast of the Conversion of St. Paul
or on the memorial of Mary Magdalen). Even in the case of a memorial, these
readings must replace those prescribed by the weekday Lectionary for that day.

Sometimes *accommodated readings* are provided to focus on a certain aspect of
the spiritual life or the saint's accomplishments. It is not necessary to use these

readings every time they are provided, unless pastoral reasons so demand. Generally it would be preferable to use the semicontinuous readings from the book assigned in the weekday Lectionary to that liturgical season.

In addition, the Common of the Saints provides *general readings* that are appropriate for various kinds of saints (martyrs, pastors, virgins) or for the saints in general. When several texts are given for the same readings, the celebrant may choose the one most suitable for the congregation. However:

1. On solemnities when three readings are assigned the first choice should be from the Old Testament, the second from the writings of the apostles, and the third from a Gospel, unless the conference of bishops gives permission for only two readings.

2. On feasts and memorials when only two readings are assigned the first choice is from the Old Testament or from the writings of the apostles and the second from a Gospel. During Easter time, however, it is customary to use the writings of the apostles for the first reading and John's Gospel for the second.

f. The guidelines above, governing the choice of readings from the Common of the Saints, also apply to ritual Masses, votive Masses, and Masses for various needs and occasions when several texts are provided for the same reading.

VIII. CHANTS BETWEEN THE READINGS

1851   9. According to the General Instruction of the Roman Missal, (nos. 36–40),[a] there is to be a song after each reading.

The more important song is the psalm following the first reading. As a rule, the psalm should be the one assigned to the reading, except for readings from the Common of the Saints, ritual Masses, votive Masses, and Masses for various needs and occasions. For these the celebrant will look to the pastoral benefit of the participants as the criterion of his choice.

To make it easier for the people to join in the psalm, some selected texts and responses have been chosen for different times of the year and for different classes of saints and these may be used in place of the assigned response if the psalm is sung.

The other song, between the second reading and the gospel, is either specified for the Mass and related to the day's gospel or may be chosen from the series of texts given for the particular season or in the Common.

During Lent the following acclamations (or similar ones) may be used before and after the verse that precedes the gospel:

> *Praise to you, Lord Jesus Christ, king of endless glory!*
> *Praise and honor to you, Lord Jesus Christ!*
> *Glory and praise to you, Lord Jesus Christ!*
> *Glory to you, Word of God, Lord Jesus Christ!*

IX. PURPOSE OF THE LECTIONARY

1852   10. On the basis of the intention of Vatican Council II, the Order of Readings provided by the Lectionary of the Roman Missal has been composed above all for a pastoral purpose. To achieve this aim, not only the foundational principles of this new Order of Readings but also the lists of texts that it provides have been discussed and revised over and over again, with the cooperation of a great many

---

    [a]   See DOL 208 nos. 1426–30.

experts in exegesis, pastoral studies, catechesis, and liturgy from all parts of the world. The Order of Readings is the fruit of this combined work.

The hope is that as this new Order becomes the source for reading and explaining sacred Scripture to the Christian people at the eucharistic celebration, a great step will be taken toward achieving the objective stated repeatedly by Vatican Council II and expressed by Pope Paul VI in these words: "All this has been planned to arouse among the faithful a greater hunger for the word of God. Under the guidance of the Holy Spirit, this hunger is meant, so to speak, to impel the people of the New Covenant toward the perfect unity of the Church. We are fully confident that under this arrangement both priest and faithful will prepare their minds and hearts more devoutly for the Lord's Supper and that, meditating on the Scriptures, they will be nourished more each day by the words of the Lord. In accord with the teachings of the Second Vatican Council, all will thus regard sacred Scripture as the abiding source of spiritual life, the foundation for Christian instruction, and the core of all theological study."[5]

CHAPTER II
DESCRIPTION OF THE ORDER OF READINGS

The following description of the Order of Readings brings out more clearly the structure of the entire Lectionary and its correlation with the liturgical year.   1853

I. ADVENT

11. 1. *Sundays.* Each gospel reading has a specific theme: the Lord's coming in glory at the end of time (First Sunday), John the Baptist (Second and Third Sundays), and the events that immediately prepared for the Lord's birth (Fourth Sunday).   1854

The Old Testament readings are prophecies about the Messiah and Messianic times, especially from the Book of Isaiah.

The selections from the writings of the apostles present exhortations and proclamations on different themes of this season.

2. *Weekdays.* Two series of readings are given: one from the beginning of Advent to 16 December, the other from 17 December to 24 December.

The first part of Advent is devoted to a semicontinuous reading of the Book of Isaiah, distributed in accord with the sequence of the book and including those important passages that are also read on Sundays. Gospel passages for these days have been chosen because of their relationship to the first reading.

Beginning on Thursday of the Second Week, the gospel passages are about John the Baptist, while the first readings either continue Isaiah or come from a text related to the day's gospel.

The gospels of the last week before Christmas are from Matthew (Chapter 1) and Luke (Chapter 1), on the events that immediately prepared for the Lord's birth. Selections for the first reading are from different books of the Old Testament that have important Messianic prophecies and a relationship to the gospel texts.

II. CHRISTMAS SEASON

12. 1. *Solemnities, Feasts, and Sundays.* For the vigil and the three Masses of Christmas, the prophetic reading is from Isaiah. These passages are from the Roman   1855

---

[5] Paul VI, Ap. Const. *Missale Romanum*, 3 April 1969 [DOL 202 no. 1362].

tradition and have been retained in various particular rites. With two exceptions, the other readings follow the Roman Missal.

The gospel of the Sunday within the octave of Christmas, the feast of the Holy Family, tells of Jesus' childhood. The other readings concern family life.

The readings for the octave of Christmas, the solemnity of Mary the Mother of God, are about the virgin Mother of God (the gospel and second reading) and about the naming of the child Jesus (the gospel and first reading, since the feast of the Holy Name is no longer in the calendar).

The readings for the second Sunday after Christmas refer to the mystery of the incarnation.

On Epiphany the apostolic reading speaks of the call of all peoples to salvation.

The readings for the Sunday after Epiphany, the feast of the Baptism of the Lord, speak of that mystery.

2. *Weekdays.* From 29 December on there is a continuous reading of the whole of 1 John, which actually begins earlier on 27 December, feast of St. John the Evangelist, and on 28 December, feast of the Holy Innocents.

The gospels present the Lord's manifestations: the events of Jesus' childhood from the Gospel of Luke (29–30 December), the first chapter of the Gospel of John (31 December – 5 January), and the significant manifestations recorded in the three Synoptic Gospels (7–12 January).

III. LENTEN SEASON

1856   13.   1.   *Sundays.* The gospel selections for the first two Sundays recount the Lord's temptations and transfiguration as recorded in the three Synoptic Gospels.

For Year A on the next three Sundays the gospels are about the Samaritan woman, the man born blind, and Lazarus. Since these passages are very important in relation to Christian initiation, they may also be used for Years B and C, especially when there are candidates for baptism. However, for pastoral reasons, many wished another choice of texts for Years B and C and alternative selections have been provided: Year B, texts from John about Christ's future glorification through his cross and resurrection; Year C, texts from Luke on conversion.

The Old Testament readings are about the history of salvation, one of the main topics of Lenten catechesis. A series of texts has been prepared for each year to present the principal elements of this history from the beginning to the promise of the New Covenant, especially readings about Abraham (Second Sunday) and about the deliverance of God's people from slavery (Third Sunday).

The selections from the writings of the apostles have been chosen so that they bear a relationship to the gospel and Old Testament readings and, as far as possible, form an appropriate connection between them.

2. *Weekdays.* The gospel and Old Testament readings were chosen for their mutual relationship and for their treatment of various themes for Lenten catechesis. Whenever possible, most of the readings from the Roman Missal were preserved. It also seemed best, however, to arrange the readings from the Gospel of John in a better sequence, since most of it used to be read without any special order. Therefore a semicontinuous reading of the Gospel of John, with a better relation to Lenten themes, begins on Monday of the Fourth Week.

Since the readings about the Samaritan woman, the man born blind, and Lazarus are assigned for Sundays only in Year A (and are optional in Years B and C), additional Masses with these texts have been inserted at the beginning of the Third,

Fourth, and Fifth Weeks. During Years B and C they may be used on any day of these weeks in place of the assigned weekday readings.

IV. EASTER SEASON

14. 1. *Sundays.* Until the Third Sunday of Easter, the gospel selections recount the appearances of the risen Christ. To avoid interrupting the narrative, the readings about the Good Shepherd, previously assigned to the Second Sunday after Easter, are now assigned to the Fourth Sunday of Easter (that is, the Third Sunday after Easter). The gospels of the Fifth, Sixth, and Seventh Sundays of Easter are excerpts from the discourse and prayer of Christ after the last supper.   1857

The first reading is from Acts, arranged in a three-year cycle of parallel and progressive selections. Thus something about the life, witness, and growth of the early Church is presented every year.

The selections from the writings of the apostles are: Year A, First Letter of Peter; Year B, First Letter of John; Year C, Revelation. These texts seem most appropriate to the spirit of the Easter season, a spirit of joyful faith and confident hope.

2. *Weekdays.* As on Sunday, the first reading is from Acts, arranged semicontinuously.

The gospel readings during Easter week tell of the Lord's appearances, with the conclusions of the Synoptic Gospels reserved for the Ascension. A semicontinuous reading of the Gospel of John follows, appropriate for the Easter theme and complementary to the Lenten readings. These readings are largely devoted to the discourse and prayer of the Lord after the last supper.

V. ORDINARY TIME

1. Arrangement and Choice of Texts

15. Ordinary Time consists of the thirty-three or thirty-four weeks that are not part of the seasons already mentioned. It begins on the Monday after the Sunday following 6 January and goes to the Tuesday before Ash Wednesday inclusive, and from the Monday after Pentecost Sunday until evening prayer of the First Sunday of Advent.   1858

This Lectionary provides Sunday and weekday readings for thirty-four weeks. But in some years there are only thirty-three weeks in Ordinary Time. In addition, some Sundays either belong to another season (the Sunday on which the Baptism of the Lord falls and Pentecost) or else are impeded by a solemnity that coincides with Sunday (for example, Holy Trinity and Christ the King).

The following guidelines should be observed for the correct use of the readings during Ordinary Time.

1. The Sunday celebrated as the feast of the Baptism of the Lord takes the place of the First Sunday in Ordinary Time. Therefore the readings for the First Week begin on the Monday after the Sunday following 6 January.

2. The Sunday following the feast of the Baptism of the Lord is the Second Sunday in Ordinary Time and the following Sundays are numbered consecutively until the beginning of Lent. The readings for the week in which Lent begins continue until Tuesday inclusive. On Ash Wednesday the Lenten readings begin.

3. The weeks of Ordinary Time begin again after Pentecost Sunday in the following order:

a. When there are thirty-four Sundays in Ordinary Time, the readings are resumed at the week immediately following the last one used before Lent. For instance, if Lent begins during the Sixth Week of Ordinary Time, then the Monday after Pentecost Sunday begins the Seventh Week of Ordinary Time. The solemnity of the Trinity takes the place of a Sunday of Ordinary Time.

b. When there are only thirty-three Sundays of Ordinary Time, the week that would normally follow Pentecost is omitted. Thus the eschatalogical readings with which the liturgical year concludes will still be read during the last two weeks of Ordinary Time. For instance, if Lent begins during the Fifth Week of Ordinary Time, the Sixth Week is omitted and the Seventh Week begins on the Monday after Pentecost.

2. Sunday Readings

1859

16. 1. *Gospel readings*: The gospel for the Second Sunday in Ordinary Time refers to the manifestation of the Lord, already celebrated on Epiphany, with the traditional passage about the wedding at Cana and two other passages from the Gospel of John.

The Third Sunday in Ordinary Time begins the semicontinuous readings of the three Synoptic Gospels. This arrangement provides a presentation of each Gospel's distinctive teaching as the Lord's life and preaching unfold.

The above arrangement and distribution of texts also allows a certain harmony between the meaning of each Gospel and the development of the liturgical year. The readings after Epiphany are concerned with the beginning of the Lord's preaching and are related to his baptism and first manifestation, which are celebrated on Epiphany and the following Sundays. At the end of the liturgical year the eschatalogical themes of these last Sundays occur in sequence because the chapters of the Synoptic Gospels that precede the passion narratives treat these themes more or less extensively.

In Year B after the Sixteenth Sunday in Ordinary Time there are five readings from Chapter 6 of the Gospel of John (the teaching on the bread of life). This insertion is only natural, since the multiplication of the bread in John parallels the same narrative in Mark. In Year C the first text in the semicontinuous reading of Luke (Third Sunday in Ordinary Time) is the introduction to his Gospel. This passage expresses the author's intention very beautifully and there seemed to be no better place for it.

2. *Old Testament readings* were chosen for their relationship to each gospel passage. This serves a twofold purpose: any extreme contrast between the readings of different Masses is avoided and at the same time the unity of Old and New Testaments is clearly shown. This relationship between the readings of the same Mass is indicated by the careful selection of the captions prefixed to the readings.

As far as possible, the choice of readings was made in such a way that they would be short and easy to grasp. But care has been taken to ensure that a large number of Old Testament texts of major significance would be read on Sundays. Such readings are distributed not according to a logical order but on the basis of what the gospel reading requires. Still, the treasury of the word of God is opened up so that all who participate in Sunday Mass will hear most of the Old Testament's principal sections.

3. *Writings of the apostles*: A semicontinuous reading of the Letters of Paul and James is presented. (The Letters of Peter and John are read during the Christmas and Easter seasons.)

Paul's First Letter to the Corinthians, since it is lengthy and discusses so many different questions, is arranged in a three-year cycle at the beginning of this season of Ordinary Time. It seemed best to divide the Letter to the Hebrews into one part for Year B and another for Year C.

All selections are short and should be quite easy for the faithful to understand.

Table II at the end of the Introduction indicates the distribution of epistles over the three-year cycle of the Sundays in Ordinary Time.[b]

4. The theme of the readings chosen for the Thirty-Fourth and last Sunday of the liturgical year is Christ the King, prefigured by David and proclaimed in the humiliations he suffered by dying for us on the cross, who governs and guides his Church until his return at the end of time.

3. WEEKDAY READINGS

17. 1. *Gospel selections*: These are arranged so that Mark is read first (First to Ninth Weeks), then Matthew (Tenth to Twentieth Weeks), and finally Luke (Twenty-Second to Thirty-Fourth Weeks). Chapters 1–12 of Mark are read in their entirety, omitting only those two passages from Chapter 6 that are read on weekdays at other times of the year. Everything not found in Mark is read from Matthew and Luke. Thus all the elements that give the different Gospels their distinctive style or that are necessary for an intelligent understanding of each Gospel are read two or three times. The eschatological teaching is complete in the Gospel of Luke and so is read at the end of the liturgical year.

2. *First reading*: This is taken in periods of weeks first from the Old then from the New Testament; the number of weeks depends on the length of the book read.

a. Extensive selections from the books of the *New Testament* are read so that the listener is given something of each letter's substance. However, passages having little pastoral relevance today have been omitted, such as those concerning glossolalia or the discipline of the early Church.

b. The limited readings from the *Old Testament* are an attempt to give something of the individual character of each book. The historical texts have been chosen for their presentation of an overall view of the history of salvation before the incarnation. Lengthy narratives could not be included; sometimes a few verses have been selected to make up a short reading. In addition the religious significance of some historical events is brought out by selections from the wisdom books that serve as introductions or conclusions to a series of historical readings.

Almost all the Old Testament books will be found in the weekday Lectionary in the Proper of Seasons. The only books omitted are the very short prophetic books (Obadiah, Zephaniah) and a poetic book not suited to reading (Song of Songs). Some texts written for edification require a lengthy reading to be understood. Of these Tobit and Ruth are read; Esther and Judith are omitted; texts from these are assigned to Sundays and weekdays at other times of the year. Table III at the end of this Introduction indicates the distribution of the biblical books over the two years of the weekdays in Ordinary Time.

c. At the end of the liturgical year the readings are from the books that correspond to the eschatological character of this period, that is, Daniel and Revelation.

----

b   The tables mentioned here and in no. 17 may be found in English editions of the Lectionary.

1860

CHAPTER III
FORMAT OF THE READINGS

1861   This edition of the Lectionary carries for each reading a textual reference, caption, and *incipit*, about which the following points should be noted.

1862   18. A. The *textual reference* (chapter and verse) is always to the Vulgate, but with an additional reference to the original Hebrew, Aramaic, or Greek text wherever there is a discrepancy. In translations either type of reference is permissible, according to the decision of the competent authority for each language. But an accurate reference to chapter and verses must always be given and may be carried in the text or in the margin.

The function of these references is to provide liturgical books with the "announcement" (*inscriptio*) of the text that must be read in the celebration, but which is not carried in this volume. This "announcement" of the text will observe the following norms, but they may be altered by decree of the competent authorities on the basis of what is customary and useful for different places and languages.

1. The formulary is always to be: *A reading from the Book of . . .*, or *Letter of . . .*, or *Gospel according to . . .*, not: *The beginning of . . .* (unless it seems advisable in some special instances) or: *Continuation of. . . .*

2. The names of the books as given in the Roman Missal are to be kept, with the following exceptions.

a. Where there are two books with the same name, the title is to be: "First Book" and "Second Book" (e.g., "of Kings," "of Maccabees") or "First Letter" and "Second Letter."

b. The title more common in current usage is to be used for the following:

I and II Samuel instead of I and II Kings;
I and II Kings instead of III and IV Kings;
I and II Chronicles instead of I and II Paralipomenon;
Ezra and Nehemiah instead of I and II Esdras.

c. The distinct titles for the sapiential books, called hitherto Books of Wisdom are: Job, Proverbs, Ecclesiastes (or in vernacular editions Qoheleth), Song of Songs, Wisdom, Ecclesiasticus (or in vernacular editions, Sirach).

d. For all the books listed as prophetic in the Vulgate the title is to be: *A reading from the Book of Isaiah, Jeremiah . . . the Prophet,* even in the case of books not regarded by some as prophetic.

e. The titles are to be *Book of Lamentations* and *Hebrews*, without mention of Jeremiah or Paul, since it is today universally agreed that these two are not the authors of the books in question.

1863   19. B. There is a *caption* prefixed to each text, chosen carefully (usually from the words of the text itself) in order to point out the main theme of the reading and, when necessary, to make the connection between the readings of the same Mass clear.

Vernacular editions are not to carry texts without such summaries. It will be up to the competent authority to decide whether the summaries in this edition should be translated or whether others are to be composed that better suit the mentality of different peoples. Wherever it seems advisable, the summary may be supplemented by a commentary that makes more explicit the general meaning of the passage.

20. C. In the present Order of Readings the *incipit* first contains the customary   1864
introductory phrase *At that time, In those days, Brothers and Sisters, Dearly Beloved,* or *Thus
says the Lord.* These words are not given when the text itself provides sufficient
indication of the time or the persons involved or where such phrases would not fit
in with the very nature of the text. For the individual languages, such phrases may
be changed or dropped by decree of the competent authorities.

After the first words of the *incipit* the Order of Readings gives the proper
beginning of the reading, with some words deleted or supplied for intelligibility, inasmuch as the text is separated from its context. When the text for a reading is made
up of nonconsecutive verses and this has necessitated changes in wording, these are
appropriately marked.

21. D. In order to facilitate the congregation's acclamation, the words for the   1865
reader *This is the word of the Lord,* or similar words suited to local custom, are to be
printed at the end of the reading for use by the reader.

CHAPTER IV
PREPARING TRANSLATIONS OF THE LECTIONARY

22. In addition to what has just been noted, especially in nos. 18–20, the following   1866
rules are to be followed in vernacular editions of the Lectionary.

All are to carry the texts explaining the *structure and aim* of the Lectionary, that
is, at least Chapter I of this Introduction.

23. The size of the Lectionary will necessitate editions in more than one volume;   1867
no particular division is prescribed.

One possibility is the ancient custom of publishing two distinct books, one for
gospels and another for epistles, i.e., readings from the Old Testament and the
apostles.

It seems best that there be a separate Sunday Lectionary, which could include
suitable excerpts from the sanctoral cycle, and a weekday Lectionary. A practical
basis for dividing the Sunday Lectionary is the three-year cycle, so that all the
readings for each year are presented in proper sequence.

But other arrangements that may be devised may be used at will.

24. Texts for the *chants* should always be adjoined to the readings, especially for   1868
the celebration of recited Masses. Separate books carrying the chants alone, however, are permitted. It is recommended that the texts be printed with divisions into
stanzas.

Whenever a text consists of different parts, the typography must make this
structure of the text clear. It is likewise recommended that even nonpoetic texts be
printed with division into sense lines to assist the proclamation of the readings,
especially by those less skilled. Whenever there is a long and short form, they
should be printed so that either one may be read with ease; if such a separation does
not seem feasible, a way is to be found to ensure that each text can be proclaimed
without mistakes.

All editions should carry a biblical index, modeled on the one in the present
volume. [. . .]c

25. The principles governing the work of translating the biblical readings and the   1869
chants between the readings are found in the Consilium instruction, 25 January

---

c   The index of readings appears at the end of the Lectionary.

1969, on preparing translations, to presidents of the conferences of bishops and of national liturgical commissions;[d] also to be observed is the declaration on the translation of provisory texts, published in *Notitiae* 5 (1969) 68,[e] which concern the obligation of submitting to the Congregation for Divine Worship for confirmation translations of even provisory texts approved for liturgical use.

233. SC DIVINE WORSHIP, **Instruction** *Decreto quo*, on editions and use of the new *Lectionary for Mass*, 25 July 1969: Not 5 (1969) 238–239.

1870   The Decree promulgating the new *Lectionary for Mass*[a] and establishing the First Sunday of Advent, 30 November 1969, as its effective date, also entrusted to the conferences of bishops the preparation of vernacular editions of this Order of Readings.

In consideration of the difficulties that such preparation will doubtless entail, this Congregation for Divine Worship judges it advisable to provide the following guidelines to direct and facilitate the work of the conferences of bishops.

1871   1.   The First Sunday of Advent 1969 is to be regarded as the first day on which the new *Lectionary for Mass* may be used, since this is also the effective date for use of the new Order of Mass. A coherent collection of liturgical texts and rites is thus provided as the means for arranging the eucharistic celebration in a way that is richer pastorally. Even so, it is permissible to introduce the new Lectionary gradually.

1872   2.   The great number of readings will require an edition of the Lectionary in more than one volume. It is left up to the conferences of bishops to make a division of the contents for each volume; ease of use in the celebration of the liturgy should be the criterion.

The division into volumes also makes possible a better scheduling of the preparation of editions.

1873   3.   Priority should be given to publishing the volumes for the order of readings on Sundays and holydays of obligation. In particular, it is best to prepare at once a volume, or part of a volume, containing Year B of the Sunday readings, since these are to be used in the coming liturgical year. The hope is that this could be done in the brief period remaining between now and 30 November. Thereafter, and at a more leisurely pace, the other volumes for subsequent years can be produced.

1874   4.   As for the order of readings for weekdays, since experimental plans are almost everywhere now being used, there is less pressure and these plans can be used for the time being until publication of a new weekday lectionary.

1875   5.   On the same basis the readings contained in the current Roman Missal for the Propers and Commons of Saints, votive Masses, and Masses for the dead can be used for the present. It is better to publish the new readings for these along with the weekday lectionary.

---

   d   See DOL 123.

   e   See DOL 124.

   a   See DOL 231.

6.   The editing of the new Order of Readings is to conform to the principles   1876
established in the instruction on translation from the Consilium, 25 January 1969.[b]
Vernacular texts do not need a second confirmation if they are taken from versions
of sacred Scripture already lawfully approved and *confirmed by the Apostolic See for use in
the liturgy*. But if they are taken from versions not yet approved or being newly
composed, they must be forwarded for confirmation to this Congregation for Divine Worship even in the case of translations that are provisory (see the declaration
on *ad interim* translations of liturgical texts, *Notitiae* 5, 1969, 69).[c]

7.   Therefore from 30 November 1969 on the new *Lectionary for Mass* will begin to   1877
go into effect in accord with what the conferences of bishops decide. Thus once the
conferences have prepared the translations and obtained any needed confirmation
from this Congregation, they are authorized to fix a suitable date on which the new
Order of Readings may or must be used.

▶   209.   SC DIVINE WORSHIP, Instruction *Constitutione Apostolica*, on the gradual carrying
           out of the Apostolic Constitution *Missale Romanum*, 20 October 1969:

           nos. 15–18:   The order of readings for Mass [nos. 1747–49].

▶   481.   SC DIVINE WORSHIP, Instruction *Calendaria particularia*, on revision of particular
           calendars and propers, 24 June 1970:

           nos. 41–42:   Biblical readings [nos. 4036–37].

▶   52.   SC DIVINE WORSHIP, Instruction (third) *Liturgicae instaurationes*, 5 September
           1970:

           no. 2:   Readings from Scripture [no. 513].

234. SC DIVINE WORSHIP, **Decree** *Ordine lectionum*, promulgating the *editio
typica* of the Latin Lectionary of the Roman Missal, 30 September 1970: AAS
63 (1971) 710.

     The Order of Readings for Mass was approved by Pope Paul VI in the Apostol-   1878
ic Constitution *Missale Romanum*, 3 April 1969,[a] and the Congregation for Divine
Worship by its decree of 25 May 1969[b] issued the list of references for the biblical
readings. The Congregation then undertook preparation of a lectionary providing
the full Latin text of all the readings.
     The Congregation now publishes this Latin edition of the Lectionary of the
Roman Missal and declares it to be the *editio typica*[c] .

▶   215.   PONTIFICAL COMMISSION FOR THE INTERPRETATION OF THE DE-
           CREES OF VATICAN COUNCIL II, Reply, on the General Instruction of the
           Roman Missal no. 42, 11 January 1971.

---

   b   See DOL 123.

   c   See DOL 124.

   a   See DOL 202 [no. 1362].

   b   See DOL 231.

   c   See DOL 232, for the Introduction to the *Lectionary for Mass*, which was reprinted in this Latin
Lectionary.

▶ 169. SC CLERGY, *General Catechetical Directory*, 11 April 1971.

no. 17: Ministry of the word in the Church [no. 1099].

▶ 318. SYNOD OF BISHOPS 1971, *The Ministerial Priesthood*, 30 November 1971:

Part II, no. 1: Ministry of the word by priests [no. 2571].

▶ 329. SC BISHOPS, *Directory on the Pastoral Ministry of Bishops*, 22 February 1973:

nos. 55, 59: Preaching and the homily [nos. 2642, 2643].

235. SC DIVINE WORSHIP, *Lectionary of the Roman Missal*, volume 3, **Introduction** *Volumen tertium*, June 1972: Vatican Polyglot Press, 1972.

1879 The third volume of the Lectionary of the Roman Missal supplies the readings for celebrations of the saints and for ritual Masses, Masses for various needs and occasions, votive Masses, and Masses for the dead.

1880 1. In celebrations of the saints:

a. On solemnities and feasts the readings must always be those given in the Proper or Common; for solemnities and feasts of the General Roman Calendar, proper readings are always assigned.

b. On memorials the weekday Lectionary is normally used.

But sometimes proper readings are assigned, that is, readings on the life of the saint or on the mystery celebrated in the Mass; these readings must be read in place of the readings for the same day in the weekday Lectionary. Whenever such instances occur, they are expressly noted at the proper place in this Lectionary.

For other cases, the readings of a memorial are used only when special considerations, especially of a pastoral kind, make this advisable. At times "accommodated" readings are given, that is, readings that bring out some particular feature of a saint's spiritual life or apostolate. But for the most part, references are given to reading in the Commons in order to facilitate choice. These, however, are merely suggestions: in place of an accommodated reading or the particular readings proposed from a Common, any other reading from the Common referred to may be selected.

c. In all celebrations of saints, the readings may be selected not only from the Commons to which reference is given in each case, but also from the Common of Holy Men and Women, whenever there is special reason to do so.

d. When particular calendars change the rank of a celebration, care must be taken that solemnities have three readings, the first from the Old Testament (during Easter from Acts or Revelation) with responsorial psalm, the second from the New Testament, the third from the Gospels.

1881 2. In the Commons, for ritual and votive Masses and Masses for various needs and occasions, the responsorial psalm assigned to the first reading and the *Alleluia* verse assigned to the gospel seem to be those most appropriate, but in both cases it is permissible to choose another from the same series.

There is nothing given in the places mentioned after the second reading. When, however, before the gospel there is only one reading taken from the series for the second reading, a suitable responsorial psalm should be selected from among those given after each of the first readings.

3.   In the case of votive Masses the preferred readings during the Easter season are   1882
provided for those occasions on which votive Masses are allowed according to the
provisions of the General Instruction of the Roman Missal.[a]

▶   248.   SC DIVINE WORSHIP, Circular Letter *Eucharistiae participationem*, on the eucharistic prayers, 27 April 1973:

nos. 14:   Comments before the readings [no. 1988].
       15:          The homily [no. 1989].

▶   276.   SC DIVINE WORSHIP, *Directory for Masses with Children*, 1 November 1973:

nos. 41–48:   Biblical readings and homily [nos. 2174–81].

236. PAUL VI, **Apostolic Exhortation** *Evangelii nuntiandi*, on evangelization in the modern world, 8 December 1975: AAS 68 (1976) 5–76 (excerpts).

42.   Secondly, it is not superfluous to emphasize the importance and necessity of   1883
preaching. "And how are they to believe in him of whom they have not heard? And
how are they to hear without a preacher? . . . Faith, then, comes by hearing and
hearing by the word of God."[69] This law once laid down by the Apostle Paul still
retains its full force and power today.

Preaching, the spoken proclamation of God's message, is indeed always indispensable. We are well aware that today's people seem to be sated with talk, often
tired of listening, and, what is worse, to be hardening themselves against words.
We are also aware that many psychologists and sociologists express the view that
our contemporaries have passed beyond a culture of the word, which is now
ineffective and useless, and now live in the culture of the image. These facts should
certainly impel us, for the purpose of transmitting the message of the Gospel, to
employ the modern resources this civilization has produced. The positive efforts
already made in this sphere seem sound and promising; we cannot but praise them
and encourage their further development. The distaste produced these days by so
much empty talk and the greater emphasis on many other forms of communication
must not, however, obscure the importance of the spoken word or cause a loss of
confidence in it. Especially when it is the bearer of the power of God, the word
retains its power and effectiveness.[70] This is why Paul's axiom, "Faith comes from
hearing,"[71] remains relevant: it is the word that is heard that leads to belief.

43.   Preaching that proclaims the Gospel can take many forms, which a burning   1884
zeal for souls will suggest and vary almost infinitely. In fact there are innumerable
events and situations in human life that offer the opportunity for a discreet but
incisive statement of what the Lord wishes to say in this or that particular circum-

---

[a]   See GIRM nos. 326–334 [DOL 208 nos. 1716–24].

[69]   Rom 10:14, 17.

[70]   See 1 Cor 2:1–5.

[71]   Rom 10:17.

stance. A person simply needs a genuine spiritual sensitivity to read God's message in the events of life. Above all in these times when the liturgy renewed by the Council has given greatly increased value to the liturgy of the word, it would be a mistake not to see in the homily an important and very adaptable instrument of evangelization. Of course it is necessary to know and put to good use the requirements and the strengths of the homily, so that it will reach its full pastoral effectiveness. But it is particularly necessary for each individual to be convinced of this effectiveness and to bring to it the dedication of a total love. When integrated in a special way into the eucharistic celebration, from which it receives its proper force and vigor, this kind of preaching certainly has a particular role in evangelization, because it expresses the sacred minister's profound faith and is suffused with love. The faithful assembled so as to form a paschal Church, celebrating the feast of the Lord present in their midst, expect much from this preaching and will benefit greatly from it. But it must be simple, clear, direct, well adapted, profoundly dependent on the Gospel, faithful to the magisterium, animated by the balanced apostolic ardor that is of its essence, full of hope, fostering belief, and productive of peace and unity. Many parochial or other communities live and are held together thanks to the Sunday homily, when it possesses such qualities.

Let us add that, in virtue of the same liturgical reform, the eucharistic celebration is not the only proper occasion for the homily. The homily has a place and must not be neglected in the celebration of all the sacraments, at paraliturgies, and in assemblies of the faithful. It will in every case be a privileged moment for proclaiming the word of the Lord.

237. JOHN PAUL II, **Apostolic Constitution** *Scripturarum thesaurus*, declaring the *Nova Vulgata Bibliorum sacrorum editio* (Neo-Vulgate) to be the *editio typica* and promulgating it, 25 April 1979: AAS (1979) 557–559; Not 15 (1979) 233–235.

1885   The treasure of the Scriptures contains God's saving message and St. Augustine says rightly: "The Scriptures, coming from that city from which we are pilgrims, exhort us to live rightly" (*Enarr. in Ps.* 90, 2, 1: PL 37, 1159). The Church has always justly held this treasure in highest honor and safeguarded it with particular care. From its very beginnings it has never failed to ensure that the Christian people have the fullest opportunity of coming to know the word of God, especially in the liturgy, where "sacred Scripture is of the greatest importance" (SC art. 24).[a] Therefore the Church in the West has given preference to that version usually called the Vulgate, composed in large measure by the renowned doctor of the Church, St. Jerome, and "established in the Church by its use for so many centuries" (Council of Trent, sess. 4: *Enchiridion biblicum* 21). With regard to this highly esteemed version, the Church has taken pains over the preparation of a critical text through the edition, still in process, by the monks of the Abbey of St. Jerome *in Urbe*, which our predecessor Pius XI established for this purpose (Apostolic Constitution *Inter praecipuas*, 15 June 1933: AAS 26 [1934] 85ff.).

In our own days, however, Vatican Council II, reaffirming the honor shown to the Vulgate edition (DV no. 22),[b] and intent on a readier understanding of the Psalter in the liturgy of the hours, decreed that the work of revising the Psalter,

---

[a]   DOL 1 no. 24.

[b]   See DOL 14 no. 225.

already well begun, "is to be finished as soon as possible and is to take into account the style of Christian Latin . . . and the entire tradition of the Latin Church" (SC art. 91).ᶜ

These considerations moved our predecessor Paul VI to establish, before the end of the Council, 29 November 1965, a special pontifical commission to carry out the mandate of the Council and to revise all the books of sacred Scripture in order to provide the Church with the kind of Latin edition that would match the progress in biblical studies and that especially would contribute to the liturgy. Pope Paul directed that in the work of revision "there is to be respect for the letter of the ancient text of the Vulgate where it accurately reflects the original texts, in the way that contemporary critical texts do; where it departs from the original or gives a less faithful translation, the Vulgate is to be carefully corrected. To this end Christian biblical Latinity is to be used, so that a right balance will be achieved between a respect for tradition and the sound requirements of contemporary literary criticism" (see Paul VI, Address, 23 December 1966: AAS 49 [1967] 53–54).

The text resulting from this revision, which was more extensive in some Old   1886
Testament books not done by St. Jerome, has been published between 1969 and 1977 in separate volumes; it is now ready in the *editio typica* in one volume. This Neo-Vulgate edition can serve as the *editio typica* on which to base vernacular versions intended for liturgical and pastoral use. Also, in the words of Paul VI, "we may be permitted to think that the edition will serve as a sound basis for biblical studies . . . especially in places where it is difficult to have access to specialized libraries or to scholarly studies (see Paul VI, Address, 22 December 1977: AAS 70 [1978] 43).

In the past the Church regarded the Vulgate edition as a sufficient resource for imparting the word of God to the Christian people. The Neo-Vulgate certainly will be all the more so. This is a work that Paul VI earnestly desired but did not live to see completed. John Paul I devotedly continued it and had decided to send the books of the Pentateuch, edited by the Pontifical Commission, as a gift to the bishops who will soon meet in the city of Puebla. It is a work that we ourself have long awaited, along with many people in the Catholic world. It is our joy now to present the printed edition to the Church.

Therefore by this Apostolic Constitution we declare to be *typica* the *Nova Vulgata*   1887
Bibliorum sacrorum editio and we promulgate it especially for use in the liturgy and, as we have said, as suited to other areas.

It is our will that this Apostolic Constitution remain always in effect and that it be exactly observed by all concerned, anything to the contrary notwithstanding.

238. JOHN PAUL II, **Address** to the Pontifical Commission for the Neo-Vulgate, on the occasion of the publication of the *editio typica* of the Neo-Vulgate, 27 April 1979: Not 15 (1979) 236–237 (Italian).

Before all else allow me to express my great joy today on receiving the official   1888
presentation of the *editio typica* of the Neo-Vulgate version of the holy Bible. My joy is like that of the harvester finally reaping the rich fruits of long and careful labors.

My thoughts must turn at this moment to the unforgettable figure of Pope Paul VI, to whom is due all the merit and honor of having undertaken this project.

ᶜ   DOL 1 no. 91.

Today this definitive publication marks the term of that project, which he followed, encouraged, and brought to the very threshold of completion. His untimely death and the even more sudden death of Pope John Paul I have resulted in my becoming the one to promulgate for the entire Church the results of a labor that preceded my pontificate.

In any case, thanks be to God, who never leaves his works unfinished.

Special thanks go to you, the officials and members of the Pontifical Commission for the Neo-Vulgate, and to all those who have put their abilities, time, and love at the service of an undertaking at once scholarly and pastoral. You have for a long time devoted your research and your untiring energies to a work that will surely remain for ages to come such an eloquent sign of the Church's solicitude for the written word of God, "of whose fullness we have all received" (Jn 1:16), because it is "the word of salvation" (Acts 13:26).

1889   With the Neo-Vulgate the children of the Church have in their hands yet another means that, especially in celebration of the liturgy, will assist a more secure and precise approach to the fonts of revelation; scientific studies also have at their disposal a new and authoritative point of reference.

I should like to think that St. Jerome himself is pleased with this achievement! The Neo-Vulgate not only stands as a sign of continuity with his work, rather than of its replacement, but it is the product of a keenness and a passion the equal of his own. Further, the knowledge of languages and exegesis stamp the new version with a faithfulness certainly the equal of Jerome's, which has stood the test of more than fifteen centuries of history. Certainly St. Jerome remains a master of doctrine and of Latin, as well as of spirituality. He who, at the commission of Pope Damasus, dedicated his entire life to studying and meditating on the sacred text knows well what that costs, but also how one who is bent over the Scriptures is uplifted. It is a cause for rejoicing that for many Christians what he understood and what you understand has come true, namely, what he wrote to the virgin Eustochium: "Sleep creeps up on the one holding the book, but the sacred page raises the nodding head" (Ep. 22, *Ad Eustoch.* 17).

My wish is that this work you have brought to completion will be really fruitful for the life of the Church and will intensify the saving encounter of the faithful with the Lord, serving to satisfy that "hunger for the word" spoken of by the prophet Amos (2:11) and so sharply felt, it seems, in our times.

▶   76.   JOHN PAUL II, Apostolic Exhortation *Catechesi tradendae*, on catechesis in our time, 16 October 1979:

no. 48:   The homily [no. 611].

Section 6. General Intercessions

SUMMARY (DOL 239–240). The Constitution on the Liturgy art. 53 included another instance of restoring an ancient usage, the "universal prayer" or "prayer of the faithful." In English designated as the general intercessions, this element of the reform has become a welcome and dynamic element in liturgical celebrations.

The present section consists largely of cross-references to other pertinent documents of this collection. The specific text is the Consilium's study of this restored part of the Mass, the second edition, which has official status, and includes an Appendix on the history of this prayer (DOL 239). The other text concerns the general intercessions during the Lent of 1966 (DOL 240).

▶   1.   VATICAN COUNCIL II, Constitution on the Liturgy *Sacrosanctum Concilium*, 4
            December 1963:

            art. 53:   Restoration of the universal prayer [no. 53].
                  54:                    Vernacular for the universal prayer [no. 54].

▶   23.   SC RITES (Consilium), Instruction (first) *Inter Oecumenici*, 26 September 1964:

            no. 56:   Beginning the use of the universal prayer [no.
                                         315].

239. CONSILIUM, *The Universal Prayer or Prayer of the Faithful*, 1st ed., *pro manuscripto*, 13 January 1965; 2nd ed. 17 April 1966: Vatican Polyglot Press, 1966.*

INTRODUCTION

1890   The Constitution on the Liturgy has taught and decreed (art. 53) the following on the universal prayer or prayer of the faithful: "Especially on Sundays and holydays of obligation there is to be restored, after the gospel and the homily, 'the universal prayer' or 'the prayer of the faithful.' By this prayer, in which the people are to take part, intercession will be made for holy Church, for the civil authorities, for those oppressed by various needs, for all people, and for the salvation of the entire world."[a]

On the same point the Congregation of Rites' instruction on the orderly carrying out of the Constitution on the Liturgy, 26 September 1964, has this to say (no. 56): "In places where the universal prayer or prayer of the faithful is already the custom, it shall take place before the offertory, after the *Oremus*, and, for the time being, with formularies in use in individual regions. The celebrant is to lead the prayer at either his chair, the altar, the lectern, or the edge of the sanctuary. A deacon, cantor, or other suitable minister may sing the intentions or intercessions. The celebrant takes the introduction and concluding prayer, this being ordinarily the *Deus refugium nostrum et virtus* (Missale Romanum, Orationes diversae no. 20) or another prayer more suited to particular needs. In places where the universal prayer or prayer of the faithful is not the custom, the competent territorial authority may decree its use in the manner already indicated and with formularies approved provisorily by that authority."[b]

This present booklet, composed under the care and effort of the Consilium, has as its purpose to give illustrative samples of such texts in order to provide the competent ecclesiastical authority with models for the correct preparation, in its own region, of formularies or with criteria for its approval of such formularies. The series of texts presented here are therefore not to be taken as obligatory.

A French translation is printed alongside the Latin text in order to facilitate the work of the territorial authority in the preparation of vernacular texts. This arrangement shows to what extent intelligent adaptations may be made in keeping with the idiom and rules of each language.

---

    *   Text here is that of the 2nd edition.

    a   DOL 1 no. 53.

    b   DOL 23 no. 348.

The samples of sets of intentions provided here generally correspond to the sets of chants for Mass in the *Graduale simplex* (Vatican Polyglot Press, Vatican City, 17 April 1966).

CHAPTER I
PRACTICAL DIRECTORY

§ I. NATURE AND PASTORAL VALUE OF THE PRAYER
OF THE FAITHFUL

1.   "Universal prayer" is a term for a prayer or intercession directed to God, made   1891
at the invitation of the proper minister and by the faithful as a group. This prayer makes intercession for the various needs of the Church, especially the universal Church, and of the whole world.

2.   Thus this prayer has three noteworthy characteristics: 1892
    a.   *It is a petition addressed to God.* Therefore it is not the expression of adoration or thanksgiving alone; nor is it in praise of some saint or a summary to give instruction on truths about religious obligations or the nature of the Mass.
    b.   *It is a petition to God chiefly for blessings of a universal kind:* on behalf of the whole Church, the world, all those "beset by various needs"; nevertheless it is proper also to pray for the faithful actually making up the assembly.
    c.   *It belongs to the whole congregation* ("with the people taking part"), because the assembly responds to the minister's invitations and does not through a single *Amen* simply conclude petitions made by the minister alone .

3.   There is a place for this prayer not simply during Mass, but also in popular   1893
devotions and in the other rites of the liturgy, in keeping with what the Constitution on the Liturgy has described. Firm in its faith in the communion of saints and in its own all-embracing vocation, the gathered Church in offering this prayer stands as the great entreater and advocate appointed for all humanity. The holy people of God exercise their royal priesthood to the fullest above all by sharing in the sacraments, but also by joining in this prayer. Of its nature this supplication still belongs only to the faithful, not to catechumens.

4.   The place proper to the prayer of the faithful is at the end of every celebration   1894
of the word of God; as a rule it takes place even if the eucharistic sacrifice is not to follow (see the instruction of 26 September 1964, nos. 37 and 73 c).[c]

    The reason is that this prayer is the fruit, as it were, of the working of the word of God in the hearts of the faithful: instructed, stirred and renewed by the word, all stand together to offer prayer for the needs of the whole Church and the whole world.

    Thus there is an analogy: sacramental communion is the conclusion and, in regard to the people's participation, the climax of the liturgy of the eucharist; the prayer of the faithful, according to the witness of antiquity, appears as the conclusion and, in regard to the people's participation, the climax of the entire liturgy of the word. This is why the Constitution (art. 54)[d] and the Instruction cited (no. 57),[e]

---

    [c]   See DOL 23 nos. 329 and 365.

    [d]   See DOL 1 no. 54 [The Vatican text reverses the SC and InterOec references].

    [e]   See DOL 23 no. 349.

when dealing with use of the vernacular in the liturgy, both first of all make mention of the readings and of this prayer.

But the prayer can also be seen in another way as a hinge between the two parts of the Mass: it terminates the liturgy of the word in which God's wonderful works and the Christian calling are brought to mind; it ushers in the liturgy of the eucharist by stating some of those general and particular intentions for which the sacrifice is to be offered.

1895   5.   The prayer of the faithful is to be put into use as often as possible, so that it may "be restored especially on Sundays and holydays of obligation" (SC art. 53)[f] and also on weekdays at all Masses celebrated with a large number of people present.

§ II. PARTS AND MINISTERS

1896   6.   The prayer of the faithful consists of several parts: the announcement or statement of the intentions; the responses of the assembly; the concluding formularies. Another part that may be included is an introductory commentary.

1897   7.   It is the celebrant's responsibility to motivate the people in regard to this prayer by introductory comments on its liturgical and pastoral significance. Such an introduction, normally brief and addressed not to God but to the people, may touch on the liturgical season or on the theme of the feast or of the saint being celebrated, and it should connect these with the ensuing prayer. But an introduction may be omitted for a good reason, especially when the prayer of the faithful immediately follows the homily.

1898   8.   In the style of the ancient Roman usage, the priest himself may propose the intentions to the people. But, in accord with *Inter Oecumenici* (no. 56),[g] this function usually belongs to the deacon.

In Masses with no deacon present the function should be assigned to some other suitable person assisting (e.g., a commentator) or to the celebrant or one of the concelebrants.

If the intentions are set to music, which is desirable, the minister or the person assisting must be able to sing properly.

When the celebrant himself does not announce the intentions, he responds along with the congregation and does not continue Mass until the universal prayer is over, thus following the rule given by *Inter Oecumenici* in the case of confirmation or marriage celebrated within Mass (nos. 66 and 72).[h]

1899   9.   After the priest's introductory comments (designated in the formulas of this booklet as "Section A"), there are usually four sets of intentions in any prayer of the faithful (excepting the cases in no. 10), namely, for:

B. the needs of the Church universal, e.g., for the pope, the bishops and pastors of the Church, missions, Christian unity, vocations to the priesthood and religious life (Section B);

C. national or world affairs, e.g., peace, leaders of government, good weather, the safety of crops, elections, economic crises, etc. (Section C);

---

f   See DOL 1 no. 53.

g   See DOL 23 no. 348.

h   See DOL 23 nos. 358 and 364.

D. those beset by poverty or tribulation, e.g., for those absent, the persecuted, the unemployed, the sick and infirm, the dying, prisoners, exiles, etc. (Section D);

E. the congregation and members of the local community, e.g., those in the parish preparing for baptism, confirmation, orders, marriage, for pastors, for a coming parish mission, for first communicants, etc. (Section E).

At least one intention from each set is to be announced.

10. In such votive celebrations as weddings or funerals more scope is allowed for the appropriate votive intention, but never by completely omitting the general intentions.   1900

11. *As to structure,* the intentions *usually are expressed in one of three forms* (as is indicated in the historical summary in this booklet):   1901

a. the full form ("Let us pray *for. . .that"*), which states those to be prayed for and what is to be prayed for. An example is the invitations to prayer or first part of each of the solemn prayers on Good Friday;

b. a first partial form ("Let us pray *that. . ."*), which immediately mentions the favor to be requested, referring in only one word to the persons prayed for. An example is the petitions of the final section of the Litany of the Saints;

c. a second partial form ("Let us pray *for. . .*), which states only those being prayed for. Examples are some of the litanic "deprecations" in both the East and the West.

12. Of utmost importance is the part of the prayer of the faithful involving the congregation's participation. For this to be real and active it is better that it be repeated with each invitation to pray. There are four ways of doing so: 1902

a. a short acclamation, always the same in the same celebration; this is the easiest form of participation and established by the long usage known by the name "litany";

b. participation through silent prayer during a suitable pause; though seemingly passive this silent participation, tested by its Roman usage in the solemn prayers, can contribute a great deal to prayer;

c. the communal recitation of a rather long intercessory formulary; to avoid boredom, however, it is necessary that there be variety in the texts and that the faithful have written copies of them;

d. finally, a combination of the first and second: after a brief silence, the deacon in a second, very short invitation calls for the congregation's acclamation. This way can be used on certain more solemn occasions.

Without doubt the first way has the most to recommend it, even though it is right that there be complete freedom to use any of the others.

13. Because the Constitution on the Liturgy calls for participation by the people and this is really the principal element in the prayer of the faithful, it is completely out of place in Masses with a congregation for only the choir or ministers to respond to the one announcing the intentions.   1903

14. The conclusion of the prayer belongs to the one presiding (see *Inter Oecumenici* no. 56).[i] As a rule, the conclusion takes place only once at the end of the whole prayer and usually in the form of a concluding prayer, limited to asking God to hear the petitions poured forth. This concluding prayer should in no way be a repetition   1904

---

[i]   See DOL 23 no. 348.

of the opening prayer of the day. But in votive celebrations, where most of the petitions relate to the votive intention (see no. 10), the priest's concluding prayer may also express this special intention.

§ III. RESPECTING FREEDOM IN THE USE OF THE PRAYER OF THE FAITHFUL

1905   15. In order that the prayer of the faithful may be an expression of the authentic prayer of the Church as universal yet at home in every place and period, there must be a strong preference for the freedom to vary formularies and match them to the character of regions or peoples.

1906   16. Greater conformity can be required for the concluding part and a degree of uniformity in the people's responses for individual nations or neighboring regions sharing the same language. More freedom is left in regard to the choice of petitions and the ways of participation. But such freedom must respect the essential properties of the prayer of the faithful already stated.

1907   17. For the Roman Rite as a whole, the Consilium sets out the *principles* and *rules* governing the right arrangement of the prayer of the faithful.

1908   18. But it is for the territorial bodies of bishops and, where applicable, for local Ordinaries to approve formularies (see *Inter Oecumenici* no. 56)[i] and to provide pastors with an ample collection of intentions to choose from.

1909   19. It is proper to leave it to the pastor of a church:

a. to choose from among the many approved formularies for intentions those to be announced for each set;

b. to add a few other intentions of his own composition, provided he respects the rule on keeping the four classes of intention indicated in no. 9 and writes out the text ahead of time.

1910   20. To ensure that the prayer of the faithful will not become an aggravation to the people because of its length, the competent authority may stipulate the maximum number of intentions for any Mass, if this seems warranted. But it will be permissible to exceed this number on a given occasion, e.g., at a celebration of the word, at a pilgrimage, or at some extraordinary gathering.

CHAPTER II
SAMPLES FOR COMPOSING A PLAN FOR THE UNIVERSAL PRAYER

1911   There is no need to translate the samples given into the various languages. It is better that the texts be made to suit the character or language of each people.

The term *oratio communis* or *oratio fidelium* itself can be quite readily expressed by synonyms, for example, *prex* or *deprecatio universalis*. The expressions *oratio communis* or *oratio fidelium* are retained in documents because they are the accepted terms in antiquity and because of their *technical* meaning. Even so, a literal translation of them does not seem to be the best translation: the whole Mass is a universal prayer of participation and the Lord's Prayer is distinctively the prayer of the faithful.

---

i   See DOL 23 no. 348.

These various samples do not rule out other styles of composing the prayer of the faithful, especially in regions where this prayer is already the practice.[1] The formularies assigned for the various seasons or feasts are offered merely as examples and others may be substituted at the discretion of the conferences of bishops. In individual formularies the sequence of intentions (B,C,D,E), although generally preferable, is not entirely obligatory (see formulary 52 for weddings): e.g., in votive celebrations it will sometimes be better to begin the prayer of the faithful with the votive intentions, which are more on the minds of the congregation, so as to go from these particular intentions to the more general. [. . .][a]

APPENDIX I
HISTORY OF THE UNIVERSAL PRAYER OR
PRAYER OF THE FAITHFUL

1.   The prayer of the faithful, which still exists in almost all rites and seems at one time to have existed in all, very probably had an apostolic or even a Jewish origin. That is true even if the text of 1 Timothy cited by the Constitution on the Liturgy[1] is not a specific reference to this particular form of liturgical petition but a generic reference to the Christian's obligation to pray.

1912

2.   We find a more explicit link with the liturgical prayer of the faithful in its technical sense at the end of the Letter of Pope St. Clement written before the end of the first century. After a homiletic exhortation to the Corinthians, the successor of St. Peter invites them: "Let us entreat the Creator of all things with urgent petition and supplication that through his beloved Son Jesus Christ he preserve intact those counted among his elect throughout the world."

1913

After this brief appeal to the Corinthians, Clement immediately begins a great petition addressed to God — for the people of God, those afflicted by various needs, for pardon for sin, for peace, for rulers — then concludes with a magnificent doxology.

3.   But, as is well known, we find the first explicit mention of the prayer of the faithful in 150 A.D. as a part of the liturgy following the homily or the rite of baptism, before the kiss of peace and the eucharistic sacrifice. In his *Apologia I* St. Justin Martyr writes that [on Sunday after the reading of Scripture and the homily of the one presiding] "we all stand together and offer prayers" (67). On the occasion of baptism, "we bring [the one newly baptized] into the assembly and offer communal prayers for ourselves, for the one baptized, and for all others wherever they may be. We pray that we may become worthy adherents to the truth, spend our lives in good works, and keep the commandments so that we may reach eternal salvation" (65). Justin makes a distinction between these "universal prayers" of the whole assembly and the "eucharist and prayer" that "after the kiss of peace the one presiding utters over the bread and wine" and at whose conclusion the people respond: *Amen*.

1914

---

¹   For example, certain regions have the custom of proposing intentions in the manner used in the final part of the Litany of the Saints.

ª   Samples of formularies in Latin with French translation follow here in the booklet, 16–159.

¹   "I exhort therefore that first of all there be supplications, prayers, intercessions, and thanksgiving for all people; for rulers and for all that are in authority; that we may lead a quiet and peaceable life in all godliness and uprightness. For this is good and acceptable in the sight of God our Savior, whose will is that all should be saved and come to know the truth" (1 Tm 2:1–4) [see DOL 1 no. 53].

1915 4. In the early years of the third century, with similar words Hippolytus of Rome in his *Traditio apostolica* directs that after receiving baptism the neophytes "then pray together with all the people, for they do not do so before they have received all these things [the rites of baptism]." Hippolytus indicates that the kiss of peace and the offering of the bread and wine then follow.[2]

1916 5. *Many of the Fathers make frequent allusions* to the universal prayer (in the West: Cyprian, Tertullian, Ambrose, Arnobius, Augustine, Siricius; in the East: Clement of Alexandria, Dionysius of Alexandria, Origen, Athanasius, Chrysostom, and others). Even though in some texts it is not clear whether the subject is this part of the liturgy of the Mass, in many others it is.

But as far as the specific form of the prayer and its intentions is concerned, the statements of Fathers of the second and fourth century, are ambiguous. Tertullian in passing reminds Christians "to pray also for rulers, their ministers and officers, the state of the world, the peace of its affairs, and the delay of its end" (*Apologeticum* 39, 2). And Ambrose: "prayer is requested for the people, for rulers, for others" (*De sacramentis* 4, 14).

1917 6. The solemn prayers concluding the liturgy of Good Friday are the oldest surviving text and the oldest form of the prayer of the faithful in the Roman Rite. Baumstark and Jungmann assign the text to the third century; St. Prosper of Aquitaine in the fifth century clearly refers to it. Later use of this prayer was limited to Holy Week, but at the beginning of the eighth century Roman Ordinal 24 is evidence of its continuance in use not only on Good Friday but also on the Wednesday of Holy Week.

As we know, in these solemn prayers there is a sequence of nine intentions: for the Church, the pope, all ranks of the people of God, the emperor, catechumens, those with various needs, heretics and schismatics, Jews, and pagans. Their form is as follows:

a. Nine times the priest himself invites the congregation to prayer, announcing the intention in the fuller form: "Let us pray . . . for . . . that."

b. After each invitation, at the direction of the deacon, the people kneel and pray in silence.

c. Then, again at the deacon's direction, all rise and the priest, exercising his proper function, recites aloud the concluding collect addressed to God.

d. Finally, the people acclaim their assent to the concluding collect with their *Amen.*

1918 7. The *litany* is another form of the universal prayer that was current in the East earlier and that the Roman liturgy adopted at the end of the fifth century. It is a formulary of "deprecation" in which:

a. The deacon announces the intentions in a way shorter than in the solemn Roman prayers, either in the longer form, "Let us pray . . . for . . . that," or in the short form, "Let us pray that. . ., or in the shorter form, "Let us pray for . . .," without mention of what is to be prayed for, but only of the beneficiaries of the prayer. As the formularies of petition become shortened their number greatly increases and new ones appear: for the fruits of the earth, benefactors, the dead, etc.; for the assembly there are individual intentions for pardon for sin, protection by the angels, a Christian way of life, a happy death, etc.

b. The people respond to each invitation of the deacon with a very short acclamation of petition; as the number of intentions increases this is repeated as

---

[2] B. Botte, ed. (Münster, 1963) 54; (Paris, 1946) 53.

many as fifteen or twenty times (the *Testamentum Domini* in a fifth-century Syrian text) or even thirty-five times (the same litany of the *Testamentum Domini* in a text of the Ethiopian liturgy).

    c. The priest, conflating a number of intentions into a series, makes three, two, or even one collect of the people's prayers at the end of the whole litany.[3]

8. It is hard to say whether this kind of litany is the primitive form of the   1919 universal prayer in the Eastern, especially the Syrian, liturgies. Its composition in some Eastern texts seems to date from the third century. Whatever its origins, this form was in full use throughout the East at the end of the fourth century.

    In the following centuries this form also spread remarkably throughout the West, often being substituted for the original local form of the prayer of the faithful. A literal translation of Greek formularies appeared in the Celtic-Germanic litany called the *Deprecatio Sancti Martini* and the Ambrosian litany *Divinae pacis*,[4] still used in Milan during Lent. In Rome the *Deprecatio Gelasii Papae*, much superior in style, was introduced at the end of the fifth century and from the outset, or soon thereafter, was placed at the *Introit* of the papal Mass. Except during Holy Week, it supplanted the ancient Roman form of the prayer of the faithful, until it itself was reduced, before the end of the seventh century, to the simple acclamation, *Kyrie, eleison*.

9. It is clear that the prayer of the faithful was not only part of the Mass but was   1920 a *conclusion of every major noneucharistic celebration.*[5] Its oldest Roman form remains at the end of the liturgy of the word on Good Friday. Use of the litany at the end of the morning and evening offices continues in the Byzantine, Armenian, and other rites; this also was at one time the Roman usage, the traces of which are the weekday and Sunday *preces* of the divine office.

10. In the fourth century, first in the East and later in Rome, the practice began of   1921 the *priest's intercession* at the end of the anaphora or in the midst of the canon. It is a recapitulation of the intentions and in many cases of the very words of the prayer of the faithful. The practice is abundantly documented and continues in all rites, except the Mozarabic.[6]

11. *In the Visigothic liturgy of Spain* (and in the Gallican liturgies), a distinctive form of   1922 the prayer seems to have existed. It comprised an exhortation prefacing the particular announcements of intentions or a general invitation to prayer addressed to the congregation (the Gauls referred to it as the "preface of the Mass").

---

   [3] See M. Righetti, *Storia liturgica* v. 3 (2nd ed., Milan, 1956) 264. The first legislation on this matter is in canon 19 of the Council of Laodicea in the middle of the fourth century (before A.D. 381): "After the addresses of the bishops the first thing must be the prayer over the catechumens; after the catechumens have left, come the prayers over penitents. Once these have left . . . the prayers of the faithful are to be completed, one, namely the first, in silence, the second and third with the customary acclamations. Then the sign of peace is given . . . and the sacrifice offered" (Hefele-Leclerq, *Histoire des Conciles* 1, 1010).

   [4] The last part of the Litany of the Saints seems to have had the same origin (see H. Bishop, *Liturgica historia* 142). These litanies, of obscure origin, were used in the Carolingian period as a common petition of the faithful, but in processions, not at Mass.

   [5] "All the major nonliturgical *synaxes*, that is, assemblies for readings and prayers without celebration of the eucharist, for example, morning prayer and evening prayer, were ended with a prayer of the faithful" (P. Borella, *Il rito ambrosiano*, Brescia, 1964) 164.

   [6] But the Mozarabic rite makes mention of those making the offering at the time when the gifts are offered at the altar, that is, at what we call the offertory.

1923   12. In regions where the Roman Rite displaced the Gallican rites, the Sunday use of the prayer of the faithful, often at the end of the liturgy of the word before the eucharist, apparently never ceased.

        There is evidence of this use in France from the Council of Lyons in A.D. 517, which refers to "the prayer of the people said after the gospel"; also from a commentary on the Mass by the Pseudo-Germain of Paris in the seventh century, which discusses a diaconal litany combined with a priest's prayer.

        Very probably formularies from these Gallican usages passed into the Roman Mass; the texts exist in documents of the ninth to the eleventh century, Germanic and Lotharingian (the Missal of Leofric of Exeter), Celtic and Anglo-Saxon (the Drummond Missal, the York Gospel Book).

1924   13. From the beginning of the 10th century in Germanic and Gallican collections of canon law a canon is repeated that is said to be taken from a council at Orleans: "On Sundays and feast days after the sermon in the Mass the priest must exhort the people to offer together to the Lord prayers for various needs, in keeping with the teaching of the apostles: for their king, bishop, and the pastors of their churches, for peace, against the plague, for those of the parish sick in bed, for the recently deceased. During each petition the people are to say the Lord's Prayer in silence, while the priest is to say solemnly the prayer expressing the need pertinent to each intention. After this the sacrifice is celebrated."[7]

1925   14. Different twelfth-century formularies of the prayer of the faithful survive from Germany and Bohemia; among them a special place belongs to one that Honorius of Autun wrote in his homiliary entitled *Speculum Ecclesiae*. The formulary begins in this way: "Brothers, you must not stand here idle, but pray for yourselves and for the entire holy Church of God, that he . . . will deign to give it peace, etc." The fourteen, long intention announcements concern: the Church and the clergy (4), the king and judges (2), those beset by needs (5), the whole Christian people (1), the celebrant (1), and the assembly (1). The conclusion is: "Come now and raise your prayers aloud to heaven and sing God's praises: *Kyrie, eleison*."

1926   15. This or similar texts seems to be the source of several, late-medieval formularies for announcing intentions (called in France *Formules du Prône* or *Prières du Prône*). There is evidence of these or even the actual texts from the thirteenth to the sixteenth century from nearly all regions of the Roman Rite: Spain, France, England, Germany, Iceland, Poland, Bohemia, and also from the city of Siena in Italy. The Sienese evidence is as follows: "Weekly . . . on Sunday . . . he asks the people to pray for peace, for those entering or in God's service, that God may allow them . . . and us so to live in this world that with them we may share in the kingdom of heaven. For those also who are sick in soul or in body, that . . . . Then he urges the people to pray for the souls of the dead . . . . And he tells them to sing the Lord's Prayer and the clergy to recite a psalm . . . ."

        In the late-medieval centuries the priest recited twelve or even fifteen intention announcements in the vernacular, using the fuller form: "Pray (or let us pray) *for . . . that . . .*"; then one or two psalms and prayers were often said by the clergy alone, while the people silently recited the Lord's Prayer.

        There is no evidence up to now of such a practice in Rome.

1927   16. From the time of the sixteenth-century Reformers and especially after the Council of Trent, in many regions this medieval form of the universal prayer underwent major changes.

---

    [7]   Mansi 8, 361. PL 132, 224; 140, 658; 161, 193.

Suddenly or gradually these prayers disappeared in Italy, Spain, and Poland, as the new books of the Roman liturgy and different forms of popular devotion were introduced.

In Germany St. Peter Canisius in 1556 composed a beautiful formulary addressed to God by the whole assembly, which replaced the medieval prayers until the present century. Then it was revised in the form of a litany, with the people taking a very active part and often, in the style of the Canisian formulary, after the announcement of the intentions by the presiding priest or commentator.

In France in the 17th century the *Preces pronai* (as they were then called) were given an inappropriate place before the homily and were encumbered with purely didactic elements. In the next centuries they were reduced little by little to a mere vestige of what they had been and this remained the case until the present.

17.   Bossuet, however, was still speaking of the great importance of the prayer of the faithful when in 1687 he wrote in the second part of his catechism for the instruction of the people of his diocese: "Why is it better to hear the parish Mass rather than another? Because at this Mass there is an assembly of the faithful. For any other reason? Because at the parish Mass the *prières du prône* take place. What are they? They consist of two main parts. What are they? The first is the prayer of the faithful that God prescribes for the whole Church, for pastors, for rulers, for the sick, for the afflicted, and for all the needs of the people of God, both general and special. Is such a prayer heard by God? By all means, especially when it is the communal prayer of the pastor and all the faithful gathered together in the assembly."[8,a]   1928

240. SC RITES (Consilium), **Communication** *Sacra Rituum Congregatio*, on a special intention for incorporation into the prayer of the faithful for Lent 1966, 24 February 1966: Not 2 (1966) 94.

The Congregation of Rites at the command of Pope Paul VI announces that throughout Lent of this year whenever the universal prayer or prayer of the faithful is to be said at Mass it should incorporate the following intercession for peace: "That a just peace and concord may come to people who are grievously afflicted by war or civil upheaval."   1929

Note. As the problems of today worsen, it would be well to add to the above intention one asking that all the faithful may feel themselves obligated, as members joined in one family, to help their brothers and sisters in spirit and in deed.

This is to be the second among the intentions established for Lent (in the sequence established by the Consilium it would be under C)[a] and the text is to be composed according to the different styles of announcing those intentions, for example: "For the peace and concord of nations, that a just peace . . . let us pray to the Lord."

▶   508.   SC RITES (Consilium), Instruction *Musicam sacram*, on music in the liturgy, 5 March 1967:

---

   8   *Catéchisme du Diocèse de Meaux* (Paris, 1687) Part 2, 4–5.

   a   A second part of the Appendix provides Gregorian chant models for the faithful's response.

   a   This refers to the models for the prayer of the faithful on p. 42 of the booklet of the Consilium [see DOL 239 no. 1899].

no. 30: Chant for the general intercessions [no. 4151].

▶ 39. SC RITES (Consilium), Instruction (second) *Tres abhinc annos*, 4 May 1967:

no. 6: Intentions of the general intercessions [no. 452].

▶ 326. SC CLERGY, General Directory *Peregrinans in terra*, on the pastoral ministry in tourism, 30 April 1969:

II, 3, B, c: General intercessions [no. 2617].

▶ 275. SC DIVINE WORSHIP, Instruction *Actio pastoralis*, on Masses with special groups, 15 May 1969:

no. 6 h: General intercessions [no. 2127].

▶ 208. SC RITES (Consilium); SC DIVINE WORSHIP, General Instruction of the Roman Missal, 1st ed. 6 April 1969; 4th ed. 27 March 1975.

nos. 45–47:	General intercessions [nos. 1435–37].
61, 132:	Deacon's role [nos. 1451, 1522].
66, 151:	Reader's role [nos. 1456, 1541].
70:	Women's role [no. 1460].
220:	Mass without congregation [no. 1610].
272:	Lectern, place for general intercessions [no. 1662].

▶ 52. SC DIVINE WORSHIP, Instruction (third) *Liturgicae instaurationes*, 5 September 1970:

nos. 3 g:	General intercessions [no. 521].
7 b:	Women's role [no. 525].

▶ 426. SC DIVINE WORSHIP, General Instruction of the Liturgy of the Hours, 2 February 1971:

nos. 94:	General intercessions of a Mass joined with morning prayer [no. 3524].
96:	At a Mass joined with evening prayer [no. 3526].

▶ 216. SC DIVINE WORSHIP, Notification *Instructione de Constitutione*, on the Roman Missal . . ., 14 June 1971:

no. 4 a: Use of the vernacular in the Mass [no. 1773].

▶ 301. SC DIVINE WORSHIP, *Rite of Christian Initiation of Adults*, Introduction, 6 January 1972:

no. 36: Active participation of the newly baptized [no. 2363].

▶ 535. SC DIVINE WORSHIP, *Ordo cantus Missae*, Introduction, 24 June 1972:

no. 12: General intercessions [no. 4291].

▶ 248. SC DIVINE WORSHIP, Circular Letter *Eucharistiae participationem*, on the eucharistic prayers, 27 April 1973:

no. 16: General intercessions [no. 1990].

▶   276.   SC DIVINE WORSHIP, *Directory for Masses with Children*, 1 November 1973:

    nos. 22:   Responding to the general intercessions [no. 2155].
         29:               Their prior preparation [no. 2162].
         36:               Illustrating [no. 2169].

Section 7. The Eucharistic Prayer

SUMMARY (DOL 241–251). The Constitution on the Liturgy did not explicitly address the subject of the eucharistic prayer, which, however, quickly became a major point of concern in the revision of the Roman Missal. This is clear from the numerous cross-references within the present section and from the 11 specific texts on this central part of the eucharistic celebration.

—The major documents here concern the liturgical texts. With regard to the three new eucharistic prayers added to the new Order of Mass, there is their decree of promulgation (DOL 241), the detailed norms for the use of each (DOL 242), a letter of the Consilium on the significance of the new anaphoras (DOL 243), and a set of guidelines to assist relevant liturgical catechesis (DOL 244). To the eucharistic prayers for general use were added the Eucharistic Prayers for Masses with Children and for Masses of Reconciliation (on the occasion of the 1975 Holy Year). The decree of approval (DOL 249) and the Introductions to these Prayers (DOL 250) are presented here, together with a letter extending the period of their use (DOL 251).

—The subsidiary documents are an address of Paul VI (DOL 246), norms guiding the composition of new eucharistic prayers (DOL 245), a decree on mention of the bishop's name during the eucharistic prayer (DOL 247), an important circular letter on the new eucharistic prayers and on the possibility of the creation and adaptation of other eucharistic prayers by the conferences of bishops (DOL 248).

▶ 23. SC RITES (Consilium), Instruction (first) *Inter Oecumenici*, 26 September 1964:

nos. 48 f: Doxology at end of canon [no. 340].
57 c: Vernacular in the dialogues and acclamations [no. 349].

▶ 531. SC RITES (Consilium), Decree *Edita Instructione*, promulgating the chants for the Roman Missal, 14 December 1964:

Chants for the Roman Canon [no. 4255].

▶ 110. SECRETARIAT OF STATE, Letter *Ho l'honore*, on concession of the preface in the vernacular, 27 April 1965.

▶ 117. PAUL VI, Concession *ad experimentum* of the vernacular in the canon, 31 January 1967.

▶ 508. SC RITES (Consilium), Instruction *Musicam sacram*, on music in the liturgy, 5 March 1967:

nos. 29 c, 34:   Singing during the eucharistic prayer [nos. 4150, 4155].

▶ 39. SC RITES (Consilium), Instruction (second) *Tres abhinc annos*, 4 May 1967:

nos. 7 b, c: Priest's genuflections during the canon [no. 453].
10:              Canon said aloud or sung [no. 456].
11–12:   Gestures during the canon [nos. 457–458].
28 a: Canon in the vernacular [no. 474].

▶ 179. SC RITES (Consilium), Instruction *Eucharisticum mysterium*, on worship of the eucharist, 25 May 1967:

no. 21:   Canon of the Mass [no. 1250].

▶ 41. CONSILIUM, Letter *Dans sa récente allocution*, on issues of the reform, 21 June 1967:

no. 7:   Translation of the canon [no. 486].

▶ 118. CONSILIUM, Communication *Aussitôt après*, on the translation of the Roman Canon, 10 August 1967.

241. SC RITES (Consilium), **Decree** *Prece eucharistica*, promulgating three new eucharistic prayers and eight prefaces, 23 May 1968: Not 4 (1968) 156.

1930   Through the eucharistic prayer in the celebration of Mass the Church, out of obedience to the Lord's commandment, "Do this in memory of me" (1 Cor 11:24–25), has always continued to do what Christ did at the Last Supper and to offer thanks to the merciful Father for the wonderful works he has wrought in Christ to carry out the plan of salvation. For the sake of a greater richness and variety, many of the conferences of bishops, the faithful, and liturgical scholars have had the desire that, while retaining the traditional and revered Roman Canon, the Latin Church, like other Churches, should have other eucharistic prayers as well.

By papal mandate the Consilium has therefore prepared three new eucharistic prayers, supplementing them with an expanded series of prefaces. As a part of the eucharistic prayer, these prefaces bring out in more detail and proclaim the mystery of salvation during the course of the liturgical year.

The Congregation of Rites has reviewed the texts prepared by the Consilium and Pope Paul VI has approved them and authorized their publication for use in all churches of the Latin rite, beginning with 15 August, the feast of the Assumption of the Blessed Virgin Mary.

The conferences of bishops are to give approval to translations of these texts, in keeping with the conciliar Constitution *Sacrosanctum Concilium* (art. 36, §§ 3 and 4)[a] and the Instruction *Inter Oecumenici* (nos. 29 and 30);[b] the *acta* of the conferences, together with the translations themselves, are to be sent in the usual way to the Consilium for approval, that is to say, confirmation, by the Apostolic See.

242. SC RITES (Consilium), **Norms**, on the use of Eucharistic Prayers I – IV, 23 May 1968: Not 4 (1968) 157–160.

EUCHARISTIC PRAYER I

I.   Eucharistic Prayer I, that is, the Roman Canon, may always be used; its use is particularly suited to days assigned a proper *In union with the whole Church* or a proper *Bless and approve*; to feasts of the apostles and saints mentioned in this Prayer; also to Sundays, unless pastoral reasons call for a different eucharistic prayer.[R1]   1931

II.   The norms to be followed in concelebration and for singing this prayer are in the *Rite of Concelebration* (7 March 1965) nos. 35–42.   1932

EUCHARISTIC PRAYER II

I.   Because of its distinctive features, Eucharistic Prayer II, is better suited to weekdays or to special occasions.   1933

Even though it has a corresponding preface, it may also be used with different ones, especially those summarizing the mystery of salvation, for example, the Sunday prefaces for Ordinary Time and the common prefaces.

In the celebration of a Mass for the dead, the special formulary may be inserted at its proper place, namely, before the *Remember our brothers and sisters*.[R2]

ᵃ   See DOL 1 no. 36.

ᵇ   See DOL 23 nos. 321 and 322.

R1   Query: When the canon of the Mass is said aloud, may the congregation make the response, *Amen?* Reply: The celebrant alone must recite the canon; it is a sacerdotal prayer. Therefore it belongs to him alone to recite during it the conclusions *Through Christ our Lord* with their *Amen*. But it is hard to stop the congregation from spontaneously saying the *Amen* to the various conclusions. If they are requested not to, there is the fear that they may not join in the response to the final doxology. It seems best therefore not to bother the people if they respond during the canon: Not 4 (1968) 136, no. 114. See also DOL 208 no. 1712, note R58.

R2   1. Query: When may the special formulary for the dead in Eucharistic Prayers II and III be used? Reply: The problem arose because the rubric for Eucharistic Prayer III read this way: "When this Prayer is used . . ." (see *Preces eucharisticae et praefationes*, Vatican Polyglot Press, 1967, 35). This rubric has been clarified in the new Order of Mass (GIRM no. 322 b [DOL 208 no. 1712]) and reads simply: "When Mass is

1934   II. In concelebration:

1. The *Lord, you are holy indeed* is recited by the celebrant alone, with hands extended.

2. From the *Let your Spirit* through the *May all of us who share* all the concelebrants recite everything in unison and in the following manner:

   a. the *Let your Spirit*, with hands outstretched toward the offerings, then joining their hands at the end;

   b. the *Before he was given up* and *When supper was ended*, with hands joined and bowing their heads at *gave you thanks*;

   c. the words of the Lord, with right hand outstretched toward the bread and the chalice, if this seems appropriate; at the elevation they look toward the host and the chalice, then bow deeply;

   d. the *In memory of his death*, with hands outstretched;

   e. the *May all of us who share*, while bowing deeply and with hands joined.

3. The intercessions for the living, *Lord, remember your Church*, and for the dead, *Remember our brothers and sisters*, may be assigned to one of the concelebrants, who recites them alone, with hands outstretched.

4. The concluding doxology is recited by the celebrant alone or together with all the concelebrants.

5. The celebrant begins the memorial acclamation after the consecration, with the words, *Let us proclaim the mystery of faith*; the congregation continues it, using the announced formulary.

1935   III. The following parts of this Prayer may be sung: *Before he was given up to death, When supper was ended, In memory of his death and resurrection*, the concluding doxology.

---

celebrated for any of the dead." Therefore the special embolism for the dead may be used in any Mass that is celebrated for a deceased person or in which there is a special memorial of the deceased. The point of the law is to facilitate carrying out the GIRM no. 316 [DOL 208 no. 1706] on moderation in the use of Masses for the dead: Not 5 (1969) 325, no. 4.

2. Query: In the part of Eucharistic Prayer II that begins with the words *In memory of his death and resurrection* the expression *to stand in your presence and serve you* seems to be an allusion to the parable of the Pharisee and the publican (see Lk 18:9–14). Is this not a sufficient reason to introduce some variation into the liturgical text? Reply: No. The expression in question, taken verbatim from the text of Hippolytus, is in no way an allusion to the biblical parable of the Pharisee and the publican; rather it has chiefly a priestly meaning. The Ethiopian version is clearer (*nous tenir avant toi et te servir comme prêtres* in the translation in Botte's edition p. 17). These words derive from the Old Testament, especially from Deuteronomy: Not 8 (1972) 194.

3. Query: Eucharistic Prayer II also has the passage *Remember Lord . . . together with N. our Pope, N. our Bishop, and all the clergy*. Why not also "the laity and religious"? Reply: That paragraph, after the style of the Roman Canon, affirms only the communion of the hierarchy. The general structure of the Roman Canon provides a clearer understanding of the issue. Because the eucharistic prayers are diverse in doctrinal content, their diversity, as adding an accessory value, seems quite useful. Furthermore, Eucharistic Prayer II is *shorter*: Not 8 (1972) 194–195.

4. Query: ". . . I request of the Congregation for Divine Worship permission to transfer the text of the preface for Eucharistic Prayer II to a place after the *Sanctus*, making it a *post-Sanctus*. The reason for this transfer is that if the celebrant chooses another preface of the season or of the saints the beginning of the anaphora of St. Hippolytus is not read. Thus this anaphora is considerably shortened and a good part (the beginning) of this beautiful eucharistic prayer is lost." Reply of the Congregation: 1. The structure of Eucharistic Prayer II does not allow using its texts like movable pieces that can fit in anywhere. The first part of the anaphora (the preface) is a giving of thanks, the function of which is to introduce the singing of the *Sanctus*. In no way, then, could it be placed after the *Sanctus* as a means of recovering this beautiful text. 2. Even when it is introduced by another preface as permitted by the rubrics of the Missal, Eucharistic Prayer II retains its unity because every preface, in its own way, takes up the theme of thanksgiving. Nor is this Prayer thereby truncated; the eucharistic prayer has to be viewed in its present totality (preface, *Sanctus*) and not in its distinct literary origins: Not 9 (1973) 246.

EUCHARISTIC PRAYER III

I.   Eucharistic Prayer III may be used with any of the prefaces; like the Roman   1936
Canon, it is to have precedence on Sundays and holydays. In this prayer it is
permissible to use the special formulary for a deceased person, to be inserted at its
proper place, namely, after the *In mercy and love unite all your children wherever they may
be*.[R3]

II. In concelebration: 1937
     1.   The *Father, you are holy indeed* is recited by the celebrant alone, with hands
outstretched.
     2.   From the *And so, Father* through the *Look with favor on your Church's offering* all
the concelebrants recite everything in unison and in the following manner:
          a.   the *And so, Father*, with hands outstretched toward the offerings; after
          the words, *at whose command we celebrate this eucharist*, they join their hands;
          b.   the *On the night he was betrayed* and *When supper was ended*, with hands
          joined and bowing their heads at *gave you thanks*;
          c.   the words of the Lord, with right hand outstretched toward the bread
          and the chalice, if this seems appropriate; at the elevation they look toward
          the host and the chalice, then bow deeply;
          d.   the *Father calling to mind*, with hands outstretched;
          e.   the *Look with favor*, while bowing deeply and with hands joined.
     3.   The intercessions, *May he make us* and *Lord may this sacrifice*, may be assigned
to one of the concelebrants, who recites them alone, with hands outstretched.
     4.   The concluding doxology is recited by the celebrant alone or together with
all the concelebrants.
     5.   The celebrant begins the memorial acclamation after the consecration, with
the words, *Let us proclaim the mystery of faith*; the congregation continues it, using the
announced formulary.

III. The following parts of this Prayer may be sung: the *On the night he was betrayed*,   1938
When supper was ended, the concluding doxology.

EUCHARISTIC PRAYER IV

I.   Eucharistic Prayer IV has an unchangeable preface and presents a more com-   1939
plete summary of the history of salvation. It may be used whenever a Mass does
not have a proper preface; its use is particularly suited to a congregation of people
with a more developed knowledge of Scripture.
     The special formulary for a deceased person cannot be inserted into this Prayer
because of its distinctive structure.

II. In concelebration: 1940
     1.   The preface and the *Father, we acknowledge* through *bring us the fullness of grace*
are recited by the celebrant alone, with hands outstretched.
     2.   From the *Father, may this Holy Spirit* through the *Lord, look upon this sacrifice* all
the concelebrants recite everything in unison and in the following manner:
          a.   the *Father, may this Holy Spirit*, with hands outstretched toward the
          offerings; after the words, *an everlasting covenant*, they join their hands;

[R3]   See DOL 208 no. 1445, note R14.

b. the *While they were at supper* and *In the same way*, with hands joined and bowing their heads at *gave you thanks*, which in this prayer is said only before the consecration of the wine;

c. the words of the Lord, with right hand outstretched toward the bread and the chalice, if this seems appropriate; at the elevation they look toward the host and the chalice, then bow deeply;

d. the *Father, we now celebrate*, with hands outstretched;

e. the *Lord, look upon this sacrifice*, while bowing deeply and with hands joined.

3. The intercession, *Lord, remember those*, may be assigned to one of the concelebrants, who recites it alone, with hands outstretched.

4. The concluding doxology is recited by the celebrant alone or together with all the concelebrants.

5. The celebrant begins the memorial acclamation after the consecration, with the words, *Let us proclaim the mystery of faith*; the congregation continues it, using the announced formulary.

1941   III. The following parts of this Prayer may be sung: the *While they were at supper, In the same way, Father, we now celebrate*, the concluding doxology.

243. CONSILIUM, Letter *La publication* of Cardinal B. Gut to presidents of the conferences of bishops and of national liturgical commissions, on the new eucharistic prayers, 2 June 1968: Not 4 (1968) 146–148.*

1942   The publication of the new eucharistic prayers for the Roman liturgy, truly as a new canticle placed on the lips of the praying Church by the Holy Spirit, gives me the welcome opportunity of communicating for the first time as President of the Consilium with Your Excellency and, through you, with all the venerable bishops, clergy, religious and faithful of your country, especially with those who wholeheartedly dedicate themselves to the progress of an intelligent, orderly and dynamic renewal of the liturgy in the spirit of the Council and the postconciliar documents.

With this letter it is my sincere pleasure to enclose copies of the three new anaphoras and the eight new prefaces, together with some "Guidelines" which may be found useful. These latter may help Your Excellency in providing a sense of direction in showing the clergy and faithful the reasons for this innovation, its significance, and basic principles. These indications can also be of assistance in regulating a fruitful and prudent implementation of these Prayers.

All this will allow Your Excellency to broaden the catechesis on the Mass, and in particular on the eucharistic prayer, which has already been initiated with the introduction of the vernacular for this part of the eucharistic celebration. The Church shows her concern for a celebration which is more alive and which fosters better participation, as well as her concern for an ever deepening appreciation of the eucharistic mystery, by presenting a wealth and variety of themes and aspects for catechesis.

Moreover, this new publication follows the express wish of the Holy See, which, even with the changes in personnel, still remains quite definite in asserting

---

* English text from the Consilium.

that the prescription of the Council for "an accurate, general reform of the liturgy" (Constitution on the Sacred Liturgy art. 21)[a] be brought to implementation.

The Council's decision is gradually becoming more and more everyone's desire. The reports received from every part of the world together with the results of the Consilium's inquiry on liturgical reform, as well as the living testimony of the delegates of the episcopal conferences at the Synod of Bishops, all attest to the fervor of efforts in every country to give new "spirit and truth" to prayer. There is clear evidence of the satisfaction, and often the enthusiasm, of the faithful who have become dynamic and vocal participants in the sacred actions and more aware of their vocation and their priesthood.   1943

I wish to express the wholehearted gratitude of the Consilium for all these endeavors, as well as for the various surveys, statistics, desires, goodwill, and encouragement manifested so many times by individual bishops, priests, and faithful, or by episcopal conferences.

It would also be appreciated if Your Excellency would be so kind as to assure all those in contact with the pastoral dimensions of the liturgy that the Consilium is not insensitive to the difficulties which they encounter and wishes to serve their needs, giving the liturgy that characteristic of perennial youth desired and indicated by the Holy Father himself (Address to the Consilium Fathers, 13 October 1966, *Notitiae*, no. 23, 305).[b]   1944

The field in which the conscientious experts of the Consilium have patiently and quietly labored for four years is beginning to give forth its fruits. The eucharistic prayers are the most precious of these, but will not be the last.

Some rites are already in experimentation in various regions and others will follow, we hope within a short time. In this way the Consilium hopes to respond to the trust of the episcopacy and to the legitimate expectations of pastors and faithful by continuing to labor in the spirit and method of these years.

Above all, the Consilium hopes that it may continue to rely on the reciprocal, and so necessary, understanding and cooperation of each country's hierarchy. What needs to be promoted is an *orderly* progress, one which both corresponds to the needs of men of today and develops the thrust of solid tradition, and which is adapted to the possibilities of acceptance and to the level of preparation of the faithful. The law of *gradual* progress, foreseen at the outset of the Consilium's work, still seems to be valid. What causes turmoil is not the path of progress itself, but the undertaking of experiments which have not been sufficiently studied nor inserted into an organic plan of the general reform of the liturgy.

For this reason, allow me to renew the exhortation so often made by my venerable predecessor, His Eminence, Giacomo Cardinal Lercaro, to await the rites prepared by the Consilium and to study those adaptations which would seem appropriate and useful.

May this new gift to the Church be the guarantee of these intentions and desires, as I ask Your Excellency to express to all the members of your episcopal conference my fraternal greeting and my sincere encouragement in pursuing the path opened by the Council, which is so rich in promise.

---

[a] See DOL 1 no. 21.

[b] See DOL 84.

244. CONSILIUM, **Guidelines** *Au cours des derniers mois*, to assist catechesis on the anaphoras of the Mass, 2 June 1968: Not 4 (1968) 148–155 (French).

1945   The conferences of bishops during the last several months have acted on the concession of the vernacular for the canon of the Mass.[a] A still further step forward comes about now with the introduction of new anaphoras into the Roman liturgy. Its spiritual and pastoral purpose is clear: to open more lavishly to priests and faithful, in the way they celebrate Mass, the biblical treasures of the Christian life and those traditional in the universal Church and to assist in their being understood and vitally assimilated. In their celebrations priests and people will thus be able to achieve the ideal of full, active, inward, and outward participation that the Council has set as the aim of the reform of the liturgy.[b] Through this new usage regarding anaphoras the Church intends to further one objective: that for every priest, baptized person, and community the celebration of the eucharistic sacrifice may become in reality "the source and the summit of all the Church's worship and of the entire Christian life."[1]

Therefore for the introduction of this new usage an intense preliminary and accompanying catechesis is indispensable. It must be both instructional and spiritual and should be given first to the clergy, then to the better prepared groups, then to all the faithful.

The preparation of the clergy must be more technical, yet always pointed to assisting them in their pastoral mission. Catechesis of the people must as far as possible avoid historical explanations and difficult theological points, those above all that are still controverted among theologians themselves. The catechesis should rather go immediately to the meaning of the prayers as they actually are today and to their bearing on everyday life.

The main points of focus for the people's catechesis in the anaphoras are those that follow.

1. GENERAL MEANING OF THE ANAPHORA

1946   First, to explain to the people because of its newness the terminology that the particular language will adopt to designate the anaphora ("anaphora," "eucharistic prayer," "canon," etc.).

"Anaphora" means the great prayer recited as the central part of the Mass unfolds, going from the *The Lord be with you . . .*, *Lift up your hearts . . .* to the *Through him, with him, . . . all honor and glory is yours for ever and ever.*

A prayer of thanksgiving and praise to the Father, as well as of petitions addressed to him, the anaphora is recited over the bread and wine; during it, in imitation of the Lord Jesus and in obedience to his command, come the repetition and reactualization of what he did at the last supper and after it, the sharing in his body and blood in communion.

2. ESSENTIALS OF THE ANAPHORA

1947   They consist in a central core and its further elaborations.

---

[a]   See DOL 117.

[b]   See DOL 1 no. 14.

[1]   Instr. EuchMyst no. 3 e [DOL 179 no. 1232]. See also LG no. 11 [DOL 4 no. 141]; SC art. 41 [DOL 1 no. 41]; PO nos. 2, 5, 6 [DOL 18 nos. 257, 260, 261]; UR no. 15 [DOL 6 no. 187].

a. The core is the narrative-reactualization of what Jesus did at the last supper, leaving out only the breaking of the bread and the communion, which come at the final part of the Mass.

Jesus, having taken the bread: 1. pronounced over it a prayer of thanks and praise to the Father; 2. broke the bread and gave it to his disciples; 3. said: "Do this in memory of me," that is, as a celebration that calls to mind and contains what I am and what I have done for you.

Jesus did the same regarding the chalice.

These elements in every case constitute the core of the anaphora, which consists therefore of:

1. a hymn consisting of thanksgiving and praise to the Father for his gifts, those of the redemption above all (in the Roman Canon this is the preface);

2. the narrative of Jesus' actions and the words he spoke in instituting the eucharist (in the Roman Canon, the *The day before he suffered*. . .).

3. The point, however, is not a mere narrative of things past, but a narrative intended to reactualize what Jesus did. For this reason the prayer of supplication is also addressed to the Father, asking that he make the narrative effective by sanctifying the bread and wine, that is, concretely by making them become the body and blood of Christ (in the Roman Canon, the *Bless and approve our offering*. . .), to the end that we who receive them may be made holy by these gifts (in the Roman Canon, the *Look with favor on these offerings*. . .).

4. Jesus had said that we were to do all this "in memory" of him, that is, as a celebration recalling and containing what he has done for us. This has bearing on our redemption and principally on his redeeming death on the cross, because his actions involved above all his body, given for us, and his blood, shed for our sins. Inasmuch as it is a "memorial" that makes the body given for us and the blood shed for our sins to be present, the celebration of the eucharist involves a sacrificial offering. This is why the anaphora includes a prayer offering the holy gifts "in memory" of the passion, death, and resurrection (in fact of the whole plan of Christ's redemption). In the Roman Canon this is the *Father, we celebrate the memory of Christ.* . . .

5. The anaphora has its termination in a doxology to which all the people reply: *Amen!*

b. Three elements further elaborate this central core: 1948

1. The *Sanctus* in which all the people take part as a conclusion to the triumphal hymn of thanks, the preface.

2. The intercessory prayers on behalf of those for whose intentions the sacrifice is offered; this is a logical extension of the concept of offering sacrifice for someone's benefit (in the Roman Canon: the *We offer them for* . . .; *Father, accept this offering* . . .; *Remember, Lord, those who have died* . . .; and the *Though we are sinners.* . . .

3. The commemoration of the saints, which the intercessory prayers develop.

3. VARIETY OF ANAPHORA TEXTS

In the different liturgies, especially those of the East, the tradition includes a   1949
rich variety in the texts for the eucharistic prayers. They evince common elements as well as differences, some of which, on secondary points, are considerable.

1950   1. Sometimes the common elements occupy a different place in the different eucharistic prayers. In the Roman Canon, for example, the petition addressed to the Father that the bread and wine become the body and blood of Christ (the *Bless and approve our offering*. . .) occurs before the institution narrative; in the anaphoras deriving from the liturgy of Antioch it occurs, instead, after the institution narrative; in the ancient liturgy of Alexandria it probably occurred before, as in the Roman Canon, but in later texts from this Church it occurs twice, once before and once after the institution narrative. In the Roman Canon the intercessory prayers for the living occur before and those for the dead after the institution narrative; in the Alexandrian tradition both occur before and in the Antiochene, after. Thus the make-up of the anaphora consequent on the placement of its different elements may vary on certain points and its structure may vary in degree of clarity.

1951   2. A second basis of differentiation rests on the fact that in certain liturgical traditions nearly all the anaphora elements are fixed, not varying with different feasts; this is the case in the East. In other traditions certain important elements do vary with the feasts. In the Roman Canon the preface is variable (and on a few occasions the *Father, accept this offering*. . .); in the Hispanic and Gallican traditions, the entire text, excepting the institution narrative, varies with the feasts.

1952   3. A third variable is the degree of emphasis given to certain ideas.

1953   4. A fourth is style, as to degrees of conciseness, solemnity, the use of metaphor or of Scripture, etc.

Each Eastern Church usually has more than one and sometimes several anaphoras, alternating their use according to circumstances.

Such a variety in the tradition of anaphoras throughout the entire Church is a genuine treasure: one anaphora complements another; one allows for a better expression of certain ideas than is possible in the same completeness and manner in all.

4. New Anaphoras in the Roman Liturgy

1954   The Holy See has introduced three new anaphoras into the Roman liturgy in response to the wishes of many bishops, reaffirmed at the recent Synod of Bishops, and in the interest of making possible in the central part of the eucharistic celebration a better proclamation of God's blessings and a better recollection of the history of salvation.

With these added to the Roman Canon — hereafter "Eucharistic Prayer I" — the Roman liturgy will from now on have four anaphoras.

Why this new departure? To consider the variety of anaphoras in the tradition of the universal Church is to realize that one anaphora alone cannot contain all the pastoral, spiritual, and theological richness to be hoped for. A multiplicity of texts must make up for the limitations of any one of them. This has always been the course taken by all the Christian Churches, the Roman alone excepted; they have all had and continue to have a variety of anaphoras, sometimes a great variety. In adding three new anaphoras to the Roman Canon, the Church's intent here too has been to enrich the Roman liturgy pastorally, spiritually, and liturgically.

5. CHARACTERISTICS OF THE ANAPHORAS OF THE ROMAN LITURGY

1. The Roman Canon

1955   In the order of its elements and thus in its structure, the distinguishing features of the Roman Canon are: a. it places before the institution narrative the petition that the bread and wine may become the body and blood of Christ (the *Bless and approve our offering*); b. it places the intercessory prayers for the living before and those for the dead after the institution narrative and separates the two lists commemorating the saints; c. as in the Hispanic and Gallican traditions, it varies according to feasts the first part of the canon, the preface (and on a few occasions the *Father, accept this offering*).

In the existing Roman Canon its unity and the logical sequence of its ideas are not immediately or readily perceptible. It leaves the impression of a series of discrete, merely juxtaposed prayers; it requires a degree of reflection for a grasp of their unity.

On the other hand, the varying of the prefaces on different feasts endows the first part of the Roman Canon with a rich variety. The new prefaces that the liturgical reform has introduced open the way to taking fuller advantage of this spiritual and pastoral potential.

As to themes, it is a characteristic of the Roman Canon throughout to stress the offering of gifts and the plea to God to accept them in our favor.

The Roman Canon also has its distinctive style, deeply imbued with the Roman taste for a certain gravity and for a simultaneous redundance and brevity.

The Roman Canon has an important value as a theological, liturgical, and spiritual document of the Latin Church. It existed certainly by the beginning of the fifth century; from the beginning of the seventh it has remained practically unaltered; later it became the single canon in the entire Latin Church.

2. CRITERIA FOLLOWED BY THE THREE NEW ANAPHORAS

a. *Continuity of thought and clarity of structure.* This is due to the natural and easily grasped connection between parts and ideas. The *structure*, accordingly, is basically the same in the three new anaphoras:

    1. preface (variable in Anaphoras II and III, fixed in IV) with the *Sanctus* at the end;

    2. transition from the *Sanctus* to the consecratory epiclesis, that is, the petition addressed to the Father that through the action of the Holy Spirit the bread and wine may become the body and blood of Christ. The transition is very short in Anaphora II, somewhat short in III, long in IV;

    3. consecratory epiclesis;

    4. institution narrative;

    5. anamnesis, that is, the "memorial" of the passion and of the whole "mystery" of Christ and the offering up of the divine victim;

    6. prayer that the offering will be received and that the communion will be fruitful;

    7 and 8. commemoration of the saints and the intercessions (Anaphora III); intercessions and commemoration of the saints (Anaphoras II and IV).

    9. concluding doxology.

The main difference between this structure and that of the Roman Canon itself is that in these three new anaphoras the commemoration of the saints and the intercessory prayers have all been grouped together into the second part of the anaphoras, rather than occurring, as in the Roman Canon, partly before and partly after the institution narrative. This rearrangement, modeled on the Antiochene tradition, confers a much greater clarity on the new formularies, since the distinct parts fall into a natural sequence. They continue to be Roman in style, however, especially in their placement of the consecratory epiclesis before the institution narrative.

1956

1957   b. *Variety*. The general structure is common to the three new anaphoras, but each one has its own destinctive characteristics — spiritual, pastoral, and stylistic — in relation both to each other and to the Roman Canon. This means the avoidance, to the extent possible, of a repetition of concepts, words, and phrases from the Roman Canon itself in the three anaphoras or, in one of them, of those from another.

The result for the Roman liturgy is a notable enrichment, including, among other things, a fuller expression of the theology of: the eucharist, the history of salvation, both in general and about the people of God and the Church, the role of the Holy Spirit in the Church, particularly in the eucharist. The universalist and ecumenical viewpoints of Vatican II and of the so-called theology of the world have in these anaphoras a restrained, biblical, but real echo. All of this still takes nothing away from their clearly traditional character.

Anaphora II is intentionally short, made up of simple ideas. The anaphora of Hippolytus (from the beginning of the 3rd century) is the inspiration of its style and much of its phrasing.

Anaphora III is intended to be of medium length, with a clear structure and readily perceptible transition from one part to another. It is suited for use with any of the traditional or new Roman prefaces because of an identical import in structure and style.

The particular feature of Anaphora IV is that before the institution narrative it presents, in an orderly and somewhat developed way, a complete synthesis of the history of salvation, following the model of the Antiochene tradition. This requires the preface to be limited to the themes of creation in general and the creation of the angels, the two first stages in the history of salvation; this history is then carried further, beginning with the creation of man, in the prayer between the *Sanctus* and the epiclesis. Further, the preface with this anaphora must always be the same: it could change with feasts and treat other things only to the detriment of the exposition of the history of salvation — compact but complete, ordered, and free of repetitions — that this anaphora intends.

In our view it is very important pastorally that the faithful from time to time hear this kind of orderly and complete summary of the history of salvation; it can serve as a general framework within which they can later locate the many details of this history as they hear them on other occasions.

6. GUIDELINES FOR USING THE ANAPHORAS

1958   The choice of one of the four anaphoras of the Roman liturgy cannot be regulated by criteria fixing and restricting the use to a particular feast and liturgical season. The fact is that they are written in the style of the Roman tradition: this does not develop throughout the anaphora a theme related to the mystery celebrated but in the preface alone sets out one aspect of the theme.

The supreme criteria must therefore be pastoral. This involves two points in particular: the possibility of using along with these new prayers the existing texts proper to the great feasts; the correspondence of the prayer chosen to the intellectual and spiritual capacities of the faithful.

These two principles allow for the following guidelines.

1959   1. The Roman Canon, which may always be used, must take precedence on feast days that have proper texts as part of the anaphora (the preface, the *In union with the whole Church*, the *Father, accept this offering*). In the Roman tradition these are the texts that bring into the anaphora the distinctive feature of the day. The Roman Canon should, in addition, also be used on the feast days of the saints it mentions.

2. Because of its conciseness and comparative simplicity, Eucharistic Prayer II   1960
can be used to advantage on weekdays and in Masses with children, young people,
and small groups. Its simplicity also makes it a good starting point for catechesis on
the different elements of the eucharistic prayer.

It includes its own preface, which should be used with the rest of the
prayer. But use of a corresponding preface is permissible, that is, one concisely
expressing the mystery of salvation: for example, the new prefaces given for Ordinary Time and the new common prefaces.

3. Eucharistic Prayer III may be joined with any preface already existing in   1961
the Roman Missal. On Sundays, therefore, this prayer and the Roman Canon could
be alternated.

4. Eucharistic Prayer IV must be used just as it is, without any change even of   1962
the preface. Further, because it comprises a rather detailed summary of the history
of salvation and as such presupposes a somewhat superior knowledge of Scripture,
it should be given preference for use with groups having a better foundation in
Scripture, whenever a preface connected with other parts of the canon is not obligatory.

After the model of the Roman Canon, with its elements proper to certain
celebrations (the *Father, accept this offering*), the new eucharistic prayers make provision
for a special embolism, to be inserted among the intercessory prayers at the celebration of Mass for a deceased person. This embolism may be added in Anaphoras II
and III, but not in IV, since it would break up the unitary structure of this anaphora.

CONCLUSION

These are the guidelines followed in the preparation of the new eucharistic   1963
prayers. It has seemed useful also to offer them as an introduction to the new texts
for a better understanding of their true nature and purpose. We hope and expect
that they will thus contribute to fostering the devotion of the faithful, to enhancing
their participation in the celebration of the eucharist, and, in a concrete way, to
improving their formation and life as Christians.

245. CONSILIUM, **Declaration** *In conficiendis*, on certain points regarding
the eucharistic prayers, 6 November 1968: Not 4 (1968) 356.

In preparing translations of the new eucharistic prayers the following are to be   1964
observed:

1. Pope Paul VI has decided to grant the wish of many that in the formularies
of consecration the Lord's words are to have a uniform format. The purpose is to
make their recitation easier for priests, especially in concelebration.

Accordingly, in the new eucharistic prayers the words of the Lord are to be
printed in this way:

> *At the consecration of the bread*:
> Take this all of you and eat it:
> this is my body
> which will be given up for you.

> *At the consecration of the wine*:
> Take this, all of you, and drink from it:
> this is the cup of my blood,
> the blood of the new and everlasting covenant.
> It will be shed for you and for all
> so that sins may be forgiven.
> Do this in memory of me.

The words of the Lord are to be printed in a typeface bolder than that in the rest of the text, in keeping with what is laid down in the Congregation of Rites' Instruction *Eucharisticum mysterium* no. 21, b.[a]

1965
   2. In these same new eucharistic prayers, at least in editions of the canon for use by bishops, after the words *N. our Bishop* in the intercessions the words *and me, your unworthy servant* are to be inserted. Usage of these words conforms to that of the Roman Canon [Eucharistic Prayer I] when a bishop celebrates the Mass.

▶ 123. CONSILIUM, Instruction *Comme le prévoit*, on translation of liturgical texts, 25 January 1969:

   no. 33:   Translation of consecratory prayers, anaphoras, prefaces [no. 870].

246. PAUL VI, **Address** to a meeting sponsored by the national liturgical commission of Italy on the theme: The Eucharistic Prayer in the Celebration of Mass, 7 February 1969: Not 5 (1969) 61–64 (Italian; excerpts).

1966
   [. . .] What is central in our heart at this moment and what we wish to share with you, because you are the experts responsible at the diocesan and national level for the furtherance of the liturgy, is a threefold directive as an ever more effective model for your activity, which we perceive already to be in line with our own wishes.

1967
   Work together as one, we say before all else. [. . .] If your activity, in the way it is already evolving, remains always closely bonded to the progress of national liturgical life; if it is not hampered by useless delays in creating problems and suggesting their solutions or in anticipating difficulties; if, in a word, your activity continues to be conducted with an ever watchful and prompt sense of responsibility, everything can proceed smoothly. You will avoid unwarranted resistance, dangerous divisions, unauthorized experiments; you will address the requirements of contemporary needs with the unifying force of adherence to tradition so that all measures will be in accord with a sound renewal.

1968
   Work well, we say to you secondly. We know that for you work is a title of honor, besides being your declared commitment. But there is need to emphasize this strongly, so that the effort you have all exerted so far and continue to exert, which is in process of producing in a short time remarkable results in programs and initiatives, may always remain at peak intensity.
   To work well means to instill into the souls of priests and laity the value — not merely ritual, but theological, pastoral, and ascetical — of the liturgical reform in general and now of the eucharistic prayers in particular. The aim is both that the

---

   [a] See DOL 179 no. 1250.

spirituality of our beloved clergy will profit from them and that the faithful will be led to a more intense participation in the eucharistic sacrifice, in such a way, for example, that they will not limit themselves to joining in the acclamation after the consecration, but will adopt an inner attitude of spiritual offering as an exercise of their own royal priesthood.

To work well means to create as companion to the new liturgical texts a sufficient deepening in the knowledge of the Bible, the Fathers, and Christian spirituality. This is to be achieved by means of a vast effort of cooperation in which experts in the specific disciplines make their proper contribution and a well-planned use of the media of communication.

To work well means to strive not only that the broad lines of liturgical reform are followed but also that the process shows absolute faithfulness to all its details regarding gestures, voice, diction, the ministers, readers, servers, cantors (how dear to our heart is liturgical singing and how far, sad to say, it remains from the rich results we look for).

To work well means to bring out completely — we emphasize *completely* — the traditions present in the liturgical texts and all the more so now that we are entering into the august, stark, sacred, majestic, awesome sanctuary of the eucharistic prayers. Of old the "Discipline of the Secret" sought to shield these prayers for a long time from intrusion or irreverence; they deserve, therefore, all the most sensitive attention of devotion, doctrine, and literary expression in the vernacular. On this point it will be advisable to proceed with patience, without haste, and above all with a measure of humility, enlisting the cooperation of many, not just theologians and liturgists, but also those skilled in literature and style. The goal is for the translations to be documents of acknowledged and transparent beauty that can stand the stern test of time because of their aptness, balance, elegance, and richness in expression and language, as befits the inner wealth of their content.

To work with clarity, we say finally. The bishops of Italy look to you; so do the   1969
simple people who have within themselves a sense of God; with a critical, perhaps distrustful eye, so do the champions of culture and art; so do the young, who show signs of a renewed interest in the liturgy. Do not disappoint the expectations that from all sectors of the Christian people are fixed on your activity. At the same time do not close yourselves off from one group in order to satisfy others. The liturgy teaches universality; it does not divide but unites; it does not set up barriers but fuses hearts in prayer and love. We are alluding to cases, more or less underground, that by fragmenting the celebration of the liturgy into various categories of the faithful, even to the point of individual homes or private groups, run the risk of causing the loss of the spirit of catholicity, the union in one faith that binds the Church together. *Lex orandi, lex credendi*, as everyone well knows; but, sadly, particularism in prayer can turn out to be an adulteration of the *sensus Ecclesiae*, of the lived and suffered *patrimonium fidei*. We allude, furthermore, to youth Masses. These are in themselves excellent and are to be wholeheartedly encouraged. But only where they are free of polemical motivation vis-à-vis other Masses and altogether removed from novelties that under pretext of adapting the Mass to today's mentality pervert the celebration, impoverishing it as to ritual, texts, music and singing, length, and the homily.

You, however, must make the distinctions required, must realize that the confidence placed in you is an expectation of great things from your work, above all by reason of the directness and clarity with which you are able to answer, without harmful confusion, the profound and multiple needs of the Christian people.

▶   202.   PAUL VI, Apostolic Constitution *Missale Romanum,* approving the new Roman
          Missal, 3 April 1969:

                              The eucharistic prayer [no. 1360].

▶   208.   SC RITES (Consilium); SC DIVINE WORSHIP, General Instruction of the Ro-
          man Missal, 1st ed. 6 April 1969; 4th ed. 27 March 1975:

          Introduction no. 2:   Eucharistic prayers [no. 1377].
          nos. 48:   Liturgy of the eucharist [no. 1438].
                54–55:   Eucharistic prayer [nos. 1444–45].
                108–110:   Rites for the eucharistic prayer [nos. 1498–1500].
                134–135:   Deacon's role [nos. 1524–25].
                168–191:   Eucharistic prayer at concelebrations [nos.
                                  1558–81].
                223:            At Mass without congregation [no. 1613].
                235 e: Incensation at consecration [no. 1625].
                322:            Choice of the eucharistic prayer [no. 1712].

▶   52.   SC DIVINE WORSHIP, Instruction (third) *Liturgicae instaurationes,* 5 September
          1970:

          no. 4:   Eucharistic prayer [no. 522].

247. SC DIVINE WORSHIP, Decree *Cum de nomine,* on mention of the bishop's name in the eucharistic prayer, 9 October 1972: AAS 64 (1972)
692–694; Not 8 (1972) 347–349.

1970   Since the Roman Missal has no directive on expressing the bishop's name in
          the eucharistic prayer, many Ordinaries and even conferences of bishops have
          asked this Congregation about those whose names are to be mentioned.

              Mention of the bishop in the eucharistic prayer is not simply or mainly a
          matter of honor but of communion and charity: to point to him as the steward of
          the grace of the supreme priesthood[1] or to pray for divine help on behalf of his
          person and ministry within the eucharistic celebration, the summit of all the
          Church's activity and the fount from which all its power flows.[2]

              Such considerations obviously apply also to those who, whether marked by
          episcopal consecration or not, preside over some community of the people of God
          that is not yet established as a diocese. Consequently the following are prescribed.

1971   1.   In the eucharistic prayer these persons must be named:

              a.   the bishop of the diocese;

              b.   a bishop still retaining administration of one diocese after being transferred
          to another see;

              c.   an apostolic administrator — whether the see is vacant or not — with
          either a temporary or permanent appointment, who is a bishop and actually is
          fully exercising his office, especially in spiritual matters;

              d.   a vicar and prefect apostolic;

---

    [1]   See LG no. 26 [DOL 4 no. 146].

    [2]   See SC art. 10 [DOL 1 no. 10].

e. a prelate and an abbot *nullius* having jurisdiction over a territory not attached to any diocese.

2. In addition, it is *permitted* to name in the eucharistic prayer coadjutor and auxiliary bishops who assist the bishop of the diocese in ruling it and others, as long as they have received the episcopal character. If there are many such, they are remembered collectively, without mention of their names, after the name of the proper Ordinary as indicated in no. 1.   1972

3. In other, exceptional circumstances the Apostolic See is to be consulted.   1973

4. As to the formulary to be used: 1974

a. In remembering the bishop, vicar or prefect apostolic, and the prelate or abbot *nullius*, depending on which one it is, the formulary will be: *together with N. our Bishop (Vicar, Prelate, Prefect, Abbot)*.

b. If names are to be grouped together, the diocesan bishop's name is always mentioned first, then the next name, thus: *together with N. our Bishop and N. . . .*; or when several are to be mentioned collectively: *together with N. our Bishop and his assistant bishops*.

c. When a priest celebrates Mass in a different territory but for a group of the faithful of his own diocese (vicariate or prefecture, prelature or abbey *nullius*), as, for example, on the occasion of a pilgrimage, the formulary will be: *together with N. our Bishop (Vicar, Prelate, Prefect, Abbot)* and *N. the Bishop of this Church*.

d. When a bishop celebrates Mass:

— within the boundaries of his own Church, he may associate his coadjutor or auxiliary bishops with himself in this way: *together with me your unworthy servant and my assistant bishops;*

— outside the boundaries of his own Church, the formulary will be: *together with my brother N. Bishop (or Prelate, Prefect, etc.) of this Church and me your unworthy servant.*

The Congregation for Divine Worship after consultation with the Congregation for Bishops and the Pontifical Commission for the Revision of the Code of Canon Law decreed these directives. Pope Paul VI on 5 September 1972 approved and confirmed them by his authority, ordering that all concerned observe them.

All things to the contrary notwithstanding.

248. SC DIVINE WORSHIP, **Circular Letter** *Eucharistiae participationem* to presidents of the conferences of bishops, on the eucharistic prayers, 27 April 1973: Not 9 (1973) 193–201.

1. To provide for the faithful's participating in the eucharist with consciousness   1975
of what they are doing, with devotion, and full involvement[1] is the main objective
of the reform of the liturgy and in particular of the recent revision of the Roman
Missal, carried out in keeping with the directives of Vatican Council II.[2] Clearly a
distinctive feature of the Missal, promulgated by authority of Pope Paul VI, is the
rich collection of texts to choose from in the many cases when an option is granted.

---

[1] See SC art. 48 [DOL 1 no. 48].

[2] See Paul VI, Ap. Const. *Missale Romanum*, 3 April 1969 [DOL 202].

This applies to readings taken from sacred Scripture, chants, the general intercessions and acclamations for the use of the entire community of the faithful, even the *presidential* prayers, including the eucharistic prayers. Three new texts of these, in addition to the Roman Canon of ancient tradition, have been approved for use.[3]

1976   2.   The reason for supplying such a wide choice of texts and the purpose intended in the revision of formularies are pastoral in nature, namely, to ensure unity and variety in liturgical prayer. By using texts given in the Roman Missal, the different Christian communities gathered together to celebrate the eucharist have the experience that they themselves constitute the Church praying with the same faith and the same formularies of prayer. Such communities, especially with use of the vernacular, also are sharing in the opportunity for the one mystery of Christ to be proclaimed in a variety of ways. In addition, the faithful individually can also more readily raise their hearts to the Lord in supplication and thanks[4] and have a more spiritually effective share in the celebrations.

1977   3.   Even though several years have passed since the promulgation of the Roman Missal, it has not yet been possible to bring it fully into celebrations with the people because in many countries the immense work of translating requires yet more time.[5] In addition, quite often there is a lack of knowledge on the means of increasing the pastoral effectiveness of celebrations and in arranging the Mass insufficient attention is given to the general spiritual good of the assembly.[6]

1978   4.   During this period, however, many have felt the desire for even greater adaptation of the eucharistic celebration through the composition of new formularies, including new eucharistic prayers. They maintain that the options given in the present Order of Mass regarding the *presidential* prayers and the four eucharistic prayers do not yet fully meet the needs of different groups, regions, and peoples. Consequently this Congregation has many times received the petition for the approval (or for the permission to grant approval) and for the use of new texts for the presidential and eucharistic prayers that are composed in accord with the contemporary mentality and idiom.

In addition during the last few years a number of authors of different languages and countries have published their own compositions of eucharistic prayers as theoretical models. Another frequent occurrence, in spite of its proscription by Vatican Council II[7] and prohibitions by the bishops, is that priests are using privately composed texts.

1979   5.   Against this background this Congregation, at the direction of Pope Paul VI and employing experts from around the world, has carefully studied the issue, and its implications, of composing new eucharistic prayers or of granting to the conferences of bishops the power to approve them. The conclusions of this study have been submitted to the Fathers of this Congregation in a plenary session, to the judgment of other Congregations involved, and finally to Pope Paul. After all the factors have been fully weighed, the decision is that at this time it is not advisable to grant to the conferences of bishops a general permission to compose or approve

---

    [3]   See ibid. [DOL 202 no. 1360].

    [4]   See GIRM no. 54 [DOL 208 no. 1444].

    [5]   On the principles on which translations must be based, see Consilium, Instr., 25 Jan. 1969 [DOL 123].

    [6]   See GIRM no. 313 [DOL 208 no. 1703].

    [7]   See SC art. 22, § 3 [DOL 1 no. 22].

new eucharistic prayers. On the contrary, it is judged that the wiser course is to counsel a more complete catechesis on the real nature of the eucharistic prayer.[8] For the eucharistic prayer as the high point of the celebration must also be the high point of a more profound catechesis. It seems equally necessary that there be fuller instruction on the resources available for priests to intensify the faithful's participation through the use both of the norms established by current liturgical law and of the formularies provided in the Roman Missal.

6.   There are therefore to be only four eucharistic prayers, those, namely, con-   1980
tained in the revised Roman Missal; it is unlawful to use any other prayer that is composed without leave of the Apostolic See or that does not have its approval. The conferences of bishops and the bishops individually are urgently requested that by using compelling reasons they lead priests to respect the one practice of the Roman Church: this course will be a service to the good of the Church itself and to the correct carrying out of the liturgical celebration.

Moved by a pastoral love for unity, the Apostolic See reserves to itself the right to regulate a matter so important as the discipline of the eucharistic prayers. The Apostolic See will not refuse to consider lawful needs within the Roman Rite and will accord every consideration to the petitions submitted by the conferences of bishops for the possible composition in special circumstances of a new eucharistic prayer and its introduction into the liturgy. The Apostolic See will set forth the norms to be observed in each case.

7.   Now that this decision has been announced, it seems worthwhile to offer some   1981
considerations that can make its meaning clearer and its execution easier. Some points have to do with the nature and importance of the eucharistic prayer in liturgical tradition, especially the Roman tradition; others concern possibilities for adapting the celebration to individual groups without altering the text of the eu-charistic prayer in any way.

8.   The eucharistic prayer of its nature is "the high point of the entire celebra-   1982
tion." It is a prayer of thanksgiving and sanctification, having as its purpose "that the whole congregation join Christ in acknowledging the great things God has done and in offering the sacrifice."[9] This prayer is spoken by the ministerial priest as the spokesman of the voice of God addressed to the people and of the voice of the people raising their hearts and minds to God. Therefore only the sound of the prayer must be heard, as the assembly gathered to celebrate the liturgy maintains a reverent silence.

The character of the eucharistic prayer that must have precedence therefore is that it is a giving of thanks for the entire mystery of salvation or for some feature of that mystery being celebrated in the liturgy according to the different days, feasts, seasons, or rites. Its catechetical character, directed toward bringing out special features of a particular celebration, is secondary.[10]

So that those sharing in the eucharist might better thank God and bless him, in the revision of the Roman Missal "the eucharistic prayer has been enriched with a great number of prefaces — drawn from the early tradition of the Roman Church or recently composed — in order that the different facets of the mystery of salvation

---

   [8]   See Card. Benno Gut, Letter to the conferences of bishops, 2 June 1968, and guidelines to facilitate catechesis on the anaphoras [DOL 243 and 244].

   [9]   GIRM no. 54 [DOL 208 no. 1444].

   [10]   See ibid. no. 55 a [DOL 208 no. 1445].

will stand out more clearly and that there will be more and richer themes of thanksgiving."[11]

For the same reason, as well, the priest presiding at the eucharist is authorized to introduce the eucharistic prayer with a brief comment,[12] designed to point out to the people its thanksgiving themes. This is done in a way best suited to the actual assembly, so that the community may come to perceive the connection between its own life and the history of salvation and may derive greater benefit from celebrating the eucharist.

1983   9.   Similarly, as to the purpose and make-up or structure of the eucharistic prayer, its supplicatory or intercessory aspect must be viewed as secondary. The reformed liturgy puts the emphasis on this aspect particularly in the general intercessions, which, in a form more flexible and suited to the circumstances, expresses petitions for the Church and for all people and their needs. Even so, the new liturgical books also provide various intercessory formularies in special celebrations, above all in ritual Masses, for incorporation into each of the eucharistic prayers in a way conformed to their respective structures.[13] This arrangement both brings out the reason for the particular and precise celebration and signifies that the prayer is being offered in communion with the entire Church.[14]

1984   10.   In addition to the variations just listed, whose purpose is to link thanksgiving and intercession more closely to the celebration, the Roman tradition contains certain formularies to be used *infra actionem* (within the eucharistic prayer) on the chief solemnities of the liturgical year in order to make more explicit the commemoration of the mystery of the Lord being celebrated.[15]

Clearly, then, it is characteristic of the Roman tradition both to attach great importance to the immutability of texts and to make room for appropriate variations. The reason for the one is that the faithful by hearing the same text repeatedly are more readily united with the celebrant in prayer; for the other, that a few variations in the text are welcome and useful because they fix the attention, stir devotion, and enhance the prayer with phrases proper to the occasion.

Regarding the variable elements mentioned in nos. 8–10, a similar arrangement may be made and the Apostolic See's confirmation of it sought by the conferences of bishops for their region, bishops for the proper of their diocese, and the competent authority for the proper of a religious family.

1985   11.   Supreme importance must be attached to the ecclesial dimension in the celebration of the eucharist. For in the eucharistic celebration "the unity of all believers who form one body in Christ is both expressed and brought about"[16] and "the

---

[11]   Paul VI, Ap. Const. *Missale Romanum*, 3 April 1969 [DOL 202 no. 1360].

[12]   See GIRM no. 11 [DOL 208 no. 1401].

[13]   Thus in addition to the place for inserting names in the *Remember, Lord*, Eucharistic Prayer I, the Roman Canon, has a special *Remember, Lord* for godparents in Masses for the Christian initiation of adults. There are also special formularies for the *Father, accept this offering* for use from the Mass of the Easter Vigil until the Second Sunday of Easter and in Masses for adult candidates for baptism and newly baptized, those confirmed, those ordained, bride and bridegroom, religious making profession, those consecrated to a life of virginity. Eucharistic Prayers II, III, and IV have special embolisms for newly baptized adults, religious making profession, and those consecrated to a life of virginity.

[14]   See GIRM no. 55 g [DOL 208 no. 1445].

[15]   See the proper *In union with the whole Church* for Christmas and Christmas week, for Epiphany, for the Mass of the Easter Vigil and used until the Second Sunday of Easter, for the Ascension, for Pentecost.

[16]   LG no. 3 [DOL 4 no. 137].

celebration of Mass is itself a profession of faith; in that celebration the entire Church recognizes and gives expression to itself."[17] These points stand out clearly in the eucharistic prayer itself, in which it is not some private person or merely a local community addressing God, but the "one, single Catholic Church" existing in the many particular Churches.[18] Where eucharistic prayers not approved by competent church authority are used, it is by no means unusual for distress and dissension to arise, whereas the eucharist should be the "sign of unity" and "bond of charity."[19] For there are many who complain about the excessively subjective tone of such texts. Since they subscribe to the eucharistic prayer by their *Amen* at the end, those participating in the celebration have in fact the right for it not to be interspersed or filled with the personal views of the one who composed it or recites it.

This shows the necessity of using only those texts of the eucharistic prayer that, being approved by lawful authority in the Church, clearly and completely express an ecclesial outlook.

12. In the eucharistic prayer, because of its nature, it is not always or easily possible to achieve a precise adaptation to the different groups or circumstances and a complete expression of its catechetical function. These are to be achieved in those parts and formularies of the liturgical service that allow or require variation.   1986

13. Those who prepare and preside over celebrations are reminded, first of all, of the options granted by the General Instruction of the Roman Missal.[20] In certain cases they may choose Mass formularies and the texts for the various parts of the Mass (such as the readings, prayers, and chants) "that correspond as fully as possible to the needs, spiritual preparation, and mentality of the participants."[21] Nor must they forget that other documents, promulgated after publication of the General Instruction, provide further norms and guidelines for celebrations that have vitality and are suited to pastoral needs.[22]   1987

14. Among elements favoring a fuller adaptation that are within the power of individual celebrants may be mentioned the introductions, the homily, and the general intercessions.   1988

First, the introductions. They are ways of leading the faithful to a more thorough grasp of the meaning of the sacred rites or certain of their parts and to an inner participation in them. Particularly important are the introductions that the General Instruction assigns to be prepared and spoken by the priest: the comments introducing the faithful to the day's Mass before the celebration, to the liturgy of the word before the readings, and to the eucharistic prayer before the preface; the comments concluding the whole rite before the dismissal.[23] Prominence should also be given to those introductions that the Order of Mass provides for certain rites, for example, the introductions to the penitential rite and the Lord's Prayer. By their very nature such introductions do not require that they be given verbatim in the

---

[17] Secretariat for Christian Unity, Instr. *In quibusdam rerum circumstantiis*, 1 June 1972 [DOL 155 no. 1045].

[18] See LG no. 23: AAS 57 (1965) 27; ConstDecrDecl 134.

[19] See Augustine, *In Ioannis Evangelium* Tr. 26, 13: CCL 36, 266. SC art. 47 [DOL 1 no. 47].

[20] See GIRM nos. 314–324 [DOL 208 nos. 1704–14].

[21] GIRM no. 313 [DOL 208 no. 1703].

[22] See SCDW, Instr. *Actio pastoralis*, 15 May 1969 [DOL 275]; Instr. *Memoriale Domini*, 29 May 1969 [DOL 260]; Instr. *Sacramentali Communione*, 29 June 1970 [DOL 270].

[23] See GIRM no. 11 [DOL 208 no. 1386].

form they have in the Missal; consequently it may well be helpful, at least in certain cases, to adapt them to the actual situation of a community. But the way any of these introductions is presented must respect the character proper to each and not turn into a sermon or homily. There must be a concern for brevity and the avoidance of a wordiness that would bore the participants.

1989   15. The homily must also be mentioned. It is "a part of the liturgy"[24] by which the word of God proclaimed in the liturgical assembly is explained to help the community present. It is given in a way that is suited to the community's capacity and way of life and that is relevant to the circumstances of the celebration.

1990   16. Finally much is to be made of the general intercessions, which in a sense is the community's response to the word of God proclaimed and received. To ensure its effectiveness care must be taken that the intentions made on behalf of the whole world's needs are suited to the gathered assembly; this means that there be a certain flexibility proportioned to the nature of this prayer in the preparation of the intentions.

1991   17. For the celebration to belong to the community and to be vital requires more than choosing texts. The one presiding and others with a special role in the celebration must have a precise sense of the different styles of verbal communication that are involved in the readings, homily, introductions, and the like.[25]

    In reciting prayers, and particularly the eucharistic prayer, the priest is to avoid, on the one hand, a monotonous, uninflected style and, on the other, a style of speech and actions too personal and dramatic. As the one presiding over the rite, the priest should by his speech, singing, and actions help those taking part to form a true community that celebrates and lives out the memorial of the Lord.

1992   18. In order to ensure the full impact of the words and greater spiritual profit, attention must always be given, as so many desire, to the sacred silence that at stated times must be observed as a part of the liturgy.[26] This will allow all the participants, according to the nature and reason for the period of silence, either to reflect on their own lives, to meditate briefly on what they have heard, or to praise and entreat God in their hearts.[27]

1993   19. In view of what has here been said it is possible to wish and hope that pastors, rather than bringing novelties of text and rite into the liturgy, will instead apply themselves fully to leading the faithful to a better understanding of the character, structure, and elements of celebration, especially of the eucharistic prayer, and to an ever more complete and aware participation. The power and effectiveness of the liturgy does not consist merely in the newness and variety of its elements, but in a deeper communion with the mystery of salvation that becomes present and active in the liturgical rites. Accordingly, only in the professing of one faith and the outpouring of one prayer to God can the faithful attain their own salvation and enter into communion with each other.

---

24   SC art. 52 [DOL 1 no. 52].

25   See GIRM no. 18 [DOL 208 no. 1408].

26   See SC art. 30 [DOL 1 no. 30]. SCR, Instr. MusSacr, 5 March 1967, no. 17 [DOL 508 no. 4138].

27   See GIRM no. 23 [DOL 208 no. 1413].

Pope Paul VI, on 18 April 1973, approved and confirmed by his own authority the contents of this Circular Letter, prepared by the Congregation, and ordered its publication.

249. SC DIVINE WORSHIP, **Decree** *Postquam de Precibus*, approving the Eucharistic Prayers for Masses with Children and for Masses of Reconciliation, 1 November 1974: Not 11 (1975) 4–6.

After the publication of the circular letter on eucharistic prayers by this   1994
Congregation, 27 April 1973,[a] some conferences of bishops and some individual bishops from various parts of the world presented a request to the Apostolic See to obtain new eucharistic prayers for Masses that are celebrated with children and for Masses of reconciliation.

The *Directory for Masses with Children*, published 1 November 1973, stated as a general recommendation that the presidential prayers composed for adults should be so adapted in Masses with children that the children will consider them to be expressions of their own religious experience.[1] But with regard to the most sublime of the presidential prayers, namely, the eucharistic prayer, the same document stipulated that only the four approved eucharistic prayers were to be used even with children "until the Apostolic See makes other provision for Masses with children."[2]

Further, on the occasion of the Holy Year a special eucharistic prayer seemed to be particularly useful and appropriate. Such a prayer might also be used at penitential services, especially since its basic theme includes various aspects that reach their high point in the thanksgiving and blessing of the eucharistic prayer.

Pope Paul VI considered these legitimate requests and made this Congregation responsible for preparing some special forms of the eucharistic prayer for the occasions mentioned.

Three drafts of eucharistic prayers for Masses with children and two for Masses of reconciliation were therefore prepared and submitted to the Pope for his judgment. On 26 October 1974 he decreed the following:

1.   The eucharistic prayers contained in this booklet are approved *as an experiment*   1995
and *for three years*, that is, until the end of 1977. The Eucharistic Prayer for Masses of Reconciliation may be used when there are special celebrations with the theme of reconciliation and penance, especially during Lent and on the occasion of a pilgrimage or a religious meeting.

The texts, however, may not be inserted into official editions of the Roman Missal.[b]

---

[a]   See DOL 248.

[1]   See SCDW, *Directory for Masses with Children* no. 51 [DOL 276 no. 2184].

[2]   Ibid. no. 52 [DOL 276 no. 2185].

[b]   This is the first of several variants in the text of the Decree and the Introduction in Not 11 (1975) 4–12 from the text in the photocopied booklet of 1 November 1974 from SCDW. These will be indicated as "Nov.'74":
    Nov.'74: "These texts, however, may not be published in official editions nor are they to be inserted into the Roman Missal."

1996   2.   The eucharistic prayers in question are sent to presidents of the conferences of bishops who request them. Each conference of bishops may choose *only one* eucharistic prayer for Masses with children and *one* for Masses of reconciliation.[3]

1997   3.   A translation of the text chosen by the conference of bishops[c] is to be approved and submitted to this Congregation for confirmation. It may be used only after confirmation by the Apostolic See.

     The translation of the text may be made with a degree of freedom in order that it correspond fully to the requirements and idiom of the respective language. It may differ somewhat from the Latin texts, in accordance with nos. 9–11 of the Introduction to the Eucharistic Prayers for Masses with Children. The *structure* of the eucharistic prayer, however, and the meaning of the text are to be maintained; the formularies of consecration, which must be the same in all eucharistic prayers, are to be translated *faithfully* and *literally*.

1998   4.   Use of a eucharistic prayer for Masses with children is restricted to Masses that are celebrated with children alone or Masses at which the majority of the participants are children.[4]

     A community of children means one so considered by the *Directory for Masses with Children*, that is, one consisting of children who have not yet reached the age referred to as preadolescence.[5]

     Those who receive the faculty for experimental use of the eucharistic prayers in question are bound to the exact observance of the conditions already stated.

250. SC DIVINE WORSHIP, *Eucharistic Prayers for Masses with Children and for Masses of Reconciliation,* **Introduction**, 1 November 1974: Not 11 (1975) 7–12.

EUCHARISTIC PRAYERS FOR MASSES WITH CHILDREN

INTRODUCTION

1999   1.   The texts of the eucharistic prayer adapted for children must contribute toward their taking part more fruitfully in Masses for adults.

     Thus the *Directory for Masses with Children* establishes that some texts of the Mass are never to be altered for children "lest the difference between Masses with children and Masses with adults become too great." Among such texts are the "acclamations and responses of the people to the priest's greetings."[1] The dialogue for the preface of these eucharistic prayers is therefore always the same as in Masses for adults and the same holds for the *Sanctus*, apart from what is stated in nos. 18 and 23.

---

     [3]   The Holy See, however, will give every consideration, in individual cases, to reasonable requests for the use of more than one of these prayers (from a communication from the papal Secretariat of State, 26 Jan. 1975, Prot. N. 272908).

     [c]   Nov.'74: "A translation of the text chosen by the conference of bishops is to be made."

     [4]   See SCDW, *Directory for Masses with Children* no. 19 [DOL 276 no. 2152].

     [5]   See ibid. no. 6 [DOL 276 no. 2139].

     [1]   *Directory for Masses with Children* no. 39 [DOL 276 no. 2172].

2. In keeping with the Apostolic Constitution *Missale Romanum*, the words of the Lord in every formulary of the canon are also exactly the same.[2]   2000

3. Before the words *Do this in memory of me* a sentence has been introduced, *Then he said to them*, in order to make clearer for children the distinction between what is said over the bread and wine and what refers to the celebration's being repeated.   2001

4. Each of the three eucharistic prayers for Masses with children contains, with a very few exceptions, all those elements that, according to the General Instruction of the Roman Missal no. 55,[a] make up the eucharistic prayer.   2002

5. Not only do they contain the required elements, but they also express those elements that, following tradition, have always been expressed, for example, in the anamnesis or the epiclesis, but in a simpler style of language, suited to the understanding of children.   2003

6. Although a simpler style of language was adopted, the authors always had in mind the importance of avoiding the danger of childish language, which would jeopardize the dignity of the eucharistic celebration, especially if it affected the words to be said by the celebrant himself.   2004

7. Because the principles of active participation are in some respects even more significant for children, the number of acclamations in the eucharistic prayers for Masses with children has been increased, in order to enlarge this kind of participation and make it more effective.[3] This has been done without obscuring the nature of the eucharistic prayer as a *presidential* prayer.   2005

8. Because it is very difficult for only one eucharistic prayer to be used throughout the world in Masses with children, in view of cultural differences and the mentality of various peoples, it seemed appropriate to propose at least three texts differing in character (explained in nos. 23–25).   2006

TRANSLATION OF THESE PRAYERS INTO VARIOUS LANGUAGES

9. It is for the conference of bishops to choose one of the drafts proposed here and to see that the text is translated into the vernacular so that it corresponds fully to pastoral, pedagogical, and liturgical needs. This text must be approved by the conference of bishops and sent to the Apostolic See for confirmation.[b]   2007

10. It is strongly recommended that this work of translation be given to a group of men and women with competences not only in the area of liturgy, but also of pedagogy, catechetics, language, and music.   2008

11. The committee of translators should always remember that in this case the Latin text is not intended for liturgical use. Therefore it is not to be merely translated.   2009

The Latin text does determine the purpose, substance, and general form of these prayers and these elements should be the same in the translations into the

---

[2] See Paul VI, Ap. Const. *Missale Romanum* [DOL 202 no. 1360].

[a] See DOL 208 no. 1445.

[3] See Directory for Masses with Children no. 22 [DOL 276 no. 2155].

[b] Nov.'74: "This text may not be introduced into liturgical use before having the confirmation of the Apostolic See."

various languages. Features proper to Latin (which never developed a special style of speaking with children) are never to be carried over into the vernacular texts intended for liturgical use: specifically, the Latin preference for compound sentences, the somewhat ornate and repetitious style, and the so-called cursus. The style of the vernacular text is in every aspect to be adapted to the spirit of the respective language as well as to the manner of speaking with children in each language concerning matters of great importance. These principles are all the more pertinent in the case of languages that are far removed from Latin, especially non-Western languages. An example of translation for each eucharistic prayer in one of the Western languages is provided as a possible aid to the translator.

2010   12. In translating these texts careful distinction should be made between the several literary genres that occur in the eucharistic prayer, namely, the preface, the intercessions, acclamations, etc., in keeping with the sound principles laid down in the instruction of 25 January 1969 for the translation of liturgical texts.[4]

2011   13. In addition, the conferences of bishops should see that new *musical settings* in keeping with the culture of the region are prepared for the parts of the prayers to be sung by the children.

LITURGICAL USE OF THESE PRAYERS

2012   14. Use of these prayers is strictly limited to Masses celebrated with children. But the right of the bishop as determined in the *Directory for Masses with Children*[5] remains intact.

2013   15. From the three texts of the eucharistic prayer the one that seems best suited to the circumstances of the children[c] should be chosen: either the first for its greater simplicity, the second for its greater participation, or the third for the variations it affords.

2014   16. Introducing new acclamations into liturgical use is made easier if a cantor or one of the children leads and then all repeat the acclamations in song or recitation. Care should be taken in the preparation of texts in the vernacular, however, that acclamations have a simple introduction, for example, use of a cue word to invite the acclamation.

2015   17. In place of the new acclamations found in these eucharistic prayers, the conferences of bishops may introduce others, provided these convey the same spirit.

2016   18. It is necessary that children too learn to sing or recite the *Sanctus*, but the rule remains in effect that sometimes it is permissible to use "with the melodies appropriate translations accepted by competent authority, even if these do not agree completely with the liturgical texts, in order to facilitate the participation of the children."[6] Wherever, among the various peoples, responsorial singing is the custom, the conference of bishops may also allow responsorial singing of the *Sanctus*.

---

    [4] See Consilium, Instr. on the translation of liturgical texts for celebrations with a congregation, 25 Jan. 1969 [DOL 123].

    [5] See *Directory for Masses with Children* no. 19 [DOL 276 no. 2152].

    [c] Nov. '74: ". . . the children of each particular country."

    [6] *Directory of Masses with Children* no. 31 [DOL 276 no. 2164].

19. The place for the acclamation by the faithful at the end of the consecration has   2017
been slightly changed. This is done for pedagogical reasons. In order that the
children may clearly understand the connection between the words of the Lord, *Do
this in memory of me*, and the anamnesis by the priest celebrant, the acclamation,
whether of memorial or of praise, is not made until after the anamnesis has been
recited.

20. To encourage participation by the children, it is permissible, in keeping with   2018
the *Directory for Masses with Children*, to insert special reasons for giving thanks before
the dialogue for the preface.[7] The regulations of the *Directory* no. 33 also apply for
participation by means of gestures and postures.[d] Above all, great stress should be
placed on inner participation, and what is said in no. 23 about the celebration as
festive, familial, and meditative is especially true of the eucharistic prayer.[e]

21. To encourage this inner participation, which should be a matter of deepest   2019
concern for pastors of children, careful catechetical instruction must precede and
follow the celebration. Among the texts that this catechesis will rightly clarify for
the children, a preeminent place belongs to the eucharistic prayers, which will be
used at the high point in the celebration.[8]

22. The rubrics for the individual eucharistic prayers appearing in the Latin text   2020
are all to be incorporated into the vernacular text.[f]

Special rubrics for concelebration as are found in the four eucharistic prayers
already in use are lacking in these prayers. In view of the psychology of children it
seems better to refrain from concelebration when Mass is celebrated with them.

A. Eucharistic Prayer I

23. In order to accustom the children more easily to the *Sanctus*, Eucharistic Prayer I   2021
divides it into the two parts concluded by the acclamation, *Hosanna in the highest*. In
keeping with no. 16, these acclamations may be sung or recited by repeating them
after a cantor or one of the children. The third time the entire *Sanctus* may be sung
by all. After the anamnesis of Prayer I, one of the acclamations approved for the
four eucharistic prayers may be used in place of the simpler acclamation given in
the text.

B. Eucharistic Prayer II

24. In Eucharistic Prayer II, except for the *Sanctus* and the acclamation after the   2022
anamnesis, other optional acclamations may be substituted. The acclamations that
have been inserted after the words of the Lord spoken over the bread and the wine
must be regarded as a shared meditation on the eucharistic mystery and sung as
such.

C. Eucharistic Prayer III

25. In Eucharistic Prayer III variable parts are indicated for only one occasion,   2023
namely, for the Easter season. It is intended, however, that similar variable parts be

---

7   See *Directory of Masses with Children* no. 22 [DOL 276 no. 2155].

d   See DOL 276 no. 2166.

e   See DOL 276 no. 2156.

8   See *Directory for Masses with Children* no. 12 [DOL 276 no. 2145].

f   Nov.'74: "22. The rubrics for the individual eucharistic prayers are given in the Latin text only. All
of them are to be inserted in the vernacular text."

approved by the conference of bishops for other seasons and occasions and, after the requisite confirmation by the Apostolic See, put into use in keeping with the circular letter on eucharistic prayers no. 10.[9] In preparing these texts care should be taken to ensure the due correlation of their three parts (preface, part after the *Sanctus*, epiclesis).

After the consecration, the same acclamation occurs three times in the same way in order that the character of praise and thanksgiving belonging to the entire eucharistic prayer may be conveyed to the children.

EUCHARISTIC PRAYERS FOR MASSES OF RECONCILIATION
INTRODUCTION

2024   1.   The intentions for the celebration of the Holy Year have been proposed on many occasions by Pope Paul VI and it seems appropriate for these intentions to resound repeatedly in liturgical celebrations, especially in the sacrifice of the Mass, including the eucharistic prayer. For this reason two texts of the eucharistic prayer have been prepared to shed light on aspects of reconciliation, insofar as they may be the object of thanksgiving.

2025   2.   The conference of bishops may choose one text to be used in its territory during the Holy Year for Masses when celebrations express the intentions of the year. The texts may also be used after the Holy Year in Masses when the mystery of reconciliation is the special theme set before the faithful.

2026   3.   These proposed texts contain all the elements that make up a eucharistic prayer in accordance with the General Instruction of the Roman Missal no. 55.[8] The order of these elements is the same as in Eucharistic Prayers II-IV of the Roman Missal.

2027   4.   The rubrics are given in the Latin texts. To assist those who are to prepare translations, a version in a Western language is added for each prayer. When a eucharistic prayer is published in a vernacular language, the rubrics are also to be printed.

In the text of the prayers the parts to be recited by concelebrants are indicated and the rubrics given for concelebration.[h]

251. SC SACRAMENTS AND DIVINE WORSHIP, Letter *Sacrum hoc Dicasterium* to presidents of the conferences of bishops, on extension of the use of the Eucharistic Prayers for Masses with Children and of Reconciliation, 10 December 1977: Not 13 (1977) 555-556.

2028   This Congregation, at the direction of Pope Paul VI, carefully submitted for his judgment the results of the consultation with several conferences of bishops on the use of the Eucharistic Prayers for Masses with Children and of Reconciliation.

Those conferences of bishops that had received the faculty to use these prayers have nearly unanimously rendered a favorable judgment on their use. But some

---

[9]   See AAS 65 (1973) 344 [DOL 248 no. 1984].

[8]   See DOL 208 no. 1445.

[h]   Nov.'74 gives these rubrics here as part of the Introduction.

have petitioned that use of the prayers be extended beyond the end of the present year 1977, because the time between the beginning and end of the concession has been short. This, of course, lessened the possibility for pastors to make an evaluation of the pastoral effectiveness of this experiment.

Pope Paul has graciously authorized that use of the Eucharistic Prayers for Masses with Children and of Reconciliation be extended for another three-year period, namely, until the end of 1980. The same conditions as before are to be observed both by conferences of bishops already possessing the faculty and by conferences that with approval from the Holy See wish to introduce use of these prayers into their own countries.

As it has the pleasure of communicating this matter to you, this Congregation thinks it advisable to recall several conditions absolutely required for the introduction and use of these prayers.

1.   Use of any eucharistic prayer for Masses with children is restricted to those   2029
Masses celebrated for them alone or at which they make up the majority of those participating (see the booklet issued under the auspices of the Congregation for Divine Worship, entitled *Preces Eucharisticae pro Missis cum pueris et de reconciliatione*, Rome, 1 November 1974, p. 2, no. 4).[a]

2.   Eucharist Prayers for Masses of Reconciliation may be used when there are   2030
special celebrations on the themes of reconciliation and penance, especially during Lent, and on the occasion of a pilgrimage or a religious meeting (ibid., p. 2, no. 1).[b]

3.   The texts are issued "provisorily" and "as an experiment." Therefore they   2031
cannot be published in official editions nor incorporated into the Roman Missal (ibid., p. 2, no. 1).[c]

4.   It will be up to the Holy See, after the experiment, to provide definitive texts   2032
so that they may be incorporated into the Roman Missal.

Meanwhile the conferences of bishops assisted by those liturgical commissions   2033
lawfully set up in accord with the provisions of the Constitution on the Liturgy art. 44,[d] to work out effective aids (texts, melodies, especially for the acclamations) toward an active and informed participation by children in celebrations with them. The purpose of such celebrations is never to be lost sight of: "It is always necessary to keep in mind that such eucharistic celebrations must lead the children toward the celebration of Mass with adults, especially the Masses at which the Christian community must come together on Sundays" (*Directory for Masses with Children* no. 21).[e]

Conferences of bishops that have not yet introduced the Eucharistic Prayers for Masses with Children and of Reconciliation and that intend to petition from the Holy See the faculty for their use ought to take note that this concession will terminate at the end of 1980.

    [a]   See DOL 249 no. 1998.

    [b]   See DOL 249 no. 1995.

    [c]   See DOL 249 no. 1995.

    [d]   See DOL 1 no. 44.

    [e]   DOL 276 no. 2154.

SECTION 8. COMMUNION

SUMMARY (DOL 252–273). The Constitution on the Liturgy art. 55 emphasized the importance of full participation in the eucharistic celebration through communion and with hosts consecrated at the same Mass; it also restored for certain occasions the usage of communion under both kinds. In the course of carrying out the liturgical reform other issues related to communion arose and were the occasion of twenty-two interventions of the Holy See. This section arranges the relevant texts into three subsections, on the ministers and rite of communion, communion under both kinds, and the eucharistic fast.

SECTION 8. COMMUNION: A. MINISTER AND RITES

SUMMARY (DOL 252–267). There are 16 documents.

—On the ministers of communion the principal document is an instruction of the Congregation for the Discipline of the Sacraments giving the general rules (DOL 259). The 1969 Latin text of *Fidei custos* was not published officially and this is the first English translation to be published. Significant is the development of church discipline given here on women religious (DOL 253, 255, 256) and on laypersons (DOL 257, 258, 262, 263) as eucharistic ministers.

—On the rites for communion there is an early decree promulgating a new formulary for ministering communion (DOL 252) and one modifying the rites for communion in hospitals (DOL 254). On the special issue of the manner of receiving communion in the hand there is a 1969 instruction (DOL 260), a letter to conferences of bishops petitioning this permission (DOL 261), and a 1976 letter to all the conferences on the practice (DOL 267). Other important texts are the decree of promulgation and the introductions to the rites for communion outside Mass (DOL 265, 266).

—Finally, there is a major text that covers both special eucharistic ministers and the rites of communion, the 1973 Instruction *Immensae caritatis*, on facilitating communion (DOL 264).

▶ 1. VATICAN COUNCIL II, Constitution on the Liturgy *Sacrosanctum Concilium*, 4 December 1963:

art. 55: Fuller participation in the Mass by use of hosts consecrated at the same Mass [no. 55].

252. SC RITES, **Decree** *Quo actuosius*, promulgating a new formulary for the distribution of communion, 25 April 1964: AAS 56 (1964) 337–338.

2034   In order that the people may more actively and beneficially take part in the sacrifice of the Mass and profess their faith in the eucharistic mystery in the very act of receiving communion, numerous requests have been submitted to Pope Paul VI for a more appropriate formulary for the distribution of communion.

Graciously welcoming such requests, the Pope has established that in the distribution of communion, in place of the formulary now in use, the priest is simply to say: *The body of Christ* and the people are to answer: *Amen*, then receive communion. This is to be followed whenever communion is distributed, both within and outside Mass.

All things to the contrary notwithstanding, even those worthy of special mention.[1]

253. SC EXTRAORDINARY AFFAIRS, **Rescript** (Brazil), authorizing certain women religious to give communion, 24 April 1965.[*]

2035   Pope Paul VI in an audience granted to the undersigned Secretary of the Congregation for Extraordinary Affairs grants the favor requested (of permitting women religious in the parishes of Nisia Floresta and Taipu, Brazil, to distribute communion) under the following conditions.

1. When the sacred minister of the eucharist is to be absent for a foreseen period of at least eight days.

2. The faculty is granted only for use in the community chapel and on behalf of the religious and of all who regularly attend the chapel.

3. The eucharist is to be distributed by one or more women religious, designated for this ministry by the local Ordinary.

4. The sacrament of the eucharist is to be distributed after all have recited together the *Confiteor* and the *Lord I am not worthy*; the religious who distribute communion are permitted to say the words: *The body of Christ.*

5. This faculty is to be used only with the express permission of the Ordinary and under his supervision.

6. The faculty is granted *as an experiment* for one year, unless the Holy See has, before the expiration of that period, made some more definite arrangement.

All things to the contrary notwithstanding.[a]

---

[1] By kind concession of the Pope the present decree may be put into practice at once; it must be put into practice by all beginning with Pentecost Sunday.

[*] Text, CommRel 45 (1966) 337–338 (Portuguese).

[a] The ritual, as determined by Eugenio de Araújo Sales, Apostolic Administrator of Natal, is given in CommRel in a note, p. 338.

▶   23.   SC RITES (Consilium), Instruction (first) *Inter Oecumenici*, 26 September 1964:

nos. 48 i: Rites for communion [no. 340].
      60:            Communion more than once a day [no. 352].

254. SC RITES, **Decree** *Cum hac nostra aetate*, on communion in hospitals, 14 February 1966: AAS 58 (1966) 525–526; Not 2 (1966) 327.

In our own times the prevailing practice is for frequent or daily communion   2036
even among the sick in hospitals. But there is some inconvenience attendant on
this practice, in view of the new architecture of hospitals and their internal regimen.
Therefore, in order that communion may be more easily and quickly administered
to many sick people, the Congregation of Rites has thought it well for the prescriptions of the Roman Ritual, Title 5, ch. 4, no. 28, to be altered in favor of the
procedure that follows.

1. In single-building hospitals with a chapel the priest administering is to   2037
recite in the chapel all the prayers required by the Roman Ritual before and after
the communion of the sick. Using the formulary for communion, he is then to
distribute the eucharist to the patients in their rooms.

2. But in hospitals with many wings the eucharist is to be carried reverently   2038
from the chapel and placed on a table prepared at a fitting and convenient place in
each building. There, after reciting the prayers required before and after communion of the sick, the priest distributes communion in the way already stated.

After receiving the report made on these points by the Cardinal Prefect, Pope
Paul VI ratified and confirmed these changes and kindly granted their use whenever
circumstances require.

255. SC PROPAGATION OF THE FAITH, **Rescript** (Canada) to the Vicar Apostolic of Grouard, Alberta, on the rite to be followed by women religious authorized to give communion, 31 May 1966.*

The religious superior carrying out the rite recites with the sisters and the   2039
people the *Confiteor* (omitting the *To you, Father*) and the *Lord, I am not worthy*. After she
has given communion to herself, she distributes the hosts, saying to each communicant: *The body of Christ*; each responds: *Amen*. The religious superior is to wear the
religious habit, wash her hands before communion, and purify her fingers in the
lavabo dish afterward.

---

* Prot. N. 5106/65; see CLD 6, 560–561.

256. SC DISCIPLINE OF THE SACRAMENTS, **Rescript** (Canada) to the Bishop of Hauterive, Quebec, allowing religious to give communion, 11 November 1966.*

2040   The Bishop of Hauterive humbly requests Your Holiness for the faculty to allow the superiors of nonclerical men religious and of women religious in his diocese to give communion to themselves and to the other religious and those of the faithful who may be present; but only in the chapel of the religious house and if no priest or deacon is available.

Reply: The Congregation of the Sacraments, in virtue of special faculties granted to the Cardinal Prefect by Pope Paul VI and considering the special circumstances involved, grants to the petitioner, 11 November 1966, the special faculty requested. The conditions are that it is foreseen that no sacred minister will be available for some days; that all danger of irreverence to the blessed sacrament is precluded; that every safeguard surrounds use of this faculty; and especially that the instruction sent by this Congregation in its letter of 7 May 1966 to the apostolic nuncio of Canada be followed.

All things to the contrary notwithstanding. This concession is valid for three years.

▶   179.   SC RITES (Consilium), Instruction *Eucharisticum mysterium*, on worship of the eucharist, 25 May 1967:

nos. 31–41:   Communion of the people [nos. 1260–70].

257. SC DISCIPLINE OF THE SACRAMENTS, **Rescript** (West Germany) to the conference of bishops, on distribution of communion by laypersons, 28 November 1967 and 14 February 1968.*

2041   Following on a decision made in September 1967, the German conference of bishops requested the Holy See that lay people be allowed to distribute holy communion.

The Congregation for the Discipline of the Sacraments granted this request for three years through the rescript Prot. N. 2199/67, dated 28 November 1967 and 14 February 1968.

By this rescript local Ordinaries received authorization for the following.

1. Local Ordinaries may depute fit persons of the male sex to distribute holy communion *during Mass*, on condition that there is no other way to keep the distribution of communion from lasting too long.

2. Local Ordinaries may depute fit persons of the male sex to give communion to themselves and others in churches and public oratories *outside Mass*, as well as to bring communion to the sick, on condition that no sacred minister is expected to be available for several days.

3. Local Ordinaries may depute superiors of religious houses of men or of cloistered communities of women engaged in some apostolate in the diocese to give

---

*   Prot. N. 2350/66; see CLD 6, 561.

*   Prot. N. 2199/67; text in ArchKathKRecht 137 (1968) 221–222.

communion in the house chapel to themselves, the members of the community, and also any of the faithful who may be present, whenever no sacred minister is expected to be available for several days.

258. SC EVANGELIZATION OF PEOPLES, Rescript (Antilles) to the Archbishop of Kingston, Jamaica, allowing laypersons to give communion, 28 November 1968.*

Petition: The Ordinary of the Archdiocese of Kingston, Jamaica, as president of   2042
the conference of bishops of the Antilles, in his own name and that of all the Ordinaries of that conference, humbly requests of Your Holiness the faculty for each one of them to allow in his territory (in accord with the norms laid down in the Instruction *Fidei custos*, 10 March 1966, on the minister of eucharistic communion in the absence of a priest or deacon[a]) that persons who are declared to be qualified in that Instruction and are so designated by the Ordinary may distribute communion and also bring it to the sick.

Reply: In virtue of faculties granted to it by Pope Paul VI, the Congregation for the Evangelization of Peoples or the Propagation of the Faith, after considering the petition, kindly grants the favor as requested.

This concession is valid for three years.

▶   208.   SC RITES (Consilium); SC DIVINE WORSHIP, General Instruction of the Roman Missal, 1st ed. 6 April 1969; 4th ed. 27 March 1975.

nos. 56, 115–119:	Rites for communion [nos. 1446, 1505–09].
60:	Ministry of the priest [no. 1450].
61, 137–138:	Ministry of the deacon [nos. 1451, 1527–28].
68:	Special ministers [no. 1458].
192–206:	Communion at concelebrated Masses [nos. 1582–96].
224–230:	At Masses without a congregation [nos. 1614–20].
237–239:	Purification of the vessels [nos. 1627–29].
289–296:	Vessels [nos. 1679–86].

259. SC DISCIPLINE OF THE SACRAMENTS, Instruction *Fidei custos*, on special ministers to administer communion, 30 April 1969.*

As guardian of the faith, the Church carefully preserves the deposit of that   2043
faith unchanged throughout the ages. But when special circumstances and new demands arise, the Church changes prudently and at the same time magnanimously the purely canonical norms it has legislated. For the prescriptions of canon law must always be adapted to serve the Church's purpose, the salvation of souls, so that as

---

  * Prot. N. 6445/68; see CLD 6, 649–650.

  a See DOL 259.

  * The original Latin text was never published by the Congregation. A translation of the first version of 10 March 1966 appears in CLD 7, 645–648; this DOL translation is based on the 1969 version sent to presidents of the conferences of bishops.

times and conditions demand, these laws may continue to be effective and to be relevant to the regulation of all the Church's activity.

Today the conditions of human life are changing at an extremely rapid pace. The Church cannot disregard, among other things, the limitations and obstacles facing it as a result of the scarcity of ordained ministers in some regions at a time when pastoral needs are increasing and there is a demand for many forms and programs of pastoral ministry.

In his pastoral concern Pope Paul VI has decided to accede to the desires of the faithful by carefully amending the existing law. Therefore, because of present needs, in addition to the ministers already specified in can. 845, special ministers are constituted in order that they may give communion to themselves and to the faithful.

By authority of the Pope, therefore, the following norms on administering communion according to the Latin rite are laid down in the interest of right order.

2044   1.   The following authorities, who are called "pastors" in this Instruction, may for the good of their subjects ask the Congregation for the Discipline of the Sacraments or the Congregation for the Evangelization of Peoples or the Propagation of the Faith for the faculty to permit fit persons to administer communion to themselves and to the faithful: residential bishops; coadjutors who have been given all episcopal rights and duties; abbots with jurisdiction; prelates who are local Ordinaries; vicars capitular; apostolic administrators; vicars and prefects apostolic, even if they do not have episcopal orders. They may use this faculty:

a.   whenever a minister indicated in can. 845 is not available;

b.   whenever the usual minister is unable to administer communion without difficulty because of poor health, advanced age, or the demands of the pastoral ministry;

c.   whenever the number of faithful wishing to receive communion is so great that the celebration of Mass would take too long.

2045   2.   Once they have been given this faculty, the pastors specified in no. 1 may delegate it to auxiliary bishops, vicars general, episcopal vicars, and episcopal delegates.

2046   3.   A suitable person, as specified in no. 1, is to be chosen in this order of preference: subdeacons, clerics in minor orders, those who have received tonsure, men religious, women religious, male catechists (unless, in the prudent judgment of the pastor, a male catechist is preferable to a woman religious), laymen, laywomen.

2047   4.   Specifics:

a.   In oratories of religious communities, both of men and of women, the pastors in no. 1 may obtain the faculty to permit unordained men superiors and women superiors, or the substitutes of either, to give communion, observing every caution, to themselves and their subjects and to the faithful who may be present; also to bring communion to the sick residing in the house.

b.   In orphanages, residences, schools, and institutions in the broadest sense run by either men religious or women religious, the pastors in no. 1 may be given the faculty allowing unordained men superiors or directors and women superiors, or the substitutes of either, or even a lay Christian of proven piety, to give communion to themselves, to those belonging to their own institution, and to others of the faithful present for any reason; also to bring communion to the sick.

5.   A lay Christian who is to be chosen as a special minister of communion should   2048
be outstanding in Christian life, in faith, and in morals, and one whose mature age
warrants the choice and who is properly trained to carry out so exalted a function.
A woman of outstanding piety may be chosen in cases of necessity, that is, whenever another fit person cannot be found.

6.   A fit person whom the bishop chooses by name to administer communion is to   2049
receive a mandate from the bishop according to the rite prepared for commissioning
a minister and must carry out the distribution of communion in keeping with the
liturgical norms.

6 bis.[a] The pastors mentioned in no. 1 may also obtain from the Congregation   2050
mentioned the faculty to grant that parish priests, pastors of quasi-parishes, parochial vicars, rectors of churches, and other priests having the care of souls may
appoint a fit person, according to the precedence determined in no. 3, to distribute
communion on a particular occasion in cases of necessity.

7.   In the administration of communion there must be caution against any danger   2051
of irreverence to the blessed sacrament, which must be shown the highest honor.

8.   The Congregation for the Discipline of the Sacraments and for the Evangeliza-   2052
tion of Peoples grants the faculty in question for three years to the pastors in no. 1
who rightfully request it.

9.   After the three-year period, such pastors are not to fail to create a report to the   2053
two Congregations on the practical results and whether there has really been a
contribution to the good of souls.

▶   275. SC DIVINE WORSHIP, Instruction *Actio pastoralis*, on Masses with special
      groups, 15 May 1969:

      no. 7:   Communion [no. 2128].

260. SC DIVINE WORSHIP, **Instruction** *Memoriale Domini*, on the manner of giving communion, 29 May 1969: AAS 61 (1969) 541–545; Not 5 (1969) 347–351.

In celebrating the memorial of the Lord, the Church bears witness by means of   2054
the rite itself to its faith in and adoration of Christ, present in the sacrifice and given
as food to those sharing in the table of the eucharist.

The Church therefore has an intense concern to ensure the worthy celebration
and fruitful reception of the eucharist through an exact fidelity to the tradition that
has evolved and come down to us, enriching the Church's practice and life. The
pages of history show that the manner of celebrating and receiving the eucharist
has taken many forms. At the present, with a view to meeting the spiritual and
psychological needs of today's people more effectively, many and major changes in
rite have been introduced into the eucharistic celebration. As for the discipline
governing the way in which the faithful share in the sacrament, communion under
the form of both bread and wine, when certain circumstances obtain, has been

---
    [a] This paragraph, 6 bis, is an addition by the Congregation in the Circular Letter *Textuum novae facultatis*
to presidents of the conferences of bishops, 10 January 1970.

brought back from the disuse into which it had fallen after once being quite general in the Latin rite. (The disuse had become universal at the time of the Council of Trent, which supported it with dogmatic teaching and defended it as suited to the conditions of that era.[1])

These measures of reform have made the sign value of the eucharistic meal and the full carrying out of Christ's command more explicit and striking. At the same time, however, the more complete sharing in the eucharistic celebration, of which sacramental communion is the sign, has prompted a desire in some quarters during the last several years to return to that usage whereby the eucharistic bread is placed in the hand of the faithful, who communicate by putting the host into their own mouth.

Moreover such a rite has even been put into practice in some communities and locales, even though the Apostolic See's approval has not been sought beforehand and in some cases the necessary preparation of the faithful has not been provided.

2055   It is quite true that ancient usage at times allowed the faithful to receive this divine food in the hand and to put it into their own mouth. It is also true that in the earliest years they could take the blessed sacrament away with them from the place of worship, principally in order that they might use it as viaticum in case they had to face danger for the sake of professing their faith.

But it is also true that the laws of the Church and the writings of the Fathers give ample witness to a supreme reverence and utmost caution toward the eucharist. "No one . . . eats that flesh who has not first adored it";[2] everyone receiving it is warned: ". . . Receive it with care that nothing of it be lost to you";[3] "For it is the body of Christ."[4]

Further, the care and ministry of the Lord's body and blood were entrusted in a special way to the sacred ministers or to those deputed for this: "After the one presiding has completed the prayers and the people have all responded together, those whom it is our custom to call 'deacons' distribute for participation by all present the bread, wine, and water in which thanksgiving has been offered and they also bring them to those who are absent."[5]

Thus quite early the function of bringing the eucharist to those absent was assigned exclusively to sacred ministers as a precautionary measure to ensure the reverence due to Christ's body and to meet the needs of the faithful. With the passage of time as the truth of the eucharistic mystery, its power, and Christ's presence in it were more deeply understood, the usage adopted was that the minister himself placed the particle of the consecrated bread on the tongue of the communicant. This measure was prompted by a keen sense both of reverence toward the sacrament and of the humility with which it should be received.

2056   In view of the overall contemporary situation of the Church, this manner of distributing communion must be retained. Not only is it based on a practice handed down over many centuries, but above all it signifies the faithful's reverence for the eucharist. Such a practice in no way takes away from the personal dignity of those

---

[1]   See Council of Trent, sess. 21, *Doctrina de communione sub utraque specie et parvulorum*: Denz-Schön 1726–27; sess. 22, *Decretum super petitionem concessionis calicis*: Denz-Schön 1760.

[2]   Augustine, *Enarrationes in Psalmos* 98, 9: PL 37, 1264.

[3]   Cyril of Jerusalem, *Catecheses mystagogicae* 5, 21: PG 33, 1126.

[4]   Hippolytus, *Traditio apostolica* n. 37: B. Botte, ed. (1963) 84.

[5]   Justin Martyr, *Apologia* 1, 65: PG 6, 427.

coming to so great a sacrament and it is a part of the preparation that is a prerequisite for the fruitful reception of the Lord's body.[6]

The reverence involved is a sign of sharing not "in ordinary bread and wine"[7] but in the Lord's body and blood; in virtue of this communion "the people of God share the benefits of the paschal sacrifice, renew the new covenant made once and for all by God with humanity in the blood of Christ, and in faith and hope foreshadow and anticipate the eschatological banquet in the Father's kingdom."[8]

Further, this way of distributing communion, which must now be regarded as the normal practice, more effectively ensures that communion is distributed with the required reverence, decorum, and dignity; that there is less danger of disrespect for the eucharistic elements, in which "in a unique way Christ is present, whole and entire, God and man, substantially and continuously";[9] finally, that the caution is exercised which the Church has always counseled regarding the particles of the consecrated bread: "What you might permit to fall, think of as being the loss of a part of your own body."[10]

When, therefore, a few conferences of bishops and some individual bishops petitioned that the practice of placing the consecrated bread in the hand of the faithful be allowed in their territories, Pope Paul VI decided that all the bishops of the Latin Church be asked individually for their opinion on the advisability of introducing this rite. A change in so important a matter that has its basis in an ancient and honored tradition does not simply affect discipline, but can also bring with it the dangers that, it is feared, may arise from the new way of administering communion. In particular, these dangers are both the possibility of a lessening of reverence toward the august sacrament of the altar, its profanation, and the watering down of the true doctrine of the eucharist.   2057

Three questions, therefore, were presented to the bishops; their replies to them, received up to 12 March 1969, were as follows: 2058

1. Do you think that a positive response should be given to the request to allow the rite of receiving communion in the hand?

In favor:	567
Opposed:	1,233
In favor with reservations:	315
Invalid votes:	20

2. Are you in favor, provided the local Ordinary agrees, of prior experiments with this new rite in small communities?

In favor:	751
Opposed:	1,215
Invalid votes:	70

3. Are you of the opinion that the faithful, after well-planned catechetical preparation, would welcome this new rite?

---

6   See Augustine, *Enarrationes in Psalmos* 98, 9: PL 37, 1264–65.

7   See Justin Martyr, *Apologia* 1, 66: PG 6, 427. See also Irenaeus, *Adversus haereses* 1, 4, c. 18, n. 5: PG 7, 1028–29.

8   SCR, Instr. EuchMyst no. 3 a [DOL 179 no. 1232].

9   Ibid. no. 9 [DOL 179 no. 1238].

10   Cyril of Jerusalem, *Catecheses mystagogicae* 5, 21: PG 33, 1126.

Yes:	835
No:	1,185
Invalid votes:	128

The answers given show that by far the greater number of bishops think that the discipline currently in force should not at all be changed. And if it were to be changed, it would be an offense to the sensibilities and spiritual outlook of these bishops and a great many of the faithful.

2059   In a way appropriate to the seriousness of the matter and the importance of the issues raised, Pope Paul VI has considered the thoughts and recommendations of the bishops, "whom the Holy Spirit has made the guardians over" the Churches.[11] His judgment is not to change the long-accepted manner of administering communion to the faithful.

The Apostolic See earnestly urges bishops, priests, and faithful, therefore, to obey conscientiously the prevailing law, now reconfirmed, in view of the judgment rendered by the majority of the Catholic episcopate, the form in use in the actual rite of the liturgy, and the general good of the Church itself.

2060   Wherever the contrary practice, that is, of communion in the hand, has already come into use, the Apostolic See, in order to assist the conferences of bishops to fulfill a pastoral responsibility often made more difficult by the contemporary state of affairs, entrusts to the same conferences of bishops the duty and task of evaluating any possible special circumstances. This, however, is with the proviso both that they prevent any possible lack of reverence or false ideas about the eucharist from being engendered in the attitudes of the people and that they carefully eliminate anything else unacceptable.

2061   In order that this usage will be rightly dealt with, the conferences of bishops in these cases will, after previous careful study, come to a decision by secret ballot. To carry, their decision must receive two-thirds of the votes cast. The conferences will then submit their decision to the Holy See for the requisite confirmation[12] and will also annex an accurate report of the reasons that led to the decision.[R1] Mindful of that bond existing between the various local Churches and between each of them and the universal Church, the Holy See will carefully weigh each case in the interest of the general good, the building up of all, and the increase in faith and devotion that comes from mutual example.

By apostolic authority Pope Paul VI, on 28 May 1969, duly approved this Instruction, prepared at his command. He directed also that it be brought to the attention of the bishops by the presidents of the conferences of bishops.

All things to the contrary notwithstanding.

---

[11] See Acts 20:28.

[12] See CD no. 38, 4 [DOL 7 no. 199].

[R1] Query: From different parts of the world it has been asked whether communion in the hand of the faithful is permissible at will or whether the priest needs some indult for this. Also whether the faculty to grant such an indult belongs to the Ordinary or to the conference of bishops in each country. Reply: The norm contained in the Instruction on the manner of giving communion, *Memoriale Domini*, remains in full force, namely: "[Text here quoted]." Therefore not even the Ordinary, much less a priest, may overstep this disposition of the law: Not 8 (1972) 343.

261. SC DIVINE WORSHIP, **Letter** *En réponse à la demande* to presidents of those conferences of bishops petitioning the indult for communion in the hand, 29 May 1969: AAS 61 (1969) 546–547 (French); Not 5 (1969) 351–353 (French).*

In reply to the request of your conference of bishops regarding permission to give communion by placing the host on the hand of the faithful, I wish to communicate the following.   2062

Pope Paul VI calls attention to the purpose of the Instruction *Memoriale Domini* of 29 May 1969,[a] on retaining the traditional practice in use. At the same time he has taken into account the reasons given to support your request and the outcome of the vote taken on this matter. The Pope grants that throughout the territory of your conference, each bishop may, according to his prudent judgment and conscience, authorize in his diocese the introduction of the new rite for giving communion. The condition is the complete avoidance of any cause for the faithful to be shocked and any danger of irreverence toward the eucharist.

The following norms must therefore be respected.

1. The new manner of giving communion must not be imposed in a way that would exclude the traditional practice. It is a matter of particular seriousness that in places where the new practice is lawfully permitted every one of the faithful have the option of receiving communion on the tongue and even when other persons are receiving communion in the hand. The two ways of receiving communion can without question take place during the same liturgical service. There is a twofold purpose here: that none will find in the new rite anything disturbing to personal devotion toward the eucharist; that this sacrament, the source and cause of unity by its very nature, will not become an occasion of discord between members of the faithful.   2063

2. The rite of communion in the hand must not be put into practice indiscriminately. Since the question involves human attitudes, this mode of communion is bound up with the perceptiveness and preparation of the one receiving. It is advisable, therefore, that the rite be introduced gradually and in the beginning within small, better prepared groups and in favorable settings. Above all it is necessary to have the introduction of the rite preceded by an effective catechesis, so that the people will clearly understand the meaning of receiving in the hand and will practice it with the reverence owed to the sacrament. This catechesis must succeed in excluding any suggestion that in the mind of the Church there is a lessening of faith in the eucharistic presence and in excluding as well any danger or hint of danger of profaning the eucharist.   2064

3. The option offered to the faithful of receiving the eucharistic bread in their hand and putting it into their own mouth must not turn out to be the occasion for regarding it as ordinary bread or as just another religious article. Instead this option must increase in them a consciousness of the dignity of the members of Christ's Mystical Body, into which they are incorporated by baptism and by the grace of the eucharist. It must also increase their faith in the sublime reality of the Lord's body   2065

---

* AAS and Not note that "to the conferences requesting the indult, the SCDW sent this letter, composed in the language of the conference." There is, however, no such English version. See note b of this document.

[a] See DOL 260.

and blood, which they touch with their hand. Their attitude of reverence must measure up to what they are doing.

2066 4.   As to the way to carry out the new rite: one possible model is the traditional usage, which expresses the ministerial functions, by having the priest or deacon place the host in the hand of the communicant. Alternatively, it is permissible to adopt a simpler procedure, namely, allowing the faithful themselves to take the host from the ciborium or paten. The faithful should consume the host before returning to their place; the minister's part will be brought out by use of the usual formulary, *The body of Christ*, to which the communicant replies: *Amen*.

2067 5.   Whatever procedure is adopted, care must be taken not to allow particles of the eucharistic bread to fall or be scattered. Care must also be taken that the communicants have clean hands and that there comportment is becoming and in keeping with the practices of the different peoples.

2068 6.   In the case of communion under both kinds by way of intinction, it is never permitted to place on the hand of the communicant the host that has been dipped in the Lord's blood.

2069 7.   Bishops allowing introduction of the new way of receiving communion are requested to send to this Congregation after six months a report on the result of its concession.[b]

262. SC DISCIPLINE OF THE SACRAMENTS, Rescript (U.S.A.) to the Bishop of Duluth, Minnesota, authorizing lay people to give communion, 25 June 1969.*

2070   The Bishop of Duluth, prostrate at the feet of Your Holiness, humbly requests the faculty to allow qualified persons to distribute holy communion in the churches and public oratories of his diocese in order to assist the priest lest Mass last too long.

On 25 June 1969 the Congregation for the Discipline of the Sacraments, in virtue of special faculties granted by Pope Paul VI, after having heard the recitals, grants the petitioner the special faculty in keeping with the terms of the request, provided qualified persons are chosen by name by the bishop and in the rite

---

b   The *Summarium Decretorum* on confirmation of the decisions of conferences of bishops in *Notitiae* lists the granting of this faculty to the following English-speaking conferences (in each case reference is made to the present document as found in AAS and Not):

South Africa	3 February 1970
Canada	12 February 1970
Rhodesia (Zimbabwe)	2 October 1971
Zambia	11 March 1974
New Zealand	24 April 1974
Australia	26 September 1975
England and Wales	6 March 1976
Papua and New Guinea	28 April 1976
Ireland	4 September 1976
Pakistan	29 October 1976
U.S.A.	17 June 1977
Scotland	7 July 1977
Malaysia and Singapore	3 October 1977

*   Prot. N. 1220/69; see *Jurist* 29 (1969) 465; CLD 7, 650–651.

prescribed they receive a mandate from the bishop. All danger of irreverence to the blessed sacrament is to be removed, all the precautions in the exercise of this faculty are to be followed, and in other respects the prescriptions of the Instruction *Fidei custos*, issued by this Congregation on 30 April 1969,[a] are to be observed.

All things to the contrary notwithstanding. The present grant is to remain in effect *for three years*.

263. SC DISCIPLINE OF THE SACRAMENTS, **Rescript** (U.S.A.) to the conference of bishops, authorizing laypersons to give communion, 9 March 1971.*

The president of the episcopal conference of the United States humbly asks, in the name of the Ordinaries of that country, the faculty to permit:

2071

1. qualified persons to give holy communion to themselves, distribute it to other members of the faithful, and bring it to the sick, in churches and public oratories, in the absence of an ordinary minister of communion or if the latter is impeded by age, bad health, or the pastoral ministry;

2. lay superiors of religious communities or those who take their place to give holy communion to themselves and distribute it to the members, the faithful who may be present, and the sick, in the oratory of the religious house and in the same circumstances;

3. qualified persons to assist the celebrating priest in the administration of the holy eucharist during Mass in churches and public oratories, when a very lengthy distribution of communion cannot otherwise be avoided.

In virtue of special faculties given it by His Holiness Pope Paul VI, the Congregation for the Discipline of the Sacraments on 9 March 1971, granted these faculties — after considering the facts and in accord with the request — to the petitioner and the individual (Ordinaries) of the United States, provided the suitable persons mentioned in the petition are chosen by name by their own Ordinary and receive a mandate from him, together with the lay superiors or their substitutes. Any danger of irreverence of the holy eucharist is to be avoided, every caution is to be exercised in the use of these faculties, and in other matters the Instruction *Fidei custos*,[a] issued by this Congregation on 30 April 1969, is to be followed.

2072

Anything to the contrary notwithstanding.

Valid for a year.[b]

---

[a] See DOL 259.

* Text, BCL Newsletter 7 (1971) 273.

[a] See DOL 259.

[b] Extended indefinitely at the pleasure of the Holy See, 18 January 1972: BCL Newsletter 8 (1972) 1.

264. SC DISCIPLINE OF THE SACRAMENTS, Instruction *Immensae caritatis*, on facilitating reception of communion in certain circumstances, 29 January 1973: AAS 65 (1973) 264–271; Not 9 (1973) 157–164.

2073 The proof of his boundless charity that Christ the Lord left to his Bride the Church, namely, the inexpressible and supreme gift of the eucharist, requires us to deepen our appreciation of this great mystery and to share ever more fully in its saving power. Accordingly, the Church, in its pastoral zeal and care, has repeatedly made practical laws and timely statements of doctrine aimed at furthering devotion toward the eucharist, the summit and center of Christian worship.

The new conditions of the present seem to demand that, without prejudice to the supreme reverence due to so great a sacrament,[1] access to communion be made easier, so that by sharing more fully in the effects of the sacrifice of the Mass, the faithful may more willingly and intensely give themselves to God and to the good of the Church and of all humanity.

The first measures to be taken are meant to prevent reception of communion from becoming either impossible or difficult because there are not enough ministers. Measures must be taken, secondly, to prevent exclusion of the sick from this great comfort of the spirit, the reception of communion, because of their inability to observe the law of fast, even in its current less severe form. Finally, it seems advantageous in certain instances to allow the faithful who request it to receive communion a second time on the same day.

In response therefore to the preferences of several conferences of bishops, the following norms are issued on:

1. special ministers for distributing communion;

2. broader faculty to receive communion twice in a day;

3. mitigation of the eucharistic fast in favor of the sick and the elderly;

4. devotion and reverence toward the blessed sacrament whenever the host is placed in the hand.

1. SPECIAL MINISTERS OF THE EUCHARIST

2074 There are several situations in which a shortage of ministers of communion has been pointed out:

— within Mass because of a great crowd of people or some disability of the celebrant;

— outside Mass when distance makes it difficult to bring communion, especially as viaticum to the sick in danger of death; or when the sheer number of

---

[1] See Council of Trent, sess. 13, *Decretum de SS. Eucharistiae Sacramento* cap. 7: Denz-Schön 1646–47: "It is unfitting to take part in any sacred function without holiness. Assuredly, therefore, the more that Christians perceive the sacredness and divinity of this heavenly sacrament, the more must they take every care not to come to receive it without reverence and holiness, especially since we have the frightening words of St. Paul: 'For those who eat and drink unworthily, eat and drink damnation to themselves, not discerning the Lord's body' (1 Cor 11:29). Those wishing to receive communion must be reminded of St. Paul's command: 'Let a man examine himself' (1 Cor 11:28). Church usage makes it clear that such an examination is needed because those conscious of mortal sin, no matter how contrite they may regard themselves, must not go to the eucharist without sacramental confession beforehand. This Council decrees that, when confessors are available, this practice must always be observed by all Christians, including priests obliged by office to celebrate Mass. A priest who in case of necessity has celebrated Mass without confessing beforehand must go to confession as soon thereafter as possible." See also Congregation of the Council, Decr. *Sacra Tridentina Synodus*, 20 Dec. 1905: AAS 38 (1905–06) 400–406. SCDF, *Pastoral Norms on Giving General Sacramental Absolution*, 16 June 1972, Norm I [DOL 361 no. 3039].

sick people, especially in hospitals or similar institutions, requires several ministers.

In order, then, that the faithful who are in the state of grace and rightly and devoutly wish to share in the sacred meal may not be deprived of this sacramental aid and solace, Pope Paul VI has decided it opportune to authorize special ministers who will be empowered to give communion to themselves and others of the faithful, under the exact and specified conditions here listed.

I.   Local Ordinaries possess the faculty enabling them to permit fit persons, each   2075
chosen by name as a special minister, in a given instance or for a set period or even permanently, to give communion to themselves and others of the faithful and to carry it to the sick residing at home:

    a.   whenever no priest, deacon, or acolyte is available;

    b.   whenever the same ministers are impeded from administering communion because of another pastoral ministry, ill-health, or old age;

    c.   whenever the number of faithful wishing to receive communion is so great that the celebration of Mass or the giving of communion outside Mass would take too long.

II.   The same local Ordinaries possess the faculty of granting individual priests in   2076
the course of their ministry the power to appoint, for a given occasion, a fit person to distribute communion in cases of genuine necessity.

III.   The local Ordinaries also may delegate these faculties to auxiliary bishops,   2077
episcopal vicars, and episcopal delegates.

IV.   The fit person referred to in nos. I and II will be designated according to the   2078
order of this listing (which may be changed at the prudent discretion of the local Ordinary): reader, major seminarian, man religious, woman religious, catechist, one of the faithful — a man or a woman.

V.   In the oratories of communities of both men and women religious the office of   2079
distributing communion in the circumstances stated in no. I may rightly be assigned to the nonordained superior of men religious or to the superior of women religious or to their vicars.

VI.   If there is time, it is advisable that the fit person chosen by the local Ordinary   2080
as a minister of communion and the person, referred to in no. II, appointed by a priest having this faculty, should receive a commission (*mandatum*) according to the rite annexed to this Instruction.[2] This minister is to carry out the distribution of communion in keeping with liturgical norms.

Because these faculties have been granted exclusively in favor of the spiritual   2081
good of the faithful and for cases of genuine need, let priests remember that such faculties do not release them from the obligation of giving the eucharist to the faithful who lawfully request it and especially of bringing and administering it to the sick.

The faithful who are special ministers of communion must be persons whose good qualities of Christian life, faith, and morals recommend them. Let them strive to be worthy of this great office, foster their own devotion to the eucharist, and show an example to the rest of the faithful by their own devotion and reverence

---

   2   The *editio typica* of this rite was published separately [see DOL 343].

toward the most august sacrament of the altar. No one is to be chosen whose appointment the faithful might find disquieting.

2. A MORE EXTENSIVE FACULTY TO RECEIVE COMMUNION TWICE IN ONE DAY

2082   The discipline now in force permits the faithful to receive communion a second time on the same day:

— on Saturday evening or the evening before a holyday of obligation, when they are fulfilling the obligation to assist at Mass, even if they have received communion that morning;[3]

— at the second Mass of Easter Sunday and in one of the day Masses on Christmas, even if they have received communion at the Mass of the Easter Vigil or at the Mass at Midnight on Christmas;[4]

— also at the evening Mass on Holy Thursday, even if they have also received communion at the chrism Mass.[5]

Over and above those listed, there are other situations of the same type that favor a second communion. The reasons for granting a new faculty therefore must here be set out in detail.

2083   Like a provident mother, the Church has established from centuries-old practice and has received into its canon law a norm according to which it is lawful for the faithful to receive communion only once a day. That norm remains unchanged and is not to be disregarded simply for reasons of devotion. Any ill-advised desire to repeat communion must be countered by the truth that the more devoutly a person approaches the holy table the greater the power of that sacrament which feeds, strengthens, and expresses faith, charity, and the rest of the virtues.[6] For the faithful are to go forth from the liturgical celebration to do works of charity, religion, and the apostolate "so that what they have received by faith and sacrament in the celebration of the eucharist they will hold to by the way they live."[7]

2084   There may however be special circumstances in which the faithful who have already received communion on the same day or in which priests who have celebrated Mass attend some community's celebration. It will be lawful for these faithful and these priests to receive communion a second time in the following situations:

1. at ritual Masses in which the sacraments of baptism, confirmation, anointing of the sick, orders, and marriage are administered, as well as at Masses in which there is a first communion;[8]

2. at Masses for the consecration of a church or an altar, for a religious profession, for the conferral of a "canonical mission";

3. at the Masses for the dead on the occasion of the funeral, news of the death, the final burial, or the first anniversary;

---

[3]   See SCR, Instr. EuchMyst, 25 May 1967 no. 28 [DOL 179 no. 1257].

[4]   See ibid.

[5]   See ibid.; SCR, Instr. InterOec, 26 Sept. 1964, no. 60 [DOL 23 no. 352]; Instr. *Tres abhinc annos*, 4 May 1967, no. 14 [DOL 39 no. 460].

[6]   See ST 3a, 79. 7 ad 3; 8 ad 1.

[7]   SCR, Instr. EuchMyst no. 13 [DOL 179 no. 1242].

[8]   See GIRM no. 329 [DOL 208 no. 1719].

4. at the principal Mass celebrated in a cathedral or parish church on the solemnity of Corpus Christi and on the day of a pastoral visitation; at a Mass celebrated on the occasion of a major religious superior's canonical visitation to a particular religious house or chapter;

5. at the principal Mass at a eucharistic or Marian congress, whether international or national, regional or diocesan;

6. at the principal Mass of any kind of meeting, pilgrimage, or people's mission;[R2]

7. at the administration of viaticum, when communion may be given to the members of the household and the friends of the sick person who are present.

8. Over and above the cases already mentioned, the local Ordinary is allowed to grant for a single occasion the faculty to receive communion twice on the same day whenever, because of truly special circumstances, a second reception is warranted on the basis of this Instruction.

3. MITIGATION OF THE EUCHARISTIC FAST IN FAVOR OF THE SICK AND THE ELDERLY

First, it remains firm and established that one of the faithful to whom viaticum is administered in danger of death is not bound by any precept of fast.[9] Also remaining in force is the concession made by Pius XII on the basis of which "the sick, even though not bedridden, may without any time limit take nonalcoholic drinks and either liquid or solid medicines before celebrating Mass and receiving communion."[10]   2085

As for food and drink serving as nourishment, that tradition must be preserved according to which the eucharist was to be taken "before all food," as Tertullian says,[11] as a sign of the excellence of the sacramental food.

To give recognition to the dignity of the sacrament and to stir up joy at the coming of the Lord, it is well to observe a period of silence and recollection. It is a sufficient sign of devotion and respect on the part of the sick if they direct their mind for a brief period to this great mystery. The duration of the eucharistic fast, that is, of abstaining from food or alcoholic drink, is reduced to approximately a quarter of an hour for: 2086

1. the sick in health-care facilities or at home, even if they are not bedridden;

2. the faithful of advanced years, whether they are confined to their homes because of old age or live in homes for the aged;

3. sick priests, even if not bedridden, and elderly priests, as regards both celebrating Mass and receiving communion;

4. persons caring for, as well as the family and friends of, the sick and elderly who wish to receive communion with them, whenever such persons cannot keep the one-hour fast without inconvenience.

[R2] See DOL 223 no. 1796, note R3, Query 2.

[9] See CIC can. 858, § 1.

[10] Pius XII, Motu Proprio *Sacram Communionem*, 19 March 1957, no. 4: AAS 49 (1957) 178.

[11] Tertullian, *Ad uxorem* 2,5: PL 1, 1408.

4. DEVOTION AND REVERENCE TOWARD THE EUCHARIST
IN THE CASE OF COMMUNION IN THE HAND

2087   Ever since the Instruction *Memoriale Domini* three years ago, some of the conferences of bishops have been requesting the Apostolic See for the faculty to allow ministers distributing communion to place the eucharistic bread in the hand of the faithful. The same Instruction contained a reminder that "the laws of the Church and the writings of the Fathers give ample witness of a supreme reverence and utmost caution toward the eucharist"[12] and that this must continue. Particularly in regard to this way of receiving communion, experience suggests certain matters requiring careful attention.

2088   On the part of both the minister and the recipient, whenever the host is placed in the hand of a communicant there must be careful concern and caution, especially about particles that might fall from the hosts.

The usage of communion in the hand must be accompanied by relevant instruction or catechesis on Catholic teaching regarding Christ's real and permanent presence under the eucharistic elements and the proper reverence toward this sacrament.[13]

The faithful must be taught that Jesus Christ is Lord and Savior and that therefore the worship of *latria* or adoration belonging to God is owed to Christ present in this sacrament. They are also to be instructed not to omit after communion the sincere and appropriate thanksgiving that is in keeping with their individual capacities, state, and occupation.[14]

Finally, to the end that their coming to this heavenly table may be completely worthy and fruitful, the faithful should be instructed on its benefits and effects, for both the individual and society, so that their familial relationship to the Father who gives us our "daily bread,"[15] may reflect the highest reverence for him, nurture love, and lead to a living bond with Christ, in whose flesh and blood we share.[16]

Pope Paul VI approved this Instruction, confirmed it with his authority, and ordered its publication, setting the day of publication as its effective date.

▶   343.   SC DIVINE WORSHIP, *Rite of Commissioning Special Ministers of Holy Communion*, Introduction, 29 January 1973.

---

[12]   SCDW, Instr. *Memoriale Domini*, 29 May 1969 [DOL 260 no. 2055], which remains in force.

[13]   See SC art. 7 [DOL 1 no. 7]. SCR, Instr. EuchMyst no. 9 [DOL 179 no. 1238]. SCDW, Instr. *Memoriale Domini*, the words "they must prevent any possible lack of reverence or false opinions about the eucharist from taking root in the minds of the people" [DOL 260 no. 2060].

[14]   See Paul VI, Addr. to members of the Permanent Council on International Eucharistic Congresses [DOL 182].

[15]   See Lk 11:3.

[16]   See Heb 2:14.

265. SC DIVINE WORSHIP, **Decree** *Eucharistiae Sacramentum*, promulgating the *editio typica* of rites for holy communion and worship of the eucharist outside Mass, 21 June 1973: AAS 65 (1973) 610; Not 9 (1973) 306–307.

The sacrament of the eucharist was entrusted by Christ to his Bride the Church, as spiritual nourishment and as a pledge of eternal life. The Church continues to receive this gift with faith and love.

2089

The celebration of the eucharist in the sacrifice of the Mass is the true origin and purpose of the worship shown to the eucharist outside Mass. The principal reason for reserving the sacrament after Mass is to unite, through sacramental communion, the faithful unable to participate in the Mass, especially the sick and the aged, with Christ and the offering of his sacrifice.

In turn, eucharistic reservation, which became customary in order to permit the reception of communion, led to the practice of adoring this sacrament and offering to it the worship of *latria* that is due to God. This cult of adoration is based on valid and solid principles; furthermore, the Church itself has instituted public and communal forms of this worship.

The rite of Mass has already been revised. The Instruction *Eucharisticum Mysterium*, published 25 May 1967, has set out the norms "on the practical arrangement of the worship of this sacrament even after Mass and on its correlation with the proper arrangement of the Mass in conformity with the directives of Vatican Council II and other pertinent documents of the Apostolic See."[1] Now the Congregation for Divine Worship has revised the rites that bear the title *Holy Communion and Worship of the Eucharist outside Mass*.

These rites, approved by Pope Paul VI, are now published in this edition, which is declared to be the *editio typica*. They are to replace the rites that appear in the Roman Ritual at the present time. They may be used at once in Latin; they may be used in the vernacular from the day set by the conferences of bishops for their territory, after the conferences have prepared a vernacular version and have obtained the confirmation of the Holy See.

2090

Anything to the contrary notwithstanding.

266. SC DIVINE WORSHIP, *Holy Communion and Worship of the Eucharist outside Mass*, Chapter 1, Holy Communion outside Mass, **Introduction**, 21 June 1973: Vatican Polyglot Press (1973) 11–15; Not 9 (1973) 311–316.

CHAPTER I
HOLY COMMUNION OUTSIDE MASS[a]

INTRODUCTION

I. The Relationship Between Communion Outside
Mass and the Sacrifice

13. Sacramental communion received during Mass is a more complete participation in the eucharistic celebration. This truth stands out more clearly, by force of

2091

---

[1] SCR, Instr. EuchMyst no. 3 g [DOL 179 no. 1232].

[a] For the General Introduction of the document and ch. 3, see DOL 279.

the sign value, when after the priest's communion the faithful receive the Lord's body and blood from the same sacrifice.[1] Therefore, recently baked bread should ordinarily be consecrated in every eucharistic celebration for the communion of the faithful.

2092   14. The faithful are to be led to the practice of receiving communion during the actual eucharistic celebration.

Priests, however, are not to refuse to give communion to the faithful who ask for it even outside Mass.[2]

In fact it is proper that those who are prevented from being present at the community's celebration should be refreshed with the eucharist. In this way they may realize that they are united not only with the Lord's sacrifice but also with the community itself and are supported by the love of their brothers and sisters.

Pastors should take care that the sick and the elderly be given the opportunity, even if they are not gravely ill or in imminent danger of death, to receive the eucharist often, even daily, especially during the Easter season. It is lawful to minister communion under the form of wine to those who cannot receive the consecrated bread.[3]

2093   15. The faithful should be instructed carefully that, even when they receive communion outside Mass, they are closely united with the sacrifice that perpetuates the sacrifice of the cross. They are sharers in the sacred banquet in which "through the communion of the body and blood of the Lord, the people of God share the benefits of the paschal sacrifice, renew the new covenant with us made once and for all by God in Christ's blood, and in faith and hope foreshadow and anticipate the eschatological banquet in the Father's kingdom, as they proclaim the death of the Lord until he comes."[4]

II. THE TIME OF COMMUNION OUTSIDE MASS

2094   16. Communion may be given outside Mass on any day and at any hour. It is proper, however, to schedule the hours for giving communion, with a view to the convenience of the faithful, so that the celebration may take place in a fuller form and with greater spiritual benefit. Nevertheless:

a.   On Holy Thursday communion may be given only during Mass; communion may be brought to the sick at any hour of the day.

b.   On Good Friday communion may be given only during the celebration of the passion of the Lord; communion may be brought at any hour of the day to the sick who cannot participate in the celebration.

c.   On Holy Saturday communion may be given only as viaticum.[5]

---

[1]   See SC art. 55 [DOL 1 no. 55].

[2]   See SCR, Instr. EuchMyst no. 33 a [DOL 179 no. 1262].

[3]   See ibid. nos. 40–41 [DOL 179 no. 1269–70].

[4]   Ibid. no. 3 a [DOL 179 no. 1232].

[5]   See MR, *Missa vespertina in Cena Domini,* 243; *Celebratio Passionis Domini* 250, no. 3; *Sabbato Sancto* 265 [RM, Holy Thursday, *Evening Mass of the Lord's Supper;* Good Friday, *Celebration of the Lord's Passion* no. 3; Holy Saturday].

III. The Minister of Communion

17. It belongs first of all to the priest and the deacon to minister holy communion   2095
to the faithful who ask to receive it.[6] It is most fitting, therefore, that they give a
suitable part of their time to this ministry of their order, depending on the needs of
the faithful.

It also belongs to an acolyte who has been properly instituted to give communion as a special minister when the priest and deacon are absent or impeded by
sickness, old age, or pastoral ministry or when the number of the faithful at the
holy table is so great that the Mass or other service may be unreasonably prolonged.[7]

The local Ordinary may give other special ministers the faculty to give communion whenever it seems necessary for the pastoral benefit of the faithful and no
priest, deacon, or acolyte is available.[8]

IV. The Place of Communion Outside Mass

18. The place where communion outside Mass is ordinarily given is a church or   2096
oratory in which the eucharist is regularly celebrated or reserved, or a church,
oratory, or other place where the local community regularly gathers for the liturgical assembly on Sundays or other days. Communion may be given, however, in
other places, including private homes, when it is a question of the sick, prisoners, or
others who cannot leave the place without danger or serious difficulty.

V. Regulations for Giving Communion

19. When communion is given in a church or oratory, a corporal is to be placed on   2097
the altar, which is already covered with a cloth, and there are to be two lighted
candles as a sign of reverence and festiveness.[9] A communion plate is to be used.

When communion is given in other places, a suitable table is to be prepared
and covered with a cloth; candles are also to be provided.

20. The minister of communion, if he is a priest or deacon, is to be vested in an alb,   2098
or a surplice over a cassock, and a stole.

Other ministers should wear either the liturgical vesture that may be traditional in their region or attire that is in keeping with this ministry and has been
approved by the Ordinary.

The eucharist for communion outside a church is to be carried in a pyx or other
covered vessel; the vesture of the minister and the manner of carrying the eucharist
should be appropriate and in accord with local circumstances.

21. In giving communion, the custom of placing the particle of consecrated bread   2099
on the tongue of the communicant is to be maintained because it is based on a
tradition of several centuries.

Conferences of bishops, however, may decree, once their decision has been
confirmed by the Apostolic See, that communion may also be given in their territories by placing the consecrated bread in the hand of the faithful, provided any

---

6   See SCR, Instr. EuchMyst no. 31 [DOL 179 no. 1260].

7   See Paul VI, Motu Proprio *Ministeria quaedam*, 15 Aug. 1972, no. VI [DOL 340 no. 2931].

8   See SCDS, Instr. *Immensae caritatis*, 29 January 1973, 1, nos. I and II [DOL 264 nos. 2075–76].

9   See GIRM no. 269 [DOL 208 no. 1659].

danger is prevented of engendering in the attitudes of the faithful irreverence or false ideas about the eucharist.[10]

The faithful, furthermore, must be taught that Jesus Christ is Lord and Savior and that therefore the worship of *latria* or adoration belonging to God is owed to Christ present in this sacrament.[11]

In either case, communion must be given by the authorized minister, who shows the particle of consecrated bread to the communicants and gives it to them, saying: *The body of Christ*, to which the communicants reply: *Amen.*

In the case of communion under the appearance of wine, the regulations of the Instruction *Sacramentali Communione* of 29 June 1970 are to be followed exactly.[12]

2100   22. Fragments remaining after communion are to be reverently gathered and placed in the ciborium or in a vessel with water.

Likewise, if communion is given under the appearance of wine, the chalice or other vessel is to be washed with water.

The water used for cleansing the vessels may be drunk or poured out in a suitable place.

VI. Dispositions for Communion

2101   23. The eucharist, which continuously makes the paschal mystery of Christ to be present among us, is the source of every grace and of the forgiveness of sins. Nevertheless, those who intend to receive the body of the Lord must approach it with a pure conscience and proper dispositions of soul if they are to receive the effects of the paschal sacrament.

On this account the Church prescribes "that those conscious of mortal sin, even though they think themselves to be contrite, must not go to the holy eucharist without sacramental confession beforehand."[13] When there is a case of necessity and no confessor is available, they are first to make an act of perfect contrition with the intention of confessing individually, at the proper time, the mortal sins that they cannot confess at present.

It is desirable that those who receive communion daily or very often go to the sacrament of penance at regular intervals, depending on their circumstances.

The faithful also should look upon the eucharist as a remedy that frees them from their daily faults and preserves them from mortal sins; they should also receive an explanation of how to make use of the penitential parts of the liturgy, especially at Mass.[14]

2102   24. Communicants are not to receive the sacrament unless they have fasted for one hour from solid food and beverages, with the exception of water.

The period of the eucharistic fast, that is, abstinence from food or alcoholic drink, is reduced to about a quarter of an hour for:

1. the sick who are living in hospitals or at home, even if they are not confined to bed;

---

[10]   See SCDW, Instr. *Memoriale Domini*, 29 May 1969, [DOL 260 no. 2060].

[11]   See SCDS, Instr. *Immensae caritatis* no. 4 [DOL 264 no. 2088].

[12]   See no. 6 [DOL 270 no. 2115].

[13]   See Council of Trent, sess. 13, *Decr. de Eucharistia* 7: Denz-Schön 1646–47; sess. 14, *Canones de sacramento Paenitentiae* 9: Denz-Schön 1709. SCDF, *Pastoral Norms on Giving General Sacramental Absolution*, 16 June 1972, Preface and Norm VI [DOL 361 nos. 3038 and 3044].

[14]   See SCR, Instr. EuchMyst no. 35 [DOL 179 no. 1264].

2. the faithful of advanced age, even if not bedridden, whether they are confined to their homes because of old age or live in a nursing home;

3. sick priests, even if not bedridden, or elderly priests, whether they are to celebrate Mass or to receive communion;

4. persons caring for, as well as the family and friends of, the sick or the elderly who wish to receive communion with them, whenever such persons cannot keep the one-hour fast without inconvenience.[15]

25. The union with Christ, to which the sacrament is directed, should be extended to the whole of Christian life. Thus the faithful, constantly reflecting upon the gift they have received, should carry on their daily work with thanksgiving, under the guidance of the Holy Spirit, and should bring forth fruits of rich charity.

2103

In order to continue more surely in the thanksgiving that in the Mass is offered to God in an eminent way, those who have been nourished by communion should be encouraged to remain for some time in prayer.[16,R3]

▶ 276. SC DIVINE WORSHIP, *Directory for Masses with Children*, 1 November 1973:

nos. 53–54:   Rite of communion [nos. 2186–87].

267. SC SACRAMENTS AND DIVINE WORSHIP, Letter *Instructione "Memoriale Domini"* to presidents of the conferences of bishops, on communion in the hand, 17 March 1976.*

After the Instruction *Memoriale Domini* on the manner of giving holy communion had been published as well as liturgical norms on the same point, the Apostolic See since 1969 has granted to petitioning conferences of bishops, in accord with *Memoriale Domini*, the faculty of giving communion in the hand of the faithful (see AAS, 1969, pp. 541–547).[a]

2104

By reason of orders from above, this Congregation respectfully requests the conferences of bishops that have received the faculty in question kindly to indicate the results of the favor in relation to the pastoral and liturgical life in dioceses.

The reasons for returning to the ancient and established practice of placing the consecrated bread on the hand were indeed sound and remain so. But at the same time some appeals have reached this Congregation, deploring acts lacking reverence toward the eucharist and other abuses. Such matters provide growing evidence of the need of an insistent and careful catechesis so as to guide the faithful toward liturgical reform.

In this situation, therefore, I earnestly request that, after appropriate consultation with Ordinaries, you make a precise report on all points pertinent to the

---

[15] See SCDS, Instr. *Immensae caritatis* no. 3 [DOL 264 no. 2086].

[16] See SCR, Instr. EuchMyst no. 38 [DOL 179 no. 1267].

[R3] [Prior to the present document]. Query: Have the formularies to be used for communion outside Mass been changed (e.g., the *Confiteor, Behold the Lamb of God*) ? Reply: No. In distributing communion outside Mass the formularies given in the *Ordo Missae* (nos. 133–135) must be used (including the *Confiteor* and the absolution [*Ordo Missae* no. 3]) until other provisions are made: Not 6 (1970) 264, no. 40.

* SCSDW, Prot. N. CD 355/76.

[a] See DOL 260 no. 2061.

introduction of the new usage for giving communion. In this way the Pope will himself be able to obtain as complete a knowledge as possible about this matter.

My request is that the report in question be submitted to this Congregation not later than Christmas of the current year, 1976.

Section 8. Communion: B. Communion under Both Kinds

SUMMARY (DOL 268–270). The principal text in this section is the Introduction of the *Rite of Communion under Both Kinds* (DOL 268), which was promulgated in 1965 by the same decree that promulgated the *Rite of Concelebration*. The practice was gradually broadened and the 1970 Instruction *Sacramentali Communione* (DOL 270) presents general church discipline as it now stands in the General Instruction of the Roman Missal. A subsidiary text here is a reply on a query in a particular instance of communion under both kinds (DOL 269).

▶   1.   VATICAN COUNCIL II, Constitution on the Liturgy *Sacrosanctum Concilium*, 4
          December 1964:

          art. 55:   Restoring communion under both kinds in certain
                                  instances [no. 55].

▶   222. SC RITES AND CONSILIUM, Decree *Ecclesiae semper*, promulgating the *editio typica*
          of the rites of concelebration and of communion under both kinds, 7 March
          1965.

268. SC RITES AND CONSILIUM, *Rite of Communion under Both Kinds,* **Introduction**, 7 March 1965: Vatican Polyglot Press, 1965, 51–52.

2105   1.   The dogmatic principles laid down by the Council of Trent remaining intact,
        communion under both kinds may be allowed, at the discretion of the bishops, for:

        1. those ordained at the Mass of their ordination;

        2. the deacon and subdeacon exercising their ministries at a pontifical or
        solemn Mass;[R4]

        3. an abbess at the Mass in which she is blessed;

        4. those consecrated to a life of virginity at the Mass of their consecration;

        5. those professed at the Mass of their religious profession, provided they
        pronounce their vows during Mass;

        6. the bride and bridegroom at their wedding Mass;

        7. adults newly baptized at the Mass following their baptism;

        8. adults newly confirmed at the Mass of their confirmation;[R5]

        9. baptized persons newly received into the full communion of the Catholic
        Church;

        10. those mentioned in nos. 3–6 at Masses celebrating their jubilees;

        11. priests who are present at major celebrations and are not able to celebrate
        or concelebrate; lay brothers who are present at a concelebration in religious
        houses.[R6]

[R4] 1. Query: Is it permissible according to the intent of the *Rite* no. 1:2 for the deacon to receive
communion under both kinds when he assists alone at the celebration of Mass? Reply: Yes, at a sung
Mass. The words of the *Rite* "at a pontifical or solemn Mass" restrict communion under both kinds for the
deacon to a sung Mass: Not 1 (1965) 189, no. 56.
    2. Query: On the basis of an analogy with the *Rite of Concelebration* (no. 15 [DOL 223 no. 1808]): may
priests functioning as deacon and subdeacon at a solemn Mass receive communion under both kinds, even
if they have already celebrated Mass or will do so? Reply: No. The general law (CIC can. 857) on not
receiving communion twice on the same day remains in force. The cases in the *Rite of Concelebration* no. 15
[DOL 223 no. 1808] and the Instruction [InterOec] no. 60 [DOL 23 no. 352] are to be regarded as a
relaxation of the law that applies only to those cases explicitly determined. The case cited here involves
exclusively a true deacon or subdeacon exercising his ministry: Not 1 (1965) 307, no. 86.

[R5] Query: Are the words *"adults* newly confirmed" to be taken in the juridic sense of CIC can. 745, § 2,
2, namely, to mean persons who possess the use of reason, or in the everyday sense, namely, to mean those
who have at least reached the age of puberty? Reply: To mean those who have reached the age of puberty:
Not 1 (1965) 143, no. 36.

[R6] Query: When "lay brothers" are referred to in regard to communion under both kinds: a. is the
reference only to those acting as servers at a concelebrated Mass; b. or to all professed lay brothers who
are participants at the concelebrated Mass? Reply: To a: No; to b: Yes: ibid., no. 37.

In each case the choice of the rite to be used from those given later in this ritual belongs to the bishops.[a]

PRIOR CATECHESIS

2.   For the faithful who take part in the rite or are present at it, pastors should take care to call to mind as clearly as possible Catholic teaching according to the Council of Trent (sess. 21, ch. 1–3) on the manner of communion. Above all they should instruct the people that according to Catholic faith "Christ whole and entire as well as the genuine sacrament are received even under one kind only; that, therefore, as far as the effects are concerned, those who receive in this manner are not deprived of any grace necessary for salvation" (ibid., ch. 3).[b]   2106

Pastors are also to explain that the Church has power in its stewardship of the sacraments, provided their substance remains intact. The Church may make those rules and changes that, in view of the different conditions, times, and places, it decides to be in the interest of reverence for the sacraments or the well-being of the recipients (see ibid., ch. 2). At the same time the faithful should be encouraged to take part more intensely in a sacred rite in which the sign of the eucharistic meal stands out more explicitly.

PREPARATIONS

3.   The following are to be prepared for distributing communion under both kinds: 2107

a.   If communion is received from the chalice with a tube, silver tubes are needed for the celebrant and each communicant. There should also be a container of water for purifying the tubes.

b.   If communion is given with a spoon, only one spoon is necessary.

c.   If communion is given by intinction, care is to be taken that the eucharistic bread is not too thin or too small, but a little thicker than usual so that after being partly dipped into the precious blood it can still easily be given to the communicant.

269. SC RITES, **Reply** to a query, on communion under both kinds to members of secular institutes on the day of their profession, 8 July 1965: Not 2 (1966) 132.

The Congregation of Rites has been requested to make the pertinent declaration on: whether communion may be given under both kinds even to members of secular institutes on the day of their profession, in the way that the new law allows this for the professed in the Mass of their religious profession, provided they pronounce their vows during Mass.[a]   2108

The same Congregation, after thorough consideration, has replied: Yes, provided the profession itself is made during Mass.

---

a   The ritual is substantially the same as is now found in GIRM nos. 244–252 [DOL 208 nos. 1634–42].

b   The *editio typica* mistakenly referred to ch. 1–9 and here to ch. 9. The correct references are ch. 1–3 and here ch. 3 [Denz-Schön 1726–29 and 1729. See GIRM no. 241, note 69 [DOL 208 no. 1631].

a   See DOL 268 no. 2105.

Pope Paul VI in an audience on 8 July 1965 has approved and confirmed this reply.

▶   179. SC RITES (Consilium), Instruction *Eucharisticum mysterium*, on worship of the eucharist, 25 May 1967:

no.   32:   Communion under both kinds [no. 1261].

▶   208. SC RITES (Consilium); SC DIVINE WORSHIP, General Instruction of the Roman Missal, 1st ed. 6 April 1969; 4th ed. 27 March 1975:

nos. 240–252:   Communion under both kinds [no. 1630–42].

▶   275. SC DIVINE WORSHIP, Instruction *Actio pastoralis*, on Masses with special
groups, 15 May 1969:

no.   7:   Communion under both kinds [no. 2128].

▶   261. SC DIVINE WORSHIP, Letter *En réponse à la demande* to petitioning conferences of
bishops, on communion in the hand, 29 May 1969:

no.   6:   Communion by intinction [no. 2068].

270. SC DIVINE WORSHIP, **Instruction** *Sacramentali Communione*, extending the practice of communion under both kinds, 29 June 1970: AAS 62 (1970) 664–666; Not 6 (1970) 322–324.

2109   That sacramental communion brings the faithful more completely into the celebration of the eucharist is the teaching of the Church's entire tradition. For through communion the faithful come to share more completely in the eucharistic sacrifice. They take part, that is, not simply by faith and the prayers they utter or simply by an affective, spiritual union with Christ offered on the altar, but by receiving Christ himself sacramentally so as to obtain for themselves a fuller share in the effects of his holy sacrifice.

To the end that the fullness of the sacramental sign in the eucharistic banquet would be more striking for the faithful,[1] Vatican Council II decreed that in certain instances, to be determined by the Apostolic See, the faithful could receive communion under both kinds.[2] This was without prejudice to those dogmatic principles laid down by the Council of Trent to teach that Christ, whole and entire, as well as the genuine sacrament are received under the form of either bread or wine.[3]

The will of Vatican Council II in this regard has been gradually put into practice,[4] as the preparation of the faithful has gone forward, in order to ensure richer results in devotion and spiritual profit from this change in eucharistic discipline.

---

[1] See GIRM no. 240 [DOL 208 no. 1630].

[2] See SC art. 55 [DOL 1 no. 55].

[3] See Council of Trent, sess. 21, *Decr. de Communione eucharistica* cap. 1–3: Denz-Schön 1725–29.

[4] See SCR, Decr. *Ecclesiae semper*, 7 March 1965 [DOL 222]; Instr. EuchMyst, 25 May 1967, no. 32 [DOL 179 no. 1261]. GIRM nos. 76 and 242 [DOL 208 nos. 1466 and 1632; this reference in AAS is given as nos. 76–242, obviously an error; even the relevance of no. 76 is unclear, Ed.].

Subsequently there has been a growing desire to increase the instances in which administration of communion under both kinds would be allowed, according to the different situations in the various parts of the world and among different peoples.

Having considered the petitions of many bishops and conferences of bishops, as well as of superiors of religious families, this Congregation, at the direction of Pope Paul VI, therefore decrees the following regarding permission to administer communion under both kinds.

1.   Communion may be distributed under both kinds, at the discretion of the Ordinary, in those cases determined by the Apostolic See, according to the list in the Appendix to this document.   2110

2.   The conferences of bishops moreover have the power to decide to what extent and under what considerations and conditions Ordinaries are empowered to grant communion under both kinds in other instances that are of special significance in the spiritual life of any community or group of the faithful.   2111

3.   Within such limits, Ordinaries may designate the particular instances, but on condition that they grant permission not indiscriminately but for clearly defined celebrations and that they point out matters for caution. They are also to exclude occasions when there will be a large number of communicants. The groups receiving this permission must also be specific, well ordered, and homogeneous.   2112

4.   The local Ordinary may grant this permission for all churches and oratories in his territory; the Ordinary of religious, for all houses of his institute.   2113

Both must ensure observance of the norms laid down by the Apostolic See or the conference of bishops. Before granting the permission, they must have assurance that all measures can be carried out that will safeguard the holiness of the sacrament.

5.   The necessary catechesis must precede admission of the faithful to communion under both kinds in order that they will have a clear knowledge of the meaning of this rite.   2114

6.   For a fitting administration of communion under both kinds care must be taken that all is done with proper reverence and that the rite outlined in the General Instruction of the Roman Missal nos. 244–251[a] is observed.   2115

The character of the particular liturgical assembly as well as the age, circumstances, and preparation of the communicants should be considered, then the choice should be made of the way of giving communion that ensures its being done with dignity, devotion, propriety, and the avoidance of the danger of irreverence.

Among the ways of communicating prescribed by the General Instruction of the Roman Missal, receiving from the chalice itself ranks first. Even so, it is to be chosen only when everything can be carried out in fitting order and with no danger of irreverence toward the blood of Christ. When they are available, other priests or deacons or even acolytes should be chosen to present the chalice. The method of communicating in which the communicants pass the chalice to one another or go directly to the chalice to take Christ's blood must be regarded as unacceptable.

Whenever none of the ministers already mentioned is available, if the communicants are few and are to receive communion under both kinds by drinking

---

[a]   DOL 208 nos. 1634–41.

directly from the chalice, the priest himself distributes communion, first under the form of bread, then under the form of wine.

Otherwise the preference should be for the rite of communion under both kinds by intinction: it is more likely to obviate the practical difficulties and to ensure the reverence due the sacrament more effectively. Intinction makes access to communion under both kinds easier and safer for the faithful of all ages and conditions; at the same time it preserves the truth present in the more complete sign.

On 26 June 1970 Pope Paul VI approved and confirmed this Instruction and ordered it to be made public.[b]

---

[b]   The APPENDIX to *Sacramentali Communione*: "Instances determined by the General Instruction of the Roman Missal (no. 242) when communion may be given under both kinds" is in AAS 62 (1970) 666–667, Not 6 (1970) 325–326, and in DOL 208 no. 1632 in the emended (1975) form given by the GIRM, with variants from the Appendix in notes.

Section 8. Communion: C. Eucharistic Fast

SUMMARY (DOL 271–273). The general discipline on the fast before communion was amended in the case of priest celebrants by a 1964 decree of the Holy Office (DOL 271) and for both priests and the faithful by a concession of Paul VI announced viva voce during a session of the Council (DOL 272). The text of the *Catechism of St. Pius X* was emended to reflect this change (DOL 273). Other points concerning the discipline of the eucharistic fast are given in the important cross-references of this section.

▶   103.   PAUL VI, Motu Proprio *Pastorale munus*, on the powers and privileges of bishops, 30 November 1963:

I, 3:   Dispensation in cases of bination and trination [no. 714].

271. SC HOLY OFFICE, Decree *In Apostolica Constitutione*, on the eucharistic fast for priests celebrating Mass, 10 January 1964: AAS 56 (1964) 212.

2116   In the Apostolic Constitution *Christus Dominus* of 6 January 1953, as well as in the Motu Proprio *Sacram Communionem* of 19 March 1957, new norms were laid down shortening the time for the eucharistic fast to three hours for solid foods and alcoholic drinks and to one hour for nonalcoholic drinks.

Both documents stated that the period of one hour or three hours was to be calculated by reference to the time *before communion* for the faithful and *before Mass* for priest celebrants.

It has now been decided to abolish this distinction in the computation of time: even for priests celebrating Mass the period of eucharistic fasting is to be counted from the moment they are to receive communion in the Mass and no longer from the moment they are to begin Mass.

The present Decree was passed by the Fathers of the Congregation of the Holy Office in plenary session on Wednesday, 18 December 1963. At an audience granted to the Assessor of the same Congregation, 23 December 1963, Pope Paul VI kindly approved the decree and ordered its publication.

272. PAUL VI, Concession, on the eucharistic fast, announced at a public session of Vatican Council II, 21 November 1964: AAS 57 (1965) 186.

2117   In view of the difficulties in many places regarding the eucharistic fast, Pope Paul VI, acceding to the requests of the bishops, grants that the fast from solid food is shortened to one hour before communion in the case of both priests and faithful. The concession also covers use of alcoholic beverages, but with proper moderation being observed.

273. SC COUNCIL, Notification *Come è noto*, on the eucharistic fast in the *Catechism of St. Pius X*, 18 June 1965: AAS 57 (1965) 666 (Italian).

2118   As is well known, in public session of Vatican Council II on 21 November 1964 (AAS 57 [1965] 186),[a] Pope Paul VI announced a new concession in regard to the eucharistic fast.

In keeping with that concession this Congregation, with the agreement of the Congregation of the Holy Office and the approval of Pope Paul, has determined that the wording for no. 339 of the Catechism of St. Pius X be replaced by the following:

— *In what does the eucharistic fast consist?*

---

[a]   See DOL 272.

— *The eucharistic fast consists in abstaining from all food and drink for one hour before communion.*

▶ 105. PAUL VI, Motu Proprio *De Episcoporum muneribus*, on norms for the power of dispensation, 15 June 1966:

    no. 20:   Dispensation from eucharistic fast reserved to Holy See [no. 750].

▶ 275. SC DIVINE WORSHIP, Instruction *Actio pastoralis*, on Masses with special groups, 15 May 1969:

    no. 10 c: Eucharistic fast [no. 2131].

▶ 264. SC DISCIPLINE OF THE SACRAMENTS, Instruction *Immensae caritatis*, on facilitating communion, 29 January 1973:

    no. 3:   Mitigation of the eucharistic fast for the sick and elderly [nos. 2085–86].

▶ 266. SC DIVINE WORSHIP, *Holy Communion and Worship of the Eucharist outside Mass*, Chapter 1, Holy Communion, Introduction, 21 June 1973:

    no. 24:   Eucharistic fast [no. 2102].

SECTION 9. SPECIAL DIRECTORIES

SUMMARY (DOL 274–276). The Constitution on the Liturgy art. 38 decreed: "Provisions shall also be made . . . for legitimate variations and adaptations to different groups . . . provided the substantial unity of the Roman Rite is preserved." This sound principle is reflected in the 3 texts in this section. The first is a particular reply permitting the use of sign language in Masses for the deaf (DOL 274). But the major documents are the two directories, for Masses with special groups (DOL 275) and for Masses with children (DOL 276). Both are of great significance in the liturgical reform as they make provision for a true adaptation of the eucharistic celebration to the participants in accord with their number, age, spiritual needs, and their character as constituting the actual liturgical assembly.

274. CONSILIUM, **Reply** (U.S.A.) to Archbishop J. F. Dearden, President of the Bishops' Commission on the Liturgical Apostolate, on Mass for the deaf, 10 December 1965.*

2119   On 8 July this year, the question of Mass for congregations of deaf persons was submitted to the Consilium by the American Bishops' Commission on the Liturgical Apostolate.

In November, suggestions concerning the question were approved by the Bishops of the Consilium and the matter was put before the Holy Father on 2 December.

The question revolved around the use of sign language. It was asked whether it were fitting: 1. that the readings should be communicated to the people by means of signs; 2. that the deaf people should reply, in those parts pertaining to the congregation, by means of signs.

It was asked in general whether sign language could be used in all those parts of the Mass that were in the vernacular, and more specifically: (a) whether texts proffered by the celebrant could be at the same time spoken *and* signified with his hands; (b) whether in those texts that were said together by the celebrant and by the people, the people could follow the sign language of the celebrant, they themselves also using the sign language.

With great willingness and kindness, the Holy Father has given his full approval to these suggestions, and has said moreover that sign language could be used with and by deaf people throughout the liturgy, whenever it was judged to be pastorally desirable.[R1]

275. SC DIVINE WORSHIP, **Instruction** *Actio pastoralis*, on Masses with special groups, 15 May 1969: AAS 61 (1969) 806–811; Not 6 (1970) 50–55.

2120   The pastoral activity of the Church sets as one of its chief aims the instruction of the faithful about their deeper involvement in the ecclesial community. In this way through celebrations, especially of the liturgy, all will endeavor to join themselves to their brothers and sisters in the communion of the Church, both universal and local.

For the liturgical assembly, presided over by one possessing the power of calling together the people of God, guiding them, teaching them, and making them holy, is the sign and the instrument of all humanity's unity and above all of the Church's unity with Christ.[1]

That is achieved and is experienced in the shared celebration of the eucharist, especially on Sundays and holydays, around the bishop and within the assembly of the parish, whose pastor is the bishop's representative.[2]

2121   But pastoral care also has as its purpose and direction particular groups. This is not for the sake of creating *ecclesiolae* or privilege, but to serve the faithful's particu-

---

* Text, *The Jurist* 26 (1966) 388–389; Bishops' Commission on the Liturgical Apostolate *Newsletter* 2 (1966) 30–31.

R1 See DOL 23 no. 296, note R1, Query 2.

1 See LG no. 1: AAS 57 (1965) 5; ConstDecrDecl 93; SC art. 83 [DOL 1 no. 83].

2 See LG nos. 26, 28 [DOL 4 nos. 146, 148]; SC art. 41–42 [DOL 1 nos. 41–42]. SCR, Instr. EuchMyst nos. 26–27, 25 May 1967 [DOL 179 nos. 1255–56].

lar needs or to deepen the Christian life in accord with the requirements and capacities of the members of these groups. This brings the advantages that spring from a special spiritual or apostolic, common bond and from the desire to help one another toward spiritual growth.

From experience pastoral activity teaches how much good having their own celebrations can do for these groups. For when these celebrations have proper and wise planning and direction they are no obstacle to parish unity; instead they serve the parish's missionary activity by their power to achieve closer contact with some of the people or to deepen the formation of others.

Furthermore, the source of the vitality of these groups lies in the combination, during what are called prayer meetings, of the shared study of Christian truth and the members' shared intention of conforming their pattern of life to this truth. For the meetings are conducted in settings and on terms congenial to the group, especially the reading and meditating on God's word, and the celebration of the eucharist often completes and, as it were, crowns them.

Among these groups at the present time the desire to take part in the eucharistic celebration is intense. For this reason it seemed to be the right moment to provide norms regulating this celebration in such a way that it will always be carried out with order, exactness, and decorum for the spiritual advantage of those taking part and with respect for the proper nature of religious worship.

1.   Careful thought should be given to the question of whether, all things being considered, a eucharistic celebration in each instance is truly an advantage to pastoral activity or whether a religious celebration of another type is advisable.   2122

2.   It is right to include the following among those special groups for whose benefit the eucharist may be celebrated: 2123

    a.   groups gathered to make a retreat, to devote a day or more to religious or pastoral studies, to conduct meetings on the apostolate of the laity or on the apostolate of other kinds of associations;

    b.   meetings of any sector of the parish for the purpose of pastoral activity;

    c.   groups of the faithful who live in places far from the parish church and gather at stated times to attend to their own spiritual formation;

    d.   groups of the faithful of the same category who meet at fixed times for instruction or religious formation especially suited to them;

    e.   gatherings in the home, around the sick or elderly who are house-bound and can never take part in the celebration of the eucharist; included are neighbors and others taking care of such people;

    f.   gatherings in the home on the occasion of a wake or other special religious occasion.

3.   In most cases the eucharistic celebration for special groups is to be held in a place of worship.   2124

4.   The faculty of allowing a eucharistic celebration for special groups to take place outside a place of worship is reserved to the local Ordinary or, for his own houses, to the Ordinary of religious. But, especially when it is a question of private homes or institutions, they are to grant this faculty only if the place is suitable and decent.[3] A bedroom is always excluded.[4]   2125

---

   [3]   See GIRM no. 253 [DOL 208 no. 1643].

   [4]   See Paul VI, Motu Proprio *Pastorale munus*, 30 Nov. 1963, [I] no. 7 [DOL 103 no. 718]. Secretariat of State, Pontifical Rescript *Cum admotae*, 6 Nov. 1964, no. 4 [DOL 141 no. 942].

Furthermore, care must be taken that the concern for a more spacious and finer place does not lead to deliberate favoritism toward certain families and so to the restoration under another guise of the privileges that the Constitution on the Liturgy repudiates.[5]

2126   5.   The fundamental principles given by the Instruction *Eucharisticum mysterium* are to be kept in mind, especially:[6]

a.   The eucharistic sacrifice and the sacred meal form part of the same mystery in such a way that the closest theological and sacramental bond joins the one with the other.

b.   No Mass is to be regarded as a celebration belonging exclusively to a particular group, but as the celebration of the Church, at which the priest presides over the entire liturgy in exercising his function as the Church's minister.

c.   Every measure is to be taken to ensure that, in regard to the proper arrangement of the place, the condition of the articles used, and the comportment of the people, the worship of adoration rightly owed to God himself is shown to the sacrament of the eucharist.

2127   6.   In order to facilitate a eucharistic celebration truly suited to the circumstances of the occasion and the people, each of its parts is to be properly arranged, with the general norms and the following principles as criteria.

a.   The participation of the faithful should be encouraged to the utmost, with attention paid to the circumstances of the celebration and the means of achieving that participation.

b.   Before the celebration some time may be devoted to meditation on Scripture or to an instruction on a spiritual topic.

c.   In addition to making introductory comments, the celebrant may speak briefly on the liturgy of the word before the readings and on the liturgy of the eucharist before the preface; he also may say something before the dismissal of the faithful. But he is to refrain from comments during the eucharistic prayer.

d.   What is prescribed under "f" and "h" here remaining intact and with the exception of what is spoken by a "commentator," the faithful are to refrain from making reflections, exhortations, or the like during the celebration.

e.   In the liturgy of the word, depending on the actual situation, texts may be chosen that are more suited to the particular celebration, provided they are chosen from the texts of an approved lectionary.

f.   One of the participants (man or woman) may proclaim the readings before the gospel; but only a priest or a deacon when one is present may read the gospel.

g.   In the homily the priest is to make mention of this particular celebration and to explain the relationships existing between the assembly presently gathered and the local and universal Church.

h.   The general intercessions, always with respect for their religious character, may be adapted to the special circumstances. Care is to be taken, however, against complete omission of the general intentions for the Church, the world, brothers and sisters beset by needs, and the assembly present. Those present at the rite may add some particular intention, properly prepared ahead of time.

2128   7.   Sacramental communion makes participation in the eucharistic celebration more complete and wholehearted.

---

[5]   See SC art. 32 [DOL 1 no. 32].

[6]   SCR, Instr. EuchMyst no. 3 [DOL 179 no. 1232].

As to the manner of distributing communion, the usage lawfully in practice in each diocese should be followed. As for communion under both kinds,[R2] the rules of the General Instruction of the Roman Missal are to be followed.[7] This form of communion, however, is not permitted in Masses celebrated in a private home, except when viaticum is being given.[8]

8. To further the faithful's participation, there is some advantage, especially in certain circumstances, to be gained from singing, since this increases a sense of unity. Nevertheless in this matter too the norms for singing and music in sacred celebrations are to be respected and everything excluded that would conflict with the holiness of the rite and the devotion of the faithful. 2129

9. There must also be caution against introducing the adaptations permitted only for special groups into celebrations in the church for a general congregation. 2130

10. As to prerequisites for the celebration of the eucharist with these special groups outside a place of worship, and particularly in private homes, the following are to be observed. 2131

a. The faculty mentioned in no. 4 is not to be granted, except in particular instances, for Sundays and holydays of obligation. Otherwise the parish liturgical assembly might be deprived of that ministry of priests and participation of the people which would benefit the life and unity of the community.

b. If the priest celebrant is not the pastor, he should advise the pastor ahead of time. The pastor is to make a report on these celebrations to the bishop.

c. The norms regarding the eucharistic fast are to be observed; there is therefore never to be any sort of meal or banquet preceding the Mass. If there is one afterward, the table for it, as far as possible, is not to be the one on which the eucharist has been celebrated.

d. The eucharistic bread is to be unleavened, the only kind permitted in the Latin rite, and baked in the same shape that is customary for other Masses.

e. The time of celebration should not be very late at night.

f. In the case of family celebrations, those reasonably seeking to take part should not be excluded.

11. There must also be a wise choice of the form of celebration and, with due respect for liturgical laws, of the elements best suited to the situation. Therefore: 2132

R2 In regard to communion under both kinds, Not 6 (1970) 49 has this introductory note: The present Instruction had first been sent to the presidents of the conferences of bishops and of national liturgical commissions, 15 May 1969 (Prot. 77/69). Later it was published in AAS 61 (1969) 806–811. At that time the text was reviewed and in a few places emended in conformity with requests or suggestions submitted by the conferences of bishops, almost all of which were incorporated. The one exception, however, was anything related to broadening the concession of communion under both kinds. It is true that eucharistic celebration in small groups provides a more suitable occasion for communion under both kinds. Nevertheless precisely in such conditions numerous, highly publicized abuses have occurred, some so serious that they gave the impression of endangering faith in Christ's real presence as well as the adoration and respect due to the eucharist. This must be a matter of serious concern to the Apostolic See.

Accordingly, even though pastoral considerations might make a more liberal concession of communion under both kinds desirable, the unwelcome features sometimes accompanying it at present cannot be ignored. This does not rule out a favorable response to the wishes of so many pastors and faithful in the near future, once the abuses denounced have been at last removed.

7 See GIRM nos. 240–243 [DOL 208 nos. 1630–33].

8 See SCR, Instr. EuchMyst nos. 32, 6; 41 [DOL 179 nos. 1261; 1270].

a. Texts for use in the Mass are to be taken exclusively from the Roman Missal or from authorized supplements. Any substitution for these texts, with the exception of the directive in no. 6 e, is ruled out as something arbitrary.

b. The altar furnishings, vessels, and vestments in number, design, and quality are to conform to existing laws.[9]

c. The prescriptions for an ordinary eucharistic celebration apply to the celebrant's gestures and the ceremonies as well as the standing, kneeling, and sitting of those present.

2133   In conclusion, pastors are earnestly urged to weigh thoroughly the effectiveness of these celebrations for spiritual formation. For they are worthwhile only if they bring those who take part to know the Christian mystery more profoundly, to be more devoted to divine worship, to be more involved in the ecclesial community, and to be more committed to works of the apostolate and of charity among their brothers and sisters.

In these days there are those who think themselves to be renewed because of their display of sometimes mindless *novelties* or their concoction of arbitrary styles of liturgical celebration. But priests, diocesan and regular, truly concerned about the welfare of the faithful, know full well that the way of a lasting and sanctifying pastoral activity is to be found in steadfast and magnanimous loyalty to the will of the Church as expressed in its precepts, norms, and structures.

Anything that departs from this pattern, even if it has a specious attractiveness, is in fact spiritually upsetting to the faithful and makes the ministry of priests lifeless and sterile.

This Instruction, prepared at Pope Paul VI's direction by the Congregation for Divine Worship and approved by him, shall henceforth regulate all celebrations of Mass with special groups.

▶ 51. SECRETARIAT OF STATE, Letter to Bishop A. Mistrorigo, on the prayer of the community, August 1970.

Youth Masses [no. 508].

276. SC DIVINE WORSHIP, *Directory for Masses with Children, Pueros baptizatos,* 1 November 1973: AAS 66 (1974) 30–46; Not 10 (1974) 5–21.

INTRODUCTION

2134   1. The Church must show special concern for baptized children who have yet to be fully initiated through the sacraments of confirmation and eucharist as well as for children who have only recently been admitted to holy communion. Today the circumstances in which children grow up are not favorable to their spiritual progress.[1] In addition parents sometimes scarcely fulfill the obligations they accepted at the baptism of their children to bring them up as Christians.

---

[9] See GIRM nos. 268–270; 290–296; 297–310 [DOL 208 nos. 1658–60; 1680–86; 1687–1700].

[1] See SCC, *General Catechetical Directory* no. 5: AAS 64 (1972) 101–102.

2.   In the upbringing of children in the Church a special difficulty arises from the   2135
fact that liturgical celebrations, especially the eucharist, cannot fully exercise their
inherent pedagogical force upon children.[2] Although the vernacular may now be
used at Mass, still the words and signs have not been sufficiently adapted to the
capacity of children.

In fact, even in daily life children do not always understand all their experiences with adults but rather may find them boring. It cannot therefore be expected
of the liturgy that everything must always be intelligible to them. Nonetheless, we
may fear spiritual harm if over the years children repeatedly experience in the
Church things that are barely comprehensible: recent psychological study has established how profoundly children are formed by the religious experience of infancy and early childhood, because of the special religious receptivity proper to those
years.[3]

3.   The Church follows its Master, who "put his arms around the children . . .   2136
and blessed them" (Mk 10:16). It cannot leave children in the condition described.
Vatican Council II had spoken in the Constitution on the Liturgy about the need of
liturgical adaptation for various groups.[4] Soon afterwards, especially in the first
Synod of Bishops held in Rome in 1967, the Church began to consider how participation by children could be made easier. On the occasion of the Synod, the President of the Consilium for the Implementation of the Constitution on the Liturgy
said explicitly that it could not be a matter of "creating some entirely special rite
but rather of retaining, shortening, or omitting some elements or of making a better
selection of texts."[5]

4.   All the details of eucharistic celebration with a congregation were determined   2137
in the General Instruction of the revised Roman Missal published in 1969. Then this
Congregation began to prepare a special Directory for Masses with Children, as a
supplement to the General Instruction. This was done in response to repeated
petitions from the entire Catholic world and with the cooperation of men and
women specialists from almost every nation.

5.   Like the General Instruction of the Roman Missal, this Directory reserves some   2138
adaptations to the conferences of bishops or to individual bishops.[6]

Some adaptations of the Mass may be necessary for children in a given country
but cannot be included in a general directory. In accord with the Constitution on the
Liturgy art. 40,[a] the conferences of bishops are to propose such adaptations to the
Apostolic See for introduction into the liturgy with its consent.

6.   The Directory is concerned with children who have not yet entered the period   2139
of preadolescence. It does not speak directly of children who are physically or
mentally handicapped, because a broader adaptation is sometimes necessary for
them.[7] Nevertheless, the following norms may also be applied to the handicapped,
with the necessary changes.

---

[2] See SC art. 33 [DOL 1 no. 33].

[3] See SCC, *General Catechetical Directory* no. 78 [DOL 169 no. 1107].

[4] See SC art. 38 [DOL 1 no. 38]. See also SCDW, Instr. *Actio pastoralis*, 15 May 1969 [DOL 275].

[5] "De Liturgia in prima Synodo Episcoporum": Not 3 (1967) 368.

[6] See nos. 19, 32, 33 of this Directory.

[a] See DOL 1 no. 40.

[7] See the Order of Mass with deaf and mute children of German-speaking regions approved, that is,
confirmed by this Congregation, 26 June 1970 (Prot. N. 1546/70).

2140 7. The first chapter of the Directory (nos. 8–15) gives a kind of foundation by considering the different ways in which children are introduced to the eucharistic liturgy. The second chapter briefly treats Masses with adults in which children also take part (nos. 16–19). Finally, the third chapter (nos. 20–54) treats at greater length Masses with children in which only some adults take part.

CHAPTER I
THE INTRODUCTION OF CHILDREN TO THE EUCHARISTIC
CELEBRATION

2141 8. A fully Christian life is inconceivable without participation in the liturgical services in which the faithful, gathered into a single assembly, celebrate the paschal mystery. Therefore, the religious initiation of children must be in harmony with this purpose.[8] The Church baptizes children and therefore, relying on the gifts conferred by this sacrament, it must be concerned that once baptized they grow in communion with Christ and each other. The sign and pledge of that communion is participation in the eucharistic table, for which children are being prepared or led to a deeper realization of its meaning. This liturgical and eucharistic formation may not be separated from their general education, both human and Christian; indeed it would be harmful if their liturgical formation lacked such a basis.

2142 9. For this reason all who have a part in the formation of children should consult and work together toward one objective: that even if children already have some feeling for God and the things of God, they may also experience in proportion to their age and personal development the human values that are present in the eucharistic celebration. These values include the community activity, exchange of greetings, capacity to listen and to seek and grant pardon, expression of gratitude, experience of symbolic actions, a meal of friendship, and festive celebration.[9]

Eucharistic catechesis, dealt with in no. 12, should develop such human values. Then, depending on their age and their psychological and social situation, children will gradually open their minds to the perception of Christian values and the celebration of the mystery of Christ.[10]

2143 10. The Christian family has the greatest role in instilling these Christian and human values.[11] Thus Christian education, provided by parents and other educators, should be strongly encouraged in relation to the liturgical formation of children as well.

By reason of the duty in conscience freely accepted at the baptism of their children, parents are bound to teach them gradually how to pray. This they do by praying with them each day and by introducing them to prayers said privately.[12] If children, prepared in this way even from their early years, take part in the Mass with their family when they wish, they will easily begin to sing and to pray in the liturgical community and indeed will already have some initial idea of the eucharistic mystery.

If the parents are weak in faith but still wish their children to receive Christian formation, they should be urged at least to communicate to their children the

---

8 See SC art. 14, 19 [DOL 1 nos. 14, 19].

9 See SCC, *General Catechetical Directory* no. 25 [DOL 169 no. 1100].

10 See GE no. 2 [DOL 13 no. 216].

11 See ibid. no. 3: AAS 58 (1966) 731; ConstDecrDecl 392.

12 See SCC, *General Catechetical Directory* no. 78 [DOL 169 no. 1107].

human values mentioned already and, when the occasion arises, to participate in meetings of parents and in noneucharistic celebrations held with children.

11. The Christian communities to which the individual families belong or in which the children live also have a responsibility toward children baptized in the Church. By giving witness to the Gospel, living communal charity, and actively celebrating the mysteries of Christ, the Christian community is an excellent school of Christian and liturgical formation for the children who live in it.   2144

Within the Christian community, godparents or other persons noted for their dedicated service can, out of apostolic zeal, contribute greatly to the necessary catechesis in the case of families that fail in their obligation toward the children's Christian upbringing.

Preschool programs, Catholic schools, and various kinds of associations for children serve these same ends in a special way.

12. Even in the case of children, the liturgy itself always exerts its own inherent power to instruct.[13] Yet within religious-education programs in the schools and parishes the necessary importance should be given to catechesis on the Mass.[14] This catechesis should be directed to the child's active, conscious, and authentic participation.[15] "Suited to children's age and capabilities, it should, by means of the main rites and prayers of the Mass, aim at conveying its meaning, including what relates to taking part in the Church's life."[16] This is especially true of the text of the eucharistic prayer and of the acclamations by which the children take part in this prayer.   2145

The catechesis preparing children for first communion calls for special mention. In it they should learn not only the truths of faith regarding the eucharist but also how from first communion on — after being prepared according to their capacity by penance — they can as full members of Christ's Body take part actively with the people of God in the eucharist, sharing in the Lord's table and the community of their brothers and sisters.

13. Various kinds of celebrations may also play a major role in the liturgical formation of children and in their preparation for the Church's liturgical life. By the very fact of such celebrations children easily come to appreciate some liturgical elements, for example, greetings, silence, and common praise (especially when this is sung together). But care must be taken that the instructive element does not become dominant in these celebrations.   2146

14. Depending on the capacity of the children, the word of God should have a greater and greater place in these celebrations. In fact, as the children's spiritual capacity develops, celebrations of the word of God in the strict sense should be held frequently, especially during Advent and Lent.[17] These will help greatly to develop in the children an appreciation of the word of God.   2147

---

[13] See SC art. 33 [DOL 1 no. 33].

[14] See SCR, Instr. EuchMyst, 25 May 1967, no. 14 [DOL 179 no. 1243].

[15] See SCC, *General Catechetical Directory* no. 25 [DOL 169 no. 1100].

[16] See SCR, Instr. EuchMyst no. 14 [DOL 179 no. 1243]. SCC, *General Catechetical Directory* no. 57 [DOL 169 no. 1104].

[17] See SC art. 35, 4 [DOL 1 no. 35].

2148   15. While all that has been said remains true, the final purpose of all liturgical and eucharistic formation must be a greater and greater conformity to the Gospel in the daily life of the children.

CHAPTER II
MASSES WITH ADULTS IN WHICH CHILDREN ALSO PARTICIPATE

2149   16. In many places parish Masses are celebrated, especially on Sundays and holy-days, at which a good many children take part along with the large number of adults. On such occasions the witness of adult believers can have a great effect upon the children. Adults can in turn benefit spiritually from experiencing the part that the children have within the Christian community. The Christian spirit of the family is greatly fostered when children take part in these Masses together with their parents and other family members.

Infants who as yet are unable or unwilling to take part in the Mass may be brought in at the end of Mass to be blessed together with the rest of the community. This may be done, for example, if parish helpers have been taking care of them in a separate area.

2150   17. Nevertheless, in Masses of this kind it is necessary to take great care that the children present do not feel neglected because of their inability to participate or to understand what happens and what is proclaimed in the celebration. Some account should be taken of their presence: for example, by speaking to them directly in the introductory comments (as at the beginning and the end of Mass) and at some point in the homily.

Sometimes, moreover, if the place itself and the nature of the community permit, it will be appropriate to celebrate the liturgy of the word, including a homily, with the children in a separate, but not too distant, room. Then, before the eucharistic liturgy begins, the children are led to the place where the adults have meanwhile celebrated their own liturgy of the word.

2151   18. It may also be very helpful to give some tasks to the children. They may, for example, bring forward the gifts or perform one or other of the songs of the Mass.

2152   19. If the number of children is large, it may at times be suitable to plan the Mass so that it corresponds more closely to the needs of the children. In this case the homily should be directed to them but in such a way that adults may also benefit from it. Wherever the bishop permits, in addition to the adaptations already provided in the Order of Mass, one or other of the particular adaptations described later in the Directory may be employed in a Mass celebrated with adults in which children also participate.

CHAPTER III
MASSES WITH CHILDREN IN WHICH ONLY A FEW ADULTS PARTICIPATE

2153   20. In addition to the Masses in which children take part with their parents and other family members (which are not always possible everywhere), Masses with children in which only a few adults take part are recommended, especially during the week. From the beginning of the liturgical reform it has been clear to everyone that some adaptations are necessary in these Masses.[18]

---

[18]   See no. 3 of this Directory.

Such adaptations, but only those of a more general kind, will be considered later (nos. 38–54).

21. It is always necessary to keep in mind that these eucharistic celebrations must lead children toward the celebration of Mass with adults, especially the Masses at which the Christian community must come together on Sundays.[19] Thus, apart from adaptations that are necessary because of the children's age, the result should not be entirely special rites, markedly different from the Order of Mass celebrated with a congregation.[20] The purpose of the various elements should always correspond with what is said in the General Instruction of the Roman Missal on individual points, even if at times for pastoral reasons an absolute *identity* cannot be insisted upon.

2154

OFFICES AND MINISTRIES IN THE CELEBRATION

22. The principles of active and conscious participation are in a sense even more significant for Masses celebrated with children. Every effort should therefore be made to increase this participation and to make it more intense. For this reason as many children as possible should have special parts in the celebration: for example; preparing the place and the altar (see no. 29), acting as cantor (see no. 24), singing in a choir, playing musical instruments (see no. 32), proclaiming the readings (see nos. 24 and 47), responding during the homily (see no. 48), reciting the intentions of the general intercessions, bringing the gifts to the altar, and performing similar activities in accord with the usage of various peoples (see no. 34).

2155

To encourage participation, it will sometimes be helpful to have several additions, for example, the insertion of motives for giving thanks before the priest begins the dialogue of the preface.

In all this, it should be kept in mind that external activities will be fruitless and even harmful if they do not serve the internal participation of the children. Thus religious silence has its importance even in Masses with children (see no. 37). The children should not be allowed to forget that all the forms of participation reach their high point in eucharistic communion, when the body and blood of Christ are received as spiritual nourishment.[21]

23. It is the responsibility of the priest who celebrates with children to make the celebration festive, familial, and meditative.[22] Even more than in Masses with adults, the priest is the one to create this kind of attitude, which depends on his personal preparation and his manner of acting and speaking with others.

2156

The priest should be concerned above all about the dignity, clarity, and simplicity of his actions and gestures. In speaking to the children he should express himself so that he will be easily understood, while avoiding any childish style of speech.

The free use of introductory comments[23] will lead children to a genuine liturgical participation, but these should be more than mere explanatory remarks.

---

[19]   See SC art. 42 and 106 [DOL 1 nos. 42 and 106].

[20]   See "De Liturgia in prima Synodo Episcoporum": Not 3 (1967) 368.

[21]   See GIRM no. 56 [DOL 208 no. 1446].

[22]   See no. 37 of this Directory.

[23]   See GIRM no. 11 [DOL 208 no. 1401].

It will help him to reach the hearts of the children if the priest sometimes expresses the invitations in his own words, for example, at the penitential rite, the prayer over the gifts, the Lord's Prayer, the sign of peace, and communion.

2157   24. Since the eucharist is always the action of the entire ecclesial community, the participation of at least some adults is desirable. These should be present not as monitors but as participants, praying with the children and helping them to the extent necessary.

With the consent of the pastor or rector of the church, one of the adults may speak to the children after the gospel, especially if the priest finds it difficult to adapt himself to the mentality of children. In this matter the norms soon to be issued by the Congregation for the Clergy should be observed.[b]

Even in Masses with children attention is to be paid to the diversity of ministries so that the Mass may stand out clearly as the celebration of a community.[24] For example, readers and cantors, whether children or adults, should be employed. In this way a variety of voices will keep the children from becoming bored.

PLACE AND TIME OF CELEBRATION

2158   25. The primary place for the eucharistic celebration for children is the church. Within the church, however, a space should be carefully chosen, if available, that will be suited to the number of participants. It should be a place where the children can act with a feeling of ease according to the requirements of a living liturgy that is suited to their age.

If the church does not satisfy these demands, it will sometimes be suitable to celebrate the eucharist with children outside a place of worship. But in that case the place chosen should be appropriate and worthy of the celebration.[25]

2159   26. The time of day chosen for Masses with children should correspond to the circumstances of their lives so that they may be most open to hearing the word of God and to celebrating the eucharist.

2160   27. Weekday Mass in which children participate can certainly be celebrated with greater effect and less danger of boredom if it does not take place every day (for example, in boarding schools). Moreover, preparation can be more careful if there is a longer interval between diverse celebrations.[R3]

---

   [b]   See DOL 344.

   [24]   See SC art. 28 [DOL 1 no. 28].

   [25]   See GIRM no. 253 [DOL 208 no. 1643].

   [R3]   Query: Is the practice of a daily Mass for children to be repudiated? Reply: In some boarding schools or in Catholic schools it has been the practice to bring the children to daily Mass. After publication of the Directory for Masses with Children some are asking themselves about the meaning to be taken from the Directory no. 27: "[Text quoted]." The issue depends on custom and on the pastoral prudence of the teachers. But these are the intentions of the Directory. 1. To be avoided is the children's looking on participation in daily Mass as merely a matter of obedience to some rule and their abandoning it once their school days end. 2. Children must be guided toward an understanding of the full meaning of the Mass and its parts. For this it is necessary that they become accustomed to its various forms of prayer and celebration. The Directory expresses its intent quite clearly in no. 27: "[Text of paragraph two quoted]." This correlates with the statements in nos. 13–15, which discuss celebrations of various types so that the daily life of the children is ever more permeated with the Gospel and they understand the elements of the liturgy that prepare them to take part more fully in the Mass. 3. The celebration of Mass is an activity of the entire community. Therefore, the active participation of children is to be furthered to the utmost. They accordingly ought to have a part in the preparation for Mass, which can be accomplished more surely if "there is a longer interval between diverse celebrations."

   Daily Mass is not in itself to be made light of. Indeed "the faithful should be invited to take part in

Sometimes it will be preferable to have common prayer, to which the children may contribute spontaneously, or else a common meditation, or a celebration of the word of God. These are ways of continuing the eucharistic celebrations already held and of leading to a deeper participation in subsequent celebrations.

28. When the number of children who celebrate the eucharist together is very great, attentive and conscious participation becomes more difficult. Therefore, if possible, several groups should be formed; these should not be set up rigidly according to age but with regard for the children's progress in religious formation and catechetical preparation.   2161

During the week such groups may be invited to the sacrifice of the Mass on different days.

PREPARATION FOR THE CELEBRATION

29. Each eucharistic celebration with children should be carefully prepared beforehand, especially with regard to the prayers, songs, readings, and intentions of the general intercessions. This should be done in discussion with the adults and with the children who will have a special ministry in these Masses. If possible, some of the children should take part in preparing and ornamenting the place of celebration and preparing the chalice with the paten and the cruets. Presupposing the appropriate internal participation, such activity will help to develop the spirit of community celebration.   2162

SINGING AND MUSIC

30. Singing must be given great importance in all celebrations, but it is to be especially encouraged in every way for Masses celebrated with children, in view of their special affinity for music.[26] The culture of various peoples and the capabilities of the children present should be taken into account.   2163

If possible, the acclamations should be sung by the children rather than recited, especially the acclamations that form part of the eucharistic prayer.

31. To facilitate the children's participation in singing the *Gloria, Credo, Sanctus,* and *Agnus Dei,* it is permissible to use with the melodies appropriate vernacular texts, accepted by competent authority, even if these do not correspond exactly to the liturgical texts.[27]   2164

32. The use of "musical instruments can add a great deal" in Masses with children, especially if they are played by the children themselves.[28] The playing of instruments will help to sustain the singing or to encourage the reflection of the children; sometimes in their own fashion instruments express festive joy and the praise of God.   2165

Care should always be taken, however, that the musical accompaniment does not overpower the singing or become a distraction rather than a help to the chil-

---

Mass often on weekdays as well, even daily" (SCR, Instr. EuchMyst no. 29 [DOL 179 no. 1258]). But in the case of children this should be regarded as a goal toward which liturgical and catechetical instruction tends by the use of sound pedagogy and progressive guidance, not by the flat imposition of a duty: Not 11 (1975) 125–126.

[26]   See GIRM no. 19 [DOL 208 no. 1409].

[27]   See SCR, Instr. MusSacr, 5 March 1967, no. 55 [DOL 508 no. 4176].

[28]   SCR, Instr. MusSacr no. 62 [DOL 508 no. 4183].

dren. Music should correspond to the purpose intended for the different periods at which it is played during the Mass.

With these precautions and with due and special discretion, recorded music may also be used in Masses with children, in accord with norms established by the conferences of bishops.[R4]

GESTURES

2166   33. In view of the nature of the liturgy as an activity of the entire person and in view of the psychology of children, participation by means of gestures and posture should be strongly encouraged in Masses with children, with due regard for age and local customs. Much depends not only on the actions of the priest,[29] but also on the manner in which the children conduct themselves as a community.

If, in accord with the norm of the General Instruction of the Roman Missal,[30] a conference of bishops adapts the congregation's actions at Mass to the mentality of a people, it should take the special condition of children into account or should decide on adaptations that are for children only.

2167   34. Among the actions that are considered under this heading, processions and other activities that involve physical participation deserve special mention.

The children's entering in procession with the priest can serve to help them to experience a sense of the communion that is thus being created.[31] The participation of at least some children in the procession with the Book of the Gospels makes clear the presence of Christ announcing the word to his people. The procession of children with the chalice and the gifts expresses more clearly the value and meaning of the preparation of the gifts. The communion procession, if properly arranged, helps greatly to develop the children's devotion.

VISUAL ELEMENTS

2168   35. The liturgy of the Mass contains many visual elements and these should be given great prominence with children. This is especially true of the particular visual elements in the course of the liturgical year, for example, the veneration of the cross, the Easter candle, the lights on the feast of the Presentation of the Lord, and the variety of colors and liturgical appointments.

In addition to the visual elements that belong to the celebration and to the place of celebration, it is appropriate to introduce other elements that will permit children to perceive visually the wonderful works of God in creation and redemption and thus support their prayer. The liturgy should never appear as something dry and merely intellectual.

2169   36. For the same reason, the use of art work prepared by the children themselves may be useful, for example, as illustrations of a homily, as visual expressions of the intentions of the general intercessions, or as inspirations to reflection.

    [R4]   See DOL 38 no. 443, note R32.

    [29]   See no. 23 of this Directory.

    [30]   See GIRM no. 21 [DOL 208 no. 1411].

    [31]   See GIRM no. 24 [DOL 208 no. 1414].

SILENCE

37. Even in Masses with children "silence should be observed at the designated   2170
times as part of the celebration"[32] lest too great a place be given to external action.
In their own way children are genuinely capable of reflection. They need some
guidance, however, so that they will learn how, in keeping with the different
moments of the Mass (for example, after the homily or after communion[33]), to
recollect themselves, meditate briefly, or praise God and pray to him in their
hearts.[34]

Besides this, with even greater care than in Masses with adults, the liturgical
texts should be proclaimed intelligibly and unhurriedly, with the necessary pauses.

PARTS OF THE MASS

38. The general structure of the Mass, which "is made up as it were of the liturgy   2171
of the word and the liturgy of the eucharist," should always be maintained, as
should certain rites to open and conclude the celebration.[35] Within individual parts
of the celebration, the adaptations that follow seem necessary if children are truly
to experience, in their own way and according to the psychological patterns of
childhood, "the mystery of faith . . . by means of rites and prayers."[36]

39. Some rites and texts should never be adapted for children lest the difference   2172
between Masses with children and the Masses with adults become too pronounced.[37] These are "the acclamations and the responses to the priest's greeting,"[38] the Lord's Prayer, and the Trinitarian formulary at the end of the blessing
with which the priest concludes the Mass. It is urged, moreover, that children
should become accustomed to the Nicene Creed little by little, the right to use the
Apostles' Creed indicated in no. 49 remaining intact.

A. INTRODUCTORY RITE

40. The introductory rite of Mass has as its purpose "that the faithful coming   2173
together take on the form of a community and prepare themselves to listen to God's
word and celebrate the eucharist properly."[39] Therefore every effort should be made
to create this disposition in the children and not to jeopardize it by any excess of
rites in this part of Mass.

It is sometimes proper to omit one or other element of the introductory rite or
perhaps to expand one of the elements. There should always be at least some
introductory element, which is completed by the opening prayer. In choosing individual elements, care should be taken that each one be used from time to time and
that none be entirely neglected.

---

32   GIRM no. 23 [DOL 208 no. 1413].

33   See SCR, Instr. EuchMyst no. 38 [DOL 179 no. 1267].

34   See GIRM no. 23 [DOL 208 no. 1413].

35   GIRM no. 8 [DOL 208 no. 1398].

36   SC art. 48 [DOL 1 no. 48].

37   See no. 21 of this Directory.

38   GIRM no. 15 [DOL 208 no. 1405].

39   GIRM no. 24 [DOL 208 no. 1414].

B. Reading and Explanation of the Word of God

2174   41. Since readings taken from holy Scripture "form the main part of the liturgy of the word,"[40] even in Masses celebrated with children biblical reading should never be omitted.

2175   42. With regard to the number of readings on Sundays and holydays, the decrees of the conferences of bishops are to be observed. If three or even two readings appointed on Sundays or weekdays can be understood by children only with difficulty, it is permissible to read two or only one of them, but the reading of the gospel should never be omitted.

2176   43. If all the readings assigned to the day seem to be unsuited to the capacity of the children, it is permissible to choose readings or a reading either from the Lectionary of the Roman Missal or directly from the Bible, but taking into account the liturgical seasons. It is recommended, moreover, that the individual conferences of bishops see to the composition of lectionaries for Masses with children.

   If, because of the limited capabilities of the children, it seems necessary to omit one or other verse of a biblical reading, this should be done cautiously and in such a way "that the meaning of the text or the intent and, as it were, style of the Scriptures are not distorted."[41]

2177   44. In the choice of readings the criterion to be followed is the quality rather than the quantity of the texts from the Scriptures. A shorter reading is not as such always more suited to children than a lengthy reading. Everything depends on the spiritual advantage that the reading can bring to the children.

2178   45. In the biblical texts "God is speaking to his people . . . and Christ is present to the faithful through his own word."[42] Paraphrases of Scripture should therefore be avoided. On the other hand, the use of translations that may already exist for the catechesis of children and that are accepted by the competent authority is recommended.

2179   46. Verses of psalms, carefully selected in accord with the understanding of children, or singing in the form of psalmody or the *Alleluia* with a simple verse should be sung between the readings. The children should always have a part in this singing, but sometimes a reflective silence may be substituted for the singing.

   If only a single reading is chosen, the singing may follow the homily.

2180   47. All the elements that will help explain the readings should be given great consideration so that the children may make the biblical readings their own and may come more and more to appreciate the value of God's word.

   Among such elements are the introductory comments that may precede the readings[43] and that by explaining the context or by introducing the text itself help the children to listen better and more fruitfully. The interpretation and explanation of the readings from the Scriptures in the Mass on a saint's day may include an account of the saint's life, not only in the homily but even before the readings in the form of an introduction.

---

[40]   GIRM no. 33 [DOL 208 no. 1423].

[41]   RM, *Lectionary for Mass*, Introduction no. 7 d [DOL 232 no. 1849].

[42]   GIRM no. 33 [DOL 208 no. 1423].

[43]   See GIRM no. 11 [DOL 208 no. 1401].

When the text of the readings lends itself to this, it may be helpful to have the children read it with parts distributed among them, as is provided for the reading of the Lord's passion during Holy Week.

48. The homily explaining the word of God should be given great prominence in all Masses with children. Sometimes the homily intended for children should become a dialogue with them, unless it is preferred that they should listen in silence.

49. If the profession of faith occurs at the end of the liturgy of the word, the Apostles' Creed may be used with children, especially because it is part of their catechetical formation.

C. PRESIDENTIAL PRAYERS

50. The priest is permitted to choose from the Roman Missal texts of presidential prayers more suited to children, so that he may truly associate the children with himself. But he is to take into account the liturgical season.

51. Since these prayers were composed for adult Christians, however, the principle simply of choosing from among them does not serve the purpose of having the children regard the prayers as an expression of their own life and religious experience.[44] If this is the case, the text of prayers of the Roman Missal may be adapted to the needs of children, but this should be done in such a way that, preserving the purpose of the prayer and to some extent its substance as well, the priest avoids anything that is foreign to the literary genre of a presidential prayer, such as moral exhortations or a childish manner of speech.

52. The eucharistic prayer is of the greatest importance in the eucharist celebrated with children because it is the high point of the entire celebration.[45] Much depends on the manner in which the priest proclaims this prayer[46] and on the way the children take part by listening and making their acclamations.

    The disposition of mind required for this central part of the celebration and the calm and reverence with which everything is done must make the children as attentive as possible. Their attention should be on the real presence of Christ on the altar under the elements of bread and wine, on his offering, on the thanksgiving through him and with him and in him, and on the Church's offering, which is made during the prayer and by which the faithful offer themselves and their lives with Christ to the eternal Father in the Holy Spirit.

    For the present, the four eucharistic prayers approved by the supreme authority for Masses with adults and introduced into liturgical use are to be employed until the Apostolic See makes other provision for Masses with children.[c]

D. RITES BEFORE COMMUNION

53. When the eucharistic prayer has ended, the Lord's Prayer, the breaking of bread, and the invitation to communion should always follow,[47] that is, the elements that have the principal significance in the structure of this part of the Mass.

2181

2182

2183

2184

2185

2186

   [44] See Consilium, Instr. on translations of liturgical texts for celebrations with a congregation, 25 Jan. 1969, no. 20 [DOL 123 no. 857].

   [45] See GIRM no. 54 [DOL 208 no. 1444].

   [46] See nos. 23 and 37 of this Directory.

   [c] See DOL 249 and 250.

   [47] See no. 23 of this Directory.

E. Communion and the Following Rites

2187   54. Everything should be done so that the children who are properly disposed and who have already been admitted to the eucharist may go to the holy table calmly and with recollection and thus take part fully in the eucharistic mystery. If possible, there should be singing, suited to the children, during the communion procession.[48]

The comments that precede the final blessing[49] are important in Masses with children. Before they are dismissed they need some repetition and application of what they have heard, but this should be done in a very few words. In particular, this is the appropriate time to express the connection between the liturgy and life.

At least sometimes, depending on the liturgical seasons and different occasions in the children's life, the priest should use more expanded forms of blessing, but at the end should always retain the Trinitarian formulary with the sign of the cross.[50]

*   *   *   *   *

2188   55. The contents of the Directory have as their purpose to help children readily and joyfully to encounter Christ together in the eucharistic celebration and to stand with him in the presence of the Father.[51] If they are formed by conscious and active participation in the eucharistic sacrifice and meal, they should learn day by day, at home and away from home, to proclaim Christ to others among their family and among their peers, by living the "faith, that works through love" (Gal 5:6).

This Directory was prepared by the Congregation for Divine Worship. On 22 October 1973, Pope Paul VI approved and confirmed it and ordered that it be published.

▶   250. SC DIVINE WORSHIP, *Eucharistic Prayers for Masses with Children. . .*, Introduction, 1 November 1974.

---

48   See SCR, Instr. MusSacr no. 32 [DOL 508 no. 4153].

49   See GIRM no. 11 [DOL 208 no. 1401].

50   See no. 39 of this Directory.

51   See RM, Eucharistic Prayer II.

SECTION 10. WORSHIP OF THE EUCHARIST OUTSIDE MASS

SUMMARY (DOL 277–279). The many cross-references in this section indicate that the general documents on the eucharist have repeatedly expressed the rightfulness of the worship of Christ present in the eucharist and the norms for this adoration and the other ways of honoring this sacrament. There are 3 specific texts.

—The major text here is from *Holy Communion and Worship of the Eucharist outside Mass*, the General Introduction and the introductions on the various forms of eucharistic worship (DOL 279).

—Subsidiary texts are a letter of Paul VI on the subject of eucharistic worship (DOL 277) and a declaration of the Congregation for the Doctrine of the Faith on particles of consecrated hosts (DOL 278).

▶ 103.   PAUL VI, Motu Proprio *Pastorale munus*, on the powers and privileges of bishops, 30 November 1963:

II, no. 5:   Eucharistic reservation in the bishop's chapel [no. 743].

▶ 31.   CONSILIUM, Letter *Le renouveau liturgique*, on furthering liturgical reform, 30 June 1965:

no. 7:   Tabernacle for reservation [no. 416].

▶ 542.   SC RITES, Reply to a query, on the tabernacle, 3 July 1965.

▶ 176.   PAUL VI, Encyclical *Mysterium fidei*, 3 September 1965:

nos. 56–63:   Eucharistic worship outside Mass [nos. 1200–07].

▶ 32. CONSILIUM, letter *L'heureux développement*, on problems in the reform of the liturgy, 25 January 1966:

no. 6:   Placement of tabernacle [no. 428].

▶ 179. SC RITES (Consilium), Instruction *Eucharisticum mysterium*, on worship of the eucharist, 25 May 1967:

nos. 49–51:   Reasons for reservation [nos. 1278–80].
     52–57:   Place for reservation [nos. 1281–86].
     58:                     Eucharistic devotions [no. 1287].
     59:                     Eucharistic processions [no. 1288].
     60–66:   Exposition [nos. 1289–95].
     67:                     Eucharistic congresses [no. 1296].

277. PAUL VI, **Epistle** *Saluberrimum Sacramentum Eucharistiae* to Rev. Roland Huot, Superior General of the Priests of the Blessed Sacrament, on worship of the eucharist outside Mass, 10 January 1969: AAS 61 (1969) 169–171.

2189   The most salutary sacrament of the eucharist stands as the center of the Church's life because it contains really, truly, and substantially the author of grace himself. Therefore it takes hold of the minds of believers in such a way that they understand, not by force of elaborate argument but by a kind of insight into the reality, that they should offer to this sacrament the worship of adoration. The effect of this exercise of worship is the expression and increase of the virtue of religion by which the believing spirit acknowledges its all-transcending creator and his lordship and strives for the attitude of submissive reverence proper to the creature. This adoration is shown even through the body, which is offered as a "living sacrifice, holy and acceptable to God."[1] As St. Thomas Aquinas writes, "In all acts of worship what is exterior is related to what is interior as to the more important element. Therefore exterior adoration takes place because of the interior, namely, in order that the signs of humility that we manifest through the body may stir our affections to subject themselves to God."[2]

---

[1]   Rom 12:1.

[2]   ST 2a2ae, 84.2.

Those who, like the religious congregation that you, dear son, govern, and other similar associations, dedicate their service to adoration of Christ the Lord present in the blessed sacrament, offer a shining confirmation of faith against those who deny God by their teaching or way of life or who, while appearing to keep the faith, attach scant importance to it.

But for a fuller understanding of this matter it is necessary to take into consideration that adoration is not to be isolated from the sacrament in its entirety, that is, from the mystery of salvation "which is Christ . . . the hope of glory."[3] This is to say that the eucharist must be viewed not only in regard to what relates to the real presence, but "in all its fullness, both in the celebration of Mass and in the worship of the sacred elements reserved after Mass in order to extend the grace of the sacrifice."[4] The reason, therefore, that adorers continue worship of the eucharist outside Mass is that they may more fully share in the effects of the sacrifice and be empowered to take part in it more effectively. In order that this help from heaven may be more abundantly poured forth on daily life, the practice of the virtues is also necessary. When indeed we offer the homage of devout service to Christ hidden in the august sacrament, we receive an increase in the theological virtues of faith, hope, and charity. These give to the soul the right dispositions enabling it "with due devotion to celebrate the memorial of the Lord and to receive frequently the bread given us by the Father."[5]   2190

Further, this adoration, which, as we have said, continues the grace of the eucharistic sacrifice, has a beneficial effect on the entire community of the Church. For the prayers offered to him who is "God with us" there on the altar are truly "catholic," because they bear upon the whole Church and the whole world. History teaches this to be so: our predecessor Pope Clement VIII in the year 1592 authorized and promoted the Forty-Hours devotion to be observed successively in the churches of Rome in order to beseech heavenly aid for the human family in extremely trying times.[6] Accordingly, this adoration is not primarily a fulfillment of the devout aspirations of individuals, but rather stirs the spirit "to cultivate a 'social' love by which we place the common good before the good of the individual, make our own the interests of the community, of the parish, of the entire Church, and extend our charity to the whole world, because we know that the members of Christ are everywhere."[7]

Therefore let religious institutes and associations that, by their own law, approved by the Church, have as their entrusted service the offering of the worship of adoration to the sacrament of the eucharist realize that they fulfill a most exalted responsibility and do so in the name of the entire Church. Provided they live up to their vocation with devotion, fidelity, and constancy, the life of religious as well as those dedicated to contemplation alone or engaged in apostolic works "stands as a sign that can and should effectively draw the members of the Church . . . and points out to all people the towering greatness of the strength of Christ in glory and the boundless power of the Holy Spirit."[8]   2191

---

[3] Col 1:27.

[4] SCR, Instr. EuchMyst no. 3 g [DOL 179 no. 1232].

[5] SCR, Instr. EuchMyst no. 50 [DOL 179 no. 1279].

[6] See *Bullarium Romanum* 5, 1 (Rome, 1751) 412.

[7] Paul VI, Encycl. *Mysterium fidei* no. 69 [DOL 176 no. 1213].

[8] LG no. 44: AAS 57 (1965) 50–51; ConstDecrDecl 177.

There is, therefore, no reason for the members who perform this outstanding service to grow fainthearted in these times, as though, as some allege, the issue were a "devotion become obsolete" and they were wasting time because other works have greater urgency. They must be convinced that as of old so also now the Church has an absolute need of those who "adore" the sacrament "in spirit and in truth";[9] they must, as is right, apply all diligence to ensure an exact following of the teachings and precepts we have given on this matter in both the Encyclical *Mysterium fidei* and the Instruction *Eucharisticum mysterium*.

▶ 208. SC RITES (Consilium); SC DIVINE WORSHIP, General Instruction of the Roman Missal, 1st ed. 6 April 1969; 4th ed. 27 March 1975:

nos. 276–277: Place for eucharistic reservation [nos. 1666–67].

▶ 182. PAUL VI, Address to a special audience, on eucharistic worship, 1 March 1972:

Eucharistic congresses [no. 1304].

278. SC DOCTRINE OF THE FAITH, Declaration *Cum de fragmentis*, on particles of the consecrated hosts, 2 May 1972: Not 8 (1972) 277.

2192
Regarding hosts left over after communion, several queries have been directed to the Apostolic See. Therefore this Congregation, after consultation with the Congregations for the Discipline of the Sacraments and for Divine Worship, has decided on the following response.

After communion, the left-over hosts, as well as any particles that may have fallen from them and that still have the form of bread, are to be reserved or consumed with the reverence due to the eucharistic presence of Christ. Further, with regard to any other eucharistic fragments, the prescriptions on purifying the chalice and paten are to be observed as they are given in the General Instruction of the Roman Missal nos. 120, 138, 237–239[a] and in the Order of Mass with a congregation no. 138 and without a congregation no. 31. Hosts not consumed at once are to be carried by an authorized minister to the place where the blessed sacrament is reserved (see General Instruction of the Roman Missal no. 276).[b]

▶ 340. PAUL VI, Motu Proprio *Ministeria quaedam*, on tonsure, minor orders, subdiaconate, 15 August 1972:

VI: The acolyte as special minister of the eucharist [no. 2931].

▶ 265. SC DIVINE WORSHIP, Decree *Eucharistiae sacramentum*, promulgating the *editio typica* of rites for holy communion and the worship of the eucharist outside Mass, 21 June 1973.

---

[9] See Jn 4:23.

[a] See DOL 208 nos. 1510, 1528, 1627–29.

[b] See DOL 208 no. 1666.

279. SC DIVINE WORSHIP, *Holy Communion and Worship of the Eucharist outside Mass*, **General Introduction** and Chapter 3, **Introductions**, 21 June 1973: Vatican Polyglot Press, 1973.

GENERAL INTRODUCTION

I. Relationship Between Eucharistic Worship outside Mass and the Eucharistic Celebration

1.   The celebration of the eucharist is the center of the entire Christian life, both for the universal Church and for the local congregations of the Church. "The other sacraments, like every other ministry of the Church and every work of the apostolate, are linked with the holy eucharist and have it as their end. For the eucharist contains the Church's entire spiritual wealth, that is, Christ himself. He is our Passover and living bread; through his flesh, made living and life-giving by the Holy Spirit, he is bringing life to people and in this way inviting and leading them to offer themselves together with him, as well as their labors and all created things."[1]

2.   "The celebration of the eucharist in the sacrifice of the Mass," moreover, "is truly the origin and the purpose of the worship that is shown to the eucharist outside Mass."[2] Christ the Lord "is offered in the sacrifice of the Mass when he begins to be sacramentally present as the spiritual food of the faithful under the appearance of bread and wine"; "after the sacrifice has been offered . . . as long as the eucharist is reserved in churches and oratories, Christ is truly the Emmanuel, that is, 'God with us.' Day and night he is in our midst; full of grace and truth, he dwells among us."[3]

3.   No one therefore may doubt "that all the faithful show this holy sacrament the veneration and adoration that is due to God himself, as has always been the practice recognized in the Catholic Church. Nor is the sacrament to be less the object of adoration on the grounds that it was instituted by Christ the Lord to be received as food."[4]

4.   In order to give right direction and encouragement to devotion to the sacrament of the eucharist, the eucharistic mystery must be considered in all its fullness, both in the celebration of Mass and in the worship of the sacrament reserved after Mass in order to extend the grace of the sacrifice.[5]

II. Purpose of Eucharistic Reservation

5.   The primary and original reason for reservation of the eucharist outside Mass is the administration of viaticum. The secondary ends are the giving of communion and the adoration of our Lord Jesus Christ present in the sacrament. The reservation of the sacrament for the sick led to the praiseworthy practice of adoring this heavenly food that is reserved in churches. This cult of adoration has a sound and

2193

2194

2195

2196

2197

---

[1]   PO no. 5 [DOL 18 no. 260].

[2]   SCR, Instr. EuchMyst no. 3 e [DOL 179 no. 1232].

[3]   Ibid. no. 3 b and Paul VI, Encycl. *Mysterium fidei* no. 67 [DOL 176 no. 1211].

[4]   SCR, Instr. EuchMyst no. 3 f [DOL 179 no. 1232].

[5]   See ibid. no. 3 g [DOL 179 no. 1232].

firm foundation, especially since faith in the real presence of the Lord has as its natural consequence the outward, public manifestation of that belief.[6]

2198   6.   In the celebration of Mass the chief ways in which Christ is present in his Church emerge clearly one after the other. First, he is present in the very assembly of the faithful, gathered together in his name; next, he is present in his word, with the reading and explanation of Scripture in the church; also in the person of the minister; finally, and above all, in the eucharistic elements. In a way that is completely unique, the whole and entire Christ, God and man, is substantially and permanently present in the sacrament. This presence of Christ under the appearance of bread and wine "is called real, not to exclude the other kinds of presence as though they were not real, but because it is real par excellence."[7]

Consequently, on the grounds of the sign value, it is more in keeping with the nature of the celebration that, through reservation of the sacrament in the tabernacle, Christ not be present eucharistically from the beginning on the altar where Mass is celebrated. That presence is the effect of the consecration and should appear as such.[8]

2199   7.   The consecrated hosts are to be frequently renewed and reserved in a ciborium or other vessel, in a number sufficient for the communion of the sick and of others outside Mass.[9]

2200   8.   Pastors should see that churches and public oratories where, in conformity with the law, the holy eucharist is reserved, are open every day for at least several hours, at a convenient time, so that the faithful may easily pray in the presence of the blessed sacrament.[10]

III. Place of Eucharistic Reservation

2201   9.   The place for the reservation of the eucharist should be truly preeminent. It is highly recommended that the place be suitable also for private adoration and prayer so that the faithful may readily and fruitfully continue to honor the Lord, present in the sacrament, through personal worship.

This will be achieved more easily if the chapel is separate from the body of the church, especially in churches where marriages and funerals are celebrated frequently and in churches where there are many visitors because of pilgrimages or the artistic and historical treasures.

2202   10.   The holy eucharist is to be reserved in a solid tabernacle. It must be opaque and unbreakable.[R1] Ordinarily there should be only one tabernacle in a church; this may be placed on an altar or if not on an altar, at the discretion of the local Ordinary, in some other noble and properly ornamented part of the church.[11]

---

6   See ibid. no. 49 [DOL 179 no. 1278].

7   Paul VI, Encycl. *Mysterium fidei* no. 39 [DOL 176 no. 1183].

8   See SCR, Instr. EuchMyst 55 [DOL 179 no. 1284].

9   See GIRM nos. 285, 292 [DOL 208 nos. 1675, 1682].

10   See SCR, Instr. EuchMyst no. 51 [DOL 179 no. 1280].

R1   See DOL 179 no. 1281, note R4.

11   See ibid. nos. 52–53 [DOL 179 nos. 1281–82].

The key to the tabernacle where the eucharist is reserved must be kept most carefully by the priest in charge of the church or oratory or by a special minister who has received the faculty to give communion.[R2]

11. The presence of the eucharist in the tabernacle is to be shown by a veil or in another suitable way determined by the competent authority.   2203

According to traditional usage, an oil lamp or lamp with a wax candle is to burn constantly near the tabernacle as a sign of the honor shown to the Lord.[12]

IV. COMPETENCE OF THE CONFERENCES OF BISHOPS

12. It is for the conferences of bishops, in the preparation of particular rituals in accord with the Constitution on the Liturgy (art. 63, b),[c] to accommodate this title of the Roman Ritual to the needs of individual regions so that, once the *acta* of the conferences have been confirmed by the Apostolic See, the ritual may be followed in the respective regions.   2204

In this matter it will be up to the conferences:

a. to consider carefully what elements, if any, from the traditions of individual peoples may be retained or introduced, provided they are compatible with the spirit of the liturgy; the conferences are then to propose to the Apostolic See adaptations considered useful or necessary that will be introduced with its consent;

b. to prepare translations of texts that are truly accommodated to the character of various languages and the mentality of various cultures; they may add texts, especially for singing with appropriate melodies.[†]

CHAPTER III
FORMS OF WORSHIP OF THE EUCHARIST

79. The eucharistic sacrifice is the source and culmination of the whole Christian life. Therefore devotion, both private and public, toward the eucharist even outside Mass that conforms to the norms laid down by lawful authority is strongly advocated.   2205

In structuring these devotional exercises account should be taken of the liturgical seasons so that they accord with the liturgy, are in some way derived from it, and lead the people back to it.[1]

80. When the faithful adore Christ present in the sacrament, they should remember that this presence derives from the sacrifice and has as its purpose both sacramental and spiritual communion.   2206

[R2] On this point Not 9 (1973) 333 comments on the relationship between the reformed ritual and the canonical rules now in force: The norms contained in the reformed Roman Ritual and approved by Pope Paul VI amend, as required, the prescriptions of the *Codex Iuris Canonici* and other laws hitherto in force or repeal them; other laws that are neither repealed nor amended in the new Ritual remain valid and firm. Accordingly, in regard to the custody of the eucharist [see Introduction no. 10] the 26 May 1938 Instruction of the Congregation of the Sacraments, *Nullo unquam*, (AAS 30 [1938] 198) continues to apply.

[12] See SCR, Instr. EuchMyst no. 57 [DOL 179 no. 1286].

[c] See DOL 1 no. 63.

[†] The Latin text has the following footnote here: The text of the psalms and New Testament books are quoted from the edition by the Pontifical Commission for the Neo-Vulgate [see DOL 237]. Liturgical texts that are used in respect of a man, may be used with a change of gender for a woman also. And in either case the singular may be changed into the plural.

[1] See SCR, Instr. EuchMyst no. 58 [DOL 179 no. 1287].

Therefore, the devotion prompting the faithful to visit the blessed sacrament draws them into an ever deeper share in the paschal mystery and leads them to respond gratefully to the gift of him who through his humanity constantly pours divine life into the members of his Body. Abiding with Christ the Lord, they enjoy his intimate friendship and pour out their hearts before him for themselves and for those dear to them and they pray for the peace and salvation of the world. Offering their entire lives with Christ to the Father in the Holy Spirit, they derive from this sublime colloquy an increase of faith, hope, and charity. Thus they foster those right dispositions that enable them with due devotion to celebrate the memorial of the Lord and receive frequently the bread given us by the Father.

Therefore, the faithful should strive to worship Christ the Lord in the blessed sacrament in a manner fitting in with their own way of life. Pastors should show the way by example and by word encourage their people.[2]

2207   81. Prayer before Christ the Lord sacramentally present extends the union with Christ that the faithful have reached in communion. It renews the covenant that in turn moves them to maintain by the way they live what they have received through faith and the sacrament. They should strive to lead their whole lives in the strength of this heavenly food, as sharers in the death and resurrection of the Lord. All should be eager to do good works and to please God, so that they may seek to imbue the world with the Christian spirit and, in all things, even in the midst of human affairs, to become witnesses of Christ.[3]

1. EXPOSITION OF THE HOLY EUCHARIST

INTRODUCTION

I. Relationship between Exposition and Mass

2208   82. Exposition of the holy eucharist, either in a ciborium or in a monstrance, leads us to acknowledge Christ's marvelous presence in the sacrament and invites us to the spiritual union with him that culminates in sacramental communion. Therefore it is a strong encouragement toward the worship owed to Christ in spirit and in truth.

In such exposition care must be taken that everything clearly brings out the meaning of eucharistic worship in its correlation with the Mass. There must be nothing about the appointments used for exposition that could in any way obscure Christ's intention of instituting the eucharist above all to be near us to feed, to heal, and to comfort us.[4]

2209   83. During the exposition of the blessed sacrament, celebration of Mass in the body of the Church is prohibited.

In addition to the reasons given in no. 6, the celebration of the eucharistic mystery includes in a higher way that inner communion to which exposition is meant to lead the faithful.

If exposition of the blessed sacrament goes on for a day or for several successive days, it should be interrupted during the celebration of Mass, unless it is

---

[2]   See ibid. no. 50 [DOL 179 no. 1279].

[3]   See ibid. no. 13 [DOL 179 no. 1242].

[4]   See ibid. no. 60 [DOL 179 no. 1289].

celebrated in a chapel separate from the area of exposition and at least some of the faithful remain in adoration.[5]

II. REGULATIONS FOR EXPOSITION

84. Genuflection in the presence of the blessed sacrament, whether reserved in the tabernacle or exposed for public adoration, is on one knee.

2210

85. For exposition of the blessed sacrament in the monstrance, four to six candles are lighted, as at Mass, and incense is used. For exposition of the blessed sacrament in the ciborium, at least two candles should be lighted and incense may be used.

2211

LENGTHY EXPOSITION

86. In churches where the eucharist is regularly reserved, it is recommended that solemn exposition of the blessed sacrament for an extended period of time should take place once a year, even though this period is not strictly continuous. In this way the local community may meditate on this mystery more deeply and adore.

2212

This kind of exposition, however, may take place, with the consent of the local Ordinary, only if there is assurance of the participation of a reasonable number of the faithful.[6]

87. For any serious and general need, the local Ordinary is empowered to order prayer before the blessed sacrament exposed for a more extended period of time in those churches to which the faithful come in large numbers.[7]

2213

88. Where there cannot be uninterrupted exposition because there is not a sufficient number of worshipers, it is permissible to replace the blessed sacrament in the tabernacle at fixed hours that are announced ahead of time. But this may not be done more than twice a day, for example, at midday and at night.

2214

The following form of simple reposition may be observed: the priest or deacon, vested in an alb, or a surplice over a cassock, and a stole, replaces the blessed sacrament in the tabernacle after a brief period of adoration and a prayer said with those present. The exposition of the blessed sacrament may take place again, in the same manner and at a scheduled time.[8]

BRIEF PERIOD OF EXPOSITION

89. Shorter expositions of the eucharist are to be arranged in such a way that the blessing with the eucharist is preceded by a reasonable time for readings of the word of God, songs, prayers, and a period for silent prayer.[9]

2215

Exposition merely for the purpose of giving benediction is prohibited.

ADORATION IN RELIGIOUS COMMUNITIES

90. According to the constitutions and regulations of their institute, some religious communities and other groups have the practice of perpetual eucharistic adoration or adoration over extended periods of time. It is strongly recommended that they pattern this holy practice in harmony with the spirit of the liturgy. Then, with the whole community taking part, the adoration before Christ the Lord, will consist of readings, songs, and religious silence to foster effectively the spiritual life of the

2216

---

[5]   See ibid. no. 61 [DOL 179 no. 1290].

[6]   See ibid. no. 63 [DOL 179 no. 1292].

[7]   See ibid. no. 64 [DOL 179 no. 1293].

[8]   See ibid. no. 65 [DOL 179 no. 1294].

[9]   See ibid. no. 66 [DOL 179 no. 1295].

community. This promotes between the members of the religious house the spirit of unity and mutual love that the eucharist signifies and effects, and gives the worship due to the sacrament a more sublime expression.

The form of adoration in which one or two members of the community take turns before the blessed sacrament is also to be maintained and is highly commended. Through it, in accordance with the nature of the institute as approved by the Church, the worshipers adore Christ the Lord in the sacrament and pray to him in the name of the entire community and Church.

III. Minister of Exposition

2217   91. The ordinary minister for exposition of the eucharist is a priest or deacon.[R3] At the end of the period of adoration, before the reposition, he blesses the congregation with the sacrament.

In the absence of a priest or deacon or if they are lawfully impeded, the following persons may publicly expose and later repose the eucharist for the adoration of the faithful:

a.   an acolyte or special minister of communion;

b.   upon appointment by the local Ordinary, a member of a religious community or of a pious association of laymen or laywomen which is devoted to eucharistic adoration.

Such ministers may open the tabernacle and also, as required, place the ciborium on the altar or place the host in the monstrance. At the end of the period of adoration, they replace the blessed sacrament in the tabernacle. It is not lawful, however, for them to give the blessing with the sacrament.

2218   92. The minister, if he is a priest or deacon, should vest in an alb, or a surplice over a cassock, and a stole. Other ministers should wear either the liturgical vestments that are used in the region or the vesture that is befitting this ministry and is approved by the Ordinary.

The priest or deacon should wear a white cope and humeral veil to give the blessing at the end of adoration, when the exposition takes place with the monstrance; in the case of exposition in the ciborium, he should put on the humeral veil. [. . .]

2. EUCHARISTIC PROCESSIONS

2219   101. In processions in which the eucharist is carried through the streets solemnly with singing, the Christian people give public witness to faith and to their devotion toward this sacrament.[R4]

[R3]   For nos. 91, 92, 97, 99, 100, see DOL 309 no. 2536, note R1.

[R4]   Query: Is it lawful to have a blessed sacrament procession inside the church? Reply: No. In some places there was a custom of sometimes having processions inside the church. The rite of holy communion and worship of the eucharist outside Mass does not discuss these explicitly. But when dealing with the blessed sacrament procession it considers only processions "through the streets" (no. 104), "from one church to another" (no. 107), with "decoration of the streets" (no. 104). Those inside the church are not truly "processions." The case of the evening Mass on Holy Thursday is irrelevant. No "procession" follows it, but rather only the solemn transfer of the blessed sacrament to the place of repose. Contrary to the custom in question, the Introduction, which strongly recommends the procession on Corpus Christi, clearly states: "If the procession [text quoted] appropriate places" (no. 102). This is to be carried out either by celebration of Mass or by adoration of the blessed sacrament, accompanied by Scripture readings, singing, a homily, and a period of meditation: Not 11 (1975) 64.

But it is for the local Ordinary to decide on both the advisability of such processions in today's conditions and on the time, place, and plan for them that will ensure their being carried out with decorum and without any loss of reverence toward this sacrament.[12]

102. The annual procession on the solemnity of Corpus Christi, or on a convenient day near this feast, has a special importance and meaning for the pastoral life of the parish or city. It is therefore desirable to continue this procession, in accordance with the law, when today's circumstances permit and when it can truly be a sign of common faith and adoration.

    In the principal districts of large cities there may be additional eucharistic processions for pastoral reasons at the discretion of the local Ordinary. If the procession cannot be held on the solemnity of Corpus Christi, it is fitting to hold some kind of public celebration for the entire city or its principal districts in the cathedral church or other convenient places.

2220

103. It is fitting that a eucharistic procession begin after the Mass and the host to be carried in the procession is consecrated at this Mass. A procession may also take place, however, at the end of a lengthy period of public adoration that has been held after Mass.

2221

104. Eucharistic processions should be arranged in accordance with local customs in regard to the decoration of the streets and the order followed by the participants. In the course of the procession there may be stations where the eucharistic blessing is given, if there is such a custom and some pastoral advantage recommends it. Songs and prayers should be planned with the purpose of expressing the faith of the participants and the centering of their attention on the Lord alone. [. . .]

2222

3. EUCHARISTIC CONGRESSES

109. Eucharistic congresses have been introduced into the life of the Church in recent years as a special manifestation of eucharistic worship. They should be considered as a kind of "station" to which a particular community invites an entire local Church or to which an individual local Church invites other Churches of a single region or nation or even of the entire world. The purpose is that together the members of the Church join in the deepest profession of some aspect of the eucharistic mystery and express their worship publicly in the bond of charity and unity.

    Such congresses should be a genuine sign of faith and charity by reason of the total participation of the local Church and the association with it of the other Churches.

2223

110. Both the local Church and other Churches should undertake studies beforehand concerning the place, theme, and program of the congress. These studies are meant to lead to the consideration of genuine needs and to foster the progress of theological studies and the good of the local Church. Specialists in theological, biblical, liturgical, pastoral, and humane studies should help in this research.

2224

111. In preparation for a eucharistic congress, the concentration should be on the following:

    a. a thorough catechesis, accommodated to the capacity of different groups, concerning the eucharist, especially as the mystery of Christ living and working in the Church;

2225

---

[12] See SCR, Instr. EuchMyst no. 59 [DOL 179 no. 1288].

b. more active participation in the liturgy in order to encourage a reverent hearing of the word of God and the spirit of mutual love and community;[13]

c. research into the means and the pursuit of social action for human development and the just distribution of goods, including the temporal, following the example of the primitive Christian community.[14] The goal is that every eucharistic table may be a center from which the leaven of the Gospel spreads as a force in the growth of contemporary society and as the pledge of the future kingdom.[15]

2226   112. The celebration of the congress should be planned on the basis of the following criteria.[16]

a. The celebration of the eucharist should be the true center and high point of the congress, to which all the programs and the various devotional services should be directed.

b. Celebrations of the word of God, catechetical meetings, and public conferences should be planned to investigate thoroughly the theme of the congress and to set out more clearly the ways for carrying out its practical implications.

c. There should be an opportunity for common prayers and extended adoration in the presence of the blessed sacrament exposed at designated churches that are especially suited to this form of piety.

d. The regulations concerning eucharistic processions[17] should be observed for the procession in which the blessed sacrament is carried through the streets of the city to the accompaniment of public hymns and prayers, taking into account local, social, and religious conditions.

▶   330. SC BISHOPS, Decree, *Apostolatus maris*, on the pastoral care of seamen and ship passengers, 24 September 1977:

Part II, I no. 7:   Eucharistic reservation aboard ship [no. 2669].

▶   335. SC CATHOLIC EDUCATION, Instruction *In ecclesiasticam futurorum sacerdotum*, on liturgical formation in seminaries, 3 June 1979:

Appendix, no. 41:   Worship of the eucharist outside Mass [no. 2882].

▶   See also Chapter 7, Section 2. Places of worship.

13   See SC art. 41–52 [DOL 1 nos. 41–52].

14   See Acts 4:32.

15   See SC art. 47 [DOL 1 no. 47]; UR no. 15 [DOL 6 no. 187].

16   See SCR, Instr. EuchMyst no. 67 [DOL 179 no. 1296].

17   See nos. 101–108 of this document.

SECTION 11. MASS INTENTIONS AND STIPENDS

SUMMARY (DOL 280–287). In this area there have been certain changes in church discipline. There are 8 relevant documents.

—Paul VI's Motu Proprio *Firma in traditione* (DOL 287) dealt with the general matter of Mass offerings; it had been preceded by a notification of the Secretariat of State (DOL 284) and a letter of the Congregation for Religious and Secular Institutes (DOL 286) announcing the papal intention to change the existing discipline.

—The subsidiary documents in this section deal with particular points: the Mass *pro populo* (DOL 283), binated Masses (DOL 280, 282, 285), the series called Gregorian Masses (DOL 281).

▶ 103. PAUL VI, Motu Proprio *Pastorale munus*, on the powers and privileges of bishops, 30 November 1963:

I, nos. 11–12: Reduction or suppression of funded Masses [nos. 722–723].

280. SC SEMINARIES AND UNIVERSITIES, **Rescript** (U.S.A.), permitting a stipend for a binated Mass, to assist seminaries, 16 September 1965.*

2227   In an audience of 6 July 1965 granted to the undersigned Cardinal Prefect of the Sacred Congregation of Seminaries and Universities, Pope Paul VI, in view of the economic hardships under which the seminaries of some nations labor, has kindly granted the following for five years: to priests celebrating Mass in their respective dioceses the local Ordinaries may grant the faculty to accept offerings for binated Masses on feast days and ferials on the condition, however, that the same Most Reverend Prelates contribute the offerings to the diocesan seminary as well as to other diocesan needs. This power is also granted to provide for the inconvenience and poverty of the celebrating priests insofar as may be necessary.

It will be very praiseworthy if the local Ordinaries shall be pleased to remit part of these offerings to the Sacred Congregation of Seminaries and Universities to provide a subsidy to poorer seminaries.

▶ 225. SC COUNCIL, Reply to a query, on the stipend at a concelebrated Mass, 18 April 1966.

281. SC COUNCIL, **Declaration** *Tricenario Gregoriano*, on the continuity of Gregorian Masses, 24 February 1967: AAS 59 (1967) 229–230.

2228   The series of thirty Gregorian Masses may be interrupted because of some unforeseen obstacle (for example, sudden illness) or other justifiable cause (for example, celebration of a funeral or wedding Mass). The disposition of the Church preserves those intercessory fruits of this series that the practice of the Church and the devotion of the faithful have attributed to the thirty Masses. But the priest celebrant has a firm obligation to complete their celebration as soon as possible.

In this very important matter the Ordinary is to guard against the intrusion of abuses.

▶ 107. SC BISHOPS, Index of quinquennial faculties granted to local Ordinaries, 1 January 1968.

SC Clergy: Possibility of transferring the obligation for funded Masses [no. 760].

---

* Text, CLD 6, 558–559.

282. SC CATHOLIC EDUCATION, **Rescript** (U.S.A.), permitting a stipend for two Masses on a weekday, 24 July 1969.*

In view of the economic hardships by which seminaries in some countries are   2229
pressed, Pope Paul VI, on 24 October 1968, again graciously granted for a five-year
period that local Ordinaries may give the priests who celebrate Mass in their
diocese the faculty to accept stipends for two Masses on weekdays, on condition,
however, that the bishops assign the stipends to the diocesan seminary and also to
other diocesan needs, after having provided, if need be, for the priest celebrant's
inconvenience and poverty.

Very worthy of praise are those local Ordinaries who wish to give some part of
these stipends to the Congregation for Catholic Education to provide help to poor
seminaries.

283. SC CLERGY, **Decree** *Litteris Apostolicis*, on the obligation of celebrating
the Mass *pro populo*, 25 July 1970: AAS 63 (1971) 943–944; Not 6 (1970) 380.

In virtue of the Motu Proprio *Mysterii Paschalis* of Pope Paul VI, 14 February   2230
1969ª (AAS 61 [1969] 222), the new General Roman Calendar took effect on 1
January 1970.

Serious reasons dictated the change or suppression of a number of things
previously contained in the Calendar, as the commentary on the new calendar
explains.ᵇ Therefore, in view of present circumstances and after ascertaining the
wishes of the conferences of bishops, the Congregation for the Clergy by papal
mandate establishes the following concerning the obligation of celebrating the
Mass *pro populo*.

The obligation binding on pastors to offer the Mass *pro populo* is established for
each and every Sunday and all holydays of obligation observed in the place. Rescripts hitherto granted and involving a lesser obligation remain valid until their
date of expiration.

The effective date for these matters is 1 January 1971.

▶   104.   PONTIFICAL COMMISSION FOR THE INTERPRETATION OF THE DE-
              CREES OF VATICAN COUNCIL II, Reply, on the Motu Proprio *Pastorale munus* I,
              nos. 11–12, 1 July 1971.

284. SECRETARIAT OF STATE, **Notice** *Quo clarius*, on the application of
Mass intentions, 29 November 1971: AAS 63 (1971) 841.

More precise regulation is planned in regard to the serious and delicate matter   2231
of the celebration and application of Masses for the intention of those making
offerings. It is also proposed to establish balanced criteria for weighing and resolving future requests that — in exceptional cases — may be presented regarding the
reduction, condonation, and commutation of Mass obligations. Therefore Pope Paul

---

    *   Letter, Prot. N. 688/63, to National Conference of Catholic Bishops (U.S.A.); text, CLD 7, 616.

    ª   See DOL 440; AAS and Not wrongly give 15 Feb. as date of this Motu Proprio.

    ᵇ   The commentary was published in the *editio typica* of the GNLYC, but not as an official document.

VI has decided to reserve to himself, but only provisorily and temporarily, all questions concerning this matter. The Pope at the same time has decreed the suspension, from 1 February 1972, of all faculties hitherto granted, general or personal, for whatever reason and to whatever physical or moral person, either in virtue of the law or by himself or his predecessors, whether immediately, even orally, or through the curial congregations. Those faculties alone are untouched that are granted to bishops by the Motu Proprio *Pastorale munus*, 30 November 1963, [I] nos. 11 and 12.[a]

By papal mandate those affected in any way by this new arrangement are now given timely notification of these matters. The effective date of this arrangement is the date already mentioned, 1 February 1972. All things to the contrary notwithstanding, even those deserving special mention.

285. SC RELIGIOUS AND SECULAR INSTITUTES, **Rescript** (Germany), permitting religious priests to accept a stipend for binated or trinated Masses, 10 January 1972.*

2232
The Archbishop of Munich and Freising, president of the conference of bishops of Germany, humbly requests extension of the rescript Prot. N. 7919/61, 17 December 1966. This granted the power to allow the religious priests of Germany to accept stipends for a second and third Mass they celebrate, on condition that these stipends in their entirety be at the disposal of the major religious superiors. The petition is made because the reasons for it continue.

Et Deus, etc. . . .

In virtue of faculties granted by Pope Paul VI, the Congregation for Religous and Secular Institutes, after considering the recitals, grants as a favor the extension of the rescript cited, in keeping with the terms of the petition, for another five years.

All things to the contrary notwithstanding.

286. SC RELIGIOUS AND SECULAR INSTITUTES, **Letter** to Rev. P. Arrupe, President of the Union of Superiors General, on Mass intentions, 15 January 1972.*

2233
I must inform you that Pope Paul VI has decided to reserve to himself, but provisorily and for the time being, all powers concerning the reduction, condonation, and commutation of Mass stipends and of the obligations pertaining to the application or celebration of Masses. At the same time he suspends all general and particular faculties hitherto granted by the law itself, by him personally, or by his predecessors, whether directly or through the curial congregations, whatever the time or the reason for the grant and whether it was made to a physical or a moral

---

[a] See DOL 103 nos. 722–723.

* Prot. N. 7919/61; text in ArchKathKRecht 141 (1972) 195–196.

* Prot. N. Sp. R. 161/72; text in CommRel 53 (1972) 78 (Italian).

person. The only faculties excepted are those granted to bishops in the Motu Proprio *Pastorale munus* [I] nos. 11 and 12.[a]

The effective date of this papal decision is 1 February 1972, "all things to the contrary notwithstanding, even those deserving special mention."

In keeping with this decision, the superiors of all religious institutes shall submit to this Congregation, not later than Easter 1972, a detailed listing of all faculties possessed by themselves or their subjects regarding the reduction, condonation, or commutation of Mass stipends and of the obligations pertaining to the application or celebration of Masses.

I therefore request that you kindly bring these matters to the attention of the superiors general of the Union.

287. PAUL VI, **Motu Proprio** *Firma in traditione*, on faculties regarding Mass stipends, 13 June 1974: AAS 66 (1974) 308–311.

In the established tradition of the Church, the faithful, moved by an ecclesial and religious sense, join to the eucharistic sacrifice a kind of sacrifice of their own, as a way of taking part more intensely. They thus do their share to provide for the Church's needs, especially the support of its ministers. This practice is in accord with the spirit of the Lord's words: "The laborer . . . is worthy of his hire" (Lk 10:7), which St. Paul alludes to in 1 Timothy (5:18) and in 1 Corinthians (9:7–14).   2234

By this practice the faithful associate themselves more closely with Christ's act of offering himself as victim and in so doing experience its effects more fully. The Church has not only approved the practice but has encouraged it, regarding it as a sign of the union of the baptized with Christ and of the people with the priest, who carries out his ministry for their benefit.

To safeguard this sound understanding and to protect it against any possible distortion, appropriate norms have been laid down over the course of the centuries. Their purpose has been that the worship that the people desired to offer generously to God would in fact be carried out with a corresponding dutifulness and magnanimity. But because of the varying circumstances of the times and of human society, it sometimes becomes morally impossible — therefore somewhat inequitable — to satisfy in full the Mass obligations asked for and accepted. The Church in such cases is therefore forced to make a proper review of such obligations; at the same time it takes pains to remain consistent in this matter and to keep faith with the donors.

With the chief consideration being the drawing up of balanced norms to regulate Mass stipends (a matter serious and calling for great prudence), we decided through the notification issued by the Secretary of State or Papal Secretary, 29 November 1971 (AAS 63 [1971] 841),[a] to reserve to ourself all decisions to be made concerning petitioned reductions, condonations, and commutations of Mass stipends. We also suspended, from 1 February 1972, all faculties, no matter to whom or how granted.   2235

Now, however, we think it time to terminate that reservation, since the ends for which this arrangement was introduced have been achieved on all major points. We propose that the regulation of this matter be based on a new foundation and

---

[a]   See DOL 103 nos. 722–723.

[a]   See DOL 284.

not be impeded in any way by inaccurate interpretations relying on what might have been lawful in the past. It has therefore been decided to do away with any remaining elements of the former faculties.

We do, nonetheless, intend to meet in some way the needs that our brothers in the episcopate must sometimes deal with. Taking into account, therefore, the tested experience deriving from the use of the faculties granted to bishops by the Motu Proprios *Pastorale munus* (AAS 56 [1964] 5–12)[b] and *De Episcoporum muneribus* (AAS 58 [1966] 467–472),[c] we have judged it advisable to grant certain faculties to those who share with us in the pastoral ministry of the Church.

Accordingly, after thoroughly weighing the matter, we establish and decree, *motu proprio* and from the fullness of our apostolic authority, the following for the universal Church.

2236   I.   The reservation, contained in the notification of the Secretariat of State, 29 November 1971, ceases on 1 July 1974. From that date therefore the congregations of the Roman Curia are empowered to resume their competency in this matter; but they are to adapt its exercise to the new, more precise norms that are enjoined on them individually. From 1 July 1974, accordingly, any petitions regarding the matter in question are to be directed to the curial congregations.

2237   II.   As regards Mass stipends, from the same date all faculties hitherto in force, no matter how granted or acquired, are definitively revoked. These, then, cease to exist: faculties granted to any person, physical or moral, by ourself or our predecessors, even *viva voce*, by the Roman Curia or by any other authority, in virtue of privilege, indult, dispensation, or on any other grounds, particular law not being excepted; faculties acquired in virtue of the communication of privileges, of custom — even particular, centuries-old, or immemorial — of prescription, or on any other grounds.

After this revocation, we establish that henceforth only the following faculties are in force:

     a.   the faculties now granted to the congregations of the Roman Curia, referred to in no. I;

     b.   the faculties contained in the Motu Proprio *Pastorale munus* and in the "Index of Faculties" customarily given to local Ordinaries and papal legates;

     c.   the new faculties that the present Motu Proprio grants to bishops, treated in no. III.

2238   III.   Also from 1 July we grant the following faculties to those persons mentioned in the Motu Proprio *Pastorale munus*, under the same conditions that it lays down:

     a.   the faculty to permit priests binating or trinating in the diocese to apply these Masses, when they have received a stipend that is being given over to needs predefined by the diocese; the faculty to permit them to apply the Masses in keeping with those intentions for which otherwise a condonation or even a simple reduction would have to be requested. This faculty does not cover binated concelebrated Masses, treated in the Declaration of the Congregation for Divine Worship, 7 August 1972, no. 3 b (AAS 64 [1974] 561–563),[d] since for such Masses a stipend under any title is forbidden;

     b.   the faculty of reducing, at a ratio corresponding to the diminished revenues, an obligation incumbent on cathedral or collegiate chapters, to apply the

---

   b   See DOL 103.

   c   See DOL 105.

   d   See DOL 226 no. 1816.

conventual Mass daily on behalf of benefactors, with the exception, however, of one conventual Mass each month;

c. the faculty of transferring Mass obligations, for a proportionate reason, to days, churches, or altars other than those stipulated in the terms establishing funded Masses.

The effective date for these norms is 1 July 1974.

We command that all matters decreed by this Motu Proprio are established and ratified, all things to the contrary notwithstanding, even those deserving most special mention.

CHAPTER THREE

THE OTHER SACRAMENTS AND THE SACRAMENTALS

SUMMARY (DOL 288–417). The Constitution on the Liturgy in its third chapter places the profound, theological meaning of the sacraments and sacramentals as the basis for the importance of their liturgical expression and the faithful's participation in them; it also establishes the rules for use of the vernacular to enhance participation (art. 59–63). The Constitution then treats the revision first of the liturgy of baptism, confirmation, penance, anointing of the sick, orders, marriage. The Council also directs that there be a revision of the sacramentals and mentions in particular blessings, rites of consecration to virginity and religious profession, funerals. In 1979 the section of the Roman Pontifical on blessings remained the only revision yet to be completed. Chapter Three of *Documents on the Liturgy* in its ten sections presents the documents implementing this part of the Constitution.

Section 1. The Sacraments and the Sacramentals in General

SUMMARY (DOL 288–291). The most important texts here are those given as cross-references. From the Constitution on the Liturgy itself and the Dogmatic Constitution on the Church themes relevant to liturgical catechesis were developed in other major documents: the sacraments presuppose faith; in them Christ is present and active; their celebration engages the exercise of the universal and the ministerial priesthood. The 4 specific texts in this section reflect papal teaching:

—A letter of the Secretariat of State treats "the Church as sacrament and the sacraments of the Church" (DOL 288).

—From the popes themselves there are two addresses of Paul VI on pastoral aspects of sacramental life (DOL 289–290) and one of John Paul II on sacramental discipline in the Church's life (DOL 291).

▶   1.   VATICAN COUNCIL II, Constitution on the Liturgy *Sacrosanctum Concilium*, 4
         December 1963:

         art. 7:   Christ's presence in the sacraments [no. 7].
               27–40   General principles of reform of the liturgy [nos.
                                       27–40].
               59–63   Liturgy of the sacraments and the sacramentals
                                       [nos. 59–63].
               79:                     Sacramentals and blessings [no. 79].

▶   23.   SC RITES (Consilium), Instruction (first) *Inter Oecumenici*, 26 September 1964:

         nos. 6:   Sacramental life [no. 298].
               35:                     Equality of all the faithful [no. 327].
               61:                     Use of the vernacular [no. 353].
               76–77:   Sacramentals [nos. 368–369].

▶   4.   VATICAN COUNCIL II, Dogmatic Constitution on the Church *Lumen gentium*, 21
          November 1964:

          nos. 10–11:   Universal priesthood of the faithful in the sacra-
                                       ments [nos. 140–141].

▶   176. PAUL VI, Encyclical *Mysterium fidei*, 3 September 1965:

          no. 38:   Christ's active presence in sacraments [no. 1182].

288. SECRETARIAT OF STATE, **Letter** to Bishop C. Rossi, President of the Italian Liturgical Commission, on the occasion of the 17th National Liturgical Week of Italy (Pavia, 29 August - 2 September 1966), on the theme: The Church as Sacrament and the Sacraments of the Church, 18 August 1966: Not 2 (1966) 293–295 (Italian).

2239   There is soon to be celebrated at Pavia, under the aegis of the Centro di Azione
Liturgica, executive arm of the bishops' liturgical commission, the 17th National
Week of Pastoral Liturgy, on the theme: the Church as sacrament and the sacra-
ments of the Church. In cordially conveying this information Your Excellency
requested to have again this year an expression of approval and the blessing of Pope
Paul VI for this important event. [. . .]

The Pope is particularly pleased with the choice of theme. Proposed this year
for the reflection of so many esteemed scholars, this theme in its very formulation
reflects its inspiration by the theological teaching of Vatican Council II. With a
renewed clarity the Council has reasserted a teaching that goes back to the luminous insights of the ancient Fathers of both the Greek and the Latin Church.

2240   The very first paragraph of the Dogmatic Constitution *Lumen gentium* says of the
Church that "in Christ it is like the sacrament or sign and the instrument of
intimate union with God and of the unity of the entire human race" (LG no. 1; see
also no. 9). The Church is "loved with an everlasting love" (Jer 31:3) by the heavenly Father and has been made to be his people and Christ's Mystical Body. Thus it
exists in the world both as the striking symbol of that love in which God has given
us all things (see Rom 8:32) and as the effective, universal instrument of salvation.
Because salvation is the result of the capital grace of the divine Savior's human

nature, it is to be found normally and fully in the Catholic Church alone as the Church is the Mystical Body of Christ, its Head. It belongs therefore to the Catholic Church to communicate and to spread salvation to all the generations of the human family and in all the ages and places that are part of human history.

The sacramentality of the Church rests on its mission to continue Christ's work, to extend it, and to be identified with Christ himself. The Church's sacramentality achieves constant actualization, adapted to all peoples of all times, in the individual sacraments, which were instituted by Christ and entrusted to the Church as sources for sanctifying the essential and most decisive moments of human existence. Vatican Council II has given prominence to the ecclesiological aspect of the sacraments (see LG nos. 10–11).[a] It has reasserted its supreme importance from the point of view of the entire Church, not merely of the particular needs, however legitimate, of individual souls. Baptism, the first sacrament, by bestowing on the faithful their first configuration to Christ's priesthood fashions the spiritual organism and the membership of the Church. From baptism all the other sacraments have their origin and supreme among them is the eucharist, which holds the Church together by the bonds of Christ's own charity. To his followers Christ communicates and spreads his own attitudes of love toward his heavenly Father and of selflessness toward his brothers and sisters.

It is the warm wish of Pope Paul that from a close, comparative study of the various conciliar documents, the coming liturgical week may achieve effective results on both the theoretical and practical level. He calls special attention to the duty of serious and concrete preaching that leads to an ever better understanding of the key place of the sacraments in the context of ecclesial life. He urges as well the duty of a profound catechetical formation at all levels. This must enlighten Christians, right from their first steps within the community of the Church. They must learn about the riches that God puts at their disposal by means of the sacramental system and about their obligation to situate their lives within the light of the individual sacraments. They must learn to base their lives on the implications of these sacraments for the sake both of the good of the Church and of their own complete imitation of the divine model, Jesus Christ. [. . .]   2241

▶   508.   SC RITES (Consilium), Instruction *Musicam sacram*, on music in the liturgy, 5 March 1967:

nos. 43–45:   Chants in the sacraments and sacramentals [nos. 4164–66].

▶   168.   PAUL VI, Solemn Profession of faith, 30 June 1968:

no. 19:   The sacraments of faith [no. 1095].

▶   208.   SC RITES (Consilium); SC DIVINE WORSHIP, General Instruction of the Roman Missal, 1st ed. 6 April 1969; 4th ed. 27 March 1975.

nos. 326–334:   Ritual Masses for the sacraments and sacramentals [nos. 1716–24].

---

[a]   See DOL 4 nos. 140–141.

289. PAUL VI, **Address** to a meeting of the presbyterate of Rome, on pastoral effectiveness in the ritual use of the sacraments, 29 October 1970: Not 6 (1970) 377–379 (Italian; excerpt).

2242   [. . .] It is easy for us to reflect on something else that is new and that is expressed in the theme of your meeting: the new pastoral ministry of the sacraments. The newness in this area is based mainly on the reform of the liturgy. You are well aware of this. But two considerations justify this claim to a newness that goes beyond the merely ritual applications. One point concerns theological coherence, the other pastoral effectiveness. There is an obvious usefulness, even a need, of a theological rethinking, above all regarding the very concept of a sacrament as a divine action completed by a human action, with the divine as the principal cause of grace, the human as the instrumental cause and condition.[2]

The mysterious encounter between the divine, transcendent activity and a human, ministerial activity is something that deserves a continuous reflection, a wonderful rebirth, a constant vivid realization. One reason is that the existential character of this encounter and its frequent repetition requires this unbroken attention, this ever-new discovery, if we wish to keep the celebration of the sacraments from deteriorating into an almost superstitious formalism. A further reason is that this theological reflection is called for by the nature of a sacrament: we know its nature is to be a symbol, a sign of an intervention and of an effective bestowal of divine grace. To be a sign means to be a kind of language; it means that in the outward elements themselves a sacrament declares a theme, chosen by Christ, for inexhaustible thought. That thought leads to an encounter with a divine thought, telling us that Christ wishes to make us grasp something of the mystery with which he desires to associate us.

A sacrament's being a sign means that with regard to sacramental life our minds must continually be intent on penetrating what the sacramental symbol signifies. Take baptism: St. Paul urges us to pass from the outward perception of the visible sign to the inner understanding of what it signifies, namely, something that takes place in a specific communication of grace, that is, of the mysterious divine life within our lowly human life. He writes to the Romans (6:3–4): "Do you not know that as many of us as have been baptized into Jesus Christ have been baptized into his death? We are therefore buried with him by baptism into death; that as Christ is raised up from the dead by the glory of the Father, we also should walk in newness of life."

What profound and amazing supernatural truths the eucharistic symbols, bread and wine, make us think of — and first among them the unity of the Church (ST 3a, 73. 3). What fullness of love marriage reminds us of, as it has become the sign of the love between Christ and the Church for which he gave his life. And so on.

2243   The meaning constituting the new mentality with which we must celebrate the sacraments consists in a completely dignified manner of celebrating that reflects a faith eager and glad about the ministry (is it always so in practice?). But more than that, it consists in a catechesis adapted to every sacrament. In our religious customs it might be said that first communion alone is surrounded with such attentiveness.

The renewed pastoral ministry must study and put into practice much more pertinent methods for the celebration of the rest of the sacraments. Pedagogy for the sacraments must be more developed in the pastoral life. The effectiveness causing grace is entirely and principally from God, working within the sacramental

---

[2] See A. Ciappi, OP, *De sacramentis in communi* (Berruti, Rome, 1957).

act (*ex opere operato*, in the words of the theologians), but the effectiveness as instrument and condition for the mysterious divine action depends on the human being (*ex opere operantis*). It depends on the minister, on the recipient, and on the ecclesial community taking part in the celebration and administration of the sacraments (see PO no. 13).[a]

What then is required of you if the pastoral ministry of the sacraments is to be renewed? A better catechetical and spiritual preparation, a more complete celebration, as both a rite and community act, and on the part of both ministers and faithful. Also a more conscious application of the sacramental reality to life as it is lived: the purpose of the sacrament is lasting moral effects. [. . .]

▶   169.   SC CLERGY, *General Catechetical Directory*, 11 April 1971.

      nos. 57, 106:   Catechesis of the sacraments [nos. 1104, 1111].

▶   318.   SYNOD OF BISHOPS, *The Ministerial Priesthood*, 30 November 1971:

      Part Two, I, no. 1:   The priest and the sacraments [no. 2571].

▶   329.   SC BISHOPS, *Directory on the Pastoral Ministry of Bishops*, 22 February 1973:

      nos. 87–89:   The bishop and the sacraments [no. 2657–59].

▶   130.   SC DIVINE WORSHIP, Circular letter *Dum toto terrarum*, on the translation of the forms of the sacraments, 25 October 1973.

▶   100.   SC DIVINE WORSHIP, Report to Synod of Bishops, September 1974.

      Sacraments and preaching [no. 701].

290. PAUL VI, **Address** to the bishops of Switzerland, on the liturgy and the sacraments, 1 December 1977: AAS 70 (1978) 102–107; Not 13 (1977) 618 (French; excerpt).

[. . .] Thanks to the intense work of preparation and revitalization, the renewed liturgy has flourished beautifully in your country, with the welcome participation of the people. That is heartening. Protect the primary purpose of the liturgy, which is the glory of God and the manifestation of salvation through the liturgical celebration. We hope that the Catholics of Switzerland will derive great benefit from the pastoral letter that your conference is in the process of completing on "the Christians's Sunday." We have also in mind the praiseworthy efforts in the cause of better preparation for the sacraments. On this point, the norms issued by the Apostolic See to ensure the authenticity and right balance of the reform by preventing the neglect of important elements may not be disregarded. An example is the individual confession of sins, including confession by children preparing for first communion. Pastors must understand that such confession is in accord with the law and set aside a place and time for it. [. . .]

2244

---

a   See DOL 18 no. 265.

291. JOHN PAUL II, **Address** to bishops of Canada, excerpt on the sacramental discipline of the Church, 17 November 1978: AAS 71 (1979) 32–36; Not 14 (1978) 562–566 (English; excerpt).

2245   [. . .] At the same time, as bishops we are urged to a deep pastoral concern for the sacred discipline common to the whole Church.[7] This brings with it a need for a sensitivity to the delicate and sovereign action of the Holy Spirit in the life of our people and a humble realization that this action is accomplished in a special way through the ministry of the bishops, who, united with the entire episcopal college and with Peter its head, are promised the assistance of the Holy Spirit, so that they may effectively lead the faithful to salvation.

At this moment in the life of the Church there are two particular aspects of sacramental discipline that are worthy of the special attention of the universal Church and I wish to mention them in order to assist bishops everywhere. These matters form part of that general discipline of which the Apostolic See has prime responsibility and in which the Pope wishes to sustain his brethren in the episcopate and to offer a word of encouragement and pastoral orientation for the spiritual well-being of the faithful. These two matters are the practice of first confession before first communion and the question of general absolution.

2246   After some initial experimentation had been conducted, Paul VI in 1973 reiterated the discipline of the Latin Church in regard to first confession.[a] In a spirit of exemplary fidelity, numerous bishops, priests, deacons, religious, teachers, and catechists set out to explain the importance of a discipline which the supreme authority of the Church had confirmed and to apply it for the benefit of the faithful. Ecclesial communities were comforted to know that the universal Church gave renewed assurance about a pastoral matter on which, previously, honest divergence of opinion existed. I am grateful to you for your own vigilance in this regard and ask you to continue to explain the Church's solicitude in maintaining this universal discipline, so rich in doctrinal background and confirmed by the experience of so many local Churches. With regard to children who have reached the age of reason, the Church is happy to guarantee the pastoral value of having them experience the sacramental expression of conversion before being initiated into the eucharistic sharing of the paschal mystery.

2247   As Supreme Pastor, Paul VI manifested similar deep solicitude for the great question of conversion in its sacramental aspect of individual confession. In an *Ad limina* visit earlier this year he referred at some length to the Pastoral Norms[b] governing the use of general absolution,[8] showing that these norms are in fact linked to the solemn teaching of the Council of Trent concerning the *divine precept* of individual confession. Once again he indicated the altogether *exceptional* character of general absolution. At the same time he asked the bishops to help their priests "to have an ever-greater appreciation of the splendid ministry of theirs as confessors. . . . Other works, for lack of time, may have to be postponed or even abandoned, but not the confessional."[c] I thank you for what you have done and will do to show the importance of the Church's wise discipline in an area that is so intimately linked with the work of reconciliation. In the name of the Lord Jesus, let us give

---

[7] See LG no. 23.

[a] See DOL 379.

[b] See DOL 361.

[8] Address, 20 April 1978, to bishops from the United States [DOL 378].

[c] DOL 378 no. 3139.

assurance, in union with the whole Church, to all our priests of the great supernatural effectiveness of a persevering ministry exercised through auricular confession, in fidelity to the command of the Lord and the teaching of his Church. And once again let us assure all our people of the great benefits derived from frequent confession. I am indeed convinced of the words of my predecessor Pius XII: "Not without the inspiration of the Holy Spirit was this practice introduced into the Church."[9]

▶   76.   JOHN PAUL II, Apostolic Exhortation *Catechesi tradendae*, 16 October 1979:

no. 23:   Catechesis and the sacraments [no. 609].

▶   See also Chapter 1, Section 8. Ecumenism.

[9]   AAS 35 (1943) 235.

Section 2. Baptism

SUMMARY (DOL 292–302). The conciliar Constitution devoted several articles to this first, foundational sacrament: the restoration of the adult catechumenate (art. 64–65); revision of the various rites of baptism (art. 66–69); blessing of the baptismal water at every baptism (art. 70). In addition to its important cross-references, the present section contains 11 texts through which the conciliar decisions have been carried out, and especially in regard to new rites.

—On the rite of baptism for children there is a decree promulgating the first *editio typica* (DOL 292) and a declaration about the second *editio typica* (DOL 293), as well as the General Introduction to Christian Initiation (DOL 294) and the Introduction to the *Rite of Baptism for Children* (DOL 295). There is also a decree extending the *vacatio legis* for the use of the new rite (DOL 296).

—On the rites of Christian initiation of adults there is the decree promulgating the first *editio typica* (DOL 300), the Introduction of the *Rite of Christian Initiation of Adults* (DOL 301), and from the Congregation for Divine Worship reflections on Chapter Four of this rite (DOL 302).

—Issues connected with the rites of baptism are treated in replies from the Congregation for the Doctrine of the Faith on the time for baptizing children (DOL 297) and from the Congregation for Divine Worship on whether baptism should be administered to children in the hospital or in their parish (DOL 298); though particular, these replies have universal implications. There is also a letter from the Congregation for Religious on ministers of baptism (DOL 299).

▶ 1. VATICAN COUNCIL II, Constitution on the Liturgy *Sacrosanctum Concilium*, 4 December 1963:

art. 61:   Use of the vernacular [no. 61].
64:     Adult catechumenate [no. 64].
66–69:   Rites of baptism [nos. 66–69].
70:     Blessing of baptismal water [no. 70].

▶ 23. SC RITES (Consilium), Instruction (first) *Inter Oecumenici*, 26 September 1964:

nos. 61:   Use of the vernacular [no. 353].
62–63:   Omissions in supplying ceremonies of baptism [nos. 354–355].

▶ 17. VATICAN COUNCIL II, Decree on the Missionary Activity of the Church *Ad gentes*, 17 December 1965:

no. 17:   Catechumenate and Christian initiation [no. 249].

▶ 140. SECRETARIAT FOR CHRISTIAN UNITY, Ecumenical Directory I, 14 May 1967:

nos. 48:   Eastern Orthodox Christians as godparents [no. 1002].
57:     Catholics as witnesses at the baptism of other Christians [no. 1011].

292. SC DIVINE WORSHIP, **Decree** *Ordinem Baptismi parvulorum*, promulgating the *editio typica* of the rite of baptism for children, 15 May 1969: AAS 61 (1969) 548; Not 5 (1969) 221.

2248   Vatican Council II decreed that the rite of baptism for children in the Roman Ritual was to be revised in order that: the rite might be better adapted to the actual condition of children; the role and responsibilities of parents and godparents might be more clearly expressed; suitable adaptations might be made for the baptism of a large number of people; suitable adaptations might likewise be made for a great number of recipients or for baptism administered by catechists in mission areas or by others in circumstances when the ordinary minister is unavailable; a rite would be composed to make it clear that children baptized according to the shorter rite have already been received into the Church (SC art. 67–69).[a]

This revision has been carried out by the Consilium for the Implementation of the Constitution on the Sacred Liturgy. By his apostolic authority Pope Paul VI has approved and ordered the publication of this new rite of baptism for children to replace the rite given in the Roman Ritual.

Therefore this Sacred Congregation, acting on the express mandate of the Pope, promulgates this rite and sets 8 September 1969 as its effective date.[b]

---

 [a] See DOL 1 nos. 67–69.

 [b] The first *editio typica* was published by the Vatican Polyglot Press in 1969. See DOL 293.

293. SC DIVINE WORSHIP, **Declaration** *Cum necesse sit*, on the second *editio typica* of the rite of baptism for children, 29 August 1973: Not 9 (1973) 268.

Since there is need for a second printing of the *Ordo baptismi parvulorum*, pub-   2249
lished in 1969, it seemed opportune to prepare a second, emended and expanded
edition of this rite. The more important changes are the following:

1.   Page 7 no. 2: instead of *a nativa hominum condicione* [from their natural human
condition] the text is *de potestate tenebrarum erepti* [rescued from the power of
darkness].ª

2.   Page 8 no. 5: after the word *homines* [people] the text adds, *ab omni culpae labe, tum
originali tum personali abluit eosque* [washes away every stain of sin, both original and
personal, and makes us. . .].ᵇ

3.   Page 15 no. 1: the words *habere et* [to have and] are deleted.ᶜ

4.   Page 85 no. 221: instead of *a potestate tenebrarum* [from the power of darkness] the
text has *ab originalis culpae labe nunc* [from the stain of original sin you now].ᵈ

Some other, less important emendations have been introduced into titles and
rubrics in order that there might be a closer correspondence to the words and style
found in the liturgical books published since 1969.ᵉ

By his authority Pope Paul VI has approved this second edition of the rite of
baptism for children. The Congregation for Divine Worship now issues it and
declares it to be the *editio typica*.

Incorporation of the emendations and additions made in the rite of baptism for
children into future vernacular editions is entrusted to the responsibility of the
conferences of bishops.

All things to the contrary notwithstanding.

294. SC DIVINE WORSHIP, *Christian Initiation*, **General Introduction,** 2nd
editio typica: Vatican Polyglot Press, 1973.*

1.   Through the sacraments of Christian initiation men and women are freed from   2250
the power of darkness. With Christ they die, are buried, and rise again. They
receive the Spirit of adoption that makes them God's sons and daughters and with
the entire people of God they celebrate the memorial of the Lord's death and
resurrection.¹

2.   Through baptism men and women are incorporated into Christ. They are   2251
formed into God's people and they obtain forgiveness of all their sins. They are

---

ª   From the General Introduction to Christian Initiation no. 2 [DOL 294 no. 2251].

ᵇ   Ibid. no. 5 [DOL 294 no. 2254].

ᶜ   From the *Rite of Baptism for Children*, Introduction no. 1 [DOL 295 no. 2285].

ᵈ   From ch. 7, texts for the rite of baptism for children, the alternate prayer of exorcism.

ᵉ   These and other variants are given in notes to the pertinent documents; see DOL 294 note *.

*   Variants in the 1969 edition are noted, with the designation "OBP '69."

¹   See AG no. 14 [DOL 17 no. 246].

rescued from the power of darkness and brought to the dignity of adopted children,[2,b] a new creation through water and the Holy Spirit. Hence they are called and are indeed the children of God.[3] Signed with the gift of the Spirit in confirmation, Christians more perfectly become the image of their Lord and are filled with the Holy Spirit. They bear witness to him before all the world and are working to bring the Body of Christ to its fullness as soon as possible.[4] Finally, they come to the table of the eucharist to eat the flesh and drink the blood of the Son of Man so that they may have eternal life[5] and show forth the unity of God's people. By offering themselves with Christ, they share in his universal sacrifice: the entire community of the redeemed offered to God by their High Priest.[6] They pray for a greater outpouring of the Holy Spirit so that the whole human race may be brought into the unity of God's family.[7] Thus the three sacraments of Christian initiation closely combine to bring the faithful to the full stature of Christ and to enable them to carry out the mission of the entire people of God in the Church and in the world.[8]

I. DIGNITY OF BAPTISM

2252   3.   Baptism is the door to life and to the kingdom of God. Christ offered this first sacrament of the New Law to all that they might have eternal life.[9] He entrusted this sacrament and the Gospel to his Church when he told his apostles: "Go, make disciples of all nations, and baptize them in the name of the Father, and of the Son, and of the Holy Spirit."[10] Baptism is therefore, above all, the sacrament of that faith by which men and women, enlightened by the Spirit's grace, respond to the Gospel of Christ. That is why the Church believes it is its most basic and necessary duty to inspire all, catechumens, parents of children still to be baptized, and godparents, to that true and living faith by which they hold fast to Christ and enter into or confirm their commitment to the New Covenant. To accomplish this, the Church prescribes the pastoral instruction of catechumens, the preparation of the children's parents, the celebration of God's word, and the profession of baptismal faith.

2253   4.   Further, baptism is the sacrament by which men and women are incorporated into the Church, built up together in the Spirit into a house where God lives,[11] into a holy nation and a royal priesthood.[12] It is a sacramental bond of unity linking all who have been signed by it.[13] Because of that unchangeable effect (signified in the Latin liturgy by the anointing of the baptized person with chrism in the presence of God's people), the rite of baptism is held in highest honor by all Christians. It may

---

2   See Col 1:13; Rom 8:15; Gal 4:5. See also Council of Trent, sess. 6, *Decr. de iustificatione* cap. 4: Denz-Schön 1524.

b   OPB '69: "are brought from their natural human condition to the dignity of adopted children."

3   See 1 Jn 3:1.

4   See AG no. 36 [DOL 17 no. 253].

5   See Jn 6:55.

6   See Augustine, *De civitate Dei* 10, 6: PL 41, 284. LG no. 11 [DOL 4 no. 141]; PO no. 2 [DOL 18 no. 257].

7   See LG no. 28 [DOL 4 no. 148].

8   See LG no. 31.

9   See Jn 3:5.

10   Mt 28.19.

11   See Eph 2:22.

12   See 1 Pt 2:9.

13   See UR no. 22 [DOL 6 no. 189].

never lawfully be repeated once it has been validly celebrated, even if by Christians from whom we are separated.

5.   Baptism, the cleansing with water by the power of the living word,[14] washes   2254
away every stain of sin, original and personal,[c] makes us sharers in God's own
life[15] and his adopted children.[16] As proclaimed in the prayers for the blessing of
the water, baptism is a cleansing water of rebirth[17] that makes us God's children
born from on high. The blessed Trinity is invoked over those who are to be baptized. Signed in this name, they are consecrated to the Trinity and enter into communion with the Father, the Son, and the Holy Spirit. They are prepared for this
high dignity and led to it by the scriptural readings, the prayer of the community,
and the threefold profession of faith.

6.   Far superior to the purifications of the Old Law, baptism produces these effects   2255
by the power of the mystery of the Lord's passion and resurrection. Those who are
baptized are united to Christ in a death like his.[18] They are buried with him in
death, they are given life again with him, and with him they rise again.[19] For
baptism recalls and effects the paschal mystery itself, because by means of it we
pass from the death of sin into life. Its celebration, therefore, should reflect the joy
of the resurrection, especially when it takes place during the Easter Vigil or on a
Sunday.

II. OFFICES AND MINISTRIES OF BAPTISM

7.   Christian instruction and the preparation for baptism are a vital concern of   2256
God's people, the Church, which hands on and nourishes the faith it has received
from the apostles. Through the ministry of the Church, adults are called by the
Holy Spirit to the Gospel and infants are baptized in the faith of the Church and
brought up in it. Therefore it is most important that catechists and other lay people
should work with priests and deacons in preparing for baptism. In the actual celebration, the people of God (represented not only by the parents, godparents, and
relatives, but also, as far as possible, by friends, neighbors, and some members of
the local Church) should take an active part. Thus they will show their common
faith and express their joy as the newly baptized are received into the community
of the Church.

8.   It is a very ancient custom of the Church that adults are not admitted to   2257
baptism without a godparent, a member of the Christian community who will assist
them at least in the final preparation for baptism and after baptism will help them
persevere in the faith and in their lives as Christians.

In the baptism of children, as well, a godparent is to be present in order to
represent the expansion of the spiritual family of the one to be baptized and the
role of the Church as a mother. As occasion offers, the godparent helps the parents
to lead the child to profess the faith and to show this by living it.

---

[14]   See Eph 5:26.

[c]   OPB '69 lacks "washes . . . personal."

[15]   See 2 Pt 1:4.

[16]   See Rom 8:15; Gal 4:5.

[17]   See Ti 3:5.

[18]   See Rom 6:4–5.

[19]   See Eph 2:5–6.

2258   9.   At least in the final rites of the catechumenate and in the actual celebration of baptism, the godparent's part is to testify to the faith of the adult candidate or, together with the parents, to profess the Church's faith, in which the child is being baptized.

2259   10.   Therefore the godparent, chosen by the catechumen or the family, must, in the judgment of the pastor, be qualified to carry out the proper liturgical functions mentioned in no. 9, that is:

    1.   be mature enough to undertake this responsibility;

    2.   be initiated with the three sacraments of initiation, baptism, confirmation, and eucharist;

    3.   be a member of the Catholic Church, canonically free to carry out this office. A baptized and believing Christian from a separated Church or Community may act as a godparent or Christian witness along with a Catholic godparent, at the request of the parents and in accordance with the norms laid down for various ecumenical cases.[d]

2260   11.   The ordinary ministers of baptism are bishops, priests, and deacons. In every celebration of this sacrament they should remember that within the Church they act in the name of Christ and by the power of the Holy Spirit. They should therefore be diligent in the ministry of the word of God and in the celebration of the sacrament. They must avoid any action that the faithful could rightly regard as favoritism.[20]

2261   12.   Bishops are the chief stewards of the mysteries of God and leaders of the entire liturgical life in the Church committed to them.[21] They thus direct the conferring of baptism, by which a sharing in the kingly priesthood of Christ is granted.[22] Therefore they should personally celebrate baptism, especially at the Easter Vigil. The preparation and baptism of adults is entrusted to them in a special way.

2262   13.   It is the duty of pastors to assist the bishop in the instruction and baptism of the adults entrusted to their care, unless the bishop makes other provisions. It is also their duty, with the assistance of catechists or other qualified lay people, to prepare the parents and godparents of children with appropriate pastoral guidance and to baptize the children.

2263   14.   Other priests and deacons, since they are cooperators in the ministry of bishops and parish priests (pastors), also prepare candidates for baptism and, by the invitation or consent of the bishop or parish priest (pastor), celebrate the sacrament.

2264   15.   The celebrant may be assisted by other priests and deacons and also by the laity in those parts that pertain to them, especially if there is a large number to be baptized. Provision for this is made in various parts of the rite.

2265   16.   In imminent danger of death and especially at the moment of death, when no priest or deacon is available, any member of the faithful, indeed anyone with the right intention, may and sometimes must administer baptism. If it is a question only of danger of death, then the sacrament should be administered by a member of the

---

    [d]   See DOL 147 nos. 1002, 1011.

    [20]   See SC art. 32 [DOL 1 no. 32]; GS no. 29.

    [21]   See CD no. 15 [DOL 7 no. 194].

    [22]   See LG no. 26 [DOL 4 no. 146].

faithful if possible, according to the shorter rite (nos. 157–164). Even in this case a small community should be formed to assist at the rite or at least one or two witnesses should be present if possible.

17. All laypersons, since they belong to the priestly people, and especially parents   2266
and, by reason of their work, catechists, midwives, family or social workers or nurses of the sick, as well as physicians and surgeons, should be thoroughly aware, according to their capacities, of the proper method of baptizing in case of emergency. They should be taught by parish priests, deacons, and catechists. Bishops should provide appropriate means within their diocese for such instruction.

III. REQUIREMENTS FOR THE CELEBRATION OF BAPTISM

18. The water used in baptism should be true water and clean, both for the sake of   2267
the authentic sacramental symbolism and for hygienic reasons.

19. The baptismal font, or the vessel in which on occasion the water is prepared   2268
for the celebration of the sacrament in the sanctuary, should be spotlessly clean and of pleasing design.

20. If the climate requires, provision should be made for the water to be heated   2269
beforehand.

21. Except in the case of necessity, the priest or deacon is to use only water that   2270
has been blessed for the rite. The water blessed at the Easter Vigil should, if possible, be kept and used throughout the Easter season to signify more clearly the relationship between the sacrament of baptism and the paschal mystery. Outside the Easter season, it is desirable that the water be blessed for each occasion, in order to express clearly through the words of blessing the mystery of salvation that the Church recalls and proclaims. If the baptistery is supplied with running water, the blessing is given to the water as it flows.

22. Either the rite of immersion, which is more suitable as a symbol of participa-   2271
tion in the death and resurrection of Christ, or the rite of infusion may lawfully be used in the celebration of baptism.

23. The words for conferring baptism in the Latin Church are: I BAPTIZE YOU IN   2272
THE NAME OF THE FATHER, AND OF THE SON, AND OF THE HOLY SPIRIT.

24. For celebrating the liturgy of the word of God a suitable place should be   2273
provided in the baptistery or in the church.

25. The baptistery is the area where the baptismal font flows or has been placed. It   2274
should be reserved for the sacrament of baptism and should be a place worthy for Christians to be reborn in water and the Holy Spirit. It may be situated in a chapel either inside or outside the church or in some other part of the church easily seen by the faithful; it should be large enough to accommodate a good number of people. After the Easter season, the Easter candle should be given a place of honor in the baptistery, so that when it is lighted for the celebration of baptism the candles of the newly baptized may easily be lighted from it.

26. In the celebration the parts of the rite that are to be celebrated outside the   2275
baptistery should be carried out in different areas of the church that most conveniently suit the size of the congregation and the several stages of the baptismal liturgy. When the baptistery cannot accommodate all the catechumens and the

congregation, the parts of the rite that are customarily celebrated inside the baptistery may be transferred to some other suitable area of the church.

2276   27. As far as possible, all recently born babies should be baptized at a common celebration on the same day. Except for a good reason, baptism should not be celebrated more than once on the same day in the same church.

2277   28. Further details concerning the time for baptism of adults and children will be found in the respective rites. But at all times the celebration of the sacrament should make prominent its paschal character.

2278   29. Parish priests (pastors) must carefully and without delay record in the baptismal register the names of those baptized, the minister, parents and godparents, and the place and date of baptism.

IV. ADAPTATIONS BY THE CONFERENCES OF BISHOPS

2279   30. According to the Constitution on the Liturgy (art. 63, b),[e] it is within the competence of the conferences of bishops to compose for their local rituals a section corresponding to this one in the Roman Ritual, adapted to the needs of their respective regions. After it has been confirmed by the Apostolic See, it may be used in the regions for which it was prepared.

In this connection, it is the responsibility of the conferences of bishops:

1. to decide on the adaptations mentioned in the Constitution on the Liturgy, art. 39;[f]

2. carefully and prudently to weigh what elements of a people's distinctive traditions and culture may suitably be admitted into divine worship and so to propose to the Apostolic See other adaptations considered useful or necessary that will be introduced with its consent;

3. to retain distinctive elements of any existing local rituals, as long as they conform to the Constitution on the Liturgy and correspond to contemporary needs, or to modify these elements;

4. to prepare translations of the texts that genuinely reflect the characteristics of various languages and cultures and to add, whenever helpful, music suitable for singing;

5. to adapt and augment the Introductions contained in the Roman Ritual, so that the ministers may fully understand the meaning of the rites and carry them out effectively;

6. to arrange the material in the various editions of the liturgical books prepared under the guidance of the conferences of bishops so that these books may be best suited for pastoral use.

2280   31. Taking into consideration especially the norms in the Constitution on the Liturgy art. 37–40, 65,[g] the conferences of bishops in mission countries have the responsibility to judge whether certain initiation ceremonies in use among some peoples can be adapted for the rite of Christian baptism and to decide whether these ceremonies are to be incorporated into it.

---

e   See DOL 1 no. 63.

f   See DOL 1 no. 39.

g   See DOL 1 nos. 37–40, 65.

32. When the Roman Ritual for baptism provides several optional formularies,   2281
local rituals may add other formularies of the same kind.

33. The celebration of baptism is greatly enhanced by the use of song. It stimulates   2282
a sense of unity among those present, it fosters their praying together, and it
expresses the joy of Easter that should permeate the whole rite. Conferences of
bishops should therefore encourage and help specialists in music to compose settings for the liturgical texts regarded as suitable for congregational singing.

V. ADAPTATIONS BY THE MINISTER OF BAPTISM

34. Taking into account existing circumstances and other needs, as well as the   2283
wishes of the faithful, the minister should make full use of the various options
allowed in the rite.

35. In addition to the adaptations that are provided in the Roman Ritual for the   2284
dialogue and blessings, the minister may make other adaptations for special circumstances. These adaptations will be indicated more fully in the Introductions to the
rites of baptism for adults and for children.

295. SC DIVINE WORSHIP, *Rite of Baptism for Children,* **Introduction,** 2nd
editio typica: Vatican Polyglot Press, 1973.*

INTRODUCTION

I. IMPORTANCE OF BAPTIZING CHILDREN

1.   The term "children" or "infants" refers to those who have not yet reached the   2285
age of discernment and therefore cannot profess personal faith.[a]

2.   From the earliest times, the Church, to which the mission of preaching the   2286
Gospel and of baptizing was entrusted, has baptized not only adults but children as
well. Our Lord said: "Unless a man is reborn in water and the Holy Spirit, he cannot
enter the kingdom of God."[1] The Church has always understood these words to
mean that children should not be deprived of baptism, because they are baptized in
the faith of the Church, a faith proclaimed for them by their parents and godparents, who represent both the local Church and the whole society of saints and
believers: "The whole Church is the mother of all and the mother of each."[2]

3.   To fulfill the true meaning of the sacrament, children must later be formed in   2287
the faith in which they have been baptized. The foundation of this formation will
be the sacrament itself that they have already received. Christian formation, which
is their due, seeks to lead them gradually to learn God's plan in Christ, so that they
may ultimately accept for themselves the faith in which they have been baptized.

---

*   Variants in the 1969 edition are noted, with the designation "OBP '69."

[a]   OBP '69: "cannot have or profess personal faith."

[1]   Jn 3:5.

[2]   Augustine, *Ep.* 98, 5: PL 33, 362.

II. MINISTRIES AND ROLES IN THE CELEBRATION OF BAPTISM

2288   4.   The people of God, that is, the Church, made present by the local community, has an important part to play in the baptism of both children and adults.

Before and after the celebration of the sacrament, the child has a right to the love and help of the community. During the rite, in addition to the ways of congregational participation mentioned in the General Introduction to Christian Initiation no. 7,[b] the community exercises its duty when it expresses its assent together with the celebrant after the profession of faith by the parents and godparents. In this way it is clear that the faith in which the children are baptized is not the private possession of the individual family, but the common treasure of the whole Church of Christ.

2289   5.   Because of the natural relationships, parents have a ministry and a responsibility in the baptism of infants more important than those of the godparents.

1.   Before the celebration of the sacrament, it is of great importance that parents, moved by their own faith or with the help of friends or other members of the community, should prepare to take part in the rite with understanding. They should be provided with suitable means such as books, letters addressed to them, and catechisms designed for families. The parish priest (pastor) should make it his duty to visit them or see that they are visited; he should try to gather a group of families together and prepare them for the coming celebration by pastoral counsel and common prayer.

2.   It is very important that the parents be present at the celebration in which their child is reborn in water and the Holy Spirit.

3.   In the celebration of baptism, the father and mother have special parts to play. They listen to the words addressed to them by the celebrant, they join in prayer along with the congregation, and they exercise a genuine ministry when: a. they publicly ask that the child be baptized; b. they sign their child with the sign of the cross after the celebrant; c. they renounce Satan and recite the profession of faith; d. they (and especially the mother) carry the child to the font; e. they hold the lighted candle; f. they are blessed with the prayers formulated specifically for mothers and fathers.

4.   A parent unable to make the profession of faith (for example, not being a Catholic) may keep silent. Such a parent, when making the request for the child's baptism is asked only to make arrangements or at least to give permission for the child's instruction in the faith of its baptism.

5.   After baptism it is the responsibility of the parents, in their gratitude to God and in fidelity to the duty they have undertaken, to assist the child to know God, whose adopted child it has become, to prepare the child to receive confirmation and participate in the holy eucharist. In this duty they are again to be helped by the parish priest (pastor) by suitable means.

2290   6.   Each child may have a godfather (*patrinus*) and a godmother (*matrina*), the word "godparents" is used in the rite to describe both.

2291   7.   In addition to what is said about the ordinary minister of baptism in the General Introduction to Christian Initiation nos. 11–15,[c] the following should be noted:

---

    b   See DOL 294 no. 2256.

    c   See DOL 294 nos. 2260–64.

1. It is the duty of the priest to prepare families for the baptism of their children and to help them in the task of Christian formation that they have undertaken. It is the duty of the bishop to coordinate such pastoral efforts in the diocese, with the help also of deacons and lay people.

2. It is also the duty of the priest to arrange that baptism is always celebrated with proper dignity and, as far as possible, adapted to the circumstances and wishes of the families concerned. All who perform the rite of baptism should do so with exactness and reverence; they must also try to be understanding and friendly to all.

III. TIME AND PLACE FOR THE BAPTISM OF CHILDREN

8.   As for the time of baptism, the first consideration is the welfare of the child,   2292
that it may not be deprived of the benefit of the sacrament; then the health of the mother must be considered, so that, if at all possible, she too may be present. Then, as long as they do not interfere with the greater good of the child, there are pastoral considerations, such as allowing sufficient time to prepare the parents and to plan the actual celebration in order to bring out its true character effectively. Accordingly:

1.   If the child is in danger of death, it is to be baptized without delay, in the manner laid down in no. 21.

2.   In other cases, as soon as possible—if need be, even before the child is born, the parents should be in touch with the parish priest (pastor) concerning the baptism, so that proper preparation may be made for the celebration.

3.   An infant should be baptized within the first weeks after birth. The conference of bishops may, for sufficiently serious pastoral reasons, determine a longer interval of time between birth and baptism.

4.   When the parents are not yet prepared to profess the faith or to undertake the duty of bringing up their children as Christians, it is for the parish priest (pastor), keeping in mind whatever regulations may have been laid down by the conference of bishops, to determine the time for the baptism of infants.[d]

9.   To bring out the paschal character of baptism, it is recommended that the   2293
sacrament be celebrated during the Easter Vigil or on Sunday, when the Church commemorates the Lord's resurrection. On Sunday, baptism may be celebrated even during Mass, so that the entire community may be present and the relationship between baptism and eucharist may be clearly seen; but this should not be done too often. Regulations for the celebration of baptism during the Easter Vigil or at Mass on Sunday will be set out later.

10.   So that baptism may clearly appear as the sacrament of the Church's faith and   2294
of incorporation into the people of God, it should normally be celebrated in the parish church, which must have a baptismal font.

11.   After consulting the local parish priest (pastor), the bishop may permit or   2295
direct that a baptismal font be placed in another church or public oratory within the parish boundaries. In these places, too, the right to celebrate baptism belongs ordinarily to the parish priest (pastor).

12.   Except in case of danger of death, baptism should not be celebrated in private   2296
homes.

---

[d]   On the time of baptism see DOL 297.

2297 13. Unless the bishop decides otherwise (see no. 11), baptism should not be celebrated in hospitals, except in cases of emergency or for some other compelling pastoral reason. But care should always be taken that the parish priest is notified and that the parents are suitably prepared beforehand.[e]

2298 14. While the liturgy of the word is being celebrated, it is desirable that children should be taken to some other place. But provision must be made for the mothers or godmothers to attend the liturgy of the word; the children should therefore be entrusted to the care of other women.

IV. STRUCTURE OF THE RITE OF BAPTIZING CHILDREN

A. ORDER OF BAPTISM CELEBRATED BY THE ORDINARY MINISTER

2299 15. Baptism, whether for one child, or for several, or even for a larger number, should be celebrated by the ordinary minister and with the full rite when there is no immediate danger of death.

2300 16. The rite begins with the reception of the children. This is to indicate the desire of the parents and godparents, as well as the intention of the Church, concerning the celebration of the sacrament of baptism. These purposes are expressed in action when the parents and the celebrant trace the sign of the cross on the foreheads of the children.

2301 17. Then the liturgy of the word is directed toward stirring up the faith of the parents, godparents, and congregation and toward praying in common for the fruits of baptism before the sacrament itself. This part of the celebration consists of the reading of one or more passages from holy Scripture; a homily, followed by a period of silence; the general intercessions, with its concluding prayer, drawn up in the style of an exorcism, to introduce either the anointing with the oil of catechumens or the laying on of hands.

2302 18. In the celebration of the sacrament:

1. The immediate preparation consists of:

   a. the solemn prayer of the celebrant, which, by invoking God and recalling his plan of salvation, blesses the water of baptism or makes reference to its earlier blessing;

   b. the renunciation of Satan on the part of parents and godparents and their profession of faith, to which is added the assent of the celebrant and the community; and the final interrogation of the parents and godparents.

2. The sacrament itself consists of the washing in water by way of immersion or infusion, depending on local custom, and the invocation of the blessed Trinity.

3. The completion of the sacrament consists, first, of the anointing with chrism, which signifies the royal priesthood of the baptized and enrollment into the company of the people of God; then of the ceremonies of the white garment, lighted candle, and *ephpheta* rite (the last of which is optional).

2303 19. Before the altar to prefigure the future sharing in the eucharist, the celebrant introduces and all recite the Lord's Prayer, in which God's children pray to their Father in heaven. Finally, a prayer of blessing is said over the mothers, fathers, and all present, to ask the outpouring of God's grace upon them.

---

[e] See DOL 298.

B. Shorter Rite of Baptism

20. In the shorter rite of baptism designed for the use of catechists,[3] the reception   2304
of the children, the celebration of the word of God, or the instruction by the
minister, and the general intercessions are retained. Before the font, the minister
offers a prayer invoking God and recalling the history of salvation as it relates to
baptism. After the baptismal washing, an adapted formulary is recited in place of
the anointing with chrism and the whole rite concludes in the customary way. The
omissions, therefore, are the exorcism, the anointing with oil of catechumens and
with chrism, and the *ephphetha* rite.

21. The shorter rite for baptizing a child in danger of death and in the absence of   2305
the ordinary minister has a twofold structure:

1. At the moment of death or when there is urgency because of imminent
danger of death, the minister,[4] omitting all other ceremonies, pours water (not
necessarily blessed but real and natural water) on the head of the child and pronounces the customary formulary.[5]

2. If, however, it is prudently judged that there is sufficient time, several of
the faithful may be gathered together and, if one of them is able to lead the others
in a short prayer, the following rite may be used: an explanation by the minister of
the sacrament, a short set of general intercessions, the profession of faith by the
parents or one godparent and the pouring of the water with the customary words.
But if those present are uneducated, the minister of the sacrament should recite the
profession of faith aloud and baptize according to the rite for use in danger of
death.

22. In danger of death, the priest or deacon may also use this shorter form if   2306
necessary. If there is time and he has the sacred chrism, the parish priest (pastor) or
other priest enjoying the same faculty should not fail to confer confirmation after
baptism. In this case he omits the postbaptismal anointing with chrism.

V. ADAPTATIONS BY CONFERENCES OF BISHOPS OR BY BISHOPS

23. In addition to the adaptations provided for in the General Introduction (nos.   2307
30–33), the baptismal rite for infants admits other variations, to be determined by
the conferences of bishops.

24. As is indicated in the Roman Ritual, the following matters are left to the   2308
discretion of the conferences:

1. As local customs may dictate, the questioning about the name of the child
may be arranged in different ways: the name may have been given already or may
be given during the rite of baptism.

2. The anointing with oil of catechumens may be omitted (nos. 50, 87).

3. The formulary of renunciation may be made more pointed and detailed
(nos. 57, 94, 121).

4. If the number to be baptized is very great, the anointing with chrism may
be omitted (no. 125).

5. The *ephphetha* rite may be retained (nos. 64, 101).

---

[3]   See SC art. 68 [DOL 1 no. 68].

[4]   See General Introduction to Christian Initiation no. 16 [DOL 294 no. 2265].

[5]   See ibid. no. 23 [DOL 294 no. 2272].

2309   25. In many countries parents are sometimes not ready for the celebration of baptism or they ask for their children to be baptized even though the latter will not afterward receive a Christian education and will even lose the faith. Since to instruct such parents and to inquire about their faith in the course of the rite itself is not enough, conferences of bishops may issue pastoral directives, for the guidance of parish priests (pastors), to determine a longer interval between birth and baptism.

2310   26. It is for the bishop to decide for his diocese whether catechists may give the homily on their own or only by reading a written text.

VI. ADAPTATIONS BY THE MINISTER

2311   27. During meetings to prepare the parents for the baptism of their children, it is important that the instruction should be supported by prayer and religious rites. For this the various elements provided in the rite of baptism for the celebration of the word of God will prove helpful.

2312   28. When the baptism of children is celebrated as part of the Easter Vigil, the ritual should be arranged as follows:

 1. At a convenient time and place before the Easter Vigil the rite of receiving the children is celebrated. The liturgy of the word may be omitted at the end, according to circumstances, and the prayer of exorcism is said, followed by the anointing with oil of catechumens.

 2. The celebration of the sacrament (nos. 56–58, 60–63) takes place after the blessing of the water, as is indicated in the rite of the Easter Vigil.

 3. The assent of the celebrant and community (no. 59) is omitted, as are the presentation of the lighted candle (no. 64) and the *ephphetha* rite (no. 65).

 4. The conclusion of the rite (nos. 67–71) is omitted.

2313   29. If baptism takes place during Sunday Mass, the Mass for that Sunday is used, or, on the Sundays of the Christmas season and of Ordinary Time, the Mass for the Baptism of Children,[f] and the celebration takes place as follows:

 1. The rite of receiving the children (nos. 33–43) takes place at the beginning of Mass and the greeting and penitential rite of the Mass are omitted.

 2. In the liturgy of the word:

  a. The readings are taken from the Mass of the Sunday. But in the Christmas season and in Ordinary Time they may also be taken from those given in the Lectionary for Mass (III, 474–489)[g] or in this baptismal rite (nos. 44, 186–215).

  When a ritual Mass is prohibited, one of the readings may be taken from the texts provided for the celebration of baptism for children, with attention paid to the pastoral benefit of the faithful and the character of the liturgical day.[h]

  b. The homily is based on the sacred texts, but should take account of the baptism that is to take place.

---

 [f]   OBP '69: "29. If baptism takes place during Sunday Mass, the Mass for that Sunday is used and the celebration takes place as follows:"

 [g]   English edition (1969), Readings nos. 757–761.

 [h]   OBP '69: "a. The readings are taken from the Mass of the Sunday or, for special reasons, from those provided in the baptismal rite."

c. The *Credo* is not said, since the profession of faith by the entire community before baptism takes its place.

d. The general intercessions are taken from those used in the rite of baptism (nos. 47–48). At the end, however, before the invocation of the saints, petitions are added for the universal Church and the needs of the world.

3. The celebration of baptism continues with the prayer of exorcism, anointing, and other ceremonies described in the rite (nos. 49–66).

4. After the celebration of baptism, the Mass continues in the usual way with the presentation of the gifts.

5. For the blessing at the end of Mass, the priest may use one of the formularies provided in the rite of baptism (nos. 70, 247–249).

30. If baptism is celebrated during Mass on weekdays, it is arranged in basically   2314
the same way as on Sunday, but the readings for the liturgy of the word may be
taken from those that are provided in the rite of baptism (nos. 44, 186–194,
204–215).

31. In accordance with the General Introduction no. 34,[i] the minister may make   2315
some adaptations in the rite as circumstances require, such as:

1. If the child's mother died in childbirth, this should be taken into account in
the opening instruction (no. 36), general intercessions (nos. 47, 217–220), and final
blessing (nos. 70, 247–248).

2. In the dialogue with the parents (nos. 37–38, 76–77), their answers should
be taken into account: if they have not answered *Baptism*, but *Faith*, or *The grace of
Christ*, or *Entrance into the Church*, or *Everlasting life*, then the minister does not begin by
saying *Baptism*, but uses *Faith*, or *The grace of Christ*, and so forth.

3. The rite of bringing a child already baptized to the church (nos. 165–185),
which has been drawn up for use only when the child has been baptized in danger
of death, should be adapted to cover other contingencies, for example, when children have been baptized during a time of religious persecution or temporary disagreement between the parents.

(N.B. 1. The texts of the psalms and of the New Testament are taken from the Neo-
Vulgate edition of the Bible. 2. Liturgical texts written in the masculine gender can
be changed to the feminine; those written in the singular can be changed to the
plural.)

296. SC DIVINE WORSHIP, **Decree** *Petentibus nonnullis Conferentiis,* extending
the *vacatio legis* of the *Rite of Baptism for Children*, 10 July 1969: AAS 61 (1969)
549–550; Not 5 (1969) 222.

Several conferences of bishops have requested that the *vacatio legis* until 8   2316
September 1969 for the new *Rite of Baptism for Children* be extended so that the work
of translation of the rite might proceed at a calmer pace and pastoral action might
be planned more effectively. At the direction of Pope Paul VI, this Congregation for
Divine Worship decrees that the new *Rite of Baptism for Children,* promulgated on 15
May 1969, is to become effective on 29 March, that is, Easter Sunday 1970. But this
applies in such a way that from 8 September 1969 use of either the new rite or the

---

[i] See DOL 294 no. 2283.

rite contained in the Roman Ritual or Pontifical is discretionary; from 29 March 1970 use of the new rite is obligatory.

Furthermore, once the individual conferences of bishops have prepared a vernacular translation and received this Congregation's confirmation, they are authorized to set a suitable effective date earlier than 29 March 1970 for the new *Rite of Baptism for Children.*

All things to the contrary notwithstanding.

297. SC DOCTRINE OF THE FAITH, **Reply** (Togo) of Cardinal F. Seper to Bishop B. Henrion, of Dapango, on the time for the baptism of children, 13 July 1970: Not 7 (1971) 69–70 (French).

2317
In its letter to you on 15 February 1967 replying to your proposal about restoring the catechumenate for children, the Congregation for the Doctrine of the Faith advised you of its intention to pursue study of the issue, but without prejudice to the traditional practice or the need to insist on the parents' responsibility.

I am now able to pass on to you the conclusions of the study commission appointed for this matter. These conclusions have been approved by the cardinals of this Congregation and ratified by Pope Paul VI on 19 June 1970.

The following points, therefore, have been decided.

2318
I. *In the case of infants of:*

    1. Practicing Christians:

        a. The guide is to be the Introduction of the new *Rite of Baptism,* especially in what concerns the preparation of parents.[a]

        b. The normal desire of devout parents is for their child to be born into the life of the children of God *as soon as possible.*[b]

    2. Non-Christian parents or nonpracticing Christian parents: N.B. "Nonpracticing" should be understood in this case to mean Christians who are polygamous, unmarried, married lawfully but lapsed altogether from the regular practice of the faith, or those who request their child's baptism as a purely social convention.

        a. It is essential to bring them to a recognition of their responsibilities.

        b. It is also essential to evaluate the sufficiency of the guarantees concerning the Catholic upbringing of the children. These guarantees are given by some member of the family or by the godfather or godmother or by the support of the Christian community. (By guarantees we mean that there is a well-founded hope of a Catholic upbringing.)

        c. If the conditions are sufficient in the judgment of the pastor, the Church can go ahead with the baptism, because the children are baptized in the faith of the Church.

        d. If the conditions are insufficient, there is the possibility of proposing to the parents: the enrollment of the child with a view to its being baptized later; further pastoral meetings as a way of preparing them for the rite of reception of their child for baptism.

---

    a   See DOL 295 no. 2289.

    b   See DOL 295 no. 2292.

II. *In the case of adults and of children, as these terms are defined in CIC* can. 745 par. 1–2:   2319

The catechumenate is to be restored in keeping with the will of Vatican Council II and with the adaptations that are left to the decision of the conferences of bishops.

298. SC DIVINE WORSHIP, **Reply** (Rome) of Cardinal B. Gut to Cardinal A. Dell'Acqua, Vicar of the Diocese of Rome, on the baptism of children in hospitals or in their parishes, 19 August 1970: Not 7 (1971) 61–63 (Italian).

This Congregation has received the letter, dated 7 July 1970 (Prot. N. 9289/70), with the request of Your Eminence to know its mind regarding application in the Diocese of Rome of the new legislation on administering baptism for children.   2320

You make reference in particular to the "Notice" of 24 June 1970, which urges the faithful to celebrate baptism as a rule in the parish not in hospitals, "except in cases of emergency or for some other compelling pastoral reason."[a] Some have thought this to be at variance with art. 154 of the Roman Synod, promulgated 29 June 1966.

After a full report of the problem to Pope Paul VI, I have the responsibility to communicate the following reply.

1. The recent "Notice" does not seem to be at variance with the Roman Synod.   2321

The main reason is that the matter involved is something altogether new and in a context different from that considered by the Roman Synod. The *Rite of Baptism for Children* amounts to a reordering of the disciplinary, liturgical, and ritual elements in the baptism of infants. A new act of legislation is involved that supplants the previous one. Naturally, since a law for the entire Church is at issue, this law has its source in a papal act, which brings about the repeal of previous legislation. The decree prefixed to the *Rite* clearly states the Pope's approval and the mandate of promulgation *nomine Summi Pontificis.*

Even leaving aside the juridic consideration, the new arrangement is not in conflict with the Roman Synod. The Synod granted to the Cardinal Vicar the faculty to allow (*concedere poterit*) baptisms in hospitals. The *Rite of Baptism for Children* nos. 11 and 13 contains an equivalent expression: "the bishop . . . may *permit* or *direct* that a baptismal font be placed in a church or public oratory within the parish boundaries" (no. 11).[b] The new discipline in a sense extends to the entire Church what had been a particular arrangement for Rome.

If, in the spirit of the new *Rite of Baptism for Children,* the Cardinal Vicar has thought it wise to modify previous procedures, he has in fact used a right deriving from the Synod and from the Introduction of the new *Rite of Baptism for Children.*

2. This Congregation values highly the intense effort to reestablish the sense of belonging to a parish and the spirit of community, which the *Rite of Baptism* strongly emphasizes. The parish must always be viewed as the center of the spiritual and sacramental life and the parish community as the natural familial setting for initiation into the sacraments, upbringing in the faith, and the development of the Christian personality.   2322

---

a   The text of this is given in Not 7 (1971) 59–61.

b   DOL 295 no. 2295.

2323   3.   Given the situation of big cities and of Rome in particular, it would seem that from a pastoral point of view the new arrangements may be put into effect gradually as prudent judgment suggests.

a.   Chaplains, sisters, and anyone else in more immediate contact with parents will give their wholehearted support to the request that people center their interests on the parish. For the newcomers of the Christian family are reborn to the life of grace within the Christian community that by nature is first.

b.   Measures must therefore be taken to ensure that parents in turning back to the parish will find there a welcoming ambience, a preparation, and a kind of celebration that meet the demands of the new *Rite of Baptism*. Contact with the parish must not be a mere formality that can be just as well taken care of at the hospital. This applies most of all to what concerns the pastoral preparation of parents, which should be started, if at all possible, before the child's birth.

c.   Even so, in certain instances a hospital church or chapel can well serve as a strong support for the pastoral ministry of the parish in regard to baptism. It is not so much a question of the mere number of baptisms administered at the hospital; rather the continuing presence of a zealous chaplain, with proper help and in responsible cooperation with the pastor involved, can contribute to a suitable preparation of the parents for the baptism of the child.

d.   The Cardinal Vicar must make the choice of hospitals to be given permission to have a baptismal font on a case-by-case basis. He must take into consideration the condition of the people who use the hospitals and their spiritual needs. Thus it will be necessary to issue precise norms and to establish clearly defined conditions concerning the regulation of pastoral work, the way places of worship are to be arranged, the carrying out of the rite with all the planning required for its true worthiness. The permission must be firmly denied whenever it is foreseen that such conditions cannot be fulfilled. The vicariate offices responsible must ascertain whether or not such conditions exist.

e.   As far as possible, conferral of individual baptisms must be avoided in favor of a community celebration, which better brings out the sense of the family of God. To this end days and schedules should be set when baptism can be administered so as to take care of all recently born infants.

f.   The ritual and pastoral directives must be put into effect wherever baptism is administered, either by right or by privilege. This applies also to the patriarchal basilicas.

299. SC RELIGIOUS AND SECULAR INSTITUTES, **Letter** to Rev. P. Arrupe, SJ, President of the Union of Superiors General, on baptism by nonclerical men religious and women religious, 12 October 1970 (Italian).*

2324   I wish to inform you that Pope Paul VI has agreed to approve the following. Outside mission territories in the continued absence of a regular minister of baptism, nonclerical men religious and women religious may administer this sacrament. They are to observe the "Rite of Baptism for Children Administered by a Catechist" from the *Rite of Baptism for Children*, promulgated by the Congregation for Divine Worship, 15 May 1969.[a]

---

   *   Text, CommRel 52 (1971) 188–189.

   [a]   See DOL 295.

The indult is granted upon the request of local Ordinaries, who must submit the case in question to the Congregation for the Sacraments. The granting of the faculty is subject to the following conditions:

a. In the locale involved no regular minister (priest or deacon) is present. It is for the national conference of bishops to decide whether this continued absence (physical or moral) for all or part of a country is a fact.

b. The nonclerical men religious and the women religious must be eighteen years of age, have made their first religious profession or accepted an equivalent obligation, and they must also have received sufficient catechetical instruction.

In granting this indult the national conference of bishops and the individual local Ordinaries are reminded that they must see to the observance of those norms of the *Codex Iuris Canonici* not explicitly repealed by the *Rite of Baptism for Children*, regarding godparents, the time, the place, and the recording of the baptism.   2325

Finally, a nonclerical man religious or a woman religious who has administered baptism has the obligation of carefully recording the baptism as soon as possible, in keeping with the norms of the *Codex Iuris Canonici* and the Instruction *Sacrosanctum* of the Congregation of the Sacraments.   2326

I request you to notify the superiors general concerned of the aforementioned concession.

▶   153.   SECRETARIAT FOR CHRISTIAN UNITY, Reply (Colombia), on non-Catholic Christians as godparents, 3 December 1970.

▶   169.   SC CLERGY, *General Catechetical Directory*, 11 April 1971:

nos. 57:   Catechesis for baptism [no. 1104].
      130:           Adult catechumenate [no. 1114].

300. SC DIVINE WORSHIP, **Decree** *Ordinis Baptismi adultorum*, promulgating the new rite of Christian initiation of adults, 6 January 1972: AAS 64 (1972) 252; Not 8 (1972) 68.

The Second Vatican Council prescribed the revision of the rite of baptism of adults and decreed that the catechumenate for adults, divided into several stages, should be restored. By this means the time of the catechumenate, which is intended as a period of well-suited instruction, would be sanctified by liturgical rites to be celebrated at successive intervals of time.[a] The Council likewise decreed that both the solemn and simple rites of adult baptism should be revised, with proper attention to the restored catechumenate.[b]   2327

In observance of these decrees, the Congregation for Divine Worship prepared a new rite for the Christian initiation of adults, which Pope Paul VI has approved. The Congregation now publishes it and declares the present edition to be the *editio typica*, to replace the rite of baptism of adults now in the Roman Ritual. It likewise decrees that this new rite may be used in Latin at once and in the vernacular from the day to be appointed by the conference of bishops after it has prepared a translation and had it confirmed by the Apostolic See.

---

a   See DOL 1 no. 64.

b   See DOL 1 no. 66.

All things to the contrary notwithstanding.

301. SC DIVINE WORSHIP, *Rite of Christian Initiation of Adults,* **Introductions,** 6 January 1972: Vatican Polyglot Press, 1972.*

INTRODUCTION

2328   1.   The rite of Christian initiation described below is designed for adults who, after hearing the mystery of Christ proclaimed, consciously and freely seek the living God and enter the way of faith and conversion as the Holy Spirit opens their hearts. By God's help they will be strengthened spiritually during their preparation and at the proper time will receive the sacraments fruitfully.

2329   2.   This rite includes not only the celebration of the sacraments of baptism, confirmation, and the eucharist, but also all the rites of the catechumenate. A catechumenate, endorsed by the ancient practice of the Church and adapted to contemporary missionary work throughout the world, was so widely requested that the Second Vatican Council decreed its restoration, revision, and adaptation to local traditions.[1]

2330   3.   So that it will be accommodated more closely to the work of the Church and to the circumstances of individuals, parishes, and missions, the rite of initiation first gives the complete or usual form, intended for the preparation of a large number of people (see nos. 68–239). By making simple changes, pastors may adapt this form for the preparation of one person. Then, for special cases, there is the simple form, which may be carried out in one celebration (see nos. 240–273) or in several celebrations (see nos. 274–277), as well as a short form for those in danger of death (see nos. 278–294).

I. STRUCTURE OF THE INITIATION OF ADULTS

2331   4.   The initiation of catechumens is a gradual process that takes place within the community of the faithful. Together with the catechumens, the faithful reflect upon the value of the paschal mystery, renew their own conversion, and by their example lead the catechumens to obey the Holy Spirit more generously.

2332   5.   The rite of initiation is suited to the spiritual journey of adults, which varies according to the many forms of God's grace, the free cooperation of the individuals, the action of the Church, and the circumstances of time and place.

2333   6.   On this journey, besides periods for making inquiry and for maturing (see no. 7) there are stages or "steps": the progress of the catechumen is, as it were, a passage through a gateway or the climbing of another "step."

      a.   First stage [catechumenate]: at the point of initial conversion, they wish to become Christians and are accepted as catechumens by the Church.

---

    *   Translation based on the emended, second printing of the *editio typica* (Vatican Polyglot Press, 1974); this also carries the General Introduction to Christian Initiation, not carried in the first printing (1972).

    [1]   See SC art. 64–66 [DOL 1 nos. 64–66]; AG no. 14 [DOL 17 no. 246]; CD no. 14 [DOL 7 no. 193].

b. Second stage [final preparation]: when their faith has grown and the catechumenate is almost completed, they are admitted to a more intense preparation for
the sacraments.

c. Third stage [sacraments of initiation]: after the spiritual preparation is
completed, they receive the sacraments of Christian initiation.

These three stages, "steps," or "gateways" are to be considered as the major,
more intense moments of initiation and are marked by three liturgical rites: the first
by the rite of entrance into the order of catechumens, the second by the election or
enrollment of names, and the third by the celebration of Christian initiation.

7.   The stages lead to the periods for making inquiry and maturing; alternatively,   2334
the periods may also be considered to prepare for the stages.

a. The first period consists of inquiry on the part of the candidates and of
evangelization and the precatechumenate on the part of the Church. It ends with
entrance into the order of catechumens.

b. The second period, which begins with this entrance into the order of catechumens and which may last for several years, includes catechesis and the rites
connected with catechesis. It comes to an end on the day of election.

c. The third period, shorter in length, ordinarily coincides with the Lenten
preparation for the Easter celebration and the sacraments. It is a time of purification
and enlightenment.

d. The final period goes through the whole Easter season and is devoted to the
postbaptismal catechesis or mystagogy. It is a time for deepening the Christian
experience, for gaining spiritual fruit, and for entering more closely into the life and
unity of the community of the faithful.

Thus there are four continuous periods: the precatechumenate, marked by the
hearing of the first preaching of the Gospel; the catechumenate, set aside for a
complete catechesis; the period of purification and enlightenment (Lenten preparation) for a more intense spiritual preparation; and the period of postbaptismal
catechesis or mystagogy, marked by the new experience of sacraments and community.

8.   The whole initiation must bear a strong paschal character, since the initiation   2335
of Christians is the first sacramental sharing in the death and rising of Christ and
since, in addition, the period of purification and enlightenment ordinarily coincides
with Lent[2] and the postbaptismal catechesis or mystagogy with the Easter season.
In this way Lent achieves its full force as a more intense preparation of the elect and
the Easter Vigil is considered the proper time for the sacraments of initiation.[3]
Because of pastoral needs, however, the sacraments of initiation may be celebrated
outside these seasons.

A. Evangelization and Precatechumenate

9.   Although the rite of initiation begins with admission to the catechumenate,   2336
the preceding period or precatechumenate is of great importance and as a rule
should not be omitted. It is a time of evangelization: faithfully and constantly the
living God is proclaimed and Jesus Christ whom he has sent for the salvation of all.
Thus those who are not yet Christians, their hearts opened by the Holy Spirit, may
believe and be freely converted to the Lord and commit themselves sincerely to

---

[2]   See SC art. 109 [DOL 1 no. 109].

[3]   This amends CIC can. 790.

him. For he is the way, the truth, and the life who fulfills all their spiritual expectations, indeed infinitely surpasses them.[4]

2337   10. From evangelization, completed with the help of God, come faith and initial conversion; these cause a person to feel called away from sin and drawn into the mystery of God's love. The whole period of the precatechumenate is set aside for this evangelization, so that the genuine will to follow Christ and seek baptism may mature.

2338   11. During this period, catechists, deacons, and priests, as well as laypersons, are to give a suitable explanation of the Gospel to the candidates. They are to receive help and attention so that with a purified and clearer intention they may cooperate with God's grace. Meetings of the candidates with families and groups of Christians may then more easily be arranged.

2339   12. In addition to the evangelization that is proper to this period, the conferences of bishops may provide, if necessary and according to local circumstances, a preliminary manner of receiving interested inquirers ("sympathizers"): those who, even though they do not fully believe, show some inclination toward the Christian faith.

   1. Such a reception, if it takes place, will be carried out without any ritual celebration; it is the expression not yet of faith, but of a right intention.

   2. The reception will be adapted to local conditions and opportunities. Some candidates need to see evidence of the spirit of Christians that they are striving to understand and experience. For others, however, whose catechumenate has been delayed for one reason or another, some first outward act on their part or on the community's is appropriate.

   3. The reception will be held at a meeting or gathering of the local community, on an occasion suitable for friendly conversation. An inquirer or "sympathizer" is introduced by a friend and then welcomed and received by the priest or some other worthy and suitable member of the community.

2340   13. During the precatechumenate period, pastors should help inquirers with prayers suited to them.

B. Catechumenate

2341   14. The rite described as the "entrance into the order of catechumens" is of the utmost importance. Assembling publicly for the first time, the candidates make their intention known to the Church and the Church, carrying out its apostolic mission, admits those who intend to become members. God showers his grace on them, as this celebration manifests their desire publicly and marks their reception and first consecration by the Church.

2342   15. For this step to be taken it is required that in the candidates the beginnings of the spiritual life and the fundamentals of Christian teaching be already established.[5] There must be evidence of the first faith that was conceived during the period of the precatechumenate, of an initial conversion and intention to change their lives and to enter into a relationship with God in Christ. Consequently, there must also be evidence of the first stirrings of repentance and a start to the practice of calling upon God in prayer, and some first experience of the company and the spirit of Christians.

---

[4]   See AG no. 13.

[5]   See AG no. 14 [DOL 17 no. 246].

16. With the help of the sponsors (see no. 42), catechists, and deacons, it is the   2343
responsibility of pastors to judge the external indications of these dispositions.[6] It is
also their duty, in view of the power of sacraments already validly received (see
General Introduction to Christian Initiation no. 4),[a] to see that no baptized person
seeks for any reason whatever to be baptized again.

17. After the celebration of the rite, the names are written at once in the register of   2344
catechumens, along with the names of the minister and sponsors and the date and
place of admission.

18. From this time on, the catechumens, who have been welcomed by the Church   2345
with a mother's love and concern and are joined to the Church, are now part of the
household of Christ;[7] they are nourished by the Church on the word of God and
sustained by liturgical celebrations. They should be eager, then, to take part in the
liturgy of the word and to receive blessings and sacramentals. When two catechumens marry or when a catechumen marries an unbaptized person, an appropriate
rite is to be used.[8] One who dies during the catechumenate receives a Christian
burial.

19. The catechumenate is an extended period during which the candidates are   2346
given pastoral formation and are trained by suitable discipline.[9] In this way, the
dispositions manifested at their entry into the catechumenate are brought to maturity. This is achieved in four ways:

   1. A suitable catechesis provided by priests, deacons, or catechists and other
laypersons, planned to be gradual and complete in its coverage, accommodated to
the liturgical year, and enriched by celebrations of the word, leads the catechumens
not only to an appropriate acquaintance with dogmas and precepts but also to
personal knowledge of the mystery of salvation in which they desire to participate.

   2. Familiar with living the Christian way of life and helped by the example
and support of sponsors and godparents and the whole community of the faithful,
the catechumens learn to pray to God more easily, to witness to the faith, to keep
alive in all their activities the expectation of Christ, to follow supernatural inspiration in their deeds, and to exercise charity toward neighbor to the point of self-
renunciation. Thus formed, "new converts set out on a spiritual journey. Already
sharing through faith in the mystery of Christ's death and resurrection, they pass
from the old to a new nature made perfect in Christ. This transition, which brings
with it a progressive change of outlook and conduct, should become evident together with its social consequences and should be gradually effected during the
time of the catechumenate. Since the Lord in whom they believe is a sign of
contradiction, converts often experience divisions and separations, but they also
taste the joy that God gives without measure."[10]

   3. By suitable liturgical rites, the Church like a mother helps the catechumens
on their journey, cleanses them little by little and strengthens them with God's
blessing. It is recommended that celebrations of the word be arranged for their
benefit and they may also attend the liturgy of the word with the faithful, thus

---

[6]   See AG no. 13.

[a]   See DOL 294 no. 2253.

[7]   See LG no. 14; AG no. 14 [DOL 17 no. 246].

[8]   See *Rite of Marriage* nos. 55–56.

[9]   See AG no. 14 [DOL 17 no. 246].

[10] See AG no. 13.

better preparing themselves for participation in the eucharist in time to come. Ordinarily, however, when they are present in the assembly of the faithful, they should be dismissed in a friendly manner before the liturgy of the eucharist begins, unless there are difficulties in this. For they must await their baptism, which will bring them into the priestly people and empower them to participate in Christ's new worship.

4. Since the Church's life is apostolic, catechumens should also learn how to work actively with others to spread the Gospel and build up the Church by the testimony of their lives and the profession of their faith.[11]

2347   20. The period of time appropriate for the catechumenate depends on the grace of God and on various circumstances, such as the program of instruction for the catechumenate, the number of catechists, deacons, and priests, the cooperation of the individual catechumens, the means necessary to reach the place of the catechumenate and to spend time there, and the help of the local community. Nothing, therefore, can be settled a priori. The bishop has the responsibility of setting the period of time and directing the discipline of the catechumenate. It is recommended that the conferences of bishops, after considering the conditions of their people and region,[12] regulate this matter in greater detail.

C. PERIOD OF PURIFICATION AND ENLIGHTENMENT (LENTEN PREPARATION)

2348   21. The time of purification and enlightenment of the catechumens customarily coincides with Lent. Both in its liturgy and in its liturgical catechesis, Lent is a commemoration of baptism or a preparation for it and a time of penance;[13] it renews the community of the faithful together with the catechumens and makes them ready to celebrate the paschal mystery, which the sacraments of initiation apply to each individual.[14]

2349   22. The second stage of initiation begins the period of purification and enlightenment, marked by a more intense preparation of heart and spirit. At this stage the Church makes the "election," that is, the choice and admission of the catechumens who because of their dispositions are worthy to take part in the next celebration of the sacraments of initiation. This stage is called election because the admission made by the Church is founded on the election by God, in whose name the Church acts. It is also called the enrollment of names because the candidates, as a pledge of fidelity, write their names in the book of those who have been elected.

2350   23. Before the election is celebrated, the candidates are expected to have a conversion of mind and conduct, a sufficient acquaintance with Christian teaching, and a sense of faith and charity. A decision on their suitableness is also required. Later, in the actual celebration of the rite, the manifestation of their intention and the decision of the bishop or his delegate should take place in the presence of the community. It is thus clear that the election, which enjoys such great solemnity, is the turning point in the whole catechumenate.

2351   24. From the day of their election and admission, catechumens are called the "elect." They also are called *competentes* ("competitors"), because they vie with each

---

[11]   See AG no. 14 [DOL 17 no. 246].

[12]   See SC art. 64 [DOL 1 no. 64].

[13]   See SC art. 109 [DOL 1 no. 109].

[14]   See AG no. 14 [DOL 17 no. 246].

other or compete to receive Christ's sacraments and the gifts of the Holy Spirit. They are also called *illuminandi* ("those to be enlightened"), because baptism itself has the name "illumination" and sheds the light of faith on the newly baptized. In our times other terms may be used that, depending on regions and cultures, are better suited to popular understanding and the idiom of the language.

25. During this period, a more intense spiritual preparation, which involves interi-   2352
or recollection more than catechesis, is intended to purify hearts and minds by the examination of conscience and by penance and also to enlighten those hearts and minds with a deeper knowledge of Christ the Savior. This is accomplished in various rites, especially in the scrutinies and presentations.

1. The "scrutinies," which are celebrated solemnly on Sundays, have the twofold purpose mentioned above: to reveal anything that is weak, defective, or sinful in the hearts of the elect, so that it may be healed, and to reveal what is upright, strong, and holy, so that it may be strengthened. For the scrutinies are intended to free from sin and the devil and to give strength in Christ, who is the way, the truth, and the life of the elect.

2. The "presentations," by which the Church hands on to the elect its ancient texts of faith and prayer, namely, the creed and the Lord's Prayer, are intended to enlighten the elect. The creed, recalling the wonderful works of God for the salvation of the human race, suffuses the vision of the elect with the light of faith and joy. In the Lord's Prayer, they recognize more fully the new spirit of adoption by which they will call God their Father, especially in the midst of the eucharistic assembly.

26. In immediate preparation for the sacraments: 2353

1. The elect should be instructed to rest from their ordinary work as far as possible on Holy Saturday, spend the time in prayer and inner recollection, and fast according to their ability.[15]

2. That same day, if there is a meeting of the elect, some of the immediately preparatory rites may be celebrated, such as the recitation of the creed, the *ephphetha* rite, the choosing of a Christian name, and, if it is to be done, the anointing with the oil of catechumens.

D. Sacraments of Initiation

27. The sacraments of baptism, confirmation, and eucharist are the final stage in   2354
which the elect come forward and, with their sins forgiven, are admitted into the people of God, receive the adoption of the children of God, are led by the Holy Spirit into the promised fullness of time, and, in the eucharistic sacrifice and meal, have a foretaste of the kingdom of God.

A. CELEBRATION OF THE BAPTISM OF ADULTS

28. The celebration of baptism, which reaches its high point in the washing with   2355
water and invocation of the Holy Trinity, is preceded by the blessing of the water and the profession of faith, which are intimately linked to the rite of washing with water itself.

29. The blessing of the water expresses the religious meaning of water as God's   2356
creation and shows forth to all present the beginnings of God's saving mystery; it recalls the unfolding of the paschal mystery and the use of water for its sacramental accomplishment, while during it the Holy Trinity is invoked for the first time.

---

[15] See SC art. 110 [DOL 1 no. 110].

2357   30. In the rites of renunciation and profession of faith the same paschal mystery, already commemorated in the blessing of the water and soon to be professed briefly by the celebrant in the words of baptism, is proclaimed in the active faith of those to be baptized. For adults are not saved unless, coming forward of their own accord, they have the will to accept God's gift by their belief. They are receiving the sacrament of faith, which is not only the faith of the Church, but also the faith of each one of them; and it is expected that it will be active in each one of them. As they are baptized, far from receiving so great a sacrament merely passively, they enter into a covenant with Christ by an act of their own will, renouncing error and holding fast to the true God.

2358   31. After professing in living faith Christ's paschal mystery, they come forward immediately to receive that mystery as expressed in the washing with water; upon their professing faith in the Holy Trinity, the Trinity, invoked by the celebrant, acts to number the elect among the adopted children of God and to make them part of the people of God.

2359   32. Therefore the washing with water should be given its full importance in the celebration of baptism: it is the sign of the mystical sharing in Christ's death and resurrection that brings about in those who believe in his name death to sin and rising to eternal life. Accordingly, either immersion or infusion should be chosen for the rite, whichever suits individual cases better, so that in different traditions and circumstances there will be a clear understanding that this washing is not just a purification rite but the sacrament of being joined to Christ.

2360   33. The anointing with chrism after baptism is a sign of the royal priesthood of the baptized and their enrollment into the company of the people of God. The white garment is a symbol of their new dignity and the lighted candle shows their vocation to live as befits children of light.

B. CELEBRATION OF THE CONFIRMATION OF ADULTS

2361   34. According to the ancient practice preserved in the Roman liturgy, adults are not to be baptized without receiving confirmation immediately afterward (see no. 44), unless serious reasons prevent this. This combination signifies the unity of the paschal mystery, the link between the mission of the Son and the outpouring of the Holy Spirit, and the connection between the two sacraments through which the Son and the Spirit come with the Father to those baptized.

2362   35. Accordingly, confirmation is conferred after the explanatory rites of baptism, the postbaptismal anointing being omitted (no. 224).

C. THE NEOPHYTES' FIRST SHARING IN THE EUCHARIST

2363   36. Lastly, the eucharist is celebrated. For the first time and with full right the neophytes take part in it. This is the culminating point of their initiation. For in this eucharist the neophytes, who have been raised to the dignity of the royal priesthood, have an active part in both the general intercessions and, as far as possible, in the presentation of the gifts. With the whole community they take part in the celebration of the sacrifice and they say the Lord's Prayer, thus giving expression to the spirit of adoption as God's children that they have received in baptism. Then, by receiving the body that was given and the blood that was shed, they confirm the gifts they have received and have a foretaste of the eternal banquet.

E. Period of Postbaptismal Catechesis or Mystagogy

37. After this last stage has been completed, the community along with the neo-   2364
phytes grows in perceiving more deeply the paschal mystery and in making it part
of their lives by meditation on the Gospel, sharing in the eucharist, and doing
works of charity. This is the final period of initiation, the time of the neophytes'
mystagogy or postbaptismal catechesis.

38. The neophytes acquire a truly more complete and more fruitful grasp of the   2365
"mysteries" by the newness of what they have heard and above all by the experience of the sacraments they have received. For they have been renewed in mind,
tasted more deeply the good word of God, received the fellowship of the Holy
Spirit, and discovered the beauty of the Lord. Out of this experience, which belongs
to Christians and grows as it is lived, they derive a new sense of the faith, the
Church, and the world.

39. Just as the freshness with which they come to the sacraments enlightens the   2366
neophytes' understanding of the Scriptures, so also it increases their knowledge of
other people and thus has an impact on their experience of community. As a result
their interaction with the rest of the faithful is made easier and more beneficial. The
period of postbaptismal catechesis is of utmost importance so that the neophytes,
with the help of their godparents, may enter into closer ties with the other faithful
and bring to the others a renewed vision and fresh energies.

40. Since the distinctive character and force of this period issue from the new,   2367
personal experience of the sacraments and of the community, the chief setting for
the postbaptismal catechesis or mystagogy is the Masses called Masses for neophytes, that is, the Sunday Masses of the Easter season. In these celebrations,
besides meeting with the community and sharing in the mysteries, the newly
baptized will find the readings of the Lectionary particularly appropriate for them,
especially the readings of Year A. For this reason, the whole local community
should be invited to these Masses, along with the neophytes and their godparents.
The texts of these Masses may be used even when Christian initiation is celebrated
outside the usual time.

II. MINISTRIES AND OFFICES

41. The people of God, represented by the local Church, besides attending to what   2368
is stated in the General Introduction to Christian Initiation no. 7,[b] should always
understand and show that the initiation of adults is its concern and the business of
all the baptized.[16] Therefore the community must always be fully prepared in the
pursuit of its apostolic vocation to give help to those who are searching for Christ.
In the various circumstances of daily life, even as in the apostolate, all the followers
of Christ have the obligation of spreading the faith according to their abilities.[17]
Hence, the entire community must help the candidates and catechumens throughout the whole period of their initiation, during the precatechumenate, the catechumenate, and the period of postbaptismal catechesis or mystagogy. In particular:

    1. During the period of evangelization and precatechumenate, the faithful
should remember that for the Church and its members the supreme purpose of their

---

  b See DOL 294 no. 2256.

  16 See AG no. 14 [DOL 17 no. 246].

  17 See LG no. 17 [DOL 4 no. 144].

apostolate is to bring Christ's message to the world by word and deed and to communicate his grace.[18] They should therefore show themselves ready to open up the spirit of the Christian community to the candidates and to welcome them into their homes, personal conversation, and some community gatherings.

2.   The faithful should seek to be present at the celebrations of the catechumenate whenever possible and should take an active part in the responses, prayers, singing, and acclamations.

3.   On the day of election, because it is a day of growth for the community, the faithful should be sure to give honest and carefully considered testimony about the catechumens.

4.   During Lent, the period of purification and enlightenment, the faithful should be present at and attentive to the rites of the scrutinies and presentations and give the catechumens the example of their own renewal in the spirit of penance, faith, and charity. At the Easter Vigil, they should attach great importance to renewing their own baptismal promises.

5.   The faithful should take part in the Masses for neophytes during the period immediately after baptism, welcome the neophytes with open arms in charity, and help them to feel more at home in the community of the baptized.

2369   42.   Any candidate seeking admission as a catechumen is accompanied by a sponsor, that is, a man or woman who has known and assisted the candidate and stands as a witness to the candidate's moral character, faith, and intention. It may happen that this sponsor is not the one who will serve as godparent for the periods of purification, enlightenment, and mystagogy; in that case, another person takes the sponsor's place in the role of godparent.

2370   43.   But on the day of election, at the celebration of the sacraments, and during the period of mystagogy the candidate is accompanied by a godparent.[19] This is a person chosen by the candidate on the basis of example, good qualities, and friendship, delegated by the local Christian community, and approved by the priest. It is the responsibility of the godparent to show the candidate how to practice the Gospel in personal and social life and to be for the candidate a bearer of Christian witness and a guardian over growth in the baptismal life. Chosen before the candidate's election, the godparent fulfills this office publicly from the day of the election, testifying to the community about the candidate. The godparents continue to be important during the time after reception of the sacraments when the neophyte needs to be assisted to remain true to the baptismal promises.

2371   44.   The bishop,[20] in person or through his delegate, sets up, regulates, and promotes the pastoral formation of catechumens and admits the candidates to their election and to the sacraments. It is to be hoped that, presiding if possible at the Lenten liturgy, he will himself celebrate the rite of election and, at the Easter Vigil, the sacraments of initiation. Finally, as part of his pastoral care, the bishop should depute catechists, truly worthy and properly prepared, to celebrate the minor exorcisms.[21]

---

[18]   See AA no. 6.

[19]   See General Introduction to Christian Initiation no. 8 [DOL 294 no. 2257].

[20]   See ibid. no. 12 [DOL 294 no. 2261].

[21]   In this case CIC can. 1153 is abrogated.

45. Priests, besides their usual ministry exercised in any celebration of baptism,   2372
confirmation, and the eucharist,[22] have the responsibility of attending to the pastoral and personal care of the catechumens,[23] especially those who seem hesitant and
weak. With the help of deacons and catechists, they are to provide instruction for
the catechumens; they are also to approve the choice of godparents and gladly listen
to and help them. Finally, priests should be diligent in the correct celebration and
adaptation of the rites throughout the entire course of Christian initiation (see no.
67).

46. The priest who baptizes an adult or a child of catechetical age should, when   2373
the bishop is absent, also confer confirmation, unless this sacrament is to be given at
another time (see no. 56).[24]

    When there is a large number to be confirmed, the minister of confirmation
may associate priests with himself to administer the sacrament.

    These priests:

    a. must have a particular function or office in the diocese, that is, they must
    be vicars general, episcopal vicars or delegates, district or regional vicars, or
    those who by mandate of the Ordinary hold equivalent offices;

    b. or must be the parish priests (pastors) of the places where confirmation is
    celebrated, pastors of the places where the candidates belong, or priests who
    did special work in the catechetical preparation of those to be confirmed.[25]

47. Deacons, if they are available, should be ready to help. If the conference of   2374
bishops has decided in favor of having permanent deacons, it should see to it that
there are enough of them to ensure that the stages, periods, and exercises of the
catechumenate take place in all the places where pastoral needs require.[26]

48. Catechists have an important office for the progress of the catechumens and   2375
for the growth of the community. As often as possible, they should have an active
part in the rites. When they are teaching, they should see that their instruction is
filled with the spirit of the Gospel, adapted to the liturgical signs and the cycle of
the Church's year, suited to the needs of the catechumens, and as far as possible
enriched by local traditions. When deputed by the bishop, they may perform the
minor exorcisms (see no. 44) and the blessings[27] contained in the ritual nos.
113–124.

III. TIME AND PLACE OF INITIATION

49. As a general rule, pastors should make use of the rite of initiation in such a   2376
way that the sacraments themselves are celebrated at the Easter Vigil and the
election takes place on the First Sunday of Lent. The rest of the rites are spaced on
the basis of the arrangement already described (nos. 6–8, 14–40). For pastoral
needs of a more serious nature, however, it is lawful to arrange the schedule for the
entire rite differently, as will be detailed later (nos. 58–62).

---

22   See General Introduction to Christian Initiation nos. 13–15 [DOL 294 nos. 2262–64].

23   See PO no. 6 [DOL 18 no. 261].

24   See *Rite of Confirmation*, Introduction no. 7, b [DOL 305 no. 2516].

25   See ibid. no. 8 [DOL 305 no. 2517].

26   See LG no. 26; AG no. 16.

27   See SC art. 79 [DOL 1 no. 79].

A. Lawful or Customary Times

2377 50. The following should be noted about the time of celebrating the rite of entrance into the order of catechumens:

1. It should not be too early, but should be delayed until the candidates, according to their own dispositions and situation, have had sufficient time to conceive an initial faith and to show the first signs of conversion (see no. 15).

2. In places where the number of candidates is smaller than usual, there should be a delay until a large enough group is formed for catechesis and the liturgical rites.

3. Two dates in the year, or three if necessary, are to be fixed as normally the best times for carrying out this rite.

2378 51. The rite of election or enrollment of names should as a rule be celebrated on the First Sunday of Lent. For convenience it may be anticipated somewhat or even celebrated during the week.

2379 52. The scrutinies should take place on the Third, Fourth, and Fifth Sundays of Lent, or, if necessary, on the other Sundays of Lent or even on more convenient weekdays. Three scrutinies should be celebrated. The bishop may dispense from one of them for serious reasons or even from two in extraordinary circumstances. When, for lack of time, the election is held early, the first scrutiny is also to be held early; in this case, however, care is to be taken not to prolong the period of purification and enlightenment beyond eight weeks.

2380 53. By ancient usage, the presentations, since they take place after the scrutinies, are part of the same period of purification and enlightenment. They are celebrated during the week. The presentation of the creed to the catechumens takes place during the week after the first scrutiny; the presentation of the Lord's Prayer during the week after the third scrutiny. For pastoral reasons, however, to enrich the liturgy in the period of the catechumenate, the presentations may be transferred and celebrated during the catechumenate as a kind of "rite of passage" (see nos. 125–126).

2381 54. On Holy Saturday, when the elect refrain from work (see no. 26) and spend their time in recollection, the various, immediately preparatory rites may be celebrated: the catechumen's recitation of the creed, the *ephphetha* rite, the choosing of a Christian name, and even the anointing with the oil of catechumens (see nos. 193–207).

2382 55. The sacraments for the initiation of adults are to be celebrated at the Easter Vigil itself (see nos. 8, 49). If there is a large number of catechumens, the sacraments are given to the majority that night and may be given to the rest on days within the Easter octave, whether at the principal church or at a mission station. In this case either the Mass of the day or the ritual Mass for Christian Initiation may be used with the readings from the Easter Vigil.

2383 56. In certain cases, confirmation may be postponed until near the end of the period of postbaptismal catechesis, for example, Pentecost Sunday (see no. 237).

2384 57. On all the Sundays of Easter after the first, the "Masses for neophytes" are to be celebrated. The entire community and the newly baptized with their godparents should be urged to attend (see no. 40).

B. Outside the Customary Times

58. The rite of initiation is normally arranged so that the sacraments will be   2385
celebrated during the Easter Vigil. Because of unusual circumstances and pastoral
needs, however, the rite of election and the rites during the period of purification
and enlightenment may be held outside Lent and the sacraments may be celebrated
outside the Easter Vigil or Easter Sunday. Even in ordinary circumstances, but only
for serious pastoral needs (for example, if there is a very large number of persons to
be baptized), it is lawful to choose another time, especially the Easter season, to
celebrate the sacraments of initiation. The program of initiation during Lent, however, must be maintained. When this is done, even though the time of its insertion
into the liturgical year is changed, the structure of the entire rite, with its properly
spaced intervals, remains the same. But the following adjustments are to be made.

59. As far as possible, the sacraments of initiation are to be celebrated on Sunday,   2386
using, as occasion suggests, the Sunday Mass or the proper ritual Mass (see no. 55).

60. The rite of entrance into the order of catechumens is to take place when the   2387
time is right, as explained in no. 50.

61. The election is to be celebrated about six weeks before the sacraments of   2388
initiation so that there is sufficient time for the scrutinies and the presentations.
Care should be taken that the celebration of the election does not fall on a solemnity of the liturgical year. The readings assigned in the ritual itself are to be used and
the Mass texts will be those of the day or of the ritual Mass for Election or
Enrollment of Names.

62. The scrutinies should not be celebrated on solemnities, but on Sundays or even   2389
on weekdays, with the usual intervals and use of the readings given in the ritual
itself. The Mass texts will be those of the day or of the ritual Mass (see no. 374).

63. The rites should be celebrated in the places appropriate to them as indicated in   2390
the ritual. Consideration should be given to special needs that arise in secondary
stations of mission territories.

IV. ADAPTATIONS BY CONFERENCES OF BISHOPS USING THIS ROMAN RITUAL

64. In addition to the adaptations envisioned in the General Introduction to Chris-   2391
tian Initiation nos. 30–33,[c] the rite of initiation of adults allows for the conferences
of bishops to decide on other adaptations.

65. The conferences have discretionary power to make the following decisions: 2392

    1. to establish, where it seems advisable, some method of receiving well-dis-
posed inquirers ("sympathizers") prior to the catechumenate (see no. 12);

    2. to insert, where paganism is widespread, the first exorcism and the first
renunciation into the rite of entrance into the order of catechumens (nos. 79–
80);

    3. to decree that the tracing of the sign of the cross upon the forehead be
replaced by making that sign before the forehead, in areas where the act of
touching may not seem proper (no. 83);

---

[c] See DOL 294 nos. 2279–82.

4. to decree that in the rite of entrance into the order of catechumens (no. 88) candidates receive a new name wherever it is the practice of non-Christian religions to give a new name to initiates immediately;

5. to allow within the same rite (no. 89), according to local customs, subsidiary rites that symbolize reception into the community;

6. to establish during the period of the catechumenate, in addition to the usual rites (nos. 106–124), "rites of passage": for example, anticipating the presentations (nos. 125–126), the *ephphetha* rite, the catechumens' recitation of the creed, or even the anointing with the oil of catechumens (nos. 127–129);

7. to decree the omission of the anointing with the oil of catechumens (no. 218) or its transferral to the immediately preparatory rites (nos. 206–207) or its use during the period of the catechumenate as a kind of "rite of passage" (nos. 127–132);

8. to make the formularies of renunciation more specific and detailed (see nos. 80, 217).

V. ADAPTATIONS BY THE BISHOP

2393   66. It pertains to the bishop for his own diocese:

1. to set up the formation program of the catechumenate and to lay down norms according to local needs (see no. 44);

2. to decree whether and when, as circumstances warrant, the whole rite of initiation may be celebrated outside the customary times (see no. 58);

3. to dispense, on the basis of some serious obstacle, from one scrutiny or, in extraordinary circumstances, even from two (see no. 240);

4. to permit the simple rite to be used in whole or in part (see no. 240);

5. to depute catechists who are truly worthy and properly prepared to give the exorcisms and blessings (see nos. 44, 48);

6. to preside at the rite of election and to ratify, personally or through a delegate, the admission of the elect (see no. 44).

VI. ADAPTATIONS BY THE MINISTER

2394   67. It is for the celebrant to use fully and intelligently the freedom which is given to him either in the General Introduction to Christian Initiation no. 34[d] or in the rubrics of the rite itself. In many places the manner of acting or praying is intentionally left undetermined or two alternatives are offered, so that the celebrant, according to his prudent pastoral judgment, may accommodate the rite to the circumstances of the candidates and others who are present. The greatest freedom is left in the introductions and intercessions, which may always be shortened, changed, or even expanded with new intentions in order to fit the circumstances or special situation of the candidates (for example, a sad or joyful event occurring in a family) or of the others present (for example, joy or sorrow common to the parish or civic community).

The celebrant will also adapt the texts by changing the gender and number as required.

_____

[d] See DOL 294 no. 2283.

CHAPTER I
RITE OF THE CATECHUMENATE ARRANGED IN STAGES

FIRST STAGE: ENTRANCE INTO THE ORDER OF CATECHUMENS

68. The rite by which those intending to become Christians are received as cate-   2395
chumens is celebrated when, after hearing the first proclamation of the living God,
they have an initial faith in Christ the Savior. This presupposes the first evangelization, the beginning of conversion and faith and of a sense of the Church, previous
contact with a priest or some members of the community, and preparation of the
candidates for this liturgical rite.

69. Before the candidates' entry into the order of catechumens, which will take   2396
place on determined days during the year suited to local conditions, a period should
be set aside long enough, in proportion to varying needs, to evaluate and to purify,
if necessary, the candidates' motives for conversion.

70. It is desirable that the entire Christian community or some part of it, consisting   2397
of friends and acquaintances, catechists and priests, take an active part in the
celebration.

71. The sponsors should also attend in order to present to the Church the candi-   2398
dates they have brought.

72. The rite, which consists of the reception of the candidates, the liturgy of the   2399
word, and their dismissal, may also be followed by the eucharist.

PERIOD OF THE CATECHUMENATE AND ITS RITES

98. The catechumenate or pastoral formation of catechumens should be long   2400
enough — several years if necessary — for their conversion and faith to become
strong. For it is by instruction in the whole of the Christian life and a sufficiently
prolonged probation that catechumens are properly initiated into the mysteries of
salvation, the practice of an evangelical way of life, and the liturgical rites that will
be celebrated. This will bring them into the life of faith, liturgy, and charity belonging to the people of God.

   At the discretion of the local Ordinary, on the basis of the spiritual preparation
of the candidate, the period of the catechumenate may in particular cases be shortened; in altogether singular cases it may even be completed all at once (see no. 240).

99. During this period of presenting Catholic teaching in its completeness to the   2401
catechumens, the instruction should be of a kind that enlightens faith, directs the
heart toward God, fosters participation in the liturgy, inspires apostolic activity, and
nurtures a life completely in accord with the spirit of Christ.

100. There should be celebrations of the word of God, adapted to the liturgical   2402
season, that contribute both to the instruction of the catechumens and to the needs
of the community (see nos. 106–108).

101. The first or minor exorcisms, which are of positive content and composed in   2403
the form of a prayer, place before the catechumens the real nature of Christian life,
the struggle between flesh and spirit, the importance of self-denial for reaching the
blessedness of God's kingdom, and the unending need for God's help (see nos.
109–118).

2404   102. The blessings are a sign of God's love and of the Church's tender care. They are bestowed on the catechumens so that, even though as yet they do not have the grace of the sacraments, they may still receive from the Church courage, joy, and peace to continue the difficult journey they have begun (see nos. 119–124).

2405   103. Through the years of advancing from one catechetical gathering to the next, rites can be used at certain points to symbolize the catechumens' onward passage. Therefore, to this end it is allowed to anticipate the presentation of the creed and Lord's Prayer and the *ephphetha* rite, rites for which there may not always be time at the final preparation of the *competentes* (see nos. 125–126). It is also possible, wherever helpful or desired, to anticipate celebrations of anointing with the oil of catechumens (see nos. 127–132).

2406   104. During this period the catechumens should give thought to finding the godparents who will present them to the Church on the day of their election (see General Introduction to Christian Initiation nos. 8–10;[e] also here no. 43).

2407   105. From time to time during the year, the entire group that is concerned in the initiation of the catechumens should assemble for some celebrations of the catechumenate and for the rites of passage (see nos. 125–132). This involves priests, deacons, catechists, sponsors, godparents, friends and neighbors.

SECOND STAGE: RITE OF ELECTION OR ENROLLMENT OF NAMES

2408   133. At the beginning of the Lenten season, during which the final preparation for sacramental initiation takes place, the "election" or "enrollment of names" is celebrated. In this rite the Church hears the testimony of the godparents and catechists, the catechumens reaffirm their intention, and the Church evaluates their state of preparation and decides whether they may receive the Easter sacraments.

2409   134. The catechumenate ends with the celebration of the election, thus completing the lengthy formation of the mind and heart. To be enrolled among the elect catechumens must have an enlightened faith and a deliberate intention to receive the sacraments of the Church. After their election, they are encouraged to follow Christ with greater generosity.

2410   135. The election is the focal point of the Church's concern for the catechumens. The bishop, priests, deacons, catechists, godparents, and the whole community, according to their particular responsibility and in their own way, should give very careful consideration and a decision on the matter of the instruction and progress of the catechumens. Then they should surround the elect with prayer, so that the entire Church may lead them to encounter Christ.

2411   136. The godparents are chosen beforehand by the catechumens; the choice should be made with the consent of the priest and those chosen should, as far as possible, be accepted for their role by the local community. The godparents exercise their ministry publicly for the first time in this rite. They are called at the beginning of the rite and come forward with the catechumens (no. 143); they testify on behalf of the catechumens before the community (no. 144); if desired, they write their names with the catechumens in the book of the elect (no. 146).

2412   137. To ensure the authenticity of the proceedings, there should be a deliberation on the suitability of the candidates before the liturgical rite is celebrated. This is

---

    e See DOL 294 nos. 2257–59.

done by those involved in the training of the catechumens — priests, deacons, and catechists — and by the godparents and delegates of the local community. If circumstances permit, the assembly of catechumens may also take part. This deliberation may take various forms, depending on local conditions and pastoral needs. The acceptance of the candidates should be announced by the celebrant during the liturgical rite.

138. The celebrant is the bishop or his delegate. However much or little he was involved in the preceding deliberation, it is his responsibility to show in the homily or during the rite the religious and ecclesial meaning of the election. He has the responsibility of announcing the Church's decision before all present and hearing their judgment if this is so desired; of asking the catechumens to give a personal expression of their intention; and, acting in the name of Christ and his Church, of admitting the elect. He should open to all the divine mystery shown in the call of the Church and in its liturgical celebration. He should remind the faithful to give good example to the elect, and, together with them, to prepare themselves for the Easter solemnities.   2413

139. The sacraments of initiation are celebrated during the Easter solemnities and preparation for them is part of the distinctive character of Lent. Accordingly, the rite of election should normally take place on the First Sunday of Lent. The time for the final preparation of the *competentes* should coincide with the Lenten season. The celebration of Lent will benefit the elect by reason of its liturgical structure and the participation of the community. For urgent pastoral reasons, however, especially in secondary mission stations, it is permitted to celebrate the rite during the preceding or following week.   2414

PERIOD OF PURIFICATION AND ENLIGHTENMENT AND ITS RITES

152. This period normally falls in Lent and begins with the election. During this time, the catechumens and the local community give themselves to spiritual recollection so that they may prepare themselves for the feast of Easter and for the sacraments of initiation. To this end the scrutinies, the presentations, and the immediately preparatory rites are provided for them.   2415

SCRUTINIES AND PRESENTATIONS

153. The scrutinies and presentations take place during the Lent that precedes the sacraments of initiation. The spiritual and catechetical preparation of the elect, or *competentes* , is completed by these rites and is continued throughout the entire period of Lent.   2416

I. Scrutinies

154. The purpose of the scrutinies is mainly spiritual; they are concluded by exorcisms. The scrutinies are intended to purify the catechumens' minds and hearts, to strengthen them against temptation, to purify their intentions, and to make firm their decision, so that they may become more closely united with Christ and make progress in their efforts to love God more deeply.   2417

155. The *competentes* must have the intention of arriving at an intimate knowledge of Christ and his Church and they are expected particularly to progress in sincere self-knowledge through a serious appraisal of self and true penance.   2418

2419 156. The rite of exorcism is celebrated by priests and deacons. The elect, having learned from the Church as from their mother about the mystery of Christ who frees from sin, are freed in this rite from the effects of sin and from the influence of the devil; they are strengthened in their spiritual journey and they open their hearts to receive the gifts of the Savior.

2420 157. In order to inspire a desire for purification and redemption by Christ, three scrutinies are held. Their purpose is twofold: to teach the catechumens gradually about the mystery of sin, from which the whole world and every person longs to be delivered and thus saved from its present and future consequences; to fill their spirit with an understanding of Christ the Redeemer, the living water (see the gospel about the Samaritan woman), the light of the world (see the gospel about the man born blind), the resurrection and the life (see the gospel about the raising of Lazarus). From the first to the final scrutiny there should be progress in the recognition of sin and the desire for salvation.

2421 158. The scrutinies, with a priest or deacon presiding over the community, are to be celebrated in such a way that the faithful too may benefit from the liturgy of scrutinies and join in praying for the elect.

2422 159. The scrutinies ought to take place during the Masses for the Scrutinies held on the Third, Fourth, and Fifth Sundays of Lent; the readings from Year A with their chants are used, as given in the Lectionary.[f] If for pastoral reasons this cannot be done on the proper Sundays, other Lenten Sundays or even suitable weekdays may be chosen. The first Mass of the scrutinies is always that of the Samaritan woman, the second of the man born blind, and the third of Lazarus.

THIRD STAGE: CELEBRATION OF THE SACRAMENTS OF INITIATION

2423 208. When the initiation of adults is celebrated at the proper time, that is, during the Easter Vigil, the sacraments are conferred after the blessing of the water, as noted in the order of the Easter Vigil no. 44.

2424 209. If it takes place outside the customary time (see Introduction nos. 58–59), the celebration should be filled with the Easter spirit (General Introduction to Christian Initiation no. 6);[g] and the ritual Mass from the Missal is to be used (see also no. 388).

CELEBRATION OF BAPTISM

2425 210. Even when the sacraments of initiation are celebrated outside the Easter season, the rite of blessing the water is to be included (see General Introduction to Christian Initiation no. 21).[h] This blessing by its recital of the wondrous works of God calls to mind the mystery of his love from the very beginning of the world and the creation of the human race. Then, by its invocation of the Holy Spirit and proclamation of Christ's death and resurrection, the blessing impresses on the mind newness of life through the Lord's cleansing water of regeneration by which we share in his death and resurrection and receive the holiness of God.

2426 211. The renunciation of Satan and the profession of faith form one rite, which achieves its full effect in the baptism of adults. For baptism is the sacrament of that

---

[f] In the English edition (1969), the readings are nos. 28, 31, and 34.

[g] See DOL 294 no. 2255.

[h] See DOL 294 no. 2270.

faith by which catechumens hold fast to God and at the same time receive new birth from him. A proper prelude to their washing therefore is the act by which the catechumens, as was prefigured in the first covenant with the patriarchs, utterly renounce sin and Satan in order to commit themselves for ever to the promise of a savior and the mystery of the Trinity. By this act, made before the celebrant and the community, they express the intention, which has matured during the period of the catechumenate, to enter into the New Covenant with Christ. They have embraced this faith as divinely handed down by the Church and as adults are baptized in it.

212. The anointing with the oil of catechumens that occurs between the renuncia-   2427
tion and the profession of faith may be anticipated for pastoral need and liturgical benefit (see nos. 206–207).

In this case, it should signify the need of God's strength so that the persons who are being baptized, despite the bonds of their past life and overcoming the opposition of the devil, may determinedly take the step of professing their faith and hold to it without faltering throughout their entire lives.

PERIOD OF POSTBAPTISMAL CATECHESIS OR MYSTAGOGY

235. To strengthen the first steps of the neophytes, it is desirable for the community   2428
of the faithful, their godparents, and their pastors to give them thoughtful and friendly help continually. The greatest care should be taken that they experience a full and joyful welcome into the community.

236. Throughout the Easter season at Sunday Mass special places in the congrega-   2429
tion are to be reserved for the neophytes. All the neophytes should make an effort to take part in these Masses along with their godparents. The homily and, where appropriate, even the general intercessions, should take account of their presence and their needs.

237. To close the period of postbaptismal catechesis, some sort of celebration should   2430
be held at the end of the Easter season near Pentecost Sunday; festivities in keeping with local custom may accompany the occasion.

238. On the anniversary of their baptism the neophytes should be gathered togeth-   2431
er in order to give thanks to God, to share with one another their spiritual experi-ences, and to renew their commitment.

239. To establish pastoral contact with these new members of his Church, the   2432
bishop, particularly if he was unable to preside at the sacraments of initiation himself, should arrange at least once a year to meet the recently baptized neo-phytes, if possible, and to preside over a eucharistic celebration with them. At this Mass they may receive holy communion under both kinds.

CHAPTER II
SIMPLE RITE FOR THE INITIATION OF AN ADULT

240. In extraordinary circumstances when a candidate has been unable to go   2433
through all the stages of initiation or when the local Ordinary, convinced that the candidate's Christian conversion is sincere and that he or she is religiously mature, decides that the candidate may receive baptism without delay, the Ordinary, in individual cases, can allow the use of the simple rite given here. In this rite either all the rites are carried out at once (nos. 245–273), or permission is given to have, in addition to the celebration of the sacraments, one or another of the rites of the catechumenate or of the period of purification and enlightenment (nos. 274–277).

2434   241. Having already chosen a godparent (see Introduction no. 43) and having become acquainted with the local community (see ibid. nos. 12 and 19, § 2), the candidate must have an adequate period of instruction and preparation before baptism in order to purify his or her motives for seeking baptism and to grow stronger in conversion and faith.

2435   242. The rite expresses not only the presentation and welcoming of the candidate but also the candidate's clear and firm resolve to request Christian initiation and the Church's approval. Then, following an appropriate liturgy of the word, comes the celebration of all the sacraments of initiation.

2436   243. Normally the rite is celebrated within Mass. Appropriate readings are to be chosen. The rest of the Mass texts are to be taken from the ritual Mass for Christian Initiation or from some other Mass. After being baptized and confirmed the candidate shares in the celebration of the eucharist for the first time.

2437   244. As far as possible, the celebration ought to be on a Sunday (see Introduction no. 59), involving the active participation of the local community.

*   *   *

2438   274. In extraordinary circumstances, such as disease, old age, change of domicile, or a long journey, when: a. the candidate could not begin the catechumenate with an appropriate rite, or began it and could not complete it with all its rites; b. and for other reasons it would be harmful to his or her spiritual welfare if through the use of this simple rite he or she were deprived of the benefits of a longer preparation — then, with the bishop's permission, it would be important to add one or more elements of the complete rite to the simple rite.

2439   275. This augmented rite allows a new candidate to catch up with those who are more advanced, through the addition of some of the initial ceremonies for the complete rite (such as entrance into the catechumenate, minor exorcisms, blessings, and the like); or it allows an individual who began with the others to receive the rites he or she missed (such as election, rite of purification and illumination, and the sacraments of initiation).

2440   276. Adaptations may be made with pastoral judgment, relating the complete rite and the augmented rite in this way:

    1. by adding, for example, rites from the catechumenate (nos. 106–132) and the presentations (nos. 183–192);

    2. by dividing and enlarging the rite of reception (nos. 245–251) or the liturgy of the word (nos. 252–256). In the rite of reception, nos. 245–247 can be expanded on the model of the rite of forming catechumens nos. 73–97; nos. 248–249 can be made to accommodate the rite of election by dropping nos. 246–247, when this is warranted. In the liturgy of the word, nos. 253–255 may be adapted to one or other of the scrutinies (nos. 160–179), and so on;

    3. by using part of the simple rite in place of some of the ceremonies in the complete rite; or, when "inquirers" or "sympathizers" are received (see Introduction, no. 12, § 3), by joining the rite of entrance into the catechumenate (nos. 73–93) with the rite of election (nos. 143–151).

2441   277. When this augmented rite is used, care should be taken that:

    1. the candidate has received a full catechesis;

    2. the rite is celebrated with the active participation of a congregation;

3. after receiving the sacraments the neophyte benefits from a period of post-baptismal catechesis, insofar as this is possible.

CHAPTER III
SHORT RITE FOR THE INITIATION OF AN ADULT IN DANGER OF DEATH OR AT THE POINT OF DEATH

278. Anyone, catechumen or not, who is in danger of death may be baptized with the short rite that follows (nos. 283–294), as long as such a person is not at the point of death and is able to hear and answer the questions.   2442

279. One already admitted as a catechumen must make a promise to complete the usual catechesis upon recovering. One not a catechumen must give serious indication of being converted to Christ and of renouncing pagan worship and must not be seen to be attached to anything that conflicts with the moral life (for example, "simultaneous" polygamy, etc.). The person must also make a promise to go through the complete cycle of initiation upon recovering.   2443

280. This short rite is particularly suited for use by catechists and laypersons.   2444

   In a case of emergency, however, a priest or a deacon may use this rite. Normally the priest and deacon are to use the simple rite (nos. 240–273), making adaptations as required by place and time.

   If the sacred chrism is at hand and there is time, a priest who baptizes should confer confirmation after the baptism; in this case the postbaptismal anointing with chrism is omitted (no. 263).

   Also whenever possible the priest or deacon, as well as a catechist or layperson having permission to distribute communion, should give the eucharist to the person newly baptized. In this case the sacrament may be brought before the celebration of the rite and placed reverently on a table covered with a white cloth.

281. When a person is at the point of death or when time is pressing because death is imminent, the minister, omitting everything else, pours natural water (even if not blessed) on the head of the sick person, while saying the usual sacramental form (see General Introduction to Christian Initiation no. 23).[i]   2445

282. If persons who were baptized in proximate danger of death or at the point of death should recover their health, they should be given a suitable formation, be received at the church at a fitting time, and be given the rest of the sacraments of initiation. In such a case the guidelines given in nos. 295–305 are followed, with the necessary changes.   2446

CHAPTER IV
PREPARING UNCATECHIZED ADULTS FOR CONFIRMATION AND THE EUCHARIST

295. The following pastoral suggestions concern adults who were baptized as infants but did not receive further catechetical formation and did not receive confirmation and the eucharist. They may also be applied to similar cases, especially that of an adult baptized in danger or at the point of death.   2447

---

   i   See DOL 294 no. 2272.

Even if these adults have not yet heard the message of the mystery of Christ, their status differs from that of catechumens since they have already become members of the Church and children of God by baptism. Hence their conversion is based on the baptism they have already received and they must develop strength from that source.

2448   296. As in the case of catechumens, the preparation of these adults requires a considerable time (see Introduction no. 21 [19]) because their faith, infused in baptism, must grow and take deep root in them through suitable discipline, a catechesis adapted to their needs, contact with the community of the faithful, and their participation in certain liturgical rites.

2449   297. For the most part the plan of catechesis corresponds to the one laid down for catechumens (see Introduction no. 19, § 1). But in the process of catechesis the priest, deacon, or catechist should take account of the special status of these adults as already baptized.

2450   298. The Christian community, as it does for catechumens, should help these adults by its love and prayer and by testifying to their suitability when it is time for them to be admitted to the sacraments (Introduction nos. 4, 19 § 2, 23).

2451   299. A sponsor presents these adults to the community. During the time of their formation each of them chooses a godparent approved by the priest. The godparent works with the adult as the representative of the community and has the same responsibilities as a godparent towards a catechumen (see Introduction no. 43). The godparent chosen at this time can be the same as the one who was godparent at the baptism, provided the person is truly capable of carrying out this responsibility.

2452   300. The period of preparation is made holy by means of liturgical celebrations. The first of these is the rite by which the adults are welcomed into the community and acknowledge themselves to be part of it since they are already sealed with baptism.

2453   301. From this time onward they take part in celebrations of the liturgy of the word — both those of the whole Christian assembly and those intended for catechumens.

2454   302. As a sign of God's activity in this work of preparation, some of the rites belonging to the catechumenate, suited to the condition and spiritual needs of these adults, can be used to advantage. Among these are the presentation of the creed, the Lord's Prayer, and the Gospels.

2455   303. This period of catechesis should be properly related to the liturgical year; this is especially true of its final phase, which should as a rule coincide with Lent. During this season these adults will gather at certain times to hold penitential services that will lead to the celebration of the sacrament of penance.

2456   304. The climax of their entire formation will normally be the Easter Vigil. At that time the adults will make profession of their baptismal faith, receive the sacrament of confirmation, and take part in the eucharist. If, because the bishop or special minister of that sacrament is not present, confirmation cannot be given at the Easter Vigil, it is to be celebrated as soon as possible and, if this can be arranged, during the Easter season.

2457   305. These adults will complete their Christian formation and become fully integrated into the community by experiencing the period of postbaptismal catechesis with the neophytes.

CHAPTER V
RITE OF INITIATION FOR CHILDREN OF CATECHETICAL AGE

306. This rite is intended for children, unbaptized as infants, who have reached the   2458
age of reason and are of catechetical age and who have been brought by their
parents or guardians for Christian initiation or have come of their own accord with
parental permission. Such children are suitable candidates if they are already capable of receiving and nurturing a personal faith and of recognizing an obligation in
conscience. They cannot yet, however, be treated as adults because, being children,
they are dependent on their parents or guardians and are still strongly influenced by
their companions and their social surroundings.

307. The initiation of these children requires both a conversion, which is personal   2459
and somewhat developed according to their age, and the assistance of the education
needed at this age. From then on their initiation is to be adapted both to the
spiritual progress of the candidates, that is, their growth in faith, and to the catechetical instruction they receive. Accordingly, as with adults, their initiation is to be
extended over several years, if need be, before they receive the sacraments. It is also
divided into different stages and periods and is marked by liturgical rites.

308. The children's progress in the formation they receive depends as much on the   2460
help and example of their companions as on their parents. This should be taken into
account.

    a. Generally the children to be initiated belong to a group of their compan-
ions who are already baptized and are preparing for confirmation and eucharist.
Therefore, their initiation is based on this catechetical group and shares in its
progress.

    b. It is to be hoped that the children will also receive as much help and
example as possible from their parents, who must assent to their initiation and to
their leading a Christian life from this time forward. The period of initiation will
also provide a good opportunity for the family to have contact with priests and
catechists.

309. According to circumstances, it is of considerable advantage to form a group of   2461
several children who are in this same situation for the celebrations belonging to this
rite, in order that they may help one another in their progress as catechumens.

310. In regard to the time for these celebrations, it is desirable that as far as possible   2462
the final period of preparation coincides with Lent and that the sacraments themselves are celebrated at the Easter Vigil (see Introduction no. 8). Before the children
are admitted to the sacraments at Easter, it should be established that they are ready
for the sacraments and that the occasion is compatible with the program of catechetical instruction they are receiving. As far as possible, the candidates should
come to the sacraments of initiation when their baptized companions are receiving
confirmation or eucharist.

311. The celebrations should take place with the active participation of a congrega-   2463
tion, made up of a suitable number of the faithful, the parents, family, members of
the catechetical group, and a few adult friends. When children of this age are
initiated, it is generally desirable not to have the whole parish community present;
it is enough to have it represented.

312. The conferences of bishops may adapt and add to the rite given here in order   2464
to meet local needs and conditions more fully, as well as to provide greater pastoral

opportunities. The adult rite of the presentations (nos. 103, 125, 181–192) may be adapted to the age of the children and added. When this rite is translated, the instructions and prayers should be adapted to the understanding of children. Furthermore, in addition to a prayer already translated from the Roman Ritual, the conference of bishops may also approve an alternative prayer that says the same things in a way better adapted to children (General Introduction to Christian Initiation no. 32).[j]

2465   313. Ministers using this rite should freely and wisely use the options given to them in the General Introduction to Christian Initiation nos. 34–35[k] and in the Introductions to the *Rite of the Baptism for Children* no. 31[l] and the *Rite of Christian Initiation of Adults* no. 67.

FIRST STAGE: ENTRANCE INTO THE ORDER OF CATECHUMENS

2466   314. This rite is celebrated with a small but active congregation so that the children will not be distracted by a large group (see no. 311). When possible, the candidates' parents or guardians should be present. If they cannot come, they should indicate that they have given consent to their children. Their place should be taken by "sponsors" (Introduction no. 42), suitable members of the Church who act on this occasion for the parents and present the children.

2467   315. The celebration takes place in the church or in a place that, according to the age and understanding of the children, can help them to experience a warm welcome. According to the circumstances, the first part, the introductory rite, is celebrated at the entrance of the church or of the other site. The second part, the liturgy of the word, is celebrated in the church or in a specially chosen place.

SECOND STAGE: PENITENTIAL RITES OR SCRUTINIES

2468   330. These penitential rites, which are among the main events of the catechumenate for children, are a kind of scrutiny, similar to those in the adult rite (nos. 152–180). Since both are alike in purpose, the guidelines given for scrutinies (nos. 25 § 1, 154–159) may be used and adapted.

2469   331. Since the scrutinies normally belong to the final period of preparation for baptism, these penitential rites require that the children already exhibit a degree of faith and understanding approaching that required for baptism.

2470   332. The catechumens take part in these rites along with their godparents and members of the catechetical groups. Everything is to be adapted to those present, so that the penitential celebrations are also of benefit to those who are not catechumens. During this celebration some children who have already been baptized and are members of the catechetical group may receive the sacrament of penance for the first time. In this case, care should be taken to include instructions, intentions for the prayers, and gestures that are appropriate for these children.

2471   333. The penitential rites are celebrated during Lent, if the catechumens are to be initiated at Easter; if not, at the most suitable time. At least one celebration is held, and if it can be conveniently done, a second should be added. The texts for the

---

    j   See DOL 294 no. 2281.
    k   See DOL 294 nos. 2283–84.
    l   See DOL 295 no. 2315.

second celebration are to be composed on the model of the first, but for the intercessions and prayer of exorcism the texts given in nos. 164, 171, 178 are used, with
appropriate modifications.

THIRD STAGE: CELEBRATION OF THE SACRAMENTS OF INITIATION

343. To show forth the paschal character of baptism, this sacrament should be   2472
celebrated at the Easter Vigil or on Sunday, when the Church recalls the Lord's
resurrection (see *Rite of Baptism for Children*, Introduction no. 9),[m] taking into consideration what has been outlined in no. 310.

344. Baptism is celebrated during the Mass in which the neophytes are to share in   2473
the eucharist for the first time. Confirmation is given at the same celebration by the
bishop or by the priest who baptizes.

345. If baptism is celebrated at a time other than the Easter Vigil or Easter Sunday,   2474
the Mass of the day or the ritual Mass for Christian Initiation is used. The readings
are chosen from among those given in no. 388. The readings of the Sunday or feast
may be used instead.

346. All the catechumens are to be accompanied by their own godparent, chosen by   2475
themselves and approved by the priest (see Introduction no. 43).

APPENDIX

RITE OF RECEIVING BAPTIZED CHRISTIANS INTO
THE FULL COMMUNION OF THE CATHOLIC CHURCH

INTRODUCTION

1.   The rite for the reception of one born and baptized in a separated Ecclesial   2476
Community into the full communion of the Catholic Church,[1] according to the
Latin rite, is arranged so that no greater burden than necessary is demanded for
reception into communion and unity[2] (see Acts 15:28).

2.   In the case of Eastern Christians who enter into the fullness of Catholic com-   2477
munion, nothing more than a simple profession of Catholic faith is required, even if
they are permitted, upon recourse to the Apostolic See, to transfer to the Latin rite.[3]

3.   a.   The rite should be seen as a celebration of the Church, with its climax in   2478
eucharistic communion. For this reason the rite of reception is generally celebrated
within Mass.

  b. Anything that has the appearance of triumphalism should be carefully
avoided and the manner of celebrating this Mass should be precisely defined. Both
the ecumenical implications and the bond between the candidate and the parish
community should be considered. Often it will be more appropriate to celebrate the

---

[m] See DOL 295 no. 2293.

[1] See SC art. 69 b [DOL 1 no. 69]; UR no. 3 [DOL 6 no. 183]. Secretariat for Christian Unity,
Ecumenical Directory I no. 19 [DOL 147 no. 973].

[2] See UR no. 18.

[3] See OE nos. 25 and 4.

Mass with only a few relatives and friends. If for a serious reason Mass cannot be celebrated, the reception should take place where possible during a liturgy of the word. The person to be received into full communion should be consulted about the form of reception.

2479   4.   If the reception is celebrated outside Mass, the connection with eucharistic communion should be made clear. Mass should be celebrated as soon as possible, so that the newly received person may participate fully with other Catholics for the first time.

2480   5.   Baptized Christians are to receive both doctrinal and spiritual preparation, according to pastoral requirements in individual cases, for their reception into the full communion of the Catholic Church. They should grow in their spiritual adherence to the Church where they will find the fullness of their baptism.

During the period of preparation the candidate may share in worship according to the norms of the Ecumenical Directory.[a]

Any treatment of the candidates as though they were catechumens is to be absolutely avoided.

2481   6.   No abjuration of heresy is required of one born and baptized outside the visible communion of the Catholic Church, but only the profession of faith.[4]

2482   7.   The sacrament of baptism may not be repeated and conditional baptism is not permitted unless there is a prudent doubt about the fact or validity of the baptism already received. If after serious investigation it seems necessary — because of such prudent doubt —to confer baptism again conditionally, the minister should explain beforehand the reasons why baptism is conferred conditionally in this instance and he should administer it in the private form.[5]

The local Ordinary shall determine, in individual cases, what rites are to be included or excluded in conditional baptism.

2483   8.   It is the office of the bishop to receive baptized Christians into full communion. But the priest to whom he entrusts the celebration of the rite has the faculty of confirming the candidate during the rite of admission,[6] unless the latter has already been validly confirmed.

2484   9.   If the profession of faith and reception take place within Mass, the candidates, according to their own conscience, should confess their sins beforehand. They should first inform the confessor that they are about to be received into full communion. Any confessor who is lawfully approved may hear such a confession.

2485   10.   At the reception, candidates should be accompanied if possible by a sponsor, that is, the person who has had the chief part in bringing them into full communion or in preparing them. Two sponsors may be permitted for each candidate.

2486   11.   In the eucharistic celebration during which reception takes place or, if the reception takes place outside Mass, in the Mass that follows, communion may be received under both kinds by those received into communion, by their sponsors,

---

    [a]   See DOL 147 nos. 979–985; 1009–10.

    [4]   See Secretariat for Christian Unity, Ecumenical Directory I, nos. 19 and 20 [DOL 147 nos. 973 and 974].

    [5]   See ibid. nos. 14–15 [DOL 147 nos. 968–969].

    [6]   See *Rite of Confirmation*, Introduction no. 7 [DOL 305 no. 2516].

parents, and spouses, if they are Catholics, by lay catechists who have instructed them, and also by all Catholics present, if the numbers or other circumstances make it feasible.

12. Conferences of bishops may accommodate the rite of reception to various circumstances, in accord with the Constitution on the Liturgy art. 63.[b] The local Ordinary, moreover, may adapt the rite, enlarging or shortening it in view of special personal or local circumstances.[7]   2487

13. The names of those received into full communion should be recorded in a special book, with the date and place of baptism also noted.   2488

▶   329.   SC BISHOPS, *Directory on the Pastoral Office of Bishops,* 22 February 1973:

         no.   72:   Catechumenate [no. 2644].

302. SC DIVINE WORSHIP, **Reflections** on the *Rite of Christian Initiation of Adults,* Chapter 4, 8 March 1973: Not 9 (1973) 274–278 (Italian).

1.   Baptism cannot be repeated.[1] By reason of the indelible baptismal character, permanent membership in Christ and the Church cannot be nullified or completely lost, even if the person baptized is not reared in the faith or does not live up to the obligations of the faith or even expressly renounces it.   2489

2.   Baptism received as an infant in virtue of the faith of the Church must later be lived personally. The baptized must accept Christ's call, profess the faith belonging to them, deepen this faith more and more, and express it in works of charity. Catechesis[2] must help them and it has the further function of fitting the recipients into the concrete life of the community, that is, of bringing believers into the community's apostolic work and liturgical life. Such a postbaptismal catechesis is therefore in no way a catechumenate. Thus the term "catechumenate" is not to be used in this context,[3] but is to be reserved to true catechumens. The term "election" is likewise to be avoided, because the persons involved have already received God's election in baptism.   2490

3.   The psychological condition of noncatechized Catholics may resemble that of catechumens. Accordingly, their catechesis may rightly follow the same order of instructions as that for catechumens; but the sacraments already received must be taken into account.[4]   2491

      If the sponsor for baptism (or confirmation) has died or is no longer part of the community, another of its members can take special care of the candidate.[5]

---

   [b]   See DOL 1 no. 63.

   [7]   See Secretariat for Christian Unity, Ecumenical Directory I, no. 19 [DOL 147 no. 973].

   [1]   See Denz-Schön 110–111, 123, 1617.

   [2]   See *Rite of Christian Initiation of Adults* no. 296 [DOL 301 nos. 2448].

   [3]   Notice also that the *Rite of Receiving Baptized Christians into the Full Communion of the Catholic Church* no. 5 says: "Any treatment of the candidates as though they were catechumens is to be absolutely avoided" [DOL 301 no. 2480].

   [4]   See *Rite of Christian Initiation of Adults* nos. 296–298 [DOL 301 nos. 2448–50].

   [5]   See ibid. no. 299 [DOL 301 no. 2451].

LITURGICAL RITES FOR THE CATECHESIS OF THE BAPTIZED

2492   Catechesis addresses and takes in the whole person. It can thus be most helpful if catechesis is given a visible expression and is deepened by means of liturgical rites.[6] But since the people involved are baptized Christians and even fully "initiated," such rites must not be viewed as an extension of those of the catechumenate. They are rather a manifestation and explanation of an already accomplished reality in order to better the understanding of its significance. If, then, anyone wishes to use some of the rites from the *Rite of Christian Initiation of Adults,* which are permitted?

1. RITE OF WELCOME INTO THE COMMUNITY

2493   The rite "by which adults are welcomed into the community"[7] must be kept in clear distinction from the rite "of entrance into the order of catechumens."[8] Only some of the elements of this rite of entrance may be used. For example: the candidates express the willingness to make a serious effort to deepen their faith; the persons wishing to assist them (sponsors) express readiness to do so; the sign of the cross is used as a reminder of the signing of the forehead before baptism, but with a different text. The bringing of the candidates into the Church must be conducted in such a way that it does not have the appearance of being the first incorporation into the community, which would be a gesture contrary to fact; it must appear rather as a new and more conscious entrance into the living community.

    The "rite of election or enrollment of names,"[9] which for catechumens is a sign of their beginning the last period of probation, has no relevance to the baptized. The only way it might be used is as an expression of their written agreement to a serious catechetical effort.

2. LITURGIES OF THE WORD

2494   Liturgies of the word are celebrations appropriate even for noncatechized Christians.[10] These liturgies do not simply present the history of salvation but teach how to celebrate it; they lead to prayer that centers on those searching for faith and preparing themselves for participation in the Mass.

    The baptized, even those noncatechized, who take part in the Mass are not to be dismissed like catechumens before the liturgy of the eucharist. They have the right to take part, even if in some cases it may be advisable to introduce them to the eucharistic celebration gradually. They also already have the right to a postbaptismal catechesis.

3. PRESENTATION

2495   In coordination with the particular steps in the catechetical preparation of the candidates, there could be a place assigned in the different liturgies of the word for the "presentation of the creed, the Lord's Prayer, and the Gospels."[11]

---

[6] See ibid. nos. 300–303 [DOL 301 nos. 2452–55].

[7] See ibid. no. 300 [DOL 301 no. 2452].

[8] See ibid. nos. 68–97 [DOL 301 nos. 2395–99].

[9] See ibid. nos. 133–151 [DOL 301 nos. 2408–14].

[10] See ibid. no. 301 [DOL 301 no. 2453].

[11] See ibid. nos. 302; [DOL 301 no. 2454], 181–182 .

4. Penitential Services

The scrutinies, which for catechumens are combined with the major exorcisms, are meant to purify the mind and heart, to give help against temptation, and to strengthen the will to be converted and to hold fast to God.[12]

2496

To replace the scrutinies for catechumens, penitential services could be held in the case of the baptized[13] as a preparation leading them to a beneficial reception of the sacrament of penance. Accordingly, the rites could be like the penitential rites of the early Church: special prayers and blessing accompanied by the laying on of hands.

If deemed advisable, it is possible also to permit prayers like those for the exorcisms, supplicatory in form, but necessarily avoiding any allusion to original sin and mentioning only personal sin and temptation. The grace of baptism must always be kept in mind — received once, it is meant always to be lived more fully.[14]

5. Sacrament of Penance

With St. Augustine the early Church regarded the sacrament of penance as a "second baptism." On completion of the cycle of catechesis modeled on the progress of the catechumenate, the sacrament of penance could therefore occupy the place similar to that of baptism.[15]

2497

But only certain elements of the immediately preparatory and explanatory rites of baptism may be kept:

a. The "recitation of the creed"[16] before or after the sacrament of penance.

b. The presentation of the lighted baptismal candle after the sacrament of penance.[17]

Other elements cannot be included:

a. The *ephphetha* rite;[18] a person already baptized must make the profession of faith without any special preparatory rite: such a person already possesses the right to praise God and to turn to him in prayer.

b. The anointings;[19] in no way whatsoever may the prebaptismal anointing with the oil of catechumens or the postbaptismal anointing be used. Both are strictly bound up with baptism in its true and literal meaning.

Further, the use of the oil of catechumens is envisioned exclusively for catechumens, as is clear from the prayer used to bless it.[20]

---

12   See ibid. no. 154 [DOL 301 no. 2417].

13   See ibid. no. 303 [DOL 301 no. 2455].

14   What follows here in no. 5 applies to the anointings with the oil of catechumens, seen in the *Rite of Christian Initiation of Adults* nos. 127–132 as occurring during the period of the catechumenate and as connected with the exorcisms.

15   See *Rite of Christian Initiation of Adults* nos. 193–226.

16   See ibid. nos. 193–199.

17   See ibid. no. 226.

18   See ibid. nos. 200–202.

19   See ibid. nos. 206–207, 218, 224.

20   See ibid. no. 207; also *Rite of Blessing the Oil of Catechumens and of the Sick and of Consecrating the Chrism* no. 22. Other anointings with the oil of catechumens have with good reason been abolished, for example, the anointing of newly ordained priests and the anointing of bells.

The anointing with chrism is one of the signs that explain the conferral of baptism; the text for it speaks clearly of baptism just conferred.[21]

c.   The white garment:[22] this is put on immediately after baptism and explains the baptism just completed.

6. (Confirmation and) Eucharist

2498   After the reception of the sacrament of penance, the administration of confirmation (if not already received) and the eucharist follow, if possible on the Easter Vigil.[23]

If confirmation has already been received, prominence should be given to the renewal of the baptismal promises in an especially solemn celebration of the eucharist, the culmination of the catechetical process.[24]

Even afterwards, however, it is advisable to continue to watch over the Christian formation of those who have been catechized until they are able to direct their own Christian life.

▶   67.   SYNOD OF BISHOPS, "Message to the People of God," 28 October 1977:

Part II, nos. 7–11:   Catechesis [nos. 587–591].

---

[21]   See *Rite of Christian Initiation of Adults* no. 224.

[22]   See ibid. no. 225.

[23]   See ibid. no. 304 [DOL 301 no. 2456].

[24]   See ibid. nos. 217 and 219.

Section 3. Confirmation

SUMMARY (DOL 303–308). The Constitution on the Liturgy art. 71 decreed the revison of
the rite of confirmation in a way that would bring out more clearly the close relationship of
this sacrament with the whole process of Christian initiation. Some provisional measures
were taken in accord with the intent of the Council and in 1971 the revised rite was
published. The present section comprises 6 documents.

—The principal texts are Paul VI's apostolic constitution approving the new rite and
determining the essential elements of the sacrament (DOL 303), the decree promulgating
the rite (DOL 304), and the introduction to the new rite itself (DOL 305).

—The subsidiary texts are a communication on the effective date of the new rite (DOL
307)and official replies on the essential gesture in the conferral of the sacrament (DOL 306)
and on the authorized minister (DOL 308).

▶   103.   PAUL VI, Motu Proprio *Pastorale munus*, on the powers and privileges of bishops, 30 November 1963:

    I, no. 13:   Confirmation in danger of death by chaplains of hospitals, orphanages, or prisons [no. 724].

▶   1.   VATICAN COUNCIL II, Constitution on the Liturgy *Sacrosanctum Concilium*, 4 December 1963:

    art. 71:   Revision of the rite of confirmation [no. 71].

▶   20.   PAUL VI, Motu Proprio *Sacram Liturgiam*, on putting into effect some prescriptions of the Constitution on the Liturgy, 25 January 1964:

    art. IV: Confirmation during Mass [no. 282].

▶   23.   SC RITES (Consilium), Instruction (first) *Inter Oecumenici*, 26 September 1964:

    nos. 61:   Use of the vernacular [no. 353].
       64–67:   Rite of confirmation [nos. 356–359].

▶   328.   SC BISHOPS, Instruction *Sacra Congregatio pro Episcopis*, on pastoral ministry to migrants, 22 August 1969:

    nos. 38 and 39, § 4:   Confirmation in danger of death by chaplains [nos. 2632 and 2633].

▶   169.   SC CLERGY, *General Catechetical Directory*, 11 April 1971:

    no. 57:   Catechesis for confirmation [no. 1104].

303. PAUL VI, **Apostolic Constitution**, *Divinae consortium naturae*, approving the new rite of confirmation, 15 August 1971: AAS 63 (1971) 657–664; Not 7 (1971) 333–339.

2499   The sharing in the divine nature received through the grace of Christ bears a certain likeness to the origin, development, and nourishing of natural life. The faithful are born anew by baptism, strengthened by the sacrament of confirmation, and finally are sustained by the food of eternal life in the eucharist. By means of these sacraments of Christian initiation, they thus receive in increasing measure the treasures of divine life and advance toward the perfection of charity. It has rightly been written: "The body is washed, that the soul may be cleansed; the body is anointed, that the soul may be consecrated; the body is signed, that the soul too may be fortified; the body is overshadowed by the laying on of hands, that the soul may be enlightened by the Spirit; the body is fed on the body and blood of Christ, that the soul may be richly nourished by God."[1]

Conscious of its pastoral charge, the Second Vatican Ecumenical Council devoted special attention to these sacraments of initiation. It prescribed that the rites should be revised in a way that would make them more suited to the understanding of the faithful. Since the *Rite of Baptism for Children*, revised at the mandate of the Council and published at our command, is already in use, it is now fitting to publish

---

[1]   Tertullian, *De resurrectione mortuorum* 8, 3: CCL 2, 931.

a rite of confirmation, in order to show the unity of Christian initiation in its true light.

In fact, careful attention and application have been devoted in these last years   2500
to the task of revising the manner of celebrating this sacrament. The aim of this work has been that "the intimate connection of this sacrament with the whole of Christian initiation may stand out more clearly."[2] But the link between confirmation and the other sacraments of initiation is more easily perceived not simply from the fact that their rites have been more closely conjoined; the rite and words by which confirmation is conferred also make this link clear. As a result the rite and words of this sacrament "express more clearly the holy things they signify and the Christian people, as far as possible, are able to understand them with ease and take part in them fully, actively, and as befits a community."[3]

For that purpose, it has been our wish also to include in this revision what concerns the very essence of the rite of confirmation, through which the faithful receive the Holy Spirit as Gift.

The New Testament shows how the Holy Spirit was with Christ to bring the   2501
Messiah's mission to fulfillment. On receiving the baptism of John, Jesus saw the Spirit descending on him (see Mk 1:10) and remaining with him (see Jn 1:32). He was led by the Spirit to undertake his public ministry as the Messiah, relying on the Spirit's presence and assistance. Teaching the people of Nazareth, he showed by what he said that the words of Isaiah, "The Spirit of the Lord is upon me," referred to himself (see Lk 4:17–21).

He later promised his disciples that the Holy Spirit would help them also to bear fearless witness to their faith even before persecutors (see Lk 12:12). The day before he suffered, he assured his apostles that he would send the Spirit of truth from his Father (see Jn 15:26) to stay with them "for ever" (Jn 14:16) and help them to be his witnesses (see Jn 15:26). Finally, after his resurrection, Christ promised the coming descent of the Holy Spirit: "You will receive power when the Holy Spirit comes upon you; then you are to be my witnesses" (Acts 1:8; see Lk 24:49).

On the feast of Pentecost, the Holy Spirit did indeed come down in an extraordinary way on the apostles as they were gathered together with Mary the mother of Jesus and the group of disciples. They were so "filled with" the Holy Spirit (Acts 2:4) that by divine inspiration they began to proclaim "the mighty works of God." Peter regarded the Spirit who had thus come down upon the apostles as the gift of the Messianic age (see Acts 2:17–18). Then those who believed the apostles' preaching were baptized and they too received "the gift of the Holy Spirit" (Acts 2:38). From that time on the apostles, in fulfillment of Christ's wish, imparted to the newly baptized by the laying on of hands the gift of the Spirit that completes the grace of baptism. This is why the Letter to the Hebrews listed among the first elements of Christian instruction the teaching about baptism and the laying on of hands (Heb 6:2). This laying on of hands is rightly recognized by reason of Catholic tradition as the beginning of the sacrament of confirmation, which in a certain way perpetuates the grace of Pentecost in the Church.

This makes clear the specific importance of confirmation for sacramental initia-   2502
tion, by which the faithful "as members of the living Christ are incorporated into

---

[2]   SC art. 71 [DOL 1 no. 71].

[3]   SC art. 21 [DOL 1 no. 21].

him and configured to him through baptism and through confirmation and the eucharist."⁴ In baptism, the newly baptized receive forgiveness of sins, adoption as children of God, and the character of Christ by which they are made members of the Church and for the first time become sharers in the priesthood of their Savior (see 1 Pt 2:5, 9). Through the sacrament of confirmation those who have been born anew in baptism receive the inexpressible Gift, the Holy Spirit himself, by whom "they are endowed . . . with special strength."⁵ Moreover, having been signed with the character of this sacrament, they are "more closely bound to the Church"⁶ and "they are more strictly obliged to spread and defend the faith, both by word and by deed, as true witnesses of Christ."⁷ Finally, confirmation is so closely linked with the holy eucharist⁸ that the faithful, after being signed by baptism and confirmation, are incorporated fully into the Body of Christ by participation in the eucharist.⁹

2503   From ancient times the conferring of the gift of the Holy Spirit has been carried out in the Church through various rites. These rites have undergone many changes in the East and the West, but always keeping as their meaning the conferring of the Holy Spirit.

In many Eastern rites it seems that from early times a rite of chrismation, not yet clearly distinguished from baptism,¹⁰ prevailed for the conferring of the Holy Spirit. That rite continues in use today in the greater part of the Churches of the East.

In the West there are very ancient witnesses concerning the part of Christian initiation that was later distinctly recognized to be the sacrament of confirmation. There are directives for the performance of many rites after the baptismal washing and before the eucharistic meal — for example, anointing, the laying on of the hand, consignation¹¹ — contained both in liturgical documents¹² and in many testimonies of the Fathers. Consequently, in the course of the centuries, problems and doubts arose as to what belonged with certainty to the essence of the rite of confirmation. Worth mentioning, however, are at least some of the elements that, from the thirteenth century onward, in the ecumenical councils and in papal documents, cast considerable light on the importance of anointing, but at the same time did not allow the laying on of hands to be forgotten.

---

⁴ AG no. 36 [DOL 17 no. 253].

⁵ LG no. 11 [DOL 4 no. 141].

⁶ Ibid.

⁷ Ibid. See also AG no. 11 [DOL 17 no. 245].

⁸ See PO no. 5 [DOL 18 no. 260].

⁹ See ibid.

¹⁰ See Origen, De principiis 1, 3, 2: GCS 22, 49ff.; Comm. in Ep. ad Rom. 5, 8: PG 14, 1038. Cyril of Jerusalem, Catech. 16, 26; 21, 1–7: PG 33, 956; 1088–93.

¹¹ See Tertullian, De Baptismo 7–8: CCL 1, 282ff. B. Botte, ed., La tradition apostolique de Saint Hippolyte: Liturgiewissenschaftliche Quellen und Forschungen 39 (Münster, W., 1963) 52–54. Ambrose, De Sacramentis 2, 24; 3, 2, 8; 6, 2, 9: CSEL 73, 36; 42; 74–75; De mysteriis 7, 42: CSEL 73, 106.

¹² Mohlberg LibSacr 75. H. Lietzmann, ed., Das Sacramentarium Gregorianum nach den Aachener Urexemplar: Liturgiegeschichtliche Quellen 3 (Münster, W., 1921) 53ff. M. Ferotin, ed., Liber Ordinum: Monumenta Ecclesiae Liturgica V (Paris, 1904) 33ff. Mohlberg MissGall 67C. Vogel and R. Elze, Le Pontifical Romano-Germanique du dixième siècle: Le Texte II: Studi e Testi 227 (Vatican City, 1963) 109. M. Andrieu, Le Pontifical Romaine du XIIe siecle in Le Pontifical Romain au Moyen-Age v. 1: Studi e Testi 86 (Vatican City, 1938) 247ff., 289; Le Pontifical de la Curie Romaine au XIIIe siècle, ibid. v. 2: Studi e Testi 87 (Vatican City, 1940) 452ff.

Our predecessor Innocent III wrote: "The anointing of the forehead with   2504
chrism signifies the laying on of the hand, the other name for which is
confirmation, since through it the Holy Spirit is given for growth and strength."[13]
Another of our predecessors, Innocent IV, mentions that the apostles conferred the
Holy Spirit "through the laying on of the hand, which confirmation or the anointing of the forehead with chrism represents."[14] In the profession of faith of Emperor
Michael Palaeologus read at the Council of Lyons II mention is made of the sacrament of confirmation, which "bishops confer by the laying on of hands, anointing
with chrism those who have been baptized."[15] The Decree for the Armenians,
issued by the Council of Florence, declares that the "matter" of the sacrament of
confirmation is "chrism made of olive oil . . . and balsam"[16] and, quoting the words
of the Acts of the Apostles concerning Peter and John, who gave the Holy Spirit
through the laying on of hands (see Acts 8:17), it adds: "in the Church in place of
that laying on of the hand, confirmation is given."[17] The Council of Trent, though it
had no intention of defining the essential rite of confirmation, designated it simply
by the term "the holy chrism of confirmation."[18] Benedict XIV made this declaration: "Therefore let this be said, which is beyond dispute: in the Latin Church the
sacrament of confirmation is conferred by using sacred chrism or olive oil mixed
with balsam and blessed by the bishop, and by the sacramental minister's tracing
the sign of the cross on the forehead of the recipient, while the same minister
pronounces the words of the form."[19]

Taking account of these declarations and traditions, many theologians maintained that for valid administration of confirmation only the anointing with chrism,
done by placing the hand on the forehead, was required. Nevertheless, in the rites
of the Latin Church a laying of hands on those to be confirmed prior to anointing
them with chrism was always prescribed.

With regard to the words of the rite by which the Holy Spirit is given, it   2505
should be noted that already in the primitive Church Peter and John, in order to
complete the initiation of those baptized in Samaria, prayed that they might receive
the Holy Spirit and then laid hands on them (see Acts 8:15–17). In the East the first
traces of the expression *seal of the gift of the Holy Spirit* appeared in the fourth and
fifth centuries.[20] The expression was quickly accepted by the Church of Constantinople and still is in use in Byzantine-Rite Churches.

In the West, however, the words of the rite that completes baptism were less
settled until the twelfth and thirteenth centuries. But in the twelfth-century Roman
Pontifical the formulary that later became the common one first occurs: "I sign you

---

[13]   Innocent III, *Ep. "Cum venisset"*: PL 215, 285. The profession of faith that the same Pope imposed on
the Waldenses has these words: "We regard confirmation by the bishop, that is, the laying on of hands, to
be holy and to be received with reverence": PL 215, 1511.

[14]   Innocent IV, *Ep. "Sub Catholicae professione"*: Mansi 23, 579.

[15]   Council of Lyons II: Mansi 24, 71.

[16]   *Epistolae Pontificiae ad Concilium Florentinum spectantes*: G. Hofmann, ed., *Concilium Florentinum* v. 1, ser. A,
part II (Rome, 1944) 128.

[17]   Ibid. 129.

[18]   CT 5, Act. II, 996.

[19]   Benedict XIV, *Ep. "Ex quo primum tempore"* 52: *Benedicti XIV . . . Bullarium*, v. 3 (Prati, 1847) 320.

[20]   Cyril of Jerusalem, *Catech.* 18, 33: PG 33, 1056. Asterius, Bishop of Amasea, *In parabolam de filio prodigo*,
in the "Library of Photius," Cod. 271: PG 104, 213. See also *Epistola cuiusdam Patriarchae Constantinopolitani ad
Martyrium, Episcopum Antiochenum*:PG 119, 900.

with the sign of the cross and confirm you with the chrism of salvation. In the name of the Father and of the Son and of the Holy Spirit."[21]

2506   From what we have recalled, it is clear that in the administration of confirmation in the East and the West, though in different ways, the most important place was occupied by the anointing, which in a certain way represents the apostolic laying on of hands. Since this anointing with chrism is an apt sign of the spiritual anointing of the Holy Spirit who is given to the faithful, we wish to confirm its existence and importance.

As regards the words pronounced in confirmation, we have examined with the consideration it deserves the dignity of the respected formulary used in the Latin Church, but we judge preferable the very ancient formulary belonging to the Byzantine Rite. This expresses the Gift of the Holy Spirit himself and calls to mind the outpouring of the Spirit on the day of Pentecost (see Acts 2:1–4, 38). We therefore adopt this formulary, rendering it almost word for word.

2507   Therefore, in order that the revision of the rite of confirmation may, as is fitting, include even the essence of the sacramental rite, by our supreme apostolic authority we decree and lay down that in the Latin Church the following are to be observed for the future.

THE SACRAMENT OF CONFIRMATION IS CONFERRED THROUGH THE ANOINTING WITH CHRISM ON THE FOREHEAD, WHICH IS DONE BY THE LAYING ON OF THE HAND, AND THROUGH THE WORDS: BE SEALED WITH THE GIFT OF THE HOLY SPIRIT.[a]

But the laying of hands on the elect, carried out with the prescribed prayer before the anointing, is still to be regarded as very important, even if it is not of the essence of the sacramental rite: it contributes to the complete perfection of the rite and to a more thorough understanding of the sacrament. It is evident that this prior laying on of hands differs from the later laying on of the hand in the anointing of the forehead.

2508   Having established and declared all these elements concerning the essential rite of the sacrament of confirmation, we also approve by our apostolic authority the rite for the same sacrament. This has been revised by the Congregation for Divine Worship, after consultation with the Congregations for the Doctrine of the Faith, for the Discipline of the Sacraments, and for the Evangelization of Peoples on the matters that are within their competence. The Latin edition of the rite containing the new sacramental form will come into effect as soon as it is published; the editions in the vernacular languages, prepared by the conferences of bishops and confirmed by the Apostolic See, will come into effect on the date to be laid down by each conference. The old rite may be used until the end of the year 1972. From 1 January 1973, however, only the new rite is to be used by those concerned.

We intend that everything that we have laid down and prescribed should be firm and effective in the Latin Church, notwithstanding, where relevant, the apostolic constitutions and ordinances issued by our predecessors, and other prescriptions, even those worthy of special mention.

---

[21] M. Andrieu, *Le Pontifical Romain du XIIe siècle* in *Le Pontifical Romain au Moyen-Age*, v. 1: *Studi e testi* 86 (Vatican City, 1938) 247.

[a] Latin: ACCIPE SIGNACULUM DONI SPIRITUS SANCTI.

304. SC DIVINE WORSHIP, **Decree** *Peculiare Spiritus Sancti donum*, promulgating the *editio typica* of the new rite of confirmation, 22 August 1971: AAS 64 (1972) 77; Not 7 (1971) 332.

In the sacrament of confirmation the apostles and the bishops, who are their   2509
successors, hand on to the baptized the special gift of the Holy Spirit, promised by
Christ the Lord and poured out upon the apostles at Pentecost. Thus the initiation
in the Christian life is completed so that believers are strengthened by power from
heaven, made true witnesses of Christ in word and deed, and bound more closely to
the Church.

To make "the intimate connection of this sacrament with the whole of Christian initiation" clearer, Vatican Council II decreed that the rite of confirmation was
to be revised.[1]

Now that this work has been completed and approved by Pope Paul VI in the
Apostolic Constitution *Divinae consortium naturae* of 15 August 1971,[a] the Congregation for Divine Worship has published the new *Rite of Confirmation*. It is to replace the
rite now in use in the Roman Pontifical and Ritual. The Congregation declares the
present edition to be the *editio typica*.

All things to the contrary notwithstanding.

305. SC DIVINE WORSHIP, *Rite of Confirmation,* **Introduction**, 22 August
1971: Vatican Polyglot Press, 1971.

INTRODUCTION

I. DIGNITY OF CONFIRMATION

1.   Those who have been baptized continue on the path of Christian initiation   2510
through the sacrament of confirmation. In this sacrament they receive the Holy
Spirit whom the Lord sent upon the apostles on Pentecost.

2.   This giving of the Holy Spirit conforms believers more fully to Christ and   2511
strengthens them so that they may bear witness to Christ for the building up of his
Body in faith and love. They are so marked with the character or seal of the Lord
that the sacrament of confirmation cannot be repeated.

II. OFFICES AND MINISTRIES IN THE CELEBRATION OF CONFIRMATION

3.   One of the highest responsibilities of the people of God is to prepare the   2512
baptized for confirmation. Pastors have the special responsibility to see that all the
baptized reach the completion of Christian initiation and therefore that they are
carefully prepared for confirmation.

Adult catechumens who are to be confirmed immediately after baptism have
the help of the Christian community and, in particular, the formation that is given
to them during the catechumenate. Catechists, sponsors, and members of the local

---

[1]   See SC art. 71 [DOL 1 no. 71].

[a]   See DOL 303.

Church participate in the catechumenate by means of catechesis and community celebrations of the rites of initiation. For those who were baptized in infancy and are confirmed only as adults the plan for the catechumenate is used with appropriate adaptations.

The initiation of children into the sacramental life is ordinarily the responsibility and concern of Christian parents. They are to form and gradually increase a spirit of faith in the children and, at times with the help of catechism classes, prepare them for the fruitful reception of the sacraments of confirmation and the eucharist. The role of the parents is also expressed by their active participation in the celebration of the sacraments.

2513   4.   Pains should be taken to give the liturgical service the festive and solemn character that its significance for the local Church requires. This will be achieved above all if the candidates are gathered together for a community celebration of the rites. All the people of God, represented by the families and friends of the candidates and by members of the local community, will be invited to take part in such a celebration and will endeavor to express their faith by means of the effects the Holy Spirit has produced in them.

2514   5.   As a rule there should be a sponsor for each of those to be confirmed. These sponsors bring the candidates to receive the sacrament, present them to the minister for the anointing, and will later help them to fulfill their baptismal promises faithfully under the influence of the Holy Spirit whom they have received.

In view of contemporary pastoral circumstances, it is desirable that the godparent at baptism, if available, also be the sponsor at confirmation; CIC can. 796, no. 1 is therefore amended. This change expresses more clearly the link between baptism and confirmation and also makes the function and responsibility of the sponsor more effective.

Nonetheless the option of choosing a special sponsor for confirmation is not excluded. Even the parents themselves may present their children for confirmation. It is for the local Ordinary to determine diocesan practice in the light of local conditions and circumstances.[R1]

2515   6.   Pastors will see that the sponsors, chosen by the candidates or their families, are spiritually fit to take on this responsibility and have these qualities:

   a.   sufficient maturity to fulfill their function;

   b.   membership in the Catholic Church and their own reception of Christian initiation through baptism, confirmation, and eucharist;

   c.   freedom from any impediment of law to their fulfilling the office of sponsor.

2516   7.   The primary minister of confirmation is the bishop. Normally a bishop administers the sacrament so that there will be a clearer reference to the first pouring forth of the Holy Spirit on Pentecost: after the apostles were filled with the Holy Spirit, they themselves gave the Spirit to the faithful through the laying on of hands. Thus the reception of the Spirit through the ministry of the bishop shows the close bond

---

[R1]   Query: Is a sponsor still required for confirmation? Reply: According to the *Rite of Confirmation*, Introduction no. 5, *as a rule*, that is, apart from exceptional cases, there should be a sponsor. But three possibilities are presented; they are not listed as equivalent, but in a certain order of precedence, the preferred way coming first. It is *desirable* [text paraphased]. Nonetheless the option of choosing a special sponsor for confirmation is *not excluded*. Even the parents themselves may present their children for confirmation. It is up to the local Ordinary, in his pastoral prudence and "in the light of local circumstances" to decide on "the diocesan practice." In exceptional circumstances he may even permit a person to receive confirmation without a sponsor: Not 11 (1975) 61–62.

that joins the confirmed to the Church and the mandate received from Christ to bear witness to him before all.

The law gives the faculty to confirm to the following besides the bishop:

a. apostolic administrators who are not bishops, prelates or abbots *nullius*, vicars and prefects apostolic, vicars capitular, within the limits of their territory and while they hold office;

b. priests who, in virtue of an office they lawfully hold, baptize an adult or a child old enough for catechesis or receive a validly baptized adult into the full communion of the Church;

c. in danger of death, provided a bishop is not easily available or is lawfully impeded: pastors and parochial vicars; in their absence, their associate pastors; priests who are in charge of special parishes lawfully established; administrators; substitute and assistant priests (coadjutors);[1] in the absence of all of the preceding, any priest who is not disqualified by censure or canonical penalty.

8. On the basis of true need and a special reason, as sometimes is present because of the large number of those to be confirmed, the minister of confirmation mentioned in no. 7 or the extraordinary minister designated by special indult of the Apostolic See or by law may associate other priests with himself in the administration of this sacrament.   2517

It is required that these priests:

a. either have a particular function or office in the diocese, being, namely, vicars general, episcopal vicars or delegates, district or regional vicars,[2] or those who by mandate of the Ordinary are counted as equal to these *ex officio*;

b. or be the pastors of the places where confirmation is conferred, pastors of the places where the candidates belong, or priests who have had a special part in the catechetical preparation of the candidates.

III. CELEBRATION OF THE SACRAMENT

9. The sacrament of confirmation is conferred through the anointing with chrism on the forehead, which is done by the laying on of the hand, and through the words: BE SEALED WITH THE GIFT OF THE HOLY SPIRIT.   2518

The laying of hands on the candidates with the prayer, *All-powerful God*, does not pertain to the valid giving of the sacrament. But it is still to be regarded as very important: it contributes to the complete perfection of the rite and to a more thorough understanding of the sacrament.

The priests who may at times be associated with the principal minister in conferring the sacrament join him in the laying of hands on all the candidates, but say nothing.

The whole rite presents a twofold symbolism. The laying of hands on the candidates by the bishop and the concelebrating priest represents the biblical gesture by which the gift of the Holy Spirit is invoked and in a manner well suited to the understanding of the Christian people. The anointing with chrism and the accompanying words express clearly the effect of the giving of the Holy Spirit. Signed with the perfumed oil, the baptized receive the indelible character, the seal of the Lord, together with the gift of the Spirit that conforms them more closely to Christ and gives them the grace of spreading "the sweet odor of Christ."

---

[1] See CIC can. 451, 471, 476, 216 § 4, 472, 474, 475.

[2] See CIC can. 217 § 1.

2519   10. The chrism is consecrated by the bishop in the Mass that is celebrated as a rule on Holy Thursday for this purpose.[a]

2520   11. Adult catechumens and children who are baptized at an age when they are old enough for catechesis should ordinarily be admitted to confirmation and the eucharist at the same time as they receive baptism. If this is impossible, they should receive confirmation at another community celebration (see no. 4). Similarly, adults who were baptized in infancy should, after suitable preparation, receive confirmation and the eucharist at a community celebration.

With regard to children, in the Latin Church the administration of confirmation is generally delayed until about the seventh year. For pastoral reasons, however, especially to implant deeply in the lives of the faithful complete obedience to Christ the Lord and a firm witnessing to him, the conferences of bishops may set an age that seems more suitable. This means that the sacrament is given, after the formation proper to it, when the recipients are more mature.

In this case every necessary precaution is to be taken to ensure that in the event of danger of death or serious problems of another kind children receive confirmation in good time, so that they are not left without the benefit of this sacrament.

2521   12. Persons who are to receive confirmation must have already received baptism. Moreover, those possessing the use of reason must be in the state of grace, properly instructed, and capable of renewing the baptismal promises.

The conference of bishops has responsibility for determining more precisely the catechetical resources for the preparation of candidates for confirmation, especially children.

In the case of adults, those principles are to be followed, with the required adaptations, that apply in the individual dioceses to admitting catechumens to baptism and eucharist. Measures are to be taken especially for catechesis preceding confirmation and for the association of the candidates with the Christian community and with individual Christians. Such association is to be of a kind that is effective and sufficient as a practical help for the candidates to achieve formation toward both bearing witness by Christian living and carrying on the apostolate. It should also assist the candidates to have a genuine desire to share in the eucharist (see *Rite of Christian Initiation of Adults*, Introduction no. 19[b]).

Sometimes the preparation of baptized adults for confirmation coincides with preparation for marriage. In such cases, if it is foreseen that the conditions for a fruitful reception of confirmation cannot be satisfied, the local Ordinary will judge whether it is better to defer confirmation until after the marriage.

If one who has the use of reason is confirmed in danger of death, there should, as far as possible, be some spiritual preparation beforehand, suited to the individual situation.

2522   13. Confirmation takes place as a rule within Mass in order that the fundamental connection of this sacrament with all of Christian initiation may stand out in clearer light. Christian initiation reaches its culmination in the communion of the body and blood of Christ. The newly confirmed therefore participate in the eucharist, which completes their Christian initiation.

---

[a] See DOL 459.

[b] See DOL 301 no. 2346.

If the candidates for confirmation are children who have not received the eucharist and are not being admitted to first communion at this liturgical celebration or if there are other special circumstances, confirmation should be celebrated outside Mass. When this occurs, there is first to be a celebration of the word of God.

When confirmation is given during Mass, it is fitting that the minister of confirmation celebrate the Mass or, better, concelebrate it, especially with those priests who may be joining him in administering the sacrament.

If the Mass is celebrated by someone else, it is proper that the bishop preside over the liturgy of the word, doing all that the celebrant normally does, and that he give the blessing at the end of Mass.

Great emphasis should be placed on the celebration of the word of God that introduces the rite of confirmation. It is from the hearing of the word of God that the many-sided work of the Holy Spirit flows out upon the Church and upon each one of the baptized and confirmed. Through this hearing of his word God's will is made known in the life of Christians.

Great importance is likewise to be attached to the saying of the Lord's Prayer. Those to be confirmed will recite it together with the congregation — either during Mass before communion or outside Mass before the blessing — because it is the Spirit who prays in us and in the Spirit the Christian says: "Abba, Father."

14. The pastor should record in a special book the names of the minister, those confirmed, parents, and sponsors, and the date and place of confirmation. This is in addition to the notation in the baptismal register to be made according to the requirements of the law.   2523

15. If the pastor of the newly confirmed person was not present, the minister should promptly inform him of the confirmation, either personally or through a representative.   2524

IV. ADAPTATIONS PERMITTED IN THE RITE OF CONFIRMATION

16. By virtue of the Constitution of the Liturgy (art. 63 b),[c] conferences of bish-   2525
ops have the right to prepare in particular rituals a section bearing the same title as the present title IV on confirmation in the Roman Pontifical. This is to be adapted to the needs of the individual parts of the world and it is to be used once the *acta* of the conference have been reviewed by the Apostolic See.[3]

17. The conference of bishops will consider whether, in view of local circum-   2526
stances and the culture and traditions of the people, it is opportune:

a. to make suitable adaptations of the formularies for the renewal of baptismal promises and professions, either following the text in the rite of baptism or accommodating these formularies so that they are more in accord with the circumstances of the candidates for confirmation;

b. to introduce a different manner for the minister to give the sign of peace after the anointing, either to each individual or to all the newly confirmed together.

---

c   See DOL 1 no. 63.

3   See *Rite of Baptism for Children*, General Introduction to Christian Initiation nos. 30–33 [DOL 294 nos. 2279–82].

2527   18. The minister of confirmation may introduce some explanations into the rite in individual cases in view of the capacity of the candidates for confirmation. He may also make appropriate accommodations in the existing texts, for example, by expressing these in a kind of dialogue, especially with children.

When confirmation is given by a minister who is not a bishop, whether by concession of the general law or by special indult of the Apostolic See, it is fitting for him to mention in the homily that the bishop is the original minister of the sacrament and to explain the reason why priests receive the faculty to confirm from the law or by an indult of the Apostolic See.

V. PREPARATIONS

2528   19. The following should be prepared for the administration of confirmation:

a.   when confirmation is given within Mass, the vestments prescribed for the celebration of Mass both for the bishop and for any assisting priests who concelebrate with him. If the Mass is celebrated by someone else, the minister of confirmation as well as any priests joining him in administering the sacrament should take part in the Mass wearing the vestments prescribed for administering confirmation: alb, stole, and, for the minister, the cope; these also are the vestments worn when confirmation is given outside Mass;

b.   chairs for the bishop and the priests assisting him;

c.   vessel (or vessels) for the chrism;

d.   Roman Pontifical or Roman Ritual;

e.   when confirmation is given within Mass, the requisites for celebration of Mass and for communion under both kinds, if it is to be given;

f.   the requisites for the washing of hands after the anointing of those to be confirmed.

▶   301.   SC DIVINE WORSHIP, *Rite of Christian Initiation of Adults*, Introduction, 6 January 1972:

nos. 34–35:	Confirmation of adults [nos. 2361–62].
56:	Confirmation on Pentecost [no. 2383].
295–305:	Preparation of baptized, non-catechized adults for confirmation and eucharist [nos. 2447–57].

306. PONTIFICAL COMMISSION FOR THE INTERPRETATION OF THE DECREES OF VATICAN COUNCIL II, Reply to a query, on the essential sacramental gesture for confirmation, 9 June 1972: AAS 64 (1972) 526; Not 8 (1972) 281.

2529   The Fathers of the Pontifical Commission for the Interpretation of the Decrees of Vatican Council II have decided to reply in this way to the following query proposed in their plenary session, thus:

Query: According to the Apostolic Constitution *Divinae consortium naturae*, 15 August 1971,[a] must the minister in carrying out the act of anointing with chrism lay his outstretched hand on the head of the one being confirmed or is an anointing with the thumb sufficient?

---

a   See DOL 303 no. 2507.

Reply: To the first, no; to the second, yes, according to the document. The intent is: anointing with chrism done as described sufficiently expresses the laying on of hands.

Pope Paul VI in an audience granted to the undersigned, 9 June 1972, confirmed the decision given, approved it, and ordered its publication.

307. SC DIVINE WORSHIP, **Communication** *La Sacra Congregazione*, on effective dates for the new rites of confirmation and of institution to ministries, 8 December 1972.*

The Congregation for Divine Worship announces:

1.   *Rite of confirmation.* By reason of what is laid down by the Apostolic Constitution *Divinae consortium naturae*, 15 August 1971, the new *Rite of Confirmation* must be used throughout the Church, whether in Latin or in the vernacular, beginning on 1 January 1973.[a]   `2530`

2.   *Rite for conferring ecclesial ministries and for candidates for holy orders.* In accord with the Motu Proprio *Ministeria quaedam*[b] and the Motu Proprio *Ad pascendum*,[c] 15 August 1972, new rites have been prepared, namely: the *Rite of Institution of Readers and Acolytes*; of *Admission to Candidacy as Deacons and Priests*; of *Commitment to Celibacy*. The effective date for the use of these rites in Latin is 1 January 1973. They may be used in the vernacular after their translation has been approved by the conferences of bishops and confirmed by the Holy See.   `2531`

308. PONTIFICAL COMMISSION FOR THE INTERPRETATION OF THE DECREES OF VATICAN COUNCIL II, **Reply** to a query, on the minister of confirmation, 25 April 1975: AAS 67 (1975) 348; Not 11 (1975) 176.

The Fathers of the Pontifical Commission for the Interpretation of the Decrees of Vatican Council II have decided to reply in this way to the following queries, proposed to them in their plenary session: `2532`

I
(MINISTER OF CONFIRMATION)

Query: Does the faculty in the *Rite of Receiving Baptized Christians into the Full Communion of the Catholic Church*, Introduction no. 8,[a] and in the *Rite of Confirmation*, Introduction no. 7 b,[b] include also the case of the readmission of an apostate from the faith who has not been confirmed? The faculty in question permits the priest

---

*   Text, OR 15 Dec. 1972, 2 (Italian).
a   See DOL 303.
b   See DOL 340.
c   See DOL 319.
a   See DOL 301 no. 2483.
b   See DOL 305 no. 2516.

deputed by the bishop for the reception to confirm the candidate as part of the reception rite.

Reply: Yes.

[. . .]

Pope Paul VI, at an audience granted to the undersigned [President of the Commission], 25 April 1975, confirmed these decisions, approved them, and ordered their publication.

▶ 132. SC DIVINE WORSHIP, Letter to the English-speaking conferences of bishops, approving the translation of the sacramental form of confirmation, 5 May 1975.

▶ 330. SC BISHOPS, Decree *Apostolatus maris*, on the pastoral care of seamen and ship passengers, 24 September 1977:

Part II, I, no. 8:   Confirmation aboard ship [no. 2669].

Section 4. Holy Orders

SUMMARY (DOL 309-335). The Constitution on the Liturgy not only called for a revision of the rites of ordination (art. 76) but also explicitly recognized the many forms of genuine liturgical ministry exercised in the liturgical assembly (art. 28–29). This fact, as well as other elements of the ecclesiology of the Council, is reflected in the distinction between the present section and the following section on ministries other than those of the ordained. The consideration of the sacrament of orders is divided into three subsections that reflect the conciliar teaching on sacred orders, the revision of the rites of ordination, the liturgical aspects of conciliar and postconciliar emphases in the area of pastoral ministry, and the increased attention to liturgical formation in seminaries, in accord with the Constitution (art. 15–17).

Section 4. Holy Orders: A. The Sacrament Itself

SUMMARY (DOL 309–323). By reason of postconciliar developments, in the Latin Church there are now three sacred orders, episcopacy, presbyterate, and diaconate, including the permanent diaconate; the order of subdeacons and the minor orders have been suppressed in the general discipline of the Latin Church (see DOL 340). The 15 texts here presented reflect this development.

—On the diaconate the major documents include a motu proprio of Paul VI on the sacred order of diaconate (DOL 319) and another on restoration of the permanent diaconate in the Latin Church (DOL 309). There is also a letter of the Congregation for Catholic Education on formation of permanent deacons (DOL 314) and a group of replies giving official interpretations on the powers of deacons (DOL 310, 311, 316, 320). The two remaining texts are particular responses, on deacons assisting at marriages (DOL 312) and on the permanent diaconate in the Society of African Missions (DOL 313).

—On the priesthood there are excerpts from the study issued by the Synod of Bishops, *The Ministerial Priesthood* (DOL 318), from the declaration of the Congregation for the Doctrine of the Faith on the ordination of women (DOL 321), and from two letters of John Paul I (DOL 322, 323). In addition there is the publication of the texts for priests' renewal of their commitment to celibacy (DOL 315) and an excerpt regarding liturgical celebrations from the norms for the laicization of priests issued by the Congregation for the Doctrine of the Faith (DOL 317).

▶ 4. VATICAN COUNCIL II, Dogmatic Constitution on the Church *Lumen gentium,* 21 November 1964:

        nos. 21, 26–27:   Bishops [nos. 145, 146–147].
            28:          Priests [no. 148].
            29:          Deacons [no. 149].

▶ 7. VATICAN COUNCIL II, Decree on the Pastoral Office of Bishops *Christus Dominus,* 28 October 1965:

        nos. 11–12, 14–15:   Diocesan bishops [nos. 191–192, 193–194].
            30:          Pastors of parishes [no. 196].
            38:          The conferences of bishops [no. 199].

▶ 18. VATICAN COUNCIL II, Decree on the Ministry and Life of Priests *Presbyterorum Ordinis,* 7 December 1965:

        nos. 2–8:   Ministry of priests [nos. 257–263].

▶ 199. SC RITES, Decree (Rome), on the deacon at Mass, 12 January 1966.

▶ 11. PONTIFICAL CENTRAL COMMISSION FOR COORDINATING POSTCONCILIAR WORKS AND FOR INTERPRETING THE DECREES OF VATICAN COUNCIL II, Reply to a query, on *Perfectae caritatis* no. 10 § 2, 10 June 1966.

309. PAUL VI, **Motu Proprio** *Sacrum Diaconatus Ordinem*, restoring the permanent diaconate in the Latin Church, 18 June 1967: AAS 59 (1967) 697–704 (excerpt).

2533   The holy order of diaconate has been held in high honor by the Church ever since primitive apostolic times. St. Paul is a witness to this as he addresses greetings explicitly to deacons along with bishops[1] and instructs Timothy on the virtues and spiritual qualities required of deacons if they are to be judged worthy of their ministry.[2]

      The Second Ecumenical Vatican Council mentioned the diaconate with honor in the Constitution *Lumen gentium*, thus continuing the ancient practice. After treating bishops and presbyters, the Council in the same document discussed this third level of holy orders, explaining its dignity and listing its offices. But the Council saw very well that "as the discipline of the Latin Church currently stands, these diaconal functions supremely necessary to the Church's life, can be carried out only with great difficulty in many places." In a desire to deal more effectively with a matter of such importance, the Council wisely decreed that "henceforth it will be permissible to restore the diaconate as a distinct and permanent rank of the hierarchy."[3]

2534   Many diaconal functions, especially in mission lands, are in practice often entrusted to laymen. Nevertheless "to make their ministry more effective through sacramental grace, it is advantageous to strengthen and bind closer to the altar

    [1] See Phil 1:1.

    [2] See 1 Tm 3:8–13.

    [3] LG no. 29 [DOL 4 no. 149].

through the apostolic tradition of the laying on of hands those men who are actually exercising diaconal functions . . . ."[4] Such a course of action will serve very well to put the distinctive nature of this order in its proper light. It is not to be regarded simply as a step on the way to priesthood; rather it is endowed with its own indelible character and special grace in such a way that those who are called to the diaconate are empowered for a permanent service to the "mysteries of Christ and the Church."[5]

The restoration of the permanent diaconate throughout the Latin Church is not a matter of obligation, because "it belongs to the various sorts of competent, territorial bodies of bishops to decide, with papal approval, whether and where it may be advantageous to create permanent deacons for the care of souls."[6] Nevertheless we regard it as not only helpful but imperative to issue clear and precise norms about this matter. They will adapt the permanent diaconate to the new prescriptions of the Council and set forth in advance the right conditions not only for a more effective planning of the diaconal ministry but also for relating the formation of the candidates more closely to their own different modes of life, to the obligations they share, and to their sacred dignity.   2535

First, then, unless an exception is noted, we confirm all those things that the Code of Canon Law lays down on deacons' rights and obligations, both those common to all clerics and those proper to deacons. We rule that these rights and obligations apply also to those who are to remain deacons permanently. In addition, for deacons we also lay down what follows.

V

22. According to Vatican Council II's Constitution *Lumen gentium*,[a] it belongs to deacons, insofar as the local Ordinary has assigned them these functions: 2536

1. to assist the bishop and priest during liturgical services in regard to all those matters assigned to the deacon by the liturgical books for the various rites;

2. to administer baptism solemnly and to supply the ceremonies that were omitted in either an infant or adult baptism;

3. to reserve the eucharist and to give communion to himself and others; to bring viaticum to the dying; to give benediction with the monstrance or ciborium;

4. to assist at marriages in the name of the Church, when no priest is available, and, with the bishop's or pastor's delegation, to impart the nuptial blessing; the other requirements of CIC being observed and can. 1098 remaining in force,[8] whenever the canons speak of a priest, the text is also to be taken as applying to a deacon;

5. to administer sacramentals and preside at funeral and burial rites;

6. to read the books of Scripture to the faithful, to instruct and exhort the congregation;

---

4   AG no. 16 [DOL 17 no. 248].

5   See LG no. 41: AAS 57 (1965) 46; ConstDecrDecl 168.

6   LG 29 [DOL 4 no. 149].

a   See LG no. 29 [DOL 4 no. 149].

8   CIC can. 1095, § 2 and 1096.

7. to preside at offices of worship and at prayer services, when no priest is present;

8. to lead celebrations of the word, especially in places where there is a lack of priests;

9. to perform, in the name of the hierarchy, duties of charity and administration, and works of social service;

10. to act as the lawful authority, in the name of the pastor and the bishop, over isolated Christian communities;

10. to encourage and help with the apostolic works of the laity.[R1]

2537   23. All these services are to be carried out in full communion with the bishop and his presbyterate, that is, under their authority; they exercise their charge over the local faithful through the deacon.

2538   24. Deacons are, insofar as is possible, to take part in pastoral councils.

VI

2539   25. As servants of the mysteries of Christ and the Church, deacons are to refrain from every vice and to be intent on pleasing God in all things, "prepared to do every good work"[9] for the salvation of souls. Because of the order they have received, they should far surpass others in the liturgical life, dedication to prayer, divine service, obedience, charity, and chastity.

2540   26. It shall be up to the conferences of bishops to lay down norms for fostering the spiritual life of deacons, both the celibate and the married. But it is for local Ordinaries to ensure that all deacons:

1. devote time to the word of God by assiduous reading and thoughtful meditation;

2. often, even daily if possible, take part in the sacrifice of the Mass, be strengthened by the sacrament, and make visits of devotion;

3. frequently purify their spirit through the sacrament of penance and prepare for its worthy reception by a daily examination of conscience;

4. honor and love the Virgin Mary, Mother of God, with deep devotion.

R1 Query: Some religious communities have inquired whether, when there are priests present, a deacon may lawfully: a. preside at the divine office as hebdomadarian; b. give benediction; c. give the homily. Reply: a. The phrase "a priest or deacon" in GILH nos. 254 and 256 [DOL 426 nos. 3684 and 3686] and in the rubrics of the Ordinary of the Liturgy of the Hours, in no way implies that a deacon may exercise the office of presiding when priests are present, even though the texts in question do not carry the phrase "in the absence of a priest." The mind of the legislator is that the deacon is ordained to assist the priest or to substitute when there is no priest. Accordingly, on the basis of the current norms a deacon is not to preside at the celebration of the office when priests are present. On the other hand, a deacon certainly does carry out the office of presiding in a group of women religious or laity or when there are priests who are lawfully impeded (they are sick, elderly, etc.). b. Similarly in *Holy Communion and Worship of the Eucharist outside Mass* nos. 91, 92, 97, 99, 100, the phrase "a priest or deacon" even when there is no explicit use of the phrase "or in the absence of a priest" in no way means that the deacon, who is an ordinary minister for exposition, may give benediction when there are priests present. The right practice and the exceptions are the same as in the preceding paragraph. c. The deacon is an ordinary minister of the word of God, just as he is for the celebration of baptism and for the giving of communion. As such he may lawfully give the homily after the proclamation of the gospel, as indicated in GIRM no. 61, which adds "sometimes" [DOL 208 no. 1451]. Accordingly, the deacon may fulfill his proper office in the preaching of the word of God without completely supplanting priests in the work of instructing the faithful: Not 12 (1976) 46–47.

9 2 Tm 2:21.

27. It is highly fitting that permanent deacons daily recite at least some part of the divine office, to be designated by the conference of bishops.   2541

28. Diocesan deacons must make a retreat at least every three years in some religious house or place of prayer designated by the local Ordinary.   2542

29. Deacons are not to neglect study, especially the study of sacred doctrine. They are to read the books of the Bible faithfully. They are to devote themselves to the ecclesiastical disciplines in order to equip themselves to explain Catholic teaching correctly to others and to be better prepared to give guidance and support to the faithful. To these ends, deacons are to be called together at regularly scheduled meetings for the discussion of issues involving their life and ministry.   2543

30. Because of the distinctive nature of the ministry committed to them, deacons are obliged to show respect and obedience toward the bishop. Bishops in turn are to esteem these servants of the people of God and to treat them with fatherly charity. When any deacon with good reason resides outside his own diocese for any length of time, he is to submit to the supervision and authority of the local Ordinary in these matters involving diaconal duties and functions.[10]   2544

31. In matters of dress, deacons are to follow local custom as determined by the norms of the conference of bishops.   2545

VII

32. To establish the permanent diaconate in a religious community of men is a right proper to the Holy See and it alone examines and approves the decisions of general chapters in this regard.[b]   2546

310. PONTIFICAL COMMISSION FOR THE INTERPRETATION OF THE DECREES OF VATICAN COUNCIL II, **Reply** to a query, on the Motu Proprio *Sacrum Diaconatus Ordinem* no. 22, 26 March 1968: AAS 60 (1968) 363.

The Fathers of the Pontifical Commission for the Interpretation of the Decrees of Vatican Council II have decided to reply in this way to the following query, proposed to them in plenary session: 2547

Query: Does a deacon who is not a permanent deacon but intends to go on to priesthood have those functions that are listed in the Constitution *Lumen gentium*, 21 November 1964, no. 29[a] and in the Motu Proprio *Sacrum Diaconatus Ordinem*, 18 June 1967, no. 22?[b]

Reply: Yes.

Pope Paul VI at an audience granted to the undersigned [President of the Commission], 26 March 1968, confirmed this decision, approved it, and ordered its publication.

---

[10] *Ius Orientalium, De personis* can. 87: AAS 49 (1957) 462.

[b] See DOL 313.

[a] See DOL 4 no. 149.

[b] See DOL 309 no. 2536.

311. PONTIFICAL COMMISSION FOR THE INTERPRETATION OF THE DECREES OF VATICAN COUNCIL II, **Reply** to a query regarding the Motu Proprio *Sacrum Diaconatus Ordinem* no. 22, § 4, 4 April 1969: AAS 61 (1969) 348.

2548   The Fathers of the Pontifical Commission for the Interpretation of the Decrees of Vatican Council II have decided to reply in this way to the following query, proposed to them in plenary session:

Query: On the basis of a comparison with the Constitution *Lumen gentium*, 21 November 1964, no. 29,ᵃ in the Motu Proprio *Sacrum Diaconatus Ordinem*, 18 June 1967, no. 22, § 4ᵇ does the phrase *ubi deest sacerdos* (when no priest is available) place a condition for the validity of a deacon's receiving delegation to assist at a marriage?

Reply: No, the phrase in question does not amount to a requisite for validity.

Pope Paul VI at an audience granted to the undersigned [President of the Commission], 4 April 1969, confirmed this decision, approved it, and ordered its publication.

312. SC DISCIPLINE OF THE SACRAMENTS, **Letter** to the president of the conference of bishops of the U.S.A., on a permanent deacon's assisting at a marriage, 30 August 1968.*

2549   Because it is a matter that will probably be of general interest to the hierarchy, I wish to inform you of a decision given by the Sacred Congregation for the Sacraments on 30 August 1968 (N. 1660/68) about the assistance of a deacon at a marriage with delegation from the bishop or pastor.

The Holy See states that, after publication of the Motu Proprio *Sacrum Diaconatus Ordinem* of 18 June 1967, deacons *permanenter constituti* can assist at marriages under the conditions specified in no. V of this document.ᵃ

These norms cannot be applied to deacons who are preparing for the priesthood.

Previous to the Motu Proprio *Sacrum Diaconatus Ordinem*, no deacon could validly assist at a marriage.

▶   208.   SC RITES (Consilium); SC DIVINE WORSHIP, General Instruction of the Roman Missal, 1st ed. 6 April 1969; 4th ed. 27 March 1975:

nos. 59–61:	Offices and ministries of holy orders [nos. 1449–51].
127–141:	Functions of the deacon [nos. 1517–31].

ᵃ   See DOL 4 no. 149.

ᵇ   See DOL 309 no. 2536.

*   Text CLD 7, 689.

ᵃ   See DOL 309 no. 2536.

313. SC EVANGELIZATION OF PEOPLES, **Rescript** (Society of African Missions) to Rev. Theo van Asten, Superior General, granting establishment of the permanent diaconate in that Society, 5 July 1969.*

Very Reverend Father:

It has been your wish to put before this Congregation in due time a request having as its purpose that, in conformity with the Motu Proprio *Sacrum Diaconatus Ordinem,*[a] this Congregation approve the unanimous resolution of the general chapter of your Society that "the permanent diaconate be established in the Society."

2550

I am pleased to inform you that this Congregation, after careful consideration of the desire expressed by your general chapter, has decided that the reasons agreed upon by the chapter are sound. Having in mind also the Decree *Ad gentes* no. 16,[b] the Congregation through this letter therefore gladly gives its approval to the permission requested, "all requirements of the law being respected."

In informing you of this decision, I draw your attention to two points.

1. It is better for the diaconate to be conferred only on those who have made their permanent commitment in the Society.

2. For young deacons who have already entered the Society as brothers, the period of special formation for the diaconate may be shortened. This takes into account the formation they have already received in the novitiate and during the years of probation or the first years of their religious life.

In the case of those who enter the Society with the intention from the outset of becoming deacons, the overall period of formation cannot be less than three years (see *Sacrum Diaconatus Ordinem* no. 9).

In the case of brothers who are already older, that is, over thirty-five years of age, a particular program of formation for the diaconate is to be arranged for them in keeping with the directives of *Sacrum Diaconatus Ordinem* (nos. 14 and 15) and with their own individual needs.

314. SC CATHOLIC EDUCATION, **Letter** *Come è a conoscenza* to apostolic nuncios, on formation for the permanent diaconate, 16 July 1969.*

As is well known, Pope Paul VI, through the Motu Proprio *Sacrum Diaconatus Ordinem,*[a] has granted permission for the restoration in the Latin Church of the permanent diaconate. This is in accord with the express intention of Vatican Council II.[b]

2551

As soon as some conferences of bishops requested such a permission for their own countries, it became a matter of urgent necessity to formulate norms for the preparation of candidates to the permanent diaconate.

---

* Text, CommRel 51 (1970) 269–270 (French).

a See DOL 309 no. 2546.

b See DOL 17 no. 248.

* Text, *Enchiridion Vaticanum* 3, 10th ed. (Edizioni Dehoniane, Bologna, 1976) nos. 1408–12 (Italian).

a See DOL 309 no. 2535.

b See DOL 4 no. 149.

As the first measure to be taken, each conference of bishops should set up a committee of experts, if it has not yet done so. This committee's task should be a thorough study based on the requirements of its own country to determine whether there are solid grounds for introducing the permanent diaconate and what is the most effective way of doing so.

The committee's study will do well to take as criteria the basic principles already expressed in *Sacrum Diaconatus Ordinem*.

2552 　　　We are facing a problem that is new for our times and it is not a simple matter to set up in advance a *ratio studiorum* and a formation program for candidates for the permanent diaconate.

The first need is to determine the functions belonging to the deacon as one who is midway between priest and people. Various conferences of bishops define such functions differently, as became clear during the debates in the hall of the Council.

It is also necessary to keep in mind that diaconal candidates can be of two categories, as both the Council[1] and *Sacrum Diaconatus Ordinem* have envisioned:[c] young men committed to celibacy and older men who are already married and are engaged in a profession or occupation. Another sort of difference involves the ministry intended for these deacons. The same formation cannot be imposed for deacons destined to work in mission areas or the developing countries and those who are to exercise their functions in countries of a more advanced and developed culture.

It is thus up to each conference of bishops to decide the type or types of diaconate that seem best designed for the needs of the country and, consequently, to decide what kind of preparation the candidates should receive.

2553 　　　Since there will be different kinds of formation, it follows that the structure for programs of study must also be varied.

For young men committed to celibacy, attention must be directed to special institutes with formal courses of study and with a spiritual formation that will prepare the candidates for their future ministry as deacons. On the other hand, for married men the courses must be compatible with their employment responsibilities; thus it should be possible to organize evening courses or study-weeks over a fairly extended period of time. In the case of married men, there is a need to take into account the education some already have and to accelerate the courses accordingly. Others, however, with hardly more than an elementary education will clearly need courses of much longer duration. In any event, a hasty or superficial preparation is to be ruled out absolutely: the functions of deacons, as laid down by both the Constitution *Lumen gentium* (no. 29)[d] and the Motu Proprio (no. 22)[e] are so important that they demand a solid and effective formation.

Deacons must, in fact, prepare catechumens for baptism, explain and comment on the word of God in preaching, prepare the faithful for marriage and respect all the regulations affecting this sacrament, take the place of the priest, when there is none, in preparing the faithful for death and in administering viaticum.

Such functions call for a doctrinal formation far superior to that of the simple catechist, one that in a way is comparable to that of the priest.

---

[1]　See LG no. 29 [DOL 4 no. 149].

[d]　See DOL 4 no. 149.

[e]　See DOL 309 no. 2536.

The appropriate courses should include the study of: 2554

a. Sacred Scripture. This should include all those ideas that will equip deacons to understand the word of God and explain it to the faithful in a way aimed at
growth in the spiritual life. The deacon must be capable of giving the homily and
presiding at the liturgy of the word, when there is no priest.

b. Doctrine. This course of study should be like that provided in catechetical
institutes for religious who are not priests. A possible model is the course developed
by the Christian Brothers or by those advanced courses in religion given for the
better-educated laity. Further, the emphasis must be biblical and kerygmatic. It will
be best not to dwell on controverted points, but simply to indicate them through
readings chosen from the Fathers, theologians, and spiritual writers.

c. Morality. This should center on personal, social, and political morality and
be at the level of courses for catechists or for the members of Catholic Action.

d. Canon law. Concentration should be on the canon law of marriage and on
pastoral practice in preparing the faithful to receive this sacrament.

e. Liturgy. This may be incorporated into the course on doctrine; it includes
material on the carrying out of liturgical rites.

f. Technical instruction. This is to prepare the candidates for specific activities
of ministry and covers psychology, catechetical pedagogy, oratory, singing, how to
set up Catholic organizations, church management, how to keep current the registers of baptisms, confirmations, marriages, funerals, etc.

Future deacons must obviously not be required to have the entire complement   2555
of courses that make up the indispensable qualification of candidates for the priesthood (for example, church history, a full course in canon law, philosophy). Nevertheless in some parts of the world, and particularly for deacons who are to serve in
cities, it is advisable that they complete their education through those disciplines
that peculiar local circumstances demand. Examples are the study of non-Christian
religions, ecumenism, key philosophical issues, particularly those of current interest, the study of certain economic or political questions, etc.

It will thus be up to the bishops of each country to decide on what combination of disciplines the ministry of deacons in that country requires.

There is, finally, a need to remember that the educational formation of deacons
is not completed at the moment of their ordination; plans must be made for a
"permanent," that is, continuing formation, either through courses of renewal specifically for deacons or through their participation in study-weeks intended for
priests.

315. SC DIVINE WORSHIP, **Publication** *Sacra Congregatio pro Clericis* of the
text for the renewal of commitment to priestly service, 6 March 1970: Not 6
(1970) 86–87.

The Congregation for the Clergy recently sent (4 November 1969) a circular   2556
letter to presidents of the conferences of bishops "on the continuing education and
formation of the clergy, especially the younger clergy."

This document has these words on page 7: "In order to strengthen this spiritual
life and the sense of priesthood, it is most desirable that on Holy Thursday morning
every priest — whether or not he is actually present at the chrism Mass — renew
the act by which he committed himself to Christ and by which he promised to carry
out the priesthood's responsibilities, especially to observe celibacy and obedience to

his bishop (or religious superior). Also that in his spirit he celebrate the gift, sealed by the sacrament of orders, that is his calling to the service of the Church."

In recent times the chrism Mass has undergone several changes.

In 1956, with the transfer of the Mass of the Lord's Supper to the evening hours, a complete plan for the chrism Mass was composed. The texts referred throughout to the holy oils: the older texts, as might be expected, to the chrism and the later texts to the oil of the sick.

In 1967 the entire liturgy of the chrism Mass was revised in order that it would more clearly express the concept of the priesthood, whose institution is commemorated on Holy Thursday.

This idea is now given a more coherent and profound expression. Formerly at the chrism Mass in each diocese chosen representatives of the clergy gathered around the bishop. The same principle continues, but the hope is that on this day all priests may take part in the Mass, so that it "serves as a manifestation of the communion of the presbyters with their bishop."

If the number of priests is not too great, all may concelebrate with the bishop; otherwise the concelebrants are to be selected either from different parts of the diocese or from among the different heads of diocesan programs.

It is well for those who do not concelebrate to receive communion and under both kinds, even if they have already celebrated Mass for the benefit of the faithful or will do so later.

2557   The new elements of this liturgy of the chrism are in the forthcoming Roman Missal and Pope Paul VI in promulgating them has decreed that they be put into use on Holy Thursday of this year, 26 March. These new elements are the renewal of commitment to priestly service and the preface.

Promises of Commitment. Just as religious annually renew the vows of their profession, so also it is proper that priests renew the promises made to the bishop at their ordination. The bishop entreats the congregation to pray for his priests and for himself.

Preface. The preface recalls the institution of the ministerial priesthood, over and above the royal priesthood of believers, and lists its duties: to offer sacrifice; to bear the message of salvation; to make people holy through the sacraments; to be an example by their virtue. Priests are to strive constantly to conform themselves to Christ by faith and an undivided love.

These few words contain the whole program of pastoral life and personal sanctification for the one who is Christ's priest and the minister of the Church.

After their commemoration of the priesthood in the chrism Mass with the bishop and their self-renewal through the renewal of their commitment, the priests return to their people and with the entire parish "family" joyously celebrate the Lord's Supper in the evening.

The new texts mentioned are here presented.

AT THE CHRISM MASS

2558   The bishop concelebrates this Mass with his presbyterate and during it blesses the oils. It serves as an expression of the communion between the priests and their bishop. It therefore is of great advantage that, if at all possible, all the priests take part in the Mass and receive communion, even under both kinds. As a sign of the unity of the diocese's presbyterate, the priests who concelebrate with the bishop are to be from different sectors of the diocese.

In the homily the bishop is to urge his priests to be loyal to the fulfillment of their office and to invite them to make a public renewal of their commitment to priestly service.

316. PONTIFICAL COMMISSION FOR THE INTERPRETATION OF THE DECREES OF VATICAN COUNCIL II, **Reply** to a query, on the pastoral powers of permanent deacons, 19 July 1970: AAS 62 (1970) 570.

The Fathers of the Pontifical Commission for the Interpretation of the Decrees   2559
of Vatican Council II have decided to reply in this way to the following queries, proposed to them in their plenary session:

I
(GENERAL DELEGATION GRANTED TO A DEACON TO
ASSIST AT MARRIAGES)

Query: In regard to general delegation or permission to assist at marriages, granted in accord with can. 1095, § 2, may a deacon who is permanently and lawfully assigned to some parish be considered on the basis of the intent of can. 1096, § 1 as the equivalent of curates with respect to the parish of their assignment?

Reply: Yes. [. . .]

Pope Paul VI at an audience granted to the undersigned [President of the Commission], 19 July 1970, confirmed these decisions, approved them, and ordered their publication.

▶   474.   PAUL VI, Homily, on St. Teresa of Avila, Doctor of the Church, 27 September
1970:

Women and hierarchical offices [no. 3962].

317. SC DOCTRINE OF THE FAITH, **Norms**, to be used by the curia of a diocese or of a religious institute to prepare cases for reduction to the lay state with dispensation from the obligations of holy orders, 13 January 1971: AAS 63 (1971) 303–308 (excerpt).

VI. CONDITIONS TO BE OBSERVED BY A DISPENSED PRIEST

2.   As to the celebration of the dispensed priest's canonical marriage, the Ordinary   2560
is to ensure personally that any public celebration or display is excluded and that the marriage takes place before an approved priest, without witnesses or, if necessary, with two witnesses. Record of the marriage is to be kept in the secret files of the curia.

It belongs to the local Ordinary of the diocesan or religious petitioner's place of residence along with the petitioner's own diocesan or religious superior to decide how the dispensation as well as the celebration of his marriage are to be kept secret; or, how, with proper precautions, they are to be divulged to the petitioner's relatives, friends, and employer in order to safeguard his good name and the economic and social rights deriving from his new state as a married layman.

2561   The Ordinary charged with informing the petitioner of the rescript is to urge him earnestly to take part in the life of the people of God in a way consonant with his new way of life, to give good example, and to show himself to be a loving son of the Church. At the same time the Ordinary is to inform the petitioner that any priest reduced to the lay state and dispensed from his obligations is barred from:

      a. exercising any function of holy orders, except those indicated in can. 882 and 892, § 2;

      b. exercising any liturgical function in celebrations with a congregation, in a place where his condition is known, and from ever giving the homily; [. . .].

▶   426. SC DIVINE WORSHIP, General Instruction of the Liturgy of the Hours, 2 February 1971:

nos. 17, 20–25:	Responsibilities of ordained ministers [nos. 3447, 3450–55].
31 a:	Cathedral and collegiate chapters [no. 3461].
47, 54, 190, 197, 254–257:	Offices of ordained ministers [nos. 3477, 3484, 3620, 3627, 3684–87].

▶   169. SC CLERGY, *General Catechetical Directory*, 11 April 1971:

no. 57:	Catechesis for holy orders [no. 1104].

318. SYNOD OF BISHOPS 1971, **Study** *The Ministerial Priesthood* (*Ultimis temporibus*), 30 November 1971: AAS 63 (1971) 898–922 (excerpt).

DESCRIPTION OF THE SITUATION

2562   3. Vatican Council II emphasized the preeminence of the proclamation of the Gospel, which through faith must lead to the fullness of the celebration of the sacraments. But current thinking about the religious situation fosters doubts in many minds concerning the meaning of the ministry of the sacraments and *divine worship*. Many priests, who are not in the midst of their own identity crisis, are asking themselves another question: What methods must be used for sacramental practice to be an expression of faith really affecting the whole of personal and social life and to keep Christian worship from being wrongly reduced to a mere external *ritualism*?

    Priests are very concerned with the image that the Church seems to present to the world. At the same time they are deeply conscious of the singular "dignity of the human person" and therefore want to bring about a change within the Church itself in interpersonal relationships, in relations between person and institutions, and in the very structures of authority.

2563   4. Relationships between bishops and priests and between priests themselves are also growing more difficult by the very fact that the exercise of the ministry is becoming more diversified. Present-day society is divided into many groups having diverse interests, which call for differing skills and forms of apostolate. This gives rise to problems concerning the brotherhood of priests, their sharing a common outlook, and their coordination of ministries.

Happily the recent Council recalled the traditional and fruitful teaching on the universal priesthood of the faithful (see LG no. 10).[a] But as a kind of backwash certain issues arise that seem to obscure the position of the priestly ministry in the Church and that deeply trouble the minds of some priests and faithful. Many activities that in the past were reserved to priests — for instance, catechetics, the administration of communities, and even those in the liturgy — are today quite frequently carried out by laypersons. On the other hand, many priests, for reasons already mentioned, are trying to involve themselves in the condition of life of laypersons. Hence a number of questions are being asked: Does the priestly ministry have any specific nature? Is this ministry necessary? Is the priesthood permanent? What does being a priest mean today? Would it not be enough for the service of the Christian communities to have presidents designated for the preservation of the common good, without sacramental ordination, and exercising their office for a fixed period?

7.   We know that there are some parts of the world in which the contemporary   2564
profound cultural change has hitherto been less felt and that the questions raised earlier are not being asked everywhere, nor by all priests, nor in the same way. But since communications between individuals and peoples have today become more frequent and more rapid, we judge it good and opportune to examine these questions in the light of faith and to give humbly but in the strength of the Holy Spirit some principles for finding more *concrete* answers to them. Although this response must be applied differently according to the situation in individual parts of the world, it will have the force of truth for all those faithful and priests who live in conditions of greater tranquility. Therefore, ardently desiring to strengthen the witness of faith, as brothers we urge all the faithful to strive to contemplate the Lord Jesus living in his Church and to realize that he wishes to work in a special way through his ministers; they will thus be convinced that the Christian community cannot fulfill its complete mission without the ministerial priesthood. Let priests realize that the bishops truly share their anxieties and desire to share them even more.

* * *

Prompted by this desire, the Synod Fathers, in the spirit of the Gospel, following closely the teaching of Vatican Council II and considering also the documents and addresses of Pope Paul VI, intend to set forth briefly some of the principles in the Church's teaching on the ministerial priesthood that are at present more urgent, together with guidelines for pastoral practice.

PART ONE
PRINCIPLES OF DOCTRINE

1. CHRIST, ALPHA AND OMEGA.

Jesus Christ, the Son of God and the Word, "whom the Father sanctified and   2565
sent into the world" (Jn 10:36) and who was marked with the seal of the fullness of the Holy Spirit (see Lk 4:1, 18–21; Acts 10:38), proclaimed to the world the Good News of reconciliation between God and humankind. His preaching as a prophet, confirmed by miracles, reaches its summit in the paschal mystery, the supreme word of that divine love with which the Father addressed us. On the cross Jesus showed himself to the utmost to be the Good Shepherd who laid down his life for his sheep in order to gather them into that unity of which he himself is the center (see Jn 10:15ff., 11:52). Exercising a supreme and unique priesthood by his self-offering, he

---

[a]   See DOL 4 no. 140.

surpassed, by fulfilling them, all the ritual priesthoods and holocausts of the Old Testament and indeed of the pagans. In his sacrifice he took on himself the miseries and sacrifices of people of every age and also the efforts of those who suffer in the cause of justice or who are daily oppressed by misfortune. He took on himself the endeavors of those who abandon the world and attempt to reach God by asceticism and contemplation, as well as the labors of those who sincerely spend their lives for a better present and future society. He bore the sins of us all on the cross; rising from the dead and being made Lord (see Phil 2:9–11), he reconciled us to God; and he laid the foundation of the people of the New Covenant, that is, of the Church.

He is the "one Mediator between God and humanity, the man Christ Jesus" (1 Tm 2:5), "for in him were created all things" (Col 1:16; see Jn 1:3ff.) and everything is brought together under him, as Head (see Eph 1:10). Being the image of the Father and the manifestation of the unseen God (see Col 1:15), he emptied himself and was raised up and therefore brought us into that communion with the Holy Spirit which he lives with the Father.

When therefore we speak of the priesthood of Christ, we should have before our eyes a unique, incomparable reality, which includes the prophetic and royal office of the incarnate Word of God.

Jesus Christ thus signifies and manifests in many ways the presence and effectiveness of the love with which God has first loved us. The Lord himself, constantly influencing the Church by his Spirit, stirs up and fosters the response of all those who offer themselves to this freely given love.

2. COMING TO CHRIST IN THE CHURCH.

2566   The way to the person and mystery of Christ stands always open in the Holy Spirit through the Scriptures understood in the living tradition of the Church. All the Scriptures, especially the New Testament, must be interpreted as intimately interlinked and interrelated because they have a single inspiration. The books of the New Testament are not of such differing value that some of them can be reduced to mere late inventions.

A personal and immediate relationship with Christ in the Church must still for the faithful of today sustain their whole spiritual lives.

3. THE CHURCH FROM CHRIST THROUGH THE APOSTLES.

2567   Christ founded on the apostles the Church that he had declared he would build on Peter (see LG no. 18). Two of the Church's characteristics are already manifested in the apostles: in the body of the twelve both communion in the Spirit and the origin of the hierarchical ministry are already present (see AG no. 5). For that reason, the New Testament writings speak of the Church as founded on the apostles (see Rv 21:14; Mt 16:18). This was concisely expressed by ancient tradition: "The Church from the apostles, the apostles from Christ, Christ from God."[1]

The Church, founded on the apostles, sent into the world to be a pilgrim there, was established as the sacrament of the salvation that came to us from God in Christ. In the Church, Christ is present and at work on behalf of the world as Savior, in order that the love offered by God to us might be met by our response. In and through the Church the Holy Spirit stirs up impulses of generous free will by which we participate in the very work of creation and redemption.

---

[1] Tertullian, *De praescriptione haer.* 21, 4. See also Clement of Rome, *Ep. 1 Ad Cor.* 42, 1–4. Ignatius of Antioch, *Ad Magn.* 4 and passim. Irenaeus, *Adv. haer.* 4, 21, 3. Origen, *De principiis* 4, 2, 1. Serapion, Bishop of Antioch, in Eusebius, *Hist. eccl.* 6, 12.

4. THE ORIGIN AND NATURE OF THE HIERARCHICAL MINISTRY.

The Church, which through the gift of the Spirit is endowed with an organic   2568
structure, participates in different ways in the offices of Christ as priest, prophet,
and king, in order to carry out its mission of salvation in his name and by his power
as a priestly people (see LG no. 10).[b]

The New Testament writings make it clear that an apostle and a community of
believers united with one another by a mutual link under Christ as Head and the
influence of his Spirit form part of the original, irreplaceable structure of the
Church. The twelve apostles exercised their mission and functions and "they had
helpers in their ministry (see Acts 6:2–6, 11:30, 13:1, 14:23, 20:17; 1 Thes 5:12–13;
Phil 1:1; Col 4:11 and passim). Further, in order that the mission assigned to them
might continue after their death, they passed on to their immediate cooperators, as
a kind of testament, the duty of perfecting and consolidating the work they had
begun (Acts 20:25–27; 2 Tm 4:6 taken together with 1 Tm 5:22; 2 Tm 2:2; Ti 1:5; St.
Clement of Rome *Ad Cor.* 44:3). They charged these co-workers to attend to the
whole flock in which the Holy Spirit placed them to shepherd the Church of God
(see Acts 20:28). The apostles appointed such men and made provision that, when
they died, others of proven character would take up their ministry (see St. Clement
of Rome *Ad Cor.* 44:2) " (LG no. 20).

The letters of St. Paul show that he was conscious of acting by Christ's mission
and mandate (see 2 Cor 5:18ff.). Those powers of the Apostle for the care of the
Churches that could be communicated were handed on to others (see 2 Tm 1:6) and
they in turn were obliged to hand them on to yet others (see Ti 1:5).

This essential structure of the Church — consisting of the flock and the shepherds appointed for this purpose (see 1 Pt 5:1–4) — according to the tradition of the
Church itself always has been and remains the norm. Precisely as a result of this
structure, the Church can never remain closed in on itself and is always subject to
Christ as its origin and Head.

Among the various charisms and services, the priestly ministry of the New
Testament, which continues Christ's function as mediator and which in essence and
not merely in degree is distinct from the universal priesthood of the faithful (see LG
no. 10),[c] alone perpetuates the essential work of the apostles. By effectively proclaiming the Gospel, by gathering together and leading the community, by forgiving sins, and especially by celebrating the eucharist, it makes Christ, the Head of
the community, present in the exercise of his work of human redemption and of
giving full glory to God.

By virtue of the sacrament of orders, which confers an anointing of the Holy
Spirit and configures them to Christ (see PO no. 2),[d] bishops and, at a subordinate
level, priests become sharers in the offices of sanctifying, teaching, and governing.
The exercise of these functions is determined more precisely by hierarchical communion (see LG nos. 24, 27–28).[e]

The priestly ministry reaches its summit in the celebration of the eucharist,
which is the source and center of the Church's unity. Only a priest is able to act in
the person of Christ in presiding over and effecting the sacrificial banquet in which
the people of God are associated with Christ's offering (see LG no. 28).[f]

---

[b]   See DOL 4 no. 140.

[c]   See DOL 4 no. 140.

[d]   See DOL 18 no. 257.

[e]   See DOL 4 nos. 147–148.

[f]   See DOL 4 no. 148.

The priest is a sign of the divine, eternal plan, proclaimed and effective today in the Church. He makes Christ, the Savior of us all, sacramentally present among his brothers and sisters, in both their personal and social lives. He is the guarantor both of the first proclamation of the Gospel for the gathering together of the Church and of the ceaseless renewal of the Church once it has already been gathered together. Without the presence and activity of that ministry received by the laying on of hands with prayer, the Church cannot have full certainty of its fidelity and visible continuity.

5. PERMANENCE OF THE PRIESTHOOD.

2569   By the laying on of hands a gift of the Holy Spirit that cannot be lost is communicated (see 2 Tm 1:6). This reality configures the ordained minister to Christ the Priest, consecrates him (see PO no. 2),[8] and makes him a sharer in Christ's mission under its two aspects of authority and service.

That authority does not belong to the minister as his own: it is a manifestation of the *exousia* (that is, power) of the Lord, by which the priest is an ambassador of Christ in the eschatological work of reconciliation (see 2 Cor 5:18–20). He also assists in turning human freedom toward God for the building up of the Christian community.

The lifelong permanence of this *reality and sign*, the existence of which pertains to the faith and which is referred to in the Church's tradition as the priestly character, expresses the fact that Christ associated the Church with himself in an irrevocable way for the salvation of the world and that the Church commits itself to Christ in a definitive way for the carrying out of his work. The minister, whose life bears the seal of the gift received through the sacrament of orders, reminds the Church that the gift of God is decisive. In the midst of the Christian community, which, in spite of its defects, lives by the Spirit, the minister is a pledge of the salvific presence of Christ.

This special participation in Christ's priesthood does not disappear even if a priest for ecclesial or personal reasons is dispensed or removed from the exercise of his ministry.

PART TWO
GUIDELINES FOR THE PRIESTLY LIFE AND MINISTRY

2570   Considering the priestly mission in the light of the mystery of Christ and the communion of the Church, the Fathers of this Synod, united with Pope Paul VI and conscious of the present anxieties of bishops and priests in the fulfillment of the responsibility they share, offer the following guidelines to clarify certain issues and to bring encouragement.

I. PRIESTS IN THE MISSION OF CHRIST AND THE CHURCH

1. MISSION: EVANGELIZATION AND SACRAMENTAL LIFE.

2571   a. "By their vocation and ordination, the priests of the New Testament are indeed set apart in a certain sense within the midst of the people of God. But this is so, not that they may be made distant from this people or from any human being, but that they may be totally dedicated to the work for which the Lord has raised them up" (PO no. 3). Priests thus find their identity to the extent that they fully live the Church's mission and exercise it in different ways in communion with the entire people of God, as pastors and the Lord's ministers in the Spirit, in order to

---

8   See DOL 18 no. 257.

fulfill by their work the plan of salvation in history. "Since through their ministry — consisting above all in the eucharist as this builds up the Church — they enter into communion with Christ the Head of the Church and bring others into that communion, they cannot help but experience how much remains unachieved for the full measure of Christ's Body and how much is yet to be added for its continual growth" (AG no. 39).[h]

b. Priests are sent to all people and their mission must begin with the preaching of God's word. "Priests have for their first responsibility the proclaiming of God's Gospel to all. . . . The saving word gives birth to faith in the hearts of nonbelievers and nurtures it in the heart of believers" (PO no. 4).[i] The goal of evangelization is "that all who are made children of God by faith and baptism should come together to praise God in the midst of his Church, to take part in the sacrifice, and to eat the Lord's Supper" (SC art. 10).[j] If rightly understood, the ministry of the word leads to the sacraments and to the Christian life, as it is practiced in the visible community of the Church and in the world.

The sacraments are celebrated in conjunction with the proclamation of God's word and thus develop faith by strengthening it with grace. The sacraments cannot be treated lightly, since through them the word achieves its fuller effect, namely, communion in the mystery of Christ.

Let priests then perform their ministry in such a way that the faithful will "with great eagerness frequent those sacraments that were instituted to nourish the Christian life" (SC 59).[k]

An enduring evangelization and well-ordered sacramental life of the community demand, by their nature, a *diakonia* of authority, that is, a service to unity and the duty of providing leadership in charity. Thus the mutual relationship between evangelization and the celebration of the sacraments is clearly seen in the mission of the Church. A separation between the two would divide the heart of the Church to the point of imperiling the faith, and the priest, who is dedicated to the service of unity in the community, would be gravely distorting his ministry.

To unite evangelization with sacramental life belongs always to the ministerial priesthood and every priest must keep that carefully in mind. Yet the application of this principle to each priest's life and ministry must be made with discretion, for the exercise of the priestly ministry often needs in practice to take different forms in order that it may better meet the special or new situations in which the Gospel is to be proclaimed.

c. Although the pedagogy of faith demands that people be gradually initiated into the Christian life, the Church must nevertheless always proclaim to the world the Gospel in its entirety. Each priest shares in the special responsibility of preaching the whole of the word of God and of explaining it according to the faith of the Church.

The proclamation of the word of God is the announcement in the power of the Spirit of the wonderful works of God and the calling of all to share in the paschal mystery and to introduce it as a leaven into *concrete* human history. That proclamation is God's action in which the power of the Holy Spirit gathers the Church together interiorly and exteriorly. By evangelization the minister of the word prepares the ways of the Lord with great patience and faith, conforming

---

h   DOL 17 no. 256.

i   DOL 18 no. 259.

j   DOL 1 no. 10.

k   DOL 1 no. 59.

himself to the various and differently evolving conditions of the life of individuals and of peoples.

The Church is impelled by the need to keep in view both the personal and social aspects of the proclamation of the Gospel as the source of an answer to all the more fundamental human problems (see CD no. 13). Thus the Church not only preaches conversion to God to individuals but, as the conscience of humanity, also addresses society itself, in the best way it can. The Church thus exercises a prophetic function in society's regard, while at the same taking pains over its own inner renewal.

The experiences of life, whether of people in general or of priests, must be kept in mind and always interpreted in the light of the Gospel, but they cannot be either the sole or the principal norm of preaching.

d. Salvation, which is effected through the sacraments, does not come from ourselves but is the gift of God. This is why the action of Christ, the one Priest and Mediator, has primacy in his Body, which is the Church.

Since the sacraments are truly sacraments of faith (see SC art. 59),[1] they require conscious and free participation by every Christian who has the use of reason. This makes clear the great importance of preparation and of a disposition of faith on the part of the person who receives the sacraments; it also makes clear the necessity for a witness of faith in his entire life on the part of the minister and especially in the way he values and celebrates the sacraments themselves.

To bishops and, in the cases established by law, to the conferences of bishops is committed the responsibility of authentically promoting, in accordance with the norms given by the Holy See, pastoral activity and liturgical reform better adapted to each region and also of determining the criteria for admission to the sacraments. These criteria, which must be applied by priests, are likewise to be explained to the faithful, so that those who request a sacrament are made more aware of their own responsibility.

3. THE SPIRITUAL LIFE OF PRIESTS.

2572

[. . .] Just as Christ, anointed by the Holy Spirit, was moved by his deep love for his Father to give his life for us, so the priest, consecrated by the Holy Spirit, and in a special way made like Christ the Priest, dedicates himself to the work of the Father performed through the Son. Thus the whole rule for the priest's life is expressed in the words of Jesus: "And for their sake I consecrate myself, that they also may be consecrated in truth" (Jn 17:19).

Priests are to imitate the example of Christ who was continually in prayer and to be led by the Holy Spirit in whom we cry: "Abba, Father." They thus must give themselves to the contemplation of the word of God and each day take the opportunity to examine the events of life in the light of the Gospel. Thus having become faithful and attentive hearers of the word, they will become true ministers of the word. Let them be assiduous in personal prayer, in the liturgy of the hours, in frequent reception of the sacrament of penance, and especially in devotion to the mystery of the eucharist. Even if the eucharist should be celebrated without participation by the faithful, it nevertheless remains the center of the life of the entire Church and at the heart of priestly existence.

With his mind raised to heaven and sharing in the communion of saints, the priest should frequently turn to Mary the Mother of God, who received the Word of God with perfect faith, and daily ask her for the grace of conforming himself to her Son. [. . .]

---

[1]   See DOL 1 no. 59.

II. PRIESTS IN THE COMMUNION OF THE CHURCH

1. RELATIONS BETWEEN PRIESTS AND THEIR BISHOP.

Priests will adhere more faithfully to their mission the more they know and   2573
show themselves to be faithful to ecclesial communion. Thus the pastoral ministry,
which is exercised by bishops, priests, and deacons, is an eminent sign of this
ecclesial communion, because to serve it they have received a special mandate.

But in order that this ministry may really become a sign of communion, the
concrete conditions in which it is exercised must be regarded as of greatest importance.

Vatican Council II in the Decree *Presbyterorum Ordinis,* expressed the guiding
principle that the very unity of consecration and mission requires the hierarchical
communion of priests with the order of bishops. That principle is considered fundamental to a practical restoration or renewal, with full confidence, of the mutual
relationship between the bishop and the presbyterium over which he presides. The
principle must be put into practice more concretely, especially through the concern
shown by bishops.

The service of authority on the one side and on the other the exercise of an
obedience that is not merely passive should be carried out in a spirit of faith,
mutual charity, filial and friendly confidence, and constant and patient dialogue.
Thus the collaboration and *responsible* cooperation of priests with the bishop will be
sincere, friendly, and at the same time supernatural (see LG no. 28; CD no. 15; PO
no. 7).ᵐ [. . .]

3. RELATIONS BETWEEN PRIESTS AND LAITY.

Let priests remember "confidently to entrust to the laity duties in the service of   2574
the Church, allowing them freedom and room for action. In fact, on suitable occasions, they should invite them to undertake works on their own initiative" (PO no.
9). The laity, "likewise sharing their cares, should help their priests by prayer and
action to the extent possible, so that their priests can more readily overcome
difficulties and be able to fulfill their responsibilities with greater effect" (ibid).

It is necessary to keep always in mind the special character of the Church's
communion in order that, in accordance with the recognized duties and charisms of
each person, personal freedom may be properly coordinated with the unity of life
and activity belonging to the people of God. [. . .]

* * *

Rescript of 30 November 1971: AAS 63 (1971) 897.

Pope Paul VI has carefully examined the two documents containing the pro-   2575
posals expressed by the Second General Assembly of the Synod of Bishops on the
themes, "The Ministerial Priesthood" and "Justice in the World," which had been
put before the Assembly for study.

As he has already announced in his address at the general audience of 24
November, it is the Pope's decision that the aforementioned documents be made
public.

The Pope now accepts and confirms all the conclusions in the two documents
that conform to the current norms: in particular, he confirms that in the Latin
Church there shall continue to be observed in its entirety, with God's help, the
present discipline of priestly celibacy.

ᵐ   DOL 4 no. 148; DOL 7 no. 194; DOL 18 no. 262.

The Pope reserves to himself to examine carefully in due course whether the proposals — and which of them — contained in the recommendations of the Synodal Assembly should become precepts or simply guidelines.

319. PAUL VI, **Motu Proprio** *Ad pascendum*, laying down norms regarding the order of diaconate, 15 August 1972: AAS 64 (1972) 534–540; Not 9 (1973) 9–16.

2576
For the nurture and constant increase of the people of God, Christ the Lord instituted in the Church a variety of ministries that work for the good of the whole Body.[1]

Since the apostolic age itself the diaconate has had a distinctive and superior rank among these ministries and has always been held in great honor by the Church. Explicit testimony of this is given by the Apostle St. Paul both in his Letter to the Philippians, in which he sends his greetings not only to the bishops but also to the deacons,[2] and in his Letter to Timothy, in which he highlights the qualities and virtues that deacons must have in order to be proved worthy of their own ministry.[3]

Later, when the early writers of the Church acclaim the dignity of deacons, they do not fail to extol also the spiritual qualities and virtues required for the carrying out of that ministry, namely, fidelity to Christ, moral integrity, and obedience to the bishop.

St. Ignatius of Antioch declares that the office of the deacon is none other than "the ministry of Jesus Christ, who was with the Father before all ages and has been manifested in the final time."[4] He also remarks: "The deacons too, who are ministers of the mysteries of Jesus Christ, should please all in every way, for they are not servers of food and drink, but ministers of the Church of God."[5]

St. Polycarp of Smyrna exhorts deacons to be "disciplined in all things, merciful, diligent, walking according to the truth of the Lord, who became the servant of all."[6] The author of the *Didascalia Apostolorum*, recalling the words of Christ, "Anyone who wants to be great among you must be your servant,"[7] addresses the following fraternal exhortation to deacons: "Accordingly you deacons also should act in such a way that, if there should be a need that calls on you even to lay down your life for someone, you would do so. . . . If the Lord of heaven and earth served us and suffered and sustained everything on our behalf, should we not do this all the more for others, since we are imitators of him and have been given the place of Christ?"[8]

When moreover the writers of the first centuries give instruction on the importance of the diaconal ministry, they offer many examples of the manifold important duties entrusted to deacons and clearly show how much authority they possessed in

---

[1] See LG no. 18: AAS 57 (1965) 21–22; ConstDecrDecl 124.

[2] See Phil 1:1.

[3] See 1 Tm 3:8–13.

[4] Ignatius of Antioch, *Ad Magnesios* 4, 1: Funk PA 1, 235.

[5] *Idem, Ad Trallianos* 2, 3: Funk PA 1, 245.

[6] Polycarp of Smyrna, *Ep. ad Philippenses* 5, 2: Funk PA 1, 301–303.

[7] Mt 20:26–27.

[8] *Didascalia Apostolorum* 3, 13, 2–4: Funk DidConst 1, 214.

the Christian communities and how great their contribution was to the apostolate. The deacon is described as "the ear, mouth, heart, and soul of the bishop."[9] The deacon is at the service of the bishop in order that the bishop may serve the whole people of God and take care of the sick and the poor;[10] he is correctly and rightly called "one who shows love for orphans, for the devout and for the widowed, one who is fervent in spirit, one who shows love for what is good."[11] Furthermore, he is entrusted with the duty of taking the eucharist to the sick confined to their homes,[12] of conferring baptism,[13] and of attending to preaching the word of God in accordance with the will and intention of the bishop.

Accordingly, the diaconate flourished in a wonderful way in the Church and at the same time gave an outstanding witness of love for Christ and for neighbor through the performance of works of charity,[14] the celebration of sacred rites,[15] and in pastoral service.[16]

Exercise of the office of deacon enabled those who were to become presbyters to give proof of themselves, to display the merit of their work, and to acquire preparation — all of which were requirements for receiving the dignity of the priesthood and the office of pastor.

As time went on, the discipline concerning this holy order was changed. The prohibition against conferring ordination without observing the established sequence of orders was strengthened, but there was a gradual decrease in the number of those who, instead of advancing to a higher order, preferred to remain deacons all their lives. As a consequence, the permanent diaconate almost entirely disappeared in the Latin Church. It is hardly necessary to mention what was decreed by the Council of Trent when it proposed to restore the sacred orders in accordance with their own nature as ancient functions within the Church.[17] But it was only much later that the idea matured of restoring this important order also as a truly permanent rank. Our predecessor Pius XII briefly alluded to this matter.[18] Finally, Vatican Council II supported the wishes and requests that, where this would lead to the good of souls, the permanent diaconate should be restored as an intermediate order between the higher ranks of the Church's hierarchy and the rest of the people of God. The permanent diaconate was meant to be an expression of the needs and desires of the Christian communities, a driving force for the Church's service or *diakonia* toward the local Christian communities, and a sign or sacrament of the Lord Christ himself, who "came not to be served but to serve."[19]

2577

---

[9]   Ibid. 2, 44, 4: Funk DidConst 1, 138.

[10]   See *Traditio Apostolica* 39 and 34: B. Botte, ed., *La Tradition Apostolique de Saint Hippolyte, Essai de reconstruction* (Münster, 1963) 87 and 81.

[11]   *Testamentum D. N. Iesu Christi* 1, 38: I. E. Rahmani, ed. and tr. (Mainz, 1899) 93.

[12]   See Justin Martyr, *Apologia* 1, 65, 5 and 67, 5: G. Rauschen, ed., *S. Iustini Apologiae duae* (2nd ed., Bonn, 1911) 107 and 111.

[13]   See Tertullian, *De Baptismo* 17, 1: CCL, *Tertulliani Opera*, Part 1 (1954) 291.

[14]   See *Didascalia Apostolorum* 2, 31, 2: Funk DidConst 1, 112. See also *Testamentum D. N. Iesu Christi* 1, 31: I. E. Rahmani, ed. and tr. (Mainz, 1899) 75.

[15]   See *Didascalia Apostolorum* 2, 57, 6 and 58, 1: Funk DidConst 1, 162, 166.

[16]   See Cyprian, *Epistolae* 15 and 16: G. Hartel, ed. (Vienna, 1871) 513–520. See also Augustine, *De catechizandis rudibus* 1, cap. 1, 1: PL 40, 309–310.

[17]   See Council of Trent, sess. 23, cap. 1–4: Mansi 33, 138–140.

[18]   See Pius XII, Address to participants in the second meeting of Catholics from around the world, on the lay apostolate, Rome, 5 Oct. 1957: AAS 49 (1957) 925.

[19]   Mt 20:28.

2578   For this reason, at the third session of the Council, in October 1964, the Fathers ratified the principle of the restoration of the diaconate and in the following November the Dogmatic Constitution *Lumen gentium* was promulgated. In article 29 of this document a description is given of the principal characteristics proper to that state: "At a lower level of the hierarchy are deacons, who receive the laying on of hands 'not unto priesthood but only for a ministry of service.' Strengthened by sacramental grace, they have as their service for the people of God, in communion with the bishop and the presbyterate, the *diakonia* of liturgy, word, and charity."[20]

The same Constitution made the following declaration about permanency in the rank of deacon: "As the discipline of the Latin Church currently stands, these diaconal functions, supremely necessary to the Church's life, can be carried out in many places only with great difficulty. Henceforth, therefore, it will be permissible to restore the diaconate as a distinct and permanent rank of the hierarchy."[21]

2579   This restoration of the permanent diaconate required however that the instructions of the Council be more profoundly examined and that there be mature deliberation concerning the juridical status of both the celibate and the married deacon. Similarly, it was necessary that matters connected with the diaconate of those who are to become priests should be adapted to contemporary conditions, so that the time of diaconate would furnish the proof of way of life, of maturity, and of aptitude for the priestly ministry that ancient discipline demanded from candidates for the presbyterate.

Thus on 18 June 1967, we issued the Motu Proprio *Sacrum Diaconatus Ordinem*, by which suitable canonical norms for the permanent diaconate were established.[22] On 17 June of the following year, through the Apostolic Constitution *Pontificalis Romani recognitio*,[23] we authorized the new rite for the conferring of the sacred orders of deacons, presbyters, and bishops and at the same time defined the matter and the form of the ordination itself.

2580   Now that we are proceeding further as today we promulgate the Motu Proprio *Ministeria quaedam*,[a] we consider it advisable to issue certain norms concerning the diaconate. We also desire that candidates for the diaconate should know what ministries they are to exercise before ordination and when and under what considerations they are to take upon themselves the obligations of celibacy and liturgical prayer.

Since entrance into the clerical state is deferred until diaconate, there no longer exists the rite of first tonsure, by which a layman used to become a cleric. But a new rite is introduced by which one who aspires to ordination as deacon or presbyter publicly manifests his will to offer himself to God and the Church, so that he may exercise a sacred order. The Church in accepting this offering chooses and calls him to prepare himself to receive a sacred order. In this way he is properly admitted into the ranks of candidates for the diaconate or presbyterate.

There is a particular reason why the ministries of reader and acolyte should be entrusted to those who, as candidates for sacred orders, desire to devote themselves to God and to the Church in a special way. For the Church, which "never ceases to

---

[20]   LG no. 29 [DOL 4 no. 149].

[21]   LG no. 29 [DOL 4 no. 149].

[22]   See DOL 309.

[23]   See DOL 324 [dated, 18 June 1968].

[a]   See DOL 340.

receive the bread of life from the table both of God's word and of Christ's body and to offer it to the faithful,"[24] considers it to be very advantageous that, both by study and· by gradual exercise of the ministry of the word and of the altar, candidates for sacred orders should through intimate contact understand and reflect on the double aspect of the priestly office. The result is that the genuineness of ministry becomes especially striking: the candidates are to approach holy orders fully aware of their vocation, "fervent in spirit, serving the Lord . . . constant in prayer, and aware of the needs of the faithful."[25]

We have weighed every aspect of the question thoroughly, sought the opinion of experts, consulted with the conferences of bishops and taken their views into account; we have taken counsel with our esteemed brothers who are members of the sacred congregations competent in this matter. By our apostolic authority we therefore decree the following norms, amending, if and insofar as is necessary, the provisions of the Code of Canon Law now in force, and we promulgate them with this Motu Proprio.

I.   a.   A rite is hereby introduced for the admission of candidates for ordination   2581
as deacons and presbyters. In order that this admission be properly made, the free petition of the aspirant, drawn up and signed by his own hand, is required, as well as the acceptance by the competent ecclesiastical superior given in writing, through which the election by the Church is effected.

Professed members of clerical religious institutes who are preparing for the priesthood are not bound to this rite.

b.   The competent superior for this acceptance is the Ordinary (the bishop and, in clerical institutes of perfection, the major superior). Those can be accepted who give signs of an authentic vocation and, endowed with good moral qualities and free from mental and physical defects, wish to dedicate their lives to the service of the Church for the glory of God and the good of souls. It is necessary that those who aspire to the transitional diaconate already have completed at least their twentieth year and have begun their course of theological studies.

c.   In virtue of being accepted, the candidate must care for his vocation in a special way and deepen it. He also acquires the right to the necessary spiritual assistance by which he can develop his vocation and submit unconditionally to the will of God.

II.   Candidates for the permanent diaconate and for the transitional diaconate, as   2582
well as candidates for the presbyterate itself, are to receive the ministries of reader and acolyte, unless they have already done so, and are to exercise them for a suitable period, in order to be better disposed for the future service of the word and of the altar.

Dispensation from receiving these ministries on the part of such candidates is reserved to the Holy See.

III.   The liturgical rites by which admission of candidates for ordination as deacons   2583
and presbyters takes place and by which the aforementioned ministries are conferred should be performed by the Ordinary of the aspirant (the bishop and, in clerical institutes of perfection, the major superior).

IV.   The intervals (interstices) established by the Holy See or by the conferences of   2584
bishops between the conferring, during the course of theological studies, of the

---

[24]   DV no. 21 [DOL 14 no. 224].

[25]   Rom 12:11–13.

ministry of readers and that of acolytes, and between the ministry of acolytes and the order of deacons, must be observed.

2585 V. Before ordination candidates for the diaconate shall give to the Ordinary (the bishop and, in clerical institutes of perfection, the major superior) a declaration drawn up and signed in their own hand, by which they testify that they are about to receive the order freely and of their own accord.

2586 VI. The special consecration to celibacy observed for the sake of the kingdom of heaven and its obligation for candidates to the priesthood and for unmarried candidates to the diaconate are in truth connected with the diaconate. The public commitment to celibacy before God and the Church is to be celebrated, even by religious, in a special rite, which is to precede ordination to the diaconate. Celibacy taken on in this way is a diriment impediment to entering marriage.

In accordance with the traditional discipline of the Church, a married deacon who has lost his wife cannot (*inhabiles sunt*) enter a new marriage.[26]

2587 VII. a. Deacons called to the presbyterate are not to be ordained until they have completed the course of studies prescribed by the norms of the Apostolic See.

b. In regard to the course of theological studies to precede the ordination of permanent deacons, the conferences of bishops, with attention to the local situation, will issue the proper norms and submit them for the approval of the Congregation for Catholic Education.

2588 VIII. In conformity with the General Instruction of the Liturgy of the Hours nos. 29–30:[b]

a. Deacons called to the priesthood are obliged by reason of their ordination to celebrate the liturgy of the hours.

b. It is most fitting that permanent deacons should each day recite at least a part of the liturgy of the hours, to be determined by the conference of bishops.

2589 IX. Entrance into the clerical state and incardination into a diocese are brought about by ordination to the diaconate.

2590 X. The rite of admission as candidates for ordination to the diaconate and priesthood and of the special consecration of celibacy will be published soon by the competent department of the Roman Curia.

2591 TRANSITIONAL NORMS: Candidates for the sacrament of orders who have already received first tonsure before the promulgation of this Motu Proprio retain all the duties, rights, and privileges of clerics. Those who have been promoted to the order of subdiaconate are held to the obligations taken on in regard to both celibacy and the liturgy of the hours. But they must celebrate once again their public commitment to celibacy before God and the Church by the new special rite preceding ordination to the diaconate.

All the matters decreed by us in this Letter, issued *motu proprio*, we order to be confirmed and ratified, anything to the contrary notwithstanding. We also determine their effective date to be 1 January 1973.

▶ 247. SC DIVINE WORSHIP, Decree *Cum de nomine*, on the bishop's name in the eucharistic prayer, 9 October 1972.

---

[26] See Paul VI, Motu Proprio *Sacrum Diaconatus Ordinem* no. 16: AAS 59 (1967) 701.

[b] See DOL 426 nos. 3459–60.

▶   329.   SC BISHOPS, *Directory on the Pastoral Ministry of Bishops*, 22 February 1973.

▶   171.   SC DOCTRINE OF THE FAITH, Declaration *Mysterium Ecclesiae*, on Catholic teaching about the Church, 24 June 1973:

        no. 6:   The Church's association with Christ's priesthood [nos. 1125–28].

320. PONTIFICAL COMMISSION FOR THE INTERPRETATION OF THE DECREES OF VATICAN COUNCIL II, **Reply** to a query, on the powers of a deacon regarding the sacramentals and blessings, 13 November 1974: AAS 66 (1974) 667; Not 11 (1975) 36.

The Fathers of the Pontifical Commission for the Interpretation of the Decrees of Vatican Council II have decided to reply in this way to the following query, proposed to them in plenary session.

2592

Query: According to the norms of CIC can. 1147, § 1, the Dogmatic Constitution *Lumen gentium* no. 29,[a] and the Motu Proprio *Sacrum Diaconatus Ordinem* no. 22,[b] is the deacon authorized to impart constitutive blessings or blessings of invocation and to administer the sacramentals, and to what extent?

Reply: The deacon is authorized to impart only those blessings and administer only those sacramentals that are granted to him explicitly by the law.[R2]

---

    a   See DOL 4 no. 149.

    b   See DOL 309 no. 2536.

  R2   The following commentary was added in Not 11 (1975) 36–39:
The conciliar Constitution *Lumen gentium* no. 29 states with regard to the deacon: "The deacon's duties, following assignment by competent authority [text quoted, DOL 4 no. 149]."
These functions are more specifically determined by Paul VI's Motu Proprio *Sacrum Diaconatus Ordinem* [no. V; DOL 309 no. 2536] and later by certain of the reformed liturgical books. Our present interest is in the points referring to the deacon's faculty regarding the sacraments to "bless and administer." Thus the deacon is allowed to give the blessing in administering communion and viaticum (*Holy Communion and Worship of the Eucharist outside Mass* nos. 17 [DOL 266 no. 2095], 39, 54), at exposition of the blessed sacrament (ibid. nos. 97–99), at the celebration of baptism (*Rite of Baptism for Children*, General Introduction to Christian Initiation no. 11 [DOL 294 no. 2260], of marriage (*Rite of Marriage* nos. 53, 47, 50), and of funerals (*Rite of Funerals* nos. 19 [DOL 416 no. 3391], 33, 53).
Consequently, some have asked whether the deacon's competency may be extended to the giving of other blessings, for example, the blessing of religious articles (medals, rosaries), of throats on St. Blase Day, etc., or to other sacramentals not mentioned in the documents already cited. On the other hand CIC can. 1147, par. 4 states: "Deacons and readers have the power to give validly and lawfully only those blessings expressly permitted them by the law." The query therefore was proposed to the PCIDV, which gave the reply here reported. The PCIDV has indicated to the SCDW the reasons on which it based its reply. With the consent of the PCIDV we report these reasons so that the import of the reply may be clearly understood.
[Italian] "The statement of the conciliar principle, contained in the Dogmatic Constitution *Lumen gentium* no. 29, must be applied in the liturgical books, as has also been the case with other competencies assigned in a general way to the deacon in the same conciliar text. For example 'to carry viaticum to the dying, officiate at funerals and burial rites, assist at and bless marriages' [DOL 4 no. 149].
"The function of the legislative authority applying the principles is called for by no. 29 of the Constitution itself, which reads: '*Diaconi est, prout ei a competente auctoritate assignatum fuerit.*' The *prout* means precisely 'insofar as,' 'to the extent that' the authority agrees. Thus among the *liturgical functions* belonging to the deacon *by virtue of ordination* and in addition to those blessings assigned to him by the law, he may give the blessings *within the rites of those sacraments or sacramentals for which he is the minister.* As for other blessings or sacramentals *we are to look to the liturgical books already published or to be published later.*
"Therefore to set the limits of the exercise of the deacon's office does not belong to the PCIDV but to the responsible curial congregations. They are empowered to establish norms for the reservation of the sacramentals and of blessings, establishing the conditions and limits of the deacon's powers.
"It is likewise inopportune to make a list of blessings to be assigned to the deacon; the same can be

Pope Paul VI at an audience granted to the undersigned [President of the Commission], 13 November 1974, confirmed this decision, approved it, and ordered its publication.

▶   161. PAUL VI, Epistle "We write" to Dr. D. Coggan, Archbishop of Canterbury, on the ordination of women, 30 November 1975.

▶   162. PAUL VI, Epistle "As the tenth" to Dr. D. Coggan, Archbishop of Canterbury, on the ordination of women, 23 March 1976.

321. SC DOCTRINE OF THE FAITH, Declaration *Inter insigniores*, on the question of the admission of women to the ministerial priesthood, 15 October 1976: AAS 69 (1977) 98–116 (excerpts).

INTRODUCTION
THE ROLE OF WOMEN IN MODERN SOCIETY AND THE CHURCH

2593   Among the more striking characteristics of our present age, Pope John XXIII, in his Encyclical *Pacem in terris* of 11 April 1963, pointed out "the part that women are now taking in public life. . . . This is a development that is perhaps growing more rapidly among Christian nations, but is also happening extensively, if more slowly,

---

said of sacramentals, since, in addition, new ones may be established by the Holy See and the conferences of bishops.

"Furthermore, it is not correct to posit a distinction differentiating sacramentals and blessings: every blessing is, at base, a sacramental. Admittedly with the reform of the liturgy profound changes have come about relative to earlier discipline: deacons have been placed on a par ritually with priests in regard to the administration of some of the sacraments and sacramentals. Even for baptism the deacon has become an ordinary minister, whereas before he was the extraordinary minister. On the other hand, there are some sacramentals that it seems a deacon cannot administer: for example, the blessing of an abbot, consecration to a life of virginity, institution to ministries. This is because of the status of the persons who through these blessings are consecrated to divine worship and to the Church's worship. The tradition of the Eastern Churches contrasts sharply with the concessions made in the Latin rite to deacons: blessings are reserved exclusively to the bishop and the priest; the deacon assists the priest at the eucharist and — except in an emergency — is not the minister of baptism, since its administration is conjoined with that of confirmation.

"It has further been remarked that the expansion of the deacon's powers implies a diminishing of the status of the priest, with a consequent equivalence of functions in the matter being considered. Extending the deacon's faculties runs the risk also of lessening in the eyes of the faithful the sense of the grandeur of the sacerdotal character and even of the value of the sacraments and sacramentals. To limit the expansion of the deacon's faculties would mean a closer adherence to the principle confirmed in the same no. 29 of *Lumen gentium* that the deacon receives 'the laying on of hands not unto priesthood but only for a ministry of service' [DOL 4 no. 149]. Thus it seems advisable to hold to the current canonical and liturgical norms contained in CIC can. 1147, § 4, in *Lumen gentium* no. 29, and in the other postconciliar documents, even if there are no objections of a doctrinal nature that might prevent the granting of further faculties to deacons.

"The expression *cetera sacramentalia* (other sacramentals) of *Lumen gentium* cannot be taken to mean *omnia sacramentalia* (all the sacramentals). Nor does the rule of law apply: if the deacon is competent for the greater — to administer certain sacraments (in fact only baptism is involved since the distribution of the eucharist does not make the deacon the *minister* of the eucharist) — therefore he is competent for the less, that is, to administer sacramentals and give blessings.

"According to this reply, therefore, the norms given in the liturgical books must be observed. The deacon has the power to celebrate blessings and sacramentals accordingly as the law grants this. The reformed ritual for blessings, which is now being prepared, will settle the matter in more detail." See also DOL 309 no. 2536, note R1.

among nations that are heirs to different traditions and imbued with a different culture."[1] Along the same lines, Vatican Council II, listing in its Pastoral Constitution *Gaudium et spes* the forms of discrimination touching the basic rights of the person that must be overcome and eliminated as contrary to God's plan, gives first place to discrimination based upon sex.[2] The equality resulting from overcoming discrimination will secure the building of a human society that is not leveled out and uniform but harmonious and unified, if men and women contribute to it their own resources and dynamic energies, as Pope Paul VI has recently stated.[3] [. . .]

For some years now some of those Christian communities that separated from the Apostolic Roman See in the 16th century or later have been admitting women to the pastoral office on a par with men. This initiative has led to petitions and writings by members of these communities and similar groups, directed toward making this admission a general thing; other communities have taken an opposite stand. Clearly this is a matter of ecumenical importance about which the Catholic Church must make its thinking known and all the more so because in various quarters the issue has been raised whether the Church too could modify its discipline and admit women to priestly ordination. Even some Catholic theologians have intensified the debate, appealing to studies not only in the sphere of exegesis, patristics, and church history but also in the historical development of institutions and customs, of sociology, and of psychology. As a result, the various arguments capable of clarifying this important problem have been submitted to a critical examination. Since we are dealing with a controversy that, at least in its present form, classical theology scarcely touched upon, the protagonists run the risk of neglecting essential considerations.

In execution of a mandate received from Pope Paul VI and echoing the thought he himself made in his letter of 30 November 1976,[6] the Congregation for the Doctrine of the Faith therefore judges that this must be restated: the Church, in fidelity to the example of the Lord, does not consider itself authorized to admit women to priestly ordination. The Congregation also thinks it timely in view of the current situation to explain this position of the Church. Some will perhaps view the position with displeasure but its positive value will become apparent in the long run, since it can be of help in deepening understanding of the roles proper to men and to women.

I. THE CHURCH'S CONSTANT TRADITION

The Catholic Church has never held that priestly or episcopal ordination can be validly conferred on women. A few heretical, especially Gnostic, sects in the first centuries presumed to entrust exercise of the priestly ministry to women. This innovation was immediately noted and condemned by the Fathers as a departure, unacceptable in the Church.[7] It is true that the writings of the Fathers give evidence of the undeniable taint of prejudice against women; nevertheless, it should be noted that this prejudice had hardly any influence on their pastoral activity and still less

2594

2595

1   AAS 55 (1963) 267–268.

2   See GS no. 29: AAS 58 (1963) 1048–49; ConstDecrDecl 721.

3   See Paul VI, Address to members of the study commission on the role of women in society and in the Church and members of the council for the Year of the Woman, 18 April 1975: AAS 67 (1975) 266.

6   See AAS 68 (1976) 599–600, 600–601 [Epistles to the Archbishop of Canterbury, DOL 161, 162].

7   Irenaeus, *Adv. haereses* 1, 14, 2: PG 7, 580–581; Harvey 1, 114–122. Tertullian, *De praescript. haeretic.* 41, 5: CCL 1, 221. Firmilian of Caesarea in Cyprian, *Ep.* 75: CSEL 3, 817–818. Origen, *Fragmenta in 1 Cor* 74: *Journal of Theological Studies* 10 (1909) 41–42. Epiphanius, *Panarion* 49, 2–3; 78, 23, and 79, 2–4: GCS 31, 243–244; 37, 473, and 477–479.

on their spiritual direction. But aside from such considerations, which were inspired by the spirit of the times, there is clear record — especially in the canonical documents of the Antiochene and Egyptian traditions — that only men were called to the properly sacerdotal order and ministry because of the one, main reason: the Church's intention to preserve faithfully the model for sacerdotal ministry that the Lord Jesus Christ willed and that the apostles preserved exactly.[8]

The same conviction animated medieval theologians,[9] even if, in their desire to clarify by reason the truths of faith, the scholastics often resorted to arguments on this point that modern scholars would have difficulty in admitting or would even rightly repudiate. From the Middle Ages to the present, the issue, it seems, was not raised again; the practice had been accepted unquestionably by all, enjoying, so to speak, the rights of prescription.

The Church's tradition in the matter has thus been so firm throughout the ages that the magisterium had no need to interpret a principle that had not been attacked, or to defend a law that had not been challenged. But whenever there was occasion for its expression this tradition served as a witness of the Church's intent to conform to the model left by the Lord.

The Churches of the East have faithfully held to the same tradition. Their unanimity on this point is all the more remarkable since on many other questions they readily agree that each Church has its own, different law. Today, as well, these same Churches refuse to have any part in the demands aimed at the ordination of women to the priesthood. [. . .]

IV. THE ACTIONS OF CHRIST AND THE APOSTLES AS PERMANENT NORMS

2596   [. . .] Those who support the legitimacy of change in the matter turn to the way the Church regulates sacramental discipline. It is, of course, pointed out in our day especially how conscious the Church is of the power it has over the sacraments, even though they were instituted by Christ, and that it has used this power through the years to make the sacraments more explicit as signs and to specify the conditions of their conferral. All evidence of this is clear from recent decrees of Pius XII and Paul VI.[12] Nevertheless careful attention must also be given to the fact that this power, although real, has definite limits. On this point Pius XII remarked: "The Church has no power over the substance of the sacraments, that is to say, over what Christ the Lord determined, as the sources of revelation attest, to be the prescribed elements in the sacramental sign."[13] This had already been taught by the Council of Trent, which declared: "In its stewardship of the sacraments, provided their substance remains untouched, the Church has always possessed the power to make the rules and changes that it judges to be advantageous, according to different conditions, times, and places, to the well-being of the recipients and the respect due to the sacraments themselves."[14]

---

[8]   See *Didascalia Apostolorum* c. 15: R.H. Connolly, ed., 133 and 142. *Constitutiones Apostolicae* 3, c. 6, nn. 1–2; c. 9, nn. 3–4: Funk DidConst 1, 191; 201. John Chrysostom, *De sacerdotio* 2,2: PG 48, 633.

[9]   See Bonaventure, *In 4 Sent.*, dist. 25, art. 2, q. 1: Quaracchi edition, v. 4, 649. Richard of Middleton, *In 4 Sent.*, dist. 25, art. 4, no. 1: Venice edition, 1499, folio 177ʳ. John Duns Scotus, *In 4 Sent.*, dist. 25: *Opus Oxoniense*, Vivès edition, vol. 19; *Reportata Parisiensia*, Vivès edition, vol. 24, 369–371. Durandus of Saint-Pourçain, *In 4 Sent.*, dist. 25, q. 2: Venice edition, 1571, folio 364ᵛ.

[12]   See Pius XII, Ap. Const. *Sacramentum Ordinis*, 30 Nov. 1947: AAS 40 (1948) 5–7. Paul VI, Ap. Const. *Divinae consortium naturae*, 15 Aug. 1971 [DOL 309]; Ap. Const. *Sacram Unctionem*, 30 Nov. 1972 [DOL 408].

[13]   Pius XII, Ap. Const. *Sacramentum Ordinis*: loc. cit. 5.

[14]   Council of Trent, sess. 21, cap. 2: Denz-Schön 1728.

Moreover, it must not be overlooked that the sacramental signs have not been chosen, so to speak, by artificial convention. In many respects, they are natural signs because they incorporate the connatural symbolism of actions and things. More than this, however, the sacramental signs are principally meant to link the person of a later period to the supreme event of the history of salvation, in order to enable that person to understand, through all the Bible's wealth of pedagogy and symbolism, what kind of grace they signify and produce. Thus the eucharist is not simply a familial meal; it is at the same time the memorial making Christ's sacrifice present and *actual* anew, and is also the Church's offering of his sacrifice. So too the ministerial priesthood is not simply a pastoral charge; it involves also the continuation of those functions that Christ committed to the apostles and of the powers belonging to those functions. Adaptation to the times and to secular culture cannot therefore go so far as to create a substantial break in that sacramental relationship with the events constitutive of the Christian religion and with Christ himself.

In these matters it is finally the Church, expressing itself through the magisterium, that decides what is unchangeable and what is subject to change. The reason the Church judges that certain changes are inadmissible is its own consciousness of being bound by the way Christ acted. In such cases the Church is not at all influenced by a misguided antiquarianism, but is in fact keeping faith with its Lord. Only in this light can the true reason for the Church's decision be understood. [. . .]

Therefore the practice of the Church possesses normative force. Underlying the fact that priestly ordination is bestowed only on males is a tradition unbroken throughout all of history, universal in East and West, having as its purpose to suppress abuses at once. This norm, based on Christ's example, has been respected and continues to be respected because it is seen as conformed to God's plan with regard to his Church.

V. THE MINISTERIAL PRIESTHOOD IN THE LIGHT OF THE MYSTERY OF CHRIST

After this review of the Church's norm and its basis, it seems useful and timely to explain this norm by showing its fittingness in the light of theological reflection: that males alone have been called to receive sacerdotal ordination has an intimate correlation with the genuine nature of the sacrament of orders and its specific reference to the mystery of Christ. This is not meant as a conclusive argument but as an explanation of doctrine through the correspondence between different truths of faith (*analogia fidei*).

2597

The Church's constant teaching, repeated and clarified by Vatican Council II[a] and again recalled by the 1971 Synod of Bishops[b] and by the Congregation for the Doctrine of the Faith in its Declaration of 24 June 1973,[c] declares that the bishop or the priest, in the exercise of his ministry, does not act in his own name, *in persona propria*, rather he represents Christ, who acts through him: "The priest truly acts in the place of Christ," as St. Cyprian already wrote in the third century.[15] It is this power to represent Christ that St. Paul considered as characteristic of his apostolic office (see 2 Cor 5:20; Gal 4:14). The supreme expression of this representation is found in the altogether special form it assumes in the celebration of the eucharist, the source and center of the Church's unity and the sacrificial meal in which the

---

[a]   See, e.g., DOL 1 no. 33; DOL 4 no. 148; DOL 18 no. 257.

[b]   See DOL 318 no. 2568.

[c]   See DOL 171 no. 1126.

[15]   Cyprian, *Ep.* 63, 14: PL 4, 397; G. Hartel, ed., *Omnia opera* (CSEL) v. 3, 713.

people of God are joined to the sacrifice of Christ: the priest, who alone has the power to perform it, then acts not only through the effective power conferred on him by Christ, but *in persona Christi*,[16] taking the role of Christ, to the point of being his very image, when he pronounces the words of consecration.[17]

The Christian priesthood is therefore of a sacramental nature: the priest is a sign whose supernatural effectiveness comes from the ordination received, but a sign that must be perceptible[18] and with a signification that the faithful must be able to recognize with ease. The whole sacramental system is in fact based upon natural signs that have a power of symbolism congenial to the human mind. "Sacramental signs," says St. Thomas, "represent what they signify by a natural resemblance."[19] The same natural resemblance is required in persons as in things. When Christ's role in the eucharist is to be expressed sacramentally, the required "natural resemblance" between Christ and his minister would be lacking if the role of Christ were not taken by a man. It would then be difficult to see in the minister the image of Christ, since Christ himself was and remains a man. [. . .]

2598   [. . .] But the counterargument may be raised that the priest, especially when he presides at the liturgical and sacramental functions, equally represents the Church: he acts in its name with "the intention of doing what the Church does." In this sense the theologians of the Middle Ages said that the minister also acts *in persona Ecclesiae*, that is, in the name of the entire Church and in order to represent the Church. No matter what the degree of the faithful's participation in a liturgical service, the priest celebrates in the name of the entire Church, praying in the name of all and, in the Mass, offering the sacrifice of the entire Church, since in the new Passover, the Church under visible signs through the ministry of the priest offers Christ's sacrifice.[20] Since, then, the priest also represents the Church "herself," would it not be possible to think that the Church's being represented by a woman is consistent with the meaning of sign already given? Admittedly the priest represents the Church, which is the Body of Christ. But he does so precisely because he first represents Christ himself, who is the Head and Shepherd of the Church. Vatican Council II[21] used this phrase to make more precise and to complete the expression *in persona Christi*. It is in this quality that the priest presides over the Christian assembly

---

[16]   See SC art. 33: ". . .by the priest, who presides over the assembly in the person of Christ" [DOL 1 no. 33]. LG no. 10: "The ministerial priest, by the sacred power he possesses, builds up and guides the priestly people; acting in the person of Christ, he makes present the eucharistic sacrifice and offers it to God in the name of all the people . . ." [DOL 4 no. 140]. LG no. 28: "By virtue of the sacrament of orders, in the image of Christ the eternal High Priest . . . they exercise their sacred function above all in the eucharistic worship or celebration of Mass, by which, acting in the person of Christ . . ." [DOL 4 no. 148]. PO no. 2: ". . . priests, by the anointing of the Holy Spirit, are marked with a distinct sacramental character and are so configured to Christ the Priest that they have the power to act in the person of Christ the Head" [DOL 18 no. 257]. PO no. 13 "as ministers of the sacred, above all in the sacrifice of the Mass, priests in a particular way represent the person of Christ . . ." [DOL 18 no. 265]. See also Synod of Bishops 1971, *The Ministerial Priesthood* Part I, no. 4 [DOL 318 no. 2568]. SCDF, Declaration on Catholic Teaching about the Church, 24 June 1973, no. 6 [DOL 171 no. 1126].

[17]   ST 3a, 83. 1 ad 3: ["just as the celebration of this sacrament is an image representative of the cross itself" ibid., ad 2] "so also on the same grounds the priest bears the image of Christ, in whose person and power he pronounces the words in order to consecrate."

[18]   Clearly arguing against women's ordination, St. Thomas says: "Because the sacrament is a sign made up of those things done in the sacramental celebration, there must be not only a reality but a reality having signification" (*In 4 Sent.*, dist. 25, q. 2, art. 2, *quaestiuncula* 1, Reply).

[19]   Ibid., art. 2, *quaestiuncula* 1 ad. 4.

[20]   See Council of Trent, sess. 22, cap. 1: Denz-Schön 1741.

[21]   LG no. 28: "Exercising within the limits of their authority the function of Christ as Shepherd and Head . . ." [DOL 4 no. 28]. PO no. 2: "Thus they have the power to act in the person of Christ the Head" [DOL 18 no. 257]. PO no. 6: "the office of Christ the Head and Shepherd" [DOL 18 no. 261]. See also Pius XII, Encycl. *Mediator Dei*: "The minister of the altar stands in the person of Christ as Head, offering in the

and celebrates the eucharistic sacrifice in which the whole Church offers and is itself wholly offered.[22] [. . .]

VI. THE MINISTERIAL PRIESTHOOD EXPLAINED BY THE MYSTERY OF THE CHURCH

It is relevant to recall that problems arising out of the theology of the sacraments, especially when they concern the ministerial priesthood, as is the case here, cannot be solved except in the light of revelation. The human sciences, however valuable their contribution in their own domain, are inadequate in such a matter, since they cannot encompass the realities of faith: the properly supernatural content of these realities is beyond their competence.

How much the Church, unique in its nature and its structures, differs from other societies must not be disregarded. The pastoral charge in the Church is normally linked to the sacrament of orders: it is not a mere polity comparable to the modes of authority found in the civil sphere. It is not granted by the people's free choice, even if the term "election" is sometimes applied to one being entrusted with a pastoral charge. For it is only through the laying on of hands and the prayer of the successors of the apostles that the election is confirmed as being from God and that the Holy Spirit, given in ordination, makes the recipient a sharer in the governing power of Christ, the supreme Shepherd (see Acts 20:28). Thus the office is a work of service and love: "If you love me, feed my sheep."

It is not therefore clear how it is possible to propose the admission of women to the priesthood in virtue of the equality of rights that society recognizes and that holds good also for Christians. To this end use is sometimes made of the text quoted already from the Letter to the Galatians (3:28), which says that in Christ there is no longer any distinction between men and women. But this passage does not concern ministries, but only affirms the universal calling to divine adoption, which is the same for all. Moreover, and above all, to number ministry among human rights would be to err extremely about the very nature of the ministerial priesthood: baptism endows no one with any right to receive public ministry in the Church. The priesthood is conferred not for anyone's personal honor or advantage, but for service to God and the Church. It in fact corresponds to a special, completely freely-given calling: "You have not chosen me, I have chosen you and have appointed you . . ." (Jn 15:16; see Heb 5:4).

It is sometimes stated or it is written in books and periodicals that some women feel that they have a vocation to the priesthood. Such an attraction, however noble and understandable, still does not suffice for a genuine vocation. A vocation cannot be reduced to a mere personal leaning, which can remain purely subjective. Since the priesthood is a particular ministry over which the Church has received charge and control, authentication by the authority and faith of the Church is so indispensable here as to be a constitutive part of the vocation: Christ chose "those he wanted" (Mk 3:13). On the other hand, there is a universal vocation of all the baptized to the exercise of the royal priesthood by offering their lives to God and by giving witness for his praise.

Women who express a desire for the ministerial priesthood are doubtless motivated by the desire to serve Christ and the Church. And it is not surprising that, at a time when they are becoming more aware of having been the victims of discrimina-

2599

2600

---

name of all the members": AAS 39 (1947) 556. Synod of Bishops 1971 *The Ministerial Priesthood* Part I, no. 4: "He makes Christ present as Head of the community" [DOL 318 no. 2568].

[22]   Paul VI, Encycl. *Mysterium fidei*, 3 Sept. 1965 [DOL 176 no. 1175].

tion in society, they should desire the ministerial priesthood itself. But it must not be forgotten that the priesthood does not form part of the rights of the individual, but stems from the plan forming the mystery of Christ and of the Church. The priestly office cannot become the goal of social advancement; no merely human progress of society or of the individual can of itself give access to it, since it is of an entirely different order.

It therefore remains for us to meditate more deeply on the nature of the real equality of the baptized, which is one of the great affirmations of Christianity. Equality is in no way identity, for the Church is a Body differentiated by the diversity of its members and in that Body each individual has his or her role. The roles must be kept distinct and not be confused; they do not favor the superiority of some vis-à-vis others, nor do they provide an excuse for jealousy. The only more perfect gift, which can and must be desired, is love (see 1 Cor 12:13). The greatest in the kingdom of heaven are not those persons who are ministers but those persons who are saints. [. . .]

322. JOHN PAUL II, Epistle *Magnus dies* to the bishops of the Church, on the priesthood, 8 April 1979: AAS 71 (1979) 389–393 (excerpts).

2601   The great day is drawing near when, concelebrating on Holy Thursday with our brothers in the priesthood, we shall again reflect on the greatness of Christ's gift that makes us sharers in his eternal priesthood. On that day, prior to celebrating the Mass of the Lord's Supper, we shall gather together in our cathedrals to renew before him who became for us "obedient unto death"[1] in complete self-giving to the Church, his Bride, our own gift of self exclusively to the service of Christ in the same Church. [. . .]

[. . .] In fact the gift of the sacramental fullness of the priesthood is greater than all the toils and also all the sufferings involved in our pastoral ministry in the episcopate.

Vatican Council II reminded us and clearly explained that this ministry, while being a personal duty for each of us, is nevertheless something that we carry out in the brotherly communion of the whole of the Church's college or "body" of bishops. While it is right that we should address every human being, and especially every Christian as "brother," this word takes on an altogether special meaning with regard to us bishops and our mutual relationships: in a certain sense it goes back directly to that brotherhood that gathered the apostles around Christ and to that friendship with which Christ honored them and through which he united them to one another, as is attested by the words of John's Gospel already quoted [Jn 15:15ff.].

2602   Therefore, Revered and Dear Brothers, we must express the wish, today especially, that everything that Vatican Council II so wonderfully renewed in our awareness will take on an ever more mature character of collegiality, both as the source of our collaboration (*collegialitas effectiva*) and as the sign of a fraternal bond of sentiments (*collegialitas affectiva*), in order to build up Christ's Mystical Body and deepen the unity of the whole people of God. As you gather in your cathedrals, with the

---

[1]   Phil 2:8.

diocesan and religious priests who make up the presbyterium of your local Churches, your dioceses, you will receive from them — as the liturgy provides[a] — the renewal of the promises that they placed in your hands as their bishops on the day of their priestly ordination. With this in mind, I am sending priests a letter meant for them that — as I hope — will enable you and them to live even more deeply on the basis of this unity, the mysterious bond that joins us in the one priesthood of Jesus Christ, brought to completion with the sacrifice of the Cross, by which he merited entrance "into the sanctuary."[5] Revered Brothers, I hope that these words of mine addressed to priests at the beginning of my ministry in the See of St. Peter, will also help you increasingly to strengthen that communion and unity of the whole presbyterium[6] that have their basis in our collegial communion and unity in the Church.

323. JOHN PAUL II, **Epistle** *Novo incipiente* to all the priests of the Church, on the priesthood, 8 April 1979: AAS 71 (1979) 393–417 (excerpts).

1. FOR YOU I AM A BISHOP, WITH YOU I AM A PRIEST

At the beginning of my new ministry in the Church, I feel a deep need to speak to you, all of you without any exception, the priests, both diocesan and religious, who are my brothers by virtue of the sacrament of orders. From the very beginning I wish to express my faith in the vocation that unites you to your bishops in a special communion of sacrament and ministry, through which the Church, the Mystical Body of Christ, is built up. To all of you therefore who, by virtue of a special grace and through a singular gift of our Saviour, bear "the burden of the day and the heat"[1] in the midst of the many tasks of the priestly and pastoral ministry, I have addressed my thoughts and my heart from the moment when Christ called me to this See, where St. Peter, with his life and his death, had to respond right to the end to the question: "Do you love me? Do you love me more than these others do?"[2]

2603

I think of you all the time, I pray for you, with you *I seek the ways of spiritual union and collaboration*, because by virtue of the sacrament of orders that I also received [. . .] you are my brothers. And so, adapting the words of St. Augustine, I want to say to you today: "For you I am a bishop, with you I am a priest."[3] Today, in fact, the special circumstance of the proximity of Holy Thursday impels me to share with you the thoughts that I enclose in this letter. This annual feast of our priesthood unites the whole presbyterium of each diocese around its bishop in the concelebration of the eucharist.[a] On this day all priests are invited to renew, before their own bishop and together with him, the promises they made at their priestly ordination. This fact enables me, together with all my brothers in the episcopate, to be joined to you in a special unity and especially to be in the very heart of the mystery of Jesus Christ, the mystery in which all of us share.

---

a   See DOL 315.

5   Heb 9:12.

6   See LG no. 20.

1   See Mt 20:12.

2   See Jn 21:15ff.

3   "Vobis enim sum episcopus, vobiscum sum christianus" (*Serm.* 340, 1): PL 38, 1483.

a   See DOL 315.

Vatican Council II, which put such explicit emphasis on the collegiality of the episcopate in the Church, also gave a new form to the life of communities of priests, joined together by a special bond of brotherhood and united to the bishops of the respective local Church. The whole priestly life and ministry serve to strengthen that bond and deepen it. A particular responsibility for the various tasks that this life and ministry involve is taken on by the priests' councils. In accord with the thought of the Council and the Motu Proprio *Ecclesiae Sanctae*[4] of Paul VI, these should be an active force in every diocese. All this is meant to ensure that each bishop, in union with his presbyterium, can serve the great cause of evangelization ever more effectively. Through this service the Church lives out its mission, indeed its very nature. The importance of the unity of priests with their own bishop on this point is confirmed by the words of St. Ignatius of Antioch: "Strive to do all things in the harmony of God, with the bishop presiding to represent God, with the presbyters representing the council of the apostles, and the deacons, so dear to me, being concerned with the service of Jesus Christ entrusted to them."[5] [. . .]

3. "CHOSEN FROM THE PEOPLE . . . APPOINTED TO ACT ON BEHALF OF THE PEOPLE"[7]

2604 Vatican Council II elaborated the concept of the priesthood in greater detail as, in the course of its teaching, the Council presented the priesthood as a kind of outward expression of the inner powers or "dynamics" that give form to the responsibility that the entire people of God have in the Church. We should all turn back especially to the Constitution *Lumen gentium* and reread carefully the relevant paragraphs. The mission of the people of God is carried out through the sharing in the office and mission of Jesus Christ himself, which, as we know, has a threefold character: it is the mission and office of prophet, priest, and king. If we look into the conciliar texts accurately, it is clear that we should speak of the threefold character of Christ's service and mission, not of three diverse offices. In fact, the three aspects are closely linked to one another, explain one another, condition one another, and clarify one another. Consequently, it is from the unity of these three elements that our sharing in Christ's mission and office takes its origin. As Christians, members of the people of God, and subsequently, as priests, sharers in the hierarchical order, we take our origin from the combination of the mission and office of our Master, who is prophet, priest, and king, in order to bear witness to him in a special way in the Church and before the world.

The priesthood in which we share through the sacrament of orders, which has been "imprinted" on our souls for ever through a special sign from God, that is, the "character," remains in explicit relationship with the common priesthood of the faithful, that is, the priesthood of all the baptized, but at the same time it differs from that priesthood "in essence and not only in degree."[8] In this way the words of the author of the Letter to the Hebrews about the priest, who has been "chosen from the people . . . appointed to act on behalf of the people,"[9] take on their full meaning.

At this point, it is better to reread once more the whole of this classical conciliar text, which expresses the basic truth on the theme of our vocation in the Church: "[Text of LG no. 10 quoted, DOL 4 no. 140]."

---

4   Paul VI, Motu Proprio *Ecclesiae Sanctae* I, art. 15.

5   Ignatius of Antioch, *Ep. ad Magnesios* 6, 1: Funk PA 1, 235.

7   Heb 5:1.

8   LG no. 10 [DOL 4 no. 140].

9   Heb 5:1.

4. THE PRIEST AS A GIFT OF CHRIST FOR THE COMMUNITY

We would do well also to give full value not only to the theoretical meaning   2605
but also to the authentic functioning and effect of that mutual "relation" existing
between the hierarchical priesthood and the priesthood shared by all the faithful.
They differ not only in degree but also in essence because of the richness of the
very priesthood of Christ. This is the one center and the one source both of the
participation that belongs to all the baptized and of the other participation that is
reached through a distinct sacrament, the sacrament of orders. This sacrament, dear
brothers, is specifically for us, the effect of the special grace of vocation and the
basis of our identity. By virtue of its very nature and of everything that it produces
in our life and activity, the sacrament of orders serves to make the faithful aware of
the priesthood they all share and to live it.[11] The sacrament reminds them that they
are the people of God and enables them "to offer spiritual sacrifices"[12] through
which Christ himself makes us an everlasting gift to the Father.[13] This takes place,
above all, when the priest "by the sacred power he possesses, . . . acting in the
person of Christ (*in persona Christi*), makes present the eucharistic sacrifice and offers
it to God in the name of all the people,"[14] as we read in the conciliar text already
quoted.

Our sacramental priesthood is therefore a "hierarchical" and at the same time a
"ministerial" priesthood. It constitutes a special ministry, that is, a ministry of
"service" to the community of believers. It does not however take its origin from
that community, as though it were the community that "called" or "delegated." The
sacramental priesthood is truly a gift for the good of this community and comes
from Christ himself, from the fullness of his priesthood. This fullness finds its
expression in the fact that Christ, while making everyone capable of offering the
spiritual sacrifice, calls certain ones and empowers them to be ministers of his own
sacramental sacrifice, the eucharist — in the offering of which all the faithful share
and into which all the spiritual sacrifices of the people of God are incorporated.

Conscious of these truths, we understand how our priesthood is "hierarchical,"
that is to say, connected with the power of gathering and guiding the priestly
people[15] and how for this very reason it is "ministerial." We carry out that office
through which Christ himself unceasingly serves the Father in the work of our
salvation. Our entire priestly existence is and must be deeply characterized as
service, if we wish to celebrate the eucharistic sacrifice genuinely *in persona Christi*.
[. . .]

▶   See also Chapter Seven, Section 3. Vestments.

11   See Eph 4:11ff.

12   See 1 Pt 2:5.

13   See ibid. 3:18.

14   LG no. 10 [DOL 4 no. 140].

15   See LG no. 10 [DOL 4 no. 140].

Section 4. Holy Orders: B. Ordinations

SUMMARY (DOL 324–325). The Constitution on the Liturgy art. 76 decreed the revision of the ceremonies and texts of the ordination rites. In addition to the numerous cross-references in the present section, there are 2 major texts on the rites.

—An apostolic constitution of Paul VI reviewed the teaching of the Church on the three sacred orders that constitute the hierarchy of the Church and approved the new rites for the ordination of deacons, presbyters, and bishops, declaring what was the essential sacramental formulary in each case (DOL 324).

—The Congregation of Rites issued the decree promulgating the *editio typica* of these new rites prepared by the Consilium (DOL 325). Unlike the subsequent editions of the liturgical rites, the *editio typica* of the ordination rites was published without the introductions (*praenotanda*) to the rites that are envisioned by the Constitution on the Liturgy art. 63 b.

▶   103.   PAUL VI, Motu Proprio *Pastorale munus*, on the powers and privileges of bishops, 30 November 1963:

          I, no. 18:   Place and times for ordinations [no. 729].

▶   1.   VATICAN COUNCIL II, Constitution on the Liturgy *Sacrosanctum Concilium*, 4 December 1963:

          art. 76:   Revision of ordination rites [no. 76].

▶   23.   SC RITES (Consilium), Instruction (first) *Inter Oecumenici*, 26 September 1964:

          nos. 61 b: Use of the vernacular in ordinations [no. 353].
               68:                      Rite of episcopal consecration [no. 360].

▶   112.   SC RITES, Enumeration *Constitutio de sacra Liturgia* of the parts of ordination in the vernacular, 17 July 1965.

▶   224.   SC RITES, Reply (Zamora, Mexico), on concelebration at priests' ordination, 26 November 1965.

▶   117.   PAUL VI, Concession, allowing, *ad experimentum*, the vernacular in the canon of the Mass and in ordinations, 31 January 1967.

▶   39.   SC RITES (Consilium), Instruction (second) *Tres abhinc annos*, 4 May 1967:

          no.   28 b: Use of the vernacular in ordinations [no. 474].

▶   41.   CONSILIUM, Letter *Dans sa récente allocution* to presidents of the conferences of bishops, on reform of the liturgy, 21 June 1967.

          no.   7:   Translation of the canon and of the ordination rites [no. 486].

324. PAUL VI, Apostolic Constitution *Pontificalis Romani recognitio*, approving new rites for the ordination of deacons, priests, and bishops, 18 June 1968: AAS 60 (1968) 369–373; Not 4 (1968) 209–213.

2606   The revision of the Roman Pontifical is prescribed in a general way by the Second Vatican Ecumenical Council[1] and is also governed by the specific conciliar directive ordering the revision of "both the ceremonies and texts" of the ordination rites.[2]

          Among the rites of ordination the first to be considered are those that constitute the hierarchy through the sacrament of orders, conferred in its several degrees. "The divinely established ecclesiastical ministry is exercised at different levels by those who from antiquity have been called bishops, presbyters, and deacons."[3]

          The revision of the rites for ordinations is to follow the general principles that must direct the entire reform of the liturgy according to the decrees of Vatican Council II. But in addition a supreme criterion for that revision must be the clear

-----
   [1]   See SC art. 25 [DOL 1 no. 25].
   [2]   SC art. 76 [DOL 1 no. 76].
   [3]   LG no. 28 [DOL 4 no. 148].

teaching of the Dogmatic Constitution on the Church concerning the nature and effects of the sacrament of orders.[a] This teaching must of course receive expression through the liturgy itself in its own way, because "the texts and rites should be so drawn up that they express more clearly the holy things they signify and that the Christian people, as far as possible, are able to understand them with ease and to take part in the rites fully, actively, and as befits a community."[4]

The Council teaches that episcopal consecration bestows the fullness of the sacrament of orders, that fullness of power, namely, which in both the Church's liturgical practice and the language of the Fathers is called the high priesthood, the summit of the sacred ministry. But episcopal consecration, together with the office of sanctifying, also confers the offices of teaching and governing, offices that of their very nature can be exercised only in hierarchic communion with the head of the college and its members. For from tradition, expressed especially in liturgical rites and in the usage of the Church of both East and West, it is clear that the laying on of hands and the words of consecration bestow the grace of the Holy Spirit and impress a sacred character in such a way that bishops in an eminent and visible way carry on the role of Christ himself as teacher, shepherd, and high priest and act in his person.[5]

To these words must be added a number of important doctrinal points con- 2607
cerning the apostolic succession of bishops and their functions and duties. Even if these themes are already present in the rite of episcopal consecration, it still seems that they must be better and more precisely expressed. To ensure this, it was judged appropriate to take from ancient sources the consecratory prayer that is found in the document called the *Apostolic Tradition of Hippolytus of Rome*, written at the beginning of the third century. This consecratory prayer is still used, in large part, in the ordination rites of the Coptic and West Syrian liturgies. Thus in the very act of ordination there is a witness to the harmony of tradition in East and West concerning the apostolic office of bishops.

With regard to presbyters, the following should be especially recalled from the acts of the Council: "Even though they do not possess the fullness of the priesthood and in the exercise of their power are subordinate to the bishops, priests are nevertheless linked to the bishops in priestly dignity. By virtue of the sacrament of orders, in the image of Christ the eternal High Priest (see Heb 5:1–10 and 7–24, 9:11–28), they are consecrated to preach the Gospel, to shepherd the faithful, and to celebrate divine worship as true priests of the New Testament."[6] Elsewhere the Council says: "By ordination and the mission they receive from the bishops, presbyters are promoted to the service of Christ the Teacher, Priest, and King. They share in his ministry of unceasingly building up the Church on earth into the people of God, the Body of Christ, and the temple of the Holy Spirit."[7] In the ordination of presbyters, as formerly given in the Roman Pontifical, the mission and grace of the presbyter as a helper of the episcopal order were very clearly described. Yet it seemed necessary to reduce the entire rite, which had been divided into several parts, to a greater unity and to express more strikingly the central part of the ordination, that is, the laying on of hands and the consecratory prayer.

---

[a] See DOL 4 nos. 145–149.

[4] SC art. 21 [DOL 1 no. 21].

[5] See LG no. 21 [DOL 4 no. 145].

[6] LG no. 28 [DOL 4 no. 148].

[7] PO no. 1: AAS 58 (1966) 991; ConstDecrDecl 619–620.

Finally, with regard to deacons, in addition to the content of our Motu Proprio *Sacrum Diaconatus Ordinem*, issued 18 June 1967,[b] the following should be especially recalled: "At a lower level of the hierarchy are deacons, who receive the laying on of hands 'not unto priesthood, but only for a ministry service' (*Constitutions of the Church of Egypt* 3, 2). Strengthened by sacramental grace, they have as their service for the people of God, in communion with the bishop and his college of presbyters, the *diakonia* of liturgy, word, and charity."[8] In the ordination of deacons a few changes had to be made to satisfy the recent prescriptions about the diaconate as a distinct and permanent grade of the hierarchy in the Latin Church or to achieve a greater simplicity and clarity in the rites.

2608   Among the other documents of the magisterium pertaining to sacred orders, we consider one worthy of particular mention, namely, the Apostolic Constitution *Sacramentum Ordinis* published by our predecessor, Pius XII, 30 November 1947. In this Constitution he declared that "the sole matter of the sacred orders of diaconate and presbyterate is the laying on of hands; likewise the sole form is the words determining the application of this matter, which unequivocally signify the sacramental effects — namely, the power of orders and the grace of the Holy Spirit — and are accepted and used as such by the Church."[9] After this, the document determines which laying on of hands and which words constitute the matter and form in the conferring of each order.

It was necessary in the revision of the rite to add, delete, or change certain things, in order either to restore the texts of the rite to the form they had in antiquity, to clarify expressions, or to bring out more clearly the effects of the sacraments. We therefore think it necessary, so as to remove all controversy and avoid perplexity of conscience, to declare what are to be held as the essentials in each revised rite. By our supreme apostolic authority we decree and establish the following with regard to the matter and form in the conferring of each order.

2609   In the ordination of deacons, the matter is the laying of the bishop's hands on the individual candidates that is done in silence before the consecratory prayer; the form consists in the words of the consecratory prayer, of which the following belong to the essence and are consequently required for validity: LORD, SEND FORTH UPON THEM THE HOLY SPIRIT, THAT THEY MAY BE STRENGTHENED BY THE GIFT OF YOUR SEVENFOLD GRACE TO CARRY OUT FAITHFULLY THE WORK OF THE MINISTRY.[c]

2610   In the ordination of presbyters, the matter is likewise the laying of the bishop's hands on the individual candidates that is done in silence before the consecratory prayer; the form consists in the words of the consecratory prayer, of which the following belong to the essence and are consequently required for validity: ALMIGHTY FATHER, GRANT TO THESE SERVANTS OF YOURS THE DIGNITY OF THE PRIESTHOOD. RENEW WITHIN THEM THE SPIRIT OF HOLINESS. AS CO-WORKERS WITH THE ORDER OF BISHOPS MAY THEY BE FAITHFUL

---

[b]   See DOL 309.

[8]   LG no. 29 [DOL 4 no. 149].

[9]   AAS 40 (1948) 6.

[c]   Latin: Emitte in eos, Domine, quaesumus, Spiritum Sanctum, quo in opus ministerii fideliter exsequendi munere septiformis tuae gratiae roborentur.

TO THE MINISTRY THAT THEY RECEIVE FROM YOU, LORD GOD, AND BE
TO OTHERS A MODEL OF RIGHT CONDUCT.[d]

Finally, in the ordination of a bishop, the matter is the laying of hands on the   2611
head of the bishop-elect by the consecrating bishops, or at least by the principal
consecrator, that is done in silence before the consecratory prayer; the form consists
in the words of the consecratory prayer, of which the following belong to the
essence and are consequently required for validity: SO NOW POUR OUT UPON
THIS CHOSEN ONE THAT POWER WHICH IS FROM YOU, THE GOVERNING
SPIRIT WHOM YOU GAVE TO YOUR BELOVED SON, JESUS CHRIST, THE
SPIRIT GIVEN BY HIM TO THE HOLY APOSTLES, WHO FOUNDED THE
CHURCH IN EVERY PLACE TO BE YOUR TEMPLE FOR THE UNCEASING
GLORY AND PRAISE OF YOUR NAME.[e]

This rite for the conferring of the orders of diaconate, presbyterate, and episco-   2612
pate has been revised by the Consilium for the Implementation of the Constitution
on the Sacred Liturgy "with the employment of experts and with the consultation
of bishops, from various parts of the world."[10] By our apostolic authority we
approve this rite so that it may be used in the future for the conferral of these
orders in place of the rite now found in the Roman Pontifical.

It is our will that these our decrees and prescriptions be firm and effective now
and in the future, notwithstanding, to the extent necessary, the apostolic constitutions and ordinances issued by our predecessors and other prescriptions, even those
deserving particular mention and amendment.

325. SC RITES (Consilium), **Decree** *Per Constitutionem Apostolicam*, promulgating the rites for the ordination of deacons, presbyters, and bishops, 15
August 1968: Vatican Polyglot Press, 1968.

Through the Apostolic Constitution *Pontificalis Romani recognitio*, 18 June 1968,   2613
Pope Paul VI approved in place of the previous rite in the Roman Pontifical the new
rite to be used henceforth for the conferral of the orders of diaconate, presbyterate,
and episcopate.[a] This rite had been revised by the Consilium, employing experts
and consulting with the bishops from the various parts of the world.

In virtue of the powers given it by Pope Paul VI therefore this Congregation of
Rites by the present Decree issues and declares to be the *editio typica* that part of the
Roman Pontifical containing these new rites for the conferral of the orders of
diaconate, presbyterate, and episcopate.

It is further established that until 6 April 1969, that is, Easter Sunday, either
these new rites of ordination or those presently in the Roman Pontifical may be
used; after that date only the new rites are to be used.[R1]

---

[d]   Latin: Da, quaesumus, omnipotens Pater, in hos famulos tuos Presbyterii dignitatem; innova in
visceribus eorum Spiritum sanctitatis; acceptum a te, Deus, secundi meriti munus obtineant, censuramque
morum exemplo suae conversationis insinuent.

[e]   Latin: Et nunc effunde super hunc Electum eam virtutem, quae a te est, Spiritum principalem,
quem dedisti dilecto Filio tuo Iesu Christo, quem ipse donavit sanctis Apostolis, qui constituerunt Ecclesiam per singula loca, ut sanctuarium tuum, in gloriam et laudem indeficientem nominis tui.

[10]   SC art. 25 [DOL 1 no. 25].

[a]   See DOL 324 no. 2612.

[R1]   Query: How is the ordination of subdeacons to be carried out? Reply: The rite for the ordination of
subdeacons has not yet been revised. Therefore conferral of this order is to be according to the rite as

All things to the contrary notwithstanding.

▶   335.   SC CATHOLIC EDUCATION, Instruction *In ecclesiasticam futurorum sacerdotum*, on liturgical formation in seminaries, 3 June 1979:

nos. 37–42:   Ordinations [nos. 2816–21].

given in the Roman Pontifical, even if in the one liturgical service deacons and presbyters as well as subdeacons are to be ordained. The ordination of subdeacons thus is to be carried out after the opening prayer of the Mass; the Litany of the Saints is to be sung according to its new form; the reading of the mandate given in the Roman Pontifical may be omitted. When deacons or priests are ordained in the same liturgical service, the subdeacons cannot be assigned the "charge" (*pensum*) of reciting one nocturn of the divine office for the bishop: Not 5 (1969) 327, no. 9. See DOL 340.

SECTION 4. HOLY ORDERS: C. THE PASTORAL OFFICE

SUMMARY (DOL 326–331). From 6 texts dealing with the pastoral responsibilities of bishops, priests, and deacons this subsection presents excerpts pertinent to their life and ministry in relation to the liturgy itself and to its pastoral aspects.

—The *Directory on the Pastoral Ministry of Bishops* (DOL 329) includes many sections of importance to the liturgy.

—In addition there are texts on specific pastoral-liturgical matters. An address of Paul VI considers the bishop's obligations regarding the liturgy (DOL 331). There is a directory on the pastoral ministry to tourists (DOL 326), a papal letter and a curial directory on the ministry to migrants (DOL 327 and 328), a decree on the pastoral care of seamen and ship passengers (DOL 330).

▶ 21. PAUL VI, Address to bishops of Italy, on liturgical reform, 14 April 1964.

▶ 7. VATICAN COUNCIL II, Decree on the Pastoral Office of Bishops *Christus Dominus*, 28 October 1965.

▶ 18. VATICAN COUNCIL II, Decree on the Ministry and Life of Priests *Presbyterorum Ordinis*, 7 December 1965.

326. SC CLERGY, **General Directory** *Peregrinans in terra*, on the pastoral ministry in tourism, 30 April 1969: AAS 61 (1969) 3605 (excerpts).

II. PASTORAL PRACTICE[32]

3. WORK OF THE DIOCESES

A. GENERAL NORMS. [. . .]

2614 1. There is a need to heighten awareness, especially with the aid of preaching and catechesis, of tourism's positive values, both human and Christian, in order that there will be joyous participation and communion with the Easter of the Lord.

2615 4. The Christian's formation regarding tourism is completed by celebration of the eucharist, "the fount and apex of the whole Christian life."[45] In the eucharist tourists and those engaged in the tourist industry offer to God the divine Victim and with him themselves[46] according to their respective situations — the first, one of pleasure, relaxation, their special enjoyment of the gift of creation; the others, one of service to their brothers and sisters.

From receiving Christ's body in communion they derive the strength by which, remaining close to baptismal, therefore, moral grace,[47] they are fit to carry out the apostolate that the Church entrusts to and expects of them. *As a channel for unity and peace*, tourism finds its central support in the eucharist, the *sign of unity* and *bond of peace* for the people of God[48] and the fontal cause of the freedom that is able to accomplish so much good.

Moreover, by sharing in the eucharist Christians, like the pilgrims to Emmaus (see Lk 24:05), will be able more readily to recognize as brothers and sisters in Christ their companion tourists, those whom they meet in their travels, or those whom they serve.

B. PARTICULAR NORMS. [. . .]

2616 It is the responsibility of the local Ordinary: [. . .]

b. *As to the ministry of priests*: [. . .]

---

[32] Since this General Directory regards pastoral activity concerned with problems raised by tourism for the Church and since it is directed to bishops in that they are the ones responsible for the care of souls, clearly the proposals in the Directory are related essentially to questions regarding the apostolate as regulated by the bishops. In the drawing up of these various directive norms serious consideration has been given to pastoral experience in many countries in the world.

[45] LG no. 11; see also no. 3 [DOL 4 no. 141; also no. 137].

[46] See LG no. 11 [DOL 4 no. 141].

[47] See ST 3a, 79.1 and 5.

[48] See Augustine, *In Ioannem Tract.* 26, n. 13: PL 35, 1613. See also 1 Cor 10:17, 12:12 and 27; Rom 12:6. ST 3a, 82.7 ad 2. LG nos. 3 and 11 [DOL 4 nos. 137 and 141].

— to grant to pastors, in view of the international features of tourism and of making the administration of the sacrament of penance easier, the faculty of delegating priests temporarily resident in their parishes, providing these already have regular faculties in their own diocese, to hear confessions even of foreign tourists, but at set times; [. . .]

— to remind priests travelling to carry with them the oils for anointing of the sick.[a]

c. *As to worship in places for tourists*:   2617

— to ensure the worthiness of the place of worship, considering the good effect that it exercises on all when it is kept up properly;

— to ensure celebrations of the liturgy, at convenient hours, with care, and with preaching suited to the spiritual needs of visitors;[57]

— to promote celebration of Mass on Sundays and holydays and administration of the sacrament of penance, by means of timely announcements, using bulletins and signs and, where applicable, several languages;[58]

— to encourage on Sundays and holydays (and their vigils) evening Masses and celebration of at least one evening Mass on weekdays in parishes where there are vacation places.

Also when there is such a weekday liturgy it will be advantageous, as experience teaches, to have a short homily;

— after statistics have been carefully reviewed, to weigh the advisability of celebrating Mass on holydays and Sundays beginning with evening prayer I of the Sunday or vigil;[59]

— to ensure the celebration of Mass on Sundays and holydays in camping grounds, at a convenient and prechosen site, and, where possible, by means of "chapels on wheels"; also to encourage the presence of special groups to offer Christian witness to the tourists;

— to ensure that pastors, especially on Sundays and holydays, arrange for assistance to be provided by visiting priests or those resident temporarily in their parishes;

— to prescribe that in the general intercessions during the tourist season there be a mention both of those who are on vacation, in order to appeal to them to fulfill their Christian obligations, and of those who cannot enjoy a vacation because they are poor or because tourism is their occupation;

— to arrange for places of worship to be open all day in order to encourage the devotion of the faithful and to enable them to enjoy viewing any special works of art that might be there;

— to take measures that a portion of the church collection be assigned to services necessary for the care of souls or to further the dialogue with tourists;

— to urge monasteries of contemplatives to bring the help of their prayers to the pastoral ministry regarding tourism.

d. *As to religious tourism*:   2618

---

a   See DOL 407.

57   See SCR, Instr. EuchMyst no. 19 [DOL 179 no. 1248]. See also GS no. 44.

58   See SC Council, Circular Letter N. 104132, 19 March 1966 [DOL 446].

59   See SCR, Instr. EuchMyst no. 28 [DOL 179 no. 1257]; cf., by analogy, OE no. 15 [DOL 5 no. 169].

— to ensure that religious tourism (pilgrimages) is highly regarded by safeguarding its spiritual element or the sacred character of locally traditional feasts;

— to promote esteem for shrines existing in the diocese in view both of the great contribution the shrines themselves make to the administration of the sacraments of penance and the eucharist and the considerable influence they exercise on nonpracticing tourists.

2619   e. *As to the Christian people*: [. . .]

— to see to the proper appreciation of the treasures of Christian art in the diocese by providing clear information on their religious significance; toward this end the spiritual and cultural training of tour guides should be promoted, as well as the thorough preparation of technical devices useful for an appreciation of the works of art or to explain the Christian life;[63] [. . .]

— to ensure, even by making particular mention of it in preaching every Sunday or holyday, that the faithful are rightly instructed regarding Christian conduct on the highways so that their driving does not endanger the lives of others;[64]

— to promote the use of an SOS sign in automobiles, already a useful practice in some countries, in order to facilitate religious assistance in case of serious accident.

2620   f. *As to those in the tourist business*: [. . .]

— to persuade hotel owners of the advantages of placing a Bible in every room, as is now done in some countries, and if possible, in the languages of the majority of tourists and with the fraternal cooperation of the ministers of worship of Christians separated from us.

2621   g. *As to other Christians separated from us*:

— besides those things already mentioned: a. to provide non-Catholic Christians with places of worship, in keeping with the norms of the Ecumenical Directory;[67] b. to invite those having the care of souls to direct non-Catholic Christians to their own minister or place of worship, if there is one, in the spirit of the prescriptions of the Ecumenical Directory (nos. 53 and 54 for Eastern Christians,[68] nos. 62 and 63 for other Christians[69]). [. . .]

4. RELIGIOUS ASSISTING IN PASTORAL WORK OF TOURISM

2622   Religious, inasmuch as "they serve the good of the whole Church in accord with their calling and the grace given to them,"[74] have the power to provide their own strong assistance to the pastoral ministry in tourism. This they can do either by offering their prayers (see no. 23) or by teaching according to their capabilities or

---

63   See Paul VI, OR, 24 Jan. 1969.

64   See GS no. 30. See also Paul VI: AAS 57 (1965) 907–909.

67   See Ecumenical Directory I, on Eastern Christians, no. 52: "[Text quoted: DOL 147 no. 1006] "; on other Christians, no. 61, "[Text quoted: DOL 147 no. 1015]."

68   See ibid. nos. 53, 54 "[Text quoted: DOL 147 nos. 1006, 1007]."

69   See ibid. nos. 62, 63: "[Text quoted: DOL 147, nos. 1016, 1017]."

74   LG no. 28 [DOL 4 no. 148].

also by putting their media of social communication at the disposal of this ministry. [. . .]

5. DEACONS IN PASTORAL MINISTRY TO TOURISTS

Where the permanent diaconate has been restored by the conferences of bishops with papal consent (see *Sacrum Diaconatus Ordinem I*, 1), the assistance of permanent deacons, under the leadership of their superiors, will also be very valuable in the practice of pastoral ministry to tourists. "Strengthened by sacramental grace, they have as their service for the people of God, in communion with the bishop and his presbyterate, the *diakonia* of liturgy, word, and charity"[77] and so are valued cooperators. But that they be such, it is very necessary that the diocese make provision for their special training also in this pastoral field. [. . .]

2623

---

327. PAUL VI, **Motu Proprio** *Pastoralis migratorum cura*, on the pastoral care of migrants, 15 August 1969: AAS 61 (1969) 601–603.

The pastoral care of migrants has always been the object of the maternal concern of the Church, which throughout the age has never failed in its assistance to those who, like Christ with the holy family in Egypt, have been forced to leave their native land.

2624

Striking evidence of this care is the Apostolic Constitution *Exsul Familia*, which our predecessor Pope Pius XII issued on 1 August 1952.[1] This must be regarded as the principal papal directive of recent times on the problem.

The Fathers of Vatican Council II were fully aware of the seriousness and importance of this matter. Moved by the intention of making better and more effective provision for the spiritual care of migrants, they considered every facet of this problem, especially those that involve religion and that are therefore directly linked with the Church's own purpose — to provide for the salvation of souls.

In particular, the Council advocated special concern for those of the faithful "who because of their situation in life — for example exiles and refugees — are unable to avail themselves sufficiently of the ordinary pastoral care enjoyed by others, but are practically without it." The Council then urgently appealed to the conferences of bishops, especially national conferences, "to examine the more pressing problems affecting such people and provide and promote means and agencies designed for their spiritual care."[2] The Council also addressed these further words of exhortation to bishops: "Let them show that they have a deep concern for all their people, whatever their age, their social status, or their country of origin, toward the native-born, foreigners, and transients."[3]

It is obviously not possible to carry out this pastoral ministry without taking into account the spiritual heritage and the culture of the migrants themselves. In this regard, their native language is of utmost importance, since through it these people express their thoughts, their attitudes, and their religious life. There is, however, an obvious need for caution: even lawful diversity and adaptation to

2625

---

[77] LG no. 29 [DOL 4 no. 149]. See also Motu Proprio *Sacrum Diaconatus Ordinem*, 18 June 1967, I, nos. 1 and 2.

[1] AAS 44 (1952) 649ff.

[2] CD no. 18.

[3] CD no. 16.

various national groups must not turn out to be detrimental to that unity that all in the Church are called to share: "For by one Spirit we are all baptized into one Body, whether we are Jews or Gentiles, slaves or free."[4] "For you are all one in Christ Jesus."[5]

Accordingly, it is the duty of the Apostolic See, taking as its own the concerns of the Council, to provide bishops and the conferences of bishops with the resources for taking the proper measures in regard to the spiritual care of migrants. These people are not entrusted to the bishops' pastoral ministry simply like the rest of the faithful; because of their peculiar situation in life they require an attention that really matches their own needs.

2626   There is a further consideration. The radically changed conditions in which contemporary migration occurs have caused an increasing need for a revision of the norms on this matter issued by the Apostolic See and for adjusting such norms to today's new situation. In other words, it is necessary to fashion into a new and improved plan the program and structure on which the work of ministry to migrants is based. This will particularly involve the practical application to this work of the extensive experience already gained and of the common efforts of all concerned. Therefore bishops will have the power, as required by different circumstances of time and place, to use the various special forms of the apostolate that practice has proved effective. The broad area of the apostolate to migrants requires a correct assessment by all and an intense concentration of all resources. Therefore, it is absolutely necessary that in addition to the priests assigned to this ministry, religious and the laity also contribute with their combined cooperation.

We have deliberated on these matters and given careful consideration to the opinions of the various conferences of bishops and the members of the Congregation for Bishops. In consequence we now decree, *motu proprio* and by our apostolic authority, that the pastoral norms on the spiritual care of migrants in the Apostolic Constitution *Exsul Familia* are to be appropriately revised by the Congregation for Bishops. We therefore assign to the Congregation the task of promulgating these revised norms by means of a special instruction.[a]

328. SC BISHOPS, **Instruction** *Sacra Congregatio pro Episcopis*, on the pastoral ministry to migrants, 22 August 1969: AAS 61 (1969) 614–643 (excerpts).

CHAPTER III
NATIONAL CONFERENCES OF BISHOPS

[. . .]

2627   24. § 1. The various forms of migration involved today in the increased travel throughout the world and the classes of people — seafarers, air travellers, itinerants — present new pastoral problems. They also involve unfamiliar considerations bearing on the spiritual life, psychology, economics, and administration. This is especially the case with exiles, refugees, or migrants who leave overpopulated regions seeking to better their lives.

---

[4]   1 Cor 12:13–14.

[5]   Gal 3:28.

[a]   See DOL 328.

§ 2. To obtain the help necessary to solve these problems as effectively as the resources permit, it is advisable for the conferences of bishops and local Ordinaries to set aside an annual "Migrants' Day."[44]

§ 3. The principal objectives of this observance are: that the members of the people of God, according to the capacities of each, will recognize, out of a consideration of the divine plan of salvation, their own responsibilities and will do their part to promote the causes involved in the area of migration; that all the faithful will through prayer plead for God's help to obtain vocations; that the devoted apostolate of priests will be strengthened; and that the Christian faith of the migrants will remain strong and be deepened. [. . .]

CHAPTER IV
LOCAL ORDINARIES

[. . .]

B. Local Ordinaries Where There Are Migrants

32. In accordance with the norms of Vatican Council II,[51] local Ordinaries are not to refuse to accept into the liturgy the use of the migrants' own native language. [. . .]

2628

33. [. . .] § 1. Where there is a large number of migrants using the one language, whether they are permanent residents or transients, the erection of a personal parish may be advisable, its limits to be established by the local Ordinary.[52]

2629

§ 4. Whenever it seems inadvisable to erect either a personal parish or a mission with the care of souls, either *sui iuris* or attached to a parish, provision is to be made for the spiritual care of migrants through a chaplain or mission priest of the same language, with a preestablished territory for the exercise of his ministry.

34. § 1. Each chaplain or mission priest for migrants must, as far as possible, be given a church or chapel or a semipublic oratory in order to carry out his sacred ministry.

2630

§ 2. Otherwise the local Ordinary is to issue norms making it possible for such a chaplain or mission priest to carry out his ministry freely and fully in another church, including a parish church.

CHAPTER V
CHAPLAINS OR MISSION PRIESTS FOR MIGRANTS
AND THEIR DELEGATES

A. Chaplains or Mission Priests

[. . .]

---

44   See Ap. Const. *Exsul Familia* Tit. II, art. 49.

51   See SC art. 38 [DOL 1 no. 38]. Instr. EuchMyst no. 19 [DOL 179 no. 1248].

52   See CD no. 32. Paul VI, Motu Proprio *Ecclesiae Sanctae* no. 21, § 3: "The diocesan bishop by his own authority, after hearing the priests' council, has the power to erect or suppress parishes or to reorganize them in any way whatsoever. But he must act in such a way that the matter is properly disposed by the competent authority in cases where there are agreements between the Apostolic See and the civil government or vested rights belonging to physical or moral persons."

2631   37. § 2. During his tenure a chaplain or mission priest for migrants is subject to the jurisdiction of the local Ordinary in both the exercise of his ministry and in matters of church discipline.

2632   38. A chaplain or mission priest given charge of a personal parish[58] possesses parochial power as well as all the rights and duties that are proper to pastors (parish priests) according to the norms of the general law. Even though he lacks territorial jurisdiction, such a priest also has the faculty of administering the sacrament of confirmation to his subjects who are at the point of death.[59]

2633   39. § 1. A chaplain or mission priest who has been assigned a mission involving pastoral care[60] possesses his own proper powers and by analogy is equivalent to a pastor (parish priest).

§ 2. His power is personal, that is, to be exercised only over the persons of migrants of the same language and within the limits of his mission.

§ 3. The same power is to be considered as being coextensive in law with that of the local pastor (parish priest).[61] Therefore for celebration of the sacraments, including marriage, any migrant may go either to the chaplain or mission priest for migrants of the same language or to the local pastor (parish priest).[62]

§ 4. Finally, in addition to all those things that the general law grants to pastors (parish priests), there are other rights and obligations belonging to a chaplain or mission priest for migrants:

Among his rights the following are to be included:

a.   the power to administer to his subjects, that is, to the faithful of the same language, the sacrament of confirmation, as regulated by the Decree *Spiritus Sancti munera*;

b.   the power to assist validly at a marriage in which one of the spouses is of the same language as himself, within the limits of his assigned territory, all the requirements of the law being observed, including the prescription of the *Codex Iuris Canonici* on lawfulness[63] and the norms for the investigations concerning the state of the prospective spouses.[64]

Among his obligations the following are to be included:

a.   the same duties in exercising his ministry on behalf of the faithful of his own language as are proper to a pastor (parish priest) according to the norms of the *Codex Iuris Canonici;*[65] [. . .]

c.   he is not however bound by the obligation of celebrating the Mass *pro populo* required by the general law.

---

[58]   See art. 33, § 1 of this Instruction.

[59]   From an audience given by Pope Paul VI, 30 April 1968.

[60]   See Ap. Const. *Exsul Familia* Tit. II, art. 34, 35.

[61]   See ibid., art. 36.

[62]   See ibid., art. 39.

[63]   See CIC can. 1097.

[64]   See SC Sacraments, Instr.: AAS 33 (1941) 297–307.

[65]   See CIC can. 467–469.

40. § 1. In a place where he cannot establish a mission with the care of souls, the 2634
local Ordinary is to grant to a chaplain or mission priest faculties adequate for
migrants of the same language and resident in a definite sector[69] to have the help of
the sacred ministry.

§ 2. In such a situation bishops are to make sure that the rights and functions
of the chaplain or mission priest for migrants are precisely defined and are coordinated with the responsibility of the local pastor (parish priest).

42. Chaplains or mission priests for migrants are to be loyal in spirit and action 2635
and to adapt themselves to the diocese where they exercise the ministry, whatever
the juridic status they are given and whatever the assistance they provide for
migrants through the mandate of the local Ordinary. [. . .] They are to be faithful in
attending the conferences on moral and liturgical matters. [. . .]

B. DELEGATES OF CHAPLAINS OR OF MISSIONARY PRIESTS

47. § 1. The delegate must ensure: 2636

b. that there is utmost care for the worthiness and cleanliness of churches,
chapels, or oratories and of all sacred furnishings, especially in regard to reservation of the blessed sacrament and the celebration of Mass;

d. that sacred services are carried out according to the prescriptions of the
liturgical laws and the decrees of the Congregation for Divine Worship; that
ecclesiastical property is carefully managed and the obligations attached to it
are rightly fulfilled, especially Mass obligations; that the entries are correctly
made in parish registers and that these are kept safe [. . .].

329. SC BISHOPS, *Directory on the Pastoral Ministry of Bishops* (*Ecclesiae imago*), 22
February 1973: Vatican Polyglot Press, 1973 (excerpts).

PART I
FUNDAMENTAL PRINCIPLES OF THE MINISTRY AND LIFE OF BISHOPS

CHAPTER I
NATURE AND MISSION OF THE CHURCH AS THEY DEFINE THE MINISTRY

2. The Church is in Christ as *sacrament*, that is, as sign and instrument of 2637
intimate union with God and of the unity of the whole human race, so that those
who believe may have access to the Father through Christ in the one Spirit (see Eph
2:18). Thus the universal Church manifests itself as "a people gathered together in
the unity of the Father and of the Son and of the Holy Spirit."[1]

[. . .] Of the many elements and aspects of the universal Church, some appear
to be especially significant for a closer insight into the character and duties of the
bishop within the context of the local Church, which should be as complete a
reflection of the universal Church as possible.[3]

---

69   See art. 33, § 4 of the Instruction.

1   Cyprian, *De orat. dom.* 23: PL 4, 553.

3   See AG no. 20.

2638   5. *Priestly character of the Church.* All the people of God share in the prophetic, priestly, and kingly office of Christ, but some among them are specially consecrated in a further way and share in the priesthood of Christ to the point of exercising the sacred ministry, both to further the glory of God and to lead their brothers and sisters toward a richer share in the divine life.[8]

CHAPTER III
CHARACTERISTICS OF THE MINISTRY OF BISHOPS

2639   14. As a member of the Church and as one who functions as head and pastor of the Christian people, the bishop must combine in himself the qualities of being at once father and brother, student of Christ and teacher of the faith, son of the Church and, in a certain way, father in the Church, since he is the minister of the spiritual rebirth of Christians (see 1 Cor 4:15).

2640   15. Of the two sides of the bishop's identity, the one derives from baptism and confirmation, through which he shares with the rest of the people of God in the universal priesthood of the faithful, the other derives from the fullness of the sacrament of orders, through which he shares in the ministerial and hierarchic priesthood (different from the other priesthood in kind not only in degree) as Christ's vicar or vicegerent in order to form and shepherd the people of God.[1]

Bishops have the responsibility of teaching the word of God with authority and bearing witness to it, of guarding it faithfully and interpreting it authentically.[2] They are to preside over Christian worship in the person of Christ and to be stewards of the mysteries of God.[3] It is their responsibility to gather together and rule the local Churches,[4] to choose and direct their assistants in the sacred ministry,[5] to pass judgment on the soundness and rightful exercise of charisms.[6] Through the Holy Spirit given to them by episcopal ordination, bishops "have been made true and authentic teachers of the faith, sanctifiers, and shepherds."[7]

2641   16. Placed at the summit of the sacred ministry, the bishop exists as a living sign of Christ's presence in his Church, as one bearing witness to the word of God and communicating God's life through the sacraments. The bishop exists also as a sign of the Church's presence in the world, as one leading the members of the Mystical Body of Christ in the work of redemption and salvation that all the faithful must carry out in the world.[8]

---

[8]   See LG no. 13; PO no. 2 [DOL 18 no. 257].

[1]   See LG nos. 10, 26–27 [DOL 4 nos. 146–147].

[2]   See LG nos. 24–25.

[3]   See LG no. 26 [DOL 4 no. 146].

[4]   See LG no. 27 [DOL 4 no. 147].

[5]   See LG nos. 28–29 [DOL 4 nos. 148–149].

[6]   See LG no. 12.

[7]   See CD no. 2.

[8]   See LG no. 21 [DOL 4 no. 145].

PART III
MINISTRY OF THE BISHOP IN THE LOCAL CHURCH
[. . .]

SECTION I
THE VARIOUS MINISTRIES OF A BISHOP

CHAPTER I
THE BISHOP AS TEACHER IN THE COMMUNITY OF FAITH

I. TEACHING OFFICE OF THE BISHOP

THE IMPORTANCE AND OBLIGATION OF PREACHING

55. "Among the principal duties of bishops, the preaching of the Gospel occupies   2642
the preeminent place. Bishops are the heralds of faith who lead new disciples to
Christ. They are the authentic teachers, that is, teachers endowed with Christ's
authority, who preach to the people committed to them the truths that must be
believed and put into practice. Under the light of the Holy Spirit, bishops explain
that faith, bringing forth from the treasure of revelation both new things and old
(see Mt 13:52), making faith bear fruit and by their vigilance warding off any errors
that threaten their flock (see 2 Tm 4:1–4)."[1]

Like St. Paul, therefore, the bishop himself is one set apart for the Gospel of
God (see Rom 1:1), its defender (see Phil 1:16), and its bold herald (see Rom 1:6). He
is thus appointed as the authoritative teacher of his flock, the witness of faith, the
guardian and judge in all matters of faith and morals.

The bishop is bound to devote himself to the ministry of the word (see Acts
6:4), meditating on it with reverence, proclaiming it with confidence.[2] Unless legitimately prevented, he preaches the word of God personally, with Scripture as his
source and guide,[3] so that all may offer the obedience of faith to God revealing
himself.[4]

He keeps his priests always aware that the special and absolutely necessary
duty of the pastor of souls is to preach the word of God.

TEACHING IN THE HOMILY

59. The proper form of preaching for an already evangelized community is the   2643
homily. The bishop preaches it during the celebration of the liturgy in a simple,
familiar way suited to the understanding of all, calling to mind from the sacred text
the wonderful works of God and the mysteries of Christ and instructing the faithful in the laws of Christian living.

Since the homily comes after the sacred reading in the liturgy, which is the
summit and source of the whole life of the Church,[7] it excels all other forms of
preaching and in a certain way includes them, especially *catechesis*. Even if the bishop
himself can but rarely and with difficulty perform the task of catechesis in a formal
way, the homily gives him an effective opportunity to bring out briefly and pointedly from the liturgy of the day primary truths of the Christian faith, unless
pastoral reasons suggest something else.

---

[1]   LG no. 25.

[2]   See DV no. 1 [DOL 14 no. 218].

[3]   See DV no. 21 [DOL 14 no. 224].

[4]   See DV no. 5.

[7]   See SC art. 10 [DOL 1 no. 10].

In order that he may more easily touch the hearts of the faithful and draw them to the truth, the bishop must above all understand the mentality, customs, circumstances, dangers, and prejudices of the individuals and groups he addresses. He must constantly adapt his method of teaching to their capacity, character, and needs so that each one may be able to share joyfully in the sources of salvation (see Is 12:3) and the treasures of sacred doctrine.

FORMS OF THE CATECHUMENATE

2644   72. The bishop sees to it that throughout his diocese the catechumenate for adults about to be admitted to the sacraments of Christian initiation is established and carried out in keeping with the norms laid down by competent ecclesiastical authority.[19]

Besides the catechetical preparation of the families of children to be baptized,[20] the bishop, in cooperation with his confreres in the regional or national conferences, is to arrange for some type of catechumenate for children, adolescents, and adults baptized in infancy, so that they may be formed step by step toward Christian maturity in faith through a schedule of catechesis and education planned to coordinate with the sacraments of penance, eucharist, confirmation, and marriage.[21]

CHAPTER II
THE BISHOP AS HIGH PRIEST IN THE COMMUNITY OF
RELIGIOUS WORSHIP

2645   75. Just as in the early Church the apostles devoted themselves "to prayer and to the ministry of the word" (Acts 6:4), so likewise bishops, successors of the apostles, exercising the ministry of Christ the High Priest, gather their Churches together to worship God through prayer and the celebration of the eucharist.[1]

The ministry of the bishop, the high priest and presiding member of the community gathered for prayer, has always held and still holds the first place in the Church. By its very nature this ministry, even though closely linked to them, is ranked above the ministries of teaching and ruling, since the bishop's office of sanctifying in the person of Christ, the supreme and eternal High Priest, stands as the summit and source of the other ministries.[2]

I. THE BISHOP AND PRAYER

THE BISHOP'S PRIESTLY OFFICE

2646   76. The bishop possesses the fullness of that priesthood which he shares with other ministers of the community of the faithful. As he is an instrument of the supreme and eternal Priest, therefore, "the faithful's life in Christ in some way derives from and depends on him."[3]

---

[19]   See SC art. 64–66 [DOL 1 nos. 64–66]; CD no. 14 [DOL 7 no. 193]; AG no. 14 [DOL 17 no. 246]. RR, *Rite of Christian Initiation of Adults* [DOL 301]. SCC, *General Catechetical Directory* no. 130 [DOL 169 no. 1114].

[20]   See RR, *Rite of Baptism for Children*, Introduction no. 7 [DOL 295 no. 2291].

[21]   See RR, *Rite of Confirmation*, Introduction nos. 3, 12 [DOL 305 nos. 2512, 2521]; *Rite of Marriage*, Introduction no. 5 [DOL 349 no. 2973]. SCC, *General Catechetical Directory* nos. 77–97: AAS 64 (1972) 145–146; Addendum [DOL 169 nos. 1115–20].

[1]   See LG nos. 20, 21, 26 [DOL 4 nos. 145, 146].

[2]   See CD no. 15 [DOL 7 no. 194]; SC nos. 10, 41 [DOL 1 nos. 10, 41]; PO no. 5 [DOL 18 no. 260].

[3]   SC art. 41 [DOL 1 no. 41].

Conscious of his office, the bishop therefore sees himself above all as the steward of the sacred mysteries and directs his offices of teacher and shepherd to them.[4] The bishop's supreme concern, then, is that he and his Church devote themselves to the worship of God and fulfill the priestly office, the supreme act of the new people of God, the holy nation, the royal priesthood (see 1 Pt 2:4–10),[5] which they exercise most specially at the liturgical assemblies. The whole dignity of episcopacy and its supreme position in the Church have as their reason the fullness of the sacred power with which it has been endowed.[6]

FOSTERING CONSTANCY IN PRAYER

77. The bishop devotes his unflagging energy to making his whole diocese grow together into a praying community "that perseveres with one accord in prayer" (Acts 1:14; see Acts 2:42 and 46) and adores the Father "in spirit and in truth" (Jn 4:23). Like the apostles in the upper room (see Acts 1:13), the bishop presides over this community, showing the way by his own example.

2647

The bishop offers visible witness to this above all when he presides in person at the Christian baptism of adults, confirmation, the conferring of holy orders, and the celebration of the eucharist.

THE BISHOP'S OWN PRIESTLY ACTS

78. In carrying out the sacred rites the bishop by his devoutness and gravity clearly shows himself to the faithful as a true high priest,[7] "who is taken from among them and made their representative before God to offer gifts and sacrifices for sins" (Heb 5:1). He finds joy in celebrating the divine mysteries with his people as often as possible, well aware that every community around the altar under the sacred ministry of the bishop is "a symbol of that charity and unity of the Mystical Body, without which there can be no salvation."[8] By his example he emphasizes the fact that "a communal celebration involving the presence and active participation of the faithful . . . is to be preferred to a celebration that is individual and, as it were, private."[9]

2648

STRIVING AFTER CHRISTIAN PERFECTION

79. Praying for his people and working for them both alone and through his priestly co-workers, the bishop pours out upon the faithful in many ways and in abundance the fullness of Christ's holiness and stirs their resolve to strive, all in their separate ways of life, for Christian perfection.[10]

2649

II. The Bishop and the Liturgy

IMPORTANCE OF THE LITURGY

80. The bishop should ensure that in his diocese the liturgy, which is the common and public worship of the people of God, is celebrated with as much dignity as possible and with an aware, reverent, and fruitful participation by all, with the sacred minister presiding, and with observance of the prescribed norms. Preaching

2650

---

4   See LG no. 26 [DOL 4 no. 146]; CD no. 15 [DOL 7 no. 194].

5   See LG no. 10 [DOL 4 no. 140].

6   See LG no. 21 [DOL 4 no. 145].

7   See CD no. 15 [DOL 7 no. 194].

8   LG no. 26 [DOL 4 no. 146].

9   SC art. 27 [DOL 1 no. 27].

10   See LG nos. 26, 40, 41.

must lead to the liturgy and the liturgy, especially that of the eucharist, must lead in turn to a familial communion in charity, both spiritual and material.

LITURGICAL RITES IN THE CATHEDRAL AND IN OTHER DIOCESAN CHURCHES

2651   81. a. In order that all the clergy and the faithful may regard the cathedral church as the center of divine worship in the diocesan community, the bishop himself frequently presides over the divine mysteries and the liturgy of the hours celebrated by the cathedral chapter, especially on Sundays and other more solemn feasts of the year. He also tries to make the liturgical life of the cathedral church preeminent in its beauty, its observance of liturgical laws, and the fervor of the Christian people, so that the cathedral may clearly stand out as the mother and teacher of the other churches of the diocese.[11]

b. The bishop is glad, however, to exercise his office of high priest also at other places of worship in the diocese and to be present at Mass, especially in parishes, either on the occasion of pastoral visitations or whenever the faithful attend in large numbers or priests meet, so that the faithful become ever more conscious of their union with the bishop as the one presiding over the Church at prayer.

LITURGICAL INSTRUCTION OF THE FAITHFUL

2652   82. As high priest and chief moderator of divine worship in the local Church, the bishop is responsible for directing the whole liturgical life of the diocese, for animating and protecting it.[12] It is up to him also to further the liturgical instruction of the faithful with the assistance of appropriate commissions and agencies (e.g., on liturgy, music, art, etc.),[13] and of pastors and other priests, religious, and lay people trained for this work and dedicated to the apostolate of the liturgy.

LITURGICAL DIRECTORIES

2653   83. In his own conference of bishops, the bishop contributes his views and his support to the preparation and faithful observance in his diocese of a "Liturgical Directory," a "Book of Prayers," and a "Directory for the Administration of the Sacraments," conformed to the instructions of the Holy See.

ADAPTATION AND EXPERIMENTAL FORMS IN THE LITURGY

2654   84. With his confreres in the conference of bishops, the bishop investigates liturgical adaptations, to be made in accord with the law, that are consonant with the culture and traditions of a given people and with particular pastoral needs.[14]

Likewise, should the good of souls truly demand it, the bishop, respecting the norms laid down by the Holy See, shares in the prudent and candid deliberation of the conference of bishops on the advisability of testing new liturgical practices. The purpose of this testing is that the energy and warmth of faith may show their vitality in the creation of new and striking liturgical forms, more clearly expressing the mentality and fulfilling the expectations of contemporary people and bringing out the community-character of religion.

---

[11]   See SC art. 41 [DOL 1 no. 41].

[12]   See SC art. 22, 26 [DOL 1 nos. 22, 26]; CD no. 15 [DOL 7 no. 194].

[13]   See SC art. 45–46 [DOL 1 nos. 45–46]. SCR, Instr. MusSacr no. 68 [DOL 508 no. 1189]. SCC, Circular letter to the conferences of bishops on the care of the historico-artistic heritage of the Church, 11 April 1971 [DOL 541 no. 4331].

[14]   See SCDW, Instr. *Liturgicae instaurationes*, 5 Sept. 1970, no. 12 [DOL 52 no. 530].

MASSES IN HOMES OR WITH SPECIFIC GROUPS

85. To meet the genuine needs of his people, not to establish *ecclesiolae* or special privileges, the bishop has authorization to allow, on particular, set occasions, celebration of the eucharist with special groups, outside a place of worship, or even in private, family homes.[15]

2655

SPECIAL OBSERVANCE OF SUNDAY

86. a. The bishop takes great care that the faithful properly recognize, honor, and celebrate Sunday as the true "day of the Lord," on which the Church gathers together to renew the memory of the Lord's paschal mystery by listening to the word of God, offering the sacrifice of the Lord, and also by sanctifying the day with prayer, charity, and rest from work.[16] The bishop therefore takes special interest in the rites celebrated on Sundays by congregations gathered in various churches and also in the sacraments, e.g., baptism and confirmation, that are administered by preference on this day and with as large an attendance of the faithful as possible.

2656

b. In addition, he strives to have pastors, whenever possible, invite the faithful and give them the necessary catechesis to celebrate in church with clergy or religious, certain parts of the liturgy of the hours, evening prayer, for example.[17]

c. The bishop directs that "on Sundays and holydays the celebrations that take place in other churches or oratories must be coordinated with the celebrations in parish churches so that they contribute to the overall pastoral program. It is indeed preferable that small, nonclerical religious communities and other such communities, especially those that work in the parish, take part in the parish Mass on these days. As to the hours and the number of Masses to be celebrated in parishes, the convenience of the parish community should be kept in mind and the number of Masses not so multiplied as to do harm to pastoral effectiveness."[18] Hence the bishop, after hearing everyone concerned, has a schedule of services drawn up for all the churches and public oratories of the diocese.

d. He is also concerned that, in whatever place divine worship is available, services are scheduled for the convenience of those who leave early on Sunday morning or on holydays of obligation for the sake of recreation, exercise, or leisure, or because they must go to work. Therefore in places where they gather or along the way, at railway stations and airports or at places that are always open (such as shopping centers, radio stations, industrial plants, etc.), Mass should be celebrated at convenient hours on Sundays and holydays and also, if need be, on the preceding evening.

e. Finally, it is up to the bishop to see that pastors make proper provision for the faithful coming from places where a different language is spoken, especially in the churches of larger cities and in populous vacation centers. These faithful are to have the opportunity to assist at Mass celebrated according to their own practices and in their own language or, in case there are many languages, in the majority language or in Latin. The hour of this Mass should be posted at the doors of all the churches and if possible in railway and bus stations, hotels, and similar places.[19]

---

15   See SCDW, Instr. on Masses with special groups, 15 May 1969 [DOL 275].

16   See SC art. 102, 106 [DOL 1 nos. 102, 106].

17   See SC art. 99, 100 [DOL 1 nos. 99, 100].

18   SCR, Instr. EuchMyst, 25 May 1967, no. 26 [DOL 179 no. 1255].

19   See SCDW, Instr. EuchMyst no. 19 [DOL 179 no. 1248].

CELEBRATION OF THE SACRAMENTS

2657   87. Whenever the sacraments are celebrated, the bishop, as the one responsible for regulating their administration according to the norms established by competent authority, sees to it that the ministers and faithful understand and express the religious meaning of the sacraments for both the individual and the community. That meaning is the sacraments' share in the power to sanctify through the paschal mystery of Christ and his sacrifice offered to the Father. Therefore:

a. The bishop exercises vigilance that preaching and pastoral practice relating to the sacraments, especially baptism, penance,[20] the eucharist,[21] and marriage, are in complete harmony with the Church's teaching.

b. He sees to it that these sacraments are celebrated by all rightly, carefully, and with the greatest reverence, in keeping with the rites recently restored by the Apostolic See and adapted, within the limits allowed, by the individual conferences of bishops; the proper instruction of priests and faithful is a prerequisite.

c. The bishop, who alone is the primary minister of the sacrament of confirmation,[22] insists on proper preparation of candidates and, as far as possible, himself confers the sacrament with all solemnity in the presence of the assembled community.

d. When the bishop confers the orders of diaconate, priesthood, and, when there is occasion, episcopacy, he knows that then above all he is exercising his ministry as head and servant of the community of the faithful. As a way of building up the people of God, he sees that the rites of ordination are celebrated with proper solemnity and the presence of the faithful in the cathedral or, if it seems advisable, in other churches of the diocese. The aim is that Christian families will have a high regard for the vocation to the sacred ministry and by their prayer and efforts assist those who have been divinely called.

e. Concerning the matter of sacramental sharing with other, separated Christians, he sees to it that the norms set down by the Apostolic See are exactly observed.[23]

OUTWARD SOLEMNITY OF THE SACRAMENTS AND SACRAMENTALS

2658   88. In the celebration of the sacraments and sacramentals, "apart from the distinction between persons according to their liturgical function and sacred orders and the due honors to be given to civil authorities provided by liturgical laws, no special honors are to be paid in the liturgy to any private persons or classes of persons, whether in the ceremonies or by external display."[24]

Unless the conference of bishops has taken the laudable step of establishing a uniform standard for the entire region, the bishop throughout his diocese sees to the mitigation and standardization, if not the abolition, of the practice, where it exists, of requiring fees from the faithful — Mass stipends excepted — on the occasion of the celebration of the sacraments and sacramentals. At the same time, he does not neglect to point out the meaning and value of the faithful's offerings

---

²⁰   See SCDF, Pastoral Norms on General Absolution [DOL 361].

²¹   See SCDS, Instr. on facilitating holy communion, 29 Jan. 1973 [DOL 264].

²²   See LG no. 26 [DOL 4 no. 146]. RR, *Rite of Confirmation*, Introduction [DOL 305 no. 2516].

²³   See SecCU, Ecumenical Directory I nos. 42–50, 55–59 [DOL 147 nos. 996–1004, 1009–13]; *idem,* Declaration on shared eucharistic celebrations, 7 Jan. 1970 [DOL 150]; *idem,* Instr. on admitting other Christians to eucharistic communion in the Catholic Church, 1 June 1972 [DOL 155].

²⁴   SC art. 32 [DOL 1 no. 32].

made to God and disbursed by the Church for divine worship, the support of its ministers, and the relief of the poor.[25]

THE BISHOP'S EXAMPLE IN RECEIVING THE SACRAMENTS

89. As head and model of priests and faithful, the bishop gives example in receiving the sacraments, for which his need is no different from that of any other member of the Church. When he himself is seriously ill, he takes special care to receive the anointing of the sick and to have holy viaticum brought to him, with clergy and people accompanying. He does all he can to arrange for the communal celebration of the last rites and funerals for priests and he presides whenever possible at priests' funerals.

2659

III. Popular Devotions

PROPER REGULATION OF FORMS OF DEVOTION

90. To increase devotion in the entire people of God, the bishop earnestly recommends and fosters the adoration offered to Christ the Lord. He promotes and regulates acts of veneration toward the Blessed Virgin Mary and the other saints in such a way that these devotions "accord with the sacred liturgy, are in some way derived from it, and lead the people to it, since in fact by its very nature the liturgy far surpasses any of them."[26] Therefore:

2660

a. With the greatest care he fosters the adoration, both within and outside Mass, of Christ the Lord substantially present in the eucharist,[27] as well as devotion to the Sacred Heart of Jesus.[28] He makes sure that the construction and placement of the tabernacle meet liturgical norms; he sees to it that churches and public oratories are open for eucharistic worship to suit the convenience of the faithful.

b. The bishop takes care that the sacred shrines erected in honor of God, the Blessed Virgin Mary, and the saints effectively serve the spiritual life of the diocese in every way, with all hindrances removed and even the suggestion of money-making eliminated. This calls for his vigilance over the liturgical celebrations held in these places and his regulation of pilgrimages, so that everything leads to the greatest spiritual growth, especially from the preaching of the word of God and the administration of the sacraments.

c. The bishop does not forbid any of the good and useful things belonging to the popular celebrations and amusements occurring in the course of the year on feasts proper to a place or of the universal calendar (e.g., those of a patron saint or the Blessed Virgin Mary, Christmas, Easter, etc.). Rather he perfects them and properly directs the religious aspect, imbuing it with elements of sound faith, supernatural devotion, and Christian teaching. Accordingly, he guards against expressions of popular religion that conflict with Christian truth or the mind of the Church, and puts an end to those that exist, but at the same time he prudently opens the way to new forms of devotion.

d. He takes precautions against the intrusion into devotional practices or liturgical celebrations of forms of prayer, song, or music that are harmful to the true Christian spirit or introduce a semblance or suggestion of the profane. Therefore

---

[25] See ST 2a2ae, 86.2. PO nos. 20, 21. Synod of Bishops 1971, *The Ministerial Priesthood* Part II, no. 4 [DOL 318 no. 2568].

[26] SC art. 13 [DOL 1 no. 13].

[27] See SCR, Instr. EuchMyst nos. 50, 58 [DOL 179 nos. 1279, 1287].

[28] See Pius XI, Encycl. *Miserentissimus Redemptor*, 8 May 1928: AAS 20 (1928) 165–178. Pius XII, Encycl. *Haurietis aquas*, 15 May 1956: AAS 48 (1956) 309–353. Paul VI, Apostolic Epistle, *Investigabiles divitias Christi*, 6 Feb. 1965 [DOL 453].

the texts of the vernacular prayers and songs for the faithful's sharing in the liturgy, unless they have already been assigned or approved by the Apostolic See or the national conference of bishops, require the bishop's approval, attesting that they are of a biblical and liturgical inspiration and therefore sound and beneficial for use even in the faithful's private prayer.

PRESERVING AND FOSTERING POPULAR DEVOTIONS

2661   91. The sound desire to promote liturgical life carries with it the desire to preserve, foster, and even spread those devotions that express and nourish the spirit of prayer. This is especially true if they reflect holy Scripture and the liturgy or were originated by saints or are ancient witnesses to a tradition of faith and devotion.

If texts for such devotions are to be changed or adapted, either as regards their theology or literary style, especially when they are translated into the vernacular, the advice of theologians and those skilled in pastoral work, psychology, pedagogy, and the humanities should be sought as required by the norms of the conference of bishops, which is competent to allow new texts for the entire territory. Every bishop should follow the same procedure in regard to his own diocese.

a.   Among the devotions to be reverently preserved and spread among Christian families and communities, the holy rosary of Mary stands out. It has been ceaselessly recommended by the popes as a kind of compendium of the Gospel and therefore as a model devotional practice recommended for the Church[29] and splendidly confirmed by the practice of the saints. The bishop may not change the mysteries of the rosary, in view of its universal use, without consulting the conference of bishops and the Holy See.

b.   Also to be preserved and encouraged are the devout meditation on the Lord's passion known as the Way of the Cross and certain novenas, especially those that precede liturgical solemnities (for example, Pentecost and Christmas), for they are rich in true Christian devotion. If there is a need for change, the procedures already mentioned apply.

c.   Also to be encouraged are biblical paraliturgies, that is, vigils consisting of public reading of sacred Scripture, with meditation on it and intervals of prayer and song.

CHAPTER IV
THE BISHOP PRESIDING OVER THE COMMUNITY OF CHARITY

ARTICLE I. WORKS OF CHARITY

LINKS BETWEEN CHARITY AND LITURGY

2662   131. In order that the souls of the faithful may be imbued with Christian charity and that they may be drawn to its practical consequences, the bishop strives to have them realize that as they share actively and intelligently in it, the liturgy itself, especially the eucharist, calls them to an active charity. They express this awareness by the offering of money and of other gifts at the eucharistic celebration during the presentation of the gifts, which on certain occasions should take on greater solemnity. For the same purpose the bishop may suggest other ways to the faithful, either as a preparation for the eucharistic celebration or as a thanksgiving, especially on Sundays and holydays, for example, to visit the sick, prisoners, needy families, and institutions, to contribute something for local or outside needs, to make offerings for works of charity or of divine worship.

----

29   See Paul VI, Ap. Exhort., *Recurrens mensis octobris*, 7 Oct. 1969 [DOL 464].

CHAPTER VI
THE BISHOP IN THE DIOCESAN SYNOD AND IN THE PASTORAL VISITATION

I. Diocesan Synod

CELEBRATION OF THE SYNOD

165. The synodal assembly expresses and affirms its sense of community first in its   2663
celebrations of the liturgy, especially the eucharist; these celebrations are, as it were,
the center of the synod and as many of the faithful as possible should take part in
them. The liturgy of the word has an intimate connection with these solemn rites
and suitable homilies are therefore given to explain the synod's meaning and its
program. Talks also can be given to the people gathered for the divine liturgy to
throw light on the fundamentals of doctrine and pastoral action that have bearing
on the work of the synod. [. . .]

II. Pastoral Visitation

PASTORAL VISITATION OF PARISHES

168. The principal reason for visitation of the parishes is that the bishop may come   2664
in contact with people — clergy, religious, and laity. Everything done in the visitation should serve this purpose.

   During the visitation of the parishes, therefore, among other things, the bishop
endeavors:

    a. to celebrate Mass and preach the word of God;

    b. to confer the sacrament of confirmation solemnly, during Mass if possible;
    [. . .]

    g. to visit the sick whenever he has the chance. [. . .]

SECTION II
STRUCTURES OF THE LOCAL CHURCH AND
THE BISHOP'S CO-WORKERS IN THE PASTORAL MINISTRY

CHAPTER I
DIOCESAN STRUCTURES

II. The Parish

DIOCESAN OFFICE OR COMMISSION FOR NEW PARISHES

178. Unless it seems more useful to establish a special permanent diocesan office,   2665
the bishop may set up a commission whose function it will be, in consultation with
the priests' council and the other commissions concerned, to handle all matters that
pertain to the erection of new parishes and the building of churches.

   This commission should be as representative as possible of the entire diocesan
community. It conscientiously and devotedly approaches the question of erecting
parishes and building churches as a common endeavor and as far as possible assumes the burdens and funding of the program.

ESTABLISHING AUXILIARY CHURCHES AND ORATORIES

180. In addition to parish churches, the bishop promotes the erection of auxiliary   2666
churches and oratories in areas where people live or gather in large numbers,
especially for health or recreation, and also along highways and at train or bus
stations and airports. Where this is not possible, he buys or leases private buildings
suited to sacred worship and other needs of the ecclesial community.

The construction or adaptation of these buildings should observe the laws of good taste and beauty proper to places of worship.

SOME REQUISITES FOR THE BUILDING OF CHURCHES

2667   181. In the building of churches, especially parish churches, the bishop ensures the blending of devotion and art, mindful of both fittingness and poverty, attractiveness and utility. He carefully avoids anything suggesting eccentric novelty or violating rather than enhancing the sacredness of the place and the devotion of the faithful.[12]

Finally, in the building, renovating, or furnishing of churches he exercises caution against excessive expenditure and burdening the parish with huge loans. It would be incongruous to put dead stones ahead of the Church's charity and apostolic work, which, if necessary, must take precedence over the magnificence of buildings. Nevertheless, "the church, the house of prayer, must be well cared for and suited to prayer and liturgy. There the eucharist is celebrated and reserved and the faithful gather for worship. There the presence of the Son of God, our Savior offered on the altar of sacrifice for us, is treasured as the aid and solace of the faithful."[13]

COLLECTIONS FOR NEW PLACES OF WORSHIP

2668   182. Prudently and in a way appealing to their sense of faith, the bishop brings the people of God to a realization of the duty they have to supply the resources for the work of erecting new parishes and constructing new buildings for worship and for charity in the diocese. For this purpose he may institute special-collection days on which the collection may be brought with the gifts to the altar during Mass, thus signifying the active participation of the people. He may also impose fees for administrative services, the sacraments and sacramentals being always excluded.

In order to form the mentality of the faithful correctly and to collect funds, an association may be formed that reflects the attitudes and wishes of the community.

In this matter the bishop takes every precaution that pastoral care does not give way to the quest for money; rather, the spirit of poverty and faith characteristic of the Church must stand out clearly for all to see.

330. SC BISHOPS (Pontifical Commission on Migrants and Travelers), **Decree** *Apostolatus maris*, on the pastoral care of seamen and ship passengers, 24 September 1977: AAS 69 (1977) 737–746 (excerpt).

PART TWO

I

FACULTIES FOR PRIESTS ENGAGED IN THE MINISTRY
TO SEAMEN AND SHIP PASSENGERS

2669   The faculties and privileges listed here are given, during their tenure and from the beginning of any voyage, to chaplains in the apostolate of the sea who engage in this ministry to seafarers, whether in port or at sea.

The following faculties are of particular importance:

---

[12]   See SC art. 122–127 [DOL 1 nos. 122–127].

[13]   PO no. 5 [DOL 18 no. 260].

1.   to celebrate Mass twice on weekdays and, if genuine pastoral need requires, three times on Sundays and holydays;

2.   to celebrate Mass at any hour of the day and to give communion in the evening, for a good reason and observing the prescriptions of law;

3.   to celebrate Mass outside a place of worship, but in a worthy and decent place — but never in a bedroom — on a particular occasion for a good reason, but on a regular basis only for a more serious reason;

4.   to celebrate Mass at sea and on rivers, with all necessary precautions being taken;

5.   to use electric lights in place of candles when Mass is celebrated aboard ship, as often as necessity demands;

6.   to celebrate a second Mass during the evening hours of Holy Thursday in churches and public or semipublic oratories when a pastoral reason requires; also to celebrate Mass during the morning hours in case of genuine need and only for the faithful who cannot in any way take part in the evening Mass;

7.   to reserve the eucharist in a lawfully erected chapel on a ship, but only after obtaining an apostolic indult from the Holy See, through this Pontifical Commission;

8.   to administer the sacrament of confirmation during a voyage to any sailor, child, or adult aboard, on condition that there is no bishop available who is in communion with the Apostolic See and it is foreseen that the person to be confirmed, because of age, ignorance of the language, or the local conditions, would only receive this sacrament ashore with great difficulty; all the other requirements of law are also to be observed;

9.   to absolve during a voyage all penitents from the censure incurred, according to the *Codex Iuris Canonici* can. 2350, § 1, for procuring an abortion; other requirements of the law are to be observed;

10. to absolve during a voyage penitents on board for any reason from the censures and penalties treated in the *Codex Iuris Canonici* can. 2314, if such penitents, after having culpably fallen away from the Catholic faith or communion, contritely seek reconciliation with the Church;[1]

11. whenever impeded for any reason whatever from carrying out his ministry and when recourse to a local Ordinary or national director is impossible, to delegate any priest on board as a passenger to serve as chaplain and during the voyage to minister to the seamen and other passengers, with full use of the faculties proper to chaplains.

II

AS FOR PRIVILEGES, THE FOLLOWING ARE ESPECIALLY LISTED

1.   Seamen are permitted to fulfill their Easter duty any time during the year, after they have received proper instruction or catechesis in regard to the precept of annual communion.

2.   Seamen are dispensed from the law of fast and abstinence in the Apostolic Constitution *Paenitemini* ch. III, II, §§ 2 and 3. But it is suggested that when they take advantage of this dispensation they compensate by some appropriate act of devotion and that as far as possible they keep both fast and abstinence on Good Friday.

3.   All those who are aboard ship for any reason as well as those who have any dealings with the ship are dispensed during the voyage from the law of fast and

2670

---

1   See Ecumenical Directory I no. 19 [DOL 147 no. 973].

abstinence given in the Apostolic Constitution *Paenitemini* ch. III c, II §§ 2 and 3, but with the qualification in the preceding number being observed.

4.   Provided they have gone to confession and received communion, the faithful aboard ship may gain a plenary indulgence on the titular feast of the chapel and on 2 August, if they devoutly visit the chapel lawfully erected on the ship and recite there the Lord's Prayer and the Creed for the pope's intention.

5.   Under the same conditions, on 2 November they may also gain once a plenary indulgence applicable only to the dead by devoutly visiting the chapel and reciting the Lord's Prayer and Creed for the pope's intention.

The indulgences in nos. 4 and 5 may also be gained, with the fulfillment of the same conditions, by seamen and their relatives and by members of the apostolate of the sea, either in chapels or oratories of the circles "Stella Maris" or in oratories of other centers of the apostolate of the sea.

331. PAUL VI, **Address** to the bishops of Lombardy, excerpt on the bishop's duties regarding the liturgy, 21 April 1977: Not 13 (1977) 199 (Italian).

2671   Finally, the bishop is the priest of the liturgy. Here too the field for his work is seen to be as vast as it is prominent because it is imperative that, among other things, the bishop put to ever better use the great conciliar reform. In the liturgy the communitary dimension has been recovered and the theme of active and conscious participation stressed. The bishop's duty will therefore be that of using to fullest advantage, and of leading others to do the same, every single liturgical celebration in the Church. His purpose must be that the celebration matches the themes already mentioned and takes its proper place within the context of his overall pastoral ministry. The relevant opportunities are many. We must, for example, address ourselves to the different social and professional groups. We must be attentive not only to correct diction and respect for the sacred texts, but also to liturgical song, in accord with a tradition that the Church not only must not let die, but must increase and enrich with new, attractive compositions. The Church of St. Ambrose, we are pleased to note, offers us examples of this tradition that are models of incomparable beauty and instructive power.

▶   67.   SYNOD OF BISHOPS, 1977, "Message to the People of God," 28 October 1977:

no.   14 b: Catechesis [no. 594].

Section 4. Holy Orders: D. Priestly Formation

SUMMARY (DOL 332–335). The Constitution on the Liturgy art. 15–17 addressed the liturgical formation of seminarians in the context of the general principles on furthering active participation in the liturgy. The conciliar concern was reflected notably in Paul VI's *Sacram Liturgiam* and the Instruction *Inter Oecumenici*, cross-referenced here. There are 4 texts devoted to the subject of this subsection:

—In 1965 the Congregation of Seminaries and Universities prepared a lengthy instruction on liturgical formation in seminaries (DOL 332). But this document remained largely a dead letter. The successor to the earlier Congregation, the Congregation for Catholic Education, issued a similar instruction in a somewhat improved form in 1979 (DOL 335).

—Extracts on liturgical formation of clergy are presented from a circular letter of the Congregation for the Clergy (DOL 333) and from the *Basic Plan for Priestly Formation* issued by the Congregation for Catholic Education (DOL 334).

▶ 1. VATICAN COUNCIL II, Constitution on the Liturgy Sacrosanctum Concilium, 4 December 1963:

art. 15–17: Liturgical formation of clerics [nos. 15–17].
     18: Liturgical life of priests [no. 18].

▶ 20. PAUL VI, Motu Proprio *Sacram Liturgiam*, on putting into effect some prescriptions of the Constitution on the Liturgy, 25 January 1964:

art. I: Liturgical formation of the clergy [no. 279].

▶ 23. SC RITES (Consilium), Instruction (first) *Inter Oecumenici*, 26 September 1964:

nos. 11–12: Liturgical formation of clerics [nos. 303–304].
     14–17: Liturgical formation for the spiritual life of clerics [nos. 306–309].

▶ 17. VATICAN COUNCIL II, Decree on the Missionary Activity of the Church *Ad gentes*, 7 December 1965:

no. 16: Seminaries in mission Churches [no. 248].

332. SC SEMINARIES AND UNIVERSITIES, Instruction *Doctrina et exemplo*, on the liturgical formation of future priests, 25 December 1965: Vatican Polyglot Press, n.d.*

FOREWORD

2672 1. By his teaching and example the Lord Jesus strove during his public life to accustom his disciples to the practice of prayer in common. Not only did he attend temple services with them so as to be present at the rites of the Mosaic Law, but he also taught them the words of the Lord's Prayer and gave them the model of the great eucharistic prayer, two of the main constitutive elements of the Church's public prayer. Consequently, bishops in the Church have always taken care to preside personally at the liturgy and to watch diligently over its celebration and the sound development of its various forms.

2673 2. Abiding by these traditional principles, the modern popes have been especially attentive to the teaching of liturgy in seminaries and to the formation of seminarians in the office they will later discharge in the public celebration of prayer. Furthermore, the conciliar Constitution on the Liturgy *Sacrosanctum Concilium* devoted special attention to this formation, which is to be continued through the whole course of ecclesiastical studies and which priests themselves must continue and develop throughout their priestly life. Only pastors thoroughly steeped in the theory and practice of liturgy will be able to teach the faithful and bring them to an intelligent and fervent participation in the various liturgical celebrations of the Christian community.

2674 3. The liturgy in its earthly form expresses, calls to mind, and keeps continually new the mystery of salvation, the paschal mystery. As a result the splendor of the liturgy has many distinctive qualities: The liturgy is:

---

* Text reprinted from *Seminarium* 1 (1966) 37–65.

— a public manifestation of the unfailing holiness of the Church and one of the clearest signs of its divine origin;

— a cry to the Father springing from the Church's heart under the inspiration of the Holy Spirit;

— perfect praise and adoration in spirit and in truth, rendering in Christ and through Christ all honor and glory to God;

— an unfailingly effective instrument for our purification and sanctification;

— the most fitting and universal teaching program for the training and formation of the Church's children;

— the luminous and affective contemplation of the entire treasure of revelation;

— not only a powerful form of the active apostolate, but also the most extensive and surest program for the apostolate of prayer;

— the preeminent actuation of supernatural charity, grounded in the communion of saints, for the full attainment of the living unity of the Church;

— finally, an anticipation of the eternal praise already begun in heaven, with which it constitutes a single, integrated worship and toward which it tends unfalteringly as its own culmination.

4.   To recognize this far-reaching significance of the liturgy is to discover at the same time the special properties it has to influence the total formation of aspirants to the priesthood. In particular: 2675

— The foundation of the whole liturgy is Christ the Priest, and especially his redemptive sacrifice, unceasingly actual in the most holy eucharist.

— The liturgy is above all a sacred activity that the Church carries out and directs to God. All the Church's other functions of sanctifying and teaching in the service of people, important as they are, are but consequences of this primary purpose or means to attain it.

— Celebration of liturgy is always through an act at once internal and external: external, because it is public; internal, because it is truthful and sincere. The thoughts and sentiments of the minister and those present do not alone make up that interiority: it includes as present the inner life of all the members of the Church, because in every true liturgical rite the Church offers the sign and the expression of its entire life.

— Liturgical participation ought above all to be supernatural, rooted therefore in faith, hope, and charity. Moreover, its special efficacy does not depend on a theatrical setting or on the participants' numbers, but on the consuming ardor of their spiritual life and union with God.

— Liturgical worship as the public act of the Church is necessarily hierarchical and, as a result, subject to the prescriptions of competent authority. Personal preference and disobedience to prescriptions of law, in consequence, alter the nature of the act from being liturgical; no longer is it the worship of the Church but the private worship of one person or of some faction.

5.   The attention and interest of seminarians must therefore be awakened and rightly directed toward the liturgy by their being shown how liturgical life enriches them spiritually and equips them to fulfill their future pastoral ministry.   2676

6.   The liturgy, first of all, enriches the future minister's own life — doctrinally, spiritually, even humanly.   2677

As the act of redemption made present, the liturgy brings together in the unity of one and the same living celebration the exercise of faith as well as of all theological knowledge and moral action; the carrying out of this one work brings into a unity the many facets of Christian life. Liturgy as teaching embodied in sign, while taking nothing away from the objectiveness of faith and its supporting theological science, raises theology from the level of theoretical knowledge to the level of living worship. Liturgy as the celebration of mysteries has a sublime power to create and deepen a sense of the divine and an effectiveness to train the spirit in reverence toward God's transcendence.

Liturgy thus forestalls a fragmented and uncoordinated teaching of the theological disciplines and opens the way to their being actually applied in future ministry. The light deriving from the liturgy endows the ecclesiastical disciplines with new power: the study of Scripture discovers the *sensus plenior*; dogmatic theology expresses itself in adoration; moral theology leads to devotion; history becomes a proclamation of divine providence; canon law seeks to perceive the demands of love.

2678   7.   In the development of the seminarian's spiritual life, the liturgy has its first influence as an ascetical training. Because it makes the seminarians actual participants in Christ's paschal mystery, the liturgy imposes: the discipline of conscientious observance of the rites; the renunciation of the self, which all but disappears and is absorbed within a communal action; the purification of heart needed to pass through symbols to the mystery they cloak and conceal.

Secondly, the liturgy is the foremost school of prayer, providing its subject matter and fundamental dispositions, as well as its most complete formulations and broadest intentions.

Finally, the liturgy is a school of the supernatural contemplation that comes into being under the inspiration of the Holy Spirit, in the darkened light of the mystery of faith, joining us to God through sacred signs, yet not revealing God fully, so that in the soul the desire for a fuller union remains alive and increases.

2679   8.   Even at the level simply of human culture the liturgy develops the seminarians. A foreshortened acquaintance with human affairs is a defect often alleged against future ministers of the Gospel. Because of the long years of seclusion during their training, they live isolated from other people and have virtually no work experience. For this liturgy provides an effective remedy.

As a task to be fulfilled the liturgy calls upon those powers needed for action, impelling the young cleric to put into practice not only his newly gained learning, but also his energies and natural talents. As the carrying out of a communal undertaking, the liturgy develops his social powers, giving him a sense of community and of his place in it, as well as a feeling for discipline and communion with his confreres. To a high degree it fosters a sense of service, moderation, and right judgment.

In its use of the arts and styles of poetry and music, the liturgy is a singular school that over the centuries has trained the master artists and inspired their genius to create masterpieces. The liturgy thus enriches the life of those who will keep alive in their spirit zeal for the house of God.

2680   9.   Besides enriching the seminarians themselves, the liturgical life, in a special manner, is the proper preparation of spirit for a productive priestly ministry. Liturgy rightly celebrated through the conjoined devotion of celebrant and faithful has an acknowledged apostolic power. Only if the priest has been so trained that he himself clearly perceives the meaning and force of the liturgy will he be able to present the sacred rites to the faithful with the required understanding, love, and prudence and, in accord with the Church's prescriptions and without any kind of dilution, adapt them to the different groups with whom he celebrates the liturgy.

10. Furthermore, this formation will uncover the full riches of the liturgical texts   2681
and rites that will support the preaching of the priest each day and give that preaching its peculiar and rightful place at the very center of the celebration.

A burning dedication to the liturgy will have as its effect the priest's bringing together connaturally in every liturgy the attentiveness of mind, the peace, and the ardor that make the celebration beautiful and beneficial for the spiritual development of the gathered faithful.

11. The liturgical education of seminarians, then, must be regarded as so important   2682
and weighty a matter that Vatican Council II unreservedly declared that there could be no hope for the people's spiritual progress (i.e., that they would receive the Christian spirit from the liturgy as its first source) "unless the pastors themselves become thoroughly imbued with the spirit and power of the liturgy and make themselves its teachers." Therefore, this Congregation has determined to publish the kind of instruction needed on the liturgical training of clergy: a reminder, namely, and expansion of the relevant principles and precepts running through both the conciliar Constitution and the Instruction *Inter Oecumenici*.[†]

CHAPTER I
FOSTERING THE LITURGICAL LIFE IN THE SEMINARY

12. The bishop is responsible for the liturgical training of his clergy. He will, then,   2683
exercise a careful vigilance both in appointing teachers and in insisting on exact observance of this Instruction. Should it be necessary, he will introduce into the seminary without delay a complete revamping of liturgical practice conformed to the model to be set forth in this Instruction.

13. Officials and professors of the seminary, as the bishop's proxies and the execu-   2684
tors of his commands, will diligently undertake to carry out, each in his own sphere, the various phases of liturgical training and for greater effectiveness will join willingly in a cooperative effort.

ART. 1. SACRED CELEBRATIONS IN GENERAL

14. In accord with the importance the Church attaches to the liturgy, the sacrifice   2685
of the Mass and the divine office are to be celebrated in the seminary with the greatest care possible. Only then will the seminarians' liturgical life match the will of the Council as set forth in the Constitution on the Liturgy.

15. The language of the liturgy in the Mass and divine office in seminaries will be   2686
Latin, the language of the Latin Church, which all clerics are required to know (SC art. 36, § 1 and art. 101, § 1).[a] It will be advisable, however, to use the vernacular in the celebration of Mass on some specified days (for example, once a week) — to the extent permitted by the lawful authority for each region and confirmed by the Holy See — so that the clergy will be better prepared for the vernacular celebrations in

---

[†] Consequently this Instruction is faithful to the Constitution *Sacrosanctum Concilium* (4 Dec. 1963: AAS 56 [1964] 97–134) and the Instruction *Inter Oecumenici* (26 Sept. 1964: AAS 56 [1964] 887–900). Citations from these correspond to their paragraph numbers, using the sigla CC for the Constitution and IE for the Instruction. [This edition substitutes its own sigla, SC and InterOec; the text quoted in the preceding sentence is from SC art. 14 (DOL 1 no. 14)].

[a] See DOL 1 nos. 36 and 101.

the parishes. Thus use of the vernacular must never become the general practice at the expense of Latin. In granting the use of the vernacular, the Church does not intend that clerics think themselves freed from going to the sources or that in their preparation for the priesthood they neglect even slightly the universal language of the Latin Church.

2687   16. "Liturgical celebrations shall be carried out as perfectly as possible. Therefore:

a. "Rubrics shall be observed exactly and ceremonies carried out with dignity, under the careful supervision of superiors and with the required preparation beforehand.

b. "Clerics shall frequently exercise the liturgical functions proper to their order, i.e., of deacon, subdeacon, acolyte, reader, as well as those of commentator and cantor" (InterOec no. 13).[b]

2688   17. All celebrations should be carried out not only meticulously but also with attention to the integrity and beauty due to the performance of divine service. In this way future pastors will train themselves to a manner of life that will set them apart and will increase in the faithful an interest in and a taste for prayer and a sense of the sacred and its demands.

2689   18. If there is not one already, a prefect of ceremonies is to be appointed who will teach each person his part and see to it that everything is done with dignity and decorum. In instructing the clerics regarding their functions, he should use the texts of the law so that the clerics themselves may know how to use them as the needs of priestly ministry require. Moreover, as often as it seems necessary there should be rehearsals, especially as regards the less frequently used rites when the clerics are to participate in sacred celebrations at the cathedral church.

2690   19. "Seminary churches and chapels, all sacred furnishings and vestments shall bear the mark of genuine Christian art, including the contemporary," (InterOec no. 13 c).[c] Efforts are to be made to provide an organ for the church, if possible (see SC art. 120).[d]

2691   20. In keeping with the intent of the Constitution and liturgical law, all seminarians should actively participate in the liturgical rites and particularly in congregational singing; those with the ability should join the *schola cantorum*.

2692   21. The primary source of liturgical chants is to be the treasury of Gregorian chant. "The Church acknowledges Gregorian chant as distinctive of the Roman liturgy; therefore, other things being equal, it should be given pride of place in liturgical services" (SC art. 116).[e]

The seminary *schola cantorum* also has for its use chants from the rich repertoire of classical and modern polyphony, which by its close adherence to texts and genuine devotion graces the liturgy of the Church and provides praises worthy of God (see ibid.).[f]

---

[b]   DOL 23 no. 305.

[c]   DOL 23 no. 305.

[d]   See DOL 1 no. 120.

[e]   DOL 1 no. 116.

[f]   See DOL 1 no. 116.

22. Even though special care must be taken that the seminarians have a strong loyalty to the treasury of music proper to the Church universal (see SC art. 112, 114),[g] nevertheless, steps must also be taken for them to learn to use the liturgical repertoire composed in the native language of their own people and approved by the competent territorial authority (see SC art. 118).[h]

2693

ART. II. THE MYSTERY OF THE EUCHARIST

23. As the center of all spiritual life, Mass should be celebrated every day of the week and all the seminarians should take part. The celebration should take different forms, in order to bring out more clearly the diverse functions in the liturgical assembly and to make it possible for all the students to take an active part. The ideal should be to introduce the clerics by actual practice to the different forms for Masses that they will have to celebrate with parish congregations.

2694

24. On Sundays and on other greater feasts, the celebration shall be a sung Mass, with all in the house participating, and, when possible, preferably with a deacon and even with a subdeacon. As will be made clear later, there is to be a homily at the Mass and the students are to be urged to receive communion. With the Ordinary's consent, it is desirable that priests of the seminary who do not have some outside ministry concelebrate as an expression of the oneness of the priesthood and the sacrifice.

2695

25. Clerics should take part in the liturgy at the cathedral at least on the more solemn feasts and particularly when the clergy of the city are also present. Since all the faithful "should hold in great esteem the liturgical life of the diocese centered around the bishop, especially in his cathedral church" (SC art. 41),[i] seminarians shall be the first example of this. For the Mass of the bishop with his priests and ministers gathered around the altar with him is the preeminent manifestation of the life of the diocese. In the performance of liturgical functions in the cathedral, seminarians should also be employed as ministers to exercise the order corresponding to their assigned liturgical ministries.

2696

ART. III. DIVINE OFFICE

26. It is eminently right that seminarians, even those not yet bound to the divine office, celebrate communally lauds in the morning and vespers in the evening, and at the right time of day for these hours. Officials of the seminary should, as far as possible, also take part. It will be advantageous to substitute these hours, explicitly given pride of place by Vatican Council II (SC art. 89),[j] for the customary morning and evening prayers; by reciting the psalms together the students will acquire a taste for and an acquaintance with the divine office (InterOec no. 16).[k] On major feasts lauds and vespers are to be sung in their entirety.

2697

27. Even though as a rule the recitation of vespers should take precedence over recitation of compline, now and then the choice should be for compline when it fits in better with the time of day. Even if compline is not recited in common, the students would do well to make parts of it their private prayer before retiring.

2698

---

g See DOL 1 nos. 112, 114.

h See DOL 1 no. 118.

i DOL 1 no. 41.

j See DOL 1 no. 89.

k See DOL 23 no. 308.

2699   28. A practice to be recommended is the introduction occasionally of one of the little hours, e.g., terce before morning classes, sext before the noon meal, none before afternoon classes.

2700   29. Unless there is some impediment (e.g., the seminary's being far away), the seminarians should, when the opportunity arises, take part in vespers or the other hours of the office that the bishop celebrates with the faithful, especially in the cathedral (InterOec no. 16).[l]

2701   30. Care is to be taken in drawing up a daily schedule for the seminary to afford clerics in major orders a sufficient and convenient time to fulfill their office obligation properly (InterOec no. 16).[m] They are also to be urged to the communal celebration recommended by the Council (SC art. 99)[n] and this is to be carried out not only with exact observance but with the perfection due to divine service.

2702   31. So that in the psalmody the minds of the seminarians may match the music and words, provision is to be made for instruction, suited to their age and capacities, in the right understanding of the psalms and, as the conciliar Constitution affirms, in the dignity due to the singing of God's praises (SC art. 83–86, 88, 90).[o]

CHAPTER II
LITURGICAL SPIRITUALITY

2703   32. A worthy and becoming celebration of sacred rites in the seminary is obviously not enough; a spiritual formation of the seminarians is needed that in the present teaches them to take part in the liturgy with knowledge, intensity, and profit and for the future instructs them how from it to nourish their own spiritual life and to share it with others (see SC art. 11, 17, 18; InterOec no. 14).[a]

2704   33. No proper instruction in liturgical spirituality is possible unless the professors themselves make the liturgy the source of their own spiritual life and hold fast to it as the source of an integral and genuine Christian spirit. That is an indispensable requirement for all engaged in clergy education.

2705   34. Such training belongs also in minor seminaries and high schools; in fact its beginnings are in the education given in the home and in the parish. It does not limit itself to the superficial, but seeks to impart a love for liturgical matters and an intense interest in them. Liturgical education in no small measure has its grounding in human education and should be connected naturally with it as its crowning.

2706   35. Clergy education in the spirit of the liturgy should take into consideration not only those initiated from childhood into the liturgical and spiritual life but also those introduced to it only as adults. Christ's paschal mystery, renewed by the liturgy, communicated in the sacraments, and the model for every life, should be proclaimed in a way suited to each person (see SC art. 5–7; InterOec no. 6).[b]

---

[l]   See DOL 23 no. 308.

[m]   See DOL 23 no. 308.

[n]   See DOL 1 no. 99.

[o]   See DOL 1 nos. 83–86, 88, 90.

[a]   See DOL 1 nos. 11, 17, 18; DOL 23 no. 306.

[b]   See DOL 1 nos. 5–7; DOL 23 no. 298.

36. Care shall therefore be taken that during liturgical celebrations the superior or another qualified priest preach a homily of a kind defined in the Instruction *Inter Oecumenici* (nos. 53–55).ᶜ The homily is never to be omitted on Sundays and holydays of obligation; it is strongly recommended for weekday Masses during Lent; even a daily homily is desirable, provided it is very short.

2707

37. For spiritual reading seminarians are to read, in addition to the Scriptures, not only modern ascetical and mystical works, but also the writings of the Fathers and books dealing with the sacrifice of the Mass and the liturgical year, and, in general, with whatever is conducive to fostering a genuine liturgical spirituality. Spiritual directors will encourage their charges toward such reading, in keeping with individual needs and temperaments, and will assist them in the selection of books. Furthermore, they will teach the students to become familiar with theological and ascetical literature about the sacrifice of the Mass and the way of close personal union with it.

2708

38. Spiritual directors should take care to make use of the sacramental gifts bestowed in the liturgy to develop the souls of their charges in Christian perfection. Directors are to give the liturgy precedence over all other aids and, like the Church which sees liturgy at the very heart of spirituality, they will assist the spirit of seminarians to enter deeply into the mystery of Christ — renewed and in a sense made actual again in the liturgy — as their guide and the companion of their work. An intelligent and intense participation in the public worship of the Church will be the necessary sustenance and the principal resource for the spiritual life of clerics.

2709

39. Clerics should be instilled with the duty of adoration and special devotion toward the body and blood of Christ really present under the eucharistic appearances. They should be counseled in such practices as thanksgiving after Mass, the reception of holy communion whenever they can, daily visits to the blessed sacrament.

2710

40. Liturgical life in no way spurns or impedes personal meditation, but rather prompts it and nourishes it with scriptural and liturgical texts (InterOec no. 14),ᵈ a point that is to be emphasized to the seminarians and brought home with examples.

2711

41. Other devotions practiced in the seminary by law or custom are to be held in due honor and not, by misguidedly alleging the liturgy as the reason, rashly dropped. Nevertheless liturgy takes precedence, "since by its very nature it far surpasses them" (SC art. 13; InterOec no. 17).ᵉ With proper regard for the liturgical seasons, such devotions should be so related to the liturgy that they harmonize with it and are seen as somehow deriving from it (SC art. 13).ᶠ

2712

42. The spirit of the liturgy should profoundly mark the seminary's regimen and manner of life (see SC art. 17)ᵍ and the passage of time should be marked by the prominence of the Lord's Day and the cycle of the liturgical year. Sunday should really be the principal feast day, standing out not only by the solemn celebration of the liturgy but also by the community's joyfulness and its rest from work-a-day tasks. Community observance is to be encouraged with regard to devout practices

2713

ᶜ See DOL 23 nos. 345–347.

ᵈ See DOL 23 no. 306.

ᵉ DOL 1 no. 13; DOL 23 no. 309.

ᶠ See DOL 1 no. 13.

ᵍ See DOL 1 no. 17.

deriving from custom or Christian usage that fit in with the various seasons of the liturgical year (InterOec no. 14).[h]

2714   43. Whatever belongs to the worship of God in any way must be treated devoutly and reverently. Therefore, silence and recollection should be observed in the chapel; proper marks of reverence should be shown to sacred Scripture, the Book of the Gospels, the missal, and the sacred vessels. Moreover, the same reverence marking sacred rites should also be carried over as part of the tone of the whole way of life.

CHAPTER III
PRACTICAL TRAINING FOR THE LITURGY

ART. I. PASTORAL FORMATION

2715   44. From the outset seminarians must be prepared step by step, as they mature, for the sacred ministries to which the Church calls them. The aim therefore is that they become acquainted with the various ways of exercising these ministries. Especially during the last two years of seminary, they should be sent out to the parishes on one Sunday every month to help the parish priests.

2716   45. The parishes chosen should be those where the liturgical life better accords with the Church's wishes. It is supremely important that clerics learn respect and reverence for the liturgy and find out from experience the wisdom of the norms established by lawful authority.

2717   46. They are also to learn, however, the special hardships besetting those parishes that lack sacred ministers and where, from necessity, the priest is practically alone in the performance of liturgical celebrations. At the same time, they should be instilled with the duty the priest has, in keeping with the tradition of the Church, to train the assistants required for a simple yet becoming performance of liturgical rites.

2718   47. Clerics should be prepared for the difficult role of commentator in the parish liturgy. They should learn to discharge that office with proper prudence and seriousness, care being taken that they understand that the commentator should never become an obstacle between the celebration going on at the altar and the assembly of the faithful called to participate in it. Priests expert in this field will carefully observe and evaluate the student's attempts at this function.

2719   48. The seminarians, one by one or in groups, should learn by practice how to prepare a complete parish celebration. They should design a plan for proper liturgical catechesis of the faithful and should devote themselves to studying the text of the Sunday Mass, ponder the readings, and prepare reflections on them. They should determine in advance which songs, in keeping with liturgical laws, are best suited to the day's liturgy. Through rehearsals, they should instruct the readers and other ministers of the liturgical assembly.

2720   49. After due preparation, the clerics should also exercise their ministry in the liturgy of the sacraments of Christian initiation and of marriage and in rites for the dead. Consequently, they should learn the rubrics necessary for the valid and worthy administration of the various sacraments. They should likewise learn a method of stirring up and fostering the faithful's inward and outward sharing in the liturgy of the sacraments.

---

[h]   See DOL 23 no. 306.

50. Clerics must be thoroughly instructed that the liturgy does not exhaust the total activity of the Church (SC art. 9–11);[a] aided by the texts of Vatican II, they are also to learn how the various pastoral functions should be linked with the liturgy (InterOec no. 7).[b]

Art. II. Training for Sacred Music

51. "Sacred song closely bound to the text forms a necessary or integral part of the solemn liturgy" (SC art. 112).[c] Its study, then, is not an empty quest for the beautiful, because any kind of liturgical formation that neglects sacred song is necessarily deficient. And so "great importance is to be attached to the teaching and practice of music in seminaries and in the novitiates and houses of study of religious of both sexes. . . . To impart this instruction, those in charge of teaching sacred music are to receive thorough training" (SC art. 115).[d]

52. Sacred music must be numbered among the disciplines necessary for the right training of seminarians and, therefore, must be taught for a sufficient number of hours and with a well-planned program beginning with the first courses of study and continuing through theology. Students are required to undergo an annual examination in music as in other disciplines. Every seminary should therefore have a trained professor of sacred music, who is to be a full-fledged member of the faculty.

53. All the seminarians should acquire an adequate knowledge of Gregorian melodies, especially the best known. Frequent use will enable the seminarians to know by heart the chants, both the simple and the more elaborate, in traditional use by the Christian people.

54. They should also acquire the basic principles for directing a choir so that they may be able to lead at least the *Kyrie* chant and the psalmody and to direct the singing of liturgical texts in the vernacular.

55. The students should also be taught other types of music and they should be instructed in the authentic religious song of the people, not only the modern but also that preserved in the oral tradition of their own people.

56. If it does not already exist, in each seminary a *schola cantorum* should be formed under the direction of a trained choir master. The *schola* must observe the norms for liturgical music given by the competent authority.

57. Seminarians already able to play the organ should diligently continue their training in the seminary and should receive help for this in every way possible. Those with special talents should be sent, after completion of their studies, to a graduate school of music to finish their training.

58. There should be an effort to provide enough pianos and small organs so that students will have the chance to practice. To improve the performance of liturgical singing it will also be helpful to provide the seminary with such learning resources as tapes and records.

2721

2722

2723

2724

2725

2726

2727

2728

2729

---

[a] See DOL 1 nos. 9–11.

[b] See DOL 23 no. 299.

[c] DOL 1 no. 112.

[d] DOL 1 no. 115.

2730   59. It is of great importance that the speaking style of a priest — whether he is praying, talking, or reading — be polished and have a clear and pleasing sound. Accordingly, in addition to the course in music there should be a separate course in elocution, under the care of a professor really expert in this art.

ART. III. TRAINING IN SACRED ART

2731   60. The norms on respecting and preserving the treasury of sacred music handed down to us apply in due measure to the other sacred arts. As a consequence, the seminary officials responsible must always keep in mind the conciliar Constitution art. 129: "During their philosophical and theological studies, clerics are to be taught about the history and development of sacred art and about the sound principles on which the productions of its works must be grounded. In consequence they will be able to appreciate and preserve the Church's treasured monuments and be in a position to offer good advice to artists who are engaged in producing works of art."[e]

2732   61. If there is not already provision in the curriculum for sacred or Christian art, training of this kind shall be given the students at least through a series of lectures. These may well be given by laity of the diocese who are experts in this field, even those not belonging to the faculty. All exhibits of sacred art, both ancient and modern, should be seriously discussed and evaluated in the seminary.

2733   62. Seminary officials will take care that the students acquire firsthand knowledge of the diocesan art treasures and of the best modern works. Their training must be such that later there will be no reason to lament, through fault of the clergy, the sale, destruction, or any diminution of the sacred patrimony of Church art, a heritage entrusted to the vigilance of the clergy (SC art. 126).[f]

2734   63. The principles that Vatican Council II set down regarding sacred art and the plans for constructing and decorating churches (SC art. 122–128; see InterOec nos. 90–99)[g] should be carefully taught and explained. In addition, the students should be shown the prevailing norms of this branch of knowledge; the emphasis should not be on contradictions and discrepancies discernible on minor points but on bringing out for reflection the spirit animating past and current church documents on this matter.

CHAPTER IV
THE COURSE OF LITURGICAL STUDIES

2735   64. Whether considered in itself or in the total program of the other branches of the theological course, the place set aside for the courses in liturgy has already been defined in the conciliar Constitution in these words: "The study of liturgy is to be ranked among the compulsory and major courses in seminaries and religious houses of study; in theological faculties it is to rank among the principal courses. It is to be taught under its theological, historical, spiritual, pastoral, and canonical aspects. Moreover, other professors, while striving to expound the mystery of Christ and the history of salvation from the angle proper to each of their own subjects, must nevertheless do so in a way that will clearly bring out the connection between their

---

[e]   DOL 1 no. 129.

[f]   See DOL 1 no. 126.

[g]   See DOL 1 nos. 122–128; DOL 23 nos. 382–391.

subjects and the liturgy, as also the underlying unity of all priestly training" (SC art. 16).[a]

65. In order that this branch of knowledge in the training of candidates for the priesthood receive the emphasis it deserves, the course in liturgical studies shall occupy one hour a week through the four years of the curriculum for theology. In order to meet the special academic needs of seminaries in different regions, liturgical studies can be taught from the start of the philosophy curriculum and be completed in three or even in two years, provided the number of hours already stipulated is exactly respected and the subject matter covered in all its parts.

2736

66. The professor chosen is to be highly qualified, in theology and history especially, possessed of a clear grasp of pastoral issues, and imbued with a sense of the Church's public prayer. Accordingly, local Ordinaries should see to it that, as soon as possible, the seminary have a professor well prepared in this discipline (see InterOec no. 11),[b] and therefore one who is trained for his position in a graduate school specializing in liturgy.

2737

67. The sacred liturgy is to be taught in its theological and historical as well as in its spiritual, pastoral, and canonical aspects (SC art. 16).[c] Consequently, to clarify the course in liturgy and to expedite carrying it out, an *Appendix* to this Instruction furnishes a syllabus of topics recommended for classes, as well as directions regarding the method to be followed in dealing with the various subjects. The authority competent according to law, however, has the right to rearrange and redistribute the material over the years of the course, provided the minimum coverage required is not shortened in any way.

2738

68. All professors in the theology courses should keep in mind the recommendation of the Council, namely, that the principal branches of knowledge should, from considerations proper to the object of each discipline, develop in correlation with the mystery of Christ and the history of salvation, in such a way that the relation of these disciplines to the liturgy and to the unity of priestly training becomes absolutely clear (SC art. 16).[d] Above all, then, the development of sacramental theology should consist in themes soundly proven from the history of liturgy and should explain them by ample use of liturgical texts.

2739

Since the public prayer of the Church revolves around sacred Scripture as its pivot, the function of biblical studies will be to make it directly possible for the students to acquire a deeper and firmer understanding of the major texts for the liturgy and to deepen their love and devotion toward such texts (see SC art. 24, 90).[e]

69. In order that professors may not lack resources necessary for proper education and for scholarly writing, seminary officials should see to it that the library is supplied with a wealth of necessary and useful books in the area of liturgy: editions of liturgical collections, writings of the Fathers, compilations of decrees on matters liturgical, noteworthy commentaries on the liturgy, and books dealing with the biblical, theological, historical, canonical, and ascetical aspects of liturgy. It will be

2740

---

[a] DOL 1 no. 16.

[b] See DOL 23 no. 303.

[c] See DOL 1 no. 16.

[d] See DOL 1 no. 16.

[e] See DOL 1 nos. 24, 90.

the duty of the liturgy professor, moreover, to lead the students to go deeply into the sources themselves and to recommend to them the more recent and worthwhile books.

* * * *

After consultation with the Consilium and with the approval of the Congregation of Rites, the Congregation of Seminaries and Universities has planned and drawn up this Instruction, intended for the proper liturgical formation of seminarians. Pope Paul VI has ratified and approved it and ordered its publication; all things to the contrary notwithstanding.

APPENDIX
OUTLINES FOR A COURSE IN LITURGICAL STUDIES
(see Instruction ch. IV, no. 67)

PART I
ELEMENTS AND PRINCIPLES

Art. I. Nature of the Liturgy and its Importance to the Church's Life

2741 The course in liturgy should best begin with a short consideration of Christ's priesthood, redemption, sacrifice, and the work of sanctifying he has carried out through his teaching and sacraments.

There should then be a review, with commentary, of the teaching in the conciliar Constitution on the Liturgy art. 5–13, with stress on the points the Council wished to instill.

These, therefore, are the topics to be treated:

1. the nature of liturgy, which is the carrying out of the work of salvation completed by Christ and in which the Mystical Body of Jesus Christ, Head and members, offers full public worship to God; why, therefore, the liturgy stands as the exercise of Jesus Christ's priestly office (SC art. 7);[a]

2. the paschal mystery of Christ's passion, resurrection, and ascension that the Church celebrates in the liturgy (art. 6), and "from which all the sacraments and sacramentals draw their power" (art. 61);[b]

3. the place of the liturgy in the economy of salvation: "The wonderful works of God among the people of the Old Testament were a prelude" to the saving work of Christ (art. 5),[c] because "all these were our examples" (1 Cor 10:6); Christ completed his own work once and for all when he was born of woman, made under the Law, when he suffered under Pontius Pilate and rose on the third day; the Church will preach the Gospel until the end of time, will celebrate the eucharist, administer the other sacraments, in full awareness of Christ's presence, especially in the liturgy (art. 6–7);[d] the liturgy on earth is a foretaste of that liturgy in heaven when God will be all in all (art. 8).[e]

---

[a] See DOL 1 no. 7.

[b] DOL 1 no. 61.

[c] DOL 1 no. 5.

[d] See DOL 1 nos. 6–7.

[e] See DOL 1 no. 8.

Further points:

4. the liturgy uses perceptible, sacred signs to signify divine realities and through these signs, each in its own way, brings about human sanctification (art. 7, 33);[f]

5. as the exercise of Christ's priestly office, the liturgy includes a twofold movement: from God to us to sanctify us; from us to God as our adoration in spirit and in truth;

6. Christian liturgy, therefore, is not simply the complement of natural worship, but its expansion and transformation;

7. the liturgy, even though not being the totality of the Church's activity, is "the summit toward which the Church's activity is directed; at the same time it is the fount from which all the Church's power flows." This point needs further elaboration, based on the Constitution (art. 9–13).[g]

ART. II. THE AUTHORITY COMPETENT IN MATTERS OF LITURGY AND IN LITURGICAL LAW

1. On historical grounds the professor will show that laws on liturgy, i.e., the Church's public prayer, have always been in the hands of the hierarchy and belong to the hierarchy *iure divino*; also that over the centuries the exercise of that right has taken different forms.

2. The professor will explain the distinctive character of the hierarchy's right over the liturgy, which means the power to set forth the conditions of authenticity for the Church's prayer and for the sacred safeguarding of the trust received from the Lord.

3. After a review of Tridentine legislation, the professor should present and explain what Vatican Council II inaugurated with regard to liturgical law, especially in the Constitution art. 22,[h] pointing out the respective competence of the Holy See, the bishops, and the "conferences" of bishops.

4. Something should be said on the subject of liturgical books of both the Latin and Eastern Churches: norms on these publications; the revision envisioned by the Constitution; the books of the local Churches or religious orders; editions in the vernacular; rubrics, the need for them and the criteria for interpreting them.

5. There should be an outline of the fonts of liturgical law: the decrees of the ecumenical councils and of the popes, the decrees, replies, and instructions of the curial congregations, the *Codex Iuris Canonici*, and custom. Here again criteria of interpretation should be covered.

ART. III. CHARACTER OF THE LITURGY AS A HIERARCHIC ACTION OF THE COMMUNITY

1. There should be a presentation, guided by the Constitution art. 26–32 and 41–42,[i] of principles regarding the liturgical assembly as a holy people gathered in right order under the bishop. Such principles are to be elucidated from the teaching of sacred Scripture, examples in the early Church, and patristic texts.

2742

2743

---

[f]   See DOL 1 nos. 7, 33.

[g]   See DOL 1 nos. 9–13.

[h]   See DOL 1 no. 22.

[i]   See DOL 1 nos. 26–32 and 41–42.

2. Pointing out the diversity of members and functions marking the liturgical assembly, the professor is to outline the roles of celebrant, ministers, servers, choir, and congregation.

3. He is to explain the role of the faithful and their active participation in accord with the intent of the Constitution and of recent papal decrees.

4. He should show the preeminence of the bishop's role according to the teaching of the Constitution on the Liturgy and the Dogmatic Constitution on the Church *Lumen gentium*.

ART. IV. INSTRUCTIVE AND PASTORAL CHARACTER OF THE LITURGY

2744   1. As the Council says, "In the liturgy God is speaking to his people and Christ is still proclaiming his Gospel. And the people are responding to God by both song and prayer" (art. 33).[j]

2. In the liturgy, therefore, Scripture or the word of God holds first place, whether as read for all to hear or as sung by the whole assembly. The professor will treat at length the use of Scripture, both in the readings and in chants based on it, and he should also say something about the nonbiblical readings and hymns composed by the Church. He is to present the general principles on Bible services, the homily, and catechesis and show the primacy of Scripture for an understanding of the signs, actions, and prayers of the liturgy (see SC art. 24).[k]

3. The professor will take time to show the distinctive contribution and function of sacred song in the liturgy. He should go over the different types of sacred song: psalmody for singing the psalms and biblical canticles; hymnody that leaves greater latitude for meditation; the doxologies and acclamations, etc. Historical examples should be used to explain the dialogue between celebrant and congregation.

4. There should be a treatment of the different prayer styles: those of the celebrant (the oration, thanksgiving, narrative formularies, blessing, exorcism, silent prayers) and those of the congregation (the Lord's Prayer, prayer in silence, litanies).

5. There should be a brief history of sacred music: its origin, and early development; well-founded historical information on Gregorian chant, its spread, development, corruption, and restoration; other styles of sacred music approved by the Church should also receive attention.

6. A further topic is liturgical languages: the history of relevant church discipline in East and West; the way versions of the Bible, especially from Greek into Latin, have shaped Christian language; the place of Greek in the origins of liturgy and of Latin as a revered tradition in the Church of the West.

On the basis of history and of the various liturgical languages, the professor will then bring out the threefold criterion governing church law and usage in this matter: to set apart some sacred language, i.e., one sufficiently separated from a secular language as intended for sacred use and as hieratic in character; to preserve unity by the intangible bond of the style of praying; to endow the rites with a clarity sufficient to ensure the participation of the faithful.

---

j   DOL 1 no. 33.

k   See DOL 1 no. 24.

7.   Because the liturgy uses not just words but also signs "chosen by Christ or the Church to signify invisible, divine realities" (SC art. 33),[1] there should also be lectures on the gestures called for in liturgical prayer and on the articles used in liturgical worship. Instruction on gestures and posture, their meaning and spiritual impact, should derive from Scripture, the writings of the Fathers, and the teaching of St. Thomas Aquinas. Every care is to be taken to see that such instruction does not remain in the abstract but is put into use in the daily liturgy. It will be helpful to review the symbolism, especially the biblical symbolism, of the natural materials in use in the liturgy, especially those that are sacramental signs: light, water, bread, wine, oil, incense, etc.

8.   In the course of explaining the rite for the dedication of a church, following the Constitution art. 122–128,[m] there should be a theological treatment of places reserved for worship and the function of their different parts: the altar, places for eucharistic reservation, celebrant's chair, the lectern (ambo), place for the choir and organ, the baptistery, place for the congregation, and the place for the liturgy of penance.

9.   The students should receive assistance to apply what they learn in other courses toward an appreciation of the history and norms of sacred art. Christian iconography should be discussed as well as the requirements that sacred art must meet in these times in order to benefit the Christian people.

10.   All of this serves to show the teaching quality of the liturgy and how "although it is above all things the worship of the divine majesty, it likewise contains rich instruction for the faithful" (SC art. 33).[n] The force of the axiom, *lex orandi est lex credendi*, should be brought out and a basis given for discriminating between things that the Church in its liturgy presents to the faithful for belief and those that are of a kind not stamped by the authority of the magisterium.

ART. V. IDEAS ON THE HISTORY OF LITURGY

The history of liturgy is of such great importance that Vatican Council II and the popes have unhesitatingly asserted its primary influence on the contemporary liturgical reform. The orderly treatment of the individual liturgical services and the sacraments should therefore give due emphasis to the history of each rite for a better understanding of current liturgical usage and for a clearer and more certain sacramental theology.   2745

A more readily understandable development of the lecture material will be aided by the presentation of an outline of the progression and periods of all of liturgical history.

1.   Origins: through the use of the New Testament books, a description of the liturgical assembly in the apostolic age. Students are to be introduced to the sources on the liturgy of the early centuries; fortunately the texts are readily available: the *Didachē*, Clement of Rome, Justin, Irenaeus, Tertullian, Hippolytus of Rome, Cyprian, the *Didascalia* and *Apostolic Constitutions*, the *Euchologion* attributed to Serapion, the *Peregrinatio Egeriae* [Aetheriae], selected texts from the early anaphoras, and the patristic catecheses. This will bring out that Christian worship was something new,

---

    ^l   DOL 1 no. 33.

    ^m   See DOL 1 nos. 122–128.

    ⁿ   DOL 1 no. 33.

even though it will be necessary to point out what elements the early Church took from both Jewish prayer and from profane usage.

2.   Variety of Liturgical Languages or Families. Because the liturgies of the different Churches developed gradually with their own laws and texts, it will be well to outline the liturgical families of the East and West, touching on their origin, history, and individual character.

A principal objective should be to show clearly a common bond between the various rites; in the treatment of each individual liturgical service, especially those for the sacraments, the texts and rites from other liturgies should be brought in that will enrich doctrine and feed devotion.

3.   Progress and Spread of the Roman Liturgy up to the 13th Century. The first topic should be the local liturgy of Rome itself, as known from authentic records. A list of sources should be given and they should be referred to during lectures on theology and liturgy: sacramentaries, Roman Ordinals, the *Liber pontificalis*, papal letters, the sermons of St. Leo and St. Gregory, etc.

Next to be covered is the spread of the Roman rite, particularly in the Carolingian period, throughout Italy, Gaul, Germany, Spain, and elsewhere, always with local accretions, as is clear from medieval sacramentaries and missals and especially from the Romano-Germanic Pontifical.

That period was not only one of composition of new prayers for the priest, but also of the creation of many, many hymns and private prayers. Out of the numerous books needed for solemn and communal liturgies were fashioned missals *plenaria* and breviaries for private recitation.

4.   Work of the Council of Trent Reforming Abuses and Promoting Liturgical Unity. There should be a review of Tridentine decrees on divine worship and an account of how, at the mandate and according to the intent of the Council, the popes revised the liturgical books and disseminated them so effectively that they remained in use until present times.

5.   Liturgical Progress in the 17th and 18th Centuries. This should cover particularly eucharistic devotion, the careful observance of rites, the pastoral efforts in different regions toward the faithful's liturgical understanding and participation. There should be mention of the liturgical renewal in France and elsewhere during the 18th century, whose valid elements are to be indicated; but the frequently disordered, unlawful, and reprehensible motivation is also to be made plain.

6.   It should be shown how St. Pius X, Pius XI, and Pius XII through a progression of measures prepared and began the liturgical reform that was espoused by Vatican Council II.

Then this reform itself should be reviewed, its pastoral focus and outlook brought to light. There is to be an examination of the documents following up the Constitution and a stress on the need for development in the direction of variety, especially in the case of mission territories.

PART II
MASS AND WORSHIP OF THE EUCHARIST

Art. I. General Ideas on the Mass to Be Given to Students

2746   1.   An explanation is to be given of the various terms used in ancient documents and in different liturgies to refer to the Mass.

2.   There should then be a sound exposition of the texts of the New Testament on the institution of the eucharist, including their comparison with Jewish texts on the Passover meal and on other parallels that prefigure the eucharistic celebration.

3.   The derivation of the chief elements of the Mass, shared in all liturgies, should be shown from the documents of Christian antiquity so that they can be more clearly perceived in today's celebration and better explained to the faithful.

Ideally students should read primitive texts taken from the Fathers or from ancient liturgical books.

4.   As to the Roman Missal, the literary provenance of modern liturgical books should be traced: sacramentaries, books of epistles and gospels, the Mass Antiphonal, the Roman Ordinals, medieval missals. There should then be a brief conspectus of the history of the Roman Missal and the *Ritus servandi* with their successive revisions.

5.   Because of the diverse forms of celebration for the Roman Mass, there should be a short description of the papal Mass, the pontifical Mass, the solemn Mass, the Mass "with deacon," the sung Mass with celebrant alone, the Mass said with a congregation, the private Mass. Guidelines should be given, in keeping with the Constitution (SC art. 48)[a] and the new rubrics, on how the faithful may participate not only actively but with devotion and awareness.

6.   Concelebration in the tradition of East and West and in current usage is to receive a full development as to its specific character.

Art. II. Norms for a Correct Presentation of the Individual Parts of the Mass to the Students

1.   Preliminaries should include a view of the conditions required by law for the celebration of Mass, plus a brief history of the priest's vestments.   2747

2.   It should be brought out clearly that "the two parts that, in a certain sense, go to make up the Mass, namely, the liturgy of the word and the liturgy of the eucharist, are so closely connected with each other that they form but one single act of worship" (SC art. 56).[b]

3.   The parts assigned to each participant in the Mass — celebrant, ministers, congregation, the choir — are to be distinguished.

4.   Not only rubrics but also decrees and pastoral norms issued by the bodies of bishops are to be taken into account and presented and explained accurately.

5.   The professor is to deal at length with the separate rites of the Mass, then restore or connect them to the flow of the whole celebration so that all the rites stand out clearly: the entrance rite, the progress of the liturgy of the word toward the gospel and homily, the parts of the presentation of the gifts, the genius and style of the canon, the rites preparing for communion, etc.

Historical considerations as well as a comparison, to the extent possible, with the rites of other liturgies, are to elucidate each of the rites.

---

[a]   See DOL 1 no. 48.

[b]   See DOL 1 no. 56.

6.   The professor should call special attention to the reforms introduced into the Mass and in particular to what concerns the homily, prayer of the faithful, and communion under both kinds.

7.   Guidelines should be given for catechesis that is designed to lead the faithful to a more fruitful participation.

8.   In dealing with the liturgy of the word, the professor will discuss also those forms of celebration of the word recommended in the Constitution art. 35, § 4.c

Art. III. Worship of the Eucharist outside Mass

2748   Since the worship of the eucharist outside Mass has greatly increased in the Latin Church, this development should be carefully explained in its relationship to the Mass as sacrifice.

The topics involved are eucharistic communion outside Mass and eucharistic reservation as to its theological and pastoral basis and the requirements of law governing it.

Eucharistic devotion and its principal expressions should be treated: processions, exposition, Forty Hours devotions, benediction. This should be done with careful avoidance of any scorn for these forms of devotion (see Paul VI, Encyclical *Mysterium fidei*).d At the same time, the recommendation of the Constitution (SC art. 13)e should be recalled and an explanation given of how such devotions "should be so fashioned that they harmonize with the liturgy, are in some way drawn from it, and lead the people to it" (ibid).f

PART III
THE OTHER SACRAMENTS; SACRAMENTALS

2749   Treatment of the Roman Ritual and Pontifical should be based on the texts themselves with a view to bringing out the teaching they contain; the history of the rites should aid in their explanation and comprehension. Every phase should end with a study of pastoral issues to prepare candidates for the priesthood for their future pastoral ministry. Local rituals should be dealt with, in keeping with the Constitution art. 63.a

Art. I. Christian Initiation

2750   Christian initiation, comprising the catechumenate, baptism, confirmation, and first communion, must receive careful treatment because it is the basic catechesis for children and because an immense number of adults throughout the world go through the same process of initiation.

1.   There is to be a full historical treatment of the liturgy of baptism and the liturgical catechumenate that will result in a right understanding and elucidation of the new rite for conferring baptism through stages.

---

c   See DOL 1 no. 35.

d   See DOL 176 nos. 1154 and 1207.

e   See DOL 1 no. 13.

f   DOL 1 no. 13.

a   See DOL 1 no. 63.

2.   The resources for bringing out the meaning of the baptismal rites should be the catechesis of the Fathers, the Lenten liturgy, the texts of the chrism Mass, and above all the texts for the Easter Vigil and for Easter Week.

3.   There should be emphasis on pastoral duties regarding the preparation of adult catechumens and the parents of infants as well as the baptismal celebration itself.

4.   Ancient and modern forms for celebrating baptism should be brought out and in that context there should be precise pastoral instruction on their importance and the results to be looked for from these celebrations in the life of the parish and the people.

5.   The rite of confirmation should be handled by means of the same resources and method so as to bring out the distinctive force of this sacrament and its close connection with baptism.

Details should be given on the pastoral measures needed for preparing people to receive the sacrament beneficially, with attention to any directives of the bishop in this regard.

6.   There should be a brief treatment of the eucharist in its character as the crown of the sacraments of initiation and on the admission of children to first communion.

Art. II. Orders

The treatment and explanation of the ordination rites should be sufficient for a   2751
better appreciation of the history of the sacrament of orders as it is today. It is a matter to be decided whether this topic is better dealt with during the course of liturgical studies or left to be studied phase by phase as the seminarians are promoted to each order.

In any case the professor of liturgy should be responsible at least for laying out the general principles for an understanding of the text of the Pontifical and for putting the individual orders into the context of the Church's tradition.

The ordination rites should be explained historically, as they existed in Christian antiquity and in the Roman and the Gallican liturgical traditions and their intermixture. To the extent possible there should be a word about ordination in the Eastern Churches.

The primary emphasis should be on episcopal ordination, so as to establish clearly that all orders stand in relation to episcopacy and that priests are co-workers of the bishop, invested with a ministry subordinate to his [*secundi meriti munus*].

On the diaconate more must be said than formerly, in order that what Vatican Council II determined in the Dogmatic Constitution *Lumen gentium* will be understood.[b]

Art. III. Marriage and the Life of Virginity

There should be a history of the rites of marriage, pointing up their many   2752
regional and cultural variants and showing how they have been adapted to suit the religious and political customs of different peoples.

Because New Testament and patristic teaching correlates the nature and knowledge of Christian marriage and the life of virginity, the two liturgies, of marriage and of consecration to a life of virginity in the Roman Pontifical, ought be studied together.

---

b   See LG no. 29 [DOL 4 no. 149].

Art. IV. Monastic Liturgy

2753   The same rite of consecration together with the ancient rites of monastic profession in their details will bring out the way religious life constitutes a special state in the Church (see LG ch. 6).[c]

Art. V. Penitential Liturgies

2754   The lectures will treat of public penance in the discipline of the early Church through texts from the Roman Pontifical and show which elements were incorporated into the Lenten liturgy. Private penance and the liturgy for it will be discussed briefly.

Art. VI. Liturgy for the Sick

2755   In regard to texts and rites as well as pastoral practice, those parts of the ritual should be brought out that describe visitation of the sick and the sacrament of anointing. The sacrament should be dwelt on and its history brought out in support of the restoration ordered by Vatican Council II (SC art. 73–75).[d]

Art. VII. Liturgy of Christian Death

2756   The liturgy for the dead should also be a course topic, with parts on viaticum, the rites for commending the soul, and funerals. Those aspects that call to mind the paschal mystery should have prominence. The seminarians should be trained in the pastoral ministry for the dying and for funerals.

Art. VIII. Sacramentals

2757   1.   One topic should be processions and their religious significance, with pilgrimages being explained as a distinctive type of procession.

2.   There should be a brief history of the blessings in the Roman Ritual. The emphasis should be on their meaning and usefulness for sanctifying daily life. The clerics should be instilled with reverence and respect toward all the lawful forms of devotion through which Christians profess their faith by the way they live. At the same time clerics should be advised of the caution to be exercised against the intrusion of abuses or superstitions.

PART IV
SANCTIFYING THE TIME

2758   The first subject should be the Lord's Day, "the foundation and core of the whole liturgical year" (SC art. 106).

Art. I. Sunday

2759   1.   Much is to be made of Sunday, with the Constitution (SC art. 106) as the source for explaining its nature and elements. Historical arguments should show that it is the Easter of each week and so closely linked with the beginnings of the Church that "by a tradition handed down from the apostles it took its origin from the very day of Christ's resurrection."[a]

---

[c]   See DOL 4 no. 45.

[d]   See DOL 1 nos. 73–75.

[a]   DOL 1 no. 106.

2.   Serious attention should be devoted to pastoral methods that will bring about a genuine sanctification of this day in a way that all the faithful will actually observe in practice.

3.   The Sundays in Ordinary Time make available to the faithful the riches of the word of God. Accordingly, it is necessary that the seminarians learn how, in keeping with liturgical law, to further celebration of these Sundays faithfully and with care and to give their celebration precedence over everything else.

Art. II. The Liturgical Year

1.   The treatment of the liturgical year must provide for the students a concise and   2760
orderly summary of the findings of history on this matter.

2.   First is to come the history of Easter and its cycle: the fifty-day Easter season, Holy Week, the season of preparation, above all Lent. But history is not enough; the students should receive the kind of instruction that will make the paschal mystery alive in their own souls and prepare them for pastoral ministry and the furtherance of the reform intended by Vatican Council II (SC art. 102, 104, 110).[b]

3.   Next comes the Christmas-Epiphany cycle, with a consideration of its history and spiritual meaning.

4.   The rogation and ember days should be explained briefly, as well as the feasts of the Lord more recently introduced into the calendar: Holy Trinity, Corpus Christi, Sacred Heart, Christ the King, etc.

5.   The veneration of the Blessed Virgin in the Church should be treated histori- cally (SC art. 103);[c] her principal feasts throughout the year should be reviewed.

6.   As to the saints commemorated during the liturgical year, the teaching of the Constitution (art. 104)[d] is to be recalled. Also to be treated are the origin and development of the cult of martyrs and other saints, reverence for their burial place or relics, the place Christian life gives to veneration of the saints.

Art. III. Sanctifying the Hours of the Day: the Divine Office

1.   The Church honors the duty of praising God committed to it by Christ not   2761
only in celebrating the eucharist but in other ways as well, above all by fulfilling the divine office (SC art. 83).[e]

2.   There should be a demonstration from history of how important the hours of the office are for sanctifying the day and its parts and for obeying properly Christ's command to pray without ceasing. The symbolism of each hour as found in early spiritual writers is to be brought out.

3.   There should be an explanation of the special significance attached by the Council to lauds and vespers, the double "hinge of the whole office" (SC art. 89).[f]

---

b   See DOL 1 nos. 102, 104, 110.

c   See DOL 1 no. 103.

d   See DOL 1 no. 104.

e   See DOL 1 no. 83.

f   DOL 1 no. 89.

4.   It should be stressed how the Church has made this daily prayer its own, so that it is "truly the voice of a bride addressing her bridegroom" (SC art. 84).[g] As an explanation, the students should receive themes taken from patristic commentaries on the psalms and should be shown the titles attached from Christian antiquity to specific psalms and preserved in ancient psalter collections.

5.   History and canon law should be brought in to show how Church discipline has deputed priests and others in a distinct way to carry out this sublime prayer (SC art. 84, 95, 96, 98).[h]

6.   The community character of the office should be made clear; the usual condition for its celebration and the part of the people should be described.

7.   The traditions of the different Churches regarding the structure and celebration of the office should be noted, a brief history of the Roman Breviary given, and reference made to its reform in the 16th and 20th centuries.

333.   SC CLERGY, **Circular Letter** *Inter ea* to presidents of the conferences of bishops, on continuing education and formation of the clergy, especially the younger clergy, 4 November 1969: AAS 62 (1970) 123–134 (excerpts).

GENERAL CONSIDERATIONS

[. . .]

2762   5.   The *intellectual* formation of priests, planned with order and coherence, should include not simply a review but a deepening in those primary disciplines to which they have already devoted long efforts. Among theological topics, emphasis should be on those having greater bearing on the spiritual life and pastoral ministry. *Advances* in theology and *new pastoral issues* should receive thorough attention, especially on points on which the Church's living magisterium has made any sort of pronouncement. Finally, there must be special concern to connect the established body of doctrine and the results of experience in pastoral ministry.

Accordingly the list of postordination studies should include the following: sacred Scripture, patristics, documents of the Church's tradition — with the decrees of the magisterium from councils and popes having particular prominence — liturgy, the established works of theologians, *practica* in the pastoral, catechetical, homiletic, and educational fields, and themes on the social teaching of the Church. [. . .]

2763   9.   [. . .] To strengthen his spiritual life and sense of the priesthood it is strongly recommended that on the morning of Holy Thursday every priest, whether present at the chrism Mass or not, renew the act by which he dedicated himself to Christ and promised to carry out his priestly obligations, especially to observe celibacy and to render obedience to his bishop (or religious superior). Let every priest celebrate in his heart the gift, consecrated by orders, of his calling to service in the Church.[a]

---

[g]   DOL 1 no. 84.

[h]   See DOL 1 nos. 84, 95, 96, 98.

[a]   See DOL 315.

11. A strong spiritual life and sound theological knowledge enliven and nurture *pastoral* motivation and ministry, an effective administration of the sacraments, a convincing preaching of God's word, and every form of pastoral charity: in short, the entire service for which priests have received ordination.[8] [. . .]

2764

334. SC CATHOLIC EDUCATION, *Basic Plan for Priestly Formation (In Synodo Episcopali),* 6 January 1970: AAS 62 (1970) 321–384 (excerpts).

INTRODUCTION

3. CONCEPT OF THE CATHOLIC PRIESTHOOD AS THE PROPER GOAL OF PRIESTLY FORMATION

The goal proper to priestly formation rests on the concept of the Catholic priesthood. That concept has its origins in divine revelation as explained by the unbroken tradition and the teaching office of the Church. This teaching on the priesthood, which must give any plan for priestly formation its distinctive force and direction, can be drawn from the very words of Vatican Council II.

2765

[. . .] Presbyters share in Christ's priesthood in a way differing from the faithful: "Even though they do not possess the fullness of the priesthood and in the exercise of their powers are subordinate to the bishops, priests are nevertheless linked to the bishops in priestly dignity. By virtue of the sacrament of orders, in the image of Christ the eternal High Priest (see Heb 5:1–10, 7:24, 9:11–28), they are consecrated to preach the Gospel, to shepherd the faithful, and to celebrate divine worship as true priests of the New Testament."[13] On this basis, therefore, their *ministerial priesthood* surpasses the universal priesthood of the faithful: through the ministerial priesthood some members in the Church, the Body of Christ, are made like Christ the Head and elevated "to the service of Christ the Teacher, Priest, and King, having a part in that ministry of his by which the Church is being continually built up here on earth to be the people of God, the Body of Christ, and the temple of the Holy Spirit."[14] [. . .]

The *priestly ministry* as Vatican Council II explains it is carried out principally in the *ministry of the word* and the *work of sanctifying people.* "No one can be saved except by first having believed. Priests, therefore, as the co-workers of the bishops, have for their first responsibility the proclaiming of God's Gospel to all,"[28] fulfilling the Lord's command: "Going therefore into the whole world, preach the Gospel to every creature" (Mt 16:16). Priests carry out that command when "by their goodness in associating with people, they lead them to glorify God; preaching openly, they proclaim the mystery of Christ to nonbelievers; they catechize or they explain the Church's teaching; they make an effort to deal with contemporary problems under the light of Christ."[29]

The ministry of the word, however, has as its goal to bring people to faith and the sacrament of salvation; it reaches its high point in the eucharistic celebration. "Priests exercise their sacred function above all in eucharistic worship or celebration of Mass, by which, acting in the person of Christ and proclaiming his mystery,

---

8 See RP, *Ordination of Priests.* LG no. 28 [DOL 4 no. 148].

13 LG no. 28 [DOL 4 no. 148].

14 PO no. 1.

28 PO no. 4 [DOL 18 no. 259]; see also LG no. 28 [DOL 4 no. 148].

29 PO no. 4.

they unite the prayers of the faithful with the sacrifice of their Head and until the Lord's coming (see 2 Cor 11:26) make present again and apply in the sacrifice of the Mass the single sacrifice of the New Testament, namely, that of Christ offering himself once to the Father as spotless victim (see Heb 9:11–28). For the repentant or for the sick among the faithful they exercise the ministry of reconciliation and alleviation and they present the needs and the prayers of the faithful to God the Father" (see Heb 5:1–3).[30] Accordingly the ministry of preaching is of its nature meant to be completed by the ministry of sanctifying, by which the priest, acting in the person of Christ, contributes his part to building up the Church.

The priest is the leader of the gathered people of God through evangelical preaching, through the sacraments, and above all by the eucharistic celebration. [. . .]

4. ACTIVITY AND LIFE OF THE PRIEST IN THE CONTEMPORARY WORLD

2766   The *role of the priest* as the Church has defined it in its essentials is carried out today in *entirely new conditions*, which show themselves in new human needs and in contemporary culture.

Contemporary human needs are defined particularly by reason of a higher evaluation of the human person and a progressive change in the religious sense. If not actually and explicitly at least by action, people today recognize their own human dignity, their rights to betterment, to express their minds freely, and to have a part in their own and the world's advancement. As a fuller human mastery of the world is established, with the major, concomitant social changes, less stock than formerly is put in the conventional forms of Christian life. It is true that amid universal change there are some Christian groups that give evidence of a more personal type of religious life, apparent from their particular reverence toward the word of God and the liturgy and from a more maturely developed conscience. Yet at the same time there is a daily increase in the number of those who are partly or completely losing the contact they should have with the Church and are tending toward a type of naturalistic religion and ethic. [. . .]

II. PASTORAL CARE OF VOCATIONS

[. . .]

2767   9.   Every necessary step to obtain vocations from God must be promoted, above all the prayers Christ himself called for (see Mt 9: 39; Lk 18:2). There must be both private prayers and community prayer at certain appropriate times during the liturgical year and on more solemn occasions to be fixed by ecclesiastical authority. This is the purpose especially of the World Day of Prayer for Vocations established by the Holy See and scheduled annually for celebration by the Church worldwide.[56] [. . .]

---

[30]   LG no. 28 [DOL 4 no. 148].

[56]   See the letter of Card. H. I. Cicognani, Secretary of State, to Card. G. Pizzardo, Prefect of the SC Seminaries and Universities, 23 Jan. 1964.

III. MINOR SEMINARIES[60] AND OTHER INSTITUTIONS
OF LIKE PURPOSE

[. . .]

14. [. . .] The primary and necessary element in the spiritual formation of the   2768
students is the liturgical life, shared in with an ever increasing awareness as they
advance in age. Also important are other devotions, daily or of the season, established in the seminary rules. Such devotional practices are to be suited to Christian
young men and all are to take part in them cheerfully and willingly.[69]

IV. MAJOR SEMINARIES

20. The major seminary receives students who, having completed their preparato-   2769
ry studies, seek a priestly formation properly so-called. For the purpose of the
seminary is to develop the candidates' vocation more clearly and completely and to
form, on the model of our Lord Jesus Christ, Teacher, Priest, and Pastor, real pastors, preparing them for the ministry of teaching, sanctifying, and shepherding the
people of God.[75]

---

[60] Vatican Council II expressed its thoughts on the *major* seminary, the institution immediately designed for the priesthood and regarded as necessary. The Council also looked at that institution, widespread up to now, called a minor seminary. The Council decided that it must be entirely reformed, but that
it continues to have a purpose even in our day and to be favorable to the nurturing of the seeds of a
vocation. That the minor seminary may better measure up to its important objective under current
conditions, the Council issued a few but very apposite norms for it. They are designed to give this
institution a distinctive structure, consonant with its nature and purpose. They do not give it the form of a
kind of scaled-down major seminary; that would not serve the purpose of providing properly either for
study or for a true freedom regarding vocations. Even while endorsing the minor seminary, the Council
does not deny that some may and even properly should explore other avenues to encourage vocations to
the priesthood. The only proviso is that this does not hurt the minor seminary as an institution and that
new experiments are prudently and seriously planned toward their objective and are not simply a dis-
guised way of abandoning that end. For it is the Church's conviction — as is clear from its teaching,
experience, and practice — that even in boyhood some signs of a divine vocation are discernible and these
call for careful and sensitive care.

[69] See OT no. 8 [DOL 12 no. 213]; SC art. 13, 14, 17 [DOL 1 nos. 13, 14, 17]. See also GE nos. 2, 4.
Pius XII Ap. Exhort. *Menti Nostrae*, 23 Sept. 1950: AAS 42 (1950) 671, 689. Paul VI, Address *Il Concilio* to the
bishops of Italy, 6 Dec. 1965: *Insegnamenti di Paolo VI*, v. 3, 710. SC Sacraments, Instr. *Postquam Pius* to the
episcopate, on daily communion in seminaries and other ecclesiastical institutions, 8 Dec. 1938. SCR,
Instr. InterOec, 26 Sept. 1964, nos. 14, 15, 17, 18 [DOL 23 nos. 306, 307, 309, 310]; Instr. EuchMyst, 25 May
1967 [DOL 179].

[75] See OT no. 4 [DOL 12 no. 212].

VIII. SPIRITUAL FORMATION[99]

[. . .]

2770   52. Daily celebration of the eucharist, completed in sacramental communion received freely and worthily, is to be the center of the entire life of the seminary and the students are to take part in it devoutly. For by taking part in the sacrifice of the Mass, "the fount and apex of the whole Christian life,"[121] the seminarians share in Christ's charity, drawing from this abundant source the supernatural power for their own spiritual life and apostolic labor.

The eucharistic sacrifice and indeed the whole of the liturgy, in keeping with the intent of *Sacrosanctum Concilium*, are therefore to occupy such a principal place in the seminary that they stand out clearly as "the summit toward which the activity of the Church is directed and at the same time as the fount from which all the Church's power flows."[122]

A sound variety is to be provided in the manner of celebrating the liturgy. This is to be done in such a way that the students derive from it not only spiritual progress, but also a practical preparation right from their seminary years for their future liturgical ministry and apostolate.[123]

2771   53. Formation for eucharistic training must be intimately joined with formation for the divine office. Through it priests "pray to God in the name of the Church for all the people in their care and indeed for the whole world."[124] The students are therefore to learn the Church's own way of prayer through a pertinent introduction to sacred Scripture, to the psalms, and other biblically inspired prayers, through frequent community recitation of some part of the office (for example, morning prayer and evening prayer). The end in view is that they grasp with a deeper, more reverent understanding the word of God speaking in the psalms and throughout the

---

[99]   Under this heading are given the main elements of the priest's spiritual life that the students are gradually to acquire. They may be summarized as follows:

The students' spiritual life takes its form from Christ the Priest, to whom their vocation unites future priests in a particular way. Because they must "share in one and the same priesthood of Christ" (PO no. 7 [DOL 18 no. 262]), it is essential that they be configured to him not simply by ordination but in their whole spirit. This occurs by their gradually taking on through daily effort the evangelical form of life. They especially dedicate themselves to Christ and follow him "who was a virgin (see Mt 8:20; Lk 9:58), who by his obedience unto the death of the cross (see Phil 2:8) redeemed us and made us holy" (PC no. 1).

Grounded ever more deeply in faith, hope, and charity, they are to open themselves to the Holy Spirit and seek to acquire the habit of prayer especially from the liturgy and their contemplation of God's word. Nurturing their spirituality by a faithful use of the sacraments, they are to seek to develop all the virtues in due proportion, so that they may become in the Mystical Body of Christ "worthy ministers of the Head" (PO no. 12). They will be brought along toward a sense of the Church and their future role as apostles in such a way as to be able, under the bishop's authority and in a spirit of service, to contribute their own simple and fraternal cooperation as part of the diocesan clergy. Led by pastoral charity they are to learn to perceive changes in human society with a quick and open mind and to read the signs of the times and in the light of God's will (see PO no. 14 [DOL 18 no. 266]) to unite their inner life with their outward activity. In this way the exercise of the apostolate will make them holy and even though living on earth, they will show that they are not of this world (see LG no. 41).

[121]   LG no. 11 [DOL 4 no. 141].

[122]   SC art. 10 [DOL 1 no. 10]. See also SCR, Instr. EuchMyst [DOL 179].

[123]   See OT no. 8 [DOL 12 no. 213]; SC art. 17–19 [DOL 1 nos. 17–19]; PO no. 5 [DOL 18 no. 260]; AG no. 19. SCR, Instr. InterOec nos. 14–15 [DOL 23 nos. 307–308]. See also Pius XII, Encycl. *Mediator Dei*, 20 Nov. 1947: AAS 39 (1947) 547ff.; Ap. Exhort. *Menti Nostrae*, 25 Sept. 1950: AAS 42 (1950) 666ff., 691. John XXIII, Encycl. *Sacerdotii Nostri primordia*, 1 Aug. 1959: AAS 51 (1959) 561ff. Paul VI, Addr. *Voi avete* to the participants in the "13th Week on Pastoral Orientations," Rome, 6 Sept. 1963: *Insegnamenti di Paolo VI*, v. 1, 121 and 122; Encycl. *Mysterium fidei*, 3 Sept. 1965 [DOL 176 nos. 1205ff.].

[124]   PO no. 5 [DOL 18 no. 260].

liturgy and that at the same time they are trained to honor faithfully in their life as priests the obligation of the divine office.[125]

But this part of liturgical formation cannot be called complete unless it convinces the students of the strict connection between the liturgy and life's daily work, with its requirements of an apostolate and a genuine witness to a living faith that works through charity.[126]

54. In order to live their life as priests rightly and faithfully, the students must gradually, in proportion to their age and maturity, acquire a settled form of life, protected by solid virtues; otherwise they will not be able to remain truly and perseveringly loyal to Christ and the Church.

2772

A priest must: [. . .]

b. find Christ habitually in the close communion of prayer;

c. learn to hold fast to the word of God in Scripture with loving faith and then to communicate it to others;

d. have a strong desire to visit and adore Christ sacramentally present in the eucharist and to find joy in this; [. . .].

55. Daily conversion to the following of Christ and the spirit of the Gospel is absolutely necessary. The virtue of penance must therefore be instilled into future priests, with aid of community penitential services for both their own formation and the instruction of others. The seminarians are to strive continuously to achieve out of love for Christ a desire for a crucified life and purification of heart. They are to pray fervently for the help of the grace necessary, therefore, and above all to become accustomed to the frequent reception of the sacrament of penance, in which each one's struggles are in a sense consecrated. Each one is therefore to have his own spiritual director, to whom in simplicity and trust he is to lay bare his conscience in order to be more securely guided in the way of the Lord.[129] [. . .]

2773

56. The way to the priesthood is by steps and the sign of these steps is the institution of minor orders, which empower for particular ecclesiastical functions, after a proper intellectual and spiritual initiation.[a] [. . .]

2774

57. Following the example and counsel of Christ (see Mt 6:6, 14:13; Mk 6:30 and 46), who amid the labors of every day gladly sought solitude in order to spend time with the Father rapt in prayer, the seminarians should desire to cultivate "a life hidden with Christ in God (see Col 3:3) as the source of a pressing love of neighbor for the salvation of the world and the building up of the Church."[131] [. . .]

2775

XII. THEOLOGICAL STUDIES

[. . .]

---

[125]   See SC art. 17, 90 [DOL 1 nos. 17, 90]. SCR, Instr. InterOec nos. 14–17 [DOL 23 nos. 306–309]. See also Pius XII Encycl. *Mediator Dei*: AAS 39 (1947) 547ff., 572ff. John XXIII, Ap. Exhort. *Sacrae Laudes*, 6 Jan. 1962: AAS 54 (1962) 69; Addr. *Flagrantissima voluntas* to students in Rome, 28 Jan 1960: AAS 52 (1960) 275ff.

[126]   See SC art. 10 [DOL 1 no. 10].

[129]   See Pius XII, Encycl. *Mystici Corporis*, 29 June 1943: AAS 35 (1943) 235; Ap. Exhort. *Menti Nostrae*, 23 Sept. 1950: AAS 42 (1950) 674. John XXIII, Encycl. *Sacerdotii Nostri primordia*: AAS 51 (1959) 574–575. Paul VI, Ap. Const. *Paenitemini*, 17 Nov. 1966 [DOL 358].

[a]   See DOL 340 nos. 2922, 2926–28.

[131]   PC no. 6.

2776   79. *Liturgy* is now to be regarded as one of the major disciplines. Therefore it is to be taught not only under its canonical aspect, but especially under its spiritual and pastoral aspects in correlation with the other disciplines. The aim is that the students will perceive above all how the mysteries of salvation are present and at work in the celebrations of the liturgy. Moreover, by a clear explanation of the liturgical texts and rites of both East and West, the liturgy is to stand out plainly as a primary *locus theologicus*, giving expression to the Church's faith and spirituality.[163]

Finally, the norms for the reform of the liturgy are to be set clearly before the students so that they may better understand the adaptations and changes decreed by the Church. A further end is that they are able also to perceive other adaptations that may rightly be hoped for. Moreover in the serious and complex problems currently being debated in various places, the students should be enabled to distinguish what is changeless in the liturgy, as of divine institution, from what is changeable.[164] [. . .]

XVI. STRICTLY PASTORAL FORMATION[196]

2777   94. [. . .] The kind of strictly pastoral formation to be given must be adapted to regional conditions: in some places Christian life is flourishing; others are marked by the neglect or abandonment of religion; others are divided into different confessions or diverse religions. Pastoral formation must look primarily to catechetics and homiletics, the celebration of the sacraments, spiritual direction for the various

---

[163]   See OT no. 16 [DOL 12 no. 214]. See also SC art. 2, 10, 14, 15, 16 [DOL 1 nos. 2, 10, 14, 15, 16]; OE no. 4 [DOL 5 no. 164].

[164]   See SC art. 23 [DOL 1 no. 23]. SCR, Instr. InterOec nos. 11–12 [DOL 23 nos. 303–304]. Paul VI, Addr. *Facile concisere* to the Consilium, 14 Oct. 1968 [DOL 92 no. 672].

[196]   As the present section will show more precisely, this part of the formation demands that in the course of their studies the seminarians not only hold fast to Christ the Redeemer with an apostolic love but also that "in the things of God and the things of this world they are so formed as to be in truth a leaven in the world for the strengthening and growth of the Body of Christ" (PC no. 11). Thus the students are gradually to acquire a pastoral spirit and, learning the doctrinal norms, they are to strive through an appropriate praxis to develop in themselves those capacities by which they can be effective channels of Christ's grace and teaching for people of all conditions.

This presupposes well-designed plans for contact between the seminary and both the Church and civil community, which are the proper field for apostolic activity. The seminary, on the one hand, must not be regarded as so closed off that the students feel themselves removed from the real conditions of people and of life, as though these were something alien to themselves. But on the other hand, the seminary must not be regarded as so open that students regard every kind of experience as their right. Everything must be carried out in the light of the truth, that is, in view of their future life as priests, correctly understood and embraced.

In the interest of more effective results from this formation, superiors must be careful to establish practical norms that really answer the requirements of the life of study and prayer and that preserve a true hierarchy of values. It is above all up to the superiors to train the future priest in the wise use of his freedom; they are to permit only such new approaches as really contribute to the intrinsic purpose of pastoral formation. The candidates for the priesthood will cheerfully accept such policies as long as the sincerely sought objective of their common efforts is kept clearly before them at all times and explained in intelligent conferences by the superiors.

A further requirement of a practical preparation for the apostolate is that the students be introduced to a successful cooperation with both the priests of the diocese and the laity, so that they will grow in a knowledge of the pastoral situation. They are to have in mind the teaching of Vatican Council II that sets forth the position of the laity in the Church (LG ch. 4) and explains their distinctive role (AA ch. 3). Then, under the direction of experienced supervisors, the seminarians are gradually to associate with apostolic groups of the laity and to study their special and distinctive function in the Body of Christ in its true nature. With a right appreciation for the need of the apostolic work of the laity (PO no. 9; AA no. 25), the students are to learn both how to set out for the laity in its true light the exalted service they fulfill in the Church and to perform their own priestly office for the service of the laity in a way that makes clear the genuine dignity and complementarity of both states.

states of life, parish administration, pastoral contact with non-Catholics and non-believers, and other matters necessary for the building up of the Body of Christ.[198]
[. . .]

98. Depending on the location of the seminary, the number of students, and other   2778
circumstances, those kinds of training practices are to be chosen during the year
which seem most helpful: teaching catechism; taking part in parish liturgies on
Sundays and holydays; visiting the sick, the poor, and prisoners; assisting priests in
their ministry to youth and to workers, etc.

The amount of time to be devoted to such activities must be balanced with the
requirements of study. Further, they are to be carried on in the light of theological
principles and with reflection. Experienced and prudent priests are to supervise
them: these are to give assignments to each of the students; instruct them in a
method; work alongside the students; set up a review with them designed to evaluate their experiences and to provide them with sound advice. In this way these
activities will do no harm to the spiritual and intellectual formation of the students
but will instead be an effective aid.

335. SC CATHOLIC EDUCATION, Instruction *In ecclesiasticam futurorum sa-cerdotum*, on liturgical formation in seminaries, 3 June 1979: Not 15 (1979) 526–566.

The renewal of the ecclesiastical formation of future priests as Vatican Council   2779
II directed is a matter that has for the past several years engaged the efforts of the
Congregation for Catholic Education. The objective has been to provide the conferences of bishops with the needed assistance; the present *Instruction on Liturgical Formation in Seminaries* is now added to the various directives and pedagogical aids already
produced for the purpose intended.[a] The Instruction seeks to offer suitable directives and norms so that the liturgical life and the study of the liturgy in institutions
for priestly formation might be better adapted to modern needs. The great importance that the liturgy occupies in the Church's life demands that through prolonged, careful training and study of the liturgy contemporary candidates for the
priesthood are equipped to carry out properly the liturgical responsibilities of their
pastoral ministry.

INTRODUCTION

A. IMPORTANCE OF THE LITURGY IN PRIESTLY FORMATION

1. The importance of the liturgy in priestly formation is clear to all. Priests are   2780
consecrated to God by the bishop to preach the Gospel and to shepherd the faithful
and, after being made in a special way sharers in Christ's priesthood, to preside over
liturgical celebration in the person of Christ the Head, who in the liturgy continually exercises his priestly office for us through the Holy Spirit.[1] The liturgy, "making
the work of our redemption a present reality," is the outstanding means "whereby

---

[198] See OT no. 19 [DOL 12 no. 215]; AG no. 16; PC no. 18; OE no. 4 [DOL 5 no. 164]. See also Pius XII,
Ap. Const. *Sedes sapientiae*, 31 May 1956: AAS 48 (1956) 363ff. John XXIII, Addr. *L'ultimo incontro* to seminari-
ans, 10 Aug. 1962: AAS 54 (1962) 584ff. Paul VI, Addr. *Voi avete* to the participants in "the 13th Week on
Pastoral Orientations," 6 Sept. 1963: *Insegnamenti di Paolo VI*, v. 1, 117ff.

[a] See DOL 332 and 334.

[1] See PO nos. 2, 5, 9, 12.

the faithful may express in their lives and manifest to others the mystery of Christ and the real nature of the true Church."[2] Continued dedication to the liturgy and to its study will therefore bring to future priests a more solid knowledge and firmness in their faith and will open the way to their own vital experience of the Church.

2781   2.   All genuine liturgical formation includes both doctrine and practice. As a "mystagogical" formation, the practice is obtained first and mainly through the students' actual liturgical life, into which they are daily more deeply initiated through celebrating the liturgy together. Such a careful and practical initiation is the foundation of all further liturgical study and its possession is a prerequisite for the academic discussions of liturgical questions.

B. TIMELINESS OF THE PRESENT INSTRUCTION

2782   3.   Especially at the present time, formation in the liturgy has its own particular importance. New liturgical books have now been published in accord with the norms of the liturgical reform decreed by Vatican Council II. It is therefore necessary to promote the correct instruction of future priests in order that they may be capable of understanding clearly the character and import of the reformed liturgy, of integrating it with their spiritual life and way of acting, and of communicating it properly to the faithful.[3]

2783   4.   Furthermore, greater emphasis on liturgical formation in seminaries is needed also to address the new pedagogical problems arising out of the growing secularization of society. This creates an obstacle to people's understanding the true liturgy and makes them less capable of an intense liturgical involvement and participation. Even students themselves notice this difficulty and thus often express a desire for a deeper and more authentic liturgical life.

2784   5.   In the Constitution *Sacrosanctum Concilium*[4] and the Decree *Optatam totius*,[5] Vatican Council II itself stated the urgent need for a relevant liturgical formation. More recently this Congregation's *Basic Plan for Priestly Formation*[6] reaffirmed this. Its norms, taken from documents of the Church, provided the conferences of bishops with useful guidelines for deciding on particular prescriptions related to local needs in their own programs of priestly formation regarding liturgy.[7]

Requests have been coming to this Congregation from various parts of the world to issue more complete pedagogical norms, based on recent experience, that would concern both the correct regulation of liturgical life in seminaries and the teaching of the liturgy.

C. NATURE OF THIS INSTRUCTION

2785   6.   Because of such consideration, this Congregation, after consultation with the Congregation for the Sacraments and Divine Worship, decided to issue the present Instruction. It is meant to complement the *Basic Plan* and to have the same weight as to its binding force.[8] It intends to set out only matters of general application,[9]

---

²   SC art. 2 [DOL 1 no. 2].

³   See SC art. 14 [DOL 1 no. 14].

⁴   See SC art. 15–17 [DOL 1 nos. 15–17].

⁵   See OT nos. 4, 8, 16, 19 [DOL 12 nos. 212–215].

⁶   See *Basic Plan for Priestly Formation* nos. 14, 52, 53, 79, 94, 98 [DOL 334 nos. 2768, 2770–71, 2776–77].

⁷   See PO no. 1.

⁸   See *Basic Plan*, Preliminary remarks, no. 2.

⁹   See ibid. no. 7.

leaving it up to the conferences of bishops to see to any further, needed development of this matter or to choose the more suitable course when alternatives are given.[10]

A further purpose of the present Instruction is to provide for programs of priestly formation that are being prepared or revised a better explanation of material pertinent to the study of liturgy in the seminary and to the seminary's liturgical planning and life.

7.   In the norms that the Instruction prescribes it considers the two goals of liturgical formation: the practical (mystagogical), that is, the correct and orderly celebration of the liturgy; the theoretical (doctrinal), that is, the clear presentation of the science of liturgy, taught as one of the major theological disciplines.   2786

PART ONE
LITURGICAL LIFE OF SEMINARIES

1. GENERAL PRINCIPLES FOR PROMOTING THE LITURGICAL LIFE OF SEMINARIES

A. Special Introduction into the Liturgical Life in a Preliminary Period of Training

8.   "So that the seminarians' spiritual formation can rest upon a firmer basis and they can embrace their vocation with a decision maturely weighed,"[11] it is currently the practice of bishops to establish at the beginning of the first year of seminary life an appropriate period of time for a more intense spiritual training. It is recommended for this period that those students entering a seminary for the first time receive a suitable, short introduction into the liturgy. They need this in order to participate profitably in the spiritual life of the seminary from the very beginning. The program should include some catechesis about the Mass, the liturgical year, the sacrament of penance, and the liturgy of the hours.   2787

B. Pedagogical Principles for Initiation into the Liturgical Life

9.   An authentic initiation or *mystagogia* should mainly explain the foundation of the entire liturgical life: the history of salvation, the paschal mystery of Christ, the genuine nature of the Church, the presence of Christ in liturgical celebrations, the hearing of the word of God, the spirit of prayer, of adoration, and of thanksgiving, and the expectation of the coming of the Lord.[12]   2788

10. § 1. The celebration of the liturgy, as the prayer of the Church, embodies the very nature of the Church in such a way that the celebration itself moves all to a unity of voice and heart and it is at the same time a celebration that is fully communal and fully personal. Indeed, "the spiritual life is not limited to participation in the liturgy."[13] For liturgical and personal devotion support and complement each other. Individual communion in prayer with Christ leads to fuller, conscious, and devout participation in the liturgy; personal devotion in turn receives its model and support from liturgical life.   2789

---

[10]   See ibid. no. 3.

[11]   OT no. 12.

[12]   See SC art. 5–8 [DOL 1 nos. 5–8].

[13]   SC art. 12 [DOL 1 no. 12].

Thus in the seminary both the liturgy and personal spirituality are to be fostered and properly integrated.[14] According to local needs, the emphasis will be either on the community and its proper spirituality, if this is not adequately understood, or else on personal devotion,[15] if this is held in lower esteem.

§ 2. Devotional practices endorsed by the Church should be so fashioned that they harmonize with the liturgical seasons, accord with the liturgy, in a certain way derive from it, and lead the students to it.[16]

§ 3. From sharing more intensely in the liturgical life, the students should learn to foster an interior life and gradually acquire a deep spirit of meditation and spiritual conversion. Furthermore, liturgical instruction should convince the students of the close connection between the liturgy and the daily life of priest and people, since the liturgy inspires the apostolate and requires a genuine witness to a living faith that works through charity.[17]

2790   11. The understanding of the liturgy that is considered necessary for a priest and that seminarians must acquire demands a continuous contact with Scripture, as the Constitution *Sacrosanctum Concilium* recommends,[18] and also some acquaintance with the writings of the Fathers of the Church.[19] The students will gradually acquire the proper habit of mind as they progress in their studies, in the spiritual life, and in participation in liturgical celebrations, especially in the liturgy of the hours and in celebrations of God's word.[20] Measures must also be taken that through the efforts mentioned and also through special study the seminarians are introduced to an understanding of the liturgy's symbolic mode of expression, which through sensible signs, words, and gestures signifies, and in the case of the sacraments actually causes, divine realities.

C. Seminary Community Gathered for Liturgical Celebration

2791   12. A liturgical celebration makes any Christian community so solidly firm that its members become "one in heart and soul" (Acts 4:32); much more, then, in a seminary should it unify the community and develop a spirit of community in the students. Their formation has as its very purpose that through ordination they will share in the one priesthood, that they will be as one in their sense of the priesthood, that they will become co-workers of their bishop and remain closely united to him, and that they will exercise a ministry of building up the Church. Thus, the liturgical celebration in the seminary is to be such that its communal and supernatural nature will shine forth and that it will thus truly be a source and bond of the community life that is proper to the seminary and particularly suited to prepare the students for the unity of the priesthood.[21]

The rector and the professors should take care to celebrate the liturgy along with their students, and so show them clearly the communal nature of the liturgy and its riches. Professors who do not reside in the seminary should sometimes also

---

[14]   See OT no. 8 [DOL 12 no. 213].

[15]   See *Basic Plan* no. 54 [DOL 334 no. 2772].

[16]   See SC art. 13 [DOL 1 no. 13].

[17]   See SC art. 10–11 [DOL 1 nos. 10–11]. *Basic Plan* no. 53 [DOL 334 no. 2771].

[18]   See SC art. 24, 90 [DOL 1 nos. 24, 90].

[19]   See *Basic Plan* nos. 54ff.

[20]   See ibid. no. 53 [DOL 334 no. 2771].

[21]   See ibid. nos. 46 and 47.

be given the opportunity to join with the priests and students of the seminary and to participate in the liturgical services.

The students not only should take an active part in the liturgy, but should also be invited to work with their professors in planning it.

13. The seminarians should have concrete experience of the mystery of the Church as hierarchical, namely, as having an ordered variety of members and distinct ministries. To this purpose it is helpful that in the seminary there be deacons, acolytes, and readers who are imbued with the spirituality of their own offices and who exercise their ministries in the liturgical services.[22] Thus the proper office of the ministerial priesthood will be clear to all the students, as well as the offices of deacon, reader, and acolyte.

2792

In each seminary there should be a *schola cantorum*, in accord with the provisions of the Instruction *Musicam sacram* no. 19.[b]

14. Although it would be better for the entire community as a rule to gather to participate in the liturgy together, it will sometimes be useful to have some liturgical celebrations with small groups. This might be with those students who have recently entered the seminary and are in need of liturgical catechesis, as mentioned in no. 8, or, in regional seminaries, with the students from the same diocese, or there may be some other basis. Caution should be exercised, however, to ensure that such groups do not harm the unity of the entire community and that the prescriptions of the Holy See are followed.[23]

2793

15. Every means must therefore be taken to ensure that the authentic, ecclesial nature of a liturgical assembly stands out clearly. The seminary community, however, is a part of the Church, which is a community distinct and set apart from other communities and groups. The seminary community must therefore be an expression of the Church itself and must be open to the whole ecclesial community. Consequently, it should at times join in parish liturgical celebrations, especially on special occasions and, above all, in solemn celebrations at which the bishop presides.

2794

The liturgical life of the diocese centered around the bishop is recommended to all the faithful[24] and is all the more necessary for those who are to be the bishop's future co-workers. Therefore, on major solemnities, especially the Easter triduum, and on other occasions established by diocesan tradition, it is right that, either in the cathedral or in another church where the bishop celebrates the liturgy, the seminarians, above all deacons, be with their own bishop and carry out around him those ministries that are theirs by ordination or institution. There could be some difficulty in this practice for seminaries where the students come from different dioceses. Sometimes opportunities should be provided for them to participate in the life of their own diocese and to minister alongside their own bishop in the liturgy. But in keeping with tradition they should also learn to serve the local Church and the bishop in the place where they are.

---

[22]   See SC art. 28 [DOL 1 no. 28].

[b]   See DOL 508 no. 4140.

[23]   See SCDW, Instr. on Masses with special groups, 15 May 1969 [DOL 275].

[24]   See SC art. 41 [DOL 1 no. 41].

D. CELEBRATION ITSELF

2795   16. The students should remember that liturgical services are not private functions but are celebrations of the Church. They belong to the whole Body of the Church and show forth and produce that Body; that is why these celebrations are governed by the laws of the Church.[25] Therefore the celebration of the liturgy in seminaries must be exemplary with regard to the rites, the spiritual and pastoral aspects,[26] and fidelity to liturgical laws and texts as well as to the norms laid down by the Apostolic See and the conferences of bishops.

2796   17. To introduce the students into the riches of the liturgy with greater spiritual profit and to give them a practical preparation for their future ministry, a sound variety in the way of celebrating and participating in the liturgy should be fostered.[27] This variety concerns the ways of celebrating Mass, celebrations of the word, penitential or baptismal celebrations, and the plan for rites of blessing. Variety also extends to the degree of solemnity in the rites and their adaptation to various circumstances and exigencies, as such adaptations are permitted or recommended in the liturgical books and in the prescriptions of the Apostolic See.

Variety also involves the art of making the right choice from among the different options provided in the liturgical books or also of choosing, composing, and using new texts adapted to various occasions (for instance, the intentions of the general intercessions or the introductory comments). It is the duty of the seminary faculty not only to help and lead the students, but also to correct them patiently, in such a way as to form in them the true concept of the liturgy that is based on the mind and teaching of the Church. This is the most effective way to teach future priests how to take advantage pastorally of the many possibilities provided by the reformed liturgy and at the same time to respect proper limits.

2797   18. The concern for variety just mentioned must never draw attention away from the need to grasp deeply and intimately those elements of the liturgy that belong to the part that, being of divine institution, is unchangeable.[28] The structure of the liturgy always remains the same and many gestures and texts, especially those of greater importance, are often repeated. Therefore, the students are to be helped toward a deeper insight into these parts of the liturgy and to meditate on them and think about them. They need to learn how to derive from them continually new food for the spirit and to savor it.

2798   19. A good knowledge of Latin and of Gregorian chant is extremely useful for the students. There is a need to safeguard for the faithful the opportunity to join together in song and prayer at international gatherings, as Vatican Council II envisioned.[29] It is also right that future priests have a thorough grounding in the tradition of the Church at prayer, understand the authentic meaning of texts, and thus be able to explain vernacular translations by comparing them to the original.

---

[25] See SC art. 23 and 26 [DOL 1 nos. 23 and 26].

[26] See no. 46 of this Instruction.

[27] See *Basic Plan* no. 52 [DOL 334 no. 2770].

[28] See SC art. 21 [DOL 1 no. 21].

[29] See SC art. 54 [DOL 1 no. 54].

E. Preparing the Students for the Pastor's Liturgical Office

20. Great care should be exercised to prepare the students for the office of pastor   2799
and presider at the liturgical assembly of the faithful; they are to be taught all the
matters related to proper celebration of the liturgy, especially the Mass.[30] But a
twofold distortion must be avoided. 1. The students should not consider and experience the celebration of the liturgy as mere practice for learning their future pastoral roles. On the contrary, they must participate fully, consciously, and intensely in
the liturgical mysteries here and now in terms of their actual situation. 2. They are
not to choose those liturgical texts that in their mind might seem suitable for the
faithful who will be under their future pastoral care. Rather they should here and
now experience all the riches of the Church's prayer so that, possessing such riches,
they will later be able to communicate them to the faithful.

21. The students should try to apply to their pastoral training the things they   2800
experience and learn in the seminary. For their proximate introduction into their
role in the liturgy, particularly their being sent to exercise their different functions
in parish celebrations, the best times are some suitable occasions during the academic year, but mainly vacation times. Then for their more intense training there
should be a period near the end of the theology course when the future priests, as a
rule already ordained to the diaconate, have more extensive opportunities to exercise the liturgical ministry. The seminary faculty or diocesan directors of liturgy
must guide and moderate in order to ensure that this training serves its purpose and
contributes to the students' preparation.[31]

2. NORMS FOR THE SPECIFIC LITURGICAL RITES

A. Mass and Worship of the Eucharist

22. The eucharistic sacrifice is to stand out clearly to the students as the true   2801
source and apex of the entire Christian life. It is their way of sharing in the love of
Christ as they derive from the Mass the supernatural strength for their spiritual
lives and for their apostolic labor.[32] In accord with the different liturgical days,
frequent explanation of this point in the homily will be helpful, because there is
such need to instill in the students an attitude toward the eucharist that they may
not have acquired prior to their entrance into the seminary. As future presbyters
they must be convinced of the idea that in celebrating the eucharistic sacrifice the
priest fulfills his chief office. For in this sacrifice our redemption is continuously
exercised and the priest, joined to the act of Christ the Priest, offers himself entirely
to God each day.[33]

23. Daily celebration of the eucharist, completed in sacramental communion re-   2802
ceived freely and worthily, is to be the center of the entire life of the seminary and
the students are to take part with a full sense of its significance.[34]

Without prejudice to the exceptions noted in no. 14, the Mass must be an act
of the entire seminary community. In it each and every person is to share according
to his status. Priests who live in the seminary and are not bound by pastoral

---

[30]   See SCR, Instr. EuchMyst, 25 May 1967, no. 20 [DOL 179 no. 1249].

[31]   See *Basic Plan* nos. 94, 97, 99.

[32]   See LG no. 11 [DOL 4 no. 141]; PC no. 6. *Basic Plan* no. 52 [DOL 334 no. 2770]. John Paul II, Encycl.
Redemptor hominis, 4 March 1979 [DOL 191 no. 1330].

[33]   See PO no. 13 [DOL 18 no. 265].

[34]   See *Basic Plan* no. 52 [DOL 334 no. 2770].

obligation to celebrate Mass somewhere else should concelebrate. Deacons, acolytes, and readers should carry out their proper functions.[35]

It is desirable that in every Mass some parts be sung.[36]

2803   24. Communion has a fuller form as a sign when received under both kinds.[37]
Therefore this is recommended in seminaries, but with the observance of the norms
of the General Instruction of the Roman Missal and of the bishops.[c]

2804   25. During vacations the students express their spiritual maturity and love for
their priestly vocations by regularly and constantly attending weekday Mass.

2805   26. In view of contemporary practices in some places, seminarians should be made
aware of how strongly the Church advises priests to celebrate Mass daily, even if
they are not bound to do so by a pastoral obligation or even if the faithful cannot
be present. The celebration is always an act of Christ and the Church offered to
God for the salvation of the whole world.[38]

2806   27. Taking part in the Mass with the proper reverence and the inspiration of faith
will bring the students to a more ardent devotion to the holy eucharist, in accord
with the intent of the Encyclical Letter *Mysterium fidei* and the Instruction *Eucharisticum mysterium*.[39] Both recommend the practice of spending some time in prayer after
communion and visiting the chapel during the day to pray before the blessed
sacrament. Indeed, on some days of the year there may be exposition of the blessed
sacrament, in accord with the norms contained in the same Instruction[40] and the
directives of the local Ordinary.

In arranging seminary chapels, the tabernacle in which the holy eucharist is
reserved is to be located in a place that favors private visits, so that the students will
not neglect to honor our Lord in the blessed sacrament fruitfully and easily even by
private adoration.[41]

B. Liturgy of the Hours

2807   28. The reformed liturgy of the hours[42] has opened up great spiritual riches for the
praying Church, especially for priests, deacons, religious obliged to choir, and all
the people of God, who are strongly invited to take part in it.[43] Therefore, in
seminaries not only those bound to recite it, namely, priests and deacons, but also

---

[35]   See nos. 10 and 41 of this Instruction.

[36]   See SCR, Instr. MusSacr, 5 March 1967 [DOL 508 no. 4148]. See also GIRM [DOL 208 no. 1409].

[37]   See SCR, Instr. EuchMyst, 25 May 1967, no. 32: "In this form . . . a fuller light shines on the sign
of the eucharistic banquet. Moreover there is a clearer expression of that will by which the new and
everlasting covenant is ratified in the blood of the Lord and of the relationship of the eucharistic banquet
to the eschatological banquet in the Father's kingdom" [DOL 179 no. 1261].

[c]   See DOL 208 nos. 1630–42.

[38]   See PO no. 13 [DOL 18 no. 265]. Paul VI, Encycl. *Mysterium fidei*, 3 Sept. 1965, no. 32 [DOL 176 no.
1176].

[39]   See Paul VI, Encycl. *Mysterium fidei* nos. 64–71 [DOL 176 nos. 1208–15]. SCR, Instr. EuchMyst nos.
38, 50 [DOL 179 nos. 1267, 1279]. See also RR, *Holy Communion and Worship of the Eucharist outside Mass* [DOL
279 nos. 2208–18]. PO no. 18 [DOL 18 no. 267].

[40]   See Instr. EuchMyst nos. 62–66 [DOL 179 nos. 1291–95].

[41]   See Instr. EuchMyst no. 53 [DOL 179 no. 1282].

[42]   See Paul VI, Ap. Const. *Laudis canticum*, 1 Nov. 1970 [DOL 424].

[43]   See GILH nos. 20, 22, 26–27 [DOL 426 nos. 3450, 3452, 3456–57].

the entire body of students are to show great esteem toward the liturgy of the hours.

29. Accordingly the celebration of the hours is to be fostered in the seminary and it should often be sung, especially on Sundays and holydays. It is appropriate that the one presiding should assist the students with short introductory comments. By such means the seminarians will gradually develop a taste, an understanding, and a love for the divine office. They will learn to derive from it the support for their personal prayer and contemplation, with the result that the liturgy of the hours and other lawful devotional practices will be combined harmoniously, not be mutually exclusive.

2808

30. At their proper times of day, lauds as morning prayer and vespers as evening prayer are as a rule to be celebrated in common. "By the venerable tradition of the universal Church, they are the two hinges on which the daily office turns."[44]

2809

Wherever possible, night prayer is to be recited before the students retire to their rooms and, when it is not possible to recite it in common, they should be counseled to say it in private.

Where it is the practice to gather in common for some other prayers during the day, it is useful to celebrate daytime prayer at that time.

Especially on the vigils of Sundays and solemnities, it is laudable to celebrate the office of readings and to do so at least occasionally by means of the "extended vigil," as described in *The Liturgy of the Hours*.[d]

Finally, during retreats the celebration of the entire office with each of the hours celebrated at its proper time is an appropriate way to observe the periods of prayer.

31. The minds of the students must be carefully formed so that at the time of their ordination as deacons they will willingly and with a proper understanding accept from the Church the mandate to celebrate daily the entire liturgy of the hours. For the Church deputes this task to those who share in sacred orders "so as to ensure at least in their persons the regular carrying out of the duty of the whole community and the unceasing continuance of Christ's prayer in the Church."[45]

2810

Seminary superiors must, then, remind the students that for a proper initiation into the divine office they need, besides the actual experience of its celebration, a distinct kind of preparation. They must have a thorough acquaintance with the principles set forth in the General Instruction of the Liturgy of the Hours. In addition they must acquire an understanding of the psalms, so that, in the light of the New Testament and tradition, they learn how to perceive the mystery of Christ in the psalms and to derive from the texts support for their personal prayer.[46]

C. Sunday and the Liturgical Year

32. Whether seminarians participate in the Mass at the seminary or are sent out into parishes, Sunday should be for them, both in the celebration of the liturgy and throughout the day, "the first holyday of all." It must be presented to the students and instilled in them as the joyful celebration of the paschal mystery.[47]

2811

---

[44] SC art. 89 [DOL 1 no. 89].

[d] See GILH no. 73 [DOL 426 no. 3503].

[45] GILH no. 28 [DOL 426 no. 3458]. See also PO no. 13 [DOL 18 no. 265].

[46] See *Basic Plan* no. 53 [DOL 334 no. 2771].

[47] See SC art. 106 [DOL 1 no. 106].

In the seminary the yearly cycle of Christ's mysteries should be celebrated with special fervor, in keeping with the intent of the Constitution *Sacrosanctum Concilium*.[48]

Therefore, it must be ensured that in addition to the celebration of Mass and the liturgy of the hours, according to the norms of the liturgical books, the seminary celebration of Sunday and the main feasts of our Lord, of the Blessed Virgin Mary, and of the saints take on a festive character that will make them days of gladness.

Special importance is to be given to the celebration of the saints from the diocese — or from the region, in the case of a regional seminary. The life and spirit of these saints should be explained to the students. Care should also be taken about the proper celebration of the feast of the dedication of the cathedral and the anniversary of the local bishop's ordination.

The principal concern, however, is preparation for these celebrations through a catechesis of a kind that at once meets the present needs of those who are students today and their future needs as priests. The pastoral value of popular customs should be included in this catechesis. The entire liturgical year should serve through both celebration of the liturgy and the students' way of life as a spiritual journey toward sharing in the mystery of Christ.

2812   33. A truly complete formation of the students is required in order that throughout their years of preparation in the seminary they may experience richer and more developed forms of the liturgical celebrations of the seasons and solemnities of the liturgical year. After their ordination to the sacerdotal ministry the celebration of feasts will increase their work as pastors and they will be obliged to repeat these celebrations in various places, often in more simplified form, as provided for in the liturgical books. Clearly, then, the way the students experience the liturgy in the seminary will serve as a model to guide their future pastoral ministry and as a foundation to support their meditation and teaching about the liturgical year.

2813   34. A correct and relevant pedagogy about the liturgical cycle cannot overlook a particular contemporary characteristic that, especially in some places where faith is weaker, seems to impede a full understanding of the sacred seasons and feasts. Attention must be directed toward those students who before their entry into the seminary did not have a fervent and deep experience of the liturgical year. They need to be helped toward a supernatural sense of the liturgical year and made capable of acquiring a deeper recognition of its salvific events and of receiving the graces connected with them.

D. Sacrament of Penance

2814   35. In the spiritual life of future priests, great importance is to be given to the sacrament of penance. Because it is a sacrament, of all penitential acts it is the one most capable of developing in them those dispositions that the imitation of Christ and the spirit of the Gospel require: a conversion that is daily more complete, purity of heart, and the virtue of penance with its readiness for a crucified life.

2815   36. The students, therefore, should often receive the sacrament of reconciliation to acquire the grace they need for their daily spiritual struggles.[49] Frequent confession "is not a mere ritual repetition or psychological exercise, but a serious striving to

---

48   See SC art. 102–105, 108–111 [DOL 2 nos. 102–105, 108–111].

49   See *Basic Plan* no. 55 [DOL 334 no. 2773].

perfect the grace of baptism so that, as we bear in our body the death of Jesus Christ, his life may be seen in us ever more clearly."[50]

Reception of the sacrament of reconciliation is a very personal act, to be carried out individually. Its liturgical character is always to be retained and, as a rule, it is to be distinct from spiritual direction. The frequency of confession is to be decided by each person with his own confessor, following the traditions of masters of spirituality and the laws of the Church.

Furthermore, to point out more clearly the ecclesial nature of penance[51] it will be useful on occasion, especially during Lent and during retreats, to have a liturgical penitential service, based on what is proposed in the Roman Ritual, either without sacramental confession or else with confession and individual absolution. But when there is confession the freedom of each person is to be respected.

E. Celebration of Ordinations and the Preparatory Rites

37. The Church treats candidates for the priesthood in the way it treats candidates for Christian initiation, that is, accompanying them in their journey not only with doctrinal and spiritual formation, but also with rites.

2816

When there is sufficient evidence of the maturity of the rightly motivated intention of the aspirants, they are invited during the course of their studies and in accord with the norms set by the conference of bishops, to give public expression to their intention. The bishop gives in writing his acceptance of the aspirants, in virtue of which their election by the Church becomes effective. He then celebrates the rite of their admission to candidacy for ordination as deacons and priests.[52]

During the course of theological studies,[53] these same candidates "unless they have already done so, are to receive the ministries of reader and acolyte and are to exercise them for a suitable period, in order to be better disposed for the future service of the word and of the altar."[54] They are to observe between the two ministries the interval (interstices) established or to be established by the Apostolic See or the conference of bishops.

38. The celebration of these rites and the instruction preparing for them offer the students the opportunity to help each other by prayer, to acquire a better appreciation of the meaning, importance, and duties of the ministries they are about to receive, and to deepen the spirituality required for the carrying out of their different ministries and orders. The more important elements for such spiritual and doctrinal preparation will be readily apparent from the prescriptions in the Motu Proprios *Ad pascendum*[55] and *Ministeria quaedam*.[56]

2817

The rites are to be celebrated with the entire community of the seminary, if possible, taking part, either in the candidates' parish or in the seminary.

39. The celebration of the ordination of deacons and priests sometimes in the home parish of the candidates or a parish where they have already exercised some ministry will have good pastoral results. But these ordinations are in fact occasions

2818

---

[50]   RR, *Rite of Penance*, Introduction no. 7 [DOL 368 no. 3072]. See also John Paul II, Encycl. *Redemptor hominis* no. 20 [DOL 191 no. 1331].

[51]   See RR, *Rite of Penance*, Introduction no. 22 [DOL 368 no. 3087].

[52]   See Paul VI, Motu Proprio *Ad pascendum* I and III [DOL 319 nos. 2581 and 2583].

[53]   See ibid. IV [DOL 319 no. 2584].

[54]   Ibid. II [DOL 319 no. 2582].

[55]   See ibid. I c [DOL 319 no. 2581].

[56]   See *Ministeria quaedam* nos. V and VI [DOL 340 nos. 2930 and 2931].

of joy for the entire community of the diocese. All therefore should be informed of these ordinations and invited to them. Their celebration demands therefore careful and worthy preparation, so that priests, deacons, seminarians, and the faithful will gather round the bishop.

2819   40. Sacred ordinations deeply affect the life of the whole seminary community. Not only the ordinands, but all the seminarians should be instructed beforehand with the necessary catechesis about the rites and texts. This will help them to acquire the authentic teaching on the priesthood and the spiritual essence of the apostolic life.

2820   41. Readers and acolytes ought to exercise their offices. Before they are called to the priesthood, deacons should exercise ministries of their order for some time, either in the seminary or in some parish or, better still, at the side of their bishop.

2821   42. Since the Church has made considerable changes in the discipline and rites for the steps leading to the priesthood, seminary faculties are, of course, reminded to renew their thinking and style of formational work so that this new discipline will more surely achieve good results.

PART TWO
TEACHING LITURGY IN SEMINARIES

A. General Principle

2822   43. There is a first, elementary introduction to the liturgy to be held, according to the requirements of different places, as soon as the students enter the seminary, as already mentioned in no. 9 of this Instruction.[57] In addition, the conferences of bishops are to arrange that in their own program of priestly formation the course in liturgy has a place in the four-year theological curriculum that fulfills the prescription of the Constitution *Sacrosanctum Concilium* art. 16: "The study of liturgy is to be ranked among the compulsory and major courses in seminaries and religious houses of studies; in theological faculties it is to rank among the principal subjects. It is to be taught under its theological, historical, spiritual, pastoral, and canonical aspects."[e] These requirements, which are elaborated in the *Basic Plan* no. 79,[f] must be understood in the genuine sense and put into effect as the following paragraphs indicate.

B. Proper Object and Purpose of the Course

2823   44. The course in liturgy is to be taught in such a way that it meets contemporary needs. In this regard the main concerns are to be for the theological, pastoral, and ecumenical spheres.

        a. The strict connection between the liturgy and the teachings of faith has a special importance for the correct liturgical formation of future priests. This must be clearly pointed out as the course in liturgy develops. Above all in prayer the Church expresses its faith, so that *legem credendi lex statuat supplicandi* ("let the rule of prayer declare the rule of faith").[58] Therefore, the *lex supplicandi* is not only to be

---

[57]   This first liturgical initiation can be made a part of the "Introductory Course in the Mystery of Christ and the History of Salvation" referred to in the Decree *Optatam totius* no. 14 and the *Basic Plan* no. 62.

    e   DOL 1 no. 16.

    f   See DOL 334 no. 2776.

[58]   See Prosper of Aquitaine, *Indiculus* c. 8: Denz-Schön 246.

observed in such a way that the *lex credendi* is not endangered, but those in turn pursuing theology must carefully investigate the tradition of divine worship, particularly when they study the nature of the Church and the doctrine and discipline of the sacraments.

b. With regard to the pastoral aspect, it is of the highest importance that the liturgical reform promoted by Vatican Council II be correctly and fully grasped by future priests in the light of sound doctrine and of both the Western and the Eastern tradition. The norms for the reform of the liturgy are to be set clearly before the students so that they may better understand the adaptations and changes decreed by the Church. A further end is that they are enabled also to perceive other adaptations that may rightly be hoped for. Moreover in the serious and complex problems currently being debated in various places, the students should be taught to distinguish what is changeless in the liturgy, being of divine institution, from what is changeable.[59]

c. The ecumenical dialogue promoted by Vatican Council II also requires a careful preparation in the science of liturgy. This dialogue gives rise to many difficult liturgical issues and the students must be equipped to evaluate them properly.

C. Scope of the Course in Liturgy and the Method for Teaching It

45. Each conference of bishops is responsible for determining in its own formation program the way the liturgy is to be taught in the seminary. The *Appendix* to this Instruction contains, as a model, a list of the main points that probably should be treated. Here only the more general norms are stated.

2824

46. The foremost need is that the liturgical celebrations in what concerns their texts and their rites and signs are explained to the students.

2825

The prayers and other texts proclaimed in the liturgy are to be explained in a way that sheds light on their wealth of doctrine and spirituality. It will often not be enough to read them in vernacular translation; the original texts must be used and explained with the help of sacred Scripture and the tradition of the Fathers. Furthermore, the literary genre of Christian euchology and especially of the psalms is not easily understood without developing a measure of education in the humanities.

The professor must carefully provide the students with an explanation of the General Instructions found as preliminaries in the Roman Missal and *The Liturgy of the Hours*. This also applies to the Introductions found at the beginning of each major section of the Roman Ritual. These documents provide the theological doctrine, the pastoral rationale, and the spiritual aspect not only of the rites in general but also of their individual components. These documents, moreover, often propose a variety of ways of carrying out the same rite. The professor should therefore develop the judgment of the students in a way that will give them the ability later to know how to make a choice among the various options according to different circumstances. He should also help them to understand why the rubrics often use the terms *as a rule, according to circumstances, it is commendable to do this or that*, etc.

47. Since today the historical part of the liturgy has assumed great importance,[60] there is good reason for the lectures to go carefully into the history of the rites. This will provide a better perception of their meaning and the ability to distinguish

2826

---

59   See *Basic Plan* no. 79 [DOL 334 no. 2776]. SC art. 21 [DOL 1 no. 21].

60   See no. 44 of this Instruction.

between unchangeable elements, divinely instituted, and other elements "that not only may but ought to be changed with the passage of time if they have suffered from the intrusion of anything out of harmony with the inner nature of the liturgy or have become pointless."⁶¹ It should be pointed out how in various circumstances the Church has displayed its pastoral skill by taking into account the different customs and cultures of peoples. Sacramental theology, moreover, especially from studying the historical documents of the rites, can derive much benefit and acquire greater clarity and certitude.

2827   48. The historical examination of the rites should give due importance to the traditions of the Eastern Churches: "For, distinguished as they are by their venerable antiquity, they are bright with the tradition that was handed down from the apostles through the Fathers and that forms part of the divinely revealed and undivided heritage of the universal Church."⁶² Pastoral considerations also are a motive for all to acquire a knowledge of the Eastern liturgies.

2828   49. Over and above the treatment of the single liturgical rites, however, a theological explanation of the nature of the liturgy itself, following the mind of the Constitution *Sacrosanctum Conilium* art. 5 to 11 is of the greatest advantage. To achieve this objective seminarians are to receive a deep understanding of the paschal mystery of Christ "the fount from which all sacraments and sacramentals draw their power,"⁶³ the history of salvation,⁶⁴ and Christ's presence in the liturgy.⁶⁵ Also the concept of sign must be gone into thoroughly, since the liturgy uses perceptible things to signify unseen, divine realities,⁶⁶ in order that through these signs, in a way proper to each, human sanctification might be brought about.⁶⁷ From these signs it must be made clear how the liturgical assembly is the expression of God's Church as it is the people of God, both endowed with unity and structured by a diversity of ministries.⁶⁸

2829   50. For a deeper theological treatment of the liturgy as well as for the resolution of many problems confronting pastors in planning and promoting the liturgy, much importance is to be attached to the established findings of the contemporary social sciences, such as anthropology, sociology, linguistics, the comparative history of religions, etc. On many points these disciplines are enlightening, but only within the limits set by the supernatural nature of the liturgy. What must be cultivated in the students is a good judgment, so that they become capable of soundly evaluating the importance of such disciplines and at the same time of avoiding anything that would tend to diminish the full, supernatural import of Catholic worship.

In the use of these sciences, the following norm should be observed: "Rather than multiplying the number of courses, new problems or new considerations are to be skillfully integrated with the established courses."⁶⁹

---

⁶¹   SC art. 21 [DOL 1 no. 21].

⁶²   OE no. 1.

⁶³   SC art. 61 [DOL 1 no. 61].

⁶⁴   See SC art. 5 [DOL 1 no. 5].

⁶⁵   See SC art. 6–7 [DOL 1 nos. 6–7].

⁶⁶   See SC art. 33 [DOL 1 no. 33].

⁶⁷   See SC art. 7 [DOL 1 no. 7].

⁶⁸   See SC art. 26–32; 41–42 [DOL 1 nos. 26–32; 41–42].

⁶⁹   *Basic Plan* no. 80.

D. Qualifications of the Professor of Liturgy and Relationship of the Liturgy to Other Courses in the Seminary

51. In the interest of proper teaching, there ought to be in each seminary a special professor thoroughly trained to teach liturgy and, if at all possible, at one of the institutes devoted to liturgical studies.[70] He should be one who has done special studies in theology and history and who has a firm grasp of pastoral issues and a sense of the public prayer of the Church. He should perceive his own work not simply as academic and technical, but as mystagogical, that is, as leading the students into the liturgical life and into its spiritual character.

2830

52. In a special way the professors of sacred Scripture should be mindful of how much richer a selection of biblical readings the reformed liturgy offers to the faithful and that all liturgical celebrations and signs derive their meaning from holy Scripture.[71] As a consequence, it will be necessary that future priests receive a more complete understanding of the books of the Bible and the history of salvation. That means not only developing a knowledge of exegesis, but also "that warm and living love for Scripture to which the venerable tradition of both Eastern and Western rites gives testimony."[72]

2831

53. Progress in the study of liturgy will be greatly furthered by its coordination with the other disciplines, as Vatican Council II recommends.[73] For example, especially in the treatment of sacramental theology and practice there should be close cooperation between the liturgy professor and the professors of dogmatics, moral and pastoral theology, and canon law. There should be frequent conversations as an aid to their working together toward the same goal, their avoiding needless repetition of topics, or their presenting conflicting views.

2832

54. In arranging the syllabus for the theological courses, the objective should be that, if possible, liturgical topics will be dealt with at the same time as the closely related theological topics. For instance, at the time that ecclesiology is taught, the course on liturgy develops the theological meaning of the Church's prayer, and so forth.

In some seminaries it perhaps might be useful to have the liturgy professor also teach the entire theology of sacraments, provided he is qualified in both sacramental theology and liturgiology.

2833

55. Careful attention must also be given to a clear indication of those elements and aspects from the course on liturgy essential to that theological synthesis which, according to the *Basic Plan* no. 63, is the result expected from the whole course of studies. This synthesis must be explicitly articulated at the last stage of the years of theological study.

2834

E. Music and Sacred Art

56. Since sacred music is of such importance in liturgical celebrations, experts in music must give the students the instruction, including practical instruction, re-

2835

---

[70] See SC art. 15 [DOL 1 no. 15]. SCR, Instr. InterOec, 26 Sept. 1964, no. 11 [DOL 23 no. 303].

[71] See SC art. 24 [DOL 1 no. 24].

[72] SC art. 24 [DOL 1 no. 24].

[73] See SC art. 16: "Moreover, other professors, while striving to expound the mystery of Christ and the history of salvation from the angle proper to each of their own subjects, must nevertheless do so in a way which will clearly bring out the connection between their subjects and the liturgy, as also the underlying unity of all priestly training." See also OT no. 16 [DOL 12 no. 214]. *Basic Plan* no. 90.

quired for their future roles in presiding and leading liturgical celebrations. Their teaching should be guided not only by the talents of the individual students, but also by the new methods in general use in schools of music that assist the students' progress. But attention must above all center on giving the seminarians not simply musical or instrumental skills, but a genuine formation of mind and sensitivity. Then they will have an appreciative familiarity with the best musical works of the past and the ability to recognize in contemporary efforts compositions that have sound merit as sacred music.[74]

2836   57. Likewise, "during their philosophical and theological studies clerics are to be taught about the history and development of sacred art and about the sound principles on which the production of its works must be grounded. In consequence, they will be able to appreciate and preserve the Church's treasured monuments and be in a position to offer good advice to artists who are engaged in producing works of art."[75] Christian archaeology in fact has much to contribute to the understanding of the liturgical life and faith of the early Church.

2837   58. Finally, it is extremely necessary that the students learn communication skills, as well as the use of the media. It is essential in liturgical celebrations that the faithful understand not only what the priest says in the homily or in the presidential prayers, but also what he is meant to express by gesture and action. Formation in communication skills is of such high importance in the reformed liturgy that it deserves very special consideration.

F. Practical Pastoral Introduction to the Liturgical Ministry

2838   59. Practical pastoral introduction to the liturgical ministry must be imparted in a way matching the students' progress and at specifically determined times throughout the whole course of study;[76] it reaches its peak during the final year of study. After sharing in the sources of a genuinely Christian spirit from the seminary liturgical life, those soon to be priests will receive a more concrete formation adapted to the special circumstances in which they will be exercising their ministry. During this time of practical formation, there must be insistence on the pastoral norms and instructions that the bishops have issued in regard to preparation for the sacraments and their administration. In order to give this formation, the seminary professors should consult the liturgical commission of the diocese or region.

The students' own adaptation to local conditions and liturgical law requires that they also learn and appreciate the various forms of popular devotion endorsed by church authority.[77]

G. Advanced Studies in Liturgy for Some Students

2839   60. In order that dioceses might have priests well qualified to teach liturgy and to direct diocesan liturgical commissions, candidates capable of such responsibilities must be prepared. After completion of their general seminary training and some time spent in pastoral work, priests appointed by their bishops are to be sent to one

---

[74]   See SC art. 112–121 [DOL 1 nos. 112–121]. SCR, Instr. MusSacr [DOL 508 nos. 4173–74].

[75]   SC art. 129 [DOL 1 no. 129].

[76]   See nos. 20–21 of this Instruction.

[77]   See SC art. 13 [DOL 1 no. 13].

of the liturgical institutes established by the Holy See or by the conferences of bishops.[78] This is particularly urgent in those places where, in the judgment of competent church authorities, a more thorough liturgical adaptation is needed.

H. Liturgical Formation in the Continuing Education of Priests

61. The directive of Vatican Council II requires that after the regular course of study priestly formation is to be completed and continued;[79] this includes liturgical formation. The value of this is that the course of the regular seminary training cannot exhaust the riches of the liturgy. Contemporary circumstances are an added reason, because the changes in mores and in society are so rapid that it is not possible to anticipate during the seminary either future pastoral problems that must be faced or theological controversies that may arise. Another factor not to be overlooked is the way that periodicals, congresses, and the media spread opinions that also affect the liturgy. These opinions give rise to difficult problems that priests must deal with because such problems have a bearing on their own everyday concerns.

Conclusion

62. The reform of the liturgy is the source of continuously increasing good results. This is not surprising, since the liturgy contributes most to the faithful's expressing in their lives and showing to others the mystery of Christ and the real nature of the Church. More than the other faithful, priests and seminarians must realize that they have received this blessing, since in the liturgy they acquire a keener and more intense experience of the priesthood and its demands. They are invited to imitate what they handle. Therefore, the assiduous pursuit and practice of the liturgy ceaselessly recall to their minds the goal toward which all their apostolic labors tend. A further result is that all the striving in their studies, pastoral practice, and spiritual life gradually grows into a profoundly integrated unity.

APPENDIX
LIST OF IMPORTANT ISSUES IN THE LITURGICAL FORMATION IN SEMINARIES

CONTEMPORARY NEED FOR A PROFOUND LITURGICAL FORMATION

1. The Constitution *Sacrosanctum Concilium* establishes the norm that "the study of the liturgy is to be ranked among the compulsory and major courses in seminaries and religious houses of study; in theological faculties it is to rank among the principal courses. It is to be taught under its theological, historical, spiritual, pastoral, and canonical aspects."[1]

The course in liturgy is therefore to be taught in such a way as to meet contemporary needs.

a. The reform of the liturgy, begun by Vatican Council II and now successfully put into effect, must be understood in practice, in the light of the liturgical tradition not only of the West but also of the Eastern Churches.[2]

2840

2841

2842

---

[78] See *Basic Plan* no. 85.

[79] See OT no. 22. *Basic Plan* nos. 100–101.

[1] SC art. 16 [DOL 1 no. 16].

[2] See *Basic Plan* no. 79 [DOL 334 no. 2776].

b. Vatican Council II advocated adaptation of the liturgy according to the genius and traditions of the various peoples.[3] That requires a more extensive and detailed study of the liturgy, both historically and theologically, in order to ensure that no harm is done to an authentic and genuine liturgical spirit.

c. In the ecumenical dialogue many difficult problems exist that have their origin in the liturgy: on doctrine, concerning the Mass, orders, and the other sacraments; on pastoral practice, in ways described in the Ecumenical Directory[a] and in other documents issued by the Apostolic See.

d. Finally, and principally, since the *legem credendi lex statuat supplicandi*, liturgical tradition must be researched in a way that will throw light on contemporary doctrinal and disciplinary debate about the mystery of Christ and the sacraments. Moreover, the liturgy, which through prayer brings the students to the source of the Christian mystery, becomes the sustenance of their spiritual life and is a powerful force unifying the different courses of the theological curriculum.

FORCE OF THE LIST

2843   2. This list of topics is not meant to serve as a rigid framework for setting up the unalterable outline of the curriculum for liturgical formation. On the contrary that formation requires a plan that meets actual circumstances.

In compliance with the *Basic Plan for Priestly Formation*, the seminarians' training should begin with an introduction into the mystery of Christ and the history of salvation. The purpose of this is "to enable the students to appreciate the idea, order, and apostolic purpose of their ecclesiastical studies and at the same time to help them to deepen their faith and understand more completely their priestly vocation."[4] This purpose cannot be achieved unless at the same time they are given a proper introduction to the liturgy. This may be part of the introductory course or else a course apart, given at the very beginning of the curriculum of studies. This introduction should explain the role of the liturgy in the economy of salvation, in the life of the Church, and in the spiritual life of each Christian. At the very beginning it would be extremely useful to give the students a brief explanation of the Mass and of the major hours of the divine office.

2844   3. The order of the topics on this list also may be changed in the interest of coordinating them with the other theological disciplines and the life of the seminary itself. For instance, a deeper study of the first chapter of the Constitution on the Liturgy will have greater impact for students who have already acquired some of the basics of theology. It may also be practical to treat the liturgical year and its seasons at the time they are actually being celebrated. Coordination of the liturgical study of the sacraments with their theological study also has great advantages.

2845   4. All the material on this list is not presented as though the liturgy professor should include it all in his lectures. He is to make a selection of themes that will allow his students a view of the essentials of the liturgy; but he should avoid omissions that would be harmful to the preparation of future priests. The more detailed questions not dealt with in the lectures should be proposed to the seminarians for personal study or for study in small groups, a method of proven effectiveness in other disciplines.

---

[3] See SC art. 37–40 [DOL 1 nos. 37–40].

[a] See DOL 147.

[4] *Basic Plan* no. 62.

5.   The liturgy professor must keep in mind that he is the one chiefly responsible   2846
for leading the students to a thorough study of those liturgical texts that they must
fully master in order to be celebrants capable of bringing the faithful to an aware
and intense sharing in the mystery of Christ.

6.   The repeated recommendation in this list of a return to ancient sources is to be   2847
understood as the ideal to be pursued. Its realization, of course, depends on the
resources available to the individual seminaries.

PROPER COORDINATION OF LITURGY WITH OTHER SEMINARY COURSES

7.   There should be careful attention to the harmonious and coherent coordina-   2848
tion of the liturgy course with the other seminary courses, as this Instruction states
in nos. 52–56. Moreover, many topics are interconnected, especially on the doctrine
of the sacraments and their pastoral administration, and should be treated either by
the liturgy professor or by other professors in a way that avoids omissions or
useless repetition. On the contrary, such topics are an opportunity for interdiscipli-
nary cooperation designed for a deeper and more beneficial presentation of the
same topic in its liturgical, dogmatic, canonical, historical, and pastoral dimensions.

PART ONE
ELEMENTS AND PRINCIPLES

ARTICLE I. NATURE OF THE LITURGY AND IMPORTANCE
IN THE CHURCH'S LIFE

8.   A useful preliminary is an introduction into the idea of worship, from an   2849
anthropological and psychological viewpoint, that is, as an attitude of the human
spirit and a phenomenon present, though in a distorted way, even in secularized
societies.

9.   The Christian liturgy, however, completes and transcends such a notion of   2850
worship. This will be made clear by exposition and commentary explaining the
teaching of the Constitution *Sacrosanctum Concilium* art. 5–13. The points to be made
are:

a.   The nature of the liturgy: "Rightly, then, the liturgy is considered as an
exercise of the priestly office of Jesus Christ. In the liturgy, by means of signs
perceptible to the senses, human sanctification is signified and brought about in
ways proper to each of these signs; in the liturgy the whole public worship is
performed by the Mystical Body of Christ Jesus, that is, by the Head and his
members."[5]

b.   The paschal mystery of Christ's passion, resurrection, and ascension that
the Church celebrates in the liturgy[6] and that is the source "from which all the
sacraments and sacramentals draw their power."[7]

c.   The place of the liturgy in the economy of salvation: "The wonderful
works of God among the people of the Old Testament were a prelude" to the saving
work of Christ,[8] because "all these were our examples";[9] Christ completed his own
work once and for all when he was born of woman, became subject to the Law,

---

[5]   SC art. 7 [DOL 1 no. 7].

[6]   See SC art. 6 [DOL 1 no. 6].

[7]   SC art. 61 [DOL 1 no. 61].

[8]   SC art. 5 [DOL 1 no. 5].

[9]   1 Cor 10:11.

suffered under Pontius Pilate, and rose on the third day; the Church will preach the Gospel until the end of time, will celebrate the eucharist, administer the other sacraments, in full awareness of Christ's presence, especially in the liturgy;[10] the liturgy on earth is a foretaste of that liturgy in heaven when God will be all in all.[11]

d. The liturgy uses sacred signs perceptible to the senses to signify divine realities and through these signs, in a way proper to each, brings about human sanctification.[12]

e. As the exercise of Christ's priestly office, the liturgy includes a twofold movement: from God to us to sanctify us; from us to God as our adoration in spirit and in truth.[13]

f. The liturgy, even though not being the totality of the Church's activity, is "the summit toward which the Church's activity is directed; at the same time it is the fount from which all the Church's power flows." This point needs further elaboration based on the Constitution.[14]

ARTICLE II. NATURE OF THE LITURGY AS A HIERARCHIC ACTION AND THE ACTION OF A COMMUNITY; ALSO LITURGICAL LAW

2851   10. There should be a presentation, guided by the Constitution art. 26–32 and 41–42, of principles regarding the liturgical assembly, namely, the holy people called together and ordered under the leadership of the bishop (or of the priest who stands in his place). These principles should be developed from the teaching of sacred Scripture, the examples of the early Church, and the texts of the Fathers.

Furthermore, it is useful to add something about the conditions under which it is lawful to celebrate the liturgy quasi-privately.

2852   11. Emphasis should be given to the diversity of members and functions that a liturgical assembly requires. Thus the roles of celebrant, ministers, choir, and people are to be outlined. The role of the faithful and their active participation should be explained in keeping with the mind of Vatican Council II and at the same time the distinction between the universal priesthood of all the baptized and the ministerial priesthood in virtue of which the presiding priest presides at the liturgical assembly "in the person of Christ."[15]

2853   12. The preeminent office of the bishop is to be explained on the basis of the Constitition *Lumen gentium*.[b]

2854   13. By means of a brief review, the professor should demonstrate how liturgical laws have always been the responsibility of the hierarchy; how this belongs to the hierarchy by divine law; and how, in the course of time, there have been different ways of fulfilling this law.

---

[10]   See SC art. 6–7 [DOL 1 nos. 6–7].

[11]   See SC art. 8 [DOL 1 no. 8].

[12]   See SC art. 7 and 13 [DOL 1 nos. 7 and 13].

[13]   See SC art. 5–7 [DOL 1 nos. 5–7].

[14]   See SC art. 9–13 [DOL 1 nos. 9–13].

[15]   See John Paul II, Encycl. *Redemptor hominis*, 4 March 1979: AAS 71 (1979) 311; Epistle to all priests in the Church, 8 April 1979 [DOL 323 no. 2605].

[b]   See DOL 4 nos. 146–147.

The current disposition of things, as decreed in the Constitution art. 22, is then to be indicated by bringing out the roles of the Apostolic See, the conferences of bishops, and the local bishop.[c]

14. Likewise, a historical exposition is to show why the Church, even from the most ancient times, gradually forbade improvisation in the composition and offering of prayers in the liturgy and why today it has imposed limits on flexibility, variations, and experimentation.   2855

Article III. Instructive and Pastoral Nature of the Liturgy

15. "In the liturgy God is speaking to his people and Christ is still proclaiming his Gospel. And the people are responding to God by both song and prayer."[16] The first part of the liturgy is, therefore, given over to sacred Scripture, that is, the word of God, either read and listened to by all or sung by the assembly. The professor will elaborate on the use of Scripture both in the readings and in the songs taken from them, mentioning also nonbiblical readings and hymns composed by the Church. He is to present the principles on Bible services, the homily, and catechesis and show how important Scripture is for an understanding of the signs, actions, and prayers of the liturgy.[17]   2856

16. Thorough attention is to be given to explaining the distinctive value of sacred song and its function in the liturgy. Points to be covered are: the diverse styles of song, psalmody for the psalms and biblical hymns, hymnody, doxologies, acclamation, etc. The dialogue between the celebrant and the assembly should be explained through use of examples.   2857

17. The types of prayer of both the priest and the people should be explained: in the first instance, for example, collects, thanksgiving, blessings, exorcisms, narrative formularies, prayers said inaudibly; in the second, the Lord's Prayer, silent prayer, litanies, etc.   2858

18. If possible, there should be a brief history of sacred song, its origins, and early development, and a history of the nature of Gregorian chant. There should also be mention of other traditionally accepted styles and the principles in the instruction of the Congregation of Rites, 5 March 1967, on music in the liturgy should be explained.[d]   2859

19. Next there is the topic of liturgical language. This involves a brief history of the practice of both the West and the East. According to his own abilities, the professor shows how the translations of the sacred books, especially from Greek into Latin, have shaped Christian language and some of the principles governing contemporary translation into the vernacular.   2860

20. The liturgy, however, uses not only words but also signs "that have been chosen by Christ or by the Church to signify invisible divine reality."[18] Thus the lectures should touch on gestures and physical bearing in liturgical prayer and on articles used in liturgical worship. There should be instruction from Scripture and

---

[c]   See DOL 1 no. 22.

[16]   See SC art. 33 [DOL 1 no. 33].

[17]   See SC art. 24 [DOL 1 no. 24].

[d]   See DOL 508.

[18]   SC art. 33 [DOL 1 no. 33].

the Fathers regarding the psychological influence of gestures and postures. This explanation should not be left in the abstract but put to use in the liturgy. Even if done briefly, it is helpful to explain the meaning, especially the biblical meaning, of each of the natural elements used in the liturgy, such as light, water, bread, wine, oil, incense, etc., with particular attention to those that are sacramental signs.

2862   21. Today there are some who are trying to strip liturgical worship of its sacred character and are therefore of the wrong opinion that sacred articles and furnishings are to be discarded in favor of things in everyday, common use. Thus there is need to repudiate such an opinion as a distortion of the genuine nature of the liturgy.[19]

2863   22. There should be a theological explanation about the places of worship and their meaning and a discussion of the rite for the dedication of a church. Other points include the functions of the altar, tabernacle, celebrant's chair, lectern (ambo), and baptistery.

2864   23. The students should be helped to apply their other courses to an appreciation of the history and laws of sacred art. There should be a discussion of Christian iconography and of the requirements contemporary sacred art must respect in order to serve the Christian people.

2865   24. All of this should serve to bring out the instructive character of the liturgy and how, although the liturgy is above all things the worship of the divine majesty, it also contains rich instruction for the faithful.[20] This implies that sufficient attention is given to the axiom, *legem credendi lex statuat supplicandi* ("let the law of prayer declare the law of belief"). It also implies that the students learn the criteria for discriminating between matters that the Church in its liturgy presents to the faithful for belief and those that are of a kind that the Church's magisterium does not stamp with its own authority.

2866   25. In the sense already stated in the Instruction no. 50, attention should be given to social sciences like anthropology and psychology in order to face the problems to today's people and to show pastors ways of solving them.

ARTICLE IV. ELEMENTS ON THE HISTORY OF THE LITURGY

2867   26. The presentation of the individual celebrations and sacraments should emphasize the history of each rite in order to bring out the meaning of modern liturgical usage and to clarify and support sacramental theology.

It will serve the cause of clarity in the development of the lectures to repeat frequently an outline of the stages and ages of the entire history of the liturgy and to point out the interconnection between the liturgy and Christian spirituality.

If possible, there should be an introduction describing Jewish prayer at the time of Christ, especially in the synagogue, in private homes, and in the Passover celebration, so that the seminarians may recognize that Christian prayer bears both a resemblance to Jewish prayer and something new.

Next there should be a description of the liturgical assembly at the time of the apostles. Ideally also the students will be exposed to the liturgical sources of the first centuries (for instance, the *Didachē*, Clement of Rome, Justin, Irenaeus, Tertullian, Hippolytus of Rome, Cyprian, the *Didascalia* and the *Apostolic Constitutions*,

---

[19]   See Paul VI, Addr. to the Consilium, 14 Oct. 1968 [DOL 92 no. 675].

[20]   See SC art. 33 [DOL 1 no. 33].

the *Pilgrimage of Hygeria* [Aetheria]) and to texts selected from the early anaphoras and the catecheses of the Fathers.

27. Since the laws and texts of the liturgy gradually evolved in the Churches in various regions, it would be useful at this point to trace the different liturgical families, both of the East and of the West, and to state briefly their origin, history, and character. This is especially important in areas where there are many faithful of the Eastern Churches.

2868

The relationship between the rites should also be brought out clearly. But the treatment of the individual liturgical celebrations, especially the sacraments, should include the texts and rites of different liturgies in order to enhance the teaching and inspire devotion.

28. There is to be an explanation of the Council of Trent's correction of liturgical abuses and promotion of liturgical unity. The Tridentine decrees on the liturgy are to be presented and the students shown how, at the mandate of this Council and in accord with its intent, the popes had the liturgical books revised and so widely disseminated that they remained in use until our own time. In addition it would be useful to give an account of the liturgical progress made during the 16th and 17th centuries, in spite of difficulties, especially through the contribution of historical learning. Thus devotion to the eucharist, careful observance of rubrics, pastoral programs undertaken in various places for the faithful's understanding and participation, prepared the way for the renewal in our century that Pope St. Pius X began and that Vatican Council II has everywhere furthered.

2869

29. It would be most useful to outline for the students the series of documents putting this liturgical reform gradually into effect, so that they will understand it more thoroughly.

2870

PART TWO
MASS AND EUCHARISTIC WORSHIP

Article I. General Notions to Be Taught

30. Before all else the New Testament texts about the institution of the eucharist are to be thoroughly presented and compared with the texts for Jewish prayers used in daily life and in the Passover supper, as well as with other forms of evidence prefiguring the eucharistic institution.

2871

31. A short history of the Mass should bring out the elements of the Mass common in all the liturgies, so that these might be more clearly perceived in the present-day eucharistic celebration and be more effectively pointed out to the Christian people.

2872

It is desirable that the students, where possible, actually read some of the early Mass texts, either selected from works of the Fathers or taken from the ancient liturgies. Collections of such texts are today available in many good anthologies.

Especially in areas where there are faithful of the Eastern rites, the seminarians should receive some idea about the Mass in those rites, particularly from a spiritual point of view.

32. The various forms of celebrating Mass should be described: stational Masses; the basic form of Mass with a congregation; Mass without a congregation. The offices and ministries of the celebrant, concelebrants, ministers, choir, and people

2873

should be outlined, as set out in the General Instruction of the Roman Missal, issued in 1970.[e]

2874   33. Special, detailed explanation should be devoted to concelebration and its current practice, on the basis of the Eastern and the Latin traditions.

2875   34. The General Instruction chapters 4–5 should be followed in a review of the requisite conditions for celebration dictated not simply by tradition and law, but by the needs of the human spirit and human nature.[f] This involves such points as places of worship, the altar and its adornment, vessels, vestments, etc.

ARTICLE II. NORMS FOR A CORRECT EXPLANATION OF THE INDIVIDUAL PARTS OF RITES AND OF THE MASS

2876   35. The professors are to bring out the two parts that, in a certain sense, go to make up the Mass, namely, the liturgy of the word and the liturgy of the eucharist, which are so closely connected as to form but one single act of worship.[21]

2877   36. The professor should explain clearly and distinctly the individual rites of the Mass, giving to each its proper importance: the entrance rite; the progress of the readings in the liturgy of the word toward the gospel, the homily, and the general intercessions; the parts of the preparation of the gifts; the character and structure of the entire eucharistic prayer; the rites preparing for communion; the concluding rites.

As far as possible, the individual rites should be explained through a consideration of their history and a comparison with the rites of other liturgies.

2878   37. The same method particularly applies to the articulation and explanation of the component elements of the eucharistic prayer.[22]

2879   38. There is to be a historical, theological, and pastoral treatment of communion under both kinds.

2880   39. On the basis of the Instruction *Eucharisticum mysterium*, 25 May 1967,[g] guidelines should be given for instructing the faithful toward a more beneficial participation in the Mass and for showing them how the eucharist is the center of the entire sacramental system.

2881   40. In discussing the liturgy of the word, the professor should bring in those celebrations of the word advocated in the Constitution on the Liturgy art. 35, 4.[23]

ARTICLE III. EUCHARISTIC WORSHIP OUTSIDE MASS

2882   41. The worship of the eucharist outside Mass has greatly increased over the centuries. Therefore care must be taken to explain this in relationship to the sacrifice of the Mass itself and in conformity with the previously mentioned Instruc-

---

[e]   See DOL 208 nos. 1448–63.

[f]   See DOL 208 nos. 1464–1670.

[21]   See SC art. 56 [DOL 1 no. 56].

[22]   See GIRM no. 55 [DOL 208 no. 1445]. See also SCDW, Circular Letter on the eucharistic prayers, 27 April 1973 [DOL 248].

[g]   See DOL 179 nos. 1234–44.

[23]   See SCR, Instr. InterOec, 26 Sept. 1964, nos. 37–39 [DOL 23 nos. 329–331].

tion of 25 May 1967. There should also be a review of the part of the Roman Ritual entitled *Holy Communion and Worship of the Eucharist outside Mass*, issued 21 June 1973.[h]

Other necessary topics are reception of communion outside Mass, reservation of the blessed sacrament, including the theological and pastoral reason for it and the canonical requirements.

Then there should be a treatment of eucharistic devotions and their principal expressions: processions, exposition of the blessed sacrament, eucharistic congresses. The two documents mentioned endorse these and regulate their use in such a way that they derive from the Mass and lead the faithful to participate in the sacrifice and communion.

PART THREE
OTHER SACRAMENTS AND THE SACRAMENTALS

42. The lectures on the revised Roman Pontifical and Ritual should be based on the texts themselves and their Introductions, in order to bring out the teaching they contain. The explanation and understanding of the rites will be assisted by giving their history. A pastoral concern should mark the entire treatment, so that the candidates for the priesthood will be prepared for the future exercise of their pastoral ministry.   2883

ARTICLE I. CHRISTIAN INITIATION

43. Christian initiation includes the rite of the catechumenate, the sacraments of baptism and confirmation, and first communion. Care in its explanation is demanded because Christian initiation is the foundation of catechesis for children and because throughout the world countless adults commit themselves to the same process of initiation.   2884

44. The history of the baptismal liturgy and of the liturgical catechumenate should therefore be developed in order to ensure a proper understanding and clear idea of the rite. The meaning of the baptismal rites themselves should be brought out through the liturgy of Lent, the text of the chrism Mass, and the rites and texts of the Easter Vigil and of Easter Week.   2885

45. The students should be urged and guided toward reading the baptismal catecheses of the Fathers, which are readily available today in editions both in the original and in the vernacular.   2886

46. It would be well to point out both in ancient and more recent usage the practice of celebrating the anniversary of baptism. This is an opportunity for careful pastoral instruction on the importance of such a celebration and of the spiritual benefits to parishes and the faithful that may rightly be expected as a result.   2887

47. With the same resources and method, the rite of confirmation should be explained on the basis of Pope Paul VI's Apostolic Constitution *Divinae consortium naturae*, 15 August 1971,[i] in order to bring out both the import of this sacrament and its close connection with baptism.   2888

In a special way either the liturgy professor or the professor of pastoral theology must explain the pastoral programs for the preparation and beneficial celebration

---

[h] See DOL 279 nos. 2193–96.

[i] See DOL 303.

of confirmation and, at the same time, indicate any regulations about this matter laid down by the conference of bishops or the local Ordinary.

2889   48.   It is useful also to touch on the eucharist as the high point of the sacraments of initiation and on the admission of children to first communion.

Article II. Sacrament of Orders and Various Ministries

2890   49.   The rite and discipline of the sacrament of orders and of the various other ministries of the Church must be presented and explained in greater detail since, at the direction of Vatican Council II, they have been so radically revised. It is a matter to be decided whether this is better dealt with during the course of liturgical studies or left to be studied phase by phase as the seminarians are promoted to each of the ministries or orders.

Clearly, however, the liturgy professor is responsible at least for presenting the texts of the revised Roman Pontifical and for explaining through historical tradition the Apostolic Constitution *Pontificalis Romani*, 18 June 1968,[j] and the Motu Proprios *Sacrum Diaconatus Ordinem*, 18 June 1967,[k] and *Ad pascendum* and *Ministeria quaedam*, 15 August 1972.[l]

If possible, something should be said about the rites of ordination used in the Eastern Churches; this is especially important in those areas where there are many of the faithful of these Churches.

2891   50.   The rite of ordination of a bishop should be explained correctly so that it will be clear that all the orders and ministries have reference to the bishop and especially that priests are co-workers of the bishop and are next to him in rank and dignity.

Article III. Marriage and Virginity

2892   51.   A history of the rite of marriage is to be given, with an indication of its variety and characteristics in different regions. It should be shown how the rite has always been adapted to the religious and civil customs of diverse peoples. There should be a description of the texts and the readings that the revised ritual contains.

Because New Testament and patristic teaching correlates the nature and knowledge of Christian marriage and the life of virginity, the two liturgies, of marriage and of consecration to a life of virginity, in the revised Roman Pontifical should be studied together.

Article IV. Liturgy of Religious Consecration

2893   52.   A brief presentation of the rite of consecration to a life of virginity and the rite of religious profession will show how religious life constitutes a special state in the Church, as Vatican Council II teaches in the Dogmatic Constitution *Lumen gentium*.[24]

Article V. Liturgy of Penance

2894   53.   For a better grasp of both the sacrament and other penitential acts, the students should be given a historical outline of penitential liturgy and discipline.

---

j   See DOL 324.

k   See DOL 309.

l   See DOL 319 and 340.

24   See LG ch. 6.

With the help of the revised Roman Ritual and of the Pastoral Norms issued by the Congregation for the Doctrine of the Faith, 16 June 1972,[m] the rite of the sacrament of penance should be explained. There should be a clear statement of the conditions required for giving general absolution.

The penitential character of the Lenten liturgy should be brought out, as also the importance of the penitential rite at the beginning of Mass and the norms for penitential services in the documents already cited.

Article VI. Liturgy of the Sick

54. There should be an explanation of the Apostolic Constitution *Sacram Unctionem*, 30 November 1972,[n] and of *Pastoral Care of the Sick: Rites of Anointing and Viaticum* in the revised Roman Ritual.[o] It would be well to show from the history of liturgy the grounds for the reform of this rite as decreed by Vatican Council II.[25]

2895

Article VII. Liturgy of Christian Death

55. The liturgy course should also treat the liturgy for the dying and the dead: viaticum, rite of commendation of the dying, and, finally, the funeral rites. Proper emphasis should be given to all the elements in these rites that express the paschal mystery. The students should be taught how to choose suitable texts from those abundantly provided in the new Ritual. They should be instructed about the pastoral care of the dying and the pastoral importance of funeral celebrations.

2896

Article VIII. Sacramentals

56. Processions and their religious significance should be treated, with pilgrimages being explained as a distinctive type of procession, having their own pastoral value.

2897

57. A brief history and a theology of blessings should be given. The emphasis should be on their meaning and usefulness for sanctifying daily life. The students should be instilled with reverence and respect toward all the lawful forms of devotion through which Christians profess their faith in their way of life. At the same time, the seminarians should be advised about the caution to be exercised against the intrusion of abuses and superstitions.

2898

PART FOUR
SANCTIFICATION OF TIME

58. The first topic treated here should be Sunday, "the foundation and core of the whole liturgical year."[26]

2899

Article I. Sunday

59. The highest importance must be attached to Sunday, with its meaning and elements explained from the Constitution on the Liturgy.[27] Through historical arguments, it is to be shown that Sunday is the weekly Easter, so closely joined to the

2900

---

[m] See DOL 361.

[n] See DOL 408.

[o] See DOL 410.

[25] See SC art. 73–75 [DOL 1 nos. 73–75].

[26] SC art. 106 [DOL 1 no. 106].

[27] See ibid.

beginnings of the Church that by a tradition handed down from the apostles it takes its origin from the very day of Christ's resurrection.[28]

2901   60. There should be thorough discussion of the pastoral methods for truly keeping this day holy, as all the faithful are obliged to do.

2902   61. The Sundays in Ordinary Time make available to the faithful the riches of the word of God. Accordingly, it is necessary that the seminarians learn how, in keeping with liturgical law, to further celebration of these Sundays faithfully and with care.

ARTICLE II. LITURGICAL YEAR

2903   62. The students receive instruction throughout the year from their superiors and professors on the intelligent and devout celebration of seasons and feasts as these occur. Nevertheless, the lectures should present an orderly and coherent summary of the liturgical year in the light of history and on the basis of Pope Paul VI's Motu Proprio *Mysterii paschalis*, 14 February 1969.[p]

2904   63. The major topic should be the history and spiritual character of Easter and the Easter season — that is, the fifty days after Easter that culminate in the solemnity of Pentecost — the Easter triduum, and the preparation for Easter, that is, Lent. The teaching aim should be to lead all the seminarians to live the paschal mystery with intense interiority and to prepare them for their paschal ministry.

2905   64. Next comes the Christmas-Epiphany cycle, with a consideration of its history and spiritual meaning.

2906   65. There should be a brief explanation of those solemnities of the Lord that were introduced into the liturgical year in more recent times: Holy Trinity, Corpus Christi, Sacred Heart, Christ the King, etc.

2907   66. The veneration of the Blessed Virgin in the Church should be treated historically;[29] her principal feasts throughout the year should be reviewed.

2908   67. As to the saints commemorated during the liturgical year, the teaching of the Constitution is to be recalled.[30] Also to be treated are the origin and development of the cult of martyrs and other saints, reverence for their burial place or relics, the place Christian life gives to veneration of the saints.

ARTICLE III. SANCTIFICATION OF THE HOURS OF THE DAY AND THE LITURGY OF THE HOURS

2909   68. To dispose the students rightly for the devout and beneficial celebration of the divine office, the professor of liturgy is responsible for presenting the General Instruction that serves as a preliminary to the book of the liturgy of the hours promulgated by Paul VI on 1 November 1970.[q]

2910   69. The emphasis should be on the doctrinal part of that General Instruction (Chapter 1), and in particular the obligation of offering praise that Christ entrusted

---

[28]   See ibid.

[p]   See DOL 440.

[29]   See SC art. 103 [DOL 1 no. 103].

[30]   See SC art. 104 [DOL 1 no. 104].

[q]   See DOL 424 and 426.

to the Church and that it fulfills not only by celebrating the eucharist but also in other ways, especially by the divine office.[31]

70. The testimony in the Acts of the Apostles and in the Church's tradition should   2911
be presented as evidence of the great importance of the hours of the office for the sanctification of the entire day and its parts and for the fulfillment of Christ's command to pray always. The symbolic import of each of the hours is to be brought out clearly from the early spiritual writers and from the prayers found in the liturgy of the hours.

71. There should be an explanation of the special significance attached by the   2912
Council to morning prayer and evening prayer, the double "hinge of the whole office."[32]

72. It is to be made clear how the Church has made this daily prayer its own as   2913
truly "the voice of a bride addressing her bridegroom, the very prayer that Christ himself, together with his Body, addresses to his Father."[33]

73. Special attention should be given to develop the students' devotion to the   2914
psalms through the lectures in exegesis by the professor of sacred Scripture and through acquainting them with the psalm titles and with the prayers in *The Liturgy of the Hours*.[34]

74. On the basis of the decrees of Vatican Council II,[35] there should be an explana-   2915
tion of the communal nature of the divine office, of the general invitation of all the faithful to take part in it, and also of the mandate especially deputing priests and others to celebrate this marvelous song of praise.

75. It would be useful to mention something about the traditions of the different   2916
Churches regarding the structure and celebration of the office and also to give a brief historical description of the Roman office and its various reforms from the 16th century to the present.

31   See SC art. 81 [DOL 1 no. 81].

32   SC art. 89 [DOL 1 no. 89]. See GILH nos. 37–54 [DOL 426 nos. 3467–84].

33   SC art. 84 [DOL 1 no. 84]. See GILH nos. 15–16 [DOL 426 nos. 3445–46].

34   See GILH nos. 100–135 [DOL 426 nos. 3530–65].

35   See SC art. 84–100 [DOL 1 nos. 84–100]; PO nos. 6 and 13 [DOL 18 nos. 261 and 265]; LG no. 41. GILH nos. 20–37 [DOL 426 nos. 3450–67].

Section 5. Ministries

SUMMARY (DOL 336–346). The Constitution on the Liturgy art. 29 explicitly recognizes that servers, readers, commentators, and members of the choir also exercise a genuine liturgical ministry. But the concept and reorganization of ministries has had a much more evolved development, especially since 1972.

—The major texts are the 1972 Motu Proprio *Ministeria quaedam* of Paul VI, which suppressed first tonsure and the major order of subdiaconate and reorganized the former minor orders as ministries (DOL 340), and texts consequent upon this new discipline for the Latin Church: the decree of promulgation and the rite of institution to the ministries of reader and acolyte (DOL 341 and 342), a particular reply on the question of delegation to administer the rite of institution (DOL 345), and a letter to the conferences of bishops on the question of inaugurating further new ministries (DOL 346). The rite of commissioning special ministers of communion is also included here (DOL 343).

—Subsidiary documents include two addresses of Paul VI to altar servers (DOL 336, 338), a decree authorizing nondeacons to read the gospel of Christ's passion (DOL 337), an excerpt of a letter on the missionary activity of the laity (DOL 339), and a letter addressed to the bishops of Germany on lay participation in the preaching office (DOL 344).

▶   1.   VATICAN COUNCIL II, Constitution on the Liturgy *Sacrosanctum Concilium,* 4 December 1963:

art. 29:   Liturgical ministry of servers, readers, commentators, and choir [no. 29].

336. PAUL VI, **Address** to the Piccolo Clero, the altar servers of Rome, 25 April 1964.*

2917   We must make special mention of the main group that makes up this great audience and for which the celebration of this Mass was arranged: the Piccolo Clero of Rome. [. . .]

The message of the Pope on your behalf will suffice to remind your parents, pastors, curates, teachers, representatives of the Society, Fanciulli cattolici, of the importance of the Piccolo Clero. First of all, this is the religious importance of altar boys for divine worship. You are well aware of this and adults also realize it very well, especially the good priests. How could a beautiful religious rite take place without you? It is not possible, particularly now when we are short of adult clergy. We must rely on our noisy little altar boys. But you are not noisy, restless, and unruly during sacred rites; rather you are very good, at least if someone prepares and directs you. As a matter of fact, many times it is one of your own number, older and more experienced, who trains you so well. You yourselves above all give to everyone good example of quiet, attentive, and devout behavior in church. You know how to do all your tasks: to make the responses at Mass, to ring the bells, to serve as acolytes, to walk in procession, and even to sing. Singing is the hardest, but also the most beautiful thing of all, and once you have learned it, it is something you like and enjoy.

You are good altar boys, we said, and you are important. What would the Church do to conduct its services with dignity without you? You are well aware of this, because you are pleased that a responsible part in the liturgical rites has been entrusted to you. If there is any rivalry among you, it is to be the first to arrive and to receive some important or difficult part to perform. Realize that you contribute to something serious and sacred; and it is so: you are doing honor to God.

So true is this that the ecumenical Council (you know, don't you, what the Council is? the meeting of all the world's bishops with the pope) has turned its attention to you in the Constitution on the Liturgy. Above all the Council repeated over and over the necessity of the people's participation in the official prayer of the Church. And the Council remembered you: in the Constitution on the Liturgy art. 29 it declared that you too, the young servers at the altar, exercise a true liturgical ministry.[a]

That is not all: your presence in the liturgical rites suggests other values that are worthy of attention. There is, for example, a social and communitarian aspect. Dear sons of our Christian families and of the Christian family that is the Church, where you are, the community is immediately conscious of itself, it becomes a community, it comes closer together. By your innocence, your joyfulness, your willingness to love and to serve you move the community to become united. [. . .]

---

*   Text, OR 26 April 1964, 1 (Italian; excerpts).

a   See DOL 1 no. 29.

▶   23.   SC RITES (Consilium), Instruction (first) *Inter Oecumenici,* 26 September 1964:

      nos. 50, 52:   Readers or servers for the readings [nos. 342, 344].
           56:           Role of the cantor or other minister for the general intercessions [nos. 348].

337. SC RITES, Decree *Plures locorum,* authorizing nondeacons to read the gospel of Christ's passion, 25 March 1965: AAS 57 (1965) 413–414.

Many local Ordinaries, in view of the difficulty of having three deacons or three priests to read the gospel of the Lord's passion in keeping with the Instruction of 26 September 1964, nos. 50 and 51,[a] have petitioned the Apostolic See for the permission to depute three readers or three qualified servers when necessary.   2918

In reply the Congregation of Rites, using the faculties given to it by Pope Paul VI, grants that in the absence of one, two, or even three deacons or priests, other clerics or even laypersons may read the gospel of the Lord's passion, but they are to wear liturgical garb.

▶   17.   VATICAN COUNCIL II, Decree on the Church's Missionary Activity *Ad gentes,* 7 December 1965:

      no. 17:   Liturgical celebration for commissioning catechists [no. 249].

▶   32.   CONSILIUM, Letter *L'heureux développement,* on problems in the reform of the liturgy, 25 January 1966:

      no. 7:   Women serving at the altar [no. 429].

▶   508.   SC RITES (Consilium), Instruction *Musicam sacram,* on music in the liturgy, 5 March 1967:

      nos. 13, 24–26:   Liturgical ministries [nos. 4134, 4145–47].
         19–20, 22–23:   Choir members [nos. 4140–41, 4143–44].
         21:           Cantor [no. 4142].

338. PAUL VI, Address to a pilgrimage of altar servers from various parts of Europe, 30 March 1967: AAS 59 (1967) 349–354; Not 3 (1967) 136–137 (French).

Dear sons, in your beautiful white albs you present us with a splendid sight that is a joy to our eyes and our heart. We are happy to address a few words to you, in response to the request expressed in your name by your friend and protector in Rome, the Cardinal Archpriest of St. Peter's.   2919

His words introducing you to us suggest the thought that the whiteness of your vestments is a reflection of the whiteness of your souls. Your contact with the altar sustains and develops in your souls, faith, devotion, purity, and all the virtues that are pleasing to God.

---

  a   See DOL 23 nos. 342 and 343.

You will remember the young man in the gospel who had faithfully cultivated those same virtues since childhood. The evangelist tells us that Jesus looked upon him with love: *Iesus, intuitus eum, dilexit eum,* "Looking on him, Jesus loved him."[1]

We believe that we see the Savior's look also resting upon each one of you with special favor. Are you not the ones who come so very near to him as you serve at the altar? Is it then surprising that his call to an even greater nearness to him should at some time — as has just been said to us — sound in the hearts of some of you?

Dear sons, the charge that we wish to commit to you consists in two points: be faithful to carry out in exemplary fashion the liturgical functions assigned to you; listen to the voice of Christ if he graciously calls you to follow him more closely.

2920 To be faithful: that is a whole program for life. As you know the word "faithfulness" includes the word "faith." To revivify that faith at the tombs of the Apostles is the reason you have come to Rome. In that faith St. Paul summarized his whole life as an apostle when he came to the end of his earthly life: *fidem servavi,* "I have kept the faith," he said to his disciple Timothy.[2] I have been faithful to God, to Christ, to the Church. I have been faithful to my calling, to the ministry entrusted to me. May such a faithfulness be yours and may it be particularly true of those concerns involved in your functions as servers at the altar.

You might at times think that the liturgy is made up of a lot of minor details: posture, genuflections, bows, handling the censer, missal, cruets, etc. It is then that you must remember the words of Christ in the gospel: "He that is faithful in the smallest things is faithful also in the great."[3] Moreover, in the liturgy nothing is little, when we realize the greatness of the one to whom it is directed.

Therefore, dear sons, be outstanding in faithfulness toward carrying out your sacred functions. To that devote your attention, all your heart, and all your love.

Next, listen to the divine call. We will share with you one of our worries. In the face of the vastness of the task of evangelization that the modern world sets before us, we often put the question to ourself: How are we going to find enough priests, enough religious to meet this need? Does it not seem as though God is calling in vain — that today's young people have no wish to hear him; that they no longer have the taste for God, the response to the ideal, the attraction toward sacrifice?

Dear sons, a good number of those older than you have resoundingly repudiated such fears. May it come true that a great many of you also will follow in their footsteps! Be on your guard against letting the voice that calls you go unheard and unanswered. Pray ardently that from among your ranks Christ may choose many to carry on his priesthood. [. . .]

▶ 179. SC RITES (Consilium), Instruction *Eucharisticum mysterium,* on worship of the eucharist, 25 May 1967:

nos. 32, 7 and 8 a: Ministers receiving communion under both kinds [no. 1261].

▶ 550. SC RITES (Consilium), Instruction *Pontificalis ritus,* on simplification of pontifical rites and insignia, 21 June 1968:

---

1   Mk 10:21.

2   2 Tm 4:7.

3   Lk 16:10.

nos. 9, 25–26:   Minor ministers in pontifical celebrations [nos. 4466, 4482–83].

▶   208.   SC RITES (Consilium); SC DIVINE WORSHIP, General Instruction of the Roman Missal, 1st ed. 6 April 1969; 4th ed. 27 March 1975:

nos. 65–73:   Particular ministries [nos. 1455–63].
    142–147:   Acolyte's functions [nos. 1532–37].
    148–149:   Reader's functions [nos. 1538–39].
    242, §§ 5, 7, 8a: Communion under both kinds for ministers [no. 1632].
    301:              Vestments of ministers [no. 1691].

339. SC EVANGELIZATION OF PEOPLES, **Letter** *Notre temps* to local Ordinaries, on the missionary activity of the laity, 17 May 1970 (excerpts).*

INTRODUCTION

Our age has rightly been called the age of the laity because of the increasing importance of their activity in the Church.

Vatican Council II acknowledges this fact when speaking of the dignity of lay people, their role in the Church, and also their rights and duties. [. . .]

II. MISSIONARY ACTIVITY

B. SERVICE FOR SALVATION

3. PARTICIPATION IN THE MINISTERIAL PRIESTHOOD

In many communities there are still other occasions for the laity to help in the   2921
conservation and propagation of the faith according to their ability and individual charism. Together with priests and religious they can provide catechetical training for children and catechumens. In the liturgy they can proclaim and, according to the circumstances, explain holy Scripture. They can share in the ministry of the eucharist, preserving the body of Christ in the tabernacle and distributing it to the faithful and to the sick, according to the directives of the local hierarchy. [. . .]

▶   215.   PONTIFICAL COMMISSION FOR INTERPRETATION . . . VATICAN II, Reply, on the General Instruction of the Roman Missal no. 42 (the homily), 11 January 1971.

▶   426.   SC DIVINE WORSHIP, General Instruction of the Liturgy of the Hours, 2 February 1971:

nos. 253, 257–260:   Particular ministries [nos. 3683, 3687–90].

▶   169.   SC CLERGY, *General Catechetical Directory,* 11 April 1971:

nos. 114–115:   Catechists [nos. 1112–13].

---

* English text, OREng 17 Sept. 1970, 6–8.

340. PAUL VI, **Motu Proprio** *Ministeria quaedam,* on first tonsure, minor orders, and the subdiaconate, 15 August 1972: AAS 64 (1972) 529–534; Not 9 (1973) 4–8.

2922   Certain ministries were established by the Church even in the most ancient times for the purpose of suitably giving worship to God and for offering service to the people of God according to their needs. By these ministries, the offices to be carried out in the liturgy and the practice of charity, deemed suitable to varying circumstances, were entrusted to the faithful. The conferring of these functions often took place by a special rite, in which, after God's blessing had been implored, a Christian was established in a special class or rank for the fulfillment of some ecclesiastical function.

Some of these functions, which were more closely connected with the liturgical celebration, slowly came to be considered as a training in preparation for the reception of sacred orders. As a result, the offices of porter, reader, exorcist, and acolyte were called minor orders in the Latin Church in relation to the subdiaconate, diaconate, and priesthood, which were called major orders. Generally, though not everywhere, these minor orders were reserved to those who received them as steps toward the priesthood.

Nevertheless, since the minor orders have not always been the same and many functions connected with them, as at present, have also been exercised by the laity, it seems fitting to reexamine this practice and to adapt it to contemporary needs. What is obsolete in these offices will thus be removed and what is useful retained; also anything new that is needed will be introduced and at the same time the requirements for candidates for holy orders will be established.

2923   While Vatican Council II was in preparation, many bishops of the Church requested that the minor orders and subdiaconate be revised. Although the Council did not decree anything concerning this for the Latin Church, it stated certain principles for resolving the issue. There is no doubt that the norms laid down by the Council regarding the general and orderly reform of the liturgy[1] also include those areas that concern ministries in the liturgical assembly, so that the very arrangement of the celebration itself makes the Church stand out as being formed in a structure of different orders and ministries.[2] Thus Vatican Council II decreed that "in liturgical celebrations each one, minister or layperson, who has an office to perform, should do all of, but only, those parts which pertain to that office by the nature of the rite and the principles of liturgy."[3]

With this assertion is closely connected what was written a little earlier in the same Constitution: "The Church earnestly desires that all the faithful be led to that full, conscious, and active participation in liturgical celebrations called for by the very nature of the liturgy. Such participation by the Christian people as 'a chosen race, a royal priesthood, a holy nation, a purchased people' (1 Pt 2:9; see 2:4–5) is their right and duty by reason of their baptism. In the reform and promotion of the liturgy, this full and active participation by all the people is the aim to be considered before all else. For it is the primary and indispensable source from which the faithful are to derive the true Christian spirit and therefore pastors must zealously

---

[1]   See SC art. 62 [DOL 1 no. 62]; see also art. 21 [DOL 1 no. 21].

[2]   See GIRM no. 58 [DOL 208 no. 1448].

[3]   SC art. 28 [DOL 1 no. 28].

strive in all their pastoral work to achieve such participation by means of the necessary instruction."[4]

Among the particular offices to be preserved and adapted to contemporary needs are those that are in a special way more closely connected with the ministries of the word and of the altar and that in the Latin Church are called the offices of *reader* and *acolyte* and the subdiaconate. It is fitting to preserve and adapt these in such a way, that from this time on there will be two offices: that of reader and that of acolyte, which will include the functions of the subdiaconate.

In addition to the offices universal in the Latin Church, the conferences of bishops may request others of the Apostolic See, if they judge the establishment of such offices in their region to be necessary or very useful because of special reasons. To these belong, for example, the ministries of *porter, exorcist,* and *catechist,*[5] as well as others to be conferred on those who are dedicated to works of charity, where this ministry has not been assigned to deacons.

It is in accordance with the reality itself and with the contemporary outlook that the above-mentioned ministries should no longer be called minor orders; their conferral will not be called *ordination,* but *institution.* Only those who have received the diaconate, however, will be clerics in the true sense and will be so regarded. This arrangement will bring out more clearly the distinction between clergy and laity, between what is proper and reserved to the clergy and what can be entrusted to the laity. This will also bring out more clearly that mutuality by which "the universal priesthood of believers and the ministerial or hierarchic priesthood, though they differ from one another in essence and not only in degree, are nonetheless interrelated: each of them in its own special way is a sharing in the one priesthood of Christ."[6]   2924

After weighing every aspect of the question, seeking the opinion of experts, consulting with the conferences of bishops and taking their views into account, and after taking counsel with our esteemed brothers who are members of the congregations competent in this matter, by our apostolic authority we enact the following norms, amending — if and insofar as is necessary — provisions of the *Codex Iuris Canonici* now in force, and we promulgate them through this Motu Proprio.   2925

I.   First tonsure is no longer conferred; entrance into the clerical state is joined to the diaconate.   2926

II.   What up to now were called minor orders are henceforth to be called *ministries.*   2927

III.   Ministries may be assigned to lay Christians; hence they are no longer to be considered as reserved to candidates for the sacrament of orders.   2928

IV.   Two ministries, adapted to present-day needs, are to be preserved in the whole Latin Church, namely, those of reader and acolyte. The functions heretofore assigned to the subdeacon are entrusted to the reader and the acolyte; consequently, the major order of subdiaconate no longer exists in the Latin Church. There is, however, no reason why the acolyte cannot be called a subdeacon in some places, at the discretion of the conference of bishops.   2929

---

4   SC art. 14 [DOL 1 no. 14].

5   See AG no. 15: AAS 58 (1966) 965; ConstDecrDecl 574; see also AG no. 17 [DOL 17 no. 249].

6   LG no. 10 [DOL 4 no. 140].

2930   V.   The reader is appointed for a function proper to him, that of reading the word of God in the liturgical assembly. Accordingly, he is to proclaim the readings from sacred Scripture, except for the gospel in the Mass and other sacred celebrations; he is to recite the psalm between the readings when there is no psalmist; he is to present the intentions for the general intercessions in the absence of a deacon or cantor; he is to direct the singing and the participation by the faithful; he is to instruct the faithful for the worthy reception of the sacraments. He may also, insofar as may be necessary, take care of preparing other faithful who are appointed on a temporary basis to read the Scriptures in liturgical celebrations. That he may more fittingly and perfectly fulfill these functions, he is to meditate assiduously on sacred Scripture.

Aware of the office he has undertaken, the reader is to make every effort and employ suitable means to acquire that increasingly warm and living love[7] and knowledge of Scripture that will make him a more perfect disciple of the Lord.

2931   VI.   The acolyte is appointed in order to aid the deacon and to minister to the priest. It is his duty therefore to attend to the service of the altar and to assist the deacon and the priest in liturgical celebrations, especially in the celebration of Mass; he is also to distribute communion as a special minister when the ministers spoken of in the *Codex Iuris Canonici* can. 845 are not available or are prevented by ill health, age, or another pastoral ministry from performing this function, or when the number of communicants is so great that the celebration of Mass would be unduly prolonged. In the same extraordinary circumstances an acolyte may be entrusted with publicly exposing the blessed sacrament for adoration by the faithful and afterward replacing it, but not with blessing the people. He may also, to the extent needed, take care of instructing other faithful who on a temporary basis are appointed to assist the priest or deacon in liturgical celebrations by carrying the missal, cross, candles, etc., or by performing other such duties. He will perform these functions more worthily if he participates in the holy eucharist with increasingly fervent devotion, receives nourishment from it, and deepens his knowledge about it.

As one set aside in a special way for the service of the altar, the acolyte should learn all matters concerning public divine worship and strive to grasp their inner spiritual meaning: in that way he will be able each day to offer himself entirely to God, be an example to all by his gravity and reverence in church, and have a sincere love for the Mystical Body of Christ, the people of God, especially for the weak and the sick.

2932   VII.   In accordance with the ancient tradition of the Church, institution to the ministries of reader and acolyte is reserved to men.[R1]

---

[7]   See SC art. 24 [DOL 1 no. 24]; DV no. 25 [DOL 14 no. 227].

[R1]   Clarification on the Motu Proprio *Ministeria quaedam:* "In reporting to their readers the two recent Motu Proprios *Ministeria quaedam* and *Ad pascendum* [DOL 319] (on the new discipline for *sacred ministries,* supplanting first tonsure, minor orders, and subdiaconate, and on admission to the diaconate) the press in various nations has made conflicting comments on *Ministeria quaedam* no. VII, which reserves to men institution as a reader or acolyte. On this point it is well to remark that the Motu Proprio *Ministeria quaedam* has opened up to laymen admission to those ministries that, as minor orders, have hitherto been reserved to clerics. On the question of women's exercising certain liturgical offices, the Motu Proprio had no intention of introducing anything new and has adhered to the prevailing norms. In any case, it would be ill-advised to anticipate or to predetermine what might be established in the future, after the study of women's part in the community life of the Church. During the 1971 Synod of Bishops, some bishops expressed the hope for such a study. As the Rev. P. Dezza has explicitly stated at the press conference of 14 Sept. at which he introduced the two papal documents, nothing therefore prevents women's continuing to be deputed for public readings during liturgical celebrations, as they have been doing for several years on the basis of the GIRM, published 3 April 1969 [see DOL 208 no. 1460]. For this function a formal and canonical institution to ministry by the bishop is not required. Similarly, according to the norms now in

VIII.   The following are requirements for admission to the ministries: 2933

    a.   the presentation of a petition that has been freely made out and signed by the aspirant to the Ordinary (the bishop and, in clerical institutes, the major superior) who has the right to accept the petition;

    b.   a suitable age and special qualities to be determined by the conference of bishops;

    c.   a firm will to give faithful service to God and the Christian people.

IX.   The ministries are conferred by the Ordinary (the bishop and, in clerical   2934
institutes, the major superior) through the liturgical rite *De institutione lectoris* and *De institutione acolythi* as revised by the Apostolic See.

X.   An interval, determined by the Holy See or the conferences of bishops, shall   2935
be observed between the conferring of the ministries of reader and acolyte whenever more than one ministry is conferred on the same person.

XI.   Unless they have already done so, candidates for ordination as deacons and   2936
priests are to receive the ministries of reader and acolyte and are to exercise them for a suitable time, in order to be better disposed for the future service of the word and of the altar. Dispensation from receiving these ministries on the part of such candidates is reserved to the Holy See.

XII.   The conferring of ministries does not bring with it the right to support or   2937
remuneration from the Church.

XIII.   The rite of institution of readers and acolytes will soon be published by the   2938
competent department of the Roman Curia.

    The effective date of these norms is 1 January 1973.

    We command as established and confirmed whatever this Motu Proprio has decreed, all things to the contrary notwithstanding.

▶   319.   PAUL VI, Motu Proprio *Ad pascendum,* norms on the diaconate, 15 August 1972:

                Ministries of reader and acolyte [no. 2580].

        no.   IV: Intervals (interstices) in the conferral of ministries [no. 2584].

341. SC DIVINE WORSHIP, **Decree** *Ministeriorum disciplina,* promulgating the *editio typica* of the rite of institution of readers and acolytes, 3 December 1972: AAS 65 (1973) 274–275; Not 9 (1973) 17.

    The discipline for ministries was established by Pope Paul VI on 15 August   2939
1972 through the Motu Proprio *Ministeria quaedam;* on the same day the norms were laid down for the diaconate, whether transitional or permanent, through the Motu Proprio *Ad pascendum.* The Congregation for Divine Worship has therefore duly pre-

---

effect, bishops may always request the Holy See for the authorization of women as special ministers of holy communion. This is the accurate meaning of the Motu Proprio *Ministeria quaedam"* (OR 6 Oct. 1972): Not 9 (1973) 16.

pared the rite of institution of readers and acolytes, the rite of admission to candidacy for ordination as deacons and priests, and the rite of commitment to celibacy.

Pope Paul VI by his authority has approved these rites and ordered their publication for use in Latin beginning on 1 January 1973. They are to be used in the vernacular beginning on a date to be established by the conferences of bishops for their own regions, after they have approved the translations and have obtained the Apostolic See's confirmation.

342. SC DIVINE WORSHIP, *Institution of Readers, Institution of Acolytes, Admission to Candidacy for Ordination as Deacons and Priests, Commitment to Celibacy,* **Introductions,** 3 December 1972: Vatican Polyglot Press, 1972.

CHAPTER I
INSTITUTION OF READERS

INTRODUCTION

2940   1.   The bishop or the major superior of a clerical religious institute carries out the institution of readers, either within Mass or at a celebration of the word of God.

2941   2.   The readings are taken in whole or in part from the liturgy of the day or, alternatively, from the texts provided in this ritual. [. . .]

CHAPTER II
INSTITUTION OF ACOLYTES

INTRODUCTION

2942   1.   The bishop or the major superior of a clerical religious institute carries out the institution of acolytes, within Mass.

2943   2.   The readings are taken in whole or in part from the liturgy of the day or, alternatively, from the texts provided in this ritual. [. . .]

CHAPTER III
ADMISSION TO CANDIDACY FOR ORDINATION AS
DEACONS AND PRIESTS

INTRODUCTION

2944   1.   The rite of admission to candidacy for ordination as deacons and priests is celebrated when there is clear evidence that the aspirants' properly formed intention has sufficiently matured.

Those who have made profession in a clerical religious institute are not bound to the celebration of this rite.

2945   2.   The aspirants must make a public expression of the intention to receive holy orders. The bishop, in turn, or the major superior of a clerical religious institute, gives the public acceptance of this intention.

2946   3.   The rite of admission may be celebrated on any day, but preferably on the greater feast days, in a church or other suitable place and either within Mass or at a celebration of the word of God. Because of its character this rite is never combined with ordinations or with the institution of readers or of acolytes.

4.   The readings are taken, in whole or in part, from the liturgy of the day or,   2947
alternatively, from those provided in this ritual. [. . .]

CHAPTER IV
COMMITMENT TO CELIBACY

1.   Religious included, candidates for the priesthood and unmarried candidates for   2948
the diaconate must make a public acceptance of celibacy before they go on to the
rite of ordination as deacons. [. . .]

▶   307.   SC DIVINE WORSHIP, Communication *La Sacra Congregazione,* on the effective
date of the new rites of confirmation and of institution to ministries, 8 December
1972.

343. SC DIVINE WORSHIP, *Rite of Commissioning Special Ministers of Holy Communion,* **Introduction,** 29 January 1973: Not 9 (1973) 165–167.

RITE OF COMMISSIONING A SPECIAL MINISTER OF HOLY COMMUNION

1.   When the local Ordinary or his delegate[1] deputes anyone in particular circum-   2949
stances as a special minister of holy communion, that person should receive a
mandate according to the following rite.[2] This rite may take place either within or
outside Mass, with a congregation present. [. . .]

RITE OF COMMISSIONING A MINISTER OF HOLY COMMUNION ON A SINGLE OCCASION

10.   When anyone is deputed in cases of genuine need to distribute holy commun-   2950
ion,[3] that person should receive a mandate according to the following rite.

ON THE RITE TO BE OBSERVED BY A SPECIAL MINISTER IN DISTRIBUTING HOLY COMMUNION

13.   The special minister who is to distribute communion is to wear either the   2951
liturgical vestment in use locally or clothing befitting this sacred ministry. [. . .]

15.   In giving communion outside Mass a special minister observes the rite set forth   2952
in the Roman Ritual.

▶   279.   SC DIVINE WORSHIP, *Holy Communion and Worship of the Eucharist outside Mass,*
Chapter 3, Eucharistic Worship, Introductions, 21 June 1973.

nos. 91–92:   Minister for exposition of the blessed sacrament
[nos. 2217–18].

---

[1]   See Instr. *Immensae caritatis* 1, nos. I and VI [DOL 264 nos. 2075, 2080].

[2]   The texts for the rite, which are given for the case of one man being commissioned, may be adapted in gender for the case of a woman or in number for the case of several persons.

[3]   See Instr. *Immensae caritatis* 1, nos. II and VI [DOL 264 nos. 2076, 2080].

344. SC CLERGY, **Letter** of Cardinal J. Wright to Cardinal J. Döpfner, President of the German conference of bishops, on preaching by the laity, 20 November 1973.*

2953   The noble duty of taking part in the Church's saving mission rests on all the faithful; this is the mind of Vatican Council II. For this reason the general synod of the West German dioceses decided to urge the laity toward wholehearted dedication of their apostolic efforts within the family of the Church. Prompted by this laudable ideal, the participants in the synod, meeting 3–7 January 1973 in the cathedral of Würzburg, called for lay participation in the preaching office in the Church. They expressed their decision in these words: "Lay people must have a part in proclaiming the word of God: by witnessing to their faith during the liturgy; after receiving canonical mission, by giving the sermon or conference at liturgical services; in exceptional cases, by giving the homily during Mass" (*Die Beteilung der Laien an der Verkündigung* no. 3).

In the name of the bishops of West Germany, Your Eminence has on 22 February 1973 sent that resolution to this Congregation, with the request for the appropriate, required permission of the Holy See.

2954   This Congregation had already treated the point in the past at a plenary meeting. Nevertheless, keeping in mind the reply of the Fathers of the Pontifical Commission for the Interpretation of the Decrees of Vatican Council II, 11 January 1971,[a] the Congregation along with other curial congregations has again dealt fully with this proposal, consulting especially with the Congregations for the Doctrine of the Faith and for Divine Worship and with the Council for the Laity.

2955   The Congregation gladly acknowledges that the apostolate of the laity in both the world and the Church, so often emphasized and endorsed by Vatican Council II, has by now a long tradition in Germany. Unquestionably, approval must be given to that sincere cooperation that the laity are giving to the ordained ministers in all the works of evangelization. By reason of the people of God's shared responsibility for proclaiming the word of God, the German synod's desire is that such cooperation extend also to the office of preaching at liturgical services.

We must, however, note the Council's teaching that the preaching office in the Church belongs first of all to the bishops as the teachers vested with authority, then to priests as the bishops' cooperators, and finally to deacons. Accordingly, the Council teaches that there is an intimate connection between holy orders and the preaching office. The theme of the people of God's shared responsibility for proclaiming his word must therefore be understood of the people of God as constituted hierarchically, that is, through the sacrament of holy orders.

2956   For this reason it will be readily understood that we of the Congregation have been confronted by the same problem discussed and debated within the German conference of bishops and the sessions of the synod. That problem is: whether extending the office of preaching to the laity will obscure the essential distinction existing between the ministerial priesthood of priests and the universal priesthood of all believers. The problem would be intensified if use of the permission were to develop not as the exception but as the rule. This applies especially to lay preaching

---

*   Prot. 144823/1; text in ArchKathKRecht 142 (1973) 480–482.

a   See DOL 215.

during the Mass: the liturgy of the word and the liturgy of the eucharist are so closely connected that they form but a single act of worship[b] and in the Mass of the community the priest exercises not only his ministry of word and sacrifice but also his office as pastor of the people.

In order therefore that in liturgical services the office of preaching will be fulfilled by ordained ministers, vocations to the priesthood and the diaconate must be promoted through every available means. We are deeply convinced that in this regard bishops must leave no measure untried; this is an essential element of their pastoral concern.

We recognize, however, the special circumstances of the German dioceses, especially the shortage of clergy and the urgent need to provide for the care of souls. Therefore, in the manner here to be indicated, laypersons may be deputed for the office of preaching at liturgical services on the grounds of serving either as substitutes or as assistants.

1.   In places lacking a priest or deacon, bishops are to choose laypersons who will be empowered to give a homily during the celebration of the word of God so that on Sundays and holydays of obligation the faithful may receive help to sanctify the day.

    2957

2.   a.   During a Mass the celebrant normally gives the sermon.

    2958

    b.   But a celebrant may be physically or morally prevented from fulfilling this function, no other priest or deacon may be available, and thus the faithful may be deprived of the spiritual help coming from the word of God. In such a case of compelling or reasonable need, bishops have the power to grant to laypersons the faculty to preach even during a Mass.

    c.   Bishops are empowered to grant the same faculty when on a particular occasion (for example, celebrations on behalf of the Christian family, to promote works of charity or foreign missions, or other celebrations at the discretion of the bishop) laypersons are available who have special qualifications and whose words are likely to be especially effective.

3.   If circumstances permit, the celebrant gives an introduction or conclusion to sermons by the laity.

    2959

4.   To empower them to exercise the office of preaching at liturgical services, laypersons need to receive from the bishop a canonical mission, that is, delegation.

When the faculty to preach is to be of extended duration and in those cases indicated in no. 2, b and c, the bishop in person is to bestow the canonical mission. He may grant the faculty to subdelegate this canonical mission only to assistant bishops, vicars general, and episcopal vicars.

The bishop has the power to revoke the canonical mission for what he judges to be well-founded reasons.

5.   The appointment of laypersons must follow to the letter the rules to be issued by the conference of bishops. Criteria of selection must be, besides the requisite knowledge, a Christian manner of life and docility toward the Church's magisterium and lawful local pastors.

    2960

---

[b]   See DOL 1 no. 56.

2961   6.   In the case of those who have returned from the clerical to the lay state, the norms of the Congregation for the Doctrine of the Faith (AAS 63 [1971] 308, no. 4 b) apply.ᶜ

2962   7.   The present rules, amending *Codex Iuris Canonici* can. 1342, § 2, are given as an experiment and will remain in effect as the petition requests for four years. At the end of this period the conference of bishops will submit a report of the results to the Holy See.

2963   8.   Because of the seriousness of the matter, each bishop of West Germany before putting the present faculties into effect must first hear the opinion of the priests' council.

Pope Paul VI has graciously approved the present rules, trusting that, with any kind of abuse being prevented, this apostolic concession will truly serve to the advantage of the faithful of Germany.

345. SC DIVINE WORSHIP, **Letter** of Cardinal J.R. Knox to Bishop R. Coffy, President of the French bishops' committee on liturgy, on delegation for the rite of institution to ministry, 7 June 1974 (French).*

2964   The issue involved is one of ministries (of reader or of acolyte) and not of holy orders; their conferral or institution belongs to an Ordinary. Therefore, he has the power to delegate without an indult from the Apostolic See.

346. SC SACRAMENTS AND DIVINE WORSHIP, **Letter** *Novit profecto* to presidents of the conferences of bishops, on new ministries to be established by the conferences of bishops, 27 October 1977.*

2965   As Your Excellency well knows, a much debated issue of our times is that of admitting the laity to carry out forms of ministry. This is especially so after Vatican Council II's exposition in many documents of the teaching on the place of the laity in the Church's apostolate and after the conciliar exhortation that "they too take an active part in the saving work of the Church according to their own abilities and the needs of the times" (LG no. 33).

Many documents of the Holy See during recent years have given impetus to lay Catholics to participate in the pastoral activity of the Church. Notable in this regard is the Motu Proprio *Ministeria quaedam:* after abolishing minor orders and making diaconal ordination the way of admission into the clergy, this document sanctioned new forms of ministry, *issuing not from holy orders but from ecclesial institution.*ᵃ

Ministeria quaedam further establishes the ministries of reader and acolyte for the entire Latin Church: but it also adds: "Besides the offices universal in the Latin Church, the conferences of bishops may request others of the Apostolic See, if they

---

ᶜ   See DOL 317 no. 2561.

*   SCDW, Prot. N. 221/69.

*   SCSDW, Prot. N. 1837/77.

ᵃ   See DOL 340 no. 2924.

judge the establishment of such offices in their region to be necessary or very useful because of special reasons."[b]

In keeping with the options granted by *Ministeria quaedam,* a number of conferences of bishops have requested the establishment of further ministries. Therefore Pope Paul VI has ordered the Congregation for the Sacraments and Divine Worship to prepare a plan for the establishment of new ministries, not connected with holy orders, that might be introduced into the practice of the Latin Church. The power also would be granted to confer these ministries on women, especially women religious.

A commission made up of experts in the matter and of representatives of the curial congregations involved has given careful consideration to this rather complex issue. Then on 22–23 November 1976 the same issue was submitted to examination by the cardinals and bishops, members of the Congregation for the Sacraments and Divine Worship, who were meeting in Rome for a plenary session. From these consultations it became clear that various questions and obstacles made it inadvisable at this time to establish new ministries in the universal Church. The opinion that prevailed was the position of those who recommended a delay on this matter until there should be more information on the effects and development of local experiments.

This being the case, and with the determinations of *Ministeria quaedam* being duly respected, Pope Paul VI has decided to grant to conferences of bishops requesting it from the Apostolic See permission to establish new ministries that they deem truly necessary or very useful in their own regions. Accordingly, the episcopates concerned may send the petition to this Congregation. They are to set forth the reasons for such a request together with the statutes containing one by one and distinctly the norms on the choice, spiritual and cultural formation, duties and activities of the new ministers, as well as the plan proposed to guide and help them pastorally in the practice of their distinct ministries.

It need hardly be mentioned that these new ministries may also be conferred on women.

▶   See also Chapter Six. Music

[b]   See DOL 340 no. 2923.

2966

Section 6. Marriage

SUMMARY (DOL 347–357). The Constitution on the Liturgy art. 77–78 decreed a revision of the rite of marriage and made quite explicit the possibilities for adaptation of the rite to different cultures and peoples. Vatican Council II's marked attention to ecumenism has also been significantly reflected in the postconciliar discipline regarding mixed marriages. The present section therefore has two subsections.

Section 6. Marriage: A. The Rite of Marriage

SUMMARY (DOL 347–350). The new rite of marriage revised according to the conciliar directive appeared in 1969. The major texts here are the decree promulgating the rite (DOL 348) and the introduction to the rite itself (DOL 349). In addition there is a particular reply on the nuptial blessing (DOL 347) and an address of John Paul II on the sacrament of marriage (DOL 350).

▶   1.   VATICAN COUNCIL II, Constitution on the Liturgy *Sacrosanctum Concilium*, 3
        December 1963:

        art. 36, 63 a: Use of the vernacular [nos. 36, 63].
              77–78:   Rite of marriage [nos. 77–78].

▶   20. PAUL VI, Motu Proprio *Sacram Liturgiam*, on putting into effect some prescriptions
        of the Constitution on the Liturgy, 25 January 1964:

        art. V: Marriage within or outside Mass [no. 283].

▶   23. SC RITES (Consilium), Instruction (first) *Inter Oecumenici*, 26 September 1964:

        nos. 61 a: Use of the vernacular [no. 353].
              70–75:   Rite of marriage [nos. 362–367].

▶   4.   VATICAN COUNCIL II, Dogmatic Constitution on the Church *Lumen gentium*, 21
        November 1964:

        no. 11:   Sacrament of marriage and family life [no. 141].

▶   16. VATICAN COUNCIL II, Decree on the Apostolate of the Laity *Apostolicam actuosi-
        tatem*, 18 November 1965:

        no. 11:   Family life and the apostolate [no. 245].

347. SC RITES, **Reply** (Holland), on the nuptial blessing during "closed
times," 24 November 1965: Not 2 (1966) 181.

2967   His Excellency Jan G. M. Bluyssen, Titular Bishop of Aeto and Vicar General
of 's-Hertogenbosch, in the name of all Ordinaries of Holland, submitted the following query to the Congregation of Rites for the appropriate reply.

        In view of the *Codex Iuris Canonici* can. 1108, §§ 2 and 3 of the Instruction of the
Congregation of Rites, 26 September 1964, nos. 70–75,[a] may the solemn nuptial
blessing be given during a closed time without permission of the local Ordinary?

        After thoroughly considering the matter, the same Congregation replied: Yes,
but provided the Instruction mentioned, no. 75, is observed.

▶   19. VATICAN COUNCIL II, Pastoral Constitution *Gaudium et spes*, 7 December 1965:

        nos. 48–52:   Dignity of marriage and of the family [nos.
                               271–273].

▶   105. PAUL VI, Motu Proprio *De Episcoporum muneribus*, on norms for the power of
        dispensation, 15 June 1966:

        IX no. 17:   Dispensation from the canonical form of marriage
                               [no. 748].

▶   179. SC RITES (Consilium), Instruction *Eucharisticum mysterium*, on worship of the eu-
        charist, 25 May 1967:

_____

a   See DOL 23 nos. 362–367.

nos. 32, 2 and 11:   Communion under both kinds [no. 1261].
            36:        Communion of the bride and groom [no. 1265].

▶   309.   PAUL VI, Motu Proprio *Sacrum Diaconatus Ordinem*, restoring the permanent diaco-
           nate in the Latin Church, 18 June 1967:

    no. 22, 4:   Deacon assisting at marriage [no. 2536].

▶   312.   CONGREGATION FOR THE DISCIPLINE OF THE SACRAMENTS, Letter to
           U.S. conference of bishops, on permanent deacons assisting at a marriage, 30
           August 1968.

348. SC RITES, **Decree** *Ordo celebrandi Matrimonium*, promulgating the *editio typica* of the rite of marriage, 19 March 1969: Not 5 (1969) 203.

The rite for celebrating marriage has been revised according to the norms of   2968
the Constitution on the Liturgy, in order that this rite might be enriched, more
clearly signify the grace of the sacrament, and impart a knowledge of the obligation
of the married couple.[a] This revision has been carried out by the Consilium for the
Implementation of the Constitution on the Sacred Liturgy. By his apostolic authority, Pope Paul VI has approved this rite and ordered its publication. Therefore this
Congregation, acting on the express mandate of the Pope, publishes this rite and
directs that it be used from 1 July 1969.

349. SC RITES, *Rite of Marriage,* **Introduction**, 19 March 1969: Vatican Polyglot Press, 1969; Not 5 (1969) 216–220.

INTRODUCTION

IMPORTANCE AND DIGNITY OF THE SACRAMENT OF MARRIAGE

1.   In virtue of the sacrament of marriage, married Christians signify and share in   2969
the mystery of the unity and fruitful love that exists between Christ and his
Church;[1] they thus help each other to attain holiness in their married life and in
welcoming and rearing children; and they have their own special place and gift
among the people of God.[2]

2.   A marriage is established by the marriage covenant, the irrevocable consent   2970
that the spouses freely give to and receive from each other. This unique union of a
man and woman and the good of the children impose total fidelity on each of them
and the unbreakable unity of their bond. To make the indissoluble marriage covenant a clearer sign of this full meaning and a surer help in its fulfillment, Christ the

---

   a   See DOL 1 no. 77.

   1   See Eph 5:32.

   2   See 1 Cor 7:7. LG no. 11 [DOL 4 no. 141].

Lord raised it to the dignity of a sacrament, modeled on his own nuptial bond with the Church.[3]

2971   3.   Christian couples, therefore, are to strive to nourish and develop their marriage by undivided affection, which wells up from the fountain of divine love: in a merging of the human and the divine, they remain faithful in body and in mind, in good times as in bad.[4]

2972   4.   By their very nature, the institution of marriage and wedded love have as their purpose the procreation and education of children and find in them their ultimate crown. Children are the most precious gift of a marriage and contribute most to the well-being of the parents. Therefore, married Christians, without in any way considering the other purposes of marriage of less account, should be steadfast and ready to cooperate with the love of the Creator and Savior, who through them will constantly enrich and enlarge his own family.[5]

2973   5.   A priest should bear in mind these doctrinal principles, both in his instructions to those preparing to be married and when giving the homily during the marriage ceremony; he should relate the homily to the text of the sacred readings.[6]

The bridal couple should, if necessary, be given a review of these fundamentals of Christian doctrine; then the catechesis for marriage should include the teachings on marriage and the family, on the sacrament itself and its rites, prayers, and readings. In this way the bridegroom and the bride will receive far greater benefit from the celebration of the sacrament.

2974   6.   In the celebration of marriage (which normally should be within Mass), certain elements should be stressed. The first is the liturgy of the word, which brings out the importance of Christian marriage in the history of salvation and the duties and responsibilities it involves for the sanctification of the couple and their children. Also to be emphasized are: the consent of the contracting parties, which the priest asks and receives; the special nuptial blessing on the bride, by which the priest implores God's blessing on the marriage covenant; and, finally, the reception of holy communion by the groom and the bride and by others present, which above all is the source of love and lifts us up into communion with our Lord and with one another.[7]

2975   7.   Priests should first of all strengthen and nourish the faith of those about to be married, for the sacrament of marriage presupposes and demands faith.[8]

CHOICE OF RITE

2976   8.   In a marriage between a Catholic and a baptized person who is not a Catholic, the rite of marriage outside Mass (nos. 39–54) shall be used. If the situation warrants and if the local Ordinary gives permission, the rite for celebrating marriage within Mass (nos. 19–38) may be used, except that communion is not given to the non-Catholic, since the general law does not allow it.

---

[3]   See GS no. 48 [DOL 19 no. 271].

[4]   See GS nos. 48, 49 [DOL 19 nos. 271,272].

[5]   See GS nos. 48 [DOL 19 no. 271], 50.

[6]   See SC art. 52 [DOL 1 no. 52]. SCR, Instr. InterOec, 26 Sept. 1964, no. 54 [DOL 23 no. 346].

[7]   See AA no. 3 [DOL 16 no. 232]; LG no. 12 [DOL 4 no. 142].

[8]   See SC art. 59 [DOL 1 no. 59].

In a marriage between a Catholic and one who is not baptized, the rite in nos. 55–66 of the ritual is to be followed.

9.   Furthermore, priests should show special consideration for those who take part in liturgical celebrations or hear the Gospel only on the occasion of a wedding, either because they are not Catholics or because they are Catholics who rarely if ever take part in the eucharist or who apparently have lost their faith. Priests after all are ministers of Christ's Gospel to everyone.

2977

10. In the celebration of marriage, apart from the liturgical laws providing for due honors to civil authorities, there is to be no preferential treatment of any private persons or classes of person, whether in the ceremonies or by external display.[9]

2978

11. Whenever marriage is celebrated during Mass, white vestments are worn and the wedding Mass is used. If the marriage is celebrated on a Sunday or solemnity, the Mass of the day is used with the nuptial blessing and the special final blessing according to the circumstances.

2979

The liturgy of the word as adapted to the marriage celebration, however, is a highly effective means for the catechesis on the sacrament of marriage and its duties. Therefore when the wedding Mass may not be held, one of the readings from the texts provided for the marriage celebration (nos. 67–105) may be chosen, except from Holy Thursday to Easter, on the solemnities of Epiphany, Ascension, Pentecost, or Corpus Christi, or on holydays of obligation. On the Sundays of the Christmas season and in Ordinary Time, the entire wedding Mass may be used in Masses that are not parish Masses.

When a marriage is celebrated during Advent or Lent or other days of penance, the parish priest should advise the couple to take into consideration the special nature of these liturgical seasons.

PREPARATION OF LOCAL RITUALS

12. Without prejudice to the faculty spoken of in no. 17 for regions where the Roman Ritual for marriage is used, particular rituals shall be prepared, suitable for the customs and needs of individual areas, in conformity with the norms of the Constitution on the Liturgy art. 63 b and 77.[a] Decisions on this matter are to be reviewed by the Apostolic See.

2980

In making adaptations, the following points must be remembered.

13. The formularies of the Roman Ritual may be adapted or, as the case may be, supplemented (including the questions before the consent and the actual words of consent).

2981

When the Roman Ritual has several optional formularies, local rituals may add others of the same type.

14. Within the actual rite of the sacrament of marriage, the arrangement of parts may be varied. If it seems more suitable, even the questions before the consent may be omitted as long as the assisting priest asks for and receives the consent of the contracting parties.

2982

---

   [9]   See SC art. 32 [DOL 1 no. 32].

   [a]   See DOL 1 nos. 63 and 77.

2983   15. After the exchange of rings, the crowning or veiling of the bride may take place according to local custom.

In any region where the joining of hands or the blessing or exchange of rings does not fit in with the practice of the people, the conference of bishops may allow these rites to be omitted or other rites substituted.

2984   16. As for the marriage customs of nations that are now receiving the Gospel for the first time, whatever is good and is not indissolubly bound up with superstition and error should be sympathetically considered and, if possible, preserved intact. Such things may in fact be taken over into the liturgy itself, as long as they harmonize with its true and authentic spirit.[10]

RIGHT TO PREPARE A COMPLETELY NEW RITE

2985   17. Each conference of bishops may draw up its own marriage rite suited to the usages of the place and people and approved by the Apostolic See. A necessary condition, however, is that in the rite the priest assisting at such marriages must ask for and receive the consent of the contracting parties[11] and the nuptial blessing should always be given.[12]

2986   18. Among peoples where the marriage ceremonies customarily take place in the home, sometimes over a period of several days, their customs should be adapted to the Christian spirit and to the liturgy. In such cases the conference of bishops, according to the pastoral needs of the people, may allow the sacramental rite to be celebrated in the home.[R1]

---

10   See SC art. 37 [DOL 1 no. 37].

11   See SC art. 77 [DOL 1 no. 77].

12   See SC art. 78 [DOL 1 no. 78].

R1   SCDW, Guidelines "Music in the Marriage Liturgy":
The *Rite of Marriage* has restored a genuinely liturgical tone to the wedding celebration. Since its introduction, from many quarters, regions, and peoples, the Congregation for Divine Worship has been requested for an evaluation, in the context of the liturgy, of some musical compositions that continue in widespread use and are regarded as "traditional" for weddings. Specific examples cited are: Mendelssohn's "Wedding March," Wagner's "Wedding March," Handel's "Largo," Gounod's "Ave Maria," Schubert's "Ave Maria," Stradella's "Aria di Chiesa." The Congregation has questioned thirteen international experts on this point, nine musicians and four liturgists. From their replies certain guidelines have emerged. We think it useful to present a synthesis of these in order to provide a general way for addressing this problem.
      1. The experts questioned have for the most part expressed a negative opinion, not questioning the intrinsic artistic worth of the pieces, but judging them unsuited to use in the liturgy. To accept such music without qualification would mean continuing something now out of date.
      2. It is possible that use and the passage of time have invested such compositions with the quality of being sacred. Nevertheless, there is a duty and a need to give preference to melodies and songs meant not just for listening but for genuine community participation. This is what the norms and spirit of the reform of the liturgy require.
      3. The pieces in question at this point belong to the past and to a repertoire that liturgically is nonfunctional, obsolete in style, and in need of gradual reform. We must look to the concern of Vatican Council II that every element of the liturgical celebration fit into it harmoniously and we must remember that, as the conciliar Constitution states (SC art. 112 [DOL 1 no. 112]), sacred music will be holy to the degree that it is closely bound to the actual liturgical rite as a more pleasing expression of prayer and an aid to the community's union of spirit. Such considerations impose the task of gradually replacing the old musical compositions with a repertoire matching the conciliar legislation and the norms of the Instruction *Musicam sacram* [DOL 508]. This music must be adapted to the level of the people's culture, to socio-musical development, and above all to the level of liturgical formation. The work is a matter at once of music and of pastoral liturgy.
      4. According to the Constitution on the Liturgy art. 39 and 119 [DOL 1 nos. 39 and 119] and the Instruction *Musicam sacram* no. 12 [DOL 508 no. 4133], it belongs to the competent, ecclesiastical territorial authority — the conference of bishops — to decide on the adaptation, within established limits,

▶ 208. SC RITES (Consilium); SC DIVINE WORSHIP, General Instruction of the Roman Missal, 1st. ed. 6 April 1969; 4th ed. 27 March 1975:

no. 242, § 2, 11:   Communion under both kinds at weddings.

▶ 169. SC CLERGY, *General Catechetical Directory*, 11 April 1971:

nos. 59:   Catechesis for marriage [no. 1106].
      78:          Catechesis by parents [no. 1107].

▶ 305. SC DIVINE WORSHIP, *Rite of Confirmation*, Introduction, 22 August 1971:

no. 12:   Confirmation and marriage [no. 2521].

350. JOHN PAUL II, **Address** to delegates of the committee of the Centre de Liaison des Equipes de Recherche and to members of the council of the Fédération Internationale d'Action Familiale, on Christian marriage, 3 November 1979: Not 15 (1979) 673–674 (French; excerpt).

It is of primary importance for Christians that they raise the level of discourse by looking immediately to the theological aspect of the family and, consequently, by dwelling on the sacramental reality of marriage. That sacramentality is intelligible only in the light of the history of salvation. This history has the character of being a history of covenant and of communion, first between Yahweh and Israel, then between Jesus Christ and the Church, which is now the Church in expectation of the eschatological covenant. The Council states precisely: "The Savior of all, Bridegroom of the Church, comes forward to meet Christian spouses through the sacrament of marriage" (GS 48, § 2). Christian marriage is related to the history of the covenant as being at once its memorial, its actualization, and its prophecy. St. Paul calls it "a great mystery." When they marry, Christian spouses not only begin a saga of their own, even in the sense of their own sanctification and mission; they also begin a saga that involves them in a responsible way in the great saga of the history of salvation.

2987

Their marriage is a *memorial*: the sacrament gives them the grace and the duty to bring to mind the great works of God and to bear witness to them for their children. Their marriage is an *actualization*: it gives them the grace and the duty of putting into effect in the here and now the demands of a forgiving and redemptive love, both toward each other and toward their children. Their marriage is a *prophecy*: it gives them the grace and duty of living out the hope of their future encounter with Christ and of being witnesses to that hope.

of liturgical texts and in particular the music for them. According to the recent Third General Instruction no. 3 c [DOL 52 no. 517], it belongs to the conference of bishops and, when there are no general norms, to the bishops within their own dioceses: to establish a collection of songs intended for special groups; to decide whether in practice the various musical forms are in keeping with the spirit of the liturgical rites and with the character of each particular phase of the rites. The criterion is that the music does not interfere with the participation of the entire assembly, but rather fixes the mind's attention and the heart's sentiments on the sacred rites.

5. The most important task of all continues to be education in the new liturgical point of view that is being advanced by the current reform. That reform sees sacred music and singing as having the noble ministerial purpose of furthering the faithful's complete and active participation as a community and of being at the same time a necessary and integrating element of the solemn liturgy (SC art. 112 [DOL 1 no. 112]): Not 7 (1971) 110–111. See also Not 8 (1972) 25–29.

2988   It is quite true that every sacrament brings with it a share in the nuptial love of Christ for the Church. But in marriage the mode and substance of this participation are specific. The mode is the way in which the spouses share in it precisely as spouses, that is, the two as one couple. This is so true that the primary and immediate effect of the sacrament of marriage (*res et sacramentum*) is not supernatural grace itself but the Christian marriage bond: a communion specifically Christian because it represents the mystery of Christ's incarnation and the mystery of covenant. The substance of their participation in Christ's life is also specific: marital love involves a totality, embracing all the components of the person — the drives of body and instinct, the power of sense and emotion, the longings of mind and will. That love is bent on a deeply personal unity that, surpassing the union in one flesh, leads to the formation of but one heart and one soul. That love demands its being unbreakable and faithful in an absolute, mutual self-giving. That love opens the way to fruitfulness (see the Encyclical *Humanae vitae*). Briefly, it is a matter of all the normal qualities of natural marital love but with a new signification. This signification not only purifies those qualities and strengthens them, but elevates them to the level of being the expression of distinctively Christian values.

       Such is the exalted point of view that Christian spouses are to adopt: it means for them their dignity, their strength, their challenge, and their joy.

SECTION 6. MARRIAGE: B. MIXED MARRIAGES

SUMMARY (DOL 351–357). The developments on the issue of mixed marriages, including their liturgical celebration, are reflected in the major texts here: an instruction of the Congregation for the Doctrine of the Faith (DOL 351); Paul VI's Motu Proprio *Matrimonia mixta* (DOL 354), along with two official interpretations on its provisions (DOL 355 and 357), and a decree specifically for Christians of the Eastern Churches (DOL 352). From the ecumenical dialogue on mixed marriage there is a liturgical excerpt (DOL 356). Finally, a particular rescript reflects church discipline on the assistance of a non-Catholic pastor at a marriage in a Catholic church (DOL 353).

▶   5.   VATICAN COUNCIL II, Decree on the Eastern Churches *Orientalium Ecclesiarum*, 21 November 1964:

no.   18:   Marriage with non-Catholic Eastern Christians [no. 172].

351. SC DOCTRINE OF THE FAITH, Instruction *Matrimonii sacramentum*, on mixed marriages, 18 March 1966: AAS 58 (1966) 235–239 (excerpt).

2989   The sacrament of marriage was established by Christ the Lord as a sign of his own union with the Church. For marriage to have its full sacred power and to become in truth for the spouses that great mystery (see Eph 5:32) by which in their intimacy of life they become a sign of Christ's love in giving himself for all, it absolutely demands full and complete harmony between the spouses, especially in matters of religion. [. . .] Therefore the Church exercises the utmost care and vigilance to see that Catholics marry Catholics. [. . .]

2990   III.   In the celebration of mixed marriages the canonical form, as stipulated in can. 1094, must be observed. This is a requirement for the validity of a marriage.

          In the event of problems, the Ordinary is to refer the case with all its details to the Apostolic See.

2991   IV.   With regard to the liturgical form, amending can. 1102 § 2 and can. 1109, § 3, it is granted to local Ordinaries to allow mixed marriages also to be celebrated with all the rites, the usual blessings, and a sermon.

2992   V.   Any marriage celebration before a Catholic priest and a non-Catholic minister who together carry out their respective rites is absolutely forbidden.

          However, on completion of the religious ceremony, nothing stands in the way of the non-Catholic minister's offering words of congratulation and encouragement and reciting prayers with the non-Catholics who are present. Such arrangements are allowed on approval by the local Ordinary and with the necessary precautions to avoid any danger of shocking the people.

▶   105.   PAUL VI, Motu Proprio *De Episcoporum muneribus*, on norms for the power of dispensation, 15 June 1966:

IX no. 18 c: *Sanatio in radice* in mixed marriages [no. 749].

352. SC EASTERN CHURCHES, Decree *Crescens matrimoniorum*, on mixed marriages between Catholics and non-Catholic Eastern Christians, 22 February 1967: AAS 59 (1967) 165–166.

2993   There has been a growing frequency of mixed marriages between Eastern Catholics and other Eastern non-Catholics Christians in the Eastern patriarchates and eparchies, as well as in Latin dioceses, and with this increase a need to meet the resultant problems. On this account Vatican Council II decreed: "To prevent invalidity in the case of marriages between Eastern Catholics and baptized Eastern non-Catholics and to provide for the stability and sanctity of marriage and for family peace, this Council decrees that for such marriages the canonical form is obligatory only as to their lawfulness; for their validity the presence of a sacred minister suffices, as long as the other requirements of law are met" (OE no. 18).[a]

In the special conditions now prevailing, mixed marriages between Latin-rite Catholics and Eastern non-Catholic Christians are taking place and the differences in canonical discipline are engendering many serious problems both in the East and in the West. Therefore requests have come to Pope Paul VI from various places asking that he consent to make canonical practice uniform, granting to Latin-rite Catholics what has been established for Eastern-rite Catholics.

Pope Paul VI, after thorough consideration and investigation, has decided to honor the requests and desires directed to him. He has graciously granted that, in all parts of the world, when Catholics of either the Latin or an Eastern rite enter into a marriage with Eastern non-Catholic Christians, the canonical form for the celebration of these marriages binds only in regard to lawfulness; for validity the presence of an ordained minister suffices, as long as the other requirements of law are observed. The reasons for this concession are: to prevent invalid marriages between Latin-rite Catholics and non-Catholic Christians of the Eastern rites; to provide for the stability and sanctity of marriage; to increase charity between the Catholic faithful and the Eastern faithful separated from us.   2994

Care must be taken under the supervision of the bishops that such marriages are accurately recorded as soon as possible in the prescribed registers. The same also applies to the marriages that, in accord with the provisions of the conciliar Decree on the Eastern Churches no. 18,[b] Eastern Catholics contract with baptized, Eastern non-Catholics.   2995

In the interest of the sanctity of marriage, non-Catholic ministers are respectfully and urgently requested to cooperate in seeing to it that a record of the wedding is made in the register pertaining to the Catholic party, whether of the Latin or an Eastern rite.

Further, local Ordinaries dispensing from the matrimonial impediment of mixed religion are also granted the faculty of dispensing from the obligation of observing the canonical form for lawfulness whenever there are problems that in their prudent judgment require such a dispensation.   2996

Pope Paul VI has directed the Congregation for the Eastern Churches, over which he himself presides, that this important decision and concession be published. Accordingly, the same Congregation, after consultation with the Congregation for the Doctrine of the Faith, has drawn up the present decree by mandate of Pope Paul for publication in the *Acta Apostolicae Sedis*.   2997

So that this new discipline may become known to all concerned, whether they belong to a Catholic rite or are Orthodox Christians, the present Decree will take effect on 25 March 1967, the Feast of the Annunciation of the Blessed Virgin Mary.

▶   147.   SECRETARIAT FOR CHRISTIAN UNITY, Ecumenical Directory I, 14 March 1967:

        nos. 49 and 58:   Witnesses at mixed marriages [nos. 1003 and 1012].

---

a   DOL 5 no. 172.

b   See DOL 5 no. 172.

▶ 312. SC DISCIPLINE OF THE SACRAMENTS, Letter to U.S. conference of bishops, on permanent deacons assisting at a marriage, 30 August 1968.

353. SC DOCTRINE OF THE FAITH, Rescript (U.S.A.) to Archbishop Leo Binz (Saint Paul-Minneapolis, U.S.A.), on a mixed marriage in a church in the presence of a Lutheran minister, 3 September 1968.*

2998   In your letter of 1 July 1968 Your Excellency requested dispensation from the canonical form of marriage along with the dispensation from the matrimonial impediments of mixed religion and disparity of cult. The marriage was to be contracted between *N.N.*, a Catholic woman and *N.N.*, a non-Catholic man. The parties, who have already made the canonical promises, request that the *marriage ceremony take place in a Catholic church with the father of the non-Catholic party*, who is a Lutheran minister, assisting.

    I wish to inform you on this matter that after duly considering all the circumstances this Congregation has decided that it cannot grant this request. To date there *has never been* exception on this point, in spite of numerous similar petitions. If necessary Your Excellency may employ the dispensation from the canonical form in order that *the parties may enter into the marriage in a non-Catholic church*, in the presence of a non-Catholic minister.

354. PAUL VI, Motu Proprio *Matrimonia mixta*, on mixed marriages, 31 March 1970: AAS 62 (1970) 257–263 (excerpts).

2999   Mixed marriages — that is, marriages between a Catholic party and a non-Catholic party, baptized or nonbaptized — have always been dealt with by the Church as a serious part of its responsibility. [. . .]

3000   The Church recognizes that mixed marriages, which are the consequence of diversity of religions and the division of Christians, with rare exceptions do not contribute to the reestablishment of the unity of Christians. Many problems are inherent in a mixed marriage itself, because a degree of division is introduced into the living nucleus of the Church, as the Christian family is so rightly called; within the family, obedience to the teachings of the Gospel is made harder because of differences in matters of religion, especially with regard to taking part in the Church's worship and the upbringing of children. [. . .]

3001   The Church does not attach equal value in either its teaching or its laws to a marriage between a Catholic and a baptized non-Catholic and a marriage between a Catholic and a nonbaptized partner. For, as Vatican Council II has declared, those who, although not Catholics, "believe in Christ and have received baptism rightly are established in a true, even though incomplete, communion with the Catholic Church."[1] Eastern Christians, baptized outside the Catholic Church, although separated from communion with us, possess genuine sacraments in their own Churches,

---

  * SCDF, Prot. N. 3218/68m.

  [1] UR no. 3: AAS 57 (1965) 93; ConstDecrDecl 248. See also LG no. 15: AAS 57 (1965) 19–20; ConstDecrDecl 119–120.

especially priesthood and eucharist, which join them with us by a very close bond.[2] In a marriage between the baptized, a true sacrament, there exists a certain sharing in spiritual goods that is missing in a marriage between a baptized spouse and one who is not.

Even so, the problems that are present in mixed marriages between the baptized must not be disregarded. For there is often a difference of opinion between them on: the character of marriage as a sacrament; the proper meaning of a marriage celebrated in the Church; the interpretation of moral principles relevant to marriage and the family; the limits set by the obedience due to the Catholic Church; the scope of ecclesiastical authority. Plainly these difficult problems can only be solved fully when Christian unity is restored. [. . .]   3002

Furthermore, in a mixed marriage the Catholic party is bound by the obligation not only to remain staunch in the faith but also as far as possible to see that the children are baptized, brought up in the same faith, and given all the helps for their eternal salvation that the Catholic Church provides for its members. [. . .]   3003

In view of all this, it will surprise no one that the canonical discipline regarding mixed marriages cannot be uniform and must be adjusted to meet the different circumstances of individual cases. This applies to the canonical form for marriage, the liturgical celebration, the pastoral care to be provided to the spouses and their children, depending on the different situations of the spouses or their degree of ecclesiastical communion. [. . .]   3004

By way of preface we state that Eastern Catholics who marry baptized non-Catholics or the nonbaptized are not subject to the norms about to be laid down by this Motu Proprio. As to the marriages of Catholics of any rite with Eastern Christians who are not Catholics, the Church has already recently issued rules[6] and we wish them to remain in effect.   3005

Our motive is that ecclesiastical discipline on mixed marriages be improved and that, while respecting the prescriptions of the divine law, canon law provide for the different situations of spouses, in keeping with the mind of Vatican Council II as expressed in the Decree *Unitatis redintegratio*[7] and the Declaration *Dignitatis humanae*.[8] We have also taken into account the desires expressed in the Synod of Bishops. Therefore by our authority and after long deliberation we establish and decree the norms that follow. [. . .]

8.   Mixed marriages must be contracted with the canonical form, which is required for validity, but without prejudice to the prescription in the Decree *Crescens matrimoniorum*, issued 22 February 1967 by the Congregation for the Eastern Churches.[9]   3006

9.   When serious problems stand in the way of observing the canonical form, local Ordinaries have the right to dispense from the canonical form in a mixed marriage. It belongs to the conference of bishops to establish norms for uniformity and lawfulness in the granting of this dispensation in its own region or territory; some public manner of celebrating the marriage, however, must be maintained. [. . .]   3007

---

2   See UR 13–18: AAS 57 (1965) 100–104; ConstDecrDecl 262–268.

6   See OE no. 18 [DOL 5 no. 172]. SCEC, Decr. *Crescens matrimoniorum* [DOL 352].

7   See UR [DOL 6].

8   AAS 58 (1966) 929–946; ConstDecrDecl 511–532.

9   See DOL 352 no. 2994.

3008   11. As to the liturgical form of celebrating mixed marriages, if this is to be taken from the Roman Ritual, the rite to be used must be from the *Rite of Marriage* promulgated by our authority. This holds whether it is a marriage between a Catholic and a baptized non-Catholic (*Rite* nos. 39–54) or a marriage between a Catholic and a nonbaptized partner (*Rite* nos. 59–66). In a marriage between a Catholic and a baptized non-Catholic, it is permissible in particular cases, with the consent of the local Ordinary, to use the rites for celebrating a marriage within Mass (*Rite* nos. 19–38); the general law regarding eucharistic communion, however, must be observed.

3009   12. The conferences of bishops are to inform the Apostolic See about whatever they have decreed according to their own competence about mixed marriages.

3010   13. A marriage celebration in the presence of a Catholic priest or deacon and a non-Catholic minister who together carry out their own respective rites is forbidden. Nor is it allowed to have, before or after the Catholic celebration, a second religious celebration with the purpose of giving or renewing the matrimonial consent. [. . .]

3011   14. Local Ordinaries and pastors are to ensure that the Catholic partner and the children born of a mixed marriage are not deprived of the spiritual help needed to fulfill their obligations of conscience. They are to encourage the Catholic partner to be ever mindful of the Catholic faith as a gift and to bear personal witness "with meekness, fear, and a clear conscience."[10] They are to help the husband and wife to develop the unity of their marital and family life, which, in the case of Christians, is grounded on their baptism. Therefore it is strongly recommended that Catholic bishops and pastors establish contacts with ministers of other religious communities and that these contacts be marked by genuine honesty and enlightened trustfulness.

3012   17. Any instance of special difficulty or doubt regarding the application of these norms requires recourse to the Apostolic See.

Whatever we have decreed by this Motu Proprio, we command as confirmed and established and as effective from 1 October 1970, all things to the contrary notwithstanding.

355. PONTIFICAL COMMISSION FOR THE INTERPRETATION OF THE DECREES OF VATICAN COUNCIL II, **Reply** to a query, on the Motu Proprio *Matrimonia mixta* no. 9, 11 February 1972: AAS 64 (1972) 397.

3013   The Fathers of the Pontifical Commission for the Interpretation of the Decrees of Vatican Council II have decided to reply in this way to the queries presented to them in their plenary session:

I

Query: In keeping with the Motu Proprio *Matrimonia mixta*, 31 March 1970, may the local Ordinary grant a dispensation from the canonical form for celebration of a mixed marriage if one partner is a Catholic and the other person was baptized

---

[10]   1 Pt 3:15–16.

in the Catholic Church, but fell away and was converted to another non-Catholic confession?

Reply: Yes, provided serious difficulties stand in the way of observing the canonical form. [. . .]

Pope Paul VI in an audience granted to the undersigned [President of the Commission], 11 February 1972, confirmed these decisions, approved them, and ordered their publication.

356. SECRETARIAT FOR CHRISTIAN UNITY, *Final Report: Theology of Marriage and the Problems of Mixed Marriages 1971–1977*: Dialogue between the Lutheran World Federation, The World Alliance of Reformed Churches, and the Secretariat for Christian Unity of the Roman Catholic Church, 14 January 1978.*

VI. STATEMENT AND DISCUSSION OF THE NORMS OF THE CATHOLIC CHURCH REGARDING MIXED MARRIAGES

A. Norms of the Catholic Church on Mixed Marriages

3. THE LITURGICAL FORM[a]

86. The canonical form normally coincides with the liturgical form of the celebration of marriage. In the case of a marriage of a Catholic with a baptized person, two possibilities are envisaged: 3014

a. a celebration without a Mass, according to the rite of the *Ordo celebrandi matrimonium* of 1969, nos. 39–54, in the framework of a liturgy of the word, followed by the exchange of promises and the blessing of the spouses;

b. alternatively, with the consent of the local Ordinary, a celebration during Mass, according to the same *Ordo* nos. 19–38; but in this case for the distribution of communion the rules concerning intercommunion must be observed.[b]

87. Paragraph 13 of *Matrimonia mixta*[c] is intended to prevent a form of celebration which might be to the detriment of sound ecumenism instead of promoting it; or else one that might cause doctrinal confusion. This paragraph forbids a simultaneous celebration in two different rites or a non-Catholic celebration preceding or following the Catholic one, if this includes a fresh expression or renewing of the marriage vows. In fact, since the Church considers as valid the exchange of vows of the spouses in the presence of a Catholic priest or deacon, another exchange of vows, either before or after, would be like performing a second marriage, for a marriage is made effective through a single act.   3015

---

*   English text published by USCC Publications Office, Washington, D.C., 1978 (excerpt).

a   See DOL 351 no. 2991, 352 no. 2994, and 354 no. 3008.

b   See DOL 147 nos. 992–999, 1009; DOL 150 and 155.

c   See DOL 354 no. 3010.

357. PONTIFICAL COMMISSION FOR THE INTERPRETATION OF THE DECREES OF VATICAN COUNCIL II, **Reply** to a query, on dispensing from the canonical form of marriage, 9 April 1979: AAS 71 (1979) 632.

3016   The Fathers of the Pontifical Commission for the Interpretation of the Decrees of Vatican Council II have decided to reply as follows to the queries presented to them at a plenary meeting:

On Dispensing from the Canonical Form of Marriage

Query: I. In granting a dispensation from the canonical form in mixed marriages according to the Motu Proprio *Matrimonia mixta*,[a] may the diocesan bishop limit the extent of the grant by the addition of clauses regarding validity?

II. If the answer to I is affirmative, can nonobservance of such clauses have the effect of making the marriage invalid because it lacked the canonical form?

III. In the situation described in no. II may the diocesan bishop render a declaration of nullity in the manner of a special case on the basis of the Motu Proprio *Causas matrimoniales* no. XI, provided the proofs mentioned in no. X are present?

Reply: Yes to I, II, and III.

At an audience granted 9 April 1979 to the undersigned [President of the Commission], Pope John Paul II confirmed this decision, approved it, and ordered it published.

▶   See also Chapter One, Section 8. Ecumenism.

[a] See DOL 354 no. 3007.

Section 7. Penance

SUMMARY (DOL 358–390). The Constitution on the Liturgy art. 72 decreed a revision of the liturgy of the sacrament of penance and in art. 110 also touched on the qualities of penitential practices in general. The sacrament itself and the penitential character inherent in the Christian life are prominent in other conciliar documents. The present section in its four subsections reflects the developments since the Council on the practice of Christian penance, on the sacrament, on the particular issue of children's first confession, and on indulgences, a traditional element of the Church's teaching that has some liturgical relevance.

Section 7. Penance: A. Christian Penance

SUMMARY (DOL 358–359). Pope Paul VI's Apostolic Constitution *Paenitemini* gives both a comprehensive doctrinal review of the place of the virtue and practice of penance in the Christian life and revises penitential observances in the Church. The excerpts from the doctrinal exposition, which notably integrates the conciliar documents, as well as the disciplinary norms provide a setting for the liturgy of the sacrament of reconciliation and penitential services and for the penitential elements in the liturgical year (DOL 358). A subsidiary text adds an official reply interpreting one of the norms of *Paenitemini* (DOL 359).

▶   1.   VATICAN COUNCIL II, Constitution on the Liturgy *Sacrosanctum Concilium*, 4
      December 1963:

      art. 109–110:   Lent, the special penitential season [nos. 109–110].

358. PAUL VI, **Apostolic Constitution** *Paenitemini*, on Christian penance, 17
February 1966: AAS 58 (1966) 177–198 (excerpts).

3017   "Repent and believe the Gospel."[1] These words of the Lord seem to us to bear
repeating: Vatican Council II has reached its successful conclusion and now the
Church advances on its journey with quickened step, so to speak. For we look on
the duty to teach all our children, indeed all people of these times who are sensitive
to religion, the implications and importance of the Lord's command to repent as
deserving a high place among the serious and pressing issues facing our pastoral
concern. The more complete awareness of the nature of the Church and of its links
with the world provided by the Council prompts us to honor that duty.

        During the Council the Church, in its intent to reflect more deeply on the
mystery of its own being, gave a clear statement of what it is. It looked deeply into
the elements of its nature — the human and the divine, the visible and the invisible,
the transitory and the everlasting. Pondering deeply, first of all, the bonds linking it
with Christ and his saving work, the Church set out more clearly the obligation that
forms part of God's call to all its members, namely, to share in Christ's own mission,
including its aspect of atonement.[2]

        The Church has grown in its awareness that, even though it is holy and
without reproach from the standpoint of God's design,[3] it is made up of members

---

    [1] Mk 1:15.

    [2] See LG no. 5: ". . . The Church, endowed with the gifts of its holy Founder and faithfully
observing his commandments of charity, humility, and renunciation, has received the mission of proclaiming and establishing among all peoples the kingdom of Christ and of God; the Church indeed stands as the
seed and beginning of that kingdom on earth . . . ." no. 8: "Christ accomplished the work of redemption
amid poverty and persecution; so too the Church is summoned to walk the same path, so that it may bring
to all the effects of salvation. Christ Jesus, 'being in the form of God . . . emptied himself and took to
himself the form of a slave' (Phil 2:6–7) and for our sake 'though he was rich, yet became poor' (2 Cor
8:9); so too the Church, although for its mission it needs human resources, is not established to seek
earthly glory, but by its example to spread humility and self-renunciation . . . ." See also AA no. 1.

    [3] See Eph 5:27.

subject to sin. It knows that they are in continuous need of conversion and reform,[4] not only inward and personal, but outward and social.[5] Finally, the Church
also gave more careful consideration to its mission vis à vis the earthly city.[6] For in
teaching people the right way of using the world and of consecrating its concerns, it
at the same time urged on them a saving restraint, ensuring that, in their journey to
their heavenly home, they would not be impeded by their involvement in the
things of earth.[7]

Motivated by such considerations, we repeat today to our sons and daughters
the words first spoken by Peter to the people after Pentecost: "Repent . . . for the
remission of sins";[8] we wish also today to address to all peoples the words once
addressed to the people of Lystra: "Turn to the living God."[9] [. . .]

I

In the light of Christ human beings gain a new vision, the recognition of the   3018
holiness of God and the wickedness of sin.[36] Through Christ's word and message
they perceive how they are invited to turn to God and how pardon is granted. They
receive these gifts in full through baptism. Fashioning its recipients in the likeness
of the Lord's passion, death, and resurrection,[37] baptism, so to speak, stamps the
whole of human life with the seal of Christ's mystery.

Following in the Lord's footsteps, all who bear the name Christian must deny
themselves, take up their cross, and share in his suffering. Thus transformed into

---

4   See LG no. 8: "Christ, 'holy, blameless, undefiled' (Heb 7:26), knew no sin (see 2 Cor 5:21), but
came solely to seek pardon for the sins of his people (see Heb 2:17); the Church, on the other hand, having
sinners in its midst, is at the same time holy and in need of cleansing, and so is unceasingly intent on
repentance and reform." See also UR no. 4: "God has enriched the Catholic Church with every revealed
truth and all the means of grace. Nevertheless its members do not live with all the intensity they should,
with the result that the Church does not appear in all its splendor to other Christians separated from us
and to all the world and the growth of God's kingdom is slowed. All Catholics ought to strive therefore
for Christian perfection and to endeavor, according to their individual state, that the Church, bearing in its
body Jesus' humility and mortification (see 2 Cor 4:10; Phil 2:5–8) may be purified more and more and
renewed. Then at last Christ will present the Church to himself, glorious and without spot or wrinkle (see
Eph 5:27)." See UR no. 7: "Genuine ecumenism does not exist without interior conversion. For newness of
mind (see Eph 4:23), self-abnegation, and the generous outpouring of charity are the source of the
progress and intensification of the desire for unity." UR no. 8: "This conversion of heart and holiness of
life, accompanied by public and personal prayer for Christian unity, must be regarded as the soul of the
entire ecumenical movement and deserves to be called spiritual ecumenism."

5   See SC art. 110: "During Lent penance should not be only inward and individual, but also outward
and social" [DOL 1 no. 110].

6   See GS, especially no. 40.

7   See 1 Cor 7:31: "For the fashion of this world passes away." Rom 12:2: "Do not be conformed to
this world." See UR no. 6: ". . . Christ summons the Church in its pilgrim journey to the continuous
reformation it always needs as a human and earthly institution" [DOL 6 no. 185]. See LG no. 8: "'In its
pilgrimage the Church walks with God's consolation on one side and the world's persecution on the other'
(St. Augustine De civ. Dei 17, 51, 2: PL 41, 614) and proclaims the cross and death of the Lord until he comes
(see 1 Cor 11:26)." LG no. 9: ". . . As it passes through trials and tribulation, the Church is strengthened
by the power of God's grace pledged in the Lord's promise: that in the frailty of the flesh it would not fall
away from fidelity but would remain his worthy Bride; that under the influence of the Holy Spirit it
would never cease to renew itself until through the cross it comes into the light that knows no setting."
See also GS nos. 37, 39, 93.

8   Acts 2:38.

9   Acts 14:15. See Paul VI, Address to the United Nations, 4 Oct. 1965: AAS 57 (1965) 885.

36   See Lk 5:8, 7:36–50.

37   See Rom 6:3–11; Col 2:11–15, 3:1–4.

the image of Christ's death, they are empowered to receive as a reward a share in the glory of his resurrection.[38] Moreover, in such a condition Christians must no longer live for themselves[39] but for God, who has loved them and given himself for them.[40] They must live as well for their neighbor so that "they may fill up in their flesh what remains of the afflictions of Christ, for the sake of his Body, which is the Church."[41]

The Church is conjoined to Christ by the closest bonds. Therefore the repentance of all the faithful also bears a close relationship to the whole human community. For it is not only as an original gift that the faithful receive *metanoia* in the Church through baptism; through the sacrament of penance in the Church that same gift is restored and strengthened for those members who have sinned. "Those who receive the sacrament of penance obtain from God's mercy pardon for having offended him, and at the same time reconciliation with the Church, which they have wounded by their sins and which by charity, example, and prayer seeks their conversion."[42] In the Church the expiatory penance imposed in the sacrament on each penitent becomes by special title a share in Christ's own atonement. The general law of the Church joins to this penitential work other such works that the faithful perform and the sufferings they bear in patience.[43]

From all of this the service of always bearing the Lord's "mortification" in body and spirit[44] becomes an intimate part of the entire life of the baptized at all times and in all its aspects. [. . .]

---

[38] See Phil 3:10–11; Rom 8:17.

[39] See Rom 6:10, 14:8; 2 Cor 5:15; Phil 1:21.

[40] See Gal 2:20. See also LG no. 7: "All his members must be made like Christ until he is formed in them (see Gal 4:19). Therefore we are all taken up into the mysteries of his life, configured to him, dead and raised again with him, until we reign together with him (see Phil 3:21; 2 Tm 2:11; Eph 2:6; Col 2:12; etc.). Pilgrims still on earth and amid trials and persecution following in his footsteps, we are joined to his sufferings like the Body to the Head, suffering with him, so that we may be glorified with him (see Rom 8:17)."

[41] Col 1:24. See AG no. 36: "From this renewed spirit prayers and penitential works are offered willingly to God so that by his grace the effort of missionaries will achieve good results." See also OT no. 2 [DOL 12 no. 211].

[42] LG no. 11, which continues: "By the sacred anointing of the sick and the prayer of priests the entire Church commends the sick to the suffering and glorified Lord, asking that he lighten their suffering and save them (see Jas 5:14, 16); the Church exhorts them, moreover, to contribute to the welfare of the whole people of God by associating themselves willingly with Christ's passion and death (see Rom 8:17; Col 1:24; 2 Tm 2:11–12; 1 Pt 4:13) " [DOL 4 no. 141]. See also PO no. 5: "Priests instruct the faithful to offer the divine victim to the Father in the sacrifice of the Mass and with him to make an offering of their own life. In the spirit of Christ the Good Shepherd priests guide the faithful to bring their sins with contrite heart to the Church in the sacrament of penance for the sake of an ever more complete conversion to the Lord . . ." [DOL 18 no. 260]. PO no. 6: "Further, an ecclesial community by charity, prayer, example, and penitential practices fulfills a true form of motherhood by bringing souls to Christ" [DOL 18 no. 261].

[43] Thomas Aquinas, *Quaestiones quodlibetales* 3, qu. 13, art. 28: "It seems quite right that the priest not burden a penitent with the weight of a heavy penance. A small fire would be quickly put out if many logs were piled onto it; so too it might happen that the small spark of contrition just kindled in a penitent would be put out because of the heaviness of a penance and the sinner might fall into complete despair. Thus it is better for the priest to point out to the penitent what a heavy penance ought to be imposed for his sins, but then in fact to impose something that the penitent is capable of bearing. From performing this the penitent may learn to perform the greater works of penance that the priest would not attempt to impose. The expiation of the penitent over and above what has been expressly enjoined acquires greater value in atoning for past sins by reason of that general charge the priest expresses in the words: 'May whatever good you do profit you for the remission of sins.' Thus it is a praiseworthy practice that many priests use these words of the longer form of absolution."

[44] See 2 Cor 4:10.

III

The Church emphasizes that in the practice of the virtue of penance the first 3019
consideration is its religious and spiritual character; this is what helps even today's
people to perceive what God is, what his rights over his human creature are, and
what the salvation brought by Christ means. At the same time, however, the
Church urges all believers to combine their inner conversion to God with outward
acts of bodily mortification.

a. The Church stresses, first of all, the practice of penance by all through
fulfillment of the duties of their state in life and the patient bearing both of the
hardships of each day's struggle inherent in our life on earth and of the troubling
uncertainties of that life.[56]

b. Some of the Church's members, however, labor under sickness, disease,
poverty, and other misfortunes or "suffer persecution for the sake of righteousness." They are advised to learn how to unite their sufferings with Christ in
patience. In this way they will not only more fully live up to their obligation to do
penance, but also will be blessed by a life sustained by divine grace and that
happiness promised in the Gospel to them and their brothers and sisters."[57]

c. Priests and those who profess the evangelical counsels must honor in an
even higher degree the obligation to deny self. For priests bear a deeper imprint of
Christ's own character and religious follow the Lord's "emptying himself" more
intensely and strive with greater helps and more effectively for the fullness of
charity.[58]

---

[56] See LG no. 34. ". . . If carried out in the Spirit, all their works, their prayers and apostolic
endeavors, their ordinary married and family life, their daily occupation, their physical and mental
relaxation, and even the hardships of life, when patiently borne, become spiritual sacrifices acceptable to
God through Jesus Christ (see 1 Pt 2:5). All these are most fittingly offered to the Father along with the
offering of the body of the Lord in the celebration of the eucharist. Thus as adorers acting in holiness in all
things, the laity consecrate the world itself to God" [DOL 4 no. 151]. LG no. 36: ". . . He shared this
power with his disciples so that they too may be established in kingly freedom, by self-abnegation and a
holy life may overcome the reign of sin in themselves (see Rom 6:12), and also, serving Christ in others,
may by humility and patience lead their brothers and sisters to that King, to serve whom is to reign." LG
no. 41: "In all types of life and duties all those pursue the same kind of holiness who are led by the Spirit
of God and, obeying the voice of the Father, adoring him in spirit and in truth, follow Christ, poor,
humble, and bearing the cross, so that they may be rewarded by sharing in his glory." See also GS no. 4.

[57] See LG no. 41: "To unite themselves in a special way to Christ suffering for the world's salvation is
the lesson to be learned by all those who are burdened by poverty, illness, disease, and other hardships or
who suffer persecution for the sake of righteousness: those whom Christ called blessed and whom 'the
God of all grace, who has called us unto his eternal glory in Christ Jesus, after they have suffered awhile,
will make perfect, establish, and strengthen' (1 Pt 5:10)."

[58] See PO no. 12: "[Priests] consecrated by the Spirit's anointing and sent forth by Christ, mortify the
works of the flesh in themselves." PO no. 13: "They seek to kill in themselves vices and lusts; . . . The
leaders of communities are faithful to the ascesis proper to pastors, renouncing their own comfort . . . ."
See also PO nos. 16 and 17. See LG no. 41: "As those who ex officio pray and offer sacrifice for their people
and the entire people of God, knowing what they do and imitating what they touch, they are not to be
deterred even by apostolic cares, perils, and hardships, but rather through these they are to rise to a higher
holiness for the service of the whole Church of God by nurturing and fostering their activity from
contemplation."
See AG no. 24: "One who is sent enters into the life and mission of him who emptied himself
taking the form of a slave (Phil 2:7). Therefore he must be ready to remain faithful for life to his vocation,
to renounce self and all that he owns, and to 'become all things to all men' (1 Cor 9:22)."
See LG no. 42: "Like a mother, the Church rejoices to find in its midst men and women who follow
more closely and exemplify more clearly the Savior's self-giving by embracing poverty in the freedom of
God's children and by renouncing their own will: those, namely, who submit themselves to another
human being for the sake of God in matters of perfection beyond what is of precept, so that they may
more completely model themselves on Christ's obedience."
See PC no. 7: "In the Mystical Body of Christ, in which 'all the members do not have the same
function' (Rom 12:4), a place apart, whatever the demands of the apostolate, will always belong to those
institutes totally dedicated to contemplation, those, namely, whose members in solitude and silence, in

The Church nevertheless appeals to all the faithful together that they obey the Lord's command to repent not only through the hardships and setbacks bound up with the nature of daily life, but also by acts of bodily mortification.[59]

3020 With a view therefore of reminding its children of the precept of penance and urging its observance, the Apostolic See intends to revise the Church's penitential practice in a way suited to the times.

It will be up to the wisdom and pastoral concern of the bishops to meet and to issue norms, in view of their knowledge of their regions and people, that will serve as an effective means to attain the end proposed. These norms, however, must be in line with those that follow.

The Church is intent especially upon expressing the three principal ways, longstanding in its practice, which make it possible to fulfill the divine command to repent. These are prayer, fasting, and works of charity — even though fast and abstinence have had a privileged place. These ways of penance have been shared by all the centuries; yet in our own time there are particular reasons advanced in favor of one way of penance above the others, depending on circumstances.[60] For example, in the richer nations stress is placed on the witness of self-denial so that Christians will not become worldly;[61] another emphasis is the witness of charity

---

constant prayer and willing penance, devote themselves entirely to God." PC no. 12: "Religious therefore, striving to remain faithful to their profession, must believe in the words of the Lord and, trusting in God's help rather than in their own resources, practice mortification and discipline over their senses." PC no. 13: "[Voluntary poverty] is a share in Christ's poverty; for our sake he being rich became poor so that by his lacking all we would have much" (see 2 Cor 8:9; Mt 8:20). PC no. 14: "By their profession of obedience religious offer absolute dedication of their own will as a sacrifice to God and are united with greater constancy and sureness to the divine salvific will." PC no. 25: ". . . Religious are to spread Christ's Gospel throughout the world by the completeness of their faith, their charity for God and neighbor, their love of the cross, and their hope of future glory."

See OT no. 2: "This Council endorses the well-tested means of general cooperation in the work of vocations, namely, fervent prayer, Christian penance . . ." [DOL 12 no. 211]. OT no. 8: ". . . They [seminarians] should live Christ's paschal mystery in such a way as to be able to lead the people to be entrusted to them to enter into it" [DOL 12 no. 213]. OT no. 9: ". . . With special care [major seminarians] are to be trained in priestly obedience, in the ideal of a life of poverty, and in a spirit of self-denial, so that they will develop the attitude of readily renouncing even things that are lawful but not expedient and of modeling themselves on Christ crucified."

[59] See LG no. 42: ". . . All the faithful must apply themselves unfailingly . . . to prayer, self-denial, active service of others, and the practice of the virtues." LG no. 42 ". . . all must be prepared to confess Christ before the world, and to follow him in the way of the cross amid the persecutions that the Church will never be without."

See SC art. 9: "Before people can come to the liturgy they must be called to faith and conversion . . . . Therefore the Church announces the good tidings of salvation to those who do not believe, so that all may know the true God and Jesus Christ whom he has sent and may be converted from their ways, doing penance (see Jn 17:3; Lk 24:27; Acts 2:38). To believers, also, the Church must ever preach faith and penance . . ." [DOL 1 no. 9]. SC art. 12: "We learn from the same Apostle that we must always bear about in our body the dying Jesus so that the life also of Jesus may be made manifest in our bodily frame (see 2 Cor 4:10–11). This is why we ask the Lord in the sacrifice of the Mass that 'receiving the offering of the spiritual victim, he may fashion us for himself as an eternal gift' (prayer over the gifts, Monday within the octave of Pentecost) " [DOL 1 no. 12]. SC art. 104: "By celebrating their passage from earth to heaven the Church proclaims the paschal mystery achieved in the saints who have suffered and been glorified with Christ; it proposes them to the faithful as examples drawing all to the Father through Christ and pleads through their merits for God's favors" [DOL 1 no. 104].

[60] See SC art. 110: "The practice of penance should be fostered in ways that are possible in our times and in different regions and according to the circumstances of the faithful; it should be encouraged by the authorities mentioned in art. 22" [DOL 1 no. 110].

[61] See Rom 12:2: "Do not be conformed to this world." See also Mk 2:19; Mt 9:15. GS no. 37: "The Church of Christ acknowledges that human progress can be an aid to human happiness. At the same time, however, in its trust in the plan of the Creator, it is impelled to repeat the words of St. Paul: 'Do not be conformed to this world' (Rom 12:2), which means the spirit of vanity and wickedness that perverts

toward others, even those in foreign lands, who are suffering poverty and hunger.[62]

In the poorer countries, it will be more pleasing and acceptable to God, as well as of greater advantage to the members of Christ's Body, if, while not neglecting the chance to advance greater social equality, the people prayerfully offer their wretchedness to God the Father, in devout and intimate union with the sufferings of Christ.

The Church, then, retains the outward practice of penance that for centuries has been observed canonically, including fast and abstinence, in places where it is preferable to follow this ancient practice. At the same time, however, it judges that the other ways of penance should be sealed by the authority of Church prescription wherever it may seem advisable to the conferences of bishops to substitute the practice of prayer and the works of charity for the observance of fast and abstinence.

It is also the decision of the Apostolic See[63] to establish certain days and seasons that in the course of the liturgical year more fully express Christ's paschal mystery[64] or are required by special needs of the Church.[65] The purpose is to join all the faithful together in a kind of shared celebration of penance.

---

human endeavor, meant for the service of God and neighbor, into an instrument of sin."

[62] See Rom 15:26–27; Gal 2:10; 2 Cor 8:9; Acts 24:17. See also GS no. 88: ". . . It belongs to the entire people of God, with the bishops leading by word and example, to lessen the misery of the age as much as possible and to do so, in keeping with the established practice of the Church, not just from their surplus but from their substance. This is to forestall that human scandal of some nations — and quite often those populated by a majority bearing the name of Christian — having an abundance of materialities while others do not even have the necessities of life but are suffering in hunger, disease, and in every imaginable misery."

[63] See SC art. 105: "Finally, in the various seasons of the year and according to its traditional discipline, the Church completes the formation of the faithful by means of devout practices for soul and body, by instruction, prayer, and works of penance and mercy" [DOL 1 no. 105].

[64] See SC art. 107: "The liturgical year is to be so revised that the traditional customs and discipline of the sacred seasons are preserved or restored to suit the conditions of modern times; their specific character is to be retained, so that they duly nourish the devotion of the faithful who celebrate the mysteries of Christian redemption and above all the paschal mystery" [DOL 1 no. 107].
    On Lent as a preparation for the celebration of this paschal mystery, see SC art. 109: "Lent is marked by two themes, the baptismal and the penitential. By recalling or preparing for baptism and by repentance this season disposes the faithful, as they more diligently listen to the word of God and devote themselves to prayer, to celebrate the paschal mystery. The baptismal and penitential aspects of Lent are to be given greater prominence in both liturgy and liturgical catechesis. Hence: a. More use is to be made of the baptismal features proper to the Lenten liturgy; some of those from an earlier era are to be restored as may seem advisable. b. The same is to apply to the penitential elements. As regards catechesis, it is important to impress on the minds of the faithful not only the social consequences of sin but also the essence of the virtue of penance, namely, detestation of sin as an offense against God; the role of the Church in penitential practices is not to be neglected and the people are to be exhorted to pray for sinners" [DOL 1 no. 109].
    On the paschal mystery's being celebrated each week, see SC art. 102: "The Church is conscious that it must celebrate the saving work of the divine Bridegroom by devoutly recalling it on certain days throughout the course of the year. Every week, on the day which the Church has called the Lord's Day, it keeps the memory of the Lord's resurrection . . ." [DOL 1 no. 102]. See also SC art. 106 [DOL 1 no. 106] and Eusebius, De solemnitate paschali 12: PG 24, 705: "Every Sunday we receive life from the sanctified body of Christ, our saving pasch, and our soul receives the seal of his precious blood"; ibid.: PG 1, 701: "Moses' followers sacrificed the Passover lamb once a year . . . we of the New Covenant celebrate our Passover every Sunday . . . . The Gospel teaching commands that we do these things not just once a year but continually and daily. We therefore celebrate every week the Passover that is ours, carrying out on that day of salvation the mysteries of the true Lamb, who has redeemed us. See John Chrysostom, In Ep. 1 ad Tim. 5:3: PG 62, 529–530: "The mystery celebrated in the Easter triduum contains nothing more than the mystery we celebrate at this moment: that mystery is one even as the grace of the Holy Spirit is one. Why then, you say, is that time called Easter? Because that is the time when Christ suffered for us. No one therefore should approach the Easter celebrations and other celebrations differently: for the one power is present. . . . The Easter celebrations do in fact have one thing additional: they were the days when our

Therefore the following matters are declared and decreed.

3021   I.   § 1. All the faithful are obliged by divine law to do penance.

3022   II.   § 1. Lent retains its penitential character.

§ 2. The days of penance that must be observed as obligatory throughout the Church are: every Friday of the year and Ash Wednesday or, alternatively in the case of diversity of rites, the first day of the Great Lent. The substantial observance of these days is of grave obligation.[a]

§ 3. Without prejudice to the faculties given in nos. VI and VIII, for the practice of penance on these days abstinence is to be observed every Friday of the year, unless it is a holyday of obligation; fast and abstinence are to be observed on Ash Wednesday — or, in the case of a diversity of rite, on the first day of the Great Lent — and on Good Friday.

3023   III.   § 1. The law of abstinence bans the eating of meat, but not of eggs, milk-products, or sauces made with animal fats.

§ 2. The law of fast prescribes a single full meal each day; it does not rule out taking some food in the morning and evening, following accepted local customs as to the amount and kind of food.

3024   IV.   The law of abstinence is binding on those who have completed their fourteenth year; the law of fast is binding on all from their twenty-first to their sixtieth birthday. As to those under twenty-one, pastors and parents are to take special pains that they be led to develop a genuine sense of penance.

3025   V.   All privileges and both general and particular indults are abolished. These norms change nothing with regard to the vows of any person, physical or moral, or the constitutions or rule of any religious or other approved institute.

3026   VI.   § 1. On the basis of the Decree on the Pastoral Office of Bishops *Christus Dominus* no. 38, 4,[b] it belongs to the conferences of bishops to:

    a.   transfer for a good reason the penitential days, always, however, respecting Lent:

    b.   substitute for fast and abstinence other forms of penance, especially works of charity and devotional practices.

§ 2. The conferences of bishops are to report to the Apostolic See, for its information, what they decree in this matter.

3027   VII.   Without prejudice to the power of dispensation that, also according to the Decree *Christus Dominus* no. 8 b, belongs to each bishop, a pastor also, for a good reason and observing the prescriptions of Ordinaries, may grant either to individuals or to particular families, a dispensation or mitigation of the fast and abstinence in favor of other devotional acts. The superior of a clerical religious order or institute has the same power with regard to his own subjects.

---

salvation began, the days when Christ was sacrificed. But as far as the mystery contained is concerned those celebrations have no preeminence."

[65] See Acts 13:3: "And when they had fasted and prayed and laid hands on them, they sent them away."

  [a] See DOL 359.

  [b] See DOL 7 no. 199.

VIII. In the Eastern Churches the right to determine days of fast and abstinence   3028
belongs, in keeping with the conciliar Decree on the Eastern Catholic Churches no.
23, to the patriarch with his synod or to the supreme authority in each Church,
acting with his council of hierarchs.

IX.   § 1. It is strongly recommended that besides more frequent use of the sacra-   3029
ment of penance, bishops and other pastors earnestly promote, especially during
Lent, special works of penance, for the sake of expiation or petition.

§ 2. All the faithful are strongly urged to become deeply committed to the
Christian spirit of penance as an incentive to works of charity and repentance.

X.   § 1. The effective date for these prescriptions — promulgated by way of   3030
exception in *L'Osservatore Romano* — is Ash Wednesday of this year, that is, on 23
February 1966.

§ 2. Wherever special privileges and any kind of indult, whether general or
particular, have hitherto been in effect, a *vacatio legis* of six months from the date of
promulgation is to be considered as granted.

It is our will that these our decrees and prescriptions are now and in the
future to be established and effective, notwithstanding, where necessary, apostolic
constitutions, ordinances, and other prescriptions of our predecessors, even those
deserving of special mention and amendment.

359. SC COUNCIL, **Reply** to a query, on the Apostolic Constitution
Paenitemini no. II, § 2, 24 February 1967: AAS 59 (1967) 229.

Query: I. Should the *substantial* observance of the penitential days that the   3031
Apostolic Constitution *Paenitemini* in its legislative part, no. II § 2,[a] declares to be a
grave obligation be taken to mean each individual day of obligatory penance prescribed for the whole Church?

II. Or rather should it be taken to mean the overall observance of the penitential days with the prescribed practices?

Reply: With the approval of Pope Paul VI, the Congregation of the Council has
replied:

To I: No.

To II: Yes. In other words a person sins gravely by the omission, without any
excuse, of a considerable portion, quantitatively or qualitatively, of the overall
prescribed penitential observance.

▶   442.   SC RITES (Consilium), General Norms for the Liturgical Year and for the Calendar, 21 March 1969:

no.   27:   Lenten penance [no. 3793].

▶   330.   SC BISHOPS, Decree *Apostolatus maris*, on the pastoral care of seamen and ship
passengers, 24 September 1977:

Part II, nos. 2–3:   Dispensation from the law of fast and abstinence
[no. 2670].

---

a   See DOL 358 no. 3022.

SECTION 7. PENANCE: B. SACRAMENT OF PENANCE IN GENERAL

SUMMARY (DOL 360–378). The revision of the rites and formularies of the sacrament decreed by the Constitution on the Liturgy art. 72 gave rise to the 19 specific texts presented here and there are also 20 cross-references on relevant doctrinal, pastoral, disciplinary, and liturgical points.

—The documents on the sacrament itself include six addresses of Pope Paul VI (DOL 363, 371, 372, 373, 376, 378), a letter from the Secretariat of State representing Pope Paul's reflections on the sacrament of reconciliation (DOL 374), three interventions of the Congregation for the Doctrine of the Faith occasioned by a profanation of the sacrament (DOL 364, 365, 366), and two texts concerning the use of the sacrament by religious (DOL 360, 362).

—The documents on the revision of the rite consist of the decree of promulgation (DOL 367), the introduction to the new rite (DOL 368), an address of Pope Paul in which he described the new rite to a general audience (DOL 369), and a letter to the French episcopate on the preparation of vernacular versions (DOL 370).

—On the specific pastoral issue of general absolution the Congregation for the Doctrine of the Faith issued a set of pastoral norms (DOL 361), a reflection on the introduction to the new rite, in a letter to the American bishops (DOL 375), and a reply to a query (DOL 377).

▶   103.   PAUL VI, Motu Proprio *Pastorale munus*, on the powers and privileges of bishops, 30 November 1963:

I, no. 14:   Bishops' powers to grant faculties to confessors [no. 725].

II, nos. 2–4:   Bishops' privileges as confessors [nos. 740–742].

▶   1.   VATICAN COUNCIL II, Constitution on the Liturgy *Sacrosanctum Concilium*, 4 December 1963:

art. 35:   Celebrations of the word in Lent [no. 35].

36, 63:   Use of the vernacular in the sacrament [nos. 36, 63].

72:                       Rite of penance [no. 72].

▶   23.   SC RITES (Consilium), Instruction (first) *Inter Oecumenici*, 26 September 1964:

nos. 38–39:   Celebrations of the word during Lent [nos. 330–331].

▶   141.   SECRETARIAT OF STATE, Pontifical Rescript *Cum admotae*, on faculties delegated to religious superiors, 6 November 1964:

I, no. 12:   Regarding confessions of religious [no. 945].

▶   4.   VATICAN COUNCIL II, Dogmatic Constitution on the Church *Lumen gentium*, 21 November 1964:

no. 11:   Sacrament of penance [no. 141].

▶   18.   VATICAN COUNCIL II, Decree on the Ministry and Life of Priests *Presbyterorum Ordinis*, 7 December 1965:

nos. 13, 18:   Sacrament of penance in the life of priests [nos. 265 and 267].

▶   358.   PAUL VI, Apostolic Constitution *Paenitemini*, on Christian penance, 17 February 1966:

I: Sacrament of penance [no. 3018].

III, art. IX, § 1:   Frequent use of the sacrament [no. 3029].

▶   178.   SC DOCTRINE OF THE FAITH, Letter *Cum Oecumenicum Concilium*, on erroneous interpretations of Vatican II, 24 July 1966:

no. 7:   Sacrament of penance [no. 1227].

▶   179.   SC RITES (Consilium), Instruction *Eucharisticum mysterium*, on worship of the eucharist, 25 May 1967:

no. 35:   Penance and communion [no. 1264].

▶   309.   PAUL VI, Motu Proprio *Sacrum Diaconatus Ordinem*, restoring the permanent diaconate in the Latin Church, 18 June 1967:

no. 26:   Deacons' frequent use of the sacrament [no. 2540].

▶ 326. SC CLERGY, General Directory *Peregrinans in terra*, on the pastoral ministry in tourism, 30 April 1969:

II. 3. B, b:	Power of confessors [no. 2616].
II. 3. B, c:	Confessions on holydays [no. 2617].
II. 3. B, d:	Confessions at places of pilgrimage [no. 2618].

▶ 334. SC CATHOLIC EDUCATION, *Basic Plan for Priestly Formation*, 6 January 1970:

no. 55:	Frequent use of the sacrament of penance [no. 2773].

360. SC RELIGIOUS AND SECULAR INSTITUTES, **Decree** *Dum canonicarum legum recognitio*, establishing norms for the use and administration of the sacrament of penance, especially in the case of women religious, 8 December 1970: AAS 63 (1971) 318–319.

During the present process of revising canon law, the Congregation for Religious and Secular Institutes in plenary session has thought it advisable for several pressing reasons to review certain issues regarding the use and administration of the sacrament of penance, particularly in the case of women religious. The Congregation has also considered the issue of the suitability of a religious for profession in a certain special instance.   3032

After thoroughly considering these points, the Fathers in plenary assembly, 26–27 October 1970, decided to decree what follows.

1.   Because they have a special bond with the Church that "unceasingly seeks repentance and reform" (LG no. 8), religious are to place high value on the sacrament of penance. This sacrament restores and strengthens in the Church's members who have sinned the gift of *metanoia*, that is, conversion, to Christ's kingdom which was first received in baptism (see Apostolic Constitution *Paenitemini*: AAS 58 [1966] 179–180).[a] It confers from God's mercy pardon for offending him and at the same time reconciliation with the Church, which we injure by sinning (see LG no. 11).[b]   3033

2.   Religious are thus to place equally high value on the frequent reception of the sacrament. For that increases self-knowledge and humility, contributes a salutary discipline of soul, and causes an abundance of grace. These and other effects are powerful aids to more rapid progress along the way of virtue; in addition they bring growth to the general good of the whole community (see Encycl. *Mystici Corporis*: AAS 35 [1943] 235).   3034

3.   Intent on developing their own union with God, therefore, religious are to endeavor to receive the sacrament of penance frequently, that is, twice a month. Superiors are to be concerned about promoting this practice and are to ensure that the members of the community have the opportunity for sacramental confession at least every other week and more often if they wish.   3035

4.   Specifically with regard to women religious: 3036

---

   [a] See DOL 358 no. 3018.

   [b] See DOL 4 no. 141.

a.   As a safeguard for complete freedom of conscience, all women religious, novices included, may lawfully and validly make their sacramental confession to any priest who is approved in the place to hear confessions; the priest needs no special jurisdiction (CIC can. 876) or appointment.

b.   Nevertheless, in the interest of the community's well-being, monasteries of contemplatives, houses of formation, and communities with many religious are to have an ordinary confessor. Of these, at least the monasteries and houses of formation are also to have an extraordinary confessor, but there is no obligation to go to either confessor.

c.   For other communities appointment of an ordinary confessor is permissible if special circumstances suggest this in the judgment of the Ordinary and on the basis of the community's prior request or consent.

d.   The local Ordinary is to choose with care confessors who possess the requisite maturity and necessary qualifications. He is to decide on the number, age, and period of appointment of these confessors; he is to proceed with their appointment or reappointment after conferring previously with the community involved.

e.   Those prescriptions of canon law are suspended that are contrary to the foregoing dispositions or are incompatible with them or, in view of them, are pointless and irrelevant.

3037   5.   To the extent that they are applicable, the points decreed in no. 4 are in effect also for nonclerical communities of men. [. . .]

In an audience on 20 November granted to the Secretary of this Congregation, Pope Paul VI graciously approved these dispositions and ordered that they be effective immediately, without any formula of execution, and remain so until the revised code of canon law has been promulgated.

▶   169.   SC CLERGY, *General Catechetical Directory*, 11 April 1971:

no.   57:   Catechesis for the sacrament of penance [no. 1104].

▶   301.   SC DIVINE WORSHIP, *Rite of Christian Initiation of Adults*, Introductions, 6 January 1972:

nos. 303, 332:   Sacrament of penance in the context of Christian initiation [nos. 2455, 2470].

Appendix, no. 9:   Sacrament of penance in the reception of a baptized Christian into the full communion of the Church [no. 2484].

361. SC DOCTRINE OF THE FAITH, Pastoral Norms *Sacramentum Paenitentiae*, on general absolution, 16 June 1972: AAS 64 (1972) 510–514; Not 8 (1972) 312–317.

3038   The sacrament of penance was instituted by Christ the Lord so that sinners might receive pardon from God's mercy for having offended him and at the same time reconciliation with the Church.[1] Christ instituted the sacrament when he

---
[1]   See LG no. 11 [DOL 4 no. 141].

bestowed on his apostles and their lawful successors the power of loosing and binding sins.[2]

The Council of Trent's solemn teaching is that for an integral and complete pardon of sins three acts are required of the penitent as parts of the sacrament: contrition, confession, and expiation. The Council also taught that the priest's absolution is a judicial act and that by divine law it is necessary for penitents to confess to a priest all those mortal sins and their specifying moral circumstances that they remember after a careful examination of conscience.[3]

Many local Ordinaries are today concerned on two accounts. The one is the difficulty their people are having about individual confession because of the present shortage of priests in some regions. The second concern is certain erroneous theories regarding the doctrine on the sacrament of penance and the unwarranted practice of giving a single general absolution for sins confessed only in a generic way. They therefore have requested the Holy See, in the interest of the true nature of the sacrament of penance, to remind the Christian people of the norms necessary for the proper use of this sacrament and to issue new norms for the current situation.

After thoroughly studying these problems and keeping in mind the Instruction of 25 March 1944 from the Apostolic Penitentiary, this Congregation makes the following declarations.

I.   The teaching of the Council of Trent must continue to be held firmly as   3039
doctrine and applied exactly in practice. Therefore a practice that has arisen in some places must be repudiated, namely, presuming to satisfy through only a collective or so-called communal confession the precept of the sacramental confession of mortal sins in order to receive absolution. In addition to the divine precept stated at the Council of Trent, a cogent reason for this repudiation is the important benefit for the faithful that, as the experience of centuries attests, comes from individual confession made and received properly. Individual, complete confession and the receiving of absolution remain the only ordinary way for the faithful to obtain reconciliation with God and the Church, unless physical or moral impossibility excuses them from this manner of confessing.

II.   By reason of special conditions occasionally arising, there can indeed be cases   3040
when it is lawful or even necessary to give general absolution to many penitents without prior individual confession.

The main instance of this is imminent danger of death and the lack of time for a priest or priests, even if available, to hear the confession of individual penitents. In such a situation, any and every priest has the faculty to give general absolution; if there is time, he should preface this with a very brief exhortation that each person be sure to make an act of contrition.

III.   In addition to the case of danger of death, general absolution of many of the   3041
faithful who have only confessed generically, but have been rightly disposed for penance, is lawful when there is a serious need. This means a case in which, given the number of penitents, not enough confessors are available to hear the individual confessions properly within a reasonable time, with the result that, through no fault of their own, the faithful would be forced to be for a long time without the grace of the sacrament or without communion. Such a situation may occur in mission lands particularly, but in other places as well and in groups of people to whom the serious need mentioned clearly applies.

---

[2]   See Jn 20:22ff.

[3]   See Council of Trent, sess. 14, *Canones de sacramento paenitentiae* 4, 6–9: Denz-Schön 1704, 1706–09.

When confessors can be made available, however, the procedure is not lawful solely on the basis of a large number of penitents, for example, at some great festival or pilgrimage.[4]

3042   IV.   Local Ordinaries and priests, to the extent that it applies to them, have a serious obligation in conscience to make sure that there is not a scarcity of confessors because some priests neglect this important ministry,[5] involving themselves rather in secular concerns or in less important ministries, especially when these could be provided by deacons or qualified lay people.

3043   V.   It belongs exclusively to the local Ordinary, after consultation with other members of the conference of bishops, to make the judgment on whether the conditions stated already[6] are verified and therefore to decide when it is lawful to give general absolution.

If, apart from the instances established by the local Ordinary, any other serious need arises for giving general absolution, a priest is bound first, whenever possible, to have recourse to the local Ordinary in order to give the general absolution lawfully. If this is not possible, he is to inform the same Ordinary as soon as possible of the need in question and of the fact of the absolution.

3044   VI.   With respect to the faithful, it is absolutely required for the reception of general sacramental absolution that they have the proper dispositions. This means that they repent individually of their sins, have the intention of refraining from them, are resolved to rectify scandal or injuries they may have caused, intend to make an individual confession in due time of those serious sins they cannot at the present time confess. Priests are to take pains to instruct the faithful about these dispositions and conditions that are prerequisites for the sacrament to have its effect.

3045   VII.   Unless there is a good reason preventing it, those who receive pardon for serious sin through general absolution are to go to auricular confession before any further reception of general absolution. And unless a moral impossibility stands in the way, they are absolutely bound to go to a confessor within one year. For the precept binding every one of the faithful binds them as well, namely, to confess individually to a priest at least once a year all those grave sins not hitherto confessed one by one.[7]

3046   VIII.   Priests are to instruct the faithful that they are forbidden, if they are burdened with mortal sin and there are sufficient confessors available, to put off by design or neglect fulfilling the obligation of individual confession in expectation of an occasion when a general absolution will be given.[8]

3047   IX.   To enable the faithful to fulfill without difficulty the obligation of individual confession, steps are to be taken to ensure that there are confessors available in places of worship on days and at times assigned for the convenience of the faithful.

---

[4]   See Proposition 29 among those condemned by Innocent XI, 2 March 1679: Denz-Schön 2159.

[5]   See PO nos. 5, 13 [DOL 18 nos. 260, 265]; CD no. 30 [DOL 7 no. 196].

[6]   In Norm III.

[7]   See Lateran Council IV, cap. 21 and Council of Trent, *Doctrina de Sacramento Paenitentiae* cap. 5, *De confessione*, and can. 7–8: Denz-Schön 812; 1679–83 and 1707–08. See also SC Holy Office, Proposition 11 condemned in the Decr. of 24 Sept. 1665: Denz-Schön 2031.

[8]   See Apostolic Penitentiary, Instr. of 25 March 1944.

In the case of places so far distant from each other that the priest can visit them only once in a while during the year, this should be the arrangement: if at all possible, on each occasion he is to hear the confessions of some group of penitents; he bestows general sacramental absolution on the other penitents, as long as the conditions already given are verified.[9] But the procedure should be such that, if possible, all the faithful have the opportunity for individual confession at least once a year.

X.   The faithful should receive thorough instruction that liturgical celebrations and communal penitential services are extremely useful as a preparation for a more beneficial confession and for amending their life. But care must be taken against confusing such celebrations or services with sacramental confession and absolution.

    3048

Each penitent who makes an individual confession during such services is to receive absolution individually from the confessor involved. In any instance when sacramental absolution is to be given collectively, its bestowal is to follow the special rite established by the Congregation for Divine Worship.[10] The rite is to be completely separated from Mass.

XI.   Persons who are actually a scandal to the faithful may receive general sacramental absolution along with the others provided they are seriously repentant and resolved to remove the scandal. They are not, however, to go to communion until in the judgment of a confessor whom they must consult personally they have removed the scandal.

    3049

As to absolution from reserved censures, the canonical norms currently in force are to be followed; the next individual confession is used in computing the time period for recourse to the competent authority.

XII.   On the subject of frequent, "devotional" confession, priests are not to dare to discourage the faithful from this practice. On the contrary, they are to extol its great benefits for the Christian life[11] and to make it clear that they are always ready to hear such confessions whenever the faithful reasonably request. What must be absolutely avoided is the restriction of individual confession to mortal sins alone. That would deprive the faithful of an important effect of confession and would injure the good name of those who receive the sacrament individually.

    3050

XIII.   Sacramental absolutions given collectively that do not respect the norms just given are to be considered a grievous abuse. All pastors are to guard carefully against it out of a sense of the moral responsibility placed on them to protect the good of souls and the dignity of the sacrament of penance.

    3051

In an audience granted to the undersigned Cardinal Prefect of the Congregation for the Doctrine of the Faith, 16 June 1972, Pope Paul VI expressly approved these Norms and ordered that they could be promulgated at once.

---

[9]   See Norm III.

[10]   However, until promulgation of this rite [see DOL 369, 370] the words now prescribed for sacramental absolution are to be used and obviously in the plural.

[11]   See Encycl. *Mystici Corporis*: AAS 35 (1943) 235.

362. SC EASTERN CHURCHES, **Decree** *Orientalium Religiosorum*, granting faculties to religious of the Eastern Churches, 27 June 1972: AAS 64 (1972) 738–743 (excerpt).

3052   The superiors general of Eastern religious, in their concern for the expeditious and effective progress of the renewal of religious life in accord with the mind of Vatican Council II, have submitted to the Apostolic See petitions for the favor of certain broader faculties. [. . .]

This Congregation for the Eastern Churches, at the mandate of Pope Paul VI, now publishes the following faculties that have been granted to religious of the Eastern Churches.

3053   6.   Intent on developing their own union with God, therefore, religious are to endeavor to receive the sacrament of penance at least twice a month (see CIC can. 138, § 1, no. 3). Superiors are to be concerned about promoting this practice and are to ensure that the members of the community have the opportunity for sacramental confession at least every other week and more often if they wish (see CIC can. 138, § 2).

3054   7.   Specifically with regard to women religious:

a.   As a safeguard for complete freedom of conscience, all women religious, novices included, may validly and lawfully make their sacramental confession to any priest who is approved in the place to hear confessions; the religious discipline of the community, however, is not to be upset. The local Hierarch is to guard against abuses in this matter and by his care and prudence suppress any that may occur, while respecting freedom of conscience.

b.   In the interest of the community's well-being, monasteries of the contemplative life, houses of formation, and larger communities are to have an ordinary confessor. Of these at least the monasteries and houses of formation are also to have an extraordinary confessor, but there is no obligation to go to either confessor.

c.   For other communities appointment of an ordinary confessor is permissible if special circumstances suggest this in the judgment of the local Hierarch.

d.   The local Hierarch is to choose with care confessors who possess the requisite maturity and necessary qualifications. He is to decide on the number, age, and the period of appointment or reappointment after conferring previously with the community involved.

e.   Those prescriptions of canon law are suspended that are contrary to the foregoing dispositions or are incompatible with them or, in view of them, are pointless and irrelevant.

3055   8.   To the extent that they are applicable, the points decreed in no. 7 are in effect also for nonclerical communities of men. [. . .]

3056   23.   Religious who are priests and have received from the major superior of an exempt, clerical religious institute the faculty to hear confessions may hear the confessions of religious and novices in all religious houses and elsewhere.

363. PAUL VI, **Address** to a general audience, on the sacrament of reconciliation, 19 July 1972: Not 8 (1972) 305–307 (Italian).

The promulgation of some "Pastoral Norms on General Sacramental Absolution," 16 June 1972, by the Congregation for the Doctrine of the Faith is something you are probably aware of.[a] If not, it will be to your advantage to become acquainted with these norms, because they concern the discipline of the sacrament of penance. They thus involve one of the fundamental issues of Christian life — reconciliation. Reconciliation of one who has sinned, first of all, with God, through the restoration (or the improvement) of the state of grace, that is, of the supernatural life in one who has lost (or weakened) it. Reconciliation, as well, with the Church through readmission to its communion, if, unhappily, the sin committed brought with it a complete or partial exclusion from a living incorporation in the Mystical Body of Christ, which is the Church. As you see, we are dealing with an essential and vital issue bearing on our personal relationship with the process of our own salvation.

3057

What is the issue? It is the sacrament of penance, which entails confession because of a rule deriving from Christ, from the tradition of the Church, and from the ecumenical councils, both Lateran Council IV (A.D. 1215) and the Council of Trent (sess. 14, ch. 8). Confession requires a minister, the priest authorized to hear confessions and thus give absolution. But in some places there are no priests or there are so few or they come so infrequently (in mission lands, for example) that there is neither the means nor the time for the normal exercise of this ministry. Is it not possible to make up for this by means of a general absolution without individual confessions? Furthermore, in some places has there not already been introduced so-called communal confession, that is, a penitential service by an assembly of the faithful who all together receive sacramental absolution without individual, auricular confession?

3058

The reply given by the Congregation for the Doctrine of the Faith followed upon much study and consultation, reflection on the interpretation of the obligation deriving from Christ's merciful will, a responsible and pastorally-inspired evaluation of the genuine well-being of the Church and the faithful and of the duty and importance of the ministry of priests. That reply is as follows. First: the rule of the Council of Trent remains in force and calls for exact observance on the part of priests and faithful (among whom are the priests themselves), namely, as heretofore, absolution from mortal sins requires prior self-accusation.[b] The law remains. Secondly: as already established in law, in certain cases of imminent danger of death (for example, fire, shipwreck, war, etc.) when there is no time to hear individual confessions, "any and every priest has the faculty to give general absolution."[c] Necessity and emergency prevail over the usual rule. Third, and this is something new: "In addition to the case of danger of death, general absolution of many of the faithful who have only confessed generically, but have been rightly disposed for penance, is lawful if there is a serious need. This means a case in which, given the number of penitents, not enough confessors are available to hear the individual confessions properly within a reasonable time, with the result that, through no fault of their own, the faithful would be forced to be for a long time without the grace of the sacrament or without communion. Such a situation may occur in mission lands, but in other places as well and in groups of people to whom the

---

[a]   See DOL 361.

[b]   See DOL 361 no. 3039.

[c]   DOL 361 no. 3040.

serious need mentioned clearly applies. When confessors can be made available, however, the procedure is not lawful solely only on the basis of a large number of penitents, for example, at some great festival or pilgrimage. . . . The rite is to be completely separated from Mass."d

3059   Other prescriptions that are worth knowing and meant to be precisely and clearly explained to the faithful complete this new discipline. This discipline will evoke from all who have a sense of the authentically Catholic pastoral life a two-fold reaction. One is admiration and joy over the loving care of the Church, which, like a mother, is so concerned to be as generous as possible in dispensing the treasures of grace. The second is appreciation and hope. For these norms are a reminder of the unique importance of the dark drama of sin in human existence (a drama the seriousness of which contemporary laxism seeks to discount entirely) and they are also an authoritative and inspiring confirmation given to the people of God of the mystery of repentance carried out through confession.

Ours is an age that desperately needs to recover a clear, well-founded moral consciousness and that yearns for liberation from the force that most interiorly and oppressively holds people prisoner. For this age it is surely providential to have this reminder of the reality of the sacramental grace of penance. If sin is slavery and death, then the recovery of the sense of sin and recourse to God's remedy of pardon is a matter to be reflected on and to be celebrated with the interest and enthusiasm we reserve to the major happenings of life and of history. We address ourself to you, our brothers in the priesthood, called to be physicians of souls, confidants, masters, psychiatrists of grace, in the extremely effective and at the same time delicate and grave ministry of confession. We address ourself to all of you, the faithful sons and daughters of the Church, both to those who have the happy experience of this sacrament and to those who may have been held back from it by a deep-rooted pride or by groundless fears. We exhort all of you to have esteem, reverence, gratitude, and desire for this "ministry of reconciliation" (2 Cor 5:18), which truly means the paschal joy of resurrection.

364. SC DOCTRINE OF THE FAITH, **Declaration** *Sacra Congregatio*, in defense of the dignity of the sacrament of penance, 23 March 1973: AAS 65 (1973) 678.

3060   The Congregation for the Doctrine of the Faith, in virtue of the special power given to it by Pope Paul VI, makes the following decisive declaration. From this day a *latae sententiae* excommunication reserved to no one is incurred by those who, with contempt for the sacrament of penance, make a tape or recording of sacramental confessions, whether genuine or feigned, by use of any kind of mechanical device, or publish confessions obtained in this manner. The same excommunication applies to all who give formal cooperation in this matter. The prescriptions of CIC can. 889, 890, and 2369 remain unchanged.

---

d   DOL 361 nos. 3041 and 3048.

365. SC DOCTRINE OF THE FAITH, **Declaration** *Allo scopo*, on the dignity of the sacrament of penance, 23 March 1973.*

In the interest of ensuring absolutely the respect due to the sacrament of   3061
penance and the secrecy of confession, the Church has been obliged to threaten
with very serious penalties anyone who might profane the sacrament and violate its
secrecy.

At the present time the forthcoming publication of a book with the transcriptions of genuine or feigned sacramental confessions has been widely announced. Therefore the Congregation for the Doctrine of the Faith, in virtue of the power committed to it by Pope Paul VI, declares that anyone who profanes the sacrament of penance by making a recording of genuine or even feigned confessions and anyone giving formal cooperation to such or similar publications, whether as an author or collaborator, by that fact is outside the communion of the Church, that is, ipso facto excommunicated. Such a person, however, if rightly disposed, may be absolved from the censure by any priest lawfully authorized to hear confessions.

366. SC DOCTRINE OF THE FAITH, **Note** *Essendo pervenute*, on the authentic interpretation of the Declaration *Sacra Congregatio* of 23 March 1973, 24 March 1973.*

Because of questions reaching it on the application of the Declaration of 23   3062
March 1973, the Congregation for the Doctrine of the Faith makes the following
clarifications.

1.   The moral judgment of complete repudiation of the profanation committed against the sacredness of confession and the secrecy due to the administration of the sacrament remains intact; it applies also to anyone who has given formal cooperation to such an act, even prior to the Declaration. The threatened excommunication comes into effect from the moment publication takes place.

2.   The censure is incurred not only by the authors and editors, should they not take steps to withdraw their publication from circulation and sale, but also by those who take part in advertising or distributing the publication.

367. SC DIVINE WORSHIP, **Decree** *Reconciliationem inter Deum et homines*, promulgating the *editio typica* of the new rite of penance, 2 December 1973: AAS 66 (1974) 172–173; Not 10 (1974) 42–43.

Reconciliation between God and his people was brought about by our Lord   3063
Jesus Christ in the mystery of his death and resurrection (see Rom 5:10). The Lord
entrusted the ministry of reconciliation to the Church in the person of the apostles
(see 2 Cor 5:18ff.). The Church carries out this ministry by bringing the good news
of salvation to people and by baptizing them in water and the Holy Spirit (see Mt
28:19).

---

*   Text, OR 24 March 1973, 1 (Italian).

*   Text, OR 25 March 1973, 1 (Italian).

Because of human weakness, however, Christians "leave [their] first love" (see Rv 2:4) and even break off their friendship with God by sinning. The Lord therefore instituted a special sacrament of penance for the pardon of sins committed after baptism (see Jn 20:21–23) and the Church has faithfully celebrated the sacrament throughout the centuries — in varying ways, but retaining its essential elements.

Vatican Council II decreed that "the rite and formularies for the sacrament of penance are to be revised so that they may more clearly express both the nature and effect of this sacrament."[1] In view of this the Congregation for Divine Worship has carefully prepared the new *Rite of Penance* so that the celebration of the sacrament may be more fully understood by the faithful.

3064   In this new rite, besides the *Rite for Reconciliation of Individual Penitents*, a *Rite for Reconciliation of Several Penitents* has been drawn up to emphasize the relation of the sacrament to the community. This rite places individual confession and absolution in the context of a celebration of the word of God. Furthermore, for special occasions a *Rite for Reconciliation of Several Penitents with General Confession and Absolution* has been composed in accordance with the Pastoral Norms on General Sacramental Absolution, issued by the Congregation for the Doctrine of the Faith, 16 June 1972.[2]

The Church is deeply concerned with calling the faithful to continual conversion and renewal. It desires that the baptized who have sinned should acknowledge their sins against God and their neighbor and have heartfelt repentance for them; it takes pains to prepare them to celebrate the sacrament of penance. For this reason the Church urges the faithful to attend penitential celebrations from time to time. This Congregation has therefore made regulations for such celebrations and has proposed examples or models that conferences of bishops may adapt to the needs of their own regions.

3065   Pope Paul VI has by his authority approved the *Rite of Penance* prepared by the Congregation for Divine Worship and ordered it to be published. It is to replace the pertinent titles of the Roman Ritual hitherto in use. The *Rite* in its Latin original is to come into force as soon as it is published; vernacular versions, from the day determined by the conferences of bishops, after they have approved the translation and received confirmation from the Apostolic See.

368. SC DIVINE WORSHIP, *Rite of Penance*, **Introduction**, 2 December 1973: Vatican Polyglot Press, 1974.

INTRODUCTION

I. MYSTERY OF RECONCILIATION IN THE HISTORY OF SALVATION

3066   1. The Father has shown forth his mercy by reconciling the world to himself in Christ and by making peace for all things on earth and in heaven by the blood of Christ on the cross.[1] The Son of God made man lived among us in order to free us

---

1   SC art. 72 [DOL 1 no. 72].

2   See DOL 361.

1   See 2 Cor 5:18ff.; Col 1:20.

from the slavery of sin[2] and to call us out of darkness into his wonderful light.[3] He therefore began his work on earth by preaching repentance and saying: "Repent and believe the Gospel" (Mk 1:15).

This invitation to repentance, which had often been sounded by the prophets, prepared people's hearts for the coming of the kingdom of God through the voice of John the Baptist, who came "preaching a baptism of repentance for the forgiveness of sins" (Mk 1:4).

Jesus, however, not only exhorted people to repentance so that they would abandon their sins and turn wholeheartedly to the Lord,[4] but welcoming sinners, he actually reconciled them with the Father.[5] Moreover, he healed the sick in order to offer a sign of his power to forgive sin.[6] Finally, he himself died for our sins and rose again for our justification.[7] Therefore, on the night he was betrayed and began his saving passion,[8] he instituted the sacrifice of the New Covenant in his blood for the forgiveness of sins.[9] After his resurrection he sent the Holy Spirit upon the apostles, empowering them to forgive or retain sins[10] and sending them forth to all peoples to preach repentance and the forgiveness of sins in his name.[11]

The Lord said to Peter: "I will give you the keys of the kingdom of heaven, and whatever you bind on earth will be bound in heaven, and whatever you loose on earth will be loosed also in heaven" (Mt 16:19). In obedience to this command, on the day of Pentecost Peter preached the forgiveness of sins by baptism: "Repent and let every one of you be baptized in the name of Jesus Christ for the remission of sins" (Acts 2:38).[12] Since then the Church has never failed to call people from sin to conversion and through the celebration of penance to show the victory of Christ over sin.

2.   This victory is first brought to light in baptism where our fallen nature is crucified with Christ so that the body of sin may be destroyed and we may no longer be slaves to sin, but rise with Christ and live for God.[13] For this reason the Church proclaims its faith in "one baptism for the forgiveness of sins."

                                                                                3067

In the sacrifice of the Mass the passion of Christ is again made present; his body given for us and his blood shed for the forgiveness of sins are offered to God again by the Church for the salvation of the world. For in the eucharist Christ is present and is offered as "the sacrifice which has made our peace"[14] with God and in order that "we may be brought together in unity"[15] by his Holy Spirit.

---

²   See Jn 8:34–36.

³   See 1 Pt 2:9.

⁴   See Lk 15.

⁵   Lk 5:20 and 27–32, 7:48.

⁶   See Mt 9:2–8.

⁷   See Rom 4:25.

⁸   See RM, Eucharistic Prayer III.

⁹   See Mt 26:28.

¹⁰   See Jn 20:19–23.

¹¹   See Lk 24:47.

¹²   See Acts 3:19 and 26, 17:30.

¹³   See Rom 6:4–10.

¹⁴   See RM, Eucharistic Prayer III.

¹⁵   See RM, Eucharistic Prayer II.

Furthermore, our Savior Jesus Christ, when he gave to his apostles and their successors power to forgive sins, instituted in his Church the sacrament of penance. Its purpose is that the faithful who fall into sin after baptism may be reconciled with God through the restoration of grace.[16] The Church "possesses both water and tears: the water of baptism, the tears of penance."[17]

II. RECONCILIATION OF PENITENTS IN THE CHURCH'S LIFE

THE CHURCH, BOTH HOLY AND ALWAYS IN NEED OF PURIFICATION

3068   3.   Christ "loved the Church and gave himself up for it to make it holy" (Eph 5:25–26) and he united the Church to himself as a bride.[18] He filled it with his divine gifts,[19] because it is his Body and his fullness; through the Church he spreads truth and grace upon all.

The members of the Church, however, are exposed to temptation and often fall into the wretchedness of sin. As a result, "whereas Christ, 'holy, harmless, undefiled' (Heb 7:26), knew no sin (see 2 Cor 5:21) but came solely to seek pardon for the sins of his people (see Heb 2:17), the Church, having sinners in its midst, is at the same time holy and in need of cleansing, and so is unceasingly intent on repentance and reform."[20]

PENANCE IN THE CHURCH'S LIFE AND LITURGY

3069   4.   The people of God accomplish and perfect this continual repentance in many different ways. They share in the sufferings of Christ[21] by enduring their own difficulties, carry out works of mercy and charity,[22] and adopt ever more fully the outlook of the Gospel message. Thus the people of God become in the world a sign of conversion to God. All this the Church expresses in its life and celebrates in its liturgy when the faithful confess that they are sinners and ask pardon of God and of their brothers and sisters. This happens in penitential services, in the proclamation of the word of God, in prayer, and in the penitential parts of the eucharistic celebration.[23]

In the sacrament of penance the faithful "obtain from God's mercy pardon for having offended him and at the same time reconciliation with the Church, which they have wounded by their sins and which by charity, example, and prayer seeks their conversion."[24]

---

[16]   See Council of Trent, sess. 14, *De sacramento Paenitentiae* cap. 1: Denz-Schön 1668 and 1670; can. 1: Denz-Schön 1701.

[17]   Ambrose, *Ep.* 41, 12: PL 16, 1116.

[18]   See Rv 19:7.

[19]   See Eph 1:22–23. LG no. 7: AAS 57 (1965) 9–11; ConstDecrDecl 100–102.

[20]   LG no. 8: AAS 57 (1965) 12; ConstDecrDecl 106.

[21]   See 1 Pt 4:13.

[22]   See 1 Pt 4:8.

[23]   See Council of Trent, sess. 14, *De sacramento Paenitentiae*: Denz-Schön 1638, 1740, 1743. SCR, Instr. EuchMyst, 25 May 1967, no. 35 [DOL 179 no. 1264]; GIRM, nos. 29, 30, 56 a, b, g [DOL 208 nos. 1419, 1420, 1446].

[24]   LG no. 11 [DOL 4 no. 141].

RECONCILIATION WITH GOD AND WITH THE CHURCH

5.   Since every sin is an offense against God that disrupts our friendship with him,   3070
"the ultimate purpose of penance is that we should love God deeply and commit
ourselves completely to him."[25] Therefore, the sinner who by the grace of a merciful God embraces the way of penance comes back to the Father who "first loved us"
(1 Jn 4:19), to Christ who gave himself up for us,[26] and to the Holy Spirit who has
been poured out on us abundantly.[27]

      "The hidden and gracious mystery of God unites us all through a supernatural
bond: on this basis one person's sin harms the rest even as one person's goodness
enriches them."[28] Penance always therefore entails reconciliation with our brothers
and sisters who remain harmed by our sins.

      In fact, people frequently join together to commit injustice. But it is also true
that they help each other in doing penance; freed from sin by the grace of Christ,
they become, with all persons of good will, agents of justice and peace in the world.

SACRAMENT OF PENANCE AND ITS PARTS

6.   Followers of Christ who have sinned but who, by the prompting of the Holy   3071
Spirit, come to the sacrament of penance should above all be wholeheartedly converted to God. This inner conversion embraces sorrow for sin and the intent to lead
a new life. It is expressed through confession made to the Church, due expiation,
and amendment of life. God grants pardon for sin through the Church, which
works by the ministry of priests.[29]

a. Contrition

      The most important act of the penitent is contrition, which is "heartfelt sorrow
and aversion for the sin committed along with the intention of sinning no more."[30]
"We can only approach the kingdom of Christ by *metanoia*. This is a profound
change of the whole person by which we begin to consider, judge, and arrange our
life according to the holiness and love of God, made manifest in his Son in the last
days and given to us in abundance" (see Heb 1:2; Col 1:19 and passim; Eph 1:23 and
passim).[31] The genuineness of penance depends on this heartfelt contrition. For
conversion should affect a person from within toward a progressively deeper enlightenment and an ever-closer likeness to Christ.

b. Confession

      The sacrament of penance includes the confession of sins, which comes from
true knowledge of self before God and from contrition for those sins. However, the
inner examination of heart and the outward accusation must be made in the light of
God's mercy. Confession requires on the penitent's part the will to open the heart to
the minister of God and on the minister's part a spiritual judgment by which, acting

---

      [25]   Paul VI, Ap. Const. *Paenitemini*, 17 Feb. 1966: AAS 58 (1966) 179. See also LG no. 11 [DOL 4 no.
141].

      [26]   See Gal 2:20; Eph 5:25.

      [27]   See Ti 3:6.

      [28]   Paul VI, Ap. Const. *Indulgentiarum doctrina*, 1 Jan. 1967, no. 4 [DOL 386 no. 3158]. See also Pius XII,
Encycl. *Mystici Corporis*, 29 June 1943: AAS 35 (1943) 213.

      [29]   See Council of Trent, sess. 14, *De sacramento Paenitentiae*, cap. 3: Denz-Schön 1673–75 [the *ed. typica*
erroneously cites cap. 1].

      [30]   Ibid., cap. 4: Denz-Schön 1676.

      [31]   Paul VI, Ap. Const. *Paenitemini*, 17 Feb. 1966: AAS 58 (1966) 179.

in the person of Christ, he pronounces his decision of forgiveness or retention of sins in accord with the power of the keys.[32]

c. Act of Penance

True conversion is completed by expiation for the sins committed, by amendment of life, and also by rectifying injuries done.[33] The kind and extent of the expiation must be suited to the personal condition of penitents so that they may restore the order that they have upset and through the corresponding remedy be cured of the sickness from which they suffered. Therefore, it is necessary that the act of penance really be a remedy for sin and a help to renewal of life. Thus penitents, "forgetting the things that are behind" (Phil 3:13), again become part of the mystery of salvation and press on toward the things that are to come.

d. Absolution

Through the sign of absolution God grants pardon to sinners who in sacramental confession manifest their change of heart to the Church's minister; this completes the sacrament of penance. For in God's design the humanity and loving kindness of our Savior have visibly appeared to us[34] and so God uses visible signs to give salvation and to renew the broken covenant.

In the sacrament of penance the Father receives the repentant children who come back to him, Christ places the lost sheep on his shoulders and brings them back to the sheepfold, and the Holy Spirit resanctifies those who are the temple of God or dwells more fully in them. The expression of all this is the sharing in the Lord's table, begun again or made more ardent; such a return of children from afar brings great rejoicing at the banquet of God's Church.[35]

NEED AND BENEFIT OF THIS SACRAMENT

3072   7.   Just as the wounds of sin are varied and multiple in the life of individuals and of the community, so too the healing that penance provides is varied. Those who by grave sin have withdrawn from communion with God in love are called back in the sacrament of penance to the life they have lost. And those who, experiencing their weakness daily, fall into venial sins draw strength from a repeated celebration of penance to reach the full freedom of the children of God.

a.   To obtain the saving remedy of the sacrament of penance, according to the plan of our merciful God, the faithful must confess to a priest each and every grave sin that they remember after an examination of conscience.[36]

b.   Moreover, the frequent and careful celebration of this sacrament is also very useful as a remedy for venial sins. This is not a mere ritual repetition or psychological exercise, but a serious striving to perfect the grace of baptism so that, as we bear in our body the death of Jesus Christ, his life may be seen in us ever more clearly.[37] In confession of this kind, penitents who accuse themselves of venial faults should try to be more closely conformed to Christ and to follow the voice of the Spirit more attentively.

---

[32] See Council of Trent, sess. 14, *De sacramanto Paenitentiae* cap. 5: Denz-Schön 1679.

[33] See ibid. cap. 8: Denz-Schön 1690–92. Paul VI, Ap. Const. *Indulgentiarum doctrina*, nos. 2–3 [DOL 386 nos. 3156–57].

[34] See Ti 3:4–5.

[35] See Lk 15:7, 10 and 32.

[36] See Council of Trent, sess. 14, *De sacramento Paenitentiae* can. 7–8: Denz-Schön 1707–08.

[37] See 2 Cor 4:10.

In order that this sacrament of healing may truly achieve its purpose among the faithful, it must take root in their entire life and move them to more fervent service of God and neighbor.

The celebration of this sacrament is thus always an act in which the Church proclaims its faith, gives thanks to God for the freedom with which Christ has made us free,[38] and offers its life as a spiritual sacrifice in praise of God's glory, as it hastens to meet the Lord Jesus.

III. OFFICES AND MINISTRIES IN THE RECONCILIATION OF PENITENTS

ROLE OF THE COMMUNITY IN THE CELEBRATION OF PENANCE

8.   The whole Church, as a priestly people, acts in different ways in the work of reconciliation that has been entrusted to it by the Lord. Not only does the Church call sinners to repentance by preaching the word of God, but it also intercedes for them and helps penitents with a maternal care and solicitude to acknowledge and confess their sins and to obtain the mercy of God, who alone can forgive sins. Further, the Church becomes itself the instrument of the conversion and absolution of the penitent through the ministry entrusted by Christ to the apostles and their successors.[39]

3073

MINISTER OF THE SACRAMENT OF PENANCE

9.   a.   The Church exercises the ministry of the sacrament of penance through bishops and priests. By preaching God's word they call the faithful to conversion; in the name of Christ and by the power of the Holy Spirit they declare and grant the forgiveness of sins.

In the exercise of this ministry priests act in communion with the bishop and share in his power and office as the one who regulates the penitential discipline.[40]

b.   The competent minister of the sacrament of penance is a priest who has the faculty to absolve in accordance with canon law. All priests, however, even though not approved to hear confessions, absolve validly and lawfully any penitents without exception who are in danger of death.

3074

PASTORAL EXERCISE OF THIS MINISTRY

10.   a.   In order that he may fulfill his ministry properly and faithfully, understand the disorders of souls and apply the appropriate remedies to them, and act as a wise judge, the confessor must acquire the needed knowledge and prudence by constant study under the guidance of the Church's magisterium and especially by praying fervently to God. For the discernment of spirits is indeed a deep knowledge of God's working in the human heart, a gift of the Spirit, and an effect of charity.[41]

b.   The confessor should always show himself to be ready and willing to hear the confessions of the faithful whenever they reasonably request this.[42]

c.   By receiving repentant sinners and leading them to the light of the truth, the confessor fulfills a paternal function: he reveals the heart of the Father and reflects the image of Christ the Good Shepherd. He should keep in mind that he has

3075

---

38   See Gal 4:31.

39   See Mt 18:18; Jn 20:23.

40   See LG no. 26 [DOL 4 no. 146].

41   See Phil 1:9–10.

42   See SCDF, Pastoral Norms for General Absolution, 16 June 1972, Norm XII [DOL 361 no. 3050].

been entrusted with the ministry of Christ, who accomplished the saving work of human redemption by mercy and by his power is present in the sacraments.[43]

d. Conscious that he has come to know the secrets of another's conscience only because he is God's minister, the confessor is bound by the obligation of preserving the seal of confession absolutely unbroken.

PENITENTS

3076   11. The parts that penitents themselves have in the celebration of the sacrament are of the greatest importance.

When with proper dispositions they approach this saving remedy instituted by Christ and confess their sins, their own acts become part of the sacrament itself, which is completed when the words of absolution are spoken by the minister in the name of Christ.

In this way the faithful, even as they experience and proclaim the mercy of God in their own life, are with the priest celebrating the liturgy of the Church's continual self-renewal.

IV. CELEBRATION OF THE SACRAMENT OF PENANCE

PLACE OF CELEBRATION

3077   12. The locations for the ministration of the sacrament of penance and the place of the confessor are those prescribed by canon law.

TIME OF CELEBRATION

3078   13. The reconciliation of penitents may be celebrated in all liturgical seasons and on any day. But it is right that the faithful be informed of the day and hours at which the priest is available for this ministry. They should be encouraged to approach the sacrament of penance at times when Mass is not being celebrated and preferably at the scheduled hours.[44]

Lent is the season most appropriate for celebrating the sacrament of penance. Already on Ash Wednesday the people of God hear the solemn invitation, "Turn away from sin and be faithful to the Gospel." It is therefore fitting to have several penitential services during Lent, so that all the faithful may have an opportunity to be reconciled with God and their neighbor and so be able to celebrate the paschal mystery in the Easter triduum with renewed hearts.

LITURGICAL VESTMENTS

3079   14. With respect to liturgical vestments in the celebration of penance, the norms laid down by the local Ordinaries are to be followed.

A. RITE FOR RECONCILIATION OF INDIVIDUAL PENITENTS

PREPARATION OF PRIEST AND PENITENT

3080   15. Priest and penitents should prepare themselves above all by prayer to celebrate the sacrament. The priest should call upon the Holy Spirit so that he may receive enlightenment and charity; the penitents should compare their own life with the example and commandments of Christ and then pray to God for the forgiveness of their sins.

---

[43]   See SC art. 7 [DOL 1 no. 7].

[44]   See SCR, Instr. EuchMyst, 25 May 1967, no. 35 [DOL 179 no. 1264].

WELCOMING THE PENITENT

16. The priest should welcome penitents with fraternal charity and, if need be, address them with friendly words. The penitent then makes the sign of the cross, saying: *In the name of the Father, and of the Son, and of the Holy Spirit. Amen.* The priest may also make the sign of the cross with the penitent. Next the priest briefly urges the penitent to have confidence in God. Penitents who are unknown to the priest are advised to inform him of their state in life, the time of their last confession, their difficulties in leading the Christian life, and anything else that may help the confessor in the exercise of his ministry.

3081

READING OF THE WORD OF GOD

17. Next, the occasion may be taken for the priest, or even the penitent, to read a text of holy Scripture, or this may be done as part of the preparation for the actual celebration of the sacrament. For through the word of God Christians receive light to recognize their sins and are called to conversion and to confidence in God's mercy.

3082

PENITENT'S CONFESSION AND ACCEPTANCE OF THE PENANCE

18. Next comes the penitent's confession of sins, beginning with the general confession formulary, *I confess to almighty God,* if this is the custom. If necessary, the confessor assists the penitent to make a complete confession; he also encourages the penitent to repent sincerely for offenses against God; finally he offers practical advice for beginning a new life, and, where necessary, gives instruction on the duties of the Christian life .

3083

A penitent who has been the cause of harm or scandal to others is to be led by the priest to resolve to make due restitution.

Next, the priest imposes an act of penance or expiation on the penitent; this should serve not only as atonement for past sins but also as an aid to a new life and an antidote for weakness. As far as possible, therefore, the penance should correspond to the seriousness and nature of the sins. This act of penance may suitably take the form of prayer, self-denial, and especially service to neighbor and works of mercy. These will underline the fact that sin and its forgiveness have a social aspect.

PENITENT'S PRAYER AND THE PRIEST'S ABSOLUTION

19. Next, through a prayer for God's pardon the penitent expresses contrition and the resolution to begin a new life. It is advantageous for this prayer to be based on the words of Scripture.

3084

Following the penitent's prayer, the priest extends his hands, or at least his right hand, over the head of the penitent and pronounces the formulary of absolution, in which the essential words are: I ABSOLVE YOU FROM YOUR SINS IN THE NAME OF THE FATHER AND OF THE SON AND OF THE HOLY SPIRIT. As he says the final phrase the priest makes the sign of the cross over the penitent. The form of absolution (see no. 46) indicates that the reconciliation of the penitent comes from the mercy of the Father; it shows the connection between the reconciliation of the sinner and the paschal mystery of Christ; it stresses the role of the Holy Spirit in the forgiveness of sins; finally, it underlines the ecclesial aspect of the sacrament, because reconciliation with God is asked for and given through the ministry of the Church.

PROCLAMATION OF PRAISE AND DISMISSAL OF THE PENITENT

20. After receiving pardon for sin, the penitent praises the mercy of God and gives him thanks in a short invocation taken from Scripture. Then the priest bids the penitent to go in peace.

3085

The penitent continues the conversion thus begun and expresses it by a life renewed according to the Gospel and more and more steeped in the love of God, for "love covers over a multitude of sins" (1 Pt 4:8).

SHORTER RITE

3086   21. When pastoral need dictates, the priest may omit or shorten some parts of the rite but must always retain in their entirety the penitent's confession of sins and acceptance of the act of penance, the invitation to contrition (no. 44), and the formularies of absolution and dismissal. In imminent danger of death, it is sufficient for the priest to say the essential words of the form of absolution, namely: I ABSOLVE YOU FROM YOUR SINS IN THE NAME OF THE FATHER, AND OF THE SON, AND OF THE HOLY SPIRIT.

B. Rite for Reconciliation of Several Penitents with Individual Confession and Absolution

3087   22. When a number of penitents assemble at the same time to receive sacramental reconciliation, it is fitting that they be prepared for the sacrament by a celebration of the word of God.

Those who will receive the sacrament at another time may also take part in the service.

Communal celebration shows more clearly the ecclesial nature of penance. The faithful listen together to the word of God, which as it proclaims his mercy invites them to conversion; at the same time they examine the conformity of their lives with that word of God and help each other through common prayer. After confessing and being absolved individually, all join in praising God together for his wonderful deeds on behalf of the people he has gained for himself through the blood of his Son.

If necessary, several priests should be available in suitable places to hear individual confessions and to reconcile the penitents.

INTRODUCTORY RITES

3088   23. When the faithful have gathered, a suitable hymn may be sung. Then the priest greets them and, if necessary, he or another minister gives a brief introduction to the celebration and explains the order of service. Next he invites all to pray and after a period of silence completes the opening prayer.

CELEBRATION OF THE WORD OF GOD

3089   24. The sacrament of penance should begin with a hearing of God's word, because through his word God calls his people to repentance and leads them to a true conversion of heart.

One or more readings may be chosen. If more than one are read, a psalm, another suitable song, or a period of silence should be inserted between them, so that the word of God may be more deeply understood and heartfelt assent may be given to it. If there is only one reading, it is preferable that it be from a gospel.

Readings should be chosen that will:

a.   let God's voice be heard, calling his people back to conversion and ever closer conformity with Christ;

b.   call to mind the mystery of our reconciliation through the death and resurrection of Christ and through the gift of the Holy Spirit;

c.   bring to bear on people's lives God's judgment of good and evil as a light for the examination of conscience.

25. The homily, taking as its source the scriptural text, should lead the penitents to examine their conscience and to turn away from sin and toward God. It should remind the faithful that sin works against God, against the community and one's neighbors, and against the person of the sinner. Therefore it would be good to recall: 3090

    a. the infinite mercy of God, greater than all our sins, by which again and again he calls us back to himself;

    b. the need for inner repentance, by which we are genuinely prepared to make reparation for sin;

    c. the social dimension of grace and sin whose effect is that in some way the actions of individuals affect the whole Body of the Church;

    d. the duty of expiation for sin, which is effective because of Christ's expiation and requires especially, in addition to works of penance, the exercise of true charity toward God and neighbor.

26. After the homily a suitable period of silence should be allowed for an examination of conscience and the awakening of true contrition for sin. The priest or a deacon or other minister may help the faithful with brief considerations or a litany, adapted to their background, age, etc. 3091

If it should seem suitable, the community's examination of conscience and awakening of contrition may take the place of the homily. But in this case the text of Scripture that has just been read should serve as the starting point.

RITE OF RECONCILIATION

27. At the invitation of the deacon or other minister, all kneel or bow down and say a form of general confession (for example, the prayer, *I confess to almighty God*). Then they stand, if this seems useful, and join in a litany or suitable song to express confession of sins, heartfelt contrition, prayer for forgiveness, and trust in God's mercy. Finally, they say the Lord's Prayer, which is never omitted. 3092

28. After the Lord's Prayer the priests go to the places assigned for confession. The penitents who desire to confess their sins go to the priest of their choice. After they have accepted a suitable act of penance, the priest absolves them, using the formulary for the reconciliation of an individual penitent. 3093

29. When the confessions are over, the priests return to the sanctuary. The priest who presides invites all to make an act of thanksgiving to praise God for his mercy. This may be done in a psalm or hymn or litany. Finally, the priest concludes the celebration with one of the prayers in praise of God for this great love. 3094

DISMISSAL OF THE PEOPLE

30. After the prayer of thanksgiving the priest blesses the faithful. Then the deacon or the priest himself dismisses the congregation. 3095

C. Rite for Reconciliation of Penitents with General Confession and Absolution

DISCIPLINE OF GENERAL ABSOLUTION

31. An individual, complete confession and the receiving of absolution remain the only ordinary way for the faithful to obtain reconciliation with God and the Church, unless physical or moral impossibility excuses from this kind of confession. 3096

Special, occasional circumstances may render it lawful and even necessary to give general absolution to a number of penitents without their previous individual confession.

In addition to the case of danger of death, general absolution for many of the faithful who have only confessed generically, but have been rightly disposed for penance, is lawful if there is a serious need. This means a case in which, given the number of penitents, not enough confessors are available to hear the individual confessions properly within a reasonable time, with the result that, through no fault of their own, the faithful would be forced to be for a long time without the grace of the sacrament or without communion. Such a situation may occur in mission lands particularly, but in other places as well and in groups of people to whom the serious need mentioned clearly applies.

When confessors can be made available, however, the procedure is not lawful solely on the basis of a large number of penitents, for example, at some great festival or pilgrimage.[45]

3097   32. It belongs exclusively to the local Ordinary, after consultation with other members of the conference of bishops, to make the judgment on whether the conditions stated already are verified and therefore to decide when it is lawful to give general absolution.

If, apart from the instances established by the local Ordinary, any other serious need arises for giving general absolution, a priest is bound first, whenever possible, to have recourse to the local Ordinary in order to give the general absolution. If this is not possible, he is to inform the same Ordinary as soon as possible of the need in question and of the fact of the absolution.[46]

3098   33. With respect to the faithful, it is absolutely required for the reception of general sacramental absolution that they have the proper dispositions. This means that they repent individually of their sins, have the intention of refraining from them, are resolved to rectify scandal or injuries they may have caused, and intend to make an individual confession in due time of those serious sins they cannot at the present time confess. Priests are to take pains to instruct the faithful about these dispositions and conditions that are prerequisites for the sacrament to have its effect.[47]

3099   34. Unless there is a good reason preventing it, those who receive pardon for serious sin through general absolution are to go to auricular confession before any further reception of general absolution. And unless a moral impossibility stands in the way, they are absolutely bound to go to a confessor within one year. For the precept binding every one of the faithful binds them as well, namely, to confess individually to a priest at least once a year all those grave sins not hitherto confessed one by one.[48]

RITE OF GENERAL ABSOLUTION

3100   35. For the reconciliation of penitents by general confession and absolution in the cases provided by law, everything takes place as described already for the reconciliation of several penitents with individual confession and absolution, with the following exceptions.

---

[45]   SCDF, Pastoral Norms for General Absolution, 16 June 1972, Norm III [DOL 361 no. 3041].

[46]   Ibid. Norm V [DOL 361 no. 3043].

[47]   Ibid. Norms VI and XI [DOL 361 nos. 3044 and 3049].

[48]   Ibid. Norms VII and VIII [DOL 361 nos. 3045 and 3046].

a. After the homily or during it, the faithful who seek general absolution are to be instructed to dispose themselves properly, that is, to have a personal sorrow for sins committed and the resolve to avoid committing them again; the intention to repair any scandal and harm caused and likewise to confess in due time each one of the grave sins that they cannot confess at present.[49] Some expiatory penance should be proposed for all to perform; individuals may add to this penance if they wish.

b. The deacon, another minister, or the priest then calls upon the penitents who wish to receive absolution to show their intention by some sign (for example, by bowing their heads, kneeling, or giving some other sign determined by the conferences of bishops). They should also say together a form of general confession (for example, the prayer, *I confess to almighty God*), which may be followed by a litany or a penitential song. Then the Lord's Prayer is sung or said by all, as indicated in no. 27.

c. Then the priest pronounces the invocation that expresses prayer for the grace of the Holy Spirit to pardon sin, proclamation of victory over sin through Christ's death and resurrection, and the sacramental absolution given to the penitents.

d. Finally, the priest invites the people to give thanks, as indicated in no. 29 and, omitting the concluding prayer, he immediately blesses and dismisses them.

V. PENITENTIAL SERVICES

NATURE AND STRUCTURE

36. Penitential services are gatherings of the people of God to hear God's word as an invitation to conversion and renewal of life and as the message of our liberation from sin through Christ's death and resurrection. The structure of these services is the same as that usually followed in celebrations of the word of God[50] and given in the *Rite for Reconciliation of Several Penitents*.   3101

It is appropriate, therefore, that after the introductory rites (song, greeting, and opening prayer) one or more biblical readings be chosen with songs, psalms, or periods of silence inserted between them. In the homily these readings should be explained and applied to the congregation. Before or after the readings from Scripture, readings from the Fathers or other writers may also be selected that will help the community and each person to a true awareness of sin and heartfelt sorrow, in other words, to bring about conversion of life.

After the homily and reflection on God's word, it is desirable that the congregation, united in voice and spirit, pray together in a litany or in some other way suited to general participation. At the end the Lord's Prayer is said, asking God our Father "to forgive us our sins as we forgive those who sin against us . . . and deliver us from evil." The priest or the minister who presides concludes with a prayer and the dismissal of the people.

BENEFIT AND IMPORTANCE

37. Care must be taken to ensure that the faithful do not confuse these celebrations with the celebration of the sacrament of penance.[51] Penitential services are very helpful in promoting conversion of life and purification of heart.[52]   3102

It is desirable to arrange them especially for these purposes:

---

[49]   See ibid. Norm VI [DOL 361 no. 3044].

[50]   See SCR, Instr. InterOec, 26 Sept. 1964, nos. 37–39 [DOL 23 nos. 329–331].

[51]   See SCDF, Pastoral Norms for General Absolution, Norm X [DOL 361 no. 3048].

[52]   Ibid.

— to foster the spirit of penance within the Christian community;

— to help the faithful to prepare for individual confession that can be made later at a convenient time;

— to help children gradually to form their conscience about sin in human life and about freedom from sin through Christ;

— to help catechumens during their conversion.

Penitential services, moreover, are very useful in places where no priest is available to give sacramental absolution. They offer help in reaching that perfect contrition that comes from charity and that enables the faithful to receive God's grace through a desire for the sacrament of penance in the future.[53]

VI. ADAPTATIONS OF THE RITE TO VARIOUS REGIONS AND CIRCUMSTANCES

ADAPTATIONS BY THE CONFERENCES OF BISHOPS

3103   38. In preparing particular rituals, the conferences of bishops have the authority to adapt the rite of penance to the needs of individual regions so that, after confirmation of the conference's decisions by the Apostolic See, the rituals may be used in the respective regions. It is the responsibility of the conferences of bishops in this matter:

a. to establish regulations for the discipline of the sacrament of penance, particularly those affecting the ministry of priests and the reservation of sins;

b. to determine more precisely regulations about the place proper for the ordinary celebration of the sacrament of penance and about the signs of repentance to be shown by the faithful before general absolution (see no. 35);

c. to prepare translations of texts adapted to the character and language of each people; also to compose new texts of prayers for use by the faithful and the minister, keeping the essential sacramental formulary intact.

COMPETENCE OF THE BISHOP

3104   39. It is for the diocesan bishop:

a. to regulate the discipline of penance in his diocese,[54] even to the extent of adapting the rite according to the rules proposed by the conference of bishops;

b. to determine, after consultation with the other members of the conference of bishops, when general sacramental absolution may be permitted under the conditions laid down by the Holy See.[55]

ADAPTATIONS BY THE MINISTER

3105   40. It is for priests, and especially parish priests (pastors):

a. in celebrating reconciliation with individuals or with a community, to adapt the rite to the concrete circumstances of the penitents. They must preserve the essential structure and the entire form of absolution, but if necessary they may omit some parts of the rite for pastoral reasons or enlarge upon them, may select the texts of readings or prayers, and may choose a place more suitable for the celebration according to the regulations of the conference of bishops, so that the entire celebration may be enriching and effective;

b. to schedule and prepare occasional penitential services during the year, especially in Lent. In order that the texts chosen and the order of the celebra-

---

[53]   See Council of Trent, sess. 14, *De sacramento Paenitentiae* cap. 5: Denz-Schön 1677.

[54]   See LG no. 26 [DOL 4 no. 146].

[55]   See SCDF, Pastoral Norms for General Absolution, Norm V [DOL 361 no. 3043].

tion may be adapted to the conditions and circumstances of the community or group (for example, children, sick persons, etc.), priests may be assisted by others, including the laity;

c. to decide to give general sacramental absolution preceded by only a generic confession, when a grave need not provided for by the diocesan bishop arises and when recourse to him is not possible. They are obliged to notify the Ordinary as soon as possible of such a need and of the fact that absolution was given.

APPENDIX II
SAMPLES OF PENITENTIAL SERVICES

PLANNING PENITENTIAL SERVICES

1. Penitential services, already discussed in the *Rite of Penance* (nos. 36–37), are extremely helpful in advancing the life of both individuals and communities toward the spirit and virtue of penance and toward a preparation for a more beneficial celebration of the sacrament of penance. But measures are to be taken to ensure that the faithful do not confuse these celebrations with sacramental confession and absolution.[1]

　　3106

2. Penitential services, and particularly those arranged for special groups and occasions, are to take carefully into account the specific kind of life, manner of expression, and intellectual capacities of the congregation. Thus it shall be the responsibility of liturgical commissions[2] and each Christian community to prepare penitential services in such a way that the texts chosen and the rite observed are suitable according to the group involved and the particular occasion.

　　3107

3. As a help in this matter several different samples of penitential services are here given. They are, however, to be taken as models, to be adapted to the proper and distinctive conditions of each community.

　　3108

4. Sometimes these services will include the sacrament of penance. In such cases after the readings and the homily the rite for reconciling several penitents with individual confession and absolution is to be used (*Rite of Penance* nos. 54–59) or, in those special cases for which the law provides, the rite for general confession and absolution (*Rite of Penance* nos. 60–63).

　　3109

369. PAUL VI, **Address** to a general audience, on the new rite of penance, 3 April 1974: Not 10 (1974) 225–227 (Italian; excerpt).

We must not be indifferent and certainly not distrustful toward the invitation the Church is now addressing to us to reform our way of thinking and therefore also our religious practice relative to the sacrament of penance, which from now on we will do better to speak of as the sacrament of reconciliation. By that we mean, first, reconciliation with God; this is something we are familiar with even if it will always be a reason for endless and joyous wonder. We mean also reconciliation

　　3110

---

[1]　See SCDF, Pastoral Norms on General Absolution, 16 June 1972, Norm X [DOL 361 no. 3048].

[2]　See SCR, Instr. InterOec no. 39 [DOL 23 no. 331].

with the Church; the sacrament of penance brings us back to the Church from the condition of being sick and dead members to that of being healthy and alive. It is at this point that a new matter for reflection begins, offered to our ecclesial consciousness by the publication of the new *Rite of Penance*, a text promulgated as a result of the conciliar reform of the liturgy.[a] The reflection is this: just as our every personal failure has its impact on our own essential and vital relationship with God, so too that failure has its impact on our relationship with the community, which in an analogous sense is also essential and vital and which binds us to Christ's Mystical Body, that is, with the holy and living Church whose members we are. As is always the case in our religious world, we find here too those experiences characteristic of life, the experiences of wonder and joy. To be a holy and living part of the Church of God, of redeemed humanity: Brothers and children, we would do well to devote particular attention to this theme of the sacrament of penance, reformed in spirit and in rite. We are talking precisely about the supreme interest of our life, our own salvation.

We are dealing with walking on the edge of two great abysses [. . .]. The one is that of sin; today's mentality is blinding itself to the existence of sin and blocking out the dizzying sight of sin's lethal and fearsome depths. The other abyss is that of love, of goodness, of mercy, of grace, of resurrection: it is what God offers to our freedom at the level of redemption and of the sacramental activity of the Church.

3111   A second point. This freedom of ours, which either suddenly but more often gradually must turn itself toward the ocean of salvation, is at this point called, we repeat, conversion. Our powers of soul are submerged in their own disordered attitudes, prone to their own egocentric, lower instincts. Conversion means a choice, a direction, a turning of those powers to the good, to life, to God, who, like the good shepherd in the gospel, comes in search of us. Conversion is the personally decisive moment of *metanoia*, of repentance, the moment of remorse, of contrition. It is distinctive of contrition to add purer and more valid motives to the conscious regret for personal failure. These are the motives of seeing sin as an offense against God and as a sundering of ecclesial communion: they go beyond the consideration of the debasing of the individual dignity of a person made in God's image.

3112   A third point concerns the rite of penance, the practical "how is it done." In this respect the reform of the liturgy has had noteworthy developments. For it envisions three possible forms of reconciliation. The first is the reconciliation of an individual, which continues as always, but with a new emphasis on the demand for personal dispositions and on the relationship to the word of God. Through God's word the blessed message of his kindness comes to us and towards God's word we must direct our souls, as they first are converted then justified. This form of reconciliation is the accustomed one, but enriched by a greater awareness, seriousness, listening, and so to speak, by a new outpouring of divine love and of our own inexpressible joy in the knowledge of being restored to divine life. We will never reach the point of saying enough in defense of the sacrament of reconciliation: for us sinners it is a renewed baptism of supernatural rebirth.

The second way of reconciliation is that of a communal preparation followed by individual confession and absolution. It combines the two values of being a community act and a personal act. It is a preferable form of reconciliation for our people when it is possible but it usually presupposes the presence of many ministers of the sacrament and this is not always easy. Still, we hope that especially for homogeneous groups — children, youth, workers, the sick, pilgrims, etc. — it may

---

    [a] See DOL 367 and 368.

become the normal way of celebration, since it involves a more complete preparation and a more structured service.

Then there is the third way, a collective form of reconciliation with a single, general absolution. This form, however, is by way of exception, of necessity, in cases sanctioned by the bishops, and with the continuing obligation of individual accusation of grave sins, that is, mortal sins, at a later time.

You have already heard these things repeatedly and you will hear them again.   3113
You will also hear the clarification and correction of certain inaccurate reports that have been circulated regarding the new rite of penance, for example, that confessionals have been eliminated. The confessional must remain: it serves as the protective screen between the minister and the penitent, as a guarantee of the absolute reserve imposed on their communication and proper to it. (Remember what Guitton wrote about the Abbé Guillaume Pouget, an exceptional priest, a master of the spiritual life, and most perceptive thinker. He was a Vincentian and all kinds of people, many of them famous and highly placed, visited him in his own room — in Paris, Rue de Sèvres 85 — and ended up going to confession there, because he was blind: see J. Guitton, *Portrait de M. Pouget*, Gallimard, 1941; *Dialogues avec M. Pouget*, Grasset, 1954.)

But regarding this theme we wish to recommend, very simply, two things that we think to be extremely important. The first is for all: namely, that they give or, if necessary, restore to the sacrament of penance the essential role belonging to it in the Christian life. In practice there is no redeeming of human frailty, we can say, and there is no true vocation to follow Christ and to spiritual perfection that does not derive from the serious and wise use of this sacrament of humility and joy. The second thing is for priests: namely, to urge on them high regard for the care of souls, its patient practice, and its art. These all belong to their ministry. This is not a matter of giving to the priest, so to speak, an "integralist" or individualistic course to follow, removed from the great problems of community and society. It is rather a matter of priests' faithfulness to their distinctive calling as ministers of grace and specialists in the art of healing souls, even more so than today's psychologists and psychiatrists. We offer these two burning recommendations accompanied by our apostolic blessing. (See R. Guardini, *La coscienza*, Morcelliana, Brescia; *Valore e attualità del Sacr. della Penitenza*, Pianazzi e Triacra, Pas-Verlag, 1974).

370. SC DOCTRINE OF THE FAITH, Letter to Cardinal F. Marty, President of the conference of bishops of France, on the preparation of vernacular editions of the rite of penance, 3 June 1974.*

Regarding the preparation in the vernacular of new rituals for penance, the   3114
Congregation for the Doctrine of the Faith deems it important and even indispensable that such liturgical books all include an *integral and faithful* translation of the *Praenotanda* of the new *Ordo Paenitentiae*. This text in fact provides doctrinal and disciplinary principles that apply to the whole Church. It therefore stands as the obligatory reference point and provides a clear setting for adaptations that the various conferences of bishops judge to be necessary.

· SCDF, Prot. 274/64.

371. PAUL VI, **Address** to a general audience, on the sacrament of reconciliation, 26 February 1975: Not 11 (1975) 65–66 (Italian).

3115   We choose for today the important topic of the place that the sacrament of penance holds in the plan of salvation. There is a corresponding question with historical roots going back to the third century and more recently to the controversy with the Protestants. That question is whether in the system of the Christian faith there exists a sacrament of repentance after baptism. Can a Christian falling into sin after baptism still have any recourse to the mercy of God? Those baptized have the priceless benefit of divine grace, that is, of the joining of their life, through Christ's merits, with the inexpressible, transcendent life of God (see 2 Pt 1:4). Can the sins of such persons still find pardon once they have shattered and betrayed that vital union? Christians are by definition the faithful. If, alas, they do not remain faithful, can they presume, or at least hope, to be readmitted into the state of grace? Presupposing inexhaustible goodness on God's part, is the contrition of sinners, based on faith, enough for their return to the life-giving friendship of God and the communion of the Church?

And here is the first truth, paradoxical but no less real: on the level of God's goodness the possibility does exist for the pardon of the sins even of Christians, which after baptism take on a greater, more abhorrent seriousness. We know this and rejoice in it: that possibility does exist. Bound by too narrow and literal an interpretation of a single text in Hebrews — "For if we sin willfully after we have received the knowledge of the truth, there remains no more sacrifice for sins" (10:26) — the early Church in some places was reluctant to acknowledge the forgiveness of some, more serious and scandalous sins, like apostasy, murder, and adultery. The teaching and the discipline regarding penance evolved, however, especially after the persecution of Decius when first Pope Cornelius then St. Cyprian in Carthage acknowledged that the *lapsi* (those who to escape torture had sacrificed to the gods) could be admitted to penance and be reconciled if genuinely repentant (see A. Saba, *Storia della Chiesa* 1, 166. St. Cyprian, *De Lapsis*: PL 4, 463–494. G. Mercati, *Le Lettere di S. Cornelio papa*, etc.). Was there not a solid basis for this development in the Lord's words (Mt 16:19; 18:18 and 22: *usque ad septuagies septies*; Jn 20:23) ? This saving generosity inspired the development of penitential practices in which, as we shall see, contrition has a constant importance. These practices also gave rise to sacramental confession, which since last year's publication of the new *Rite of Penance* by the Congregation for Divine Worship,[a] has had a ritual form meeting the criteria of Vatican Council II. The *Rite of Penance* ranks undoubtedly with the most significant recent liturgical and pastoral legislation and, we hope, with the most effective documents of reform and of moral and spiritual reconciliation. We urge you to study this new rite.

There is great reason for us to fix our attention, our amazement, and our joy on the fact that Christ has obtained for us through the institution of the sacrament of penance pardon for sins after baptism (see Denz-Schön 1601, 1701), sins that are so senseless and deserving reproach. This truly is an act of infinite kindness and mercy, an intervention of God's own power (see Mk 2:7) to restore souls to new and divine life.

By our faith and devotion let us give to this sacrament or, if necessary, give back to it, the gratitude, the rejoicing that it deserves.

---

[a]   See DOL 368.

372. PAUL VI, **Address** to a general audience, on the conditions for receiving the sacrament of penance, 5 March 1975.*

We continue our current passage along the simple but salutary path of our   3116
catechism, the Catholic teaching we share together.

Responsive to the spirituality distinctive of Lent and to the insistent summons of the Holy Year, we have the present and continuing duty to fix our attention on the act and precise moment of our own conversion, that is, on the sacrament of penance, which we are accustomed to call confession.

All of us know what this involves and we are not going to repeat the catechism lesson on this topic. But it is so important and so controverted that we do not think it superfluous to recall some aspects of this topic. First of all, we have not yet said anything about the divine, transcendent, supernatural element in this sacrament. That part is something tremendous, because it restores grace, that is, it revives the divine life. This is what counts most in our souls. At this time we must recall that God's saving intervention demands certain conditions on the part of the recipient. We all know what these are. The sacramental causality of penance is not something automatic or magical. It involves an encounter having as its prerequisites amenability, receptivity, a predisposition, a particular, human collaboration.

These prerequisites constitute the problem on the human side, the encounter with the gift of divine grace offered by the sacrament of penance. On this point a whole moral and religious psychology could be elaborated.

Here we simplify the immense work of analysis opened up by the topic to   3117
stress the two cardinal points in this area of the Catholic discipline of penance. The first has the difficult and somber name, "contrition," coming from the Council of Trent. This Council devoted a great deal of study to this element in Catholic teaching; we find its essential formulation repeated in our catechism. Trent says: "Contrition, which holds the primary place among the penitent's acts, is sorrow of soul and detestation for the sin committed, with the intention of not sinning again" (Denz-Schön 1676). Sorrow of soul is not an easy, nor a pleasant matter. It issues from a consciousness of something from which a person ordinarily seeks to draw back, the consciousness of sin. That in turn presupposes faith in the relationship existing between our life and the unbreakable and abiding law of God. In these times a secularizing, sometimes worse than pagan morality has taken root. It cauterizes the moral conscience after having extinguished the sense of religion. Sin — that immeasurable, mysterious repercussion of disordered human activity upon God — no longer has any standing; it signifies nothing. Human activity in its most exalted meaning no longer has for its point of reference either God's law or God's goodness. Rather its direction lies elsewhere: utility, self-interest, pleasure, success, the absolute independence of the will, the feelings, and subjective caprice. No longer is there any room in the central, inner depths of the human heart for contrition, remorse at having offended God. The heart is closed off hermetically by the unyielding seals of radical worldliness.

We will not stop to describe the danger, the harm, the penalties of this moral petrification. They are obvious to anyone with a simple eye or a professional eye on the deterioration of modern life. We prefer to speak about the revivifying effectiveness of contrition when its motives are the offense committed against God's goodness, on the one hand, and the ugliness of sin's wickedness on the other; that is, when, in the language of theology, contrition is "perfect." Contrition so understood is already in itself the reason for God's pardon, when it is accompanied

---

    * Text, OR 6 March 1975, 1 (Italian).

by the resolve to receive the sacrament of penance as soon as possible (see St. Thomas Aquinas, Suppl. 5, 1). A letter from a religious has suggested that we call the attention of our listeners to this providential way of obtaining the Lord's mercy for anyone who is in danger of death and without the possibility of the help of the minister of the sacrament (see Denz-Schön 1677). It is something to be aware of.

3118   The other cardinal point in this material is confession. Confession is the self-accusation made by a person seeking God's pardon of personal sins and the details of their moral kind and circumstances, to a minister authorized to hear and absolve the penitent. It appears to be a fearful business and a fearful penalty. So it is for anyone who has not had the experience of the humility that discovers the voice of truth and justice speaking within and the liberating, comforting hope of sacramental absolution. The moments of a sincere confession are perhaps among the sweetest, most consoling, most decisive moments of life. Whatever the case, this for us is a turning point in our own salvation: we may apply to it the well-known statement of Augustine: "He who created you without you, will not save you without you" (*Serm.* 169, 11: PL 38, 923).

This moment of our Christian life must also be looked on with childlike humility and mature courage.

373. PAUL VI, **Address** to a general audience, on the ministerial aspect of the sacrament of penance, 12 March 1975.*

3119   The Lent we are now celebrating in preparation for Easter and the nearness of that holy, dramatic feast oblige us to complete our own catechetical review with a call to the spirit of penance. This cannot be missing in any person who regards Easter as a central event in our religious practice and as a responsibility to enter into the mystery of salvation through an intense, personal participation (see Ap. Const. *Paenitemini* IX, 2).ª

The spirit of penance demands by its own inner logic a definite practice of penance, formerly seriously binding all of the faithful; in our own times this has become more flexible and more limited in its obligatory acts (for those held to it, for example, fasting is obligatory only on two days, Ash Wednesday and Good Friday). This, however, does not abolish the fact that the three other penitential practices are all the more recommended for voluntary acceptance by all the faithful: prayer, mortification, and doing works of charity.ᵇ

There remains, however, one traditional and obligatory sacramental act characterizing and enriching this season of conversion and expiation. As all know, this is the act of confession, the act of penance par excellence. The recent liturgical reform has resulted in valuable norms and instruction regarding confession. These too we assume are well known, but we also recommend both that they be made widely known by the Church's pastors and teachers and studied and reflected on by the ecclesial community and the faithful individually.

3120   In our talk with you today we summon your attention to the ministerial aspect of this sacrament of penance. Currently there is an erroneous emphasis that would put aside the ritual and ecclesial discipline that this sacrament necessarily includes.

---

*   Text, OR 13 March 1975, 1 (Italian).

ª   See DOL 358 no. 3029.

ᵇ   See DOL 358 no. 3020.

It insists rather on the usual, in itself excellent but incomplete, defense of the inner, intensely personal characteristics required and produced by a genuine repentance in the soul of anyone who has grasped the need and nature of conversion. This is the conversion of heart to God and the renewed conjunction with divine life of a soul that had fallen into sin and therefore death. It is worth observing that this inner, intimate, profound, secret, intense aspect of the sinner's reconciliation with God is today not only preserved but demanded even more than ever (given the highly developed conscience of today's people and the simplifying of public and personal asceticism by the ecclesial rules now in effect). This personal reconciliation of the sinner with God is possible at all times and in cases of emergency suffices to obtain the revivifying pardon of grace through an act of perfect contrition, as the catechism teaches. But we must remember that an act of perfect contrition must include, at least implicitly, the resolve to seek out, as soon as possible, the authorized ministry of the priest, endowed with the awesome power to forgive sins and to reconcile with God and with the living community of the Church those who have been unfaithful.

At this point it is useful to note that sin, if serious, breaks the bond of the sinner with God, but also has another negative effect. Especially and publicly in the early centuries, the Church has attached great importance to this effect. It is the shattering of the social and spiritual bond of the sinner with the Church community. Sin is not only an offense against God and the ruin of the person committing it; sin also wounds ecclesial communion (see *Rite of Penance* no. 5).^c So much so that the Code of Canon Law attaches to certain, specific grave sins excommunication, that is, exclusion, ipso facto (canonists say *latae sententiae*) of an unfaithful member of the Church from sharing in the benefits of ecclesial charity. Sin thus also injures the Church and this damage redounding upon the one guilty of the offense results in the sinner's being, so to speak, cut off from the flow of life that means union with the living organism of the Church. This is the case even if the Church does not actually exercise an act of formal rejection, that is, pronounce sentence of excommunication. 3121

We bring up this sad possibility to underline the need for the priest's ministry. This is human in its expression and limitations, but suprahuman in its power to make effective the divine words of which the priest is minister: "Whose sins you shall forgive they are forgiven them and whose sins you shall retain they are retained" (Jn 20:23). What a sublime Gospel!

It is a most precious and consoling Gospel, a Gospel that obliges and a Gospel running throughout the discipline of the holy Church of God. This Gospel suggests to us two recommendations. The first is to priests (it would deserve a quite long and interesting discourse). Brothers in the priesthood, deepen your practice of this ministry of salvation, become its dedicated specialists. It is most delicate and most demanding, but noble, the direct channel of grace, a true therapy for souls, a source of light and of wisdom, an inexhaustible way to spread good, a school of experience and humility for the ministry itself. Do not neglect it, do not bungle it, never, never desecrate it. Make it become your patient and wise exercise of the charity belonging to the priest. 3122

The second recommendation is to all the faithful. Have trust in sacramental confession. It is an event, first difficult then sweet, that embodies hope in God's mercy. You are careful to choose a qualified physician for the health of your body, a wise psychoanalyst for the health of your mind; know also how to choose, if you can, a spiritual physician, one who is discreet, wise, and good, a real dispenser of

---

^c   See DOL 368 no. 3070.

comfort, of counsel, of admonition, of grace: the grace of the resurrection, the grace of Easter.

374. SECRETARIAT OF STATE, **Letter** of Cardinal J. Villot to Bishop C. Manziana, on the occasion of the 26th National Liturgical Week of Italy (Florence, 25–29 August 1975) on the theme: Reconciled with the Father in Christ and in the Church, 31 July 1975: Not 11 (1975) 220–222 (Italian).

3123   Pope Paul VI has learned with intense satisfaction that the 26th National Liturgical Week, sponsored, as usual, by the Centro di Azione Liturgica and to be held at Florence, will have as its theme: Reconciled with the Father in Christ and in the Church.

This theme is obviously one close to Pope Paul's heart because of the supreme importance of the sacrament of reconciliation in the life of the Church and of individual Christians. He is well aware that since promulgation of the new rite of penance many new programs have begun in the dioceses of Italy, designed to explain the theology and pastoral practice of the new rite and to advance its ever more intelligent use in the Christian life. All of this became part of the pastoral plan of the Italian conference of bishops, which in its 11th general assembly last year approved an important document, "Evangelization and the Sacrament of Penance." The Pope himself has repeatedly turned to this vital topic in his addresses to general audiences in connection with the Holy Year, with Lent, and with the promulgation of the new rite of penance and its gradual employment.[a] He is therefore quite happy that the liturgical week offers the occasion for some reflections that he thinks relevant both to the focus of pastors and to the life of the faithful.

THEME OF THE LITURGICAL WEEK

3124   The week's theme contains before all else the words "Reconciled with the Father." It is right to emphasize the most genuine meaning of reconciliation and so, as was St. Paul's mind, to put the primary emphasis on God's goodness. It is he who first loves us, who first comes to meet us so that we may allow ourselves to be reconciled with him, our Father. This is the origin of our own obligation to be converted, that is, to reverse ourselves and turn to him, who is infinite mercy. Actually mercy as term and as concept so fills the books of the Bible, especially the Book of Psalms, that it has become a characteristic and irreplaceable element in Christian speech and thought to indicate not simply the love of God for human beings, but the distinctive quality of divine love that unceasingly expresses itself and imprints itself in spite of the unworthiness of those who are its recipients.

"Reconciled with the Father in Christ," the theme continues. Christ the Lord, with his blood shed on the cross, is in truth at the center of the mystery of reconciliation. This accordingly is identical with the mystery of human liberation and redemption from the most real and profound form of slavery, the slavery of sin. There can never be enough emphasis on the active presence of Christ, who, through the sacramental sign of reconciliation, actualizes and repeatedly confirms the healing, elevating, and sanctifying powers of the paschal mystery, in the passage from darkness to the sublime light of the divine life.

Any reference to the Father's mercy and the redemption worked by Christ the Lord must open up naturally into a special attention to the Holy Spirit. The risen Christ promised the Spirit to his apostles, along with the power to forgive and to

---

[a]   See, for example, DOL 369, 371, 372, 373, 490.

retain sins; of the Holy Spirit the liturgy says, in its wonderful summary: *He is our forgiveness* (Saturday of the 7th Week of Easter, prayer over the gifts).

Accordingly, the sacrament bears the light of the very life of the blessed Trinity: as point of departure — the Father who first loved us, Christ who has given himself for us, the Holy Spirit poured forth upon us abundantly; and as term — the Father who welcomes his repentant children on their return to him, Christ who then places on his shoulders the lost sheep to return it to the sheepfold, the Holy Spirit who resanctifies his temple or makes his dwelling place in it warmer and more imtimate. We have only to allow ourselves to be suffused by that indescribable light of the mystery of the Trinity in order to grasp the greatness of the sacrament of reconciliation, in order to increase faith in its sacramental effectiveness, and in order to celebrate its rite with confident surrender and active commitment.

"Reconciled with the Father in Christ and the Church." The theme of the Florence meeting concludes. Here we could bring to bear the beautiful language in which the Introduction of the new rite, fashioned out of Pauline, patristic, and conciliar texts presents the Church. The Church appears as bringing about people's conversion when, by Christ's command, it reconciles them to God. The Church also appears as being, in its sinful members, the subject of that conversion and as feeling itself constantly obliged to that conversion in all the manifestations of its own life.[b]

PASTORAL MINISTRY OF THE SACRAMENT

These points are meant to prompt the participants to go deeper, under the guidance of the leaders of the liturgical week, into the major theological and spiritual principles concerning penance as these have been stated by the Council of Trent and remain valid and binding. But in addition it is not out of place to emphasize also other factors that take on great significance in the celebration of this sacrament.   3125

Pope Paul addresses a word especially to priests, so that they will love their ministry, prepare their people through catechesis, and be always ready to hear confessions. The new rite offers many opportunities to give the sacrament its full due, especially in the setting of a celebration of God's word. Nothing, however, will be as important as the availability of pastors and their fidelity to the confessional. Even though the new rite envisages its eventual redesign, approved by lawful authority, the confessional retains its entire important function, particularly, in Pope Paul's words, "as it serves as the protective screen between the minister and the penitent, as a guarantee of the absolute reserve imposed on their communication and proper to it" (Address to a general audience, 3 April 1974).[c]

FREQUENT CONFESSION

The Pope desires, further, to call to the attention of all — priests, religious, and faithful — the frequent use of this sacrament. Regrettably, there are some who have little regard for frequent confession; that, however, is not the mind of the Church. The new rite also recommends frequent confession, portraying it as a renewed commitment to increase the grace of baptism and as the occasion and stimulus for a closer conformity to Christ and of increasing docility to the voice of the Holy Spirit.[d] Also, as Pope Paul underlined in his apostolic exhortation on Christian joy "frequent confession remains a privileged source of holiness, peace, and joy" (AAS 67 [1975] 312).   3126

---

b   See DOL 368 nos. 3066–70.

c   DOL 369 no. 3113.

d   See DOL 368 no. 3072.

The Pope, finally, places a special emphasis on children's confession, particularly their first confession. This must always precede their first communion even if an extended period between the two is helpful. From the earliest years an evangelization must begin that will make ever stronger and more conscious the support of a living faith for their celebration of the sacrament and above all for a sure and consistent way of living the Christian life.

All these topics and others of pastoral importance will doubtless be treated and fully explored during the work of the liturgical week. For this reason it is Pope Paul's hope that the week will be profitable spiritually, to the end that all the participants will derive from it an impetus for their generous apostolate.

375. SC DOCTRINE OF THE FAITH, Letter (U.S.A.), commenting on the Pastoral Norms for General Absolution, 14 January 1977.*

3127   1.   The Pastoral Norms for General Absolution[a] were developed to assist pastors in confronting those existing situations in the life of the Church which are attended by extraordinary circumstances. They are not intended to provide a basis for convoking large gatherings of faithful for the purpose of imparting general absolution, in the absence of such extraordinary circumstances.

3128   2.   As the recent letter of the Congregation for the Sacraments and Divine Worship (October 29, 1976; Prot. N. 936/76) states, for the licit use of general absolution all the conditions specified in Norm III of the above-mentioned Pastoral Norms[b] must be simultaneously verified. This means that the large number of penitents for whom there are insufficient confessors would be deprived of sacramental grace or holy communion for a long time and without any fault of their own. In ordinary circumstances, the faithful would be able to provide for their proper reception of the sacrament of penance in the normal way if not during, then before or after the large gatherings mentioned.

3129   3.   The examples explicitly mentioned in Norm III as inappropriate situations for the use of general absolution — the large crowds foreseen on the occasions of festivals and pilgrimages, when arrangements for confessions can prudently be provided for — would *a fortiori* implicitly exclude the convocation of a large crowd for the primary purpose of giving general absolution.

3130   4.   Norm VI explicitly requires the diligent reminder that the penitent's sincere intention to bring his serious sins to individual confession within a reasonable time is a condition necessary for validity.[c]

3131   5.   Norm X clearly indicates that communal celebrations of the sacrament of penance must be distinct from the celebration of Mass.[d]

3132   6.   Norm XI explicitly calls for the penitent to have a serious intention to remove scandal, where that may be present, before receiving general sacramental absolu-

---

· Text, BCL Newsletter 13 (1977) 57–58, excerpt of the letter, SCDF, Prot. 274/64, to the NCCB.

a   See DOL 361.

b   See DOL 361 no. 3041.

c   See DOL 361 no. 3044.

d   See DOL 361 no. 3048.

tion. Moreover, the norm also clearly states that before one receives holy communion in this case, such scandal must have been removed in accord with the personal judgment of one's individual confessor.[e] This norm will certainly find some application in the case of divorced Catholics who have remarried outside the Church.

376. PAUL VI, **Address** to a general audience, on penance as the "sacrament of resurrection and peace," 23 March 1977: Not 13 (1977) 149–150 (Italian; excerpt).

The nearness of Easter summons us to a duty that is the mark of every faithful Catholic's participation in the celebration of the great feast of the redemption: the duty of confession, that is, of receiving the sacrament of penance, personally and honestly, accusing ourselves of our sins with humble repentance and a firm purpose of amendment. This is a serious law of the Church and it remains in force. [. . .]

3133

We must therefore point to a certain growing failure to keep up the practice of this sacrament that is often accompanied by a marked departure from fidelity and active involvement in ecclesial life. This is greatly disturbing to anyone, whether priest or simple faithful, who loves the mystico-sociological reality of the mystery of our incorporation into Christ, the mystery of grace and of salvation. We are completely and always in need of this sacrament. It is not only canon law that tells us this (see CIC can. 906). So does the least awareness of the profound rebirth affected in us by baptism with the resulting obligation to develop out of this rebirth a personal, integral, and higher life of moral virtue. So does the experience of the spiritual benefits that confession — especially when its use is a constant in the development of the spiritual life — ensures for those who seek to be strong and faithful in living up to their religion (see A. Manzoni, *La Morale cattolica*, 1, ch. 8).

We will not follow this simple allusion with a defense of confession. [. . .] We will say merely that such a defense is possible and obvious for anyone who calls to mind the words of the risen Christ, uttered on the very evening of his resurrection, when he appeared to his disciples in the upper room: "'Peace be unto you: as my Father has sent me, so I send you.' When he had said this, he breathed on them and said to them: 'Whose sins you shall forgive, they are forgiven them and whose sins you shall retain, they are retained'" (Jn 20:21–23). Such was the institution of the sacrament of penance; thus from the outset it is of its nature the sacrament of resurrection of souls that were dead, then brought back to life, the sacrament of life, of peace, and of joy.

We would simply urge our brother priests who are authorized to administer the sacrament of penance that they give to the pastoral practice, sealed and supported by the sacrament, the importance it demands, as well the care and the spirit of wisdom and sacrifice it deserves. Confession is the sacrament of healing par excellence and the sacrament of instruction for formation in the Christian life at all its levels (see the review *Seminarium* no. 3, 1973).

3134

We would also urge all the faithful to rid themselves of any misgiving that the current sacramental discipline may suggest about going to confession. The Church does, in certain, special instances, now permit general absolution. But we are to remember that this permission stands as an exception; it does not remove the obligation of personal confession; it is not intended to deprive us of the experience, the benefits, or the value of confession. As a school of moral wisdom, confession

---

[e] See DOL 361 no. 3049.

forms in the mind the ability to discern good from evil. As a training ground for spiritual vigor, it develops the will in consistency, in positive virtue, in the fulfillment of difficult duties. As a dialogue on Christian perfection, confession helps the discovery of personal vocation and the strengthening of the resolve to fidelity and growth in the sanctification belonging to each individual. May this Easter bring to each of you the blessing of celebrating it with a good confession. Along with communion, this is the great gift of Easter (see the always relevant *Catechismus ex Decreto Concilii Tridentini ad Parochos. De Poenit. Sacramento*, and the recent Pastoral Norms on General Absolution of the Congregation for the Doctrine of the Faith, 16 June 1972, AAS 64, 1972, 510ff.).[a]

▶ 334. SC BISHOPS, Decree *Apostolatus maris*, on the pastoral ministry to seamen and ship passengers, 24 September 1977:

Part II, I, nos. 9–10: Absolution from censures no. [2679].

▶ 68. PAUL VI, Address to the bishops of Holland, on celebrating in faith and joy, 17 November 1977:

Sacrament of penance [no. 598].

377. SC DOCTRINE OF THE FAITH, Reply (U.S.A.) to a query, on general absolution, 20 January 1978: Not 14 (1978) 6–7 (English).*

A QUESTION ABOUT GENERAL ABSOLUTION

3135   In the case of a certain ecclesiastical jurisdiction "X," special penitential services in preparation for Easter were planned, specifying places and times in which general absolution would be given, together with provision for preparation of the people for such services. This pastoral plan was favorably received by the faithful, and general absolution was given in the presence of several priests, some of whom were also penitents. Is the case described above in conformity with the norms for general absolution?

RESPONSE

The Congregation for the Doctrine of the Faith replies that the case described does not conform to the 1972 *Normae pastorales circa absolutionem sacramentalem generali modo impertiendam* (AAS vol. 64, pp. 510–514) because the conditions listed for the use of the extraordinary practice of general absolution are not necessarily verified.

3136   1. Norm III requires that the faithful, too large in number for the small number of priests to hear their individual confessions properly within a suitable period of time, would have to go without sacramental grace or holy communion for a long time and through no fault of their own.[a]

    The case described does not offer any reason why the faithful could not find other opportunities for confession and holy communion, which are normally

---

    [a] See DOL 361.

    * English text, SCDF, Prot. N. 274/64, also in BCL Newsletter 14 (1968) 114.

    [a] See DOL 361 no. 3041.

offered on a regular basis in their parishes; such a reason might be present, for example, where a priest could visit a remote mission station only infrequently.

2.   Norm IV requires that bishops and priests dispose the arrangement of pastoral   3137
duties so that a sufficient number of priests will be available for the ministry of
sacramental confession.[b]

The case described does not offer any reason why the available priests could
not arrange for the normal confession procedures according to nos. 15–21 and
22–30 of the *Ordo Paenitentiae*.[c]

378. PAUL VI, **Address** to bishops of the United States from New York, on
the sacrament of penance in the Church's teaching, 20 April 1978: Not 14
(1978) 205–207 (English).

For a few moments we would like to reflect with you on a fundamental aspect   3138
of the Gospel: Christ's call to conversion. This theme of conversion was announced
by John the Baptist: "Reform your lives" (Mt 3:2). These words were later spoken
by Jesus himself (see Mt 4:17). And just as the apostles had learned this message
from the Lord, so they were instructed by him to make it the content of their
preaching (see Lk 24:27). On the very day of Pentecost, faithful to the command of
Jesus, Peter proclaimed conversion for the forgiveness of sins (see Acts 2:38). And
St. Paul also says clearly: "I preached a message of reform and of conversion to God
(Acts 26:19).

Dear Brothers, this call to conversion has come down to us from the Lord
Jesus: it is meant for our own lives and for our incessant and fearless proclamation
to the world. On a former occasion we said that conversion is a whole program
linked with the renewing action of the Gospel (see *General Audience*, 9 November
1977). As such, conversion constitutes the goal to be achieved by our apostolic
ministry: to awaken a consciousness of sin in its perennial and tragic reality, a
consciousness of its personal and social dimensions, together with a realization that
"grace has far surpassed sin" (Rom 5:20); and to proclaim salvation in Jesus Christ.

Today we wish to speak to you, your fellow bishops, and brother priests in   3139
America, particularly about certain sacramental aspects of conversion, certain dimensions of the sacrament of penance or of reconciliation. Six years ago, with our
special approval and by our mandate, the Sacred Congregation for the Doctrine of
the Faith promulgated Pastoral Norms regulating general sacramental absolution.
This document, entitled *Sacramentum Paenitentiae*, reiterated the solemn teaching of the
Council of Trent concerning the divine precept of individual confession. The document also acknowledged the difficulty experienced by the faithful in some places in
going to individual confession because of a lack of priests. Provisions were made for
general absolution in cases of grave necessity, and the conditions constituting this
grave necessity were clearly specified (*Norm 3*).[a]

---

  [b]   See DOL 361 no. 3042.

  [c]   See DOL 368 nos. 3080–86 and 3087–95.

  [a]   See DOL 361 no. 3041.

It was then reserved to the Ordinary, after consultation with other members of the episcopal conference, to judge whether the necessary conditions determined by the Apostolic See and specified in Norm 3 were in fact present.[b] Ordinaries were not authorized to change the required conditions, to substitute other conditions for those given, or to determine grave necessity according to their personal criteria, however worthy. *Sacramentum Paenitentiae* recognized in effect that the norms governing the basic discipline of the Church's ministry of reconciliation were a matter of special concern to the universal Church and of regulation by her supreme authority. What is so important in the application of the norms is the general effectiveness of the basic ecclesial ministry of reconciliation in accordance with the intention of Christ the Savior. In the life of the Church general absolution is not to be used as a normal pastoral option or as a means of confronting any difficult pastoral situation. It is permitted only for the extraordinary situations of grave necessity as indicated in Norm 3. Just last year we drew attention publicly to the altogether *exceptional* character of general absolution (see *General Audience*, 23 March 1977).[c]

Brethren, we also recall the words of our bicentennial letter to the bishops of America: "We ask for supreme vigilance in the question of auricular confession" (AAS 68 [1976] 410).[d] And today we add explicitly: we ask for faithful observance of the norms. Fidelity to the communion of the universal Church requires it; at the same time this fidelity will be the guarantee of the supernatural effectiveness of your ecclesial mission of reconciliation.

Moreover, we ask you, the bishops, to help your priests to have an ever greater appreciation of this splendid ministry of theirs as confessors (see LG no. 30). The experience of centuries confirms the importance of this ministry. And if priests deeply understand how closely they collaborate, through the sacrament of penance, with the Savior in the work of conversion, they will give themselves with ever greater zeal to this ministry. More confessors will readily be available to the faithful. Other works, for lack of time, may have to be postponed or even abandoned, but not the confessional. The example of St. John Vianney is not outmoded. The exhortation of Pope John in his Encyclical *Sacerdotii Nostri Primordia* is still extremely relevant.

We have repeatedly asked that the capital function of the sacrament of penance be safeguarded (see *General Audience*, 3 April 1974, 12 March 1975).[e] And two years ago, when we beatified the Capuchin Father Leopoldo da Castelnovo, we pointed out that he reached the highest holiness through a ministry dedicated to the confessional. We believe that conditions in the Church today — in your own dioceses as elsewhere — are ripe for a more diligent and fruitful use of the Sacrament of Penance, in accordance with the *Ordo Paenitentiae*, and for a more intensive ministry on the part of priests, with the consequent fruits of greater holiness and justice in the lives of priests and faithful. But the full actuation of this renewal depends, under God's grace, on your own vigilance and fidelity. It requires constant guidance on your part and strong spiritual leadership. Moreover, with regard to the practice of frequent confession we ask you to recall to your priests and religious and laity — to all the faithful in search of holiness — the words of our predecessor Pius XII: "Not without the inspiration of the Holy Spirit was this practice introduced into the Church" (AAS 35 [1943] 235).

---

[b] See DOL 361 no. 3041.

[c] See DOL 376 [no. 3134].

[d] DOL 60 no. 561.

[e] See DOL 373.

Another important aspect of the penitential discipline of the Church is the   3140
practice of first confession before first communion. Our appeal here is that the
norms of the Apostolic See be not emptied of their meaning by contrary practice. In
this regard we repeat words we spoke last year to a group of bishops during their *ad
limina* visit: "The faithful would be rightly shocked that obvious abuses are tolerat-
ed by those who have received the charge of the 'episcopate,' which stands for,
since the earliest days of the Church, vigilance and unity" (AAS 69 [1977] 473).

There are many other aspects of conversion that we would like to speak to you
about. But we shall conclude by urging you to take back to your people an uplifting
message of confidence, which is: "Christ Jesus our hope" (1 Tm 1:1). In the power of
his resurrection, through the strength of his word, exhort the faithful to continue
the life-long process of conversion, well aware that: "Eye has not seen, ear has not
heard, nor has it so much as dawned on man what God has prepared for those who
love him" (1 Cor 2:9).

▶   291. JOHN PAUL II, Address to Canadian bishops, on sacramental discipline, 17
           November 1978.

▶   191. JOHN PAUL II, Encyclical *Redemptor hominis*, 4 March 1979:

           no.   20:   Eucharist and penance [no. 1331].

▶   192. JOHN PAUL II, Address to the bishops of Bengal, on the eucharist and penance,
           26 April, 1979:

                               Eucharist and penance. [no. 1333].

▶   335. SC CATHOLIC EDUCATION, Instruction *In ecclesiasticam futurorum sacerdotum*, on
           liturgical formation in seminaries, 3 June 1979:

           no.   35:   Penance [no. 2814].

▶   75.   JOHN PAUL II, Address to the bishops of the U.S.A., on bishops as guardians
           and promotors of the liturgy, 5 October 1979.

Section 7. Penance: C. First Confession of Children

SUMMARY (DOL 379–382). Pastoral-liturgical catechesis and adaptation of the liturgy for children gave rise to the particular issue of children's first confession. The 4 texts here represent curial interventions indicating that first confession must precede first communion. The Congregation for the Discipline of the Sacraments published a declaration (DOL 379); the Congregation for the Clergy and for the Sacraments and Divine Worship conjointly issued two letters to the conferences of bishops (DOL 380, 381), and to the second annexed a reply to an explicit query on first confession (DOL 382).

▶   169.   SC CLERGY, *General Catechetical Directory*, 11 August 1971:

> ADDENDUM   First confession and first communion of
>   children [nos. 1115–20].

379. SC DISCIPLINE OF THE SACRAMENTS, Declaration *Sanctus Pontifex*, on children's confession prior to their first communion, 24 May 1973: AAS 65 (1973) 410.

3141   Pope St. Pius X, basing himself on the prescription of canon 21 of Lateran Council IV, ruled through the Decree *Quam singulari*, 8 August 1916 (AAS 2 [1910] 577–583), that children were to receive the sacraments of penance and the eucharist as soon as they reached the age of reason. Put into practice throughout the universal Church, this precept has yielded many good results for the Christian life and spiritual perfection and continues to do so.

The "Addendum" to the General Catechetical Directory, promulgated by the Congregation for the Clergy, 11 April 1971 (AAS 64 [1972] 97–176), confirmed the practice in which children's first communion is preceded by the sacrament of penance in these words: "Having weighed all these points and keeping in mind the common and general practice, which per se cannot be derogated without the approval of the Apostolic See, and also having heard the conferences of bishops, the Holy See judges it fitting that the practice now in force in the Church of putting confession ahead of first communion should be retained" (no. 5).[a]

The same document took into consideration new practices introduced in some regions whereby reception of the eucharist was permitted before reception of the sacrament of penance. The document merely permitted the continuation of these experiments for the time being if "they have first communicated with the Holy See, which will gladly listen to them, and if they are of one mind with the Holy See" (ibid.).

3142   The Congregations for the Discipline of the Sacraments and for the Clergy have considered this matter thoroughly and taken into account the views of the conferences of bishops. With the approval of Pope Paul VI, therefore, the two Congregations by the present document declare that an end must be put to these experiments — which now have gone on for three years — to coincide with the close of the school year 1972–73 and that thereafter the Decree *Quam singulari* must be obeyed everywhere by all.

380. SC SACRAMENTS AND DIVINE WORSHIP and SC CLERGY, Letter to the conferences of bishops, on children's first confession before first communion, 30 April 1976.[*]

3143   The Holy See has received a formal *quaesitum* from the Redemptorist Fathers, among many, which puts in concrete terms the pleas contained in countless letters

---

[a]   DOL 169 no. 1120.

[*]   English text from the Congregations, Prot. N. 152516/II.

from parents, priests, bishops, and even children regarding the confusion created in some areas by an unduly elastic interpretation of the Decree *Quam singulari*, which stipulated that "the obligation to satisfy both the precept of confession and that of communion begins . . . at the age of reason" (reaffirmed by the joint Declaration of the Sacred Congregations for the Sacraments and for the Clergy of 25 May 1973)[a] and by a perhaps unduly narrow interpretation of the application of the letter of the Secretary of State to the 26th National Liturgical Week of Italy, held in Florence, 25–29 August 1975, in which the Holy Father placed "particular accent on the confession of children and especially on first confession, which ought always to precede first communion, even if at a judicious separation from it."[b]

Accordingly, rather than reply individually to the letters received from parents, priests, and individual bishops, we have been authorized to publish an official and approved reply to the *quaesitum* thus submitted.

The Congregations believe that the requirement of catechesis for the sacra-   3144
ments of penance and the eucharist, with the order of reception suggested in the traditional phrasing "confession and communion," except in cases clearly calling for exception, is binding on the universal Church. This norm is not only for the spiritual good of the children and the peace of mind of their parents, but also for the spiritual strengthening of the Church, in the context of the general reform of the sacrament of penance.

It has been decided by the Holy See that previous information concerning the forthcoming publication of the *quaesitum* and its officially approved response be sent to the presidents of those hierarchies who [sic], for whatever reason, found the previous Declaration embarrassing to their time schedules or to the personal opinions of some of their religious educators.

It is understood, and we are instructed to say, that such previous notification is not intended to reopen any aspect of the mind of the Holy See as expressed in *Quam singulari*, the Declaration of 1973, or the Letter to the Liturgical Week in Florence.

We are confident that the whole matter will be better appreciated in the context of the general reform of the sacrament of reconciliation and that the presidents of the national conferences will be eager to support the efforts of the Holy See to revivify the sacrament of penance and inculcate in the faithful from childhood the meaning of reconciliation, all with pastoral patience but fidelity to the general law of the Church.

We are grateful to the many bishops and directors of religious education who   3145
have written Rome to encourage a program intensifying the relationship between individual spiritual formation, beginning at the earliest age, and priestly work, and which at the same time reinforces, in accordance with the Holy Father's repeated pleas, recourse to the sacrament of penance, even for confessions of devotion.

We are particularly grateful to those hierarchies who [sic] either in their letters or visits to the Holy See have manifested their acceptance of the doctrine and discipline established by Pope St. Pius X, recognizing the grave danger of which we are witnesses of a return, which can be documented, to not a few of the unfortunate practices which prompted his action in *Quam singulari*. Among these are the refusal of absolution to children who wish to go to confession. Such children were often guided to the sacrament by their own parents or priests and then confounded by other teachers of religion who impeded their free access to the sacrament. In this connection, we owe a special word of gratitude to those priests who, on their own

---

[a]   See DOL 379 [correct date is 24 May 1973].

[b]   DOL 374 no. 3126.

or because of the initiatives taken by the Holy See, have increased their devotion to the delicate but extremely important apostolate of spiritual guidance of children within the confessional.

Many of these have taken the trouble to write to the Holy See declaring openly the need to put an end to the present confusion. It has been our general policy not to reply to individual parents whose children have been refused catechesis for first confession, or at most have been offered the opportunity for private instruction, thus creating the impression that they are somehow exceptional or morally in a special situation. We have not replied to such letters because of the confidence that the hierarchy and clergy would speedily remedy this situation by means which would not, on the one hand, interfere with the freedom of the child or, on the other, make him the object of the taunts of his companions who are often capable of little cruelties toward those who would go to confession while the others neglect the sacrament.

3146   We are particularly charged with recalling that whereas social, economic, and cultural conditions may differ from nation to nation, human nature remains fundamentally the same and the general norms governing those sacraments which are bound up with the ennobling of it are universal.

We are fully respectful of the desire of the representatives of the Holy See and of the officials of the national conferences of bishops to be at the same time the interpreters and defenders, insofar as possible, of the positions of the hierarchies at whose service they are and to defend their credibility, but at the moment there is an urgent need for the defense, with reason and kindness, of the credibility of the Holy See, its congregations, its secretary of state and the authority of the Holy Father himself, without whose personal and official approbation no decrees are issued, as is well known, by the individual dicasteries. This fact is sometimes forgotten by individual theologians or coordinators of religious education in the articles they publish and the conferences they give, all to the great confusion of the faithful and clergy.

The *quaesitum* referred to above and the corresponding official reply will be posted as soon as possible.

381. SC SACRAMENTS AND DIVINE WORSHIP and SC CLERGY, Letter *In quibusdam Ecclesiae partibus* to the conferences of bishops, on children's first confession prior to first communion, 31 March 1977.*

3147   In some parts of the Church and in some centers for catechetics, even though the Declaration *Sanctus Pontifex* was published on 24 May 1973 jointly by the Sacred Congregations for the Discipline of the Sacraments and for the Clergy (see AAS 65, 1973, 410),ᵃ dissension and doubts still remain about the ecclesiastical discipline relevant to children's receiving the sacrament of penance before they receive their first communion. Many inquiries and requests have come to this Apostolic See from bishops, priests, and parents. One apostolic religious institute, exercising its ministry in many countries, has posed the question explicitly: after the promulgation of the Declaration, is it still lawful for first communion to precede first confession as a

---

*   SCSDW and SCC, Prot. N. 2/76.
ᵃ   See DOL 379.

general rule in those parishes where this practice has been in force for the last several years?

Moreover, recent surveys by the Congregation for the Sacraments and Divine Worship have established the need of inculcating the Church's norms regarding this issue and also the timeliness of explaining again, to the extent required, the mind and force of this declaration. This is done by giving an official reply to the query raised by the religious institute already mentioned (see appendix).[b]

It is certainly not necessary to explain the reason for publishing the Declaration. All are fully aware of the grave disturbance, created by some opinions based on psychological and pedagogical reasons, that was undermining the accepted practice of the Church. It is interesting to note, however, that, before the Decree *Quam singulari* (see AAS 2, 579), according to the general opinion, children who reached a certain age could be admitted to confession, but not to communion; now, conversely, it is claimed that children may receive communion, but that it is not right for confession to precede. The Decree *Quam singulari* itself placed the origin of the regrettable practice in question in the failure to settle clearly the age of discretion suited to receiving the sacraments: "The abuses we censure spring from this, that the age of discretion was not properly or correctly settled and that some assign one age for confession and another for the eucharist." For this reason in no. 1 of the legislative section, the Decree prescribes that there is only one age for these sacraments and that when it is reached, the obligation begins of receiving both according to the designated order, i.e., confession before communion: "The age of discretion both for confession and for communion is the age at which the child begins to reason, i.e., around the seventh year, either before or after. That is the time when the obligation begins of fulfilling the precept both of confession and of communion."[1]

3148

That confession should precede communion is clear from the order in which these two sacraments are listed in the Decree, as well as from the fact that the repudiated abuses concerned the admission not to confession but rather to communion.

3149

The need for safeguarding and protecting worthy participation in the eucharist has compelled the Church to introduce as the norm in its discipline and pastoral practice that confession should precede communion. In this way it respects the right of the faithful — both adults and children — to receive the sacrament of reconciliation.

Moreover, St. Paul's admonition (see 1 Cor 11:28) truly establishes a directive norm that applies even to children. They too, therefore, should examine their conscience before receiving the eucharist. But often children are not able to examine their conscience clearly and surely without help; they will be able to do so more easily and safely if the assistance of a priest confessor is available to them. Many children feel troubled by small and unimportant things, while others may fail to recognize or make little of more serious faults.

Another consideration is the impossibility, if confession does not precede first communion, of respecting the precept of canon 854 of the Code of Canon Law, which assigns the judgment about the sufficient disposition for first communion to the priest.

---

[b]   See DOL 382.

[1]   The strict obligation of confession should, of course, be understood according to the accepted teaching of the Church.

It is further to be remembered what many good pastors have learned from their catechetical and ministerial experience, namely, the great benefits and saving power that first confession has in the life of children if it is carefully prepared, properly adapted to their age and their capacity to perceive spiritual things, and carefully administered.

When they arrive at the age of discretion, children already possess in the Church the right to receive both sacraments. It would be an absurd and unjust discrimination and a violation of conscience if they were prepared for and admitted only to communion. It is not enough to say that children have the right to go to confession, if this right is excluded in practice.

3150   When children are sufficiently instructed and are aware of the special nature of these two sacraments, it will not be difficult for them to go first to the sacrament of reconciliation, which — in a simple but fundamental way — arouses in them the awareness of moral good and evil and aids them to bring a more mature disposition to their happy meeting with Christ in the eucharist. A deep conviction about the need of the greatest purity for the reception of the eucharist worthily, if prudently and properly instilled in children right from the time of their first communion, will accompany them for the rest of their lives and lead to a greater esteem for, and a more frequent use of, the sacrament of reconciliation. Pope Paul VI taught this in the letter he wrote through the Secretary of State on the occasion of the 26th Liturgical Week celebrated in Florence: "The Pope, finally, places a special emphasis on children's confession, particularly their first confession. This must always precede their first communion even if an extended period between the two is helpful. From the earliest years an evangelization must begin that will make ever stronger and more conscious the support of a living faith for their celebration of the sacrament and above all for a sure and consistent way of living the Christian life."[c]

It may well be remarked that the special conditions of society and culture in different countries are not a legitimate reason for establishing a different discipline. Human nature is basically the same everywhere and the goals of spiritual development that belong to the sacrament are set equally before everyone. And indeed, whatever their social or cultural situation, if children can receive the eucharist in a conscious way, suited to their age, they can also have an equal awareness of sin and ask God's pardon in confession.

Finally, one must remember that the reform and reinvigoration of the sacrament of penance so needed today and so desired by pastors in the universal Church, cannot come about unless it has its foundation and beginning in the careful and effective preparation and reception of the sacraments of Christian initiation.

382. SC SACRAMENTS AND DIVINE WORSHIP and SC CLERGY, **Reply** to a query, on first confession and first communion, 20 May 1977: AAS 69 (1977) 427; Not 13 (1977) 603.*

3151   After the Declaration of 24 May 1973,[a] is it still lawful for first communion to precede first confession as a general rule in those parishes where this practice has been in force for the last several years? The Congregations for the Sacraments and

---

  c   DOL 374 no. 3126.

  *   Annex to DOL 381.

  a   See DOL 379.

Divine Worship and for the Clergy, with the approval of Pope Paul VI, have replied: No, in accord with the mind of the Declaration.

That mind is that a year from promulgation of the Declaration there be an end to all experiments in which first communion is received without prior reception of the sacrament of penance and that the discipline of the Church return to the spirit of the Decree *Quam singulari*.

▶   291.   JOHN PAUL II, Address to Canadian bishops, on sacramental discipline, 17 November 1978.

Individual confession [no. 2247].

Section 7. Penance: D. Indulgences

SUMMARY (DOL 383–390). The conciliar documents do not treat the topic of indulgences. The major text here is Pope Paul VI's review of the Church's traditional teaching and revision of its discipline (DOL 386). His apostolic constitution led to the decree promulgating a revised *Enchiridion Indulgentiarum*, which incorporated the papal norms (DOL 389, 390). The subsidiary texts deal with particulars: the papal blessing (DOL 383, 387), blessed religious articles (DOL 384), a prayer before the divine office (DOL 385), and the gaining of indulgences by religious and members of pious associations (DOL 388).

▶   103.   PAUL VI, Motu Proprio *Pastorale munus*, on the powers and privileges of bishops,
            30 November 1963:

        I, no. 30:   Granting faculty to erect indulgenced stations of
                                           the cross [no. 737].

383. APOSTOLIC PENITENTIARY, **Decree** *Sanctissimus D.N. Paulus*, allowing newly ordained priests to bestow the papal blessing, 5 November 1964:
AAS 56 (1964) 953.

3152   Pope Paul VI has received favorably the requests presented to him on behalf of
newly ordained priests. In order to show his fatherly solicitude in their regard, he
has kindly consented to rule that every newly ordained priest on the occasion of his
first solemnly celebrated Mass may impart once, using the formulary in the Roman
Ritual and outside of Rome, the papal blessing, to which a plenary indulgence is
attached. The indulgence may be gained by all the faithful who, after receiving the
sacraments of penance and the eucharist, devoutly assist at that first Mass, receive
the papal blessing reverently, and pray for the intentions of the pope.

            The present favor will be in effect perpetually from the present date and
without any apostolic brief being sent.

            All things to the contrary notwithstanding.

384. APOSTOLIC PENITENTIARY, **Declaration** *Sacra Paenitentiaria Apostolica*, on the indulgences attached to blessed religious articles, 6 March 1965:
AAS 57 (1965) 547.

3153   The Apostolic Penitentiary declares that all priests who, in virtue of the faculty
granted them by the Instruction for the orderly carrying out of the Constitution on
the Liturgy,[a] duly bless the religious articles indicated in the Roman Ritual, tit. IX,
ch. 10, no. 4 and ch. 11, no. 2 and the following, using the prescribed formulary, also
confer on the same articles the indulgences now in effect, until other dispositions
are made.

            A report of this was made to Pope Paul VI at an audience granted to the
undersigned Cardinal Penitentiary Major on 2 February 1965. The Pope approved
this Declaration, confirmed it, and allowed its publication; at the same time he
kindly ruled that its effective date is 7 March 1965.

            ---

            [a]   See DOL 23 no. 369.

385. APOSTOLIC PENITENTIARY, **Decree** *Die 31 Ianuarii 1966*, attaching indulgences to a prayer before divine office, 31 January 1966: AAS 58 (1966) 332.

INDULGENCES FOR A PRAYER BEFORE
RECITATION OF THE OFFICE

Lord God we offer this sacrifice of praise to your divine majesty. United in devoted service to your servant Paul, our Pope, we entreat your boundless mercy that you who have gladdened your Church by the celebration of the Second Vatican Ecumenical Council may grant that its salutary effects will increase throughout the world. Through Christ our Lord. Amen.

3154

31 January 1966

To clerics, and to men and women religious who devoutly recite this prayer before the divine office, the Little Office of the Blessed Virgin Mary, or some other in keeping with their own constitution, Pope Paul VI has graciously agreed to the granting of the following indulgences: 1. a partial indulgence of fifty days *to be gained by those with at least inner contrition;* 2. a plenary indulgence *to be gained, under the usual conditions, once a month if they have recited this prayer daily throughout the entire month. This concession is to be effective from this day* in perpetuity.

Anything to the contrary notwithstanding.

386. PAUL VI, **Apostolic Constitution** *Indulgentiarum doctrina*, on indulgences, 1 January 1967: AAS 59 (1967) 5–24.

I

1. The teaching and practice regarding indulgences prevailing for centuries in the Catholic Church rest on divine revelation as their firm foundation.[1] This revelation, handed on by the apostles, "develops in the Church under the influence of the Holy Spirit" as ". . . with the passage of the centuries the Church advances toward the fullness of divine truth until in it God's words are wholly accomplished."[2]

3155

In the interest of a right understanding of the teaching on indulgences and its sound application it is our responsibility to call attention to certain truths. The whole Church, enlightened by God's word, has always believed these truths and, both through pastoral practice and doctrinal statements, the bishops, successors of the apostles, and above all the popes, successors of St. Peter, have taught them down through the years and do so still.

2. As divine revelation teaches, punishment inflicted by God's holiness and justice is the consequence of sin. Such punishment is to be borne in this world through the pain, miseries, and hardships of the present life, above all through death,[3] or in

3156

---

[1]   See Council of Trent, sess. 25, *Decr. de indulgentiis*: "The power of granting indulgences has been given to the Church by Christ and the Church has used this divinely bestowed power even from its earliest days . . .": Denz-Schön 1835. See Mt 28:18.

[2]   DV no. 8 [DOL 14 no. 221]. See also Vatican Council I, Dogmatic Const. De fide catholica *Dei Filius*, cap. 4, De fide et ratione: Denz-Schön 3020.

[3]   See Gn 3:16–19: "To the woman he said: 'I will greatly multiply your pain in childbearing: in pain you shall bring forth children. Yet your desire shall be for your husband and he shall rule you.' To the man he said: 'Because you have listened to your wife and have eaten from the tree of which I commanded that

the world to come through the fire and torments of hell or the pains of purgatory.⁴ The faithful of Christ have thus always had the conviction that the path of evil has many stumbling blocks and that it is a rough and thorny path, lethal to those who follow it.⁵

A just and merciful judgment of God enjoins such punishments: they are meant to purge the soul, to protect the inviolability of the moral order, and to restore the divine glory to its full majesty. With respect to the last point, every sin involves the upsetting of the general order that in his inexpressible wisdom and boundless charity God has laid out; sin also involves the destruction of supreme values, pertaining both to the individual sinner and the entire human community. To the mind of Christians of every era it has been absolutely clear that sin is a transgression of the divine law, but over and above that, even if not directly and flagrantly, a contempt or neglect toward the personal friendship between God and each person;⁶ that it is a real and never adequately measured offense against God, an ungrateful rejection of God's love offered to us in Christ. For Christ has called us his friends, not his servants.⁷

3157   3.   For the complete pardon of sins and for their reparation, as it is called, it is thus necessary that a genuine conversion of spirit restore friendship with God and make expiation for the affront to his wisdom and goodness. But more than that, it is necessary that all the values, personal, social, and those forming part of the general order that sin has undermined or destroyed, be fully reestablished, either through voluntary, punitive reparation or through the bearing of those punishments decreed by God's just and absolutely holy wisdom. The sanctity and splendor of God's glory will thus be made to shine forth throughout the world. For the fact and the

---

you were not to eat of it, cursed is the ground because of you. In toil you shall eat of it all the days of your life. It shall bring forth to you thorns and thistles. . . . In the sweat of your face you shall eat bread till you return to the ground, for out of it you were taken. You are dust, and to dust you shall return.'"
See also Lk 19:41–44; Rom 2:9; 1 Cor 11:30.
See Augustine, *Enarr. in Ps. 58* 1, 13: "Every iniquity, great or small, must be punished, whether by the sinner's repentance or by God's vengeance.": CCL 39, 739; PL 36, 701.
See ST 1a2ae, 87.1: "Since sin is an act that lacks due order, it is clear that whoever sins is in conflict with some kind of order. Therefore the sinner is repressed by that order. Such repression is what punishment is."

⁴ See Mt 25:41–42: "Depart from me, you accursed, into the everlasting fire prepared for the devil and his angels. For I was hungry and you did not feed me." See also Mk 9:42–43; Jn 5:28–29; Rom 2:9; Gal 6:6–8.
See Council of Lyons II, sess. 4, *Professio fidei Michaelis Palaeologi imperatoris*: Denz-Schön 856–858.
See Council of Florence, *Decr. pro Graecis*: Denz-Schön 1304–06.
See Augustine, *Enchiridion* 66, 17: "Many things seem in this life to be forgiven and to go unavenged by punishment, but their punishment is being kept for the hereafter. For it is not in vain that the day on which the judge of the living and the dead is to come bears the name 'judgment day.' On the other hand, some things are avenged in this life, but if they are remitted they will cause no suffering in the world to come. Thus with regard to certain temporal punishments exacted of sinners in this life, St. Paul advises those whose sins are pardoned how to avoid such punishments being stored up until the end: 'If we would judge ourselves we should not be judged. But when we are judged, we are chastened by the Lord that we should not be chastened by the world' (1 Cor 11:31–32).": Scheel, ed. (Tübingen, 1930) 42; PL 40, 263.

⁵ See *Hermes Pastor*, Mand. 6, 1, 3: Funk PA 1, 487.

⁶ See Is 1:2–3: "I have reared and brought up sons, but they have rebelled against me. The ox knew its owner and the ass its master's crib; but Israel does not know, my people do not understand." See also Dt 8:11 and 32, 15ff.; Ps 105 [106]:21 and 118 [119] passim; Wis 7:14; Is 17:10 and 44:21; Jer 33:8; Ex 20:27.
See DV no. 2: "Thus by this revelation the unseen God (see Col 1:15; 1 Tm 1:17) speaks to us as his friends from the abundance of his love (see Ex 33:11; Jn 15:14–15) and communicates with us (see Bar 3:38) in order to invite us and welcome us into a communion with him.": AAS 58 (1966) 818; ConstDecr-Decl 424; see also DV no. 21 [DOL 14 no. 224].

⁷ See Jn 15:14–15. See also GS no. 22: AAS 58 (1966) 1042; ConstDecrDecl 709–710; AG no. 13: AAS 58 (1966) 962; ConstDecrDecl 568.

severity of punishment manifest the folly and wickedness of sin and its evil consequences.

The teaching on purgatory clearly shows that punishments to be borne or the
remnants of sin to be purged can remain and often do remain even after the sin has
been pardoned.[8] For in purgatory the souls of the dead who "have died truly
repentant in God's love, before they have atoned for their sins and omissions by the
worthy fruits of repentance"[9] are cleansed after death by the fires of purgatory. The
prayers of the liturgy point to the same fact: the Christian community from earliest
times in the celebration of the eucharist has used these prayers to plead "that we
who are justly afflicted for our sins may mercifully be delivered for the glory of
your name."[10]

All of us, pilgrims in this world, commit at least light and, as they are called,
daily sins;[11] we are all therefore in need of God's mercy for deliverance from sin's
penal consequences.

II

4.   The hidden and gracious mystery of God's design unites us all through a   3158
supernatural bond: on this basis one person's sin harms the rest even as one person's goodness enriches them.[12] As a result, the faithful help one another to attain
this supernatural destiny. The sign of their communion is expressed in Adam: his

---

   [8]   See Nm 20:12: "And the Lord said to Moses and Aaron: 'Because you did not believe in me, to
sanctify me in the eyes of the people of Israel, therefore you should not bring this assembly into the land
that I have given them.'"
      See Nm 27:13–14: "And when you have seen it, you also shall be gathered to your people, as your
brother Aaron was gathered, because you rebelled against my word in the wilderness of Zith, to sanctify
me in the waters before their eyes."
      See 2 Sm 12:13–14: "And David said to Nathan: 'I have sinned against the Lord.' And Nathan said
to David: 'The Lord also has put away your sin; you shall not die. Nevertheless, because by this deed you
have utterly scorned the Lord, the child that is born to you shall die.'"
      See Innocent IV, *Instructio pro Graecis*: Denz-Schön 838.
      See Council of Trent, sess. 6, can. 30: "Let anyone be anathema who would say that after having
the grace of justification a sinner receives pardon for sin and release from the debt of eternal punishment
in such a way that no debt of temporal punishment remains, to be acquitted in this life or in the world to
come in purgatory, before the sinner's admittance to the kingdom of heaven is possible.": Denz-Schön
1580; see also Denz-Schön 1689, 1693.
      See Augustine *In Io. Ev. tract.* 124, 5: "We are obliged to suffer in this life even after our sins have
been pardoned, although original sin was the reason why we have fallen into this plight. For punishment
lasts longer than sin so that sin is not regarded lightly, as would be the case were the punishment ended
with the end of the sin. Thus even when sin no longer holds us bound to eternal damnation, temporal
punishment still is binding on us, either as a sign of the misery we have earned, as a corrective against a
sinful life, or as an exercise in the patience we need": CCL 36, 683–684; PL 35 1972–73.

   [9]   Council of Lyons II, sess. 4: Denz-Schön 856.

   [10]   See MR, Septuagesima Sunday, collect: We ask you, O Lord, hear the prayers of your people: that
we who are justly afflicted for our sins may mercifully be delivered for the glory of your name."
      See MR, Monday of the First Week of Lent, prayer over the people: "Loosen, O Lord, the bonds of
our sins and graciously prevent whatever we have deserved because of them."
      See MR, Third Sunday of Lent, prayers after communion: "O Lord, graciously deliver from all
guilt and peril those whom you favor with a share in so great a mystery."

   [11]   See Jas 3:2: "We all fail in many things."
      See 1 Jn 1:8: "If we say we have no sin, we deceive ourselves and the truth is not in us." On this
text the Council of Carthage comments: "The Council also has decided with regard to the words of St.
John the Apostle "[Text quoted]" to anathematize anyone of the opinion that they are to be taken to mean
that we should say we have sinned as a sign of humility, not as a statement of truth.": Denz-Schön 228.
      See Council of Trent, sess. 6, *Decr. de iustificatione* cap. 2: Denz-Schön 1537.
      See LG no. 40: "Because we all offend in many matters (see Jas 3:2), we are continually in need of
God's mercy and must pray daily 'Forgive us our sins' (Mt 6:12).": AAS 57 (1965) 45; ConstDecrDecl 166.

   [12]   See Augustine, *De bapt. contra Donat.* 1, 28: PL 43, 124.

sin passes to us all on the basis of procreation. But the far greater and more complete source, foundation, and model of this supernatural bond is Christ: communion with him is the vocation God has given to us all.[13]

3159   5.   This means that Christ "who was without sin" "suffered for us ";[14] "he was wounded for our offenses, crushed for our sins . . . by his stripes we were healed."[15]

Following in Christ's footsteps,[16] his faithful have always sought to assist each other along the road to the Father by prayer, spiritual kindnesses, and penitential expiation. The more ardent the charity motivating them, the more closely they have followed Christ in his suffering by bearing their own cross in atonement for their own sins and the sins of others and with the conviction that in the eyes of the Father of mercies they could be of service to the salvation of their brothers and sisters.[17] This, of course, is the ancient dogma of the communion of saints, namely,

----

[13]   See Jn 15:5: "I am the vine, you are the branches: all who abide in me and I in them bear much fruit."

See 1 Cor 12:27: "Now you are the Body of Christ and every one of you a member of it." See also 1 Cor 1:9–10 and 17; Eph 1:20–23, 4:4.

See LG no. 7 [DOL 4 no. 139].

See Pius XII, Encycl. *Mystici Corporis*: "The communication of Christ's Spirit is the basis . . . for the Church's becoming, so to speak, the plenitude and complement of the Redeemer: in the Church Christ in a sense reaches his fulfillment in all things (see Thomas Aquinas, *Comm. in epist ad Eph*. 1, lect. 8). In this statement we have touched on the reason why . . . the mystical Head who is Christ and the Church that on earth acts in his person as another Christ, form the one new being in which heaven and earth are joined to continue the saving work of the cross: when we say Christ, we mean the Head and the Body, the whole Christ.": Denz-Schön 3813; AAS 35 (1943) 230–231.

See Augustine, *Enarrat. in Ps. 90*, 1: "Our Lord Jesus Christ is the total, complete man, both Head and Body: we acknowledge the Head in that man who was born of the Virgin Mary. . . . He is the Head of the Church. The Body of this Head is the Church, not the Church in this place but the Church here and the Church universal. Nor is it just the Church of today, but the Church from the time of Abel down to those to be born until the end of time who will believe in Christ, the entire holy people belonging to the one city. That city is Christ's Body and Christ is its Head.": CCL 39, 1266; PL 37, 1159.

[14]   See 1 Pt 2:22 and 21.

[15]   See Is 53:4–6 with 1 Pt 2:21–25. See also Jn 1:29; Rom 4: 25 and 5:9ff.; 1 Cor 15:3; 2 Cor 5:21; Gal 1:4; Eph 1:7ff.; Heb 1: 3, etc.; 1 Jn 3:5.

[16]   See 1 Pt 2:21.

[17]   See Col 1:24: "Now I rejoice in my sufferings for your sake and in my flesh I complete what is lacking in Christ; afflictions for the sake of his Body, that is the Church."

See Clement of Alexandria, *Lib. Quis dives salvetur* 42: St. John the Apostle urges a young thief to repentance, exclaiming: "I will be responsible to Christ for you. If necessary, I will gladly undergo your death, even as the Lord took on death for our sake. I will give my life as the substitute for yours.": GCS, *Clemens* 3, 190; PG 9, 650.

See Cyprian, *De lapsis* 17, 36: "We believe that the merits of the martyrs and the words of the just have great power before the judge — but at the coming of judgment day, when, after the end of the present world, Christ's people will stand before his throne." "Whatever the martyrs have entreated and the priests have done for them can bring merciful forgiveness and be favorable on behalf of those who repent, work, and plead.": CSEL 3, 249–250 and 263; PL 4:495 and 508.

See Jerome, *Contra Vigilantium* 6: "You say in your book that while we are alive we can pray for each other, but after we have died no one's prayer for another is to be heard: you say this especially because the martyrs could not do so even using the avengement of their own blood as an appeal (Rv 6:10). But if the apostles and martyrs when still in the body and in need of being concerned about themselves can pray for others, how much more so after their crown, their victory, and their triumph?": PL 23, 359.

See Basil the Great, *Homilia in Martyrem Julittam* 9: "We must weep therefore with those who weep. When you see others grieving out of repentance for their sins, shed tears with them, share in their grieving. The evils in others will enable you to correct what is wrong is yourselves. For those who shed scalding tears for the sins of their neighbors are healed themselves as they weep for others. . . . Grieve over sin: it is the sickness of the soul, the death of the deathless soul; sin calls for sorrow and unremitting laments.": PG 31, 258–259.

See John Chrysostom, *In epist. ad Philipp*. 1, hom. 3, 3: "Therefore let us not as a matter of course grieve over those who die nor rejoice over the living. What then? Let us grieve over sinners not only as they die but while they live; let us rejoice over the just not only while they live but also after they have

that the life of each of God's children is in Christ and through Christ conjoined with the life of all other Christians.[18] That sublime bond exists in the supernatural unity of the Mystical Body of Christ and constitutes the one mystical person.[19]

That is the basis of the "treasury of the Church."[20] The treasury of the Church is not to be likened to a centuries-old accumulation of material wealth. It means rather the limitless and inexhaustible value that the expiations and merits offered by Christ have in the eyes of God for the liberation of all humanity from sin and for the creation of communion with the Father. The treasury of the Church is Christ the Redeemer himself: in him the atonement and merit of his redemption exist and are at work.[21] Added to this treasure is also the vast, incalculable, ever increasing value in God's eyes of the prayers and good works of the Blessed Virgin Mary and all the saints. As they followed Christ through the power of his grace, they became holy and they have accomplished a work pleasing to the Father. As a result, in working out their own salvation they have also contributed to the salvation of their comembers in Christ's Mystical Body.

"All those who belong to Christ, possessing his Spirit, come together into the one Church and are joined together in Christ (see Eph 4:16). The union between those who are still pilgrims and their brothers and sisters who have died in the peace of Christ is therefore not broken, but rather strengthened by a communion in spiritual blessings; this has always been the faith of the Church. Because those in heaven are more closely united with Christ, they ground the whole Church more

---

died.": PG 62, 203.

See ST 1a2ae, 87.8: "If we speak of an expiatory punishment, one that we take on ourselves, then there are instances where one person bears the punishment due to another by reason of a bond between them. . . . If we are speaking of a punishment as it is inflicted for sin and as it has a fully penal quality, then a person is punished only for his own sin, because sinning is a personal act. If we speak of a punishment that is remedial, here too it may happen that a person is punished for another's sin. We have already determined that adversities in regard to possessions or even the body itself are in a way punitive remedies pointed toward salvation. Hence there is nothing against someone's being afflicted with such punishments either by God or by man for another's sin."

[18] See Leo XIII, Encycl. Epistle *Mirae caritatis:* "The communion of saints means precisely . . . the communication of mutual help, expiation, prayers, and kindnesses. This communication takes place between all the faithful, whether those in the bliss of heaven, those bound by the fires of purification, or those still on their earthly pilgrimage; all together they form the one city, whose Head is Christ and whose charter is charity.": *Acta Leonis XIII* 22 (1902) 129; Denz-Schön 3363.

[19] See 1 Cor 12:12–13: "For as the body is one and has many members and all the members of that one body, being many, are one body, so also is Christ. For by one Spirit we are all baptized into one Body."

See Pius XII, Encycl. *Mystici Corporis:* "Thus [Christ] in some way lives in the Church so that the Church is like Christ's other self. Writing to the Corinthians, St. Paul asserts this when, without qualification, he calls the Church 'Christ' (see 1 Cor 12:12); he does so in imitation of his Master, who had cried out to Paul when he was the scourge of the Church: 'Saul, Saul, why do you persecute me?' (see Acts 9:4, 22:7, 26:14). To take it on the word of St. Gregory of Nyssa, St. Paul frequently calls the Church 'Christ' (see *De vita Moysis:* PG 44, 385); and you know well, revered brothers, the saying of Augustine 'Christ preaches Christ' (see *Sermones* 354, 1: PL 39, 1563).": AAS 35 (1943) 218.

See ST 3a, 48.2 ad 1 and 49.1.

[20] See Clement VI, Jubilee Bull *Unigenitus Dei Filius:* "The only begotten Son of God . . . gained a treasure for the Church militant . . . Christ entrusted this treasury to be dispensed to the faithful . . . through St. Peter, the bearer of the keys of heaven, and his successors, Christ's vicars on earth . . . The merits of the Blessed Mother of God and of all the elect from the first of the just to the last are recognized as supplementing the building up of this treasury . . .": Denz-Schön 1025, 1026, 1027.

See Sixtus IV, Encycl. Epistle *Romani Pontificis:* ". . . We who have received the fullness of power from on high, wishing to bring help and suffrage to the souls in purgatory from the universal Church's treasury, which consists of the merits of Christ and the saints and is entrusted to us . . .": Denz-Schön 1406.

See Leo X, Decr. *Cum postquam* to Cajetan de Vio, Papal Legate: ". . . to distribute the treasury of the merits of Jesus Christ and the saints . . .": Denz-Schön 1448; see Denz-Schön 1467 and 2641.

[21] See Heb 7:23–25, 9:11–28.

firmly in holiness . . . and in many ways contribute to its upbuilding (see 1 Cor 12:12–27). For after they have been received into their heavenly home and are present to the Lord (see 2 Cor 5:8), through him and with him and in him they do not cease to intercede with the Father for us, showing forth the merits they have won on earth through the one Mediator between God and us (see 1 Tm 2:5), by serving God in all things and filling up in their flesh those things that are lacking of the sufferings of Christ for his Body which is the Church (see Col 1:24). Thus their familial concern brings great aid to our weakness."[22]

Thus between all the faithful — those in the bliss of heaven, those expiating for their sins in purgatory, and those still pilgrims on earth — there exists the continuing bond of charity and a rich interchange of all those good actions that, as atonement is made for the sins of the entire Mystical Body, appeases divine justice. At the same time divine mercy is moved to grant pardon in order that contrite sinners may more speedily reach complete possession of the blessings of God's family.

III

3160   6.   Aware of these truths right from its beginnings, the Church recognized and understood various ways of applying to its individual members the effects of the Lord's redemption, as well as ways for all its members to cooperate in the salvation of the others. This was how the whole Body of the Church was to be fitly joined together in righteousness and holiness for the full coming of God's kingdom, when he will be all things in all.

The apostles themselves urged their disciples to pray for the salvation of sinners.[23] The Church has unfailingly preserved this practice of its earliest days.[24] This has especially occurred in the pleas of penitents for the intercession of the entire community[25] and in suffrages on behalf of the dead, above all by the offering of the eucharistic sacrifice.[26] Also from earliest times in the Church the practice has

---

[22]   LG no. 49 [DOL 4 no. 157].

[23]   See Jas 5:16: "Confess your faults one to another and pray one for another, that you may be healed. The effectual, fervent prayer of a righteous man avails much."
    See 1 Jn 5:16: "If anyone sees another commit a sin not deserving of death, he shall ask and God will give life for those whose sin is not unto death."

[24]   See Clement of Rome, Ad Cor. 56.1: "Let us therefore also pray for those who are involved in any kind of sin, that restraint and humility may be given to them. Not that they should yield to us but to God's will. Thus the remembrance of them before God and the saints will be profitable to them and effective.": Funk PA 1, 171.
    See Martyrium S. Polycarpi 8, 1: Finally he had finished his prayer, in which he had mentioned all those who at any time had come into contact with him, the small and the great, the famous and the unknown, and those belonging to the entire Catholic Church throughout the world, . . .": Funk PA 1, 321, 323.

[25]   See Sozomen, Hist. Eccl. 7, 16, who says that in public penance after the celebration of Mass, penitents in the Church at Rome "cast themselves on the ground in groans and laments. Then the bishop, coming toward them in tears, also prostrates himself; and, confessing as one, the whole assembly of the Church weeps. Then the bishop rises first and bids the prostrate penitents rise. After prayers for the penitent sinners, as is proper, the bishop dismisses them.": PG 67, 1462.

[26]   See Cyril of Jerusalem, Catechesis 23 (mystag. 5) 9, 10: "[We pray] then also for our deceased holy fathers and bishops and collectively for all who lived their lives among us. For we believe that this will be a great help to those souls for whom we pray while the holy and majestic victim lies in our presence." Confirming his point by the example of a crown being fashioned for an emperor to obtain his pardon for those driven into exile, Cyril concludes his sermon, saying: "Similarly in praying to God for the dead, even if they were sinners, we do not present him with a crown; rather we offer Christ who was sacrificed for our sins, pleading with the merciful God to relent and be gracious both to them and to us.": PG 33, 1115 and 1118.
    See Augustine, Confessiones 9, 12, 32: PL 32, 777; 9, 11, 27: PL 32, 775; Sermones 172, 2: PL 38, 936; De

existed of offering to God for the salvation of sinners good works, and in particular those that are more difficult for human frailty.[27] Because the sufferings of martyrs for the faith and for God's law were held in such high esteem, penitents used to ask their intervention so that, assisted by the merits of these confessors of the faith, they would more quickly be granted reconciliation by the bishops.[28] The high value set on the prayers and good works of the just led to the statement that the help of the whole Christian people cleansed, purified, and redeemed the penitent.[29]

In all of this, however, there was no thought that the individual members of the Church were acting through their personal powers for the pardon of the sins of others. The belief rather was that the Church itself precisely as it is the one Body joined to Christ as Head made expiation in its individual members.[30]

The Church of the Fathers held the absolute conviction that it carried out this salvific work in the communion of its pastors and under their authority; the Holy Spirit placed them as bishops to shepherd the Church of God.[31] Upon careful consideration of all the issues, the bishops established the manner and measure of expiation to be offered. They even gave permission for the satisfaction of canonical penances by means of other works perhaps less onerous, suited to the good of the whole community or contributing to devotion. Such works were to be performed by penitents themselves or even in some cases by others of the faithful.[32]

---

cura pro mortuis gerenda 1, 3: PL 40, 593.

[27] See Clement of Alexandria, *Lib. Quis dives salvetur* 42 [St. John the Apostle at the conversion of the young thief]. "Now pleading with God, now struggling along with the young man by prolonged fasts and with many sweet words softening his spirit, John did not give up, as they say, until he had brought him by persevering constancy into the Church . . .": GCS 17, 189–190; PG 9, 651.

[28] See Tertullian, *Ad martyres* 1, 6: "Some in the Church who lacked this pardon used to request it of the martyrs in prison.": CCL 1, 3; PL 1, 695.
See Cyprian, *Epist* 18 (or 12), 1: "We must, I think, do something about our brothers and sisters who have received certificates of pardon [*libelli pacis*] from the martyrs . . . that after the imposition of penance, they may come to the Lord with the pardon that they sought to receive through letters written to us by the martyrs.": CSEL 3, 2, 523–524; PL 4, 265; see also *idem, Epist.* 19 (or 13), 2: CSEL 3, 2, 525: PL 4, 267.
See Eusibius of Caesarea, *Hist. Eccl.* 1, 6, 42: GCS, *Eus.* 2, 2, 610; PG 20, 614–615.

[29] See Ambrose, *De paenitentia* 1, 15: ". . . One who is rescued from sin by the prayers and tears of the people and purged inwardly is like one who is cleansed by the words of a whole people and washed by their tears. For Christ's gift to his Church so that one may be redeemed by all; the Church received the gift of Christ's own coming so that all would be redeemed by one.": PL 16, 511.

[30] See Tertullian, *De paenitentia* 10, 5–6: "The Body can find no joy in the trouble of one member, the whole must grieve together and seek for a remedy. The Church is in each one and the Church is Christ: therefore when you plead with your brothers and sisters, you plead with Christ and entreat him. So too when they shed tears over you, Christ is sorrowing, Christ is imploring the Father. What a son asks is always readily obtained.": CCL 1, 337; PL 1, 1356.
See Augustine, *Enarrat. in Ps.* 85, 1: CCL 39, 1176–77; PL 37, 1082.

[31] See Acts 20:28. See also Council of Trent, sess. 23, *Decr. de sacramento ordinis* cap. 4: Denz-Schön 1768. Vatican Council I, sess. 4. Dogm. Const. De Ecclesia *Pastor aeternus* cap. 3: Denz-Schön 3061. LG no. 20: AAS 57 (1965) 23; ConstDecrDecl 126–128.
See Ignatius of Antioch, *Ad Smyrnaeos* 8, 1: "Let no one do anything related to the Church except joined to the bishops.": Funk PA 1, 283.

[32] See Council of Nicaea I, can. 12: ". . . those who by fear and tears and patience and good works give proof of their conversion in deed and in attitude, rightly will be received into the communion of prayers when the preestablished time of their probation is up, together with whatever work the bishop has the right to determine in kindness concerning them. . . .": Mansi 2, 674.
See Council of Neo-Caesarea can. 3: Mansi 2, 540.
See Innocent I, *Epist.* 25, 7, 10: PL 29, 559.
See Leo the Great, *Epist.* 159, 6: PL 54, 1138.
See Basil the Great, *Epist.* 217 (canonica 3), 74: "A person who has fallen into the sins mentioned may by repenting become good again and the one who has been entrusted by God with the power of binding and loosing may, in view of the greatness of the sinner's repentance, show clemency in reducing the time of punishment. This clemency would not deserve condemnation because the accounts in Scrip-

IV

3161   7.   Thus in the Church the abiding conviction has continued that the pastors of the Lord's flock could free the faithful from the remains of their sins by applying the merits of Christ and the saints. That conviction led gradually over the centuries through the inspiration of the Holy Spirit, who is the constant life-source of the people of God, to the practice of indulgences. The practice represents development, not departure, in the doctrine and discipline of the Church;[33] it is a new blessing, deriving from revelation as its root, introduced for the advantage of the faithful and of the whole Church.

The practice of indulgences spread gradually. It became a clear element in the history of the Church, above all when the popes decreed that certain works conducive to the good of the entire Church community "were to be regarded as having value for every kind of penance."[34] Further, the popes, "relying on the mercy of almighty God . . . and on the merits and authority of his apostles," granted "out of the fullness of apostolic power" not only full and generous, but absolute pardon for sins to the faithful who, "after true repentance and confession," performed such works.[35]

For "the only-begotten Son of God . . . gained a treasury for the Church militant. Christ entrusted this treasury to be dispensed for the well-being of the faithful through St. Peter, the bearer of the keys of heaven, and his successors, Christ's vicars on earth. This treasury is to be applied with mercy to those who are repentant and have confessed, on the basis of proper and reasonable causes, in some cases for total and in others for partial remission of the temporal punishment due to sin. The application may be either universal or for a particular case (according to what, in the Lord, the popes decide to be best). The merits of the blessed Mother of God and of all the saints . . . are recognized as supplementing these riches of the treasury of the Church."[36]

3162   8.   "Indulgence" is the name proper to this remission of the temporal punishment due to sins already forgiven as to their culpable element.[37]

---

ture teach us that those who do penance with greater ardor quickly receive God's mercy.": PL 32, 803. See Ambrose, *De paenitentia* 1, 15 (in note 29).

[33]   See Vincent of Lérins, *Commonitorium primum* 23: PL 50, 667–668.

[34]   See Council of Clermont, can. 2: "If anyone out of devotion alone and not to gain honor or money goes to Jerusalem to liberate the Church of God, that journey is to be regarded as a complete act of penance.": Mansi 20, 816.

[35]   See Boniface VIII, Bull *Antiquorum habet*: "The reliable records of the ancients show that great pardons and indulgences for sins were granted to those journeying to St. Peter's Basilica in Rome. Therefore . . ., regarding with favor all and each one of these pardons and indulgences as established, we confirm and approve them by apostolic authority. Relying on the mercy of almighty God and the merits of his apostles, on the counsel of our brothers, and on the fullness of our own apostolic power, we will and do grant this year and every future one-hundredth year not only full and generous pardon, but absolute pardon for sins to all . . . who devoutly journey to those basilicas, after repenting and confessing. . . .": Denz-Schön 868.

[36]   Clement VI, Jubilee Bull *Unigenitus Dei Filius*: Denz-Schön 1025, 1026, 1027.

[37]   See Leo X, Decr. *Cum postquam*: ". . . we have decided to inform you that the Roman Church, which the other Churches are obliged to look to as a mother, has taught the following. The pope, successor of St. Peter the keybearer and the vicar of Jesus Christ on earth, possesses the power of the keys. Those keys are able to open the kingdom of heaven by taking away impediments to heaven existing in the faithful, namely, sin and the temporal punishment due to actual sin. The sin is taken away through the sacrament of penance; the temporal punishment, due according to divine justice for actual sins, through an ecclesiastical indulgence. Therefore to the faithful, who by the union of charity are Christ's members, whether they are in this life or in purgatory, the pope can, for reasonable cause, grant indulgences out of the superabundance of the merits of Christ and the saints. In granting an indulgence by his apostolic authority on behalf of both the living and the dead, the pope can distribute the treasury of the merits of Christ and

An indulgence has certain features in common with other methods and means of taking away the remnants of sin, but at the same time is clearly distinct from the others.

This means that in the case of an indulgence the Church, using its power as minister of Christ the Lord's redemption, not only offers prayer, but authoritatively dispenses to the faithful rightly disposed the treasury of the expiatory works of Christ and the saints for the remission of temporal punishment.[38]

The purpose intended by ecclesiastical authority in granting indulgences is not only to help the faithful to pay the penalties due to sin, but also to cause them to perform works of devotion, repentance, and charity — especially works that contribute to the growth of faith and the good of the community.[39]

The faithful who apply indulgences as suffrages for the dead are practicing charity in a superior way and with their thoughts on the things of heaven are dealing more virtuously with the things of earth.

The Church's magisterium has defended and declared this teaching in various documents.[40] The practice of indulgences has sometimes been infected with abuses.

---

the saints, confer an indulgence by way of absolution, or transfer it by way of suffrage, as is customary. Therefore all, both the living and the dead, who have truly gained all such indulgences are freed from the temporal punishment due according to God's justice for their actual sins in the measure equal to the indulgences they have gained.": Denz-Schön 1447–48.

[38]   See Paul VI, Letter *Sacrosancta Portiunculae*: "An indulgence granted by the Church to penitents is an expression of the wonderful communion of saints that mystically binds together by the one bond of Christ's charity the Blessed Virgin Mary and the assembly of Christ's faithful, whether triumphant in heaven, abiding in purgatory, or journeying on earth. An indulgence given through the Church either lessens or completely wipes out the punishment that in some way prevents us from attaining a closer union with God. Therefore the faithful who are repentant find in this special form of ecclesial charity the present help by which they may put off their old self and become a new being 'which is renewed in knowledge after the image of him that created it' (Col 3:10).: AAS 58 (1966) 633–634.

[39]   See ibid.: "The Church reaches out to those faithful of Christ who, moved by repentance, seek to achieve after sin this *metanoia* by striving for that holiness which they first put on through their baptism in Christ. The Church by granting indulgences lends the support and assistance of a maternal embrace to its weak and frail children. An indulgence is not therefore an easy way out, whereby we may avoid the repentance required for sins. Rather it is a support that all the faithful, fully conscious in humility of their sins, find in the Mystical Body of Christ, which 'by charity, example, and prayer seeks their conversion' (LG no. 11).": AAS 58 (1966) 632.

[40]   Clement VI, Jubilee Bull *Unigenitus Dei Filius*: Denz-Schön 1026.
     Clement VI, Letter *Super quibusdam*: Denz-Schön 1059.
     Martin V, Bull *Inter cunctas*: Denz-Schön 1266.
     Sixtus IV, Bull *Salvator noster*: Denz-Schön 1398.
     Sixtus IV, Encycl. Epistle *Romani Pontificis provida*: "Wishing through our letters to correct . . . such scandals and errors . . ., we have written to . . . prelates that they explain to the faithful the meaning of the plenary indulgence granted by us as a suffrage on behalf of the souls in purgatory. It does not mean that through this indulgence the faithful are discouraged from devout and good works; it means that the indulgence can be helpful as a suffrage for the salvation of souls. In that way the indulgence would profit these souls as though devout prayers were said and alms given in behalf of their salvation. We did not and do not intend, nor would we wish the inference to be made, that the indulgence does no more good or has no more effect than almsgiving and prayer or that almsgiving and prayer do as much good or have as great an effect as an indulgence by way of suffrage. We very well know that there is a great difference between prayer or almsgiving and such an indulgence. We stated that the indulgence has its effect '*perinde*' meaning 'in that way,' ' *ac si*,' that is, in the way that prayer and almsgiving have an effect. And because prayer and almsgiving have their effect as suffrages offered for souls, in our desire to bring help and suffrage to the souls in purgatory, we, to whom the fullness of power has been given from above, have granted the indulgence in question out of the treasury of the universal Church, which consists in the merits of Christ and the saints and has been entrusted to us. . . .": Denz-Schön 1405–06.
     Leo X, Bull *Exsurge Domine*: Denz-Schön 1467–72.
     Pius VI, Const. *Auctorem fidei* prop. 40: "The statement that 'an indulgence in its precise meaning amounts to the remission of a part of that penance that had been established canonically' — as though to say that an indulgence besides being simply the remission of a canonical punishment does not have the effect of pardoning the temporal punishment due according to divine justice for actual sins — is false,

This has happened because "rash and excessive indulgences" have led to contempt for the keys of the Church and to the weakening of penitential expiation,[41] and because "fraudulent appeals for money" have brought curses upon the very name of indulgences.[42] The Church, however, uprooting and correcting abuses, "teaches and prescribes that the practice of indulgences, so beneficial to the Christian people and sanctioned by the authority of the sacred councils, must be preserved; the Church anathematizes those who state that indulgences are useless or who deny the Church's power to grant them."[43]

3163   9.   The Church today still invites all its children to weigh well and reflect on the real effectiveness of the practice of indulgences in fostering the life of individuals and of the Christian community as a whole.

To mention only the main points: this practice teaches us first "how evil and bitter it is to forsake . . . the Lord God."[44] For when the faithful gain indulgences they realize that by their own powers they cannot atone for the evil that they have afflicted upon themselves and the entire community by sinning; they therefore are moved to a healthy humility.

Next, the practice of indulgences teaches us the closeness of the union in Christ that binds us together and the extent to which the supernatural life of each person can contribute to others so that they too may be united more easily and more closely to the Father. Thus the practice of indulgences effectively enkindles charity in us and is an exceptional exercise of charity when it brings help to those asleep in Christ.

3164   10.   In addition, the usage of indulgences builds up confidence and hope for full reconciliation with God the Father. Yet this occurs in such a way that the practice provides no basis for negligence nor in any way lessens the concern to develop those dispositions required for full communion with God. Indulgences are indeed freely given favors, but they are granted both to the living and the dead only on fulfillment of certain conditions: to gain them the requirement in some cases is the performance of good works, in others the faithful's having the necessary disposi-

---

rash, contemptuous of the merits of Christ, and long ago included in the condemnation of Luther's art. 19.": Denz-Schön 2640.

    Ibid.: "Likewise the continuation of that proposition: 'the scholastics, puffed up by their subtleties, have proposed the misunderstood treasury of the merits of Christ and the saints and have replaced the clear notion of absolution from canonical penalty with the confused and false notion of the application of merits — as though to say that the treasury of the Church, the source of the pope's granting indulgences, does not consist in Christ's and the saints' merits' — is false, rash, contemptuous of the merits of Christ and the saints, and long ago included in the condemnation of Luther's art. 17.": Denz-Schön 2641.

    Ibid., prop. 42: "Likewise what follows: 'still more lamentable is the intention that this fanciful application be transferred to the dead' — is false, rash, offensive to the devout, contemptuous of the popes and the practice and mind of the Church universal, leading to the error qualified as heretical in Peter of Osma, and also already condemned in Luther's art. 22.": Denz-Schön 2642.

    Pius XI, Indiction of the Extraordinary Holy Year *Quod nuper*: ". . . mercifully in the Lord we grant and impart a full indulgence of all punishment due for sin to those who have first obtained remission and pardon of each of their own sins.": AAS 25 (1933) 8.

    Pius XII, Indiction of the Universal Jubilee *Iubilaeum maximum*: "We mercifully in the Lord grant and impart a full indulgence and pardon for all punishment due to sin to all the faithful during the course of this Holy Year who, after they have duly atoned for their sins through the sacrament of penance and received communion, . . . devoutly visit . . . the Roman basilicas . . . and recite . . . prayers.": AAS 41 (1949) 258–259.

[41] See Lateran Council IV, cap. 62: Denz-Schön 819.

[42] See Council of Trent, *Decr. de indulgentiis*: Denz-Schön 1835.

[43] Ibid.

[44] Jer 2:19.

tions, namely, love for God, hatred toward sin, trust in the merits of Christ the Lord, and the firm belief that the communion of saints is of great advantage to the faithful.

Nor must we omit that in gaining an indulgence the faithful submit themselves with docility to the lawful pastors in the Church, above all to the successor of St. Peter, the bearer of the keys of heaven. Christ himself has commanded these pastors to feed and shepherd his Church.

Thus it is that the salutary establishment of indulgences contributes in its own way toward presenting the Church to Christ without stain or wrinkle, but holy and undefiled,[45] and joined wondrously together in Christ by the supernatural bond of charity. Through indulgences the members of the Church in its state of purification advance more rapidly toward the heavenly Church. Therefore through indulgences the kingdom of Christ is being increasingly and more quickly established "till we all come into the unity of this faith and of the knowledge of the Son of God unto the point of our full perfection, according to the measure of the fullness of Christ himself."[46]

11. On the grounds of such truths, the Church once more recommends to its faithful the practice of indulgences as one dear to the Christian people throughout the many centuries and in our own times as well. At the same time the Church intends to take nothing away from other methods of sanctification and purification: above all the sacrifice of the Mass and the sacraments, and particularly the sacrament of penance, next the many helps that are included under the name of sacramentals, and finally devotional, penitential, and charitable works. All of these have in common that they sanctify and purify all the more effectively the closer a person is joined by charity to Christ the Head and to the Church his Body. The primacy of charity in the Christian life receives further confirmation by the teaching on indulgences. For they cannot be gained without genuine conversion (*metanoia*) and union with God, to which the performance of prescribed works is annexed. Thus the remission of penalties from the distribution of the Church's treasury is incorporated under the primacy of charity, which is maintained.

The Church appeals to the faithful not to abandon or make light of the traditions of the Fathers but to receive them reverently as a precious possession of the Catholic family and to honor those traditions. Nevertheless, the Church permits every person to use these resources of purgation and sanctification in the full freedom belonging to God's children. The Church ceaselessly reminds all the faithful of those things that must have priority in order to attain salvation because they are either the necessary things or the better and more effective.[47]

The Church at this time has seen fit to introduce new elements and decree new norms with regard to indulgences in order to enhance the value of this practice and the esteem for it.

    3165

---

[45]   See Eph 5:27.

[46]   Eph 4:13.

[47]   See Thomas Aquinas, *In 4 Sent.* dist. 20, q. 1, a. 3, quaestiuncula 12.2 ad 2 (ST, Suppl., 25.2 ad 2): ". . . although such indulgences are of great worth for the remission of punishment, still, other works are more meritorious regarding the essence of our eternal reward: and this is infinitely better than the remission of temporal punishment."

V

3166   12. The following norms introduce changes into the discipline of indulgences that are suited to the times and take into account the wishes of the conferences of bishops.

The regulations regarding indulgences in the *Codex Iuris Canonici* and the decrees of the Holy See remain unchanged to the extent that they are compatible with the new norms.

The formulation of these norms has been concerned mainly with three points: to fix a new measure for partial indulgences; to lessen the number of plenary indulgences; to reduce and organize into a simpler and worthier form the matters related to indulgences attached to objects and places ("real and local" indulgences).

In regard to partial indulgences, in place of the ancient measure in days and years a new standard or measure has been set. According to it the act of the member of the Church who performs the indulgenced work is the criterion.

For by such an act the faithful can gain — in addition to merit, the chief effect of a good act — the remission of temporal punishment. That remission will be in proportion to the charity of the one acting and the value of the work done. Therefore it was decided to take this remission of punishment acquired by the faithful through their act as the measure of the remission of punishment that the supreme authority in the Church generously adds in the form of a partial indulgence.

As to plenary indulgences, it seemed advisable to reduce their number in a way that would be conducive to the faithful's right evaluation of them and helpful to their gaining them by being disposed in the required way. For the usual receives scant attention; the plentiful is not highly valued. Also many of the faithful need a time sufficient for a right preparation to gain a plenary indulgence.

As to "real" and "local" indulgences, two things were necessary: a severe reduction in their number; the suppression of the very terms. The reason for the second is to make it clear that the Christian's acts are the subject of indulgences, not things or places; these are merely the occasions for gaining indulgences. Members of pious associations can gain the indulgences belonging to such associations by performing the prescribed works; the use of insignia is not a requirement.

NORMS

3167   N. 1. An indulgence is the remission in the eyes of God of the temporal punishment due to sins whose culpable element has been taken away. The faithful who are rightly disposed and observe the definite, prescribed conditions gain this remission through the help of the Church, which, as the minister of redemption, authoritatively distributes and applies the treasury of the expiatory works of Christ and the saints.

3168   N. 2. An indulgence is either plenary or partial accordingly as it frees a person either in whole or in part from the temporal punishment due to sins.

3169   N. 3. Both partial and plenary indulgences are always applicable to the dead as suffrages.

3170   N. 4. Henceforth a partial indulgence shall be designated by the words "partial indulgence" alone without any indication of days or years being added.

N. 5. Any of the faithful who, being at least inwardly contrite, perform a work carrying with it a partial indulgence, receive through the Church the remission of temporal punishment equivalent to what their own act already receives.

3171

N. 6. A plenary indulgence may be gained only once on any day; the rule in N.18 regarding those on the verge of death is an exception.

A partial indulgence may be gained many times a day unless something different is explicitly stated.

3172

N. 7. The requirements for gaining a plenary indulgence are the performance of the indulgenced work and the fulfillment of three conditions: sacramental confession; eucharistic communion; prayer for the pope's intentions. A further requirement is the exclusion of all attachment to sin, even venial sin.

Unless this unqualified disposition and the three conditions are present, the indulgence will be only partial; the prescription of N. 11 for those impeded is an exception.

3173

N. 8. The three conditions may be carried out several days preceding or following performance of the prescribed work. But it is more fitting that communion and prayer for the pope's intentions take place on the day this work is performed.

3174

N. 9. Several plenary indulgences may be gained on the basis of a single sacramental confession; only one may be gained, however, on the basis of a single communion and prayer for the pope's intentions.

3175

N. 10. The condition requiring prayer for the pope's intentions is completely satisfied by reciting once the Our Father and Hail Mary for his intentions; nevertheless all of the faithful have the option of reciting any other prayer suited to their own devotion and their reverence for the pope.

3176

N. 11. The faculty granted confessors by CIC can. 935 to commute for the benefit of those who are impeded either the prescribed work or the required conditions remains in force. But local Ordinaries may also grant to the faithful subject to them in keeping with canon law and who reside in places where they cannot go to confession or communion at all or can do so only with great hardship that they may gain a plenary indulgence without actual confession and communion, provided they have inner contrition and the resolution to receive these sacraments as soon as possible.

3177

N. 12. The division of indulgences into "personal," "real," and "local" is no longer used. This is to make it clear that the subject of indulgences is the Christian's act, even though such an act sometimes has a connection with a particular object or place.

3178

N. 13. The *Enchiridion indulgentiarum* is to be revised in such a way that indulgences will be attached only to major prayers and devotional, penitential, and charitable works.

3179

N. 14. Lists and compilations of indulgences belonging to religious orders, congregations, societies of common life, secular institutes, and pious associations of the faithful shall be revised as soon as possible. This will result in the possibility of gaining a plenary indulgence only on special days fixed by the Holy See after a proposal in this regard has been made by the highest religious superior or by the local Ordinary in the case of pious associations.

3180

3181   N. 15. On 2 November a plenary indulgence, applicable exclusively to the dead, may be gained in all churches as well as in all public oratories and in all semipublic oratories — by those with a right to use them.

In all parish churches a plenary indulgence may be gained on two days in the year: the titular feast of the church and either on 2 August, the day of the "Portiuncula" indulgence or on another suitable day to be fixed by the Ordinary.

All the aforementioned indulgences may be gained either on the days already stipulated or, with the Ordinary's consent, on the Sunday preceding or following such days.

Other indulgences attached to churches or oratories shall be revised as soon as possible.

3182   N. 16. The prescribed work for gaining an indulgence attached to a church or oratory is a devout visit there, which includes the recitation of the Lord's Prayer and the Creed (*Pater* and *Credo*).

3183   N. 17. All the faithful gain a partial indulgence in devoutly using religious articles (crucifixes, crosses, rosaries, scapulars, medals) properly blessed by any priest.

All the faithful devoutly using a religious article blessed by the pope or by any bishop may also gain a plenary indulgence on the feast of the Apostles Peter and Paul; but they must add the profession of faith, recited in any approved formulary.

3184   N. 18. It may happen that one of the faithful in danger of death is unable to have a priest to administer the sacraments and to impart the apostolic blessing with its attached plenary indulgence, mentioned in CIC can. 468, § 2. In such a case, the Church, like a devoted mother, graciously grants such a person who is properly disposed a plenary indulgence to be gained at the hour of death. The one condition is the practice of praying for this all during life. Use of a crucifix or cross is recommended for the gaining of this indulgence.

The faithful may gain this plenary indulgence at the hour of death even if they have already gained another plenary indulgence on the same day.

3185   N. 19. The norms issued on plenary indulgences and especially those listed in N. 6, are applied also to those plenary indulgences that by custom hitherto have been called *toties quoties* indulgences.

3186   N. 20. Like a devoted mother, the Church in its special concern for the faithful departed establishes that in every sacrifice of the Mass suffrages are most lavishly offered on behalf of the dead; any privilege in this matter is suppressed.

3187   The effective date for the new norms regulating the gaining of indulgences is three months from the date on which this Apostolic Constitution appears in the *Acta Apostolicae Sedis*.

Indulgences attached to religious objects that are not mentioned in this Apostolic Constitution are suppressed three months after its publication in the *Acta Apostolicae Sedis*.

The revisions mentioned in N. 14 and N. 15 must be submitted to the Apostolic Penitentiary within one year. Two years from the date of this Apostolic Constitution indulgences that have not received confirmation will become null.

We will these our decrees and prescriptions to be and to remain established and in effect, notwithstanding, to the extent necessary, the constitutions and apos-

tolic ordinances issued by our predecessors, and other prescriptions, even those
worthy of special mention and amendment.

387. APOSTOLIC PENITENTIARY, **Decree** *Sanctissimus D. N. Paulus*, granting indulgences for the 19th centenary of the martyrdom of St. Peter and St.
Paul in Rome, 28 June 1967: AAS 59 (1967) 764.

Pope Paul VI issued on 22 February 1967 the Apostolic Exhortation *Petrum et*   3188
Paulum Apostolos on the occasion of the 19th centenary of the martyrdom in Rome of
the blessed Princes of the Apostles. Later, in order that the faithful might profit
more abundantly from celebrating this anniversary, the Pope has graciously granted, at an audience given to the undersigned Cardinal Penitentiary Major, 10 June
1967, the following favors, which will be in effect from 29 June 1967, the feast of
Saints Peter and Paul, until the same date in 1968: 1. To every local Ordinary, in
keeping with CIC can. 914 (see can. 315) — or if he is impeded, to a bishop to be
rightly designated in his place — the *faculty* to impart, with the prescribed formulary, the *papal blessing with a plenary indulgence attached.* He may do this once during the
jubilee celebration, on a day when the profession of faith is recited in the cathedral
or other church, according to the formulary for more solemn use. The plenary
indulgence may be gained by the faithful who, after confessing, receiving communion, and reciting for the pope's intention the Our Father and Hail Mary, or another
prayer suiting their devotion, assist devoutly at this sacred ceremony and reverently
receive the papal blessing. 2. *A plenary indulgence,* under the same conditions, to be
gained by the faithful: a. once, when on another suitable feast they similarly recite
the profession of faith in other churches and oratories; b. also once, when on a fixed
date, to be chosen from any of the more solemn feasts, they say the same profession
of faith in the family home, in the centers of Catholic associations, in schools, in
factories, in hospitals, and in all assemblies or meetings.

All things to the contrary notwithstanding.

388. APOSTOLIC PENITENTIARY, **Norms** *Ut haec S. Paenitentiaria,* on the
gaining of indulgences by members of religious institutes and pious associations, 1967.*

ON THE REVISION OF INDULGENCES FOR RELIGIOUS

FOR RELIGIOUS INSTITUTES AND PIOUS ASSOCIATIONS

This Sacred Penitentiary is to decide "those special days" on which alone   3189
plenary indulgences can be granted, according to Norm 14 of the Apostolic Constitution *Indulgentiarum doctrina.*ᵃ For this purpose the superior general (in the case of a
religious institute) or the local Ordinary (in the case of a pious association of the
faithful) will kindly present a list of only certain, preferred days on which they
wish a plenary indulgence to be granted.

The days in question are to be listed in descending order of preference.

 ˑ   Text, CommRel 47 (1966) 172–173.

 ᵃ   See DOL 386 no. 3180.

3190   Be advised that this Sacred Penitentiary already intends to grant a plenary indulgence on the following days.

I. FOR A RELIGIOUS INSTITUTE

A. For the entire institute:
1. the feast day of the titular or principal patron;
2. the feast day of the saint or the blessed who founded the institute;
3. at the time of a general chapter.

B. For individual houses:
1. the feast day of the principal patron of the house;
2. the feast days of the saints or the blessed whose bodies or special relics are reserved there;
3. at the conclusion of a canonical visitation.

C. For the individual members:
1. the day of their entrance into the novitiate;
2. the day of their first profession;
3. the day of their final profession;
4. the twenty-fifth, fiftieth, sixtieth, and seventy-fifth anniversary of their first profession.

II. FOR A PIOUS ASSOCIATION OF THE FAITHFUL

1. the feast day of the titular or principal patron;
2. the day of a member's enrollment.

In the case of a pious association of the faithful, its principal activities of devotion, religious culture, and charity are to be indicated.

For Churches or Oratories

3191   This Sacred Penitentiary is to decide what indulgences may be confirmed or granted for the first time to a church or oratory envisioned by the last section of Norm 15 of the Apostolic Constitution *Indulgentiarum doctrina*.[b] For this purpose the following questions are to be answered:

1. Have indulgences already been granted to the church or oratory? If so, a text of these is to be presented.
2   What is the *titular* of the church or oratory?
3. Is the body or a special relic of any saint or blessed reserved in the church or oratory? If so, is it the object of a special *cultus*?
4. What feast day is celebrated with the greatest number of the faithful an attendance?

389. APOSTOLIC PENITENTIARY, Decree *In Constitutione Apostolica*, promulgating the new authentic edition of the *Enchiridion indulgentiarum*, 29 June 1968: AAS 60 (1968) 413–414.

3192   In the Apostolic Constitution *Indulgentiarum doctrina* of 1 January 1967 we read: "The Church at this time has seen fit to introduce new elements and decree new

---

b   See DOL 386 no. 3181.

norms with regard to indulgences in order to enhance the value of this practice and the esteem for it."[a]

Norm 13 of the Constitution establishes this: "The *Enchiridion indulgentiarum* is to be revised with a view to attaching indulgences only to major prayers and devotional, penitential, and charitable works."[b]

In obedience to the will of Pope Paul VI as expressed both through the Apostolic Constitution *Indulgentiarum doctrina* and through later enactments, this Apostolic Pentitentiary has carefully seen to the compilation of a new *Enchiridion indulgentiarum*.

After receiving the report of the undersigned Cardinal Penitentiary Major at an audience on 14 June 1968, Pope Paul VI has on 15 June 1968 approved the new *Enchiridion indulgentiarum* printed by the Vatican Press. He has ordered it to be the authoritative collection; suppressed are all general grants of indulgences not incorporated into the new *Enchiridion* as well as all the legislation on indulgences of the *Codex Iuris Canonici*, of apostolic letters, even motu proprios, and of decrees of the Holy See that are not included among the Norms for indulgences in this *Enchiridion*.

All things to the contrary notwithstanding, even those meriting explicit mention.

390. APOSTOLIC PENITENTIARY, *Enchiridion indulgentiarum*, **Norms** on Indulgences, 29 June 1968: Vatican Polyglot Press, June 1968; 2nd emended printing, October 1968.

NORMS ON INDULGENCES

1. An indulgence is the remission in the eyes of God of the temporal punishment due to sins whose culpable element has been taken away. The faithful who are rightly disposed and observe the definite, prescribed conditions gain this remission through the help of the Church, which, as the minister of redemption, authoritatively distributes and applies the treasury of the expiatory works of Christ and the saints.[1]   3193

2. An indulgence is either plenary or partial, that is, it frees a person either from all or from some of the temporal punishment due to sins.[2]   3194

3. No one gaining an indulgence may apply it to other living people.[3]   3195

4. Both partial and plenary indulgences are always applicable to the dead as suffrages.[4]   3196

5. Henceforth a partial indulgence shall be designated with the words "partial indulgence" alone without any indication of days or years being added.[5]   3197

---

[a] DOL 386 no. 3165.

[b] DOL 386 no. 3179.

[1] Ap. Const. *Indulgentiarum doctrina* N. 1 [DOL 386 no. 3167].

[2] Ibid. N. 2 [DOL 386 no. 3168].

[3] See CIC can. 930.

[4] Ap. Const. *Indulgentiarum doctrina* N. 3 [DOL 386 no. 3169].

[5] Ibid. N. 4 [DOL 386 no. 3170].

3198   6.   Any of the faithful who, being at least inwardly contrite, perform a work carrying with it a partial indulgence, receive through the Church the remission of temporal punishment equivalent to what their own act already receives.[6]

3199   7.   The division of indulgences into "personal," "real," and "local" is no longer used. This is to make it clear that the subject of indulgences is the Christian's act, even though such an act sometimes has a connection with a particular object or place.[7]

3200   8.   To the pope has been entrusted the distribution of the entire spiritual treasury of the Church. Only those others to whom the law explicitly grants this may by ordinary power grant indulgences.[8]

3201   9.   Requests on points related to the granting and use of indulgences are to be addressed to only one agency in the Roman Curia, the Apostolic Penitentiary. This is without prejudice, however, to the Congregation for the Doctrine of the Faith's right of overseeing whatever involves dogmatic teaching on indulgences.[9]

3202   10.   Those below the pope may not:

a.   assign to others the power to grant indulgences, unless they have an explicit indult from the Apostolic See to do so;

b.   attach a further indulgence to the same work already indulgenced by the Apostolic See or by someone else, unless new requisite conditions are prescribed.[10]

3203   11.   Diocesan bishops and their equivalents in law possess from the outset of their pastoral office the right to:

§ 1.   grant partial indulgences to persons or in the places subject to their jurisdiction.[11§1]

§ 2.   bestow the papal blessing with a plenary indulgence, using the prescribed formulary, three times a year on solemn feasts that they will designate, even if they only assist at the solemn Mass.[11§2]

3204   12.   Metropolitans may grant partial indulgences in their suffragan dioceses just as in their own.[12]

3205   13.   Patriarchs may grant partial indulgences in every place, even those exempt, of their patriarchate, in churches of their own rite outside the boundaries of their patriarchate, and everywhere in the world in favor of their own people. Archbishops major have the same power.[13]

---

[6]   Ibid. N. 5 [DOL 386 no. 3171].

[7]   Ibid. N. 12 [DOL 386 no. 3178].

[8]   See CIC can. 912.

[9]   See Paul VI, Ap. Const. *Regimini Ecclesiae universae*, 15 Aug. 1967, no. 113: AAS 59 (1967) 923.

[10]   See CIC can. 913.

[11§1]   See CIC Can. 349, § 2, 2°. Motu Proprio *Cleri sanctitati*, 2 June 1957, can. 396. § 2, 2°; can. 364, § 3, 3°; can 367, § 2, 1°, and can. 391: AAS 49 (1957) 541ff.

[11§2]   See CIC can. 914. See also Motu Proprio *Suburbicariis sedibus*, 11 April 1962, II, 2: AAS 54 (1962) 255.

[12]   See CIC can. 274. Motu Proprio *Cleri sanctitati* can. 319, 6° and can. 320, § 1, 4°.

[13]   See Motu Proprio *Cleri sanctitati* 283, 4°; see also can. 326, § 1, 10° (can. 319, 6°) and § 2.

14. Cardinals possess the power to grant partial indulgences in every place or institution and in favor of those persons subject to their jurisdiction or protection. They may do the same elsewhere, but only regarding indulgences to be gained by the people present on each occasion.[14]

3206

15. § 1. No book, booklet, or pamphlet listing indulgences granted is to be published without permission of the local Ordinary or local Hierarch.

    § 2. The publication, in no matter what language, of an authentic collection of prayers and devotional works to which the Apostolic See has attached indulgences requires the express permission of the same Apostolic See.[15]

3207

16. Those who have requested of the pope the granting of indulgences in favor of all the faithful are bound by the obligation, under pain of nullification of the favor granted, to send to the Apostolic Penitentiary authentic copies of the concessions given to them.[16]

3208

17. An indulgence attached to any feast is regarded as transferred to the day to which the same feast or its external observance is lawfully transferred.[17]

3209

18. To gain an indulgence attached to a particular day any required visit to a church or oratory may be made from noon of the day preceding until midnight at the end of the assigned day.[18]

3210

19. All the faithful gain a partial indulgence in devoutly using religious articles (crucifixes, crosses, rosaries, scapulars, medals) properly blessed by any priest.

    All the faithful devoutly using a religious article blessed by the pope or any bishop may also gain a plenary indulgence on the feast of the Apostles Peter and Paul; but they must add the profession of faith recited in any approved formulary.[19]

3211

20. § 1. Indulgences attached to the visiting of a church do not expire if the church is razed and then rebuilt within fifty years on the same or virtually the same site and under the same name.

    § 2. An indulgence attached to the use of a religious article expires only when the article itself ceases to exist or is sold.[20]

3212

21. Like a devoted mother, the Church in its special concern for the faithful departed establishes that in every sacrifice of the Mass suffrages are most lavishly offered on behalf of the dead; any privilege on this matter is suppressed.[21]

3213

22. § 1. To be capable of gaining indulgences a person must be baptized, not excommunicated, in the state of grace at least at the end of the prerequisite works, and subject to the jurisdiction of the one granting the indulgence.

3214

---

[14] See CIC can. 239 and Motu Proprio *Cleri sanctitati* can. 185, § 1, 24°.

[15] See CIC can. 1388.

[16] See CIC can. 920.

[17] See CIC can. 922. See also *Codex Rubricarum* nos. 356–359: AAS 52 (1960) 657.

[18] See CIC can. 923.

[19] Ap. Const. *Indulgentiarum doctrina* N. 17 [DOL 386 no. 3183].

[20] See CIC can. 924.

[21] Ap. Const. *Indulgentiarum doctrina* N. 20 [DOL 386 no. 3186].

§ 2. Actually to gain indulgences the person must have at least the general intention of doing so and must perform the acts enjoined at the time stipulated and in the manner required according to the tenor of the grant.[22]

3215   23. Unless somthing different is obvious from the tenor of the concession, indulgences granted by a bishop may be gained by his subjects outside his territory and by all those present in his territory, whether visitors, nonpermanent residents, or exempt religious.[23]

3216   24. § 1. A plenary indulgence may be gained only once on any day.

§ 2. A member of the faithful may, however, gain a plenary indulgence at the hour of death even after having gained one already on the same day.

§ 3. A partial indulgence may be gained many times a day, unless something different is explicitly stated.[24]

3217   25. The prescribed work for gaining a plenary indulgence attached to a church or oratory is a devout visit there, which includes the recitation of the Lord's Prayer and the Creed (*Pater* and *Credo*).[25]

3218   26. The requirements for gaining a plenary indulgence are the performance of the indulgenced work and fulfillment of three conditions: sacramental confession, eucharistic communion, and prayer for the pope's intentions. A further requirement is the exclusion of all attachment to sin, even venial sin.

Unless this unqualified disposition and the three conditions are present, the indulgence will only be partial; the prescriptions in N. 34 and N. 35 for those impeded are exceptions.[26]

3219   27. The three conditions may be carried out several days preceding or following performance of the prescribed work. But it is more fitting that communion and prayer for the pope's intentions take place on the day the work is performed.[27]

3220   28. Several plenary indulgences may be gained on the basis of a single sacramental confession; only one may be gained, however, on the basis of a single communion and prayer for the pope's intentions.[28]

3221   29. The condition requiring prayer for the pope's intentions is completely satisfied by reciting once the Our Father and Hail Mary for his intentions; nevertheless all the faithful have the option of reciting any other prayer suited to their own devotion and their reverence for the pope.[29]

3222   30. The norms issued on plenary indulgences, and especially those listed in N. 24, § 1, are applied also to those plenary indulgences that by custom hitherto have been called *toties quoties* indulgences.[30]

---

[22] See CIC can. 925; see CIC can. 2262.

[23] See CIC can. 927.

[24] Ap. Const. *Indulgentiarum doctrina* N. 6 [DOL 386 no. 3172]. See also ibid. N. 18 [DOL 386 no. 3184].

[25] Ibid N. 16 [DOL 386 no. 3182].

[26] Ibid N. 7 [DOL 386 no. 3173].

[27] Ibid N. 8 [DOL 386 no. 3174].

[28] Ibid N. 9 [DOL 386 no. 3175].

[29] Ibid N. 10 [DOL 386 no. 3176].

[30] Ibid N. 19 [DOL 386 no. 3185].

31. An indulgence cannot be attached to a work to which a person is obliged by law or precept. Nevertheless a person who performs a work imposed as such a penance in confession and which may also be indulgenced can at the one time both satisfy the sacramental penance and gain the indulgence.[31]

3223

32. An indulgence annexed to any prayer may be gained no matter what the language of recitation, provided the accuracy of the translation is supported by a declaration either of the Apostolic Penitentiary or of one of the Ordinaries or Hierarchs in the region where the language of the translation is in general use.[32]

3224

33. To gain indulgences it suffices to recite a prayer alternating with another person or to follow it mentally as another recites it.[33]

3225

34. Confessors are empowered to commute either the prescribed work or the necessary conditions in favor of those for whom these are impossible because of the existence of some legitimate obstacle.[34]

3226

35. Local Ordinaries or Hierarchs may also grant to the faithful subject to them, in keeping with canon law, and who reside in places where they cannot go to confession or communion at all or can do so only with great hardship that they may gain a plenary indulgence without actual confession and communion, provided they have inner contrition and the resolution to go to these sacraments as soon as possible.[35]

3227

36. Many can gain the indulgences attached to public prayers simply by raising their minds and devotion to God as they are present with other of the faithful praying in the same place. In the case of private prayers it is enough for people to go over them mentally and express them in some sign or even simply to read them without pronouncing the words.[36]

3228

▶   330. SC BISHOPS, Decree *Apostolatus maris*, on the pastoral ministry to seamen and ship passengers, 24 September 1977:
         Part II, II, nos. 4–5:   Indulgences [no. 2670].

▶   See also Chapter Five, Section 7. Holy Years.

---

[31] See CIC can. 932.

[32] See CIC can. 934, § 2.

[33] See CIC can. 934, § 3.

[34] See CIC can. 935.

[35] Ap. Const. *Indulgentiarum doctrina* N. 11 [DOL 386 no. 3177].

[36] See CIC can. 936.

SECTION 8. RELIGIOUS LIFE

SUMMARY (DOL 391–406). After its general consideration of sacramentals and blessings, the Constitution on the Liturgy in art. 80 particularly decreed the revision of rites that relate to those of the faithful who embrace a state of life dedicated to the evangelical counsels. The conciliar teaching in *Lumen gentium* and *Perfectae caritatis* on religious in the Church also gave renewed prominence and a more profound understanding of the place of the liturgy in the life of religious. Both the ritual reform and the place of liturgy in the renewal of religious life are covered in the two following subsections.

SECTION 8. RELIGIOUS LIFE: A. RITES

SUMMARY (DOL 391–399). The texts here reflect the carrying out of the Constitution on the Liturgy art. 80, decreeing revision of rites related to the life of Christian perfection.

—On religious profession there are 5 texts: the decree promulgating a new rite (DOL 391), the introduction to the rite itself (DOL 392), a reply on the formulary of profession (DOL 393), a letter to superiors general as well as a set of guidelines regarding each institute's adaptation of the new rite (DOL 396, 397).

—On consecration to a life of virginity there is the decree promulgating a new rite and the introduction to the rite (DOL 394, 395).

—On the abbatial blessing there is the decree promulgating a new rite for the blessing of an abbot and an abbess and the introductions to each of these rites of blessing (DOL 398, 399).

▶ 1. VATICAN COUNCIL II, Constitution on the Liturgy *Sacrosanctum Concilium*, 4 December 1963:

art. 55: Communion under both kinds at the Mass of religious profession [no. 55].

80: Rite of religious profession [no. 80].

▶ 4. VATICAN COUNCIL II, Dogmatic Constitution on the Church *Lumen gentium*, 21 November 1964:

no. 45: Rite of religious profession [no. 156].

▶ 179. SC RITES (Consilium), Instruction *Eucharisticum mysterium*, on worship of the eucharist, 25 May 1967:

no. 32, 4 and 11: Communion under both kinds for religious on the day of their profession, for women religious on their jubilee, for an abbess at the Mass of blessing, for those being consecrated to a life of virginity at the Mass of consecration [no. 1261].

▶ 208. SC RITES (Consilium); SC DIVINE WORSHIP, General Instruction of the Roman Missal, 1st ed. 6 April 1969; 4th ed. 27 March 1975:

no. 242, 4: Communion under both kinds for religious on the days noted above [no. 1632].

391. SC DIVINE WORSHIP, **Decree** *Professionis ritus*, promulgating the new rite of religious profession, 2 February 1970: AAS 62 (1970) 553; Not 6 (1970) 113.

3229   The rite of profession by which religious, in commitment to the evangelical counsels, vow themselves to God, has been revised in accord with the intent of the Constitution on the Liturgy. The life dedicated to God by the bonds of religious life has always held a place of high honor in the eyes of the Church, which from the earliest centuries has surrounded the act of religious profession with liturgical rites. The Fathers of Vatican Council II directed that a rite of religious profession and renewal of vows be drawn up that would contribute to greater unity, simplicity, and dignity and that, apart from exceptions in particular law, it should be adopted by those who make their profession or renewal of vows within Mass (art. 80).[a]

Carrying out this directive, the Consilium has composed the present rite of religious profession; Pope Paul VI by his apostolic authority has approved it and ordered that it be incorporated into the Roman Ritual and published. Consequently this Congregation for Divine Worship, at the explicit mandate of the Pope, promulgates this rite.

The conferences of bishops (where applicable, through the joint commission of nations of the same language) are to see to the careful vernacular translations of the rite, after consultation with the conferences of major religious superiors in each country.

The rite of profession must be an expression of the identity and spirit of the individual religious family. Therefore each religious institute should adapt this rite

---
[a] See DOL 1 no. 80.

in such a way that the ritual clearly brings out the institute's special character, then send the rite to this Congregation as soon as possible for confirmation.

All things to the contrary notwithstanding.

392. SC DIVINE WORSHIP, *Rite of Religious Profession*, **Introduction**, 2 February 1970: Vatican Polyglot Press, 1970; emended reprint, 1975.*

INTRODUCTION

I. NATURE AND IMPORT OF RELIGIOUS PROFESSION

1.   In response to God's call many Christians dedicate themselves to his service and to the welfare of humanity through the sacred bonds of religious life and seek to follow Christ more closely through the evangelical counsels.[1] This leads to the grace of baptism achieving richer results in them.[2]

3230

2.   The Church has always esteemed the religious life, which, under the guidance of the Holy Spirit, has taken various forms in the course of history.[3] It has raised religious life to the rank of a canonical state and approved a great number of religious institutes and protected them by wise legislation.[4]

3231

For it is the Church that receives the vows of those who make religious profession, begs God's grace for them by its public prayer, puts them in God's hands, blesses them, and unites their offering with the eucharistic sacrifice.[5]

II. RITES FOR THE DIFFERENT STAGES OF RELIGIOUS LIFE

3.   The steps by which religious dedicate themselves to God and the Church are these: novitiate, first profession (or other sacred bonds), and final profession. The constitutions of religious institutes add to these a renewal of vows.

3232

4.   The novitiate, the beginning of religious life,[6] is a time of testing for both novice and community. Entry into the novitiate should be marked by a rite in which God's grace is sought for the special purpose of the period. This rite should, of its

3233

---

   *   The text here is based on this second printing, which carries the following note: "It is necessary to reprint the *Order professionis religiosae*, first published in 1970. Therefore it seemed advisable to provide this reprint with certain minor changes:

   1. The texts of the psalms and of the New Testament have been taken from the Neo-Vulgate edition of the Bible.

   2. There are some emendations of titles and rubrics in order that these might more closely correspond to the language and style found in the liturgical books published since 1969.

   3. The liturgical texts can be adapted to fit particular situations by a change in gender or number.

   [1]   See LG no. 43; PC no. 1.
   [2]   See LG no. 43.
   [3]   See ibid.; PC no. 1.
   [4]   See LG no. 45 [DOL 4 no. 156]; PC no. 1.
   [5]   See LG no. 45 [DOL 4 no. 156].
   [6]   See SCRSI, Instr. *Renovationis causam*, 6 Jan. 1969, no. 13: AAS 61 (1969) 113.

nature, be restrained and simple, celebrated in the presence only of the religious community. It should take place outside Mass.

3234   5.   First profession then follows. Through temporary vows made before God and the Church the novices promise to observe the evangelical counsels. Such vows may be taken within Mass, but without special solemnity. The rite of first profession provides for the bestowal of insignia of the religious life and the habit, following the very ancient custom of giving the habit at the end of the period of probation, since the habit is a sign of consecration.[7]

Where a promise or some other kind of bond takes the place of profession,[8] the proper setting for the rite is some suitable liturgical service, such as a liturgy of the word, a part of the liturgy of the hours, especially morning prayer or evening prayer, or, if circumstances require, the eucharistic sacrifice itself.

3235   6.   After the period prescribed by law, final profession is made, by which religious bind themselves permanently to the service of God and the Church. Perpetual profession reflects the unbreakable union between Christ and his Bride, the Church.[9]

It is very fitting that the rite of final profession should take place within Mass, with due solemnity and in the presence of the religious community and the people.[10] The rite consists of these parts:

a.   the calling or asking of those to be professed (this may be omitted if desired);

b.   the homily or address, which reminds the people and those to be professed of the value of religious life;

c.   the examination by which the celebrant or superior asks those who are to be professed whether they are prepared to be consecrated to God and to follow the way of perfect charity, according to the rule of their religious family;

d.   the litanies, in which prayer is offered to God the Father and the intercession of the Blessed Virgin Mary and all the saints is invoked;

e.   the profession, made in the presence of the Church, the lawful superior of the institute, the witnesses, and the congregation;[R1]

---

[7]   See PC no. 17.

[8]   See LG no. 44. SCRSI, Instr. *Renovationis causam*, 6 Jan. 1969, nos. 2, 7: AAS 61 (1969) 105–106, 110–111.

[9]   See LG no. 44.

[10]   See SC art. 80 [DOL 1 no. 80].

[R1]   Query: May either the bishop or the priest who presides at the eucharistic celebration receive the profession of women religious? Reply: The ritual for religious profession, part two, no. 39 states: "After the prayer, two already professed sisters, as determined by the custom of the community, take their place at the superior's chair and stand there as the witnesses. Those making profession go to the superior one by one and read the profession formulary . . . ." No. 69 gives practically the same rubric: "Those making profession go to the superior one by one and read the profession formulary." In the minds of some this procedure is unbecoming when, as the rite of profession itself recommends, profession is made during Mass and all the more so if a bishop presides at the eucharist. They propose as reasons the hierarchic and sacramental nature of the Church (see LG nos. 25, 45), which receives expression in the celebration of the liturgy, above all the Mass (see SC art. 46 [DOL 1 no. 46]; EuchMyst no. 16 [DOL 179 no. 1245]).
    The matter has been given considerable thought and when asked for its opinion the Congregation for Religious answered in this way: "This Congregation does not regard as valid or cogent the reasons advanced to justify a modification of the rite at its most important point, when the competent superiors receive the candidates' vows and, in the Church's name, incorporate those professed into the religious community" (14 Oct. 1974, Prot N. 5898/69).
    The following are the reasons underlying the Congregation's reply:
    "1. The general law and jurisprudence.
    "a. In virtue of CIC can. 572, § 1, 6°, the condition for the validity of religious profession is

    f. the solemn blessing or consecration of the professed, by which the Church ratifies their profession through a liturgical consecration, asking the heavenly Father to pour forth upon them the gifts of the Holy Spirit;

    g. the presentation of the insignia of profession, if this is the custom of the religious family, as outward signs of perpetual dedication to God.

7.   In some religious communities vows are renewed at fixed times in accordance with the constitutions.   3236

This renewal of vows may take place within Mass, but without solemnity, especially if renewal of vows is frequent or annual.

A liturgical rite has place only in the case of renewal of vows that has the force of law. In many religious communities, however, the custom of renewing vows has become established as an exercise of devotion. It may be carried out in many ways; but the practice of doing publicly within Mass what belongs to private devotion is not to be encouraged. If it seems appropriate to renew vows publicly on special anniversaries, for example, the twenty-fifth or fiftieth year of religious life, the rite for the renewal of vows may be used with the necessary adaptations.

---

its acceptance by the lawful superior. This necessarily involves a superior or superioress belonging to the religious institute and more precisely designated by its individual constitutions. These superiors in receiving public vows, personally or through a delegate, are acting in the name of the Church and of their own community.

    "b. Profession is both the first moment and the act constitutive of a relationship between the institute and the one professed that will be lifelong. It is therefore reasonable that no outsider be interposed at the very point when this relationship is being established.

    "c. The canonists' teaching is unanimous in reserving to the superiors belonging to the institute the right of receiving profession. So much so that in institutes of diocesan rank, which are subject to the local Ordinary in a particular way, it is not the bishop who receives profession but the superiors of the institutes.

    "2. Recent documents of the Holy See.

    "a. The *Rite of Religious Profession* establishes explicitly that the vows of men religious are to be pronounced before their superior, even if he is not a priest, no matter who the celebrant is (bishop or simple priest). The same rule is repeated for the profession of women religious.

    "b. The directive in the rite of consecration to a life of virginity when combined with final profession is that it is for the superioress to receive the vows, even though it belongs to the bishop to preside at the ceremony. These rites make very precise the part of the superior, who receives the profession of vows, and the part of the bishop (or priest celebrant), to whom is reserved the consecratory prayer over the newly professed. Presiding at the eucharistic celebration and the rites surrounding profession is one thing; receiving the vows is quite another.

    "3. Points of a liturgical nature.

    "a. There seems no reason to exclude making profession outside Mass.

    "b. The teaching on the sacramental and hierarchic structure of the Church has not been compromised in any way; the lawful superiors, in the meaning of CIC can. 572, act precisely in the name of the institute as approved by the Church itself.

    "c. It would be relevant to recall the common teaching, one that Vatican Council II built on and reaffirmed in both *Lumen gentium* and *Perfectae caritatis*: religious profession is in continuity with baptismal grace and the baptismal character. The profession of the evangelical counsels is therefore one of those spiritual sacrifices that Christians offer in the exercise of their baptismal priesthood and that takes on a sacramental and liturgical form when it is exercised within a community of celebration that unites itself to Christ's sacrifice.

    "In the new *Rite* it is necessary to coordinate the rightly planned functions of the two distinct ministers with their two distinct ministries. These two are required by the composite mystical reality that the rite conjoins in the one celebration. The minister of the eucharist, head of the liturgical community, brings to completion in the sacrament the sacrifice that profession expresses as it is pronounced in the hands of the minister proper to it. The *sacerdos*, therefore, whether bishop or priest, is a minister less suited to being the bearer of the sign of a structure and a communion that do not derive from holy orders. Yet he is the irreplaceable minister precisely as president of the liturgical community, gathered around him and constituted hierarchically, even though he does not carry out ministries that are assigned to others.

    "This liturgically exact point of view should put into focus the proper title under which the *sacerdos* and the superior as such take their parts and the subordination of the ministry of the superior to that of the *sacerdos*": Not 11 (1975) 62–64.

3237   8. Since all these rites have their own special character, each demands a celebration of its own. The celebration of several rites within the same liturgical service is to be absolutely excluded.

III. MASS FOR THE RITE OF RELIGIOUS PROFESSION

3238   9. Whenever religious profession, and especially final profession, takes place within Mass, it is appropriate to choose one of the ritual Masses for the day of religious profession from the Roman Missal or from approved propers. In the case of a Sunday of Advent, Lent, or Easter, of any solemnity, or of Ash Wednesday and all of Holy Week, the Mass is that of the day; but the special formularies for the professed during the eucharistic prayer and the final blessing may be retained.

3239   10. Since the liturgy of the word for the rite of profession can be an important aid to bringing out the meaning of religious life and its responsibilities, it is lawful, when the Mass for the day of religious profession may not be used, to take one reading from the special list of readings for the rite of profession. But this may not be done during the Easter triduum, on the solemnities of Christmas, Epiphany, Ascension, Pentecost, or Corpus Christi, or on other solemnities of obligation.

3240   11. White vestments are worn for the ritual Mass for the day of religious profession.

IV. ADAPTATIONS TO BE MADE BY INDIVIDUAL INSTITUTES

3241   12. The norms governing the rite of initiation (nos. 1–13 of the ritual) are not of obligation unless this is clearly stated (as in the prohibition of having the rite within Mass, no. 2) or the nature of the rite so demands (as in the rule that the rite should be restrained and simple, no. 3).

3242   13. All who make or renew their religious profession within Mass must use the rites of temporary profession, final profession, or renewal of vows, unless they possess a particular right in this matter.[11]

3243   14. Religious families should adapt the rite so that it more clearly reflects and manifests the character and spirit of each institute. For this purpose the faculty of adapting the rite is given to each institute; its decisions are then to be reviewed by the Apostolic See.

In making adaptations in the rite of profession, the following points should be especially respected:

a. The rite must take place immediately after the gospel.

b. The arrangement of parts must remain intact, but some parts may be omitted or others of a similar nature substituted.

c. A liturgical distinction between perpetual profession and temporary profession or renewal of vows must be strictly maintained. What is proper to one rite may not be inserted into another.

d. As is stated in the pertinent places, many formularies in the rite of profession may be changed, and in fact must be, to reflect more clearly the character and spirit of each institute. Where the Roman Ritual offers several optional formularies, particular rituals may add others of the same kind.

---

[11]   See SC art. 80 [DOL 1 no. 80].

15. Profession in the presence of the blessed sacrament, prior to communion, is not   3244
in harmony with a true understanding of the liturgy. Henceforth, then, new religious communities are forbidden to adopt the practice. Institutes that follow this
practice on the basis of a particular law are urged to discontinue it.

Similarly, all religious following a rite proper to them are instructed to embrace
and follow authentic liturgical forms, putting aside anything in conflict with the
principles of the liturgical reform. This is the way to achieve that simplicity, dignity, and closer unity that the Council has so strongly endorsed.[12]

RITE OF A RELIGIOUS PROMISE

I. General Rules for the Rite of a Religious Promise

1. Some religious institutes find it desirable for the novices, upon completing the   3245
canonical year of novitiate, not to take temporary vows but to bind themselves to
the institute only by a special promise or other temporary bond, either for some
years or until the time of final profession.[1]

2. Although the promise or other temporary bond are of their very nature   3246
different from religious vows, they nevertheless have reference to the three evangelical counsels and in some fashion are a preparation for profession.[2] It is therefore
highly desirable that they take place in a setting of fervent prayer; indeed, the
Church does not hesitate to allow the promise to be made within a suitable liturgical service, such as a celebration of the word of God or the liturgy of the hours,
especially at morning or evening prayer, or, if circumstances so dictate, even within
the eucharistic sacrifice.

3. In arranging the rite of a promise, the greatest care should be taken to maintain   3247
its distinct character, avoiding the inclusion of what is proper to religious profession. In the composition of formularies, the choice of readings, and the use of
liturgical signs, therefore, all that by force of law or by ancient custom belongs to
the rite of religious profession should be avoided.

4. The taking of the promise is a ceremony mainly internal to the religious   3248
community. The primary purpose of the promise is that the candidate gain further
experience of the religious life and be tested by the institute. Consequently, the rite
should be carried out with a corresponding simplicity.

393. SC RELIGIOUS AND SECULAR INSTITUTES, **Reply** to a query, on
the formulary of religious profession, 14 February 1973: Not 9 (1973) 283
(Italian).*

[Query: Is an individual candidate for profession free to compose the profession formulary? What are the elements that must be retained in the formulary?]

---

12   See SC art. 80 [DOL 1 no. 80].

1   See SCRSI, Instr. *Renovationis causam*, 6 Jan. 1969, nos. 2, 7, 34: AAS 61 (1969) 105–106, 110–111,
118–119.

2   See ibid., nos. 7, 35: AAS 61 (1969) 110–111, 119.

*   SCRSI, Prot. N. 16935/72.

3249   1.   The rite published by the Congregation for Divine Worship prescribes that the *formula professionis* must be submitted for the approval of the Congregation for Religious and Secular Institutes.[a] This being so, it is not possible to maintain that the composition of the formulary for pronouncing religious vows can be left up to the personal initiative of the individual candidates. The formulary must thus be substantially the same for the entire institute, since the duties and rights resulting from the profession are the same.

3250   2.   A further, quite obvious consequence is that no formulary may ever omit certain elements that are intrinsic to the profession of public vows (CIC can. 1308, par. 1). The import of this statement is that the vows, which are made to God, include chastity, poverty, and obedience; the correlative obligations are understood to be accepted, "according to the rule or the constitutions"; there is to be a mention of the name or office of the one who receives the profession in the name of the Church; there is to be a statement of the time period for which the vows are made.

Provided these essential requirements are respected, every religious institute may revise its own formulary of profession and adapt it to the requirements of its own distinctive form of spirituality.

3251   3.   As long as what has been stated is respected, the individual candidates for profession may, with the superior's agreement, add some expression of their personal intention or devotion either at the end or the beginning of the approved formulary. Such additions, however, must be unostentatious, sensible, and in keeping with the seriousness and solemnity of the act of profession itself.

394. SC DIVINE WORSHIP, **Decree** *Consecrationis virginum*, promulgating the *editio typica* of the rite of consecration to a life of virginity, 31 May 1970: AAS 62 (1970) 650; Not 6 (1970) 313.

3252   The rite of consecration to a life of virginity is counted among the most precious treasures in the Roman liturgy. For holy virginity is above all a sublime gift that Christ Jesus bequeathed to his Bride, the Church. As a consequence, from the time of the apostles, virgins have dedicated their chastity to God, thus gracing the Mystical Body of Christ and enriching it with a wonderful fruitfulness. In its maternal care the Church from the earliest ages, as the Fathers attest, has kept the practice of putting its seal through a consecratory prayer upon the devout and exacting resolve of virgins. In the course of time this consecration has become a received part of the Roman Pontifical, supplemented by other sacred ceremonies to give clearer expression that holy virgins stand as an image of the Church's espousal to Christ.

Vatican Council II decreed that the rite of consecration to a life of virginity also undergo revision (see SC art. 80).[a]

In obedience to this directive the Consilium has drawn up the present rite; Pope Paul VI by his apostolic authority has approved it and ordered its publication. Therefore, at the express mandate of the Pope, this Congregation for Divine Worship promulgates it, establishing that, once it has been suitably adapted, if

---

[a]   See DOL 392 no. 3243.

[a]   See DOL 1 no. 80.

necessary, its effective date is 6 January 1971 for those nuns who by law are entitled to use it.

Vernacular translations prepared by the conferences of bishops as well as adaptations of the rite are to be sent for confirmation to this Congregation as soon as possible.

All things to the contrary notwithstanding.

395. SC DIVINE WORSHIP, *Rite of Consecration to a Life of Virginity,* **Introduction**, 31 May 1970: Vatican Polyglot Press, 1970.

INTRODUCTION

I. NATURE AND IMPORT OF CONSECRATION TO VIRGINITY

1.   The custom of consecrating women to a life of virginity flourished even in the   3253
early Church. It led to the formation of a solemn rite constituting the candidate a sacred person, a surpassing sign of the Church's love for Christ, and an eschatological image of the world to come and the glory of the heavenly Bride of Christ. In the rite of consecration the Church reveals its love of virginity, begs God's grace on those who are consecrated, and prays with fervor for an outpouring of the Holy Spirit.

II. THE MAIN DUTIES OF THOSE CONSECRATED

2.   Those who consecrate their chastity under the inspiration of the Holy Spirit do   3254
so for the sake of a more fervent love of Christ and of greater freedom in the service of their brothers and sisters.

They are to spend their time in works of penance and of mercy, in apostolic activity, and in prayer, according to their state of life and spiritual gifts.

To fulfill their duty of prayer they are strongly advised to recite the liturgy of the hours each day, especially morning prayer and evening prayer. In this way, by joining their voice to those of Christ the High Priest and of his Church, they will offer unending praise to their heavenly Father and pray for the salvation of the whole world.

III. THOSE WHO MAY BE CONSECRATED

3.   This consecration may be received by nuns or by women living in the world.   3255

4.   In the case of nuns it is required: 3256

a. that they have never married or lived in public or flagrant violation of chastity;

b. that they have made their final profession, either in the same rite or on an earlier occasion;

c. that their religious family uses this rite because of long-established custom or by new permission of the competent authority.

5.   In the case of women living in the world it is required: 3257

a. that they have never married or lived in public or flagrant violation of chastity;

b. that by their age, prudence, and universally attested good character they give assurance of perseverance in a life of chastity dedicated to the service of the Church and of their neighbor;

c. that they be admitted to this consecration by the bishop who is the local Ordinary.

It is for the bishop to decide on the conditions under which women living in the world are to undertake a life of perpetual virginity.

IV. THE MINISTER OF THE RITE

3258   6.   The minister of the rite of consecration is the bishop who is the local Ordinary.

V. THE FORM OF THE RITE

3259   7.   For the consecration of women living in the world the rite described in Chapter I of this ritual is to be used.

For the consecration of nuns the rite found in Chapter II of this ritual is to be followed. This integrates religious profession with the consecration. For a good reason, however, these two rites may be separated, for example, when this is in accordance with long-established custom. But care should be taken not to duplicate parts of the rite; the two liturgical services should be so arranged that the rite of religious profession omits any prayer of consecration, retaining only those elements that belong to religious profession. But the prayer, *Loving Father, chaste bodies* and the ritual elements with a nuptial significance (for example, the presentation of the ring) are to be reserved for the rite of consecration.

The rite consists of these parts:

a.   the calling of the candidates;

b.   the homily or address, instructing the candidates and the people on the grace of viginity;

c.   the examination by which the bishop asks the candidates about their readiness to persevere in their intention and to receive the consecration;

d.   the litanies, in which prayer is offered to God the Father and the intercession of the Blessed Virgin Mary and all the saints is invoked;

e.   the renewal of the intention of chastity (or the making of religious profession);

f.   the solemn blessing or consecration by which the Church asks our heavenly Father to pour out the gifts of the Holy Spirit on the candidates;

g.   the presentation of the insignia of consecration as outward signs of a spiritual dedication.

VI. MASS FOR THE CONSECRATION TO A LIFE OF VIRGINITY

3260   8.   It is appropriate to use the ritual Mass for the day of consecration to a life of virginity. On a solemnity or a Sunday of Advent, Lent, or the Easter season the Mass of the day is used, but the special formularies for the eucharistic prayer and the final blessing may be used.

3261   9.   The liturgy of the word for the rite of consecration to a life of virginity can be a help in understanding the importance and place of virginity in the Church. Therefore it is lawful, when the Mass for the day of consecration to a life of virginity is not permitted, to take one reading from the special list of readings for this rite. But this may not be done during the Easter triduum, on the Solemnities of Christmas, Epiphany, Ascension, Pentecost, or Corpus Christi, or on other solemnities of obligation.

3262   10.   White vestments are worn for the ritual Mass for the day of consecration.[R2]

[R2]   The following queries were submitted to the SCDW on the rite of consecration.

Queries: 1. Is it true that the *Rite of Consecration to a Life of Virginity* is reserved to nuns taking solemn vows, members of women's secular institutes, and virgins living in the world and that the *Rite of*

Religious Profession is the only rite open to women religious taking simple vows?

2. If women religious of simple vows use the *Rite of Religious Profession*, can they be regarded as consecrated in the same way as women who receive consecration to a life of virginity? Can it be said that there are degrees of consecration? If so, what constitutes the supreme or highest degree, the rite used or the nature of the vows?

3. Is a vow required for consecration or does any commitment, like a promise, accepted by the Church suffice?

4. Is consecration the consequence of temporary or of final profession?

5. Is the rite of consecration restricted to women or is it also open to men belonging to secular institutes? If to women, is this for historical or for cultural reasons or is the possibility of consecration based on the nature of women?

6. An article in *L'Osservatore Romano* on the new rite of religious profession stated that profession is a consecration truly and literally. How is this to be explained, since in the new rites oil is not used whereas it is used in consecrations in the strict sense?

7. Does the prayer of blessing in the *Rite of Religious Profession* possess essentially the same value as that in the *Rite of Consecration to a Life of Virginity*?

The Relator of the study group that prepared both rites in question answered point by point.

Reply: 1. The *Rite of Consecration to a Life of Virginity* (hereafter OCV) is in fact restricted to nuns, women belonging to secular institutes, and other laywomen. This is clear from an accurate reading of the OCV, Introduction no. 3. Perhaps it is surprising that in our times one category of women religious (nuns) is admitted to consecration and another (sisters) is excluded and yet consecration has been opened up to members of secular institutes and laywomen. A rejected proposal was that sisters belonging to institutes of perpetual vows be allowed to choose, on the basis of their own preference, either the *Rite of Religious Profession* (hereafter OPR) or the OCV. The present disposition of the matter assuredly is based on sound and well-considered reasons. Nevertheless it seems correct and reasonable to envision the possibility of future development of the present legislation. An ecclesiastical law — expressed at present solely in the new Roman Pontifical — is involved, which as such is subject to exceptions as a result of the petitions of individual religious institutes. That should not cause us to overlook a remarkable step forward: the fact that the OCV, until a short time ago a very rare privilege, has now been extended even to laywomen. With respect to the second part of the question, the two things must be looked at differently. First, the OPR is the basic rite for *all* women religious (in fact many nuns taking solemn vows prefer to follow the OPR). Secondly, the *periti* of the Consilium had been informed by the SC Religious that in all probability the distinction between simple and solemn vows would disappear in the future code of canon law. The OPR was therefore drawn up without in any way applying that distinction. The OPR centers on the *perpetuity* and *totality* of the gift of self.

2. Yes, of course. Women religious making perpetual vows by using the OPR are truly *consecrated*, according to the intention of the Church and the words of the rite. As to the second part of the question: there do not appear to be degrees of consecration, determined by the different rites used. The consecratory language of the OPR ch. III, is no less "strong" than that of the OCV ch. II.

3. Strictly speaking, for consecration a vow is not necessary, in the technical sense that "vow" has taken on in the last centuries. Rather the essential requirements are the person's intention of self-offering to God in a total and perpetual way and the Church's acceptance of that intention. That seems to be the criterion behind the OCV, Introduction, no. 5 c.

4. A person receives consecration from perpetual profession and the accompanying liturgical act of the Church (the consecratory prayer). This is the requirement of the very nature of consecration, which presupposes totality and perpetuity; today's canonists and liturgists are in complete agreement on this point. In the OPR ch. II (temporary profession) such terms as "consecration" or "consecrated" are not used; they are kept exclusively for ch. III (final profession).

5. There is in the OPR an advance regarding men. If they have embraced the religious life, the Church also pronounces over them on the day of their final profession a solemn prayer of consecration and regards them as consecrated men (LG ch. 4 provides a sound doctrinal foundation on this point). But no rite has been composed for laymen paralleling that of consecration to a life of virginity open to laywomen. That is undoubtedly due in great measure to historical and cultural reasons and to a tradition that reaches back almost to the era of the apostles. We do not know about the future. It is possible that the attitude of the faithful may evolve to the point that there will be a consecration of men like that of women. At present the presuppositions for this do not seem to exist. This is probably the present mind of the Church — of both pastors and people. There is no evidence that a petition in regard to men has ever been made.

6. In effect the OPR and OCV are rites having the nature of genuine consecrations. We should not restrict the term "consecration" to rites in which oil is used. To judge whether or not a rite contains a consecration, it is necessary to look above all to the intention of the Church and to consider whether the requisites for the concept of consecration (total and permanent dedication to God . . .) exist in the thing

▶   127.   SC DIVINE WORSHIP, Letter *Die 2 februarii*, on the vernacular translation of the
           rite of religious profession, 15 July 1970.

396. SC DIVINE WORSHIP, **Letter** *Le 2 février* to superiors general of religious orders, on the adaptation of the *Rite of Religious Profession*, 15 July 1970:
Not 6 (1970) 318–319 (French).

3263   On 2 February 1970 this Congregation for Divine Worship, by order of Pope
        Paul VI, promulgated the *Ordo professionis religiosae*.ᵃ

        As you know, this rite responds to a directive of Vatican Council II: "A rite of
        religious profession and renewal of vows shall be drawn up with a view to achiev-
        ing greater unity, simplicity, and dignity. Apart from exceptions in particular law,
        this rite should be adopted by those who make profession or renewal of vows
        within Mass" (SC art. 80).ᵇ

        In incorporating this *Rite of Religious Profession* into an official liturgical book, the
        Roman Ritual, the Holy See intended that — except for cases of particular law — it
        should became the rite universally used by all who make profession within Mass or
        would like to do so.

        The *Rite of Religious Profession* has been drawn up so as to blend a necessary unity
        of structure with a broad openness to adaptation to the varying circumstances of
        the different communities. This feature is combined with the fact that the *Rite* is the
        result of a long period of cooperation between the Consilium, the Congregation for
        Religious, and a number of religious families (they received the proposal for the
        new rite in 1968). In consequence there is every hope that the *Rite of Religious Profession*
        will prove to be the effective instrument to achieve the "greater unity" that the
        Council looked for in this matter.

3264   Some communities have already sent in their profession rite, in a form revised
        and properly adapted on the basis of the *Rite of Religious Profession*. On the part of both
        the communities submitting the rite and the *periti* of this Congregation, however,
        certain questions have emerged with respect to the principles and method to be
        followed in the work of adaptation. It therefore has seemed advisable to provide
        some guidelines to facilitate this work.ᶜ

        This Congregation is confident that your own institute will be eager to devote
        careful attention to the adaptation of the *Rite of Religious Profession* and in a way that

---

or person involved. Thus the use or nonuse of oil is secondary. Use of oil in most consecrations is
explained by the fact that the Church regards anointing to be a rite strikingly expressive of its own
intention. But in truth in the liturgy the oils are often signs expressing a consecration already accomplished in virtue of other liturgical acts. For example, in the rites of baptism and ordination to priesthood
the actual consecration comes before the anointings of the head of the newly baptized and of the hands of
the newly ordained. Both anointings are clear expressions of the inner effects accomplished by the coming
of the Holy Spirit. The anointing of the sick — the single New Testament anointing and certainly of
divine-apostolic origin — does not fall into the category of a properly consecratory rite. Consecration to a
life of virginity has always been looked on, even canonically, as a genuine consecration, yet as a rule oils
have never been used in it. Likewise oil is not used in the ordination of a deacon, the consecratory
character of which seems indisputable.
    7.   Yes. That has always been the intention of those responsible for this area of the liturgy: Not
7 (1971) 107–110.
    ᵃ   See DOL 391, 392.
    ᵇ   DOL 1 no. 80.
    ᶜ   See DOL 397.

respects the structural unity of the Roman rite and brings out, as required, the spirituality proper to your own religious family.

397. SC DIVINE WORSHIP, **Guidelines** *Les principales indications,* on the adaptation of the *Rite of Religious Profession,* 15 July 1970: Not 6 (1970) 319–322 (French).

The chief guidelines for adaptation of the *Rite of Religious Profession* were set out   3265
in the Introduction of the *Rite* itself (ch. IV: Adaptations proper to each institute, nos. 12–15).[a] These guidelines, possessing normative force, are quite clear and need no elaboration, except for a few supplementary notes.

1.   Methodologically, it is important to note that the work must consist in an   3266
adaptation of the *Rite of Religious Profession* of a kind that gives adequate expression to the spirituality proper to the institute. The work must consequently proceed with the *Rite* as the point of departure and by inserting at the pertinent places elements proper to the institute.

Thus it would be the wrong way around to take as the working base the institute's former book of ceremonies and incorporate elements of the *Rite of Profession* here and there.

2.   Those religious institutes that, because of their geographic extent or other   3267
factors, wish to compose a Latin adaptation on the basis of the *editio typica* can, of course, do so at once.

On the other hand, those institutes that wish to compose an adaptation directly in a modern language must do so on the basis of *official* translations of the *Ordo professionis.* To prepare such official translations is the right and duty of the conferences of bishops, with the collaboration of the associations of religious; the Congregation for Divine Worship must give confirmation and approval of such translations (see Decree of the Congregation for Divine Worship, 2 February 1970).[b]

3.   Before incorporating its own elements into the *Rite,* each institute must carry   3268
out a critical review of such elements, that is, verify their accord with the general principles of liturgical reform (the Constitution *Sacrosanctum Concilium*), of religious life (the Constitution *Lumen gentium* and the Decree *Perfectae Caritatis*), of the relationship with the modern world (the Constitution *Gaudium et spes*). In truth, some recurring ideas in the ceremonial books of religious are hard to reconcile with the theology of the religious life set forth in the great conciliar documents.[1]

4.   The places most open to the incorporation of proper elements in the *Rite of*   3269
Religious Profession are many and for the most part indicated by the phrase *his vel similibus verbis, hac vel simili prece,* etc. In substituting a proper formulary for one in the *Rite,* take care that it is of the same literary genre. Take particular care to respect in prayers the style and proper rules of Roman euchology, as well as doctrinal content.

---

a   See DOL 392 nos. 3241–44.

b   See DOL 391.

1   This critical review should be taken to mean that each community conducts it in the light of the purposes, spirit, and tradition of its own institute. Such elements are different depending on whether it is a community of apostolic life, of contemplative life, or of mixed life.

3270   5.   The intent of the phrases *his vel similibus verbis, hoc vel alio modo* is to facilitate the work of adaptation by each institute and to favor a proper diversity. For this reason, in many cases, especially where the texts express thoughts pertaining to persons, the institutes would do well to retain corresponding phrases.

3271   6.   Under no consideration must the adaptation impoverish the *Rite of Profession*.

     a.   As to biblical texts, it is not right to keep one or two and completely disregard the rest. Rather each institute should consider whether to add others so as to shed light on its own spirituality or activity (missions, education, nursing, etc.).

     b.   Similarly, when the *Rite of Profession* provides an option between two prayers, for example, for the solemn prayer of consecration, this option must be understood in relation to an actual celebration and not as involving a choice made once for all celebrations so that one of the alternative prayers is flatly excluded. Rather, in this matter, as in similar instances, the general principle must be kept in view: "Where the Roman Ritual offers several optional formularies, particular rituals may add others of the same kind" (*Rite of Profession*, Introduction no. 14 d).^c [c]

3272   7.   As to liturgical considerations, by the fact that the habit is bestowed *within Mass* (see *Rite*, Part I, nos. 31 and 137) with the intent of its becoming the sign proclaiming the religious state, the habit itself becomes sacred and needs no special blessing.

     Still, should there be a wish to bless the habit, it is to be done *outside Mass*, as the *Rite* indicates elsewhere in the case of women religious (see *Rite*, Part II, nos. 15–16).

3273   8.   Even if it is made up of several parts, the habit must be regarded as a single unit. It is therefore better to give the habit in one act and to use a single formulary.

     Thus the practice of giving each part with its own formulary is to be discouraged.

     As to the formulary for giving the habit, certain expressions recurring in the ceremonial books of religious are to be avoided, those, namely, that today sound archaic or fulsome or that employ Scripture in an unsound sense.

3274   9.   In the Litany of the Saints institutes are to avoid introducing an excessive number of saints of their own or grouping them before all the other saints. The addition of saints' names is to limit itself to these most representative and to insert the names where they belong according to the structure of the Litany of the Saints.

3275   10.   Each institute must submit to this Congregation for Divine Worship (Piazza Pio XII 10, Roma) its own work of adaptation of the *Rite of Religious Profession*:

     a.   in a complete, organized way, that is, containing all the rites, from entrance into the novitiate through final profession;

     b.   in an integral form, without excessive cross-references;

     c.   The stages that religious pass through from the novitiate through final profession differ from one institute to another. Therefore in adapting the *Rite of Profession* to the individual "curriculum" of formation, it clearly will not always be possible to retain the order of numbering in the *Rite*. For example, many institutes prefer to place the *Rite of a Religious Promise*, an Appendix in the *Rite*, immediately after the initiation rite. The main point is that the whole be organized and coherent. For the convenience of the reviewers, it is desirable

---

     ^c See DOL 392 no. 3243.

that there be a reference to the numbering arrangement of the *Rite*, either in the margin or as a footnote, using, for example, the following sigla:

Pr   = Praenotanda;
Op I = Ordo Professionis, Pars Prior;
Op II = Ordo Professionis, Pars Altera;
RP   = Ritus Promissionis;
Ap   = Appendice;

These should be followed by the paragraph numbers of the *Rite*, in arabic numerals.

d. in four copies and a clear format;

e. with a report giving the reasons for the adaptations and the changes decided on.

398. SC DIVINE WORSHIP, **Decree** *Abbatem et Abbatissam*, promulgating the *editio typica* of the rite of blessing of an abbot or abbess, 9 November 1970: AAS 63 (1971) 710–711; Not 7 (1971) 32.

The blessing of an abbot or abbess of a monastery after their canonical election   3276
is a traditional rite in the Church's liturgy. It is meant to show that the whole religious community is praying for God's grace to come upon the person they have chosen to lead them along the way to perfection. In the course of the centuries this rite took on different forms for different times and places. In our own day, therefore, it seems fitting that these traditional rites be revised by removing from them what no longer suits our modern mentality, so that they may express more clearly the spiritual responsibilities of the head of a religious family.

The present revision of the rite of blessing of an abbot and abbess was approved by Pope Paul VI, 19 October 1970. This Congregation for Divine Worship now publishes it to replace the existing rite in the Roman Pontifical.

The Latin text may be used as soon as it is published.

The conferences of bishops should ensure that translations are prepared and should set an effective date for their use after these have been duly confirmed by the Holy See.

399. SC DIVINE WORSHIP, *Rite of Blessing of an Abbot and an Abbess*, **Introduction**, 9 November 1970: Vatican Polyglot Press, 1970.

RITE OF BLESSING OF AN ABBOT

INTRODUCTION

1. The blessing of an abbot should take place, if possible, in the presence of a   3277
gathering of religious and, if circumstances permit, of the faithful. The blessing should take place on a Sunday or major feast day; for pastoral reasons another day may be chosen.

3278   2.   The rite of blessing is usually celebrated by the bishop of the place where the monastery is situated. For a good reason, and with the consent of the bishop of the place, the abbot-elect may receive the blessing from another bishop or abbot.

3279   3.   Two religious from his monastery assist the abbot-elect.

3280   4.   It is desirable that the religious assisting the abbot-elect, the abbots, priest-religious, and other priests present concelebrate the Mass with the officiating prelate and the abbot-elect.

3281   5.   If the abbot-elect receives the blessing in his own abbey at the hands of another abbot, the officiating abbot may ask the newly blessed abbot to preside at the concelebration of the eucharistic liturgy. Otherwise the officiating prelate presides and the new abbot takes first place among the concelebrants.

3282   6.   The officiating prelate and all the concelebrants wear the vestments required for Mass, together with pectoral cross and dalmatic. If the assisting religious do not concelebrate, they wear choir dress or surplice.

3283   7.   The blessing of ring, pastoral staff, and miter normally takes place at some convenient time before the actual blessing of the abbot.

3284   8.   Besides what is needed for the concelebration of Mass and for communion under both kinds, there should also be prepared:
     a.   the Roman Pontifical;
     b.   the Rule;
     c.   the pastoral staff;
     d.   the ring and the miter for the abbot-elect, if they are to be presented to him.

3285   9.   During the liturgy of the word, the officiating prelate should sit in the official chair; the abbot-elect should sit between the assisting religious in a suitable place within the sanctuary.

3286   10.   As a rule, the blessing takes place at the chair. To enable the faithful to participate more fully, a seat for the officiating prelate may be placed before the altar or in some other suitable place; the seats for the abbot-elect and the religious assisting him should be so arranged that the religious and the faithful may have a clear view of the ceremony.

RITE OF BLESSING OF AN ABBESS

INTRODUCTION

3287   1.   The blessing of an abbess should take place, if possible, in the presence of a gathering of women religious and of the faithful. The blessing should take place on a Sunday or major feast day; for pastoral reasons another day may be chosen.

3288   2.   The blessing is performed as a rule by the bishop of the place where the monastery is situated. For a good reason, and with the consent of the bishop of the place, the abbess-elect may receive the blessing from another bishop or an abbot.

3289   3.   The abbess-elect, assisted by two religious from her monastery, is given a place in the sanctuary, outside the enclosure, so that she may be near the bishop or prelate who gives the blessing and so that all present, nuns and faithful, may see the ceremony and take part in it.

4.   Besides what is needed for the celebration of Mass, there should also be   3290
prepared:

   a.   the Roman Pontifical;

   b.   the Rule and, if it is to be presented, the ring;

   c.   a chalice or chalices sufficiently large for communion under both kinds.

5.   The blessing usually takes place at the chair. To enable the faithful to partici-   3291
pate more fully, a seat for the bishop or prelate who gives the blessing may be placed before the altar or in some other suitable place; the seats for the abbess-elect and the religious assisting her should be so arranged that the nuns and faithful may have a clear view of the ceremony.[R3]

[R3]   Query: May the abbatial blessing contained in the *Rite of Blessing of an Abbot and an Abbess* be used for titular abbots? Reply: The abbatial blessing in the *Rite of Blessing of an Abbot and an Abbess* may be used only for abbots who, after their canonical election, actually rule over some community. Thus this blessing cannot be given to abbots who have no ruling power over a community, even if they may rightfully possess the title of abbot on various, mainly historical grounds (e.g., if they are in charge of a church that brings with it the abbatial title). The Decree of 9 Nov. 1970 by which the Congregation for Divine Worship promulgated this *Rite* speaks only of the rite for *an abbot who presides over a religious community*. In any case the entire rite signifies and expresses that "the whole religious community is praying for God's grace to come upon the person they have chosen to lead them along the way of perfection" (ibid. [DOL 398 no. 3276]). Its use therefore for a titular abbot would result in a sham and in an empty ceremony, used merely for the sake of external solemnity: Not 13 (1977) 601.

Section 8. Religious Life: B. Liturgy and Religious Life

SUMMARY (DOL 400–406). The texts here reflect the prominence given to the liturgy as the preeminent source of the religious life.

—Excerpts dealing with the liturgy are given from two formal documents, Pope Paul VI's apostolic exhortation on the renewal and an instruction of the Congregation for Religious and Secular Institutes addressed particularly to contemplatives (DOL 402).

—The remaining texts are addresses of Paul VI, one to superiors general of women religious (DOL 400) and others to Benedictines (DOL 401, 403, 405, 406).

▶ 1. VATICAN COUNCIL II, Constitution on the Liturgy *Sacrosanctum Concilium*, 4 December 1963:

art. 98: Religious obliged to divine office [no. 98].
101, § 2: Vernacular in the divine office of religious [no. 101].

▶ 20. PAUL VI, Motu Proprio *Sacram Liturgiam*, on putting into effect some prescriptions of the Constitution on the Liturgy, 25 January 1964:

art. VIII: Divine office of religious [no. 286].

▶ 23. SC RITES (Consilium), Instruction (first) *Inter Oecumenici*, 26 September 1964:

nos. 4: Active participation [no. 296].[R1]
18: Liturgical formation of religious [no. 310].
59: Lay religious' knowledge of Latin chants [no. 351].
84: Divine office of religious [no. 376].

▶ 176. PAUL VI, Encyclical *Mysterium fidei*, on the eucharist, 3 September 1965:

no. 71: Eucharist in religious life [no. 1215].

▶ 7. VATICAN COUNCIL II, Decree on the Pastoral Office of Bishops *Christus Dominus*, 28 October 1965:

no. 35, 4: Pastoral office of the bishop toward religious [no. 197].

▶ 10. VATICAN COUNCIL II, Decree on the Appropriate Renewal of Religious Life *Perfectae caritatis*, 28 October 1965.

400. PAUL VI, **Address** to the 14th congress of major superioresses, excerpt on the importance of the liturgy in the renewal of religious life, 16 May 1966: AAS 58 (1966) 488–492; Not 2 (1966) 210–211 (Italian).

3292 [. . .] We should like to point out to you in particular three directions to follow in this process of generous love toward the Church.

Above all there is the ever more conscious participation in the liturgy, as the conciliar decree on the renewal of religious life has stated. This decree says that religious "with heart and voice should carry out the liturgy, especially the mystery of the eucharist, in accord with the mind of the Church, and from that abundant source nurture their spiritual life."[7]

Second, there is the intimate knowledge of the inspired books of the Old and above all the New Testament, following the Council's invitation: "They should turn daily to sacred Scripture, there to learn by reading and meditation the 'surpassing knowledge of Jesus Christ' . . . ."[8] Thus strengthened at the table of the divine Law and the sacred altar, they are to love Christ's members as brothers and sisters and to

---

[R1] See DOL 23 no. 296, note R1 on opening the screen during Mass in monasteries of cloistered nuns: Not 2 (1965) 190, no. 57.

[7] PC no. 6 [DOL 10 no. 204].

[8] Phil 3:8.

respect and love their pastors with a filial spirit. They should more and more live and be of one mind with the Church, totally dedicated to its mission."[9]

Third, we recommend a sense of community. Given the solid foundations we have mentioned, this cannot be missing. For of its nature the liturgy, and especially the eucharistic life, nurtures the charity of Christ's individual members, preventing devotion from atrophying in the sterility of individualism and sentimentalism. The knowledge of Scripture, as it affords a broad vision of the history and development of the people of God, cannot help but bring a conception of the sense of community that is open, solid, and fruitful. Nowhere is there greater possibility for the shining example of a sense of community than in the communities of religious. They take as their distinctive characteristic the common life, open to the eyes of all as a witness of Christ's presence. *Ubi caritas et amor, Deus ibi est. Congregavit nos in unum Christi amor.*

▶   11.   PONTIFICAL COMMISSION FOR COORDINATING POSTCONCILIAR WORK AND INTERPRETING THE DECREES OF VATICAN COUNCIL II, Response to a query, on the ordination of members of institutes of religious brothers, 10 June 1966.

401. PAUL VI, **Address** to Benedictine abbots, excerpt on liturgy and contemplation, 30 September 1966: AAS 58 (1966) 884–889; Not 2 (1966) 311.

▸3   [. . .] To contemplate, that is, to be intent on God in thought and in love, is an act of a kind that in some way all must practice. Praying to God must engage the soul's higher faculties, the powers, namely, of thought and of love. An act of divine worship is meaningless without a necessarily concomitant, interior effort on the part of the person praying. Some are of the opinion that the participants in a liturgical service are exempt from such an effort. It is as though a liturgical service could free the individual faithful from eliciting at the same time a personal act. This would amount to the same thing as the individual singers in a choir being freed from the need to join their voices with the voices of the others. You, on the contrary, are perfectly aware how thoroughly the liturgy demands and encourages an inner, spiritual striving that brings the person praying to contemplation. You certainly remember the words of the Encyclical *Mediator Dei*, which we must always keep before us: "The liturgy does not suppress the deepest sentiments of individual Christians; the opposite is true: it reenforces and intensifies them."[6] [. . .]

Make the liturgy the object of your foremost efforts with a kind of mystical and burning intensity. Now that the Council has been completed, above all integrate the liturgy and the devotion it nourishes with the conciliar norms for uniform observance. To this purpose, permit us to remind you that the norms we ourself have recently issued through the Pontifical Letter *Sacrificium laudis*[a] regarding the use of Latin in the divine office apply also to monks. Do not regard us as having imposed a new burden by these norms; rather our intent was to safeguard your own ancient tradition and to protect your own treasury of culture and spirituality. [. . .]

▶   386.   PAUL VI, Apostolic Constitution *Indulgentiarum doctrina*, on indulgences, 1 January 1967:

---

9   PC no. 6 [DOL 10 no. 204].

6   AAS 39 (1947) 567.

a   See DOL 421.

Norm 14:   List of indulgences proper to religious orders and congregations [no. 3180].

▶ 508. SC RITES (Consilium), Instruction *Musicam sacram*, on music in the liturgy, 5 March 1967:

nos. 40:   Divine office sung by religious [no. 4161].
      41:          Language of the divine office of religious [no. 4162].
      49:          Latin and religious [no. 4170].

▶ 179. SC RITES (Consilium), Instruction *Eucharisticum Mysterium*, on worship of the eucharist, 25 May 1967:

nos. 26:   Religious communities and the parish Sunday Mass [no. 1255].
      32, 4, 10, and 11: Communion under both kinds for religious [no. 1261].

▶ 208. SC RITES (Consilium); SC DIVINE WORSHIP, General Instruction of the Roman Missal, 1st ed. 6 April 1969; 4th ed. 27 March 1975:

no. 242, 4, 8 b, 10,
      11, and 14: Communion under both kinds and religious [no. 1632].

▶ 326. SC CLERGY, General Directory *Peregrinans in terra*, on the pastoral ministry in tourism, 30 April 1969:

II, no. 4:   Aid from religious in this ministry [no. 2622].

402. SC RELIGIOUS AND SECULAR INSTITUTES, Instruction *Venite seorsum*, on the contemplative life and the enclosure of nuns, 15 August 1969: AAS 61 (1969) 674–690 (excerpts).

I

3294 I. Withdrawal from the world for a life more centered on the solitude of prayer is a distinctive way of living and expressing Christ's paschal mystery: death for the sake of resurrection. [. . .]

All the faithful are called to follow Christ in the preaching of his saving Gospel; they must contribute to the building up of the earthly city, becoming like a leaven to transform it into the family of God.[16] This is the sense in which the follower of Christ remains in the world (see Jn 17:15). This responsibility, however, does not express the total mystery of the Church: the same Church that is established for the service of God and all people[17] is also, and preeminently, the gather-

---

[16] See GS no. 40: "The Church . . . exists as a leaven and as the soul of human society that must be renewed in Christ and transformed into the family of God."

[17] GS nos. 3, 40–45 speaks of the service of all people in their earthly cares; AG no. 12 states: "The Church claims no other authority than that of ministering, with God's help, to all people in charity and faithful service." But the Church's primary service is for eternal salvation; see LG no. 48: "Christ . . . has established his Body which is the Church as the universal sacrament of salvation." See also LG no. 5.

ing of all the redeemed, of those, namely, who through baptism and the other sacraments have already passed over from this world to the Father.[18] The Church is indeed "eager to act" yet at the same time "intent on contemplation," in such a way that "the human is directed and subordinated to the divine, the visible to the invisible, action to contemplation."[19] It is therefore right and necessary that some of the faithful specifically express in their lives this contemplative side of the Church, retiring into solitude, as recipients of this grace from the Holy Spirit,[20] in order to give themselves up to God alone in assiduous prayer and voluntary penance."[21]
[. . .]

II

To those things that are founded on Christ's paschal mystery as shared in by the Church must be added the theme that recollection and quiet are essential to safeguard and facilitate the encounter with God in prayer.[24] The manner of life of those dedicated completely to contemplation seeks to remove all that can divide the spirit. Therefore its direction is to give the opportunity to achieve the fullness of personality that is marked by the unity of a deeper dedication to the God it seeks and of a more complete concentration upon him.

3295

That search for God, for which a person must renounce all possessions (see Lk 14:33), takes place above all in reading and meditating on the Scriptures (see *Perfectae*

---

[18]   See LG nos. 2, 7, etc.

[19]   SC art. 2 [DOL 1 no. 2].

[20]   See GS no. 38: "The gifts of the Spirit are diverse: calling some to give clear witness to the longing for a heavenly home and to keep that witness alive within the human family . . . ."

[21]   Patristic tradition teaches that the contemplative life is a special expression of Jesus' own prayer in solitude on the mountain, which prefigured the contemplative life. See John Cassian: "He retired alone on the mountain to pray, thus teaching us by his example . . . that we too must go apart alone" (*Collationes* 10, 6, 4: PL 49, 826). Jerome: "Seek Christ in solitude; pray alone on the mountain with Jesus" (*Ep. ad Paulinum* 58, 4, 2: CSEL 54, 532). Isidore of Seville: "His spending the night on the mountain out of a desire for prayer was a symbol of the contemplative life" (*Different.* lib. 2, 2, 34: PL 83, 91). Pseudo-Jerome: "When he prayed, he exemplified the contemplative life; when he sat down to teach he showed the active life . . . . He went to the mountain to pray and went out to the crowds, showing both forms of life together" (PL 30, 571). Walafridus Strabo: "When he went up to the mountain, he demonstrated the contemplative life" (*Expos. in IV Evang.*: PL 114, 872). Paschasius Radbertus: "That we give ourselves up to God alone in contemplation, that is, on the mountain" (*Expos. in Matth.*: PL 120, 522). William, Abbot of St. Theodoric: "Jesus himself lived [the solitary life] most deeply and the disciples yearned for it when he was with them: when those with him on the mountain had seen the glory of his transfiguration, Peter immediately thought that it would be good to be there always" (*Ad fratres de Monte Dei* 1, 1: PL 184, 310). Amadeus of Lausanne: "On the mountain with Moses and Elias he provided us with a mirror, so that we can contemplate what we seek face to face" (*Hom.* 3: G. Bavaud, ed., SC 72, 90–92). LG no. 46: "Religious should be intent on making the Church more and more a sign to believers and unbelievers of Christ in contemplation on the mountain . . . and always obedient to the will of the Father who sent him."
In the East John Climacus (*Scala Paradisi* gr. 1: PG 88, 632–644) and in the West Ambrose (*Ep.* 27, 1–3 and 28, 1, 8: PL 16, 1047, 1051, 1053) and others after him have accommodated themes in Exodus to the monastic life. See also Jerome to Eustochium: "Follow Moses in the desert and enter into the promised land" (*Ep.* 22, 24: PL 22, 410; CSEL 54, 177).

[24]   See Hos 2:14: "I will charm her and bring her into the wilderness and speak tenderly to her." Augustine: "It is difficult to see Christ in a crowd. Our spirit needs a degree of solitude; we see God by a kind of solitary concentration. The crowd means noise; this vision seeks quiet" (*In Io. Tract.* 17, 5: PL 35, 1533). Guigo I the Carthusian: "Now when the moment of his passion was at hand, he left his apostles to pray alone, instructing us by this example how advantageous solitude is to prayer, since he did not wish to pray in the company of others, not even apostles (*Consuetudines* 80, 10: PL 153, 758). John of the Cross: "[For prayer] it is well to choose a solitary, even desolate place, so that the spirit may firmly and directly ascend to God, not hindered or held back by the things of the senses. . . . This is why our Savior chose for prayer places that were lonely and undistracting to the senses, (thus giving us an example), but that, like the mountains rising above the earth, lifted up the soul" (*Ascent of Mount Carmel* III, 39, 2; see also *Spiritual Canticle* B, 35, 1).

caritatis no. 6). The companion of prayer must therefore be the reading of Scripture "so that there may be a conversation between God and ourselves: 'when we pray we speak to him; when we read the Scriptures he speaks to us'" (see Const. *Dei Verbum* no. 25; Ambrose, *De officiis ministrorum* 1, 20, 88: PL 16, 50). [. . .]

III

3296   [. . .] If contemplatives exist, so to speak, in the heart of the world, they exist much more in the heart of the Church.[30] The prayer of contemplatives, above all their taking part in the eucharistic sacrifice and their celebration of the liturgy of the hours, is the carrying out of the foremost responsibility of that praying community which is the Church, namely, giving glory to God. Their prayer is the worship by which "a precious sacrifice of praise" is offered to the Father through the Son in the Holy Spirit.[31] Through this sacrifice those who give themselves to it are brought into the mystery of the sublime colloquy that Christ the Lord carries on unceasingly with the heavenly Father and that in the bosom of the Father expresses Christ's infinite love for him. The prayer of contemplatives, finally, is the summit toward which the entire Church aspires.[32] Because they give expression to the Church's innermost life, therefore, contemplatives are essential to the completeness of its presence.[33] [. . .]

Religious dedicated solely to contemplation assist the Church's missionary activity, "because it is God who when asked sends laborers for his harvest, opens the minds of non-Christians to hear the Gospel, and makes the word of salvation take root in their hearts."[36] In the solitude where they devote themselves to prayer, contemplatives do not forget their brothers and sisters. If they have withdrawn from close contact with others, it is not to seek quiet for their own comfort, but to share in a more all-embracing way in the toils, travails, and hopes of all.[37]

---

[30]   See Paul VI: "We wish these islands of the hidden life, of penance, and meditation to know . . . that they are neither forgotten, nor cut off from the community life of God's Church; rather that they form its heart, they increase its richness in spirituality, they elevate its prayer, support its charity, have their part in its sufferings, its labors, its apostolate, its hopes, and build up its merits" (Addr. 2 Feb. 1966: *Insegnamenti di Paolo VI*, v. 6 [1966] 56).

[31]   PC no. 7 [DOL 10 no. 205]. John of the Cross: "More than all other works combined . . . is a little of this pure love precious to God and the soul and a help to the Church. Mary Magdalen hid herself in the desert for thirty years to give herself totally to this love . . . so great to the Church is the benefit and importance of this pure love. . . . It was ultimately for such a love that we have been created" (*Spiritual Canticle* B, 28, 2–3).

[32]   See SC art. 10: "Toward God's glorification all other activities of the Church are directed as toward their end" [DOL 1 no. 10]. See also GS no. 76; AA no. 2.

[33]   See AG no. 18: "The contemplative life is to be everywhere renewed because it belongs to the completeness of the Church's presence." See John XXIII: "The contemplative life! . . . It forms one of the basic structures of the Church, an element present throughout the Church's two-thousand year history" (Addr. to Trappists, 20 Sept. 1960: AAS 52 [1960] 896).

[36]   AG no. 40. See also Const. *Umbratilem*: AAS 16 (1924) 389. SCR, Decr. to proceed with the canonization of St. Teresa Margaret Redi, 2 Feb. 1934: ". . . her soul fixed to the cross with Christ by the supreme martyrdom of the heart, she gains for herself and others the rich effects of the redemption. In the Church these are the purest and most exalted souls — those that by suffering, loving, and praying do service to all by their silent apostolate.": AAS 26 (1934) 106.

[37]   See Paul VI: "Does this physical, exterior, social isolation separate you from the Church? I come to say to you: be mindful of how much the Church thinks of you; you are not forgotten and therefore the separation that would be the hardest — spiritual separation — does not exist. Why? Because you are the object of special attention, of remembrance. Need we say more? The Church is mindful of you: you have given yourselves to this kind of life in order to be in continuous dialogue with the Lord, in order to be ready to hear his voice more clearly and to let our poor human voice sound with greater purity and intensity. You have made this contact between heaven and earth the single project of your life. You contemplatives have dedicated yourselves to God's taking possession of your soul. The Church therefore

IV

The mystery of the contemplative life therefore is momentous; the privileged   3297
place it occupies in the economy of salvation stands out clearly from the foregoing
consideration; on a completely distinctive basis this life flourishes among cloistered
nuns. By·their identity these women are a more striking symbol of the mystery of
the Church as the "unspotted Bride of the unspotted Lamb."[38] Sitting at the Lord's
feet to hear his word (see Lk 10:39) in silence and seclusion, they savor and seek
those things that are above, where their life is hidden with Christ in God, until with
their Bridegroom they will appear in glory.[39] The woman's part is to treasure the
word rather than to proclaim it to the ends of the earth (although she can also be
called to do this to good effect). Her role is to come to a profound inner knowledge
of the word and to make it bear fruit in a way that is life-giving, clear, and proper to
her. The mature woman is more sensitive to the needs of others and feels them
deeply. She gives fuller expression to the fidelity of the Church towards its Bridegroom[40] and at the same time possesses a sense of the fruitfulness of the contemplative life. Thus as its liturgy attests,[41] the Church has always had a special regard
for Christian virgins. As a sign of the particular divine desire toward them,[42] the
Church has carefully protected both their separation from the world and the monastic enclosure.[43]

Mention of the Blessed Virgin Mary cannot be omitted here. She received the
Word of God within, conceiving Christ "first with the full faith of her spirit before
conceiving him in her womb."[44] Mary stands as a garden locked, a fountain sealed,

---

sees in you the most exalted expression of its own being: in a certain way, you are at the top" (Addr. to
Aventine Camaldolese nuns, 23 Feb. 1968: *Vita monastica* no. 85, p. 68). *Idem:* "You are given not merely a
place in the Catholic Church, but, as the Council says, a responsibility; you are not separated from the
great communion of the family of Christ; you are specialists . . ." (Addr. to superiors of Benedictine
nuns, 28 Oct. 1966: AAS 58 [1966] 1159–60). Vatican Council II has put the matter sublimely: "Let no one
think that by their consecration religious become either estranged from other human beings or useless
citizens of the earthly city. For even if at times they do not *live* immediately among their contemporaries,
religious keep others present to themselves in a higher way in the heart of Christ and cooperate spiritually
with them. In this way the building up of the earthly city rests always on the Lord and is directed toward
him, lest those labor in vain who build it" (LG no. 46). Teresa of Avila: "Persuade the sisters to be ever
intent on asking God to assist those who labor for the Church" (*Way of Perfection,* title for ch. 3). *Idem:* "If in
this way we can in any way reach God, we shall be his defenders even though we are in a cloister. . . . If your
prayers and longings and penance and fasts are not done for the purpose I refer to, realize that then you
are not acting for or fulfilling the purpose for which the Lord has brought you here" (ibid. nos. 5, 10).

[38]   LG no. 6.

[39]   See ibid.

[40]   See LG no. 6: "The Church . . ., which Christ willed to join to himself with an unbreakable bond
. . . and to be subject to himself in love and fidelity . . . ."

[41]   The Western liturgy adapts and applies nuptial symbolism only to holy women, thus illustrating
that their holiness is, so to speak, the result of their spiritual marriage with their Bridegroom and Lord. On
the other hand, the liturgy never uses — as it does in the case of men — the themes of the "new man" or
those referring to a mode of becoming sharers with Christ as Priest, Pontiff, and Prophet. Also since the
fourth century the religious profession of women has been treated as a special ceremony distinct from that
of monks: for the *veiling of virgins,* which must be regarded as an adaptation of the *veiling* of brides, turns the
ceremony into a kind of wedding.

[42]   See Dt 4:24; 2 Cor 11:2: "I feel a divine jealousy toward you, for I betrothed you in Christ to
present you as a pure bride to her one husband."

[43]   See Caesar of Arles, *Reg. ad Virg.* (Approved by Pope Hormisdas): PL 67: 1107. Council of Epauna
(A.D. 517) can. 38: CCL 148 A, 34. Boniface VIII, Const. *Periculoso* (A.D. 1298). Council of Trent, sess. 25,
Decr. de Regularibus cap. 5. CIC can. 597–603 and 2342. Pius XII, Ap. Const. *Sponsa Christi.* SC Religious, Instr.
Inter praeclara and *Inter cetera.*

[44]   Augustine, *Serm.* 215: PL 38: 1074.

a gate closed (see Song of Solomon 4:12; Ez 44:1–2), "in her faith and charity, as the type and exemplar of the Church."[45] The holy Virgin is the model of the contemplative life; by right and the ancient tradition of both East and West the liturgy applies these words of the Gospel to her: "Mary has chosen the better part" (Lk 10:38–42).[46]

V

3298   There is another point of excellence in this mystery of the contemplative life: the value of the sign and the witness that gives contemplatives, whom God sets apart for prayer, a share in all "ministry of the word,"[47] even though this does not involve the ministry of actual preaching. [. . .]

VII
RULES ON THE PAPAL ENCLOSURE OF NUNS

3299   8.   In addition to cases governed by particular indults of the Holy See, entrance into the cloister is allowed: [. . .]

> e.   to the priest with his ministers in order to administer communion to the sick or to conduct funeral ceremonies. Entrance is permitted also to a priest in order to offer assistance to those who are burdened with long or grave illness;

> f.   to a priest with his ministers for liturgical processions, if this is requested by the superioress. [. . .]

403. PAUL VI, **Address** to Benedictine abbots and conventual priors taking part in a congress of the Benedictine Confederation, excerpt on liturgical prayer, 1 October 1970: Not 6 (1970) 347.

3300   Liturgical prayer is a major resource; nothing can replace it; it continuously forms the pattern of the interior life and sustains it. This prayer has as its center and foundation the celebration of the eucharistic sacrifice and the recitation of the divine office, the *opus Dei* par excellence. The Benedictines are committed to liturgical prayer as the preeminent and preferred occupation of their life and as their particular concern. If every consecrated person must be, to use the vernacular, a "specialist about God," this above all applies to you, beloved members of the Order of St. Benedict. You must conduct yourselves during the long hours dedicated to the divine office in such a way that you may draw near to the divine majesty through a spirit that is free from passing things, silent, and austere; that you may readily enter into dialogue with God in joy and adoration, drawn by the example of Christ's prayer. As our predecessor Pius XII said in the Encyclical *Mediator Dei*: "Taking human nature, the Word of God inaugurated for this earthly exile the hymn that is sung in heaven for ever. As we must humbly admit, 'we do not know how to pray as we ought, but the Spirit himself intercedes for us with sighs beyond words'

---

[45]   LG no. 53.

[46]   This Lucan passage has been used as the text for the gospel on feasts of the Blessed Virgin Mary since the sixth century in both East and West: for example, the Dormition or Assumption of Mary (see B. Capelle, "La fête de l'Assomption dans l'histoire liturgique," *Ephemerides theologicae Lovanenses* 3 [1926] 33–45).

[47]   See Acts 6:2, 4: "It is not right that we give up preaching the word of God to serve tables. . . . But we will devote ourselves to prayer and to the ministry of the word."

(Rom 8:26). And in us Christ also through the Spirit pleads with the Father. This exalted dignity of the Church's prayer must be matched by our own concentrated devotion." The same Encyclical continues with the following words taken from your own Rule of St. Benedict: "'Let us arise to sing the psalms in such a way that our spirit is in harmony with our voice' (ch. 19). Thus the issue is not mere recitation or singing, which, no matter how correct in terms of the musical and ritual rules, reach only the ear. The issue rather is the ascent of mind and heart to God, so that, joined to Christ, we may give ourselves and all our acts to him."[1]

▶ 360. SC RELIGIOUS AND SECULAR INSTITUTES, Decree *Dum canonicarum legum recognitio*, establishing norms on the sacrament of penance for religious, on the sacrament of penance, 8 December 1970.

▶ 426. SC DIVINE WORSHIP, General Instruction of the Liturgy of the Hours, 2 February 1971:

        nos. 24, 26, 31 b, 32:   Liturgy of the hours and religious [nos. 3454, 3456, 3461, 3462].

404. PAUL VI, Apostolic Exhortation *Evangelica testificatio*, on the renewal of the religious life, 29 June 1971: AAS 63 (1971) 497–526 (excerpt).

1. The evangelical witness of the religious life clearly shows to the eyes of the world the primacy given to love for God and does this so strikingly that we must give thanks to the Holy Spirit. Like our predecessor John XXIII before the celebration of Vatican Council II, we wish now in simplicity to express to you our own high hopes and then those of all the bishops and members of the Church. The basis for this hope is the spiritual magnanimity of those men and women who have consecrated their lives to the Lord by keeping the spirit and practice of the evangelical counsels. Our hope also is to help you to walk your chosen path as Christ's followers, faithful to the teaching of Vatican Council II.   3301

IV

42. Beloved religious, how could you not long to know more intimately the one for whom you live and whom you wish to make known to others? Prayer joins you to him. If prayer is no longer sweet for you, you will again experience a desire for it by bringing yourself back to it in humility. Do not forget the evidence of history: the index to vigor or apathy in religious life is fidelity to prayer or its neglect.   3302

43. Prayer means the discovery of intimate familiarity with God, the desire to adore him, the will to make intercession. The experience of Christian holiness attests to the effectiveness of prayer; in it God shows himself to the mind and heart of his servants. The gifts of the Spirit are manifold, but their effect is always the same. We taste that close and true knowledge of God without which we cannot grasp the value of the Christian or religious life, nor possess the power for progress fitted with joyous hope toward those things that do not pass away.   3303

44. The Holy Spirit doubtless also bestows on you the grace to find God in the hearts of others, teaching you to love them as brothers and sisters. The Spirit helps   3304

---

[1] AAS 39 (1947) 573–574.

you to discern signs of his love in the fabric of the events of your life. If, then, in humility we attend to people and to our surroundings, the Spirit of Jesus enlightens us and enriches us with his wisdom, so long as we are deeply filled with a spirit of prayer.

3305   45. An imbalance "between the general conditions of life and the requisites for knowledge and contemplation,"[53] is this not one of the tragedies of the times? Many people, including many of the young, have lost the meaning of life and are anxiously looking for the contemplative side of their own being, not knowing that Christ, through his Church, can respond to their yearning. Such considerations must impel you to give serious thought to what people rightfully expect of you. You have explicitly and unequivocally taken on the responsibility of living a life in the service of the Word, "the true light that enlightens everyone."[54] You must accordingly be aware of the importance of prayer in your life and learn to devote yourselves to it eagerly. Daily prayer, carried on faithfully, for each one of you is a primary requirement: this is why it must be given first place in your constitutions and in life.

3306   46. Spiritual people are aware that periods of silence are the prerequisites for divine love and for this a degree of solitude is usually necessary to hear God *speaking to the heart*.[55] But a silence that is mere absence of noise and speech and that is incapable of restoring spiritual vitality must be warned against; it could even be contrary to the love of others at a time when contact with them is called for. The real search for close union with God imposes the need for the silence of the whole person; this is true both of those for whom God must be found amid noise and turmoil, and of those dedicated to contemplation.[56] For silence is prerequisite for faith, hope, and for a love for God that is receptive to the gifts of the Holy Spirit and a love for neighbor that is open to the mystery of other persons.

3307   47. Is there any need to recall the special importance in your communities of the Church's liturgy, the center of which is the eucharistic sacrifice, the conjunction of inner prayer with outward worship?[57] At your religious profession the Church has joined you as an offering with the eucharistic sacrifice.[58] This offering must stand daily as the truth and be continuously made actual. The main source for that to happen is Christ's body and blood in communion, which keeps constant your burning willingness to love even to the point of sacrificing your life.[59]

3308   48. Of its nature the eucharist, a "sacrament of love, a sign of unity, a bond of charity,"[60] is the center of your communities, which have come together in the name of the eucharist. Consistent with this is the public gathering of your communities in the chapel, where the presence of the eucharist at once signifies and causes the reality that must be the main responsibility of every religious family and of every Christian gathering. Through the eucharist we unceasingly proclaim the

---

[53]   GS no. 8: AAS 58 (1966) 1030; ConstDecrDecl 690.

[54]   Jn 1:9.

[55]   See Hos 2:14.

[56]   See SCRSI, Instr. *Venite seorsum*: AAS (1969) 674–690. Message to the Synod of Bishops from monks dedicated to the contemplative life, 10 Oct. 1967: DocCath 64 (1967) 1907–10.

[57]   See SC [DOL 1].

[58]   See *Rite of Religious Profession* [DOL 392].

[59]   See PC no. 15: AAS 58 (1966) 709; ConstDecrDecl 347.

[60]   SC art. 47 [DOL 1 no. 47].

Lord's death and resurrection and prepare ourselves for his glorious Second Coming. It is a constant reminder to you of the sufferings of body and spirit by which Christ was afflicted, but which he bore willingly even to agony and death on the cross. Your own hardships provide the opportunity of undergoing patiently with Christ and of offering to the Father the many misfortunes and unjust torments that afflict our brothers and sisters and that can receive meaning only from Christ's sacrifice seen in the light of faith.

49. Thus the world is also present within your life, dedicated to prayer and self-   3309
giving, as the Council has forcefully stated: "Let no one think that by their consecration religious become either estranged from other human beings or useless people in the earthly city. For even if at times they do not live immediately among their contemporaries, religious keep others present to themselves in a higher way in the heart of Christ and cooperate spiritually with them. In this way the building up of the earthly city rests always on the Lord and is directed toward him, lest those labor in vain who build it."[61]

50. The participation in the fulfillment of the Church's task is impossible, as the   3310
Council insists, unless religious accept and advance the Church's endeavors and plans in the "biblical, liturgical, dogmatic, pastoral, ecumenical, missionary, and social fields."[62] With great concern for doctrine and its concomitant pastoral activity, you will devote yourselves to the work, mindful that exemption of religious refers most of all to internal matters and you will not withdraw yourselves from the bishop's jurisdiction to which you are subject. This jurisdiction belongs to bishops *as the fulfillment of their pastoral office and right order in the care of souls require.*[63] You more than others must always keep in mind that the Church's activity continues Christ's activity on behalf of all only to the degree that you follow the way of life of Christ himself, who brings all things back to the Father: "All are yours and you are Christ's and Christ is God's."[64] For your vocation immediately and effectively directs you along the way toward the eternal kingdom. Through the spiritual struggles that are inevitable in any genuinely religious life you "offer a clear and surpassing witness that the world cannot be transformed and offered to God without the spirit of the beatitudes."[65]

▶   362.   SC EASTERN CHURCHES, Decree *Orientalium Religiosorum*, faculties for religious of the Eastern Churches, 27 June 1972.

▶   432.   SC DIVINE WORSHIP, Notification *Universi qui Officium*, on the liturgy of the hours in certain religious communities, 6 August 1972.

▶   226.   SC DIVINE WORSHIP, Declaration *In celebratione Missae*, on concelebration, 7 August 1972.

nos. 1 and 3 a: In religious communities [nos. 1814 and 1816].

▶   264.   SC DISCIPLINE OF THE SACRAMENTS, Instruction *Immensae caritatis*, on facilitating communion, 29 January 1973:

---

[61]   LG no. 46: AAS 57 (1965) 52; ConstDecrDecl 180.

[62]   PC no. 2 c: AAS 58 (1966) 703; ConstDecrDecl 335.

[63]   See CD no. 35, 3: AAS 58 (1966) 691; ConstDecrDecl 311.

[64]   1 Cor 3:22–23. See GS no. 37: AAS 58 (1966) 1055; Const DecrDecl 731.

[65]   LG no. 31: AAS 57 (1965) 37; ConstDecrDecl 152.

<table>
<tr><td>1, no. V:</td><td>Men and women religious as special ministers of the eucharist [no. 2079].</td></tr>
</table>

▶ 329. SC BISHOPS, *Directory on the Pastoral Ministry of Bishops*, 22 February 1973:

<table>
<tr><td>no. 86 b:</td><td>Religious communities and the parish Mass [no. 2656].</td></tr>
</table>

▶ 279. SC DIVINE WORSHIP, *Holy Communion and Worship of the Eucharist outside Mass*, Chapter 3, Eucharistic Worship, Introductions, 21 June 1973:

<table>
<tr><td>no. 90:</td><td>Eucharistic adoration in religious communities [no. 2216].</td></tr>
</table>

405. PAUL VI, **Address** to Benedictine monks and nuns meeting in Rome, excerpt on liturgy and monastic spirituality, 1 October 1973: AAS 65 (1973) 546–550.

3311   [. . .] We are well aware of the great care with which you have considered the liturgy during your current meeting. We are filled with joy at your dedication and your intense desire to take steps for your own revered tradition to flourish and continue; it forms an essential part of your spiritual life and down through the ages it has always been an asset to the life of the Church. We know that you are experiencing some anxiety about the vital power, the deep significance, and the advantages deriving from the liturgical reform you have carried out. Added to this anxiety is a fear that these very advantages may not be as completely appreciated as they deserve. The fear is increased by the fact that different attitudes have emerged in the vast family of St. Benedict regarding the rite to be followed in the liturgy of the hours. The issue is whether in your different monasteries the rite should be uniform or have a form peculiar to each monastery.

This is a matter of great significance, as it touches both your constant historical and spiritual tradition, your own monastic ties with each other. These ties would no longer be strengthened by a single form of the liturgy, but would be expressed in many, differing voices, so that in celebrating the praises of God you would no longer be *una voce dicentes*. Accordingly, as is your own preference, there must be a thorough review of this issue in all its ramifications, before a decision on appropriate norms that have preceptive force. [. . .]

Not only must you fulfill the responsibility of liturgical prayer, whose importance is so great, but also of private prayer, on which Vatican Council II has given such excellent instruction.[6] St. Benedict in his Rule is regarded as treating of this in the chapter entitled, *De reverentia orationis*: "We must beseech the Lord God of all with all humility and pure devotion."[7]

3312   The exhortations of your father and lawgiver are in no way irrelevant to these times when things develop and change so rapidly. As of old so also now you must form a "school of the Lord's service."[8] This means that your monasteries must be of such a character that those who enter may there learn to serve God and to remain faithful to that service. This includes above all divine worship, the putting into

---

6   See SC art. 12 [DOL 1 no. 12].

7   Ch. 20. See P. Delatte, *Commentaire sur la Règle de Saint Benoît*, Paris, 217.

8   *Rule of St. Benedict*, prologue.

practice of the virtue of religion that we have already touched on and the work of sanctification.

Regarding worship, it is well to stress one particular point: as you attend to the liturgy with the care and devotion it deserves, that sweet voice of the Church singing resounds and never ceases within your walls. Even our contemporaries are sensitive to the indescribable and uplifting power that is present in song and that gives expression in sweet melody to feelings of adoration, praise, repentance, and pleading. As to the work of sanctification, think over this statement of Augustine: "Let not only your voice sound God's praises, but let your deeds match your voices."[9]

Although you are withdrawn from the world, in order to give yourselves up to God, you are still set apart for the Gospel of God.[10] That hidden apostolic fruitfulness spoken of by the Council[11] spreads from your monasteries to the Church and to human society. It should be likened to a leaven that, by God's power, brings about the renewal of the world. [. . .]

406. PAUL VI, **Address** to abbots prior of the Benedictine Confederation, excerpt on choral prayer, 23 September 1977: AAS 69 (1977) 669; Not 13 (1977) 486.

[. . .] We see you here in your great numbers as an image of that choir whose task is to praise God and to pour forth prayers for others to the Lord. In the cenobitic form of life that St. Benedict established and that must have as its goal the perfection of charity, clearly a great importance must be given to the virtue of religion. The *opus Dei* belonging to this virtue is at the same time a kind of instrument for the sanctification of each of you. If therefore you derive your spiritual powers from this source, you do carry out the divine office with joy, and each one of you can repeat these words of St. Augustine: "My psalter, my joy" (*Enarr. in Ps.* 137, 3: PL 37, 1775). After the Church's inauguration of the liturgical reform originating in Vatican Council II, it is for you to contribute your efforts so that, as far as it is in your power, the liturgy will be carried out worthily and the faithful will better understand it and take a more active part in it.

3313

---

9   *Enarr. in Ps.* 166, 2: PL 37, 1899.

10   See Rom 1:1.

11   See PC no. 7 [DOL 10 no. 205].

Section 9. Sacraments of the Sick

SUMMARY (DOL 407–412). The Constitution on the Liturgy art. 73–75 discussed the sacrament that, as it noted, may more properly be called the "anointing of the sick" and decreed revision of the rites for the pastoral care of the sick.

—The texts on the rite include Paul VI's apostolic constitution approving it (DOL 408), the decree of promulgation (DOL 409), the introduction to the rite (DOL 410), and a decree extending the delay in its obligatory use (DOL 411).

—The subsidiary texts are a decree on priests carrying the oil of the sick when traveling (DOL 407) and a homily given by Paul VI when he celebrated a communal anointing of the sick (DOL 412).

▶   1.   VATICAN COUNCIL II, Constitution on the Liturgy *Sacrosanctum Concilium*, 4
          December 1963:

          nos. 73, 75:   Anointing of the sick [nos. 73, 75].
                74:            Sacraments of the sick [no. 74].

▶   23.   SC RITES (Consilium), Instruction (first) *Inter Oecumenici*, 26 September 1964:

          nos. 61 a: Use of the vernacular [no. 353].
                68:           Combined rite of anointing of the sick and viati-
                              cum [no. 360].

407. SC RITES, **Decree** *Pientissima Mater Ecclesia*, granting local Ordinaries
the power to allow priests to carry with them the oil of the sick, 4 March
1965: AAS 57 (1965) 409.

3314   Like a tender mother, the Church provides its sons and daughters who are in
danger of death with means to assist them to triumph in their final struggle.

Today there are more serious and unexpected dangers to life. In order therefore
to assist in the eternal salvation of the faithful in their last agony, many bishops
have submitted the request to the Pope that, CIC can. 946 notwithstanding, he
consent to grant to all priests the permission to carry the oil of the sick with them,
especially when using the various means of transportation to travel.

At an audience granted 4 March 1965, the undersigned Cardinal Prefect of the
Congregation of Rites reported on the matter to Pope Paul VI. In consideration of
the special circumstances set before him, the Pope has graciously granted to local
Ordinaries the power to allow priests to carry with them, as situations may suggest,
the duly blessed oil of the sick; the oil is to be kept safely and reverently.

▶   179. SC RITES (Consilium), Instruction *Eucharisticum mysterium*, on worship of the eu-
          charist, 25 May 1967:

          nos. 32, 6:   Viaticum under both kinds [no. 1261].
                39:           Communion received as viaticum [no. 1268].

▶   208. SC RITES (Consilium); SC DIVINE WORSHIP, General Instruction of the Ro-
          man Missal, 1st ed. 6 April 1969; 4th ed. 27 March 1975:

          no. 242, 6:   Viaticum under both kinds [no. 1632].

▶   326. SC CLERGY, General Directory *Peregrinans in terra*, on the Pastoral Ministry in
          Tourism, 30 April 1969:

          II, 3, B, b: Priests traveling and carrying the oil of the sick
                              [no. 2616].

408. PAUL VI, **Apostolic Constitution** *Sacram Unctionem infirmorum*, on the sacrament of anointing of the sick, 30 November 1972: AAS 65 (1973) 5–9; Not 9 (1973) 52–55.

The Catholic Church professes and teaches that the anointing of the sick is one of the seven sacraments of the New Testament, that it was instituted by Christ our Lord, "intimated in Mark (6:13) and through James, the apostle and the brother of the Lord, recommended to the faithful and made known: 'Is there anyone sick among you? Let him send for the presbyters of the Church and let them pray over him, anointing him with oil in the name of the Lord. The prayer of faith will save the sick man and the Lord will raise him up. If he has committed any sins, they will be forgiven him' (Jas 5:14–15)."[1]

3315

From ancient times there is evidence of the anointing of the sick in the Church's tradition, particularly in the liturgical tradition, both in the East and in the West. Worthy of special note are the letter that Innocent I, our predecessor, addressed to Decentius, Bishop of Gubbio,[2] and also the ancient prayer used for blessing the oil of the sick, "Lord, . . . send the Holy Spirit, our Helper and Friend . . . ." This prayer was inserted in the eucharistic prayer[3] and is still preserved in the Roman Pontifical.[4]

3316

In the course of the centuries of liturgical tradition, the parts of the body to be anointed with holy oil were more explicitly defined in different ways. Several formularies of prayer were added to accompany the anointings and these are contained in the liturgical books of various Churches. In the Church of Rome during the Middle Ages the custom prevailed of anointing the sick on the senses with the formulary: *Per istam sanctam Unctionem, et suam piissimam misericordiam, indulgeat tibi Dominus quidquid deliquisti,* with the name of each sense added.[5]

In addition, the teaching concerning the sacrament of anointing is expounded in the documents of the ecumenical Councils of Florence, Trent especially, and Vatican II.

After the Council of Florence had described the essential elements of the sacrament of the anointing of the sick,[6] the Council of Trent declared that it was of divine institution and explained what is taught in the Letter of James concerning holy anointing, especially about the reality signified and the effects of the sacrament: "This reality is in fact the grace of the Holy Spirit, whose anointing takes away sins, if any still remain, and the remnants of sin; this anointing also raises up and strengthens the soul of the sick person, arousing a great confidence in the divine mercy; thus sustained, the sick person may more easily bear the trials and hardships of sickness, more easily resist the temptations of the devil 'lying in wait

---

[1] Council of Trent, sess. 14, *De extrema unctione* cap. 1 (see also can. 1): CT 7, 1, 355–356; Denz-Schön 1695, 1715.

[2] Innocent I, Ep. *Si Instituta Ecclesiastica* cap. 8: PL 20, 559–561; Denz-Schön 216.

[3] Mohlberg LibSacr 61. *Le Sacramentaire Grégorien,* J. Deshusses, ed. (Spicilegium Friburgense 16; Fribourg, 1971) 172. See also *La Tradition Apostolique de Saint Hippolyte,* B. Botte, ed. (Liturgiewissenschaftliche Quellen und Forschungen 39; Münster in W., 1963) 18–19. *Le Grand Euchologie du Monastère Blanc,* E. Lanne, ed., (*Patrologia Orientalis* 28, 2; Paris, 1958) 392–395.

[4] See PR, *Ordo benedicendi Oleum Catechumenorum et Infirmorum et conficiendi chrisma* (Vatican City, 1971) 11–12 [See RM, Appendix II, *Rite of Blessing of Oils* no. 20].

[5] See M. Andrieu, *Le Pontifical Romain au Moyen-Age*: v. 1, *Le Pontifical Romain du XIIe siècle: Studi e Testi* 86 (Vatican City, 1938) 267–268; v. 2, *Le Pontifical Romain de la Curie Romaine au XIIIe siècle: Studi e Testi* 87 (Vatican City, 1940) 491–492.

[6] *Decr. pro Armeniis*: G. Hofmann, *Conc. Florent.* I-II, 130; Denz-Schön 1324ff.

for his heel' (Gn 3:15), and sometimes regain bodily health, if this is expedient for the health of the soul."[7] The same Council also declared that these words of the apostle state with sufficient clarity that "this anointing is to be given to the sick, especially those who are in such a serious condition as to appear to have reached the end of their life. For this reason it is also called the sacrament of the dying."[8] Finally, the Council declared that the presbyter is the proper minister of the sacrament.[9]

Vatican Council II adds the following: "'Extreme unction,' which may also and more properly be called 'anointing of the sick,' is not a sacrament for those only who are at the point of death. Hence, as soon as any one of the faithful begins to be in danger of death from sickness or old age, the fitting time for that person to receive this sacrament has certainly already arrived."[10] The use of this sacrament is a concern of the whole Church: "By the sacred anointing of the sick and the prayer of its presbyters, the whole Church commends the sick to the suffering and glorified Lord so that he may raise them up and save them (see Jas 5:14–16). The Church exhorts them, moreover, to contribute to the welfare of the whole people of God by associating themselves willingly with the passion and death of Christ (see Rom 8:17; Col 1:24; 2 Tm 2:11–12; 1 Pt 4:13)."[11]

3317 All these considerations had to be weighed in revising the rite of anointing in order better to adapt to present-day conditions those elements that were subject to change.[12]

We have thought fit to modify the sacramental form in such a way that, by reflecting the words of James, it may better express the effects of the sacrament.

Since olive oil, which has been prescribed until now for the valid celebration of the sacrament, is unobtainable or difficult to obtain in some parts of the world, we have decreed, at the request of a number of bishops, that from now on, according to circumstances, another kind of oil can also be used, provided it is derived from plants and is thus similar to olive oil.

As regards the number of anointings and the parts of the body to be anointed, it has seemed opportune to simplify the rite.

3318 Therefore, since this revision in certain points touches upon the sacramental rite itself, by our apostolic authority we establish that the following is to be observed for the future in the Latin rite:

THE SACRAMENT OF THE ANOINTING OF THE SICK IS GIVEN TO THOSE WHO ARE SERIOUSLY ILL BY ANOINTING THEM ON THE FOREHEAD AND HANDS WITH BLESSED OLIVE OIL OR, ACCORDING TO CIRCUMSTANCES, WITH ANOTHER BLESSED PLANT OIL AND SAYING ONCE ONLY THESE WORDS: "THROUGH THIS HOLY ANOINTING MAY THE LORD IN HIS LOVE AND MERCY HELP YOU WITH THE GRACE OF THE HOLY SPIRIT. MAY THE LORD WHO FREES YOU FROM SIN SAVE YOU AND RAISE YOU UP."[a]

---

[7] Council of Trent, sess. 14, *De extrema unctione* cap. 2: CT 7, 1, 356; Denz-Schön 1696.

[8] Ibid., cap. 3: CT ibid.; Denz-Schön 1698.

[9] Ibid.: CT ibid.; Denz-Schön 1697, 1719.

[10] SC art. 73 [DOL 1 no. 73].

[11] LG no. 11 [DOL 4 no. 141].

[12] See SC art. 1 [DOL 1 no. 1].

[a] Latin: Per istam sanctam unctionem et suam piissimam misericordiam adiuvet te Dominus gratia Spiritus Sancti, ut a peccatis liberatum te salvet atque propitius allevet.

In case of necessity, however, it is sufficient that a single anointing be given on the forehead or, because of the particular condition of the sick person, on another suitable part of the body while the whole sacramental form is said.

The sacrament may be repeated if the sick person recovers after being anointed and then again falls ill or if during the same illness the person's condition becomes more serious.

Having made these decisions and declarations about the essential rite of the sacrament of the anointing of the sick, by our apostolic authority we also approve the *Ordo Unctionis infirmorum eorumque pastoralis curae*, which has been revised by the Congregation for Divine Worship. At the same time, where necessary we amend the prescriptions of the Code of Canon Law or other laws hitherto in force or we repeal them; other prescriptions and laws, which are neither repealed nor amended by the above-mentioned rite, remain valid and in force. The Latin edition containing the new rite will come into force as soon as it is published; the vernacular editions, prepared by the conferences of bishops and confirmed by the Apostolic See, will come into force on the dates to be laid down by the individual conferences. The old rite may be used until 31 December 1973. From 1 January 1974, however, only the new rite is to be used by those concerned.

We intend that everything we have laid down and prescribed should be firm and effective in the Latin rite, notwithstanding, where relevant, the apostolic constitutions and ordinances issued by our predecessors and other prescriptions, even if worthy of special mention.

409. SC DIVINE WORSHIP, **Decree** *Infirmis cum Ecclesia*, promulgating the *editio typica* of the rites for the pastoral care of the sick, anointing and viaticum, 7 December 1972: AAS 65 (1973) 275–276; Not 9 (1973) 51.

When the Church cares for the sick, it serves Christ himself in the suffering members of his Mystical Body. When it follows the example of the Lord Jesus, who "went about doing good and healing all" (Acts 10:38), the Church obeys his command to care for the sick (see Mk 16:18).

The Church shows this solicitude not only by visiting those who are in poor health but also by raising them up through the sacrament of anointing and by nourishing them with the eucharist during their illness and when they are in danger of death. Finally, the Church offers prayers for the sick to commend them to God, especially in the last crisis of life.

To make the meaning of the sacrament of anointing clearer and more evident, Vatican Council II decreed: "The number of the anointings is to be adapted to the circumstances; the prayers that belong to the rite of anointing are to be so revised that they correspond to the varying conditions of the sick who receive the sacrament."[1] The Council also directed that a continuous rite be prepared according to which the sick person is anointed after the sacrament of penance and before receiving viaticum.[2]

3319

3320

---

[1] SC art. 75 [DOL 1 no. 75].

[2] See SC art. 74 [DOL 1 no. 74].

In the Apostolic Constitution *Sacram Unctionem infirmorum* of 30 November 1972, Pope Paul VI established a new sacramental form of anointing and approved the *Ordo Unctionis infirmorum eorumque pastoralis curae*.ᵃ The Congregation for Divine Worship prepared this rite and now issues it, declaring this to be the *editio typica* so that it may replace the pertinent sections that are now in the Roman Ritual.

410. SC DIVINE WORSHIP, *Pastoral Care of the Sick: Rites of Anointing and Viaticum*, **Introduction**, 7 December 1972: Vatican Polyglot Press, 1972.

GENERAL INTRODUCTION

I. HUMAN SICKNESS AND ITS MEANING IN THE MYSTERY OF SALVATION†

3321 1. Suffering and illness have always been among the greatest problems that trouble the human spirit. Christians feel and experience pain as do all other people; yet their faith helps them to grasp more deeply the mystery of suffering and to bear their pain with greater courage. From Christ's words they know that sickness has meaning and value for their own salvation and for the salvation of the world. They also know that Christ, who during his life often visited and healed the sick, loves them in their illness.

3322 2. Although closely linked with the human condition, sickness cannot as a general rule be regarded as a punishment inflicted on each individual for personal sins (see Jn 9:3). Christ himself, who is without sin, in fulfilling the words of Isaiah took on all the wounds of his passion and shared in all human pain (see Is 53:4–5). Moreover, when we undergo afflictions, Christ is still pained and tormented in his members, made like him. Still, our afflictions seem but momentary and slight when compared to the greatness of the eternal glory for which they prepare us (see 2 Cor 4:17).

3323 3. Part of the plan laid out by God's providence is that we should fight strenuously against all sickness and carefully seek the blessings of good health, so that we may fulfill our role in human society and in the Church. Yet we should always be prepared to fill up what is lacking in Christ's sufferings for the salvation of the world as we look forward to creation's being set free in the glory of the children of God (see Col 1:24; Rom 8:19–21).

Moreover, the role of the sick in the Church is to be a reminder to others of the essential or higher things. By their witness the sick show that our mortal life must be redeemed through the mystery of Christ's death and resurrection.

3324 4. The sick person is not the only one who should fight against illness. Doctors and all who are devoted in any way to caring for the sick should consider it their duty to use all the means which in their judgment may help the sick, both physically and spiritually. In so doing, they are fulfilling the command of Christ to visit the sick, for Christ implied that those who visit the sick should be concerned for the whole person and offer both physical relief and spiritual comfort.

ᵃ See DOL 408 nos. 3318–19.

† Scriptural texts of the New Testament are from the edition of the Pontifical Commission for the Neo-Vulgate.

II. CELEBRATION OF THE SACRAMENTS FOR THE SICK AND THE DYING

A. ANOINTING OF THE SICK

5.   The Lord himself showed great concern for the bodily and spiritual welfare of   3325
the sick and commanded his followers to do likewise. This is clear from the Gospels, and above all from the existence of the sacrament of anointing, which he
instituted and which is made known in the Letter of James. Since then the Church
has never ceased to celebrate this sacrament for its members by the anointing and
the prayer of its priests, commending those who are ill to the suffering and glorified
Lord, that he may raise them up and save them (see Jas 5:14–16). Moreover, the
Church exhorts them to associate themselves willingly with the passion and death
of Christ (see Rom 8:17),[1] and thus contribute to the welfare of the people of God.[2]

Those who are seriously ill need the special help of God's grace in this time of
anxiety, lest they be broken in spirit and, under the pressure of temptation, perhaps
weakened in their faith.

This is why, through the sacrament of anointing, Christ strengthens the faithful who are afflicted by illness, providing them with the strongest means of support.[3]

The celebration of this sacrament consists especially in the laying on of hands
by the priests of the Church, the offering of the prayer of faith, and the anointing of
the sick with oil made holy by God's blessing. This rite signifies the grace of the
sacrament and confers it.

6.   This sacrament gives the grace of the Holy Spirit to those who are sick: by this   3326
grace the whole person is helped and saved, sustained by trust in God, and
strengthened against the temptations of the Evil One and against anxiety over
death. Thus the sick person is able not only to bear suffering bravely, but also to
fight against it. A return to physical health may follow the reception of this sacrament if it will be beneficial to the sick person's salvation. If necessary, the sacrament
also provides the sick person with the forgiveness of sins and the completion of
Christian penance. [4]

7.   In the anointing of the sick, which includes the the prayer of faith (see Jas   3327
5:15), faith itself is manifested. Above all this faith must be made actual both in the
minister of the sacrament and, even more importantly, in the recipient. The sick
person will be saved by personal faith and the faith of the Church, which looks
back to the death and resurrection of Christ, the source of the sacrament's power
(see Jas 5:15),[5] and looks ahead to the future kingdom that is pledged in the
sacraments.

RECIPIENTS OF THE ANOINTING OF THE SICK

8.   The Letter of James states that the sick are to be anointed in order to raise them   3328
up and save them.[6] Great care and concern should be taken to see that those of the

---

   [1]   See also Col 1:24; 2 Tm 2:11–12; 1 Pt 4:13.

   [2]   See Council of Trent, sess. 14, *De extrema unctione* cap. 1: Denz-Schön 1695. LG no. 11 [DOL 4 no.
141].

   [3]   See Council of Trent, sess. 14, *De extrema unctione*, prooem.: Denz-Schön 1694 [The *editio typica*
erroneously refers to cap. 1.]

   [4]   See ibid. and cap. 2: Denz-Schön 1694 and 1696.

   [5]   See Thomas Aquinas, *In IV Sententiarum* d. 1, q. 1, a. 4, quaestiuncula 3.

   [6]   See Council of Trent, sess. 14, *De extrema unctione* cap. 2: Denz-Schön 1696.

faithful whose health is seriously impaired by sickness or old age receive this sacrament.[7]

A prudent or reasonably sure judgment, without scruple, is sufficient for deciding on the seriousness of an illness;[8] if necessary a doctor may be consulted.

3329   9.   The sacrament may be repeated if the sick person recovers after being anointed[a] or if during the same illness the person's condition becomes more serious.

3330   10.   A sick person may be anointed before surgery whenever a serious illness is the reason for the surgery.

3331   11.   Elderly people may be anointed if they have become notably weakened even though no serious illness is present.

3332   12.   Sick children may be anointed if they have sufficient use of reason to be strengthened by this sacrament.

3333   13.   In public and private catechesis, the faithful should be educated to ask for the sacrament of anointing and, as soon as the right time comes, to receive it with full faith and devotion. They should not follow the wrongful practice of delaying the reception of the sacrament. All who care for the sick should be taught the meaning and purpose of the sacrament.

3334   14.   The sacrament of anointing may be conferred upon sick people who, although they have lost consciousness or the use of reason, would, as Christian believers, probably have asked for it were they in control of their faculties.[9]

3335   15.   When a priest has been called to attend those who are already dead, he should not administer the sacrament of anointing. Instead, he should pray for them, asking that God forgive their sins and graciously receive them into the kingdom. But if the priest is doubtful whether the sick person is dead, he may give the sacrament conditionally (no. 269).[10]

MINISTER OF THE ANOINTING OF THE SICK

3336   16.   The priest is the only proper minister of the anointing of the sick.[11]

This office is ordinarily exercised by bishops, parish priests (pastors) and their assistants, priests who are responsible for the sick or aged in hospitals, and superiors of clerical religious institutes.[12]

3337   17.   These ministers have the pastoral responsibility both of preparing and helping the sick and others who are present, with the assistance of religious and laity, and of celebrating the sacrament.

---

[7]   See SC art. 73 [DOL 1 no. 73].

[8]   See Pius XI, Epistle *Explorata res*, 2 February 1923: AAS 15 (1923) 103–107.

[a]   See DOL 408 no. 3318: "The sacrament may be repeated if the sick person recovers after being anointed *and again falls ill . . .*", italicized words omitted here in no. 9.

[9]   See CIC can. 943.

[10]   See CIC can. 941.

[11]   See Council of Trent, sess. 14, *De extrema unctione* cap. 3 and can. 4: Denz-Schön 1697 and 1719. CIC can. 938.

[12]   See CIC can. 938.

The local Ordinary has the responsibility of supervising celebrations at which sick persons from various parishes or hospitals may come together to receive the sacrament.

18. Other priests also confer the sacrament of anointing with the consent of the ministers mentioned in no. 16. Presuming such consent in a case of necessity, a priest need only inform the parish priest (pastor) or hospital chaplain later.   3338

19. When two or more priests are present for the anointing of a sick person, one of them may say the prayers and carry out the anointings, saying the sacramental form. The others may take the remaining parts, such as the introductory rites, readings, invocations, or instructions. Each priest may lay hands on the sick person.   3339

REQUIREMENTS FOR CELEBRATING THE ANOINTING OF THE SICK

20. The matter proper for the sacrament is olive oil or, according to circumstances, other oil derived from plants.[13]   3340

21. The oil used for anointing the sick must be blessed for this purpose by the bishop or by a priest who has this faculty, either from the law or by special concession of the Apostolic See.   3341

The law itself permits the following, besides a bishop, to bless the oil of the sick:

    a. those whom the law equates with diocesan bishops;

    b. in case of true necessity, any priest.[14]

The oil of the sick is ordinarily blessed by the bishop on Holy Thursday.[15]

22. If a priest, in accord with no. 21 b, is to bless the oil during the rite, he may bring the unblessed oil with him, or the family of the sick person may prepare the oil in a suitable vessel. If any of the oil is left after the celebration of the sacrament, it should be absorbed in cotton or cotton wool and burned.   3342

If the priest uses oil that has already been blessed (either by the bishop or by a priest), he brings it with him in the vessel in which it is kept. This vessel, made of suitable material, should be clean and should contain sufficient oil (soaked in cotton or cotton wool for convenience). In this case, after celebrating the sacrament the priest returns the vessel to the place where it is kept with proper respect. He should make sure that the oil remains fit for use and should replenish it from time to time, either yearly when the bishop blesses the oil on Holy Thursday or more frequently if necessary.

23. The sick person is anointed on the forehead and on the hands. It is appropriate to divide the sacramental form so that the first part is said while the forehead is anointed, the latter part while the hands are anointed.   3343

In case of necessity, however, it is sufficient that a single anointing be given on the forehead or, because of the particular condition of the sick person, on another suitable part of the body, while the whole sacramental form is said.

---

[13]   See *Rite of Blessing the Oil of Catechumens and of the Sick and of Consecrating Chrism*, Introduction no. 3 [DOL 459 no. 3863].

[14]   See ibid. no. 8 [DOL 459 no. 3868].

[15]   See ibid. no. 9 [DOL 459 no. 3869].

3344   24. Depending on the culture and traditions of different peoples, the number of anointings may be increased and the places to be anointed may be changed. Directives on this should be included in the preparation of particular rituals.

3345   25. The following is the sacramental form with which the anointing of the sick is given in the Latin rite: THROUGH THIS HOLY ANOINTING MAY THE LORD IN HIS LOVE AND MERCY HELP YOU WITH THE GRACE OF THE HOLY SPIRIT. MAY THE LORD WHO FREES YOU FROM SIN SAVE YOU AND RAISE YOU UP.

B. Viaticum for the Dying

3346   26. When in their passage from this life Christians are strengthened by the body and blood of Christ in viaticum, they have the pledge of the resurrection that the Lord promised: "Those who eat my flesh and drink my blood have eternal life, and I will raise them up on the last day" (Jn 6:54).

When possible, viaticum should be received within Mass so that the sick person may receive communion under both kinds. Communion received as viaticum should be considered a special sign of participation in the mystery that is celebrated in the eucharist: the mystery of the death of the Lord and his passage to the Father.[16]

3347   27. All baptized Christians who are able to receive communion are bound to receive viaticum by reason of the precept to receive communion when in danger of death from any cause. Priests with pastoral responsibility must see that the celebration of this sacrament is not delayed, but that the faithful are nourished by it while still in full possession of their faculties.[17]

3348   28. It is also desirable that during the celebration of viaticum Christians renew the faith professed at their baptism, by which they became adopted children of God and coheirs of the promise of eternal life.

3349   29. The ordinary ministers of viaticum are the parish priest (pastor) and his assistants, the priest who is responsible for the sick in hospitals, and the superior of a clerical religious institute. In case of necessity, any other priest with at least the presumed permission of the competent minister may give viaticum.

If no priest is available, viaticum may be brought to the sick by a deacon or by another member of the faithful, either a man or woman, who by the authority of the Apostolic See has been duly appointed by the bishop to give the eucharist to the faithful. In this case, a deacon follows the rite prescribed in the ritual; other ministers use the rite they ordinarily follow for distributing communion, but with the special words given in the ritual for the rite for viaticum.

C. Continuous Rite

3350   30. For special cases, when sudden illness or some other cause has unexpectedly placed one of the faithful in proximate danger of death, a continuous rite is provided by which the sick person may be given the sacraments of penance, anointing, and the eucharist as viaticum in a single celebration.

If death is imminent and there is not enough time to celebrate the three sacraments in the manner already described, the sick person should be given an

---

[16]   See SCR, Instr. EuchMyst, 25 May 1967, nos. 36, 39, 41 [DOL 179 nos. 1265, 1268, 1270]. Paul VI, Motu Proprio *Pastorale munus*, 30 Nov. 1963, no. 7: AAS 56 (1964) 7. CIC can. 822, 4.

[17]   See SCR, Instr. EuchMyst no. 39 [DOL 179 no. 1268].

opportunity to make a sacramental confession, even if it has to be a generic confession. After this the person should be given viaticum, since all the faithful are bound to receive this sacrament if they are in danger of death. Then, if there is sufficient time, the sick person should be anointed.

The sick person who, because of the nature of the illness, cannot receive communion should be anointed.

31. If the sick person is to be strengthened by the sacrament of confirmation, nos. 234, 237, 245, and 286 of this ritual should be consulted.

In danger of death, provided the bishop is not easily available or is lawfully impeded, the law gives the faculty to confirm to the following: parish priests (pastors) and parochial vicars; in their absence, associate pastors (curates), priests who are in charge of special parishes lawfully established, administrators, substitute priests, and assistant priests (coadjutors); in the absence of all of the preceding, any priest who is not under censure or canonical penalty.[18]

III. OFFICES AND MINISTRIES FOR THE SICK

32. If one member suffers in the Body of Christ, which is the Church, all the members suffer with that member (1 Cor 12:26).[19] For this reason, kindness shown toward the sick and works of charity and mutual help for the relief of every kind of human want are held in special honor.[20] Every scientific effort to prolong life[21] and every act of care for the sick, on the part of any person, may be considered a preparation for the Gospel and a sharing in Christ's healing ministry.[22]

33. It is thus especially fitting that all baptized Christians share in this ministry of mutual charity within the Body of Christ by doing all that they can to help the sick return to health, by showing love for the sick, and by celebrating the sacraments with them. Like the other sacraments, these too have a community aspect, which should be brought out as much as possible when they are celebrated.

34. The family and friends of the sick and those who take care of them in any way have a special share in this ministry of comfort. In particular, it is their task to strengthen the sick with words of faith and by praying with them, to commend them to the suffering and glorified Lord, and to encourage them to contribute to the well-being of the people of God by associating themselves willingly with Christ's passion and death.[23] If the sickness grows worse, the family and friends of the sick and those who take care of them have the responsibility of informing the parish priest (pastor) and by their kind words of prudently disposing the sick for the reception of the sacraments at the proper time.

35. Priests, particularly parish priests (pastors) and the others mentioned in no. 16, should remember that it is their duty to care for the sick by personal visits and other acts of kindness.[24] Especially when they give the sacraments, priests should stir up the hope of those present and strengthen their faith in Christ who suffered

3351

3352

3353

3354

3355

---

18   See *Rite of Confirmation*, Introduction no. 7 c [DOL 305 no. 2516].

19   See LG no. 7 [DOL 4 no. 139].

20   See AA no. 8: AAS 58 (1966) 845; ConstDecrDecl 474.

21   See GS no. 18 [DOL 19 no. 269].

22   See LG no. 28 [DOL 4 no. 148].

23   See LG no. 21 [DOL 4 no. 145].

24   See CIC can. 468, 1.

and is glorified. By bringing the Church's love and the consolation of faith, they comfort believers and raise the minds of others to God.

3356   36. It is important that all the faithful, and above all the sick, be aided by suitable catechesis in preparing for and participating in the sacraments of anointing and viaticum, especially if the celebration is to be carried out communally. In this way they will understand more fully what has been said about the anointing of the sick and about viaticum, and the celebration of these sacraments will nourish, strengthen, and manifest faith more effectively. For the prayer of faith that accompanies the celebration of the sacrament is nourished by the profession of this faith.

3357   37. When the priest prepares for the celebration of the sacraments, he should ask about the condition of the sick person. He should take this information into account, for example, in planning the rite, in choosing readings and prayers, and in deciding whether he will celebrate Mass when viaticum is to be given. As far as possible, he should arrange all this with the sick person and the family beforehand, when he explains the meaning of the sacraments.

IV. ADAPTATIONS BELONGING TO THE CONFERENCES OF BISHOPS

3358   38. In virtue of the Constitution on the Liturgy (art. 63 b),[b] the conferences of bishops have the right to prepare a section in particular rituals corresponding to the present section of the Roman Ritual and adapted to the needs of the different parts of the world. This section is for use in the regions concerned once the *acta* have been reviewed by the Apostolic See.

The following are the responsibilities of the conferences of bishops in this regard.

a. to decide on the adaptations dealt with in the Constitution on the Liturgy art. 39;[c]

b. to weigh carefully and prudently what elements from the traditions and culture of individual peoples may be appropriately admitted into divine worship, then to propose to the Apostolic See adaptations considered useful or necessary that will be introduced with its consent;[d]

c. to retain elements in the rites of the sick that may now exist in particular rituals, as long as they are compatible with the Constitution on the Liturgy and with contemporary needs; or to adapt any of these elements;

d. to prepare translations of the texts so that they are truly adapted to the genius of different languages and cultures and to add, whenever appropriate, suitable melodies for singing;

e. to adapt and enlarge, if necessary, this Introduction in the Roman Ritual in order to encourage the conscious and active participation of the faithful;

f. to arrange the material in the editions of liturgical books prepared under the direction of the conferences of bishops in a format that will be as suitable as possible for pastoral use.

3359   39. Whenever the Roman Ritual gives several alternative texts, particular rituals may add other texts of the same kind.

---

b   See DOL 1 no. 63.

c   See DOL 1 no. 39.

d   See DOL 1 no. 40.

V. ADAPTATIONS BY THE MINISTER

40. The minister should take into account the particular circumstances, needs, and   3360
desires of the sick and of other members of the faithful and should willingly use the
various possibilities that the rites provide.

    a. The minister should be especially aware that the sick tire easily and that
their physical condition may change from day to day and even from hour to hour.
For this reason the celebration may be shortened if necessary.

    b. When there is no group of the faithful present, the priest should remember
that the Church is already present in his own person and in the one who is ill. For
this reason he should try to offer the sick person the love and help of the Christian
community both before and after the celebration of the sacrament. He may ask
another Christian from the local community to do this if the sick person will accept
this help.

    c. Sick persons who regain their health after being anointed should be en-
couraged to give thanks for the favor received by participating in a Mass of thanksgiving or by some other suitable means.

41. The priest should follow the structure of the rite in the celebration, while   3361
adapting it to the place and the people involved. The penitential rite may be part of
the introductory rite or take place after the reading from Scripture. In place of the
thanksgiving over the oil, the priest may give an instruction. This alternative
should be considered when the sick person is in a hospital and other sick people
present do not take part in the celebration of the sacrament.

▶   264.   SC DISCIPLINE OF THE SACRAMENTS, Instruction *Immensae caritatis*, on facilitating communion, 29 January 1973:

1, Introduction:	Viaticum and special ministers of communion [no. 2074].
2, no. 7:	Communion a second time on the same day as viaticum [no. 2084].
3:	Mitigation of eucharistic fast for the sick [no. 2086].

▶   329.   SC BISHOPS, *Directory on the Pastoral Ministry of Bishops*, 22 February 1973:

no. 89:	Bishops receiving the sacraments of the sick [no. 2659].

▶   266.   SC DIVINE WORSHIP, *Holy Communion and the Worship of the Eucharist outside Mass*,
Chapter 1, Holy Communion, Introduction, 21 June 1973:

no. 16:	Communion of the sick during the Easter triduum [no. 2094].

411. SC DIVINE WORSHIP, **Decree** *Constitutio Apostolica*, extending the *vacatio legis* for the *Pastoral Care of the Sick: Rites of Anointing and Viaticum*, 10 January
1974: AAS 66 (1974) 100; Not 10 (1974) 36.

    The Apostolic Constitution *Sacram Unctionem infirmorum* of Pope Paul VI, 30   3362
November 1972, established that the use of *Pastoral Care of the Sick: Rites of Anointing*

and Viaticum revised by this Congregation was to be obligatory for all beginning with 1 January 1974.[a]

Several conferences of bishops have requested however that the *vacatio legis* for the new rite be extended in order that they may prepare the vernacular versions without pressure. Therefore this Congregation for Divine Worship, at the mandate of Pope Paul VI, decrees the following.

3363   1.   Use of the new *Ordo Unctionis infirmorum eorumque pastoralis curae* is already permitted for celebrations in Latin.

3364   2.   The conferences of bishops are to ensure that the translation of the new rite is finished as quickly as possible and to fix a date, after their own approval and the Apostolic See's confirmation of the translation, on which its use becomes obligatory. From the effective date of the vernacular edition, only the new rite for the anointing of the sick shall be used whether in Latin or in the vernacular.

All things to the contrary notwithstanding.

412. PAUL VI, **Homily** at a communal anointing of the sick during Mass in St. Peter's Square, 5 October 1975: Not 11 (1975) 257–258 (Italian).

3365   The sacrament of anointing of the sick, which we are administering to some of you today, was instituted and handed down to us as an efficacious sign of Christ's redemptive love that intends to heal chiefly the soul yet without leaving out the body. By its conferral the Church does not of course claim to replace medical care and the rite is altogether removed from those pseudoreligious ideas and practices that belong to the realm of superstition. As you know the Church's activity is on a higher, supernatural level, that of the sacraments. These are efficacious signs of the intervention of Christ, the Savior and divine Physician, in our life and in our physical and spiritual needs. At the same time, however, the sacrament of anointing includes a meaning that is deeply human and that can be summed up in these words of St. Paul: "Contribute to the needs of the saints . . . weep with those who weep . . . seek to do good" (Rom 12:13ff.). And today we cannot but make our own his other words: "Who is weak and I am not weak?" (2 Cor 11:29). Nor can we forget the explicit evidence on this sacrament that James the Apostle has given us: "Is there anyone sick among you? Let him send for the presbyters of the Church and let them pray over him, anointing him with oil in the name of the Lord. The prayer of faith will save the sick man and the Lord will raise him up. If he has committed any sins, they will be forgiven" (Jas 5:14–15).

Here as in the other sacraments the Church's main concern is, of course, the soul, pardon for sin, and the increase of God's grace. But also, to the extent that it is up to the Church, its desire and intent is to obtain relief and, if possible, even healing for the sick. Taking as our grounds the Lord's own words, passed on by the apostles, and prompted by their sentiments of charity, we have recently endorsed the reform of the rite of anointing. The revision's intent was to make the overall purposes of the rite clearer and to lead to a wider availability of the sacrament and to extend it — within reasonable limits — even beyond cases of mortal illness.

As the humble representative of Christ, we are therefore here today in order to administer a sacrament. We once more commend this sacrament to our brothers and

---

a   DOL 408 no. 3319.

our sons, the bishops and priests; they bear the trust of ministering to this chosen portion of the Church, namely, the sick.

Section 10. Funerals

SUMMARY (DOL 413–418). The Constitution on the Liturgy art. 81 decreed a revision of the rite of funerals that would reflect the paschal character of the Christian's death and allow for adaptation to the various cultures and regions; art. 82 directed a revision of the rite for children's funerals.

—The major texts here, then, are the decree promulgating the new rite (DOL 415) and the introduction to the rite (DOL 416).

—Besides the several important cross-references, there are also 4 other specific texts bearing on the liturgy for the dead: a 1963 instruction of the Holy Office on cremation (DOL 413), a particular decree from the Congregation of Rites on celebrating a funeral Mass on Saturday evening (DOL 414), a letter and a decree of the Congregation for the Doctrine of the Faith on the canonical issue of the Christian burial of Catholics involved in irregular marriages at the time of their death (DOL 417, 418).

413. SC HOLY OFFICE, **Instruction** *Piam et constantem*, on cremation, 8 May 1963: AAS 56 (1964) 822–823.

3366   The reverent, unbroken practice of burying the bodies of the faithful departed is something the Church has always taken pains to encourage. It has surrounded the practice with rites suited to bringing out more clearly the symbolic and religious significance of burial and has threatened with penalties those who might attack this sound practice. The Church has especially employed such sanctions in the face of hate-inspired assaults against Christian practices and traditions by those who, imbued with the animosity of their secret societies, sought to replace burial by cremation. This practice was meant to be a symbol of their antagonistic denial of Christian dogma, above all of the resurrection of the dead and the immortality of the soul.

   Such an intent clearly was subjective, belonging to the mind of the proponents of cremation, not something objective, inherent in the meaning of cremation itself. Cremation does not affect the soul nor prevent God's omnipotence from restoring the body; neither, then, does it in itself include an objective denial of the dogmas mentioned.

   The issue is not therefore an intrinsically evil act, opposed *per se* to the Christian religion. This has always been the thinking of the Church: in certain situations where it was or is clear that there is an upright motive for cremation, based on serious reasons, especially of public order, the Church did not and does not object to it.

   There has been a change for the better in attitudes and in recent years more frequent and clearer situations impeding the practice of burial have developed. Consequently, the Holy See is receiving repeated requests for a relaxation of church discipline relative to cremation. The procedure is clearly being advocated today, not out of hatred of the Church or Christian customs, but rather for reasons of health, economics, or other reasons involving private or public order.

   It is the decision of the Church to accede to the requests received, out of concern primarily for the spiritual well-being of the faithful, but also out of its awareness of other pressures. The Church therefore establishes the following.

3367 1. All necessary measures must be taken to preserve the practice of reverently burying the faithful departed. Accordingly, through proper instruction and persuasion Ordinaries are to ensure that the faithful refrain from cremation and not discontinue the practice of burial except when forced to do so by necessity. For the Church has always maintained the practice of burial and consecrated it through liturgical rites.

3368 2. It has seemed the wiser course, however, to relax somewhat the prescriptions of canon law touching on cremation, for two reasons. One is so that difficulties arising from contemporary circumstances may not be unduly increased; the other, so that the need for dispensation from the pertinent laws may not arise too often. Accordingly, the stipulations of CIC can. 1203, par. 2 (on carrying out a person's will to be cremated) and of can. 1240, par. 1, no. 5 (on the denial of ecclesiastical burial to a person who has left such a directive) no longer have universal binding force, but only in those cases in which it is clear that the reason for choosing cremation was either a denial of Christian dogmas, the animosity of a secret society, or hatred of the Catholic religion and the Church.

3.   From this it follows that the sacraments or public prayers are not to be refused   3369
to those who have chosen cremation unless there is evidence that their choice was
made on the basis of the anti-Christian motives just listed.

4.   The devout attitude of the faithful toward the ecclesiastical tradition must be   3370
kept from being harmed and the Church's adverse attitude toward cremation must
be clearly evident. Therefore the rites of ecclesiastical burial and the ensuing
suffrages may never be carried out at the place of cremation itself, not even simply
to accompany the body as it is being brought there.

The cardinals in charge of safeguarding matters of faith and morals reviewed this Instruction in
a plenary meeting on 8 May 1963. Pope Paul VI at an audience granted to the Cardinal Secretary of
the Holy Office on 5 July 1963 has agreed to approve it.

▶   1.   VATICAN COUNCIL II, Constitution on the Liturgy *Sacrosanctum Concilium*, 4
          December 1963:

          art. 81:   Revision of rite of funerals [no. 81].
                82:         Funeral of children [no. 82].

▶   23.   SC RITES (Consilium), Instruction (first) *Inter Oecumenici*, 26 September 1964:

          no. 61 d: Use of the vernacular at funerals [no. 353].

414. SC RITES, **Decree** (Avila, Spain), on a funeral Mass in the evening of a
vigil, 15 October 1965: Not 2 (1966) 181.

          His Excellency Sancho Moro, Bishop of Avila, Spain has presented the follow-   3371
ing query to the Congregation of Rites:
          When funeral rites are held in the evening on the vigil of any liturgical day on
which the funeral Mass is forbidden, may the funeral Mass, without singing, be
celebrated?
          After receiving the opinion of the liturgical commission and thoroughly con-
sidering the matter, the Congregation replied: Yes.

▶   208. SC RITES (Consilium); SC DIVINE WORSHIP, General Instruction of the Ro-
          man Missal, 1st ed. 6 April 1969; 4th ed. 27 March 1975:

          nos. 335–341:   Masses for the dead [nos. 1725–31].

415. SC DIVINE WORSHIP, **Decree** *Ritibus exsequiarum*, promulgating the
editio typica of the rite of funerals, 15 August 1969: Not 5 (1969) 423–424.

          By means of the funeral rites it has been the practice of the Church, as a tender   3372
mother, not simply to commend the dead to God but also to raise high the hope of
its children and to give witness to its own faith in the future resurrection of the
baptized with Christ.
          Vatican Council II accordingly directed that the funeral rites be revised in such
a way that they would more clearly express the paschal character of the Christian's

death and also that the rites for the burial of children would have a proper Mass (SC art. 81–82).[a]

The Consilium prepared the desired rites and put them into trial use in different parts of the world. Now Pope Paul VI by his apostolic authority has approved and ordered the publication of these rites as henceforth obligatory for all those using the Roman Ritual.

Also by order of Pope Paul this Congregation for Divine Worship promulgates the *Rite of Funerals*, stipulating that its effective date is 1 June 1970.

The Congregation further establishes that until 1 June 1970 when Latin is used in celebrating funerals there is an option to use either the present rite or the rite now in the Roman Ritual; after 1 June 1970 only this new *Rite of Funerals* is to be used.

Once the individual conferences of bishops have prepared a vernacular version of the rite and received its confirmation from this Congregation, they have authorization to fix any other, feasible effective date prior to 1 June 1970 for use of the *Rite of Funerals*.

All things to the contrary notwithstanding.

416. SC DIVINE WORSHIP, *Rite of Funerals*, **Introduction**, 15 August 1969: Vatican Polyglot Press, 1969.

INTRODUCTION

3373   1.   At the funerals of its children the Church confidently celebrates Christ's paschal mystery. Its intention is that those who by baptism were made one body with the dead and risen Christ may with him pass from death to life. In soul they are to be cleansed and taken up into heaven with the saints and elect; in body they await the blessed hope of Christ's coming and the resurrection of the dead.

The Church therefore offers the eucharistic sacrifice of Christ's Passover for the dead and pours forth prayers and petitions for them. Because of the communion of all Christ's members with each other, all of this brings spiritual aid to the dead and the consolation of hope to the living.

3374   2.   As they celebrate the funerals of their brothers and sisters, Christians should be intent on affirming their hope for eternal life. They should not however give the impression of either disregard or contempt for the attitudes or practices of their own time and place. In such matters as family traditions, local customs, burial societies, Christians should willingly acknowledge whatever they perceive to be good and try to transform whatever seems alien to the Gospel. Then the funeral ceremonies for Christians will both manifest paschal faith and be true examples of the spirit of the Gospel.

3375   3.   Although any form of empty display must be excluded, it is right to show respect for the bodies of the faithful departed, which in life were the temple of the Holy Spirit. This is why it is worthwhile that there be an expression of faith in eternal life and the offering of prayers for the deceased, at least at the more significant times between death and burial.

---

   [a] See DOL 1 nos. 81–82.

Depending on local custom, such special moments include the vigil at the home of the deceased, the laying out of the body, and the carrying of the body to the place of burial. They should be marked by the gathering of family and friends and, if possible, of the whole community to receive in the liturgy of the word the consolation of hope, to offer together the eucharistic sacrifice, and to pay last respects to the deceased by a final farewell.

4. To take into account in some degree conditions in all parts of the world, the present rite of funerals for adults is arranged on the basis of three models: 3376

     a. The first envisions three stations, namely, at the home of the deceased, at the church, and at the cemetery.

     b. The second covers only two stations, at the church and at the cemetery.

     c. The third involves only one station, which is at the home of the deceased.

5. The first model for a funeral is practically the same as the former rite in the Roman Ritual. It includes as a rule, at least in country places, three stations, namely, at the home of the deceased, at the church, and at the cemetery, with two processions in between. Especially in large cities, however, processions are seldom held or are inconvenient for various reasons. As for the stations at home and at the cemetery, priests sometimes are unable to lead them because of a shortage of clergy or the distance of the cemetery from the church. In view of these considerations, the faithful must be urged to recite the usual psalms and prayers themselves when there is no deacon or priest present. If that is impossible, the home and cemetery stations are to be omitted.   3377

6. In this first model the station at the church consists as a rule in the celebration of the funeral Mass; this is forbidden only during the Easter triduum, on solemnities, and on the Sundays of Advent, Lent, and the Easter season. Pastoral reasons may on occasion require that a funeral be celebrated in the church without a Mass (which in all cases must if possible be celebrated on another day within a reasonable time); in that case a liturgy of the word is prescribed absolutely. Therefore the station at the church always includes a liturgy of the word, with or without a Mass, and the rite hitherto called "absolution" of the dead and henceforth to be called "the final commendation and farewell."[R1]   3378

7. The second funeral plan consists of only two stations, namely, at the cemetery, that is, at the cemetery chapel, and at the grave. This plan does not envision a eucharistic celebration, but one is to take place, without the body present, before the actual funeral or after the funeral.   3379

[R1] 1. Query: Must there be an absolution only when the body is present or may there also be one after other Masses for the dead? Reply: The *Codex rubricarum* no. 401 remains in force; an absolution is appropriate but only when the body is present: Not 1 (1965) 254.

    2. Query: How should a funeral be conducted during the Easter triduum? Reply: 1. A funeral Mass may not be celebrated during the Easter triduum or on Holy Thursday morning. The basis for the query is the language of the GIRM no. 336: "The funeral Mass has first place among the Masses for the dead and may be celebrated on any day except solemnities that are days of obligation and the Sundays of Advent, Lent, and the Easter season" [text revised in the 1975 ed. of RM; see DOL 208 no. 1726]. There is no mention of the Easter triduum. But the point is clear from other parts of the Roman Missal, as the explanation given in Not 10 (1974) 145–146 has already pointed out [see DOL 208 no. 1726, note R63, Query 2]. To give further clarification there is in the *editio altera* of the Roman Missal (which will be described in the next issue of *Notitiae*) an addition to no. 336 among the days on which a funeral Mass is forbidden: "Holy Thursday and the Easter triduum" [see DOL 208, no. 1726]. 2. When a funeral has to be held on the days in question, the proper thing is to have a celebration of the word with the rite of farewell, as the *Rite of Funerals* no. 6 provides. Readings are to be chosen suited to the liturgical season. There may be singing during the celebration. Communion, however, may not be distributed (see MR 243, 250 no. 2, 265, Holy Saturday): Not 11 (1975) 288.

3380   8.   A funeral rite, following the third model, to be celebrated in the deceased's home may perhaps in some places be regarded as pointless. Yet in certain parts of the world it seems needed. In view of the many diversities, the model purposefully does not go into details. At the same time it seemed advisable at least to set out guidelines so that this plan might share certain elements with the other two, for example, the liturgy of the word and the rite of final commendation or farewell. The detailed directives will be left to the conferences of bishops to settle.

3381   9.   In the future preparation of particular rituals conformed to the Roman Ritual, it will be up to the conference of bishops either to keep the three models or to change their arrangement or to omit one or other of them. For it is quite possible that in any particular country one model, for example, the first with its three stations, is the only one in use and as such the one to be kept. Elsewhere all three may be needed. The conference of bishops will make the arrangements appropriate to what particular needs require.

3382   10.   After the funeral Mass the rite of final commendation and farewell is celebrated.

     The meaning of the rite does not signify a kind of purification of the deceased; that is what the eucharistic sacrifice accomplishes. Rather it stands as a farewell by which the Christian community together pays respect to one of its members before the body is removed or buried. Death, of course, always has involved an element of separation, but Christians as Christ's members are one in him and not even death can part them from each other.[1]

     The priest's opening words are to introduce and explain this rite, a few moments of silence are to follow, then the sprinkling with holy water and the incensation, then a song of farewell. Not only is it useful for all to sing this song, composed of a pertinent text set to a suitable melody, but all should have the sense of its being the high point of the entire rite.

     Also to be seen as signs of farewell are the sprinkling with holy water, a reminder that through baptism the person was marked for eternal life, and the incensation, signifying respect for the body as the temple of the Holy Spirit.

     The rite of final commendation and farewell may only be held during an actual funeral service, that is, when the body is present.

3383   11.   In any celebration for the deceased, whether a funeral or not, the rite attaches great importance to the readings from the word of God. These proclaim the paschal mystery, they convey the hope of being gathered together again in God's kingdom, they teach remembrance of the dead, and throughout they encourage the witness of a Christian life.

3384   12.   In its good offices on behalf of the dead, the Church turns again and again especially to the prayer of the psalms as an expression of grief and a sure source of trust. Pastors are therefore to make an earnest effort through an effective catechesis to lead their communities to a clearer and deeper grasp of at least some of the psalms provided for the funeral liturgy. With regard to other chants that the rite frequently assigns on pastoral grounds, they are also to seek to instill a "warm and living love of Scripture"[2] and a sense of its meaning in the liturgy.

---

[1]   See Simeon of Thessalonica, *De ordine sepulturae*: PG 155, 685 B.

[2]   SC art. 24 [DOL 1 no. 24].

13. In its prayers the Christian community confesses its faith and makes compassionate intercession for deceased adults that they may reach their final happiness with God. The community's belief is that deceased children whom through baptism God has adopted as his own have already attained that blessedness. But the community pours forth its prayers on behalf of their parents, as well as for all the loved ones of the dead, so that in their grief they will experience the comfort of faith.   3385

14. The practice of reciting the office for the dead on the occasion of funerals or at other times is based in some places on particular law, on an endowment for this purpose, or on custom. The practice may be continued, provided the office is celebrated becomingly and devoutly. But in view of the circumstances of contemporary life and for pastoral considerations, a Bible vigil or celebration of God's word (nos. 27–29) may be substituted.   3386

15. Funeral rites are to be granted to those who have chosen cremation, unless there is evidence that their choice was dictated by anti-Christian motives, as set forth in the Holy Office's Instruction on cremation, 8 May 1963, nos. 2–3.[3]   3387

The funeral is to be celebrated according to the model in use in the region. It should be carried out in a way, however, that clearly expresses the Church's preference for the custom of burying the dead, after the example of Christ's own will to be buried, and that forestalls any danger of scandalizing or shocking the faithful.

The rites usually held in the cemetery chapel or at the grave may in this case take place within the confines of the crematorium and, for want of any other suitable place, even in the crematorium room.[4] Every precaution is to be taken against the danger of scandal or religious indifferentism.

OFFICES AND MINISTRIES TOWARD THE DEAD

16. In the celebration of a funeral all the members of the people of God must remember that to each one a role and an office is entrusted: to relatives and friends, funeral directors, the Christian community as such, finally, the priest, who as the teacher of faith and the minister of comfort presides at the liturgical rites and celebrates the eucharist.[R2]   3388

17. All should also be mindful, and priests especially, that as they commend the deceased to God at a funeral, they have a responsibility as well to raise the hopes of those present and to build up their faith in the paschal mystery and the resurrection of the dead. They should do so in such a way, however, that as bearers of the tenderness of the Church and the comfort of faith, they console those who believe without offending those who grieve.   3389

18. In preparing and planning a funeral, priests are to keep in mind with delicate sensitivity not only the identity of the deceased and the circumstances of the death, but also the grief of the bereaved and their needs for a Christian life. Priests are to be particularly mindful of those who attend the liturgical celebration or hear the Gospel because of the funeral, but are either non-Catholics or Catholics who never or seldom take part in the eucharist or have apparently lost the faith. Priests are, after all, the servants of Christ's Gospel on behalf of all.   3390

---

[3] See AAS 56 (1964) 822–823 [DOL 413 nos. 3368–69].

[4] Cf. DOL 413 no. 3370.

[R2] See DOL 223 no. 1794, note R2.

3391   19. Except for the Mass, a deacon may conduct all the funeral rites. As pastoral needs require, the conference of bishops, with the Apostolic See's permission, may even depute a layperson for this.

When there is no priest or deacon, it is recommended that in funerals according to the first model laypersons carry out the stations at the home and cemetery; the same applies generally to all vigils for the dead.

3392   20. Apart from the marks of distinction arising from a person's liturgical function or holy orders and those honors due to civil authorities according to liturgical law,[4] no special honors are to be paid in the celebration of a funeral to any private persons or classes of persons.

ADAPTATIONS BELONGING TO THE CONFERENCES OF BISHOPS

3393   21. In virtue of the Constitution on the Liturgy (art. 63 b),[b] the conferences of bishops have the right to prepare a section in particular rituals corresponding to the present section of the Roman Ritual and adapted to the needs of the different parts of the world. This section is for use in the regions concerned, once the *acta* of the conferences have been reviewed by the Apostolic See.

In making such adaptations it shall be up to the conferences of bishops:

1. to decide on the adaptations, within the limits laid down in the present section of the Roman Ritual;

2. to weigh carefully and prudently which elements from the traditions and culture of individual peoples may be appropriately admitted and accordingly to propose to the Apostolic See further adaptations considered to be useful or necessary that will be introduced into the liturgy with its consent;[c]

3. to retain elements of particular rituals that may now exist, provided they are compatible with the Constitution on the Liturgy and contemporary needs, or to adapt such elements;

4. to prepare translations of the texts that are truly suited to the genius of the different languages and cultures and, whenever appropriate, to add suitable melodies for singing;

5. to adapt and enlarge this Introduction in the Roman Ritual in such a way that the ministers will fully grasp and carry out the meaning of the rites;

6. in editions of the liturgical books to be prepared under the direction of the conferences of bishops, to arrange the material in a format deemed to be best suited to pastoral practice; this is to be done in such a way, however, that none of the contents of this *editio typica* are omitted.

When added rubrics or texts are judged useful, these are to be set off by some typographical symbol or mark from the rubrics and texts of the Roman Ritual.

3394   22. In drawing up particular rituals for funerals, it shall be up to the conferences of bishops:

1. to give the rite an arrangement patterned on one or more of the models, in the way indicated in no. 9;

2. to replace the formularies given in the basic rite with others taken from those in chapter VI, should this seem advantageous;

---

    [4]   See SC art. 32 [DOL 1 no. 32].

    [b]   See DOL 1 no. 63.

    [c]   See DOL 1 no. 40.

3. to add different formularies of the same type whenever the Roman Ritual provides optional formularies (following the rule given in no. 21, 6);

4. to decide whether laypersons should be deputed to celebrate funerals (see no. 19);

5. to decree, whenever pastoral considerations dictate, omission of the sprinkling with holy water and the incensation or to substitute another rite for them;

6. to decree for funerals the liturgical color that fits in with the culture of peoples, that is not offensive to human grief, and that is an expression of Christian hope in the light of the paschal mystery.

FUNCTION OF THE PRIEST IN PREPARING AND PLANNING THE CELEBRATION

23. The priest is to make willing use of the options allowed in the rite, taking into consideration the many different situations and the wishes of the family and the community.

3395

24. The rite provided for each model is drawn up in such a way that it can be carried out with simplicity; nevertheless the rite supplies a wide selection of texts to fit various contingencies. Thus, for example:

3396

1. As a general rule all texts are interchangeable, in order to achieve, with the help of the community or the family, a closer reflection of the actual circumstances of each celebration.

2. Some elements are not assigned as obligatory, but are left as optional additions, as, for example, the prayer for the mourners at the home of the deceased.

3. In keeping with liturgical tradition, a wide freedom of choice is given regarding the texts provided for processions.

4. When a psalm listed or suggested for a liturgical reason may present a pastoral problem, another psalm may be substituted. Even within the psalms a verse or verses that seem to be unsuitable from a pastoral standpoint may be omitted.

5. The texts of prayers are always written in the singular, that is, for one deceased male. Accordingly, in any particular case the text is to be modified as to both gender and number.

6. In prayers the lines within parentheses may be omitted.

25. Like the entire ministry of the priest to the dead, celebration of the funeral liturgy with meaning and dignity presupposes a view of the priestly office in its inner relationship with the Christian mystery.

3397

Among the priest's responsibilites are:

1. to be at the side of the sick and dying, as is indicated in the proper section of the Roman Ritual;

2. to impart catechesis on the meaning of Christian death;

3. to comfort the family of the deceased, to sustain them amid the anguish of their grief, to be as kind and helpful as possible, and, through the use of the resources provided and allowed in the ritual, to prepare with them a funeral celebration that has meaning for them;

4. finally, to fit the liturgy for the dead into the total setting of the liturgical life of the parish and his own pastoral ministry.

417. SC DOCTRINE OF THE FAITH, **Letter** *Complures Conferentiae Episcopales* to presidents of the conferences of bishops, on ecclesiastical burial for Christians involved in an irregular marriage, 29 May 1973.*

3398   Several conferences of bishops and many local Ordinaries have requested of this Congregation a relaxation of the discipline in force regarding the ecclesiastical burial of those faithful who at the time of their death are involved in an irregular marriage.

The Congregation carefully reviewed the opinions and recommendations that have come in on this subject and in 1972 held a plenary meeting to discuss them.

At this meeting the Fathers decided, with the approval of Pope Paul VI, that celebration of ecclesiastical burial should be made easier for those Catholics to whom it had been denied by the provisions of canon 1240.

As an amendment of this canon to the extent required, a new set of regulations will be promulgated as soon as possible.[a] On the basis of the new arrangement the celebration of liturgical funeral rites will no longer be forbidden in the case of the faithful who, even though involved in a clearly sinful situation before their death, have maintained allegiance to the Church and have given some evidence of repentance. A necessary condition is that there be no public scandal for the rest of the faithful.

It will be possible to lessen or forestall such scandal to the faithful and the ecclesiastical community to the extent that pastors explain in an effective way the meaning of a Christian funeral. Then the majority will see the funeral as an appeal to God's mercy and as the Christian community's witness to faith in the resurrection of the dead and life eternal.

Through this letter I request that you kindly inform the Ordinaries of your conference of bishops that the text of the new decree on ecclesiastical burial will be published soon and will become effective immediately on the date of its publication.

418. SC DOCTRINE OF THE FAITH, **Decree** *Patres Sacrae Congregationis*, on ecclesiastical burial, 20 September 1973: AAS 65 (1973) 500.

3399   The Fathers of the Congregation for the Doctrine of the Faith in plenary meetings on 14–15 November 1972 have decreed in regard to ecclesiastical burial: a funeral is not to be forbidden for public sinners if before death they have given some evidence of repentance and there is no danger of scandal to others of the faithful.

On 17 November 1972, at an audience granted to the undersigned Cardinal Prefect, Pope Paul VI confirmed and approved this decree and ordered its publication, thus repealing to the extent required canon 1240 par. 1; all things to the contrary notwithstanding.

▶   163.   SC DOCTRINE OF THE FAITH, Decree *Accidit in diversis regionibus*, on Mass for deceased non-Catholics, 11 June 1976.

---

*   SCDF, Prot. N. 1284/66.

a   See DOL 418.

▶   173.   SC DOCTRINE OF THE FAITH, Letter *Recentiores Episcoporum Synodi* to the confer-
          ences of bishops, on eschatology, 17 May 1979.

CHAPTER FOUR

THE DIVINE OFFICE

SUMMARY (DOL 419–439). The Constitution on the Liturgy devoted its fourth chapter to the divine office, reviewing the theological significance (art. 83–86), laying down norms for its revision (art. 95–100), defining a new discipline on its obligatory character (art. 95–100) and on the language to be used (art. 101). The direction given by the Constitution was taken up immediately both in other conciliar documents and in the documents during the interim prior to publication of the revised version of the office in 1971. The present chapter, accordingly, as its first two sections has one on the divine office prior to publication of *The Liturgy of the Hours* and one on this new book. Because carrying out the official prayer of the Church to perfection has always been the special commitment of the monastic orders, there is a third section on the monastic office.

Section 1. Office Prior to 1971

SUMMARY (DOL 419–423). The 18 cross-references here indicate how in the conciliar documents, the general instructions on the reform, as well as in more particular directives the spirit and intent of the Constitution on the Liturgy were immediately acted upon. There are also the 5 texts specifically addressing the celebration of the divine office.

—Paul VI in a letter to superiors general of institutes bound to choir developed the theological import of their celebration of the office (DOL 421); he also granted suppression of the hour of prime (DOL 419).

—The Congregation of Rites issued a particular reply to queries on the choral office (DOL 420).

—The Congregation of Religious significantly indicated approval of the proposal of the Visitation nuns to replace the Office of the Blessed Virgin Mary with the divine office (DOL 422) and also issued a reply to mendicant orders on the choral office (DOL 423).

▶   103. PAUL VI, Motu Proprio *Pastorale munus*, on the powers and privileges of bishops, 30 November 1963:

I, nos.   24–25:   Reduction of the choral office [nos. 731–732].
          26:            Commutation of the divine office [no. 733].

▶   1.   VATICAN COUNCIL II, Constitution on the Liturgy *Sacrosanctum Concilium*, 4 December 1963:

art. 83–101:   Divine office [nos. 83–101].

▶   20.   PAUL VI, Motu Proprio *Sacram Liturgiam*, on putting into effect some prescriptions of the Constitution on the Liturgy, 25 January 1964:

art. VI: Omission of prime and choice of one minor hour [no. 284].
      VII: Commutation of the divine office [no. 285].
      VIII: Liturgical value of little offices in religious institutes [no. 286].
      IX: Language of the office [no. 287].

▶   23.   SC RITES AND CONSILIUM, Instruction (first) *Inter Oecumenici*, 26 September 1964:

nos. 16:   Divine office in major seminaries [no. 308].
      17:               In houses of formation of religious [no. 309].
      78:               Choral office [no. 370].
      79:               Dispensation and commutation [no. 371].
      80–84:   Little offices [nos. 372–376].
      85–89:   Language of divine office [nos. 377–381].

▶   109. SC RITES, Reply (Capuchins), on the recitation of the divine office in the vernacular by lay brothers, 9 January 1965.

419. PAUL VI, **Concession** regarding the omission of prime for communities bound to choir, 2 June 1965: Not 1 (1965) 272.

3400   "On 2 June 1965 (Prot. N. 43991/65) Pope Paul VI granted that members of religious communities 'bound to choir' may be excused from the obligation of including prime in the recitation of the divine office, whether chorally or privately. Execution of this indult is left to the prudent judgment of the religious superiors general."[R1] [. . .]

▶   10.   VATICAN COUNCIL II, Decree on the Appropriate Renewal of Religious Life *Perfectae caritatis*, 28 October 1965:

no.   9:   Divine office in monasteries and religious communities [no. 207].

420. SC RITES, **Reply** to queries (Dom G. B. Franzoni, Rome), on the divine office, 8 November 1965: Not 2 (1966) 182–183.

Dom Giovanni Battista Franzoni, Abbot Ordinary of St. Paul's in Rome, has respectfully submitted to the Congregation of Rites the following queries for appropriate solution.

3401

1. Is the versicle *Fidelium animae* to be omitted at the canonical hour immediately preceding the conventual Mass or at the end of vespers when exposition and benediction of the blessed sacrament are to follow immediately?

2. Does the rule in the *Ritus servandus in celebratione Missae* no. 22, on omitting the prayers at the foot of the altar whenever some other liturgical service has immediately preceded, apply only to those rites at which the priest who is to celebrate Mass has presided? Or is its scope wider, so that it must be applied even in the case where the priest who is to celebrate Mass has not presided or was not even present at the rite preceding: for example, the case of the conventual Mass celebrated after terce?

3. The choral dress proper to monks of the Order of St. Benedict is the cowl; thus the query: Is it permissible for priests present at the conventual Mass to assist the celebrant in distributing communion after simply putting on a stole over the cowl, not a surplice, as is the ancient monastic practice still in use in the distribution of palms on Palm Sunday and of candles on Candlemas Day?

4. If the procession should be omitted on one or other of the rogation days, must the Litany of the Saints with its versicles and prayers be said in choir without procession or is it to be omitted even in choir?

The same Congregation, after hearing the decision of the liturgical commission and deliberating on these points, has decided to reply as follows:

To I: No.

To II: No to the first part; Yes to the second.

To III: No.

To IV: According to the *Codex rubricarum* no. 83, the local Ordinary is to establish special services of prayer, during which the Litany of the Saints is to be recited.

▶   114.   SC RITES AND SC RELIGIOUS, Instruction *In edicendis normis*, on the language to be used in celebrations of religious, 23 November 1965.

▶   18.   VATICAN COUNCIL II, Decree on the Ministry and Life of Priests *Presbyterorum Ordinis*, 7 December 1965:

         nos. 5, 13:   Divine office in the life of priests [nos. 260, 265].

▶   332.   SC SEMINARIES AND UNIVERSITIES, Instruction *Doctrina et exemplo*, on liturgical formation in seminaries, 25 December 1965:

         nos. 26–31:   Divine office [nos. 2697–2702].
         Appendix, art. 3:   Sanctifying the hours of the day [no. 2743].

▶   385.   APOSTOLIC PENITENTIARY, Decree *Die 31 ianuarii*, on indulgenced prayer before divine office, 31 January 1966.

▶   143.   SC RELIGIOUS, Decree *Religionum laicalium*, on faculties delegated to religious superiors, 31 May 1966:

I, no. 9:   Dispensation of the office obligation for nuns [no. 953].

▶   106. PAUL VI, Motu Proprio *Ecclesiae Sanctae*, on norms for carrying out certain of the conciliar decrees, 6 August 1965:

II, no. 20:   Divine office of religious brothers and sisters [no. 756].

421. PAUL VI, Epistle *Sacrificium laudis* **to superiors general of clerical religious institutes bound to choir, on the celebration of the divine office, 15 August 1966: Not 2 (1966) 252–255.**

3402   The sacrifice of praise is the offering of lips honoring the Lord in psalms and hymns, devoutly consecrating the hours, the days, and the years as times of worship, with the sacrifice of the eucharist as its center, like a shining sun, drawing all the rest to itself. Your religious families in their dedication to God have always held this sacrifice of praise in high esteem, wisely recognizing that nothing should take precedence over so holy an activity. Clearly it has been the source of great glory to the Creator of all things and of the highest service to the Church. Through this sure and dedicated manner of prayer you have given a lesson that divine worship is essential in the life of the human community.

Letters from some of you and reports from other sources, however, have made us aware that — speaking only of the Latin rite — your houses or provinces have introduced diverse practices into the celebration of the liturgy. Some of them are deeply attached to Latin while others prefer the vernacular in the choral office; some here and there are in favor of replacing the Gregorian chant with modern music; some have even pressed for doing away with Latin altogether.

We must admit to being quite disturbed and troubled by these demands; they raise the questions of where such an attitude and hitherto unheard of discontent have come from and why they have spread.

You surely have the experience of our unquestionable love and esteem for your religious families. They have often won our admiration by the evidence of their marked devotion and their contributions to culture. We count it a joy to have any legitimate and proper occasion to show kindness to them, to accede to their desires, and to contribute to their betterment.

3403   But the matters we have referred to are occurring after Vatican Council II has deliberately and solemnly issued its decision on this matter (see SC art. 101, § 1)[a] and after the instructions pursuant to this decision have published their clear norms. First the General Instruction *on the correct carrying out of the Constitution on the Liturgy*, 26 September 1964, has decreed: "In reciting the divine office in choir clerics are bound to retain the Latin language" (no. 85).[b] Another instruction, with the heading *On the language to be used in celebrations of the divine office and the "conventual" or "community" Mass in religious houses*, 23 November 1965, confirms that precept and at the same time takes account of the spiritual benefits for the faithful and the special conditions prevailing in mission territories.[c] Until therefore the law prescribes oth-

---

    a   See DOL 1 no. 101.
    b   DOL 23 no. 377.
    c   See DOL 114 nos. 792, 793, 798.

erwise, these laws remain in force and demand the obedience that must be the special merit of religious, as the beloved sons of the Church.

It is not a matter merely of keeping the Latin language in the choral office, although this has its own importance since Latin deserves to be safeguarded as an abundant source of culture and a rich treasury for devotion. But the issue is to keep intact the grace, the beauty, and the inherent strength of these prayers and chants. The issue is the choral office, uttered "sweetly by the voices of the Church singing" (Augustine, *Conf.* 9, 6: PL 32, 769), your heritage from your founders, your masters, and your saints — the luminaries of your communities. Do not make light of the traditions of your forefathers, which through the ages have been your glory. The ideal of the choral office has been one of the chief reasons for the continued existence and welcome increase of your communities. It is astounding, therefore, that in the face of the agitation of the moment some think that this ideal is to be discarded.

In the present state of affairs what voice, what song could replace the formularies of Catholic devotion that you have used up to this point? You must weigh carefully and reflect lest a worse state of affairs follow on the repudiation of that glorious heritage. What must be feared is that the choral office will be reduced to some unstructured mode of praying that you above all will find vapid and boring. There is also the question of whether people who want to take part in the liturgy will go to your churches in such numbers if they will no longer hear there the ancient language, natural to the liturgical prayers, accompanied by a chant full of gravity and grace. We appeal, therefore, to all involved to think carefully about what they wish to cast aside and not to allow that fountain to run dry from which they have so plentifully drunk until now.

Undoubtedly the Latin language confronts the novices of your institute with a problem, sometimes a major problem. But as you well know this problem is not to be regarded as insuperable, especially for you who, being more removed from the affairs and noise of the world, can more readily devote yourselves to learning. In any case, those prayers, marked by their ancient merit and noble majesty, will serve to attract to you young men with a vocation to be close to the Lord. Conversely, take away the language that transcends national boundaries and possesses a marvelous spiritual power and the music that rises from the depths of the soul where faith resides and charity burns — we mean Gregorian chant — and the choral office will be like a snuffed candle; it will no longer shed light, no longer draw the eyes and minds of the people. 3404

Dearest sons, the demands already mentioned involve such serious issues that at the present time we cannot accede to them by amending the norms of the Council and of the instructions cited. We earnestly urge you therefore to consider every side of this complex matter. Out of our good will and high esteem for you we cannot permit something that could be the cause of your own downfall, that could be the source of serious loss to you, and that surely would afflict the Church of God with sickness and sadness. Even if you are reluctant, allow us to defend your real interests. The Church has introduced the vernacular into the liturgy for pastoral advantage, that is, in favor of those who do not know Latin. The same Church gives you the mandate to safeguard the traditional dignity, beauty, and gravity of the choral office in both its language and its chant.

With open and untroubled spirit, therefore, obey the commands that a great love for your own ancient observances itself suggests, but that also a father's love for you proposes, and that concern for divine worship commends.

422. SC RELIGIOUS, **Letter** to the mothers superior of Visitation monasteries and to all Visitation nuns, on replacing the Little Office of the Blessed Virgin Mary with the divine office, 29 January 1967: Not 3 (1967) 114 (French).

3405   The Congregation of Religious has noted with satisfaction the result of the survey conducted in Visitation monasteries on replacing the Little Office of the Blessed Virgin with the divine office.

The Congregation of Religious has noted with satisfaction the result of the

Most of you have decided to request this change for the sake of conforming to the mind of the Council and of Pope Paul VI's Motu Proprio *Ecclesiae Sanctae*.[a] You may be sure that you will derive rich benefits for your own sanctification and for the sanctification of others. By this step you will be more closely united to the liturgical prayer of the universal Church and you will be responding more loyally to the urgent appeal that the Vicar of Christ continually addresses to contemplatives: to address God with greater fervor and persistence in order to obtain the grace of faith and salvation for today's world.

3406   I.   In virtue of the powers granted by Pope Paul VI, the Congregation of Religious, after consultation with the Consilium, grants to the petitioning monasteries permission to adopt the Roman Breviary as soon as they are, in the judgment of the local Ordinary, capable of reciting it properly.

3407   II.   The Congregation permits monasteries that have expressed this desire to continue to recite the Little Office of the Blessed Virgin. If later any such monasteries request it, permission to adopt the Roman Breviary will be granted.

3408   III.   The Order of the Visitation of Mary will be obliged to recite or sing only the following parts of the divine office: matins of one nocturn consisting of three psalms and three readings, lauds, terce, sext, none, vespers, compline.

3409   IV.   The office may be celebrated in the vernacular if two-thirds of the members of the conventual chapter agree.

3410   V.   The office for feasts proper to the Visitation Order will be settled later.

▶   508.   SC RITES (Consilium), Instruction *Musicam sacram*, on music in the liturgy, 5 March 1967:

        nos. 37–41:   Chant for the divine office [nos. 4158–62].

▶   179.   SC RITES AND CONSILIUM, Instruction *Eucharisticum mysterium*, on worship of the eucharist, 25 May 1967:

        no.   17:   Divine office not to be celebrated during Mass [no. 1246].

▶   309.   PAUL VI, Motu proprio *Sacrum Diaconatus Ordinem*, restoring the permanent diaconate in the Latin Church, 18 June 1967:

        no.   27:   Deacons' participation in divine office [no. 2541].

▶   119.   SC RELIGIOUS, Reply (Capuchins), on the vernacular in the divine office, 20 September 1967.

---

[a]   See DOL 106 no. 756.

► 122. SECRETARIAT OF STATE, Letter to the Cistercian abbot of Hauterive, on Latin in the liturgy, 14 June 1968.

423. SC RELIGIOUS AND SECULAR INSTITUTES, **Rescript** (mendicant orders), on recitation of the divine office in common, 31 May 1969.*

This Congregation has received many petitions concerning the choral recita- 3411
tion of the divine office. As you know, it submitted the issue for study to a commission set up expressly for this purpose and made up of five superiors general or their deputies.

The commission's conclusions and proposals have been weighed with the greatest care and attention by the Congregation and then submitted to Pope Paul VI for approval.

At an audience granted to the undersigned Cardinal Prefect of the Congregation, 13 May 1969, the Pope has kindly given approval to what follows.

1. The Congregation for Religious and Secular Institutes grants to mendicant 3412
orders that they may lawfully recite the divine office in common rather than in choir if a special general chapter should so decide.

2. a. To the general chapter of mendicant orders wishing to keep the obligation 3413
of reciting the divine office in choir the same Congregation grants permission to make particular exceptions. In such a case the chapter is to decide which hour may be recited in common rather than in choir and on the place for reciting it outside choir.

   b. Whenever, in special circumstances and for serious reasons approved by the general chapter, any community is unable to carry out the entire divine office in choir or in common, the superior general with his council is to stipulate which canonical hours must be recited in choir or in common. In addition, the individual religious remain under the obligation of reciting privately those parts of the divine office that they have not satisfied in choir or in common.

3. It is unlawful to replace the divine office with other forms of prayer, even if 3414
these have been duly chosen by a community. Such a substitution is contrary to the prescriptions of Vatican Council II and the Holy See will absolutely not grant a dispensation on this point.

This communication is sent to you, Most Reverend Father, for your information and direction.

► 126. SC DIVINE WORSHIP, Norms *In confirmandis actis*, on uniform translation of liturgical texts, 6 February 1970:

   no. 1 c: Texts of the divine office [no. 889].

► 51. SECRETARIAT OF STATE, Letter to Bishop A. Mistrorigo, on the prayer of the community, August 1970:

   no. 1:   Divine office of priests [no. 503].

---

* SCRSI, Letter, Prot. N. R.S.1506/69, to the minister general of the Capuchins; Latin text, CommRel 15 (1970) 182–184.

▶   See also Chapter Five, Section 5. Particular calendars and propers.

Section 2. The Liturgy of the Hours

SUMMARY (DOL 424–436). The extensive work of revision that restructured and enriched the celebration of the liturgy of the hours was completed in 1970. A first group of texts here concern *The Liturgy of the Hours*; a second group, the celebration of the office.

—The major texts on *The Liturgy of the Hours* are Paul VI's apostolic constitution approving it (DOL 424), the decree accompanying the doctrinal, pastoral, and liturgical introduction (DOL 425), this General Instruction of the Liturgy of the Hours itself (DOL 426), and the decree promulgating the four volumes of *The Liturgy of the Hours* (DOL 427). In addition there are related subsidiary texts on the development of optional patristic lectionaries (DOL 428, 433), on provisional chants (DOL 429), on the use of the former breviary in Holy Week of 1972 by those not yet having the new book (DOL 430). There is also an authentic interpretation of a passage in the General Instruction (DOL 431) and a note on vernacular editions of *The Liturgy of the Hours* (DOL 434).

—Regarding celebration of the liturgy of the hours there is an excerpt from an address of John Paul II in New York (DOL 436), a letter of the Secretariat of State on the Church's prayer (DOL 435), and a notification of the Congregation for Divine Worship to contemplative communities on the spirit of the General Instruction and on certain adaptations (DOL 432).

424. PAUL VI, **Apostolic Constitution** *Laudis canticum*, promulgating the revised book of the liturgy of the hours, 1 November 1970: AAS 63 (1971) 527–535; Not 7 (1971) 146–152.

3415   The hymn of praise that is sung through all the ages in the heavenly places and was brought by the High Priest, Christ Jesus, into this land of exile has been continued by the Church with constant fidelity over many centuries, in a rich variety of forms.

The liturgy of the hours gradually developed into the prayer of the local Church, a prayer offered at regular intervals and in appointed places under the presidency of a priest. It was seen as a kind of necessary complement by which the fullness of divine worship contained in the eucharistic sacrifice would overflow to reach all the hours of daily life.

The book of the divine office, gradually enlarged by many additions in the course of time, became a suitable instrument for the sacred service for which it was designed. Since over the generations a good many changes were introduced in the form of celebration, including the practice of individual recitation, it is not strange that the breviary, as it was sometimes called, underwent many transformations, sometimes affecting the principles of its arrangement.

3416   The Council of Trent, unable, because of shortness of time, to complete the reform of the breviary, left this matter to the Apostolic See. The Roman Breviary, promulgated in 1568 by our predecessor St. Pius V, achieved above all what was so urgently needed, the introduction of uniformity in the canonical prayer of the Latin Church, after this uniformity had lapsed.

In subsequent centuries many revisions were made by Sixtus V, Clement VIII, Urban VIII, Clement XI, and other popes.

In 1911 St. Pius X promulgated a new breviary, prepared at his command. The ancient custom was restored of reciting the 150 psalms each week and the arrangement of the psalter was entirely revised to remove all repetitions and to harmonize the weekday psalter and the cycle of biblical readings with the offices of saints. In addition, the office of Sunday was raised in rank and dignity to take general precedence over feasts of saints.

The whole work of liturgical revision was undertaken again by Pius XII. For both private and public recitation of the office he permitted the use of the new translation of the psalter prepared by the Pontifical Biblical Institute and in 1947 established a special commission with the responsibility of studying the question of the breviary. In 1955 all the bishops throughout the world were questioned about this matter. The fruits of this labor and concern were first seen in the decree on the simplification of the rubrics, published 23 March 1955, and in the regulations for the breviary issued by John XXIII in the *Codex rubricarum* of 1960.

Though only a part of the liturgical reform came under his seal, Pope John XXIII was aware that the fundamental principles on which the liturgy rests required further study. He entrusted this task to the Second Vatican Ecumenical Council, which in the meantime he had convoked. The result was that the Council treated the liturgy as a whole, and the hours in particular, with such thoroughness and skill, such spirituality and power, that there is scarcely a parallel to the Council's work in the entire history of the Church.

3417   While Vatican Council II was still in session, it was our concern that after the promulgation of the Constitution on the Liturgy, its decrees should be put immediately into effect. For this purpose we established a special commission within the Consilium for the Implementation of the Constitution on the Liturgy. With the help of scholars and specialists in the liturgical, theological, spiritual, and pastoral disciplines, the Consilium worked with the greatest zeal and diligence over a period of seven years to produce the new book for the liturgy of the hours.

The principles underlying it, its whole arrangement, as well as its individual parts were approved by the Consilium and also by the 1967 Synod of Bishops, after consultation with the bishops of the whole Church and a very large number of pastors, religious, and laity.

It will be helpful here, then, to set out in detail the underlying principles and the structure of the liturgy of the hours.

1.   As required by the Constitution *Sacrosanctum Concilium*, account was taken of the   3418
circumstances in which priests engaged in apostolic works find themselves today.[a]

The office has been drawn up and arranged in such a way that not only clergy but also religious and indeed laity may participate in it, since it is the prayer of the whole people of God. People of different callings and circumstances, with their individual needs, were kept in mind and a variety of ways of celebrating the office has been provided, by means of which the prayer can be adapted to suit the way of life and vocation of different groups dedicated to the liturgy of the hours.

2.   Since the liturgy of the hours is the means of sanctifying the day, the order of   3419
this prayer was revised so that in the circumstances of contemporary life the canonical hours could be more easily related to the chronological hours of the day.

For this reason the hour of prime was suppressed; morning prayer and evening prayer, as hinges of the entire office, were assigned the most important role and now have the character of true morning and evening prayer; the office of readings retains its character as a night office for those who celebrate it during the night, but it is suitable for any hour of the day; the daytime prayer is so arranged that those who choose only one of the hours for midmorning, midday, and midafternoon may say the one most suitable to the actual time of day, without losing any part of the four-week psalter.

3.   To ensure that in celebrating the office mind and voice may be more easily in   3420
harmony and that the liturgy of the hours may become in reality "a source of devotion and nourishment for personal prayer,"[1] in the new book, the amount of obligatory daily prayer has been considerably reduced, but variety in the texts has been notably increased and many aids to meditation on the psalms provided, for example, the captions, antiphons, psalm-prayers, and optional periods of silence.

4.   In accordance with the ruling by the Council,[2] the weekly cycle of the psalter   3421
has been replaced by an arrangement of the psalms over a period of four weeks, in the new version prepared by the Commission for the Neo-Vulgate edition of the Bible, which we ourselves established. In this new arrangement of the psalms a few of the psalms and verses that are somewhat harsh in tone have been omitted, especially because of the difficulties anticipated from their use in vernacular celebration. In addition, new canticles from the Old Testament have been added to morning prayer in order to increase its spiritual richness and canticles from the New Testament now enhance the beauty of evening prayer.

---

[a]   See DOL 1 no. 88.

[1]   SC art. 90 [DOL 1 no. 90].

[2]   SC art. 91 [DOL 1 no. 91].

3422   5.   In the new cycle of readings from holy Scripture there is a more ample selection from the treasury of God's word, so planned as to harmonize with the cycle of readings at Mass.

    The passages provide in general a certain unity of theme and have been chosen to present, in the course of the year, the principal stages in the history of salvation.

3423   6.   In accordance with the norms laid down by the Council, the daily reading from the works of the Fathers and of ecclesiastical writers has been revised in such a way that the best of the writings of Christian authors, especially of the Fathers, is included. Besides this, an optional lectionary will be prepared with a fuller selection from the spiritual riches of these writers, as a source of even more abundant benefits.

3424   7.   Anything that is not in harmony with historical truth has been removed from the text of the liturgy of the hours. On this score, the readings, especially biographies of the saints, have been revised in such a way that, first and foremost, the spiritual portrait of the saints and their significance for the life of the Church emerge and are placed in their true context.

3425   8.   Intercessions (*preces*) have been added to morning prayer to express the consecration of the day and to offer prayer for the day's work about to begin. There is also a short act of supplication at evening prayer, drawn up in the form of general intercessions.

    The Lord's Prayer has been restored to its position at the end of these prayers. Since the Lord's Prayer is also said at Mass, this change represents a return in our time to early Christian usage, namely, of saying this prayer three times in the day.

3426   Now that the prayer of holy Church has been reformed and entirely revised in keeping with its very ancient tradition and in the light of the needs of our day, it is to be hoped above all that the liturgy of the hours may pervade and penetrate the whole of Christian prayer, giving it life, direction, and expression and effectively nourishing the spiritual life of the people of God.

    We have, therefore, every confidence that an appreciation of the prayer "without ceasing"[3] that our Lord Jesus Christ commanded will take on new life. The book for the liturgy of the hours, distributed as it is according to seasons, continually strengthens and supports that prayer. The very celebration of the liturgy of the hours, especially when a community gathered for this purpose expresses the genuine nature of the praying Church and stands as a wonderful sign of that Church.

    Christian prayer above all is the prayer of the whole human community, which Christ joins to himself.[4] Everyone shares in this prayer, which is proper to the one Body as it offers prayers that give expression to the voice of Christ's beloved Bride, to the hopes and desires of the whole Christian people, to supplications and petitions for the needs of all humanity.

    This prayer takes its unity from the heart of Christ, for our Redeemer desired "that the life he had entered upon in his mortal body with supplications and with his sacrifice should continue without interruption through the ages in his Mystical Body, which is the Church."[5] Because of this, the prayer of the Church is at the

---

   [3] See Lk 18:1 and 21:36; 1 Thes 5:17; Eph 6:18.

   [4] See SC art. 83 [DOL 1 no. 83].

   [5] Pius XII, Encycl. *Mediator Dei*, 20 Nov. 1947, no. 2: AAS 39 (1947) 522.

same time "the very prayer that Christ himself, together with his Body, addresses to the Father."[6] As we celebrate the office, therefore, we must recognize our own voices echoing in Christ, his voice echoing in us.[7]

To manifest this quality of our prayer more clearly, "the warm and living love for holy Scripture"[8] that permeates the liturgy of the hours must come to life in all of us, so that Scripture may indeed become the chief source of all Christian prayer. In particular, the praying of the psalms, which continually ponders and proclaims the action of God in the history of salvation, must be grasped with new warmth by the people of God. This will be achieved more readily if a deeper understanding of the psalms, in the meaning in which they are used in the liturgy, is more diligently promoted among the clergy and communicated to all the faithful by means of appropriate catechesis. The wider range of Scripture readings provided not only in the Mass but also in the new liturgy of the hours will enable the history of salvation to be constantly recalled and its continuation in the life of the human race to be effectively proclaimed.

The life of Christ in his Mystical Body also perfects and elevates the personal life of each member of the faithful. Any conflict therefore between the prayer of the Church and personal prayer must be entirely excluded; rather the relationship between them must be strengthened and enlarged. Mental prayer should draw unfailing nourishment from readings, psalms, and the other parts of the liturgy of the hours. The recitation of the office should be adapted, as far as possible, to the needs of living and personal prayer, so that as the General Instruction provides, rhythms and melodies are used and forms of celebration chosen that are more suited to the spiritual needs of those who pray it. If the prayer of the divine office becomes genuine personal prayer, the relation between the liturgy and the whole Christian life also becomes clearer. The whole life of the faithful, hour by hour during day and night, is a kind of *leitourgia* or public service, in which the faithful give themselves over to the ministry of love toward God and neighbor, identifying themselves with the action of Christ, who by his life and self-offering sanctified the life of all humanity.   3427

The liturgy of the hours clearly expresses and effectively strengthens this sublime truth, embodied in the Christian life.

For this reason the hours are recommended to all Christ's faithful members, including those who are not bound by law to their recitation.

Those who have received from the Church the mandate to celebrate the liturgy of the hours are to complete its entire course faithfully each day, respecting as far as possible the actual time of day; first and foremost, they are to give due importance to morning and evening prayer.   3428

Those who are in holy orders and are marked in a special way with the sign of Christ the Priest, as well as those consecrated in a particular way to the service of God and of the Church by the vows of religious profession, should not only be moved to celebrate the hours through obedience to law, but should also feel themselves drawn to them because of the intrinsic excellence of the hours and their pastoral and ascetical value. It is extremely desirable that the public prayer of the Church be offered by all from hearts renewed, in acknowledgment of the inherent need within the whole Body of the Church: as the image of its Head, the Church must be described as the praying Church.

---

6   SC art. 84 [DOL 1 no. 84].

7   See Augustine, *Enarrat. in Ps. 85*, 1: CCL 39, 1176.

8   SC art. 24 [DOL 1 no. 24].

May the praise of God reecho in the Church of our day with greater grandeur and beauty by means of the new book for the liturgy of the hours, which now by Apostolic authority we sanction, approve, and promulgate. May it join the praise sung by saints and angels in the court of heaven. May it go from strength to strength in the days of this earthly exile and soon attain the fullness of praise that throughout eternity will be given "to the One who sits upon the throne and to the Lamb."[9]

3429   We decree that this new book for the liturgy of the hours may be put into use as soon as it is published. Meanwhile, the conferences of bishops are to see to the preparation of editions of this liturgical work in the vernacular and, after approval, that is, confirmation, of these editions by the Apostolic See, are to fix the date when the vernacular editions may or must be used, either in whole or in part. Beginning on the effective date for use of these versions in vernacular celebrations, only the revised form of the liturgy of the hours is to be followed, even by those who continue to use Latin.

For those however who, because of advanced age or for special reasons, experience serious difficulties in observing the new rite it is lawful to continue to use the former Roman Breviary, in whole or in part, with the consent of their Ordinary, and exclusively in individual recitation.

We wish that these decrees and prescriptions be firm and effective now and in the future, notwithstanding, to the extent necessary, apostolic constitutions and ordinances issued by our predecessors, and other prescriptions, even those deserving explicit mention and amendment.

425. SC DIVINE WORSHIP, **Decree** *Cum editio*, accompanying the General Instruction of the Liturgy of the Hours, 2 February 1971: Vatican Polyglot Press, 1971, p. 5.

3430   The edition of volumes for the divine office, that is, the *Liturgia Horarum*, needs more time for completion because of the magnitude of the work and other related problems. Therefore, by express mandate of Pope Paul VI, this Congregation has provided for the prior and separate publication of the *Instructio generalis de Liturgia Horarum*; it will later be incorporated into Volume 1 of the *Liturgia Horarum*.

Because of this, priests, religious, and faithful, both individually and in groups meeting for study or prayer, will have ample opportunity to become familiar with the nature of this new book of the Church at prayer, the structure marking the liturgy of the hours, the norms regulating its celebration, and the spiritual treasures it will place in the hands of the people of God.

---

[9] Rv 5:13.

426. SC DIVINE WORSHIP, **General Instruction of the Liturgy of the Hours**, 2 February 1971: Vatican Polyglot Press, 1971.

CHAPTER I
IMPORTANCE OF THE LITURGY OF THE HOURS OR
DIVINE OFFICE IN THE LIFE OF THE CHURCH

1.   Public and common prayer by the people of God is rightly considered to be among the primary duties of the Church. From the very beginning those who were baptized "devoted themselves to the teaching of the apostles and to the community, to the breaking of the bread, and to prayer" (Acts 2:42). The Acts of the Apostles give frequent testimony to the fact that the Christian community prayed with one accord.[1]

    The witness of the early Church teaches us that individual Christians devoted themselves to prayer at fixed times. Then, in different places, it soon became the established practice to assign special times for common prayer, for example, the last hour of the day when evening draws on and the lamp is lighted, or the first hour when night draws to a close with the rising of the sun.

    In the course of time other hours came to be sanctified by prayer in common. These were seen by the Fathers as foreshadowed in the Acts of the Apostles. There we read of the disciples gathered together at the third hour.[2] The prince of the apostles "went up on the housetop to pray, about the sixth hour" (10:9); "Peter and John were going up to the temple at the hour of prayer, the ninth hour" (3:1); "about midnight Paul and Silas were praying and singing hymns to God" (16:25).

2.   Such prayer in common gradually took the form of a set cycle of hours. This liturgy of the hours or divine office, enriched by readings, is principally a prayer of praise and petition. Indeed, it is the prayer of the Church with Christ and to Christ.

I. PRAYER OF CHRIST

CHRIST THE INTERCESSOR WITH THE FATHER

3.   When the Word, proceeding from the Father as the splendor of his glory, came to give us all a share in God's life, "Christ Jesus, High Priest of the new and eternal covenant, taking human nature, introduced into this earthly exile the hymn of praise that is sung throughout all ages in the halls of heaven."[3] From then on in Christ's heart the praise of God assumes a human sound in words of adoration, expiation, and intercession, presented to the Father by the Head of the new humanity, the Mediator between God and his people, in the name of all and for the good of all.

4.   In his goodness the Son of God, who is one with his Father (see Jn 10:30) and who on entering the world said: "Here I am! I come, God, to do your will" (Heb 10:9; see Jn 6:38), has left us the lesson of his own prayer. The Gospels many times show us Christ at prayer: when his mission is revealed by the Father;[4] before he

3431

3432

3433

3434

---

[1]   See Acts 1:14, 4:24, 12:5 and 12. See also Eph 5:19–21.

[2]   See Acts 2:1–15.

[3]   SC art. 83 [DOL 1 no. 83].

[4]   See Lk 3:21–22.

calls the apostles;[5] when he blesses God at the multiplication of the loaves;[6] when he is transfigured on the mountain;[7] when he heals the deaf-mute;[8] when he raises Lazarus;[9] before he asks for Peter's confession of faith;[10] when he teaches the disciples how to pray;[11] when the disciples return from their mission;[12] when he blesses the little children;[13] when he prays for Peter.[14]

The work of each day was closely bound up with his prayer, indeed flowed out from it: he would retire into the desert or into the hills to pray,[15] rise very early[16] or spend the night up to the fourth watch[17] in prayer to God.[18]

We are right in thinking that he took part both in public prayers: in the synagogues, which he entered on the Sabbath "as his custom was;"[19] in the temple, which he called a house of prayer;[20] and in the private prayers that for devout Israelites were a daily practice. He used the traditional blessings of God at meals, as is expressly mentioned in connection with the multiplication of the loaves,[21] the last supper,[22] and the meal at Emmaus.[23] He also joined with the disciples in a hymn of praise.[24]

To the very end of his life, as his passion was approaching,[25] at the last supper,[26] in the agony in the garden,[27] and on the cross,[28] the divine teacher showed that prayer was the soul of his Messianic ministry and paschal death. "In the days of his life on earth he offered up prayers and entreaties with loud cries and tears to the one who could deliver him from death and because of his reverence his prayer was heard" (Heb 5:7). By a single offering on the altar of the cross "he has made

---

5   See Lk 6:12.

6   See Mt 14:19, 15:36; Mk 6:41, 8:7; Lk 9:16; Jn 6:11.

7   See Lk 9:28–29.

8   See Mk 7:34.

9   See Jn 11:41ff.

10   See Lk 9:18.

11   See Lk 11:1.

12   See Mt 11:25ff.; Lk 10:21ff.

13   See Mt 19:13.

14   See Lk 22:32.

15   See Mk 1:35, 6:46; Lk 5:16. See also Mt 4:1 and par.; Mt 14:23.

16   See Mk 1:35.

17   See Mt 14:23 and 25; Mk 6:46 and 48.

18   See Lk 6:12.

19   See Lk 4:16.

20   See Mt 21:13 and par.

21   See Mt 14:19 and par.; Mt 15:36 and par.

22   See Mt 26:26 and par.

23   See Lk 24:30.

24   See Mt 26:30 and par.

25   See Jn 12:27ff.

26   See Jn 17:1–26.

27   See Mt 26:36–44 and par.

28   See Lk 23:34 and 46; Mt 27:46; Mk 15:34.

perfect forever those who are being sanctified" (Heb 10–14). Raised from the dead, he lives for ever, making intercession for us.[29]

II. PRAYER OF THE CHURCH

COMMANDMENT TO PRAY

5.   Jesus has commanded us to do as he did. On many occasions he said: "Pray," "ask," "seek"[30] "in my name."[31] He taught us how to pray in what is known as the Lord's Prayer.[32] He taught us that prayer is necessary,[33] that it should be humble,[34] watchful,[35] persevering, confident in the Father's goodness,[36] single-minded, and in conformity with God's nature.[37]   3435

Here and there in their letters the apostles have handed on to us many prayers, particularly of praise and thanks. They instruct us on prayer in the Holy Spirit,[38] through Christ,[39] offered to God,[40] as to its persistence and constancy,[41] its power to sanctify,[42] and on prayer of praise,[43] thanks,[44] petition,[45] and intercession for all.[46]

CHRIST'S PRAYER CONTINUED BY THE CHURCH

6.   Since we are entirely dependent on God, we must acknowledge and express this sovereignty of the Creator, as the devout people of every age have done by means of prayer.   3436

Prayer directed to God must be linked with Christ, the Lord of all, the one Mediator[47] through whom alone we have access to God.[48] He unites to himself the whole human community[49] in such a way that there is an intimate bond between the prayer of Christ and the prayer of all humanity. In Christ and in Christ alone human worship of God receives its redemptive value and attains its goal.

---

29   See Heb 7:25.

30   Mt 5:44, 7:7, 26:41; Mk 13:33, 14:38; Lk 6:28, 10:2, 11:9, 22:40 and 46.

31   Jn 14:13ff., 15:16, 16:23ff. and 26.

32   See Mt 6:9–13; Lk 11:2–4.

33   See Lk 18:1.

34   See Lk 18:9–14.

35   See Lk 21:36; Mk 13:33.

36   See Lk 11:5–13, 18:1–8; Jn 14:13, 16:23.

37   See Mt 6:5–8, 23:14; Lk 20:47; Jn 4:23.

38   See Rom 8:15 and 26; 1 Cor 12:3; Gal 4:6; Jude 20.

39   See 2 Cor 1:20; Col 3:17.

40   See Heb 13:15.

41   See Rom 12:12; 1 Cor 7:5; Eph 6:18; Col 4:2; 1 Thes 5:17; 1 Tm 5:5; 1 Pt 4:7.

42   See 1 Tm 4:5; Jas 5:15ff.; 1 Jn 3:22, 5:14ff.

43   See Eph 5:19ff.; Heb 13:15; Rv 19:5.

44   See Col 3:17; Phil 4:6; 1 Thes 5:17; 1 Tm 2:1.

45   See Rom 8:26; Phil 4:6.

46   See Rom 15:30; 1 Tm 2:1 ff.; Eph 6:18; 1 Thes 5:25; Jas 5: 14 and 16.

47   See 1 Tm 2:5; Heb 8:6, 9:15, 12:24.

48   See Rom 5:2; Eph 2:18, 3:12.

49   See SC art. 83 [DOL 1 no. 83].

3437   7.   There is a special and very close bond between Christ and those whom he makes members of his Body, the Church, through the sacrament of rebirth. Thus, from the Head all the riches belonging to the Son flow throughout the whole Body: the communication of the Spirit, the truth, the life, and the participation in the divine sonship that Christ manifested in all his prayer when he dwelt among us.

Christ's priesthood is also shared by the whole Body of the Church, so that the baptized are consecrated as a spiritual temple and holy priesthood through the rebirth of baptism and the anointing by the Holy Spirit[50] and are empowered to offer the worship of the New Covenant, a worship that derives not from our own powers but from Christ's merit and gift.

"God could give us no greater gift than to establish as our Head the Word through whom he created all things and to unite us to that Head as members. The results are many. The Head is Son of God and Son of Man, one as God with the Father and one as man with us. When we speak in prayer to the Father, we do not separate the Son from him and when the Son's Body prays it does not separate itself from its Head. It is the one Savior of his Body, the Lord Christ Jesus, who prays for us and in us and who is prayed to by us. He prays for us as our priest, in us as our Head; he is prayed to by us as our God. Recognize therefore our own voice in him and his voice in us."[51]

The excellence of Christian prayer lies in its sharing in the reverent love of the only-begotten Son for the Father and in the prayer that the Son put into words in his earthly life and that still continues without ceasing in the name of the whole human race and for its salvation, throughout the universal Church and in all its members.

ACTION OF THE HOLY SPIRIT

3438   8.   The unity of the Church at prayer is brought about by the Holy Spirit, who is the same in Christ,[52] in the whole Church, and in every baptized person. It is this Spirit who "helps us in our weakness" and "intercedes for us with longings too deep for words" (Rom 8:26). As the Spirit of the Son, he gives us "the spirit of adopted children, by which we cry out: Abba, Father" (Rom 8:15; see Gal 4:6; 1 Cor 12:3; Eph 5:18; Jude 20). There can be therefore no Christian prayer without the action of the Holy Spirit, who unites the whole Church and leads it through the Son to the Father.

COMMUNITY CHARACTER OF PRAYER

3439   9.   It follows that the example and precept of our Lord and the apostles in regard to constant and persevering prayer are not to be seen as a purely legal regulation. They belong to the very essence of the Church itself, which is a community and which in prayer must express its nature as a community. Hence, when the community of believers is first mentioned in the Acts of the Apostles, it is seen as a community gathered together at prayer "with the women and Mary, the mother of Jesus, and his brothers" (Acts 1:14). "There was one heart and soul in the company of those who believed" (Acts 4:32). Their oneness in spirit was founded on the word of God, on the communion of charity, on prayer, and on the eucharist.[53]

---

[50]   See LG no. 10 [DOL 4 no. 140].

[51]   Augustine, *Enarrat. in Ps. 85*, 1: CCL 39, 1176.

[52]   See Lk 10:21, the occasion when Jesus "rejoiced in the Holy Spirit and said: 'I thank you, Father . . . .'"

[53]   See Acts 2:42 Gr.

Though prayer in private and in seclusion[54] is always necessary and to be encouraged[55] and is practiced by the members of the Church through Christ in the Holy Spirit, there is a special excellence in the prayer of the community. Christ himself has said: "Where two or three are gathered together in my name, I am there in their midst" (Mt 18:20).

III. LITURGY OF THE HOURS

CONSECRATION OF TIME

10. Christ taught us: "You must pray at all times and not lose heart" (Lk 18:1). The Church has been faithful in obeying this instruction; it never ceases to offer prayer and makes this exhortation its own: "Through him (Jesus) let us offer to God an unceasing sacrifice of praise" (Heb 15:15). The Church fulfills this precept not only by celebrating the eucharist but in other ways also, especially through the liturgy of the hours. By ancient Christian tradition what distinguishes the liturgy of the hours from other liturgical services is that it consecrates to God the whole cycle of the day and the night.[56]   3440

11. The purpose of the liturgy of the hours is to sanctify the day and the whole range of human activity. Therefore its structure has been revised in such a way as to make each hour once more correspond as nearly as possible to natural time and to take account of the circumstances of life today.[57]   3441

Hence, "that the day may be truly sanctified and the hours themselves recited with spiritual advantage, it is best that each of them be prayed at a time most closely corresponding to the true time of each canonical hour."[58]

LITURGY OF THE HOURS AND THE EUCHARIST

12. To the different hours of the day the liturgy of the hours extends[59] the praise and thanksgiving, the memorial of the mysteries of salvation, the petitions and the foretaste of heavenly glory that are present in the eucharistic mystery, "the center and high point in the whole life of the Christian community."[60]   3442

The liturgy of the hours is in turn an excellent preparation for the celebration of the eucharist itself, for it inspires and deepens in a fitting way the dispositions necessary for the fruitful celebration of the eucharist: faith, hope, love, devotion, and the spirit of self-denial.

PRIESTHOOD OF CHRIST IN THE LITURGY OF THE HOURS

13. In the Holy Spirit Christ carries out through the Church "the task of redeeming humanity and giving perfect glory to God,"[61] not only when the eucharist is celebrated and the sacraments administered but also in other ways and especially when the liturgy of the hours is celebrated.[62] There Christ himself is present — in   3443

---

54 See Mt 6:6.

55 See SC art. 12 [DOL 1 no. 12].

56 See SC art. 83–84 [DOL 1 nos. 83–84].

57 See SC art. 88 [DOL 1 no. 88].

58 SC art. 94 [DOL 1 no. 94].

59 See PO no. 5 [DOL 18 no. 260].

60 CD no. 30 [DOL 7 no. 196].

61 SC art. 5 [DOL 1 no. 5].

62 See SC art. 83 and 98 [DOL 1 nos. 83 and 98].

the gathered community, in the proclamation of God's word, "in the prayer and song of the Church."[63]

SANCTIFICATION OF GOD'S PEOPLE

3444   14. Our sanctification is accomplished[64] and worship is offered to God in the liturgy of the hours in such a way that an exchange or dialogue is set up between God and us, in which "God is speaking to his people . . . and his people are responding to him by both song and prayer."[65]

Those taking part in the liturgy of the hours have access to holiness of the richest kind through the life-giving word of God, which in this liturgy receives great emphasis. Thus its readings are drawn from sacred Scripture, God's words in the psalms are sung in his presence, and the intercessions, prayers, and hymns are inspired by Scripture and steeped in its spirit.[66]

Hence, not only when those things are read "that are written for our instruction" (Rom 15:4), but also when the Church prays or sings, faith is deepened for those who take part and their minds are lifted up to God, in order to offer him their worship as intelligent beings and to receive his grace more plentifully.[67]

PRAISING GOD WITH THE CHURCH IN HEAVEN

3445   15. In the liturgy of the hours the Church exercises the priestly office of its Head and offers to God "without ceasing"[68] a sacrifice of praise, that is, a tribute of lips acknowledging his name.[69] This prayer is "the voice of a bride addressing her bridegroom; it is the very prayer that Christ himself, together with his Body, addresses to the Father."[70] "All who render this service are not only fulfilling a duty of the Church, but also are sharing in the greatest honor of Christ's Bride for by offering these praises to God they are standing before God's throne in the name of the Church, their Mother."[71]

3446   16. When the Church offers praise to God in the liturgy of the hours, it unites itself with that hymn of praise sung throughout all ages in the halls of heaven;[72] it also receives a foretaste of the song of praise in heaven, described by John in the Book of Revelation, the song sung continually before the throne of God and of the Lamb. Our close union with the Church in heaven is given effective voice "when we all, from every tribe and tongue and people and nation redeemed by Christ's blood (see Rv 5:9) and gathered together into the one Church, glorify the triune God with one hymn of praise."[73]

The prophets came almost to a vision of this liturgy of heaven as the victory of a day without night, of a light without darkness: "The sun will no more be your light by day, and the brightness of the moon will not shine upon you, but the Lord will be your everlasting light" (Is 60:19; see Rv 21:23 and 25). "There will be a single

---

63   SC art. 7 [DOL 1 no. 7].

64   See SC art. 10 [DOL 1 no. 10].

65   SC art. 33 [DOL 1 no. 33].

66   See SC art. 24 [DOL 1 no. 24].

67   See SC art. 33 [DOL 1 no. 33].

68   1 Thes 5:17.

69   See Heb 13:15.

70   SC art. 84 [DOL 1 no. 84].

71   SC art. 85 [DOL 1 no. 85].

72   See SC art. 83 [DOL 1 no. 83].

73   LG no. 50 [DOL 4 no. 158]; SC art. 8 and 104 [DOL 1 nos. 8 and 104].

day, known to the Lord, not day and night, and at evening there will be light" (Zech 14:7). Already "the end of the ages has come upon us (see 1 Cor 10:11) and the renewal of the world has been irrevocably established and in a true sense is being anticipated in this world."[74] By faith we too are taught the meaning of our temporal life, so that we look forward with all creation to the revealing of God's children.[75] In the liturgy of the hours we proclaim this faith, we express and nourish this hope, we share in some degree the joy of everlasting praise and of that day that knows no setting.

PETITION AND INTERCESSION

17. But besides the praise of God, the Church in the liturgy of the hours expresses   3447
the prayers and desires of all the faithful; indeed, it prays to Christ, and through him to the Father, for the salvation of the whole world.[76] The Church's voice is not just its own; it is also Christ's voice, since its prayers are offered in Christ's name, that is, "through our Lord Jesus Christ," and so the Church continues to offer the prayer and petition that Christ poured out in the days of his earthly life[77] and that have therefore a unique effectiveness. The ecclesial community thus exercises a truly maternal function in bringing souls to Christ, not only by charity, good example, and works of penance but also by prayer.[78]

The concern with prayer involves those especially who have been called by a special mandate to carry out the liturgy of the hours: bishops and priests as they pray in virtue of their office for their own people and for the whole people of God;[79] other sacred ministers, and also religious.[80]

18. Those then who take part in the liturgy of the hours bring growth to God's   3448
people in a hidden but fruitful apostolate,[81] for the work of the apostolate is directed to this end, "that all who are made children of God by faith and baptism should come together to praise God in the midst of this Church, to take part in the sacrifice, and to eat the Lord's Supper."[82]

Thus by their lives the faithful show forth and reveal to others "the mystery of Christ and the real nature of the true Church. It is of the essence of the Church to be visible yet endowed with invisible resources, eager to act yet intent on contemplation, present in this world yet not at home in it."[83]

In their turn the readings and prayers of the liturgy of the hours form a wellspring of the Christian life: the table of sacred Scripture and the writings of the saints nurture its life and prayers strengthen it. Only the Lord, without whom we can do nothing,[84] can, in response to our request, give power and increase to what

---

[74] LG no. 48.

[75] See Rom 8:19.

[76] See SC art. 83 [DOL 1 no. 83].

[77] See Heb 5:7.

[78] See PO no. 6 [DOL 18 no. 261].

[79] See LG no. 41.

[80] See no. 24 of this Instruction.

[81] See PC no. 7 [DOL 10 no. 205].

[82] SC art. 10 [DOL 1 no. 10].

[83] SC art. 2 [DOL 1 no. 2].

[84] See Jn 15:5.

we do,[85] so that we may be built up each day in the Spirit into the temple of God,[86] to the measure of Christ's fullness,[87] and receive greater strength also to bring the good news of Christ to those outside.[88]

HARMONY OF MIND AND VOICE

3449   19. Mind and voice must be in harmony in a celebration that is worthy, attentive, and devout, if this prayer is to be made their own by those taking part and to be a source of devotion, a means of gaining God's manifold grace, a deepening of personal prayer, and an incentive to the work of the apostolate.[89] All should be intent on cooperating with God's grace, so as not to receive it in vain. Seeking Christ, penetrating ever more deeply into his mystery through prayer[90] they should offer praise and petition to God with the same mind and heart as the divine Redeemer when he prayed.[R1]

IV. PARTICIPANTS IN THE LITURGY OF THE HOURS

A. CELEBRATION IN COMMON

3450   20. The liturgy of the hours, like other liturgical services, is not a private matter but belongs to the whole Body of the Church, whose life it both expresses and affects.[91] This liturgy stands out most strikingly as an ecclesial celebration when, through the bishop surrounded by his priests and ministers,[92] the local Church celebrates it. For "in the local Church the one, holy, catholic, and apostolic Church is truly present and at work."[93] Such a celebration is therefore most earnestly recommended. When, in the absence of the bishop, a chapter of canons or other priests celebrate the liturgy of the hours, they should always respect the true time

---

[85]   See SC art. 86 [DOL 1 no. 86].

[86]   See Eph 2:21–22.

[87]   See Eph 4:13.

[88]   See SC art. 2 [DOL 1 no. 2].

[89]   See SC art. 90 [DOL 1 no. 90]. *Rule of St. Benedict* ch. 19.

[90]   See PO no. 14 [DOL 18 no. 266]; OT no. 8 [DOL 12 no. 213].

[R1]   Query: When a person recites the liturgy of the hours, do the readings have to be pronounced or simply read? Reply: *It is enough simply to read them.* The conciliar Constitution on the Liturgy says nothing about an obligation to oral recitation when a person says the office alone, although there was a difference of opinion on this among the conciliar Fathers. They decreed a reform of the breviary not for the purpose of shortening the time for prayer but of giving all who celebrate the liturgy of the hours a better time for prayer. Accordingly, all the documents treating of the reform of the divine office urge that "the mind be attuned to the voice" and that "the prayer of the Church be a source of devotion and nourishment also for personal prayer" (SC art. 90 [DOL 1 no. 90]). This calls for the reading of Scripture and the Fathers as well as the recitation of the psalms, in which God is speaking to his people and they are responding (see SC art. 33 [DOL 1 no. 33]), to consist "not in a cursory reading of a breviary" (see Schema of SC, *Modi a Patribus Conciliaribus propositi, a Commissione de sacra Liturgia examinati* vol. 4, *De Officio Divino*, 13) but in personal meditation. Otherwise even if there is a recitation of the hours, there is no penetration by the word of God nor true prayer. The true course is "that as we celebrate the office, we must recognize our own voices echoing in Christ, his voice echoing in us" (Paul VI, Ap. Const. *Laudis canticum* [DOL 424 no. 3426]). This is the way for the liturgy of the hours to be a personal prayer, sincere and effective, a source of devotion, the sustenance of the spiritual life and of each day's apostolic labors. Then the relationship between the Church's prayer and personal prayer is strengthened and mental prayer has an unfailing source in the readings, the psalms, and other parts of the liturgy of the hours (see ibid. [DOL 424 no. 3427]). Sometimes a surer guarantee for this objective of the liturgy of the hours in individual recitation may be to omit the oral recitation of each word, especially in the case of the readings: Not 9 (1973) 150.

[91]   See SC art. 26 [DOL 1 no. 26].

[92]   See SC art. 41 [DOL 1 no. 41].

[93]   CD no. 11 [DOL 7 no. 191].

of day and, as far as possible, the people should take part. The same is to be said of collegiate chapters.

21. Wherever possible, other groups of the faithful should celebrate the liturgy of the hours communally in church. This especially applies to parishes — the cells of the diocese, established under their pastors, taking the place of the bishop; they "represent in some degree the visible Church established throughout the world."[94]

3451

22. Hence, when the people are invited to the liturgy of the hours and come together in unity of heart and voice, they show forth the Church in its celebration of the mystery of Christ.[95]

3452

23. Those in holy orders or with a special canonical mission[96] have the responsibility of initiating and directing the prayer of the community; "they should expend every effort so that those entrusted to their care may become of one mind in prayer."[97] They must therefore see to it that the people are invited, and prepared by suitable instruction, to celebrate the principal hours in common, especially on Sundays and holydays.[98] They should teach the people how to make this participation a source of genuine prayer;[99] they should therefore give the people suitable guidance in the Christian understanding of the psalms, in order to progress by degrees to a greater appreciation and more frequent use of the prayer of the Church.[100]

3453

24. Communities of canons, monks, nuns, and other religious who celebrate the liturgy of the hours by rule or according to their constitutions, whether with the general rite or a particular rite, in whole or in part, represent in a special way the Church at prayer. They are a fuller sign of the Church as it continuously praises God with one voice and they fulfill the duty of "working," above all by prayer, "to build up and increase the whole Mystical Body of Christ, and for the good of the local Churches."[101] This is especially true of those living the contemplative life.

3454

25. Even when having no obligation to communal celebration, all sacred ministers and all clerics living in a community or meeting together should arrange to say at least some part of the liturgy of the hours in common, particularly morning prayer and evening prayer.[102]

3455

26. Men and women religious not bound to a common celebration, as well as members of any institute of perfection, are strongly urged to gather together, by themselves or with the people, to celebrate the liturgy of the hours or part of it.

3456

---

[94] See art. 42 [DOL 1 no. 42]. See also AA no. 10 [DOL 16 no. 236].

[95] See SC art. 26 and 84 [DOL 1 nos. 26 and 84].

[96] See AG no. 17.

[97] CD no. 15 [DOL 7 no. 194].

[98] See SC art. 100 [DOL 1 no. 100].

[99] See PO no. 5 [DOL 18 no. 260].

[100] See nos. 100–109 of this Instruction.

[101] CD no. 33; see also PC nos. 6, 7, 15 [DOL 10 nos. 204, 205, 209]; AG no. 15 [DOL 17 no. 247].

[102] See SC art. 99 [DOL 1 no. 99].

3457 27. Lay groups gathering for prayer, apostolic work, or any other reason are encouraged to fulfill the Church's duty[103] by celebrating part of the liturgy of the hours. The laity must learn above all how in the liturgy they are adoring God the Father in spirit and in truth;[104] they should bear in mind that through public worship and prayer they reach all humanity and can contribute significantly to the salvation of the whole world.[105]

Finally, it is of great advantage for the family, the domestic sanctuary of the Church, not only to pray together to God but also to celebrate some parts of the liturgy of the hours as occasion offers, in order to enter more deeply into the life of the Church.[106]

B. Mandate to Celebrate the Liturgy of the Hours

3458 28. Sacted ministers have the liturgy of the hours entrusted to them in such a particular way that even when the faithful are not present they are to pray it themselves with the adaptations necessary under these circumstances. The Church commissions them to celebrate the liturgy of the hours so as to ensure at least in their persons the regular carrying out of the duty of the whole community and the unceasing continuance of Christ's prayer in the Church.[107]

The bishop represents Christ in an eminent and conspicuous way and is the high priest of his flock; the life in Christ of his faithful people may be said in a sense to derive from him and depend on him.[108] He should, then, be the first of all the members of his Church in offering prayer. His prayer in the recitation of the liturgy of the hours is always made in the name of the Church and on behalf of the Church entrusted to him.[109]

United as they are with the bishop and the whole presbyterium, priests are themselves representative in a special way of Christ the Priest[110] and so share the same responsibility of praying to God for the people entrusted to them and indeed for the whole world.[111]

All these ministers fulfill the ministry of the Good Shepherd who prays for his sheep that they may have life and so be brought into perfect unity.[112] In the liturgy of the hours that the Church sets before them they are not only to find a source of devotion and a strengthening of personal prayer,[113] but must also nourish and foster pastoral missionary activity as the fruit of their contemplation to gladden the whole Church of God.[114]

3459 29. Hence bishops, priests, and other sacred ministers, who have received from the Church the mandate to celebrate the liturgy of the hours (see no. 17), should recite

---

[103] See SC art. 100 [DOL 1 no. 100].

[104] See Jn 4:23.

[105] See GE no. 2 [DOL 13 no. 216]; AA no. 16 [DOL 16 no. 238].

[106] See AA no. 11 [DOL 16 no. 237].

[107] See PO no. 13 [DOL 18 no. 265].

[108] See SC art. 41 [DOL 1 no. 41]; LG no. 21 [DOL 4 no. 145].

[109] See LG no. 26 [DOL 4 no. 146]; CD no. 15 [DOL 7 no. 194].

[110] See PO no. 13 [DOL 18 no. 265].

[111] See PO no. 5 [DOL 18 no. 260].

[112] See Jn 10:11, 17:20 and 23.

[113] See SC art. 90 [DOL 1 no. 90].

[114] See LG no. 41.

the full sequence of hours each day, observing as far as possible the true time of day.

They should, first and foremost, attach due importance to those hours that are, so to speak, the two hinges of the liturgy of the hours, that is, morning prayer and evening prayer,[a] which should not be omitted except for a serious reason.

They should faithfully pray the office of readings, which is above all a liturgical celebration of the word of God. In this way they fulfill daily a duty that is peculiarly their own, that is, of receiving the word of God into their lives, so that they may become more perfect as disciples of the Lord and experience more deeply the unfathomable riches of Christ.[115]

In order to sanctify the whole day more completely, they will also treasure the recitation of daytime prayer and night prayer, to round off the whole *Opus Dei* and to commend themselves to God before retiring.

30. It is most fitting that permanent deacons recite daily at least some part of the liturgy of the hours, to be determined by the conference of bishops.[116]   3460

31. a. Cathedral and collegiate chapters should celebrate in choir those parts of the liturgy of the hours that are prescribed for them by the general law or by particular law.   3461

In private recitation individual members of these chapters should include those hours that are recited in their chapter,[R2] in addition to the hours prescribed for all sacred ministers.[117]

b. Religious communities bound to the recitation of the liturgy of the hours and their individual members should celebrate the hours in keeping with their own particular law; but the prescription of no. 29 in regard to those in holy orders is to be respected.

Communities bound to choir should celebrate the whole sequence of the hours daily in choir;[118] when absent from choir their members should recite the hours in keeping with their own particular law; but the prescriptions in no. 29 are always to be respected.

32. Other religious communities and their individual members are advised to celebrate some parts of the liturgy of the hours, in accordance with their own situation, for it is the prayer of the Church and makes the whole Church, scattered throughout the world, one in heart and mind.[119]   3462

---

[a]   See DOL 1 no. 89.

[115]   See DV no. 25 [DOL 14 no. 227]; PO no. 13 [DOL 18 no. 265].

[116]   See Paul VI, Motu Proprio *Sacrum Diaconatus Ordinem*, 18 June 1967, no. 27 [DOL 309 no. 2541].

[R2]   Query: What should the arrangement be in celebrating the liturgy of the hours in cathedral chapters? Reply: The GILH nos. 76 and 31 regulate the celebration of the liturgy of the hours in chapters of canons: "[Text quoted, nos. 76 and 31]." Particular law is to determine in detail which hours must be celebrated by the chapter; the individual members who are absent from the capitular celebration must recite such hours privately. The greatest care is to be taken to celebrate the hours at the corresponding natural time of day, with solemnity and the participation of the people. There is to be no combining of more than one hour at the same celebration. Now that the GILH has been published, it is required that the practice of chapters be made to conform to it. If necessary there is to be a revision of the capitular statutes and approval by the authority competent to give it. The aim is that the service to the liturgy rendered by the chapter reflect the documents of the liturgical reform: Not 8 (1972) 192.

[117]   See SCR, Instr. InterOec no. 78 b [DOL 23 no. 370].

[118]   See SC art. 95 [DOL 1 no. 95].

[119]   See Acts 4:32.

This recommendation applies also to laypersons.[120]

C. STRUCTURE OF THE CELEBRATION

3463   33. The structure of the liturgy of the hours follows laws of its own and incorporates in its own way elements found in other Christian celebrations. Thus it is so constructed that, after a hymn, there is always psalmody, then a long or short reading of sacred Scripture, and finally prayer of petition.

In a celebration in common and in private recitation the essential structure of this liturgy remains the same, that is, it is a conversation between God and his people. Celebration in common, however, expresses more clearly the ecclesial nature of the liturgy of the hours; it makes for active participation by all, in a way suited to each one's condition, through the acclamations, dialogue, alternating psalmody, and similar elements. It also better provides for the different literary genres that make up the liturgy of the hours.[121] Hence, whenever it is possible to have a celebration in common, with the people present and actively taking part, this kind of celebration is to be preferred to one that is individual and, as it were, private.[122] It is also advantageous to sing the office in choir and in community as opportunity offers, in accordance with the nature and function of the individual parts.

In this way the Apostle's exhortation is obeyed: "Let the word of Christ dwell in you in all its fullness, as you teach and counsel each other in all wisdom by psalms, hymns, and spiritual canticles, singing thankfully to God in your hearts" (Col 3:16; see Eph 5:19–20).

CHAPTER II
SANCTIFICATION OF THE DAY: THE DIFFERENT LITURGICAL HOURS

I. INTRODUCTION TO THE WHOLE OFFICE

3464   34. The whole office begins as a rule with an invitatory. This consists in the verse, *Lord, open my lips. And my mouth will proclaim your praise*, and Ps 95. This psalm invites the faithful each day to sing God's praise and to listen to his voice and draws them to hope for "the Lord's rest."[1]

In place of Ps 95, Ps 100, Ps 67, or Ps 24 may be used as circumstances may suggest.

It is preferable to recite the invitatory psalm responsorially as it is set out in the text, that is, with the antiphon recited at the beginning, then repeated, and repeated again after each strophe.

3465   35. The invitatory is placed at the beginning of the whole sequence of the day's prayer, that is, it precedes either morning prayer or the office of readings, whichever of these liturgical rites begins the day. The invitatory psalm with its antiphon may be omitted, however, when the invitatory is the prelude to morning prayer.

3466   36. The variation of the invitatory antiphon, to suit the different liturgical days, is indicated at its place of occurrence.

---

[120]   See SC art. 100 [DOL 1 no. 100].

[121]   See SC art. 26, 28–30 [DOL 1 nos. 26, 28–30].

[122]   See SC art. 27 [DOL 1 no. 27].

[1]   See Heb 3:7 - 4:16.

II. MORNING PRAYER AND EVENING PRAYER

37. "By the venerable tradition of the universal Church, lauds as morning prayer   3467
and vespers as evening prayer are the two hinges on which the daily office turns;
hence they are to be considered as the chief hours and celebrated as such."[2]

38. As is clear from many of the elements that make it up, morning prayer is   3468
intended and arranged to sanctify the morning. St. Basil the Great gives an excellent
description of this character in these words: "It is said in the morning in order that
the first stirrings of our mind and will may be consecrated to God and that we may
take nothing in hand until we have been gladdened by the thought of God, as it is
written: 'I was mindful of God and was glad' (Ps 77:4 [Jerome's translation from
Hebrew]), or set our bodies to any task before we do what has been said: 'I will pray
to you, Lord, you will hear my voice in the morning; I will stand before you in the
morning and gaze on you' (Ps 5:4–5)."[3]

Celebrated as it is as the light of a new day is dawning, this hour also recalls
the resurrection of the Lord Jesus, the true light enlightening all people (see Jn 1:9)
and "the sun of justice" (Mal 4:2), "rising from on high" (Lk 1:78). Hence, we can
well understand the advice of St. Cyprian: "There should be prayer in the morning
so that the resurrection of the Lord may thus be celebrated."[4]

39. When evening approaches and the day is already far spent, evening prayer is   3469
celebrated in order that "we may give thanks for what has been given us, or what
we have done well, during the day."[5] We also recall the redemption through the
prayer we send up "like incense in the Lord's sight," and in which "the raising up of
our hands" becomes "an evening sacrifice."[6] This sacrifice "may also be interpreted
more spiritually as the true evening sacrifice that our Savior the Lord entrusted to
the apostles at supper on the evening when he instituted the sacred mysteries of the
Church or of the evening sacrifice of the next day, the sacrifice, that is, which,
raising his hands, he offered to the Father at the end of the ages for the salvation of
the whole world."[7] Again, in order to fix our hope on the light that knows no
setting, "we pray and make petition for the light to come down on us anew; we
implore the coming of Christ who will bring the grace of eternal light."[8] Finally, at
this hour we join with the Churches of the East in calling upon the "joy-giving
light of that holy glory, born of the immortal, heavenly Father, the holy and blessed
Jesus Christ; now that we have come to the setting of the sun and have seen the
evening star, we sing in praise of God, Father, Son, and Holy Spirit. . . ."

40. Morning prayer and evening prayer are therefore to be accorded the highest   3470
importance as the prayer of the Christian community. Their public or communal
celebration should be encouraged, especially in the case of those who live in community. Indeed, the recitation of these hours should be recommended also to individual members of the faithful unable to take part in a celebration in common.

---

[2] SC art. 89 a [DOL 1 no. 89]; see also art. 100 [DOL 1 no. 100].

[3] Basil the Great, *Regulae fusius tractatae* resp. 37, 3: PG 31, 1014.

[4] Cyprian, *De oratione dominica* 35: PL 4, 561.

[5] Basil the Great, *Regulae fusius tractatae* resp. 37, 3: PG 31, 1015.

[6] See Ps 141:2.

[7] John Cassian, *De institutione coenob.* 3, 3: PL 49, 124, 125.

[8] Cyprian, *De oratione dominica* 35: PL 4, 560.

3471   41. Morning prayer and evening prayer begin with the introductory verse, *God, come to my assistance. Lord, make haste to help me.* There follows the *Glory to the Father,* with *As it was in the beginning* and *Alleluia* (omitted in Lent). This introduction is omitted at morning prayer when the invitatory immediately precedes it.

3472   42. Then an appropriate hymn is sung immediately. The purpose of the hymn is to set the tone for the hour or the feast and, especially in celebrations with a congregation, to form a simple and pleasant introduction to prayer.

3473   43. After the hymn the psalmody follows, in accordance with the rules laid down in nos. 121–125. The psalmody of morning prayer consists of one morning psalm, then a canticle from the Old Testament and, finally, a second psalm of praise, following the tradition of the Church.

      The psalmody of evening prayer consists of two psalms (or two parts of a longer psalm) suited to the hour and to celebration with a congregation and a canticle from the letters of the apostles or from the Book of Revelation.

3474   44. After the psalmody there is either a short reading or a longer one.

3475   45. The short reading is provided to fit the day, the season, and the feast. It is to be read and received as a true proclamation of God's word that emphasizes some holy thought or highlights some shorter passages that may be overlooked in the continuous cycle of Scripture readings.

      The short readings are different for each day of the psalter cycle.

3476   46. Especially in a celebration with a congregation, a longer Scripture reading may be chosen either from the office of readings or the Lectionary for Mass, particularly texts that for some reason have not been used. From time to time some other more suitable reading may be used, in accordance with the rules in nos. 248–249 and 251.

3477   47. In a celebration with a congregation a short homily may follow the reading to explain its meaning, as circumstances suggest.

3478   48. After the reading or homily a period of silence may be observed.

3479   49. As a response to the word of God, a responsorial chant or short responsory is provided; this may be omitted. Other chants with the same purpose and character may also be substituted in its place, provided these have been duly approved by the conference of bishops.

3480   50. Next is the solemn recitation of the gospel canticle with its antiphon, that is, the Canticle of Zechariah at morning prayer and the Canticle of Mary at evening prayer. Sanctioned by age-old popular usage in the Roman Church, these canticles are expressions of praise and thanksgiving for our redemption. The antiphon for each canticle is indicated, according to the character of the day, the season, or the feast.

3481   51. After the canticle, at morning prayer come the petitions for the consecration of the day and its work to God and at evening prayer, the intercessions (see nos. 179–193).

3482   52. After the petitions or intercessions the Lord's Prayer is said by all.

53. Immediately after the Lord's Prayer there follows the concluding prayer, which   3483
for weekdays in Ordinary Time is found in the psalter and for other days in the
proper.

54. Then, if a priest or deacon is presiding, he dismisses the congregation with the   3484
greeting, *The Lord be with you*, and the blessing as at Mass. He adds the invitation, *Go
in peace*. R. *Thanks be to God*. In the absence of a priest or deacon the celebration
concludes with *May the Lord bless us*, etc.

III. OFFICE OF READINGS

55. The office of readings seeks to provide God's people, and in particular those   3485
consecrated to God in a special way, with a wider selection of passages from sacred
Scripture for meditation, together with the finest excerpts from spiritual writers.
Even though the cycle of scriptural readings at daily Mass is now richer, the treasures of revelation and tradition to be found in the office of readings will also
contribute greatly to the spiritual life. Bishops and priests in particular should prize
these treasures, so that they may hand on to others the word of God they have
themselves received and make their teaching "the true nourishment for the people
of God."[9]

56. But prayer should accompany "the reading of sacred Scripture so that there   3486
may be a conversation between God and his people: 'we talk with God when we
pray, we listen to him when we read God's words.'"[10] For this reason the office of
readings consists also of psalms, a hymn, a prayer, and other texts, giving it the
character of true prayer.

57. The Constitution on the Liturgy directs that the office of readings, "though it   3487
should retain its character as a night office of praise when celebrated in choir, shall
be adapted so that it may be recited at any hour of the day; it shall be made up of
fewer psalms and longer readings."[11]

58. Those who are obliged by their own particular law and others who commend-   3488
ably wish to retain the character of this office as a night office of praise (either by
saying it at night or very early in the morning and before morning prayer), during
Ordinary Time choose the hymn from the selection given for this purpose. Moreover, for Sundays, solemnities, and certain feasts what is said in nos. 70–73 about
vigils must be kept in mind.

59. Without prejudice to the regulations just given, the office of readings may be   3489
recited at any hour of the day, even during the night hours of the previous day, after
evening prayer has been said.

60. If the office of readings is said before morning prayer, the invitatory precedes   3490
it, as noted (nos. 34–36). Otherwise it begins with the verse, *God, come to my assistance*
with the *Glory to the Father, As it was in the beginning*, and the *Alleluia* (omitted in Lent).

61. Then the hymn is sung. In Ordinary Time this is taken either from the night   3491
selections, as already indicated (nos. 34–36), or from the morning selections, depending on what the true time of day requires.

---

⁹   RP, Ordination of Priests no. 14.

¹⁰   Ambrose, *De officiis ministrorum* 1, 20, 88: PL 16, 50. See also DV no. 25 [DOL 14 no. 227].

¹¹   SC art. 89 c [DOL 1 no. 89].

3492   62. The psalmody follows and consists of three psalms (or parts in the case of longer psalms). During the Easter triduum, on days within the octaves of Easter and Christmas, on solemnities and feasts, the psalms are proper, with their proper antiphons.

         On Sundays and weekdays, however, the psalms and their antiphons are taken from the current week and day of the psalter. On memorials of the saints they are similarly taken from the current week and day of the psalter, unless there are proper psalms or antiphons (see nos. 218ff.).

3493   63. Between the psalmody and the readings there is, as a rule, a verse, marking a transition in the prayer from psalmody to listening.

3494   64. There are two readings: the first is from the Scriptures, the second is from the writings of the Fathers or church writers, or else is a reading connected with the saints.

3495   65. After each reading there is a responsory (see nos. 169–172).

3496   66. The scriptural reading is normally to be taken from the Proper of Seasons, in accordance with the rules to be given later (nos. 140–155). On solemnities and feasts, however, it is taken from the proper or the common.

3497   67. On solemnities and feasts of saints a proper second reading is used; if there is none, the second reading is taken from the respective Common of Saints. On memorials of saints when the celebration is not impeded, the reading in connection with the saint replaces the current second reading (see nos. 166 and 235).

3498   68. On Sundays outside Lent, on days within the octaves of Easter and Christmas, and on solemnities and feasts the *Te Deum* is said after the second reading with its responsory but is omitted on memorials and weekdays. The last part of this hymn, that is, from the verse, *Save your people, Lord* to the end, may be omitted.

3499   69. The office of readings normally concludes with the prayer proper to the day and, at least in recitation in common, with the acclamation, *Let us praise the Lord.* R. *And give him thanks.*

IV. VIGILS

3500   70. The Easter Vigil is celebrated by the whole Church, in the rites given in the relevant liturgical books. "The vigil of this night," as St. Augustine said, "is of such importance that it could claim exclusively for itself the name 'vigil,' common though this is to all the others."[12] "We keep vigil on that night when the Lord rose again and inaugurated for us in his humanity that life . . . in which there is neither death nor sleep. . . . Hence, the one whose resurrection we celebrate by keeping watch a little longer will see to it that we reign with him by living a life without end."[13]

3501   71. As with the Easter Vigil, it was customary to begin certain solemnities (different in different Churches) with a vigil. Among these solemnities Christmas and Pentecost are preeminent. This custom should be maintained and fostered, according to the particular usage of each Church. Whenever it seems good to add a

---

[12]   Augustine, *Sermo Guelferbytanus* 5: PL Suppl 2, 550.

[13]   Ibid.: PL Suppl 2, 552.

vigil for other solemnities or pilgrimages, the general norms for celebrations of the word should be followed.

72. The Fathers and spiritual writers have frequently encouraged Christians, espe-   3502
cially those who lead the contemplative life, to pray during the night. Such prayer expresses and awakens our expectation of the Lord's Second Coming: "At midnight the cry went up: 'See, the bridegroom is coming, go out to meet him'" (Mt 25:6). "Keep watch, then, for you do not know when the master of the house is coming, whether late or at midnight or at cockcrow or in the morning, so that if he comes unexpectedly he may not find you sleeping" (Mk 13:35–36). All who maintain the character of the office of readings as a night office, therefore, are to be commended.

73. Further, since in the Roman Rite the office of readings is always of a uniform   3503
brevity, especially for the sake of those engaged in apostolic work, those who desire, in accordance with tradition, to extend the celebration of the vigils of Sundays, solemnities, and feasts should do so as follows.

First, the office of readings is to be celebrated as in *The Liturgy of the Hours* up to the end of the readings. After the two readings and before the *Te Deum* canticles should be added from the special appendix of *The Liturgy of the Hours*. Then the gospel should be read; a homily on the gospel may be added. After this the *Te Deum* is sung and the prayer said.

On solemnities and feasts the gospel is to be taken from the Lectionary for Mass; on Sundays, from the series on the paschal mystery in the appendix of *The Liturgy of the Hours*.

V. DAYTIME HOURS

74. Following a very ancient tradition Christians have made a practice of praying   3504
out of private devotion at various times of the day, even in the course of their work, in imitation of the Church in apostolic times. In different ways with the passage of time this tradition has taken the form of a liturgical celebration.

75. Liturgical custom in both East and West has retained midmorning, midday, and   3505
midafternoon prayer, mainly because these hours were linked to a commemoration of the events of the Lord's passion and of the first preaching of the Gospel.

76. Vatican Council II decreed that these lesser hours are to be retained in   3506
choir.[14,R3]

The liturgical practice of saying these three hours is to be retained, without prejudice to particular law, by those who live the contemplative life. It is recommended also for all, especially those who take part in retreats or pastoral meetings.

77. Outside choir, without prejudice to particular law, it is permitted to choose   3507
from the three hours the one most appropriate to the time of day, so that the tradition of prayer in the course of the day's work may be maintained.

78. Daytime prayer is so arranged as to take into account both those who recite   3508
only one hour and those who are obliged, or desire, to say all three hours.

79. The daytime hours begin with the introductory verse, *God come to my assistance*   3509
with the *Glory to the Father, As it was in the beginning,* and the *Alleluia* (omitted in Lent).

---

[14]   See SC art. 89 [DOL 1 no. 1].

[R3]   See DOL 426 no. 3461, note R2.

Then a hymn appropriate to the hour is sung. The psalmody is next, then the reading, followed by the verse. The hour concludes with the prayer and, at least in recitation in common, with the acclamation, *Let us praise the Lord.* R. *And give him thanks.*

3510   80. Different hymns and prayers are given for each of the hours so that, in keeping with tradition, they may correspond to the true time of day and thus sanctify it in a more pointed way. Those who recite only one hour should therefore choose the texts that correspond to the true time of day.

In addition, the readings and prayers vary in keeping with the character of the day, the season, or the feast.

3511   81. Two psalmodies are provided: the current psalmody and the complementary psalmody. Those who pray one hour should use the current psalmody. Those who pray more than one hour should use the current psalmody at one hour and the complementary psalmody at the others.

3512   82. The current psalmody consists of three psalms (or parts in the case of longer psalms) from the psalter, with their antiphons, unless directions are given to the contrary.

On solemnities, the Easter triduum, and days within the octave of Easter, proper antiphons are said with three psalms chosen from the complementary psalmody, unless special psalms are to be used or the celebration falls on a Sunday, when the psalms are those from the Sunday of Week I of the psalter.

3513   83. The complementary psalter consists of three sets of three psalms, chosen as a rule from the Gradual Psalms.

VI. NIGHT PRAYER

3514   84. Night prayer is the last prayer of the day, said before retiring, even if that is after midnight.

3515   85. Night prayer begins like the other hours, with the verse, *God, come to my assistance,* the *Glory to the Father, As it was in the beginning,* and the *Alleluia* (omitted in Lent).

3516   86. It is a laudable practice to have next an examination of conscience; in a celebration in common this takes place in silence or as part of a penitential rite based on the formularies in the Roman Missal.

3517   87. The appropriate hymn follows.

3518   88. After evening prayer I of Sunday the psalmody consists of Ps 4 and Ps 134; after evening prayer II of Sunday it consists of Ps 91.

On the other days psalms are chosen that are full of confidence in the Lord; it is permissible to use the Sunday psalms instead, especially for the convenience of those who may wish to pray night prayer from memory.

3519   89. After the psalmody there is a reading, followed by the responsory, *Into your hands.* Then, as a climax to the whole hour, the Canticle of Simeon, *Lord, now you let your servant go in peace* follows, with its antiphon.

3520   90. The concluding prayer then follows, as it appears in the psalter.

91. After the prayer the blessing, *May the all-powerful Lord* is used, even in private recitation.

3521

92. Finally, one of the antiphons in honor of the Blessed Virgin Mary is said. In the Easter season this is always to be the *Regina caeli*. In addition to the antiphons given in *The Liturgy of the Hours*, others may be approved by the conferences of bishops.[15]

3522

VII. COMBINING THE HOURS WITH MASS OR WITH EACH OTHER

93. In particular cases, if circumstances require, it is possible to link an hour more closely with Mass when there is a celebration of the liturgy of the hours in public or in common, according to the norms that follow, provided the Mass and the hour belong to one and the same office. Care must be taken, however, that this does not result in harm to pastoral work, especially on Sundays.

3523

94. When morning prayer, celebrated in choir or in common, comes immediately before Mass, the whole celebration may begin either with the introductory verse and hymn of morning prayer, especially on weekdays, or with the entrance song, procession, and celebrant's greeting, especially on Sundays and holydays; one of the introductory rites is thus omitted.

3524

The psalmody of morning prayer follows as usual, up to, but excluding, the reading. After the psalmody the penitential rite is omitted and, as circumstances suggest, the *Kyrie*; the *Gloria* then follows, if required by the rubrics, and the celebrant says the opening prayer of the Mass. The liturgy of the word follows as usual.

The general intercessions are made in the place and form customary at Mass. But on weekdays, at Mass in the morning, the intercessions of morning prayer may replace the daily form of the general intercessions at Mass.

After the communion with its communion song the Canticle of Zechariah, *Blessed be the Lord*, with its antiphon from morning prayer, is sung. Then follow the prayer after communion and the rest as usual.

95. If public celebration of a daytime hour, whichever corresponds to the time of day, is immediately followed by Mass, the whole celebration may begin in the same way, either with the introductory verse and hymn for the hour, especially on weekdays, or with the entrance song, procession, and celebrant's greeting, especially on Sundays and holydays; one of the introductory rites is thus omitted.

3525

The psalmody of the hour follows as usual up to, but excluding, the reading. After the psalmody the penitential rite is omitted and, as circumstances suggest, the *Kyrie*; the *Gloria* then follows, if required by the rubrics, and the celebrant says the opening prayer of the Mass.

96. Evening prayer, celebrated immediately before Mass, is joined to it in the same way as morning prayer. Evening prayer I of solemnities, Sundays, or feasts of the Lord falling on Sundays may not be celebrated until after Mass of the preceding day or Saturday.

3526

97. When a daytime hour or evening prayer follows Mass, the Mass is celebrated in the usual way up to and including the prayer after communion.

3527

When the prayer after communion has been said, the psalmody of the hour begins without introduction. At the daytime hour, after the psalmody the short reading is omitted and the prayer is said at once and the dismissal takes place as at

---

[15] See SC art. 38 [DOL 1 no. 38].

Mass. At evening prayer, after the psalmody the short reading is omitted and the Canticle of Mary with its antiphon follows at once; the intercessions and the Lord's Prayer are omitted; the concluding prayer follows, then the blessing of the congregation.

3528   98.   Apart from Christmas eve, the combining of Mass with the office of readings is normally excluded, since the Mass already has its own cycle of readings, to be kept distinct from any other. But if by way of exception, it should be necessary to join the two, then immediately after the second reading from the office, with its responsory, the rest is omitted and the Mass begins with the *Gloria*, if it is called for; otherwise the Mass begins with the opening prayer.

3529   99.   If the office of readings comes immediately before another hour of the office, then the appropriate hymn for that hour may be sung at the beginning of the office of readings. At the end of the office of readings the prayer and conclusion are omitted and in the hour following the introductory verse with the *Glory to the Father* is omitted.

CHAPTER III
DIFFERENT ELEMENTS IN THE LITURGY OF THE HOURS

I. PSALMS AND THEIR CONNECTION WITH CHRISTIAN PRAYER

3530   100. In the liturgy of the hours the Church in large measure prays through the magnificent songs that the Old Testament authors composed under the inspiration of the Holy Spirit. The origin of these verses gives them great power to raise the mind to God, to inspire devotion, to evoke gratitude in times of favor, and to bring consolation and courage in times of trial.

3531   101. The psalms, however, are only a foreshadowing of the fullness of time that came to pass in Christ the Lord and that is the source of the power of the Church's prayer. Hence, while the Christian people are all agreed on the supreme value to be placed on the psalms, they can sometimes experience difficulty in making this inspired poetry their own prayer.

3532   102. Yet the Holy Spirit, under whose inspiration the psalms were written, is always present by his grace to those believers who use them with good will. But more is necessary: the faithful must "improve their understanding of the Bible, especially of the psalms,"[1] according to their individual capacity, so that they may understand how and by what method they can truly pray through the psalms.

3533   103. The psalms are not readings or prose prayers, but poems of praise. They can on occasion be recited as readings, but from their literary genre they are properly called *Tehillim* ("songs of praise") in Hebrew and *psalmoi* ("songs to be sung to the lyre") in Greek. In fact, all the psalms have a musical quality that determines their correct style of delivery. Thus even when a psalm is recited and not sung or is said silently in private, its musical character should govern its use. A psalm does present a text to the minds of the people, but its aim is to move the heart of those singing it or listening to it and also of those accompanying it "on the lyre and harp."

3534   104. To sing the psalms with understanding, then, is to meditate on them verse by verse, with the heart always ready to respond in the way the Holy Spirit desires.

---

[1] SC art. 90 [DOL 1 no. 90].

The one who inspired the psalmist will also be present to those who in faith and love are ready to receive his grace. For this reason the singing of psalms, though it demands the reverence owed to God's majesty, should be the expression of a joyful spirit and a loving heart, in keeping with their character as sacred poetry and divine song and above all with the freedom of the children of God.

105. Often the words of a psalm help us to pray with greater ease and fervor, whether in thanksgiving and joyful praise of God or in prayer for help in the throes of suffering. But difficulties may arise, especially when the psalm is not addressed directly to God. The psalmist is a poet and often addresses the people as he recalls Israel's history; sometimes he addresses others, including subrational creatures. He even represents the words as being spoken by God himself and individual people, including, as in Ps 2, God's enemies. This shows that a psalm is a different kind of prayer from a prayer or collect composed by the Church. Moreover, it is in keeping with the poetic and musical character of the psalms that they do not necessarily address God but are sung in God's presence. Thus St. Benedict's instruction: "Let us reflect on what it means to be in the sight of God and his angels, and let us so stand in his presence that our minds are in harmony with our voices."[2]   3535

106. In praying the psalms we should open our hearts to the different attitudes they express, varying with the literary genre to which each belongs (psalms of grief, trust, gratitude, etc.) and to which biblical scholars rightly attach great importance.   3536

107. Staying close to the meaning of the words, the person who prays the psalms looks for the significance of the text for the human life of the believer.   3537

It is clear that each psalm was written in its own individual circumstances, which the titles given for each psalm in the Hebrew psalter are meant to indicate. But whatever its historical origin, each psalm has its own meaning, which we cannot overlook even in our own day. Though the psalms originated very many centuries ago among an Eastern people, they express accurately the pain and hope, the unhappiness and trust of people of every age and country, and sing above all of faith in God, of revelation, and of redemption.

108. Those who pray the psalms in the liturgy of the hours do so not so much in their own name as in the name of the entire Body of Christ. This consideration does away with the problem of a possible discrepancy between personal feelings and the sentiments a psalm is expressing: for example, when a person feels sad and the psalm is one of joy or when a person feels happy and the psalm is one of mourning. Such a problem is readily solved in private prayer, which allows for the choice of a psalm suited to personal feelings. The divine office, however, is not private; the cycle of psalms is public, in the name of the Church, even for those who may be reciting an hour alone. Those who pray the psalms in the name of the Church nevertheless can always find a reason for joy or sadness, for the saying of the Apostle applies in this case also: "Rejoice with the joyful and weep with those who weep" (Rom 12:15). In this way human frailty, wounded by self-love, is healed in proportion to the love that makes the heart match the voice that prays the psalms.[3]   3538

109. Those who pray the psalms in the name of the Church should be aware of their full sense (*sensus plenus*), especially their Messianic sense, which was the reason for the Church's introduction of the psalter into its prayer. This Messianic sense was fully revealed in the New Testament and indeed was affirmed publicly by   3539

---

²   *Rule of St. Benedict* ch. 19.

³   See *Rule of St. Benedict* ch. 19.

Christ the Lord in person when he said to the apostles: "All that is written about me in the law of Moses and the prophets and the psalms must be fulfilled" (Lk 24:44). The best-known example of this Messianic sense is the dialogue in Matthew's Gospel on the Messiah as Son of David and David's Lord,[4] where Ps 110 is interpreted as Messianic.

Following this line of thought, the Fathers of the Church saw the whole psalter as a prophecy of Christ and the Church and explained it in this sense; for the same reason the psalms have been chosen for use in the liturgy. Though somewhat contrived interpretations were at times proposed, in general the Fathers and the liturgy itself had the right to hear in the singing of the psalms the voice of Christ crying out to the Father or of the Father conversing with the Son; indeed, they also recognized in the psalms the voice of the Church, the apostles, and the martyrs. This method of interpretation also flourished in the Middle Ages; in many manuscripts of the period the Christological meaning of each psalm was set before those praying by means of the caption prefixed. A Christological meaning is by no means confined to the recognized Messianic psalms but is given also to many others. Some of these interpretations are doubtless Christological only in an accommodated sense, but they have the support of the Church's tradition.

On the great feasts especially, the choice of psalms is often based on their Christological meaning and antiphons taken from these psalms are frequently used to throw light on this meaning.

II. ANTIPHONS AND OTHER AIDS TO PRAYING THE PSALMS

3540 110. In the Latin tradition of psalmody three elements have greatly contributed to an understanding of the psalms and their use as Christian prayer: the captions, the psalm-prayers, and in particular the antiphons.

3541 111. In the psalter of *The Liturgy of the Hours* a caption is given for each psalm to explain its meaning and its import for the personal life of the believer. These captions are intended only as an aid to prayer. A quotation from the New Testament or the Fathers of the Church is added to foster prayer in the light of Christ's new revelation; it is an invitation to pray the psalms in their Christological meaning.

3542 112. Psalm-prayers for each psalm are given in the supplement to *The Liturgy of the Hours* as an aid to understanding them in a predominantly Christian way. An ancient tradition provides a model for their use: after the psalm a period of silence is observed, then the prayer gives a resumé and resolution of the thoughts and aspirations of those praying the psalms.

3543 113. Even when the liturgy of the hours is recited, not sung, each psalm retains its own antiphon, which is also to be said in private recitation. The antiphons help to bring out the literary genre of the psalm; they highlight some theme that may otherwise not attract the attention it deserves; they suggest an individual tone in a psalm, varying with different contexts: indeed, as long as farfetched accommodated senses are avoided, antiphons are of great value in helping toward an understanding of the typological meaning or the meaning appropriate to the feast; they can also add pleasure and variety to the recitation of the psalms.

3544 114. The antiphons in the psalter have been designed to lend themselves to vernacular translation and to repetition after each strophe, in accordance with no. 125.

---

4   See Mt 22:44ff.

When the office of Ordinary Time is recited, not sung, the quotations printed with the psalms may be used in place of these antiphons (see no. 111).

115. When a psalm may be divided because of its length into several sections within one and the same hour, an antiphon is given for each section. This is to provide variety, especially when the hour is sung, and also to help toward a better understanding of the riches of the psalm. Still, it is permissible to say or sing the complete psalm without interruption, using only the first antiphon.   3545

116. Proper antiphons are given for each of the psalms of morning prayer and evening prayer during the Easter triduum, on the days within the octaves of Easter and Christmas, on the Sundays of the seasons of Advent, Christmas, Lent, and Easter, on the weekdays of Holy Week and the Easter season, and from the 17th to the 24th of December.   3546

117. On solemnities proper antiphons are given for the office of readings, morning prayer, the daytime hours, and evening prayer; if not, the antiphons are taken from the common. On feasts the same applies to the office of readings and to morning prayer and evening prayer.   3547

118. Any memorials of the saints that have proper antiphons retain them (see no. 235).   3548

119. The antiphons for the Canticles of Zechariah and of Mary are taken, during Ordinary Time, from the Proper of Seasons, if they are given there; if not, they are taken from the current week and day of the psalter. On solemnities and feasts they are taken from the proper if they are given there; if not, they are taken from the common. On memorials without proper antiphons the antiphon may be taken at will either from the common or from the current week.   3549

120. During the Easter season *Alleluia* is added to all antiphons, unless it would clash with the meaning of a particular antiphon.   3550

III. WAYS OF SINGING THE PSALMS

121. Different psalms may be sung in different ways for a fuller grasp of their spiritual meaning and beauty. The choice of ways is dictated by the literary genre or length of each psalm, by the language used, whether Latin or the vernacular, and especially by the kind of celebration, whether individual, with a group, or with a congregation. The reason for using psalms is not the establishment of a fixed amount of prayer but their own variety and the character proper to each.   3551

122. The psalms are sung or said in one of three ways, according to the different usages established in tradition or experience: directly (*in directum*), that is, all sing the entire psalm, or antiphonally, that is, two choirs or sections of the congregation sing alternate verses or strophes, or responsorially.   3552

123. At the beginning of each psalm its own antiphon is always to be recited, as noted in nos. 113–120. At the end of the psalm the practice of concluding with the *Glory to the Father* and *As it was in the beginning* is retained. This is the fitting conclusion endorsed by tradition and it gives to Old Testament prayer a note of praise and a Christological and Trinitarian sense. The antiphon may be repeated at the end of the psalm.   3553

3554   124. When longer psalms occur, sections are marked in the psalter that divide the parts in such a way as to keep the threefold structure of the hour; but great care has been taken not to distort the meaning of the psalm.

It is useful to observe this division, especially in a choral celebration in Latin; the *Glory to the Father* is added at the end of each section.

It is permissible, however, either to keep this traditional way or to pause between the different sections of the same psalm or to recite the whole psalm and its antiphon as a single unit without a break.

3555   125. In addition, when the literary genre of a psalm suggests it, the divisions into strophes are marked in order that, especially when the psalm is sung in the vernacular, the antiphons may be repeated after each strophe; in this case the *Glory to the Father* need be said only at the end of the psalm.

IV. PLAN FOR THE DISTRIBUTION OF THE PSALMS IN THE OFFICE

3556   126. The psalms are distributed over a four-week cycle in such a way that very few psalms are omitted, while some, traditionally more important, occur more frequently than others; morning prayer and evening prayer as well as night prayer have been assigned psalms appropriate to these hours.[5]

3557   127. Since morning prayer and evening prayer are particularly designed for celebration with a congregation, the psalms chosen for them are those more suited to this purpose.

3558   128. For night prayer the norm given in no. 88 has been followed.

3559   129. For Sunday, including its office of readings and daytime prayer, the psalms chosen are those that tradition has particularly singled out as expressions of the paschal mystery. Certain psalms of a penitential character or connected with the passion are assigned to Friday.

3560   130. Three psalms (78, 105, and 106) are reserved for the seasons of Advent, Christmas, Lent, and Easter, because they throw a special light on the Old Testament history of salvation as the forerunner of its fulfillment in the New.

3561   131. Three psalms (58, 83, and 109) have been omitted from the psalter cycle because of their curses; in the same way, some verses have been omitted from certain psalms, as noted at the head of each. The reason for the omission is a certain psychological difficulty, even though the psalms of imprecation are in fact used as prayer in the New Testament, for example, Rv 6:10, and in no sense to encourage the use of curses.

3562   132. Psalms too long to be included in one hour of the office are assigned to the same hour on different days so that they may be recited in full by those who do not usually say other hours. Thus Ps 119 is divided in keeping with its own internal structure and is spread over twenty-two days during daytime prayer, because tradition has assigned it to the day hours.

3563   133. The four-week cycle of the psalter is coordinated with the liturgical year in such a way that on the First Sunday of Advent, the First Sunday in Ordinary Time,

---

[5]   See SC art. 91 [DOL 1 no. 91].

the First Sunday of Lent, and Easter Sunday the cycle is always begun again with Week I (others being omitted when necessary).

After Pentecost, when the psalter cycle follows the series of weeks in Ordinary Time, it begins with the week indicated in the Proper of Seasons at the beginning of the appropriate week in Ordinary Time.

134. On solemnities and feasts, during the Easter triduum, and on the days within   3564
the octaves of Easter and Christmas, proper psalms are assigned to the office of readings from those with a tradition of use at these times and their relevance is generally highlighted by the choice of antiphon. This is also the case at daytime prayer on certain solemnities of the Lord and during the octave of Easter. At morning prayer the psalms and canticle are taken from the Sunday of the Week I of the psalter. On solemnities the psalms at evening prayer I are taken from the *Laudate* Psalms, following an ancient custom. At evening prayer II on solemnities and at evening prayer on feasts the psalms and canticle are proper. At daytime prayer on solemnities (except those already mentioned and those falling on Sunday) the psalms are taken from the Gradual Psalms; at daytime prayer on feasts the psalms are those of the current week and day of the psalter.

135. In all other cases the psalms are taken from the current week and day of the   3565
psalter, unless there are proper antiphons or proper psalms.

V. CANTICLES FROM THE OLD AND NEW TESTAMENTS

136. At morning prayer between the first and the second psalm a canticle from the   3566
Old Testament is inserted, in accordance with custom. In addition to the series handed down from the ancient Roman tradition and the other series introduced into the breviary by St. Pius X, several other canticles have been added to the psalter from different books of the Old Testament, in order that each weekday of the four-week cycle may have its own proper canticle and on Sunday the two sections of the Canticle of the Three Children may be alternated.

137. At evening prayer, after the two psalms, a canticle of the New Testament is   3567
inserted, from the letters of the apostles or the Book of Revelation. Seven canticles are given for each week of the four-week cycle, one for each day. On the Sundays of Lent, however, in place of the *Alleluia* Canticle from the Book of Revelation, the canticle is from the First Letter of Peter. In addition, on the solemnity of the Epiphany and the feast of the Transfiguration the canticle is from the First Letter to Timothy; this is indicated in those offices.

138. The gospel Canticles of Zechariah, of Mary, and of Simeon are to be treated   3568
with the same solemnity and dignity as are customary at the proclamation of the gospel itself.

139. Both psalmody and readings are arranged in keeping with the received rule of   3569
tradition that the Old Testament is read first, then the writings of the apostles, and finally the gospel.

VI. READINGS FROM SACRED SCRIPTURE

A. READING OF SACRED SCRIPTURE IN GENERAL

140. The reading of sacred Scripture, which, following an ancient tradition, takes   3570
place publicly in the liturgy, is to have special importance for all Christians, not only in the celebration of the eucharist but also in the divine office. The reason is

that this reading is not the result of individual choice or devotion but is the planned decision of the Church itself, in order that in the course of the year the Bride of Christ may unfold the mystery of Christ "from his incarnation and birth until his ascension, the day of Pentecost, and the expectation of blessed hope and of the Lord's return."[6] In addition, the reading of sacred Scripture in the liturgical celebration is always accompanied by prayer in order that the reading may have greater effect and that, in turn, prayer — especially the praying of the psalms — may gain fuller understanding and become more fervent and devout because of the reading.

3571   141. In the liturgy of the hours there is a longer reading of sacred Scripture and a shorter reading.

3572   142. The longer reading, optional at morning prayer and evening prayer, is described in no. 46.

B. Cycle of Scripture Readings in the Office of Readings

3573   143. The cycle of readings from sacred Scripture in the office of readings takes into account both those special seasons during which by an ancient tradition particular books are to be read and the cycle of readings at Mass. The liturgy of the hours is thus coordinated with the Mass in such a way that the scriptural readings in the office complement the readings at Mass and so provide a complete view of the history of salvation.

3574   144. Without prejudice to the exception noted in no. 73, there are no readings from the Gospel in the liturgy of the hours, since in the Mass each year the Gospel is read in its entirety.

3575   145. There are two cycles of biblical readings. The first is a one-year cycle and is incorporated into *The Liturgy of the Hours*; the second, given in the supplement for optional use, is a two-year cycle, like the cycle of readings at weekday Masses in Ordinary Time.

3576   146. The two-year cycle of readings for the liturgy of the hours is so arranged that each year there are readings from nearly all the books of sacred Scripture as well as longer and more difficult texts that are not suitable for inclusion in the Mass. The New Testament as a whole is read each year, partly in the Mass, partly in the liturgy of the hours; but for the Old Testament books a selection has been made of those parts that are of greater importance for the understanding of the history of salvation and for deepening devotion.

The complementarity between the readings in the liturgy of the hours and in the Mass in no way assigns the same texts to the same days or spreads the same books over the same seasons. This would leave the liturgy of the hours with the less important passages and upset the sequence of texts. Rather this complementarity necessarily demands that the same book be used in the Mass and in the liturgy of the hours in alternate years or that, if it is read in the same year, there be some interval in between.

3577   147. During Advent, following an ancient tradition, passages are read from Isaiah in a semicontinuous sequence, alternating in a two-year cycle. In addition, the Book of Ruth and certain prophecies from Micah are read. Since there are special readings from 17 to 24 December (both dates included), readings for the Third Week of Advent which fall on these dates are omitted.

---

[6]   SC art. 102 [DOL 1 no. 102].

148. From 29 December until 5 January the readings for Year I are taken from the   3578
Letter to the Colossians (which considers the incarnation of the Lord within the
context of the whole history of salvation) and the readings for Year II are taken
from the Song of Songs (which foreshadows the union of God and humanity in
Christ): "God the Father prepared a wedding feast for God his Son when he united
him with human nature in the womb of the Virgin, when he who is God before all
ages willed that his Son should become man at the end of the ages."[7]

149. From 7 January until the Saturday after the Epiphany the readings are eschato-   3579
logical texts from Isaiah 60–66 and Baruch. Readings remaining unused are omitted
for that year.

150. During Lent the readings for the first year are passages from Deuteronomy and   3580
the Letter to the Hebrews. Those for the second year review the history of salvation
from Exodus, Leviticus, and Numbers. The Letter to the Hebrews interprets the Old
Covenant in the light of the paschal mystery of Christ. A passage from the same
letter, on Christ's sacrifice (Heb 9:11–28), is read on Good Friday; another, on the
Lord's rest (Heb 4:1–16), is read on Holy Saturday. On the other days of Holy Week
the readings in Year I are the third and fourth Songs of the Servant of the Lord and
extracts from Lamentations; in Year II the prophet Jeremiah is read, as a type of
Christ in his passion.

151. During the Easter season, apart from the First and Second Sundays of Easter   3581
and the solemnities of the Ascension and Pentecost, there are the traditional readings from the First Letter of Peter, the Book of Revelation, and the Letters of John
(for Year I), and from the Acts of the Apostles (for Year II).

152. From the Monday after the feast of the Baptism of the Lord until Lent and   3582
from the Monday after Pentecost until Advent there is a continuous series of
thirty-four weeks in Ordinary Time.

　　　This series is interrupted from Ash Wednesday until Pentecost. On the Monday after Pentecost Sunday the cycle of readings in Ordinary Time is resumed,
beginning with the week after the one interrupted because of Lent; the reading
assigned to the Sunday is omitted.

　　　In years with only thirty-three weeks in Ordinary Time, the week immediately
following Pentecost is dropped, in order to retain the readings of the last weeks,
which are eschatological readings.

　　　The books of the Old Testament are arranged so as to follow the history of
salvation: God reveals himself in the history of his people as he leads and enlightens them in progressive stages. This is why prophetic books are read along with the
historical books, but with due consideration of the period in which the prophets
lived and taught. Hence, the cycle of readings from the Old Testament contains, in
Year I, the historical books and prophetic utterances from the Book of Joshua as far
as, and including, the time of the exile. In Year II, after the readings from Genesis
(read before Lent), the history of salvation is resumed after the exile up to the time
of the Maccabees. Year II includes the later prophets, the wisdom literature, and the
narratives in Esther, Tobit, and Judith.

　　　The letters of the apostles not read at special times are distributed through the
year in a way that takes into account the readings at Mass and the chronological
order in which these letters were written.

7　Gregory the Great, *Homilia 34 in Evangelia*: PL 76: 1282.

3583   153. The one-year cycle is shortened in such a way that each year special passages from sacred Scripture are read, but in correlation with the two-year cycle of readings at Mass, to which it is intended to be complementary.

3584   154. Proper readings are assigned for solemnities and feasts; otherwise the readings are taken from the respective Common of Saints.

3585   155. As far as possible, each passage read keeps to a certain unity. In order therefore to strike a balance in length (otherwise difficult to achieve in view of the different literary genres of the books), some verses are occasionally omitted, though omissions are always noted. But it is permissible and commendable to read the complete passage from an approved text.

C. Short Readings

3586   156. The short readings or "chapters" (*capitula*) are referred to in no. 45, which describes their importance in the liturgy of the hours. They have been chosen to give clear and concise expression to a theme or an exhortation. Care has also been taken to ensure variety.

3587   157. Accordingly, four weekly series of short readings have been composed for Ordinary Time. They are incorporated into the psalter in such a way that the reading changes during the four weeks. There are also weekly series for the seasons of Advent, Christmas, Lent, and Easter. In addition there are proper short readings for solemnities, feasts, and some memorials, as well as a one-week series for night prayer.

3588   158. The following determined the choice of short readings:

      a. in accordance with tradition, exclusion of the Gospels;

      b. respect for the special character of Sunday, or even of Friday, and of the individual hours;

      c. use only of the New Testament for the readings at evening prayer, following as they do a New Testament canticle.

VII. READINGS FROM THE FATHERS AND CHURCH WRITERS

3589   159. In keeping with the tradition of the Roman Church the office of readings has, after the biblical reading, a reading from the Fathers or church writers, with a responsory, unless there is to be a reading relating to a saint (see nos. 228–239).

3590   160. Texts for this reading are given from the writings of the Fathers and doctors of the Church and from other ecclesiastical writers of the Eastern and Western Church. Pride of place is given to the Fathers because of their distinctive authority in the Church.

3591   161. In addition to the readings that *The Liturgy of the Hours* assigns to each day, the optional lectionary supplies a larger collection, in order that the treasures of the Church's tradition may be more widely available to those who pray the liturgy of the hours. Everyone is free to take the second reading either from *The Liturgy of the Hours* or from the optional lectionary.

3592   162. Further, the conferences of bishops may prepare additional texts, adapted to the traditions and culture of their own region,[8] for inclusion in the optional lection-

---

    8 See SC art. 38 [DOL 1 no. 38].

ary as a supplement. These texts are to be taken from the works of Catholic writers, outstanding for their teaching and holiness of life.[a]

163. The purpose of the second reading is principally to provide for meditation on the word of God as received by the Church in its tradition. The Church has always been convinced of the need to teach the word of God authentically to believers, so that "the line of interpretation regarding the prophets and apostles may be guided by an ecclesial and catholic understanding."[9]

3593

164. By constant use of the writings handed down by the universal tradition of the Church, those who read them are led to a deeper reflection on sacred Scripture and to a relish and love for it. The writings of the Fathers are an outstanding witness to the contemplation of the word of God over the centuries by the Bride of the incarnate Word: the Church, "possessing the counsel and spirit of its Bridegroom and God,"[10] is always seeking to attain a more profound understanding of the sacred Scriptures.

3594

165. The reading of the Fathers leads Christians to an understanding also of the liturgical seasons and feasts. In addition, it gives them access to the priceless spiritual treasures that form the unique patrimony of the Church and provide a firm foundation for the spiritual life and a rich source for increasing devotion. Preachers of God's word also have at hand each day superb examples of sacred preaching.

3595

VIII. READINGS IN HONOR OF SAINTS

166. The "hagiographical" readings or readings in honor of saints are either texts from a Father of the Church or another ecclesiastical writer, referring specifically or rightly applicable to the saint being commemorated, or the readings are texts from the saint's own writings, or are biographical.

3596

167. Those who compose particular propers for saints must ensure historical accuracy[11] as well as genuine spiritual benefit for those who will read or hear the readings about the saints. Anything that merely excites amazement should be carefully avoided. Emphasis should be given to the individual spiritual characteristics of the saints, in a way suited to modern conditions; stress should also be laid on their contribution to the life and spirituality of the Church.

3597

168. A short biographical note, simply giving historical facts and a brief sketch of the saint's life, is provided at the head of the reading. This is for information only and is not for reading aloud.

3598

IX. RESPONSORIES

169. Its responsory follows the biblical reading in the office of readings. The text of this responsory has been drawn from traditional sources or freshly composed, in order to throw new light on the passage just read, put it in the context of the history of salvation, lead from the Old Testament to the New, turn what has been

3599

---

[a]   See DOL 428, 431, and 433.

[9]   Vincent of Lérins, *Commonitorium* 2: PL 50, 640.

[10]   Bernard of Clairvaux, *Sermo 3 in vigilia Nativitatis* 1: PL 183 (ed. 1879) 94.

[11]   See SC art. 92 c [DOL 1 no. 92].

read into prayer and contemplation, or provide pleasant variety by its poetic beauty.

3600 170. A pertinent responsory also follows the second reading. It is less closely linked with the text of the reading, however, and thus makes for a greater freedom in meditation.

3601 171. The responsories and the portions to be repeated even in private recitation therefore retain their value. The customary reprise of the whole responsory may be omitted when the office is not being sung, unless the sense requires this repetition.

3602 172. In a similar but simpler way, the responsory at morning prayer, evening prayer, and night prayer (see nos. 49 and 89), and the verse at daytime prayer, are linked to the short reading as a kind of acclamation, enabling God's word to enter more deeply into the mind and heart of the one listening or reading.

X. HYMNS AND OTHER NONBIBLICAL SONGS

3603 173. A very ancient tradition gives hymns the place in the office that they still retain.[12] By their mystical and poetic character they are specifically designed for God's praise. But they also are an element for the people; in fact more often than the other parts of the office the hymns bring out the proper theme of individual hours or feasts and incline and draw the spirit to a devout celebration. The beauty of their language often adds to this power. Furthermore, in the office hymns are the main poetic element created by the Church.

3604 174. A hymn follows the traditional rule of ending with a doxology, usually addressed to the same divine person as the hymn itself.

3605 175. In the office for Ordinary Time, to ensure variety, a twofold cycle of hymns is given for each hour, for use in alternate weeks.

3606 176. In addition, a twofold cycle of hymns has been introduced into the office of readings for Ordinary Time, one for use at night and the other for use during the day.

3607 177. New hymns can be set to traditional melodies of the same rhythm and meter.

3608 178. For vernacular celebration, the conferences of bishops may adapt the Latin hymns to suit the character of their own language and introduce fresh compositions,[13] provided these are in complete harmony with the spirit of the hour, season, or feast. Great care must be taken not to allow popular songs that have no artistic merit and are not in keeping with the dignity of the liturgy.

XI. INTERCESSIONS, LORD'S PRAYER, AND CONCLUDING PRAYER

A. The Prayers or Intercessions at Morning Prayer and Evening Prayer

3609 179. The liturgy of the hours is a celebration in praise of God. Yet Jewish and Christian tradition does not separate prayer of petition from praise of God; often enough, praise turns somehow to petition. The Apostle Paul exhorts us to offer

---

[12] See SC art. 93 [DOL 1 no. 93].

[13] See SC art. 38 [DOL 1 no. 38].

"prayers, petitions, intercessions, and thanksgiving for all: for kings and all in authority, so that we may be able to live quiet and peaceful lives in all reverence and decency, for this is good and acceptable before God our Savior, who wishes all to be saved and to come to the knowledge of the truth" (1 Tm 2:1–4). The Fathers of the Church frequently explained this as an exhortation to offer prayer in the morning and in the evening.[14]

180. The general intercessions, restored in the Mass of the Roman Rite, have their place also at evening prayer, though in a different fashion, as will be explained later.

3610

181. Since traditionally morning prayer puts the whole day in God's hands, there are invocations at morning prayer for the purpose of commending or consecrating the day to God.

3611

182. The word *preces* covers both the intercessions at evening prayer and the invocations for dedicating the day to God at morning prayer.

3612

183. In the interest of variety and especially of giving fuller expression to the many needs of the Church and of all people in relation to different states of life, groups, persons, circumstances, and seasons, different intercessory formularies are given for each day of the four-week psalter in Ordinary Time and for the special seasons of the liturgical year, as well as for certain feasts.

3613

184. In addition, the conferences of bishops have the right to adapt the formularies given in the book of the liturgy of the hours and also to approve new ones,[15] in accordance with the norms that follow.

3614

185. As in the Lord's Prayer, petitions should be linked with praise of God and acknowledgment of his glory or with a reference to the history of salvation.

3615

186. In the intercessions at evening prayer the last intention is always for the dead.

3616

187. Since the liturgy of the hours is above all the prayer of the whole Church for the whole Church, indeed for the salvation of the whole world,[16] universal intentions should take precedence over all others, namely, for: the Church and its ministers; secular authorities; the poor, the sick, and the sorrowful; the needs of the whole world, that is, peace and other intentions of this kind.

3617

188. It is permissible, however, to include particular intentions at both morning prayer and evening prayer.

3618

189. The intercessions in the office are so arranged that they can be adapted for celebration with a congregation or in a small community or for private recitation.

3619

190. The intercessions in a celebration with a congregation or in common are thus introduced by a brief invitation, given by the priest or minister and designating the single response that the congregation is to repeat after each petition.

3620

191. Further, the intentions are phrased as direct addresses to God and thus are suitable for both common celebration and private recitation.

3621

---

14   Thus, for example, John Chrysostom, *In Epist. ad Tim 1*, Homilia 6: PG 62, 530.

15   See SC art. 38 [DOL 1 no. 38].

16   See SC art. 83 and 89 [DOL 1 no. 83 and 89].

3622   192. Each intention consists of two parts; the second may be used as an alternative response.

3623   193. Different methods can therefore be used for the intercessions. The priest or minister may say both parts of the intention and the congregation respond with a uniform response or a silent pause, or the priest or minister may say only the first part of the intention and the congregation respond with the second part.

B. LORD'S PRAYER

3624   194. In accord with ancient tradition, the Lord's Prayer has a place suited to its dignity, namely, after the intercessions at morning prayer and evening prayer, the hours most often celebrated with the people.

3625   195. Henceforth, therefore, the Lord's Prayer will be said with solemnity on three occasions during the day: at Mass, at morning prayer, and at evening prayer.

3626   196. The Lord's Prayer is said by all after a brief introduction, if this seems opportune.

C. CONCLUDING PRAYER

3627   197. The concluding prayer at the end marks the completion of an entire hour. In a celebration in public and with a congregation, it belongs by tradition to a priest or deacon to say this prayer.[17]

3628   198. In the office of readings, this prayer is as a rule the prayer proper to the day. At night prayer, the prayer is always the prayer given in the psalter for that hour.

3629   199. The concluding prayer at morning prayer and evening prayer is taken from the proper on Sundays, on the weekdays of the seasons of Advent, Christmas, Lent, and Easter, and on solemnities, feasts, and memorials. On weekdays in Ordinary Time the prayer is the one given in the four-week psalter to express the character of these two hours.

3630   200. The concluding prayer at daytime prayer is taken from the proper on Sundays, on the weekdays of the seasons of Advent, Christmas, Lent, and Easter, and on solemnities and feasts. On other days the prayers are those that express the character of the particular hour. These are given in the four-week psalter.

XII. SACRED SILENCE

3631   201. It is a general principle that care should be taken in liturgical services to see that "at the proper times all observe a reverent silence."[18] An opportunity for silence should therefore be provided in the celebration of the liturgy of the hours.

3632   202. In order to receive in our hearts the full sound of the voice of the Holy Spirit and to unite our personal prayer more closely with the word of God and the public voice of the Church, it is permissible, as occasion offers and prudence suggests, to have an interval of silence. It may come either after the repetition of the antiphon at the end of the psalm, in the traditional way, especially if the psalm-prayer is to be

---

17   See no. 256 of this Instruction.

18   SC art. 30 [DOL 1 no. 30].

said after the pause (see no. 112), or after the short or longer readings, either before or after the responsory.

Care must be taken to avoid the kind of silence that would disturb the structure of the office or annoy and weary those taking part.

203. In individual recitation there is even greater freedom to pause in meditation on some text that moves the spirit; the office does not on this account lose its public character.   3633

CHAPTER IV
VARIOUS CELEBRATIONS THROUGHOUT THE YEAR

I. MYSTERIES OF THE LORD

A. Sunday

204. The office of Sunday begins with evening prayer I, which is taken entirely from the four-week psalter, except those parts that are marked as proper.   3634

205. When a feast of the Lord is celebrated on Sunday, it has a proper evening prayer I.   3635

206. The way to celebrate Sunday vigils, as circumstances suggest, has been discussed in no. 73.   3636

207. It is of great advantage to celebrate, when possible, at least evening prayer with the people, in keeping with a very ancient tradition.[1]   3637

B. Easter Triduum

208. For the Easter triduum the office is celebrated in the way set forth in the Proper of Seasons.   3638

209. Those who take part in the evening Mass of the Lord's Supper or the celebration of the Lord's passion on Good Friday do not say evening prayer on either day.   3639

210. On Good Friday and Holy Saturday the office of readings should be celebrated publicly with the people before morning prayer, as far as this is possible.   3640

211. Night prayer for Holy Saturday is said only by those who are not present at the Easter Vigil.   3641

212. The Easter Vigil takes the place of the office of readings. Those not present at the solemn celebration of the Vigil should therefore read at least four of its readings with the chants and prayers. It is desirable that these be the readings from Exodus, Ezekiel, St. Paul, and from the Gospel. The *Te Deum* follows, then the prayer of the day.   3642

213. Morning prayer for Easter Sunday is said by all. It is fitting that evening prayer be celebrated in a more solemn way to mark the ending of so holy a day and to commemorate the occasions when the Lord showed himself to his disciples. Great care should be taken to maintain, where it exists, the particular tradition of cele-   3643

---

[1] See SC art. 100 [DOL 1 no. 100].

brating evening prayer on Easter Sunday in honor of baptism. During this there is a procession to the font as the psalms are being sung.

C. EASTER SEASON

3644   214. The liturgy of the hours takes on a paschal character from the acclamation, *Alleluia* that concludes most antiphons (see no. 120), from the hymns, antiphons, and special intercessions, and from the proper readings assigned to each hour.

D. CHRISTMAS SEASON

3645   215. On Christmas eve it is fitting that by means of the office of readings, a solemn vigil be celebrated before Mass. Night prayer is not said by those present at this vigil.

3646   216. Morning prayer on Christmas Day is said as a rule before the Mass at Dawn.

E. OTHER SOLEMNITIES AND FEASTS OF THE LORD

3647   217. In arranging the office for solemnities and feasts of the Lord, what is said in nos. 225–233 should be observed, with any necessary changes.

II. THE SAINTS

3648   218. The celebrations of the saints are arranged so that they do not take precedence over those feast days and special seasons that commemorate the mysteries of salvation.[2] Nor are they allowed to break up the sequence of psalms and biblical readings or to give rise to undue repetitions. At the same time, the plan makes proper provision for the rightful honoring of the individual saints. These principles form the basis for the reform of the calendar, carried out by order of Vatican Council II, and for the plan for celebrating the saints in the liturgy of the hours that is described in the following paragraphs.

3649   219. Celebrations in honor of the saints are either solemnities, feasts, or memorials.

3650   220. Memorials are either obligatory memorials or, when not so classified, optional memorials. In deciding on the merits of celebrating an optional memorial in an office to be celebrated with the people or in common, account should be taken of the general good or of the genuine devotion of the congregation, not simply that of the person presiding.

3651   221. When more than one optional memorial falls on the same day, only one may be celebrated; the rest are omitted.

3652   222. Only solemnities are transferred, in accordance with the rubrics.

3653   223. The norms that follow apply to the saints entered in the General Roman Calendar and to those with a place in particular calendars.

3654   224. Where proper parts are not given, they are supplied from the respective Common of Saints.

1. ARRANGEMENT OF THE OFFICE FOR SOLEMNITIES

3655   225. Solemnities have an evening prayer I on the preceding day.

---

[2] See SC art. 111 [DOL 1 no. 111].

226. At evening prayer I and II, the hymn, the antiphons, the short reading with its   3656
responsory, and the concluding prayer are proper. Where anything proper is missing, it is supplied from the common.

In keeping with an ancient tradition, at evening prayer I both psalms are as a
rule taken from the *Laudate* Psalms (Ps 113, 117, 135, 146, 147 A, 147 B). The New
Testament canticle is noted in its appropriate place. At evening prayer II the psalms
and canticles are proper; the intercessions are either proper or from the common.

227. At morning prayer, the hymn, the antiphons, the short reading with its re-   3657
sponsory, and the concluding prayer are proper. Where anything proper is missing,
it is supplied from the common. The psalms are to be taken from the Sunday of
Week I of the four-week psalter; the intercessions are either proper or from the
common.

228. In the office of readings, everything is proper: the hymn, the antiphons and   3658
psalms, the readings and the responsories. The first reading is from Scripture; the
second is about the saint. In the case of a saint with a purely local cult and without
special texts even in the local proper, everything is taken from the common.

At the end of the office of readings the *Te Deum* and the proper prayer are said.

229. At daytime prayer, the hymn of the weekday is used, unless other directions   3659
are given. The psalms are from the Gradual Psalms with a proper antiphon. On
Sundays the psalms are taken from the Sunday of Week I of the four-week psalter
and the short reading and concluding prayer are proper. But on certain solemnities
of the Lord there are special psalms.

230. At night prayer, everything is said as on Sundays, after evening prayer I and II   3660
respectively.

2. Arrangement of the Office for Feasts

231. Feasts have no evening prayer I, except those feasts of the Lord that fall on a   3661
Sunday. At the office of readings, at morning prayer, and at evening prayer, all is
done as on solemnities.

232. At daytime prayer, the hymn of the weekday is used. The weekday psalms   3662
with their antiphons are said, unless a special reason or tradition requires a proper
antiphon; this will be indicated as the case occurs. The reading and concluding
prayer are proper.

233. Night prayer is said as on ordinary days.   3663

3. Arrangement of the Office for Memorials

234. In the arrangement of the office there is no difference between obligatory and   3664
optional memorials, except in the case of optional memorials falling during privileged seasons.

A. MEMORIALS DURING ORDINARY TIME

235. In the office of readings, at morning prayer, and at evening prayer: 3665

a.   the psalms and their antiphons are taken from the current week and day,
unless there are proper antiphons or proper psalms, which is indicated as the
case occurs;

b.   the antiphon at the invitatory, the hymn, the short reading, the antiphons
at the Canticles of Zechariah and of Mary, and the intercessions must be those

of the saint if these are given in the proper; otherwise, they are taken either from the common or from the current week and day;

c. the concluding prayer from the office of the saint is to be said;

d. in the office of readings, the Scripture reading with its responsory is from the current cycle. The second reading is about the saint, with a proper responsory or one taken from the common; if there is no proper reading, the patristic reading for the day is used. The *Te Deum* is not said.

3666 236. At daytime prayer and night prayer, all is from the weekday and nothing is from the office of the saint.

B. MEMORIALS DURING PRIVILEGED SEASONS

3667 237. On Sundays, solemnities, and feasts, on Ash Wednesday, during Holy Week, and during the octave of Easter, memorials that happen to fall on these days are disregarded.

3668 238. On the weekdays from 17 to 24 December, during the octave of Christmas, and on the weekdays of Lent, no obligatory memorials are celebrated, even in particular calendars. When any happen to fall during Lent in a given year, they are treated as optional memorials.

3669 239. During privileged seasons, if it is desired to celebrate the office of a saint on a day assigned to his or her memorial:

a. in the office of readings, after the patristic reading (with its responsory) from the Proper of Seasons, a proper reading about the saint (with its responsory) may follow, with the concluding prayer of the saint;

b. at morning prayer and evening prayer, the ending of the concluding prayer may be omitted and the saint's antiphon (from the proper or common) and prayer may be added.

C. MEMORIAL OF THE BLESSED VIRGIN MARY ON SATURDAY

3670 240. On Saturdays in Ordinary Time, when optional memorials are permitted, an optional memorial of the Blessed Virgin Mary may be celebrated in the same way as other memorials, with its own proper reading.

III. CALENDAR AND OPTION TO CHOOSE AN OFFICE OR PART OF AN OFFICE

A. CALENDAR TO BE FOLLOWED

3671 241. The office in choir and in common is to be celebrated according to the proper calendar of the diocese, of the religious family, or of the individual churches.[3] Members of religious institutes join with the community of the local Church in celebrating the dedication of the cathedral and the feasts of the principal patrons of the place and of the wider geographical region in which they live.[4]

3672 242. When clerics or religious who are obliged under any title to pray the divine office join in an office celebrated in common according to a calendar or rite different from their own, they fulfill their obligation in respect to the part of the office at which they are present.

---

[3] See General Norms for the Liturgical Year and the Calendar no. 52 [DOL 442 no. 3818].

[4] See ibid. no. 52 c [DOL 442 no. 3818].

243. In private celebration, the calendar of the place or the person's own calendar   3673
may be followed, except on proper solemnities and on proper feasts.[5]

B. Option to Choose an Office

244. On weekdays when an optional memorial is permitted, for a good reason the   3674
office of a saint listed on that day in the Roman Martyrology, or in an approved
appendix to it, may be celebrated in the same way as other memorials (see nos.
234–239).

245. For a public cause or out of devotion, except on solemnities, the Sundays of   3675
the seasons of Advent, Lent, and Easter, Ash Wednesday, Holy Week, the octave of
Easter, and 2 November, a votive office may be celebrated, in whole or in part: for
example, on the occasion of a pilgrimage, a local feast, or the external solemnity of a
saint.

C. Option to Choose Texts

246. In certain particular cases there is an option to choose texts different from   3676
those given for the day, provided there is no distortion of the general arrangement
of each hour and the rules that follow are respected.

247. In the office for Sundays, solemnities, feasts of the Lord listed in the General   3677
Calendar, the weekdays of Lent and Holy Week, the days within the octaves of
Easter and Christmas, and the weekdays from 17 to 24 December inclusive, it is
never permissible to change the formularies that are proper or adapted to the
celebration, such as antiphons, hymns, readings, responsories, prayers, and very
often also the psalms.

In place of the Sunday psalms of the current week, there is an option to
substitute the Sunday psalms of a different week, and, in the case of an office
celebrated with a congregation, even other psalms especially chosen to lead the
people step by step to an understanding of the psalms.

248. In the office of readings, the current cycle of sacred Scripture must always be   3678
respected. The Church's intent that "a more representative portion of the holy
Scriptures will be read to the people in the course of a prescribed number of
years"[6] applies also to the divine office.

Therefore the cycle of readings from Scripture that is provided in the office of
readings must not be set aside during the seasons of Advent, Christmas, Lent, and
Easter. During Ordinary Time, however, on a particular day or for a few days in
succession, it is permissible, for a good reason, to choose readings from those
provided on other days or even other biblical readings: for example, on the occasion
of retreats, pastoral gatherings, prayers for Christian unity, or other such events.

249. When the continuous reading is interrupted because of a solemnity or feast or   3679
special celebration, it is allowed during the same week, taking into account the
readings for the whole week, either to combine the parts omitted with others or to
decide which of the texts are to be preferred.

250. The office of readings also offers the option to choose, with a good reason,   3680
another reading from the same season, taken from *The Liturgy of the Hours* or the
optional lectionary (no. 161), in preference to the second reading appointed for the

---

⁵   See ibid. Table of Liturgical Days nos. 4 and 8 [DOL 442 no. 3825].

⁶   SC art. 51 [DOL 1 no. 51].

day. On weekdays in Ordinary Time and, if it seems opportune, even in the seasons of Advent, Christmas, Lent, and Easter, the choice is open for a semicontinuous reading of the work of a Father of the Church, in harmony with the biblical and liturgical context.

3681 251. The readings, prayers, songs, and intercessions appointed for the weekdays of a particular season may be used on other weekdays of the same season.

3682 252. Everyone should be concerned to respect the complete cycle of the four-week psalter.[7] Still, for spiritual or pastoral advantage, the psalms appointed for a particular day may be replaced with others from the same hour of a different day. There are also circumstances occasionally arising when it is permissible to choose suitable psalms and other texts in the way done for a votive office.

CHAPTER V
RITES FOR CELEBRATION IN COMMON

I. OFFICES TO BE CARRIED OUT

3683 253. In the celebration of the liturgy of the hours, as in all other liturgical services, "each one, minister or layperson, who has an office to perform, should do all of, but only, those parts which pertain to that office by the nature of the rite and the principles of liturgy."[1]

3684 254. When a bishop presides, especially in the cathedral, he should be attended by his college of priests and by ministers and the people should take a full and active part. A priest or deacon should normally preside at every celebration with a congregation and ministers should also be present.[R4]

3685 255. The priest or deacon who presides at a celebration may wear a stole over the alb or surplice; a priest may also wear a cope. On greater solemnities the wearing of the cope by many priests or of the dalmatic by many deacons is permitted.

3686 256. It belongs to the presiding priest or deacon, at the chair, to open the celebration with the introductory verse, begin the Lord's Prayer, say the concluding prayer, greet the people, bless them, and dismiss them.

3687 257. Either the priest or a minister may lead the intercessions.

3688 258. In the absence of a priest or deacon, the one who presides at the office is only one among equals and does not enter the sanctuary or greet and bless the people.

3689 259. Those who act as readers, standing in a convenient place, read either the long readings or the short readings.

3690 260. A cantor or cantors should intone the antiphons, psalms, and other chants. With regard to the psalmody, the directions of nos. 121–125 should be followed.

3691 261. During the gospel canticle at morning prayer and evening prayer there may be an incensation of the altar, then of the priest and congregation.

---

7 See nos. 100–109 of this Instruction.

1 SC art. 28 [DOL 1 no. 28].

R4 For nos. 254 and 256 see DOL 309 no. 2536, note R1.

262. The choral obligation applies to the community, not to the place of celebration,   3692
which need not be a church, especially in the case of those hours that are celebrated
without solemnity.

263. All taking part stand during: 3693
  a. the introduction to the office and the introductory verses of each hour;
  b. the hymn;
  c. the gospel canticle;
  d. the intercessions, the Lord's Prayer, and the concluding prayer.

264. All sit to listen to the readings, except the gospel.   3694

265. The assembly either sits or stands, depending on custom, while the psalms and   3695
other canticles (with their antiphons) are being said.

266. All make the sign of the cross, from forehead to breast and from left shoulder   3696
to right, at:
  a. the beginning of the hours, when *God, come to my assistance* is being said;
  b. the beginning of the gospel, the Canticles of Zechariah, of Mary, and of
  Simeon.
      The sign of the cross is made on the mouth at the beginning of the invitatory,
at *Lord, open my lips.*

II. SINGING IN THE OFFICE

267. In the rubrics and norms of this Instruction, the words "say," "recite," etc., are   3697
to be understood to refer to either singing or recitation, in the light of the principles
that follow.

268. "The sung celebration of the divine office is more in keeping with the nature of   3698
this prayer and a mark of both higher solemnity and closer union of hearts in
offering praise to God. . . . Therefore the singing of the office is earnestly recommended to those who carry out the office in choir or in common."[2]

269. The declarations of Vatican Council II on liturgical singing apply to all liturgi-   3699
cal services but in a special way to the liturgy of the hours.[3] Though every part of it
has been revised in such a way that all may be fruitfully recited even by individuals, many of these parts are lyrical in form and do not yield their fuller meaning
unless they are sung, especially the psalms, canticles, hymns, and responsories.

270. Hence, in celebrating the liturgy singing is not to be regarded as an embellish-   3700
ment superimposed on prayer; rather, it wells up from the depths of a soul intent on
prayer and the praise of God and reveals in a full and complete way the community
nature of Christian worship.
      Christian communities of all kinds seeking to use this form of prayer as fre-
quently as possible are to be commended. Clerics and religious, as well as all the
people of God, must be trained by suitable catechesis and practice to join together
in singing the hours in a spirit of joy, especially on Sundays and holydays. But it is
no easy task to sing the entire office; nor is the Church's praise to be considered
either by origin or by nature the exclusive possession of clerics and monks but the

---

  [2] SCR, Instr. MusSacr, 5 March 1967, no. 37 [DOL 508 no. 4158]. See also SC art. 99 [DOL 1 no. 99].

  [3] See SC art. 113 [DOL 1 no. 113].

property of the whole Christian community. Therefore several principles must be kept simultaneously in mind if the sung celebration of the liturgy of the hours is to be performed correctly and to stand out in its true nature and splendor.

3701   271. It is particularly appropriate that there be singing at least on Sundays and holydays, so that the different degrees of solemnity will thus come to be recognized.

3702   272. It is the same with the hours: all are not of equal importance; thus it is desirable that those that are the true hinges of the office, that is, morning prayer and evening prayer, should receive greater prominence through the use of singing.

3703   273. A celebration with singing throughout is commendable, provided it has artistic and spiritual excellence; but it may be useful on occasion to apply the principle of "progressive solemnity." There are practical reasons for this, as well as the fact that in this way the various elements of liturgical celebration are not treated indiscriminately, but each can again be given its connatural meaning and genuine function. The liturgy of the hours is then not seen as a beautiful memorial of the past demanding intact preservation as an object of admiration; rather it is seen as open to constantly new forms of life and growth and to being the unmistakable sign of a community's vibrant vitality.

The principle of "progressive solemnity" therefore is one that recognizes several intermediate stages between singing the office in full and just reciting all the parts. Its application offers the possibility of a rich and pleasing variety. The criteria are the particular day or hour being celebrated, the character of the individual elements comprising the office, the size and composition of the community, as well as the number of singers available in the circumstances.

With this increased range of variation, it is possible for the public praise of the Church to be sung more frequently than formerly and to be adapted in a variety of ways to different circumstances. There is also great hope that new ways and expressions of public worship may be found for our own age, as has clearly always happened in the life of the Church.

3704   274. For liturgical celebrations sung in Latin, Gregorian chant, as the music proper to the Roman liturgy, should have pride of place, all other things being equal.[4] Nevertheless, "the Church does not exclude any type of sacred music from liturgical services as long as the music matches the spirit of the service itself and the character of the individual parts and is not a hindrance to the required active participation of the people."[5] At a sung office, if a melody is not available for the given antiphon, another antiphon should be taken from those in the repertoire, provided it is suitable in terms of nos. 113 and 121–125.

3705   275. Since the liturgy of the hours may be celebrated in the vernacular, "appropriate measures are to be taken to prepare melodies for use in the vernacular singing of the divine office."[6]

3706   276. But it is permissible to sing the various parts in different languages at one and the same celebration.[7]

---

[4] See SC art. 116 [DOL 1 no. 116].

[5] SCR, Instr. MusSacr no. 9 [DOL 508 no. 4130]. See also SC art. 116 [DOL 1 no. 116].

[6] SCR, Instr. MusSacr no. 41 [DOL 508 no. 4162]; see also nos. 54–61 [DOL 508 nos. 4175–82].

[7] See ibid. no. 51 [DOL 508 no. 4172].

277. The decision on which parts to choose for singing follows from the authentic structure of a liturgical celebration. This demands that the significance and function of each part and of singing should be fully respected. Some parts by their nature call for singing:[8] in particular, acclamations, responses to the greetings of priest and ministers, responses in litanies, also antiphons and psalms, the verses and reprises in responsories, hymns and canticles.[9]

3707

278. Clearly the psalms are closely bound up with music (see nos. 103–120), as both Jewish and Christian tradition confirm. In fact a complete understanding of many of the psalms is greatly assisted by singing them or at least not losing sight of their poetic and musical character. Accordingly, whenever possible singing the psalms should have preference, at least for the major days and hours and in view of the character of the psalms themselves.

3708

279. The different ways of reciting the psalms have been described in nos. 121–123. Varying these ways should depend not so much on external circumstances as on the different genres of the psalms to be recited in the same celebration. Thus the wisdom psalms and the narrative psalms are perhaps better listened to, whereas psalms of praise and thanksgiving are of their nature designed for singing in common. The main consideration is to ensure that the celebration is not too inflexible or elaborate nor concerned merely with formal observance of rules, but that it matches the reality of what is celebrated. The primary aim must be to inspire hearts with a desire for genuine prayer and to show that the celebration of God's praise is a thing of joy (see Ps 147).

3709

280. Even when the hours are recited, hymns can nourish prayer, provided they have doctrinal and literary excellence; but of their nature they are designed for singing and so, as far as possible, at a celebration in common they should be sung.

3710

281. The short responsory after the reading at morning prayer and evening prayer (see no. 49) is of its nature designed for singing and indeed for congregational singing.

3711

282. The responsories following the readings in the office of readings by their very nature and function also call for their being sung. In the plan of the office, however, they are composed in such a way that they retain their power even in individual and private recitation. Responsories set to simpler melodies can be sung more frequently than those responsories drawn from the traditional liturgical books.

3712

283. The longer readings and the short readings are not of themselves designed for singing. When they are proclaimed, great care should be taken that the reading is dignified, clear, and distinct and that it is really audible and fully intelligible for all. The only acceptable melody for a reading is therefore one that best ensures the hearing of the words and the understanding of the text.

3713

284. Texts that are said only by the person presiding, such as the concluding prayer, can be sung gracefully and appropriately, especially in Latin. This, however, will be more difficult in some languages, unless singing makes the texts more clearly audible for all.

3714

---

[8] See ibid. no. 6 [DOL 508 no. 4127].

[9] See ibid. nos. 16 a and 38 [DOL 508 nos. 4137 and 4159].

427. SC DIVINE WORSHIP, **Decree** *Horarum Liturgia*, promulgating the *editio typica* of the book for the liturgy of the hours, 11 April 1971: AAS 63 (1971) 712; Not 7 (1971) 145.

3715   Through the liturgy of the hours, which from longstanding practice it celebrates throughout each day, the Church fulfills the Lord's command to pray without ceasing and at the same time offers praise to God the Father and intercedes for the salvation of the world.

    Vatican Council II accordingly attached great importance to this established practice of the Church and intended its renewal. Therefore the Council took pains to ensure the proper reform of this manner of praying. Its intent was that priests and the other members of the Church might, in the present-day circumstances, carry out the office better and more completely (see SC art. 84).[a]

    This work of reform has been brought to its conclusion and approved by Pope Paul VI through the Apostolic Constitution *Laudis canticum*, 1 November 1970.[b] The Congregation for Divine Worship has therefore seen to the publication of the book composed in Latin for the celebration of the liturgy of the hours according to the Roman Rite. It declares the edition now being issued to be the *editio typica*.[c]

    Anything to the contrary notwithstanding.

▶   216.   SC DIVINE WORSHIP, Notification on the Roman Missal, the book for the liturgy of the hours, the General Calendar, 14 June 1971:

    nos. 3, 4 c: Liturgy of the hours [nos. 1772, 1773].

428. SC DIVINE WORSHIP, **Notice** *Annis praeteritis*, on the patristic lectionary for optional use, October 1971: Not 7 (1971) 289.

3716   During the last several years some conferences of bishops have received permission to approve for use in the celebration of the divine office special collections of texts chosen from the Fathers or ecclesiastical writers. The purpose was to enrich the celebration of the office and to prepare a new liturgy of the hours by means of lawful experimentation.

    This concession was made "until a new corpus of patristic readings for the liturgy of the hours should be approved."

    Now that the General Instruction of the Liturgy of the Hours has been promulgated through the Apostolic Constitution *Laudis canticum*, 1 November 1970,[a] however, the collections in question must be brought into line with the norms in the General Instruction: "Further, the conferences of bishops may prepare additional texts, suited to the traditions and culture of their own region, for inclusion in the optional lectionary as a supplement. These texts are to be taken from the works of *Catholic* writers, *outstanding for their teaching and holiness of life* " (no. 162; see also nos. 160 and 161).[b]

---

  [a] See DOL 1 no. 84.

  [b] See DOL 424.

  [c] See DOL 434, on vernacular editions; DOL 125 no. 884 note R3, on the completeness of vernacular editions.

  [a] See DOL 424.

  [b] See DOL 426 no. 3592; also nos. 3590–91.

429. SC DIVINE WORSHIP, **Norms** *Novo Liturgiae Horarum* on texts for *ad interim* use in the divine office and the Mass, especially in sung celebrations, 11 November 1971: Not 7 (1971) 379–383.

I. DIVINE OFFICE

Since the new book for the liturgy of the hours has now been published, books   3717
must be prepared for the sung celebration of the divine office in Latin. The Congregation for Divine Worship is already engaged in this task, but a certain amount of time is necessary for its completion.

Meantime several communities of canons or religious desiring to have sung celebrations in Latin of the divine office or a part of it have made this inquiry: whether the reformed structure of the liturgy of the hours may be used while retaining *ad interim* the *Breviarium Romanum* and the *Antiphonale sacrosanctae Romanae Ecclesiae pro diurnis Horis*, published under St. Pius X. There are, moreover, others who are still waiting for vernacular editions of the *Liturgia Horarum* or for whom the volumes in Latin are not available, but who wish to follow the new rite for the liturgy of the hours. They have made the same inquiry regarding the celebration of the divine office, whether chorally or individually.

Accordingly the Congregation for Divine Worship with the approval of Pope Paul VI offers the plan here outlined, until publication of the new books. The plan is designed to adapt the celebration of the reformed structure of the liturgy of the hours by those who use the old liturgical books *ad interim* whether in choir, in common, or in private.

The plan proposed for adapting the former office to the new liturgy of the hours must be viewed as a completely temporary solution; it has been drawn up solely for the purpose of meeting the peculiar situation of this transitional period. The plan must in no way be seen as a substitute for the book of the liturgy of the hours, for although use of the book is as yet not possible, in the future its use in its entirety will be required in view of its spiritual wealth and variety and the explicit norm of the Church (see Ap. Const. *Laudis canticum*).[a]

The intent of the reformed book is not to shorten, but to foster prayer — marked by tranquility of spirit, interspersed with silent intervals, and shared in preferably by a community — that is attentive and devout because the correspondence of the office with the true time of day is made easier.

Those communities especially for which at least one copy of the reformed book is readily available are not to omit using those new elements of the liturgy of the hours that can be carried out by a single minister, for example, the readings, prayers, intercessions.

INVITATORY

The place for the invitatory is at the beginning of the entire round of daily   3718
prayer, that is, it comes before either the office of readings or morning prayer, whichever service begins the day. The invitatory consists of the verse *Domine labia* and the psalm with its antiphon.

OFFICE OF READINGS

℣ *Deus in adiutorium, Gloria, Alleluia* (omitted during Lent). When the office of   3719
readings precedes morning prayer, then, as noted, the invitatory comes before it.

Morning hymn.

---

a   See DOL 424 no. 3429.

The psalmody: three psalms with their antiphons.

The verse introducing the readings, without *Pater noster*.

The readings are as follows:

a. In the case of an office with three nocturns, the biblical reading is formed by making one reading out of the three of the first nocturn; the patristic reading, by making one reading out of the three of the second nocturn.

After each reading there is a responsory, chosen at will; it is said after the second reading even when the *Te Deum* is to be said.

b. In the case of an office with only one nocturn, there is only the biblical reading — composed in the way indicated — and, when there is one, the reading related to the saint.

The *Te Deum*, recited only on Sundays outside Lent, on the days of the octave of Easter and Christmas, and on solemnities and feasts, may conclude with the verse *Aeterne fac . . . .*

Prayer of the day.

V. *Benedicamus Domino.*

R. *Amen.*

MORNING PRAYER

3720   V. *Deus in adiutorium, Gloria, Alleluia.*

All of this is omitted when morning prayer is celebrated as the first hour of the day; in this case the invitatory is said.

Hymn

Psalmody: one of the first three psalms from morning prayer is said, then the canticle, then the final psalm, all with their antiphons.

Capitulum without the R. *Deo gratias.*

Short responsory from prime or terce, without the V. and R.

Benedictus with its antiphon.

Preces: some of the invocations or verses from the *preces* from the formularies of the weekday *preces* of morning prayer are said.

Pater noster. Prayer of the day without the *Oremus*.

If a priest or deacon presides, he blesses the congregation as at Mass and says the dismissal formulary: *Ite in pace*. R. *Deo gratias.*

The conclusion in the absence of a priest or deacon or in private recitation is: *Dominus nos benedicat, et ab omni malo defendat, et ad vitam perducat aeternam.* R. *Amen.*

MIDDAY HOUR

3721   V. *Deus in adiutorium, Gloria, Alleluia.*

Hymn, psalms, and *capitulum* of terce, sext, or none, depending on the time the office is said.

The short responsory is not said, but the V. and R. following it are.

Prayer of the day, preceded by Oremus and closed with the short conclusion.

V. *Benedicamus Domino.* R. *Deo gratias.*

EVENING PRAYER

3722   V. *Deus in adiutorium, Gloria, Alleluia.*

Hymn.

Psalmody: three of the five psalms for evening prayer, with their antiphons.

But on Sundays two of these three psalms are to be Ps 109 [110] *Dixit Dominus* and Ps. 113 [114] *In exitu* (up to but not including the verse *Non nobis*).

Capitulum, without the R. *Deo gratias.*

Short responsory from either sext or none, without the V. and R.

Magnificat with its antiphon.

Preces chosen from the invocations belonging to the final section of the Litany of the Saints.

Pater noster, prayer, blessing, and dismissal as in morning prayer.

NIGHT PRAYER

V. *Deus in adiutorium, Gloria, Alleluia.*   3723

An examination of conscience is recommended; it may be incorporated as a community celebration into the penitential rite and follow the formularies used at Mass.

Hymn: *Te lucis.*

Psalmody:

a. on Sundays and solemnities: the first and third (or just the second) psalm for Sunday night prayer;

b. on other days: one of the psalms for night prayer of the day. But, in keeping with the rule in the General Instruction of the Liturgy of the Hours no. 88,[b] the psalms for Sunday night prayer may always be used.

Capitulum. Short responsory without the V. and R. , antiphon, *Nunc dimittis*, then the prayer, preceded by the *Oremus*, and with the short conclusion.

Blessing: *Noctem quietam*, as found at the beginning of night prayer.

Marian antiphon: In the Easter season this is the *Regina caeli*; at other times it may be one of the following: *Alma Redemptoris Mater, Ave Regina caelorum, Salve Regina, Sub tuum praesidium*, or others approved by the conferences of bishops.

The verse, prayer, and the *Divinum auxilium* are omitted.

II. MASS

Until publication of the book *Ordo cantus Missae*,[c] now in press, those who wish   3724
to celebrate Mass with Gregorian chant may still use the established collection in the *Graduale Romanum* of St. Pius X.

Note however:

1. For the final Sundays in Ordinary Time: the plan for each Sunday in Ordinary Time may be substituted for the chants assigned for the Twenty-third Sunday after Pentecost; or a "proper" may be put together out of the chants of the various Sundays in Ordinary Time.

The same applies to the Sundays following the Third Sunday after Epiphany.

2. For celebrations of the saints, chants from those in the *Graduale Romanum* or the pertinent ones from the Common of the Saints may be used.

---

b   See DOL 426 no. 3518.

c   See DOL 534 and 535.

430. SC DIVINE WORSHIP, **Guidelines** *Sacra Congregatio pro Cultu Divino,* on celebrating the liturgy of the hours during Holy Week and the Easter octave, for those using the former breviary, 3 March 1972: Not 8 (1972) 96–99 (excerpt).

3725   The Congregation for Divine Worship on 11 November 1971 issued "Norms" regarding *ad interim* texts for use in the celebration of the divine office by those who still have the former liturgical books.[a]

Those "Norms" must also be followed in the special offices of Holy Thursday, Good Friday, Holy Saturday, and the Easter octave.

3726   In order to facilitate adaptation on these days to the new structure of the liturgy of the hours, however, the following plan for the office is outlined here.

1. In all the offices the overall structure described in the General Instruction of the Liturgy of the Hours must be followed.

2. Parts that are not considered to be propers are taken from the Ordinary for the passion season and the Easter season.

3. At morning prayer, evening prayer, and night prayer there is this substitution for the short responsory: for the Easter triduum, the antiphon *Christus factus est;* for the Easter octave, the antiphon *Haec dies.*

4. For all the hours the *Gloria Patri* is said as usual at the end of the psalms.

5. On the Second Sunday of Easter (in albis) *the office is said as on other days during the octave with the parts proper to this Sunday.*

6. Structure of the office. [. . .]

431. SC DOCTRINE OF THE FAITH, **Declaration,** on the authentic interpretation of the General Instruction of the Liturgy of the Hours, no. 162, 9 July 1972 (Italian).*

3727   For Catholic authors the norm establishes that they be "outstanding for their teaching and holiness of life."[a] That necessarily limits the choice to authors whose life and teaching can unreservedly be held up to the faithful and clearly advises us *not,* as a general rule, *to choose* the texts of *living authors.*

432. SC DIVINE WORSHIP, **Notification** *Universi qui Officium,* on the liturgy of the hours for certain religious communities, 6 August 1972: Not 8 (1972) 254–258.

3728   All who are celebrating the divine office according to the new books for the liturgy of the hours are, as they say themselves, discovering richer resources for nurturing their spiritual life; from it they are deriving a new motivation for renewing the way they celebrate God's praises.

---

[a]   See DOL 429.

*   Prot. 640/72, quoted in Not 8 (1972) 249 [see DOL 433 no. 3737].

[a]   See DOL 426 no. 3592.

But some religious communities, mainly contemplative, desire a larger collection of the psalms to be recited each day, especially in the office of readings. They also would like to have the right to vary the psalms for the three minor hours. Some have even requested permission to retain the Roman Breviary.

This Congregation stresses the importance of those who in solitude and silence, in constant prayer and willing penance, offer to God a sublime sacrifice of praise,[1] imaging Christ in contemplation on the mountain.[2] At the same time, although favoring their desires and wishes, the Congregation strongly encourages these religious to enter worthily, attentively, and devoutly into that colloquy between God and humankind to which they are deputed by the law of the Church;[3] to celebrate the liturgy with a dedication of spirit and resolve of mind to be the embodiment of the Church as it is a community of prayer.[4]

The solemnity with which they carry out the liturgy of the hours is also at issue. That highlights the importance attached to the public prayer of the Church as it is gathered together with Christ its Bridegroom in the Holy Spirit and addresses praise to the Father. The solemnity of the office is evidence also that those who, so to speak, exist in the very heart of the Church, value the Church's prayer, that is, the prayer of Christ and his Body to the Father,[5] and that they look on that prayer as the extension and reminder of the eucharistic celebration through all the hours of the day. The solemnity is also the sign that these religious regard the exchange or dialogue between God and his children as something not to be interrupted during the day and that they are more completely fulfilling the duty of working toward the building up and growth of Christ's Mystical Body, as well as toward the well-being of the particular Churches — a primary concern of those leading the contemplative life.[6]   **3729**

I.   Toward the realization of these ideals the Constitution *Sacrosanctum Concilium* made certain decrees that are suited to the integration of the liturgy of the hours into the fabric of the Christian life and that are consistent with the Church's tradition: **3730**

1.   Because the purpose of the office is to sanctify the day, the hours are to be returned to the true time of day corresponding to them (art. 88).[a]

2.   By the ancient tradition of the universal Church lauds as morning prayer and vespers as evening prayer are the two hinges on which the daily office turns; hence they are to be considered as the chief hours and celebrated as such (art. 89 a).[b]

3.   The hour known as matins shall be made up of fewer psalms and longer readings (art. 89 c).[c]

---

[1]   See PC no. 7 [DOL 10 no. 205].

[2]   See LG no. 46.

[3]   See SC no. 84 [DOL 1 no. 84]. GILH nos. 17, 24, 31 b [DOL 426 nos. 3447, 3454, 3461; Not and EDL erroneously cite GILH 31 b as 316!].

[4]   See GILH nos. 9, 24 [DOL 426 nos. 3439, 3454].

[5]   See SC art. 85 [DOL 1 no. 85].

[6]   See GILH no. 24 [DOL 426 no. 3454].

[a]   See DOL 1 no. 88.

[b]   See DOL 1 no. 89.

[c]   See DOL 1 no. 89.

4. The hour of prime is to be suppressed (art. 84 d).[d]

5. Readings from sacred Scripture shall be so arranged that the riches of God's word may be easily accessible in greater measure (art. 92 a).[e]

6. Readings excerpted from the works of the Fathers, doctors, and ecclesiastical writers shall be better selected (art. 92 b).[f]

The General Instruction of the Liturgy of the Hours has accurately carried out the conciliar mandate. All who are the special representatives of the praying Church, religious communities above all, would be obliged to adhere willingly to the letter and spirit of the new liturgy of the hours in celebrating the office were it not for the obstacle of those legitimate reasons indicated in the decree of the Congregation for Divine Worship, issued on 11 November 1971.[g]

3731   In order, however, that the spirit of the new liturgy of the hours may not fail to be understood by some people, serious thought must be devoted to those elements in the General Instruction that contribute to achieving a more complete celebration. These elements are the following:

a. An understanding and spiritual savoring of the psalms (see GILH nos. 100–109):[h] this will lead to their being sung or recited in such a way that those who pray them will experience what may be called the spiritual fragrance and beauty of the psalms.

b. Sung celebration of the divine office: to those who carry out the office in choir or in common the sung office is strongly recommended as more consistent with the nature of this way of prayer and as a sign of greater solemnity and of a deeper inner union of hearts in giving voice to God's praises. The singing of the office should be put into practice according to the laws and customs of each community; but there must be care at least to suggest the principle of "progressive solemnity" (see no. 273).[i]

c. In order to allow the voice of the Holy Spirit to be heard inwardly and to bind personal prayer more closely to the word of God and the public prayer of the Church, prudently interspersed periods of silence are to be observed (see no. 202)[j] after each psalm, once the antiphon has been repeated, and after both the long and the short readings.

d. As the laws or traditions of each community permit, the office of readings is to keep its character as nocturnal praise (see nos. 57–58);[k] especially on Sundays and more solemn days, a vigil may be added. This is especially suited to those who live the contemplative life; the Fathers and spiritual writers have repeatedly exhorted them to nocturnal prayer to express and awaken the expectation of the Lord's Second Coming. All therefore who retain its nocturnal character for the office of readings are to be commended (see no. 72).[l]

---

[d]   See DOL 1 no. 84.

[e]   See DOL 1 no. 92.

[f]   See DOL 1 no. 92.

[g]   See DOL 429.

[h]   See DOL 426 nos. 3530–39.

[i]   See DOL 426 no. 3703.

[j]   See DOL 426 no. 3632.

[k]   See DOL 426 nos. 3487–88.

[l]   See DOL 426 no. 3502.

e.   Where possible, psalm-prayers are to be put to use; they help those praying the psalms to perceive especially their Christian interpretation. The psalm-prayers are those which, in keeping with an ancient tradition, are said after the psalm is completed and a period of silence has ensued, as a resumé and resolution of the sentiments of those praying the psalms (see no. 112).[m] Collections of such prayers may still be composed and submitted to the Holy See for approval before the supplement to *The Liturgy of the Hours* is published.

f.   In addition to the readings provided in *The Liturgy of the Hours*, particular lectionaries may be composed that are adapted to the special spiritual needs of religious communities; prior submission for the Holy See's approval is required.

In regard to readings, especially the readings from Scripture, the understanding of which is the reason for all other readings, note that they are an encounter and dialogue with God. They are the praise of the goodness of the one who through his word, passed down to us in Christ and in the Church, has ushered us into the eternal colloquy of his love. This is the clear explanation of why the readings in the liturgy may also be regarded as the praise of God (see nos. 140 and 29).[n] But in order for the readings to be genuine prayer as they are proclaimed, every care must be exercised that they are read clearly and distinctly and in such a way as to be truly intelligible to all (see no. 283).[o] The only acceptable melody for sung readings is one that ensures that the texts are heard and understood.

II.   Against this background, the adaptations that follow may be introduced into   3732
the structure of the liturgy of the hours when special groups wish to prolong the celebration of the hours, especially the office of readings.

A. OFFICE OF READINGS

During the week: six psalms may be said, thus: three psalms of Week I (or II),   3733
followed by the biblical reading of the day with its responsory; three psalms of the same day for Week III (or IV), followed by the patristic reading of the day with its responsory.

On Sundays and holydays there may be six psalms and three canticles for a pro-longed vigil, in the way already outlined, namely: three psalms and a biblical reading with its responsory; three psalms and a patristic reading with its responsory; three canticles, a gospel, the *Te Deum*.

B. DAYTIME HOURS

The General Instruction of the Liturgy of the Hours establishes that the hours   3734
of terce, sext, and none may be retained by those who live the contemplative life, but without prejudice to particular law (no. 76).[p] Accordingly, those who celebrate these three minor hours may substitute for the supplementary psalmody, except on Sundays, the following psalms: *at terce*: the psalms of the current week for the daytime hour; *at sext*: the psalms of the preceding week for the daytime hour; *at none*: the psalms of the following week for the daytime hour.

Introduction of the changes indicated requires the consent of the community,   3735
expressed by two-thirds of the secret votes cast being in favor.

---

m   See DOL 426 no. 3542.

n   See DOL 426 nos. 3570 and 3459.

o   See DOL 426 no. 3713.

p   See DOL 426 no. 3506.

The Congregation for Divine Worship after consultation with the Congregation for Religious and Secular Institutes, has drawn up these norms. Pope Paul VI approved them on 5 August 1972 and ordered their publication.[R5]

All things to the contrary notwithstanding.

433. SC DIVINE WORSHIP, **Note** *Mense octobris anni 1971*, on optional readings from the Fathers in the liturgy of the hours, October 1972: Not 8 (1972) 249–250.

3736   In October 1971 the Congregation for Divine Worship published through *Notitiae* (no. 66, p. 289)[a] a kind of caution regarding the prescription of the General Instruction of the Liturgy of the Hours no. 162 on the preparation of optional "patristic" readings in lectionaries for the divine office.

     The caution was aimed at collections of readings from the "Fathers" that were being circulated in such places as Belgium, France, Italy, and the United States, either unofficially or under the sponsorship of the conferences of bishops; it was permissible to use such collections until the complete publication of *The Liturgy of the Hours*. Now that this book has appeared, however, the rules given in the General Instruction of the Liturgy of the Hours no. 162 for the choosing of readings must be followed. "The conferences of bishops may prepare additional texts, suited to the traditions and mentality of their own region, for inclusion in the optional lectionary

---

[R5]   In response to several queries on the celebration of the liturgy of the hours as adapted to the office of certain religious communities, particularly of monks and nuns, it is helpful to present the following more precise details. They form a useful complement to the rules given by the Notification of 6 Aug. 1972 (Not 8 [1972] 257).

     A. Office of readings.
        1. *During the week*: On Thursday of Week II, replace Ps 44 in the first part of the office with Ps 34, divided into three sections: vv. 2–8, 9–15, 16–23. This is to avoid repeating Ps 44, which occurs also on Thursday of Week IV.
        2. *For solemnities and feasts*: The three psalms of the first part of the office are from the proper or the common. For the psalms in the second part, take *ad libitum* those of the office of readings from one of the four Sundays; this should be done in such a way as to avoid repeating one psalm already in the first part or in another hour of the day. (For example, do not choose for the second part of this office the psalms [1, 2, and 3] of the first Sunday for several feasts of the Lord on which Ps 2 already occurs [2 Feb., 25 March, 14 Sept., Christ the King, 25 Dec.]. Similarly the office of the third Sunday is incompatible with the solemnity of Christ the King [Ps 145], just as the office of the fourth Sunday is with the psalms for the Dedication of a Church or of the Common of the Blessed Virgin [Ps 24] or with those of the Baptism of the Lord [Ps 66]).
        3. *Verse before the second reading*: Use the verse indicated in the office from which the psalms for the second part are chosen. In a case of duplication, during the principal seasons, take one of the verses indicated for terce, sext, and none. Thus: on Monday and Thursday: the verse of terce; on Tuesday and Friday: the verse of sext; on Wednesday, Saturday, and Sunday: the verse of none.
        4. *Verse before the gospel on a vigil*: it is replaced by the dialogue preceding the gospel, as at Mass: greeting, announcement of the reading, acclamation.

     B. The little hours.
        1. *On solemnities and Sundays*: Use the supplementary psalmody (Gradual Psalms).
        2. On other days: Use the following psalms: at terce: the psalms of the current day of the week for the daytime hour; at sext: psalms of the corresponding day in the previous week; at none: psalms of the corresponding day in the following week.
     This rule if applied to the Saturdays of Weeks II and IV would result in a repetition of Ps 34 at sext and none (on the Saturday of the first and second week). To avoid this duplication use the following psalms after the portion of Ps 119: at terce: Ps 34, divided into two parts, vv. 2–11 and 12–23; at sext: Ps 61 and Ps 64; at none: Ps 45, divided into two parts, vv. 2–10 and 11–18: Not 10 (1974) 39–40.

     [a]   See DOL 428.

as a supplement. These texts are to be taken from the works of Catholic writers, outstanding for their teaching and holiness of life."[b]

The recent declaration of the Congregation for the Doctrine of the Faith (9 July   3737
1972, Prot. 640/72) explains this prescription more precisely: "For Catholic authors the norm establishes that they be 'outstanding for their teaching and holiness of life.' That necessarily limits the choice to authors whose life and teaching can unreservedly be held up to the faithful and clearly advises us *not*, as a general rule, *to choose* the texts of *living authors*."[c]

Some editors in preparing lectionaries have sought to respect the prescription by marking with an asterisk or by a preliminary notation readings taken from living authors or from authors who are non-Catholics or clearly not outstanding for their "teaching and holiness of life." The intent was to indicate that such selections were suitable only for personal meditation or private use, not for celebration of the divine office.

Now, however, such a measure seems completely inadequate: it does not in fact eliminate the danger of the ambiguity easily resulting from an intermingling of readings that are allowed with those not allowed in the celebration of the liturgy of the hours.

Careful consideration of all the factors involved makes it apparent that a clear   3738
distinction between editions of books is, if not necessary, at least highly advisable: one should contain collections of the "Fathers" for celebration of the divine office; a different book should contain the collections of writers that are useful for private reading or meditation.

Such collections may rightly be marked by a broader freedom of selection; but the collections of readings from the "Fathers," that is, texts for use in celebrating the liturgy, must conform exactly to the norms laid down.

434. SC DIVINE WORSHIP, Note *Liturgiae Horarum interpretationes*, on vernacular editions of *The Liturgy of the Hours*, 15 January 1973: Not 9 (1973) 3.

Translations of the *Liturgia Horarum* for publication in the vernacular are being   3739
assiduously prepared in all parts of the world. Publishers are taking different approaches in trying to overcome the technical problems arising from the fact that the four volumes are so large. Even with the *editio typica* the printers were faced with the same difficulty; they could find no other solution but to make each of the volumes self-contained, with the result that some parts had to be repeated in all the volumes.

Is there any way to avoid this? That is up to production editors and typographers. Whatever procedure is adopted, however, it is supremely important not to burden priests with an edition that would make the recitation of the office of readings difficult: for example, if they had to use two volumes at the same time, one for the office of readings and the other for the daytime hours, or had to deal with other similar solutions.

Any such measure will certainly be troublesome and will provide a ready excuse for neglecting the office of readings, which is an integral part of the liturgy

---

[b]   DOL 426 no. 3592.

[c]   DOL 431 no. 3727.

of the hours. Daily reading of the Fathers, in addition to the readings from Scripture, is held to be among the principal new elements in the reformed divine office; it "will contribute greatly to the spiritual life" both for those consecrated to the Lord in a special way and for the faithful generally (see GILH no. 55).[a]

In order that ordained ministers may faithfully fulfill the mandate received from the Church to carry out the entire daily course of the liturgy of the hours, they need to be provided with the practical means of doing so, namely, an edition easy to use. Responsibility for this is in the hands of the editors and publishers.

▶   335. SC CATHOLIC EDUCATION, Instruction *In ecclesiasticam futurorum sacerdotum*, on liturgical formation in seminaries, 3 June 1979:

> nos. 28–31:   Liturgy of the hours [nos. 2807–10].
> Appendix, nos. 68–75: Sanctification of the day and the liturgy of the hours [nos. 2909–16].

435. SECRETARIAT OF STATE, **Letter** of Cardinal A. Casaroli to Bishop C. Manziana, on the occasion of the 30th National Liturgical Week of Italy (Casale-Monferrato, 27–31 August 1979), with the theme: The Church That Prays in Time, August 1979: Not 15 (1979) 597–600 (Italian).

3740   Pope John Paul II has been pleased to learn that the 30th National Liturgical Week of Italy, to be celebrated at Casale-Monferrato, a diocese rich in ancient Christian traditions, will have as its theme the liturgy of the hours.

It is gratifying to the Pope to see in such a meeting the continued study of the several documents on the liturgical reform intended by Vatican Council II, with a view to their deeper understanding. Such an effort will help the great number of participants to grasp more fully the spirit of the reform of the liturgy and to transfer it, in all its forms and expressions, into the life of the entire ecclesial community and of each one of its members.

3741   The need of both pastors and people for such a reflection and, so to speak, pause for meditation is obvious to everyone. It comes after the intense period of activity carrying out the liturgical reform, during which the texts and rites have largely been recast with a view to making the liturgy more accessible and simple, but at the same time richer and more varied.

Pastors must have a profound grasp of the genuine meaning of the liturgy, so that they may safeguard its character as "a sacred action surpassing all others" (SC art. 7);[a] also so that they may protect it against a desacralization that stains, contaminates, and cheapens everything, as well as against a ritualism that could trivialize the surging vitality awakened in the Church by the passage of the Holy Spirit, the Creator (see SC art. 43).[b]

As for the people, their desire is to receive a way of participating ever more fully in the reformed liturgy with calm awareness and to find in the liturgy a solid basis on which to revitalize the substance of their faith ever more intensely; to find also an authentic source from which they are to draw the quiet ardor of their prayer each day.

---

[a]   See DOL 426 no. 3485.

[a]   DOL 1 no. 7.

[b]   See DOL 1 no. 43.

Because of such considerations and grounds the meeting's theme as articulated in the keynote, "The Church That Prays in Time," seems to the Pope to be of special interest. There are two reasons. The first is that it calls for a recognition of the fundamental importance of the divine office as the primary expression of the "public and common prayer" (GILH no. 1)[c] not only of the clergy and of those with a special mandate for it, but of the Church as a whole. The second reason is that the theme implicitly reaffirms the irreplaceable value of the encounter with God through prayer, in every moment and in every situation of human existence.

It is no accident that the Congregation for Catholic Education in its recent instruction on liturgical formation in seminaries states that "the reformed liturgy of the hours has opened up great spiritual riches for the praying Church . . . for all the people of God, who are strongly invited to take part in it" (no. 28)[d] . The document also intends that the students develop "a taste, an understanding, and a love for the riches of the office . . . and derive from it the support for their personal prayer and contemplation" (no. 29).[e] In this way they will later become masters in the special field of their own apostolate.

To understand, to love, to have a taste for the office: the Pope wishes to draw the attention of all the participants in the liturgical week to those three ideas.

First and foremost, to understand: there is not always and in everyone the genuine knowledge of the office concisely provided by Paul VI's Apostolic Constitution *Laudis canticum*[f] and more extensively by the General Instruction of the Liturgy of the Hours.[g] To understand means to perceive the office as the ecclesial prayer of adoration and praise to the Father, with and through Christ, in the Holy Spirit. To understand means to see it as the extension and prolongation of the eucharistic mystery through the great themes that are the marks and rhythm of the eucharistic celebration: remembrance, thanksgiving, offering, reconciliation with God. As the theme of the liturgical week suggests, to understand the office means to look on it as sanctifying time, that basic element in which our existence unfolds and in which for each one of us in some way the wonderful works of God accomplishing our salvation in history live again and are renewed. The "hinges" upon which God's wonderful works are purposefully set are the hour of morning prayer — God creates the world and recreates it in the risen Christ, and of evening prayer — God redeems the world from sin in the "blessed passion" of Christ the Lord, "the sun of righteousness" (Mal 4:2), "the splendor of the Father's glory" (Heb 1:3).   3742

To love the office. The General Instruction (no. 29)[h] calls to mind the daily obligation for all who have received the mandate to carry out the office; it repeats the daily duty of choral recitation by cathedral and collegial chapters;[i] it emphasizes the office's being recommended to religious and laity[j] as a joyous moment of encounter with God, as a song of love for the God who has himself dictated the words of the song and who in some way suggests its melody. Love the office because it makes those who pray it to be "one heart and one mind" in reciting or   3743

---

[c]   See DOL 426 no. 3431.

[d]   DOL 335 no. 2807.

[e]   DOL 335 no. 2808.

[f]   See DOL 424.

[g]   See DOL 426.

[h]   See DOL 426 no. 3459.

[i]   See DOL 426 no. 3461.

[j]   See DOL 426 no. 3461–62.

singing the same psalms, in hearing and meditating on the same biblical and patristic readings, and in the petitions of the same prayers.

3744   Finally, to have a taste for the divine office. It is particularly necessary to develop a taste for the psalms, these wonderful songs that are always relevant in the concreteness and richness of their sentiments of awe, praise, repentance, and trusting surrender. There is a need to find delight in community recitation of the office, in singing it in any of the variety of forms possible. To have a taste for the office also means for its *veritas temporis*, the appositeness to the moment that integrates it into life and sanctifies its rhythms and cadences. To savor the office in this sense means to have the ever more profound conviction that this prayer as it marks the hours of the day is not flight from the world of real life but a working along with God to bring about the world's salvation. It is altogether consistent with the logic of this thrust of the office that many communities of young people are gathering on their own initiative to celebrate the principal hours of the office. From this they are deriving great benefit, because their encounter with God enriches their encounter with each other and makes it fruitful.

The liturgical week at Casale will achieve the aim of its observance if it makes an effective contribution to understanding, loving, and savoring the office, as well as to restoring gradually the celebration of evening prayer in parishes on Sundays and holydays and to inaugurating little by little the celebration of morning prayer, particularly on special occasions. [. . .]

436. JOHN PAUL II, **Address** at St. Patrick's Cathedral, New York City, excerpt on the liturgy of the hours as community prayer, 3 October 1979: Not 15 (1979) 607–608 (English).

3745   St. Paul asks: "who will separate us from the love of Christ?"

As long as we remain what we are this morning — a community of prayer united in Christ, an ecclesial community of praise and worship of the Father — we shall understand and experience the answer: that no one — nothing at all — will ever separate us from the love of Christ. For us today, the Church's morning prayer is a joyful, communal celebration of God's love in Christ.

The value of the liturgy of the hours is enormous. Through it all the faithful, but especially the clergy and religious, fulfill a role of prime importance: Christ's prayer goes on in the world. The Holy Spirit himself intercedes for God's people (see Rom 8:27). The Christian community, with praise and thanksgiving, glorifies the wisdom, the power, the providence, and the salvation of our God.

In this prayer of praise we lift up our hearts to the Father of our Lord Jesus Christ, bringing with us the anguish and hopes, the joys and sorrows of all our brothers and sisters in the world.

And our prayer becomes likewise a school of sensitivity, making us aware of how much our destinies are linked together in the human family. Our prayer becomes a school of love — a special kind of Christian consecrated love, by which we love the world, but with the heart of Christ.

Through this prayer of Christ to which we give voice, our day is sanctified, our activities transformed, our actions made holy. We pray the same psalms that Jesus prayed and come into personal contact with him — the person to whom all Scripture points, the goal to which all history is directed.

In our celebration of the word of God, the mystery of Christ opens up before us and envelops us. And through union with our Head, Jesus Christ, we become ever more increasingly one with all the members of his Body. As never before, it becomes possible for us to reach out and embrace the world, but to embrace it with Christ: with authentic generosity, with pure and effective love, in service, in healing, and in reconciliation.

The efficacy of our prayer renders special honor to the Father because it is made always through Christ and for the glory of his name: "We ask this through our Lord Jesus Christ, your Son, who lives and reigns with you and the Holy Spirit, one God, for ever and ever."

As a community prayer and praise, with the liturgy of the hours among the highest priorities of our day — each day — we can be sure that nothing will separate us from the love of God that is in Christ Jesus our Lord.

Section 3. Monastic Orders

SUMMARY (DOL 437–439). Reverence for tradition and a concern to respond to the particular needs of certain monastic communities are evident in the 3 texts presented.

—In a reply the Consilium authorized experiments aimed at adaptations in the celebration of the office (DOL 437).

—In a letter to major superiors of three monastic orders the Congregation for Divine Worship gave directions for the work of revising their office and calendar (DOL 438).

—In a decree the Congregation for the Sacraments and Divine Worship approved for the Order of St. Benedict the new *Thesaurus Liturgiae Horarum Monasticae* (DOL 439).

437. CONSILIUM, **Rescript** (Benedictines), regarding experiments with the monastic office, 17 October 1967.*

3746   Right Reverend Father,

The Consilium has received your petition, dated 2 October, and made in the ·name of all the superiors of the English Benedictine Congregation, requesting powers to experiment with the structure of the divine office in choir.

I have pleasure in informing you that the Consilium grants you these powers. The details of the grant are as follows.

1. Each monastic community shall assemble for prayer at least three times a day.

2. Every hour of the divine office shall comprise psalms, lessons, a hymn, and a prayer.

3. The lessons shall be selected by the local superior, in consultation with the community.

4. The cursus of the psalms shall be so arranged that every week between 75 and 100 psalms shall be recited; the entire psalter shall be covered in four weeks, though certain psalms will occur with greater frequency.

5. Little hours and compline can be said out of choir, if found expedient.

6. This arrangement is granted to the monasteries of the English Benedictine Congregation, subject to the following conditions.

a. A list of the monasteries that propose to make use of this concession must be presented to the Consilium.

b. The concession is granted as an experiment for one year, commencing on 15 November 1967, and is to be renewed annually. In May of next year each monastery must submit a report to the Consilium on its use of this concession.

c. No publicity may be given to these experiments in any public or private publication, without the express permission of the Consilium.

d. These experiments shall come to an end when other provision is made by competent authority.

▶   403.   PAUL VI, Address to Benedictine abbots, on liturgical prayer, 1 October 1970.

438. SC DIVINE WORSHIP, **Letter** *Facendo seguito* to the Reverends Rembert Weakland, Abbot Primate OSB, Vincent Hermans, Procurator General OCSO, and Battista Gregorio, Procurator General SOCist, on the divine office and calendar of monastic orders, 8 July 1971.*

3747   Following up on several recent discussions, we take the opportunity to set forth some ideas in order to make clear the thinking of this Congregation with regard to the divine office and calendar for monastic orders.

3748   1.   Once the period of experiment is terminated, this Congregation wishes monastic orders to come to a decision on the fundamental elements of the *Ordo Liturgiae*

---

*   Private. Prot. N. 2919/67.

*   Private. Prot. NN. 1305, 1306, 1307/71; text in *Acta Curiae Generalis Ordinis Cistercensis*, nova series no. 21 (1972) 21–22.

Horarum in such a way that the entire monastic family will have a common basis both for the structure of the office and for its celebration.

2.   This common basis may make provision for several forms of celebration, so   3749
that all communities, in accord with their character and the external works in which they are engaged, may again be unified in the common basis of celebrating the divine office.

3.   This Congregation considers that the monastic orders ought to safeguard their   3750
characteristic form of prayer — at a measured pace, in common, and somewhat prolonged.

With regard to the psalter in particular, this Congregation recommends the preparation of three plans: one on the lines laid down in the *Rule of St. Benedict* (but possibly modified in details); another, distributing the psalter *over the period of one week*; a third, *over a period of two weeks*.

Plans based on a distribution of the psalms over a period of three or four weeks would seem to fall outside the spirit of the *Rule*.

For monks simply to adopt the prayer of the pastoral clergy, as set out in the *Liturgia Horarum* of the Roman Rite, would deprive the spiritual life of the Church of that distinctive note contributed by the monastic orders.

4.   Particular law will be able to provide norms that will meet the requirements of   3751
the circumstances or the needs of individual communities.

5.   This Congregation would be grateful if the liturgical commissions of each of   3752
the three branches of the monastic family would be kind enough to work together in an endeavor to find a common ground of agreement on the form of their prayer in the divine office.

439. SC SACRAMENT AND DIVINE WORSHIP, **Decree** *Operi Dei,* approving for the entire Benedictine Order the *Thesaurus Liturgiae Horarum Monasticae* and all its parts, 10 February 1977: Not 13 (1977) 157–158.

CONFEDERATION OF THE ORDER OF ST. BENEDICT

The *Opus Dei*, St. Benedict pointed out in his monastic rule, must have prece-   3753
dence over everything else. The desire of his religious family is that this principle, honored through the centuries, should take on a new vigor adapted to the conditions and needs of our age. For communities of monks and nuns as they carry out the public prayer of the Church in the liturgy of the hours not only foster their own spiritual life by establishing a continuing, intense communion with God, but also are an image of the praying Church. The Church, gathered together with Christ its Bridegroom in the Holy Spirit and turned toward the Father, praises him, offers up Christ's saving worship, and fulfills its duty of cooperating through prayer in building up and bringing to salvation the whole human family.

Consequently, the Confederation of the Order of St. Benedict, welcoming the principles established by Vatican Council II for the reform of the liturgy of the hours and for endowing it with new vitality and spiritual force, has carefully composed a *Thesaurus Liturgiae Horarum* through the studies and efforts of the liturgical commission charged with this work. The purpose of the *Thesaurus* is that there may be an aid and a model for each community of monks and nuns as the basis for its own renewal, suited to its region, and for its own more fruitful celebration of the divine office.

The Most Reverend Dom Rembert G. Weakland, Abbot Primate of the Confederation, in his letter of 11 November 1976, earnestly requests approval of the aforementioned *Thesaurus*.

Having considered the petition, the Congregation for the Sacraments and Divine Worship is pleased, in virtue of the powers granted by Pope Paul VI, to confirm the Latin text of the *Thesaurus Liturgiae Horarum Monasticae* as given in the copy submitted and as consisting in its several parts: *Directory* for the divine office, *Introduction*, the four plans for the psalter, Proper of Seasons, Proper of Saints, and Common of Saints.

▶   See also Chapter Three, Section 8: B. Liturgy and Religious Life.

CHAPTER FIVE

THE LITURGICAL YEAR

SUMMARY (DOL 440–499). The Constitution on the Liturgy in its fifth chapter dealt with the reform of the liturgical year. It recalled the significance and implications of the primacy of the celebration of the paschal mystery (art. 102, 105, 106), recognized the legitimate but subordinate place of the veneration of the Blessed Virgin and the saints (art. 103, 104, 111); it set out, accordingly, the principles for the revision of the liturgical year (art. 107–110). The seven sections of the present chapter reflect how the teaching and decrees of the Constitution have been applied.

Section 1. General Principles

SUMMARY (DOL 440–443). The 4 texts here are on the revision of the General Calendar: Paul VI's motu proprio approving the norms and calendar for the liturgical year (DOL 440), the decree promulgating the norms and the new calendar (DOL 441), the text of those general norms (DOL 442), and notification on an *ad interim* arrangement for the year 1971 (DOL 443).

▶   1.   VATICAN COUNCIL II, Constitution on the Liturgy *Sacrosanctum Concilium*, 8
         December 1963:

         art. 102–111:   The liturgical year [nos. 102–111].

▶   23. SC RITES (Consilium), Instruction (first) *Inter Oecumenici*, 26 September 1964:

         nos. 6:   The liturgical year [no. 298].
         14, 17:   Liturgical life of the clergy in the framework of
                                the liturgical year [nos. 306, 309].
         55:                    The homily and the liturgical year [no. 347].

440. PAUL VI, **Motu Proprio** *Mysterii paschalis*, approving the general norms
for the liturgical year and the new General Roman Calendar, 14 February
1969: AAS 61 (1969) 222–226; Not 5 (1969) 159–162.

3754   Celebration of the paschal mystery is of supreme importance in Christian
worship and the cycle of days, weeks, and the whole year unfold its meaning: this
is the teaching so clearly given us by Vatican Council II. Consequently, as to both
the plan of the Proper of Seasons and of Saints and the revision of the Roman
Calendar it is essential that Christ's paschal mystery receive greater prominence in
the reform of the liturgical year, for which the Council has given the norms.[1]

                                    I

3755   With the passage of centuries, it must be admitted, the faithful have become
accustomed to so many special religious devotions that the principal mysteries of
the redemption have lost their proper place. This was due partly to the increased
number of vigils, holydays, and octaves, partly to the gradual overlapping of various seasons in the liturgical year.

         But it is also clear that our predecessors St. Pius X and John XXIII laid down
several rules aimed at restoring Sunday to its original rank and its place of esteem in
the mind of all as the "first holyday of all."[2] They also renewed the celebration of Lent.

         It is true as well that our predecessor Pius XII decreed[3] for the Western Church
restoration of the Easter Vigil, as the occasion for the people of God to reaffirm their
spiritual covenant with the risen Lord during the celebration of the sacraments of
Christian initiation.

         Faithful to the teaching of the Fathers and of the tradition of the Catholic
Church, these popes rightly perceived the true nature of the liturgical year's cycle.
It is not simply the commemoration of the historical events by which Christ Jesus
won our salvation through his death and a calling to mind of the past that instructs
and nurtures the faithful, even the simplest, who meditate on it. They taught also
that the cycle of the liturgical year "possesses a distinct sacramental power and
efficacy to strengthen Christian life."[4] This is also our own mind and teaching.

---
[1]   SC art. 102–111 [DOL 1 nos. 102–111].

[2]   SC art. 106 [DOL 1 no. 106].

[3]   SCR, Decr. *Dominicae Resurrectionis*, 9 Feb. 1951: AAS 43 (1951) 128–129.

[4]   SCR, Decr. *Maxima redemptionis nostra mysteria*, 16 Nov. 1955: AAS 47 (1955) 839.

Thus as we celebrate the "sacrament of the birth of Christ"[5] and his appearance in the world, it is right and proper for us to pray that "through him who is like us outwardly, we may be changed inwardly."[6] And that while we are celebrating his passage from death to life, we ask God that those who are reborn with Christ may "by their life hold fast to the sacrament they have received by faith."[7] In the words of Vatican Council II, "recalling the mysteries of redemption, the Church opens to the faithful the riches of the Lord's powers and merits, so that these are in some way made present in every age in order that the faithful may lay hold on them and be filled with saving grace."[8]

The purpose of the reordering of the liturgical year and of the norms accomplishing its reform, therefore, is that through faith, hope, and love the faithful may share more deeply in "the whole mystery of Christ as it unfolds throughout the year."[9]

II

We do not see as a conflict with this theme the splendor of feasts of the Blessed Virgin Mary, "who is joined by an inseparable bond to the saving work of her Son,"[10] and of memorials of the saints, which are rightly considered as the birthdays of "the martyrs and victors who lead us."[11] Indeed "the feasts of the saints proclaim the wonderful work of Christ in his servants, and display to the faithful fitting examples for their imitation."[12] Further, the Catholic Church has always firmly and securely held that the feasts of the saints proclaim and renew Christ's paschal mystery.[13]

3756

Undeniably, however, over the course of the centuries more feasts of the saints were introduced than was necessary; therefore the Council pointed out: "Lest the feasts of the saints take precedence over the feasts commemorating the very mysteries of salvation, many of them should be left to be celebrated by a particular Church or nation or religious family; those only should be extended to the universal Church that commemorate saints of truly universal significance."[14]

To put these decrees of the Council into effect, the names of some saints have been deleted from the General Calendar and permission was granted to restore the memorials and veneration of other saints in those areas with which they have been traditionally associated. The removal of certain lesser-known saints from the Roman Calendar has allowed the addition of the names of martyrs from regions where the Gospel spread later in history. In consequence, the single catalogue displays in equal dignity as representatives of all peoples those who either shed their blood for Christ or were outstanding in their heroic virtues.

For these reasons we regard the new General Calendar drawn up for the Latin rite to be more in keeping with the spirituality and attitudes of the times and to be a

---

5   Leo the Great, *Sermo XXVII in Nativitate Domini* 7, 1: PL 54, 216.

6   See MR, collect, Epiphany [RM, opening prayer, Baptism of the Lord].

7   MR, collect, Tuesday of Easter Week [RM, opening prayer, Monday of the octave of Easter].

8   SC art. 102 [DOL 1 no. 102].

9   SC art. 102 [DOL 1 no. 102].

10   SC art. 103 [DOL 1 no. 103].

11   See *Syriac Breviary* (5th Century), B. Mariani, ed., (Rome, 1956) 27.

12   SC art. 111 [DOL 1 no. 111].

13   See SC art. 104 [DOL 1 no. 104].

14   SC art. 111 [DOL 1 no. 111].

clearer reflection of the Church's universality. In this last regard, the Calendar carries the names of the noblest of men and women who place before all the people of God striking examples of holiness and in a wide diversity of forms. The immense spiritual value of this to the whole Christian people hardly needs mention.

3757   After carefully considering before the Lord all these matters, with our apostolic authority we approve the new Roman Calendar drawn up by the Consilium and also the general norms governing the arrangement of the liturgical year. The effective date for them is 1 January 1970. In accordance with the decrees that the Congregation of Rites has prepared in conjunction with the Consilium, they will remain in force until the publication of the duly reformed Roman Missal and Breviary.

We decree all we have established *motu proprio* in this Letter to be valid and confirmed, notwithstanding, to the extent necessary, the constitutions and apostolic ordinations issued by our predecessors, as well as other directives, even those worthy of explicit mention and amendment.

441. SC RITES, Decree *Anni liturgici ordinatione*, promulgating the *editio typica* of the General Roman Calendar, 21 March 1969: Not 5 (1969) 163–164.

3758   The arrangement of the liturgical year and the General Roman Calendar have been approved by Pope Paul VI through the Motu Proprio *Mysterii paschalis celebratio-nem*, 14 February 1969.[a] This Congregation of Rites, by special mandate of the Pope, now promulgates them, fixing as their effective date 1 January 1970.

During the waiting period for the new breviary and missal revised according to the norms of the Constitution on the Liturgy, the new General Calendar is to be adapted to the liturgical books now in force as follows:

3759   a.   Liturgical days entered in the Calendar as "solemnities" are to be celebrated as feasts of the first class; "feasts," as feasts of the second class; "memorials," as feasts of the third class. If such memorials fall on the weekdays of Advent between 17 December and 24 December, on the days within the octave of Christmas, or on the weekdays of Lent, their celebration is optional and consists solely in a commemoration at the end of lauds, with antiphon, verse, and prayer. In arranging the observance of weekdays, the norms now in force are to be observed.

3760   b.   The feasts of the Baptism of the Lord and of Christ the King are to be celebrated on the days newly assigned to them; even in 1969 the feast of the Holy Family is to be observed on the Sunday within the octave of Christmas.

3761   c.   Feasts that have been removed from the General Calendar are no longer to be celebrated universally in the Roman Rite, but are to be kept if they are in particular calendars.

3762   d.   Saints' days listed as optional memorials in the new Calendar are to be observed accordingly. The celebration is to be like a feast of the third class. But if they occur on the weekdays of Advent between 17 December and 24 December, the days within the octave of Christmas, or the weekdays of Lent, they are observed as a commemoration at the end of lauds, with antiphon, verse, and prayer.

---

a   See DOL 440 no. 3757.

e.   Saints' days assigned to a new date in the revised Calendar shall continue to be   3763
celebrated on the day listed in the current liturgical books.

f.   Saints' days newly entered in the revised Calendar are to be observed as   3764
optional memorials, with the use either of texts from the common or of one of the
Masses assigned in the Roman Missal for certain regions.

Accordingly, appended to the reformed General Calendar there is a general   3765
calendar for *ad interim* use, that is, until promulgation of the new liturgical books.

Finally, it seemed consistent with the revision of the Calendar also to revise the
Litany of the Saints. Two forms are published: the longer one for use in public
intercessions and processions, the shorter form for use in rites that are incorporated
in a Mass.[b]

These two forms of the litany, which may be used optionally at once, become
mandatory on 1 January 1970.

All those concerned should endeavor to make diocesan or religious calendars   3766
and the propers of Masses and offices harmonize with the General Calendar, using
as criteria the norms on the structure of the liturgical year. These calendars and
propers, which are subject to approval by the Apostolic See, will become effective
at the same time as the reformed missal and breviary.

All things to the contrary notwithstanding.

442. SC RITES (Consilium), **General Norms for the Liturgical Year and
the Calendar**, 21 March 1969: Vatican Polyglot Press, 1969.*

CHAPTER ONE
THE LITURGICAL YEAR

1.   Christ's saving work is celebrated in sacred memory by the Church on fixed   3767
days throughout the year. Each week on the day called the Lord's Day the Church
commemorates the Lord's resurrection. Once a year at Easter the Church honors
this resurrection and passion with the utmost solemnity. In fact through the yearly
cycle the Church unfolds the entire mystery of Christ and keeps the anniversaries
of the saints.

During the different seasons of the liturgical year, the Church, in accord with
traditional discipline, carries out the formation of the faithful by means of devotional practices, both interior and exterior, instruction, and works of penance and
mercy.[1]

---

b   The *editio typica* of the General Roman Calendar and the Norms, also included as "official" documents, the calendar for *ad interim* use (pp. 40–49) and the revised forms of the Litany (pp. 33–39). A
preliminary note classified the rest of the contents (pp. 53–177) as "unofficial"; they consisted of commentaries prepared by the Consilium on the reformed liturgical year, the new General Calendar, and the
revised Litany of the Saints. In 1975 ICEL made available an English version of both the official and the
unofficial documents.

*   The translation is based on the text in MR, 2nd *editio typica*, 1975, which incorporates changes made
by the 1st *editio typica* of MR, 1970 and adds a few others. Variants are carried in footnotes and are
designated CR (*Calendarium Romanum*) or also MR'70. For a list of variants see Not 6 (1970) 192 and 11
(1975) 309; for a list of *corrigenda* of CR see Not 5 (1969) 303.

1   See SC art. 102–105 [DOL 1 nos. 102–105].

3768 2. The principles given here may and must be applied to both the Roman Rite and all others; but the practical rules are to be taken as pertaining solely to the Roman Rite, except in matters that of their nature also affect the other rites.[2]

TITLE I: LITURGICAL DAYS

I. The Liturgical Day in General

3769 3. Each day is made holy through the liturgical celebrations of the people of God, especially through the eucharistic sacrifice and the divine office.

The liturgical day runs from midnight to midnight, but the observance of Sunday and solemnities begins with the evening of the preceding day.

II. Sunday

3770 4. The Church celebrates the paschal mystery on the first day of the week, known as the Lord's Day or Sunday. This follows a tradition handed down from the apostles and having its origin from the day of Christ's resurrection. Thus Sunday must be ranked as the first holyday of all.[3]

3771 5. Because of its special importance, the Sunday celebration gives way only to solemnities or feasts of the Lord. The Sundays of the seasons of Advent, Lent, and Easter, however, take precedence over all solemnities and feasts of the Lord. Solemnities occurring on these Sundays are observed on the Saturday preceding.

3772 6. By its nature, Sunday excludes any other celebration's being permanently assigned to that day, with these exceptions:

    a. Sunday within the octave of Christmas is the feast of the Holy Family;

    b. Sunday following 6 January is the feast of the Baptism of the Lord;

    c. Sunday after Pentecost is the solemnity of the Holy Trinity;

    d. the last Sunday in Ordinary Time is the solemnity of Christ the King.

3773 7. In those places where the solemnities of Epiphany, Ascension, and Corpus Christi[a] are not observed as holydays of obligation, they are assigned to a Sunday, which is then considered their proper day in the calendar. Thus:

    a. Epiphany, to the Sunday falling between 2 January and 8 January;

    b. Ascension, to the Seventh Sunday of Easter;

    c. the solemnity of Corpus Christi, to the Sunday after Trinity Sunday.[R1]

III. Solemnities, Feasts, and Memorials

3774 8. As it celebrates the mystery of Christ in yearly cycle, the Church also venerates with a particular love Mary, the Mother of God, and sets before the devotion of the faithful the memory of the martyrs and other saints.[4]

---

[2] See SC art. 5 [DOL 1 no. 5].

[3] See SC art. 106 [DOL 1 no. 106].

[a] CR: "SS. Eucharistiae" for "SS. Corporis et Sanguinis Christi."

[R1] Query: In regions where the solemnities of Epiphany, Ascension, and Corpus Christi are transferred to Sunday, how is the celebration of Mass and office to be structured? Reply: Considering the declaration made by the Congregation of Rites in 1968 (See Not 4 [1968] 279 [DOL 456]), beginning in 1970 when the solemnities mentioned are transferred to Sunday, their celebration observes the following calendar: [calendar and offices follow]: Not 5 (1969) 326–327, no. 8.

[4] See SC art. 103–104 [DOL 1 nos. 103–104].

9.   The saints of universal significance have celebrations obligatory throughout   3775
the entire Church. Other saints either are listed in the General Calendar for optional celebration or are left to the veneration of some particular Church, region, or
religious family.[5]

10.   According to their importance, celebrations are distinguished from each other   3776
and named as follows: solemnities, feasts, memorials.

11.   Solemnities are counted as the principal days in the calendar and their obser-   3777
vance begins with evening prayer I of the preceding day. Some also have their own
vigil Mass for use when Mass is celebrated in the evening of the preceding day.

12.   The celebration of Easter and Christmas, the two greatest solemnities, con-   3778
tinues for eight days, with each octave governed by its own rules.

13.   Feasts are celebrated within the limits of the natural day and accordingly do   3779
not have evening prayer I. Exceptions are feasts of the Lord that fall on a Sunday in
Ordinary Time and in the Christmas season[b] and that replace the Sunday office.[R2]

14.   Memorials are either obligatory or optional. Their observance is integrated into   3780
the celebration of the occurring weekday in accord with the norms set forth in the
General Instructions of the Roman Missal and the Liturgy of the Hours.[c]

       Obligatory memorials occurring on Lenten weekdays may only be celebrated
as optional memorials.

       Should more than one optional memorial fall on the same day, only one may
be celebrated; the others are omitted.

15.   On Saturdays in Ordinary Time when there is no obligatory memorial, an   3781
optional memorial of the Blessed Virgin Mary is allowed.

IV. Weekdays

16.   The days following Sunday are called weekdays. They are celebrated in   3782
different ways according to the importance each one has.

       a.   Ash Wednesday and the days of Holy Week, from Monday to Thursday
inclusive, have precedence over all other celebrations.

       b.   The weekdays of Advent from 17 December to 24 December inclusive and
all the weekdays of Lent have precedence over obligatory memorials.

       c.   All other weekdays give way to solemnities and feasts and are combined
with memorials.

---

   [5]   See SC art. 111 [DOL 1 no. 111].

   [b]   CR lacks "and in the Christmas season."

   [R2]   Query: For the feast of the Holy Family and of the Baptism of the Lord should evening prayer I be
celebrated? Reply: Yes. (see *General Norms for the Liturgical Year and the Calendar* no. 13). As is clear from the
table of precedence (ibid. no. 59, 6), Sundays of the Christmas season are equivalent in rank to Sundays in
Ordinary Time and the feasts of the Lord that fall on such Sundays have an evening prayer I: Not 5 (1969)
325, no. 5; here the word No appeared at the beginning of the Reply but was later corrected to Yes, ibid.
402.

   [c]   CR and MR'70: "in the general instructions for Mass and the divine office."

TITLE II: THE YEARLY CYCLE

3783   17. By means of the yearly cycle the Church celebrates the whole mystery of Christ, from his incarnation until the day of Pentecost and the expectation of his coming again.[6]

I. Easter Triduum

3784   18. Christ redeemed us all and gave perfect glory to God principally through his paschal mystery: dying he destroyed our death and rising he restored our life. Therefore the Easter triduum of the passion and resurrection of Christ is the culmination of the entire liturgical year.[7] Thus the solemnity of Easter has the same kind of preeminence in the liturgical year that Sunday has in the week.[8]

3785   19. The Easter triduum begins with the evening Mass of the Lord's Supper, reaches its high point in the Easter Vigil, and closes with evening prayer on Easter Sunday.

3786   20. On Good Friday[9] and, if possible, also on Holy Saturday until the Easter Vigil,[10] the Easter fast is observed everywhere.[d,R3]

3787   21. The Easter Vigil, during the holy night when Christ rose from the dead, ranks as the "mother of all vigils."[11] Keeping watch, the Church awaits Christ's resurrection and celebrates it in the sacraments. Accordingly, the entire celebration of this vigil should take place at night, that is, it should either begin after nightfall or end before the dawn of Sunday.[e]

II. Easter Season

3788   22. The fifty days from Easter Sunday to Pentecost are celebrated in joyful exultation as one feast day, or better as one "great Sunday."[12]

These above all others are the days for the singing of the *Alleluia*.

---

[6]   See SC art. 102 [DOL 1 no. 102].

[7]   See SC art. 5 [DOL 1 no. 5].

[8]   See SC art. 106 [DOL 1 no. 106].

[9]   See Paul VI, Ap. Const. *Paenitemini*, 17 Feb. 1966, II, §3 [DOL 358 no. 3022].

[10]   See SC art. 110 [DOL 1 no. 110].

[d]   CR adds: "The celebration of the Lord's passion takes place on Good Friday during the afternoon hours."

[R3]   Query: In the Roman Missal for Good Friday this rubric appears in no. 1: "Today and tomorrow the Church, on the basis of an age-old tradition, refrains altogether from celebrating the sacraments." Should this be taken to mean all the sacraments or only the sacrifice of the Mass? Reply: The rubric should be taken to refer only to the celebration of Mass. The words "refrains altogether from celebrating the sacraments" derive from a letter of Pope Innocent I to Decentius, in which there is the statement: "It is universally known that on these two days (that is, Friday and Saturday) the apostles were in mourning and were hiding for fear of the Jews; their fasting on these days is so certain that it is the Church's tradition to refrain altogether on those days from celebrating the sacraments" (*Ep*. 25, 4: PL 20, 555B–556A). In keeping with the practice of the first centuries, the holy fast of Easter that is observed on Good Friday and, if possible, on Holy Saturday until the Easter Vigil (see General Norms. . . . no. 20) includes also fasting, that is, refraining from the eucharistic celebration. This is the explanation and meaning of rubric no. 1 on Good Friday: Not 13 (1977) 602.

[11]   Augustine, *Sermo* 219: PL 38, 1088.

[e]   CR: "beginning after nightfall and ending before the dawn of Sunday."

[12]   Athanasius, *Epist. fest.* 1: PG 26, 1366.

23. The Sundays of this season rank as the paschal Sundays and, after Easter Sunday itself, are called the Second, Third, Fourth, Fifth, Sixth, and Seventh Sundays of Easter. The period of fifty sacred days ends on Pentecost Sunday.

3789

24. The first eight days of the Easter season make up the octave of Easter and are celebrated as solemnities of the Lord.

3790

25. On the fortieth day after Easter the Ascension is celebrated, except in places where, not being a holyday of obligation, it has been transferred to the Seventh Sunday of Easter (see no. 7).R4

3791

26. The weekdays after the Ascension until the Saturday before Pentecost inclusive are a preparation for the coming of the Holy Spirit.

3792

III. LENT

27. Lent is a preparation for the celebration of Easter. For the Lenten liturgy disposes both catechumens and the faithful to celebrate the paschal mystery: catechumens, through the several stages of Christian initiation; the faithful, through reminders of their own baptism and through penitential practices.[13]

3793

28. Lent runs from Ash Wednesday until the Mass of the Lord's Supper exclusive.

The *Alleluia* is not used from the beginning of Lent until the Easter Vigil.

3794

29. On Ash Wednesday, a universal day of fast,[14] ashes are distributed.R5

3795

30. The Sundays of this season are called the First, Second, Third, Fourth, and Fifth Sundays of Lent. The Sixth Sunday, which marks the beginning of Holy Week, is called Passion Sunday (Palm Sunday).

3796

31. Holy Week has as its purpose the remembrance of Christ's passion, beginning with his Messianic entrance into Jerusalem.

At the chrism Mass on Holy Thursday morning the bishop, concelebrating Mass with his body of priests, blesses the oils and consecrates the chrism.

3797

IV. CHRISTMAS SEASON

32. Next to the yearly celebration of the paschal mystery, the Church holds most sacred the memorial of Christ's birth and early manifestations. This is the purpose of the Christmas season.

3798

33. The Christmas season runs from evening prayer I of Christmas until the Sunday after Epiphany or after 6 January, inclusive.

3799

R4   Query: Since the vigil for the Ascension has been suppressed, what are the Mass and office for this day? Reply: The Mass is of the preceding Sunday; the office, for 1970, is that in the Roman Breviary, namely, of the vigil: Not 5 (1969) 325, no. 7.

13   See SC art. 109 [DOL 1 no. 109].

14   See Paul VI, Ap. Const. *Paenitemini*, 17 Feb. 1966, II §3 [DOL 358 no. 3022].

R5   Query: May the following be done outside Mass: the blessing and distribution of ashes (Ash Wednesday), of palms (Palm Sunday), and of candles (Presentation) ? Reply: For pastoral reasons the blessing and distribution of ashes may take place outside Mass (see MR, 180 [RM, rubric at the end of the Ash Wednesday Mass]). The other two rites are inseparably connected with the celebration of Mass, having the character of a procession as a solemn entrance rite: Not 10 (1974) 80, no. 2.

3800   34. The Mass of the vigil of Christmas is used in the evening of 24 December, either before or after evening prayer I.

    On Christmas itself, following an ancient tradition of Rome, three Masses may be celebrated: namely, the Mass at Midnight, the Mass at Dawn, and the Mass during the Day.[R6]

3801   35. Christmas has its own octave, arranged as follows:

    a.   Sunday within the octave is the feast of the Holy Family;

    b.   26 December is the feast of Saint Stephen, First Martyr;

    c.   27 December is the feast of Saint John, Apostle and Evangelist;

    d.   28 December is the feast of the Holy Innocents;

    e.   29, 30, and 31 December are days within the octave;

    f.   1 January, the octave day of Christmas, is the solemnity of Mary, Mother of God. It also recalls the conferral of the holy Name of Jesus.

3802   36. The Sunday falling between 2 January and 5 January is the Second Sunday after Christmas.[R7]

3803   37. Epiphany is celebrated on 6 January, unless (where it is not observed as a holyday of obligation) it has been assigned to the Sunday occurring between 2 January and 8 January (see no. 7).

3804   38. The Sunday falling after 6 January is the feast of the Baptism of the Lord.

V. Advent

3805   39. Advent has a twofold character: as a season to prepare for Christmas when Christ's first coming to us is remembered; as a season when that remembrance directs the mind and heart to await Christ's Second Coming at the end of time. Advent is thus a period for devout and joyful expectation.

3806   40. Advent begins with evening prayer I of the Sunday falling on or closest to 30 November and ends before evening prayer I of Christmas.[R8]

3807   41. The Sundays of this season are named the First, Second, Third, and Fourth Sundays of Advent.

3808   42. The weekdays from 17 December to 24 December inclusive serve to prepare more directly for the Lord's birth.

[R6] 1. Query: May the Mass of the vigil of Christmas be celebrated in the morning on 24 December? Reply: No. The Mass is the Mass of the weekday. The idea of a vigil has been completely altered; vigils in the former way of observance no longer exist. Now in the evening of the day preceding certain solemnities the vigil's proper Mass is celebrated as already part of the solemnity; thus it is a festive Mass: Not 5 (1969) 405, no. 21.

    2. Query: May the Christmas Mass at Midnight be celebrated in the evening of the Christmas vigil? Reply: The Christmas Mass at Midnight must be celebrated around midnight so that the celebration is authentic as to time. For the evening Mass in fulfillment of the precept the text to be used is that for the vigil Mass, as indicated in the rubrics of the Missal (MR 153 [RM, Christmas, Vigil Mass]: "This Mass is celebrated during the afternoon of 24 December, whether before or after evening prayer I of Christmas"): Not 10 (1974) 80, no. 1.

[R7] Query: What Mass is to be celebrated on the Second Sunday after Christmas? Reply: The Mass to be provided by the reformed Roman Missal; otherwise, the Mass in the current Roman Missal for the Sunday after Christmas: Not 5 (1969) 325, no. 6.

[R8] Query: Is a commemoration of the weekday to be made on solemnities that fall during Advent or Lent? Reply: No. There is no commemoration either in the Mass or in the office: Not 5 (1969) 405, no. 19.

VI. Ordinary Time

43. Apart from those seasons having their own distinctive character, thirty-three   3809
or thirty-four weeks remain in the yearly cycle that do not celebrate a specific
aspect of the mystery of Christ. Rather, especially on the Sundays, they are devoted
to the mystery of Christ in all its aspects. This period is known as Ordinary Time.

44. Ordinary Time begins on Monday after the Sunday following 6 January and   3810
continues until Tuesday before Ash Wednesday inclusive. It begins again on Monday after Pentecost and ends before evening prayer I of the First Sunday of Advent.

 This is also the reason for the series of liturgical texts found in both the Roman
Missal and *The Liturgy of the Hours* (Vol. III – IV), for Sundays and weekdays in this
season.[f]

VII. Rogation and Ember Days

45. On rogation and ember days the practice of the Church is to offer prayers to   3811
the Lord for the needs of all people, especially for the productivity of the earth and
for human labor, and to give him public thanks.

46. In order to adapt the rogation and ember days to various regions and the   3812
different needs of the people, the conferences of bishops should arrange the time
and plan of their celebration.

 Consequently, the competent authority should lay down norms, in view of
local conditions, on extending such celebrations over one or several days and on
repeating them during the year.

47. On each day of these celebrations the Mass should be one of the votive Masses   3813
for various needs and occasions[g] that is best suited to the intentions of the petition-
ers.[R9]

CHAPTER II
THE CALENDAR

TITLE I: CALENDAR AND CELEBRATIONS TO BE ENTERED

48. The arrangement for celebrating the liturgical year is governed by the calendar: 3814
the General Calendar, for use in the entire Roman Rite, or a particular calendar, for
use in a particular Church or in families of religious.

49. In the General Calendar the entire cycle of celebrations is entered: celebrations   3815
of the mystery of salvation as found in the Proper of Seasons, of those saints having
universal significance who must therefore be celebrated by everyone or of saints
who show the universality and continuity of holiness within the people of God.

---

 [f] CR and MR'70: "in both the Breviary and the Missal."

 [g] CR and MR'70: "one of the votive Masses."

 [R9] Query: How should rogation days and ember days be celebrated? Reply: In regard to the time and
the manner of celebration, the directives of the conferences of bishops or of the individual bishops are to
be followed. On the former rogation and ember days the Mass and office were those of the weekday or of
the saints. But the bishop or the conference of bishops has the power to order special celebrations on those
days; the celebrations may be varied, e.g., for rural or for urban settings, and may relate to different
themes, like the harvest, peace, the unity of the Church, the spread of the faith, etc. In this case the votive
Mass suited to the occasion is celebrated: Not 5 (1969) 405.

Particular calendars have more specialized celebrations, arranged to harmonize with the general cycle.[1] The individual Churches or families of religious should show a special honor to those saints who are properly their own.

Particular calendars, drawn up by the competent authority, must be approved by the Apostolic See.

3816   50. The drawing up of a particular calendar is to be guided by the following considerations:

a. The Proper of Seasons (that is, the cycle of seasons, solemnities, and feasts that unfold and honor the mystery of redemption during the liturgical year) must be kept intact and retain its rightful preeminence over particular celebrations.

b. Particular celebrations must be coordinated harmoniously with universal celebrations, with care for the rank and precedence indicated for each in the Table of Liturgical Days. Lest particular calendars be enlarged disproportionately, individual saints may have only one feast in the liturgical year. For persuasive pastoral reasons there may be another celebration in the form of an optional memorial marking the transfer or discovery of the bodies of patrons or founders of Churches or of families of religious.

c. Feasts granted by indult may not duplicate other celebrations already contained in the cycle of the mystery of salvation, nor may they be multiplied out of proportion.

3817   51. Although it is reasonable for each diocese to have its own calendar and propers for the Mass and office, there is no reason why entire provinces, regions, countries, or even larger areas may not have common calendars and propers, prepared with the cooperation of all the parties involved.

This principle may also be followed in the case of the calendars for several provinces of religious within the same civil territory.

3818   52. A particular calendar is prepared by inserting in the General Calendar special solemnities, feasts, and memorials proper to that calendar:

a. in a diocesan calendar, in addition to celebrations of its patrons and the dedication of the cathedral,[R10] the saints and the blessed who bear some special

---

[1]   See SCDW, Instr. *Calendaria particularia*, 24 June 1970 [DOL 481].

[R10]   1. Query: Must the anniversary of the dedication of a co-cathedral church be celebrated throughout the diocese? Reply: No. Celebration of the anniversary of the dedication of the cathedral church is observed on the annual date of the consecration in the cathedral itself with the rank of a solemnity; in other churches of the diocese, with the rank of a feast. When co-cathedrals exist in a diocese, the anniversary of their dedication is observed in the dedicated church *alone*, not throughout the diocese. The reason is that the title of co-cathedral is usually given to churches on the basis of some special importance they have had in the history of the diocese. But there is only one cathedral church, the symbol of the unity of the local Church, and only its dedication ought to be celebrated throughout the diocese. But when one diocese has been formed from many former dioceses each of which retains a certain measure of individual unity — e.g., having a curia and chapter — each may celebrate the anniversary of its own cathedral: Not 9 (1973) 152.
2. Not 8 (1972) 103 gives the following commentary on no. 52 a, annual celebration of the dedication of a church. The annual observance of the dedication of a church celebrates the mystery of the living Church, that is, the people of God in pilgrimage to the new Jerusalem. The reformed rite for the dedication of a church, soon to be published [see DOL 547], sets out the norms that follow; their purpose is to give due importance to this annual celebration, while at the same time ensuring its harmony with the liturgical cycle and with the elements of popular devotion.
I.   *Anniversary of the dedication of the cathedral.* The anniversary celebration of the dedication of a cathedral church is to be observed on the date of the church's consecration, with the rank of a solemnity in the cathedral itself and of a feast in the other churches of the diocese. When this date is impeded perpetually, the celebration is assigned to the nearest unimpeded date. It is desirable that the faithful of the entire diocese come together on the day of the celebration to celebrate the eucharist with the bishop.

connection with that diocese, for example, as their birthplace, residence over a long period, or place of death;

b. in the calendar of religious, besides celebrations of their title,[R11] founder, or patron, those saints and blesseds who were members of that religious family or had some special relationship with it;

c. in a calendar for individual churches, celebrations proper to a diocese or religious community, those celebrations that are proper to that church and are listed in the Table of Liturgical Days and also the saints who are buried in that church. Members of religious communities should join with the community of the local Church in celebrating the anniversary of the dedication of the cathedral and the principal patrons of the place and of the larger region where they live.

53. When a diocese or religious family has the distinction of having many saints and blessed, care must be taken not to overload the calendar of the entire diocese or institute. Consequently:　　　　　　　　　　　　　　　　　　　　　　3819

a. The first measure that can be taken is to have a common feast of all the saints and the blessed of a given diocese or religious family or of some category.

b. Only the saints and blessed of particular significance for an entire diocese or religious family may be entered in the calendar with an individual celebration.

c. The other saints or blessed are to be celebrated only in those places with which they have closer ties or where their bodies are buried.

54. Proper celebrations should be entered in the calendar as obligatory or optional memorials, unless other provisions have been made for them in the Table of Liturgical Days or there are special historical or pastoral reasons. But there is no reason why some celebrations may not be observed with greater solemnity in some places than in the rest of the diocese or religious community.　　　　　　　　　　3820

55. Celebrations entered in a particular calendar must be observed by all who are bound to follow that calendar. Only with the approval of the Apostolic See may celebrations be removed from a calendar or changed in rank.　　　　　　　　3821

TITLE II: THE PROPER DATE FOR CELEBRATIONS

56. The Church's practice has been to celebrate the saints on the date of their death ("birthday"), a practice it would be well to follow when entering proper celebrations in particular calendars.　　　　　　　　　　　　　　　　　　3822

II. *Anniversary of a particular church.* One of the following days may be chosen for the celebration of the dedication of a particular church: a. the anniversary date of its consecration, when traditionally this day is marked as a festive day for the people or for a community, as, for example, in monastic churches; b. the Sunday nearest the anniversary date, if it is a Sunday in Ordinary Time; c. the Sunday before the solemnity of All Saints, in order to focus on the bond between the Church on earth and the Church in heaven. The choice is to be made once and for all by the local community, with the bishop's approval. In the case of a church with an unknown date of dedication, the choice is between the Sunday before the solemnity of All Saints and 25 October. In a church that is built on the site of an earlier, consecrated church, but that has itself not been dedicated, the anniversary of the earlier dedication may be celebrated on a date to be chosen according to the norms just given.

R11 Query: Must the title of church be changed when it presents a historical problem or is no longer listed in the General Calendar? Reply: No. Every church retains its title and celebrates the corresponding feast even if the General Calendar no longer carries the title. At the time of the study preparatory to a revision of the particular calendars, the question of titles might well be brought up and dealt with in the light not only of historicity but also of the spiritual and pastoral values affecting the faithful: Not 5 (1969) 404, no. 18.

Even though proper celebrations have special importance for individual local Churches or religious families, it is of great advantage that there be as much unity as possible in the observance of solemnities, feasts, and obligatory memorials listed in the General Calendar.

In entering proper celebrations in a particular calendar, therefore, the following are to be observed.

a. Celebrations listed in the General Calendar are to be entered on the same date in a particular calendar, with a change in rank of celebration if necessary.

This also applies to diocesan or religious calendars when celebrations proper to an individual church alone are added.

b. Celebrations for saints not included in the General Calendar should be assigned to the date of their death. If the date of death is not known, the celebrations should be assigned to a date associated with the saint on some other grounds, such as the date of ordination or of the discovery or transfer of the saint's body; otherwise it is celebrated on a date unimpeded by other celebrations in that particular calendar.[a]

c. If the date of death or other appropriate date is impeded in the General Calendar or in a particular calendar by another obligatory celebration, even of lower rank, the celebrations should be assigned to the closest date not so impeded.

d. If, however, it is a question of celebrations that cannot be transferred to another date because of pastoral reasons, the impeding celebration should itself be transferred.[b]

e. Other celebrations, called feasts granted by indult, should be entered on a date more pastorally appropriate.

f. The cycle of the liturgical year should stand out with its full preeminence, but at the same time the celebration of the saints should not be permanently impeded. Therefore, dates that most of the time fall during Lent and the octave of Easter, as well as the weekdays between 17 December and 31 December, should remain free of any particular celebration, unless it is a question of optional memorials, feasts found in the Table of Liturgical Days under no. 8 a, b, c, d, or solemnities that cannot be transferred to another season.

The solemnity of Saint Joseph (19 March), except where it is observed as a holyday of obligation, may be transferred by the conferences of bishops to another day outside Lent.

3823 57. If some saints or blessed are listed in the calendar on the same date, they are always celebrated together whenever they are of equal rank, even though one or more of them may be more proper to that calendar. If one or other of these saints or blessed is to be celebrated with a higher rank, that office alone is observed and the others are omitted, unless it is appropriate to assign them to another date in the form of an obligatory memorial.

3824 58. For the pastoral advantage of the people, it is permissible to observe on the Sundays in Ordinary Time those celebrations that fall during the week and have special appeal to the devotion of the faithful, provided the celebrations take prece-

---

[a] CR lacks the entire second sentence.

[b] CR for 56 c and d has: "c. If, however,the date of death is unknown, the celebration should be assigned to another date proper to the same saint on other grounds, e.g., date of ordination, of the discovery or transfer of the saint's body, or else to a date in the particular calendar not impeded by other celebrations. d. But if the date of death is impeded by another celebration of higher or equal rank in the General Calendar or the particular calendar, the celebration should be assigned to the closest date not so impeded."

dence over these Sundays in the Table of Liturgical Days. The Mass for such celebrations may be used at all the Masses at which a congregation is present.[R12]

59. Precedence among liturgical days relative to the celebration is governed solely by the following table. 3825

TABLE OF LITURGICAL DAYS
ACCORDING TO THEIR ORDER OF PRECEDENCE

I

1. Easter triduum of the Lord's passion and resurrection.

2. Christmas, Epiphany, Ascension, and Pentecost.

Sundays of Advent, Lent, and the Easter season.

Ash Wednesday.

Weekdays of Holy Week from Monday to Thursday inclusive.

Days within the octave of Easter.

3. Solemnities of the Lord, the Blessed Virgin Mary, and saints listed in the General Calendar.

All Souls.

4. Proper solemnities, namely:

a. Solemnity of the principal patron of the place, that is, the city or state.

b. Solemnity of the dedication of a particular church and the anniversary.

c. Solemnity of the title of a particular church.

d. Solemnity of the title, or of the founder, or of the principal patron of a religious order or congregation.

II

5. Feasts of the Lord in the General Calendar.[c,R13]

[R12] 1. Query: May the anniversary of the dedication of a church and the solemnity of the patron or title of a church be transferred to a Sunday? Reply: *Yes*, in the following case: the Sunday is in Ordinary Time or in the Christmas season and the anniversary is of a *particular* church or the solemnity is of the *principal* patron of a specific place or of the title of a *particular* church. All Masses with a congregation may be the Mass for such celebrations (see General Norms . . . no. 58). *No*, if the transfer would be to a Sunday of Advent, Lent, or the Easter season, or to one on which any solemnity of the Lord, of Mary, or of the saints listed in the General Calendar falls; or if the celebration involves the anniversary of the dedication of the *cathedral* church or the patron of a region or nation or a secondary patron: Not 5 (1969) 404, no. 16.

2. Query: May the anniversary of the dedication of the cathedral be celebrated on a Sunday in Ordinary Time? Reply: No. The case involves celebrating a *particular feast of the Lord* throughout a diocese (see General Norms . . . no. 52 a, c). In the table of liturgical days (no. 5) only feasts of the Lord listed in the *General Calendar* take precedence over Sundays of the Christmas season and Sundays in Ordinary Time; proper feasts do not and the celebration of the dedication of the cathedral church is a proper feast (Table . . . no. 8 b). The basis for this rule is to safeguard the special character of Sunday and to prevent it from being supplanted by other celebrations. However, *an instance may happen*, for example, on the occasion of a renovation or a special anniversary, when the bishop of a diocese wishes to stress the importance of the cathedral as the symbol of the unity of the local Church by bringing together the entire diocesan community at the same celebration. Often this is possible only on a Sunday. In such an instance the bishop may use the power granted him by the GIRM no. 332: "In cases of serious need or pastoral advantage, at the direction of the local Ordinary or with his permission, an appropriate Mass may be celebrated on any day except solemnities, the Sundays of Advent, Lent, and the Easter season, on days within the octave of Easter, on All Souls, Ash Wednesday, and during Holy Week" [DOL 208 no. 1722]: Not 11 (1975) 61.

c CR lacks "in the General Calendar."

[R13] (59, 3 and 5). Query: [This year] 14 September and 9 November will fall on a Sunday in Ordinary Time. What should the celebrations be on these dates? Reply: On 14 September, the feast of the Triumph of the Cross; on 9 November, the feast of the Dedication of St. John Lateran: Not 10 (1974) 40, no. 3.

6.   Sundays of the Christmas season and Sundays in Ordinary Time.

7.   Feasts of the Blessed Virgin Mary and of the saints in the General Calendar.

8.   Proper feasts, namely:

a.   Feast of the principal patron of the diocese.

b.   Feast of the anniversary of the dedication of the cathedral.

c.   Feast of the principal patron of a region or province, or a country, or of a wider territory.

d.   Feast of the title, founder, or principal patron of an order or congregation and of a religious province, without prejudice to the directives in no. 4.

e.   Other feasts proper to an individual church.

f.   Other feasts listed in the calendar of a diocese or of a religious order or congregation.

9.   Weekdays of Advent from 17 December to 24 December inclusive.

Days within the octave of Christmas.

Weekdays of Lent.

III

10. Obligatory memorials in the General Calendar.

11. Proper obligatory memorials, namely:

a.   Memorial of a secondary patron of the place, diocese, region, or province, country or wider territory, or of an order or congregation and of a religious province.

b.   Obligatory memorials listed in the calendar of a diocese, or of an order or congregation.[d]

12. Optional memorials; but these may be celebrated even on the days listed in no. 9, in the special manner described by the General Instructions of the Roman Missal and of the Liturgy of the Hours.[e]

In the same manner obligatory memorials may be celebrated as optional memorials if they happen to fall on the Lenten weekdays.

13. Weekdays of Advent up to 16 December inclusive.

Weekdays of the Christmas season from 2 January until the Saturday after Epiphany.

Weekdays of the Easter season from Monday after the octave of Easter until the Saturday before Pentecost inclusive.

Weekdays in Ordinary Time.

3826   60. If several celebrations fall on the same day, the one that holds the highest rank according to the preceding Table of Liturgical Days is observed. But a solemnity impeded by a liturgical day that takes precedence over it should be transferred to the closest day not listed in nos. 1–8 in the table of precedence; the rule of no. 5 remains in effect. Other celebrations are omitted that year.[f,R14]

---

d   CR and MR'70: "11 b. Other obligatory memorials proper to an individual church." 11 c is as 11 b here.

e   CR and MR'70: "in the instructions for the Mass and the office."

f   CR: "60. If several celebrations coincide on the same day, the one that holds the highest rank according to the preceding table is observed.

"But: a. If the coincidence is permanent, solemnities and feasts, as well as memorials of a particular calendar that are impeded throughout a diocese, a family of religious or its province, are assigned to the nearest day unimpeded by a solemnity or feast. Memorials of the General Calendar that are impeded in a particular calendar or memorials of a diocese of family of religious that are impeded only in a particular

61. If the same day were to call for celebration of evening prayer of that day's   3827
office and evening prayer I of the following day, evening prayer of the day with the
higher rank in the Table of Liturgical Days takes precedence; in cases of equal rank,
evening prayer of the actual day takes precedence.[R15]

▶   93.   PAUL VI, Address to a consistory, on the liturgy, 28 April 1969.

New General Calendar [no. 676].

443. SC DIVINE WORSHIP, Notification *In decreto*, on the calendar for
1971, 17 May 1970: Not 6 (1970) 193.

The decree of publication for the liturgical General Calendar made the provi-   3828
sion that the Calendar, in its definitive formulation, would have the force of law
upon publication of the Roman Breviary and Missal as revised according to the
decrees of Vatican Council II.[a]

This Congregation promulgated the Latin *editio typica* of the Roman Missal on
26 March 1970 and committed the preparation of the vernacular editions to the
conferences of bishops, which are also to stipulate the effective date for these
vernacular editions.[b]

As for the Roman Breviary, the preparatory work is coming to an end.

Clearly, however, preparation of the vernacular editions of the Roman Missal
within the year 1970 is impossible. Therefore it is hereby established that both the
ad interim General Calendar and *ad interim* particular calendars are to continue in use
also during the year 1971.

▶   216.   SC DIVINE WORSHIP, Notification *Instructione de Constitutione*, on the Roman
Missal, the book for the liturgy of the hours, the General Calendar, 14 June
1971:

nos. 5–6:   General Calendar [nos. 1774–75].

---

church are omitted. b. If the coincidence is just on a particular occasion, a solemnity that is impeded by a
liturgical day having precedence is transferred to the nearest day that is not one of those listed in nos. 1–8
of the table of precedence. Other celebrations are omitted that year."

[R14]   Query: What is the method for transferring solemnities impeded by a liturgical day that takes
precedence? Reply: The general rule is that impeded solemnities are transferred to the nearest day (see
General Norms . . . no. 60). But solemnities that happen to fall on the Sundays of Advent and Lent
sometimes are not transferrable to the day following: for example, when the solemnity of Saint Joseph or
of the Annunciation of the Lord fall on Palm Sunday and then would have to be celebrated two weeks
later. Accordingly, to ease such problems the General Norms no. 5 establish that solemnities that during
Advent and Lent may fall on a Sunday are to be celebrated as a rule on the preceding Saturday. But when
the Saturday is not free of those celebrations listed in the table of precedence nos. 1–8, the general
principle in no. 60 may be followed: Not 6 (1970) 405, no. 44. See also DOL 442 no. 3824, note R12.

[R15]   The text for the Litany of the Saints published in CR (pp. 32–39) was emended in 1970:
The following changes are to be incorporated into the Litany of the Saints.
    1. *The name* Saint John the Baptist *is to be placed immediately after the name* Saint Elijah [English:
Abraham, Moses, and Elijah] *and before the name of Saint Joseph.*
    2. *The name* Saint Stanislaus (*Bishop and Martyr*) *is to be inserted after the name of Saint Boniface and before
the name of Saint Thomas Becket. This second change applies, however, only to the Litany in the form for use in solemn
supplications:* Not 6 (1970) 375.

[a]   See DOL 441 no. 3758.

[b]   See DOL 213 no. 1765.

▶   335. SC CATHOLIC EDUCATION, Instruction *In ecclesiasticam futurorum sacerdotum*, on liturgical formation in seminaries, 3 June 1979:

Appendix, nos. 62–67: The liturgical year [nos. 2903–08].

SECTION 2. THE LORD'S DAY

SUMMARY (DOL 444–452). The Constitution on the Liturgy describes Sunday, the Lord's Day, as the "first holyday of all," the "foundation and core of the whole liturgical year" (art. 106). The 21 cross-references here as well as the specific texts on Sunday indicate the work of those in charge of the liturgical reform to ensure that all Catholics would celebrate properly this special day of the ecclesial assembly. The 9 specific texts may be grouped in order of importance.

—First are documents of a general import on the traditional meaning of Sunday: a letter of Paul VI to a national eucharistic congress (DOL 450), a letter of the Secretariat of State on the occasion of a national liturgical week (DOL 451), and an address of Paul VI to pilgrims (DOL 452).

—Concerning the new discipline of the celebration of the Sunday Mass on Saturday evening there are four texts: a letter of the Congregation of Rites announcing the directives of the Congregation of the Council (DOL 444), an early application of these in a rescript to the German bishops (DOL 445), a declaration on the evening Mass for 23 December 1967 (DOL 447), and a note clarifying arrangements when a holyday falls on Saturday or Monday (DOL 448).

—The particular issue of the participation of tourists in the Sunday Mass is treated in a letter of the Congregation of the Council to local Ordinaries (DOL 446). Paul VI in an address to French bishops spoke of Sunday celebrations without a priest (DOL 449).

▶   103.   PAUL VI, Motu Proprio *Pastorale munus*, on the powers and privileges of bishops, 30 November 1963:

  I,   no. 2:   Granting faculty for trination on Sunday [no. 713].

▶   1.   VATICAN COUNCIL II, Constitution on the Liturgy *Sacrosanctum Concilium*, 4 December 1963:

  art. 35:   Celebrations of the word on Sunday [no. 35].

▶   20.   PAUL VI, Motu Proprio *Sacram Liturgiam*, putting into effect some prescriptions of the Constitution on the Liturgy, 25 January 1964:

  art. III: Homily obligatory on Sunday [no. 281].

▶   23.   SC RITES (Consilium), Instruction (first) *Inter Oecumenici*, 26 September 1964:

  nos. 15:   Sunday Mass in major seminaries [no. 307].
        18:                     In religious houses [no. 310].
        37-38:   Celebrations of the word on Sunday [nos. 329-330].
        53:                     Homily obligatory on Sunday [no. 345].

▶   5.   VATICAN COUNCIL II, Decree on the Eastern Catholic Churches *Orientalium Ecclesiarum*, 21 November 1964:

  no. 15:   Sunday Mass obligation [no. 169].

444. SC RITES, Letter *Impetrata prius* to Cardinal P. Ciriaci, Prefect of the Congregation of the Council, regarding Sunday Mass on Saturday evening, 25 September 1965: Not 2 (1966) 14.

3829   Many local Ordinaries have received from the Congregation of the Council the faculty of allowing the faithful of their dioceses to fulfill on Saturday evening or on the evening before a holyday of obligation the precept of hearing Mass[R1] and have

R1   A report carried in *La Civiltà cattolica* 115, no. 3 (1964) 94 is of interest for the history of this faculty. "Vatican Radio news, 12 June [1964], broadcast the following announcement: 'The faithful may fulfill the obligation to hear Mass also by assisting at its celebration on Saturday evening in churches specifically designated by the local ecclesiastical authority. The Congregation of the Council, at the request of the local Ordinaries, has granted the faculty by which Mass may be celebrated after Saturday's first vespers in fulfillment of the Sunday obligation. The designation of the hours, places, and churches for the application of this faculty is left to the discretion of local Ordinaries. The faculty is already in effect in some dioceses of Italy, Switzerland, and Argentina'[2][2It has also recently been granted to Catholics of Israel, where as is well known, Sunday is treated as a work day . . . .] Vatican Radio on 16 June [1964] broadcast the following clarification: 'Not all have understood the proper limitations of the announcement we have broadcast relative to the indults granted by the Congregation of the Council in particular places where there are special religious needs, due in part to the contemporary growth in tourism. It is therefore necessary to clarify the matter through the following specifics: 1. There has been no change in the general nature of the Church's discipline regarding the Sunday precept: namely, Sunday is the day consecrated to the Lord, by both a community act of reverence and an act of worship obligatory for each individual. 2. The precept includes a twofold obligation, the positive one of hearing Mass and the negative one of refraining from servile work. 3. At the request of some diocesan Ordinaries the faculty of satisfying the Sunday precept by hearing Mass on Saturday evening has been granted for the purpose of making it easier to fulfill this obligation, to eliminate the deplorable failure to do so, and to make up for the regrettable shortage of clergy wherever this or other similar reasons exist. 4. The granting of this faculty is still rather uncommon and remains an exception to the general law, according to which the discipline of the Church

then petitioned this Congregation of Rites for use of the liturgical text proper to the Sunday or holyday following.

In view of the reasonableness of the Ordinaries' petition and in the interest of simplifying both concessions of the Apostolic See, this Congregation of Rites makes the following request of Your Eminence: whenever the Congregation of the Council grants to local Ordinaries the power to allow the faithful of their dioceses to satisfy the Sunday or holyday precept, will it kindly mention in the pertinent rescript that in such instances, by mandate of the Congregation of Rites, the *Sunday or holyday liturgical texts are to be used* and that the homily and prayer of the faithful *are not* to be omitted, in keeping with the intent of the Congregation of Rites' Instruction of 26 September 1964, nos. 53–56.[a,R2]

▶ 414. SC RITES, Decree (Avila), on a funeral Mass in the evening of a vigil, 15 October 1965.

445. SC COUNCIL, **Rescript** (Germany), allowing the Sunday Mass on Saturday evening, 19 October 1965.[*]

The president of the conference of bishops of Germany, on behalf of the individual local Ordinaries, humbly requests of Your Holiness the faculty to allow, in special cases, anticipation of the Sunday or holyday Mass on the evening before; also the indult for the faithful assisting at this Mass to satisfy the prescription of the *Codex Iuris Canonici* can. 1248.

3830

The reason for the request is the shortage of priests, particularly in the regions where there are displaced persons, and the heavy travel of the populace on weekends. The petition also requests that Ordinaries be given the power to designate the churches and persons to which the indult is applicable.

In view of the recitals, the Congregation of the Council graciously grants all the local Ordinaries of Germany the faculties indicated in the petition for five years and on a trial basis. The conditions are: in conformity with the Instruction of 26 September 1964, nos. 53ff.,[a] the liturgical texts for the following day must be used and there must be a homily and prayer of the faithful; steps are to be taken to ensure that the faithful firmly retain the idea that Sunday is a day set apart for the Lord.

stays unchanged; ever since the apostolic age the Church has regarded Sunday to be the Lord's Day'."

[a] See DOL 23 nos. 345–348.

[R2] Query: When by indult of the Apostolic See, a Mass celebrated on the evening before satisfies the Sunday or holyday precept, which Mass is to be said? Reply: It is best to say the Sunday or holyday Mass and to include a homily and the prayer of the faithful: Not 1 (1965) 307, no. 87.

[*] Text, ArchKathKRecht 135 (1966) 253–254.

[a] See DOL 23 nos. 345–348.

446. SC COUNCIL, **Circular Letter** *Omnibus in comperto* to local Ordinaries, on tourists' participation in Sunday and holyday Masses, 19 March 1966: Not 2 (1966) 185–189.

3831   It is a well-known fact that tourism is constantly increasing even in regions of low economic growth.

The rate of internal travel in the individual countries alone has doubled since 1958; the number of international tourists exceeds 100 million — with 80 million of them in Europe.

Tourism, therefore, as a primary and complicated issue affecting modern people, clearly amounts to a new life style.

If enjoyed in the right spirit, pleasure trips are conducive to relaxation and restoration of the powers of both mind and body. Furthermore, they contribute to culture by means of foreign travel, which develops the human spirit and enriches all concerned through their contact with each other.[1]

But the number of travelers also demands that pastoral care be adapted to the obvious needs involved, especially with regard to observance of the Lord's Day. This means the celebration of Masses with a homily in the various languages and the assignment of enough priests to hear tourists' confessions in their own languages.

3832   Pope Paul VI has many times put before the consideration of the bishops the importance and seriousness of tourism as it involves pastoral care. He has urged them not to remain tied to traditional methods but to seek new approaches that answer that pastoral concern committed to the Church by our Savior.[2] The individual ecclesiastical authorities in the Church have received from God the grave obligation of dedication to the spiritual care of those faithful who reside even temporarily in their dioceses or parishes and of carrying out a ministry adapted to the contemporary requirements for well-planned pastoral care.[3]

The result will be that the freedom truly belonging to tourists will not give rise to dissipation or separation from God. Rather this new "social fact"[4] will possess the power to produce its beneficent effects upon the work of ministry and to avoid other negative effects.

Thus after urging local Ordinaries to "show their care toward all people of whatever . . . nation, . . . to the native born, to foreigners, and to visitors,"[5] the Fathers of Vatican Council II add: "There is to be a pursuit of pastoral methods adapted to support the spiritual life of those who travel for the sake of relaxation. The conferences of bishops, especially national conferences, are to study the more pressing problems related to such people and to take steps to provide and to support . . . suitable resources and agencies for their spiritual care that are designed to meet the situation of the time, the place, and the people involved. They are to keep in mind above all the norms that the Apostolic See has established or will establish."[6]

---

[1]   See GS nos. 54, 61.

[2]   See Paul VI, Addr. to participants in the Third Symposium on Tourism: OR 7 June 1964.

[3]   See Paul VI, Address proclaiming St. Martha as patron of hotel workers: OR 8 March 1964.

[4]   Paul VI, Address on the feast of the Assumption, 1963: OR 17–18 Aug. 1963.

[5]   CD no. 16.

[6]   CD no. 18.

The Church does not have a *passive* attitude toward this social fact. The reverse   3833
is true: the Church views as its proper responsibility the effort to ensure the employment of the most careful measures wherever tourism exists.

In addition it will be advantageous to encourage through well-attended meetings more programs of a cultural and recreational kind that dispose people to listen
to the word of God.[7]

But all such activities have as their ultimate objective that the faithful go to
church.[8] Therefore it will be necessary whenever an assembly is made up mostly of
foreigners *to establish*, at the discretion of the local Ordinaries,[9] *separate and complete
liturgical services, namely, the Sunday and holyday Mass, with the obligatory homily,*[10] *confessions,
or other celebrations in the house of God, in the language of the majority of the tourists, and, if
possible, with priests of the same language assisting.*[11]

The fact is that in many dioceses where there are health resorts or other
vacation centers the number of residents is increasing greatly. Happily also the
attendance at the sacrifice of the Mass is high and there is a quite remarkable
reception of the sacraments, even by visitors.

This is clear proof of the degree to which true Christians are together sharing
in the love of God[12] and are thus forming the one family in Christ as children of the
Father of us all.[13]

On the other hand it is not unusual that at liturgical services and preaching   3834
tourists assist like strangers, ill at ease. That is utterly in conflict with the spirit of
the Council; an ecumenical spirit that can have no other basis than the mutual
charity that, as the *bond of perfection*, unites all the faithful.

Furthermore, as we have said, tourism is an excellent opportunity for the
faithful to become acquainted with other members of Christ, of conversing with
them, and of having a direct experience of the endless variety within the Church.

All of that will only be possible, however, if the resident Christian communities in tourist centers welcome with the open arms of charity tourists of every
tongue and nation as friends and as brothers and sisters. Tourism offers a priceless
opportunity for a community apostolate that, as the Decree on the Apostolate of
the Laity *Apostolicam Actuositatem* no. 10 recommends, gathers in all the forms of
human diversity and integrates them into the universality of the Church. Even the
spirit of ecumenism, to which the Council gave new impetus, and religious freedom
have broad opportunities for practice in centers of tourism;[14] obviously nothing can
advance the ecumenical spirit more than contacts between those who engage in
dialogue. In this way the Church in which "the laity . . . have the right . . . to
receive from their bishops . . . especially the assistance of the word of God and of
the sacraments"[15] will be seen in its true light, as the Body of Christ, in which there

---

7   See Paul VI, Addr. to the participants in the Third Symposium on Tourism: OR 7 June 1964.

8   See John XXIII, Addr. to participants in the first meeting, under the sponsorship of the Congregation of the Council, on the theme: "Tourism and the Pastoral Ministry," 19 Feb. 1963: AAS 55 (1963)
232–238.

9   See SC art. 22, 36, 39 [DOL 1 nos. 22, 36, 39]; CD no. 15 [DOL 7 no. 194].

10   See SC art. 14, 52, 54 [DOL 1 nos. 14, 52, 54].

11   See CD nos. 23, 30.

12   See LG no. 49: AAS 57 (1965) 54; ConstDecrDecl 184.

13   See LG no. 51 [DOL 4 no. 159].

14   See DH nos. 3, 6.

15   LG no. 37 [DOL 4 no. 153].

is neither "Jew nor Greek, slave nor free, because all are one in Christ" (Gal 3:28; Col 3:11).

3835 Esteemed Brothers, we therefore commend that you put into effect the points established in the Constitution on the Liturgy *Sacrosanctum Concilium* (art. 14, 52, and 54) and in the Decree on the Pastoral Office of Bishops *Christus Dominus* (nos. 16, 23, 30), as well as those that we have recalled to your attention.

Vacation travel will then really become a time for relaxing the powers of body and soul. It will also have the power to contribute to contemporary culture, to the bonds between peoples, and to the establishment of peace among all nations.[16]

As for the exact and careful implementation of the present recommendations, the Church asks everyone that "all . . . be done in love" (1 Cor 16:14).

May this be obtained from God through the apostolic blessing that Pope Paul VI gladly bestows as a pledge of heavenly gifts and a sign of his fatherly good wishes on the bishops and all pastors, above all on those engaged in this endeavor of salvation. [. . .]

▶ 239. CONSILIUM, *The Universal Prayer or Prayer of the Faithful*, 17 April 1966:

Introduction and no. 5: Use especially on Sunday (nos. 1890, 1895).

▶ 508. SC RITES, Instruction *Musicam sacram*, on music in the liturgy, 5 March 1967:

nos. 27:	Sung Mass on Sunday [no. 4148].
37:	Sung office on Sunday [no. 4158].
41:	Participation of the faithful in Sunday Mass [no. 4162].

▶ 147. SECRETARIAT FOR CHRISTIAN UNITY, Ecumenical Directory I, 14 May 1967:

no. 47:	Occasional participation of a Catholic in the Sunday liturgy of separated Eastern Christians [no. 1001].

▶ 179. SC RITES (Consilium), Instruction *Eucharisticum mysterium*, on worship of the eucharist, 25 May 1967:

nos. 17:	Avoiding the scattering of the Christian community on Sunday [no. 1246].
25–28:	Sunday eucharistic celebration [nos. 1254–57].

447. SC RITES, Declaration *Cum Dominica IV Adventus*, on the evening Mass for 23 December 1967, 12 December 1967: Not 3 (1967) 428.

3836 Because the Fourth Sunday of Advent falls this year, 1967, on the vigil of Christmas, the Mass of the vigil is said. In those places where by apostolic indult Mass is celebrated on Saturday evening, 23 December, in fulfillment of the precept for the Sunday following, the Congregation of Rites declares that the evening Mass

---

[16] See Paul VI, Addr. to participants of all nations in the meeting on tourism sponsored by the United Nations, 31 Aug. 1963: AAS 55 (1963) 746–749.

to be said is not the Mass of the vigil of Christmas, but that of the Fourth Sunday of Advent.

▶ 242. SC RITES (Consilium), Norms, on use of Eucharistic Prayers I–IV, 23 May 1968:

     Use on Sunday [nos. 1931, 1933, 1936, 1940].

▶ 440. PAUL VI, Motu Proprio *Mysterii paschalis*, approving the norms for the liturgical year and the new General Calendar, 14 February 1969:

     Dignity of Sunday [no. 3755].

▶ 442. SC RITES (Consilium), General Norms for the Liturgical Year and the Calendar, 21 March 1969:

nos. 1:	The Lord's Day [no. 3767].
4–7:	Sunday [nos. 3770–73].
58:	Celebrations transferred to Sunday [no. 3824].
59:	Sunday in the table of precedence [no. 3825].

▶ 208. SC RITES (Consilium); SC DIVINE WORSHIP, General Instruction of the Roman Missal, 1st ed. 6 April 1969: 4th ed. 27 March 1975:

nos. 31:	*Gloria* on Sunday except in Advent and Lent [no. 1421].
42:	Homily obligatory on Sunday [no. 1432].
44:	Profession of faith on Sunday [no. 1434].
75:	Community celebration of Sunday [no. 1465].
77:	Mass with congregation on Sunday [no. 1467].
315:	Choice of the Sunday Mass [no. 1705].
318:	Biblical readings on Sunday [no. 1708].
322:	Use of eucharistic prayers on Sunday [no. 1712].

▶ 326. SC CLERGY, General Directory *Peregrinaus in terra*, on pastoral ministry in tourism, 30 April 1969:

| II, B, c: | Sunday Mass on Saturday [no. 2617]. |

▶ 294. SC DIVINE WORSHIP, *Christian Initiation*, General Introduction, 29 August 1973:

| no. 6: | Baptism preferably celebrated on Sunday [no. 2255]. |

▶ 295. SC DIVINE WORSHIP, *Rite of Baptism for Children*, Introduction, 29 August 1973:

| no. 9: | Celebration on Sunday even within Mass [no. 2293]. |

▶ 275. SC DIVINE WORSHIP, Instruction *Actio pastoralis*, on Masses with special groups, 15 May 1969:

| no. 10 a: | Masses on Sunday [no. 2131]. |

▶ 232. SC DIVINE WORSHIP, *Lectionary for Mass*, Introduction, 25 May 1969:

| nos. 2–3: | Biblical readings on Sunday [nos. 1844–45]. |
| 7: | Choice of biblical readings on Sunday [no. 1849]. |

15-16:	Readings for Sundays in Ordinary Time [nos. 1858-59].

▶ 209. SC DIVINE WORSHIP, Instruction *Constitutione Apostolica*, the gradual carrying out of the Apostolic Constitution *Missale Romanum* (3 April 1969), 20 October 1969:

no. 8 d:	Possibility of only two readings on Sunday [no. 1740].

▶ 481. SC DIVINE WORSHIP, Instruction *Calendaria particularia*, on revision of particular calendars and propers, 24 June 1970:

no. 2 a:	No particular celebrations on Sunday [no. 3997].

▶ 283. SC CLERGY, Decree *Litteris Apostolicis*, on the Mass *pro populo*, 25 July 1970.

▶ 426. SC DIVINE WORSHIP, General Instruction of the Liturgy of the Hours, 2 February 1971:

nos. 23:	Liturgy of the hours on Sunday [no. 3453].
68:	*Te Deum* on Sunday, except in Lent [no. 3498].
73:	Sunday vigil [no. 3503].
96:	Evening prayer I of Sunday [no. 3526].
129:	Choice of psalms on Sunday [no. 3559].
158 b:	Short readings on Sunday [no. 3588].
204-207:	Sunday celebration of the liturgy of the hours [nos. 3634-37].
237:	No memorial on Sunday [no. 3667].
247:	Choice of other psalms on Sunday [no. 3676].
271:	Sung office on Sunday [no. 3701].

▶ 429. SC DIVINE WORSHIP, Norms *Novo Liturgiae Horarum*, on texts for *ad interim* use, 11 November 1971:

Te Deum on Sunday [no. 3719].
Chants for the final Sundays in Ordinary Time [no. 3724].

▶ 301. SC DIVINE WORSHIP, *Rite of Christian Initiation of Adults*, Introductions, 6 January 1972:

nos. 25, 62:	Scrutinies on Sunday [nos. 2352, 2389].
59:	Sacraments of initiation on Sunday [no. 2386].
244:	Simple rite of initiation of an adult on Sunday [no. 2437].
343:	Initiation of children of catechetical age on Sunday [no. 2472].

▶ 432. SC DIVINE WORSHIP, Notification *Universi qui Officium*, on the liturgy of the hours for religious, 6 August 1972:

Longer office of readings on Sunday [no. 3733].

▶ 329. SC BISHOPS, *Directory on the Pastoral Ministry of Bishops*, 22 February 1973:

nos. 81:	Sunday celebrations at the cathedral [no. 2651].
86:	Liturgical celebrations on Sunday [no. 2656].

▶   276.   SC DIVINE WORSHIP, *Directory for Masses with Children*, 1 November 1973:

nos. 16:   Children at Sunday Mass in the parish [no. 2149].
       20:                    Adults at Masses for children on Sunday [no.
                             2153].
       42:                    Number of readings on Sunday [no. 2175].

448. SC DIVINE WORSHIP, **Note** *Instructio "Eucharisticum mysterium,"* on the Mass of a Sunday or holyday anticipated on the preceding evening, May 1974: Not 11 (1974) 222–223.

The Instruction *Eucharisticum mysterium* no. 28 states: "Where indult of the Apos-   3837
tolic See permits fulfillment on the preceding Saturday evening of the obligation to
participate in the Sunday Mass, . . . the Mass is to be celebrated as assigned in the
calendar for the Sunday and the homily and general intercessions are not to be
omitted."[a]

This is the general norm. But when a holyday of obligation falls on a Saturday
or a Monday, a question arises. For on the evening of the first festive day (the
Saturday or the Sunday) there is a case of the coincidence of two liturgical days
because "the observance of Sunday and solemnities begins with the evening of the
preceding day" (General Norms for the Liturgical Year and the Calendar no. 3).[b]
Also at the same celebration some of the people are there to fulfill the precept for
the actual day; others, to fulfill the precept for the following day. For example, it
can happen that on the evening of the Fourth Sunday of Advent when it falls on 24
December there is at the one time an evening Mass of the Sunday and of the vigil of
Christmas. Similarly, when Christmas falls on Saturday, in the evening there is a
simultaneity between the Mass of Christmas and the anticipated Mass of the Holy
Family.

These and like cases cannot be resolved by means of a general rule because of
differing pastoral considerations and the different customs of the faithful.

Accordingly the following guidelines may be offered.

1.   The general principle governing celebration of the Mass for a day of precept   3838
anticipated in the evening is that given in the Instruction *Eucharisticum mysterium* no.
28.

2.   In the case of a Sunday following a holyday or vice versa, the best way to   3839
achieve completeness in the observance of the entire liturgical day is to apply to the
celebration of an evening Mass what is laid down in the case of evening prayer,
namely: "If the same day were to call for celebration of evening prayer of that day's
office and evening prayer I of the following day, evening prayer of the day with the
higher rank in the Table of Liturgical Days takes precedence; in cases of equal rank,
evening prayer of the actual day takes precedence" (General Norms for the Liturgical Year and the Calendar no. 61).[c]

---

[a]   DOL 179 no. 1257.

[b]   DOL 442 no. 3769.

[c]   DOL 442 no. 3827.

3840　3.　On vigils of solemnities having a special vigil Mass (Christmas, Nativity of Saint John the Baptist, Saint Peter and Saint Paul, Assumption) this Mass is said even if the vigil falls on a Sunday.

3841　4.　In the light of pastoral circumstances, the local Ordinary is to indicate at the beginning of the year in the diocesan liturgical calendar the practice to be followed throughout the diocese; when pastoral reasons seem to dictate preference of the one Mass over the other, he may even, if necessary, depart from what has been said in the present document.

449. PAUL VI, **Address** to the bishops of Central France, on Sunday assemblies without a priest, 26 March 1977: Not 13 (1977) 151–152 (French; excerpt).

3842　　You are faced also with the issue of Sunday assemblies without a priest in rural areas. There the village forms a kind of natural unity, both social and religious, that it would be dangerous to give up or to scatter. We understand the sense of this very well and the advantages that can be gained for the participants' exercise of responsibility and the village's vitality. Today's preference is for communities that keep their human dimension, provided they have sufficient resources, are alive, and are not ghettos. We therefore say to you: proceed judiciously, but without multiplying this type of Sunday assembly, as though it were the ideal solution and the last chance! First of all, you share the strong conviction that there is a need to choose carefully the assembly leaders, lay or religious, and to prepare them; this measure alone brings out the truth that the priest's role is of paramount importance. Furthermore, the goal must always be celebration of the sacrifice of the Mass, the only true actualization of the Lord's paschal mystery. Above all let us all realize that these Sunday assemblies could never be enough to rebuild communities that are alive and outreaching amid a populace that is barely Christian or in process of dropping the observance of Sunday. A further prerequisite is to create other gatherings of friendship and study, as well as teams of priests and the better-trained laity. These are designed to assist the people around them to form bonds of charity and to take a firmer grip on their familial, educational, professional, and spiritual responsibilities.

450. PAUL VI, **Epistle** *Piscariensium civitas* to Cardinal J. Colombo, Archbishop of Milan, on the occasion of the 19th National Eucharistic Congress of Italy (Pescara, 11–18 September 1977), on the theme: The Lord's Day Is the Weekly Easter of the People of God, 4 August 1977: AAS 69 (1977) 565–567; Not 13 (1977) 357–359 (excerpt).

3843　　The city of Pescara will soon have the eyes of all the Catholics of Italy fixed on it: there our beloved country will celebrate the 19th National Eucharistic Congress. [. . .] The special theme proposed for this congress seems particularly suited to promote divine worship and to nurture eucharistic devotion: it is a theme intrinsic to the liturgical reform introduced by Vatican Council II. This is the theme's formulation, offering in a few words a great deal for reflection: "The Lord's Day Is the Weekly Easter of the People of God." The words are completely in accord with the following statement of the Council: "By a tradition handed down from the apostles

and having its origin from the very day of Christ's resurrection, the Church celebrates every eighth day . . . . For on this day Christ's faithful must gather together
so that, by hearing the word of God and taking part in the eucharist, they may call
to mind the passion, the resurrection, and the glorification of the Lord Jesus and
may thank God who 'has begotten them unto a living hope' again through the
resurrection of Jesus Christ from the dead (1 Pt 1:3)."[1] Christ's entire paschal
mystery is involved, his death, his glorious resurrection from death, and his ascension into heaven. Thus on the Lord's Day the ecclesial community, gathered as one
around the Lord who called its members out of darkness into his sublime light, not
only must devoutly call those saving events to mind, but, with the help of divine
grace, bring them to bear on its members. That is accomplished above all through
their participation in the eucharistic sacrifice, a participation they express most
clearly by receiving the Lord's body in communion.

The Lord's Day thus retains its great importance in the Christian life even in   3844
these times when many factors draw people away from those things that are above.
The very ancient work entitled the *Didascalia Apostolorum* contains words that in our
own day seem to retain their force, in spite of the great changes since they were
written: "Because you are Christ's members, do not scatter from the church by not
coming together. You who have Christ as your Head present and communing with
you according to his promise, do not neglect your Savior or separate him from his
members. Do not shatter or scatter the Body of Christ nor put the earthly needs of
your life ahead of the word of God. Instead on the Lord's Day, putting all else aside,
run together to the church."[2]

Without any doubt making holy the Lord's Day, that is, celebrating the weekly
Easter, will make the heavenly gift received have a hidden, but powerful influence
on personal and public life. Because they are nourished by the eucharistic meal, the
faithful possess the power enabling them to bear witness to Christ in their home
life and in the wider human society. Moreover, from the eucharist flow peace and
concord, since those who feed on it become as the one body.[3] Social tensions are not
resolved by violence, by exploitation, by killing, but above all by wills bent on
peace and prepared for self-giving. This sublime sacrament makes such a resolve
strong and unwavering. [. . .]

451. SECRETARIAT OF STATE, **Letter** of Cardinal J. Villot to Bishop C.
Manziana, on the occasion of the 28th National Liturgical Week of Italy, on
the theme: The Lord's Day Is the Lord of Days (Pescara, 29 August–2
September 1977), August 1977: Not 13 (1977) 468–471 (Italian; excerpt).

Particularly welcome to Pope Paul VI is the announcement that the 28th Na-   3845
tional Liturgical Week will be held this year at Pescara, 29 August–2 September, in
the same place and with the same theme as the national eucharistic congress.[a] The
liturgical week will thus serve as a kind of preparation and also prelude for the
congress. In this circumstance the Pope sees a sign of the unity of purpose and the
effective cooperation that must always inspire pastoral activity; he sees as well a

---

[1]   SC art. 106 [DOL 1 no. 106].

[2]   2, 59, 2: Funk DidConst 1, 170.

[3]   See 1 Cor 10:17.

[a]   See DOL 450.

further demonstration of the exemplary consistency with which the Centro di Azione Liturgica, organizer of the week, is fulfilling its charge in full cooperation with the Italian bishops and with their directives.

Pope Paul desires especially to stress the capital importance of the theme of the Lord's Day, stated in the program for the liturgical week in the pointed expression of Pseudo-Eusebius of Alexandria: "The Lord's Day is the lord of days" (PG 86, 416). The unique primacy of Sunday over the other days of the week is due in fact, as the Council teaches us, to the grandeur and centrality of the mystery that, since the era of the apostles, has been the object of this "first holyday of all," so utterly Christian. The mystery is the paschal mystery of Christ, who died and rose again to liberate us from sin, to share with us his own life, and to establish us in the blessed hope of a final meeting with him in his Father's house (see SC art. 106).[b] Accordingly, although holydays other than Sunday can and do vary from country to country, there is absolutely no difference regarding Sunday: the entire Church is together in the celebration on this day of its weekly Easter.

Pope Paul is therefore pleased that the program for the liturgical week, by applying a methodology already suggested by the conciliar Constitution art. 16,[c] provides first of all for a careful examination of the concrete situation and then proposes an intense study both of the history of Sunday and of the mystery celebrated; this is the only way to derive well-directed and sound approaches for practical and effective pastoral action.

Taking the point of departure provided by the theme and the program, Pope Paul would like to emphasize certain of their elements that are much on his own mind.

3846   1.   First of all is the basic meaning that Sunday has always had for Christians: that they come together in a worship assembly to hear the word of God and to take part in the eucharist. The paschal mystery includes and requires such a gathering together because it is the mystery of Christ the Redeemer and he came to gather again the children of God who had been scattered (see Jn 11:52). As the sign of celebrating this mystery, the Sunday also requires that Christians be found together, present actively at the rite that is sacred par excellence and that in the one act of worship, the Mass, combines the word and the eucharist into the closest union (see SC art. 56).[d]

There is no Sunday without a worshiping assembly and no assembly without the word of God and the eucharist. Not the eucharist alone or the word alone: already in the third century the *Didascalia apostolorum* held the two to be inseparable, in this statement: "What excuse before God will those have who do not come together on the Lord's Day to hear the word of God and to receive that divine food that endures for eternity?" (Funk DidConst 2, 59.3). Apropos, Pope Paul in a recent address dealing with the problem of the priestless Sunday assembly, where there is a serious clergy shortage, has forcefully declared that "these Sunday assemblies without the eucharist could never be enough to rebuild Christian communities that are alive and outreaching" and that "the goal must always be celebration of the sacrifice of the Mass, the only true actualization of the Lord's paschal mystery" (OR, 27 March 1977, 2).[e]

---

    b   See DOL 1 no. 106.

    c   See DOL 1 no. 16.

    d   See DOL 1 no. 56.

    e   See DOL 449 no. 3842.

2.   Sunday liturgical assemblies have greater impact to the degree that they are   3847
well attended, structured, and pastorally alive. Therefore the Pope wishes to recall
the practical directives of the Instruction *Eucharisticum mysterium*. These give preeminence on Sunday to the Mass of the bishop in the cathedral and of the pastor in the
parish. The directives suggest that the Masses in particular churches or oratories be
coordinated with the parish Mass; but also that members of religious communities
and other special groups give preference to attendance at the Mass of the parish
community. These guidelines also urge the eventual reduction of the number of
Masses with a view to fostering the formation of large, close-knit assemblies and
ending any fragmentation into small groups (see *Eucharisticum mysterium* nos. 25–27).[f]

3.   The emphasis on the Mass as the central Sunday celebration, however, must   3848
not create the idea that the celebration of the Lord's Day consists exclusively in the
Mass. It is true that the Mass is the privileged moment of the Sunday; it is also true
that the entire day "has as its purpose not only rest for the body and relaxation of
the spirit," as Pope Paul has said recently, "but also and above all refreshment of
soul" (OR, 25–26 July 1977, 1). It is up to those engaged in the pastoral ministry to
lead the faithful to set high value on all those forms and considerations that enter
naturally into the Christian meaning of Sunday. They are all bound up with the
richness of the Sunday's paschal implications for faith, hope, and charity: to make
family life more intense and close; to expand the joys of friendship; to do the works
of charity; to visit the sick; to go to pray in cemeteries. . . .

      In regard, again, to the liturgical week, the Pope realizes how much of the time
during it is given over to celebrations, prayer, congregational singing by the whole
assembly. He therefore has great hopes for the effective measures to be taken, the
experiments to be encouraged, the exertion of every effort toward restoring to the
Sunday celebration its crowning liturgical touch, the celebration of vespers, the
evening sacrifice of praise to Christ the Redeemer (see SC art. 100).[g] In that way
Sunday, the Lord's Day, will indeed be the lord of days. [. . .]

452. PAUL VI, **Address** to pilgrims at Pescara, on Sunday as the weekly
Easter of the people of God, 25 April 1978: Not 14 (1978) 208 (Italian;
excerpt).

      This gathering is an overwhelming sight, a striking exemplification of what the   3849
human community is called to be when it opens itself up to welcome Christ as
Master and Lord and accepts his invitation to sit with him at the common table,
where he breaks the one bread for all. That bread is food for a new life and the
inexhaustible source for a hope that is arduous. This gathering is a sight that,
although in a less solemn way, must be repeated every Sunday in our parishes
through the contribution of all and especially the young, in order to provide for
each person an opportunity to meet Christ and to meet brothers and sisters. Such an
encounter should be a reassuring comfort to the spirit after the experience of the
difficulties of being surrounded by the harshness of workaday life.

      The attention of those taking part in the eucharistic congress last September
had as its focus the meaning of Sunday as the "weekly Easter of the people of
God." At that time we expressed the wish that the congress would signal "the time

---

f   See DOL 179 nos. 1254–56.

g   See DOL 1 no. 100.

of the community's new attachment to the living and loyal observance of this vital commandment" because "in the blessed, repeated remembrance of the Easter of salvation that the Sunday Mass is" we must recognize the "pivotal point of the life of religion." We renew that wish today, in the hope that Sunday may come to be regarded and lived as "the Lord's Day." He stands ready to redeem from within the profaneness of time, directing its inexorable march toward the joyful expectation of its blessed completion in the glorious Second Coming of Christ. Around the euchar-istic table, by listening to the word of God and by breaking the divine bread together, the community is restored; it rediscovers itself; it eases its rising tensions; it regains confidence and equips itself to return with renewed enthusiasm to its task of "consecrating the world," its specific Christian mission (see LG no. 34).

▶ 335. SC CATHOLIC EDUCATION, Instruction *In ecclesiasticam futurorum sacerdotum*, on liturgical formation in seminaries, 3 June 1979:

no. 32: Celebration of Sunday [no. 2811].
Appendix, nos. 58–61: Instruction about Sunday [nos. 2899–2902].

Section 3. Temporal Cycle

SUMMARY (DOL 453–461). There are 20 cross-references here to other documents on the cycle of celebrations of the mysteries of the Lord. There are 9 texts on specific elements of the temporal cycle.

—On the mysteries of the Lord there is a letter of Paul VI on the Sacred Heart (DOL 453), a declaration of the Congregation of Rites on transferring Epiphany, Ascension, and Corpus Christi to Sunday (DOL 456), and from the Congregation for the Sacraments and Divine Worship, a decree on the celebration of the Baptism of the Lord (DOL 460).

—On Lent there are two addresses of Paul VI (DOL 455, 461).

—On Holy Week there is a decree promulgating provisional texts in 1965 (DOL 454), a rescript to the Antilles on celebrating the blessing of oils on Wednesday (DOL 457), and the decree of promulgation and the introduction of a revised rite for blessing the oils and consecrating the chrism (DOL 458, 459).

▶ 1. VATICAN COUNCIL II, Constitution on the Liturgy *Sacrosanctum Concilium*, 4 December 1963:

art. 38: Celebrations of the word during Lent [no. 38].
102, 106–108: Proper of Seasons [nos. 102, 106–108].
109–110: Lent [nos. 109–110].
Appendix: Fixed date for Easter [no. 131].

▶ 23. SC RITES, Instruction (first) *Inter Oecumenici*, 26 September 1964:

nos. 38–39: Celebrations of the word during Lent [nos. 330–331].
60: Communion at Masses on Easter and Christmas [no. 352].

453. PAUL VI, **Apostolic Epistle** *"Investigabilies divitias Christi,"* marking the second centenary of the feast, on the liturgical cult of the Sacred Heart, 6 February 1965: AAS 57 (1965) 298–301.

3850   "The unfathomable riches of Christ,"[1] poured out from his pierced side when in dying on the Cross he reconciled all humanity to the Father, have been so clearly manifested through the ever spreading devotion to the Sacred Heart of Christ in these last centuries as to yield the happiest results for the benefit of the Church.

Our most merciful Savior, appearing, it is related, to the chosen nun Margaret Mary Alacoque in the town of Paray-le-Monial, asked insistently that all people in a public outpouring of prayer should venerate his heart, "wounded for love of us," and make reparation for the wrongs of every sort against him. Devotion to the Sacred Heart, which already existed in some places through the efforts of St. John Eudes, took on a marvellous vitality among clergy and laity and spread to almost every continent on earth.

Accordingly the Holy See crowned this widespread veneration when Pope Clement XIII in response to the requests of the bishops of Poland and of the Archconfraternity of the Sacred Heart in Rome approved on 6 February 1765 the decree issued on 6 January 1765 by the Congregation of Rites and granted a liturgical feast of the Sacred Heart with its own Mass and office to the Polish nation and to the Archconfraternity of the Sacred Heart.[2]

The result was that seventy-five years after the humble religious of the Order of the Visitation had passed over into the joys of heaven the liturgical feast of the Sacred Heart with its proper rites was already being celebrated. The feast was celebrated not only by the king, bishops, and faithful of Poland, and by the members of the Archconfraternity of the Sacred Heart, but also by the Visitation nuns, the whole city of Rome, the bishops and queen of France, the superior and members of the Society of Jesus. Thus the feast quickly spread to the whole Church and produced the fruits of holiness in the souls of the faithful.

3851   Now, at the time of the second centenary of these marvellous beginnings, we have with joy noted the solemn celebrations held in commemoration of the occasion and above all in the Diocese of Autun, where Paray-le-Monial is situated, and

---

[1] Eph 3:8.

[2] See Pius XII, Encycl. *Haurietis aquas*: AAS 48 (1956) 341. A. Gardellini, *Decreta authentica S.R.C.*, v. 2 (1856) no. 4324; v. 3, no. 4579, 2.

specifically in the church of that town. This is now the center of devout pilgrimages in honor of the sacred place where, it is believed, the secrets of the Heart of Jesus were revealed and from which they have spread throughout the world.

Our own wish and desire is that with this opportunity offered, you, Esteemed Brothers, the bishops of God's Church, and the people committed to your care, will fittingly observe the institution of the feast, with its meaning placed in the clearest possible light. This may be done either through conferences for a full and effective explanation to the faithful of the sublime, spiritual themes of theology that manifest the infinite treasures of the love of the Sacred Heart or through special services that will deepen the attachment of the faithful to this priceless devotion. The aim is that all Christians, prompted by a renewed spirit, will offer due homage to the Sacred Heart, atone by their constantly more fervent offerings for sins of every kind, and fashion the whole pattern of their lives in keeping with a genuine charity, "the fulfillment of the law."[3]

The Most Sacred Heart of Jesus, "burning furnace of charity," is the symbol and manifest image of that eternal love by which "God so loved the world as to give his only Son."[4] We thus hold it for certain that these devout commemorations will do much to deepen perception and comprehension of the riches of divine love. We are equally sure that all the faithful will derive from them the special strength to conform their lives earnestly to the Gospel, to reform their conduct so as to put into practice the precepts of God's law.

Above all we desire the veneration of the Sacred Heart of Jesus, whose most excellent gift is the eucharist, to be heightened through participation in that sacrament. For in the eucharistic sacrifice the same Savior, "living ever to make intercession for us,"[5] is immolated and received whose heart was opened by the soldier's lance, to shed upon all humanity the stream of precious blood and water. In this sacrament, the crown and center of all the others, "we taste the sweetness of the spirit at its source and bring to mind that most sublime charity that Christ demonstrated in his passion."[6] Thus, in the words of St. John Damascene, we must "approach Christ with burning desire . . . so that the fire of that desire, made to flame up by the spark of his love, may burn away our sin and light up our hearts; so that we may catch fire from contact with that divine fire and be deified."[7]

3852

These, then, are the reasons especially why it seems to us that the cult of the Sacred Heart, which, sad to say, has waned for some people, should flourish more each day; why all should hold it in esteem as a preemiment and approved form of devotion toward Christ Jesus, "the King and center of all hearts, who is the Head of the Body, his Church, . . . the beginning, the firstborn from the dead in order that in everything he might hold the first place."[8] There is a pressing need today for this devotion, especially in view of the prescriptions of Vatican Council II.

The Council strongly endorses "popular devotions of the Christian people . . . above all when they are ordered by the Apostolic See."[9] Therefore, it seems, this should be the particular message preached: that everything rests on adoring and being at one with Christ Jesus and especially on the mystery of the eucharist,

---

3   See Rom 13:10.

4   Jn 3:16.

5   Heb 7:25.

6   Thomas Aquinas, *Opusculum* 57.

7   John Damascene, *De fide orthodoxa* 4, 13: PG 94, 1150.

8   Col 1:18.

9   SC art. 13 [DOL 1 no. 13].

which, like the other rites of the liturgy, "is the source for achieving human sanctification in Christ and God's glorification, the end to which all the Church's other activities are directed."[10]

▶ 228. CONSILIUM, Note, on the epistle for Saturday after the Third Sunday of Lent, 28 February 1965.

454. SC RITES (Consilium), **Decree** *Quamplures Episcopi*, promulgating the text of changes in the Order of Holy Week, 7 March 1965: AAS 57 (1965) 412–413.

3853

Many bishops, now that Holy Thursday is near, have petitioned the Apostolic See for the faculty to concelebrate the chrism Mass. Through this concelebration priests from the different parts of the diocese will gather round the bishop and concelebrate with him both the eucharist and the blessing of the oils. This will highlight the unity of priests with the bishop, as well as the bishop's central place in the liturgical life of the diocese as "the high priest of his flock, the faithful's life in Christ in some way deriving from and depending on him" (SC art. 41).[a]

The Constitution on the Liturgy, however, provides (art. 57, § 1, 1, a)[b] that, once the rite of concelebration has been published, each bishop has the faculty to concelebrate the chrism Mass. It has therefore been deemed advisable to take the following steps: to revise the texts of the chrism Mass somewhat so that they are more in line with the purpose of this Mass; and, even before the definitive reform that is to be carried out in due time as part of the revision of the whole Roman Pontifical, to simplify the rite for the blessing of the oils so that it may be more readily incorporated into the day's celebration and may facilitate the active participation of the faithful.

Also, in view of the introduction of certain changes in the Order of Holy Week, it has seemed well to modify a phrase here and there in the solemn prayers for Good Friday so that they may be more in accord with the mind and decrees of Vatican Council II regarding ecumenism.

Accordingly, by mandate of Pope Paul VI, the Consilium has carefully studied and prepared the changes mentioned for incorporation into the Order of Holy Week. The Congregation of Rites, with the Pope's approval, has decreed that these changes are to be published for obligatory use by all beginning with Holy Week of this year 1965.[c]

All things to the contrary notwithstanding.

▶ 337. SC RITES, Decree *Plures locorum*, on nondeacons reading the gospel of Christ's passion, 25 March 1965.

▶ 146. PAUL VI, Epistle *Nous nous apprêtons* to Christophoros, Patriarch of Alexandria, on a common date for Easter, 31 March 1966.

---

10 SC art. 10 [DOL 1 no. 10].

a DOL 1 no. 41.

b See DOL 1 no. 57.

c This text was published as, *Variationes in Ordinem Hebdomadae sanctae inducendae*: Vatican Polyglot Press, 1965.

▶   179.   SC RITES (Consilium), Instruction *Eucharisticum mysterium*, on worship of the eucharist, 25 May 1967:

       no.   59:   Eucharistic procession on Corpus Christi [no. 1288].

▶   107.   SC BISHOPS, Index of quinquennial faculties granted to local Ordinaries, 1 January 1968:

       SC Rites, no. 2:   Faculty to bless oils with the presence of available priests and ministers [no. 762].

455. PAUL VI, **Address** to a general audience, on the liturgical pedagogy of Lent, 28 February 1968: Not 4 (1968) 89–90 (Italian).

Today, Ash Wednesday, is the beginning of Lent, that is, a season dominated by the liturgy. In a rich array of texts, prayers, rites, and ascetical practices Lent unfolds a season that the voice of the recent Council in an altogether special way recommends the Church to value highly (see *Sacrosanctum Concilium* art. 109–110).[a] That, dear visitors, is what we are doing for you now, by turning above all to a statement that stands as a general principle of the Christian life, namely: "The Church's liturgy is a vast reservoir for human instruction, Christian guidance, the mastery over our lives. It is a reservoir that up to now has scarcely been tapped" (Jungmann).

3854

The liturgy teaches us how to live, indeed causes us to live, provided it is understood and shared in. We might call to mind the manner and the power of its directing us to God, of its making us one with Christ, and of its giving us the *sensus Ecclesiae*. We might readily again find reflected in the celebration of the liturgy the guiding thoughts for our own weekly conversations regarding the Church, the faith, and most recently the Catholic laity. The liturgy is the life of the Mystical Body in act; clearly the whole spiritual life does not consist solely in participation in the liturgy (see *Sacrosanctum Concilium* art. 12),[b] but the liturgy "is the primary and indispensable source from which the faithful are to derive the true Christian spirit" (ibid. art. 14).[c]

What, then, are the themes of the liturgical pedagogy of Lent?

3855

There are many and they are woven into a long poem that reaches its climax in a drama of tragedy and triumph in the celebration of the paschal mystery. In the Lenten liturgy, as in a catechism, we can review as a first theme the true human condition. This is presented to us against a background light, the light of God. As it is reflected on the human being, God's creature and masterpiece, that light reveals havoc, restlessness, conflict between flesh and spirit, deformity, the need of restoration along with the inability to achieve it, radical unhappiness, that is, sin, and therefore the human need to be saved, redeemed, called back to life again. This doleful reality provides the pattern of the other Lenten themes. Prominent among them is prayer, born of a stricken and humbled conscience that only the hope in Christ as Savior and Mediator draws back from despair, from that cynicism and bewilderment of absurdity and moral anarchy that so often express the condition of

---

   [a]   See DOL 1 nos. 109–110.

   [b]   See DOL 1 no. 12.

   [c]   DOL 1 no. 14.

the contemporary soul. Along with prayer there is repentance, the expression of a sorrow in the soul that is impelled to translate itself into outward signs of penance and expiation. Let us recognize how the discipline of the Lenten fast gave expression with a realistic severity to the needs of a conscience that was convinced of its own state of guilt. Now the fast is no longer obligatory, except on Ash Wednesday and Good Friday (see *Paenitemini* II, § 3);[d] for everyone, however, there remains the obligation to do penance, to which the liturgy of Lent so urgently summons us.

3856   There is another, consequent theme: the hearing of the word of God. The first message it receives is one of repentance, but then suddenly this hearing brings us the first lines in the divine plan of salvation. It is in the word of God that we have the proclamation of the truth that is life, the proclamation of faith, of mercy, of the means of our rebirth, above all of baptism.

3857   From this a further dominant theme emerges.

The "baptismal elements" belong properly to the Lenten liturgy and run throughout its catechesis, its prayer, and its rites. To remember baptism means for us to remember that we are Christians, how we became Christians, and why we remain Christians. Christ emerges, therefore, as the focal point of this pedagogy of the liturgy. He is not a merely ideal and abstract Christ, but the Christ in the twofold reality of his historical appearance, culminating in his passion and resurrection, and of his saving mission. In making us participate through the sacraments in his life as man and God, Christ's mission infuses a new source of life into us — grace, the Holy Spirit, through whom we live and are Christians.

Such is the picture of Lent and we must not forget it, not be satisfied to look at it as outsiders, with a distracted and casual glance. The pedagogy of the liturgy is, so to speak, existential; it is meant to become a human reality, to be personalized, to cast all of us under its salutary spell. That spell will free us from the many other spells cast on us by the senses and the world and will lead us to live in the reality of Christ.

456. SC RITES (Consilium), **Declaration** *Cum recentioribus temporibus*, on the office and Mass in countries where Epiphany, Ascension, and Corpus Christi are transferred to Sunday, 18 October 1968: Not 4 (1968) 279.

3858   In recent years some conferences of bishops have obtained from the Apostolic See permission to transfer to Sunday the solemnities of Epiphany, Ascension, and Corpus Christi, with suppression of the obligation of the precept on the days proper to these feasts. This has resulted in several rubrical problems regarding the structure for the celebration of Mass and divine office.

To make better provision for these cases during the interval before revision of the Roman Breviary and Missal, this Congregation of Rites declares that in the places where the feasts in question are no longer holydays of obligation, the following calendar is to be observed, beginning in 1969: [Calendar and *ordo* for Mass and office follow.]

---

    d   See DOL 358 no. 3022.

457. SC EVANGELIZATION OF PEOPLES, **Rescript** (Antilles), allowing the blessing of oils on the evening of the Wednesday of Holy Week, 14 January 1969.*

Petition: The president of the conference of bishops of the Antilles, in the name   3859
of all the Ordinaries of the said conference, humbly asks that in these territories the
holy oils may be blessed also during the evening of Wednesday of Holy Week.

Reply: The Congregation for the Evangelization of Peoples or for the Propagation of the Faith, in virtue of faculties granted to it by Pope Paul VI, and in view of
the recitals, graciously grants the favor as requested. The present grant is valid for
five years.

▶   440.   PAUL VI, Motu Proprio *Mysterii paschalis*, approving the norms for the liturgical
                year and the new General Calendar, 14 February 1969.

                            Restoration of Sunday [no. 3755].

▶   441.   SC RITES (Consilium), Decree *Anni liturgici*, promulgating the *editio typica* of the
                General Roman Calendar, 21 March 1969:

                            Interim adaptations [nos. 3759–60].

▶   442.   SC RITES (Consilium), General Norms for the Liturgical Year and the Calendar,
                21 March 1969:

                nos. 1:   The various liturgical seasons [no. 3767].
                     7:          Solemnities of Epiphany, Ascension, and Corpus
                                 Christi on Sunday [no. 3773].
                     17–47:   Yearly cycle [nos. 3783–3814].
                     59:         Table of precedence [no. 3825].

▶   208.   SC RITES (Consilium); SC DIVINE WORSHIP, General Instruction of the Ro-
                man Missal, 1st ed. 6 April 1969; 4th ed. 27 March 1975.

                nos. 314–316:   Choice of Mass corresponding to the liturgical
                                 days [nos. 1704–06].

▶   232.   SC DIVINE WORSHIP, *Lectionary for Mass*, Introduction, 25 May 1969:

                nos. 3:   Lectionary for Sundays and holydays [no. 1845].
                     4:          Weekday lectionary [no. 1846].
                     11–17:   Lectionary for the cycle of seasons [nos. 1854–60].

▶   315.   SC DIVINE WORSHIP, Publication *Sacra Congregatio pro Clericis* of the text for the
                renewal of priestly promises and the special preface on Holy Thursday, 6 March
                1970.

---

* Prot. N. 6444/68; see CLD 7, 35–36.

458. SC DIVINE WORSHIP, **Decree** *Ritibus Hebdomadae sanctae,* promulgating the *editio typica* of the rite of blessing the oil of catechumens and of the sick and of consecrating chrism, 3 December 1970: AAS 63 (1971) 711; Not 7 (1971) 89.

3860   After the rites for Holy Week in the Roman Missal had been revised as required, it seemed appropriate that the rite used in the chrism Mass for the blessing of the oil of catechumens and of the sick and for the consecration of the chrism as it now stands in the Roman Pontifical should also be changed.

     The Congregation for Divine Worship has therefore revised this rite and upon its approval by authority of Pope Paul VI promulgates it. The Congregation decrees its use from now on in place of the present rite in the Roman Pontifical.

     The conferences of bishops have the responsibility of preparing vernacular editions and submitting them for confirmation by this Congregation.

     All things to the contrary notwithstanding.

459. SC DIVINE WORSHIP, *Rite of the Blessing of Oils,* and *Rite of Consecrating the Chrism,* **Introduction,** 3 December 1970: Vatican Polyglot Press, 1971.

INTRODUCTION

3861   1.   The bishop is to be looked on as the high priest of his flock. The life in Christ of his faithful is in some way derived from and dependent upon the bishop.[1]

     He concelebrates the chrism Mass with priests from the different parts of his diocese and during it consecrates the chrism and blesses the other holy oils. This Mass is therefore one of the chief expressions of the fullness of the bishop's priesthood and is looked on as a symbol of the close bond between the bishop and his priests. For the chrism the bishop consecrates is used to anoint the newly baptized and to trace the sign of Christ on those to be confirmed; the oil of catechumens is used to prepare and dispose them for baptism; the oil of the sick, to strengthen them amid their infirmities.

3862   2.   The Christian liturgy has adopted the Old Testament usage of anointing kings, priests, and prophets with consecratory oil because they prefigured Christ, whose name means "the anointed of the Lord."

     Similarly, the chrism is a sign that Christians, incorporated by baptism into the paschal mystery of Christ, dying, buried, and rising with him,[2] are sharers in his kingly and prophetic priesthood and that by confirmation they receive the spiritual anointing of the Spirit who is given to them.

     The oil of catechumens extends the effects of the baptismal exorcisms: it strengthens the candidates with the power to renounce the devil and sin before they go to the font of life for rebirth.

     The oil of the sick, for the use of which James is the witness,[3] provides the sick with a remedy for both spiritual and bodily illness, so that they may have strength to bear up under evil and obtain pardon for their sins.

---

[1] See SC art. 41 [DOL 1 no. 41].

[2] See SC art. 6 [DOL 1 no. 6].

[3] See Jas 5:14.

I. THE OILS

3.   The matter suitable for a sacrament is olive oil or, according to local conditions,   3863
another oil extracted from plants.

4.   The chrism is made of oil and some aromatic substance.   3864

5.   The chrism may be mixed either in private prior to the consecration or by the   3865
bishop during the liturgical rite itself.

II. THE MINISTER

6.   Consecration of the chrism belongs exclusively to a bishop.   3866

7.   If the conference of bishops decides to retain its use, the oil of catechumens is   3867
blessed by the bishop together with the other oils at the chrism Mass.

  However, in the case of the baptism of adults, priests have the faculty to bless
the oil of catechumens before the anointing at the designated stage in the catechumenate.

8.   The oil to be used in the anointing of the sick, must be blessed for this purpose   3868
by a bishop or else by a priest who has this faculty in virtue of the law itself or of
its special concession to him by the Holy See.

  In virtue of the law itself the following may bless the oil for use in the
anointing of the sick:

  a.   those who are the equivalent in law to a diocesan bishop;

  b.   in a case of true necessity, any priest.

III. TIME OF THE BLESSING

9.   The blessing of the oil of the sick and of catechumens and the consecration of   3869
the chrism are carried out by the bishop as a rule on Holy Thursday at the proper
Mass to be celebrated in the morning.

10.   If it is difficult for the clergy and people to gather on that day, the blessing may   3870
be advanced to an earlier day, but still close to Easter. The proper chrism Mass is
always used.

IV. PLACE OF THE BLESSING WITHIN THE MASS

11.   In keeping with longstanding practice in the Latin liturgy, the blessing of the   3871
oil of the sick takes place before the end of the eucharistic prayer; the blessing of
the oil of catechumens and the consecration of the chrism, after communion.

12.   For pastoral reasons, however, it is permissible for the entire rite of blessing to   3872
take place after the liturgy of the word, according to the rite described below.

▶   426.   SC DIVINE WORSHIP, General Instruction of the Liturgy of the Hours, 2
        February 1971:

        nos. 204–217:   Celebration of the mysteries of the Lord [nos.
                             3634–47].

▶   181.   PAUL VI, Address to a general audience on the feast of Corpus Christi, 7 June
        1971.

▶   430.   SC DIVINE WORSHIP, Guidelines *Sacra Congregatio pro Cultu Divino*, on the liturgy
        of the hours in Holy Week, 3 March 1972.

▶ 279. SC DIVINE WORSHIP, *Holy Communion and Worship of the Eucharist outside Mass*, Chapter 3, Introduction, 21 June 1973.

  no. 102:   Eucharistic procession on the feast of Corpus Christi [no. 2220].

▶ 160. SECRETARIAT FOR CHRISTIAN UNITY, Letter *Le deuxième Concile du Vatican* to presidents of the conferences of bishops, on a fixed date for Easter, 18 May 1975.

▶ 185. PAUL VI, Homily at Bolsena, on the International Eucharistic Congress at Philadelphia, 8 August 1976.

▶ 164. SECRETARIAT FOR CHRISTIAN UNITY, Letter *Dans ma lettre*, on a common celebration of Easter, 15 March 1977.

460. SC SACRAMENTS AND DIVINE WORSHIP, **Decree** *Celebratio Baptismatis Domini*, on the celebration of the Baptism of the Lord, 7 October 1977: Not 13 (1977) 477.

3873   The celebration of the Baptism of the Lord has been given a place of honor through the reform of the General Roman Calendar, which has assigned it to the Sunday after Epiphany. This is meant to facilitate observance of the feast by the whole Christian community gathered together on that Sunday, since in the history of salvation and in the liturgical year this feast has highly important doctrinal, pastoral, and ecumenical dimensions.

But in places where the solemnity of the Epiphany is not a holyday of obligation and is therefore assigned to the Sunday falling between 2 January and 8 January, it often happens that the feast of the Baptism of the Lord coincides with the solemnity of the Epiphany and thus cannot be observed.

In consideration of many petitions on this point and with the approval of Pope Paul VI, this Congregation for the Sacraments and Divine Worship decrees:

In places where the solemnity of the Epiphany is to be transferred to the Sunday falling on 7 January or 8 January, with the result that the feast of the Baptism of the Lord would be omitted, this feast is to be transferred to the Monday immediately following that Sunday.

All things to the contrary notwithstanding.

461. PAUL VI, **Address** to a general audience, on Lent, a "sacramental" time, 8 February 1978: Not 14 (1978) 62–64 (Italian; excerpt).

3874   The Church has always given a normative importance to the sequence of time in the annual chronological cycle and during the year presents in an orderly pattern the elements of its spiritual and ascetical teaching. Lent is a special phase, a privileged phase, and today happily marks its liturgical beginning. We need to turn to this traditional practice of the Church that invests the calendar with a particular authority and gives a spiritual meaning to the passage of time. No member of the faithful may be indifferent to the succession of the days as they change with the sun and the seasons, as if all were the same and there were no need to live them in different ways. We know very well how much help comes from the weekly arrangement of days in which even civil law makes the first day of the week a day of rest and the Christian is bound to a particular religious observance: to take part in the *synaxis*, the community's liturgical assembly, celebrating the sacred word and the eucharistic sacrifice. Vatican Council II has reaffirmed this law according to which "the Lord's Day is the first holyday of all and should be proposed to the devotion of the faithful and taught to them in such a way that it may become in fact a day of joy and of freedom from work" (SC art. 106).[a] We know this; we would do well to regard this norm as decisive for our religious and civil conduct. The same norm, further, leads us to give even greater prominence to the period preceding and preparing for Easter, the season of Lent.

Lent is a period of preparation for the sacraments and first of all, in the case of catechumens, for baptism. In the case of Christians already baptized Lent is supposed to be not merely a reminder of the first sacrament received, cleansing and regenerating them, but a psychological and moral renewal in virtue of that baptism. For this sacrament includes with the acceptance of faith a way of life consistent with faith because, by the logic of the spiritual principle enunciated by St. Paul, "The just live by faith" (Rom 1:17). The living out of baptism is a continuing process of development and practice. Lent also has as its objective the reconciliation of the repentant. The entire teaching on sin committed after baptism has in Lent its primary articulation and also reaches its inexpressible effect, which consists in the peace of a conscience restored to God's friendship through the sacrament of penance. Lenten preparation then receives its crown in the predispositions for Easter, when the eucharistic sacrifice will open to the faithful the way to communion with Christ himself, "the paschal lamb sacrificed" for us (1 Cor 5:7).

3875

These sacraments are the focal point for the practice and transformation of the Christian's life. That life is marked by an intensifying of the religious spirit, of mortification, and of charity. The listening to the word of God becomes more attentive and frequent. It may be true that today there are no longer large congregations at Lenten courses. But every thoughtful Christian must find the time and the means to attend at least an Easter preparation preached for some special group. The fact is that this form of preaching fortunately has become widespread and readily available. Through it the lamp of prayer is rekindled, almost spontaneously, or better, through the hidden encounter with the Holy Spirit made present in the soul. This fills the atmosphere of Lent with its own special light of both remorse and joy.

What remains of the Lenten obligation of abstinence and fast? Is nothing left of that season that once was so demanding, so strict, and so . . . ritualized? Except for the two fast days still obligatory for those capable (that is, Ash Wednesday, today, and Good Friday, the "great and bitter day"), the strict obligation of former years has been abolished by the Church in its sensitivity to changed conditions and the demands of modern life.[b] Yet for strong and faithful spirits what does remain is all the more worthy of being kept carefully in mind. Two elements supply for the former fast: personal austerity in regard to food, amusements, and work and love of neighbor — the suffering, the needy, those expecting our help, our pardon. All of this is left, along with the obligation of abstaining from meat on Friday during Lent. Thus this Lenten program, varying with the individual, voluntary, and not always easy, demands our effort (what children call their *fioretto* [Lenten sacrifice]), our austerity. This alone makes the Christian life strong and genuine.

3876

---

a   DOL 1 no. 106.

b   See DOL 358 no. 3022.

Let it be an austerity in opposition to the self-indulgence of the times, not ostentatious in its practice (see Mt 6:1ff.), but unaffected and reenforcing our Christian repentance!

Section 4. Sanctoral Cycle

SUMMARY (DOL 462–479). The Constitution on the Liturgy in proposing the guiding principles for the celebrations of saints during the liturgical year considers first the special veneration shown to Mary (art. 103), then treats the celebration of the other saints (art. 104). Accordingly this section is divided into two subsections.

Section 4. Sanctoral Cycle: A. The Blessed Virgin Mary

SUMMARY (DOL 462–468). There are 7 texts concerned with the veneration of the Mother of God in the Church.

—The major texts are all from Paul VI and together they form an important presentation of the place that Mary holds in the Church's worship, especially in the light of the teaching of Vatican Council II's Dogmatic Constitution on the Church, chapter eight. Pope Paul devoted an encyclical and an apostolic exhortation to the rosary, "the resumé of the Gospel" (DOL 462, 464). From another apostolic exhortation on the meaning of the special title, "Mary, Mother of the Church," there are excerpts pertaining to the liturgy (DOL 463). Especially significant is the apostolic exhortation *Marialis cultus*, which is a thorough review and development of the proper theology of the liturgical *cultus* directed to Mary (DOL 467). Pope Paul's views are also conveyed in a letter of the Secretariat of State on Mary in the Church's worship and life (DOL 468).

—The subsidiary texts, from the Congregation for Divine Worship, are a note on the celebration of the Immaculate Conception in 1974 (DOL 465) and norms on the crowning of Marian images (DOL 466).

▶ 1.   VATICAN COUNCIL II, Constitution on the Liturgy *Sacrosanctum Concilium*, 4
       December 1963:

       art. 103:   Marian feasts [no. 103].

▶ 4.   VATICAN COUNCIL II, Dogmatic Constitution on the Church *Lumen gentium*, 21
       November 1964:

       nos. 66–67:   Veneration of Mary in the Church [nos. 160–161].

▶ 6.   VATICAN COUNCIL II, Decree on Ecumenism *Unitatis redintegratio*, 21 November
       1964:

       no. 15:   Veneration of Mary in Eastern Churches not in
                                    union with Rome [no. 187].

▶ 31. CONSILIUM, Letter *Le renouveau liturgique*, on furthering liturgical reform, 30 June
       1965:

       no. 8:   Veneration of Mary in churches (images and sta-
                                    tues) [no. 417].

▶ 12. VATICAN COUNCIL II, Decree on Priestly Formation *Optatam totius*, 28 October
       1965:

       no. 8:   Marian devotion [no. 213].

▶ 17. VATICAN COUNCIL II, Decree on the Ministry and Life of Priests *Presbyterorum
       Ordinis*, 7 December 1965:

       no. 18:   Marian devotion [no. 267].

462. PAUL VI, Encyclical *Christi Matri*, **on the rosary, 15 September 1966:**
AAS 58 (1966) 745–749 (excerpt).

3877   The rosary of Christ's Mother is woven like a mystical pattern into the days of
October through a longstanding practice of the Christian people. Following the
example of our predecessors, we summon all the Church's children to offer special
acts of devotion to the Blessed Virgin this year. The danger of more widespread and
serious disaster threatens the human family, since, particularly in Southeast Asia,
the bloody struggles and savagery of war continue. We thus have a somber reminder to do all that is in our power to safeguard peace. [. . .]

3878   By the urging of our own pastoral charge we are obliged to ask for divine help.
Peace, "a blessing so immense that even in earthly and mortal affairs there is no
news more welcome, no goal more sought after, no state of affairs more joyful"[3]
must be obtained from the Prince of Peace.[4] The constant practice of the Church
has been to fly to Mary his Mother, its ever present intercessor in times of uncertainty and fear. Therefore we too turn to her our own thoughts, yours, our Es-

---

³   Augustine, *De civ. Dei* 19, 11: PL 41, 637.
⁴   See Is 9:6.

teemed Brothers, and those of all the faithful. As St. Irenaeus says, "she has become for the whole human race the cause of salvation."[5] Nothing seems to us more timely and advantageous than that the suppliant voices of the whole Christian family be raised to the Mother of God, under the invocation "Queen of Peace," so that she may bestow the gifts of her maternal goodness amid so many and such great troubles and afflictions. Earnest, constant prayer is to be addressed to her whom, during Vatican Council II with the approval of the Fathers and the Catholic world, we have again proclaimed as Mother of the Church, its spiritual parent. This ratifies a doctrinal theme handed down from the past. For she, as the Mother of the Savior, Augustine teaches "is clearly the Mother of his members."[6] St. Anselm, among others, concurs: "Can any dignity be more highly valued than your being the Mother of those whose father and brother Christ consented to become?"[7] Our predecessor Leo XIII used the same title of Mary: "She is truly the Mother of the Church."[8] It is therefore not in vain that during today's frightening troubles we place our hope in her.

As evil increases, the devotion of the people of God must also increase. There-   3879
fore, Esteemed Brothers, our deep desire is that under your leadership, exhortation, and influence the people's pleas be addressed to this most compassionate Mother during the month of October, as we have said, through the devout recitation of the rosary. This form of prayer is well suited to the people of God, most acceptable to the Mother of God, and most effective in imploring God's gifts. If not in so many words, certainly by implication Vatican Council II has thoroughly impressed the praying of the rosary on the minds of the Church's children, in these words: "They are to treasure those Marian devotions and practices commended over the centuries by the Church's magisterium."[9]

Such an effective service of prayer has great power to repel evil and to ward off calamities, as the history of the Church clearly testifies. But in addition it richly nurtures the Christian life: "Above all it strengthens Catholic faith, which is revitalized through the recital on the sacred mysteries, and raises the mind to those truths God has imparted."[10]

Accordingly, during October, dedicated to Our Lady of the Rosary, let prayers be doubled and petitions pour forth, so that by her intercession the dawn of true peace may at last shine upon us, including peace in the practice of religion, which, sad to say, not all people are today free to profess. In particular it is our wish that 4 October, the anniversary of our journey in the cause of peace to the United Nations, be observed throughout the Catholic world this year as "a day of prayer for peace." It shall be your responsibility, Esteemed Brothers, out of your zeal for religion, for which you are to be commended, and the urgency of the issue, of which you are well aware, to prescribe services of prayer. Through them, priests, religious, the laity, and in a special way children, whose innocence sets them apart, the sick, and the suffering, are on that day to plead with the Mother of God and of the Church. We too on that day, in St. Peter's Basilica, at the tomb of the Prince of Apostles, will pray to the Virgin Mother of God, the defender of the Christian cause and the mediator of peace. Thus in all the lands of the earth the one resound-

---

5   Irenaeus, *Adv. haer.* 3, 22: PG 7, 959.

6   Augustine, *De sanct. virg.* 6: PL 40, 399.

7   Anselm, *Or.* 47: PL 158, 945.

8   Leo XIII, Ep. Encycl. *Adiutricem populi christiani*, 5 Sept. 1895: *Acta Leonis* 15 (1896) 302.

9   LG no. 67 [DOL 4 no. 161].

10   Pius XI, Encycl. *Ingravescentibus malis*, 29 Sept. 1937: AAS 29 (1937) 378.

ing voice of the Church will storm heaven. For, as St. Augustine says, "the many languages spoken by the mouth are but one in the faith of the heart."[11] [. . .]

463. PAUL VI, Apostolic Exhortation *Signum magnum*, on Mary, Mother of the Church, 13 May 1967: AAS 59 (1967) 465–475 (excerpts).

3880   The great sign that St. John the Apostle saw in the heavens, "A woman clothed with the sun,"[1] is with good reason interpreted by the liturgy of the Catholic Church to refer to the Blessed Virgin, who by the grace of Christ the Redeemer is the Mother of us all. [. . .]

The many witnesses in sacred Scripture, in the Fathers, in the Constitution *Lumen gentium*, in pronouncements of recent popes support the truth that Mary, the Mother of God and of the Redeemer, is "linked with him by a close and unbreakable bond"[9] and has received a unique "role . . . in the mystery of the incarnate Word and his Mystical Body,"[10] that is, "in the plan of salvation."[11] Accepting these, we see clearly that the Virgin Mother of God not only as "his most holy Mother who took part in the mysteries of Christ,"[12] but also as "the Mother of the Church"[13] "is to be justly honored by a special veneration in the Church"[14] and especially "a liturgical cultus."[15]

There need be no fear that the reform of the liturgy — now progressing under the motto "The rule of faith establishes the rule of prayer"[16] — enjoins any diminution on the "altogether singular"[17] veneration that is due to the Blessed Virgin because of her eminent privileges, above all her dignity as the Mother of God. Conversely, there need be no fear that an increased liturgical or personal veneration of the Mother of God could either obscure or lessen the worship of "adoration offered equally to the Word incarnate, the Father, and the Holy Spirit."[18] [. . .]

3881   I. [. . .] Because the splendor of virtue is so brilliant in Mary, it is the first duty of those who recognize in Christ's Mother a perfect expression of the Church to bind themselves to her more closely in offering thanks to God on high. He has done great things in her for the good of the whole human race and there is no way to thank him enough. A second duty also falls upon all the faithful, that of offering the veneration of praise, honor, and love to that most faithful servant of the Lord. For in God's wise and gentle governance the free consent of Mary's will and her

---

[11]   Augustine, *Enarrat in Ps. 54*, 11: PL 36, 636.

[1]   See Rv 12:1.

[9]   See LG no. 53: AAS 57 (1965) 58; ConstDecrDecl 197.

[10]   LG no. 54: ibid. 59; 192–193.

[11]   LG no. 55: ibid. 59; 113.

[12]   LG no. 66 [DOL 4 no. 160].

[13]   Paul VI, Addr. in St. Peter's to the conciliar Fathers, on the feast of the Presentation of Mary, at the end of the third session of the Council: AAS 56 (1964) 1016.

[14]   LG no. 66 [DOL 4 no. 160].

[15]   LG no. 67 [DOL 4 no. 161].

[16]   Pius XII, Encycl. *Mediator Dei*: AAS 39 (1947) 541.

[17]   See LG no. 66 [DOL 4 no. 160].

[18]   LG no. 66 [DOL 4 no. 160].

generously given efforts have contributed much to accomplishing the divine purposes and continue to contribute to bringing about human salvation.[33] All the
faithful may thus make their own this prayer of St. Anselm: "Glorious Queen, may
it be given to us to rise up to Jesus your Son, who has willed to come down to us
through you."[34]

II. [. . .] We hold it as certain, Esteemed Brothers, that the Church's contempo-   3882
rary teaching on the veneration to be offered to the Blessed Virgin as a mark of
praise, thanks, and love is clearly in accord with the Gospel's teaching as interpreted and developed unequivocally by tradition in both East and West. Our hopes
therefore are raised that this Apostolic Exhortation will be welcomed gladly as a
means of fostering devotion to Mary. And that not only the Christians entrusted to
our care will so receive it but also those who, although not within the full communion of the Catholic Church, nonetheless are one with us in honoring and venerating
the Virgin Mary as the Mother of God's Son.

May the Immaculate Heart of Mary shine as an example of perfect love for   3883
God and neighbor before the eyes of all Christians. May her heart lead them to
share in the holy sacraments of the Church that free and defend the souls of the
faithful from sin. May it move them to atone for the numberless affronts to God's
majesty. May her Immaculate Heart be the sign of unity and a force toward the
strengthening of the bonds of charity between all Christians in the one Church of
Jesus Christ, which "under the teaching of the Holy Spirit cherishes [the Virgin
Mary] with filial devotion as its beloved Mother."[52]

Moreover, this year is the silver jubilee of the date, 31 October 1942, on which
our predecessor Pius XII in a radio broadcast to the Portuguese people solemnly
consecrated the Church and the human race to the Immaculate Heart of Mary[53] (a
consecration we renewed on 21 November 1964).[54] We therefore exhort all the
Church's members to consecrate themselves again individually to the Immaculate
Heart of the Mother of the Church; that, translating the clear import of this act of
filial love into their lives, they conform their conduct more and more to God's will
and, devoutly imitating the example of their heavenly Queen, serve her as true
children. [. . .]

▶   179.   SC RITES, Instruction *Eucharisticum mysterium*, on worship of the eucharist, 25
           May 1967:

           no. 29:   Participation of the faithful in weekday Masses on
                                 feasts of Mary [no. 1258].

▶   309.   PAUL VI, Motu Proprio *Sacrum Diaconatus Ordinem*, restoring the permanent diaco-
           nate in the Latin Church, 18 June 1967:

           no. 26, 4:   Deacon's Marian devotion [no. 2540].

---

[33]   See LG no. 56: AAS 57 (1965) 60; ConstDecrDecl 195.

[34]   Anselm, *Or.* 54: PL 158, 961.

[52]   LG no. 53: AAS 57 (1965) 59; ConstDecrDecl 192.

[53]   See *Discorsi e Radiomessaggi di S.S. Pio XII*, v. 4, 260–262; also AAS 34 (1942) 345–346.

[54]   See AAS 56 (1964) 1017.

▶ 440. PAUL VI, Motu Proprio *Mysterii paschalis,* approving the norms for the liturgical year and the General Calendar, 14 February 1969:

Feasts of Mary [no. 3756].

▶ 442. SC RITES (Consilium), General Norms for the Liturgical Year and the Calendar, 21 March 1969:

nos. 8:   Celebrations in honor of Mary [no. 3774].
     15:            Marian office on Saturday in Ordinary Time [no. 3781].
     35 f: Solemnity of Mary, Mother of God, 1 January [no. 3801].
     59, 3 and 7:   Table of Liturgical Days [no. 3825].

▶ 208. SC RITES (Consilium); SC DIVINE WORSHIP, General Instruction of the Roman Missal, 1st ed. 6 April 1969; 4th ed. 27 March 1975.

nos. 234 a: Bowing the head at name of Mary [no. 1624].
     278:          Images of Mary in churches [no. 1668].
     316 c: Memorials of Mary [no. 1706].
     329 c: Votive Masses in honor of Mary[R1] [no. 1719].

464. PAUL VI, **Apostolic Exhortation** *Recurrens mensis octobris,* on the rosary, 7 October 1969: AAS 61 (1969) 649–654 (excerpt).

3884   The return of October gives us the opportunity once again to urge the whole Christian people to use that form of prayer so deeply rooted in Catholic piety, which has lost none of its importance vis à vis contemporary problems. We speak of the recitation of Mary's rosary.

This year we propose to all our children an intention that seems to us more urgent and serious than ever, namely, the establishment of peace between individuals and nations.

Some progress has been made and there are glimmers of real hope. Yet civil war still rages, there are signs of impending crises, we even see conflict between Christians, who profess the one Gospel of love.

Right within the Church itself there is dissension between its members, accusing and condemning one another. Therefore we must at this time exert every effort and plead for peace.

An anniversary that instills greater confidence also prompts us, the four-hundredth anniversary of our predecessor St. Pius V's Apostolic Letter *Consueverunt romani Pontifices.* At a time of great upheaval for the Church and evil for society the Pope settled the makeup of the rosary in a way suited to every era.

[R1] 1. Query: The celebration of Mary, Queen of Apostles is assigned by numerous particular calendars to the Saturday after Ascension. In places where the solemnity of the Ascension is transferred to the following Sunday, should Mary, Queen of Apostles be celebrated on the Saturday after the Sixth or after the Seventh Sunday of the Easter season? Reply: Wherever there is a celebration of Mary, Queen of Apostles, it should be observed on a Saturday after Ascension: a. on the Saturday after the Sixth Sunday of the Easter season where the Ascension is celebrated on Thursday of that week; b. on the Saturday after the Seventh Sunday where the Ascension is assigned to the Sixth Sunday: Not 14 (1978) 52.

2. The text for the feast of Mary, Mother of the Church, was published in Not 9 (1973) 382–383 and incorporated into MR, 2nd *editio typica* (1975) 867–869.

As we faithfully guard this holy heritage, the source of strength and courage for the Christian people, we at the same time exhort clergy and people to beg God by the Blessed Virgin Mary's intercession to bring about peace and reconciliation between all individuals and peoples. [. . .]

I.   [. . .] The prayers by which we plead for peace are worthwhile precisely   3885
because nothing can take their place as a way to that goal. Through them we are joining ourselves to Christ, in whom we receive all gifts,[2] in order to accept the mission of peace. And for this there is no other course than to use the priceless intercession of Mary, his Mother, who, as the Gospel teaches "found favor with God."[3]

The simple maiden of Nazareth became the mother of the "Prince of Peace,"[4] the one whose birth was accompanied by the angels heralding peace[5] and who himself proclaimed publicly: "Blessed are the peacemakers, for they shall be called the children of God."[6] The Gospel shows that Mary was concerned about seeing to and alleviating human needs: in the village of Cana she did not hesitate to become the suppliant in order to ensure the guests' enjoyment at the wedding feast.[7] How then, if we plead with her sincerely, could she fail to intercede for us to obtain peace, a gift so much more sublime?

Vatican Council II gave us timely instruction that Mary continues her intercession with her Son on behalf of her children still on life's journey.[8] Christ generously heeded her when she said ingenuously: "They have no wine." How could he not show the same generosity to her plea: "They have no peace"?

II.   Everyone of us must strive for justice and peace "to the utmost of our powers   3886
and resources."[9] Therefore it will be the responsibility of every Christian to ask Mary to pray with us and for us that the Lord may give us the peace that the world cannot give.[10] Moreover, as we meditate on the mysteries of the rosary we are enabled, like Mary, to acquire the spirit of the peacemakers through intimate and continued contact with Jesus and an imitation of the mysteries of his redemptive life. [. . .]

III.   [. . .] May the continued contemplation of the mysteries of our salvation   3887
fashion you after the image of Christ and the example of Mary as bearers of peace. May Mary's rosary — both in the form given us by St. Pius V and in other forms adapted, with the approval of lawful authority, to today's mentality — lead to what our predecessor John XXIII longed for: the public and universal supplication for the ordinary and the special needs of the Church, of nations, and of the whole world.[20]

---

²   See Rom 8:32.

³   Lk 1:30.

⁴   Is 9:5.

⁵   See Lk 2:14.

⁶   Mt 5:9.

⁷   See Jn 2:15.

⁸   See LG no. 62: AAS 57 (1965) 63; ConstDecrDecl 199–200.

⁹   Paul VI, Encycl. *Populorum progressio* no. 75: AAS 59 (1967) 294.

¹⁰   See MR, collect of the Mass for Peace.

²⁰   John XXIII, Apostolic Letter *Il Religioso convegno*, 29 Sept. 1961: AAS 53 (1961) 646.

3888   This crown of prayer stands as a kind of "compendium of the Gospel"[21] and thus as "an expression of the Church's own devotion."[22]

Through this way of prayer to Mary, the holy Mother of God and our Mother, we will contribute to the realization of this desire of the Council: "Let all the faithful pour forth their unceasing prayers to the Mother of God and our own Mother. Let them plead that she who aided the Church in its beginnings by her prayers may now, as she is exalted in heaven above all the angels and saints, intercede with her Son within the communion of saints. Let them pray for this until the entire family of peoples, whether bearing the Christian name or still unaware of their Savior, are gathered together with peace and concord into the one people of God, unto the glory of the holy and undivided Trinity."[23] [. . .]

▶   481.   SC DIVINE WORSHIP, Instruction *Calendaria particularia*, on revision of particular calendars and propers, 24 June 1970:

   nos. 34:   Mary, titular of a church [no. 4029].
         35:          Solemnity of Mary as titular of a church [no. 4030].

▶   426.   SC DIVINE WORSHIP, General Instruction of the Liturgy of the Hours, 2 February 1971:

   no. 240:   Marian office on Saturdays in Ordinary Time [no. 3670].

▶   169.   SC CLERGY, *General Catechetical Directory*, 11 April 1971:

   Part V, no. 78:   Children's prayer to Mary [no. 1107].

▶   318.   SYNOD OF BISHOPS, *The Ministerial Priesthood*, 30 November 1971:

   Part II, I, no. 3: Priests' devotion to Mary [no. 2572].

▶   535.   SC DIVINE WORSHIP, *Ordo cantus Missae*, Introduction, 24 June 1972:

   I. Reform of the
   Graduale Romanum: Neo-Gregorian compositions for the feast of the Immaculate Conception [no. 4278].

465. SC DIVINE WORSHIP, Note *Anno 1974*, on the solemnity of the Immaculate Conception in 1974, 20 January 1973: Not 9 (1973) 71.

3889   In 1974 the solemnity of the Immaculate Conception of the Blessed Virgin Mary falls on the Second Sunday of Advent.

---

[21]   Card. J. G. Saliège, *Voilà ta Mère*, pages mariales recueillies et présentées par Mgr. Garrone (Toulouse, Apostolat de la Prière, 1958) 40.

[22]   Paul VI, Addr., 23 July 1963, to those attending the third Dominican meeting on the rosary: *Insegnamenti di Paolo VI*, v. 1 (1963) 464.

[23]   LG no. 69: AAS 57 (1965) 66–67; ConstDecrDecl 206.

According to the norms of the General Roman Calendar this solemnity of the Blessed Virgin Mary should be moved ahead to Saturday (see General Norms for the Liturgical Year and the Calendar no. 5).[a]

Because of the request of a number of bishops, Pope Paul VI grants that at the discretion of the conference of bishops the liturgical celebration of the Immaculate Virgin Mary may be observed in 1974 on 8 December, in spite of this being a Sunday of Advent.

The homily and general intercessions are to stress the sense of the Advent season.

The faculty is published at this time in order to inform those editing liturgical calendars well in advance.

▶   477.   SC DIVINE WORSHIP, Norms *Patronus, liturgica acceptione*, on patron saints, 19 March 1973:

nos. 1 and 4:   Mary as patron [nos. 3971 and 3974].

466. SC DIVINE WORSHIP, **Norms** *Pluries decursu temporis*, on crowning images of the Blessed Virgin, 25 March 1973: AAS 65 (1973) 280–281; Not 9 (1973) 266–267.*

Often in history the Christian people have earnestly asked and received permission to place a crown upon some particular image of the Blessed Virgin Mary. The reason for this is that "Mary, as the Mother of God, placed by grace next to her Son above all angels and saints, has shared in the mysteries of Christ and is justly honored by a special veneration in the Church."[1] The rite given in the Roman Pontifical stands as permanent evidence of the tradition of crowning her images.   3890

By mandate of Pope Paul VI the Congregation for Divine Worship lays down the following norms for the coronation rite.

1.   Only images of the Blessed Virgin, whether paintings or statues, may be crowned; the image of a saint or blessed may not.   3891

When an image portrays Mary with our Savior Jesus Christ, both figures must be crowned.

2.   Images to be crowned must be those specially revered by the Christian people, so that the rite does in fact express the attachment and devotion of the people to the Mother of the Lord.   3892

3.   The rite for crowning an image that is the object of devotion in a particular place must as a rule be conducted by the bishop of that place. He follows the rite as given in the Roman Pontifical.   3893

The crown used must be gracefully made and have the beauty of a noble simplicity and genuine art.

---

[a]   See DOL 442 no. 3771.

*   The text in both AAS and Not appears as part II with norms on patron saints; see DOL 407.

[1]   LG no. 66 [DOL 4 no. 160].

3894   4.   For the crowning of an image "in the name and by the authority of the pope," which is done by a papal legate, the requirement is that the image is regarded as having truly special significance for the Church or for some nation or region.

To obtain authorization for such a crowning, the following *documents* must be sent well ahead of time to the Congregation for Divine Worship:

    a.   the petition either of the bishop or of the conference of bishops (depending on whether the image involved is venerated in a diocese or in a region or nation);

    b.   a brief historical summary about the image itself and of the people's devotion in its regard;

    c.   ecclesiastical or civil proceedings, requests, lists of signatures, to accompany the petition and serve as evidence of the will of the Christian people.

3895   5.   The faculty for the crowning is granted by means of a decree of this Congregation and an apostolic letter sent in the form of a brief.

▶   156.   PAUL VI AND SHENOUDA III, (Patriarch of Alexandria), Joint Statement, 19 March 1973:

Veneration of the Blessed Virgin [no. 1051].

467. PAUL VI, Apostolic Exhortation *Marialis cultus*, on rightly grounding and increasing Marian devotion, 2 February 1974: AAS 66 (1974) 113–168; Not 10 (1974) 153–197.

3896   That Marian devotion should grow has been an object of our unceasing efforts ever since we were raised to the chair of Peter. Our intent has been to give expression to the mind of the Church in this regard and to the promptings of our own heart. But in addition we have been influenced in this course because this form of piety is, obviously, a privileged element of the life of worship that combines the highest reaches of wisdom and the virtue of religion and that is therefore a principal obligation of the people of God.[1]

In view of that obligation we have continued to encourage and further the great work of liturgical reform that the Second Vatican Ecumenical Council undertook. There can be no doubt that there was a special divine providence involved in the fact that the first document of the Council, approved and signed *in the Holy Spirit* by ourself and the conciliar Fathers, was the Constitution *Sacrosanctum Concilium*. And this document has as its purpose to reform and enrich the liturgy and to make the faithful's participation in the divine mysteries more beneficial.[2] Since the time of the Council the objective of much that we have done in our pontificate has been to give a more effective form to the worship owed to God. Evidence of these efforts is the promulgation over the last several years of many liturgical books of the Roman Rite, reformed according to the principles and norms of the Council. For this we thank the Lord, the giver of all good gifts, and we also thank the conferences of bishops and the bishops individually for assisting in various ways in the preparation of the liturgical books.

---

[1]   See Lactantius, *Divinae Institutiones* 4; 3, 6–10: CSEL 19, 279.

[2]   See SC art. 1–3, 11, 21, 48 [DOL 1 nos. 1–3, 11, 21, 48].

There is joy and gratitude in our soul as we reflect on the work already accomplished and the first successes of the liturgical reform, which will increase with the growth in understanding of the reform in its primary and basic ideals and with its right practice. At the same time we consider it our duty to foster with watchful care any undertaking related to the progress of the *cultus* through which the Church adores "in spirit and in truth" (see Jn 4:24) Father, Son, and Holy Spirit, "honors with special love Mary, the Mother of God,"³ and keeps the memory of the martyrs and the other saints with reverent marks of devotion.

As we have already pointed out, devotion to Mary fits into the pattern, so to   3897
speak, of the *cultus* that rightfully deserves to be called *Christian*, because from Christ it has its origin and effectiveness, in Christ it has its complete and pure form of expression, and through Christ it leads to the Father in the Holy Spirit. The progress we seek in that devotion is characteristic of the piety proper to the Church. The truth is that the devotion involved in showing veneration to Mary expresses her connection with the divine plan for the redemption of humanity. Mary is thus venerated under a special title corresponding to each role she has within that divine plan⁴ and the sound and proven progress in venerating the Mother of God follows of necessity the path of the authentic development of Christian worship. Furthermore, the very history of this devotion demonstrates that "the various forms of Marian devotion sanctioned by the Church, within the limits of sound orthodoxy,"⁵ have been created and have flourished properly, that is, in subordination to the worship offered to Christ. This worship has given to Marian devotion its origin, meaning, and ultimate purpose. That continues to be true in our own era: the contemporary Church, in its reflections on the mystery of Christ and on its own nature, has seen at the origins of the first and as the fulfillment of the second a Woman, the Virgin Mary, Mother of Christ and Mother of the Church. A deeper insight into the office entrusted to Mary is translated into the joyful veneration offered to her and the reverence of adoration directed toward God's plan. For his will is that in his family, the Church, and consequently in every home, there be a woman present to watch over it, inspired by the hidden will to serve, and "gently to guide its steps until the coming of the glorious day of the Lord."⁶

The pattern of contemporary change has had an impact on social behavior, on   3898
the perceptions of peoples, on styles in literature and the arts, on the methods of social communication, even on the ways of expressing religious attitudes. Moreover, certain practices of worship that not long ago seemed suitable as expressions of the religious feelings of individuals or of Christian communities are today regarded as inadequate or less relevant, because they are bound up with past conceptions of social life and culture. At the same time, many are in search of new ways to express the unchangeable bond that exists between creatures and their Creator, between God's children and their Father. This may lead to some being upset for a time. Yet those who reflect on such issues with a sense of trust in God will see that many of the directions taken by contemporary devotion (for example, concern for the interior rather than for externals) are an aid to the growth of Christian devotion in general and to Marian devotion in particular. The result will be that as the present age listens attentively to the voice of tradition and reflects on the advances

---

³ SC art. 103 [DOL 1 no. 103].

⁴ See LG no. 66 [DOL 4 no. 160].

⁵ LG no. 66 [DOL 4 no. 160].

⁶ Preface, votive Mass of Mary, Mother of the Church [text published in Not 9 (1973) 382–383 and incorporated in MR, 1975, 868].

in theology and other disciplines, it will contribute its own paean of praise to her whom, in her own prophetic words, "all generations will call blessed" (see Lk 1:48).

We thus regard it to be part of our apostolic ministry to expound in a kind of colloquy with you, Esteemed Brothers, certain themes relative to the place the Blessed Virgin Mary holds in the Church's worship. Vatican Council II[7] and we ourself[8] have already touched on such themes; yet we do not think it pointless to deal with them once more. For this is a way to discuss problems and especially to advance the devotion toward the Virgin Mary that originates from the Word of God as its cause and is carried out in the Spirit of Christ.

We intend: (I) to dwell on certain issues concerning the connection between the liturgy and the *cultus* of the Mother of God; (II) to propose considerations and directive norms suited to foster the lawful progress of this *cultus*; and finally, to offer some thoughts on renewing an eager, more thoughtful recitation of the rosary, a practice constantly counseled by our predecessors and of longstanding usage among the Christian people.

I

3899   1.   Turning to consider the place of Mary in Christian worship, we must look first to the liturgy. Besides being rich in doctrinal content, it has an incomparable pastoral power and stands as a proven model for other forms of worship. We would prefer to examine the different liturgies of East and West, but for the purposes of the present Apostolic Exhortation we will look only at the books of the Roman Rite. For only this rite has been reformed throughout in keeping with the practical norms issued by Vatican Council II,[9] including the ways of expressing veneration for Mary. We must, accordingly, carefully examine and evaluate the Roman Rite.

3900   2.   Before the reform of the Roman liturgy itself, the General Calendar was carefully revised. The calendar was drawn up with the purpose of giving proper emphasis to celebration of the work of salvation on fixed days; the entire mystery of Christ from his incarnation to the awaiting of his coming in glory was arranged over the course of the liturgical year.[10] The calendar thus more appropriately and closely integrates the commemoration of Mary into the annual cycle of her Son's mysteries.

3901   3.   During Advent the liturgy frequently brings Mary to mind. On 8 December the solemnity of the Immaculate Conception recalls the preparation for the Savior's coming at its origins (See Is 11:1 and 10) and also the happy beginning of the Church in its beauty without spot or wrinkle.[11] But in addition during Advent the Blessed Virgin is remembered especially on the weekdays from 17 to 24 December and in a particular way on the Sunday before Christmas. On this day the readings are the ancient prophecies about the Virgin Mother and the Messiah[12] and the

---

7   See LG 66–67 [DOL 4 nos. 160–161]; SC art. 103 [DOL 1 no. 103].

8   See Ap. Exhort. *Signum magnum* [DOL 463].

9   See SC no. 3 [DOL 1 no. 3].

10   See SC art. 102 [DOL 1 no. 102].

11   See RM, preface of the Immaculate Conception.

12   MR, *Ordo lectionum Missae* (ed. *typica*, 1969) 8 [Lectionary for Mass, Fourth Sunday of Advent, Reading I: Year A, Is 7:10–14: The virgin shall conceive; Year B, 2 Sm 7:1–5, 8:11–16: The Lord will make the house of David secure forever; Year C, Mi 5:1–4: Out of you will be born the one who is to rule over

gospel narratives are about the imminent birth of Christ and of John the Baptist.[13]

4.   The faithful who carry the spirit of Advent from the liturgy into their own   3902
lives perceive the inexpressible love in the Virgin Mother's welcoming of her
Son.[14] Thus the Advent liturgy leads them to keep her before their own eyes as a
model and to prepare the way for the coming Savior, "watching in prayer, their
hearts filled with wonder and praise."[15] It is also well to note that in the Advent
liturgy there is a link between the remembrance of Christ's mother and the awaiting of the Messiah and the remembrance of Christ's Second Coming. Thus the
liturgy provides a clear and normative model for balance in worship that precludes
any tendency (such as is present in some forms of popular devotion) to separate
Marian devotion from its necessary point of reference, which is Christ. The result is
that, as liturgists have affirmed, Advent can be seen to be a season singularly suited
to offering veneration to the Mother of God. We fully support this judgment and
proposal and desire their acceptance and observance everywhere.

5.   The Christmas season stands as a continuing remembrance of that divine,   3903
virginal, and salvific motherhood by which "without losing her virginity Mary gave
the world its savior."[16] On Christmas itself, as it adores the Savior, the Church also
honors his glorious Mother. On Epiphany, as it celebrates the universal call to
salvation, the Church gazes on the Virgin, the true Seat of Wisdom and Mother of
the King, presenting for the Magi's adoration the Redeemer of all peoples (see Mt
2:11). On the feast of the Holy Family (the Sunday within the octave of Christmas)
the Church, full of reverence, reflects on the home life at Nazareth of the Son of
God and Son of Man with his Mother Mary and with the just man Joseph (see Mt
1:19).

    In the revised arrangement of the Christmas season we should all, it seems to
us, turn with one mind to the restored solemnity of the Mother of God. This feast
was entered into the calendar in the liturgy of the city of Rome for the first day of
January. The purpose of the celebration is to honor the role of Mary in the mystery
of salvation and at the same time to sing the praises of the unique dignity thus
coming to "the Holy Mother . . . through whom we have been given the gift of
receiving the author of life."[17] This same solemnity also offers an excellent opportunity to renew the adoration rightfully to be shown to the newborn Prince of
Peace, as we once again hear the good tidings of great joy (see Lk 2:14) and pray to
God through the intercession of the Queen of Peace for the priceless gift of peace.
Because of these considerations and the fact that the octave of Christmas coincides
with a day of hope, New Year's Day, we have assigned to it the observance of the
World Day of Peace.[a] This observance gains increasing approval and has already
had good effects in the hearts of many people.

Israel].

   [13] Ibid. [Lectionary for Mass, Fourth Sunday of Advent, Gospel, Year A, Mt 1:18–24: Jesus was born
of Mary, who was betrothed to Joseph, a relative of David; Year B, Lk 1:26–38: You shall conceive and
bear a son; Year C, Lk 1:39–45: Why should it happen that I am honored with a visit from the mother of
my Lord?].

   [14] See RM, preface II for Advent.

   [15] Ibid.

   [16] RM, Eucharistic Prayer I the *In union with the whole Church* for Christmas and its octave.

   [17] RM, 1 January, entrance antiphon and opening prayer.

   [a] See DOL 497, no. 4097.

3904   6.   Along with the Marian celebrations of the Immaculate Conception and of
Mary, Mother of God, we must also consider the ancient feasts observed on 25
March and 15 August.

For the celebration of the incarnation, the General Roman Calendar has with
good reason restored the ancient title *In Annuntiatione Domini*. But the celebration is
really at the same time a festival of Christ and of the Virgin: a celebration honoring
the Word who became the "Son of Mary" (Mk 6:3) and the Virgin who became the
Mother of God. With respect to Christ, the liturgies of East and West, with their
inexhaustible riches, celebrate this solemnity as a remembrance of the *fiat* that the
incarnate Word uttered as he came into this world: "I come to do your will, O God"
(Heb 10:7; Ps 39:8–9). Thus it is a commemoration of the beginning of the redemption and of the indissoluble espousal uniting divine and human nature in the person
of the Word. As for Mary, the celebration is the feast of the new Eve, of the
obedient and faithful maiden who with the generous utterance of her own *fiat* (see
Lk 1:38) has been made the Mother of God through the working of the Holy Spirit,
as well as truly the Mother of the living and the true Ark of the Covenant, the
temple of God, because her body received the one Mediator (see 1 Tm 2:5). Thus
the solemnity of the Annunciation is the recollection of the moment in time that
was the high point in the dialogue concerning our salvation initiated by God with
us; the day is also the memorial of the Virgin's freely given consent and of her
cooperation in the carrying out of the divine plan for human redemption.

On 15 August we celebrate the glorious Assumption of Mary into heaven. It is
the festival honoring the fullness of blessedness that was her destiny, the glorification of her immaculate soul and virginal body that completely conformed her
to the risen Christ. This is a celebration that offers to the Church and to all humanity an exemplar and a consoling message, teaching us the fulfillment of our highest
hopes: their own future glorification is happily in store for all those whom Christ
has made his own brothers and sisters by taking on their "flesh and blood" (Heb
2:14; see Gal 4:4). The solemnity of the Assumption is continued on into the
celebration of the Queenship of Mary on the octave day. She who is enthroned next
to the King of Ages is contemplated as the radiant Queen and interceding Mother.[18]

These then are the four solemnities that in their high rank as liturgical celebrations bring out the main truths related to the simple handmaid of the Lord.

3905   7.   After the review of these solemnities, it is also necessary to list those feasts
related to the remembrance of events of salvation in which the Blessed Virgin is
closely associated with her Son. Thus there is the feast of the Birth of Mary (8
September), "who brought the dawn of hope and salvation to the world."[19] The
liturgy of the Visitation (31 May) celebrates the Blessed Virgin Mary's bearing the
Son in her womb[20] and going to Elizabeth to offer the help of her love and to
proclaim the mercy of God her Savior.[21] The memorial of Our Lady of Sorrows (15
September) provides an occasion to recall vividly the supreme, decisive moment in
the history of salvation and also to venerate the Mother sharing in her Son's
sufferings as she stood at the foot of the cross.[22]

The feast for 2 February, with the restored title *In Praesentatione Domini*, should
be deeply pondered for a thorough grasp of the rich realities it contains as a

---

18   See RM, 22 August, opening prayer.

19   RM, 8 September, prayer after communion.

20   See RM, 31 May, opening prayer.

21   See ibid., opening prayer and prayer over the gifts.

22   See RM, 15 September, opening prayer.

combined remembrance of Son and Mother. For it is a celebration of the mystery of salvation accomplished by Christ with Mary at his side as Mother of the suffering Servant of Yahweh, as the one fulfilling the charge belonging to ancient Israel, and as the prototype of the new people of God, who again and again are afflicted in their faith and hope by torment and persecution (see Lk 2:21–35).

8.   The reformed General Roman Calendar particularly emphasizes the celebra-   3906
tions mentioned. Yet it also includes another category of celebrations, those, namely, that, while based on a local *cultus*, have spread and have appealed to many people
(11 February, Our Lady of Lourdes; 5 August, Dedication of Saint Mary Major). To
such observances should be added others that began as celebrations proper to
religious communities, but then became so widespread that they were rightly regarded as ecclesial (16 July, Our Lady of Mount Carmel; 7 October, Our Lady of the
Rosary). Finally, we should add those celebrations (excluding the apocryphal) that
present realities containing a powerful force of example and that are surrounded by
venerable tradition, particularly dear to Eastern Christians (21 November, Presentation of Mary), or that are evidence of strong currents in contemporary devotion
(Saturday after the Second Sunday after Pentecost, the Immaculate Heart of Mary).

9.   We must not forget that the General Roman Calendar does not exhaust the   3907
Marian celebrations. Carefully respecting liturgical norms and with the devout and
willing consent of the faithful, particular calendars include Marian feasts of the
various local Churches. And we must also mention the permission to make frequent
liturgical commemoration of the Virgin through the memorial of Mary on Saturday.
This ancient and we might say humble memorial is now made particularly convenient and diversified because of the flexible structure of the present Calendar and
the numerous texts for the memorial supplied by the Roman Missal.

10.   In this Apostolic Exhortation our intent is not to review the entire contents of   3908
the new Roman Missal. Rather, since we set out to review the reformed books of
the Roman Rite,[23] it is well for us to go over certain of their pertinent features and
themes. We wish first of all to point out that, in a wonderful correspondence to the
Eastern liturgies,[24] the eucharistic prayers of the Roman Missal place great emphasis on the memory of the Blessed Virgin. In the ancient Roman Canon, which
remembers the Mother of God in words full of rich teaching and devout worship
we read: *In union with the whole Church we honor Mary the ever-virgin Mother of Jesus Christ,
our Lord and God.* Similarly, Eucharistic Prayer III, a new addition, expresses the desire
of those who pray it that together with the Mother they may share in the inheritance belonging to the children: *May he make us an everlasting gift to you and enable us to
share in the inheritance of your saints, with Mary, the virgin Mother of God.*

      This daily remembrance, at the very center of the sacrifice of the Mass, ought
to be seen as conveying in a special way the veneration offered by the Church to
the "blessed of the Most High" (see Lk 1:28).

11.   The texts of the newly reformed Roman Missal contain these main Marian   3909
themes of Roman euchology: her immaculate conception and fullness of grace, her
divine motherhood, her absolute and fruitful virginity, her being the temple of the
Holy Spirit, her cooperation in the mission of her Son, her holiness as a shining
exemplar, her compassionate intercession, her assumption into heaven, her dignity

---

      [23]   See no. 1 of this Apostolic Exhortation [no. 3899; AAS gives a wrong page reference].

      [24]   Among the many anaphoras, the following may be noted as highly esteemed in the East: *Anaphora
Marci Evangelistae,* A. Hänggi and I. Pahl, eds., (Fribourg, Editions Universitaires, 1968) 107; *Anaphora Iacobi
fratris Domini graeca,* ibid. 257; *Anaphora Ioannis Chrysostomi,* ibid. 229.

as Queen and Mother. From the perusal of the Missal's texts we see clearly that all of these are themes received in continuous and complete doctrinal consistency with the past. Other, somewhat new themes have entered the Missal that reveal a similar coherence with contemporary theological developments. This is the case, for example, with the theme "Mary, Mother of the Church"; it has often and in different ways been woven into the texts of the Missal, even as there are many different relationships existing between Christ's Mother and the Church. Such texts include: in the Virgin's immaculate conception recognition of the beginnings of the Church as Christ's Bride without spot or wrinkle;[25] in the dogma of the assumption, the perception of the already accomplished beginning as well as the picture of that final result for the Church as a whole still to be achieved[26] in the mystery of the divine maternity, the acknowledgment of Mary as Mother of the Head and members of the Mystical Body, so that the holy Mother of God is simultaneously to be proclaimed the caring Mother of the Church.[27]

Whenever it directs its gaze to the Church, whether in the beginning or in the present, the liturgy invariably finds Mary. Thus she remained with the apostles, joining in prayer with them,[28] and the liturgy sees her now also present and at work, wishing to live the mystery of Christ along with the Church: . . . *May your Church with her* [Mary] *be united to Christ in his suffering and so come to share in his rising to new life.*[29] As it sings God's praises the liturgy sees Mary as intent on glorifying God with the Church: . . . *with Mary may we praise you for ever.*[30] Because it is worship calling continuously for practical application in life, the liturgy prays for the power to translate devotion to Mary into steadfast and sorrowing love for the Church; thus, in the wonderful phrasing of the prayer after communion for 15 September: *As we honor the compassionate love of the Virgin Mary, may we make up in our own lives, for the good of the Church, whatever is lacking in the sufferings of Christ.*

3910   12. The Lectionary for Mass is one of the books of the Roman Rite that must be viewed as especially enriched because of the reform of the liturgy since Vatican Council II. This applies both to the number of texts added and to the teachings they contain. The texts are sources of the word of God, which is always "living and active" (Heb 4:12). The reason for such a large collection of texts is that through the pattern of the three-year cycle the entire history of salvation would be recounted and the mystery of Christ proclaimed more fully. From this it naturally and logically follows that the Lectionary should contain a greater number of Old and New Testament readings referring to the Blessed Virgin. But this increased number in no way evidences any lack of balanced judgment: only those readings have been included that in varying degrees bear a Marian sense, on the grounds either of their clear literal meaning or of a careful interpretation, supported by teachings of the Church's magisterium or of sound tradition. It is further necessary to consider that such readings occur not only on feasts of Mary but also in many other cases: for example, on some of the Sundays of the liturgical year;[31] in the celebration of ritual

---

[25]   See RM, 8 December, preface.

[26]   See RM, 15 August, preface.

[27]   See RM, 1 January, prayer after communion.

[28]   See RM, Common of the Blessed Virgin Mary 6, Easter season, opening prayer.

[29]   RM, 15 September, opening prayer.

[30]   RM, 31 May, opening prayer. The same idea is present in preface II of the Blessed Virgin Mary: *In celebrating the memory of the Blessed Virgin Mary, it is our special joy to echo* HER *song of thanksgiving.*

[31]   See Lectionary for Mass: Third Sunday of Advent (Year C, Zeph 3:14–18 a); Fourth Sunday of Advent (see note 12); Sunday in the octave of Christmas (Year A, Mt 2, 13–15 and 19–23; Year B, Lk 2:22–40; Year C, Lk 2:41–52); Second Sunday after Christmas (Jn 1:1–18); Seventh Sunday of Easter (Year

Masses that profoundly touch the sacramental life of Christians and their choice of vocation;[32] finally, in Masses for various occasions, both happy and sad, in Christian experience.[33]

13. The reformed book for the divine office, *The Liturgy of the Hours*, also contains striking evidence of devotion toward the Mother of the Lord. This is seen first in the hymns, some of which are literary masterpieces, for example, Dante's prayer to the Virgin.[34] There are also: the antiphons of night prayer that end each day's round of prayer with fuller, more ardent sentiments of petition to Mary and to which are added the *Sub tuum praesidium*, the well-known trope of such revered antiquity and sublime sentiments; the intercessions of morning prayer, which so often trustingly appeal to the Mother of God; finally, the many choice pages of Marian devotion from authors of the early Christian centuries, the Middle Ages, and more recent times.

3911

14. The Roman Missal, the Lectionary for Mass, and *The Liturgy of the Hours*, which should be seen as the basic books for the entire liturgical prayer of the Roman Rite, honor the memory of the Virgin with frequent expressions of veneration. Yet other liturgical books in many other passages express intense love and prayerful appeal to the Mother of God. The Church calls upon the Mother of grace before the washing of the candidates in the saving waters of baptism.[35] The Church implores Mary's prayers on behalf of mothers who in their great gratitude for the gift of motherhood go joyfully to be churched.[36] The Church holds her up as model for its sons and daughters who in embracing religious life make profession to follow Christ[37] or receive consecration to a life of virginity;[38] and the Church asks her maternal aid for all of them.[39] It offers its earnest prayer to her for its members who are near death.[40] It asks her intervention on behalf of those whose eyes have been closed to the light of time and who stand before Christ, the Light of eternity.[41] Finally, the Church prays through Mary's intercession for the gentle comforting of those who, burdened with bitter grief, weep in faith over the departure of their loved ones.[42]

3912

A, Acts 1:12–14); Second Sunday in Ordinary Time (Year C, Jn 2:1–12); Tenth Sunday in Ordinary Time (Year B, Gn 3:9–15); Fourteenth Sunday in Ordinary Time (Year B, Mk 6:1–6).

[32] See Lectionary for Mass: Mass for the Preparation and Baptism of Adults, Presentation of the Lord's Prayer, Reading II, 2: Gal 4, 4–7; Mass for Christian Initiation apart from the Easter Vigil, Gospel 7: Jn 1:1–5, 9–14, and 16–18; Mass for Marriage, Gospel 7: Jn 2:1–11; Mass for Consecration to a Life of Virginity and Religious Profession, Reading I, 7: Is 61:9–11; Gospel 6: Mk 3:31–35; Lk 1:26–38. See also *Rite of Consecration to a Life of Virginity* no. 130; *Rite of Religious Profession*, Part Two, no. 145.

[33] See Lectionary for Mass: Mass for Refugees and Exiles, Gospel 1: Mt 1:13–15 and 19–23; Mass in Thanksgiving, Reading I, 4: Zeph 3:14–15.

[34] See *La Divina Commedia: Paradiso* canto 33, 1–9; see LH, Memorial of Mary on Saturday, hymn for the office of readings.

[35] See *Rite of Baptism for Children* no. 48; *Rite of Christian Initiation of Adults* no. 214.

[36] See RR, tit. VII, ch. 3, Blessing of a woman after childbirth.

[37] See *Rite of Religious Profession*, Part One, nos. 57–67.

[38] See *Rite of Consecration to a Life of Virginity* no. 16.

[39] See *Rite of Religious Profession*, Part One, nos. 62 and 142; Part Two, nos. 67 and 158; *Rite of Consecration to a Life of Virginity* nos. 18 and 20.

[40] See *Pastoral Care of the Sick: Rites of Anointing and Viaticum* nos. 143, 146, 147, 150.

[41] See RM, Various Prayers for the Dead, [I4] For Relatives, Friends, and Benefactors, opening prayer.

[42] See *Rite of Funerals* no. 226.

3913   15. This survey of newly reformed liturgical books prompts us to declare and
affirm with gratifying assurance that the the post-Vatican II reform has, as was the
aim of the liturgical movement, viewed the Virgin Mary in her place as part of the
entire mystery of Christ; it has recognized, in keeping with the convictions of
tradition, the unique place belonging to her in Christian worship as the holy Mother of God and the cherished companion of the Redeemer.

Nor could it have been otherwise. Anyone considering the course of Christian
worship readily perceives that in both East and West the most excellent and splendid expressions of devotion to Mary developed either within the liturgy itself or as
attached to it.

We should in fact notice that the universal Church's contemporary veneration
of Mary derives from and continues the devotion that the Church has at all times
shown toward Mary in its zeal for the truth and in its ever watchful use of worthy
forms of worship. Tradition, which is always living because of the unfailing presence of the Spirit and the continuous listening to the word of God, is the abiding
source of the contemporary Church's motives, arguments, and inspiration for the
veneration it offers to the Virgin. The sublimest evidence and most solid record of
this living tradition is the liturgy.

3914   16. Continuing with the conciliar teaching on Mary and the Church, we turn to
reflect on the reason for the special relationships existing between Mary and the
liturgy: how Mary has become the exemplar of that sense of reverent devotion with
which the Church celebrates the divine mysteries and expresses them in its way of
life. The basis of Mary's being the model in this respect is the Church's view of her
as the foremost instance and illustration of faith, charity, and absolute union with
Christ,[43] in other words, of that inner attitude with which the Church, joined to its
Lord as a beloved Bride, calls upon him and through him offers its worship to the
eternal Father.[44]

3915   17. Mary is the *Virgin who listens*, welcoming the word of God with faith. The faith
we speak of was the condition of her becoming the Mother of God and the path to
that exalted place. In the words of St. Augustine's insight, "the Blessed Mary
brought forth in faith the one whom she had conceived in faith."[45] When the angel
had put an end to her hesitancy (see Lk 1:34–37), "full of faith, and conceiving
Christ in her soul before conceiving him in her womb, she said, 'Behold the handmaid of the Lord, be it done unto me according to your word' (Lk 1:38)."[46] That
faith was the reason for her blessedness and the guarantee that the promise to her
would be kept: "And blessed is she who believed that what was spoken to her from
the Lord would come about" (Lk 1:45). As the first participant in the beginnings of
Christ's incarnation and its privileged witness, she treasured through her faith the
memory of his infancy and pondered its events in her heart (see Lk 2:19, 51). The
Church follows Mary in this: above all in the liturgy it listens to the word of God,
welcomes it, proclaims and reveres it; the Church gives it to Christ's faithful as the
bread of life;[47] in the light of that word, the Church reads the signs of the times,
interprets human events, and lives its life.

---

[43]   See LG no. 63: AAS 57 (1965) 64; ConstDecrDecl 201.

[44]   See SC art. 7 [DOL 1 no. 7].

[45]   Augustine, *Sermo.* 215, 4: PL 38, 1074.

[46]   Ibid.

[47]   See DV no. 21 [DOL 14 no. 224].

18. Mary is the *Virgin who prays*. This is exemplified by her visitation. She went to the mother of John the Baptist and gave voice to the praise of God and to her own humility, faith, and hope in her canticle, the *Magnificat* (see Lk 1:46–55). Mary's chief prayer and the song of the Messianic age brings together the festive joy of the ancient and the new Israel. As St. Irenaeus seems to suggest, the Canticle of Mary combined both the joy of Abraham at the vision of Christ's day (see Jn 8:56)[48] and the voice of the Church in its prophetic role: "In her joy Mary cried out, prophesying in the name of the Church, 'My soul proclaims the greatness of the Lord.'"[49] The Canticle of Mary has indeed become a prayer shared by the entire Church throughout all the ages.

At Cana as well Mary shows herself as the Virgin who prays. There by her gentle, caring prayer she had pointed out to her Son simply an earthly need; a heavenly grace was the effect she achieved: Jesus performed the first of his signs and thus strengthened the disciples' faith in him (see Jn 2:1–12).

Finally, Mary appears as the *Virgin who prays* during the last period of her life. The Apostles "with one accord devoted themselves to prayer, together with the women and Mary the Mother of Jesus and with his brethren" (Acts 1:14). Thus it is right to see Mary praying in the infant Church and it remains right to see her praying now: although she has been received into heaven, she does not fail in her office of interceding and saving.[50] The Church also is a virgin who prays, bringing before the Father each day the needs of its children "and unceasingly engaged in praising the Lord and interceding for the salvation of the whole world."[51]

19. Mary is the *Virgin who is a mother*. "In faith and obedience and as a virgin whom the power of the Holy Spirit had overshadowed, she gave birth to the Son of the Father."[52] God willed this unique and marvelous divine motherhood to be the figure and exemplar of the fecundity of the virgin Church that also becomes a mother: "By preaching and baptizing it brings forth children conceived of the Holy Spirit and born of God, into a new and immortal life."[53] Thus the Fathers of the Church were right in teaching that the Church in the sacrament of baptism somehow continues Mary's virginal motherhood. We may offer one example of this teaching from our predecessor St. Leo the Great; in one of his Christmas sermons he says: "[Christ] placed in the baptismal font the source of his own origin in the womb of the Virgin: the power of the most High and the overshadowing of the Holy Spirit [see Lk 1:35] that caused Mary to give birth to the Savior now cause the water to give rebirth to the believer."[54] And if we want to find the same idea in liturgical sources, we can cite the very beautiful *Illatio* [preface] of the Mozarabic liturgy: "[Mary] carried life in her womb; the Church, in the baptismal font. In the body of Mary Christ put on flesh; in the waters of the Church the baptized put on Christ."[55]

3916

3917

---

[48] See Irenaeus, *Adversus haereses* 4, 7, 1: PG 71, 990–991; SC 100, part 2, 454–458.

[49] Irenaeus, *Adversus haereses* 3, 10, 2: PG 7, 1, 873; SC 34, 164.

[50] See LG no. 62: AAS 57 (1965) 63; ConstDecrDecl 199.

[51] SC art. 83 [DOL 1 no. 83].

[52] LG no. 63: AAS 57 (1965) 64; ConstDecrDecl 201.

[53] LG no. 64: AAS 57 (1965) 64; ConstDecrDecl 201–202.

[54] Leo the Great, *Tractatus 25* (In Nativitate Domini) 5: CCL 138, 123: SC 22 bis, 132; see also *Tractatus 29* (In Nativitate Domini) 1: CCL 138, 147; SC 22 bis, 178; *Tractatus 63* (De Passione Domini) 6: CCL 138, 386; SC 74, 82.

[55] M. Férotin, *Le Liber Mozarabicus Sacramentorum* col. 56.

3918   20. Finally, Mary is the *Virgin who makes her offering to God*. The presentation of Jesus in the temple illustrates this (see Lk 2:22–35). Under the guidance of the Holy Spirit, the Church sees in this event, besides the fulfillment and observance of the laws on offering the firstborn (see Lv 12:6–8), something related to the history of the mystery of salvation. The Church perceives in the presentation the continuation of the offering par excellence that the Word made flesh on coming into the world made to God (see Heb 10:5–7) and sees the announcement of universal salvation, as Simeon, calling Jesus the light revealing God to the nations and the glory of Israel (see Lk 2:32), recognizes the Messiah and the Savior of all. The Church also understands the event as a prophetic reference to Christ's passion: the words of Simeon, associating in the one prophetic utterance the Son as the "sign of contradiction" (Lk 2:24) and the Mother whose heart would be pierced by a sword (see Lk 2:35), were brought to fulfillment on Calvary. The particular note of this mystery of salvation, considered in its various aspects, is that through the presentation it leads the mind to the final outcome, the cross. Especially since the Middle Ages, the Virgin carrying her Son to Jerusalem to present him to the Lord (see Lk 2:28 [22]) has represented for the Church that will of offering which surpassed the ordinary meaning of the rite. St. Bernard's gentle urging addressed to Mary is evidence of this interpretation: "Offer your Son, holy Virgin, and give back to the Lord the fruit of your womb. Offer for our reconciliation the holy victim who is pleasing to God."[56]

This association of Mother with Son in the work of redemption[57] had its supreme moment on Calvary. There Christ "offered himself without blemish to God" (Heb 9:14) and Mary, standing by the cross (see Jn 19:25), "suffered intensely with her only begotten Son and united herself as his Mother to his sacrifice, consenting with love to the offering of the victim who was born of her,"[58] whom she also offered to the eternal Father.[59] In order to continue the sacrifice of the cross throughout the ages, the divine Savior of humankind established the eucharistic sacrifice, the memorial of his death and resurrection, and gave it to the Church, his Bride.[60] The Church in turn gathers the faithful especially on the Lord's Day, to celebrate the Lord's Passover until he comes.[61] The Church does so in communion with the saints, above all with the Blessed Virgin,[62] imitating her burning charity and pure faith.

3919   21. But even as she is the model for the Church as a whole in its worship of God, Mary is clearly also the *teacher of devotion* for individual Christians. They have studied her in order to make their lives like hers a worship of God and to make worship a part of their lives. As early as the fourth century St. Ambrose expressed to the faithful his own wish that they might possess Mary's attitude of singing God's

---

[56]   Bernard of Clairvaux, In purificatione B. Mariae, *Sermo* 3, 2: PL 183, 370; *S. Bernardi Opera*, J. Leclercq and H. Rochits, eds., v. 4 (Rome, 1966) 342.

[57]   See LG no. 57: AAS 57 (1965) 61; ConstDecrDecl 196.

[58]   LG no. 58: AAS 57 (1965) 61; ConstDecrDecl 197.

[59]   See Pius XII, Encycl. *Mystici Corporis*: AAS 35 (1943) 247.

[60]   See SC art. 47 [DOL 1 no. 47].

[61]   See SC art. 102 and 106 [DOL 1 nos. 102 and 106].

[62]   ". . . graciously remember all those who have pleased you throughout the ages, the holy fathers, patriarchs, prophets, apostles [. . .] and the holy and glorious Mother of God and all the saints [. . .]. May they be mindful of our wretchedness and poverty and offer to you with us the awesome, unbloody sacrifice.": *Anaphora Iacobi fratris Domini syriaca; Prex Eucharistica*, A. Hänggi and I. Pahl, eds. (Fribourg, Editions Universitaires, 1968) 274.

praises: "May the mind of Mary be in all to magnify the Lord; her spirit, to rejoice in God."[63] But above all Mary is the model of the kind of worship that makes the life of each person become an offering made to God. All can learn this ancient and uninterrupted teaching from the Church, but also by listening to Mary herself, whose answer to God's message was "Behold the handmaid of the Lord, be it done unto me according to your word" (Lk 1:38). Her words were a kind of anticipation of that beautiful petition of the Lord's Prayer, "Thy will be done" (Mt 6:10). For all Christians Mary's assent is a lesson and an example of how bowing to the Father's will becomes the path and the aid toward personal holiness.

22. It is extremely useful to note that the Church with variety and effectiveness   3920
has translated its many links with Mary into forms of worship. From the Church's vision of the sublime dignity of the Virgin whom the power of the Holy Spirit made the Mother of God comes a deep veneration. From contemplation of her spiritual motherhood that extends to all the members of the Mystical Body comes an ardent love. From its experience of her intercession as its advocate and help[64] comes supplication full of trust. From reflection on the simple handmaiden graced with the dignity of being the Queen of mercy and the Mother of grace comes the Church's work of charity. From its gaze upon the holiness and virtues of Mary, full of grace, comes an earnest following of her example. From the Church's "contemplation, as in a flawless image, of that which the Church itself desires and hopes wholly to be"[65] comes a profoundly moving awe. Finally, a dedicated sense of its own vocation results in the Church's perceiving in the companion of the Redeemer, who already fully shares in the fruits of the paschal mystery, the prophetic fulfillment of what belongs to its own future destiny until that day when it will become the Bride, without spot or wrinkle (see Eph 5:27), adorned for the Bridegroom, Jesus Christ (see Rv 21:2).

23. Esteemed Brothers, we have reviewed the devotion that the liturgical tradition   3921
of the universal Church and the reformed Roman Rite show to the holy Mother of God. We have recalled how the liturgy offers us the golden rule of Christian devotion because of its preeminence as divine worship. We have brought to mind how the Church in celebrating the divine mysteries takes on an attitude of faith and love that in every way is like the attitude of the Blessed Virgin. Such considerations create a clear realization of the pertinence of Vatican Council II's exhortation to all the Church's members "to foster wholeheartedly the *cultus* — especially the liturgical *cultus* — of the Blessed Virgin."[66] It is our own wish that this appeal will everywhere receive unqualified assent and conscientious fulfillment in practice.

II

24. Vatican Council II also teaches that in addition to the liturgical *cultus* other   3922
forms of devotion are to be promoted, especially those having the approval and endorsement of the magisterium.[67] But the faithful's devotion and acts of veneration toward the Mother of God have also taken different forms, corresponding to historical and local circumstances and the varying attitudes and cultures of peoples. One result is that the forms expressing devotion and subject to the conditions of

---

63   Ambrose, *Expositio Evangelii secundum Lucam* 2, 26: CSEL 32, v. 4, 55; SC 45, 83–84.

64   See LG no. 62: AAS 57 (1965) 63; ConstDecrDecl 200.

65   SC art. 103 [DOL 1 no. 103].

66   See LG no. 67 [DOL 4 no. 161].

67   See LG no. 67 [DOL 4 no. 161].

the times seem in need of a reform that will eliminate the ephemeral, retain what is of enduring value, and integrate those truths of faith that have been reached from theological investigation and affirmed by the Church's magisterium. The conferences of bishops, particular Churches, religious orders and congregations, communities of the faithful must therefore develop genuine and effective courses of action and at the same time address the issue of revising the form and practice of devotion toward the Virgin Mary. But it is our desire that in this matter there be respect for tradition and openness to the legitimate demands of our contemporaries. Accordingly it seems right, Esteemed Brothers, that we point out certain principles for dealing with the issue.

3923   25. First of all, it is of great advantage that the practices of Marian devotion clearly evince their intrinsically Trinitarian and Christological character. From its essential direction and meaning Christian worship is offered to Father, Son, and Holy Spirit — or, as the liturgy itself puts it, to the Father, through Christ, in the Spirit. On this basis Christian worship itself, although in a profoundly different way, includes first and in a unique manner the Mother of the Savior, then the saints; this is how the Church proclaims the paschal mystery in those who have suffered and been glorified with Christ.[68] In the Virgin Mary all things are related to Christ and depend on Christ: God the Father chose her from all eternity as a Mother of complete holiness and the Holy Spirit adorned her with gifts given to no one else. Nor has genuinely Christian devotion ever failed to stress the unbreakable bond and necessary relationship between the Virgin and the divine Savior.[69] Our own thought is that there is something here especially in keeping with the direction of contemporary spirituality, which is almost wholly concerned with and fixed on the "problem of Christ."[70] In every expression of devotion to the Virgin Mary particular importance must be attached to the Christological aspect and practice must be so shaped that it is related to God's plan in which "the origins of the Virgin . . . were foreordained along with the incarnation of the divine Savior."[71] Without any doubt this will help devotion to Jesus' Mother to become more sound and effective and a powerful means toward achieving "unity in faith and in knowledge of the Son of God, to reach the perfection that is measured by the fullness of Christ" (Eph 4:13). In addition, such a course will contribute much to increasing the worship owed to Christ himself, because, in keeping with the constant understanding of the Church, reasserted in our own times,[72] "service to the handmaid is referred to her master; thus service to the Mother, redounds to her Son; [. . .] homage to the Queen, passes on to the King."[73]

3924   26. To this instruction on the Christological nature of Marian devotion we think it useful to join another pertinent exhortation. In devotion to Mary one of the absolutely necessary elements of faith must receive the importance it deserves, namely, the Person and action of the Holy Spirit. Theological study and the liturgy itself have together shown that the influence on the Virgin of Nazareth is one of the Holy

---

[68]   See SC art. 104 [DOL 1 no. 104].

[69]   See LG no. 66 [DOL 4 no. 160].

[70]   See Paul VI, Addr., 24 April 1970, in the church dedicated to "Nostra Signora di Bonaria" at Cagliari: AAS 62 (1970) 300.

[71]   Pius IX, Apostolic Letter *Ineffabilis Deus: Pii IX Pontificis Maximi Acta* 1, 1 (Rome, 1854) 599. See also V. Sardi, *La solenne definizione del dogma dell' Immacolato concepimento di Maria Santissima. Atti e documenti . . .* (Rome, 1904–05) v. 2, 302.

[72]   See LG no. 66 [DOL 4 no. 160].

[73]   Ildefonsus of Toledo, *De virginitate perpetua sanctae Mariae* cap. 12: PL 96, 108.

Spirit's interventions in the history of salvation. The Fathers of the Church and ecclesiastical writers, for example, have attributed Mary's sanctification from its beginnings to the influence of the Holy Spirit; Mary was "fashioned and formed into a new creature" by the Spirit.[74] In pondering over the passages of the Gospel — "the Holy Spirit will come upon you and the power of the Most High will over-shadow you" (Lk 1:35) and "she was found to be with child of the Holy Spirit . . .; that which is conceived in her is of the Holy Spirit" (see Mt 1:18, 20) — those authors have seen in the intervention of the Holy Spirit an act that consecrated Mary's virginity and made it fruitful[75] and transformed her into "the abode of the King" or the "bridal chamber of the Word,"[76] the "temple" or "tabernacle of the Lord,"[77] the "Ark of the Covenant" or "the Ark of Sanctification."[78] All such titles echo the Bible. In looking to the deeper meaning of the incarnation, these same writers have seen in the hidden bond between the Holy Spirit and Mary a kind of betrothal. Prudentius describes this in poetic words: "The unwed Virgin is wedded to the Holy Spirit."[79] They have also given her the title "sacred repository of the Holy Spirit."[80] The title brings out the sacred nature of the Virgin who became the permanent dwelling of the Spirit. Their consideration of the teaching on the Holy Spirit as Paraclete has led these authors to see the Spirit as the source of the fullness of grace that was given to Mary (see Lk 1:28) and the wealth of gifts that have ennobled her. They have thus attributed to the Holy Spirit the faith, hope, and charity that inspired the Virgin's heart, the strength that sustained her obedience to God's will, the moral courage that supported her in her suffering at the foot of the cross.[81] They also have recognized in her prophetic *Magnificat* (see Lk 1:46–55) the special influence of the Holy Spirit, who had spoken in ages past through the prophets.[82] Finally, from their contemplation of Mary persevering in prayer with the apostles in the upper room where the Holy Spirit was about to come down upon

74   See LG no. 56: AAS 57 (1965) 60; ConstDecrDecl 194. See also the authors cited in LG note 176 [ConstDecrDec note 5].

75   See Ambrose, *De Spiritu Sancto* 2, 37–38: CSEL 79, 100–101. John Cassian, *De incarnatione Domini* 2, cap. 2: CSEL 17, 247–249. Bede the Venerable, *Homelia* 1, 3: CCL 122, 18 and 20.

76   Ambrose, *De institutione virginis* cap. 12, 79: PL 16 (ed. 1880) 339; *Epistula* 30, 3 and *Epistula* 42, 7: PL 16 (ed. 1880) 1107 and 1175; *Expositio evangelii secundum Lucam* 10, 132: SC 52, 200. Proclus of Constantinople, *Oratio* 1, 1 and *Oratio* 5, 3: PG 65, 681 and 720. Basil of Seleucia, *Oratio* 39, 3: PG 85, 433. Andrew of Crete, *Oratio* 4: PG 97, 868. Germanus I of Constantinople, *Oratio* 3, 15: PG 98, 305.

77   See Jerome, *Adversus Iovinianum* 1, 33: PL 23, 267. Ambrose, *Epistula* 63, 33: PL 16 (ed. 1880) 1249; *De institutione virginis* cap. 17, 105: PL 16 (1880) 346; *De Spiritu Sancto* 3, 79–80: CSEL 79, 182–183. Sedulius, *Hymnus* "A solis ortus cardine," vv. 13–14: CSEL 10, 164. *Hymnus Acathistos* strophe 23: I.B. Pitra, ed., *Analecta Sacra* 1, 261. Proclus of Constantinople, *Oratio* 1, 3: PG 65, 684; *Oratio* 2, 6: PG 65, 700. Basil of Seleucia, *Oratio* 4: PG 97, 868. John Damascene, *Oratio* 4, 10: PG 96, 677.

78   See Severus of Antioch, *Homilia* 57: PatrOr 8, 357–358. Hesychius of Jerusalem, *Homilia de sancta Maria Deipara*: PG 93, 1464. Chrysippus of Jerusalem, *Oratio in sanctam Mariam Deiparam* 2: PatrOr 19, 338. Andrew of Crete, *Oratio* 5: PG 97, 896. John Damascene, *Oratio* 6, 6: PG 96, 672.

79   Prudentius, *Liber Apotheosis* vv. 571–572: CCL 126, 97.

80   See Isidore of Seville, *De ortu et obitu Patrum* cap. 67, 111: PL 83, 148. Ildefonsus of Toledo, *De virginitate perpetua sanctae Mariae* cap. 10: PL 96, 95. Bernard of Clairvaux, *In Assumptione B. Virginis Mariae, Sermo* 4, 4: PL 183, 428; *In Nativitate B. Virginis Mariae*: PL 183, 442. Peter Damian, *Carmina sacra et preces* 2, Oratio ad Dei Filium: PL 145, 921. Antiphon, *Beata Dei Genitrix Maria: Corpus antiphonalium officii*, R.J. Hesbert, ed. (Rome, 1970) v. 4, no. 6314, p. 80.

81   See Paulinus the Deacon, *Homilia* 1, *In Assumptione B. Mariae Virginis*: PL 95, 1567. *De Assumptione sanctae Mariae Virginis*, attributed to Paschasius Radbertus nn. 31, 42, 57, 83: A. Ripberger, ed., in *Spicilegium Friburgense* 9 (1962) 72, 76, 84, 96–97. Eadmer of Canterbury, *De excellentia Virginis Mariae* cap. 4–5: PL 159, 562–567. Bernard of Clairvaux, *In laudibus Virginis Matris, Homilia* 4, 3: *Sancti Bernardi Opera*, J. Leclercq and H. Rochais, eds., v. 4 (Rome, 1966) 49–50.

82   See Origen, *In Lucam Homilia* 7, 3: PG 13, 1817; SC 87, 156. Cyril of Alexandria, *Commentarius in Aggaeum prophetam* cap. 19: PG 71, 1060. Ambrose, *De fide* 4, 9, 113–114: CSEL 78, 197–198; *Expositio evangelii secundum Lucam* 2, 23 and 27–28: CSEL 32, part 4, 53–54 and 55–56. Severian of Gabala, *In mundi creationem*

the young Church (see Acts 1:12–14, 2:1–4) these authors have enriched the beautiful theme "Mary-Church" with new insights.[83] But above all they have implored
the Virgin's intercession that they might receive from the Holy Spirit the power to
beget Christ in their own souls. As evidence of this there is a prayer of St. Ildefonsus, outstanding for its meaning and its powerful expressiveness: "I pray you, I pray
you, O holy Virgin, that I may have Jesus through that Spirit by whom you begot
him. May my soul receive Jesus through that Spirit by whom your flesh conceived
him. . . . May I live Jesus in that Spirit in whom you now adore him as your Lord
and gaze on him as your Son."[84]

3925   27. Some say that many of the more recent devotional texts do not adequately
reflect all of Catholic teaching on the Holy Spirit. It is up to the scholars to judge
the merits of this allegation and to weigh its implications. Our own concern is
rather to encourage all, especially pastors and theologians, that with discerning and
precise study they look thoroughly into the work of the Spirit in the history of
salvation. They should then take the measures necessary for the books and texts of
Christian devotion to give clear expression to the life-giving activity of the Spirit.
Such an endeavor will bring into prominence the meaning of the hidden bond
between the Spirit of God and the Virgin Mary and their joint influence on the
Church. These teachings of faith, more deeply penetrated, will bring progress to the
practice of a greatly intensified devotion.

3926   28. With respect to these devotional practices, the testimony of the faithful's
reverent homage to the Mother of God, there is a further need to bring out clearly
and explicitly the place Mary holds in the Church: "after Christ the highest and to
us the nearest."[85] The very structure of churches of the Byzantine Rite represents
this high place graphically and, as it were, physically. The parts of the church and
the ikons are arranged so that the Annunciation is portrayed above the central door
of the ikonostasis and the glorious *Theotokos* on the apse wall. This clearly expresses
how the consent of the handmaid of the Lord opens the way for the human race to
return to God and how the holy Mother points out the route of that journey. This
symbolism, in which the church building itself portrays the place of Mary in the
mystery of the Church, is rich in meaning and seems to demand that the various
types of devotion to Mary develop everywhere in an ecclesial direction and with an
ecclesial outlook.

    The recollection of the basic concepts that Vatican Council II proposed on the
nature of the Church — "the family of God, the people of God, the kingdom of
God, the Mystical Body of Christ"[86] — will undoubtedly have as a result that the
faithful will more readily perceive Mary's mission and office in the mystery of the
Church and her superior place within the communion of saints. A further effect will
be that the faithful will more deeply appreciate that familial bond of union be-

---

oratio 6, 10: PG 56, 497–498. Antipater of Bosra, *Homilia in Sanctissimae Deiparae Annuntiationem* 16: PG 85, 1785.

[83]   See Eadmer of Canterbury, *De excellentia Virginis Mariae* cap. 7: PL 159, 571. Amadeus of Lausanne, *De Maria Virginea Matre, Homila* 7: PL 188, 1337; SC 72, 184.

[84]   Ildefonsus of Toledo, *De virginitate perpetua sanctae Mariae* cap. 12: PL 96, 106.

[85]   LG no. 54: AAS 57 (1965) 59; ConstDecrDecl 193. See also Paul VI, Addr. to the Fathers of Vatican II, at the end of the second session, 4 December 1963: AAS 56 (1964) 37.

[86]   LG nos. 6, 7–8, 9–17: AAS 57 (1965) 8–9, 9–12, 12–21; Const DecrDecl 77, 77–78, 78–85.

tween them as the Virgin's children — "for she cooperates with maternal love in begetting and rearing them"[87] — and as also the Church's children — "we are born of the Church's womb, nursed by its milk, given life by its Spirit."[88] Thus Mary and the Church work together to bring forth Christ's Mystical Body: "Each is Christ's Mother, but neither begets the whole [Body] without the other."[89] Still another result of this recollection will be the faithful's more clearly perceiving the Church's worldwide activity as the extension of Mary's own care and solicitude. The Virgin's love was expressed in action in the home at Nazareth, in the visit to Elizabeth, at Cana, on Calvary — all events of salvation having the greatest ecclesial importance. This love is continued and expressed in the Church's own motherly care and solicitous will that all people come to a knowledge of the truth (see 1 Tm 2:4); in its watching over the little ones, the needy, and the weak, in its unceasing efforts to strengthen social peace and harmony, in its sustained dedication and striving that all people come to share in the salvation that Christ won for them through his death. By reason of this perception, love for the Church will become love for Mary and vice versa: neither the Church nor Mary can exist without each other, as Chromatius of Aquileia perceptively observes: "The Church . . . was first gathered together in the upper room with Mary the Mother of Jesus and with his brethren. We cannot therefore even call it the Church unless Mary the Mother of the Lord and his brethren are with it."[90] In conclusion, we repeat that devotion to the Blessed Virgin must bear the mark of its intrinsically ecclesiological import. That will lead to the proper planning and concentration of efforts for a sound renewal of the forms of that devotion and the texts expressing it.

29. To the themes already expressed, which originate in a reflection on the relationship of the Virgin Mary with God, Father, Son, and Holy Spirit, we wish to add some directive norms based on the conception and intent of the Council's teaching.[91] These are biblical, liturgical, ecumenical, and anthropological norms; they need to be kept in view whenever practices of devotion are revised or created, in order that there may be a deeper and sharper perception of the bond that joins us to the Mother of Christ and our Mother within the communion of saints.   3927

30. Today there is a recognition that Christian devotion everywhere requires the incorporation of biblical content and themes. Progress in biblical studies, the more widespread reading of Scripture, the forceful lesson of tradition, and the inner prompting of the Holy Spirit all influence contemporary Christians and teach them to use the Bible more and more as the primary prayer book and to draw from it solid practical guidance and examples. Devotion and reverence toward Mary cannot in any way be out of harmony with this universal trend in Christian life;[92] on the contrary, Marian devotion must derive new vitality and sure help from this biblical emphasis. The Scriptures wonderfully reveal the divine plan for human salvation and in so doing are filled with the mystery of the Savior and from Genesis to Revelation contain the most unmistakable teachings on the one who was the the Savior's Mother and companion. But we should in no way wish to limit the influence of the Bible to the passages or symbols carefully selected from the sacred books; much more is involved. A biblical orientation demands that the language   3928

---

[87]   LG no. 63: AAS 57 (1965) 64; ConstDecrDecl 201.

[88]   Cyprian of Carthage, De catholicae Ecclesiae unitate 5: CSEL 3, 214.

[89]   Isaac of Stella, Sermo 51, In Assumptione B. Mariae: PL 194, 1863.

[90]   Chromatius of Aquileia, Sermo 30, 1: SC 164, 134.

[91]   See LG nos. 66–69: AAS 57 (1965) 65–67; ConstDecrDecl 203–206.

[92]   See DV no. 25 [DOL 14 no. 227].

and themes of the biblical books be incorporated into the formularies of prayer and the texts for the chants. Above all it requires Marian devotion to be so completely permeated with the major themes of the Christian message that as the faithful revere the Seat of Wisdom, they in turn may be enlightened by the Word of God and led to live their lives in accord with the precepts of Wisdom incarnate.

3929   31. We have already discussed the veneration the Church pays to the Mother of God in the liturgy. The topic now is other forms of devotion and the ideas on which they must be based; therefore we need to call to mind the prescription of the Constitution *Sacrosanctum Concilium*. In endorsing Christian popular devotions it adds: "These devotions should be so fashioned that they harmonize with the liturgical seasons, accord with the liturgy, are in some way derived from it, and lead the people to it, since, in fact, the liturgy by its very nature far surpasses any of them."[93] This is a wise and clear law, but its application seems difficult, especially in regard to devotion to Mary, which has such a broad range of expressions. The law demands of those in charge of local communities great effort and pastoral wisdom and constancy; it demands of the faithful, good will, ready to receive directive norms and measures that, because their source is the genuine nature of Christian worship, require a change of certain age-old practices that have to some degree obscured that genuine nature.

On this point we may mention two attitudes that in pastoral use and practice may result in frustrating the rule of Vatican Council II. The first is the attitude of some engaged in the pastoral ministry who, rejecting popular devotions *a priori* suppress them (whereas in fact, when rightly conducted, they are endorsed by the magisterium). Such people thus create a vacuum they cannot fill. Clearly they forget that the Council did not direct the elimination of popular devotions but rather their harmonization with the liturgy.

The second is the attitude of those who, not following sound liturgical and pastoral principles, combine popular devotions and services of the liturgy into one, in mixed or "hybrid" celebrations. It sometimes happens that parts of a novena or similar devotion are incorporated into the offering of the eucharistic sacrifice. The danger resulting is that the memorial of the Lord may no longer stand as the highpoint for the gathering of the Christian community but may be simply the setting for some popular devotion. We wish to remind those acting in this way of the conciliar norm: popular devotions must be subordinated to the liturgy, not intermingled with it. Wise pastoral ministry sets out clearly and explains the inherent nature of liturgical services; it extolls and promotes popular devotions in such a way as to adapt them to the needs of individual ecclesial communities and to direct them toward contributing to the liturgy.

3930   32. The ecclesial character in Marian devotion is the reason for the Church's concerns about this devotion and chief among these concerns today is the restoration of the unity of Christians. Devotion toward the Mother of God is therefore accompanied by an awareness of the anxieties and the initiatives of the ecumenical movement; in other words, that devotion itself becomes ecumenical, and on many grounds.

First of all, in this regard Catholics are at one with their brothers and sisters of the Orthodox Churches. In these Churches devotion toward the Blessed Virgin takes forms that are filled with striking poetic inspiration and sublime doctrine, as

---

[93]   SC art. 13 [DOL 1 no. 13].

they venerate with a special love the Mother of God under the title of Hope of Christians.[94] Catholics are also joined to the Anglicans in this matter. Many outstanding Anglican theologians of the past have explained the solid basis in Scripture regarding the *cultus* of the Mother of our Lord and contemporary Anglican theologians give greater expression to the importance of Mary's place in the Christian life. In glorifying God with the words of the Virgin (see Lk 1:46–55), Catholics are also linked with other Christians of the Churches of the Reformation, who have a burning love of the Scriptures.

Further, reverence to the Mother of Christ and of Christians provides Catholics with a natural and frequent occasion for asking her to intercede with her Son that all the baptized may come together to form the one people of God.[95] It is likewise the Catholic Church's intention to preserve undiminished the special character proper to Marian devotion,[96] but also carefully to avoid any exaggeration that might lead other Christians to a mistaken idea about the Church's genuine teaching[97] and to suppress any mode of veneration that is at variance with orthodox Catholic practice. Finally, Marian devotion becomes a path toward Christ, the source and center of all ecclesial communion, because it is of the nature of that devotion that "as we honor the Mother her Son . . . receives the recognition, the love, and the glory that are his due."[98] And all who confess Christ as God and Lord, Savior and only Mediator (see 1 Tm 2:5) are called to be united to each other, with him in the unity of the Holy Spirit.[99]

33. We are fully aware that serious differences exist between the point of view of a   3931
great many Christians of other Churches and Ecclesial Communities and Catholic teaching "on . . . Mary's role in the work of salvation"[100] and in consequence on the veneration to be offered to her. But the same power of the Most High that overshadowed the Virgin of Nazareth (see Lk 1:35) is at work upon the ecumenical movement and is bringing about its good effects. We therefore wish to express our own hope that the veneration of the simple handmaid of the Lord, to whom he that is mighty has done great things (see Lk 1: 49), will, even if gradually, cease to be an obstacle and become rather an opening and, as it were, a meeting point for achieving the unity of all those who believe in Christ. For we rejoice to observe that a more precise understanding of Mary's role in the mystery of Christ and the Church on the part also of Christians separated from us is smoothing the progress toward such a meeting point. In the village of Cana Mary obtained by her request Jesus' first miracle (see Jn 2:1–12); in our own times she has the power to hasten by her intercession the time when Christ's followers will reach complete communion. Support for our hope comes from the thought of our predecessor Leo XIII, who stated that the cause of Christian unity "is an office that belongs properly to Mary's spiritual motherhood. For Mary has brought forth those who belong to Christ only in the one faith and love. It could not be otherwise. 'Is Christ divided?' (1 Cor 1:13)

---

94   See *Officium magni canonis paracletici*, *Magnum Orologion* (Athens, 1963) 558; also the liturgical *kanones* and *troparia* passim: see Sophronios Eustradiadou, *Theotokarion* (Chennevières-sur-Marne, 1931) 9, 19.

95   See LG no. 69: AAS 57 (1965) 66–67; ConstDecrDecl 206.

96   See LG no. 66 [DOL 4 no. 160].

97   See LG no. 67 [DOL 4 no. 161].

98   LG no. 66 [DOL 4 no. 160].

99   See Paul VI, Addr. in St. Peter's to the Fathers of Vatican II, 21 November 1964: AAS 56 (1964) 1017.

100   UR no. 20: AAS 57 (1965) 105; ConstDecrDecl 270.

and must we not all live the life of Christ as one so that 'we may bear fruit for God' (Rom 7:4) ?''[101]

3932   34. On the question of venerating Mary careful attention must be paid to the well-established findings of the social sciences. This will contribute to removing one of the causes of the problems surrounding Marian devotion. That cause is the conflict of themes of Marian devotion with contemporary anthropological views and the profoundly altered psychological condition of contemporary human life and activity. As many devotional books and articles show, it is obviously difficult to integrate ideas about Mary into contemporary life situations. This is true in particular about the place of women. In family life, civil law and social progress are giving women equality with men and authority over the family. In politics, women in many countries have achieved the power to participate equally with men in civil affairs. In society generally, women are emerging from the narrow circle of the home to take ever expanding active roles. In the area of culture, they are obtaining new opportunities for intellectual pursuits and authority.

Some people see as a result that veneration of Mary is foreign to all this and that choosing her as an example is a problem. They comment that the scope of her own life was too narrow when compared to the wide range of contemporary possibilities for involvement. We urge theologians, those in charge of Christian communities, and all the faithful to give this problem the consideration it deserves. At the same time it seems advisable that we ourself address our own efforts to a solution by offering several suggestions.

3933   35. First of all, the reason the Church proposes Mary as an example to be imitated is not the life she led and much less the *social and cultural* conditions of that life, which now are all but extinct. The reason is rather that in the concrete situation of her life she adhered completely and with a full sense of her responsibility to God's will (see Lk 1:38); she received his word and carried it out; her way of life was anchored in charity and the will to serve; in a word, she was the first and most perfect follower of Christ. These are what constitute her universal and unending power of example.

3934   36. We would further note that the problems mentioned are closely linked to certain characteristics of the idea of Mary in the popular mind or in literature. They are not the marks of the idea of Mary found in the Gospels nor marks of the doctrinal themes that have been derived and developed from the slow and serious work of explaining the revealed word of God. Generations of Christians in different social and cultural circumstances saw in Mary the ideal and role of the New Woman, the perfect Christian, who in herself combined and epitomized the events typical particularly of a woman's life, because she is a wife and a mother. They saw the Mother of Jesus as the prototype of woman's condition and as the foremost model of evangelical life. And these generations expressed their sentiments in ways consistent with the outlook and imagery of their own times. There is scarcely any reason for surprise at all this. As the Church surveys the long history of Marian devotion, it rejoices at the correspondence between the *cultus* and its own era. But the Church does not tie itself down to the ways of thought or expression proper to any particular age nor to the underlying anthropological views. The Church understands why certain forms of *cultus*, worthwhile in themselves, are less suited to people who belong to another epoch and another culture.

---

[101]   Leo XIII, Encyclical Epistle, *Adiutricem populi: Acta Sanctae Sedis* 28 (1895–1896) 135.

38. After our statement of directive norms for the effective promotion of Marian   3935
devotion, a warning seems necessary about certain altogether mistaken forms of
Marian devotion. By its own authoritative declaration Vatican Council II has already forbidden theological opinions about Mary or forms of Marian devotion that
go beyond the bounds of sound doctrine or liturgy, as well as a reductionism that
would diminish her stature and role. The Council furthermore reproved certain
deviations in devotion: a mindless credulity, that is, a concern for external ritual
rather than for a serious religious commitment; sheer, passing feeling, utterly foreign to the spirit of the Gospel, which requires an enduring and tireless commitment.[106] We reaffirm these strictures, because we are dealing with forms of devotion
that are incompatible with Catholic faith and therefore have no place in Catholic
worship. A careful defense against such errors and unsound practices will have
many good effects on devotion to Mary. That devotion will become more willing
and genuine because it rests on solid ground: study of the sources of divine revelation and respect for the teachings of the Church's magisterium far surpass an
excessive interest in novelty or sensational happenings. That devotion will also be
objective, that is, based on historical truth: all that is fanciful or false will be removed.
The devotion will also be consonant with sound doctrine; there will be no proposal
of a diminished image of Mary or of one that is exaggerated and that for this very
reason would obscure her true portrait as given by the Gospels. That devotion,
finally, will be *pure in its motives*: anything that suggests base self-interest will be kept
out of the sanctuary.

39. We wish to add confirmation, if that is possible, to the truth that the ultimate   3936
objective of devotion to Mary is to give glory to God and to move the faithful to
complete conformity in life and conduct to God's will. The Church's children,
joining their voices in praise of Jesus' Mother to the voice of the unnamed woman
in the Gospel, cry out together to him: "Blessed is the womb that bore you and the
breast that nursed you" (Lk 11:27). When they do so they must give careful heed to
the divine Master's sober reply: "Rather blessed are they who hear the word of God
and keep it" (Lk 11:28). His answer redounds to the high praise of the Virgin Mary,
according to several of the Fathers' interpretation,[107] to which Vatican Council II
added its own confirmation.[108] Jesus' reply is also an exhortation to us that we live
in accord with God's commandments and recalls these other teachings of the Savior: "Not everyone who says to me 'Lord, Lord' will enter the kingdom of heaven,
but whoever does the will of my Father who is in heaven will enter into the
kingdom of heaven" (Mt 7:21). "You are my friends if you do what I command
you" (Jn 15:14).

III

40. We have set out certain principles designed to give Marian devotion new   3937
vitality. Now it is for the conferences of bishops, the heads of local communities,
and the superiors of religious institutes to establish wisely the proper kind of
devotional practices to honor the Blessed Virgin. It is also their responsibility to
assist those who desire to introduce new practices out of genuine zeal and interest
in the welfare of the faithful. For many reasons it seems to us worthwhile to discuss

---

[106] See LG 67 [DOL 4 no. 161].

[107] See Augustine, *In Iohannis Evangelium, Tractatus* 10, 3: CCL 36, 101–102; *Epistula* 243, *Ad Laetum* 9: CSEL
57, 575–576. Bede the Venerable, *In Lucae Evangelium expositio* 4, 11, 28: CCL 120, 237; *Homelia* 1, 4: CCL 122,
26–27.

[108] See LG no. 58: AAS 57 (1965) 61; ConstDecrDecl 197.

two forms of devotion practiced especially in the West and treated many times by the Apostolic See: the Angelus and the Rosary. [. . .]

3938   41. Our words here on the Angelus have only one purpose: to repeat a simple, but pressing appeal that the custom of reciting this prayer be kept. It is not in any need of revision. After the passage of so many centuries the Angelus still retains the power and beauty it has from the simplicity of its structure and its derivation from Scripture. Moreover in its historical origins it is linked to prayer for the blessings of peace. Liturgically the hours of its occurrence consecrate the various times of the day. The Angelus also is a reminder of the paschal mystery, since we pray that having received the message of Christ's incarnation, *we may be brought by his passion and cross to the glory of his resurrection.*[109] Many of the practices once accompanying its recitation have been suppressed or are obsolete, but these are minor matters; unchanged are the power of the Angelus as a contemplation of the incarnation, the significance of the angelic salutation to Mary, and its plea for her compassionate intercession. Further, even though times have changed, many people still retain regular moments in the morning, at noon, and in the evening as times to mark the course of the day's activities with a pause for prayer.

3939   48. Contemporary scholarship has provided a fuller understanding of the connections between liturgical worship and the rosary. One result is that the rosary must be regarded as an offshoot of the liturgy and for this reason received as its name "our Lady's psalter." Through it the less educated faithful were enabled to associate themselves with the whole Church's song of praise and intercession. On the other hand, it must be acknowledged that the use of the rosary arose in the late Middle Ages, a period when, as the genuine spirit of the liturgy waned, the people fell away from liturgical worship to a degree, in favor of a kind of outward devotion to Christ's humanity and the Blessed Virgin Mary. Not long ago one result was that some wanted to count the rosary as a liturgical rite; conversely, in their concern to prevent the errors of the past in pastoral ministry, others were wrongfully spurning the rosary. We can readily resolve the issue in the light of the teaching of Vatican Council II's Constitution *Sacrosanctum Concilium.* Its import is that liturgical celebrations and the devotional practice of the rosary are seen to be neither in opposition nor on an equal plane.[114] Every form of prayer becomes more effective to the degree that its inherent force and character are preserved. Since the preeminence of the services of the liturgy has been established, there will be no difficulty in recognizing the rosary as the kind of devotion that is readily compatible with the liturgy. In a way similar to the liturgy, the rosary has the character of being a community prayer; it is nurtured by Scripture; it is completely centered on the mystery of Christ. The two types of prayer are, it is true, on levels that are intrinsically different. Yet both the anamnesis of the liturgy and the meditations of the rosary focus on those same saving events whose author is Christ. Under the veil of signs, the liturgy brings about the representation and hidden workings of the chief mysteries of our redemption. Through devout meditation the rosary calls to mind these same mysteries and moves the will to accept from them a way of life. Once a distinction in essence between the two is granted, it is immediately clear that the rosary is a devotion that finds its origin in the liturgy and that, if practiced according to its authentic spirit, leads naturally to the liturgy, while yet remaining outside the threshold of the liturgy itself. Since its meditations on the mysteries of Christ accustom the faithful to reflect on these, the rosary has the power to dispose their

---

[109] RM, Fourth Sunday of Advent, opening prayer. Similar thoughts are contained in the opening prayer for 25 March, which may be substituted in the recitation of the Angelus.

[114] See SC art. 13 [DOL 1 no. 13].

minds to celebrate the same mysteries in the rites of the liturgy and then to keep the memory of them alive throughout the day. To recite the rosary during a liturgical service, however, is a misguided practice, which unfortunately still prevails in some places. [. . .]

52. Pursuing the intention of our predecessors, we wish at this time to recommend earnestly the family rosary. Vatican Council II has declared that the family, the primary, living cell of society, "by the loyalty of its members to each other and their praying to God together shows itself to be a sanctuary of the Church in the home."[115] The Christian family therefore stands out, so to speak, as the Church of the household,[116] if together its members, in proportion to their individual role and condition, promote justice; if they practice the works of mercy; if they dedicate themselves to serving their neighbor, participate in the apostolate of the wider local community, and take part in the services of the liturgy;[117] finally, if they pray to God as a family. If this last is not true, then the life of the home must be said to lack the distinguishing mark of the Christian family. For this reason, while the theological concept of the family as the Church of the household is being recovered, there must be a corresponding effort on everyone's part to restore to homes the practice of praying together.

53. In keeping with the directives of Vatican Council II, the General Instruction of the Liturgy of the Hours rightly includes the family among those groups to which the celebration of the divine office in common is particularly appropriate: "It is of great advantage for the family, the domestic sanctuary of the Church, not only to pray together to God but also to celebrate some parts of the liturgy of the hours as occasion offers, in order to enter more deeply into the life of the Church."[118] Every possible measure must be taken to bring this directive increasingly and willingly into effect in Christian families.

54. Next to the liturgy of the hours (in which family prayer can reach its highest realization) the rosary must surely be counted among those "prayers in common" to which the Christian family is invited. Our own intention and strong desire is that when the family members gather for prayer, they often and gladly make use of the rosary. We are well aware that the changed conditions of modern life are not favorable to bringing all the family together in the home. Even if there is such a gathering, it is hard, for many reasons, to turn it into an occasion for prayer. We admit the difficulty. But under the pressure of conditions of place and *mores*, the Christian's responsibility is not to be overcome, but to overcome; not to surrender but to act with courage. Thus Christian families that wish to live up to the responsibility of their vocation and to translate the devotion proper to the family into living action must strive with all their energies to remove the obstacles to the family gathering and family prayer.

56. Esteemed Brothers, we wish near the end of our Apostolic Exhortation to emphasize in a summary the theological eminence of Marian devotion and to recapitulate its pastoral power to renew the Christian way of life.

   The Church's devotion to Mary forms part of the very nature of Christian worship. The honor always and everywhere paid to Mary — from Elizabeth's

3940

3941

3942

3943

---

115   AA no. 11 [DOL 16 no. 237].

116   See LG no. 11 [DOL 4 no. 141].

117   See AA no. 11 [DOL 16 no. 237].

118   GILH no. 27 [DOL 426 no. 3457].

salutation of blessing (see Lk 1:42–45) to today's expressions of praise and petition — is a shining witness that the Church's own law of prayer (*lex orandi*) serves as an invitation to give firmer support in our consciousness to the law of faith (*lex credendi*). Conversely, the Church's law of faith requires that its law of prayer regarding Christ's Mother be everywhere in full effect. Devotion to Mary is deeply rooted in the revealed word of God and solidly supported in the following truths of Catholic teaching. The dignity of Mary is unique: she is "the Mother of God's Son, therefore the most beloved daughter of the Father and the repository of the Holy Spirit; by this gift of surpassing grace she stands far above all creatures in heaven and on earth."[119] She cooperated in those events that were of the highest importance in the work of redemption that her Son accomplished. Hers is a holiness that, though full from the moment of her immaculate conception, yet increased more and more as she obeyed the Father's will and walked along the path of suffering (see Lk 2:34–35, 2:41–52; Jn 19:25–27) in faith, hope, and charity that grew without interruption. Hers is a unique role and place among the people of God, since she is at once the most exalted member, shining model, and loving Mother. Her intercession is unceasing and effective; because of it, even though assumed into heaven, she is near the faithful who call on her and she is near to those who do not even know they are her children. Finally, her glory ennobles the entire human race; in the wonderful verse of Dante Alighieri "You are that Woman who so ennobles human nature that its Creator did not disdain to become a human creature."[120] Mary does belong to our race, she is truly a daughter of Eve, although free of Eve's sin; she is truly our sister, who in an earthly life of humility and poverty shared fully in our own lot.

To these truths we add this consideration. Devotion to Mary has its ultimate explanation from God's inscrutable, free will. Because God is love, eternal and divine (see Jn 4:7–8 and 16), the counsel of his love is the basis of all he does. He has loved Mary and done great things to her (see Lk 1:49). He has loved her for himself and he has loved her for our sake. He has given her to himself and he has given her to us.

3944   57. Christ is the only way leading to the Father (see Jn 14:4–11). Christ stands as the supreme model on whose image his followers must pattern their life (see Jn 13:15), so that they have the same mind in themselves that was also in him (see Phil 2:15), must live his own life and possess his Spirit (see Gal 2:20; Rom 8:10–11). These truths have always been the Church's teaching and therefore care must be taken that nothing occurs in the pastoral ministry that conflicts with this teaching. At the same time, taught by the Holy Spirit and in possession of the experience acquired over the ages, the Church acknowledges that devotion to Mary, subordinated to devotion toward the divine Redeemer and related to it, possesses great power and efficacy in the pastoral sphere and for the renewal of the Christian life. The reason for this effectiveness is readily grasped. Further, the manifold role of Mary toward the people of God is a truly supernatural reality that exists in the Body of the Church in an intense and beneficial way. It is useful to reflect on all the aspects of Mary's role; all of them, in proportion to their individual kind of power, have the one purpose, namely, to give to all her children the spiritual lineaments of her only begotten Son. Thus the maternal intercession of the Virgin, her example of holiness, and the divine grace within her, stand for the human race as the evidence of things to be hoped for.

---

[119] LG no. 53: AAS 57 (1965) 58–59; ConstDecrDecl 192.

[120] *La Divina Commedia: Paradiso* 33, 4–6.

Mary's office of motherhood impels the people of God to take refuge in her with the trust of children. She offers herself as one eagerly ready to hear their prayers with maternal love and to come to their rescue with her powerful help.[121] This is why it is the practice of the faithful to call upon her as "Comforter of the afflicted," "Health of the sick," "Refuge of sinners"; they ask for comfort when they suffer, relief when they are sick, the strength that frees from slavery when they have sinned. And she who is free from all stain of sin truly guides her children so that they overcome sin with resolute will.[122] We must repeat again and again that this deliverance from evil and the slavery of sin (see Mt 6:13) have to be seen as the necessary precondition for any Christian moral reformation.

The example of holiness presented by Mary causes the faithful to raise their eyes to her "who shines more brightly than the entire community of the elect as the exemplar of virtue."[123] [. . .]

Devotion to Christ's Mother provides the faithful with the opportunity for growth in God's grace and that growth must be kept as the supreme goal of every form of pastoral activity. It is impossible to pay due honor to her who is full of grace without honoring divine grace itself, that is, God's friendship, his communion with the soul, and the indwelling of the Holy Spirit. God's grace has a profound effect on us and conforms us to the image of his Son (see Rom 8:29; Col 1:18). Relying on an experience supported by the evidence of the centuries, the Catholic Church acknowledges in Marian devotion a powerful help offered to people in their quest for attaining the fullness of life. Mary the New Woman stands next to Christ the New Man, in whose mystery alone is light shed on the human mystery itself.[124] We receive a kind of pledge of assurance that the divine plan for human salvation has already been fulfilled in a person of the human race, that is, in Mary. Often our contemporaries go back and forth between anxiety and hope; a sense of their insignificance casts them down yet they aspire to the infinite; their spirit is in turmoil as the enigma of death pierces their heart and perplexes their mind; imprisoned by loneliness, they long in boredom and weariness for communion with others. To them we say that the Blessed Virgin Mary, both in the hardships of her own life on earth and in her blessedness in heaven, offers a serene view of life and possesses words that are made to give courage. She promises hope in place of anguish, communion in place of loneliness, peace in place of turmoil, gladness and beauty in place of boredom and weariness, the expectation of eternal realities in place of earthly craving, life in place of death.

58. Esteemed Brothers, we have thought it well to discourse at length on devotion to the Mother of God: it is part of the complete meaning of Christian worship. Such an exposition was required by the seriousness of a topic that theologians have in recent years subjected to thorough examination and rethinking and in some cases have made controversial. It is comforting to us that the Apostolic See's efforts and your own to carry out the directives of the Council, and in particular those on liturgical reform, have made significant contributions to a more profound adoration of God, Father, Son, and Holy Spirit, and to the faithful's growth in Christian living. We observe with reassurance that the reformed Roman liturgy emerges as a witness to the Church's devotion to the Virgin Mary. We are confident that the directive norms laid down to advance and increase this devotion will be wholeheartedly put into practice.

3945

---

[121]   See LG nos. 60–63: AAS 57 (1965) 62–64; ConstDecrDecl 198–201.

[122]   See LG no. 65: AAS 57 (1965) 64–65; ConstDecrDecl 202–203.

[123]   LG no. 65: AAS 57 (1965) 64; ConstDecrDecl 202.

[124]   See GS no. 22: AAS 58 (1966) 1042–44; ConstDecrDecl 709.

468. SECRETARIAT OF STATE, **Letter** of Cardinal J. Villot to Bishop C. Manziana, on the occasion of the 27th National Liturgical Week of Italy (Bologna, 30 August – 3 September 1976), on the theme: "Mary in the Church's Worship and Life," August 1976: Not 12 (1976) 404–406 (Italian; excerpts).

3946   Pope Paul, as everyone knows, has always had deep concern for Marian devotion and has made continuing efforts to increase it and to make it ever more authentic, in all its expressions, on the basis of the broad fundamentals of Christian faith and within the framework of the Church's life. To this purpose he issued two years ago the Apostolic Exhortation *Marialis cultus*; his intention was "to advance the devotion toward the Virgin Mary that originates from the Word of God as its cause and is carried out in the Spirit of Christ" (see AAS 66 [1974] 116).[a] He has therefore noted with satisfaction how the program for the liturgical week sets before us the precise theme followed by *Marialis cultus*, that is, the rich doctrinal content, developed gradually from the beginning of the Church until the present, in the celebrations and texts of the Marian liturgy.[. . .]

3947   A further point in the program that the Pope wishes to stress as worthy of particular attention concerns the relationship between Mary and the Church. This involves Mary's mission in the mystery of the Church and her eminent place within the communion of saints (see *Marialis cultus* no. 28).[b] This mission is related to Mary's unique presence within the mystery of Christ and the hidden bonds between the Holy Spirit and the Virgin of Nazareth. It had been already clearly expressed and reaffirmed by Vatican Council II (see LG ch. 8), but Pope Paul desired to ratify it with his own authority when, at the close of the third period of the Council and concomitantly with promulgation of *Lumen gentium*, he proclaimed Mary as "Mother of the Church," that is, of the entire people of God, both the faithful and their shepherds (see AAS 56 [1964] 1014–17). The Pope repeats his exhortation made on that occasion so that the Blessed Virgin may be even more honored and invoked under that title by the Christian people. Mary "Mother of the Church" also now has a liturgical expression in the new votive Mass incorporated into the second *editio typica* of the Roman Missal (see RM, 2nd *ed. typica* [1975] 867–869).[c]

3948   A third point that the Pope views with pleasure is that along with the liturgical *cultus* of the Virgin, popular devotions also will come under discussion. The basic spontaneity of such devotions receives timely and effective enrichment, from new forms that arise out of genuine religious inspiration and pastoral sensitivity. Then they can and must contribute to making Marian devotion what *Marialis cultus* sets as the ideal: solid in its foundations, authentic in its historical background, conformed to doctrine, clear in its motivation. Then it will be of such a nature that it can become, even if only gradually, no longer an obstacle to the union of all Christians in Christ, but in fact an opening and meeting ground for that union (see *Marialis cultus* nos. 33 and 38).[d] [. . .]

> [a] DOL 467 no. 3898.
>
> [b] See DOL 467 no. 3926.
>
> [c] See Not 9 (1973) 382–383.
>
> [d] DOL 467 nos. 3931 and 3935.

Section 4. Sanctoral Cycle: B. The Saints and the Blessed

SUMMARY (DOL 469–479). There are 11 texts in this subsection.

—The documents having a general import include an instruction from the Congregation of Rites and its revised version from the Congregation for Divine Worship, on celebrations of those newly canonized or beatified (DOL 472, 476), a text of a new rite of canonization (DOL 473), and norms on patron saints (DOL 477).

—The remaining documents concern particular celebrations: a decree of the Congregation of Rites on the feast of St. Joseph in 1967 (DOL 471); a communication of the Congregation for the Sacraments and Divine Worship on All Saints in 1975 (DOL 478); a letter of Pope Paul VI and a decree of the Congregation of Rites on St. Benedict, Patron of Europe (DOL 469, 470); homilies of Paul VI on St. Teresa of Avila and St. Catherine of Siena, the first women proclaimed doctors of the Church (DOL 474, 475); a letter of the Congregation for the Sacraments and Divine Worship on the celebration of St. Stanislaus as an obligatory memorial (DOL 479).

▶ 1. VATICAN COUNCIL II, Constitution on the Liturgy *Sacrosanctum Concilium*, 3 December 1963:

art. 104, 111: Celebrations of the saints [nos. 104, 111].

469. PAUL VI, Apostolic Letter *Pacis nuntius*, declaring St. Benedict the patron of Europe, 26 October 1964: AAS 56 (1964) 965–967.

3949   Messenger of peace, architect of European unity and mentor of its civilization, above all herald of the Christian religion and father of Western monasticism are the well-earned titles honoring St. Benedict, Abbot. At a time when, with the fall of the enfeebled Roman Empire, some regions of Europe were slipping into the Dark Ages and others still lacked civilization and spiritual blessings, St. Benedict by the intense efforts of his own unwavering virtue brought about a shining new dawn on the European continent. For with the cross, the book, and the plough he brought, personally and through his sons, Christian civilization to the peoples spread from the Mediterranean to Scandinavia, from Ireland to Poland (see AAS, 1947, 453).

Through the cross, that is the law of Jesus Christ, he established and fostered the institutions of private and public life. It is well to mention in this regard the *Opus Dei*, that is, the fixed and constant round of prayer, by which he instilled the truth that the worship of God is of supreme importance in human affairs. In this way he created a spiritual unity in Europe so that peoples diverse in language, race, and culture regarded themselves as the one people of God. Through the loyal efforts of the monks schooled in the lessons of so great a father, that unity became a distinguishing characteristic of the Middle Ages. Such unity, which St. Augustine calls the "form of all beauty" (see *Ep.* 18, 2: PL 33, 85), was gradually shattered by lamentable turns of history; all those of good will are today striving to recover it.

Through the book, that is, the education of the mind, the same revered patriarch who gave so many monasteries their origin and their vitality, preserved with assiduous care the literary masterpieces of antiquity at a time when the humanities were shrouded in darkness; he passed these documents on to posterity and devotedly studied their teaching.

Through the plough, that is farming and other resources, he changed vast uncultivated lands into orchards and fields of grain. In the process and under the motto *ora et labora* he joined work to prayer and added a new dignity to human labor.

3950   It was therefore with good reason that Pope Pius XII called St. Benedict the "Father of Europe" (see AAS, 1947, 453), for he inspired the people of that continent with the love and desire for the right order that is the foundation of all life in society. It was also Pius XII's hope that through the intercession of this heroic man God would show favor to the efforts of those who seek to draw the same nations together with the bonds of true community. The same happy result was the deep desire that prompted John XXIII's loving devotion to this cause. We ourself warmly approve the measures designed to foster unity between the nations of Europe. For this reason we have willingly acceded to the requests to declare St. Benedict the patron of Europe that have been addressed to us from many parts of Europe by cardinals, archbishops, bishops, superiors general of religious orders and congregations, and by outstanding members of the laity. We have the opportunity to make a public declaration of this heavenly patronage today as we reconsecrate to God, in honor of the Blessed Virgin Mary and St. Benedict, the church of Monte Cassino.

Destroyed by the ravages of World War II in 1944, it has now been rebuilt by the power of an invincible devotion.

We happily consecrate this church today, following the example of many of our predecessors who themselves over the centuries have dedicated this center of religion and the monastic life, so renowned as the burial place of St. Benedict.

May this great saint support our aspirations. As once he dispelled the darkness with the light of Christ and brought the blessings of peace, may he now watch over the interests of Europe and by his intercession promote their greater progress. Therefore on the basis of the consultation, study, and sound decision of the Congregation of Rites we establish and declare by the fullness of our apostolic authority and in virtue of this Apostolic Letter that St. Benedict, Abbot is the chief patron before God of all Europe. He is accorded all the liturgical honors and privileges belonging to the principal patrons of places. [. . .]

470. SC RITES, **Decree** (dioceses of Europe) *Sanctum Benedictum*, promulgating the new texts for the feast of St. Benedict, Patron of Europe, 26 May 1965: Not 1 (1965) 157.

Saint Benedict, Abbot, through the Apostolic Letter *Pacis nuntius*, 24 October 1964 (see AAS, 1964) 965–967),[a] was established and declared by Pope Paul the principal patron of Europe, in order that its well-being might be under his care and advanced by his intercession.   3951

In order to heighten the solemnity of the liturgical celebration of his patronage, the Congregation of Rites, in virtue of faculties received from Pope Paul VI, has composed a proper Mass of St. Benedict, Patron of Europe, and has approved the text as given in the attached copy.

The observance according to the rubrics of the feast of St. Benedict, Abbot, on 21 March with the rank of third class remains unchanged. But in addition the Congregation grants that annually on 11 July in each of the churches and oratories of Europe the Mass of St. Benedict, Patron of Europe may be celebrated as a votive Mass of the second class. When 11 July falls on a Sunday, only two Masses of the patronage, as votive Masses of the second class, are permitted, in conformity with the *Codex rubricarum* no. 360.

▶   31.   CONSILIUM, Letter *Le renouveau liturgique*, on furthering liturgical reform, 30 June 1965:

        no.   8:   Veneration of the saints in churches (images and statues) [no. 417].

471. SC RITES, **Decree** (Urbis et Orbis) *Cum proximo anno*, on the feast of St. Joseph in 1967, 13 May 1966: Not 2 (1966) 180.

Next year, 1967, the feast of St. Joseph, Husband of the Blessed Virgin Mary, Confessor, and Patron of the Universal Church would have to be transferred from 19 March to 3 April according to the rules of the rubrics, because the Second   3952

ᵃ   See DOL 469 no. 3950.

Sunday of Passiontide (Palm Sunday) falls on 19 March. Therefore many local Ordinaries have petitioned this Congregation of Rites for the celebration of the feast of St. Joseph on 18 March.

At an audience granted 9 May 1966 to the undersigned Cardinal Prefect of the Congregation for a report on the matter, Pope Paul VI has acceded to the petitions and decreed that next year, 1967, the office and Mass of St. Joseph, Husband of the Blessed Virgin Mary, Confessor, and Patron of the Universal Church are to be celebrated on 18 March; in other respects the rubrics remain unchanged.

▶ 179. SC RITES, Instruction *Eucharisticum mysterium*, on worship of the eucharist, 25 May 1967:

no. 29: The faithful's participation on weekdays in certain feasts of the saints [no. 1258].

472. SC RITES, **Instruction** *Ad solemnia*, on celebrations in honor of the saints and the blessed, within a year of their canonization or beatification, 12 September 1968: AAS 60 (1968) 602.

3953 1. For celebrations, usually in the form of a triduum, in honor of a saint or blessed *within a year* of canonization or beatification a particular indult of the Congregation of Rites is required (*Codex Rubricarum* nos. 338 a and 339).

3954 2. Each day during such a celebration votive Masses of the new saint or blessed are permitted on all liturgical days except those listed in the table of precedence nos. 1–10 (*Codex Rubricarum* no. 91) and on the weekdays of Lent and on those of Advent from 17 December to 23 December.

The votive Masses are celebrated with *Gloria*; the *Credo* is not said unless the day itself is a Sunday or holyday of obligation or there is a large attendance at the Mass.

3955 3. Daily during these celebrations evening prayer of the new saint or blessed may be celebrated and without commemorations; this satisfies the obligation of the divine office for evening prayer that day.

Evening prayer of the saint or blessed is prohibited on the days listed in the table of precedence nos. 1–10 (*Codex Rubricarum* no. 91) and also on the weekdays of Lent and those of Advent from 17 December to 23 December.

3956 4. It is a praiseworthy practice to bring such celebrations to a close with the *Te Deum* and benediction with the blessed sacrament on the last day.

3957 5. To encourage veneration and devotion toward those recently canonized or beatified the Apostolic Penitentiary grants a *plenary indulgence* that may be gained once by the faithful who, after confession and communion and recitation of the *Our Father* and *Hail Mary* for the pope's intention, devoutly visit a church or oratory where the celebrations are held and there say the *Our Father* and the *Creed*. It grants a *partial indulgence* to those who are at least inwardly contrite and devoutly make the same kind of visit during the days of the celebration.[a]

---

a For the revision of this Instruction see DOL 476.

▶   440.   PAUL VI, Motu Proprio *Mysterii paschalis*, approving the norms for the liturgical year and the General Calendar, 14 February 1969:

Feasts of the saints [no. 3756].

▶   441.   SC RITES (Consilium), General Norms for the Liturgical Year and the Calendar, 21 March 1968:

nos. 8–14:   Celebrations in honor of the saints [nos. 3774–80].
59, 3, 4, 6, and 8: Table of Liturgical Days [no. 3825].

▶   208.   SC RITES (Consilium); SC DIVINE WORSHIP, General Instruction of the Roman Missal, 4th ed. 27 March 1975:

nos. 234 a: Bowing the head at the mention of the saint's name in whose honor the Mass is being celebrated [no. 1624].
278:             Images of the saints in churches [no. 1668].
316 c: Optional memorials of the saints and popular devotion [no. 1706].
329 c: Votive Masses in honor of the saints [no. 1719].

▶   93.   PAUL VI, Address to a consistory, excerpt on the liturgy, 28 April 1969:

Celebrations of the saints [no. 676].

473. SC DIVINE WORSHIP, New **rite** of canonization used for the first time at the canonization of St. Julie Billiart, 22 June 1969: Not 5 (1969) 292–293.

On the occasion of Pope Paul VI's solemn canonization on 22 June 1969 of Blessed Julie Billiart, Virgin, Foundress of the Sisters of the Blessed Virgin Mary, the new rite outlined here was used with the Pope's approval.   3958

1.   During the procession to the altar the entrance antiphon is sung by the choir and the whole congregation alternately.

2.   Upon reaching the altar and reverencing it, the pope goes directly up to the altar and kisses it, then goes to the chair. The prayers at the foot of the altar are omitted.

3.   Once the pope has reached the chair, the Cardinal Postulator of the Cause together with the Consistorial Advocate approaches the pope and requests the canonization:

Holy Father, the Church asks that through you the Blessed N. be enrolled in the catalogue of saints and be called Saint by all Christ's faithful.

4.   The Secretary of Apostolic Letters to Princes responds in the pope's name by inviting those present to pray earnestly to God before the pope proceeds to the solemn proclamation.

5.   The first cardinal deacon says: *Let us kneel.* All kneel. The pope kneels at the prie-dieu. The singing of the Litany of the Saints follows (in its new form). At the end, the *Agnus Dei* being omitted, these are sung at once:

Kyrie eleison (three times).

Christe eleison (three times).

Kyrie eleison (three times).

6.   Only the pope stands and says the prayer:

We ask you O Lord to hear the prayers of your people and let the light of your Holy Spirit enlighten our minds: so that what we do by our service may be pleasing to you and contribute to the growth of your Church.

7.   When the prayer is finished, the first cardinal deacon says: *Let us rise.* All rise and stand with head uncovered. The pope sits and, having taken the miter, pronounces the formulary of canonization.

For the honor of the holy and undivided Trinity, the exaltation of the Catholic faith, and the growth of Christian life, by authority of our Lord Jesus Christ, of the blessed Apostles Peter and Paul, and our own, after long deliberation and frequent prayer for divine help, and with the counsel of many of our brother bishops, we decree and define Blessed N. to be a saint and we enroll him/her in the catalogue of saints, declaring that he/she is to be honored among the saints with reverent devotion throughout the universal Church.

In the name of the Father and of the Son and of the Holy Spirit.

All answer: *Amen.*

8.   Then the Cardinal Postulator of the Cause, together with the Consistorial Advocate, approaches the chair again and thanks the pope:

Holy Father, in the name of holy Church I thank you for the pronouncement you have made and ask that you decree an apostolic letter on the canonization.

The pope answers: *We so decree.*

9.   The Cardinal Postulator of the Cause and the Consistorial Advocate then leave the chair and the pope begins the *Gloria*. The Mass continues in the usual way.

10.   At the presentation of the gifts the members of the postulation of the cause of canonization offer gifts to the pope.

▶   481. SC DIVINE WORSHIP, Instruction *Calendaria particularia*, on revision of particular calendars and propers, 24 June 1970.

474. PAUL VI, **Homily**, on St. Teresa of Avila, Doctor of the Church, 27 September 1970: AAS 62 (1970) 590–594 (Italian; excerpts).

3959   We have conferred on St. Teresa of Avila the title of doctor of the Church or, better, we have acknowledged her right to this title. [. . .]

The meaning of this act is very clear. It is an act that deliberately intends to bring light and its symbol might well be a lamp burning before the simple, majestic figure of St. Teresa. The light in question includes both the rays of the title of doctor shining on her and the rays that the same title sheds on us.

The light of this title shines on Teresa to bring out her unmistakable qualities that have already received full recognition in the past. First and above all is her holiness of life. This is a value that has had official recognition since 12 March 1622 (St. Teresa had died thirty years earlier) and the celebrated canonization ceremony in which our predecessor Gregory XV enrolled in the catalogue of saints, along with

Teresa, Ignatius Loyola, Francis Xavier, and Isidore the Farmer, the glories of Catholic Spain, and Philip Neri of Florence and Rome. A second, but outstanding quality is "the eminence of her teaching."

St. Teresa's teaching is resplendent with the charism of truth, its conformity with Catholic faith, its service for the spiritual life. Another mark of her teaching, particularly worthy of note, is the charism of wisdom. It brings to mind the most appealing and at the same time the most mysterious characteristic of St. Teresa, Doctor of the Church, namely, the influence of divine inspiration on this giant among mystical writers. What was the source of her teaching? Undoubtedly it was her intelligence, cultural and spiritual education, reading, discussions with eminent masters of theology and the spiritual life, a remarkable sensitivity, constant and intense asceticism, contemplation; one source, in a word, was her response to grace, welcomed into a soul extraordinarily rich and ready for the experience of prayer. But was that the sole source of "the eminence of her teaching." Must we not also take note at the same time in St. Teresa of acts, events, states of which she was not the initiator but the passive subject and which are mystical in the full sense of the word, to be attributed to an extraordinary intervention of the Holy Spirit? Without question we are in the presence of a soul clearly the subject of extraordinary divine initiatives that make themselves felt and that, in her characteristic literary style, St. Teresa then describes with simplicity, accuracy, and overwhelming power. [. . .]

For a long time it has been acknowledged with, we may say, unanimous assent, that it is St. Teresa's special privilege to be a mother and teacher for persons dedicated to the spiritual life. She is a mother full of a captivating simplicity and a teacher of astonishing profundity. The agreement of a long line of saints, theologians, the faithful, and scholars attests to these qualities. Today we have ratified them in order that, honored with the title of doctor, she may have a more authoritative role in her own religious family, the praying Church, and the world, bringing her past and ever present message: the message of prayer.

Made more brilliant and piercing today, the message of prayer is the ray of light that the title of doctor of the Church now conferred on her also sheds upon us. May this message reach us, the children of the Church, at a time of great striving for reform and renewal in liturgical prayer. May it reach us as we are tempted by the noise and pressures of the world around us to surrender to the concerns of modern life and to lose the real treasures of our souls for the sake of seductive earthly treasures. May this message come to us, children of our own times, when not only the practice of conversing with God, but the sense of the need and duty to adore him and call on him are being lost. May it come to us, this message that is the music and song of the soul filled with grace and open to communing with God in faith, hope, and charity. For today the probing of psychoanalysis is picking apart the fragile and complex structure we are, not in order to evoke the responses of a pained but redeemed humanity but in order to give vent to the confused moans of its animal subconscious and the clamor of its untamed passions and despondent anguish. May we hear the sublime and simple message of prayer from the wise Teresa, who urges us to search for "the great good that God does to a soul as he prepares it for the ardent practice of mental prayer, . . . since, it seems to me, mental prayer is nothing else but a conversation between friends, in which again and again we speak, one to one, with him whom we know loves us."[2]

This, then, is the message of St. Teresa of Jesus, Doctor of the Church; let us heed it and make it our own.

We must add two other points that seem to us to be important.

3960

3961

---

[2] *Vida* 8, 4 – 5.

3962   The first is to note that St. Teresa is the first woman on whom the Church has bestowed the title of doctor of the Church. This fact brings to mind, however, the stern words of St. Paul: *Mulieres in ecclesiis taceant;*[3] even today these words mean that women are not meant to exercise in the Church the hierarchic offices of teacher and minister. Has St. Paul's command now been flouted?

        We can answer that question with a clear No. In fact the issue is not a title that implies hierarchical functions of the magisterium; at the same time, however, we ought to emphasize that this does not in any way mean a lessening of esteem for the sublime mission that women have as part of the people of God.

        On the contrary, as they become part of the Church by baptism, women share in the universal priesthood of all the faithful. That deputes and obliges women to "profess before all the faith they have received from God through the Church."[4] In so professing their faith, many women have reached the loftiest heights, to the point even that their words and writings have become a light and a guide for their brothers. Their light was intensified every day in intimate contact with God, even in the most sublime forms of mystical prayer, for which St. Francis de Sales does not hesitate to say women have a special capacity. That light became life in an exalted way for the good and the service of others.

        Thus the Council wished to acknowledge the high degree of cooperation with divine grace that is the vocation of women in order to establish the kingdom of God on earth. In extolling the mission of women, the Council forthrightly invites their cooperation "to prevent the downfall of humanity," "to reconcile men with life," "to save the peace of the world."[5] [. . .]

475. PAUL VI, **Homily**, on St. Catherine of Siena, Doctor of the Church, 4 October 1970: AAS 62 (1970) 673–678 (Italian; excerpts).

3963   Spiritual exaltation fills us as we proclaim the humble and wise Dominican virgin, Catherine of Siena, a doctor of the Church. We find a precedent or we should say a justification in the sheer joy felt by Jesus Christ when, in St. Luke's words, "He rejoiced in the Spirit and said: 'I thank you, Father, Lord of heaven and earth, that you have hidden these things from the wise and understanding and revealed them to the little ones. For such, Father, was your gracious will.'"[1] [. . .]

        God's preference for what is insignificant and even scorned in the eyes of the world had already been proclaimed by Christ when, in sharp contrast with the world's values, he acclaimed as blessed and as the heirs of his kingdom the poor, the afflicted, the meek, those hungering for justice, the pure of heart, the peacemakers.[4]

        We do not intend to linger over showing how in Catherine's life and work the beatitudes have been exemplified with a superb fidelity and beauty. [. . .]

        Instead we think it pertinent at this time to bring out, even if briefly, the second of the reasons that in the Church's judgment justify bestowing the title of

---

   [3]   1 Cor 14:34.

   [4]   LG ch. 2, no. 11 [DOL 4 no. 141].

   [5]   Vatican Council II, "Message to Women."

   [1]   Lk 10:21; see Mt 11:25–26.

   [4]   See Mt 5:3–10.

doctor of the Church on the illustrious daughter of the city of Siena. That reason is the distinctive excellence of her teaching. [. . .]

What shall we say of the eminence of Catherine's teaching? In her writings — her *Letters*, a notable number of which are extant, her *Dialogues* or *Libro della Divina Dottrina*, and her *orationes* — we will not find the apologetic power or the theological mastery that mark the works of the great luminaries of the ancient Church in East and West. Neither could we expect of the uneducated virgin of Fontebranda the lofty speculations of systematic theology that have immortalized the medieval scholastic masters. It is true that her writings reflect in a surprising degree the theology of St. Thomas Aquinas; but even so his thought is there, stripped of its technical terminology. Instead, what is striking in this saint is her infused wisdom: a wisdom full of light, profundity, and an intoxicating grasp of divine truths and the mysteries of faith contained in the books of the Old and New Testament. Her assimilation of these truths and these mysteries was, it is true, helped by her singular natural gifts; but clearly in itself it is a prodigy, its cause, a charism of the wisdom of the Holy Spirit, a mystical charism.

3964

In her writings Catherine of Siena presents a shining model of those charisms of exhortation, the "word of wisdom" and the "word of knowledge" that St. Paul pointed out as working in some of the faithful in the primitive Christian communities. He wished the use of these gifts to be properly controlled, cautioning that they were not given merely for the benefit of the recipients, but much more for the good of the whole Body of the Church. For in that Body, he explains: "It is the one and the same Spirit who apportions to each individual as he wishes."[6] Thus the benefit of the spiritual treasures the Holy Spirit bestows must redound to the good of all the members of Christ's Mystical Body.[7]

Pius II in the Bull of Canonization declared: "She did not acquire her teaching on her own; she was a disciple before she was a teacher."[8] In truth Catherine's works are filled with the rays of a superhuman wisdom, with pressing appeals to imitate Christ in all the mysteries of his life and passion, and with guidance for the practice of the virtues proper to each person's state of life. Her *Letters* are like so many sparks of a mystical fire, kindled in her burning heart by the infinite Love who is the Holy Spirit.

What, then, are the characteristics, the dominant themes of her ascetical and mystical teaching? It seems to us that, imitating the "glorious Paul,"[9] whose vigorous and driving style she so often reflects, Catherine is the mystic of the incarnate Word and especially of Christ crucified. She was the advocate of the redemptive power of the adorable blood of the Son of God, shed on the cross with lavish love for the salvation of all human generations.[10] Catherine saw the Savior's blood as flowing continuously in the sacrifice of the Mass and in the sacraments, through the priest's ministry, to cleanse and enrich Christ's entire Mystical Body. We could thus call Catherine the mystic of Christ's Mystical Body, that is, of the Church.

3965

---

[6]   1 Cor 12:11.

[7]   See 1 Cor 11:5; Rom 12:8; 1 Tm 6:2; Ti 2:15.

[8]   M. H. Laurent, OP, *Proc. Cast.* 521–530. Italian tr., I. Taurisano, OP, *S. Caterina di Siena* (Rome, 1948) 665–673.

[9]   *Dialogues* ch. 11 (G. Cavallini, ed., 1968, 27).

[10]   *Dialogues* ch. 127 (ed. cit., 325).

But for her the Church is a true mother, to whom it is right to be submissive, to offer respect and help. She dared to say: "The Church is none other than Christ himself."[11] [. . .]

What kind of renewal and reform did she intend for the Church? Assuredly not the subversion of its essential structures, rebellion against its pastors, a life given over to personal charisms, arbitrary novelties in worship and practice, as some people would wish today. On the contrary Catherine repeatedly affirms that the beauty of Christ's Bride will be restored and that reform must be achieved "not through warfare, but through peace and tranquility, through the humble and continuous prayer, the sweat, and the tears of God's servants."[18] What she intended before all else is an interior reform and only then an outward reform, but always in communion with the lawful representatives of Christ and in filial obedience to them. [. . .]

▶ 426. SC DIVINE WORSHIP, General Instruction of the Liturgy of the Hours, 2 February 1971:

nos. 218–219: Celebration of the saints [nos. 3648–49].

476. SC DIVINE WORSHIP, Norms, on celebrations in honor of any saint or blessed held at an appropriate time after the canonization or beatification, 15 October 1972.*

3966   1.   For celebrations in honor of a saint or blessed, usually held *at an opportune time* after the canonization, a particular indult of the Congregation for Divine Worship is required.

3967   2.   Daily during these celebrations votive Masses of the new saint or blessed are permitted, except on the days listed in the table of precedence nos. 1–4 (General Norms for the Liturgical Year and the Calendar no. 59, I).[a]

These Masses are celebrated with *Gloria*; the *Credo* is optional, in keeping with the rule in the General Instruction of the Roman Missal no. 44.[b]

3968   3.   Daily celebration of the liturgy of the hours of the new saint or blessed is also permitted; it satisfies the obligation of the divine office for the day (see General Instruction of the Liturgy of the Hours no. 245).[c]

3969   4.   The hymn *Te Deum* on the final day is a suitable conclusion for the celebrations.

If a votive Mass of the new saint or blessed is celebrated, the *Te Deum* is sung after the distribution of communion is over (the last part of the *Te Deum* may be omitted, namely, from the verse, *Save your people, Lord*, to the end).

---

[11] *Letter* 171 (P. Misciatelli, ed., v. 3, 89).

[18] *Dialogues* ch. 15, 86 (ed. cit., 44, 197).

* Text not published (see EDL p. 414, note a). The text of the norms is an emendation of the Instruction *Ad solemnia* [DOL 472].

[a] See DOL 442 no. 3825.

[b] See DOL 208 no. 1434.

[c] See GILH 426 no. 3675.

5.   The faithful who, after confession and communion and the recitation of the   3970
Our Father and *Hail Mary* or another prayer for the pope's intentions, devoutly visit
the churches or public oratories where the celebrations are held and there recite the
Our Father and the *Creed* may gain a *plenary indulgence* once. A *partial indulgence* is granted
to those who are at least inwardly contrite and devoutly make the same kind of
visit during the same period (Apostolic Penitentiary, 12 October 1968, N.
1528/68/R).

▶   329.   SC BISHOPS, *Directory on the Pastoral Ministry of Bishops*, 22 February 1973:

      nos. 90–91:   Popular devotions [nos. 2660–61].

477. SC DIVINE WORSHIP, **Norms** *Patronus, liturgica acceptione*, on patron
saints, 19 March 1973: AAS 65 (1973) 276–279; Not 9 (1973) 263–266.*

1.   A patron in the liturgical sense of the term means the Blessed Virgin Mary, a   3971
saint, or a blessed who because of an ancient tradition or lawful custom is celebrated as a protector, that is, as an advocate before God.

2.   A patron is distinct from a title or titular of a church, a religious congregation,   3972
or a community, even though the term "title" implies patronage.

3.   There are patrons of: 3973
      a.   *places* (a nation, region, diocese, state, city or town, parish);
      b.   *religious families;*
      c.   *moral persons, sodalities, institutes,* and *organizations,* ecclesiastical and civil.

CHOICE OF A PATRON
4.   The *Blessed Virgin Mary*, under any title received in the liturgy, *the angels*, and *the*   3974
saints may be chosen as patrons. The blessed may not, without a special indult of the
Apostolic See.[1] The choice of a Divine Person is always excluded.[2]

5.   There may be only one patron. It is lawful, however, to choose two or more   3975
saints as patrons if they are listed together in the calendar.
      In the past for special reasons another saint has sometimes been taken as a
secondary patron. From now on as a rule there is to be only one.

6.   Patrons of places are to be chosen by the clergy and faithful, that is, by those   3976
to be placed under the saint's protection.
      Patrons of religious families, moral persons, sodalities, institutes, and organiza-
tions are to be chosen by those involved, that is, by the members who make up the
respective groups.[3]
      The choice of a patron is to be made either by ballot or vote or by petition or
the collection of signatures.

---

   *   The text in both AAS and Not appears as part I with norms on crowning Marian images; see DOL
466.
   [1]   See CIC can. 1278.
   [2]   See SCDW, Instr. *Calendaria particularia*, 24 June 1970, no. 28 [DOL 481 no. 4023].
   [3]   See SCDW, Instr. *Calendaria particularia* no. 30 [DOL 481 no. 4025].

APPROVAL

3977   7.   Choice of a patron requires the approval of the competent authority: the *bishop* for a diocese; the *conference of bishops* for an ecclesiastical province, a region, or a nation; the *provincial chapter* for a province of religious and the *general chapter* for an entire religious institute. In the case of moral persons, sodalities, institutes, or organizations that are international the matter is to be submitted to the Holy See.

CONFIRMATION

3978   8.   The choice and approval of a patron require confirmation by the Congregation for Divine Worship.[4]

To obtain this confirmation the following documents must be sent to the Congregation:

a.   petition of the local ecclesiastical authority or, where applicable and possible, of the civil authority;

b.   *acta*, petitions, lists of signatures that endorse the choice and are evidence of it, as well as a report expressing the reasons for the choice;

c.   proof that the competent authority has approved the choice.

3979   9.   Confirmation is granted through a decree of the Congregation and, in the case of patrons of a more extensive geographical area, also by means of an apostolic letter in the form of a brief.

3980   10.   The *cultus* and devotion toward a patron already formally established or accepted from time immemorial may have ceased in the course of time or it may happen that nothing certain is known about the saint. In such a case a new patron may be chosen after thorough deliberation. The requirements already laid down are followed.[5]

LITURGICAL CELEBRATION OF A PATRON

3981   11.   A liturgical celebration belongs only to patrons duly chosen or accepted by immemorial tradition. No special liturgical right belongs to other saints who are called patrons only in a wide sense, purely out of devotion.[6]

3982   12.   The celebration of the patron of a city or town, of a moral person, an institute, or an organization is observed with the rank of *solemnity*. Such a solemnity has *precedence* over all feasts in the General Calendar or in a particular calendar and over a Sunday of the Christmas season or a Sunday in Ordinary Time.

The celebration of the patron of a diocese, province, region, or nation and the patron of a province of religious is observed with the rank of a *feast*.[7] As pastoral reasons may suggest, however, for example, when the patron has great importance for the history of a certain region or is the object of great devotion for the faithful, the celebration may have the rank of a solemnity.[8] The patron of a place or of a wider area must be celebrated even by religious[9] and those who have their own calendar.

---

[4]   See ibid.

[5]   See ibid. no. 33 [DOL 481 no. 4028].

[6]   See ibid. no. 29 [DOL 481 no. 4024].

[7]   See General Norms for the Liturgical Year and the Calendar no. 59 [DOL 442 no. 3825].

[8]   SCDW, Instr. *Calendaria particularia* no. 8 [DOL 481 no. 4003].

[9]   See General Norms for the Liturgical Year and the Calendar no. 52 c [DOL 442 no. 3818]. SCDW, Instr. *Calendaria particularia* no. 16 d [DOL 481 no. 4011].

13. In their own right religious institutes may celebrate with the rank of a solemnity either their patron or their title or their founder who is a saint.[a] But, in special circumstances they may petition that a second one of these celebrations have the rank of a solemnity.

3983

14. Secondary patrons formally established in the past are to be celebrated with the rank of an obligatory memorial.[10]

3984

15. The following are no longer to be honored as patrons: those established in the past because of peculiar historical circumstances; those chosen in the past either because of some extraordinary event, for example, a plague, war, or other disaster, or because of a special, but now extinct *cultus*.[11]

3985

478. SC SACRAMENTS AND DIVINE WORSHIP, **Communication** *Domenica prossima*, on the evening Mass for 1 November in 1975, 29 October 1975: Not 11 (1975) 349 (Italian).

Next Sunday will mark the application for the first time of the norm providing for celebration of All Souls on a Sunday (see *Missale Romanum* 635). That is in accord with the directive of the Constitution on the Liturgy. "The rite of funerals should express more clearly the paschal character of Christian death."[a]

3986

Queries have come from different places about the Mass to be celebrated on the evening of 1 November.

As already published at the appropriate time in *Notitiae* 10 (1974) 222–223,[b] in the case of the concurrence of two days of obligation the evening Mass is that of the liturgical day higher in rank. Therefore in the case at hand the Mass celebrated on 1 November is to be the Mass for the solemnity of All Saints (see *Missale Romanum*, "Tabula dierum liturgicarum," 1, 3, p. 110).[c]

479. SC SACRAMENTS AND DIVINE WORSHIP, **Circular Letter** *Summus Pontifex* to presidents of the conferences of bishops and of national liturgical commissions, on the celebration of St. Stanislaus, Bishop and Martyr, 11 April in the General Roman Calendar, 29 May 1979: Not 15 (1979) 308–309.

Pope John Paul II, on the occasion of the ninth centenary of the death of St. Stanislaus, Bishop and Martyr, sent on 8 May 1979, to the bishops and the whole people of God in Poland, the Apostolic Letter *Rutilans agmen*. This lays down that the celebration of St. Stanislaus is to appear in the General Roman Calendar from now

3987

---

^a See DOL 481 no. 4007.

¹⁰ SCDW, Instr. *Calendaria particularia* no. 16 d [DOL 481 no. 4011].

¹¹ See ibid. no. 32 [DOL 481 no. 4027].

^a See DOL 1 no. 81.

^b See DOL 448 nos. 3838, 3839.

^c See DOL 442 no. 3825.

on with the rank of an obligatory memorial, rather than its previous rank of an optional memorial.

On the occasion of informing you of this decision, this Congregation considers it opportune also to provide certain guidelines in this matter.

3988   1.   Beginning with the next liturgical year, 1979–80, any *ordo* for Mass and the divine office published for the use of a diocese or religious family is to indicate the newly decreed rank for the celebration in honor of St. Stanislaus. The same rank is to be noted in any new liturgical book yet to be prepared under the supervision of the conferences of bishops.

3989   2.   The new rank of celebration involves no change in the date of celebration or the texts of the Roman Missal and *The Liturgy of the Hours* that are to be used.

a.   The date assigned to the celebration of St. Stanislaus remains the same, namely, 11 April, as in the General Roman Calendar.

b.   The texts to be used in the Mass and office remain the same, those, namely, in the Roman Missal and *The Liturgy of the Hours*.

3990   3.   Wherever, according to the norm of a particular law, St. Stanislaus is celebrated on a different date or with a different rank, the celebration will retain this date and rank.

►   See also Chapter Five, Section 5. Particular calendars and propers.

Section 5. Particular Calendars and Propers

SUMMARY (DOL 480–483). A revision of the diocesan and religious' calendars and propers for Mass and the liturgy of the hours became necessary because, following the Constitution on the Liturgy art. 111, the General Norms for the Liturgical Year and the Calendar restricted the number of saints in the General Calendar to those of universal significance, but at the same time noted: "The individual Churches or families of religious should show a special honor to those saints who are properly their own" (no. 49).

There are 4 texts on the process of revision. The Congregation for Divine Worship issued first an instruction on provisional adaptation of particular calendars (DOL 480), then a definitive instruction on the revision of calendars and propers (DOL 481). In 1974 the same Congregation sent a letter to bishops and religious general superiors containing norms to expedite the work of revision (DOL 482). Finally, the Congregation for the Sacraments and Divine Worship found it necessary, because the work had not been completed on schedule, to issue in 1977 a reminder and repeat the norms given in 1974 (DOL 483).

▶ 111. CONSILIUM, Instruction *Popularibus interpretationibus*, on translations of propers of dioceses and religious families, 1–2 June 1965.

▶ 441. SC RITES (Consilium), Decree *Anni liturgici ordinatione*, promulgating the *editio typica* of the General Roman Calendar, 21 March 1969:

> Conforming particular calendars and propers to the universal calendar [no. 3766].

▶ 442. SC RITES (Consilium), General Norms for the Liturgical Year and the Calendar, 21 March 1969:

> nos. 49–56:   Particular calendars [nos. 3815–22].
> 59:   Table of precedence [no. 3825].

480. SC DIVINE WORSHIP, **Instruction** *Decreto Sacrae Congregationis Rituum*, on the interim adaptation of particular calendars, 29 June 1969: Not 5 (1969) 283.

3991   The Decree of the Congregation of Rites promulgating the new General Roman Calendar establishes that proper calendars for offices and Masses are to be revised by "using as criteria the norms on the structure of the liturgical year."[a] To facilitate and safeguard this work, the Congregation for Divine Worship intends to issue pertinent guidelines and norms.[b]

Meanwhile *for the year* 1970 and until the *editio typica* of the individual liturgical books has been completed, the following are to be observed.

3992   1   Celebrations that a particular calendar has in common with the General Calendar are to be carried out in the manner indicated in the General Calendar.

3993   2   Proper celebrations presently listed in particular calendars are to be retained and the manner of observing them is to be the same as that of celebrations retained in the General Calendar, that is:

a.   Feasts of the first class retained in the new Table of Liturgical Days as solemnities are to become solemnities.

b.   Feasts of the second class retained in the new Table of Liturgical Days as feasts are to be celebrated as feasts.

c.   Feasts of the third class are to be regarded as obligatory memorials. For the year 1970, should one of these coincide with an obligatory memorial of the General Calendar, the celebrant has the option of choosing either one.

d.   Commemorations become optional memorials when they fall on a day allowing an optional memorial; otherwise (that is, when these commemorations fall on the date of a solemnity, feast, or obligatory memorial) they are to be omitted.

3994   3   The norms just listed are to be applied also to any feasts of the blessed that may belong to particular calendars.

---

[a]   DOL 441 no. 3766.
[b]   See DOL 481.

481. SC DIVINE WORSHIP, **Instruction** *Calendaria particularia*, on the revision of particular calendars and of the propers for offices and Masses, 24 June 1970: AAS 62 (1970) 651–663; Not 6 (1970) 349–370.

Particular calendars as well as the propers for offices and Masses should at this   3995
time be revised so that the principles and norms used in revising the Roman Missal[1] and Breviary are also applied to particular calendars and to the propers of offices and Masses.

Now that the new General Calendar has been published,[2] the liturgical year is arranged in such a way that there is a closer coordination between the cycle of seasons and the cycle of saints. In accord with the directive of Vatican Council II only those of the saints who are judged to have real significance for the universal Church have been included in the General Calendar.

It remains, therefore, to carry out the rest of the Council's directive, namely, that appropriate celebrations of other saints should be observed only in those places where special reasons justify their being honored, that is, in the individual countries, dioceses, and religious institutes to which these saints more properly belong.[3]

For this purpose and also in response to the many queries already proposed, the Congregation for Divine Worship deems it opportune to issue the present Instruction; it will serve as a means of carrying out the work of revision more securely and easily.

CHAPTER I
GENERAL NORMS

1.   Individual Churches and religious institutes should show special honor to the   3996
saints belonging to them and particular calendars are to coordinate those celebrations with the general cycle.[4]

2.   The Proper of Seasons, that is, the cycle of seasons, solemnities, and feasts that   3997
brings out in detail and honors the entire mystery of redemption during the liturgical year, is always to be observed intact and to have proper precedence over particular celebrations.[5] Therefore:

a.   On Sundays any permanent particular celebration is per se forbidden.[6]

b.   The days during which Lent and the octave of Easter frequently occur and also 17 December to 31 December are to be kept free of particular celebrations. Exceptions are optional memorials, the feasts mentioned in the Table of Liturgical Days no. 8 a, b, c, d,[a] or solemnities not transferable to another season.[7]

c.   Celebrations allowed by indult, that is, celebrations that have no strictly proper reason for inclusion in a particular calendar, must not duplicate celebrations

---

[1]   See GNLYC [DOL 442]. GIRM, Introduction [DOL 208 no. 1376].

[2]   See Paul VI, Motu Proprio *Mysterii paschalis*, 14 Feb. 1969 [DOL 440].

[3]   See SC art. 111 [DOL 1 no. 111].

[4]   See GNLYC no. 49 [DOL 442 no. 3815].

[5]   See GNLYC no. 50 [DOL 442 no. 3816].

[6]   See GNLYC no. 6 [DOL 442 no. 3772].

[a]   See DOL 442 no. 3825.

[7]   See GNLYC nos. 56ff. [DOL 442 nos. 3822–24].

already in the cycle of the mystery of salvation and they must not be too numerous.[8] Special reasons must support the retention of old celebrations of this kind or the introduction of new ones.

3998   3.   There is to be only one celebration a year honoring any particular saint. Where persuasive pastoral reasons exist, however, a second celebration is allowed, in the form of an optional memorial, for the transfer or discovery of the body of a patron saint or the founder of a particular Church or religious institute or for a special event in the life of the same saints (e.g., their conversion).[9] Any existing remembrances at regular intervals (e.g., on a set day each month or week) of the same mystery or saint are to be suppressed.

3999   4.   Thorough theological, historical, and pastoral research is a necessary prerequisite to the revision of particular calendars and propers.[10] Therefore Ordinaries or other lawful authorities will see to the appointment of a commission of experts in these fields.

Consultation with the clergy and people concerned, or with the members of religious institutes, must be part of the process of editing new calendars. Such calendars are to be approved by the competent authority and to be submitted for the confirmation of this Congregation for Divine Worship *within five years* of the publication of the new Roman Missal and Breviary.[b,R1]

Once approved in the way indicated, a calendar must be followed by all those for whom it is obligatory; there can be no subsequent change without the Apostolic See's consent.

4000   5.   Once the calendar and proper for a diocese or religious institute have been duly revised, Ordinaries are to ensure that the calendars, propers, indults, and privileges belonging to individual churches and to the provinces of religious that are subject to their jurisdiction are also properly revised. The principles and norms to be used for this are those set forth in the present Instruction.

4001   6.   Particular calendars and the propers for offices and Masses are to be sent to this Congregation in *three* typed copies and with one copy of the former calendar and proper attached. The material sent is to include:

a.   a short but clear presentation of the reasons for introducing the individual changes, especially where these depart from the norms of the present Instruction;

---

8   See GNLYC no. 50 c [DOL 442 no. 3816].

9   See GNLYC no. 50 b [DOL 442 no. 3816].

10   See SC art. 23 [DOL 1 no. 23].

b   See DOL 482.

R1   On this requirement the SCDW published the following: The Instruction *on the revision of particular calendars and the propers of offices and Masses,* issued 24 June 1974, required that all calendars and propers be submitted for confirmation "*within five years* of the publication date of the new Roman Missal and the Breviary" (AAS 62 [1970] 652; Not 6 [1970] 352). The new Roman Missal was in fact published on 26 March 1970 and *The Liturgy of the Hours* on 11 August 1971. Therefore on 11 April 1976 the available time for the completion of the revision of propers will come to an end. The work is actually underway everywhere, in national, regional, and diocesan liturgical commissions and in the particular Churches and the religious institutes. This is the status up to 1 April 1973 [report by countries, regions and religious communities follows]: Not 9 (1973) 284.

b. in the case of new offices or Masses, a clear indication of those parts that are taken from other, already approved offices or Masses and of those that are entirely new compositions.[R2]

CHAPTER II
PROPER CELEBRATIONS AND CALENDARS

A. PARTICULAR CELEBRATIONS

7. The proper celebrations entered in particular calendars are those that must be observed *ipso iure* or those granted by indult.   4002

8. Proper celebrations of a region, nation, or wider geographical area: 4003

— feast of the principal patron; but for pastoral reasons this may be observed as a solemnity;

— memorial of the secondary patron;

— other celebrations of saints or the blessed who are duly listed in the Roman Martyrology or its Appendix and who have a special relationship to the region, nation, or wider geographical area.

9. Proper celebrations of a diocese: 4004

— feast of the principal patron; but for pastoral reasons, this may be observed as a solemnity;

— feast of the anniversary of the dedication of the cathedral;

— memorial of the secondary patron;

— celebrations of saints or the blessed who are duly listed in the Roman Martyrology or its Appendix and who belong to the diocese in a particular way, for example, because it was their place of origin, long-time residence, or place of death or because of a *cultus* from time immemorial that still continues.

10. Proper celebrations belonging to a town or a city: 4005

— solemnity of the principal patron;

— memorial of the secondary patron.

11. Proper celebrations belonging to an individual church: 4006

— solemnity of the anniversary of its dedication, if it is consecrated;

— solemnity of its title;

— memorial of a saint or a blessed listed in the Roman Martyrology or its Appendix whose burial place is in that church.

12. Proper celebrations belonging to a religious institute: 4007

[R2] After the report noted at no. 3999, note R1, the SCDW concludes: A long way yet remains before all the countries, dioceses, and religious institutes put the reform of the liturgy fully into effect. A look at the statistics suffices. There are 117 conferences of bishops, many of them combined under one name and organization; some do not use a liturgical proper, especially where the Churches are of recent foundation. There are 2172 residential sees in the whole Church, 222 institutes of men religious, 1162 of women religious. The number of propers to be revised is still large and the time to complete the revision not really long. Even so, it will be possible to complete the work within the time stipulated, and even before then, because, with God's help, all those assigned to prepare the texts are working tirelessly. Is it possible that by the Holy Year 1975 we will have all the propers revised and published in the vernacular? All texts, both for Masses and offices, must be presented to the Congregation for Divine Worship in Latin and in their vernacular version. As to the Latin, note that the new version from the Pontifical Commission for the Neo-Vulgate Edition must be used for the psalms and all the New Testament books: Not 9 (1973) 287.

a. Of the entire institute:

— solemnity or feast of its title;

— solemnity or feast of its canonized founder;

— solemnity or feast of the principal patron of an order or congregation;

— feast of a beatified founder;

— memorial of a secondary patron;

— celebrations of saints and the blessed who were members of the order or congregation, in keeping with the rule in no. 17 a.

b. Of individual provinces:

— feast of the title or principal patron;

— memorial of the secondary patron;

— celebrations of saints and the blessed who had some special connection with the province, in keeping with the rule in no. 17 b.

Regarding celebrations of a title, a canonized founder, and a principal patron, religious are to remember that only one of these may be listed in the calendar as a solemnity and the others are to be observed as feasts.[c] As in the case of the revision of the proper calendar, the choice in this matter belongs to the supreme authority in the religious institute.

B. PARTICULAR CALENDAR AND CELEBRATIONS TO BE INCLUDED

4008   13. A particular calendar is formed by the insertion of particular celebrations into the General Calendar. A particular calendar may be a calendar for a country or region, for a diocese, or for a religious institute.

4009   14. A national calendar or, depending on the circumstances, a regional calendar is drawn up for an entire nation or region. It includes those celebrations, both proper and allowed by indult, that do not exist in the General Calendar or that are to be observed with a higher rank in the particular calendar.

This is a way of assigning appropriate celebrations in the particular countries or regions to saints who are important in the national or regional religious history, particularly because of their teaching or apostolate.

4010   15. a. Each diocese or ecclesiastical territory equivalent in law to a diocese (see CIC can. 293, § 1 and can. 319) has a diocesan calendar.

b. Drawing up a diocesan calendar means adding to the General Calendar:

— celebrations, both proper and by indult, belonging to the entire country, the region, and wider geographical area;

— celebrations, both proper and by indult, belonging to the entire diocese.

c. The calendars of any place, church or oratory, as well as of religious congregations and institutes lacking their own religious calendar, are all drawn up in coordination with the diocesan calendar, with celebrations, both proper and by indult, added.

4011   16. a. The following have a religious calendar:

— orders of men; their calendar must also be followed by any nuns and sisters belonging to the same order and by its tertiaries who live in community and make simple vows;

---

[c] See DOL 477 no. 3983.

— religious congregations, societies, and institutes of pontifical rank, if they are in any way obliged to celebrate the divine office.

b. Drawing up a religious calendar means inserting into the General Calendar celebrations both proper and granted by indult to the order or congregation.

c. The calendar of each religious province and each church or oratory of the order or congregation is drawn up in coordination with the religious calendar, with celebrations, both proper and by indult, added.

d. Members of religious institutes join with the local Church in celebrating the anniversary of the dedication of the cathedral and the feast of the principal patrons of both the place and the wider area in which they reside.[11,R3]

17. When any diocese or religious family holds the distinction of having many canonized or beatified members, care is to be taken not to have a disproportionate number in the calendar of the entire diocese or institute. Therefore:

a. A special celebration is assigned only to the saints or the blessed who have special significance for an entire diocese (e.g., those who founded it or brought honor to it by their martyrdom or outstanding merits) or for an entire religious

4012

---

[11] See GNLYC no. 52 c [DOL 442 no. 3818].

[R3] Query: May religious who have a proper calendar celebrate the Mass and the liturgy of the hours according to the calendar of the local Church, the diocese, the region, or the country in which they reside? Reply: We must recall the norms in the different liturgical books on this point.
   1. *What a proper calendar means*
       Particular calendars contain proper celebrations coordinated harmoniously with the general cycle. The individual Churches or religious institutes should honor those saints belonging to them in a special way (see GNLYC no. 49 [DOL 442 no. 3815]). Drawing up a particular calendar means inserting into the General Calendar feasts and memorials that are proper (see GNLYC no. 52 [DOL 442 no. 3818]). Religious, however, are obliged to celebrate the anniversary of the dedication of the cathedral of their diocese of residence and the principal patron of the place and wider region of their residence (see GNLYC no. 52 c [DOL 442 no. 3818]).
   2. *Liturgy of the hours*
       a. The office in choir and in common must be carried out according to the proper calendar of the religious (GILH no. 241 [DOL 426 no. 3671]).
       b. Private recitation may follow either the calendar of the place or the proper calendar, except on solemnities and proper feasts (GILH no. 243 [DOL 426 no. 3673]).
   3. *Mass*
       a. On solemnities the priest is obliged to follow the calendar of the church where he celebrates Mass.
       b. On Sundays, the weekdays of Advent, the Christmas season, Lent, and the Easter season, on feasts and obligatory memorials:
           — in a Mass with a congregation the priest is to follow the calendar of the church where he celebrates;
           — in a Mass without a congregation he may choose either the calendar of the church or his own calendar.
       Taken together, these points lead to the following conclusions.
   1. In individual celebration of the liturgy of the hours or of Mass religious may follow either their own calendar or that of the local Church.
   2. In celebrating *in choir* or *in common* they must per se always follow their own calendar. Still, it seems right to commend the wish of certain religious communities to enter more closely into the life and prayer of the local Church. The Congregation for Divine Worship has therefore allowed certain religious institutes to follow the calendar of the diocese, but with the addition of their own proper celebrations. To foster unity among the members of the same religious institute, however, the choice between their own and the diocesan calendar (with their own celebrations added) is not to be left up to the individual but is to be made at least within a region or country by the authorized superiors.
   3. Following a proper calendar may entail certain differences from the calendar of a region or nation, especially with regard to the proper dates for celebrations or the rank of certain celebrations. In such cases it seems preferable that the religious of that region or country adapt their proper calendar to conform to that of the country or region. In celebrations with a congregation they are obliged to do so: Not 9 (1973) 151–152.

institute (e.g., the principal martyrs or the saints or the blessed who have graced the institute by their outstanding merits).

b. Celebrations of other saints and the blessed are to be restricted to those places to which they have closer ties or which are their place of burial.[12] A collective celebration may be added to the calendar of a diocese or religious institute for all the saints or the blessed belonging to them or for a certain class (e.g., martyrs, bishops, etc.).

The points just laid down are to be observed, with the necessary modifications, in drawing up national calendars or calendars for a wider area.

4013   18. A critical study is to be made concerning all the saints and the blessed who are to be entered in a calendar in order to ensure the historical authenticity of their life and work as well as of the origin and the spread of their *cultus*. For this purpose there is to be consultation with experts on matters of local hagiography and of hagiographical collections in modern critical editions. In cases where any doubts remain, the whole matter may be referred to this Congregation.

4014   19. The revision of particular calendars is to include expunging the names of saints about whom little or nothing is known historically except such names. The same is true of saints' names that in the past were entered in a calendar because of some special reason but now have little or no relevance to the diocese or religious institute.

4015   20. In modern times the boundaries of dioceses have often been redrawn. Therefore, the diocesan calendar is to retain the names of saints of every area that makes up the new diocese only if such saints are of general significance for the entire new diocese.

C. PROPER DAY FOR CELEBRATIONS

4016   21. If at all possible, their exact date of death is to be assigned to saints. If that date is unknown, the celebration is assigned a date belonging to the saint on some other grounds, for example, the date of the discovery, exhumation, or transfer of the body or the date of canonization. Otherwise the date assigned is one on which there are no other celebrations in the particular calendar.

The traditional date is retained, however, when a saint is already listed in the calendar and the date of celebration is so closely linked with the faithful's devotion, popular traditions, or civil custom that it cannot be easily changed.[13]

4017   22. Celebrations that are called "celebrations by indult" are to be assigned to a day best suited pastorally.

4018   23. The following are to be respected whenever proper celebrations need to be harmonized with celebrations of the universal Church:

a. Solemnities listed in the General Calendar for the same date are to be observed, unless there is some different directive (see no. 36).

b. Feasts listed in the General Calendar for the same date are to be kept also in particular calendars and the proper feast coinciding on the same date transferred to the nearest free date. There is an exception when the date of the proper feast is so

---

12   See GNLYC no. 53 c [DOL 442 no. 3819].

13   See GNLYC no. 56 c [DOL 442 no. 3822].

connected with local custom or popular devotion that it cannot be transferred without serious inconvenience.

c. A proper memorial is to take precedence over a universal, optional memorial. In some cases, however, a proper memorial may take precedence even over a universal, obligatory memorial. This is done either by changing the universal memorial into an optional memorial and in the calendar combining it with the proper memorial of the same rank on the same date or by transferring the universal memorial to a later date, if this seems preferable.

D. RANK OF CELEBRATIONS

24. Celebrations that are to be listed in particular calendars *ipso iure* as solemnities or feasts are explicitly listed in the Table of Liturgical Days.[d] These have already been discussed in nos. 8–12.   4019

Unless special historical or pastoral reasons stand in the way, other proper celebrations are to be entered in the calendar as either obligatory or optional memorials.[14]

An optional memorial offers the choice between the office and Mass of the weekday and those of a saint, and therefore does not in any way interfere with a celebration of the saints. Rather, it permits the necessary adaptation in the arrangement of the celebration of a liturgical day to the spiritual needs, devotion, preparation, and mentality of those taking part. Use of the optional memorial therefore will be of great advantage to the preparation of calendars, especially in cases where a great number of saints have to be incorporated into them.

25. The observance of some celebrations in a particular place may have greater solemnity than in the entire diocese or religious institute.[15] Through a wise application of this distinction calendars will better meet special needs and circumstances.   4020

26. If any of the saints or the blessed are mentioned together in a calendar, they are to be celebrated together whenever they are celebrated with the same rank, even though one of them or several are more relevant to a particular calendar. When one or more of these saints or blessed are to be celebrated with a higher rank, only the office for them is observed; the celebration of the others is omitted, unless there is some reason for assigning another date to them for celebration as an obligatory memorial.[16]   4021

E. TITLES OF THE SAINTS

27. The following titles are suppressed: "Confessor and Bishop," "Confessor, Nonbishop," "Neither Virgin nor Martyr," "Widow"; the following are the titles to be attached to the names of saints, as in the General Calendar: 4022

a. titles of received usage: Apostle (Evangelist), Martyr, Virgin.

b. titles designating rank in the hierarchy: Bishop (Pope), Priest, Deacon.

c. titles indicating that the saint belonged to a religious institute: Abbot (Monk), Religious.

---

[d] See DOL 442 no. 3825.

[14] See GNLYC no. 54 [DOL 442 no. 3820].

[15] See GNLYC no. 54 [DOL 442 no. 3820].

[16] See GNLYC no. 16 [DOL 442 no. 3782].

"Abbot" is assigned as a title to saints belonging to an order having the office of abbot, even to saints who were priests, e.g., St. Bernard. Men religious who were not priests are assigned the title "Religious." Women who were married prior to entering religious life are assigned the title "Religious"; other women religious are assigned the traditional title "Virgin."

In the General Calendar no special title follows the names of lay saints who were not martyrs or virgins. But particular calendars may use certain designations that suggest in some way the saints' state in life (e.g., "King," "Father," "Mother," etc.).

CHAPTER III
CELEBRATIONS IN PARTICULAR

A. PATRONS AND TITLES

4023   28. Only saints, that is, those who are lawfully honored by this title, may be chosen as patrons of countries, regions, dioceses, places, religious institutes, and moral persons; the blessed may not be patrons without an apostolic indult.[17] The choice of a Divine Person is always excluded.

4024   29. A liturgical celebration as patron is accorded only to saints chosen and appointed in accord with ancient usage or accepted as such by an immemorial tradition. No special liturgical right belongs to other saints who are called patrons only in a wide sense, purely out of devotion.

4025   30. The choice of a patron is to be made by the clergy and people; it is for the bishop or other competent ecclesiastical authority to approve the choice. The choice and the approval require the confirmation of the Congregation for Divine Worship.[18]

In the case of a patron of an order, congregation, or religious institute or one of its provinces, the choice is to be made by the members involved and the competent authority for the religious gives the approval. The choice and its approval require the confirmation of the Congregation for Divine Worship.

4026   31. From now on there is to be only one principal patron. Another may be added as a secondary patron for some particular reason. As far as possible, the same is to hold for patrons already appointed; the requirements in nos. 32 and 33 are to be taken into account.

The choice of two or more saints as principal patrons is permitted if they are listed together in the calendar.

4027   32. The following are no longer to be honored as patrons: a primary or secondary patron established in the past because of peculiar historical circumstances; also those chosen either because of some extraordinary event, e.g., a plague, war, or other disaster, or because of a special, but now extinct *cultus*.

4028   33. The prescriptions in no. 30 being observed, a new patron may be chosen, after thorough deliberation and consultation with those concerned, whenever the *cultus* and devotion toward a patron duly chosen or received from time immemorial have ceased or whenever nothing is known for sure about the patron.

---

[17]   See CIC can. 1278. See also SCR, *Decreta authentica* no. 526, 23 March 1630, no. 1.

[18]   See SCR, *Decreta authentica* no. 526, 23 March 1630, nos. 2–3.

34. Churches may have as their titles: the Trinity; our Lord Jesus Christ, invoked under one of the mysteries of his life or name that are already part of the liturgy; the Blessed Virgin Mary, also under some designation taken up into the liturgy; the angels; saints listed in the Roman Martyrology or properly canonized, but not the blessed, without an apostolic indult.[19]

4029

Just as there is to be only one principal patron, from now on there is to be only one title for a church, except in the case of saints listed together in the calendar.

Whenever it is decided to change the title of a church, the rules laid down in no. 33 on patrons are followed.

35. The solemnity of one of the titles of the Blessed Virgin Mary that is not in the General Calendar or a particular calendar is observed either on 15 August or on another date in those calendars on which there is a Marian celebration that fits in better with the particular title, for example, by reason of great pilgrimages, popular traditions, etc.

4030

The same method is to be followed in the choice of a date for the solemnity of titles of the Lord not listed in the General Calendar or a particular calendar.

B. SOLEMNITIES WITH THE HOLYDAY PRECEPT SUPPRESSED

36. Solemnities to which the holyday precept is attached are celebrated, even when the Apostolic See has abolished the precept, on their date in the General Calendar, except when they must or may be transferred to another date according to the General Norms for the Liturgical Year and the Calendar.[20]

4031

Should any conference of bishops judge it advisable to assign to one of these solemnities, e.g., All Saints, another date that fits in better with local traditions or the culture of a people, the conference may propose the matter to the Apostolic See.

37. When solemnities for which the holyday precept has been abolished are assigned a proper date other than the one in the General Calendar, they must also be listed in particular calendars on that same date.

4032

C. ROGATION AND EMBER DAYS

38. It is for the conference of bishops to decide for its own region how the celebrations corresponding to the rogation and ember days are to be observed. The conference is therefore to decide the time and number of days for rogations and also the time, number, and purpose of the days corresponding to the ember days.

4033

For such days the conference is likewise to specify which votive Masses are to be used on those days from among those given in the new edition of the Roman Missal for various needs and occasions.[21]

---

[19] PR (ed. 1961), *Ordo ad ecclesiam dedicandam et consecrandam* [see also DOL 547 no. 4372].

[20] See GNLYC nos. 7 and 56 f at the end [DOL 442 nos. 3773 and 3822].

[21] See GNLYC nos. 46–47 [DOL 442 nos. 3812–13].

CHAPTER IV

REVISION OF PROPERS OF MASSES AND OFFICES

A. PROPERS OF MASSES

4034   39. In the revision of the proper texts for Masses it is useful to make a distinction between texts belonging to the Missal and those belonging to the Lectionary.

4035   40. The texts of the Missal are: the entrance antiphon, opening prayer, prayer over the gifts, preface, communion antiphon, prayer after communion. The solemn blessing or prayer over the people may also be included.

a. The point of the entrance antiphon is to direct the thoughts of the congregation to the meaning of the celebration.[22] The text should be such that it can be recited whenever it is not sung and can serve as a basis for the priest's introductory instruction. The communion antiphon should in some way express the place of communion within the eucharistic mystery.

b. Among the prayers, only the opening prayer has direct bearing on the saint being celebrated. It is well to give prominence to the saint's characteristics, some aspect of the saint's spiritual life or apostolate, without resorting to trite phrases, e.g., about miracles or establishing a religious institute. The prayer over the gifts and the prayer after communion, however, bear directly on the eucharistic mystery; any mention of the saint must only be incidental. The new Roman Missal provides samples of prayers over the people and solemn blessings that may replace the usual final blessing on certain days or occasions.

c. The preface must express the proper theme of thanksgiving that characterizes the days or seasons to which the preface belongs. It does not have the literary form of a petition but of praise glorifying God through Christ the Lord because of some particular element in the mystery of salvation.

Any proper preface is to be included with the text of the Mass to which it belongs.

4036   41. With regard to the readings, care must be taken that on solemnities there are three; that the Old Testament is not read during the Easter season; that proper readings assigned for a Mass always have a proper responsorial psalm and a proper acclamation or verse before the gospel.[23]

4037   42. The newly reformed Roman Missal and Lectionary contain many texts in the commons that may be used to advantage in revising propers, especially when the propers do not contain texts that should be kept because of their spiritual or pastoral importance or because of their antiquity.

B. PROPERS OF OFFICES

4038   43. A very important element and characteristic of the divine office is the reading about the life of the saint or from ecclesiastical writers that is to be composed or selected for every solemnity, feast, or memorial. This reading may be drawn from the writings of the Fathers or ecclesiastical writers; for the offices of the saints and the blessed, it may be an excerpt from their own writings or a statement on the

---

[22] See GIRM nos. 25, 26, 29 [DOL 208 nos. 1415, 1416, 1419].

[23] See GIRM nos. 37–38 [DOL 208 no. 1427–28].

marks of their spiritual life or apostolate. A biographical sketch appears as a preliminary to this reading, but it is not to be read as part of the office.

Preparation or revision of the hagiographical readings are to ensure that they are short and restrained (e.g., usually not more than one hundred twenty words). Generalities are to be avoided and anything false or odd deleted or corrected.

As an aid to meditation on the text, the reading is to have with it an appropriate responsory, either proper or from a common.

44. Other elements that can give the office its character as a proper, especially on solemnities and feasts, are the invitatory, the antiphons, especially in morning and evening prayer, and the intercessions (*preces*). Any existing proper hymns may be kept, but with the emendations as required. The prayer is always the same as the opening prayer of the Mass.

For the revision or the new composition of these parts there are many texts in the reformed Roman Breviary that may be used.

C. FORMAT OF OFFICES AND MASSES

45. The Latin and the vernacular *editio typica* of the Roman Missal and Breviary should serve as guides for the format of the proper of offices and Masses. This applies to the general layout, the typography for the texts and headings, and the designation of the books of the Bible and the writings of the Fathers.

46. It is practical for editions of the Roman Missal and Roman Breviary for a country or wider region to print celebrations proper to the entire country or region at their place among the celebrations of the General Calendar and to print in an appendix celebrations proper only to a particular section, for example, a locale or diocese.

47. To make proper provision for texts sung in the Mass and office, there is to be an indication of the melodies that may be employed in view of the norms governing the style of the particular chants and the options to substitute one text for another. For Masses there is to be an indication of the psalm for the entrance and the communion and the antiphon and psalm to be sung at the presentation of the gifts.

CHAPTER V
LITURGICAL PRIVILEGES AND INDULTS

48. Privileges and indults conflicting with the new norms for the liturgy are to be considered as revoked. If, however, any Ordinary deems it necessary to renew one or other of these privileges and indults, he is to make a proper request for this, indicating the reasons.

Privileges and indults not in conflict with the new norms continue in force; these too, however, must be revised in order to ensure their safe continuance.

49. It will be the responsibility of every Ordinary to transmit to this Congregation for review and renewal, in addition to the particular calendar and propers of offices and Masses, a list of privileges in liturgical matters (a copy of the document of concession is to be attached).

50. In the printed copies of propers, a list of liturgical privileges is to be included so that this is available to anyone using the proper.

4039

4040

4041

4042

4043

4044

4045

On 23 June 1970 Pope Paul VI graciously approved this entire Instruction and each of its parts and directed that it be carefully carried out by all concerned.

▶ 426. SC DIVINE WORSHIP, General Instruction of the Liturgy of the Hours, 2 February 1971:

| nos. 167: | Readings about the saints in particular propers [no. 3597]. |
| 241–243: | Office according to a proper calendar [nos. 3671–73]. |

▶ 216. SC DIVINE WORSHIP, Notification *Instructione de Constitutione*, on the Roman Missal, the book for the liturgy of the hours, the General Calendar, 14 June 1971:

| no. 6: | Particular calendars [no. 1775]. |

▶ 248. SC DIVINE WORSHIP, Circular Letter *Eucharistiae participationem*, on the eucharistic prayers, 27 April 1973:

| no. 10: | Insertions proper to dioceses and religious institutes [no. 1984]. |

482. SC DIVINE WORSHIP, **Letter** *Novo Calendario Romano* to bishops and general superiors of religious, to speed up preparation of the particular calendars of dioceses and religious institutes, as well as of proper texts for the Roman Missal and *The Liturgy of the Hours*, February 1974: Not 10 (1974) 87–88.

4046   After promulgation of the General Roman Calendar (which is now included in the reformed Roman Missal), this Congregation issued norms to be followed in drawing up proper calendars for each country, region, diocese, or religious institute. These are in the "Instruction on the revision of particular calendars and the proper of offices and Masses," 24 June 1970.[a]

Calendars and the propers of Masses and offices are to be prepared, according to the norm of that Instruction no. 4, "within five years of the publication of the new Roman Missal and Breviary."[b]

Since the Roman Missal has been published as well as *The Liturgy of the Hours* in the *editio typica* of 16 April 1971, calendars and propers must be prepared by 16 April 1976.[c] This Congregation is confident, however, that the work will move more quickly and that within the year 1974 all calendars and propers, both of dioceses and religious institutes, will have been revised and confirmed.

For the completion of this work the Congregation considers it useful to recall the rules to be followed.

4047   1.   The revisers of calendars and propers are to keep in mind the norms given in the General Instructions of the Roman Missal and of the Liturgy of the Hours, the

---

a   See DOL 481.

b   DOL 481 no. 3999.

c   Decree of promulgation dated 11 April 1971; see DOL 427.

General Norms for the Liturgical Year and the Calendar, and the Instruction on particular calendars.

They will also need some familiarity with the reformed liturgical books in order to grasp how the norms mentioned have been applied in the editing of those books, especially in the case of euchological texts.

2.   Careful theological, historical, and pastoral research by experts in these disciplines must precede the revision of calendars and propers.   4048

3.   The diocese or religious institute most closely associated with offices and Masses common to several dioceses or religious institutes or to both dioceses and religious institutes should compose the texts and the others involved accept them. There should not be different texts for such Masses and offices unless special considerations indicate othewise.   4049

4.   Once they have been revised after consultation with the clergy, faithful, and members of religious communities concerned, calendars and propers are to receive their approval from the competent territorial authority (the national conference of bishops for the calendar and the propers of a country; the local Ordinary for a diocesan calendar; the superior general for the calendar of a religious institute). They are then to be submitted to this Congregation for confirmation. Three copies of the Latin text and of the translation are to be sent, as well as: 4050

— a report of the work done;

— the criteria followed;

— the names of experts involved;

— a copy of the former calendar and propers.

483. SC SACRAMENTS AND DIVINE WORSHIP, **Norms** *Calendaria et Propria*, on particular calendars and the propers of Masses and offices, December 1977: Not 13 (1977) 557–558.

Calendars and the propers of Masses and offices were to be prepared and confirmed, according to the norm of the Instruction *Calendaria particularia*, 24 June 1970, no. 4, within five years of the date of publication of the new Roman Missal and of the Breviary.[a]   4051

Yet six years after the *editio typica* of both the Roman Missal and *The Liturgy of the Hours*, the work of revising the calendars and propers of both dioceses and religious institutes is still not finished.

In order that the work in question may be completed as quickly as possible by all those involved, this Congregation considers it useful to recall the principles and norms already issued on this matter.

[Text of February 1974 repeated in full: see DOL 482]

---

[a]   See DOL 481 no. 3999.

Section 6. Holy Years

SUMMARY (DOL 484–494). The texts in this section could have been presented in conjunction with those in Chapter Three, Section 7, B, on indulgences. They are placed instead in the chapter on the liturgical year in order to indicate more than the penitential aspect of the observance of holy years. This observance, first of all, marks the whole liturgical cycle during the year as a period of special grace; second the two Holy Years of 1966 and 1975 were occasions of euchological enrichment of the Roman liturgy (see DOL 207, 249–251, 487, 493).

Section 6. Holy Years: A. Jubilee of 1966

SUMMARY (DOL 484–489). This subsection includes Paul VI's apostolic constitution declaring the Jubilee (DOL 484) and motu proprio extending it (DOL 489), two texts on indulgences from the Apostolic Penitentiary (DOL 485, 486), and from the Congregation of Rites a decree promulgating the Mass of the Jubilee (DOL 487) and a decree on its celebration on days of the first class (DOL 488).

484. PAUL VI, **Apostolic Constitution** *Mirificus eventus*, declaring and promulgating an extraordinary Jubilee, 1 January – 29 May 1966, in all the dioceses of the Catholic world, 7 December 1965: AAS 57 (1965) 945–951 (excerpts).

4052   A wonderful occurrence has just come to an end, the Second Vatican Ecumenical Council, to which the whole Catholic family and even the entire human community has for four years ever more intently directed its thoughts and interest. That singular event seems to us to demand that the memory of the extensive conciliar sessions become lasting for all; further and more importantly, that Christians be imbued with a willingness to observe the Council's teachings.

As we have already announced, nothing seemed to us a more effective means for the purpose intended than the celebration of an extraordinary Jubilee. We regarded this as the best measure, first, for bringing about the public thanksgiving assuredly due to God for the rich gifts showered on his Church, both during the anxious yet joyous period of preparation and during the four years of the Council's lively and successful deliberations. We chose the Jubilee, second, to ask for divine blessings upon the present period especially, when the current wave of joy and expectancy among people permits us to hope that they will be immensely benefited by the Council. [. . .]

Walking in the footsteps of our predecessors and on the basis of consultation with our esteemed brothers, the cardinals of the holy Roman Church, by the authority of almighty God, of the blessed apostles Peter and Paul, and by our own, for the glory of God, the salvation of souls, and the advancement of the Catholic Church — we therefore declare by this letter, we promulgate, and we wish to be taken as declared and promulgated an extraordinary Jubilee in each and all the dioceses of the Catholic world, to begin on 1 January 1966 and to end on the feast of Pentecost, 29 May 1966.

Having thus announced this special period of heavenly salvation and this opening of the fonts of heavenly graces, we regard it as our duty to set forth the principal objectives we seek from the opportunity thus provided.

4053   Like our predecessors in similar situations, we look above all for a marked change of heart on the part of the faithful that must be deeply interior. This means their cultivation of the virtue of repentance, accompanied by sacramental confession, by which they are washed, as it were, by Christ's precious blood. This change cannot take place unless Christians, in order to be raised up, are joined as closely as possible to the divine Redeemer, who through the unbloody renewal of the sacrifice of the cross and through the access he gives us to his eucharistic body builds up our souls and brings them to perfection, so that we may reach a real and genuine share in the divine life. Thus we have solid hope that the Jubilee promulgated may move the best of Christians to ever greater heights and all good Christians to fulfill the duties of daily life in keeping with God's commandments. May it also come to pass during this time of devotion that those who are separated from the source of grace, and especially those who have unwisely forgotten or rejected faith in God, may use the special opportunity now given to them and make their peace with God. [. . .]

The Council we have just closed has deserved the title "the Council on the Church," since in it the Bride of Christ has reflected deeply on the God-given mandate to care for souls. Similarly, we regard the announced Jubilee to have as its specific purpose that in all the faithful, both of the hierarchic and the lay order, the *sensus Ecclesiae* should increase and that there be a more enlightened and intense awareness of this in the minds of all. It is absolutely imperative, therefore, that during the coming Jubilee the Church, following the course we once said the

Council must follow, not fail "to look deeply into itself; meditate on the mystery of its own being; thoroughly examine the teaching on its origin, its nature, its fulfillment of its mandate, its purpose. Even though it is well known to the Church and has been elaborated and disseminated during the past century, that teaching can never be said to be completely mastered and understood."[3]

We are firmly convinced that there can be no surer way of accomplishing these   4054
salutary proposals than having the jubilee celebration in each diocese centered and, so to speak, housed in the cathedral church, with the bishop, the father and shepherd of the flock entrusted to him, as the central figure.

The diocesan cathedral, which in its architectural and artistic beauty often stands as a splendid affirmation of our ancestors' zeal for art and religion, has as its primary mark of dignity that, as the ancient name itself signifies, it houses the *cathedra* of the bishop. The bishop's chair is like a link with the unity, order, power, and truth-bearing magisterium of Peter. This also is why the cathedral church, in the majesty of its building, is a symbol of the spiritual temple that is built up in souls and is resplendent with the glory of divine grace. As St. Paul says: "We are the temple of the living God."[4] The cathedral, furthermore, should be regarded as the express image of Christ's visible Church, praying, singing, and worshiping on earth. The cathedral should be regarded as the image of Christ's Mystical Body, whose members are joined together in an organism of charity that is sustained by the outpouring of God's gifts. We read in the feast of the Dedication of a Church according to the Ambrosian Rite: "This is the mother of all, ennobled by the number of her children. Daily through the Holy Spirit she brings them forth unto God. The whole world is filled with her offspring. She offers them up to heaven on their cradle, the cross. This is that sublime city standing on a mountaintop visible to all, shining before all eyes."[5]

In keeping with the symbolism of the cathedral, then, the faithful during the coming Jubilee should go there individually or in groups to assist at the liturgy, or to listen to preaching, or to gain the special remission of the punishment due to sin that by tradition are called indulgences.

The Jubliee, as we have said, must be celebrated with the bishop as its central, sustaining figure and we urge all to gather round him in great numbers as true children of the Church.

At the conclusion of the Council the bishops returned to their sees burning   4055
with a holy zeal, intent on inspiring their people to put the conciliar teachings into practice. Accordingly, let the faithful in every diocese, both priests and all the Christian people, express gratitude to their bishop for his conscientious and unflagging work during the Council. Let them give him renewed evidence of their filial reverence and loyalty. Let them above all pledge their cooperation in prayer, their way of life, and their self-sacrifice. In a word, clergy, religious, and laity of every kind, bound together in unity, should eagerly submit themselves to the wise and fatherly rule of their bishops. To borrow the words of Vatican Council II, the bishops "should sanctify the Churches entrusted to them in such a way that their Churches will fully manifest the sense of Christ's universal Church."[6]

---

3   Paul VI, Encycl. *Ecclesiam suam*, 6 Aug. 1964: AAS 56 (1964) 611.

4   2 Cor 6:16.

5   *Missale Ambrosianum*, preface for the feast of the Dedication of a Church.

6   CD no. 15 [DOL 7 no. 194].

The bishop, in turn, by his authority presides in the cathedral over the assemblies of the Christian family under his care, gives them standards for carrying out the apostolate, enkindles their fervor to do the works of charity and to pray. What he thus achieves is that in the chief church of the diocese the outward celebration of the liturgy becomes a striking manifestation of the people's inner union in mind and heart and of the harmony between the flock and its shepherd.

In the cathedral during the coming days of salvation the bishop is to provide special series of sermons explaining the decrees of Vatican Council II, missions, and special services for clergy and laity, especially during Lent as a preparation for Easter. These programs are meant to arouse in all the earnest desire for self-renewal. [. . .]

485. APOSTOLIC PENITENTIARY, Decree *Cum plures Episcopi*, on the indulgences of the extraordinary Jubilee of 1966, 20 December 1965: AAS 57 (1965) 1018.

4056   Many bishops have urgently requested that the jubilee indulgences granted to the faithful by the Apostolic Constitution *Mirificus eventus* might also be gained by those for whom it is difficult to go to the cathedral church because of particular circumstances of place or of time. Therefore, Pope Paul VI, through the decree of this Penitentiary, has graciously given to all local Ordinaries who judge that it will contribute to the success of the Jubilee the faculty of designating, in addition to the cathedral, one or more churches of the diocese where the faithful may gain the indulgences of the Jubilee.

486. APOSTOLIC PENITENTIARY, Declaration *Cum non pauci*, on the indulgences for the extraordinary Jubilee of 1966, 5 January 1966: AAS 58 (1966) 105–106.

4057   Many local Ordinaries have presented problems or queries regarding the jubilee indulgences granted by the Apostolic Constitution *Mirificus eventus*. Therefore, at the explicit mandate of Pope Paul VI, this Penitentiary, in order to dispel all perplexities about the meaning of the Constitution, declares that a plenary indulgence may be gained by all the faithful who go to confession and communion and pray for the pope's intention:

4058   1. as often as they attend at least three lectures on the decrees of Vatican Council II in a church or other suitable place;

4059   2. as often as they devoutly attend at least three of the sermons for a parish mission in any church;

4060   3. in keeping with the norm of the decree of the Apostolic Penitentiary, 20 December 1965,[a] as often as they devoutly assist at a Mass celebrated with some solemnity by any bishop in the cathedral or in another church designated by the local Ordinary;

4061   4. once only during the time of the extraordinary Jubilee, if they devoutly visit the cathedral or another church designated by the local Ordinary, in

---

[a]   See DOL 485.

accord with the same decree, and there recite the profession of faith in any lawfully approved form;

5. if they devoutly receive the papal blessing imparted once, on the occasion of the principal jubilee celebration, by the local bishop or by his coadjutor or auxiliary or even by another bishop rightfully delegated to do so. 4062

If the local Ordinary should wish to designate one or more other churches in addition to the cathedral for the gaining of the jubilee indulgences, it would be well for him to choose principal churches of the diocese, for example, the primary church of a deanery or some major shrine. 4063

Further, it is particularly desirable that the lectures on the decrees of Vatican Council II, which should be held in each parish church or elsewhere, culminate in a pilgrimage to the cathedral or to another church designated by the local Ordinary in accord with the same decree. All the faithful of the same sector or of the same category should try to go there together if at all possible.

In virtue of CIC can. 935 all confessors have the power to commute the works of devotion just indicated for the gaining of the indulgences in favor of those of the faithful who are prevented from performing them by reason of some legitimate obstacle.

487. SC RITES, Decree *Extraordinarium Iubilaeum*, promulgating the Mass for the Jubilee of 1966, 6 January 1966: Not 2 (1966) 42.

The extraordinary Jubilee that Pope Paul VI declared and promulgated for celebration as a kind of crown of Vatican Council II in all the dioceses of the Catholic world has been planned in such a way that "it should be centered and, so to speak, housed in the cathedral, with the bishop, the father and pastor of the flock entrusted to him, as the central figure" (Motu Proprio *Mirificus eventus*).[a] It is appropriate, then, that the liturgical texts for use in the main eucharistic celebrations of this Jubilee more pointedly reflect and give prominence to the important idea of the bishop and the Church. 4064

The Mass texts that the present Decree promulgates may be used: 4065

1. whenever, Mass is celebrated with some solemnity by any bishop in the cathedral or, in accord with the decree of the Apostolic Penitentiary, 20 December 1965,[b] in another church designated by the local Ordinary, for those faithful who come to such churches in order to gain the jubilee indulgences;

2. whenever Mass is celebrated in any church at the conclusion of a mission or of the special lectures on the decrees of Vatican Council II, as specified in the declaration of the Apostolic Penitentiary, 5 January 1966;[c]

3. whenever Mass is celebrated for the faithful belonging to the same place or category who come as a body to the cathedral or, as in no. 1, to another church designated by the local Ordinary, at the end of a mission or of special lectures on the decrees of Vatican Council II.

---

[a] See DOL 484 no. 4054; *Mirificus eventus* is an apostolic constitution, not a motu proprio.

[b] See DOL 485.

[c] See DOL 486 nos. 4058–59.

The Masses in question are to be celebrated in white vestments and with the rank of votive Masses of the second class, in accord with the *Codex rubricarum* no. 343. The *Credo* is always to be said, even if the celebration does not fall on a Sunday.

All things to the contrary notwithstanding.

▶   115.   CONSILIUM, Communication *Per Litteras Apostolicas*, on norms for translation of the Mass of the Jubilee, 21 January 1966.

488. SC RITES, **Decree** *Plures sacrorum Antistites*, on celebrating the Mass for the extraordinary Jubilee on liturgical days of the first class, 1 March 1966: Not 2 (1966) 94.

4066   Many bishops have pointed out to the Apostolic See that it is mainly on Sundays and holydays that the faithful go to the cathedral, or other churches designated by the local Ordinary, to gain the jubilee indulgences. They have consequently earnestly requested that the Mass text that the Congregation of Rites approved on 6 January 1966[a] and granted for use on such occasions as a votive Mass of the second class might be used even on liturgical days of the first class.

In virtue of faculties granted by Pope Paul VI and in consideration of the special situation pointed out, the Congregation of Rites kindly grants the request as a favor and in keeping with the terms of the recitals; all of Holy Week, Easter Sunday, Ascension, and Pentecost Sunday are excluded. In all other respects the rubrics are to be observed.

All things to the contrary notwithstanding.

489. PAUL VI, **Motu Proprio** *Summi Dei beneficio*, extending the extraordinary Jubilee of 1966, 3 May 1966: AAS 58 (1966) 337–341 (excerpts).

4067   Through God's gracious kindness the extraordinary Jubilee declared through the Apostolic Constitution *Mirificus eventus* in December 1965[a] has been welcomed with unbelievable approval by people of all nations. We can hardly express the joy this brings to our heart. This acceptance is a clear expression of how highly the Christian people regard the practices of religion and devotion. The acceptance is a reflection also of the high hopes that Vatican Council II, ended last year, has raised in the hearts of the faithful, of the intense interest it has aroused, and of the resolve to a better life it has inspired. This acceptance is also an expression of the veneration its children have for the Church and of their love for it as the tender mother of all, their protector, and their teacher.

4068   We have received reports from many places of how faithfully the measures proposed in *Mirificus eventus* have been carried out. The faithful have flocked to the churches, above all to the diocesan cathedral, to hear instructions on the teachings of the Council, or to go to confession or to receive the eucharist. At the same time they have surrounded with special respect the shepherds and fathers of their dioceses, returned from the Council and exhorting them to moral renewal. Undoubted-

---

[a]   See DOL 487.

[a]   See DOL 484.

ly these things will be the source of the greatest benefits not only for individual souls and the Catholic Church, but also for the entire human community.

But in some places the works proposed in *Mirificus eventus* could not be carried out, as was anticipated, within the time assigned, because of the great size of the region involved, the lack of priests, or other reasons.   4069

In order that the faithful in their care not be deprived of rich spiritual advantages, the Ordinaries of such places have therefore requested us to extend the limits of the extraordinary Jubilee promulgated in December 1966 for a longer period. We have gladly decided to accede to this request, since nothing is more important to us than that the Church's children share ever more fully in the limitless merits of the Redeemer and, strengthened by that help, continue in their effort to live a more upright life. Therefore, trusting in God's mercy and the authority of the apostles Peter and Paul, in virtue of the power to bind and to loose committed to us by God, we extend for the whole Catholic world the extraordinary Jubilee declared by the Apostolic Constitution *Mirificus eventus*. It will thus be prolonged from 29 May 1966, its scheduled expiration date, to the end of 8 December 1966, the feast of the Immaculate Conception. We rule that, like the purposes of the Jubilee, its privileges, faculties, and favors also remain the same. We remind all those concerned to consult *Mirificus eventus* often, so that nothing that belongs to the Jubilee will be forgotten [. . .]

Section 6. Holy Years: B. The Holy Year 1975

SUMMARY (DOL 490–494). There are 5 documents here: from Paul VI in 1973 an address and a letter announcing the forthcoming Jubilee (DOL 490, 491) and the papal bull proclaiming it (DOL 494), from the Apostolic Penitentiary a decree on the jubilee indulgences (DOL 492), and from the Council for the Holy Year with the Congregation for Divine Worship, the rite for celebrating the Jubilee in the local Churches during the year prior to its celebration in Rome (DOL 493).

490. PAUL VI, **Address** in St. Peter's, announcing the Holy Year 1975, 9 May 1973: AAS 65 (1973) 322–325 (Italian; excerpts).

4070   We wish today to make an announcement to you that we think important for the spiritual life of the Church. It is this. After prayer and reflection we have decided next year, 1975, to celebrate the Holy Year, in keeping with the twenty-five year cycle established for it by our predecessor Paul II, through the Bull *Ineffabilis Providentia*, 17 April 1470. [. . .]

We have asked ourself whether such a tradition as this should be continued in our times. They are so different from ages past and so affected, on the one hand, by the ways of religion that Vatican Council II introduced into ecclesial life and, on the other hand, by the indifference in practice of such a great portion of today's world toward the ritual of past centuries. But we were immediately convinced that celebration of the Holy Year can indeed be integrated coherently with the spiritual themes of the Council, which it is our obligation to put into effect. But we are also sure that the Holy Year is consistent with and can contribute to the tireless and loving effort that the Church devotes to the moral needs of our times, to the expression of its deepest aspirations, and even to a genuine sympathy for some of the manifestations of the spirit of this age. [. . .]

4071   The Holy Year has as its specific purpose a personal, inner, and therefore in some ways, outward renewal. The Holy Year is meant to be an available yet at the same time extraordinary form of therapy that must bring spiritual health to every conscience and, as a consequence, to social attitudes, at least to some degree. This is the general idea of the coming Holy Year and it is embodied in another central idea that is more particular and directed toward practice: the idea of reconciliation.

The term "reconciliation" connotes as its opposite, separation. What sort of separation must we overcome in order to achieve the reconciliation that is the condition for the hoped-for renewal of the Jubilee? What kind of separation? Perhaps it is enough simply to state the theme-word "reconciliation" in order to make us realize that our life is beset by too much separation, too much disharmony, too much disorder for us to be able to enjoy the gifts of individual and collective life as they are ideally meant to be.

Before all else we are in need of reestablishing a genuine, vital, and happy relationship with God, of being reconciled in humility and in love with him. From this first and constitutive harmony, the entire world of our experience can then be the expression of a need for reconciliation and can have its full impact in charity and justice to other persons in whom we will immediately acknowledge the right to be called our brothers and sisters. Reconciliation then can develop in other limitless and real spheres of existence: the community of the Church itself, society, politics, ecumenism, peace . . . . If God permits us to celebrate the Holy Year, it will present many relevant ideas for us to elaborate.

4072   At this moment we limit ourself to one important point about the structure of this Holy Year. According to centuries-old custom, the Holy Year has Rome as its focal point and so will this one, but with one new departure. The prescribed conditions for gaining the particular spiritual benefits will this time be granted to the local Churches ahead of time. Thus each local Church throughout the world will be able to begin immediately to take advantage of this great opportunity for renewal and reconciliation and so to prepare better for its culminating and decisive period to be celebrated in Rome in the year 1975. This Roman observance will give its accustomed meaning to the traditional pilgrimage to the tombs of Peter and Paul for those who can and wish to undertake it. The important and salutary Jubilee of repentance and spirituality, involving the entire Church and marked by the grant-ing of special indulgences, will begin on the coming feast of Pentecost, 10 June 1973. In former Holy Years the extension of such indulgences took place after the celebrations at Rome; in this one it will precede them. It will be clear to everyone that this innovation also involves the intention of showing, through a more mani-fest and effective communion, respect for the local Churches, the living members of the single, universal Church of Christ. [. . .]

491. PAUL VI, **Epistle** *Iniziandosi ufficialmente* to Cardinal M. de Fürstenberg, on the great universal Jubilee declared for 1975, 31 May 1973: AAS 65 (1973) 357–360 (Italian).

The offical beginning in all the Churches of the world of that great surge of spiritual renewal that will culminate in Rome during 1975 is 10 June 1975, Pentecost. We therefore wish to lay before you, Lord Cardinal, whom we have put in charge of the Central Committee for the Holy Year, the objectives we have in mind, the spirit we should like to see prevail in those who respond to our invitation, and the results we hope can be achieved through the grace of the Holy Spirit, in whose name and under whose light we now set out on this course.

4073

As we have stated ever since our first announcement on 9 May 1973,[a] through this Jubilee we intend the renewal of people and their reconciliation with God. Both occur above all at the deep level of that inner sanctuary where conscience receives the call to conversion or *metanoia* through faith and repentance[1] and to the search for the fullness of charity.

God himself in his boundless mercy, after redeeming the world through Jesus Christ his Son, calls all of us without exception to share in the effects of the redemption[2] and through his Holy Spirit intervenes to bring about his salvation in them.[3]

The Church's conviction is that only God's inner action can bring about recon-ciliation between people. This is the social dimension of the New Covenant that must extend to all sectors and levels of life in the relationships between individuals, families, groups, classes, nations. To the extent possible to human frailty and the imperfection of earthly institutions, that reconciliation is meant to become a leaven of peace and universal unity.

The Church is accordingly committed to bring it about that the power of Christ's redemption will strengthen the bonds of faith and charity, in the blood of his cross,[4] between the faithful, within dioceses, parishes, religious communities, and other centers of the Christian life and apostolate, as well as within the Churches still separated from us. Then the Pentecost of grace will become also the Pentecost of a new mutual love.

Such is the spirit we hope to see pervade the whole celebration of the Holy Year.

---

[a] See DOL 490.

[1] See Mk 1:15.

[2] See 1 Tm 2:4.

[3] See Rom 8:10ff.

[4] See Col 1:20.

4074   For this reason, too, we look for a rediscovery of the value of penitential practices as a sign and means of grace and as a commitment to that interior renewal that in the sacrament of penance — used and administered in accord with the Church's rules — receives its full effectiveness so that individuals and communities may again find their way along the path of salvation.[5]

    In our view, the pilgrimage may well be the expression, the occasion, and, as it were, the synthesis of all these practices, which have as their crown the celebration of the eucharist. In the genuine tradition of Christian asceticism pilgrimages have always had devotion and expiation as their motives. The pilgrimage can still today be inspired by the same motives, both when it takes a form like the ancient pilgrimages to Rome and when it involves use of the modern media of communication.

    It is essential that the mark of the pilgrimage, besides prayer and penance, be the practice of love of neighbor. For that is a clear proof of love for God[6] and it must be expressed in spiritual and corporal works of mercy toward those most in need by the faithful individually, by their associations, by ecclesial communities and institutions. In this way the Holy Year will extend the Church's charity and will be a portent of a renewal and a reconciliation that is universal in scope.

4075   In order that the purposes stated may be more readily achieved, it is our wish that the practice of the pilgrimage be carried out in all the local Churches, in cathedrals, in national and diocesan shrines. Such pilgrimages can serve as intermediary steps that will eventually, in 1975, lead to Rome, the visible center of the universal Church. At Rome groups representing the local Churches will end this journey of renewal and reconciliation, will venerate the tombs of Peter and Paul, renew their loyalty to the Church of Peter; and we, please God, will have the joy of welcoming them with open arms and together with them will bear witness to the Church's unity in faith and charity.

    It is our burning desire that in this journey to "the wells of salvation"[7] our children in full union with the Church of Peter will be joined, in ways possible to them, by other followers of Christ and by all those who, along different and seemingly distant paths, seek out the one God with upright conscience and good will.[8]

    The specific programs for the Holy Year pilgrimage and other practices aimed at furthering renewal and reconciliation will be drawn up for the local Churches by the conferences of bishops, with proper consideration being given both to local mentalities and customs and to the true purposes of the Holy Year as we have here stated them.

    On our part, we ask of pilgrims that, after praying for our own intentions and those of the college of bishops, they take part locally in a solemn, community celebration or spend time in meditation before the Lord and at the end recite or sing the Lord's Prayer and the *Credo* and a prayer to the Blessed Virgin Mary.

    Through these sincere and simple expressions the faithful in the local Churches will make actual a real conversion and will profess their willingness to continue and to become stronger in charity toward God and neighbor. In reply, so to speak, as the lowly servant of Christ the Redeemer, we will duly grant the *donum indulgentiae*. Also to be recipients of this gift are those of our children who cannot take part in the Holy Year pilgrimage because they are prevented by illness or some

---

[5]   See Acts 16:17.

[6]   See 1 Jn 4:20, 21, 3:14.

[7]   See Is 12:3.

[8]   See Acts 17:27.

other serious reason; they have only to join it in spirit through the offering of their prayers and sufferings.

Through the Holy Year the Church, exercising its "ministry of reconciliation"[9] offers a choice opportunity, a special invitation, because all whom the Church's word reaches and, more importantly — as is the object of our most fervent desires and prayers — those whom the inner, inexpressible touch of grace reaches, have the way to share in Christian joy, the effect of the saving power of the Redeemer.

We end this letter by expressing the hopes we place in the celebration of the coming Holy Year. These, we repeat, are renewal and reconciliation as inner realities and as the actualization of unity, mutual love, and peace that from souls renewed and reconciled in Christ will spread within the Church and toward the whole human community, through the channels of charity whose fruits are justice, goodness, mutual pardon, the gift of self and of personal possessions for the sake of others. In a word, our hope and our expectation is that a renewed Christian sense of human existence will purify souls and will permeate the world for the salvation of all.

These, Lord Cardinal, are the matters we wished to inform you of on the eve of an important period of the history of the Church in our own times, the symbol of which, at the proper moment, will be the opening of the Holy Door. We ask you to share these thoughts with our brothers in the episcopate. We bless you and all those whom our summons reaches, from the fullness of the heart of a father and of the humble servant of the servants of God.

492. APOSTOLIC PENITENTIARY, **Decree** *E.mus Cardinalis Praeses*, stating the requirements to gain the "donum Indulgentiae" in the various local Churches on the occasion of the Holy Year, 24 September 1973: AAS 65 (1973) 615.

The Cardinal President of the Central Council for the Celebration of the Holy Year has requested the Apostolic Penitentiary to lay down the requirements for gaining the *donum Indulgentiae* promised by Pope Paul VI[a] in order to foster the spirit of reconciliation and renewal that are the themes of this Holy Year.

In virtue of the mandate of the Pope, the Apostolic Penitentiary grants the following, namely, that from the First Sunday of Advent 1973 until the date of the opening of the Holy Year in Rome, the faithful of the various local Churches can gain:

1. a plenary indulgence, at times to be fixed by the conferences of bishops, if they make a pilgrimage to the cathedral, or to other churches designated by the local Ordinary, for a solemn, community celebration;[b]

2. a plenary indulgence, likewise at times to be fixed by the conferences of bishops, if as part of a group (for example, of students, family members, fellow artisans or workers, members of pious associations) they visit the cathedral or other churches designated by the local Ordinary and remain there in prayerful meditation for an appropriate interval, to be concluded with the recitation or

4076

4077

---

[9]   See 2 Cor 5:18.

[a]   See DOL 491 no. 4075.

[b]   See DOL 490 no. 4072.

singing of the Lord's Prayer and the Apostles' Creed and a prayer to the Blessed Virgin Mary;

3. a plenary indulgence if, should illness or other serious cause keep them from taking part in a pilgrimage, they join it in spirit and offer their prayer and suffering to God.^{c}

For the Diocese of Rome, which should clearly be an example and incentive to the other ecclesial communities in this matter, the Apostolic Penitentiary decrees that the times and ways for gaining the plenary indulgence of the Jubilee are to be decided by the Cardinal Vicar of Rome.

All things to the contrary notwithstanding.

493. CENTRAL COUNCIL FOR THE HOLY YEAR and SC DIVINE WORSHIP, *Order for the Celebration of the Holy Year in the Local Churches,* **Introduction**, 1973: Not 9 (1973) 347–349; Vatican Polyglot Press, 1973.^{R1}

INTRODUCTION

4078   1.   The Holy Year is a year of grace in a special sense. For it is a time when the people of God draw near to the sources of salvation with a new and deeper purpose in order to reach spiritual renewal. This renewal is meant to make them more and more a priestly and prophetic people, a holy people, reflecting and bearing witness to the holiness of Christ himself, their Head.

Such a renewal takes place first of all in the local Churches, that is, the dioceses. With the bishop leading, the faithful of these Churches are invited to live

---

^{c} See DOL 491 no. 4075.

^{R1} Not 19 (1973) 345–346 has the following introductory note: The celebration of the Holy Year in the local Churches declared by Pope Paul VI is meant as a spiritual journey so that the faithful by stages, as in a pilgrimage, may come to a deeper understanding of the mystery of Christ and more intensely experience his immeasurable riches.

The pilgrim journey of the Holy Year leads the people of God to an experience of the mystery of the divine will. Wishing to save us all, God reveals himself "in many and various ways" (Heb 1:1); "when the fullness of time had come he sent his Son, the Word made flesh, anointed by the Holy Spirit, to preach the Gospel to the poor, to heal the contrite of heart" (see SC art. 5 [DOL 1 no. 5]) and to proclaim "liberty to the captives and the opening of the prison to those who were in chains, to proclaim the year of the Lord's favor" (see Is 61:1–2). Christ not only has uttered the call to salvation but has carried out the work of redemption, above all through his paschal mystery, in which "by dying, he destroyed our death and by rising restored our life" (MR, Easter Preface I). "For it was from the side of Christ as he slept the sleep of death on the cross that there came forth the sublime sacrament of the whole Church" (SC art. 5 [DOL 1 no. 5]). The Church continuously carries out the work of salvation, therefore, chiefly by means of the sacraments. Their hinges are: *baptism,* which incorporates us into Christ's paschal mystery; the *eucharist,* which is the perpetual memorial of Christ's death and resurrection, the sacrament of worship, the sign of unity, the bond of charity, the paschal meal (see SCR, Instr. EuchMyst, 25 May 1967, no. 3 [DOL 179 no. 1232]); *penance,* by which the faithful "obtain from God's mercy pardon for having offended him and at the same time reconciliation with the Church, which they have wounded by their sins" (LG no. 11 [DOL 4 no. 141].

The "journey of salvation" that today's Church continues by means of the liturgy and unfolds by means of the liturgical year is proposed for the particular Churches during the Holy Year in seven stages or periods of time. They may be observed over the course either of one week or of a longer time and even on individual, designated days. The high points are the call to repentance (stage III), the celebration of the sacraments of reconciliation (stage V) and of the eucharist (stage VII). In every case, all the elements are to be adapted to suit local situations and the pastoral requirements of assemblies of the faithful. [. . .]

In addition to the Introduction given here, Not ibid. 350–391 also includes other selections from the *Ordo Anni Sancti celebrandi in Ecclesiis particularibus* (Vatican Polyglot Press, 1973).

during the Jubilee in such a way that they strive toward genuine conversion. If they are more open and docile to the word of God, they will also be better prepared for reconciliation both with God and with their brothers and sisters in Christ, "through whom we have now received our reconciliation" (see Rom 5:11).

Dying for us and rising from the dead, Christ Jesus was made the minister of our reconciliation with the Father. He now continues to be offered through the ministry of the Church (see 2 Cor 5:18–19), which through the Holy Year urgently repeats St. Paul's summons: "We implore you, be reconciled to God" (2 Cor 5:20).

The closer we come to God in reconciliation, encountering the Father of kindness and mercy, the more we find in him the motive and the desire to be reconciled with each other during our journey on earth so that we may together traverse the way to our Father's house.

The clearest "sign" of this reconciliation is Christ's sacrifice. By eating one and the same bread and drinking the chalice together, the faithful individually and as communities prepare a gift for their brothers and sisters that is a mutual inspiration toward genuine love for the Church.

2. The path toward reconciliation within the local Churches has as its striking complement the path to Rome: that is, to the Church that was taught the Gospel by Peter and Paul and was hallowed by their blood. "Every Church, that is, all the faithful wherever they may be, must be in agreement with the Church of Rome because of its preeminence: in this Church the apostolic tradition has been always preserved by the faithful everywhere."[1]   **4079**

The result will be an intensification of the desire for building up the unity of the Mystical Body with the pope and with all his brother bishops of every race, language, and nation. Hunger and thirst after justice will be renewed. The resolve of the "peacemakers" will grow more ardent and their efforts to relieve the world's needs will quicken.

3. It is especially necessary that the spiritual journey of the Holy Year be in keeping with the spirit of the liturgy. Accordingly, the liturgical mystery and the sacraments of penance and the eucharist are to be regarded as the main supports for the attainment both of reconciliation with God and neighbor and of the self-renewal that the faithful individually and as ecclesial communities must achieve.   **4080**

4. As means of realizing such goals, certain reflections are here offered to the conferences of bishops, as aids for planning spiritual programs during the period of the Holy Year.   **4081**

These guidelines, however, may be adapted to the situation of the particular countries and to special assemblies of the faithful who take part in liturgies for the Jubilee. Such adaptations are to take into account and respect the educational and religious development of individuals and groups, their mentality, preferences, and requests.

5. The main concern of bishops must be to provide the faithful with the opportunity to receive spiritual renewal by means of the history of salvation as the Church reenacts it in the liturgy. There are suggestions and recommendations about catechesis on the more important themes that should be unfolded during the Holy Year. These are found principally in the readings of the Masses for the Sundays of 1973–1974 (*Path of Salvation*).   **4082**

---

[1] Irenaeus, *Adversus haereses* 3, 3, 2.

4083   6.   A general outline regarding the *Path of Reconciliation* during the Holy Year (*Week of Reconciliation*) is offered as a plan arranged over seven periods of time; the plan rests mainly on the two sacraments of Christian renewal, penance and the eucharist.

     This plan, however, is open to greater elaboration in order that the jubilee rites may be celebrated at the time of the liturgical year that is more apt to move the will, namely, Lent and the Easter season. The plan may also be compressed into a shorter period.

4084   7.   When communities or the individual faithful are unable to be present at all the rites if these are spaced over an entire year, the celebrations may be held in different periods throughout the Holy Year.

     A major concern of bishops should be that the desired purpose of the Holy Year is achieved in the most effective way possible, depending on the different situations and places. Then it will have a pronounced effect on the life and activities of the faithful and of civil society.

4085   8.   The specific plan offered here, designed in order that the faithful will undertake the spiritual journey of the Holy Year with greater fervor, may be adapted to different groups of people and put into effect at different periods of the year.

4086   9.   During the Holy Year the local Churches may engage in other programs not indicated here. The supreme goal is that the communities of the individual dioceses achieve the conversion and renewal for which the Holy Year is at once the source and the favorable time.

4087   10.   As they seek for self-renewal during the Holy Year, let the people of God not forget those who have gone before them in this earthly life.

     The effects of charity that the faithful achieve and, once reconciled with God, increase through constancy in seeking renewal, will also redound to the benefit of the dead: those who wait in expectation of the vision of God are assisted by the devout prayers and good works of the living to reach the home of the blessed more quickly.

     Accordingly, in all churches and places of worship, as the Holy Year gives impetus to the fervor of the faithful, those religious services are recommended that the Church prescribes as ways of imploring God's help for the faithful departed. Masses and prayers for the dead are of chief importance.

4088   11.   Prayers for the pope, as a bond of unity between all the Churches, should always be part of the liturgical celebrations attended by all the people and also of popular devotions. [. . .]

494. PAUL VI, **Bull** *Apostolorum limina*, declaring the Holy Year 1975 at Rome, 23 May 1974: AAS 66 (1974) 289–307 (excerpts).

4089   The *Apostolorum limina* designates the holy places of Rome, where the tombs of the apostles Peter and Paul are properly safeguarded and devoutly venerated. Through Peter and Paul, our "holy fathers," Rome became not only "the disciple of truth"[1] but also its teacher and the center of Catholic unity. Now as the celebration

---

[1]   See Leo the Great, *Sermo* 82, 1: PL 54, 422.

in Rome of the universal Jubilee draws near, these shrines of the apostles shine as a clear beacon, beckoning the minds of the faithful.

Through the course of the centuries the shrines of Peter and Paul have always moved the Christian people to a fervent faith and to bear witness to ecclesial communion, because in its foundation on the apostles by Christ Jesus[2] the Church recognizes its own identity and nature and in that foundation possesses the cause of its unity. [. . .]

I

The Holy Year 1975 seems to us to involve all the primary and chief motives of past Jubilees and to summarize them in the two themes that we set for it when first announcing the Holy Year in an address on 9 May 1973.[13] These themes are *renewal* and *reconciliation*. We have presented them for the reflection of pastors and faithful as they were to celebrate the Jubilee in the local Churches; we have also addressed our own exhortations and catechesis to these themes. But the spiritual aspirations they both proclaim and the profound and important realities they express will be more vividly brought to realization in Rome. There the pilgrims to the tombs of the apostles Peter and Paul and to the monuments of other martyrs will more readily come in contact with the ancient sources of the Church's faith and life. The goal will be that they turn back to God in repentance, find their charity strengthened, and enter into closer union with their brothers and sisters through God's grace.

    4090

Renewal and reconciliation involve before all else the inner life, for the root of every good and, unfortunately, of every evil lies in the deepest recesses of the soul. Conversion must therefore take place within as a *metanoia*, that is, a change of course, a change in each person's attitudes, choices, and way of living.

But also in regard to the Church as a whole, ten years after the end of Vatican Council II, the coming Holy Year seems to us to stand as the terminus of one period, devoted to self-examination and reform, and as the beginning of a new period when the Church must be built up by developments in matters of theology, spirituality, and pastoral activity. This whole endeavor must have as its basis the foundations laid and consolidated with so much effort during the past years in accord with the principles of new life in Christ and of the communion of all of us in him, who has reconciled us with the Father in his blood.[14]

The pilgrim journey to Rome of pastors and faithful representing all the local Churches will be a symbol of a new spiritual journey by which Christians will devote themselves to conversion and mutual reconciliation.

We are mindful of that sign of the inner, spiritual attitude of such pilgrims and of the effort with which the Christian people they represent are striving to renew their spiritual energies. As the steward of the word and grace of reconciliation, we therefore grant, to the extent that it is within our power, the *donum indulgentiae* to all those who undertake the pilgrimage to Rome as well as to those who are unable to do so but who join this pilgrimage in spirit. [. . .]

---

    [2]   See Rv 21:14.

    [13]   See Paul VI, Address to a general audience at St. Peter's in which he announced a universal Jubilee for 1975, 9 May 1973 [DOL 490 no. 4070].

    [14]   See 2 Cor 5:18–20; Rom 5:10.

II

4091   From the Church's very ancient practice it is clear that an indulgence, attached to a variety of Christian penitential works and practices, was granted in a special way on the occasion of pilgrimages to the places sanctified by the life, death, and resurrection of Christ our Redeemer and by the apostles' witness to faith. We are now carrying on this ancient, revered tradition, in keeping with the principles and norms that we have laid down in the Apostolic Constitution *Indulgentiarum doctrina*[16] and here briefly recall.

        Christ is our "Righteousness" and so he fittingly bears the title, our "Pardon." Because we are the minister of Christ the Redeemer, in keeping with the Church's established practice we happily extend the gift of pardon to those faithful who, after turning back to God with their whole heart, bear genuine living witness of their will to remain joined to God and neighbor by charity and to grow in it through their repentance, devotion, and help of others.[17] Their share in the gift of pardon derives from the fullness of the treasury of salvation that Christ the Redeemer himself established; "in him the atonement and merit of his redemption exist and are at work."[18] Christ's fullness, of which we have all received,[19] is the explanation of that "ancient dogma of the communion of saints, namely, that the life of each of God's children is in Christ and through Christ conjoined with the life of all other Christians. That sublime bond exists in the supernatural unity of the Mystical Body of Christ and constitutes the one mystical person."[20]

        "The hidden and gracious mystery of the divine plan unites us all through a supernatural bond: on this basis one person's sin harms the rest even as one person's goodness enriches them."[21] Using its power as the servant of Christ the Lord's redemption, the Church in conferring an indulgence imparts to the faithful within the communion of saints a share of Christ's fullness[22] and lavishly puts at their disposal the means of salvation.

        Thus, embracing and helping its weak and frail children like a mother, the Church bears them up; they find support as the whole Mystical Body of Christ works for their conversion by charity, example, and prayer. The faithful who are repentant experience in this special type of ecclesial charity a powerful help to cast off the old creature and put on the new: that is what true conversion and renewal mean.[23] "The purpose intended" by the Church "in granting indulgences is not only to help the faithful to pay the penalties due to sin, but also to cause them to perform works of devotion, repentance, and charity — especially works that contribute to the growth of faith and the good of the community."[24]

---

16   Paul VI, Ap. Const. *Indulgentiarum doctrina* [DOL 386].

17   See Paul VI, Epistle *Iniziandosi ufficialmente* to Card. M. de Fürstenberg . . ., 31 May 1973 [DOL 491 no. 4075].

18   Ap. Const. *Indulgentiarum doctrina* no. 5 [DOL 386 no. 3159].

19   See Jn 1:16.

20   Ap. Const. *Indulgentiarum doctrina* no. 5 [DOL 386 no. 3159]. See ST 3a, 48.2 ad 1 and 49.1.

21   Ibid. no. 4 [DOL 386 no. 3158].

22   See ibid. no. 8 [DOL 386 no. 3162].

23   See Paul VI, Epistle *Sacrosancta Portiunculae ecclesia* to Rev. C. Koser, on the seventh centenary of the Portiuncula Indulgence granted to St. Francis by Pope Honorius III, 14 July 1966: AAS 58 (1966) 631–634.

24   Ap. Const. *Indulgentiarum doctrina* no. 8 [DOL 386 no. 3162].

III

As the spokesman, therefore, of the Church's maternal attitude, we bestow the gift of a plenary indulgence on all those rightly disposed faithful who, after receiving the sacrament of penance and communion, pray for the intentions of the pope and the college of bishops:

1. if they make a pilgrimage to one of the patriarchal basilicas of Rome (namely, the Basilicas of St. Peter, of St. Paul-outside-the-Walls, the Archbasilica of St. John Lateran, the Basilica of St. Mary Major), or to another church or site in Rome designated by the competent authority, and there devoutly participate in a liturgical rite, especially the Mass, or in some other devotion (for example, the stations of the cross or the rosary);

2. if they visit, in a group or singly, one of the four patriarchal basilicas, and those only, for a period of meditation to be concluded with the Lord's Prayer, a profession of faith in any lawfully approved formulary, and a prayer to the Blessed Virgin Mary;

3. when prevented by illness or another serious reason from making a pilgrimage to Rome, if they join it in spirit wherever they are and offer prayers and their suffering to God;

4. when in Rome they are prevented by sickness or another serious reason from their own (ecclesial, familial, or social) community's liturgical celebration, other devotion, or visit to a basilica, as indicated in nos. 1 and 2, if they unite themselves in spirit with their community and offer prayers and their suffering to God.

During the year of the Jubilee, furthermore, other grants of indulgences remain in effect; but the rule that a plenary indulgence may be gained only once on any day stands.[25] All indulgences are always applicable to the dead in the form of a suffrage.[26]

For the same reasons, namely, to offer the faithful the fullest help for salvation and to serve the interests of pastors, especially confessors, we rule that confessors who take part in a jubilee pilgrimage may use those faculties they have received from the lawful authority in their own diocese[27] to hear the confessions, en route or in Rome, of Christians making the pilgrimage with them and of others who may join these pilgrims for confession. The right of the penitentiaries of the patriarchal basilicas regarding the confessionals there, however, remains intact.[28] These penitentiaries will receive special faculties from the Apostolic Penitentiary.

IV

We have already pointed out that the two main objectives for the Holy Year are spiritual renewal in Christ and reconciliation with God, also that both involve not only the inner life of each individual, but also the entire Church, and even, in some way, the whole human community. We therefore earnestly urge all those involved to reflect on these aims, to take the measures necessary to further them, and to contribute their cooperation so that the Holy Year may in truth result in achieving the renewal of the Church and in speeding the march toward the prize

4092

4093

---

[25] See *Ench. Indulg.* Norm 24, § 1 [DOL 390 no. 3216].

[26] See ibid. Norm 4 [DOL 390 no. 3196].

[27] See Motu Proprio *Pastorale munus* I, no. 14 [DOL 103 no. 725].

[28] See *Prima Synodus Romana*, 1960, art. 63.

that, in accord with the mind of Vatican Council II looking to the future, is especially dear to our heart. This is that penance, purification of spirit, and thus conversion to God have as their effect the increase of the Church's apostolic activity. [. . .]

A decade after Vatican Council II began the great and salutary work of reform in the areas of pastoral ministry, the practice of penance, and the liturgy, we think that now is the time to review this work and to increase its effects. With attention to those matters that have been firmly sanctioned by the Church's authority, the aim must be to examine the many different experiments carried out throughout the Church and to decide which ones should be regarded as really sound and legitimate. These are then to be put into full practice with great zeal, in keeping with the norms and methods that pastoral wisdom and the inspiration of genuine devotion suggest.

From Christian communities all over the world, throngs of pilgrims, both pastors and faithful, will come to Rome, joined in a common eagerness to receive the true gifts of Christ's grace and love. That will certainly provide excellent opportunities for presenting, sharing, comparing, and testing a wide variety of experiences, studies, and opinions. This will be especially the case if congresses and meetings are held, involving different levels of ecclesial communities and groups of experts, and combining the practice of prayer with the commitment to the apostolate.

We wish here to mention a particular need to find the right balance, as has already taken place on the liturgy in a remarkable way, that must prevail among the various elements of the contemporary pastoral ministry: namely, between tradition and the task of finding what is new; between the nature of the Christian apostolate as inherently religious and a practical effectiveness in all the areas of social life; between that spontaneity of action in the apostolate usually called charismatic and fidelity to the laws resting on the mandate of Christ and the bishops of the Church. Such laws, enacted by the Church and continually adapted to the different historical eras, permit particular experiments within the Christian community to be accepted in such a way that they are an advantage, not an obstacle, to the building up of the Body of Christ, which is the Church.[33] [. . .]

We also wish to point to the ever more pressing need of furthering the type of apostolate that addresses the conditions proper to each place and category of people. It should be carried out in such a way that it is not in conflict with the Church's necessary and traditional institutions, the diocese and the parish, but rather is integrated with them and brings the leaven of the Gospel into all the forms of the life of contemporary society — especially regarding workers, intellectuals, and the young. These new social forms often differ from the forms of ecclesial life received from our forebears, and seem alien to communities of the faithful bound together through prayer, faith, and charity.

It will be likewise necessary to give thought to methods of catechesis and of preaching the word of God that meet contemporary needs so that effective measures can be devised. Special attention must be given to the care required to ensure that the media of social communication contribute to human and Christian betterment for both individuals and communities. [. . .]

VII

4094   We wish, finally, to declare and to proclaim that reconciliation between Christians is one of the most important objectives of the Holy Year. Indeed, before all peoples are one day led to restoration to the grace of God *our Father*, it is essential to restore the unity of those already believing in Jesus Christ and accepting him as the

---

[33]   See Rom 15:2; 1 Cor 14:3; Eph 4:12.

Lord of mercy who delivers us and joins us together by the Spirit of love and truth. Therefore the Jubilee, which the Catholic Church has made part of its customs and usage as a most favorable period for the right renewal of individuals, can also serve as a period for advancing the unity of Christians.

We call to mind the teaching of Vatican Council II that commitment to the reconciliation of Christians and every effort on its behalf as well as all genuine ecumenism must necessarily derive from a change of heart. The very desire for Christian communion reaches its maturity from renewal of spirit, from self-denial, the full exercise of love, and fidelity to revealed truth.[38]

From that truth the whole ecumenical movement has its meaning and true motivation. The Catholic Church goes along with the ecumenical movement as far as it can and through that movement the Churches and Communities not yet fully joined with the Apostolic See search and long for that full communion that Christ prayed for. The responsibility and duty of the entire Church is to restore this unity in an integral communion of Churches.[39] The "year of grace" in this sense offers an opportunity for special repentance over the divisions between Christians, an occasion for renewal as it means the deeper experience of the life of holiness in Christ, an advance toward the hoped-for reconciliation through more frequent dialogues and the sound cooperation of Christians in working to achieve the world's salvation: "That they also may be in us, so that the world may believe."[40] [. . .]

On the occasion of the Holy Year 1975 the following liturgical texts were published: Eucharistic Prayers for Reconciliation [see DOL 249–251]; Mass for Reconciliation (Masses for Various Needs and Occasions, 22bis, *Missale Romanum*, 2nd *editio typica*, 1975 [see DOL 207]).

---

[38]   See UR no. 7: AAS 57 (1965) 97; ConstDecrDecl 256.

[39]   See UR no. 5: AAS 57 (1965) 96; ConstDecrDecl 255.

[40]   Jn 17:21.

Section 7. Other Documents

SUMMARY (DOL 495–499). The texts here are on particular points that bear some relation to the liturgical year. Three are on the annual World Day of Peace, an excerpt from a written message of Paul VI announcing its observance (DOL 497) and two texts on its liturgical celebration (DOL 498, 499). There are also two decrees of the Congregation of Rites, one adding a new invocation of the Holy Spirit to the Divine Praises (DOL 495) and one ordering the prayer *pro Papa* in the Mass on 30 June 1964 (DOL 496).

495. SC RITES, **Decree** *Piae invocationes*, on a new invocation of the Holy Spirit, the Paraclete, 25 April 1964: AAS 56 (1964) 338.

4095   Devout invocations in praise of God, our Lord Jesus Christ, and the Blessed Virgin Mary had their origin as ways of reparation for offenses against these names. But in time, because of the faithful's devotion, the character of praise became dominant and many petitions were added. In order that each person of the Trinity might receive acknowledgment in praise and supplication through this form of prayer, many requests have been presented to Pope Paul VI for the addition of an explicit invocation of the Holy Spirit.

Welcoming these requests, the Pope has ordered that in the Divine Praises, a reparation against blasphemy that begins with *Blessed be God*, the invocation *Blessed be the Holy Spirit, the Paraclete* is to be added in the eighth place, after the invocation *Blessed be Jesus in the most holy sacrament of the altar*.

All things to the contrary notwithstanding.

496. SC RITES, **Decree** *Die 30 Iunii*, prescribing the collect *pro Papa* on 30 June 1964, the anniversary of Paul VI's coronation, 9 May 1964.*

4096   On 30 June, the anniversary of Pope Paul VI's coronation and the feast of the Commemoration of St. Paul the Apostle, the collect *pro Papa* is to be said under separate conclusion at all Masses, whether sung or recited, no matter what rank the celebration has. All other rubrics are to be observed.

If a different Mass is celebrated on that same date, the collect *pro Papa* is to be said along with the collect of that Mass under a single conclusion.

497. PAUL VI, **Message** (written) to all people "of good will," urging their observance on 1 January of a World Day of Peace, 8 December 1967: AAS 60 (1967) 1097–1102 (Italian; excerpt).

4097   We address ourself to all people of good will in order to urge them to observe the "World Day of Peace" on the first day of the civil year, 1 January 1968. Our hope is that thereafter this observance would be repeated at the beginning of the calendar that marks and measures the passage of human life through time. The observance should be a symbol of hope and of promise for the reign of peace with its just and beneficent order over the course of the year to come. [. . .]

To you, our Esteemed Brothers in the episcopate. And to you, beloved sons and daughters, the faithful of the Catholic Church.

We also address the invitation just announced, namely, to dedicate a special observance on the first day of the civil year, 1 January 1968, to reflection and resolve about peace.

Such an observance must not change the liturgical calendar, which sets aside New Year's Day for veneration of Mary the Mother of God and the Holy Name of Jesus. But of course these holy and tender religious remembrances must shed their light of goodness, wisdom, and hope upon the petition, meditation, and efforts that

---

* Text, OR 10 May 1964, 8.

we direct toward the great and longed for gift of peace that the world so badly needs. [. . .]

498. CONSILIUM, **Publication** of liturgical texts for celebration of the World Day of Peace, 1969, December 1968: Not 4 (1968) 366 and 377.

Celebration of the World Day of Peace, 1 January 1969, will center on the theme, "The Advancement of Human Rights." To assist pastors and to make prayer meetings more effective, a group of liturgical texts has been assembled that may be used in keeping with the different situations and types of celebration.

4098

We present the French version of the texts in this four-part collection. [Texts follow.]

IV
VOTIVE MASS FOR PEACE

On 1 January throughout the world the Mass for the octave day of Christmas must be celebrated. But wherever there is a special celebration for peace, the votive Mass "for Peace" may be celebrated, at the discretion of the local Ordinary. This Mass may also be said as a votive Mass of the second class on days free of any obligatory feast.

499. SC SACRAMENTS AND DIVINE WORSHIP, **Letter** *Honori mihi duco*, to presidents of the conferences of bishops, on the norms for celebration of the World Day of Peace in 1978, 24 November 1977: Not 13 (1977) 609.

I have the honor of sending you the norms for celebrating Mass on the occasion of the World Day of Peace, which is observed annually on 1 January or on another day set by the conference of bishops.

4099

Wherever *there is some special celebration for peace*, the Mass for peace may be celebrated with the local Ordinary's permission; the texts are those in the Roman Missal (see MR, 2nd *editio typica*, 1975, 821–823 [RM, Mass for Peace and Justice]).

Special texts bearing on the theme proposed for each year will be sent beforehand as sample formularies for the general intercessions in the Mass for Peace.

CHAPTER SIX

MUSIC

SUMMARY (DOL 500–538). The Constitution on the Liturgy in chapter six did not limit itself to a strong and clear statement of the integral place music holds in the liturgical celebration; it also described the role of Gregorian chant, polyphony, the religious songs of the people, the setting of vernacular liturgical texts to music, and the playing of the organ and other musical instruments. The texts in the present chapter indicate the care during the reform of the liturgy to follow the direction given by the Constitution and the great intensity of the effort to make music contribute its distinctive enrichment to Catholic worship.

Section 1. General Documents

SUMMARY (DOL 500–528). There are 15 cross-references to more general documents and 29 texts specifically devoted to music in the liturgy.

—The major text is the instruction published in 1967 by the Congregation of Rites with the Consilium (DOL 508). It is a comprehensive treatment of music in worship and its contents have been adapted for use in all the new liturgical books.

—Two other important general statements are from the Consilium, one to the Italian episcopate (DOL 512), the other on the occasion of an international congress on liturgical music (DOL 515).

—In order to facilitate the use of Gregorian chant by the faithful the Congregation for Divine Worship made available a booklet with a basic repertoire of chants; the Congregation's accompanying letter and the introduction to *Iubilate Deo* are presented here (DOL 523, 524).

—This section also provides 24 other texts from Paul VI or the Secretariat of State that were addressed to particular groups or occasioned by special events. Together these texts contain a rich body of teaching on the importance of music in the liturgy.The texts are connected with the following organizations or occasions: the International Association of Sacred Music (DOL 500, 506, 522, 525); Universa Laus (DOL 502, 505, 507, 511); the Italian Society of Saint Cecilia (DOL 514, 519, 520, 528); the Review *Musica Sacra* (DOL 503); Italian congresses on sacred music (DOL 521, 526, 527); meetings of the members of church choirs (501, 509, 513, 516, 518) or the Little Singers (DOL 504, 510, 517).

500. PAUL VI, **Epistle** (autograph) *Nobile subsidium*, establishing canonically the Consociatio Internationalis Musicae Sacrae (CIMS; International Association of Sacred Music), 22 November 1963: AAS 56 (1964) 231–234.

4100   That noble support of the liturgy, the art of sacred music, has been in the past and remains still a major concern of the Apostolic See, as papal documents clearly attest, because music has always served as a special aid to devotion. The subject has been dealt with at length in St. Pius X's Motu Proprio *Tra le sollecitudini dell' officio pastorale*, 22 November 1913, Pius XI's Apostolic Constitution *Divini cultus sanctitatem*, 20 December 1928, Pius XII's Encyclical *Musicae sacrae disciplina*, 25 December 1955, and the norms of the same Pope's Instruction on Sacred Music and Liturgy, 3 September 1958. More recently Pope John XXIII, reminding us all of the measures taken by his predecessors, gave particular encouragement to the study and development of sacred music. His Epistle *Iucunda laudatio*, 8 December 1961, may be mentioned; it was addressed to Eugenio Anglés Pamies, President of the Pontifical Institute of Sacred Music on the occasion of the fiftieth anniversary of its foundation. Vatican Council II also included the matter of sacred music among the many topics it dealt with.[a]

      The manifold objectives of these popes included the following: to create closer ties between those dedicated to the art of sacred music and the Apostolic See; to put at the service of the Apostolic See an international institute that would keep it abreast of the needs of sacred music and also carry out the measures taken by the supreme authority of the Church in regard to sacred music; in a particular way, to provide missionaries with help for the solution of the difficult and important problem of music in mission lands and to coordinate efforts in this direction; finally, to promote publication of works on sacred music and studies of the Church's musical heritage.

      In his directives already mentioned,[1] our predecessor Pius XII recommended the increase of societies dedicated to sacred music and that they be formed into associations nationally and internationally in order to advance the study and art of sacred music.

      Carrying out this desire and acceding to the many similar wishes expressed by the bishops of several countries, we have decided and, by force of this autograph letter, decree the following.

4101   I.   The Consociatio Internationalis Musicae Sacrae is established canonically in the form of a "moral person," with its headquarters in Rome.

4102   II.   Its patron is the Cardinal Prefect *pro tempore* of the Congregation of Rites.

4103   III.   The objective for the Consociatio is to promote cooperation and concerted action of as many people as possible throughout the world and within every country for the cultivation of sacred music and its progress in accord with the Church's directives.

4104   IV.   Members of the Consociatio are of two kinds, members *iure proprio* and aggregate members.

      a.   The institutes of sacred music approved by the Apostolic See and the societies of sacred music recognized by ecclesiastical authority are members *iure proprio*.

---

    [a]   See DOL 1 nos. 112–121.

    [1]   Pius XII, Instruction on Sacred Music and the Liturgy, no. 117.

b.   Other institutes and societies accepted by the Consociatio's board of governors are aggregate members.

c.   Under the conditions laid down by the same board of governors, individuals may also be enrolled as aggregate members.

V.   The organization of the Consociatio consists of a general council, a board of governors, and a secretariat.   4105

a.   The general council consists of all those assembled for the meetings of the Consociatio.

b.   The board of governors, which presides over the general council and the Consociatio itself, is made up of a president and two vice-presidents. After being proposed by the general council, these three are appointed by the pope and hold office for three years, that is, until the next international meeting on sacred music, held in keeping with no. VI b.

c.   The secretariat consists of the secretary and the treasurer. Both are appointed by the board of governors; they have no fixed term and must reside in Rome.

VI.   a.   The general council has the supreme authority and makes all decisions on the business of the Consociatio. It reviews and approves the reports on the work done by the board of governors. It is responsible for the budget and the financial report.   4106

b.   The general council meets as a rule every three years at the international meeting on sacred music, unless another arrangement should seem advisable.

c.   In the general council all representatives of the members *iure proprio* as well as a delegate from each country, to be chosen by the bishops, have a decisive vote; all representatives have a consultative vote and may be nominated for offices.

VII.   The function of the board of governors is to carry out the decisions of the general council.   4107

VIII.   The secretariat deals with all the functions usual for the offices of a secretary and a treasurer, under the supervision of the president or, if necessary, of the two vice-presidents together. All concerned take full responsibility for their actions.   4108

IX.   The president or, if he is unable to do so, the two vice-presidents act in the name of the Consociatio.   4109

X.   The treasury of the Consociatio consists of membership contributions, donations and bequests of benefactors, profits from its publications.   4110

XI.   The board of governors must draw up bylaws carrying out these statutes and place them before the general council for debate and approval.   4111

We order and establish these statutes, all things to the contrary notwithstanding.

▶   1.   VATICAN COUNCIL II, Constitution on the Liturgy *Sacrosanctum Concilium*, 4 December 1963:

art. 36 § 1:	Use of the vernacular in a certain number of chants [no. 36].
39:	Competence of bodies of bishops regarding music [no. 39].
99:	Sung choral office or office in common [no. 99].

112–121:   Music [nos. 112–121].

▶   20.   PAUL VI, Motu Proprio *Sacram Liturgiam*, on putting into effect some prescriptions of the Constitution on the Liturgy, 25 January 1964:

art. II: Diocesan music commission [no. 280].

▶   79.   CONSILIUM, Letter *Le sarei grato* to papal nuncios and apostolic delegates, on the reform of the liturgy, 25 March 1964:

no. 3:   Repertoire of religious songs in the vernacular [no. 618].

501. PAUL VI, **Address** to the Institut Grégorien of Paris, on Gregorian chant, 6 April 1964 (French; excerpt).*

4112   After your celebration of the liturgy together here in the Vatican Basilica, we are happy to receive you and offer a few words of encouragement. [. . .]

The Pope's satisfaction in welcoming you this morning is not caused simply by the freshness of your youth; it rests on the privileged place you hold in the Church's liturgy.

By performing Gregorian chant, named for Pope St. Gregory the Great, you are ensuring a great beauty for the liturgical services of the Roman Church. This unison style of singing possesses in an eminent degree, as our predecessors have stressed, all the qualities called for by religious music. It enriches the splendor of the rites, it fosters the assembly's unity of spirit, and it disposes the assembly to praise God more perfectly.

Almost as much applies to polyphony, to the degree that it is free of anything theatrical, the meaning of the words remain understandable to the people listening, and the melody matches the liturgical rite it accompanies. [. . .]

Some of you may be uneasy about future applications of the Constitution on the Liturgy, which was adopted by the conciliar Fathers and which we promulgated on 4 December 1963. Those who are uneasy should read over again the passages on liturgical singing in this wonderful document, particularly these words. "The treasure of liturgical music is to be preserved and fostered with great care" (SC art. 114).[a]

There is, of course, a complete work of adaptation to be accomplished. But we know that you are generous, well disposed, and prepared for it by your gifts, your studies, your zeal; that you are thus faithful to the apt words of St. Augustine that are your motto: "Singing is for lovers" (*Serm.* 336, 1). Simply to see you is assurance of the love inspiring all of you. [. . .]

▶   23.   SC RITES (Consilium), Instruction (first) *Inter Oecumenici*, 26 September 1964:

nos. 42:   Approval of new chants in the vernacular for the celebrant and the ministers [no. 334].
57:                         Vernacular in sung Masses [no. 349].
97:                         Place for choir and organ [no. 389].

---

*   Text, OR 8 April 1964.
[a]   DOL 1 no. 114.

502. CONSILIUM, **Letter** to Bishop Charrière of Fribourg (Switzerland), on the occasion of the 4th Musical Study Week, on liturgical singing after Vatican Council II, 21 August 1965 (French).

To the organizers and speakers at the study week on singing in the reform of   4113
the liturgy and to all the participants, I send warm good wishes.

Cantare amantis est. This is the reason we want a liturgy that transforms the heart of the people of God into burning love for the Lord. We also want singing that raises the people's prayer on the wings of beauty, art, and inspiration.

Study the past if you wish a better future. But above all make sure that the style of song in the new liturgical awareness of the people of God does not lead to a loss of the past but that it is worthy of the sound and holy tradition of the Church and of divine worship to which the Church humbly devotes its service. [. . .]

▶   113.   PAUL VI, Address to translators of liturgical texts, 10 November 1965:

Translations in liturgical singing [no. 787].

▶   332.   SC SEMINARIES AND UNIVERSITIES, Instruction *Doctrina et exemplo*, on liturgical formation in seminaries, 25 December 1965:

nos. 51–59:   Musical training in the seminary [nos. 2722–30].

503. SECRETARIAT OF STATE, **Letter** of Cardinal A. Cicognani to the Review *Musica Sacra*, on the occasion of its tenth anniversary, excerpt on music in the liturgical reform, 1965: Not 2 (1966) 65 (Italian).

The conciliar norms have solemnly reconfirmed the full importance of "the   4114
ministerial function supplied by sacred music in the service of the Lord" (SC art. 112).[a] At the same time, these norms have opened up for those dedicated to sacred music new vistas and new problems, particularly concerning the faithful's active participation in public prayer by means of singing. That participation imposes a search for new forms of expression more closely adapted to the people's prayer. But it also demands that in every musical composition the values of genuine art are safeguarded. We must never forget that together with its religious inspiration sacred music must also possess, in the words of St. Pius X, that basic quality "integrity of form" (*Acta Pii X*, v. 1, 77). There is no other way for music to honor its exalted duty of bringing solemnity and beauty to liturgical celebrations and of leading souls to a closer contact with the divine.

To enable composers, at this stage of research and experiment, to hear the word of authority; to call their attention once more to the apostolic value of their contribution; to encourage their good efforts and arouse new energies in them — these are the important services that today more than ever await the work of the respected journal *Musica Sacra*.[1]

▶   32.   CONSILIUM, Letter *L'heureux développement*, on problems in the reform of the liturgy, 25 January 1966:

---

[a]   DOL 1 no. 112.

[1]   *Musica Sacra* no. 1, 1965, 4–5.

nos. 4:   Choirs [no. 426].
        5:                           Sacred quality of church music [no. 427].

▶   134. SC RITES (Consilium), Decree *Cum nostra aetate*, on editions of the liturgical
        books, 27 January 1966:

        no. 10:   Editions of books of Gregorian chant [no. 928].

504. PAUL VI, **Address** to the annual meeting of "Little Singers" (Loreto,
13–17 April 1966), excerpt on contributing to the solemnity of liturgical
worship, 18 April 1966: Not 2 (1966) 155–156 (French).

4115   You express this candor and innocent *joie de vivre* in your songs. You are the
"Little Singers" and that is also a reason why you are at home here: the Church
loves these songs and encourages those who are dedicated to them. [. . .]

        We salute you in a special way just after the great ecumenical Council held in
Rome. For among a great many other things, singing in the Church — as someone
has surely told you — was a concern of the Council. In particular the Council has
declared: "The treasure of sacred music is to be preserved and fostered with great
care. Choirs must be diligently developed. . . . Musicians and singers, *especially young
boys*, must be given a genuine liturgical training" (SC art. 114, 115).[a]

        Dear Little Singers, you see that the Council concerned itself with you. Now it
is your turn to be concerned with the Council, that is, to put its directives into
practice so that with always greater worthiness you may fulfill the function you
have been called on to carry out: to enrich the worship that the Church offers to
God in the liturgy.

        That calls for effort, work, many rehearsals, much patience. But you are doing
this for God and nothing in the whole world is better than working for God. [. . .]

505. SECRETARIAT OF STATE, **Letter** of Archbishop A. Dell'Acqua to J.
Gelineau, SJ, on the foundation of Universa Laus, 11 May 1966: Not 2
(1966) 199 (French).

4116   Pope Paul VI was pleased to receive the letter addressed to him by yourself and
by Don Luigi Agustoni and Erhard Quack, on the outcome of your meeting at
Lugano, and informing him of the foundation of an international study group,
called Universa Laus.

        Pope Paul has viewed this as a timely step at this period when the application
of the conciliar directives in the field of liturgical song and music raises so many
sensitive issues.

        The Pope also is pleased to extend to the newly established organization his
wishes for success and with fatherly encouragement he sends to its three presidents
and to all its members the apostolic blessing requested.

---

        [a] DOL 1 nos. 114, 115.

506. SECRETARIAT OF STATE, **Letter** of Cardinal A. Cicognani to Archbishop W. E. Cousins of Milwaukee, on the occasion of the Fifth International Meeting on Sacred Music (Milwaukee-Chicago, 21–28 August 1966), 12 August 1966: Not 2 (1966) 292–293 (English).

The Fifth International Congress of Sacred Music, to be held under the auspices of the "Consociatio Internationalis Musicae Sacrae" in collaboration with the Church Music Association of America, is most important because it will be the first such conference since the close of the Second Vatican Ecumenical Council.

4117

The Holy Father takes deep interest in the deliberations of this Congress, because it was he who established the "Consociatio" by his letter *Nobile subsidium Liturgiae* of 22 November 1963,[a] entrusting to it the responsibility of organizing these international congresses to promote progress and wise development in this important field.

The Fifth Congress has rightly been concentrated upon the great problems of sacred music arising from the decisions of the Council. In particular, various study sessions, directed by experts from the different nations and with invited specialists, including some not of the Catholic faith, will be devoted to studying in depth the theological, psychological, historical, and pastoral foundations of these principal problems. It is only by profound meditation upon these fundamental problems that an equitable application of the high directives of the Council can be made, thus avoiding hasty or improvised solutions which may, in the future, damage the very cause they seek to promote.

Among the consequences flowing from the conciliar decisions in the field of sacred music, outstanding is the extraordinary production of studies concerning the essential relations between religion and the musical art. It is fitting, then, that the Congress's study session should begin with this subject.

Other problems exist, however, of more immediate practical application. The most important of these, without a doubt, is the admission into the liturgy of the vernacular languages, as sanctioned by the Vatican Council in order to favor more active participation in the liturgy by the faithful. On this point, as well as on the others, the Congress will remain faithful to the Constitution on the Liturgy, which lays down general fundamental rules, permits certain concessions, clearly defines the motives underlying them and the limits within which they must be maintained.

4118

His Holiness is pleased to note that in its public sessions and practical executions, the Congress will illustrate the basic principle of the conciliar Constitution on the Liturgy, that, namely, of inserting all new liturgico-musical elements into those magnificent achievements which the Church created and has faithfully preserved throughout her long history. The Council called these the "treasury of sacred music" and commanded that it "be conserved and promoted with the greatest care."[b] Such conservation and promotion are evidently not intended to take place outside that environment in which and for which sacred music was born, but rather within the practical liturgical execution, for "the glory of God and the sanctification of the faithful,"[c] which the Constitution itself defines as the final purpose of sacred music.

Confident that the deliberations of the Congress, by God's assistance and guidance, will contribute richly toward the fulfillment of the decisions of the Sec-

---

[a] See DOL 500.

[b] See DOL 1 no. 114.

[c] See DOL 1 no. 112.

ond Vatican Council, and toward the momentous cause of sacred music, the Holy Father willingly imparts to Your Excellency, to the organizers of and all those participating in the Congress, his special, paternal Apostolic Blessing.

▶   84.   PAUL VI, Address to the members of the Consilium, 13 October 1966:

Music in the liturgy [no. 635].

507. CONSILIUM, Necessary **clarification** *Nell'aprile scorso*, on Universa Laus and the Consociatio Internationalis Musicae Sacrae, October 1966: Not 2 (1966) 249–251 (Italian).

4119   Last April seventy scholars, both priests and laypersons, of different nationalities, who are involved in the current reform of singing and music in the liturgy, met at Lugano. This was the fifth successive year that they organized such meetings, which combined study of liturgico-musical problems and celebrations of the liturgy.

At the end of the April meeting, the participants, with the approval of His Excellency Angelo Jelmini, Apostolic Administrator of Lugano, and with the support of the Most Reverend Raymond Tschudy, Abbot of Einsiedeln and president of the liturgical commission of Switzerland, agreed to found an association with the title Universa Laus, an International Study Group on Song and Music in the Liturgy.

On 21 April the board or "Praesidium" was elected and was made up of three scholars: the priests Fr. Luigi Agustoni and Joseph Gelineau, SJ, and Mr. Erhard Quack. On the same day these three sent Pope Paul VI a letter announcing the foundation of the Group, and expressing filial devotion, and requesting the apostolic blessing for themselves, the members, and the enterprise itself. On 11 May the Pope had the Secretariat of State respond with a cordial letter of good wishes and fatherly encouragement, as is usual in such instances.

This letter appeared in several periodicals, was partially reported as a note in a press release on the meeting at Lugano, and was published in *Notitiae* (no. 18, 1966, 199), official organ of the Consilium.[a]

Someone who was neither an officer nor a member of Universa Laus had the idea and expressed it in writing that the letter amounted to the Holy See's *official* approval of an association that, even though it came into being with the full, required authorization and consent of the competent authority, still originated through private initiative. Obviously this is incorrect: to give official approval for an organization of this kind the Holy See would have addressed itself to the local ecclesiastical authority and in the correct juridical form.

4120   It is well known that in the area of sacred music there already exists the Consociatio Internationalis Musicae Sacrae (CIMS), established 22 November 1963[b] and having its secretariat in Rome, Piazza S. Agostino 20 A. The purpose of the Consociatio is to join together all associations for sacred music, both present and future, receiving them as members and coordinating their activities in keeping with the Church's directives.

ᵃ   See DOL 505.

ᵇ   See DOL 500.

According to the statutes of the Consociatio, the member associations may even be international. In fact, the current state of the liturgical reform practically demands this. For there are mixed commissions, in accord with the Holy See's wishes, for the liturgical or pastoral problems of all the regions with the same language; international or transnational associations for music in the service of the liturgy are also useful and in some cases even necessary.

Universa Laus belongs to this type of association, with its own precise sphere, objectives, and methods, which are all clearly settled in its own statutes. After final completion of its structure and organization, Universa Laus will, of course, become a member of the Consociatio. This is the sense of a further communication on 13 July 1966 to Monsignor Johann Overath, representing the Consociatio, and to Joseph Gelineau, SJ, representing Universa Laus.

Therefore we are authorized to state that on the Holy See's part there has been   4121
no condemnation of Universa Laus nor is there any possibility of one, as has been recently and rashly claimed. Nor has there been any order given to suppress it, since Universa Laus is not a duplication (which would be useless and harmful) of the Consociatio. Rather it is an autonomous and distinct organization, with clearly defined interests, which exists, lives, and works in the same way as the other musical associations confederated under the Consociatio. It too will be joined to the Consociatio at the proper time, in harmony of purpose and activity.

The priests and laity who founded Universa Laus in their shared goals and their love of the liturgy have earned the Church's commendation. They may continue in holy joy the valuable work they have begun under the direction of the competent authority and in conformity with the Constitution on the Liturgy.

▶   38.   CONSILIUM, Editorial *Mécanique et Liturgie*, on mechanical devices in the liturgy, January 1967.[R1]

508. SC RITES, **Instruction** *Musicam sacram*, on music in the liturgy, 5 March 1967: AAS 60 (1967) 300–320; Not 3 (1967) 87–105; Vatican Polyglot Press (n. d.).

PREFACE

1.   Sacred music is one of the elements of liturgical reform that Vatican Council II   4122
considered thoroughly. The Council explained the role of music in divine worship and set out many principles and rules in the Constitution on the Liturgy, which has an entire chapter on the subject.

2.   The recently begun reform of the liturgy is already putting the conciliar enact-   4123
ments into effect. The new norms relative to the faithful's active participation and the structuring of the rites, however, have given rise to some problems about music and its ministerial function. It seems necessary to solve these in order to bring out more clearly the meaning of the relevant principles of the Constitution on the Liturgy.

3.   By mandate of Pope Paul VI the Consilium has carefully examined these   4124
problems and drawn up the present Instruction. It is not a collection of all the

---

[R1]   See also DOL 38 no. 443, note R32.

legislation on sacred music, but a statement simply of the principal norms that seem most needed at the present time. The Instruction also stands as a continuation and complement of the earlier Instruction of the Congregation of Rites on the correct carrying out of the Constitution on the Liturgy, which was also prepared by the Consilium and issued 26 September 1964.[a]

4125   4.   The reasonable expectation is that in welcoming and carrying out these norms pastors, composers, and the faithful, will strive with one accord to achieve the genuine purpose of sacred music, "which is the glory of God and the sanctification of the faithful."[1]

a.   Music is "sacred" insofar as it is composed for the celebration of divine worship and possesses integrity of form.[2]

b.   The term "sacred music" here includes: Gregorian chant, the several styles of polyphony, both ancient and modern; sacred music for organ and for other permitted instruments, and the sacred, i.e., liturgical or religious, music of the people.[3]

I.   GENERAL NORMS

4126   5.   A liturgical service takes on a nobler aspect when the rites are celebrated with singing, the ministers of each rank take their parts in them, and the congregation actively participates.[4] This form of celebration gives a more graceful expression to prayer and brings out more distinctly the hierarchic character of the liturgy and the specific make-up of the community. It achieves a closer union of hearts through the union of voices. It raises the mind more readily to heavenly realities through the splendor of the rites. It makes the whole celebration a more striking symbol of the celebration to come in the heavenly Jerusalem.

Pastors are therefore to strive devotedly to achieve this form of celebration. They would do well even to adapt to congregational celebrations without singing the distribution of functions and parts that more properly belongs to sung services. They are to be particularly careful that there are enough necessary, qualified ministers and that the people's active participation is helped.

The truly successful preparation of a liturgical celebration is to be achieved through the cooperation, under the parish priest (pastor) or rector, of all who have a part in the rites themselves and in the pastoral and musical elements of the celebration.

4127   6.   To give its true structure to the celebration of the liturgy requires, first, the proper assignment of functions and the kind of execution in which "each one, minister or layperson, who has an office to perform, does all of, but only, those parts which pertain to that office by the nature of the rite and the principles of liturgy."[5] But an additional requirement is exact fidelity to the meaning and character of each part and of each song. To achieve this end it is above all necessary that those parts

---

[a]   See DOL 23.

[1]   SC art. 112 [DOL 1 no. 112].

[2]   See St. Pius X, Motu Proprio *Tra le sollecitudini*, 22 Nov. 1903, no. 2: *Acta Sanctae Sedis* 36 (1903–04) 332.

[3]   See SCR, Instr. on sacred music and the liturgy, 3 Sept. 1958, no. 4: AAS 50 (1958) 633.

[4]   See SC art. 113 [DOL 1 no. 113].

[5]   SC art. 28 [DOL 1 no. 28].

which of their nature call for singing are in fact sung and in the style and form demanded by the parts themselves.

7.   The amount of singing determines the gradations between the most solemn form of liturgical celebrations, in which all the parts calling for singing are sung, and the most simple form, in which nothing is sung. For the choice of parts to be sung, those should be first that of their nature are more important and particularly those sung by the priest or other ministers and answered by the congregation or sung by the priest and congregation together. Later other parts, for the congregation alone or the choir alone, may be added gradually.   4128

8.   Whenever a choice of people for a sung liturgical celebration is possible, those with musical talent should obviously be preferred. This is particularly the case with the more solemn liturgical services, those involving more difficult music, or those to be broadcast on radio or television.[6]   4129

When no such choice is possible and the priest or minister does not have the voice to sing properly, he may recite, audibly and clearly, one or other of the more difficult parts belonging to him. This, however, is not to be done merely to suit the personal preference of the priest or minister.

9.   The choice of the style of music for a choir or congregation should be guided by the abilities of those who must do the singing. The Church does not exclude any type of sacred music from liturgical services as long as the music matches the spirit of the service itself and the character of the individual parts[7] and is not a hindrance to the required active participation of the people.[8]   4130

10. It is advisable that there be as much suitable variety as possible in the forms of celebration and the degree of participation in proportion to the solemnity of the day and of the assembly, in order that the faithful will more willingly and effectively contribute their own participation.   4131

11. The real solemnity of a liturgical service, it should be kept in mind, depends not on a more ornate musical style or more ceremonial splendor but on a worthy and reverent celebration. This means respect for the integrity of the rites, that is, carrying out each of the parts in keeping with its proper character. More ornate styles of singing and greater ceremonial splendor are obviously sometimes desirable, when they are possible. But it would be in conflict with the genuine solemnity of a liturgical service if such things were to cause any element of the service to be omitted, altered, or performed improperly.   4132

12. The Apostolic See alone has authority to establish, in accord with the norms of tradition and particularly of the Constitution on the Liturgy, those general principles that stand as the foundation for sacred music. The various lawfully-constituted territorial bodies of bishops and the bishops themselves have authority to regulate sacred music within the already defined limits.[9]   4133

---

⁶   See SCR, Instr. on sacred music and the liturgy, 3 Sept. 1958, no. 95: AAS 30 (1958) 656–657.

⁷   See SC art. 116 [DOL 1 no. 116].

⁸   See SC art. 28 [DOL 1 no. 28].

⁹   See SC art. 22 [DOL 1 no. 22].

II. THOSE WITH A ROLE IN LITURGICAL CELEBRATIONS

4134 13. Liturgical services are celebrations of the Church, that is, of the holy people united in proper order under a bishop or priest.[10] In a liturgical service the priest and his ministers have a special place because of holy orders; the servers, reader, commentator, and choir members, because of the ministry they perform.[11]

4135 14. Acting in the person of Christ, the priest presides over the gathered assembly. The prayers he sings or recites aloud are spoken in the name of the entire people of God and of all in the assembly;[12] therefore all present must listen to them with reverence.

4136 15. The faithful carry out their proper liturgical function by offering their complete, conscious, and active participation. The very nature of the liturgy demands this and it is the right and duty of the Christian people by reason of their baptism.[13]

This participation must be:

a. internal, that is, the faithful make their thoughts match what they say and hear, and cooperate with divine grace;[14]

b. but also external, that is, they express their inner participation through their gestures, outward bearing, acclamations, responses, and song.[15]

The faithful are also to be taught that they should try to raise their mind to God through interior participation as they listen to the singing of ministers or choir.

4137 16. A liturgical celebration can have no more solemn or pleasing feature than the whole assembly's expressing its faith and devotion in song. Thus an active participation that is manifested by singing should be carefully fostered along these lines:

a. It should include especially the acclamations, responses to the greetings of the priest and the ministers and responses in litanies, the antiphons and psalms, the verses of the responsorial psalm, and other similar verses, hymns, and canticles.[16]

b. Pertinent catechesis as well as actual practice should lead the people gradually to a more extensive and indeed complete participation in all the parts proper to them.

c. Some of the congregational parts may be assigned to the choir alone, however, especially when the people are not yet sufficiently trained or melodies for part-singing are used. But the people are not to be excluded from the other parts proper to them. The practice of assigning the singing of the entire Proper and Ordinary of the Mass to the choir alone without the rest of the congregation is not to be permitted.

4138 17. At the proper times a holy silence is also to be observed.[17] That does not mean treating the faithful as outsiders or mute onlookers at the liturgical service; it means

---

[10] See SC art. 26 and 41–42 [DOL 1 nos. 26 and 41–42]; LG no. 28 [DOL 4 no. 148].

[11] See SC art. 29 [DOL 1 no. 29].

[12] See SC art. 33 [DOL 1 no. 33].

[13] See SC art. 14 [DOL 1 no. 14].

[14] See SC art. 11 [DOL 1 no. 11].

[15] See SC art. 30 [DOL 1 no. 30].

[16] See SC art. 30 [DOL 1 no. 30].

[17] See SC art. 30 [DOL 1 no. 30].

rather making use of their own sentiments to bring them closer to the mystery being celebrated. Such sentiments are evoked by the word of God, the songs and prayers, and the people's spiritual bond with the priest as he recites the parts belonging to the celebrant.

18. Those of the faithful who are members of religious societies for the laity should receive special training in sacred song, in order that they may make an effective contribution to sustaining and furthering the congregation's participation.[18] But the training of all the people in this regard is to be carried out thoroughly and patiently as part of their complete liturgical formation. It should be suited to their age, condition, way of life, and stage of religious development and should begin from the very first years of their schooling in the primary grades.[19]

4139

19. Because of the liturgical ministry it exercises, the choir (*cappella musica; schola cantorum*) should be mentioned here explicitly.

4140

The conciliar norms regarding reform of the liturgy have given the choir's function greater prominence and importance. The choir is responsible for the correct performance of the parts that belong to it, according to the differing types of liturgical assembly and for helping the faithful to take an active part in the singing.

Therefore:

a. Choirs are to be developed with great care, especially in cathedrals and other major churches, in seminaries, and in religious houses of study.

b. In smaller churches as well a choir should be formed, even if there are only a few members.

20. Over the centuries the choirs of basilicas, cathedrals, monasteries, and other major churches have won high praise because they have preserved and developed the priceless treasury of sacred music. By means of rules issued specifically for them and reviewed and approved by the Ordinary such choirs are to be continued in order to carry out liturgical celebrations with greater solemnity.

4141

Nevertheless choir directors and parish priests (pastors) or rectors of churches are to ensure that the congregation always joins in the singing of at least the more simple parts belonging to them.

21. Especially where even a small choir is not possible, there must be at least one or more cantors, thoroughly trained to intone at least the simpler chants that the congregation sings and to lead and sustain the singing.

4142

Even in churches having a choir it is better for a cantor to be present for those celebrations that the choir cannot attend but that should be carried out with some degree of solemnity and thus with singing.

22. Depending on the established customs of peoples and on other circumstances, a choir may be made up of men and boys, of all men or all boys, of both men and women, and, where the situation really requires, even of all women.

4143

23. According to the design of the particular church, the place for the choir is to be such that:

4144

a. its status as a part of the community with a special function is clearly evident;

---

[18]   See SCR, Instr. InterOec, 26 Sept. 1964, nos. 19 and 59 [DOL 23 nos. 311 and 351].

[19]   See SC art. 19 [DOL 1 no. 19]. SCR, Instr. on sacred music and the liturgy, 3 Sept. 1958, nos. 106–108: AAS 50 (1958) 660.

    b. the performance of its liturgical ministry is facilitated;[20]

    c. full, that is, sacramental, participation in the Mass remains convenient for each of the members.

When there are women members, the choir's place is to be outside the sanctuary.

4145   24. In addition to musical training, choir members should receive instruction on the liturgy and on spirituality. Then the results of the proper fulfillment of their liturgical ministry will be the dignity of the liturgical service and an example for the faithful, as well as the spiritual benefit of the choir members themselves.

4146   25. Diocesan, national, and international associations for sacred music, especially those approved and repeatedly endorsed by the Apostolic See,[b] are to offer help for both the artistic and spiritual training of choirs.

4147   26. The priest, ministers, servers, choir members, and commentator are to sing or recite the parts assigned to them in a fully intelligible way, in order to make it easier and obvious for the congregation to respond when the rite requires. The priest and the ministers of every rank should join their own voices with those of the entire assembly in the parts belonging to the congregation.[21]

III. SINGING DURING MASS

4148   27. As far as possible, eucharistic celebrations with the people, especially on Sundays, should by preference take the form of a Mass with singing, even more than once in the same day.

4149   28. The distinction between the solemn, the high, and the low Mass, sanctioned by the 1958 Instruction (no. 3) remains in force, according to tradition and current law. But for pastoral reasons degrees of solemnity for the sung Mass are proposed here in order that it will become easier, in accord with each congregation's capability, to make the celebration of Mass more solemn through the use of singing.

These degrees must be so employed, however, that the first may always be used without the others, but the second and third never without the first. Thus in all cases the faithful are to be brought to take part fully in the singing.

4150   29. To the first degree belong:

    a. in the entrance rites

      — the priest's greeting and the congregation's response;

      — the opening prayer.

    b. in the liturgy of the word

      — the gospel acclamations.

    c. in the liturgy of the eucharist

      — the prayer over the gifts;

      — the preface, with the opening dialogue and the *Sanctus*;

      — the Lord's Prayer, with the invitation and embolism;

      — the greeting *May the peace of the Lord*;

---

    [20] See SCR, InterOec no. 97 [DOL 23 no. 389].

    [b] See DOL 500.

    [21] See SCR, InterOec no. 48 b [DOL 23 no. 340].

— the prayer after communion;

— the final dismissal.[R2]

30. To the second degree belong: 4151

    a. *Kyrie, Gloria, Agnus Dei*;

    b. profession of faith;

    c. general intercessions.[R3]

31. To the third degree belong: 4152

    a. songs for the entrance procession and for communion;

    b. chants after a lesson or epistle;

    c. *Alleluia* before the gospel;

    d. songs for the presentation of the gifts;

    e. the Scripture readings, except when it seems better not to have them sung.

32. In some places there is the lawful practice, occasionally confirmed by indult, of   4153
substituting other songs for the entrance, offertory, and communion chants in the
Graduale. At the discretion of the competent territorial authority this practice may
be kept, on condition that the songs substituted fit in with those parts of the Mass,
the feast, or the liturgical season. The texts of such songs must also have the
approval of the same territorial authority.

33. The assembly of the faithful should, as far as possible, have a part in singing   4154
the Proper of the Mass, especially by use of the simpler responses or other appropriate melodies.[R4]

[R2] Query: In the Instruction on music in the liturgy no. 29 c, do the dismissal formularies to be sung
include the priest's blessing? Reply: According to the recently reformed rite the final dismissal of the Mass
consists of the greeting of the congregation, the blessing, and the dismissal. According to the rubrics
presently in force, which reserve the singing of the blessing to a bishop, the greeting would be sung, the
blessing recited, and the dismissal also sung. The incongruity of such a procedure, however, is obvious —
the most important element, the blessing, would have the least solemnity. Previously the incongruity was
less striking, because the blessing came last and stood alone, separated from the dismissal formulary by
the silent recitation of the prayer *Placeat*. But now the blessing comes between the other two sung elements
and it seems out of place to switch back and forth between singing and recitation. Therefore in view of the
new arrangement of the elements or the rite of concluding the Mass, it seems proper in the interest of
uniformity for a priest also to sing the blessing at a sung Mass. Two melodies are provided here [301–303]
for the final blessing for insertion in the proper place and the parts reserved for a bishop are indicated. The
first melody is coordinated with the festive and ferial tones for prayers; the other, with the tone *ad libitum*:
Not 3 (1967) 300, no. 105.

[R3] Query: Is the invitation, *Let us pray* still to be used before the offertory? Reply: No. The general
intercessions preceding the offertory antiphon have as their introduction the priest's invitation to prayer.
Thus the *Let us pray* in question would be a duplication. This is why the *Variationes in Ordinem Missae
inducendae* have emended the *Ordo Missae* no. 18. In the interest of uniformity, the point applies to all
Masses, even when there are no general intercessions: Not 3 (1967) 303, no. 106.

[R4] Query: Many have inquired whether the rule still applies that appears in the Instruction on sacred
music and the liturgy, 3 Sept. 1958, no. 33: "In low Masses religious songs of the people may be sung by
the congregation, without prejudice, however, to the principle that they be entirely consistent with the
particular parts of the Mass." Reply: That rule has been superseded. What must be sung is the Mass, its
Ordinary and Proper, not "something," no matter how consistent, that is imposed on the Mass. Because
the liturgical service is one, it has only one countenance, one motif, one voice, the voice of the Church. To
continue to *replace the texts of the Mass being celebrated* with motets that are reverent and devout, yet out of
keeping with the Mass of the day (for example, the *Lauda Sion* on a saint's feast) amounts to continuing an
unacceptable ambiguity: it is to cheat the people. Liturgical song involves not mere melody, but words,
text, thought, and the sentiments that the poetry and music contain. Thus texts must be those of the
Mass, not others, and singing means singing the Mass not just singing during Mass: Not 5 (1969) 406.

Of all the chants for the Proper the one coming between the readings as a gradual or responsorial psalm is particularly significant. It is intrinsically a part of the liturgy of the word and thus is to be sung with the whole assembly sitting, listening, and even, if possible, taking part.

4155   34. When there is to be part-singing for the chants of the Ordinary of the Mass, they may be sung by the choir alone in the customary way, that is, either a cappella or with instrumental accompaniment. The Congregation, however, must not be altogether left out of the singing for the Mass.

In other cases the chants of the Ordinary may be divided between choir and congregation or between one part of the congregation and another. The singing is then done by alternating verses or in any other way that takes in most of the entire text. It is important in any such arrangement, however, to attend to the following. Because it is a profession of faith, the *Credo* is best sung by all or else sung in a manner that allows the congregation's proper participation. Because it is an acclamation concluding the preface, the *Sanctus* should as a rule be sung by the entire assembly along with the priest. Because it accompanies the breaking of the bread, the *Agnus Dei* may be repeated as often as necessary, especially in concelebrations and it is appropriate as well for the congregation to have a part in it, at least by singing the final *Grant us peace.*

4156   35. The congregation should join the priest in singing the Lord's Prayer.[22] When it is in Latin, it is sung to the traditional melodies; the melodies for singing it in the vernacular must have the approval of the competent territorial authority.

4157   36. Any one of the parts of the Proper or the Ordinary in a low Mass may be sung. Sometimes it is even quite appropriate to have other songs at the beginning, at the presentation of the gifts, and at the communion, as well as at the end of Mass. It is not enough for these songs to be "eucharistic" in some way; they must be in keeping with the parts of the Mass and with the feast or liturgical season.

IV. SINGING THE DIVINE OFFICE

4158   37. Celebration of the divine office in song is more in keeping with the nature of this prayer and a sign of both higher solemnity and closer union of hearts in praising God. In keeping with the explicit wish of the Constitution on the Liturgy,[23] therefore, the singing of the office is strongly recommended to those who carry it out in choir or in common.

At least on Sundays and holydays it would be well for them to sing some part of the office, especially morning prayer and evening prayer, the two principal hours.

Other clerics living together in centers of study or coming together for retreats or for other meetings should take the opportunity to sanctify their assemblies through the singing of some parts of the divine office.

4159   38. In the singing of the divine office both the law in force for those bound to choir and particular indults remain unchanged. But the principle of "progressive" solemnity is applicable; namely, the parts that of their nature are more directly designed for singing (dialogues, hymns, verses, canticles) are sung and the other parts recited.

---

[22]   See SCR, Instr. InterOec no. 48 g [DOL 23 no. 340].

[23]   See SC art. 99 [DOL 1 no. 99].

39. The faithful are to be invited, and also instructed through proper catechesis, to   4160
celebrate some parts of the divine office together on Sundays and holydays, especially evening prayer or whatever other hours are customary in different places or
groups. All the faithful, especially the better educated, are to be guided through
proper instruction to use the psalms in their Christian meaning for prayer. In this
way the faithful will be led gradually to a fuller appreciation and use of the
Church's public prayer.

40. Formation in the use of the psalms is particularly important for members of   4161
institutes professing the evangelical counsels, in order that they may possess a rich
resource for nurturing their spiritual life. They should, if possible, celebrate the
principal hours of the office, and even with singing, so that they will take part more
completely in the public prayer of the Church.

41. Clerics must retain Latin in the choral celebration of the office, in conformity   4162
with the norm of the Constitution on the Liturgy that is based on the centuries-old
tradition of the Latin rite.[24]

The Constitution on the Liturgy,[25] however, also makes provision for the
faithful, nuns, and other nonclerical members of institutes professing the evangelical counsels to use the vernacular in the office. Attention should therefore be given
to providing melodies for the vernacular singing of the divine office.

V. SACRED MUSIC IN THE CELEBRATION OF THE SACRAMENTS AND
SACRAMENTALS, IN SPECIAL SERVICES OF THE LITURGICAL YEAR, IN
CELEBRATIONS OF THE WORD OF GOD, AND IN POPULAR DEVOTIONS

42. The Council has stated as a principle that whenever rites according to their   4163
specific nature make provision for communal celebration involving the presence
and active participation of the faithful, this way of celebrating them is to be preferred to a celebration that is individual and, so to speak, private.[26] From this it
follows that singing becomes very important, in that it more strikingly expresses
the "ecclesial" aspect of a celebration.

43. Certain celebrations of the sacraments and sacramentals are particularly sig-   4164
nificant in the life of a parish community: confirmations, ordinations, marriages, the
consecration of a church or altar, funerals, etc. As far as possible, therefore, they
should be carried out with singing, so that even the solemnity of the rite may
contribute to a greater pastoral effectiveness. Every precaution is to be taken, however, against introducing into a celebration under the guise of solemnity anything
merely profane or out of keeping with divine worship; this applies particularly to
marriages.[R5]

44. Celebrations that have a distinctive character in the course of the liturgical   4165
year should also be marked by greater solemnity through singing. The rites of Holy
Week should be given a unique solemnity; through the celebration of the paschal
mystery these rites lead the faithful to the very center of the liturgical year and of
the liturgy itself.

---

[24]   See SC art. 101, §1 [DOL 1 no. 101]. SCR, Instr. InterOec no. 85 [DOL 23 no. 377].

[25]   See SC art. 101, §§2 and 3 [DOL 1 no. 101].

[26]   See SC art. 27 [DOL 1 no. 27].

[R5]   See DOL 349 no. 2986, note R1.

4166   45. Suitable melodies are also to be provided for the liturgy of the sacraments and sacramentals and for other special services of the liturgical year. These melodies are meant to favor a more solemn celebration even in the vernacular, in keeping with the norms of the competent authority and the capability of each liturgical assembly.

4167   46. Music also has great power to nurture the faithful's devotion in celebrations of the word of God and in popular devotions.

The model for celebrations of the word of God[27] should be the liturgy of the word at Mass.[28] Among the important resources for popular devotions are the psalms, musical works taken from the treasury of the past and the present, the religious songs of the people, the playing of the organ and other suitable instruments.

Musical pieces that no longer have a place in the liturgy, but have the power to touch religious feeling and to assist meditation on the sacred mysteries are very well suited for use in popular devotions and especially in celebrations of the word of God.[29]

VI. LANGUAGE FOR USE IN SUNG LITURGIES;
PRESERVING THE TREASURY OF SACRED MUSIC

4168   47. According to the Constitution on the Liturgy, "particular law remaining in force, the use of the Latin language is to be preserved in the Latin rites."[30]

At the same time "use of the mother tongue . . . frequently may be of great advantage to the people."[31] Therefore "the competent ecclesiastical authority . . . is empowered to decide whether and to what extent the vernacular is to be used. . . . The *acta* of the competent authority are to be approved, that is, confirmed by the Apostolic See."[32]

These norms being observed exactly, there should be a wise use of the kind of participation that is best suited to the capabilities of each assembly.

Pastors should see to it that, in addition to the vernacular, "the faithful are also able to say or to sing together in Latin those parts of the Ordinary of the Mass belonging to them."[33]

4169   48. Once the vernacular has been introduced into the Mass, local Ordinaries should determine whether it is advisable to retain one or more Masses in Latin, particularly sung Masses. This applies especially to great cities in churches with a large attendance of faithful using a foreign languages.

4170   49. The norms of the Congregation of Seminaries and Universities on liturgical formation in seminaries[c] are to be observed in regard to use of Latin or of the vernacular in liturgical celebrations in a seminary.

---

27   See SCR, Instr. InterOec nos. 37–39 [DOL 23 nos. 329–331].

28   See SCR, Instr. InterOec no. 37 [DOL 23 no. 329].

29   See no. 53 of this Instruction.

30   SC art. 36, § 1 [DOL 1 no. 36].

31   SC art. 36, § 2 [DOL 1 no. 36].

32   SC art. 36, § 3 [DOL 1 no. 36].

33   SC art. 54 [DOL 1 no. 54]. SCR, Instr. InterOec no. 59 [DOL 23 no. 351].

c   See DOL 332 no. 2686.

The norms in the Motu Proprio *Sacrificium laudis*, 15 August 1966,[d] and this Congregation's instruction on the language for religious in celebrating the divine office and the conventual or community Mass, 23 November 1965,[e] are to be followed in their liturgical services by the members of institutes professing the evangelical counsels.

50. In liturgies to be celebrated in Latin: 4171

a. Because it is proper to the Roman liturgy, Gregorian chant has pride of place, all other things being equal.[34] Proper use should be made of the melodies in the *editiones typicae* of this chant.

b. "It is desirable also that an edition be prepared containing simpler melodies for use in small churches."[35]

c. Other kinds of melodies, either for unison or part-singing and taken from the traditional repertoire or from new works, are to be held in respect, encouraged, and used as the occasion suggests.[36]

51. In view of local conditions, the pastoral good of the faithful, and the idiom of   4172 each language, parish priests (pastors) are to decide whether selections from the musical repertoire composed for Latin texts should be used not only for liturgies in Latin but also for those in the vernacular.

52. To preserve the treasury of sacred music and to encourage new styles of sacred   4173 song, "great importance is to be attached to the teaching and practice of music in seminaries, in the novitiates and houses of study of religious of both sexes, and also in other Catholic institutions and schools" and particularly in institutes of higher studies specifically established for this purpose.[37] Especially to be promoted are the study and use of Gregorian chant; its distinctive qualities make it an important foundation for a mastery of sacred music.

53. New compositions are to conform faithfully to the principles and rules here set   4174 forth. "They are to have the qualities proper to genuine sacred music; they are not to be limited to works that can be sung only by large choirs, but are to provide also for the needs of small choirs and for the active participation of the entire assembly of the faithful."[38]

Those parts of the traditional treasury of music that best meet the require-ments of the reformed liturgy are to receive attention first. Then experts are to study the possibility of adapting other parts to the same requirements. Finally, parts that are incompatible with the nature of the liturgical service or with its proper pastoral celebration are to be transferred to an appropriate place in popular devo-tions and particularly in celebrations of the word of God.[39]

---

[d] See DOL 421.

[e] See DOL 114.

[34] See SC art. 116 [DOL 1 no. 116].

[35] SC art. 117 [DOL 1 no. 117].

[36] See SC art. 116 [DOL 1 no. 116].

[37] SC art. 115 [DOL 1 no. 115].

[38] SC art. 121 [DOL 1 no. 121].

[39] See no. 46 of this Instruction.

VII.   COMPOSING MUSICAL SETTINGS FOR VERNACULAR TEXTS

4175   54. Translators of texts to be set to music should take care to combine properly
conformity to the Latin and adaptability to the music. They are to respect the idiom
and grammar of the vernacular and the proper characteristics of the people. Composers of new melodies are to pay careful heed to similar guidelines, as well as the
laws of sacred music.

The competent territorial authority must accordingly see to it that experts in
music and in Latin and the vernacular form part of the commission charged with
preparing translations and that their cooperation enters into the work from the very
outset.

4176   55. The competent territorial authority will decide whether vernacular texts traditionally associated with certain melodies may be used, even though these texts do
not correspond exactly to the approved translations of liturgical texts.

4177   56. Of special importance among the melodies to be composed for vernacular texts
are those that belong to the priest and ministers for singing alone, together with the
congregation, or in dialogue with the congregation. Composers of these melodies
are to study whether the corresponding traditional melodies of the Latin liturgy
may suggest melodies for use with the same texts in the vernacular.

4178   57. New melodies for the priest and ministers must receive the approval of the
competent territorial authority.[40]

4179   58. The bodies of bishops concerned are to see to it that there is a single vernacular
translation for a single language used in different regions. It is advisable also to
have, as far as possible, one or more common melodies for the priest's and ministers' parts and for the congregation's acclamations and responses. This will foster a
shared way for people of the same language to take part in the liturgy.

4180   59. In their approach to a new work, composers should have as their motive the
continuation of the tradition that provided the Church a genuine treasury of music
for use in divine worship. They should thoroughly study the works of the past,
their styles and characteristics; at the same time they should reflect on the new laws
and requirements of the liturgy. The objective is that "any new form adopted
should in some way grow organically from forms already existing"[41] and that new
works will become a truly worthy part of the Church's musical heritage.

4181   60. New melodies for the vernacular texts obviously require a period of testing in
order to become firmly established. But their use in church purely for the sake of
trying them out must be avoided, since that would be out of keeping with the
holiness of the place, the dignity of the liturgy, and the devotion of the faithful.

4182   61. The attempt to adapt sacred music in those areas that possess their own musical tradition, especially mission lands, requires special preparation on the part of
musicians.[42] The issue is one of harmoniously blending a sense of the sacred with
the spirit, traditions, and expressions proper to the genius of those peoples. All
involved must possess a sufficient knowledge of the Church's liturgy and musical

---

[40]   See SCR, Instr. InterOec no. 42 [DOL 23 no. 334].

[41]   SC art. 23 [DOL 1 no. 23].

[42]   See SC art. 119 [DOL 1 no. 119].

tradition as well as of the language, the popular singing, and the other cultural expressions of the people for whom they labor.

VIII.   SACRED INSTRUMENTAL MUSIC

62. Musical instruments either accompanying the singing or played alone can add a great deal to liturgical celebrations.   4183

"The pipe organ is to be held in high esteem, for it is the traditional musical instrument that adds a wonderful splendor to the Church's ceremonies and power-fully lifts up the spirit to God and to higher things.

"But other instruments also may be admitted for use in divine worship, with the knowledge and consent of the competent territorial authority. . . . This may be done, however, only on condition that the instruments are suitable, or can be made suitable, for sacred use, are in accord with the dignity of the place of worship, and truly contribute to the uplifting of the faithful."[43]

63. One criterion for accepting and using musical instruments is the genius and traditions of the particular peoples. At the same time, however, instruments that are generally associated and used only with worldly music are to be absolutely barred from liturgical services and religious devotions.[44] All musical instruments accepted for divine worship must be played in such a way as to meet the requirements of a liturgical service and to contribute to the beauty of worship and the building up of the faithful.   4184

64. Musical instruments as the accompaniment for singing have the power to support the voice, to facilitate participation, and to intensify the unity of the worshiping assembly. But their playing is not to drown out the voice so that the texts cannot be easily heard. Instruments are to be silent during any part sung by the priest or ministers by reason of their function.   4185

65. As accompaniment for the choir or congregation the organ and other lawfully acceptable instruments may be played in both sung and read Masses. Solo playing is allowed at the beginning of Mass, prior to the priest's reaching the altar, at the presentation of the gifts, at the communion, and at the end of Mass.[f]   4186

With the appropriate adaptations, the same rule may be applied for other liturgical services.

66. Solo playing of musical instruments is forbidden during Advent, Lent, the Easter triduum, and at services and Masses for the dead.   4187

67. It is, of course, imperative that organists and other musicians be accomplished enough to play properly. But in addition they must have a deep and thorough knowledge of the significance of the liturgy. That is required in order that even their improvisations will truly enhance the celebration in accord with the genuine char-acter of each of its parts and will assist the participation of the faithful.[45]   4188

---

[43]   SC art. 120 [DOL 1 no. 120].

[44]   See SCR, Instr. on music and the sacred liturgy, 3 Sept. 1958, no. 70: AAS 50 (1958) 652.

[f]   See DOL 208 no. 1402, note R1.

[45]   See nos. 24–25 of this Instruction.

IX. COMMISSIONS IN CHARGE OF PROMOTING SACRED MUSIC

4189   68. Diocesan music commissions make an important contribution to the promotion of sacred music as part of the program of pastoral liturgy in the diocese.

      As far as possible, therefore, every diocese is to have such a commission to work in close conjunction with the diocesan liturgical commission.

      For greater efficiency it will be better in most cases to combine the two commissions into one, made up of experts in each field.

      It is also strongly recommended that, when it is considered helpful, several dioceses establish a single commission to carry out a unified program in an entire region through a coordinated use of resources.

4190   69. The liturgical commission recommended for bodies of bishops[46] is also to have responsibility for music and should accordingly include musical experts in its membership. It would also be well for this commission to establish contacts not only with the diocesan commissions but also with other associations of the region that are involved with sacred music. This applies also to the institutes of pastoral liturgy mentioned in the same article of the Constitution.

      At an audience granted to Cardinal Arcadio M. Larraona, Prefect of this Congregation, 9 February 1967, Pope Paul VI approved the present Instruction, confirmed it by his authority, and commanded its publication, setting 14 May 1967, Pentecost Sunday, as its effective date.

      All things to the contrary notwithstanding.

509. PAUL VI, **Address** to choirs from France, on preserving the treasury of sacred music, 5 April 1967: Not 4 (1967) 134–135 (French).

4191   We wish now to direct a special greeting to the pilgrimage of liturgical choirs from France, organized by the Institut Supérieur de Musique Sacrée of the Institut Catholique of Paris.

      Since your visit three years ago,[a] dear sons and daughters, an interesting period of research and study has ensued for all who, like yourselves, are dedicated to sacred music. In conformity with the Council's directives, singing in the vernacular has taken its place alongside singing in Latin. Even the change of your own name from the Institut Grégorien to the Institut Supérieur de Musique Sacrée is one sign of this development.

      Some people have managed to misinterpret the import of the new directions taken and have been more anxious to destroy and suppress than to preserve and to foster growth.

      But as we said last year in welcoming the Benedictine abbesses of Italy, "the Council is not to be viewed as some sort of cyclone, as a revolution that would displace received ideas and practices and open the way to unthinkable and rash novelties. No, the Council is not a revolution but a renewal" (AAS 58 [1966] 1156).

      In their formulation of the Constitution on the Liturgy, the conciliar Fathers made their intent absolutely clear: not to empty the Church's treasury of sacred music, but to enrich it; not to separate fidelity to tradition and openness to renewal

---

46   See SC art. 44 [DOL 1 no. 44].

a   See DOL 501.

but to unite the two; in a word, like the scribe in the gospel, to combine with a sound balance the old and the new — the *nova et vetera* (Mt 13:52).

With particular reference to the traditional chant, the Congregation of Rites' recent Instruction *Musicam sacram* sheds a clear light on the function and need of choirs and *scholae cantorum* in the aftermath of the Council. The Instruction thus explicitly recommends "the study and use of Gregorian chant; its distinctive qualities make it an important foundation for a mastery of sacred music" (no. 52).[b]

We are well aware, dear children, that you are dedicated, in a spirit of complete docility to the Church, to promoting both the traditional song of the Church — Gregorian chant and polyphony — and new musical compositions in French, and we compliment you for that. May you thus be enabled to contribute more and more toward bringing to liturgical celebrations those marks of sublimity and beauty that are such a help for people to draw nearer to God.

510. PAUL VI, **Address** to the 11th International Meeting of the Federation of Little Singers, 9 July 1967: Not 4 (1967) 305–308 (excerpts).

[Italian] [. . .] Jesus calls you to sing and to sing for him. We could say that   4192
Jesus needs your voices and takes great delight in them. Do you remember his triumphal entry into Jerusalem and then into the temple? The people, among them little children, sang a hymn in honor of Jesus, recognized as the Messiah sent by God. And when the enemies of the Lord wanted to silence those voices of jubilation, the Lord himself spoke in defense of those acclaiming him (see Mt 21:16; Lk 19:40). Yes, Jesus calls you to sing, to sing for him. He calls you today through the Church: remember that during the Council right here in this basilica the Church thought about you and even directed that school children be trained in sacred music. There is even an explicit word setting you aside as special; the Constitution on the Liturgy says that boys especially, *"imprimis pueris,"* should be given special liturgical training in sacred music (see SC art. 115).[a]

It is important, most important, my dear children, that the Church's prayer, the prayer of the Christian community, of the faithful, have added to it the beauty of your voices, from the youngest to the oldest; that they lift up this prayer and make it audible in heaven and on earth. Remember, you have a great task in the Church's spiritual life. If you sing the Lord's praises and the Church's pleas, you hold a very important and beautiful place among all the members of the Church. It is the Pope who tells you this in the name of Jesus: and in his name the Pope encourages and blesses you.

[French] Now a word to you, dear Little Singers, of the French language. They   4193
tell us that this morning you are in the majority. What we wish to tell you is that you must not only sing, but *why* you must sing.

Singing can have many purposes: to amuse and please oneself or others; to express oneself and be admired. Singing, can also have as its purpose, as it does for you, to praise God and beautify liturgical worship.

But there is an even more beautiful and deeper reason. We offer it to you by quoting the great doctor of the Church, St. Augustine: "Singing is for lovers — *Cantare amantis est."*

---

b   DOL 508 no. 4173.

a   See DOL 1 no. 115.

That, dear children, is why you must sing and sing well: because you love Jesus and wish to honor and please him. He has made you his children, his brothers, and his friends. He has brought you nearer than others to his Church's liturgy. Show him your thanks, your love, and your appreciation of his gifts. Offer in return your own gift, your own offering, that of your voice and your efforts to train it and make it always more worthy to sing his praises.

Perhaps you ask yourselves, now that the Mass is being sung in your native tongue, why they still make you learn the Latin chants. But on a day like this it is easy for you to understand why: you are gathered here with others from so many different countries and are glad to be able to join together in singing the same chants in the Latin Church's traditional language.

You choristers are the ones to whom is entrusted in part the beautiful mission of preserving among the Christian people the use and knowledge of Gregorian chant. Alongside it now, yet never meant to replace it entirely, is the use of vernacular singing.

Learn how to devote yourselves eagerly and cheerfully to both forms of singing, as the Church desires and as the Council solemnly charges you to do.

4194   [German] To each of you, dear Little Singers, God has given a voice, clear and beautiful. At the celebration of the liturgy, whenever you sing on Sundays and holydays you unite your many voices into a single great song for the glory of God and the joy of his people.

Your singing forms you into a young community, bound together by your difficult and exacting rehearsals, but also by your joy and honor when you have sung well in the liturgy. The exalted art of singing demands great effort. You must sacrifice many things that could delight your young hearts. But that is a valuable lesson for a lifetime. It will teach you that your singing is service: it is a task that, as you perform it with generous joy, allows you to do something great and beautiful for God and for your brothers and sisters.

4195   [English] Besides singing all together, you must also sing *well*. This is not easy; it demands much practice and hard work. But it is possible, and therefore you must practice and work so as to make your singing as perfect as you can.

Your song is your gift to God and you strive to make that gift as beautiful and attractive as it can possibly be. In this way your singing will gain merit in the eyes of God, who will not fail to reward your efforts, your good will, and your search for perfection in his service.

4196   [Spanish] With your participation in the Church's liturgy [. . .] you are anticipating in a way the liturgy of the blessed in heaven. In a vision full of symbols and images St. John portrays Christ's glorification as the spotless Lamb receiving blessing and thanks on the throne of glory. First there are the representatives of redeemed humanity, with harps and perfumed robes of gold, who sing a new canticle: "You ransomed people for God from every tribe and tongue and have made them a kingdom." Then come myriads of angels who sing: "The Lamb who was slain is worthy to receive honor and glory and blessing." And finally all creatures of the earth, the heavens, and the sea sing in unison: "To him who sits upon the throne and to the Lamb blessings and honor and glory and might for ever and ever" (see Rv ch. 5).

Dear children, in taking part in the Church's *laus perennis* with your sweet voices, you are able to capture as it were the canticle of all creation and offer it to Christ for whom all of it was made. Through your songs and melodies you make the sweet voice of the beloved Bride, the Church, rise up to the Bridegroom, Christ.

You are like the angels at Bethlehem proclaiming to the community of the elect the presence of the Savior. You are the glory of Christ; you are the joy of the Church.

511. CONSILIUM, **Letter** of Cardinal G. Lercaro to Archbishop E. Delgado Gómez, Archbishop of Pamplona, on the occasion of the study week on sacred music organized by Universa Laus (Pamplona, 28 August–3 September 1967), August 1967: Not 3 (1967) 350–351 (Spanish; excerpt).

[. . .] Such measures as this [study week] are today more necessary than ever   4197
in order that by continued efforts, the liturgy may regain its innate solemnity and through that solemnity succeed in bringing its sanctifying power to the active and conscious participation of the holy people of God. The introduction of the vernacular into the Church's official worship, new pastoral needs, the higher aspirations of our contemporaries demand, along with the revered and priceless musical heritage of tradition, development of a new patrimony of sacred music that combines inspiration, dignity, and purpose. This new music must be both pleasing and strong, artistically genuine, contemporary in spirit, and worthy of the sanctuary. Because the task is both difficult and delicate, demanding an ecclesial, that is, universal cooperation of resources and programs, I am firmly convinced that meetings or study weeks bringing together a common striving for the best and an exchange of the most varied experiences are indispensable. This is especially so where study is combined with model celebrations of the liturgy, as the programs and statutes of Universa Laus direct. Only in such an arrangement can our own pathways join the pathway of the Lord. [. . .]

512. CONSILIUM, **Letter** to the Italian conference of bishops, on liturgical music, 2 February 1968: Not 4 (1968) 95–98 (Italian).

This Office has received the report on "The pastoral results of the liturgical   4198
reform in Italy." [. . .]

A reading of this report clearly reveals the energy and generosity with which the dioceses of Italy have striven to bring about the liturgical reform intended by the Council. The results achieved have great value and deserve the highest praise. But considerable work still remains for the liturgy to reach deeply into the lives of the faithful and in particular to fill the young with a profound sense of the supernatural life and of divine mystery, made present through the texts, rites, singing, and sacred signs of the liturgy.

Because reform of the liturgy is on the threshold of its most important and urgent phase, permit me, following Pope Paul VI's wishes, to state several points that are to be of particular concern at this stage.

1. For the reformed liturgy to speak to people in a language that touches their   4199
souls more deeply and persuasively, it is absolutely necessary to bring about the greatest possible growth in *sacred music* and especially in congregational *singing*.

Where its continuance is decided, celebration in Latin will bring about a loving care for the precious heritage of Gregorian chant and also of sacred polyphony and of the superior compositions of modern music.

In any event we must not lose the important ecclesial bond that consists of a solid repertoire in Gregorian chant and therefore in Latin. The national liturgical commission is responsible for a program that will include the *Credo* and the *Pater noster* among the Gregorian melodies that the people should know well (see SC art. 54; the Instructions *Inter Oecumenici* no. 59; and *Musicam sacram* no. 47).[a]

Vernacular celebration will have to create gradually a new musical repertoire that is adapted to the accent and rhythm of the Italian language and that by its inspiration, beauty, and soundness of form will come up to the level of the traditional musical heritage.

No liturgical celebration, whether in a splendid cathedral or in the most humble country parish, must be without at least a minimum of singing, if only of the *Sanctus* and the Lord's Prayer.

Pope Paul earnestly desires, therefore, that singing be increased in every diocese and in a way suited to today's forms of worship and to today's needs. The study and practice of singing should increase above all in seminaries and in religious institutes, as well as in Catholic associations (see the Instruction *Musicam sacram* no. 18).[b]

Commissions and associations for sacred music should be revitalized and promoted in every way possible and should work with the liturgical commissions in complete accord about programs, objectives, and activities.

The Pope's special expectation is the reestablishment or the creation of a national organization responsible for music and singing in the service of worship, fulfilling a function carried out for so many years by the estimable Associazione Italiana di Santa Cecilia. Such an agency must not interfere with the work proper to those particular entities already working so successfully in many regions and dioceses. Rather its function is to coordinate, to set up programs, to carry out joint efforts in a spirit of cooperation and always in complete harmony with the bishops' commission for the liturgy (see the Instruction *Musicam sacram* nos. 25 and 69).[c]

This new "Santa Cecilia" must also organize meetings, congresses, study and work weeks or days, to the end that a new breath of life and of grace will return and surround the altars of our liturgical assemblies with beautiful liturgical singing of the people as in the best periods of the past.

4200   2.   The *scholae cantorum* must also take up with new energies their service for the splendor of worship; or, where they do not exist, they must be established, even in small parishes (see the Instruction *Musicam sacram* no. 19 b).[d] As we all know, the choir's purpose is twofold, to lead and sustain the congregation's singing and to supply for the congregation's inability to sing because of the nature of the music or because of circumstances. Thus the role of the choir is not ruled out, provided the prescription of *Musicam sacram* nos. 16 c and 20 is safeguarded and respected, namely that *the congregation is not prevented but instead assisted* in every way to take its proper part.[e]

---

  [a]   See DOL 1 no. 54; DOL 23 no. 351; DOL 508 no. 4168.

  [b]   See DOL 508 no. 4139.

  [c]   See DOL 508 nos. 4146 and 4190.

  [d]   See DOL 508 no. 4140.

  [e]   See DOL 508 nos. 4137 and 4141.

3.   Measures should be taken to train cantors (see the Instruction *Musicam sacram*   4201
no. 21)[f] and for this purpose courses or special classes should be established. Although they should not be too young, adolescents and young men should be
chosen, or even mature men, who have the ability and the religious understanding
to intone and direct the songs of the assembly or to sing their own parts in responsorial singing. Their example will be an invitation and an encouragement for men,
who often take no part in the singing in church.

4.   The professional training of *parish organists* should not be neglected. The sound   4202
of the organ is extremely helpful, even indispensable, for worship in an assembly of
the people, to help sustain the singing and to create an atmosphere of festiveness,
joyous serenity, and recollection during the celebration, in keeping with the established norms.

5.   Another enterprise is very dear to Pope Paul: the preparation and training of   4203
young *readers* to proclaim the word of God in the readings and *to direct* and *animate* the
assembly. Suitable courses are also needed for them.

     Readers do not improvise. They must have relevant instruction, practice cor-
rect, modulated, clear, and expressive diction and learn how to use the microphone
so as not to disturb the spirit of silence and quiet listening. The reader's charge
becomes ever more important because the vernacular makes the texts more understandable, and thus listened to, followed, and appreciated by the faithful. Moreover, the greater variety of texts makes it difficult at times for the people to have
copies from which to follow what is read by the reader or priest at the pulpit or
altar. A clear proclamation of the texts will thus be of great service toward making
the word of God in liturgical celebration richer and more appreciated.

6.   Particular care must be shown for the support and development of associations   4204
or groups of Little Singers, so that their "high, clear, and innocent" voices will fill
liturgical celebrations. "The Church's prayer, the prayer of the Christian community, of the faithful, will have added to it the beauty of their voices from the youngest
to the oldest; they will lift up this prayer and make it audible in heaven and on
earth" (Paul VI, 9 July 1967).[g]

7.   Finally, it is the Pope's intense hope that, along with the beauty of singing, the   4205
altar will be surrounded by the *artistic beauty* of gestures "that reveal,"[h] of the
ceremonies, of the workmanship and grace of the furnishings (see Paul VI, Address
to the meeting on "Sacred art and liturgy," 4 January 1967).[i] Not a cold correctness
about ceremony, but a sensitive love and a delicate, faith-filled attentiveness toward
all that relates to the worship of the Lord is the means by which we must bring
perfection and beauty to the carrying out of the sacred rites.

     Altar boys and young readers are to be trained in reverent, respectful, and
graceful comportment. They should have a sense of order and exactness that comes
from recollection and the spirit of faith. They will then be the most fragrant and
promising blossoms around the altar of the Lord.

     Associations for altar boys and readers must, therefore, be the object of the
greatest concern of the clergy, who, by every means, are to foster the development,
efforts, and training of these groups.

---

f   See DOL 508 no. 4142.

g   DOL 510 no. 4192.

h   See DOL 42.

i   See DOL 539 no. 4318.

The Consilium sends these modest guidelines as a reflection of the thought and wishes of Pope Paul VI. In so doing it expresses the warmest wishes that their implementation will mark a further advance in the liturgico-musical reform so happily begun and that all the flourishing dioceses of Italy may find in this reform the source of the genuine Christian spirit and of a profound sense of religion.

513. PAUL VI, **Address** to the 8th International Meeting of Church Choirs (Loreto, 17–21 April 1968), 22 April 1968: Not 4 (1968) 142–144 (Italian; excerpt).

4206   [. . .] The Ecumenical Council's solemn endorsement of the Christian people's active participation in liturgical celebrations, and also in regard to singing, has opened new pathways for the future of sacred music. That does not imply the rejection of the Church's great musical tradition; the Council called this "a treasure of inestimable value," which "is to be preserved and fostered with great care."[a] The point is rather an enrichment of this heritage through the addition of new elements and new values. In other words, beloved sons, the Church awaits from you the creation of new expressions of the art of music, the search for new forms that are worthy of the past and that will be the means for the choir, not to replace the congregation in liturgical prayer, but rather to assist and sustain active participation. As you can see, a vast field lies before you; yours is an immense responsibility, worthy of the most noble effort.

There is so much we would wish to say to you on a topic close to our heart: we put our hopes in you and base our great expectations on your talent and cooperation. But we are satisfied by our certainty that even these brief highlights will meet in you a ready willingness and a warm, generous resolve.

Strive, then, beloved sons, to be ever faithful to the exalted ideal set before you and to be ever conscious of the duties it imposes. [. . .]

514. PAUL VI, **Address** to the participants in the general meeting of the Associazione Italiana di Santa Cecilia of Italy, on sacred music, handmaiden of the liturgy, 18 September 1968: Not 4 (1968) 269–273 (Italian).

4207   We gladly address our words to you and do so with our thanks and our praise for the spirit in which you receive them. We speak out of respect and affection for you personally; out of the unremitting awareness and concern demanded by our pontifical and pastoral office for the liturgy, "summit and source of the Church's life" (see SC art. 10);[a] out of our need of you, who represent the high purposes of your own movement and the promotion of both community in the life of religion and splendor in divine worship. We need an Associazione Italiana di Santa Cecilia that with sound balance is at once intelligently faithful to the Church's glorious musical and choral traditions and consciously open to the emerging demands both of a religious worship that is always living and improving and of a pastoral-liturgical ministry that is up-to-date, effective, and fruitful.

---

        [a]   See DOL 1 nos. 112, 114.

        [a]   See DOL 1 no. 10.

Your own program enters into an important phase in the history of the reform so wisely promoted by Vatican Council II. Good results have already been achieved in the area of your own concern. In Italy as in other countries the Christian people are now singing more in their worship assemblies. New texts and new melodies are being grafted onto the ancient, majestic tree; they are the promise of new branches growing under the breath of the spiritual spring that today so clearly and deeply marks the Church's life.

Yet this reform is not without obstacles that also involve sacred music and song. Moreover, there is a failure at times to hold in due honor the priceless musical heritage; the new styles of music are not always in keeping with the Church's magnificent and revered tradition, which is so sound even at the level of culture. On the one hand, musical compositions are offered that, although simple and easy to perform, are either uninspired or lacking in any nobility. On the other hand, musical experiments are going on here and there that are completely unauthorized and outlandish and that must cause anyone to be puzzled and suspicious. It is up to you, therefore, to make your own contribution to the sensitive and pressing tasks of reflection and sound judgment, of support or correction, as the case may require. 4208

In carrying out that mission you must above all not lose sight of the function of sacred music and liturgical singing. The alternative is the futility of every attempt at reform and the impossibility of correct and appropriate use of the different structural resources for this noble and sacred endeavor. These resources are, as you well know, Gregorian chant, sacred polyphony, and modern music; the organ and other instruments; the Latin and vernacular texts; the ministers, choir, and congregation; official liturgical song and the religious music of the people (see SC ch. 6; SCR, Instruction on music in the liturgy, 1967).[b]

Music and song are servants of worship and are its subordinates. Accordingly they must always possess the qualities befitting their place: grandeur yet simplicity; solemnity and majesty; the least possible unworthiness of the absolute transcendence of God, to whom they are directed, and of the human spirit, which they are meant to express. Music and song must possess the power to put the soul in devout contact with the Lord, arousing and expressing sentiments of praise, petition, expiation, thanksgiving, joy as well as sorrow, love, trust, peace. There is a limitless range for every kind of inspiring melody and the most varied harmony.

Since that is the essential function for sacred music, what ground is there for allowing anything shabby or banal or anything that caters to the vagaries of aestheticism or is based on the prevailing excesses of technology? The last, it is true, reflects one of the characteristics of the age (which of course is called in all that belongs to it to be brought to God); but it needs the intervention of genuine art to be taken into the sphere of the sacred.

Vocal and instrumental music that is not at once marked by the spirit of prayer, dignity, and beauty, is barred from entrance into the world of the sacred and the religious. The assimilation and sanctification of the secular, which is today a distinguishing mark of the Church's mission in the world, clearly has limits; this is all the more the case when the issue is to invest the secular with the sacredness belonging to divine worship. We need hardly recall that the Council of Trent in the disciplinary Decree "On the conduct of the Mass," forbids every style of music "in which the organ or the singing introduces anything lascivious or impure." Not everything that is "outside the temple" (*profanum*) is fit to be brought through its doors. 4209

---

[b] See DOL 1 nos. 112–121; DOL 508.

There is no reason to think that such remarks are meant to place limits that would stifle the creativity of the artist or composer or the no-less inspired creativity of the performer. Neither are these words meant to bar the instrumental or vocal music typical of the culture and customs of peoples of non-Western civilizations. The primary purpose of sacred music is to evoke God's majesty and to honor it. But at the same time music is meant to be a solemn affirmation of the most genuine nobility of the human person, that of prayer. These exalted purposes are the basis for limitless new musical compositions that are unmistakably marked by the charism of creative freedom and the stamp of genuine art. But the same considerations also afford an understanding of and appreciation for Gregorian chant and polyphony. These are religious and human values of the past whose permanent, ever present value and incomparable perfection would be difficult to deny.

4210   One particular function of sacred song is to give greater impact to the texts offered for the understanding and appreciation of the faithful in order to enliven their faith and warm their devotion (see St. Pius X, *Tra le sollecitudini*).

The word and song of the heart, the word spoken and sung, this is a theme forming part of the broader, richer theme of contemplation and the liturgy, of the internal and the external in divine worship. The theme involves the core of human nature itself and therefore runs through the history of the many forms, especially the Christian forms, of religio-cultural human experience. St. Augustine (see *De Musica*; *Conf.* 9, 6 and 10, 33; *Ep.* 166, 5, 13; *Retract.* 1, 11) and St. Thomas Aquinas (ST 2a2ae, 91.3) were but two of the spiritual masters keenly aware of that theme.

To overcome the difficulties and to avoid the aberrations possible will require, first of all, choosing (drawing the *nova et vetera* from the treasury of faith and art) and preparing texts well suited by both their solidly religious and sublimely inspired content and their worthy and graceful literary expression. These texts must then be set to music and performed with careful fidelity, avoiding the excess of obscuring the texts by useless redundancies and annoying prolixity belonging to another age and the defect of impoverishing the texts. The ideal must be to achieve between the *cantus* and the *res quae canitur* (St. Augustine, *Conf.* 10) the mutual and effective complementarity that is the surest way to raise minds and hearts to God.

4211   Finally, we wish also to touch on the community role of sacred and religious song; this is bound up with the social aspect of the liturgy so strongly and rightly emphasized today.

Liturgical song involves the Church as a whole: a "community of hearts" that expresses itself "in a single voice" (St. Clement, *Ad Corinth.* 34, 7) and that singing strengthens and reenforces. Sacred music that properly fulfills this function has the power to produce great results for Christian and human solidarity, for charity and communion in Christ. Moreover, fidelity to the purpose of music as fostering community will succeed in keeping out styles appealing only to an elite and as such incompatible with a music that must be "popular" because it is the music of a people, the people of God.

Song also, however, involves the Church in its organic structure; it must therefore cause that essential structure, reflected in the hierarchical and communal character of the entire liturgy, also to be strikingly clear in the music. Over the wide extent of the universal priesthood of all the faithful the Holy Spirit distributes his gifts in great diversity; similarly, in the worship assembly he confers the ministry of choirs, of children and adults, the ministry of the composer, the organist, the choir director. These are your ministries, beloved sons, and they involve many roles to attend to, many functions to keep vital. Through them the singing will develop in a fitting and orderly way, corresponding to each individual's office and making the service itself resplendent because of its cooperation and harmony, the building up of all together in the Church, and the forming of all together into a living temple for the honor and glory of the Father.

Beloved sons, such are the supreme purposes of your mission. It has been our wish to make you dwell on them because of our love, but even more because of the responsibility of our apostolic office. We have gone over them again as the basic criteria that must in practice inspire your work; we are sure that you will not draw away from their beckoning light and energizing force. May you also be helped by the realization that your mission is great and beneficial in the eyes of the Church, which by singing expresses and strengthens the Christian people's faith, and also in the eyes of the world, the world of today that is so in need of a beautiful and undaunted witness to religious realities, to the sacred, to God.

515. CONSILIUM, **Letter** of Cardinal B. Gut, to Cardinal J. P. Cody, Archbishop of Chicago, on the occasion of the National Congress of Diocesan Liturgical Commissions and Music Commissions of the United States (Chicago, 20–22 November 1968), 7 November 1968: Not 4 (1968) 388–389 (English).

May I take this opportunity, through your kindness, to greet all those attend-   4212
ing the national meeting of representatives from diocesan liturgical and music commissions in the United States.

I should like to express the Consilium's appreciation and praise for the wonderful work carried out in so many parts of the United States by the diocesan commissions. In this, special tribute must be paid to the Bishops' Committee on the Liturgy, which has always sought to make the liturgical reform a truly pastoral renewal.

Nor is it out of place to make special reference to the diocese which is host to this year's meeting, namely, the Archdiocese of Chicago. The energetic initiatives carried out in the Chicago Archdiocese to deepen the knowledge of the liturgy among the clergy, religious, and faithful and to provide practical aids for a fuller participation in the Church's worship are widely known throughout the Christian world.

As the members of the music and liturgical commissions come together to discuss the new eucharistic prayers and prefaces and the statement of the Music Advisory Board, "The Place of Music in Eucharistic Celebrations," in a spirit of fraternal collaboration, I draw their attention to two points.

Firstly, at this stage of the liturgical reform, in our liturgical celebrations and   4213
educational programs we must above all concern ourselves with the *spiritual depth* of the renewal. We have already seen many modifications in the layout of our churches and many changes in the texts and actions of our rites. It is to be hoped that further reforms concerning the Mass and the Ritual will be published in the coming year. Already there has been widespread preparation for these rites and in many places study has been undertaken of those adaptations which would seem appropriate and useful. But in all of this we should keep clearly in our minds that the purpose of all pastoral activity concerning the liturgy is that the paschal mystery of Christ may be expressed in men's lives. To this all our efforts and prayers must be directed.

4214   *Secondly*, to attain this end, a high level of communication and cooperation between all those engaged in the liturgical reform is vital. This is why the liturgy- and music-commission members have come together this November in Chicago. The extent to which the liturgical renewal penetrates into every sphere of life will depend to a large extent on these men and women.

We are all aware from our personal experience of the difficulties involved in liturgical reform, but we must never become discouraged. Speaking of the Church's worship, our Holy Father Pope Paul VI has referred to the perennial youth of the liturgy. The eucharistic prayers which are to be discussed in Chicago are evidence of this: they bear witness to the life which is breathed into the Church by the Spirit of Christ. Life generates life: these prayers are the first verses of a new canticle on the Church's lips. Building on the sure foundations of the Church's tradition and not rejecting the heritage of the past, they will at the same time call forth other verses of this canticle, other hymns and other innumerable and unceasing songs: the songs of the liturgy of perennial youth.

▶   123.   CONSILIUM, Instruction *Comme le prévoit*, on translation of liturgical texts for celebrations with a congregation, 25 January 1969:

nos. 36:   Translation of texts meant to be sung [no. 873].
     37:           Translation of liturgical hymns [no. 874].

516. PAUL VI, Address to the 9th International Meeting of Church Choirs, 14 April 1969: Not 5 (1969) 135–138 (Italian; excerpt).

4215   [. . .] You understand, then, the great and genuine usefulness, even the neces- sity, of your service to the Church, the assembly of the faithful gathered at the altar of holy mysteries. For this reason, and returning to what we had the opportunity of saying to you on an earlier occasion, we wished to welcome you again with all the fullness of our fatherly love and with the burning hope we have in our heart. We wished to express our thanks to you, and in the name of the whole Church, for what you are doing in the cause of sacred singing. You are not only taking the path set by the noblest and purest tradition, but also willingly following the direction given to sacred music by Vatican Council II and by the current measures of the Apostolic See, issued through the congregations of the Roman Curia.

4216   As we mentioned in last year's audience, a vast area lies open for your activity: "The Church awaits from you the creation of new expressions of the art of music, the search for new forms that are worthy of the past and that will be the means for the choir, not to replace the congregation in liturgical prayer, but rather to assist and sustain active participation. . . . Yours is an immense responsibility, worthy of the most noble effort" (OR 24 April 1968).[a] The Constitution on the Liturgy chap- ter 6 makes it clear that the Council's concern was to enhance sacred singing through every means possible: the promotion of choirs (art. 114);[b] the recognition of Gregorian chant as the chant proper to the Roman liturgy, holding pride of place (see art. 116),[c] yet not to the exclusion of polyphony when this fits in with the

---

[a]   DOL 513 no. 4206.
[b]   See DOL 1 no. 114.
[c]   See DOL 1 no. 116.

spirit of a liturgical service (see ibid.);[d] the use of the people's own religious music, so that "the faithful may raise their voices in song" (art. 118).[e] The Council has above all stressed the point that religious music possesses a distinctive value because it adds delight to prayer, fosters oneness of spirit, and invests the rites with greater solemnity (art. 112).[f]

Beloved sons, the line of march has thus been clearly traced out before you. We are sure that the Church Choirs here present, as well as the numerous, happy groups of Little Singers, are and will continue to be exact in following that line for the sake of the contribution of singing to the growth of liturgical life. But as significant, promising, and encouraging as your presence is, it does not make us forget that the guidance of the Holy See and the norms of Vatican Council II are not always and everywhere being followed. Too many voices remain still, not joining in the singing that is also a joyous profession of faith in Christ. Too many liturgical celebrations altogether lack those mystical stirrings that a genuinely religious music communicates to the open and perceptive souls of the faithful. Sometimes as well there are questionable innovations here and there. But the sacred song that the Church makes its own continues to possess the hidden and strong power of the liturgy itself. This visible expression of the invisible mysteries of redemption and salvation is not only a help for personal union with God; it is the participation in the unique, great, and eternal worship that the Spirit and the Bride offer to the heavenly Father (see Rv 21:2–3, 22:17). This worship offers the sacrifice of the spotless Lamb and unites itself to the hymn of unceasing praise that joins earth to heaven and that in heaven will know no end. [. . .]

517. SECRETARIAT OF STATE, **Letter** of Cardinal J. Villot to Cardinal J. Garibi y Rivera, Archbishop of Guadalajara (Mexico), on the occasion of the 12th International Congress of Little Singers (Guadalajara, 27 December 1969–1 January 1970), December 1969: Not 6 (1970) 309–310 (Spanish; excerpt).

[. . .] During the last seventy years, from St. Pius X to Vatican Council II and since then, the Apostolic See has expressed itself repeatedly on the place of sacred music in the liturgy. As a result the documents issued on this topic constitute a very sizable doctrinal corpus. Anyone interested in the theme should pause attentively over this teaching in order to penetrate and take hold of its riches (see SC ch. 6; the Instruction *Musicam sacram*, 5 March 1967).[a]

4217

Moreover, the serious problems now besetting sacred music and thus disturbing the harmony belonging to it could be solved by taking as the key the doctrinal principles and practical guidelines contained in the conciliar and postconciliar documents.

It can never be sufficiently emphasized that sacred music is an integral part of the liturgy: it shares in the essence of the liturgy and becomes part of the very mystery of the liturgical celebration.

---

d   See DOL 1 no. 116.

e   DOL 1 no. 118.

f   See DOL 1 no. 112.

a   See DOL 1 nos. 112–121; DOL 508.

For this reason singing and music above all stand in the service of the text and by bringing out its meaning have the power to make the text itself more effective.

When the music graces a text and becomes a meaningful and expressive commentary on it, the text is elucidated and conveys more clearly the mystery that its words contain.

This was the experience of St. Augustine: "I confess that I take delight in the melodies that enliven your own word when they are sung by a sweet and well-trained voice. Not so that I may remain fixed in the music, but so that I may arise again when I wish. . . . When I recall the tears I shed at hearing the singing of your Church at the beginning of my conversion and when I notice that I still am deeply moved not by the singing but by what the singing is about, when the words are sung with a clear voice and with proper expression, I recognize anew the great value of church music" (*Conf.* 10, 33).

In this regard the participants in the Congress, so at home in the world of music, will readily think of relevant examples created in the past by Gregorian chant, sacred polyphony, and more recent music. . . .

4218   Our own times also provide other musical forms. Clearly, every contemporary art must remain always in search of new styles with which to offer God the homage of beauty.

Thus the art of music also is in the midst of writing a new chapter in its own history to be added to the earlier chapters on sacred music. The Church raises no a priori objection against new musical compositions that can fit into the liturgical service and its different parts, and on condition that the techniques and styles of these new compositions are not means of intruding what is inherently profane into the domain of the sacred.

When contemporary compositions exhibit the characteristics of genuine art, the Church will not hesitate to welcome them. Exception would have to be made should it become evident that such music contained anything that would lessen dignity and that thus made it unfit for the exalted service of divine worship (see Pius XII, Encycl. *Musicae sacrae disciplina* ch. 2, art. 8).

4219   In view of the light shed by the Council on the theme of the people's participation, a congress on music could not of course fail to contribute to the cause of determining a solution to the problem of participation in the singing of the liturgy.

Everyone is aware that the liturgical reform makes room for the congregation's singing, but without excluding, even in the same service, the part proper to the choir. In addition to fulfilling its own proper function, the choir must be a guide and help for the congregation to take part in the singing. Even when the people's singing cannot achieve an ideal musical perfection, it remains a participation of unquestionable spiritual value.

Choirs should recognize that the liturgy is an essentially communal act of the entire assembly, present and formed hierarchically, with all having a proper, active role, not to be equated or confused with others. While respecting artistic demands, the choirs must give positive help to ensure the assembly's active participation in the singing. This is the only way for the choir's part to be the source of genuine art in the liturgy.

4220   The objectives intended will be achieved by work on two levels: the musical and the liturgical.

Little need be said about the musical preparation: the artistic perfection achieved by the musical performances of the member groups of the International Federation of Little Singers is universally recognized.

A few words may be said about the liturgical aspect. A more immediate and active participation in the liturgy calls for and even demands a sense of the sacred, a knowledge of the significance of feasts, liturgical seasons, and rites. Because the singer's work is directed to the text, an understanding of its content, in itself and in its context, is always desirable.

Preparation of this kind is a necessary prerequisite for the opening of the spirit to the knowledge of what singing as the service of God is meant to achieve.

The singing will become a true harmony to the degree that it is a blending of skilled technique and of a genuinely religious spirit that allows the voice to become the devout expression to the soul. [. . .]

518. PAUL VI, **Address** to the 10th International Congress of Church Choirs, 6 April 1970: Not 6 (1970) 154–157 (Italian; excerpts).

[. . .] Your wish is for a word from the Pope. His word can be nothing else but an echo of the Church's recent declarations on the relationship between music and liturgy (in the Constitution on the Liturgy and the various instructions on carrying it out, particularly that on sacred music, 5 March 1967[a]). His word is an echo also of what the Church has said on the role that you as choirs are called to fulfill in order to bring an ever greater splendor and devotion to the celebration of the sacred mysteries.   4221

The study of such documents clearly establishes that the charge the Church entrusts to music, its composers and performers, remains, as it has always been, one of great importance and highest purpose. Music is meant to give expression to forms of beauty that during the celebration of the liturgy will accompany the unfolding of the sacred rites and adorn the various types of the Church's prayer with the vibrant harmonies of song. Music makes the splendor of God's own countenance shine on the assembly gathered in Christ's name. The spiritual power of art helps to raise the heart more readily to the cleansing and sanctifying encounter with the luminous reality of the sacred and thus to be best disposed to celebrate the mystery of salvation and to share deeply in its effects.

The documents referred to have accordingly provided a place for every kind of choral group, from the choirs of the great basilicas, noble cathedrals, and historic monasteries, to the modest *scholae* of the small parishes (see *Musicam sacram* no. 19).[b] So that no liturgy may be devoid of singing, the Instruction on sacred music has urged that whenever even a small choir is not possible "there must be one or more cantors to intone at least the simpler chants that the congregation sings and to lead and sustain that singing" (*Musicam sacram* no. 21).[c]

Your presence is needed at all levels; besides your service as a group, the support that each of you individually can give to your own church and parish takes away nothing from your function, your tastes, your good will. Your function as choirs continues to be invaluable, indeed irreplaceable: you have only to recall the Instruction's solemn assertion that, in pursuance of the conciliar norms on liturgical   4222

---

   [a] See DOL 508.

   [b] See DOL 508 no. 4140.

   [c] DOL 508 no. 4142.

reform, the role of choirs, *cappelle musicale,* or *scholae,* has taken on "even greater prominence and importance" (*Musicam sacram* no. 19).[d] Carry out your mission with joy, with love, with reverence, and with dedication. The sphere for your proper function is immense: if the hope is that the entire assembly take part in the sacred rites by singing, it is at the same time realistic to recognize that the choir has a preeminent function on the musical plane. Only the choir has the ability to provide a proper performance of the more solemn chants, those, for example, of the entrance procession, the presentation of the gifts, the communion, and the verses of the responsorial psalm. At the same time do not cut yourselves off from the requirements of the rites or forget the needs of the congregation. Do not shut yourselves up, contrary to God's will, in narcissistic complacency over your singing virtuosity and artistic abilities. Rather, know well how to give real guidance to the assembly, as the Instruction intends, by inspiring the people to sing, by raising the level of their taste, by arousing their desire to take part. Give to the celebrations solemnity, joy, unity. This is a priceless service that you are giving to the Church, especially to the clergy, and to its worship assemblies; you must devote all your power to that service.

4223   You also will be able to put under the rubric of this "service" all that relates to your musical repertoire. This is a precious treasure of history, art, and faith that the Church has always cherished as a cultural expression and as a component of the spiritual life.

Today, however, not everything in this treasury may be put to use on a regular basis. The best in this heritage must remain in the repertoire of church choirs. To this end the repertoire must be adapted to the new requirements of the liturgy, or, where that is not possible, used in paraliturgies — celebrations of the word of God, Bible vigils, or even in special, nonliturgical performances; this is the wise directive of the Instruction (see *Musicam Sacram* nos. 46, 53).[e] The vernacular repertoire in certain countries is clearly only at its first stages and musicians, composers, and singers of future generations have an unlimited opportunity: the challenge is to combine all the musical technique of choirs with making available to the people melodies they can sing. Musicians are already directing their talents to these new problems. It is for you to execute their compositions; when they conform to the Church's directive norms and the canons of art, you should perform such compositions gladly. The purpose is to provide a beginning for the great work ahead for sacred music, especially after the adoption of the new Roman Missal and its elements that will enrich the traditional liturgical heritage. You must be able to welcome what is new with humility and inner freedom, dissociating yourselves, if necessary, from those attitudes that pretend to represent the changeless tradition of the Church but which in fact do not. A spirit of openness, of amenability, of adaptability is the expression of the ministerial purpose that, as we have said, is your calling and that makes your singing worthy of the highest praise. [. . .]

▶   52.   SC DIVINE WORSHIP, Instruction (third) *Liturgicae instaurationes,* 5 September
         1970:

         nos. 3 c: Congregational singing [no. 517].
               7 c: Women as cantors and organists [no. 525].

---

[d]   DOL 508 no. 4140.

[e]   See DOL 508 nos. 4167, 4174.

519. PAUL VI, **Address** to women religious taking part in the National Convention of the Associazione Italiana di Santa Cecilia, 15 April 1971: Not 7 (1971) 241–243 (Italian; excerpt).

[. . .] Our wish is to leave you with one counsel: always give first place, as the 4224
main concern for yourselves and for others, to the *sensus Ecclesiae*. Otherwise, instead of helping to deepen charity, singing can be a source of disturbing, diluting, and profaning the sacred and even of creating division among the faithful. The *sensus Ecclesiae* will mean your grasping in obedience, prayer, and the interior life the sublime and elevating reasons for our musical endeavors. The *sensus Ecclesiae* means also the deep study of papal and conciliar documents in order always to be aware of the criteria that regulate the liturgical life. [. . .] The *sensus Ecclesiae*, finally, will mean discernment in what concerns the music of the liturgy: not everything is valid, not everything is lawful, not everything is good. In the liturgy the sacred must come together with the beautiful in a harmonious and devout synthesis that allows the assemblies with their different capabilities fully to express their faith for the glory of God and the building up of the Mystical Body.

Know therefore how to make a judicious, wise, impartial choice of sacred 4225
songs. Guided by the Church's norms, your own liturgical sensitivities, as well as by study and the cultivation of taste, you will thus be able to develop a definitive corpus of Italian liturgical songs that for decades to come will be on the lips of the faithful and in their hearts.

The Constitution on the Liturgy has counseled musicians to produce "compositions having the qualities proper to genuine sacred music. The texts . . . must always be consistent with Catholic teaching; indeed they should be drawn chiefly from holy Scripture and liturgical sources" (SC art. 121).[a] It will be necessary to judge whether new sacred compositions really match these standards and to decide whether they are inspired musically merely by some passing vogue and devoid of either spiritual or artistic value. Let your own concern be to choose for the liturgy the kinds of music that in actual use combine the dignity of art and the spirit of prayer. As to texts, the excerpt from the Council is explicit: the effort must be to have something really sound, rejecting those expressions that in some cases do honor neither to the sacred meaning nor to the right usage of the Italian language and create graceless, trite expressions more typical of a slogan than of a prayer.

Other texts and music, making no claim to admittance into the church, do answer modern needs, expecially those of the young. They may be used on other occasions of relaxation or of meetings for reflection and study, so that singing may be a means of increasing enthusiasm. But the liturgy is "an exercise of the priestly office of Jesus Christ . . . the action of Christ the priest and of his Body which is the Church" (SC art. 7);[b] it demands, therefore, only what is most suited to its proper and sublime character. Here is the place for exercising the *sensus Ecclesiae* that must guide your judgment and your choices. [. . .]

ADDENDUM*

It is absolutely true to say *how very, very dear to our heart is the success of your* 4226
Association and the mission facing you. That mission is to give to the Church's song,

---

    [a] DOL 1 no. 121.

    [b] DOL 1 no. 7.

    * Text in Not 9 (1973) 141–143 (Italian): informal words of Pope Paul at the same audience, before the official address itself, which alone was printed in OR.

to liturgical song, to congregational song, new expressions that involve not just small groups but the great mass of the Christian people.

We see in the question of sacred music three major issues of our own ministry.

LITURGICAL ISSUE

4227   The first is the issue of the liturgy. In the recent years of the liturgical reform, the Church has put enormous efforts into preparing for the Christian people laws, formularies, words, a responsible role. . . . But there is more to be done. What is this reform if it remains silent, if no song is sung, if there is no *Alleluia* like the one you have just allowed me to hear? Such a reform would be something prosaic; it would be a fact and could perhaps survive like everything else but without your own and the people's liturgical and sacred song it would never have its full effect and, I believe, would not lead the faithful to growth in grace.

MUSICAL ISSUE

4228   The second aspect [. . .] involves the art of music.

How much criticism we have read and continue to read, even very recently, in the daily and weekly newspapers . . . . They carp at the repertoire, ancient, classical, and contemporary alike . . . at the language, both Latin and the vernacular . . . at the style, Gregorian, polyphonic, or modern . . . .

The Church welcomes all musical forms and expressions, provided they bear the genuine qualities of sacred music.

Vatican Council II has clearly endorsed the *nova et vetera*. We too, avoiding condemnation yet defending and preserving the repertoire of tradition and the sound heritage of art, must also continue with new advances, hoping that they come from able masters.

You are teachers of singing and music. We appeal to you to give us, besides the traditional repertoire a new literature of sacred music for the people that possesses style and art. We remember hearing St. Alphonsus's Christmas carol, *Tu scendi dalle stelle*. What could be more childlike than this? . . . Yet it is most profound.

We hope for a new flourishing of songs for the people. . . They have the power to give to our prayer the charism not just of music, but also of poetry, of the enthusiasm that should accompany the expression of prayer and make it sing.

PASTORAL ISSUE

4229   Without sacred song, can a parish community be alive, possess a full, beautiful, ecclesial, and baptismal life? The *pastoral issue* is not just to bring about singing on the part of a small group, the *schola* of musicians, but of the great mass of people — children, all the women, all the men, the way they do in the Northern countries. When the Germans come to Rome, all the men sing and their voices can be clearly heard. . . . I do not remember ever hearing men in Italy sing with such gusto. [. . .]

I conclude these introductory words by speaking of the charge that has been entrusted to the Associazione Italiana di Santa Cecilia and that you religious have willingly accepted. Try to make those in your own religious family share in it, those in the parishes, those in the communities where you live. It is of the utmost importance. *Is there singing? Then there is prayer. Is there prayer? Then people are going to church and religion is alive. Is there religion? Then there is faith and there is salvation.* This is a logical chain, even though it seems a paradox, and it has its own significance. *If there is singing, then religious life is vigorous in a community.* And if that is the case, we can be sure that God's mercy has graces and gifts in store for that community.

I remember that pastoral visits in the Diocese of Milan often brought me to districts that were completely Communist, yet the choirs were full of young people who came to sing. Thus singing *has a marvelous power of attraction*; it is a beautiful, natural bond, full of warmth.

520. PAUL VI, **Homily** at the Mass for the Congress of the Associazione Italiana di Santa Cecilia observing the centenary of the birth of Lorenzo Perosi, 24 September 1972: Not 8 (1972) 307–311.

[. . .] We wish now to say something in approval and recognition of the fact   4230
that your Congress intends to commemorate the centenary of the birth of the great, the unforgettable Monsignor Lorenzo Perosi, Lifetime Master Director of our Sistine Chapel.

This centenary comes at a momentous time for the Church. Maestro Perosi, with his marvelous musical inspiration, was the key figure in the liturgical movement sponsored by our predecessor St. Pius X. By his admirable compositions and the influence of his own genius, Monsignor Perosi brought sacred music back to its place as the sincere and worthy expression of divine worship, freeing it from a certain decadence that had beset it in the period immediately previous to his work.

Perosi had the ability to follow exactly the course set by St. Pius X in the Motu Proprio *Tra le sollecitudini* no. 2: "Sacred music must possess in an eminent degree the qualities proper to the liturgy and specifically *holiness, integrity of form*, and . . . *universality*."

During the reform of the liturgy intended by the Council, Perosi, it seems to us, has still something to say to those dedicated to sacred music. It is above all this: the worship of the Lord and the sacred words that veil "mystery," yet somehow reveal the awesome supernatural realities, must be graced with musical forms as perfect as a creature can make them. Genius is the gift of God and he distributes his gifts as he sees fit. But even when the human spirit cannot reach the heights of genius, it cannot and must not omit any effort to achieve that perfection in form and in sacredness that belongs to church music. Moreover, in their search for new styles musicians must take into consideration the character of the celebration, the place of worship, the assembly, the divine majesty as the object and end of the musical composition. Composers must also be mindful of the traditions of the Church that Lorenzo Perosi served well and faithfully by the dedication of his artistic talents and entire life.

It is therefore right for the Church solemnly to remember its own priest and to put his art, the motivation of his musical inspiration, and his dedication before the attentive consideration of all who put their artistic talents at the service of divine worship.

From the outset of our pontifical service and particularly from the time we   4231
turned our efforts to the carrying out of the liturgical reform we have not missed any chance to endorse the task of promoting, in every possible way, congregational singing in the celebration of the sacred mysteries. We have done so not only in official documents, in instructions, in the norms of the new liturgical books, but also in our conversations with the various categories of the people of God: in exhortations to our brothers in the episcopate, to liturgical commissions, to associations for sacred music, to your own association, to *scholae cantorum*, Church Choirs, and to the Little Singers.

But today before such a distinguished gathering of experts in sacred music we must renew this appeal.

There is a human need to bring the best in the human person to the worship of God and to express our love to God with all the human faculties. Life itself is full of the joyous expressions of song, as St. John Chrysostom remarked: "A mother sings as she rocks her baby to sleep in her arms. The traveller sings . . . as he walks in the heat of the day. The farmer sings as he tends his vines, gathers or presses the grapes, or does any other work. Sailors sing as they row, . . . they sing alone or together, seeking through song to ease their fatigue. Thanks to singing the spirit bears with the hardest suffering" (*Expos. in Ps.* 41, 1: PG 55, 156–157). If song is on our lips so often in the joyous and sad moments of life, should it not also sustain us Christians "as we work out our salvation"?

Song is a demand and an expression of love. This is how St. Augustine puts it: "Singing arises from joy and if we look closer at it, from love. *Canticum res est hilaritatis et si diligentius consideremus, res est amoris"* (*Sermo* 34, 1: PL 38, 210). "To sing and make music belong to lovers. *Cantare et psallere negotium esse solet amantium"* (*Sermo* 33, 1: PL 38, 207).

As a natural sign of love, song has an indispensable part in Christian worship. For this is the service of charity, of that love on which, as the prayer of the Mass reminds us, "rests the foundation of all law." Because "we wish to sing about the one we love" (St. Augustine, *Sermo* 34, 6: PL 38, 211), our love for God expresses itself in song. Love and praise go hand in hand, as again Augustine says: "To love and to praise, to praise in loving, to love in praising. *Amare et laudare, laudare in amore, amare in laudibus* (*Enarr. in Ps. 147*, 3: PL 37, 1916).

4232   But singing also expresses and nurtures our love for one another. Singing fashions a community, as the harmony of voices fosters the harmony of hearts. It eliminates differences of age, origin, and social class and it brings everyone into one accord in praising God, Creator of the universe and Father of us all. This is why the Council urges that "the people's own religious songs are to be encouraged with care so that in sacred devotions as well as during services of the liturgy itself . . . the faithful may lift their voices in song" (SC art. 118).[a] The liturgy is the act of the entire Church, the sacrament of unity, that is, the holy people, united and ordered under their bishops (see SC art. 26).[b] The liturgy belongs to the whole ecclesial Body and that is why the fundamental objective of the liturgical reform is the active participation of the faithful in the worship due to the Lord and offered to him. The singing of the community is one of the most necessary elements to achieve this goal. Congregational singing must therefore regain all its power and stand in the first place. Regrettably, sometimes we do not see the wonderful sight of an entire assembly fully taking part in the singing. "Too many voices remain still, not joining in the singing. Too many liturgical celebrations altogether lack those mystical stirrings that a genuinely religious music communicates to the open and perceptive souls of the faithful." These were our words to the 9th Meeting of Church Choirs (14 April 1969).[c]

4233   A serious responsibility rests on those charged with the pastoral ministry and in particular on those who have been given talent by God. They must help and support the faithful's participation in the liturgy through simple songs, through the search for new forms worthy of the past, through esteem for the ancient musical heritage. They must see to it that the music is matched to the different moments of the celebration and to the seasons of the liturgical year; that the music has the

---

[a]   DOL 1 no. 118.

[b]   See DOL 1 no. 26.

[c]   DOL 516 no. 4216.

power to express the sacred and to touch the religious sensibilities of people of our own times.

Let not the Savior have to address to any of you the reproof in today's gospel: "Why stand you all the day idle?" Rather try to welcome with good will the invitation to work in his vineyard for a task that holds such a high place in the Church's heart. Let song become the song of a Christian life, as again St. Augustine urges: "Sing with the voice, sing with the mouth, sing with the heart, sing with your upright lives. 'Sing to the Lord a new song, his praise in the assembly of the faithful.' The singer himself is the praise he must sing. Do you wish to praise God? You yourselves are to be his praise. And you will be if you live rightly" (*Sermo* 34, 6: CCL 41, 426).

▶   55.   PAUL VI, Address to a general audience, proposing a decalogue of prayer, 22 August 1973:

art. X: Sacred song and music [no. 548].[R6]

521. SECRETARIAT OF STATE, **Letter** of Cardinal J. Villot to Cardinal G. Siri, Archbishop of Genoa, on the occasion of a national meeting on sacred music (Genoa, 26–30 September 1973), September 1973: Not 9 (1973) 301 (Italian; excerpt).

We must avoid and bar from liturgical celebrations profane types of music,   4234
particularly singing with a style so agitated, intrusive, and raucous that it would disturb the serenity of the service and would be incompatible with its spiritual, sanctifying purposes. A broad field is thus opened for pastoral initiative, the effort, namely, of leading the faithful to participate with voice and song in the rites, while at the same time protecting these rites from the invasion of noise, poor taste, and desacralization. Instead there must be encouragement of the kind of sacred music that helps to raise the mind to God and that through the devout singing of God's praises helps to provide a foretaste of the liturgy of heaven.

Pope Paul VI therefore invites all composers of sacred music to devote themselves completely to supplying music for the Church's liturgy that is truly alive and contemporary, yet without disregarding the ancient heritage, as a source of inspiration, enlightenment, and direction. The liturgical reform still in progress offers to composers "an opportunity to test their own abilities, their inventiveness, their pastoral zeal" (Address to the Cecilians, 24 September 1972); the reform initiates "a new epoch for sacred music" (Address to a general audience, 22 August 1973).[a] The Church awaits a new spring in the art of sacred music that will also interpret the ritual texts in their vernacular versions.

Finally, it remains Pope Paul's firm expectation that Gregorian chant will be preserved and performed in monasteries, religious houses, and seminaries as a privileged form of sung prayer and as an element of the highest cultural and instructional value. He notes the many requests worldwide to preserve the Latin, Gregorian singing of the *Gloria, Credo, Sanctus, Pater noster,* and *Agnus Dei.* The Pope again recommends, therefore, that every appropriate measure be taken to transform this desire into fact and that these ancient melodies be treasured as the voice of the

---

[R6]   See commentary, "Liturgie et chant grégorien": Not 9 (1973) 302–303.

[a]   DOL 55 no. 548.

universal Church and continue to be sung as expressions and demonstrations of the unity existing throughout the ecclesial community.

522. PAUL VI, **Address** at an audience for choir members, on the occasion of the tenth anniversary of the Consociatio Internationalis Musicae Sacrae, 12 October 1973.[*]

4235   It is always a joy for us to be able to address the problems of sacred music, which is of such major importance for the Church's life. Today we greet the members of the Consociatio Internationalis Musicae Sacrae,[a] who are recognized as experts in the field of music. In so doing we wish again to repeat to them how concerned we are that their work, by reason of an objective and ever deepening study, may always follow the guidelines traced by the Holy See to further the success of the liturgical reform.

Only recently we called attention to this point: a new era is opening up for sacred music.[b] Even though it is an era full of hope, it is not going to develop without difficulties and crises. In order to contribute to their successful solution, it is important that the Consociatio exercise the function that the times impose: the simultaneous function of preservation and development. It is important to preserve, at least in certain centers of specialization, the heritage of sacred music and song that belongs distinctively to the Latin Church. It is also necessary to instruct the faithful in the creation of a union between worship and a mode of musical expression, particularly liturgical singing, that is suited to worship. Furthermore, we must all commend the concern of those who are striving to keep in the repertoire of customary liturgical song at least the several texts that have always and everywhere been sung in Latin and in Gregorian chant. These texts make communal song possible even for people of different countries at certain special occasions in Catholic worship. The *Gloria*, *Credo*, and *Sanctus* of the Mass are examples.

4236   But we referred also to development. New vistas have opened up for the Church's music and for sacred song as the result of the reform of the liturgy launched by the Council. A new flowering is today awaited for the art of religious music because in every country the vernacular has been brought into liturgical worship. The vernacular must not be allowed to lack the beauty and expressiveness that lie within the power of genuinely religious music and singing suited to the texts. As it traced out the liturgical-pastoral demands, the Council made the pertinent reminder that "the Church approves of all forms of genuine art possessing the qualities required and admits them into divine worship" (Constitution on the Liturgy art. 112).[c] It is up to you, therefore, to put all your efforts at the service of music for the vernacular texts in order to ensure its worthiness and beauty and to enable all the people to take part effectively and beneficially in the Church's prayer.

You are devoting yourselves with love to the spiritual and artistic heritage handed down from the past. Formed at the cost of so much effort, this precious treasure must be a guide and an encouragement for your own activity.

---

[*] Text, OR 13 Oct. 1973, 1 (French).

[a] See DOL 500.

[b] See DOL 55 no. 548.

[c] DOL 1 no. 112.

From this very moment we must develop the sources of a new progress in music at the service of worship. This is to guarantee for the Church of today and of tomorrow a sacred music that is vital and contemporary, worthy to take its place alongside the music of past ages. [. . .]

523. SC DIVINE WORSHIP, **Letter** *Voluntati obsequens* to bishops, accompanying the booklet *Iubilate Deo*, 14 April 1974: Not 10 (1974) 123–126.

Pope Paul VI has expressed often, and even recently, the wish that the faithful of all countries be able to sing at least a few Gregorian chants in Latin (for example, the *Gloria, Credo, Sanctus, Agnus Dei*).[1] In compliance, this Congregation has prepared the enclosed booklet *Iubilate Deo*, which provides a short collection of such Gregorian chants.

4237

I have the honor and office of sending you a copy of this booklet as a gift from the Pope himself. I also take this occasion to commend to your own pastoral concerns this new measure intended to ensure the carrying out of the prescription of Vatican Council II: "Steps should be taken enabling the faithful to say or to sing together in Latin those parts of the Ordinary of the Mass belonging to them."[2]

Whenever the faithful pray together as a community, they show at once the complex diversity of a people gathered "from every tribe, language, and nation" and their unity in faith and charity. The diversity stands out in the many languages lawfully used in the liturgy and in the song settings suited to those languages. The languages and songs convey the religious spirit of each particular people, along with the identical teachings of faith; the different types of music correspond to the culture and traditions of each people. The unity of faith, on the other hand, stands out in a marked manner through the use of Latin and Gregorian chant. This, as we all well know, has through the ages been the accompaniment for the liturgy of the Roman Rite; it has nurtured faith and devotion; it has achieved such perfection that the Church rightly regards it as a special heritage of incomparable excellence; finally, it has been acknowledged by Vatican Council II as "the chant distinctive of the Roman liturgy."[3]

Undoubtedly one of the principal aims of the reform of the liturgy is the promotion of congregational singing, in order to give fuller expression to the festive, communal, and familial character of the liturgy. "A liturgical service takes on a nobler aspect when the rites are celebrated with singing, the ministers of each rank take their parts in them, and the congregation actively participates."[4] The issue is a major concern for those agencies charged with the reform of the liturgy and one that faces its own problems and obstacles. Thus, as it has often done before, the Congregation for Divine Worship appeals for the furtherance and growth of congregational singing.

4238

---

[1] See Paul VI, Address to a general audience, 22 Aug. 1973 [DOL 55 no. 548]; Address to the CIMS, 12 Oct. 1973 [DOL 522 no. 4235]. Secretariat of State, Letter to the Associazione Italiana di Santa Cecilia, 30 Sept. 1973 [DOL 521 no. 4234].

[2] SC art. 54 [DOL 1 no. 54].

[3] SC art. 116 [DOL 1 no. 116].

[4] Instr. MusSacr, 5 March 1967, no. 5 [DOL 508 no. 4126].

4239   As to singing in the vernacular: the reform of the liturgy also "offers to composers an opportunity to test their own abilities, their inventiveness, their pastoral zeal."[5] Thus composers of both the music and the words must be inspired and encouraged to put all their energies and abilities at the service of this noble cause. This is the means toward the creation of songs for the people that are truly worthy to become part of the praise of God, the liturgical rites, or popular devotions, because the songs are expressions of faith and of genuine art. The Council's inauguration of the reform of the liturgy set a new ideal and a new goal for the Church's musical practice and for sacred song: "A new flowering is today awaited in the art of religious music because in every country the vernacular has been brought into liturgical worship. The vernacular must not be allowed to lack the beauty and expressiveness that lie within the power of genuinely religious music and singing suited to the texts."[6]

4240   In its successful progress the reform of the liturgy does not reject nor can it spurn the entire past, but "is to preserve its heritage with great care."[7] The liturgical renewal holds in high esteem whatever good the past contains and whatever advantage it brings to the spheres of religion, culture, and art; at the same time it safeguards all those elements that can be of service in strengthening and making clearer to all the bond between believers. Thus the enclosed short collection of Gregorian chants should meet this need and cause the faithful to draw closer together and to unite themselves in unanimity with all their brothers and sisters in the faith as well as with the living tradition of ages past. Thus the intent to increase singing in large gatherings of the faithful must include concern for Latin Gregorian chants.

    That need is all the more pressing in view of the proximity of the Holy Year 1975, a time when the faithful of different languages, nations, and races will gather in large numbers to worship the Lord together.

4241   Lastly, there must be particular attention to keeping a sound balance between vernacular singing and Gregorian chant, especially on the part of those who, because of their office, are more involved in the Church's life and therefore more keenly aware of that life. Accordingly the Pope urges "that Gregorian chant be preserved and performed in monasteries, religious houses, and seminaries as a privileged form of sung prayer and as an element of the highest cultural and instructional value."[8] Moreover, the study and use of Gregorian chant "because of its distinctive qualities are an important foundation for a mastery of sacred music."[9]

4242   In sending you this gift of Pope Paul, I have thought it opportune to restate his frequently expressed mind and intention that the conciliar Constitution on the Liturgy be fully and exactly put into practice. After you have consulted the established diocesan and national agencies responsible for the liturgy, music, pastoral work, and catechetics, you will decide on the most practical method for the faithful to learn and to sing the Latin chants in the booklet *Iubilate Deo*. You will also establish the means for the agencies mentioned to promote the preservation and use

---

    [5] See Instr. MusSacr no. 54 [DOL 508 no. 4175]. Paul VI, Addr. to the Associazione Italiana di Santa Cecilia, 24 Sept. 1972 [Not has as the date 23 Oct.].

    [6] Paul VI, Address to the CIMS, 12 Oct. 1973 [DOL 522 no. 4236].

    [7] SC art. 114 [DOL 1 no. 114].

    [8] Secretariat of State, Letter of Card. J. Villot to the Associazione Italiana di Santa Cecilia, 30 Sept. 1973 [DOL 521 no. 4234].

    [9] Instr. MusSacr no. 52 [DOL 508 no. 4173].

of the Gregorian chant. These steps will provide the liturgical reform with new possibilities for contributing to the building up of the whole Church.

The present volume may be published and a vernacular translation added for a better understanding of the Latin text.

524. SC DIVINE WORSHIP, Booklet *Iubilate Deo*, Preface, 11 April 1974: Vatican Polyglot Press, 1974.

THE BOND OF UNITY . . .

In the Constitution on the Liturgy, after urging that the vernacular take a proper place in liturgical celebration, Vatican Council II adds this directive: "Nevertheless steps should be taken enabling the faithful to say or to sing together in Latin those parts of the Ordinary of the Mass belonging to them."[1]

4243

With this intention, Pope Paul VI on several recent occasions has expressed the desire that Gregorian chant accompany the eucharistic celebrations of the people of God and lend its strong support to these celebrations with its pleasing music and also that the voice of the faithful be heard in both Gregorian and vernacular singing.[2]

The present short volume is a response to the Pope's wishes. It is a collection of the simpler melodies for the faithful to sing together — particularly on the occasion of the Holy Year.

In this way Gregorian chant will continue to be a bond that forms the members of many nations into a single people, gathered together in Christ's name with one heart, one mind, and one voice. This living unity, symbolized by the union of voices that speak in different languages, accents, and inflections is a striking manifestation of the diversified harmony of the one Church. As St. Ambrose exclaims: "How close the bond of unity is when so many people join together in the one chorus. They are like the different strings of the harp that yet produces one melody. The harpist may often make mistakes while playing on just a few strings, but the artist who is the Holy Spirit never makes a mistake while playing on the hearts of a whole people."[3]

May God grant that the desire shared by all will be successfully realized, namely, that the heart of the Church at prayer will have a joyful, resounding voice throughout the world in these pleasing and reverent melodies.[R7]

---

[1]　SC art. 54 [DOL 1 no. 54].

[2]　See Paul VI, Address to a general audience of the CIMS, 12 Oct. 1973 [DOL 522 no. 4235]. See also Secretariat of State, Letter of Card. J. Villot to the meeting of the Associazione Italiana di Santa Cecilia, Genoa, 26–30 Sept. 1963 [DOL 521 no. 4234].

[3]　Ambrose, *Explanationes psalmorum* in Ps. 1:9: PL 14, 925.

[R7]　Commentary in Not 10 (1974) 122: The Congregation for Divine Worship has seen to the publication of the small, but beautifully made volume, *Iubilate Deo* (Vatican Polyglot Press, 54 pp., 11 x 16 cm., printed in black and red, four illustrations inserted from liturgical codices of the Vatican Library, cover title stamped in gold with the first notes of the melody for *Iubilate*, the offertory antiphon of the Second Sunday after Epiphany and the First Sunday after Easter from the old Roman Gradual; see *Ordo cantus Missae* nos. 88 and 89). The volume is a collection of the simpler Gregorian chants that the faithful should know, in keeping with the mind of the Constitution on the Liturgy and the desire expressed by Pope Paul VI on numerous occasions. The volume has been sent in the Pope's name to each of the bishops and superiors general of religious, along with a letter of the Congregation for Divine Worship, which is reprinted in this number of *Notitiae* [See DOL 523].

The first section of *Iubilate Deo* bears the title *Cantus Missae* and supplies all the chants for the

525. SECRETARIAT OF STATE, **Letter** of Cardinal J. Villot to the Archbishop of Salzburg, on the occasion of the 6th International Congress of the CIMS (Salzburg, 26 August–2 September 1974), August 1974: Not 10 (1974) 344–345 (German; excerpt).

4244   [. . .] The efforts of the Consociatio Internationalis Musicae Sacrae on behalf of the preservation of church music and Gregorian chant are known to all. This chant in particular remains for the Church a heritage of inestimable value and of great educational significance.

Ever since he began his pontificate, Pope Paul VI has missed no opportunity to urge composers, pastors, and the faithful to devote all their energies to the furtherance of congregational singing. As the decrees of Vatican Council II are being carried out, the liturgical celebrations are taking on new forms, which call for the understanding and active participation of the faithful. Among these new measures singing is a distinctive factor for the furtherance of participation. It contributes a quality of warmth and festiveness to the liturgy, it both expresses and strengthens a spirit of unity, it helps to bring the whole person into the celebration of the sacred mysteries.

It is absolutely essential that congregational songs, which must be inspired by art, beauty, and devotion, become part of the liturgy in the vernacular: for the majority of the faithful this is the usual form of religious celebration.

Pope Paul wishes to recall the directive he has in past years already put before the Consociatio Internationalis Musicae Sacrae, namely, that it devote all its energies to serving the liturgical reform.

4245   "A new flowering is today awaited for the art of sacred music because in every country the vernacular has been brought into liturgical worship. The vernacular must not be allowed to lack the beauty and expressiveness that lie within the power of genuinely religious music and of singing suited to the texts."[a]

The Consociatio must work in close cooperation with the authorized agencies of the conferences of bishops; they have the responsibility, under the guidance of the liturgical books and the directives of the Holy See, for planning and promoting the liturgy in their respective countries. In this way the Consociatio will be able to offer a valuable service to the Holy See in its concern to carry out the reform of the liturgy. And by acting at the same time as an intermediary for the development of new initiatives and the exchange of experiences the Consociatio has an opportunity to serve the entire Church. One basis for such cooperation is the project to be discussed at the coming meeting, namely, to prepare in many languages a collection of songs that would make it possible for the faithful to join together in God's praises, particularly as representatives of all peoples gather for the celebrations of the Holy Year. [. . .]

Ordinary of the Mass along with the responses incorporated into the new Roman Missal; these are already well known in the vernacular but hardly at all in Latin.

Under the title *Cantus varii,* the second part of the volume contains chants for various celebrations (eucharistic chants, hymns, and canticles, Marian antiphons, the *Te Deum,* etc.).

Although reduced to a minimum, this selection will be extremely useful if the faithful learn the chants contained in the volume, as the Pope and the Congregation for Divine Worship intend. As the preface of the volume says: "In this way [text quoted] devout melodies."

[a]   DOL 522 no. 4236.

526. SECRETARIAT OF STATE, **Letter** of Cardinal J. Villot, on the occasion of the 21st National Congress on Sacred Music sponsored by the Associazione Italiana di Santa Cecilia (Vicenza, 26–29 September 1974) with the theme: Music in Evangelization, 13 September 1974: Not 10 (1974) 345–347 (Italian; excerpt).

Evangelization is an absolute, basic duty of the Church. In its wisdom and by the authority bestowed on it by its divine Founder, the Church chooses the most effective means to bring people the message of salvation, to lead them to a knowledge of God's mysteries and gifts, to guide them in the practice of the supernatural life. In the proclamation of God's word the liturgy holds a preeminent place; Vatican Council II calls the liturgy, by reason of its teaching and pastoral qualities, "the primary and indispensable source from which the faithful are to derive the true Christian spirit" (SC art. 14).[a] In the liturgy, in turn, singing takes on special importance: it is an expression of God's praises, of spirits lifted toward him, and of hearts made one.

4246

Since the earliest times the Church has ennobled singing by making it an integrating part of the liturgical service and a means of evangelization. St. Paul's exhortation to the Ephesians may be cited on this point: "Be filled with the Spirit, addressing one another in psalms and hymns and spiritual songs, singing and making melody to the Lord with all your heart" (Eph 5:18–19). Singing has also often been the means chosen to proclaim and spread the truth and to put down error. Thus St. Ambrose, an outstanding advocate of singing as part of his pastoral ministry, writes: "What could be more impressive than the faith in the Trinity daily professed by the voices of all the people? They vie with each other to profess their faith and they learn through the verses to proclaim Father, Son, and Holy Spirit. Thus those who before could scarcely be called pupils have now all become teachers" (*Sermo contra Auxentium* 34: PL 16, 1017–18). And again: "In the singing of the psalms teaching and enjoyment compete; the one who sings with joy gains instruction at the same time. Lessons taught through force do not last long; but what you have learned with pleasure, once impressed on your mind, is never lost" (*Enarratio in Ps. 1, 10*: PL 14, 925–926).

His illustrious disciple, St. Augustine, echoes Ambrose in the *Confessions*. After recalling the emotion the hymns and canticles of the Ambrosian liturgy awakened in him (see *Conf.* 9, 6: PL 32, 769–770), Augustine says with reference to the sacred texts: "I perceive that these holy words fill my soul with a greater devotion when they are sung than when they are not; the many different sentiments of the soul find in song and voice their own echo and are stirred by I know not what hidden power" (*Conf.* 10, 33: PL 32, 799–800).

A return to this same tradition is marked by the liturgical reform's restoration of responsorial singing. This provides the relevant advantages of opening the way for the entire assembly's participation, of joining together in one voice the minds and hearts of all present, and of instilling in even the most simple people a theme that by its multiple repetition becomes, so to speak, a spiritual souvenir of the celebration they took part in. St. John Chrysostom commented in his own day: "The psalm we have sung has blended our many different voices and from them has raised on high a single, harmonious chorus. Young and old, rich and poor, men and women, slaves and freemen — we have all taken part in the same melody. . . . Nor is it just those present that the song has joined together, but also the dead with the living: the Psalmist himself has sung with us" (*Homilia de studio praesentium* 2: PG 63, 486–487).

---

[a]   DOL 1 no. 14.

4247   As Pope Paul himself has said, sacred music worthy of the name is "a powerful humanizing as well as a spiritualizing instrument. For it draws us near to God, who is light and peace and harmony, fruitful and alive. Raising us up to him, it refines the human spirit, quiets its restlessness and anxiety, puts it into a state of order and serenity" (*Insegnamenti di Paolo VI*, vol. 4, 1966, p. 582). All the parts of the Mass are in themselves already a form of evangelization, because they revivify faith and transform it into adoration. But in singing and music the parts of the Mass can find a powerful and expressive way to foster the participation of the faithful. This also is the reason for the earnest recommendation of singing to proclaim God's gift and to arouse fervor in celebrations of all the sacraments and especially in the liturgy of the word, which is a preparation for the sacrament itself. Singing is added to the liturgy of the hours with all the more reason because of the wealth of psalms and hymns in it and because of its choral structure.

        The Pope's desire therefore is that there will be at least the basic minimum of singing in celebrations with a congregation and that every church will be filled with the sound of music. For music lifts those present up to God, fulfills their deepest aspirations, reenforces their communion in faith and charity. Centers for catechetics, retreats, pastoral meetings, and prayer should resound with hymns and songs. But for these the privileged place is the church itself: its sacredness, deriving from the sacramental presence of the living God, and its atmosphere of silence give the church the power to elicit in the faithful the need to unite their voices in a conjoined expression of faith.

527. SECRETARIAT OF STATE, **Letter** of Cardinal J. Villot to Cardinal C. Ursi, Archbishop of Naples, on the occasion of the 22nd National Congress on Sacred Music (Naples, 22–26 September 1976), on the theme: Music and Parish Life, September 1976: Not 12 (1976) 407–410 (Italian).

4248   Pope Paul VI has welcomed the request, expressed in your letter of 16 August on behalf of the organizers of the 22nd Congress on Sacred Music, Naples, 22–26 September, for a message of encouragement regarding the theme proposed this year by the Associazione Italiana di Santa Cecilia: Music and Parish Life. The Pope has directed me to express before all else his satisfaction at the choice of subject. It provides an especially pastoral focus, because it invites the participants to reflect on the part music must play in the normal development of parish life and on the qualities required today for music to have the power to correspond to the many pastoral aspects of parish life.

        Furthermore, the Pope finds this theme particularly timely and urgent now that the agencies of the Church responsible for carrying out the will of Vatican Council II have advanced the cause of liturgical reform "by so drawing up texts and rites that they express more clearly the holy things they signify and that the Christian people, as far as possible, are able to understand them with ease and to take part in the rites fully, actively, and as befits a community" (SC art. 21).[a]

        Conscious of the important part music has always played in the Church's liturgical celebrations, the conciliar Fathers in decreeing the reform of the liturgy have insisted that "the treasure of sacred music is to be preserved and fostered with great care" (SC art. 114)[b] and have emphasized that "its ministerial function in the

---

    [a]   DOL 1 no. 21.

    [b]   DOL 1 no. 114.

service of the Lord adds delight to prayer, fosters oneness in spirit, and invests the rites with greater solemnity" (SC art. 112).[c]

The continuing revision of liturgical texts and the impressive addition of new   4249
compositions, the fuller liturgical participation required of the faithful, the prominent role assigned to the choir, the adoption of the vernacular — all these are
factors that bring home the need to add new melodies to a rich Gregorian, polyphonic, and popular heritage of abiding value. The Instruction *Musicam sacram*, 5
March 1967,[d] has already provided direction and standards to fill an existing gap
that could create the impression that the reform of the liturgy is incomplete and
lacking in the song that it requires and deserves.

Experts in sacred music thus have before them an immense field of action and
a challenging responsibility: to undertake with rekindled ardor the work of creating
and renewing music for the liturgy. The Pope gladly acknowledges the praiseworthy efforts already exerted to make sacred music match the new liturgical and
pastoral demands. This is true of composers, of those charged with forming choirs
where there have been none or with improving choirs already existing, and of those
charged with promoting the instruction of the faithful so that they join in the parts
of the singing belonging to them.

Yet there is still a long way to go. Sacred song must reach the artistic ideal and
sublimity required of it. It must be the bearer of a religious message that has the
power to elicit from the faithful the spiritual responses matching the Church's
liturgical texts and rites. Sacred song must well up from the depths of the soul and
express fully the communal character of Christian worship (see General Instruction
of the Liturgy of the Hours no. 270).[e] Consequently, it is obviously impossible for
the composition of such a vast, complex musical repertoire to be the product of
hasty improvisation. Instead it will have to be the product of gradual growth,
proceeding apace with the enlightenment of the minds of composers by the Lord's
mysteries and the touching of their hearts. The spark of inspiration so struck will
cause the music designed as the accompaniment and stimulus of the prayer of the
people of God to be created in an atmosphere of deeply Christian spirituality and of
a genuine experience of faith.

The faithful, as well, and in particular choir members, must attain and deepen
a spiritual perceptiveness that is not satisfied with a few, often sentimental hymns,
out of keeping with the spirit of the liturgy, but is attuned to appreciate the beauty
and expressive power of sacred song. According to the goal set by St. Ambrose, they
must develop the attitude "of delight in the Church's harmonious song and in the
people's voices and holy lives that rest upon unity in singing God's praises. . . .
Then they will find joy . . . in hearing this people, the musical instrument played
by God, resounding with the notes of divine revelation and with the Holy Spirit's
inner inspiration" (*Hexaemeron* 3, 1, 5).

Long and taxing labor is involved in the process of making sacred music   4250
advance apace with the liturgical and pastoral ministry. The primary center of such
labor is the parish, which provides the setting for its concrete realization. Thus
music in the parish is the commendable focus of the coming congress on sacred
music, with the related objective of providing practical guidelines and of giving
new impetus to the various projects underway in this area.

---

[c] DOL 1 no. 112.

[d] See DOL 508.

[e] See DOL 426 no. 3700.

The unifying life-source of the parish is the sacrifice of the Mass, "center and high point of the whole life of the Christian community" (CD no. 30).[f] Therefore the spiritual and apostolic effectiveness of the parish depends on the intensity of the faithful's living Christ's mysteries that are renewed sacramentally in the liturgy and that the faithful should bring to bear on Christian life and evangelization.

We cannot forget that today more than ever a parish seeking to be like the leaven in the dough and the light illuminating the entire house must extend its own vitality to many levels. The parish is first of all the community of believers, keenly aware of their baptismal life and committed to showing by their actions their loyalty to Christ the Lord. But the parish includes also catechumens, those who are weak in faith, and those who are Christians in name only. In a word the parish comprises whole groups in need of a catechesis initiating them into Christ's mysteries and the Church's liturgy. And within the parish there are also nonbelievers, those who have not received and welcomed the message of the Gospel and who make up the mission sector of the parish community. Sacred music has a specific message to bring to each of these different categories of people.

For the community of believers the message is ecclesial unity in the joy of the Holy Spirit. St. Basil writes: "The singing of the psalms is a channel for the unifying power of charity; singing brings the faithful into the harmony of being one choir with one heart" (*Homilia in Ps.* 1, 2). Such unity makes possible the experience of the joy of the Holy Spirit. Thus the singing does not mean merely learning new melodies; the songs become a catechesis deepening the faithful's knowledge of the texts and the spiritual content of the mysteries they celebrate in song.

For Christians still weak in faith, as well as for nonbelievers, an assembly enthusiastically singing God's praises has the power to be a herald of goodness, of religious devotion, and of a convinced, lived faith. A short time after his conversion and still full of remorse over the music of the dance and worldly songs, St. Augustine asked himself whether church music might be a danger for weak souls; his conclusion: "When I recall the tears I shed at hearing the singing of your Church at the beginning of my conversion and when I notice that I still am deeply moved, not by the singing but by what the singing is about, if the words are sung with a clear voice and with proper expression, I recognize anew the great value of church music. . . . I tend to approve singing in the Church for the purpose of raising a weak soul to devotion by means of the delights that touch it through the sound of music" (*Conf.* 10:33).

4251   The intrinsic purpose of music is the twofold task of evoking and expressing the most beautiful feelings of the human heart. Sacred music is music that possesses the power to raise the human heart to the heights of perceiving some reflection of God's goodness and beauty. Liturgical and evangelizing music is music that has the further power to make the Christian people one chorus united in order to praise God and proclaim their own faith. The sound of such music has the power to touch God's heart and to announce to the world the joyous hope of the Christian good news.

Pope Paul VI therefore renews his repeated endorsement of the tireless promotion of sacred singing in the parishes through the formation of capable choirs that will also give support to congregational singing. He also again recommends a patient and continuing training of all the faithful so that they may be able to share in the celebration of the holy mysteries as a community and as a singing community. [. . .]

---

f   DOL 7 no. 196.

528. PAUL VI, **Homily** in St. Peter's, excerpt to members of the Associazione Italiana di Santa Cecilia, 25 September 1977: Not 13 (1977) 475 (Italian).

There is no need for us to make a defense of sacred singing to you. No one is in a better position to grasp and appreciate the importance and singular value of your choirs' service to the Church. Without you the liturgy would be missing a strong support and the people's prayer would be missing one wing in its ascent to God. There still is reason, however, to recall that Vatican Council II has opened new paths for the future of sacred music. For in establishing that the first place in liturgical singing belongs to the assembly the Council has still not lessened the role of the choir. In fact the choir's responsibility has come into greater prominence and importance, since choirs must act as a support, a model, and an inspiration for music that is more noble and more ennobling, as the Instruction *Musicam sacram* has said.[a] Because they are at the service of divine worship, your talents and your art are not meant only for yourselves and your listeners, but are the means of glorifying God, an expression and profession of faith. This amounts to saying that your song is prayer. Thus our exhortation to you is: sing well not just with your voice but above all with your heart. For it is the heart that gives value to the praises that issue from your lips; only by welling up from the heart can your song rise to God as a worthy expression of the praise due to him.

Dearest children, we cannot end this meeting without calling your attention again to an ancient adage that stands as a motto for you and as a remembrance of today's celebration: *Bis orat qui bene cantat:* "He who sings well prays doubly." The intensity that prayer gains from song increases its ardor and its power.

Sing, then; sing with both voice and heart. Make everyone see how beautiful it is to pray in song, as you do, with the Church and for the Church. Spread joy, goodness, light. May you keep your souls always filled with fervor and sincerity, so that your lips may always be worthy to celebrate the praises of the Lord in whose honor you sing.

▶   335.   SC CATHOLIC EDUCATION, Instruction *In ecclesiasticam futurorum sacerdotum*, on liturgical formation in seminaries, 3 June 1979:

          no.   58:   Music [no. 2837].

---

[a]   See DOL 508 no. 4140.

4252

SECTION 2. CHANTS FOR MASS

SUMMARY (DOL 529–538). The 10 documents presented here represent the practical application of the attention given by the Constitution on the Liturgy to the active participation
of the faithful, the fulfillment of their proper function by all members of the assembly, the
enrichment of the repertoire of sacred music. Notable in the present section are the numerous cross-references to the General Instruction of the Roman Missal.

—The principal texts deal with four new collections of Latin chants: the *Kyriale simplex*, its
decree of promulgation and introduction are given (DOL 529, 530); for the chants of the
Roman Missal, the decree of promulgation (DOL 531); for *The Simple Gradual*, the decree
promulgating the first edition (DOL 532), its introduction (DOL 533), the decree promulgating the second edition (DOL 536) and its introduction (DOL 537); for the *Ordo cantus
Missae*, the decree of promulgation and the introduction (DOL 534, 535).

—In addition there is a note from the Congregation for Divine Worship on music in
vernacular editions of the Roman Missal (DOL 538).

529. SC RITES (Consilium), **Decree** *Quum Constitutio*, promulgating the *editio typica* of the *Kyriale simplex*, 14 December 1964: AAS 57 (1965) 407.

4253   Because the Constitution on the Liturgy has decreed the preparation of an edition of the simpler Gregorian melodies,[a] the Consilium has carefully compiled a new collection of such melodies for the Ordinary of the Mass.

     In virtue of the faculties given to it by Pope Paul VI, the Congregation of Rites has approved this suitably revised collection of Gregorian melodies for the Ordinary of the Mass, as contained in the attached copy. The Congregation has also declared it to be the authorized collection and granted permission for its use.

     All things to the contrary notwithstanding.

530. SC RITES (Consilium), *Kyriale simplex*, **Introduction**, 14 December 1964: Vatican Polyglot Press, 1965.

4254   The Second Vatican Ecumenical Council in the Constitution on the Liturgy art. 117 has decreed: "It is desirable that an edition be prepared containing the simpler melodies . . . ."[a]

     The present *Kyriale simplex*, responding to the pastoral concern of the Council, supplements the *Kyriale Vaticanum* with the simpler melodies. The present text is not meant to disparage the more complex selections in the *Kyriale Vaticanum*. These may be used in churches where different pastoral considerations recommend their continuance.

     The simpler melodies here provided are those given in the *Editio Vaticana* or in other sources in the Roman, Ambrosian, or Mozarabic Rites. This allows everyone to make a more extensive use of the heritage of the ancient rites, yet the combination of elements from different rites does not indiscriminately and wrongly confuse them. Only in the case of the *Gloria* from the Ambrosian Rite is there a more simple concluding *Amen*; this is not inconsistent with the true ancient usage. There should be no surprise that in our own times these melodies have other uses outside Mass; this in no way detracts from their primary use, which is for the Mass itself.

     The arrangement of the *Kyriale* places the antiphons *Asperges me* and *Vidi aquam* first, followed by five simple settings for the Ordinary of the Mass. There is no intrinsic relationship between these five and the different ranks of the liturgical days. The first of the settings in particular meets the wishes of the Council: "Steps should be taken enabling the faithful to say or sing together in Latin those parts of the Ordinary of the Mass belonging to them" (SC art. 54).[b] But each of the parts is numbered sequentially in order to make it easier, as desired, to have an Ordinary made up of selections from the different settings.

     Following the five settings of the Ordinary, the chant for the dismissal rite (*Ite, Missa est* and *Benedicamus Domini*) is given with only one chant tone in conformity with the current rubrics of the Roman Missal. The last item is the tones for the *Credo*.

     The individual invocations of the *Kyrie* may properly be assigned to two or three cantors or groups of singers.

---

    [a]   See DOL 1 no. 117.

    [a]   DOL 1 no. 117.

    [b]   DOL 1 no. 54.

For the *Agnus Dei* the whole congregation may sing only the responses *miserere nobis* and *dona nobis pacem*, rather than the whole.

An *Appendix* contains two tones for use by the congregation in singing the *Pater noster* with the celebrant.

531. SC RITES (Consilium), Decree *Edita Instructione*, promulgating chants for the Roman Missal, 14 December 1964: AAS 57 (1965) 408.*

After the publication of the Instruction on the correct carrying out of the   4255
Constitution on the Liturgy,[a] certain chants for inclusion in the Roman Missal seemed necessary or useful both for compliance to the Instruction and for the rite of concelebration.

The Consilium has thus carefully compiled the present collection of melodies, which may be used experimentally. In virtue of the faculties given to it by Pope Paul VI, this Congregation of Rites has approved, declared to be authorized, and sanctioned for experimental use the attached collection of Gregorian melodies that are needed in the Roman Missal by reason of the Instruction mentioned and the rite of concelebration.

All things to the contrary notwithstanding.

▶   508.   SC RITES (Consilium), Instruction *Musicam sacram*, on music in the liturgy, 5
            March 1967:

            nos. 27–36:   Singing in the celebration of Mass [nos. 4148–57].
                 65–66:   Instrumental music at Mass [no. 4186–87].

532. SC RITES (Consilium), Decree *Sacrosancti Oecumenici*, promulgating the *editio typica* of *The Simple Gradual*, 3 September 1967: Not 3 (1967) 311.

The Second Vatican Ecumenical Council in the Constitution on the Liturgy   4256
decreed the preparation of an edition of simpler Gregorian melodies for use in smaller churches (SC art. 117).[a] Its purpose is to bring about more effectively the active participation of all the people in the sacred rites celebrated with singing. In obedience to this decree, the Consilium has carried out the composition of the *Graduale simplex* for use in smaller churches. It contains the simpler chants for the Proper of the Mass, which may be used in place of the more complex melodies of the *Graduale Romanum*.

The Congregation of Rites grants that this *Simple Gradual*, approved by Pope Paul VI, may be used at will in smaller churches. It permits this use as regulated by the norms given in *The Simple Gradual* itself, unless some future legislation determines otherwise.

All things to the contrary notwithstanding.

---

*   The chants themselves were published as: *Cantus qui in Missali Romano desiderantur, iuxta Instructionem ad exsecutionem Constitutionis de sacra Liturgia recte ordinandam et iuxta ritum concelebrationis*, Vatican Polyglot Press, 1965.

a   See DOL 23.

a   See DOL 1 no. 117.

533. SC RITES (Consilium), *The Simple Gradual*, **Introduction**, 3 September 1967: Vatican Polyglot Press, 1967; Not 3 (1967) 312–315.

INTRODUCTION

I. NATURE OF THIS EDITION

4257   1.   In the desire to further sacred singing and the active participation of the faithful in sung liturgies, the Second Vatican Ecumenical Council decreed in its Constitution on the Liturgy that, besides the *editio typica* of the Gregorian melodies, "an edition . . . containing the simpler melodies for use in small churches" also be prepared (SC art. 117).[a] In obedience to the conciliar Fathers' intentions, experts have prepared the present edition for the required chants of the Proper of the Mass. It is designed for those churches where a correct rendition of the more complex chants of the *Graduale Romanum* would prove difficult.

4258   2.   The *Graduale Romanum* should be held in high esteem in the Church because of its admirable artistic and devotional qualities; its standing is to remain undiminished. Consequently its continued use is earnestly desired in those churches that have a choir with the *musical training* required to perform the more complex melodies properly.

Even in smaller churches using the *The Simple Gradual* it is preferable to keep certain selections from the *Graduale Romanum*, especially the easier ones or those more familiar through long usage among certain peoples.

4259   3.   Thus there is no reason to use one book to the exclusion of the other. In fact a combination of settings taken from each source can result in greater and welcome variety.

4260   4.   Discriminating use of *The Simple Gradual*, therefore, will not at all impoverish the treasury of Gregorian melodies but will enrich it. This applies, first of all, to the choice of texts, because it introduces into use in the liturgy some texts not given until now in the Roman Missal. It applies, second, to the melodies, because *The Simple Gradual* provides new melodies deriving from the authentic body of Gregorian sources. It applies, thirdly, to pastoral considerations, because *The Simple Gradual* makes sung celebrations possible even for small congregations.

II. CRITERIA EMPLOYED

4261   5.   In order to make possible a nobler, that is, a sung celebration of the eucharist and to ensure the faithful's participation, there is an absolute need for simpler melodies.

4262   6.   For these, however, the more complex melodies in the *Graduale Romanum* could not be the source: under no consideration could it have been right to drop notes or groups of notes (*melismas*) from those melodies. Nor did it seem consistent with the task at hand to compose original, neo-Gregorian melodies for texts of the Roman Missal.

4263   7.   Consequently authentic melodies, answering the intended purpose, have been carefully selected from the deposit of Gregorian chants both in the extant *editiones typicae* and in manuscript sources of the Roman Rite and other Latin rites.

---

   a   DOL 1 no. 117.

8.   This selection of chants, however, has given rise to a new set of texts, since   4264
only in rare cases did a chant melody exist as the setting for words now in the
Roman Missal. Quite often, however, the text of an antiphon taken from a psalm
has no simple melody and the text could not be given as an antiphon. But it does
appear as a verse within the psalm that is sung after the antiphon.

   *Since musical considerations alone governed the choice of the new texts, they may in no way be
used without music.*

III. COMPONENTS OF THE CHANTS

9.   The entrance, offertory, and communion chants are made up of an antiphon,   4265
verse, and reprise of the antiphon.

10.   The chants between the readings, depending on the season of the liturgical   4266
year, are made up of:

   a.   a responsorial psalm, with psalm verse or *Alleluia* as the response;

   b.   a psalm without a response, traditionally called a "tract";

   c.   an *Alleluia* with psalm verses for the seasons when the *Alleluia* is sung or
   another gospel acclamation without *Alleluia* for the period from Septuagesima
   to Easter.

IV. STRUCTURE OF THE MASS FORMULARIES

11.   In the Proper of Seasons not every Sunday has its own proper chants; instead   4267
there are one or more formularies for each liturgical season that may be used on the
Sundays throughout that season.

   Each feast of the Lord does have proper chants.

12.   In the Proper of Saints there are proper chants for the feasts that have prece-   4268
dence when they coincide with a Sunday.

13.   The arrangement of the Common of Saints corresponds to the common in the   4269
Roman Missal, in such a way, however, that only one formulary is given for each
class of saints. But this formulary has several chants for the different parts of the
Mass, thus providing the option to use whichever chant is best suited to a particular
saint.

V. PERSONS NEEDED FOR THE SINGING OF THE CHANTS OF THE SIMPLE GRADUAL

14.   The guiding principle is set forth in the Constitution on the Liturgy: "Each   4270
one, minister or layperson, who has an office to perform, should do all, but only,
those parts which pertain to that office by the nature of the rite and the principles
of liturgy" (SC art. 28).[b] Therefore, in the case of *The Simple Gradual*:

   a.   Antiphons are intoned by a cantor, who also leads the psalms, with the
congregation responding. Psalms may also be sung by the choir.

   b.   Antiphons and the response to the psalms between the readings should be
sung by the entire congregation. The congregation's part may, however, sometimes
be assigned to the choir; but it is better that the whole assembly sing at least the
response to the psalms between the readings, in view of their nature and of the fact
that they are easy to sing.

VI. USE OF THE SIMPLE GRADUAL

15.   The entrance, offertory, and communion antiphons are sung with one verse or   4271
with several as the circumstances suggest.

---

   b   DOL 1 no. 28.

An antiphon is repeated after the verses of a psalm. But there is an option regarding versicles, even including omission of some of them, provided the versicles retained express a complete thought. The verses for the entrance and communion antiphon conclude with *Gloria parti* and *Sicut erat*, combined to make up one whole verse, as is indicated in the text where the common tones are found.

In singing a psalm two elements in the psalm tone in particular are to be respected: the beginning (*initium*), which connects the ending of the antiphon with the intonation of the psalm; the termination, which connects the ending of the psalm tone with the beginning of the antiphon.

4272   16.   The following is the arrangement of the chants between the readings.

a.   During seasons when the *Alleluia* is used, a psalm with a psalm verse as the response and the *Alleluia* with at least one psalm verse are sung; or else a psalm alone with the *Alleluia* as the response.

b.   During seasons when the *Alleluia* is not used, a psalm with a psalm verse as response and, optionally, an antiphon as the gospel acclamation with at least one verse are sung; or else a psalm without response, that is, a tract, and, optionally the gospel acclamation as just described.

c.   During the Easter Season a psalm with the *Alleluia* as the response is sung; or else the *Alleluia* with its psalm.

When two psalms of the same genre are given, it suffices to choose one of them.

When a psalm has more than five verses, at least five, chosen at will, are always sung.

4273   17.   When more than one formulary is given for the same season, the choice of one of them is optional, according to what seems best for the occasion. Some parts may even be chosen from one formulary and some from another.

4274   18.   At communion Ps 33 [34] *I will bless the Lord*, with the response *Alleluia* or *Taste and see*, may always be sung.

▶   120.   CONSILIUM, Communication *Instantibus pluribus*, on norms for the translation of the *Graduale simplex*, 23 January 1968.

▶   242.   SC RITES (Consilium), Norms on use of Eucharistic Prayers I–IV, 23 May 1968:

> Parts that may be sung [nos. 1932, 1935, 1938, 1941].

▶   208.   SC RITES (Consilium); SC DIVINE WORSHIP, General Instruction of the Roman Missal, 4th ed. 27 March 1975:

nos.		
18:	Texts read or sung [no. 1408].	
19:	Importance of singing [no. 1409].	
62:	Singing by the assembly [no. 1452].	
63:	Choir, musicians, organist [no. 1453].	
67:	Psalmist [no. 1457].	
73:	Participation of all concerned in the preparation of the music [no. 1463].	
272:	Lectern, place for singing the responsorial psalm [no. 1662].	
274:	Place for choir, organ, and other musical instruments [no. 1664].	
324:	Choice of chants [no. 1714].	

Chants for the Mass:
nos. 25–26, 83:	Entrance song [nos. 1415–16, 1473].
30, 87:	*Kyrie* [no. 1420, 1477].
31, 87:	*Gloria* [nos. 1421, 1477].
36–40, 90, 92–93:	Chants between readings [nos. 1426–30, 1480,1482–83].
43–44, 98:	*Credo* [no. 1433–34, 1488].
45–47, 99:	General intercessions [nos. 1435–36, 1489].
50, 100:	Presentation of the gifts [nos. 1440, 1490].
55 b, 108:	*Sanctus* [nos. 1445, 1498].
55 (end):	Memorial acclamations [no. 1445].
56 a, 110–111:	Lord's Prayer [nos. 1446, 1500–01].
56 e, 113:	*Agnus Dei* [nos. 1446, 1503].
56 i, 119:	Communion song [nos. 1446, 1509].
56 j, 121:	Song after communion [nos. 1446, 1511].

▶ 275. SC DIVINE WORSHIP, Instruction *Actio pastoralis*, on Masses with special groups, 15 May 1969:

no. 8:   Singing [no. 2129].

▶ 429. SC DIVINE WORSHIP, Norms *Novo Liturgiae Horarum*, on texts for *ad interim* use, 11 November 1971.

II: At Mass [no. 3724].

534. SC DIVINE WORSHIP, Decree *Thesaurum cantus gregoriani* promulgating the *editio typica* of the *Ordo cantus Missae*, 24 June 1972: AAS 65 (1973) 274; Not 8 (1972) 215.

The treasury of Gregorian chant has been passed on to us by tradition and Vatican Council II has explicitly declared in the Constitution on the Liturgy that it must be reverently preserved and put to proper use (SC art. 114 and 117).[a]   4275

To carry out this decision, especially after the publication of new liturgical books revised in keeping with the mind of the Council, this Congregation for Divine Worship has thought it advisable to provide certain directives. They are intended to adapt the *Graduale Romanum* to new conditions and to ensure that no text of the authentic Gregorian chant is lost.

By virtue of the mandate of Pope Paul VI, this Congregation decrees therefore that those who celebrate the eucharist in Latin are to observe the following new plan in arranging the chants for Mass.

All things to the contrary notwithstanding.

---

[a]   See DOL 1 nos. 114 and 117.

535. SC DIVINE WORSHIP, *Ordo cantus Missae*, **Introduction**, 24 June 1974:
Vatican Polyglot Press, 1972.*

INTRODUCTION

I. REFORM OF THE GRADUALE ROMANUM

4276   Reform of the General Calendar and of the liturgical books, particularly the
Roman Missal and Lectionary, has resulted in the need also to make a number of
changes and adaptations in the *Graduale Romanum*. Thus, the suppression of several
celebrations in the liturgical year — for example, the season of Septuagesima, the
octave of Pentecost, the ember days — required taking out the corresponding
Masses. Transference of saints to a different liturgical season entailed making appropriate modifications. The introduction of new Masses called for supplying new
proper chants. And the new plan of biblical readings required transferring a number
of texts (for example, communion antiphons) to other days more closely connected
with the readings.

The criterion for the present rearrangement of the *Graduale* is the prescription
in the Constitution on the Liturgy art. 114: "The treasure of sacred music is to be
preserved and fostered with great care."[a] The revision has thus done no harm to the
authentic corpus of Gregorian chant, but has in some ways enhanced it, since by
eliminating certain later imitations, giving a more appropriate place to ancient texts,
and adding certain norms the revision makes use of this corpus easier and more
varied.

4277   The first concern was to retain the authentic Gregorian treasure in its entirety.
Chants for Masses no longer forming part of the liturgical year have been employed
to compose other Masses (for example, Masses for the weekdays of Advent, for the
weekdays between Ascension and Pentecost); or have replaced other chants that
were repeated often during the year (for example, during Lent or on the Sundays in
Ordinary Time); or, when their style permitted, have been assigned to celebrations
of the saints.

In addition, nearly twenty authentic Gregorian chants that, because of changes
in the course of time, had fallen into disuse have been brought back into the
repertoire. Measures have also been taken against the distortion or mutilation of
any authentic chant; when elements have been removed that were not suited to a
particular liturgical season, for example, in an antiphon text of the *Alleluia* having
notes that form an integral part of the melody.

4278   The elimination, particularly in the case of saints' feasts, of passages that are
late, neo-Gregorian imitations means that only authentically Gregorian chants remain. Nevertheless it remains permissible, for those who wish, to keep and to sing
neo-Gregorian melodies. None has been completely eliminated from the *Graduale Romanum*; in fact for several of received usage no substitution has been made (for example, chants for the solemnities of the Sacred Heart, Christ the King, the Immaculate
Conception). On the other hand, melodies from the authentic corpus and, where
possible, connected with the same text, have replaced neo-Gregorian melodies.

---

* Title of the volume: *Missale Romanum ex decreto Sacrosancti Oecumenici Concilii Vaticani II instauratum
auctoritate Pauli Pp. VI promulgatum, Ordo cantus Missae.*

[a] DOL 1 no. 114.

Finally, the authentic Gregorian repertoire, freed of the nonauthentic melodies,   4279
was carefully allocated throughout the *Graduale* in order to avoid excessive repetition of the same texts and to replace them with other beautiful selections that
appear only once during the year. The utmost care was given in this regard to enrich
the commons, assigning to them all the chants not proper to any particular saint
and thus available for all the saints of the same class. The commons have been
further supplemented with many chants deriving from the Proper of Seasons that
were seldom used. The rubrics make provision as well for use of the newly arranged
commons for the sake of greater flexibility in meeting pastoral needs.

For pastoral reasons also there is an option regarding the chants for the Proper
of Seasons: namely, as circumstances suggest, to replace the text proper to a day
with another text belonging to the same season.

The norms for the singing of the Mass in the front of the *Graduale Romanum*
have also been revised and emended in a way that brings out more clearly the
function of each particular chant.

II. RITES TO BE FOLLOWED IN SINGING THE MASS

1.   When the congregation has gathered and while the priests and ministers are   4280
going to the altar, the entrance antiphon begins. Its intonation may be shorter or
longer as the circumstances warrant; better still, the whole assembly may begin the
chant together. Thus the asterisk in the *Graduale* marking off the part to be intoned
is to be regarded merely as a guide.

When the choir has sung the antiphon, the cantor or cantors sing the verse,
then the choir repeats the antiphon.

The alternation between antiphon and versicles may go on as long as is necessary to accompany the entrance procession. The final repetition of the antiphon,
however, may be preceded by the *Gloria Patri* and *Sicut erat*, sung as the one, final
versicle. When the *Gloria Patri* and *Sicut erat* have a special musical termination, this
must be used with each of the other verses.

If the *Gloria Patri* and the repetition of the antiphon would cause the chant to
last too long, the *Gloria Patri* is omitted. When the procession is short, only one
psalm verse is used or even the antiphon alone, without verse.

Whenever a liturgical procession precedes the Mass, the entrance antiphon is
sung as the procession enters the church or is even omitted, as the liturgical books
indicate in each case.

2.   Each acclamation of the *Kyrie* may be assigned to a different cantor or part of   4281
the choir or congregation. Each acclamation is as a rule sung twice, but may be sung
more than twice, especially by reason of the music itself, as is indicated in no. 491.

Each acclamation is preceded by a brief invocation when the *Kyrie* is sung as
part of the penitential rite.

3.   The hymn *Gloria in excelsis* is intoned by the priest or, if more convenient, by the   4282
cantor. It is sung either by cantors and choir alternating or by two choirs antiphonally. The division of the verses indicated by a double line in the *Graduale* need not be
followed, if a better division, compatible with the music, is devised.

4.   Whenever there are two readings before the gospel, the first — usually from   4283
the Old Testament — is chanted according to the lesson or prophecy tone, with the
usual termination for the final period. The conclusion *Verbum Domini* also is sung
with the same final termination; then all sing the acclamation *Deo gratias* in the
manner usual for the end of lessons.

4284   5.   The gradual response is sung after the first reading by the cantors or the choir. The verse is sung all the way through by the cantors. To be disregarded, therefore, is the asterisk in the *Graduale* indicating the choir's coming in at the end of the gradual verse, the *Alleluia* verse, and the last verse of the tract. When it seems appropriate, the first part of the response may be repeated as far as the verse.

During the Easter season the gradual response is omitted and the *Alleluia* is sung in the way that will be indicated later.

4285   6.   The second reading, from the New Testament, is sung in the epistle tone with its proper termination; the second reading may also be sung in the tone of the first reading. The conclusion *Verbum Domini* is sung according to the melody given among the common tones; all then sing the acclamation *Deo gratias*.

4286   7.   Either the *Alleluia* or tract follows the second reading. The arrangement for the *Alleluia* is this: the cantors sing the entire *Alleluia* and its neumes, then the choir repeats it. But the whole may be sung once by all, should this seem desirable. The cantors sing the verse all the way through; after the verse all repeat the *Alleluia*.

During Lent the tract replaces the *Alleluia*. Two parts of the choir sing the verses antiphonally or the cantors alternate with the choir. The final verse may be sung by all together.

4287   8.   When there is a sequence, it is sung in alternation either by the cantors with choir or by the two parts of the choir; the final *Amen* is omitted. When the *Alleluia* and its verse are not sung, the sequence is omitted.

4288   9.   Whenever there is only one reading before the gospel, it is followed by either the gradual responsory or the *Alleluia* with its verse. During the Easter season one or the other *Alleluia* is sung.

4289   10.   The conclusion *Verbum Domini*, in the way given among the common tones, follows the proper termination of the singing of the gospel; all then sing the acclamation, *Laus tibi, Christe*.

4290   11.   The *Credo* is sung as a rule either by all together or in alternation.

4291   12.   The singing of the general intercessions follows local custom.

4292   13.   After the offertory antiphon, versicles may be sung, depending on tradition; but they also may be omitted, including the *Domine, Iesu Christe* in a Mass for the dead. After each verse there is a repetition of the part of the antiphon marked for repetition.

4293   14.   After the preface, all sing the *Sanctus* and after the consecration all join in the memorial acclamation.

4294   15.   After the doxology of the eucharistic prayer, all sing the acclamation, *Amen*. Then the priest alone pronounces the invitation for the Lord's Prayer and all sing it with him. The priest alone continues with the embolism and all join in the concluding doxology.

4295   16.   During the breaking of the bread and the commingling, the invocation *Agnus Dei* is sung by the cantors and answered by all. The *Agnus Dei* may be repeated in a way conforming to the music as often as is necessary to accompany the breaking of the bread. At the last repetition the conclusion is *dona nobis pacem*.

17. The communion antiphon is begun as the priest receives the body of the Lord. It is sung in the same way as the entrance antiphon, but with proper provision for the cantors to receive communion.

4296

18. After the final blessing by the priest, the deacon sings the *Ite, missa est* and all join in the acclamation, *Deo gratias*.

4297

III. USE OF THE ORDO CANTUS MISSAE

19. A great variety of readings has been introduced into the Roman Missal, but the chants for Mass received from tradition cannot be changed. Accordingly, the same chant formulary is used with the different readings in the Lectionary for the three-year cycle (A, B, C) established for Sundays.

4298

For weekdays the chants of the previous Sunday are used again, both with the readings assigned to each day of the special seasons — Advent, Lent, and Easter — and with the first reading for Ordinary Time, in its two-year cycle (I and II).

Chants closely related to the readings should, of course, be appropriately transferred for use with these readings.

20. After each basic formulary, changes that need to be made in the Proper of Seasons are indicated in the *Ordo cantus Missae* by means of the following symbols:

4299

A, B, C for Sundays, solemnities, and certain feasts;

I and II with arabic numerals adjoined in parentheses for the weekdays (7 is the numeral for Saturday); arabic numerals alone for the weekdays of the other seasons.

These symbols are references to the section of the *Ordo* (nos. 136–141) that lists all the changes together.

21. As its principal norm, this *Ordo cantus Missae* has the aim of respecting the arrangement of the Roman Missal as faithfully as possible. This is the reason for the transferral or change of some chant formularies.

4300

COMMUNION PSALMS

22. The numbering of the psalms and their verses is that of the Neo-Vulgate edition (Vatican Polyglot Press, 1969). The format of the verses and their parts is that of the *Liturgia Horarum* (Vatican Polyglot Press, 1971).

4301

23. An asterisk attached to a psalm number indicates that the antiphon is not from the psalter and therefore that the psalm is provided as an option. In such a case another psalm may be substituted at will, for example, Ps 33 [34], which by an ancient tradition is used at communion.

4302

When this psalm is given as the psalm at communion, no particular verses are usually suggested, since all the verses are so relevant.

▶ 523. SC DIVINE WORSHIP, Letter *Voluntati obsequens*, accompanying *Iubilate Deo*, 14 April 1974.

▶ 524. SC DIVINE WORSHIP, Booklet *Iubilate Deo*, Introduction, 14 April 1974.

536. SC DIVINE WORSHIP, **Decree** *Cantus faciliores,* promulgating the 2nd *editio typica* of the *Graduale simplex*, 22 November 1974: Not 11 (1975) 292.[R1]

4303   The simpler chants belonging to the Ordinary and the Proper of Mass were published in the *Kyriale simplex* of 1964[a] and the *Graduale simplex* of 1967.[b] The purpose of these chants was to fulfill the precepts of Vatican Council II's Constitution on the Liturgy requiring an edition of the simpler Gregorian melodies for use in smaller churches (SC art. 117).[c]

The purpose of these chants was to fulfill the precepts of Vatican Council II's Constitution on the Liturgy requiring an edition of the simpler Gregorian melodies for use in smaller churches (SC art. 117).

Since that time, after the revision of the General Roman Calendar, of the psalter in the Neo-Vulgate edition, and of the liturgical books for the celebration of Mass, a new arrangement of the chants of the *Graduale Romanum* appeared in the *Ordo cantus Missae* of 1972.[d] This edition emended and supplemented the *Graduale simplex* and *Kyriale simplex*, which are now put into a one-volume edition.

The Congregation for Divine Worship now releases this edition, approved by Paul VI, and declares it to be the *editio typica*, authorized for liturgical use according to the norms in the *Graduale* itself.

All things to the contrary notwithstanding.

537. SC DIVINE WORSHIP, *Graduale simplex* (2nd *editio typica*), **Introduction**, 22 November 1974: Vatican Polyglot Press, 1975.

INTRODUCTION

I. NATURE OF THIS EDITION

1–4.   [Text as in 1st edition.[a]]

II. CRITERIA EMPLOYED

5–9.   [Text as in 1st edition nos. 5–8.[b]]

[R1]   Not 11 (1975) 291 has this commentary: The *Graduale simplex* was first published in 1967. Previous to it came publication of the *Kyriale simplex* and the *Cantus qui in Missali Romano desiderantur* (1965). Later, after the new *Missale Romanum* and *Ordo Lectionum Missae* were issued, the corresponding *Ordo cantus Missae* (1972) appeared. In view of all this a new edition of the *Graduale simplex* has been prepared with modifications and a new arrangement of its contents to conform to the books mentioned. In addition the *Kyriale simplex*, *Graduale simplex*, and some elements of the *Ordo cantus Missae* (particularly those pertaining to the chants for the Ordinary of the Mass) have been combined into the one work.

Therefore the Introduction reprinted here has also been revised at several points. The volume contains three main sections: I. Chants in the Ordinary of the Mass; II. *Kyriale simplex*; III. *Graduale simplex*. This in turn includes: the Proper of Seasons, the Proper of Saints, the commons, ritual Masses, Masses for various needs and occasions, liturgy for the dead (Masses and funerals). Finally, there are also common tones, an appendix with chants for the sprinkling with holy water, for the general intercessions, for communion, and with a selection of other chants (*Tantum ergo, Veni creator, Te Deum,* Marian antiphons) and the Litany of the Saints.

   [a]   See DOL 529 and 530.

   [b]   See DOL 532 and 533.

   [c]   See DOL 1 no. 117.

   [d]   See DOL 534 and 535.

   [a]   See DOL 533 nos. 4257–60.

   [b]   See DOL 533 nos. 4261–64.

III. CHANTS OF THE *KYRIALE SIMPLEX*

10. Its parts are so arranged as to form five simple settings for the Ordinary of the   4304
Mass; but there is no intrinsic relationship between the five settings and the
different ranks of the liturgical days. The first of the settings in particular meets this
requirement of the Council: "Steps should be taken enabling the faithful to say or
sing together in Latin those parts of the Ordinary of the Mass belonging to them"
(SC art. 54).ᶜ But each of the parts is numbered sequentially in order to make it
easier, as desired, to have an Ordinary made up of selections from the different
settings.

11. At the end of the hymn *Gloria in excelsis* taken from the Ambrosian Rite, there is   4305
a more simple *Amen*; this is not inconsistent with the true ancient usage.ᵈ

12. Rather than singing the entire *Agnus Dei*, the congregation may simply respond   4306
with the *miserere nobis* and *dona nobis pacem*.ᵉ

IV. COMPONENTS OF THE CHANTS

13–14. [Text as in 1st edition, nos. 9–10.ᶠ]

V. STRUCTURE OF THE MASS SETTINGS

15. [Text as in 1st edition no. 11.ᵍ]

16. In the Proper of Saints there are proper chants for the celebrationsʰ that have   4307
precedence when they coincide with a Sunday.

17. The arrangement of the Commons of Saints corresponds to the commonsⁱ in   4308
the Roman Missal, in such a way, however, that only one formulary is given for
each class of saints. But this formulary has several chants for the different parts of
the Mass, thus providing the option to use whichever chant is best suited to a
particular saint.

VI. PERSONS NEEDED FOR THE SINGING OF THE CHANTS OF THE *GRADUALE SIMPLEX*

18. [Text as in 1st edition no. 14.ʲ]

VIII. USE OF THE *GRADUALE SIMPLEX*

19. [Text as in 1st edition no. 15.ᵏ]

20. The following is the arrangement of the chants between the readings: 4309

When there are two readings before the gospel:

a.   Outside Lent and the Easter season, the responsorial psalm is sung after the
first reading; after the second reading, the psalm with *Alleluia* as the verse or the
antiphon *Alleluia* with its own verses.

ᶜ   DOL 1 no. 54.

ᵈ   See DOL 530 no. 4254.

ᵉ   Nos. 10–12 are a revision of the 1964 *Kyriale simplex*, Introduction; see DOL 530 no. 4254.

ᶠ   See DOL 533 nos. 4265–66.

ᵍ   See DOL 533 no. 4267.

ʰ   1st ed.: "feasts" for "celebrations" [DOL 530 no. 4268].

ⁱ   1st ed.: "common" for "commons" in both places here [DOL 533 no. 4269].

ʲ   See DOL 533 no. 4270.

ᵏ   See DOL 533 no. 4271.

b. During Lent, after the first reading, the first responsorial psalm is sung; after the second, either the second responsorial psalm or an antiphon of acclamation or a tract.

c. During the Easter season, after the first reading the first or second psalm with *Alleluia* as the verse is sung; after the second reading, either the second psalm with *Alleluia* as the verse or the antiphon *Alleluia* with its verses.

Whenever there is only a single reading before the gospel, a single chant may be chosen at will from those appropriate to the reading.

At least five verses of a psalm, chosen at will, are always sung, whenever more than five are given.

4310   21. [Text for the first paragraph as in 1st edition no. 17.[1]]

At communion the singing of Ps. 33 [34] *I will bless the Lord*, with the response *Alleluia* or *Taste and see*, is always permitted.

But, as is indicated at the end of this volume, p. 462, other suitable chants may be chosen at will.[m]

538. SC DIVINE WORSHIP, Note *Passim quaeritur*, on the music for inclusion in vernacular editions of the Roman Missal, May 1975: Not 11 (1975) 129–132.

4311   From several quarters this question has been raised: Is music for sung Masses *obligatory* in new vernacular editions of the Roman Missal for the celebrant's use?

Certain recent editions do provide the music for the celebrant's chant; others do not. The result is the growing practice of Masses with no singing, not even of those parts that by preference should be sung, namely, "those to be sung by the priest or ministers with the people responding or by the priest and people together" (GIRM no. 19).[a]

4312   1. The reply to the question proposed is an unqualified yes. Like both the former and the new Roman Missal (see its *Appendix*), the various national or regional, vernacular editions must provide for the Ordinary of the Mass the music to be sung by the celebrant, the ministers, and the congregation or choir.

4313   2. *Which parts of the Mass are to be sung?*

We will confine ourselves to the Ordinary of the Mass. The best way to respond to the question is to look at what can be gathered from received usage, the melodies supplied in the *editio typica* of the *Missalis Romani*, and the literary genre of the particular parts of the Mass.

a. *Traditional usage.* The Missal in received usage until 1970 carried the following music for the Ordinary of the Mass:

Four intonations for the *Gloria*, one for the *Credo*.

All the prefaces, with both the solemn and the simple tone.

The *Pater noster*, with two melodies.

---

[1]   See DOL 533 no. 4273.

[m]   The second paragraph replaces and adds to 1st ed., no. 18 [see DOL 533 no. 4274].

[a]   DOL 208 no. 1409.

The *Ite, Missa est*, with six melodies, the *Benedicamus Domino* with four, and the *Requiescat in pace*.

An appendix carried optional chants for intoning the *Gloria* and *Credo*, for prefaces, the *Ite, Missa est Benedicamus Domino*, and for the *Asperges*.

In addition, the chant books, namely, the *Graduale Romanum* and its companion volume, the *Liber usualis*, contained melodies for other texts, for example, for the singing of collects.

b. The *editio typica* of the current Roman Missal (1970) in its Appendix has music for the Ordinary of the Mass, namely, for:

The greeting formularies at the beginning of Mass.

The acclamations after the readings.

The preface tones (simple and solemn).

The eucharistic prayers.

The doxology of the eucharistic prayers (two tones).

The *Pater noster* (two tones).

The tone for the embolism.

The tone for the final blessing.

But also to be kept in mind for a correct idea about the singing is the *Ordo cantus Missae*, published in 1972. It provides music for a number of other formularies, namely, for:

The sign of the cross at the beginning of Mass.

The tones for the opening prayer.

The tones for readings.

A third tone for the *Pater noster*.

The *Pax Domini*.

The solemn blessings and prayer over the people.

The bishop's blessing.

Nor should we forget that the monks of Solesmes, out of their own zeal and initiative, have published a booklet containing melodies for the entire Mass.

c. *Literary genre*. Not all these melodies must be contained in vernacular editions of the Missal, since a further consideration is the literary genre of the liturgical texts and the idiom of each language. Thus some texts sung in Latin do not lend themselves to vernacular singing.

The following are reasonable, general criteria:

Invitations or brief instructions by the celebrant or deacon are *spoken* rather than sung.

Readings are *proclaimed* rather than sung. But it is useful to sing the final phrase of the first and second reading and particularly the opening dialogue and final phrase of the gospel reading.

There is great *advantage* to the singing of prayers, and above all the most exalted of them, the *preface* leading up to the singing of the *Sanctus*, surely ought to be sung.

Acclamations by all means should be sung.

The chants of the Mass, namely, the *Gloria, Sanctus, Agnus Dei*, also should be sung. But these are not at issue here, since music for them is printed in the books intended for the use of the congregation.

3.   *Practically speaking* the formularies for the Ordinary of the Mass that should be   4314
provided with music in vernacular editions of the Roman Missal are:

The greetings.

Acclamations:

> *The Lord be with you. And also with you.*
>
> *A reading from the Gospel according to N. Glory to you, O Lord.*
>
> *This is the word of the Lord. Praise to you, Lord Jesus Christ.*
>
> *Let us proclaim the mystery of faith* and the corresponding three acclamations.
>
> *For the kingdom.*

The prefaces.

The parts of the eucharistic prayers that may be sung.

The *Lord's Prayer* with its embolism.

Lord, Jesus Christ, you said to your apostles (because it introduces the greeting, *May the peace of the Lord*).

The simple and a solemn tone for the final blessing.

A tone for the bishop's blessing.

The Mass is ended and *Thanks be to God.*

Besides the melodies listed for the Ordinary of the Mass, the former and, to some extent, the current Missal supplied music for various celebrations in the yearly cycle, for the *Exsultet*, for example. Such melodies should also be composed and incorporated into new vernacular missals.

4315   4.   *One melody or several?*

The former Missal carried two or more melodies.

That standard may still be followed. But too many melodies cause confusion. For these "official" melodies are meant to facilitate the participation of the people in the sung Mass. When melodies are multiplied, the congregation does not learn them readily and in particular finds it difficult to answer the acclamations.

4316   5.   *Is the music to be put in an appendix to the Missal or in the text itself?*

In the text, and with the passage to which the music belongs. This is the more practical course, preferable to consigning it to the Appendix as the *editio typica* does.

An exceptional situation arises when the same edition of the Missal must serve several regions or nations with diverse musical traditions. In such a case the music would have to be in a separate fascicle as an appendix in the volume. But this remains the exception.

When the music is printed with the passages to which it belongs, it has the added advantage of reminding the priest celebrant that these parts of the Mass are *as a rule* to be sung; this is all to the good for the solemnity and effectiveness of the celebration.

From now on, therefore, the vernacular editions of the Missal submitted for confirmation by the Congregation for Divine Worship must carry *suitable melodies* for all the parts mentioned, especially of the Ordinary, that should be sung or may be sung.

▶   On singing in other celebrations, see Chapters Three and Four.

CHAPTER SEVEN

ART AND FURNISHINGS

SUMMARY (DOL 539–554). In its seventh and final chapter the Constitution on the Liturgy discussed the general norms of sacred art and the care to be taken for the beauty and becomingness of all the material things used in the liturgy. This final chapter of *Documents on the Liturgy*, accordingly, presents a section of general texts on sacred art, then specific sections on places of worship and on vestments.

Section 1. General Documents

SUMMARY (DOL 539–541). The general texts are an address of Paul VI on the relationship of art to the liturgy (DOL 539), his address on the significance of the Council with regard to sacred art (DOL 540), and a circular letter of the Congregation for the Clergy on safeguarding the Church's artistic heritage (DOL 541).

▶ 1.   VATICAN COUNCIL II, Constitution on the Liturgy *Sacrosanctum Concilium*, 4
         December 1963:

         art. 39:   Competence of bodies of bishops regarding the
                                arts in the liturgy [no. 39].
               122–130:   Art and furnishings [nos. 122–130].[a]

▶ 20.   PAUL VI, Motu Proprio *Sacram Liturgiam*, on putting into effect some prescriptions
         of the Constitution on the Liturgy, 25 January 1964:

         art. II: Diocesan commission on sacred art [no. 280].

▶ 23.   SC RITES (Consilium), Instruction *Inter Oecumenici* (first), 26 September 1964:

         nos. 13 c: Sacred art in major seminaries [no. 305].
              18:              Sacred art in religious houses of formation [no.
                               310].

▶ 19.   VATICAN COUNCIL II, Pastoral Constitution on the Church in the Modern
         World *Gaudium et spes*, 7 December 1965:

         no. 62:   Contemporary art [no. 275].

▶ 332. CONGREGATION OF SEMINARIES AND UNIVERSITIES, Instruction *Doctrina
         et exemplo*, on liturgical formation in seminaries, 25 December 1965:

         nos. 60–63:   Training in sacred art [nos. 2731–34].

539. PAUL VI, **Address** to participants in a national congress of diocesan
liturgical commissions of Italy, on liturgy and sacred art, 4 January 1967:
Not 3 (1967) 33–36 (Italian; excerpt).

4317   Along with others from the world of art, we should also honor those repre-
         senting the world of liturgy, and in particular the members of the Commissione
         Episcopale Italiana per la Liturgia and all those delegates of the diocesan commis-
         sions for liturgy and for sacred art.

             In so doing we have the pleasure of singling out the authorized and qualified
         spokesmen of those agencies of the church hierarchy. The conciliar Constitution on
         the Liturgy *Sacrosanctum Concilium* has summoned the existing commissions to a new
         vitality and has commanded their creation where they do not exist.[a] The present
         meeting is a reason for our own satisfaction and hope, since it is our responsibility
         to ensure that the conciliar decisions are effectively implemented. It is pleasant to
         note that this first postconciliar meeting in Italy concerns the carrying out of one of
         the important conciliar decisions. That decision has a practical and canonical im-
         port, but it also involves an issue of principle, namely, the relationship between
         liturgy and sacred art. The Council prescribes that both the regional and diocesan

         ―――――――――
         [a] See DOL 1 nos. 43–46.

liturgical commission enlist the help "of experts in liturgical science, music, art, and pastoral practice" (SC art. 44).[b] The Council at the same time suggests that the three commissions of liturgy, music, and art "work in closest collaboration; indeed it will often be best to fuse the three of them into one single commission" (SC art. 46).[c]

This reaffirms a principle supported by the whole of Catholic tradition, name-   4318
ly, that the celebration of the liturgy has an aesthetic aspect. Liturgy and art are sisters. There are profound reasons not only justifying but to a degree demanding that expressions of both the sacred and the artistic surround the liturgical act — the Church's communal, official prayer and the renewal of mysteries in which God's action is present and God's presence is actual. You are all aware of such reasons and, particularly in this era of renewal, are reflecting on them in order to have a clear idea and sound criterion for the why and how of the close relationship that must exist between Catholic worship and sacred art. Worship must give to the expressions of art a content that they could not otherwise aspire to and that completely fills them with a vibrant movement toward pure and absolute beauty. Sacred art, in turn, must bring to worship its purest and fullest gift, the gift of an expression that transcends words, that somehow embodies the spiritual and spiritualizes the material. Jesus Christ has appeared in order to be in our midst as the visible image of the invisible God (see Col 1:15; Jn 1:17 and 14:9; 2 Tm 1:10, etc.). For the institution of the eucharist, Jesus also wanted "a large upper room furnished" (Lk 22:12) and wanted to make use of the festive setting of the Jewish Passover meal ("giving thanks, he blessed . . ."; see *La Maison Dieu* 87, L. Ligier, "De la cène de Jésus à l'anaphore de l'Eglise"). Ever since then the Christian liturgy's connatural setting has been a ritual that is external, decorous, sung, full of poetry, filled with remembrance, symbolism, promise, and blessing. Therefore the liturgy has spoken the language of sacramental signs, utterly simple in themselves yet calling for an appreciation, a recognition, and a celebration that the community of the faithful, in the most sacred and worthy manner possible, offers to the mystery present.

Reflection on the origins of the marriage between liturgy and art, particularly   4319
on the eucharistic practice of the early Church, will encourage us to defend that union in our own time as the source of our worship's outward expressions of the sacred. Theological research into the essence of the eucharistic liturgy does lead to a recognition of the primacy of the sacrament itself, because its purpose is the unity of the Mystical Body and because it is par excellence the sacrament of charity (ST 3a, 73.2 and 3). But that does not in any way justify arbitrarily stripping church-established worship of the sacral and aesthetic forms that surround it and present it to the people of God. Such a course would do more than cast aside the elements of art gracing divine worship; it would trivialize the meaning of the mystery celebrated, undermine the principles of community prayer, and could lead ultimately to doubt or even denial of the reality of the sacrament of the eucharist.

The return to sources, however, will also teach us to reexamine the relationship mentioned between liturgy and art in order to strengthen that bond wherever it may have become weakened or altered. We should be guided by the preeminent purpose of the conciliar Constitution on the Liturgy, to restore to the people of God active participation in the celebration of worship. That task involves certain norms that art must take as its own if it wishes to rise to the sacral status that Catholic worship assigns to it and expects of it. The primary norm is that sacred art be functional, that is, the felicitous expression of what the liturgy is meant to be, the

---

[b]   DOL 1 no. 44.

[c]   DOL 1 no. 46.

worship of God and the language of the community at prayer. It may be true that the incorporation of art into liturgy imposes on art a number of strictures and prescriptions, which implies that art may claim a greater and in a sense fuller freedom apart from liturgy. We must acknowledge such a broader range of choices because liturgy, especially the pastoral liturgy intended by the Council, clearly does not exhaust the immeasurable fruitfulness of art, even when devoted only to its religious expression.

4320   But permit us to pass over at this time the many thoughts your presence suggests and to conclude this most welcome meeting with two recommendations. First, to the liturgists among you: strive to put the reform of the liturgy into practice with wisdom, willingness, and effectiveness. Keep away from the arbitrary in liturgy and keep away from obstructionist criticisms. Show people what the Council stands for in regard to prayer. Show them what the Catholic Church stands for, that in it the law of charity is expressed, with loyalty and good will, in the law of obedience. Conversely, show people by your deeds that the law of obedience is completely on the side of the law of charity. In this era that is stifling prayer, faith, the eschatological expectation of a future destiny, Providence holds out to us a golden opportunity we must not lose: to give art to the people again, to give them back a sense of the genuine life of religion. You who are the directors and members of diocesan liturgical commissions, be assured that the Pope is gratified for your disciplined, willing, and intense work and that great hopes are placed in you for a renaissance of the liturgy and therefore of the Christian life among the Italian people.

4321   To those of you who are dedicated to sacred art we say that there is a need to give a more careful and effective attention to preserving and renewing the immense and priceless patrimony of religious art in Italy. Make this effort; it is a duty and the time to honor it is now. We feel sure that the civil authorities charged with the preservation of works of art will have no wish to exclude you, hinder you, or ignore you in the awesome and delicate work of safeguarding our artistic treasures. Rather they will wish to help you to preserve and honor such works for the sake not only of aesthetic appreciation, but above all of the people's devotion; this was the reason these treasures were conceived and created in the first place. You will also receive help, please God, to add to these treasures beautiful works of your own inspiration that will show that creativity in sacred art has not died out among the people of Italy.

In conclusion, the Church has need of saints, yes, but also of artists, of skilled and good artists. Both saints and artists are a witness of the living Spirit of Christ. Yours is the trust and the privilege of giving to the Church new artists who will express and advance the holiness of the Church.

▶   208.   SC Rites (Consilium); SC DIVINE WORSHIP, General Instruction of the Roman Missal, 1st ed. 6 April 1969; 4th ed. 27 March 1975.

nos. 287–288:	Liturgical furnishings in general [nos. 1677–78].
289–296:	Vessels [nos. 1679–86].
311–312:	Other articles used in church [nos. 1701–02].

▶   275.   SC DIVINE WORSHIP, Instruction *Actio pastoralis*, on Masses with special groups, 15 May 1969.

| no. 11 b: | Furnishings, vessels, vestments [no. 2132]. |

540. PAUL VI, **Address** to the Pontifical Commission for Sacred Art in Italy, on the conciliar spring and sacred art, 17 December 1969: Not 6 (1970) 3–6 (Italian; excerpt).

[. . .] The conciliar spring has also come with its promise of progress to the   4322
choice garden of sacred art; the plough of the Council has turned over this garden for new growth. We have great hope of progress; we could ask for nothing better than that sacred art flourish anew under the breath of the Holy Spirit whom the Church has called upon for all its vital activity in this historic period.

COUNCIL OF NICAEA II

We wish to point out how the Council has spoken explicitly of sacred art. But   4323
it is interesting to note that this is not the first time that the topic has come up in a council of the Church. We all know how, in 787 A.D., the Council of Nicaea II by its teaching put an end to the Iconoclastic Controversy in the East and then throughout the Church. The Council vindicated the legitimacy of sacred images on the one hand and, on the other, the place of icons and everything connected with their veneration in worship as purely relative and symbolic. The honor showed to images has reference not so much to them as to their "prototype," that is, to the person and the truth they represent. Their purpose is to raise the spirit beyond the figure to what the figure stands for (see Denz-Schön 600–601). The teaching is absolutely clear to us all, but at this historic period and in the present spiritual climate the teaching is most timely as a safeguard against any idolatrous tendency regarding images and as a guarantee of the legitimacy invested by tradition in the creations of sacred art, of its symbolic and didactic role, and of its power to develop and grow (see St. Basil, *De Spiritu Sancto* 18: PG 32, 149).

COUNCIL OF TRENT

The Council of Trent again took up the issue in order to correct ambiguous   4324
expressions of the scholastics (see ST 3a, 25.3) and to counteract certain contrary Protestant positions by reaffirming the propriety of honoring images (see Denz-Schön 1823); the Council also added the customary defense of the worth and usefulness of sacred art (see Bossuet, passages on "Le culte dû aux images": *Oeuvres compl.* 8, 21–29; 7, 429–443, ed. 1846). There is an entire body of literature in history, theology, apologetics, and aesthetics that shows us the Church's justification and wisdom in regard to this exquisite and sublime outward expression of the spirit. The Church entrusts art with a mediating role, analogous, we might say, to the role of the priest or, perhaps better, to that of Jacob's ladder descending and ascending. Art is meant to bring the divine to the human world, to the level of the senses, then, from the spiritual insight gained through the senses and the stirrings of the emotions, to raise the human world to God, to his inexpressible kingdom of mystery, beauty, and life. In making use of its many perceptible signs, the liturgy shows its own artistic vocation; when it is well understood and properly celebrated, the liturgy superbly fulfills this vocation in both beauty of form and profundity of content.

VATICAN COUNCIL II

Vatican Council II in the Constitution on the Liturgy devotes the whole of   4325
chapter 7 to sacred art in its relation to liturgy. The Council thus gives art a new impetus that will, we hope, mean its setting out on new and promising paths. An added reason for hope is that the new directions of these paths are marked by the freedom that Pius XII's Encyclical *Mediator Dei* affirms authoritatively as the right of art itself even more than of the artist: "We must not scorn and out of prejudice sweepingly reject contemporary forms and creations; it is surely necessary to give

free scope to the art of our own times, while avoiding through a sound balance both excessive realism and exaggerated symbolism and while taking into consideration the Christian community rather than the personal views and tastes of artists" (AAS, 1947, 590. See SC art. 123ᵃ).

4326   This leads us to conclude by encouraging you to act in such a way that, under the aegis of the liturgy, that is, divine worship, a bond of union, an alliance, will be reestablished between modern art and the life of religion. This should contribute to restore to art its two greatest and most characteristic values. The first is beauty, perceptible beauty (*id quod visum placet*: a beauty grasped in the integrity, proportion, and purity of the work of art; ST 1a, 39.1). The second is that indefinable but vibrant value, the artistic spirit, the lyrical experience in the artist that is reflected in his work. The alliance between art and the life of religion will also succeed in giving again to the Church, the Bride of Christ, a voice that love inspires and that inspires love.

There is a second concluding point to which Vatican Council II attributes particular importance. Before anticipating a new epiphany for sacred art, as though it could spontaneously give itself a new birth and new creativity, we must take pains with the formation of artists. As always we must begin with the education of the person (see SC art. 127).ᵇ [. . .]

▶   52.   SC DIVINE WORSHIP, Instruction (third) *Liturgicae instaurationes*, 5 September 1970:

nos. 8:   Vessels and furnishings [no. 526].
     9:          Place of the eucharist [no. 527].
     10:         Arrangement and decoration of places of worship [no. 528].

541. SC CLERGY, **Circular Letter** *Opera artis* to presidents of the conferences of bishops, on the care of the Church's historical and artistic heritage, 11 April 1971: AAS 63 (1971) 315–317.

4327   Works of art, the most exalted expressions of the human spirit, bring us closer and closer to the divine Artisan[1] and with good reason are regarded as the heritage of the entire human family.[2]

The Church has always held the ministry of the arts in the highest esteem and has striven to see that "all things set apart for use in divine worship are truly worthy, becoming, and beautiful, signs and symbols of the supernatural world."[3] The Church through the centuries has also safeguarded the artistic treasures belonging to it.[4]

ᵃ   See DOL 1 no. 123.

ᵇ   See DOL 1 no. 127.

[1]   See SC art. 122 [DOL 1 no. 122].

[2]   See Pius XII, *Discorsi e Radio messaggi*, Ed. pol. Vat., v. 15, 448. SC Clergy, General Directory on the Pastoral Ministry in Tourism: AAS 61 (1969) 366.

[3]   SC art. 122 [DOL 1 no. 122].

[4]   See *La Legislazione ecclesiastica sull'Arte*, Card. C. Costantini, ed., "Fede e Arte" 5 (1957) 359ff. SC Council, letters on this subject, especially 30 Dec. 1952: AAS 45 (1953) 101–102; *Regolamento relativo al prestito di opera d'arte di proprietà della Santa Sede*: AAS 57 (1965) 677ff. GIRM ch. 5, "Arrangement and Furnishing of

Accordingly, in our own times as well, bishops, no matter how hard pressed by their responsibilities, must take seriously the care of places of worship and sacred objects. They bear singular witness to the reverence of the people toward God and deserve such care also because of their historical or artistic value.

It grieves the faithful to see that more than ever before there is so much unlawful transferal of ownership of the historical and artistic heritage of the Church, as well as theft, confiscation, and destruction.

Disregarding the warnings and legislation of the Holy See,[5] many people have made unwarranted changes in places of worship under the pretext of carrying out the reform of the liturgy and have thus caused the disfigurement or loss of priceless works of art.

In some places church buildings no longer serving their original purpose are in such a state of neglect that grave harm is being done to the local ecclesiastical heritage and works of art.

In its responsibility for the administration of the artistic patrimony of the Church,[6] this Congregation has taken cognizance of these facts and circumstances. It therefore urges the conferences of bishops to lay down regulations applying to this extremely important matter.

Meanwhile the Congregation rightfully issues the following reminders and decrees.

1. "In commissioning artists and choosing works of art that are to become part of a church, the highest artistic standard is to be set in order that art may aid faith and devotion and be true to the reality it is to symbolize and the purpose it is to serve."[7]   4328

2. Works of art from the past are always and everywhere to be preserved so that they may lend their noble service to divine worship and their help to the people's active participation in the liturgy.[8]   4329

3. Each diocesan curia is responsible for measures to ensure that, in conformity with the norms set by the local Ordinary, rectors of churches, after consultation with experts, prepare an inventory of places of worship and of the contents that are of artistic or historical importance. This is to be an itemized inventory that lists the value of each entry. Two copies are to be drawn up, one to be kept by the church and the other by the diocesan curia. It would be well for another copy to be sent by the curia to the Vatican Library. The inventory should include notations on changes that have taken place in the course of time.   4330

4. Mindful of the legislation of Vatican Council II[9] and of the directives in the documents of the Holy See,[10] bishops are to exercise unfailing vigilance to ensure that the remodeling of places of worship by reason of the reform of the liturgy is carried out with the utmost caution. Any alterations must always be in keeping with the norms of the liturgical reform and may never proceed without the approv-   4331

Churches for the Eucharistic Celebration" [nos. 253–280; DOL 208 nos. 1643–70].

    [5] See Consilium, Letter of the president, 30 June 1965, no. 8 [DOL 31 no. 417]; SCR, InterOec ch. 5, nos. 90–99 [DOL 23 nos. 382–391]; GIRM nos. 257ff. [DOL 208 nos. 1647–69].

    [6] See Paul VI, Ap. Const. *Regimini Ecclesiae Universae* no. 70: AAS 59 (1967) 911–912.

    [7] GIRM no. 254 [DOL 208 no. 1644].

    [8] See SC art. 124 [DOL 1 no. 124].

    [9] See SC art. 44, 45, 46, 126 [DOL 1 nos. 44, 45, 46, 126].

    [10] See SCR, Instr. EuchMyst no. 24 [DOL 179 no. 1253].

al of the commissions on sacred art, on liturgy, and, when applicable, on music, or without prior consultation with experts. The civil laws of the various countries protecting valuable works of art are also to be taken into account.

4332   5.   Attending to the norms of the Directory *Peregrinans in terra* on the pastoral ministry in tourism,[11] local Ordinaries are to make sure that holy places and objects of celebrated artistic merit are made more accessible to all; they bear witness to the Church's life and history. Nevertheless even sacred edifices of artistic value remain places of worship and tourists must not in any way disturb the liturgical celebrations.

4333   6.   Should it become necessary to adapt works of art and the treasures of the past to the new liturgical laws,[12] bishops are to take care that the need is genuine and that no harm comes to the works of art. The norms and criteria in no. 4 of this document are also to be followed. When it is judged that any such works are no longer suited to divine worship, they are never to be given over to profane use. Rather they are to be set up in a fitting place, namely, in a diocesan or interdiocesan museum, so that they are accessible to all who wish to look at them. Similarly, ecclesiastical buildings graced by art are not to be treated with neglect even when they no longer are used for their original purpose. If they must be sold, buyers who can take proper care of them are to be given preference (see CIC can. 1187).

4334   7.   Precious objects, especially votive offerings, are not to be disposed of without permission of the Holy See, in keeping with CIC can. 1532. The penalties in can. 2347–2349 continue to apply to those transferring ownership of such objects unlawfully; such persons cannot be absolved until they have made restitution for the losses incurred. Petitions submitted to obtain the permission in question are to state clearly the decision of the commissions on sacred art, on liturgy, and, when applicable, on music, as well as the opinion of experts. In each instance, the applicable civil laws are to be respected.

This Congregation has full confidence that sacred works of art will everywhere be treated reverently and safeguarded and that in their efforts to promote new works in keeping with the mentality of every age the bishops will use those works to aid the faithful's active and effective participation in the liturgy.

▶   335.   SC CATHOLIC EDUCATION, Instruction *In ecclesiasticam futurorum sacerdotum*, on liturgical formation in seminaries, 3 June 1979:

no. 57:   Sacred art [no. 2836].

11   See AAS 61 (1969) 373–376 [DOL 326 nos. 2617, 2619].
12   See GIRM no. 254 [DOL 208 no. 1644].

Section 2. Places of Worship

SUMMARY (DOL 542–548). The major texts concern the revised rite for the dedication of a church and of an altar, which reflects the conciliar teaching of both the Constitution on the Liturgy and the Dogmatic Constitution on the Church. The documents are the decree of promulgation (DOL 546) and the introduction of the new rite (DOL 547). The subsidiary texts are on particular points: replies on the tabernacle (DOL 542) and an altar facing the people (DOL 543); a motu proprio of Paul VI on the papal altar (DOL 544), a decree of the Congregation of Rites on the title of minor basilica (DOL 545), and a faculty from the Congregation for Bishops allowing priests to consecrate an altar (DOL 548).

▶ 1. VATICAN COUNCIL II, Constitution on the Liturgy *Sacrosanctum Consilium*, 4 December 1963:

> art. 124:   Works of art; building of churches [no. 124].
>   125:   Sacred images [no. 125].
>   128:   Revision of legislation on sacred art [no. 128].

▶ 23. SC RITES (Consilium), Instruction (first) *Inter Oecumenici*, 26 September 1964:

> nos. 90–99:   Building of churches and altars to ensure liturgical participation [nos. 382–391].

▶ 31. CONSILIUM, Circular Letter *Le renouveau liturgique*, on furthering liturgical reform, 30 June 1965:

> nos. 6:   Altar facing the people [no. 415].
>   7:   Tabernacle for reservation [no. 416].
>   8:   Sacred images [no. 417].

542. SC RITES, **Reply** to a query, on the tabernacle and baldachin, 3 July 1965: Not 1 (1965) 308, no. 90.

4335   Query: Must there be a veil covering the tabernacle where the blessed sacrament is reserved whenever above the tabernacle there is a baldachin decorated with a cloth of white or of the color of the day's office?

Reply: No (SCR, 3 July 1965, Prot. N. 33/65).

543. SC RITES, **Reply** to a query (Washington), on an altar facing the people, 16 July 1965: Not 2 (1966) 183.

4336   His Excellency Philip Matthew Hannan, Titular Bishop of Hierapolis, Auxiliary Bishop and Vicar General of Washington, has respectfully submitted the following queries to the Congregation of Rites for the proper solution:

1. Is permission of the local Ordinary needed to erect an altar facing the people?

2. May all priests celebrate Mass facing the people without permission of the Ordinary or the pastor?

After thoroughly weighing the matter, the Congregation has given the following reply to the queries raised.

To 1. Yes.

To 2. Yes.

▶ 18. VATICAN COUNCIL II, Decree on the Ministry and Life of Priests *Presbyterorum Ordinis*, 7 December 1965:

> no. 5:   Beauty of the church [no. 260].

▶ 19. VATICAN COUNCIL II, Pastoral Constitution on the Church in the Modern World *Gaudium et spes*, 7 December 1965:

no. 62:   Welcoming new art forms into the sanctuary [no. 275].

▶   32.   CONSILIUM, Letter *L'heureux développement*, on problems in the reform of the liturgy, 25 January 1966:

no. 6:   Altar facing the people and the tabernacle [no. 428].

544. PAUL VI, **Motu Proprio** *Peculiare ius*, on the use of the papal altar in the Roman patriarchal basilicas, 8 February 1966: AAS 58 (1966) 119–122; Not 2 (1966) 201–204.

The special law regulating use of the papal altar in the patriarchal basilicas at both Rome and Assisi is a clear indication of the marks of singular honor to be accorded those basilicas in that they belong to the pope by a kind of personal title.   4337

In virtue of this special right, the pope alone may officiate at the main altar of these basilicas. No one else may do so without his explicit permission.[1]

The apparent origin of this privilege is the ancient usage of reserving the main altar in a cathedral to the bishop alone as a clear sign that all the faithful of a diocese came together in the one faith, were loyal to the one pastor, and gathered around the one altar. Thus St. Ignatius of Antioch writes: "The body of our Lord Jesus Christ is one, the chalice holding his blood is one, the altar is one, just as there is one bishop with his priests and deacons, my fellow servants."[2]

A longstanding custom in Rome set aside the altars of the basilicas for the pope. These basilicas belonged to the *Patriarchium*, that is, to the papal see, and documents from the Middle Ages designate them as the basilicas "of the Patriarchate."[3]

The rule was not as strict at the beginning as it is today. Thus in the fifth century our predecessor Pope Simplicius instituted the practice of having priests of the titulars of certain sections of Rome celebrate the liturgy during the week at the Basilicas of St. Peter, St. Paul, and St. Lawrence;[4] we know that later this applied also to the Basilica of St. Mary Major. There is also evidence that in the ninth century the arrangement for divine worship on weekdays had the seven cardinal priests celebrating in each of the four patriarchal basilicas.[5] In the middle of the eighth century at St. John Lateran the seven cardinal bishops of the suburbicarian dioceses carried out the liturgy during the week. They also were entrusted by our predecessor Stephen III with the celebration of the liturgy on individual Sundays *super altare S. Petri.*[6]

But as times and conditions changed, it gradually came about that the rule reserving use of a papal altar to the pope alone was strictly enforced. Finally it

---

[1]   See CIC can. 823, § 3.

[2]   Ignatius of Antioch, *Ad Phil.* 4; see also *Ad Magn.* 7; *Ad Smyrn.* 8.

[3]   See *Descriptio Lateranensis Ecclesiae* cap. 9: R. Valentini and G. Zucchetti, eds., *Codice Topografico della Città di Roma* 3 (Rome, 1946) 344.

[4]   See L. Duchesne, ed., *Liber Pontificalis* 1 (Paris, 1886) 249.

[5]   See *Descriptio Lateranensis Ecclesiae.*

[6]   See L. Duchesne, ed., *Liber Pontificalis* 1, 478.

received definitive formulation in the law that our predecessor Benedict XIV laid down[7] and that the *Codex Iuris Canonici* incorporated.

4338   Contemporary conditions, however, seem to demand that we broaden this privilege in the Roman basilicas. The first consideration is that on the Church's more solemn feasts, that is, when there is a large attendance of people in church, it is best that Mass be celebrated at an elevated and central place. Then, in conformity with the will of Vatican Council II, "the location of the altar will be truly central so that the attention of the whole congregation naturally focuses there."[8] Second, in these times well-attended Catholic congresses or meetings for various purposes are often held in Rome and the participants should gather at least once for the liturgy in a church large enough to accommodate a huge number of people. Third, more than ever before throngs of Christians from all over the world come to Rome out of devotion. We must provide a clearly visible altar for them, since their main interest is to visit the patriarchal basilicas and take part in the Mass there.

Amending the law in force, therefore, we grant that others besides the pope may celebrate the eucharistic sacrifice at a papal altar. The following are the required conditions.

4339   1.   Clearly no concession is made regarding the same basilica at which the pope himself has decided to celebrate on the same day.

And since this situation is most likely to occur in the Basilica of St. Peter, permission will rarely be given to celebrate Mass at the papal altar.

4340   2.   The present concession applies exclusively to the patriarchal basilicas in Rome, namely: the Archbasilica of the Lateran and the Basilicas of St. Peter, St. Paul, St. Mary Major, and St. Lawrence-outside-the-Walls.

4341   3.   Those who may make use of this concession are:

a.   in his own basilica, the cardinal archpriest of the basilica or, if he should be absent from Rome or impeded, a bishop taking his place or delegated by him;

b.   in the Archbasilica of the Lateran, the cardinal vicar of Rome or a bishop he delegates;

c.   in the Basilica of St. Paul, the abbot in charge;

d.   in the Basilica of St. Lawrence-outside-the-Walls, the "commendatory abbot";

e.   in any Roman patriarchal basilica, any bishop leading a large pilgrimage.

f.   With regard to the Roman patriarchal basilicas, it is not our intention to curtail in any way the privileges that some prelates now enjoy on some major feast days.

4342   4.   The reason for granting this permission must in every case be a very large gathering of the faithful: because of the Church's solemn feasts of the first class; because of congresses or meetings held on various subjects; because of a great pilgrimage to Rome.

4343   5.   To prevent the multiplying of concessions, we judge it sufficient that they be granted only by the person in charge of a patriarchal basilica.

---

[7]   See *Fontes Iuris Canonici*.

[8]   SCR, Instr. InterOec, 26 Sept. 1964, no. 91 [DOL 23 no. 383].

We command as established and confirmed whatever we have decreed by this Letter given *motu proprio*, all things to the contrary notwithstanding.

▶ 147. SECRETARIAT FOR PROMOTING CHRISTIAN UNITY, Ecumenical Directory I, 14 May 1967:

nos. 36:	Place for ecumenical services [no. 990].
52, 61:	Sharing use of churches [nos. 1006, 1015].

▶ 179. SC RITES (Consilium), Instruction *Eucharisticum Mysterium*, on worship of the eucharist, 25 May 1967:

nos. 24:	Arrangement of churches [no. 1253].
52 –57:	Place of eucharistic reservation [nos. 1281–86].

▶ 107. SC BISHOPS, Index of quinquennial faculties granted to local Ordinaries, 1 January 1968:

III, no. 1:	Faculty to allow priests to consecrate altars [no. 761].

545. SC RITES (Consilium), **Decree** *Domus Dei*, on the title of minor basilica, 6 June 1968: AAS 60 (1968) 536–539.

The house of God in its adornment and beauty has always been the object of the Church's concern. In accord with the conditions of time, place, and the various peoples, the Church has thus continually issued the norms needed to ensure respect for places of worship and to enhance their dignity. Moreover, it is Christian faith and devotion that have contributed so much to making the churches built in the course of the centuries more beautiful and worthy. The popes have bestowed favors on the more celebrated churches and among these favors the title of minor basilica has existed now for more than a century. This title bears an intrinsic relationship to that of major basilica, given to the patriarchal basilicas only since the eighteenth century.

4344

The patriarchal basilicas, as everyone knows, are regarded and are in fact parts of the Lateran Patriarchate. The Archbasilica of the Holy Savior [St. John Lateran], "head, mother, and mistress of all churches,"[1] is the pope's cathedral; the Basilicas of St. Peter, St. Paul, St. Lawrence-outside-the-Walls, and St. Mary Major are held in a special way to be papal churches.

The mind of Vatican Council II is that all ecclesiastical practices must be adapted to contemporary conditions and needs. After obtaining the opinion and advice of experts and fully deliberating the whole issue, the Congregation of Rites has therefore come to the decision that the title of minor basilica should indeed be retained but with a new and fuller meaning. This is intended to link the churches of this title more closely to the Chair of Peter and to make them centers of special liturgical and pastoral ministry.

To achieve this objective, the Congregation of Rites has carefully revised and appropriately emended the conditions, obligations, and concessions attached to the title for those churches that will receive it in the future.

---

[1] *Descriptio Lateranensis Ecclesiae* 2: R. Valentini and G. Zucchetti, eds., *Codice Topografico della Città di Roma* 3 (Rome, 1946) 335. See Peter Damian, *Epistularum* lib. 2, 1: PL 144, 255–256.

I. CONDITIONS

4345   1.   A church must be worthy of the title because of its notable size and beauty; its design must also exactly conform to liturgical laws.ª

4346   2.   It must be a consecrated church.ᵇ

4347   3.   It must enjoy a certain prestige in the diocese, for example, because it houses the body or some special relic of a canonized saint, because a celebrated image receives special veneration there, or because the church itself is prominent in some extraordinary event of diocesan religious history.

4348   4.   The church should serve as a central source of the pastoral and religious life:

        a.   The liturgy and above all celebration of the eucharist must be carried out to perfection as an example for other churches in the observance of liturgical laws and in the faithful's active participation.

        b.   There is to be a choir and a director of music to ensure the faithful's participation.²

        c.   Priests are to be assigned to the church in sufficient numbers and confessors are to be available at set times to meet the needs of penitents.

        d.   Preaching is to be frequent, not just limited to the homily on Sundays and holydays.

II. OBLIGATIONS

4349   5.   In the basilica special courses of instruction, series of conferences, and other such programs are to further the religious formation of the faithful.ᶜ

4350   6.   Of all the activities and programs of the basilica, studying and making known the documents expressing the mind of the pope and the magisterium of the Church are to receive special emphasis.

4351   7.   In the basilica special solemnity is to mark the celebration of:

        a.   feast of the Chair of Peter (22 Feb.);

        b.   feast of Peter and Paul, Apostles (29 June);

        c.   anniversary of the elevationᵈ of the pope.

    ª   Later emendations by the Congregation for Divine Worship are noted with the designation SCDW. Here SCDW adds: "and the church must have been consecrated."

    ᵇ   SCDW: "2. As to structure and design, the church is to be conducive to the proper celebration of the liturgical services and to bringing about the faithful's active participation."

    ²   See Instr. MusSacr nos. 19–22 [DOL 508 nos. 4140–43].

    ᶜ   SCDW: "5. The documentation submitted to this Congregation to request the title of major basilica must include the following:
        a.   the petition of the local Ordinary, even in the case of exempt churches;
        b.   an indication of whether there are other basilicas in the diocese and their names;
        c.   the *nihil obstat* of the conference of bishops;
        d.   brochures, books, and photographs that adequately show the design, structure, and condition of the church;
        e.   answers to the attached questionnaire."
    Nos. 5–11 of the Decree are SCDW nos. 6–11.

    ᵈ   SCDW: "election."

8.   As may seem advisable, in every basilica especially on holydays, one or more   4352
of the Masses, recited or sung, is to be in Latin.[3] When sung, such Masses are to
have Gregorian melodies or sacred polyphony performed with great care and attention.[e]

9.   The facade of the basilica should carry the arms of the pope or the Apostolic   4353
See.

III. CONCESSIONS

10.   The faithful may gain a plenary indulgence under the usual conditions by   4354
visiting the basilica on the following days:

    a.   feast of Peter and Paul, Apostles (29 June);

    b.   feast of the titular;

    c.   Dedication of St. Mary of the Portiuncula (2 Aug.);

    d.   one day chosen at will during the year.

11.   The *Credo* may be said at Masses in which a pilgrimage or a large number of   4355
people take part.[f]

12.   The papal symbol, that is, the crossed keys, may be used on the basilica's   4356
banners, furnishings, and seal.

13.   The rector of the basilica has the right to wear over the rochet a black mozzetta   4357
(cape) of silk with red piping and buttons.

14.   Every effort is to be made to bring churches already having the title of basilica   4358
into line with the conditions and obligations in nos. 1–9.

15.   For any church, even one exempt, the local Ordinary must be the one to   4359
submit the petition for the title of minor basilica and he is to vouch for the existence of the requisite conditions. In the petition he will indicate how many basilicas
already exist in the diocese and their names. Finally, petitions are to be accompanied by brochures, books, and photographs that adequately show the design, structure, and condition of the church.[g]

    At an audience granted to the undersigned Secretary of the Congregation of
Rites, 6 June 1968, Pope Paul VI approved the present Decree and by his apostolic
authority confirmed it. The Pope stipulated that from now on the title of minor
basilica will be granted to churches that fulfill the conditions listed and that can
carry out the obligations entailed by the title.

▶   208.   SC RITES (Consilium); SC DIVINE WORSHIP, General Instruction of the Ro-
          man Missal, 1st ed. 6 April 1969; 4th ed. 27 March 1975:

          nos. 253–280:   Arrangement and furnishing of churches for the
                              celebration of the eucharist [nos. 1643–70].

---

   [3]   See SC art. 54 [DOL 1 no. 54]. Instr. InterOec no. 59 [DOL 23 no. 351]; Instr. MusSacr no. 48 [DOL
508 no. 4169].

   [e]   SCDW adds: "As warranted, Masses should also be celebrated for larger groups of pilgrims in their
vernacular."

   [f]   SCDW omits no. 11.

   [g]   SCDW omits nos. 14–15.

▶ 279. SC SACRAMENTS AND DIVINE WORSHIP, *Holy Communion and Worship of the Eucharist outside Mass*, Introduction, 21 June 1973:

nos. 9–11:   Place of reservation [nos. 2201–03].

▶ 159. SECRETARIAT FOR CHRISTIAN UNITY, *Ecumenical Collaboration at the Regional and Local Levels*, 22 February 1975.

III, D: Shared premises [nos. 1066–69].

546. SC DIVINE WORSHIP, **Decree** *Dedicationis ecclesiae*, promulgating the *editio typica* of the rite of dedication of a church and an altar, 29 May 1977: Not 13 (1977) 364–365.

4360   The rite for the dedication of a church and an altar is rightly considered to be among the most solemn of liturgical services. A church is the place where the Christian community is gathered to hear the word of God, to offer intercession and praise to him, and above all to celebrate the holy mysteries, and it is the place where the holy sacrament of the eucharist is kept. Thus it stands as a special kind of image of the Church itself, which is God's temple built from living stones. And the altar of a church, around which the holy people gather to take part in the Lord's sacrifice and to be refreshed at the heavenly meal, stands as a sign of Christ himself, who is the priest, the victim, and the altar of his own sacrifice.

These rites, found in the second book of the Roman Pontifical, were revised and simplified in 1961. Nevertheless it was judged necessary to revise the rites again and to adapt them to contemporary conditions in view of the purpose and the norms of the liturgical reform that Vatican Council II set in motion and fostered.

Pope Paul VI by his authority has approved the new *Ordo dedicationis ecclesiae et altaris* prepared by the Congregation for the Sacraments and Divine Worship. He has ordered it published and prescribed that it replace the rites now in the second book of the Roman Pontifical.

This Congregation, by mandate of the Pope, therefore publishes this *Ordo dedicationis ecclesiae et altaris*. In the Latin text it will be in effect as soon as it appears; in the vernacular, it will take effect, after the translations have been confirmed and approved by the Apostolic See, on the day determined by the conferences of bishops.

Anything to the contrary notwithstanding.

547. SC SACRAMENTS AND DIVINE WORSHIP, *Rite of Dedication of a Church and an Altar*, **Introductions**, 29 May 1977: Vatican Polyglot Press, 1977.

CHAPTER ONE
RITE OF LAYING THE FOUNDATION STONE OR
BEGINNING WORK ON THE BUILDING OF A CHURCH

INTRODUCTION

1.   When the building of a new church begins, it is desirable to celebrate a rite to ask God's blessing for the success of the work and to remind the people that the structure built of stone will be a visible sign of the living Church, God's building that is formed of the people themselves.[1]

4361

In accordance with liturgical tradition, this rite consists of the blessing of the site of the new church and the blessing and laying of the foundation stone. When there is to be no foundation stone because of the particular architecture of the building, the rite of the blessing of the site of the new church should still be celebrated in order to dedicate the beginning of the work to God.

2.   The rite for the laying of a foundation stone or for beginning a new church may be celebrated on any day except during the Easter triduum. But the preference should be for a day when the people can be present in large numbers.

4362

3.   The bishop of the diocese is rightly the one to celebrate the rite. If he cannot do so himself, he shall entrust the function to another bishop or a priest, especially to one who is his associate and assistant in the pastoral care of the diocese or of the community for which the new church is to be built.

4363

4.   Notice of the date and hour of the celebration should be given to the people in good time. The parish priest (pastor) or others concerned should instruct them in the meaning of the rite and the reverence to be shown toward the church that is to be built for them.

4364

It is also desirable that the people be asked to give their generous and willing support in the building of the church.

5.   Insofar as possible, the area for the erection of the church should be marked out clearly. It should be possible to walk about without difficulty.

4365

6.   In the place where the altar will be located, a wooden cross of suitable height is fixed in the ground.

4366

7.   For the celebration of the rite the following should be prepared:

4367

— The Roman Pontifical and Lectionary;

— chair for the bishop;

— depending on the circumstances, the foundation stone, which by tradition is a rectangular cornerstone, together with cement and the tools for setting the stone in the foundation;

— container of holy water with sprinkler;

— censer, incense boat and spoon;

---

[1]   See 1 Cor 3:9. LG no. 6 [DOL 4 no. 138].

— processional cross and torches for the servers.

Sound equipment should be set up so that the assembly can clearly hear the readings, prayers, and instructions.

4368   8.   For the celebration of the rite the vestments are white or of some festive color. The following should be prepared:

— for the bishop: alb, stole, cope, miter, and pastoral staff;

— for the priest, when one presides over the celebration: alb, stole, and cope;

— for the deacons: albs, stoles, and, if opportune, dalmatics;

— for other ministers: albs or other lawfully approved dress.

CHAPTER TWO
DEDICATION OF A CHURCH

INTRODUCTION

I. NATURE AND DIGNITY OF CHURCHES

4369   1.   Through his death and resurrection, Christ became the true and perfect temple[1] of the New Covenant and gathered together a people to be his own.

This holy people, made one as the Father, Son, and Holy Spirit are one, is the Church,[2] that is, the temple of God built of living stones, where the Father is worshiped in spirit and in truth.[3]

Rightly, then, from early times "church" has also been the name given to the building in which the Christian community gathers to hear the word of God, to pray together, to receive the sacraments, and to celebrate the eucharist.

4370   2.   Because the church is a visible building, it stands as a special sign of the pilgrim Church on earth and reflects the Church dwelling in heaven.

When a church is erected as a building destined solely and permanently for assembling the people of God and for carrying out sacred functions, it is fitting that it be dedicated to God with a solemn rite, in accordance with the ancient custom of the Church.

4371   3.   The very nature of a church demands that it be suited to sacred celebrations, dignified, evincing a noble beauty, not mere costly display, and it should stand as a sign and symbol of heavenly realities. "The general plan of the sacred edifice should be such that in some way it conveys the image of the gathered assembly. It should also allow the participants to take the place most appropriate to them and assist all to carry out their individual functions properly."[a] Moreover, in what concerns the sanctuary, the altar, the chair, the lectern, and the place for the reservation of the blessed sacrament, the norms of the General Instruction of the Roman Missal are to be followed.[4]

---

[1]   See Jn 2:21.

[2]   See Cyprian, *De oratione dominica* 23: PL 4, 553. LG no. 4: AAS 57 (1965) 7; ConstDecrDecl 96.

[3]   See Jn 4:23.

[a]   DOL 208 no. 1647.

[4]   See GIRM nos. 253, 257, 258, 259–267, 271, 272, 276–277 [DOL 208 nos. 1643, 1647, 1648, 1649–57, 1661, 1662, 1666–67]. See also Roman Ritual, *Holy Communion and Worship of the Eucharist outside Mass* nos. 6 and 9–11 [DOL 279 nos. 2198 and 2201–03].

Also, the norms must be observed that concern things and places destined for the celebration of other sacraments, especially baptism and penance.[5]

II. Titular of a Church and the Relics of the Saints to Be Placed in It

4.   Every church to be dedicated must have a titular. This may be: the Blessed   4372
Trinity; our Lord Jesus Christ invoked according to a mystery of his life or a title
already accepted in the liturgy; the Holy Spirit; the Blessed Virgin Mary, likewise
invoked according to some appellation already accepted in the liturgy; one of the
angels; or, finally, a saint inscribed in the Roman Martyrology or in a duly approved
Appendix. A blessed may not be the titular without an indult of the Apostolic See.
A church should have one titular only, unless it is a question of saints who are listed
together in the Calendar.[b]

5.   The tradition in the Roman liturgy of placing relics of martyrs or other saints   4373
beneath the altar should be preserved, if possible.[6] But the following should be
noted:

   a.   Such relics should be of a size sufficient for them to be recognized as parts
of human bodies. Hence excessively small relics of one or more saints must not be
placed beneath the altar.

   b.   The greatest care must be taken to determine whether the relics in question
are authentic. It is better for an altar to be dedicated without relics than to have
relics of doubtful authenticity placed beneath it.

   c.   A reliquary must not be placed upon the altar or set into the table of the
altar; it must be placed beneath the table of the altar, as the design of the altar
permits.

III. Celebration of the Dedication

MINISTER OF THE RITE

6.   Since the bishop has been entrusted with the care of the particular Church, it is   4374
his responsibility to dedicate to God new churches built in his diocese.

   If he cannot himself preside at the rite, he shall entrust this function to another
bishop, especially to one who is his associate and assistant in the pastoral care of
the community for which the church has been built or, in altogether special circumstances, to a priest, to whom he shall give a special mandate.

CHOICE OF DAY

7.   A day should be chosen for the dedication of the new church when the people   4375
can be present in large numbers, especially a Sunday. Since the theme of the dedication pervades this entire rite, the dedication of a new church may not take place on
days on which it is altogether improper to disregard the mystery then being commemorated: the Easter triduum, Christmas, Epiphany, Ascension, Pentecost, Ash
Wednesday, the weekdays of Holy Week, and All Souls.

MASS OF THE DEDICATION

8.   The celebration of the eucharist is inseparably bound up with the rite of the   4376
dedication of a church; when a church is dedicated therefore the liturgical texts of

---

[5] See *Rite of Baptism for Children* no. 25 [DOL 295 no. 2309]; *Rite of Penance* no. 12 [DOL 368 no. 3077].

[b] See DOL 481 no. 4029.

[6] See GIRM no. 266 [DOL 208 no. 1656].

the day are omitted and texts proper to the rite are used for both the liturgy of the word and the liturgy of the eucharist.

4377   9.   It is fitting that the bishop concelebrate the Mass with the priests who take part with him in the rite of dedication and those who have been given charge over the parish or the community for which the church has been built.

OFFICE OF THE DEDICATION

4378   10.   The day on which a church is dedicated is kept as a solemnity in that church.

The office of the dedication of a church is celebrated, beginning with evening prayer I. When the rite of depositing relics takes place, it is highly recommended to keep a vigil at the relics of the martyr or saint that are to be placed beneath the altar; the best way of doing this is to have the office of readings, taken from the respective common or proper. This vigil should be properly adapted to encourage the people's participation, but the requirements of the law are respected.[7]

PARTS OF THE RITE

A. Entrance into the Church

4379   11.   The rite of the dedication begins with the entrance into the church; this may take place in one of the three following ways; the one best suited to the circumstances of time and place is to be used.

— *Procession* to the church to be dedicated: all assemble in a nearby church or other suitable place, from which the bishop, the ministers, and the congregation proceed to the church to be dedicated, praying and singing.

— *Solemn entrance*: if the procession cannot take place or seems inopportune, the community gathers at the entrance of the church.

— *Simple entrance*: the congregation assembles in the church itself; the bishop, the concelebrants, and the ministers enter from the sacristy in the usual way.

Two rituals are most significant in the entrance into a new church:

a.   The handing over of the church: representatives of those who have been involved in the building of the church hand it over to the bishop.

b.   The sprinkling of the church: the bishop blesses water and with it sprinkles the people, who are the spiritual temple, then the walls of the church, and finally, the altar.

B. Liturgy of the Word

4380   12.   Three readings are used in the liturgy of the word. The texts are chosen from those in the Lectionary (nos. 704 and 706) for the rite of the dedication of a church.

The first reading is always, even during the Easter season, the passage of Nehemiah that tells of the people of Jerusalem gathered in the presence of the scribe Ezra to hear the proclamation of the law of God (Neh 8:1–4a, 5–6, 8–10).

4381   13.   After the readings the bishop gives the homily, in which he explains the biblical readings and the meaning of the dedication of a church.

The profession of faith is always said. The general intercessions are omitted, since the Litany of the Saints is sung in their place.

---

[7]   See GILH nos. 70–73 [DOL 426 nos. 3500–03].

C. Prayer of Dediction and the Anointing of the Church and the Altar

Depositing of the Relics of the Saints

14. If it is to take place, the relics of a martyr are deposited after the singing of the Litany of the Saints, to signify that the sacrifice of the members has its source in the sacrifice of the Head.[8] When relics of a martyr are not available, relics of another saint may be deposited in the altar.   4382

Prayer of Dedication

15. The celebration of the eucharist is the most important and the one necessary rite for the dedication of a church. Nevertheless, in accordance with the tradition of the Church in both East and West, a special prayer of dedication is also said. This prayer is a sign of the intention to dedicate the church to the Lord for all times and a petition for his blessing.   4383

Rites of Anointing, Incensing, Covering, and Lighting the Altar

16. The rites of anointing, incensing, covering, and lighting the altar express in visible signs several aspects of the invisible work that the Lord accomplishes through the Church in its celebration of the divine mysteries, especially the eucharist.   4384

    a. *Anointing* of the altar and the walls of the church:

    — The anointing with chrism makes the altar a symbol of Christ, who, before all others, is and is called "The Anointed One"; for the Father anointed him with the Holy Spirit and constituted him the High Priest so that on the altar of his body he might offer the sacrifice of his life for the salvation of all.

    — The anointing of the church signifies that it is given over entirely and perpetually to Christian worship. In keeping with liturgical tradition, there are twelve anointings, or, where it is more convenient, four, as a symbol that the church is an image of the holy city of Jerusalem.

    b. *Incense* is burned on the altar to signify that Christ's sacrifice, there perpetuated in mystery, ascends to God as an odor of sweetness and also to signify that the people's prayers rise up pleasing and acceptable, reaching the throne of God.[9]

    The incensation of the nave of the church indicates that the dedication makes it a house of prayer, but the people of God are incensed first, because they are the living temple in which each faithful member is a spiritual altar.[10]

    c. *The covering of the altar* indicates that the Christian altar is the altar of the eucharistic sacrifice and the table of the Lord; around it priests and people, by one and the same rite but with a difference of function, celebrate the memorial of Christ's death and resurrection and partake of his supper. For this reason the altar is prepared as the table of the sacrificial banquet and adorned as for a feast. Thus the dressing of the altar clearly signifies that it is the Lord's table at which all God's people joyously meet to be refreshed with divine food, namely, the body and blood of Christ sacrificed.

---

   8 See RM, Common of Martyrs 8, prayer over the gifts. Ambrose, *Epistula* 22:13: PL 16, 1023: "Let the triumphant victims rest in the place where Christ is victim: he, however, who suffered for all, upon the altar; they, who have been redeemed by his sufferings, beneath the altar." See Ps. Maximus of Turin, *Sermo* 78: PL 57, 689–690. Rv 6:9: "I saw underneath the altar the souls of all the people who had been killed on account of the word of God, for witnessing to it."

   9 See Rv 8:3–4.

  10 See Rom 12:1.

d. *The lighting of the altar*, which is followed by the lighting of the church, reminds us that Christ is "a light to enlighten the nations";[11] his brightness shines out in the Church and through it in the whole human family.

D. Celebration of the Eucharist

4385   17. After the altar has been prepared, the bishop celebrates the eucharist, the principal and the most ancient part of the whole rite,[12] because the celebration of the eucharist is in the closest harmony with the rite of the dedication of a church:

— For the celebration of the eucharistic sacrifice achieves the end for which the church was built and the altar erected and expresses this end by particularly clear signs.

— Furthermore, the eucharist, which sanctifies the hearts of those who receive it, in a sense consecrates the altar and the place of celebration, as the ancient Fathers of the Church often assert: "This altar should be an object of awe: by nature it is stone, but it is made holy when it receives the body of Christ."[13]

— Finally, the bond closely connecting the dedication of a church with the celebration of the eucharist is likewise evident from the fact that the Mass for the dedication has its own preface, which is a central part of the rite itself.

IV. ADAPTATION OF THE RITE

ADAPTATIONS WITHIN THE COMPETENCE OF THE CONFERENCES OF BISHOPS

4386   18. The conferences of bishops may adapt this rite, as required, to the character of each region, but in such a way that nothing of its dignity and solemnity is lost.

However, the following are to be respected:

a. The celebration of the Mass with the proper preface and prayer for a dedication must never be omitted.

b. Rites that have a special meaning and force from liturgical tradition (see no. 16) must be retained, unless weighty reasons stand in the way, but the wording may be suitably adapted if necessary.

With regard to adaptations, the competent ecclesiasical authority is to consult the Holy See and introduce adaptations with its consent.[14]

ADAPTATIONS WITHIN THE COMPETENCE OF THE MINISTERS

4387   19. It is for the bishop and for those in charge of the celebration of the rite:

— to decide the manner of entrance into the church (see no. 11);

— to determine the manner of handing over the new church to the bishop (no. 11);

— to decide whether to have the depositing of relics of the saints. The decisive consideration is the spiritual good of the community; the prescriptions in no. 5 must be followed.

It is for the rector of the church to be dedicated, helped by those who assist him in the pastoral work, to decide and prepare everything concerning the readings, singing, and other pastoral aids to foster the fruitful participation of the people and to ensure a dignified celebration.

---

[11]   Lk 2:32.

[12]   See Pope Vigilius, *Epistula ad Profuturum episcopum* 4: PL 84, 832.

[13]   John Chrysostom, *Homilia 20 in 2 Cor.* 3: PG 61, 540.

[14]   See SC art. 40 [DOL 1 no. 40].

V. Pastoral Preparation

20. In order that the people may take part fully in the rite of dedication, the rector   4388
of the church to be dedicated and others experienced in the pastoral ministry are to
instruct them on the import of the celebration and its spiritual, ecclesial, and evangelizing power.

Accordingly, the people are to be instructed about the various parts of the
church and their use, the rite of dedication, and the chief liturgical symbols employed in it. Thus led by suitable pastoral resources to a full understanding of the
meaning of the dedication of a church through its rites and prayers, they will take
an active, intelligent, and devout part in the sacred service.

VI. Requisites for the Dedication of a Church

21.   For the celebration of the rite the following should be prepared: 4389

a. *In the place of assembly*:

— The Roman Pontifical;

— processional cross;

— if relics of the saints are to be carried in procession, the items indicated
in no. 24 a.

b. *In the sacristy or in the sanctuary or in the body of the church to be dedicated*, as each
situation requires:

— The Roman Missal;

— The Lectionary;

— container of water to be blessed and sprinkler;

— containers with the chrism;

— towels for wiping the table of the altar;

— if needed, a waxed linen cloth or waterproof covering of the same size
as the altar;

— basin and jug of water, towels, and all that is needed for washing the
bishop's hands and those of the priests after they have anointed the walls
of the church;

— linen gremial;

— brazier for burning incense or aromatic spices; or grains of incense and
small candles to burn on the altar;

— censer, incense boat and spoon;

— chalice, corporal, purificators, and hand towel;

— bread, wine, and water for the celebration of Mass;

— altar cross, unless there is already a cross in the sanctuary or the cross
that is carried in the entrance procession is to be placed near the altar;

— altar cloth, candles, and candlesticks;

— flowers, if opportune.

22. It is praiseworthy to keep the ancient custom of hanging on the walls of the   4390
church crosses made of stone, brass, or other suitable material or of having the
crosses carved on the walls. Thus twelve or four crosses should be provided, depending on the number of anointings (see no. 16), and fixed here and there at a
suitable height on the walls of the church. Beneath each cross a small bracket
should be fitted and in it a small candlestick is placed, with a candle to be lighted.

4391   23. For the Mass of the dedication the vestments are white or of some festive color. The following should be prepared:

— for the bishop: alb, stole, chasuble, miter, pastoral staff, and pallium, if the bishop has the right to wear one;

— for the concelebrating priests: the vestments for concelebrating Mass;

— for the deacons: albs, stoles, and dalmatics;

— for other ministers: albs or other lawfully approved dress.

4392   24. If relics of the saints are to be placed beneath the altar, the following should be prepared:

a. *In the place of assembly*:

— reliquary containing the relics, placed between flowers and lights. When the simple entrance is used, the reliquary may be placed in a suitable part of the sanctuary before the rite begins;

— for the deacons who will carry the relics to be deposited: albs, red stoles, if the relics are those of a martyr, or white in other cases, and, if available, dalmatics. If the relics are carried by priests, then in place of dalmatics chasubles should be prepared.

The relics may also be carried by other ministers, vested in albs or other lawfully approved dress.

b. *In the sanctuary*:

— a small table on which the reliquary is placed during the first part of the dedication rite.

c. *In the sacristy*:

— a sealant or cement to close the cover of the aperture. In addition, a stonemason should be on hand to close the depository of the relics at the proper time.

4393   25. The record of the dedication of the church should be drawn up in duplicate, signed by the bishop, the rector of the church, and representatives of the local community; one copy is to be kept in the diocesan archives, the other in the archives of the church. Where the depositing of relics takes place, a third copy of the record should be made, to be placed at the proper time in the reliquary.

In this record mention should be made of the day, month, and year of the church's dedication, the name of the bishop who celebrated the rite, also the titular of the church and, where applicable, the names of the martyrs or saints whose relics have been deposited beneath the altar.

Moreover, in a suitable place in the church, an inscription should be placed stating the day, month, and year when the dedication took place, the titular of the church, and the name of the bishop who celebrated the rite.

VII. ANNIVERSARY OF THE DEDICATION

A. ANNIVERSARY OF THE DEDICATION OF THE CATHEDRAL CHURCH

4394   26. In order that the importance and dignity of the local Church may stand out with greater clarity, the anniversary of the dedication of its cathedral is to be celebrated, with the rank of a solemnity in the cathedral itself, with the rank of a feast in the other churches of the diocese, on the date on which the dedication of the church recurs.[15] If this date is always impeded, the celebration is assigned to the nearest date open.

---

[15]   See GNLYC, Table of Liturgical Days, I, 4 b and II, 8 b [DOL 442 no. 3825].

It is desirable that in the cathedral church on the anniversary the bishop concelebrate the eucharist with the chapter of canons or the priests' senate and with the participation of as many of the people as possible.[R1]

B. ANNIVERSARY OF THE DEDICATION OF A PARTICULAR CHURCH

27. The anniversary of a church's dedication is celebrated with the rank of a solemnity.[16]   4395

CHAPTER THREE
DEDICATION OF A CHURCH IN WHICH MASS IS ALREADY BEING CELEBRATED REGULARLY

INTRODUCTION

1. In order to bring out fully the symbolism and the significance of the rite, the opening of a new church and its dedication should take place at one and the same time. For this reason, as was said before, care should be taken that, as far as possible, Mass is not celebrated in a new church before it is dedicated (see chapter two, nos. 8, 15, 17).   4396

Nevertheless in the case of the dedication of a church where the sacred mysteries are already being celebrated regularly, the rite set out in this chapter must be used.

Moreover, a clear distinction exists in regard to these churches. In the case of those just built the reason for a dedication is obvious. In the case of those standing for some time the following requirements must be met for them to be dedicated:

— that the altar has not already been dedicated, since it is rightly forbidden both by custom and by liturgical law to dedicate a church without dedicating the altar, for the dedication of the altar is the principal part of the whole rite;

— that there be something new or notably altered about the edifice, relative either to its structure (for example, a total restoration) or its status in law (for example, the church's being ranked as a parish church).

2. All the directions given in the Introduction to chapter two apply to this rite, unless they are clearly extraneous to the situation which this rite envisages or other directions are given.   4397

This rite differs chiefly from that described in chapter two on these points:

a. The rite of opening the doors of the church (see chapter two, no. 34 or no. 41) is omitted, since the church is already open to the community; consequently, the entrance takes the form of the simple entrance (see chapter two, nos.43–47). However, in the case of dedicating a church closed for a long time and now being opened again for sacred celebrations, the rite of opening the doors may be carried out, since in this case it retains its point and significance.

b. The rite of handing over the church to the bishop (see chapter two, no. 33 or no. 40 or no. 47), depending on the situation, is either to be followed, omitted, or adapted in a way relevant to the condition of the church being dedicated (for example, it will be right to retain it in dedicating a church built recently; to omit it in dedicating an older church where nothing has been changed in the structure; to adapt it in dedicating an older church completely restored).

[R1] See DOL 442 no. 3818, note R10.

[16] See GNLYC, Table of Liturgical Days, I, 4 b [DOL 442 no. 3825].

    c. The rite of sprinkling the church walls with holy water (see chapter two, nos. 48–50), purificatory by its very nature, is omitted;

    d. All the rites belonging to the first proclamation of the word of God in a church (see chapter two, no. 53) are omitted; thus the liturgy of the word takes place in the usual way. A different, pertinent reading is chosen in place of Neh 8:1–4a and its responsorial psalm, Ps 19b: 8–9, 10, 15 (see chapter two, no. 54 a).

CHAPTER FOUR
RITE OF DEDICATION OF AN ALTAR

INTRODUCTION

I. NATURE AND DIGNITY OF THE ALTAR

4398   1.   From meditating on God's word, the ancient Fathers of the Church did not hesitate to assert that Christ was the victim, priest, and altar of his own sacrifice.[1] For in the Letter to the Hebrews Christ is presented as the High Priest who is also the living altar of the heavenly temple;[2] and in the Book of Revelation our Redeemer appears as the Lamb who has been sacrificed[3] and whose offering is taken by the holy angel to the altar in heaven.[4]

THE CHRISTIAN IS ALSO A SPIRITUAL ALTAR

4399   2.   Since Christ, Head and Teacher, is the true altar, his members and disciples are also spiritual altars on which the sacrifice of a holy life is offered to God. The Fathers seem to have this in mind. St. Ignatius of Antioch asks the Romans quite plainly: "Grant me only this favor: let my blood be spilled in sacrifice to God, while there is still an altar ready."[5] St. Polycarp exhorts widows to lead a life of holiness, for "they are God's altar."[6] Among others, St. Gregory the Great echoes these words when he says: "What is God's altar if not the souls of those who lead good lives? . . . Rightly, then, the heart of the just is said to be the altar of God."[7]

    In another image frequently used by the writers of the Church, Christians who give themselves to prayer, offer petitions to God, and present sacrifices of supplication, are the living stones out of which the Lord Jesus builds the Church's altar.[8]

THE ALTAR, TABLE OF THE SACRIFICE AND THE PASCHAL MEAL

4400   3.   By instituting in the form of a sacrificial meal the memorial of the sacrifice he was about to offer the Father on the altar of the cross, Christ made holy the table where the community would come to celebrate their Passover. Therefore the altar is the table for a sacrifice and for a banquet. At this table the priest, representing Christ the Lord, accomplishes what the Lord himself did and what he handed on to his disciples to do in his memory. The Apostle clearly intimates this: "The blessing cup that we bless is a communion with the blood of Christ and the bread that we

---

[1]   See Epiphanius, *Panarium* 2, 1, *Haeresis* 55: PG 41, 979. Cyril of Alexandria, *De adoratione in spiritu et veritate* 9: PG 68, 647.

[2]   See Heb 4:14, 13:10.

[3]   See Rv 5:6.

[4]   See RM, Order of Mass, no. 96.

[5]   Ignatius of Antioch, *Ad Romanos* 2:2: Funk PA 1:255.

[6]   Polycarp, *Ad Philippenses* 4:3: Funk PA 1:301.

[7]   Gregory the Great, *Homiliarum in Ezechielem* 10, 19: PL 76, 1069.

[8]   See Origen, *In librum Iesu Nave*, Homilia 9, 1: SC 71, 244 and 246.

break is a communion with the body of Christ. The fact that there is only one loaf means that though there are many of us, we form a single Body because we all have a share in this one loaf."[9]

THE ALTAR, SIGN OF CHRIST

4.   The Church's children have the power to celebrate the memorial of Christ and   4401
take their place at the Lord's table anywhere that circumstances might require. But it is in keeping with the eucharistic mystery that the Christian people erect a permanent altar for the celebration of the Lord's Supper and they have done so from the earliest times.

The Christian altar is by its very nature properly the table of sacrifice and of the paschal banquet. It is:

— a unique altar on which the sacrifice of the cross is perpetuated in mystery throughout the ages until Christ comes;

— a table at which the Church's children gather to give thanks to God and receive the body and blood of Christ.

In every church, then, the altar "is the center of the thanksgiving that the eucharist accomplishes"[10] and around which the Church's other rites are, in a certain manner, arrayed.[11]

At the altar the memorial of the Lord is celebrated and his body and blood given to the people. Therefore the Church's writers have seen in the altar a sign of Christ himself. This is the basis for the saying, "The altar is Christ."

THE ALTAR AS HONORING MARTYRS

5.   All the dignity of the altar rests on its being the Lord's table. Thus the martyr's   4402
body does not bring honor to the altar; rather the altar does honor to the martyr's tomb. For it is altogether proper to erect altars over the burial place of martyrs and other saints or to deposit their relics beneath altars as a mark of respect and as a symbol of the truth that the sacrifice of the members has its source in the sacrifice of the Head.[12] Thus "the triumphant victims come to their rest in the place where Christ is victim: he, however, who suffered for all is on the altar; they who have been redeemed by his sufferings are beneath the altar."[13] This arrangement would seem to recall in a certain manner the spiritual vision of the Apostle John in the Book of Revelation: "I saw underneath the altar the souls of all the people who have been killed on account of the word of God, for witnessing to it."[14] His meaning is that although all the saints are rightly called Christ's witnesses, the witness of blood has a special significance that only the relics of martyrs beneath the altar express in its entirety.

II. Erecting an Altar

6.   It is desirable that in every church there be a fixed altar and that in other places   4403
set apart for sacred celebrations there be either a fixed or a movable altar.

---

9   See 1 Cor 10:16–17.

10   GIRM no. 259 [DOL 208 no. 1649].

11   See Pius XII, Encycl. *Mediator Dei*: AAS 39 (1947) 529.

12   See RM, Common of Martyrs 8, prayer over the gifts.

13   Ambrose, *Epistula* 22, 13: PL 16, 1023. See Ps. Maximus of Turin, *Sermo* 78: PL 57, 689–690.

14   Rv 6:9.

A fixed altar is one so constructed that it is attached to the floor so that it cannot be moved; a movable altar can be transferred from place to place.[15]

4404   7.   In new churches it is better to erect only one altar so that in the one assembly of the people of God the single altar signifies the one Savior Jesus Christ and the one eucharist of the Church.

But an altar may also be erected in a chapel (somewhat separated, if possible, from the body of the church) where the tabernacle for the reservation of the blessed sacrament is situated. On weekdays when there is a small gathering of people Mass may be celebrated at this altar.

The merely decorative erection of several altars in a church must be entirely avoided.

4405   8.   The altar should be freestanding so that the priest can easily walk around it and celebrate Mass facing the people. "It should be so placed as to be a focal point on which the attention of the whole congregation centers naturally."[16]

4406   9.   In accordance with received custom in the Church and the biblical symbolism connected with an altar, the table of a fixed altar should be of stone, indeed of natural stone. But, at the discretion of the conference of bishops, any becoming, solid, and finely wrought material may be used in erecting an altar.

The pedestal or base of the table may be of any sort of material, provided it is becoming and solid.[17]

4407   10.   The altar is of its very nature dedicated to the one God, for the eucharistic sacrifice is offered to the one God. This is the sense in which the Church's practice of dedicating altars to God in honor of the saints must be understood. St. Augustine expresses it well: "It is not to any of the martyrs, but to the God of the martyrs, though in memory of the martyrs, that we raise our altars."[18]

This should be made clear to the people. In new churches statues and pictures of saints may not be placed above the altar.

Likewise, when relics of saints are exposed for veneration, they should not be placed on the table of the altar.

4408   11.   It is fitting to continue the tradition in the Roman liturgy of placing relics of martyrs or other saints beneath the altar.[19] But the following should be noted.

a.   Such relics should be of a size sufficient for them to be recognizable as parts of human bodies. Hence excessively small relics of one or more saints must not be placed beneath an altar.

b.   The greatest care must be taken to determine whether the relics in question are authentic. It is better for an altar to be dedicated without relics than to have relics of doubtful authenticity placed beneath it.

c.   A reliquary must not be placed on the altar or set into the table of the altar, but placed beneath the table of the altar, as the design of the altar permits.

---

[15]   See GIRM nos. 265, 261 [DOL 208 nos. 1655, 1651].

[16]   GIRM no. 262 [DOL 208 no. 1652].

[17]   See GIRM no. 263 [DOL 208 no. 1653].

[18]   Augustine, *Contra Faustum* 20, 21: PL 42, 384.

[19]   See GIRM no. 266 [DOL 208 no. 1656].

When the rite of depositing relics takes place, it is highly recommended to keep a vigil at the relics of the martyr or saint, in accordance with the provisions of chapter two, no. 10.

III. CELEBRATION OF THE DEDICATION

MINISTER OF THE RITE

12. Since the bishop has been entrusted with the care of the particular Church, it is his responsibility to dedicate to God new altars built in his diocese.   4409

If he cannot himself preside at the rite, he shall entrust the function to another bishop, especially to one who is his associate and assistant in the pastoral care of the community for which the new altar has been erected or, in altogether special circumstances, to a priest, to whom he shall give a special mandate.

CHOICE OF DAY

13. Since an altar becomes sacred principally by the celebration of the eucharist, in fidelity to this truth the celebration of Mass on a new altar before it has been dedicated is to be carefully avoided, so that the Mass of dedication may also be the first eucharist celebrated on the altar.   4410

14. A day should be chosen for the dedication of a new altar when the people can be present in large numbers, especially a Sunday, unless pastoral considerations suggest otherwise. However, the rite of the dedication of an altar may not be celebrated during the Easter triduum, on Ash Wednesday, the weekdays of Holy Week, and All Souls.   4411

MASS OF THE DEDICATION

15. The celebration of the eucharist is inseparably bound up with the rite of the dedication of an altar. The Mass is the Mass for the dedication of an altar. On Christmas, Epiphany, Ascension, Pentecost, and on the Sundays of Advent, Lent, and the Easter season, the Mass is the Mass of the day, with the exception of the prayer over the gifts and the preface, which are closely interwoven with the rite itself.   4412

16. It is fitting that the bishop concelebrate the Mass with the priests present, especially with those who have been given charge over the parish or the community for which the altar has been erected.   4413

PARTS OF THE RITE

A. Introductory Rites

17. The introductory rites of the Mass of the dedication of an altar take place in the usual way except that in place of the penitential rite the bishop blesses water and with it sprinkles the people and the new altar.   4414

B. Liturgy of the Word

18. It is commendable to have three readings in the liturgy of the word, chosen, according to the rubrical norm, either from the liturgy of the day (see no. 15) or from those in the Lectionary for the rite of the dedication of an altar (nos. 704 and 706).   4415

19. After the readings, the bishop gives the homily, in which he explains the biblical readings and the meaning of the dedication of an altar.   4416

After the homily, the profession of faith is said. The general intercessions are omitted, since the Litany of the Saints is sung in their place.

C. Prayer of Dedication and the Anointing of the Altar

Depositing of the Relics of the Saints

4417   20. If it is to take place, the relics of martyrs or other saints are placed beneath the altar after the Litany of the Saints. The rite is meant to signify that all who have been baptized in the death of Christ, especially those who have shed their blood for the Lord, share in Christ's passion (see no. 5).

Prayer of Dedication

4418   21. The celebration of the eucharist is the most important and the one necessary rite for the dedication of an altar. Nevertheless, in accordance with the universal tradition of the Church in both East and West, a special prayer of dedication is also said. This prayer is a sign of the intention to dedicate the altar to the Lord for all times and a petition for his blessing.

Rites of Anointing, Incensing, Covering, and Lighting the Altar

4419   22. The rites of anointing, incensing, covering, and lighting the altar express in visible signs several aspects of the invisible work that the Lord accomplishes through the Church in its celebration of the divine mysteries, especially the eucharist.

    a. *Anointing* of the altar: The anointing with chrism makes the altar a symbol of Christ, who, before all others, is and is called "The Anointed One"; for the Father anointed him with the Holy Spirit and constituted him the High Priest so that on the altar of his body he might offer the sacrifice of his life for the salvation of all.

    b. *Incense* is burned on the altar to signify that Christ's sacrifice, there perpetuated in mystery, ascends to God as an odor of sweetness, and also to signify that the people's prayers rise up pleasing and acceptable, reaching the throne of God.[20]

    c. The *covering* of the altar indicates that the Christian altar is the altar of the eucharistic sacrifice and the table of the Lord; around it priests and people, by one and the same rite but with a difference of function, celebrate the memorial of Christ's death and resurrection and partake of his supper. For this reason the altar is prepared as the table of the sacrificial banquet and adorned as for a feast. Thus the dressing of the altar clearly signifies that it is the Lord's table at which all God's people joyously meet to be refreshed with divine food, namely, the body and blood of Christ sacrificed.

    d. The *lighting* of the altar teaches us that Christ is "a light to enlighten the nations";[21] his brightness shines out in the Church and through it in the whole human family.

D. CELEBRATION OF THE EUCHARIST

4420   23. After the altar has been prepared, the bishop celebrates the eucharist, the principal and the most ancient part of the whole rite,[22] because the celebration of the eucharist is in the closest harmony with the rite of the dedication of an altar:

    — For the celebration of the eucharistic sacrifice achieves the end for which the altar was erected and expresses this end by particularly clear signs.

---

[20] See Rv 8:3–4: An angel "who had a golden censer, came and stood at the altar. A large quantity of incense was given to him to offer with the prayers of all the saints on the golden altar that stood in front of the throne; and so from the angel's hand the smoke of the incense went up in the presence of God and with it the prayers of the saints."

[21] Lk 2:32.

[22] See Pope Vigilius, *Epistula ad Profuturum Episcopum* 4: PL 84, 832.

— Furthermore, the eucharist, which sanctifies the hearts of those who receive it, in a sense consecrates the altar, as the ancient Fathers of the Church often assert: "This altar should be an object of awe: by nature it is stone, but it is made holy when it receives the body of Christ."[23]

— Finally, the bond closely connecting the dedication of an altar with the celebration of the eucharist is likewise evident from the fact that the Mass for the dedication has its own preface, which is a central part of the rite itself.

IV. ADAPTATION OF THE RITE

ADAPTATIONS WITHIN THE COMPETENCE OF THE CONFERENCES OF BISHOPS

24. The conferences of bishops may adapt this rite, as required, to the character of each region, but in such a way that nothing of its dignity and solemnity is lost.

However, the following are to be respected:

a. The celebration of the Mass with its proper preface and prayer of dedication must never be omitted.

b. Rites that have a special meaning and force from liturgical tradition (see no. 22) must be retained, unless weighty reasons stand in the way, but the wording may be suitably adapted if necessary.

With regard to adaptations, the competent ecclesiastical authority is to consult the Holy See and introduce adaptations with its consent.[24]

4421

ADAPTATIONS WITHIN THE COMPETENCE OF THE MINISTERS

25. It is for the bishop and for those in charge of the celebration of the rite to decide whether to have the depositing of relics of the saints; in so doing, they are to follow what is laid down in no. 11 and they are to take as the decisive consideration the spiritual good of the community and a proper sense of liturgy.

It is for the rector of the church in which the altar is to be dedicated, helped by those who assist him in the pastoral work, to decide and prepare everything concerning the readings, singing, and other pastoral aids to foster the fruitful participation of the people and to ensure a dignified celebration.

4422

V. PASTORAL PREPARATION

26. The people are to be informed in good time about the dedication of a new altar and they are to be properly prepared to take an active part in the rite. Accordingly, they should be taught what each rite means and how it is carried out. For the purpose of giving this instruction, use may be made of what has been said earlier about the nature and dignity of an altar and the meaning and import of the rites. In this way the people will be imbued with the rightful love that is owed to the altar.

4423

VI. REQUISITES FOR THE DEDICATION OF AN ALTAR

27. For the celebration of the rite the following should be prepared:

— The Roman Missal;

— The Lectionary;

— The Roman Pontifical;

— the cross and the Book of the Gospels to be carried in the procession;

— container with the water to be blessed and sprinkler;

— container with the holy chrism;

4424

---

23 John Chrysostom, *Homilia 20 in 2 Cor.* 3: PG 61, 540.

24 See SC art. 40 [DOL 1 no. 40].

— towels for wiping the table of the altar;

— if needed, a waxed linen cloth or other waterproof covering of the same size as the altar;

— basin and jug of water, towels, and all that is needed for washing the bishop's hands;

— linen gremial;

— brazier for burning incense or aromatic spices; or grains of incense and small candles to burn on the altar;

— censer, incense boat and spoon;

— chalice, corporal, purificators, and hand towel;

— bread, wine, and water for the celebration of Mass;

— altar cross, unless there is already a cross in the sanctuary, or the cross that is carried in the entrance procession is to be placed near the altar;

— altar cloth, candles, and candlesticks;

— flowers, if opportune.

4425   28. For the Mass of the dedication the vestments are white or of some festive color, The following should be prepared:

— for the bishop: alb, stole, chasuble, miter, pastoral staff, and pallium, if the bishop has the right to wear one;

— for the concelebrating priests: the vestments for concelebrating Mass;

— for the deacons: albs, stoles, and, if opportune, dalmatics;

— for other ministers: albs or other lawfully approved dress.

4426   29. If relics of the saints are to be placed beneath the altar, the following should be prepared:

     a. *In the place from which the procession begins*:

— a reliquary containing the relics, placed between flowers and lights. But as circumstances dictate, the reliquary may be placed in a suitable part of the sanctuary before the rite begins;

— for the deacons who will carry the relics to be deposited: albs, red stoles, if the relics are those of a martyr, or white in other cases, and, if available, dalmatics. If the relics are carried by priests, then, in place of dalmatics, chasubles should be prepared. Relics may also be carried by other ministers, vested in albs or other lawfully approved dress.

     b. *In the sanctuary*:

— a small table on which the reliquary is placed during the first part of the dedication rite.

     c. *In the sacristy*:

— a sealant or cement to close the cover of the aperture. In addition, a stonemason should be on hand to close the depository of the relics at the proper time.

4427   30. It is fitting to observe the custom of enclosing in the reliquary a parchment on which is recorded the day, month, and year of the dedication of the altar, the name of the bishop who celebrated the rite, the titular of the church, and the names of the martyrs or saints whose relics are deposited beneath the altar.

A record of the dedication is to be drawn up in duplicate and signed by the bishop, the rector of the church, and representatives of the local community; one copy is to be kept in the diocesan archives, the other in the archives of the church.

CHAPTER FIVE
RITE OF BLESSING A CHURCH

INTRODUCTION

1.   Since sacred edifices, that is, churches, are permanently set aside for the cele-   4428
bration of the divine mysteries, it is right for them to receive a dedication to God.
This is done according to the rite in chapters two and three for dedicating a church,
a rite impressive for its striking ceremonies and symbols.

Private oratories, chapels, or other sacred edifices set aside only temporarily for
divine worship because of special conditions, more properly receive a blessing,
according to the rite described below.

2.   As to the structure of the liturgy, the choice of a titular, and the pastoral   4429
preparation of the people, what is said in the Introduction to chapter two, nos. 4–5,
7, 20, is to be followed, with the necessary modifications.

A church or an oratory is blessed by the bishop of the diocese or by a priest
delegated by him.

3.   A church or an oratory may be blessed on any day, apart from the Easter   4430
triduum. As far as possible a day should be chosen when the people can be present
in large numbers, especially a Sunday, unless pastoral considerations suggest otherwise.

4.   On days mentioned in the Table of Liturgical Days, nos. 1–4,[a] the Mass is the   4431
Mass of the day; but on other days the Mass is either the Mass of the day or the
Mass of the titular of the church or oratory.

5.   For the rite of the blessing of a church or an oratory all things needed for the   4432
celebration of Mass are prepared. But even though it may have already been blessed
or dedicated, the altar should be left bare until the beginning of the liturgy of the
eucharist. In a suitable place in the sanctuary the following also should be prepared:

— container of water to be blessed and sprinkler;

— censer, incense boat and spoon;

— The Roman Pontifical;

— altar cross, unless there is already a cross in the sanctuary, or the cross that
is carried in the entrance procession is to be placed near the altar;

— altar cloth, candles, candlesticks, and flowers, if opportune.

6.   When at the same time as the church is blessed the altar is to be consecrated,   4433
all those things should be prepared that are listed in chapter four, no. 27 and no. 29,
if relics of the saints are to be deposited beneath the altar.

7.   For the Mass of the blessing of a church the vestments are white or of some   4434
festive color. The following should be prepared:

— for the bishop: alb, stole, chasuble, miter, pastoral staff;

— for a priest: the vestments for celebrating Mass;

— for the concelebrating priests: the vestments for concelebrating Mass;

— for the deacons: albs, stoles, and dalmatics;

— for other ministers: albs or other lawfully approved dress.

---

[a]   See DOL 442 nos. 3825.

CHAPTER SIX
RITE OF BLESSING AN ALTAR

INTRODUCTION

4435   1.   "A fixed altar is one so constructed that it is attached to the floor so that it cannot be moved; a movable altar can be transferred from place to place."[1]

    A fixed altar is to be dedicated according to the rite described in chapter four. A movable altar also deserves religious respect because it is a table set aside solely and permanently for the eucharistic banquet. Consequently, before a movable altar is put to use, if it is not dedicated, it should at least be blessed with the following rite.[2]

4436   2.   A movable altar may be constructed of any solid material that the traditions and culture of different regions determine to be suitable for liturgical use.[3]

4437   3.   To erect a movable altar what is laid down in the Introduction to chapter four, nos. 6–10, is to be followed, with the necessary modifications. However, it is not permissible to place the relics of saints in the base of a movable altar.

4438   4.   It is appropriate that a movable altar be blessed by the bishop of the diocese or by the priest who is rector of the church.

4439   5.   A movable altar may be blessed on any day, except Good Friday and Holy Saturday. As far as possible, a day should be chosen when the people can be present in large numbers, especially a Sunday, unless pastoral considerations suggest otherwise.

4440   6.   In the rite of blessing a movable altar the Mass is the Mass of the day.

4441   7.   The altar should be left bare until the beginning of the liturgy of the eucharist. Hence a cross (if need be), an altar cloth, candles, and everything else necessary to prepare the altar should be on hand at a convenient place in the sanctuary.

CHAPTER SEVEN
RITE OF BLESSING A CHALICE AND PATEN

INTRODUCTION

4442   1.   The chalice and paten for offering, consecrating, and receiving the bread and wine[1] have as their sole and permanent purpose the celebration of the eucharist and are therefore "sacred vessels."

4443   2.   The intention to devote these vessels entirely to the celebration of the eucharist is expressed in the presence of the community through a special blessing, which is preferably to be imparted within Mass.

---

[1] GIRM no. 261 [DOL 208 no. 1651].

[2] See GIRM no. 265 [DOL 208 no. 1655].

[3] See GIRM no. 264 [DOL 208 no. 1654].

[1] See GIRM no. 289 [DOL 208 no. 1679].

3.   Any priest may bless a chalice and paten, provided they have been made in   4444
conformity with the norms given in the General Instruction of the Roman Missal
nos. 290–295.ª

4.   If only a chalice or only a paten is to be blessed, the text should be modified   4445
accordingly.

548. SC BISHOPS, **Faculties** granted local Ordinaries until promulgation
of a new Code of Canon Law: faculty for the consecration of an altar by a
priest, 9 July 1977.*

II

FROM THE CONGREGATION FOR THE
SACRAMENTS AND DIVINE WORSHIP

The faculty to depute priests (whenever possible, those possessing some eccle-   4446
siastical rank) to consecrate an immovable, fixed altar; they are to follow the rite
and text of the revised Roman Pontifical.ª

ª   See DOL 208 nos. 1680–85.

*   Text, CommRel 58 (1977) 365.

ª   See DOL 547.

Section 3. Vestments and Vesture

SUMMARY (DOL 549–554). The Constitution on the Liturgy touched on the vestments befitting the liturgy in art. 124 and 128 and in art. 130 recommended restriction in the use of pontificals. Both the cross-references and the texts in the present section reflect the carrying out of the intention of the Council.

—From Paul VI there are two motu proprios, on the use of pontificals (DOL 549) and on the pallium (DOL 554). Implementing the first, the Congregation of Rites with the Consilium issued an instruction on the simplification of pontifical rites and insignia (DOL 550). Extending the movement toward simplification in the externals of ecclesiastical life, the Secretariat of State published an instruction on the vesture, titles, and insignia of cardinals, bishops, and lesser prelates (DOL 551) and the Congregation for the Clergy, a circular letter on choral vesture (DOL 552). There is also a text of the Congregation for Divine Worship granting use of a new style of vestment for Mass, the chasuble-alb (DOL 553).

▶ 1.   VATICAN COUNCIL II, Constitution on the Liturgy *Sacrosanctum Concilium*, 4
         December 1963:

     art. 124:   Beauty of vestments and sacred ornaments [no.
                                124].
         128:                   Material and design of vestments. [no. 128].
         130:                   Pontifical insignia [no. 130].

▶ 23.   SC RITES (Consilium), Instruction (first) *Inter Oecumenici*, 26 September 1964:

     nos. 13 c: Liturgical vestments in major seminaries [no. 305].
         18:                    In religious houses of formation [no. 310].

▶ 39.   SC RITES (Consilium), Instruction (second) *Tres abhinc annos*, 4 May 1967:

     nos. 25–27:   Vestments [nos. 471–473].

▶ 147.   SECRETARIAT FOR CHRISTIAN UNITY, Ecumenical Directory I, 14 May
         1967:

     nos. 37, 51 b, 60:   Choral vesture permitted in ecumenical celebrations
                                [nos. 991, 1005, 1014].

▶ 179.   SC RITES (Consilium), Instruction *Eucharisticum mysterium*, on worship of the eu-
         charist, 25 May 1967:

     no. 24:   Material and design of vestments [no. 1253].

549. PAUL VI, **Motu Proprio** *Pontificalia insignia*, on the use of pontificals, 21
June 1968: AAS 60 (1968) 374–377; Not 4 (1968) 224–226.

4447
     Pontifical insignia have been created and approved by the Church over the
course of the centuries in order to give to the faithful a clear and visible expression
of the bishop's sacred office. That expression occurs notably in the solemn presentation of these insignia within the rite of episcopal ordination or consecration by
the use of formularies that describe the pastoral charge entrusted to the bishop over
his people. Particularly in the Middle Ages, many authors have written treatises on
these insignia that bring out both their pastoral and their spiritual symbolism. The
pontificals bring out the bishop's rank and power: he is the shepherd and teacher of
his people, commanded to guide and to feed them; he is "to be looked on as the
high priest of his flock, the faithful's life in Christ in some way deriving from and
depending on him."[1]

     For several centuries the pontifical insignia belonged exclusively to bishops;
gradually, however, they were granted to other ecclesiastics. Some of these were
assistants to the bishops in the pastoral ministry; others were prelates, for example,
abbots in their monasteries or territories who possessed some jurisdiction exempt
from the local bishop; others were clergy, either individually or as a class, who were
given some symbol of rank or honor. The result is that today there are many clergy
who do not possess episcopal rank yet on various grounds and in different degrees
have the privilege of using pontificals. This privilege is regulated by the prescriptions of the *Codex Iuris Canonici*, the Motu Proprio *Inter multiplices* of our predecessor St.

---

[1] SC art. 41 [DOL 1 no. 41].

Pius X, 21 February 1905, and the Apostolic Constitution *Ad incrementum* of our predecessor Pius XI, 15 August 1934.

The recent Second Vatican Ecumenical Council has, however, shed new light **4448** on the dignity and office of bishops in the Church and has brought out more sharply the distinction between bishops and priests of secondary rank. Moreover in treating of the liturgy the Council has ruled that "rites should be marked by a noble simplicity . . . they should be within the people's power of comprehension and as a rule not require much explanation."[2] For the elements taken up into the liturgy are signs that point to unseen divine realities;[3] the faithful must therefore be able to grasp them readily and, as far as possible, immediately, in order that they may lead to heavenly things.

In its norms relevant to the reform of the liturgy, the Council was therefore consistent in ruling that "the use of pontifical insignia should be reserved to those ecclesiastical persons who have episcopal rank or some definite jurisdiction."[4] We should take into consideration the mentality and conditions of our own era, which attaches great importance to the authenticity of signs and to the real need that liturgical rites be marked by a noble simplicity. Accordingly it is very necessary to restore authenticity to the use of pontifical insignia as expressions of the rank and the charge of those who shepherd the people of God.

To carry out the intention of the Council, therefore, we decree the following by our apostolic authority, *motu proprio*, and of set purpose.

1.   In conformity with the directives of the Constitution on the Liturgy art. 130, **4449** we command that from now on besides bishops only those prelates are to use pontifical insignia who although of nonepiscopal rank have actual jurisdiction, namely:

   a.   papal legates;

   b.   abbots and prelates with jurisdiction over a territory separate from any diocese (see CIC can. 319, § 1; can. 325);

   c.   apostolic administrators with a permanent appointment (can. 315, § 1);

   d.   abbots regular with jurisdiction, after they have received the abbatial blessing (can. 625).

2.   Even if they do not have episcopal rank, the following are to use pontifical **4450** insignia, except for the bishop's chair and staff:

   a.   apostolic administrators with a temporary appointment (can. 351, § 2, 2°; see also can. 308);

   b.   vicars and prefects apostolic (can. 308).

3.   The prelates listed in nos. 1 and 2 possess the rights mentioned only within **4451** their own territory and during their tenure. Abbots primate and abbots general of monastic congregations during their tenure, however, may use pontificals in all the monasteries of their order or congregation. Other abbots regular with jurisdiction possess the same right within every monastery of their order, but upon consent of the abbot or conventual prior of that monastery.

---

   [2]   SC art. 34 [DOL 1 no. 34].

   [3]   See SC art. 33 [DOL 1 no. 33].

   [4]   SC art. 130 [DOL 1 no. 130].

4452   4.   Blessed abbots regular, once they have ceased their ruling office, and titular abbots may use pontificals within any monastery of their order or congregation, but upon consent of the abbot or conventual prior of that monastery.

4453   5.   Other prelates not having episcopal rank who were named before the present Motu Proprio continue to possess the privileges they now enjoy regarding use of certain pontificals, as granted them by law either individually or as members of a class. They may, however, give up such privileges of their own accord, in keeping with the provisions of the law.

4454   6.   In view both of the recent decrees of the Council and of the principles already here explained on preserving the authenticity of signs in the liturgy, prelates named in the future will no longer possess the right to use pontificals; those in nos. 1 and 2 are exceptions.

4455   7.   What has been said here regarding prelates applies as well to any clergy who use pontificals no matter what their entitlement.

4456   8.   The effective date for the matters decreed by this Motu Proprio is 8 September 1968.

Whatever has been laid down by this Motu Proprio we command as settled and ratified, all things to the contrary notwithstanding, even those deserving explicit mention.

550. SC RITES, Instruction *Pontificalis ritus*, on the simplification of pontifical rites and insignia, 21 June 1968: AAS 60 (1968) 406–412; Not 4 (1968) 246–252.

4457   Esteem for the pontifical rites and care over them are matters of centuries-old standing. These rites provide a symbol of the honor by which the bishop's dignity is to be acknowledged in the Church and they place clearly before the faithful the mystery of the Church itself.

The *Caeremoniale Episcoporum*, a collection of the norms required for pontifical celebrations made by papal authority, is evidence of the Church's continuing attentiveness regarding rites to be celebrated by a bishop.

The *Caeremoniale* preserves venerable traditions belonging to the ancient celebrations in which priests, deacons, and ministers perform their ministry when a bishop presides and the congregation of the faithful is present. In many places, however, it contains matters that are obsolete and not in keeping with our own times.

Reform of the liturgy was meant to bring the rites once again to a noble simplicity and to authenticity as signs. Once begun many bishops insistently requested that pontifical celebrations and insignia also be simplified.

Not everything in the *Caeremoniale Episcoporum* can be revised before completion of the definitive reform of the Order of Mass, the divine office, and the liturgical year. But careful reflection on the matter led to the conclusion that it is now timely to establish certain measures that, while preserving the dignity of pontifical rites, will also mark them with simplicity. Therefore the following matters are ordered to be changed or introduced at once.

I. PRIESTS AND MINISTERS IN A CELEBRATION
WITH THE BISHOP

PRIESTS AND MINISTERS IN A CONCELEBRATED MASS

1.   The preeminent manifestation of the Church is most clearly expressed in the   4458
eucharist at which the bishop presides, surrounded by his college of priests and
ministers, with the people taking an active part. To show this more clearly it is
especially fitting, now that concelebration has been restored, for priests to be
present with the bishop at a solemn celebration and concelebrate with him, in
accord with an ancient tradition in the Church.

So that priests who hold some higher rank may have more opportunity to
concelebrate with the bishop:

a.   One of the concelebrants may perform the function of assistant priest.

b.   When no deacons are present, two of the concelebrants may replace assistant deacons.[1]

B. ASSISTANT PRIEST AND DEACONS

2.   It belongs to the assistant priest to stand by the bishop's side as he reads.   4459
When the bishop is not at the altar, however, a server holds the book in front of
him.

3.   As a rule, priests of higher rank assist the bishop at the chair. It is permissible,   4460
however, for a deacon to do so and to perform the ministries of the assistant
deacons; if necessary, the deacon and subdeacon of the Mass may fulfill these
functions.

C. DEACONS AND SUBDEACONS

4.   At a celebration with a bishop presiding, the reality of orders and ministries   4461
should stand out clearly. Therefore, deacons and subdeacons, if any are present,
should not be excluded from serving as the deacon at the altar and the subdeacon
for Mass.

5.   Several deacons, clad in their proper vestments, may exercise their ministry,   4462
each taking a part of this ministry.

6.   When a bishop celebrates a Mass without singing, it is fitting that he be   4463
assisted by at least one deacon, vested in amice, alb, cincture, and stole; the deacon
reads the gospel and assists at the altar.[2]

7.   If all the deacons and subdeacons called for by the rubrics are not available on   4464
Holy Thursday at the chrism Mass, fewer suffice. If none at all are available, some
of the concelebrating priests are to carry the oils.

D. CANONS PRESENT IN CHOIR

8.   At a pontifical Mass of a bishop the canons are always to wear a canon's choral   4465
vesture.

E. LESSER MINISTERS

9.   Ministers who assist the bishop at the throne are not to wear a cope.   4466

---

[1]   See *Rite of Concelebration* no. 18 and 19.

[2]   See *Ritus servandus in celebratione Missae* (1965) no. 44.

II. CHAIR OR THRONE OF THE BISHOP

4467   10. The honored and traditional name for the chair of the bishop is the *cathedra*.

4468   11. From now on there is to be no baldachin over the bishop's chair; but the valuable works of art from the past are to be preserved with utmost care. Further, existing baldachins are not to be removed without consultation with the commissions on liturgy and art.

4469   12. Depending on the design of each church the chair should have enough steps leading up to it for the bishop to be clearly visible to the faithful and truly to appear as the one presiding over the whole community of the faithful.

4470   13. In all cases there is to be only a single episcopal chair and the bishop who sits on it is the one who is celebrating or presiding pontifically at the celebration. A chair is also to be provided in a convenient place for any other bishop or prelate who may be present, but it is not to be set up as a *cathedra*.

III. SIMPLIFICATION OF SOME OF THE PONTIFICAL VESTURE AND INSIGNIA

4471   14. A bishop who wears an alb as required by the rubrics need not wear the rochet under the alb.

4472   15. Use of the following is left to the bishop's choice:
    a. buskins and sandals;
    b. gloves, which may be white on all occasions if he prefers;
    c. the morse (*formale*) worn over the cope.

4473   16. The following are to be dropped:
    a. the episcopal tunicle previously worn under the dalmatic;
    b. the silk lap-cloth (*gremial*); another gremial is retained, if it serves a purpose, e.g., for the performance of anointings;
    c. the candle (*bugia*) presented to the bishop for readings, unless it is needed;
    d. the cushion for kneeling during the rites.

4474   17. In keeping with ancient tradition, the bishop is to retain the dalmatic when he celebrates solemnly. In addition he is to wear it in a recited Mass at the consecration of a bishop, the conferral of orders, the blessing of an abbot or an abbess, the blessing and consecration of virgins, the consecration of a church and an altar. But for a reasonable cause he may omit wearing the dalmatic under the chasuble.

4475   18. In each liturgical service a bishop is to use only one miter, plain or ornate depending on the character of the celebration.

4476   19. Any bishop who, with the consent of the local bishop, celebrates solemnly may use the episcopal staff.

4477   20. Only a single cross is to be carried in a procession, to increase the dignity of the cross and its veneration. If an archbishop is present, the cross will be the archiepiscopal cross, to be carried at the head of the procession, with the image of Christ crucified facing forward. The recommended practice is to stand the processional cross near the altar so that it serves as the altar cross. If this is not done, the processional cross is put away.

IV. THINGS TO BE CHANGED OR ELIMINATED IN
EPISCOPAL RITES

A. PUTTING ON AND TAKING OFF VESTMENTS

21.   In any liturgical ceremony a bishop vests and unvests in a side chapel or, if   4478
there is none, in the sacristy, at the chair, or, if more convenient, in front of the
altar. Vestments and insignia, however, are not to be laid on the altar.

22.   When a bishop presides in a side chapel at an hour of the office suited to the   4479
time of day, he wears the chasuble right from the start of the office.

B. THE BOOK OF THE GOSPELS

23.   The Book of the Gospels, preferably distinct from the book of other readings,   4480
is carried by the subdeacon at the beginning of Mass. After the bishop celebrant has
kissed the altar and the Book of the Gospels, this is left on the altar at the middle.
After saying the prayer, *Almighty God, cleanse my heart*, the deacon takes the Book of
the Gospels before asking the bishop's blessing for the singing of the gospel.

C. LITURGY OF THE WORD IN A MASS AT WHICH A BISHOP PRESIDES WITHOUT CELEBRATING

24.   When, in keeping with no. 13, a bishop presides at a Mass without celebrating,   4481
he may do all those things in the liturgy of the word that usually belong to the
celebrant.

D. THINGS TO BE ELIMINATED

25.   The bishop is no longer greeted by a genuflection but by a bow. In carrying out   4482
their service the ministers stand rather than kneel before him, unless kneeling is
more practical.

26.   The washing of the bishop's hands within a liturgical rite is carried out by   4483
acolytes or clerics, not by members of the bishop's household.

27.   All prescriptions in the *Caeremoniale Episcoporum* on forming a circle of assistants   4484
in front of the bishop or on certain parts recited in alternation are abolished.

28.   Also to be abolished is the previous tasting of the bread, wine, and water   4485
prescribed in the *Caeremoniale*.

29.   If a bishop presides at a canonical hour before Mass, he omits those preparato-   4486
ry prayers for Mass that the *Caeremoniale* prescribes during the chanting of the
psalms [lib. II, cap. viii, no. 9].

30.   In a Mass at which a bishop presides without celebrating, the celebrant, not   4487
the bishop, blesses the water to be poured into the chalice at the offertory.

31.   The bishop may omit use of the miter and staff as he goes from one place to   4488
another when there is only a short space between them.

32.   A bishop does not use the miter, unless he already has it on, for the washing of   4489
the hands and the receiving of incensation.

E. BLESSINGS BY A BISHOP

33.   The blessing after the homily mentioned in the *Caeremoniale* is abolished.   4490

34.   When, in keeping with the provisions of law, a bishop bestows it, the papal   4491
blessing with its formularies replaces the usual blessing at the end of Mass.

4492   35. The cross is not to be brought to an archbishop when he gives the blessing.

4493   36. A bishop is to take the staff before he begins the blessing formulary, so that
this is not interrupted. Thus in this instance the raising and extension of the hands
prescribed in the *Ritus servandus* no. 87, are omitted.

An archbishop is to put the miter on before the blessing.

4494   37. After the blessing, the bishop, with miter and staff, reverences the altar, as he
is leaving. If he has the right to wear the pallium, he does not take it off at the altar
but in the sacristy.

V. PRELATES OF LESS THAN EPISCOPAL RANK; OTHER CLERICS; OTHER LITURGICAL RITES

4495   38. All the points in this Instruction on simplifying pontifical vesture, insignia,
and rites and on matters to be eliminated or modified apply in due measure to
prelates or clerics of less than episcopal rank who by law or by privilege are entitled
to certain pontifical insignia.

4496   39. The suppressions and changes that have been decreed here apply also to all
liturgical services celebrated by other clerics.

Pope Paul VI on 10 June 1968 approved this Instruction drawn up by the
Congregation of Rites and the Consilium, confirmed it by his authority, and ordered
its publication, setting 8 September 1968, the feast of the Birth of the Blessed
Virgin Mary, as its effective date.

551. SECRETARIAT OF STATE, Instruction *Ut sive sollicite,* on the vesture,
titles, and insignia of cardinals, bishops, and lesser prelates, 31 March 1969:
AAS 61 (1969) 334–340.

4497   In conscientious fulfillment of his obligation to watch over the universal
Church and in his efforts to carry out the directives and teachings of Vatican
Council II, Pope Paul VI has devoted his attention even to the outward symbols of
ecclesiastical life. His intention has been to adapt such externals to the altered
conditions of the present time and to relate them more closely to the spiritual
values they are meant to signify and to enhance.

The issue at hand is disquieting to our contemporaries. It involves harmoniz-
ing, without giving in to conflicting, extreme demands, propriety and dignity with
simplicity, practicality, and the spirit of humility and poverty. These qualities must
above all characterize those who, by their admittance to ecclesiastical office, have
received a clear duty of service to the people of God.

Prompted by such considerations, the Pope in the last two years has seen to the
issuance of norms on the dress and other prerogatives of cardinals (see SC Ceremo-
nies, Decree, 6 June 1967, Prot. N. 3711), the Motu Proprio *Pontificalis Domus,* 28
March 1968, on the composition of the papal household, the Motu Proprio
Pontificalia insignia, 21 July [June] 1968, on pontificals,[a] and the related Decree of the
Congregation of Rites, Prot. N. R.32/968, on the same date.[b]

---

a   See DOL 549; AAS mistakenly has 21 July 1968 as the date.

b   See DOL 550 [the document is an instruction, not a decree].

Pope Paul, however, wished to change even more extensively the regulations on the vesture, titles, and coats-of-arms of cardinals, bishops, and prelates of lesser rank. He therefore ordered a special commission of cardinals and the papal Secretary of State to study the issue thoroughly, taking into account both established custom, contemporary usage, and the spiritual values connected with various symbols of ecclesiastical life, even though they are external nonessentials.

The consultation of this commission is the basis of the present Instruction. In an audience granted to me, the Cardinal Secretary of State, 28 March 1969, Pope Paul VI approved this Instruction and set 13 April 1969, Low Sunday, as its effective date.

All things to the contrary notwithstanding, even those deserving explicit mention.

PART ONE
DRESS

A. CARDINALS

1.   The following continue in use: the cassock of red wool or similar material, with   4498
sash, piping, buttons, and stitching of red silk; the mozzetta of the same material
and color as the cassock but without the small hood.
     The *mantelletta* is abolished.

2.   The black cassock with piping and red-silk stitching, buttonholes, and but-   4499
tons, but without the oversleeves, also continues in use.
     The elbow-length cape, trimmed in the same manner as this cassock, may be
worn over it.

3.   The sash of red watered-silk, with silk fringes at the two ends, is to be worn   4500
with both the red cassock and the red-trimmed black cassock.
     The sash with tassels is abolished.

4.   When the red cassock is worn, red stockings are also worn, but are optional   4501
with the red-trimmed black cassock.

5.   The dress for ordinary or everyday use may be the plain black cassock. The   4502
stockings worn with it are to be black. The red *collare* [rabat or rabbi] and the
skullcap of red watered-silk may be worn even with the plain black cassock.

6.   The red watered-silk biretta is to be used only with choral dress, not for   4503
everyday wear.

7.   Use of the red watered-silk cloak [*ferraiuolo*] is no longer obligatory for papal   4504
audiences and ceremonies held with the pope present. Its use is also optional in
other cases, but should always be restricted to particular solemn occasions.

8.   The great cloak of red wool [*tabarro*] is abolished. In its place a decent black   4505
cloak, even with cape, may be used.

9.   The red cardinalatial hat [*galero*] and the red plush hat are abolished. But the   4506
black plush hat remains in use, to which, when warranted, red and gold cord and
tassels may be added.

10. Use of red shoes and buckles, even silver buckles on black shoes, is abolished.   4507

4508   11. The rochet of linen or similar material is retained. The surplice or cotta is never to be worn over the rochet.

4509   12. The *cappa magna*, without ermine, is no longer obligatory; it can be used only outside Rome, on very solemn occasions.

4510   13. The cord and chain for the pectoral cross are retained. But the cord is to be worn only with the red cassock or sacred vestments.

B. BISHOPS

4511   14. By analogy with what has been laid down for cardinals, bishops keep the purple cassock, the mozzetta without the small hood, and the black cassock with red piping and buttons.

The mozzetta may be worn anywhere, even by titular bishops.

The purple *mantelletta* or cloak is abolished.

The red-trimmed black cassock with its other red ornaments is no longer obligatory as ordinary dress. The small cape may be worn over it.

4512   15. With regard to the sash, stockings, ordinary dress, *collare* [rabat], skullcap, biretta, *ferraiuolo*, cloak [*tabarro*], buckles, rochet, *cappa magna*, cord and chain for the pectoral cross, the rules laid down in nos. 3–8 and 10–13 are to be followed.

4513   16. The black plush hat with green cord and tassels, which is to be the same for all bishops, both residential and titular, is retained.

4514   17. Like all other bishops, those appointed from religious orders and congregations will use the purple cassock and the black cassock, with or without red trimmings.

C. LESSER PRELATES

4515   18. The higher-ranking prelates of the offices of the Roman Curia who do not have episcopal rank, the auditors of the Rota, the promoter general of justice, and the defender of the bond of the Apostolic Signatura, apostolic protonotaries *de numero*, papal chamberlains, and domestic prelates retain the purple cassock, the purple *mantelletta*, the rochet, the red-trimmed black cassock without cape, the purple sash with fringes of silk at the two ends, the purple *ferraiuolo* (nonobligatory), and the red tuft on the biretta.

The silk sash with tassels, purple stockings, and shoe-buckles are abolished.

4516   19. For supernumerary apostolic protonotaries and for honorary prelates of His Holiness, the purple *mantelletta*, the silk sash with tassels, purple stockings, shoe-buckles, and the red tuft on the biretta are all abolished.

The purple cassock, the red-trimmed black cassock without cape, and the silk sash with fringes are retained. If necessary, the unpleated surplice [cotta] may be worn over the purple cassock, in place of the rochet.

The purple *ferraiuolo*, although not obligatory, is retained for supernumerary apostolic protonotaries, but not for honorary prelates of His Holiness.

4517   20. Chaplains of His Holiness keep the purple-trimmed black cassock with purple sash and other ornaments. It is to be worn also in sacred ceremonies.

The purple cassock, the purple *mantellone*, the sash with tassels, and shoe-buckles are abolished.

PART II
TITLES AND COATS-OF-ARMS

21. The titles called "titles of kinship," which the pope uses in reference to cardi-   4518
nals, bishops and other ecclesiastics, will be limited to the following: for a cardinal,
"Our Esteemed Brother"; for a bishop, "Esteemed Brother"; for others, "Beloved
Son."

22. For cardinals the title "Eminence" and for bishops, "Excellency," may still be   4519
used and the adjectival phrase "Most Reverend" added.

23. The simple titles "Lord Cardinal" and the Italian *Monsignore* may be used to   4520
address a cardinal and a bishop either orally or in writing.

24. "Most Reverend" may be added to the title *Monsignore* in addressing bishops.   4521

25. For the prelates listed in no. 18, "Most Reverend" may also be added to the   4522
title *Monsignore*.

    For the dean of the Roman Rota and the secretary of the Apostolic Signatura,
the title "Excellency" may be used but without "Most Reverend." The same applies
to the vice-chamberlain of the Holy Roman Church.

26. For supernumerary apostolic protonotaries, honorary prelates, and chaplains of   4523
His Holiness the title *Monsignore*, preceded where applicable by "Reverend," may be
used.

27. In formal letters, the expressions "kissing the sacred purple," "kissing the   4524
sacred ring" may be omitted.

28. Cardinals and bishops are granted the right to have a coat-of-arms. The use of   4525
coats-of-arms must conform to the rules of heraldry and must be simple and clear.

    The episcopal staff and the miter in coats-of-arms is suppressed.

29. Cardinals are allowed to have their coats-of-arms affixed to the outside of their   4526
titular or diaconal church.

    The portrait of the titular cardinal is to be removed from such churches. Inside,
near the main door, a plaque is permitted with the name of the titular cardinal
inscribed in a manner suited to the style of the building.

ADDITIONAL PROVISIONS

30. With regard to the dress and titles of cardinals and patriarchs of the Eastern   4527
rites, the traditional usages of their individual rite is to be followed.

31. Patriarchs of the Latin rite who are not cardinals are to dress like other bishops.   4528

32. Papal legates, whether bishops or not, are to conform to the rules already given   4529
for bishops.

    But within their own jurisdiction they may use the sash, skullcap, biretta, and
ferraiuolo of watered silk.

    They will be accorded the title "Esteemed Brother" referred to in no. 21, only
if they are bishops.

4530   33. Prelates *nullius*, abbots *nullius*, apostolic administrators, vicars and prefects apostolic who are not bishops may dress like bishops.

4531   34. In the matter of forms of address conferences of bishops may lay down suitable rules conforming to local usages, but they are to take into account the norms and rules contained in the present Instruction.

4532   35. Concerning the dress and titles of canons, holders of benefices, and pastors, the Congregation for the Clergy will issue pertinent rules for the future that are in keeping with the reason for this Instruction, namely, to reduce everything in this matter to a simpler form.ᶜ

▶   208. SC RITE; SC DIVINE WORSHIP, General Instruction of the Roman Missal, 1st ed. 6 April 1969; 4th ed. 27 March 1975:

nos. 81:   Liturgical vestments of the priest and ministers [no. 1471].
        161:              Concelebrants' vestments [no. 1551].
        297–310:   Liturgical vestments [nos. 1687–1700].

▶   275. SC DIVINE WORSHIP, Instruction *Actio pastoralis*, on Masses with special groups, 15 May 1969:

no. 11 b: Liturgical vestments [no. 2132].

▶   52.   SC DIVINE WORSHIP, Instruction (third) *Liturgicae instaurationes*, 5 September 1970:

no. 8:   Vestments [no. 526].

552. SC CLERGY, Circular Letter *Per Instructionem*, on the reform of choral vesture, 30 October 1970: AAS 63 (1971) 314–315; Not 8 (1972) 36–37.

4533   The Instruction *Ut sive sollicite*, which the Cardinal Secretary of State issued on 31 March 1969 by order of Pope Paul VI, directed this Congregation for the Clergy to make rules, consistent with that Instruction, for the choral vesture and titles of canons, holders of benefices, and pastors.[1]

        This Congregation has consulted the Latin-rite conferences of bishops concerned, compared their decisions, and submitted them to review by the papal Secretariat of State. The Congregation in virtue of the present Circular Letter now entrusts to the same conferences of bishops the task of simplifying choral vesture. They are to be guided by the following universal rules:

4534   1.   This Letter abolishes all, even centuries-old and immemorial privileges, in keeping with the directives of the Motu Proprio *Pontificalia insignia*, 21 June 1968,[2] and the Instruction *Ut sive sollicite*, 31 March 1969.[3]

ᶜ   See DOL 552.

[1]   No. 35 [DOL 551 no. 4532].

[2]   See AAS 60 (1968) 374–377 [DOL 549].

[3]   See AAS 61 (1969) 334–340 [DOL 551].

2.   Only those canons who are bishops may wear the purple mozzetta. Other   4535
canons are to wear a black or grey mozzetta with purple trim. Clerics holding
benefices are to wear a black or grey mozzetta and pastors are to use only the stole.

3.   Canons, clerics holding benefices, and pastors are also forbidden to use any of   4536
the following insignia, which are still in use in some places: the *mantelletta*, the sash
with tassles, red stockings, shoes with buckles, purple cloak, rochet, miter, staff,
ring, pectoral cross.

4.   Everything in the Apostolic See's documents already mentioned concerning   4537
cardinals and bishops applies also, in due proportion, to other categories of ecclesiastics.

Each conference of bishops is given the power to put into effect gradually,
while respecting the requirements of law, the aforementioned directives contained
in the documents of the Apostolic See and in the present Letter.

▶   426.   SC DIVINE WORSHIP, General Instruction of the Liturgy of the Hours, 2
            February 1971:

     no.   255:   Vestments of priests and deacons [no. 3685].

553. SC DIVINE WORSHIP, **Concession** *La Sacrée Congrégation*, allowing use
of the chasuble-alb, 1 May 1971; Not 9 (1973) 96–98 (French).*

A petition conforming to the General Instruction of the Roman Missal no.   4538
304[a] has been addressed to the Congregation for Divine Worship to authorize
wearing of the chasuble-alb with the stole over it in liturgical celebrations. This is a
loose-fitting priestly vestment that entirely envelops the celebrant's body and thus
replaces the alb.

1.   This proposal seems to be consistent with the general principles on liturgical   4539
vestments, as determined by the General Instruction of the Roman Missal no. 297.[b]
In particular:

     a.   The prominence given to the stole by reason of its being worn over the
chasuble-alb puts due emphasis on the hierarchic ministry of the priest, namely, his
role as presiding over the assembly *in persona Christi* (See Introduction no. 4; Text no.
60).[c]

     b.   Since it is so ample that it covers the celebrant's entire body, the chasuble-
alb maintains the sacredness of things used in the liturgy and adds an element of
beauty, if it is of graceful design and good material.

2.   Taking into account the diversity in pastoral situations, the Congregation for   4540
Divine Worship therefore authorizes use of this vestment under the following
conditions.

---

* SCDW, Prot. N. 1937/71, to France; the same concession was extended to other conferences of
bishops.
   [a]   See DOL 208 no. 1694.
   [b]   See DOL 208 no. 1687.
   [c]   See DOL 208 nos. 1379; 1450.

a. For the usual celebration of Mass, particularly in places of worship, the traditional liturgical vestments are to continue in use: the amice (when needed to cover the neck completely), the alb, the stole, and the chasuble, as required by the General Instruction nos. 81 a, 298, and 299.[d] It is preferable to ensure the observance of this prescription, but at the same time not to refuse to meet legitimate needs of the present day.

b. For concelebration, the General Instruction (no. 161)[e] has confirmed the faculty granted to concelebrants, except for the principal concelebrant, to wear just the alb with the stole over it. This makes for a certain simplicity but at the same time respects the dignity and sacredness of the liturgical service. It is proper in concelebrations that the principal concelebrant wear the vestments listed here in no. 2 a.

c. The chasuble-alb may be worn in concelebrations for Masses with special groups, for celebrations outside a place of worship, and for other similar occasions where this usage seems to be suggested by reason of the place or people involved.

d. As to color, the only requirement for use of the chasuble-alb is that the stole be of the color assigned to the Mass.

4541   3.   We should add that the approval of a new type of vestment must not put an end to the creativity of artisans and vestment makers regarding the design or the material and color of vestments. But all their efforts must respect the twofold requirement formulated by the General Instruction no. 297[f] and repeated here in no. 1 a and b: to give proper emphasis to the celebrant's ministry and to ensure the sacredness and beauty of the vestments.

▶   266.   SC DIVINE WORSHIP, *Holy Communion and Worship of the Eucharist outside Mass*, Chapter 2, Holy Communion, 21 June 1973:

no.   20:   Vestments of the minister of communion [no. 2098].

▶   279.   SC DIVINE WORSHIP, *Holy Communion and Worship of the Eucharist outside Mass*, Chapter 3, Forms of Worship.

nos. 88:   Vestments for simple repositions [no. 2214].
       92:                        Vestments for exposition [no. 2218].

554. PAUL VI, **Motu Proprio** *Inter eximia episcopalis*, on the pallium, 11 May 1978: AAS 70 (1978) 441–442; Not 14 (1978) 319–320.

4542   The pallium, received from the revered tomb of St. Peter,[1] is deservedly included among the special insignia of the bishop's office. It is one of those marks of honor that the Apostolic See has from earliest times accorded to Churches and their

---

d   See DOL 208 nos. 1471 and 1688.

e   See DOL 208 no. 1551.

f   See DOL 208 no. 1687.

1   See PR, pars prima, *ed. typica* (Rome, 1962) 62.

heads, first throughout Europe, then throughout the world. The pallium, "a symbol of archiepiscopal power,"[2] "belongs *de iure* only to an archbishop,"[3] since, through its bestowal the fullness of the pontifical office is conferred along with the title of archbishop."[4] As historical records show,[5] however, the popes have continued the early practice of honoring episcopal sees with the dignity of the archiepiscopal pallium as a grant in perpetuity in order to enhance the standing of such Churches because of the renown of the place, the antiquity of the Churches, and their unfailing reverence toward the See of Peter. Furthermore, the popes have also followed the practice of conferring the pallium as a personal privilege to reward the exceptional merits of illustrious bishops.[6]

Vatican Council II, however, has decreed that new and effective norms are to specify the rights and privileges of metropolitans.[7] We have accordingly decided to revise the privileges and practices related to the granting of the pallium in order that it might serve as a distinctive symbol of the power of the metropolitan.[8]

We have received and taken into consideration the opinions of the Roman curial congregations involved and of the commissions for the revision of the code of canon law and of the Eastern code of canon law. Of set purpose and by our own supreme apostolic authority, we now decree that for the entire Latin Church the pallium hereafter belongs exclusively to metropolitans and the Latin-rite patriarch of Jerusalem.[9] We abolish all privileges and customs now applying either to particular Churches or to certain bishops as a personal prerogative.

4543

As to the Eastern Churches, we repeal canon 322 of the Motu Proprio *Cleri sanctitati*.[10]

We permit archbishops and bishops who already have received the pallium, however, to use it as long as they continue as pastors of the Churches now entrusted to them.

In the case of the episcopal ordination of a pope-elect who is not yet a bishop, wearing of the pallium is granted by law to the cardinal dean of the college of cardinals[11] or else to that cardinal to whom the rite of ordination is assigned according to the Apostolic Constitution *Romano Pontifici eligendo*.[12]

The effective date for these norms is the date of their publication in the *Acta Apostolicae Sedis*.

We command that whatever has been decreed by this Motu Proprio is ratified and established, all things to the contrary notwithstanding, even those deserving explicit mention.

[2]   CIC can. 275.

[3]   Benedict XIV, *De Synodo dioecesana* lib. 2, 6, no. 1.

[4]   Benedict XIV, Ap. Const. *Ad honorandum*, 27 March 1754, § 17.

[5]   See Benedict XIV, *De Synodo dioecesana* loc. cit.

[6]   See Benedict XIV, Ap. Const. *Inter conspicuos*, 29 Aug. 1744, no. 18.

[7]   See CD no. 40: AAS 58 (1966) 694; ConstDecrDecl 318.

[8]   See CIC can. 275.

[9]   See Pius IX, Apostolic Letter *Nulla celebrior*, 23 July 1947: *Acta Pii IX*, pars. 2, vol. 1, 62.

[10]   See AAS 49 (1957) 529.

[11]   See CIC can. 239, § 2.

[12]   See AAS 67 (1975) 644–645.

APPENDIX

DOCUMENT TITLES BY DATE OF ISSUE

Date	Source, Designation, Subject	DOL
8 May 1963	SC HOLY OFFICE, Instruction *Piam et constantem*, on cremation.	413
22 November 1963	PAUL VI, Epistle (autograph) *Nobile subsidium*, establishing the CIMS.	500
30 November 1963	PAUL VI, Motu Proprio *Pastorale munus*, on the powers and privileges of bishops.	103
4 December 1963	VATICAN COUNCIL II, Constitution on the Liturgy *Sacrosanctum Concilium*.	1
4 December 1963	PAUL VI, Address to the Fathers at the end of the second period of the Council.	2
4 December 1963	VATICAN COUNCIL II, Decree on the Media of Social Communication *Inter mirifica*.	3
10 January 1964	SC HOLY OFFICE, Decree *In Apostolica Constitutione*, on eucharistic fast for priests.	271
15 January 1964	PAUL VI, Apostolic Exhortation *E peregrinatione*, on prayer for Christian unity.	144
25 January 1964	PAUL VI, Motu Proprio *Sacram Liturgiam*, on putting into effect some prescriptions of the Constitution on the Liturgy.	20
29 February 1964	SECRETARIAT OF STATE, Letter *Mi onore di communicare* to the Consilium, on its organization and work.	77
25 March 1964	CONSILIUM, Letter *Le sarei grato* to papal nuncios and apostolic delegates, on reform of the liturgy.	79
6 April 1964	PAUL VI, Address to choir members, on Gregorian chant.	501
14 April 1964	PAUL VI, Address to bishops of Italy, on liturgical reform.	21
21 April 1964	PONTIFICAL BIBLICAL COMMISSION, Instruction *Sancta Mater Ecclesia*, on the historical truth of the Gospels.	227
25 April 1964	SC RITES, Decree *Quo actuosius*, promulgating a new formulary for communion.	252
25 April 1964	PAUL VI, Address to altar servers.	336
25 April 1964	SC RITES, Decree *Piae invocationes*, on a new invocation of the Holy Spirit.	495
9 May 1964	SC RITES, Decree *Die 30 Iunii*, on the collect *pro Papa* for 30 June 1964.	496
23 June 1964	PAUL VI, Address to a consistory, on carrying out reform of the liturgy.	22
6 August 1964	PAUL VI, Encyclical *Ecclesiam suam*, excerpt on preaching.	195
26 September 1964	SC RITES (Consilium), Instruction (first) *Inter Oecumenici*, on carrying out the Constitution on the Liturgy.	23
16 October 1964	CONSILIUM, Letter *Consilium ad exsequendum* to the conferences of bishops, on uniform translations in a language common to several countries.	108

26 October 1964	PAUL VI, Apostolic Letter *Pacis nuntius*, declaring St. Benedict patron of Europe.	469
29 October 1964	CONSILIUM, Remarks of Cardinal G. Lercaro at a papal audience for the Consilium.	80
29 October 1964	PAUL VI, Address to the members of the Consilium.	81
5 November 1964	APOSTOLIC PENITENTIARY, Decree *Sanctissimus D. N. Paulus*, on papal blessing by newly ordained priests.	383
6 November 1964	SECRETARIAT OF STATE, Pontifical Rescript *Cum admotae*, on faculties delegated to religious superiors.	141
21 November 1964	VATICAN COUNCIL II, Dogmatic Constitution on the Church *Lumen gentium*.	4
21 November 1964	VATICAN COUNCIL II, Decree on the Eastern Catholic Churches *Orientalium Ecclesiarum*.	5
21 November 1964	VATICAN COUNCIL II, Decree on Ecumenism *Unitatis redintegratio*.	6
21 November 1964	PAUL VI, Concession, on eucharistic fast	272
14 December 1964	SC RITES (Consilium), Decree *Quum Constitutio*, promulgating the *editio typica* of the *Kyriale simplex*.	529
14 December 1964	SC RITES (Consilium), *Kyriale simplex*, Introduction.	530
14 December 1964	SC RITES (Consilium), Decree *Edita Instructione*, promulgating the chants for the Roman Missal.	531
1964–1969	CONSILIUM, List of members.	78
7 January 1965	SECRETARIAT OF STATE, Letter *Compio il venerato incarico*, on the respective competences of the SC Rites and the Consilium.	82
9 January 1965	SC RITES, Reply (Capuchins), on recitation of the divine office by lay brothers.	109
13 January 1965	PAUL VI, Address to a general audience, on the recent Constitution on the Liturgy.	24
27 January 1965	SC RITES (Consilium), Decree *Nuper edita Instructione*, on the new Order of Mass and rites of celebration.	196
6 February 1965	PAUL VI, Apostolic Epistle "*Investigabiles divitias Christi*," on the Sacred Heart.	453
15 February 1965	SC RITES, Letter to publishers, on corrections for rubrics of the *Missale Romanum*.	197
28 February 1965	CONSILIUM, Note, on the epistle for the Saturday after the 3rd Sunday of Lent.	228
1 March 1965	PAUL VI, Address to pastors and Lenten preachers of Rome.	25
4 March 1965	SC RITES, Decree *Pientissima Mater Ecclesia*, on priests' carrying the oil of the sick.	407
6 March 1965	APOSTOLIC PENITENTIARY, Declaration *Sacra Paenitentiaria Apostolica*, on indulgenced religious articles.	384
7 March 1965	PAUL VI, Remarks at the Angelus, on beginning of the vernacular in the liturgy.	26
7 March 1965	SC RITES (Consilium), Decree *Ecclesiae semper*, promulgating the *editio typica* of the rites of concelebration and of communion under both kinds.	222
7 March 1965	SC RITES (Consilium), *Rite of Concelebration*, Introduction.	223
7 March 1965	SC RITES (Consilium), *Rite of Communion under Both Kinds*, Introduction.	268
7 March 1965	SC RITES (Consilium), Decree *Quamplures Episcopi*, on changes in Holy Week.	454
17 March 1965	PAUL VI, Address to a general audience, on reactions to the reform of the liturgy.	27
25 March 1965	SC RITES, Decree *Plures locorum*, on nondeacons reading the gospel of Christ's passion.	337
29 March 1965	CONSILIUM, Letter *Ordo agendorum* to the conferences of bishops, requesting a report on the first steps of the reform.	28
24 April 1965	SC EXTRAORDINARY AFFAIRS, Rescript (Brazil), on women religious distributing communion.	253
27 April 1965	SECRETARIAT OF STATE, Letter *Ho L'onore*, on Pope Paul VI's concession of the preface in the vernacular.	110
26 May 1965	SC RITES, Decree (dioceses of Europe) *Sanctum Bene-*	470

dictum, on texts for feast of St. Benedict, Patron of Europe.

1–2 June 1965	CONSILIUM, Instruction *Popularibus interpretationibus*, on translations of propers of dioceses and religious families.	111
2 June 1965	PAUL VI, Concession, on omission of prime.	419
10 June 1965	PAUL VI, Address to eucharistic congress at Pisa.	174
15 June 1965	CONSILIUM, Declaration *Passim quandoque*, on liturgical experimentation.	29
18 June 1965	SC COUNCIL, Notification *Come è noto*, on eucharistic fast in the *Catechism of St. Pius X.*	273
24 June 1965	PAUL VI, Address to a consistory, on the beginnings of liturgical reform.	30
30 June 1965	CONSILIUM, Letter *Le renouveau liturgique* to the conferences of bishops, on furthering liturgical reform.	31
3 July 1965	SC RITES, Reply, on tabernacle with baldachin.	542
8 July 1965	SC RITES, Reply, on communion under both kinds for members of secular institutes.	269
16 July 1965	SC RITES, Reply (Washington), on altar facing the people.	543
17 July 1965	SC RITES, Enumeration *Constitutio de sacra Liturgia* of the parts of rites of ordination in the vernacular.	112
19 July 1965	PAUL VI, Epistle *Pastoralem Episcoporum Hollandiae* to Cardinal B. Alfrink, on the Dutch bishops' pastoral on the eucharist.	175
21 August 1965	CONSILIUM, Letter to Bishop Charrière, on liturgical singing.	502
3 September 1965	PAUL VI, Encyclical *Mysterium fidei*, on the eucharist.	176
14 September 1965	CONSILIUM, *Masses for the Fourth Period of Vatican Council II*, Introduction and Order of Celebration	198
16 September 1965	SC SEMINARIES AND UNIVERSITIES, Rescript (U.S.A.), on stipend for a bination.	280
25 September 1965	SC RITES, Letter *Impetrata prius* to Cardinal P. Ciriaci, on Sunday Mass on Saturday evening.	444
15 October 1965	CONSILIUM, Note *Prima phasis renovationis*, on *ad interim* weekday lectionaries.	229
15 October 1965	SC RITES, Decree (Avila), on a funeral Mass in the evening of a vigil.	414
19 October 1965	SC COUNCIL, Rescript (Germany), allowing Sunday Mass on Saturday evening.	445
28 October 1965	VATICAN COUNCIL II, Decree on the Pastoral Office of Bishops *Christus Dominus.*	7
28 October 1965	VATICAN COUNCIL II, Decree on the Appropriate Renewal of Religious Life *Perfectae caritatis.*	10
28 October 1965	VATICAN COUNCIL II, Decree on Priestly Formation *Optatam totius.*	12
28 October 1965	VATICAN COUNCIL II, Declaration on Christian Education *Gravissimum educationis.*	13
8 November 1965	SC RITES, Reply (Dom Franzoni), on the divine office.	420
10 November 1965	PAUL VI, Address to translators of liturgical texts.	113
18 November 1965	VATICAN COUNCIL II, Dogmatic Constitution on Divine Revelation *Dei Verbum.*	14
18 November 1965	VATICAN COUNCIL II, Decree on the Apostolate of the Laity *Apostolicam actuositatem.*	16
23 November 1965	SC RITES and SC RELIGIOUS, Instruction *In edicendis normis*, on the language to be used in celebrations of religious.	114
24 November 1965	SC RITES, Reply (Holland), on nuptial blessing in "closed times."	347
26 November 1965	SC RITES, Reply (Zamora, Mexico), on concelebration at priests' ordination.	224
7 December 1965	VATICAN COUNCIL II, Decree on the Church's Missionary Activity *Ad gentes.*	17
7 December 1965	VATICAN COUNCIL II, Decree on the Ministry and Life of Priests *Presbyterorum Ordinis.*	18
7 December 1965	VATICAN COUNCIL II, Pastoral Constitution on the	19

Church in the Modern World *Gaudium et spes.*

7 December 1965	PAUL VI, Apostolic Constitution *Mirificus eventus*, declaring the extraordinary Jubilee of 1966.	484
10 December 1965	CONSILIUM, Reply (U.S.A.), on Mass for the deaf.	274
14 December 1965	SC RELIGIOUS, Notice, on religious in the liturgical apostolate.	142
20 December 1965	APOSTOLIC PENITENTIARY, Decree *Cum plures Episcopi*, on indulgences of the Jubilee of 1966.	485
25 December 1965	SC SEMINARIES AND UNIVERSITIES, Instruction *Doctrina et exemplo*, on the liturgical formation of future priests.	332
1965	SECRETARIAT OF STATE, Letter to the review *Musica Sacra*, on liturgical music.	503
5 January 1966	APOSTOLIC PENITENTIARY, Declaration *Cum non pauci*, on the indulgences for the Jubilee of 1966.	486
6 January 1966	SC RITES, Decree *Extraordinarium Iubilaeum*, promulgating the Mass for the Jubilee of 1966.	487
12 January 1966	SC RITES, Decree (Rome), on the deacon at Mass.	199
21 January 1966	CONSILIUM, Communication *Per Litteras Apostolicas*, on norms for translation of the Mass of the Jubilee.	115
25 January 1966	CONSILIUM, Letter *L'heureux développement* to the conferences of bishops, on problems in the reform of the liturgy.	32
27 January 1966	SC RITES (Consilium), Decree *Cum, nostra aetate*, on editions of the liturgical books.	134
31 January 1966	APOSTOLIC PENITENTIARY, Decree *Die 31 Ianuarii*, on indulgenced prayer before office.	385
5 February 1966	SC RITES, Reply, on omitting the prayers at the foot of the altar.	200
8 February 1966	PAUL VI, Motu Proprio *Peculiare ius*, on use of the papal altar.	544
14 February 1966	SC RITES, Decree *Cum hac nostra aetate*, on communion in hospitals.	254
17 February 1966	PAUL VI, Apostolic Constitution *Paenitemini*, on Christian penance.	358
24 February 1966	SC RITES (Consilium), Communication *Sacra Rituum Congregatio*, on special intention for Lent 1966.	240
1 March 1966	SC RITES, Decree *Plures sacrorum Antistites*, on the jubilee (1966) Mass on days of the first class.	488
18 March 1966	SC DOCTRINE OF THE FAITH, Instruction *Matrimonii sacramentum*, on mixed marriages.	351
19 March 1966	SC COUNCIL, Circular Letter *Omnibus in comperto* to local Ordinaries, on tourists at Sunday Masses.	446
24 March 1966	PAUL VI and MICHAEL RAMSEY (Archbishop of Canterbury), Joint Statement.	145
25 March 1966	PAUL VI, Epistle *Vox laetitiae* to Cardinal P. Richaud, on the eucharistic congress at Bordeaux.	177
27 March 1966	PAUL VI, Homily, on themes and objectives of the Council regarding reform of the liturgy.	33
31 March 1966	PAUL VI, Epistle *Nous nous apprêtons* to Christophoros, Patriarch of Alexandria, on a common date for Easter.	146
6 April 1966	PAUL VI, Address to a general audience, on participation in Holy Week.	34
16 April 1966	PAUL VI, Address to Latinists.	116
17 April 1966	CONSILIUM, *The Universal Prayer or Prayer of the Faithful* (2nd ed.).	239
18 April 1966	SC COUNCIL, Reply, on the stipend for a concelebrated Mass.	225
18 April 1966	PAUL VI, Address to the International Federation of Little Singers.	504
3 May 1966	PAUL VI, Motu Proprio *Summi Dei beneficio*, extending the extraordinary Jubilee of 1966.	489
11 May 1966	SECRETARIAT OF STATE, Letter, on the foundation of Universa Laus.	505
13 May 1966	SC RITES, Decree *Cum proximo anno*, on feast of St. Joseph in 1967.	471

16 May 1966	PAUL VI, Address to major superioresses, on liturgy and religious life.	400
31 May 1966	SC RELIGIOUS, Decree *Religionum laicalium*, on faculties delegated to religious superiors.	143
31 May 1966	SC PROPAGATION OF THE FAITH, Rescript (Canada), on the rite of communion distributed by women religious.	255
10 June 1966	PONTIFICAL CENTRAL COMMISSION FOR COORDINATING POSTCONCILIAR WORK . . ., Reply, on the Decree *Christus Dominus* no. 38, section 4.	8
10 June 1966	PONTIFICAL CENTRAL COMMISSION FOR COORDINATING POSTCONCILIAR WORK . . ., Reply, on the Decree *Perfectae caritatis*.	11
15 June 1966	PAUL VI, Motu Proprio *De Episcoporum muneribus*, on norms for the power of dispensation.	105
24 July 1966	SC DOCTRINE OF THE FAITH, Letter *Cum Oecumenicum Concilium* to the conferences of bishops, on erroneous interpretations of Vatican II.	178
5 August 1966	SC RITES, Letter *Non latet sane* to the conferences of bishops, on royalties for Latin liturgical books.	135
6 August 1966	PAUL VI, Motu Proprio *Ecclesiae Sanctae*, on norms for carrying out certain of the conciliar decrees.	106
12 August 1966	SECRETARIAT OF STATE, Letter to Archbishop W. E. Cousins, on sacred music.	506
15 August 1966	PAUL VI, Epistle *Sacrificium laudis* to religious superiors, on the divine office.	421
18 August 1966	SECRETARIAT OF STATE, Letter to Bishop C. Rossi, on Church and sacraments.	288
10 September 1966	ADMINISTRATION OF THE PATRIMONY OF THE HOLY SEE, Letter to the conferences of bishops, on royalties for liturgical books.	136
15 September 1966	PAUL VI, Encyclical *Christi Matri*, on the rosary.	462
30 September 1966	PAUL VI, Address to abbots, on liturgy and contemplation.	401
13 October 1966	CONSILIUM, Remarks of Cardinal G. Lercaro at a papal audience for the Consilium.	83
13 October 1966	PAUL VI, Address to the members of the Consilium.	84
October 1966	CONSILIUM, Clarification *Nell'aprile scorso*, on Universa Laus and the CIMS.	507
11 November 1966	SC DISCIPLINE OF THE SACRAMENTS, Rescript (Canada), on religious distributing communion.	256
29 December 1966	SC RITES (Consilium), Declaration *Da qualche tempo*, repudiating arbitrary innovations.	35
December 1966	CONSILIUM, Editorial *Expériences liturgiques*, on experimentation.	36
1 January 1967	PAUL VI, Apostolic Constitution *Indulgentiarum doctrina*, on indulgences.	386
4 January 1967	SC RITES (Consilium), Press Conference, on the Declaration of 29 December 1966.	37
4 January 1967	PAUL VI, Address to diocesan liturgical commissions, on liturgy and sacred art.	539
29 January 1967	SC RELIGIOUS, Letter to Visitation nuns, on replacing the Little Office with the divine office.	422
31 January 1967	PAUL VI, Concession, allowing, *ad experimentum*, vernacular in the canon of the Mass and in ordinations.	117
January 1967	CONSILIUM, Editorial *Mécanique et Liturgie*, on mechanical devices in the liturgy.	38
January 1967	CONSILIUM, Note *Lectionarium feriale*, on the lectionary of the Consilium.	230
22 February 1967	SC EASTERN CHURCHES, Decree *Crescens matrimoniorum*, on mixed marriages of Eastern Christians.	352
24 February 1967	SC COUNCIL, Declaration *Tricenario Gergoriano*, on Gregorian Masses.	281
24 February 1967	SC COUNCIL, Reply, on *Paenitemini* no. II, section 2.	359
5 March 1967	SC RITES (Consilium), Instruction *Musicam sacram*, on music in the liturgy.	508
30 March 1967	PAUL VI, Address to altar servers.	338

5 April 1967	PAUL VI, Address to choirs of France, on preserving the treasury of sacred music.	509
19 April 1967	CONSILIUM, Remarks of Cardinal G. Lercaro at a papal audience for the Consilium.	85
19 April 1967	PAUL VI, Address to the members of the Consilium.	86
4 May 1967	SC RITES (Consilium), Instruction (second) *Tres abhinc annos*, on carrying out the Constitution on the Liturgy.	39
13 May 1967	PAUL VI, Apostolic Exhortation *Signum magnum*, on Mary, Mother of the Church.	463
14 May 1967	SECRETARIAT FOR CHRISTIAN UNITY, Ecumenical Directory, Part I, *Ad totam Ecclesiam*.	147
18 May 1967	SC RITES (Consilium), Decree *Per Instructionem alteram*, on changes in the Order of Mass.	201
25 May 1967	SC RITES (Consilium), Instruction *Eucharisticum mysterium*, on worship of the eucharist.	179
15 June 1967	CONSILIUM, Letter to the conferences of bishops, requesting survey of results of the reform.	40
18 June 1967	PAUL VI, Motu Proprio *Sacrum Diaconatus Ordinem*, restoring the permanent diaconate in the Latin Church.	309
21 June 1967	CONSILIUM, Letter *Dans sa récente allocution* to the conferences of bishops, on issues of the reform.	41
28 June 1967	APOSTOLIC PENITENTIARY, Decree *Sanctissimus D.N. Paulus*, on indulgences for 19th centenary of the martyrdom of St. Peter and St. Paul.	387
9 July 1967	PAUL VI, Address to the International Federation of Little Singers.	510
6 August 1967	PAUL VI, Motu Proprio *Pro comperto sane*, on diocesan bishops as members of the curial congregations.	87
10 August 1967	CONSILIUM, Communication *Aussitôt après* to the conferences of bishops, on the translation of the Roman Canon.	118
15 August 1967	PAUL VI, Apostolic Constitution *Regimini Ecclesiae universae*, on reform of the Roman Curia.	88
August 1967	CONSILIUM, Letter to Archbishop E. Delgado Gómez, on sacred music.	511
3 September 1967	SC RITES (Consilium), Decree *Sacrosancti Oecumenici Concilii*, promulgating the *editio typica* of *The Simple Gradual*.	532
3 September 1967	SC RITES (Consilium), *The Simple Gradual*, Introduction.	533
20 September 1967	SC RELIGIOUS, Rescript (Capuchins), on the vernacular in the divine office.	119
17 October 1967	CONSILIUM, Rescript (Benedictines), on monastic office.	437
28 October 1967	PAUL VI and ATHENAGORAS I (Patriarch of Constantinople), Joint Statement.	148
28 November 1967	SC DISCIPLINE OF THE SACRAMENTS, Rescript (Germany), on laity distributing communion.	257
8 December 1967	PAUL VI, Message (written), on 1 January as World Day of Peace.	497
12 December 1967	SC RITES, Declaration *Cum Dominica IV Adventus*, on evening Mass for 23 December 1967.	447
30 December 1967	SECRETARIAT OF STATE, Rescript *Cum notae causae*, delaying effective date of *Regimini Ecclesiae universae*.	89
1967	APOSTOLIC PENITENTIARY, Norms *Ut haec S. Paenitentiaria*, on gaining indulgences.	388
1 January 1968	SC BISHOPS, Index of quinquennial faculties granted to local Ordinaries.	107
8 January 1968	ADMINISTRATION OF THE PATRIMONY OF THE HOLY SEE, Letter to the conferences of bishops, on royalties for liturgical books.	137
9 January 1968	PAUL VI, Epistle *Nell'atto in cui* to Cardinal G. Lercaro, at the end of his term of office.	90
23 January 1968	CONSILIUM, Communication *Instantibus pluribus*, on norms for the translation of the *Graduale simplex*.	120
January 1968	CONSILIUM, Editorial *Des gestes qui révèlent*, on gestures in the liturgy.	42

2 February 1968	CONSILIUM, Letter to the Italian bishops, on liturgical music.	512
5 February 1968	PONTIFICAL COMMISSION FOR INTERPRETATION . . . VATICAN II, Reply, on the Decree *Christus Dominus* and the Motu Proprio *Ecclesiae Sanctae.*	9
5 February 1968	PONTIFICAL COMMISSION FOR INTERPRETATION . . . VATICAN II, Reply, on the Constitution *Dei Verbum* no. 21.	15
28 February 1968	PAUL VI, Address to a general audience, on the pedagogy of Lent.	455
26 March 1968	PONTIFICAL COMMISSION FOR INTERPRETATION . . . VATICAN II, Reply, on *Sacrum Diaconatus Ordinem* no. 22.	310
22 April 1968	PAUL VI, Address to the 8th International Meeting of Church Choirs.	513
26 April 1968	PAUL VI, Address to Latinists, on Latin and the vernacular in the Church.	121
23 May 1968	SC RITES (Consilium), Decree *Prece eucharistica*, promulgating three new eucharistic prayers and eight prefaces.	241
23 May 1968	SC RITES (Consilium), Norms, on use of Eucharistic Prayers I–IV.	242
2 June 1968	CONSILIUM, Letter *La publication* to the conferences of bishops, on the new eucharistic prayers.	243
2 June 1968	CONSILIUM, Guidelines *Au cours des derniers mois*, on catechesis for the anaphoras.	244
6 June 1968	SC RITES (Consilium), Decree *Domus Dei*, on the title of minor basilica.	545
14 June 1968	SECRETARIAT OF STATE, Letter to the Cistercian Abbot of Hauterive, on Latin in the liturgy.	122
18 June 1968	PAUL VI, Apostolic Constitution *Pontificalis Romani recognitio*, approving new ordination rites.	324
21 June 1968	PAUL VI, Motu Proprio *Pontificalia insignia*, on use of pontificals.	549
21 June 1968	SC RITES (Consilium), Instruction *Pontificalis ritus*, on simplification of pontifical rites and insignia.	550
29 June 1968	APOSTOLIC PENITENTIARY, Decree *In Constitutione Apostolica*, promulgating the new edition of the *Enchiridion indulgentiarum.*	389
29 June 1968	APOSTOLIC PENITENTIARY, *Enchiridion indulgentiarum*, Norms.	390
30 June 1968	PAUL VI, Solemn Profession of Faith (Credo of the People of God).	168
16 July 1968	PAUL VI, Epistle *Inclitae Columbiae* to Cardinal G. Lercaro, on the International Eucharistic Congress at Bogotá.	180
15 August 1968	SC RITES (Consilium), Decree *Per Constitutionem Apostolicam*, promulgating new rites of ordination.	325
30 August 1968	SC DISCIPLINE OF THE SACRAMENTS, Letter to U.S. conference of bishops, on permanent deacons assisting at a marriage.	312
3 September 1968	SC DOCTRINE OF THE FAITH, Rescript (U.S.A.), on a mixed marriage before a Lutheran minister.	353
12 September 1968	SC RITES (Consilium), Instruction *Ad solemnia*, on celebrations of the newly canonized.	472
18 September 1968	PAUL VI, Address to Cecilians, on music.	514
6 October 1968	SECRETARIAT FOR CHRISTIAN UNITY, Note *In questi ultimi mesi*, on application of the Ecumenical Directory	149
14 October 1968	CONSILIUM, Remarks of Cardinal B. Gut at an audience for the Consilium.	91
14 October 1968	PAUL VI, Address to the members of the Consilium.	92
18 October 1968	SC RITES (Consilium), Declaration *Cum recentioribus temporibus* on Epiphany, Ascension, Corpus Christi transferred to Sunday.	456
6 November 1968	CONSILIUM, Declaration *In conficiendis*, on the eucharistic prayers.	245

7 November 1968	CONSILIUM, Letter to Cardinal J. P. Cody, on music	515
28 November 1968	SC EVANGELIZATION OF PEOPLES, Rescript (Antilles), on laity distributing communion.	258
December 1968	CONSILIUM, Publication of liturgical texts for World Day of Peace, 1969.	498
10 January 1969	PAUL VI, Epistle *Saluberrimum Sacramentum Eucharistiae* to Rev. R. Huot, on eucharistic worship outside Mass.	277
14 January 1969	SC EVANGELIZATION OF PEOPLES, Rescript (Antilles), on blessing of oils on Wednesday of Holy Week.	457
25 January 1969	CONSILIUM, Instruction *Comme le prévoit*, on translation of liturgical texts for celebrations with a congregation.	123
7 February 1969	PAUL VI, Address to a liturgical congress, on the eucharistic prayer.	246
14 February 1969	PAUL VI, Motu Proprio *Mysterii paschalis*, approving the norms for the liturgical year and the new General Roman Calendar.	440
19 March 1969	SC RITES (Consilium), Decree *Ordo celebrandi Matrimonium*, promulgating the *editio typica* of the rite of marriage.	348
19 March 1969	SC RITES (Consilium), *Rite of Marriage*, Introduction.	349
21 March 1969	SC RITES (Consilium, Decree *Anni Liturgici ordinatione*, promulgating the *editio typica* of the General Roman Calendar.	441
21 March 1969	SC RITES (Consilium), General Norms for the Liturgical Year and the Calendar.	442
31 March 1969	SECRETARIAT OF STATE, Instruction *Ut sive sollicite*, on vesture, titles, and insignia of cardinals, bishops, and lesser prelates.	551
March 1969	CONSILIUM, Declaration *Circa Instructionem*, on *ad interim* translations of liturgical texts.	124
3 April 1969	PAUL VI, Apostolic Constitution *Missale Romanum*, approving the new Roman Missal.	202
4 April 1969	PONTIFICAL COMMISSION FOR INTERPRETATION ... VATICAN II, Reply, on *Sacrum Diaconatus Ordinem* no. 22, section 4.	311
6 April 1969	SC RITES (Consilium), Decree *Ordine Missae*, promulgating the new Order of Mass, with the General Instruction of the Roman Missal.	203
14 April 1969	PAUL VI, Address to the 9th International Meeting of Church Choirs.	516
25 April 1969	CONSILIUM, Rescript (India), on liturgical adaptations.	43
28 April 1969	PAUL VI, Address to a consistory, excerpt on the liturgy and on the division of SC Rites into two congregations.	93
30 April 1969	SC DISCIPLINE OF THE SACRAMENTS, Instruction *Fidei custos*, on special ministers of communion.	259
30 April 1969	SC CLERGY, General Directory *Peregrinans in terra*, on the pastoral ministry in tourism.	326
8 May 1969	PAUL VI, Apostolic Constitution *Sacra Rituum Congregatio*, establishing SC Divine Worship and SC Causes of Saints.	94
12 May 1969	SC DIVINE WORSHIP, Epistle *La Sacra Congregazione* of Cardinal B. Gut to Pope Paul VI, on the new Congregation	96
12 May 1969	PAUL VI, Epistle (autograph) *Rispondiamo subito*, in reply to Cardinal B. Gut.	97
15 May 1969	SC DIVINE WORSHIP, Instruction *Actio pastoralis*, on Masses with special groups.	275
15 May 1969	SC DIVINE WORSHIP, Decree *Ordinem Baptismi parvulorum*, promulgating the *editio typica* of the rite of baptism for children.	292
25 May 1969	SC DIVINE WORSHIP, Decree *Ordo lectionum*, promulgating the *editio typica* of the order of readings for Mass.	231

25 May 1969	SC DIVINE WORSHIP, *Lectionary for Mass,* Introduction.	232
29 May 1969	SC DIVINE WORSHIP, Instruction *Memoriale Domini,* on the manner of giving communion.	260
29 May 1969	SC DIVINE WORSHIP, Letter *En réponse à la demande* to petitioning conferences of bishops, on communion in the hand.	261
31 May 1969	SC RELIGIOUS AND SECULAR INSTITUTES, Rescript (mendicant orders), on recitation of office in common.	423
22 June 1969	SC DIVINE WORSHIP, new rite of canonization.	473
25 June 1969	SC DISCIPLINE OF THE SACRAMENTS, Rescript (U.S.A.), on laity giving communion.	262
29 June 1969	SC DIVINE WORSHIP, Instruction *Decreto Sacrae Congregationis,* on adapting particular calendars.	480
5 July 1969	SC EVANGELIZATION OF PEOPLES, Rescript (Society of African Missions), on the permanent diaconate.	313
10 July 1969	SC DIVINE WORSHIP, Decree *Petentibus nonnullis Conferentiis,* extending the *vacatio legis* of the *Rite of Baptism for Children.*	296
16 July 1969	SC CATHOLIC EDUCATION, Letter *Come è a conoscenza* to apostolic nuncios, on formation for permanent diaconate.	314
24 July 1969	SC CATHOLIC EDUCATION, Rescript (U.S.A.), on stipend for two weekday Masses.	282
25 July 1969	SC DIVINE WORSHIP, Instruction *Decreto quo,* on editions and use of the new *Lectionary for Mass.*	233
31 July 1969	PAUL VI, Address to bishops of Africa, on liturgy and cultures.	44
13 August 1969	PAUL VI, Address to a general audience, on the liturgy and personal prayer.	45
15 August 1969	PAUL VI, Motu Proprio *Pastoralis migratorum cura,* on the pastoral care of migrants.	327
15 August 1969	SC RELIGIOUS AND SECULAR INSTITUTES, Instruction *Venite seorsum,* on contemplative life and law of enclosure.	402
15 August 1969	SC DIVINE WORSHIP, Decree *Ritibus exsequiarum,* promulgating the *editio typica* of the rite of funerals.	415
15 August 1969	SC DIVINE WORSHIP, *Rite of Funerals,* Introduction.	416
20 August 1969	PAUL VI, Address to a general audience, on prayer prompted by joy and hope.	46
22 August 1969	SC BISHOPS, Instruction *Sacra Congregatio pro Episcopis,* on pastoral ministry to migrants.	328
3 September 1969	PAUL VI, Address to a general audience, on reform of the liturgy and a new spirit of prayer.	47
7 September 1969	PAUL VI, Remarks at the Angelus, on the parish and liturgical life.	48
15 September 1969	SC DIVINE WORSHIP, Declaration *Plures liturgicae,* on the translation of new liturgical texts.	125
7 October 1969	PAUL VI, Apostolic Exhortation *Recurrens mensis octobris,* on the rosary.	464
20 October 1969	SC DIVINE WORSHIP, Instruction *Constitutione Apostolica,* on the gradual carrying out of the Apostolic Constitution *Missale Romanum.*	209
4 November 1969	SC CLERGY, Circular Letter *Inter ea* to the conferences of bishops, on continuing education and formation of clergy.	333
10 November 1969	SC DIVINE WORSHIP, Letter *Cum nonnullae Conferentiae* to the conferences of bishops, on Latin appendix in vernacular Roman Missals.	210
18 November 1969	SC DIVINE WORSHIP, Declaration *Institutio Generalis Missalis Romani,* the 2nd printing of the Order of Mass; clarification of the General Instruction.	204
19 November 1969	PAUL VI, Address to a general audience, on the new Order of Mass.	211
26 November 1969	PAUL VI, Address to a general audience, on the new Order of Mass.	212

17 December 1969 — PAUL VI, Address to the Pontifical Commission for Sacred Art in Italy, on the conciliar spring and sacred art. — 540

December 1969 — SECRETARIAT OF STATE, Letter to Cardinal J. Garibi y Rivera, on music. — 517

1969–1975 — SC DIVINE WORSHIP, List of members. — 95

6 January 1970 — SC CATHOLIC EDUCATION, *Basic Plan for Priestly Formation*. — 334

7 January 1970 — SECRETARIAT FOR CHRISTIAN UNITY, Declaration *Dans ces derniers temps*, on eucharistic sharing. — 150

2 February 1970 — SC DIVINE WORSHIP, Decree *Professionis ritus*, promulgating the new rite of religious profession. — 391

2 February 1970 — SC DIVINE WORSHIP, *Rite of Religious Profession*, Introduction. — 392

6 February 1970 — SC DIVINE WORSHIP, Norms *In confirmandis actis*, on uniform translations of liturgical texts. — 126

25 February 1970 — SC DIVINE WORSHIP, Letter *Tandis que cette S. Congrégation* to the conferences of bishops, on the publication of liturgical books. — 138

6 March 1970 — SC DIVINE WORSHIP, Publication *Sacra Congregatio pro Clericis* of the text for renewal of priestly commitment. — 315

26 March 1970 — SC DIVINE WORSHIP, Decree *Celebrationes eucharisticae*, promulgating the 1st *editio typica* of the *Missale Romanum*. — 213

31 March 1970 — PAUL VI, Motu Proprio *Matrimonia mixta*, on mixed marriages. — 354

6 April 1970 — PAUL VI, Address to the 10th International Meeting of Church Choirs. — 518

10 April 1970 — SC DIVINE WORSHIP, Remarks of Cardinal B. Gut at a papal audience for the Consilium. — 98

10 April 1970 — PAUL VI, Address to the members of the Consilium. — 99

16 April 1970 — SECRETARIAT FOR CHRISTIAN UNITY, Ecumenical Directory, Part II, *Spiritus Domini*. — 151

22 April 1970 — PAUL VI, Address to a general audience, on the Church as a praying community. — 49

12 May 1970 — PAUL VI and VASKEN I (Patriarch of the Armenians), Joint Statement. — 152

15 May 1970 — SC DIVINE WORSHIP, Declaration *Nonnullae Commissiones*, on the publication of liturgical books. — 139

17 May 1970 — SC EVANGELIZATION OF PEOPLES, Letter *Notre temps* to local Ordinaries, on the missionary activity of the laity. — 339

17 May 1970 — SC DIVINE WORSHIP, Notification *In decreto*, on the calendar for 1971. — 443

31 May 1970 — SC DIVINE WORSHIP, Decree *Consecrationis virginum*, promulgating the *editio typica* of the rite of consecration to a life of virginity. — 394

31 May 1970 — SC DIVINE WORSHIP, *Rite of Consecration to a Life of Virginity*, Introduction. — 395

May 1970 — SC DIVINE WORSHIP, Presentation *Edita Institutione* of the changes in the General Instruction of the Roman Missal. — 205

2 June 1970 — PAUL VI, Address to a general audience, on the new pedagogy of the sense of community. — 50

24 June 1970 — SC DIVINE WORSHIP, Instruction *Calendaria particularia*, on revision of particular calendars and propers. — 481

29 June 1970 — SC DIVINE WORSHIP, Instruction *Sacramentali Communione*, extending communion under both kinds. — 270

13 July 1970 — SC DOCTRINE OF THE FAITH, Reply (Togo), on the time for baptism of children. — 297

15 July 1970 — SC DIVINE WORSHIP, Letter *Die 2 Februarii* to liturgical commissions, on the vernacular translation of the rite of religious profession. — 127

15 July 1970 — SC DIVINE WORSHIP, Letter *Le 2 février* to superiors general, on adaptation of the *Rite of Religious Profession*. — 396

15 July 1970	SC DIVINE WORSHIP, Guidelines *Les principales indica-tions*, on adaptation of the *Rite of Religious Profession*.	397
19 July 1970	PONTIFICAL COMMISSION FOR INTERPRETA-TION ... VATICAN II, Reply, on powers of perma-nent deacons.	316
25 July 1970	SC CLERGY, Decree *Litteris Apostolicis*, on the Mass *pro populo*.	283
19 August 1970	SC DIVINE WORSHIP, Reply (Rome), on baptism of children in hospitals.	298
August 1970	SECRETARIAT OF STATE, Letter to Bishop A. Mistro-rigo, on the prayer of the community.	51
5 September 1970	SC DIVINE WORSHIP, Instruction (third) *Liturgicae in-staurationes*, on the carrying out of the Constitution on the Liturgy.	52
27 September 1970	PAUL VI, Homily, on St. Teresa of Avila, Doctor of the Church.	474
30 September 1970	SC DIVINE WORSHIP, Decree *Ordine lectionum*, the *edi-tio typica* of the Lectionary.	234
1 October 1970	PAUL VI, Address to Benedictine abbots, on liturgical prayer.	403
4 October 1970	PAUL VI, Homily, on St. Catherine of Siena, Doctor of the Church.	475
12 October 1970	SC RELIGIOUS AND SECULAR INSTITUTES, Letter to Union of Superiors General, on baptism by religious.	299
18 October 1970	SC DIVINE WORSHIP, Comments *Praesens Missale par-vum*, accompanying the new *Missale parvum*.	214
29 October 1970	PAUL VI, Address to priests, on ritual use of the sacra-ments.	289
30 October 1970	SC CLERGY, Circular Letter *Per Instructionem* to the con-ferences of bishops, on reform of choral vesture.	552
1 November 1970	PAUL VI, Apostolic Constitution *Laudis canticum*, pro-mulgating the revised book of the liturgy of the hours.	424
9 November 1970	SC DIVINE WORSHIP, Decree *Abbatem et Abbatissam*, promulgating the *editio typica* of the rite of the abba-tial blessing.	398
9 November 1970	SC DIVINE WORSHIP, *Rite of Blessing of an Abbot and an Abbess*, Introduction	399
3 December 1970	SECRETARIAT FOR CHRISTIAN UNITY, Reply (Colom-bia), on non-Catholic Christians as godparents.	153
3 December 1970	SC DIVINE WORSHIP, Decree *Ritibus Hebdomadae sanc-tae*, promulgating the *editio typica* of rite of blessing oils.	458
3 December 1970	SC DIVINE WORSHIP, *Rite of the Blessing of Oils, Rite of Consecrating the Chrism*, Introduction.	459
8 December 1970	SC RELIGIOUS AND SECULAR INSTITUTES, Decree *Dum canonicarum legum recognitio*, establishing norms on the sacrament of penance for religious.	360
11 January 1971	PONTIFICAL COMMISSION FOR INTERPRETATION ... VATICAN II, Reply, on the General Instruction of the Roman Missal no. 42.	215
13 January 1971	SC DOCTRINE OF THE FAITH, Norms, on laicization.	317
2 February 1971	SC DIVINE WORSHIP, Decree *Cum editio*, on the Gen-eral Instruction of the Liturgy of the Hours.	425
2 February 1971	SC DIVINE WORSHIP, General Instruction of the Lit-urgy of the Hours.	426
9 March 1971	SC DISCIPLINE OF THE SACRAMENTS, Rescript (U.S.A.), on laity distributing communion.	263
11 April 1971	SC CLERGY, *General Catechetical Directory*.	169
11 April 1971	SC DIVINE WORSHIP, Decree *Horarum Liturgia*, pro-mulgating the *editio typica* of the book for the liturgy of the hours.	427
11 April 1971	SC CLERGY, Circular Letter *Opera artis* to the confer-ences of bishops, on care of the Church's historical and artistic heritage.	541
15 April 1971	PAUL VI, Address to women-religious Cecilians, on mu-sic.	519

1 May 1971	SC DIVINE WORSHIP, Concession *La Sacrée Congréga-tion*, on the chasuble-alb.	553
23 May 1971	PONTIFICAL COMMISSION FOR THE MEDIA OF SO-CIAL COMMUNICATION, Instruction *Communio et progressio*, on application of the Decree on the Media.	170
7 June 1971	PAUL VI, Address to a general audience on the feast of Corpus Christi.	181
14 June 1971	SC DIVINE WORSHIP, Notification *Instructione de Consti-tutione*, on the Roman Missal, the book for the liturgy of the hours, the General Calendar.	216
29 June 1971	PAUL VI, Apostolic Exhortation *Evangelica testificatio*, on renewal of religious life.	404
1 July 1971	PONTIFICAL COMMISSION FOR INTERPRETATION ... VATICAN II, Reply, on the Motu Proprio *Pastorale munus* I, nos. 11–12.	104
8 July 1971	SC DIVINE WORSHIP, Letter *Facendo seguito* to monastic orders, on their office and calendar.	438
15 August 1971	PAUL VI, Apostolic Constitution *Divinae consortium na-turae*, approving the new rite of confirmation.	303
22 August 1971	SC DIVINE WORSHIP, Decree *Peculiare Spiritus Sancti donum*, promulgating the *editio typica* of the rite of confirmation.	304
22 August 1971	SC DIVINE WORSHIP, *Rite of Confirmation*, Introduction.	305
30 August 1971	SECRETARIAT OF STATE, Letter to Bishop C. Rossi, on the new Roman Missal.	217
27 October 1971	PAUL VI and MAR IGNATIOS JAKOB II (Patriarch of Antioch of the Syrians), Joint Statement.	154
29 October 1971	SC DIVINE WORSHIP, Letter *Al comenzar* to conferences of bishops of Spanish-speaking countries, on trans-lations.	128
October 1971	SC DIVINE WORSHIP, Notice *Annis praeteritis*, on the optional patristic lectionary.	428
3 November 1971	PAUL VI, Address to a general audience, on the Church as a community of prayer.	53
11 November 1971	SC DIVINE WORSHIP, Norms *Novo Liturgiae Horarum*, on texts for *ad interim* use.	429
29 November 1971	SECRETARIAT OF STATE, Notification *Quo clarius*, on Mass intentions.	284
30 November 1971	SYNOD OF BISHOPS 1971, *The Ministerial Priesthood*.	318
6 January 1972	SC DIVINE WORSHIP, Decree *Ordinis Baptismi adul-torum*, promulgating the *editio typica* of the new rite of Christian initiation of adults.	300
6 January 1972	SC DIVINE WORSHIP, *Rite of Christian Initiation of Adults*, Introductions.	301
10 January 1972	SC RELIGIOUS AND SECULAR INSTITUTES, Rescript (Germany), on stipend for bination or trination.	285
15 January 1972	SC RELIGIOUS AND SECULAR INSTITUTES, Letter to Union of Superiors General, on Mass intentions.	286
11 February 1972	PONTIFICAL COMMISSION FOR INTERPRETATION ... VATICAN II, Reply, on *Matrimonia mixta* no. 9.	355
1 March 1972	PAUL VI, Address to a special audience, on eucharistic worship.	182
3 March 1972	SC DIVINE WORSHIP, Guidelines *Sacra Congregatio pro Cultu Divino*, on the liturgy of the hours in Holy Week.	430
2 May 1972	SC DOCTRINE OF THE FAITH, Declaration *Cum de fragmentis*, on consecrated particles.	278
1 June 1972	SECRETARIAT FOR CHRISTIAN UNITY, Instruction, on special instances of admitting other Christians to eucharistic communion.	155
9 June 1972	PONTIFICAL COMMISSION FOR INTERPRETATION ... VATICAN II, Reply, on the sacrament of con-firmation.	306
16 June 1972	SC DIVINE WORSHIP, Reply (Abbé Lardic), on use of the Missal of St. Pius V.	218
16 June 1972	SC DOCTRINE OF THE FAITH, Pastoral Norms *Sacra-mentum Paenitentiae*, on general absolution.	361

24 June 1972	SC DIVINE WORSHIP, Decree *Thesaurus cantus gregoriani*, promulgating the *editio typica* of the *Ordo cantus Missae*.	534
24 June 1972	SC DIVINE WORSHIP, *Ordo cantus Missae*, Introduction.	535
27 June 1972	SC EASTERN CHURCHES, Decree *Orientalium Religiosorum*, on faculties for religious.	362
June 1972	SC DIVINE WORSHIP, *Lectionary of the Roman Missal*, volume 3, Introduction.	235
9 July 1972	SC DOCTRINE OF THE FAITH, Declaration, on the interpretation of the General Instruction of the Liturgy of the Hours no. 162.	431
19 July 1972	PAUL VI, Address to a general audience, on the sacrament of reconciliation.	363
6 August 1972	SC DIVINE WORSHIP, Notification *Universi qui Officium*, on the liturgy of the hours for religious.	432
7 August 1972	SC DIVINE WORSHIP, Declaration *In celebratione Missae*, on concelebration.	226
15 August 1972	PAUL VI, Motu Proprio *Ad pascendum*, laying down norms on the diaconate.	319
15 August 1972	PAUL VI, Motu Proprio *Ministeria quaedam*, on tonsure, minor orders, subdiaconate.	340
24 September 1972	PAUL VI, Homily to Cecilians, on music.	520
9 October 1972	SC DIVINE WORSHIP, Decree *Cum de nomine*, on the bishop's name in the eucharistic prayer.	247
15 October 1972	SC DIVINE WORSHIP, Norms, on celebrations of the newly canonized (emended text).	476
October 1972	SC DIVINE WORSHIP, Note *Mense octobris anni 1971*, on optional patristic readings in the liturgy of the hours.	433
8 November 1972	SC DIVINE WORSHIP, Letter *Durante los meses* to CELAM, on certain aspects of the reform of the liturgy.	54
20 November 1972	SC DIVINE WORSHIP, Circular Letter *El 6 febrero* to Spanish-speaking conferences of bishops in Latin America, on uniform translations.	129
30 November 1972	PAUL VI, Apostolic Constitution, *Sacram Unctionem infirmorum*, on the sacrament of anointing.	408
3 December 1972	SC DIVINE WORSHIP, Decree *Ministeriorum disciplina*, promulgating the *editio typica* of the rite of institution.	341
3 December 1972	SC DIVINE WORSHIP, *Rite of Institution of Readers, . . .* Introductions.	342
7 December 1972	SC DIVINE WORSHIP, Decree *Infirmis cum Ecclesia*, promulgating the *editio typica* of the rites for the pastoral care of the sick, anointing and viaticum.	409
7 December 1972	SC DIVINE WORSHIP, *Pastoral Care of the Sick: Rites of Anointing and Viaticum*, Introduction.	410
8 December 1972	SC DIVINE WORSHIP, Communication *La Sacra Congregazione*, on effective date of new rites of confirmation and institution to ministries.	307
23 December 1972	SC DIVINE WORSHIP, Presentation *Cum, die 1 Ianuarii* of the changes in the General Instruction of the Roman Missal.	206
15 January 1973	SC DIVINE WORSHIP, Note *Liturgiae Horarum interpretationes*, on vernacular editions of *The Liturgy of the Hours*.	434
20 January 1973	SC DIVINE WORSHIP, Note *Anno 1974*, on Immaculate Conception in 1974.	465
29 January 1973	SC DISCIPLINE OF THE SACRAMENTS, Instruction *Immensae caritatis*, on facilitating communion.	264
29 January 1973	SC DIVINE WORSHIP, *Rite of Commissioning Special Ministers of Holy Communion*, Introduction.	343
14 February 1973	SC RELIGIOUS AND SECULAR INSTITUTES, Reply, on the formulary of religious profession.	393
22 February 1973	SC BISHOPS, *Directory on the Pastoral Ministry of Bishops*.	329
8 March 1973	SC DIVINE WORSHIP, Reflections, on the *Rite of Christian Intiation of Adults*.	302
19 March 1973	SC DIVINE WORSHIP, Norms *Patronus, liturgica acceptione*, on patron saints.	477
23 March 1973	SC DOCTRINE OF THE FAITH, Declaration *Sacra Con-*	364

	gregatio, on the dignity of the sacrament of penance.	
23 March 1973	SC DOCTRINE OF THE FAITH, Declaration *Allo scopo*, on the dignity of the sacrament of penance.	365
24 March 1973	SC DOCTRINE OF THE FAITH, Note *Essendo pervenute*, on interpreting the Declaration of 23 March 1973.	366
25 March 1973	SC DIVINE WORSHIP, Norms *Pluries decursu temporis*, on crowning Marian images.	466
27 April 1973	SC DIVINE WORSHIP, Circular Letter *Eucharistiae participationem*, on the eucharistic prayers.	248
9 May 1973	PAUL VI, Address in St. Peter's, announcing the Holy Year 1975.	490
10 May 1973	PAUL VI and SHENOUDA III (Patriarch of Alexandria), Joint Statement.	156
24 May 1973	SC DISCIPLINE OF THE SACRAMENTS and SC CLERGY, Declaration *Sanctus Pontifex*, on first confession of children.	379
29 May 1973	SC DOCTRINE OF THE FAITH, Letter *Complures Conferentiae Episcopales* to the conferences of bishops, on ecclesiastical burial.	417
31 May 1973	PAUL VI, Epistle *Iniziandosi ufficialmente* to Cardinal M. de Fürstenberg, on the Jubilee of 1975.	491
21 June 1973	SC DIVINE WORSHIP, Decree *Eucharistiae Sacramentum*, promulgating the *editio typica* of rites for communion and worship of the eucharist outside Mass.	265
21 June 1973	SC DIVINE WORSHIP, *Holy Communion and Worship of the Eucharist outside Mass*, Chapter 1, Holy Communion, Introduction.	266
21 June 1973	SC DIVINE WORSHIP, *Holy Communion and Worship of the Eucharist outside Mass*, General Introduction; Chapter 3, Eucharsitic Worship, Introduction.	279
24 June 1973	SC DOCTRINE OF THE FAITH, Declaration *Mysterium Ecclesiae*, on Catholic teaching about the Church.	171
22 August 1973	PAUL VI, Address to a general audience, proposing a decalogue for prayer.	55
29 August 1973	SC DIVINE WORSHIP, Declaration *Cum necesse sit*, on the 2nd *editio typica* of the rite of baptism for children.	293
29 August 1973	SC DIVINE WORSHIP, *Christian Initiation*, General Introduction (2nd ed.; 1st ed., 15 May 1969).	294
29 August 1973	SC DIVINE WORSHIP, *Rite of Baptism for Children*, Introduction (2nd ed.; 1st ed., 15 May 1969).	295
20 September 1973	SC DOCTRINE OF THE FAITH, Decree *Patres Sacrae Congregationis*, on ecclesiastical burial.	418
24 September 1973	APOSTOLIC PENITENTIARY, Decree *E.mus Cardinalis Praeses*, on the jubilee (1975) indulgences in the local Churches.	492
September 1973	SECRETARIAT OF STATE, Letter to Cardinal G. Siri, on music.	521
1 October 1973	PAUL VI, Address to Benedictines, on liturgy and monastic spirituality.	405
12 October 1973	PAUL VI, Address to choir members, on the tenth anniversary of CIMS.	522
17 October 1973	SECRETARIAT FOR CHRISTIAN UNITY, Communication *Dopo la pubblicazione*, on the Instruction of 1 June 1972.	157
25 October 1973	SC DIVINE WORSHIP, Circular Letter *Dum toto terrarum* to the conferences of bishops, on the translation of the forms of the sacraments.	130
1 November 1973	SC DIVINE WORSHIP, *Directory for Masses with Children*.	276
20 November 1973	SC CLERGY, Letter to German bishops, on preaching by the laity.	344
2 December 1973	SC DIVINE WORSHIP, Decree *Reconciliationem inter Deum et hominem*, promulgating the *editio typica* of the new rite of penance.	367
2 December 1973	SC DIVINE WORSHIP, *Rite of Penance*, Introduction.	368
1973	COUNCIL FOR THE HOLY YEAR and SC DIVINE WORSHIP, *Order for the Celebration of the Holy Year in the Local Churches*, Introduction.	493

10 January 1974	SC DIVINE WORSHIP, Decree *Constitutio Apostolica*, extending the *vacatio legis* of *Pastoral Care of the Sick: Rite of Anointing and Viaticum*.	411
25 January 1974	SC DOCTRINE OF THE FAITH, Declaration *Instauratio liturgica*, on the translation of the forms of the sacraments.	131
2 February 1974	PAUL VI, Apostolic Exhortation *Marialis cultus*, on Marian devotion.	467
February 1974	SC DIVINE WORSHIP, Letter *Novo Calendario Romano* to bishops and major superiors, on preparation of calendars of dioceses and of religious.	482
3 April 1974	PAUL VI, Address to a general audience, on the new rite of penance.	369
14 April 1974	SC DIVINE WORSHIP, Letter *Voluntati obsequens* to bishops, accompanying *Iubilate Deo*.	523
14 April 1974	SC DIVINE WORSHIP, Booklet *Iubilate Deo*, Preface.	524
23 May 1974	PAUL VI, Bull *Apostolorum limina*, proclaiming the Holy Year 1975.	494
May 1974	SC DIVINE WORSHIP, Note *Instructio "Eucharisticum Mysterium,"* on the anticipated Mass of a Sunday or holyday.	448
3 June 1974	SC DOCTRINE OF THE FAITH, Letter to Cardinal F. Marty, on the preparation of vernacular editions of the rite of penance.	370
7 June 1974	SC DIVINE WORSHIP, Letter to Bishop R. Coffy, on delegation for the rite of institution.	345
13 June 1974	PAUL VI, Motu Proprio *Firma in traditione*, on faculties regarding Mass stipends.	287
August 1974	SECRETARIAT OF STATE, Letter to the Archbishop of Salzburg, on music.	525
13 September 1974	SECRETARIAT OF STATE, Letter to the 21st National Congress on Sacred Music in Italy, on music.	526
September 1974	SC DIVINE WORSHIP, Report *Sacra Congregatio* of Cardinal J. Knox to the Synod of Bishops 1974.	100
28 October 1974	SC DIVINE WORSHIP, Notification *Conferentiarum Episcopalium*, on obligatory use of the Roman Missal.	219
1 November 1974	SC DIVINE WORSHIP, Decree *Postquam de Precibus*, approving the Eucharistic Prayers for Masses with Children and of Reconciliation.	249
1 November 1974	SC DIVINE WORSHIP, *Eucharistic Prayers for Masses with Children and of Reconciliation*, Introduction.	250
13 November 1974	PONTIFICAL COMMISSION FOR INTERPRETATION ... VATICAN II, Reply, on deacon's powers regarding sacramentals and blessings.	320
22 November 1974	SC DIVINE WORSHIP, Decree *Cantus faciliores*, promulgating the 2nd *editio typica* of the *Graduale simplex*.	536
22 November 1974	SC DIVINE WORSHIP, *Graduale simplex* (2nd *editio typica*), Introduction.	537
1 December 1974	SECRETARIAT FOR CHRISTIAN UNITY, Guidelines *Datée du 28 octobre 1965*, on *Nostra aetate* no. 14.	158
20 January 1975	PAUL VI, Epistle (autograph) *Cum proximae celebrationes*, on the centenary of the death of Dom Guéranger.	172
22 February 1975	SECRETARIAT FOR CHRISTIAN UNITY, *Ecumenical Collaboration at the Regional and Local Levels*.	159
26 February 1975	PAUL VI, Address to a general audience, on the sacrament of reconciliation.	371
5 March 1975	PAUL VI, Address to a general audience, on conditions for receiving penance.	372
12 March 1975	PAUL VI, Address to a general audience, on the ministerial aspect of penance.	373
19 March 1975	SC DOCTRINE OF THE FAITH, Decree *Ecclesiae Pastorum*, on bishops' vigilance regarding books.	140
26 March 1975	PAUL VI, Address to a general audience, on the effects of liturgical participation.	56
27 March 1975	SC DIVINE WORSHIP, Decree *Cum Missale Romanum*, on the 2nd *editio typica* of the *Missale Romanum*.	207
27 March 1975	SC DIVINE WORSHIP, General Instruction of the Roman Missal (4th ed.).	208

25 April 1975	PONTIFICAL COMMISSION FOR INTERPRETATION ... VATICAN II, Reply, on minister of confirmation.	308
5 May 1975	SC DIVINE WORSHIP, Letter to presidents of English-speaking conferences of bishops, approving the translation of the sacramental form for confirmation.	132
18 May 1975	SECRETARIAT FOR CHRISTIAN UNITY, Letter *Le deuxième Concile du Vatican* to the conferences of bishops, on a fixed date for Easter.	160
May 1975	SC DIVINE WORSHIP, Note *Passim quaeritur*, on music in vernacular editions of the Roman Missal.	538
11 July 1975	PAUL VI, Apostolic Constitution *Constans nobis*, establishing SC Sacraments and Divine Worship.	101
31 July 1975	SECRETARIAT OF STATE, Letter to Bishop C. Manziana, on reconciliation with God and the Church.	374
6 August 1975	PAUL VI, Address to a general audience, on the liturgy and renewal of Christian life.	57
5 October 1975	PAUL VI, Homily, at a communal anointing of the sick.	412
11 October 1975	SECRETARIAT OF STATE, Letter to Bishop R. Coffy, on obligatory use of the Roman Missal.	220
29 October 1975	SC SACRAMENTS AND DIVINE WORSHIP, Communication *Domenica prossima*, on the evening Mass for 1 November 1975.	478
30 November 1975	PAUL VI, Epistle "We write" to Dr. F.D. Coggan, Archbishop of Canterbury, on the ordination of women.	161
8 December 1975	PAUL VI, Apostolic Exhortation *Evangelii nuntiandi*, on evangelization.	236
1975–1979	SC SACRAMENTS AND DIVINE WORSHIP, List of members.	102
21 February 1976	PAUL VI, Epistle *Nous avons pris* to Cardinal J. Villot, on the case of Archbishop M. Lefebvre.	58
25 February 1976	VATICAN PRESS OFFICE, Reply, on the so-called Protestant influences on the Order of Mass.	221
17 March 1976	SC SACRAMENTS AND DIVINE WORSHIP, Letter *Instructione "Memoriale Domini"* to the conferences of bishops, on communion in the hand.	267
23 March 1976	PAUL VI, Epistle "As the tenth" to Dr. F. D. Coggan, Archbishop of Canterbury, on the ordination of women.	162
30 April 1976	SC SACRAMENTS AND DIVINE WORSHIP and SC CLERGY, Letter to the conferences of bishops, on first confession of children.	380
24 May 1976	PAUL VI, Address to a consistory, on loyalty to the Church and the Council.	59
5 June 1976	SC SACRAMENTS AND DIVINE WORSHIP, Letter *Decem iam annos* to the conferences of bishops, on the vernacular in the liturgy.	133
6 June 1976	PAUL VI, Epistle "To Our Venerable" to bishops of the U.S.A., on the liturgy as the soul of the Christian people.	60
11 June 1976	SC DOCTRINE OF THE FAITH, Decree *Accidit in diversis regionibus*, on Mass for deceased non-Catholics.	163
7 July 1976	PAUL VI, Epistle *Eventus religiosus* to Cardinal J. R. Knox, on the International Eucharistic Congress at Philadelphia.	183
8 August 1976	PAUL VI, Message (televised), to the International Eucharistic Congress at Philadelphia.	184
8 August 1976	PAUL VI, Homily at Bolsena, on the International Eucharistic Congress at Philadelphia.	185
August 1976	SECRETARIAT OF STATE, Letter to Bishop C. Manziana, on Mary in the Church's worship and life.	468
September 1976	SECRETARIAT OF STATE, Letter to Cardinal C. Ursi, on the 22nd National Congress on Sacred Music.	527
11 October 1976	PAUL VI, Epistle *Cum te* to Archbishop Marcel Lefebvre.	61
15 October 1976	SC DOCTRINE OF THE FAITH, Declaration *Inter insigniores*, on the ordination of women.	321
14 January 1977	SC DOCTRINE OF THE FAITH, Letter to NCCB, com-	375

menting on the Pastoral Norms for general absolution.

10 February 1977	SC SACRAMENTS AND DIVINE WORSHIP, Decree *Operi Dei*, approving the *Thesaurus Liturgiae Horarum Monasticae*.	439
16 March 1977	SECRETARIAT FOR CHRISTIAN UNITY, Letter *Dans ma lettre* to the conferences of bishops, on a common celebration of Easter.	164
23 March 1977	PAUL VI, Address to a general audience, on penance as "sacrament of resurrection and peace."	376
26 March 1977	PAUL VI, Address to bishops of France, on Sunday assemblies without a priest.	449
31 March 1977	SC SACRAMENTS AND DIVINE WORSHIP, Letter to the review *Phase*, on liturgical-pastoral ministry today.	62
31 March 1977	SC SACRAMENTS AND DIVINE WORSHIP and SC CLERGY, Letter *In quibusdam partibus Ecclesiae* to the conferences of bishops, on first confession of children.	381
18 April 1977	PAUL VI, Address to bishops of France, on gravity and dignity in the liturgy.	63
21 April 1977	PAUL VI, Address to bishops of Lombardy, on the bishop's duties regarding the liturgy.	331
29 April 1977	PAUL VI and FREDERICK DONALD COGGAN (Archbishop of Canterbury), Joint Statement.	165
30 April 1977	PAUL VI, Address at the Pontifical Greek College, on liturgical traditions as a pastoral resource.	64
20 May 1977	SC SACRAMENTS AND DIVINE WORSHIP and SC CLERGY, Reply, on first confession and first communion.	382
29 May 1977	SC SACRAMENTS AND DIVINE WORSHIP, Decree *Dedicationis ecclesiae*, promulgating the *editio typica* of the rite of dedication of a church.	546
29 May 1977	SC SACRAMENTS AND DIVINE WORSHIP, *Rite of Dedication of a Church and of an Altar*, Introductions.	547
12 June 1977	PAUL VI, Homily, on the feast of Corpus Christi.	186
27 June 1977	PAUL VI, Address to a consistory, on results of the liturgical reform.	65
9 July 1977	SC BISHOPS, Faculty for priest to consecrate an altar.	548
July 1977	SECRETARIAT OF STATE, Letter to Bishop R. Alberti, on the occasion of the second CELAM meeting on liturgy.	66
4 August 1977	PAUL VI, Epistle *Piscariensium civitas* to Cardinal J. Colombo, on the Lord's Day.	450
August 1977	SECRETARIAT OF STATE, Letter to Bishop C. Manziana, on the Lord's Day.	451
17 September 1977	PAUL VI, Homily, at a eucharistic congress in Pescara.	187
23 September 1977	PAUL VI, Address to Benedictine abbots prior, on choral prayer.	406
24 September 1977	SC BISHOPS, Decree *Apostolatus maris*, on the pastoral care of seamen and ship passengers.	330
25 September 1977	PAUL VI, Homily to Cecilians, on music.	528
7 October 1977	SC SACRAMENTS AND DIVINE WORSHIP, Decree *Celebratio Baptismatis Domini*, on celebration of the Baptism of the Lord.	460
27 October 1977	SC SACRAMENTS AND DIVINE WORSHIP, Letter *Novit profecto* to the conferences of bishops, on new ministries.	346
28 October 1977	SYNOD OF BISHOPS, 1977, "Message to the People of God."	67
17 November 1977	PAUL VI, Address to bishops of Holland, on celebrating in faith and joy.	68
24 November 1977	SC SACRAMENTS AND DIVINE WORSHIP, Letter *Honori mihi duco* to the conferences of bishops, on norms for celebrating World Day of Peace, 1978.	499
1 December 1977	PAUL VI, Address to Swiss bishops, on the liturgy and the sacraments.	290

10 December 1977	SC SACRAMENTS AND DIVINE WORSHIP, Letter *Sacrum hoc Dicasterium* to the conferences of bishops, extending the Eucharistic Prayers for Masses with Children.	251
December 1977	SC SACRAMENTS AND DIVINE WORSHIP, Norms *Calendaria et Propria*, on particular calendars and propers.	483
14 January 1978	SECRETARIAT FOR CHRISTIAN UNITY, *Final Report: Theology of Marriage and the Problems of Mixed Marriages, 1971–1977*.	356
20 January 1978	SC DOCTRINE OF THE FAITH, Reply (U.S.A.), on general absolution.	377
8 February 1978	PAUL VI, Address to a general audience, on Lent, a "sacramental" time.	461
20 April 1978	PAUL VI, Address to bishops from New York, on penance in the Church's teaching.	378
25 April 1978	PAUL VI, Address at Pescara, on Sunday as weekly Easter.	452
11 May 1978	PAUL VI, Motu Proprio *Inter eximia episcopalis*, on the pallium.	554
28 May 1978	PAUL VI, Homily, on the feast of Corpus Christi.	188
15 June 1978	PAUL VI, Address to American bishops, on the eucharistic sacrifice.	189
23 September 1978	JOHN PAUL I, Homily at St. John Lateran, excerpt on liturgical irregularities.	69
17 October 1978	JOHN PAUL II, Address (televised), excerpt on fidelity to liturgical norms.	70
17 November 1978	JOHN PAUL II, Address to Canadian bishops, on sacramental discipline.	291
23 November 1978	JOHN PAUL II, Address to Byzantine-Ruthenian bishops, on importance of the particular rites in the Church.	71
1 January 1979	JOHN PAUL II, Epistle *Le Congrès eucharistique* to Cardinal J. Knox, on the International Eucharistic Congress at Lourdes in 1981.	190
4 March 1979	JOHN PAUL II, Encyclical *Redemptor hominis*, excerpt on the eucharist.	191
8 April 1979	JOHN PAUL II, Epistle *Magnus dies* to bishops, on the priesthood.	322
8 April 1979	JOHN PAUL II, Epistle *Novo incipiente* to priests, on the priesthood.	323
9 April 1979	PONTIFICAL COMMISSION FOR INTERPRETATION ... VATICAN II, Reply, on dispensing from canonical form of marriage.	357
25 April 1979	JOHN PAUL II, Apostolic Constitution *Scripturarum thesaurus*, the Neo-Vulgate.	237
26 April 1979	JOHN PAUL II, Address to bishops of India, on the eucharist and penance.	192
27 April 1979	JOHN PAUL II, Address to the Pontifical Commission on the Neo-Vulgate, on the occasion of publication.	238
17 May 1979	SC DOCTRINE OF THE FAITH, Letter *Recentiores Episcoporum Synodi* to the conferences of bishops on eschatology.	173
29 May 1979	SC SACRAMENTS AND DIVINE WORSHIP, Circular Letter *Summus Pontifex* to the conferences of bishops, on celebration of feast of St. Stanislaus.	479
3 June 1979	SC CATHOLIC EDUCATION, Instruction *In ecclesiasticam futurorum sacerdotum*, on liturgical formation in seminaries.	335
August 1979	SECRETARIAT OF STATE, Letter to Bishop C. Manziana, on the liturgy of the hours.	435
29 September 1979	JOHN PAUL II, Homily in Dublin, on the eucharist.	193
3 October 1979	JOHN PAUL II, Address at St. Charles Seminary, Philadelphia, on liturgical prayer, the guarantee of fidelity to the Church.	72

3 October 1979	JOHN PAUL II, Address in New York, on the liturgy of the hours.	436
4 October 1979	JOHN PAUL II, Address to Ukrainian community of Philadelphia, on diversity of rites as presence of the Spirit.	73
4 October 1979	JOHN PAUL II, Address at the Civic Center, Philadelphia, on pastoral activity and active participation.	74
5 October 1979	JOHN PAUL II, Address in Chicago to bishops of the U.S.A., on bishops as guardians and promoters of the liturgy.	75
5 October 1979	JOHN PAUL II, Homily in Chicago, on the eucharist.	194
16 October 1979	JOHN PAUL II, Apostolic Exhortation *Catechesi tradendae*, on catechesis in our time.	76
3 November 1979	JOHN PAUL II, Address, on Christian marriage.	350
29 November 1979	JOHN PAUL II and DEMETRIOS I (Ecumenical Patriarch), Joint Statement.	166
29 November 1979	JOHN PAUL II, Homily at Istanbul, on full communion in the eucharist.	167

DOCUMENT NUMBERS BY CLASSIFICATION

CONCILIAR

Constitution   1

Declaration   13

Decrees   3, 5, 6, 7, 10, 12, 16, 17, 18

Dogmatic Constitutions   4, 14

Pastoral Constitution   19

PAPAL

Addresses
Paul VI

    General Audiences   24, 27, 34, 45, 46, 47, 49, 50, 53, 55, 56, 57, 181, 211, 212, 363, 369, 371, 372, 373, 376, 455, 461, 490

    Episcopate   2, 21, 22, 30, 44, 59, 63, 65, 68, 81, 84, 86, 92, 93, 99, 189, 290, 331, 378, 449

    Various   25, 64, 113, 116, 121, 174, 182, 246, 289, 336, 338, 400, 401, 403, 405, 406, 452, 501, 504, 509, 510, 513, 514, 516, 518, 519, 522, 539, 540

John Paul II   70, 71, 72, 73, 74, 75, 192, 238, 291, 350, 436

Apostolic Constitutions
Paul VI   88, 94, 101, 202, 303, 324, 358, 386, 408, 424, 484

John Paul II   237

Apostolic Epistle   453

Apostolic Exhortations
Paul VI

144, 236, 404, 463, 464, 467

John Paul II

76

Apostolic Letter

469

Bull

494

Concessions

117, 272, 419

Encyclicals
Paul VI

176, 195, 462

John Paul II

191

Epistles
Paul VI

58, 60, 61, 90, 146, 161, 162, 175, 177, 180, 183, 277, 421, 450, 491

John Paul II

190, 322, 323

Epistles (autograph)

97, 172, 500

Homilies
Paul VI

33, 185, 186, 187, 188, 412, 474, 475, 520, 528

John Paul I

69

John Paul II

167, 193, 194

Joint Statements
Paul VI

145, 148, 152, 154, 156

John Paul II

165, 166

Message, televised

184

Message, written

497

Motu Proprios

20, 87, 103, 105, 106, 287, 309, 319, 327, 340, 354, 440, 489, 544, 549, 554

Profession of Faith

168

Remarks at the Angelus

26, 48

CURIAL

Circular Letters
SC Clergy

333, 541, 552

SC Council

446

SC Divine Worship

129, 130, 248

SC Sacraments and Divine Worship

479

Communications
Consilium

115, 118, 120

SC Divine Worship

307

SC Rites

240

SC Sacraments and Divine Worship   478

Secretariat for Christian Unity   157

Concession
SC Divine Worship   553

Declarations
Apostolic Penitentiary   384, 486

Consilium   29, 124, 245

SC Council   281

SC Discipline of the Sacraments   379

SC Doctrine of the Faith   131, 171, 278, 321, 364, 365, 431

SC Divine Worship   125, 139, 204, 226, 293

SC Rites   447

SC Rites and Consilium   35, 456

Secretariat for Christian Unity   150

Decrees
Apostolic Penitentiary   383, 385, 387, 389, 485, 492

Holy Office   271

SC Bishops   330

SC Clergy   283

SC Divine Worship
Promulgation of Typical Editions   207, 213, 231, 234, 265, 292, 300, 304, 341, 367, 391, 394, 398, 409, 415, 425, 427, 458, 534, 536

Others   247, 249, 296, 411

SC Doctrine of the Faith   140, 163, 418

SC Eastern Churches   352, 362

SC Religious   143

SC Religious and Secular Institutes   360

SC Rites   252, 254, 337, 407, 470, 471, 487, 488, 495, 496

SC Rites (Consilium)
Promulgation of Typical Editions   196, 201, 203, 222, 241, 325, 348, 441, 454, 529, 531, 532

Others   134, 545

SC Sacraments and Divine Worship
Promulgation of Typical Edition   546

Others   439, 460

Decrees (Particular)
SC Rites   199, 414, 470

Directories
SC Bishops   329

SC Clergy   169, 326

SC Divine Worship   276

Secretariat for Christian Unity   147, 151

Guidelines
Consilium   244

SC Divine Worship   397, 430

Secretariat for Christian Unity   158

Instructions
General
    SC Divine Worship   52

    SC Rites (Consilium)   23, 39
Special
    Consilium   111, 123

    Holy Office   413

    Pontifical Biblical Commission   227

    Pontifical Commission for the Media
       of Social Communication   170

    SC Bishops   328

    SC Catholic Education   335

    SC Discipline of the Sacraments   259, 264

    SC Divine Worship   209, 233, 260, 270, 275, 480, 481

    SC Doctrine of the Faith   351

    SC Religious and Secular Institutes   402

    SC Rites (Consilium)   179, 472, 508, 550

    SC Rites and SC Religious   114

    SC Seminaries and Universities   332

    Secretariat for Christian Unity   155

    Secretariat of State   551

Introductions (*Praenotanda*)
SC Divine Worship   232, 235, 250, 266, 279, 294, 295, 301, 305, 342,
                                                             368, 392, 395, 399, 410, 416, 426, 459, 524, 535, 537

SC Rites (Consilium)   208, 223, 268, 349, 530, 533

SC Sacraments and Divine Worship   547

Letters
Administration of the Patrimony
   of the Holy See   136, 137

Consilium   28, 31, 32, 40, 41, 79, 108, 243, 502, 511, 512, 515

SC Catholic Education   314

SC Clergy   344, 380

SC Discipline of the Sacraments   312

SC Divine Worship   54, 127, 128, 132, 138, 210, 261, 345, 396, 438, 482,
                                                             523

SC Doctrine of the Faith   173, 178, 370, 375, 417

SC Evangelization of Peoples   339

SC Religious   422

SC Religious and Secular Institutes   286, 299

SC Rites   135, 197, 444

SC Sacraments and Divine Worship   62, 133, 251, 267, 346, 380, 499

Secretariat for Christian Unity   160, 164

Letters of the Secretariat of State   51, 66, 77, 82, 110, 122, 217, 220, 288, 374, 435,
                                             451, 468, 503, 505, 506, 517, 521, 525, 526, 527

Norms
Apostolic Penitentiary   388, 390

SC Divine Worship   126, 429, 466, 476, 477

SC Doctrine of the Faith   317, 361

SC Rites (Consilium)   242, 442

SC Sacraments and Divine Worship   483

Notes
Consilium   228, 229, 230

SC Divine Worship   433, 434, 448, 465, 538

SC Doctrine of the Faith   366

Secretariat for Christian Unity   149

Notices
SC Divine Worship   428

SC Religious   142

Notifications
SC Council   273

SC Divine Worship   216, 219, 432, 443

Secretariat of State   284

Replies
Pontifical Central Commission for
    Coordinating Postconciliar Work ...   8, 11

Pontifical Commission for the
    Interpretation of the Decrees of
    Vatican Council II   9, 15, 104, 215, 306, 308, 310, 311, 316, 320, 355,
                                             357

SC Council   225, 359

SC Religious and Secular Institutes   393

SC Rites   200, 269, 542

SC Sacraments and Divine Worship
    and SC Clergy   382

Vatican Press Office   221

Rescripts
Secretariat of State   89, 141

Rescripts or Replies (particular)
Consilium   43, 274, 437

SC Catholic Education   282

SC Council   445

SC Discipline of the Sacraments 256, 257, 262, 263

SC Divine Worship 218, 298

SC Doctrine of the Faith 297, 353, 377

SC Evangelization of Peoples 258, 313, 457

SC Propagation of the Faith 255

SC Religious 119

SC Religious and Secular Institutes 285, 423

SC Rites 109, 224, 347, 420, 543

SC Seminaries and Universities 280

Secretariat for Christian Unity 153

Various
Clarification
Consilium 507
Comments
SC Divine Worship 214
Editorials (*Notitiae*)
Consilium 36, 38, 42
Enumeration
SC Rites 112
Epistle
SC Divine Worship 96
Faculties
SC Bishops 107, 548
List of Members
Consilium 78

SC Divine Worship 95

SC Sacraments and Divine Worship 102
Liturgical Texts and Rites
Consilium 198, 239, 498

Council for the Holy Year and SC
Divine Worship 493

SC Divine Worship 315, 343, 473
Presentations
SC Divine Worship 205, 206
Press Conferences
Consilium (A. Bugnini) 37
Reflections
SC Divine Worship 302
Remarks
President of Consilium 80, 83, 85, 91, 98
Reports
SC Divine Worship 100

Secretariat for Christian Unity 356
Studies
SC Catholic Education 334

Secretariat for Christian Unity 159

Synod of Bishops 67, 318

INCIPITS

	Date	DOL
Abbatem et Abbatissam	9 November 1970	398
Accidit in diversis regionibus	11 June 1976	163
Actio pastoralis	15 May 1969	275
Ad gentes	7 December 1965	17
Ad pascendum	15 August 1972	319
Ad solemnia	12 September 1968	472
Ad totam Ecclesiam	14 May 1967	147
Al comenzar	29 October 1971	128
Allo scopo	23 March 1973	365
Anni liturgici ordinatione	21 March 1969	441
Annis praeteritis	October 1971	428
Anno 1974	20 January 1973	465
Apostolatus maris	24 September 1977	330
Apostolicam actuositatem	18 November 1965	16
Apostolorum limina	23 May 1974	494
"As the tenth"	23 March 1976	162
Au cours des derniers mois	2 June 1968	244
Aussitôt après	10 August 1967	118
Calendaria et Propria	December 1977	483
Calendaria particularia	24 June 1970	481
Cantus faciliores	22 November 1974	536
Catechesi tradendae	16 October 1979	76
Celebratio Baptismatis Domini	7 October 1977	460
Celebrationes eucharisticae	26 March 1970	213
Christi Matri	15 September 1966	462
Christus Dominus	28 October 1965	7
Circa Instructionem	March 1969	124
Come è a conoscenza	16 July 1969	314
Come è noto	18 June 1965	273
Comme le prévoit	25 January 1969	123
Communio et progressio	23 May 1971	170
Compio il venerato incarico	7 January 1965	82
Complures Conferentiae Episcopales	29 May 1973	417
Conferentiarum Episcopalium	28 October 1974	219
Consecrationis virginum	31 May 1970	394
Consilium ad exsequendum	16 October 1964	108
Constans nobis	11 July 1975	101
Constitutio Apostolica	10 January 1974	411
Constitutio de sacra Liturgia	17 July 1965	112
Constitutione Apostolica	20 October 1969	209
Crescens matrimoniorum	22 February 1967	352
Cum, admotae	6 November 1964	141
Cum de fragmentis	2 May 1972	278
Cum de nomine	9 October 1972	247
Cum, die 1 Ianuarii	23 December 1972	206
Cum Dominica IV Adventus	12 December 1967	447
Cum editio	2 February 1971	425
Cum hac nostra aetate	14 February 1966	254
Cum Missale Romanum	27 March 1975	207
Cum necesse sit	29 August 1973	293
Cum non pauci	5 January 1966	486
Cum nonnullae Conferentiae	10 November 1969	210
Cum, nostra aetate	27 January 1966	134
Cum notae causae	30 December 1967	89
Cum Oecumenicum Concilium	24 July 1966	178
Cum plures Episcopi	20 December 1965	485
Cum proximae celebrationes	20 January 1975	172
Cum proximo anno	13 May 1966	471
Cum recentioribus temporibus	18 October 1968	456
Cum te	11 October 1976	61
Da qualche tempo	29 December 1966	35
Dans ces derniers temps	7 January 1970	150

Dans ma lettre	16 March 1977	164
Dans sa récente allocution	21 June 1967	41
Datée du 28 octobre 1965	1 December 1974	158
De Episcoporum muneribus	15 June 1966	105
Decem iam annos	5 June 1976	133
Decreto quo	25 July 1969	233
Decreto Sacrae Congregationis	29 June 1969	480
Dedicationis ecclesiae	29 May 1977	546
Dei Verbum	18 November 1965	14
Die 2 Februarii	15 July 1970	127
Die 30 Iunii	9 May 1964	496
Die 31 Ianuarii	31 January 1966	385
Divinae consortium naturae	15 August 1971	303
Doctrina et exemplo	25 December 1965	332
Domenica prossima	29 October 1975	478
Domus Dei	6 June 1968	545
Dopo la pubblicazione	17 October 1973	157
Dum canonicarum legum recognitio	8 December 1970	360
Dum toto terrarum	25 October 1973	130
Durante los meses	8 November 1972	54
E peregrinatione	15 January 1964	144
Ecclesiae Pastorum	19 March 1975	140
Ecclesiae Sanctae	6 August 1966	106
Ecclesiae semper	7 March 1965	222
Ecclesiam suam	6 August 1964	195
Edita Institutione	May 1970	205
Edita Instructione	14 December 1964	531
El 6 febrero	20 November 1972	129
E.mus Cardinalis Praeses	24 September 1973	492
En réponse à la demande	29 May 1969	261
Essendo pervenute	24 March 1973	366
Eucharistiae participationem	27 April 1973	248
Eucharistiae Sacramentum	21 June 1973	265
Eucharisticum mysterium	25 May 1967	179
Evangelica testificatio	29 June 1971	404
Evangelii nuntiandi	8 December 1975	236
Eventus religiosus	7 July 1976	183
Extraordinarium Iubilaeum	6 January 1966	487
Facendo seguito	8 July 1971	438
Fidei custos	30 April 1969	259
Firma in traditione	13 June 1974	287
Gaudium et spes	7 December 1965	19
Gravissimum educationis	28 October 1965	13
Ho l'onore	27 April 1965	110
Honori mihi duco	24 November 1977	499
Horarum Liturgia	11 April 1971	427
Immensae caritatis	29 January 1973	264
Impetrata prius	25 September 1965	444
In Apostolica Constitutione	10 January 1964	271
In celebratione Missae	26 November 1965	224
In conficiendis	6 November 1968	245
In confirmandis actis	6 February 1970	126
In Constitutione Apostolica	29 June 1968	389
In decreto	17 May 1970	443
In ecclesiasticam futurorum sacerdotum	3 June 1979	335
In edicendis normis	23 November 1965	114
In questi ultimi mesi	6 October 1968	149
In quibusdam partibus Ecclesiae	31 March 1977	381
Inclitae Columbiae	16 July 1968	180
Indulgentiarum doctrina	1 January 1967	386
Infirmis cum Ecclesia	7 December 1972	409
Iniziandosi ufficialmente	31 May 1973	491
Instantibus pluribus	23 January 1968	120
Instauratio liturgica	25 January 1974	131
Institutio Generalis Missalis Romani	18 November 1969	204
Instructio Eucharisticum Mysterium	May 1974	448

Instructione de Constitutione	14 June 1971	216
Instructione Memoriale Domini	17 March 1976	267
Inter ea	4 November 1969	333
Inter eximia episcopalis	11 May 1978	554
Inter insigniores	15 October 1976	321
Inter mirifica	4 December 1963	3
Inter Oecumenici	26 September 1964	23
Investigabiles divitias Christi	6 February 1965	453
La publication	2 June 1968	243
La Sacra Congregazione	12 May 1969	96
La Sacra Congregazione	8 December 1972	307
La Sacrée Congrégation	1 May 1971	553
Laudis canticum	1 November 1970	424
Le Congrès eucharistique	1 January 1979	190
Le deuxième Concile du Vatican	18 May 1975	160
Le renouveau liturgique	30 June 1965	31
Le sarei grato	25 March 1964	79
Le 2 février	15 July 1970	396
Lectionarium feriale	January 1967	230
Les principales indications	15 July 1970	397
L'heureux développement	25 January 1966	32
Litteris Apostolicis	25 July 1970	283
Liturgiae Horarum interpretationes	15 January 1973	434
Liturgicae instaurationes	5 September 1970	52
Lumen gentium	21 November 1964	4
Magnus dies	8 April 1979	322
Marialis cultus	2 February 1974	467
Matrimonia mixta	31 March 1970	354
Matrimonii sacramentum	18 March 1966	351
Memoriale Domini	29 May 1969	260
Mense octobris anni 1971	October 1972	433
Mi onore di communicare	29 February 1964	77
Ministeria quaedam	15 August 1972	340
Ministeriorum disciplina	3 December 1972	341
Mirificus eventus	7 December 1965	484
Missale Romanum	3 April 1969	202
Musicam sacram	5 March 1967	508
Mysterii paschalis	14 February 1969	440
Mysterium Ecclesiae	24 June 1973	171
Mysterium fidei	3 September 1965	176
Nell'aprile scorso	October 1966	507
Nell'atto in cui	9 January 1968	90
Nobile subsidium	22 November 1963	500
Non latet sane	5 August 1966	135
Nonnullae Commissiones	15 May 1970	139
Notre temps	17 May 1970	339
Nous avons pris	21 February 1976	58
Nous nous apprêtons	31 March 1966	146
Novit profecto	27 October 1977	346
Novo Calendario Romano	February 1974	482
Novo incipiente	8 April 1979	323
Novo Liturgiae Horarum	11 November 1971	429
Nuper edita Instructione	27 January 1965	196
Omnibus in comperto	19 March 1966	446
Opera artis	11 April 1971	541
Operi Dei	10 February 1977	439
Optatam totius	28 October 1965	12
Ordine lectionum	30 September 1970	234
Ordine Missae	6 April 1969	203
Ordinem Baptismi parvulorum	15 May 1969	292
Ordinis Baptismi adultorum	6 January 1972	300
Ordo agendorum	29 March 1965	28
Ordo celebrandi Matrimonium	19 March 1969	348
Ordo lectionum	25 May 1969	231
Orientalium Ecclesiarum	21 November 1964	5
Orientalium Religiosorum	27 June 1972	362

Pacis nuntius	26 October 1964	469
Paenitemini	17 February 1966	358
Passim quaeritur	May 1975	538
Passim quandoque	15 June 1965	29
Pastorale munus	30 November 1963	103
Pastoralem Episcoporum Hollandiae	19 July 1965	175
Pastoralis migratorum cura	15 August 1969	327
Patres Sacrae Congregationis	20 September 1973	418
Patronus, liturgica acceptione	19 March 1973	477
Peculiare ius	8 February 1966	544
Peculiare Spiritus Sancti donum	22 August 1971	304
Per Constitutionem Apostolicam	15 August 1968	325
Per Instructionem	30 October 1970	552
Per Instructionem alteram	18 May 1967	201
Per Litteras Apostolicas	21 January 1966	115
Peregrinans in terra	30 April 1969	326
Perfectae caritatis	28 October 1965	10
Petentibus nonnullis Conferentiis	10 July 1969	296
Piae invocationes	25 April 1964	495
Piam et constantem	8 May 1963	413
Pientissima Mater Ecclesia	4 March 1965	407
Piscariensium civitas	4 August 1977	450
Plures liturgicae	15 September 1969	125
Plures locorum	25 March 1965	337
Plures sacrorum Antistites	1 March 1966	488
Pluries decursu temporis	25 March 1973	466
Pontificalia insignia	21 June 1968	549
Pontificalis ritus	21 June 1968	550
Pontificalis Romani recognitio	18 June 1968	324
Popularibus interpretationibus	1–2 June 1965	111
Postquam de Precibus	1 November 1974	249
Praesens Missale parvum	18 October 1970	214
Prece eucharistica	23 May 1968	241
Presbyterorum Ordinis	7 December 1965	18
Prima phasis renovationis	15 October 1965	229
Pro comperto sane	6 August 1967	87
Professionis ritus	2 February 1970	391
Quamplures Episcopi	7 March 1965	454
Quo actuosius	25 April 1964	252
Quo clarius	29 November 1971	284
Quum Constitutio	14 December 1964	529
Recentiores Episcoporum Synodi	17 May 1979	173
Reconciliationem inter Deum et hominem	2 December 1973	367
Recurrens mensis octobris	7 October 1969	464
Redemptor hominis	4 March 1979	191
Regimini Ecclesiae universae	15 August 1967	88
Religionum laicalium	31 May 1966	143
Rispondiamo subito	12 May 1969	97
Ritibus exsequiarum	15 August 1969	415
Ritibus Hebdomadae sanctae	3 December 1970	458
Sacra Congregatio	23 March 1973	364
Sacra Congregatio	September 1974	100
Sacra Congregatio pro Clericis	6 March 1970	315
Sacra Congregatio pro Cultu Divino	3 March 1972	430
Sacra Congregatio pro Episcopis	22 August 1969	328
Sacra Paenitentiaria Apostolica	6 March 1965	384
Sacra Rituum Congregatio	24 February 1966	240
Sacra Rituum Congregatio	8 May 1969	94
Sacram Liturgiam	5 January 1964	20
Sacram Unctionem infirmorum	30 November 1972	408
Sacramentali Communione	29 June 1970	270
Sacramentum Paenitentiae	16 June 1972	361
Sacrificium laudis	15 August 1966	421
Sacrosancti Oecumenici Concilii	3 September 1967	532
Sacrosanctum Concilium	4 December 1963	1
Sacrum Diaconatus Ordinem	18 June 1967	309

Sacrum hoc Dicasterium	10 December 1977	251
Saluberrimum Sacramentum Eucharistiae	10 January 1969	277
Sancta Mater Ecclesia	21 April 1964	227
Sanctissimus D. N. Paulus	5 November 1964	383
Sanctissimus D. N. Paulus	28 June 1967	387
Sanctum Benedictum	26 May 1965	470
Sanctus Pontifex	24 May 1973	379
Scripturarum thesaurus	25 April 1979	237
Signum magnum	13 May 1967	463
Spiritus Domini	16 April 1970	151
Summi Dei beneficio	3 May 1966	489
Summus Pontifex	29 May 1979	479
Tandis que cette S. Congrégation	25 February 1970	138
Thesaurus cantus gregoriani	24 June 1972	534
"To Our Venerable"	6 June 1976	60
Tres abhinc annos	4 May 1967	39
Tricenario Gregoriano	24 February 1967	281
Unitatis redintegratio	21 November 1964	6
Universi qui Officium	6 August 1972	432
Ut haec S. Paenitentiaria	1967	388
Ut sive sollicite	31 March 1969	551
Venite seorsum	15 August 1969	402
Voluntati obsequens	14 April 1974	523
Vox laetitiae	25 March 1966	177
"We write"	30 November 1975	161

REPLIES FROM *NOTITIAE*

(References are to paragraphs annotated with "R" footnotes)

absolution of the dead 3378
Agnus Dei
    repetition 1446
    Shalom 1446
    striking breast 1477
alcoholic priests 1674
altar, veneration of 1417
altar cross 386
altar facing the people 383
altar servers, rubrics for 1360
Ascension
    transference 3773
    vigil 3791
ashes, blessing of, outside Mass 3795
Asperges 328
Baptism of the Lord: evening prayer I 3779
bows at Mass 1624
broadcasts, delayed 1122
calendars, proper 4011
candles
    blessing 3795
    material 1659
canon of the Mass: congregational responses
    474
celebrant's place at Mass 341
celebrations of the word 329
chair, celebrant's 384
chants between readings 1360

chants for Mass 4243
choral office
    prime 370
    religious traveling 370
Christmas, vigil of 3800
Christmas season: Second Sunday 3802
cloister-screen of nuns 296
co-cathedral, dedication of 3818
commingling (Order of Mass) 1503
communion, repetition of 352, 1796
communion, rite of
    formulary outside Mass 1262, 2103
    kneeling after communion 1411
    servers 1360
communion in the hand 2061
communion under both kinds 1261, 1808, 2105,
    2128
concelebration
    binated Mass as 1807
    eucharistic prayer 1558, 1581
    funerals 1360, 1812
    incensation and veneration of altar   1810
    organist-concelebrant 1796
    permission 1794
    purifications 1810
    religious 1548
    seminary 307
    sign of peace 1810
    stipend 1812
congregation: standing, etc. 1360, 1411

consecration of the Mass: vernacular versions 1445

consecration to a life of virginity 3262

conventual/community Mass 1796

Corpus Christi 3773

deacon
blessings 2592
homilist 1360
liturgical functions 2536

dedication of a church, anniversary of 3818, 3824

dismissal rite (Order of Mass)
eucharistic exposition following 1360
music 4150

ember days, celebration of 3813

entrance song 1416

Epiphany 3773

eucharistic bread 1673

eucharistic exposition
celebration of Mass 387
deacon 2536
homily 1294
Marian prayers 1294
reposition 1294
women religious 1291

eucharistic celebrations, music for 4154

eucharistic prayer
congregational responses 1931
final doxology 1581
organ accompaniment 1402

Eucharistic Prayer I 1712

Eucharistic Prayer II 1933–34

Eucharistic Prayer III 1445, 1933

eucharistic processions 2219

eucharistic reservation 387, 2202

eucharistic wine 1674

final blessing
benediction following Mass 1360
bishop 1360, 1447
celebrant's gestures 1498

funeral Masses
concelebration 1812
days permitted 1726, 3378

general intercessions 348, 1360

genuflections at Mass 1360, 1624

gestures at Mass 1477

Gloria 1421

Good Friday: sacraments 3786

gospel reading
place 1360
vestments 342

Holy Family: evening prayer I 3779

Holy Thursday: Eucharistic Prayer II 1712

homilist, deacon as 1340, 2536

homily
funeral 345
place 1487
sign of the cross 1432
syllabus 345

hosts, particles of 1522

Immaculate Heart of Mary: Mass 1723

incensation
concelebration 1810
preparation of the gifts 1441

institution to ministry 2332

Iubilate Deo 4243

Jesus Christ the High Priest, Mass of 1723

kissing of hand/of objects 328

kneeling 1360, 1402, 1411

lectern: Masses with small groups 1662

little offices 372

Litany of the Saints, emendation of 3827

liturgical books, editions of 884

liturgy of the hours, celebration of
cathedral chapters 3461
deacon presiding 2536
religious calendar 4011
religious communities 3735

liturgy of the hours, obligation of
dispensation 370
"mental" recitation 3449

Liturgy of the Hours, The, editions of 884

Lord, I am not worthy (Order of Mass) 1472

marriage rite
instruction 366
music 1413, 2986
records and tapes 443

Mary, Queen of Apostles 3384

Mass, calendar for 4011

Mass stipend for concelebration 1807

Mass with a congregation 349

Masses for the dead
days permitted 1722
rubrics 462

Masses for various needs 1706

Masses with children, daily 2160

master of ceremonies 1360

memorial acclamation 1613

memorials, prayers of Mass on 1713

missal, place of 1360

missals, hand 1360, 1452

music
dismissal rite of Mass 4150
Ordinary of Mass 334
organ at Mass 1402, 1413
records and tapes 443
songs for Mass 4154

offertory
meaning 1439
Oremus 1340, 4151

office of readings on Sunday 464

Ordinary of Mass, music for 334

organ
accompanying eucharistic prayer 1402
following homily 1413

palms, blessing of 3795

particular calendars and propers 3999, 4001

Passion (Palm) Sunday: color 1698

patron of a church 3824

penitential rite 1477

prayer after communion: *The Lord be with you*
      1360
prayer over the gifts 1360, 1713
prayers at foot of altar 340, 1360
preface
      celebrant's gestures 1498
      proper 1712
prelates, assistant ministers of 1360
preparation of the gifts
      incensation 1441
      "offertory" and 1439
presentation of the gifts 1360, 1492
prime, suppression of 3400
profession of faith
      Easter octave 1433
      genuflection 1360
      intonation 1360
      manner of reciting 1421
purifications
      celebrant's fingers 458, 1360, 1627
      principal concelebrant 1810
      vessels 1628
reader 342, 1360
readings for Mass
      announcements of text 1479
      celebrant's role 1360, 1662
      number 1708
regulation of liturgy 312, 314
religious profession, recipient of 3235
rogation days, celebration of 3802
Roman Missal
      Latin appendix 884
      obligatory use 1752
rubrics, uniformity of 314
Sacred Heart: Mass 1723
Sanctus, polyphonic singing of 1360

Sanctus bell 1499
sign language 296
sign of peace 1502, 1810
silence after homily 1413
singing in recited Mass 340
solemn blessing (Order of Mass) 1514
solemnities
      transference 3826
      weekdays of Advent, Lent 3806
sponsor for confirmation 2514
sprinkling with holy water 328
stole, celebrant's 1689
subdeacon, ordination of 2613
Sunday Mass
      anticipation on Saturday 3829
      seminaries 307
title (titular) of a church 3818, 3824
tabernacle
      altar facing people 387
      glass 1281
tabernacle key 2202
translations, changing of 312
vernacular
      ad interim texts 883
      use in Mass 349
Veni, Sancte Spiritus: genuflection 1360
vessels, consecration of 1686
vigils 3800
votive Masses 1706, 1723
washing of hands (Order of Mass) 1442
weekdays
      Advent 1723, 3806
      Christmas season 1723
      Lent 3806
women, ministries of 2932

ABBREVIATIONS AND SIGLA

BOOKS OF THE BIBLE

Acts	Acts of the Apostles	1 Kgs	1 Kings
Am	Amos	2 Kgs	2 Kings
Bar	Baruch	Lam	Lamentations
1 Chr	1 Chronicles	Lk	Luke
2 Chr	2 Chronicles	Lv	Leviticus
Col	Colossians	Mal	Malachi
1 Cor	1 Corinthians	1 Mc	1 Maccabees
2 Cor	2 Corinthians	2 Mc	2 Maccabees
Dn	Daniel	Mi	Micah
Dt	Deuteronomy	Mk	Mark
Eccl	Ecclesiastes	Mt	Matthew
Eph	Ephesians	Na	Nahum
Est	Esther	Neh	Nehemiah
Ex	Exodus	Nm	Numbers
Ez	Ezekiel	Ob	Obadiah
Ezr	Ezra	1 Pt	1 Peter
Gal	Galatians	2 Pt	2 Peter
Gn	Genesis	Phil	Philippians
Hb	Habakkuk	Phlm	Philemon
Heb	Hebrews	Prv	Proverbs
Hg	Haggai	Ps	Psalms
Hos	Hosea	Rom	Romans
Is	Isaiah	Ru	Ruth
Jas	James	Rv	Revelation
Jb	Job	Song	Song of Songs
Jdt	Judith	Sir	Sirach
Jer	Jeremiah	1 Sm	1 Samuel
Jl	Joel	2 Sm	2 Samuel
Jgs	Judges	Tb	Tobit
Jn	John	1 Thes	1 Thessalonians
1 Jn	1 John	2 Thes	2 Thessalonians
2 Jn	2 John	Ti	Titus
3 Jn	3 John	1 Tm	1 Timothy
Jon	Jonah	2 Tm	2 Timothy
Jos	Joshua	Wis	Wisdom
Jude	Jude	Zec	Zechariah
		Zep	Zephaniah

DOCUMENTS OF VATICAN II

ALPHABETICALLY

AA	*Apostolicam actuositatem*	(Laity)
AG	*Ad gentes*	(Missions)
CD	*Christus Dominus*	(Bishops)

DV	*Dei Verbum*	(Revelation)
DH	*Dignitatis humanae*	(Religious Freedom)
GE	*Gravissimum educationis*	(Christian Education)
GS	*Gaudium et spes*	(Church, Modern World)
IM	*Inter mirifica*	(Communications)
LG	*Lumen gentium*	(Church)
NA	*Nostra aetate*	(Non-Christians)
OE	*Orientalium Ecclesiarum*	(Eastern Churches)
OT	*Optatam totius*	(Priestly Formation)
PC	*Perfectae caritatis*	(Religious Life)
PO	*Presbyterorum ordinis*	(Priesthood)
SC	*Sacrosanctum Concilium*	(Liturgy)
UR	*Unitatis redintegratio*	(Ecumenism)

CHRONOLOGICALLY

Sacrosanctum Concilium (SC) — (Constitution on the Sacred Liturgy) AAS 56 (1964) 97–138; ConstDecrDecl 3–69.

Inter mirifica (IM) — (Decree on the Instruments of Social Communication) AAS 56 (1964) 145–157; ConstDecrDecl 73–89.

Lumen gentium (LG) — (Dogmatic Constitution on the Church) AAS 57 (1965) 5–71; ConstDecrDecl 93–206.

Orientalium Ecclesiarum (OE) — (Decree on Eastern Catholic Churches) AAS 57 (1965) 76–89; ConstDecrDecl 223–246.

Unitatis redintegratio (UR) — (Decree on Ecumenism) AAS 57 (1965) 90–112; ConstDecrDecl 243–274.

Christus Dominus (CD) — (Decree on the Bishops' Pastoral Office in the Church) AAS 58 (1966) 673–701; ConstDecrDecl 277–336.

Perfectae caritatis (PC) — (Decree on the Appropriate Renewal of the Religious Life) AAS 58 (1966) 702–712; ConstDecrDecl 333–353.

Optatam totius (OT) — (Decree on Priestly Formation) AAS 58 (1966) 713–727; ConstDecrDecl 357–384.

Gravissimum educationis (GE) — (Declaration on Christian Education) AAS 58 (1966) 728–739; ConstDecrDecl 387–408.

Nostra aetate (NA) — (Declaration on the Relationship of the Church to Non-Christian Religions) AAS 58 (1966) 740–744; ConstDecrDecl 411–419.

Dei Verbum (DV) — (Dogmatic Constitution on Divine Revelation) AAS 58 (1966) 817–835; ConstDecrDecl 423–435.

Apostolicam actuositatem (AA) — (Decree on the Apostolate of the Laity) AAS 58 (1966) 837–864; ConstDecrDecl 459–508.

Dignitatis humanae (DH) — (Declaration on Religious Freedom) AAS 58 (1966) 929–946; ConstDecrDecl 511–540.

Ad gentes (AG) — (Decree on the Church's Missionary Activity) AAS 58 (1966) 947–990; ConstDecrDecl 543–615.

Presbyterorum ordinis (PO) — (Decree on the Ministry and Life of Priests) AAS 58 (1966) 990–1024; ConstDecrDecl 619–678.

Gaudium et spes (GS) — (Pastoral Constitution on the Church in the Modern World) AAS 58 (1966) 1025–1120; ConstDecrDecl 681–835.

GENERAL AND BIBLIOGRAPHICAL ABBREVIATIONS (SIGLA)

AAS	*Acta Apostolicae Sedis.* Commentarium officiale (Vatican City, 1909–)
abp.	Archbishop
addr.	address (allocution)
ap. const.	apostolic constitution
ap. exhort.	apostolic exhortation
ArchKathKRecht	*Archiv für katholisches Kirchenrecht* (Mainz, 1857–)

art.	article, articles
BCL Newsletter	Bishops' Committee on the Liturgy, National Conference of Catholic Bishops, *Newsletter*, (Washington, D.C., 1965–)
bp.	bishop
BrevRom	*Breviarium Romanum*
can.	canon
cap.	*caput, capita* [chapter(s)]
card.	cardinal
CCL	*Corpus Christianorum, Series latina* (Turnhout, Belgium, 1953–)
CELAM	Consejo Episcopal Latino-Americano
cf.	compare
ch.	chapter, chapters
CIC	*Codex Iuris Canonici* (Rome, 1918)
CIMS	Consociatio Internationalis Musicae Sacrae [International Association of Sacred Music]
CLD	*Canon Law Digest*
COeD	*Conciliorum oecumenicorum decreta* (Bologna and Freiburg, 1962)
CommRel	*Commentarium pro religiosis et missionariis* (Rome, 1920–)
Consilium	Consilium for the Implementation of the Constitution on the Liturgy
Const.	*Constitutio*
Const. Ap.	*Constitutio Apostolica* (Apostolic Constitution)
ConstDecrDecl	*Sacrosanctum Oecumenicum Concilium Vaticanum II: Constitutiones, Decreta, Declarationes* (Vatican Polyglot Press, 1966)
CSEL	*Corpus scriptorum ecclesiasticorum* (Vienna, 1866–)
CT	*Concilium Tridentinum: Diariorum, actorum, epistularum, tractatuum nova collectio*, ed. Görres Gesellschaft, 13 v. (Freiburg, 1901–38)
Denz-Schön	*Enchiridion symbolorum*, H. Denzinger, A. Schönmetzer, eds. (33rd ed., Freiburg, B., 1965)
decl.	declaration
decr.	decree
DocCath	*La Documentation catholique* (Paris, 1919–)
doctr.	*doctrina* (teaching)
ed.	edition; editor(s)
ed. cit.	*editione citata* (edition cited)
ed. typica	*editio typica*
EDL	*Enchiridion documentorum instaurationis liturgicae I* (1963–73), R. Kaczynski, ed., (Rome, 1976) [references are to paragraph numbers]
EnchVat	*Enchiridion Vaticanum* 3 v. (10th ed., Bologna, 1976)
encycl.	encyclical
ep.	*epistula* (letter)
EphLit	*Ephemerides liturgicae* (Rome, 1887–)
EuchMyst	*Eucharisticum Mysterium*, SCR and Consilium, Instr. on worship of the Eucharist, 25 May 1967 [DOL 179]
Funk DidConst	F. X. Funk, ed., *Didascalia et Constitutiones Apostolorum*, 2 v. (Paderborn, 1905)
Funk PA	F. X. Funk, ed., *Patres apostolici*, 2 v. (Tübingen, 1901)
GCS	*Die griecheschen christlichen Schriftsteller der ersten drei Jahrhunderte* (Leipzig, 1897–)
GILH	General Instruction of the Liturgy of the Hours (1971) [DOL 426]
GIRM	General Instruction of the Roman Missal (4th ed., 1975) [DOL 208]
GNLYC	General Norms for the Liturgical Year and the Calendar (1969) [DOL 442]
Gr.	Greek text of Bible
Harvey	W. Harvey, ed., *Sancti Irenaei Ep. Lugdunensis libros*

	quinque adversus haereses, 2 v. (Cambridge, 1857)
instr.	instruction
introd.	introduction
InterOec	*Inter oecumenici,* SCR, First Instruction on the correct implementation of the Constitution on the Liturgy, 26 Sept. 1964 [DOL 23]
LH	*Liturgy of the Hours*
lib.	*liber* (book)
Litt.Ap.	*Litterae Apostolicae* (Apostolic Letter)
Mansi	G. D. Mansi, *Sacrorum Conciliorum nova et amplissima collectio* 32 v. (Florence, Venice, 1757–98), repr. and continued by L. Petit and G. B. Martin 53 v. in 60 (Paris, 1889–1927; repr. Gratz, 1960–61).
Mohlberg LibSacr	L. C. Mohlberg, ed., *Liber Sacramentorum Romanae Aeclesiae ordinis anni circuli* in *Rerum ecclesiasticarum documenta, Series Maior: Fontes,* v. 4 (Rome, 1960; 2nd ed., 1968)
Mohlberg MissGoth	L. C. Mohlberg, ed., *Missale Gothicum,* ibid., v. 5 (Rome, 1961)
Mohlberg SacrVeron	L. C. Mohlberg et al., ed., *Sacramentarium Veronense,* ibid., v. 1 (Rome, 1st ed., 1956; 2nd ed., 1966; 3rd ed., 1978)
motu proprio	apostolic letter *motu proprio*
MR	*Missale Romanum*
MusSacr	SCR, Instruction *Musicam sacram,* 5 March 1967 [DOL 508]
n.	*numero* (number)
NCCB	National Conference of Catholic Bishops [U.S.]
nn.	*numeris* (numbers)
no., nos.	number, numbers
Not	*Notitiae* v. 1–5, 1965–69, Consilium; v. 6–11, 1970–75, SCDW; v. 12–, 1976–, SCSDW (Rome)
OR	*L'Osservatore Romano* (Vatican City, 1861–)
OREng	*L'Osservatore Romano,* English ed., Weekly (Vatican City, 1968–)
p., pp.	page, pages
par.	parallel passages in the Synoptic Gospels
PatrOr	*Patrologia Orientalis,* R. Graffin and F. Nau, ed. (Paris, 1903–)
PCIDV	Pontifical Commission for the Interpretation of the Decrees of Vatican Council II
PG	*Patrologiae cursus completus: Series graeca,* J. P. Migne, ed., 161 v. (Paris, 1857–66)
PL	*Patrologiae cursus completus: Series latina,* J. P. Migne, ed., 222 v. (Paris, 1844–55)
PL Suppl	*Patrologiae cursus completus: Series latina, Suppl.,* A. Hamman, ed. (Paris, 1957–)
PR	*Pontificale Romanum* (ed. 1962)
pt.	part
RM	Roman Missal or Sacramentary (English translations of the new *Missale Romanum*)
RP	*The Roman Pontifical* (1978)
RR	Roman Ritual
SC	*Sources chrétiennes,* H. de Lubac et al., ed. (Paris, 1941–)
SCB	Congregation for Bishops
SCC	Congregation for the Clergy
SCCE	Congregation for Catholic Education
SCCS	Congregation for the Causes of Saints
SCDF	Congregation for the Doctrine of the Faith
SCDS	Congregation for the Discipline of the Sacraments
SCDW	Congregation for Divine Worship
SCEC	Congregation for the Eastern Churches
SCEP	Congregation for the Evangelization of Peoples
SCR	Congregation of Rites

SCRel	Congregation of Religious
SCRSI	Congregation for Religious and Secular Institutes
SCSDW	Congregation for the Sacraments and Divine Worship
SecCU	Secretariat for Promoting Christian Unity
SecSt	Secretariat of State (Papal)
sess.	session
ST	St. Thomas Aquinas, *Summa theologiae* (Part, question, article, reply, e.g., ST 1a, 5.4 ad 1—Prima Pars, question 5. article 4, reply to argument 1)
tit.	*titulus* (title)
tr.	translation; translator
tract.	*tractatus* (treatise)
USCC	United States Catholic Conference
v. or vol.	volume(s)
vv.	verses

GENERAL INDEX

(References are to marginal paragraph numbers)

abbess, blessing of
> minister 3288
> place of recipient 3289
> proper day 3287
> requisites 3290–91
> revision of rite 3276
> see also *Blessing of an Abbot and an Abbess, Rite of*

abbot, blessing of
> concelebration 3280–81
> insignia 3283
> minister 3278
> place of recipient 3285–86
> requisites 3284
> revision of rite 3276
> vestments 3282
> see also *Blessing of an Abbot and an Abbess, Rite of*

abbots
> faculties 711, 938–950, 2044, 2050, 2238
> name in eucharistic prayer 1971
> pontifical insignia 4449, 4452
> vesture 4530

abjuration of heresy *see* heresy, abjuration of

absolution, sacramental
> completion of sacrament 3071
> formulary 3084
> general absolution
>> abuses 3051
>> censures and 3049
>> competent authority 3043, 3097, 3104
>> conditions 607, 3040–41, 3057, 3096, 3128–29
>> dispositions of penitent 3044, 3049, 3098, 3132
>> exceptional character 2247, 3134, 3139
>> Pastoral Norms 1333, 2247, 3039–51
>> priest's decision 3105
>> reception by public sinners 3049
>> rite 3048, 3100
>> separation from Mass 3048, 3131
>> subsequent confession 3130
>> unwarranted case 3135–37
> individual absolution 598, *see also* confession

absolution of the dead
> responsories 470
> usage of term 3378
> vestments 472

abstinence, law of 3023
> age 3024
> days 3022, 3876
> dispensation 3027
> Eastern Catholic Churches 3028
> other penitential practices and 3876
> privileges and indults 3025
> seamen 2670

acclamations
> Masses with children 2014–15
> participation 1405
> readings at Mass 1865
> singing in vernacular 4313
> *see also* memorial acclamation

acolyte
> eucharistic exposition 2217
> functions at Mass 1455, 1532
>> introductory rites 1533–34
>> liturgy of the eucharist 1535–37
>> place 1534
> minister of communion 2095
> *see also* altar servers

acolyte, ministry of
> candidates for orders 2580, 2582
> establishment for Latin Church 2929
> eucharistic devotion 2931
> functions 2931
> qualifications 2931
> revision 2923
> seminarians 2816, 2820

acolytes, institution of
> conditions 2933
> interstices 2935
> minister 2934, 2942
> reception by candidates for orders 2936
> reservation to men 2932
> rite 2942–43
> usage of term 2924
> see also *Institution of Readers and Acolytes, Rite of*

***Ad gentes*, application of** 758–759

adaptation 37–40
> Africa 490
> bishops and 292, 436, 2654
> celebrant's choice of texts 1987–90
> children 2136
> conferences of bishops and 40, 482, *see also* conferences of bishops
> Consilium 482

cultural traditions 2279
dangers 697
formation of local Churches 250
handicapped persons 2139
inculturation and 582
India 489
limits 410
liturgical celebrations 2796
liturgical formation in seminaries 2842
opportune time 619
petitions of bishops 446
reform of liturgy 292
study of liturgy 2823
styles of liturgy 759
unity of the Church 2625

admission to candidacy for ordination *see*
ordination, admission to candidacy for

Admission to Candidacy for Ordination as
Deacons and Priests, Commitment to
Celibacy
effective date 2531
introduction 2944–47
promulgation 2939

Advent
duration 3806
liturgy of the hours
readings 3577
memorials 3668
music 4187
place of Mary 3901–02
precedence of Sunday 3771, 3807
readings
Isaiah 1849
order 1854
provisional lectionary 1823–24
twofold character 3805
weekdays, 17–24 December 3782, 3808

Africa, liturgy in 490

agapē **in early Church** 235, 438

Agnus Dei
accompanying rite 1407
Mass with a congregation 1503
Mass without a congregation 1616
singing 1446, 2164, 4156, 4254, 4295
use of vernacular 4313

alb
common vestment 526, 1471, 1688
ministers below deacon 1691

All Saints 3986

All Souls
celebration on Sunday 3986
plenary indulgence 2770, 3181

Alleluia
Easter season 3788
independent rite 1407
Lent 1427, 3794
liturgy of the hours 3471, 3490, 3509, 3515,
3550, 3644
manner of singing 1427, 4286, 4288

Alleluia **canticle** 3567

Alleluia **verse** 1427, 1881

altar
anointing 4384
dedication to saints 4407

design and placement 128, 383, 1253,
1652–53, 4338, 4405, 4406
enclosure of relics 1656, 4373
honoring martyrs 4402
images and statues 4407
symbolism 4360, 4398, 4399, 4401
table of sacrifice and communion 1649,
4400–01

altar, blessing of
altars to be blessed 4435
Mass text 4440
minister 4438
proper day 4439
requisites 4441

altar, consecration of
priest consecrator 761, 4446
requisites 4433
see also churches, blessing of

altar, dedication of
adaptation 4421–22
catechesis preceding 4423
celebration of eucharist 4420
depositing of relics 4417
introductory rites 4414
liturgy of the word 4415–16
Mass text 4412
minister 4409
prayer of dedication 4418
proper and excluded days 4410–11
record 4327
requisites 4424–27
responsibilities of rector 4422
rites of dedication 4419
see also *Dedication of a Church and an Altar,*
Rite of

altar, fixed
consecration 1655
dedication 4435
meaning 1651, 4403, 4435

altar, incensation of
entrance rites 1417, 1475, 1519, 1553
manner 1475, 1626
preparation of gifts 1441, 1495, 1523, 1535

altar, movable
blessing 4435, 4438–41
consecrated or blessed 1655
erection 4437
material 1654, 4436
meaning 1651, 4403

altar, papal *see* papal altar

altar, portable
delegation to consecrate 734
Mass facing the people 415

altar, preparation of
acolyte 1535
presentation of the gifts 1439

altar, veneration of
adaptation 1622, 1740
bows at Mass 1624
concelebration 1553, 1598
conclusion of Mass 1515, 1531
entrance rites of Mass 1416, 1474

altar cloth 1658

altar cross *see* cross, altar

incensation at Mass 1626
placement 1660
use at Mass 1649

altar facing people
construction and design 383, 415, 428
permission of local Ordinary 4336
problems 428

altar linens, washing of 735

altar servers
Mass without a congregation 1600
fidelity 2919
functions at Mass 1458
liturgical ministry 29, 2917, 4134
training 4205
vocations 2920
women 429, 525

altar stone 1655

altar table 4406

altars, minor 385, 1657, 4404

ambo *see* lectern

amice, use of 1471, 1688

anamnesis 1445, 1956

anaphora 1946, *see also* eucharistic prayer

angels
patrons 3974
titles (titulars of churches) 4372

Angelus 3938

Anglican Communion
ecumenism 1073
Marian devotion 3930
ordination of women 1072–73
relations with Roman Church 960, 1080–90

announcements at Mass 1513, 1529

Annunciation
Mary in liturgy 3904
profession of faith 1488

anointing, Christian meaning of 3862, *see also*
chrism

anointing of the sick 141
catechesis 3356
communal celebration 3337, 3356, 3365
conditional administration 3335
continuous with penance and viaticum 74,
360, 3350
Council of Florence 3316
Council of Trent 3316
effects 1104, 3326
essential elements 3316, 3318, 3345
faith and 3327
minister
adaptations of rite 3360–61
authorized 3336, 3338
preparation of rite 3337
several priests 3339
number of anointings 74, 3344
oil 3340–42
parts anointed 3317, 3343
place among sacraments 141, 3315
purpose 3318, 3325, 3365
recipients 3328, 3365
repetition 3318, 3329–32
revision of rite
decreed 74, 3220, 3317

provisional form 360
time 73, 3316, 3333
viaticum and 74, 360

Anointing of the Sick, Rite of *see Pastoral Care*
of the Sick: Rites of Anointing and Viaticum

anointings, baptismal 2360, 2427, 2497

antemensium, blessing of 369, 720, 942

antiphons
Simple Gradual 4270–71
translations 833–834

antiphons in liturgy of the hours
Easter season 3550, 3644
gospel canticles 3480, 3564
invitatory 3464–66
Marian antiphons 3522
proper offices 4039
psalm antiphons
Christological sense 3539
daytime hours 3512, 3546–47
divisions of psalms 3545
memorials of the saints 3548
morning and evening prayer 3546–47
office of readings 3492, 3546–47, 3564
proper 3546–47
purpose 3543
repetition after strophes 3555
singing 3554
vernacular translation 3544
silence and 3632
sources 3492

apostates 973

Apostles' Creed 2182

apostolate of the laity
fields 236–237
good order 240
means 238
objectives 234–235
preaching and 2955

apostolic administrator
faculties 711, 2044, 2050, 2238
name in eucharistic prayer 1971
pontifical insignia 4449, 4451
vesture 4530

apostolic succession
communicatio in sacris 1027
Eastern Churches 187, 993
ordination of bishops 2607

art 122–127
bishop's concern 124
"conciliar spring" 4322–26
contemporary 123, 275, 1644, 4236
Church's acceptance 122–123, 4327
liturgical formation in seminaries 2731–34,
2836
liturgical norms 4319
liturgy and 1644, 4317–21, 4324
nobility 122
religion and 4326
rights of 4325

art, commissions on
consultation 126
establishment 46, 280, 4317

art, institutes of 127

art, works of
  accessibility to tourists 4332
  adaptation to reformed liturgy 4333
  bishop's concern 4327, 4333
  care of Church's patrimony 1253, 2619,
    2733, 4327–34
artists
  bishop's concern 127
  Church's patrimony 4321
  contribution to liturgy 127
  spiritual formation 4326
  standards 122, 1644, 4328
Ascension
  day of celebration 3773, 3791, 3858
  prayer for Christian unity 976
  weekdays after 3792
Ash Wednesday
  blessing of ashes 368
  celebration 3795
  fast and abstinence 3022, 3876
  liturgy of the hours 3667
  precedence 3782
ashes, blessing of
  prayers 368
  use of chasuble 472
Asperges, **vestments for** 472, 4254
assemblies of bishops 315, *see also* conferences
  of bishops
Assumption
  Mary in liturgy 3904
  vigil on Sunday 3840
audiovisuals 696, 2168–69
auxiliary bishops
  faculties 711
  name in eucharistic prayer 1972

baldachin
  bishop's chair 4468
  use of tabernacle veil 4335
baptism
  apostolate of laity 232
  bond of Christian unity 189
  Christian witness 245
  Christians separated from us 189, 964,
    2253
  communion of the Church 965, 972
  conditional administration 969, 2482
  conditions of validity 967
  conversion and 3018
  dignity 2252
  ecumenical dialogue 970–971
  effects 1104, 2251, 2254, 2502, 3067
  incorporation into the Church 141, 2253
  minister
      adaptations of rite 2311–15
      assistants 2264
      bishop 2260, 2681
      danger of death 2265, 2266, 2305
      deacon 2536
      nonclerical religious 2324–26
      ordinary 2260
  nonrepeatable 1094, 2253, 2482, 2489
  offices and ministries 2256–66
  personal commitment 2490

rite
      adaptations 2279–80, 2283–84
      alternative forms 68
      danger of death 2445
      infusion or immersion 2271
      liturgy of the word 2273
      participation of community 2256
      place in church 2274–75
      requirements 2267–78
      revision 66, 479
      supplying ceremonies 69, 354–355
  sacrament of faith 2252, 2426
  sacramental form 2272
  sacramental signs 2242, 2359
  union with paschal mystery 139, 2255
Baptism for Children, Rite of
  Consilium 637
  extension of *vacatio legis* 2316
  introduction 2285–2315
  law of the Church 2321
  promulgation 2248
  second *editio typica* 2249
baptism of adults
  action of Trinity 2358
  anniversary celebration 2431
  anointing with chrism 2360, 2427
  bishop's responsibility 2681
  celebration 2355–60, 2425–27
  godparents 2257–58
  postbaptismal catechesis 2428
  rite
      immersion or infusion 2359
      revision 66, 2327
  see also Christian initiation of adults
baptism of children
  age of child 2292, 2317
  basis of Christian formation 2287
  children of nonpracticing parents 2317
  communal celebration 2276
  danger of death 2305
  Easter Vigil 2312
  faith of the Church 2256, 2289
  hospitals and 2296, 2320–23
  ministries and roles
      community 2288
      godparents 2257–58, 2296
      ministers 2291
      parents 2289, 2311
  proper day 2293
  proper place 2294–96
  reason 2286
  rite
      celebration by ordinary minister
        2299–2303
      reception of children 2300
      revision 67–69, 2248
      shorter form 2304–06
Baptism of the Lord 3760, 3772, 3804, 3873
baptismal character
  Christian initiation 2502
  deputation for worship 141
  indelibility 2489
  universal priesthood 1125
baptismal font
  design and care of 2268

nonparochial churches 2295, 2321

baptismal promises, renewal of
celebration of viaticum 3348
Christian initiation of adults 2368
confirmation 71, 357, 2526
uncatechized Christians 2498

baptismal register
pastor's responsibility 2278
recording of confirmation 2523
religious-ministers 2326

baptismal water
blessing 70, 2270, 2355–56, 2425
care 2267, 2269

baptistery
design 128, 391, 2274
Easter candle 2274

basic Christian communities 582

basilicas, minor 4345–59

basilicas, patriarchal
celebration of baptism 2323
list 4337, 4344

bells
blessing 369
simulation 443
use at Mass 1499

Benedicamus Domino
Gregorian melodies 4254
Mass of exposition 1289

Benedict, St., Patron of Europe 3949–51

benediction *see* eucharistic benediction

Bible *see* Scripture

Bible, books of 1862

Bible vigils
promotion 35, 2661
replacement of office of the dead 3386

bidding prayers *see* general intercessions

bination
faculty 713
stipend 2227, 2229, 2238

Birth of Mary 3905

bishop
catechesis and 594
coat-of-arms 4525
collegiality 2602
concern for universal Church 255
example of holiness 146, 194, 2649
liturgical responsibilities
adaptation 292, 436, 2654
catechesis 193
celebrations in cathedral and parishes 2615, 2648, 2651
celebrations of the sacraments 2647
community aspect of liturgy 2671
eucharistic celebrations 146, 1271, 1449
eucharistic worship 1208
exclusion of discrimination 326, 2658
experiments 40, 436, 441, 530, 639, 790, 2654
leadership 442, 2261, 2650, 2652, 4055
liturgical directories 2653
liturgy of religious 753–754, 3310

ministry of word and sacraments 146, 1271
participation 277, 395, 2671
pastoral visitations
personal reception of sacraments 2659
popular devotions 2660–61
priestly formation 212, 2683–84
reform of liturgy 511, 535
regulation of liturgy 22, 289, 314, 423, 606–607, 701
revision of books 25
sacramental life of faithful 194
vigilance over books 935–937
name in eucharistic prayer 1499, 1965, 1976
pastoral office 145, 191–197, 566, 2337–68
powers and privileges 147, 710–746, 748–749, 760–763, 2235, 2238, 2639–41
preaching office 145, 153, 192, 1126, 1338, 2245, 2637, 2239–43
relations with priests 262
religious and 197, 3310
rule of diocese 147, 191–194
see also conferences of bishops; local Ordinaries, powers of

bishop, consecration of
concelebration 1798
laying on of hands 76, 145, 361

bishops, conferences of *see* conferences of bishops

bishops, ordination of
apostolic succession 2607
Apostolic Tradition of Hippolytus 2607
effects 145, 2606
rite
approval 2612
determination of essentials 2611
promulgation 2613
revision 2608

bishops, vesture of 1805, 4511–14, *see also* pontifical insignia

blessed, the
adaptation of particular calendars 3994
celebrations of the newly beatified 3953–57, 3966–70
patron saints 3974, 4023
title (titular) 4029, 4372

blessing, final *see* final blessing

blessing, nuptial *see* nuptial blessing

blessing, papal *see* papal blessing

Blessing of an Abbot and an Abbess, Rite of
introduction 3271–91
promulgation 3276
see also abbess, blessing of; abbot, blessing of

blessing of an altar *see* altar, blessing of

blessing of a church *see* churches, blessing of

Blessing of Oils and Consecrating the Chrism, Rite of
introduction 3861–72
promulgation 3860
see also oils, blessing of

blessings
    bishop 745, 4490–91
    deacon 2592
    indulgences attached 3153
    reservation 79, 369, 745
Book of the Gospels
    deacon carrying 1518
    enthronement 1346
    entrance procession 1474, 1538
    pontifical Mass 4480
    preparations for Mass 1469
    reverence 1425, 1622, 1740
    separate volume 1867
books *see* liturgical books, editions of
bows
    limitation 328
    use in Mass 1624
bread, eucharistic *see* eucharistic bread
breaking of the bread
    communion rite 1446
    concelebration 1585
    eucharistic bread 1673
    Mass with a congregation 1503
    Mass without a congregation 1616
    Masses with children 2186
breviary *see* Roman Breviary; *Liturgy of the Hours, The*
bride, crowning of 2983
broadcasts of liturgy 20, 1121–24, 1251, 4129
brothers, religious 208, 210, 2546
burial, ecclesiastical
    Christians in irregular marriages 3398
    denial of rites 3369–70
    public sinners 3399
burial of infants, rite for 82
burial of the dead
    Christian tradition 3366, 3370
    preference over cremation 3367, 3387
    see also funerals
Byzantine-Ruthenian Rite 602

Caeremoniale Episcoporum
    pontifical rites and insignia 4457
    revision 690, 693, 4457
Calendar, General Roman
    approval 3757
    celebrations
        cycle 3815
        proper days 3822
        saints 111, 3756
    effective date 1774, 3757, 3758
    interim form 1769, 1775–77, 3759–65, 3828
    liturgical year and 676
    particular calendars and 3761, 3766, 3816, 3818
    promulgation 3758
    revision 106–111, 3648, 3754, 3900
    table of precedence 3825
    universal use 3814
calendar, perpetual 131
calendars, diocesan 3817
    celebrations included 3818, 4012–14
    change of diocesan boundaries 4015

General Calendar and 3766
    norms for revision 4047–50
calendars, particular 3814
    approval 3815
    celebrations of the saints 3756
    General Roman Calendar and 3761, 3766, 3816, 3818
    individual churches 3818
    interim adaptation 1775, 3991–94
    kinds 3817
    obligatory use 3821, 3999
    purpose 3815
    readings for Mass 1881
    revision 3991
        approval 4050
        celebrations included 3818–19, 4008–15
        confirmation 4050
        day for celebrations 3822–25, 4016–18
        general norms 3816, 3995–4001
        liturgical indults 4043–45
        patrons 3982, 4023–28
        preparatory study 3999, 4048
        proper celebrations 4002–07
        rank of celebrations 3829, 4019–22
        rogation and ember days 4033
        time period 3999, 4046, 4051
        titles (titulars) 4029–30
        titles of saints 4022
    solemnities without precept 4031–32
calendars, religious 4011
    celebrations included 3818, 4012
    General Calendar and 3766
    norms for revision 4047–50
    regional 3817
Candlemas Day 368
candles
    baptism 2302, 2360
    communion outside Mass 2097
    dedication of a church 4390
    eucharistic exposition 2211
    Mass 1469, 1474
    use in all liturgical services 1659
candles, blessing of 368
candles, electric 444, 2669
candlesticks, placement of 386, 1659
canon law 2043
canon of the Mass
    parts sung 456
    recitation aloud 456, 1250
    rubrics (prior to 1969) 457–458
    translation 486
    use of vernacular 474, 816–819
    see also eucharistic prayer
canonical form of marriage
    marriage between Catholics 2985
    marriage with baptized Christians
        dispensation 3007, 3013, 3016
        obligatory 2990, 3006
    marriage with Eastern Orthodox
        Christians 172, 2993–94, 3005
canonization, rite of 3958

canons
    celebration of liturgy of the hours 95, 370,
        732, 3954
    vesture 4465, 4532, 4535–36
Canticle of Mary 3480, 3527, 3568
Canticle of Simeon 3519, 3568
Canticle of Zechariah 3480, 3524, 3568
canticles in liturgy of the hours
    distribution 3566–69
    morning and evening prayer 3473, 3480,
        3566
    night prayer 3519
    Old/New Testament 3569
    vigils 3503
cantor
    formation 4142, 4201
    liturgy of the hours 3690
    responsibilities 1454, 4201, 4221
cantor of psalm 1426, 1457
captions
    psalms 3539, 3541
    readings for Mass 1863
cardinals
    coats-of-arms 4525
    Eastern-rite 4527
    titles of address 4518–24
    vesture 4498–4510
catechesis
    age levels 1107
    bishop's role 594
    catechumenate for adults as model 588
    children 2142
    Christian community 592–593
    Christian education 217
    contemporary state 584, 608–612, 1101
    first communion 2145
    forms 588
    homily 611
    inculturation and 586
    laity and 236
    marriage and family 1106
    ministry of the word 1099
    mission of Church 608
    mystery of Christ 587
    sacraments 609, 1103–04
    sources 610
    word, memory, witness 588–590
catechesis, liturgical
    anointing and viaticum 3356
    bishop's role 193
    celebrations of the sacraments 2243
    children 1243
    commentaries 35
    dedication of an altar 4423
    dedication of a church 4388
    divine worship 540
    eucharist
        communion in the hand 2064, 2088,
            2093, 2099
        communion outside Mass 2093
        communion under both kinds 2106,
            2114
        eucharistic congresses 2225
        Masses with children 2019

        new eucharistic prayers 1943, 1945,
            1966–68
        new Order of Mass 1738
        principles 1234–44
    General Instruction of the Roman Missal
        and 1780
    integration into rites 35
    Lent 109
    participation 504, 1100
    penance 1118, 2497
    personal prayer 1100
    popular devotions 612
    psalms for the dead 3384
catechesis, postbaptismal *see* postbaptismal
    catechesis
catechesis of baptized adults
    adaptation of baptismal rites 2497
    adaptation of catechumenate 2454
    celebration of sacraments 2456, 2498, 2520
    comparison to catechumenate 2490–92
    completion 2457, 2498
    duration 2448
    godparents 2451
    liturgical celebrations 2452–53, 2494
    participation of community 2450
    plan 2449
    presentations 2495
    purpose 2447
    rite of welcome 2493
    sacrament of penance 2497
    scrutinies 2496
    sponsor 2451
    time of year 2455
Catechism of St. Pius X 2118
catechists
    catechumenate for adults 2375
    exorcisms and blessings 2371, 2393
    formation 249, 1113
    leaders of community 594
    liturgy for canonical mission 249
    preparation for baptism 2256
    shorter rite of baptism for children 2304
    spiritual life 1112
catechumenate for adults 2490
    adaptation for adult confirmation 2512
    adaptations by bishop 2393
    arrangement in stages 2395–2432
    bishop's responsibility 2371, 2644
    blessings 2404
    catechesis 1110, 2401
    catechesis of the baptized and 2490–93
    celebrations of the word 2402
    dispositions of candidates 2342–43
    duration 2347, 2400, 2433
    election *see* election
    elements 1114, 2346
    entrance *see* entrance into order of
        catechumens
    exclusion of the baptized 2343
    godparents 2406
    minor exorcisms 2403
    mission lands 246
    model for catechesis 588
    participation of community 1114, 2368,
        2407, 2512

period of purification *see* purification and enlightenment
  presentations 2352
  register of names 2344
  restoration 64, 193, 609, 2319, 2327, 2329
  scrutinies *see* scrutinies
  time of rites 2377–82, 3793

catechumenate for children of catechetical age
  adaptation of rites 2464–65
  age of children 2319, 2458
  bishop's responsibility 2644
  catechetical group 2460–61
  celebration of sacraments 2472–75
  confirmation 2520
  duration of catechesis 2459
  entrance as catechumens 2466–67
  godparents 2475
  participation of community 2463
  scrutinies 2468–71
  time 2462

catechumens
  Christian burial 2345
  election 2350
  preparation 246
  registering of names 2344
  revision of canon law 246
  rite of marriage 2345
  status in Church 246, 2345
  terms designating 2351, 2405, 2414

cathedral
  celebration of liturgy of the hours 308, 3450
  center of liturgy 41, 2651
  choir 114
  significance 1645, 4055

cathedral, dedication of 3671, 3818, 4394

cathedral chapters 95, 370

Catherine of Siena, St. 3963–65

CELAM
  Department of Liturgy 579
  Instituto Liturgico de Medellín 537
  separate liturgical commission 538

celebrant (Mass)
  action in person of Christ 33, 4135
  commentaries and introductions 1401
  personal prayers 1403
  planning of celebrations 1703
  readings 344, 1486
  vestments 1689, 1692

celebrations, liturgical *see* liturgical celebrations

celebrations, particular
  days excluded 3997
  proper/by indult 3997, 4002

celebrations, proper
  kinds 4002–07
  rank 4019
  seminaries 2811
  see also calendars, particular

celebrations by indult 3997, 4017

celebrations of the word
  absence of priest 329, 524
  catechumenate 2346, 2405, 2494
  communion outside Mass 1262

  deacon 2536
  funeral without Mass 3378
  lay homilist 2957
  liturgy of the word as model 4167
  music 4167
  obsolete musical compositions 4174, 4223
  plan 329
  replacement of office of the dead 3386
  rite of confirmation 2522
  rite of penance 3082, 3087
  uncatechized Christians
  vigils 330
  see also Bible vigils

celibacy, commitment to
  prerequisite for ordination 2948
  renewal 2556–58, 2603

cemetery, blessing of 369

censures, absolution from
  faculties of confessors 725, 2661
  reception of baptized Christians 974
  recipients of general absolution 3049

chair, bishop's 4450, 4467–70

chair, celebrant's
  design 1661
  place 384, 1161

chalice
  blessing 4443–45
  concelebration 1810
  consecration 526, 734
  dignity 1679, 4442
  material 1681
  spilling at Mass 1629

chalice veil 1470

chants between readings 1426–30, 1851
  choice 1714
  manner of singing 4284, 4286
    Ordo cantus Missae 4298
    Simple Gradual 4266, 4272, 4309
  Mass with a congregation 1480, 1482
  Mass without a congregation 1607
  Masses for various needs 1719
  Masses with children 2179
  place for proclaiming 341
  preservation of Latin chants 4298
  principles for translations 1869
  reader 1540
  recitation or omission 1429
  single reading before gospel 1428
  vernacular editions 1868

chants for Mass
  appendix of Roman Missal 4313
  choice 516
  see also communion song; entrance song; Ordinary of the Mass; *Ordo cantus Missae*

chapel of reservation 387
  altar 4404
  place in church 1282
  recommendation and use 416, 1666
  seminaries 2806
  suitableness 2200

chapels
  bishop's house 763
  minor altars 385

seminaries 305, 2690
see also oratories, blessing of

chaplains
baptism in hospitals 2323
maritime faculties 2669–70
minister of confirmation 724, 2633, 2669
ministry to migrants 2631–36

character, sacramental *see* sacramental
character

chasuble
concelebrants 1551
uses 472
vestment proper to celebrant 1689
worn with alb 1688–89

chasuble-alb 4538–40

children
age of discretion 3148
anointing of the sick 3332
catechesis on Mass 1243
Church's concern 2134–36
Eucharistic Prayers *see* Eucharistic Prayers
for Masses with Children
first confession *see* first confession of
children
funerals 3385
introduction to eucharist 2141–48
Masses with *see* Masses with children
2149–52
moral formation 1117, 2142
recipients of baptism 2285
right to sacraments 3149
rosary devotion 3879

children of catechetical age *see* catechumenate
for children of catechetical age

choir
congregation's part in singing 4137, 4141,
4155, 4200, 4219
development 114, 4140, 4141, 4200, 4216,
4221
elimination 426
function at Mass 1453
houses of study 4140
liturgical function 29, 324, 4134, 4145,
4220, 4222
membership 4143
place in church 389, 1647, 1664, 4144
responsibilities 4140, 4200, 4252
seminaries 2725, 2727, 2792, 4140
service to Church 4252
see also Church Choirs; Little Singers

choir boys 115, 4115, 4192

choir directors 1454, 4249

choir members
formation 4249
participation in Mass 389–390, 1647, 1664,
4144

choral office
daytime prayer 89
dispensation or commutation 731, 953
language
clerical communities 791–799
Latin 3402–04
monasteries of nuns 800
SC Religious and 794, 803

vernacular 101, 765
obligation 95, 370, 731, 3461, 3506
omission of prime 3400
place of celebration 3692
preservation of structure 3402–03
provisional norms 370–371
singing 3731, 4158
substitution of communal recitation
3411–14

chrism
anointing in confirmation 2518
baptismal anointing 2360, 2497
composition 3864–65
dedication of an altar 4419
dedication of a church 4384
symbolism 3862

chrism, consecration of
bishop as minister 2519, 3861, 3866
place within Mass 3871–72
preparation of chrism 3865
revision of rite 3860
time of celebration 2519, 3869–70
see also *Blessing of Oils and Consecrating the
Chrism, Rite of*

chrism Mass
concelebration with bishop 1547, 2558,
3797, 3853, 3861
day of celebration 3797
ministerial priesthood and 1379, 2557–58,
2602
renewal of priestly commitment 2557, 2603
revision of liturgy 2556, 3853, 3860

chrismation 2503

Christ, prayer of
gospel accounts 3434
intercession with the Father 3433
liturgy of the hours 83–84, 3426

Christ, presence of
eucharist *see* real presence
eucharistic celebrations 1397
liturgical celebrations 7
modes 1179–82, 1238, 1284, 1305, 1317,
2198
sacraments 1102

Christ, priesthood of
Church's association 1125, 3437
liturgy of the hours 3443
nature of liturgy 7, 550
universal and ministerial priesthood 140,
257, 2565, 2957

Christ the King
day of celebration 3760, 3772
readings for Mass 1859

Christian education 216–217

Christian initiation
missions 246
paschal character 2335
role of community 2368
stages 2331–34

Christian Initiation, **General Introduction**
1309–40, 2250–84

Christian initiation, sacraments of
children of catechetical age 2472–75
connection between 2499

effects 2250–51, 2502
sacrament of penance and 3150
time of celebration 2382, 2386, 2423–24
uncatechized Christians 2498
Christian initiation of adults
catechumenate 53, 2341–47, *see also*
catechumenate for adults
celebration of the sacraments 2354–63,
2423–32
elements 2329
evangelization and precatechumenate
2336–40
mission lands 65
multiple forms of rite 2330
offices and ministries 2368–75
place of celebration 2390
postbaptismal catechesis (mystagogy)
2364–67, 2428–32
postponement of confirmation 2383
purpose 2328
short rite 2442–46
simple rite 2433–41
structure 2331–33
times for celebration 2377–89
uncatechized adults *see* catechesis of
baptized adults
Christian Initiation of Adults, Rite of
adaptations 2391–94
introductions 2328–2475
promulgation 2327
reflections on 2489–98
Christmas
anticipated Mass (1967) 1257
morning prayer 3646
profession of faith at Mass 1488
priests' three Masses 1802, 3800
Christmas, octave of
celebrations 3801
memorials in liturgy of the hours 3668
provisional lectionary 1841
solemnities 3778
Christmas, vigil of
celebration 3501
Mass 3800, 3840
office of readings 3645
Christmas season
duration 3799
liturgy of the hours 3578–79, 3645–46
provisional lectionary 1825–29
purpose 3798
readings for Mass 1849, 1855
Christus Dominus
application on conferences of bishops 755
application on religious 753
Church
apostolic mandate 144
apostolicity 138
Eastern Churches 188
hierarchic ministry 2567
catholicity 188
celebration of paschal mystery 6
communio 162, 182, 495, 499, 501
community of prayer 497–498, 532–533,
3439
eschatological nature 157–159

eucharistic faith 1044
hierarchic structure 145–149, 2792
holiness 1095, 3068
human culture and 274
images of 138
kingdom of Christ 137
liturgy manifesting 2, 41
local/universal 483
loyalty to 553–558
mission 241
mission of atonement 3017
mystery of 137–139
mystery of eucharist and 1055, 1175
organic body 502
power from Christ 1181
priestly character 1125, 2638, 3437
primordial sacrament 1102, 2239–40
reformation continuous 185, 3068
relation to all peoples 268
tradition and 221
unity
communion of faith and worship 182
effect of eucharist 1185–88, 1235
prayer services 186
variety and 411, 602
worshiping society 134, 182
Church, prayer of
Christ's mandate 3435
Christ's presence 1179, 1238
community character 3439
continuation of Christ's prayer 3436–37
liturgy of the hours 83–84, 3426
primary duty 3431
unity from the Holy Spirit 3438
Church Choirs (association)
Church's musical treasury 4206, 4216
service to Church 4215, 4221–23
churches
accessibility
bishop's responsibility 2660
eucharistic adoration 1280, 2200
tourists 2617, 4332
arrangement for Mass 528, 1643–70
care of 260, 1253, 2636, 4366
celebration of liturgy and 438
facilities for the faithful 1670
inventory of works of art 4330
nature 4360, 4369
particular calendar 3818, 3996
proper celebrations 4006
relics 4373
shared premises 180, 1066–69
symbolism 497, 1647, 4361, 4370–71
title of minor basilica 4344–59
titles (titulars) 3972, 4372
churches, blessing of
catechesis preceding 4429
consecration of altar 4433
edifices to be blessed 4428
Mass text 4431
minister 4429
proper day 4436
requisites 4432–33
vestments 4434

churches, building of
    auxiliary 2666
    bishop's responsibility 2665–68
    cornerstone 4367
    diocesan commission 2665
    fixed altar 4403
    norms 124
    number of altars 4404
    offerings of the faithful 2658
    revision of statutes 128
    rites beginning 4361–68
    training of seminarians 2734
churches, consecration of 1645
churches, dedication of
    adaptations 4386–87, 4397
    anniversary celebration 4394–95
    anointings 4384
    bishop as minister 4374
    catechesis preceding 4388
    celebration of eucharist 4385
    churches already in use 4396
    crosses on walls 4390
    depositing of relics 4382
    entrance rite 4379
    liturgy of the hours 4378
    liturgy of the word 4380
    Mass text 4376–77
    prayer of dedication 4383
    proper days 4375
    record 4393
    requisites 4389–93
    responsibilities of rector 4387
    rites dedicating altar 4384
    see also *Dedication of a Church and an Altar,
        Rite of*
churches, design of
    general plan 1669
    norms 382–391, 4371
    remodeling
        abuses 415, 417, 4327
        bishop's responsibilities 4331
        Church's artistic heritage 1253, 4331
    tabernacle 1285
Churches, local *see* local Churches
Churches, non-Catholic 183
Churches, particular *see* particular Churches
ciborium 1682
CIMS *see* Consociatio Internationalis Musicae
    Sacrae
cincture 1471, 1688
clergy, continuing education of 18, 2762–64
clergy, diocesan 195–196
clergy, liturgical formation of 14, 303–305,
    2480, *see also* liturgical formation in
    seminaries
clerical state, entrance into 2589, 2926
cloister *see* enclosure, papal
coadjutor bishop
    faculties 711
    name in eucharistic prayer 1972
coats-of-arms
    cardinals and bishops 4525
    minor basilicas 4353

collect *pro Papa* 4096
collects *see* opening prayer; prayers
collegiality
    bishops 2602
    liturgical celebrations 483
    priests 2603
colors *see* liturgical colors
commendation, rite of 1730, 3378, 3382
commentaries
    adaptation of celebrations 1988
    editions of liturgical books 925
    liturgical catechesis 35
    Masses with children 2156, 2180
    place in Mass 520
    priest celebrant 1401
commentator
    functions at Mass 1458
    liturgical function 29, 4134
    training of seminarians 2718
commingling (Order of Mass)
    communion rite 1446
    concelebration 1586
    Mass with a congregation 1503
    Mass without a congregation 1616
Commitment to Celibacy (rite)
    effective date 2531
    introduction 2948
    promulgation 2939
    see also celibacy, commitment to
Common of Saints
    Ordo cantus Missae 4279
    readings
        general 1850
        provisional lectionary 1875
        revision of particular propers 4037
        Simple Gradual 4269, 4308
communicatio in sacris 984
    Catholics and Eastern Orthodox Christians
        attendance at liturgical services 1004
        endorsement 178, 993, 995, 1026
        eucharistic sharing 999, 1001, 1028
        godparents 1002, 1040
        marriages 1003
        precedence and vesture of ministers
            1005
        reciprocity 997, 1000
        sacramental sharing 996–998, 1000
        shared facilities 1006
    Catholics and Western Christians
        attendance at worship services 1013
        eucharistic sharing 1049–50
        godparents 1011, 1039
        limitation 1009, 1027
        liturgical offices 1010
        marriages 1012
        precedence and vesture of ministers
            1014
        sacramental sharing 1009, 1022
        shared facilities 1015
    Christian unity and 186, 992, 1021, 1025
    documents governing 1065
    goal desired 1093
    liturgical worship 985
    reception into full communion 2480

regulation by bishop 2657
communicatio in spiritualibus 983
  appropriateness 979
  reciprocity 981
  safeguards 982
  shared prayer services 1065
communion (Order of Mass)
  arrangement (prior to 1969) 459
  concelebration 1582–96
  elements 1446
  Mass with a congregation 524, 1500–12
  Mass without a congregation 1614–20
  Masses with children 2167, 2187
  see also communion antiphon; communion
    song
communion, minister of 524
  acolyte 1532, 2095
  celebrant of Mass 1260, 1507
  communion outside Mass 1262, 2093
  communion under both kinds 524, 1634,
    1636, 1639, 1641, 2115
  deacon 1527, 2095, 3349
  laypersons 524, 2041–42, 2048, 2070
  special ministers *see* special ministers of
    communion
  vestments 3401
  women religious 2035, 2039–40
communion, reception of
  approach of communicants 1412
  Catholic teaching 1631
  Christ's initiative 1316
  communion under both kinds *see*
    communion under both kinds
  communion under one kind 55, 2056–57,
    2059, 2099, 2109
  concelebrants 1587–96
  dispositions of communicants 1298–1301,
    2101
  eucharistic fast *see* eucharistic fast
  eucharistic participation 55, 1046, 1260,
    2109, 2128
  facilitation 2073–88
  formulary 340, 1507, 2034
  frequency 1266
  hosts consecrated at same Mass 55, 1284,
    1446, 2198
  in the hand *see* communion in the hand
  kneeling/standing for 1263
  Masses for the dead 1729
  outside Mass *see* communion outside Mass
  repetition on same day
    concelebration 1808
    occasions 352, 460, 1257, 2084
    traditional discipline 2083
    viaticum 1268
  sacrament of penance and 1264, 1332–33,
    1335, 2101, 3150, *see also* first confession
    of children
  short rite of Christian initiation 2444
  sick people
    form of wine alone 1269
    union with community 1270
    see also eucharistic fast; viaticum
  special occasions 1265
  thanksgiving 461, 2103

time of day 744, 939, 2669
tradition of reverence 2055, 2087
use of communion plate 1507
communion antiphon
  Mass without a congregation 1618
  reader 1542
  recitation 1446
  sources 516
communion in the hand
  ancient usage 2055
  bishop's report 2058, 2069, 2104
  catechesis preceding 2064, 2088, 2093,
    2099
  communion by intinction and 2068
  communion outside Mass 2099
  complaints of irreverence 2104
  gradual introduction 2065
  letter of indult 2062–69
  procedure 2066
  respect for traditional manner 2063
  reverence 2065, 2087–88
  safeguards 2067
communion of saints
  atonement for sin 3159
  funerals 3373
  liturgical celebrations and 157, 276
communion outside Mass
  catechesis 2093
  dispositions of communicants 2101–03
  eucharistic fast 2102
  manner of reception 2099
  minister 2095
  permission 1262
  place 2096
  relation to Mass 2091
  rite
    hospitals 2036–38
    lay minister 2035, 2039
    liturgies of the word and 524
    preparations 2097
    promulgation 2089–90
    purifications 2100
    special ministers 2952
  time of day 2094
  vestments 2098
  see also *Holy Communion and Worship of the
    Eucharist outside Mass*
communion plate 1507, 2097
communion song
  accompanying rite 1407
  choice 1714
  manner of singing 4296
  Mass with a congregation 1509
  meaning 1446
  music for vernacular 1744
  Simple Gradual 4265, 4271, 4274, 4310
communion under both kinds
  catechesis preceding 524, 1631, 2106, 2114
  concelebrants 1590–93
  concession 1389
    extension 2109–15
    restrictions 524, 2112
  deacon at concelebration 1809
  home Masses 2128

manner of administration 524, 1590–93, 1596, 1636–42, 2115
Mass with a congregation 1508
Masses with special groups 2128
ministers 524, 1527, 1536, 1634, 1636, 1639, 1641, 2115
occasions 1261, 1632, 2108, 2110
preparations 1633, 2107
priests at chrism Mass 2557–58
restoration 55, 2054, 2059
seminarians 2803
sign value 1261, 1630, 2109
trial period 435

Communion under Both Kinds, Rite of
introduction 2105–07
promulgation 1793

community, sense of
new pedagogy 499–502
hierarchy and 411, 436

community Mass
concelebration 57, 1466, 1814
language 810–811, 3403
manner of celebration 1466

competentes (catechumens) 2351, 2405, 2414

compline
celebration with congregation 468
revision 89
see also night prayer

composers
criteria 121, 4230, 4249
melodies for sacred ministers 4177
melodies for vernacular texts 4239
respect for tradition 480
responsibilities 4221, 4234

concelebrants
chairs 1810
ministerial functions 1550, 1808
number 1797–98
place 1797
vestments 473, 526, 1551, 1805, 1810, 4540

concelebration
anniversary of dedication of cathedral 4394
bishop with priests 1547, 2558, 3797, 3853, 4458
blessing of an abbot 3280–81
celebration before or after 1548
chrism Mass 2556, 2558, 3797, 3853
communion rite 1582–96
communities of priests 1276
concession 57, 1793
concluding rite 1597–98
confirmation 2522
consecration of a bishop 1798
conventual or community Mass 1466, 1814
dedication of a church 4377
eucharistic bread 1277
eucharistic prayer 1558–81, 1934, 1937, 1940
exclusion from 1546, 1801
gestures 1806–07
individual celebration and 57, 414, 1794, 1816
introductory rites 1551–54
liturgy of the word 1554–55

Masses with children 2020
norms obligatory 1799
number on same day 1276, 1544, 1795
occasions 57, 1543, 1794, 1798
place of assisting ministers 1809
preeminent manifestation of Church 1792, 1814
preparations 1810
prior catechesis 1804
recitation of texts 1806–07
regulation 57, 1353–54, 1545, 1796–97, 1816
rite decreed 57, 1793
seminaries 307, 2695, 2802
symbol of unity 57, 414, 1276, 1449, 1543, 1792, 1794
trial period for rite 435

Concelebration, Rite of
introduction 1794–1810
promulgation 1788–93

concluding prayer (liturgy of the hours) 3627–30
daytime hours 3510, 3630
morning and evening prayer 3483, 3629
night prayer 3520, 3628
office of readings 3499, 3628
options 3681
singing 3714
vigils 3503

concluding rites (Order of Mass)
elements 1447
Mass with a congregation 1529–31
Mass without a congregation 1621
omission 1516

conferences of bishops
adaptation by 40, 482
altar 1653, 4406
baptismal rites 2279–82, 2308
choral vesture 4537
Christian initiation of adults 2391–92
confirmation rite 2525–26
cultural traditions 2279
dedication of an altar 4421
dedication of a church 4386
Directory of Masses with Children 2138
eucharistic celebrations 1396, 1411, 2166
eucharistic worship 2204
funeral rites 3380–81, 3393–94
furnishings 1678
General Instruction of the Roman Missal 1740
general intercessions 1908
gestures 2392
hymns of liturgy of the hours 3608
incipit of readings 1864
introductions (*praenotanda*) 2279
liturgical books 38
liturgical colors 469, 1698
liturgy of the hours 3614
marriage rites 77, 2983
Masses with children 2033
optional patristic lectionaries 3592
particular rituals 3358
rite of anointing 3358

rite of penance 3103
rogation and ember days 3812, 4033
sign of peace 1446
transference of solemnities 4031
translations 890
vessels 1680
vestments 526, 1694–95
liturgical books and
   adaptations 38, 529, 885, 2280
   composition of new texts 3103
   copyright 934
   editio typica 919
   format 3393
   lectionaries for children 2176
   optional patristic lectionaries 3716
   particular rituals 63
   publication 485, 926, 935
   weekday lectionaries 1820
liturgical rites and
   catechesis for confirmation 2521
   duration of catechumenate 2347
   Eucharistic Prayer for Masses of
      Reconciliation 2025
   new eucharistic prayers 1979
   reception of "sympathizers" 2339,
      2392
music and
   approval 517
   eucharistic prayer 2011
   instruments 120
   Order of Mass 517, 1737
   rite of baptism 2282
   Roman Missal 1744
   vernacular texts 334, 4176, 4179
norms on
   approval of *acta* 313
   confirmation of *acta* 321
   convener 317
   enactment of decrees 320, 616
   interconference relations 755
   juridic status and power 199–201
   kinds 315, 755
   liturgical commission 44
   loyalty to Holy See 3146
   membership 288, 316
   president 218
   promulgation of decrees 323
   relations with mixed commissions
      888, 890
   reports to Consilium 615–616
   voting rights of members 319
pastoral responsibilities
   migrants 2627
   missions 252, 759
   new ministries 2923
   tourists 3832
permanent diaconate and
   dress of deacons 2545
   formation program 2551–52, 2587
   liturgy of the hours 2541, 3460
   missions 248
   restoration in territory 2535
   spiritual life of deacons 2540
regulation of liturgy 22, 288
   communicatio in sacris 186
   communion in the hand 2060–61, 2099

communion under both kinds 1632,
   2111
enactment of decrees 616
exclusion of discrimination 326
experiments 40, 405, 441, 481, 530
first confession of children 1120
General Roman Calendar 1774
introduction of vernacular 6, 617–618
lay preachers 619, 2960
liturgical centers and periodicals 423
liturgical reform 302, 669, 672
mixed marriages 3009
penitential days and practices 3026
readings for Mass 1708, 1740, 1850,
   2175
reports to Consilium 615–616
seminary course in liturgy 2822, 2824
time of baptism for children 2309
use of Order of Mass 1739
women readers 1740
translations 287, 332, 839
   ad interim lectionary 1748
   adaptations in 890
   approval 36, 485, 882–883, 913
   eucharistic prayers 1930, 2007
   eucharistic worship 2204
   Lectionary for Mass 1747, 1771, 1842,
      1870, 1877
   little offices 375
   Liturgy of the Hours 1771, 3429
   mixed commissions 888, 890
   new rites 885
   Order of Mass 1734–35
   Pastoral Care of the Sick . . . 3319, 3358,
      3364
   prayers 518, 838–861, 871
   Rite of Baptism for Children 2249, 2316
   Rite of Blessing of an Abbot or Abbess
      3276
   Rite of Blessing of Oils . . . 3860
   Rite of Christian Initiation of Adults 2327
   Rite of Consecration to a Life of Virginity
      3852
   *Rite of Dedication of a Church and an
      Altar* 4360
   Rite of Funerals 3372, 3393
   Rite of Institution of Readers . . . 2531
   Rite of Penance 3065
   Roman Missal 1742, 1746, 1754, 1765,
      1771
   Simple Gradual 832
vernacular in liturgy 36, 474, 912
   decrees on 322
   gradual introduction 618
   Mass 349
   music 334, 4176, 4179
   report to Consilium 617
confession
   benefits 2247, 3118, 3134
   bishop's vigilance 3139
   communal celebrations of penance 3093
   danger of death 3350
   essential part of sacrament 3071, 3083
   false teaching on 1227
   frequency 3050, 3072, 3126
   general absolution and 3045, 3099, 3130

ministry of priests 2247
need 562, 598
obligation 3039, 3057, 3072, 3096, 3133, 3139
pastor's responsibility 196
provision of confessors 3042, 3047
reception of baptized Christians 2484
recordings and publication of 3060–62
reform of liturgy and 3119
trust in use 3122

confessional, retention of 3113

confessors
authorized 3074
commitment to ministry 3075, 3113
commutation of requisites for indulgence 3226
danger of death 3074
jurisdiction in religious institutes 945
priests of exempt religious institutes 3056
provisions for women religious 738, 3036, 3054
qualifications 3075
seal of confession 3075

confirmation
apostolate of laity 232
candidates
age of children 2520
preparation 2512–13
qualifications 2521
Christian initiation of adults 2361
Christian witness 245
Council of Trent 2504
dignity 2510–11
effects 141, 1104, 2251, 2502, 2509
essential elements 2503–07, 2518, 2529
first communion and 2522
minister
adaptation of rite 2527
authorization by law 2516
bishop 2516, 2522, 2527, 2657
chaplains 724, 2633, 2669
danger of death 2516, 3351
Eastern Churches 167–168
emergency baptism 2306
priests assisting 2373, 2517
reception of baptized Christians 2483
rites of Christian initiation 2444, 2473
offices and ministries 2512–17
parish record 2523
postponement 2383, 2521
renewal of baptismal promises 357, 2526
rite
celebration 2518–24
danger of death 2521, 3351
provisional form 356–359
requisites 2528
revision 71, 2509
vestments 356, 358
within/outside Mass 71, 282, 356, 2522
sacramental character 2502, 2518
sacramental signs 2518
sacraments of Christian initiation 71, 2361, 2500, 2502
sponsors 2514–15

Confirmation, Rite of

adaptations 2525–27
approval 2499–2507
effective date 2530
introduction 2510–28
process of revision 2500
promulgation 2509
translation of sacramental form 910

congregation
chairs and benches for 1663
incensation at Mass 1625
kneeling, standing, sitting 1263, 1452, 1740
place in church 390, 1647
proper liturgical functions 324, 1452
see also liturgical assembly; participation

congregational singing
bishop and 114
choir's responsibility 4219
development 290, 517, 4199, 4231–33, 4244
lack of 4216
ministry of reader 2930
Ordinary of Mass in Latin 1409, 4254, 4304
pastors' responsibility 4233
reform of liturgy 4238
seminaries 2691
service to community 4232
training for 4140

Congregations, Roman *see* SC Causes of Saints; SC Clergy, etc.

Consecration of Chrism, Rite of see Blessing of Oils and Consecrating the Chrism, Rite of

consecration of the Mass
bell for elevation 1499
celebrant's bow 1624
congregation kneeling 1411
eucharistic prayer 1445
formulary of consecration 1360
Masses with children 2000–01
typography of Roman Missal 1964
incensation 1625
institution narrative 1942

consecration to a life of virginity
Church's esteem 3252, 3297
nature and import 3253
requirements of those consecrated 3254–57
rite
form 3252
liturgy of the word 3261
Mass text 3260
minister 3258
revision 80, 3252
vestments 3262

Consecration to a Life of Virginity, Rite of
adaptations 3252
introduction 3253–62
promulgation 3252

Consilium
adaptation of liturgy 482
competence 625, 634
confirmation of translations 485, 883
cooperation with national commission 478
dissolution 689
ecumenical relations 629
establishment 278, 3417
hierarchy and 1944

list of members 614
liturgical experiments 639
liturgical innovations 412
new eucharistic prayers 637, 668
new Roman Missal 675
non-Catholic observers 629
ordination rites 2612
prevention of abuses 634
Protestant observers 1787
readings for Mass 1844
responsibilities 294, 412, 613–614, 620–621,
    630, 638
results of work 624, 628, 668–669, 688, 690
rite of concelebration 1793
SC Divine Worship and 683
Synod of Bishops 637
uniform translations 764

**Consociatio Internationalis Musicae Sacrae
(CIMS)**
establishment 4100–11
Gregorian chant 4244
international composers 4117
melodies for vernacular 4245
Universa Laus and 4119–21

Constitution on the Liturgy
achievements of Vatican II 132–134, 293
implementation
    first instruction 293–391
    Sacram Liturgiam 279–289
    second instruction 445–474
    third instruction 509–531
liturgical movement and 491, 578
Magna Charta of reform 690
new vision of liturgy 437
purpose 297, 393, 431, 787, 3596
renewal of Church 392
spiritual pedagogy 394
study and fulfillment 277

contemplative life
cloistered nuns 3297
concentration on prayer 3295
expression of nature of Church 3294
liturgy and 3293
prayer of the Church 3296

contemplatives
night office 3731
place in Church 205
prayer of the Church 3728

contrition *see* penance

conventual Mass
concelebration 57, 1543, 1794, 1814
language 808–809, 1773, 3403
manner of celebration 1466
prayers at foot of altar 3401

conversion
call of Christ 3138
catechumenate 2346, 2377, 2396, 2434
children of catechetical age 2458
Church's concern 3017, 3064, 3066
confession 2247
disposition for liturgy 9, 538
ecumenism 975
effect of liturgy 580
election of catechumens 2350
eucharist 607

meaning 3112
precatechumenate 2337
reconciliation 4090
sacrament of penance 3033, 3071
sacraments 3018
uncatechized adults 2447

converts 69, 2346, *see also* reception of baptized
Christians

cope, use of
eucharistic benediction 2218
general norm 1693
minister of confirmation 2528
priests at liturgy of the hours 3685

copyright 934

cornerstone, blessing of 369, 4367, *see also*
churches, dedication of

Corpus Christi
eucharistic procession 2220
institution of feast 1207
real presence honored 1378
transference to Sunday 3773, 3858

Credo
Gregorian melodies 4254
manner of singing 4290
pilgrimages 4355
see also profession of faith

cremation
burial preferred 3369–70, 3387
funeral rites permitted 3387
relaxation of canon law 3368

crosier *see* pastoral staff

cross, altar
incensation 1626
placement 386, 1660
use required 1649

cross, archiepiscopal 4477, 4492

cross, processional
acolyte 1533
placement 1474
use 4477

cultures and traditions
Latin America 582
links with Gospel 274
liturgical adaptation 37, 490, 2279
missionary activity 244

dalmatic, use of
bishop 4474
deacon 1690, 3986

day, liturgical *see* liturgical days

daytime prayer
choice of hours 89, 3419
choral office 3506
concluding prayer 3510, 3630
Mass before or after 3525, 3527
memorials 3666
obligation
    choral 3506
    individual 3507
proper psalms 3564
purpose 3504
retention of terce, sext, none 3734
seminaries 2699

solemnities of the saints 3659
structure 3508–13
times of celebration 3505
deacon
catechetical formation 1113
celibacy 2586
functions at Mass 1451
announcements 1529
concluding rites 1529–31
general intercessions 1898
introductory rites 1518–20
liturgy of the eucharist 1523–28
liturgy of the word 1521–22
reception of communion 1527, 1589, 1594, 1634
liturgical ministries
baptism 2260, 2263
blessings 2592
catechumenate for adults 2374
celebration of Bible services 35
communion outside Mass 2095
eucharistic exposition 2217
funerals 3391
homilist 329
presiding at liturgy of the hours 3685–86
viaticum 3349
ministry of service 149, 194
obligation of liturgy of the hours 3458–59
powers 2592
vestments
dalmatic 1696
stole 1692
see also diaconate
deacon, permanent
assistance at marriage 2536, 2548, 2549, 2559
catechumenate for adults 2374
celibate/married 2552–53
communion with bishop 2537, 2544
dress 2545
formation program 2551–55
functions 2536
institution as reader, acolyte 2582
liturgy of the hours 2541, 2588, 3460
ministry to tourists 2623
pastoral councils 2538
qualities 2539
spiritual life 2540, 2542
study 2543
see also diaconate, permanent
deacon, transitional
course of studies 2587
exercise of order 2820
functions 2547
institution as reader, acolyte 2582
liturgy of the hours 2588
deacons, ordination of
celebration of diocese 2818
commitment to celibacy 2948
declaration of freedom 2528
effect 2607
prior institution to ministries 2936
rite
approval 2612

determination of essentials 2609
promulgation 2613
revision 2607–08
death
Catholic faith 1138–40
mystery of 269
death, Christian
catechesis 3397
paschal mystery 3389
prayers for the dead 158
dedication of an altar *see* altar, dedication of
dedication of a church *see* churches, dedication of
dedication of a church, celebration of 4378, 4395
Dedication of a Church and an Altar, Rite of
adaptations 4386–87, 4397, 4421–22
introductions 4361–4445
promulgation 4360
Dedication of Saint Mary Major 3906
desacralization, repudiation of 512, 640, 673, 3742, 4234
devotions, popular
biblical orientation 3928
bishop's responsibilities 2660–61
catechesis 612
endorsement 161
eucharistic worship 1336, 2205
harmony with liturgy 3929–30
Latin America 582
music 4167, 4283
norms 13, 1287
religious 757
seminaries 17, 213, 306, 309, 2712, 2789
texts 2661
diaconate
celibacy 2586
Church's esteem 2553, 2576
entrance into clerical state 2926
norms 2576–91
sacred order 2533
diaconate, permanent
formation program 2587, 2623
men religious 2546
restoration 149
Eastern Churches 171
history 2577
mission lands 248
norms 2579
optional character 2535
revision of ordination rites 2607–08
dialects 912
dioceses
liturgical life 41–42, 194
proper celebrations 3775, 3973, 3976–77, 4004, *see also* calendars, diocesan
rule of bishop 191–194
translations of propers 767–775
see also local Churches
director of liturgy 1459
Directory for Masses with Children
introduction 2134–88
success 694

see also Masses with children

discrimination, exclusion of 32, 326, 390, 1663, 2658, 2978, 3392

dismissal rite (Order of Mass)
arrangement (prior to 1969), 462
deacon 1530
formulary 1447
Mass with a congregation 1514
Mass without a congregation 1621
music 4297, 4314
structure (prior to 1969), 462

dispensations, reserved 748–749

divine office *see* liturgy of the hours

dogmatic formulas 1168–69

doxology of eucharistic prayer 1445

drums, use of 440

dying, sacraments of the 3325–49

Easter
anticipated Mass 1257
celebration of Christian initiation 2334
celebration of paschal mystery 102, 3767
common date
Eastern Catholic Churches 174
Eastern Orthodox Churches 962
Roman Catholic Church 131, 1070–71, 1078–79
fixed date 131
liturgy of the hours 3643
preeminence 3784
reform of liturgy 246

Easter candle 2274

Easter duty
confession 3133
seamen 2670

Easter octave
celebration 3790
liturgy of the hours
memorials 3667
provisional texts 3725–26
solemnities 3778

Easter Proclamation *(Exsultet)*
music for vernacular 4314
place for proclaiming 1662

Easter season
duration 3789
Gospel of John 1849
liturgy of the hours 3581, 3644
Masses for neophytes 2367
meaning 3788
postbaptismal catechesis 2335
prayer for Christian unity 976
provisional lectionary 1830–32
readings for Mass 1849, 1857
Sundays 3771, 3789

Easter triduum
culmination of year 3784
duration 3785
liturgy of the hours 3638–43
musical instruments 4187

Easter Vigil
baptism of children 2312
baptismal water 2270

bishop celebrating baptism 2681
hour of celebration 3787
office of readings 3642
preeminence 3785, 3787
renewal of baptismal promises 2368
restoration 3755
sacraments of Christian initiation 2335, 2423, 2456, 2472, 2498

Eastern Catholic Churches 162–181
eucharist 1218
holydays 169, 173
language of liturgy 177
law of fast and abstinence 3028
liturgical heritage 133, 577
Marian devotion 3926
preservation of heritage 602, 604
rites safeguarded 165
study of liturgy 2745, 2827
synods 199

Eastern Orthodox Churches
Armenian Orthodox 1038
common date for Easter 962, 1070, 1078
communicatio in sacris 187, 993–1008
devotion to liturgy 187
ecumenical prayer services 989
ecumenism 187–188
Greek Orthodox 1018, 1091–93
links with Catholic Church 187, 993
Marian devotion 187, 3930
See of St. Mark of Alexandria 1051
Syrian Orthodox 1041
validity of baptism 966
validity of sacraments 187, 993

Ecumenical Directory I
application of norms 1019–23
binding force 1031
eucharistic sharing 1028, 1048
godparents 1040
Western Christians 1029

ecumenical prayer services
churches of Eastern Christians 989–990
desirability 986–987
ecumenical meetings 976
form of celebration 989
local ecumenism 1065
place of celebration 990
themes 988
vesture and precedence 991

ecumenism
baptism and 970–971
Catholic principles 182–184
common date for Easter 131, 174, 1070–71, 1078–79
communicatio in sacris see *communicatio in sacris*
dialogue 970–971, 1063
Eastern Orthodox Churches 178–181
educational aids 1035
eucharist 1237
eucharistic faith 1216
eucharistic sharing *see* eucharistic sharing
false interpretations 1228
higher education 1034–37
instruction in principles 1034
liturgical formation in seminaries 2842

Marian devotion 3930–31
Mass for deceased non-Catholics 1074–77
ministry in tourism 2621, 3834
mixed marriages 3000, 3011, 3014–15
ordination of women 1072–73
practice 185–186
prayers for unity 1035
program of study 1037
reception of baptized Christians 2378
reconciliation 4094
renewal in the Church 185
solemn prayers of Good Friday 3853
"soul of" 975
study of liturgy 2823
theological disciplines 1036
translations of Scripture 225

ecumenism, local 1065–69

ecumenism, spiritual
prayer 1065
promotion 975

editio typica 919

elderly, the
anointing of the sick 3331
communion 2092
eucharistic fast 2085–86

election (catechumenate for adults)
acceptance of candidates 2412
bishop presiding 2371
duties of celebrant 2413
enrollment of names 2350
meaning 2349
nonapplicability to baptized 2493
participation of community 2368, 2410
purpose 2405
qualifications of candidates 2350, 2409
readings 2386
role of godparents 2411
time of celebration
    first Sunday of Lent 2376, 2378, 2498,
        2414
    other times 2385, 2388

ember days
adaptation 3810
celebration 4033
purpose 3811
votive Masses 3831

embolism (Order of Mass)
concelebration 1583
Lord's Prayer 1446
Mass with a congregation 1501
Mass without a congregation 1614
singing of doxology 4294

Enchiridion Indulgentiarum
promulgation of new edition 3192
revision 3179

enclosure, papal 3299

enrollment of names *see* election
(catechumenate for adults)

entrance antiphon (Order of Mass)
Mass without a congregation 1605
particular propers 4035
sources 516

**entrance into order of catechumens
(catechumenate for adults)**

acceptance of candidates 2343
adaptation of rite 2392
celebration of rite 2399
children of catechetical age 2466–67
nonapplicability to baptized 2343
participation of community 2397
preparatory period 2396
qualifications of candidates 2342
registering of names 2344
sponsors 2398
status of catechumens 2345
time 2377, 2387, 2495
welcoming rite 2493

entrance procession
acolyte 1533
concelebration 1552
deacon 1518
incensation 1625
Masses with children 2167
order of ministers 1472
reader 1538

entrance song (Order of Mass)
accompanying rite 1407
choice 1714
entrance procession 1473
manner of singing 1416
music for vernacular 1744
Ordo cantus Missae 4280
purpose 1415
Simple Gradual 4265, 4271

ephphetha **rite**
catechumenate for adults 2405
connection with baptism 2497

epiclesis (Order of Mass) 1445, 1956

Epiphany
day of celebration 3803
prayer for Christian unity 976
transference to Sunday 3773, 3803
    concurrence with Baptism of the Lord
        3873
    Mass and office 3858

episcopal conferences *see* conferences of
bishops

episcopate 145–147

eschatology, Catholic teaching on 1131–40

eucharist, mystery of 47–58
actuality in Mass 1171
bond of charity 1307
bread of life 1327–28
call to conversion 1335
center of Church's life 1235
center of liturgy 298, 1147, 1230
center of local Church 1236
center of sacramental life 1105
Christian initiation 2251, 2502
Christian life 1324
Church's care 2073, 2089
communion of Mystical Body 139
devotion to Sacred Heart 3852
dignity of the faithful 1211
documents of the Church 1232
dogmatic formulas 1168
ecumenism 1216–19

evangelization and 260, 560, 1325
facets 1309–11
faith of other Churches 1237
false interpretations 1143, 1154, 1226
human needs 1313–14
institution 47
mystery of Church 1043–44, 1055
mystery of faith 1159–69, 1315, 1318
other truths implied 1142
preeminence 260, 509, 605, 1716, 2193
principles of catechesis 1234–44
real presence *see* real presence
remedy for sin 2101, 3067
sacrament of penance 1330, 1332, 1335
sacramental symbolism 1184–87, 1233,
    2243
sacrifice and sacrament 1096, 1126, 1144,
    1149, 1171–78, 1306, 1312, 1317, 1319,
    1329, 2126
Scripture and 229, 267
seminarians 2801
sign and cause of unity 182, 1044,
    1185–87, 1235, 1302–03, 1307, 1326,
    1330, 1337
social aspects 1297, 1326, 1328, 2225
spiritual food 1047, 1055
spiritual wealth of Church 1323, 1334
teaching of Church 1330
transubstantiation *see* transubstantiation

eucharistic benediction
following Mass 1295
ministers 2217, 2931
vestments 2218
see also eucharistic exposition

eucharistic bread
care 1675
communion by intinction and 1633, 1810
concelebration 1277, 1810
Masses with special groups 2131
particles *see* hosts, particles of
paten for consecration 1683
qualities 523, 1672–73

eucharistic celebrations
adaptation 1978
aesthetic aspect 4319
agapē and 235, 438
arbitrary innovations 433
arrangement of churches 1253
bishop's responsibilities 146, 1271, 1449
broadcasts 1251
celebrant's responsibilities 1991
center of Christian life 1391
children *see* Masses with children
choice of texts 1703–15, 1976
Church's care 1376, 1788
combining with liturgy of the hours
    3523–28
communio of the Church 1046
communion events 1320
communion of saints 158
community and 200–201, 261, 1045, 1245,
    1247, 1404
conversion 607
distinction of ministries 1448, 1461–62,
    1813

ecclesial nature 137, 1048, 1271, 1791,
    1985, 2126
experiments 530
extension by liturgy of the hours 3442
family eucharistic meals and 433, 438
fragmentation 1969
funerals 3373
gravity and dignity 576, 1391–96
lay preaching 2956, 2958
manner of celebration 1249
meetings on Christian life 1259
ministry of priests 260
modes of Christ's presence 1378, 1397
non-Catholic participation *see communicatio
    in sacris*
observance of law 1274
office of the faithful 1452
outward signs 1395
parish life 4249
participation 48, 1393, 1975
pastors' responsibility 196
photographs 1252
place 438, 527, 1643, 1650, 2124
planning 1463, 1703
pledge of future glory 1321
private homes 438
provisional texts 3724
religious communities 3308
sacrifice of Christ 1789
seminaries 307, 2694–96, 2770, 2802
sign language for the deaf 2119
silence 1992
singing
    degrees of solemnity 4150–52
    importance 1409
    low Mass 4157
    preferred form of celebration 4148
    quality of songs 4157
    substitution of songs 4153
social effects 3844
special groups *see* Masses with special
    groups
tourists 2615
uniformity in standing, sitting, kneeling
    1410–11, 1452
unity of Church 1322–26, 2120
unity of priesthood 1790
universal priesthood 141
weekdays 1258
welcome to visitors 1248
youth Masses 508

eucharistic congresses
catechesis 2225
mode of celebration 2226
preparation 2225
purpose 1296, 2223
study programs 2224
symbols of ecclesial unity 1304

eucharistic exposition
altar decorations 2208, 2211
annual prolongation 1292, 2212
benediction 2215
celebration of Mass during 2209
duration 1293–95, 2215
forty hours 1325, 2190
genuflections 2210

interruption 1290, 1294, 2214
minister 2217, 2536, 2931
relation to Mass 1289, 2208
rite 1291
rite of reposition 2214
vestments 2218

eucharistic fast
Catechism of St. Pius X 2118
celebrants 714
communion outside Mass 2102
computation of time 2116
dispensation reserved 750
Masses with special groups 2131
mitigation 2102, 2117
priest celebrants 714, 2116
sick people 2085–86
SC Discipline of the Sacraments 653
viaticum 2085

eucharistic prayer
center of eucharistic celebration 1444
chief presidential prayer 1400
choice of text 1712
component elements 1445, 1947
introductory comments 1982
lay ministers 524
Mass of religious profession 3238
Mass with a congregation 1498–99
Mass without a congregation 1613
Masses for deceased non-Catholics 1077
Masses with children 2185
meaning 1946, 1982
music in vernacular editions 4314
name of bishop 1970–74
parts sung 456
place of deacon 1524
proper prefaces 1712
proposal of new texts 694
recitation by priest alone 522
recitation in concelebration 1558–60
regional formularies 1979
revision of Roman Missal 1360
ritual Masses 1983
structure 1983
tone of celebrant 1991
typography of Roman Missal 1964
unauthorized texts 1786, 1978, 1980, 1985
use of vernacular 474
variable elements 1950–53, 1984
variety of texts 1949
words of consecration 1360

Eucharistic Prayer I
appropriate use 1712, 1931, 1959
approval 1360
characteristics 1955
limiting of intercessions 521
recitation in concelebration 1561–68
singing 1932

Eucharistic Prayer II
anaphora of Hippolytus 1957
appropriate use 1712, 1933, 1960
approval 1360
characteristics 1957
recitation in concelebration 1569–72, 1934
singing 1935

Eucharistic Prayer III
appropriate use 1712, 1936
approval 1360
characteristics 1957
preface 1961
recitation in concelebration 1573–76, 1957
singing 1938

Eucharistic Prayer IV
appropriate use 1712, 1939, 1962
approval 1360
characteristics 1957
preface 1712, 1962
recitation in concelebration 1577–81, 1940
singing 1941

Eucharistic Prayers for Masses of Reconciliation
approval 1995
choice 1996
editions of Roman Missal 2031
elements 2026
Holy Year (1975) 2024
translation 1997
use 2028, 2030
vernacular publication 2027

Eucharistic Prayers for Masses with Children
acclamations 2005
approval 1995
choice 1996
Latin text 2009
purpose 1999
style of language 2004
three texts 2021–23
translation 1997, 2007–10
use 1998, 2012–20, 2028–29

Eucharistic Prayers II–IV
catechesis on meaning 1956–57, 1969
criteria of composition 1956–57
guildelines for catechesis 1945–63
name of bishop 1965
promulgation 1930
sacrificial nature of Mass 700

eucharistic processions
eucharistic congresses 2226
manner 2222
meaning 2219
norms 1288
time 2221

eucharistic reservation
aboard ship 2669
chapel *see* chapel of reservation
external signs 2203
home of bishop 743
place 387, 416, 1281–86, 1666–67, 2201–03
prayer 1279
purpose 1278, 2089, 2197–2200
real presence 1098, 1212, 2194
renewal of hosts 2199
shared premises and 1068
tabernacle *see* tabernacle
veil and lamp 1286

eucharistic sharing
Catholic position 1024–33, 1055
celebration of mixed marriages 3014

competent authority 1050, 1058
conditions 1009, 1022–23, 1030, 1048,
    1058–59
Eastern Christians 179
Eastern/Western Christians 1049, 1060
ecclesial communion 1055
Ecumenical Directory I 1048
expression of unity 1056
forms of the practice 1024
goal desired 1033, 1062, 1093
Protestant and Anglican Christians 1019,
    1023
special cases 1042–50, 1052–63
Western Christians 1028
eucharistic wine
care 1675
qualities 1674
water substituted 1676
eucharistic worship
bishop's responsibilities 2660
life of the Church 1302–05
perennial validity 1304
priestly life 267
promotion 1208–20
seminarians 2710, 2806
eucharistic worship outside Mass 1287–96
accessibility of churches 2200
adaptation 2204
basis 1232, 2089
contemporary relevance 2191
correlation with Mass 1289, 2089, 2190,
    2193–96, 2205
ecclesial nature 2190
eucharistic reservation 2197
forms 2205–26
forty-hours devotion 1325
historical development 1298
popular devotions 1336
prayer before blessed sacrament 2207
promulgation of rites 2089–90
real presence 1223, 2189
social implications 1213–14
visits 1279, 2206
worship of *latria* 267, 1200–07, 1232, 1304,
    1323, 2089, 2126, 2195
see also *Holy Communion and Worship of the
    Eucharist outside Mass*
eulogy, prohibition of 1728
evangelization 1883–84
eucharist 1325
liturgy 581, 701
role of music 4246–47
sacraments 600, 2571
**evangelization and precatechumenate, period
of**
meaning 2334, 2336–37
pastors' responsibility 2340
role of community 2368
"sympathizers" 2339
evening Mass 1257
concurrence of days of precept 3986
tourists 2617
see also holydays; Sunday Mass
evening prayer
canticles 3567–68

celebration in cathedral 308, 2700
celebration in common 3470
concluding formulary 3484
concluding prayer 3483, 3629
concurrence of celebrations 3827, 3839
intercessions 3425, 3610
longer reading 3572
Lord's Prayer 3624
Mass before or after 3526, 3527
memorials 3665, 3669
newly canonized saints 3955
parish celebration 100, 2656, 3451–53
principal hour 89, 3419, 3467, 3470
purpose 3468
responsory 3479, 3602, 3711
seminaries 2698, 2809
singing 3702, 3711
structure 3471–84
Sunday celebration 3634, 3627
evening prayer I
proper psalms 3564
solemnities of saints 3655–56
time of celebration 3526
evening prayer II
proper psalms 3564
solemnities of saints 3656
exorcisms
catechesis of the baptized 2496
celebration of rite 2419
exorcisms, major 2496
exorcisms, minor 2371, 2403
experiments, liturgical
bishop's regulation 481, 2654
competent authority 40, 405, 436, 441,
    530, 639, 790
conferences of bishops 405, 481
Consilium 668
innovations
    altar servers 412
    desacralization 512
    eucharistic prayers 1786, 1978
    false justification 480
    loyalty to Church and 601
    music 4208, 4216
    repudiation 23, 135, 289, 404, 413,
        433–434, 506, 510, 557, 600, 639,
        2133
    rites of Mass 439
    texts 694
    translations 480
    work of the Consilium and 412
lawful/unlawful 435–436
liturgical commissions 44, 337, 479
norms 405, 482
review in Holy Year 1975 4093
success 628
exposition see eucharistic exposition
Exsultet see Easter Proclamation
extreme unction 73, see also anointing of the
sick
family
celebration of liturgy of the hours 3457
church of the household 141, 237

formation of children 2143
holiness 271
liturgical life 237
family life, promotion of 273
family rosary 3940–42
farewell, rite of *see* final commendation, rite of
fast
Ash Wednesday 3795
Good Friday 3786
Holy Saturday 3786
law
age 3024
days 3022
dispensation 2670, 3027
Eastern Catholic Churches 3028
meaning 3023
paschal fast 110
privileges and indults 3025
other penitential practices and 3876
Fathers of the Church
optional lectionaries 3736–38
readings in liturgy of the hours 92, 3590,
3594–95
readings in penitential services 3101
study of liturgy 2790
tradition 221
understanding of Scripture 226
feasts
celebration 3779
choice of Mass 1705
readings for Mass 1709, 1850, 1880
readings in liturgy of the hours 3584
feasts of the Lord
celebration of 3779
liturgy of the hours 3635, 3547, 3667
precedence 108
feasts of the Lord on Sunday
celebration 3772–73
evening prayer I 3526
Fidelium animae 3401
final blessing (Order of Mass) 1447
archbishop 4492
Mass of religious profession 3238
Mass with a congregation 1514
Mass without a congregation 1621
Mass without a server 1601
Masses with children 2187
pontifical Mass 4491
final commendation, rite of (funerals) 1730,
3378, 3382
first communion
catechesis 2145
confirmation and 2522
need of prior confession 3149
first confession of children
age of discretion 1116
bishops' vigilance 3140
danger of delay 3145
dissension in Church 3147–48
experiments 1119–20, 3142, 3151
General Catechetical Directory 3141
retention of traditional practice 1120,
2246, 3144

St. Pius X 3141, 3143
value 3126, 3149–50
forty hours devotion 1325, 2190, *see also*
eucharistic exposition
funeral Mass
days permitted 1726, 3378
homily 1788
pastoral planning 1731
rite of final commendation 1730, 3378,
3382
second model of rite 3379
times permitted 3378
funerals
adaptation 3393–94
catechesis on psalms 3384
celebration on eve of prohibited day 3371
children 82, 3385
Christian attitude 3374
eschatology and 1136
eulogy forbidden 1728
exclusion of discrimination 3392
final commendation 1730, 3378, 3382
ministers 3390
priest's preparations 3390, 3395–96
priest's responsibilities 3389, 3397
non-Catholic or nonpracticing mourners
1731, 3390
participation of community 3388–89
paschal character 81, 3373, 3389
public sinners 3399
readings 3383
respect for body of deceased 3375
revision of rites 82, 3372
rites for those cremated 3387
three models 3376–80
Funerals, Rite of
adaptation 3393–94
introduction 3373–97
promulgation 3372
furnishings, sacred
adaptation 128, 526, 1677
Masses with special groups 2132
qualities 128, 526, 1643, 1677–78, 1701–02,
4371
revision of laws 128
seminaries 305

general absolution *see* absolution, sacramental
**General Instruction of the Liturgy of the
Hours**
liturgical formation in seminaries 2810,
2825
major principles 3731
publication 3430
General Instruction of the Roman Missal
adaptations 1740
application (*Liturgicae instaurationes*)
512–528
changes
1970 list 1371
1972 list 1372
choice of texts 1987
communion under both kinds 2115
interpretations
no. 42 1768

no. 76 1814
no. 158 1815
pastoral-liturgical life 509
promulgation 1367
purpose and scope 1359, 1396
resource for catechesis 1780
study by seminarians 2825
teaching on the Mass 699

general intercessions
adaptation 1905–08, 1990
anticipated Mass of precept 1257, 3829–30,
3837
baptism of children 2301
catechumens 1893
celebrant's part 1897–98, 1904
characteristics 1436, 1892
Christian initiation of adults 2428
conclusion 1904
congregation's part 1902–03
deacon 1522, 1898
dedication of a church 4381
eucharist prayer and 521, 1983
evening prayer 3425
freedom in use 1905–08
Good Friday prayers 1917
history 1912–28
imperated prayer 452
intentions
Christian unity 978
local community 521
minister 1437, 1898
number 1910
sequence 1436, 1899
structure 1901
votive intentions 1436, 1900
Latin Mass 1773
lauds and vespers 467
Lent (1966) 1929
litanies and 1918
manner of celebration 348
Mass with a congregation 1435, 1489
Mass without a congregation 1610
Masses with children 2155
Masses with special groups 2127
Masses with tourists 2617
nature and pastoral value 1891–95
participation 1406
parts 1896
place in liturgical celebrations 1894
reader 1541, 2930
restoration 53, 1890, 1895
singing 1890, 4291
terminology 1911
use of vernacular 54
varied uses in liturgy 1893

**General Norms for the Liturgical Year and the
Calendar**
approval 3754–57
effective date 1774
promulgation 3758
see also Calendar, General Roman;
liturgical year

General Roman Calendar *see* Calendar,
General Roman

genuflections
before blessed sacrament 2210
celebrant at Mass 453, 1623
concelebration 1806–07
pontifical Mass 4482

gestures
concelebration 1559–81, 1806–07
Masses with children 2166
Masses with special groups 2132
quality 4205
significance 487–488

Gloria **(Order of Mass)**
independent rite 1407
Mass with a congregation 1477
Mass without a congregation 1605
meaning and use 1421
singing
Amen 4304
manner 4282
Masses with children 2164
vernacular 4313

Gloria Patri 4271

Glory to the Father **(liturgy of the hours)**
3553–55

godparents 2290
catechesis of children 2144
catechumenate for adults 246, 2370
children of catechetical age 2475
choice 2259, 2406
duties 67, 2370
offices
celebration of baptism 2258
preparation for baptism 2257
rite of election 2411
qualifications 2259, 2370
separated Christians as 1002, 1011,
1039–40, 2259
sponsors at confirmation 2514
see also sponsors

Good Friday
communion outside Mass 2094
fast and abstinence 110, 3022, 3786, 3876
office of readings 3640
prayer for Christian unity 976
revision of solemn prayers 3853

gospel acclamation (Order of Mass)
Lent 1851
particular propers 4036

gospel reading (Order of Mass)
conclusion 4289
deacon's functions 1521
exclusion from liturgy of the hours 3574
gospel of Christ's passion 2918
incensation 1521, 1625
Mass with a congregation 342, 1483–85
Mass without a congregation 1608
Masses with special groups 2127
procession 1521
reverence 1425
weekdays 1846

Gospels, historical truth of 1817

Graduale Romanum
adaptation 4275

General Roman Calendar and 4276
norms for singing Mass 4279
reform 4276–79
revision of Roman Missal 1364
Simple Gradual and 4258–59, 4262

Graduale simplex
adaptation of chants 833
norms for translations 831–834
promulgation
1st *editio typica* 4256
2nd *editio typica* 4268, 4307
see also *Simple Gradual, The*

greetings at Mass
entrance rites 1418
Mass with a congregation 1476
Mass without a congregation 1603
Mass without a server 1601

Gregorian chant
bishops' promotion 4242
bond of unity 4199, 4237, 4243
chants for Roman Missal (1964) 4255
cultivation 828, 4173, 4191, 4241
desire to replace 3402
distinctive of Roman liturgy 4238
edition of simpler melodies 117, 4171,
4253, 4256–57, 4303
editions of Solesmes 1130, 4313
liturgy of the hours 3704
neo-Gregorian melodies
Ordo cantus Missae 4275
Simple Gradual 4262
Ordinary of Mass in Latin 4234–35, 4237,
4243, 4254, 4304
Ordo cantus Missae 4275, 4302
preservation 548, 3404, 4234, 4241,
4275–77, 4298
pride of place 116, 2692, 3704, 4171, 4216
seminarians 2692, 2725, 2798
Simple Gradual 4256–76
typical editions 117, 4257
value 4112, 4209, 4237
vernacular and 4241

Gregorian Masses 2228
Guéranger, Prosper 1129

habit, religious 3272–73
handicapped, the 2139
heresy, abjuration of
requirements 728
suppression 974, 2481

hierarchy
apostolate of the laity 240
sense of community and 411, 436

Hippolytus of Rome
Eucharistic Prayer II 1957
general intercessions 1915
ordination rites 2607

holiness, universal call to 154
Holy Communion and Worship of the
Eucharist outside Mass
introductions 2091–2103, 2193–2226
promulgation 2089–90

Holy Family 3772, 3801
Holy Name of Jesus 1855, 3801

holy orders
conferral outside cathedral 729
diaconate 2607
effects 1104, 2606
episcopacy 2606
exclusion of women 2595–96
hierarchic ministry 2568
meaning 141, 1104
new rites 2579
priesthood 2607
religious brothers 208, 210, 2546
rites *see* ordination, rites of
sacerdotal character
bishop 145
configuration to Christ's priesthood
257
permanence 2569
teaching of Church 1127
universal priesthood and 2604
Western, non-Catholic Churches 189

Holy Saturday
catechumens' preparation 2381
communion outside Mass 2094
night prayer 3641
office of readings 3640
paschal fast 110, 3786

Holy See
bishops and 710
conferences of bishops and 3146
liturgical experiments 441
regulation of liturgy 313
vernacular in Mass 350

Holy Spirit
charisms in the Church 232
Christian community 247
confirmation 2510–11
fulfillment of Christ's mission 2501
invocation in Divine Praises 4095
liturgical movement 43, 407, 579
Marian devotions 3924–25
paschal mystery 2361
prayer of the Church 3438
title (titular) of churches 4372
tradition 221, 3913

Holy Thursday
blessing of oils *see* oils, blessing of
chrism Mass *see* chrism Mass
communion outside Mass 2094
concelebration 57, 2556, 2558, 3797, 3853
evening Mass 2669
liturgy of the hours 3639
prayer for Christian unity 976
real presence 1378
renewal of priestly commitment 2763
repetition of communion 460

Holy Trinity 3772
holy water, sprinkling with 472, 3382, 4254
Holy Week
changes in rites (1965) 3853
Easter triduum 3784–87
liturgy of the hours
memorials 3667
provisional arrangements 465, 3725–26
participation 431–432
purpose 3797

solemnity 4165
weekdays 3782
Holy Year (1966) *see* Jubilee, extraordinary
(1966)
Holy Year (1975)
announcement 4070
declaration 4089–94
eucharistic prayer 1994, 2024
indulgences 4075, 4077, 4092
local Churches 4072, 4075, 4079
objectives 4071, 4073–76, 4078, 4090
Order for Celebration 4078–88
holydays
anticipated Mass
concession 3829–30
conditions 1257
text 3837
arrangement of readings 1845
concurrence with Sunday Mass 3838–41
Eastern Catholic Churches 169, 173
general intercessions, 53, 1895
homily 52, 281, 345
Mass *pro populo* 2230
Masses for tourists 3833
Masses with special groups 2131
observance 290, 543–544
participation in Mass 49
provision of services 291
singing 1467, 3701
suppression 4031–32
home Masses 438, 2125, 2655
homilist
catechist-minister of baptism 2310
deacon 329
laypersons 329, 513, 1768, 2957
Masses with children 2157
non-Catholics 1010
priest celebrant 1432
homily
adaptation of celebrations 1989
addressing children 2152
anticipated Mass of precept 1257, 3829–30,
3837
baptism of children 2301
bishop's teaching office 2643
catechesis 611
chrism Mass 2558
concelebration 1553
dedication of a church 4381
dialogue forbidden 513
effectiveness 1884
eucharistic celebrations 1249
funeral Mass 1728
integral part of liturgy 52, 347, 1399, 1431
liturgy of sacraments 611
Masses with children 2156, 2181
Masses with special groups 2127
ministry of the word 1099
morning and evening prayer 3477
obligatory character 52, 281, 345, 1388,
1432
penitential services 3090, 3101
place 1487
rite of marriage 362, 2973
rite of religious profession 3235

source 346
Sunday Mass in seminaries 307
vigils in liturgy of the hours 3503
see also preaching
hospitals
adaptation of rite of anointing 3361
celebration of baptism 2297
chaplains and pastors 2323
rite of communion 2036–38
hosts *see* eucharistic bread
hosts, particles of
communion in the hand 2067, 2088
falling at Mass 1629
Mass with a congregation 1510
purifications at Mass 458, 1627
houses of study
music 115
professor of liturgy 303
study of liturgy 16, 279
humeral veil 2218
hymns in the liturgy of the hours 93, 3603–08
daytime prayer 3509–10
morning and evening prayer 3472
office of readings 3491
options 3681
singing preferable 3710

illuminandi **(catechumens)** 4351
images
arrangement of churches 1668
excessive reduction 417
exclusion from altar 4407
limitation 125, 1668
placement 128
images, crowning of 3890–95
images, veneration of
lawfulness 161
theological basis 4323
Immaculate Conception 3889, 3904
Immaculate Heart of Mary 3883, 3906
imperated prayer, replacement of 452
incardination 2589
incensation
dedication of an altar 4419
dedication of a church 4384
funerals 3382
optional uses at Mass 1625
preparation of gifts 1495, 1535
rules 328
see also altar, incensation of
incense
entrance procession 1472
gospel reading 1483
symbolism 4384, 4419
incipit of readings 1864
inculturation
catechesis 586
see also adaptation
individualism 495
indulgences, doctrine of
basis
revelation 3155
teaching of Church 4091

partial indulgences
  classification 3170, 3197
  effect 3216
  meaning 3160
plenary indulgences
  applicability 3195, 3208
  meaning 3168, 3194
  requirements 3173–76, 3216–21
  toties quoties 3185, 3222
respect for tradition 3160, 3165
indulgences, practice of
  contemporary relevance 3162–65, 3167–87
  granting authority 3200–07, 3215, 3227
  lists
    publication 3207
    revision 3180, 3187
  origins 3161
  pious associations 3190
  record of concession 3208
  reform 3166
  religious institutes 3190
  revised norms 3193–3224
  works prescribed
    celebration of feasts 3188, 3208, 3957,
      3970
    commutation 3177
    pilgrimages 4091
    recitation of prayers 3154, 3224–25,
      3228
    use of religious articles 3153, 3187,
      3211
    visit to church or oratory 3182, 3191,
      3210, 3212, 4352
    works of precept 3223
indults, liturgical 4043–45
institution narrative (eucharistic prayer) 1445
Institution of Readers and Acolytes, Rite of
  effective date 2531
  introductions 2940–43
  promulgation 2939
institution to ministry
  candidates for diaconate, priesthood 2936
  celebration of rite 2817
  interstices 2584, 2935
  introduction of term 2924
  minister
    delegation 2964
    Ordinary 2934
  prerequisites 2933
  recipients' self-support 2937
  reserved to men 2932
  seminarians 2774
Instituto Litúrgico de Medellín 537
Inter Oecumenici
  Consilium 620, 624
  results 445
intercessions (eucharistic prayer) 1445
intercessions (liturgy of the hours) 3481,
  3609–23
  morning and evening prayer 3425, 3524,
    3611
  options 3681
  proper offices 4039
intercommunion *see* eucharistic sharing

International Association of Sacred Music *see*
  Consociatio Internationalis Musicae Sacrae
intervals (interstices) 2816, 2935
intinction *see* communion under both kinds
introductions (*praenotanda*)
  adaptation 2279
  particular rituals 63
  vernacular editions 884, 3114, 3358, 3393
introductory comments *see* commentaries
introductory rites (Order of Mass)
  concelebration 1551–53
  elements 1414
  functions
    acolyte 1533–34
    deacon 1518–20
  Mass with a congregation 1470–78
  Mass without a congregation 1603–06
  Masses with children 2173
invitations
  general intercessions 1892
  Masses with children 2156
  Pray, brothers and sisters 1497
invitatory (liturgy of the hours) 3464–66
  office of readings 3490
  proper offices 4039
Ite, Missa est
  Gregorian melodies 4254
  manner of singing 4297
Iubilate Deo
  preface 4243
  presentation to bishops 4237–42

jazz, exclusion of 427
Jewish-Catholic relations 1064
John XXIII
  music 4100
  unity of Christians 959
joint commissions *see* liturgical commissions,
  mixed
Joseph, St.
  feast of (1967) 3952
  solemnity of 3822
Jubilee, extraordinary (1966)
  bishops' role 4055
  days for celebration 4066
  diocesan cathedrals 4054
  extension 4067–69
  indulgences 3188, 4056–58
  Mass 812–814
  promulgation 2076, 4052, 4064–65
  purpose 4053

kissing of altar
  adaptation 1622
  celebrant at Mass 454
kissing of hand or objects 328
kneeling
  Masses with special groups 2132
  Order of Mass 1740
  reception of communion 1263
  uniformity 1410–11, 1452

Kyriale simplex
   arrangement in *Simple Gradual* 4304
   introduction 4254
   Ordo cantus Missae and 4303
   promulgation 4253–54
Kyriale Vaticanum 4254
Kyrie
   manner of singing 4254, 4280
   Mass with a congregation 1420, 1477
   Mass without a congregation 1605

laicization, norms on 2500–61, 2961
laity
   bishops and 153
   celebration of liturgy of the hours 100,
      3418, 3457
   charisms 232
   liturgical roles 240, 2921
   mission of Church 2953
   missionary activity 2921
   participation in ministry 239, 2965, *see also*
      lay ministers
   participation in preaching office 2157,
      2953–63
   place in Church 150–153
   presiding at celebrations 695
   priestly, prophetic, kingly office 151–152,
      231
   sacramentals 79
language, liturgical
   creation by use 856
   qualities 852, 854–856
   see also translations; vernacular in liturgy
last gospel, suppression of 340
Latin America
   evangelization 581
   liturgical books 895–896
   liturgical institutes 537
   liturgical reform 580–582
   new ministries 582
   popular religion 582
   separate translations 536
Latin language
   appendix to Roman Missal 1755
   choral office 792
   Gregorian chant in office 829
   liturgy of the hours 101, 377–378, 3403,
      3704, 4162
   monastic office 3293
   preservation 36, 639, 836, 1762, 3403,
      4168, 4199
   priests' knowledge 379
   reason for sacrificing 430, 836, 1762
   seminary liturgies 2686
   singing of Ordinary of Mass 54, 351, 424,
      1409, 4168, 4234–35, 4237, 4243
   study by seminarians 835, 2798, 3404
   translations 840
   unity of faith 4237
   vernacular and 835–836
Latin Mass
   minor basilicas 4352
   need to provide 424–425, 1773, 2656, 4169
   rites for singing 4280–97
Laudate **psalms** 3656

lauds
   celebration with congregation 467
   chief hour 89
   see also morning prayer
lay associations 311
lay ministers
   eucharistic exposition 2218
   funeral rites 3391, 3394
   special ministers of communion
      2041–53, 2070, 2071–72
laying on of hands
   confirmation 2501, 2503–04, 2507, 2518
   ordination rites 76, 145, 361, 2609–11
lectern (ambo)
   placement 388, 1662
   reservation of use 1458, 1662
lectionaries
   experimental form 1749
   Masses with children 2176
   regional editions 448
   religious communities 3731
lectionaries, patristic (liturgy of the hours)
   authors included 3716, 3727, 3736–38
   supplements 3592
   use 3591
lectionary, weekday
   edition of Consilium 1822–41
   provisional form 1819–21
Lectionary for Mass
   biblical index 1868
   celebrations of saints 1847
   chants between readings 1851
   date for use 1770–73, 1871, 1877
   format 1861–65
   general arrangement 1844
   increased use of Scripture 508
   introduction 1843–69
   Latin *editio typica* 1756, 1878
   Latin text (vol. 3) 1879–82
   multivolume editions 1867, 1872
   Old and New Testaments 1845
   order of readings
      criteria of arrangement 1849–50
      description 1853–65
      see also *Order of Readings*
   pastoral purpose 1852
   preparations for Mass 1470
   Propers of Saints 1875
   provisional norms 1747–50
   richness 1781
   ritual and votive Masses 1848
   Roman Missal and 4034
   Sundays and holydays 1845
   translations
      preparation 1866–69
      use 1771
   translations of Scripture 1875
   weekdays 1846
   see also readings for Mass
Lefebvre, Archbishop Marcel
   errors 552, 555, 564–568
   repentance urged 556, 563–572
   seminaries 566, 571
   statement required 570
   Tridentine Mass 569

Lent
baptismal and penitential themes 109, 246, 2348, 3022, 3793, 3857, 3875
catechesis of baptized adults 2455
catechumenate for adults 2334, 2348–53, 2412, 2422
celebration of marriage 2979
celebration of sacrament of penance 3078
Christian initiation of children 2462
duration 3794
eucharistic celebrations 3875
fast and abstinence 110, 3876
gospel acclamation 1851
liturgical pedagogy 3854–57
liturgy of the hours
memorials 3668
readings 3580
music 4187
penitential practices 110, 3029
prayer 3855
readings for Mass 1846, 1849–50, 1856
reform of liturgy 246
sacramental time 3874–76
Sundays 3771, 3795
weekdays 3782

Leonine prayers, suppression of 340

Lercaro, Cardinal Giacomo
end of tenure 667
Paul VI's defense 639

lex orandi/lex credendi
Consilium 690
Mass 1045
nature of liturgy 551
new Order of Mass 1759
new Roman Missal 1377
reform of liturgy 578, 632, 670
study of liturgy 2823

Liber precum 693

Litany of the Saints
choral office 3401
dedication of a church 4381
religious profession 3235
revised forms 3765
use by religious institutes 3274

little offices
approval of translations 374
authority for use of vernacular 375
conformity to divine office 372
public prayer of Church 98, 286, 373
replacement by divine office 3405–10

Little Singers
liturgical formation 4220
promotion 4204
service to liturgy 4115, 4192–96, 4220

liturgical apostolate
promotion 45
religious and 951

liturgical assembly
absence of priest 35, 239, 524, 3842, 3845
distinction of ministries 28, 1448
ecclesial character 2794
eucharist 260
exclusion of discrimination 32, 326–327
expression of the Church 483, 580

kneeling, standing, sitting 1740
order and structure 1647
unity 1245–46, 2120

liturgical books, editions of
adaptation by conferences of bishops 529, 885, 2280
anonymous publication 529, 934
bishops' vigilance 935–937
central collection 929
completeness 529, 926
copyright 529, 934
format 529, 693, 925, 3358, 3394
introductions *(praenotanda)* 884, 1866, 3114
Latin appendices 923
Latin *editio typica* 919
local or regional editions 335, 484, 485
norms for publishers 918–929
preliminaries
confirmation by Holy See 917
conformity to Latin *editio typica* 927
decree of promulgation 625, 919
qualities 332, 922
resources of the reform 580
royalties 930–933
vernacular *editio typica* 919
see also translations

liturgical books, revision of
aim 21
conciliar decree 25
criteria 622
cultural adaptation 38
Graduale Romanum and 4276
progress 894
review of work 693

liturgical celebrations
acts of the entire Church 26, 1100, 2795
aesthetic aspect 4318
basis of solemnity 4132
broadcasts 20, 1121–24, 1251, 4129
communal preferred 27, 4163
communion of saints 276
contemporary relevance 580
deacon presiding 2536
distinction of ministries 28, 2157, 2923, 4127, 4270
ecclesial character 41, 2120, 2795, 2923, 4134, 4211
exclusion of discrimination 32, 326, 390, 1663, 2658, 2978, 3392
faith and joy 596–598
formation of children 2135, 2146
hierarchic character 4211
languages 333
laypersons presiding 152, 239, 695
mechanical devices 443–444
music 4171, 4216
non-Catholic Churches 183, 190
participation 2923, 4136
pastoral training of seminarians 2799–2800
preeminence 7
preparation 545
priest and sacred ministers 4134
purpose 261
Scripture and 35, 2831
silence 3631, 4138

singing 4126, 4137, 4163, 4238
social nature 1271
study of liturgy 2825
training of seminarians 2719
unity of assembly 1245–46, 2791
unity of Church 483
universal call to holiness 154
variety of forms 2796
works of charity and 1101

liturgical centers
cooperation 418
definition 421
increase 507
relations with hierarchy 420

liturgical colors
chasuble-alb 4540
concelebration 1805
Masses for the dead 81, 469
rite of funerals 3394
traditional usage 1698
votive Masses 1700

liturgical commissions
catechesis for Order of Mass 1738
consultation on art and music 44, 46, 4317
establishment 44, 280, 4317
experiments 337
music commissions and 4214
reform of liturgy 536
translations 537
weekday lectionaries 1821

liturgical commissions, diocesan
celebrations of word of God 330
construction of churches 1646
reform of liturgy 580
responsibilities 339

liturgical commissions, mixed
establishment 484–485, 894
uniform translations 485, 878

liturgical commissions, national
competence 337
cooperation with the Consilium 478, 482
experiments 479
membership 336
reform of liturgy 580
smaller countries 627
translations 332, 881–883

liturgical days
concurrence of celebrations 3826–27
duration 3769
table of precedence 3825

liturgical directories 2653

liturgical experiments see experiments,
liturgical

liturgical formation
children 2141–48
faithful 311
need 14, 698
pastors' responsibilities 19
religious institutes 310
youth 508

liturgical formation in seminaries
conciliar decrees 15–17, 212–213
contemporary need 2842
eucharistic celebrations 2770

language of liturgy 4170
new discipline for orders 2821
norms 303–305, 2672–2761, 2779, 2916
prefect of ceremonies 2689
preliminary training period 2787, 2822
theological disciplines and 214
see also liturgy, study of; seminarians;
seminaries

liturgical institutes
catechesis for Order of Mass 1738
cooperation with hierarchy 789
Latin America 537

liturgical language see language, liturgical

liturgical laws
experiments 40
loyalty to Council 601
transitional period 413

liturgical life
diocese 194, 2794
parish 496, 2322–23
participation 236
promotion 41–42

liturgical ministries see ministries, liturgical

liturgical movement
Church's recognition 418
Constitution on the Liturgy and 578
culmination 491
Holy Spirit 43, 407, 579, 1357
Marian devotion 3913
Pius XII 407, 418, 579, 1357
results 437
spread 494

liturgical periodicals
meaning 422
service to reform 418, 420, 507, 789

liturgical prayer see prayer, liturgical

liturgical rites see rites

liturgical texts see texts, liturgical

liturgical traditions 577

liturgical year
adaptation 107
annual cycle 102, 3783–3813, 3995
calendars governing 3814
instructive and sacramental power 3755,
3767, 3874
norms 3754–57
paschal mystery 106, 3754, 3767, 3783
purpose 102, 3874
revision 107, 111, 676
see also Calendar, General Roman

liturgists
Latin America 537
responsibilities 4320

liturgy
authenticity 443
Christian education 216
Christ's priesthood 7, 550, 4225
Church's concern 276
communal character 4219
communal/hierarchic character 436, 441
communal/personal character 500
contemplation and 3293
conversion and 580

cultural adaptations 37–40, 490, *see also*
  adaptation
dignity and importance 5–13, 132, 550, 576
distinction of functions 324–325
distinctive qualities 2674
ecclesial character 671, 1759, 1969, 4232
evangelization 581, 701
evidence of tradition 3913
faithful's dispositions 11
foretaste of heavenly liturgy 159, 276
glory of God 2244
hierarchic character 436, 671
immutable/mutable elements 21, 2797,
  2826
instructive character 33, 394, 413, 623,
  2145, 3854
lex orandi, lex credendi see *lex orandi/lex
  credendi*
Mary and 3899–3921, 3914, 3943
ministry of sanctification 212
model of popular devotions 3921
paschal mystery 6
pastoral aspects 33, 2823
perennial youth 4214
personal prayer and 491, 494, 2789
public prayer of Church 135, 1786
relation to faith 511
renewal of Christian life 550, 4246
sanctification of life 61
social sciences and 2829
soul of Christian people 559–562
theocentric character 607
understanding of Scripture 226
words and rites 35
works of charity 2662
liturgy, reform of 21–40
adaptation *see* adaptation
application to non-Roman rites 301
attention to spiritual depth 4213
authority of the Church 1758, 1786
basis in Constitution 292
bishop's role 511, 535
continuity with past 23, 437, 624, 631,
  4240
contribution of monks 3313
cooperation 4214
critics 413, 493, 510, 575, 578, 699
eucharistic participation 1146, 1150–51,
  1975
fidelity to norms 1968
gradual process 296, 1944
introductions of revised books 884
Latin America 534–537
laws on places of worship 128
limits 634
loyalty to Council 691
manifestation of the Church 2
Marian devotion and 3945
norms 22–40, 301–339
objectives 290, 393, 430, 539, 580, 1761,
  1945, 2923
principles 5–46, 296–299
problems 419–429, 694
reactions 400–402
relation to universal Church 531
resistance to authority 672

respect for laws 495
results 300, 403, 406, 408, 435–477, 578,
  1943, 2841, 3896
review in Holy Year 1975 4093
review of modes of liturgical expression
  632
revision of texts and rites 4248, *see also*
  rites; texts, liturgical
Scripture and 1819
spirit of prayer in the Church 494–495
spiritual pedagogy 407
stability 627
transitional period 509
via media 701
liturgy, regulation of 22, 194, 288–289, 312,
  423, 446
liturgy, study of
courses 16, 303
prescription 16, 214, 279
priests 260
see also seminaries
liturgy of the eucharist (Order of Mass)
  1438–46
component elements 1438
concelebration 1556–96
dismissal of catechumens 2346
general intercessions and 1894
liturgy of the word and 56, 1239, 1398,
  2956
Mass with a congregation 1490–1512
Mass without a congregation 1611–20
uncatechized Christians 2964
liturgy of the hours
Church's tradition 3415, 3431
distribution of psalms revised 91
Eastern Churches 169, 756
ecclesial character 3450
hymns 93, 3509–10, 3472, 3491, 3603–08,
  3681, 3710
language 287, 377–381
love of 3743
non-Roman rite translations 380
personal prayer and 90, 3426–27
petition 3447, 3609
praise of God 3445–46
prayer of Christ and Church 83–85, 90,
  504, 590, 3426
prayer of the Christian community 504
priesthood of Christ 3444
revision
  decree 87
  principles 89–101, 3418–25
  results 504
sanctification of people of God 3444
spiritual formation in seminaries 2771
taste for 3744
understanding of 3742
liturgy of the hours, celebration of
calendar followed 3671–73
choice of office 3674–79
combining with Mass 513, 3523–28
conciliar principles 3730
contemplative communities 3728–35
expression of the Church 3426
hours combined 3529

in choir *see* choral office
in common 3450–57
    calendar 3671–72
    cantor 3690
    communities of priests 99
    distinction of ministries 3683
    family 3457, 3941
    functions of presider 3684–88
    intercessions 3619–20
    laity 504, 3457, 4160
    local Church 3450
    meetings of priests 3455
    mendicant orders 3411–14
    optional memorials 3650
    parish 100, 2656, 3451–53
    place 3692
    preferred manner 3463, 3745
    reader 3689
    religious communities 756, 3428, 3454,
      3456
    rubrics 3693–96
    seminaries 2807–09
    singing 100, 504, 3697–3714, 3731,
      4158–59
individual 3458–62
    calendar 3673
    public character 3633
Latin 101, 377–378, 3403, 3704, 4162
monastic dedication 3312–13, 3753
monastic office 3753
prayer of Christ and Church 3426
priests 265, 3428
progressive solemnity 3703, 3731, 4159
proper hours of day 88, 94
provisional texts 3717–23
relation to eucharist 504, 3402, 3442
sanctification of time 84, 88, 3402, 3419,
    3440–41, 3459, 3529, 3740–44
silence 3731
structure 3463
substitution for 97
union of mind and voice 3449
variations prior to 1971 465–468
vernacular 1773, 3409
liturgy of the hours, obligation of
bishops, priests, deacons 86, 2588,
    3458–59
chapters and religious communities
    3461–62
clerics in major orders 95–96, 176, 2701
daytime prayer 3506–07
dispensation and commutation 97, 285,
    371, 733
formation of seminarians 2810
permanent deacons 2541, 3460
substitution 3414
Liturgy of the Hours, The
date for use 1770–73
delay of Latin edition 3430
division of volumes 3739
effective date 3429
history of development 3417
monastic orders and 3750
promulgation 3415–29, 3715
reduction of obligatory prayer 3420

revision of proper offices 4039
supplementary readings 3575
see also General Instruction of the Liturgy
    of the Hours
liturgy of the word (Order of Mass) 1423–37
bishop presiding 4481
catechumens' participation 2345–46
concelebration 1554–55
cultivation 513
elements 1423
essential to celebration 1781
formation of children 2148
general intercessions 1894
liturgy of the eucharist and 55, 259, 396,
    513, 1239, 1398, 2956
Mass with a congregation 1479–89
Mass without a congregation 1607–10
separate for children 2150
uncatechized Christians 2453
local Churches
celebration of liturgy of the hours 3450
celebration of saints 111
diocese 191
eucharist 1236
formation in mission lands 250
Mass with bishop 1464
popular devotions 13
rule of bishop 147
universal Church and 146, 194, 483, 501,
    2637, 3450
see also particular Churches
local Ordinaries, powers of
accessibility of works of art 4332
communal anointing of the sick 3337
communicatio in sacris 186, 1021
communion under both kinds 2112
concurrence of Sunday and holyday 3841
confessors for women religious 3036
consecration of altars 4446
construction of churches 1646
discipline of concelebration 1353–54, 1545,
    1796
duration of catechumenate 2400, 2433
eucharistic exposition 2212–13
eucharistic processions 2219
eucharistic sharing 1050, 1058
foreign-language services 333
general absolution 3139
general intercessions 1908
lay ministers of communion 2041
liturgical books 936
marriage of laicized priest 2560
Mass stipends 2237
Masses with special groups 2125
minister of consecration to virginity 3258
ministry to tourists 2616
mixed marriages
    celebration 2991–92
    canonical form 3013, 3016
    impediment of mixed religion 2996
oil of the sick 3314
pastoral care of migrants 2628–30
plenary indulgences 3177, 3227
prayer books 937
provision of Latin Mass 1773, 4169

reception of baptized Christians 2487
repetition of communion 2084
sacred art and furnishings 126
shared premises 1069
special ministers of communion 2041,
    2075–77, 2095
sponsors for confirmation 2514
use of Missal of St. Pius V 1783
see also Ordinaries

Lord's Day
first holyday 106
liturgical year 102
resurrection of Christ 102
see also Sunday

Lord's Prayer
catechumenate for adults 2352
concelebration 1582
liturgy of the hours 3482, 3527, 3624–26
Mass with a congregation 1500
Mass without a congregation 1614
Masses with children 2186
meaning at Mass 1446
melodies for vernacular 4156, 4314
participation 1406
penitential services 3101
place in daily liturgy 3425, 3625
rite of confirmation 2522
rite of penance 3092, 3100
singing
    Latin chant 4199, 4254
    manner 4294

major superiors
admission to candidacy for ordination
    2945
advisability of concelebration 1545
institution to ministries 2933, 2940, 2942
vernacular in little office 375
see also Ordinaries, powers of; religious
    superiors

maniple 471

Marian antiphons 3522

maritime faculties 2669–70

marriage
apostolate of laity and 152, 237
canonical form *see* canonical form of
    marriage
catechesis 1103, 2973
celebration in closed times 367, 2967, 2979
celebration in home 2986
conjugal love 272
faith 2975
fidelity 2971
laicized priests 2560
minister assisting
    chaplain of migrants 2633
    deacon 2536, 2548, 2549, 2559
    non-Catholic minister 2992, 2998
    pastor or delegate 364
    responsibility toward non-Catholic
        guests 2977
    vestments 364, 2979
promotion 273
purpose 2971

rite
    adaptation 77, 2980–84
    choice 2976
    elements stressed 2974
    exclusion of discrimination 2978
    homily 362
    liturgy of the word 2979
    marriage of catechumens 2345
    Mass text 2979
    mixed marriages *see* marriages, mixed
    music 4164
    non-Catholic witnesses 1003, 1013
    nuptial blessing 365–366, 2967, 2979
    provisional form 362–367
    readings 2979
    revision 77, 637
    within/outside Mass 78, 283, 362, 366,
        2973, 2976, 2979
sacramental nature 271, 1106, 2969–70,
    2987–89

Marriage, Rite of
adaptation for local rituals 2980–84
introduction 2969–86
preparation of a different rite 2985–86
promulgation 2968

marriages, mixed
Anglican/Roman Catholic cooperation 1085
Church's concern 2989, 2999–3000
ecumenism and 3000, 3014–15
general norms
    canonical form 2990
    interpellations 730
    liturgical form 2991–92, 2998
marriage with baptized Christians
    canonical discipline 3004
    canonical form 3006–07, 3013, 3016
    choice of rite 2976, 3008, 3014
    minister assisting 3010, 3015
    obligations of Catholic party 3003
    pastoral assistance to spouses 3011
    true sacrament 3001
marriage with Eastern Orthodox
    Christians
    canonical form 172, 2993–94, 3005
    impediment of mixed religion 2996
    recording 2995
marriage with the nonbaptized 2997, 3001

martyrs
altar honoring 4402
liturgical year 104

Mary
Church's worship and life 3946
example for faithful 3297, 3883, 3919,
    3933–34
image of Church 103
model of Church 3926
    apostolate 3917
    faith 3915
    forms of worship 3920
    offering sacrifice 3918
    prayer 3916
mystery of Christ and Church 160–161

Mary, cultus of
adaptation 3933–34

basis 160–161, 3880, 3882, 3923, 3943
bishop's promotion 2660
Catholic teaching 417
communion of saints 158
Coptic Church 1051
Council of Ephesus 160, 187
Eastern Christians 187
ecclesial aspects 3947
ecumenical aspects 3930–31
endorsement 3879, 3897, 3921
exaggeration 3930
liturgy 161
 General Roman Calendar 3900–06
 Lectionary for Mass 3910
 liturgical year 103, 3901–05
 Liturgy of the Hours 3911
 particular calendars 3900–07
 patronage 3971, 3874
 reform of liturgy 1130, 3880
 Roman euchology 3909
 Roman Missal 3908
pastoral ministry and 3944
popular devotions
 Angelus 3938
 biblical content 3928
 Christological aspect 3923
 criteria 3935, 3948
 crowning of images 3890–95
 ecclesial character 3926
 emphasis on Holy Spirit 3924–25
 Liber precum 693
 mistaken forms 3935
 rosary 2661, 3877–79, 3884–88,
  3939–42
 social sciences and 3932–34
 Trinitarian aspect 3923
preachers 161
priestly life 267
promotion 3937
purpose 3936
themes of *Marialis cultus* 693, 3946
tradition of the Church 3913

Mary, Mother of the Church 3380–83, 3878,
3909, 3947

Mary, Mother of God 3801, 3903
votive Mass for peace 4099
World Day of Peace 4097

Mass
action of Christ and Church 265, 1232
center of Church's life 509, 1045
center of priest's life 266
Christ's presence 1182
component elements 1399–1433
doctrinal themes 1232
eucharistic catechesis 1244
false interpretations 1226
general structure 1397–98
influence on daily life 1242
liturgy of the word/of the eucharist 1239,
 1398
mystery of the Church and 1175
participation 1210
public and social nature 1176, 1222, 1232
termination of experiments 530
transubstantiation 1097

true sacrifice 1096, 1105, 1171–72, 1377
unauthorized texts 435
universal/ministerial priesthood 1240
see also eucharist, mystery of; eucharistic
 celebrations

Mass, celebration of
blind and infirm priests 464, 716–717, 721,
 940–941
chapel of reservation 4404
choice of form 1275
daily 1177, 2805
eucharistic devotion and 414
eucharistic exposition and 1290, 2209
individual 57, 265, 414, 1155, 1794, 1816
maritime faculties 719, 2669
observance of law 1274
outside a place of worship 718, 942, 1650,
 2655, 2669
priest seated 943
repetition on same day 713, 1548, 1802,
 1815, 2669, 3800
requisite articles 1671–1702
sign language for the deaf 2119
time of day 744, 939, 2669
vestments 4540

Mass, choice of texts for 1704–06
General Instruction of the Roman Missal
 1987
Masses with special groups 2132
options 447–449
readings 1850
use of *Missale parvum* 1767

Mass, forms of celebration of
concelebrated Masses 1543–98
distinction of ministries 1372
general rules 1622–42
liturgy of the hours and 3257
Mass with a congregation
 rites for singing in Latin 4280–97
 structure 1467–1542
Mass without a congregation
 language 1773
 structure 1599–1621
Mass without a server 1601
seminaries 2694, 2796

Mass, low/high/solemn 4149

Mass, offices and ministries in 1448–63

Mass, pontifical
assistant priests and deacons 4459
blessings 4490–91
concelebration 4458
deacons and subdeacons 4461–64
minor ministers 4466
simplification 4478–94
vesture of canons 4465

Mass facing the people
altar 383, 428
rearrangement of churches 415
right to celebrate 4336
tabernacle 387, 1283–84

Mass obligations
reduction 722–723, 747, 2238
transference of site 760, 2238

Mass of St. Pius V *see* Tridentine Mass

Mass *pro populo*
  chaplain for migrants 2633
  revision of calendar and 2230
Mass stipends
  binated Mass 2227, 2229, 2232, 2238
  chaplain for migrants 2636
  church discipline 2234
  concelebration 1803, 1812, 1816
  reduction of obligation 2238
  religious priests 2233
  revision of discipline 2231, 2233, 2235
  revocation of former faculties 2237
  trinated Mass 2232, 2238
Masses for the dead 1725–31
  celebration for non-Catholics 1074–77
  days permitted 1727
  dismissal rite (prior to 1969) 462
  Eucharistic Prayers II–IV 1933, 1936, 1939
  faculty of bishop 763
  limitation of use 1706
  liturgical color 469
  musical instruments 4187
  purpose 1725
Masses for neophytes
  Christian initiation 2367
  Easter season 2384
  participation of community 2368
  readings 2367
Masses for various needs 1716–24
  days permitted 1722–23
  liturgical color 1700
  readings 1718, 1848, 1850
  revision of Roman Missal 1390
  rogation and ember days 3813
  special day of prayer 1721
Masses with children
  adaptation
    bishops and conferences of bishops
      2138
    limitations 2153–54
    Masses with adults adapted 2152
    texts 1999
  adult monitors 2157
  aids to participation 2033
  bishop's regulation 2012, 2152
  children's participation 2155
  distinction of ministries 2157
  eucharistic prayer 1994, 1999–2023
  gestures 2166–67
  homilist 2157
  interval between 2160
  music 2163–65
  number of participants 2161
  offices and ministries 2155–57
  participation 2188
  parts of the Mass 2171–87
  place 2158
  preparation of celebration 2162
  readings 2174–82
  silence 2170
  time 2159
  visual elements 2168–69
Masses with special groups
  adaptation 2130
  bishop's authorization 2655

chasuble-alb 4540
  communion under both kinds 2128
  day for celebration 1256, 2131
  form of celebration 2132
  meal following 2131
  norms 2127
  place 2124
  readings 519, 1709, 2127
  time of day 2131
matins
  nocturnal character 89
  structure prior to 1971 465
  see also office of readings
mechanical devices
  Masses with children 2165
  use in liturgy 443–444, 4208
media of communication
  broadcast of rites 20, 1121–24, 1251, 4129
  Church's use 136
  liturgical formation in seminaries 2837
  liturgy and 696
memorial acclamation (Order of Mass)
  independent rite 1407
  manner of singing 4293
  Masses with children 2017
memorials 3780
  celebrations of particular calendars 4019
  choice of opening prayer 1713
  liturgy of the hours 3665–69
  provisory norm 3759
  readings for Mass 1850, 1880
memorials, obligatory
  choice of Mass 1705
  weekdays of Lent 3780
memorials, optional
  choice of Mass 1706
  concurrence 3780
  liturgy of the hours 3650–51
  provisory norm 3762
  saints in Martyrology 3674
microphone, use of 390, 443, 1663
migrants, pastoral care of 2624–36
  bishops 291, 2656
  foreign-language services 333
ministries
  diversity 231
  hierarchic
    bishops, priests, deacons 148, 2606
    origin and nature 2568
  laity and 152, 2928, 2965
  new forms 582, 2923, 2965–66
  use of term 2927
ministries, liturgical
  distinction 28
  exercise
    laicized priests 2561
    lay participants 29, 152, 695, 2917, *see
      also* lay ministers
    manner 305
  revision 2923
  tradition of Church 2922
  training of seminarians 2838

ministry of the word
elevation by liturgy 396
forms 259, 1099
ministry of sacraments and 701
source 610

ministry of word and sacrament
laity 234
missions 244
priests 212

minor hours *see* daytime prayer

minor orders
history 2922
ministries 2927
term discontinued 2924, 2927

missal, preparation of 1470

Missale parvum 1766

Missale Romanum **(Apostolic Constitution)**
consecration of the Mass 2000
gradual implementation 1732–52
Roman Missal obligatory 1786
teaching on Mass 699

mission lands
catechumenate for adults 246
musical traditions 119
native priests 251
rites of baptism 68, 2280

missionaries
Christian community and 247
native priests and 251

missionary activity
contemplatives 3296
cooperation of the faithful 253, 758
doctrinal principles 242–244
meaning 244
right organization 252

missions
Christian witness 245
meaning 243
vocations 248

miter
abbatial 3283–84
episcopal 4475
pontifical Mass 4193, 4488–89

mixed commissions *see* liturgical commissions, mixed

mixed marriages *see* marriages, mixed

monastic life, liturgy and 3311–12

monastic office
Benedictine *Thesaurus* 3753
Benedictine tradition 312, 3300
common basis of celebration 3478–79
concession of experiments 3746
particular communities 3751
psalter cycle 3750
St. Benedict 3949
uniform rite 3311
see also choral office

monastic orders
reform of liturgy 1130
renewal 207

monks
choral office 95, 207, 370, 3454
Latin in divine office 3293

Liturgy of the Hours and 3750

monstrance, material for 1682

morning prayer
canticles 3566
celebration in common 3470
concluding prayer 3483, 3629
intercessions 3425, 3524, 3611
Lord's Prayer 3624
manner of concluding 3484
Mass following 3524
memorials 3665, 3669
principal hour 89, 3419, 3467
psalms 3357, 3473
purpose 3468
reading 3572
responsory 3479, 3602, 3711
seminaries 2809
singing 3702
solemnities of the saints 3657
structure 3471–84

music 112–121, 4122–90
adaptation 119, 4182
associations 4100, 4199, 4235
authority to regulate 517, 4133
broadcasts 4129
celebrations in Latin 4171
choice of kind 4130
Church and 4100, 4130, 4217
Church's treasury
adaptation to reform 4174
enrichment 4206, 4234, 4249
preservation 114, 4112, 4115, 4118, 4191, 4248
desacralization 4234
diocesan commissions 46
editions of particular propers 4042
eucharistic prayers 2011
evangelization and 4246–47, 4251
instrumental 4183–88, 4209
integral part of liturgy 112
jazz excluded 427
liturgical formation in seminaries 115, 2722–30, 2835
liturgy of the hours
melodies for vernacular 3705
styles approved 3704
melodies for Order of Mass 1737
melodies for Roman Missal 1744
melodies for vernacular 334, 618, 4118
need of study 635
new compositions
continuity with tradition 4113, 4118, 4210, 4240
criteria 4225, 4230, 4249
development 4174, 4197, 4209, 4218
melodies for vernacular texts 4162, 4166, 4199, 4234, 4236, 4239, 4245
new era 548, 4234–36
non-Western 119, 4209
participation and 4219
power 4211, 4247
profane excluded 440
purpose 112
qualities 4114, 4125, 4208, 4234
records and tapes 443, 2165

reform of the liturgy 635, 4114, 4122–23,
    4199–4205
    liturgical issue 4227
    musical issue 4225
    nonobservance of norms 4216–17
    pastoral issue 4228
religious music of the people 118, 4125
resources for reform 4208
sacredness 112, 427, 4251
seminary professor 2724
sensus Ecclesiae and 4224
service to liturgy 113, 4100, 4123, 4125,
    4207–11, 4216, 4221, 4230, 4248
styles approved 116, 517, 3704, 4125, 4218
teaching and practice 4173
translators of texts 787, 872–873
unauthorized experiments 4208
union with rite 112
union with text 4210, 4217
uses for obsolete compositions 4167, 4174,
    4223
see also congregational singing; Gregorian
    chant; singing

music, commissions on
    establishment 280, 4189, 4190
    liturgical commissions and 44, 46, 4214,
        4317
    promotion 4200

music, institutes of 115

musical instruments
    acceptability 120, 517, 4183–84
    adaptation 440
    improvisations 4188
    mechanically operated 443
    organ *see* organ
    restrictions 427, 440
    singing and 4185–86
    solo playing 4186–87

musicians
    adaptation and 4182
    liturgical training 115, 4188
    responsibilities 4221

mystagogy *see* Christian initiation of adults

Nativity of John the Baptist 3840

Neo-Vulgate
    liturgical resource 1889
    promulgation 1885, 1888
    psalms in *Ordo cantus Missae* 4301, 4303

night prayer
    Canticle of Simeon 3568
    concluding prayer 3520, 3628
    examination of conscience 3516
    Marian antiphons 3522
    memorials 3666
    proper hour 89, 3514
    psalms 3358, 3518
    responsory 3519
    seminarians 2698, 2809
    solemnities of the saints 3660
    structure 3515–22

none 3506, 3734, *see also* daytime prayer

Nostra aetate 1064

Notitiae
    inception 628
    liturgical commentaries 634
novitiate, entrance into 3233
nuns
    choral office 95, 370, 3454
        dispensation 953
        language 800–804
    consecration to a life of virginity 3256
    contemplative life 3297
    language of conventual Mass 809
    papal enclosure 3299
nuptial blessing
    closed times 365, 2967
    rite of marriage 2979
    outside Mass 366
    within Mass 365
nuptial Mass (prior to 1969) 363–364, 463, *see
    also* marriage

offering (eucharistic prayer) 1445
offertory (Order of Mass)
    rubrics (prior to 1969) 455
    see also presentation of the gifts
offertory antiphon (Order of Mass)
    Ordo cantus Missae 4292
    Simple Gradual 4265, 4271
office of the dead
    liturgical color 469
    replacement 3386
office of readings
    adaptation 89
    combining with another hour 3529
    combining with Mass 3528
    concluding prayer 3499, 3628
    memorials 3665, 3669
    nocturnal character 3502, 3731
    psalms 3492, 3564
    purpose 3485–86
    readings 3493–97, 3678–81
    responsories 3495, 3599–3601, 3712
    seminaries 2809
    solemnities of the saints 3658
    structure 3490–99
    Te Deum 3498, 3503, 3642
    time of celebration 3487–89
    uses 3419
    vernacular editions 3739
    vigils extending 3500–03, 3733
oil of catechumens
    blessing *see* oils, blessing of
    exclusive use 2497
    symbolism 3862
oil of the sick
    blessing *see* oils, blessing of
    care 3342
    composition 3317, 3340
    priests carrying 2616, 3314
    symbolism 3862
oils, blessing of
    chrism Mass 3797
    competent minister 3341, 3867
    faculty 762
    place within Mass 3871–72
    time 3341–42, 3859, 3869–70

see also *Blessing of Oils and Consecrating the Chrism, Rite of*

Old Testament
Jewish/Catholic relations 1064
reverence of Christians 223

open-air Masses 438

opening prayer (Order of Mass)
choice of text 1713
forms of conclusion 1422
Mass with a congregation 1478
Mass without a congregation 1606
Masses with children 2184
meaning 1422
options 518
particular propers 4035
period before 1969 450–452
singing in vernacular 4313
translations 518, 838–861, 865, 871
use of only one 1422
weekdays in Ordinary Time 518

oratories, blessing of 369, 4428–34

Order for Celebration of the Holy Year 4078–88

Order of Mass
alteration forbidden 515
beginning of use 1757–60
changes (prior to 1969) 340, 453–462, 1340, 1356
characteristics 1763
liturgy of word/of eucharist 1759
nature of changes 1759
obligatory use 555
participation 1759
prior catechesis 1738
process of revision 636
promulgation 1367
"Protestant" influences 1787
provisional norms (1969) 1745
reason for changes 1761
revision decreed 50, 675, 1758
revision of Roman Missal 1361
sign of unity 569
use of Latin text 1733

Order of Readings for Mass
description 1853–65
promulgation 1842

Ordinaries, local *see* local Ordinaries, powers of

Ordinaries, powers of
application of Constitution 434
communion under both kinds 524, 2113
concelebration 57, 1353–54, 1543, 1545, 1796
institution to ministry 2934, 2940, 2942, 2964
obligation of liturgy of the hours 97, 285, 371
regulation of liturgy 446
reserved blessings 79
sacred art 124
use of Missal of 1570 1784
use of Tridentine Mass 1784, 1786
use of vernacular 101, 375, 378, 1773

Ordinary of the Mass, singing of
celebrations in Latin

Kyriale simplex 4253
Gregorian chants 54, 351, 4168, 4199, 4234–35, 4237, 4243, 4254, 4304
congregation's part 4137, 4141, 4155
manner 4155
music for vernacular Roman Missal 4312

Ordinary Time
liturgy of the hours
cycle of hymns 3605–06
readings 3582
number of weeks 1858
particular celebrations on Sunday 3824
purpose 3809
readings for Mass
arrangement and choice 1858
Sunday readings 1859
time of occurrence 3810
weekday readings 1860

ordination admission to candidacy for
distinction from institution 2946
requisites of candidates
declaration of intention 2581, 2945
qualifications 2816
rite
celebration 2944–47
establishment 2581, 2590
see also *Admission to Candidacy for Ordination as Deacons and Priests*
time of admission 2944

ordination, rites of
bishop's responsibilities 2657
essential elements
diaconate 2609
episcopacy 2611
priesthood 2610
parts in vernacular 474, 776, 816–819
promulgation 2613
revision 76, 668, 2579, 2606
seminaries 2816–21
translations 486
see also bishops _____, deacons _____, priests, ordination of

Ordo cantus Missae
chants added 4313
Kyriale simplex and 4303
preservation of treasury of chant 4277
promulgation 4275
Proper of Seasons 430, 4279
psalms 4301
rites followed 4280–97
Roman Missal and 4300
Simple Gradual and 4303
use 4298–99

organ
liturgical use 120, 4183, 4202
placement in church 389, 1665

organists
ministry 453, 4211
training 2728–29, 4188, 4202

Our Lady of Lourdes 3906
Our Lady of Mount Carmel 3906
Our Lady of Sorrows 3905
Our Lady of the Rosary 3906

pallium, use of
  pontifical Mass 4494
  reservation to metropolitans 4543
  tradition of Church 4542
papal altar
  concession of use 4338–43
  history 4337
papal blessing
  bestowal
    bishop 3203
    newly ordained priests 3152
  reservation 369
parents
  baptism of children
    celebration 67, 2289
    preparation 2311
  catechesis of unbaptized children 2460
  confirmation of children
    liturgical formation of children 2143
    preparation 2512
    sponsors 2513
  first teachers of faith 141, 542
parish
  adaptation to diverse members 4249
  children's baptism 2320–23
  choir 4229
  diocesan commission for 2665
  liturgical life 41–42, 496, 2322, 4248–51
  liturgy of the hours 100, 2656, 3451–53
  Mass 4249
  music 4248–51
  Sunday Mass 1255, 1465, 2656, 3847
parish, personal 2629
participation
  aim of liturgical reform 14, 296, 430–431,
    2923
  apostolate of laity 233, 236
  bishop's responsibility 277
  catechesis 504, 1100
  children 2141
  communion 55
  communion under both kinds 1631
  conciliar teaching 431
  congregational singing 114, 551, 4219,
    4244, 4246
  contribution of the arts 4319
  design of churches 382
  Directory for Masses with Children 2188
  effects 549
  entrance into paschal mystery 549
  eucharistic celebrations 48, 561, 1210, 1241
  general intercessions 1902
  goal of pastoral activity 605
  Inter Oecumenici and 445
  liturgy of the hours 3418
  manifestation of Church 41
  Masses with children 2155
  means of achieving 30
  new eucharistic prayers 1945
  new Order of Mass 50, 1759
  pastoral guidance 395
  prior conversion 538
  promotion 14–20, 546
  qualities 11, 432–433, 4136
  revision of liturgical year 3755

role of faithful 4136
  universal priesthood 1380
  vernacular in liturgy 399, 787
particles *see* hosts, particles of
particular Churches
  Catholic Church and 162
  celebrations of the saints 3775
  equality and dignity 163
  holydays 173
  see also local Churches
paschal candle *see* Easter candle
paschal mystery
  celebration in liturgy 6, 270
  celebrations of the saints 104
  faith and sacraments of faith 298
  fulfillment of human endeavor 270
  history of salvation 5
  Holy Week participation 432
  sacraments and sacramentals 61
passion, reading of 2918
Passion (Palm) Sunday 3796
*Pastoral Care of the Sick: Rites of Anointing
  and Viaticum*
  adaptations 3344, 3358, 3360–61
  approval 3319
  effective date 3319, 3362–64
  introduction 3321–61
  promulgation 3320
  translations 3364
pastoral-liturgical activity
  other pastoral work and 299
  promotion 43–46
  source 298
pastoral-liturgical institutes
  cooperation with bishops 338
  establishment 44, 303
  increase 507
  music commissions and 4190
Pastoral Norms for General Absolution
  bishop and 607
  commentary 3127–32
  fidelity in observing 2139
  Rite of Penance 3064
pastoral staff
  abbatial 3283–84
  episcopal 4450, 4476
  pontifical Mass 4488, 4493
pastors, responsibilities of
  accessibility of churches 2200
  administration of viaticum 1268
  assistance at marriages 364
  care of the sick 3355
  communion of the sick 1269, 2092
  congregational singing 114
  dispensation from law of fast and
    abstinence 3027
  eucharistic catechesis 1234
  eucharistic celebrations 1993
  general intercessions 1909
  liturgical catechesis 56
  liturgical formation of faithful 311
  liturgy of the hours in parish 3453
  Masses with special groups 2131–32
  planning of funerals 1731

prayer for Christian unity 978
preparation for baptism 2262
representation of bishop 42
sponsors for confirmation 2515

paten
blessing 4443–45
consecration 526, 734
dignity 1679, 4442
material 1682
size 1683

patron saints
approval 3977
choice 3974–76, 4025, 4028
confirmation 3978–80
liturgical celebration 3671, 3818, 3981–85,
4003–07, 4024
meaning 3971–73, 4023
norm of exclusion 3985, 4027
number 4026
secondary patrons 3984, 4026

penance, Christian
anointing of the sick 3326
Church's call to repentance 3017
Church's life and liturgy 3069
forms 110, 3876
Lent 3855
obligation 3021
virtue 109, 3019

Penance, Rite of
adaptations 3103–05
effective date 3065
introduction 3066–3105
promulgation 3063–65
value 3115
vernacular editions 598, 3114

penance, sacrament of
acceptance of penance 3071
bishop's regulation 3104
catechesis
baptized adults 2497
children 1118
conditions for reception 3038, 3071, 3076,
3116–18
confession *see* confession
contrition 3071, 3111, 3117
conversion *see* conversion
Council of Trent 3038
dignity 3060
Eastern Churches, 170, 179
effects 3069. 3072
eucharist and 1264, 1332–33, 1335, 2101,
3150
evolution of practice 3115
excommunication of profaners 3060–62
false interpretations 1227
importance 598, 3113, 3123
institution 3038
joined with anointing and viaticum 3351
minister
adaptations 3105
bishop 3074
pastoral responsibilities 265, 607,
3075, 3120–22, 3125, 3139
vestments 3079
see also confessor

ministry in tourism 2616
norms for religious 3036–37, 3052–56
personal/social aspects 1331, 3064
purpose 3063, 3067, 3115
regulation of discipline 3103–04
rite
communal celebrations 3048, 3131
forms 3112
place of celebration 3077
readings 3089
reconciliation of individual penitents
3080–85
reconciliation of several penitents
3087–95
reconciliation with general absolution
3096–3100
revision 72, 3063
role of community 3073
shorter rite 3086
time of celebration 3078, 3875
sacrament of reconciliation 141, 1104,
3057–59, 3121
sacrament of resurrection and peace
3133–34
sacraments of Christian initiation and 3150
SC Doctrine of the Faith 650
seminarians 2814–15

penitential practices
adaptation 110
days of penance 3022–31
Holy Year (1975) 407
norms 3021–30
obligatory character 3119
principal forms 3020
promotion 3029

penitential rite (Order of Mass)
elements 1419
Mass with a congregation 1477
Mass without a congregation 1603
night prayer and 3516
participation 1406
revision of Roman Missal 1361

penitential services
adaptation 3105, 3107
benefit and importance 3102, 3106
catechesis of the baptized 2496
distinction from sacrament 3048, 3102,
3106
inclusion of sacrament 3109
Lent 3078
nature and structure 3101
readings 3101
scrutinies and 2468–71
seminaries 2773, 2815

Pentecost
anticipated Mass (1967) 1257
celebration of vigil 3501
day of celebration 3789

people of God 140–144
Perfectae caritatis, application of 756–757
permanent diaconate *see* diaconate, permanent
Perosi, Lorenzo 4230
Peter and Paul, SS., solemnity of 3840
pews, reservation of 1663

Phase (review) 573–575
phonograph, use of 443, 2165
photographs 1252
pilgrimages
    bishop's regulation 2660
    Christian meaning 4074
    indulgences 4091
    promotion and care 2618
Pius X, St.
    age of discretion in children 3148
    first confession and communion 1120,
        3141
    sacred music 112, 440, 4100, 4230
Pius XII
    liturgical movement 407, 418, 579, 1357
    ordination rites 2608
    pastoral care of migrants 2624
    rights of art 4325
    sacred music 4100
Placeat 462
polyphony
    acceptability 116, 4112, 4209, 4216
    seminaries 2692
pontifical insignia
    norms for use 130, 4448–55
    simplification 4457–96
    tradition of Church 4447
pontifical Mass *see* Mass, pontifical 4482–89
pontifical rites, simplification of 4457–96,
pontificals *see* pontifical insignia
popular devotions *see* devotions, popular
postbaptismal catechesis (mystagogy) 2364
    bishop meeting neophytes 2432
    celebration of close 2430
    experience of community 2366, 2428
    experience of sacraments 2365
    Masses for neophytes 2367, 2429
postures *see* kneeling, standing, sitting
praenotanda see introductions
prayer
    communal/personal 533, 547
    contemporary life 538
    decalogue for 539–48
    life of the Church 132, 538
    necessity 12
    public/interior 533
prayer, liturgical
    guarantee of fidelity 603
    increase 498
    offering in name of assembly 33, 603
    see also Church, prayer of; liturgy of the
        hours
prayer, personal
    catechesis 1100
    decline 409
    liturgy of the hours 90
    relation to liturgy 491, 494, 1100
    source in joy and hope 492–493
prayer after communion (Order of Mass)
    Mass with a congregation 1512
    Mass without a congregation 1620
    meaning 1446
    particular propers 4035

use of only one 1422
prayer books, publication of 937
prayer in the liturgy of the hours *see*
    concluding prayer (liturgy of the hours)
prayer meetings 2120
prayer of Christ *see* Christ, prayer of
prayer of the Church *see* Church, prayer of
prayer of the faithful (Order of Mass)
    restoration 53
    see also general intercessions
prayer over the gifts (Order of Mass)
    Mass with a congregation 1497
    Mass without a congregation 1613
    particular propers 4035
    preparation for eucharistic prayer 1443
    use of only one 1422
prayer over the people (Order of Mass)
    concluding rite of Mass 1447
    Mass with a congregation 1514
    particular propers 4035
    translation 871
prayer services, ecumenical *see* ecumenical
    prayer services
prayers at foot of altar
    omission 342, 1335
    suppression of Ps 42 340
preaching
    avoidance of novelty 1817
    bishop's office 192, 2642, 2955
    catechesis 611
    Christ's presence 1180, 1238
    deacons 2955
    effectiveness 397
    establishment of Church 243
    laypersons 2953–63
    Lent 3875
    liturgical celebrations 35
    liturgy and 2650
    mandate of the Church 144
    ministerial/universal priesthood 2956
    ministry of priest 148, 257, 259, 1113,
        1126, 2571, 2765, 2955
    necessity 1883
    pastors 196
    preeminence 1127, 1338, 2562
    priestly formation 212
    qualities 1339
    sacraments and 259, 701, 2241, 2571
    SC Clergy 665
    source in Scripture 224, 227
    syllabuses 347
    various forms 259, 1884
    see also homily
precatechumenate
    Christian community 2338
    purpose 2337–38
    role of community 2368
    "sympathizers" 2339
preces 3612, *see also* intercessions (liturgy of the
    hours)
preface (Order of Mass)
    chrism Mass 2557
    concelebration 1558

eucharistic prayer 1444
Mass with a congregation 1498
Masses with children 2018
new texts 1360, 1930
particular propers 4035
singing in vernacular 4314
thanksgiving theme 1445, 4035
use of vernacular 486, 766
variety 1711
prefect of ceremonies 2689
prefects apostolic
faculties 711, 2044, 2050, 2238
name in eucharistic prayer 1971
prelates, vesture of 4515–17
prelates *nullius*
faculties 711, 2044, 2050, 2238
name in eucharistic prayer 1971
presbyters *see* priests
presentation of the gifts (Order of Mass)
acolyte 1535
deacon 1523
faithful's participation 1491
incensation 1625
Mass with a congregation 1490–94
Mass without a congregation 1611–12
Masses with children 2151, 2155
procedure 1439
Rite of Christian Initiation of Adults 2363
Presentation of the Lord 3905
Presentation of Mary 3906
presentation song (Order of Mass)
choice 1714
manner of singing 4292
Mass with a congregation 1490
music for vernacular 1744
preparation of the gifts 1440
Simple Gradual 4265, 4271
presentations (catechumenate)
catechesis of the baptized 2495
catechumenate for adults 2352, 2405
time 2380
presidential prayers (Order of Mass)
Masses with children 1994, 2183–85
proper to priest 1400
recitation aloud 1402
priesthood, Christ's *see* Christ, priesthood of
priesthood, ministerial
apostolicity of Church 2568
bishops 2601–02
celebration of Mass 1379
communicatio in sacris and 1028
Eastern Churches 187
eucharistic ministry 1044, 1142
hierarchical nature 2605
mission of the Church 257, 258
mystery of the Church 2599
origin 257, 1126
permanence 2569
priesthood of Christ 2597
sacerdotal character 1127
Synod of Bishops on 2562–74
universal priesthood and 140, 1125–28,
1240, 2563, 2604–05, 2765, 2956
vocations 211, 2600

women excluded 2593–2600
priesthood, universal
baptism and 140, 1125
derivation from Christ 257
diversity of ministries 4211
eucharistic celebrations 1175, 1380
eucharistic devotion 1175
ministerial priesthood and 140, 1125–28,
1240, 2563, 2604–05, 2765, 2956
sacraments 140–141, 232
women 3962
priestly commitment, renewal of 2763
priestly formation 211–215
aims 212
basic plan 2765–78
concept of priesthood 2765
Eastern Catholic Churches 164–165
importance of liturgy 15–18, 306, 2780–81
missions 248
pastoral aspects 215
preaching 212
see also liturgical formation in seminaries
Priestly Fraternity of St. Pius X 571
priests, life of
daily celebration of Mass 1197, 1272–74,
2805
eucharistic devotion 561
helps 267
liturgy of the hours 86, 504, 3428, 3458–59
Mary 267
mutual help 263
prayer 266
spiritual life 265, 2572
study of liturgy 260
priests, ministry of
action in name of people 140, 2598
care of churches 260
care of the sick and dying 3397
catechumens 2372
Christian community 261
Church's ministry 512
collegiality 2603
contemporary world 2766
cooperators of bishop 148, 194, 256–257,
260, 262, 2563, 2573
distribution 264
eucharistic celebrations 144, 260, 1322,
1450, 2568
evangelization 2571
holy orders and 257
individual celebration of Mass 57, 265,
414, 1794, 1816
ministers of baptism 2260
ministers of Christ 260, 266, 2597
ministers of communion 2081, 2095
ministers of penance 2247, 3113, 3122,
3125, 3134, 3139
missions 256
preaching office 148, 257, 259, 1113, 1126,
2571, 2765, 2955
preparations for baptism 2263
relationship with laity 2574
sacraments 257–267
sacred offices 148, 256–257, 259–261

priests, ordination of
celebration of diocese 2818
commitment to celibacy 2948
concelebration 1798, 1811
effects 2607
prior institution to ministries 2936
rite
approval 2612
determination of essentials 2610
promulgation 2613
revision 2608

prime
omission 284, 370, 376, 3400
suppression 89, 3419

privileges, liturgical 4043–45

processional cross *see* cross, processional

processions
Easter evening prayer 3643
Masses with children 2167
papal enclosure 3299
preparation of the gifts 1440

processions, eucharistic *see* eucharistic
processions

profession, religious *see* religious profession

profession of faith
baptism of adults 2355, 2357, 2426
baptism of children 2288
dedication of a church 4381
Mass with a congregation 1488
Mass without a congregation 1609
Masses with children 2182
meaning at Mass 1433
participation 1406
singing
celebrations in Latin 4199
congregation's part 4158
Masses with children 2164
see also Credo
use 1434

professor of liturgy
course in sacramental theology 2833
plan of course 2845
qualifications 303, 2830
responsibility 2846

progressive solemnity, principle of 3703, 3731,
4159

promise, religious *see* religious promise

Proper of the Mass
Gregorian chants for 4256
Simple Gradual 4257

Proper of Seasons
formation of the faithful 105
mysteries of salvation 3815
particular calendars 3816
precedence 108, 3997
traditional practices 107

propers, particular
editions 4040–42
harmony with General Calendar 3766
Latin text of Masses 1756
readings for liturgy of the hours 3597
readings for Mass 4036

revision
format 4040–42
liturgical indults 4043–45
Masses 4034–37
offices 4038–39
time period 3999, 4046, 4051

psalm-prayers (liturgy of the hours) 3542, 3731

psalms
Christian interpretation 3539
literary genre 3533, 3537
manner of praying 3534–37
musical character 3533
need of study 90, 3540, 3552
seminarians 2702, 2810
translations for singing 873
use in funerals 3384
see also chants between readings

psalms in liturgy of the hours
captions 3539, 3541
Christian interpretation 3539
current/complementary psalmody 3511,
3513
daytime prayer 3511–13
division of longer psalms 3562
Friday 3359
Glory to the Father 3553–55
history of salvation 3426
morning and evening prayer 3357, 3473
night prayer 3358, 3518
office of readings 3492, 3564
omission of Ps 58 83, 109, 3561
options 3682
personal feelings and 3538
proper 3564
psalter cycle 91, 3416, 3421, 3556–65
reservation of Ps 78 105, 106 3560
resources for meditation 3420
singing
preference for 3708
psalm tones 4271
ways 3551–55, 3709
titles in Hebrew psalter 3537
understanding 3731, 4161

Psalter, revision of 91, 1885

publishers
liturgical books 920–929
payment of royalties 930–933

purgatory 3158

**purification and enlightenment
(catechumenate)**
participation of community 2368
preparation for sacraments of initiation
2353
purpose 2352, 2415
rites 2416–22
time of celebration 2348, 2385, 2415

purifications (Order of Mass)
fingers of priest 1627
vessels 1628

pyx, material of 1682

quinquennial faculties 760–763

reader
 deacon 2536
 formation 4203, 4205
 functions at Mass 1424, 1426, 1538–42
 gospel of Christ's passion 2918
 liturgical ministry 29, 325, 4134
 liturgy of the hours 3689
 Masses with special groups 2127
 non-Catholic 1010
 woman 1460, 1740

reader, ministry of
 candidates for orders 2580, 2582
 exercise by seminarians 2820
 functions 2930
 reception by seminarians 2816
 revision 2923
 understanding of Scripture 2930

readers, institution of
 conditions 2933
 interstices 2935
 minister 2934, 2940
 reception by candidates for orders 2936
 reservation to men 2932
 rite 2940–41
 usage of term 2924
 see also *Institution of Readers and Acolytes,
  Rite of*

readings for liturgy of the hours
 character 3731
 daytime hours 3509–10
 enrichment 504
 Fathers and church writers 3423
  sources 3590–92
  value 3593–95
 gospel at vigils 3503
 history of salvation 3426
 honoring saints 3424, 4038
  biographical note 3598
  historical accuracy 92, 3424
  particular propers 3597
  texts 3596
 morning and evening prayer 3475–76
 night prayer 3519
 office of readings 3493–97, 3678–81
 optional patristic lectionary 3423
 options 3678–81
 order of occurrence 3569
 private recitation 466
 proper offices 4038
 readings for Mass and 3574–76
 revision 92
 Scripture 3422
  cycle 3573–83
  proper readings 3584
  purpose 3570
  short readings 3586–88
  shortened passages 3585
 singing 3713, 3731
 use of vernacular 474

readings for Mass
 announcement of text 1862
 approved translations 771
 avoidance of paraphrasing 2178
 captions 1863
 celebration of scrutinies 2420, 2422

 choice 1710, 1849–50
 conclusion 1865, 4283, 4289
 continuous 1709
 cycle decreed 51
 description of order 1853–65
 difficult texts 1849
 importance 1399
 incipit 1864
 Jewish/Christian relations 1064
 Latin 1773
 length 1849
 longer/shorter forms 1850, 1868
 Mass with a congregation 1479–81, 1485
 Mass without a congregation 1607
 minister 342, 1424, 1540, 2930
 new Lectionary 507
 number 1740, 1845, 1850
 omission of verses 2176
 options 519
 place for proclaiming 341, 388, 1662
 preparation of new order 1820
 principles for translations 1869
 proper/accommodated 1840, 1850, 1880
 readings for liturgy of the hours and
  3574–76
 recitation in sung Mass 343, 4313
 revision of Roman Missal 1362
 role of celebrant 344, 1486
 semicontinuous 1845, 1847
 singing 4283, 4285, 4289, 4313
 special adaptations 1715
 substitution forbidden 513
 Sunday and holyday cycle 1708, 1845
 Sundays/weekdays 1844
 vernacular proclamation 54, 4313
 weekday cycle 1709, 1846, 1860
 see also gospel reading; Lectionary for
  Mass

real presence
 effect of consecration 1284, 2198
 eucharistic worship and 1098, 1223, 2189
 faith of Church 1096, 1188–89
 false interpretations 1155, 1226
 implications 1142
 latreutic worship 267, 1200–07, 1232, 1304,
  1323, 2088, 2194–95
 Mass and 1178–90
 mystery of the eucharist 1309
 presence par excellence 1183
 sacramental signs 1141
 teaching of Church 1336, 1378
 transubstantiation 1190–99
 see also Christ, presence of

Receiving Baptized Christians ..., Rite of
 2476–88

reception of baptized Christians
 abjuration from heresy 974, 2481
 absolution from censures 973
 adaptation of rite 2487
 baptism not repeated 2482
 bishop as minister 2483
 communion under both kinds 2486
 conditional baptism exceptional 968
 confirmation
  celebration 2483

minister 2516
connection with eucharist 2378–79
Eastern Christians 164, 2477
meaning of rite 2476
preparation 2481
profession of faith 2482
reconciliation of apostates and 973
record of reception 2488
retention of canonical rite 164
revision of rite 69
sacrament of penance 2484
sponsor 2485

reciprocity
applicability 1061
communicatio in sacris 997, 1000
Ecumenical Directory I 1028

reconciliation
formulary of absolution 3084
history of salvation 3066
Holy Year (1975) 4071
meaning 4071, 4090
ministry of Church 3063, 3073
personal aspects 3121
sacrament of penance 141, 3057–59, 3070,
    3110, 3124

records and tapes, use of 443, 2165

reform of liturgy *see* liturgy, reform of

Regina caeli 3522

relics, depositing of
conditions 1656, 4373, 4408
dedication of an altar 4426
movable altar 4437
preparation 4392
record 4393, 4427
symbolism 4382

religious
authority of bishop 753
concelebration 1549
cooperation with bishop 197
eucharistic worship 1215
language of liturgy 4170
liturgical apostolate 951
liturgical life 204, 209
liturgy of the hours 98, 3428
mental prayer 757
ministers of baptism 2324–26
pastoral ministry in tourism 2622
place in Church 155–156
sacrament of penance 3033–35
special ministers of communion 2041,
    2047, 2071
study of psalms 4161

religious institutes
celebrations of saints 111, 3775
ceremonial books and Vatican II 3268
charisms 206
dedication to eucharist 2191, 2216
exemption 3310
liturgical formation 310
liturgy of the hours in common 756,
    3402–04, 3455
norms for indulgences 3190
participation in Church's life 202, 501
particular calendar 3996

proper celebrations
    founder 3983, 4007
    patron 3973, 3976–77
    title (titular) 3972
    translations of texts 767–775
public prayer of Church and 286
revision of liturgical books 203

religious institutes, clerical
faculties of superior general 938–950
language in conventual Mass 808, 810
language in divine office 791–799

religious institutes, lay
faculties of superior general 952–955
vernacular in community Mass 811
vernacular in divine office 805–807

religious life
Church's esteem 3229, 3231
contemporary relevance 3309
evangelical witness 3301

religious life, renewal of 202–209
conformity to conciliar documents 3268
cooperation with bishops 3310
eucharistic celebrations 3308
importance of liturgy 3292, 3307
prayer 3302–05
Scripture 3292
sense of community 3292
silence 3306

religious profession
nature and import 3230–31
pronouncement before blessed sacrament
    3244
relation to baptism 155
requisites of formulary 3249–51
rite
    celebration within Mass 80, 156,
        3234–35
    final profession 3235
    first profession 3234
    Litany of the Saints 3274
    Mass text 3238–39
    readings 3239
    renewal of vows 3236
    revision 80, 3263
    separation of distinct celebrations
        3237
    vestments 3240

Religious Profession, Rite of
adaptation by religious institutes 3229,
    3241–44, 3263–74, 3275
introductions 3230–48
Latin version 3267
promulgation 3229
translations 893, 3229, 3252, 3267
universal use 3263

religious promise
meaning 3246
practice 3245
rite 3234, 3247–48

religious superiors
special ministers of communion 2079
subjects' frequent confession 3035, 3053
see also major superiors; Ordinaries,
    powers of

reliquaries, placement of 4373, 4407
renunciation of Satan (baptism) 2426
responses (Order of Mass) 1405
responsorial psalm (Order of Mass)
    choice 1851
    Commons of Saints 1881
    congregation's participation 4154
    independent rite 1407
    provisory list (1969) 1750
    singing 1426
    see also chants between readings
responsories in liturgy of the hours 3599–3602
    morning and evening prayer 3479, 3602,
        3711
    night prayer 3519
    office of readings 3495, 3599–3601, 3712
    singing 3711–12
resurrection of the dead 1133–35
revelation 218–228
    false interpretations 1225
    Scripture and tradition 220
    transmittal 220–222
    words and deeds 219
ring, abbatial 3283–84, 3290
rites, revision of
    aim 21, 2500
    Church's care 1788
    Constitution on the Liturgy 638
    continuity of new with old 671, 880
    gradual process 673
    need 62
    reform of liturgy and 4248
    requirements 631
    sacraments and sacramentals 62
    teaching function 623
rites, simplification of
    criterion 1758
    decree 50, 328
    desacralization and 673
    gestures 487
    intelligibility 633, 4248
    limits 512
    purpose 134
    reform of liturgy 34
    revision of Roman Missal 1361
    substance/changing elements 50
Rites in the Church
    Catholic communion 162
    equality and dignity 3, 163, 602
    Holy Spirit 604
    norms for liturgical year 3768
    preservation 162
    retention by individual 164
    see also particular Churches
rites of passage (catechumenate) 65, 2380,
    2392, 2407
ritual Masses
    choice of readings 1710, 1850
    Christian initiation 67, 2424, 2436
    color of vestments 1700
    consecration to a life of virginity 3260
    days prohibited 1720
    dedication of an altar 4412
    dedication of a church 4376

    eucharistic prayer 1983
    Lectionary for Mass 1848
    meaning 1719
    religious profession 3238
    revision of Roman Missal 1390
    second reception of communion 2084
    weekdays in Ordinary Time 1724
rituals, particular
    introductions of Roman Ritual 63
    principles of adaptation 2279, 3271
    rite of anointing 3358–59
    rite of baptism 2281
    rite of funerals 3381
    rite of marriage 2980–84
rogation days
    adaptation 3812
    celebration 4033
    Litany of the Saints in choir 3401
    purpose 3811
    votive Masses 3813
Roman Breviary
    arrangement 3416
    history 3416
    Latin in vernacular editions 381, 923–924
    permission for use 1772, 3429
    see also Liturgy of the Hours, The
Roman Canon
    criteria of translations 820–825
    see also Eucharistic Prayer I
Roman Curia
    diocesan bishops 641
    norms on Mass stipends 2236
    reform 648–665
    Regimini Ecclesiae 666, 679
Roman Martyrology, revision of 693
Roman Missal
    chants 4313, 4255, see also Ordo cantus
        Missae
    effective date 1366, 1770–73
    Graduale Romanum and 4276
    instrument of unity 1365, 1786
    Latin editio typica
        bishop's providing in churches 1756
        music 4316
        promulgation 1374–75, 1765
        publisher 1756
        use 1741, 1765, 1770
    Lectionary and 4034–35
    lex orandi/lex credendi 1377
    Missale parvum 1766
    obligatory use 1751, 1771, 1784–86
    Ordo cantus Missae and 4300
    particular calendars and 3995
    provisory norms 1764
    qualities 506, 509, 1778, 1975–76
    result of Vatican II 597
    revision
        adaptation 1385
        background 1358
        conciliar norms 1358
        cycle of readings 1362
        eucharistic prayer 1360
        language 1390
        music 1364
        need 1357

Order of Mass 1361
    progress 693
    propers and commons 1363
    ritual Masses 1390
    sources 1383
  vernacular editions
    Dutch 597
    French 1785
    Latin text in 349, 818, 825, 923–924,
        1753–57, 1766
    music 4311, 4316
    use 1765, 1771
Roman Missal of 1570
  benefit to Church 1357
  changes in *Ordo Missae* (1965) 1341
  defense of Catholic teaching 1381
  permission to use 1751, 1772, 1782, 1784
Roman Pontifical
  revision 693, 2606
  translation of ordination rites 818
Roman Rite
  reform of liturgy 3
  respect for traditions 674
  revision of liturgy of the hours 87
Roman Ritual
  introductions 63, 2279
  progress of revision 693
Romanità 674
rosary
  compendium of the Gospel 3888
  endorsement 3879
  family rosary 3940–42
  forms 3887
  liturgical worship and 3939
  Our Lady's psalter 3939
  power 3879
  prayer for peace 3879, 3884–88
  promotion 2661
royalties 930–933
rubrics
  meaning 439
  revision of liturgical books 31

Sacram Liturgiam, application of 294
sacramental character
  baptism
    Christian initiation 2502
    deputation for divine worship 141
    indelibility 2489
    universal priesthood 1125
  confirmation 2502, 2518
  priesthood
    bishop 145
    configuration to Christ's priesthood
        257
    permanence 2569
    teaching of the Church 1127
    universal priesthood and 2604
sacramental sharing
  conditions 1009
  Eastern Christians 1026
  Western Christians 1009, 1022
  see also *communicatio in sacris*

sacramentals 79–80, 368–369
  deacon 2536, 2592
  institution by Church 60
  nature 60
  review decreed 79
  sanctification of life 1716
  singing in celebrations 4164
  use of vernacular 353
sacraments 59–78, 353–367
  catechesis 609, 1111
  Christ's presence 1102, 1182, 3365
  Church's discipline 2245
  Church's power 2596
  Church's stewardship 2106
  Eastern Churches 166, 187, 993, 1051
  ecclesial acts 580, 2240
  evangelization and 581, 600
  growth in grace 2499
  holiness of the Church 1095
  immutable/mutable elements 2106
  laity 150
  life of Mystical Body 139
  mystery of Christ in Church 1102
  pastoral ministry 2243
  preaching and 259, 701, 2241, 2571
  priestly ministry 148, 260, 2765
  sacramentality of Church 2239–40
  sacraments of faith 59, 259, 1103, 2571
  sanctification of life 1716
  sign of unity/cause of grace 1009, 1022,
      1029
  theological meaning 2242
  translation of form
    approval 905, 909
    fidelity 870, 904–908
    less-known languages 916
  unity in faith and worship 1009, 1022,
      1029
  universal priesthood 140–141, 232
sacraments, celebration of
  bishop's responsibility 2657
  catechesis 2243
  fees 2658
  homily 1884
  pastoral effectiveness 2242
  preparation 2244
  singing 4164
  training of seminarians 2720
  use of vernacular 353
sacred, sense of the 505
Sacred Heart, liturgical cult of 3850–52
saints, celebrations of
  ad interim adaptations 3993
  kinds 3649
  Lectionary for Mass 1847
  limitation 111, 3756
  liturgical year 3756, 3774
  liturgy of the hours 3648–69
    feasts 3661–63
    memorials 3665–69
    newly canonized 3968
    office of readings 3497
    transference 3652

newly canonized 3953–57, 3764, 3966–70
particular calendars
 changes 3821
 criteria 3816
 harmony with General Calendar 4018
 historical accuracy 4013
 precedence 3825
 purpose 3815
 rank 3820
 saints entered 3818–19
patron saints 3981–85
provisory dates 3763
readings for Mass 1850, 1880
solemnities 3655–60
subordination in calendar 108, 3648
titles of saints 4022
two of one saint 3998
universal/local Church 111, 676, 3775,
 3815–16, 3995

saints, titles of 4022

saints, veneration of
basis 3923
correction of abuses 159
Council of Florence 159
liturgical year 103
SC Rites 660
tradition 158

sanctuary
place of celebrant and ministers 1647
qualities 1648
space 383

sanctuary lamp 1286, 2203

Sanctus **(Order of Mass)**
acclamation 1445
adaptation of text 2016
concelebration 1558
independent rite 1407
Mass with a congregation 1498
singing
 congregation's part 4155
 manner 2016, 4293
 Masses with children 2164
 vernacular 4313

Sanctus **bell** 1499

SC Causes of Saints 679

SC Clergy
name 661
organization 662–665
preaching by laity 2954–56

SC Council 661

SC Discipline of the Sacraments
cessation 704
responsibilities 652–653

SC Divine Worship
cessation 704
establishment 678–679
first meeting 686
list of members 685
members for the Consilium 683
organization and responsibilities 680–682,
 687
report to Synod of Bishops 692–701

SC Doctrine of the Faith 648–650

SC Eastern Churches 651

SC Rites
competence 625, 634
division into two congregations 677
historico-hagiographical office 659
history 678
Judicial Section 658
responsibilities 654–655
Worship Section 657

SC Sacraments and Divine Worship
establishment and organization 702–708
list of members 709

schola cantorum see choir

Scripture
accessibility to faithful 225
catechesis 610
eucharist and 229, 267
increased use 51
Lectionary for Mass 508
life of the Church 224–228
magisterium of the Church 222
popular Marian devotions 3928
preaching 224
primacy in liturgy 24, 513, 1819, 1843,
 1852, 1885
Proper of Seasons 1849
religious life 204
revision of rites 632
rule of faith 224
study 227, 507, 1781
study of liturgy and 2790, 2831
tradition and 221–222
translations 1842, 1876
 adaptation for children 2178
 ecumenical 225
 Neo-Vulgate 1886
 original languages 869
 passages in liturgical texts 332
 readings for Mass 867, 1842, 1876
unity of books 2566

Scripture, readings from
cycle 52
increase 51
liturgy of the hours 92, 3570–88

scrutinies (catechumenate)
celebration 2421
children of catechetical age 2468–71
meaning 2496
number 2379, 2420
penitential services and 2468–71
purpose 2352, 2417–18, 2420
replacement for the baptized 2496
time 2379, 2389, 2422

seamen, pastoral care of 2669–70

Secretariat for Christian Unity
common date for Easter 1070
ecumenical progress 1032

secular institutes
communion under both kinds 2108
faculties of superior general 947

seminarians
course in elocution 2730
Gregorian chant 2798
Latin language 835, 2798

liturgical celebrations with bishop 2696, 2700, 2794
liturgical life 2683–2703
liturgical spirituality 2704–14
liturgy and education 2677
liturgy and human culture 2679
liturgy and pastoral ministry 2680–81, 2715–34
liturgy and personal prayer 2789
liturgy and spiritual life 2678
liturgy of the hours and formation 2771
mission lands 248
music 2722–30
pastoral formation 2777–78
personal prayer 2775
sacrament of penance 2814–15
sacred art 2731–34
spiritual formation 213, 2770
training for liturgical offices 2799–2800, 2838
see also liturgical formation in seminaries

seminaries
celebration of ordination rites 2816–21
concelebration 307
diversity of orders and ministries 2792
eucharistic celebrations 2771
liturgical celebrations 305, 2791–98
major/minor 2768–69
music 115
penitential services 2773
popular devotions 2712
promotion of liturgical life
    general principles 2787–2800
    specific celebrations 2801–21
right organization 212
sanctification of time 2713
study of liturgy
    advanced studies 2839
    art 2836
    compulsory course 16, 2735, 2776, 2822
    conformity to Constitution 214
    continuing education 2840
    coordination with other courses 2739, 2831–34, 2844, 2848
    history of rites 2826–27
    library resources 2740
    media of communication 2837
    music 2835
    objective 2823
    pastoral introduction 2838
    place in curriculum 2736
    plan of course 304, 2738, 2741–61, 2849–2916
    professor 15, 303, 2737, 2830
    scope and method 2824–29
    social sciences 2829
    study of Scripture 2790, 2831
theological courses 214, 2776

Septuagint 225
sequence (Order of Mass)
manner of singing 4287
use 1430
servers see altar servers
sext 3506, 3734, see also daytime prayer

shared premises
authority 1069
local ecumenism 1066–69
ship passengers, pastoral care of 2669–70
shrines 2660
sick, care of the
communion 2092
eucharistic fast 2085–86
offices and ministries 3352–57
priestly ministry 3397
reason 3323, 3325
sick, sacraments of the 3325–45
Church's concern 3320, 3325
community aspect 3353
continuous rite 3250–51
see also anointing of the sick; viaticum
sign language, use of 2119
sign of the cross
entrance rite of Mass 1418
liturgy of the hours 3696
manner 2392
sign of peace (Order of Mass)
adaptation 1740
communion rite 1446
concelebration 1584
deacon 1526
Mass with a congregation 1502
Mass without a congregation 1615
music for greeting 4313
rite of confirmation 2526
signs, sacramental
faithful's understanding 59, 580, 1104, 2242
liturgy 7
nature 2596
study of liturgy 2828
silence
communion rite 461, 1446, 1510
eucharistic celebrations 1413, 1992
liturgy of the hours 3478, 3631–33
Mass without a congregation 1620
Masses with children 2155
praying the psalms 3543
purpose 4138
sacrament of penance 3091
Simple Gradual, The
Common of Saints 4269
components of chants 4265–69
criteria of composition 4261–64
Graduale Romanum and 4250–59, 4261–62
nature of edition 4257
new texts 4264
optional texts 4273
Ordo cantus Missae and 4303
promulgation
    1st *editio typica* 4256
    2nd *editio typica* 4303
Proper of Saints 4268, 4307
Proper of Seasons 4262, 4267
psalms 4270–72
responsorial psalm 4270
singers needed 4270
sources 4262–63
use 4271–72

sin
Lenten liturgy 3855
need of confession 3059
pardon 3157
punishment 3156
sense of 3117
sickness and 3322
social consequences 109, 3121, 3137

singers
boys 115, 4115
choice 4129
liturgical formation 115, 4220
responsibilities 4221
see also Church Choirs; Little Singers

singing
antiphonal/direct/responsorial 3552
appropriate texts 121
celebrants and ministers 4147
distinction of ministries 4127
ecclesial aspect of celebration 4163, 4211, 4249
effect on Christian life 4229, 4235, 4249
enhancement of rites 113, 548, 4126
gradual introduction 4128
musical instruments and 4185–86
participation 4246
pious associations 4139
progressive solemnity of celebrations 4128
qualities 4208, 4249
reform of liturgy 4208
sensus Ecclesiae and 4224–25
styles appropriate 4132
tradition of Church 4246
union with rite 121
union with text 112, 2722
variety 4131
vernacular 113, 2693
vernacular and Gregorian chant 4241
see also congregational singing

sitting
liturgy of the hours 3693–95
Masses with special groups 2132
Order of Mass 1740
uniformity 1452

social sciences
liturgy and 2829
Marian devotions and 3932

solemn blessing (Order of Mass)
concluding rite 1447
Mass with a congregation 1514
particular propers 4035

solemnities
choice of Mass 1704
custom of vigils 3501
duration 3777–78
evening prayer I 3526
particular calendars 4031–32
provisory norm 3759
readings for liturgy of the hours 3584
readings for Mass 1709, 1850, 1880
transference 3771

solemnities of the Lord
celebration on Sunday 3772–73
liturgy of the hours 3647, 3667
titles not in General Calendar 4030

sound equipment 390, 443, 1663

special ministers of communion
appointment by priest 2076
authorization 524
communion outside Mass 1262, 2095
competent authority 2044–45, 2050
concession (U.S.A.) 2070–72
conditions for appointment 2044, 2075
duration of faculty 2052
eucharistic exposition 2218
extraordinary ministry 1325
functions at Mass 1458
laypersons 2048
mandate 2049, 2080, 2949
ministry of acolyte 2931
missionary activity of laity 2921
needs of faithful 2074
occasional 2051
order of preference 2046, 2078
qualifications 2048, 2081
regulation 562
religious 2047
rite of commissioning 2949–52
rite to be observed 2952
vesture 2951
viaticum 3349

sponsor
catechumenate for adults 2369
catechumens 2398
children of catechetical age 2466
confirmation 2514–15
reception of baptized Christians 2485

spouses
effect of sacrament 271, 2969, 2988
harmony of religion 2989
obligations 77, 2970–71

standing
liturgy of the hours 3693–95
Masses with special groups 2132
Order of Mass 1740
uniformity 1452

Stanislaus, Saint, celebration of 3987–90

stations of the cross 369, 737, 2661

statues
limitation 125, 1668
placement 128

stole
manner of wearing 1692
vestments of Mass 1689

street clothes, prohibition of 526

subdeacon
functions suppressed 1372, 2923, 2929
use of term 2929

Sunday
civil calendar 131
first holyday 106, 3755, 3770, 3845, 3874
liturgy of the hours
celebration 3634–37
evening prayer I 3526
memorials 3667
psalms 3359, 3677
singing 3701
lord of days 3845–48
precedence 106, 377, 3997
solemnities and feasts of the Lord 3772–73
weekly Easter 3767, 3770, 3843–44

Sunday Mass
  anticipation on Saturday 1257, 3829, 3837
  choice of Mass 1705
  general intercessions 53, 1895
  holyday preceding or follows 3838–41
  homily obligatory 52, 281, 345
  Masses with special groups 2131
  number and hours 1255
  obligation 106
  parish Mass 42, 1465, 2656, 3847
  participation 49, 430
  paschal mystery 106
  pastors 56
  preparation 507
  provisions for foreigners 2656
  readings 1845, 1850
  schedule supervised by bishop 2656
  seminaries 2695
  singing 1467
  tourist's participation 3831–35
  vigils 3840
  worship of community 3846
Sunday observance
  assemblies without priest 329, 3842, 3846
  bishop's responsibilities 2656
  care of tourists 2617
  Eastern Catholic Churches 169
  formation of faithful 1254
  importance 543, 3849
  Mass in Eastern church 1001
  Mass *pro populo* 2230
  norms 3847
  promotion 290
  purpose 3848
  seminaries 2713
surplice 1688
Susanna, story of 1818
"sympathizers" (catechumenate)
  duties of pastors 2340
  reception 2339, 2392
synod, diocesan 2663

tabernacle
  altar facing the people 428
  bishop's responsibility 2660
  celebration of Mass 1284
  design of churches 1285
  genuflections at Mass 1623
  lamp 1286, 2203
  place on altar 1283
  placement and design 128, 387, 428, 1667,
    2200, 2202
  single 1281, 1667, 2202
  unacceptable types 416
tabernacle key 2202
tabernacle veil 1286, 2203, 4335
Tantum ergo 1291
Te Deum
  celebrations of the newly canonized 3956,
    3969
  office of readings 3498
    Easter Vigil 3642
    vigils 3503
terce 3506, 3734, *see also* daytime prayer

Teresa of Avila, St. 3959–62
texts, liturgical
  ad interim translations 881–883
  creation in vernacular 880, 3103
  essential/secondary elements 865
  intelligibility 4248
  literary genres 862–864
  private initiatives 694
  reform of liturgy 4248
  reverence 790
  ritual signs 842
  vocal expression 1408
thematic harmony, principle of 1845–46
theological faculties
  chair of liturgy 303
  study of liturgy 16, 279
Thesaurus Liturgiae Horarum Monasticae 3753
throne
  celebrant's chair 384
  episcopal 4467–70
title (titular)
  celebration 3983, 4006–07
  change 4029
  distinction from patron 3972
  titles of the Lord 4030
titles of address 4518–24
  conferences of bishops 4531
  titles of kinship 4518
titles of the saints 4022
tonsure, first, suppression of 2580, 2926
tourism, pastoral ministry in
  norms 2614–23
  Sunday Mass 3831–35
tourists
  bishop's responsibilities 2656
  Masses in Latin 425
tract, manner of singing 4286
traditio symboli see presentations
tradition
  catechesis 610
  development 221
  magisterium of Church 222, 567
  Marian devotion 3913
  rule of faith 224
  Scripture and 222
tradition of the Fathers
  historical research 1383
  meaning 1384
  revision of Order of Mass 50, 1381
traditionalists 555
transfinalization 1155
transignification 1155
translations
  ad interim versions 881–883, 1748
  adaptation for children 2464
  approval 36, 485, 881–883, 913
  art of communication 844–845
  basis in critical texts 847
  biblical usage of terms 855
  commissions of experts 875, 877, 4175
  community prayer 857
  completeness 884

conferences of bishops *see* conferences of
  bishops
confirmation 485, 774, 911–917
criteria 332
essential/secondary elements 865
euchological formularies 870
experimental use 876
fidelity 843, 866
forms of sacraments 870, 904–908
hymns 874
integral part of rites 787, 843
Jewish/Christians relations 1064
language in common use 852
less-known languages 907
literary genres 863–864, 866, 2010
little offices 374
liturgical usage of terms 855
liturgy of the hours 101, 287
metaphors 860
multilingual countries 332
obsolete terms 862
particular texts
    Eucharistic Prayers for Masses with
      Children 1997, 2007
    Eucharistic Prayers II–IV 1964–65
    Lectionary for Mass 1747, 1771, 1842,
      1866–69, 1870, 1887
    Liturgy of the Hours, The 1771, 3429
    Order of Mass 1734–35
    propers of dioceses and religious
      765–775
    Pastoral Care of the Sick . . . 3319, 3358,
      3364
    Rite of Baptism for Children 2249, 2316
    Rite of Blessing of an Abbot or Abbess
      3276
    Rite of Blessing of Oils . . . 3860
    Rite of Christian Initiation of Adults 2327
    Rite of Confirmation 910
    Rite of Consecration to a Life of Virginity
      3852
    *Rite of Dedication of a Church and an
      Altar* 4360
    Rite of Funerals 3372, 3393
    Rite of Institution of Readers . . . 2531
    Rite of Penance 3065, 3103, 3114
    Rite of Religious Profession 893, 3229,
      3267
    Roman Canon 486
    Roman Missal 1742–43, 1746, 1754,
      1765, 1771
    Simple Gradual 832
pastoral consideration 895
prayers 518, 838–861, 871
principles 838–880, 1869
proclamation and 862, 872
psalm verses for Mass 833–834
qualities 529, 787
relation to ritual acts 863
responsibilities of translators 786–790
sacral language 854
Scripture 225, 332, 867–869, 1842, 1876,
  1886, 2178
signification of terms 850
texts for music 872–873
unauthorized changes 480

unit of meaning 849
verbatim versions 859
see also vernacular in liturgy
translations, uniform 764, 771, 788
acceptance 879, 891
bishops' consultation 332
common melodies 4179
different musical traditions and 4316
Latin America 536, 894–902
mixed commissions 485, 837, 878–879
need 484
Order of Mass 1736
parts required 889
problems 888
transubstantiation
Catholic teaching 1190–99
faith of the Church 1097
false interpretations 1155, 1226
Mass 1105
treasury of the Church
communion of saints 3159
power of pope 3200
Trent, Council of
anointing of the sick 3316
Archbishop Lefebvre 568
communion under both kinds 55, 2109
communion under one kind 1631
contrition 3117
Mass as sacrifice 1377
priestly character 1127
real presence 1188–89, 1378
sacrament of confirmation 2504
sacrament of penance 3038
sacred art 4324
veneration of saints 159
vernacular in Mass 1386
Tridentine Mass
conditions for use 555
permission for use 1751, 1772
unlawful celebration 569, 699
trination
faculty 713
stipend 2232, 2238
Trinity Sunday 3772
triumphalism 2378

Ukrainian Catholic Church 604
unity of Christians
eucharist 1237
general intercessions 978
prayer 956–959
special times of prayer 976
see also ecumenism
Universa Laus
CIMS and 4119–21
foundation 4116
universal prayer
meaning of term 1891
restoration 53
see also general intercessions
ushers 1458

Vatican Council II
adaptation 2136

aims 1
    care of migrants 2624
    Church as community of prayer 533
    communion 1388
    "Council on the Church" 4053
    ecumenism 959
    eucharistic teaching 1148–49, 1230
    false interpretations 557–558, 1224–29
    Jubilee of 1966 4052
    loyalty 553–558, 601
    Masses for Fourth Period 1342–52
    nature of Church 641, 2241, 3017, 4053
    norms on decrees 751–759
    pastoral nature 550
    preaching 2562
    reform of liturgy 430
    sacraments as ecclesial 2240
    sense of community 499
    universal priesthood 2563
    vernacular in liturgy 1387
vernacular in liturgy
    authorization 36, 4168
    beginning 399
    bishop's regulation 2661
    canon of the Mass 474
    choral office 765, 800–805, 826–830, 3402
    conferences of bishops and 36, 322, 334,
        349, 474, 617–618, 771, 4176, 4179
    Council of Trent 1386
    creation of new texts 880
    dialects excluded 912
    dioceses 767
    disquiet 424
    Eastern Churches 177
    extension of use 54, 486
    formation of readers 4203
    gradual introduction 618, 788, 1742
    Latin and 835–836, 3404
    lay religious institutes 805–807
    Lectionary for Mass 1747
    little offices 374–375
    liturgy of the hours 101, 287, 474, 4162
    love of Scripture and 1819
    Mass 54, 349
    Masses in Latin 424
    Masses with children 2164
    Masses with congregation 1773
    multilingual countries 332, 425, 912
    music
        adaptation 4118
        congregational singing 113, 4244
        Latin repertoire 4172
        melodies needed 334, 3705, 4175–84,
            4199, 4223, 4225, 4236, 4239, 4245
    Order of Mass 54, 1734
    Ordinary of Mass 4313
    ordination rites 474, 776–785
    participation 4118
    pastoral advantages 639, 787, 815, 1387,
        1762
    preface 766
    priests' knowledge of Latin and 2686
    religious institutes 768
    reports to the Consilium 617
    rite of marriage 366
    sacraments and sacramentals 63, 353

    seminaries 2686, 2693
    unauthorized uses 435
    see also translations
verse before gospel (Order of Mass)
    independent rite 1407
    seasonal variation 1428–29
vespers
    adaptation 1681, 1685
    celebration with congregation 467
    parish celebration 100
    principal hour 89
    see also evening prayer
vessels 1679–86
    adaptation 526
    blessing and consecration 1686
    deacon's functions 1523
    design 1685
    Masses with special groups 2132
    material 1680, 1684
    preparation for Mass 1470
    purification at Mass 1501, 1628
        acolyte 1537
        concelebration 1595–96
        deacon 1528
        Mass without a congregation 1619
vestments
    absolution of the dead 472
    abuses 433, 439
    adaptation 128, 526, 1691, 1694–95, 1698
    Asperges 472
    blessing of an abbot
    blessing of ashes 472
    blessing of a church 4433
    color 1697–1700
    communion outside Mass 2098
    communion rite 3401
    concelebration 473, 1551, 1805, 1810, 4540
    confirmation 356, 358, 2528
    consecration to a life of virginity 3262
    dedication of an altar 4425
    dedication of a church 4391
    design 1253, 1694, 4541
    eucharistic exposition 1294, 2214, 2218
    laying of cornerstone 4368
    liturgy of the hours 3685
    Mass 1471, 1687–1700, 4540
    Masses with special groups 2132
    material 1695
    ministers at pontifical Mass 4466
    obligatory use 526
    ornamentation 1696, 1699
    processions 1693
    religious profession 3240
    requirement 526
    rite of marriage 364, 2979
    sacrament of penance 3079
    symbolism 1687

vestments, episcopal 4471–79

vesture, ecclesiastical 991, 4357, 4515–17,
    4527–28, 4533–37

viaticum
    anointing of sick and 74, 360
    bishop's reception 2659
    catechesis 3356

communion under both kinds 3346
continuous rite 3350
deacon 2536
eucharistic fast 2085
eucharistic reservation and 2197
lawful ministers 3349
precept to receive 1268, 3347
provisional rite 360
purpose 3346
renewal of baptismal promises 3348
second reception of communion 2084
special ministers of communion 3349
time of reception 3347
see also *Pastoral Care of the Sick* . . .
vicars apostolic
faculties 711, 2044, 2050, 2238
name in eucharistic prayer 1971
Vidi aquam 4254
vigil Masses 3777, 3840
vigils
Bible services 35
dedication of a church 4378
vigils in liturgy of the hours
celebration of 1304, 3500–03, 3733
Christmas eve 3645
Easter Vigil 3642
Sunday 3636
Te Deum 3503, 3642
see also office of readings
Villot, Cardinal Jean, defense of 552
virginity *see* consecration to a life of virginity
Visitation 3905
vocations
missions 248
pastoral care 276
promotion 194, 211, 264
votive Masses
choice of readings 1850, 1880
color of vestments 1700
general intercessions 1900
kinds 1719
Lectionary for Mass 1848
provisional lectionaries 1840, 1875
World Day of Peace 4099
votive offerings 4334
votive offices 3675
vows, renewal of 3236
Vulgate
respect 225
Vatican Council II and 1885

washing of hands (Order of Mass)
Mass with a congregation 1495
Mass without a congregation 1612
pontifical Mass 4483
symbolism 1442
Week of Prayer for Christian Unity
ecumenism 976, 1065
eucharistic sharing 1033
Paul VI 959
weekdays
celebration 3759, 3782
choice of Mass 1705

days after Ascension 3792
meaning in Lectionary 1839
readings for Mass 1846, 1850
weekdays in Ordinary Time
Masses for various needs 1724
opening prayer 449, 518, 1713
provisional lectionary 1832–34
readings for Mass 1860
white garment (Christian initiation) 2360, 2497
wine *see* eucharistic wine
women
altar servers 429
choirs 4143
consecration to life of virginity 3257
contemporary issues 3933
equality in Church 2599–2600
functions in liturgical assembly 525
liturgical *ministerium* 429
Marian devotion and 3934
ministries at Mass 1460
ordination to priesthood
Anglican communion 1072–73
exclusion 2593–2600, 3962
readers at Mass 1460, 1740
role in society and Church 2593–94, 3962
special ministers of communion 2048
universal priesthood 3962
women religious
ministers of communion 2035, 2039–40
norms on sacrament of penance 3036,
3054
word of God
eucharist and 224, 229, 267, 1843
liturgical assembly 580
priestly life 265
Scripture and tradition 222
word of God, celebrations of *see* celebrations
of the word
World Council of Churches 962, 1070, 1078
World Day of Peace
date 3903
establishment 4097
liturgical texts 4098
norms for celebration 4099

youth
catechesis 584–585
liturgical formation 508, 4198
problems 585
youth Masses 508, 1969